599.094 M265h 2008
Mammals of the British Isles
: handbook

WITHDRAWN

WITHDRAWN

WITHDRAWN

MONROE COUNTY COMMUNITY COLLEGE

3 3131 00094 4219

MONROE COUNTY
COMMUNITY COLLEGE
MONROE, MICHIGAN

D1116325

MAMMALS
OF THE BRITISH ISLES:

HANDBOOK, 4TH EDITION

MAMMALS
OF THE BRITISH ISLES:

HANDBOOK, 4TH EDITION

Edited by S. Harris & D.W. Yalden

THE
Mammal
SOCIETY

Published by The Mammal Society
c/o Society for Experimental Biology
3 The Carronades
New Road
Southampton SO14 0AA

www.mammals.org.uk

© The Mammal Society 2008
Previous editions © Blackwell Scientific Publications, 1964, 1977. 1991.

All rights reserved. No part of this publication may be reproduced, stored in a
retrieval system, or transmitted, in any form or by any means, electronic,
mechanical, photocopying, recording or otherwise without the prior
permission of the copyright owner.

Copy editing by Kathleen Lyle
Design and artwork by Sally Geeve
Printed by Impress Print, Corby, UK

British Library
Cataloguing in Publication data

Mammals of the British Isles Handbook – 4th ed.
I. British Isles. Mammals
I. Harris, S. (Stephen), 1950–
II. Yalden, D.W. (Derek W.), 1940–
III. The Mammal Society
599.0941

ISBN 978-0-906282-65-6

Library of Congress
Cataloging in Publication data
Mammals of the British Isles Handbook/
edited by S. Harris & D.W. Yalden – 4th ed.

ISBN 978-0-906282-65-6
iv+799 pp.

Mammals – British Isles. Mammals. I. Harris, S. (Stephen), 1950– II.
Yalden, D.W. (Derek W.), 1940– III. The Mammal Society
QL727.H36   2008
599.0941

WITHDRAWN

MONROE COUNTY
COMMUNITY COLLEGE
MONROE, MY

3 3131 00094 4219

Contents

Preface and acknowledgements

Perhaps appropriately for a mammal handbook, this has had a long gestation. The most recent of the three previous editions, published for The Mammal Society by Blackwell Scientific Publications in 1991, has been long out of print and increasingly obsolete. As then Chairman of the Society, Professor S. Harris started to produce a new edition in 1998. Blackwell's said that they were no longer interested in publishing it, but generously handed all copyright back to the Society. New authors were recruited, and the preparation of the new edition was about 95% complete by early 2000, when a series of accidents, involving in part the sale and then resale of the publishers, delayed everything. It has taken a great deal of effort to overcome the understandable inertia and reluctance that had gathered in the last 6 years. The Mammal Society decided to publish the volume itself when the former academic publisher seemed to have lost interest, and as President of The Society, and recently retired, Dr D.W. Yalden undertook to accept the major editorial burden.

The final production of this book would have been impossible without a considerable amount of dedicated help and expertise from many other people, whom we acknowledge and thank. Firstly, all the authors have given their time and expertise in writing their accounts, and in revising them since they were first written in 1999. Their names are listed separately on p. xii–xiv, and appended to their accounts. Each systematic chapter had an expert compiler: they collated the texts within their chapters, and they are also acknowledged at the beginning of each chapter. Turning texts into a consistent style depended on the editorial skills of Kathleen Lyle. Figures, maps and photographs were scanned, trimmed and edited by Sarah Wroot. Sally Geeve compiled the texts, tables and illustrations into the well-designed pages that you are holding, and passed them to the printers. The monochrome drawings by Robert Gillmor which have survived, in many cases, from the first edition, were due for an overhaul; some have been retained, some new monochrome drawings have been added, but the main task of overhauling the portraits of the mammals was undertaken with enthusiasm by Guy Troughton. We thank him for accepting this challenge, and moreover for escalating it from monochrome drawings to a set of colour plates.

As editors, we are grateful for the backing of the Universities of Bristol and Manchester for the support we have had during the gestation of this volume; we are especially grateful to Judith Mills, who collated and archived the accounts submitted in 1999, and has unearthed them for re-use and revision in 2006–2007.

We include a new range of photographs, chosen mostly because they illustrate behaviour or other features, rather than being portraits. Again, we thank the photographers who have generously allowed us to use their work; they are acknowledged as appropriate, beside their work. Among them are Natacha Aguilar, Pia Anderwald, Mick Baines, Ian Beames, Jeremy Benney, David Burn, Brian Bevan, Norma Chapman, Peter Evans, Steve Furness, Frank Greenaway, Tony Holley, Sascha Hooker, Don Hunford, Scott Kraus, Jochen Langbein, Pat Morris, Brian Phipps, Rory Putman, Maren Reichel, Sea Mammals Research Unit, Sue Searle, David Stroud, Paul Thompson, Mark Thompson, Fernando Urgate, Derek Whiteley, Michael Woods, and Derek Yalden. We are particularly grateful to Mark Holley for permission to use some of his late father's photographs of brown hares. The authorities of the Natural History Museum (formerly the BM(NH)) and the Trustees of the National Museums of Scotland allowed us to photograph skins in their care or supplied photographs of them. A few images that we could not obtain directly from members were bought from Ardea, and we thank them too for their generosity.

S. Harris   D.W. Yalden
29 September 2007

Contributors

Marjan Addink
    National Museum of Natural History, PO Box
    9517, 2300 RA Leiden, The Netherlands
Natacha Aguilar Soto
    Department of Animal Biology, BIOECOMAC,
    University of La Laguna, 38256 La Laguna,
    Tenerife, Canary Islands
Pia Anderwald
    Sea Watch Foundation, Cynifryn, Llanfaglan,
    Caernaarfon, Gwynedd LL54 5RA
    panderwald@hotmail.com
P.A. Baker
    School of Biological Sciences, Plant Sciences
    Laboratories, The University of Reading,
    Whiteknights, Reading RG6 6AS
    p.j.baker@reading.ac.uk
S.J. Baker
    Natural England, Block 3, Government
    Buildings, Burghill Road, Westbury-on-Trym,
    Bristol BS10 6NJ
    simon.baker@naturalengland.org.uk
E. Balharry
    The Croft, Tomich, Cannich, Beauly,
    Inverness-shire IV4 7LY
    lizbalharry@btopenworld.com
L. Berge
    formerly School of Biological Sciences,
    University of Bristol, Woodland Road, Bristol
    BS8 1UG *leneberge1@hotmail.com*
R.J. Berry
    Department of Biology, University College
    London, London WC1E 6BT *rjberry@ucl.ac.uk*
J.D.S. Birks
    Swift Ecology Ltd, Glen Cottage, Lower
    Dingle, West Malvern, Worcs WR14 4BQ
    johnny.birks@swiftecology.co.uk
J.R. Boran
    Faculty of Engineering & Physical Sciences,
    University of Manchester, PO Box 88,
    Manchester M60 1QD
P.W. Bright
    School of Biological Sciences, Royal Holloway,
    University of London, Egham, Surrey
    TW20 0EX *p.bright@rhul.ac.uk*
A.P. Buckle
    School of Biological Sciences, The University
    of Reading, Whiteknights, Reading, Berkshire,
    RG6 6AJ *alan@alanbuckleconsulting.com*

David J. Bullock
    The National Trust, Heelis, Kemble Drive,
    Swindon SN2 2NA *david.bullock@national
    trust.org.uk*
T.D. Burkitt
    Coolies, Muckross, Killarney, Co. Kerry, Ireland
N.G. Chapman
    29 The Street, Barton Mills, Suffolk IP28 6AA
    ngchapman@btopenworld.com
S. Churchfield
    Department of Anatomy & Human Sciences,
    King's College London, Guy's Campus,
    London SE1 1UL *sara.churchfield@kcl.ac.uk*
P.J. Clapham
    National Marine Mammal Lab, Alaska
    Fisheries Science Center, 7600 Sand Point
    Way NE, Seattle, WA 98115, USA
    phillip.clapham@noaa.gov
M. Cole
    Scottish Natural Heritage, 12 Hope Terrace,
    Edinburgh EH9 2AS *mairi.cole@snh.gov.uk*
A. Collet
    formerly CRMM, Institut de la Mer et du
    Littoral, Port des Minimes, 1700 La Rochelle,
    France
A.S. Cooke
    Greenlawns, High Street, Bury, Huntingdon,
    Cambridgeshire PE26 2NQ
D.P. Cowan
    Central Science Laboratory, Sand Hutton, York
    YO41 1LZ *d.cowan@csl.gov.uk*
M.J. Daniels
    Deer Commission for Scotland, Great Glen
    House, Leachkin Road, Inverness IV3 8NW
    mike.daniels@dcs.gov.uk
E. Dansie
    Reindeer House, Glenmore, Aviemore,
    Inverness-shire PH22 1QU
R. Delahay
    Central Science Laboratory, Woodchester Park
    Research Unit, Nympsfield, Glos GL10 3UJ
    r.delahay@csl.gov.uk
K. Dingerkus
    Giorria Environmental Services, Ardacarha,
    Bohola, Co. Mayo, Ireland *karina@giorria.com*
C.D. Duck
    Sea Mammal Research Unit, Gatty Marine
    Laboratory, University of St Andrews, St
    Andrews, Fife KY16 8LB

N. Dunstone
    School of Biological and Biomedical Sciences,
    University of Durham, South Road, Durham
    DH1 3LE *nigel.dunstone@durham.ac.uk*
A.C. Entwistle
    Fauna & Flora International, 4th Floor,
    Jupiter House, Station Road, Cambridge, CB1
    2JD *abigail.entwistle@fauna-flora.org*
P.G.H. Evans
    Sea Watch Foundation, Cynifryn, Lllanfaglan,
    Caernaarfon, Gwynedd LL54 5RA
L. Farrell
    41 High Street, Hemingford Grey,
    Cambridgeshire PE28 BJ
J.R. Flowerdew
    Deptartment of Zoology, University of
    Cambridge, Downing Street, Cambridge CB2
    3EJ *jrf1@cam.ac.uk*
J.C.D. Gordon
    c/o Sea Mammal Research Unit, Gatty Marine
    Laboratory, University of St Andrews, St
    Andrews, Fife KY16 8LB
M.L. Gorman
    School of Biological Sciences, The University
    of Aberdeen, Zoology Building, Tillydrone
    Avenue, Aberdeen AB24 2TZ
    m.gorman@abdn.ac.uk
L.M. Gosling
    University of Newcastle, Newcastle upon
    Tyne, NE2 4HH *l.m.gosling@newcastle.ac.uk*
Martin Goulding
    mjgoulding@mjgoulding.freeserve.co.uk
Shannon Gowans
    Eckerd College, Galbraith Marine Science
    Laboratory, 4200 54th Avenue South, St.
    Petersburg, Florida 33711, USA
F. Greenaway
    frank@greenaway1.demon.co.uk
J. Gurnell
    School of Biological and Chemical Sciences,
    G.E. Fogg Building, Queen Mary, University of
    London, London E1 4NS
Ailsa J. Hall
    Sea Mammal Research Unit, Gatty Marine
    Laboratory, University of St Andrews, St
    Andrews, Fife KY16 8LB
Stephen J.G. Hall
    Department of Biological Sciences, University
    of Lincoln, Riseholme Park, Lincoln LN2 2LG
    sthall@lincoln.ac.uk
E.C. Halliwell
    Countryside Council for Wales, Maes y
    Ffynnon, Penrhosgarnedd, Bangor, Gwynedd
    LL57 2DW *l.halliwell@ccw.gov.uk*
P.S. Hammond
    Sea Mammal Research Unit, Gatty Marine
    Laboratory University of St Andrews, St
    Andrews, Fife KY16 8LB

E.J. Hare
    School of Biological and Chemical Sciences,
    G.E. Fogg Building, Queen Mary, University of
    London, London E1 4NS
    emma_j_hare@hotmail.com
S. Harris
    School of Biological Sciences, University of
    Bristol, Woodland Road, Bristol BS8 1UG
    s.harris@bristol.ac.uk
F.G. Hartley
    Pesticide Usage & Wildlife Management,
    SASA, Roddinglaw Road, Gogar, Edinburgh
    EH12 9FJ *Gill.Hartley@sasa.gov.uk*
J.S. Herman
    Department of Natural Sciences, National
    Museums of Scotland, Chambers Street,
    Edinburgh EH1 1JF
A.J.M. Hewison
    Laboratoire de Comportement et Ecologie de
    la Faune Sauvage, Institut National de la
    Recherche Agronomique BP 52627, 31326
    Castanet-Tolosan, France
    Mark.Hewison@toulouse.inra.fr
R. Hewson
    Blossom Cottage, Aboyne, Aberdeenshire
    AB34 5ER
D. Hills
    Mammal Group, Zoology Department,
    Natural History Museum, London SW7 5BD
A.R. Hoelzel
    Department of Biological and Biomedical
    Sciences, University of Durham, South Road,
    Durham DH1 3LE
Sascha K. Hooker
    Sea Mammal Research Unit, University of St
    Andrews, St Andrews, FIFE KY16 8YG
I.A.R. Hulbert
    BlueSky Telemetry Ltd, PO Box 7500,
    Aberfeldy, Perthshire PH15 2BZ
Jane Hurst
    Faculty of Veterinary Science, The University
    of Liverpool, Liverpool L69 7ZJ
A.M. Hutson
    Winkfield, Station Road, Plumpton Green,
    East Sussex BN7 3BU *hutson.t@btinternet.com*
G.R. Iason
    Macaulay Institute, Craigiebuckler, Aberdeen
    AB15 8QH UK *g.iason@macaulay.ac.uk*
D.J. Jefferies
    Greystoke, 1 Old North Road, Wansford,
    Peterborough PE8 6JR
Nancy Jennings (née Vaughan)
    1 Mendip Villas, Crabtree Lane, Dundry,
    Bristol BS41 8LN *nancy@dotmoth.co.uk*
G. Jones
    School of Biological Sciences, University of
    Bristol, Woodland Road, Bristol BS8 1UG
    Gareth.Jones@bris.ac.uk

R.E. Kenward
Bournemouth University, Poole House, Talbot Campus, Fern Barrow, Poole, Dorset BH12 5BB *reke@ceh.ac.uk*

C.M. King
University of Waikato, Department of Biological Sciences, Private Bag 3105, Hamilton, New Zealand *c.king@waikato.ac.nz*

A.C. Kitchener
National Museums of Scotland, Chambers Street, Edinburgh EH1 1JF *a.kitchener@nms.ac.uk*

S.D. Kraus
New England Aquarium, Central Wharf, Boston, MA 02110, USA *skraus@neaq.org*

X. Lambin
School of Biological Sciences, Zoology Building, Tillydrone Avenue, University of Aberdeen, Aberdeen AB24 2TZ *x.lambin@abdn.ac.uk*

J. Langbein
Chestnut Avenue, Chapel Cleeve, Minehead, Somerset, TA24 6HY UK *deer2@langbein.freeserve.co.uk*

R. Leaper
IFAW, 87-90 Albert Embankment, London SE1 7UD, UK *rleaper@ifaw.org*

Christina Lockyer
North Atlantic Marine Mammal Commission, Polar Environmental Centre, N-9296 Tromsø, Norway *christina.lockyer@nammco.no*

P.W.W. Lurz
IRES, Devonshire Building, School of Biology and Psychology, University of Newcastle, Newcastle upon Tyne NE1 7RU *p.w.w.lurz@newcastle.ac.uk*

D.W. Macdonald
Wildlife Conservation Research Unit, University of Oxford, Tubney House, Abingdon Road, Tubney, Oxon OX13 5QL *david.macdonald@zoo.oxford.ac.uk*

I.J. Mackie
School of Biological Sciences, University of Aberdeen, Tillydrone Avenue, Aberdeen AB24 2TZ *i.mackie@abdn.ac.uk*

F. Marnell
National Parks and Wildlife Service, Department of Environment, Heritage and Local Government, 7 Ely Place, Dublin 2, Ireland *ferdia.marnell@environ.ie*

A.C.W. Marsh
CSa Environmental Planning, 5F Deer Park Business Centre, Eckington, Pershore, Worcs WR10 3DN *aidan.marsh@csaenvironmental.co.uk*

A.R. Martin
British Antarctic Survey, High Cross, Madingley Road, Cambridge CB3 0ET

J.E. Matthews
Countryside Council for Wales, Plas Penrhos Campus, Penrhos Road, Bangor, Gwynedd LL57 2BX *j.matthews@ccw.gov.uk*

K. McAney
Donaghpatrick, Headford, Co. Galway, Ireland *katemcaney@vwt.org.uk*

R.A. McDonald
Central Science Laboratory, Woodchester Park Research Unit, Nympsfield, Glos. GL10 3UJ *r.mcdonald@csl.gov.uk*

J.M. Mead
Division of Mammals, National Museum of Natural History, Smithsonian Institution, Washington DC20560, USA

A.J. Mitchell-Jones
Natural England, Northminster House, Peterborough PE1 1UA *Tony.Mitchell-Jones@naturalengland.org.uk*

W.I. Montgomery
School of Biological Sciences, Queen's University Belfast, MBC, 97 Lisburn Rd, Belfast BT9 7BL *i.montgomery@qub.ac.uk*

P.A. Morris
c/o School of Biological Sciences, Royal Holloway, Egham, Surrey TW20 OEX.

Sinéad Murphy
Sea Mammal Research Unit, Gatty Marine Laboratory, University of St Andrews, St Andrews, Fife KY16 8LB *snm4@st-andrews.ac.uk*

G. Notarbartolo di Sciara
Tethys Research Institute, Milan City Aquarium, Viale G.B. Gadio 2, 20121 Milano, Italy *giuseppe@disciara.net*

V. Papastavrou
IFAW, The Old Chapel, Fairview Drive, Bristol BS6 6PW *vpapastavrou@ifaw.org*

H. Pepper
AAIS, Alice Holt Lodge, Farnham, Surrey GU10 4LH

S. Parsons
School of Biological Sciences, University of Bristol, Woodland Road, Bristol BS8 1UG

P.P. Pomeroy
Sea Mammal Research Unit, Gatty Marine Laboratory, University of St Andrews, St Andrews, Fife KY16 8LB

R.J. Putman
Keil House, Ardgour, by Fort William, Inverness-shire PH33 7AH

R.J. Quy
Wildlife Management Team, Central Science Laboratory, Sand Hutton, York YO41 1LZ *r.quy@csl.gov.uk*

P.A. Racey
School of Biological Sciences, University of Aberdeen, Tillydrone Avenue, Aberdeen AB24 2TZ

R.D. Ransome
School of Biological Sciences, University of Bristol, Woodland Road, Bristol BS8 1UG
roger.ransome@virgin.net

R. Raynor
Scottish Natural Heritage, Great Glen House, Leachkin Road, Inverness IV3 8NW
robert.raynor@snh.gov.uk

A.J. Read
Center for Marine Conservation, Nicholas School of the Environment, Duke University Marine Laboratory, Beaufort, N Carolina 28516, USA

N.J. Reeve
The Royal Parks, Holly Lodge, Richmond Park, Richmond, Surrey TW10 5HS
nreeve@royalparks.gsi.gov.uk

P. Reynolds
Capreolus Wildlife Consultancy. Motacilla, 2 West Point, Garvald, East Lothian, EH41 4LN
capreolus@gmccbroadband.org

P.W. Richardson
10 Bedford Cottages, Great Brington, Northampton NN7 4JF *PRichaBat@aol.com*

Nicola M. Rivers
Sheffield Wildlife Trust, 37 Stafford Rd, Sheffield, S2 2SF *n.rivers@wildsheffield.com and nrivers@moose-mail.com*

J.M. Russ
j.russ@abdn.ac.uk

H.W. Schofield
The Vincent Wildlife Trust, 46 High Street, Presteigne, Powys LD8 2BE
henryschofield@vwt.org.uk

J.B. Searle
Department of Biology, University of York, PO Box 373, York YO10 5YW *jbs3@york.ac.uk*

C.B. Shiel
Edenville, Kinlough, Co. Leitrim, Ireland
carolineshiel@eircom.net

R.F. Shore
Centre for Ecology and Hydrology, Lancaster Environment Centre, Library Avenue, Bailrigg, Lancaster LA1 4AP *rfs@ceh.ac.uk*

C.S. Smeenk
National Museum of Natural History, PO Box 9517, 2300 RA Leiden, The Netherlands

P.G. Smith
Ty Major, Bettws, Abergavenny NP7 7LH
peter@smithecology.co.uk

B.W. Staines
34 Manor Place, Cults, Aberdeen AB15 9QN

I.R. Stevenson
formerly Department of Biology, University of Stirling, Stirling FK9 4LA

R. Strachan
Environment Agency Wales, Llwyn Brain, Ffordd Penlan, Parc Menai, Bangor LL57 4DE
rob.strachan@environment-agency.wales.gov.uk

S.M. Swift
Drumore, Blacklunans, Blairgowrie, Perthshire PH10 7LA *Drumore1898@aol.com*

F.H. Tattersall
2 Eysey, Cricklade, Swindon SN6 6LP
fran@selectsolar.co.uk

R.K. Temple
School of Biological Science, Royal Holloway, Egham, Surrey TW20 0EX.

P.M. Thompson
Lighthouse Field Station, School of Biological Sciences, University of Aberdeen, Cromarty, Ross-shire, IV11 8YJ

R.C. Trout
Forest Research, Alice Holt Lodge, Farnham, Surrey GU10 4LH *roger.trout@forestry.gsi.gov.uk*

G.I. Twigg
6 Wentworth Way, Ascot, Berks SL5 8HU
grahamtwigg@btinternet.com

K. Van Waerebeek
CEPEC, Museo de Delfines, Pucusana, Peru

R. Waters (née Warren)
Natural England, Genesis 1, University Road, Heslington, York YO10 5ZQ
Ruth.Waters@naturalengland.org.uk

D. Waters
Institute of Integrative and Comparative Biology, L. C. Miall Building, University of Leeds, Leeds LS2 9JT *D.A.Waters@leeds.ac.uk*

B. Wilson
Scottish Association for Marine Science, Dunstaffnage Marine Laboratory, Oban, Argyll PA37 1QA *Ben.Wilson@sams.ac.uk*

G. Wilson
Central Science Laboratory, Woodchester Park Research Unit, Nympsfield, Glos GL10 3UJ
g.wilson@csl.gov.uk

G.L. Woodroffe
Finnoch, Croft Green, Sinnington, York YO62 6SJ *gordon.woodroffe@btinternet.com*

D.W. Yalden
formerly School of Life Sciences, University of Manchester, M13 9PL
d.w.yalden@manchester.ac.uk

1

Introduction

D.W. Yalden

This is the fourth edition of *The Handbook of British Mammals*, but to remove any ambiguity of its coverage, which has always been the mammals of the whole archipelago and its surrounding seas, we have rephrased the name: *Mammals of the British Isles: Handbook, 4th edition*. We aim to provide a comprehensive and authoritative coverage of all wild mammals within this area. We take the British Isles to be a geographical, not political, term. It includes the main islands of Great Britain (England, Scotland, Wales), Ireland (Northern Ireland, Republic of Ireland) and the Isle of Man. The largest island does not have a specific name that excludes surrounding islands (such as Wight, Anglesey, Hebrides, Orkney, Shetland), but we will use the term specifically for the main island, and mention the surrounding islands separately as necessary. The Channel Isles ('Iles Normandes') are not geographically part of the British Isles, nor are they part of the political entity that is the United Kingdom of Great Britain and Northern Ireland, but they are traditionally covered in accounts of the wildlife of the British Isles, and we follow that tradition. The Isle of Man equally is not politically part of the United Kingdom, neither is it covered by the term 'Great Britain and Ireland' (favoured, for instance, in the titles of various bird books), but it is assuredly part of the British Isles.

The need for this revised edition was appreciated in 1997–1998, and work on it began then under the direction of S. Harris. Authors and compilers were approached, and most had written their accounts by early 1999. A series of misfortunes (publishers taken over, bought out, change of editorial staff) meant that the contract lapsed, as did progress. The Mammal Society decided to publish the book itself in 2004, and D.W. Yalden has been largely responsible for seeing it to completion.

FORMAT FOR SPECIES ACCOUNTS

Within the systematic accounts, all species believed to have established populations in the British Isles over the last 2000 years are considered. A brief account of the fossil history of mammals is given in Chapter 3, including those species that occurred into Postglacial times – putative native species – but which became extinct before the Romans arrived. Those that have only developed ephemeral colonies or existed (so far?) for a short while in the wild are considered in Chapter 13. Within the account of each species, a standardised format is followed, though vagrants and extinct or occasional species get a briefer treatment; the categories are explained and discussed here.

CLASSIFICATION

The sequence of Orders, Families, Genera and Species is indicated by the contents list on pp. v–ix. The familiar order, which ran from Insectivora to Artiodactyla, has been changed to match current thoughts on evolution and phylogeny, particularly as summarised in [49], and following studies that have reviewed the whole of the Mammalia (e.g. [27]). Introductory notes on Order, Family and Genus summarise their content and explain recent changes.

In following [49], we introduce not only an unfamiliar sequence but some unfamiliar names, notably *Myodes* to replace *Clethrionomys*. Strictly, we should include the Pinnipedia (seals) within the order Carnivora, and combine the Cetacea with the Artiodactyla as the order Cetartiodactyla, if we accept the most recent phylogenetic analyses [27], but there are editorial and pragmatic reasons for retaining separate chapters. Molecular evidence, in particular, but also anatomical and palaeontological data, while confirming that pinnipeds form a monophyletic lineage, locates the seals Phocidae, sea lions Otariidae and walruses Odobenidae close to weasels Mustelidae within the Carnivora [1, 16]. Likewise, the Cetacea are closely related, within the Artiodactyla, to the Hippopotamidae [39]. Conversely, what we loosely group as the insectivores, and used formally to classify as the order Insectivora, are now considered to be two orders, Erinaceomorpha and Soricomorpha; these have little in common except small size, insectivorous diets, and a number of shared primitive characters which are less convincing than the derived characters that separate them, but it is convenient for us still to combine them in one chapter.

NOMENCLATURE

The current scientific name is given, along with author, date and type locality. Vernacular names are not covered by formal rules; those given largely follow [49], but popular usage in the British Isles is sometimes followed (e.g. common seal, rather than harbour seal). Synonyms that have been used in local literature, or based on British or Irish specimens, are quoted (subspecific names, however, appear under 'Variation'). Vernacular names, including those from Celtic languages where relevant to the animal's occurrence, and names for sexes and young, are given where they have some currency, but we do not provide comprehensive lists of all dialect and local names.

RECOGNITION

Principle recognition features, especially those useful in the field, are summarised, but should be read in combination with diagnostic characters given under higher categories (Order, Family, Genus) and in any associated tables.

SIGN

Confined to those of practical use in the field; well illustrated in [4] and [23]. A popular and easily accessible summary can be found in [46].

DESCRIPTION

Generally amplifies the features given under 'Recognition', including details useful in laboratory or museum conditions, and detailing differences due to sex, age and season. Reference should be made to the plates, and to standard field guides (e.g. [26, 42]. Many books, including this one, include colour photographs, and these can be very valuable, but because of differences in lighting, comparison of colour from species to species is dubious, and size is not usually evident. More detailed descriptions of appearance, skulls and teeth are given in [30]. Chromosome number and appearance is a valuable taxonomic character in many groups; karyotypes of most European mammals are reviewed in [53] and (for bats) [52].

RELATIONSHIPS

This mainly concerns taxonomic relationships, increasingly as revealed by molecular studies. Ecological relationships, particularly with nearly related species, may also be discussed.

MEASUREMENTS

Statements of size can be more misleading than helpful if age, sex and source, as well as sample size, are not specified. Mostly available data are summarised in tables; otherwise, only general indications are given. Detailed skull and tooth measurements are tabulated in [30].

VARIATION

Geographical variation is described first, starting with differences between European and British or Irish populations, then with differences between and within them. It is realised that many nominal subspecies are less distinct than once thought, and many named subspecies cannot be justified. Where they can be recognised, they are described in text or tables; otherwise nominal subspecies are just listed. Colour and other variants are mentioned.

DISTRIBUTION

In describing geographical distributions, we use a variety of formal and informal terms, as well as county and other names. Within the British Isles, there are formal terms such as Highland Scotland (Scotland north of the Highland boundary fault), Lake District, Peak District, New Forest and East Anglia (a poorly defined region which includes Norfolk, Suffolk and Essex), as well as informal phrases such as southern, midland, northern. In considering wider distributions, Palaearctic is a long-established term in zoogeography, to encompass Europe and most of Asia, north of the main mountain ranges (Caucasus–Pamirs–Himalaya–Tibetan plateau), along with a fringe of North Africa and a part of the Middle East which shares similar faunas. Europe is a less-clear term (including or excluding Russia west of the Ural Mountains and north of the Caucasus?); for present purposes it is the region, west of the borders of Russia–Byelorussia–Ukraine, covered by the recent atlas of European mammals [31].

Distribution maps, drafted by D.W. Yalden, have used the published atlas [2] for Great Britain (with some updating from [6, 40]) and relied on [19] for Ireland. In a change from previous editions, some attempt has been made to indicate status within the British Isles by shading. On these, black indicates regular or usual range; dark grey, scattered but regular occurrence; light grey, rare occurrences, vagrants, or scarce and beyond the regular range. For a few species, structured surveys allow these maps to be more nearly a density map; the captions indicate when this is so.

For wider distributions, the European atlas [31] for Europe west of Russia has been used. World maps rely heavily on those in the third edition, which were largely drawn by G.B. Corbet, and largely based on [8], but have been updated and corrected where possible, e.g. from accounts in the American Society of Mammalogist's series *Mammalian Species*.

HISTORY

The general history of the mammal fauna of Great Britain and Ireland is summarised in Chapter 3.

Information specific to the species is summarised here, including where possible information from Europe as well as the British Isles. General accounts of Pleistocene mammals for Europe in [22] and the British Isles in [47] remain useful. More recent mammalian history in the British Isles is summarised in [51].

HABITAT

Most mammals require adequate cover, as protection against predators and disturbance, and an adequate food supply. Habitat can be described generally in landscape and vegetational terms, but specific features (e.g. den sites) are also given here.

SOCIAL ORGANISATION AND BEHAVIOUR

Information is usually summarised, where available, in the following sequence: group size and structure, dispersion (home range or territory, and marking thereof), hierarchy, communication (visual, vocal, olfactory), agonistic behaviour, seasonal patterns (including dispersal and migration), burrowing, nest-building, locomotion, grooming, defence, urination/defecation and hibernation. Where systematic studies have been undertaken of behaviour in the wild, these have preference. Often captive studies or anecdotal information is all that is available; this is always interesting, but might be abnormal in the light of systematic studies. The general review of social behaviour [38] and the two-volume treatise on social use of odours in mammals [7] are valuable. Annual cycles are summarised for most species by linear charts.

FEEDING

As with behaviour, information on diet can be swamped by anecdotal data, often on unusual items, and preference is given to systematic studies with adequate sample sizes. Data are tabulated where possible. Feeding behaviour is summarised here, as well as impact on food species and food requirements.

BREEDING

Normally a brief synopsis is followed by seasonality, courtship, mating, gestation, litter size, birth, development of young through lactation to weaning, productivity. Mammalian reproduction is reviewed in [20].

POPULATION

Population size, density, age structure, survival and longevity are covered here. A set of data for Great Britain that summarises much information on density and suggests population estimates for each species is presented in [18].

MORTALITY

Covers predation, persecution and disease. Systematic data are few, but predation frequencies on small mammals are given in [44, 45] (tawny owl), [17, 24] (barn owl), [10] (small mustelids) and [50] (domestic cats). For a few species life tables are available. The impact of traffic is poorly documented, except for a few species where adequate samples of radio-tagged animals have been followed (e.g. fox, badger).

PARASITES

Ectoparasites (mainly fleas, lice, mites, ticks), endoparasites (mostly trematodes, cestodes, nematodes) and protozoans are not exhaustively listed; that would make transient records of occasional parasites seem more important than they really are. Efforts are made to summarise regular parasites and their prevalences, on the basis of adequate sampling. The information is tabulated where possible. Major diseases (bacteria, viruses) are also acknowledged.

These accounts rely heavily on the expertise of those who helped with previous editions, notably A.M. Hutson (insects), K.H. Hyatt (acarines), J. Lewis (helminths) and T. Healing (microbial parasites).

RELATIONS WITH HUMANS

This covers economic status, both as pest and game, conservation concerns, legislative status and, where relevant, maintenance in captivity, as well as study methods.

LITERATURE

This section draws attention to a few principle sources, popular or scientific monographs, for a species. The citations for detailed information in the text are collected, in numerical order, in the reference list at the end of each chapter.

Some sources which are relevant to most or all chapters, cover British and Irish mammals in general, and have underlain much of the detail, are the following:

- Arnold [2]: Distribution atlas for mammals in Great Britain, at 10 × 10 km scale, with useful analysis of ways in which records were obtained.

- Barrett-Hamilton & Hinton [5]: Major early and detailed coverage with much historical detail, unfortunately never completed – covers insectivores, bats, lagomorphs and rodents.

- Corbet [8, 9]: A systematic checklist, with brief keys and maps, of all Palaearctic mammals.

- Duff & Lawson [11]: A straightforward list of the mammals of the world; not as comprehensive as [49], but more accessible, 312 rather than 2142 pp.

- Fairley [13]: A detailed and comprehensive bibliography of Irish mammal literature.

- Fairley [14, 15]: Two accounts of Irish mammals reflecting much personal involvement; selective rather than comprehensive in their coverage.

- Hayden & Harrington [19]: A comprehensive review of Irish mammals.

- Hayssen *et al.* [20]: Update of an earlier compendium [3] of reproductive data – litter size, length of gestation, lactation, etc.

- Macdonald [25]: A comprehensive, abundantly illustrated, encyclopedia of mammals of the world, covering especially behaviour and ecology.

- McKenna & Bell [28]: A reasoned classification of genera, families and orders of mammals; being overtaken by molecular studies, but a basic reference, replacing [43].

- Millais [29]: A comprehensive three-volume account of the mammals of Great Britain and Ireland, with valuable historic information.

- Miller [30]: Taxonomic coverage of European mammals, with excellent descriptions of skulls and teeth, and tables of measurements.

- Mitchell-Jones *et al.* [31]: A distribution atlas for European mammals, at 50 × 50 km level.

- Niethammer & Krapp [33–36], continued in [12, 21, 41, 48]: A thorough and detailed handbook of European mammals, well illustrated, excellent distribution maps; in German.

- Nowak [37]: A thorough two-volume account of the world's mammals, genus by genus, each illustrated; regularly updated (currently sixth edition, seventh in preparation).

- Simpson [43]: Long accepted as the standard classification of mammals, now superseded by [28], and by new molecular work.

- Wilson & Reeder [49]: The third edition of the standard, comprehensive, listing of mammalian species, with taxonomic details (date, author, synonyms, geographic range).

The principal journals containing papers on British mammals include the following:

- *Mammal Review*, published by Blackwell Scientific Publications for The Mammal Society; mainly review articles covering all aspects of mammalogy, but with an emphasis on British mammals.

- *Journal of Zoology*, formerly *Proceedings of the Zoological Society of London*, published by Blackwell Scientific Publications for the Zoological Society of London; original research papers on all animals, including many on mammals.

- *Journal of Applied Ecology, Journal of Animal Ecology*, published by Blackwell Scientific Publications for the British Ecological Society; original research papers on all animals, respectively of applied (conservation, population management) or more theoretical ecology, including some important papers on British mammals.

- *Journal of Mammalogy*, published by the American Society of Mammalogists; emphasis on North American mammals, but increasingly global in coverage.

- *Mammalian Species*, a part-work rather than a journal, published by the American Society of Mammalogists. Each is a short (2–14 pp), comprehensive review of a named species; about 20–30 accounts published annually, so far around 800 species covered.

- *Mammalia*, published by the Museum Nationale d'Histoire Naturelle, Paris; original research papers, in French or English, and short notes, many on European mammals.

- *Mammalian Biology*, formerly *Zeitschrift für Säugetierkunde*, published by Paul Parey for the Deutsche Gesellschaft für Säugetierkunde; original research papers, mostly European mammals, now mostly in English.

- *Acta Theriologica*, published by the Polish Academy of Sciences' Mammal Research Institute at Białowieża; original research papers, in English, mostly on European mammals, though increasingly global.

REFERENCES

1 Arnason, U. *et al.* (2006) Pinnipede phylogeny and a new hypothesis for their origin and dispersal. *Molecular Phylogenetics and Evolution*, **41**, 435–354.

2 Arnold, H. (1993) *Atlas of mammals in Britain*. ITE/JNCC, HMSO, London.

3 Asdell, S.A. (1964) *Patterns of mammalian reproduction*. 2nd ed. Cornell University Press, Ithaca, NY.

4 Bang, P. & Dahlstrom, P. (1974) *Collins guide to animal tracks and signs*. Collins, London.

5 Barrett-Hamilton, G.E.H. & Hinton, M.A.C. (1911–1921) *A history of British mammals*. Gurney & Jackson, London.

6 Battersby, J. (2005) *UK mammals: species status and population trends*. JNCC/Tracking Mammals Partnership, Peterborough.

7 Brown, R.E. & Macdonald, D.W. (1985) *Social odours in mammals*. Clarendon Press, Oxford.

8 Corbet, G.B. (1978) *The mammals of the Palaearctic region: a taxonomic review*. British Museum (Natural History), London.

9 Corbet, G.B. (1984) *The mammals of the Palaearctic Region: a taxonomic review: Supplement*. British Museum (Natural History), London.

10 Day, M.G. (1968) Food habits of British stoats (*Mustela erminea*) and weasels (*M. nivalis*). *Journal of Zoology*, **155**, 485–497.

11 Duff, A. & Lawson, A. (2004) *Mammals of the world. A checklist*. A.& C. Black, London.

12 Duguy, R. & Robineau, D. (eds.) (1992) *Handbuch der Säugetiere Europas Band 6/II Pinnipedia*. Akademische Verlagsgesellschaft, Wiesbaden.

13 Fairley, J. (1984) *An Irish beast book*, 2nd edn. Blackstaff Press, Belfast.

14 Fairley, J.S. (1992) *Irish wild mammals: a guide to the literature*, 2nd ed. Privately published, J. Fairley, Galway.

15 Fairley, J. (2001) *A basket of weasels*. Privately published, J. Fairley, Belfast.

16 Flynn, J.J. & Nedbal, M.A. (1998) Phylogeny of the Carnivora (Mammalia): congruence vs compatability among multiple data sets. *Molecular Phylogenetics and Evolution*, **9**, 414–426.

17 Glue, D.E. (1974) Food of the barn owl in Britain and Ireland. *Bird Study*, **21**, 200–210.

18 Harris, S. *et al.* (1995) *A review of British mammals: population estimates and conservation status of British mammals other than cetaceans*. JNCC, Peterborough.

19 Hayden, T. & Harrington, R. (2000) *Exploring Irish mammals*. Town House, Dublin.

20 Hayssen, V., van Tienhoven, A., and van Tienhoven, A. (1993) *Asdell's patterns of mammalian reproduction: a compendium of species-specific data*. Cornell University Press, Ithaca, NY.

21 Krapp, F. (ed.) (2004). *Handbuch der Säugetiere Europas Band 4/II: Chiroptera 2*. Akademische Verlagsgesellschaft, Wiesbaden.

22 Kurten, B. (1968). *Pleistocene mammals of Europe*. Weidenfeld & Nicolson, London.

23 Lawrence, M.J. & Brown, R.W. (1974) *Mammals of Britain: their tracks, trails and signs* (revised edition). Blandford, London.

24 Love, A. *et al.* (2000) Changes in the food of British barn owls (*Tyto alba*) between 1974 and 1997. *Mammal Review*, **30**, 107–129.

25 Macdonald, D.W. & Barrett, P. (1993) *Collins field guide: Mammals of Britain and Europe*. Collins, London.

26 Macdonald, D.W. (ed.) (2001) *The new encyclopedia of mammals*. Oxford University Press, Oxford.

27 Madsen, O. *et al.* (2001) Parallel adaptive radiations in two major clades of placental mammals. *Nature*, **409**, 610–614.

28 McKenna, M. & Bell, S.K. (1997) *Classification of mammals above the species level*. Columbia University Press, New York.

29 Millais, J.G. (1904) *Mammals of Great Britain and Ireland*. Longmans Green, London.

30 Miller, G.S. (1912) *Catalogue of the mammals of Western Europe*. British Museum (Natural History), London.

31 Mitchell-Jones, A.J. *et al.* (1999) *The atlas of European mammals*. Poyser, London.

32 Niethammer, J. & Krapp, F. (eds) (1978) *Handbuch der Säugetiere Europas. Band 1/I Rodentia 1*. Akademische Verlagsgesellschaft, Wiesbaden (continued in [12, 21, 33–36, 41, 48].

33 Niethammer, J. & Krapp, F. (eds.) (1982) *Handbuch der Säugetiere Europas Band 2/I Rodentia 2*. Akademische Verlagsgesellschaft, Wiesbaden.

34 Niethammer, J. & Krapp, F. (eds.) (1986) *Handbuch der Säugetiere Europas Band 2/II Artiodactyla*. Akademische Verlagsgesellschaft, Wiesbaden.

35 Niethammer, J. & Krapp, F. (eds.) (1990) *Handbuch der Säugetiere Europas Band 3/I Insectivora, Primates*. Akademische Verlagsgesellschaft, Wiesbaden.

36 Niethammer, J. & Krapp, F. (eds.) (2001) *Handbuch der Säugetiere Europas Band 4/I Chiroptera 1*. Akademische Verlagsgesellschaft, Wiesbaden.

37 Nowak, R.M. (1999) *Walker's mammals of the world*, 6th edn. Johns Hopkins University Press, Baltimore, MD.

38 Poole, T.B. (1985) *Social behaviour in mammals*. Blackie, Glasgow.

39 Price, S.A. *et al.* (2005) A complete phylogeny of the whales, dolphins and hoofed mammals (Cetartiodactyla). *Biological Reviews*, **80**, 445–473.

40 Richardson, P. (2000) *Distribution atlas of bats in Britain and Ireland*. Bat Conservation Trust, London.

41 Robineau, D., Duguy, R. & Klima, M. (eds.) (1995) *Handbuch der Säugetiere Europas Band 6/I Cetacea*. Akademische Verlagsgesellschaft, Wiesbaden.

42 Schober, W. & Grimmberger, E. (1989) *A guide to bats of Britain and Europe*. Hamlyn, London.

43 Simpson, G.G. (1945) The principles of classification and a classification of the mammals. *Bulletin of the American Museum of Natural History*, **85**, i–xvi, 1–350.

44 Southern, H.N. (1954) Tawny owls and their prey. *Ibis*, **96**, 384–410.

45 Southern, H.N. (1970) The natural control of a population of tawny owls. *Journal of Zoology*, **162**, 197–285.

46 Strachan, R. (1995) *Mammal detective*. Whittet, London.

47 Stuart, A.J. (1982) *Pleistocene vertebrates in the British Isles*. Longman, London.

48 Stubbe, M. & Krapp, F. (eds.) (1993) *Handbuch der Säugetiere Europas Bands 5/I, 5/II Carnivora*. Akademische Verlagsgesellschaft, Wiesbaden.

49 Wilson, D.E. & Reeder, D.M. (2005) *Mammal species of the world. A taxonomic and geographic reference*. 2 vols. Johns Hopkins University Press, Baltimore, MD.

50 Woods, M. *et al.* (2003) Predation of wildlife by domestic cats *Felis catus* in Great Britain. *Mammal Review*, **33**, 174–188.

51 Yalden, D.W. (1999) *The history of British mammals*. Poyser, London.

52 Zima, J. & Horacek, I. (1985) Synopsis of karyotypes of vespertilionid bats. *Acta Universitatis Carolinae Biologica*, **1981**, 311–329.

53 Zima, J. & Král, B. (1984) Karyotypes of European mammals. III. *Acta Scientiarum Naturalium Academiae Scientiarum Bohemoslovacae Brno*, **18**, parts 7 (1–51), 8 (1–62) and 9 (1–51).

2

The mammal fauna of the British Isles in perspective

S. Harris, P.A. Morris & D.W. Yalden

The British Isles lie at the western extremity of the Palaearctic zoogeographical zone, a region that extends from Ireland across Europe, through northern Asia to the eastern tip o°f Siberia, and south to the Mediterranean coast of North Africa (roughly from 35° N to 78°N).

The British Isles, lying between 50° and 61° N, have a mammal fauna appropriate to the cool temperate part of this zone, naturally lacking species characteristic of warmer (white-toothed shrews, genet, mole-rats) or cooler (reindeer, arctic fox, lemmings) climates. Moreover, their fauna is impoverished, by comparison with nearby continental countries, due to the 8000-year isolation of the islands (Table 2.1). This characteristic is more extreme for Ireland than Great Britain, and even more so for the Isle of Man and the Scottish islands. The Channel Isles are included here although they are zoogeographically part of France; they too have impoverished mammal faunas compared with their nearest mainland.

Ireland has a terrestrial mammal fauna (i.e. excluding Cetacea) of only 31 species, of which 13 are introduced, compared with 58 in Great Britain (including 14 introductions – Table 2.2). This heavy representation of introduced mammals (42% and 24% respectively) is also a characteristic feature of the mammal faunas of Ireland and Great Britain. All Irish species occur in Great Britain, and all native British species occur in nearby European countries. However, few of the

smaller mammals occur in Ireland, and several southern species which occur in France are absent from Great Britain (see Chapter 3). Smaller mammals are particularly under-represented in Great Britain and Ireland, whose faunas are dominated by larger species.

Since the previous edition of this *Handbook,* two bats have been added to the native fauna: Nathusius' pipistrelle now breeds, having previously been recognised only as a vagrant, and soprano pipistrelle has been distinguished from common pipistrelle. One extinct native, wild boar, has re-established itself by escaping from farms (though might be regarded as feral swine, not true wild boar), and beaver is currently being considered for reintroduction. Several more vagrant bats have also been reported (Savi's and Kuhl's pipistrelles from southern Europe, little brown bat, big brown bat and silver-haired bat from North America), perhaps due to changing climate and increased travel, which increases the chances of accidental carriage, but also reflecting increased expertise and watchfulness of bat recorders.

Several species reach their northern limits within Great Britain; yellow-necked mouse, harvest mouse and dormouse are confined to the southern half (although all three occur further north elsewhere in Europe). Even the bats, despite their mobility, show restricted distributions: one is confined to southern England (grey long-eared bat), six occur in England and Wales but not Scotland (both horseshoe bats, Brandt's, Bechstein's, barbastelle, serotine), and another (noctule) only reaches southern Scotland. Except for the lesser horseshoe, bat species missing from Scotland are also absent from Ireland. These restrictions are partly due to climate, but exaggerated by the fact that northern and western Britain is higher and more acidic, so that agricultural use and natural habitats as well as rainfall and temperature alter strongly along a SE–NW gradient. Deciduous woodland, arable farmland and warmer but drier summers are more evident in the south and east, so the restriction of, for instance, dormouse to the SE half of Britain reflects a combination of these factors [4]. Productivity is also generally higher, so that bats are more numerous in SE Britain [24]. Only the

Table 2.1 Comparative numbers of native terrestrial mammal species (i.e. excluding introduced species and Cetacea) (Palaearctic and World figures from [5]).

Ireland	18
Great Britain	44
France	90
Germany	77
Europe (W of Russia)	147
Palaearctic	475
World	4325

Table 2.2 Number of mammal species in the fauna of the British Isles. *Native* species are those that breed here having arrived naturally, either across the land bridge before 8000 bp (see Chapter 3) or by flying or swimming. *Vagrants* are those (bats and seals) that occur occasionally and irregularly. The distinction between 'native' Cetacea, those occurring within continental waters, and 'vagrants', visitors from oceanic waters, is rather arbitrary. *Feral* species are former domestic mammals that have escaped and established breeding populations in the wild, notably sheep, goats, cattle and ponies. Although rabbit and fallow deer are strictly feral populations, they are included here as wild species

	Native (+ introduced)		Additional species	Vagrant	Feral	Extinct
	GB	Ireland	(small islands only)			
Insectivores	5	0 (+2)	3	–	–	–
Bats	17	9	–	6	–	–
Lagomorphs	1 (+2)	1 (+2)	–	–	–	–
Rodents	8 (+6)	2 (+4)	1	–	–	1
Carnivores	8 (+1)	4 (+2)	–	–	–	3
Pinnipeds	2	2	–	5	–	–
Ungulates	3 (+4)	0 (+3)	–	–	4	3
Marsupials	0 (+1)	0	–	–	–	–
Total	44 (+14)	18 (+13)	4	11	4	7
Cetacea	15		9		–	1

mountain hare shows a reciprocal distribution, being confined (as a native) to Ireland and Highland Scotland.

NUMERICAL COMPOSITION OF THE MAMMAL FAUNA

The absolute size of an animal population is less important scientifically, and much harder to study, than trends with time. Nevertheless, it is important to establish just how rare a 'rare species' might be; judgements about the need for conservation, the impact of various mortality factors, community structure, and the need for or merits of culling, all benefit from some estimate of absolute numbers. For a few species, counts of whole populations, or large proportions of them, have been undertaken over many years. Most breeding colonies of grey seals are counted regularly, as are red deer in Highland Scotland. The relatively few breeding colonies and hibernacula of the two horseshoe bats are also known and counted regularly. However, for most species, estimates are based on some combination of likely geographical and ecological range, densities in

suitable habitats, and relative numbers of species in large samples of e.g. bats and small mammals. First estimates for the rarer species were produced by Morris [20], extended to the full range of mammals in Great Britain in [11]. Equivalent numbers for Irish mammals have not been estimated, although a few species (e.g. lesser horseshoe bat, badger) have been enumerated, and others have been estimated here by extrapolation from British data.

For species occurring in defined areas of habitats and with reasonable density estimates for those habitats (e.g. mountain hare, squirrels, dormouse), multiplying the two gives usable estimates of total numbers. For a few species with stratified surveys, relative densities across the country and the distributions of main habitat types give good estimates of total population size (e.g. fox, badger, brown hare). For small mammals and bats, numbers of less well-known species have been estimated by comparison with species and their relative numbers in wider samples (e.g. owl pellet samples of small mammals, house visits for bats). For some species, densities in different habitats, and even their distributions, remain very uncertain (e.g. hedgehog, water shrew, weasel, stoat). The data for Great Britain are presented in Table 2.3. Despite their variable quality, these estimates provide a reasonable basis for comparisons between species, and also with birds, for which similar estimates are available [2, 7]. The estimates are of adult mammal numbers before the breeding season; figures for domestic stock also omit young (under 18 years old for humans). Some population sizes have changed since 1995, and some estimates have been improved, but these have not been altered systematically, so we retain the 1995 estimates for these comparisons; newer information is presented in species accounts where available.

A full set of estimates for all the mammal species allows some interesting comparisons (Fig. 2.1). The predictable relationship between size and abundance (larger mammals are scarcer than small ones) is very evident, but the scarcity of bats relative to equally small insectivores was unexpected [8]. Even more unexpectedly, birds are much rarer than equivalent-sized mammals, although bats are about as common as birds of similar sizes. This fits the empirical observation that the rarest birds (e.g. a few tens of bitterns, a few hundred golden eagles) are much scarcer than the rarest mammals (e.g. a few thousand otters or pine martens). In part, this reflects the fact that birds can fly to look for small patches of suitable habitat and to search widely for mates. Terrestrial mammals are much more restricted in behaviour, but their densities are around 50 times those of birds in similar habitats.

Given the inherent uncertainty in these population estimates, they must be used cautiously (note the reliability scores in Table 2.3), but one rough, reassuring, validation is available. The most abundant wild mammal appears to be the field vole, numbering about 75 million in spring. Assuming that overall numbers remain roughly stable, the number of young produced by them each year should be about equal to the number eaten by all the predators feeding on them, assuming their numbers are also correctly estimated; enough is known about the proportion of the diet contributed by field voles to most predators' diets to estimate their take. The likely annual production of young voles (around 677 million) roughly matches the estimated total dietary requirements of the predatory mammals and birds feeding on them over a year (around 744 million) [6].

This approach allows the relative abundance of each species to be compared with what might be expected for a mammal of its size, so providing an objective assessment of whether a mammal is 'too common' or 'too rare'. The former are more likely to be regarded as pests, perhaps in need of control; the latter might be in need of conservation effort [12]. On that basis, rabbit, red and roe deer seem much more abundant than predicted, whereas pine marten, wildcat and polecat are 'less abundant than they should be'. Generally, herbivores are more abundant than expected, but carnivores are rarer. Species with conservation priorities tend to be those that have observably declined, rather than being rare on this criterion (e.g. red squirrel, water vole), but the relative rarity of pine marten, wildcat and dormouse matches their conservation priority. This objective measure of conservation need reveals that the rarest species are all protected by appropriate legislation, except for harvest mouse; however, the badger, with strong legal protection, is close to being 'overabundant'.

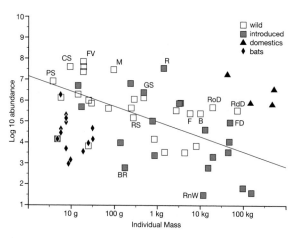

Fig. 2.1 The relationship between abundance and individual body mass for all species of terrestrial mammals in Great Britain (y = 5.023 − 0.719x). Bats and domestic mammals are also plotted, but not included in calculating the regression; they are, respectively 1–3 orders of magnitude less/more abundant than the others. Introduced species indicated in red. A few species are identified by the initials of their vernacular names (**B**adger, **B**lack **R**at, **C**ommon **S**hrew, **F**allow **D**eer, **F**ield **V**ole, **F**ox, **G**rey **S**quirrel, **M**ole, **P**ygmy **S**hrew, **R**abbit, **R**ed **D**eer, **R**ed-necked **W**allaby, **R**ed **S**quirrel, **R**oe **D**eer) (*after [8]; data in Tables 2.3 and 2.5*).

BIOMASS CONTRIBUTION

Although small species (shrews, voles, mice) dominate numerically (Table 2.3), the ecological impact of mammals is better indicated by their biomass. This is because their feeding impact on habitats is related to their sizes, not simply to numbers. Estimating biomass requires multiplying population size by a mean mass for each species, thereby compounding any errors. It is nevertheless

Table 2.3 Estimates of the population sizes and biomasses for mammals in Great Britain (from [11, 26]). Numbers indicate adults before the addition of the year's young; the young of domestic species are similarly omitted. Species are organised in order of increasing abundance. Reliability scores (1 most reliable, 5 least reliable) are explained in [11]. When this table was assembled, the soprano pipistrelle had not been recognised; current knowledge suggests that the two species are about equally numerous, so common and soprano pipistrelles are likely to number about 1 million each

Species	Population	Mass (kg)	Biomass (t)	Reliability
Greater mouse-eared bat	Extinct	0.032	0	1
Coypu	Extinct	6.25	0	1
Nathusius' pipistrelle	?	0.006	?	5
Red-necked wallaby	29	12	0.372	1
Park cattle	45	150	6.75	1
Reindeer	80	100	7	1
Chinese water deer	650	15	9.75	2
Grey long-eared bat	1 000	0.009	0.009	3
Ship rat	1 300	0.175	0.228	2
Bechstein's bat	1 500	0.01	0.015	2
Feral sheep	2 100	20	42	1
Feral ferret	2 500	0.9	2.25	5
Wildcat	3 500	4.5	15.75	3
Feral goat	>3 565	45	160.425	2
Pine marten	3 650	1.5	5.475	2
Greater horseshoe bat	>4 000	0.02	0.08	2
Barbastelle	5 000	0.008	0.04	5
Skomer vole	7 000	0.025	0.175	1
Otter	>7 350	8	58.8	3
Leisler's bat	10 000	0.025	0.25	4
Edible dormouse	10 000	0.14	1.4	3
Sika	11 500	50	575	2
Lesser white-toothed shrew	14 000	0.005	0.07	4
Lesser horseshoe bat	14 000	0.005	0.07	2
Serotine	15 000	0.032	0.48	4
Polecat	15 000	0.9	13.5	3
Brandt's bat	30 000	0.006	0.18	5
Common seal	35 000	75	2 625	2
Whiskered bat	40 000	0.006	0.24	4
Reeves' muntjac	40 000	13	520	3
Noctule	50 000	0.032	1.6	3
Grey seal	93 500	200	18 700	1
Natterer's bat	100 000	0.008	0.8	4

Table 2.3 (cont.)

Species	Population	Mass (kg)	Biomass (t)	Reliability
Fallow deer	100 000	50	5 000	4
American mink	>110 000	0.8	88	3
Daubenton's bat	150 000	0.08	1.2	4
Red squirrel	160 000	0.2	44.8	3
Brown long-eared bat	200 000	0.008	1.6	4
Red fox	240 000	6	1 440	4
Badger	250 000	10.5	2 625	2
Mountain hare	350 000	2.8	980	3
Red deer	360 000	75	27 000	2
Weasel	450 000	0.075	33.75	4
Stoat	462 000	0.25	115.5	4
Common dormouse	500 000	0.018	9	3
Roe deer	500 000	20	10 000	3
Yellow-necked mouse	750 000	0.03	22.5	4
Feral cat	813 000	3.5	2 845.5	4
Brown hare	817 500	3.3	2 697.75	2
Orkney vole	1 000 000	0.025	40	1
Water vole	1 169 000	0.3	350.55	3
Harvest mouse	1 425 000	0.006	8.55	5
Hedgehog	1 555 000	0.5	777.5	4
Water shrew	1 900 000	0.015	28.5	4
Pipistrelle	2 000 000	0.006	12	3
Grey squirrel	2 520 000	0.5	1 260	3
House mouse	>5 192 000	0.015	77.88	5
Common rat	>6 790 000	0.25	1 679.5	4
Pigmy shrew	8 600 000	0.004	34.4	4
Bank vole	23 000 000	0.02	460	3
Mole	31 000 000	0.1	3 100	3
Rabbit	37 500 000	1.5	56 250	3
Wood mouse	38 000 000	0.02	760	3
Common shrew	41 700 000	0.01	417	3
Field vole	75 000 000	0.02	2 250	4
Domestic species				
Horse	750 000	500	375 000	
Pig	853 000	150	127 950	
Cattle	3 908 900	550	2 149 895	
Sheep	20 364 600	45	913 707	
Humans	37 866 500	80	3 029 321	

Table 2.4 The composition of the terrestrial wild mammal fauna of Great Britain, by numbers of species in each order, numbers of individuals in each order, and biomass attributable to each order. Data from Table 2.3 (seals omitted)

Order	Species	Individuals	Biomass
		(thousands)	(t)
Marsupialia	1	<0.1 (<0.1%)	0.4 (<1%)
Rodentia	15	155 523.3 (54.6%)	6 217.5 (5%)
Lagomorpha	3	38 667.5 (13.6%)	59 927.7 (49%)
Insectivora	6	84 769 (29.7%)	4 357.5 (4%)
Chiroptera	14	2 620.5 (0.9%)	18.7 (<1%)
Carnivora	11	2 357 (0.8%)	7 234.5 (6%)
Artiodactyla	10	1 017.9 (0.36%)	43 320.9 (35%)
Total	60	284 955. 2 (100%)	121 077.2 (100%)

informative (Table 2.4). Lagomorphs (49% of total wild mammal biomass) and deer (35%) are much the most important, explaining better than simple numbers their economic and ecological impact, as pests, game and important prey (rabbits and hares) for predator populations. Moreover, the success of agriculture in diverting the ecosystem into supporting the human population is highlighted. Domestic species (humans included) contribute about 97% of the biomass of mammals in the British countryside, leaving only 3% made up of wild mammals. Moreover, half the latter comes from introduced species, with natives contributing only 1.4%. Among the carnivores, although stoats and weasels are the most numerous, badgers and foxes contribute much more biomass, explaining their perceived importance.

HISTORICAL COMPARISONS

The British mammal fauna has been highly modified by human activities over 10 000 years, and especially during the last 5500 years, since the beginnings of agriculture. The extensive introduction of non-native species, the extinction of larger native species (see Chapter 3) and enormous habitat changes have all impacted on faunal composition. The extent of these changes can be illustrated by a speculative comparison of the mammal fauna now present with what it might have been during the Mesolithic (9000 to 6000 years ago). At that time, humans (perhaps numbering only 2500) were hunter-gatherers

exploiting a largely forested environment. Open habitats would have been confined to river valleys, coastal areas and high ground above the natural treeline, the latter mostly in Highland Scotland. Estimating Mesolithic mammal numbers relies on comparisons with their abundance in the well-studied woodlands of the Białowieża National Park in Poland [18, 27], the best-preserved area of such habitat in Europe. Thus the comparison might alternatively be regarded as a comparison with the fauna of central Europe (Table 2.5). Changes to the bat fauna have been omitted due to lack of data. The British Mesolithic fauna would have been dominated numerically by woodland small mammals, notably common shrew, bank vole and wood mouse, but in terms of biomass, the abundant ungulates (elk, aurochs and boar as well as red and roe deer) would have predominated. Overall, wild mammals would have been about as numerous as now (249 million against 285 million), but the biomass would have been about three times greater (339 581 tonnes against 121 077 tonnes). However, the later addition of domestic species, and 36 million humans, suggests that the total mammal biomass in the British countryside today is about 20 times (6 716 950 tonnes) what it was originally. This indicates how far agriculture has changed the landscape, and how little ecological space remains for wild mammals. Some details highlight the changes: field voles were confined largely to river valley grasslands, and perhaps numbered 44 million, not 75 million as now. Conversely, the woodland rodents, bank vole and wood mouse as well as dormouse and red squirrel, would have been much more abundant, and the bank vole was probably the most numerous mammal then. Badgers and foxes are now much more abundant than they were, testimony to the suitability of agricultural land and the abundance of earthworms as well as pastoral prey (including the introduced rabbit), although it is possible that the larger predators (wolf, bear, lynx) restricted their numbers in prehistoric times.

TRENDS WITH TIME

For many purposes, changes in abundance (from year to year, perhaps, or trends over decades) may be more important than total population size. They are also more easily and reliably established. The data are patchy for British mammals, contrasting with more than 40 years of survey for common birds, longer still for some species (since 1927 for herons). Producing data on trends requires regular sampling, not necessarily every year, but this has simply not been done for most mammals. Some species, with formerly patchy distributions (including non-natives spreading from sites of introduction), show their population increases very clearly by their increasing ranges; these have been mapped at regular intervals (most clearly for grey squirrels, but also for polecat, roe, sika and muntjac). The decline of the red squirrel is equally clear from maps of its shrinking distribution. Regular monitoring of riparian sites has demonstrated the recent expansion of otter and decline of water vole. Game-bag data collated by the Game Conservancy [23] are also valuable, although influenced by changes in effort. For example, hedgehogs now have some legal protection and perhaps are not trapped (or reported as trapped) as regularly as formerly; and with more intensive rearing of pheasants, trapping to protect wild broods from stoats and weasels is less intensive [17]. Regular stratified sampling of a range of habitats and populations provides the most reliable evidence of population changes. Counts of grey seals and red deer document strong increases in populations over 40–50 years. Periodic surveys of badgers and brown hares indicate clear increases of the former but little change in the latter. The annual National Bat Monitoring and Dormouse Monitoring Programmes currently offer the best continuous runs of data for smaller species. Regular monitoring is essential to indicate when conservation is needed, confirm its success, suggest when legislation might need changing, or, conversely, monitor the success of control programmes. The Tracking Mammals Partnership, of statutory and voluntary bodies, is attempting to rectify the deficiencies in current monitoring of mammals [3].

CONSERVATION STATUS OF BRITISH MAMMALS

Unlike birds, mammals are not afforded general legal protection, and some are regarded as pests, subject to legal proscription. Householders are required to inform local authorities of the presence of house mice or rats, and those authorities are legally obliged to attempt their extermination (see Chapter 4). Agricultural and forestry pests (e.g. rabbits, grey squirrels, deer) may also be legally culled. Other species are perceived as being in need of conservation, and have legal protection (see Chapter 4), and, in some cases, Biodiversity Action Plans (BAPs) intended to promote their conservation.

EFFECTS OF LEGAL PROTECTION

Despite the lack of adequate monitoring systems for most mammals, some species have clearly undergone marked declines in numbers and/or distribution in the recent past. Giving legal protection to species perceived to be endangered is an obvious response. It was thought that grey seals numbered as few as 500 animals in 1914, leading to the imposition of a close season covering the vulnerable pupping period when cows and calves are on land for 3–4 weeks. A steady increase of around 6% per year has followed since then, perhaps indicating the success of legal protection, since hunting and disturbance of breeding colonies was a major cause of concern [13].

Legal protection for bats has been very beneficial in restricting damage to colonies, which often occur in buildings. Bats have low reproductive rates and population densities, and have been vulnerable both to direct disturbance and to the effects of treating roof timbers with pesticides. Legislation has minimised these threats, even to colonies located in private homes, although this has been somewhat controversial. Although it is not a legal requirement that householders tolerate bats in their homes, they are required to get permission from the statutory authorities before doing anything that might affect the bats or their roost. This has encouraged the recruitment of many expert amateur (and professional) bat surveyors and advisors, and has resulted in a considerable increase in knowledge of bats. Legal protection extends to underground hibernacula, as well as breeding roosts, and the two horseshoe bats have particularly benefited. Particular caves are important to them, as they hang exposed on cave walls, so they have previously suffered severely both from loss of sites and direct disturbance.

However, legal protection is less effective for species not directly threatened by human actions. Dormice, for example, have suffered from habitat

Table 2.5 Comparison of estimates for the numbers and biomass of terrestrial mammals in Great Britain in the Mesolithic period and now (from [11, 18, 27]). The total for the Recent mammal fauna includes a subtotal for feral and introduced species which are not listed separately here (but see Table 2.3). Domestic and human numbers refer to breeding 'adult' populations (over 18 years for humans) to maintain comparability with estimates for pre-breeding populations of wild mammals

Species	Mass (kg)	Mesolithic		Recent	
		Numbers	Biomass (kg)	Numbers	Biomass (kg)
Hedgehog	1.2	3 389 680	4 067 616	1 866 000	777 500
Common shrew	0.01	151 543 000	1 515 430	41 700 000	417 000
Pygmy shrew	0.004	17 492 348	69 969	8 600 000	34 400
Water shrew	0.015	1 504 369	22 566	1 900 000	28 500
Mole	0.1	28 776 130	2 877 613	31 000 000	3 100 000
Mountain hare	2.9	42 131	122 180	350 000	1 015 000
Beaver	20	80 949	1 618 980	0	0
Red squirrel	0.3	11 912 396	3 573 719	160 000	48 000
Dormouse	0.02	25 841 031	510 821	500 000	10 000
Bank vole	0.02	137 802 000	2 756 040	23 000 000	460 000
Field vole	0.03	44 083 772	1 322 513	75 000 000	2 250 000
Root vole	0.06	12 117 000	727 020	0	0
Water vole	0.3	42 371 000	12 711 300	1 169 000	350 700
Wood mouse	0.02	53 914 256	1 078 285	38 000 000	760 000
Red fox	6	72 637	435 822	240 000	1 440 000
Wolf	32	6 603	211 296	0	0
Weasel	0.075	484 244	36 318	450 000	33 750
Stoat	0.25	66 033	16 508	462 000	115 500
Polecat	0.9	110 055	99 050	15 000	13 500
Pine marten	1.5	147 474	221 211	3 650	5 475
Otter	8	22 281	178 248	7 350	58 800
Badger	10.5	13 752	144 396	250 000	2 625 000
Brown bear	255	13 207	3 367 785	0	0
Wildcat	4.5	66 033	297 149	3 500	15 750
Lynx	25	6 603	165 075	0	0
Wild boar	80	954 378	76 350 240	0	0
Roe deer	20	832 793	16 655 860	500 000	10 000 000
Elk	200	64 617	12 923 400	0	0
Red deer	100	1 253 613	125 361 300	360 000	36 000 000

Table 2.5 (cont.)

Species	Mass (kg)	Mesolithic		Recent	
		Numbers	Biomass (kg)	Numbers	Biomass (kg)
Aurochs	400	83 896	33 558 400	0	0
Humans	70	2 500	175 000	43 490 000	3 044 300 000
Horse	500			750 000	375 000 000
Pig	150			853 000	127 950 000
Cattle	550			3 908 900	2 149 895 000
Sheep	45			20 364 600	916 407 000
Total (native)		535 070 781	300 176 110	225 536 500	60 647 375
(introduced, not listed)				56 803 200	68 458 425
Total (wild + domestic)				348 698 200	6 742 657 800

loss and change, while red squirrels have declined primarily because of the spread of grey squirrels. In both cases, legislation offers protection from persecution, but this was not the main cause of their decline. Direct persecution of badgers is now illegal, and their setts are also protected, perhaps contributing to recent substantial increases in abundance. Hedgehogs now enjoy protection from malicious attack, but the effect at population level is negligible; legislation does not protect them from road traffic, mowing machines or other anthropogenic threats, which may represent a significant danger to small populations. The water vole has been granted belated protection, but only after its numbers had fallen drastically, due in part to mink predation which legislation cannot control. Clearly a more targeted approach is needed for mammal conservation, on a species-by-species basis. This is now attempted through BAPs and Species Action Plans (SAPs). Planning policy guidelines and regulations that accompany grants to assist forestry or farming now probably have more long-term implications for mammal conservation than direct legislation, although the latter does serve to highlight the intention to protect and conserve particular species.

BIODIVERSITY ACTION PLANS

There are three principal criteria for conservation that might result in BAP status. Some species are rare, either because they have limited ranges or because their density is naturally low. This is most obviously true for bats, particularly for the rarest of them (Bechstein's, grey long-eared, barbastelle). A second category of mammals are rare, and restricted to only part of their historical range, because of past persecution (pine marten, wildcat, polecat) or because of more recent human-precipitated losses (otter, reduced in England to only 6% of its range by organochlorine pesticide poisoning in the 1970s). Thirdly, some species have shown recent declines, equivalent to 50% or more over a period of 25 years. Applying these criteria can produce some anomalous results. For instance, there is good evidence that pipistrelles have declined that much in recent times, and they are therefore BAP species, despite being the commonest British bats. The much rarer (and more vulnerable) lesser horseshoe bat also qualifies as a BAP species, although it has been increasing through the 1990s, but the whiskered bat, of uncertain status and trend, does not. While polecat and pine marten were much reduced by historical persecution, they have been recovering their range and numbers during the 20th century, and do not have BAP status. Other BAP species include the brown hare, which is not a native mammal, but is characteristic of farmland, and like many farmland birds, it became less common during the 1960s and 1970s. Water voles, which have declined sharply due to habitat loss and predation by mink, and red squirrels, declining as grey squirrels advance, are two species that certainly merit their BAP status, and active conservation. Water voles have benefited from captive breeding and release in protected sites, control of mink and habitat management, especially protection of riparian strips from agricultural encroachment. It has been harder to help red squirrels, but control of grey squirrels has been attempted, most successfully on Anglesey, while red squirrel reserves in large conifer forests have also been created. The dormouse became extinct in half its former range, but captive breeding followed by release has successfully returned it to several of the counties from which it had been lost.

The most acute anomalies resulting from selecting species for BAP listing on these criteria concerned hedgehog and harvest mouse. The hedgehog was initially disqualified because evidence for its decline was considered only anecdotal and there was no statistically robust 'proof' that the level of decline exceeded the necessary threshold. Yet omitting it from BAP listing reduced the prospect of resources being channelled towards establishing the true extent of its decline, perpetuating the problem of inadequate data. For the harvest mouse, there is no statistically robust way to measure decline in population size of what is an irruptive and patchily distributed mammal. Consequently it does not qualify as a BAP species, despite surveys suggesting that it was no longer present at three quarters of the sites where it occurred 25 years earlier.

Clearly, a priority for the future is to establish better monitoring of the changing fortunes of British mammals, comparable with the system for the long-established systems for birds. A pilot study to quantify the abundance of certain species (e.g. rabbit, fox, deer), using the transects established to monitor breeding birds, shows some promise [22], but plans for a comprehensive national mammal monitoring system [16] have not so far come to fruition. The Tracking Mammals Partnership [3] aims to collate data from various monitoring schemes, but an overall strategy is lacking, as are the funds to implement it. [14] review these issues, and publish periodic overviews (e.g. [15].

BRITISH MAMMALS IN THE EUROPEAN CONSERVATION CONTEXT

It is a paradox that most of the mammals regarded as of particular conservation concern in Britain are of less concern on a European scale. Conversely, other species are very abundant here, although relatively scarce on a European scale. Of species causing most concern in Great Britain, red squirrel and dormouse are widespread and relatively abundant across Europe, although the small introduced grey squirrel population in Italy is already having a detectable negative influence on the red squirrels there [25]. Water voles are widespread and abundant, even agricultural and forestry pests, across much of Europe. Among the rarer carnivores, polecat and pine marten are also widespread, and not at risk, although the wildcat has a poorly understood distribution and status in Europe, and the possibility of genetic dilution by feral cats requires investigation. The grey long-eared, Bechstein's and barbastelle bats, although nowhere abundant, are widely distributed and there is no reason to suppose they are threatened on a European scale.

Among the most significant British species in the European context are red deer, grey seal, common seal, badger and otter. It was suggested [21] that the European red deer population (west of the former USSR) was 990 000, of which 270 000 (27%) were in Great Britain. The species has been heavily hunted, and reduced to small and fragmented populations elsewhere, as indeed it was here 200 years ago. The grey seal was estimated [1] to have a total world population of 246 700, and a European population of 121 700, of which 101 500 (respectively 41% or 83%) breed around British coasts; the British and Irish population is still thought to contribute about 40% of the world population [10]. Common seals have a wider European and world range (assuming the Pacific populations belong to the same species), but the seals around the British Isles constitute a significant part of the European total, especially because those in the North Sea have been severely affected by pollution and disease. Similarly, for the badger and otter, the large British and Irish populations comprise significant fractions of European populations which have suffered severely from persecution, pollution, road mortality and legal hunting (cf. [9, 19]).

REFERENCES

1   Anderson, S. (1991) Grey seal *Halichoerus grypus*, pp. 471–480 in Corbet, G.B. & Harris, S. *The handbook of British mammals*, 3rd ed. Blackwell Scientific Publications, Oxford.

2   Baker, H. *et al.* (2006) Population estimates of birds in Great Britain and the United Kingdom. *British Birds*, **99**, 25–44.

3   Battersby, J. (ed.) (2005) *UK mammals: species status and population trends. First report by the Tracking Mammals Partnership*. Joint Nature Conservation Committee Tracking Mammals Partnership, Peterborough.

4   Bright, P. & Morris, P. (1996) Why are dormice rare? A case study in conservation biology. *Mammal Review*, **26**, 157–187.

5   Corbet, G.B. & Hill, J.E. (1991) *A world list of mammalian species*, 3rd ed. British Museum (Natural History), London.

6   Dyczkowski, J. & Yalden, D.W. (1998) An estimate of the impact of predators on the British field vole population. *Mammal Review*, **28**, 165–184.

7   Gibbons, D.W., Reid, J.B. & Chapman, R.A. (1993) *The new atlas of breeding birds in Britain and Ireland: 1988–1991*. Poyser, London.

8   Greenwood, J.J.D. *et al.* (1996) Relations between abundance, body size and species number in British birds and mammals. *Philosophical Transactions of the Royal Society of London Series B*, **351**, 265–278.

9   Griffiths, H. & Thomas, D.H. (1993) The status of the badger *Meles meles* (L. 1758) (Carnivora, Mustelidae) in Europe. *Mammal Review*, **23**, 17–58.

10 Hammond, P.S. *et al.* (2008) Grey seal *Halichoerus grypus*, pp. 538–547, this volume.

11 Harris, S. *et al.* (1995) *A review of British mammals: population estimates and conservation status of British mammals other than Cetacea*. Joint Nature Conservation Committee, Peterborough.

12 Harris, S. *et al.* (2000) Abundance/mass relationships as a quantified basis for establishing mammal conservation priorities, pp. 101–117 in Entwistle, A. & Dunstone, N. (eds) *Priorities for the conservation of mammalian diversity. Has the panda had its day?* Cambridge University Press, Cambridge.

13 Lambert, R.A. (2002) The grey seal in Britain: a twentieth century history of a nature conservation success. *Environment and History*, **8**, 449–474.

14 Macdonald, D.W. & Tattersall, F. (2001) *Britain's mammals: the challenge for conservation*. People's Trust for Endangered Species, London.

15 Macdonald, D.W. & Tattersall, F. (2004) *The state of Britain's mammals 2004*. People's Trust for Endangered Species/Mammals Trust UK, London.

16 Macdonald, D.W. *et al.* (1998). *Proposals for future monitoring of British mammals*. Joint Nature Conservation Committee, Peterborough.

17 McDonald, R.A. & Harris, S. (1999) The use of trapping records to monitor populations of stoats *Mustela erminea* and weasels *M. nivalis*: the importance of trapping effort. *Journal of Applied Ecology*, **36**, 679–688.

18 Maroo, S. & Yalden, D.W. (2000) The Mesolithic mammal fauna of Great Britain. *Mammal Review*, **30**, 243–248.

19 Mason, C.F. & Macdonald, S.M. (1986) *Otters: conservation and ecology*. Cambridge University Press, Cambridge.

20 Morris, P. (1993) *A red data book for British mammals*. Mammal Society, London.

21 Myrberget, S. (1990) *Wildlife management in Europe outside the Soviet Union*. NINA Utreding 018, 1–47.

22 Noble, D. *et al.* (2005) *Winter mammal monitoring: a pilot study*. BTO Research Report 410 and TMS Research Report 5. British Trust for Ornithology, Thetford/The Mammal Society, London.

23 Tapper, S. (1992) *Game Heritage*. Game Conservancy Trust, Fordingbridge.

24 Walsh, A. & Harris, S. (1996) Factors determining the abundance of vespertilionid bats in Britain: geographical, land class and local habitat relationships. *Journal of Applied Ecology*, **33**, 519–529.

25 Wauters, L.A. *et al.* (1997) Replacement of red squirrels by introduced grey squirrels in Italy: evidence from a distribution survey, pp. 79–88 in Gurnell, J & Lurz, P. *The conservation of red squirrels, Sciurus vulgaris L*. People's Trust for Endangered Species, London.

26 Yalden, D.W. (1999) *The history of British mammals*. Poyser, London.

27 Yalden, D.W. (2003) Mammals in Britain – a historical perspective. *British Wildlife*, **14**, 243–251.

Red deer fighting, New Forest. A native species, much more abundant in the Mesolithic, and reduced nearly to extinction in the 19th C, but now recovered to the extent that GB hosts about a quarter of the W European population (*photo B. Phipps*).

3

History of the fauna

D.W. Yalden & A.C. Kitchener

The principal interest of fossil mammals for most mammalogists is the evidence they provide for the origin and history of the present-day mammal fauna. From this viewpoint, only the last 15 000 years are important, and this chapter concentrates on this more recent history, from the end of the Pleistocene to Roman times, 2000 years ago. However, the British Isles have also yielded significant mammal faunas of Mesozoic, Eocene–Oligocene and Pleistocene ages which are worth noticing.

MESOZOIC MAMMALS

The evolution of mammals from reptiles is well documented in the fossil record [23]: so well documented that deciding which evolutionary change heralds the emergence of the first mammal is rather arbitrary. It is conventionally accepted that the evolution of a dentary–squamosal jaw joint was a key factor (supplementing and then replacing the quadrate–articular jaw joint of reptiles and birds), and may be used to define a mammal. So defined, the first mammals appear in rocks of latest Triassic or earliest Jurassic age, about 190 million years ago. They include *Morganucodon watsoni* and *Kuehneotherium praecursorius* from South Wales. The Middle Jurassic Stonesfield quarries near Oxford are famous as the first site to yield Mesozoic mammals, contemporary with the dinosaurs; *Phascolotherium bucklandi* was described in 1828. A few teeth and jaws of Mesozoic mammals are known from additional Middle Jurassic sites in Dorset, Oxfordshire and on the Isle of Skye, giving a total of at least 12 species. The most diverse of the British Mesozoic mammal faunas come from the Early Cretaceous (formerly thought to be Late Jurassic) of the Isle of Purbeck, Dorset, where at least 28 species have been described. From the later Cretaceous there are only a few isolated teeth from Wealden deposits in SE England. These fossils are described, illustrated and thoroughly discussed by Kielan-Jaworowska *et al.* [24]. Benton *et al.* [1a] have recently reviwed Mesozoic mammal sites in Great Britain.

EOCENE–OLIGOCENE MAMMALS

Lower Eocene mammals are present in the London Clay and in the gravels immediately below it, notably at Abbey Wood, London; among them is the early horse *Hyracotherium*. Beds that range from Upper Eocene through to Lower Oligocene in age outcrop on the Isle of Wight, both at the western end at Bouldner and Headon Hill, and in the east at Whitecliff Bay, and have yielded large numbers of mammals, though mostly these are represented only by isolated teeth. The sequence of faunas and the changing habitats represented at these sites were evaluated by Hooker and co-workers [19–21]. Benton *et al.* [1a] provide a useful overview of the principal Tertiary sites in Great Britain, with full lists of species. The earlier sites have tropical forest floras and faunas, with up to 45 species present. The climate became somewhat cooler and drier into the Oligocene, but the loss of tropical forms was balanced by an influx of newer forms, so that faunal diversity was increased, with up to 77 species recorded from Headon Hill [1a].

PLEISTOCENE MAMMALS

The Pleistocene, covering roughly the last 2 million years of the geological record, was a period of alternating cold, glacial and warmer, interglacial, periods. The most recent of these warm periods, which began about 10 000 (radiocarbon) years ago (about 12 000 calendar years ago), is the Flandrian Interglacial or Holocene Period in which we are living.

Pleistocene mammals occur in a variety of sediments, including marine clays, river gravels, glacial moraines and cave infills, which often constitute localised pockets that are difficult to correlate from place to place. The fossils in these sediments, including the mammals themselves but also pollen grains, seeds, beetles and mollusc shells, may therefore be of major importance to geologists for stratigraphic correlation. For the most recent 40 000 years or so, a precise correlation can be given by measuring small amounts of radioactive carbon (^{14}C) in organic remains, giving dates (radiocarbon years before present, bp) that are close to absolute (calendar) years over the last 2000 years or so, but diverge (become younger by up to 2000 years) back towards the last ice age. In this chapter we tend to use radiocarbon dates indicated by 'BP'. Because the fossils are relatively recent, and closely related to or the same as

Table 3.1 Occurrences of mammals in Britain in the principal periods of the Pleistocene and Holocene [12,46]. Glacials in italics, interglacials in normal typeface, X – well-dated records, x – probable occurrence upon indirect evidence of dating, I – introduced

		Lower Pleistocene	Cromerian	Anglian	Hoxnian	Wolstonian	Ipswichian	Devensian	Holocene	Present
Insectivora										
Western hedgehog	*Erinaceus europaeus*		X						X	X
Pygmy shrew	*Sorex minutus/cf. minutus*		X				X		X	X
A shrew	*Sorex runtonensis*		X							
A shrew	*Sorex savini*		X							
Common Shrew	*Sorex araneus*				X		X		X	X
Water shrew	*Neomys newtoni*		X							
Common water shrew	*Neomys fodiens*						X		X	X
Greater white-toothed shrew	*Crocidura russula*						X			
Beremend shrew	*Beremendia cf. fissidens*		X							
Common mole	*Talpa europaea*		X					x	X	X
A mole	*Talpa minor/cf. minor*		X		X					
Russian desman	*Desmana moschata*		X		X					
Primates										
(Barbary) macaque	*Macaca* sp.		X		X		x			
Human	*Homo heidelbergensis*		X							
Human	*Homo sapiens*			X	X		X	X	X	X
Lagomorpha										
Steppe pika	*Ochotona pusilla*		x					X		
Hare	*Lepus* sp.		X				x			
Mountain hare	*Lepus timidus*				X	x		X	X	X
Rabbit	*Oryctolagus cuniculus*				X					I
Rodentia										
White's squirrel	*Sciurus whitei*		X							
Red squirrel	*Sciurus vulgaris*								X	X
Ground squirrel	*Spermophilus* sp.			X			X	x		
Eurasian beaver	*Castor fiber*	x	X		X		X		X	
Giant beaver	*Trogontherium cuvieri*		X		X					
A beaver	*Trogontherium minus*	x								
Common Hamster	*Cricetus cricetus*		X			x				
Schaub's dwarf hamster	*Allocricetus bursae*					x				
Steppe lemming	*Lagurus lagurus*					x				
Collared lemming	*Dicrostonyx torquatus*		x			x	X	X		
Norway lemming	*Lemmus lemmus*	x	X	X	X	x	X	X		
Bank vole	*Myodes glareolus*		X		X		X	x	X	X

Table 3.1(cont.)

		Lower Pleistocene	Cromerian	Anglian	Hoxnian	Wolstonian	Ipswichian	Devensian	Holocene	Present
Episcopal vole	*Pliomys episcopalis*		X							
A vole	*Mimomys pliocaenicus*	x								
A vole	*Mimomys blanci*	x								
A vole	*Mimomys reidi*	x								
A vole	*Mimomys newtoni*	x								
A vole	*Mimomys rex*	x								
A vole	*Mimomys pitymyoides*	x								
A vole	*Mimomys savini*		X							
A water vole	*Arvicola cantiana*		X	X	X		X	X		
Common water vole	*Arvicola terrestris*							x	X	X
A pine vole	*Pitymys arvaloides*		X		X					
Gregarious pine vole	*Pitymys gregaloides*		X							
Common vole	*Microtus arvalis/cf. arvalis*		X		X					I
Field vole	*Microtus agrestis*				X		X	X	X	X
Root vole	*Microtus oeconomus*		X	X	X	x	X	X	?	
Tundra vole	*Microtus gregalis*			X				X		
Wood mouse	*Apodemus sylvaticus*		X		X		X		X	X
Yellow-necked mouse	*Apodemus flavicollis*								X	X
Harvest mouse	*Micromys minutus*								X	X
Hazel dormouse	*Muscardinus avellanarius*			x					X	X
Garden dormouse	*Eliomys quercinus*			x						
Porcupine	*Hystrix* sp.	x								I
Carnivora										
Wolf	*Canis lupus*		X		X	x	X	X	X	
Arctic fox	*Alopex lagopus*							X		
Red fox	*Vulpes vulpes*					x	x	x	X	X
European hunting dog	*Xenocyon lycaonoides*		x							
Deninger's bear	*Ursus deningeri*		X							
Cave bear	*Ursus spelaeus*				X					
Brown bear	*Ursus arctos*						X	X	X	
Polar bear	*Ursus maritimus*							X		
Bear	*Ursus* sp.					x				
Hyaena bear	*Agriotherium* sp.	x								
English panda	*Parailurus anglicus*	x								
Weasel	*Mustela nivalis*		X						X	X
Stoat	*Mustela erminea*							x	X	X

Table 3.1(cont.)

		Lower Pleistocene	Cromerian	Anglian	Hoxnian	Wolstonian	Ipswichian	Devensian	Holocene	Present
Polecat	Mustela putorius (robusta)							x	X	X
European mink	Mustela lutreola		x							
Pine marten	Martes martes				X				X	X
Marten	Martes sp.		X							
Pannonian polecat	Pannonictis sp.		X							
Badger	Meles meles					x	X		X	X
Schlosser's wolverine	Gulo schlosseri		x							
Wolverine	Gulo gulo					x		x		
Eurasian otter	Lutra lutra								X	X
Otter	Lutra sp.		X							
A clawless otter	Aonyx reevei	x								
Corsican otter	Aonyx antiqua				x					
Perrier hyaena	Hyaena perrieri	x								
Short-faced hyaena	Hyaena brevirostris		x							
Spotted hyaena	Crocuta crocuta		X	X		X	X	x		
Greater scimitar cat	Homotherium sainzelli	x								
Lesser scimitar cat	Homotherium latidens		x							
European jaguar	Panthera gombaszogensis		x							
Leopard	Panthera pardus							x		
Lion	Panthera leo		x		X		X	x		
Jungle cat	Felis chaus		x							
Martelli's cat	Felis cf. lunensis		X							
Wildcat	Felis silvestris				X		x		X	X
Eurasian lynx	Lynx lynx							x	X	
Proboscidea										
Auvergne mastodont	Anancus arvernensis	x								
Borson's mastodon	Zygolophodon borsoni	x								
Straight-tusked elephant	Elephas antiquus		x		X	X	X			
Southern mammoth	Mammuthus meridionalis	x	x							
Steppe mammoth	Mammuthus trogontherii/ cf trogontherii		X	X						
Woolly mammoth	Mammuthus primigenius			X		X	X	X		
Perissodactyla										
Hipparion	Hipparion sp.	x								
A zebrine horse	Equus stenonis/cf. stenonis	x								
A horse	Equus bressanus/ cf. bressanus	x								

Table 3.1 (cont.)

		Lower Pleistocene	Cromerian	Anglian	Hoxnian	Wolstonian	Ipswichian	Devensian	Holocene	Present
Horse	*Equus* sp.		X							
Wild horse	*Equus ferus*			X	X	X	X	X	X	
Auvergne tapir	*Tapirus arvernensis*	x								
Christol's rhinoceros	*Dicerorhinus megarhinus*	x								
Etruscan rhinoceros	*Dicerorhinus etruscus*		X							
Merck's rhinoceros	*Stephanorhinus kirchbergensis*				X					
Steppe rhinoceros	*Stephanorhinus hemitoechus*				X		X			
Woolly rhinoceros	*Coelodonta antiquitatis*		X			X	X	X		
Artiodactyla										
Wild boar	*Sus scrofa*		X		X		x		X	
Hippopotamus	*Hippopotamus* sp.		X							
Common hippopotamus	*Hippopotamus amphibius*						X			
Verticornis deer	*Megaloceros verticornis*		X							
Giant deer	*Megaloceros giganteus*			X	X		X	X	X	
Savin's giant deer	*Megaloceros savini*	x								
A giant deer	*Megaloceros dawkinsi*		X							
Fallow deer	*Dama dama*		X		X		X			I
A bush-antlered deer	*Eucladoceros falconeri*	x								
A bush-antlered deer	*Eucladoceros sedgwicki/ cf sedgwicki*	x								
Red deer	*Cervus elaphus*		X	X	X		X	X	X	X
Broad-fronted elk	*Alces latifrons*		X							
Elk/moose	*Alces alces*							X	X	
Reindeer	*Rangifer tarandus*				X	X		X	X	I
Roe deer	*Capreolus capreolus*		X		X		x	X	X	
Cattle	cf. *Leptobos* sp.	x								
Aurochs	*Bos primigenius*				X		X		X	
Cattle/bison	*Bos* sp./*Bison* sp.			X	X	X	X	x		
Woodland bison	*Bison schoetensacki/ cf. schoetensacki*			X						
Steppe bison	*Bison priscus*=*bonasus*?						X	X		
Giant musk-ox	*Praeovibos priscus*		x							
Musk-ox	*Ovibos moschatus*							X	X	
Saiga	*Saiga tatarica*							x		
Gazelle	*Gazella* sp.	x								
English gazelle	*Gazella anglica*	x								

21

existing species, they are also important to biologists for the light they shed on the evolution of existing species and on the history of the present fauna and flora.

Within the British Isles, there is evidence of at least three glacial periods (named Anglian, Wolstonian and Devensian), though good mammal faunas are known only from the latest, Devensian, glaciation (Table 3.1), and at least three interglacials, termed Cromerian, Hoxnian and Ipswichian. However, the record of terrestrial deposits is patchy and partially obliterated by the actions of later glaciations. The deep-sea oozes contain a continuous record which suggests a much more complicated record of 20 or more cold periods [44]. Relating the patchy terrestrial record to this complete record is at present tentative, so the classical terms are retained here. Interglacial faunas are better known, probably because there were simply more mammals living here in these warmer periods, but perhaps because opportunities for fossilisation were also higher.

The early Pleistocene is poorly represented in Britain, but contains a wide diversity of species that are absent later in the Pleistocene including the extinct panda *Parailurus anglicus*, mastodons *Anancus arvernensis* and *Zygolophodon borsoni* and a tapir *Tapirus arvernensis* (Table 3.1). The Cromerian faunas uncovered in East Anglia, dating to about 350 000 BP, are the earliest good faunas, with at least 47 species including many extinct species ancestral to later, modern, ones. A monkey, *Macaca* sp., perhaps the same as the modern Barbary macaque *M. sylvana*, is a notable presence, along with the Russian desman *Desmana moschata*. However, the earliest records in Britain of some extant species, including mole, beaver, common hamster *Cricetus cricetus*, bank vole, root vole *Microtus oeconomus*, wood mouse, wolf, weasel, roe deer, fallow deer and red deer also come from these faunas. Important faunas from Boxgrove and Westbury-sub-Mendip may belong to a slightly later warm period; they include such interesting species such as European mink *Mustela lutreola*, spotted hyaena *Crocuta crocuta*, 'European jaguar' *Panthera gombaszogensis*, and lion *Panthera leo* among the carnivores, along with field vole, root vole, bank vole, wood mouse, aurochs, roe deer and rabbit. Early humans *Homo heidelbergensis* are certainly present at Boxgrove, and may have been making stone tools at Westbury-sub-Mendip.

The Anglian Glaciation has only a sparse fauna, including a ground squirrel *Spermophilus* sp., ancestral water vole *Arvicola cantiana*, narrow-headed vole *Microtus gregalis*, Norway lemming *Lemmus lemmus*, horse, reindeer and red deer.

The next, the Hoxnian, Interglacial is notable particularly for the presence of humans at Swanscombe, Kent, along with such familiar species as rabbit, fallow deer, and both macaque and desman again. Irish elk *Megalocerus giganteus*, appears for the first time, along with red and roe deer, beaver, field vole, lion, pine marten, wildcat, wild boar, wolf, cave bear *Ursus spelaeus* and straight-tusked elephant *Elephas antiquus*.

The Wolstonian Glaciation has woolly mammoth *Mammuthus primigenius*, woolly rhinoceros *Coelodonta antiquitatis*, horse, reindeer, wolverine, wolf, lion, badger, red fox, mountain hare, root vole, and collared lemming *Dicrostonyx torquatus*, Norway lemming and steppe lemming *Lagurus lagurus*. A contemporary deposit on Jersey, at La Cotte de St Brelade, has chamois *Rupicapra rupicapra* and birch mouse *Sicista betulina*, as well as collared lemming, narrow-headed vole, wolf, arctic fox *Alopex lagopus*, reindeer, horse, woolly mammoth and woolly rhinoceros.

In the Ipswichian Interglacial, fallow deer were again present, but the hippopotamus *Hippopotamus amphibius* was a characteristic member of the fauna. However, the more refined timescale now applied to the Pleistocene suggests that what were previously all collated as Ipswichian faunas include in fact faunas from three interglacials, and by implication some glacial periods have also been confused. These faunas and timescales are still being actively studied, and it is not yet possible to present a consensus.

Mammals from the last glaciation, the Devensian in Great Britain, are better known than those from earlier glaciations. The period started about 45 000 years ago with an open but not ice-covered landscape, in which herds of reindeer, horse, bison and red deer provided prey for wolf, spotted hyena, lion and brown bear. The severest weather, with an ice cap that extended as far south as the Gower Peninsula in the west and the Wash in the east, occurred in a limited period from about 25 000 to 18 000 BP. South of the ice, the fauna included such classic Ice Age species as woolly mammoth, woolly rhinoceros, reindeer, musk ox *Ovibos moschatus*, arctic fox, and collared and Norway lemmings. About 15 000 to 11 000 BP a milder interval, the Windermere Interstadial, saw such species as elk, red deer and aurochs recolonising the British Isles, though reindeer, horse and mountain hare were the main herbivores, along with such predators as wolves and humans. This is the period when Irish elk flourished in Ireland, and when the last mammoths occurred in Great Britain. A cold snap, the Younger Dryas period, lasting from 11 000 to 10 200 BP, saw saiga *Saiga tatarica* and steppe pika *Ochotona pusilla* as members of the British fauna, along with horses and reindeer as well as lemmings, root voles and narrow-headed voles, but in Ireland the Irish elk seems to have been exterminated, and red deer and aurochs retreated from Great Britain.

One important consequence of this alternating sequence of cold and warm faunas is that identifying particular isolated fossils does not tell us much about the history of any particular species in Britain. A fallow deer antler discovered in the gravels of a river terrace could belong to Cromerian, Hoxnian or Ipswichian faunas, or could have fallen off a park deer last century. It requires careful excavation, with particular care paid to the stratigraphy, to describe the history of the fauna or of any species in it. Moreover, a complete fauna of associated and obviously contemporary mammals is much more convincing evidence than an isolated specimen. Unfortunately, isolated specimens are sometimes all that we have; there is only one record of polar bear *Ursus maritimus* from England and another from Scotland, only three isolated musk ox, and four records of saiga, two of which have only uncertain dates [58].

ORIGIN OF THE PRESENT MAMMAL FAUNA

The composition of the mammal fauna now in the British Isles is the consequence of three processes: natural colonisation between the end of the last glaciation and the isolation of the isles from their nearest mainland by rising sea-levels; selective extinction, mostly caused by humans but also by climatic change; and selective introductions by humans, deliberate or accidental, since they became isles [56, 58].

NATURAL COLONISATION

The maximum extent of the ice sheet in the last (Devensian) glaciation, and the most severe climate, occurred late in the period, perhaps 25 000 to 18 000 BP. The mammals present then, including reindeer, lemmings, arctic fox and musk ox, imply conditions too severe for any of the present mammal fauna except perhaps stoat, weasel and mountain hare.

Between 15 000 and 11 000 BP, the milder interlude of the Windermere (or Allerød, in Europe) Interstadial, the ice cap melted from the Scottish mountains and birch woodland developed in southern Britain at least. During this interstadial, reindeer and Irish elk *Megaloceros giganteus* were well established in Ireland, and recent radiocarbon dating has demonstrated that red deer, brown bear, stoat and mountain hare were also present there [54]. All of these were also present then in Great Britain, where additional species included the root, field and water voles, elk *Alces alces* and aurochs *Bos primigenius*, which are

not known ever to have reached Ireland. The latest known British woolly mammoths also belong to this period [31].

The warmer conditions of the Windermere Interstadial were interrupted by a short reversion to colder conditions about 11 000 to 10 000 BP – a period recognised by archaeologists as the Younger Dryas, and termed the Loch Lomond Readvance by geologists because an ice cap reformed on some of the Scottish mountains and spread as far as Loch Lomond. Severe arctic conditions prevailed even in southern England at this time, and many species that had spread north were probably unable to survive. In Ireland, it seems certain that this caused the extinction of the Irish elk, but reindeer, collared lemming and stoat at least survived. In England, pika, Norway lemming, weasel, red fox, wild horse, and the narrow-headed, root, grey-sided *Myodes rufocanus* and water voles also occurred, being present at sites such as Ossom's Cave, Staffordshire; Robin Hood Cave, Derbyshire; Torbryan Cave, Devon; and Nazeing, Essex [41, 58]. In Scotland, wild horse, reindeer and wolf were present at Green Craig near Edinburgh [26].

The Postglacial (Flandrian or Holocene) period began with the final retreat of the ice at about 10 200 BP. It is evident both on geological grounds and from beetle faunas that the change was very rapid, an increase of average July temperatures of 8°C taking no more than 50 years. It was not the slow change that has been postulated from the floral (particularly pollen) record. Though there should be some evidence of transitional faunas, the mammals are too poorly known to provide clear evidence of them. Reindeer lingered at least to 8300 BP (Creag nan Uamh, Sutherland) and wild horse to 9330 BP (Seamer Carr, Yorkshire), and the root vole also survived into the postglacial (e.g. at Nazeing) [7, 26, 58].

However, two important Mesolithic faunas confirm the rapid establishment in Britain of temperate woodland communities. At Star Carr, Yorkshire, dated to 9500 BP [16, 30] and Thatcham, Berkshire, dated to 10 500–9600 BP [25], species such as hedgehog, beaver, roe deer, red deer, aurochs and wild boar are present (Table 2.5), matching the botanical evidence of deciduous trees at these sites. Two species in these faunas need comment. Rabbit was claimed at Thatcham, and the identification is not in question. However, this species is not otherwise present anywhere in NW Europe so early in the postglacial period, and radiocarbon dating has since confirmed that it is a recent, intrusive, specimen, dated to 270 BP. The hare at Star Carr was tentatively identified as brown hare *Lepus europaeus*; this would not be incongruent with the rest of the fauna, but would be an early record for the species in Britain. The

towards the south of its range in winter. Occurs as far south as 60 °N in Russia; would have occurred further south before human interference. Latest records in British Isles include Roddan's Port, Co. Down (10 250 BP), Darent Gravels, Kent (9760 BP), Anston Stones Cave, Yorkshire (9750 BP), Green Craig, Pentland Hills (9710 BP) and Creag nan Uamh, Sutherland (8300 BP).These early dates suggest that climatic and vegetational changes, not human hunting, caused its extinction; the well-wooded Mesolithic landscape would have been unsuitable habitat. There is no evidence to support the popular notion that reindeer survived through to the 12th century AD, to be hunted by the Vikings [7].

Irish elk (giant deer) *Megaloceros giganteus*

The Irish elk is recorded from at least 100 sites in Ireland that date to the equivalent of the Windermere Interstadial [36], and from over 50 sites in Great Britain [42]. Ten specimens have been radiocarbon dated, the latest from the famous site at Ballybetagh Bog, south of Dublin, at 10 600 BP. There are no known human sites in Ireland so early, and no evidence (tools, butchery marks) that they ever hunted the species there. Similarly, 11 specimens from the Isle of Man all date to 12 500 –11 000 BP [49]. It therefore seems that it was exterminated by the return to colder conditions in the Younger Dryas. No evidence from elsewhere in Britain, where humans were present, suggests a different pattern of extinction there; the latest there, from the river Cree, dates to 10 257 BP. However, radiocarbon dates of 7990–6816 BP, recently obtained on three specimens from the southern edge of the Ural mountains, Russia, show that it did survive elsewhere into the Postglacial period [49].

Steppe pika *Ochotona pusilla*

The steppe pika is the westernmost of the 22 or so extant species of pika, most of which frequent mountainous areas, specifically scree slopes. It has been retreating westwards on the steppes of the southern Palaearctic throughout recent history, and now occurs only in a limited area of southern Russia and Kazakhstan. In the Late Glacial it spread westwards to Belgium, France and England, where it has been found at 24 sites [15]. The latest radicarbon dates are just into the postglacial. A date of 9090 BP (Bridged Pot, Somerset) obtained on large mammal bone may be too late to date the accompanying pika in that cave, but dates of 10 180 BP (Broken Cavern, Torbryan), 10 020 BP (Great Doward Cave = Merlin's Cave, Wye Valley) and 9915 BP (Merlin's Cave) [41] suggest survival just into Postglacial times.

Root vole (northern vole) *Microtus oeconomus* (= *M. ratticeps* in older literature)

The root vole prefers wetter habitats than the field vole, but is a similar though somewhat larger grassland vole, reaching weights of 100 g. It is widely distributed across Northern Europe, south to about 50° N in Northern Germany and Poland, further south than that in Russia. There is also a relict population in N Holland at 53° N. Given this range, it is not surprising that it lasted longer in Britain than other Late Glacial species. It is recorded from at least 28 sites in Britain, but few of these records are well dated. Recent radiocarbon dates of 10 370 BP from Broken Cavern, Torbryan and 9450 BP from Merlin's Cave [41] show survival from Younger Dryas into postglacial times. Specimens from Nazeing, Essex belong in Pollen Zone V, perhaps therefore about 9500 BP, and undated specimens from Mesolithic layers in Dowel Cave and Demen's Dale Cave, Derbyshire suggest the same [57]. Price [41] reports a specimen from the Neolithic levels of Broken Cavern, Torbryan. The latest specimens come from Nornour, Isles of Scilly, apparently of Bronze Age date (around 3500 BP) [39]and from Chapel Cave, Yorkshire, also of Bronze Age [52].

Elk *Alces alces*

The elk (moose in N America) is the largest extant deer, typical of the taiga (coniferous forest) zone across the northern hemisphere. It ranges south into Poland to about 50° N. In Great Britain it is known from only about 20 postglacial sites, mostly in Scotland, and is unknown from Ireland [58]. Few examples have precise dating, but the species entered Britain in the Windermere Interstadial. There are two specimens of this date, one from Neasham, Durham, and a famous specimen from High Furlong, near Blackpool, that has spear points and other evidence of human hunting. In the Mesolithic, it occurs at Star Carr and Thatcham, dated around 9500 BP, but at few other sites. It is generally supposed to have become extinct during the Mesolithic. However, a specimen from the river Cree has been dated at 3925 BP, about Bronze Age times. Survival into Roman times in Scotland is possible, but there is no firm evidence; however, there are Gaelic names for the species (*lòn*, *miol*, *os*), implying a late survival. A supposed Roman specimen from Newstead is a misidentified red deer antler (author's data). It seems likely that human hunting and agricultural changes to the habitat in combination caused its extinction, but there is little direct evidence.

Aurochs *Bos primigenius*

The now extinct ancestor of domestic cattle was

well distributed and even abundant in postglacial Britain, with several hundred records (though dating is uncertain for most of them). The species never reached Ireland. Domestication took place in the Middle East, and the already much smaller domestic cattle were introduced by Neolithic farmers about 5500 BP; there is good genetic evidence that native aurochs did not contribute to White Park or any other of the present British breeds of cattle [51]. Aurochs bones are larger than those of domestic cattle, with a clear separation [38]. Aurochsen were present from early in the Mesolithic, being present at Star Carr and Thatcham. There are numerous Mesolithic and Neolithic records, and a number of well-dated occurrences of Bronze Age date, the latest from Galloway (3315 BP) and Charterhouse Warren Farm, Somerset (3245 BP). A number of Roman sites have possible aurochs bones, though either the dates or the identifications require confirmation (e.g. Vindolanda, Segontium). The species survived in Europe to the 17th century [28]. Historical accounts from Julius Caesar onwards refer to it as a forest animal, and the combination of hunting and loss of habitat seems likely to explain its extinction.

SELECTIVE INTRODUCTIONS

The natural colonisation of the British Isles by terrestrial mammals was only possible when they were, in fact, not isles but part of mainland Europe. This raises the important question of when the English Channel joined through to the North Sea, so ending immigration from the continent, and even more critically raises the question of whether the other islands were ever joined to Great Britain, and when, if they were, they became isolated. This is a subject reviewed at length in [56, 58].

There is no doubt that sea level was lowered, worldwide, to about 120 m below its present level at the extreme of the last glaciation, because of the volume of water locked into the ice sheets. Large areas of continental shelf were then exposed as land, including most of the present North Sea and English Channel, so Great Britain was certainly then part of Europe, and mammals were free to colonise or migrate in both directions. The Strait of Dover was carved out much earlier in the Pleistocene than the last glaciation, and the sea floor of the English Channel was probably already at its current depth. It is now 37 m below sea level, at its shallowest, so whenever the sea level rose from −120 m to −37 m may indicate when Great Britain became isolated. On the basis of curves of rising sea level from around the world, this happened by about 9500 BP, at about the time that Mesolithic hunters were camped at Star Carr. This

is much earlier than the often quoted date of 5000 BP (when present sea level was reached), and implies a limited opportunity for more southerly species to get into Britain. It is assumed that this explains the absence from the British fauna of garden dormouse *Eliomys quercinus*, common vole *Microtus arvalis*, pine vole *Pitymys subterraneus*, beech marten *Martes foina* and white-toothed shrews *Crocidura russula* and *C. leucodon*, all of which are present in northern France.

The situation further north, particularly as it affects the isolation of Orkney, Shetland, the Outer Hebrides and especially Ireland, is more complicated because, although sea level was lowered worldwide, these northern areas were themselves depressed by the weight of ice overlying them. The relative sea level around south-west Scotland seems to have been +20 m at 12 000 BP, and the present channel between south-west Scotland and Northern Ireland has a minimum depth of *c.* −55 m. On this basis, it is unlikely that Ireland was joined to Scotland at any time in the postglacial period. Yalden [55, 56] argued for a short-lived and perhaps soggy land bridge at about 8000 BP, but Devoy [14], reviewing the particular issue of land bridges across the Irish Sea, ruled out any possibility of a postglacial land bridge. This suggests that the present Irish mammal fauna either immigrated during the Windermere Interstadial, and survived the Younger Dryas in situ, or has been introduced since. A possible resolution of this problem is suggested by Wingfield [53], who argues that the weight of ice in the north would have produced a compensatory bulge in the Earth's crust further south. This bulge would have been low-lying and somewhat transitory; moreover, it would have migrated northwards as the ice cap melted. This might have allowed reindeer and Irish elk to invade Ireland during the Windermere period, along with wolf, brown bear, pygmy shrew, mountain hare and stoat. Other mammals that are presumed native to Ireland (wood mouse, wild boar, red fox, pine marten, badger, wildcat) but unlikely to have survived the Younger Dryas may have managed to arrive over the short-lived land bridge postulated by Wingfield [53], but such a bridge would have been poor habitat for the many small mammals that did not reach Ireland (common shrew, water shrew, mole, field vole, bank vole, water vole, yellow-necked mouse, dormouse) and arguably also poor for roe deer, elk and beaver.

If the likelihood of mammals reaching Ireland in the postglacial is arguable, the situation for the smaller islands is, paradoxically, clearer. Shetland, Orkney, and the Outer Hebrides are separated by channels that are more than −100 m below sea

Table 3.2 Distribution of small mammals on islands [56]

	Common vole	Field vole	Bank vole	Wood mouse	Common shrew	Pygmy shrew	Lesser white-toothed shrew	Greater white-toothed shrew
Great Britain	-	+	+	+	+	+	-	-
Ireland, Man	-	-	-a	+	-	+	-	-
Shetland, St Kilda	-	-	-	+	-	-	-	-
Orkney (Mainland)	+	-	-	+	-	-	-	-
Lewis, Barra (OH)	-	-	-	+	-b	+	-	-
N & S Uist (OH)	-	+	-	+	-	+	-	-
Coll, Tiree, Colonsay (IH)	-	-	-	+	-	-	-	-
Eigg, Muck (IH)	-	+	-	+	-	+	-	-
Raasay (IH)	-	-	+	+	+	+	-	-
Mull, Bute (IH)	-	+	+	+	+	+	-	-
Skye, Islay, Jura, Gigha, Arran (IH)	-	+	-b	+	+	+	-	-
Skomer (Wales)	-	-	+	+	+	+	-	-
Scilly	-	-	-	+	-	-	+	-
Jersey (CI)	-	-	+	+	+c	-	+	-
Sark (CI)	-	-	-	+	-	-	+	-
Alderney, Herm (CI)	-	-	-	+	-	-	-	+
Guernsey (CI)	+	-	-	+	-	-	-	+

CI, Channel Isles; IH, Inner Hebrides; OH, Outer Hebrides.
a   Bank vole now present, recent introduction.
b   Single records of common shrew, Lewis, and bank vole, Islay doubtful, need confirmation.
c   Common shrew on Jersey is S. coronatus; S. araneus elsewhere.

level, and with the added depression of the land due to the weight of ice, they can never have been joined to mainland Scotland in recent times. Their present mammal faunas (otter excepted) must be due to human introduction, sometimes deliberate but probably accidental in many cases. Corbet [8, 9] was the first to argue this thesis cogently. Previously the faunas of the small islands had been regarded as glacial relicts of previous invasions. For example, the Orkney and Guernsey voles, large forms of *Microtus arvalis*, had been interpreted as the survivors of an early invasion of the British Isles which survived on those islands though a glacial period, but were replaced on Great Britain in postglacial times by the later invading *Microtus agrestis*. This thesis is untenable; a more southern species would not reach these islands first or survive better there than a northern species. The irregularity of the fauna of the small islands also argues for an erratic rather than a systematic pattern of colonisation (Table 3.2). Field voles, common shrews and pygmy shrews occur further north in Europe than bank voles, which in turn occur further north than wood mice, so the first three should occur on most islands and the last on fewest, if the islands were repopulated naturally after the Devensian Glaciation. In fact, the wood mouse is the most widespread of these five, and it is also the one most likely to be found in houses and around buildings. As Corbet [8] argued, islands have impoverished economies, and there would have been regular trade in livestock, fodder, building materials and food, offering ample opportunity to carry small mammals as stowaways. Because the islands lack larger mammals, there would also be a considerable incentive to introduce larger species, such as red deer and rabbits for food and hedgehogs perhaps for food or for carding wool.

For the common vole on Orkney, archaeological evidence shows it to have been present, along with wood mice, for at least 4000 years [10, 11], and a comparison of the minor morphological variations of the skulls suggests that the voles are more nearly related to those from the Balkans than those from Germany [2]. Similar analyses of wood mouse skulls suggest that the populations of the Shetlands, Outer Hebrides, Ireland and some of the Inner Hebrides have been introduced from Norway, by the Vikings, rather than from Scotland [1]. However, the more recent discovery of a Mesolithic wood mouse specimen from near Dublin, with a date of 7600 BP, shows that wood mice were already present in Ireland long before the Viking colonisation [40], and the Orkney wood mice were also there long before Viking times. Genetic evidence now confirms that Orkney voles are in fact most closely related to common voles from the Pyrenean region of Iberia [18]. Similarly, Irish pygmy shrews are more closely related to Iberian ones than to English, Scottish or Manx shrews [33], and Irish pine martens also have a southern origin [13]. The paucity of genetic variation in British brown hares, by contrast with their variability elsewhere in Europe, confirms that they too were introduced, probably in Iron Age times [50].

The most obvious introductions to mainland Britain were domestic sheep and goats, neither of which was native to western Europe. They appeared with Neolithic farmers, at about 5400 BP, and domestic cattle were also brought then; probably domestic pigs were also introduced, but the archaeological evidence is less certain (pigs could have been domesticated here from wild boar). The house mouse was already associated with Neolithic farming in the Middle East, and might have been introduced to Britain in the Neolithic, but the earliest records are rather later, Iron Age, ones [3, 58]. The domestic cat has been recorded from Iron Age Orkney, much earlier than its supposed arrival with the Romans [46]. Roman and later introductions (black rat, fallow deer, rabbit, brown rat, grey squirrel, American mink,

Reeve's muntjac, water deer, sika, edible dormouse, muskrat and coypu) are treated fully elsewhere in this book.

For other islands and other species, our presumption that species are present as a result of accidental introduction is mostly speculative, and based on the erratic composition of their faunas. In particular, the Channel Isles might have been sufficiently far south to have escaped the worst effects of the Younger Dryas period, while Jersey, at least, is near enough to France and separated by a sufficiently shallow channel that one might expect all the common small mammals to have reached it. Yet it lacks any *Microtus*, pygmy shrew and water vole, and has lesser white-toothed shrew, rather than the more widespread greater white-toothed shrew, as well as wood mouse, French shrew *Sorex coronatus* and a distinctive form of bank vole. This fauna does not seem comprehensible on any basis of natural colonisation, by comparison either with the nearest mainland or with the other Channel Isles. It seems very probable then that the fauna is the result of introduction, despite the lack of direct evidence. Likewise, lesser white-toothed shrew on the Isles of Scilly and Sark, greater white-toothed shrew on Guernsey, Alderney and Herm, and bank voles on Skomer, Mull, Raasay and in SW Ireland are introductions. The field voles on North and South Uist are surely also introductions, given the absence of the species from the neighbouring large islands of Barra and Lewis. The most difficult species to explain this way is the pygmy shrew which, given the susceptibility of *Sorex* spp. to starvation, is not a likely candidate for accidental transport. It has, moreover, a very wide distribution on the Scottish isles, as well as occurring in Ireland and the Isle of Man, but the genetic evidence indicates clearly that the Irish population at least is a human introduction [33]

CONCLUSION

It is clear from this outline that we know the general pattern of postglacial colonisation of the British Isles by mammals, though we are missing some of the detail that we need for a proper understanding. In particular, we have a poor sequence of information for the smaller mammals populating smaller islands. Genetic evidence of the relatedness of several populations of small (and some larger) mammals has already clarified some of the uncertainties, and continued research will solve more of these; in particular, the genetic relationships of populations on smaller islands should be resolved by these techniques. Continued research into small-mammal faunas in caves and archaeological sites will clarify their history, as it has already for dormouse and harvest mouse (cf. Price [41] with Yalden [56, 58]). There is scope for local naturalists to help clarify the position, by uncovering documentation of early introductions and interpreting place-name evidence, but the major challenge is to discover new and reinterpret old archaeological material. The application of radiocarbon dating to large mammals has greatly improved our understanding of their history [6, 26, 27, 54]. It is now possible to obtain dates from small amounts of bone, so that small mammals can also be dated directly. This promises to revolutionise our understanding of their history during the next decade.

Further reading

There is an enormous literature on Pleistocene mammals which has fortunately been summarised by Kurtén [29] for Europe as a whole, and more specifically for the British Isles by Stuart [47] The specific question of extinctions at the end of the Pleistocene is reviewed by Stuart [48] The general topic of the origin of the mammal faunas of the British Isles is reviewed by Yalden [56, 58].

Molar tooth of woolly mammoth, from Thames Valley gravels (*photo P. Morris*).

REFERENCES

1 Berry, R.J. (1969) History in the evolution of *Apodemus sylvaticus* at one edge of its range. *Journal of Zoology*, **159**, 311–366.

1a Benton, M.J. *et al.* (2005) *Mesozoic and Tertiary fossil mammals and birds of Great Britain.* Geological Conservation Review Series No 32, JNCC, Peterborough

2 Berry, R.J. & Rose, F.E.N. (1975) Islands and the evolution of *Microtus arvalis* (Microtinae). *Journal of Zoology*, **177**, 395–409.

3 Brothwell, D. (1981) The Pleistocene and Holocene archaeology of the house mouse and related species. *Symposium of the Zoological Society of London*, **47**, 1–13.

4 Campbell, J.B. (1977) *The Upper Palaeolithic in Britain.* Clarendon Press, Oxford.

5 Clutton-Brock, J. (1986) New dates for old animals: the reindeer, the aurochs, and the wild horse in prehistoric Britain. *Archaeozoologia, Mélanges*, 111–117.

6 Clutton-Brock, J. & MacGregor, A. (1988) An end to medieval reindeer in Scotland. *Proceedings of the Society of Antiquaries of Scotland*, **118**, 23–35.

7 Charles, R. & Jacobi, R. (1994). The Late Glacial fauna from the Robin Hood Cave, Cresswell Crags: a reassessment. *Oxford Journal of Archaeology*, **13**, 1–32.

8 Corbet, G.B. (1961) Origin of the British insular races of small mammals and of the 'Lusitanian' fauna. *Nature, London*, **191**, 1037–1040.

9 Corbet, G.B. (1962) The 'Lusitanian element' in the British fauna. *Science Progress*, **50**, 177–191.

10 Corbet, G.B. (1979) Report on rodent remains, pp. 135–137 in Renfrew, C. *Investigations in Orkney.* Reports of the Research Committee of the Society of Antiquaries, **38**, London.

11 Corbet, G.B. (1986) Temporal and spatial variation of dental pattern in the voles, *Microtus arvalis*, of the Orkney Islands. *Journal of Zoology*, **208**, 395–402.

12 Currant, A. Personal communication.

13 Davison, A. *et al.* (2001) Mitochondrial phylogeography and population history of pine martens *Martes martes* compared with polecats *Mustela putorius. Molecular Ecology*, **10**, 2479–2488.

14 Devoy, R.J. (1986) Possible landbridges between Ireland and Britain: A geological appraisal. *Occasional Publications of the Irish Biogeographical Society*, **1**, 15–26.

15 Fisher, C. & Yalden, D.W. (2004) The steppe pika *Ochotona pusilla* in Britain, and a new northerly record. *Mammal Review*, **34**, 320–324.

16 Fraser, F.C. & King, J.E. (1954) Faunal remains, pp. 70–95 in Clark, J.G.D. (ed.) *Excavations at Star Carr.* Cambridge University Press, Cambridge.

17 Harris, S. *et al.* (1995) *A review of British mammals: population estimates and conservation status of British mammals, other than cetaceans.* JNCC, Peterborough.

18 Haynes, S. *et al.* (2003) Phylogeography of the common vole (*Microtus arvalis*) with emphasis on the colonization of Orkney. *Molecular Ecology*, **12**, 951–956.

19 Hooker, J.J. (1989) British mammals in the Tertiary Period. *Biological Journal of the Linnaean Society*, **38**, 9–21.

20 Hooker, J.J. (1994) Mammalian taphonomy and palaeoecology of the Bembridge Limestone Formation (Late Eocene, S. England). *Historical Biology*, **8**, 49–69.

21 Hooker, J.J. *et al.* (1995) Reconstruction of land and freshwater palaeoenvironments near the Eocene–Oligocene boundary, southern England. *Journal of the Geological Society, London*, **152**, 449–468.

22 Jenkinson, R.D.S. (1983) The recent history of the Northern Lynx, (*Lynx lynx* Linné) in the British Isles. *Quaternary Newsletter*, **41**, 1–7.

23 Kemp, T.S. (1982) *Mammal-like reptiles and the origin of mammals.* Academic Press, London.

24 Kielan-Jaworowska, Z. *et al.* (2004) *Mammals from the age*

of dinosaurs. Columbia University Press, New York.

25 King, J.E. (1962) Report on animal bones, in Wymer, J. Excavations at the Magelomosian sites at Thatcham, Berkshire, England. *Proceedings of the Prehistoric Society*, **28**, 255–361.

26 Kitchener, A.C. & Bonsall, C. (1997) AMS radiocarbon dates for some extinct Scottish mammals. *Quaternary Newsletter*, **83**, 1–11.

27 Kitchener, A.C. & Bonsall, C. (1999) Further AMS radiocarbon dates for extinct Scottish mammals. *Quaternary Newsletter*, **88**, 1–10.

28 Kowalski, K. (1967) The Pleistocene extinctions of mammals in Europe, pp. 349–364 in Martin, P.S. & Wright, H.E. (eds) *Pleistocene extinctions.* Yale University Press, New Haven, CT.

29 Kurtén, B. (1968) *Pleistocene mammals of Europe.* Weidenfeld & Nicolson, London.

30 Legge, A.J. & Rowley-Conwy, P.A. (1988) *Star Carr revisited: a re-analysis of the large mammals.* Centre for Extra-Mural Studies, Birkbeck College, University of London.

31 Lister, A.M. (1991) Late Glacial mammoths in Britain, pp. 51–59 in Barton, N., Roberts, A.J. & Roe, D.A. (eds) *The Late Glacial in north-west Europe.* CBA Research Report **77**, London.

32 McCormick, F. (1999). Early evidence for wild animals in Ireland in Benecke, N. (ed.). *The Holocene history of the European vertebrate fauna, modern aspects of research. Archäologie in Eurasien*, **6**, 355–371.

33 Mascheretti, S., *et al.* (2003) How did pygmy shrews colonize Ireland? Clues from a phylogenetic analysis of mitochondrial cytochrome b sequences. *Proceedings of the Royal Society of London Series B*, **270**, 1593–1599.

34 Mayhew, D.F. (1975) *The Quaternary history of some British rodents and lagomorphs.* PhD thesis, University of Cambridge.

35 Mitchell, G.F. (1941). The reindeer in Ireland. *Proceedings of the Royal Irish Academy*, **46B**, 183–188.

36 Mitchell, G.F. & Parkes, A.S. (1938). The giant deer in Ireland. *Proceedings of the Royal Irish Academy*, **52B**, 291–314.

37 Muller, W. (2005) The domestication of the dog – the inevitable first?, pp. 34–40 in Vigne, J.-D., Peters, J & Helmer, D. *The first steps of animal domestication.* Oxbow Books, Oxford.

38 Noddle, B. (1989) Cattle and sheep in Britain and northern Europe up to the Atlantic Period: a personal viewpoint, pp. 179–202 in Milles, A., Williams, D. & Gardner, N. (eds) *The beginnings of agriculture.* BAR International Series **496**, Oxford.

39 Pernetta, J.C. & Handford, P.T. (1970) Mammalian and avian remains from possible Bronze Age deposits on Nornour, Isles of Scilly. *Journal of Zoology*, **162**, 534–540.

40 Preece, R.C., *et al.* (1986) New biostratigraphic evidence of the Post-glacial colonization of Ireland and for Mesolithic forest disturbance. *Journal of Biogeography*, **13**, 487–509.

41 Price, C. (2003) *Late Pleistocene and Early Holocene small mammals in south west Britain.* BAR British Series 347, Archaeopress, Oxford.

42 Reynolds, R.H. (1929). *A monograph of the British Pleistocene Mammalia. Vol. III, Part III. The giant deer.* Paleontographical Society, London.

43 Savolainen, P., *et al.* (2002) Genetic evidence for an east Asian origin of domestic dogs. *Science*, **298**, 1610–1613.

44 Shackleton, N.J. *et al.* (1991) An alternative astronomical calibration of the lower Pleistocene timescale based on ODP site 677. *Transactions of the Royal Society of Edinburgh*, **81**, 252–261.

45 Simmons, I. (1995) The history of the human environment, pp. 5–15 in Vyner, B. *Moorland monuments: studies in the archaeology of north-east Yorkshire in honour of Raymond Hayes and Don Spratt.* CBA Research Report 101, York.

46 Smith, C. *et al.* (1994) Animal bone report, pp. 139–153 in Smith, B.B. (ed.). *Four millennia of Orkney prehistory,* Monograph Series 9, Society of Antiquaries of Scotland, Edinburgh.

47 Stuart, A.J. (1982) *Pleistocene vertebrates in the British Isles.* Longman, London.

48 Stuart, A.J. (1991) Mammalian extinctions in the Late Pleistocene of Northern Eurasia and North America. *Biological Reviews*, **66**, 453–562.

49 Stuart, A.J., *et al.* (2004) Pleistocene to Holocene extinction dynamics in giant deer and woolly mammoth. *Nature*, **431**, 684–689.

50 Suchentruck, F. *et al.* (2001) Little allozyme variability in brown hares *Lepus europaeus* from New Zealand and Britain – a legacy of bottlenecks? *Mammalian Biology*, **66**, 48–59.

50a Sleeman, D.P. (1986) Ireland's carnivorous mammals: problems with their arrival and survival. *Occasional Publications of the Irish Biogeographical Society*, **1**, 42-48

51 Troy, C.S. *et al.* (2001) Genetic evidence for Near-Eastern origins of European cattle. *Nature*, **410**, 1088–1091.

52 Warren, C. (2003) *The microfaunal remains from Chapel Cave, North Yorkshire.* MSc thesis, University of Bradford.

53 Wingfield, R.T.R. (1995) A model of sea-level changes in the Irish and Celtic seas during the end-Pleistocene to Holocene transition, pp. 209–242 in Preece, R.C. (ed.) *Island Britain: a Quaternary perspective.* Special Publication **96**, Geological Society, London.

54 Woodman, P. *et al.* (1997) The Irish Quaternary fauna project. *Quaternary Science Reviews*, **16**, 129–159.

55 Yalden, D.W. (1981) The occurrence of the pygmy shrew *Sorex minutus* on moorland, and the implications for its presence in Ireland. *Journal of Zoology*, **195**, 147–156.

56 Yalden, D.W. (1982) When did the mammal fauna of the British Isles arrive? *Mammal Review*, **12**, 1–57.

57 Yalden, D.W. (1992) Changing distribution and status of small mammals in Britain. *Mammal Review*, **22**, 97–106.

58 Yalden, D.W. (1999) *The history of British mammals.* Poyser, London

4

Mammals and the law

A.J. Mitchell-Jones, F. Marnell, J.E. Matthews & R. Raynor

LEGAL PROTECTION

A wide variety of laws, originating from a diversity of purposes, impinges on the protection, control, study and exploitation of the mammals of Great Britain and Ireland, resulting in a confusing picture of protection, partial protection, prohibition and restriction. In many cases, laws have been subsequently updated, by amendment Acts, Statutory Instruments or other legislation, so consulting only the original Act can give a misleading picture of the current legal situation. It is generally difficult to obtain up-to-date consolidated versions incorporating all these changes, though the recent introduction of the UK Statute Law Database (*www.statutelaw.gov.uk*) is a great step forwards. For the Republic of Ireland, Comerford [1] provides a detailed review of the major pieces of wildlife legislation and how they sit together. However, the difficulty of interpreting this legislative mixture is further compounded by the way in which the British and Irish legal systems operate through a system of decision and precedent. Only a court can decide what the law means in any particular set of circumstances. In the UK, decisions in the Crown Court (England, Wales, Northern Ireland) or Sheriff Court (Scotland) or above set legal precedents as to the meaning of any particular word or phrase and these can then be cited as authorities in subsequent cases. Decisions in lower courts thus carry no weight. Where words or phrases have not been the subject of court decisions, they are held to have their ordinary English meaning, leaving them open to further legal debate, with the House of Lords as the ultimate arbiter. The result of this system is that it is more or less impossible to give a definitive interpretation of any piece of legislation until it has been thoroughly tested in the courts. A similar system applies in Ireland, with the High Court setting precedent and the Supreme Court being the ultimate arbiter. As most wildlife legislation has received little attention from the higher courts, this leaves us with considerable difficulties in providing authoritative interpretations. This difficulty should be borne in mind when consulting this chapter – only direct quotes from the legislation can be taken as authoritative.

Further confusion is added to this picture by the differing legal systems of the components of the United Kingdom. England and Wales share a common legal system, but Scotland and Northern Ireland differ. Increased devolution in recent years has increased the extent to which these legal systems differ and this divergence is continuing. In addition, the UK Dependencies (Channel Islands and Isle of Man) have their own legal systems and are not part of the European Union except for some defined purposes.

In attempting to give a useful, detailed and practical description of the legal framework affecting mammals and our treatment of them, we have chosen to focus primarily on those pieces of legislation that are widely used rather than the arcane and obscure. We have also chosen not to cover the various welfare laws that govern the keeping of animals, wild or domestic, in captivity, other than where this relates to the taking and possession of a wild animal or where it may apply to wild mammals. A useful summary of this legislation in the UK can be found at *www.defra.gov.uk/animalh/welfare/domestic/*. The Animal Welfare Act 2006 has recently updated much of this legislation and repealed a number of older Acts. However, it applies only to England and Wales. Similarly, the acts to regulate hunting with dogs, the Protection of Wild Mammals (Scotland) Act 2002 and the Hunting Act 2004, are not covered, as these complex pieces of legislation are unlikely to affect most mammalogists.

Significant legislation to be covered includes the major pieces of general wildlife legislation. In the UK this includes the Wildlife & Countryside Act 1981 [Wildlife (Northern Ireland) Order 1985] and the Conservation (Natural Habitats &c.) Regulations 1994, [The Conservation (Natural Habitats, etc.) Regulations (Northern Ireland) 1995] together with their various amendments. A similar function is served in the Republic of Ireland by the Wildlife Act 1976, the Wildlife Amendment Act 2000 and the European Communities (Natural Habitats) Regulations 1997. Legislation referring to single species or species groups in the UK includes the Conservation of Seals Act 1970, the Protection of Badgers Act 1992, the Deer Act 1991 and the Deer (Scotland) Act 1996. We also cover the Wild

32

Mammals (Protection) Act 1996, various Orders made under the Destructive Imported Animals Act 1932 and several other pieces of legislation relating to the control of mammals. Although it is not primarily legislation affecting wild mammals, we have also covered the Animals (Scientific Procedures) Act 1986 and the equivalent legislation in the Republic of Ireland (the Cruelty to Animals Act 1876, as amended by the European Communities (Amendment of Cruelty to Animals Act, 1876) Regulations 2002), as these have an impact on some field and laboratory research techniques used by mammalogists.

The law is in a constant state of flux, with a particularly large number of changes being introduced or planned in the UK during 2007–2008. This has made it difficult to prepare a chapter that is both accurate and up to date, particularly as the interpretation and implementation of these changes will take time to mature.

INTERNATIONAL LEGISLATION

Obligation on governments with respect to wildlife protection can arise from two sources:

- *European Union directives.* These are legally binding on all Member States and their requirements must be implemented through domestic legislation, creating appropriate criminal offences if required. The European Commission has a well-established framework to check that Member States have accurately transposed the requirements of a Directive and will take infraction proceedings against Member States if necessary. The UK and Ireland have been criticised on several occasions for alleged failure to accurately transpose the requirements of Directives into domestic legislation.
- *International conventions.* Membership of these is voluntary, but they become, to a degree, binding on signatories, though it is possible for signatories to derogate from some of the requirements at time of accession (also known as entering reservations). For example, the UK is a signatory to the Bern Convention (see below), but has a reservation to allow the taking or killing of hares, stoats and weasels using methods prohibited by the convention. Enforcement of conventions is less rigorous than for directives and is generally limited to censuring governments that transgress.

The primary directives and conventions affecting the protection of mammals in the UK and Republic of Ireland are:

- **EC Directive 92/43/EEC on the Conservation of Natural Habitats and of Wild Fauna and Flora, 1992 (Habitats Directive).** This Directive introduced the system of Natura 2000 sites (Special Areas of Conservation, SACs), requiring Member States to designate protected areas for listed habitats and species. It also required Member States to implement a system of strict protection for listed species.
- **Convention on the Conservation of European Wildlife and Natural Habitats, 1979 (Bern Convention).** See *http://conventions.coe.int/Treaty/ Commun/QueVoulezVous.asp?NT=104&CM=1&C L=ENG* for details. Signatories to this convention are obliged to protect listed species (set out in several appendices with different requirements), ban indiscriminate methods of capture and undertake other activities to ensure the conservation of the habitats of protected species.
- **Convention on Migratory Species, 1979 (Bonn Convention, CMS).** This convention operates as a framework for a range of regional agreements covering particular species groups. Current agreements on mammals are the Agreement on the conservation of populations of European bats (Eurobats), the Agreement on the Conservation of Small Cetaceans of the Baltic and North Seas (ASCOBANS) and the Agreement on the Conservation of Cetaceans of the Black Sea, Mediterranean Sea and Contiguous Atlantic Area (ACCOBAMS). The UK is a Party to the first two; Ireland is a Party to Eurobats.
- **Convention on Biological Diversity, 1992 (Rio Convention, CBD).** The CBD requires Parties to develop national strategies to maintain biodiversity and undertake a range of actions aimed at maintaining or restoring biodiversity. The UK responded to this requirement by publishing the UK Biodiversity Action Plan (see *www.ukbap.org.uk*) with its associated species and habitat action plans. Mammals with individual action plans in the UK are greater and lesser horseshoe bats, barbastelle, greater mouse-eared bat, Bechstein's bat, pipistrelle, brown hare, dormouse, red squirrel, water vole and otter. The Irish government published its National Biodiversity Plan in 2002 and within that commits to developing action plans for species of highest conservation concern. A number of all-Ireland action plans have been published to date, including one for the Irish hare (see *www.npws.ie/publications*). Further all-Ireland action plans for nine bat species and for the red squirrel are drafted and are undergoing consultation. These are due to be published in 2007.

Both directives and conventions are aimed at governments rather than individuals, and so do not generally create mechanisms under which individuals can be prosecuted. However, governments can be prosecuted in the European Court of Justice if they fail to adequately transpose directives into domestic legislation. This is the end point of the infraction proceedings referred to earlier.

GENERAL WILDLIFE LEGISLATION IN THE UK

The two major pieces of UK wildlife legislation described below arise from different international obligations and overlap to a very significant extent. In some places the wording is identical, in others it differs slightly, and there are some provisions that are unique to each. Recent changes mean that the lists of protected species are now quite different, with the Habitats Regulations covering all European protected species and the Wildlife and Countryside Act covering several others. This overlap of legislation provides a rich source of confusion.

Wildlife and Countryside Act 1981 and Wildlife (Northern Ireland) Order 1985

The Wildlife and Countryside Act 1981 (WCA) transposes into UK law the Convention on the Conservation of European Wildlife and Natural Habitats (the Bern Convention). The 1981 Act has been amended several times, most recently by the Countryside and Rights of Way Act 2000 (CRoW) [England & Wales], which added the concept of recklessness to some offences and made the disturbance of Cetacea and basking sharks an offence. In Scotland, the Nature Conservation (Scotland) Act 2004 introduced some enhanced protection, such as adding recklessness to most offences and changing the law relating to snaring. In Northern Ireland, Part 1 of the Act, dealing with species protection, is replaced by the Wildlife (Northern Ireland) Order 1985 which contains similar provisions, though the list of protected species is different.

The Act deals with the protection of both sites (sites of special scientific interest, SSSIs) and species, but the relevant part for mammals is Part 1, which deals with species protection.

OFFENCES
The Act implements the requirement of the Bern Convention to ensure the special protection of species listed on Appendix II. Thus, under Section 9, it is an offence to:

- Intentionally (or recklessly, in Scotland) kill, injure or take any wild animal included in Schedule 5
- Possess or control any live or dead specimen included in Schedule 5 or anything derived from such an animal, unless it can be shown to have been legally acquired
- Intentionally or recklessly damage, destroy or obstruct access to any structure or place used for shelter or protection by a wild animal listed on Schedule 5
- Intentionally or recklessly disturb a Schedule 5 species while it is occupying a structure or place which it uses for that purpose
- Intentionally or recklessly disturb (or harass, in Scotland) a dolphin or whale (Cetacea) or a basking shark.

Schedule 5, which lists the species protected by these provisions, can be amended by Statutory Instrument (SI) by the Secretary of State and there is provision for a review every 5 years by the statutory nature conservation organisations. Species can be added or removed, added in respect of a subset of the provisions above or even added in respect of particular areas or particular times of year. The current status of Schedule 5, showing the various amendments, is shown in Table 4.1. In 2007 European protected species (EPS) were removed from all the provisions of this Act by the Conservation (Natural Habitats &c.) Amendment (Scotland) Regulations 2007 and from almost all the provisions of this Act by the Conservation (Natural Habitats &c.) (Amendment) Regulations 2007 [England & Wales], so for all practical purposes, their protection now relies on the amended Regulations. This means that the only mammals in Great Britain whose protection now depends on the WCA are pine marten, red squirrel, water vole and walrus.

In Northern Ireland, Schedule 5 included, until recently, badger, all bats (EPS), all Cetacea (EPS), pine marten, otter (EPS), common seal, grey seal and red squirrel. All EPS have now been removed from this Schedule by the Conservation (Natural Habitats &c.) (Amendment) Regulations (Northern Ireland) 2007.

The Act also implements the requirement of the Convention to protect species listed in Appendix III and to prohibit indiscriminate methods of capture. Relevant offences under Section 11 are:

- Set in position a self-locking snare calculated to cause injury to any wild animal
- Use a self-locking snare, a bow or crossbow or any explosive (other than firearm ammunition) to kill or take any wild animal
- Set, or knowingly cause or permit to be set, any snare and then fail to inspect it at least once a

Table 4.1 Schedule 5 of the Wildlife & Countryside Act 1981; animals which are protected in England, Scotland and Wales

Common name	Scientific name	Notes
Bats, horseshoe (all species)	Rhinolophidae	EPS[a]
Bats, typical (all species)	Vespertilionidae	EPS[a]
Cat, wild	*Felis silvestris*	EPS[a]
Dolphins (all species)	Cetacea	EPSb
Dormouse	*Muscardinus avellanarius*	Added in 1988, SI 288. EPS[a]
Marten, pine	*Martes martes*	Added in 1988, SI 288
Otter, common	*Lutra lutra*	EPS[a]
Porpoises (all species)	Cetacea	EPS[b]
Squirrel, red	*Sciurus vulgaris*	
Vole, water	*Arvicola terrestris*	Added in 1998, SI 878, in respect of S9(4) only.
Walrus	*Odobenus rosmarus*	Added in 1988, SI 288
Whales (all species)	Cetacea	Added in 1988, SI 288. EPS[b]

[a] Not included on Schedule 5 in Scotland and only in respect of S9(4)(b) and (c) & 9(5) in England and Wales. Correct at 1/1/07.

[b] Not included on Schedule 5 in Scotland and only in respect of S9(4A) & 9(5) in England and Wales. Correct at 1/1/07.

day (or at intervals of not more than 24 hours, in Scotland). In Scotland it is also an offence not to release or remove an animal from a snare when it is inspected.

- Set in position or use any of the following methods to injure, kill or take any wild animal listed on Schedule 6: any trap or snare, any electrical device for killing or stunning or any poisoned, poisonous or stupefying substance
- Use any of the following methods to kill or take any wild animal on Schedule 6: any automatic or semi-automatic weapon; any device for illuminating a target or sighting device for night shooting; any form of artificial light or any mirror or other dazzling device; or any gas or smoke
- Use any sound recording as a decoy for killing or taking a Schedule 6 species
- Use any mechanically propelled vehicle to pursue drive, kill or take a Schedule 6 species.

It is also an offence to knowingly cause or permit to be done any of the prohibited acts listed above. Species protected by inclusion on Schedule 6 are shown in Table 4.2. In Northern Ireland,

Schedule 6 is more extensive and contains badger, bats, hedgehog, red, fallow and sika deer, brown and Irish hare, grey and common seal, pine marten, otter and red squirrel.

Another important prohibition relevant to mammals is that it is an offence to release or allow to escape to the wild any animal which is of a kind not ordinarily resident in, or a regular visitor to, Great Britain or is listed in Schedule 9. This schedule lists a number of mammal species that have been introduced into Great Britain and are now established here. As with the other schedules, species can be added or removed by Statutory Instrument. Mammals currently listed on the schedule are shown in Table 4.3. A similar provision applies in Northern Ireland, though the only mammals included on Schedule 9 there are mink, black rat and grey squirrel. The Natural Environment and Rural Communities Act 2006 (Section 50) extended control over selected non-native species in England and Wales by making it an offence to trade in live specimens of non-native species listed by the Secretary of State. A list of banned species has not yet been published.

Table 4.2 Schedule 6 of the Wildlife & Countryside Act. Animals which may not be killed or taken by certain methods (England & Wales, Scotland). Correct at 1/1/07

Common name	Scientific name
Badger	*Meles meles*
Bats, horseshoe (all species)	Rhinolophidae
Bats, typical (all species)	Vespertilionidae
Cat, wild	*Felis silvestris*
Dolphin, bottle-nosed	*Tursiops truncatus (otherwise known as Tursiops tursio)*
Dolphin, common	*Delphinus delphis*
Dormice (all species)	Gliridae
Hedgehog	*Erinaceus europaeus*
Marten, pine	*Martes martes*
Otter, common	*Lutra lutra*
Polecat	*Mustela putorius*
Porpoise, harbour (otherwise known as Common porpoise)	*Phocoena phocoena*
Shrews (all species)	Soricidae
Squirrel, red	*Sciurus vulgaris*

DEFENCES

Once the offences have been stated in the Act, there are several defences defined that allow for otherwise illegal acts to be carried out in certain circumstances.

Wild animals

As the Act applies only to wild animals, defined as 'any animal which is or (before it was taken or killed) was living wild', it could be a defence to show that any animal involved was not a wild animal. However, the Act makes it clear that any animal is assumed to be wild unless the contrary is shown. Because they have never lived in the wild, captive-bred animals are not covered by the legislation, though it would be up to the owner to show that this was the case.

Agriculture and animal health acts

Requirements under the Agriculture Act 1947 [Agriculture (Scotland) Act 1948] or orders made under the Animal Health Act 1981 provide a defence against all offences defined in Section 9 of the WCA. Section 98 of the Agriculture Act [Section 39 in Scotland] allows the Minister of Agriculture to serve notice on landowners requiring them to control animals that are causing damage. It has been used to require landowners to control rabbits and to control deer by shooting them at night.

Possessing, selling or exchanging

A live or dead Schedule 5 species, or any part of it, may be possessed or controlled, provided the animal had not been taken or killed, or had been lawfully taken or killed, or that the animal had been lawfully sold. This allows for the keeping of specimens that were found dead, such as road casualties. It is up to the defendant to show that the defence applies, so it is advisable for anyone with a collection of protected mammals, or parts of them, to keep records of where they obtained the specimens. The Act also makes it illegal to sell, offer for sale or transport for the purpose of sale any Schedule 5 species, or parts of it, and to advertise the buying or selling of protected species. In Northern Ireland, Schedule 7 of the Wildlife (Northern Ireland) Order 1985 lists species that may not be sold alive or dead at all times; this is badger, all bats, fox, hedgehog, pine marten, otter, common and grey seal, red squirrel.

Injured and disabled animals

A disabled protected species may be captured solely for the purpose of restoring it back to health for subsequent release. Mercy killing of animals so severely injured that they have no reasonable hope of recovery is also permissible.

Prevention of serious damage

Killing or injuring a Schedule 5 species is not an offence if it can be shown that this is necessary to prevent serious damage to livestock, foodstuffs for livestock, crops, vegetables, fruit, growing timber or any form of property or to fisheries. However, this defence can only be used for 'emergency' action in situations where there was no opportunity to apply for the appropriate licence. A further related defence allows for the inadvertent capture or killing of Schedule 6 species through the use of traps, snares, electrical devices or poisonous or stupefying substances if it can be shown that these were set in position for the purpose of killing or taking, in the interests of public health, agriculture, forestry, fisheries or nature conservation, any wild animals that could be lawfully taken and that all reasonable steps were taken to avoid danger to Schedule 6 species.

Dwelling-houses

The Act contains an exception allowing the intentional disturbance of Schedule 5 species and the damaging, obstruction or destruction of places of shelter or protection in a dwelling-house. However, it remains illegal to kill, injure or take these species in dwelling-houses.

Incidental result

A defence to all the offences listed above exists for

Table 4.3 Schedule 9, Part 1 of the Wildlife and Countryside Act 1981. Animals which are established in the wild but may not be released. Correct at 1/1/07

Common name	Scientific name	Notes
Coypu	*Myocastor coypus*	
Deer, any hybrid one of whose parents or other lineal ancestors was a sika	Any hybrid of *Cervus nippon*	Sika added 1992, SI 320. Hybrids added 1999, SI 1002
With respect to the Outer Hebrides and the islands of Arran, Islay, Jura and Rum – Deer, *Cervus* (all species).	*Cervus*	Added 1999, SI 1002
Deer, any hybrid one of whose parents or other lineal ancestors was a species of *Cervus* deer	Any hybrid of the genus *Cervus*	
Deer, muntjac	*Muntiacus reevesi*	Added 1997, SI 226
Dormouse, fat	*Glis glis*	
Gerbil, Mongolian	*Meriones unguiculatus*	
Marmot, prairie (otherwise known as prairie dog	*Cynomys*	
Mink, American	*Mustela vison*	
Porcupine, crested	*Hystrix cristata*	
Porcupine, Himalayan	*Hystrix hodgsonii*	
Rat, black	*Rattus rattus*	
Squirrel, grey	*Sciurus carolinensis*	
Wallaby, red-necked	*Macropus rufogriseus*	

cases where 'the act was the incidental result of a lawful operation and could not reasonably have been avoided'. In Scotland, this defence has been replaced by the following wording: 'the unlawful act was the incidental result of a lawful operation or other activity and that the person who carried out the lawful operation or other activity took reasonable precautions for the purpose of avoiding carrying out the unlawful act, or that the person did not foresee, and could not reasonably have foreseen, that the unlawful act would be an incidental result of the carrying out of the lawful operation or other activity'. The Scottish defence only applies if the defendant stops causing any further illegal actions as soon as practically possible once he or she realises they are occurring. This defence was intended to ensure that people did not inadvertently break the law when carrying out their everyday business, but in practice is also used to allow activities, such as development (as defined in the planning legislation), that cannot be licensed, on the understanding that agreed best practice is followed.

Bats and notification

Because of their dependence on the built environment, bats had a special legal provision under the Act, requiring consultation with the Statutory Nature Conservation Organisations (SNCOs). However, the recent removal of bats from most (England & Wales) or all (Scotland, Northern Ireland) of the provisions of the Act mean that this now has little relevance.

LICENSING

Most activities that are otherwise illegal can be licensed for particular purposes. Licensable activities include killing, injuring, taking, possessing or trading protected species, using self-locking snares or any prohibited method of capture, using vehicles to pursue protected species or releasing non-native species to the wild. The purposes for which licences can be granted are:

(a) scientific or educational purposes
(b) ringing or marking
(c) conservation or introductions
(d) protecting zoological or botanical collections
(e) photography
(f) preserving public health or public safety
(g) preventing the spread of disease
(h) preventing serious damage to livestock, foodstuffs for livestock, crops, vegetables, fruit, growing timber or any form of property or to fisheries.

Selling, or advertising for sale, Schedule 5 species and releasing non-native species are also licensable, but do not need to meet any of the purposes listed above.

There is currently no purpose covering development, so, for example, it is not possible to issue a licence allowing the intentional destruction of places of shelter or protection for Schedule 5 species on development sites. Similarly, it would not be possible to license the capture and removal of Schedule 5 species from these sites. In the former case, the 'incidental result' defence (see above) can be used, but this may not stretch to the latter case as it would be hard to argue that the intentional capture of protected species was an incidental result.

Responsibility for issuing licences varies between administrations and may also be split between licensing authorities. In England, Natural England is responsible for the issue of all licences under the WCA, some on behalf of the Secretary of State. In Wales, the Countryside Council for Wales issues licences for purposes a–e above and the Welsh Assembly Government issues licences

Table 4.4 European protected species of animals on Schedule 2 of the Conservation (Natural Habitats &c.) Regulations 1994. Correct at 1/1/07

Common name	Scientific name
Bats, horseshoe (all species)	Rhinolophidae
Bats, typical (all species)	Vespertilionidae
Cat, wild	*Felis silvestris*
Dolphins, porpoises and whales (all species)	Cetacea
Dormouse	*Muscardinus avellanarius*
Otter, common	*Lutra lutra*

Table 4.4 (cont.)

Common name	Scientific name
Bat, Egyptian fruit	*Rousettus aegiptiacus*
Bear, brown	*Ursus arctos*
Beaver, European	*Castor fiber* (except Estonian, Latvian, Lithuanian, Polish, Finnish and Swedish populations)
Bison, European	*Bison bonasus*
Bucardo (Spanish ibex)	*Capra pyrenaica pyrenaica*
Chamois, Apennine	*Rupicapra pyrenaica ornata (Rupicapra rupicapra ornata)*
Chamois, Bulgarian	*Rupicapra rupicapra balcanica*
Chamois, Tatra	*Rupicapra rupicapra tatrica*
Deer, Corsican red	*Cervus elaphus corsicanus*
Desman, Pyrenean	*Galemys pyrenaicus*
Dormice	Gliridae – all species except *Glis glis and Eliomys quercinus*
Flying squirrel, Russian	*Pteromys volans (Sciuropterus russicus)*
Fox, Arctic	*Alopex lagopus*
Goat, wild	*Capra aegagrus* (natural populations)
Hamster, common	*Cricetus cricetus* (except Hungarian populations)
Hedgehog, Algerian	*Erinaceus algirus*
Lynx	*Lynx lynx* (except Estonian populations)
Lynx, Iberian	*Lynx pardinus*
Marmot, Tatra	*Marmota marmota latirostris*
Microbats	Microchiroptera
Mink, European	*Mustela lutreola*
Mouflon	*Ovis gmelini musimon (Ovis ammon musimon)* (natural populations on Corsica and Sardinia)
Mouflon, Cyprus	*Ovis orientalis ophion (Ovis gmelini ophion)*
Mouse, northern birch	*Sicista betulina*
Mouse, southern birch	*Sicista subtilis*
Otter	*Lutra lutra*
Polecat, steppe	*Mustela eversmanii*
Porcupine, crested	*Hystrix cristata*
Seal, Mediterranean monk	*Monachus monachus*
Seal, Saimaa ringed	*Phoca hispida saimensis*
Shrew, Canary	*Crocidura canariensis*
Shrew, Sicilian	*Crocidura sicula*

Table 4.7 List of Irish species protected under Schedule 5 of the Wildlife Act 1976

Common name	Scientific name	Notes
Badger	*Meles meles*	
Bat species		All species
Deer species		All species
Dolphin species		All species
Hare species		All species
Hedgehog	*Erinaceus europaeus*	
Otter	*Lutra lutra*	
Pine marten	*Martes martes*	
Porpoise species		All species
Red squirrel	*Sciurus vulgaris*	
Seal species		All species
Shrew, pygmy	*Sorex minutus*	Added 1980, S I 282
Stoat	*Mustela erminea*	Added 1980, S I 282
Whale species		All species

growing timber or any form of property or to fisheries
(h) taking or keeping protected species under strictly supervised conditions, on a selective basis and in limited numbers.

In all cases, a licence cannot be granted unless there is no satisfactory alternative and the action authorised will not be detrimental to the conservation status of the species concerned. Licences may include conditions, such as adherence to an agreed method statement, and it is an offence to contravene these conditions.

A major difference between the WCA and the Regulations is the existence of a licensing purpose that can cover development ('other imperative reasons of overriding public interest') in the Regulations. This is widely used where EPS are present on development sites.

Responsibility for issuing licences varies between administrations and may also be split between licensing authorities. In England, Natural England is responsible for the issue of all licences under the Regulations, some on behalf of the Secretary of State. In Wales, the Countryside Council for Wales issues licences for purposes a–d above and the Welsh Assembly Government issues licences for all other purposes. In Scotland, Scottish Natural Heritage issues licences for

purposes a–d and the Scottish Executive (SEERAD) issues all other licences. In Northern Ireland, all licences are issued by the Department of Environment Northern Ireland.

ENFORCEMENT OF THE WCA AND REGULATIONS

The police are the main enforcement body for wildlife offences, and in some cases local authorities may also take action. The SNCOs can give advice or assistance to the police in respect of alleged offences. The maximum fine on conviction for species offences under the WCA and Regulations is a Level 5 fine (currently £5000) per offence and/or a custodial sentence of up to 6 months. Penalties may be imposed in relation to each offence committed, so operations involving many animals or repeated offences can, in theory, accrue large fines. In addition, items which may constitute evidence of the commission of an offence may be seized and detained.

GENERAL WILDLIFE LEGISLATION IN THE REPUBLIC OF IRELAND

The legal protection of mammals in Ireland dates back over 300 years to the Deer Protection Act of 1698. The most important legislation underpinning biodiversity and nature conservation in Ireland today are the Wildlife Act 1976 (*www.irishstatutebook.ie/ZZA39Y1976.html*) and the European Communities (Natural Habitats) Regulations 1997, SI 94/1997 (*www.irishstatute book.ie/ZZSI94Y1997.html*). The former has been amended once, Wildlife (Amendment) Act 2000 (*www.irishstatute book.ie/ZZA38Y2000.html*), while the latter has been amended twice with SI 233/1998 (*www. irishstatutebook.ie/ZZS I233Y1998. html*) and SI 378/2005 (*www. environ. ie/DOEI/ DOEIPol.nsf/0/ 2b2a97f190667250802 56f0f003bc850/ $FILE/European Communities (Natural Habitats) (Amendment) Regulations, 2005.doc*).

Wildlife Acts 1976 and 2000

Although it has been extensively amended both by Regulations made under the Habitats Directive and by the Wildlife (Amendment) Act 2000 [WLAA 2000], the Wildlife Act 1976 [WLA 1976] is still the main statute governing the protection of wild mammals in the Republic of Ireland.

Chapter III relates to the protection of flora and fauna and Section 23, which deals specifically with the protection of 'wild animals (other than wild birds)', is of most relevance to mammals. Mammal species protected under the Act are listed in Schedule 5 and there is a facility for the Minister to add or remove species from this schedule. Two mammal species, the pygmy shrew and the stoat, have been added to the Schedule since it was first published. A full list of the species currently protected under Schedule 5 is given in Table 4.7.

The WLAA 2000 made a number of significant changes to Section 23 of the WLA 1976. In particular, (a) 'resting places' of Schedule 5 animals were protected for the first time, and (b) previous exemptions for the construction industry were amended so that only unintentional damage or disturbance was exempt. So now, in brief, under the Wildlife Acts 1976 and 2000, it is an offence to hunt, to injure or to wilfully interfere with or destroy the breeding or resting place of a protected wild animal.

Section 25 deals with the Minister's powers to declare by order, made from time to time as circumstances demand, that certain species of protected wild animal can be shot as 'game' species at certain times, in certain places under very strict limitations and conditions. The first of these Wild Mammal Open Season orders was made in 1977 [SI 240, 1977] and six further orders have been made since then. Table 4.8 gives the details of the current open seasons pertaining to wild mammals.

Section 26 provided for the licensing of otter hunting, hare coursing and stag hunting. Licenses ceased to be issued for otter hunting in 1990, and the WLAA 2000 repealed this part of Section 26 so that no licence can now be issued for otter hunting. Hare coursing and carted stag hunting continue under licence.

Section 32 of the WLA 1976, together with Section 40 of the WLAA 2000, regulates ringing and marking protected wild animals. Marking is defined as cutting, branding or tattooing, and ringing includes attaching 'any band, ring, microchip, tag or other marking device'.

Licensing

In certain circumstances licences can be issued to allow activities that are otherwise illegal. In particular licences can be issued under Sections 23 and 32 for the following purposes:

- to take, capture or humanely kill for scientific or educational purposes
- to photograph or video near a breeding place
- to possess an injured, disabled or orphaned wild animal
- to mark or ring.

Under Section 42 of the WLA 1976, a licence may be given allowing the scaring, capture or killing of wild birds and wild animals that are causing serious damage to food, livestock, poultry, agricultural crops and other flora and fauna.

Licence applications (including applications for derogations under the Habitats Directive – see below) are processed by the Licensing Section of the National Parks and Wildlife Service in the Department of Environment, Heritage and Local Government (see 'Permits and Licenses' at *www.npws.ie*).

Restrictions

General restrictions relating to firearms, traps, snares, poisons, decoys, lures and mechanically propelled vehicles are detailed in Sections 33–36. Statutory Instruments are published occasionally to provide further details on these restrictions. For example, SI 620, 2003 gives details of the traps, snares and nets approved 'for the purposes of Section 34 of the WLA 1976 as amended by Section 42 of the WLAA 2000.'

Introduction into the wild of certain species

Section 52 of the WLA 1976, as amended by the WLAA 2000 (subsection (7)) makes it an offence to release or allow to escape any exotic (i.e. non-native) species of animal or the spawn of such an animal, or to attempt to establish it in the wild, other than in accordance with a licence given under the Act.

Table 4.8 Irish wild mammals: open season dates and locations

Species	Dates	Location
Red deer male	1 September–31 December	Throughout the State exclusive of Co. Kerry
Red deer female and antlerless deer[a]	1 November–28 February	Throughout the State
Sika male	1 September–31 December	Throughout the State
Sika female and antlerless deer[a]	1 November–28 February	Throughout the State
Fallow male	1 September–31 December	Throughout the State
Fallow female and antlerless deer[a]	1 November–28 February	Throughout the State
Hares	26 September–28 February	Excluding the following townlands in Co. Wexford: North East Slob, North West Slob, Big Island, Beggerin Island and the Raven

[a] Antlerless deer will be construed as including any male deer without antlers, of less than 1 year, i.e. a calf.

Dangerous animals

While there is no specific legislation in Ireland regarding dangerous animals, the provisions referred to in the above paragraph are applicable to the release into the wild of dangerous animals. Furthermore, the Minister has power, under subsection (6)(a) of Section 52 of the WLA 1976 as amended by the WLAA 2000, to prohibit the possession or introduction of any species of wild animal or any part, product or derivative of such wild animal that may be detrimental to native species. This power has not yet been exercised by the Minister but regulations are being considered in the context of measures to exclude potentially invasive non-native species.

Wildlife dealers

Regulation and control of wildlife dealing and the transport, import and export of wildlife is dealt with under Part III of the WLA 1976, as amended by Part V of the WLAA 2000. In brief, only licensed wildlife dealers can sell protected wild animals (including parts or derivatives). In the interest of the conservation of a species, the Minister may by regulation temporarily control the sale or purchase of certain protected species. Section 52 (as amended by Section 56 of the WLAA 2000) covers importation of wild animals, their parts or derivatives, into the Republic of Ireland. In effect these controls only apply to imports from outside the EU.

Derogations under the Habitats Directive

Section 25 of the European Communities (Natural Habitats) Regulations, 1997, provides for derogation licences in accordance with the provisions of Article 16 of the Habitats Directive (Council Directive No 92/43/EEC).

GENERAL WILDLIFE LEGISLATION IN THE CROWN DEPENDENCIES

The Channel Isles and the Isle of Man are British Crown Dependencies, maintaining a high degree of autonomy with regard to domestic legislation, but looking to the UK for international representation and defence. They are not full members of the European Union, but have a special relationship with it. Certain European legislation applies, in accordance with Protocol 3 to the 1972 Treaty of Accession under which the UK joined the European Communities. In general, EU environmental law does not apply to the Dependencies. The Dependencies can also choose whether the UK's membership of international Conventions should extend to them, so they are not automatically members.

In the Isle of Man, the Wildlife Act 1990 contains rather similar measures to the WCA and thus gives full protection to all species of bats occurring on the island. The Act is administered by the Department of Agriculture, Fisheries and Forestry, which is responsible for issuing licences. Further information can be found at *www. gov.im/daff/countryside/wildlife/*.

In Jersey, the Conservation of Wildlife (Jersey) Law 2000 gives protection to listed species in much the same way as the WCA. The Act also prohibits specified methods of capture for listed species and contains other measures modelled fairly closely on the WCA. Protected species are all bats, Cetacea, hedgehog, seals, shrews *S. coronatus* and *C. suaveolens*, red squirrel and Jersey bank vole (*C. glareolus caesarius*). The UK's membership of the Bern and Bonn Conventions and the Convention on Biological Diversity also extends to Jersey, with the Conservation of Wildlife (Jersey) Law meeting the requirements for species and habitat protection. Jersey is also a member of the Agreement on the Conservation of Populations of European Bats (Eurobats).

The Bailiwick of Guernsey, which includes Alderney, Sark and Herm, has no specific wildlife legislation, but has extended the UK's membership of the Bonn Convention to cover the Bailiwick. Under this Convention, Guernsey is a member of both Eurobats and the Agreement on the Conservation of Small Cetaceans of the Baltic and North Seas (ASCOBANS).

SPECIFIC LEGISLATION

Some species or species groups have additional legislative protection. However, it should be borne in mind that offences against these species may also be covered by the general legislation.

Conservation of Seals Act 1970

This Act, which applies to England, Scotland and Wales, gives some limited protection to seals, which is supplemented, to a degree, by their inclusion on Schedule 3 of the Habitats Regulations. In Northern Ireland, seals are included in Schedules 5, 6 and 7 of the Wildlife (Northern Ireland) Order 1985 (see above).

Under the Conservation of Seals Act (CoSA), it is illegal to poison seals or shoot them with a firearm other than a rifle using ammunition with a bullet weight of less than 45 grains (2.9 g) and muzzle energy of less than 600 foot pounds (814 joules). The Act also defines close seasons for grey and common seals, during which time it is illegal to wilfully kill, injure or take them (Table 4.9).

This limited protection can be extended by orders made under the Act which allow the Secretary of State, after consultation with the Natural Environment Research Council (NERC),

to prohibit the killing of seals within a defined area. At present, the Conservation of Seals (England) Order 1999, prohibits the killing, injuring or taking of grey and common seals anywhere along the east coast of England from the Scottish border to Newhaven in East Sussex. The Conservation of Seals (Scotland) Order 2004 prohibits the killing injuring or taking of grey and common seals in the Moray Firth. Both these orders will remain in force until revoked.

In certain circumstances, seals may be killed or taken during the close season or in areas subject to an Order. It is not an offence to take or attempt to take a disabled seal for the purpose of tending it and releasing it when no longer disabled, or killing a seriously disabled seal that had no reasonable chance of recovery. These exceptions would allow seal rescue centres to operate throughout the year. There is also an exception for the unavoidable killing of a seal as the incidental result of a lawful action. The killing of seals interfering with fisheries is also permitted in certain circumstances. As this can be controversial, most of the wording of the exception is given:

A person shall not be guilty of an offence . . . by reason only of . . . the killing or attempted killing of any seal to prevent it from causing damage to a fishing net or fishing tackle in his possession or in the possession of a person at whose request he killed or attempted to kill the seal, or to any fish for the time being in such a fishing net, provided that at the time the seal was in the vicinity of such a net or tackle.

This can be interpreted as permitting the killing of seals in the vicinity of fishing nets or tackle, though the word 'vicinity' is not precisely defined. As with other wildlife legislation, a licensing system permits various actions that would otherwise be offences. Licences are available from the Secretary of State for the following purposes:

- *science and education:* kill or take seals in a specified area by any specified method other than strychnine
- *zoological gardens or collections:* take seals within a specified area
- *prevention of damage to fisheries, reduction of a population surplus for management purposes or use of*

Table 4.9 Close seasons for seals

Species	Dates
Common seal	1 June–31 August
Grey seal	1 September–31 December

a population surplus as a resource: kill or take seals in a specified area by any specified method other than strychnine.

As seals are on Schedule 3 of the Conservation Regulations, any licences granted under this Act cannot authorise any method of killing or taking that would be prohibited by the Regulations.

The Act contains a number of other provisions relating to the powers of constables to apprehend offenders and, more unusually, the ability of the Secretary of State to authorise people to enter upon land to obtain information or to kill seals. It also imposes a duty on the NERC to provide the Secretary of State with scientific advice on matters related to the management of seal populations. In practice, this duty is discharged through the Special Committee on Seals, which is advised by the Sea Mammals Research Unit (see *www.smru.st-and.ac.uk*).

Deer Act 1991

The Deer Act 1991, which applies to England and Wales, is a consolidation act, bringing together several pieces of earlier legislation applying to deer. A much fuller account of all the legislation affecting deer is given in [2]. The Regulatory Reform (Deer) (England and Wales) Order 2007 ('the 2007 RRO'), which comes into force in October 2007, makes certain changes to the 1991 Act and these are noted in the text. In Northern Ireland, deer are given protection by the Wildlife (Northern Ireland) Order 1985, which contains very similar provisions to the Deer Act.

The historical focus of much of the legislation relating to deer is concerned with control of their exploitation and, in particular, prevention of poaching and control of the sale of venison. This has been complicated in recent years by the development of deer farming, so the legislation has to distinguish between wild deer and farmed deer, which are kept on enclosed land and treated as livestock. Deer are not included in any of the schedules of the WCA or the Habitats Regulations, other than Schedule 9 of the WCA, which prohibits the release of certain species and their hybrids. In Northern Ireland, fallow, red and sika deer are included in Schedule 6 of the Wildlife (Northern Ireland) Order 1985, giving them protection against certain methods of capture.

The main offences defined by the Deer Act, other than those relating to trade in venison, are:

- Poaching: that is, entering land without the consent of the owner or occupier in search or pursuit of deer. This includes intentionally taking, killing or injuring deer and also

removing the carcase of any deer

- Intentionally killing deer during the close season: this does not apply to farmed deer on enclosed land.
- Killing deer at night.
- Setting in position or using for taking or killing deer any trap, snare, net or poisoned or stupefying bait.
- Using a prohibited firearm or ammunition, arrow, spear or similar missile or any missile containing a poison, stupefying drug or muscle relaxing agent to take, injure or kill any deer. Prohibited firearms and ammunition are shotguns, air weapons, any rifle with a calibre of less than .240 inches (6 mm) or a muzzle energy of less than 2305 joules and any bullet other than a soft-nosed or hollow-nosed bullet. The 2007 RRO introduces a provision permitting the use of .220 rifles with a muzzle energy of not less than 1356 joules (1000 foot pounds) and soft or hollow nosed bullets weighing not less than 3.24 g (50 grains) to kill muntjac, Chinese water deer or roe deer.
- Shooting from a mechanically propelled vehicle or using such a vehicle to drive deer. This prohibition does not apply to actions by, or with the written authority of, the occupier in relation to deer on enclosed land.

These offences are then qualified by a number of defences:

- Offences relating to killing deer in the close season (Table 4.10) or at night do not apply to anything required by the Minister under Section 98 of the Agriculture Act 1947. This provision has been used in England to allow the Minister to serve a notice on any person having the right to do so requiring them to shoot deer at night. This is done only in exceptional circumstances where deer are causing damage and other remedies have failed.
- Deer may legally be killed during the close season or at night to prevent the suffering of an injured or diseased deer. In addition, traps or nets may be used to catch these animals and they may be dispatched with a shotgun [or by any reasonable means (2007 RRO)] if they are severely injured. The 2007 RRO extends this to include any dependant deprived, or about to be deprived, of its mother.
- An authorised person (the occupier of land or anyone authorised in writing by him) may kill deer that are causing damage on his land (cultivated land, pasture or enclosed woodland) during the close season or with a shotgun of at least 12 bore loaded with

Table 4.10 Close seasons in England and Wales defined by the Deer Act 1991 and modified by the Regulatory Reform (Deer) (England and Wales) Order 2007. The Deer Act 1991 close seasons apply in Northern Ireland via the Wildlife (Northern Ireland) Order 1985.

Species	Sex	Close season dates	
		Deer Act 1991	**2007 Regulatory Reform Order (England & Wales)**
Red deer	Stag	1 May–31 July inclusive1	May–31 July inclusive
	Hind	1 March–31 October inclusive	15th March–31 October inclusive
Fallow deer	Buck	1 May–31 July inclusive	1 May–31 July inclusive
	Doe	1 March–31 October inclusive	15 March–31 October inclusive
Roe deer	Buck	1 November–31 March inclusive	1 November–31 March inclusive
	Doe	1 March–31 October inclusive	15 March–31 October inclusive
Sika	Stag	1 May–31 July inclusive	1 May–31 July inclusive
	Hind	1 March–31 October inclusive	15 March–31 October inclusive
Red/sika hybrids	Stag		1 May–31 July inclusive
	Hind		15 March–31 October inclusive
Chinese water deer	Buck		15 March–31 October inclusive
	Doe		15 March–31 October inclusive

specified ammunition. For this defence to apply, the person should show that he had reasonable grounds for believing that deer were causing damage to crops or growing timber, that further serious damage was likely and that his action was necessary to prevent such damage. This defence does not extend to night shooting.

Licences may be granted by the appropriate body (Natural England or the Countryside Council for Wales) to allow deer to be taken in the close season, during the night or using some otherwise prohibited methods of capture for the purpose of removing deer from one area to another or of taking deer alive for scientific or educational purposes. The permitted methods are the use of nets, traps, stupefying or muscle relaxing drugs and missiles carrying such drugs.

The 2007 RRO introduces new licensing purposes which will permit Natural England or the National Assembly for Wales to:

- Issue licences to kill deer during the close season for the purpose of preserving public health or public safety or conserving the natural heritage
- Issue licences to kill deer at night for the

purpose of preserving public health or public safety, conserving the natural heritage or preventing serious damage to property.

Before issuing such licences, the licensing authority must satisfy itself that there is a serious risk from the deer and that there is no satisfactory alternative solution. In addition, any action involving red, roe or fallow deer must not threaten the population of that species.

The Deer Act also contains provisions to control the sale of venison. Individuals may only sell venison to licensed game dealers and only at times of year outside the prohibited period, which relates to the close season for the species in question. Any venison offered for sale must have been killed legally. Licensed game dealers, who are licensed under the Game Act 1831 and the Game Licences Act 1860, are required to maintain record books in a set format giving details of all the venison they purchase.

Deer (Scotland) Act 1996

This consolidation Act brings together and repeals earlier legislation based on the Deer (Scotland) Act 1959. The first part of the Act defines the role of the Deer Commission for Scotland (DCS), which has a duty to further the conservation, control and sustainable management of deer in Scotland. Further details about the role and operation of this body can be found at *www.dcs.gov.uk*. The second part permits the Secretary of State to fix close seasons for all species of deer and makes provision for the killing of deer during the close season in certain circumstances. The current close seasons (Table 4.11) are carried forward from the Deer (Close Seasons) (Scotland) Order 1984.

There are several circumstances when deer may legally be killed during the close season:

- Occupiers and, when authorised in writing, employees, residents and owners and their employees may kill deer at any time on enclosed or cultivated land where they believe that serious damage will be caused to crops, pasture or human or animal foodstuffs if the deer are not killed.
- The DCS can authorise additional 'fit and competent' persons to take or kill deer on any land to prevent serious damage as defined above.
- The DCS can authorise persons to take or kill deer on any land during the close season to prevent serious damage to unenclosed land, or the natural heritage, or in the interests of public safety. Such authorisations can only be to 'fit and competent' persons and the DCS must ensure that no other reasonable means of control would be adequate.
- The DCS can authorise the shooting of deer at night to prevent serious damage to agriculture or woodland.
- Licences can be issued by the DCS to take or kill deer for scientific purposes.

The role of the DCS is further extended in Sections 7 and 8 of the Act, which introduce the concepts of Control Agreements and Control Schemes. A Control Agreement is a deer management plan drawn up by the DCS in close liaison with owners, occupiers and other interested parties aimed at preventing damage by wild deer to woodland, agriculture or the natural heritage, or to reduce the threat to public safety. Once in place, the DCS will monitor the progress of the Agreement towards the agreed objectives. If the DCS is unable to negotiate a satisfactory Agreement, or if the Agreement does not operate as planned, the DCS has the right, under Section 8, to impose a Control Scheme. This operates in a similar manner to an Agreement, but the DCS has the right to carry out any necessary deer control that owners or occupiers of land are unwilling or unable to carry out themselves. The DCS may then recover the costs of any such operations from the owners or occupiers concerned. The imposition of a Control Scheme needs the endorsement of the Secretary of State.

Part 3 of the Act defines offences in relation to deer. These include

- Taking or wilfully killing or injuring deer or removing carcasses from land, except where a legal right to do so exists (this right is usually held by owners, occupiers and persons authorised by them)
- Killing a deer otherwise than by shooting
- Taking or killing deer at night
- Using a vehicle to drive deer with the intention of taking, killing or injuring them
- Shooting deer from a moving vehicle
- Using a firearm, ammunition or other equipment to kill deer which does not comply with an Order made by the Secretary of State. This provision allows the Secretary of State to vary the list of suitable firearms and ammunition without the need to amend the Act itself.
- Possessing deer or firearms in circumstances which make it reasonable to infer that an

Table 4.11 Close seasons in Scotland defined by Order under the Deer (Scotland) Act 1996.

Species	Sex	Close season dates
Red deer, sika and red/sika hybrids	Stag	21 October–30 June inclusive
	Hind	1 February–20 October inclusive
Fallow deer	Buck	1 May–31 July inclusive
	Doe	16 February–20 October inclusive
Roe deer	Buck	21 October–31 March inclusive
	Doe	1 April–20 October inclusive

offence had been committed.

Exemptions are then provided for certain acts:

- Preventing suffering by injured or diseased deer or any dependant deprived, or about to be deprived, of its mother
- Killing deer during the close season when they are causing damage (see above)
- Certain exemptions for deer farming. For example, deer farmers are exempt from the prohibition on killing deer otherwise than by shooting and the requirement to use only approved weapons. They are also exempt from many of the controls on dealing in venison.

Part 4 of the Act deals with enforcement and the licensing of venison dealing. The police have certain rights to stop and search vehicles when they believe an offence has taken place, but in other circumstances must apply for a warrant before searching premises or people. Venison dealers must be appropriately licensed and must keep records of their game dealing in a prescribed form.

Protection of Badgers Act 1992

This consolidation Act brings together earlier legislation on badgers which was focused primarily on preventing badger digging and badger baiting. The construction of the original Badgers Act (1973) had proved inadequate to bringing successful prosecutions on numerous occasions. The Badgers Act 1991 and the Badgers (Further Protection) Act 1991 attempted to overcome these deficiencies in a number of ways, including introducing a new offence of interfering with a sett, but resulted in a confused legislative picture. To clarify matters, the 1992 Act replaced all this earlier legislation with a single consolidated Act.

The Protection of Badgers Act (PBA) applies to England, Scotland and Wales. The Nature Conservation (Scotland) Act 2004 amended certain aspects of the PBA, largely in the interest of clarity and assisting with enforcement. Northern Ireland does not have any specific badger legislation, but the badger is fully protected there as it is included in Schedules 5, 6 and 7 of the Wildlife (Northern Ireland) Order 1985 (see above).

The Act creates a number of offences:

- Wilfully killing, injuring or taking a badger, or attempting to do any of these things. Unusually, the Act also states that if there is evidence from which it could reasonably be concluded that the accused was attempting any of the prohibited acts he is presumed guilty unless he can show otherwise.
- Possessing a dead badger, including any parts or derivatives. This does not apply if the badger had not been killed or had been killed otherwise than in contravention of the Act or had been bought on the assumption that it had been acquired legally. Possessing, selling or offering for sale a live badger is also an offence.
- Cruelly ill-treating a badger, using badger tongs to kill or take a badger (or attempting to do so), digging for a badger or using a prohibited weapon to kill a badger. Prohibited weapons are any firearm other than a shotgun of at least 20 bore or a rifle with a muzzle energy of at least 160 foot pounds (217 joules) and a bullet weighing at least 38 grains (2.46 g). In the case of badger digging, the Act also states that if there is evidence from which it could reasonably be concluded that the accused was digging for a badger he is presumed guilty unless he can show otherwise.
- Intentionally or recklessly interfering with a badger sett by:
  - damaging a sett (or any part of it) or destroying it
  - obstructing access to any entrance of a badger sett
  - causing a dog to enter a badger sett
  - disturbing a badger when it is occupying a sett.

  In Scotland it is also an offence to knowingly cause or permit any of the above to be carried out.

  In the Act, a badger sett means any structure or place which displays signs indicating current use by a badger. This leaves considerable scope for interpretation.
- Marking a badger, or attaching any ring tag or other marking device. Badger marking can be licensed, and it seems that a licence is needed to mark even badgers that are in captivity because they are injured.

The Act then goes on to define a number of exceptions that permit what would otherwise be offences in certain circumstances:

- It is not an offence for a person to take and possess a disabled badger solely for the purpose of tending it, provided that the badger was disabled other than by his own act. Similarly, killing seriously injured badgers is not an offence.
- The unavoidable killing or injuring of a badger as an incidental result of a lawful action is not an offence. Similarly, damaging or obstructing a sett, or disturbing a badger occupying it, is not an offence if this was the incidental result of a lawful operation and could not reasonably have been avoided.
- Killing or taking a badger (or attempting to do

so) is not an offence if it can be shown that the action was necessary to prevent serious damage to land, crops, poultry or any other form of property. However, this defence does not apply if it was clear beforehand that such action would be needed and a licence had not been applied for. In other words, this defence only applies to emergency action.

- A similar defence to the one above also applies to interfering with setts, with a similar proviso about the need to obtain a licence if the action could be foreseen.
- A defence is also provided to allow fox hunts to temporarily stop up badger setts. However, as hunting with dogs is now illegal this defence seems unlikely to be useful and so is not described in detail.

Licence are available for a number of purposes (including development), to permit acts that would otherwise be illegal.

OTHER LEGISLATION AFFECTING MAMMALS AND MAMMALOGISTS

Agriculture Act 1947 and Agriculture (Scotland) Act 1948

Although primarily concerned with other agricultural matters, these Acts allow the Minister or Secretary of State to issue notices under Section 98 [in England & Wales] or Section 39 [in Scotland] requiring landowners to take steps to control 'pest' species on their land. The species that may be the subject of such orders are 'rabbits, hares and other rodents, deer, foxes and moles'. The notices may also require the landowner to take steps to destroy the breeding places or cover for rabbits. The Minister or Secretary of State may also issue a notice under Section 99 [England & Wales] or Section 40 [Scotland] requiring a landowner to take steps to prevent the escape of any animals kept on that land if it appears that they would cause damage.

Animals (Scientific Procedures) Act 1986 and equivalent Irish legislation

This Act applies throughout the UK, though it is administered separately in Northern Ireland. It controls any experimental or scientific procedure, known as a 'regulated procedure', on 'protected animals', which may cause that animal pain, suffering, distress or lasting harm. Currently, the definition of protected animals includes all vertebrates, except humans, and the common octopus *Octopus vulgaris*. The definition of 'regulated procedure' is quite wide and includes,

for example, the breeding of animals with genetic defects, the production of blood products, the administration of anaesthetics, feeding studies and the removal of blood or tissue (but see below for exceptions). The Home Office Inspectors can give advice on a case-by-case basis where it is not clear whether a proposed procedure would fall within the definition of a regulated procedure.

The controls of the Act do not extend to the following:

- Procedures applied to animals in the course of recognised veterinary, agricultural or animal husbandry practices. This includes clinical investigation and management as well as recognised husbandry practices used to manage or conserve animals provided they are not part of a scientific study.
- Ringing, tagging or marking of an animal for the sole purpose of enabling it to be identified providing this causes no more than momentary pain or distress and no lasting harm. This is open to a degree of interpretation, but it is generally considered that ringing, micro-chipping and ear-marking are not regulated procedures. Similarly, the taking of blood or DNA solely to establish the identity or provenance of an animal is not a regulated procedure provided the method used causes no more than momentary discomfort or distress. However, toe-clipping is considered to cause suffering in excess of the threshold and thus falls within the definition of a regulated procedure.
- The administration of drugs to animals in order to evaluate a veterinary product in accordance with Section 32 of the Medicines Act 1986.
- The humane killing of an animal for experimental purposes by an appropriate method. Suitable methods are listed in a Home Office code of practice.

The regulatory procedure under the Act is through a system of two types of licences:

- *Project licences* are issued for defined prog-rammes of work at a designated establishment, or exceptionally at a non-designated place. These licences are held by a person responsible for managing the programme of work, ensuring compliance with any licence conditions and completing licence returns.
- *Personal licences* are issued to individuals who have demonstrated that they are suitable and competent to carry out specified procedures. This normally involves attending appropriate training courses and being supervised by an existing licence holder. A personal licence is

needed to work under a project licence and does not, in itself, permit any programme of work.

The use of animals for experimental and other scientific purposes in the Republic of Ireland

Within the Republic of Ireland, the use of live animals in scientific research and other experimental activity is strictly controlled in accordance with the Cruelty to Animals Act 1876, as amended by the European Communities (Amendment of Cruelty to Animals Act, 1876) Regulations 2002 [SI No. 566, 2002] (*www.irishstatutebook.ie/ZZSI566Y2002.html*).

Under the Act, experiments on live animals (e.g. taking blood or biopsy samples) can only be performed by persons licensed by the Minister for Health and Children and in premises registered for that purpose.

The Act, as amended:

- restricts the use of animals in experiments
- provides general requirements for the care and accommodation of experimental animals
- provides standards for breeding, supplying and user establishments
- provides that an experiment shall not be performed if another scientifically satisfactory method of obtaining the result sought, not entailing the use of an animal, is reasonably and practicably available.

It is policy in Ireland not to license any experimental activity using live animals for testing of cosmetics. See the Department of Health and Children website for further details of this legislation and contact details for licences (*www.dohc.ie/*).

Destructive Imported Animals Act 1932

Several non-native mammals are considered to be significant pests of forestry and agriculture. This Act allows for the making of Orders, limiting the importation and/or keeping of these species. Orders currently in force are:

- Musk Rats (Prohibition of Importation and Keeping) Order 1933
- Grey Squirrels (Prohibition of Importation and Keeping) Order 1937
- The Non-Indigenous Rabbits (Prohibition of Importation and Keeping) Order 1954
- The Coypus (Prohibition on Keeping) Order 1987
- The Mink Keeping (Scotland) Order 2003
- The Mink Keeping (Prohibition) (England)

Order 2004.

Unless otherwise stated, these Orders apply to the whole of Great Britain. As muskrats, coypu and non-indigenous rabbits do not currently occur in the wild, these Orders should prevent any possibility of establishment or re-establishment by prohibiting their importation or keeping in Great Britain. Unfortunately, the Orders came too late to prevent the establishment of grey squirrels or mink, but the existence of these Orders still makes it illegal to keep these species in captivity (and their release is prohibited because they are on Schedule 9 of the WCA). In general, the keeping of these prohibited species can be permitted under licence from the appropriate authority (Natural England, the Scottish Executive or the Welsh Assembly Government), though it is absolutely illegal to keep mink on any Scottish island (other than Arran) and in Caithness and Sutherland.

Natural Environment and Rural Communities Act 2006

Although it contains little primary wildlife legislation, this Act ('the NERC Act') amends a number of other Acts. In particular, it strengthens the role of wildlife inspectors under the WCA. Inspectors (appointed in England or Wales) have powers of entry into premises, other than dwellings, where they have reason to believe a wildlife crime is being, or has been, committed and are able to inspect documents or, subject to some safeguards, take samples from any animals they find there. These enforcement powers have also been extended to offences under the Destructive Imported Animals Act, the Conservation of Seals Act, the Deer Act and the Protection of Badgers Act. The NERC Act also amended the WCA and the other Acts mentioned here to standardise the time within which a prosecution must be brought. This is now within 6 months of sufficient evidence becoming available but not more than 2 years after the commission of the offence.

Pests Act 1954

This Act, and in Scotland the Agriculture (Spring Traps) Scotland Act 1969, limits the use of spring traps for vermin control to types that have been approved for that use. In Northern Ireland, the use of spring traps is governed by the Welfare of Animals Act (Northern Ireland) 1972, which makes similar provisions. A list of approved traps for England and Wales is published in the Spring Traps Approval Order 1995 and can be found at *www.defra.gov.uk/wildlife-countryside/vertebrates/ approved-traps.htm* and The Spring Traps Approval (Scotland) Order 1996 (see *www. opsi.gov.uk/ SI/si1996/Uksi_19962202_en_1.htm*). Traps approved under these Orders are generally accepted as being suitable for use in Northern Ireland once those administrations have updated their lists. Before approval, traps are subjected to tests of efficacy and humaneness.

The Pests Act also designates the whole of England, apart from the City of London and the Isles of Scilly, as a rabbit clearance area. This obliges all occupiers of land to kill rabbits on their land unless it is impracticable to do so. Occupiers also have an obligation to prevent the rabbits from causing damage elsewhere, for example by fencing them in. If this is not done, a notice can be served on the occupier under the Agriculture Act 1947 (see above) requiring them to take action against rabbits. This function is now administered by Natural England, which issues about 40 notices a year.

Prevention of Damage by Pests Act 1949

This Act, which extends to England, Scotland and Wales, requires local authorities to keep, as far as is practicable, their area free from rats and mice. To achieve this, the Act gives local authorities certain rights of entry for inspection and allows them to serve notices on owners or occupiers of property or land (other than agricultural land) requiring them to destroy rats and mice or carry out works to prevent infestations. If this is not done, the local authority can carry out the work itself and recover the costs from the owner or occupier. The Act also places a duty on occupiers of land to notify the local authority if 'substantial numbers' of rats or mice are present on the land.

Protection of Animals Act 1911, Protection of Animals (Scotland) Act 1912 and Welfare of Animals Act (Northern Ireland) 1972

Although intended primarily to prevent unnecessary cruelty to domestic animals, the Protection of Animals Acts [England & Wales, Scotland] could also apply to captive wild animals in certain situations. These Acts also outlaw the use of poisons except against small vermin (rats and mice) and make it an offence to cause unnecessary suffering during the transport of animals. In England and Wales, the provisions of this Act have been largely superseded by the Animal Welfare Act 2006.

The Welfare of Animals Act (Northern Ireland) 1972 covers similar issues with respect to cruelty, the use of poisons and the transport of animals, but also includes provisions governing the use of spring traps (see above) and a requirement to inspect any trap or snare at least once a day between sunrise and sunset.

Wild Mammals (Protection) Act 1996

This short welfare act, which applies in England, Scotland and Wales, makes it illegal to mutilate, kick, beat, nail or otherwise impale, stab, burn, stone, crush, drown, drag or asphyxiate any wild mammal with intent to inflict unnecessary suffering. Exceptions apply for the attempted killing of a seriously injured mammal (though it seems unlikely that this would include an intent to cause unnecessary suffering); the killing of a mammal injured in the course of hunting, shooting or pest control activities; or the killing by means of a lawful trap, snare, dog, bird or poison.

REFERENCES

1   Comerford, H. (2001) *Wildlife Legislation 1976–2000.* Round Hall, Dublin.

2   Parkes, C. & Thornley, J. (2000) *Deer: law and liabilities.* Swan Hill Press, Shrewsbury.

United Kingdom

Agriculture Act 1947
Agriculture (Scotland) Act 1948
Agriculture (Spring Traps) Scotland Act 1969
Animal Health Act 1981
Animal Welfare Act 2006
Animals (Scientific Procedures) Act 1986
Conservation (Natural Habitats &c.) Regulations 1994
Conservation (Natural Habitats, &c.) (Amendment) Regulations 2007
Conservation (Natural Habitats, &c.) Amendment (Scotland) Regulations 2004
Conservation (Natural Habitats &c.) Amendment (Scotland) Regulations 2007
Conservation (Natural Habitats &c.) Regulations (Northern Ireland) 1995
Conservation (Natural Habitats &c.) (Amendment) Regulations (Northern Ireland) 2007
Conservation of Seals Act 1970
Conservation of Seals (England) Order 1999
Conservation of Seals (Scotland) Order 2004
Countryside and Rights of Way Act 2000
Coypus (Prohibition on Keeping) Order 1987
Deer Act 1991
Deer (Scotland) Act 1996
Destructive Imported Animals Act 1932
Grey Squirrels (Prohibition of Importation and Keeping) Order 1937
Medicines Act 1986
Mink Keeping (Prohibition) (England) Order 2004
Mink Keeping (Scotland) Order 2003
Musk Rats (Prohibition of Importation and Keeping) Order 1933
Natural Environment and Rural Communities Act 2006
Nature Conservation (Scotland) Act 2004
Non-Indigenous Rabbits (Prohibition of Importation and Keeping) Order 1954
Pests Act 1954

Prevention of Damage by Pests Act 1949
Protection of Animals Act 1911
Protection of Animals (Scotland) Act 1912
Protection of Badgers Act 1992
Regulatory Reform (Deer) (England and Wales) Order 2007
Spring Traps Approval Order 1995
Spring Traps Approval (Scotland) Order 1996
Welfare of Animals Act (Northern Ireland) 1972
Wild Mammals (Protection) Act 1996
Wildlife & Countryside Act 1981
Wildlife (Northern Ireland) Order 1985

Republic of Ireland

Cruelty to Animals Act 1876
European Communities (Amendment of Cruelty to Animals Act, 1876) Regulations 2002
Deer Protection Act 1698
European Communities (Natural Habitats) Regulations 1997
Wildlife Act 1976
Wildlife Amendment Act 2000

British Crown Dependencies

Conservation of Wildlife (Jersey) Law 2000
Wildlife Act 1990 (Isle of Man)

European Union

Conservation of Natural Habitats and of Wild Fauna and Flora 1992 (EC Directive 92/43/EEC, Habitats Directive)

International conventions

Convention on Biological Diversity, 1992 (Rio Convention)
Convention on Migratory Species, 1979 (Bonn Convention)
Convention on the Conservation of European Wildlife and Natural Habitats, 1979 (Bern Convention)

Plate 2

A Red squirrel *Sciurus vulgaris* (winter coat) **B** Grey squirrel *Sciurus carolinensis* **C** Red squirrel *Sciurus vulgaris* (summer coat, *S. v. leucourus*) **D** Edible dormouse *Glis glis* **E** Common rat *Rattus norvegicus* **F** Ship rat *Rattus rattus*

5

Rodents
Order Rodentia

Compiled by J. Gurnell and E.J.Hare

The Rodentia is much the most diverse order of extant mammals, with >2100 species (*c*.41% of all mammal species). Distributed throughout all habitable continents, from high Arctic to tropics, even (introduced) on some sub-Antarctic islands, and including Australia, where a diverse endemic radiation of Muridae has evolved. Found in all habitats from desert and tundra to rainforest; mainly terrestrial, but includes specialised arboreal, fossorial and aquatic species. Mostly small to medium-sized mammals, of mouse to rat size (20–300 g), but ranging from harvest mouse *Micromys* at 6 g to capybara *Hydrochoerus* at 60 kg. Characterised by a distinctive dentition – a single pair of gnawing, open-rooted, incisors anteriorly in both upper and lower jaws, a gap (diastema) where canines and anterior premolars might have been, and reduced number, 3–5 pairs, of cheek-teeth (premolars and molars). Incisors grow throughout life; have thickened, often yellow-orange, enamel on the anterior surfaces but thinner enamel laterally and behind, so sharpen naturally to chisel-shaped biting edges. When incisors are biting, upper and lower cheek-teeth are not in contact; in chewing, when cheek-teeth functioning, lower jaws are retracted and lower incisors somewhat behind uppers, positioned in diastema. Characterised by complex arrangements of jaw muscles, especially masseters, differing between major groups of rodents, that facilitate this differential use of the dentition; masseters have 3 layers, superficial, lateral and deep. Superficial masseter arises on zygomatic arch, but may partly move forward on it, to side of snout (e.g. in squirrels). Infraorbital foramen, which typically carries facial nerve on to muzzle, remains small in squirrels and beavers, but is enlarged in dormice, voles, rats and mice (myomorphs) to take part of lateral masseter muscles, and very large in porcupines, coypu and other S American rodents (hystricomorphs, caviomorphs) to take part of deep masseter (Fig. 5.1). Pull of these jaw muscles forward towards snout enhances fore-and-aft chewing action. Most rodents feed on seeds and other fruits, but some are specialist herbivores, eating leaves and

Table 5.1 Characteristics of families of rodents occurring in the British Isles. These characteristics do not necessarily apply to exotic members of these families

	Sciuridae	**Castoridae**	**Gliridae**	**Cricetidae** (Arvicolinae)	**Muridae** (Murinae)	**Myocastoridae**
	Squirrels	Beaver	Dormice	Voles	Mice and rats	Coypu
Weight	250–500 g	15–40 kg	15–200 g	20–1200 g	6–300 g	5–7 kg
Tail	Bushy	Scaly, flat	Bushy	Thinly haired	Thinly haired	Scaly, round
Tail length (as % of head+body	80–90	50–60	80–90	25–60	80–120	70–80
n Cheek-teeth	5/4	4/4	4/4	3/3	3/3	4/4
Crown height	Low	Medium	Low	High	Low	High
Crown pattern	Cusped	Ridged	Low ridges	Triangles	Cusped	Ridged
Habitat	Woodland	Aquatic	Scrub, woodland	Woodland, grassland aquatic	Woodland, commensal farmland	Aquatic

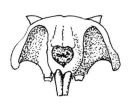
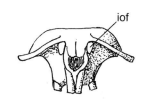
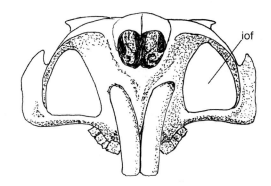

Fig. 5.1 Skulls of squirrel (left), muskrat, and coypu (right) in anterior view. The infraorbital foramen (iof) is greatly enlarged in the coypu (as also in other hystricomorphs, such as porcupines and guinea pigs), modest in the muskrat (as in other voles and mice, and dormice), but absent in squirrels (and beavers) *(drawn by D.W. Yalden)*.

stems, some are insectivorous, and a few are specialist fish-feeders. All the European species are essentially herbivorous or granivorous, though most eat some insects.

Of the 17 species considered in this handbook for the British Isles, 9 are native and 8 introduced; these include 1 native that is currently extinct (beaver), but under consideration for reintroduction, and 2 introduced species that have subsequently been exterminated (coypu described here, muskrat in Chapter 13). They belong to 6 different families, distinguished in summary form in Table 5.1. The Muridae has conventionally included as subfamilies both voles (Cricetinae or Arvicolinae) and mice and rats (Murinae); these currently raised to full family status.

FAMILY SCIURIDAE (SQUIRRELS)

A large family of *c*.289 species in 51 genera [1538], a mixture of arboreal and gliding squirrels, terrestrial marmots and ground squirrels, and intermediate chipmunks. Most diverse in SE Asia, but well represented in Eurasia and N America, less numerous in Africa and S America. Skull has simple ('sciurognath') lower jaw; infraorbital foramen small, not penetrated by jaw muscles. Cheek-teeth usually 5/4, low crowned, with low cusps, though p^3 small, sometimes absent.

GENUS *Sciurus*

A genus of typical, tree-dwelling squirrels with

Fig. 5.2 Red squirrel: moult sequence, individuals all from Hampshire, 1895–1896, respectively Jan, Feb, Apr, May, May, Jun, Jul, Aug, Aug, Sep, Oct, Nov, Dec. Tails bleach and ear tufts are lost over summer, but are replaced in autumn moult *(photo P. Morris, skins courtesy of NHM)*.

long bushy tails. *c*.28 species, most in N and C America but with 3 species in Palaearctic; 1 native and 1 introduced occur in British Isles. Teeth with p^1/p_1 very small, sometimes absent.

Red squirrel *Sciurus vulgaris*

Sciurus vulgaris Linnaeus 1758; Uppsala, Sweden. Common squirrel, brown squirrel, light-tailed squirrel; *gwiwer* (Welsh); *con, skug, feorage* (Scottish Gaelic); *iora rua* (Irish Gaelic). Note: the red squirrel of North America is a different species and genus, *Tamiasciurus hudsonicus*.

RECOGNITION

Upper fur uniformly dark but variable in colour, from deep brown to red-brown or bright chestnut to grey-brown (Plate 2). Ear tufts grow in late summer; large during winter but gradually thin to small or absent during summer (Fig. 5.2). (Larger grey squirrel may exhibit some chestnut coloration over the back and down the limbs, but is not uniform as is red squirrel, does not grow conspicuous ear tufts, has white-fringed tail.) Some red squirrels can appear (uniformly) quite grey, particularly in winter.

Skull: Shorter and deeper than grey squirrel, with relatively smaller nasal bones (Table 5.2).

FIELD SIGNS

Generally not distinguishable from grey squirrel.

Tracks and trails: Footprints show 4 toes on forefeet which point forwards, 4 closely aligned pads on palm, *c*.25 mm wide; 5 toes on hindfeet, 4 oval plantar pads and 1 hind plantar pad, *c*.40 mm long × 35 mm wide. Tracks characteristic with forefeet behind and inside the line of the larger hindfeet, stride *c*.35 cm, hops <1 m, tail held high so tail marks seldom visible. Tree bark sometimes scratched in particular places, especially on frequently used path-ways, up tree trunks or

Table 5.2 Red and grey squirrels: measurements. Lower end of ranges may include subadult animals

	Red squirrel			Grey squirrel		
	Mean	Range	n	Mean	Range	n
Head and body (mm)	220[a]	180–240		260[a]	240–285	86
Tail (mm)	180[a]	140–195		220	195–240	
Hindfeet (mm)	55[a]	49–63		>60		
Hindfeet (mm) Males	56[e]	54–59	11			
Hindfeet (mm) Females	56[e]	54–61	14			
Shin length (mm) Males				77.0[f]	55.5–84.7	150
Shin length (mm) Females				76.8[f]	62.6–84.6	118
Weight (g)						
Males	279[b]	239–340	323	532c	440–650	185
Females	278[b]	220–355	244	568c	400–720	186
Males	300[d]	260–435	58	532[f]	430–720	267
Females	296[d]	260–345	70	551[f]	430–710	240
Males	300[e]	270–360	103			
Females	307[e]	260–350[g]	109			
Condylobasal length (mm)		44–48		61.3[a]	58.1–64.4	337
Nasal length (mm)		13–16		20.8[a]	18.1–23.1	335

[*a] Broadleaved forest, Oxfordshire [339]; [b] conifer forest, E Scotland [1428]; [c] broadleaved forest, S England [1]; [d] conifer forest, E Anglia [1428]; [e] conifer forest, N England [1]; [f] conifer forest, E Anglia [1]; [g] data exclude pregnant females

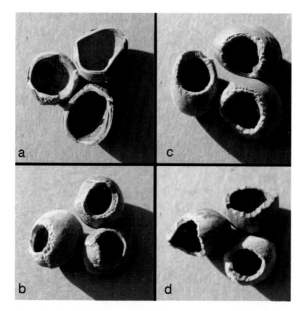

Fig. 5.3 Hazel nuts opened by various rodents. Squirrels (a) split the nuts, hazel dormice (b) cut around the hole, creating a smooth groove; wood mice (c) and bank voles (d) gnaw across the cut edge, creating a rough, grooved, internal surface. Nuts opened by bank voles show a clean outer edge, whereas wood mice create a rough surface with their upper incisors *(photos S. Searle)*.

underneath large branches.

Faeces: Cylindrical or round, slightly smaller than those of rabbit (6–8 mm diameter), dark grey to black in colour but vary according to diet; probably deposited at random.

Food: Cached during late summer and autumn; tree seeds such as hazelnuts, beech mast and acorns, as well as conifer cones, scatter-hoarded in small groups of 1–4 items just under soil surface [1498]. Fungal fruiting bodies cut and cached singly in trees to dry [919].

Feeding signs: Hazelnuts split open leaving 2 pieces of shell with clean edges (cf. mice and voles, Fig. 5.3). Characteristic 'cores' of conifer cones sometimes with associated piles of stripped scales; distinct from cones with split scales left by birds. When feeding in trees, feeding remains scattered, but sometimes clumped, for example, on tree stumps. Bark stripped from base, stem or crown of trees, particularly pole-stage trees 10–40 years old. Stem bark often left hanging in long spiral twists. Incisor tooth marks found on fungi (larger than those of mice and voles, not ragged like bird pecks or irregular and slimy like slug feeding). Terminal tips of branches frequently found scattered on ground in late winter/spring and summer.

Nests: Tree nests (dreys) sited near trunk of tree or in fork in branches; usually above *c.*6 m, may be as low as 2.5 m [1298]; dense and spherical, *c.*30 cm diameter; frequently built within dense clumps of climbing plants such as ivy [950, 1298, 1435]. Differ from bird nests in that usually include leaves (cut from living twigs), not placed out in canopy.

DESCRIPTION

Pelage: Sexes similar; colour variable. Winter coat thick, deep red to brown, grey or almost black above; thick red-brown ear tufts 2.5–3.5 cm long; dense tail, hairs uniformly dark red-brown or black, not banded. Underside pale, white or cream. Summer coat reddish brown or chestnut above; ear tufts small or absent; tail thin, chestnut to creamy white. In some forms, ear tufts and tail hairs

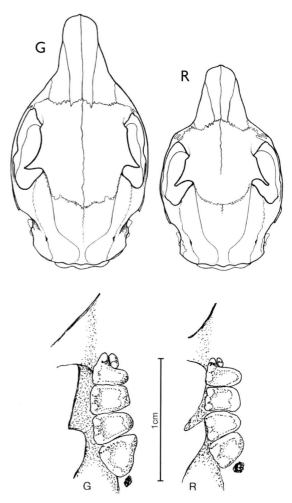

Fig. 5.4 Skulls of grey squirrel (G) and red squirrel (R) in dorsal view, showing larger size, longer muzzle of grey squirrel; inset, essentially similar upper dentitions of grey and red squirrels from below. Unlike other British rodents, squirrels have 2 upper premolars, a minute p³ and a large p⁴. (Along with canines, p¹ and p² are lost in rodents.) *(drawn by R.Gillmor (skulls) and D.W. Yalden).*

gradually bleach from winter to summer becoming blond or white from June onwards. Juveniles darker than adults.

Moult: Body fur moults twice a year; spring moult proceeds from front to back, autumn moult from back to front. Exact timing varies between individuals, particularly in relation to body condition. Ear tufts and tail hairs (from tip forwards) moult once, new hairs growing in late summer/autumn, through to December for ear tufts. Juveniles moult to appropriate summer or winter adult coat after weaning.

Anatomy: 6 sets of vibrissae on the head: above eyes, below eyes, on throat, under chin, above mouth and on nose (whiskers). Similar hairs found on feet, outer sides of forelegs, underside of body and at base of tail [454].

Nipples: 4 pairs: 1 inguinal, 1 abdominal, 2 pectoral; difficult to find in young females.

Scent glands: Associated with large mucous glands on side of mouth and sebaceous glands in the tissues of the upper and lower lips [1261]. A type of apocrinal gland also found on either side of head in chin region [454]. Urine important form of olfactory signal; vaginal secretions in oestrus females may complement urine as a sign of reproductive condition.

Skull: Smaller than that of grey squirrel (condylobasal length <50 mm, nasals <16 mm); cranium deeper and postorbital processes longer and narrower (Fig. 5.4).

Teeth: Functional cheek-teeth rooted, low-crowned, quadrate with rounded marginal cusps and concave central area, traversed by weak transverse ridges in the upper teeth; only lower and 2nd upper premolars deciduous and shed at 16 weeks of age. Wear of cheek-teeth and growth of cementum (as well as weight of eye lens) have been used to determine age [327, 772, 800, 880].

Postcranial skeleton: Shows adaptations for climbing and leaping; bones relatively light and hind limbs disproportionately long and heavy (illustrated in [1287]). Feet plantigrade; long toes (except thumbs, reduced to tubercles) with long curved claws. Well-developed tail used for balance, thermoregulation and as signalling device. Epiphyseal fusion of long bones distinguishes adults from juveniles [327, 880].

Reproductive tract: Sexes easy to separate by distance between genital opening and anus, very close in females, *c.*10 mm apart in adult males. Reproductive tract regresses in autumn and perhaps over winter if food supplies and weather poor. When active, testes are large and scrotal; scrotum sometimes darkly stained. Female tract typical Y-shape, embryo post-attachment sites sometimes visible. Vulva becomes swollen at oestrus. Weight or length of baculum in males is not an accurate method of determining age but may be used in conjunction with other techniques [327].

Chromosomes: 2n = 40, FNa = 70 and 72 (European data) [1589].

RELATIONSHIPS

Closely related to the Japanese *S. lis* and more distantly to the Persian *S. anomalus* (Caucasus and Asia Minor) [927]. No obvious sister species among the many American species of *Sciurus* [909].

MEASUREMENTS

See Table 5.2: considerable individual and seasonal variation in body weight; generally 10% increase during autumn (proportionally smaller

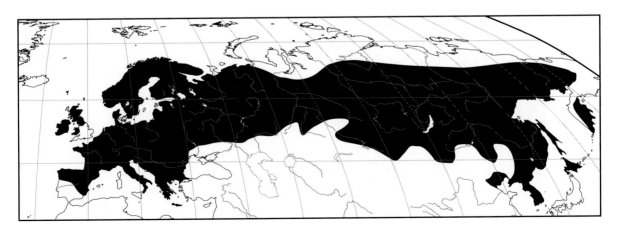

Fig. 5.5 Red squirrel *Sciurus vulgaris*: world distribution.

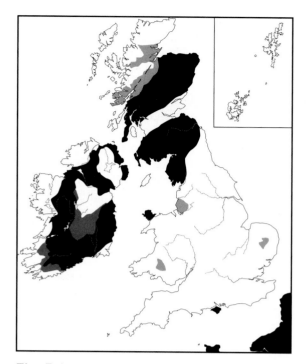

Fig. 5.6 Red squirrel *Sciurus vulgaris*: current distribution in British Isles, but shrinking.

than grey squirrel) [787]. Autumn weight increase not observed in conifer plantations [914, 918]. Weight of female not a good indicator of pregnancy.

VARIATION
Wide regional colour variation across the European range, dorsal colour ranging from dark red to black to brown to grey to 'blue' [279, 1090]. Tail, feet and ear tufts may be the same colour or contrast with the back. Underside usually white. Endemic British and Irish race, *S. v. leucourus* Kerr, 1792, said to be characterised by bleaching of the ears and tail. However, introductions of *S. v. vulgaris* from Scandinavia into Perthshire in 1793 [627, 1427] and *S. v. fuscoater* from W Europe to Lothians in 1860 (probably) and Epping Forest *c.*1910 [627, 1287], complicate this; now some squirrels exhibit bleaching but others do not. Black or melanic squirrels found in mainland Europe, rare in British Isles, as are albino forms. In mainland Europe, many populations are polymorphic and the relative proportion of colour phases (e.g. black, brown, red) varies geographically [327], seems fixed for any one region [1475, 1545]. Genetic diversity varies considerably within British Isles, no obvious phylogeographic pattern nationally, and no evolutionary divergence between haplotypes in GB and mainland Europe [75, 76]. However, red squirrel populations in Cumbria, Northumberland and Durham were found to have significant local differences in genetic structure and morphology as

a result of geographic barriers, habitat fragmentation and the 19th-century Scandinavian introductions [589–591, 915]. Large-scale 20th century afforestation in Cumbria and Northumberland has also led to significant changes in gene frequency and morphology of local populations in Cumbria [589, 590]. Small isolated population on Anglesey has reduced genetic diversity, considerably less than other GB populations [1089].

DISTRIBUTION
Widespread across Palaearctic from Ireland and Spain in W to Korea and Kamchatka in E (Fig. 5.5). In S England, present on Brownsea and Furzey islands (Dorset) and Isle of Wight. Introduced to Jersey in 19th century and thriving there. Isolated populations still present in Wales, Lancashire, N Yorkshire (Hawes and Widdale areas) and Durham. Still abundant in N Cumbria, Northumberland and large parts of Scotland and Ireland (Fig. 5.6). Absent from Isle of Man and most Scottish islands (present Arran, Bute).

HISTORY
Known from Middle Pleistocene in Europe; earliest British fossil record, Mesolithic (8710 bp), Madawg Cave, Wye Valley, also in Neolithic, Three Holes Cave, Devon [1152] and Binnel Point, Isle of Wight (*c.*4480 bp [1149]), undoubtedly native in GB; origin in Ireland more doubtful and likely to be the result of introductions. At one time ubiquitous in woodlands throughout GB and Ireland. Historically, population sizes have fluctuated widely between years. Became extinct in Ireland and S Scotland by early 18th century, and was rare in Scottish Highlands in late 18th and early 19th centuries [627, 1004]. Reintroduced to 10 sites in Scotland, mainly from England, between 1772 and 1782 [627] and to *c.*10 sites in Ireland from England between 1815 and 1856 [82]. Became very abundant between 1890 and 1910 throughout the British Isles, thereafter general decline and extinctions over large areas of England and Wales.

Introduced grey squirrel has now replaced red squirrel in much of its range. Red and grey squirrels known to have coexisted for >15–20 years in some areas, although not necessarily in the same woodland blocks [1188], but this may have hidden a slow decline such as in Hamsterley Forest, Durham [1517]. Declining distribution of red relative to grey squirrel reviewed for British Isles [899], E Anglia [1188, 1299], Wales [968], Scotland [205, 1330], and Ireland [1098]. Habitat destruction, disease and interspecific competition between red and grey squirrels all considered responsible [560, 1299, 1434]. Studies of red–grey squirrel competition in GB and Italy examined the effects of grey squirrels on behaviour, diet choice, recovery of cached tree seeds, habitat use and body growth of individual red squirrels, as well at population level [581, 1507, 1518–1520]. Grey squirrels pilfered seed caches of red squirrels during spring, leading to a lower red squirrel body mass then. No evidence of interference competition between the adults of the 2 species or food competition, although fecundity of individual female red squirrels was lower in red–grey than in red-only sites because of a lower body mass. Growth rate of young red squirrels also lower when grey squirrels present. Overall, no significant effect of grey squirrels on residency of adult red squirrels or on population turnover rate. Fewer female red squirrels bred in the summer with grey squirrels present and fewer individuals produced 2 litters/year in sites with grey squirrels. Moreover, red squirrel recruitment rate and, in the mixed broadleaf sites, juvenile residency, decreased with increasing densities of grey squirrels. In the UK, competition between the species is mediated by disease from squirrelpox virus (SQPV) infection [1233, 1245]. Grey squirrels probably brought the virus from N America [981] and are carriers of SQPV in GB (but not Italy). Virus has no effect on grey squirrels, but is invariably fatal to red squirrels [1433]. Thus appears that SQPV can cause loss of local populations of red squirrels [570]; rates of decline in red squirrel populations are 17–25 times higher in regions where SQPV is present in grey squirrel populations [1235]. Grey squirrels thought to have competitive advantage in deciduous woodland, their native habitat, where they reach higher densities than red squirrels [790] and are more efficient at digesting acorns as a result of tannin tolerance [785]. Red squirrels appear better adapted to conifer forests, but greys still utilise these woodlands, particularly where large-seeded broadleaved trees are also available [920, 922].

HABITAT

Across much of Palaearctic, found in boreal coniferous forests of Scots pine, Norway spruce and Siberian pine. In C and S Europe, also found in broadleaved woods. Mixtures of tree species provide a more reliable year-to-year seed food supply than single-species forests because of differences in mast intervals, seed size and timing of seed shed [920]. Habitat use varies with time of year in relation to food availability [1510]. Trees also provide cover from predation by aerial predators such as goshawks *Accipiter gentilis*; drey sites with spruces preferred over pines [595, 917]. Density highest in conifer mixtures dominated by pine and lowest in those dominated by Sitka spruce and in forests just reaching cone-bearing age [920]. Also found in small woods and copses. Although supposedly more timorous than grey squirrel, will readily use gardens [950]; found in urban areas in Europe.

SOCIAL ORGANIZATION AND BEHAVIOUR

Social and spatial organisation: Solitary for much of the time but communal nesting reported especially during winter and spring. Squirrels that share dreys appear to be those that are familiar with one another [664, 1503]. Dominance hierarchies among and between sexes; males not always dominant to females. Dominant animals tend to be larger and older than subordinate animals; males frequently have larger home ranges, but considerable individual variation [1503]. Adult male ranges generally larger than female. Overall, home-range size and spacing behaviour varies with habitat quality and with seasonal changes in range size relating to sexual activity, as well as changes in food availability [28, 917, 921, 923, 1499, 1504]. Average home range for both sexes varies from 1–6.6 ha in mixed deciduous woodlands, Isle of Wight and Jersey, to 9–30 ha in conifer-dominated habitats in N England and Scotland [595, 664, 914, 950]. Home ranges overlap particularly in areas of abundant food, but overlap can be small, notably between breeding females which reduce their range and deter other squirrels when suckling young [914, 923, 1499, 1504]. Densities lower than grey squirrels' in most habitats, with the exception of large conifer forests, although access to broadleaves outside the forest, as well as overall landscape structure and composition, may all play a part [787, 920]. See Population below for further details.

Aggressive acts: Include loud chucks, vigorous tail flicking and foot stamping; aggressive encounters may include high-speed chasing, tail biting and screaming [371]. Aggressive encounters between males occur when they congregate in mating chases, following a female on heat. Dominant male, at the head of following group of males, generally mates with the female [1509].

Communication and senses: Wide-angled vision and probably dichromatic colour vision; the blind spot is a slender horizontal stripe above the centre of the retina, giving minimum interference with vertical objects and clear upward vision. Vocal communication associated with typical body postures, includes loud and soft chucking calls, an explosive 'wrruhh' sound and various moans and teeth chattering. Young make shrill piping calls. Sense of smell appears highly developed.

Scent-marking: Occurs at specific places within home range (e.g. on branches or tree trunks) using urine, also secretions from glands on the chin by face-wiping behaviour [454, 664]. Scent-marks denote occupation of home range, social status and reproductive condition. Vaginal secretions as well as urine may signal females on heat, drawing males from up to 1 km away [1]. Unclear whether faeces are used as markers.

Dispersal: Takes place during autumn for juveniles and some adults. Spring dispersal also occurs, probably of animals moving away from marginal, overwintering habitats, and summer dispersal may involve juveniles born early in the year. Seasonal sex bias in dispersal; more males disperse in spring and more females in autumn [1505]. Post-breeding dispersal of adult females recorded following seasonal changes in seed availability [921]. Mass movements reported from USSR in autumns with poor food supplies [1090] but not recorded in GB.

Activity: Active all year (does not hibernate) but may remain in nest for several days during severe winter weather [1436, 1500]. Diurnal; onset of daily activity related to sunrise, but termination not related to sunset. Considerable individual variation but 1 main active phase during winter, peaking late morning, 2 phases during summer, peaking 2–4 h after sunrise and 2–4 h before sunset. Spring and autumn activity patterns intermediate between winter and summer. High winds, very hot or cold conditions and heavy rain reduce activity. May lie-up on a branch to keep cool during very hot weather. Food availability also greatly influences activity. Red squirrel thought to be more arboreal than grey squirrel [787] but this may be modified by food availability. For example, in Norway spruce plantations, 32% of the cone crop consumed by red squirrels was stripped on the ground [916]. Activity patterns described in [1298, 1436, 1500].

Movement: Across the ground a scurrying, weaving run or a series of leaps with tail held out behind. Stops frequently and sits on hind legs with head held high in an alert posture, ears erect, nose 'testing the air'. Agile climber, can move rapidly leaping from branch to branch and tree to tree, up to 4 m. Moves down tree trunks head first with frequent pauses. Escape behaviour includes moving up a tree on the far side to the observer or predator, or 'freezing' flat against tree trunk or on a branch. Able to swim.

Nests (dreys): Spherical, *c.*30 cm in diameter but sometimes larger, situated close to the trunk of a tree or in a fork in the branches, usually above 6 m, but can be lower. Often hidden by climbing plants [950, 1298, 1435]. Outer layers consist of twigs, sometimes with needles or leaves attached; inner cavity (12–16 cm diameter) lined with soft material such as moss, leaves, needles, dry grass and bark. Individuals use 2, 3 or more dreys at one time, frequently alternating dreys on consecutive nights; up to 8 used within a period of 2 weeks has been recorded [595, 914]. 2 types of nests recognised, those used during the day for rest and those slept in at night, although the latter may be used for both purposes [1503]. Drey counts may be used as crude, relative indices of population size or habitat use [1501]. Hollow trees may be used as dens, especially in broadleaved woods. Denser spruce trees rather than pines are preferred for drey location in conifer plantations [595, 917].

Grooming: Follows fixed sequence of events involving head and forepaw grooming, body grooming, hind leg scratching, hindfoot licking and tail grooming.

FEEDING

Mainly seeds, but opportunistic; wide variety of other foods taken when seeds not available – hence seasonal variation in diet. Primary foods are tree seeds, fruits, berries and fungi. Secondary foods include buds, shoots and flowers of trees; bark may be eaten in any month of the year, but usually May–July. Other green plant material, invert-ebrates (e.g. caterpillars), and lichen may be taken. No evidence that they are significant predators of birds' eggs or

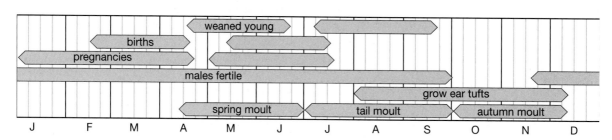

Fig. 5.7 Red squirrel: annual cycle

nestlings. Standing water may be sought in hot weather. Tree seeds may be scatter-hoarded in the autumn and fungi stashed on branches up trees [919, 1363]. Specific cache sites not learnt, although general area of caches may be; caches relocated by smell. Hoarding appears more intense in deciduous forests than coniferous forests [1435, 1498], suggested to increase the likelihood of individual survival and reproductive success [1514]. Exhibits feeding preferences according to species of tree and size of food item (e.g. Sitka spruce cones have much smaller seeds than Scots pine or Norway spruce). Habitat use follows spatial and temporal patterns of food availability [920, 923]. Bark stripped in a spiral manner from stems of coniferous trees (10–40 years old) to get at sap. Reasons for bark stripping reviewed in [781]. Foods held and rotated by forefeet while animal is squatting or hanging. Cone scales gnawed off to expose seeds, wings discarded. 60–80% of active period may be spent foraging and feeding, with more time spent foraging in coniferous than deciduous woodland [1436, 1510]. Food and foraging behaviour reviewed in [1005, 1006], energetics in [1189]. Daily energy expenditure 347 kJ in wild, Scotland [207]; less than grey squirrel, but in proportion to smaller body mass.

BREEDING

Seasonal, 2 peaks, in spring and summer. Gestation 36–42 days. Litter size 1–6, average 3. Lactation 50–70 days. Weight at birth 10–15 g [371, 455].

Breeding season can last from December–January, when males and females 9–10 months old or older become sexually active, to August–early October, when summer litters are weaned. 2 breeding peaks within a season: mating in winter and spring lead respectively to spring-born (February–April) and summer-born (May–August) litters (Fig. 5.7). 1st breeding may be delayed or missed when seed food supplies poor [557], resulting in shorter breeding season. Body weight and dominance rank in females are best predictors of fertility. Females weighing <300 g did not come into oestrus [914, 1502] and heavy females in high-quality home ranges tend to live longer and produce more offspring. Lowered density-dependent breeding success results from a greater proportion of females living in poor habitats at high density, and more non-breeding floaters at high density [1508]. Reproductive rate found to decrease with female density; density-dependent reproduction and within-sex density-dependent recruitment of juveniles thought to limit fluctuations in numbers and regulate population size [1521]. Average lifetime reproductive success

of a female red squirrel, Belgium, estimated at 5 offspring (range 1–11) [1506].

Males: Fecund for most of breeding season; period of inactivity in autumn and possibly into winter. No paternal care of young.

Females: Polyoestrous, in heat for only 1 day during each oestrous cycle. Adult females capable of producing 2 litters of 1–6 (occasionally more) each year when breeding starts early, but rarely achieve this potential. Summer litters usually larger than spring litters (e.g. means of 3.6 and 3.0 respectively). Mass at weaning, together with being born earlier in the season, affects likelihood of local survival in the first few months of life [1511]. Little known on juvenile dispersal behaviour and mortality. No postpartum oestrus until young almost weaned. Juveniles rarely capable of breeding until 10–12 months old, and most females wean 1st litter when 2 years old [1506]. Some females are not successful in rearing any young during a season [1506]. Some intrauterine loss; higher losses can occur during weaning. Young may be carried in mother's mouth to a new nest during suckling period.

Mating: Little prior courtship apart from mating chase, when males attracted to a female in heat by odour follow her for >1 h. Leading male in the following group tends to be heaviest, dominant and account for most matings [1509]. Mating system polygynous–promiscuous.

Young: Blind, deaf and naked at birth. Observed sex ratios c.1:1. Skin pigment appears on back and hairs emerge at 8–9 days. Hairs cover body by 21 days [371, 1285]. Lower incisors cut at 9–12 days, uppers at 31–42 days. Ears open 28–35 days, eyes open 28–30 days. Begin leaving nest and start eating solid food at c.7 weeks; weaned at 8–10 weeks but maternal protective behaviour may extend beyond weaning, e.g. young may nest with mother over winter (but more information required). Moult to adult coat at 3–4 months.

POPULATION

Pre-breeding population in GB estimated at 161 000 (30 000 England, 121 000 Scotland, 10 000 Wales), based on areas of woodland, median densities of 0.55/ha [624]. Likely to have declined further in England and Wales since then.

Densities: Long-term average densities of 0.5–1.5/ha are normal for both coniferous and deciduous forests, but year-to-year fluctuations large, affected by seed supply and weather. Very low densities, 0.02–0.2/ha, similar to Boreal forests,

Table 5.3 Red squirrel: typical densities (mean number per hectare)

Habitat type	Location	Density (n/ha)	Source
Conifer	Scotland	0.8	[1429]
	Scotland	0.3	[10076]
	Scotland	0.2	[595]
	Scotland	0.03	[595]
	Belgium	1.3	[1499]
	England	0.5	[1287]
	England	1.1	[1187]
	England	0.0–0.35	[924]
	Russia	0.8	[149]
	Sweden	0.02–0.17	[29]
	Spain	0.1	[1156]
Broadleaf	England	0.7	[1435]
	England	1.0	[664]
	Belgium	0.9	[1499]
	Spain	0.3	[1156]
	Jersey	0.62	[950]
Suburban	Jersey	0.87	[950]

Scandinavia, observed in large conifer forests in N England, Scotland [595, 920] (Table 5.3). Populations can recover from very low densities in 2–3 years. Annual cycle: numbers peak in autumn, before autumn dispersal and overwinter losses; troughs in spring before recruitment. Population dynamics of squirrels, particularly effects of food availability, reviewed in [557, 560, 920]. Urbanisation and road-building fragment habitats, can lead to decrease in population size, increased isolation and higher chances of extinction, although viable population persists in very small, highly fragmented woodlands on Jersey [950]. Woodland size, habitat composition and distance to nearest large woodland important determiners for red squirrel presence [28, 239, 1512, 1232, 1464].

Survival: Annual survival positively related to availability of autumn tree seed. On average 75–85% of juveniles disappear during their 1st winter; average annual survival improves thereafter to *c*.50%. Dispersal not sex-biased and strict philopatry rare; local competition determines

dispersal distance [1513]. In wild, mean expectation of life at 6 months of age is *c*.3 years; some individuals may live to 6–7 years; in captivity, to 10 years [1427].

MORTALITY

Starvation, very cold weather, and possibly parasitic disease in undernourished animals (see below), believed to be responsible for many deaths. Locally, SQPV may cause significant mortality. Predators include pine marten, wild cat, some owls, and raptors such as goshawks and buzzards [1134]. No direct evidence that predation significantly affects red squirrel numbers, but small populations in poorer habitats may be more vulnerable [595, 1134]. Stoats may take nestlings; foxes, cats and dogs could take squirrels when they are on the ground. Domestic cats important predators on Jersey [950]. Grey squirrels not a direct cause of mortality. Humans may influence mortalities by destroying or altering habitats, causing road casualties (e.g. [926]), or controlling populations under licence (see below).

PARASITES

See [793].

Ectoparasites: Fleas, *Monopsyllus sciurorum* specific to red squirrels, common throughout the British Isles. *Orchopeas howardii*, presumed to have been introduced from North America with the grey squirrel, sometimes found on red squirrels [142, 1285]. *Tarsopsylla octodecimdentata* found locally in NE Scotland and NE England, probably introduced with European squirrels in 1793 [266]. Ticks not specific; most common is the sheep tick, *Ixodes ricinus*. Spirochaetes *Borrelia afzelii* and *B. burgdorferi sensu lato, B. b. sensu stricto* reputedly transmitted to *Sciurus vulgaris* by ticks in Switzerland [680]. Occasional infestations by mange mites, but signs may be mistaken for sick, undernourished squirrels suffering from alopecia and heavy infestation of fleas and lice. Sucking lice include *Neohaematipinus sciuri* and *Enderleinellus nitzchi*.

Endoparasites: Helminths uncommon. Nematode *Enterobius* reported. Protozoa: intestinal *Eimeria* spp. common, causes coccidiosis; fatal epidemics ascribed to coccidiosis in Scandinavia [864], but evidence from elsewhere is lacking. Coccidiosis may be the proximate cause of death in undernourished, stressed and overcrowded animals; *E. sciurorum* is pathogenic in GB. Other protozoa include *Hepatozoon* and *Toxoplasma*.

Diseases: Bacterial infections rare but pasteurellosis *Pasteurella multicoda* detected [793]. Ringworm fungal infections *Trichophyton* sp., *Microsporum cookei* reported. Viruses isolated include parainfluenza [1473], members of the encephalomyocarditis group [1472] and SQPV (formerly termed parapoxvirus) [1241, 1264, 1240, 1242, 1421]. Infection with SQPV in this species resembles contagious pustular dermatitis in sheep (and looks like myxomatosis), found in E Anglia, Cumbria and Northumberland and most recently in grey squirrels in S Scotland (2005, 2006); the virus is pathogenic and there is a high probability of death (usually within 2 weeks) (see History, above). Reports of myxomatosis, diptheria, distemper, and 'consumption' are unfounded. Oral examinations of red squirrel corpses, UK, 1994–1998, found 2 cases where oral disease was probable cause of death [1246].

RELATIONS WITH HUMANS

Of aesthetic value, fully protected under the Wildlife and Countryside Act 1981 [1043] (see Chapter 4). Conservation status, highly vulnerable in England and Wales [624], but also at risk in Scotland and Ireland. Poisoning grey squirrels in areas where red squirrels are present is prohibited.

May cause economic damage to conifer plantations by stripping bark, particularly when densities approach 2/ha [1288]. Scots and Corsican pine damaged, as well as lodgepole pine, Norway spruce and European larch [1119, 1310]. Damage may be considerable at the local level. Stem damage often heals, forming calluses and leaving low-quality, scarred timber. Ring-barking, resulting in die-back and wind-snap, and crown damage also occur. A licence is required to control red squirrels (by cage trapping) before or during the main damage period of May–July, but poisoning is not legally permitted. Can be a nuisance locally to seed orchards or horticultural crops. Wild adult squirrels can suffer heavy mortality shortly after capture when confined to cages; probably related to stress or 'shock disease', associated with reduction in body temperature, hypoglycaemia and a reduction in adrenal glucocorticoids [984].

Has species action plan under UK Biodiversity Action Plan [745]; guidance on delivery of action plan in [1120]. Conservation methods in GB have been studied, e.g. best tree species mix, forest size and continuity. Large conifer forests (2000–5000 ha) considered ideal but smaller forests (e.g. >100 ha) can support viable populations. Continuous-cover forests not a prerequisite; clear-felling should be kept to small areas, good seed and nest trees left behind where possible (although these may be vulnerable to windthrow). Recent approaches use population dynamics models linked to geographic information systems to guide decisions on forest design and management [576, 579, 925, 1231]. Management of SQPV disease threat described for largest of 16 designated red squirrel refuge sites in England, Kielder Forest (50 000 ha) [582]. Further reviews of management for red squirrel conservation in [569, 571, 572, 916, 922, 1225, 1234] and guidelines on monitoring in [577, 580]. Translocation to reinforce dwindling populations or replace lost populations is feasible (reviewed in [1463]) but disease a potential problem [1241]. Captive breeding programme established in GB in 1995 [339]; captive management described in [340]. The red squirrel is a game animal in mainland Europe. Grey squirrel control using cage trapping effective on Anglesey, allowed red squirrels to increase and spread [1290], may be important in preventing colonisation by grey squirrels, particularly along incursion routes to refuge sites, in buffer zones. Long-term effectiveness and sustainability has still to be proven.

LITERATURE

First monograph on biology and history of red and grey squirrels [1285]. General semi-popular account [562]. Symposium proceedings giving comprehensive account of ecology and behaviour of both species in *Mammal Review* 1983; 13 (2–4). Comprehensive and comparative account of natural history of Holarctic tree squirrels [560]. Symposium on red squirrel research giving an up-to-date overview of research findings and status of red squirrel [569]. Summary species account [927].

AUTHORS
J. Gurnell, P.W.W. Lurz & E.C. Halliwell, with acknowledgement to the Forestry Commission for data on distribution.

Grey squirrel *Sciurus carolinensis*
Sciurus carolinensis Gmelin, 1788; Carolina, USA.
Neosciurus carolinensis.

American grey squirrel; *iora glas* (Irish Gaelic); cat squirrel, migratory squirrel, Eastern gray squirrel (North America).

RECOGNITION
Larger than red squirrel, body predominantly grizzled (agouti) grey, never uniformly brown, though some brown on the back and (in summer) on the flanks and limbs (Plate 2). Tail grizzled grey, fringed white, and slight ear tufts in summer. (Edible dormouse, uniformly grey, arboreal, has a localised distribution in Hertfordshire, is nocturnal and much smaller.)

Skull: Longer and shallower than that of the red squirrel, with relatively larger nasal bones (Fig. 5.4)

FIELD SIGNS
As in the red squirrel, but stride longer (*c*.45 cm).

DESCRIPTION
Pelage: Sexes similar. In summer, upper fur grey with brown tinge along mid-dorsal region and chestnut over flanks, limbs and feet (Fig. 5.8); ears without white backs or conspicuous tufts; underside pale, sharply demarcated; tail hairs grey, banded with brown and black, indistinct white fringe. Winter coat thicker, grey with yellow-brown on head and along mid-dorsal region; flanks, limbs and feet grey; ears white behind with short, brown, inconspicuous tufts; tail dark grey fringed with white. Juveniles darker grey with more brown than adult summer coat. Other pelage characteristics can be used to separate age classes [81].

Moult: Similar to red squirrel [824]. Juveniles moult to appropriate winter or summer coat at *c*.3 months of age.

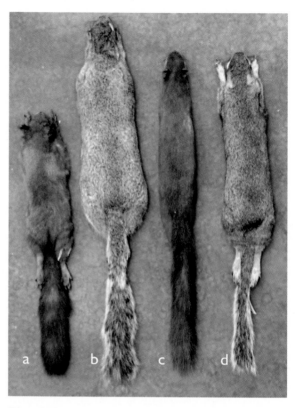

Fig. 5.8 Red and grey squirrels: winter and summer skins; red squirrels sometimes have rather grey winter coats (a), when grey squirrels are usually silver (b); grey squirrels may be rather brown in summer (d), when red squirrels are usually at their reddest (c). Both species show much individual as well as seasonal variation *(photo P. Morris, skins courtesy of NHM)*.

Nipples: 4 pairs; 1 inguinal, 1 abdominal, 2 pectoral. Become darkly pigmented with 1st pregnancy, tend to remain pigmented.

Scent glands: Probably as red squirrel; presence of mouth glands suggested by observations of behaviour [823, 1392].

Teeth: Similar to those of red squirrel (Fig. 5.4). Tooth eruption, replacement and wear, annuli in cementum (as well as eye-lens weight) used to determine age [354, 432, 451, 644].

Skeleton: Shows similar adaptations to climbing as red squirrel, although larger and more heavily built [787]. Ossification of epiphyseal cartilages distinguishes old from young animals [354, 1130]. Size of baculum useful additional indicator of age in males [801].

Reproductive tract: Similar to red squirrel. Scrotum becomes heavily pigmented, almost black, in a sexually active male [422].

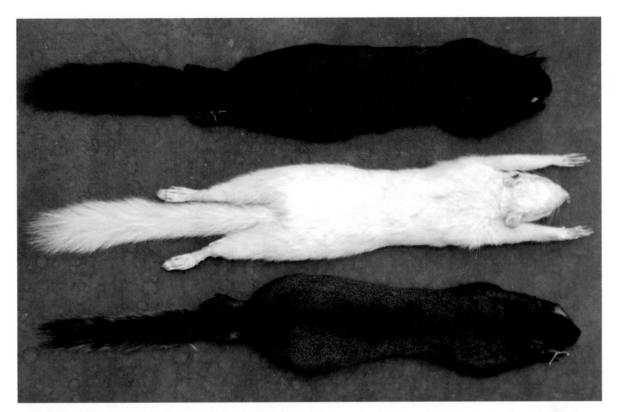

Fig. 5.9 Grey squirrel, colour variants: semimelanic (Baldock, Herts), albino (Wrotham, Kent) and melanic (Ashridge, Herts) *(photo P. Morris, skins courtesy of NHM)*.

Chromosomes: 2n = 40, FNa =76 (N America) [1589].

RELATIONSHIPS
Most closely related to *S. griseus*, the western grey squirrel (W USA).

MEASUREMENTS
See Table 5.2. Wide variation in body weight in GB, influenced by season, food supply and reproductive conditions; weights lower in late spring–summer, highest in early winter; considerable increase in body weight in some autumns, e.g. 15–25% [563, 787] (a much larger proportional increase in body weight than in red squirrels, e.g. 8–12% [787]) but may not occur in all habitats [918]. Negligible sexual dimorphism, breeding females slightly heavier than males; body weight not a good indicator of pregnancy in females nor of age unless animals very young, e.g. 4 months old and <400 g.

VARIATION
High levels of genetic variability in British grey squirrels [308, 309]. Dark grey and melanic squirrels are common in N of range in America, possibly associated with climate [357, 583]. Melanics rare in GB; reported in Buckinghamshire, Bedfordshire, Hertfordshire and Cambridgeshire, probably from melanic grey squirrels introduced to Woburn (Fig. 5.9). Albino forms rare but found in urban areas in N America; in England, reported from Essex, Kent, Surrey and Sussex. Erythristic forms with very red-brown backs occasionally found in SE England. Chestnut colouring on grey squirrels sometimes leads to confusion with red squirrels (Fig. 5.8).

DISTRIBUTION
Native to NE America (Fig. 5.10). Introduced to GB [1285] and Ireland [1098] (Fig. 5.11), as well as N

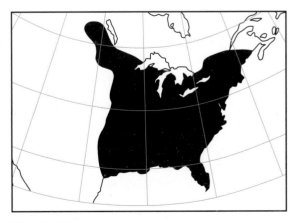

Fig. 5.10 Grey squirrel *Sciurus carolinensis*: native range; also introduced to South Africa, Tasmania.

Fig. 5.11 Grey squirrel *Sciurus carolinensis*: current range in British Isles, but expanding.

Italy [303, 1515], S Africa, Australia [560, 885, 1285].

HISTORY

Introduced from USA to *c.*30 sites in England and Wales, 1876–1929, from Canada to 3 sites in Scotland, 1892–1920, and from England to 1 site in Ireland, 1911 [1004, 1285]. Rapid expansion of range in England and Wales, 1930–1945, thereafter spread more slowly. Changing distribution reviewed for England, Scotland and Wales [899], E England [1188], NW England [908, 1298], Ireland [1098], and Scotland [205, 1330]; modelled and discussed in [1093, 1231, 1459]. Success of grey squirrel in GB partly due to ability to persist in heavily fragmented landscape [826]. Ecological replacement of red by grey squirrel discussed in red squirrel account, above.

HABITAT

In N America found in dense broadleaved forests that sometimes contain up to 10 or more tree species, providing more stable seed food supply than British broadleaved forests, which contain fewer species. Particularly associated with mature oak–hickory forests in USA.

In GB, found in wide range of habitats; most abundant in mature broadleaved forests of oak, beech, or sweet chestnut with hazel coppice. Also found in broadleaf/conifer mixtures, sometimes in mature conifer woodland but densities higher when broadleaves available nearby [431, 790, 1310, 1517], and in hedgerows, parks, gardens (Fig. 5.12) and urban areas with mature trees [434].

SOCIAL ORGANISATION AND BEHAVIOUR

Social and spatial organisation: Similar to red squirrel, hierarchical structure within and between sexes [21, 1102, 1391, 1422], but social organisation likely to be maintained by smaller inter-individual distances; densities typically much higher than those of red squirrels in broadleaf habitats, but similar to red squirrels in conifer [920, 1310, 1517]. Considerable variation in home-range size (Table 5.4), reflecting population density, food supply, woodlot size and habitat type [346, 347, 557, 560, 563, 782, 826, 1422]. Home-range size positively related to forest fragment size [826]. Relative sizes of home range as in red squirrel, males' ranges larger than females' [578, 782]. Male ranges increase up to 10-fold during spring courtship, but expand less during winter courtship [782]; females are more stable (Table 5.4). From 3–6 months old, as young become independent, range size increases quickly, overlap between mother and young decreases to *c.*50% [547]; juvenile range sizes similar to adult females [1422]. Female-biased natal philopatry results in kin clusters [578, 825]. Mothers behave the same towards both male and female young, but adult males tend to chase juvenile males more often than juvenile females, which may cause the male-biased dispersal [825]. Recent methods of home-range analysis separate high-use core areas from those visited rarely; core areas containing 60% of squirrel locations are only 30% of total range, and typically exclusive to single animals or to small groups that may share dreys [346, 782]. Large range movements rarely recorded but range sizes of juveniles prior to dispersal increase markedly, for example to 12 ha [782]; also distance of 3 km reported for juvenile taking up residence [1395].

Female and male breeding behaviour as in red squirrel. Mating system polygynous or promiscuous [307–309]. Antagonistic behaviour described [671, 1391]; fights rare but involve close contact wrestling, break off to chase; ears may become torn and bites may occur to back, rump and tail. Peaks in aggression at times of mating [821] and dispersal [822, 1106, 1422, 1423]. Communal nesting, among related females but also unrelated males, occurs in winter, probably to keep warm [598, 782, 825], and at other times of the year where the individuals again may be related females [825], or different sexes [1310]. On one occasion, 20 squirrels escaped from a single cavity in a beech tree [310].

Communication and senses: Vision similar to red squirrel; retina is two-tiered structure with the tier towards the centre of the eye composed of rods and the outer tier of cones [709]; therefore likely to be able to see in dim light. Retina cone-rich [234,

Table 5.4 Grey squirrel: average range size in mixed deciduous woodland near Oxford, 1979–1981; area (ha) likely to contain 95% of activity [346]

Season	Males	Females	Spring-born juveniles
Winter	6.6	5.4	
Spring	8.8	4.7	
Summer	11.5	6.0	6.0
Autumn	5.7	6.3	

640]. Dichromatic colour vision; uses colour cues when foraging [938]. Vocal communication has been classified into 11 different calls: buzz, kuk, quaa, moan; squeak, growl, scream, tooth-chatter, lip-smacking, muk-muk and mating call [61, 671, 819, 894–896]. Repetitive barking 'quaa' used to warn of intruders, human or otherwise. Tactile senses as red squirrel. Scent-marking and function as red squirrel; faeces may be placed at specific points in autumn [61].

Dispersal: Juveniles and some adults disperse during autumn [1423]. Road casualties increase in autumn. Mass migrations recorded in N America when densities high in autumn and food availability low [449, 1271]. Also dispersal in spring (yearlings), possibly from marginal back to preferred habitats, and in summer by spring-born young; this may contribute to bark-stripping in damage-vulnerable woodland [566, 571]. In fragmented agricultural landscapes, N America, grey squirrel distribution thought to be constrained by area requirements and dispersal ability [498]. Some studies in GB have found that dispersal is more common in June with no direct relationship to density [346].

Activity: Patterns and influence of weather and food similar to red squirrel. Much less arboreal than red squirrel in comparable habitats, but more arboreal in conifers than broadleaves [1310]. Least time spent aloft in late winter, most in midsummer.

Movement: As red squirrel, but not quite so agile.

Nests: Winter nests as red squirrel; some summer dreys are shallow platforms of twigs. Drey counts may be used as crude relative indices of population size or habitat use [348]. Holes in trees such as oak and beech used as dens; centre hollowed out and entrance gnawed to 7–10 cm diameter. Will use roof spaces of houses and outbuildings in urban and suburban areas.

Grooming: As red squirrel [671, 856].

FEEDING

Mainly tree seeds and plant material (Figs. 5.3, 5.12). Seeds preferred, including those of both broadleaf and conifer trees, but particularly large seeds such as acorns, beechnuts and chestnuts which can easily be held in the forepaws; wide range of other foods taken [1005], feeding on tree flowers in spring [782] especially noticeable through excised twigs strewn on ground. Scavenges litter bins and bird tables. No quantitative evidence that is a significant predator of birds' eggs or nestlings, although has been observed to take both; anecdotal evidence

Fig. 5.12 Grey squirrel, in winter coat, raiding bird feeder: a source of amusement to some and irritation to others *(photo B. Phipps)*.

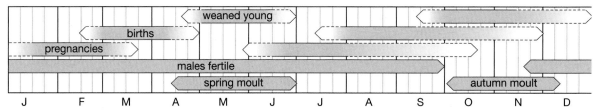

Fig. 5.13 Grey squirrel: annual cycle.

reviewed in [646]. Caching behaviour as in red squirrel, scatter-hoarding seeds when abundant in the autumn, i.e. seeds in small groups buried just below soil surface over wide areas; spacing of caches discussed in [839]. Location of specific caches not remembered although general area of caches may be; seeds relocated by smell. Tends to consume acorns of high perishability and cache those of low perishability [586]. Suggested to show specific behavioural adaptions to oaks *Quercus* sp.; bites through the radical and excises embryo of white oaks to prevent early germination [1336, 1337]. Often selects sound rather than weevil-infested acorns for caching [1335]; weevils significant dietary supplement. Nut selection improves with experience [898]. Nutritional value of bark stripping is debatable (see Relations with humans, below).

Feeding behaviour as red squirrel but on average spends much more time foraging on the ground in broadleaves than red squirrel, especially during winter months [1517]. Average proportion of foraging time spent in trees throughout year for grey squirrels in Monks Wood, Cambridgeshire, was 14% (cf. 67% for red squirrels in Lawns Wood, Cumbria) [787]. May eat 60–80 g seed/day [911]; studies of energy requirements carried out in laboratory perhaps innapplicable to free-living animals; reviewed in [809, 1189]. Daily energy expenditure in wild, Scotland, 574 kJ [207]; higher than red squirrel, but proportionate to larger mass.

BREEDING
Seasonal, usually 2 peaks, spring and summer (Fig. 5.13). Gestation 44 days [1524]. Litter size average 3 (range 1–7) [66]. Lactation 70 days. Birthweight 14–18 g.

Length of breeding season affected by food supply and weather [557, 560, 563]. Reproductive activity in males and females reviewed in [355, 1524], mating strategy in [821]. Male reproductive state assessed by visual score based on periscrotal hair and staining, and position, size and colour of testes, is a significant predictor of presence and concentration of epidermal spermatozoa [422].
Sexes: Regression of testes (e.g. from 7 to 1 g), of paired Cowper's glands (e.g. 26 to 8 mm diameter) and prostate gland (24 to 6 mm diameter) usually

occurs in autumn; stages in sexual development of male described in [422, 1036].

Female possesses twin uterine horns leading to paired ovaries; uterus in young, nulliparous female is threadlike (1.5 mm diameter) and coiled posteriorly in pelvic cavity; uterus uncoils, increases in diameter and moves up into abdomen when female approaches 10 months of age [450]. Presence of a male and adequate space necessary for induction of oestrus in female [598, 1524]. No evidence of postpartum oestrus. Copulatory plugs may be removed by female [820]. Adult female may produce 2 litters/year if breeding season starts December–February; yearlings invariably produce only 1 litter [557, 563]. Uterine losses of young may be high, to 25%, and further losses occur during weaning. If disturbed, mother may transfer young (by carrying individually in mouth) to another drey.

Mating: As in red squirrels, promiscuous or polygynous.

Young: Observed sex ratios vary, but *c*.1:1 [560]. Blind, deaf and naked at birth. Skin pigment appears on back, hairs emerge at 14 days. Hairs cover body by 20 days [1284, 1457]. Lower incisors cut 19–21 days, upper incisors 31–42 days. Ears open 28–35 days, eyes 28–30 days (*c*.90 g body weight). Begin leaving nest and start eating solid food at *c*.7 weeks [671]; weaned 8–10 weeks. Moult to adult coat at 3–4 months. Sexual maturity at 10–12 months, very rare in younger animals [1317].

POPULATION
Pre-breeding population in GB estimated at 2.52 million (2 million England, 0.2 million Scotland, 0.32 million Wales), based on areas of woodland, densities of 0.5–2.0/ha, as appropriate [624].

Densities: Long-term average densities in broadleaved forests much higher than for red squirrel; usually >2/ha and often much greater, e.g. >8/ha in oak wood, S England [563]. Densities greatly influenced by seed availability and weather [554, 557]. Density negatively related to forest fragment size [826]. Long-term densities in pure conifer habitats usually similar to red squirrel, but influenced by proximity of broadleaves [790, 920, 1310]. Annual cycle of numbers, as in red squirrel, but may be more marked with rapid changes over a few months. Complete turnover of population estimated to take >6 years in N America [67]. Population dynamics of squirrels, including effects of food availability, reviewed in [557, 561, 920].

Survival: Overwintering positively related to availability of autumn tree seed [557, 563]. Average juvenile survival (persistence) rates to 1 year vary from 0 to 50%, based on retrapped animals. Comparable annual rates for adults 50–80%, values tending to be lower for males and in conifer plantations [564, 790, 1310]. Radiotracking gives higher survival rates than re-trapping because surviving emigrants and trap-shy animals are recorded (and collared animals may sometimes be selected for good health and body weight). Shape of survival curves similar in N American and English unexploited populations [557]. In S England, mean expectation of life greatest in females at 6 months of age, i.e. 4–5 years, and in males at 18 months of age, i.e. 2–3 years [560, 563]; some females survived for 6.5 years whereas maximum recorded longevity in males was 6 years; difference may reflect residency time rather than mortality. Other studies record survival to 9 years in the wild (but <1% of population), to 20 years in captivity.

MORTALITY
Stoats, goshawks and foxes frequently kill grey squirrels; fox predation may exceed reproductive recruitment in conifer plantations [790, 1310]. Road casualties occur particularly during the autumn, and cats will kill grey squirrels. Hunted extensively throughout their range in N America, but this has little effect on population numbers. Similarly, the control of grey squirrel numbers in England (see below) has only a short-term and local effect on population levels. Humans have greatest effect on population by altering or destroying habitats. Inadequate food and severe weather important natural mortality factors, significantly influence seasonal and year-to-year population densities [557, 560]. Deaths from shock occur, as in red squirrels, but less frequently or likely, especially in animals recently captured. Mortality rates in translocated suburban [8] and forest [782] squirrels can be high

PARASITES
See [793].

Ectoparasites: Flea *Orchopeas howardii*, introduced from N America with grey squirrel, common throughout the range; red squirrel flea *Monopsyllus sciurorum* sometimes found [459, 1285]. Ticks not specific, most common being the sheep tick, *Ixodes ricinus*. Autumn mite larva *Trombicula autumnalis* attaches to exposed skin on head, elbows and underparts during summer and autumn. Infestations by mange mites uncommon. Sucking lice *Neohaematipinus sciuri*, *Hoplopleura sciuricola* and *Enderleinellus longiceps* [142] most numerous on head, back and legs [1105]. Drey fauna described in [1450]. Up to 17 species of ectoparasites found on woodland squirrels in Georgia, USA; fleas and lice possible vectors for *Bartonella* sp. [361].

Protozoan parasites: Include *Hepatozoon* and *Eimeria* [290, 1489]. Known to carry leptospirochaete bacteria [1456] and SQPV [1245]; recent work on the virus suggests SQPV represents a previously unrecognised genus of Chordopoxviridae [981, 1421]. SQPV antibodies found in serum samples from N American grey squirrels [981]. Virus particles not detected until 1994, in skin lesions on one grey squirrel from Hampshire [359], and grey squirrels generally appear clinically resistant to the disease [1433, 1434]. Field studies in UK indicate up to 100% (mean 61%) of individuals in some populations test positive to virus antibodies; grey squirrel considered vector for the disease that is lethal to red squirrels [1245]. Strategies to manage SQPV threat to red squirrels described in [582]. Virions consistent with SQPV found in grey squirrels with multiple cutaneous tumours in Florida [1412]. Microparasites include host-specific *Bartonella* species thought to have been introduced to GB with its host [160].

RELATIONS WITH HUMANS
Regarded as an attractive, mischievous animal and of amenity value by many people, but as a nuisance or a pest by others. Occasionally called a tree rat, a misleading and inappropriate name. Sometimes damages thatch or enters lofts and outbuildings, gnaws electric cables, water pipes and roof structures. Entrance holes can be blocked with wire mesh when the squirrel is not inside. Other 'nuisance' activities include taking food from bird tables or bird feeders (e.g. for chickens or pheasants), making a noise in roof spaces and taking bulbs from parks and gardens [560].

Economic damage to market gardens, orchards and arable crops can occur where sited next to good squirrel habitats and when natural squirrel foods are in short supply. Major forest pest; historical review [1273]; reviews [305, 481, 566]. Together with deer and rabbits, threatens the development of new woods [482]. Debarking damage to base, stem or crown of trees can be of economic importance and occurs particularly between May and July. Both broadleaved and conifer tree species vulnerable to damage, although thin-barked species (e.g. beech, sycamore) especially vulnerable. Small areas of damage scar over by callus growth, trunk may grow around them, lowering quality and economic value of timber. Rotting organisms will enter the wood if bark removed. If ring-barked or girdled, upper part of trunk or branch dies; growth can become distorted; top live crown may be blown out of tree (wind-snap). Beech, oak and sycamore trees at vigorous growth stage (i.e. pole-stage trees, 10–40 years old) are most vulnerable but many other species including conifers attacked [305, 566, 1310]. Larger trees tend to be more damaged than smaller ones [573, 941, 1310] and when vigour is enhanced just after thinning [789].

Damage most likely to start in areas with high densities of young squirrels [786], possibly triggered by agonistic behaviour [1391] or exploratory feeding behaviour. In some cases, bark-stripping behaviour may persist in individuals [789]. Although triggering factors are unclear, damage to individual trees and areas becomes severe primarily when high volume of phloem (but not of sugar in phloem) available for eating [566, 781, 783, 786, 788]. Trees damaged one year not always damaged in the next [573, 1310]. Damage less severe in N America, where naturally regenerating trees grow less vigorously and bark tends to be thicker [783], but some afforested landscapes in GB seriously threatened by bark stripping (e.g. [1053, 1180]). Bark strips may also be used to line dreys, dead bark normally removed in winter [566]. Has potential to become serious European forest pest; range continues to increase in N Italy towards France and Switzerland [924, 1389, 1515, 1516], where also replacing red squirrel, as in British Isles [303, 565]. Efforts to control and eradicate grey squirrel in Piedmont, 1997, stopped due to legal action [135, 1127].

Grey squirrels are controlled in GB by cage or kill trapping (regulations laid down by the Wildlife and Countryside Act 1981 and the Spring Traps Approval Order 1995), shooting (sometimes in conjunction with drey poking) or warfarin poisoning (provisions laid down by the Grey Squirrels (Warfarin) Order 1973, the Control of Pesticide Regulations 1986 and the EU Plant Protection Products Directive 91/414/EEC) [1121, 1273]. (See Chapter 4.) Poisoning effective [573] but prohibited by law in some counties: poisoning and spring trapping are not allowed in any areas where red squirrels are at risk (Wildlife and Countryside Act 1981). Damage prediction would be beneficial in reducing amount of control required [561, 784]. Control methods described in [566, 974, 1121, 1224]. Some studies carried out

on use of immunocontraception [1035, 1036], which proved acceptable to public in one survey [74], although it may only be effective as part of an integrated control strategy with other methods [1234].

Illegal to import, release or keep grey squirrels in captivity without licence from DEFRA or the Secretary of State for Scotland (Grey Squirrel (Prohibition of Importation and Keeping) Order 1937 and Wildlife and Countryside Act 1981) [1273] (see Chapter 4 for details). An important game animal in N America; up to 40 million killed annually [450].

LITERATURE
Popular account of introduction and early distribution [993]. First monograph on biology and history of red and grey squirrels [1285]. Popular accounts [1287–1289]. Popular account of both species [663]. Reviews of biology of grey and fox squirrels in N America [450, 824]. Symposium proceedings giving comprehensive account of ecology and behaviour of both species in *Mammal Review* 1983; **13** (2–4). Comprehensive and comparative account of natural history of Holarctic tree squirrels [560]. Description of the everyday lives of grey and fox squirrels [1334].

AUTHORS
J. Gurnell, R.E. Kenward, H. Pepper & P.W.W. Lurz

FAMILY CASTORIDAE (BEAVERS)

A small family of 1 genus, 2 species: Eurasian and Canadian beavers. Largest Holarctic rodent, aquatic, associated with riparian habitat in woodland. Severely hunted for fur, reduced in range and numbers by 1900, but subsequently subject to conservation measures, quotas set for hunting, and have recovered; also aided by reintroductions, especially in Europe. Eurasian beaver extinct in GB, reintroduction currently under discussion.

Eurasian beaver *Castor fiber*
Castor fiber Linnaeus, 1758; Sweden.

Afanc, llostlydan (Welsh); *dubhran losleathan* (Scottish Gaelic).

RECOGNITION
Large rodent with robust body, short neck and limbs. Uniquely adapted for semi-aquatic lifestyle with a characteristic large, flattened, scale-covered tail and webbed hindfeet to aid propulsion under water. Distinct from smaller coypu and muskrat, which have cylindrical tails, and from the otter,

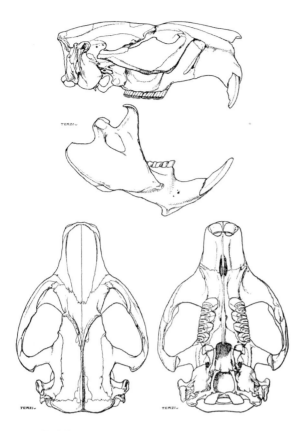

Fig. 5.14 Beaver skull *(from [995])*.

which has round, tapering, furred tail and a carnivore's head.

Skull and teeth: Distinguishable from *C. canadensis* by broader front palate and longer nasal bones (Fig. 5.14) [870]. Dental formula: $i^1/_1c^0/_0p^1/_1m^3/_3 = 20$. Large incisor teeth covered in orange enamel.

FIELD SIGNS

Tracks and trails: 5 toes on front feet not usually seen: tracks more commonly 3- or 4-toed. Distinctive webbed tracks from large hindfeet are often obliterated by dragging tail. Trails between ponds and water bodies often well used. Troughs may be found in snow on bank where animals pull out of the water.

Faeces: Rarely found, usually deposited in water. Pellets *c.*2.5–3 cm in length and width. Consist of fibrous, undigested woody material: may be connected in strings.

Nests: Bank burrows often unnoticed. Lodges constructed from woody debris (see Social organisation and behaviour, below).

Field signs: Fallen trees and stumps have characteristic ring-marking from bark stripping.

Bushes and small trees are often coppiced locally. Logs and twigs stripped of bark and tooth marks on wood chippings and debris nearby often noted. Tooth marks commonly 3–4 mm wide.

Scent mounds: Constructed of piles of mud, twigs and sticks, may reach >1 m in height and up to 30 cm in diameter.

Dams: Constructed from logs, twigs, rocks and mud in fluctuating, narrow or shallow watercourses in order to maintain sufficient water depth to cover the burrow/lodge entrance.

Feeding channels: May be cut into riverbanks to allow quick access to water and aid transport of food and building materials back to lodge. Burrows may also be excavated in river and lake banks.

DESCRIPTION

Pelage: Uniform colour, varying from yellowish to reddish brown. May appear black when wet. Long, stiff guard hairs (50–60 mm) protrude through a soft undercoat (*c.*25 mm long) to form a dense, sleek, waterproof coat. Large, flattened tail covered with scales.

Table 5.5 Beaver: measurements, showing regional variation

Head and body length (mm)	
Rhone	820–900
Elbe	800–870
Scandinavia	740–810
Tail length (mm)	
Rhone	310–380
Elbe	310–340
Scandinavia	285–335
Hindfoot length (mm)	
	160–180
Weight (kg)	
Rhone	15–38
Elbe	14.5–30
Scandinavia	12.5–30

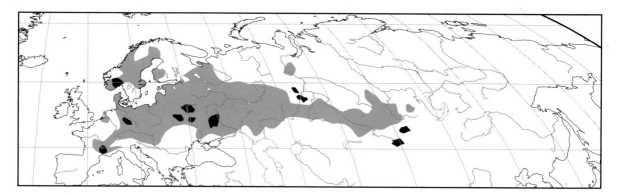

Fig. 5.15 Eurasian beaver *Castor fiber*: world distribution (black, remnant range around 1900; grey, reintroduced or recovered range).

Nipples: 2 pairs, pectoral.

Scent glands: 2 anal scent glands and 2 castor sacs. Castoreum secreted into the urine to create characteristic musky smell. Other glands are located on the soles of feet (both sexes).

Skull: Typical large rodent skull, with no infraorbital foramen (unlike coypu, muskrat); broad incisors, orange on anterior surfaces; 4 pairs cheek-teeth (p^4, m^{1-3}), all similar size and shape, oval crowns with strong cross-ridges.

Chromosomes: 2n = 48.

RELATIONSHIPS

External appearance and behaviour very similar to the N American species *C. canadensis* but differs in skull morphology and chromosome number (2n = 40 in *C. canadensis*). Naturally discrete distributions have been compromised by the introduction of *C. canadensis* to Poland, Finland and Russia. Traditional taxonomy of *C. fiber*, based on morphology and distribution, recognises 6–8 subspecies [1081, 1466, 1467] of which *C. f. fiber* (Scandinavia) thought to be closest to British animals [804]. Phylogenetic analysis using mtDNA recognised 2 lineages: eastern (Poland, Lithuania, Russia, Mongolia) and western (France, Germany, Norway); probably diverged during the last glaciation [362]. Extinct British population would have been part of western lineage.

MEASUREMENTS

See Table 5.5. British animals seem closest to morphology of Scandinavian animals.

DISTRIBUTION

Once widespread in GB and Europe, but reduced by 1900 to only 5 European and 3 Asian populations (Fig 5.15) [1081]. Populations now re-establishing in many European and Scandinavian countries across to the Urals, mainly through reintroductions [594, 934]. Asian population remains threatened. Currently extinct in GB. Proposals to reintroduce Eurasian beaver to Scotland [1265] thwarted by concerns about potential damage to European protected sites. Some currently kept in large enclosures to manage habitats in Ham Fen Reserve (Kent), Cotswold Water Park (Gloucestershire), Aigas Field Centre (Beauly, Inverness-shire) and a private estate at Bamff, Perthshire, but these are not reintroduc-tions to the wild [802]. Never present in Ireland.

HISTORY

Known in GB from the Pliocene, and in Cromerian, Hoxnian and Ipswichian Interglacials [1571]. Not present in the Windermere Interstadial, on present evidence, but recorded early in the Mesolithic (Star Carr, Thatcham) and at numerous subsequent Mesolithic, Neolithic, Bronze Age and Iron Age sites, in both England and Scotland. Rare by Roman and Saxon times; last archaeological records dated to around 900 AD [803, 1571]. About 20 English placenames thought to be based on beaver's name [50]. Documentary evidence that species survived in Wales to 1188, and in Scotland to 16th century. Review of British beavers during the Holocene [267] collates all records, suggest tentatively that might have survived to 18th century.

HABITAT

Requires year-round access to fresh water. Optimal habitat in wooded, slow-flowing broad river valley bottoms, mainly floodplains [934]. Modifies environment to colonise suboptimal habitats through dam-building behaviour [1195]. Dams (7–33/km of stream in France) are built to extend water protection around lodges, and to extend foraging opportunities [267].

SOCIAL ORGANIZATION AND BEHAVIOUR

Small family groups comprise a monogamous adult pair, young-of-year and sometimes young of the previous year. Colony size is typically 3.8±1.0 animals (smaller than the 5.2 typical for *C. canadensis* [1214]). Group sizes increase with population density.

Territories: Size varies with habitat, density and season [1081]; generally 3 km but may vary from 0.5 to 12.8 km [934].

Denning/nesting behaviour: Eurasian beavers prefer to use natural holes or burrow into the bank. Entrance below water level, leading to nest chamber *c*.0.4–0.5 m in height situated 0.3–0.7 m above the entrance. Bank burrows normally constructed in banks that are 1.5–2 m high above the burrow entrance. Bank above the nest chamber may be supplemented using woody debris if bank height is insufficient. True lodges, constructed entirely from woody debris, soil and twigs, are built where burrows or bank lodges are not options. Colonies may construct more than one lodge.

Scent-marking: Colony can use up to 7 scent mounds to mark their presence. Scent piles are marked using castor glands (spraying) and anal glands (dragging along the ground).

Vocalisation: Not conspicuous. May growl, hiss or scream.

Other communication: May slap the surface of the water with large flattened tail to warn family group of danger.

Aggressive behaviour: Lunging, sham biting and tail quivering have been noted [932] and animals may also wrestle. Will rebuild scent mounds if a neighbouring scent found.

Dispersal: Most often occurs at 1.5–2 years old. Young may return to the natal nest in the 1st year if unsuccessful in establishing a territory. Median dispersal distance 25 km, maximum 170 km [1081].

Activity: Mainly nocturnal, emerging before sunset and returning at sunrise. May exhibit diurnal activity in undisturbed areas. Active all year but may be confined to lodges and nests under ice during extreme winter conditions. May resort to a free-running circadian rhythm if isolated from daylight. Usually avoids open air in freezing temperatures. Body temperature drops by up to 4 °C in water and is raised again while grooming on land.

Locomotion: Clumsy on land but well adapted for swimming and diving. Dives last <15 min, average 5–6 min.

Other: Grooms using double claw on 2nd toe of hindfoot, which functions as a comb, or with forefeet. Capable of reingesting faeces while confined in lodge or nest.

FEEDING

Herbivorous, feeding predominantly on herbaceous vegetation in summer and bark from woody material in winter. Able to bite under water by constricting lips behind the incisors to isolate the front of the mouth.

Foraging behaviour: Generally forages within 60 m of water's edge, near the lodge. Focuses on trees <10 cm diameter. Feeding channels used to extend foraging distance inland. Most trees cut in autumn when caching food and constructing dams. Preferentially feeds on aspen, willow, poplar and alder. Conifers rarely eaten. Poor cellulose digestion (30%), therefore requires large amounts of food to obtain sufficient nutrients.

Food caching: Caches food on bottom of watercourse near lodge in winter in harsh environments.

BREEDING

Gestation 103–108 days. Litter size 1–6, average 2.7 young per litter. Lactation 2–3 months. Weight at birth 300–700 g.

Breeding season: Monoestrous, breeding mainly in December–April (oestrous cycle lasting 7–12 days). Pregnancy lasts 103–108 days, peak births in May–June. Mean litter size 2–3, sexually mature at 2 years but unlikely to breed successfully until 3rd year. Monogamous [343].

Development of young: Precocious (fully furred, eyes open at birth). Learn to swim within hours; leave nest at 1–2 months old. Weaned in 1st summer but may not disperse until 2 years old. Subadults may help rear young.

POPULATION

Numbers: Currently extinct in GB. Eurasian population currently estimated at 639 000, increased from only 1200 animals around 1900 [594, 1214].

Survival: Average lifespan 7–8 years, recorded up to 25 years [934]. Life table prepared for the English population from subfossil remains [973]. Mortality highest in 1st 6 months and at dispersal [1081]. Most common causes of mortality anthropogenic, e.g. road kills, drowning in nets. May also drown if trapped under ice or in nest by a sudden rise in water levels.

MORTALITY

Predation: Natural predators wolf, wolverine, lynx, red fox, some raptors, e.g. white-tailed eagle.

Persecution: Hunted for their pelt and castoreum, which led to extinction in GB by 16th century. Drainage of fenland may also have contributed to their loss.

Disease: Known to transmit rabies and *Giardia*. Also prone to infection with yersiniosis, avian tuberculosis, pseudotuberculosis, pneumonia, tularemia, leptospirosis and trematode flukes.

PARASITES

Ectoparasites: 'Beaver beetle', *Platypsyllus castoris* Rits, uniquely associated with *Castor* species.

Endoparasites: Gastric nematode *Travassosius rufus* Khalil found in NW European populations but absent from the Rhone and Elbe animals [870].

RELATIONS WITH HUMANS

Exploitation: Currently a valued game animal in Belarus, Estonia, Finland, Latvia, Lithuania, Norway, Russia, Sweden and Ukraine, hunted for fur and castoreum. Conversely, the subject of extensive reintroduction programmes in many European countries, and a tourist attraction in some places [594].

Legislation: Exploitation of *C. fiber* controlled through Appendix III of the Bern Convention (the Convention on the Conservation of European Wildlife and Natural Habitats). Strict protection afforded through Annex II and Annex IV of the EC Directive on the Conservation of Natural Habitats and of Wild Fauna and Flora (see Chapter 4). No specific protection currently exists under British law.

AUTHORS
M. Cole, A.C. Kitchener & D.W. Yalden

FAMILY GLIRIDAE (DORMICE)

A small family of 29 species in 9 genera; mostly Palaearctic, but 1 genus, *Graphiurus*, with 14 species in Africa; 5 in Europe, of which 1 native and 1 introduced to GB. Small, mouse–rat sized rodents, mostly arboreal, ecologically like small nocturnal squirrels (though mouse-tailed dormouse *Myomimus* is terrestrial). Dominant rodents in Eocene–Oligocene Europe, long before evolution of Muridae. Have infraorbital foramen like murids, with similar complex jaw muscles, but gut lacks caecum, cannot digest cellulose in hind gut, so dependent on more nutritious foods (insects, seeds, fruits). Have 4/4 pairs of cheek-teeth, low-crowned, with shallow transverse ridges.

GENUS *Muscardinus*

A monospecific genus, confined to W Palaearctic. Differs from other glirids in unequal sizes of cheek-teeth; premolars very small, $m^1/_1$ much longer than other molars, almost length of $m^2/_2 + m^3/_3$ combined.

Hazel dormouse *Muscardinus avellanarius*
Muscardinus avellanarius Linnaeus, 1758; Sweden. Common dormouse, sleeper; *pathew* (Welsh).

Table 5.6 Differences between two dormouse species and grey squirrel

	Hazel dormouse	**Edible dormouse**	**Grey squirrel**
Size	Small: 10–30 g, 50 mm body	Small squirrel size: 50–250 g tail 220 mm	Weight 300–600 g, body 260
Fur	Golden yellow	Grey, creamy white belly	Brown on flanks and feet in summer, hairs banded in grey and brown.
Tail	Fluffy, uniform yellow	Uniform grey or dark	Tail brown with white fringe hairs banded
Activity	Nocturnal	Nocturnal	Diurnal
In houses	Never	Often	Sometimes

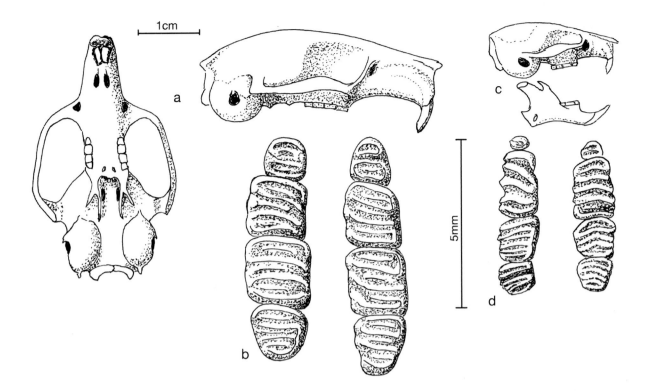

Fig. 5.16 Skulls and cheek-teeth, of edible (a, b) and hazel (c, d) dormice. Share the evident infraorbital foramen with mice and voles, but differ in having an extra cheek-tooth (p⁴/4).The molars are nearly the same size in edible dormice, whereas m¹/ı is much longer than other teeth in hazel dormice. The square angular process on the lower jaw is also characteristic (*drawn by D.W. Yalden*).

RECOGNITION

Furred, bushy tail distinctive amongst mouse-sized animals. Small size and bright golden or orange-brown pelage make it very different from the edible dormouse (Table 5.6). Juveniles greyer brown.

Skull: Readily distinguished by 4 cheek-teeth in each row, each with a unique pattern of transverse ridges (Fig. 5.16).

Fig. 5.17 Dormouse: ginger adult and greyer juvenile coats of hibernating individuals (*photo M. Woods*).

FIELD SIGNS

Standard survey method [188] involves searching for hazelnut shells which dormice open in a distinctive way [686], leaving a smooth, round hole, with oblique tooth marks around cut edge (wood mice and bank voles show radial marks of lower incisors on cut surface of hole) (Fig. 5.3). Also possible to locate by searching low-growing shrubs for nests, which are double layered, with woven bark surrounded by concentric layers of leaves, and generally have no well-defined entrance hole. Only a few species of birds make domed nests (e.g. wren), sometimes found in similar situations, but then entrance hole is distinct and lower rim of hole is reinforced with grass and fibres. Dormouse nests can be found in bramble, among dense shrub branches, in gorse and bracken. However, many nests inaccessible, built high up or in tree hollows [181, 182]. Dormouse strips honeysuckle bark for nest material, but squirrels and several bird species also do this. Advice on survey methods in [179, 189]. Readily uses nest boxes (bird, bat or those designed for dormice); these provide a way to detect presence and monitor populations [185]. Plastic tubes can be used to detect presence, but are not suitable for long-term monitoring [1046].

DESCRIPTION

Muzzle short, vibrissae very long, up to 30 mm. Eyes prominent, black; ears short, furred and rounded. Feet slender with large pads; prehensile and capable of much lateral movement at wrist and ankle; 4 functional digits on fore and hind, thumb, and hallux rudimentary. Tail almost as long as head and body, thickly furred with long hairs, giving bushy appearance.

Pelage: Soft and dense. Upper parts and tail uniform orange-brown; underside pale buff with pure white on throat, sometimes extending back as a narrow line to belly. Juveniles greyer (Fig. 5.17).

Moult: Little information; diffuse moult in autumn.

Nipples: 4 pairs; 1 pectoral, 1 abdominal, 2 inguinal.

Scent glands: Near to anus in both sexes [673] and under chin, but odour-free to human nose, contrasting with other rodents.

Teeth: 1.0.1.3/1.0.1.3. Premolars small and single-rooted, molars large, multiple-rooted, with flat crowns bearing low transverse ridges (Fig. 5.16).

Chromosomes: 2n = 46 (European data) [1589].

MEASUREMENTS

Head and body of young animals, autumn, 68–79 mm (8 in NHM), of adults, summer, *c.*80–85 mm. Tail 57–68 mm. Summer adults 16–20 g, pregnant females up to *c.*25 g. Juveniles independent at *c.*10 g. Immediately before hibernation, adults 25–35 g (record 43 g in the wild), juveniles 15–25 g [1]. Juveniles <12 g in mid October unlikely to survive hibernation [185].

VARIATION

Distinctive British race (*M. a. anglicus* Barrett-Hamilton, 1900, Bedford Purlieus, Thornhough, Northants) proposed, on basis of supposedly brighter colour; since discredited [995]. White tail-tip not uncommon, frequency *c.*10%. Albinos recorded but rare. Damaged ears and loss of part of tail are common.

DISTRIBUTION

Largely C European, from France to Urals; marginally into Turkey; absent Iberia, most of Scandinavia (Fig. 5.18). In England, widespread but patchily distributed S of line from London to Gloucester, and extending into the Welsh borders [175, 188, 189, 686]. Scattered populations Suffolk, Northamptonshire; 3 isolated populations known in Cumbria, Northumberland (Fig. 5.19). In Wales, widespread in SE and along English border, becoming much less abundant to W and N where there are scattered populations [174, 177, 686, 736]. Absent Scotland, Ireland (though brief attempt to introduce it, 19th century).

HISTORY

Ancestral *M. pliocaenicus* known from Pliocene, Poland. In Europe, *M. avellanarius* known through Middle and Upper Pleistocene [715, 851], and in England from Cromerian, Boxgrove, Sussex, [1199]. Probably an early Postglacial coloniser, arriving in GB *c.*9000 years ago; probable Mesolithic record from Chapel Cave, Yorkshire [1488] but earliest dated subfossil finds are Neolithic: Three Holes Cave (Devon), Merlin's Cave (Gwent), Dowel Cave (Derbyshire) and the Undercliff (Isle of Wight, dated 4480 bp) [1152, 1571].

Found in many more localities (>30) in C–N England in the late 19th century, present in 7 counties from which subsequently lost [1, 686]. Though relict populations might still be located, suggests loss from 1/2 former range in GB. Decline due to cessation of coppice management; woodland loss, fragmentation and conversion to plantation; loss and inappropriate management of hedgerows; and climatic change (review [185]). Reintroduction methodology developed [184]; reintroduced since 1992 to 10 counties where very rare or absent: Buckinghamshire, Bedfordshire, Cambridgeshire, Suffolk, Warwickshire, Staffordshire, Derbyshire, Nottinghamshire, Cheshire, Yorkshire [185, 186, 189].

HABITAT

Deciduous woodland with well-developed shrub layer, overgrown hedgerows, scrub and plantations where the shrub layer is suitable. Sufficient woody species diversity and low shading on the understorey are key habitat needs, providing a continuum of arboreal food sources through the summer and leading to profuse production of shrub flowers and fruits (main foods) respectively [180]. Important, but not essential, plant species in suitable habitat include hazel, oak, bramble, sweet chestnut, honeysuckle. Occupies hedgerows year-round provided they are overgrown. Hedgerows probably important for dispersal between woodlands [1, 188], but gaps in them limit movement [176]. Coniferous plantations sometimes occupied, particularly where some deciduous trees and shrubs present.

Ancient woodland (originating pre-1600) occupied more frequently than recent woodland (origin post-1600) in most regions [175, 188], in part because provide good habitat and partly because

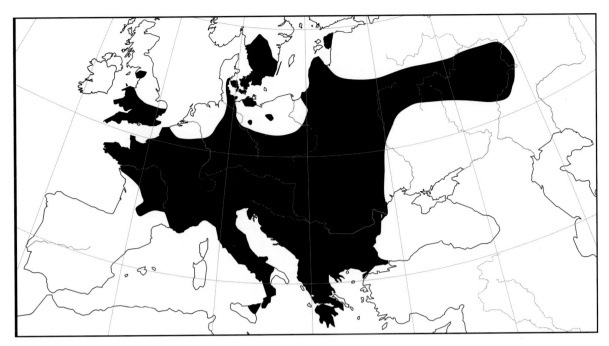

Fig. 5.18 Hazel dormouse *Muscardinus avellanarius*: Palaearctic range.

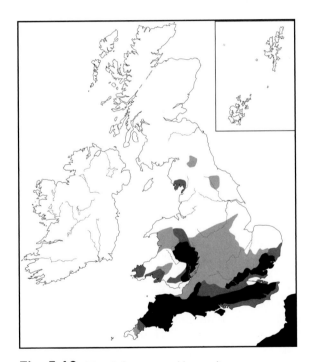

Fig. 5.19 Hazel dormouse *Muscardinus avellanarius*: range in GB.

SOCIAL ORGANISATION AND BEHAVIOUR

Social organisation: Ranges of males show little overlap when dormice are reproductively active, female ranges overlap considerably [181, 182]. Breeding males seem strongly aggressive, do not share nests [184, 1048]. Breeding males thus appear territorial, females may be partially so. A male and 1, sometimes 2, females share the same set of nests. Long-term (3-year) associations, same male and female sharing nest box in successive years, suggest long-term pair bond [1]. Nest sharing and intrasexual range overlap suggest mating system is polygynous [181, 182]. Non-breeding juveniles may remain with mother even while the latter has another litter [1, 1557]. Older literature sometimes refers to 'colonies', i.e. several animals or nests found in close proximity. Dispersion, even within apparently uniform habitat, often patchy.

Home range: Totally arboreal during summer active season. An agile climber, activity concentrated at different heights in trees and shrubs according to food availability [181, 182]. Mean home-range size in typical habitat 0.45 ha over a week, larger for males than females (radio-tracking observations [182]). Ranges larger in poor habitat, e.g. 1.2 ha for males, 0.5 ha for females at sites in Cumbria and Northumberland [1]. Travel *c.*250 m/night. Ranges are polynucleate, with multiple centres where activity concentrated about food sources, often in stands of one or a few trees [181]. In hedgerows, mean length of home range over a week was 185 m [178].

dormice are apparently poor colonists of recent woodland, especially if the latter is isolated, although sometimes abundant in scrub [369] and secondary woodland. Habitat fragmentation strongly influences distribution; more likely to be found in woods of >20 ha and in those less isolated from neighbouring woodland. In regions where woodland highly fragmented, only very large woods (>50 ha) retain dormice; in regions of high connectivity very small woods are occupied [175, 188].

Communication: Generally silent even when disturbed, but shrill squeaking noises noted during chases and aggression in captivity. Mewing and purring sounds also heard; hibernating animals may produce a wheezing sound as they wake. Neonates may emit ultrasound in the 20–30 kHz range [1].

Dispersal: Movement of marked animals, Germany, up to 1600 m for males and 700 m for females, but most remained close to point of 1st capture [1260]. Evidence from distribution in recently planted woodland and radio-tracking suggests dispersal of a few home-range diameters may be usual, with movement up to c.1700 m possible [1, 184].

Activity: Strictly nocturnal except on rare occasions; young may be active close to natal nest in daylight. Cold nights in autumn may induce diurnal activity [190] In May–August, active from soon after dusk until 0300–0400 h. In September–October, before hibernation, active all night (up to c.12 h [190]). Low ambient temperature and rain may reduce activity length [190]. Enters facultative torpor during the day in summer, when food is short or weather conditions adverse, even at ambient temperatures of up to 17 °C [1, 759]. In Mediterranean ecosystems, active season may be winter, with summer spent in aestivation [1103].

Hibernates in woven nests that are usually on the ground surface ([1, 1474]. Winter nests do not contain food stores. Hibernation very profound (Fig. 5.20); usually lasts from October to May in the UK, with intrahibernal arousals about every 8 days depending on ambient temperature; does not usually leave nest during these arousals [1].

Nests: Does not burrow. In summer, usually occupies nests above ground, up to 10 m high, but often in lower shrubs [181, 182]. Nests in which females have young may be distinguished by larger than usual size (15 cm diameter) and especially by fine internal lining of stripped bark. Newly independent young, in particular, make smaller nests, c.10 cm in diameter, often grouped only a few metres apart [684]. Frequently uses nest boxes put up for birds, occasionally found in bat boxes. Competition with birds for nest boxes apparent [760, 1250] and perhaps with *Apodemus* spp. [1]. Small boxes with a 35 mm hole facing towards trunk of tree commonly used by both sexes [1048]. A high proportion of such boxes may be used during the summer, but not normally in winter. Radio-tracking shows that individuals use 2–3 nests (in a 10-day period, probably more during whole summer) and that most natural nest sites are usually in tree hollows where these are available [182]. During hot, dry weather may not use nests at all but sleep on branches.

Grooming: Frequently watched in captivity. Rubs front paws behind head and ears, then over eyes and nose, reaching round to fur on back and sides. Finally brings tail up and forwards to comb through mouth.

FEEDING

Arboreal feeder, diet varies seasonally. In early summer, flowers and pollen normally taken, from e.g. hawthorn, honeysuckle, oak, sycamore, bramble. In midsummer, insects from oak, hazel and sycamore important. In autumn, fruits, berries and nuts, from e.g. hazel, bramble, wayfaring tree, hornbeam, sweet chestnut, yew [183, 1197]. Hazelnuts and chestnuts important prior to hibernation. In captivity, fruit and sunflower seeds accepted, but not grain; provision of water essential. Highly selective feeders, e.g. recently dehisced anthers of hawthorn flowers, ovule and nectaries of honeysuckle flowers, probably because dormouse lacks a caecum and is therefore especially poorly equipped to digest cellulose. Feed little on seeds that are chemically defended, e.g. oak, sycamore, ash [183].

BREEDING

Seasonal, usually midsummer (Fig. 5.20). Litter size typically 4–5 young (range 2–9). Gestation 22–24 days. Breeds first in year following birth, although 12.7% of litters in Lithuania born to female young-of-year [756]. Produces 1, occasionally 2, litters/year.

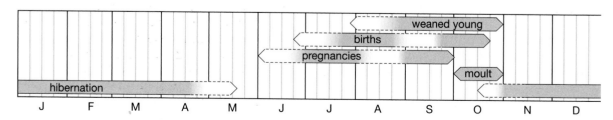

Fig. 5.20 Dormouse: annual cycle.

Season: In GB, young may be found from late May to September and exceptionally October, but usually in late July–August [185]. Timing highly variable, depending on habitat, food supply and weather. In mainland Europe, 2 main peaks of births, in late June–early July and in late July–early August [465]. At least 2 litters/year normal in Poland [1292]; 1/year normal in Germany [1476]; 2/year known in captivity [685].

Matings: Seen in captivity, accompanied by short, high-pitched squeaks. Gestation period 22–24 days.

Young: Litter size in GB averages 4.6, range 2–9, though litters of 7–9 may represent crèches [1]. Litter size 2–7, mean 3.7, in Germany [1476]; 3–6, mean 4.7, in Czechoslovakia [465]. Blind at birth, pelage well developed by 13 days, eyes open at 18 days, begin to leave nest at 30 days, independent by 40 days [1476]. May remain with mother for up to 8 weeks. 1st pelage grey, moulted at c.18 days; 2nd pelage more like adult but duller and greyer.

POPULATION

Density: Much lower than wood mice and bank voles even in good habitat. Cage trapping suggests densities of 8–10 adults/ha [1047]. Data from the National Dormouse Monitoring Programme (NDMP), based on capture of dormice in 50–150 nestboxes at >100 sites, gives average densities of c.3.5 adults/ha, pre-breeding. Most NDMP sites are good-quality habitats. Densities reach 10/ha in best habitats [180]. In Lithuania, percentage of females breeding, late breeding and incidence of 2nd litters are all density dependent [757, 758].

Population structure: In GB, population structure varies with habitat type and geographically; fewer young-of-year in woodlands where the understorey is heavily shaded, and in N GB [1].

Survival: Lives up to 6 years in captivity [685], at least 4 years recorded in marked animals in wild [753, 1260]. Ridges on molar teeth more or less worn away by 3rd year, suggesting that few survive beyond that age [910].

MORTALITY

Predation by owls probably very low compared to wood mice and bank voles. Rarely found in owl pellets or discarded bottles. Juveniles, especially, sometimes caught by cats. Weasels rarely predate dormice in nest boxes. No dormice in hibernation nests were predated, although 1 (of 30) was killed shortly before hibernation [1]. Crows and magpies seen to drop dormice. Nest containing hibernating mouse found in open below raven roost [685]. Most mortality probably occurs during hibernation, owing to insufficient fat reserves, or in early summer because of starvation. In Lithuania, winter mortality is c.60%, varying according to age [756]; annual mortality rates fairly constant [754].

PARASITES

Fleas: Rarely encountered; only *Ctenophthalmus nobilis* recorded, but other fleas of small mammals may occur; dormice may become infested with bird fleas.

Lice: Sucking louse *Schizophthirius pleurophaeus* is shared only with other Gliridae.

Mites: Follicle mite *Demodex muscardini* appears to be specific. Heavy infestations rare in the wild, more frequent in captivity.

Nematodes: Ocular disease induced by soil nematode *Rhabditis orbitalis* in a high-density population, following very wet weather and the accumulation of much organic matter in nestboxes [1243].

RELATIONS WITH HUMANS

A harmless species, vulnerable to local extinction owing to loss of its specialised habitat. Protected by Wildlife and Countryside Act 1981, as amended 1986 (Schedule 5), and subsequent European legislation (see Chapter 4). Any disturbance, trapping, etc. requires a licence. Also protected in many other European countries and all EU states (Bern Convention). Since 1990, significant conservation activity in many areas (practical advice in [191]). Since 1992, NDMP has tracked changes in relative numbers at >180 sites. Suggests that national population decline continues, especially in N areas of GB; stable in parts of S.

LITERATURE

General, illustrated accounts [187, 685, 1044]. Conservation guidelines [179, 191].

AUTHORS

P.W Bright & P.A. Morris, with acknowledgement to E. Hurrell for information from the 2nd edition.

GENUS *Glis*

A monospecific genus, confined to C Europe and Caucasus. Larger than other Gliridae, has cheek-teeth squarish, more equal in size than in *Muscardinus*. Sometimes called *Myoxus* (and family Myoxidae), but *Glis* Brisson 1767 conserved as correct name [704].

Edible dormouse *Glis glis*
Sciurus glis Linnaeus, 1766; Germany.
Fat dormouse, squirrel-tailed dormouse, grey dormouse, seven-sleeper.

RECOGNITION
More than 3 times the size of hazel dormouse, no hint of orange in the pelage (Table 5.6). More easily confused with grey squirrel because of bushy tail and greyish colour, but *Glis* generally smaller with dark brown tail lacking white fringe (Plate 2). Hindfeet smaller (<35 mm) than in a young grey squirrel of equal size. Teeth have transverse ridges.

FIELD SIGNS
Oval droppings range from pale yellow through orange to black, *c*.1 cm long × 5 mm diameter. Often deposited in characteristic large piles of 50 or more pellets. Spiral and patchy bark-stripping in tops of conifers, especially larch, in spring and early summer (often similar to grey squirrel damage).

DESCRIPTION
Squirrel-like. Head flattened, with short muzzle and long, robust vibrissae. Large, bulging black eyes; ears rounded and thin not fleshy. Legs short with sharply-clawed mobile toes. Tail bushy, almost as long as body, flattened dorsoventrally, with a median parting on the underside; frequently truncated by damage.

Upper parts greyish-brown, darkest along the spine and lighter on the flanks. Dark ring of hair around the eyes, a dark patch at the base of the vibrissae and slightly darker stripes on the outsides of the legs. Tail uniform in colour. Young animals white underneath with grey tail, older animals creamy below with browner fur and dark brown tail.

Moult: Annual, coat becoming browner with age.

Nipples: 4–6 pairs, extending from thorax to groin. Usually 5 pairs; large number an ecological adaptation to inter-annual variability in food availability [848].

Teeth: 1.0.1.3/1.0.1.3. Premolars and molars transversely ridged but with fewer ridges than in the hazel dormouse (Fig. 5.16).

Chromosomes: 2n = 62, FNa = 120 (European data)[1589].

MEASUREMENTS
Head and body 120–175 mm, tail 100–150 mm; weight *c*.60 g at weaning rising to 270 g in adults, mean adult summer weight *c*.140 g.

DISTRIBUTION
Occurs in band across C Europe, extending E to Caspian Sea, especially where beech forests predominate (Fig. 5.21). In GB confined to Chilterns and adjacent wooded areas, mostly within 35 km of Tring (Fig. 5.22). Range has increased since introduction, but only slowly. Spread appears constrained by open farmland to the west, urbanisation and forest fragmentation to the east. Illicit translocations may result in discontinuous colonisation of remote areas [1041].

HISTORY
Unknown number of individuals introduced at Tring Park, Hertfordshire, in 1902 by Walter Rothschild. Source uncertain: Hungary likely, also perhaps Switzerland or Germany [1041]. Early establishment reviewed in [1424].

HABITAT
Strongly associated with beech woodland (in GB and mainland Europe). Preferred habitat appears to be mixed deciduous woodland, especially with conifers present; also pure conifer stands. Prefers woodland canopy, does not require a dense shrub layer. Frequently lives in buildings, including occupied houses.

SOCIAL ORGANISATION AND BEHAVIOUR
Live together in loose groups, no evidence of strong hierarchical ranking. Groups of 3 or more frequently cohabit, often closely related kin [958]. Males become aggressive during the mating period and may exhibit a variety of threatening postures. Young animals lick the mother's mouth and ingest saliva and chewed food; process continues even after leaving nest. After 6 weeks, family group breaks up, although communal hibernation is frequent. These groups may be undispersed litters [810] and communal hibernation implies communication and coordination [1045].

Communication: A variety of squeaks and snuffling noises. Threatens vocally with characteristic explosive 'churring'. Distinctive, raucous squealing call emitted from high vantage points may be territorial signalling or social communication. Almost certainly uses olfactory cues: in Slovenian caves, observed following

Germany [1
in beech ma
Unlikely th;
(and only
[465]).

Young: Litt
to 13 (n =
actually be
grow, perh
birth, with
developed
young ha
rapidly, c.1
enough to
late in yea
from mot
usually m
nest and
perhaps t
places [1
earlier, ei
mass bef
tend to
overwint

POPUl
Total Br
[624]. I
animals
GB [6
showed
27% 1–
[465];
Captive
maxim
8 years
popula
marke
scale
house:

MOF
Tawny
stoats
casua
grasp
expos
anim
mast
anim

PAF
Vario
the
nest
from
seer

---

traditionally used trails underground in permanent darkness.

Home range, activity and movements: Normally arboreal; very agile climber in woodland canopy, scales smooth tree bark easily. Climbs walls and readily enters lofts of houses. Spends day in a tree-hole or a nest built close to the trunk, not out on a limb as is common among squirrels. Almost entirely nocturnal, although may be active after dawn [1207]. Home range *c*.100 m in diameter. Radio-tracking in late summer showed nightly ranges of only 0.1–0.2 ha [946], sometimes up to 0.6 ha [1045]. In Germany, males dispersed 400–1700 m and females 300–1500 m [1260]. In 100+ years since release at Tring Park, range increase averages *c*.350 m per year.

Nests: Can have several nests in home range; radio-tracked animals used up to 6 nests in 2 weeks during late summer [946]. May use old squirrel dreys or bird nests (especially pigeon) as base on which to build its own enclosed nest similar to squirrel drey. Readily uses nest boxes [1049] or substitutes made from tree guards [1046]. Nest usually includes a lining of green beech leaves, all separate, not attached to twigs, and collected fresh in the tree canopy. Inner walls of nest boxes may be shredded to provide nest lining. Nests in buildings may incorporate bits of rag and paper. Nevertheless, soft nest-lining material is usually absent; nest loose and untidy, not woven as in *Muscardinus*. Often uses nest boxes without any nesting material.

Hibernates in places with low and stable

---

temperature, especially underground (Fig. 5.23). In woodland, goes down passages from old stumps created by rotting tree roots or into crevices among roots left when trees are blown over in gales. Will also use rabbit and disused badger burrows, even old drains [1045]. Sometimes found hibernating in buildings, under floorboards, in wall cavities and in thatch or roof spaces. Hibernacula, even in damp soil, do not normally include nesting material; the animal lies curled up on bare ground; may contain 1–8

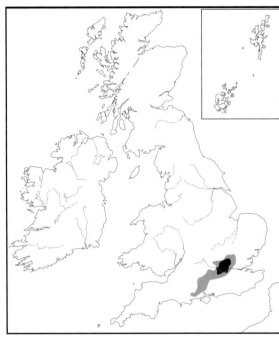

Fig. 5.22 Edible dormouse *Glis glis*: range in GB.

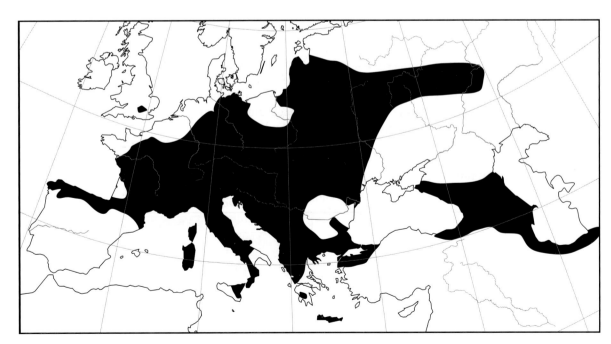

Fig. 5.21 Edible dormouse *Glis glis*: Palaearctic range.

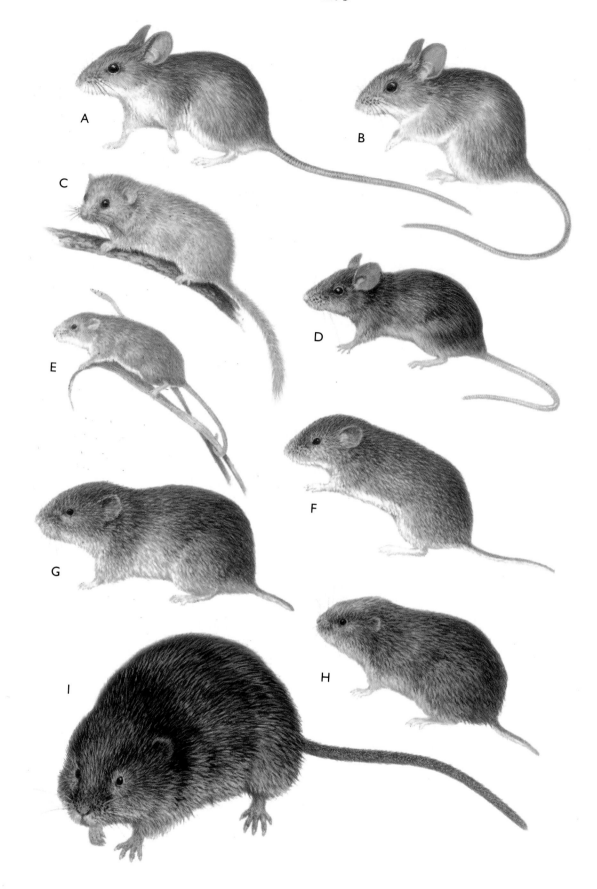

Plate 3

animals,
caught
hibernat
'hundre
tradition

Weig
nation;
[1468].
6 mont
Septem
other ye
be acti
appare
peratu
ability.
becom
progre
contin
arousa
arousa
only a
increa
from
May.
weatl
prese
sugge
activ
more
activ
Mar

FEI
Diet
avai
and
nut:
blac
app
wh
bef
in
dec
at
ba
ins
ne

F

A Yellow-necked mouse *Apodemus flavicollis* **B** Wood mouse *Apodemus sylvaticus* **C** Hazel dormouse *Muscardinus avellanarius* **D** House mouse *Mus domesticus* **E** Harvest mouse *Micromys minutus* **F** Bank vole *Myodes glareolus* **G** Orkney vole *Microtus arvalis orcadensis* **H** Field vole *Microtus agrestis* **I** Water vole *Arvicola terrestris*

FAMILY CRICETIDAE (VOLES, LEMMINGS, HAMSTERS)

A large and diverse family of mostly small mouse-like rodents, including 688 species in 130 genera as currently organised [1538]. Distributed on all continents, especially diverse in N and S America. Sometimes included in Muridae; distinctions between the 2 families blurred and complex. Infraorbital foramen obvious, part of origin for superficial masseter muscle. Differ from Muridae in having 2 rows (not 3) of cusps down molars, or zig-zag pattern of triangles derived from them. Of 11 genera present in Europe, 3 (*Myodes, Microtus, Arvicola*) native to British Isles; N American *Ondatra*, now widespread in Europe, was introduced but rapidly exterminated in British Isles (see Chapter 13).

GENUS *Myodes*

Contains 12 species of red-backed voles, more familiar as *Clethrionomys*; has a Holarctic distribution, 2 species in N America, 9 in Palaearctic and 1 in both; of 3 species in Europe, 1 native to British Isles (and another recorded as a Late Glacial fossil). Differs from *Microtus* in that molars develop roots with age, occlusal triangles more rounded. The correct generic name has been contentious; *Evotomys* was thought appropriate from *c.*1875 to the 1930s, then *Clethrionomys* was commonly used for red-backed voles from the 1930s to 2003. However, the name *Myodes*, applied to the type species *rutilus* by Pallas in 1811 and used intermittently since by Russian authors in particular, takes precedence [229].

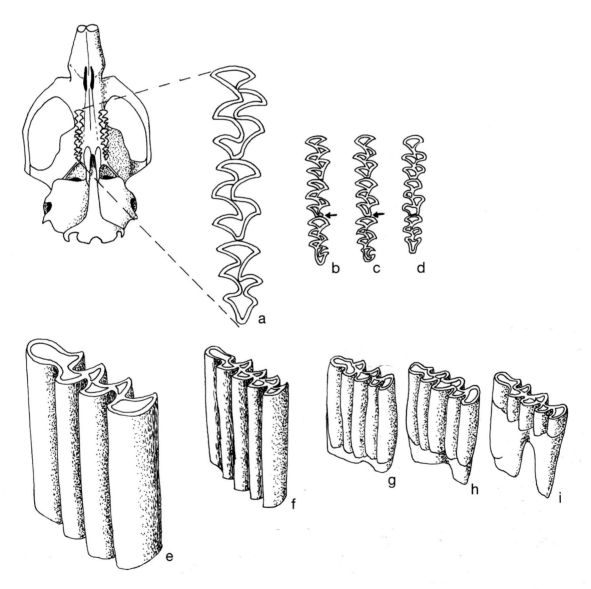

Fig. 5.25 Above, occlusal surfaces of upper right tooth-rows of water vole (a), field vole (with extra lobe on m²)(b), Orkney vole (c) and bank vole (d); below, extracted m₁, to show open-rooted condition on water vole (e) and field vole (f) (Orkney vole similar), 3 examples of bank vole (g, h, i) to show roots developing with age (*drawn by D.W. Yalden*).

Bank vole *Myodes glareolus*

Mus glareolus Schreber, 1780; Island of Lolland, Denmark.
Myodes glareolus Pallas, 1811 (renaming of *Mus glareolus*).
Clethrionomys glareolus Tilesius, 1850 (renaming of *Myodes glareolus*).
Evotomys hercynicus britannicus Miller, 1900; Basingstoke, Hampshire.
Hypudaeus hercynicus Mehlis, 1931; Harz Mountains, Germany.
Evotomys skomerensis Barratt-Hamilton, 1903; Skomer Island, Pembrokeshire, Wales.
Evotomys alstoni Barrett-Hamilton & Hinton, 1913; Tobermory, Mull, Scotland.
Evotomys caesarius Miller, 1908; St Helier, Jersey, Channel Islands.
Evotomys erica Barrett-Hamilton & Hinton, 1913; Island of Raasay, Inner Hebrides, Scotland.
Red-backed vole, wood vole, red vole.

RECOGNITION

Whole animal: Small ears and eyes, blunt nose. Chestnut-brown back, tail colour (bicoloured, lighter underneath) and length (1/2 head and body) separate it from field vole and larger water vole (Plate 3). Juveniles grey-brown, less easily distinguished from field voles but have the longer tail and more prominent ears. Discrimination of sexes easy in adults, more difficult in juvenile or sexually immature animals [567].

Skull and teeth: Skull less angular than field vole. 3 molars per jaw, loops of enamel on occlusal surfaces more rounded than in field voles (Fig. 5.25) [1563]. Molars develop distinguishable roots when >3 months old [18].

FIELD SIGNS

Tracks and trails: 4 toes on forefeet, 5 on hind; a little smaller than those of the wood mouse.

Faeces: Rounded in section, length <4 × width, smaller diameter than those of wood mouse. Usually brown-black (cf. green in field vole) but vary with diet.

Dens/nests: Tunnel systems little studied but usually arranged around a nest 2–10 cm below ground [1559], although breeding nests can also be in tree trunks. Moss, leaves, grass and feathers used for nesting material.

Other field signs: See Feeding, below.

DESCRIPTION

Pelage: Chestnut-coloured back with paler, often grey, sides; silver-grey to whitish ventral surface, border between dorsal and ventral colour well marked. Juveniles grey-brown with less contrast.

Moult: Predominantly ventral to dorsal, can be diffuse in older animals; head-to-rump moult rare [1586]. Adults moult throughout the year, seasonal peaks in spring and autumn. Young first moult at 4–6 weeks [762] and then at the next seasonal moult.

Teeth: Molars open-rooted, grow continuously as occlusal surfaces wear [1169]; length of molar roots indicates relative age [18, 585].

Table 5.7 Bank vole: measurements from Tayside and Poland

	Mean±SE 1st year (Aug–Nov)[a]	n		Mean±SE 2nd year (April)[a]	n	Range[b]
Head and body length (mm)	90.8±0.4	65		100.7±0.7	38	79–117
Tail length (mm)						33–48
Hindfoot length (mm)	16.7±0.1	60		16.8±0.1	57	17–18
Ear length (mm)						<15.0
Skull length (condylobasal) (mm)	22.1±0.1	63		23.3±0.1	32	21.6–24.9
Upper molar tooth-row	5.38±0.02	72		5.58±0.02	40	
Body weight (g)	17.7±0.3	70	Male	26.1±1.62	19	
			Female	21.9±9.12	21	

[a]Data for Tayside from [277, 282]; [b]data for Poland from [1169].

Table 5.8 Bank vole *Myodes glareolus*: subspecies in GB [277]

	M. g. glareolus	*M.g. caesarius*	*M.g. skomerensis*	*M. g. alstoni*	*M. g. erica*
Range	**Mainland**	**Jersey**	**Skomer**	**Mull**	**Raasay**
Colour in winter:					
Dorsal	Dull	Dull	Bright	Dull	Dull
Ventral	Buff	Buff	Cream	Buff	Buff
Hindfoot length (mm)	<17.8	>17.8	>17.8	>17.8	>17.8
Condylobasal length of skull (mm) of adults in spring	<24.2	>24.2	>24.2	>24.2	>24.2
Shape^a of m^3	Simple	Complex	Complex	Simple	Complex
Nasal bones: shape of posterior halves	Tapering	Tapering	Parallel-sided	Tapering	Tapering
Anterior palatal foramina: width as % length	Narrow (<30%)	Wide (>30%)	Narrow (<30%)	Medium (c.<30%)	Narrow (<30%)

^{a}m^3 either has almost no extra (4th) loop (simple condition) or a well-developed loop (complex condition).

Anatomy: Os coxa has rounded ischial angle and short, hooked pubic symphysis (neither occur in the Murinae); separated from field vole by semicircular shape of obturator foramen and absence of obturator notch; sexually dimorphic, and changes with age and parturition [263].

Nipples: 4 pairs; 2 thoracic, 2 abdominal.
Scent glands: Males have larger preputial glands than females; those of dominant males larger than those of subordinates. Preputial gland secretions contain hexadecyl acetate, an androgen-dependent substance [1350].

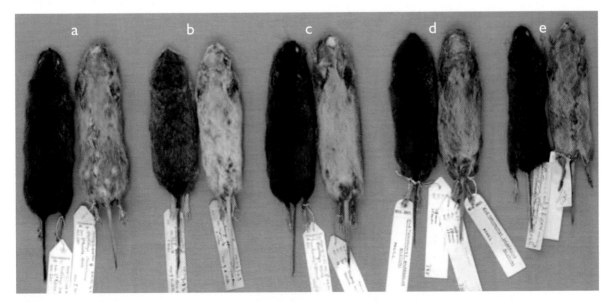

Fig. 5.26 Bank vole subspecies: (a) *M. g. caesarius* (Jersey), (b) *M. g. skomerensis* (Skomer), (c) *M. g. erica* (Raasay), (d) *M. g. alstoni* (Mull), (e) *M. g. glareolus* (Hampshire, England) *(photo P. Morris, skins courtesy of NHM)*. The island races are larger, and *skomerensis* is distinctly paler.

Skull: Delicate, rounded with shortened facial part, without frontal crest (crista frontalis) [1169].

Reproductive tract: Baculum has proximal stalk and 3 distal processes; length and width distinguish sexually mature animals from immatures [41]. Testes increase in mass on average 28-fold between breeding and non-breeding seasons, can weigh 900 mg [1226]. Female tract Y-shaped with easily distinguished ovaries at ends of uterine horns; corpora lutea appear as large cream or pink spots in ovary. Placental scars show as dark spots on uterine wall, last up to 182 days in laboratory [19]

Chromosomes: 2n = 56, FNa = 56 [118]. Primer sequences from 12 microsatellite loci have been described [68, 496].

RELATIONSHIPS
Only member of genus in GB. Distribution in Europe overlaps that of *M. rutilus* and *M. rufocanus*; counterpart in North America is *M. gapperi* [1168]. Genetic evidence (mtDNA) indicates both past and recent hybridisation between *M. rutilus* and *M. glareolus* populations, from N Fennoscandia to S Urals [325]. Laboratory studies confirm that these 2 'species' can produce fertile offspring [1097].

MEASUREMENTS
Overwintering animals increase in size with onset of breeding in spring (Table 5.7). In adults, only the lengths of hindfoot and ear are fairly constant [1169].

Body size usually greater on islands [9], also varies with latitude [277], altitude [1582] and geology [1278]. Body weight can decrease (*c*.15%) in winter [544, 1373], may vary markedly between years in populations with multi-annual population cycles [607, 609].

VARIATION
Animals in GB not distinguishable from European animals. 4 subspecies recognised from British Isles (Table 5.8), but may be extreme end of size variation seen in mainland populations, subspecific status questionable (Fig. 5.26) [1571]. Island and mainland animals are interfertile [1342]. Shape of m^3 varies in all localities, can change over time within populations [278]. Colour variants rare, not recorded from GB, but melanic, black and tan, and yellow individuals captured in mainland Europe [897]. Albinism of the tail tip occurs in 0.8% of British animals [276].

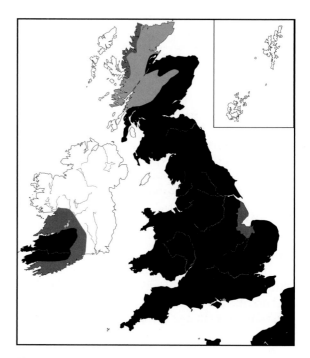

Fig. 5.28 Bank vole *Myodes glareolus*: range in British Isles. Recently introduced to Ireland and still spreading.

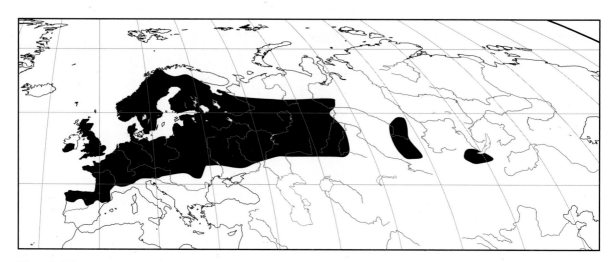

Fig. 5.27 Bank vole *Myodes glareolus*: Palaearctic range.

Fig. 5.29 Bank vole face, showing more prominent eyes and ears (cf. field vole, Fig. 5.35) *(photo P. Morris).*

DISTRIBUTION
Occurs from N of Arctic Circle to Pyrenees and Italy, from W Ireland to C Siberia; distribution discontinuous in eastern part of range (Fig 5.27); occurs to 2400 m asl in French Alps [1339].

Occurs throughout GB (Fig. 5.28), and on islands of Scalpay, Ulva, Raasay, Mull, Arran, Bute, Handa, Anglesey, Ramsey, Skomer, Wight, Hayling and Jersey; also recorded on Arran 1966–1970 [480], unconfirmed report Islay, 1974 [40]. Irish population, discovered in 1964 [1305], possibly founded by voles accidentally imported from Germany in 1920s [1300]; genetic studies confirm that founded from small, introduced population [1237]. Recorded in Cos. Waterford, Tipperary, Limerick, Galway, Clare, Cork and Kerry, in SW Ireland; estimated rate of spread *c.*3 km/year [1305]. Populations on small islands off mainland GB also likely to have been introduced.

HISTORY
Recorded from all Pleistocene interglacials since Cromerian, and possibly in last (Devensian) glaciation. MtDNA indicates bank voles in GB belong to W European phylogroup, postglacial colonisation probably occurred from C European refugia [325]. Earliest Postglacial records in GB Mesolithic; well recorded from Neolithic onwards [1152, 1571].

HABITAT
Common in mixed and deciduous mature woodland in GB (Fig. 5.29) [448]; also recorded in grasslands, deciduous and conifer plant-ations, hedgerows, fenland and road verges [95, 249, 413, 446, 834, 1023, 1072]. Thick ground cover important in all habitats [413, 834, 977]. In intensive arable areas, occurs infrequently in fields but usually present in surrounding margins, including hedgerows [805, 834, 1418, 1588, 1387]. Also occurs in isolated woodlots as small as 0.1 ha in area [435, 1580], population density may be positively correl-ated with woodlot quality [836]; may become extinct over winter in poor-quality small woods [37].

On Skomer, closely associated with dense cover of bracken and bluebells *Endymion non-scriptus* [637]. In mainland Europe, occupies same habitats as in GB but also common in taiga conifer forests and spruce plantations [1153].

SOCIAL ORGANISATION AND BEHAVIOUR
Reviewed in [483], with specific reviews on social organisation [490, 1578], spacing behaviour [484], spatial distribution, movements and dispersal [151, 152, 976, 1550, 1579] and communication [1350, 1470].

Table 5.9 Bank vole: typical home-range sizes in GB [1550]

Habitat	Season	Males		Females	
		Area (m²)	n	Area (m²)	n
Deciduous wood	All	1674	34	1292	35
Deciduous wood	All	2208	12	1124	20
Deciduous/conifer plantation	All	1497	35	600	3
Deciduous wood	Winter	1209	32	1067	26
	Summer	1398	35	953	29
Deciduous/conifer wood	Winter	380	37	261	31
	Summer	929	62	271	44

Territories: Variable home-range size in GB (Table 5.9) influenced by season, sex, sexual maturity, age, population density, habitat quality and resource availability. In non-breeding season, female home ranges often overlap, but are mutually exclusive in breeding season. Females remain site-faithful throughout the breeding season [990]; in large enclosures, mature females allow related young females to use their territory but not breed there [955]. Males have larger home ranges that overlap, even during breeding. Immatures have smaller ranges than adults. Male, and sometimes female, home-range size increases at start of breeding season [771].

Nesting: Little studied. Huddles in nests in winter, thereby conserving energy, but less commonly than wood mice [544]. Recorded to move nests within short study, but data were for only 2 animals [795].

Scent marking: Odour may be used to distinguish neighbours from strangers [1099] and kin from non-kin [845]. Males distinguish scent of females of their own race (e.g. mainland/Skomer) [497] and urine-marking patterns differ between races [743]. Chemical signals in adult male urine help maintain social organisation and act as a territorial marker [1228]. Males overmark both conspecific and heterospecific urine and faeces [1229]. Females more attracted to odour of dominant than subdominant males [843, 846], prefer odour of a mate to an unfamiliar male [844]. Scent-marking also plays a role in spacing behaviour in females [1227]. Specific site of biologically active odour(s) uncertain; preputial gland secretions (which can be passed out in urine) elicit behavioural responses but homogenates of male salivary gland and kidney also attractive to females [842].

Vocalisations: Infants call ultrasonically and audibly in the nest, with differences in intensity between races (e.g. mainland/Skomer) and changes in frequency with age. Rate and intensity of ultrasonic calling related to degree of cold stress [144] and affected by olfactory cues [769]. Adults also emit low- and high-frequency calls, especially during aggressive interactions and mating. High-frequency mating calls only emitted by males; in laboratory tests, sexually experienced males vocalise more than sexually inexperienced individuals [768].

Aggressive behaviour: In laboratory, sexually mature males defend familiar areas of cage, fight each other but not immatures; immatures are not aggressive. Male aggression and wounding greatest in breeding season, probably androgen-dependent. Mature females defend 'home' areas in cages and home ranges in large enclosures/the field [830]; aggression is greater during pregnancy and lactation [767, 829], thought to be progesterone dependent [766]. Infanticide by males and females recorded, less frequent between mutually familiar females than between same-sex or mixed-sex strangers [1581]. At above-ground bait points in the field, mutual avoidance predominates; adults dominate but rarely fight juveniles. No evidence of differences in aggression between cyclic and non-cyclic populations [613].

Dispersal: Occurs throughout the year; associated with onset of breeding and greater territoriality in both sexes in early spring and summer [151]. Subsequent dispersal predominantly by young animals, sometimes male biased [489, 1470, 1495, 1550], occurs both to and from optimal habitats [489, 901, 978], may be enhanced in degraded habitats [1054]. Dispersers not genetically distinguishable from residents [409]. Range and amount of female dispersal restricted, especially in linear habitats [2]. Hedgerows and network of ground cover both important for dispersal, particularly in intensively arable areas [1366, 1588]. Roads can reduce movements but are not complete barriers [62, 476, 1198].

Activity: Active throughout night and day, peaks at dawn and dusk in summer; less nocturnal activity in winter [44, 335, 538, 795]; there is also a variable short-term (2–6 h) activity rhythm [483].

Locomotion: Usually walk and run; active burrowers. Predominantly move on the ground but also use arboreal runways and climb hedges, although less extensively than wood mice [1019, 1146, 1380]. Males generally more arboreal than females [1550].

More sedentary than wood mice [104], movements closely associated with ground cover [795, 977]. Exploratory ability and navigation improves with age and experience [31, 483]. Movements >600 m common [33]. Bank voles return to home territories following displacement of >700 m, but homing ability poorer than that of wood mice; voles displaced 1 km did not return [1550]. Rate of return following displacement increases with repetition, suggesting that voles learn route home; olfactory and acoustic cues probably most important in homing. Activity generally reduced, use of cover increased, in presence of avian predators [230, 893]. Bank voles exposed to odour of mammalian predators in the laboratory and small-scale enclosures demonstrate anti-predatory behaviour [716, 721] but no effects on distance moved, home-range size or trapp-

Table 5.10 Bank vole: composition of diet (% volume) [604]

	Beech	Oak–ash	Oak–ash	Lime-hornbeam	Lime-hornbeam	Conifer
	PL	GB	CZ	PL	PL	S
Animal food	8	1.5	12	5	16	0.5
Seeds	41	18.5	39	38.5	28.5	0.5
of which fruits/ berries	?	10.5	?	6.5	?	14.5
Fungi	7	5	4.5	4	0.5	9
Lichens						11
Forbs	44	31.5	28.5	46	49	38
Tree leaves		12.5	11		0.5	
Dwarf shrubs						11.5
Bark			1			3.5
Root/tubers					3	
Dead leaves		20				
Various/unidentified			4.5		2	11
No. animals analysed	209	143	328	251	139	330

CZ, Czechoslovakia; GB, Great Britain; PL, Poland; S, Sweden.

ability detected in large-scale experiments [747].

FEEDING

Largely herbivorous (Table 5.9); broadly similar in diet to wood mouse but take more green leaf material (40–50% of diet), less seed and animal matter. Few studies in GB [445, 996, 1494]; general reviews of diet in Europe in [471, 604, 605]. In most detailed British study [1494], bank voles in oak/ash wood took fleshy fruits and seeds with a soft testa when available; green leaves (woody plants preferred to herbs) also important, dead leaves eaten in winter (Table 5.9). Small amounts of fungi, roots, flowers, grass, moss, and invertebrates also consumed. Young bank voles ate less seed and fruit than adults.

Diet in GB generally similar to that in C–S Europe (Table 5.9; [225, 236, 605]) although generous consumption of dead leaves may be atypical. In planted spruce forests, C Europe, fewer seeds and more fungi eaten [661]; in taiga, Scandinavia, seeds and insects hardly taken, rely on berries, fungi and lichens [603, 615]. In mixed farmland, Germany, beech flowers and rye grains important, spring–summer [5].

Seasonal and yearly variation in diet often related to availability of different foods. In beech and oak–ash forests, most animal food is eaten in spring, tree leaves in summer, fungi in summer–autumn and seeds in autumn–winter. Green leaves taken all year but less in autumn–winter; young growing plants preferred to mature and senescent ones. Large amounts of seed taken in good mast years [604]. In general, foods with high, easily extracted, energy and nutrient content preferred [603, 651, 652]. Some plants avoided because of toxic secondary metabolites [814] and mechanical constraints: seed with hard testa avoided but surrounding flesh eaten [996, 1494].

Feeds in burrows, on the ground and in trees. Seeds transported in false 'cheek pouches' [604]. Caches food [954], activity peaking late autumn–winter; seeds with relatively thin testa stored, those with thick testa eaten [43]. Beechmast scatter-hoarded in small caches (1–10 nuts), just beneath the litter layer or in tunnel walls [735]. Hazel nuts are opened with a distinctive clean-edged hole [366] (Fig. 5.3) and only the flesh of rose hips is eaten [372]. Ash keys are opened and seed extracted by splitting the pericarp down the middle from the proximal end [441].

Highly efficient digestion and assimilation of

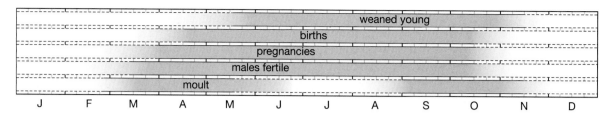

Fig. 5.30 Bank vole: annual cycle.

energy and certain minerals [471, 544, 1279], achieved in part by grinding food into very small particles [873], early degradation of cellulose in fore-stomach [1062], caecal digestion and coprophagy [874]. Refection observed in the nest [44]. Gut anatomy alters as diet changes, allowing adaptation to seasonal changes [875].

BREEDING
Reviewed in [20, 212, 254]. Breeds from March–April to September–October (but sometimes throughout winter), induced ovulation, pregnancy 18–20 days, mean litter size 4.8 (up to 7 in the wild), successive litters can be produced at 3–4-week intervals (Fig. 5.30). Females born early in breeding season can breed in same year, those born later usually breed the following spring; breeding in more than one season probably uncommon [1430]. Mating system promiscuous.

Breeding season: Over most of GB usually from March–April to September–October. On Skomer, breeding season shorter (May–September) [737]. More northerly populations tend to have shorter, more intense breeding season.

In the laboratory, photoperiod is the crucial proximate factor controlling sexual maturation [254, 1368]. In the wild, environmental and population factors also affect length of breeding season. Both supplementation of food and mild temperatures can advance onset of breeding [762, 1496]; continuation of breeding beyond October, even throughout winter, can occur, particularly when seeds are abundant [215, 437, 1154, 1320]. High population density can shorten breeding season [104, 330]; can be extended in years of low density and curtailed in years of high density in cyclic populations [1534].

Males: In laboratory, juvenile males attain sexual maturity under long photoperiods, pubertal development is arrested under short photoperiods [1368]. In the wild, testes large in spring and summer, show all stages of spermatogenesis; those >100 mg have spermatozoa [1226]. Testes usually small in late autumn–winter, spermatogenic epithelium is reduced to spermatogonia and Sertoli cells, with or without spermatocytes. Leydig

cells very much smaller in winter.

Suppression of sexual maturation in young males occurs at high densities but there may be different mechanisms for density regulation of maturation in cyclic and non-cyclic populations [484, 584].

Females: Do not have oestrous cycles in the laboratory. Ovulation induced by mating or close proximity to males; ovulation rate increases after 1st pregnancy. Females are highly fertile immediately postpartum and preferentially mate with dominant males [669]; multiple-sired litters occur [1178]. Females less receptive during lactation, mating behaviour restored after weaning [257]. 1st pregnancy more difficult to establish than subsequent ones, is easier in older animals. Priming of reproductive tract important for optimal fertility, may require production of multiple sets of corpora lutea, as can result from interrupted copulations or pregnancy block (see below) [254, 584]. Egg wastage is *c.*30%.

Introduction of strange male into cage of pregnant female can block pregnancy. Release of prolactin is blocked, leading to reduced progesterone levels and a resultant failure for embryos to implant; likely to be induced by male pheromone. Females with several generations of corpora lutea occur in the wild [169], which is consistent with but not proof of pregnancy block in free-living animals [254].

Gestation: Lasts 19–20 days in 1st pregnancy. Subsequent litters produced at 19–25 day intervals, although inter-litter interval varies between studies, habitats and with the number of suckled young [212, 254, 257]. Mean gestation length, from 12 studies, 19.6 days [703]. Mean number of corpora lutea in laboratory animals varies from 4.7 (1st pregnancy) to 5.5 (11–12th pregnancy) [254]. In wild bank voles, number of corpora lutea is 3.3–3.9, average number of placental scars 3.4–3.9, depending on season and habitat [17]. Number of placental scars sometimes exceeds number of young born: embryos can be lost in late pregnancy, or scars from previous pregnancies remain visible [19]. Lactation lasts 17–18 days [703].

In northern cyclic populations, suggested that

reproduction may be suppressed at certain times of year by high levels of mustelid (but not avian) predation [807, 828, 1212, 1577]. However, it is possible that this effect is a laboratory or methodological artifact [748, 956].

Productivity: Mean litter size from British studies is 3.53–4.11 [20]. Litter size and weaning success affected by season (peak in May–June), food availability, female body weight and age, litter succession, population density, altitude and geographical distribution, [254, 748, 830, 831, 955, 1576]. Trend to larger litters in more E populations [1585]. Average litter size from 45 studies is 4.8 [703].

Development of young: Reviewed in [472]. Young born naked, blind, with pinnae not separate from body, auditory meatus closed, toes fused, teeth not erupted. Weight at birth *c*.2 g [703, 1278]. Dorsal skin darkens at *c*.3 days, pelage appears at 4–10 days; incisors erupt days 4–7, molars days 8–12; ears open *c*.day 12, eyes *c*.day 13; pelage has adult coloration by day 15, when young run well, leave the nest for short periods and begin to feed on solid food. At *c*.18 days are weaned, weigh 9–10 g [703], thermoregulation completely developed. Independent by *c*.21 days old, subsequently increase the area over which they explore, increasingly likely to enter traps [488].

Growth rate in 1st month rapid (0.4–0.5 g/day [703, 1278]), can vary with diet, temperature and litter size. Subsequent growth when 2–3 months old is more rapid in spring-born than autumn-born animals [472]; growth retarded if dispersal prevented [975] or densities high [852]. Generally, little or no growth in winter; a few individuals grow strongly over winter, especially in mast years [608, 612].

Females can usually breed at 1.5–2 months, although pregnancy recorded in younger animals; males breed at *c*.2 months old. Females born early in breeding season can reach sexual maturity, breed in the same year, but maturation may be suppressed by high densities of adult females [213, 214, 1159] or increased density of dominant competitors [368]; those born later do not usually mature sexually until the start of next breeding season [20, 1151, 1430].

POPULATION

Numbers and density: Total GB pre-breeding population estimated to be 23 million (17.75 million England, 3.5 million Scotland, 1.75 million Wales) [624]. Trapping on 0.81 ha grids in broadleaf and mixed woodlands, 1982–1992, across GB gave May–June catches of 9.5–19.3 voles (12–24 voles/ha) and winter (mainly November–December) catches of 9–28 voles (11–34 voles/ha) [448]. In conifer woods, 7/ha (summer) and 23/ha (winter) recorded in a Sitka spruce plantation; rarely recorded in a Corsican pine plantation [951].

Hedgerows in arable landscapes in England probably contain >1/3 of the British pre-breeding population [624]. On 12 650-m farmland hedgerows, 1983–1992, average catches 5–15 voles (8–23 voles/km) (summer) and 11–22 voles (17–34 voles/km) (winter) [448]. Average monthly densities in Essex hedges, 1988–1990, 2–42 voles/km; maximum 120 voles/km [834]. Average densities in single-year studies of road verges, arable Cambridgeshire, 46 voles/km (summer) and 53 voles/km (winter) [95].

On Skomer, densities up to 475 voles/ha recorded; estimated pre-breeding population 7000; late summer population 20 000–22 000 [463, 524, 637].

Fluctuations: 2 main types of population fluctuation. Multi-annual cycles, typically lasting 3–5 years (large-scale increase and subsequent decline followed by at least one year of low density), occur in N populations [614, 1082] where winter food also abundant [719].

No evidence of multi-annual cycles in GB, but comprehensive review of British studies [20] and results from synchronous studies in multiple woods [448, 951] show annual cycles; somewhat variable, typically numbers increase during summer, peak in autumn–early winter, decline through late winter–spring. Spring declines and autumn increases observed in 65–75% and 56% of recorded populations respectively. Increases during spring and from winter to summer after winter breeding sometimes observed. Evidence of weak density-dependent regulation of numbers in both autumn and spring; seed crop has a major impact; good seed crops in autumn result in less severe spring declines and higher densities the following summer and possibly winter. Populations in deciduous woods are synchronised over the summer. Yield of tree seed may cause the synchrony, although weather may be involved. Detailed analysis of annual cycles in oak-dominated lowland forest elsewhere in Europe given in [1154].

Sex ratio: 1:1 at birth in laboratory but varies with age, can be affected by season and population density [211, 610]. In the field, sex ratio of trapped individuals generally male-biased [20].

Age determination: Growth of molar roots gives indication of age [18, 585] but growth rates vary between seasons and populations [1169]. Before roots form, shape of base of tooth and pulp cavity also indicate relative age [277, 1320]. Live-trapped animals separable into adult, subadult and juvenile on basis of pelage colour, body weight and breeding condition [567].

Age structure: Overwintering population consists predominantly of young born in late summer and autumn, sometimes contain large numbers of animals born earlier [20, 487, 488]. Overwintered population produces 1st generation in the following spring. Young born in spring–early summer suffer high mortality but those that survive may breed in the same year [488]. Autumn-born animals grow slowly, only mature sexually in next spring. Winter breeding alters this sequence and so affects the age structure of the population [1072].

Survival: Longevity is highly variable, affected by food availability, population density, weather and predation pressure [20, 147, 216, 217, 294]. Mortality in the first 6 weeks of life high (*c.*60%) [488]. Young born in spring and summer generally have a poorer survival rate over the first 4–6 months than animals born in autumn, although this can be affected by population density [20, 216]. Mortality during winter low, *c.*15%/month [488]. Most overwintered voles die by summer or late autumn; oldest individuals (18–21 months) are spring-born animals that overwinter, die in the autumn/early winter of the following year. Survival over 2 winters rare [488]. In cyclic populations, survival of cohorts depends on the phase of the multiannual cycle [1534]. In the laboratory, can live for up to 40 months [497].

Species interactions: No clear behaviourial hierarchary between wood mice and bank voles, but may be interspecific segregation [858]; activity rhythms of bank voles may be influenced by presence of wood mice [200, 538, 997]. Removal

Table 5.11 Incidence of fleas on small rodents

	Bank vole	Field vole	Orkney vole	Water vole	Wood mouse	Yellow-necked mouse	Harvest mouse	House mouse	Common rat	Ship rat	Hazel dormouse
Xenopsylla cheopis									(X)	X	
Hystrichopsylla talpae	X	X	X	X	X						
Typhloceras poppei		(X)			X		(X)				
Rhadinopsylla integella	X	X									
Rhadinopyslla isacantha	X										
Rhadinopsylla pentacantha	X	(X)			X				(X)		
Ctenophthalmus nobilis	X	X	X	X	X	X	X	(X)	X	(X)	(X)
Ctenophthalmus congener	X										
Leptopsylla segnis					(X)	(X)		X		X	
Peromyscopyslla spectabilis	X	(X)		(X)	(X)						
Amalaraeus penicilliger	X	X	X	(X)	(X)	(X)		(X)	(X)		
Nosopsyllus fasciatus	(X)	(X)		(X)	(X)	(X)	(X)	(X)	X	X	(X)
Nosopsyllus londiniensis					(X)			X	X	X	
Megabothris rectangulatus	X	X									
Megabothris turbidus	X	X			X		X	(X)	(X)		(X)
Megabothris walkeri	X	X		X	(X)			(X)	(X)		

X, regular and common; (X), occasional.

Table 5.12 Tapeworms (Eucestoda) and flukes (Digenea) recorded from some British rodents [635]

	Bank vole	Field vole	Wood mouse	Yellow-necked mouse	House mouse	Common rat
Tapeworms						
Hymenolepis diminuta			+	+	+	+ +
Rodentolepis microstoma			+		+	+
Rodentolepis straminea					+	+
Staphylocystis murissylvatici			+ +	+		
Hydatigena taeniaeformis	+ +	+ +	+ +	+ +	+ +	
Catenotaenia pusilla	+ +	+	+ +	+	+	
Skrjabomptaenia lobata	+ +		+ +	+		
Flukes						
Brachylaemus recurvum (small intestine)			+ +	+		+
Corrigia vitta (pancreas, duodenum)	+	+	+ +	+		

+, present; + +, common.

studies reveal negative impact of wood mice on bank vole numbers [406] in contrast to reports from previous descriptive studies [559]. Field voles and yellow-necked mice are behaviourally dominant over bank voles [30, 559]; competition with field voles can influence female survival, territory size and maturation of young females [367, 368].

MORTALITY

Predation: Taken by many predators [525, 710, 718, 797]. In GB, most important are tawny owl and weasel which can remove 20–40% and 1–20% respectively of standing crop [724, 796, 1324]. Tawny owls reported to take heavier individuals [1583] but juveniles seem more vulnerable to weasel predation [716, 1109]. On Skomer, barn owls take a large proportion of juveniles but relatively few adults [264]. In E Europe, martens are major predators [722]. Other important predators include adders *Vipera berus*, mink, stoats, polecats, cats and foxes [525, 717, 718, 720].

Environmental conditions affect level of predation; snow cover reduces catching efficiency of tawny owls and martens [722, 723]. Kestrels, and possibly other diurnal raptors, may detect bank voles from ultraviolet reflectance of their scent marks [813]. Environmental conditions, seed availability and population density can also affect survival [20, 488].

Disease: Little information on impact of disease on vole populations [635]. Cowpox, an orthopoxvirus, is endemic in bank voles in GB which are believed to be reservoir hosts [90, 243, 296]; it does not cause clinical signs of disease but may influence fecundity [412] and survival [231, 1404].

Pesticides and pollution: Can bioaccumulate xenobiotics [1274], has been used as biomonitor of environmental contamination [470, 1000]. Histopathological damage, impairment of reproduction, genotoxicity and acute mortality observed in either free-living voles on contaminated sites or in laboratory-held animals given environmentally realistic exposures [137, 168, 702, 1274]; effect varies between compounds and with level of exposure. May be more sensitive than other rodents to some inorganic contaminants [542, 1280]. No information that environmental contaminants cause significant impacts on populations.

PARASITES AND PATHOGENS

Ectoparasites: Various flea species recorded in GB (Table 5.11). Sucking louse *Hoplopleura acanthopus* found on voles in GB and mainland Europe [841]. Mites *Haemogamasus nidi, H. pontiger, Listrophorus leukarti, Trombicula autumnalis* common; others include *Asca affinis, Eugamasus magnus, Eulaelaps stabularis, Haemogamasus michaeli,*

Table 5.13 Nematode worms recorded from some British rodents. All are intestinal except *Pelodera strongyloides* (eyes and skin) [92]

	Bank vole	Field vole	Wood mouse	Yellow-necked mouse	House mouse	Common rat
Capillaria murissylvatici	++	+	++	+		
Trichuris muris[a]	+	+	+	+	+	
Pelodera strongyloides	++	+	++	+		
Heligmosomoides glareoli	++	+				
Heligmosomoides polygyrus	+		++	++	+	
Syphacia muris						++
Syphacia obvelata	++	+			++	
Syphacia stroma			++	++		
Aspiculuris tetraptera	+	+	+	+	+	

+, Present; ++, particularly common.

[a] Recently suggested to consist of 2 morphologically similar species *Trichurus muris* and *T. arvicolae* [410].

H. hirsutus, H. pygmaeus, Laelaps festinus, Microthrombidium pusillum and *Parasitus spinipes.* Ticks *Ixodes trianguliceps, I. apronophorus* and *I. ricinus* also infect bank voles. Blood losses due to tick feeding are 0.2%–65% but most harbour few ticks, only a few are heavily infested; feeding by ticks unlikely to affect host population dynamics directly [1372]. Bank voles acquire resistance to *I. ricinus* [342, 1175], relationship between them much investigated in mainland Europe because the tick transmits tick-borne encephalitis [855] and thought to be the primary overwintering reservoir for *Borrelia burgdorferi* (causing Lyme disease) [1372].

Helminths: See Tables 5.12 and 5.13. Orbital fluid frequently contains larval nematodes, possibly *Rhabditis* spp.

Others: Serological evidence of infection with variety of viral species [296, 764, 1080], including Puumala virus, for which bank vole is major reservoir in mainland Europe [395, 1094]. This virus causes no clinical signs of disease in voles but can be transmitted via saliva, urine and faeces to humans; causes nephropathia epidemica [1079], a relatively mild type of haemorrhagic fever with renal syndrome (HFRS); other rodent-borne hantaviruses can cause more severe, sometime fatal, types of HFRS [394].

Bacterial infections include *Rickettsia* [1182],

Mycobacterium tuberculosis var. *muris* [1527], *Mycoplasma* sp. [526], *Campylobacter fetus* [416], *C. jejuni* [929], *Yersinia* spp. [930], *Bartonella* spp. [162] and 3 other species of common enteric bacteria [636]. Infection with spirochaete *Leptospira* widespread in GB and Europe [773, 1332], highest infection rates occurring in the lightest voles [1456].

Protozoan parasites: Diverse [290, 635, 642770]. *Cryptosporidium parvum* (can cause cryptosporidiosis, a severe diarrhoeal disease) and *C. muris* detected in bank voles in GB and on Skomer; voles and other rodents may be significant reservoirs for these [218, 242, 1362]. Fungal infections *Emmonsia parva, E. crescens,* and *Trichophyton persicolor* (ringworm) recorded [379, 674, 675].

RELATIONS WITH HUMANS
Occasional forestry pest in Europe, eating seeds and seedlings, barking small trees and gnawing roots [385, 611]. Most damage occurs in winter when population densities high but food resources limited [88, 89, 867]. Bark-eating by bank voles reported in GB [776].

Management of farm habitat for bank voles (and other small mammals) reviewed in [442]. Wide field margins and those with a hedgerow favoured [1283]. Permanent and other types of set-aside relatively unattractive. Grassland management for small mammals in general needs perennial grassland with a 3-year cutting regime, 1/3 being cut each year [649].

Easily captured in live traps but require water when fed dry food [1279], may dehydrate in traps under dry conditions [1259]; ameliorated by use of apple or carrot. Capture success affected by residual odours (synthetic and those of conspecifics) in traps [568, 1017, 1277, 1419] and reproductive status [32, 38, 486]. Track registration tubes [38], radio-isotopes [15] and radio-collars used to investigate spatial dynamics; no evidence that radio-collars markedly alter behaviour or increase risk of aerial predation [827].

Survive and breed well in captivity but can develop stereotypical behaviours and polydipsia [1257, 1258]. Stereotypical behaviours reduced by environmental enrichment [271, 272] but development perhaps enhanced by genetic component [1257]. Animals brought into captivity may rapidly lay down lipid depots [419].

LITERATURE
Volume of papers on the ecology of the bank vole [1131]; volume of symposium papers on ecology and behaviour [447]; volume of symposium papers on population dynamics, dispersal, reproduction and social structure [1340]; popular account [441].

PRINCIPAL AUTHORS
R.F. Shore & E.J. Hare

GENUS *Microtus*

A large Holarctic genus of 62 species [1538], distinguished by open-rooted, continuously growing molars. Have short tails, small eyes, ears largely hidden in fur. Characteristic of grasslands in both Eurasia and N America, ranging from semi-arid grasslands (e.g around Mediterranean at 40° N and 20° N in Mexico) to tundra at 80° N. Pine voles (N America) and burrowing voles (Eurasia), formerly distinct genera (*Pitymys*, *Terricola*), now included in *Microtus*. Evolved in Pleistocene, within last 2 my, from *Mimomys*, through *Allophiomys*, which had rooted molars. Rapid and complex diversification, relationships and systematics difficult to decide. Molecular phylogeny, using mtDNA, suggests 3 main groups, the Nearctic species, the Eurasian *Terricola* and an *M. arvalis* group, but several important species lie outside these 3, including *M. gregalis*, *M. oeconomus* and *M. agrestis* [707]. Similar to larger *Arvicola*, which also has open-rooted molars, and also descended from *Mimomys*; relationships not established yet.

One species, field vole *M. agrestis*, widespread in GB, and another, common vole *M. arvalis*, marginally present, probably introduced, on Orkney and Guernsey. 2 others recorded as fossils: narrow-headed vole *M. gregalis*, in Late Pleistocene, and root vole *M. oeconomus*, may have survived to Bronze Age (see Chapter 3). No evidence that any *Microtus*, live or fossil, occurred in Ireland.

Fig. 5.31 Field voles are best surveyed by signs such as runways (here, under discarded tin) and, especially, grass clippings (*photo P. Morris*).

Field vole *Microtus agrestis*
Mus agrestis Linnaeus, 1761; Uppsala, Sweden.
Arvicola hirta Bellamy, 1839; Yealmpton, Devon.
Arvicola neglectus Jenyns, 1841; Megarnie, Perthshire.
Arvicola britannicus de Sélys, Longchamps, 1847; England.
Microtus agrestoides Hinton, 1910; Grays Thurrock, Essex; Pleistocene.
Short-tailed vole, short-tailed field mouse.

RECOGNITION
Small, greyish-brown vole, with small ears and eyes (see Fig 5.35), blunt snout and short tail (Plate 3). Colour dorsally varies from greyish to yellowish brown, never shows deep chestnut colour of bank vole. Young may be confused except that the tail is longer in the bank vole. Young water voles similar but have larger hindfeet (>21 mm) and relatively longer tails.

FIELD SIGNS
Tunnels and runways chewed through long grass, and cut remains of grass leaves and droppings within them, are good signs of presence (Fig. 5.31); quantitative assessments of vole populations can be derived from presence of signs (grass clippings most reliable) in samples of quadrats [862]. Droppings green when fresh, *c.*6–7 mm × 2–3 mm. Round nests of shredded grass, often at ground level under tussocks of grass, distinctive.

DESCRIPTION
Greyish-brown above; usually pure grey below, sometimes tinged with buff. No sexual dimorphism in colour; juveniles in 1st month of life greyer and less glossy than adults [529]. No seasonal colour change, but summer coat sparser.

Moult: In S England, several moults each year. Overwintered animals begin spring moult in February, animals born during summer have succession of moults, ultimately producing adult coat. This replaced during autumn moult, completed by October–November. No hair growth during December–January. Summer coat sparser, with coarse guard hairs; winter coat dense, with mainly fine guard hairs [14].

Skull and teeth: Skull more angular than bank vole; recognised by sharply angled prisms of cheek-teeth, which remain rootless (Fig. 5.25). Molar teeth open-rooted throughout life, continually renewed from base as worn away at the tip. Molar tooth row <7 mm (cf. similar but larger water vole, >9 mm). Additional posteromedial loop on m^2 is clearest difference from *Microtus arvalis*. Distinguished from molars of bank vole by sharp angles on grinding surface, presence of 5th loop of enamel on m^2 (Fig. 5.25).

Chromosomes: 2n = 50, FNa = 50; sex chromosomes unusually large [1589].

RELATIONSHIPS
Within *Microtus,* a distinctive species, apparently related only to juniper vole *M. juldaschi* of C Asia [707]. However, analyses of mtDNA and X and Y chromosome sequences identify 2 species

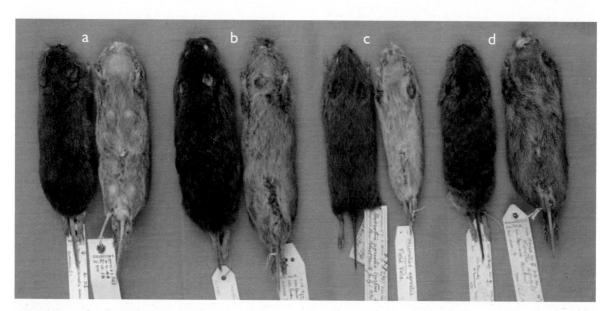

Fig. 5.32 Field vole/common vole skins, of (a) *M. arvalis sarnius* (Guernsey), (b) *M. arvalis orcadensis* (Orkney Mainland), (c) *M. agrestis hirtus* (Hampshire, England), (d) *M. agrestis neglectus* (Inverness-shire, Scotland) *(photo P. Morris, skins courtesy of NHM).*

Table 5.14 Field vole: average measurements from Loch Tay, Scotland, for adults with head and body length >90 mm. Sample size in brackets [274]

	1st year, Sept–Oct	2nd year April		All seasons	
	(both sexes)	Males	Females	Males	Females
Head and body length	102 (83)	121 (20)	115 (26)		
Skull length (condylobasal) (mm)	23.9 (118)	26.1 (17)	25.2 (21)		
Weight (g)	20.8 (118)	39.7 (20)	30.9 (25)		
Hindfoot length[a] (mm)				17.4 (101)	17 (85)

[a] All animals with head and body >90 mm.

confounded in '*Microtus agrestis*', northern form distinct from southern species, occurring Portugal–Hungary [643].

MEASUREMENTS
See Table 5.14. Males heavier than females but substantial interannual variation in mass, larger males (35.4 g) and females (32.6 g) in years of fast population growth in cyclic [245, 384] and non-cyclic populations [12]. Males may reach up to 55 g [528]. Young overwinter at *c*.17 g; spring increase in weight starts March (or earlier) for males, April for females in S England [396]. Timing of weight increase highly variable in cyclic populations [384].

VARIATION
British form not morphologically distinguishable from European populations; supposed subspecies, *M. a. hirtus* based only on average differences of colour and size, overshadowed by clinal variation within GB.

Within GB, increase in size and darkening of colour towards N: largest and darkest in Scottish Highlands ('*M.a. neglectus*', Fig. 5.32). A 4th inner ridge on m[1] is variable in all populations, but increases in size and frequency to N with sharp increase across Great Glen between C Highlands and NW Highlands; also increases significantly with altitude [274].

The following subspecific names have been proposed for Hebridean populations: *M. a. exsul* Miller, 1908 (N Uist); *M. a. mial* Barrett-Hamilton & Hinton, 1913 (Eigg); *M. a. luch* Barrett-Hamilton & Hinton, 1913 (Muck); *M. a. macgillivrayi* Barrett-Hamilton & Hinton, 1913 (Islay); *M. a. fiona* Montagu, 1922 (Gigha). Of these, only *M. a. macgillivrayi* on Islay is sufficiently distinctive to warrant recognition as a subspecies, characterised

by very dark greyish-brown ventral pelage and consistently complex m[1].

Hebridean animals mostly resemble those from W Scotland in size and colour: m[1] is mainly complex (as in the NW Highlands) in the Outer Hebrides and on Skye, Scalpay, Eigg, Luing and Islay; but simpler (as in C Highlands) on Muck, Mull, Jura, Scarba, Lismore, Gigha, Arran and Bute [282].

Differences in frequencies of 25 skeletal variants (involving skull, vertebrae, girdles and long bones) between populations from mid Wales and Oxford [128].

Colour mutants include agouti (main alternatives black or black and tan), pinkeye (normal pigmentation or red eye and pale coat), piebald (normal or white spotting on coat) [1205] and collared (a single white line running across the neck) [382]. Piebalds and pale-coated forms occasional; albinos rare and melanics very rare.

Widespread polymorphism for the presence or absence of a serum esterase (Er), controlled by 4 autosomal alleles [1270]; at high densities, animals lacking enzyme activity (Er⁻ genotype) more numerous, but survive less well in winter than Er⁺ genotypes. Thus, selective balance maintains the polymorphism. Also polymorphic for other enzymes [1270].

DISTRIBUTION
Widely distributed across W Palaearctic, from Portugal to N Cape, and E to L. Baikal (Fig. 5.33). Only *Microtus* in GB, where ubiquitous (Fig. 5.34). Occurs on most Hebridean islands, but absent from Lewis, Barra, some Inner Hebrides (S Rona, Raasay, Rhum, Colonsay, Pabay, Soay), Orkney (where replaced by *M. arvalis*) and Shetland. Also absent from Ireland, Isle of Man, Lundy, Isles of Scilly and all Channel Islands.

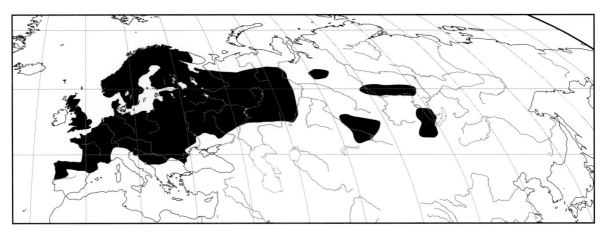

Fig. 5.33 Field vole *Microtus agrestis*: world range.

Fig. 5.34 Field vole *Microtus agrestis*: range in GB.

HISTORY

Well represented in British fossil sites from the penultimate (Wolstonian) glaciation onwards [835,1571]. Recolonised GB Late Glacial, probably absent Younger Dryas, recolonised early in Postglacial, present with lemmings at some cave sites [1152]. Genetic studies of populations from N Europe, based on mtDNA, reveal 2 lineages, derived from different glacial refugia: western form in GB, Denmark, and S to C Sweden, where meets northern form in N Sweden and Finland [705, 706]. Subfossil teeth, dated 1500–2500 bp, from Jura, Inner Hebrides, indicate slight but progressive simplification of m^1 pattern since then [278].

HABITAT

Mainly rough, often damp, ungrazed grassland, including young forestry plantations with lush growth of grass. Sparse populations occur in marginal habitats such as woodlands, hedgerow, blanket bog, dunes, scree and moorland; to >1300 m asl in the Cairngorms.

SOCIAL ORGANISATION AND BEHAVIOUR

Most information comes from Fennoscandian studies [10, 1063, 1157] with 1 study in England [906].

Home range: Space use varies between sexes, age classes, habitats, and with time and population density [390, 906, 1158].

In S Sweden, home ranges in breeding season considerably larger than those established in the non-breeding season (males, breeding season, 1434±910 m^2 (SD); non-breeding: 600±447 m^2; females, breeding season: 773±547 m^2; non-breeding season: 480±357 m^2). Area used during short periods much smaller (weekly home range *c.*150 m^2 [11]).

Significant differences in female home ranges and core areas with breeding condition (England, radio-tracking [906]). Lactating females had smallest home range (HR) and core areas (CA): (HR 67 m^2 SE 9.5; CA 32 m^2 SE 5.0), larger for perforate (HR 163 m^2 SE 21.6; CA 80 m^2 SE 36.8), largest for pregnant females (HR 230 m^2 SE 67.5; CA 140 m^2 SE 42.9); male home ranges and core areas significantly larger than for females [905]. No significant variation in male home-range size during breeding season or between years, but core areas varied between years (though not breeding season). Home ranges (but not core areas) significant smaller with higher density.

Home ranges overlap extensively during non-breeding season, but overwintered females may become territorial in spring, with onset of reproduction [390]. Mutual avoidance rather than overt aggression maintains spacing of over-wintered females [10].

Degree of female territoriality varies with stage of reproductive cycle, time of breeding season, age and relatedness between neighbours. In England, females territorial only when lactating, and core areas small. Some overlap of core areas among females at start of breeding season, perhaps due to familiarity or kin associations. Associations between females short-lived, *c.*1 breeding event [906]. As breeding season progresses, core areas became distinct, suggesting change to territorial system despite moderate to low densities, most females lactating. Different seasonal pattern in Sweden, Finland, where females breeding in year of birth had similar-sized but less exclusive home ranges than overwintered females [11], thus home range overlap increases as breeding season progresses and with population density [1158]. Reproducing mother–daughter pairs more closely spatially associated than pairs of unrelated females [1160], although no such preferential associations between sisters reproducing in the year of their birth [11].

Male spacing behaviour influenced by female density; home ranges larger and less exclusive at low than at high female density [1064]. At high male density, home-range size more variable, less competitive males occupy small ranges whereas some dominant males secure large home ranges even at high male density [1063]. In England, some males overlap during earliest spring breeding while others maintained distinct core areas (territories?). As breeding season progresses, all male core areas distinct, suggesting territoriality [905]. Males do not attempt to monopolise mating access to oestrous females, even when spatially aggregated. Large males with large home ranges father more offspring than other males. Up to 1/3 of all litters have multiple sires [1063].

Communication and senses: Olfaction important. Functional odours found in faeces (caudal glands), urine (preputial glands), and probably produced by flank glands. Individuals respond to strange odours (e.g. urine of predators) and can discriminate between own odour, that of another conspecific and that of a closely related species [256, 319, 1348, 1349]. Auditory, tactile and visual communication little studied; evidence that new objects in a vole's cage explored by all senses, but smell most important. Vocal communication conspicuous, encounters accompanied by loud chattering.

Aggression: Evidence of aggression and infanticide by females towards non-related juveniles. Infanticide committed by all reproductive classes of female, although lower by lactating females [11]. Weaning success greater for those females that are further from non-related females; no such relationship with distance to related females [1160]. Overt aggression shown by adult males in staged encounters in laboratory, and by lactating and pregnant females, particularly in nest defence; juveniles of both sexes relatively immune from attack. In laboratory colonies, a

Fig. 5.35 Field vole face, showing less prominent eyes and ears (cf. bank vole, Fig. 5.29) *(photo P. Morris)*.

single animal, usually male, becomes dominant [253, 320].

Dispersal: Young males disperse further than young females [1249]. Nearly 3 times as many young females (22%) as males (8%) disperse <1 home-range diameter, become established in the vicinity of their mother's range. Juvenile male dispersal distance decreases as total and adult female density increases but no effect of adult male density. Dispersal of subadults particularly marked in midsummer. Dispersal can be infrequent among adult field voles (<3% individuals) [1249], but rare long dispersal movements >1 km overland or by swimming may lead to the colonisation of new habitats and islands [1144]. The proportion of individuals moving different distances between birth and reproduction suggests that competition is the primary factor determining the dispersal characteristics of young and adult individuals [1249, 1250].

Activity: Generally nocturnal in summer, based on trapping studies, treadle-use monitoring and passage counters in laboratory and field [87, 386, 387, 876, 1052, 1086, 1177], but radio-tracking studies suggest that not extensively nocturnal [905]. More diurnal in winter. Juveniles tend to be more nocturnal than adults [87]. Activity peaks at dawn and dusk revealed by trapping [199]. High daytime temperatures lead to nocturnal activity in summer, cold winter nights encourage diurnal pattern [87, 312, 386, 876]. General activity levels increase in overcast or rainy conditions, but decrease when rainfall associated with low temperatures [87]. Activity levels also affected by light levels [876], and circadian rhythms entrained by daily light rhythms [593, 876, 1052]. Short-term (ultradian) activity rhythm also shown, with somewhat variable period (2–4 h) [312] as in many other *Microtus* species [948]. Ultradian rhythm has genetical basis, associated with latitudinal and population dynamic differences in Sweden [1177].

FEEDING
Herbivorous, feeding primarily on green leaves and stems of grasses [396, 602]. Mosses may contribute 20% of diet [418]. Selective feeders, but diet varies within and between vole populations. Preference palatable and nutritious plant species. Low nutrient conditions in British uplands mean that voles there must be selective feeders to maximise nutrient intake [273, 1528]. Consumption of grasses reduced in mid reproductive season, probably as a result of decreased protein content during flowering and fruiting [602]. Even though *Deschampsia* spp. are favoured species, the consumption of *D. caespitosa* reduced by 10-fold in summer, when plants are acutely toxic to field voles [13]. Tend to avoid *Dactylis glomerata*, *Eriophorum vaginatum* and *Juncus* spp.

BREEDING
Breeding seasonal, produce succession of litters (Fig. 5.36). Young born at beginning of breeding season usually reproduce the same year, some first conceiving upon weaning. Ovulation induced. Gestation 20.8 days. Litter size 1–8 (mean 5.0), varying with age, season and phase of cyclic fluctuation in cyclic populations. Weight at birth 2.2 g; lactation 14–21 days [703]. Mating promiscuous.

Length of breeding season varies, usually from about March–April to September–October although litters can be found in February. Onset of reproduction ranges from February to mid May in UK cyclic populations, with later onset following high-density years [381, 383]. Reduced breeding intensity commonly observed in midsummer [1059]. Photoperiod may trigger sexual development at start breeding season [55, 260, 543, 1328] but modified by social factors. Responsiveness to photoperiod has genetic basis, possible to select for individuals able to reproduce under short photoperiod [1329]. Vaginal perforation of weaned females hastened by direct contact with mature males [255], and females reared in presence of mature males (or exposed to their bedding) are more sexually mature (as indicated by uterine weight) [1329].

Ovulation induced [49, 172], perhaps by stimuli other than mating: e.g. virgin females may ovulate, at intervals of 3–4 days, when caged with wire-mesh maze occupied by sexually mature male

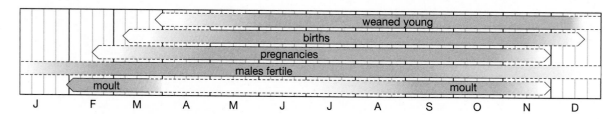

Fig. 5.36 Field vole: annual cycle.

Fig. 5.37 Field vole nestlings, in typical nest of shredded grass *(photo P. Morris).*

[998]. Consequent corpora lutea short lived [998, 999]. Removal of tactile, auditory and visual stimuli produces considerable decrease in incidence of ovulation. Strange males in laboratory block pregnancy of females previously mated with stud males (Bruce effect); may be laboratory artefact, no field evidence found in related N American *Microtus* [321].

Litter size affected by many factors including season (Fig. 5.37), weight (age) of females and their parity [383]. Litter size also increases S–N in Finland, and with different phases of Finnish and British cyclic populations [383, 1059]. Fertility declines somewhat on days 9–11 of a 14-day lactation [173]. Females may become sexually mature at *c.*4 weeks, dependent on date of birth, photoperiod and social factors.

POPULATION

Numbers: Estimated pre-breeding population, GB, 75 million (England 17.5 million; Scotland 41 million; Wales 16.5 million) [624]. Densities in optimal clear-felled areas colonised by grasses >400/ha in peak years [219, 862, 1374].

Fluctuations: GB populations show either seasonal dynamics with irregular year–year changes [605] or multi-annual cycles with 3–4 year periodicity [247, 248, 273, 862, 1133, 1365, 1390]. Non-cyclic populations appear to be variable [417, 905, 1124, 1331, 1461]. All have spring declines, rates of decline vary. 2 broad seasonal patterns: (1) decline, remain low during spring/early summer and increase late summer–autumn [273, 1461], (2) peak in early summer, decline through late summer [417, 905, 1124, 1331]. No evidence in GB of biogeographical gradient in amplitude or degree of cyclicity in population fluctuations as reported in Fennoscandia [606, 614], where northern populations tend to greater amplitude and length of cycles [1361]. Despite assertions to the contrary, no such gradient exists in continental Europe [863]. Populations in adjacent valleys, N England, may be out of phase, ripple-like spatial pattern resembling a travelling wave of vole density [861, 940]. This asynchrony exploited by predators, buffers impact of fluctuations in prey abundance. In Oxfordshire, little change in annual density, 1947–1978 [1196], but in Sussex, wide-amplitude fluctuations were observed over 6 years [1374]. Both cyclic and annual changes in numbers associated with changes in other characteristics (e.g. body weight, survival, growth and reproduction [12, 383, 384, 1059]. In recent years, consistent changes in cyclic dynamics reported both in Fennoscandia and GB; coincides with milder winters, may have dramatic cascading impacts on predators relying on high vole density in spring [139, 670].

No consensus on causes of multi-annual cycles in some areas of GB and their absence elsewhere. Predation hypothesis implicates time-delayed numerical response of weasel predation, argues that geographical gradient in relative impact of generalist and specialist predators promotes Fennoscandian gradient in cyclicity [599, 600, 606, 1447]; population cycles driven by weasel–vole interactions in N dampened by stabilising impact of generalist predators in S Fennoscandia, which respond to greater abundance by eating more voles, switching from other prey [389, 391]. Not supported from British studies [862]: variations in weasel abundance caused little variation in vole survival, showed no numerical response to vole abundance because able to exploit asynchrony of neighbouring vole populations [527, 529]. Thus arguable that predator numbers simply follow cycles in vole populations in GB but do not cause them.

Intrinsic mechanisms (genetics, behaviour) also rejected as explanations for cycles [383]. Alternative explanations include plant–herbivore interactions, with lagged changes in food quality rather than quantity, e.g. silica content [1316], scarcity of winter food [677] or pathogen–host cycles. Changes in cowpox seroprevalence and infection, and advanced vole tuberculosis infection, lag behind vole density, consistent with pathogen dynamically linked to host [219, 237].

Age structure: Age determination based on size unreliable due to varying patterns of growth. With seasonal breeding, most young recruited summer–early autumn. Most females born before June breed in year of birth, then lose weight and overwinter at size similar to subadults. Very few survive 2 winters [12, 249, 1059]. Mean monthly survival 63–73% in cyclic populations, N England [529].

MORTALITY

Preyed upon by many birds and mammals including heron, kestrel, buzzard, eagle, harrier, barn owl, tawny owl, long- and short-eared owl, fox, stoat, weasel, polecat, pine marten, American mink, wildcat and badger. Much of total annual productivity consumed by predators, estimated that 2 specialist (weasel, kestrel) and 2 generalist predators (red fox, feral cat) take 85% [364]. Small mammals, field voles in particular, the most frequently recorded prey of foxes in marginal upland (42% of scats) and upland landscapes (75%) [1522]. In lowland GB, comprised 7% of red fox diet; total mass consumed annually by foxes equivalent to 2.7–5.7 times estimated spring biomass [58]. In a cyclic British population, the contribution of *M. agrestis* to the diet of red fox in winter ranged from 0 to 100% of biomass ingested, dependent on vole density [1095]. Density fluctuations of field voles may influence those of stoats and weasels [389, 1374], although no evidence for this from GB cyclic population [527]. Field voles contribute 40% of barn owl diet, 67% of hen harrier pellets [907, 1181]. No evidence that contribution of field voles to diet of barn owls declined, 1974–1997 [907], nor support for suggestion [624] that field vole now less abundant.

PARASITES

Ectoparasites: Fleas widespread, *Ctenophthalmus nobilis*, *Megabothis turbidus*, *M. walkeri*, *Hystrichopsylla talpae* and *Amalaraeus penicilliger* common; *Rhadinopsylla integella* and *Megabothris rectangulatus* local; *R. pentacantha* and *Peromyscopsylla spectabilis* less frequent. Other rodent fleas, e.g. *Nosopsyllus fasciatus*, occasional (Table 5.11). Lice include *Haplopleura acanthopus*, a sucking louse specific to *Microtus* spp. Ticks: *Ixodes ricinus*, *I. trianguliceps*. Mites: *Trombicula autumnalis*, *Eulaelaps stabularis*, *Laelaps hilaris* and *Haemogamasus nidi* commonly found as on other rodents; hair mite *Listrophorus leukarti* more host-specific. Human ringworm fungus, *Trichophyton persicolor*, occurs in wild populations, 25% infection rate in voles from Berkshire [378, 380].

Endoparasites: Numerous protozoa [290, 374, 1533], examined especially for possible role in population cycles. In gut: *Entamoeba* spp. (non-pathogenic); intestinal flagellates include *Chilomastix*, *Hexamita*, *Trichomonas* (non-pathogenic); coccidian *Eimeria falciformis* (responsible for enteritis), shows distinct seasonal peaks in both prevalence and density of infection in early autumn, Finland, but these low before and during main crash of vole populations, late winter, presumably do not precipitate the decline [853]. See also Tables 5.12, 5.13. Prevalence of flea-borne *Trypanosoma (Herpetosoma) microti* similar between sexes, but positively related to past flea prevalence with a lag of 3 months; highest during autumn [1309]. Cowpox endemic in field voles and other rodents in GB [296]; infection fluctuates, lags 3 months behind vole abundance in cyclic populations; seroprevalence ranges 0–98% [219, 238]. In blood [54]: *Hepatozoon microti* (in leucocytes and infecting lungs and liver); tick-borne *Babesia microti* [1007]; 4 species of flea-borne *Bartonella* (previously *Grahamella*) infect erythrocytes of British field voles: *B. doshiae*, *B. taylorii*, *B. grahamii* and 4th probably a new species [1408]; tick-borne *Anaplasma phagocytophilum* [163]. Also brain (*Frankelia microtia* and *Toxoplasma gondii* [642]) and striped muscle (*Sarcocystis* sp.).

Bacterium *Leptospira interrogans*, causing leptospirosis in humans, isolated from this species [629]; infection rates in natural vole populations 21% Derbyshire, 33% Surrey [1455]. *Myobacterium microti*, causing enzootic tuberculosis in wild populations, isolated from naturally infected field voles [237]; often causes calloused skin lesions in the neck region, prevalence of such symptoms lags behind vole density by 3–6 months in cyclic UK populations [238]. *Yersinia pseudotuberculosis*, the cause of pseudotuberculosis in humans, isolated from field vole [1452] and lung lesions due to *Corynebacterium kutscheir* and *Pneumocystis carinii* described [83, 854]. In Finland, occurrence of *P. carinii* cysts highest in late autumn, related to population density.

RELATIONS WITH HUMANS

At high densities, can cause considerable damage to grassland and young plantations of fruit trees, woody-stemmed ornamental plants and forest trees. Management of grassland by cutting (3 times/year) reduced vole densities to low levels [947]. Management of grassland for field voles (and other small mammals) involves establishing perennial grass, of which 1/3 cut each year [649]. Set-aside farmland seems unattractive to field voles [442]. In arable land, thought responsible for damage to cereal crops, by cutting through the stem close to the ground and eating the stem and leaves. In 1920s–1930s, common forestry pest in

GB [375], problems now confined to deciduous but not conifer plantations.

Field voles important for conservation of avian and mammalian predators, concern expressed at loss of rough grassland in intensively arable regions (e.g [907]. Neither set-aside nor grassy field margins, managed as part of the UK government's Environmental Stewardship and Farm-management practice, particularly favourable to field voles. Grazing livestock generally reduces peak biomass of small mammals, and negative effect increases with grazing intensity [397, 1256].

A possible source of infection of ringworm [378] and jaundice (leptospirosis).

LITERATURE
Review of comparative ecology, *Microtus* and *Myodes* (= *Clethrionomys*) [703]. Popular account, with other small mammals [441].

AUTHOR
X. Lambin, with acknowledgements to J.H.W. Gipps & S.K. Alibhai, D. Evans (authors in 2nd and 3rd editions) and to R.F. Shore & J.R. Flowerdew for numerous comments and suggestions.

Orkney and Guernsey voles *Microtus arvalis*
Mus arvalis Pallas, 1779; Germany.
Microtus sarnius Miller, 1909; St Martins, Guernsey, Channel Islands.
Microtus orcadensis Millais, 1904; Pomona (=Mainland), Orkney.

Common vole (continental Europe). Many local names in Orkney: cuttick; cutoo (E Mainland); volo (Evie); voloo (Harray); vole-mouse.

RECOGNITION
Unmistakable, since the only vole present on the Orkney islands and Guernsey. Teeth differ from field vole *Microtus agrestis* in lacking posterointernal loop on m^2 (Fig. 5.25).

FIELD SIGNS
Network of runs and tunnels ramifying through the vegetation and beneath ground surface [1480]. Same tunnels used over a number of years, by successive generations of voles. Disused tunnels easily recognised since rapidly choked with spiders' webs and vegetation.

Faeces: Piles of green to black faeces deposited at latrines, dispersed at fairly regular intervals along tunnels and runs, sometimes in small side chambers.

Nests: Usually a single nest, often with several entrances and almost always underground. Generally sleeps in nest; young are born and raised in it.

Feeding remains: Grass and other herbaceous clippings found in or near active tunnels.

DESCRIPTION
Closely resembles field vole except for greater size (Tables 5.15, 5.16). Coat tends to be shorter, ears less hairy.

RELATIONSHIPS
Continental *Microtus arvalis* of earlier authors now known to comprise 2 widely sympatric sibling species with distinctive karyotypes: *M. arvalis* with 2n = 46, mostly metacentric; and *M. rossiaemeridionalis* (synonyms *epiroticus*, *subarvalis*) with 2n = 54, mostly acrocentric [952]. Voles from Orkney Mainland have the 2n = 46 karyotype [970]. Genetically, *M. arvalis* and *M. rossiaemeridionalis* closely related; social voles *M. guentheri*, *M. socialis* also belong in *arvalis* group [707].

MEASUREMENTS
See Table 5.15.

VARIATION
Island forms can be distinguished from European animals, and to a lesser extent from each other, as shown in Table 5.16. For Orkney 5 subspecies named, possibly 2 valid: *M. a. orcadensis* Millais 1904 (including *M. a. ronaldshaiensis* Hinton, 1913:

Table 5.15 Orkney vole: measurements of adults, Mainland, July–August [1]

	Males (n=39)		Females (n=38)	
	Mean	Range	Mean	Range
Head and body (mm)	122	98–134	118	97–128
Tail (mm)	39	28–44	36	27–41
Weight (g)	42	29–67	36	22–55

Table 5.16 Common vole *Microtus arvalis*: subspecies

	M. a. orcadensis	M. a. sandayensis	M. a. sarnius	M. a. arvalis
Range	Orkney: Mainland, Rousay, S. Ronaldsay	Orkney: Sanday, Westray	Guernsey	Lowland W Europe
Size	Large	Large	Large	Small
Max. skull length (mm)	30	29	28	24
Dorsal pelage	Dark	Lighter	Lighter	Lighter
Ventral colour	Strongly suffused	Lightly suffused with orange buff	Pure grey with creamy buff	± lightly suffused with creamy buff
m^1 anterior outer groove	Deep	Shallow	Deep	Moderately deep

457 (South Ronaldsay); *M. orcadensis rousaiensis* Hinton, 1913: 460 (Rousay)) and *M. a. sandayensis* Millais, 1905 (Sanday) (including *M. sandayensis westrae* Miller, 1908 (Westray)). Also *M. a. sarnius* Miller, 1909 (Guernsey).

Totally black individuals occur sporadically in Orkney. All Orkney voles characterised by large body size, much larger than most European individuals (Fig. 5.32). Though long considered an adaptation to island life, on basis of tooth size appears to have become smaller since introduction, Neolithic [281]. Neolithic samples from Westray and Orkney Mainland show that difference in m^1, now apparent between Orkney and European animals, then less pronounced [281].

DISTRIBUTION
Wide range from Spain to Caucasus, C Siberia (Fig. 5.38). In British Isles, restricted to Guernsey and 8 of Orkney islands (Fig 5.39): Mainland, Eday, Westray, Sanday, Burray, Hunda, South Ronaldsay, Rousay [154]; Neolithic remains from Holm of Westray [281] might indicate extinct population or transport by raptors. Possibly present on Shapinsay until 1906 [118], but may be a case of mistaken identity. Certainly absent by 1943 [647]. Deliberately introduced to Eday from Westray in 1987 and 1988, now considered to be established [154].

HISTORY
Guernsey population may have been introduced or may be a relict population from the end of the Pleistocene when the island was connected to continental Europe; both scenarios consistent with close relationship to adjacent continental populations indicated by epigenetic polymorphisms [126].

Orkney vole probably introduced by Neolithic settlers between c.5700 bp (earliest known settlement) and 5400 bp (earliest strata containing vole remains) [281]. Radiocarbon dates of vole bones from Westray were 4800±120 and 3590±80 years bp (OxA-1081, 1080). Argued from epigenetic characteristics that originated in SE Europe [126], but conclusion disputed [281], origin in Low Countries seemed more probable. However, molecular studies, using complete cytochrome *b* gene sequence, confirm that introduced to Orkney by Neolithic humans [630] and that they belong to same 'western' phylogenetic lineage as those from France and Spain; SW Europe therefore most likely source. Implies early movement and trade links of Neolithic people.

HABITAT
Present in most habitats in Orkney: coniferous and deciduous plantations, marsh, heather moorland, blanket bog, and rough grassland associated with cliff-tops, ditches, fence-lines, road verges and gardens. Now largely absent from arable land and from silage fields and short pastures [503, 647, 1190, 1204, 1449]. In Guernsey, more common in wet meadows than drier areas [141]. In Europe, *M. arvalis* considered more common in arable farmland than *M. agrestis*.

SOCIAL ORGANISATION AND BEHAVIOUR
Activity patterns: In captivity, Orkney voles have alternating periods of rest and activity, periodicity c.2.8 h. Captive voles under ambient conditions equally active day and night, at all times of year. Free-living voles also show regular short-term rhythm of activity (Fig. 5.15) but in addition the partition of activity between day and night (diurnality) varies seasonally.

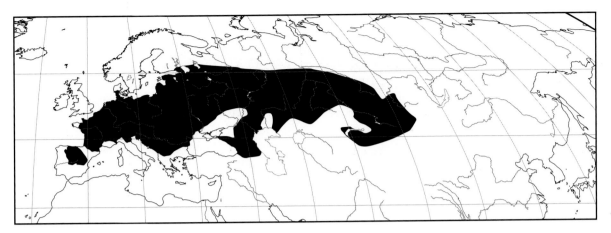

Fig. 5.38 Common vole *Microtus arvalis*: Palaearctic range.

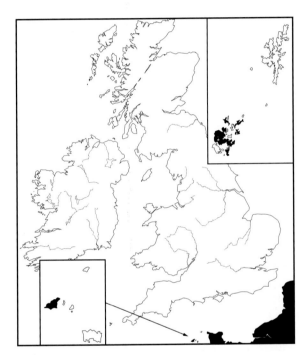

Fig. 5.39 Common vole *Microtus arvalis*: range in British Isles.

Although surface activity occurred during both day and night throughout the year, daytime activity predominated, particularly during winter [1191].

The short-term cycles of activity, with a period of *c*.3 h, also shown by short-eared owl *Asio flammeus*, the voles' principal predator. The activity cycles are synchronous both within and between the 2 species; owls appear to time hunting to coincide with peaks in vole activity [1192].

Social organisation: Radio-tracking studies indicate highly variable mating system, ranging from monogamy, where pairs occupy a largely exclusive range, with practically no overlap between the ranges of neighbouring pairs, to polygyny, where a single male overlaps the ranges of several females [1190]. Ranges are probably defended: when animals removed, vacant space rapidly occupied by neighbours. Young animals forage with their mother for some days after leaving the nest but then disperse. During the winter when densities are at their highest, voles are not associated in pairs, ranges of neighbours overlap extensively.

Home-range size varies seasonally and between habitats. Radio-tracking, Orkney, reveals ranges as large as 3700 m² for voles in overgrown drainage ditches. Mean home-range sizes at a low-density moorland site were 836 m² (males) and 619 m² (females), but only 394 m² and 296 m² at a high-density, lowland grassland site.

FEEDING
Herbivorous, feeding on the leaves, stems and roots of a wide variety of grasses and dicotyledons. Given the choice, will select heather plants treated with fertiliser and with relatively high levels of nitrogen and low levels of fibre [626].

BREEDING
On Guernsey, mating recorded in February, young difficult to distinguish from adults by August. Mean number of fetuses in 8 females was 3.3, range 2–5.

On Orkney Mainland, pregnant females found from March to November, with 60–100% pregnant in August and 30–50% in early September. Weights of male reproductive organs and numbers of stored spermatozoa declined in early September. Reproductive output varies with population density; fewer embryos resorbed in low-density populations than in higher ones; male reproductive organs weigh more at low densities.

In two captive colonies of Orkney voles, mean litter size 2.7 (508 litters [883] and 2.9 (319

Table 5.17 Orkney vole: densities in different habitats, September 1989 [1190]

Habitat	Voles/ha
Plateau blanket bog	31
Calluna moorland	31
Wet heath	100
Old peat cuttings	569
Abandoned re-seed	156
Calluna/Eriophorum	19
Rough grassland	206
Fence-line rough grass	515
Ditch rough grass	305
Re-seed	0
Swedes	0
Barley	0
Barley stubble	0

litters) with a range of 1–6. In a colony kept under ambient conditions, NE Scotland, litters born in every month of the year but with a clear peak in April–August. Gestation and lactation each last for *c*.20 days in captivity. Both males and females spend much time in the nest with the young, grooming them and retrieving them when displaced [306]. Crosses producing fertile young made between voles from Orkney and Guernsey [300] and from Orkney and Germany [1590].

POPULATION
On Orkney Mainland, population densities vary markedly between habitats (Table 5.17). No indications of regular cycles of abundance; between 1988 and 1990, no significant differences in breeding densities in any of 8 different habitats, indicating relatively stable populations [1190].

Orkney voles present in fragmented agricultural habitats until early 1940s, now absent from contemporary improved grasslands and arable crops. Probably due to the highly intensive nature of land management, in particular high stocking rates and increased silage production; there are probably fewer voles now than in the past. For example, between 1932 and 1984, 44% of the moorland on Mainland was reclaimed for agriculture [100] leading to a loss of *c*.100 000 breeding voles.

Total numbers of Orkney voles in August estimated at 3 million for Mainland, 500 000 on

Rousay, 300 000 on Westray, 200 000 on South Ronaldsay and 100 000 on Sanday [1190].

MORTALITY
Animals born in one summer usually breed in the next and then die. Autumn population thus largely young-of-year. Overwinter survival and consequent breeding densities vary markedly from year to year. Major predators of voles in Orkney are hen harriers (15% of nest deliveries, 27% of winter diet), short-eared owls (78–100% of nest deliveries, 72% of winter diet), kestrels (up to 69% of nest deliveries, 75% of winter diet [1190]) and domestic cats (100% of 1264 scats from Kingsdale, Mainland).

PARASITES
Ubiquitous rodent fleas *Amalaraeus penicilliger*, *Ctenophthalmus nobilis* and *Hystrichopsylla talpae*.

AUTHORS
M. L. Gorman & P. Reynolds

LITERATURE
Ecology in Orkney [503, 1191, 1192]; origins of Orkney voles [630].

GENUS *Arvicola*

A small genus of 3 Palaearctic species: water vole *A. terrestris* widespread, from W Europe to E Siberia, including GB, but *A. sapidus* confined to Iberia, France, *A. scherman* to France, Germany. Larger than most other voles, has small eyes, hidden ears, open-rooted molars like *Microtus*, but longer tail. Evolved from *Mimomys* in Pleistocene, as did *Microtus*, but relationships between *Microtus* and *Arvicola* uncertain.

Water vole *Arvicola terrestris*
Mus terrestris Linnaeus, 1758; Uppsala, Sweden.
Mus amphibius Linnaeus, 1758; England.
Arvicola ater MacGillivray, 1832; Scotland
Water rat, water ratten, water mole, craber, waterdog, earth hound, water campagnol.

RECOGNITION
Largest British vole (Plate 3); rat sized. Often mistaken for common rat, but has darker fur (brown or black), rounder body, much shorter, chubby face with small, protuberant eyes; tail much shorter, ears only just extend beyond the fur, and both tail and ears are darker and more hairy than in the rat. Swims frequently, dives well, usually with noisy 'plop'. Juvenile water vole resembles field vole, but head and hindfeet much larger, tail much longer. Molar row longer (>9 mm) than in other British voles (<7 mm).

Fig. 5.40 Water vole: feeding signs (a) are a valuable indication of presence, as are latrines (b) *(photos P. Morris)*.

FIELD SIGNS

Tracks and trails: Footprints show 4 toes with star arrangement, from forefoot, 5 toes from hindfoot with outer ones splayed (Fig. 9.2). Hindfeet show 5 pads (cf. 6 in common rats). Right and left tracks *c*.45 mm apart; stride averages 120 mm.

Faeces: Colour varies with food eaten and water content; usually show light green concentric circles when broken open. Typically 8–12 mm long, 3–4 mm wide, cylindrical with blunt ends; have texture of fine putty when fresh. Ranges marked with faecal latrines (March–October) deposited near the nest, burrows and favoured points where they leave or enter the water (Fig. 5.40). Latrines correlate with vole numbers, give an abundance

index of breeding colonies of water voles [933, 1050, 1556].

Runways: Usually 4–9 cm broad, within 1 m of water's edge, along densely vegetated banks of slow-flowing streams. Are pushed through or under vegetation rather than crossing open spaces. Platforms develop at water edge where voles frequently leave and enter the water. Rarely away from water, then lives almost exclusively below ground.

Burrows: 2 types: a simple, short tunnel ending in a chamber, or a complicated system of branching tunnels, multiple entrances and several chambers. Externally, burrow system can appear as a series of holes along the water's edge, at or just above the water level on steep banks, while others occur below waterline.

Nests: Usually below ground within burrow system. When water table high, nests woven into the bases of rushes, sedges or reed or at sites on higher ground. Nests lined with finely shredded grasses and reeds.

Feeding remains: Frequently found on runways as neat piles of grass, reed and sedge blades or stems of herbaceous plants; typically cut to 10-cm sections (Fig. 5.40). Where blades bitten off, imprint of the two large incisors is prominent and diagnostic, like clean secateur cut at 45° angle [1356].

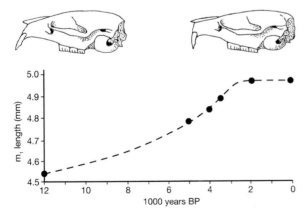

Fig. 5.41 Water vole skulls to show pro-odont (left) and orthodont (right) examples; the graph shows the increase in size since the Late Glacial *(drawn by D.W. Yalden, after [1013]).*

DESCRIPTION

Pelage: Dorsally reddish, medium or dark brown or black; melanic forms more typical for northern

Table 5.18 Water vole: measurements

	Males			Females		
	Mean	SD	n	Mean	SD	n
Breeding individuals Oxfordshire 1996–1997 [77]						
Head and body length (mm)	188.4	21.47	20	180.9	35.74	21
H&B + tail length (mm)	302.2	39.95	20	292.5	18.79	21
Hindfoot length (mm)	34.5	1.79	20	32.9	1.83	21
Weight (g)	219	76.0	20	196	68.8	21
NE Scotland [1273]						
Weight (g)	205	24.0	64	191	25.28	76

populations; grades to lighter ventral fur which is brownish or greyish white. May show partial albinism as white tail tip, paws or patch on head [1345]. Guard hairs long and glossy, shorter and denser in juveniles. Air trapped in dense fur provides thermal insulation, allowing colonisation of aquatic habitats. When excited, guard hairs erected, giving ruffled appearance.

Moult: Regular sublateral (ventral to dorsal) pattern at juvenile and adult autumn moult [847, 1091]. Animals surviving one winter usually show sublateral, rarely head-to-rump spring moult. Those surviving 2nd winter show no signs of moult, fur appears thin [884].

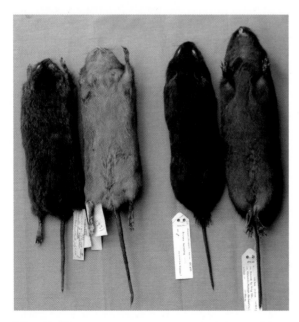

Fig. 5.42 Water vole skins, showing paler English 'A. t. brigantium' and darker Scottish 'A. t. reta' forms *(photo P. Morris, skins courtesy of NHM).*

Tail: Terete, 55–70% of head and body length.

Skull: Overwintered animals have definite nuchal crest. Temporal ridges unite in the interorbital region to form low sagittal crest.

Teeth: Molars rootless (Fig.5.25). Upper incisors usually orthodont, anterior surface enamel bright orange; sometimes pro-odont (more procumbent, assist digging) (Fig. 5.41) [1013]. Fur brushes extend from the upper lip behind the incisors downwards and close off the diastema when incisors are used for digging.

Sexes: Distance between urinary papilla and anus is not reliably sex specific. Sexing of juveniles requires eversion of penis from sheath [77]. Sebaceous scent glands on flanks of both sexes [1344, 1351], largest in breeding males (maximum in 382 males was 21 × 10 mm [884]), most active during breeding season.

Chromosomes: 2n = 36 (Edinburgh) [971], Hertfordshire [1055] and Oxford [1266]. No variation reported from GB, but in Europe Fna = 60–68 [1587].

MEASUREMENTS
See Table 5.18.

VARIATION
British animals average slightly larger than European ones (mean condylobasal length of skull 41.1 mm (n = 40) in GB, 37.5 mm (n = 10) in Scandinavia and 37.2 mm (n = 14) in Switzerland and Italy); not otherwise distinguishable from Scandinavian animals. Scottish animals generally smaller than English.

Proposed subspecies *A. amphibius reta* Miller,

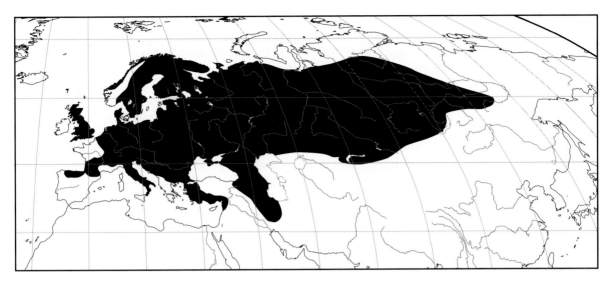

Fig. 5.43 Water vole *Arvicola terrestris*: Palaearctic range.

1910 (Aberdeen); *A. amphibius brigantium* Thomas, 1928 (Huddersfield, Yorkshire) not considered valid (Fig. 5.42).

Within GB, variation most obvious in fur colour, generally black in N and NW Scotland, brown elsewhere. Colour polymorphism is caused by single mutation at melacortin-1 receptor with simple mendelian inheritance [1138]. Nonetheless, melanic lowland populations exist in both England and Scotland; distribution and frequency of black individuals highly dynamic in time and space. *A. a. brigantium* was based upon individuals with usually projecting (pro-odont) upper incisors, but does not constitute a discrete race [284].

High frequency of partial albinism in most British populations studied [884, 1345].

DISTRIBUTION

Widespread across N Palaearctic, from N Spain, GB and Scandinavia to E Siberia (Fig. 5.43). Found throughout GB (Fig. 5.44). Present on Anglesey, Isle of Wight [1359, 1360] and several islands and islets in Sound of Jura (Reisa an-struith, Reisa Mhic Phaidean, Coiresa, and Eilean na Cille), but now absent from Bute [479], Eilean na Gamhna and Eilean Creagach near the mouth of Loch Melfort in Argyll [1405], and from most other islands. Despite wide distribution, national survey 1989–1990 [1360] reported severe decline, confirmed by repeat survey 1996–1998 [725, 1357], by then calculated at site loss of 94%. Has vanished from whole catchments in N Yorkshire [1553], Oxfordshire [78] and NE Scotland [860]. Overall, population loss even greater because number of voles at each occupied site has also decreased. One of the most rapid and serious declines of any British wild mammal during 20th century. Possible that water voles will become

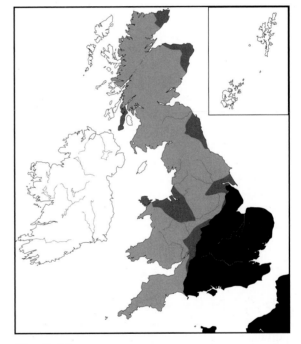

Fig. 5.44 Water vole *Arvicola terrestris*: range in GB, survey sites >20%, 10–20%, <10% occupancy [725].

confined to managed areas or parts of GB not yet affected by mink (see Mortality, below).

HISTORY

A. terrestris evolved from lower Pleistocene *Mimomys savini* through middle Pleistocene *A. cantiana*. *Arvicola* differs from *Mimomys* only in that molar teeth do not develop roots, but remain growing throughout life. Cement appeared in the angles between the prisms of the teeth, and dentine tracts spread up the front and back of the crowns, the animals and hence their teeth growing larger. Allows voles to cope with more abrasive diet

[1571]. Variation in mtDNA sequences of water voles from W Europe indicates that contemporary Scottish populations derived from Iberian glacial refugium, English and Welsh populations from E European one [1137]. Early Postglacial voles smaller, more pro-odont [1013], subsequent change might reflect Scottish form being replaced by English form (Fig. 5.41). Much more abundant in pre-Roman times (mainly fossorial form?) [725, 1571]; competition with sheep argued to be critical factor in long-term decline [725]. More recent decline, of residual population, attributed to mink predation (see Mortality, below).

HABITAT

In GB, usually found within 2 m of water's edge. Prime sites occur most frequently along densely vegetated banks of ditches, rivers, streams and marshes, generally where current slow but water present throughout the year. Populations in NE Scotland found up to 1000 m asl [860]. Along watercourses subject to mink predation, populations become restricted to small narrow waterways in headwaters of catchments away from main river [859, 860, 933, 1399]. Breeding sites in N York Moors National Park had at least 70% grass, steep banks and relatively high foliage height diversity. Grass provides food and nesting material, steep loamy and sandy banks enable voles to construct extensive burrow systems at various levels above and below waterline. Tall vegetation provides protection from avian predators [871]. Reedbed sites, S England, provide refuges from predators including mink [233]. On Scottish mainland occupies fragmented patches of exclusively riparian habitat, whereas on Scottish islands (and 1 coastal site, NW Scotland) is fossorial, colonises large areas of continuous habitat [1405]. Seasonal migration from wet to dry habitats is typical for some German and Russian populations [1104, 1532].

SOCIAL ORGANISATION AND BEHAVIOUR

Social organisation: Varies seasonally as well as, for fragmented populations, with colony size, population density and food availability [164, 1272]. In spring, co-nesting females space out, engage in fights, and losers disperse. Usually by May all breeding females occupy exclusive and defended territories. Males born early in breeding season disperse from territories by 4 months; those born later may remain near natal site during summer–autumn. In Scotland, where females rarely breed in year of birth, c.30% males and female disperse over 1st summer, while other females remain within maternal territory as non-breeders until winter [1272, 1399]. In Norfolk, some adult females, including pregnant ones, dispersed following fights with daughters [884]. When population density very high, breeding females fought much less, had overlapping and undefended home ranges. Only instances of breeding females having overlapping home ranges, lowland Scotland, were by sisters and half-sisters in a high-density population; these showed no overlap between unrelated females, based on molecular techniques [1272]. By contrast, males did not defend territories, shared large home ranges with 1–2 other males; adjusted their positions nearer oestrous females. Large males with large home ranges sire proportionately more offspring, implying that dominant males have greater access to females but cannot monopolise access to females. In populations with several males per colony, highly promiscuous with 58% of litters (n = 45) fathered by 2–3 different males [1272]. Conversely, in highly fragmented upland populations, most colonies hold a single breeding pair and monogamous; for litters for which both parents were known, 13 out of 14 mothers with at least 2 successive litters had all juveniles sired by 1 father, no cases of multiple paternities within

Table 5.19 Water vole: home-range lengths (m) derived from radio-tracking data, for breeding males and females in NE Scotland [1272]

Site	Males			Females		
	Mean	SD	n	Mean	SD	n
Black Stank	154	54.1	6	47	10.5	9
Forvie	212	6.4	2	34	4.6	4
Leet Moss	105	59.0	5	43	17.73	7
Nether Kirton	48	29.1	6	25	12.4	4
Combined data	114	48.0	19	40	14.7	24

litters (n = 30).

In Scottish uplands, occur in small, discrete colonies, median nearest-neighbour distance between colonies 0.6–0.7 km [3]; high degree of turnover with extinction and colonisation; high dispersal rates connected numerous colonies (>30) over large areas (>25 km²) [3, 1400, 1406]. High levels of genetic variability in both low-density populations in patchy habitats and populations in continuous habitats [4].

Dispersal movements frequent, extensive and take place both along waterways and overland [1405]. Inter-colony dispersal longer for both sexes in highly fragmented upland populations than in moderately fragmented Scottish lowland population: the average distances of dispersal in uplands 2.18±0.27 SE km (females), 1.65±0.27 SE km (males); in lowlands, 1.04±0.19 SE km (females), 1.50±0.25 SE km (males). In lowland NE Scotland, 11% (females) and 10% (males) of juveniles dispersed [1406] whereas 22% (males) and 16% (females) in fragmented upland population dispersed in summer of birth. Among animals larger than 100 g upon capture, corresponding proportions of dispersers were 44% of females (n = 52) and 33% of males (n = 72). Dispersal is thus female-biased in both prevalence and distance in highly fragmented populations; possibly an incest-avoidance strategy.

Home ranges: Extend linearly along banks of waterways; both males and females scent-mark at prominent latrine sites. Home-range size variable, larger for males than females (Table 5.19). Females' home-range length influenced by food availability during pregnancy but not during lactation, suggesting a territory function to minimise the risk of infanticide as well as securing access to food resources [1399]. Juveniles' home ranges generally smaller than for breeding adults. Ranges of all sexes and ages much smaller during winter than breeding season. In Oxfordshire, males roamed to 800 m, although tended to stay several days within a range of 30–40 m before changing centre of activity [77].

Scent-marking: By actively scratching flank glands with hindfeet at latrines [456] and during agonistic and sexual encounters [884]. Flank glands do not differ between sexes but were significantly correlated with individual weights. Average gland length 10.56±3.20 mm in females and 12.19±3.69 mm in males. Average width 6.87±1.81 mm and 7.75±2.39 mm in females and males respectively [77].

Aggressive behaviour: Boxing with forefeet and rolling in a clinch; more severe in males than females, involving wounding. In females, aggressive encounters begin with teeth chattering, flank scratching and tail beating. In Oxfordshire adult males seen seeking and attacking weanlings [370].

Activity: Occurs both by swimming and along runways (Fig. 5.45). Response to changes in visual cues causes flight along runways; olfactory cues cause urination, defecation and scent-marking [884]. Activity outside burrow less in winter than during rest of year. In Aberdeenshire, active every 2–4 h, and for longer during day than night [884]. Conversely, in Durham, no consistent variation in activity observed between day and night [45, 1471]. In presence of common rats, water voles inactive at night while rats foraging; compensated by increased activity during the day [1471].

Communication: When threatened or in agonistic encounters, makes arythmic calls between 2.5 and 4.4 kHz lasting *c.*0.1 s; thought to inhibit repeated approaches by conspecifics [744]. Some females avoid and others approach sounds made by conspecifics [884]. Purposeful splash diving causing an audible 'plop' also thought to warn other voles [1358].

Grooming: Involves all feet, teeth and tongue. Forefeet work from perianal region and lower flanks upwards on belly, over shoulders and then forehead.

FEEDING

Predominantly vegetarian [660, 884]; eats mainly grasses, common reeds *Phragmites*, sedges, less frequently rushes and dicotyledons (nettles *Urtica dioica* and dead nettles *Lamium album*) [45]; 227

Fig. 5.45 Water voles swim in a characteristically buoyant manner *(photo P. Morris).*

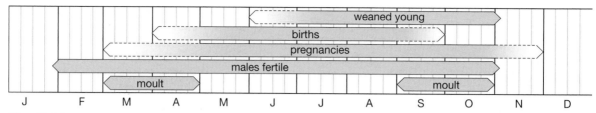

Fig. 5.46 Water vole: annual cycle.

food species recorded during 1989–1990 national survey [1369]. Very exceptionally insects, molluscs, crayfish and fish taken [645, 1057, 1238]. These protein sources, together with pollen from aquatic flowers, may be eaten by pregnant females [1358]. Equivalent of *c.*80% of body weight eaten daily. Juveniles eat fewer reeds and rhizomes than adults [660].

Usually feeds sitting on hindfeet; may eat whole stem of young grasses; more often eats only meristems, in particular nodes and base of stem of reeds. Large sections of plant remain uneaten, found as piles of often similar-length pieces since nodes equally spaced along stem (Fig. 5.40). In winter, may climb streamside shrubs to eat shoots and bark, [1358], also rhizomes and bulbs of plants such as meadow sweet *Filipendula ulmaria*. In uplands, *Potentilla erecta* a favoured herb. May store food in underground chambers as well as hay harvested in autumn, kept quite green into winter on damp floors of burrows [884].

BREEDING

Up to 5 litters, each of *c.*6 young (n = 9) born April–September in England, May–August in Scotland (Fig. 5.46) [1399]. Gestation 20–30 days [143, 645]. Mean number of corpea lutea 6.4 (n = 18, England) [1128]. Mean number of embryos 6.4 (n = 32, Scotland ([1346]), 5.7 (n = 18, England [1128]. Mean litter size 6.1 (n = 149, at 13–17 days, Norfolk [884]. Number of litters in season 1–5, mean 3.4 in Norfolk [884]; 1–5, mean 3.1 in Scotland [1272, 1399]. Weight at birth 3.5–7.5 g. Duration of lactation *c.*22 days.

Males usually fecund from February. Females polyoestrous, with postpartum oestrus and suspension of oestrus during lactation and in winter. First conceive in March–April. Weaned young occur June–October. In Aberdeenshire, females matured in year of birth only once in 5 years, no weaned young resulted [1272]. Young born naked, eyes closed. After 14 days, weigh *c.*22 g, first excursions outside nest and weaning occur about then; leave nest when mother has next litter, when at least 22 days old. Rate of growth of litters can differ widely. In Co. Durham, members of 1st litters of year attained 160 g within 5 weeks of birth, but 2nd cohort needed 12 weeks

to reach this weight [45]. Earliest maturity recorded at 77 g in females, Oxfordshire, while median weight at maturity was 110 g for voles born before July [370]. In GB, young-of-year rarely reproduce in summer of birth; in Norfolk, at most only 10% of young females lactated when population density very high [884], though all young born before July matured in their year of birth in Oxfordshire [370].

POPULATION

Density: Varies seasonally, highest in autumn and lowest in early summer before weaned young appear. In Norfolk, the number of breeding females varied from 4 to 46 per 1.6 km of waterway in different years [884]. Numbers trapped per 100 m of suitable riparian habitat ranged from 2.4 in W Lancashire [1297] and 3.3 in N York Moors National Park [1552], to 6.1 in Bure Marshes, Norfolk [884]. Fossorial water voles on Scottish Islands have a high average spring density of 2600/km^2 [1405], comparable to terrestrial populations in mainland Europe [399, 1253]. Average spring density *c.*5/km^2, Scottish lowlands [4], typically <5/km^2 during the breeding season in uplands [3]. Mean distance between adjacent colonies, lowland areas, 500 m overland [1399] but in uplands, colonies commonly >1 km apart [1]. In Scotland, 10–20% of colonies went extinct each year but similar numbers recolonised by dispersers [1402]. Where American mink present, numbers of extinctions exceed number of recolonisations, populations decline slowly to extinction [3, 871, 1403].

Sex ratio: Usually 1:1, but an excess of males at the start of winter has been reported [1347].

Survival: Few survive 2 winters, living through 3 very rare. Juveniles must reach 170 g to survive winter. Monthly survival probability 60–90%, no evidence that differs between males and females [370, 1399, 1551]. Overwintered voles disappeared in July in one study in Scotland, but persisted throughout the year in other areas.

MORTALITY
Predators include fox, otter, stoat, weasel, brown

rat, owls, herons and pike [164, 452, 728, 884, 1238, 1346]. Golden eagles regularly take water voles in Scottish Highlands [63]. In Europe, fox diet functionally related to water vole abundance [420, 1523]. However, American mink presents the most serious threat; caused local extinctions in N York Moors National Park [871, 1555], Leicestershire and Oxfordshire [1356]; determined water vole distribution in Thames catchment [78] and R. Ythan [859]; many Highland populations vulnerable to mink predation [860]. Maximum length of life in laboratory 31.5 months. Intrauterine mortality low; postnatal mortality very high.

PARASITES
Ectoparasites: Fleas *Ctenophthalmus nobilis, Hystrichopsylla talpae, Peromyscopsylla spectabilis spectabilis, Megabothris walkeri* and *M. (Gebiella) rectangularis* common, other small-mammal fleas accidental [1075]. Sucking louse *Polypax spiruga* common, not specific to water voles. Ticks: in late summer, *Ixodes ricinus* and *I. trianguliceps*, and rarely *I. apronophorus* on ears.

Endoparasites: Tapeworms; in Scotland, *Hydatigera taeniaeformis* in liver.

Diseases: *Bacillus tularense* and *Listeria monocytogenes* carried frequently by European water voles; cause tularaemia and listeriosis respectively in humans, but no cases of tularaemia recorded in GB, British water voles not been found to be carriers. *Leptospira icterohaemorrhagiae* serovar *saxkoebing*, a strain specific to voles, causes jaundice, renal failure and death in humans if untreated. Cowpox may cause skin lesions [1401]. Flea- and tick-borne *Bartonella* sp. and *Babesia microti* also prevalent

RELATIONS WITH HUMANS
In GB, rarely damages canals, dams or arable crops, though reports of damage to fish-farm pools, garden pools, undermining banks and eating vegetation [1554]. Fossorial populations, C Europe, which undergo regular population cycles, damage cultivated land periodically, every 5–8 years [1254]. Indirect persecution of water voles through rodenticide poisoning may threaten isolated urban populations [1359]; also heavy grazing of bankside vegetation, e.g. sheep numbers trebled in Dark Peak, 1930 to 1976, increased further from 78 000 to 118 000 in 1993 [24]; has restricted upland populations [1122, 1570].

Conservation management: Since 1998, has received limited legal protection under Schedule 5, Wildlife and Countryside Act 1981 (WCA) in respect of Section 9(4). Protects places of shelter or protection, but does not protect the animals themselves (but see Chapter 4). Is an offence to damage, destroy or obstruct access to water vole burrows and nests intentionally or disturb them while they are using such places. Identified for priority action under Biodiversity Steering Group Report [653] and the ensuing Species Action Plan [1560]. However, predicted to become rare except in areas not yet affected by mink. Conservation management requires mink control at certain sites together with habitat enhancement. Waterway channel, bankside, water level and vegetation management all have consequences for water voles, best practice guidelines compiled [1359].

LITERATURE
Popular account [1554]; reviews of distribution, with ecological and historical analyses [725, 1360]; status relative to mink [933]; conservation handbook [1359].

AUTHORS
G.L. Woodroffe, X. Lambin & R. Strachan

FAMILY MURIDAE
A large family of mice, rats and gerbils, *c*.731 species; in 150 genera [1538]. Largely confined to Old World (replaced in New World by Cricetidae); probably evolved in S Asia *c*.12 mya, Miocene, spread rapidly to Africa, Australia. Differ from Cricetidae in having 3 rows of cusps down upper molars (rather than 2 rows), typically 9 main cusps on m^1. Mostly seed-eaters, but diets varied, includes some insectivores, even piscivores. In British Isles, 6 species in 4 genera present, distinguished as in Table 5.20.

GENUS *Micromys*

A monospecific genus, resembling *Apodemus*; distinguished by smaller size, short muzzle, prehensile tail. Widespread across Palaearctic, from GB to Japan. Genetically isolated, a basal branch of the Murinae, perhaps closer to *Rattus* than *Apodemus* [988].

Harvest mouse *Micromys minutus*
Mus minutus, Pallas, 1771; Volga, Russia.
Mus soricinus, Hermann, 1780; Strasbourg, France.
Mus tricetus, Boddaert, 1785; Hampshire, England.
Mus minimus, White, 1789; Selborne, Hampshire.
Mus messorius, Kerr, 1792; Hampshire.

Dwarf mouse, red mouse, red ranny.

Table 5.20 Characteristics of genera of British Muridae

	Micromys	*Mus*	*Apodemus*	*Rattus*
Head and body length (mm)	50–70	70–90	80–130	150–270
Hindfoot length (mm)	13–16	16–19	19–26	30–45
Ear length (mm)	8–9	12–15	15–19	20–25
Yellow on chest	No	No	Usually	No
m^1–m^3 length (mm)	2.6–2.8	2.9–3.4	3.7–4.6	6.4–8.0
Upper incisor notched	No	Yes	No	No
No. roots on m^1	5	3	4 (–5)	5

RECOGNITION

Smallest British rodent, weighing 6 g when adult (Plate 3). Easily distinguished from other murids by blunt muzzle and small hairy ears, reminiscent of a vole's. Tail similar in length to head and body, tip very prehensile, tail does not strip when handled.

Pelage: Adult or sexually mature animals russet orange dorsally, pure white ventrally. Winter fur thicker, with dark long guard hairs dorsally. Newly independent juveniles grey-brown pelage, like house mice, but easily distinguishable by small size (*c*.4 g as opposed to *c*.7 g) and prehensile tail. Moult, juvenile to adult, produces very obvious line of new fur.

Skull: Easily distinguishable from other murids by small size, relatively short rostrum, long braincase.

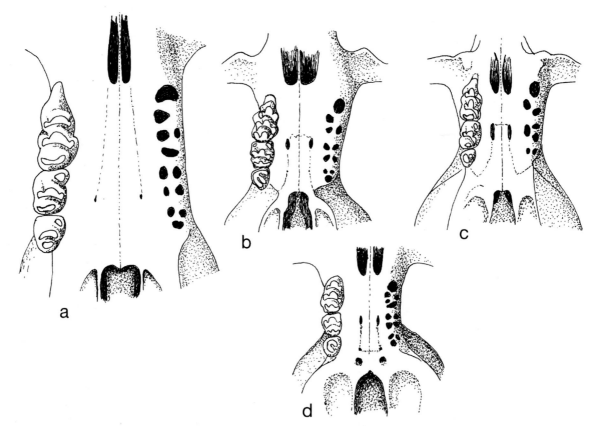

Fig. 5.47 Palates of common rat (a), wood mouse (b), house mouse (c) and harvest mouse (d). Rat and house mouse share asymmetrical first molars (m^1); these are more symmetrical in wood mouse and harvest mouse. The left molars have been removed to reveal the different numbers of alveoli; m^1 has 5 roots in *Rattus* and *Micromys*, 4 in *Apodemus*, 3 in *Mus* (*drawn by D.W. Yalden*).

Fig. 5.48 Harvest mouse: characteristic nest, suspended between grass stems *(photo D.W. Yalden)*.

Distinguished from small house-mouse skulls by having 5 roots to m^1 (Fig. 5.47), 3 to m_1, no notch in the upper incisors; molar tooth-rows <3 mm long.

FIELD SIGNS

Nests: Only British mouse that builds nests of woven grass leaves well above ground level, in stalk zone of annually growing vegetation (grass tussocks, cereals, rushes, herbs, brambles); in low grasses, may be close to ground level, but usually at height of 30–60 cm; in tall reeds, may be >1 m above ground level (Fig. 5.48). Breeding nest almost spherical, up to 10 cm in diameter; non-breeding nests smaller, usually <5 cm in diameter. Non-breeding nests may also be found at ground level amongst bales of hay or straw or on top of disused bird's nests [621]. Newly constructed nests difficult to find because green, built from living grass leaves; by early winter, brown balls of withered grass more evident. Differ from birds' nests in that woven between, not round, grass stems.

Faeces: *c*.3 mm long. Variable in colour according to contents; in summer have a high insect component. Found most frequently in resting and old breeding nests.

Unless in very large numbers, no other obvious signs of their presence, and damage to cereal ears is rarely noticeable.

DESCRIPTION

A small, slender, delicate rodent. Hind legs are not conspicuously large as in wood mice; hindfeet 12–16 mm long (see Fig. 5.51), more slender than in house mouse; outer toes adapted to climbing small stems by slight separation, can grip and hang upside down using strong prehensile tail and one foot. Small pubescent ears have a large triangular meatus, unlike other British murids. Tail weakly bicoloured, sparsely haired.

Pelage and moult: Dorsal pelage of adults consists of long dark guard hairs overlying finer russet-orange contour hairs. Ventral fur remains white in winter while the dorsal pelage is dark orange-brown. Juveniles have overall grey-brown pelage but soon start to moult into orange-brown adult pelage from haunches forward; noticeably bicoloured dorsally for a period.

Sexes: 4 pairs of nipples; very visible in female nestlings. Anogenital distance is best guide for determining the sex of older individuals, though difficult for recently independent juveniles. Adult males have thicker penis than non-breeding males, but testes rarely obvious. Sex ratio for trapped populations approximately 1:1 or shows a slight excess of males [171, 832, 850, 1215, 1326, 1433].

Scent glands: Nothing published on olfactory communication; in captivity, urine and faeces seem to be used to mark a range or territory [457, 1433].

Skull and skeleton: All parts are smaller than other British murids. Width of brain-case similar to width of zygoma, 8.6–9.6 mm. Muzzle short: distance from upper border of infraorbital foramen to tip of nasal bone less than 1/3 of distance to posterior border of occiput. Postcranial skeleton very delicate. Females have a more triangular obturator foramen in pelvis than males [197] and multiparous females have a finer ischium bone.

Teeth: m^1 has 5 roots (Fig. 5.47); m_1 has 3, of which central root very thin. Upper incisors have no notch. Fragments from owl pellets can be identified with certainty by these features. Stages of tooth wear used as ageing method [1444].

Reproductive tract: Female tract Y-shaped. Plug temporarily closes vagina after mating. Testes not obvious even during breeding season. Sperm structure unlike most Muridae in that head has no anterior hook, although sperm head flattened, asymmetrical [460].

Chromosomes 2n = 68, high for a murid [1589]

MEASUREMENTS
See Table 5.19.

VARIATION
Study of geographical variation in Europe confused by protracted winter moult from juvenile to adult pelage when animals with bicoloured dorsal pelage are common. Russian animals larger than British, over twice as heavy. Little molecular variation across whole range, from GB to Japan [1574].

Individual variation in external measurements mainly related to age, season, moults and breeding condition. At 1 week old, weight of nestlings may vary by a factor of 2; discrepancies disappear as adult weight is reached [1442]. Melanistics and albinoes not observed in wild, but small white patches in dorsal fur frequent. Variation in incidence of some skeletal characters [128]. Excessive inbreeding in captivity may result in unusual characteristics and deformities.

DISTRIBUTION
Broad range in Palaearctic from GB to Japan, patchily S to China, Taiwan (Fig. 5.49). In GB, mainly from C Yorkshire southwards, with distribution biased towards S and E. Records from N England, S Scotland, coastal strip of N Wales may represent isolated populations (Fig. 5.50); 19th-century records as far N as Banffshire questioned, but early records from Edinburgh southwards appear authentic, confirmed by later survey [622]. Evidence of at least 4 colonies in Northumberland, Durham although status there, also Isle of Wight, needs confirmation. Re-survey, 1996–1997, of 800 sites positive, 1970–1975,

recorded populations at only 29% [1252]. However in Essex the figure was 50%, subsequent surveys have found evidence in 20% of all tetrads [344].

HISTORY
Micromys is an ancient genus, probably originating in Asia. In Europe, ancestral *M. praeminutus* occurs in late Pliocene as a steppe element of the fauna. *M. minutus* recorded from Lower Pleistocene, W Germany, but thereafter absent from Europe until Late Pleistocene [1364], probably retreated to E Asia in glaciations, rapidly recolonised westwards [1574].

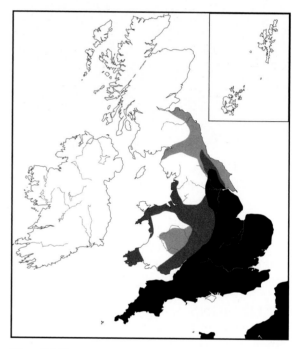

Fig. 5.50 Harvest mouse *Micromys minutus*: GB range.

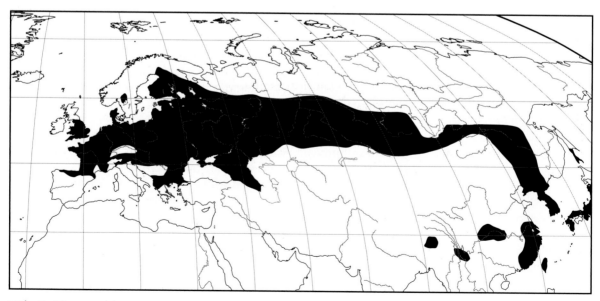

Fig. 5.49 Harvest mouse *Micromys minutus*: Palaearctic range.

Fig. 5.51 Harvest mice are light enough to climb in dead hogweed stems to reach the seeds; note the prehensile tail *(photo P. Morris)*.

Argued whether indigenous to GB; some authors considered it to be native [969], others believed it to be a Postglacial introduction [1364]. Both suggestions tenable, creation of suitable habitat by agricultural activities perhaps a prerequisite, and accidental transport of the species occurs quite frequently in GB and Europe [622, 1060]. Recent evidence of early Postglacial specimens, Wye Valley caves, seems to settle argument in favour of native status [1152].

Scarce in faunas of Roman, post-Roman and Viking age deposits [1568, 1569, 1571]. Small size, general scarcity of harvest mice in bird pellets [485, 972], militate against its recovery as a fossil.

Status in GB has been enigmatic. Described by Gilbert White in 1768, Hampshire, and by end of 19th century recorded from most counties of England, parts of S and E Scotland, but no substantiated records for Wales [622]. Generally considered rare and in decline, 20th century, until 1970s national survey showed it widely distributed and locally common; paucity of earlier records attributed to secretive nature and rarity in the pellets of predatory birds [495].

HABITAT

Favours areas of tall, dense grassy vegetation; colonises early successional stages [251]. Breeding nests may be found in long grass, reedbeds, rushes, grassy hedgerows, ditches, bramble patches and recently planted farm woodlands, cereals (with barley being least preferred) and some legume and other crops. Habitats selected and species of monocotyledon used for nest building are diverse [97, 341, 622, 742, 1176]. In areas of modern agriculture, field headlands and rough grass banks act as refuge and reservoir during winter. Even relatively new 'beetle banks' are colonised [98, 146]. Owl pellet data from the 1970s and 1990s both indicate preponderance of specimens from agricultural locations [907]. Large-scale movements necessary from such summer breeding areas as water meadows and salt marshes, which flood in winter [832]. Has been recorded from young plantations [1038] but captures in coppice [575, 648] and open or mature woodland [622] may represent overspill from adjoining areas, so long as the breeding habitat is unaffected by deer grazing [444]. Ungrazed uncut meadows or grassland cut only once a year are very suitable habitat [1444]. Occasionally recorded in rough road verges, and wasteland in urban areas [340, 622, 1125, 1398].

In winter, appears to abandon stalk zone, uses the runway systems of other small mammals, as annually growing vegetation dies back; temporary non-breeding nests built in bases of grass tussocks [623]. No evidence for normal formation of winter colonies, although concentrations of >100 recorded in ricks [1215, 1220, 1326], and harvest mice occasionally overwinter in Dutch barns [622]. Changes in the structure of the countryside are resulting in further fragmentation of the suitable habitats [834], as recorded in the recent re-survey of 800 previously known sites [86].

SOCIAL ORGANISATION AND BEHAVIOUR

An active animal whose small size allows it to climb and feed in the stalk zone (Fig. 5.51). When undisturbed, moves quietly amongst the vegetation, carefully testing the strength of the stems. When frightened, either 'freezes', attempts to escape downwards into thicker vegetation, or drops.

Home ranges: In undisturbed habitats, appears to be sedentary for much of the year; on the South Downs, Sussex, mean home-range size was 400 m² for males and 350 m² for females [1443]. Data on home ranges and population density indicate overlap of ranges. Some evidence of territoriality in the breeding season; breeding nests tend to be regularly spaced, breeding females in captive colonies frequently chase males relentlessly [1442].

Vocalisation and senses: Audible signals between individuals in the field are rare, but have been reported during courtship, mating and when population density high. Unlike many other rodents, blind youngsters often squeak audibly when disturbed, produce irregular ultrasonic pulses in the range 83–114 kHz [1443].

Hearing very acute; reacts sharply to any rustling or scraping sound up to 7 m away [1487]. Aided by the prehensile tail, has an excellent sense of balance and judgement concerning the strength of single stems of foliage. Visual acuity poor, but can detect sudden changes in silhouette from several metres.

Nothing published on olfactory communication; observations in captivity suggest that urine and faeces may be used to mark a range or territory [1442]. Enclosure studies in Finland indicate no preferences between entering clean traps or with vole or harvest mouse odours [1575].

Aggressive behaviour: Takes the form of fighting or chasing in the stalk zone or on the ground, often accompanied by vocalisation. Tail often bitten in such encounters, may be scarred or even partly lost. Bites on ears and legs, or their loss, recorded; most commonly observed in males in captivity. In a captive colony, both young and adult mice killed and partly eaten [1443].

Activity: Rhythms have been investigated in captivity; individual variation large; most studies indicate a peak of activity after dusk and close to dawn [1443], although this varies with day length. In short days animals primarily nocturnal, but in long days almost 1/2 the activity is in daylight [295] and captive colonies often show some activity throughout 24 h. Monitoring of artificial baited nests showed most activity at and after dusk [1487]. Data from numbers trapped at dawn/dusk suggests that the species is more nocturnal during summer, and diurnal during winter [1443].

Movement: Mainly by walking or climbing in the stalk zone. When frightened, will leap from stem to stem or drop to the ground.

Underground burrowing: Not common, but has been seen to make short burrows around clumps of grass roots in captivity. Can be captured during winter in traps placed in vole runways under the litter layer.

Grooming: Prehensile tail assists when grooming in the stalk zone. Often sits with hind legs on separate stalks and grooms tail and body.

FEEDING

Reputedly eats insects and seeds, but little published data on animals living in natural surroundings. In ricks during winter feeds predominantly on cereal grains [464].

Feeding behaviour: In captivity will eat fruits, seeds and berries and actively chase and consume hard- and soft-bodied insects. Will pursue and catch larger mobile insects such as butterflies and moths. In the wild, takes grain from cereal heads, often eating above ground level and leaving characteristic sickle-shaped remains. In early spring, probably eats buds, shoots and flowers when other food scarce. Analysis of faecal pellets from an urban environment showed seeds, fruit, monocotyledon and dicotyledon leaves, and insects as major dietary items, but fungi, moss, root material and other invertebrates also consumed [340].

Food requirements: High, *c.*2 g/day, due to high cost of thermoregulation. With surface area/volume ratio of 4.9 [545], daily costs of maintenance of a small harvest mouse only slightly lower than 20 g vole or mouse [501]. Mean energy budget for 7–8 g harvest mouse estimated at 29.3–36.0 kJ/day, or 4.06–4.48 kJ/g/day, from both respirometry and food consumption studies [1443]. Studies in Japan indicate that high total fat content, which does not vary seasonally, may represent its main energy reserve [1369].

BREEDING

Polyoestrous, postpartum oestrus, mating April–October, pregnancy 17–19 days, litter size 2–8. Overwintered adults and young-of-year breed, and

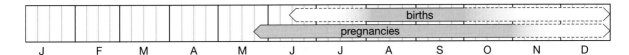

Fig. 5.52 Harvest mouse: annual cycle.

young males may have active sperm at 40 days old. New nest constructed for each litter [1443]. Males chased away from breeding nest.

Breeding season: In England, starts in May and lasts until October, even December (Fig. 5.52), depending on weather [1444], although in one volunteer survey, 74% of litters located were born August–September [620]. 50% of males fecund in late March [1215]. Cold, wet weather, particularly in the late autumn, may cause major mortality [1301]; 12% of litters found before weaning were dead [620, 1442].

Mating and gestation: Males pursue oestrous females on and above the ground for several minutes before mating takes place on the ground. Mated females lose vaginal plug quickly, become visibly pregnant 9–10 days after mating and may more than double their weight [1443] during the pregnancy of 19 days. Postpartum oestrus.

Litter sizes: Early literature (pre-1917) gave litter sizes of 4–12 (mean 6.75±0.40 from 16 published records), but in recent years 8 the maximum recorded (mean 5.4±1.60 from 62 wild litters); reasons for apparent decline unknown [620]. For captive British harvest mice, litter size 1–7 (mean 4.8) from 86 litters, 5.3 in wild litters [1443]; of 90 litters, 3 were eaten completely after disturbance. Up to 8 litters have been produced by a single female in captivity, though in the wild only 3% had 3 or more [1301].

Breeding nests: Aerial breeding nests may be found in many habitats, but principally in hedgerows, the edge of brambles, field edges, grassy banks within fields, reedbeds and scrubland. Females usually build nests in monocotyledons during late pregnancy. Nest size is usually 8–10 cm in diameter, made of green leaves from *Dactylis, Phalaris* or *Phragmites* or a range of other plant species [622]. In wild, nests are probably built mainly at night. Female sits on a stem with her hindfeet and tail, uses incisor teeth to split the distal ends of grass leaves while still attached to plant stalk. When enough leaves have been split longitudinally, she weaves them together to form outer framework of the nest and then lines it by pulling more leaves through the wall and shredding their distal ends. Finally, she

lines the very centre of the nest with fine, short cut lengths of grass or thistledown. No obvious entrance hole when nest contains young mice, although 1–2 points may be regularly used for entering and leaving nest. However, after mother abandons them at 15–16 days old, young may continue to use nest for a few more days; it becomes battered and misshapen and obvious entrance holes may develop [774, 1443]. Smaller non-breeding nests, made by males or juveniles, often have a distinct hole. Breeding nests of different females are usually spatially separated, with a minimum distance depending on the habitat type [1444], and a cluster of 2–3 breeding nests is likely to represent successive litters from one female. Over 200 nests/ha have been found in GB and almost 400/ha in Russia [1442, 1444].

Young: In captivity, usually born in early morning, but perhaps not in wild [1443]. Development described for captive mice [457, 774, 1136, 1306, 1443]. Young weigh 0.6–0.8 g at birth. Mothers suckle several times each day, subsequent growth rapid. By day 4, light brown down begins to cover the back; becomes thicker, and dark line becomes apparent dorsally. Lower and upper incisors erupt on day 7 and 8 respectively. Belly is white by day 8–9, when eyes usually open (2.5–3.5 g). Begin to leave the nest and explore at day 11.

By day 14, moult to grey/brown juvenile coat nearly complete, young capable of feeding themselves. If mother pregnant, young usually abandoned when 15–16 days old and continue to use their nest. The mother makes a new breeding nest, which may be close to the previous one.

The juvenile to adult moult may start at *c.*30 days and may be completed in 15–100 days according to season [774]. Young males may be fertile at 40–50 days and young captive females have given birth at 62 days old [1442].

POPULATION
Overwintering British population estimated at *c.*1.5 million (England 1.4 million, Wales 10 000) [624], but probably declining. Cycles of abundance occur, particularly in continental Europe [375, 994, 1443]. In GB, populations of >200/ha may be followed by low numbers the following year [1444]. Annual variations in numbers of breeding nests give index of annual mouse populations. Local populations fluctuate seasonally, peak during

November, fall steeply in February–March. Trapping at ground level becomes ineffective during early and mid summer; due either to behavioural change, perhaps associated with breeding or availability of food in the stalk zone, or to very low densities of animals. Summer samples often biased towards males, although average annual sex ratio approximately equal [1444]. Surge of juveniles recruits to trappable population, September–October; both trapping and hunting by owls are usually very successful during this period [210, 446, 1444]. Adults that have bred disappear from the population very rapidly after the termination of the breeding season. Up to 4 generations may reproduce within 1 breeding season.

Age determination and age structure: On the basis of tooth wear, maximum life span in wild is 18 months [850]. In Japan [1370], oldest of 116 mice estimated by eye-lens weight to be almost 14 months. In wild, GB, very few survive 6 months: of 454 animals marked at various ages, 30% were recaptured after 6 weeks, 13.2% after 12 weeks, 4.6% after 18 weeks, 1.5% after 24 weeks and only 0.7% after 30 weeks [1444]. Young-of-year predominate in autumn and winter populations. No animal was located both before and after a breeding season. Mice born in October survive longest, overwinter to breed the next year. In captivity, several instances of non-breeding individuals living 5 years [1443].

MORTALITY

Predators: Taken by a wide variety of vertebrates; carnivore and bird predators include mustelids, foxes, domestic cats, owls, hawks, corvids, shrikes and pheasants; blackbirds and toads take young [621]. Active intermittently throughout 24 h, so are liable to predation by both nocturnal and diurnal animals, but rarely important, mostly form <1% of diet of predators. Accounted for *c.*2% of mammal prey taken by domestic cats [1558]. Although nationally occur in only 0.8% of barn owl pellets [494], in W Sussex, where harvest mice common, barn owl diet showed seasonal cycle, from maximum of 65% of prey items in November down to <1% in June–July; mirrored inability to trap mice in these months [1442]. In Norfolk, most harvest mice eaten by barn owls are young animals, and sex ratio in pellets was 1 male:1.2 females [210]. Remains in owl pellets only useful as guide to areas where harvest mice common, unlikely to be recorded by such techniques where numbers low [495, 622].

Weather: Adverse weather towards end of breeding season kills many nestlings and young mice. Persistent rain, sudden drops in temperature and hard frosts also important causes of mortality for adult mice [1301]. In GB, highest mortality in February [1444].

Others: Changes in habitat management and modern methods of agriculture have probably reduced abundance, although relative effects of combine harvesting, insecticide spraying, stubble burning or hedge management and removal not quantified. Recent Mammal Society re-survey of historical sites indicated that suitable habitats continue to be lost, strongly associated with disappearance of harvest mice. Unfortunately, alternative habitats nearby (e.g. 'beetle banks' or other rough vegetation) not examined except in Essex, where many nearby sites were subsequently found. Sites often involved arable areas with a roadside hedge and verge incorporating rank grasses supported by bramble, blackthorn or willow herb. Increase in deer may reduce the presence of harvest mice in young and regenerating woodland [444].

PARASITES

No records of host-specific species; most data come from Europe [1301]. In GB, few ectoparasites found on specimens from ricks [1216], but several species of small-mammal flea have been recorded on the mouse or in its nests (Table 5.10; [1307, 1308]), numbers of mites and lice may be found in the short fur [142]. Infestation with tick *Ixodes trianguliceps* highest in winter, although numbers lower than on other species of small mammal with larger home ranges [1172, 1173]. Helminths reported from Europe but not GB. Protozoans *Babesia microti* and a trypan-osome recorded [290]. No fungal dermatophytes were found on 10 harvest mice examined [379].

In Europe, recorded as hosts to wide variety of bacterial, viral and fungal pathogens, some of economic importance. In Italian rice fields, excrete *Leptospira bataviae* which can cause fever in rice field workers [22]. Antibodies to hantavirus found in Russia [220]. Spirochete *Babesia burgdorferi* and helminths have been recorded in Denmark [458, 1410]. Antibodies to *Toxocara* found in harvest mice in Slovakia [353].

RELATIONS WITH HUMANS

No formal reports of harvest mice causing damage in GB; however, several instances of plague numbers causing damage in USSR [1301]; during occasional 'plague' periods in Europe, have caused serious economic damage to stored grain [375]. Reported as pests of strawberry crops, Japan [1275], may invade beet fields in Europe [751]. Even in GB, may be the most abundant small mammal in some localities, so presumably some damage attributable to them. Large numbers used to occur in unthreshed ricks during the winter [1220] and population estimates of up to 270/ha in grassland have been recorded by trapping [1444].

Habitat changes and fragmentation, such as the removal of field margins, hedgerows and wetlands, have been associated with the decline in the number of locations where harvest mice continue to be found [1126]. However, surveys in Essex of suitable nearby habitats have shown that many hold populations [344], species may continue to be under-recorded. Use of pesticides and intensive agricultural operations likely to have contributed to decline. Domestic cat predation may be of local importance.

Easy to keep in captivity, requiring little specialised attention. Breeds readily, although fighting, including tail biting, a problem in closely confined colonies [621]. High densities of non-breeding animals live agreeably, but on lowering the density, one animal usually becomes dominant, may attack others. Mated females drive away males, but consecutive litters have been raised successfully in captivity where male remained in the same cage throughout. The female may consume a disturbed litter. Diet does not seem to be an important factor in captive breeding, so long as dense vegetation is provided. Some formal reintroductions attempted (e.g. Cheshire), using captive bred animals for hard and soft releases; some populations have survived at least for several years [1230]. Aerial nests (particularly conspicuous in winter) facilitate identifying the presence of the species [622], although difficult to trap by conventional techniques during summer, when live predominantly above ground in stalk zone. Artificial baiting nests made from tennis balls with a hole cut in one side and positioned above ground level in suitable areas used to attract wild harvest mice [1487] but technique failed spectacularly in a subsequent national survey using several hundred balls, even in areas with harvest mice present. Hair tubes have potential as future survey technique [1126].

LITERATURE
Popular accounts [621, 623].

AUTHORS
R.C. Trout & S. Harris.

GENUS *Apodemus*

A Palaearctic genus of *c*.20 species; widely distributed, typically in forested areas, from Ireland to Japan. Characterised by long tail, large ears and eyes. Genetically close to *Mus*, closest relative possibly *Tokudaia osimensis*, Ryuku, Japan; probably evolved in E Asia [1341]. Replaced ecologically in N America by superficially similar *Peromyscus*, a cricetid. Of 4 species in W Europe, 2, wood mouse *A. sylvaticus* and yellow-necked mouse *A. flavicollis,* occur in British Isles.

Wood mouse *Apodemus sylvaticus*
Mus sylvaticus Linnaeus, 1758; Upsala, Sweden.
Mus intermedius Bellamy, 1839; Devon.
Mus hebridensis de Winton, 1895; Uig, Lewis, Outer Hebrides.
Mus hirtensis Barrett-Hamilton, 1899; St Kilda, Outer Hebrides.
Mus fridariensis Hinton, 1914; Fair Isle.

Long-tailed field mouse; red or hill mouse (Scotland); *llygoden y maes* (Welsh); *luch fheoir* (Scottish Gaelic); *luch fheir* (Irish Gaelic).

RECOGNITION
Dark brown upper fur, protruding eyes, large ears and long tail distinctive (Plate 3). Underside white with yellowish chest spot or streak, sometimes extensive, but never joining brown upper fur on either side of neck, distinguishing it from slightly larger yellow-necked mouse. Tail skin dark above and light below, sparsely haired; skin easily sloughed when restrained. Juveniles greyish-brown with less obvious chest spot; may be confused with house mice, but lack characteristic musky (acetamide) smell, larger feet and ears evident.

Skull and teeth: Distinguishable from house mouse and harvest mouse by long molar rows and shape of m^1 and m_1 (m^1 usually with 4 roots) (Fig. 5.47), but difficult to separate from yellow-necked mouse. Measurement of anteroposterior thickness of upper incisors and jaw length enables most skulls to be distinguished [1566].

FIELD SIGNS
Tracks and trails: Footprints have 4 toes on forefeet, 5 on hind; slightly larger than bank vole and house mouse. Overprinting common; jumping locomotion may show tail impression. Well-worn pathways sometimes visible between burrow entrances; small spoil heaps present outside freshly dug burrows. Visually obvious small objects, such as leaves or twigs, disturbed while moving [1354].

Faeces: Colour variable with food, 3–5 mm in length, larger and darker than bank vole. Randomly deposited within home range [1548] but sometimes found in groups near nests, feeding sites and cached food.

Nests: Typically of leaves and moss, within underground chamber among tree roots [730], but variable according to availability of material; also within walls, under cover in buildings, machinery and in nest boxes on trees. Weight and volume of leaves and nest depth increase with decrease in temperature in the laboratory [360].

Cached food: Left in chambers in burrow systems, field drains, garage corners. Caches often left in live traps and entrances often blocked with earth or stones [1481], particularly in autumn–winter; similar behaviour may result in blocked drainage pipes and camouflage/blocking of burrow entrances. Field caches not necessarily destroyed by ploughing [902] and sometimes present on surface.

Food remains: Left in sheltered places, e.g. under logs, between roots, in disused birds' nests, empty cans and in weedy patches in crop [1420]. Hazelnut shells opened with hole surrounded by tooth marks (Fig. 5.3). Achenes (pips) of rose hips opened to extract seed but flesh discarded; bank voles discard pips, eating flesh [372]. Seed of ash fruit ('keys') extracted through hole chewed in side of pericarp; bank vole splits pericarp wing down middle [441]. Coarse dust of 'kibblings' left behind after eating stored grain; snail shells opened by biting through shell away from spire.

Scent-marks: Not obvious; probably present on pathways [713, 714].

DESCRIPTION

Pelage: Dark brown dorsal fur grades to lighter yellow-brown on flanks; ventral fur grey-white. Some old individuals appear lighter brown, almost sandy. Yellow chest spot, if present, varies from small fleck to wide ventral suffusion but without meeting brown upper fur. Juveniles grey-brown above, grey below, with little yellow on flanks.

Moult: Variable in pattern and occurrence. Regular sublateral (ventral to dorsal) pattern in post-juvenile moult (5–7 weeks); most adults show aseasonal or autumn/winter 'patchy' moult (Fig. 5.22; [462, 1213]).

Anatomy: Mystacial and superciliary vibrissal field reaches lower ears [838]. Pelvic bones distinguish genus and sex; vary with age/reproductive history [197]. Glans penis cylindrical, spined, with ventral groove and dorsal ridge (groove possibly missing in *A. flavicollis*); baculum has proximal tapering ossified section and 3-lobed cartilaginous distal section [1537].

Nipples: 4 pairs; 3 abdominal, 1 axillary.
Scent glands: Sebaceous glands in subcaudal skin, enlarged near base of tail of males, produce white secretion; glandular development also in corners of mouth, lips and anus; goblet-shaped preputial glands (male) and clitoral glands (female) [198, 202, 203, 1350].

Skull: m^1 usually has 4 roots (Fig. 5.47), rarely 5. Accessory cusp recorded on m^3 in Ireland [777].

Reproductive tract: Usually regressed or undeveloped in winter non-breeding season. When breeding, testes large, up to 12 mm; prominent accessory glands, lagging behind testes

Table 5.21 Characters of mice of the genus *Apodemus*

Character	Wood mouse	Yellow-necked mouse
Yellow marking on chest	Narrow longitudinal streak, or absent	Broad collar, in contact with dark dorsal colour
Colour of underparts	Pale grey	Very pale grey
Length of hindfoot, without claws (mm)	19–23	22–26
Anterior–posterior diameter, upper incisors (mm)	1.10–1.30	1.45–1.65

Skulls with upper incisors measuring 1.35–1.40 mm diameter may be unidentifiable, but if molars are heavily worn will be old wood mice, and if obviously unworn will be young yellow-necks.

Table 5.22 Wood mouse: measurements of adults, Perthshire [282]

	Males			Females		
	Mean	Range	n	Mean	Range	n
Head and body length (mm)	93.6	86–103	20	91.0	81–103	13
Tail length (mm)	83.2	74–95	20	82.0	71–93	13
Hindfoot length (mm)	22.0	20.8–23.0	20	21.6	20.2–22.8	13
Ear length (mm)	15.9	14.7–17.8	17	16.1	14.6–17.3	13
Weight (g)	19.1	13–27	20	17.8	13–24	13
Condylobasal length (mm)	23.4	22.4–24.9	19	23.1	21.5–24.2	12
Upper molar tooth row (mm)	3.8	3.6–4.1	19	3.9	3.7–4.1	11

in development [53], include 'ram's horn' seminal vesicles bound to coagulating glands, partially external lobular prostate gland. Female tract Y-shaped; past attachment sites (placental scars) show as dark spots on uterine wall; corpora lutea large cream or pink spots on ovary.

Chromosomes: 2n = 48; all acrocentric (FNa = 46) [837]. Superficially similar to yellow-necked mouse but small differences such as absence of prominent

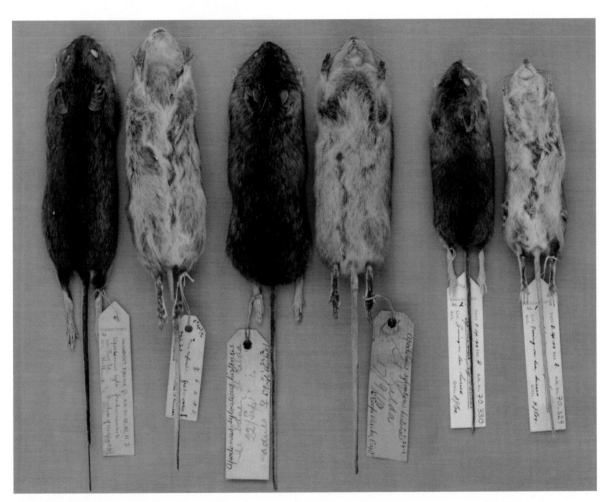

Fig. 5.53 Wood mouse, skins of subspecies *A. s. fridariensis* (Fair Isle, left), *A. s. hirtensis* (St Kilda), *A. s. sylvaticus* (Sussex, England, right) *(photo P. Morris, skins courtesy of NHM)*.

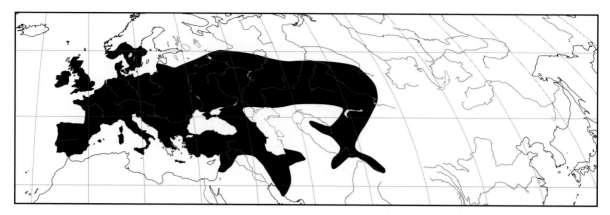

Fig. 5.54 Wood mouse *Apodemus sylvaticus*: Palaearctic range.

C-band in X chromosome [118, 377, 628]. MtDNA polymorphic [223]. Microsatellite markers described from Ukraine [59], some microsatellite loci similar to yellow-necked mouse [496].

RELATIONSHIPS

Biologically similar to yellow-necked mouse [1023, 1024]; common in woodland, though less restricted to woodland than yellow-necked mouse [559]. Centres of activity segregated from congener [1017, 1020] and behaviourally subordinate to it [252, 1016]. Genetic studies confirm monophyly of *Apodemus*, place *A. sylvaticus* close to *A. flavicollis* in subgenus *Sylvaemus* [988]. Lower mean weights in sympatry with yellow-necked mouse [16].

MEASUREMENTS

See Tables 5.20–5.22. In summer, mainland juveniles usually <15 g, adults >20 g; pregnant females up to 40 g. Winter median commonly 17–19 g, but variable [440]. Calcium-rich diet in limestone habitat increases growth/weight [1278]).

VARIATION

Much size, pelage and skeletal variation [109, 118, 329]. Most island forms distinguishable by large size (Fig. 5.53) [778]; some have high proportion with buff underside e.g. St Kilda, Lewis and Channel Isles [283, 329]. Less variation on mainland. Non-metric skeletal variation suggests 2 distinct British forms, in apparent breeding contact, but probably of different origin: E type, related to French populations, and W/N type related to island forms [117]. Size increases from N to S in Europe [16].

In woodland, frequency of normally uncommon phosphoglucomutase genotype increased in autumn, coincident with immigration from fields [877]. Uncommon genotype mobilised glycogen faster, survived worse (or emigrated

Fig. 5.55 Wood mouse *Apodemus sylvaticus*: range in British Isles. Found on most smaller islands, see Table 5.23.

more) over winter, than common genotype [878]. Variation with time on Scottish Islands [109]; frequency of non-metric variants in St Kilda mice from 1910, 1919, different from 1948, 1964, 1967; no change in Barra mice over 25 years nor from Lewis and Harris over 45 years. Silver-grey, piebald, melanistic and semi-hairless forms recorded [80, 536, 1008]; albinism of tail tip in *c.*3% of population [276].

DISTRIBUTION

Wooded and steppe zones of W Palaearctic, but not extending far into coniferous zone (Fig. 5.54). Ubiquitous in GB and Ireland except on open mountainous areas (Fig 5.55). Present on most large islands and widespread on small islands (Table 5.23).

Table 5.23 Wood mouse: records from British islands [40]

Shetland	Orkney	Inner Hebrides	Outer Hebrides	Clyde	Channel Islands	Scilly Isles	Misc.
Fair Isle	Hoy	Eigg	Lewis	Arran	Alderney	St Marys	Wight
Mainland	Shapinsay	Muck	Benbecula	Bute	Jersey	Tresco	Anglesey
Fetlar	North Ronaldsay	Tiree	Harris	Great Cumbrae	Herm		Man
West Burra	Stronsay	Skye	St Kilda		Sark		Brownsea
Yell	Mainland	Iona	North Uist		Guernsey		Hayling Island
	Sanday	Shuna	South Uist		Jethou		Walney
	Eday	Coll	Ceann Ear?				Hilbre
	Lings Holm	Lismore	Barra?				Skomer
	Graemsay	Scarba					
	Copinsay	Jura					
		Colonsay					
		Rhum					
		Canna					
		Raasay					
		Mull					
		Islay					
		Gigha					

HISTORY

Ancestral *A. dominans* present in Europe, Late Pliocene, evolved into present species by Early Pleistocene [988]. Survived through Last Glaciation in Iberian refuge, spread N and E to most of NW Europe; 3 genetically separate populations in Italy/Balkans, Sicily, N Africa [990]. Reviews [1565, 1571] suggest native to tundra faunas in Pleistocene interstadials with *Lemmus* or *Dicrostonyx*, but records may be result of muddled excavation or late intrusion by burrowing; probably formed part of British temperate deciduous woodland fauna by 9500 bp, before separation from Europe. Subfossil teeth in Mesolithic level near Dublin, 7600±500 bp [1150]. Most island populations probably introduced by humans [275]. Skeletal evidence suggests that Iceland, Faroes, Shetlands, St Kilda, Hebrides and many small Scottish island populations came from Norway (possible Viking involvement), but Mull and Colonsay (Hebrides) probably colonised from mainland [118]. However, parasitological evidence indicates mainland origin for Fair Isle (Shetland) population [1539]. Present on Orkney Mainland from Neolithic times [280]. Survival on Channel Islands through last glaciation [111] disputed on geological evidence [1565]. In Scilly Isles, now only on St Mary's and Tresco; Bronze or Iron Age remains on Nornour [1123, 1448].

HABITAT

Highly adaptable and opportunistic. Principally a woodland species [414, 440, 1038], but found in most habitats, including arable land [435, 442, 537, 1379, 1415, 1417], ungrazed grassland [251], set-aside [1382, 1208–1210, 1384–1386], agro-forestry systems [805], heather, blanket bog [865], reed beds [226, 749], fenland [446], sand dunes [287, 504], drystone walls [633, 701], hedgerows and field margins [834, 1028, 1029, 1146, 1147, 1379, 1414, 1418], road verges [95, 1125, 1198], gardens, vegetated parts of urban areas [1564] and reclaimed land, as a pioneer [592]. Probably limited in urban areas by predation and habitat fragmentation, though offset by availability of suitable gardens [56]. Considered rare above treeline on high moors and scree, except in walls or buildings, but high-altitude records occur, to 1300 m asl [1535].

In Ireland, mixed heather, grassland and bracken preferred to pure grassland, despite absence of field voles [401]. Preference for low-level cover or high-level (canopy) cover not consistent [1028, 1542]. Less abundant in 3-year-old oak coppice than younger/older growths [575].

Quality of woodland patches (tree seed availability) has varied influence on distribution; females aggregate in areas with high resources in winter and spring [1031]. Ecology in Sitka spruce plantations apparently similar to deciduous woodland [414], but shows some density-dependence in habitat utilisation [415].

Present in most crops including cereals, maize, sugar beet and beans [537, 935, 1116]. May not differentiate between use of wheat, barley and oilseed rape, but within them, small weedy patches preferred [1419]. Hedgerow favoured, particularly after harvest and over winter [935, 1432], but in general little evidence that habitat linearity (e.g. hedgerows) influences abundance of wood mice in the small-mammal community [1387]. After initial disruption of harvest [1415], can remain on bare fields over winter [537, 902, 1418], sometimes in large numbers [937]. Method of establishment of set-aside and alternative habitats available influence habitat attractiveness (density), e.g. uncut set-aside favoured and cut patches avoided [1379, 1386]. Abundance positively influenced by sward height in cereal fields in May–June [936]. Hedges and ditches influence distribution more than characteristics of field margin [1311]; area adjacent to hedgerow is avoided [727, 1386]. Abundance in Irish pastoral farm hedgerows declines with amount of land under pasture and distance from woodland, increases with increased food supply and cover [1028]. Arable farm woodland favoured when well supplied with connecting hedgerows, avoided if close to large woodlands [435]. Set-aside may be less or more attractive than crops and semi-natural habitats [1209, 1379, 1385, 1386], but uncut set-aside may provide refuge after harvest [937, 1382]. Reduced numbers in woodland heavily grazed by fallow deer *Dama dama* compared to enclosed, protected woodland [1161], although no significant reduction detected over 50 years in Wytham Wood, Oxford, where deer numbers have increased and where canopy cover, mid-cover (0.5–2.5 m) and ground vegetation have decreased [444].

SOCIAL ORGANISATION AND BEHAVIOUR

Reviews mainly related to population regulation [1030, 1469, 1542]. In winter, organisation loose, with communal nesting of both sexes (up to 3–4) [1416]. At start of breeding season, some evidence of heterosexual associations from analysis of spatial organisation [1174], observations of male–female pair bonds [468]. In cereal fields, males engage in scramble competition to mate polygynously with promiscuous females [1416]; female-defence polygyny widely reported [47, 1549, 1550]; genetic evidence of multiple paternity.

Dominance hierarchy of males reported during breeding season; uncertain whether patrol a group territory including breeding females [201, 265] or simply have overlapping home ranges [1030, 1174,

Table 5.24 Wood mouse: typical home-range sizes [47, 1415, 1416, 1550]

Habitat	Season	Males		Females	
		Area (m²)	n	Area (m²)	n
Deciduous woodland	All	2229	39	1812	25
Coniferous/deciduous woodland	All	1844	7	1072	11
	Summer	13063	3	809	19
Deciduous woodland	Summer	4485	17	1699	10
	Summer	10765	12	4009	12
Coniferous/deciduous woodland	Winter	299	13	242	11
Deciduous woodland	Winter	1294	63	1151	41
Sand dunes	Apr–Nov	36499	8	15826	9
	Dec–Mar	18832	5	12290	6
Arable fields, mainly winter wheat	Mar–Aug	14400	104	4900	32

Note also the mean home range, 6 mice of unknown sex, in winter wheat or barley: before August harvest, 7600 m²; after harvest, 4900 m². These means are not significantly different, possibly due to small sample sizes [1415].

Fig. 5.56 Wood mouse with *Cotoneaster* berries; the large ears and eyes betray its nocturnal habits *(photo P. Morris)*.

1549]. Male home ranges always overlap but in breeding season females maintain exclusive areas; in some studies, these appear to be individual or joint territories [1415, 1540, 1549]. Communal use of nest sites by females revealed by telemetry [1541]. Several dwelling-places used, but much less sensitive to disturbances than yellow-necked mice; wood mice more gregarious, forming larger groups than yellow-necked mice; the larger the groups (in both species), the more likely they are to comprise immature individuals; in winter groups may merge, unlike yellow-necked mice [323].

Home ranges: See Table 5.24. Spatial organisation variable [1550]. Home range initially small, increases with sexual maturity; autumn home ranges of juveniles remain small until following spring [1174, 1304]. Much larger in maritime dunes and arable fields than in woodland [287, 504, 1416]. Winter ranges small, overlapping within and between sexes. In breeding season, male ranges increase up to 5-fold, still overlapping both sexes; female ranges increase less, remain largely exclusive of other females [287, 1379, 1416, 1550]. In fields, when cover removed after harvest, ranges shrink dramatically [1415]. More than 10-fold variation in home-range size possible within sexes and season [1416]. Faeces deposited throughout the home range in relation to the time spent at each place, not associated with home-range boundary [1548]. Extensive use of low-level branches parallel to ground [1019].

Scent-marking: Olfactory biology well studied but relative importance of scent glands unknown

[1350]. Marking from subcaudal scent glands likely (particularly by males) during normal movements. Chemical differences in secretion between sexes and individuals indicate that species, sex and state of maturity are encoded [502, 1350]; little evidence for subcaudal gland odour being involved in territory or nest marking, self-advertisement or mate recognition [202, 203]. Passive pheromonal signals control oestrous cycles; active behavioural signals, driven by female, coordinate precopulatory and copulatory behaviour [1352]. Prefer live traps previously occupied by opposite sex; avoid traps previously holding bank voles [1419].

Vocalisation: Acoustic biology well known [1350]. Ultrasounds (>20 kHz) emitted in exploration, mating, chasing, fighting, approach to a conspecific, grooming, contact behaviour; sonic calls (<20 kHz) emitted by attacked individual, particularly during retaliation in male–male encounters. Male ultrasonic calls stimulated by odour of oestrous female, inhibited by strange male odour. Infants emit few low-frequency calls in nest but high-frequency calls emitted on removal; intensity and rate of calling increase after days 2–4, remain at high levels until days 12–15, ceasing by about day 19–24 [1315, 1350]. Rate and intensity of infant calling related to degree of cold stress on removal from nest and stage in development of homeothermy.

Other communication: Visual communications important in aggressive behaviour [551], integrated with ultrasonic and olfactory communication. Sometimes squeal audibly when stressed. Grooming near anogenital area of females used by males to obtain information about reproductive state; this information suggested to be a 'commodity' which can be bartered against female reproductive information or matings [1145, 1353].

Aggressive behaviour: Male aggression associated with breeding season [265, 857], increasing in spring [552]. Female aggression associated with lactation (in the laboratory) [548], uncommon in field [265]. Laboratory and field encounters not always aggressive [158, 265, 551, 857]; dominants commonly avoided. In the laboratory, established males and females isolate or kill strange juveniles/adolescents [438]; in the wild, juveniles are tolerated and subadults attacked [857]. Food deprivation alters aggressiveness; dominants become more subordinate and vice versa [548, 1030].

Dispersal: Recorded in adults and juveniles [732, 1031, 1032, 1497, 1542]; many adult males probably disperse throughout the year and females particularly in autumn and winter [1030, 1550]. Removal experiments in summer indicate that dispersing females attracted by low density of males or females (associated with lowered competition for food or reproductive opportunity); dispersing males attracted by greatest opportunities for copulation, regardless of absolute numbers of reproductive females [1031, 1032, 1542]. In winter, male removals result in decline in male numbers and decline in female residency but not density, indicating that area becomes less attractive; female removals made no significant change [1544]. In arable habitats, a 'balanced dispersal' model (where population regulation is density dependent, and patches of habitat vary in quality and carrying capacity, but there are no unfavourable 'sink' patches) usually fits dynamics better than a 'source–sink' model [1388].

Activity: Mainly nocturnal, biphasic in long nights (Fig. 5.56), monophasic in short nights [443, 1030], some diurnal activity above ground in summer [287, 504, 1547]. Start of activity well correlated with sunset [1547], controlled by photoperiod [387, 1030] and light intensity [388]. Last return to nest not related to sunrise [1547]; activity prolonged in poor habitat (maritime sand dune with low food availability) [504], but inhibited by poor cover, e.g. stubble fields [1415] or short grass [733], particularly on moonlit nights [795, 1547]; inhibited by combined wet and cold below 3 °C [199, 549, 550, 1547]. Active for up to 77% of night [287, 1416]. Arboreal movement, up to 5 m, common [1030, 1380]. Daily energy

expenditure 67.9 kJ/day, for individual of 20.5 g, slightly higher than other similar-sized rodents; no significant differences in daily energy expenditure across study sites (deciduous woodland and sand dune) or season, because in sand dunes and in winter, had lower body masses which offset effect of larger ranges and colder temperatures [287].

Locomotion: Walking, running, a bounding leap, or climbing. Breeding males travel at 1.4–3.4 m/min, covering up to 1200 m per night; movement greatest in sand dunes, least in woodland, and reduced outside breeding season [287, 1416]. Visually obvious small objects, such as leaves or twigs, distributed while moving; serve as 'way-marks', aid spatial navigation during exploration [1354]. In cereal fields, no correlation between breeding male weight and range size or movement, but males with largest ranges moved most [1416]. In arable habitats, males move faster than females; in winter (crop removed) females move further than males but in summer (crop growing and tall) males move further than females [937]. Lethargic movement associated with winter hypothermia [1039]; torpor induced in the laboratory by low ambient temperatures (3 °C or 12 °C) following food deprivation [1483].

Grooming: Face and ears wiped with forefeet and tail drawn through mouth; flanks and underside groomed by teeth, hindfeet cover neck, sides and underside as well [553]. Males groom females more than vice versa, likely to receive reproductive benefits in return [1145, 1353]. See also Other communication, above.

Burrow system: Sometimes complicated, probably surviving from one generation to next; extensions excavated using forefeet to dig and hindfeet to clear soil [548, 730, 794, 1030].

Nests: See Field signs, above.

SENSES
Vision good, adapted for nocturnal activity with large protruding lens to eye, insensitive to infrared and red light [265, 468, 1323]. Both shortwave- and middlewave-sensitive cones distributed uniformly across the retinal surface [1367]. Sense of smell acute; individuals discriminate between faeces or urine of others by odour alone [1547]. Hearing also acute, see Vocalisation, above. Orientation can exploit ambient magnetic field [967], see also Locomotion, above).

FEEDING
An opportunist [604, 605], taking plant and animal foods; proportions greatly affected by

habitat, season, abundance and preference [345, 504, 678, 731, 814, 1087, 1303, 1494, 1593]. Nightly diet choice changes so that amount and variation diminishes from 1st to 2nd activity period; sugars are selected for early in the night [731]. Takes seed, including acorn and sycamore (dominant most of the year); buds (especially blackberry) and dicotyledon stems (especially in early spring); live invertebrates, including caterpillars, centipedes and worms (mainly in early summer); blackberries, elderberries and fungi (in autumn) [1494], and most types of dead and dying invertebrates to varying extents [461]. More insects taken in coniferous woodland with spring–early summer peak [1012]. Invertebrates, particularly coleopterans, dominant in diet in maritime sand dunes [1593]. In sugar beet fields, earthworms important in late winter–early spring [537, 1116]; in arable fields after harvest, endosperm of sown and shed grain taken, with arthropods in spring and weed seeds and grass flowers in summer [537, 731, 1148]. Within crops, feeding places characterised by annual weeds and their remains; the seed bank is unimportant and bare ground avoided while foraging [1420]. Crop seeds preferred to weed seeds [731].

In sugar beet fields, weed seeds eaten before harvest in autumn and arthropods, mainly larvae, taken in winter; earthworms and sugar beet remains in late winter. Exceptionally, vertebrate prey may be taken, e.g. frogs [1003].

Diet varies with sex and age classes; in woodland juveniles eat less seed and subadults less animal food than adults, making up with greater variety of other foods [658, 1494]. Females ate more green plant food and less animal food than males in spring/summer [658]. Post-dispersal stinking hellebore *Helleborus foetidus* seeds naturally distributed to sheltered microsites more severely predated than those in exposed microsites; food augmentation does not reduce mouse predation. Pre-dispersal seeds appear to demand more expenditure of energy and loss of 'safety'; augmentation of natural food supplies reduces predation then [407].

BREEDING
Life cycle summarised in Fig. 5.57. Polyoestrous,

mating March–October or longer, spontaneous and induced ovulation, first pregnancy 19–20 days, subsequently 20–32 days; births occur throughout season, peak litter size June–August, mean litter size 4–7, breed from 7–8 weeks. Promiscuous: DNA microsatellite analysis indicates multiple paternity in the wild [59]; enclosure studies confirm multiple paternity in 85% of litters (n = 34), up to 4 fathers [84]. Spermatozoa from a single male compete with those from other males, but cooperate by forming distinctive aggregations (trains) of hundreds or thousands of sperm cells, significantly increasing sperm motility [363, 1037]. Telemetry confirms communal use of nests by reproductive females in the wild [1541]. Solitary and cooperative breeding females observed in enclosures; cooperation may be between related and unrelated pairs of females [475]. Reviews emphasise variability and environmental influences; female fertility limits breeding [254, 440, 1542].

Males: Seasonal cycle of testicular and accessory glands; growth in January–February, usually regress October–November [53, 254]. Testes develop fully within 28 days of weaning in laboratory [258]. Sperm head hooked anteriorly [1078]. Greater proportions of males in breeding condition when yellow-necked mice absent [959].

Females: Usually imperforate in winter; seasonal cycle (February/March–October) of vaginal perforation, usually shorter than period when sperm produced, varies with winter breeding [440, 1320]. Vagina scars over during later pregnancy, opening before parturition. Length of oestrous cycle variable; postpartum oestrus [254, 746]. Oestrous females attractive to males for <4 h [1416]. Mate after mutual investigation of ano-genital region during courtship. Several rebuffed mounting attempts precede female accepting male [553]. Early ovulations possibly not fertilised; later in the season fewer ova shed. Resorption common [1110]. Implantation at 5–6 days (primigravid), delayed in subsequent pregnancies by 1.3 days for each pup suckled. Females exclude other mice from nest. Litters usually 4–7, range 2–11. See also Parasites and pathogens, below.

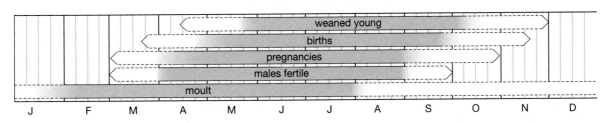

Fig. 5.57 Wood mouse *Apodemus sylvaticus*: annual cycle.

Productivity: Up to 6 successive pregnancies recorded in wild; potential for increase great; doubling of numbers each month normal. In woodland, winter breeding (early, late, or throughout) and good adult survival (associated with heavy mast crop) allows further increase, but high densities inhibit breeding [1031]; early breeding may occur without abundant seed [404] and in absence of yellow-necked mice [1022]. Winter litters usually small [1320]; size varies with geographical location and season/age [440]. Island breeding seasons usually shorter than on mainland [737].

Development: At birth, weigh 1–2 g, naked and blind; grey-brown pelage appears dorsally *c.*6 days followed by ventral white. Incisors erupt *c.*13 days, tail and hindfeet darken dorsally *c.*14 days, eyes open *c.*16 days; weaning from 18 days. Growth rate variable [436, 478, 574]. Autumn-born young develop more slowly than summer-born young [537] pups survive more than 12 h without milk or thermoregulation from mother [323]. See also Moult, above.

POPULATION
Numbers: Pre-breeding GB total estimated at 38 million; autumn *c.*114 million [624]. Local densities of 1–40/ha in mixed deciduous woodland usual, but winter increases, up to 130–200/ha or more after a good seed crop [554, 951, 1304]. In mixed arable farmland, density <1–30/ha and usually lower than surrounding woodland [537, 619, 935, 1379, 1415].

Fluctuations in numbers: Usually vary seasonally, autumn–winter peaks and spring–summer troughs [440, 951, 1025, 1026]. This pattern generally, but not always, consistent across habitats, except in arable land [935, 1379, 1384, 1414]. Harvesting and ploughing reduce densities mainly through increased predation risk or em-igration [1415]. Autumn emigration may occur from arable land to woodland [937, 1580] and road verges [1125]. Rape field centres and edges had significantly lower numbers than did barley or wheat field centres or edges; populations in arable habitats largest April–July when crop tall; in winter more mice inhabit edges of fields than centres [937]. Population dynamics generally more variable in arable crops and set-aside than in nearby woodland; numbers generally highest in woodland, lowest in set-aside, with intermediate values in field margins and crops [1379]. Density often locally food-limited [1012]; influence of winter food supply may vary between sexes [445, 1542]. Long-term studies in woodland show annual fluctuations, no evidence of longer cycles [440, 444].

Population regulation reviewed and modelled [447, 857, 951, 1025, 1027, 1032, 1379, 1542–1544]; density dependence is strong during increase but lacking in decrease; in woodland, rates of population change from summer to winter, also winter densities, higher after good seed crops; peak numbers probably limited by spatial density dependence in female reproductive activity and female territoriality. Size of autumn seed crop, in woodland, strongly influences numbers in following spring and autumn [222]. Replicated studies stress importance of spatial density-dependent inhibition of female breeding, sometimes overridden by superabundant food supply during the autumn–winter increase; role of males limited to infanticide and competition with females for food; juvenile recruitment not affected by male aggression, probably limited by spatial strife with increasing female numbers and increasing infanticide from males and females [1543]. Between study sites, numbers synchronous in both spring and autumn, probably entrained by autumn seed crop [448. 951].

Sex ratio: 1:1 at birth but adult population male-biased in live trapping [293, 555].

Age determination: 12 cusps prominent in maxillary tooth-row of young, reduce in number with age [331, 478]. Stages of wear similar to yellow-necked mouse [7, 558]. Increase in eye-lens weight [558, 541, 1163] and body weight [436, 584] also used. See also Description, Pelage; Breeding, Development of young, above.

Age structure: Late-born young predominate in autumn–winter, survive well into spring. Few adults survive from one summer to next. Mature overwintered individuals joined by juveniles from April–May onwards but survival of latter usually poor, forming small proportion until autumn when most overwintered animals disappear [440, 1021]. Significant changes in age structure associated with population reduction following pelleted molluscicide application and agricultural management [740, 741, 1281].

Survival over winter: Positively related to autumn mast crop in deciduous woodland [440, 951]. Increase in juvenile survival in summer or autumn results in peak densities in autumn–winter. Reduced survival in spring, coincident with start of breeding, increase in aggressiveness of males and formation of exclusive breeding areas by females [440, 1030, 1542]. In winter, much dispersal of both sexes occurs but immigration not necessary for autumn increase [552, 1495]. However, both sexes move away from woodland during spring decline [285, 619].

SPECIES INTERACTIONS

Often the most common small mammal, except in rough grassland when field voles may dominate [1385]. Probably competitively excludes house mouse from woodland in GB [1383], may have caused its extinction on St Kilda when human population left [129]. Hybridisation with yellow-necked mouse not successful [738]. Differs from yellow-necked mouse in later breeding season, population dynamics [1021, 1023]. Although yellow-necked mouse favours intermediate cover in woodland [961, 1020, 1023], no evidence of competitive exclusion at the habitat level. Removal experiment suggests earlier breeding by wood mouse when yellow-necked mouse removed, and vice versa, with greater use of areas of shared woodland formerly avoided [959, 1022]. Evidence for competitive interaction with bank voles equivocal. Removal experiments in Italy [406] showed reproductive condition was not affected by density of competitor, nor of conspecifics; no evidence of any habitat shift related to competitive release. However, removal of wood mouse allowed significant increase in population density of bank vole, which returned to previous density after removal ended; reverse effect, of bank vole removal on wood mouse density, not significant. Competitive effect therefore asymmetrical. Contrasts with behavioural studies at a bait point [858] which showed no clear relationship (also [477]). At low wood mouse and bank vole densities, fewer pairs of tawny owls bred, exceptionally none [1322].

MORTALITY

Predation: Predators include fox, mustelids, cat, owls, kestrel [232, 403, 492–494, 796, 796, 931]. Higher proportions of wood mice in barn owl diet in 1990s than previously, particularly in E England, suggest possible change in hunting habitat with decline in field vole [907]. Losses to avian and mammalian predators in mixed field and scrub habitats, Scandinavia, may balance annual production [389]. Domestic cat predation peaks in spring and autumn; contribute 17% of prey over year [250]; questionnaire survey suggested that wood mouse their most common prey [57]. Large proportion of population taken by tawny owls and weasels, particularly in spring in mixed deciduous woodland, Oxford, but numbers difficult to quantify [797, 1324]. Mortality from tawny owls likely to be inversely density-dependent, relatively greater at low mouse densities [1324]. Tawny owl predation selects against asymmetric individuals [466]. In Ireland, wood mouse forms *c.*70% of diet of long-eared owl, cf. only 25–50% in GB [402]; similarly, *c.*50% of barn owl prey where bank vole absent, 43% where bank vole present [1302].

Mortality increases in spring, probably reflecting combination of dispersal, increased predation and intraspecific strife [440]. In laboratory, male infanticidal tendency less if with perforate than non-perforate female; mothers can prevent infanticide by females but not by males; reproductively inactive individuals most likely to be infanticidal [1543]. See also Population, Fluctuations in numbers.

Disease: Seems not to regulate population [635]; population effects of virus and helminth infections detailed below.

PARASITES AND PATHOGENS

Reviews of parasites, disease and zoonoses [290–292, 635, 888, 1452] reveal need for more field investigations.

Ectoparasites: Fleas (see Table 5.11): many species widespread and common [142, 288, 474, 1307, 1308]. Sucking lice *Polyplax serrata* and *Hoplopleura affinis* are common and congeners *P. spinosula* (of rats) and *H. acanthopus* (of voles) also recorded. Ticks *Ixodes trianguliceps* adults, nymphs and larvae common [1172]; also *I. ricinus* larvae and nymphs. Resistance (innate and aquired) to *I. ricinus* reduced in sexually active males with high testosterone levels [676]. Mites *Laelaps agilis, Eulaelaps stabularis, Radfordia lemina* and *Trombicula autumnalis* recorded in England. Skin mite *Notoderes* spp. causes dry creamy-coloured scabs on skin. Additional records from Ireland include *Euryparasitus emarginatus, Myonussus gigas, Haemogamasus arvicolarum, H. nidi* [402, 866]. Beetle *Leptinus testaceus* is common, principally in nest; generally regarded as a scavenger [208, 403], but may be a predator [1108].

Endoparasites: See Tables 5.12 and 5.13 and [92, 887]. In S England in September, over 4 years, 91.8% of 134 wood mice carried at least 1 species of helminth and the majority (60.5%) carried 2 species [92]. Older mice carried heavier infections of cestode *Microsomacanthus crenata*, abundance also varied significantly between age cohorts from year to year; males carried heavier infections of nematode *Syphacia stroma* [92]. Irish species surveyed [402, 866]; variation and community structure described in [1009–1011]. Larval rhabditid worms occur in orbital fluid [1437]. Intestinal nematode *Heligmosmoides polygyrus* common; worm burden varies greatly between individuals, highest prevalence around April and intensity around May; high burdens occur in young, declining with age, possibly from acquired immunity and/or parasite-induced mortality [540, 541]. Infection compromises survival of young from 1 month old [539], affects population growth in enclosures [792]. More marked seasonal changes in prevalence in cereal fields than woodland [195]; infected mice more mobile, averaging 731 m at 1.6 m/min, cf. 548 m at 1.1 m/min per night if uninfected [196]. Nematode parasites of male reproductive tract may be sexually transmitted [259]. Interactions between these parasites unlikely to play dominant role in structuring the community of helminths [93].

Others: 19 species of parasitic protozoa reported [292]. Host specificity of trypanosomes not confirmed in the wild [1085]. Ringworm fungi common [379].

Bacteria: Include *Bartonella* [140], *Anaplasma (Ehrlichia) phagocytophila* [161], *Mycobacterium microti* (vole tuberculosis) [237]. Spirochaete *Leptospira* common, especially in older individuals [1456] and damp habitats [889]. Other bacteria include *Mycobacterium tuberculosis* var. *muris* and *Mycoplasma* sp. [526].

Viruses: Include louping ill [1460], hantavirus [980] and murid herpesvirus 4 (lungs and spleen) [145]. Evidence of infection with many other parasitic species [635, 764]. Cowpox *Orthopoxvirus* endemic in GB; subclinical infections could affect population dynamics [412]; show evidence of strong temporal clustering, beyond that in wood mouse populations, indicating short-lived outbreaks with transmission risk concentrated locally [231]. Infected females show delayed sexual maturation, first litter 20–30 days later [412, 1407]; transmission of cowpox virus between host species (bank voles and wood mice) is negligible despite their close cohabitation [90, 231]. Infected wood mice survive better in summer, compared with uninfected mice, but more poorly in winter; underlying causes of this contrast unclear [1404]. Infection most common in males, peak in autumn, but no clear association with age [632].

RELATIONS WITH HUMANS

Probably most common and widespread mammal on arable farmland in GB [537, 727, 1376, 1379, 1413, 1415], where heavily influenced by human activities. Combine harvesting and straw baling have little direct effect, but removal of cover greatly increases vulnerability to predation [1415]. Stubble burning causes mortality through asphyxiation. Favour weed- and invertebrate-rich areas resulting from reduced herbicide use in cereal field headlands [1417], but summer densities lower on organic wheat fields, perhaps because later sowing produces poor cover during breeding period [427]. Wood mice do not inhabit grassy margins added to the edges of cereal fields

any more than the margins of conventionally managed fields [1283]. Many subtle changes in habitat and farming practice have manipulated floral and faunal diversity and abundance, so create short-term and long-term variation in farmland habitat suitability [1379].

Chemical contamination widespread [269, 726, 727, 1276, 1282, 1375, 1376, , 1477, 1484] from exposure to heavy metals, seed dressings, slug pellets, insecticide and herbicide sprays. Laboratory results unhelpful for field prediction [1276]. Contaminants reviewed in [1274]. Blood levels of cadmium and lead are negatively correlated with haematocrit values; reduced haematicrit levels recorded from most polluted sites [1211]. Cadmium contamination explored experimentally and modelled; cadmium dose to predators increases if guts ingested as well as body tissue [1477]. Arsenic concentrations in gastrointestinal tract (including contents), liver, kidneys, spleen, lung, femur and fur higher in mice from heavily contaminated habitats; transfer to predators also likely to be through gastrointestinal tract and its contents, if consumed, but also through carcass if arsenic sequestered in fur is biologically available [392]. Genetic variation of wood mouse populations apparently unaffected by arsenic pollution [103]. Extent of contamination varies with habitat contamination but not age [392]. Sub-lethal impacts (lowered acetylcholinesterase activity) of organophosphate (deimethoate pesticide) in field and laboratory associated with impaired activity, may affect survival [332–334]. Population declines associated with application of pelleted methiocarb molluscicide [740, 741, 1281], but impact variable [1282]. Potential for secondary poisoning [461]; dead and dying slugs due to pesticide not palatable in laboratory, because of mucus secretion; residues in or on dead and dying invertebrates may be repellent. Commonly non-target victims of a range of pesticides in agricultural habitats [739], but no evidence of significant mortality. Impact of rodenticides may be under-recorded [1282]. Normal rodent control around agricultural habitats showed that 'non-target' wood mice were more exposed to rodenticides than bank voles *Myodes glareolus* or field voles *Microtus agrestis*; wood mouse numbers declined significantly after exposure, but usually recovered partially within 3 months, depending on timing relative to breeding cycle [168]. Fungicide seed treatments consumed with ingested cereal but residues lower than expected, probably because of dehusking of seeds before ingestion [65]. Denatonium benzoate (Bitrex) repellent at 100–300 μg/g [806].

Feed on stored and sown grain and seeds, especially sugar beet, but have little or no economic impact [35, 537, 631, 1115, 1116]. Feed extensively on common grass weeds of cereal crops, but significance of role as seed predator equivocal [1148]. Role, with bank vole, in woodland fruit dispersal well studied [679]. Germination of tree seeds aided by storing fruit underground, despite eating large proportions of some mast crops. Damage to sessile oak regeneration (*Quercus petraea*) limited to acorns and 1st-year seedlings.

Abundant and versatile, and thus not requiring conservation action, though review of ecology in farmland [442] suggests sympathetic habitat management would increase density and distribution.

Satisfactory breeding occurs in the laboratory but not all females may ovulate; see Breeding, above.

Possible health risks from leptospirosis (Weil's disease) through contact with urine [1452] and Lyme disease (Lyme borrelosis) through infected tick (*Ixodes ricinus*) bites [1312]; in Ireland tick abundance (but not infection rate) determined more by fallow deer than by wood mouse distribution [530].

LITERATURE
Reviews of Irish literature [402, 403], comparative ecology [1023, 1024], population regulation [1542], ecology and behaviour [447], ecology in arable farmland [1379], ecotoxicology, with other species [1274] and the genus [1078]. Also bibliographies [556, 752], semi-popular accounts [439, 441, 533] and a guide to live trapping [567].

AUTHORS
J.R. Flowerdew & F.H. Tattersall, with acknowledgements to W.I. Montgomery & G.B. Corbet.

Yellow-necked mouse *Apodemus flavicollis*
Mus flavicollis Melchior, 1834; Sielland, Denmark.
Mus sylvaticus wintoni Barrett-Hamilton, 1900; Graftonbury, Herefordshire.

RECOGNITION
In GB, yellow collar consistently complete, discernible even in juveniles as grey band, permitting easy separation from wood mouse (Table 5.20, Plate 3). Dorsally, mature adults more vivid orange-brown, and ventrally brighter white, than wood mouse. Tail usually longer than body, proportionately thicker at base than wood mouse. Adults larger, *c.*1.5 times weight of adult wood mice; more aggressive when handled, biting, urinating and vocalising more readily.

Skull: Difficult to separate from that of wood mouse, but averages larger; lower jaw 16.0–

18.8 mm long (cf. 12.3–16.4 mm in wood mouse) [1566]; greater antero-posterior thickness of upper incisors permits discrimination of most skulls (Table 5.21, [428]).

FIELD SIGNS
Footprints and faeces as in wood mouse.

DESCRIPTION
As for wood mouse except for features noted under Chromosomes, Recognition and Measurements.

RELATIONSHIPS
Morphologically so similar to wood mice, particularly in E of their European range, that interbreeding has often been claimed; not substantiated in wild [1077]. Biochemical, cytological and morphological evidence consistently confirms that they are distinct species, at least in C and W Europe [99, 324, 496, 837, 1061, 1537]. Genetic analyses [96, 268, 301, 429, 473, 988, 1186] suggest *A. flavicollis* most closely related to *A. uralensis* (= *microps*) and *A. alpicola*, then *A. sylvaticus*; these 4 species (subgenus *Sylvaemus*) more distantly related to *A. agrarius* and *A. mystacinus*. Divergence time of yellow-necked mouse from wood mouse estimated at 423 000 bp (mid Pleistocene) on basis of biochemical data [301]. In GB, breeding and biochemical studies confirm that hybridisation does not occur [738]. Recent genetic analyses comparing European and British populations suggest that latter may be valid endemic subspecies *A. f. wintoni* [323].

MEASUREMENTS
See Table 5.21.

VARIATION
Little morphological variation within the GB population; British specimens indistinguishable from those of NW Europe. Collar/chest spot variable in Europe, most evident in NW [1458]. Less genetically variable in Europe than *A. sylvaticus*, reflecting different Pleistocene history [990].

DISTRIBUTION
In Europe, extends further N than wood mouse in Scandinavia but more restricted in S and W, absent Mediterranean basin; mainly montane in S Europe (Fig. 5.58). In GB, range essentially restricted to C, E Wales, Welsh border counties, E and S England (Fig. 5.59). Noticeable gap in C England [964]. Population hotspot in Gwent [323]. Isolated record from Riding Mill, Northumberland, dated from before 1911, perhaps accidentally carried there (specimen in NHM). Uncorroborated outlying records from Cornwall, Devon, Lincolnshire and elsewhere appear suspicious. Absent Scotland,

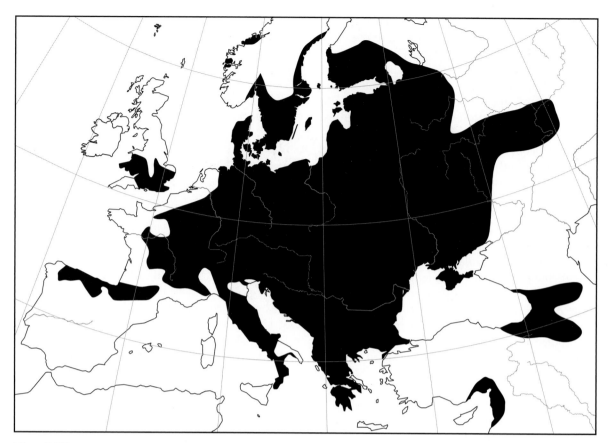

Fig. 5.58 Yellow-necked mouse *Apodemus flavicollis*: Palaearctic range.

Ireland. Within range, distribution affected by isolation of woodlands [964].

HISTORY
Following Last Glaciation, believed to have recolonised W Europe from refuge in Balkans (whereas wood mouse survived in Iberia) [989, 990]. Balkan and Turkish lineages diverged 0.4–0.6 million years ago, but less genetic diversity than in wood mouse [990]. No early records from Postglacial GB, though presumed native, an early immigrant. Recorded from Neolithic and Roman sites, Derbyshire, Lancashire, so range formerly slightly more extensive than present [1565, 1566, 1567, 1571].

HABITAT
In GB, mainly mature deciduous woods [285, 1023] (although somewhat different in parts of Europe). Associated with long-established/ancient woodland [964, 1015] and areas with higher summer temperatures, possibly linked to better tree seed production [964]. Local abundance possibly linked to tree seed availability [1572], spring abundance correlates with number of seed-producing tree species present [961]. In coppice woodland, prefers older compartments and avoids recently coppiced areas [228, 575]. Marginal habitats include

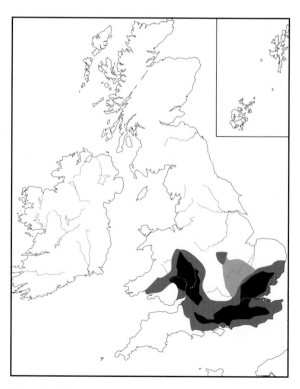

Fig. 5.59 Yellow-necked mouse *Apodemus flavicollis*: GB range.

138

coniferous woodland, hedges and rural gardens, occasionally reeds, wet woodland and heathland. Within woodland, some affinity suggested for areas of tangled understorey [1023]; structurally complex areas incorporating fallen deadwood may provide good areas for nests [323, 961].

In Europe, habitat discrimination between wood mouse and yellow-necked mouse inversely related to their morphological similarity along a NW–SE cline [639]. In E Europe, restricted to mature forest, whereas wood mouse thrives in scrub or shelter-belts [48, 588, 597, 1465]. In C Europe, restricted to montane regions [641, 969, 1056, 1247]. In W and NW Europe, may share same habitat with wood mouse [304] but absent from old fields [104, 601, 656], much as in GB.

SOCIAL ORGANISATION AND BEHAVIOUR

Social organisation: Studies using nest boxes and artificial burrows indicate extended family social structure; evidence of biparental care of young, formation of long-term pair bonds, indicating monogamy [323]. Large communal groups regularly recorded, although mixed pairs are most commonly encountered [323, 963]. Groups may benefit from social thermoregulation during winter months [323, 408]. Anecdotal evidence that group bonds are strong, no evidence of group break-up or merger [323].

Home ranges: Larger than those of wood mouse in shared habitats [1018]. Estimates of range area vary, possibly with habitat quality, but males average larger than females [1017, 1170, 1206, 1263]. Male ranges larger in breeding season than otherwise [1263]. In Europe, mean home range for adults, within and outside breeding season, estimated at 1.55 ha and 0.38 ha (males), 0.74 ha and 0.36 ha (females), respectively [1263]. In British hedgerows, have much more limited ranges [833]. Home ranges overlap between and within sexes [833, 1018], although females may defend core areas against other females [1263].

Behaviour: Similar to wood mouse [638, 1016]. Visual communication integrated with ultrasonic and olfactory communication. Olfactory and acoustic biology reviewed in [1350]. Subcaudal scent gland better developed than in wood mouse, although its functions seem similar, and may be used to scent-mark branches. Secretion differs quantitatively rather than qualitatively from that of wood mouse. Adults and infants emit ultrasonic and audible calls. Infant calls last 60 ms and are repeated 4–5/s. Commence at 56–60 kHz but fall to 40 kHz [1571]. Calls from isolated pups elicit retrieval by lactating females [1592]. Adults emit fewer, lower-frequency calls (40–50 kHz) than wood mouse. Calls often associated with social encounters, subordinate animals calling more frequently [657].

Aggressive behaviour: Generally as in wood mouse [638] but more tolerant of each other than wood mouse is of conspecifics [252, 654, 1016]. Lower levels of aggression may permit increase in numbers in early summer [1020]. Where multiple-capture traps have been used, catches of up to 10 individuals have been recorded with no evidence of intraspecific aggression [104].

Activity and movement: As in wood mouse but greater tendency to climb [638, [285, 654] though this not always apparent [1019]. Recorded in Poland at 23 m in canopy [156]. Woodland radio-tracking reveals prolonged periods spent above ground, although majority of time spent on woodland floor. Mice seen to cross a country lane via canopy links [959]. Arboreal movements may be linked to food availability on the ground and/or high density in rodent populations [659].

Residents antagonistic toward transients, which may constitute >30% of the population [1441]. Displacement movements, up to 1 km, may occur throughout year, involve both sexes [158, 1014, 1550]. Males move faster and further during breeding season [1263]. Move most, furthest, in years of low density [979].

Habitat: Greater proportion of time spent in extensive burrow systems. Most tunnels within 50 cm of surface, but some down to 150 cm, often built within tree roots or under fallen timber. Individuals may use 2 or more nests [323], with tree cavities and other above ground sites also used. Nests generally constructed of layers of leaves. Most new nests built during breeding season, those of females more substantial than males [1445]. May contain stored seeds and invertebrate food [1030]. One burrow (in Russia) contained 4 kg acorns, 4 kg hazelnuts, 150 g lime seeds, 100 g maple seeds, 150 g ash seeds [408]. Where present, artificial nest boxes often used for food storage.

Behaviour, dispersion and movements of *Apodemus* spp. reviewed in [1030, 1550].

FEEDING

Diet very similar to wood mouse [604]. In sympatric populations, interspecific overlap in diet may be 80% [662]. May be seed specialist [235, 1572], whereas wood mouse switches more readily to generalist feeding strategy; dietary divergence greatest in spring [662, 960]. Both wild-caught and laboratory-bred yellow-necks extract beech

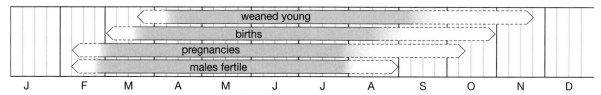

Fig. 5.60 Yellow-necked mouse: annual cycle, typically 2–3 weeks ahead of wood mouse.

seeds more efficiently, but grass seeds less efficiently, than wood mouse [655], suggesting interspecific differences in foraging strategies at least between those in different habitats.

BREEDING

Litters of 2–11 young in successive pregnancies from February or later to October (Fig. 5.60); winter breeding sporadic [1021]. Young born early in breeding season may achieve 1–2 litters the same year.

Breeding season: Duration affected by food availability, as in wood mouse [6, 505, 734]. Breeds 2–8 weeks earlier than wood mouse where they occur together [750, 1021]. Removal of wood mouse from shared woodland promotes breeding of yellow-necked mouse [1022]. In spring, males become reproductively active before females. Winter breeding thought to occur after years of high mast production [979, 1154].

Mean number of embryos throughout breeding season 5.0–6.8 in C and S Europe [147, 505, 750, 1078, 1110, 1338]. Smaller numbers at the start and end of breeding season [1110]. Losses, of 12% of all oocytes or blastocysts and 5% of all embryos, recorded [750].

Young: Weigh 2.8 g at birth, naked and blind. Eyes open at 13–16 days [1078]. Growth rates similar to wood mouse [1025]. Yellow collar visible from end of 2nd week when juvenile pelage fully developed [462]. Post-juvenile moult progresses as in wood mouse [462]. Spring-born animals may reach sexual maturity in 2–3 months [1078]. Young females may attain maturity after reaching 10 g, young males after reaching 20 g [6]. Autumn-born mice usually do not reproduce until following spring, when form most of breeding population [1021].

Sex ratio: Adult sex ratio variable, usually male biased [1021, 1111, 1338] whereas juvenile sex ratio does not differ from 1:1 [1021] in wild-caught samples.

POPULATION

In GB, typically infrequent in woodland small-mammal communities throughout much of its range but sometimes more abundant than wood mouse [559, 964]. Woodlands with these high population levels may constitute local refuges when numbers are low, and nuclei from which yellow-necked mouse disperses when numbers are increasing [559, 961, 1023]. Population growth begins with recruitment of juveniles in early summer, continues throughout the breeding season. Differences in the dynamics and regulation of wood mouse and yellow-necked mouse populations may relate to differences in social behaviour, habitat selection or responses to changing food availability. Interspecific differences possibly ameliorate the effects of interspecific competition. Perhaps much more sensitive to disturbance than wood mouse [323].

Much rarer than wood mouse in GB; estimated at 750 000 (England 662 500, Wales 87 500), on basis of density and available habitat, but patchy distribution makes this tentative [624].

Densities: > 70/ha recorded in one exceptional Gwent site [323]. More typically, maximum densities in sympatry comparable with those of wood mice, just over 50/ha [1021, 1023], and similar to densities in allopatry [979]. Temporal variation in abundance of coexisting populations of wood mouse and yellow-necked mouse may be positively correlated [559] but characteristics of annual fluctuations differ [750, 1014, 1021, 1023, 1025]. Typically reach maximum late autumn–early winter, decrease throughout winter and spring; experience high winter mortality, possibly as a result of the apparent absence of social group mergers that might help with winter social thermoregulation [323]. Variation in peak abundance between years is positively related to mast production [6, 104, 148, 1154, 1171]. This may also affect numbers breeding in the following spring [104, 734, 1023] and leads to population peaks the following autumn [979, 1154]. Spatial distribution in large forests related to productivity and distribution of trees with heavy seeds (e.g. oak and hazel) [755].

Structure: Population structure differs from wood mouse in that spring and summer populations have greater proportions of juveniles [1021, 1562].

Survival: Poor during winter, good in summer–autumn [1021]. Winter mortality more marked than in wood mouse. Few mice survive >1 year. Mean life expectancy at 1 month old is 2.9–3.6 months [147]. Dynamics and regulation of population size reviewed in [440, 1023].

Species interactions: Generally aggressive and dominant in interspecific competition experiments with wood mouse [252, 654, 1016]. Some evidence of spatial segregation in sympatric populations [1019, 1020], maintained by competitive interactions [1024]. At peaks, yellow-necked mouse depresses wood mouse numbers [656].

PARASITES

Ectoparasites: Harvest mites *Trombicula autumnalis* may be prevalent, as well as various fleas, fur mites and ticks *Ixodes* sp. Infestation levels fluctuate seasonally; independent of gregarious/solitary nesting status, gender or age class [323]. Sucking louse *Polyplax serrata* also recorded; likely that hosts similar range of ectoparasites to wood mouse. Abundance of fleas (Table 5.11) decreases as density of yellow-necked mouse increases [1333].

Endoparasites: Helminths: see Tables 5.12 and 5.13. Nematodes: evidence for pathogen-driven selection [1058]. Males appear responsible for driving infection of *Heligmosomoides polygyrus*, females have lesser role [421]. Other: in Europe, carries and is reservoir for hantaviruses [485, 913, 1065, 1291].

RELATIONS WITH HUMANS

May enter rural homes, usually over winter months, where blamed for various minor damage to internal structures and property [962]. May cause annoyance in apple stores, spoil and consume stored foods, consume seeds and interfere with electrical installations. Unlikely to damage field crops. Both inhibits and aids forest regeneration by feeding on and burying tree seeds [500, 631]. Can be bred in captivity but difficult to tame.

LITERATURE

Comprehensive treatment of ecology and behaviour of woodland rodents [447]; review of comparative ecology of wood and yellow-necked mice [1023]; most recent survey of status and distribution in GB [964].

AUTHORS
A.C.W. Marsh & W.I. Montgomery

GENUS *Mus*

A genus of *c.*38 species [1538], mostly found in SE Asia and Africa, though African species sometimes separated as *Nannomys* (formerly *Leggada*). Small mice, tails usually no longer than head and body. Distinguished by rather asymmetrical shape of m^1 (Fig. 5.47). The mostly commensal house mice of W Europe, including British Isles, were formerly regarded as one variable species, *M. musculus*. Several species now recognised, including *M. spretus* (Iberia), *M. macedonicus, spicilegus* (Balkans), which non-commensal, and a pair of commensal forms, *M. domesticus* (W) and *M. musculus* (E), which meet but scarcely interbreed along line from Denmark to Dalmatian coast, S Bulgaria. *M. domesticus*, present in British Isles, is also ancestor of all laboratory and 'fancy' mice.

House mouse *Mus domesticus*
Mus musculus Linnaeus, 1758; Uppsala, Sweden (part).

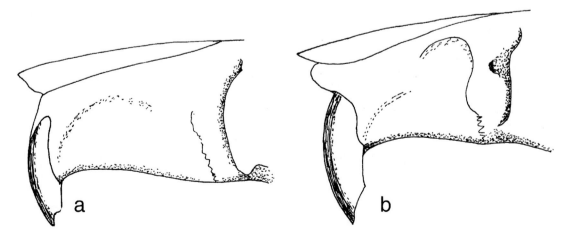

Fig. 5.61 Lateral view of incisors, showing notch in house mouse (a), not in wood mouse (b) (or other murids) (*drawn by D.W. Yalden*).

Mus domesticus Rutty, 1772; Dublin, Ireland (a *nomen nudum*).
Mus muralis Barrett-Hamilton, 1899; St Kilda, Outer Hebrides (extinct).
Mus musculus domesticus; Schwarz & Schwarz, 1943. The name *domesticus* [1262] has been conserved by Opinion 1607 of the International Commission of Zoological Nomenclature [704].

Grey mouse (usually in contrast to red mouse, *Apodemus sylvaticus*); *luch thi* (Irish Gaelic); *lugh* (Manx).

RECOGNITION
Whole animal: Dull greyish-brown dorsally, only slightly lighter ventrally (Plate 3). Juvenile wood and yellow-necked mice similarly grey, but have much longer hindfeet, broader head, larger eyes and ears. Tail slightly thicker, more prominently scaly, than other mice; tail skin not shed readily as *Apodemus*.

Skull: See Fig. 5.47. Distinguished from other mice by notched upper incisors (Fig. 5.61), and by 3 roots (rather than 4) on m^1. Both m^3 and m_3 very small, occasionally absent.

SIGN
Presence revealed by faeces, runways, footprints, smears, holes, scrapes, partially eaten food particles and damage.

Faeces: Often concentrated in favourable places; similar to wood mouse but smaller (*c.*7 mm long).

Runways and footprints: Similar to but smaller than those of wood mice; discernible along regular routes in dusty places; form small mounds of faeces, dirt, grease and urine. Dirty black smears often present along well-travelled runways. 'Loop smears' similar to but smaller than those of ship rats may be found around roof joists. Tooth marks on foods and other damaged commodities; wood mice tend to shred food and paper more than house mice. Characteristic 'stale' smell (of acetamide).

DESCRIPTION
Pelage: Rather uniform grey-brown above, slightly lighter below. Consists of long, straight overhairs, and shorted, kinked underhairs. Colour effectively determined by the overhairs, although these only *c.*20% of total number.

Moult: Periodic waves of moult spread over the body, with young hairs replacing the old ones before the latter drop out; no clear seasonal moult.

Nipples: Usually 5 pairs (3 thoracic, 2 abdominal), but variations in number common. Normally depressed, surrounded by folds of thickened hairless skin, but prominent only in lactating or aged females.

Scent glands: Scents produced in urine, some originating from the preputial and coagulating glands, and in plantar and salivary glands [203]; particularly carried in the anogenital area. Both sexes deposit urinary scent marks, but males have relatively long prepuce with brush-like hairs on the tip, and a reservoir inside the tip which holds the urine [966]; ducts of preputial glands open near the tip.

Teeth: Distinguished from other mice by distorted anterior row of cusps on m^1 and very small m^3 and m_3 (Fig. 5.47). Molar tooth wear fairly accurate method of ageing mice [891].

Reproductive tracts: Breeding can take place at any time of year, so reproductive tract does not regress. Scrotal sacs remain in contact with body cavity, testes may lie in the sacs or be retracted; their situation does not indicate breeding condition in adults.

Chromosomes: $2n = 40$, all acrocentric, individually recognisable by banding [1066]. However, fusions between centromeres (Robertsonian translocation) reported in various populations, e.g. Caithness, several Orkney islands [194, 1135, 1267]. Distinct X and Y sex chromosomes, which associate apparently end-to-end at meiosis.

RELATIONSHIPS
Closest relative the paler, shorter-tailed *M. musculus* s.s. which replaces *M. domesticus* in Scandinavia and NE of line from Denmark to Black Sea, with little overlap and very limited interbreeding [165, 192, 1179]; considered only subspecifically distinct by some [965]. *Mus spicilegus* in S Europe (which probably includes *spretus* and forms that have, probably erroneously, been called *hortulanus* and *abbotti*) also closely related, was formerly included in *M. musculus* complex [965, 1446].

MEASUREMENTS
See Table 5.20. Females slightly larger than males [110], but great variation in absolute size and bodily proportions in different environments. Mice from cold stores *c.*15% heavier than animals from houses and shops [868]. Tail a heat-regulating organ, shorter in mice from cold regions than warmer ones.

Overall body length and tail length continue to increase throughout life, albeit slowly in mature

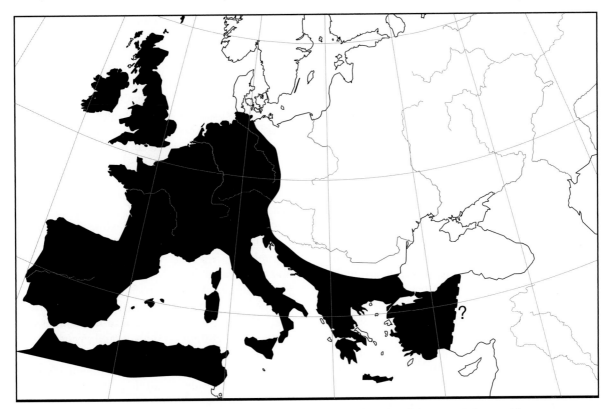

Fig. 5.62 House mouse *Mus domesticus*: European range. Introduced widely around the world.

individuals [365]. Considerable variation in size and weight among like-aged individuals in population, even among older adults [299]. Hindfoot attains almost adult length 2–3 months after birth, a good indication of body size.

VARIATION

Mice from St Kilda (now extinct), described as a distinctive species, subsequently subspecies, *M. m. muralis* [79]; had narrow mesopterygoid fossa on underside of skull. This last trait also occurs in Shetland and Faroes, and may imply common ancestry of these island races [131].

Most populations extremely variable in pelage. White ventral spotting or white belly common in some local groups and island races [80, 336, 1239]. Other colour-variants frequent, e.g. black, black-eyed white, albino, leaden and cinnamon [261, 262, 712], form the basis of extensive 'fancy mouse' and laboratory mouse breeding. Even completely hairless adults described [469].

Skeletal variation (both metrical and non-metrical) common, can be used to characterise local populations [106, 107, 318, 424, 425, 872, 1269, 1425]. Electrophoretic studies of enzyme and protein variation reveal mean heterozygosity per locus of *c*.7% among British mainland mice, island populations about 1/2 this value [115, 119, 125]. Evidence lacking that local colour forms have spread through natural selection, but some

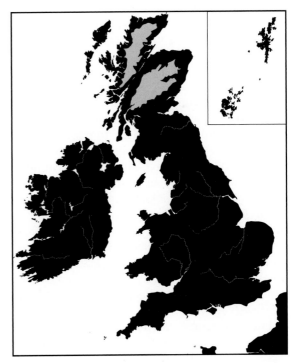

Fig. 5.63 House mouse *Mus domesticus*: range in British Isles.

'electrophoretic' variants certainly adaptive [125, 132, 1179]. Analysis of mtDNA from Irish mice revealed much polymorphism, within and between populations [1236].

DISTRIBUTION

Probably most widespread of all mammals other than humans. Besides original range (Fig. 5.62), from Nepal W to N Africa, W and S Europe, *M. domesticus* has extended its range because of its close association with human habitats, including ships. Now found in the Americas, Australasia and SE Africa. Poor competitor in natural habitats [129, 358], probably restricted in its present distribution by other small mammals (particularly in Africa). Found throughout GB and Ireland, including many small islands (Fig. 5.63).

HISTORY

Present Middle East, Last Glaciation, and associated with earliest agricultural settlements [1397]. Spread through Mediterranean region slowly, reached W Europe (France, Iberia) only in Bronze Age (while *M. musculus* spread through Balkans to N Europe) [302]. Reached GB by Iron Age, when known from Gussage All Saints, Maiden Castle (both Dorset) and Danebury (Hampshire) [1571]. Formed a small (1%) but fairly constant constituent of the Peak District small-mammal fauna in a bird roost cave from pre-Roman times onwards [170].

HABITAT

Original habitat (rock crevices in the desert steppes of Iran and C Asia) may have pre-adapted the house mouse to a commensal lifestyle [302, 1239, 1397]. However, not an obligate commensal, has become established in an enormous range of environmental conditions, living both with and without humans [113]. Worldwide, habitats range from coral atolls in the Pacific to near-Antarctic conditions on S Georgia, Brazilian shanty towns to New Zealand beech wood, Australian wheat fields to Peruvian desert, coal mines to frozen meat stores [113, 374, 433, 798, 811, 868, 1033, 1295].

In British Isles, most commonly found in buildings [688, 949, 1219, 1223, 1321, 1377] where uses structural features such as cavity walls and cracks for nesting and runways [1222]. In urban areas, found in flats, houses, warehouses, restaurants, food processing plants, shops and zoos [799, 982, 1564]. On farmland, commonly found in intensive poultry and pig units, may reach very high densities (Table 5.25). Grain silos and animal feed stores may also attract mice but their presence is unpredictable [982, 1029]. Feral mice opportunistically present in places where there are no wood mice, such as some islands (e.g. Skokholm, May [108, 129, 134, 405], Faray, Lunga [328, 711, 1438]. On mainland, avoids open fields with little cover, but makes limited use of hedges and areas close to buildings [1029, 1219, 1377].

Corn ricks used to provide an important overwintering habitat; house mouse was once the 3rd commonest species on agricultural land (after wood mouse and bank vole) [313, 1323]. Now that combine harvesting has almost completely replaced threshing, rarely trapped in arable fields or hedgerows; of 1536 individual small mammals caught on farmland in Wiltshire and Gloucestershire, only 5 were house mice [1378]. A similar process may have occurred in parts of the USA [775]. Not found in woodland in GB [1383].

SOCIAL ORGANISATION AND BEHAVIOUR

Social organisation: Very flexible according to type of habitat and population density. In most commensal situations, where food is concentrated and home ranges small, lives in territorial, mixed-sex groups comprising a single dominant male, one or several breeding females with their litters, and variable numbers of subordinate males and females, depending on density and availability of alternative sites. Females mate with dominant males, may range over several neighbouring male territories. Resident adults, particularly the dominant male, defend their territory against intruders of both sexes, but success depends on intrusion pressure and complexity of habitat, so that social structuring can range from highly isolated, inbred groups to frequent interchange of individuals between groups (reviews in [26, 69, 193, 689, 942]). In feral situations, home ranges are much greater and territories difficult to defend; adult ranges may overlap extensively and populations may approach random mating [120].

Home range: Varies enormously depending on food, cover and presence of other species [1143]. Where food is concentrated and coincident with cover, ranges can be just a few square metres, for example in cellars or chicken barns [52, 687, 1268, 1321]. By contrast, in open fields ranges are usually >100 m². Radiotelemetry revealed average ranges of 350 m² for males and 150 m² for females in agricultural fields in Queensland [840]. Trapping ranges of 120 m² in Californian hayfields increased to 365 m² where voles were absent [1162].

Communication: Primarily chemical but also acoustic. Acoustic signals (including ultrasound) important in sexual behaviour and maintaining mother–young contact [1314]. Chemical signals involved in all aspects of social behaviour (competitive, sexual, parental), regulate individual female reproductive status according to local social conditions and also used in navigation [202, 203, 693]. Although mainly nocturnal, is capable of visual discrimination between shapes, can use visual landmarks [944].

Table 5.25 House mouse: population density and range in various habitats (number of mice/ 100 m², except in ricks, where mice/100 m³). (Because house mice tend to be highly concentrated in small areas, densities/ha are misleading.)

Average no. mice/100m²	Habitat	Source
12 (max. 20)	Attic (Poland)	[1132]
14–17	Barn (USA)	[1343]
700	Chicken barn (USA)	[1268]
<4.76	Piggery (UK)	[1377]
<1500/100 m³	Ricks (UK)	[1323]
3600–10700/100 m³	Ricks (UK)	[1221]
35.3	Sunflowers (Australia)	[1255]
0.1–0.53	Hay/wheat (USA)	[1343]
0.015–0.25	Grass (island, UK)	[124]
0.6–5	Oldfield (USA)	[322]
1–1.5	Grassland (USA)	[1162]
500	Outdoor enclosure (USA)	[892]
200	Outdoor enclosure (USA)	[1118]
0.033–0.006	Beech woods (New Zealand)	[433]

Scent-marking: Deposits small streaks and spots of urine on all surfaces in its territory; repeatedly marks some sites to form urine posts which are investigated frequently by any mouse using the site [688, 694, 1203].

Urine contains high concentration of major urinary proteins, reveals information on individual identity, sex, health status and food resources of the depositor, female reproductive status or male social status, and genetic relatedness to the investigator [203, 204, 1117, 1573]. Males excrete up to 70 mg protein/ml urine, $c.10\times$ the concentration excreted by females [430, 695]. Each individual excretes unique pattern of proteins [1129, 1202]. Scent-marks used to recognise group members or intruders [699] and to advertise social dominance [517, 694, 698]. Any changes in familiar background marking alert mice to changes in their physical and social environment [688, 690–693]. Females prefer to mate with dominant males that counter-mark any scent-marks from competitor males in their territory [1193, 1194]. Dominant males deposit many more marks than subordinate males or females [337, 690–692]. Major urinary proteins stimulate competitive counter-marking between males [682]. These proteins bind two volatile male semiochemicals, 2-sec-butyl-4,5-dihydrothiazole and 3,4-dehydro-exo-brevicomin, and slowly release these volatiles from scent-marks [1201–1203]. These protein–ligand complexes are also responsible for reproductive priming effects of male urine (reviewed in [879].

Pheromones: Reproductive priming pheromones in male urine accelerate puberty in subadult females, stimulate oestrus in adults and block pregnancy in unfamiliar females mated to another male by preventing implantation (reviewed in [193, 202, 879]). Priming pheromones in the urine of non-breeding females living in groups of 3 or more inhibit puberty and oestrous cycling in other females, while the urine of pregnant or lactating females has the opposite effect (reviewed in [193, 202]). Most effects require direct contact and operate through vomeronasal system. Contact with urine marks in the environment will thus adjust female reproductive physiology according to local competition and opportunities for reproduction [697].

Dispersal: Males more likely to disperse than females, often leaving natal area at 1–2 months of age. Usually little movement ($c.5\%$) between breeding groups, although >20% of both males and females breed at different site to their birthplace [123].

Aggressive behaviour: Mutual and immediate retreat is the usual response when 2 males meet on strange territory [166]. At subsequent encounters, one mouse may hold its ground and 'freeze'; when the other retreats, makes aggressive moves towards it. However, considerable differences in aggressiveness between individuals, are more aggressive within their scent-marked home area [531, 689, 1584]. Fighting frequent when dominant territory-holding males meet, can lead to serious wounding, but established neighbours appear to avoid such encounters [690, 696, 943]. Females may be highly aggressive in defence of their nest sites [297, 689]. While males generally aim their attacks to the rump or shoulders of their opponent, females are more precipitate and attack the ventral surface [467]. Mice living ferally on Isle of May much less aggressive than those on the mainland [532].

Activity: Mainly nocturnal, but with periods of short-term activity (1–4 h) related to feeding and digestion, particularly after dusk and before dawn. Out of doors, mice begin to be caught in traps within the first 2 h of darkness. It is rare for mice to be caught by day, except in very dense populations. Both excess food and light (e.g. moonlit nights) reduce trapping success, presumably by restricting activity.

Movement: Distances of 400 m often travelled by feral animals, and individuals have been recorded moving >1 km in a single night. Commensal mice tend to centre their activity indoors, often around a single food source such as a grain hopper [27, 1219, 1223, 1143, 1183, 1377]. Movement away from fields and hedges into buildings in late autumn and winter; less marked reverse movement in spring. These movements are part of the characteristic tendency of the species to move in search of favourable conditions [761, 890, 1221, 1343]. Caged wild mice with exercise wheels may achieve 60 000 revolutions in one night (*c*.20 km).

Burrow system: Ranges from a simple 2–3 cm diameter tunnel with one or more chambers, to a complex system with several exits and chambers (*c*.10 cm in diameter), often lined with bedding material. Mice are efficient tunnellers in soft earth but readily use preformed 'tunnels' in the structure and fittings of buildings, gnawing through wood, soft plastics and wires to gain access; can enter through gaps as narrow as 1 cm.

Nests: Vary from simple pallet to enclosed sphere, made from any convenient material. Genetic differences between females in complexity of nest. Insulation of nest crucial to survival of young [928, 1546].

General: Can jump up to 60 cm and swim capably, though reluctant to enter water. Behaviour and its various components reviewed in [166, 942]. Differences in behaviour between wild and laboratory mice seem to be largely quantitative but can have important consequences for social relationships [1313]; some laboratory strains show little or no aggression [1067].

FEEDING

Omnivorous [808, 1239], though cereal grains preferred to low-carbohydrate foods [683]. Diffuse, sporadic feeders, visiting many feeding points [297]. In commensal habitats most foods are taken, particularly stored products, livestock feed and human foods [982, 1485]. Insects a substantial part of diet for wild-living island populations [108, 129]; in fields, are supplemented with crop and wild grass seeds, and green plant material [150, 672, 1530]. Can survive without drinking free water unless they are on a high-protein or high-fibre diet [423]. Daily energy demands in the wild 1.76–4.77 kJ/g [1155].

BREEDING

Litters of 5–8 are born at about monthly intervals throughout the year (indoors) or during the summer months (outdoors). Length of oestrous cycle 4–5 days. Gestation 19–20 days (extended during lactation). Mean litter size 6.5–7.5, normal range 5–8. Duration of lactation *c*.23 days [817].

Seasonality: Can breed throughout the year, indoors and outdoors, when environmental conditions are stable [73, 131, 1113, 1118, 1223, 1343, 1296]. In GB, feral populations breed only during the summer months, end March–end September. Season probably controlled mainly by temperature change, although food availability (including specific nutrients) may be important [322]; house mouse unusual in being able to breed in total darkness [193].

Mating: Sexually mature at 5–6 weeks after birth. Copulation leaves a vaginal plug which persists for 18–24 h [1479, 1531]. Little post-implantation loss, except of whole litters [85]. Oestrous cycle normally 4–5 days, up to 13 days in some individuals, others in crowded populations suppress cycling in response to pheromonal cues [202]. Postpartum oestrus within 24 h, young so conceived may not be born for up to 36 days due to delayed implantation. However, an average of 1 litter a month is normal under laboratory conditions. Females have a breeding span of 6–12 months; males *c*.18 months. The mean lifetime production of young per fertile female is *c*.40 [1480].

Litter size: Varies seasonally (early litters smaller than later ones) and in different habitats [1112, 1480]: average 5.2 in houses, 5.8 in ricks and 6.2 in cold stores [868]. Differences arise partly because numbers of ova shed increase with maternal size, but this correlation disappears in large island mice, suggesting that litter size is an adaptive character in these populations [85, 1200]. To wean a litter of 7 pups requires *c*.100 ml milk (equivalent to 1100 kJ) over a 3-week period [818].

Communal nesting: Unlike most other mammals, females in the same breeding group usually pool their litters in communal nests and nurse pups indiscriminately. Laboratory tests show that 2 females sharing are able to rear more offspring than when rearing their offspring alone [815, 816] and females prefer to share with relatives [953, 1536]. However, fewer offspring reared successfully when 3 or more females share nest [1327] and oestrous cycling is inhibited in subordinate females under such crowded conditions [202].

Sex ratio: *c*.1:1 in young animals. Proportion of mature females often increases at higher densities, possibly because of increased emigration and aggression between males [1113, 1221]. Conversely, males tend to predominate in temporary populations [1068, 1183, 1221, 1223].

Young: Born naked, blind, bright pink, weighing *c*.1.5 g. At 4 days external ears unfold; at 5–7 days, skin pigmentation becomes visible; by 8–10 days the hair is half-grown; eyes open at 13–14 days though not fully developed until 4 weeks [1314]. Start to explore outside the nest and take solid food from 17 days old, when fur full-grown and incisor teeth erupted. Fully weaned at 23 days, weight *c*.10.5 g [817].

POPULATION
Densities: See Table 5.24. British pre-breeding population estimated at *c*.5 million [624], but this is not reliable due to scarcity of data. Localised densities can be extremely high, particularly in intensive farming systems such as piggeries (densities equivalent to 476/ha reported [1377] and battery chicken barns (70 000/ha [1268] or more); however, mice often use all 3 dimensions in their environment, a factor often ignored in calculations of density per hectare. Densities much lower in dairy and arable farm buildings, domestic and business premises. Feral-living island populations usually <60/ha [124], and in hedgerows and arable fields typically <1/ha [1209, 1378]. Corn ricks used to hold high densities, up to 15/m^3 [1323].

Populations can fluctuate dramatically [115]; island populations increase *c*.8-fold during breeding season [108]. Density-dependent controls on reproduction [298] clearly sometimes overridden. 'Plagues' occur almost exclusively where little interspecific competition, usually after uncommon climatic conditions (see under Breeding, above [375, 398, 1070, 1296]).

Population structure: Commensal populations have a much higher proportion of older animals than feral-living ones [113, 1112]. Populations living in a physically limited area may have a rather rigid structure: those in small grain storage buildings in Canada each consisted of *c*.10 weaned mice of which 4–7 were reproductively active, only 1–2 being males; population size was controlled by excluding immigrants and exporting excess young [25]. However, a proportion of emigrants establish themselves elsewhere. Many studies of the social and age structure of house mice, both in large pens and under natural conditions [112, 120, 297, 892].

Survival: Laboratory mice commonly live >2 years, but wild-living mice rarely survive 2 winters. Mean life expectancy of wild mice at birth may be as little as 100 days [122]. Much variation in recapture rates in live-trapping studies; in farm buildings, 17–59% were recaptured after 6 weeks [1223, 1377], but on the Isle of Faray, Orkney, 22–60% of marked animals recaptured after 6-month interval over summer, but only 4–13% after a 6-month interval over winter [134]. On Skokholm winter survival is proportional to spring temperatures, with least winter mortality on cliffs [108].

RELATIONSHIPS WITH OTHER SPECIES
Main competitor in indoor habitats is common rat, which is avoided, particularly since rats will predate mice. Can gain access to more confined spaces than rat, which prefers more open areas such as barns and sewers. Wood mouse likely to be principal competitor in all outdoor habitats in GB, although evidence of an actual effect is circumstantial: captures of house mice outdoors, around buildings correlated negatively with captures of wood mice [1383]. Competition with wood mouse believed [129] responsible for extinction of house mouse on St Kilda after

humans left. Absence from woodland in GB assumed due to competitive exclusion by wood mouse [1383].

MORTALITY

Commensal populations are greatly affected by control measures, usually rodenticide baits and traps. Predation not a significant source of mortality, except when plagues occur [494]. No house mice in the prey of domestic cats in the Bristol area [57]. Rats probably more important predators than conventional ones such as barn owls or small carnivores [315]. Greatest hazard is probably cold [130, 765, 1107]; a drop in temperature may be fatal, particularly to an ageing animal [94]. Some low-temperature mortality is selective, producing genetic changes in exposed populations [72, 124, 133]. Direct evidence of starvation lacking except at very high densities [1068, 1069], but food shortage presumably a factor increasing the risk of death during cold. Although disease, most importantly ectromelia causing gangrene, frequently kills laboratory mice, the only reports of epidemic disease in wild mice are in plague populations [322, 1071, 1107, 1141]. Infertility and uterine oedema found in several adult females infected with harvest mites *Neotrombicula autumnalis* on Skokholm, in Wales [94]. Wild mice have very low titres of bacterial and viral antibodies.

PARASITES

Ectoparasites: Fleas *Leptopsylla segnis* and *Nosopsyllus londiniensis* specific to this species and rats, but infrequently recorded. *Ctenophthalmus nobilis* also regular and *Nosopsyllus fasciatus* recorded. Sucking louse *Polyplax serrata* recorded, as well as rat louse *P. spinosula*. Mites *Laelaps agilis*, *Myobia musculi* and *Neotrombicula autumnalis* are regular. Another 7 species reported on mice or their nesting materials from the Outer Hebrides [668].

Endoparasites: Worldwide, the most frequently recorded endoparasites are *Syphacia obvelata, Taenia taeniformis, Aspiculuris tetraptera, Hymenolepis diminuta* and *Trichuris muris* [1381]. An additional 14 species have been recorded from wild house mice in the UK [1381, 241, 242]: *Leishmania ictiohaemorrhagica, Giardia muris, Spironucleus muris, Trichomonas muris, Entamoeba muris, Eimeria falciformis, Eimeria pragensis, Pneumocystis carini, Catenotaenia pusilla, Hymenolepis stramineea, Heligmosomoides polygyrus, Syphacia stoma, Cryptosporidium parvum, Cryptosporidium muris*. Prevalences are generally <10%, but much higher for *T. muris* (74.4% [91]) and *S. obvelata* (41% [1101]). Natural infections in laboratory mice have been reviewed in [290, 1100].

Worldwide, human cases of rickettsial pox, rat-bite fever, tularaemia and murine and scrub typhus have been linked with house mice, which can also carry *Leptospira* [1001, 1456]. Favus, a skin disease caused by the fungus *Achorion quickeanum*, can be contracted through close contact with infected mice. Infections with enteric bacteria *Yersinia* spp. detected [634].

RELATIONS WITH HUMANS

Among the most widespread vertebrate pests [982], causing extensive damage, particularly to stored food products, through gnawing and contamination with droppings and urine. Only eats *c*.4 g food/day, but feeding habits very wasteful; more than 10% of the grain in corn ricks may be fragmented by mice and unsuitable for milling [1321]. Moreover, produces 50 or more droppings per day, difficult to remove economically from stored foods [499], and, together with extensive urine marking, present an important hygiene problem. Can cause significant damage to building structures, particularly by gnawing through electric cables and insulation material. In 1972, estimated that 9% of buildings in London infested by house mice [1185].

Active research into control began in World War II, on realisation that rat-control techniques were not reducing mouse depredations on stockpiled foodstuffs. Work at the Bureau of Animal Population, Oxford [1321] established basic principles and practices of control [982, 1217], stimulated studies of the biology and behaviour of wild house mice [109, 110, 114, 297].

Most control involves poisoning. Use of anticoagulant poisons seriously curbed by spread of inherited resistance to warfarin [1218]. Since early 1980s, mice in London and Birmingham, dubbed 'supermice' by the media, have developed behavioural resistance (have learned to avoid conventional rodenticide baits and traps), therefore increasingly difficult to control. Food preference is for low-carbohydrate foods such as cheese, chicken and tuna fish; avoids cereal-based products; is both a learnt and an inherited response [681]. Attempts to frighten mice by ultrasonic or electromagnetic waves have failed [36, 534].

A 'mouse fancy' was established many centuries ago in China and Japan. Some Japanese fancy mice were brought to Europe by British traders in the mid-19th century. A national Mouse Club was established in GB in 1895, and mouse shows are still held. The two main groups of fancy mice are Self (with coats of a single colour: black, fawn, silver, champagne, etc.) and Marked (dutch, tan, variegated, etc.); *c*.700 combinations recognised [270].

As early as 1664, Robert Hooke used a mouse to study the effects of increased air pressure. William Harvey employed mice in his anatomical studies. However, the modern history of laboratory mouse breeding started in 1907 when a Harvard student, C.C. Little, began to study the inheritance of coat colour under the supervision of W.E. Castle [116, 1051]. Is the most widely used species in scientific research and testing; 1.5 million laboratory mice were used in scientific procedures in the UK during 1996 [729]. Studies of mtDNA show that laboratory and fancy mice are *Mus domesticus*, although they also contain traits apparently derived from other *Mus* species.

LITERATURE
Entertaining account of studies of house mouse in grain stores [297]. Comprehensive reference works [23, 114, 453, 535]. General accounts with special reference to life history, social and population structures [69, 110, 115, 121, 127, 1239]. An introduction to fancy mice [270] and to housing mice in captivity [729]; characteristics of different laboratory strains [426]; reviews of control techniques [982] and of mouse traps [351].

AUTHORS
R.J. Berry, F.H. Tattersall & J. Hurst

GENUS *Rattus*

A mostly Asian genus of 66 species of rats, several of which are important commensal pests, especially common rat *R. norvegicus* and ship rat *R. rattus* (found worldwide, including British Isles), and *R. exulans* in Pacific. Larger, more robust, than *Mus*, cusps on molars tending to merge into cross-ridges, resembling, but less extreme, various gerbils Gerbillinae. Formerly called *Epimys*. Genetically, a basal group within Murinae, not especially close to *Mus*, but related to other SE Asian genera, e.g. *Maxomys*, *Niviventer* [1341].

British species difficult to distinguish reliably (see text), and colour misleading (hence names black rat, brown rat best avoided).

Common rat *Rattus norvegicus*
Mus norvegicus Berkenhout, 1769; GB.
Mus decumanus Pallas, 1779; Europe.
Mus hibernicus Thompson, 1837; Rathfriland, Co. Down, Ireland.

Brown rat, Norway rat, sewer rat.

RECOGNITION
Large size, relatively pointed muzzle and long scaly tail (a little shorter than head and body length) preclude confusion with mice, voles and squirrels. Hindfeet of young much broader and a little longer than those of adult mice (>27 mm as opposed to 22–25 mm for *Apodemus*), tail relatively much thicker. Distinguished from ship rat by relatively smaller eyes and smaller ears which are finely furred compared with the almost hairless ears of ship rat (Plate 2); tail relatively shorter and thicker than that of ship rat and usually dark above and pale beneath, against the ship rat's uniformly dark tail. In water easily confused with water vole but muzzle more pointed, ears more prominent and tail longer.

Skull (Fig. 5.64): Very similar to that of ship rat but somewhat heavier and more angular; supraorbital ridges tend to be parallel over cranium (curved in ship rat). Distinguishable from water vole by rooted, tuberculate molars (Fig. 5.47) and from squirrel by only 3 cheek-teeth in each row and large infraorbital foramen (Fig. 5.1).

Footprints: 4 toes on forefeet, 5 on hind; in normal walking or trotting, impression of forefoot always overprinted by hindfoot. Tracks similar to mice, but much larger. Cannot be distinguished from ship rat and difficult to separate from water vole. Squirrel footprints show all toes pointing forward and large claws. Prints sometimes seen clearly in soft mud and snow, frequently accompanied by tail swipes, which are also apparent in dusty environments such as grain stores.

Faeces: Produces *c*.40 pellets a day; coarse

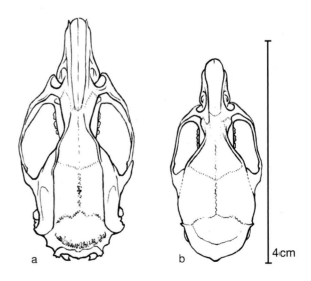

Fig. 5.64 Skulls of (a) common rat and (b) ship rat from above; the braincase is parallel-sided in the common rat, rounded in the ship rat.

Fig. 5.65 Common rat; young (just weaned), looking rather like a mouse, but betrayed by its large bulky hindfeet; hindfeet in rodents gain adult size earlier than other parts of their anatomy *(photo P. Morris)*.

textured, average 12 mm long, often tapering to a point at one or both ends; frequently deposited in groups (ship rat droppings are rather thinner, usually have rounded ends and tend to be deposited singly; those of water voles smaller, with rounded end and smooth texture). Faeces of the 2 rat species can be distinguished by microscopic examination of hairs in the droppings [1462].

Burrows: Generally 6–9 cm in diameter, often on sloping ground, banks or sides of ditches, or beneath cover such as flat stones, logs or tree roots. Earth dug from burrow remains in heap close to entrance.

Runs: May show as slight linear depressions in grass or other low vegetation or as well-worn trails of bare, trampled earth. May be 5–10 cm wide, continuous (rabbit runs discontinuous, showing as series of depressions in grass). Runs in buildings show as dark, greasy smears on wood or brickwork. To practised eye, runs often main clue to presence of this secretive species.

Damage: Common in rat-infested areas; rats gnaw many materials (including foam insulation, electric cables and some grades of aluminium) to gain access to food and harbourage and not to keep their continually growing incisors short as some believe. Main cause of incisor wear is grinding them together to keep them sharp [350].

DESCRIPTION

Pelage: Fur of adults somewhat shaggy, grey-brown above and pale grey beneath (Plate 2), but melanics common in some populations. May have white blaze or stripe mid-ventrally. Fur of juveniles from weaning to *c*.3 months (<100 g body weight) shorter, sleeker and greyer than adults (Fig. 5.65). Clear moult patterns sometimes evident in animals reaching maturity. Sparse fur on tail (skin also) dark dorsally and pale ventrally. No sexual difference in pelage.

Nipples: 6 pairs; 3 axillary, 3 abdominal.

Chromosomes: 2n = 42, FNa = 62 [1589].

MEASUREMENTS

Head and body *c*.110 mm at weaning, increasing to 280 mm or more (see Table 5.20). Condylobasal length of skull up to 54 mm in large adults. Weight from 40 g at weaning to 600 g; largest recorded 794 g [882]. Males slightly larger than females. Growth occurs throughout normal lifespan of 1–2 years.

VARIATION

Little variation over vast geographical range (Fig. 5.66). Melanics comprise 1–2% of some populations, e.g. in London [1491]. Albinism rare in wild; variety of laboratory and fancy rats (albino, hooded, etc.) very wide.

DISTRIBUTION

In urban areas throughout most of world, although restricted to coastal areas and inland settlements along rivers in subtropical and tropical Africa, Asia and S America (Fig. 5.66). In N America, still extending range N into parts of

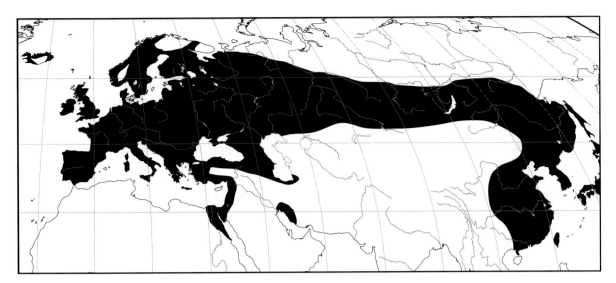

Fig. 5.66 Common rat *Rattus norvegicus*: Palaearctic range, but also introduced worldwide, especially in cooler climates.

Canada. In cultivated land and away from human habitation, only in temperate regions and tropical islands where few or no indigenous competitors. Found throughout British Isles except in most exposed mountain regions and a few of smaller offshore islands (present on majority of small islands) [1002]. Perhaps more common in E, especially E–SE England, where extensive cereal growing occurs (Fig. 5.67).

HISTORY
Probably originated in steppes of C Asia; spread across Europe and into British Isles during 18th century (largely replacing ship rat which present since Roman times). Exact date of introduction to GB uncertain, thought to have been around 1720 [1571] in shipping from Russia. Thereafter spread rapidly, reaching Scotland before 1754. (Arrived in Norway 1762; assumption, perpetuated in specific name *norvegicus*, that came to GB from there is erroneous.) Arrived in N America *c.*1740. Has not replaced ship rat everywhere (e.g. California and some other states in USA). Is perhaps being replaced in urban areas of S Asia by lesser bandicoot rat, *Bandicota bengalensis* [912]. Arrived New Zealand before ship rat, was abundant and widespread, but now less widespread than ship rat, displaced by it, perhaps in combination with stoat predation [798].

HABITAT
Highly adaptable and versatile but generally limited to habitats where competing species are few or absent or where food is augmented by human activity. Typically found associated with farm buildings, refuse tips, sewers, urban waterways and warehouses, but occurs in

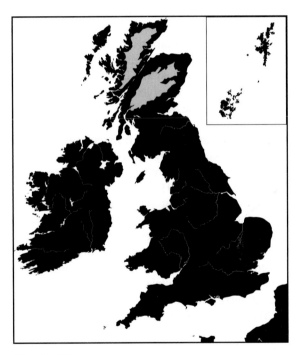

Fig. 5.67 Common rat *Rattus norvegicus*: range in British Isles.

hedgerows and ditches around cereals, outdoor pig units, pheasant feeders and cover crops such as kale. Also favours field margins around root crops such as sugar beet, stubble, turnips, swedes. Prefers areas with dense groundcover close to water. Populations independent of humans occur in many coastal habitats, particularly salt marshes; on many islands (e.g. Isle of Man, Rum, Lundy), occupy grassland as well as all types of coastline. Attempts to eradicate rats from some offshore islands (e.g. Lundy, Canna, Ailsa Craig) to protect seabird colonies.

when crop sold. Population may then disperse entirely, only to return after next harvest [700]. Alternatively, intensive livestock units may provide constant food and harbourage all year round, enabling numbers to remain more stable [221]. Colonies along field margins subject to most disruption due to harvesting, ploughing and hedge-trimming; timing of such events varies with crop and weather conditions. Despite these events, such colonies can survive, expand throughout winter, by utilising food distributed for game birds. Prolonged severe weather more likely to affect rats living entirely outdoors than those regularly venturing inside buildings.

Sex ratio: In favourable environments, such as farm buildings, tends to be slightly biased towards females; of 2133 trapped on 24 farms in S England, 53.3% were female [1164]. However, on individual farms, particularly with small populations, there may be a heavy bias towards one sex.

Age determination: Broadly, body weight increases with age, but relationship found in laboratory studies seldom applies to free-living animals, which suffer varying food availability and quality. Age at death can be determined from eye-lens weight [618], enabling age structures of populations to be determined retrospectively.

Age structure: Variable, depending on local conditions of resource availability and population density. Thus, in rapidly growing populations, >70% may be less than 8 weeks old, while in stable populations the same percentage may be mature adults (>16 weeks old). Breeding may be continuous in both states, lower presence of juveniles in stable populations results from higher juvenile mortality or dispersal of young adults.

Survival: Mortality of young in nest and just after emergence in saturated populations thought to be 99% per annum. Few rats therefore live >1 year.

MORTALITY

Predation: Young rats susceptible to most predators, but aggressive nature of large rats may deter smaller predators, such as weasels and owls; largest taken by barn owls weighed only 164 g [1040]. Established populations less vulnerable to predation than rats on the move. Cats may prevent invasion of farm buildings by rats but cannot eliminate an established population [376], possibly because they too will not often take rats of >200 g [244]. Highest published incidence in fox stomachs was 13% [886]. Of 11 farmland rats that were radio-tracked, 2 died from poisoning, 2 crushed by motor vehicles, 5 killed by predators

(fox, stoat, cat), 2 died from unknown causes [1393]. Rats with the smallest ranges (<0.1 ha) are most likely to be poisoned and those with large ranges (*c.*1 ha) to be taken by predators [289].

Persecution: Almost universally hated and reviled by humans in western countries, but tolerated in the East. Greatest cause of mortality in W likely to be deliberate poisoning, which can lead to the extinction of entire populations in a few weeks or less. Stories of rats jumping at people's throats are exaggerated misinterpretations. Cornered rats jump to escape, not to attack.

Disease: Infections with some serotypes of *Salmonella* sometimes fatal; baits containing cultures of the bacterium were used to control rat populations. Unfortunately, resistance developed quickly and infection then transmitted back to humans. Infection with *Mycoplasma pulmonis* implicated in respiratory disease and middle ear disease, the latter causing loss of balance and tendency to keep turning in circles.

PARASITES AND PATHOGENS

Fleas: Primary host for *Nosopsyllus fasciatus* (predominant species), *Xenopsylla cheopis*, *Ctenophthalmus nobilis nobilis* and *C. n. vulgaris*. Occasional reports of cat, dog and mole fleas, presumably by cross-infection with adults from primary host.

Ticks: *Ixodes* spp. sometimes found; heavy infestations of concern because ticks carry spirochaete responsible for Lyme disease in humans [1319].

Sucking lice: *Polyplax spinosula* found on 38% (n = 510) of rats from farmsteads in England and Wales [1525].

Mites: Burrowing mites *Notoedres notoedres*, *N. muris* and surface-dwelling mites *Myobia musculi*, *Mycoptes musculinus* frequent.

Helminths: *Syphacia muris* common (67%, n = 215), *Nippostrongylus brasiliensis*, *Capillaria* spp. and *Hymenolepis diminuta* were found in, respectively, 23%, 23% and 22% of rats [1525].

Others: Leptospirosis possibly the most common disease transmissible to humans from rats in GB. Previously reported that 50–70% of rats infected, most recent study (1991–1993) found only 14% (n = 259) infected with *Leptospira* spp. [1526], but only 1/2 of those carried the *icterohaemorrhagiae* serovar, the type considered responsible for Weil's disease. *Salmonella*, gut parasite which causes food poisoning in humans, common, but recent survey of farm rats failed to detect it [1525]. Other parasites carried by rats in GB, potentially causing human disease, are *Cryptosporidium parvum* (cryptosporidiosis), *Toxoplasma gondii* (toxoplasmosis), *Coxiella burnetii* (Q fever) and hantavirus.

Common rats transmit plague and typhus elsewhere in the world, but because they usually live outside rather than inside houses, probably less important vectors than ship rats.

RELATIONS WITH HUMANS

Although a recent companion, its adaptability and generalist habits enable it to thrive close to human settlements worldwide. Noted as a pest more of stored foodstuffs than standing crops. Losses result primarily from contamination with excreta and hairs rather than through consumption: 10 rats produce 146 000 droppings and 54 l of urine in a year [985]. In GB, Prevention of Damage by Pests Act 1949 requires notification of local authority of substantial numbers of rats. Very important as vector of some human diseases, particularly leptospirosis, to people who risk contact with contaminated water. In N America, concern that sylvatic plague could be transmitted to rats and then to humans has led to vigorous control campaign [157]. Also an important as predator of 'desirable' wildlife, especially seabirds and their eggs on islands [136].

Earliest attempts to control common rats used non-specific, fast-acting poisons, such as arsenious oxide, red squill and later (*c.*1930) zinc phosphide; none of these used today in GB, were considered inhumane or too dangerous, subsequently withdrawn or use restricted. Moreover, often produced symptoms before lethal dose had been ingested, so rats refused to eat any more (conditioned taste aversion). Since *c.*1950, chemical control has used anticoagulant baits, which interfere with production of clotting factors, resulting in fatal haemorrhage. Anticoagulants produce symptoms of poisoning ≥ 2 days, by which time a lethal dose has been ingested and bait shyness (aversion) does not affect the outcome. Treatments with such baits can eradicate an entire population in <3 weeks, if all consume bait without too much delay. However, some populations became resistant, via an inherited trait, to the earliest anticoagulant, warfarin. Subsequently, more potent versions, difenacoum and bromadiolone, were developed [587], but some populations again developed some resistance [945]. The most potent anticoagulants, brodifacoum and flocoumafen, currently effective, but toxicity to other animals has led to restrictions on their use. Continued, uncontrolled use of anticoagulants may result in widespread appearance of resistant rats, particularly as alternative rodenticides unavailable or difficult to use. Conversely, resistant rats appear to be less fit than susceptibles, requiring additional vitamin K in order to maintain normal blood clotting [533]. Hence, banning the use of anticoagulant formulations, if practicable, should lead to resistant strains dying out.

Irrespective of anticoagulant resistance, most rats survive poison treatments because they eat little or no bait [1165]. Improved productivity from modern farming methods, yielding abundant foods for rats (cereals and animal feedstuffs), results in baits being ignored. Also, bait containers, traps and other equipment employed to control rats may be avoided through 'new object' reaction; human odour on those objects may also discourage rats [1396]. Consequently, troublesome populations difficult to control, and techniques used may inadvertently put other wildlife at increased risk of injury or death. Non-lethal means of reducing rat numbers likely to be successful only in the long term, best aimed at lowering carrying capacity of habitat by denying rats access to food and cover. Proofing of buildings and barriers around commodities often advocated, rarely considered cost-effective. Repellents, whether chemical, ultrasonic or electromagnetic, not so far reliably effective.

On the credit side, has served for many decades as a laboratory animal. Laboratory rats are docile, respond to regular handling. Captive wild rats, even if hand-reared from very young, become jumpy and difficult to handle at an early age.

LITERATURE
Sound popular account [1451]; personal account [625]; exceptionally well-referenced account with emphasis on control [982]; broad account of most rodent pests and their control throughout the world [209].

AUTHORS
R.J. Quy & D.W. Macdonald

Ship rat *Rattus rattus*
Mus rattus Linnaeus, 1758; Sweden.
Mus alexandrinus Desmarest, 1819; Egypt.
Mus frugivorus Rafinesque, 1814; Sicily.

Black rat, roof rat, house rat, alexandrine rat.

RECOGNITION
Very similar to common rat, but relatively larger eyes and ears, and longer, thinner, unicoloured tail distinguish it at close quarters (Plate 2). In the hand, ears seen to be thinner, almost hairless

(common rat has rather furry ears). Guard hairs on back and flanks, also vibrissae, proportionately very much longer than common rat, giving somewhat spiky appearance when seen against a light background. Black fur not diagnostic: many ship rats are brown, and a proportion of common rats are black.

Skull: Very similar to that of common rat; may be distinguished by rounded, flask-shaped, outline of cranium and smaller, lighter construction (Fig. 5.64). Cusps on molars teeth more distinct, less merged into transverse ridges, than common rat, but difficult to distinguish, confused by wear.

FIELD SIGNS
Footprints: Indistinguishable from common rat.

Faeces: Average *c*.9 mm long, tend to be smaller than common rat, having rounded rather than pointed ends. In large samples (>50), droppings of the 2 species can be distinguished with 95% confidence on the basis of the relationship between length (l) and diameter (d), those of ship rat being proportionately thinner. If d/l 0.31–0.37, likely to be ship rat; if d/l 0.42–0.46, common rat [317].

Burrows: Similar to those of common rat, made very occasionally.

Runs: Greasy smears develop in places where rats pass frequently. Loop smears (i.e. those left on vertical surfaces beneath joists or other obstructions where rats pass) broken rather than continuous as with common rat. This characteristic appears diagnostic.

DESCRIPTION
Pelage typically grey-brown above, pale grey beneath, but may be completely black, or grey-brown above and creamy white beneath. In the last colour form there is usually a sharp demarcation between the belly and flanks, whereas in other colour forms gradation occurs. Numerous long guard hairs on flanks and dorsum. Skin and bristles on tail uniformly dark grey to black.

Nipples: Variable but often 5 pairs; 2 pairs axillary, 3 pairs abdominal.

Chromosomes: 2n = 38, Fna = 58 [1589]. (A form with 2n = 42 in SE Asia should probably be considered specifically distinct, as *R. diardii*.)

RELATIONSHIPS
Very closely related species, formerly classed as subspecies of *R. rattus*, also associate with humans in SE Asia, e.g. *R. argentiventer* (rice fields), *R. tiomanicus* (oil palms), *R. diardii* and *R. tanezumi* (urban areas).

MEASUREMENTS
Growth can continue throughout life; head and body of old individuals may reach 240 mm and tail up to 260 mm. Weight may reach 280 g but adults usually weigh 150–200 g. Males generally larger than females.

VARIATION
Pelage colour polymorphic in most populations, with 3 forms: all black (*rattus* type), brown with grey belly (*alexandrinus* type) and brown with creamy white belly (*frugivorus* type). Frequencies vary geographically and in different habitats; black usually dominant in N and urban areas, others in S and rural areas, do not constitute geographically definable subspecies.

In London in 1941–1943, 56% were black, 24% white-bellied, 18% grey-bellied and 2% intermediate [1492], but proportions fluctuate.

DISTRIBUTION
In urban areas throughout tropics and subtropics, extending to many small villages and even remote farms, but does not live away from buildings except on islands where there are few or no indigenous competitors, e.g. in Caribbean and Pacific. Present in many towns in temperate regions, but tends to be restricted to ports in cooler temperate areas (Fig. 5.69).

Formerly widespread in GB but now largely replaced by common rat. Most mainland records refer to small, transient groups accidentally introduced in merchandise [1454]. Suspected that there may be ship rats along both banks of the Thames, and there is a long-standing population at Tilbury [983].

Not known whether the species still exists on Alderney and Sark. Recorded on Lundy I., Bristol Channel, in the 1990s [1318] but both it and common rat eradicated by 2005 because of their predation on seabird eggs. Larger population flourishes on Shiant Is., Hebrides, where up to 1000 animals were estimated on the 2 islands [791]. On Lambay I., off Dublin, ship rat coexists with common rat [105, 1482]. May also be present further S, in Wexford and Waterford [105]. Fragility of the species in GB emphasised by most recent estimate of total population at 1300 animals [624].

HISTORY
Probably one of the first mammals to associate with early humans. May have spread from India to Egypt in the 4th century BC and thence along trade routes into Europe, reaching GB during

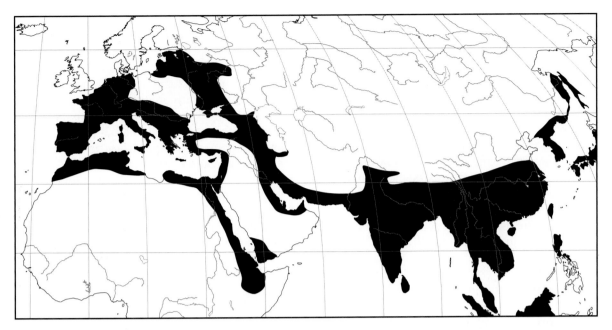

Fig. 5.69 Ship rat *Rattus rattus*: Palaearctic and Oriental range, but also introduced worldwide, especially in warmer climates.

Roman times [39]. In other parts of the world, e.g. C Africa, has spread during 20th century, following increasing urbanisation.

In GB, well-stratified remains recorded in Roman sites at London, York and Wroxeter, dated 3rd–5th centuries ad [39]. Possibly died out during Saxon times, present again by 10th century (e.g. York [1088, 1571]). Probably widespread in human habitation in GB and Ireland until gradually replaced by common rat, beginning in 18th century. By 1956, restricted to major ports, a few inland towns and some small islands [101]; by 1961 only in a few seaports [102]. Not recorded in Manchester since 1978, Bristol since 1980, Liverpool, Glasgow and Aberdeen since 1983. Disappearance has often coincided with demolition of dockside seed or flour mills, where rats were difficult to control with rodenticides. Elsewhere contraction has been due to habit of living only within buildings, making it more vulnerable to control measures than the common rat.

HABITAT

In GB, mainly restricted to dockside warehouses, food-processing plants, etc., but has also occurred in supermarkets, restaurants and modern department stores. Does not live out of doors in towns. Favours buildings with cavity walls, wall panelling and false ceilings where it can move unseen. Occupies rocks and cliffs on Shiants, Lundy (formerly) and Channel Islands where also said to live in trees [51]. Commonly nests in trees in tropical environments.

SOCIAL ORGANISATION AND BEHAVIOUR

Social organisation: Lives in groups each dominated by a male; more or less linear male hierarchy but less well-defined female hierarchy. Intruders attacked and usually driven off but may be accepted if persistent [400].

Scent-marking: Observed to rub cheeks and ventral surface on branches [400].

Aggressive behaviour: Agonistic encounters within groups are common, particularly after

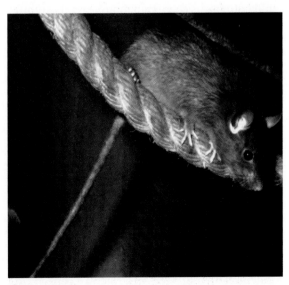

Fig. 5.70 Ship rat: the longer tail and smaller size facilitate climbing (*photo P. Morris*).

feeding. Attacks more often initiated by females than males; males inhibited from attacking females. Encounters end with appeasement or flight, physical injury rare. Most common form of attack termed 'broadsiding' in which one rat approaches another, turning sideways and pushing its opponent with hindquarters; opponent may respond with similar action. Fighting may also involve rolling and wrestling, leaping on to an opponent and 'boxing', as in common rat. Most essential component of appeasement involves mouth-to-mouth contact [400].

Activity: Predominantly nocturnal but may become active in daylight in undisturbed habitats or when food is scarce.

Movement: Similar to common rat but tends to move much more rapidly. Typically, sprints along ledges, overhead pipes or beams, then pauses motionless at a vantage point before sprinting again. Extremely agile climber (Fig. 5.70); able to cope equally with thin wire (vertical or horizontal), brickwork and vertical pipes, provided they are sited against a wall. Can swim, but unlike common rat does not often enter water voluntarily.

Senses: Similar to common rat but sight better. Reacts less strongly to unfamiliar objects than common rats and may enter traps on first night of setting.

FEEDING
Omnivorous, but often more vegetarian than common rats and notably partial to fruit [1561]. Most agricultural crops – particularly cereals – are eaten, and in the tropics sugar cane, coconuts, cocoa and even oranges and coffee berries. On Lundy, stomachs contained more vegetable matter and fewer animal remains than those of common rat.

BREEDING
Females sexually mature at c.90g. Average litter size 6.9 on shore, 7.5 on ships in Port of London [1492]. Number of embryos correlated with body weight of female. Intrauterine mortality 25% in London. Most breeding in London from mid March to mid November. Litter rate c.3–5 per year. Gestation period 21 days [780], but 23–29 days for lactating females [400].

POPULATION
Densities vary greatly with environment. In scrubland, Cyprus, 5–12/ha recorded [1493]; in a residential area of Freetown, Sierra Leone, 52/ha [881]. Turnover is fast; annual mortality c.91–97% [312].

MORTALITY
In urban situations, domestic cat probably chief predator, but in agricultural and natural environments outside British Isles ship rats taken by most mammalian, avian and reptilian predators. Frequently said that common rats will fight with and kill ship rats, and this has been demonstrated in confined colonies [70]. However, they are sympatric over much of their range (as they were on Lundy); doubtful whether common rat under natural conditions ever preys significantly on ship rat. Replacement of ship rat by the larger common rat in many temperate regions is probably due to the common rat's greater ability to withstand cold and to hunt for food under adverse conditions. In the tropics, ship rat well able to hold its own, and has displaced common rat as the common species in New Zealand.

PARASITES
See Table 5.11. Fleas *Nosopsyllus londiniensis*, *N. fasciatus*, *Leptopsylla segnis* and *Xenopsylla cheopis* recorded, all common; *Ctenophthalmus nobilis* recorded as casual. Occasionally imports of ship rats have brought exotic species such as *Xenopsylla brasiliensis* and *X. astia*. Sucking louse *Polyplax spinosula* known from this species.

Diseases: Widely held belief that ship rat was responsible for transmitting the Black Death of the 14th century has been challenged on several grounds, not least because bubonic plague cannot diffuse adequately in a cool temperate climate [1453]. Along with common rat, ship rat is a competent plague carrier but a high proportion of both species succumb to the disease so neither is a satisfactory reservoir species. Ship rats appear to carry the same diseases and parasites as common rats.

RELATIONS WITH HUMANS
Has developed marked ability to live in association with humans; much better adapted to living in buildings than common rat and consequently a more important urban pest in many areas. Often occurs in residential areas of tropical towns, living within houses; has been known to gnaw the soles of the residents' feet while they slept. Damage and fouling in stored foodstuffs widespread. A serious pest of agriculture on islands (notably in Pacific and Caribbean, but also in Cyprus and elsewhere) attacking most crops, but particularly coconuts, sugar cane and cocoa. An important vector of plague and typhus, principally in the East.

AUTHORS
G.I. Twigg, A.P. Buckle & D.J. Bullock, with acknowledgement to R. Quy.

Fig. 5.71 Coypu: now only present in zoo collections, as, here, Edinburgh *(photo D.W. Yalden)*.

FAMILY MYOCASTORIDAE

A monospecific family, closely related to other families of S American rodents, Echimyidae (spiny mice) and Capromyidae (huitias), sometimes included in them. Like all S American caviomorphs (guinea-pig allies), has very large infraorbital foramina (only comparable European rodent is porcupine *Hystrix cristata*), through which part of deep masseter muscles pass, to originate on side of muzzle; help draw lower jaw up and forwards in chewing. Has 4 cheek-teeth in each jaw, with strong cross-crests (superficially like beaver, *Castor*, but that lacks enlarged infraorbital foramen).

Coypu *Myocastor coypus*
Mus coypus Molina, 1782; R. Maipo, Chile.
Nutria.

RECOGNITION

Adults unmistakable from large size: full-grown males frequently weigh >7 kg. Superficially rat-like with tapering cylindrical tail but nose blunt with widely spaced nostrils and hindfeet webbed; anterior surface of incisors orange. In GB, now only found in captivity (Fig. 5.71).

SIGN

Footprints: Hind footprint up to 15 cm long with imprint of web often visible. Up to 5 claw marks visible in fore and hind footprints. Shallow tail scrape, up to 2 cm wide, sometimes found.

Faeces: Long, usually dark brown or green, cylindrical, often slightly curved with fine longitudinal striations, deposited in water or at random on the bank. From 2 × 7 mm at 2 weeks to 11 × 70 mm at full adult size.

Burrows and nests: Excavates complex burrow systems in ditch banks; one described in S America was 6 m deep [1293]. Can have several entrances at water level, 20 cm in diameter; some may open in level ground beyond the bank; nest chambers within may be empty or contain quantities of plant material. Often lie up close to water, under a bush or in dense vegetation. Small shallow nests 30 cm in diameter lined with dead leaves. Larger structures, resembling swan nests, occasionally built in reedbeds.

Runs: Bare of vegetation when intensively used, 15 cm wide; lead from regularly used 'climb-outs' at water's edge to complex network away from bank.

Feeding remains: Usually in or near water. Distinguished from water voles by much larger amounts and the presence of paired crescentic incisor marks on food items (roots, leaf blades, etc.) up to 17 mm wide. Coypus produce short, productive 'lawns' by intensive grazing of grasses next to water courses. Excavation for roots (e.g. docks *Rumex* spp.) and rhizomes conspicuous in winter.

DESCRIPTION

Adapted for semi-aquatic existence: partially webbed hindfeet (5th toe not included in web), valvular nostrils, small pinnae, underfur that remains dry during submersion. Long powerful claws on forefeet used for grooming, holding food and excavating burrows and food.

Pelage: Glossy brown and yellow-brown guard hair, in adults dense and up to 80 mm long on dorsal surface, 35 mm long and sparse on ventral surface. Soft grey underfur 20–25 mm deep, more dense ventrally. Prominent white vibrissae up to 130 mm long.

Nipples: Normally 4 pairs along dorsolateral body line; sometimes teats missing or bitten off; sometimes 5 pairs. High position of teats sometimes regarded as adaptation to semi-aquatic habit, but young are normally suckled on nests, not in water.

Scent glands: Males have large anal gland lying ventral to rectum and extruded during marking; female gland smaller (Table 5.25).

Genitalia: See [650]. In adult males, penis 4–5 cm anterior to anus; useful criterion for adulthood is whether penis can be fully everted. In females vulva immediately posterior to urinary papilla and anterior to anus; closed by a membrane in juveniles. Vulva opens at parturition and during oestrus but the membrane reforms, almost completely, during pregnancy.

Skull: Large infraorbital foramen in robust, flared zygomatic arch (Figs. 5.1, 5.72).

Teeth: Dental formula 1.0.1.3/1.0.1.3. 2nd molar erupts at 3 months, 3rd at 6 months and fully in place by 1 year. Premolar and molars wear to a uniformly flat grinding surface with complex infundibular pattern that changes as attrition proceeds. Incisors wider in males than females (Table 5.25).

Chromosomes: 2n = 42, FNa = 80 [1589].

MEASUREMENTS
See Table 5.26.

VARIATION
5 subspecies recognised in S America [1096]; *M. c. bonariensis* Geoffroy is most widespread (Argentina, Uruguay, Paraguay, S Brazil) and British coypus most closely resembled it. Numerous colour varieties, including albinos and melanics, bred for fur production, particularly in Poland [519]. Some variation in coat colour of wild coypus in GB: occasional animals 'sandy' or grey; 2–3 out of >30 000 seen during the 1980s had patches of white fur, 1 embryo (out of many thousands) was completely white.

DISTRIBUTION
Native to S half of S America: Bolivia, S Brazil, Paraguay, Uruguay, Argentina, C–S Chile [1096]. Substantial feral populations from escapes and

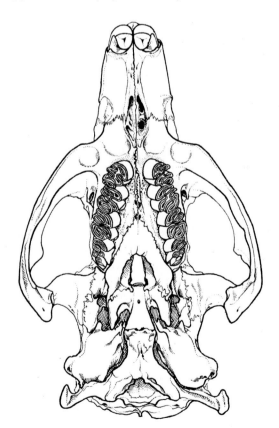

Fig. 5.72 Coypu skull, ventral view.

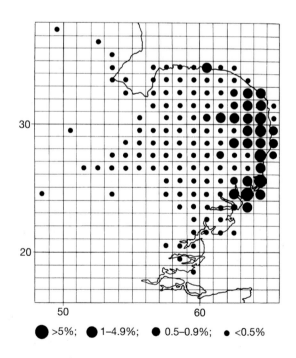

● >5%;　● 1–4.9%;　● 0.5–0.9%;　· <0.5%

Fig. 5.73 Coypu: distribution and abundance, 1970–1989, shown by captures during the eradication campaign [1].

Table 5.26 Coypu: measurement of adults >100 weeks old [1]

	Males			Females		
	Mean	SD	n	Mean	SD	n
Total weight (kg)	6.47	0.88	646	6.02	1.06	918
Eviscerated weight (kg)	5.74	0.84	391	4.87	0.67	495
Hindfoot length (minus claw) (mm)	136	5	655	129	5	922
Head and body length (mm)	603	29	82	593	28	99
Anal gland weight (g)	12.0	3.8	397	3.8	1.2	493
Lower incisor width (mm)	15.1	0.9	409	13.4	0.7	518
Length of molar tooth-row (mm)	30.8	1.8	404	30.5	1.7	511

introductions [885] in N America (mainly Louisiana), Europe [1002]. Smaller scattered populations in countries of former USSR, Middle East, Africa and Japan. In GB, eradicated by a trapping campaign.

The map (Fig. 5.73) shows the distribution of >120 000 coypus caught in control trapping or killed in other ways, such as road deaths, between 1970 and when they became extinct in GB in 1989. During that time <10 individuals were found outside the area shown; isolated individuals were caught in Grimsby, Humberside and at Castleton, Derbyshire.

HISTORY

Imported for fur farming *c.*1929. At least 49 farms established, escapes reported from 1/2 of them. All farms discontinued by 1945 but by 1944 a feral population had become established on R. Yare near Norwich [869]. By 1965, had extended throughout E Anglia and W to Lincolnshire, Huntingdon and Peterborough (now Cambridgeshire), and Hertfordshire [314, 316, 1083]. Isolated colony near Slough disappeared *c.*1954 [1083]. Population peaked at estimated 200 000 by 1962 [1083]. Numbers reduced by extensive control campaign, starting in 1962, and the very severe winter of 1962–1963. By 1970, restricted to Norfolk and Suffolk [506] and numbered 2000 individuals [522]. Population changes from 1970 until the last animal was caught in 1989 detailed in Population, below.

HABITAT

Most found in extensive fen, reed swamp and other marshland communities of E Norfolk and E Suffolk, and in areas of extensive grazing marsh in these counties. Brackish coastal marshes also supported moderate population densities. Smaller numbers found along small streams and in isolated ponds; most lowland river valleys in GB could have supported coypus.

SOCIAL ORGANISATION AND BEHAVIOUR

Social organisation: Polygynous mating system. At high and moderate densities, females live in kin groups, initiated by female colonising a patch of suitable habitat, expanding as daughters establish partially overlapping ranges. At very high densities, daughters disperse when kin groups meet. Males disperse as young adults and, when fully grown, compete for exclusive access to groups of females. A colonial habit with an alpha female and alpha male has also been described [1486]; the male was subordinate to the female except during mating, and the rest of the colony was equally subordinate to these 2. At low density, radio-tracking studies showed that females maintain isolated home ranges. Dominant male moved between up to 4 females. Mothers and daughters established separate ranges following the dispersal of one or both.

Dispersal: Individuals of both sexes disperse over a wide range of population densities. Out of 97 wild animals, ear tagged and released in Norfolk and at large for >6 months, 25% of males and 6% of females dispersed >4 km. Greatest distances moved were 9 km (male) and 7 km (female).

Home ranges: Initially small but increase with sexual maturity. Adult males have significantly larger ranges than adult females [515]. Ranges on grazing marsh (measured as convex polygon) where coypus stayed in or near the drainage ditches, were larger (mean 93.9 ha, SD = 69.5, n = 14) than in areas, such as in wet broadland habitat, where all the area within a home range could be utilised (mean 6.8 ha, SD = 5.5, n = 8) [515].

Communication: Eyesight appears poor. Mothers and offspring communicate with soft 'maawk' call which can be heard over large distances. Scent may be primary mode of communication. Both sexes have a well-developed anal gland which is extruded and wiped over the ground whenever an animal gets into or out of the water [520]. Urine also used for scent-marking. Faeces deposited mostly in water or at random on bank, apparently have no social significance.

Aggressive behaviour: Fights by grappling with strongly clawed forefeet, then biting at mouth and face of opponent. Fighting more common among males than females, as shown by a higher frequency of characteristic scars on the lips. More intense competition between males is consistent with the polygynous mating system. In captivity, females may attack males immediately after parturition and sometimes males are killed at this time: despite this, females often mate at postpartum oestrus.

Activity: Usually rests on nests or in burrows during the day and is active at night. When nights are very cold, remains in burrow and makes up lost time by feeding during the day [521]
.

Locomotion: Most commonly used gait is a walk, appears awkward as large webbed hindfeet are retracted. When alarmed, breaks into a bounding gallop, hindfeet making contact outside and in front of forefeet. Swims by alternate propulsive thrusts of hind legs. Dives silently or, when alarmed, with a loud splash (possibly an alarm signal).

Defence: When disturbed in or near water, swims away under the surface or lies immobile under water with legs outstretched for several minutes; probably anti-predator behaviour. If cornered will grind incisors together in a threatening display; chips of enamel may break off teeth in this process.

Grooming: Extensive and prolonged grooming behaviour using teeth, forefeet and hindfeet [1294], especially after swimming.

FEEDING

Herbivorous except for occasional feeding on freshwater mussels. Food items held in one or both forefeet while animal sits supported on hindfeet. Large items held on ground until small enough to pick up.

In E Anglia had a complex but ordered pattern of plant utilisation; fed on a wide variety of species including the tufted sedge *Carex elata*, burreed *Sparganium erectum*, great pond sedge *Carex riparia*, yellow water lily *Nuphar lutea* and reedmace *Typha* spp. [506]. Some plants such as pasture and salt-marsh grasses eaten throughout the year. Utilised a wide range of crops: grazed cereals in spring and ate mature seed heads in late summer; also *Brassica* and root crops, especially sugar beet. Most feeding done in or near the water, which is likely to be a mechanism for reducing predation risk [546]. Chemical analysis suggested that these feeding patterns were linked with seasonal variation in food quality; e.g. frequency of feeding on the leaves of the reed *Phragmites australis*, highest from midsummer to autumn, was correlated with carbohydrate content.

Is coprophagus: plant material eaten at night passes through the gut, is reingested the following day while animal is on the nests and is finally eliminated during the following night; mean retention time in the gut is thus *c.*24 h [507]. Selective feeding caused massive reduction in the area of reedswamp fringing open water in the Norfolk Broads [153]; also altered its composition by feeding on reedmace in preference to reeds [812]. Certain plants such as cowbane *Circuta virosa* and great water dock *Rumex hydrolapathum* virtually eliminated over large areas when coypus were numerous in the late 1950s [373].

BREEDING

Sexual maturity: Bred throughout the year in E Anglia. Age at which animals matured depended on season: youngest for animals born in late winter, oldest for those born in autumn. Females matured at 3–8 months, males at 4–10 months. Postpartum oestrus, thereafter females induced ovulators, although cycles often irregular in absence of a male; cycles varied from 4–47 days in captive animals [491].

Litter size: See Table 5.27. On average, fewer females born per litter than males. Young females give birth to smaller litters than older ones. In

Table 5.28 Coypu: birthweights (g) of young born in captivity that lived for at least 1 week [1]

	Mean	Range	n
Male	223	132–346	124
Female	207	111–327	105

Table 5.27 Coypu: litter size [1]

	Mean	**SD**	**n (litters)**
Males per litter at birth[a]	2.9	1.5	1107
Females per litter at birth[a]	2.6	1.6	1107
Total at birth[a]	5.5	2.0	1107
Total at birth in captivity[b]	5.4	2.2	42
Surviving 1 week after birth[b]	4.6	1.9	42
Total at birth, mothers < 15 months[a]	5.1	1.7	680
Total at birth, mothers > 15 months[a]	6.0	2.2	427

[a] From animals dissected in late pregnancy (14–19 weeks gestation).
[b] From litters conceived in the wild but born in captivity.

captivity, on average 1 offspring/litter dies within a week of birth, some of them killed by mother lying on them or abandoning them away from nest. Prenatal embryo losses are high: total losses between implantation and birth estimated at 50–60% [1073]. Significant relationship between winter severity and proportion of females that litter in the following spring: probably because females abort their litters after losing condition in cold weather [509]. About 28% of all litters are lost before week 6 of gestation. The average size of litters that survive this early loss is 6.5±2.1 (n = 358 litters in week 7 of gestation). Females also resorb individual embryos and thus reduce mean litter size to 5.4 at birth; may allow females to reduce litter size to a level they can support. Some losses of entire litters appear to be a mechanism for manipulating sex ratio of offspring [511].

Young: Born fully furred, with eyes open (Table 5.28). Have functional incisors and premolars, have been artificially weaned at 5 days. Neonates active within 1 h of birth, can be swimming within a few days.

Lactation: Lasts for 8 weeks in the wild but up to 14 in captivity [508]. Food consumption of lactating females was 63% higher than for control group [524]. In captivity, males grow faster than females, partly because males suck more from teats with the highest milk production (the 2nd and 3rd pairs of mammary glands are larger than the 1st and 4th). Within each sex, weight at weaning positively correlated with birthweight [524].

Growth: Maximum body size reached by 2 years (Table 5.26). Body size (foot length) at 2 years positively correlated with size at weaning [518].

POPULATION

Numbers: See Fig. 5.74. Population fluctuations caused mainly by variation in numbers of trappers employed and severity of winters [523]: 6 trappers 1970–1972, increased from 11 to 20 between 1973 and 1977, stayed at 20 1977–1980 and finally increased to 24 in 1981 (see Relations with humans, below). Cold winters reduced breeding success, allowed trapping to make larger impact on population.

Age structure: Altered by intensive trapping in wild population. In fenced study population, 8.2% of males and 14.7% of females reached 3 years old, compared with 0.6 and 1.7 in the wild population. Physiological longevity was 6.3±0.4 years in captivity, but in the wild less than 0.2% live to 4 years [513].

Sex ratio: Changed from 1:1.2 (female to male) at birth to 1.3:1 for adults, partly because males

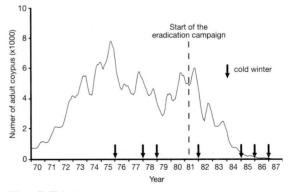

Fig. 5.74 Population size of adult coypu in England, 1970-1987, reconstructed from numbers killed in the trapping campaign and their ages at death [514].

163

more susceptible to trapping: they have larger home ranges and, unlike females, do not have periods of reduced activity around parturition.

MORTALITY

Predation: Stoats, dogs and marsh harriers were seen killing coypus. Remains of coypus seen in heron pellets and fox faeces. Dogs often badly bitten during attempts to kill coypus. Young coypus appear vulnerable and were probably taken by numerous predators including owls, hawks, mink, domestic cat and pike.

Survival of juveniles: Survival from births in autumn and early winter usually poor and those from late winter, spring and early summer did best. At most extreme, only 5% of coypus born before a cold winter survived to become adult, compared with almost 90% of those born the following April. Weaned juveniles must have experienced difficulty in excavating roots and rhizomes, the main source of food in winter, when the ground was frozen.

Adult mortality: In GB few native predators could kill full-grown coypus, so adult mortality was low apart from that caused directly by humans (e.g. trapping, shooting). Fat reserves were reduced even in mild winters [506] but adults rarely died in spite of severe frost lesions on the feet and tail; many coypus lost all or part of their tail in cold winters. However, adult coypus did perish in very severe winters such as 1946/47 and 1962/63. The fall in numbers trapped after the 1962/63 winter suggested 80–90% mortality [1083]. Dying animals were emaciated; proximate cause of death in some cases was *Yersinia pseudotuberculosis*.

PARASITES

Ectoparasites: In E Anglia [1075] 63% of coypus were infested by host-specific sucking louse *Pitrufquenia coypus* (n = 1861), the only ectoparasite also recorded from S America [957]. Of 2578 coypus, 76 (2.9%) carried ticks: 34 were *Ixodes ricinus*, 39 *I. arvicolae*, 1 *I. hexagonus*, and 2 *I. trianguliceps*. Fleas and mites very rare.

Helminths: Tapeworms *Multiceps serialis* and *Hydatigena taeniformis* and nematodes *Strongyloides papillosus* and *Trichostrongylus retortaeformis* (common in rabbit) identified from coypus [1074]. In places, up to 50% infected by liver fluke *Fasciola hepatica* [665]; overall mean infection rate of 6.4%, rose from zero at weaning to 14% in those >1.5 years [1074]. The fluke *Dicrocoelium dendriticum* also recorded.

Protozoa: 46% of coypus infected with coccidians *Eimeria*: *E. myopotami* (23%), *E. nutriae* (20%), *E. fluviatilis* (16%), *E. coypi* (11%), *E. seideli* (1%) [64]. Proportion of infected animals increased over first few weeks of life to 71%, progressively less in older classes. 2 peaks of infection, in January and June–July [64]. *Sarcocystis* sp. cysts found in muscle samples [46]. *Toxoplasma gondii* (cause of toxoplasmosis in humans and animals) isolated from coypus [666]; can probably infect all warm-blooded animals, presence in coypus did not materially increase risk to humans.

Fungi: One found with hair loss caused by ringworm *Trichophyton mentagrophytes* but 15% of apparently healthy coypus infected [1074]. *Haplosporagium paryum* (normally associated with burrowing animals such as moles and wood mice) found in lungs of 17% [1074].

Viruses: Can be infected with foot-and-mouth disease in laboratory conditions [227].

Bacteria: Small percentage in Norfolk were infected with *Yersinia pseudotuberculosies*. *Salmonella typhimurium* isolated from 8 out of sample of 12. Serology showed *Leptospira* infection in 24% of samples; *L. icterohaemorrhagiae* and *L. hebdomadis* serogroups prevalent, *L. interrogans* serovar *hardjo* isolated from tissue [1490]. Unlikely to have been significant reservoir host for cattle-associated *L. hardjo* infection, and was probably not an important source of transmission of leptospirosis to humans in GB, although possibly significant for epidemiology of disease in France [991].

RELATIONS WITH HUMANS

Extensively exploited in natural range, as captive stock and in parts of feral range [519]. Over-exploited in parts of S America [1096]; 10 million pelts a year exported up to 1910 [1248], by 1910 only 200 000 marketed. From 1920s, increasingly bred in captivity for fur, first in Argentina, then in Europe, USA and USSR. Deliberate releases in some countries, particularly USSR, to establish feral populations for fur industry.

In late 1950s, England, damage to dyke banks and river walls through burrowing and to agricultural crops and indigenous flora led, in 1962, to inclusion of coypus in Destructive Imported Animals Act 1932. Systematic control started 1962, organised by Ministry of Agriculture, Fisheries and Food (MAFF); nearly 40 500 trapped by end of 1965 [1083]. After 1965, control carried out by a consortium of Rabbit Clearance Societies and Internal Drainage Boards (IDBs). In 1971, new organisation, Coypu Control, set up; received 50% government grant, remainder of finance from

Water Authority and IDBs.

In 1977 an independent Coypu Strategy Group considered future control policy. Following its recommendations, campaign started, 1981, with objective of eradicating coypus from GB within 10 years [514]. Acknowledged that coypus were not endangered in their native range, and eradication shown to be possible [34]. Employed 24 trappers, 3 foremen and a manager, funded 50% by a government grant, 40% by Anglian Water and 10% by IDBs. Used live trapping with cage traps throughout, sometimes on baited rafts [60]. Coypus were shot, non-target species released unharmed. About 34 900 coypus were trapped or otherwise accounted for during the campaign, numbers declined rapidly [512, 516]; only 12 animals were caught in 1987 and 2 males found dead on roads in 1988. By January 1989, unlikely that breeding population remained; Coypu Control organisation disbanded. One male was trapped by MAFF research staff in December 1989 but no further evidence was found despite extensive field checks. Now certain that coypus have been successfully eradicated from GB.

Eradication campaign, based on methods used in GB, now under way in Chesapeake Bay region, Maryland, USA; by 2004 coypus removed from 6000 ha of marshland, Blackwater National Wildlife Refuge. Aimed to reverse massive environmental damage to marshland; in some areas, rapid and striking recovery documented [616]. Not yet clear whether complete eradication achievable in Chesapeake area; if not, will need continuous control to prevent re-colonisation from nearby.

LITERATURE
Non-technical summary of coypu natural history [510]; exploitation by humans [519]; eradication from GB [516].

AUTHORS
L.M. Gosling & S.J. Baker

Hazel dormouse climbing in hazel: note how the feet turn sideways in dormice, to assist in grasping twigs when climbing (*photo P. Morris*).

REFERENCES

1 Author's data.
2 Aars, J. *et al.* (1998) Bank voles in linear habitats show restricted gene flow as revealed by mitochondrial DNA (mtDNA). *Molecular Ecology,* **7**, 1383–1389.
3 Aars, J. *et al.* (2001) Water voles in the Scottish Uplands: distribution patterns of disturbed and pristine populations ahead and behind the American mink invasion front. *Animal Conservation,* **4**, 187–94.
4 Aars, J. *et al.* (2006) Widespread gene flow and high genetic variability in populations of water voles *Arvicola terrestris* in patchy habitats. *Molecular Ecology,* **165**, 1455–1466.
5 Abt, K.F. & Bock, W.F. (1998) Seasonal variations of diet composition in farmland field mice *Apodemus* spp. and bank voles *Clethrionomys glareolus. Acta Theriologica,* **43**, 379–389.
6 Adamczewska, K.A. (1961) Intensity of reproduction of the *Apodemus flavicollis* (Melchior, 1834) during the period 1954–1959. *Acta Theriologica,* **5**, 1–21.
7 Adamczewska-Andrzejewska, K.A. (1967) Age reference model for *Apodemus flavicollis* (Melchior, 1834). *Ekologia Polska Seria A,* **25**, 787–790.
8 Adams, L. *et al.* (2004) Movement and mortality of translocated urban-suburban grey squirrels. *Animal Welfare,* **13**, 45–50.
9 Adler, G.H. & Levins, R. (1994) The island syndrome in rodent populations. *Quarterly Review of Biology,* **69**, 473–490.
10 Agrell, J. (1995) *Female social behaviour, reproduction and population dynamics in a non-cyclic population of the field vole* (Microtus agrestis). PhD dissertation, Lund University.
11 Agrell, J. (1995) A shift in female social organisation independent of relatedness: an experimental study on the field vole (*Microtus agrestis*). *Behavioral Ecology,* **6**, 182–191.
12 Agrell, J. *et al.* (1992) Body weight and population dynamics: cyclic demography in a noncyclic population of the field vole (*Microtus agrestis*). *Canadian Journal of Zoology,* **70**, 494–501.
13 Agrell, J. *et al.* (1995) Delayed density-dependence in a small-rodent population. *Proceedings of the Royal Society of London Series B,* **262**, 65–70.
14 Al-Khateeb, A. & Johnson, E. (1971) Seasonal changes of pelage in the vole (*Microtus agrestis*). I. Correlation with changes in endocrine glands. *General and Comparative Endocrinology,* 16, 217–228.
15 Albov, S.A. & Serbenyuk, M.A. (1991) Doses of radioactive phosphorus (P-32) for injecting *Clethrionomys glareolus* (Rodentia, Microtinae) to detect their excrements in nature. *Zoologichesky Zhurnal,* **70**, 125–131.
16 Alcantara, M. (1991) Geographical variation in body size of the wood mouse *Apodemus sylvaticus,* L. *Mammal Review,* **21**, 143–150.
17 Alibhai, S.K. (1976) *A study of the factors governing the numbers and reproductive success of* Clethrionomys glareolus (Schreber). Ph D thesis, University of Edinburgh.
18 Alibhai, S.K. (1980) An x-ray technique for ageing bank voles (*Clethrionomys glareolus*) using the first mandibular molar. *Journal of Zoology,* **191**, 418–423.
19 Alibhai, S.K. (1982) Persistence of placental scars in the bank vole, *Clethrionomys glareolus. Journal of Zoology,* **197**, 300–303.
20 Alibhai, S.K. & Gipps, J.H.W. (1985) The population dynamics of bank voles. *Symposia of the Zoological Society of London,* **55**, 277–313.
21 Allen, D.S. & Aspey, W.P. (1986) Determinants of social dominance in eastern gray squirrels (*Sciurus carolinensis*). *Animal Behaviour,* **34**, 81–89.
22 Alston, J.M. & Broom, J.C. (1958) *Leptospirosis in man and animals.* E&S Livingstone, Edinburgh.
23 Altman, P.L. & Katz, D.D. (eds) (1979) *Inbred and genetically defined strains of laboratory animals. Part 1. Mouse and Rat.* Federal American Society of Experimental Biology, Bethesda, MD.
24 Anderson, P. *et al.* (1997) *Restoring Moorland. Peak District Moorland Management Project Phase III Report.* English Nature, Peterborough and Peak District National Park, Bakewell.
25 Anderson, P.K. (1964) Lethal alleles in *Mus musculus*: local distribution and evidence for isolation of demes. *Science,* **145**, 177–178.
26 Anderson, P.K. (1970) Ecological structure and gene flow in small mammals. *Symposia of the Zoological Society of London,* **26**, 299–325.
27 Anderson, P.K. *et al.* (1977) *Mus musculus* and *Peromyscus maniculatus*: homing ability in relation to habitat utilisation. *Canadian Journal of Zoology,* **55**, 169–182.
28 Andrén, H. & Delin, A. (1994) Habitat selection in the Eurasian red squirrel, *Sciurus vulgaris,* in relation to forest fragmentation. *Oikos,* **70**, 43–48.
29 Andrén, H. & Lemnell, P. (1992) Population fluctuations and habitat selection in the Eurasian red squirrel *Sciurus vulgaris. Ecography,* **15**, 303–307.
30 Andrzejewski, R. & Olszewski, J. (1963) Social behaviour and interspecific relations in *Apodemus flavicollis* (Melchior, 1834) and *Clethrionomys glareolus* (Schreber, 1780). *Acta Theriologica,* **7**, 155–168.
31 Andrzejewski, R. & Rajska, E. (1972) Trappability of bank vole in pitfalls and traps. *Acta Theriologica,* **17**, 155–168.
32 Andrzejewski, R. *et al.* (1971) Trappability of trap-prone and trap-shy bank voles. *Acta Theriologica,* **16**, 401–412.
33 Andrzejewski, R. *et al.* (2000) Homing and space activity in bank voles *Clethrionomys glareolus. Acta Theriologica,* **45**, 155–165.
34 Anon (1978) *Coypu: Report of the Coypu Strategy Group.* MAFF, London.
35 Anon (1980) *Field mice and sugar beet.* Leaflet 626. MAFF, Pinner.
36 Anon (1983) Ultrasonic distributors get warning letters. *Pest Management* **2**(7), 46.
37 Apeldoorn, van R.C. *et al.* (1992) Effects of habitat fragmentation on the bank vole, *Clethrionomys glareolus,* in an agricultural landscape. *Oikos,* **65**, 265–274.
38 Apeldoorn, van R. *et al.* (1993) Footprints of small mammals – a field method of sampling data for different species. *Mammalia,* **57**, 407–422.
39 Armitage, P. *et al.* (1984) New evidence of black rat in Roman London. *London Archaeologist,* **4**, 375–383.
40 Arnold, H.R. (1993) *Atlas of mammals in Britain.* HMSO, London.
41 Artimo, A. (1964) The baculurn as a criterion for distinguishing sexually mature and immature bank voles. *Annales Zoologici Fennici,* **1**, 1–6.
42 Asdell, S.A. (1965) *Patterns of mammalian reproduction.* Constable & Co., London.
43 Ashby, K.R. (1967) Studies on the ecology of field mice and voles (*Apodemus sylvaticus, Clethrionomys glareoulus* and *Microtus agrestis*) in Houghall Wood, Durham. *Journal of Zoology,* **152**, 389–413.
44 Ashby, K.R. (1972) Patterns of daily activity in mammals. *Mammal Review,* **1**, 171–185.
45 Ashby, K.R. & Vincent, M.A. (1976) Individual and population energy budgets of the water vole. *Acta Theriologica,* **21**, 499–512.
46 Ashford, R. Personal communication.
47 Attuquayefio, D.K. *et al.* (1986) Home range sizes in the wood mouse *Apodemus sylvaticus*: habitat, sex and seasonal differences. *Journal of Zoology A,* **210**, 45–53.
48 Aulak, W. (1970) Small mammal communities in Białowieża National Park. *Acta Theriologica,* **15**, 465–515.
49 Austin, C.R. (1957) Oestrus and ovulation in the field vole (*Microtus agrestis*). *Journal of Endocrinology,* **15**, IV.
50 Aybes, C. & Yalden, D.W. (1995) Place-name evidence for the former distribution and status of wolves and beavers in Britain. *Mammal Review,* **25**, 201–226.
51 Baal, H.J. (1949) The indigenous mammals, reptiles and

amphibians of the Channel Islands. *Bulletin Annuel de la Societé Jersiaise*, **15**, 101–110.

52 Baker, A.E.M. (1981) Gene flow in house mice: introduction of a new allele into free living populations. *Evolution*, **35**, 243–288.

53 Baker, J.R. (1930) The breeding season in British wild mice. *Proceedings of the Zoological Society of London*, **1930**, 113–126.

54 Baker, J.R. *et al.* (1963) Blood parasites of wild voles, *Microtus agrestis* in England. *Parasitology*, **53**, 297–301.

55 Baker, J.R. & Ranson, R.M. (1933) Factors affecting the breeding of the field mouse (*Microtus agrestis*) Part 3 – Locality. *Proceedings of the Royal Society of London*, **113**, 486–495.

56 Baker, P.J. *et al.* (2003) Factors affecting the distribution of small mammals in an urban area. *Mammal Review*, **33**, 95–100.

57 Baker, P.J. *et al.* (2005) Impact of predation by domestic cats *Felis catus* in an urban area. *Mammal Review*, **35**, 302–312.

58 Baker, P. *et al.* (2006) The potential impact of red fox *Vulpes vulpes* predation in agricultural landscapes in lowland Britain. *Wildlife Biology*, **12**, 39–50.

59 Baker, R.J. *et al.* (1999) Microsatellites indicate a high frequency of multiple paternity in *Apodemus* (Rodentia). *Molecular Ecology*, **8**, 107–111.

60 Baker, S.J. & Clarke, C.N. (1988) Cage trapping coypus (*Myocastor coypus*) on baited rafts. *Journal of Applied Ecology*, **25**, 41–48.

61 Bakken, A. (1959) Behaviour of gray squirrels. *Proceedings of the Annual Conference, Southeastern Association of Game and Fish Commissioners*, **13**, 393–406.

62 Bakowski, C. & Kozakiewicz, M. (1988) The effect of forest road on bank vole and yellow-necked mouse populations. *Acta Theriologica*, **33**, 345–353.

63 Balharry, R. Personal communication.

64 Ball, S.J. & Lewis, D.C. (1983) *Eimeria* (Protozoa: Coccidia) in wild populations of some British rodents. *Journal of Zoology*, **202**, 373–381.

65 Barber, I. *et al.* (2003) Exposure of small mammals, in particular the wood mouse *Apodemus sylvaticus*, to pesticide seed treatments. *Environmental Toxicology and Chemistry*, **22**, 1134–1139.

66 Barkalow, F.S. (1967) A record gray squirrel litter. *Journal of Mammalogy*, **48**, 141.

67 Barkalow, F.S. *et al.* (1970) The vital statistics of an unexploited gray squirrel population. *Journal of Wildlife Management*, **34**, 489–500.

68 Barker, F.S. *et al.* (2005) Highly polymorphic microsatellite loci in the bank vole (*Clethrionomys glareolus*). *Molecular Ecology Notes*, **5**, 311–313.

69 Barnard, C.J. *et al.* (1991) Of mice and kin: the functional significance of kin bias in social behaviour. *Biological Reviews*, **66**, 379–430.

70 Barnett, S.A. (1958) An analysis of social behaviour in wild rats. *Proceedings of the Zoological Society of London*, **130**, 107–52.

71 Barnett, S.A. (1975) *The rat: a study in behaviour*. University of Chicago Press, Chicago.

72 Barnett, S.A. & Dickson, R.G. (1984) Changes among wild house mice (*Mus musculus*) bred for ten generations in a cold environment, and their evolutionary implications. *Journal of Zoology*, **203**, 163–180.

73 Barnett, S.A. *et al.* (1975) House mice bred for many generations in two environments. *Journal of Zoology*, **177**, 153–69.

74 Barr, J.J.F. *et al.* (2002) Evaluation of immunocontraception as a publicly acceptable form of vertebrate pest species control: the introduced grey squirrel in Britain as an example. *Environmental Management*, **30**, 342–351.

75 Barratt, E. *et al.* (1997) Genetic structure of fragmented populations of red squirrels in Britain, pp. 61-66 in Gurnell, J. & Lurz, P.W.W. (eds.) *The conservation of red squirrels, Sciurus vulgaris, L.* PTES, London.

76 Barratt, E.M. *et al.* (1999) Genetic structure of fragmented populations of red squirrel (*Sciurus vulgaris*) in Britain. *Molecular Ecology*, **8**, S55–S63.

77 Barreto, G.R. (1998) *Analysis of a declining population of water voles, Arvicola terrestris L in England*. D Phil thesis, University of Oxford.

78 Barreto, G.R. *et al.* (1998) The role of habitat and mink predation in determining the status and distribution of water voles in England. *Animal Conservation*, **1**, 129–137.

79 Barrett-Hamilton, G.E.H. (1899) On the species of the genus *Mus* inhabiting St Kilda. *Proceedings of the Zoological Society of London*, **1899**, 77–88.

80 Barrett-Hamilton, G.E.H. & Hinton, M.A.C. (1910–21) *A history of British mammals*. Gurney & Jackson, London.

81 Barrier, M.J. & Barkalow, F.S. (1967) A rapid technique for aging gray squirrels in winter pelage. *Journal of Wildlife Management*, **31**, 715–719.

82 Barrington, R.M. (1880) On the introduction of the squirrel into Ireland. *Scientific Proceedings of the Royal Dublin Society*, NS **2**, 615–731.

83 Barrow, P.A. (1981) *Corynebacterium kutscheri* infection in wild voles (*Microtus agrestis*). *British Veterinary Journal*, **137**, 67–70.

84 Bartmann, S. & Gerlach, G. (2001) Multiple paternity and similar variance in reproductive success of male and female wood mice (*Apodemus sylvaticus*) housed in an enclosure. *Ethology*, **107**, 889–899.

85 Batten, C.A. & Berry, R.J. (1967) Prenatal mortality in wild-caught house mice. *Journal of Animal Ecology*, **34**, 453–463.

86 Battersby, J. (2005) *UK Mammals: species status and population trends*. JNCC/Tracking Mammals Partnership, Peterborough.

87 Baumler, W. (1975) Activity of some mammals in the field. *Acta Theriologica*, **20**, 365–79.

88 Baumler, W. (1998) Predicting damages of voles in forest cultivations. *Anzeiger für Schadlingskunde Pflanzenschutz Umweltschutz*, **71**, 117–120.

89 Baxter, R. & Hansson, L. (2001) Bark consumption by small rodents in the northern and southern hemispheres. *Mammal Review*, **31**, 47–59.

90 Begon, M. *et al.* (1999) Transmission dynamics of a zoonotic pathogen within and between wildlife host species. *Proceedings of the Royal Society of London Series B*, **266**, 1939–1945.

91 Behnke, J.M. & Wakelin, D. (1973) The survival of *Trichuris muris* in wild populations of its natural hosts. *Parasitology*, **67**, 157–164.

92 Behnke, J.M. *et al.* (1999) Helminth infections in *Apodemus sylvaticus* in southern England: interactive effects of host age, sex and year on the prevalence and abundance of infections. *Journal of Helminthology*, **73**, 31–44.

93 Behnke, J.M. *et al.* (2005) Do helminth parasites of wood mice interact? *Journal of Animal Ecology*, **74**, 982–993.

94 Bellamy, D. *et al.* (1973) Ageing in an island population of the house mouse. *Age and Ageing*, **2**, 235–50.

95 Bellamy, P.E. *et al.* (2000) Road verges as habitats for small mammals in Britain. *Mammal Review*, **30**, 131–139.

96 Bellinvia, E. (2004) A phylogenetic study of the genus *Apodemus* by sequencing the mitochondrial DNA control region. *Journal of Zoological Systematics and Evolutionary Research*, **42**, 289–297.

97 Bence, S.L. *et al.* (1999). Nest site selection by the harvest mouse (*Micromys minutus*) on farmland. *Aspects of Applied Biology*, **54**, 197–202.

98 Bence, S.L. *et al.* (2003). Habitat characteristics of harvest mouse nests on arable farmland. *Agriculture Ecosystems and Environment*, **99**, 179–186.

99 Benmehdi, F. *et al.* (1980) Premier rapport de la genetique biochimique des populations à la systématique des mulots de France continentale et de Corse. *Biochemical Statistics and Ecology*, **8**, 309–315 (in French).

100 Bennet, A. (1986) *An assessment of the loss of moorland on Mainland and South Ronaldsay, Orkney, 1932–1985.* Report to NCC, RSPB and WWF UK.

101 Bentley, E.W. (1959) The distribution and status of *Rattus rattus* L in the United Kingdom in 1951 and 1956. *Journal of Animal Ecology,* **28**, 299–308.

102 Bentley, E.W. (1964) A further loss of ground by *Rattus rattus* L in the United Kingdom during 1956–61. *Journal of Animal Ecology,*. **33**, 371–373

103 Berckmoes, V. *et al.* (2005) Effects of environmental pollution on microsatellite DNA diversity in wood mouse (*Apodemus sylvaticus*) populations. *Environmental Toxicology and Chemistry,* **24**, 2898–2907.

104 Bergstedt, B. (1965) Distribution, reproduction, growth and dynamics of the rodent species *Clethrionomys glareolus* (Schreber), *Apodemus flavicollis* (Melchior) and *Apodemus sylvaticus* (Linné) in Southern Sweden. *Oikos,* **16**, 132–160.

105 Berridge, D. Personal communication.

106 Berry, R.J. (1963) Epigenetic polymorphism in wild populations of *Mus musculus. Genetical Research,* **4**, 193–220.

107 Berry, R.J. (1964) The evolution of an island population of the house mouse. *Evolution,* **18**, 468–483.

108 Berry, R.J. (1968) The ecology of an island population of the house mouse. *Journal of Animal Ecology.* **37**, 445–470.

109 Berry, R.J. (1970) Covert and overt variation, as exemplified by British mouse populations. *Symposia of the Zoological Society of London,* **26**, 3–26.

110 Berry, R.J. (1970) The natural history of the house mouse. *Field Studies,* **3**, 219–262.

111 Berry, R.J. (1973) Chance and change in British long-tailed field mice (*Apodemus sylvaticus*). *Journal of Zoology,* **170**, 351–366.

112 Berry, R.J. (1978) Genetic variation in wild house mice: where natural selection and history meet. *American Scientist* **66**, 52–60.

113 Berry, R.J. (1981) Town mouse, country mouse: adaption and adaptability in *Mus domesticus* (*Mus musculus domesticus*). *Mammal Review,* **11**, 91–136.

114 Berry, R.J. (ed.) (1981) *Biology of the house mouse.* Academic Press, London.

115 Berry, R.J. (1981) Population dynamics of the house mouse. *Symposia of the Zoological Society of London,* **47**, 395–425.

116 Berry, R.J. (1984) House mouse, pp. 273–84 in Mason, I.L. (ed.) *Evolution of domesticated animals.* Longman, London.

117 Berry, R.J. (1985) Evolutionary and ecological genetics of the bank vole and wood mouse. *Symposia of the Zoological Society of London,* **55**, 1–31.

118 Berry, R.J. (1985) *The natural history of Orkney.* Collins, London.

119 Berry, R.J. (1986) Genetics of insular populations of mammals with particular reference to differentiation and founder effects in British small mammals. *Biological Journal of the Linnean Society of London,* **28**, 205–230.

120 Berry, R.J. (1986) Genetical processes in wild mouse populations. *Current Topics in Microbiology and Immunology,* **127**, 86–94.

121 Berry, R.J. & Bronson, F.H. (1992) Life history and bioeconomy of the house mouse, *Biological Review,* **67**, 519–550.

122 Berry, R.J. & Jakobson, M.E. (1971) Life and death of an island population of the house mouse. *Experimental Gerontology,* **6**, 187–197.

123 Berry, R.J. & Jakobson, M.E. (1974) Vagility in an island population of the house mouse. *Journal of Zoology,* **173**, 341–354.

124 Berry, R.J. & Jakobson, M.E. (1975) Adaption and adaptability in wild-living house mice. *Journal of Zoology,* **176**, 391–402.

125 Berry, R.J. & Peters, J. (1977) Heterogeneous heterozygosities in *Mus musculus* populations. *Proceedings of the Royal Society of London Series B,* **197**, 485–503.

126 Berry, R.J. & Rose, F.E.N. (1975) Islands and the evolution of *Microtus arvalis* (Microtinae). *Journal of Zoology,* **177**, 395–409.

127 Berry, R.J. & Scriven, P. (2005) The house mouse: a model and motor for evolutionary understanding. *Biological Journal of the Linnean Society,* **84**, 335–347.

128 Berry, R.J. & Searle, A.G. (1963) Epigenetic polymorphism of the rodent skeleton. *Proceedings of the Zoological Society of London,* **140**, 577–615.

129 Berry, R.J. & Tricker, B.J.K. (1969) Colonisation and extinction: the mice of Foula, with notes on those on Fair Isle and St Kilda. *Journal of Zoology,* **158**, 247–265.

130 Berry, R.J. *et al.* (1973) Survival of wild-living mice. *Mammal Review,* **3**, 46–57.

131 Berry, R.J. *et al.* (1978) Sub-Antarctic house mice: colonisation, survival and selection. *Journal of Zoology,* **184**, 127–141.

132 Berry, R.J. *et al.* (1979) Natural selection in house mice from South Georgia (South Atlantic Ocean). *Journal of Zoology,* **189**, 385–398.

133 Berry, R.J. *et al.* (1987) Inherited differences within an island populations of the house mouse (*Mus domesticus*). *Journal of Zoology,* **211**, 605–618.

134 Berry, R.J. *et al.* (1992) The house mice of Faray, Orkney. *Journal of Zoology,* **228**, 233–246.

135 Bertolino, S. & Genovesi, P. (2003) Spread and attempted eradication of the grey squirrel (*Sciurus carolinensis*) in Italy, and consequences for the red squirrel (*Sciurus vulgaris*) in Eurasia. *Biological Conservation,* **109**, 351–358.

136 Bertram, D.F. & Nagorsen, D.W. (1995) Introduced rats, *Rattus* spp., on the Queen Charlotte Islands: implications for seabird conservation. *Canadian Field Naturalist,* **109**, 6–10.

137 Bialonska, D. *et al.* (2002) The long-term effect of cadmium exposure through food on the postnatal development of the bank vole (*Clethrionomys glareolus* Schreber, 1780). *Folia Biologica – Krakow,* **50**, 203–209.

138 Bieber, C. (1998) Population dynamics, sexual activity, and reproduction failure in the fat dormouse (*Myoxus glis*). *Journal of Zoology,* **244**, 223–229.

139 Bierman, S.M. *et al.* (2006) Changes over time in the spatiotemporal dynamics of cyclic populations of field voles (*Microtus agrestis* L). *American Naturalist,* **167**, 583–590.

140 Birtles, R.J. *et al.* (2001) Longitudinal monitoring of bartonellosis in British wood mice and bank voles. *Epidemiology and Infection,* **126**, 323–329.

141 Bishop, I.R. & Delany, M.J. (1963) The ecological distribution of small mammals in the Channel Islands. *Mammalia,* **27**, 99–110.

142 Blackmore, D. & Owen, D.G. (1968) Ectoparasites: the significance in British wild rodents. *Symposia of the Zoological Society of London,* **24**, 197–220.

143 Blake, B.H. (1982) Reproduction in captive water voles, *Arvicola terrestris. Journal of Zoology,* **198**, 524–529.

144 Blake, B.H. (1992) Ultrasonic vocalization and body temperature maintenance in infant voles of 3 species (Rodentia, Arvicolidae). *Developmental Psychobiology,* **25**, 581–596.

145 Blasdell, K. *et al.* (2003) The wood mouse is a natural host for Murid herpesvirus 4. *Journal of General Virology,* **84**, 111–113.

146 Boatman, N. & Stoate, C. (1999) Arable farming and wildlife – can they coexist? *British Wildlife,* **10**, 260–267.

147 Bobek, B. (1969) Survival, turnover and production of small rodents in a beech forest. *Acta Theriologica,* **14**, 191–210.

148 Bobek, B. (1973) Net production of small rodents in a deciduous forest. *Acta Theriologica,* **18**, 403–434.

149 Bobyr, G. Y. (1978) A contribution to the ecology of the Altaian squirrel (*Sciurus vulgaris altaicus*). *Zoologicheskii Zhurnal,* **57**, 253–259.

150 Bomford, M. (1987) Food and reproduction of wild house mice. I. Diet and breeding seasons in various habitats on irrigated cereal farms in New South Wales. *Australian*

Wildlife Research, **14,** 183–196.

151 Bondrup-Nielsen, S. (1985) An evaluation of the effects of space use and habitat patterns on dispersal in small mammals. *Annales Zoologici Fennici,* **22,** 373–383.

152 Bondrup-Nielsen, S. & Karlsson, F. (1985) Movements and spatial patterns in populations of *Clethrionomys* species: a review. *Annales Zoologici Fennici,* **22,** 385–392.

153 Boorman, L.A. & Fuller, R.M. (1981) The changing status of reedswamp in the Norfolk Broads. *Journal of Applied Ecology,* **18,** 241–269.

154 Booth, C. & Booth, J. (1994) *The mammals of Orkney.* The Orcadian, Kirkwall, Orkney.

155 Booth, C. & Booth, J. (2005) *Sillocks, skarfies & selkies: the fish, amphibians, reptiles, birds and mammals of Orkney.* The Orcadian, Kirkwall, Orkney.

156 Borowski, S. (1962) *Apodemus flavicollis* (Melchior, 1834) in the tops of tall trees. *Acta Theriologica,* **6,** 314.

157 Bourne, J.B. (1998) Norway rat exclusion in Alberta, pp. 242–246 in Baker, R.O. & Crabb, A.C. (eds.) *Proceedings of the 18th Vertebrate Pest Conference,* University of California, Davis.

158 Bovet, J. (1962) Influence d'un effet directionel sur le retour au gîte des mulots fauve et sylvestre (*Apodemus flavicollis* Melch. et *A. sylvaticus,* L) et du campagnol roux (*Clethrionomys glareolus* Schr.) (Mammalia, Rodentia). *Zeitschrift für Tierpsychologie,* **19,** 472–488 (in French).

159 Bovet, J. (1972) On the social behaviour in a stable group of long-tailed field mice (*Apodemus sylvaticus*). *Behaviour,* **41,** 43–67.

160 Bown, K.J. *et al.* (2002) New World origins for haemoparasites infecting United Kingdom grey squirrels (*Sciurus carolinensis*), as revealed by phylogenetic analysis of bartonella infecting squirrel populations in England and the United States. *Epidemiology and Infection,* **129,** 647–653.

161 Bown, K.J. *et al.* (2003) Seasonal dynamics of *Anaplasma* (*Ehrlichia*) *phagocytophila* in a rodent–tick (*Ixodes trianguliceps*) system in the UK. *Emerging Infectious Diseases,* **9,** 63–70.

162 Bown, K.J. *et al.* (2004) Flea-borne *Bartonella grahamii* and *Bartonella taylorii* in bank voles. *Emerging Infectious Diseases,* **10,** 684–687.

163 Bown, K.J. *et al.* (2006) Sympatric *Ixodes trianguliceps* and *Ixodes ricinus* ticks feeding on field voles (*Microtus agrestis*): potential for increased risk of *Anaplasma phagocytophilum* in the United Kingdom. *Vector-borne and Zoonotic Diseases,* **6,** 404–410.

164 Boyce, C.C.K. (1991) Water vole *Arvicola terrestris,* pp 212–218 in Corbet, G.B. & Harris, S. (ed.). *Handbook of British mammals,* 3rd ed. Blackwell Scientific Publications, Oxford.

165 Bozikova, E. *et al.* (2005). Mitochondrial DNA in the hybrid zone between *Mus musculus musculus* and *Mus musculus domesticus*: a comparison of two transects. *Biological Journal of the Linnean Society,* **84,** 363–378.

166 Brain, P.F. *et al.* (eds) (1989) *House mouse aggression.* Harwood Academic, London.

167 Brainard, G.C. *et al.* (1994) Ultraviolet regulation of neuroendocrine and circadian physiology in rodents. *Vision Research,* **34,** 1521–1533.

168 Brakes, C.R. & Smith, R.H. (2005) Exposure of non-target small mammals to rodenticides: short-term effects, recovery and implications for secondary poisoning. *Journal of Applied Ecology,* **42,** 118–128.

169 Brambell, F.R. & Rowlands, I.W. (1936) Reproduction of the bank vole *Evotomys glareolus* (Schreber). I. The oestrus cycle of the female. *Philosophical Transactions of the Royal Society of London B,* **226,** 71–97.

170 Bramwell, D. *et al.* (1990) Ossom's Eyrie Cave: an archaeological contribution to the recent history of vertebrates in Britain. *Zoological Journal of the Linnean Society,* **98,** 1–25.

171 Bree, P.J.H. van & Maasson, A.W.P. (1962) Over een Winterpopulatie van de Dwergmuis *Micromys minutus* (Pallas 1778) uit Midden-Limburg. *Natuurhistorisch Maandblad,* **51,** 121–124 (in Dutch).

172 Breed, W.G. (1967) Ovulation in the genus *Microtus. Nature,* **214,** 826.

173 Breed, W.G. (1969) Oestrus and ovarian histology in the lactating vole (*Microtus agrestis*). *Journal of Reproduction and Fertility,* **18,** 33–42.

174 Bright, P.W. (1995) Distribution of the dormouse *Muscardinus avellanarius* in Wales on the edge of its range. *Mammal Review,* **25,** 101–110.

175 Bright, P.W. (1997) *Status and woodland requirements of the dormouse in England.* English Nature Research Reports. English Nature, Peterborough.

176 Bright, P.W. (1998) Behaviour of specialist species in habitat corridors: arboreal dormice avoid corridor gaps. *Animal Behaviour,* **56,** 1485–1490.

177 Bright, P.W. (2000) *Status and woodland requirements of the dormouse in Wales.* Countryside Council for Wales, Bangor.

178 Bright, P. & MacPherson, D. (2002) *Hedgerow management, dormice and biodiversity.* English Nature Research Report No. 454. English Nature, Peterborough.

179 Bright, P.W. & Morris, P.A. (1989) *A practical guide to dormouse conservation.* Occasional publication no. 11. The Mammal Society, London.

180 Bright, P.W. & Morris, P.A. (1990) Habitat requirements of dormice *Muscardinus avellanarius* in relation to woodland management in southwest England. *Biological Conservation,* **54,** 307–326.

181 Bright, P.W. & Morris, P.A. (1991) Ranging and nesting behaviour of the dormouse, *Muscardinus avellanarius,* in diverse low-growing woodland. *Journal of Zoology,* **224,** 177–190.

182 Bright, P.W. & Morris, P.A. (1992) Ranging and nesting behaviour of the dormouse, *Muscardinus avellanarius,* in coppice-with-standards woodland. *Journal of Zoology,* **226,** 589–600.

183 Bright, P.W. & Morris, P.A. (1993) Foraging behaviour of dormice, *Muscardinus avellanarius,* in two contrasting habitats. *Journal of Zoology,* **230,** 69–85.

184 Bright, P.W. & Morris, P.A. (1994) Animal translocation for conservation: performance of dormice in relation to release techniques, origin and season. *Journal of Applied Ecology,* **31,** 699–708.

185 Bright, P.W. & Morris, P.A. (1996) Why are dormice rare? – a case study in conservation biology. *Mammal Review,* 157–187.

186 Bright, P.W. & Morris, P.A. (2002) Putting dormice back on the map. *British Wildlife,* **14,** 91–100.

187 Bright, P.W. & Morris, P.A. (2005) *Dormice.* Mammal Society Series, London.

188 Bright, P.W. *et al.* (1994) Dormouse distribution: survey techniques, insular ecology and selection of sites for conservation. *Journal of Applied Ecology,* **31,** 329–339.

189 Bright, P.W. *et al.* (1996) A new survey of the dormouse *Muscardinus avellanarius* in Britain, 1993–4. *Mammal Review,* **26,** 189–195.

190 Bright, P.W. *et al.* (1996) Effects of weather and season on the summer activity of dormice *Muscardinus avellanarius. Journal of Zoology,* **238,** 521–530.

191 Bright, P.W. *et al.* (2006) *The dormouse conservation handbook.* English Nature, Peterborough.

192 Britton-Davidian, J. *et al.* (2005) Post-zygotic isolation between the two European subspecies of the house mouse: estimates from fertility patterns in wild and laboratory-bred hybrids. *Biological Journal of the Linnean Society,* **84,** 379–393.

193 Bronson, F.H. (1979) The reproductive ecology of the house mouse. *Quarterly Review of Biology,* **54,** 265–299.

194 Brooker, P. (1982) Robertsonian translocations in *Mus musculus* from NE Scotland and Orkney. *Heredity,* **48,** 305–309.

195 Brown, E.D. *et al.* (1994) *Apodemus sylvaticus* infected with *Heligmosomoides polygyrus* (Nematoda) in an arable

ecosystem: epidemiology and effects of infection on the movements of male mice. *Journal of Zoology,* **234,** 623–640.

196 Brown, E.D. *et al.* (1994) Rhythmicity of egg production by *Heligmosomoides polygyrus* (Nematoda) in wild wood mice, *Apodemus sylvaticus. Journal of Helminthology,* **68,** 105–108.

197 Brown, J. & Twigg, G.I. (1969) Studies on the pelvis of British Muridae and Cricetidae (Rodentia). *Journal of Zoology,* **158,** 81–132.

198 Brown, J.C. & Williams, J.D. (1972) The rodent preputial gland. *Mammal Review,* **2,** 105–147.

199 Brown, L.E. (1956) Field experiments on the activity of the small mammals (*Apodemus, Clethrionomys* and *Microtus*). *Proceedings of the Zoological Society of London,* **126,** 549–564.

200 Brown, L.E. (1966) Home range and movement of small mammals. *Symposia of the Zoological Society of London,* **18,** 111–142.

201 Brown, L.E. (1969) Field experiments on the movements of *Apodemus sylvaticus* L using trapping and tracking techniques. *Oecologia,* **2,** 198–222.

202 Brown, R.E. (1985) The rodents I: effects of odours on reproductive physiology (primer effects), pp.245–344 in Brown, R.E. & Macdonald, D.W. (eds.) *Social odours in mammals,* Vol 1. Clarendon Press, Oxford.

203 Brown, R.E. (1985) The rodents II. Suborder Myomorpha, pp. 345–457 in Brown, R.E. & Macdonald, D.W. (eds.) *Social odours in mammals,* Vol 1. Clarendon Press, Oxford.

204 Brown, R.E. (1995) What is the role of the immune system in determining individually distinct body odours. *International Journal of Immunopharmacology,* **17,** 655–661.

205 Bryce, J. (1997) Changes in the distributions of red and grey squirrels in Scotland. *Mammal Review,* **27,** 171–176.

206 Bryce, J. *et al.* (1997) Comparison of estimates for obtaining population estimates for red squirrels in relation to damage due to bark stripping. *Mammal Review,* **27,** 165–170.

207 Bryce, J.M. *et al.* (2001) Competition between Eurasian red and introduced Eastern grey squirrels: the energetic significance of body-mass difference. *Proceedings of the Royal Society of London Series B,* **268,** 1731–1736.

208 Buckle, A.P. (1976). Studies on the biology and distribution of *Leptinus testaceus* Muller within a community of mixed small mammal species. *Ecological Entomology,* **1,** 1–6.

209 Buckle, A.P. & Smith, R.H. (1994) *Rodent pests and their control.* CAB International, Wallingford.

210 Buckley, J. (1977) Barn owl predation on the harvest mouse. *Mammal Review,* **7,** 117–121.

211 Bujalska, G. (1983) Sex ratio, pp. 103–111 in Petrusewicz, K. (ed.) *Ecology of the bank vole. Acta Theriologica,* **28,** Suppl. 1.

212 Bujalska, G. (1983) Reproduction, pp. 148–161 in Petrusewicz, K. (ed.) *Ecology of the bank vole. Acta Theriologica,* **28,** Suppl. 1.

213 Bujalska, G. (1985) Regulation of female maturation in *Clethrionomys* species, with special reference to an island population of *Clethrionomys glareolus. Annales Zoologici Fennici,* **22,** 331–342.

214 Bujalska, G. (1995) Factors affecting breeding success in female bank voles. *Polish Ecological Studies,* **21,** 377–385.

215 Bujalska, G. (1995) Winter reproduction of *Clethrionomys glareolus* (Schreber 1780). *Polish Ecological Studies,* **21,** 387–395.

216 Bujalska, G. (1995) Winter survival in an island population of the bank vole. *Polish Ecological Studies,* **21,** 423–433.

217 Bujalska, G. & Sosnowska, D. (1995) Zonal distribution of winter survival rates in an island population of the bank vole, *Clethrionomys glareolus* (Schreber 1780). *Polish Ecological Studies,* **21,** 435–441.

218 Bull, S.A. *et al.* (1998) A survey of *Cryptosporidium* species in Skomer bank voles (*Clethrionomys glareolus skomerensis*). *Journal of Zoology,* **244,** 119–122.

219 Burthe, S. *et al.* (2006) Cowpox virus infection in *Microtus agrestis* populations: delayed density dependence and

individual risk. *Journal of Animal Ecology,* **75,** 1416–1425.

220 Butenko, A.M. *et al.* (1997) [Further study of hantavirus circulation in the Russian Federation] *Voprosy virusologii,* **42**(2), 74–76 (in Russian).

221 Butler, F.T. & Whelan, J. (1994) Population structure and reproduction in brown rats (*Rattus norvegicus*) from pig farms, Co Kildare, Ireland. *Journal of Zoology,* **233,** 277–291.

222 Butler, F.T. *et al.* Personal communication.

223 Byrne, J.M. *et al.* (1990) Some mitochondrial-DNA polymorphisms in Irish wood mice (*Apodemus sylvaticus*) and bank voles (*Clethrionomys glareolus*). *Journal of Zoology,* **221,** 299–302.

224 Calhoun, J.B. (1962) *The ecology and sociology of the Norway rat.* US Department of Health, Education and Welfare, Bethesda, MD.

225 Canova, L. & Fasola, M. (1993) Food habits and trophic relationships of small mammals in 6 habitats of the northern Po plain (Italy). *Mammalia,* **57,** 188–199.

226 Canova, L. *et al.* (1994) Comparative ecology of the wood mouse *Apodemus sylvaticus* in two differing habitats. *Zeitschrift für Säugetierkunde,* **59,** 193–198.

227 Capel-Edwards, M. (1967) Foot and mouth disease in *Myocastor coypus. Journal of Comparative Pathology,* **77,** 217–21.

228 Capizzi, D. & Luiselli, L. (1996) Ecological relationships between small mammals and age of coppice in an oak-mixed forest in central Italy. *Revue d'Ecologie: la Terre et la Vie,* **51,** 277–291.

229 Carleton, M.D. *et al.* (2003) *Myodes* Pallas, 1811, is the valid name for the genus of red-backed voles, pp. 96–98 in Averianov, A. & Abramson, N. (ed). *Systematics, phylogeny and paleontology of small mammals.* Zoological Institute, St Petersburg.

230 Carlsen, M. *et al.* (2000) Effects of predation on temporary autumn populations of subadult *Clethrionomys glareolus* in forest clearings. *Zeitschrift für Säugetierkunde,* **65,** 100–109.

231 Carslake, D. *et al.* (2005) Space-time clustering of cowpox virus infection in wild rodent populations. *Journal of Animal Ecology,* **74,** 647–655.

232 Carss, D.N. (1995) Prey brought home by two domestic cats (*Felis catus*) in northern Scotland. *Journal of Zoology,* **237,** 678–686.

233 Carter, S.P. & Bright, P.W. (2003) Reedbeds as refuges for water voles (*Arvicola terrestris*) from predation by introduced mink (*Mustela vison*). *Biological Conservation,* **111,** 371–76.

234 Carvalho, L. dos S. *et al.* (2006) Shortwave visual sensitivity in tree and flying squirrels reflects changes in lifestyle. *Current Biology,* **16,** R81–R83.

235 Castién, E. & Gosálbez, J. (1994) Habitat selection of *Apodemus flavicollis* in a *Fagus sylvatica* forest in the western Pyrenees. *Folia Zoologica,* **43,** 219–224.

236 Castién, E. & Gosálbez, J. (1996) Diet of *Clethrionomys glareolus* in the western Pyrenees (north Iberian peninsula). *Folia Zoologica,* **45,** 137–144.

237 Cavanagh, R. *et al.* (2002) *Mycobacterium microti* infection (vole tuberculosis) in wild rodent populations. *Journal of Clinical Microbiology,* **40,** 3281–3285.

238 Cavanagh, R.D. *et al.* (2004) Disease dynamics in cyclic populations of field voles (*Microtus agrestis*): cowpox virus and vole tuberculosis (*Mycobacterium microti*). *Proceedings of the Royal Society of London Series B,* **271,** 859–867.

239 Celada, C. *et al.* (1994) Occupancy of isolated woodlots by the red squirrel *Sciurus vulgaris* L in Italy. *Biological Conservation,* **69,** 177–183.

240 Central Science Laboratory (2005) *Rodent infestation in domestic properties in England, 2001.* Department for Environment, Food and Rural Affairs.

241 Chalmers, R.M. *et al.* (1994) *Cryptosporidium muris* in wild house mice (*Mus musculus*): first report in the UK. *European Journal of Protistology,* **30,** 151–155.

242 Chalmers, R.M. *et al.* (1997) The prevalence of *Cryptosporidium parvum* and *C. muris* in *Mus domesticus,*

Apodemus sylvaticus and *Clethrionomys glareolus* in an agricultural ecosystem. *Parasitological Research,* **83,** 478–482.

243 Chantrey, J. *et al.* (1999) Cowpox: reservoir hosts and geographic range. *Epidemiology and Infection,* **122,** 455–460.

244 Childs, J.E. (1986) Size dependent predation on rats (*Rattus norvegicus*) by house cats (*Felis catus*) in an urban setting. *Journal of Mammalogy,* **67,** 196–199.

245 Chitty, D. (1952) Mortality among voles (*Microtus agrestis*) at lake Vyrnwy, Montgomeryshire in 1936–39. *Philosophical Transactions of the Royal Society of London, Series B,* **236,** 505–552.

246 Chitty, D. (1954) The study of the brown rat and its control by poison, pp. 160–305 in Chitty, D. & Southern, H.N. (eds.) *Control of rats and mice,* Vol. 1. Clarendon Press, Oxford.

247 Chitty, D. (1996) *Do lemmings commit suicide? Beautiful hypotheses and ugly facts.* Oxford University Press, Oxford.

248 Chitty, D. & Chitty, H. (1962) Population trends among the voles at Lake Vyrnwy, 1932–1960. *Symposium Theriologicum Brno,* 67–76.

249 Chitty, D. & Phipps, E. (1966) Seasonal changes in survival in mixed populations of two species of vole. *Journal of Animal Ecology,* **35,** 313–32.

250 Churcher, P.B. & Lawton, J.H. (1987) Predation by domestic cats in an English village. *Journal of Zoology,* **212,** 439–455.

251 Churchfield, S. *et al.* (1997) Community structure and habitat use of small mammals in grassland of different successional age. *Journal of Zoology,* **242,** 519–530.

252 Ciháková, J. & Frynta, D. (1996) Intraspecific and interspecific behavioural interactions in the wood mouse (*Apodemus sylvaticus*) and the yellow-necked mouse (*Apodemus flavicollis*) in a neutral cage. *Folia Zoologica,* **45,** 105–113.

253 Clarke, J.R. (1956) The aggressive behaviour of the vole. *Behaviour,* **9,** 1–23.

254 Clarke, J.R. (1985) The reproductive biology of the bank vole (*Clethrionomys glareolus*) and the wood mouse (*Apodemus sylvaticus*). *Symposia of the Zoological Society of London,* **55,** 33–59.

255 Clarke, J.R. & Clulow, F.V. (1973) The effect of successive matings upon bank vole (*Clethrionomys glareolus*) and vole (*Microtus agrestis*) ovaries, pp. 160–170 in Peters, H. (ed.) *The development and maturation of the ovary and its function* (International Congress Series No. 267), Excerpta Medica, Amsterdam.

256 Clarke, J.R. & Frearson, S. (1972) Sebaceous glands in the hind quarters of the vole *Microtus agrestis. Journal of Reproduction and Fertility,* **31,** 477–481.

257 Clarke, J.R. & Hellwing, S. (1983) Fertility of the post-partum bank vole (*Clethrionomys glareolus*). *Journal of Reproduction and Fertility,* **68,** 241–246.

258 Clarke, J.R. *et al.* (1981) Seasonal breeding in voles and wood mice: coarse and fine adjustments, pp. 291–317 in Ortavant, R. *et al.* (eds.) *Photoperiodism and reproduction* (Colloq. INRA No. 6), INRA, Paris.

259 Clarke, J.R. *et al.* (2004) Sexual transmission of a nematode parasite of wood mice (*Apodemus sylvaticus*)? *Parasitology,* **128,** 561–568.

260 Clarke, R. & Kennedy, J.P. (1967) Effect of light and temperature upon gonadal activity in the vole (*Microtus agrestis*). *General and Comparative Endocrinology,* **8,** 474–488.

261 Clegg, T.M. (1963) Observations on an East Yorkshire population of the house mouse (*Mus musculus*). *Naturalist,* **885,** 39–40.

262 Clegg, T.M. (1965) *The house mouse (*Mus musculus, *L) in the South Yorkshire coal mines.* Doncaster Museum and Art Gallery, Doncaster.

263 Clevedon Brown, J. & Twigg, G.I. (1969) Studies on the pelvis in British Muridae and Cricetidae (Rodentia). *Journal of Zoology,* **158,** 81–132.

264 Clevedon Brown, J. & Twigg, G.I. (1971) Mammalian prey of the barn owl (*Tyto alba*) on Skomer Island,

Pembrokeshire. *Journal of Zoology,* **165,** 527–530.

265 Cody, C.B.J. (1982) *Studies on behavioural and territorial factors relating to the dynamics of woodland rodent populations.* DPhil. thesis, University of Oxford.

266 Coles, A. & Jessop, L. (1993) New flea records for Northumberland. *The Vasculum,* **77,** 77.

267 Coles, B. (2006) *Beavers in Britain's past.* Oxbow Books, Oxford.

268 Cooke, H.J. (1975) Evolution of the long range satellite DNAs in the genus *Apodemus. Journal of Molecular Biology,* **94,** 87–99.

269 Cooke, J.A. *et al.* (1990) The accumulation of lead, zinc, cadmium and fluoride in the wood mouse (*Apodemus sylvaticus* L). *Water Air and Soil Pollution,* **51,** 55–63.

270 Cooke, T. (1977) *Exhibition and pet mice.* Saiga, Hindhead.

271 Cooper, J.J. & Nicol, C.J. (1991) Stereotypic behavior affects environmental preference in bank voles, *Clethrionomys glareolus. Animal Behaviour,* **41,** 971–977.

272 Cooper, J.J. *et al.* (1996) Limitations on the effectiveness of environmental improvement in reducing stereotypic behaviour in bank voles (*Clethrionomys glareolus*). *Applied Animal Behaviour Science,* **48,** 237–248.

273 Cooper, M. (1991). *Diet selection and spatial dynamics in the field vole* Microtus agrestis. PhD thesis, University of Wales, Cardiff.

274 Corbet, G.B. (1960) *The distribution, variation and ecology of voles in the Scottish Highlands.* PhD thesis, University of St Andrews.

275 Corbet, G.B. (1961) Origin of the British insular races of small mammals and of the 'Lusitanian' fauna. *Nature,* **191,** 1037–1040.

276 Corbet, G.B. (1963) The frequency of albinism of the tail tip in British mammals. *Proceedings of the Zoological Society of London,* **140,** 327–330.

277 Corbet, G.B. (1964) Regional variation in the bank vole *Clethrionomys glareolus* in the British Isles. *Proceedings of the Zoological Society, London,* **143,** 191–219.

278 Corbet, G.B. (1975) Examples of short- and long-term changes in dental patterns in Scottish voles. *Mammal Review,* **5,** 17–21.

279 Corbet, G.B. (1978) *The mammals of the Palaearctic region.* British Museum (Natural History), London.

280 Corbet, G.B. (1979) Report on rodent remains, pp. 135–137 in Renfrew, C. (ed.) *Investigations in Orkney,* Society of Antiquaries/Thames & Hudson, London.

281 Corbet, G.B. (1986) Temporal and spatial variation of dental pattern in the voles *Microtus arvalis,* of the Orkney Islands. *Journal of Zoology,* **208,** 395–402.

282 Corbet, G.B. Personal communication.

283 Corbet, G.B. & Critchlow, M.A. (1986) The shrews and mice of Bardsey – a comparison with mainland animals. *Bardsey Observatory Report,* **29,** 138–141.

284 Corbet, G.B. *et al.* (1970) The taxonomic status of British water voles, genus *Arvicola. Journal of Zoology,* **161,** 301–316.

285 Corke, D. (1974) *The comparative ecology of the two British species of the genus* Apodemus *(Rodentia, Muridae).* PhD thesis, University of London.

286 Corke, D. (1977) The distribution of *Apodemus flavicollis* in Britain. *Mammal Review,* **7,** 123–130.

287 Corp, N. *et al.* (1997) Ranging behaviour and time budgets of male wood mice *Apodemus sylvaticus* in different habitats and seasons. *Oecologia,* **109,** 242–250.

288 Cotton, M.J. (1970) The comparative morphology of some species of flea larvae (Siphonaptera) associated with nests of small mammals. *Entomologist's Gazette,* **21,** 191 -204.

289 Cowan, D.P. *et al.* (2003) Ecological perspectives on the management of commensal rodents, pp. 433–439 in Singleton, G.R. *et al.* (eds) *Rats, mice and people: rodent biology and management.* Australian Centre for International Agricultural Research, Canberra.

290 Cox, F.E.G. (1970) Parasitic protozoa of British wild mammals. *Mammal Review,* **1,** 1–28.

291 Cox, F.E.G. (1979) Ecological importance of small

mammals as reservoirs of disease, pp. 213–238 in Stoddart, D.M. (ed.) *Ecology of small mammals.* Chapman & Hall, London.

292 Cox, F.E.G. (1987) Protozoan parasites of British small rodents. *Mammal Review,* **17,** 59–66.

293 Crawley, M.C. (1970) Some population dynamics of the bank vole, *Clethrionomys glareolus* and the wood mouse, *Apodemus sylvaticus* in mixed woodland. *Journal of Zoology,* **160,** 71–89.

294 Crespin, L. *et al.* (2002) Survival in fluctuating bank vole populations: seasonal and yearly variations. *Oikos,* **98,** 467–479.

295 Cross, R.M. (1970) Activity rhythms of the harvest mouse, *Micromys minutus* Pallas. *Mammalia,* **34,** 433–450.

296 Crouch, A.C. *et al.* (1995) Serological evidence for the reservoir hosts of cowpox virus in British wildlife. *Epidemiology and Infection,* **115,** 185–191.

297 Crowcroft, P. (1966) *Mice all over.* Foulis, London.

298 Crowcroft, P. & Rowe, F.P. (1958) The growth of confined colonies of the wild house-mouse (*Mus musculus* L): the effect of dispersal on female fecundity. *Proceedings of the Zoological Society of London,* **131,** 357–365.

299 Crowcroft, P. & Rowe, F.P. (1961) The weights of wild house mice (*Mus musculus* L) living in confined colonies. *Proceedings of the Zoological Society of London,* **136,** 177–185.

300 Crowcroft, W.P. & Godfrey, G. (1962) Laboratory produced hybrids of the Guernsey vole (*Microtus arvalis sarnius* Miller). *Annals and Magazine of Natural History,* **5,** 408–419.

301 Csaiki, F. *et al.* (1980) On the biochemical systematics of three *Apodemus* species. *Comparative Biochemistry and Physiology,* **65**B, 411–414.

302 Cucchi, T. *et al.* (2005) First occurrence of the house mouse (*Mus musculus domesticus* Schwarz & Schwarz 1943) in the Western Mediterranean: a zooarchaeological revision of subfossil occurrences. *Biological Journal of the Linnean Society,* **84,** 429–445.

303 Currado, I. *et al.* (1987) Note sulla presenza dello scoiattolo grigio (*Sciurus carolinensis* Gmelin, 1788) in Piemonte (Rodentia: Sciuridae). *Annales della Facoltà delle Scienze e Agraria, Torino,* **14,** 307–331 (in Italian).

304 Curry-Lindahl, K. (1959) Notes on the ecology and periodicity of some rodents and shrews in Sweden. *Mammalia,* **23,** 389–422.

305 Dagnall, J. *et al.* (1998) Bark removal damage by grey squirrels in Britain – a review, pp. 249–259 in Steele, M.A. *et al.* (eds.) *Ecology and evolutionary biology of tree squirrels.* Special Publication 6, Virginia Museum of Natural History, Martinsville, VA.

306 Dalgleish, H.M. (1986) *Parental behaviour in Orkney voles* Microtus arvalis. Honours thesis, University of Aberdeen.

307 David-Gray, Z.K. *et al.* (1998) The use of DNA fingerprinting in determining the mating system and reproductive success in a population of the introduced grey squirrel, *Sciurus carolinensis,* in southern England, pp. 43–52 in Steele, M.A. *et al.* (eds.) *Ecology and evolutionary biology of tree squirrels.* Special Publication 6, Virginia Museum of Natural History, Martinsville, VA.

308 David-Gray, Z.K. *et al.* (1999) DNA fingerprinting reveals high levels of genetic diversity in British populations of the introduced non-native grey squirrel, *Sciurus carolinensis. Journal of Zoology,* **246,** 443–486.

309 David-Gray, Z.K. *et al.* (1999) Estimating the relatedness in a population of grey squirrels, *Sciurus carolinensis,* using DNA fingerprinting. *Acta Theriologica,* **44,** 243–251.

310 Davidson, A.M. & Adams, W. (1973) The grey squirrel and tree damage. *Quarterly Journal of Forestry,* **67,** 237–47.

311 Davis, D.E. (1953) The characteristics of rat populations. *Quarterly Review of Biology,* **28,** 373–401.

312 Davis, D.H.S. (1933) Rhythmic activity in the short-tailed vole, *Microtus. Journal of Animal Ecology,* **2,** 232–238.

313 Davis, R.A. (1955) Small mammals caught near London. *London Naturalist,* **35,** 88–89.

314 Davis, R.A. (1963) Feral coypus in Britain. *Annals of Applied*

Biology, **5,** 345–348.

315 Davis, R.A. (1979) Unusual behaviour by *Rattus norvegicus. Journal of Zoology,* **188,** 298.

316 Davis, R.A. & Jenson, AG. (1960) A note on the distribution of coypu (*Myocastor coypus*) in Great Britain. *Journal of Applied Ecology,* **29,** 397.

317 Davis, R.A. & Rennison, B.D. Personal communication.

318 Davis, S.J.M. (1983) Morphometric variation of populations of house mouse *Mus domesticus* in Britain and Faroe. *Journal of Zoology,* **199,** 521–534.

319 De Jonge, G. (1980) Response to con-and hetero-specific male odours by the voles *Microtus agrestis, M. arvalis* and *Clethrionomys glareolus* with respect to competition for space. *Behaviour,* **73,** 277–303.

320 De Jonge, G. (1983) Aggression and group formation in the voles *Microtus agrestis, M. arvalis* and *Clethrionomys glareolus* in relation to intra- and inter-specific competition. *Behaviour,* **84,** 1–73.

321 de la Maza, H.M. *et al.* (1999) Exposure to strange adults does not cause pregnancy disruption or infanticide in the gray-tailed vole. *Behavioral Ecology and Sociobiology,* **45,** 107–113.

322 De Long, K.T. (1967) Population ecology of feral house mice. *Ecology,* **48,** 611–634.

323 de Mendonça, P.G. (2003) *Aspects of the social ecology of the yellow-necked mouse* Apodemus flavicollis. PhD thesis, University of Cambridge.

324 Debrot, S. & Mermod, C. (1977) Chimiotaxonomie du genre *Apodemus* Kaup, 1829 (Rodentia, Muridae). *Revue Suisse de Zoologie,* **84,** 521–526 (in French).

325 Deffontaine, V. *et al.* (2005) Beyond the Mediterranean peninsulas: evidence of central European glacial refugia for a temperate forest mammal species, the bank vole (*Clethrionomys glareolus*). *Molecular Ecology,* **141,** 727–1739.

326 Deffontaine, V. *et al.* (2006) Phylogeography and interspecific hybridization of bank and red voles (*Clethrionomys glareolus* and *rutilus*) in the Eurasian region. *Hystrix Italian Journal of Mammalogy* (N.S.) Supp. 10th International Conference Rodens & Spatium.

327 Degn, D.H. (1973) Systematic position, age criteria and reproduction of Danish red squirrels *(Sciurus vulgaris* L) *Danish Review of Game Biology,* **8,** 1–24.

328 Delany, M.J. (1961) The ecological distribution of small mammals in north-west Scotland. *Proceedings of the Zoological Society of London,* **137,** 107–126.

329 Delany, M.J. (1970) Variation and ecology of island populations of the long-tailed field-mouse (*Apodemus sylvaticus* (L.)). *Symposia of the Zoological Society of London,* **26,** 283–295.

330 Delany, M.J. & Bishop, I.R. (1960) The systematics, life history and evolution of the bank vole *Clethrionomys glareolus* Tilesius in north west Scotland. *Proceedings of the Zoological Society of London,* **135,** 409–422.

331 Delany, M.J. & Davis, P.E. (1961) Observations on the ecology and life-history of the Fair Isle field mouse *Apodemus sylvaticus fridariensis* (Kinnear). *Proceedings of the Zoological Society of London,* **136,** 439–452.

332 Dell'Omo, G. & Shore, R.F. (1996) Behavioral and physiological effects of acute sublethal exposure to dimethoate on wood mice *Apodemus sylvaticus* (I – Laboratory studies). *Archives of Environmental Contamination and Toxicology,* **31,** 91–97.

333 Dell'Omo, G. & Shore, R.F. (1996) Behavioral effects of acute sublethal exposure to dimethoate on wood mice, *Apodemus sylvaticus:* (II – Field studies on radio-tagged mice in a cereal ecosystem). *Archives of Environmental Contamination and Toxicology,* **31,** 538–542.

334 Dell'Omo, G. *et al.* (1996) The relationships between brain, serum, and whole blood ChE activity in the wood mouse (*Apodemus sylvaticus*) and the common shrew (*Sorex araneus*) after acute sublethal exposure to dimethoate. *Biomarkers,* **1,** 202–207.

335 Dell'Omo, G. *et al.* (1998) An automated system, based on

microchips, for monitoring individual activity in wild small mammals. *Journal of Experimental Zoology,* **280,** 97–99.
336 Deol, M.S. (1970) The determination and distribution of coat colour variation in the house mouse. *Symposia of the Zoological Society of London,* **26,** 239–250.
336a Deshmukh, I.K. & Cotton, M.J. (1970) The small mammals of a sand dune system. *Journal of Zoology,* **162,** 525–527.
337 Desjardins, C. *et al.* (1973) Social rank in the house mouse: differentiation revealed by ultra-violet visualisation of urinary marking patterns. *Science,* **182,** 939–941.
338 Dickinson, P. (1995) The captive care, maintenance and breeding of the red squirrel (*Sciurus vulgaris*). *Journal of the Association of British Wild Animal Keepers,* **22,** 10–23.
339 Dickinson, P. Personal communication.
340 Dickman, C.R. (1986) Habitat utilisation and diet of the harvest mouse, *Micromys minutus,* in an urban environment. *Acta Theriologica,* **31,** 249–256.
341 Dillon, P. & Brown, M. (1975) Habitat selection and nest ecology of the harvest mouse *Micromys minutus* (Pallas). *Wiltshire Natural History Magazine,* **70,** 3–9.
342 Dizij, A. & Kurtenbach, K. (1995) *Clethrionomys glareolus,* but not *Apodemus flavicollis,* acquires resistance to *Ixodes ricinus* L, the main European vector of *Borrelia burgdorferi. Parasite Immunology,* **17,** 177–183.
343 Doboszynska, T. & Zurowski, W. (1983). Reproduction of the European beaver. *Acta Zoologica Fennica,* **174,** 123–126.
344 Dobson, J. (1999) *The mammals of Essex.* Lopinga Books, Saffron Walden, Essex.
345 Don, B.A.C. (1979) Gut analysis of small mammals during a sawfly *(Cephalacia lariciphila)* outbreak. *Journal of Zoology,* **188,** 290–4.
346 Don, B.A.C. (1981) *Spatial dynamics and individual quality in a population of the grey squirrel* (Sciurus carolinensis). DPhil thesis, University of Oxford.
347 Don, B.A.C. (1983) Home range characteristics and correlates in tree squirrels. *Mammal Review,* **13,** 123–132.
348 Don, B.A.C. (1985) The use of drey counts to estimate grey squirrel populations. *Journal of Zoology,* **206,** 282–286.
349 Don, B.A.C. Personal communication.
350 Drummond, D.C. (1971) Rodents and biodeterioration. *International Biodeterioration Bulletin,* **7,** 73–79.
351 Drummond, D. (2005) *Mouse traps. A quick scamper through their long history.* North American Trap Collectors Association, Galloway.
352 Drummond, D.C. *et al.* (1977) Urban rat control: further experimental studies at Folkestone. *Environmental Health,* **85,** 265–267.
353 Dubinsky, P. *et al.* (1995) Role of small mammals in the epidemiology of toxocariasis. *Parisitology,* **110,** 187–193.
354 Dubock, A.C. (1979) Methods of age determination in grey squirrels (*Sciurus carolinensis*) in Britain. *Journal of Zoology,* **187,** 27–40.
355 Dubock, A.C. (1979) Male grey squirrel (*Sciurus carolinensis*) reproductive cycles in Britain. *Journal of Zoology,* **188,** 41–51.
356 Dubock, A.C. Personal communication.
357 Ducharme, M.B. *et al.* (1989) Thermogenic capacity in gray and black morphs of the gray squirel, *Sciurus carolinensis. Physiological Zoology,* **62,** 1273–1292.
358 Dueser, R.D. & Porter, J.H. (1986) Habitat use by insular small mammals: relative effects of competition and habitat structure. *Ecology* **67**(1), 195–201.
359 Duff, J.P. *et al.* (1996) Parapoxvirus infection of the grey squirrel. *Veterinary Record,* **138,** 527.
360 Dufour, B. (1972) Adaptations du terrier d'*Apodemus sylvaticus* à la temperature et à la lumière. *Revue Suisse de Zoologie,* **79,** 966–969 (in French).
361 Durden, L.A. *et al.* (2004) Ectoparasites of gray squirrels in two different habitats and screening of selected ectoparasites for bartonellae. *Journal of Parasitology,* **90,** 485–489.
362 Durka, W. *et al.* (2005) Mitochondrial phylogeography of the Eurasian beaver *Castor fiber* L. *Molecular Ecology,* **14,** 3843–3856.
363 Dvorakova, K. & Stopka, P. (2004) Sperm trains and mating behaviour in wood mice of the genus *Apodemus. Biology of Reproduction,* **606,** 232–232.
364 Dyczkowski, J. & Yalden, D.W. (1998). An estimate of the impact of predators on the British field vole *Microtus agrestis* population. *Mammal Review,* **28,** 165–184.
365 Dynowski, J. (1963) Morphological variability in the Białowieża population of *Mus musculus* Linnaeus, 1758. *Acta Theriologica,* **7,** 51–67.
366 East, K. (1965) Notes on the opening of hazel nuts (*Corylus avellana*) by mice and voles. *Journal of Zoology,* **147,** 223–224.
367 Eccard, J.A. & Ylönen, H. (2002) Direct interference or indirect exploitation? An experimental study of fitness costs of interspecific competition in voles. *Oikos,* **99,** 580–590.
368 Eccard, J.A. *et al.* (2002) Effects of competition and season on survival and maturation of young bank vole females. *Evolutionary Ecology,* **16,** 85–99.
369 Eden, S.M. & Eden, R.M.G. (1999) Dormice in Dorset – the importance of hedges and scrub. *British Wildlife,* **10,** 185–189.
370 Efford, M.G. (1985) *The structure and dynamics of water vole populations.* D.Phil thesis, University of Oxford.
371 Eibl-Eibesfeldt, L. (1951) Beobachtungen zur Fortplanzungsbiologie und Jugendentwicklung des Eichhörnchens *(Sciurus vulgaris* L). *Zeitschrift für Tierpsychologie,* **8,** 370–400 (in German).
372 Eldridge, M.J. (1969) Observations on food eaten by wood mice (*Apodemus sylvaticus*) and bank voles (*Clethrionomys galreolus*) in a hedge. *Journal of Zoology,* **158,** 208–209.
373 Ellis, A.E. (ed.) (1965) *The Broads.* Collins, London.
374 Elton, C. (1936) House mice (*Mus musculus*) in a coal mine in Ayrshire. *Annals and Magazine of Natural History,* **10**(17), 553–558.
375 Elton, C. (1942) *Voles, mice and lemmings.* Clarendon Press, Oxford.
376 Elton, C. (1953) The use of cats in farm rat control. *British Journal of Animal Behaviour,* **1,** 151–155.
377 Engel, W. *et al.* (1973) Cytogenetic and biochemical differences between *Apodemus sylvaticus* and *Apodemus flavicollis* possibly responsible for the failure to interbreed. *Comparative Biochemistry and Physiology,* **44B,** 1165–1173.
378 English, M.P. (1966) *Trichophyton persicolor* infection in the field vole and pipistrelle bat. *Sabouraudia,* **4,** 219–222.
379 English, M.P. (1971) Ringworm in groups of wild mammals. *Journal of Zoology,* **165,** 535–544.
380 English, M.P. & Southern, H.N. (1967) *Trichophyton persicolor* infection in a population of small wild mammals. *Sabouraudia,* 5, 302–9.
381 Ergon, T. (2003) *Fluctuating life history traits in overwintering field voles* Microtus agrestis. DrSci thesis, University of Oslo.
382 Ergon, T. Personal communication
383 Ergon, T. *et al.* (2001) Mechanisms for delayed density-dependent reproductive traits in field voles, *Microtus agrestis*: the importance of inherited environmental effects. *Oikos,* **95,** 185–197.
384 Ergon, T. *et al.* (2001) Life-history traits of voles in a fluctuating population respond to the immediate environment. *Nature,* **411,** 1043–1045.
385 Ericson, L. *et al.* (1992) Age structure of boreal willows and fluctuations in herbivore populations. *Proceedings of the Royal Society of Edinburgh Section B,* **98,** 75–89.
386 Erkinaro, E. (1961) Seasonal change of the activity of *Microtus agrestis. Oikos,* **12,** 157–163.
387 Erkinaro, E. (1970) Effect of the length of the day and twilight on the phase relationship of the 24 hour periodicity of the field mouse *Apodemus flavicollis* Melch. in natural light. *Oikos,* **13** (Suppl.), 101–107.
388 Erkinaro, E. (1973) Activity optimum in *Microtus agrestis,*

Arvicola terrestris and Apodemus flavicollis. Aquilo (Zoology), **14**, 89–92.

389 Erlinge, S. *et al.* (1983) Predation as a regulating factor on small rodent populations in southern Sweden. *Oikos*, **40**, 36–52.

390 Erlinge, S. *et al.* (1990) Social organization and population dynamics in a *Microtus agrestis* population, pp. 45–58 in Tamarin R.H., *et al.* (eds.) *Social systems and population cycles in voles.* Birkhäuser Verlag, Basel.

391 Erlinge, S. *et al.* (1991) Why are some microtine populations cyclic while others are not? *Acta Theriologica*, **36**, 63–71.

392 Erry, B.V. *et al.* (2000) Arsenic contamination in wood mice (*Apodemus sylvaticus*) and bank voles (*Clethrionomys glareolus*) on abandoned mine sites in south-west Britain. *Environmental Pollution*, **110**, 179–187.

393 Erry, B.V. *et al.* (2005) The distribution of arsenic in the body tissues of wood mice and bank voles. *Archives of Environmental Contamination and Toxicology*, **9**, 569–576.

394 Escutenaire, S. & Pastoret, P.P. (2000) Hantavirus infections. *Revue Scientifique et Technique de L'Office International des Epizooties*, **19**, 64–78.

395 Escutenaire, S. *et al.* (2000) Spatial and temporal dynamics of Puumala hantavirus infection in red bank vole (*Clethrionomys glareolus*) populations in Belgium. *Virus Research*, **67**, 91–107.

396 Evans, D.M. (1973) Seasonal variations in the body composition and nutrition of the vole *Microtus agrestis. Journal of Animal Ecology*, **42**, 1–18.

397 Evans, D.M. *et al.* (2006) To graze or not to graze? Sheep, voles, forestry and nature conservation in the British uplands. *Journal of Applied Ecology*, **43**, 499–505.

398 Evans, F.C. (1949) A population study of house mice (*Mus musculus*) following a period of local abundance. *Journal of Mammalogy*, **30**, 351–63.

399 Eviskov, V.I. *et al.* (1999) *Population ecology of the water vole (*Arvicola terrestris* L) in West Siberia. I. Population numbers, coat colour polymorphism, and reproductive effort of females. *Siberian Journal of Ecoology*, **1**, 1–11.

400 Ewer, R.F. (1971) The biology and behaviour of a free-living population of black rats (*Rattus rattus*). *Animal Behaviour Monographs*, **4**, 127–174.

401 Fairley, J.S. (1967) Woodmice in grassland at Dundrum, County Down, Northern Ireland. *Journal of Zoology*, **153**, 553–555.

402 Fairley, J.S. (1972) The fieldmouse in Ireland. *Irish Naturalists' Journal*, **17**, 152–159.

403 Fairley, J.S. (1984) *An Irish beast book,* 2nd edn. Blackstaff Press, Belfast.

404 Fairley, J.S. & Comerton, M.E. (1972) An early-breeding population of field mice *Apodemus sylvaticus* (L.) in Limekiln Wood, Athenry, Co. Galway. *Proceedings of the Royal Irish Academy*, **72l3**, 149–163.

405 Fairley, J.S. & Smal, C.M. (1987) Feral house mice in Ireland. *Irish Naturalists' Journal*, **22(7)**, 284–290.

406 Fasola, M. & Canova, L. (2000) Asymmetrical competition between the bank vole and the wood mouse, a removal experiment. *Acta Theriologica*, **45**, 353–365.

407 Fedriani, J.M. & Manzaneda, A.J. (2005) Pre-and postdispersal seed predation by rodents: balance of food and safety. *Behavioral Ecology*, **16**, 1018–1024.

408 Fedyk, A. (1971) Social thermo-regulation in *Apodemus flavicollis* (Melchior, 1934). *Acta Theriologica*, **16**, 221–229.

409 Fedyk, A. & Gebczynski, M. (1980) Genetic changes in seasonal generations of the bank vole. *Acta Theriologica*, **25**, 475–485.

410 Feliu, C. *et al.* (2000) Genetic and morphological heterogeneity in small rodent whipworms in southwestern Europe: Characterization of *Trichuris muris* and description of *Trichuris arvicolae* n. sp (Nematoda : Trichuridae). *Journal of Parasitology*, **86**, 442–449.

411 Fenn, M.G.P. & Macdonald, D.W. (1987) The contribution of field studies to stored product rodent control, pp. 107–

113 in Lawson, T.J. (ed.) *Stored products pest control*, BCPC Monograph No. 37, BCPC Publications, Thornton Heath.

412 Feore, S.M. *et al.* (1997) The effect of cowpox virus infection on fecundity in bank voles and wood mice. *Proceedings of the Royal Society of London Series B*, **264**, 1457–1461.

413 Fernandez, F.A.S. *et al.* (1994) Local variation in rodent communities of Sitka spruce plantations – the interplay of successional stage and site-specific habitat parameters. *Ecography*, **17**, 305–313.

414 Fernandez, F.A.S. *et al.* (1996) Population dynamics of the wood mouse *Apodemus sylvaticus* (Rodentia: Muridae) in Sitka spruce successional mosaic. *Journal of Zoology*, **239**, 717–730.

415 Fernandez, F.A.S. *et al.* (1999) Density-dependence in habitat utilisation by wood mice in a Sitka spruce successional mosaic: the roles of immigration, emigration, and variation among local demographic parameters. *Canadian Journal of Zoology*, **77**, 397–405.

416 Fernie, D.S. & Healing, T.D. (1976) Wild bank voles *Clethrionomys glareolus* are possibly a natural reservoir of Campylobacters, microaerophilic vibrios. *Nature, London*, **263**, 496.

417 Ferns, P.N. (1969) *Energy flux in a population of field voles,* Microtus agrestis hirtus *(Bellamy, 1839) (Muridae).* PhD thesis, University of Exeter.

418 Ferns, P.N. (1976) Diet of *Microtus agrestis* populations in South West Britain. *Oikos*, **27**, 506–511.

419 Ferns, P.N. & Adams, M.G. (1974) The effects of laboratory confinement on lipid deposition in wood mice, bank voles and field voles. *Journal of Zoology*, **174**, 524–528.

420 Ferrari, N. & Weber, J.M. (1995) Influence of the abundance of food resources on the feeding habits of the red fox *Vulpes vulpes* in Western Switzerland. *Journal of Zoology*, **236**, 117–129.

421 Ferrari, N. *et al.* (2004) The role of host sex in parasite dynamics: field experiments on the yellow-necked mouse *Apodemus flavicollis. Ecology Letters*, **7**, 88–94.

422 Ferryman, M. *et al.* (2006) Visual methods for evaluating the state of sexual development in male grey squirrels (*Sciurus carolinensis*). *Reproduction, Fertility and Development*, **18**, 283–293.

423 Fertig, D.S. & Edmonds, V.W. (1969) The physiology of the house mouse. *Scientific American*, **221**(4), 103–110.

424 Festing, M. (1972) Mouse strain identification. *Nature*, **238**, 351–352.

425 Festing, M. (1976) Phenotypic variability of the mandible shape in inbred and outbred mice. *Heredity*, **37**, 454.

426 Festing, M.F.W. (1979) *Inbred strains in biomedical research.* Macmillan, London.

427 Field, J. (1998) *Small mammal abundance in organic and intensive farmland in Gloucestershire and Wiltshire, UK.* MSc thesis, University of Reading.

428 Fielding, D.C. (1966) The identification of skulls of the two British species of *Apodemus. Journal of Zoology*, **150**, 498–500.

429 Filipucci, M.-G. *et al.* (2002) Genetic variation and evolution in the genus *Apodemus* (Muridae: Rodentia). *Biological Journal of the Linnean Society*, **75**, 395–419.

430 Finlayson, J.S. *et al.* (1963) Electrophoretic variation and sex dimorphism of the major urinary protein complex in inbred mice: a new genetic marker. *Journal of the National Cancer Institute*, **31**, 91–107.

431 Fischer, R.A. & Holler, N.R. (1991) Habitat use and relative abundance of gray squirrels in southern Alabama. *Journal of Wildlife Management*, **55**, 52–59.

432 Fisher, E.W. & Perry, A.E. (1970) Estimating ages of gray squirrels by lens-weights. *Journal of Wildlife Management*, **34**, 825–828.

433 Fitzgerald, B.M. *et al.* (1981) Spatial organisation and ecology of a sparse population of house mice (*Mus musculus*). *Journal of Animal Ecology*, **50**, 489–518.

434 Fitzgibbon, C.D. (1993) The distribution of grey squirrel

dreys in farm woodland: the influence of wood area, isolation and management. *Journal of Applied Ecology*, **30**, 736–742.

435 Fitzgibbon, C.D. (1997) Small mammals in farm woodlands: the effects of habitat, isolation and surrounding land use patterns. *Journal of Applied Ecology*, **34**, 530–539.

436 Flowerdew, J.R. (1972) The effect of supplementary food on a population of wood mice *(Apodemus sylvaticus)*. *Journal of Animal Ecology*, **41**, 553–566.

437 Flowerdew, J.R. (1973) The effects of natural and artificial changes in food supply on breeding in woodland mice and voles. *Journal of Reproduction and Fertility*, **19** (suppl.), 257–267.

438 Flowerdew, J.R. (1974) Field and laboratory experiments on the social behaviour and population dynamics of the wood mouse, *Apodemus sylvaticus*. *Journal of Animal Ecology*, **43**, 499–511.

439 Flowerdew, J.R. (1984) *Woodmice and yellow-necked mice*. Mammal Society Series. Nelson, Oswestry.

440 Flowerdew, J.R. (1985) The population dynamics of wood mice and yellow-necked mice. *Symposia of the Zoological Society of London*, **55**, 315–338.

441 Flowerdew, J. (1993) *Mice and voles*. Whittet Books, London.

442 Flowerdew, J.R. (1997) Mammal biodiversity in agricultural habitats, pp. 25–40 in Kirkwood, R.C. (ed.) *Biodiversity and conservation in agriculture, BCPC Symposium, Brighton, November 1997*, British Crop Protection Council, Farnham.

443 Flowerdew, J.R. (2000) Wood mice – small granivores/insectivores with seasonally variable patterns, pp 177–189 in Halle, S. & Stenseth, N.C. (ed.) *Activity patterns in small mammals – a comparative approach*. Ecological Studies 141, Springer-Verlag, Heidelberg.

444 Flowerdew, J.R. & Ellwood, S.A. (2001) Impacts of woodland deer on small mammal ecology. *Forestry*, **74**, 277–287.

445 Flowerdew, J.R. & Gardner, G. (1978) Small rodent populations and food supply in a Derbyshire ashwood. *Journal of Animal Ecology*, **47**, 725–740.

446 Flowerdew, J.R. *et al.* (1977) Small rodents, their habitats, and the effects of flooding at Wicken Fen, Cambridgeshire. *Journal of Zoology*, **182**, 323–342.

447 Flowerdew, J.R. *et al.* (eds.) (1985) *The ecology of woodland rodents: bank voles and wood mice*. Oxford University Press, Oxford.

448 Flowerdew, J.R. *et al.* (2004) Live trapping to monitor small mammals in Britain. *Mammal Review*, **34**, 31–50.

449 Flyger, V. (1969) The 1968 squirrel 'migration' in the eastern United States. *Proceedings of the Northeast Fish and Wildlife Conference*, **26**, 69–79.

450 Flyger, V. & Gates, J.E. (1982) Fox and gray squirrels, *Sciurus niger*, *S. carolinensis* and allies, pp. 209–229 in Chapman, J.A. & Feldhammer, G.A. (ed.) *Wild mammals of North America*. Johns Hopkins University Press, Baltimore, MD.

451 Fogl, J.G. & Mosby, H.S. (1978) Aging gray squirrels by cementum annuli in razor-sectioned teeth. *Journal of Wildlife Management*, **42**, 444–448.

452 Forman, D.W. (2005) An assessment of the local impact of native predators on an established population of British water voles *(Arvicola terrestris)*. *Journal of Zoology*, **266**, 221–226.

453 Foster, H.L. *et al.* (eds.) (1981, 1982, 1983) *The mouse in biomedical research. I. History, genetics and wild mice, II. Diseases. III Normative biology, immunology and husbandry*. Academic Press, New York.

454 Fraefel, D. (1995) Grobmorphologische und histologische Untersuchungen am Integument des Eichhörnchens *Sciurus vulgaris* L. Diplomarbeit, Zoologisches Museum, University of Zürich (in German).

455 Frank, H. (1952) Über die Jungendentwicklung des Eichhörnchens. *Zeitschrift für Tierpsychologie*, **9**, 12–22 (in German).

456 Frank, F. (1956) Das Duftmarkieren der grossen Wuhlmaus, *Arvicola terrestris* (L.). *Zeitschrift für Säugetierkunde*, **21**, 172–175 (in German).

457 Frank, F. (1957) Biologie der Zwergmaus. *Zeitschrift für Säugetierkunde*, **22**, 1–44 (in German).

458 Fransden, F. *et al.* (1995) Prevalence of antibodies to *Borrelia burgdorferi* in Danish rodents. *APMIS*, **103**, 247–253.

459 Freeman, R.B. (1941) The distribution of *Orchopeas wickhami* (Baker) (Siphonaptera), in relation to its host the American grey squirrel. *Entomologist's Monthly Magazine*, **77**, 82–89.

460 Friend, G.F. (1936) The sperms of the British muridae. *Quarterly Journal of Microscopical Science*, **78**, 419–443.

461 Fryday, S.L. *et al.* (2004) Palatability of dead earthworms and slugs to the wood mouse *(Apodemus sylvaticus)* and the potential for secondary poisoning. *Bulletin of Environmental Contamination and Toxicology*, **72**, 54–61.

462 Fullagar, P.J. (1967) Moult in field mice and the variation in the chest markings of *Apodemus sylvaticus* (Linne, 1758) and *Apodemus flavicollis* (Melchior, 1834). *Säugetierkundliche Mitteilungen*, **15**, 138–148.

463 Fullager, P.J. *et al.* (1963) The Skomer vole *(Clethrionomys glareolus skomerensis)* and long-tailed field mouse *(Apodemus sylvaticus)* on Skomer Island, Pembrokeshire, in 1960. *Proceedings of the Zoological Society of London*, **140**, 295–341.

464 Gaisler, J. *et al.* (1967) Mammals in ricks in Czechoslovakia. *Acta Societatis Naturalium Brno*, **1**, 299–348.

465 Gaisler, J. *et al.* (1977) Ecology and reproduction of Gliridae (Mammalia) in northern Moravia. *Folia Zoologica*, **26**, 213–228.

466 Galeotti, P. *et al.* (2005) Fluctuating asymmetry in body traits increases predation risks: tawny owl selection against asymmetric woodmice. *Evolutionary Ecology*, **19**, 405–418.

467 Gandelmann, R. & Svare, B. (1974) Mice: pregnancy termination, lactation and aggression. *Hormones and Behaviour*, **5**, 397–405.

468 Garson, P.J. (1975) Social interactions of woodmice *(Apodemus sylvaticus)* studied by direct observation in the wild. *Journal of Zoology*, **177**, 496–500.

469 Gaskoin, J.S. (1856) On a peculiar variety of *Mus musculus*. *Proceedings of the Zoological Society of London*, **24**, 38–40.

470 Gdula-Argasinska, J. *et al.* (2004) Further investigation of the heavy metal content of the teeth of the bank vole as an exposure indicator of environmental pollution in Poland. *Environmental Pollution*, **131**, 71–79.

471 Gebczynska, Z. (1983) Feeding habits, pp. 40–49 in Petrusewicz, K. (ed.) *Ecology of the bank vole*. *Acta Theriologica*, **28**, Supplement 1.

472 Gebczynski, M. (1983) Individual development, pp. 20–30 in Petrusewicz, K. (ed.) *Ecology of the bank vole*. *Acta Theriologica*, **28**, Supplement 1.

473 Gemmeke, H. von (1980) Proteinvariation und Taxonomie in der Gattung *Apodemus* (Mammalia, Rodentia). *Zeitschrift für Säugetierkunde*, **45**, 348–365 (in German).

474 George, R.S. (1970) Ectoparasites. *Field Studies*, **3**, 252–256.

475 Gerlach, G. & Bartmann, S. (2002) Reproductive skew, costs, and benefits of cooperative breeding in female wood mice *(Apodemus sylvaticus)*. *Behavioral Ecology*, **13**, 408–418.

476 Gerlach, G. & Musolf, K. (2000) Fragmentation of landscape as a cause for genetic subdivision in bank voles. *Conservation Biology*, **14**, 1066–1074.

477 Geuse, P. & Bauchau, V. (1985) *Apodemus sylvaticus* (Rodentia: Muridae) et *Clethrionomys glareolus* (Rodentia: Microtidae): competition ou coexistence? *Annales de la Société royale de Zoologie du Belgique*, **115**, 211–220 (in French).

478 Gibson, D.S. & Delany, M.J. (1984) The population ecology of small rodents in Pennine woodlands. *Journal of Zoology*, **203**, 63–85.

479 Gibson, J.A. (2000) Water voles. *Transactions of the Buteshire*

Natural History Society, **25,** 109.

480 Gibson, J.A. (1973) The distribution of voles on the Clyde islands. *Western Naturalist,* **2,** 40–44.

481 Gill, R.M.A. (1992) A review of damage by mammals in north temperate woods. 2. Small mammals. *Forestry,* **65,** 281–308.

482 Gill, R.M.A. *et al.* (1995) Do woodland mammals threaten the development of new woods, pp. 201–224 in Ferris-Kaan, R. (ed.) *The ecology of woodland creation.* John Wiley & Sons, London.

483 Gipps, J.H.W. (1985) The behaviour of bank voles. *Symposia of the Zoological Society of London,* **55,** 61–87.

484 Gipps, J.H.W. (1985) Spacing behaviour and male reproductive ecology in voles of the genus *Clethrionomys. Annales Zoologici Fennici,* **22,** 343–351.

485 Gligic, A. *et al.* (1992) Hemorrhagic fever with renal syndrome in Yugoslavia: Epidemiologic and epizootiologic features of a nationwide outbreak in 1989. *European Journal of Epidemiology,* **8,** 816–825.

486 Gliwicz, J. (1970) Relation between trappability and age of individuals in a population of the bank vole *(Clethrionomys glareolus). Acta Theriologica,* **15,** 15–23.

487 Gliwicz, J. (1983) Age structure, pp. 111–117 in Petrusewicz, K. (ed.) *Ecology of the bank vole. Acta Theriologica,* **28,** Supplement 1.

488 Gliwicz, J. (1983) Survival and lifespan, pp. 161–172 in Petrusewicz, K. (ed.) *Ecology of the bank vole. Acta Theriologica,* **28,** Supplement 1.

489 Gliwicz, J. (1993) Dispersal in bank voles – benefits to emigrants or to residents. *Acta Theriologica,* 38, 31–38.

490 Gliwicz, J. & Rajska-Jurgiel, E. (1983) Social organisation, pp. 134–140 in Petrusewicz, K. (ed.) *Ecology of the bank vole. Acta Theriologica,* **28,** Supplement 1.

491 Gluchowski, W. (1954) Studies on the factors governing fertility in coypu. Part one: preliminary experiments on vaginal cycles. *Annales Universitatus Mariae Curie-Sklodowska Sect. E,* **3,** 41–53.

492 Glue, D.E. (1967) Prey taken by the barn owl in England and Wales. *Bird Study,* **14,** 169–83.

493 Glue, D.E. (1970) Avian predator pellet analysis and the mammalogist. *Mammal Review,* **1,** 53–62.

494 Glue, D. (1974) The food of the barn owl in Britain and Ireland. *Bird Study,* **21,** 200–210.

495 Glue, D.E. (1975) Harvest mice as barn owl prey in the British Isles. *Mammal Review,* **5,** 9–12.

496 Gockel, J. *et al.* (1997) Isolation and characterization of microsatellite loci from *Apodemus flavicollis* (Rodentia, Muridae) and *Clethrionomys glareolus* (Rodentia, Cricetidae). *Molecular Ecology,* **6,** 597–599.

497 Godfrey, J. (1958) The origin of sexual isolation between bank voles. *Proceedings of the Royal Physical Society of Edinburgh,* **27,** 47–55.

498 Goheen, J.R. *et al.* (2003) Forces structuring tree squirrel communities in landscapes fragmented by agriculture: species differences in perceptions of forest connectivity and carrying capacity. *Oikos,* **102,** 95–103.

499 Goldenberg, N. & Rand, C. (1971) Rodents and the food industry: an in-depth analysis for a large British food handler. *Pest Control,* **39,** 24–5.

500 Golley, F.B. *et al.* (1975) The role of small mammals in temperate forests, grasslands and cultivated fields, pp. 223–241 in Golley, F.B., *et al.* (eds.) *Small mammals: their productivity and population dynamics.* Cambridge University Press, Cambridge.

501 Gorecki, A. (1971) Metabolism and energy budget in the harvest mouse. *Acta Theriologica,* **16,** 213–220.

502 Gorman, M. (1982) Social differences in the sub caudal scent gland secretion of *Apodemus sylvaticus* (Rodentia: Muridae). *Journal of Zoology,* **198,** 353–362.

503 Gorman, M. & Reynolds, P. (1993) The impact of land-use changes on voles and raptors. *Mammal Review,* **23,** 121–126.

504 Gorman, M.L. & Zubaid, A.B.M.A. (1993) A comparative study of the woodmouse *Apodemus sylvaticus* in two contrasting habitats – deciduous woodland and maritime sand-dunes. *Journal of Zoology,* **229,** 385–396.

505 Gosálbez, J. & Castién, E. (1995) Reproductive cycle, abundance and population structure of *Apodemus flavicollis* (Melchior, 1834) in the western Pyrenees. *Mammalia,* **59,** 385–396.

506 Gosling, L.M. (1974) The coypu in East Anglia. *Transactions of the Norfolk and Norwich Naturalists' Society,* **23,** 49–59.

507 Gosling, L.M. (1979) The twenty-four hour activity cycle of coypus (*Myocastor coypus*). *Journal of Zoology,* **187,** 341–367.

508 Gosling, L.M. (1980) The duration of lactation in feral coypus (*Myocastor coypus*). *Journal of Zoology,* **191,** 461–474.

509 Gosling, L.M. (1981) Climatic determinants of spring littering by feral coypus (*Myocastor coypus*). *Journal of Zoology,* **195,** 281–288.

510 Gosling, L.M. (1981) The coypu, pp. 129–135 in Boyle, C.L. (ed.) *RSPCA book of British mammals.* Collins, London.

511 Gosling, L.M. (1986) Selective abortion of entire litters in the coypu: adaptive control of offspring production in relation to quality and sex. *American Naturalist,* **127,** 772–795.

512 Gosling, L.M. (1989) Extinction to order. *New Scientist,* **1654,** 44–49.

513 Gosling, L.M. & Baker, S.J. (1982) Coypu (*Myocastor coypus*) potential longevity. *Journal of Zoology,* **197,** 285–312.

514 Gosling, L.M. & Baker, S.J. (1987) Planning and monitoring an attempt to eradicate coypus from Britain. *Symposia of the Zoological Society of London,* **58,** 99–113.

515 Gosling, L.M. & Baker, S.J. (1989) Demographic consequences of differences in the ranging behaviour of male and female coypus, pp. 154–167 in Putnam, R.J. (ed.) *Mammals as pests.* Christopher Helm, London.

516 Gosling, L.M. & Baker, S.J. (1989) The eradication of coypus and muskrats from Britain. *Biological Journal of the Linnean Society,* **38,** 39–51.

517 Gosling, L.M. & McKay, H.V. (1990) Competitor assessment by scent matching; an experimental test. *Behavioural Ecology & Sociobiology,* **26,** 415–420.

518 Gosling, L.M. & Petrie, M. (1981) The economics of social organisation, pp. 315–345 in Townsend, C.R. & Calow, P. (eds.) *Physiological ecology; an evolutionary approach to resource use,* Blackwell Scientific Publications, Oxford.

519 Gosling, L.M. & Skinner, J.R. (1984) Coypu, pp. 246–251 in Mason, I.L. (ed.) *Evolution of domesticated animals,* Longman, Harlow.

520 Gosling, L.M. & Wright, K.M.H. (1993). Scent marking and resource defence by male coypus. *Journal of Zoology,* **234,** 423–36.

521 Gosling, L.M. *et al.* (1980) Diurnal activity of feral coypus (*Myocastor coypus*) during the cold winter of 1978–9. *Journal of Zoology,* **192,** 143–6.

522 Gosling, L.M. *et al.* (1981) Continuous retrospective census of the East Anglian coypu population between 1970 and 1979. *Journal of Animal Ecology,* **50,** 885–901.

523 Gosling, L.M. *et al.* (1983) A simulation approach to investigating the response of a coypu population to climatic variation. *EPPO Bulletin,* **13,** 183–192.

524 Gosling, L.M. *et al.* (1984) Differential investment by female coypus (*Myocastor coypus*) during lactation. *Symposia of the Zoological Society of London,* **52,** 273–300.

525 Goszczynski, J. (1983) Predators, pp. 49–54 in Petrusewicz, K. (ed.) *Ecology of the bank vole. Acta Theriologica,* **28,** Supplement 1.

526 Gourley, R.N. & Wyld, S.G. (1976) Isley-type and other mycoplasmas from the alimentary tracts of cattle, pigs and rodents. *Proceedings of the Society for General Microbiology,* **3,** 142.

527 Graham, I.M. (2001) *Weasels and vole cycles: An experimental test of the specialist predator hypothesis.* PhD thesis, University of Aberdeen.

528 Graham, I.M. Personal communication.

529 Graham, I.M. & Lambin, X. (2002) The impact of weasel predation on cyclic field-vole survival: the specialist

predator hypothesis contradicted. *Journal of Animal Ecology,* **71**, 946–956.

530 Gray, J.S. *et al.* (1992). Studies on the ecology of Lyme disease in a deer forest in County Galway, Ireland. *Journal of Medical Entomology,* **29**, 915–920.

531 Gray, S.J. & Hurst, J.L. (1997) Behavioural mechanisms underlying the spatial dispersion of competitors: a comparison between two species of house mouse inhabiting different environments. *Animal Behaviour,* **53**, 511–524.

532 Gray, S.J. & Hurst, J.L. (1998) Competitive behaviour in an island population of house mice *Mus domesticus. Animal Behaviour,* **56**, 1291–1299.

533 Greaves, J.H. & Cullen-Ayres, P.B. (1988) Genetics of difenacoum resistance in the rat, pp. 389–397 in Suttie, J.W. (ed.) *Current advances in vitamin K research.* Elsevier Science, London.

534 Greaves, J.H. & Rowe, F.P. (1969) Responses of confined rodent populations to an ultrasound generator. *Journal of Wildlife Management,* **33**, 407–417.

535 Green, E. (ed.) (1966) *Biology of the laboratory mouse,* 2nd edn. McGraw-Hill, New York.

536 Green, R.E. (1977) Melanism in the wood mouse (*Apodemus sylvaticus*). *Journal of Zoology,* **182**, 157–159.

537 Green, R. (1979) The ecology of wood mice *(Apodemus sylvaticus)* on arable farmland. *Journal of Zoology,* **188**, 357–377.

538 Greenwood, P.J. (1978) Timing of activity of the bank vole (*Clethrionomys glareolus*) and the wood mouse (*Apodemus sylvaticus*) in a deciduous woodland. *Oikos,* **31**, 123–127.

539 Gregory, R.D. (1991) Parasite epidemiology and host population growth – *Heligmosmoides polygyrus* (Nematoda) in enclosed wood mouse populations. *Journal of Animal Ecology,* **60**, 805–821.

540 Gregory, R.D. (1992) On the interpretation of host-parasite ecology – *Heligmosmoides polygyrus* (Nematoda) in wild wood mouse (*Apodemus sylvaticus*) populations. *Journal of Zoology,* **226**, 109–121.

541 Gregory, R.D. *et al.* (1992) Population biology of *Heligmosmoides polygyrus* (Nematoda) in the wood mouse. *Journal of Animal Ecology,* **61**, 749–757.

542 Griffin, J.L. *et al.* (2001) High-resolution magic angle spinning H-1-NMR spectroscopy studies on the renal biochemistry in the bank vole (*Clethrionomys glareolus*) and the effects of arsenic (As^{3+}) toxicity. *Xenobiotica,* **31**, 377–385.

543 Grocock, C.A. & Clarke, J.R. (1974) Photoperiodic control of testis activity in the vole, *Microtus agrestis. Journal of Reproduction and Fertility,* **39**, 337–347.

544 Grodzínski, W. (1985) Ecological energetics of bank voles and wood mice. *Symposia of the Zoological Society of London,* **55**, 169–192.

545 Grodzínski, W. & Gorecki, A. (1967) Daily energy budgets of small rodents, pp. 295–314 in Petrusewicz, K. (ed.) *Secondary productivity of terrestrial ecosystems (principles and methods),* Vol 1. Polish Academy of Sciences, Warsaw.

546 Guichón, M.L. *et al.* (2003) Foraging behaviour of coypus *Myocastor coypus*: why do coypus consume aquatic plants? *Acta Oecologica,* **24**, 241–246.

547 Gull, J. (1977) *Movement and dispersal patterns of immature gray squirrels* (Sciurus carolinensis) *in east-central Minnesota.* MS thesis, University of Minnesota.

548 Gurnell, J. (1972) *Studies on the behaviour of wild woodmice,* Apodemus sylvaticus *(L.).* PhD. thesis, University of Exeter.

549 Gurnell, J. (1975) Notes on the activity of wild wood mice, *Apodemus sylvaticus,* in artificial enclosures. *Journal of Zoology,* **175**, 219–229.

550 Gurnell, J. (1976) Studies on the effects of bait and sampling intensity on trapping and estimating wood mice, *Apodemus sylvaticus. Journal of Zoology,* **178**, 91–105.

551 Gurnell, J. (1977) Neutral cage behavioural interaction in wild wood mice, *Apodemus sylvaticus* (Linné, 1758).

Säugetierkundliche Mitteilungen, **25**, 57–66.

552 Gurnell, J. (1978) Seasonal changes in numbers and male behavioural interaction in a population of wood mice *Apodemus sylvaticus. Journal of Animal Ecology,* **47**, 741–755.

553 Gurnell, J. (1979) *Woodland mice.* Forest Record No. 118. HMSO, London.

554 Gurnell, J. (1981) Woodland rodents and tree seed supplies. pp. 1191–1214 in Chapman, J.A. & Pursley, D. (eds.) *The worldwide furbearer conference proceedings.* Donnelly, Falls Chard, VA.

555 Gurnell, J. (1982) Trap response in woodland rodents. *Acta Theriologica,* **27**, 123–137.

556 Gurnell, J. (1982) Index to theses and dissertations relevant to the biology of *Apodemus sylvaticus, A. flavicollis* and *Clethrionomys glareolus* held in British universities. *Mammal Review,* **12**, 143–145.

557 Gurnell, J. (1983) Squirrel numbers and the abundance of tree seeds. *Mammal Review,* **13**, 133–148.

558 Gurnell, J. (1984) Determining the age of wood mice (*Apodemus sylvaticus*). *Folia Zoologica,* **33**, 339–348.

559 Gurnell, J. (1985) Woodland rodent communities. *Symposia of the Zoological Society of London,* **55**, 377–411.

560 Gurnell, J. (1987) *The natural history of squirrels.* Christopher Helm, London.

561 Gurnell, J. (1989) Demographic implications for the control of grey squirrels. pp. 131–143 in Putnam, R.J. (ed.) *Mammals as pests.* Christopher Helm, London.

562 Gurnell, J. (1994) *The red squirrel.* The Mammal Society, London.

563 Gurnell, J. (1996) The effects of food availability and winter weather on the dynamics of a grey squirrel population in southern England. *Journal of Applied Ecology,* **33**, 325–338.

564 Gurnell, J. (1996) Conserving the red squirrel, pp. 132–140 in Ratcliffe, P. & Claridge, J. (eds.) *Thetford Forest Park: the ecology of a pine forest.* Forestry Commission, Edinburgh.

565 Gurnell, J. (1996) The grey squirrel in Britain: problems for management and lessons for Europe, pp. 67–81 in Mathias, M.L., *et al.* (eds.) *European mammals.* Museu Bocage, Lisbon.

566 Gurnell, J. (1999) Grey squirrels in woodlands: managing grey squirrels to prevent woodland damage. *Enact,* **7**, 10–14.

567 Gurnell, J. & Flowerdew, J.R. (2006) *Live trapping small mammals: a practical guide,* 4th edn. The Mammal Society, London.

568 Gurnell, J. & Little, J. (1992) The influence of trap residual odour on catching woodland rodents. *Animal Behaviour,* **43**, 623–632.

569 Gurnell, J & Lurz, P.W.W. (1997) *The conservation of red squirrels,* Sciurus vulgaris L. People's Trust for Endangered Species, London.

570 Gurnell, J. & Mayle, B. (2003) Impacts and management of the grey squirrel (*Sciurus carolinensis*) in Britain and Ireland, pp. 40–45 in Bowen, C.P. (ed.) *Problems caused by non-native mammals in Britain.* People's Trust for Endangered Species, London.

571 Gurnell, J. & Pepper, H. (1988). Perspectives on the management of red and grey squirrels, pp. 92–109 in Jardine, D.C. (ed.) *Wildlife management in forests.* Institute of Chartered Foresters, Edinburgh.

572 Gurnell, J. & Pepper, H. (1993) A critical look at conserving the British red squirrel. *Mammal Review,* **23**, 127–137.

573 Gurnell, J. & Pepper, H. (1998) Grey squirrel control and damage to broadleaf woodland in England. *Quarterly Journal of Forestry,* **92**, 117–124.

574 Gurnell, J. & Reynolls, K. (1983) Growth in field and laboratory populations of wood mice *(Apodemus sylvaticus). Journal of Zoology,* **200**, 355–365.

575 Gurnell, J. *et al.* (1992) The effects of coppice management on small mammal populations, pp. 213–232 in Buckley, G.P. (ed.) *Ecology and management of coppice woodlands.* Chapman & Hall, London.

177

576 Gurnell, J. *et al.* (1997) Using geographic information systems for red squirrel conservation management, pp. 153–160 in Gurnell, J. & Lurz, P.W.W. (eds.) *The conservation of red squirrels*, Sciurus vulgaris L. People's Trust for Endangered Species, London.

577 Gurnell, J. *et al.* (2001) *Practical techniques for surveying and monitoring squirrels.* Forestry Commission Practice Note 11, Forestry Commission, Alice Holt.

578 Gurnell, J. *et al.* (2001) Spacing behaviour, kinship, and population dynamics of grey squirrels in a newly colonized broadleaf woodland in Italy. *Canadian Journal of Zoology,* **134**, 1533–1543.

579 Gurnell, J. *et al.* (2002) Conserving red squirrels (*Sciurus vulgaris*): mapping and forecasting habitat suitability using a Geographic Information Systems approach. *Biological Conservation,* **105**, 53–64.

580 Gurnell, J. *et al.* (2004) Monitoring red squirrels *Sciurus vulgaris* and grey squirrels *Sciurus carolinensis* in Britain. *Mammal Review,* **34**, 51–74.

581 Gurnell, J. *et al.* (2004) Alien species and interspecific competition: effects of introduced eastern grey squirrels on red squirrel population dynamics. *Journal of Animal Ecology,* **73**, 26–35.

582 Gurnell, J. *et al.* (2006) Squirrel poxvirus: landscape scale strategies for managing disease threat. *Biological Conservation,* **131**, 287–295.

583 Gustafson, E.J. & Vandruff, L.W. (1990) Behaviour of black and gray morphs of *Sciurus carolinensis* in an urban environment. *American Midland Naturalist,* **123**,186–192.

584 Gustafsson, T.O. (1985) Sexual maturation in *Clethrionomys. Annales Zoologici Fennici,* **22**, 303–308.

585 Gustafsson, T.O. *et al.* (1982) Determining the age of the bank vole – a laboratory study. *Acta Theriologica,* **27**, 275–282.

586 Hadj-Chikh, L.Z. *et al.* (1996) Caching decisions by grey squirrels: a test of the handling time and perishability hypotheses. *Animal Behaviour,* **52**, 941–948.

587 Hadler, M.R. & Buckle, A.P. (1992) Forty five years of anticoagulant rodenticides – past, present and future trends, pp. 149–155 in Borrecco, J.E. & Marsh, R.E. (eds.) *Proceedings of the 15th Vertebrate Pest Conference,* University of California, Davis.

588 Haitlinger, R. (1969) Morphological variability in the Wroclaw populations of *Apodemus sylvaticus. Acta Theriologica,* **14**, 285–302.

589 Hale, M.L. & Lurz, P.W.W. (2003) Morphological changes in a British mammal as a result of introductions and changes in landscape management: the red squirrel (*Sciurus vulgaris*). *Journal of Zoology,* **260**, 159–167.

590 Hale, M.L. *et al.* (2001) The impact of landscape management on the genetic structure of red squirrel populations. *Science,* **293**, 2246–2248.

591 Hale, M.L. *et al.* (2004) Patterns of genetic diversity in the red squirrel: footprints of biogeographic history and artificial introductions. *Conservation Genetics,* **5**, 167–179.

592 Halle, S. (1993) Wood mice (*Apodemus sylvaticus* L) as pioneers of recolonisation in a reclaimed area. *Oecologia,* **94**, 120–127.

593 Halle, S. & Stenseth, N.C. (1994) Microtine ultradian rhythm of activity: an evaluation of different hypotheses on the triggering mechanism. *Mammal Review,* **24**, 17–39.

594 Halley, D.J. & Rosell, F. (2002) The beaver's reconquest of Eurasia: status, population development and management of a conservation success. *Mammal Review,* **32**, 153–178.

595 Halliwell, E.C. (1997) *The ecology of red squirrels in Scotland in relation to pine marten predation.* PhD thesis, University of Aberdeen.

596 Halls, S.A. (1981) *The influence of olfactory stimuli on ultrasonic calling in murid and cricetid rodents.* PhD thesis, University of London.

597 Hamar, M. *et al.* (1966) Biometrische und Zoogeographische Untersuchungen der Gattung *Apodemus* (Kaup, 1829) in der Sozialistichen Republik Rumanien.

Acta Theriologica, **11**, 1–40 (in German).

598 Hampshire, R. (1985) *A study on the social and reproductive behaviour of captive grey squirrels* (Sciurus carolinensis). PhD thesis, University of Reading.

599 Hanski, I. & Korpimäki, E. (1995) Microtine rodent dynamics in northern Europe: parameterised models for the predator-prey interaction. *Ecology,* **76**, 840–850.

600 Hanski, I. *et al.* (1991) Specialist predators, generalist predators, and the microtine rodent cycle. *Journal of Animal Ecology,* **60**, 353–367.

601 Hansson, L. (1968) Population densities of small mammals in open field habitats in south Sweden in 1964–1967. *Oikos* ,**19**, 53–60.

602 Hansson, L. (1971) Small rodent food, feeding and population dynamics. *Oikos,* **22**, 183–198.

603 Hansson, L. (1979) Food as a limiting factor for small rodent numbers. *Oecologia,* **37**, 297–314.

604 Hansson, L. (1985) The food of bank voles, wood mice and yellow-necked mice. *Symposia of the Zoological Society of London,* **55**, 141–168.

605 Hansson, L. (1985) *Clethrionomys* food: generic, specific and regional characteristics. *Annales Zoologici Fennici,* **22**, 315–318.

606 Hansson, L. (1987) An interpretation of rodent dynamics as due to trophic interactions. *Oikos,* **50**, 308–318.

607 Hansson, L. (1990) Ultimate factors in the winter weight depression of small mammals. *Mammalia,* **54**, 397–404.

608 Hansson, L. (1991) Regional and individual variation in body growth in winter of bank voles *Clethrionomys glareolus. Acta Theriologica,* **36**, 357–362.

609 Hansson, L. (1992) Fitness and life-history correlates of weight variations in small mammals. *Oikos,* **64**, 479–484.

610 Hansson, L. (1992) Parental investment related to social systems in Microtines. *Oecologia,* **89**, 284–287.

611 Hansson, L. (1994) Bark consumption by voles in relation to geographical origin of tree species. *Scandinavian Journal of Forest Research,* **9**, 288–296.

612 Hansson, L. (1995) Size dimorphism in microtine populations – characteristics of growth and selection against large-sized individuals. *Journal of Mammalogy,* **76**, 867–872.

613 Hansson, L. (1996) Regional differences in behaviour in bank voles (*Clethrionomys glareolus*): dyadic encounters. *Behavioral Ecology and Sociobiology,* **39**, 331–334.

614 Hansson, L. & Henttonen, H. (1985) Regional differences in cyclicity and reproduction in *Clethrionomys* species: are they related. *Annales Zoologici Fennici,* **22**, 277–288.

615 Hansson, L. & Larsson, T.-B. (1978) Vole diet on experimentally managed reforestation areas in northern Sweden. *Holarctic Ecology,* **1**, 16–26.

616 Haramis, G.M. Personal communication.

617 Hardy, A.R. & Taylor, K.D. (1979) Radio-tracking of *Rattus norvegicus* on farms, pp. 657–665 in Amlaner, C.J. & Macdonald, D.W. (eds.) *A handbook on biotelemetry and radio tracking.* Pergamon Press, Oxford.

618 Hardy, A.R. *et al.* (1983) Estimation of age in the Norway rat (*Rattus norvegicus* Berkenhout) from the weight of the eyelens. *Journal of Applied Ecology,* **20**, 97–102.

619 Hare, R. Personal communication.

620 Harris, S. (1979) Breeding litter size and nestling mortality of the harvest mouse, *Micromys minutus* (Rodentia: Muridae), in Britain. *Journal of Zoology,* **188**, 437–442.

621 Harris, S. (1979) *The secret life of the harvest mouse.* Hamlyn, London.

622 Harris, S. (1979) History, distribution, status and habitat requirements of the harvest mouse (*Micromys minutus*) in Britain. *Mammal Review,* **9**, 159–171.

623 Harris, S. (1980) *The harvest mouse.* Blandford Press, Poole.

624 Harris, S. *et al.* (1995) *A review of British mammals: population estimates and conservation status of British mammals other than cetaceans.* JNCC, Peterborough.

625 Hart, M. (1982) *Rats.* Allison & Busby, London.

626 Hartley, S.E. *et al.* (1995) The effect of fertiliser and shading

on plant chemical composition and palatability to Orkney voles *Microtus arvalis orcadensis*. *Oikos,* **72,** 79–87.

627 Harvie-Brown, J.A. (1880–81) The squirrel in Great Britain. *Proceedings of the Royal Physical Society of Edinburgh* **5,** 343–8; **6,** 31–63, 115–82 (Also in book form, published by Macfarlane & Erskine, Edinburgh, 1881).

628 Hassan, N. (1984) *Chromosomal investigations on some British wild rodents.* PhD thesis, University of London.

629 Hathaway, S.C. *et al.* (1983) Identification of a reservoir of *Leptospira interrogans* serovar *Muenchen* in voles (*Microtus agrestis* and *Clethrionomys glareolus*) in England. *Zentralblatt für Bakteriologie Mikrobiologie und Hygiene Series A – Medical Microbiology Infectious Diseases Virology Parasitology,* **254,** 123–128.

630 Haynes, S. *et al.* (2003) Phylogeography of the common vole (*Microtus arvalis*) with particular emphasis on the colonization of the Orkney archipelago. *Molecular Ecology,* **12,** 951–956.

631 Hayward, G.P. & Phillipson, J. (1979) Community structure and functional role of small mammals in ecosystems, pp. 135–211 in Stoddart, D.M. (ed.) *Ecology of small mammals.* Chapman & Hall, London.

632 Hazel, S.M. *et al.* (2000) A longitudinal study of an epidemic disease in its wildlife reservoir: cowpox and wild rodents. *Epidemiology and Infection,* **124,** 551–562.

633 Healing, T.D. (1980) The dispersion of bank voles (*Clethrionomys glareolus*) and wood mice (*Apodemus sylvaticus*) in dry stone dykes. *Journal of Zoology,* **191,** 406–411.

634 Healing, T.D. Personal communication.

635 Healing, T.D. & Nowell, F. (1985) Diseases and parasites of woodland rodent populations. *Symposia of the Zoological Society of London,* **55,** 193–218.

636 Healing, T.D. *et al.* (1980) A note on some Enterbacteriaceae from the faeces of small wild British mammals. *Journal of Hygiene,* **85,** 343–345.

637 Healing, T.D. *et al.* (1983) Populations of the bank vole (*Clethrionomys glareolus*) and long-tailed field mouse (*Apodemus sylvaticus*) on Skomer Island, Dyfed. *Journal of Zoology,* **199,** 447–460.

638 Hedges, S.R. (1966) *Studies on the behaviour, taxonomy and ecology of* Apodemus sylvaticus *(L.) and* A. flavicollis *(Melchior).* PhD thesis, University of Southampton.

639 Hedges, S.R. (1969) Epigenetic polymorphism in populations of *Apodemus sylvaticus* and *A. flavicollis* (Rodentia, Muridae). *Journal of Zoology,* **159,** 425–442.

640 Heimel, J.A. *et al.* (2005) Laminar organization of response properties in primary visual cortex of the gray squirrel (*Sciurus carolinensis*). *Journal of Neurophysiology,* **94,** 3538–3554.

641 Heinrich, G. (1951) Die Deutschen Waldmaus. *Zoologische Jahrbucher Abteilung für Systematik Ökologie und Geographie der Tiere,* **80,** 99–122 (in German).

642 Hejlicek, K. & Literak, I. (1998) Long-term study of *Toxoplasma gondii* prevalence in small mammals (Insectivora and Rodentia). *Folia Zoologica,* **47,** 93–101.

643 Hellborg, L. *et al.* (2005) Analysis of sex-linked sequences supports a new mammal species in Europe. *Molecular Ecology,* **14,** 2025–2031.

644 Hench, J.E. *et al.* (1984) Age classification for the grey squirrel based on eruption, replacement, and wear of molariform teeth. *Journal of Wildlife Management,* **48,** 1409–1414.

645 Herfs, A. (1939) Uber die Fortpflanzung und Vermehrung der grossen Wuhlmaus *Arvicola terrestris* (L.). *Nachrichten für Schadlingsbekampfung,* **14,** 91–193 (in German).

646 Hewson, C. *et al.* (2004) Possible impacts of grey squirrels on birds and other wildlife. *British Wildlife,* **15,** 183–191.

647 Hewson, R. (1951) Some observations on the Orkney vole *Microtus o. orcadensis* (Millais). *North-western Naturalist,* **23,** 7–10.

648 Hicks, M.J. (1986) The effects of coppicing on small mammal populations. *Bulletin of the British Ecological Society,* **17,** 78–80.

649 Hill, D.A. *et al.* (1995) Farmland, pp. 230–266 in Sutherland, W.J. & Hill, D.A. (eds.) *Managing habitats for conservation.* Cambridge University Press, Cambridge.

650 Hillemann, H.H. *et al.* (1958) The genital system of nutria (*Myocastor coypus*). *Anatomical Record,* **139,** 515–528.

651 Hjalten, J. & Palo, T. (1992) Selection of deciduous trees by free ranging voles and hares in relation to plant chemistry. *Oikos,* **63,** 477–484.

652 Hjalten, J. *et al.* (1996) Food selection by two vole species in relation to plant growth strategies and plant chemistry. *Oikos,* **76,** 181–190.

653 HMSO (1995) *Biodiversity.* The UK Steering Group Report. 2 vols. HMSO, London.

654 Hoffmeyer, I. (1973) Interaction and habitat selection in the mice *Apodemus flavicollis* and *A. sylvaticus. Oikos,* **24,** 108–116.

655 Hoffmeyer, I. (1976) Experiments on the selection of food and foraging sites by the mice *Apodemus sylvaticus* (Linne, 1758) and *A. flavicollis* (Melchior, 1834). *Säugetierkundliche Mitteilungen,* **24,** 112–124.

656 Hoffmeyer, I. & Hansson, L. (1974) Variability in number and distribution of *Apodemus flavicollis* and *Apodemus sylvaticus*) in S Sweden. *Zeitschrift für Säugetierkunde,* **39,** 15–23.

657 Hoffmeyer, I. & Sales, G.D. (1977) Ultrasonic behaviour of *Apodemus sylvaticus* and *A. flavicollis. Oikos,* **29,** 67–77.

658 Holišová, V. (1960) Potrava mysice krovinne *Apodemus sylvaticus* L na Ceskomoravske vrchovine. *Zoologicke Listy,* **9,** 135–158 (in Czech).

659 Holišová, V. (1969) Vertical movements of some small mammals in a forest. *Zoologicke Listy,* **18,** 121–141.

660 Holišová, V. (1970) Trophic requirements of the water vole *Arvicola terrestris,* Linn., on the edge of stagnant waters. *Zoologicke Listy,* **19,** 221–233.

661 Holišová, V. & Obrtel, R. (1979) The food eaten by *Clethrionomys glareolus* in a spruce monoculture. *Folia Zoologica,* **28,** 219–230.

662 Holišová, V. & Obrtel, R. (1980) Food resource partitioning among four myomorph rodent populations coexisting in a spruce forest. *Folia Zoologica,* **29,** 193–207.

663 Holm, J. (1987) *Squirrels.* Whittet Books, London.

664 Holm, J. (1991) *The ecology of red squirrels* (Sciurus vulgaris) *in deciduous woodland.* PhD thesis, University of London.

665 Holmes, R.G. (1962) Fascioliasis in coypus (*Myocastor coypus*). *Veterinary Record,* **74,** 1552.

666 Holmes, R.G. (1977) Toxoplasmosis in coypu. *Veterinary Record,* **101,** 74–75.

667 Hoodless, A. & Morris, P.A. (1993) An estimate of population density of the fat dormouse (*Glis glis*). *Journal of Zoology,* **230,** 337–340.

668 Hora, A.M. (1934) Notes on mites collected from the Isle of Lewis, Outer Hebrides. *Parasitology,* **26,** 361–365.

669 Horne, T.J. & Ylönen, H. (1996) Female bank voles (*Clethrionomys glareolus*) prefer dominant males: but what if there is no choice? *Behavioral Ecology and Sociobiology,* **38,** 401–405.

670 Hörnfeldt, B. (2004) Long-term decline in numbers of cyclic voles in boreal Sweden: analysis and presentation of hypotheses. *Oikos,* **107,** 376–392.

671 Horwich, R.H. (1972) *The ontogeny of social behaviour in the gray squirrel,* Sciurus carolinensis. *Advances in Ethology* 8, Paul Parey, Hamburg.

672 Houtcooper, W.C. (1978) Food habits of rodents in a cultivated ecosystem. *Journal of Mammalogy,* **59,** 427–430.

673 Hrabe, V. (1971) Circumanal glands of central European Gliridae (Rodentia). *Zoologicke Listy,* **20,** 247–258.

674 Hubalek, Z. (1999) Emmonsiosis of wild rodents and insectivores in Czechland. *Journal of Wildlife Diseases,* **35,** 243–249.

675 Hubalek, Z. *et al.* (1997) Emmonsiosis of small mammals (Rodentia, Insectivora) in Southwest Moravia, Czech Republic. *Folia Zoologica,* **46,** 223–227.

676 Hughes, V.L. & Randolph, S.E. (2001) Testosterone increases the transmission potential of tick-borne parasites. *Parasitology*, **123**, 365–371.

677 Huitu, O. *et al.* (2003) Winter food supply limits growth of northern vole populations in the absence of predation. *Ecology*, **84**, 2108–2118.

678 Hulme, P.E. (1994) Postdispersal seed predation in grassland – its magnitude and sources of variation. *Journal of Ecology*, **83**, 645–652.

679 Hulme, P.E. & Hunt, M.K. (1999) Rodent post-dispersal seed predation in deciduous woodland: predator response to absolute and relative abundance of prey. *Journal of Animal Ecology*, **68**, 417–428.

680 Humair, P.F. &.Gern, L. (1998) Relationship between *Borrelia burgdorferi sensu lato* species, red squirrels (*Sciurus vulgaris*) and *Ixodes ricinus* in enzootic areas in Switzerland. *Acta Tropica*, **69**, 213–227.

681 Humphries, R.E. *et al.* (1996) The characteristics of 'behavioural resistance' and bait avoidance in house mice in the UK, pp. 157–164 in *Proceedings of Brighton Crop Protection Conference, Pests and Diseases*. British Crop Protection Council, Farnham.

682 Humphries, R.E. *et al.* (1999) Unravelling the chemical basis of competitive scent marking in house mice. *Animal Behaviour*, **58**, 1177–1190.

683 Humphries, R.E. *et al.* (2000) Cereal aversion in behaviourally-resistant house mice in Birmingham, UK. *Applied Animal Behaviour Science*, **66**, 323–333.

684 Hurrell, E. (1962) *Dormice*. Sunday Times Publications, Peterborough.

685 Hurrell, E. (1980) *The common dormouse*. Blandford Press, Poole.

686 Hurrell, E. & McIntosh, G. (1984) Mammal Society dormouse survey, January 1975–April 1979. *Mammal Review*, **14**, 1–18.

687 Hurst, J.L. (1984) *The behavioural ecology of the house mouse* (Mus domesticus). PhD thesis, University of Birmingham.

688 Hurst, J.L. (1987) The functions of urine marking in a free-living population of house mouse, *Mus domesticus* Rutty. *Animal Behaviour*, **35**, 1433–1442.

689 Hurst, J.L. (1987) Behavioural variation in wild house mice (*Mus domesticus* Rutty): a quantitative assessment of female social organisation. *Animal Behaviour*, **35**, 1846–1847.

690 Hurst, J.L. (1990) Urine marking in populations of wild house mice *Mus domesticus* Rutty. 1. Communication between males. *Animal Behaviour*, **40**, 209–222.

691 Hurst, J.L. (1990) Urine marking in populations of wild house mice *Mus domesticus* Rutty. 2. Communication between females. *Animal Behaviour*, **40**, 223–232.

692 Hurst, J.L. (1990) Urine marking in populations of wild house mice *Mus domesticus* Rutty. 3. Communication between the sexes. *Animal Behaviour*, **40**, 233–243.

693 Hurst, J.L. (1990) The network of olfactory communication operating in populations of wild house mice, pp. 401–414 in MacDonald, D.W. *et al.* (eds.) *Chemical signals in vertebrates 5*. Oxford University Press, Oxford.

694 Hurst, J.L. (1993) The priming effects of urine substrate marks on interactions between male house mice, *Mus musculus domesticus*. *Animal Behaviour*, **45**, 55–81.

695 Hurst, J.L. Personal communication.

696 Hurst, J.L. & Barnard, C.J. (1992) Kinship and social behaviour in wild house mice: effects juveniles. *Behavioral Ecology*, **3**, 196–206.

697 Hurst, J.L. & Nevison, C. (1994) Do female house mice (*Mus musculus domesticus*) regulate their exposure to reproductive priming pheromones? *Animal Behaviour*, **48**, 945–959.

698 Hurst, J.L. & Rich, R.J. (1999) Scent marks as competitive signals of mate quality, pp. 209–226 in Johnston, R.E. *et al.* (eds.) *Advances in chemical communication in vertebrates*. Plenum Press, New York.

699 Hurst, J.L. *et al.* (1993) The role of substrate odours in maintaining social tolerance between male house mice (*Mus musculus domesticus*). *Animal Behaviour*, **45**, 997–1006.

700 Huson, L.W. & Rennison, B.D. (1981) Seasonal variability of Norway rat (*Rattus norvegicus*) infestation of agricultural premises. *Journal of Zoology*, **194**, 257–260.

701 Hynes, J.A. & Fairley, J.S. (1978) A population study of fieldmice in dry-stone walls. *Irish Naturalists' Journal*, **19**, 180–184.

702 Ieradi, L.A. *et al.* (2003) Evaluation of genotoxic damage in wild rodents from a polluted area in the Czech Republic. *Folia Zoologica*, **52**, 57–66.

703 Innes, D.G.L. & Millar, J.S. (1994) Life-histories of *Clethrionomys* and *Microtus* (Microtinae). *Mammal Review*, **24**, 179–207.

704 International Committee on Zoological Nomenclature (1998) Opinion 1894. *Bulletin of Zoological Nomenclature*, **55**, 64–71.

705 Jaarola, M. & Searle, J.B. (2003) Phylogeography of field voles (*Microtus agrestis*) in Eurasia inferred from mitochondrial DNA. *Molecular Ecology*, **11**, 2613–2621.

706 Jaarola, M. & Tegelström, H. (1995) Colonization history of north European field voles (*Microtus agrestis*) revealed by mitochondrial-DNA. *Molecular Ecology*, **4**, 299–310.

707 Jaarola, M. *et al.* (2004) Molecular phylogeny of the speciose vole genus *Microtus* (Arvicolinae, Rodentia) inferred from mitochondrial DNA. *Molecular Phylogenetics and Evolution*, **33**, 747–633.

708 Jackson, J.E. (1994) The edible or fat dormouse (*Glis glis*) in Britain. *Quarterly Journal of Forestry*, **88**, 119–125.

709 Jacobs, G.H. (1981) *Comparative color vision*. Academic Press, New York.

710 Jacobsen, B.V. & Sonerud, G.A. (1993) Synchronous switch in diet and hunting habitat as a response to disappearance of snow cover in Tengmalms owl *Aegolius funereus*. *Ornis Fennica*, **70**, 78–88.

711 Jakobson, M.E. (1978) Winter acclimation and survival of wild house mice. *Journal of Zoology*, **185**, 93–104.

712 Jameson, H.L. (1898) On a probable case of protective coloration in the house mouse (*Mus musculus* L). *Zoological Journal of the Linnean Society of London*, **26**, 463–473.

713 Jamon, H. [sic] (1988) Gestion individuelle et partage social de l'espace chez *Apodemus sylvaticus* en Camargue. *Science et techniques de l'animal laboratoire*, **13**, 65–69 (in French).

714 Jamon, M. (1994) An analysis of trail-following behaviour in the wood mouse *Apodemus sylvaticus*. *Animal Behaviour*, **47**, 1127–1134.

715 Jánossy, D. (1986) *Pleistocene vertebrate faunas of Hungary*. Elsevier, Amsterdam.

716 Jedrzejewska, B. & Jedrzejewski, W. (1990) Antipredatory behavior of bank voles and prey choice of weasels – enclosure experiments. *Annales Zoologici Fennici*, 27, 321–328.

717 Jedrzejewski, W. & Jedrzejewska, B. (1992) Foraging and diet of the red fox *Vulpes vulpes* in relation to variable food resources in Białowieża National Park, Poland. *Ecography*, 15, 212–220.

718 Jedrzejewski, W. & Jedrzejewska, B. (1993) Predation on rodents in Białowieża Primeval Forest, Poland. *Ecography*, **16**, 47–64.

719 Jedrzejewski, W. & Jedrzejewska, B. (1996) Rodent cycles in relation to biomass and productivity of ground vegetation and predation in the Palearctic. *Acta Theriologica*, **41**, 1–34.

720 Jedrzejewski, W. *et al.* (1993) Winter habitat selection and feeding habits of polecats (*Mustela putorius*) in the Białowieża National Park, Poland. *Zeitschrift für Säugetierkunde*, **58**, 75–83.

721 Jedrzejewski, W. *et al.* (1993) Responses of bank voles to odours of seven species of predators: experimental data and their relevance to natural predator-vole relationships. *Oikos*, **68**, 251–257.

722 Jedrzejewski, W. *et al.* (1993) Foraging by pine marten

Martes martes in relation to food resources in Białowieża National Park, Poland. *Acta Theriologica,* **38,** 405–426.

723 Jedrzejewski, W. *et al.* (1994) Resource use by tawny owls *Strix aluco* in relation to rodent fluctuations in Białowieża National Park, Poland. *Journal of Avian Biology,* **25,** 308–318.

724 Jedrzejewski, W. *et al.* (1996) Tawny owl (*Strix aluco*) predation in a pristine deciduous forest Białowieża National Park, Poland). *Journal of Animal Ecology,* **65,** 105–120.

725 Jefferies, D.J. (ed.) (2003) *The water vole and mink survey of Britain 1996–1998 with a history of long-term changes in the status of both species and their causes.* Vincent Wildlife Trust, Ledbury.

726 Jefferies, D.J. & French, M.C. (1972) Lead concentration in small mammals trapped on roadside verges and field sites. *Environmental Pollution,* **3,** 147–156.

727 Jefferies, D.J. *et al.* (1973) The ecology of small mammals in arable fields drilled with winter wheat and the increase in their dieldrin and mercury residues. *Journal of Zoology,* **171,** 513–539.

728 Jefferies, D.J. *et al.* (1989) An enquiry into the changing status of the water vole *Arvicola terrestris* in Britain. *Mammal Review,* **19,** 111–131.

729 Jennings, M. *et al.* (1998) Refinements in rodent husbandry: the mouse. *Laboratory Animals,* **32,** 233–259.

730 Jennings, T.G. (1975) Notes on the burrow systems of wood mice (*Apodemus sylvaticus*). *Journal of Zoology,* **177,** 500–504.

731 Jensen, S.P. (1993) Temporal changes in food preferences of wood mice (*Apodemus sylvaticus* L). *Oecologia,* **94,** 76–82.

732 Jensen, S.P. (1996) Juvenile dispersal in relation to adult densities in wood mice *Apodemus sylvaticus. Acta Theriologica,* **41,** 177–186.

733 Jensen, S.P. & Honess, P. (1995) The influence of moonlight on vegetation height preference and trappability of small mammals. *Mammalia,* **59,** 35–42.

734 Jensen, T.S. (1982) Seed production and outbreaks of non-cyclic rodent populations in deciduous forests. *Oecologia (Berlin),* **54,** 184–192.

735 Jensen, T.S. (1985) Seed–seed predator interactions of European beech *Fagus sylvaticus* and forest rodents *Clethrionomys glareolus* and *Apodemus flavicollis. Oikos,* **44,** 149–156.

736 Jermyn, D.L. *et al.* (2001). *The distribution of the hazel dormouse* Muscardinus avellanarius *in Wales.* Vincent Wildlife Trust, Ledbury.

737 Jewell, P.A. (1966) Breeding season and recruitment in some British mammals confined on small islands. *Symposia of the Zoological Society of London,* **15,** 98–116.

738 Jewell, P.A. & Fullagar, P.J. (1965) Fertility among races of the field mouse (*Apodemus sylvaticus*) and their failure to form hybrids with the yellow-necked mouse (*Apodemus flavicollis*). *Evolution,* **19,** 175–181.

739 Johnson, I. (1996) Pesticide poisoning of wildlife in Britain. *British Wildlife,* **7,** 273–278.

740 Johnson, I.P. *et al.* (1991) Effects of broadcasting and of drilling methiocarb molluscicide pellets on field populations of wood mice, *Apodemus sylvaticus. Bulletin of Environmental Contamination and Toxicology,* **46,** 84–91.

741 Johnson, I.P. *et al.* (1992) Population and diet of small rodents and shrews in relation to pesticide usage, pp. 144–156 in Greig-Smith, P. *et al.* (eds.) *Pesticides, cereal farming and the environment.* HMSO, London.

742 Johnson, M. (1977) The harvest mouse: current distribution and nesting habits in Lincolnshire. *Transactions of the Lincolnshire Naturalists' Union* B, **19,** 75–77.

743 Johnson, R.P. (1975) Scent marking with urine in two races of the bank vole (*Clethrionomys glareolus*). *Behaviour,* **55,** 81–93.

744 Johst, V. (1973) Struktur und Funktion akutischer Signale der Schermaus, *Arvicola terrestris* (L.). *Forma et Functio,* **6,** 305–322 (in German).

745 Joint Nature Conservation Committee (1996) *UK strategy*

for red squirrel conservation. JNCC, Peterborough.

746 Jonsson, P & Silverin, B. (1997) The estrous cycle in female wood mice (*Apodemus sylvaticus*) and the influence of the male. *Annales Zoologici Fennici,* **34,** 197–204.

747 Jonsson, P. *et al.* (2000) Does risk of predation by mammalian predators affect the spacing behaviour of rodents? Two large-scale experiments. *Oecologia,* **122,** 487–492.

748 Jonsson, P. *et al.* (2002). Determinants of reproductive success in voles: space use in relation to food and litter size manipulation. *Evolutionary Ecology,* **16,** 455–467.

749 Jowitt, A.J.D. & Perrow, M.R. (1993) Desperately seeking . . . water shrew (*Neomys fodiens*) and harvest mouse (*Micromys minutus*) in Broadland. *Transactions of the Suffolk Naturalists' Society,* **29,** 6–11.

750 Jüdes, U. (1979) Untersuchungen zur Ökologie der Waldmaus (*Apodemus flavicollis* Linne, 1758) und der Gelbhalsmaus (*Apodemus flavicollis* Melchior, 1834) in Raum Kiel (Schleswig-Holstein). *Zeitschrift für Säugetierkunde,* **44,** 81–95; 185–195 (in German).

751 Jüdes, U. (1981) Some notes on population density of *Micromys minutus* in secondary biotype. *Zeitschrift für Säugetierkunde,* **46,** 266–268.

752 Jüdes, U. (1982) Bibliography of the genus *Apodemus* (Rodentia, Muridae). *Mammal Review,* **12,** 59–142.

753 Juškaitis, R. (1999) Life tables for the common dormouse *Muscardinus avellanarius* in Lithuania. *Acta Theriologica,* **44,** 465–470.

754 Juškaitis, R. (1999) Winter mortality of the common dormouse (*Muscardinus avellanarius*) in Lithuania. *Folia Zoologica,* **48,** 11–16.

755 Juškaitis, R. (2002) Spatial distribution of the yellow-necked mouse (*Apodemus flavicollis*) in large forest areas and its relation with seed crop of forest trees. *Mammalian Biology,* **67,** 206–211.

756 Juškaitis, R. (2003) Breeding by young-of-the-year females in common dormouse *Muscardinus avellanarius* populations in Lithuania. *Folia Zoologica,* **48,** 11–16.

757 Juškaitis, R. (2003) Late breeding in two common dormouse (*Muscardinus avellanarius*) populations. *Mammalian Biology,* **68,** 244–249.

758 Juškaitis, R. (2003) Abundance dynamics and reproductive success in the common dormouse (*Muscardinus avellanarius*) in Lithuania. *Folia Zoologica,* **52,** 239–248.

759 Juškaitis, R. (2005) Daily torpor in free-ranging common dormice (*Muscardinus avellanarius*) in Lithuania. *Mammalian Biology,* **70,** 242–249.

760 Juškaitis, R. (2006) Interactions between dormice (Gliridae) and hole-nesting birds in nestboxes. *Folia Zoologica,* **55,** 225–236.

761 Justice, K.E. (1962) *Ecological and genetical studies of evolutionary forces acting on desert populations of* Mus musculus. Arizona-Sonora Desert Museum, Tucson, AZ.

762 Kaikusalo, A. (1972) Population turnover and wintering of the bank vole, *Clethrionomys glareolus* (Schreber) in southern and central Finland. *Annales Zoologici Fennici,* **9,** 219–224.

763 Kaltwasser, M.T. & Schnitzler, H.U. (1981) Echo-location signals confirmed in rats. *Zeitschrift für Säugetierkunde,* **46,** 394–395.

764 Kaplan, C. *et al.* (1980) Evidence of infection by viruses in small British field rodents. *Journal of Hygiene,* **84,** 285–295.

765 Kaplan, H.M. *et al.* (1983) Physiology, pp. 247–292 in Foster, H.L. *et al.* (eds.) *The mouse in biomedical research,* vol. 3. Academic Press, New York.

766 Kapusta, J. (1998) Gonadal hormones and intrasexual aggressive behavior in female bank voles (*Clethrionomys glareolus*). *Aggressive Behavior,* **24,** 63–70.

767 Kapusta, J. & Marchlewska-Koj, A. (1998) Interfemale aggression in adult bank voles (*Clethrionomys glareolus*). *Aggressive Behavior,* **24,** 53–61.

768 Kapusta, J. *et al.* (1994) Sexual experience affects

behaviour of bank voles *Clethrionomys glareolus*. *Acta Theriologica*, **39**, 365–371.

769 Kapusta, J. *et al.* (1995) Home bedding modifies ultrasonic vocalization of infant bank voles. *Journal of Chemical Ecology*, **21**, 577–582.

770 Karanis, P. *et al.* (1996) A comparison of phase contrast microscopy and an immunofluorescence test for the detection of *Giardia* spp. in faecal specimens from cattle and wild rodents. *Transactions of the Royal Society of Tropical Medicine and Hygiene*, **90**, 250–251.

771 Karlsson, A.F. & Potapov, E.R. (1998) Consistency and change in bank vole (*Clethrionomys glareolus*) home ranges across a decade. *Canadian Journal of Zoology*, **76**, 1329–1334.

772 Karpukhin, I.P. & Karpukhina, N.M. (1971) Eye lens weight as a criterion of age of *Sciurus vulgaris*. *Zoologicheskii Zhurnal*, **50**, 274–277.

773 Karulin, B.E. *et al.* (1993) The bank vole, *Clethrionomys glareolus*, as the principal carrier of the agent in the forest focus of leptospirosis. *Zoologichesky Zhurnal*, **72**, 113–122.

774 Kastle, W. (1953) Die Jungendentwickicklung der Zwergmause, *Micromys minutus soricinus*, (Hermann 1780). *Säugetierkundliche Mitteilungen, Stuttgart*, **1**, 49–59 (in German).

775 Kaufman, D.W. & Kaufman, G.A. (1990) House mice (*Mus musculus*) in natural and disturbed habitats in Kansas. *Journal of Mammalogy*, **71**, 428–432.

776 Keeler, B. (1961) Damage to young plantations by the bank vole at Bernwood Forest 1958–60. *Journal of the Forestry Commission*, **30**, 55–59.

777 Kelly, P. & Fairley, J.S. (1982) An accessory cusp on the third upper molar of wood mice *Apodemus sylvaticus* from the west of Ireland. *Journal of Zoology*, **198**, 532–533.

778 Kelly, P.A. *et al.* (1982). An analysis of morphological variation in the field mouse *Apodemus sylvaticus* (L.) on some Irish islands. *Proceedings of the Royal Irish Academy*, **82**(B), 39–51.

779 Kendall, P.B. (1984) Seasonal changes of sex ratio in Norway rat (*Rattus norvegicus*) populations in Wales. *Journal of Zoology*, **203**, 288–290.

780 Kenneth, J.G. & Ritchie, G.R. (1953) *Gestation periods*, 3rd edn. Bureau of Animal Breeding, Edinburgh.

781 Kenward, R.E. (1983) The causes of damage by red and grey squirrels. *Mammal Review*, **13**, 159–166.

782 Kenward, R.E. (1985) Ranging behaviour and population dynamics of grey squirrels, pp. 319–330 in Sibly, R.M. & Smith, R.H. (eds.) *Behavioural ecology*. Blackwell Scientific Publications, Oxford.

783 Kenward, R. (1989) Bark stripping by grey squirrels in Britain and North America: why does the damage differ? pp. 144–154 in Putman, R.J. (eds.) *Mammals as pests*. Christopher Helm, London.

784 Kenward, R.E. & Dutton, J.C.F. (1996) Damage by grey squirrels. II. The value of prediction. *Quarterly Journal of Forestry*, **90**, 211–218.

785 Kenward, R.E. & Holm, J. (1993) On the replacement of the red squirrel in Britain: a phytotoxic explanation. *Proceedings of the Royal Society of London Series B*, **251**, 187–194.

786 Kenward, R.E. & Parish, T. (1986) Bark stripping by grey squirrels. *Journal of Zoology* A, **210**, 473–481.

787 Kenward, R.E. & Tonkin, M. (1986) Red and grey squirrels; some behavioural and biometric differences. *Journal of Zoology*, **209**, 279–281.

788 Kenward, R.E. *et al.* (1992) Are tree species mixtures too good for grey squirrels? pp. 243–253 in Cannell, M.G.R. *et al.* (eds.) *The ecology of mixed-species stands of trees*. Blackwell Scientific Publications, Oxford.

789 Kenward, R.E. *et al.* (1996) Damage by grey squirrels. I Bark-stripping correlates and treatment. *Quarterly Journal of Forestry*, **90**, 135–142.

790 Kenward, R.E. *et al.* (1998) Comparative demography of red squirrels (*Sciurus vulgaris*) and grey squirrels (*Sciurus carolinensis*) in deciduous and conifer woodland. *Journal of*

Zoology, **224**, 7–21.

791 Key, G. *et al.* (1998) Ship rats *Rattus rattus* on the Shiant Islands, Hebrides, Scotland. *Journal of Zoology*, **245**, 228–233.

792 Keymer, A.E. *et al.* (1991) Case-studies in population-dynamics, life-history evolution and community structure. *Acta Oecologia*, **12**, 105–118.

793 Keymer, I.F. (1983) Diseases of squirrels in Britain. *Mammal Review*, **13**, 155–158.

794 Khidas, K & Hansell, M.H. (1995) Burrowing behaviour and burrow architecture in *Apodemus sylvaticus* (Rodentia). *Zeitschrift für Säugetierkunde*, **60**, 246–250.

795 Kikkawa, J. (1964) Movement activity and distribution of small rodents *Clethrionomys glareolus* and *Apodemus sylvaticus* in woodland. *Journal of Animal Ecology*, **33**, 259–299.

796 King, C.M. (1980) The weasel *Mustela nivalis* and its prey in an English woodland. *Journal of Animal Ecology*, **49**, 127–159.

797 King, C.M. (1985) Interactions between woodland rodents and their predators. *Symposia of the Zoological Society of London*, **55**, 219–247.

798 King, C.M. (ed.) (1990) *The handbook of New Zealand mammals*. Oxford University Press, Auckland.

799 King, O.M. (1950) An ecological study of the Norway rat and the house mouse in a city block in Lawrence, Kansas. *Transactions of the Kansas Academy of Science*, **53**, 500–528.

800 Kiris, I.D. (1937) [Method and technique of age determination of the squirrel and analysis of the age group composition of squirrel populations]. *Byulleten Moskowkovo Obshchestva. Ispytatelei Prirody*, **46**, 36–42 (in Russian; French summary).

801 Kirkpatrick, C.M. & Barnett, E.M. (1957) Age criteria in male grey squirrels. *Journal of Wildlife Management*, **21**, 1–7.

802 Kitchener, A. (2001). *Beavers*. Whittet, Stowmarket.

803 Kitchener, A.C. & Bonsall, C. (1997). AMS radiocarbon dates for some extinct Scottish mammals. *Quaternary Newsletter*, **83**, 1–11.

804 Kitchener, A.C. & Lynch, J.M. (1999). *A morphometric comparison of the skulls of fossil British and extant European beavers* Castor fiber. Scottish Natural Heritage Review No. 127. Scottish Natural Heritage, Perth.

805 Klaa, K. *et al.* (2005) Distribution of small mammals in a silvoarable agroforestry system in Northern England. *Agroforestry Systems*, **63**, 101–110.

806 Kleinkauf, A. *et al.* (1999) A bitter attempt to prevent non-target poisoning of small mammals. *Mammal Review*, **29**, 201–204.

807 Klemola, T. *et al.* (1998) Does avian predation risk depress reproduction of voles? *Oecologia*, **115**, 149–153.

808 Knapka, J.J. (1983) Nutrition. pp. 51–67 in Foster, H.L. *et al.* (eds.) *The mouse in biomedical research*, vol. 4. Academic Press, New York.

809 Knee, C. (1983) Squirrel energetics. *Mammal Review*, **13**, 113–122.

810 Koenig, L. (1960) Das aktionssystem des siebenschläfers (*Glis glis* L) *Zeitschrift für Tierpsychologie*, **17**, 427–505 (in German).

811 Koford, C.B. (1968) Peruvian desert mice: water independence, competition and breeding cycle near the equator. *Science*, **160**, 552–553.

812 Kohli, E. (1981) *Untersuchung zum Eingfluss der Nutrias* (Myocaster coypus Molina) *auf die natürliche Vegetation der Camargue*. PhD thesis, University of Bern.

813 Koivula, M. *et al.* (1999) Sex and age-specific differences in ultraviolet reflectance of scent marks of bank voles (*Clethrionomys glareolus*). *Journal of Comparative Physiology A – Sensory Neural and Behavioral Physiology*, **185**, 561–564.

814 Kollmann, J. *et al.* (1998) Consistencies in post-dispersal seed predation of temperate fleshy- fruited species among seasons, years and sites. *Functional Ecology*, **12**, 683–690.

815 König, B. (1989) Behavioural ecology of kin recognition in house mice. *Ethology, Ecology and Evolution*, **1**, 99–110.

816 König, B. (1993) Maternal investment of communally

nursing female house mice (*Mus musculus domesticus*). *Behavioural Processes,* **30,** 61–74.

817 König, B. & Markl, H. (1987) Maternal care in house mice. I. The weaning strategy as a means for parental manipulation of offspring quality. *Behavioural Ecology and Sociobiology,* **20,** 1–9.

818 König, B. *et al.* (1988) Maternal care in house mice (*Mus musculus*): II. The energy cost of lactation as a function of litter size. *Journal of Zoology,* **216,** 195–210.

819 Koprowski, J.L. (1992) Do estrous female gray squirrels, *Sciurus carolinensis*, advertise their receptivity? *Canadian Field Naturalist,* **106,** 392–394.

820 Koprowski, J.L. (1992) Removal of copulatory plugs by female tree squirrels. *Journal of Mammalogy,* **73,** 572–576.

821 Koprowski, J.L. (1993) Alternative reproductive tactics in male eastern gray squirrels: 'making the best of a bad job'. *Behavioural Ecology,* **4,** 165–171.

822 Koprowski, J.L. (1993) The role of kinship in field interactions among juvenile gray squirrels (*Sciurus carolinensis*). *Canadian Journal of Zoology,* **71,** 224–226.

823 Koprowski, J.L. (1993) Sex and species biases in scent-marking behaviour by fox squirrels and eastern grey squirrels. *Journal of Zoology,* **230,** 319–356.

824 Koprowski, J.L. (1994) *Sciurus carolinensis.* Mammalian Species 480, 1–9. American Society of Mammalogists, Washington, DC.

825 Koprowski, J.L. (1996) Natal philopatry, communal nesting, and kinship in fox squirrels and gray squirrels. *Journal of Mammalogy,* **77,** 1006–1016.

826 Koprowski, J.L. (2005) The response of tree squirrels to fragmentation: a review and synthesis. *Animal Conservation,* **8,** 369–376.

827 Korpimaki, E. *et al.* (1996) Do radio-collars increase the predation risk of small rodents? *Ethology Ecology and Evolution,* **8,** 377–386.

828 Koskela, E. *et al.* (1996) Does risk of small mustelid predation affect the oestrous cycle in the bank vole, *Clethrionomys glareolus*? *Animal Behaviour,* **51,** 1159–1163.

829 Koskela, E. *et al.* (1997) Territorial behaviour and reproductive success of bank vole *Clethrionomys glareolus* females. *Journal of Animal Ecology,* **66,** 341–349.

830 Koskela, E. *et al.* (1998) Limitation of reproductive success by food availability and litter size in the bank vole, *Clethrionomys glareolus. Proceedings of the Royal Society of London Series B,* **265,** 1129–1134.

831 Koskela, E. *et al.* (1999) Experimental manipulation of breeding density and litter size: effects on reproductive success in the bank vole. *Journal of Animal Ecology,* **68,** 513–521.

832 Koskela, P. & Viro, P. (1976) The abundance, autumn migration, population structure and body dimensions of the harvest mouse in northern Finland. *Acta Theriologica,* **21,** 375–387.

833 Kotzageorgis, G.C. & Mason, C.F. (1996) Range use, determined by telemetry, of yellow-necked mice (*Apodemus flavicollis*) in hedgerows. *Journal of Zoology,* **240,** 773–777.

834 Kotzageorgis, G.C. & Mason, C.F. (1997) Small mammal populations in relation to hedgerow structure in an arable landscape. *Journal of Zoology,* **242,** 425–434.

835 Kowalski, K. & Sutcliffe, A.J. (1976) Pleistocene rodents of the British Isles. *Bulletin of the British Museum (Natural History) Geology,* **27,** 31–147.

836 Kozakiewicz, M. *et al.* (1999) Effects of habitat fragmentation on four rodent species in a Polish farm landscape. *Landscape Ecology,* **14,** 391–400.

837 Kral, B. (1970) Chromosome studies in two subgenera of the genus *Apodemus. Zoologike Listy,* **19,** 119–134.

838 Kratochvil, J. (1968) Das Vibrissenfeld der europaischen Arten der Gattung *Apodemus* Kaup, 1829. *Zoologicke Listy,* **17,** 193–209 (in German).

839 Kraus, B. (1983) A test of the optimal density-model for seed scatterhoarding. *Ecology,* **64,** 608–610.

840 Krebs, C.J. *et al.* (1995) Movements of feral house mice in agricultural landscapes. *Australian Journal of Zoology,* **43,** 293–312.

841 Kristofik, J. & Lysy, J. (1992) Seasonal dynamics of sucking lice (*Anoplura*) in small mammals (Insectivora, Rodentia) in the natural foci of infections in south-west Slovakia. *Biologia,* **47,** 605–617.

842 Kruczek, M. (1994) Reactions of female bank voles *Clethrionomys glareolus* to male chemosignals. *Acta Theriologica,* **39,** 249–255.

843 Kruczek, M. (1997) Male rank and female choice in the bank vole, *Clethrionomys glareolus. Behavioural Processes,* **40,** 171–176.

844 Kruczek, M. (1998) Female bank vole (*Clethrionomys glareolus*) recognition: preference for the stud male. *Behavioural Processes,* **43,** 229–237.

845 Kruczek, M. & Golas, A. (2003) Behavioural development of conspecific odour preferences in bank voles, *Clethrionomys glareolus. Behavioural Processes,* **64,** 31–39.

846 Kruczek, M. & Pochron, E. (1997) Chemical signals from conspecifics modify the activity of female bank voles *Clethrionomys glareolus. Acta Theriologica,* **42,** 71–78.

847 Kryltzov, A.I. (1964) Moult topography of Microtinae, other rodents and Lagomorpha. *Zeitschrift für Säugetierkunde,* **29,** 1–17.

848 Kryštufek, B. (2004) Nipples in the edible dormouse *Glis glis. Folia Zoologica,* **53,** 107–111.

849 Kryštufek, B. *et al.* (2005) Age determination and age structure in the edible dormouse *Glis glis* based on incremental bone lines. *Mammal Review,* **35,** 210–214.

850 Kubik, J. (1952) The harvest mouse *Micromys minutus* Pallas in the Białowieża National park. *Annales Universitalis Mariae Curie-Sklodowska,* **7,** 449–482.

851 Kurtén, B. (1968). *Pleistocene mammals of Europe.* Weidenfeld & Nicolson, London.

852 Kviljo, T. *et al.* (1992) Reproduction and growth in bank voles *Clethrionomys glareolus* – the effect of food quality and density manipulations in a laboratory colony. *Ecography,* **15,** 221–225.

853 Laakkonen, J. *et al.* (1998) Dynamics of intestinal coccidia in peak density *Microtus agrestis, Microtus oeconomus* and *Clethrionomus glareolus* populations in Finland. *Ecography,* **21,** 135–139.

854 Laakkonen, J. *et al.* (1999) Seasonal dynamics of *Pneumocystis carinii* in the field vole, *Microtus agrestis,* and in the common shrew, *Sorex araneus,* in Finland. *Parasitology,* **118,** 1–5.

855 Labuda, M. *et al.* (1997) Tick-borne encephalitis virus transmission between ticks cofeeding on specific immune natural rodent hosts. *Virology,* **235,** 138–143.

856 Laidler, K. (1980) *Squirrels in Britain.* David & Charles, Newton Abbot.

857 Lambin, X. (1988) Social relations in *Apodemus sylvaticus* as revealed by video-observation in the wild. *Journal of Zoology,* **216,** 587–593.

858 Lambin, X. & Bauchau, V. (1989) Contest competition between wood mice and bank voles: is there a winner? *Acta Theriologica,* **34,** 385–390.

859 Lambin, X. *et al.* (1996) *Survey of water voles and mink on the rivers Don and Ythan.* A report to Scottish Natural Heritage, ref 70/96/F1A/007.

860 Lambin, X. *et al.* (1998) *Aberdeenshire Water Vole Survey: The distribution of isolated water vole populations in the upper catchments of the rivers Dee and Don.* Scottish Natural Heritage contract report, ref C/LF1/BAT/97/2.

861 Lambin, X. *et al.* (1998) Spatial asynchrony and periodic travelling waves in cyclic field vole populations. *Proceedings of the Royal Society of London Series B,* **265,** 1491–1496.

862 Lambin, X. *et al.* (2000) Cyclic dynamics in field vole populations and generalist predation. *Journal of Animal Ecology,* **69,** 106–118.

863 Lambin, X. *et al.* (2006) Vole population cycles in northern and southern Europe: is there a need for different explanations for single pattern? *Journal of Animal Ecology,*

75, 340–349.

864 Lampio, T. (1967) Sex ratios and the factors contributing to them in the squirrel, *Sciurus vulgaris*, in Finland. *Finnish Game Research,* **29,** 5–67.

865 Lance, A.N. (1973) Numbers of wood mice (*Apodemus sylvaticus*) on improved and unimproved blanket bog. *Journal of Zoology,* **171,** 471–473.

866 Langley, R. & Fairley, J.S. (1982) Seasonal variations in infestations in a wood mouse *Apodemus sylvaticus* population in the west of Ireland. *Journal of Zoology,* **198,** 249–261.

867 Larsson, T.B. & Hansson, L. (1977) Vole diet on experimentally managed afforestation areas in northern Sweden. *Oikos,* **28,** 242–249.

868 Laurie, E.M.O. (1946) The reproduction of the house-mouse (*Mus musculus*) living in different environments. *Proceedings of the Royal Society of London Series B,* **133,** 248–281.

869 Laurie, E.M.O. (1946) The coypu (*Myocastor coypus*) in Great Britain. *Journal of Animal Ecology,* **15,** 22–34.

870 Lavrov, L.S. (1983) Evolutionary development of the genus *Castor* and taxonomy of the contemporary beavers of Eurasia. *Acta Zoolica Fennica,* **174,** 87–90.

871 Lawton, J.H. & Woodroffe, G.L. (1991) Habitat and the distribution of water voles: why are there gaps in a species' range? *Journal of Animal Ecology,* **60,** 79–91.

872 Leamy, L. (1977) Genetic and environmental correlations of morphometric traits in random bred house mice. *Evolution,* **31,** 357–369.

873 Lee, W.B. & Houston, D.C. (1993) Tooth wear patterns in voles (*Microtus agrestis* and *Clethrionomys glareolus*) and efficiency of dentition in preparing food for digestion. *Journal of Zoology,* **231,** 301–309.

874 Lee, W.B. & Houston, D.C. (1993) The role of coprophagy in digestion in voles (*Microtus agrestis* and *Clethrionomys glareolus*). *Functional Ecology,* **7,** 427–432.

875 Lee, W.B. & Houston, D.C. (1993) The effect of diet quality on gut anatomy in British voles (Microtinae). *Journal of Comparative Physiology B,* **163,** 337–339.

876 Lehmann, U. (1976) Short-term and circadian rhythms in the behaviour of the vole, *Microtus agrestis* (L.). *Oecologia (Berlin),* **23,** 185–199.

877 Leigh Brown, A.J. (1977) Genetic changes in a population of fieldmice (*Apodemus sylvaticus*) during one winter. *Journal of Zoology,* **182,** 281–219.

878 Leigh Brown, A.J. (1977) Physiological correlates of an enzyme polymorphism. *Nature,* **269,** 803–804.

879 Leinders-Zufall, T. *et al.* (2000) Ultrasensitive pheromone detection by mammalian vomeronasal neurons. *Nature,* **405,** 792–796.

880 Lemnell, P.A. (1973) Age determination in red squirrels (*Sciurus vulgaris* L). *International Congress of Game Biology,* **11,** 573–580.

881 Leslie, P.H. & Davis, D.H.S. (1939) An attempt to determine the absolute number of rats on a given area. *Journal of Animal Ecology,* **8,** 94–113.

882 Leslie, P.H. *et al.* (1952) The fertility and population structure of the brown rat *(Rattus norvegicus)* in cornricks and some other habitats. *Proceedings of the Zoological Society of London,* **122,** 187–238.

883 Leslie, P.H. *et al.* (1955) The longevity and fertility of the Orkney vole *Microtus orcadensis* as observed in the laboratory. *Proceedings of the Zoological Society of London,* **125,**115–125.

884 Leuze, C.C.K. (1976) *Social behaviour and dispersion in the water vole,* Arvicola terrestris (L.). PhD thesis, University of Aberdeen.

885 Lever, C. (1985) *Naturalized mammals of the world.* Longman, Harlow.

886 Lever, R.J. *et al.* (1957) Myxomatosis and the fox. *Agriculture,* **64,** 105–111.

887 Lewis, J.W. (1987) Helminth parasites of British rodents and insectivores. *Mammal Review,* **17,** 81–93.

888 Lewis, J.W. & Cox, F.E.G. (eds.) (1987) Proceedings of a joint meeting between the Mammal Society and the British Society for Parasitology. *Mammal Review,* **17,** 59–154.

889 Lewis, J.W. & Twigg, G.I. (1972) A study of the internal parasites of small rodents from woodland areas in Surrey. *Journal of Zoology,* **166,** 61–77.

890 Lidicker, W.Z. (1965) Comparative study of density regulation in confined populations of four species of rodents. *Research in Population Ecology,* **7,** 57–72.

891 Lidicker, W.Z. (1966) Ecological observations on a feral house mouse population declining to extinction. *Ecological Monographs,* **36,** 27–50.

892 Lidicker, W.Z. (1976) Social behaviour and density regulation in house mice living in large enclosures. *Journal of Animal Ecology,* **45,** 677–697.

893 Lima, S.L. & Dill, L.M. (1990) Behavioural decisions made under the risk of predation: a review and prospectus. *Canadian Journal of Zoology,* **68,** 619–640.

894 Lishak, R.S. (1982) Grey squirrel mating calls: a spectrographic and ontogenic analysis. *Journal of Mammalogy,* **63,** 1–3.

895 Lishak, R.S. (1982) Vocalizations of nestling gray squirrels. *Journal of Mammalogy,* **63,** 446–452.

896 Lishak, R.S. (1984) Alarm vocalizations of adult gray squirrels. *Journal of Mammalogy,* **65,** 1–4.

897 Literak, I. & Zejda, J. (1995) Color mutations of the bank vole (*Clethrionomys glareolus*) in the Czech Republic. *Folia Zoologica,* **44,** 95–96.

898 Lloyd, H.G. (1968) Observations on nut selection by a hand reared squirrel (*Sciurus carolinensis*). *Journal of Zoology,* **155,** 240–244.

899 Lloyd, H.G. (1983) Past and present distribution of red and grey squirrels. *Mammal Review,* **13,** 69–80.

900 Lofgren, O. (1995) Spatial organization of cyclic *Clethrionomys* females – occupancy of all available space at peak densities. *Oikos,* **72,** 29–35.

901 Lofgren, O. *et al.* (1996) Effect of supplemental food on a cyclic *Clethrionomys glareolus* population at peak density. *Acta Theriologica,* **41,** 383–394.

902 Loman, J. (1991) The small mammal fauna in an agricultural landscape in southern Sweden, with special reference to the wood mouse *Apodemus sylvaticus.* *Mammalia,* **55,** 91–96.

903 Lore, R. & Flannelly, K. (1977) Rat societies. *Scientific American,* **236**(5), 106–116.

904 Lore, R. & Flannelly, K. (1978) Habitat selection and burrow construction by wild *Rattus norvegicus* in a landfill. *Journal of Comparative Physiology and Psychology,* **92,** 888–896.

905 Loughran, M.F.E. (1999) *A study of the demography and social organisation of the field vole,* Microtus agrestis *in relation to food resources.* PhD thesis. University of London.

906 Loughran, M.F.E. (2006) Social organisation of female field voles *Microtus agrestis* in a population in Southern England. *Acta Theriologica,* **51,** 233–242.

907 Love, R.A. *et al.* (2000) Changes in the food of barn owls (*Tyto alba*) between 1974 and 1997. *Mammal Review,* **30,** 107–129.

908 Lowe, V.P.W. (1993) The spread of the grey squirrel (*Sciurus carolinensis*) into Cumbria since 1960 and its present distribution. *Journal of Zoology,* **231,** 663–667.

909 Lowe, V.P.W & Gardiner, A.S. (1983) Is the British squirrel (*Sciurus vulgaris leucourus* Kerr) British? *Mammal Review,* **13,** 57–67.

910 Lozan, M.N. (1961) Age determination of *Dryomys nitedula* Pall. and of *Muscardinus avellanarius* L. *Zoologicheskii Zhurnal,* **40,** 1740–1743.

911 Ludwick, R.L. *et al.* (1969) Energy metabolism of the eastern gray squirrel. *Journal of Wildlife Management,* **33,** 569–75.

912 Lund, M. (1994) Commensal rodents, pp. 23–43 in Buckle, A.P. & Smith, R.H. (eds.) *Rodent pests and their control.* CAB International, Wallingford.

913 Lundkvist, Å. *et al.* (1997) Puumala and Dobrava viruses

cause hemorrhagic fever with renal syndrome in Bosnia-Herzegovina: Evidence of highly cross-neutralizing antibody responses in early patient sera. *Journal of Medical Virology,* **53,** 51–59.

914 Lurz, P.W.W. (1995) *The ecology and conservation of the red squirrel* (Sciurus vulgaris). *in upland conifer plantations.* PhD thesis, University of Newcastle.

915 Lurz, P. (2002) A comparison of genetic and morphological variation of red squirrels in Cumbria and the north-east of England. *Carlisle Naturalist,* **10,** 12–16.

916 Lurz, P.W.W. & Garson, P.J. (1997) Forest management for red squirrels in conifer woodlands: a northern perspective, pp. 145–152 in Gurnell, J. & Lurz, P.W.W. (eds.) *The conservation of red squirrels,* Sciurus vulgaris, *L.* People's Trust for Endangered Species, London.

917 Lurz, P.W.W. & Garson, P.J. (1998) Seasonal changes in ranging behaviour and habitat choice by red squirrels (*Sciurus vulgaris*) in conifer plantations in Northern England. In Steele, M.A. *et al.* (eds.) *Ecology and evolutionary biology of tree squirrels. Special Publication, Virginia Museum of Natural History,* **6,** 79–85.

918 Lurz, P.W.W. & Lloyd, A.J. (2000) Body weights in grey and red squirrels: do seasonal weight increases occur in conifer woodland? *Journal of Zoology,* **252,** 539–543.

919 Lurz, P.W.W. & South, A.B. (1998) Cached fungi in non-native conifer forests and their importance for red squirrels (*Sciurus vulgaris* L.). *Journal of Zoology,* **246,** 468–471.

920 Lurz, P.W.W. *et al.* (1995) The ecology of squirrels in spruce dominated plantations, implications for forest management. *Forest Ecology and Management,* **79,** 79–90.

921 Lurz, P.W.W. *et al.* (1997). Effects of temporal and spatial variation in habitat quality on red squirrel *Sciurus vulgaris* dispersal behaviour. *Animal Behaviour,* **54,** 427–435.

922 Lurz, P.W.W. *et al.* (1998) Conifer species mixtures, cone crops and red squirrel conservation. *Forestry,* **71,** 67–71.

923 Lurz, P.W.W. *et al.* (2000). Effects of temporal and spatial variations in food supply on the space and habitat use of red squirrels, *Sciurus vulgaris* L. *Journal of Zoology,* **251,** 167–178.

924 Lurz, P.W.W. *et al.* (2001) Predicting grey squirrel expansion in North Italy: a spatially explicit modelling approach. *Landscape Ecology,* **16,** 407–420.

925 Lurz, P.W.W. *et al.* (2003) Planning red squirrel conservation areas: using spatially explicit population dynamics models to predict the impact of felling and forest design plans. *Forestry,* **76,** 95–108.

926 Lurz, P.W.W. *et al.* (2005) Mammals in Cumbria: examples of what publicly collected records can tell us about the distribution and ecology of our local species. *Carlisle Naturalist,* **13,** 1–15.

927 Lurz, P.W.W. *et al.* (2005) *Sciurus vulgaris. Mammalian Species,* **769,** 1–10.

928 Lynch, C.B. (1992). Clinal variation in cold adaptation in *Mus domesticus*: verification from predictions from laboratory populations. *American Naturalist,* **139,** 1219–1236.

929 Lysy, J. & Palicova, F. (1997) Small terrestrial mammals as important hosts of *Campylobacter* sp. *Biologia,* **52,** 441–443.

930 Lysy, J. & Urgeova, E. (1995) Ecological study of *Yersinia enterocolitica* isolated from small terrestrial mammals captured on the territory of the barrage system Gabcikovo. *Biologia,* **50,** 543–546.

931 Macdonald, D.W. (1977) On food preference in the red fox. *Mammal Review,* **7,** 7–23.

932 Macdonald, D.W. & Barrett, P. (1993) *Mammals of Britain and Europe.* Collins Field Guide. HarperCollins, London.

933 Macdonald, D.W. & Strachan, R. (1999) *The mink and the water vole: an analysis for conservation.* WildCRU, Oxford.

934 Macdonald, D.W. *et al.* (1995) Reintroducing the European beaver to Britain: nostalgic meddling or restoring biodiversity? *Mammal Review,* **25,** 161–200.

935 Macdonald, D.W. *et al.* (1998) *The effects of shape, location and*

management of set-aside on invertebrates and small mammals. Unpublished Report to Ministry of Agriculture, Fisheries & Food, London.

936 Macdonald, D.W. *et al.* (2000) Ecological experiments in farmland conservation, pp. 357–378 in Hutchings, M. (ed.) *Ecological consequences of habitat heterogeneity.* Blackwell Science, Oxford.

937 Macdonald, D.W. *et al.* (2000) Arable habitat use by wood mice (*Apodemus sylvaticus*). 3. A farm-scale experiment on the effects of crop rotation. *Journal of Zoology,* **250,** 313–320.

938 Macdonald, I.M.V. (1992) Grey squirrels discriminate red from green in a foraging situation. *Animal Behaviour,* **43,** 694–695.

939 Mackinnon, J.L. (1999) *Spatial dynamics of cyclic field voles,* Microtus agrestis, *populations.* PhD thesis, University of Aberdeen.

940 Mackinnon, J.L. *et al.* (2001) Scale invariant spatio-temporal patterns of field vole density. *Journal of Animal Ecology,* **70,** 101–111.

941 MacKinnon, K. (1976) *Home range, feeding ecology and social behaviour of the grey squirrel* Sciurus carolinensis *(Gmelin).* DPhil thesis, University of Oxford.

942 Mackintosh, J.H. (1981) Behaviour of the house mouse. *Symposia of the Zoological Society of London,* **47,** 337–365.

943 Mackintosh, J.L. (1970) Territory formation by laboratory mice. *Animal Behaviour,* **18,** 177–183.

944 Mackintosh, J.L. (1973) Factors affecting the recognition of territory boundaries by mice (*Mus musculus* L.). *Animal Behaviour,* **21,** 464–470.

945 MacNicoll, A.D. *et al.* (1996) The distribution and significance of anticoagulant-resistant Norway rats (*Rattus norvegicus*) in England and Wales, 1988–95, pp. 179–185 in Timm, R.M. & Crabb, A.C. (ed.) *Proceedings of the 17th Vertebrate Pest Conference.* University of California, Davis, CA.

946 MacPherson, D & Morris, P.A. Personal communication.

947 MacVicar, H.J. & Trout, R.C. (1994) Vegetation management to manipulate field vole (*Microtus agrestis*) populations in grassy plantations, pp. 302–305 in Haggar, R.J. & Peel, S. (eds.) *Grassland management and nature conservation.* British Grassland Society Occasional Symposium No. 28, Leeds.

948 Madison, D. (1985) Activity rhythms and spacing, pp. 373–419 in Tamarin, R.H. (ed.) *Biology of New World* Microtus. Special Publication 8, American Society of Mammalogists, Lawrence, KS.

949 MAFF (1982) *Mouse control in poultry houses.* Leaflet 757. MAFF Publications, Alnwick.

950 Magris, L. (1998) *The ecology and conservation of the red squirrel* (Sciurus vulgaris) *on Jersey, CI.* PhD thesis, Queen Mary & Westfield College, University of London.

951 Mallorie, H. & Flowerdew, J.R. (1994) Woodland small mammal population ecology in Britain. A preliminary review of the Mammal Society survey of wood mice (*Apodemus sylvaticus*) and bank voles (*Clethrionomys glareolus*), 1982–87. *Mammal Review,* **24,** 1–15.

952 Malygin, V.M. (1983) *Systematics of the common voles.* Nauka, Moscow.

953 Manning, C.J. *et al.* (1992) Communal nesting patterns in mice implicate MHC genes in kin recognition. *Nature,* **360,** 581–583.

954 Mappes, T. (1998) High population density in bank voles stimulates food hoarding after breeding. *Animal Behaviour,* **55,** 1483–1487.

955 Mappes, T. *et al.* (1995) Reproductive costs and litter size in the bank vole. *Proceedings of the Royal Society of London Series B,* **261,** 19–24.

956 Mappes, T. *et al.* (1998) Breeding suppression in voles under predation risk of small mustelids: laboratory or methodological artifact? *Oikos,* **82,** 365–369.

957 Marelli, C.A. (1932) El nuevo y especie, *Pitrufquenia coypus* de Malofago de la Nutria Chilena. *La Charca,* **3,** 7–9 (in Spanish).

958 Marin, G. & Pilastro, A. (1994) Communally breeding dormice, *Glis glis*, are close kin. *Animal Behaviour*, **47**, 1485–1487.

959 Marsh, A. (1999) *The national yellow-necked mouse survey report*. The Mammal Society, London.

960 Marsh, A.C.W. (1999) *Factors determining the range and abundance of the yellow-necked mouse* Apodemus flavicollis *in Great Britain*. PhD thesis, University of Bristol.

961 Marsh, A.C.W. & Harris, S. (2000) Partitioning of woodland habitat resources by two sympatric species of *Apodemus*: lessons for the conservation of the yellow-necked mouse (*A. flavicollis*) in Britain. *Biological Conservation*, **92**, 275–283.

962 Marsh, A.C.W. & Harris, S. (2000) Living with yellow-necked mice. *British Wildlife*, **11**, 168–174.

963 Marsh, A.C.W. & Morris, P.A. (2000) The use of dormouse *Muscardinus avellanarius* nest boxes by two species of *Apodemus* in Britain. *Acta Theriologica*, **45**, 443–453.

964 Marsh, A.C.W. *et al.* (2001) The yellow-necked mouse *Apodemus flavicollis* in Britain: status and analysis of factors affecting distribution. *Mammal Review*, **31**, 203–227.

965 Marshall, J.T. (1986) Systematics of the genus *Mus*. *Current Topics in Microbiology and Immunology*, **127**, 12–18.

966 Maruniak, J.A. *et al.* (1975) Adaptations for urinary marking in rodents: prepuce length and morphology. *Journal of Reproduction and Fertility*, **44**, 567–570.

967 Mather, J.G. & Baker, R.R. (1981) Magnetic sense of direction in woodmice for route-based navigation. *Nature*, **291**, 152–5.

968 Matthews, J.E. (2000) Red squirrels (Sciurus vulgaris) *on the island of Anglesey, North Wales: past, present and future*. MPhil thesis, University of London.

969 Matthews, L.H. (1952) *British mammals*. Collins, London.

970 Matthey, R. (1951) La formule chromosomique de *Microtus orcadensis* Mill. *Revue Suisse de Zoologie*, **58**, 201–213 (in French).

971 Matthey, R. (1956) Cytologie chromosomique comparée et systematique des Muridae. *Mammalia*, **20**, 93–123.

972 Mayhew, D. (1977) Avian predators as accumulators of fossil mammal material. *Boreas*, **6**, 25–31.

973 Mayhew, D.F. (1978) Age structure of a sample of subfossil beavers (*Castor fiber* L.), pp. 495–505 in Butler, P.M. & Joysey, K.A. (eds.) *Development, function and evolution of teeth*. Academic Press, London.

974 Mayle, B. *et al.* (2004) Controlling grey squirrel damage to woodlands. *Forestry Commission Practice Note*, **4**, 1–12.

975 Mazurkiewicz, M. (1972) Density and weight structure of populations of the bank vole in open and enclosed areas. *Acta Theriologica*, **17**, 455–465.

976 Mazurkiewicz, M. (1983) Spatial organisation of the population. pp. 117–127 in Petrusewicz, K. (ed.) *Ecology of the bank vole. Acta Theriologica*, **28**, Suppl. 1.

977 Mazurkiewicz, M. (1994) Factors influencing the distribution of the bank vole in forest habitats. *Acta Theriologica*, **39**, 113–126.

978 Mazurkiewicz, M. & Rajska, E. (1975) Dispersion of young bank voles from their place of birth. *Acta Theriologica*, **20**, 71–81.

979 Mazurkiewicz, M. & Rajska-Jurgiel, E. (1998) Spatial behaviour and population dynamics of woodland rodents. *Acta Theriologica*, **43**, 137–161.

980 McCaughey, C. *et al.* (1996) Evidence of hantavirus in wild rodents in Northern Ireland. *Epidemiology and Infection*, **117**, 361–365.

981 McInnes, C.J. *et al.* (2006) Genomic characterization of a novel poxvirus contributing to the decline of the red squirrel (*Sciurus vulgaris*) in the UK. *Journal of General Virology*, **87**, 2115–2125.

982 Meehan, A.P. (1984) *Rats and mice: their biology and control*. Rentokil, East Grinstead.

983 Meehan, A.P. Personal communication.

984 Merson, M.H. *et al.* (1978) Characteristics of captive gray squirrels exposed to cold and food deprivation. *Journal of Wildlife Management*, **42**, 202–205.

985 Meyer, A.N. (1994) Rodent control in practice: food stores, pp. 273–290 in Buckle, A.P. & Smith, R.H. (eds.) *Rodent pests and their control*. CAB International, Wallingford.

986 Meyer, A.N. *et al.* (1995) National commensal rodent survey 1993. *Environmental Health*, **103**, 127–135.

987 Meyer-Lucht, Y. & Sommer, S. (2005) MHC diversity and the association to nematode parasitism in the yellow-necked mouse (*Apodemus flavicollis*). *Molecular Ecology*, **14**, 2233–2243.

988 Michaux, J.R. *et al.* (2002) Phylogeny of the genus *Apodemus* with a special emphasis on the subgenus *Sylvaemus* using the nuclear IRBP gene and two mitochondrial markers: cytochrome *b* and 12S rRNA. *Molecular Phylogenetics and Evolution*, **23**, 123–136.

989 Michaux, J.R. *et al.* (2004) Phylogeographic history of the yellow-necked fieldmouse (*Apodemus flavicollis*) in Europe and in the Near and Middle East. *Molecular Phylogenetics and Evolution*, **32**, 788–798.

990 Michaux, J.R. *et al.* (2005) So close and so different: comparative phylogeography of two small mammal species, the yellow-necked fieldmouse (*Apodemus flavicollis*) and the woodmouse (*Apodemus sylvaticus*) in the Western Palearctic region. *Heredity*, **94**, 52–63.

991 Michel, V. *et al.* (2001) Role of the coypu (*Myocastor coypus*) in the epidemiology of leptospirosis in domestic animals and humans in France. *European Journal of Epidemiology*, **17**, 11–21.

992 Middleton, A.D. (1930) The ecology of the American grey squirrel (*Sciurus carolinensis* Gmelin) in the British Isles. *Proceedings of the Zoological Society of London*, **1930**, 809–843.

993 Middleton, A.D. (1931) *The grey squirrel*. Sidgwick & Jackson, London.

994 Migula, P. *et al.* (1970) Vole and mouse plagues in south eastern Poland in the years 1945–1967. *Acta Theriologica*, **15**, 233–252.

995 Miller, G.S. (1912) *Catalogue of the mammals of western Europe*. British Museum (Natural History), London.

996 Miller, R.S. (1954) Food habits of the wood mouse *Apodemus sylvaticus* (Linne 1758) and the bank vole *Clethrionomys glareolus* (Schreber 1780) in Wytham Wood, Berkshire. *Säugetierkundliche Mitteilungen*, **2**, 109–114.

997 Miller, R.S. (1955) Activity rythyms in the wood mouse *Apodemus sylvaticus* and bank vole *Clethrionomys glareolus*. *Proceedings of the Zoological Society of London*, **125**, 505–519.

998 Milligan, S.R. (1974) Social environment and ovulation in the vole, *Microtus agrestis. Journal of Reproduction and Fertility*, **41**, 35–47.

999 Milligan, S.R. (1975) Mating, ovulation and corpus luteum functions in the vole, *Microtus agrestis. Journal of Reproduction and Fertility*, **42**, 35–44.

1000 Milton, A. & Johnson, M. (1999) Biomonitoring of contaminated mine tailings through age accumulation of trace metals in the bank vole (*Clethrionomys glareolus*). *Journal of Environmental Monitoring*, **1**, 219–225.

1001 Minnette, H.P. (1964) Leptospirosis in rodents and mongooses on the island of Hawaii. *American Journal of Tropical Medicine and Hygiene*, **13**, 826–832.

1002 Mitchell-Jones, A.J. *et al.* (1999) *The atlas of European mammals*. Poyser, London.

1003 Moffat, C.B. (1928) The field mouse. *Irish Naturalists' Journal*, **11**, 106–109.

1004 Moffat, C.B. (1938) The mammals of Ireland. *Proceedings of the Royal Irish Academy* B, **44**, 1–128.

1005 Moller, H. (1983) Foods and foraging behaviour of red (*Sciurus vulgaris*) and grey (*Sciurus carolinensis*) squirrels. *Mammal Review*, **13**, 81–98.

1006 Moller, H. (1986) Red squirrels (*Sciurus vulgaris*) feeding in a Scots pine plantation in Scotland. *Journal of Zoology*, **209**, 1–84.

1007 Molyneux, D.H. (1969) The morphology and life history of *Trypanosoma* (*Hespetosoma*) *microti* of the field vole *Microtus agrestis*. *Annals of Tropical Medicine and Parasitology*,

63, 229–44.

1008 Montgomery, S.S.J. & Montgomery, W.I. (1985) A new semi-hairless mutant of the wood mouse, *Apodemus sylvaticus. Journal of Zoology A,* **207,** 626–628.

1009 Montgomery, S.S.J. & Montgomery, W.I. (1988) Cyclic and non-cyclic dynamics of helminth parasites of wood mice, *Apodemus sylvaticus. Journal of Helminthology,* **62,** 78–90.

1010 Montgomery, S.S.J. & Montgomery, W.I. (1989) Spatial and temporal variation in the infracommunity structure of helminths of *Apodemus sylvaticus* (Rodentia: Muridae). *Parasitology,* **98,** 145–150.

1011 Montgomery, S.S.J. & Montgomery, W.I. (1990) Structure, stability and species interactions in helminth communities. *International Journal for Parasitology,* **20,** 225–242.

1012 Montgomery, S.S.J. & Montgomery, W.I. (1990) Intrapopulation variation in the diet of the wood mouse *Apodemus sylvaticus. Journal of Zoology,* **222,** 641–651.

1013 Montgomery, W.I. (1975) On the relationship between sub-fossil and recent British water voles. *Mammal Review,* **5,** 23–29.

1014 Montgomery, W.I. (1977) *Studies on the ecology of two sympatric species of* Apodemus *(Rodentia: Muridae).* PhD thesis, University of Manchester.

1015 Montgomery, W.I. (1978) Studies on the distribution of *Apodemus sylvaticus* (L.) and *A. flavicollis* (Melchior) in Britain. *Mammal Review,* **8,** 177–184.

1016 Montgomery, W.I. (1978) Intra- and interspecific interactions of *Apodemus sylvaticus* (L.) and *A. flavicollis* (Melchior) under laboratory conditions. *Animal Behaviour,* **26,** 1247–1254.

1017 Montgomery, W.I. (1979) An examination of interspecific, sexual and individual biases affecting rodent capture in Longworth traps. *Acta Theriologica,* **24,** 35–45.

1018 Montgomery, W.I. (1979) Trap-revealed home range in sympatric populations of *Apodemus sylvaticus* and *A. flavicollis. Journal of Zoology,* **189,** 535–540.

1019 Montgomery, W.I. (1980) The use of arboreal runways by the woodland rodents, *Apodemus sylvaticus* (L.), *A. flavicollis* (Melchior) and *Clethrionomys glareolus* (Schreber). *Mammal Review,* **10,** 189–195.

1020 Montgomery, W.I. (1980) Spatial organisation in sympatric populations of *Apodemus sylvaticus* and *A. flavicollis* (Rodentia: Muridae). *Journal of Zoology,* **192,** 379–401.

1021 Montgomery, W.I. (1980) Population structure and dynamics of sympatric *Apodemus* species (Rodentia: Muridae). *Journal of Zoology,* **192,** 351–377.

1022 Montgomery, W.I. (1981) A removal experiment with sympatric populations of *Apodemus sylvaticus* (L.) and *A. flavicollis* Melchior (Rodentia: Muridae). *Oecologia,* **51,** 123–132.

1023 Montgomery, W.I. (1985) Interspecific competition and the comparative ecology of two congeneric species of mice, pp. 126–187 in Cook, L.M. (ed.) *Case studies in population biology,* Manchester University Press, Manchester.

1024 Montgomery, W.I. (1989) *Peromyscus* and *Apodemus*: patterns of similarity in ecological equivalents, pp. 293–365 in Kirkland, G.L. & Layne, J.N. (eds.) *Advances in the Study of* Peromyscus *(Rodentia).* Texas Tech University Press, Lubbock, TX.

1025 Montgomery, W.I. (1989) Population regulation in the wood mouse, *Apodemus sylvaticus.* I. Density-dependence in the annual cycle of abundance. *Journal of Animal Ecology,* **58,** 465–475.

1026 Montgomery, W.I. (1989) Population regulation in the wood mouse, *Apodemus sylvaticus.* II. Density-dependence in spatial distribution and reproduction. *Journal of Animal Ecology,* **58,** 477–494.

1027 Montgomery, W.I. (1989) Population parameters, spatial division and niche breadth in two *Apodemus* species sharing a woodland habitat, pp. 45–57 in Morris, D.W. *et* al. (eds.) *Patterns in the structure of mammalian communities.* Texas Tech University Press, Lubbock, TX.

1028 Montgomery, W.I. & Dowie, M. (1993) The distribution and population regulation of wood mouse *Apodemus sylvaticus* on field boundaries of pastoral farmland. *Journal of Applied Ecology,* **30,** 783–791.

1029 Montgomery, W.I. & Dowie, M. (1993) The distribution of the wood mouse *Apodemus sylvaticus* and the house mouse *Mus domesticus* on farmland in north-east Ireland. *Irish Naturalists' Journal,* **24,** 199–203.

1030 Montgomery, W.I. & Gurnell, J. (1985) The behaviour of *Apodemus. Symposia of the Zoological Society of London,* **55,** 89–115.

1031 Montgomery, W.I. *et al.* (1991) Dispersion in the wood mouse *Apodemus sylvaticus*: variable resources in time and space. *Journal of Animal Ecology,* **60,** 179–192.

1032 Montgomery, W.I. *et al.* (1997) Spatial regulation and population growth in the wood mouse *Apodemus sylvaticus*: experimental manipulations of males and females in natural populations. *Journal of Animal Ecology,* **66,** 755–768.

1033 Moojen, J. (1981) Rodent control in Rio de Janeiro. *Pest Control,* December, 17–18.

1034 Moore, C.L. (1981) An olfactory basis for maternal discrimination of sex of offspring in rats (*Rattus norvegicus*). *Animal Behaviour,* **29,** 383–386.

1035 Moore, H.D.M. (1997) On developing an immunocontraceptive vaccine for the grey squirrel, pp. 127–132 in Gurnell, J.& Lurz, P.W.W. (eds.) *The conservation of red squirrels,* Sciurus vulgaris *L.* People's Trust for Endangered Species, London.

1036 Moore, H.D.M. *et al.* (1997) Immunocontraception in rodents: a review of the development of a sperm-based immunocontraceptive vaccine for the grey squirrel (*Sciurus carolinensis*). *Reproduction, Fertility and Development,* **9,** 125–129.

1037 Moore, H. *et al.* (2002) Exceptional sperm cooperation in the wood mouse. *Nature,* **418,** 174–177.

1038 Moore, N.P. *et al.* (2003) Small mammals in new farm woodlands. *Mammal Review,* **33,** 101–104.

1039 Morris, P.A. (1968) Apparent hypothermia in the wood mouse *(Apodemus sylvaticus). Journal of Zoology,* **155,** 235–236.

1040 Morris, P. (1979) Rats in the diet of the barn owl (*Tyto alba*). *Journal of Zoology,* **189,** 540–545.

1041 Morris, P. (1997) *The edible dormouse.* The Mammal Society, London.

1042 Morris, P.A. (1997) Review of the fat dormouse (*Glis glis*) in Britain. *Natura Croatica,* **6,** 163–176.

1043 Morris, P.A. (1993) *The red data book for British mammals.* The Mammal Society, London.

1044 Morris, P. (2004) *Dormice.* Whittet, Stowmarket.

1045 Morris, P.A. & Hoodless, A. (1992) Movements and hibernaculum site in the fat dormouse (*Glis glis*). *Journal of Zoology,* **228,** 685–687.

1046 Morris, P.A. & Temple, R.K. (1998) 'Nest tubes': a potential new method for controlling numbers of the edible dormouse (*Glis glis*) in plantations. *Quarterly Journal of Forestry,* **92,** 201–205.

1047 Morris, P.A. & Whitbread, S. (1986) A method for trapping the dormouse (*Muscardinus avellanarius*). *Journal of Zoology,* **210,** 642–644.

1048 Morris, P.A. *et al.* (1990) Use of nestboxes by the dormouse *Muscardinus avellanarius. Biological Conservation,* **51,** 1–13.

1049 Morris, P.A. *et al.* (1997) Studies of the edible dormouse (*Glis glis*) in British woodlands – some preliminary results. *Quarterly Journal of Forestry,* **91,** 321–326.

1050 Morris, P.A. *et al.* (1998) Estimating numbers of the water vole *Arvicola terrestris*: a correction to the published method. *Journal of Zoology,* **246,** 61–62.

1051 Morse, H.C. (ed.) (1978) *Origins of inbred mice.* Academic Press, New York.

1052 Mossing, T. (1975) Measuring small mammal locomotory

activity with passage counters. *Oikos,* **26,** 237–249.

1053 Mountford, E.P. & Peterken, G.F. (1999) Effects of stand structure, composition and treatment on bark-stripping of beech by grey squirrels. *Forestry,* **72,** 379–386.

1054 Mukhacheva, S.V. & Lukyanov, O.A. (1997) Migratory mobility of a population of the bank vole (*Clethrionomys glareolus* Schreber, 1780) in a gradient of technogenic factors. *Russian Journal of Ecology,* **28,** 30–35.

1055 Muldal, S. (1950) A list of vertebrates observed at Bayfordbury, 1949–1950. *Report, John Innes Horticultural Institution,* **41,** 39–41.

1056 Müller, J.P. (1972) Die Verteilung der Kleinsäuger auf die Lebensraume an einen Nordhang im Churer Rheintal. *Zeitschrift für Säugetierkunde,* **37,** 257–286 (in German).

1057 Muller-Bohme, H. (1939) Beitrage zur Anatomie, Morphologie und Biologie der grossen Wuhlmaus (*Arvicola terrestris* L., *Arvicola terrestris sherman* Shaw). Gleichzeitig ein Versuch zur Losung ihrer Rassenfrage. *Arbeiten der Kaiserlichen Biologischen Reichensanstalt – Land-Fortwirtschaft,* **21,** 363–453 (in German).

1058 Musolf, K. *et al.* (2004) Evolution of MHC-*DRB* class II polymorphism in the genus *Apodemus* and a comparison of *DRB* sequences within the family Muridae (Mammalia: Rodentia). *Immunogenetics,* **56,** 420–426.

1059 Myllymäki, A. (1977) Demographic mechanisms in the fluctuation populations of the field vole (*Microtus agrestis*). *Oikos,* **40,** 407–418.

1060 Naber, F. (1982) Erste vonst van der dwergmaus *Micromys minutus* (Pallas, 1771) op Terschelling. *Lutra,* **25,** 95–96 (in Dutch).

1061 Nascetti, G. & Filipucci, M.G. (1984) Genetic variability and divergence in Italian populations of *Apodemus sylvaticus* and *Apodemus flavicollis* (Rodentia, Muridae). *Supplemento alle Ricerche di Biologia della Selvaggina,* **9,** 75–83.

1062 Naumova, E.I. *et al.* (1998) New approaches to investigate feeding and digestive system in herbivorous mammals. *Zoologichesky Zhurnal,* **77,** 20–29.

1063 Nelson, J. (1994) *Determinants of spacing behaviour, reproductive success and mating system in male field voles, Microtus agrestis.* PhD dissertation, University of Lund, Sweden.

1064 Nelson, J. (1995) Determinants of male spacing behavior in microtines – an experimental manipulation of female spatial-distribution and density. *Behavioral Ecology and Sociobiology,* **37,** 217–223.

1065 Nemirov, K. *et al.* (2003) Genetic characterization of new Dobrava hantavirus isolate from Greece. *Journal of Medical Virology,* **69,** 408–416.

1066 Nesbitt, M.N. & Francke, U. (1973) A system of nomenclature for band patterns of mouse chromosomes. *Chromosomes,* **41,** 145–158.

1067 Nevison, C.M. *et al.* (1999) Strain-specific effects of cage enrichment in male laboratory mice (*Mus musculus*). *Animal Welfare,* **8,** 361–379.

1068 Newsome, A.E. (1969) A population study of house-mice temporarily inhabiting a South Australian wheat field. *Journal of Animal Ecology,* **38,** 341–359.

1069 Newsome, A.E. (1969) A population study of house-mice permanently inhabiting a reed-bed in South Australia. *Journal of Animal Ecology,* **38,** 361–377.

1070 Newsome, A.E. & Corbett, L.K. (1975) Outbreaks of rodents in semi-arid and arid Australia: causes, preventions, and evolutionary considerations, pp. 117–53 in Prakash, I. & Ghosh, P.K. (eds.) *Rodents in desert environments.* Junk, The Hague.

1071 Newsome, A.E. & Crowcroft, W.P. (1971) Outbreaks of house mice in South Australia in 1965. *CSIRO Wildlife Research,* **61,** 41–47.

1072 Newson, R. (1963) Differences in numbers, reproduction and survival between two neighbouring populations of the bank vole (*Clethrionomys glareolus*). *Ecology,* **44,** 111–120.

1073 Newson, R.M. (1966) Reproduction in the feral coypu (*Myocastor coypus*). *Symposia of the Zoological Society of London,* **15,** 323–334.

1074 Newson, R.M. (1968) Parasites occurring on the coypu since its introduction to Britain. *Bulletin of the Mammal Society of the British Isles,* **29,** 13–14.

1075 Newson, R.M. & Holmes, R.G. (1968). Some ectoparasites of the coypu in eastern England. *Journal of Animal Ecology,* **37,** 471–481.

1076 Nieder, L. *et al.* (1982) Burrowing and feeding behaviour in the rat. *Animal Behaviour,* **30,** 837–844.

1077 Niethammer, J. (1969) Zur Frage der Introgression bei den Waldmäusen *Apodemus sylvaticus* und *A. flavicollis* (Mammalia, Rodentia). *Zeitschrift für Zoologische Systematik und Evolutionforschung,* **7,** 77–127 (in German).

1078 Niethammer, J. & Krapp, P. (ed.) (1978) *Handbuch der Säugetiere Europas, Band 1, Rodentia I. (Sciuridae, Castoridae, Gliridae, Muridae).* Akademische Verlagsgesellschaft, Wiesbaden (in German).

1079 Niklasson, B. *et al.* (1995) Temporal dynamics of Puumala virus-antibody prevalence in voles and of Nephropathia Epidemica incidence in humans. *American Journal of Tropical Medicine and Hygiene,* **53,** 134–140.

1080 Niklasson, B. *et al.* (1999) A new picornavirus isolated from bank voles (*Clethrionomys glareolus*). *Virology,* **255,** 86–93.

1081 Nolet, B.A. (1997) Management of the beaver (*Castor fiber*): towards restoration of its former distribution and ecological function in Europe. *Nature and Environment* No. **86.** Council of Europe, Strasbourg.

1082 Norrdahl, K. & Korpimäki, E. (2002) Changes in population structure and reproduction during a 3-yr population cycle of voles. *Oikos,* **96,** 331–345.

1083 Norris, J.D. (1967) A campaign against feral coypus (*Myocastor coypus*) in Great Britain. *Journal of Applied Ecology,* **4,** 191–199.

1084 Nott, H.M.R. & Sibly, R.M. (1993) Responses to novel food: the effect of social rank. *Crop Protection,* **12,** 89–94.

1085 Noyes, H.A. *et al.* (2002) Host specificity of *Trypanosoma (Herpetosoma)* species: evidence that bank voles (*Clethrionomys glareolus*) carry only one *T. (H.) evotomys* 18S rRNA genotype but wood mice (*Apodemus sylvaticus*) carry at least two polyphyletic parasites. *Parasitology,* **124,** 185–190.

1086 Nygren, J. (1978) Individual influence on diurnal rhythms of activity in cycling and non-cycling populations of the field vole, *Microtus agrestis* L. *Oecologia,* **35,** 231–239.

1087 Obrtel, R. & Holisova, V. (1979) The food eaten by *Apodemus sylvaticus* in a spruce monoculture. *Folia Zoologica,* **28,** 299–310.

1088 O'Connor, T.P. (1992) Pets and pests in Roman and Medieval Britain. *Mammal Review,* **22,** 107–113.

1089 Ogden, R. *et al.* (2005) Genetic management of the red squirrel, *Sciurus vulgaris*: a practical approach to regional conservation. *Conservation Genetics,* **6,** 511–525.

1090 Ognev, S.I. (1940) *Animals of the USSR and adjacent countries. 4 Rodents.* Moscow, Leningrad. English translation (1960), Israel Program for Scientific Translations, Jerusalem.

1091 Ognev, S.I. (1950) *Animals of the USSR and adjacent countries. 7 Rodents.* Moscow, Leningrad. English translation (1964), Israel Program for Scientific Translations, Jerusalem.

1092 Okon, E.E. (1972) Factors affecting ultrasound production in infant rodents. *Journal of Zoology,* **168,** 139–148.

1093 Okubo, A. *et al.* (1989) On the spatial spread of the grey squirrel in Britain. *Proceedings of the Royal Society of London Series B,* **238,** 113–125.

1094 Olsson, G.E. *et al.* (2002) Demographic factors associated with hantavirus infection in bank voles (*Clethrionomys glareolus*). *Emerging Infectious Diseases,* **8,** 924–929.

1095 O'Mahony, D. *et al.* (1999) Generalist fox predation on cyclic field vole populations in Britain. *Ecography,* **22,** 575–

581.

1096 Osgood, W.H. (1943) Mammals of Chile. *Field Museum Natural History Publications Zoology Series,* **30,** 131–134.

1097 Osipova, O.V. (2006) Interspecific hybrids of *Clethrionomys* voles bred in laboratory. *Hystrix Italian Journal of Mammalogy* (N.S.) Supp. 10th International Conference Rodens & Spatium.

1098 O'Teangana, D. *et al.* (2000) Distribution and status of the red squirrel (*Sciurus vulgaris*) and grey squirrel (*Sciurus carolinensis*) in Ireland. *Mammal Review,* **30,** 45–56.

1099 Owadowska, E. (1999) The range of olfactory familiarity between individuals in a population of bank voles. *Acta Theriologica,* **44,** 133–150.

1100 Owen, D. (1972) *Common parasites of laboratory rodents and lagomorphs.* HMSO, London.

1101 Owen, D. (1976) Some parasites and other organisms of wild rodents in the vicinity of an SPF unit. *Laboratory Animal,* **10,** 271–278.

1102 Pack, J.C. *et al.* (1967) Influence of social hierarchy on gray squirrel behaviour. *Journal of Wildlife Management,* **31,** 720–728.

1103 Panchetti, F. *et al.* (2004) Activity patterns of the common dormouse (*Muscardinus avellanarius*) in different Mediterranean ecosystems. *Journal of Zoology,* **262,** 289–294.

1104 Panteleyev, P.A. (1968) *Population ecology of the water vole.* Moscow. (In Russian; English translation National Lending Library, 1971).

1105 Parker, J.C. & Holliman, R.B. (1972) A method of determining ectoparasitic densities on gray squirrels. *Journal of Wildlife Management,* **36,** 1227–1234.

1106 Pasitschniak-Arts, M. & Bendell, J.F. (1990) Behavioural differences between locally recruiting and dispersing gray squirrels, *Sciurus carolinensis. Canadian Journal of Zoology,* **68,** 935–941.

1107 Pearson, O.P. (1963) History of two local outbreaks of feral house mice. *Ecology,* **44,** 540–549.

1108 Peck, S.B. (1982) A review of the ectoparasitic *Leptinus* beetles of North America (Coleoptera: Leptinidae). *Canadian Journal of Zoology,* **60,** 1517–1527.

1109 Pekkarinen, P. & Heikkila, J. (1997) Prey selection of the least weasel *Mustela nivalis* in the laboratory. *Acta Theriologica,* **42,** 179–188.

1110 Pelikan, J. (1967) Resorption rate in embryos of four *Apodemus* species. *Zoologicke Listy,* **16,** 325–342.

1111 Pelikan, J. (1970) Sex ratio in three *Apodemus* species. *Zoologicke Listy,* **19,** 23–34.

1113 Pelikan, J. (1981) Patterns of reproduction in the house mouse. *Symposia of the Zoological Society of London,* **47,** 205–229.

1114 Pelikan, K. (1967) Analysis of three population dynamical factors in *Apodemus flavicollis. Zeitschrift für Säugetierkunde,* **31,** 31–37.

1115 Pelz, H.-J. (1979) Die Waldmaus, *Apodemus sylvaticus* L auf Ackerflachen: Populationsdynamik, Saatschiden und Abwehrmbglichkeiten. *Zeitschrift für Angewandte Zoologie,* **66,** 261–280 (in German).

1116 Pelz, H.-J. (1989) Ecological aspects of damage to sugar-beet seeds by *Apodemus sylvaticus,* pp 34–48 in Putman, R.J. (ed.) *Mammals as pests.* Chapman & Hall, London.

1117 Penn, D. *et al.* (1998) Influenza infection neutralizes the attractiveness of male odour to female mice (*Mus musculus*). *Ethology,* **104,** 685–694.

1118 Pennycuik, P.R. *et al.* (1986) Variation in numbers in a house mouse population housed in a large outdoor enclosure: seasonal fluctuations. *Journal of Animal Ecology,* **55,** 371–391.

1119 Pepper, H. perssonal communication.

1120 Pepper, H. & Patterson, G. (1998) *Red squirrel conservation.* Forestry Commission Practice Note 5. Forestry Commission, Edinburgh.

1121 Pepper, P. & Currie, F. (1998) *Controlling grey squirrel damage to woodlands.* Forestry Commission Practice Note 4.

Forestry Commission, Edinburgh.

1122 Perkins, H.M. & Mallon, D.P. (1999) *The water vole in Derbyshire.* Derbyshire Wildlife Trust, Elvaston Castle, Derby.

1123 Pernetta, J.C. & Handford, P. (1970) Mammalian and avian remains from possible Bronze Age deposits on Nornour, Isles of Scilly. *Journal of Zoology,* **162,** 534–540.

1124 Perrin, M.R. (1971) *Exploratory behaviour as related to trapping results in the vole* Microtus agrestis *(Bellamy 1839).* PhD thesis, University of Exeter.

1125 Perrow, M. (1994) Roadside verges for small mammals. *British Wildlife,* **5,** 312–313.

1126 Perrow, M. & Jowitt, A. (1995). What future for the harvest mouse? *British Wildlife,* **6,** 356–365.

1127 Perry, D. (2004) Animal rights and environmental wrongs: the case of the grey squirrel in northern Italy. *Essays in Philosophy,* **5.**

1128 Perry, J.S. (1943) Reproduction in the water vole *Arvicola amphibius* Linn. *Proceedings of the Zoological Society of London,* **112,** 118–130.

1129 Pes, D. *et al.* (1999) How many major urinary proteins are produced by the house mouse *Mus domesticus*? pp. 149–161 in Johnston, R.E. *et al.* (eds.) *Advances in chemical communication in vertebrates.* Plenum Press, New York.

1130 Petrides, G.A. (1951) Notes on age determination in squirrels. *Journal of Mammalogy,* **32,** 111–112.

1131 Petrusewicz, K. (ed.) (1983) *Ecology of the bank vole. Acta Theriologica,* **28,** Supplement 1.

1132 Petrusewicz, K. & Andrzejewski, R. (1962) Natural history of a free-living population of house mice (*Mus musculus* Linnaeus), with particular reference to groupings within the population. *Ekologia Polska – Seria A,* **10**(5), 85–119.

1133 Petty, S.J. (1992) *Ecology of the tawny owl* Strix aluco *in the spruce forests of Northumberland and Argyll.* PhD thesis, Open University.

1134 Petty, S.J. *et al.* (2003). Predation of red squirrels by northern goshawk in a conifer forest in northern England: can this limit squirrel numbers and create a conservation dilemma? *Biological Conservation,* **111,** 105–114.

1135 Pialek, J. *et al.* (2005) Chromosomal variation in the house mouse: a review. *Biological Journal of the Linnean Society,* **84,** 535–563.

1136 Piechocki, R. (1958) Die Zwergmaus *Micromys minutus* Pallas. (Die Neu Brehm-Bucherei, n.22) Ziemsen, Wittenberg Lutherstadt (in German).

1137 Piertney, S.B. *et al.* (2005) Phylogeographic structure and postglacial evolutionary history of water voles (*Arvicola terrestris*) in the United Kingdom. *Molecular Ecology,* **14,** 1435–1444.

1138 Piertney, S.B. *et al.* Personal communication.

1139 Pilastro, A. *et al.* (1994) Factors affecting body mass of young fat dormice (*Glis glis*) at weaning and by hibernation. *Journal of Zoology,* **234,** 13–23.

1140 Pilastro, A. *et al.* (1996) Age-related reproductive success in solitary and communally nesting female dormice (*Glis glis*). *Journal of Zoology,* **239,** 601–608.

1141 Piper, S.E. (1928) The mouse infestation of Buena Vista lake basin, Kern County, California, September, 1926, to February, 1927. *Department of Agriculture, State of California, Monthly Bulletin,* **17,** 538–560.

1142 Platt, F.B.W. & Rowe, J.J. (1964) Damage by the edible dormouse (*Glis glis* L.) at Wendover Forest (Chilterns). *Quarterly Journal of Forestry,* **58,** 228–233.

1143 Pocock, M.J.O. *et al.* (2005) Dispersal in house mice. *Biological Journal of the Linnean Society,* **84,** 565–583.

1144 Pokki, J. (1981) Distribution, demography and dispersal of the field vole, *Microtus agrestis,* in the Travminne archipelago, Finland. *Acta Zoologica Fennica,* **164,** 1–48.

1145 Polechova, J. & Stopka, P. (2002) Geometry of social relationships in the Old World wood mouse (*Apodemus sylvaticus*). *Canadian Journal of Zoology,* **80,** 1383–1388.

1146 Pollard, E. & Relton, J. (1970) Hedges V: A study of small mammals in hedges and cultivated fields. *Journal of Applied Ecology*, **7**, 549–557.

1147 Poulton, S.M.C. (1994) Small mammal populations in hedgerows: the relationship with seed and berry production, pp. 133–138 in Boatman, N. (ed.) *Field margins: Integrating agriculture and conservation*. BCPC Monograph No. 58, British Crop Protection Council, Farnham.

1148 Povey, F.D. *et al.* (1993) Predation of annual grass weed seeds in arable field margins. *Annals of Applied Biology*, **122**, 323–328.

1149 Preece, R.C. (1986) Faunal remains from radio-carbon-dated soils within landslip debris from the Undercliff, Isle of Wight, Southern England. *Journal of Archaeological Science*, **13**, 189–200.

1150 Preece, R.C. *et al.* (1986) New biostratigraphic evidence of the post-glacial colonization of Ireland and for Mesolithic forest disturbance. *Journal of Biogeography*, **13**, 487–509.

1151 Prévot-Julliard, A. *et al.* (1999) Delayed maturation in female bank voles: optimal decision or social constraint? *Journal of Animal Ecology*, **68**, 684–697.

1152 Price, C.R. (2003) *Late Pleistocene and early Holocene small mammals in south west Britain*. BAR British Series **347**, 1–105, Archaeopress, Oxford.

1153 Pucek, M. (1983) Habitat preference, pp. 31–40 in Petrusewicz, K. (ed.) *Ecology of the bank vole. Acta Theriologica*, **28**, Suppl. 1.

1154 Pucek, Z. *et al.* (1993) Rodent population dynamics in a primeval deciduous forest (Białowieża National Park) in relation to weather, seed crop, and predation. *Acta Theriologica*, **38**, 199–232.

1155 Pulliam, H.R. *et al.* (1969) Bioelimination of tracer zinc-65 in relation to metabolic rates in mice, pp. 125–730 in Nelson, D.J. & Evans, F.C. (ed.) *Radioecology*. US Department of Commerce, Springfield, VA.

1156 Purroy, F.J. & Rey, J.M. (1974) Estudio ecologico y sistematico de la ardilla (*Sciurus vulgaris*) en Novarra. *Boletin de la Estación Central de Ecologia*, **3**, 71–82.

1157 Pusenius, J. (1996) *Intraspecific interactions, space use and reproductive success in the field vole*. PhD dissertation, University of Jyvaskyla, Finland.

1158 Pusenius, J. & Viitala, J. (1993) Varying spacing behaviour of breeding field voles, *Microtus agrestis*. *Annales Zoologici Fennici*, **30**, 143–152.

1159 Pusenius, J. & Ylönen, H. (1994) The effects of confinement on demography and spacing behaviour in the bank vole *Clethrionomys glareolus*. *Annales Zoologici Fennici*, **31**, 335–341.

1160 Pusenius, J. *et al.* (1998) Matrilineal kin clusters and their effect on reproductive success in the field vole *Microtus agrestis*. *Behavioral Ecology*, **9**, 85–92.

1161 Putman, R.J. *et al.* (1989) Vegetational and faunal change in an area of heavily grazed woodland following relief of grazing. *Biological Conservation*, **47**, 13–32.

1162 Quadagno, D.M. (1968) Home range size in feral house mice. *Journal of Mammalogy*, **49**, 149–151.

1163 Quere, J.P. & Vincent, J.P. (1989) Age-determination in wood mice (*Apodemus sylvaticus* L., 1758) by dry-weight of the lens. *Mammalia*, **53**, 287–293.

1164 Quy, R.J. Personal communication.

1165 Quy, R.J. *et al.* (1992) The influence of stored food on the effectiveness of farm rat control, pp. 291–300 in *Brighton Crop Protection Conference – Pests and Diseases*. British Crop Protection Council, Farnham.

1166 Quy, R.J., *et al.* (1994) Predicting the outcome of rodenticide trials against Norway rats living on farms, pp. 133–137 in Halverson, W.S. & Crabb, A.C. (eds.) *Proceedings of the 16th Vertebrate Pest Conference*. University of California, Davis, CA.

1167 Quy, R.J. *et al.* (1995) Control of a population of Norway rats resistant to anticoagulant rodenticides. *Pesticide Science*, **45**, 247–256.

1168 Raczynski, J. (1983) Taxonomic position, geographical range and the ecology of distribution, pp. 3–11 in Petrusewicz, K. (ed.) *Ecology of the bank vole. Acta Theriologica*, **28**, Suppl. 1.

1169 Raczynski, J. (1983) Morphological variability and taxonomic differentiation, pp. 11–20 in Petrusewicz, K. (ed.) *Ecology of the bank vole. Acta Theriologica*, **28**, Suppl 1.

1170 Radda, A. (1969) Untersuchungen über den Aktionsraum von *Apodemus flavicollis* (Melchior). *Zoologicke Listy*, **18**, 11–12 (in German).

1171 Radda, A. *et al.* (1969) Bionomische und Ökologische Studien an Österreichischen Populationen der Gelbhalsmaus (*Apodemus flavicollis* (Melchior, 1834)) durch Markierungsfang. *Oecologia (Berlin)*, **3**, 351–373 (in German).

1172 Randolph, S.E. (1975) Seasonal dynamics of a host parasite system: *Ixodex tranguliceps* (Acarina, Ixodidae) and its small mammal hosts. *Journal of Animal Ecology*, **44**, 425–449.

1173 Randolph, S.E. (1975) Patterns of distribution of the tick *Ixodes tranguliceps* Birula on its hosts. *Journal of Animal Ecology*, **44**, 451–474.

1174 Randolph, S.E. (1977) Changing spatial relationships in a population of *Apodemus sylvaticus* with the onset of breeding. *Journal of Animal Ecology*, **46**, 653–676.

1175 Randolph, S.E. (1994) Density dependent acquired resistance to ticks in natural hosts, independent of concurrent infection with *Babesia microti*. *Parasitology*, **108**, 413–419.

1176 Rands, D.G. (1979) The distribution of the harvest mouse (*Micromys minutus*) in Bedfordshire. *Bedfordshire Naturalist*, **33**, 13–16.

1177 Rasmuson, B. *et al.* (1977) Genetically controlled differences in behaviour between cycling and non-cycling populations of field vole (*Microtus agrestis*). *Hereditas*, **87**, 33–42.

1178 Ratkiewicz, M. & Borkowska, A. (2000) Multiple paternity in the bank vole (*Clethrionomys glareolus*): field and experimental data. *Zeitschrift für Säugetierkunde*, **65**, 6–14.

1179 Raufaste, N. *et al.* (2005). Inferences of selection and migration in the Danish house mouse hybrid zone. *Biological Journal of the Linnean Society*, **84**, 593–616.

1180 Rayden, T.J. & Savill, P.S. (2004) Damage to beech woodlands in the Chilterns by the grey squirrel. *Forestry*, **77**, 250–253.

1181 Redpath, S.M. *et al.* (2002) Field vole *Microtus agrestis* abundance and hen harrier *Circus cyaneus* diet and breeding in Scotland. *Ibis*, **144**, E33–E38.

1182 Rehacek, J. *et al.* (1992) Susceptibility of some species of rodents to Rickettsiae. *Folia Parasitologica*, **39**, 265–284.

1183 Reimer, J.D. & Petras, M.L. (1968) Some aspects of commensal populations of *Mus musculus* in Southwestern Ontario. *Canadian Field Naturalist*, **82**, 32–42.

1184 Rennison, B.D. & Dubock, A.C. (1978) Field trials of WBA 8119 (PP 581, brodifacoum) against warfarin-resistant infestations of *Rattus norvegicus*. *Journal of Hygiene*, **80**, 77–82.

1185 Rennison, B.D. & Shenker, A.M. (1976) Rodent infestation in some London boroughs in 1972. *Environmental Health*, **84**, 9–10.

1186 Reutter, B.A. *et al.* (2003) Cytochrome *b* haplotype divergences in west European *Apodemus*. *Mammalian Biology*, **68**, 153–164.

1187 Reynolds, J.C. (1981) *The interaction of red and grey squirrels*. PhD thesis, University of East Anglia.

1188 Reynolds, J.C. (1985) Details of the geographic replacement of the red squirrel (*Sciurus vulgaris*) by the grey squirrel (*Sciurus carolinensis*) in eastern England. *Journal of Animal Ecology*, **54**, 149–162.

1189 Reynolds, J.C. (1985) Autumn/winter energetics of Holarctic tree squirrels: a review. *Mammal Review*, **15**, 137–150.

1190 Reynolds, P. (1992) *The impact of changes in land use in Orkney on the vole Microtus arvalis and its avian predators*. PhD thesis, University of Aberdeen.

1191 Reynolds, P. & Gorman, M.L. (1994) Seasonal variation in the activity patterns of the Orkney vole *Microtus arvalis orcadensis*. *Journal of Zoology,* **233,** 605–616.

1192 Reynolds, P. & Gorman, M.L. (1999) The timing of hunting in short-eared owls (*Asio flammeus*) in relation to the activity patterns of Orkney voles (*Microtus arvalis orcadensis*) *Journal of Zoology,* **247,** 371–379.

1193 Rich, T.J. & Hurst, J.L. (1998) Scent marks as reliable signals of the competitive ability of mates. *Animal Behaviour,* **56,** 727–735.

1194 Rich, T.J. & Hurst, J.L. (1999) The competing counter-marks hypothesis: reliable assessment of competitive ability by potential mates. *Animal Behaviour,* **58,** 1027–1037.

1195 Richard, P.B. (1983) Mechanisms and adaptations in the constructive behaviour of beaver (*Castor fiber* L). *Acta Zoolica Fennica,* **174,** 105–108.

1196 Richards, C.G.J. (1985) The population dynamics of *Microtus agrestis* in Wytham, 1949 to 1978. *Acta Zoologica Fennica,* **173,** 35–38.

1197 Richards, C.G.J. *et al.* (1984) The food of the common dormouse, *Muscardinus avellanarius*, in south Devon. *Mammal Review,* **14,** 19–28.

1198 Richardson, J.H. *et al.* (1997) Are major roads a barrier to small mammals? *Journal of Zoology,* **243,** 840–846.

1199 Roberts, M.B. & Parfitt, S.A. (1999) *Boxgrove. A Middle Pleistocene hominid site at Eartham Quarry, Boxgove, West Sussex.* Vol. 17. English Heritage Archaeological Reports, London.

1200 Roberts, R.C. (1981) Genetical influences on growth and fertility. *Symposia of the Zoological Society of London,* **47,** 231–254.

1201 Robertson, D.H.L. *et al.* (1993) Extraction, characterization, and binding analysis of two pheromonally active ligands associated with major urinary protein of house mouse (*Mus musculus*). *Journal of Chemical Ecology,* **19,** 1405–1416.

1202 Robertson, D.H.L. *et al.* (1997) Molecular heterogeneity of urinary proteins in wild house mouse populations. *Rapid Communications in Mass Spectrometry,* **11,** 786–790.

1203 Robertson, D.H.L. *et al.* (1998) Ligands of urinary lipocalins from the mouse: uptake of environmentally derived chemicals. *Journal of Chemical Ecology,* **24,** 1127–1140.

1204 Robertson, J.G.M. (1977) *Population density and reproduction in* Microtus arvalis orcadensis. Honours thesis, University of Aberdeen.

1205 Robinson, R. (1970) Homologous mutants in mammalian coat colour variation. *Symposia of the Zoological Society of London,* **26,** 251–269.

1206 Rodl, P. (1974) Beitrag zur Kenntnis der Raumaktivität von *Apodemus flavicollis* Melch. und *Clethrionomys glareolus* Schreb. *Lynx,* **16,** 46–60 (in German).

1207 Rodolfi, G. (1994) Dormice, *Glis glis*, activity and hazelnut consumption. *Acta Theriologica,* **39,** 215–220.

1208 Rogers, L.M. & Gorman, M.L. (1995) The diet of the wood mouse *Apodemus sylvaticus* on set-aside land. *Journal of Zoology,* **235,** 77–83.

1209 Rogers, L.M. & Gorman, M.L. (1995) The population dynamics of small mammals living in set-aside and surrounding semi-natural and crop land. *Journal of Zoology,* **236,** 451–464.

1210 Rogers, L.M. & Gorman, M.L. (1995) The home-range size of wood mice *Apodemus sylvaticus* living in set-aside and surrounding semi-natural and crop land. *Journal of Zoology,* **237,** 675–678.

1211 Rogival, D. *et al.* (2006) Metal blood levels and hematological characteristics in wood mice (*Apodemus sylvaticus* L) along a metal pollution gradient. *Environmental Toxicology and Chemistry,* **25,** 149–157.

1212 Ronkainen, H. & Ylönen, H. (1994) Behavior of cyclic bank voles under risk of mustelid predation – do females avoid copulations? *Oecologia,* **97,** 377–381.

1213 Rood, J.P. (1965) Observations on the life cycle and variation of the long-tailed field mouse *Apodemus sylvaticus* in the Isles of Scilly and Cornwall. *Journal of Zoology,* **147,**
99–107.

1214 Rosell, F. *et al.* (2005) Ecological impacts of beavers *Castor fiber* and *Castor canadensis* and their ability to modify ecosystems. *Mammal Review,* **35,** 248–276.

1215 Rowe, F.P. (1958) Some observations on harvest mice from the corn ricks of a Hampshire farm. *Proceedings of the Zoological Society of London,* **131,** 320–323.

1216 Rowe, F.P. (1961) Ectoparasites found on harvest mice. *Proceedings of the Zoological Society of London,* **137,** 627.

1217 Rowe, F.P. (1981) Wild house mouse biology and control. *Symposia of the Zoological Society of London,* **47,** 575–589.

1218 Rowe, F.P. & Redfern, R. (1965) Toxicity tests on suspected warfarin resistant house mice (*Mus musculus* L) *Journal of Hygiene,* **63,** 417–425.

1219 Rowe, F.P. & Swinney, T. (1977) Population dynamics of small rodents in farm buildings and on arable land. *EPPO Bulletin,* **7,** 431–437.

1220 Rowe, F.P. & Taylor, E.J. (1958) The numbers of harvest mice (*Micromys minutus*) in corn ricks. *Proceedings of the Zoological Society of London,* **142,** 181–185.

1221 Rowe, F.P. *et al.* (1963) The numbers and movements of house mice (*Mus musculus* L) in the vicinity of four corn ricks. *Journal of Animal Ecology,* **32,** 87–97.

1222 Rowe, F.P. *et al.* (1983) Reproduction of the house mouse (*Mus musculus*) in farm buildings. *Journal of Zoology,* **199,** 259–269.

1223 Rowe, F.P. *et al.* (1987) Recolonisation of the buildings on a farm by house mice. *Acta Theriologica,* **32,** 3–19.

1224 Rowe, J. (1980) *Grey squirrel control.* Forestry Commission Leaflet No. 56. HMSO, London.

1225 Rowe, J. (1983) Squirrel management. *Mammal Review,* **13,** 173–182.

1226 Rowlands, I.W. (1936) Reproduction of the bank vole (*Evotomys glareolus* Schreber) II – Seasonal changes in the reproductive organs of the male. *Philosophical Transactions of the Royal Society of London Series B,* **226,** 99–120.

1227 Rozenfeld, F.M. & Denoel, A. (1994) Chemical signals involved in spacing behavior of breeding female bank voles (*Clethrionomys glareolus* Schreber 1780, Microtidae, Rodentia). *Journal of Chemical Ecology,* **20,** 803–813.

1228 Rozenfeld, F.M. & Rasmont, R. (1987) Urine marking in bank voles (*Clethrionomys glareolus* Schreber 1780, Microtidae, Rodentia) in relation to their social rank. *Canadian Journal of Zoology,* **65,** 2594–2601.

1229 Rozenfeld, F.M. & Rasmont, R. (1991) Odor cue recognition by dominant male bank voles, *Clethrionomys glareolus. Animal Behaviour,* **41,** 839–850.

1230 Rudd, P. Personal communication.

1231 Rushton, S.P. *et al.* (1997) Modelling the distribution of the red and grey squirrel at the landscape scale: a combined GIS and population dynamics approach. *Journal of Applied Ecology,* **34,** 1137–1154.

1232 Rushton, S.P. *et al.* (1999) Modelling the distribution of red squirrels (*Sciurus vulgaris*) on the Isle of Wight. *Animal Conservation,* **2,** 111–120.

1233 Rushton, S.P. *et al.* (2000) Modelling the spatial dynamics of parapoxvirus disease in red and grey squirrels: a possible cause of the decline in the red squirrel in the United Kingdom? *Journal of Applied Ecology,* **37,** 997–1012.

1234 Rushton, S.P. *et al.* (2002) Modelling the impacts and costs of grey squirrel control regimes on the viability of red squirrel populations. *Journal of Wildlife Management,* **66,** 683–697.

1235 Rushton, S.P. *et al.* (2006) Disease threats posed by alien species: the role of a poxvirus in the decline of the native red squirrel in Britain. *Epidemiology and Infection,* **134,** 521–533.

1236 Ryan, A.W. *et al.* (1993) Polymorphism, localization and geographical transfer of mitochondrial DNA in *Mus musculus domesticus* (Irish house mice). *Heredity,* **70,** 75–81.

1237 Ryan, A. *et al.* (1996) Mitochondrial DNA in bank voles *Clethrionomys glareolus* in Ireland: Evidence for a small founder population and localized founder effects. *Acta*

Theriologica, 41, 45–50.

1238 Ryder, S.R. (1962) *Water voles.* Sunday Times, London.

1239 Sage, R.D. (1981) Wild mice, pp 39–90 in Foster, H.L. *et al* (eds.) *The mouse in biomedical research,* Vol. 1. Academic Press, New York.

1240 Sainsbury, A.W. & Gurnell, J. (1995) An investigation into the health and welfare of red squirrels, *Sciurus vulgaris,* involved in reintroduction studies. *Veterinary Record,* **137,** 367–370.

1241 Sainsbury, A.W. & Gurnell, J. (1998) The health of red squirrels *Sciurus vulgaris* in translocation studies, p. 416 in *Proceedings of the 1998 AAZV and AAWV Joint Conference.*

1242 Sainsbury, A.W. & Ward, L. (1996) Parapoxvirus infection in red squirrels. *Veterinary Record,* **138,** 400.

1243 Sainsbury, A.W. *et al.* (1996) Ocular disease associated with *Rhabditis orbitalis* in a common dormouse (*Muscardinus avellanarius*). *Veterinary Record,* **139,** 192–193.

1244 Sainsbury, A.W. *et al.* (1997) Recent developments in the study of parapoxvirus, pp. 105–108 in Gurnell, J. & Lurz, P.W.W. (eds.) *The conservation of red squirrels,* Sciurus vulgaris L. People's Trust for Endangered Species, London.

1245 Sainsbury, A.W. *et al.* (2000) Grey squirrels have high seroprevalence to a paraoxvirus associated with deaths in red squirrels. *Animal Conservation,* **3,** 229–233.

1246 Sainsbury, A.W. *et al.* (2004) Oral disease in free-living red squirrels (*Sciurus vulgaris*) in the United Kingdom. *Journal of Wildlife Diseases,* **40,** 185–196.

1247 Saint Girons, M.C. (1973) *Les mammifères de France et du Benelux.* Doin, Paris (in French).

1248 Samkow, J.A. & Trubezkoij, G.W. (1974) Nutriazucht jenseits der Grenzen. *Deutsche Peltztierzuchter,* **48,** 130–132 (in German).

1249 Sandell, M. *et al.* (1990) Natal dispersal in relation to population density and sex ratio in the field vole, *Microtus agrestis. Oecologia (Berlin),* **83,** 145–149.

1250 Sandell, M. *et al.* (1991) Adult philopatry and dispersal in the field vole *Microtus agrestis. Oecologia (Berlin),* **86,** 153–158.

1251 Sara, M. *et al.* (2005) Exploitation competition between hole-nesters (*Muscardinus avellanarius,* Mammalia and *Parus caeruleus,* Aves) in Mediterranean woodlands. *Journal of Zoology,* **265,** 347–357.

1252 Sargent, G. (1999) Harvest mouse in trouble. *Mammal News,* **111,** 1.

1253 Saucy, F. (1994) Density dependence in time series of the fossorial form of the water vole, *Arvicola terrestris. Oikos,* **71,** 381–392.

1254 Saucy, F. (1999) The water vole as a pest: ecological variation, demography and population dynamics, pp. 25–42 in Cowan, P.D. & Feare, C.J. (eds.) *Advances in vertebrate pest management.* Filander Verlag, Furth.

1255 Saunders, G. (1986) Plagues of the house mouse in South Eastern Australia, pp. 173–176 in *Proceedings of the 12th Vertebrate Pest Conference.* University of California, Davis, CA.

1256 Schmidt, N.M. *et al.* (2005) Effects of grazing intensity on small mammal population ecology in wet meadows. *Basic and Applied Ecology,* **6,** 57–66.

1257 Schoenecker, B. & Heller, K.E. (2000) Indication of a genetic basis of stereotypies in laboratory-bred bank voles (*Clethrionomys glareolus*). *Applied Animal Behaviour Science,* **68,** 339–347.

1258 Schoenecker, B. *et al.* (2000) Development of stereotypies and polydipsia in wild caught bank voles (*Clethrionomys glareolus)* and their laboratory-bred offspring. Is polydipsia a symptom of diabetes mellitus? *Applied Animal Behaviour Science,* **68,** 349–357.

1259 Schon, I. & Korn, H. (1992) Causes and magnitude of body weight changes in trap-confined bank voles, *Clethrionomys glareolus. Journal of Zoology,* **227,** 319–322.

1260 Schulze, W. (1970) Beitrage zum Vorkommen und zur Biologie der Haselmaus (*Muscardinus avellanarius* L) und des Siebenschläfers (*Glis glis* L) in Sudharz. *Hercynia,* **7,** 354–371 (in German).

1261 Schumacher, S. (1924) Eine Lippenplatte beim Eichhörnchen *(Sciurus vulgaris* L) *Anatomischer Anzeiger,* **58,** 75–80 (in German).

1262 Schwarz, E. & Schwarz, H.K. (1943) The wild and commensal stocks of the house mouse (*Mus musculus* L). *Journal of Mammalogy,* **24,** 59–72.

1263 Schwarzenberger, T. von & Klingel, H. (1995) Range utilisation and activity of radio-collared yellow-necked mice, *Apodemus flavicollis* Melchior, 1934. *Zeitschrift für Säugetierkunde,* **60,** 20–32.

1264 Scott, A.C. *et al.* (1981) Parapoxvirus infection of the red squirrel *(Sciurus vulgaris). Veterinary Record,* **109,** 202.

1265 Scottish Natural Heritage (2005) *Application to the Scottish Executive by Scottish Natural Heritage for a licence under section 16(4) of the Wildlife and Countryside Act 1981, as amended, to release European beaver,* Castor fiber, *for a trial re-introduction in Knapdale, Argyll: response to the Minister's letter of 20 December 2002.* Scottish Natural Heritage, Edinburgh.

1266 Searle, J.B. Personal communication.

1267 Searle, J.B. *et al.* (1993) Further studies of a staggered hybrid zone in *Mus musculus domesticus* (the house mouse). *Heredity,* **71,** 523–531.

1268 Selander, P.K. (1970) Behavioural and genetic variation in natural populations. *American Zoologist,* **10,** 53–66.

1269 Self, G.S. & Leamy, L.J. (1978) Heritability of quasi-continuous skeletal traits in a random-bred population of house mice. *Genetics,* **88,** 109–120.

1270 Semeonoff, R. & Robertson, W. (1968) A biochemical and ecological study of plasma esterase polymorphisms in natural populations of the field vole, *Microtus agrestis* L. *Biochemical Genetics,* **1,** 205–27.

1271 Seton, E.I. (1920) Migrations of the gray squirrel *(Sciurus carolinensis). Journal of Mammalogy,* **1,** 53–58.

1272 Shahrul, A. (1998) *Spacing pattern and mating system in water voles (*Arvicola terrestris) *in north east Scotland.* DPhil thesis, University of Aberdeen.

1273 Sheail, J. (1999) The grey squirrel (*Sciurus carolinensis*) – a UK historical perspective on a vertebrate pest species. *Journal of Environmental Management,* **55,** 145–156.

1274 Sheffield, S.R. *et al.* (2001) Rodentia and Lagomorpha, pp. 215–314 in Shore, R.F. & Rattner, B.A. (eds.) *Ecotoxicology of wild mammals.* Wiley, London.

1275 Shiraishi, S. (1964) Damage of mice and voles on the fruit of strawberries under the plastic cover culture and their control. *Science Bulletin of the Faculty of Agriculture, Kyushu University,* **21,** 89–96.

1276 Shore, R.F. & Douben, E.T. (1994) Predicting ecotoxicological impacts of environmental contaminants on terrestrial small mammals. *Reviews of Environmental Contamination and Toxicology,* **134,** 49–89.

1277 Shore, R.F. & Yalden, D.W. (1991) The effect of different lubricant oils on capture success in Longworth traps. *Journal of Zoology,* **225,** 659–662.

1278 Shore, R.F. *et al.* (1992) The effect of variation in calcium intake on the growth of wood mice and bank voles. *Oecologia,* **92,** 130–137.

1279 Shore, R.F. *et al.* (1992) The effect of varying calcium intake on calcium metabolism in wild rodent species. *Journal of Zoology,* **227,** 29–42.

1280 Shore, R.F. *et al.* (1995) Impacts of an environmentally-realistic intake of cadmium on calcium, magnesium and phosphate metabolism in bank voles *Clethrionomys glareolus. Archives of Environmental Contamination and Toxicology,* **29,** 180–186.

1281 Shore, R.F. *et al.* (1997) The impacts of molluscicide pellets on spring and autumn populations of wood mice *Apodemus sylvaticus. Agriculture, Ecosystems and Environment,* **64,** 211–217.

1282 Shore, R.F. *et al.* (2003) Agricultural pesticides and mammals in Britain, pp. 37–50 in Tattersall, F. & Manley, W. (eds.) *Conservation and conflict: mammals and farming in Britain.* Linnean Society Occasional Publication 4, Westbury Publishing, Otley, Yorkshire.

1283 Shore, R.F. *et al.* (2005) Will Environmental Stewardship enhance small mammal abundance on intensively managed farmland? *Mammal Review*, **35**, 277–284.

1284 Shorten, M. (1950) Some aspects of the biology of the grey squirrel *(Sciurus carolinensis)* in Great Britain. *Proceedings of the Zoological Society of London*, **121**, 427–451.

1285 Shorten, M. (1954) *Squirrels.* Collins, London.

1286 Shorten, M. (1954) The reaction of the brown rat towards changes in its environment, pp. 307–334 in Chitty, D. & Southern, H.N. (eds.) *Control of rats and mice,* Vol. 2. Clarendon Press, Oxford.

1287 Shorten, M. (1962) *Red squirrels. Animals in Britain,* vol. 6. Sunday Times, London.

1288 Shorten, M. (1962) *Grey squirrels. Animals in Britain,* vol. 5. Sunday Times, London.

1289 Shorten, M. (1962) Squirrels, their biology and control. *MAFF Bulletin,* **184**, 1–44.

1290 Shuttleworth, C. *et al.* (2002) *Red squirrel* Sciurus vulgaris *L. conservation on Anglesey, North Wales.* Mentor Mon, Llangefni, Anglesey.

1291 Sibold, C. *et al.* (2001) Dobrava hantavirus causes hemorrhagic fever with renal syndrome in central Europe and is carried by two different *Apodemus* mice species. *Journal of Medical Virology,* **63**, 158–167.

1292 Sidorowicz, J. (1959) Über Morphologie und Biologie der Haselmaus *(Muscardinus avellanarius* L.) in Polen. *Acta Theriologica,* **3**, 75–91 (in German).

1293 Sierra De Soriano, B. (1960) Elementos constituvos de una habitaction de *Myocastor coypus bonariensis* (Geoffroy). *Revista de la Facultad de Humanidades y Ciencias, Universidad de la Republica, Uruguay,* **18**, 257–276 (in Spanish).

1294 Sierra De Soriano, B. (1961) Algunos modelos de las actividades en *Myocastor coypus bonariensis* (Geoffroy) ('nutria') en cautiverio. *Revista de la Facultad de Humanidades y Ciencias, Universidad de la Republica, Uruguay,* **19**, 261–269 (in Spanish).

1295 Singleton, G.R. (1989) Population dynamics of an outbreak of house mice *(Mus domesticus)* in the mallee wheatlands of Australia – hypothesis of plague formation. *Journal of Zoology,* **219**, 495–515.

1296 Singleton, G.R. *et al.* (2005) One hundred years of eruptions of house mice in Australia – a natural biological curio. *Biological Journal of the Linnean Society,* **84**, 617–62.

1297 Singleton, J.D. (1984) *An ecological study of* Arvicola terrestris *in west Lancashire.* MPhil thesis, Liverpool Polytechnic.

1298 Skelcher, G. (1994) *The spread of grey squirrels into red squirrel populated woodlands in North-West England.* MPhil thesis, University of London.

1299 Skelcher, G. (1997) The ecological replacement of red by grey squirrels, pp. 67–78 in Gurnell, J.& Lurz, P.W.W. (eds.) *The conservation of red squirrels,* Sciurus vulgaris *L.* People's Trust for Endangered Species, London.

1300 Sleeman, P. (1997) Mammals and mammalogy, pp. 241–262 in Foster, J.W. (ed.) *Nature in Ireland.* Lilliput Press, Dublin.

1301 Sleptsov, M.M. (1948) The biology of *Micromys minutus ussuricus* Barr, Ham. *Fauna i Ekologiya Gryzunov,* **2**, 69–100.

1302 Smal, C.M. (1990) The diet of the barn owl *Tyto alba* in southern Ireland with reference to a recently introduced prey species – the bank vole *(Clethrionomys glareolus). Bird Study,* **34**, 113–125.

1303 Smal, C.M. & Fairley, J.S. (1980) Food of wood mice *(Apodemus sylvaticus)* and bank voles *(Clethrionomys glareolus)* in oak and yew woods in Killarney, Ireland. *Journal of Zoology,* **191**, 413–418.

1304 Smal, C.M. & Fairley, J.S. (1982) The dynamics and regulation of small rodent populations in the woodland ecosystems of Killarney, Ireland. *Journal of Zoology,* **196**, 1–30.

1305 Smal, C.M. & Fairley, J.S. (1984) The spread of the bank vole *Clethrionomys glareolus* in Ireland. *Mammal Review,* **14**, 71–78.

1306 Smirnov, P.K. (1959) The postembryonic development of the harvest mouse *(Micromys minutus* Pallas). *Nauchnye, Docklady Vysshei Ahkoly, Biologi Nauki,* **3,** 76–78.

1307 Smit, F.G.A.M. (1957) Siphonaptera. *Handbook for the identification of British insects,* **1**(16), 1–94.

1308 Smit, F.G.A.M. (1957) The recorded distribution and hosts of Siphonaptera in Britain. *Entomologist's Gazette,* **8**, 45–75.

1309 Smith, A. *et al.* (2005) Trypanosomes, fleas and field voles: ecological dynamics of a host-vector-parasite interaction. *Parasitology,* **131,** 355–365.

1310 Smith, D.F.E. (1999) *Grey squirrel,* Sciurus carolinensis, *population dynamics and feeding biology in a conifer forest.* PhD thesis, University of London.

1311 Smith, H. *et al.* (1993) *The conservation management of arable field margins.* English Nature Science 18. English Nature, Peterborough.

1312 Smith, H.V., *et al.* (1991) A Lyme borrelosis human serosurvey of asympotomatic adults in Ireland. *Zentralblatt für Bakteriologie,* **275**, 382–389.

1313 Smith, J. *et al.* (1994) Comparing behaviour in wild and laboratory strains of the house mouse: levels of comparison and functional inference. *Behavioural Processes,* **32,** 79–86.

1314 Smith, J.C. (1981) Senses and communication. *Symposia of the Zoological Society of London,* **47**, 367–393.

1315 Smith, J.C. & Sales, G.D. (1980) Ultrasonic behaviour and mother–infant interactions in rodents, pp. 105–133 in Smotherman, W & Bell, R. (eds.) *Maternal influences and early behaviour.* Spectrum Publications, New York.

1316 Smith, M.J. *et al.* (2006) Delayed density-dependent season length alone can lead to rodent population cycles. *American Naturalist,* **167**, 695–704.

1317 Smith, N.B. & Barkalow, F.S. (1967) Precocious breeding of the gray squirrel. *Journal of Mammalogy,* **48**, 326–330.

1318 Smith, P.A. *et al.* (1993) The ship rat *(Rattus rattus)* on Lundy, 1991. *Journal of Zoology,* **231**, 689–695.

1319 Smith, R.P. *et al.* (1993) Norway rats as reservoir hosts for Lyme disease spirochetes on Monhegan Island, Maine. *Journal of Infectious Diseases,* **168,** 687–691.

1320 Smyth, M. (1966) Winter breeding in woodland mice, *Apodemus sylvaticus,* and voles, *Clethrionomys glareolus* and *Microtus agrestis,* near Oxford. *Journal of Animal Ecology,* **35,** 471–85.

1321 Southern, H.N. (1954) *Control of rats and mice,* vol. 3. *House mice.* Oxford University Press, Oxford.

1322 Southern, H.N. (1970) The natural control of a population of tawny owls *(Strix aluco). Journal of Zoology,* **162**, 197–285.

1323 Southern, H.N. & Laurie, E.M.O. (1946) The house-mouse *(Mus musculus)* in corn ricks. *Journal of Animal Ecology,* **15,** 134–149.

1324 Southern, H.N. & Lowe, V.P.W. (1982) Predation by tawny owls *(Strix aluco)* on bank voles *(Clethrionomys glareolus)* and wood mice *(Apodemus sylvaticus). Journal of Zoology,* **198**, 83–102.

1325 Southern, H.N. *et al.* (1946) Watching nocturnal animals by infra-red radiation. *Journal of Animal Ecology,* **37**, 75–97.

1326 Southwick, C.H. (1956) The abundance and distribution of harvest mice *(Micromys minutus)* in corn ricks near Oxford. *Proceedings of the Zoological Society of London,* **126**, 449–452.

1327 Southwick, C.H. (1958) Population characteristics of house mice living in English corn ricks: density relationships. *Proceedings of the Zoological Society of London,* **131**, 163–175.

1328 Spears, N. & Clarke, J.R. (1986) Effect of male presence and of photoperiod on the sexual maturation of the field vole *(Microtus agrestis). Journal of Reproduction and Fertility,* **78**, 231 – 8.

1329 Spears, N. & Clarke, J.R. (1988) Selection in field voles *(Microtus agrestis)* for gonadal growth under short photoperiods. *Journal of Animal Ecology,* **57,** 61–70.

1330 Staines, B. (1986) The spread of grey squirrels *(Sciurus carolinensis* Gm) into north-east Scotland. *Scottish Forestry,*

40, 190–196.

1331 Stanford, W. (1996) *The influence of female social behaviour on the population dynamics of the field vole* Microtus agrestis. PhD thesis, University of London.

1332 Stanko, M. *et al.* (1996) Occurrence of antibodies to leptospira in small mammals in Eastern Slovakia. *Veterinarini Medicina,* **41,** 373–377.

1333 Stanko, M. *et al.* (2002) Mammal density and patterns of ectoparasite species richness and abundance. *Oecologia,* **131,** 289–295.

1334 Steele, M.A. & Koprowski, J.L. (2001) *North American tree squirrels.* Smithsonian Institution Press, Washington, DC.

1335 Steele, M.A. *et al.* (1996) Caching and feeding decisions by *Sciurus carolinensis*: response to weevil-infested acorns. *Journal of Mammalogy,* **77,** 305–314.

1336 Steele, M. *et al.* (2005). Selection, predation and dispersal of seeds by tree squirrels in temperate and boreal forests: are tree squirrels keystone granivores? pp. 205–211 in Forget, P.-M. *et al.* (eds.) *Seed fate.* CAB International, Wallingford.

1337 Steele, M.A. *et al.* (2006) The innate basis of food-hoarding decisions in grey squirrels: evidence for behavioural adaptions to the oaks. *Animal Behaviour,* **71,** 155–160.

1338 Steiner, H.M. (1968) Untersuchungen über die Variabilität und Bionomie der Gattung *Apodemus* (Muridae, Mammalia) der Donau-Auen von Stockerau (Niederösterreich). *Zeitschrift für Wissenschaftliche Zoologie,* **177,** 1–96 (in German).

1339 Stenseth, N.C. (1985) Geographical distribution of *Clethrionomys* species. *Annales Zoologici Fennici,* **22,** 215–219.

1340 Stenseth, N.C. (1985) *Clethrionomys* biology: population dynamics, dispersal, reproduction and social structure. *Annales Zoologici Fennici,* **22,** 215–395.

1341 Steppan, S.J. *et al.* (2005) Multigene phylogeny of the Old World mice, Murinae, reveals distinct geographic lineages and the declining utility of mitochondrial genes compared to nuclear genes. *Molecular Phylogenetics and Evolution,* **37,** 370–388.

1342 Steven, D.M. (1955) Untersuchungen uber die britischen Formen von *Clethrionomys. Zeitschrift für Säugetierkunde,* **20,** 70–74 (in German).

1343 Stickel, L.F. (1979) Population ecology of house mice in unstable habitats. *Journal of Animal Ecology,* **48,** 871–887.

1344 Stoddart, D.M. (1969) Daily activity cycle of the water vole (*Arvicola terrestris*). *Journal of Zoology,* **159,** 538–540.

1345 Stoddart, D.M. (1970) Tail tip and other albinisms in the voles of the genus *Arvicola* Lacepede 1799. *Symposia of the Zoological Society of London,* **26,** 271–282.

1346 Stoddart, D.M. (1971) Breeding and survival in a population of water voles. *Journal of Animal Ecology,* **40,** 487–494.

1347 Stoddart, D.M. (1974) Recruitment and sex ratio in a semi-isolated population of *Arvicola terrestris* (L.), pp. 346–365 in Kratochvil, J. & Obital, R. (eds.) *Proceedings of the International Symposium on Species and Zoogeography of European Mammals,* Prague.

1348 Stoddart, D.M. (1982) Does trap odour influence estimation of population size of the short-tailed vole, *Microtus agrestis? Journal of Animal Ecology,* **51,** 375–386.

1349 Stoddart, D.M. (1982) Demonstration of olfactory discrimination by the short-tailed vole, *Microtus agrestis. Animal Behaviour,* **30,** 293–304.

1350 Stoddart, D.M. & Sales, G.M. (1985) The olfactory and acoustic biology of wood mice, yellow-necked mice and bank voles. *Symposia of the Zoological Society of London,* **55,** 117–139.

1351 Stoddart, D.M. *et al.* (1975) Evidence for social differences in the flank gland organ secretion of *Arvicola terrestris* (Rodentia: Microtinae). *Journal of Zoology,* **177,** 529–540.

1352 Stopka, P. & Macdonald, D.W. (1998) Signal interchange during mating in the wood mouse (*Apodemus sylvaticus*): the concept of active and passive signalling. *Behaviour,* **135,** 31–249.

1353 Stopka, P. & Macdonald, D.W. (1999) The market effect in the wood mouse, *Apodemus sylvaticus*: Selling information on reproductive status. *Ethology,* **105,** 969–982.

1354 Stopka, P. & Macdonald, D.W. (2003) Way-marking behaviour: an aid to spatial navigation in the wood mouse (*Apodemus sylvaticus*). *BMC Ecology,* **3,** 1–9.

1355 Storch, G. (1978) *Glis glis* (Linnaeus, 1766) – Siebenschläfer. In Niethammer, J.B. & Krapp, F. (eds.) *Handbuch der Säugetiere Europas I. (1).* Akademische Verlagsgesellschaft, Wiesbaden (in German).

1356 Strachan, C. *et al.* (1998) The rapid impact of resident American Mink on water voles: case studies in lowland England. In: *Behaviour and ecology of riparian mammals.* Zoological Society of London & The Mammal Society Symposia, **71,** 339–357.

1357 Strachan, C. *et al.* (2000) *Preliminary report on the changes in the water vole population of Britain as shown by the national surveys of 1989–1990 and 1996–1998.* Vincent Wildlife Trust, London.

1358 Strachan, R. (1997). *Water voles.* Whittet, London.

1359 Strachan, R. (1998) *Water vole conservation handbook.* Environment Agency/English Nature/WildCRU, Oxford.

1360 Strachan, R. & Jefferies, D.J. (1993) *The water vole* Arvicola terrestris *in Britain 1989–90, its distribution and changing status.* Vincent Wildlife Trust, London.

1361 Strann, K.B. *et al.* (2002) Is the heart of Fennoscandian rodent cycle still beating? A 14-year study of small mammals and Tengmalm's owls in northern Norway. *Ecography,* **25,** 81–87.

1362 Sturdee, A.P. *et al.* (1999) Detection of *Cryptosporidium* oocysts in wild mammals of mainland Britain. *Veterinary Parasitology,* **80,** 273–280.

1363 Sulkava, S. & Nyholm, E.S. (1987) Mushroom stores as winter food of the red squirrel, *Sciurus vulgaris*, in northern Finland. *Aquillo* Ser. Zool., **25,** 264–270.

1364 Sutcliffe, A.J. & Kowalski, K. (1976) Pleicestocene rodents of the British Isles. *Bulletin of the British Museum (Natural History) Geology,* **27,** 31–147.

1365 Swann, R.L. & Etheridge, B. (1995) A comparison of breeding success and prey of the common buzzard *Buteo buteo* in two areas of northern Scotland. *Bird Study,* **42,** 37–43.

1366 Szacki, J. *et al.* (1993) The influence of landscape spatial structure on small mammal movements. *Acta Theriologica,* **38,** 113–123.

1367 Szel, A. *et al.* (1994) Different patterns of retinal cone topography in two genera of rodents, *Mus* and *Apodemus. Cell and Tissue Research,* **276,** 143–150.

1368 Tahka, K.M. *et al.* (1997) Photoperiod-induced changes in androgen receptor expression in testes and accessory sex glands of the bank vole, *Clethrionomys glareolus. Biology of Reproduction,* **56,** 898–908.

1369 Takada, Y. (1993) Body fat of mice, *Apodemus, Mus* and *Micromys. Honyurui Kagaku,* **32,** 107–115.

1370 Takada, Y. (1996) Eye lens weight as an age indicator in the harvest mouse, *Micromys minutus* and age structure of wild populations. *Honyurui Kagaku,* **36,** 45–52.

1371 Talleklint, L. & Jaenson, T.G.T. (1995) Is the small mammal (*Clethrionomys glareolus*) or the tick vector (*Ixodes ricinus*) the primary overwintering reservoir for the Lyme borreliosis spirochete in Sweden. *Journal of Wildlife Diseases,* **31,** 537–540.

1372 Talleklint, L. & Jaenson, T.G.T. (1997) Infestation of mammals by *Ixodes ricinus* ticks (Acari: Ixodidae) in south-central Sweden. *Experimental and Applied Acarology,* **21,** 755–771.

1373 Tanton, M.T. (1969) The estimation and biology of populations of the bank vole (*Clethrionomys galreolus* Schr.) and wood mouse (*Apodemus sylvaticus* L.). *Journal of Animal Ecology,* **38,** 511–529.

1374 Tapper, S. (1979) The effects of fluctuating vole numbers (*Microtus agrestis*) on a population of weasels (*Mustela nivalis*) on farmland. *Journal of Animal Ecology,* **48,** 603–617.

1375 Tarrant, K.A. (1988) Histological identification of the effects of pesticides on non-target species, pp. 313–317 in Greaves, M.P. *et al.* (eds.) *Field methods for the study of environmental effects of pesticides.* BCPC Monograph No. 40. BCPC Publications, Croydon.

1376 Tarrant, K.A. *et al.* (1990) Effects of pesticide applications on small mammals in arable fields, and the recovery of their populations. pp. 173–182 in *Brighton Crop Protection Conference, Pests and Diseases.* British Crop Protection Council, Farnham.

1377 Tattersall, F.H. (1999) House mice and wood mice in and around an agricultural building. *Journal of Zoology,* **249,** 469–472.

1378 Tattersall, F.H. Personal communication.

1379 Tattersall, F.H. & Macdonald, D.W. (2003) Wood mice in the arable ecosystem, pp. 82–96 in Tattersall, F. & Manley, W. (eds.) *Conservation and conflict: mammals and farming in Britain.* Linnean Society Occasional Publication, London.

1380 Tattersall, F.H. & Whitbread, S. (1994) A trap-based comparison of the use of arboreal vegetation by populations of bank vole (*Clethrionomys glareolus*), wood mouse (*Apodemus sylvaticus*) and dormouse (*Muscardinus avellanarius*). *Journal of Zoology,* **233,** 309–314.

1381 Tattersall, F.H. *et al.* (1994) A review of the endoparasites of wild house mice *Mus domesticus. Mammal Review,* **24,** 61–71.

1382 Tattersall, F.H. *et al.* (1997) Small mammals on one-year set-aside. *Acta Theriologica,* **42,** 329–334.

1383 Tattersall, F.H. *et al.* (1997) Experimental colonisation of contrasting habitats by house mice. *Zeitschrift für Säugetierkunde,* **62,** 350–358.

1384 Tattersall, F.H. *et al.* (1999) Does the method of set-aside establishment affect its use by wood mice? *Journal of Zoology,* **249,** 472–476.

1385 Tattersall, F.H. *et al.* (1999) Small mammals on set-aside blocks and margins. *Aspects of Applied Biology,* **54,** 131–138.

1386 Tattersall, F.H. *et al.* (2001). Habitat use by wood mice (*Apodemus sylvaticus*) in a changeable arable landscape. *Journal of Zoology,* **255,** 487–494.

1387 Tattersall, F.H. *et al.* (2002) Is habitat linearity important for small mammal communities on farmland? *Journal of Applied Ecology,* **39,** 643–652.

1388 Tattersall, F.H. *et al.* (2004) Balanced dispersal or source–sink – do both models describe wood mice in farmed landscapes? *Oikos,* **106,** 536–550.

1389 Tattoni, C. *et al.* (2005) Using GRASS and spatial explicit population dynamics modelling as a conservation tool to manage grey squirrel (*Sciurus carolinensis*) in Northern Italy. *International Journal of Geoinformatics,* **1,** 71–78.

1390 Taylor, I. (1994) *Barn owls. Predator-prey relationships and conservation.* Cambridge University Press, Cambridge.

1391 Taylor, J.C. (1966) Home range and agonistic behaviour in the grey squirrel. *Symposia of the Zoological Society of London,* **18,** 229–235.

1392 Taylor, J.C. (1977) The frequency of grey squirrel (*Sciurus carolinensis*) communication by use of scent marking points. *Journal of Zoology,* **183,** 534–545.

1393 Taylor, K.D. (1978) Range of movement and activity of common rats (*Rattus norvegicus*) on agricultural land. *Journal of Applied Ecology,* **15,** 663–677.

1394 Taylor, K.D. & Quy, R.J. (1978) Long distance movements of a common rat (*Rattus norvegicus*) revealed by radio-tracking. *Mammalia,* **42,** 63–71.

1395 Taylor, K.D. *et al.* (1971) Movements of the grey squirrel as revealed by trapping. *Journal of Applied Ecology,* **8,** 123–146.

1396 Taylor, K.D. *et al.* (1974) The reactions of captive wild rats to human odour and to the odour of other rats. *Mammalia,* **38,** 581–590.

1397 Tchernov, E. (1984) Commensal animals and human sedentism in the Middle East, pp. 91–115 in Clutton-Brock, J. & Grigson, C. (eds.) *Animals in archaeology. 3: Early herders and their flocks.* BAR International Series **202,** Oxford.

1398 Teagle, W.G. (1964) The harvest mouse in the London area. *London Naturalist,* **43,** 136–149.

1399 Telfer, S. (1996) *Distribution and demography of fragmented water vole* Arvicola terrestris (L.) *populations within the river Ythan catchment.* MSc thesis, University of Aberdeen.

1400 Telfer, S. (2000) *Dispersal and metapopulation dynamics in water vole populations.* PhD thesis, University of Aberdeen.

1401 Telfer, S. Personal communication.

1402 Telfer, S. & Lambin, X.L. Personal communication.

1403 Telfer, S. *et al.* (2001) Metapopulation processes and persistence in remnant water vole populations. *Oikos,* **95,** 31–42.

1404 Telfer, S. *et al.* (2002) The effects of cowpox virus on survival in natural rodent populations: increases and decreases. *Journal of Animal Ecology,* **71,** 558–568.

1405 Telfer, S. *et al.* (2003) Demographic and genetic structure of fossorial water voles (*Arvicola terrestris*) on Scottish islands. *Journal of Zoology,* **259,** 23–29.

1406 Telfer, S. *et al.* (2003) Parentage assignment detects frequent and large-scale dispersal in water voles. *Molecular Ecology,* **12,** 1939–1949.

1407 Telfer, S. *et al.* (2005) Infection with cowpox decreases female maturation rates in wild populations of woodland rodents. *Oikos,* **109,** 317–322.

1408 Telfer, S. *et al.* (2007) Contrasting dynamics of *Bartonella* spp. in cyclic field vole populations: the impact of vector and host dynamics. *Parasitology,* **134,** 413–425.

1409 Telle, H.J. (1966) Beitrage zur Kenntnis der Verhaltenswerise von Ratten verfleichend dargestellt bei *Rattus norvegicus* und *R. rattus. Zeitschrift für Angewandte Zoologie,* **53,** 129–196 (in German).

1410 Tenora, F. *et al.* (1991) Helminths of small rodents in Denmark. *Helminthologia (Bratislava),* **28,** 151–154.

1411 Terkel, J. *et al.* (1979) Ultrasonic cries from infant rats stimulate prolactin release in lactating mothers. *Hormones and Behaviour,* **12,** 95–102.

1412 Terrell, S.P. *et al.* (2002) An epizootic of fibromatosis in gray squirrels (*Sciurus carolinensis*) in Florida. *Journal of Wildlife Diseases,* **38,** 305–312.

1413 Tew, T.E. (1989) *The behavioural ecology of the wood mouse* (Apodemus sylvaticus) *in the cereal field ecosystem.* DPhil thesis, University of Oxford.

1414 Tew, T.E. (1994) Farmland hedgerows: habitat corridors or irrelevant? A small mammal's perspective, pp. 80–94 in Watt, T.A. & Buckley, G.P. (ed.) *Hedgerow management and nature conservation.* Wye College Press, Wye.

1415 Tew, T.E. & Macdonald, D.W. (1993) The effects of harvest on arable wood mice *Apodemus sylvaticus. Biological Conservation,* **65,** 279–283.

1416 Tew, T.E. & Macdonald, D.W. (1994) Dynamics of space use and male vigor amongst wood mice, *Apodemus sylvaticus,* in the cereal ecosystem. *Behavioural Ecology and Sociobiology,* **34,** 337–345.

1417 Tew, T.E. *et al.* (1992) Herbicide application affects microhabitat use by arable wood mice (*Apodemus sylvaticus*). *Journal of Applied Ecology,* **29,** 532–539.

1418 Tew, T.E. *et al.* (1994). Field margins and small mammals, pp. 85–94 in *Field margins: Integrating agriculture and conservation.* BCPC Monograph, Brighton.

1419 Tew, T.E. *et al.* (1994) Temporal changes in olfactory preference in murid rodents revealed by live-trapping. *Journal of Mammalogy,* **75,** 750–756.

1420 Tew, T.E. *et al.* (2000) Arable habitat use by wood mice (*Apodemus sylvaticus*). 2. Microhabitat. *Journal of Zoology,* **250,** 305–311.

1421 Thomas, K. *et al.* (2003) A novel poxvirus lethal to red squirrels (*Sciurus vulgaris*). *Journal of General Virology,* **84,** 3337–3341.

1422 Thompson, D.C. (1978) The social system of the grey squirrel. *Behaviour,* **64,** 305–328.

1423 Thompson, D.C. (1978) Regulation of a northern grey squirrel (*Sciurus carolinensis*) population. *Ecology,* **59,** 708–715.

1424 Thompson, H.V. (1953) The edible dormouse (*Glis glis*) in England, 1902–1951. *Proceedings of the Zoological Society of London,* **122**, 1017–1024.

1425 Thorpe, R.S. (1981) The morphometrics of the mouse: a review. *Symposia of the Zoological Society of London,* **47,** 85–125.

1426 Timmermans, P.J.A. (1978) *Social behaviour in the rat.* PhD thesis, Catholic University of Nijmegen.

1427 Tittensor, A.M. (1975) *The red squirrel. Forest Record,* No. 101. HMSO, London.

1428 Tittensor, A. (1977) Grey squirrel *Sciurus carolinensis,* pp. 164–72 in Corbet, G.B. & Southern, H.N. (eds.) *Handbook of British mammals,* 2nd edn. Blackwell Scientific Publications, Oxford

1429 Tittensor, A. (1977) Red squirrel *Sciurus vulgaris.* pp. 153–64 In Corbet, G.B. & Southern, H.N. (eds.) *Handbook of British mammals,* 2nd edn. Blackwell Scientific Publications, Oxford.

1430 Tkadlec, E. & Zejda, J. (1998) Density-dependent life histories in female bank voles from fluctuating populations. *Journal of Animal Ecology,* **67**, 863–873.

1431 Toal, M.E. *et al.* (2002) Modeling cadmium dynamics in the guts and tissues of small mammals: dose implications for predators. *Environmental Toxicology and Chemistry,* **21**, 2493–2499.

1432 Todd, I.A. *et al.* (2000) Arable habitat use by wood mice (*Apodemus sylvaticus*). 1. Macrohabitat. *Journal of Zoology,* **250**, 299–303.

1433 Tompkins, D.M. *et al.* (2002) Parapoxvirus causes a deleterious disease in red squirrels associated with UK population declines. *Proceedings of the Royal Society of London Series B,* **269**, 529–533.

1434 Tompkins, D.M. *et al.* (2003). Ecological replacement of native red squirrels by invasive greys driven by disease. *Ecology Letters,* **6**, 189–196.

1435 Tonkin, J.M. (1983) *Ecology of red squirrels (*Sciurus vulgaris L.*) in mixed woodland.* PhD thesis, University of Bradford.

1436 Tonkin, J.M. (1983) Activity patterns of the red squirrel (*Sciurus vulgaris*). *Mammal Review,* **13**, 99–111.

1437 Trapido, H. Personal communication.

1438 Triggs, G.S. (1991) The population ecology of house mice on the Isle of May. *Journal of Zoology,* **225**, 449–468.

1439 Trilar, T. (1997) Ectoparasites from the nests of the fat dormouse (*Myoxus glis*) in Slovenia. *Natura Croatica,* **6**, 409–421.

1440 Trilar, T. *et al.* (1994) Identification of a natural cycle involving *Rickettsia typhi* infection of *Monopsyllus sciurorum* fleas from the nests of the fat dormouse (*Glis glis*). *European Journal of Epidemiology,* **10**, 757–762.

1441 Trojan, P. (1965) Intrapopulation relations and regulation of numbers in small forest rodents. *Ekologia Polska Seria A,* **13,** 143–168.

1442 Trout, R.C. (1976) *An ecological study on populations of wild harvest mice (*Micromys minutus (Pallas)). PhD thesis, University of London.

1443 Trout, R.C. (1978) A review of studies on captive harvest mice (*Micromys minutus* (Pallas)). *Mammal Review,* **8**, 159–175.

1444 Trout, R.C. (1978) A review of studies on populations of wild harvest mice (*Micromys minutus* (Pallas)). *Mammal Review,* **8**, 143–158.

1445 Truszkowski, J. (1974) Utilization of nest boxes by rodents. *Acta Theriologica,* **19,** 441–452.

1446 Tucker, P.K. *et al.* (2005) Phylogenetic relationships in the subgenus *Mus* (genus *Mus,* family Muridae, subfamily Murinae): examining gene trees and species trees *Biological Journal of the Linnean Society,* **84,** 653–662.

1447 Turchin, P. & Hanski, I. (1997) An empirically based model for latitudinal gradient in vole population dynamics. *American Naturalist,* **149,** 842–874.

1448 Turk, F.A. (1978) The animal remains from Nornour: a synoptic view of the finds, pp 99–103 in Butcher, S. (ed.) *Excavations at Nornour, Isles of Scilly, 1969–73, the pre-Roman settlement, Cornish Archaeology,* **17**, 29–112.

1449 Turner, D.T.L. (1965) A contribution to the ecology and taxonomy of *Microtus arvalis* on the island of Westray, Orkney. *Proceedings of the Zoological Society of London,* **144**, 143–150.

1450 Twigg, G.I. (1966) Notes on the invertebrate fauna of some grey squirrel dreys. *Entomologist,* **99**, 51–53.

1451 Twigg, G.I. (1975) *The brown rat.* David & Charles, London.

1452 Twigg, G.I. (1980) A review of the occurrence in British mammals of the major organisms of zoonotic importance. *Mammal Review,* **10**, 139–149.

1453 Twigg, G. (1984) *The Black Death: a biological reappraisal.* Batsford, London.

1454 Twigg, G.I. (1992) The black rat *Rattus rattus* in the United Kingdom in 1989. *Mammal Review,* **22**, 33–42.

1455 Twigg, G.I & Cuerdon, C.M. (1966) Leptospirosis in British mammals: initial survey results. *Journal of Zoology,* **150**, 494–508.

1456 Twigg, G.I. *et al.* (1968) Leptospirosis in British wild mammals. *Symposia of the Zoological Society of London,* **24**, 75–98.

1457 Uhlig, H.G. (1955) The gray squirrel. Its life history, ecology and population characteristics in West Virginia. *Pitman-Robertson Project* 31-R, Commission of West Virginia.

1458 Ursin, E. (1956) Geographical variation in *A. sylvaticus* and *A. flavicollis* (Rodentia, Muridae) in Europe with special reference to Danishard Latvian populations. *Biologiska Skrifter Kongelige Dansk Videnskabernes Selskabs,* **8**, 1–46.

1459 Usher, M.B. *et al.* (1992) An American invasion in Britain: the case of the native and the alien squirrel. *Conservation Biology,* **6**, 108–115.

1460 Varma, M.G.R. & Page, R.J.C. (1966) The epidemiology of louping ill in Ayrshire, Scotland: ectoparasites of small mammals 1. (Siphonaptera). *Journal of Medical Entomology,* **3**, 331–335.

1461 Varty, N. (1987). *A study of range and activity in the short tailed vole* (Microtus agrestis) *by live trapping and telemetry.* PhD thesis, Kings College, University of London.

1462 Vasquez, A.W. (1961) Structure and identification of common food-contaminating hairs. *Journal of the Association of Official Analytical Chemists,* **44,** 754–779.

1463 Venning, T. *et al.* (1997) An experimental study on translocating red squirrels to Thetford Forest, pp. 133–143 in Gurnell, J. & Lurz, P.W.W. (eds.) *The conservation of red squirrels,* Sciurus vulgaris, *L.* People's Trust for Endangered Species, London.

1464 Verboom, B. & Van Apeldoorn, R. (1990) Effects of habitat fragmentation on the red squirrel, *Sciurus vulgaris* L. *Landscape Ecology,* **4**, 171–176.

1465 Vereschagin, N.K. (1959) *Mammals of the Caucasus. History of the formation of the fauna.* Akademii Nauk, Leningrad.

1466 Veron, G. (1992) Étude morphométrique et taxonomique de genre *Castor. Bulletin de Museum National d'Histoire Naturelle, Paris.* 4e sér. **14**, 829–853 (in French).

1467 Veron, G. (1992) Histoire biogéographique du castor d'Europe, *Castor fiber* (Rodentia, Mammalia). *Mammalia,* **56,** 87–108 (in French).

1468 Vietinghoff-Reisch, A. von (1960) Der Siebenschläfer (*Glis glis* L.). *Monographien der Wildsäugetiere,* **14**, 1–196 (in German).

1469 Viitala, J. & Hoffmeyer, I. (1985) Social organisation in *Clethrionomys* compared with *Microtus* and *Apodemus*: Social odours, chemistry and biological effects. *Annales Zoologici Fennici,* **22**, 359–371.

1470 Viitala, J. *et al.* (1994) Different dispersal in *Clethrionomys* and *Microtus. Annales Zoologici Fennici,* **31**, 411–415.

1471 Vincent, M.A. (1974) *Energy utilisation and activity patterns of the vole Arvicola terrestris amphibius* (L.). PhD thesis, University of Durham.

1472 Vizoso, A.D. *et al.* (1964) Isolation of a virus resembling encephalormyocarditis from a red squirrel. *Nature,* **201**, 849–50.

1473 Vizoso, A.D. *et al.* (1966) Isolation of unidentified agents capable of morphologically transforming hamster cells in vitro. *Nature*, **209**, 1263–4.

1474 Vogel, P. & Frey, H. (1995) L'hibernation du muscardin *Muscardinus avellanarius* (Gliridae, Rodentia) en nature: nids, fréquence des réveils et température corporelle. *Bulletin Société Vaudoise des Sciences Naturelles, Lausanne*, **83**, 217–230.

1475 Voipio, P. (1970) Polymorphism and regional differentiation in the red squirrel (*Sciurus vulgaris*). *Annales Zoologici Fennici*, **7**, 210–215.

1476 Wachtendorf, W. (1951) Beitrage zur Ökologie und Biologie der Haselmaus (*Muscardinus avellanarius*) im Alpenvorland. *Zoologische Fahrbücher Abteilung Systematik*, **80**, 189–203.

1477 Walker, L.A. *et al.* (2002) The importance of the gut and its contents in the prey as a source a of cadmium to predators. *Environmental Toxicology and Chemistry*, **21**, 76–80.

1478 Wallace, M.E. (1981) The breeding, inbreeding and management of wild mice. *Symposia of the Zoological Society of London*, **47**, 183–204.

1479 Wallace, M.E. & Hudson, C.A. (1969) Breeding and handling small wild rodents: a method study. *Laboratory Animals*, **3**, 107–117.

1480 Wallis, S.J. (1981) Notes on the ecology of the Orkney vole (*Microtus arvalis orcadensis*). *Journal of Zoology*, **195**, 532–536.

1481 Wallis, S.J. (1983) Note on the movement of stones by the common shrew [sic], *Apodemus sylvaticus. Journal of Zoology*, **200**, 300–302.

1482 Walsh, P.M. (1988) Black rats *Rattus rattus* (L.) as prey of short-eared owls *Asio flammeus* (Pontopiddan) on Lambay Island, Co. Dublin. *Irish Naturalists' Journal*, **22**, No.12.

1483 Walton, J.B. & Andrews, J.F. (1981) Torpor induced by food deprivation in the wood mouse *Apodemus sylvaticus. Journal of Zoology*, **194**, 260–263.

1484 Walton, K.C. (1988) Environmental fluoride and fluorosis in mammals. *Mammal Review*, **18**, 77–90.

1485 Ward, R.J. (1981) Diet and nutrition. *Symposia of the Zoological Society of London*, **47**, 255–266.

1486 Warkentin, M.J. (1968) Observations on the behaviour and ecology of the nutria in Louisiana. *Tulane Studies in Zoology*, **15**, 10–17.

1487 Warner, L.J. & Batt, G.T. (1976) Some simple methods for recording wild harvest mouse (*Micromys minutus*) distribution and activity. *Journal of Zoology*, **179**, 226–229.

1488 Warren, C. (2003) *The microfaunal remains from Chapel Cave, North Yorkshire, as a reflection of local environmental change.* MSc thesis, University of Bradford.

1489 Watkins, B.M. & Nowell, F. (1991) *Hepatozoon* in grey squirrels (*Sciurus carolinensis*) trapped near Reading, Berkshire. *Journal of Zoology*, **224**, 101–112.

1490 Watkins, S.A. *et al.* (1985) The coypu as rodent reservoir of *Leptospira* infection in Great Britain. *Journal of Hygiene*, **95**, 409–417.

1491 Watson, J.S. (1944) The melanic form of *Rattus norvegicus* in London. *Nature*, **154**, 334–335.

1492 Watson, J.S. (1950) Some observations on the reproduction of *Rattus rattus* L. *Proceedings of the Zoological Society of London*, **120**, 1–12.

1493 Watson, J.S. (1951) *The rat problem in Cyprus.* Colonial Research Publication. No.9, HMSO, London.

1494 Watts, C.H.S. (1968) The foods eaten by wood mice (*Apodemus sylvaticus*) and bank voles (*Clethrionomys glareolus*) in Wytham Woods, Berkshire. *Journal of Animal Ecology*, **37**, 25–41.

1495 Watts, C.H.S. (1969) The regulation of wood mouse (*Apodemus sylvaticus*) numbers in Wytham Woods, Berkshire. *Journal of Animal Ecology*, **38**, 285–304.

1496 Watts, C.H.S. (1970) Effect of supplementary food on breeding in woodland rodents. *Journal of Mammalogy*, **51**, 169–171.

1497 Watts, C.H.S. (1970) Long distance movement of bank voles and wood mice. *Journal of Zoology*, **161**, 247–256.

1498 Wauters, L.A. & Casale, P. (1996) Long-term scatterhoarding by Eurasian red squirrels (*Sciurus vulgaris*). *Journal of Zoology*, **238**, 195–207.

1499 Wauters, L.A. & Dhondt, A.A. (1985) Population dynamics and social behaviour of red squirrel populations in different habitats. pp. 311–318 in *Proceedings of the XVII Congress of the International Union of Game Biologists,* Brussels.

1500 Wauters, L. & Dhondt, A.A. (1987) Activity budget and foraging behaviour of the red squirrel (*Sciurus vulgaris*, Linnaeus 1758) in a coniferous habitat. *Zeitschrift für Säugetierkunde*, **52**, 341–353.

1501 Wauters, L.A. & Dhondt, A.A. (1988) The use of red squirrel (*Sciurus vulgaris*) dreys to estimate population density. *Journal of Zoology*, **214**, 179–187.

1502 Wauters, L. & Dhondt, A.A. (1989) Body weight, longevity and reproductive success in red squirrels (*Sciurus vulgaris*). *Journal of Animal Ecology*, **58**, 637–651.

1503 Wauters, L. & Dhondt, A.A. (1990) Nest-use by red squirrels (*Sciurus vulgaris* Linnaeus, 1758). *Mammalia*, **54**, 377–389.

1504 Wauters, L. & Dhondt, A.A. (1992) Spacing behaviour of red squirrels, *Sciurus vulgaris*: variation between habitats and the sexes. *Animal Behaviour*, **43**, 297–311.

1505 Wauters, L. & Dhondt, A.A. (1993) Immigration pattern and success in red squirrels. *Behavioural Ecology and Sociobiology*, **33**, 159–167.

1506 Wauters, L.A. & Dhondt, A.A. (1995) Lifetime reproductive success and its correlates in female Eurasian red squirrels. *Oikos*, **72**, 402–410.

1507 Wauters, L.A. & Gurnell, J. (1999) The mechanism of replacement of red squirrels by grey squirrels: a test of the interference competition hypothesis. *Ethology*, **105**, 1053–1071.

1508 Wauters, L.A. & Lens, L. (1995) Effects of food availability and density on red squirrel (*Sciurus vulgaris*) reproduction. *Ethology*, **76**, 2460–2469.

1509 Wauters, L. *et al.* (1990) Factors affecting male mating success in red squirrels (*Sciurus vulgaris*). *Ethology, Ecology and Evolution*, **2**, 195–204.

1510 Wauters, L. *et al.* (1992) Activity budget and foraging behaviour or red squirrels (*Sciurus vulgaris*) in coniferous and deciduous habitats. *Journal of Zoology*, **227**, 71–86.

1511 Wauters, L. *et al.* (1993) Body mass at weaning and juvenile recruitment in the red squirrel. *Journal of Animal Ecology*, **62**, 280–286.

1512 Wauters, L.A. *et al.* (1994) Space use and dispersal in red squirrels in fragmented habitats, *Oikos*, **69**, 140–146.

1513 Wauters, L.A. *et al.* (1994) Survival and lifetime reproductive success in dispersing and resident red squirrels. *Behavioral Ecology and Sociobiology*, **34**, 197–201.

1514 Wauters, L.A. *et al.*(1995) Fitness consequences of hoarding in the Eurasian red squirrel. *Proceedings of the Royal Society of London Series B*, **262**, 277–281.

1515 Wauters, L.A. *et al.* (1997) Replacement of red squirrels by introduced grey squirrels in Italy: evidence from a distribution survey, pp. 79–88 in Gurnell, J. & Lurz, P.W.W. (ed.)*The conservation of red squirrels,* Sciurus vulgaris L. People's Trust for Endangered Species, London.

1516 Wauters, L.A. *et al.* (1997) Grey squirrel *Sciurus carolinensis* management in Italy – squirrel distribution in a highly fragmented landscape. *Wildlife Biology*, **3**, 117–124.

1517 Wauters, L.A. *et al.* (2000) The interspecific effects of grey squirrels (*Sciurus carolinensis*) on the space use and population dynamics of red squirrels (*S. vulgaris*) in conifer plantations. *Ecological Research*, **15**, 271–284.

1518 Wauters, L.A. *et al.* (2001) Effects of spatial variation in food availability on spacing behaviour and demography of Eurasian red squirrels. *Ecography*, **24**, 525–538.

1519 Wauters, L.A. *et al.* (2001) Does interspecific competition with grey squirrels affect the foraging behaviour and food choice of red squirrels. *Animal Behaviour*, **61**, 1079–1091.

1520 Wauters, L.A. *et al.* (2002) Interspecific competition of grey on reds: do grey squirrels deplete tree seeds cached by red squirrels. *Behavioral Ecology and Sociobiology*, **51**, 360–367.

1521 Wauters, L.A. *et al.* (2004) Within-sex density dependence and population dynamics of red squirrels *Sciurus vulgaris*. *Journal of Animal Ecology*, **73**, 11–25.

1522 Webbon, C.C. *et al.* (2006) Macroscopic prey remains in the winter diet of foxes *Vulpes vulpes* in rural Britain. *Mammal Review*, **36**, 85–97.

1523 Weber, J.M. & Aubrey, S. (1993) Predation by foxes *Vulpes vulpes* on the fossorial form of the water vole *Arvicola terrestris*, in western Switzerland. *Journal of Zoology*, **229**, 553–559.

1524 Webley, G.E. & Johnson, E. (1983) Reproductive physiology of the grey squirrel (*Sciurus carolinensis*). *Mammal Review*, **13**, 149–154.

1525 Webster, J.P. & Macdonald, D.W. (1995) Parasites of wild brown rats (*Rattus norvegicus*) on UK farms. *Parasitology*, **111**, 247–255.

1526 Webster, J.P. *et al.* (1995) Prevalence of *Leptospira* spp. in wild brown rats (*Rattus norvegicus*) on UK farms. *Epidemiology and Infection*, **114**, 195–201.

1527 Wells, A.Q. (1946) The murine type of tubercle bacillus (the vole acid-fast bacillus). *Special Report Series, Medical Research Council*, **259**, 1–48.

1528 Wheeler, P. (2005) The diet of field voles *Microtus agrestis* at low population density in upland Britain. *Acta Theriologica*, **50**, 483–492.

1529 Whishaw, I.Q. & Whishaw, G.E. (1996) Conspecific aggression influences food carrying: studies on a wild population of *Rattus norvegicus*. *Aggressive Behavior*, **22**, 47–66.

1530 Whitaker, J.O. (1966) Food of *Mus musculus, Peromyscus maniculatus bairdi*, and *Peromyscus leucopus* in Vigo county, Indiana. *Journal of Mammalogy*, **47**, 473–486.

1531 Whittingham, D.G. & Wood, M.J. (1983) Reproduction physiology, pp. 137–64 in Foster, H.L. (ed.) *The mouse in biomedical research*, vol. 3. Academic Press, New York.

1532 Wieland, H. (1973) Beitrage zur Biologie und zum Massenwechsel der grossen Wuhlmaus (*Arvicola terrestris* L.). *Zoologisches Jahrbuch, Abteilung Systematik*, **100**, 351–428 (in German).

1533 Wiger, R. (1977) Some pathological effects of endoparasites on rodents with special reference to the population ecology of microtines. *Oikos*, **29**, 598–606.

1534 Wiger, R. (1982) Roles of self regulatory mechanisms in cyclic populations of *Clethrionomys* with special reference to *Clethrionomys glareolus* – a hypothesis. *Oikos*, **38**, 60–71.

1535 Wilkinson, D.M. (1987) Montane wood mice *Apodemus sylvaticus* and their relevance to some Quaternary fossil assemblages. *Journal of Zoology*, **212**, 347–377.

1536 Wilkinson, G.S. & Baker, A.E.M. (1988) Communal nesting among genetically similar house mice. *Ethology*, **77**, 103–114.

1537 Williams, S.L. *et al.* (1980) Glans penes and bacula of five species of *Apodemus* (Rodentia: Muridae) from Croatia, Yugoslavia. *Mammalia*, **44**, 245–258.

1538 Wilson, D.E. & Reeder, D.M. (2005) *Mammal species of the world; a taxonomic and geographical reference*, 3rd edn. John Hopkins University Press, Baltimore, MD.

1539 Wilson, K. *et al.* (1998) Origin of an insular population of the wood mouse based on parasitological evidence. *Journal of Wildlife Diseases*, **34**, 150–154.

1540 Wilson, W.L. (1992) *Behavioural ecology and population regulation of the woodmouse* (Apodemus sylvaticus). PhD thesis, The Queen's University of Belfast.

1541 Wilson, W.L. *et al.* (1992) Range use in female wood mice (*Apodemus sylvaticus*) in deciduous woodland. pp. 549–560 in Preide, I.G. and Swift, S.M. (eds.) *Wildlife telemetry. Remote monitoring and tracking of animals, Proceedings of the 4th International Conference on Wildlife Telemetry*. Ellis Horwood, Chichester.

1542 Wilson, W.L. *et al.* (1993) Population regulation in the wood mouse *Apodemus sylvaticus* (L.). *Mammal Review*, **23**, 65–92.

1543 Wilson, W.L. *et al.* (1993) Infanticide and maternal defence in the wood mouse *Apodemus sylvaticus*. *Ethology Ecology and Evolution*, **5**, 365–370.

1544 Wilson, W.L. *et al.* (1996) The effects of experimental removal of male wood mice (*Apodemus sylvaticus*) on both male and female numbers. *Journal of Zoology*, **239**, 379–382.

1545 Wiltafsky, Von H. (1978) *Sciurus vulgaris* Linnaeus 1758 – Eichhörnchen. pp. 86–104 in *Handbuch der Säugetiere Europas*. Akademische Verlagsgesellschaft,Wiesbaden (in German).

1546 Wolffe, J.L. & Barnett, S.A. (1977) Effects of cold on nest-building by wild and domestic mice, *Mus musculus*, L *Biological Journal of the Linnean Society of London*, **9**, 73–85.

1547 Wolton, R.J. (1984) Individual recognition by olfaction in the wood mouse, *Apodemus sylvaticus*. *Behaviour*, **88**, 191–199.

1548 Wolton, R.J. (1985) A possible role for faeces in range-marking by the wood mouse, *Apodemus sylvaticus*. *Journal of Zoology* A, **206**, 286–291.

1549 Wolton, R.J. (1985) The ranging and nesting behaviour of wood mice, *Apodemus sylvaticus* (Rodentia, Muridae), as revealed by radiotracking. *Journal of Zoology* A, **206**, 203–224.

1550 Wolton, R.J. & Flowerdew, J.R. (1985) Spatial distribution and movements of wood mice, yellow-necked mice and bank voles. *Symposia of the Zoological Society of London*, **55**, 249–275.

1551 Woodall, P.F. (1977) *Aspects of the ecology and nutrition of the water vole*. DPhil thesis, University of Oxford.

1552 Woodroffe, G.L. (1988). *Ecology of riverside mammals*. MPhil thesis, University of York.

1553 Woodroffe, G.L. (1994) The water vole – some aspects of its ecology. *British Wildlife*, **5**, 296–303.

1554 Woodroffe, G.L. (2000) *The water vole*. The Mammal Society, London.

1555 Woodroffe, G.L. *et al.* (1990) The impact of feral mink *Mustela vison* on water voles *Arvicola terrestris* in the North Yorkshire Moors National Park. *Biological Conservation*, **51**, 49–62.

1556 Woodroffe, G.L. *et al.* (1990) Patterns in the production of latrines by water voles and their use as indices of abundance in population surveys. *Journal of Zoology*, **220**, 439–445.

1557 Woods, D. Personal communication

1558 Woods, M. *et al.* (2003) Predation of wildlife by domestic cats (*Felis catus*) in Great Britain. *Mammal Review*, **33**, 174–188.

1559 Wrangel, H.V. von (1939) Beiträge der Rötelmause, *Clethrionomys glareolus* (Schreber). *Zeitschrift für Säugetierkunde*, **14**, 54–93 (in German).

1560 WVSG (1997) *Species action plan for the United Kingdom – water vole* Arvicola terrestris. DOE/EA.

1561 Yabe, T. (1979) The relationship of food habits and ecological distributions of the Norway rat (*Rattus norvegicus*) and the Roof rat (*Rattus rattus*). *Japanese Journal of Ecology*, **29**, 235–244.

1562 Yalden, D.W. (1971) A population of the yellow-necked mouse, *Apodemus flavicollis*. *Journal of Zoology*, **164**, 244–250.

1563 Yalden, D.W. (1977) *The identification of remains in owl pellets*. Occasional publication, The Mammal Society, London.

1564 Yalden, D.W. (1980) Urban small mammals. *Journal of Zoology*, **191**, 403–406.

1565 Yalden, D.W. (1982) When did the mammal fauna of the British Isles arrive? *Mammal Review*, **12**, 1–57.

1566 Yalden, D.W. (1983) Yellow-necked mice (*Apodemus flavicollis*) in archaeological contexts. *Bulletin of the Peakland Archaeological Society*, **33**, 24–29.

1567 Yalden, D.W. (1984) The yellow-necked mouse, *Apodemus flavicollis*, in Roman Manchester. *Journal of Zoology*, **203**, 285–288.

1568 Yalden, D.W. (1992) Changing distribution and status of small mammals in Britain. *Mammal Review*, **22**, 97–106.

1569 Yalden, D.W. (1995) Small mammals from Viking-age Repton. *Journal of Zoology*, **237**, 655–657.

1570 Yalden, D.W. (1997) The current status of the water vole *Arvicola terrestris* in the Peak District. *Naturalist,* **122**, 83–88.

1571 Yalden, D. (1999) *The history of British mammals.* Poyser, London.

1572 Yalden, D.W. & Shore, R.F. (1991) Yellow-necked mice *Apodemus flavicollis* at Woodchester Park, 1968–1989. *Journal of Zoology,* **224**, 329–332.

1573 Yamazaki, K. *et al.* (1999) Origin, functions and chemistry of H-2 regulated odorants. *Genetica,* **104**, 235–240.

1574 Yasuda, S.P. *et al.* (2005) Phylogeographic patterning of mtDNA in the widely distributed harvest mouse (*Micromys minutus*) suggests dramatic cycles of range contraction and expansion during the mid- to late Pleistocene. *Canadian Journal of Zoology,* **83**, 1411–1420.

1575 Ylönen, H. (1990) Spatial avoidance between the bank vole *Clethrionomys glareolus* and the harvest mouse *Micromys minutus*: an experimental study. *Annales Zoologici Fennici,* **27**, 313–320.

1576 Ylönen, H. & Eccard, J.A. (2004) Does quality of winter food affect spring condition and breeding in female bank voles (*Clethrionomys glareolus*)? *Ecoscience,* **11**, 1–5.

1577 Ylönen, H. & Ronkainen, H. (1994) Breeding suppression in the bank vole as antipredatory adaptation in a predictable environment. *Evolutionary Ecology,* **8**, 658–666.

1578 Ylönen, H. & Viitala, J. (1985) Social organisation of an enclosed winter population of the bank vole *Clethrionomys glareolus*. *Annales Zoologici Fennici,* **22**, 353–358.

1579 Ylönen, H. & Viitala, J. (1991) Social overwintering and food distribution in the bank vole *Clethrionomys glareolus*. *Holarctic Ecology,* **14**, 131–137.

1580 Ylönen, H. *et al.* (1991) Seasonal dynamics of small mammals in an isolated woodlot and its agricultural surroundings. *Annales Zoologici Fennici,* **28**, 7–14.

1581 Ylönen, H. *et al.* (1997) Infanticide in the bank vole (*Clethrionomys glareolus*): Occurrence and the effect of familiarity on female infanticide. *Annales Zoologici Fennici,* **34**, 259–266.

1582 Yoccoz, N.G. & Mesnager, S. (1998) Are alpine bank voles larger and more sexually dimorphic because adults survive better? *Oikos,* **82**, 85–98.

1583 Zalewski, A. (1996) Choice of age classes of bank voles *Clethrionomys glareolus* by pine marten *Martes martes* and tawny owl *Strix aluco* in Białowieża National Park. *Acta Oecologica,* **17**, 233–244.

1584 Zegeren, K. van (1980) Variation in aggressiveness and the regulation of numbers in house mouse populations. *Netherlands Journal of Zoology,* **30**, 635–770.

1585 Zejda, J. (1966) Litter size in *Clethrionomys glareolus* (Schreber 1780). *Zoologicke Listy,* **15**, 193–206.

1586 Zejda, J. & Mazak, V. (1965) Cycle de changement du pelage chez le compagnol roussatre, *Clethrionomys glareolus* Schreber, 1780 (Microtidae, Mammalia). *Mammalia,* **29**, 577–597 (in French).

1587 Zejda, J. & Pelikan, J. (1969) Movements and home ranges of some rodents in lowland forests. *Zoologicke Listy,* **18**, 143–162.

1588 Zhang, Z.B. & Usher, M.B. (1991) Dispersal of wood mice and bank voles in an agricultural landscape. *Acta Theriologica,* 36, 239–245.

1589 Zima, J & Král, B. (1984) Karyotypes of European mammals 2. *Acta Scientiarum, Naturalium Academiae Scientiarum Bohemoslovacae,* **18**, 62.

1590 Zimmermann, K. (1959) *Taschenbuch unsurer wildle-benden Säugetiere.* Urania-Verlag; Leipzig (in German).

1591 Zippelius, H.M. (1974) Ultraschall-laute nestjunger Mäuse. *Behaviour,* **49**, 197–204 (in German).

1592 Zippelius, H.M. & Schleidt, W. (1956) Ultraschall-laute bei jungen Mausen. *Naturwissenschaften,* **43**, 502 (in German).

1593 Zubaid, A. & Gorman, M.L. (1991) The diet of wood mice *Apodemus sylvaticus* living in a sand dune habitat in north-east Scotland. *Journal of Zoology,* **225**, 227–232.

Edible dormouse, adult being handled. Thick gloves are essential! The large eyes indicate nocturnal habits, as do the luxuriant whiskers (*photo P. Morris*).

Plate 4

A Brown hare *Lepus europaeus* **B** Rabbit *Oryctolagus cuniculus* **C** Brown hare *L. europaeus* leveret
D Rabbit *O. cuniculus* kit **E** Irish hare *Lepus timidus hibernicus* **F** Mountain hare *L. timidus* (summer coat)
G Mountain hare *L. timidus* (winter coat)

6

Order Lagomorpha
Rabbits and hares

Compiled by D.P. Cowan

A small order of herbivorous mammals with only 2 extant families, Ochotonidae (pikas) and Leporidae (rabbits and hares), though a 3rd family, Prolagidae, became extinct in recent times. Only leporids now occur in the British Isles, though 1 species of ochotonid occurred in Late Glacial times (see Chapter 3). Share with rodents enlarged, open-rooted, anterior incisors, adapted for gnawing, but differ in having a small 2nd pair of upper incisors. Once classified as a small suborder (Duplicidentata) of Rodentia (with the majority as suborder Simplicidentata), in recognition of this feature. Increasing evidence of a long, separate, fossil history back to at least the Eocene, if not Palaeocene, along with the realisation that such features have often evolved in parallel in different groups of mammals, led to the separation of Lagomorpha as a separate order. Molecular evidence supports the concept that Rodentia and Lagomorpha are related to each other (so the ever-growing incisors may be part of their common inheritance), but also confirms that their separation was an ancient event [32, 235].

FAMILY LEPORIDAE

A family of *c*.11 genera, 61 species, of rabbits and hares [440]. Small–medium-sized herbivores, often abundant and ecologically important as pests and prey; naturally found worldwide except for Australasia, and by introduction even there. Two genera, *Oryctolagus* and *Lepus*, occur in the British Isles. Share large–very large ears, long plantigrade hindfeet much longer than forefeet, and use of caecotrophy – ingesting soft faecal pellets during day, passing hard pellets at night – to achieve similar digestive efficiency to ruminants' use of complex stomach, chewing cud.

GENUS *Oryctolagus*

A genus of just 1 species, the European rabbit *O. cuniculus*. Differs from *Lepus* particularly in ecological and reproductive characters – dependent on burrows, young altricial (naked, blind, deaf, helpless at birth), and much more social, usually living in communal burrow system (warren). Somewhat smaller than *Lepus,* ears and hindlimbs shorter, skull with narrower internal nares (Table 6.1). Appears more similar to American cottontail rabbits *Sylvilagus* [75], but molecular analyses suggest that not especially closely related, and *Oryctolagus* seems rather to be related to the Asian and African genera *Caprolagus, Bunolagus* and *Pentalagus* [327].

Rabbit *Oryctolagus cuniculus*
Lepus cuniculus Linnaeus, 1758; Germany.
Coney, conying (obsolete); *cwningen* (Welsh); *coinean* (Scottish Gaelic); *coinín* (Irish Gaelic); *conning* (Manx).

Male – buck; female – doe; young – kits or kittens.

Table 6.1 Identification of lagomorphs

	Rabbit	**Brown hare**	**Mountain hare**
Overall colour	Sandy brown	Reddish brown	Sandy or grey-brown (usually white in winter)
Upper surface of tail	Black and white	Black and white	White
Tips of ears	Dark brown	Black	Black
Length of ears from notch (mm)	60–70	90–105	60–80
Length of hindfeet (mm)	75–95	130–155	125–170

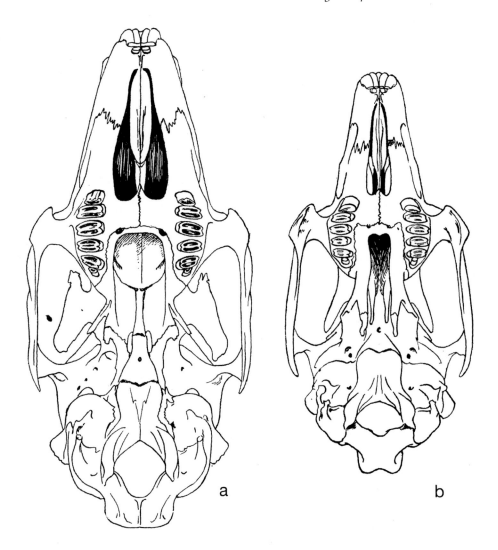

Fig 6.1 Skulls of (a) brown hare *Lepus europaeus* and (b) rabbit *Oryctolagus cuniculus* in palatal views. Note wider internal nares, shorter more triangular supraorbital process, in the hare *(from [264])*.

RECOGNITION

Whole animal: Smaller than brown and mountain hares; ears without black tips, hind legs shorter in relation to body than any hare (Plate 4). Usually flees showing white under tail (brown hare shows black tail-top) (Table 6.1).

Skull: Long bony palate and narrower posterior nares distinctive (short palate, broad nares in hares) (Fig 6.1), suture delimiting interparietal bone persists throughout life (fuses in hares); supraorbital process elongate, narrow (broad triangle in hares).

FIELD SIGNS

Tracks and trails: Footprints in snow characterised by long prints of hindlimbs and small round prints of forefeet. Leaps with one foreleg ahead of the other at slow speeds, but forelimbs tending to move together as speed increases. At high speed, hind prints lie ahead of those of forefeet. Jumping mode of progression reflected in their runs between cover, through and along fences and hedges, to grazing areas; depressions ('jumps' or 'beats') are 20–30 cm apart.

Burrows: Especially prevalent on slopes, banks, etc. where drainage more efficient. Entrances 10–50 cm in diameter, usually enter burrow at shallow angle to horizontal, although 'bolt' or 'pop' holes may be vertically above burrow. Single-entrance nesting burrows, known as stops, may be found, and also lying-up places. Annual weeds, nettles and coarse grasses encouraged by the loose soil and high nitrogen levels on and around burrows. Elder a feature of well-established burrow systems. Horseshoe-shaped scrapes in the ground much in evidence in areas occupied by rabbits.

Faeces: Not always distinguishable from hare's, but usually much smaller, black; size and friability depend on diet. May be found in 'latrines', i.e. dense aggregations of pellets, often on prominent features such as anthills [82, 282]. Also associated with scrapes.

DESCRIPTION

Sexes alike but female has narrower head; profile from ears to nose slightly less rounded than in male. Eyes with iris less yellow than hares; pupil round. Ears and hindlimbs long. 5 digits present on forelimbs, 4 on hindlimbs.

Pelage: Greyish-brown, but much variation (see Variation). Guard hairs banded brown and black (or grey). Nape of neck (woolly fur) and scrotum reddish, chest-patch brown, rest of underparts white or grey. Juveniles frequently with white star on forehead, rarely seen in adults. Long black vibrissae. Feet, including soles, furred and buff coloured. Ears lack the black tips of hares.

Moult: Once yearly; begins in March on face then spreads over back; replacement of underfur not complete until October–November. (Sometimes moult in head region resembles fur replacement, in region of eyes, following recovery from myxomatosis.)

Teeth: Dental formula 2.0.3.3/1.0.2.3. Middle 4 cheek-teeth (p^3, p^4, m^1, m^2) with double-oval pattern to crowns, 1st (p^2) and last (m^3) simpler; adapted for lateral chewing movements, lower jaws narrower than upper jaws.

Genitalia: Testes regress outside breeding season; larger in dominant individuals [28, 46]. Lie in subcutaneous scrotal sacs, can be withdrawn into abdomen. No os penis nor a true glans. Penis short and points backwards in relaxed state. Female tract Y-shaped, fusiform ovaries $c.0.5 \times 1.5$ mm. Corpora lutea easily recognised as translucent spots on ovary surface.

Nipples: 5 pairs, inguinal to pectoral.

Scent glands: Socially significant odours in urine, and in secretions from submandibular (chin) gland, Harderian glands situated deep within the orbit of the eye, inguinal glands in pouches on both sides of penis/vulva, and paired anal glands [27].

Chromosomes: 2n = 44, FNa = 76.

RELATIONSHIPS

Consigned to its own genus since separation, 1874, from *Lepus*; readily distinguished from *Lepus* by altricial young, burrowing habit, numerous

Fig 6.2 Wild rabbit showing symptoms of advanced myxomatosis *(photo P. Morris)*.

skeletal characters. Closely resembles American *Sylvilagus*, but molecular data suggest this due to convergence; is more closely related to Asian and African species [327].

Ecological relationships important and complex. Much illuminated by consequences of original myxomatosis epidemic 1953–1955 (Fig. 6.2), but reflect importance of rabbit in British ecosystems.

Plants: Exclusion of rabbits known to cause major changes in flora [425, 426], but full impact of rabbit grazing not fully appreciated until advent of myxomatosis. Removal of rabbits resulted in increase in height and cover of herbs and grass; increase in plant variety, especially palatable and economically useful grasses and legumes; increase in woody plant seedling abundance; increased plant flowering; faster plant succession due to enhanced seed germination and seedling establishment [370, 374].

Greater plant variety observed immediately post-myxomatosis, including profuse flowering of rare or less common species. In continued absence of rabbits, these plants rapidly succeeded by more dominant grass and woody species; large areas of chalk downland reverted to scrub [385, 386]. Where grazing remained absent, scrub and grassland developed into woodland [370, 389].

On acid grasslands, species not favoured by rabbits include *Anthoxanthum odoratum* and *Rumex acetosella*. Rabbit-favoured species include *Festuca rubra*, *Agrostis capillaris*, *Vicia sativa*, *Trifolium repens* [90]. In moor and heathland habitats, heavy to severe rabbit grazing can remove *Calluna vulgaris, Vaccinum myrtillus, Nardus stricta, Deschampsia caespitosa.* Results in succession by grass heathland, dominated by *Agrostis–Festuca* spp., *Deschampsia flexuosa* and *Carex arenaria.* Under continued heavy grazing, grasses eventually replaced by moss-dominated vegetation and finally lichens [112, 114].

Changes in vegetation can also result in soil destabilisation, sometimes producing screes, and in degradation of coastal sand dune systems [113, 342].

Animals: Increased vegetation height following myxomatosis benefited snails, woodlice, spiders, marbled white butterfly *Melanargia galathea*, Lulworth skipper *Thymelicus actaeon*, six-spot burnet moth *Zygaena filipendulae* and small mammals, especially short-tailed vole *Microtus agrestis*. Honeybees *Apis mellifera* benefited briefly from the abundance of flowers until succession by grasses [370].

Sand lizards *Lacerta agilis* lost breeding sites. Adonis blue *Lysandra bellargus* and large blue *Maculinea arion* butterflies suffered population reductions. Dependent relationship between short sward, caused by rabbit grazing, and red ant *Myrmica sabuleti*, which rears the larvae of the large blue, resulted in its extinction from GB in 1979 [370, 387].

Birds associated with short-sward grasslands (woodlark *Lullula arborea*, lapwing *Vanellus vanellus*, chough *Pyrrhocorax pyrrhocorax*, stone curlew *Burhinus oedicnemus*, wheatear *Oenanthe oenanthe*) declined post-myxomatosis. Succession to tall-sward grassland followed by scrubland initially benefited skylark *Alauda arvensis* and meadow pipit *Anthus pratensis*; then linnet *Acanthis cannabina*, yellowhammer *Emberiza citrinella* and whitethroat *Sylvia communis* [370].

Brown hares *Lepus europaeus* increased dramatically in certain areas post-myxomatosis, due largely to increased leveret survival as a result of increased cover; direct grazing competition and reduced transmission of stomach worm from rabbits to hares were less important in enhancing hare numbers [20, 267].

Wildcats *Felis sylvestris* exploit prey according to availability, and where abundant (E Scotland) rabbits can be >90% of diet, largely as young rabbits or diseased adults [78]. In W Scotland, rabbits less common, only a minor food [163]. Possible that prey availability, particularly rabbits, may limit wildcat numbers; declines reported post-myxomatosis [106]. Red foxes *Vulpes vulpes* are generalised predators, not reliant on rabbit populations [229]. Immediately after myxomatosis, fox populations increased due to the

abundance of diseased rabbits, generally followed by poor productivity as rabbits suddenly disappeared, but partially countered by a switch to voles (see above) as a major prey item [166, 218, 229]. Of mustelids, stoat *Mustela erminea* suffered the most marked population declines after myxomatosis, have recovered in line with recovery of rabbits [375]. Weasel *Mustela nivalis* took advantage of vole abundance. Impact of myxomatosis on pine marten *Martes martes*, polecat *Mustela putorius* and badger *Meles meles* unknown, thought not to be substantial, although all take rabbits [138, 285, 370], and now known that rabbit constitutes up to 85% of polecat diet [33]. Availability of rabbits important for breeding female mink *Mustela vison* [234].

Birds (tawny owl *Strix aluco*, barn owl *Tyto alba*, short-eared owl *Asio flammeus*, kestrel *Falco tinnuculus*) that heavily predate upon small rodents variously affected by changes in rodent populations as a consequence of myxomatosis. Some species had good breeding years while mice and vole populations increased (see above), but suffered poor breeding during subsequent years when rodents decreased due to increased predation by other predators, such as fox [361, 370]. Breeding success of red kites *Milvus milvus* declined catastrophically post-myxomatosis, uncertain whether related to rabbit abundance [93]. More recent studies show rabbits to be less important than sheep carrion for red kites in Wales [94], but are 70% of diet in N Scotland [437]. Common buzzard *Buteo buteo* suffered widescale breeding failure post-myxomatosis [268, 409]; breeding success still strongly related to rabbit abundance [13, 136, 372]. Can form up to 72% of golden eagle *Aquila chrysaetos* diet, but breeding success is not dependent upon rabbit abundance [59, 423].

MEASUREMENTS

Adult head and body up to 400 mm. Adult weight (i.e. when skeletal growth has ceased) 1200–2000 g. Stomach and intestines represent *c.*20% of live weight. Hindfoot length 85–100 mm; ear length (from occiput) 65–75 mm.

VARIATION

Much variation in pelage in British Isles, from light sandy colour to dark grey and totally melanic. Colour variants often associated with fewer guard hairs than regular pelage. Melanic forms not uncommon [343] but albinos rare on mainland. Melanism more frequent in absence of ground predators (e.g. islands/large enclosures). However, island populations often reflect introduction of domestic varieties, e.g. piebald, skewbald and long-haired forms common on Skokholm and formerly Inner Farne island. Island rabbits

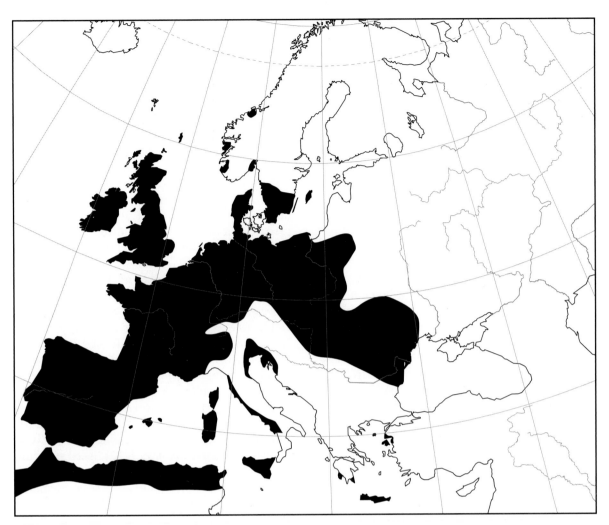

Fig. 6.3 Rabbit *Oryctolagus cuniculus*: European distribution (by introduction, found also in Australia, New Zealand and on many islands).

generally smaller than on mainland. Flashes of white sometimes occur, most frequently on forelimbs and over shoulders. Distinct genetic variants associated with domestic rabbits, therefore with feral populations that now occur widely, including in British Isles [146].

DISTRIBUTION

Originally Iberia and S France [76, 146], but now spread or introduced into most of W Europe (but only in S Scandinavia, and largely absent from Italy, Balkans) (Fig. 6.3). Also introduced into Australia, New Zealand, Chile, islands off USA and elsewhere [120, 123].

Widespread in GB and Ireland and on most islands (Fig. 6.4), but absent from the Isles of Scilly, Rhum, Tiree and some of the small Scottish islands such as Gunna, Sanday (Western Isles) and most of the Treshnish isles. In 1970, 59% of farm holdings had rabbits on cultivable land compared with 94% before the advent of myxomatosis in 1953 [227]. Surveys of the UK have found

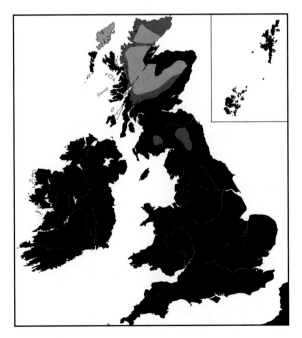

Fig. 6.4 Rabbit *Oryctolagus cuniculus*: distribution in the British Isles.

205

increases in both distribution and abundance since 1970 [209, 405], although a survey in Scotland in 2000 showed no overall change in rabbit abundance on farmland since the early 1990s [150]. Most widespread in E and SE England and Wales; most abundant in E and SE England, SE and E Scotland, and coastal Highlands and islands.

HISTORY

Present in Spain and S France since at least Mid Pleistocene, *c*.300 000 bp, presumed endemic there; distinct genetic subtypes there, not found in domestic or introduced rabbits elsewhere, present and stable over 11 000 years [146]. Present in GB at the interglacial sites of post-Cromerian Boxgrove and Hoxnian Swanscombe (Middle Pleistocene) [450]. Supposed Mesolithic record, Thatcham, Berkshire [204], radiocarbon dated to only 270 bp. Apparently absent from Neolithic, Iron Age, Roman and Anglo-Saxon sites. Introduced to England and Ireland by Normans; subsequent history documented in [347]. Earliest warrens, England, Isles of Scilly, 1176; Ireland, Lambay Island 1191, Connacht 1204; extensive warrens in N Ireland by 17th century [205]. Initially confined to managed warrens, often on islands; protected from predators and supplied with additional food. Slow increase in truly wild populations mostly in coastal areas and lowland heaths, e.g. Breckland, Norfolk. Substantial increase in wild populations from *c*.1750 onwards when changes in agriculture created favourable habitat and increasing interest in game gave rise to intensive predator control. Catastrophic decline in numbers on advent of myxomatosis in 1953 [392].

HABITAT

Most suitable habitat is short grassland, either natural, as on dry heaths and machair, or closely grazed agricultural pastures, with secure refuge (burrows, boulders, hedgerows, scrub, woodland) in close proximity to feeding areas. Occurs up to treeline if land well drained and suitable refuge available. Size and distribution of burrow systems dependent on soil type [296, 331, 332]. In loose soils, select sites with some supporting structures (roots of trees or shrubs) to help protect against collapsing burrows [292]. Burrow systems larger (more interconnected entrances) on chalk than on sand [86]. Never abundant in large coniferous plantations, except on peripheral areas and along fire breaks and rides.

SOCIAL ORGANISATION AND BEHAVIOUR

Home ranges: Generally small, 0.3–0.7 ha, but varies according to habitat and availability of resources, including food, shelter, cover from predators and breeding sites [82, 132, 185, 186]. Male ranges larger than those of females, except under conditions of low rabbit density and abundant high-quality food [96]. Evidence of longer movements (up to 500 m from refuge) at low densities, especially after abrupt changes in environment (e.g. at harvest). However, when feeding on cultivated fields, rarely move more than 50 m from cover; optimal distance *c*. 25 m. Perhaps reflects trade-off of risks from different types of predators [88], supported by evidence that move up to 3 times further from refuge in areas where predators under rigorous control, compared to rabbits at sites with predators [18].

Social groups and use of burrows: Social behaviour extensively studied in enclosures, especially in Australia [231, 275, 276, 278, 279], and in free-living populations [86, 277, 295, 358, 360]. Many populations subdivided into stable social groups based on shared access amongst females to one or more burrow systems, this group-living habit reflecting patchy distribution of nest sites [83]. However, where burrow construction is relatively easy, e.g. on sand-dune systems [86, 206], or where extensive areas of scrub are available for cover [432], social structure much looser. Within social groups, hierarchies amongst males reflect priority of access to females. Hence, dominant males sire the majority of offspring in their group [92]. Dominant females have priority of access to best nest sites. Competition between females for access to such sites can lead to serious injury and death [276]. At high densities, subordinate females may be forced to use single-entrance breeding stops away from main burrow systems [129], which are particularly susceptible to predation by badgers and foxes [273]. Juveniles born into large social groups occupying large burrow systems suffer higher levels of cat predation [294] and disease [81], although larger burrows offer increased protection against underground predators, e.g. ferrets [80]. Rabbit's distinctive burrowing habit a key factor in its success, principally by affording protection for altricial young in underground nests; need for safe nest sites has shaped social organisation of the species [83]. Infanticide by rival females reported in competition for breeding stops [212]. Not all rabbits use burrows all the time, e.g. Kolb [206] showed that most young rabbits rarely used burrows during summer, when ground cover most abundant. In arid Australian climate, burrow use only slightly greater in winter (53%) than in summer (38%) [269]. No evidence, despite popular theories, that surface living has increased in response to myxomatosis.

Territories: Group territories established during bouts of mutual paw-scraping and parallel run displays by males from adjacent groups, along territory boundaries [28, 82]. Most scrapes are created in this way, rather than as a result of feeding on roots. Hence, density of scrapes highest in areas of overlap between home ranges of bucks from adjacent social groups [82]. Territories also maintained by use of odour [267, 281–283]. Although territories are not exclusive, more than 90% of sexual interactions are within social groups [82] and up to 93% of offspring are sired by males from the social group into which they are born [92]. Females more aggressive towards juveniles than males, who often protect juveniles during chases by females [280]. Adult female aggression biased towards juvenile females; adult males will also interrupt aggression between adult females [82, 282].

Dispersal and migration: Dispersal distances >4 km recorded. Juvenile males disperse more frequently than juvenile females [85, 105, 213, 295]. Half of females first breed in their natal social groups, but only around 25% of males, on a chalk downland site in Oxfordshire; dispersal amongst adults rare in this population, but also male biased [85]. These patterns confirmed elsewhere by genetic analyses [92, 371, 428].

Scent-marking: Chin and anal gland secretions particularly involved in territorial behaviour [26, 27, 281–283]. Information concerning sexual status, individual and group recognition contained in urine and inguinal gland secretions [26, 153, 154]. Some active components of secretions identified, especially of anal gland [133, 155]. Faecal pellets from latrines elicit greater deposition of further pellets than non-latrine pellets [356]. Female urine shown to have 'primer' effects on growth and development of males [29].

Acoustic communication: Equivocal evidence that distress screams upon capture by a predator or thumping of hindfeet in presence of predator serve a warning function [40].

Other communication: Some visual signalling during reproduction and aggressive behaviour [360]. Flashing of white underside of tail may serve to warn other individuals during flight from a predator.

Activity: Crepuscular and nocturnal, but diurnal if undisturbed. Strong wind and heavy rain reduce activity, as does bright moonlight [207].

FEEDING

Eat wide range of herbage, especially grasses. Favour young, succulent leaves and shoots, select more nutritious species, e.g. of *Festuca* grasses [31, 316, 350, 439]. Winter wheat preferred to maize, and dicotyledons in mixed cultivated areas; no preference between winter wheat or winter barley varieties [25, 68]. For broadleaved or simple grass swards, short-term rate of intake in captive 'wild' rabbits increases asymptotically with sward length. During summer months, free-living wild rabbits select the shortest swards, which provide the lowest rates of intake, suggesting that foraging habitat is selected by anti-predator considerations rather than by maximising rate of food intake [196]. During times of food shortage, however, rabbits will maximise their food intake rates, and select those parts of the plant with higher nitrogen content [328]. Fasting endurance, winter, estimated at 2–8 days, depending upon availability of body reserves of fat and protein [39]. No strong evidence of direct competition for food with brown hare [68].

Refection: Rabbits, like other leporids, produce a special type of faecal pellet that is soft, covered in mucus and ingested directly from the anus [170] (sometimes termed caecotrophy, to distinguish it from coprophagy which includes re-ingestion of normal faeces). Soft pellets produced mostly while less active during daylight hours [359]. Gut morphology varies according to diet quality (influenced by season and soil type) and reproductive status [348].

BREEDING

Breeding season mainly January–August, when a succession of litters, usually of 3–7 young, produced at a minimum interval of about 30 days.

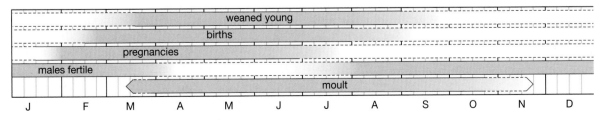

Fig. 6.5 Rabbit: annual cycle.

Males: Testes weight increases during winter–early spring, thereafter declines to minimum in autumn [42, 45, 333]. Epididymal smears may be devoid of spermatozoa in July–September [45].

Females: Proportion of pregnant females may be high in January (Fig. 6.5). Time of onset of breeding primarily determined by day length [42], but also influenced by severity of winter and body mass [329]. End of breeding season related to population density. In high-density, pre-myxomatosis, populations, season was January/February–June, with about 5% of females pregnant in other months. Season extended in post-myxomatosis low-density populations, with some out-of-season breeding as formerly. Pre-myxomatosis breeding season lasted 15–17 weeks [45]; immediately post-myxomatosis 22 weeks or more [224]. Does will copulate at approximately 7-day intervals even while pregnant [152, 182, 274]. Ovulation is induced by copulation; no oestrous cycle. If mating fails to fertilise shed ova, 14-day pseudopregnancy ensues. Gestation lasts c.30 days, postpartum oestrus normal, females usually pregnant within 24 h of parturition. No lactation anoestrus, as is common in domestic rabbit.

Productivity: Within season, number of ova shed increases at each pregnancy, up to peak in June, declines thereafter; also positively related to body weight of doe. Litter size varies according to environment. Massive prenatal mortality of entire sets of embryos can occur through intrauterine absorption [44, 45]. Such loss is characteristic of high-density populations (up to 60% loss), also occurs to lesser degree in low-density populations [225]. Live offspring produced per female per year, 10–11 in high-density populations [44], >30 in 1958 post-myxomatosis, c.20 in many expanding rabbit populations [228]. Litter size unchanged in Lincolnshire from 1967 through to 1985, suggesting that increase in litter size occurs only at very low population density [403]. Productivity strongly influenced by soil type; 14 young per female born on sandy sites, 22 on clay, 20 on chalk [402]. Subordinate females, usually yearlings, have shorter breeding seasons than dominant, generally older individuals, and suffer higher occurrence of total loss of embryos.

Development of young: Prenatal and postnatal sex ratios 1:1, although greater maternal investment in male offspring during gestation reflected in higher birthweights of males [41]. Young born in nests composed of grass or moss, lined with belly fur, situated in blind tunnels within main burrow system or in stops. Occasionally breed above ground in dense vegetation. One visit per night to suckle young, for only a few minutes [57]. Entrance to stop carefully sealed with soil and vegetation after suckling. Young blind at birth, very sparsely furred. Eyes open around 10 days. Weight at birth 30–35 g, at weaning 150–200 g. Growth rate from weaning to adult body weight, c.1000 g, is c.10 g/day [86, 358, 427], but much lower (c.5 g/day) in original range in S France and Iberia [330]. Begin to appear at burrow entrances around 18 days old and weaned at c.21–25 days. Extended maternal care up to 6–7 weeks of age reported for last litters in season [230]. Males fecund at c.4 months; females can breed at c.3–5 months, at a weight of c.830 g, although only young from early litters breed during season of birth.

POPULATION

Numbers: Vary seasonally; relatively stable over winter (<1–15/ha), followed by highly variable summer peaks (<1–40/ha) [396]. Summer peaks highest on sandy soils. Overwinter numbers higher on sand and chalk than on clay soils. By mid 1990s, population had grown to about 37 million [147], increasing at around 1% per annum but still below pre-myxomatosis densities [408]. Some evidence of decline, late 1990s–early 2000s, perhaps reflecting arrival of rabbit haemorrhagic disease (RHD); upward trend may have subsequently resumed [24]. Census method described in [314].

Sex ratio: Variable, may be female biased in group-living populations [82, 294], but varies with sampling method. In general warren-based methods, such as ferreting, produce female-biased samples, whereas others, such as cage trapping and night shooting, produce male-biased samples [37, 352].

Age determination: Proximal fusion of tibia distinguishes adults from juveniles (<9 months of age) in both live and dead animals [421]. Ageing can also be based on bodyweight up to c.1000 g [358, 427], eye-lens weight [431] and epiphyseal ossification in the lumbar vertebrae up to 26 months [401]. Length of supraorbital ridge can indicate year classes, but is subject to greater variation than eye-lens weight [208].

Age structure: Reflects seasonal cycle, with young recruited into the population during the breeding season. Adult/juvenile ratio, November–December, ranged from 1:0.8 to 1:3.0 [228].

Survival: Productivity high, but recruitment from 1965 to 1973 low, in many rabbit populations, indicating mortality of 70–92% in young-of-year

[227]. Mortality rate around 95% during 1st year of life calculated for population on chalk downland [87]. Annual adult mortality 45–65% in same population. Female life expectancy 13 weeks at 4–8 weeks old, rising to 77 weeks in middle of 3rd year [84]. Early-born young survive significantly better than others; in general, juvenile survival highly density-dependent [84, 86, 105, 294, 444]. Lack of adequate food (quality and/or quantity) sometimes influences growth and survival [86, 130, 131]. Juvenile survival for females higher than [84], or similar to [445], that of males.

MORTALITY

Predation: Foxes, stoats, polecats and wild cats prey on all ages; badgers, buzzards, weasels and domestic cats on young animals. Predation by other species (e.g. owls, great black-backed gull, raven, crow) more occasional. Rabbit abundance higher in areas where predator control practised [16]; although causal relationship between rabbit numbers and predation rate not firmly established, suggestion that foxes can regulate rabbit numbers, but only below a critical density [15, 406].

Disease: Myxoma virus arrived in GB during 1953, from France, reached Ireland in 1954 [388]. Virus isolated from forest rabbit *Sylvilagus brasiliensis,* S America, in which it causes a mild, non-lethal disease, used in experiments (GB, Skokholm, Australia), to control rabbits. Disease highly specific (possible that a few hares infected [245]; Fig. 6.2). Spread throughout the country during the next 2 years causing more than 99% mortality [385]. Principle vector in British Isles is European rabbit flea *Spilopsyllus cuniculi* (Dale), not mosquitoes as elsewhere (e.g. Australia) [67, 271, 272]. Virulence of disease, measured by survival time and mortality rate [257], has since declined [338] through increased transmissability of weaker strains [256]. Genetic resistance in rabbit populations confirmed [336, 337] and increasing. Disease endemic; major outbreaks still occur twice annually in most populations, during spring and especially late summer/autumn [339]. Most recent estimate of mortality during outbreaks 5–33% [406]. Eventual outcome of interaction between selection pressures concerning virulence and resistance uncertain, current evidence suggests variable but continuing decline in levels of mortality [334, 336, 337].

Rabbit haemorrhagic disease (RHD), also known as viral haemorrhagic disease (VHD) or rabbit calicivirus disease (RCD) in Australia, entered UK domestic rabbit population in 1992, wild rabbit population in 1994 [71]. A calicivirus, similar but not identical to European brown hare syndrome (EBHS). Environmentally resistant; viral particles are viable for weeks, and may be distributed by air, contact species or inanimate objects. First reported in China in 1984, this highly contagious disease spread to Italy in 1986 via the commercial rabbit trade, where it spread throughout Europe into wild populations. Is specific to *Oryctolagus cuniculus,* causing gross lesions of acute necrotising hepatitis, disseminated intravascular coagulation, and congestion or haemorrhaging, particularly of the lungs; death usual within 30 h post-infection in susceptible rabbits. Disease peaks in late autumn–winter [399]. Does not affect rabbits <6–8 weeks of age. Many UK rabbits immune, perhaps due to exposure to widespread, putatively non-pathogenic RHD-like virus strains, but proportion of susceptible rabbits very variable locally [69, 70, 407]. Mortality rates approximately 30%, with no significant age or sex bias, although may have a geographical component which depends upon the prevalence of the putative non-pathogenic strain [434].

Infection by coccidial parasites *Eimeria* spp., especially *E. stiedai,* can cause >10% mortality among juveniles up to *c.*4 months old, but incidence in them highly density dependent [36, 62, 81, 364].

Wild rabbits are potential carriers of VTEC *Escherichia coli* 0157 and have been implicated as a source of human infection [14]. Wild rabbits residing in close proximity to cattle excreting *E. coli* 0157 can also act as vectors for the disease [344].

PARASITES

Endoparasites: At least 10 helminth and 11 protozoan parasites. Of the helminths, *Graphidium strigosum* and *Trichostrongylus retortaeformis* most common. Burdens of *G. strigosum* increase with age of host, correlate to stomach size [348], but do not adversely affect health. *T. retortaeformis* burdens decrease with age, suggesting immune development, but in young rabbits can affect growth, condition and overwinter survival, due to high prevalence in autumn–winter. Nematode *Passalurus ambiguus* and cestodes *Cittotaenia pectinata, C. denticulata,* although common, have no detectable detrimental effects [34, 36]. Rabbits with myxomatosis can have significantly larger burdens of *T. retortaeformis, P. ambiguus* and *C. pectinata,* suggesting virally induced immuno-suppression [216].

Ectoparasites: Flea *Spilopsyllus cuniculi* specific to rabbit, usually very abundant, especially on ears. Seasonal variation in numbers [258], reproduction of flea being linked to breeding cycle of rabbit through blood hormone levels [251]. Flea locates host using olfactory cues in host's urine [412].

Urine from nestling rabbits contains a kairomone which enhances copulation, impregnation and development of fleas [341]. 14 other species of flea found on rabbit, but all stragglers originating from other mammals, such as hedgehogs, voles, rats and mice [253].

33 species of mites recorded, but most believed to be accidentally acquired. More regular are larval harvest mites *Trombicula autumnalis, Listrophorus gibbus* which scavenge skin secretions and hair scales, mange mites *Psorotes equi* and *Cheyletiella parasitivorax*. Mites typically found in ears and around genitalia [252]. Sucking louse *Haemodipsus ventricosus* regular.

Others: Isolated records of rabbits infected with leptospirosis *Leptospira* spp., syphilis *Treponema* spp. and encephalitozoonosis *Encephalitozoon cuniculi* [262, 410, 441]. Rabbits potentially implicated in the spread of Johne's disease (*Mycobacterium avium paratuberculosis*) in ruminants [64].

RELATIONS WITH HUMANS

Damage and management: Cause damage to a wide variety of agricultural crops, including cereals, roots, pasture, horticulture and forestry [72, 73, 135, 307]. Bark of many trees eaten, especially during periods of snow cover. Rabbits a major cause of failure of natural generation of forest trees [424]. Pre-myxomatosis, rabbits were the major vertebrate pests of agriculture, annual cost of damage estimated to be £50 million at 1952 prices [392]. Increasing numbers, as mortality due to myxomatosis declines, cause an increasing problem. Rabbit trapping for food and fur once an important industry (£1.5 million contribution to agricultural economy in 1952) but now mainly pursued as a pest [389]. Damage most severe when heavily grazes early growth of crop, particularly winter-planted cereals [25, 89]. Cause *c.* £115 million of damage annually to British agricultural industry [353]. This loss averages between 0.33% and 1% yield loss per rabbit/ha on winter wheat [97], grass [98] or spring barley [99]. Approximately £5 million spent per annum to manage the rabbit problem on agricultural holdings, with about $\frac{1}{2}$ of this spent managing rabbits on arable crops; about $\frac{3}{4}$ is spent on gassing and fencing [353].

Recommended method of control is gassing when burrows are accessible; population reductions 65–78% following single treatment, hence repetition advised [335, 340]. Ferreting burrows, traditional method of bolting rabbits into nets or in front of guns, yields 30–50% reductions, according to size of burrow systems [80]. Shooting, snares and traps also used. Limited efficacy of shooting demonstrated in New Zealand [438]. Control aimed at removing adults best performed over winter [351] although age and sex biases inherent in different techniques can influence effectiveness and optimal timing [352]. Non-lethal measures include the use of fences, both permanent and electric [246–248] and, for forestry, repellents [302]. Poison baiting widely used in Australia and New Zealand but illegal in UK. Methods of management reviewed in [308, 322, 353, 400]; effectiveness of control operations assessed in [390].

LITERATURE

Thompson and Worden [392] gives a general account of wild rabbit biology, Lockley [232] a description of the social life of an enclosed rabbit colony, Sheail [347] a history of the wild rabbit in GB, Cowan [79] a popular account of the natural history of wild rabbits, Tittensor and Lloyd [397] a concise account of rabbit biology and management, and Thompson and King [391] a comprehensive and worldwide review of rabbit ecology.

AUTHORS
D.P. Cowan & F.G. Hartley

GENUS *Lepus*

A genus of 29 [66] to 32 [440] species of hares. Morphologically, ecologically and genetically a very uniform genus of small herbivores whose ecology, physiology and anatomy resemble that of small ungulates. Species hard to discriminate, so taxonomy very uncertain. Characterised by large ears, very short tails and long hind legs, and by living in open habitats, where they rely on good eyesight, camouflage and the ability to flee to avoid predators (rather than cover or burrows). Widespread across the Holarctic and into Africa and S Asia; introduced elsewhere (e.g. New Zealand, S America). Two species occur in British Isles: native mountain hare *L. timidus* and anciently introduced brown hare *L. europaeus*; arguable that Irish hare *L. hibernicus* should be regarded as a species distinct from *L. timidus*.

Brown hare *Lepus europaeus*

Lepus europaeus Pallas 1778; Burgundy, France.
Lepus capensis Petter 1961 and later authors, not of Linnaeus 1758.
Hare; European hare; *sgwamog, ysgyfarnog* (Welsh); *gearr* (Scottish Gaelic); *mwaagh, cleaysh-liauyr* (Manx Gaelic).

Male – buck or jack; female – doe or jill; young – leveret.

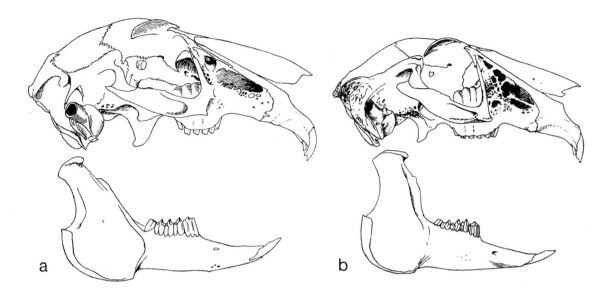

Fig. 6.6 Skulls of brown hare *Lepus europaeus* (a) and mountain hare *Lepus timidus* (b) in lateral view, showing the wider curve of the incisors, with roots extending back into the maxilla, in the mountain hare, and the different proportions of the anterior part of the zygomatic arch (*from [264]*).

RECOGNITION

Whole animal: Much larger than rabbit, with longer limbs, longer black-tipped ears, and overall russet colour (rabbit rather greyish brown (see Table 6.1). Also larger, ears longer and with more extensive black tips, than mountain hare (which is sandy- or grey-brown, not russet) (Plate 4). Leaping stride when running fast (lope, rather than rabbit's scuttle), tail normally held down, so black and white dorsal surface visible (Plate 4)).

Skull and teeth: Shorter bony palate and wider nasal passage than rabbit (Fig. 6.1), supraorbital process broadly triangular. Very similar to mountain hare, but root of upper incisor more tightly curved, restricted to premaxilla (more gently curved, originates in maxilla in mountain hare) (Fig. 6.6).

FIELD SIGNS

Tracks and trails: Trails evident across fields. Tracks with side-by-side impressions of long hindfeet (15 cm long, 4–5 claw prints visible), placed ahead of staggered oval prints of forefeet (4 cm long, 4 claws); soles fully furred, so no pad prints visible (cf. rodents, carnivores).

Faeces: Similar spheroidal pellets to rabbit's, but usually larger (1 cm), more flattened; usually brown rather than black.

Forms: Rests in shallow depression (form) in vegetation (Fig. 6.7). On ploughed fields, form may be dug about 10 cm into the ground.

Fig. 6.7 Brown hare in its form (*photo A.J.F. Holley*).

DESCRIPTION

Pelage: Reddish-brown, agouti (speckled with black) dorsally, buff on flanks, pale yellow on cheeks and inside of limbs [158]; mane of longer hair on chest deep russet, not speckled black (Plate 4). Belly white; tail white with broad black dorsal stripe. In low light, pale margins of down-turned tail and white backs of ears below their black tips stand out [173]. Dorsal fur in summer dense, slightly wavy; consists of underfur (15 mm), pile hair (24–27 mm) and guard hair (32–35 mm). In winter, fur longer, redder, with grey area on rump; fur on face and ears whiter. Pelage of leverets similar to that of adults [158].

Moult: Spring (March–June) and autumn (July–October) moults are preceded by fading of pelage. Moulting begins at nape, mid-back and head, spreads downwards and backwards. Leverets first moult at *c*.900 g, and undergo 2 moults before acquiring adult winter pelage [158].

Anatomy: Vibrissae white, black, or black with white tips [158]. Eyes large, brown, with rounded pupil; have tapetum, eyeshine at night pink. Digestive tract has simple stomach but large caecum containing cellulose-digesting bacteria, which digest material that autocoprophagy (refection) allows hares to absorb [170].

Nipples: 4 pairs; 1 pectoral, 3 inguinal.

Scent glands: Odours produced by lachrymal and Harderian glands in the orbits, submandibular glands, anal glands and inguinal glands; latter lie either side of genitalia, are larger in does than bucks. Odours probably important in sexual behaviour and convey individual identity [27].

Skull: See Figs. 6.1, 6.6. Fluctuating asymmetry in non-metric skull parameters, an indicator of overall fitness, is negatively correlated with genetic diversity [149].

Reproductive tract: Uterus bicornuate. Placental scars can be used to estimate litter sizes, fade over winter [47, 143]. Testes held intra-abdominally mid September–early November [219].

Chromosomes: 2n = 48 [304], as in all *Lepus* [327].

RELATIONSHIPS

L. europaeus more closely related to *L. capensis* (Sardinia, Africa, SW Asia) and other African hares than to other European species (*L. granatensis* (S Iberian peninsula, Majorca), *L. corsicanus* (including *L. castroviejoi*) (S Italy, Sicily, Corsica; NW Spain) and *L. timidus* [265, 303, 440]; previously considered conspecific with *L. capensis* [306] but now separated; they differ in size, proportions, colour, and genetics [303].

Replaced in Spain, S of R. Ebro, by *L. granatensis*, and in S Italy by *L. corsicanus;* also at higher altitudes (e.g. Alps) and latitudes (e.g. Scandinavia) by mountain hare *L. timidus.* Hybrids between brown and mountain hare fertile, but rare [346]. Argued that brown hare displacing mountain hare, S Sweden, by hybridisation [393]. In N Spain, some brown hares contain mtDNA from mountain hares, presumed relict from distribution in Late Glacial [3]; similar report from Denmark [124]. Hybrids with mountain hare occur in Switzerland, about 8% of brown hares sampled [369]; occasionally suspected in GB [15]. Unclear whether rabbits and brown hares compete directly for food [68, 178].

MEASUREMENTS

See Table 6.2.

Table 6.2 Measurements of adult brown hares from England [1]

	Mean	Range	SD	n
Head and body length (mm)	550	490–610	20	250
Tail length (mm)	70	40–100	10	246
Hindfoot length (mm)	145	124–156	5	251
Ear length (mm)	101	87–111	4	121
Body weight (kg)				
Adult males	3.32	2.23–4.10	0.25	116
Adult females	3.69	2.62–4.56	0.32	134

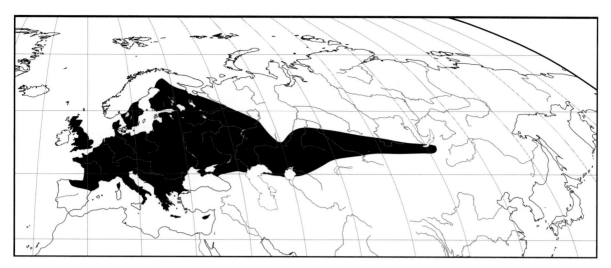

Fig. 6.8 Brown hare *Lepus europaeus*: Palaearctic distribution (also, by introduction, in N & S America, Australia, New Zealand).

VARIATION

British hares described as a subspecies (*L. e. occidentalis* de Winton 1898, type locality Moorhampton, Hereford, England) on the basis of darker colour, but not clearly separable from those in mainland Europe. Genetically, show very little variation in GB [368]. Grey, melanistic, leucistic (white, but black ear tips, tail top), albino, and sandy-coloured forms reported. In Europe, genetically more variable; rather uniform protein heterozygosity suggests gene flow, even to partially isolated populations [148].

DISTRIBUTION

Native to much of Europe, mainly N of Alps, but has spread extensively with agriculture, into Siberia as far as Lake Baikal (Fig. 6.8). Introduced to S Sweden, British Isles; also to E Canada, NE United States, S South America (Argentina, S Brazil, Chile), much of W Australia, New Zealand and various smaller islands [66, 121, 217]. 'Natural' range hard to specify because of spread through agricultural habitats as they expanded, and because of extensive introductions and restocking as a game animal.

Found throughout GB (Fig. 6.9) and on following Scottish islands: Orkney (Rousay, Mainland), Inner Hebrides (Tiree, Skye, Scalpay, Staffin, Coll, Luing, Mull, Islay, Gigha), Clyde islands (Arran, Bute, and occasionally Davaar). Introduced to Isle of Man; also naturalised in NW Ireland (Donegal, Fermanagh, Londonderry, Tyrone) after introductions for coursing, but local, scarce relative to Irish hare [324].

In Scotland, Derbyshire, and Isle of Man, where farmland gives way to *Calluna* moor, is replaced by mountain hare above *c.*300 m [111, 450]. In New Zealand, where is the only *Lepus* sp., occupies typical mountain hare habitat up to 2000 m [118, 121].

HISTORY

An animal of open steppe, survived Last Glaciation around Black Sea. Molecular evidence suggests 2 lineages, which separated about 245 kya, one survived in Balkans, other in Anatolia [202]; spread in Postglacial N of mountain chains to Germany, France, into Spain as far S as R. Ebro, and into N Italy [3, 202], but failed to reach GB, Scandinavia. Scant genetic variation in GB confirms that introduced (from Netherlands or

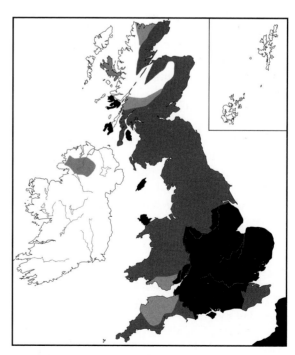

Fig. 6.9 Brown hare *Lepus europaeus*: distribution in the British Isles.

Denmark?) [368], probably in Iron Age, though archaeological evidence is inconclusive; certainly present from Roman times onwards [450]. Limited introductions to N Ireland, mid–late 19th century [324].

HABITAT
Throughout Europe, most common in arable areas where cereal growing predominates [211, 250]. Prefers cultivated areas (wheat, sugar beet, peas) to non-cultivated areas (pasture, set-aside, woodland) [43, 239]. Needs some permanent cover [293]; survival, but not production, of leverets is higher in mixed agricultural areas than in cereal monocultures [145]. Therefore, large-scale farming with a low diversity of crops and large fields is less suitable than farming that provides food and shelter all year round in small fields [260, 293, 345, 380]. In mixed farming, prefers cattle-grazed pasture and fallow in most seasons, for both feeding and resting; avoids sheep pasture except in winter [354]. Prefers strips of uncultivated land in arable fields [127]; creating such strips and windbreaks, and increasing crop diversity, can lead to dramatic increases in numbers of hares [349].

Prefers short vegetation for feeding at night [162] but areas with more cover for resting [261] and for occasional feeding during the day [173]. As well as fields, uses woods, shelter-belts, and hedgerows for resting during the day, particularly in winter [380]. In N Ireland, prefers improved grassland, which is also preferred habitat of Irish hare; niche overlap almost complete [324]. Pastures are used for feeding in summer when cereals are too mature to be eaten [380], but high densities of livestock, especially sheep, deter brown hares from some pastures [21, 354]. Human settlement reduces numbers [48], and habitat improvement may lead to increased numbers only if numbers of predators are low [363].

Worldwide, occupy diverse open habitats with low vegetation, such as moor, salt marsh, alpine grassland, steppe, near desert, pampas, sand dunes, marshes and alpine fellfield [66, 217]. Tolerates mean annual temperatures of 3–30 °C and annual rainfall of 200–1200 mm [199].

SOCIAL ORGANISATION AND BEHAVIOUR
Territories: No evidence of territorial behaviour: home ranges overlap [55]. Home range size is 20–190 ha (Table 6.3): night range may be 50% larger than day range [239, 354]. Within home ranges, European hares move seasonally [239, 354, 447] with seasonal changes in food supply and cover [325, 380]. May commute 1.7 km between feeding areas and forms at dawn and dusk [167], or forms

may be near to feeding areas [325].

Forms: May provide shelter and protection from predators; often give a good view of surroundings and are close to a route for unobserved retreat. May arrange vegetation near their forms, perhaps to improve visibility [175]. To reduce risk of predation or harassment from conspecifics, often back-track along their trails several times before returning to forms. Where hunted, are flushed from their forms more readily than where not hunted [188].

Scent-marking: Bucks scent-mark by rubbing clumps of vegetation with their chins and by urinating on their feet and kicking backwards. When guarding does, bucks lift their tails to release scent from anal and inguinal glands. Near-oestrus does followed by bucks shake their tails to release scent as a signal to the buck. Bucks and does touch noses [173].

Vocalisations: Vocalises only when in physical danger [173]; then emits a harsh shriek.

Other communication: Bucks and does hold their tails up so that white underside is visible when urinating and defecating. Does with leverets also raise their tails, perhaps as a signal [173]. When approached by red foxes in the open, adults adopt a bipedal stance facing the fox to signal to it that it has been seen, and therefore has little chance of catching them [174]. May similarly 'flag' white under-tail to humans [451].

Aggressive behaviour: Dominant bucks guard near-oestrus does from subordinates which they bite and chase off, and supplant subordinate bucks which are guarding does. Dominants thus obtain

Fig. 6.10 Brown hares fighting, the female (left) rejecting the advances of the male *(photo A.J.F. Holley)*.

Table 6.3 Home range sizes of brown hares determined by radio-tracking

Location	Habitat	Method of calculation	No. of months animals tracked	n	Mean home range size (min–max) (ha)	Source
England	Agricultural land	90 isopleth	1–7	15	38 (16–78)	[380]
Oxfordshire	Agricultural land	MCP	2	85	25 (0.3–106)	[43]
East Anglia	Conifer plantation	MCP	12	34	c.46	[447]
Somerset	Agricultural land	MCP	2	127	36±26 (active) 19±13 (rest)	[354]
Netherlands	Arable land	MCP	1–14	10	26 (8–60)	[55]
Netherlands	Cattle pasture	MCP	1–14	10	26 (8–60)	[55]
France	Intensive arable land	95 MCP	<5	20	190 (80–315)	[239]
France	Intensive arable land	MCP	>6	21	110 (39–295)	[325]
Hungary	Agricultural land (1) forest (2)	MCP	1–6	12	37 (1) 45 (2)	[210]
New Zealand	Sub-alpine grassland	MCP	<12	21	53 (30–70)	[297]

n, number of animals tracked; MCP, minimum convex polygon.

more matings than subordinates [172]. Does may be attended by one or more bucks for up to 5 days before the day of oestrus, dominant buck remains within 5 m of doe's daytime form. Near-oestrus, but unreceptive, females drop their ears in a threatening posture or box guarding bucks if they approach closely (Fig. 6.10; [173]). Boxing and chasing occur throughout the breeding season [176].

During breeding season, dispersion determined by that of does, which often form groups when feeding, and then spend less time vigilant than solitary animals, as corporate vigilance is increased in groups [55, 239, 266]. Vigilance is also related to sward height: individuals spend less time vigilant after harvest than before [239]. Increased group size does not normally lead to intraspecific aggression, but if preferred food is in a small patch, aggression may increase and social hierarchies may form, containing both bucks and does [220, 266]. In food-related aggressive encounters, animals first adopt threat postures (facing one another, ears back, sometimes drumming front feet on ground), then box [220]. Brown hares chase corvids [173].

Dispersal: Immigration occurs into areas over which shooting has taken place [249, 362]. Of 23 tagged 5-week-old leverets recovered in the Netherlands, all but one moved <1 km in 19 months [55]. Of 24 tagged 2–7-month-old animals in France, none dispersed [325]. In another study, 55% of leverets remained near their place of birth, while 33% dispersed on average 4.5 km at 4–6 months old [47]. Low levels of allozyme differentiation between separate populations of European hares suggest that dispersal is common [148].

Activity: Mainly nocturnal, spends 2/3 of night-time feeding [144]. Leaves its form up to 3 h before sunset in summer, and usually in 1 h before or after sunset in winter [176]. Returns up to 1 h before sunrise in winter, up to 5 h after sunrise in summer [173]. In New Zealand, brown hares move around near their forms during daytime

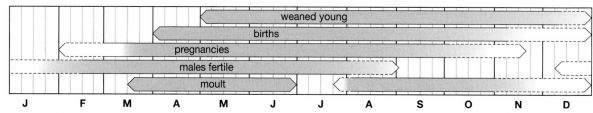

Fig. 6.11 Brown hare: annual cycle.

[297]; in a conifer plantation in E Anglia, were regularly active during the day and inactive at night [447].

Locomotion: Bucks spend more time running [144], have larger summer home ranges, and move further within them than does [447].

Others: Locomotor play in leverets consists mainly of 'streaking' or running conspicuously up and down a familiar path ('race track' [118]), sometimes with tail held up, occasionally jumping. Each leveret in a litter has its own separate path; paths converge at site where littermates meet each evening [173].

Grooming carried out in a crouched position [173], usually soon after re-entering the form for the day [118].

FEEDING

Eat grasses, herbs and arable crops (particularly young cereals, but also maize, peas, beans, sugar beet, and ears of cereals [68]. Wild grasses and herbs preferred to cultivated forms [126]; in France, field horsetail *Equisetum arvense* is particularly sought in summer [68]. Grasses form up to 90% of diet in winter, are very important all year, although in summer herbs form 40–60% of the diet [60]. Wild grasses form a large part of the diet of European hares in conifer plantations [447]. Shrubs browsed [177] if snow makes grazing difficult. May select between varieties of agricultural crops [162]. One variety of oilseed rape *Brassica napus*, if eaten in excess, can cause death [381].

Autocoprophagy: During the day while resting in form, employs autocoprophagy (re-ingestion of soft droppings called caecotrophs); takes droppings directly into its mouth from the anus, while sitting on its haunches [118]. During late afternoon, may also reingest some of hard pellets [170]. Hard pellets, made up of coarse material filtered out from softer material, are passed at night while feeding, away from form.

Food requirements: Wild hares, E Anglia, estimated to need 2310 kJ/day in summer and 2835 kJ/day in winter [249]. Captive animals consume approximately 500 g of food (3164 kJ) daily [284].

BREEDING
See Fig. 6.11

Each doe gives birth to *c*.3 litters of leverets February–October; pregnancy is rare October–December. Gestation 41–42 days. Litter size 1–4 (small litters early and late in the season; Table 6.4). Lactation lasts at least 23 days.

Males: Testes attain peak weight (10 g each) February–July, then decline until September, remain at minimum size (2 g) until November when begin to grow. Viable sperm present in all months except October–November, maximal January–June [219].

Females: Ovulation induced by mating, which takes place postpartum (Fig. 6.12). Occasional prepartum mating can lead to superfetation in which litters of embryos of 2 different ages are present in the uterus [226]. Before giving birth, does may spend 2 weeks or more alone near prospective birth site, or may solicit attention from bucks while keeping away from site of birth [173].

Prenatal losses variable, high at start and middle of breeding season [315]. Early in season,

Fig. 6.12 Brown hares copulating, January 1999 – by no means confined to 'Mad March Hares' *(photo A.J.F. Holley)*.

Table 6.4 Monthly changes in mean litter size and percentage of adult females pregnant in the brown hare, based on gross examination and counts of fetuses

	Norfolk		Norfolk		Scotland		Netherlands		Poland	
n	83		293 (Feb) 42 (May)		1569		235*		212	
Source	[219]		[249]		[168]		[54]		[315]	
	Mean	%	Mean	%	Mean	%	Mean	%	Mean	%
January	1.0	40	–	–	2.0	11	1.4	68	1.0	20
February	1.2	65	1.0	54	2.2	47	2.1	86	1.4	85
March	2.1	77	–	–	2.7	83	2.7	73	2.6	54
April	3.6	100	–	–	3.1	94	3.1	100	4.0	75
May	3.6	100	1.9	62	3.2	92	3.3	89	3.5	59
June	3.2	100	–	–	2.9	81	3.0	80	3.1	75
July	2.8	62	–	–	2.6	81	3.0	62	3.5	83
August	1.0	59	–	–	2.3	58	2.6	78	2.9	53
September	–	0	–	–	2.0	44	2.6	22	3.5	17
October	–	0	–	–	2.0	27	–	0	–	0
November	–	0	–	–	1.8	11	–	0	–	0
December	–	0	–	–	1.8	4	–	0	–	0

n, number of does examined; *, only healthy animals included in sample.

Cambridgeshire, 37% of pregnancies showed pre-implantation losses and 14% of litters were lost post-implantation [226]. Gestation lasts 37–44 days [56], but due to superfetation, intervals between successive births can be shorter [63]. Conception and birth dates can be estimated from size and weight of fetuses [56].

Productivity: Mating and breeding take place almost all year round [144, 219] (Fig 6.12). Average annual production of young per doe is 4–12 in Europe [54, 143, 300]. Does produce 1–4 litters each year in Sweden and Denmark, but 3 most common [125, 143]. Populations may be limited by recruitment [109], which in turn may be limited by food resources [143, 249].

In GB about 4% [219] and in France about 14% [47] of does breed in their year of birth. Most adult females reproduce each year (95% in France [47], 80% in Denmark [143]), but % females pregnant and litter size vary seasonally (Table 6.4) and between years. Females reproducing in their year of birth average fewer and smaller litters than older females [47].

Onset of breeding controlled by photoperiod [244], varies little between individuals. Breeding success related to weather, breeding season extended in mild autumns [168]. Litter size related to ambient temperature [115, 170] and number of leverets born negatively related to adult female density [125].

Development of leverets: Precocial: well furred, eyes open, mobile, weigh 100 g at birth (Netherlands, 101 g, range 80–130 g; Poland, 107 g, range 65–155 g; USSR, 105 g, range 80–140 g [56]; Austria, 121 g in captivity [141]). Soon after giving birth, does move 200–300 m away from leverets, thereafter visit them only to suckle. Leverets move a few metres away from each other in the next few days, eventually disperse to c.100 m from their birthplace; meet up about 30 min after sunset, spend about 10 min in locomotor play, then gather at their birthplace where, without moving except to groom themselves and each other, await the doe. Leverets approach the doe when she arrives to suckle them about 50 min after sunset,

Table 6.5 Estimated density of brown hares (numbers /ha)

Location	Habitat	Harvesting?	Density (ha^{-1})	Method	No. of years	Source
Oxfordshire	Agricultural land	No	0.2–1.0[s]	Spotlight count	3	[43]
East Anglia	Conifer plantation	No	0.1	Faecal pellet count	2	[447]
Mid-Ulster	Agricultural land	No	0.03	Point transect spotlight count	1	[324]
France	Agricultural land	No	0.4–0.7	Point transect spotlight count	5	[47]
France	Agricultural land	Yes	0.15	Point transect spotlight count	5	[47]
N France	Arable land	Yes	0.1–0.2[s]	Point transect spotlight count and total catch	?	[325]
Poland land	Agricultural land	Yes	0.08–0.28[a]	Strip transect count	4	[293]
N Italy	Poplar plantation	No	0.53[s], 0.38[a]	Total catch	7	[261]
N Italy	Agricultural land	No	0.11[s], ca. 0.3[a]	Total catch	21	[260]
Slovakia	Agricultural land before modification	Yes	0.4[s]	?	4	[349]
Slovakia	Agricultural land after modification	Yes	0.7[s]	?	44	[349]
Illumo Island, Denmark	Agricultural land	No	3.4	Total catch	–	[2]
New Zealand	Sub alpine grassland	?	2–3	?	?	[297]
Australia	?	?	0.02–0.06	Estimate		[199]

s = spring, **a** = autumn.

sometimes approach other passing adults [173]. If birthplace no longer suitable, doe and leverets meet up to 100 m away [58]. Nursing takes 1–5 min, once every 24 h. If disturbed during suckling, doe leads leverets away with her tail held up. Doe removes urine from leverets, possibly to reduce the risk of predation. After suckling, leverets again disperse [53, 173].

Leverets spend time exploring their surroundings in 1st 10 days of life, start grazing when 13–17 days old. Lactation continues for

c.35 days (longer, >67 days, for last litter of season) [53], but start taking a little solid food from 2nd week, increases sharply by 5th week, but milk still supplies most energy [141]. Cannot remain in energy balance at temperatures below 8 °C in 1st week, reduce metabolic rate and body temperature; by 2nd week, have grown enough to maintain growth [141]. After 35 days, weaning, can reach 1031 g in captivity [141], but in wild weigh 300 g, after 2 months 700 g, attain adult weight after 6 months [49].

POPULATION

Numbers: Pre-breeding numbers in GB estimated at 1.3–2 million [383] and at 817 520±137 251 (95% confidence limits [189]). Densities (Table 6.5) assessed by total catches [2], line transect counts [189], strip transect counts [301], point transect counts [19, 305, 324], and other methods [214, 447]. Can be counted when animals are inactive during the day, or when they are active at dusk, dawn, or at night (with spotlights [305]).

Fluctuations: Little information on annual fluctuations. Game bag records suggest slow decline in numbers through 1960s–1970s in GB [382], matched in recent decades by declines in many other European countries [355]. Reason(s) for apparent decline not clear; disease, increased predation, or changes in farming methods or shooting effort all suggested [20, 378, 380]; agricultural intensification felt most probable basic cause, but not clear if acting through changes in food, cover, or increased vulnerability to predation [355]. No decline in New Zealand [121]. Recent records from hunting packs suggest that numbers may have stabilised in England since 1983 [12], perhaps increased since late 1990s [379].

Numbers shot in England were high during 1960s, perhaps as consequence of reduced rabbit abundance following 1954 myxomatosis outbreak. Reduced rabbit grazing may have led to habitat change or may be direct interactions between the species [20]. In England, some game bag records show evidence of quasi-cycles with an average period of 8–10 or 11–15 years [376]. More hares shot in warm years than in cooler years [19].

Sex ratio: In embryos, male:female ratio of 1.22:1 [115]. Bucks may also predominate among adults (1.32:1 in a non-harvested island population [2]. Data from harvested populations may be confused by unintentional bias towards hunting does [309].

Age determination: Three methods used: distal end of ulna remains unossified in animals <7 months old, can be used to separate young animals from adults [415]; eye-lens weight can be used to determine the age of animals <454 days old, and allows older animals to be classed as adult [367]; periosteal growth lines on lower mandible are suitable for ageing adults in years [128].

Age structure: About 50% of the autumn population consists of young animals [299], although this varies between populations (32–82% [211]; 60% [415]).

Survival: Adult annual survival varies (0.55 for males, 0.50 for females (a non-harvested population [2, 240]), 0.51 with harvesting, 0.56 without (a declining population, France [241]), 0.51 (Poland and Sweden), 0.42 (Germany [51]), 0.40 (France [299]), 0.34 (the Netherlands [51]). Annual recruitment weak, so population growth highly sensitive to adult mortality [241].

In France, survival between birth and start of shooting season (September–November) is 0.23–0.5 [300]. Yearling survival in a non-harvested population depends on sex, body mass and weather conditions [2, 240]. Survival of leverets born early in the breeding season is very low: only 16% of conceptions in January–April result in a surviving animal the following spring. Leverets conceived at end of breeding season have much higher chance of survival [219]. 32–53% of hand-reared leverets died within a week of release for restocking [242].

Mean lifespan 2.00–2.92 years [241]. Oldest marked brown hare recaptured in the wild was 12.5 years old, and 5% of recaptured animals were >5.5 years old [310].

MORTALITY

Predation: Main predator in Europe and Australia is red fox *Vulpes vulpes* [199]; may limit population growth and density of brown hares [223, 326, 365]. In England, 80–100% of annual production of leverets taken by red foxes [326]; in Poland, 10% taken in an area of very low red fox density and intensive predator control [311], 18% from an area of lower hare density and higher red fox density [134]. May comprise 30–50% of red fox diet [134, 326]; predation may cause up to 50% of adult hare mortality, predation by foxes increases when small mammals are scarce in Poland [134]. Also taken by brown bears *Ursus arctos*, stoats *Mustela erminea*, mink *Mustela vison*, polecats *Mustela putorius*, wolverines *Gulo gulo*, lynxes *Lynx lynx*, badgers *Meles meles*, goshawks *Accipiter gentilis*, golden eagles *Aquila chrysaetos* and eagle owls *Bubo bubo* [199, 222].

Disease: Coccidiosis (caused by protozoan *Eimeria* sp.) particularly common in young animals, and the most common cause of death in the British Isles; reaches seasonal peak in autumn, when populations are high and humid conditions favour transmission [304, 435]. Leporine dysautonomia (caused by an unknown toxin, damaging the nervous system) has replaced pseudotuberculosis as 2nd most common cause of death in the British Isles [137, 435].

Pseudotuberculosis (caused by bacterium *Yersinia pseudotuberculosis*) common in winter, W and NW France, affects over 20% of animals found dead [304]; in Austria, *Y. pseudotuberculosis* isolated from only 2 of 1800 animals examined [291]; in Denmark, proportion of hares infected is positively correlated with density [321]. Tuberculosis *Mycobacterium bovis* reported from one brown hare, New Zealand [74].

EBHS, a calcivirus infection, affects mainly adult animals in autumn [104]. Causes death 5–24 h after first symptoms [357], which include blood in body cavity, congestion of the liver, spleen and kidneys, and loss of balance [65]. The disease was identified in 48% of European hares found dead in Sweden [139], is common in Germany [108] and elsewhere in Europe. In Croatia in 1986, 30 000 animals are estimated to have died of EBHS [357].

Amyloidosis with associated inflammatory lesions may cause death in wild European hares [436].

PARASITES AND PATHOGENS
Ectoparasites: Rabbit fleas *Spilopsyllus cuniculi,* ticks *Ixodes ricinus* and *Dermacentor reficulatus*, lice *Haemodipsus lyriocephalus* and *H. setonii*, mites *Listrophorus gibbus*, and *Dermanyssus* sp. occur [50, 254, 304].

Helminths: 95% of brown hares shot in Poland were infected with helminths. Trematode *Fasciola hepatica* found in liver [91]. Nematode *Graphidium strigosum* common in stomach [197], occurs in brown hares only where sympatric with its primary host, the rabbit [52]. Nematodes *Trichuris sylvilagi* and *Trichostrongylus retortaeformis* and cestodes *Andrya rhopalocephala, Mosgovoyia pectinata* and *Cittattonia pectinata* found in intestine [91, 197, 255].

Others: Infections from bacteria *Pasteurella* sp., *Leptospira interrogans* and *Francisella tularensis* recorded [151, 304]. 60% of brown hares in the Netherlands infected with bacterium *Treponema pallidum*, which causes syphilis [233]. Protozoan *Pneumocystis carinii* found in lungs of young animals [313]. Taphylococcosis and toxoplasmosis occur in adults [321].

RELATIONS WITH HUMANS
An important game animal; >5 million harvested annually in Europe [66].

In GB, driven shoots mostly confined to areas with red fox control and high brown hare density (0.1–0.4/ha), usually in February; can reduce populations by 30–70% [362]. Estimated that 390 000 shot each year in GB, and *c.*137 000 export licences issued [383]. No close season, but cannot legally be sold 1 March–31 July. Are also hunted with beagles and harriers, coursed with greyhounds or other dogs, but these methods reduce populations by <7%. Also killed by poaching [362], agricultural machines [242] and cars [55]; effects on populations unknown. Heavy metals, organochlorines, and polychlorinated biphenyls found in brown hares [61, 263].

Can be a significant pest on sugar beet, horticultural crops and plantations of young trees or shrubs, and has been persecuted as a pest of pasture in Australia [199].

Because of suspected decline in GB, has been included in UK Biodiversity Action Plan [11]; states that requirements of brown hares should be considered in reviews of habitat management schemes, and that legislation on shooting and selling be reviewed. Target is to maintain range, expand populations, double spring numbers by 2010.

PRINCIPAL AUTHOR
N. Jennings.

LITERATURE
Monographs by Péroux [304 and Zorner [452]; a popular account by Tapper [377].

Mountain hare/Irish hare *Lepus timidus*
Lepus timidus Linnaeus, 1758; Uppsala, Sweden.
Lepus timidus scoticus, Hilzheimer, 1906; Northern Scotland, Scotland.
Lepus timidus hibernicus, Bell, 1837; Ireland.
Blue hare; varying hare; variable hare; Arctic hare; white hare; *maigheach-gheal* (Scottish Gaelic); *giorria* (Irish Gaelic).

Male – buck, jack; female – doe, jill; young – leveret

RECOGNITION
Whole animal: In summer pelage, distinguishable from brown hare by smaller size, shorter ears, greyer coat (except in Ireland) without black grizzling, and all-white tail (Plate 4). Coat of leverets during 1st autumn is dark grey/brown. In winter, mostly white or in transitional pelage (except in Ireland).

Skulls and teeth: Skulls of both British hares distinguished from rabbit by wider posterior nasal opening and fusion of interparietal to supraoccipital bone (Fig. 6.1). In mountain hare, root of upper incisor extends behind suture with premaxilla into maxilla (confined to premaxilla in brown hare) (Fig. 6.6).

FIELD SIGNS

Tracks and trails: Communally used trails through long vegetation most conspicuous on moorland, usually orientated up and down hill; made and maintained by hares biting off vegetation. Sheep and cattle tracks, paths, and roads leading in required directions also commonly used. Footprints resemble those of brown hare, long hindfeet placed ahead of forefeet. Hindfeet, being heavily furred, produce a broader print than brown hare's, particularly in snow.

Faeces: Often fibrous, varying in colour from brown through grey-green to green-yellow; 0.5–1.3 cm in diameter, not distinguishable from brown hare's, and sometimes not from rabbit's, although rabbit faeces are generally smaller, darker, sometimes smeared black and clumped. Leveret faeces usually yellow/green, small, 0.3–0.8 cm. Faeces mostly deposited at random while feeding, may be clumped at conspicuous landmarks, such as isolated boulders, where hares pause during travel.

Forms: Forms are well-marked depressions, commonly in old heather, rushes, hedgerows (in Ireland) or other dense vegetation. Provide concealment from above, often hiding 80–90% of the sitting hare. Wind speed within form reduced by about 90% compared with 1 m above [384]. Forms unlined, vegetation maintained in topiarised state over many years [116]; in open habitats, generally placed to ensure excellent view of surrounding landscape. In woodland, forms generally found beneath piles of brash or collapsed tree trunks. During winter snow-lie, uses shallow scrapes in snow or lies up among boulders. Occasionally, especially leverets, uses holes, abandoned dens or burrows in peat.

DESCRIPTION

Sexes: Alike, but male has broader, squarer head. Ears are shorter and narrower than brown hare's with a black tip 30 mm long on the exterior surface and *c*.5 mm long on the interior. Dark brown iris of leverets turn a prominent yellowish in adults. Hindfeet are long with hairy soles and widely spreading toes.

Pelage: Wide variation in colour. In Scotland, winter pelage mostly white, but wide variation from pure white through to patchy brown, especially on head and back (Fig 6.13). In summer–autumn, generally dusky brown with grey-blue underfur showing through ('blue hare'), particularly on flanks, can vary from sandy-brown through light to dark grey-brown. Irish hares rarely completely change colour in winter, though

Fig. 6.13 Mountain hare in winter coat, Peak District. There is much individual and annual variation in whiteness; patches of grey or brown fur often remain on the head and along the back *(photo D.W. Yalden)*.

usually white on feet, belly. In summer, are more reddish-brown than Scottish race, closer to brown hare, but without the black grizzling (Plate 4).

Pelage has 3 main constituents; underfur *c*.15 mm long, grey proximally, brown towards the top; pile hair *c*.25 mm, dark grey with a brown subterminal band 2–4 mm wide and a black tip; and guard hairs, *c*.40 mm, which protrude sparsely through the pile hair, particularly on rump [156]. Marked differences in overall colouring are due to variation in colour and width of subterminal bands of pile hair. Underside grey, demarcation line indistinct. Head, mane on chest and upper surfaces of feet brown, although white hairs from winter coat persist on hindfeet to June or beyond [156]. Leverets darker throughout. Colour variants include albino, black (principally a population in Caithness) and pale sandy coloured.

Moult: Two annual moults; brown to white or grey-white (mid October–January, mostly completed by December) and white to brown (mid February–late May, although traces of summer coat usually visible in field in March) [117]. For *L. timidus*, there are 2 morphs of winter coat: white = W (dominant) and blue = w [30]. In blue morphs, which include those in Scotland, pelage in winter rarely reaches pure white. Moult to winter pelage begins on feet, progresses upwards

Table 6.6 Body mass of adult mountain hares in NE Scotland, Ireland, Swedish islands and mainland Norway

	Males		Females		Source
	Mean (kg)	n	Mean (kg)	n	
NE Scotland	2.6	338	2.9	428	[116]
Ireland	3.2	9	3.6	5	[442]
Sweden (islands)	2.7		3.1		[6]
Norway	2.9–3.7 (range, both sexes)		2.9–3.7 (range, both sexes)		[414]

and forwards to head; spring moult in reverse order [119]. Winter moult initiated by shorter day length, so timing constant, but progress related to air temperature, speed variable [198, 418]. At high altitudes, with greater snow-lie, turn white earlier and more completely than at lower altitudes, late young may not acquire a full winter coat [418]. Moult faster in warm than cold spring, females more rapidly than males [119, 418]. Conflicting evidence that dominant males may moult earlier [119, 413]. Irish hares may moult to a piebald coat in winter or may not whiten at all, although instances of almost total whitening are known [23, 122].

Scent glands: As in brown hare, inguinal glands lie in a pouch either side of anus, produce a yellow-orange secretion with a musky smell, which forms visible brown crystals adhering to fur. Submandibular glands may be used for scent-marking, occasionally seen rubbing chin on twig.

Chromosomes: $2n = 48$ [140], as in all *Lepus*.

RELATIONSHIPS

Lepus timidus probably conspecific with Arctic hare *L. arcticus* and Alaskan *L. othus* [75, 77]; close phylogenetic relationship confirmed using mtDNA analysis [417]. Species and subspecies have been distinguished on basis of cranial morphometric measurements [10, 75], but classification on this basis, or distinction of subspecies on the basis of pelage characteristics, must be considered doubtful given the wide variability within as well as between populations. Genetic analysis using mtDNA suggests that closer to S European *Lepus* (*L. granatensis, L. corsicanus*) than *L. europaeus* [3, 312]. *L. t. hibernicus* differs genetically from other *L. timidus*, including *L. t. scoticus*, by about 4% (*L. timidus* differs from *L. europaeus* by about 9%); has many genetic variants found in no other *L. timidus*, implying long isolation, perhaps meriting specific status [181].

In Europe, predominantly a species of mixed forest; in Scotland, traditionally associated with open heather moorlands; in Ireland, occupies agricultural land and moorland at all altitudes. By contrast, brown hares are associated with arable areas, particularly where cereal cropping predominates, and rabbits are associated with areas of short grass, dry heaths, machairs and closely-grazed agricultural pastures.

Mountain hare and brown hare remain separate despite the many opportunities to hybridise where their ranges overlap. In captivity, partially fertile hybrids of intermediate form can be created [346]. Hybridisation demonstrated in Sweden [395], with transfer of mtDNA from maternal *L. timidus* to *L. europaeus* [394]. In Switzerland, apparently stable hybridisation, in both directions, about 14% of *L. timidus* are hybrids

Table 6.7 Measurements of mountain hares [23]

	Scotland (n = 45)		Ireland (n = 27)	
	Mean	Range	Mean	Range
Head and body (mm)	502	457–545	545	521–559
Tail (without hairs) (mm)	60	43–80	74	65–83
Hindfeet (with claws) (mm)	142	127–155	156	149–168
Ear (to notch) (mm)	70	63–80	75	69–81

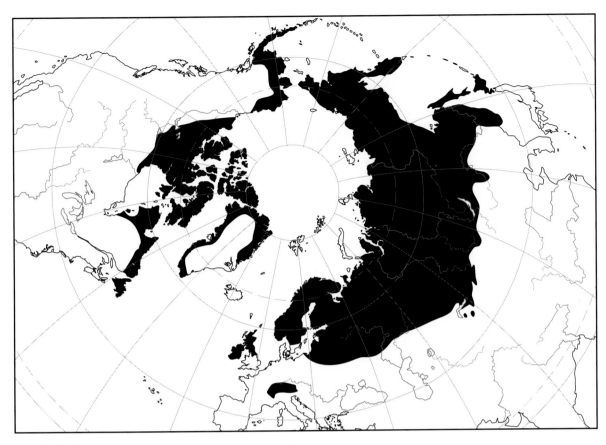

Fig. 6.14 Mountain hare *Lepus timidus*: world distribution.

[369]; hybridisation suspected, but rare, in Scotland [15]. Although no longer present in Iberia, mountain hare mtDNA (relict of Late Glacial range) persists in 3 other hare species including *L. europeaus*. [259]; similar report of *L. timidus* mtDNA in Danish *L. europaeus* [124].

MEASUREMENTS
See Tables 6.6, 6.7

Dimorphic, like all other Leporidae; adult female *c.*10% heavier than adult male [116, 160], especially March–June when pregnant. Smaller in Scotland than in Ireland or mainland Scandinavia, although similar to hares on Swedish coastal islands. Leverets separable from adults on size until *c.*4 months. Beyond *c.*4 months, palpation of head of tibia enables separation of <10-month-old leverets from adults by presence of epiphyseal notch [414]. Dried eye-lens weight also separates leverets from adults [117, 414] and cohorts identifiable by counting periosteal growth lines in the mandible [190]. Highest % body fat in January, before onset of reproductive season, twice that in August [411]. Body condition affects number of young weaned [8].

DISTRIBUTION
Broad circumpolar distribution in tundra, taiga

and boreal forest habitats. An isolated population remains in the Alps (Fig. 6.14). In the British Isles, indigenous in the Highlands of Scotland and

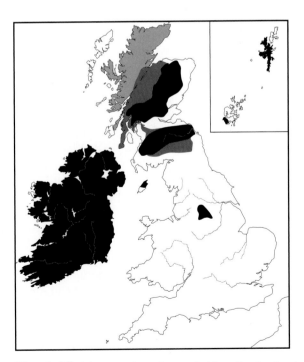

Fig. 6.15 Mountain hare *Lepus timidus*: distribution in the British Isles.

throughout Ireland. Occurs at all altitudes, but numerically concentrated in NE Scotland above 300 m asl, where strip burning management on grouse moors dominated by *Calluna vulgaris* also favours mountain hares. Patchily distributed and at low densities on moors in W and N Scotland. Occurrence elsewhere, including S Scotland, Peak District, island populations on Shetland, Hoy (Orkney), Lewis, Harris, Skye, Raasay, Scalpay and Jura and Isle of Man are all due to introductions, mainly in the 19th century (Fig 6.15). Former populations of N Wales, Eigg and Islay now extinct. Range in Peak District increased from 1971 to 1984 [448, 449], and further to 2001 [237]. Irish hares introduced into SW Scotland in about 1923 and Scottish hares to Ireland (Londonderry) in the 19th century [22], and the Isle of Man in 1910 [111]; these populations still extant. Present on Irish islands of Rathlin (Co. Antrim), Mutton (Co. Clare), Calf (Co. Cork), Magee (Co. Down), N Bull and Lambay (Co. Dublin), Abbey and Valencia (Co. Kerry), Achill and Clare (Co. Mayo).

HISTORY

Suggested from molecular evidence that originated about 3 mya, when ancestral hare immigrated from N America into Eurasia [327]. Earliest fossil *Lepus* in Europe from early middle Pleistocene, definite *L. timidus* from last interglacial.

Earliest record in GB, from S Derbyshire, dated to 12 600–12 950 bp. However, during maximum of Devensian Glaciation, 25 000–15 000 bp, Arctic fox and lemmings certainly present, suspected that mountain hares also present then [450]. Assumed that once widespread, uncertain whether range reduced by spread of woodland, Mesolithic, or by brown hare, later than Iron Age.

In Ireland, endemic *L. t. hibernicus* present from late Pleistocene, fossils dated to 28 240 bp and 12 190 bp [446]; must have survived through Nahanagan cold period after colonising Ireland much earlier in Pleistocene, or in Woodgrange Interstadial, while sea levels still low [450]. Genetic evidence suggests that been present since last interglacial, so survived glacial maximum as well as Nahanagan stage [181]. Is genetically very variable, implying large, diverse population throughout last glaciation, but also very distinctive, and not close genetically to Scottish population [142, 181]. Earliest mention is in *De mirabilibus sacræ scripturæ*, written about 650 AD by the Irish ecclesiastic Augustin [23].

HABITAT

Highest densities of hares in Scotland most common on open heather moorland [419, 420]. In such habitats, plant communities containing high proportions of grass species and/or pioneer heather preferred [164]. In more fragmented landscapes, where heather moorland, upland pastures and woodlands form an intimate mosaic, variously prefer grass mires in summer [317], upland pastures or woodlands [185] relative to their availability. Moorland therefore not a prerequisite for their presence. Occupancy of woodlands related to presence of a field layer [185], and moorlands recently planted with native trees not significantly selected [317].

Irish hares known to occupy a wide range of habitats including uplands [416], lowland bogs [419], agricultural grassland [100, 200, 433] and coastal grasslands [443] but avoid intensively farmed areas [103]. Mature silage fields and those containing stock consistently avoided, while crops selected early in growing season and after harvesting [200]. In limited area where brown hares also numerous, habitat selection (improved grassland) and use overlap almost completely [324].

In Peak District, mountain hares occupy ground above 130 m asl, are found on *Calluna–Eriophorum* communities rather than grassland [238, 448]. Similarly, mountain hares occupy ground at higher altitudes on Isle of Man [111].

SOCIAL ORGANISATION AND BEHAVIOUR

Home range: Not defended, consequently not territorial. Home-range size varies according to sex, season, habitat occupied and available green biomass [165, 186, 200, 442] (Table 6.8). Males have larger home ranges than females, and ranges larger in breeding season than non-breeding/winter seasons. Home ranges of adult females in pastoral or wooded habitats smaller than those in moorland, and range size negatively correlated with available green biomass of grass [186]; tiny ranges, 14 ha, for Irish hares on improved grassland [323]. Larger ranges in moorland (Table 6.8) may be a behavioural response to maximise a preferred food resource (grass, see Feeding, below) that is sparsely distributed. Home range comprises a night-feeding area on the lower slopes and a day-resting place uphill and among long vegetation. Tend to move uphill during June–October, distances varying from 200 m to 2.5 km and increases in altitude from 23 m to 370 m [165]. Day and night feeding areas can be separated by as much as 2 km with a difference in altitude of up to 200 m.

Scent-marking: Keen sense of smell [116]. Nostrils have tactile organs similar to those of rabbits [169]. Test and mark prominent rocks and vegetation.

Table 6.8 Home-range size (ha) of Scottish and Irish mountain hares occupying a variety of habitats. Variation between studies likely due to field and analytical methodologies

	Males	**Females**	**Source**
Moorland	113	89	[165]
Mixed upland landscape			[185]
Moorland		17	
Forestry plantation		10	
Upland pasture		7	
Upland landscape: moorland with new native plantation and grass-mire	21	15	[317]
Saltmarsh/dune	46	21	[442]
Farmland	29	12	[200]
Farmland, active	29	21	[323]

Vocalisations: A high-pitched, penetrating scream, only heard when animal in distress.

Agonistic behaviour: See [116, 165, 413]. Females dominate males in all seasons. During early spring, males follow females while feeding. If male approaches too closely, female first adopts threatening posture, and eventually may attack vigorously with forefeet. Dominant males may approach more females than do subdominants; latter often chased away. Fights between males usually involve hares of similar rank. Leverets are chased away by adults of both sexes, eventually succeed in feeding with groups of adult hares. If disturbed, leverets seek cover nearby or crouch, while adults flee.

Activity: Active predominantly at night, but much of their behaviour can be watched at dawn and dusk, particularly during summer. Often graze in groups; group size varies according to season but not time of day [200]. Groups >100 have been recorded on Irish airports [109] but this is exceptional; occasionally up to 70 hares observed at perimeter of snowfields and on sheltered slopes during strong winds with drifting snow.

Dispersal and migration: Little information on adults or leverets available from radio-tracking and capture–mark–recapture studies; 5 juveniles had home ranges encompassing area of birth, furthest adult move only 5 km [117].

Refection: All hares, like rabbits, void 2 types of pellets, the normal hard pellets and soft, unformed mucosal pellets picked up directly from the anus and ingested. Soft pellets are derived from the emptying of the deeper part of the caecum and their formation can be quick [107, 170]. Regardless of season, soft faeces generally voided during daylight, when hares inactive, commencing with sunrise, start of feeding rhythm [116, 157, 298]. Soft faeces contain more water, more protein and less fibre than hard pellets [298], process *per se* important for hare's nitrogen balance [180]. Hares produce 33–450 (mean 208) dry pellets per day, predominantly at night when feeding [116].

FEEDING

Diet composition of mountain hares varies according to season, physiological status and habitat occupied [102, 116, 157, 184, 187, 195, 373, 442].

In Scotland, heather *Calluna vulgaris* is the main food (36–90%) (Fig. 6.16), the remainder of the diet comprising mainly grasses (8–56%) and small components of rush and sedge species (0–11%), *Vaccinium myrtillus* (0–9%), *Eriophorum* spp. (0–35%) and other unidentified dicotyledons (1–7%) [116, 157, 195]. Grasses include *Deschampsia flexuosa, D. caespitosa, Nardus stricta* and *Festuca* and *Agrostis* spp. Also eats bark and twigs of gorse, willow, rowan, juniper and birch, especially in winter [318]. Seasonal shift in diet, from mainly heather in winter to mainly grasses during summer [116, 157, 187, 195, 319]. Diet composition depends on habitat. Though *Calluna* dominant component on moorland, especially in winter, in other habitats, where *Calluna* is less prevalent or even absent, grasses, rushes and

Fig. 6.16 The sharp incisors of hares enable them to trim shrubs such as heather *Calluna* very tightly, producing a topiary effect. Note thin scatter of droppings in foreground *(photo D.W. Yalden)*.

sedges form most of diet; especially true in Ireland [102, 184, 366, 373, 442]. Graminoids are heavily selected in relation to their availability [187].

During summer, reproductively active females and leverets may avoid eating plants such as heather which contain high concentrations of digestion-reducing/inhibiting plant phenolics, in favour of graminoids [195, 319]. Detailed studies of diet selection relative to availability demonstrate that hares are actually reluctant browsers, avoiding heather and preferring grasses, regardless of habitat or season [187].

Heavy grazing by mountain hares over 30 years maintained a *Callunetum* in a condition resembling pioneer heather [429]. On a smaller scale, continual heavy grazing produces conspicuous short, lawn-like bushes of heather (Fig. 6.16); shoots maintain a juvenile appearance and contain more nitrogen and phosphorus than the surrounding heather [270].

BREEDING

Strongly seasonal, mating January–June, gestation concurrent with lactation, females producing several litters of 1–4 offspring, usually March–August. In Ireland, young born as early as January and as late as October [110] (Fig 6.17). No mountain hare is known to have reproduced in its year of birth. Mating seldom observed [116] but groups of several male hares form around an oestrous female, simultaneously chasing and attempting to mount. Females rebuff and box males, one or more of which will eventually successfully copulate. Male members of the group do not normally fight one another during the chases but may attempt to defend the female by chasing away other males [1, 116].

Males: During summer of birth, testes of young males fail to develop. Thereafter, all males show strong seasonal cycle of testis and epididymal mass; begin to increase December, reach peak February–May, regress to minimum July–November, when they are abdominal.

Females: Gestation 50 days, ovulation induced by mating; females re-enter oestrus within 6–7 h postpartum [171]. In Scotland, season of births

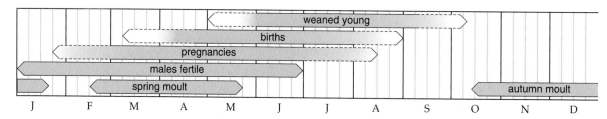

Fig. 6.17 Mountain hare: annual cycle for Scottish hares [117].

226

lasts mid March–mid August [116, 159, 191], corresponding to matings from late January–early/mid June [116, 191] (Fig. 6.17). These are extreme dates, vary between years. Overall season controlled via photoperiod which acts via secretion of melatonin from the pineal organ [194], but much variability within populations and between years [161] remains due to environmental variation [8, 116].

Ovaries smaller, appear more homogeneous, during non-reproductive period, September–January or February. Enlarge from about 17 × 6 mm in non-pregnant does to about 20 × 10 mm during pregnancy [116]; slightly larger in adults than young females. Before ovulation, follicles develop from <1 mm in diameter to 5 mm prior to rupture. During pregnancy, corpora lutea increase in size, appear as pink or red globular masses occupying most of volume of ovaries. Degenerate to yellowish, often streaky masses, forming brown persistent 'scars'.

Productivity: In Scotland, number of litters per doe per year theoretically 4 [161], calculated as 3.7 [116]. In a smaller, detailed study, only 48% of 27 females produced as many as 3 litters [193]. Prenatal mortality higher in young females breeding for 1st time, and in 1st litter in each year in all females; declines in later litters. Successful production of an early litter results in fewer offspring in final litter [193]. Early litters smaller than later ones, typically increasing from 1 born per fertile female early in the breeding season, to 2–3 offspring in later litters [116, 193]. Total productivity, offspring born per female per year, ranges from 4.3 to 6.3 [116, 161, 193], but variable between years, as is their survival.

Fig. 6.18 Leverets are precocial, left hidden by their mothers. Those of mountain hares (being grey) look even more like young rabbits than do brown hares; but a young rabbit this size would have run away *(photo D. Whiteley).*

Development of young: Born fully furred, eyes open, weighing *c*.90–100 g [116, 191]. Period between birth and weaning poorly known, but like other hare species, presumably receive little maternal care other than suckling visits (Fig. 6.18). Mammary tissue declines after *c.* 4 weeks, i.e. halfway through subsequent pregnancy, although for final litter lactation is extended [116]. Growth rate of wild leverets, NE Scotland, 14 or 18 g/day [160, 191], until reaching 1.5 kg, when growth rate slows. Surviving early-born leverets much larger than late-born leverets, due to longer growth period [191].

POPULATION

In Scotland, estimated at 300 000–360 000 [147], but considered to be declining [24]. In N Ireland, varies between 8500–21 000 [100, 101, 103] and maximum of 69 700–97 000 [398]. Large variation may reflect different survey techniques and/or large fluctuations in population numbers. In England, Peak District population was estimated at 500 [147], improved sampling and genuine increase suggest nearer 10 000 [238].

Density: Highest densities, Scotland, 200/km^2, more usually 30–69/km^2, occur in E on heather moors overlying base-rich rocks, lowest densities (2–5/km^2) occur in W on low-lying moors over poor acidic rocks [419, 420]. Densities of Irish hares commonly vary from 5 to 19/km^2 [433, 442], depending on habitat, although higher densities, 25–129/km^2, recorded [200]. In N Ireland, densities apparently lower, from 0.2/km^2 in intensively farmed areas to 1.0/km^2 in unimproved farmland [100, 103] though night-time road transects give higher densities, from 2.13/km^2 [290] to 5.87/km^2 [398]. In Peak District, late winter densities estimated from line transects at 60/km^2 (heather), 52/km^2 (cotton-grass), 28/km^2 (acid grassland) [238, 430].

In Scandinavia, mainland densities *c*.3/km^2 [221], but on heather-dominated, predator-free coastal islands off Sweden, reach unusually high densities of 400/km^2 [7].

Population fluctuations: Mountain hare populations in Scotland show unstable population dynamics [116, 420]. Time series of game bag data suggest 'weak' cyclicity in *c.* ½ of populations studied, with periodicity of cycles 9.5 years [376] or varying from 5 to 15 years [286]. Negative relationships between intensities of infection with nematode *Trichostrongylus retortaeformis* and hare fecundity [287] or condition [288, 289] have potential to destabilise population dynamics, but alternative hypotheses such as nutritional or predator limitation not tested. In Scandinavian forests, populations show 3–4-year fluctuations [5, 203], suspected to be due to predators switching to hares from depleting supply of voles [4, 179, 243]. On Swedish coastal islands, population crashes may be due to predation [9], parasites, starvation, or weather [7]. Limited evidence for fluctuations in Irish populations [398].

MORTALITY

In 1st year, main periods of natural leveret mortality, due to all causes, were August–November and January–April [116, 192]. Deaths attributed to disease or starvation outweighed predation on a Scottish grouse moor, mostly of smaller leverets [192]. Main period of adult mortality, January–May [116, 192], primarily due to shooting by gamekeepers or organised shoots in winter months. Predation by wildcats, dogs, stoats and golden eagles relatively common, but main predators in Scotland and Ireland are foxes. Other recorded predators include sea eagles and hen harriers, and buzzards which take leverets [116, 422].

PARASITES

Ectoparasites: Include rabbit flea *Spilopsyllus cuniculi*, sheep tick *Ixodes ricinus*, sucking louse *Haemodipsus leporis* and hair mite *Listrophorus gibbosus* [254].

Endoparasites: Include 5 species of helminth (Table 6.9). No lungworms found in 193 carcasses examined [38]. Adult mountain hares from woodland have intensities of infection of *Trichostrongylus retortaeformis* 4 times higher than hares from moorlands [183]. Coccidia *Eimeria* spp. occurred in 93% of mountain hares, and tapeworms *Cittotaenia* spp. in 29% [197].

Others: Yersiniosis *Yersinia pseudotuberculosis*

detected in mountain hare [236] and myxomatosis found sporadically in Irish hares [95].

RELATIONS WITH HUMANS

Historically considered as small game, with little commercial value as a source of skins, meat, or shooting revenue, hence no systematic management. Large numbers shot during organised shoots, usually in winter, are becoming increasingly commercialised for sporting revenue. Most carcasses exported. Still extensively coursed in Ireland [323]. Where local densities are high, can damage agricultural crops [116] and have serious impact on native and non-native tree establishment [318]; at moderate densities, trees unaffected [320].

Listed in Annexe V of the EC 1992 Habitats Directive (EC 92/43/EEC) as a species of 'community interest whose taking in the wild may be subject to management measures'. Effectively, this prohibits or restricts certain methods of capture, such as unselective live-trapping or night shooting (see Chapter 4). Now absent from several areas of W Scotland where formerly abundant, due to afforestation of heather moors, or excessive grazing of heather. Current threat to local populations posed by eradication by shooting, because considered a possible reservoir of louping ill, a tick-borne viral disease affecting red grouse [201, 215]. The Irish hare also receives protection under various provisions of the Irish Wildlife Act 1976 and the Wildlife (Amendment) Act 2000. Similar legislation in N Ireland led to introduction of Special Protection Order for Irish hares in 2004, and prevents certain activities associated with coursing.

AUTHORS

G.R. Iason, I.A.R. Hulbert, R. Hewson & K. Dingerkus

Table 6.9 Endoparasites in mountain hares (n = 193) collected 1984–1985 in NE Scotland [38]

Species	Incidence	Mean intensity of infection	Maximum intensity of of infection
	(%)	(no./hare)	(no./hare)
Trichostrongylus retortaeformis	88.1	3639	25 000
Trichostrongylus axei	8.3	236	750
Passalurus ambiguus	0.5	20	20
Mosgovoyia pectinata	13.5	13	107
Paranoplocephala wimerosa	1.0	1	1

REFERENCES

1   Author's data.

2   Abildgard, F. *et al.* (1972) The hare population (*Lepus europaeus* Pallas) of Illumø Island, Denmark. A report on the analysis of the data from 1957–1970. *Danish Review of Game Biology*, **6**, 1–32.

3   Alves, P.C. *et al.* (2003) Ancient introgression of *Lepus timidus* mtDNA into *L. granatensis* and *L. europaeus* in the Iberian Peninsula. *Molecular Phylogenetics and Evolution*, **27**, 70–80.

4   Angelstam, P.E. *et al.* (1984) Role of predation in short-term fluctuations of some birds and mammals in Fennoscandia. *Oecologia*, **62**, 199–208.

5   Angelstam, P. *et al.* (1985) Synchronous short-term population fluctuations of some birds and mammals in Fennoscandia – occurrence and distribution. *Holarctic Ecology*, **8**, 285–298.

6   Angerbjörn, A. (1981) Winter food as a limiting factor of dense mountain hare populations on islands, a comparative study, pp. 529–535 in Myers, K. & MacInnes, C.D. (eds.) *Proceedings of the World Lagomorph Conference, University of Guelph, Ontario.* IUCN, Gland.

7   Angerbjörn, A. (1983) Proximate causes of mountain hare population crashes: a review. *Finnish Game Research*, **41**, 29–38.

8   Angerbjörn, A. (1986) Reproduction of mountain hares (*Lepus timidus*) in relation to density and physical condition. *Journal of Zoology*, **208**, 559–568.

9   Angerbjörn, A. (1989) Mountain hare populations on islands: effects of predation by red fox. *Oecologia*, **81**, 335–340.

10 Angerbjörn, A. & Flux, J.E.C. (1995) *Lepus timidus. Mammalian Species*, **495**, 1–11.

11 Anonymous (1995) *Biodiversity: the UK action plan.* HMSO, London.

12 Anonymous (1999) Lowland research. *Game Conservancy Review*, **30**, 74–81.

13 Austin, G.E. & Houston, D.C. (1997) The breeding performance of the buzzard *Buteo buteo* in Argyll, Scotland and a comparison with other areas in Britain. *Bird Study*, **44**, 146–154.

14 Bailey, J.R. *et al.* (2002) Wild rabbits – a novel vector for vero cytotoxigenic *Escherichia coli* (VTEC) 0157. *Communicable Disease and Public Health*, **5**, 74–75.

15 Ballhary, E. *et al.* (1994) *Hybridisation in British mammals.* Joint Nature Conservation Committee Report **154**, 1–42. JNCC, Peterborough.

16 Banks, P. (2000) Can foxes regulate rabbit populations? *Journal of Wildlife Management*, **64**, 401–406.

17 Banks, P. *et al.* (1998) Ecological costs of feral predator control: foxes and rabbits. *Journal of Wildlife Management*, **62**, 766–772.

18 Banks, P. *et al.* (1999) Behavioural, morphological and dietary response of rabbits to predation risk from foxes. *Oikos*, **85**, 247–256.

19 Barnes, R.F.W. & Tapper, S.C. (1985) A method for counting hares by spotlight. *Journal of Zoology*, **206**, 273–276.

20 Barnes, R.F.W. & Tapper, S.C. (1986) Consequences of the myxomatosis epidemic in Britain's rabbit (*Oryctolagus cuniculus* L.) population on the numbers of brown hares (*Lepus europaeus* Pallas). *Mammal Review*, **16**, 111–116.

21 Barnes, R.F.W. *et al.* (1983) Use of pastures by brown hares. *Journal of Applied Ecology*, **20**, 179–185.

22 Barrett-Hamilton, G.E.H. (1894) Notes on the introduction of the brown hare into Ireland. *Irish Naturalist*, **7**, 69–76.

23 Barrett-Hamilton, G.E.H. & Hinton, M.A.C. (1910) *A history of British mammals.* Gurney & Jackson, London.

24 Battersby, J.E. (2005) *UK Mammals: species, status and population trends* JNCC/Tracking Mammals Partnership, Peterborough.

25 Bell, A.C. *et al.* (1998). The effect of rabbit (*Oryctolagus cuniculus*) grazing damage on the growth and yield of winter cereals. *Annals of Applied Biology*, **133**, 431–442.

26 Bell, D.J. (1980) Social olfaction in lagomorphs. *Symposia of the Zoological Society of London*, **45**, 141–164.

27 Bell, D.J. (1985) The rabbits and hares: order Lagomorpha, pp. 507–530 in Brown, R.E. & MacDonald, D.W. (eds.) *Social odours in mammals*, vol. 2. Clarendon Press, Oxford.

28 Bell, D.J. (1986) Social effects on physiology in the European rabbit. *Mammal Review*, **16**, 131–137.

29 Bell, D.J. & Mitchell S. (1984) Effects of female urine on growth and sexual maturation in male rabbits. *Journal of Reproduction and Fertility*, **71**, 155–160.

30 Bergengren, A. (1969) On genetics, evolution and history of distribution of the heath-hare, a distinct population of the arctic hare, *Lepus timidus* L. *Viltrevy*, **6**, 381–460.

31 Bhadresa, R. (1977) Food preferences of rabbits *Oryctolagus cuniculus* at Holkham sand dunes, Norfolk. *Journal of Applied Ecology*, **14**, 287–291.

32 Bininda-Emonds, O.R.P. *et al.* (2007) The delayed rise of present-day mammals. *Nature*, **446**, 507–512.

33 Birks, J. (1999) Polecats are on their way back. *Mammal News*, **119**, 10–11.

34 Boag, B. (1985) The incidence of helminth parasites from the rabbit (*Oryctolagus cuniculus*) in Eastern Scotland. *Journal of Helminthology*, **59**, 61–69.

35 Boag, B. (1988) Observations on the seasonal incidence of myxomatosis and its interactions with helminth parasites in the European rabbit (*Oryctolagus cuniculus*). *Journal of Wildlife Diseases*, **24**, 450–455.

36 Boag, B. (1989) Population dynamics of parasites of the wild rabbit, pp.186–195 in Putman, R.J. (ed.) *Mammals as pests.* Chapman & Hall, London.

37 Boag, B. (1992) Observations on the variation in the sex ratio of wild rabbits (*Oryctolagus cuniculus*) in eastern Scotland. *Journal of Zoology*, **227**, 338–342.

38 Boag, B. & Iason, G.R. (1986) The occurrence and abundance of helminth parasites of the mountain hare *Lepus timidus* (L) and the wild rabbit *Oryctolagus cuniculus* (L.) in Aberdeenshire, Scotland. *Journal of Helminthology*, **60**, 92–98.

39 Boos, M. *et al.* (2005) Body condition assessment and prediction of fasting endurance in wild rabbits (*Oryctolagus cuniculus*). *Wildlife Research*, **32**, 75–83.

40 Boyce, J. (1985) *The defence against predation in the European wild rabbit*, Oryctolagus cuniculus. PhD thesis, University of Aberdeen.

41 Boyd, I.L. (1985) Investment in growth by pregnant wild rabbits: relation to litter size and sex of the offspring. *Journal of Animal Ecology*, **54**, 137–47.

42 Boyd, I.L. (1986) Effects of daylength on the breeding season in male rabbits. *Mammal Review*, **16**, 125–30.

43 Bradshaw, E.L. (1993) *Social and ecological determinants of food availability in the brown hare*, Lepus europaeus *Pallas.* DPhil thesis, University of Oxford.

44 Brambell, F.W.R. (1942) Intra-uterine mortality of the wild rabbit *Oryctolagus cuniculus* (L.). *Proceedings of the Royal Society of London, Series B*, **130**, 462–79.

45 Brambell, F.W.R. (1944) The reproduction of the wild rabbit *Oryctolagus cuniculus* (L.). *Proceedings of the Zoological Society of London*, **114**, 1–45.

46 Bray, G.C. & Bell, D.J. (1984) Physiological correlates of social status in the domestic rabbit, *Oryctolagus cuniculus* L. *Acta Zoologica Fennica*, **172**, 23–24.

47 Bray, Y. (1998) *Vers une meilleure connaissance des flux démographiques chez le lièvre d'Europe* (Lepus europaeus). PhD thesis, University of Bourgogne (in French).

48 Bresiński, W. (1983) The effect of some habitat factors on the spatial distribution of a hare population during

the winter. *Acta Theriologica,* **28**, 435–441.

49 Broekhuizen, S. (1971) Age determination and age composition of hare populations, pp. 477–486 in *Transactions of the X Congress of Game Biologists, Paris.*

50 Broekhuizen, S. (1971) On the occurrence of hare lice, *Haemodipsus* spp. (Anoplura, Hoplopleuridae) on hares, *Lepus europaeus,* in the Netherlands. *Zeitschrift für Parasitenkunde,* **36**, 158–168.

51 Broekhuizen, S. (1979) Survival in adult European hares. *Acta Theriologica,* **24**, 465–473.

52 Broekhuizen, S. & Kemmers, R. (1976) The stomach worm, *Graphidium strigosum* (Dujardin) Railliet & Henry, in the European hare, *Lepus europaeus* Pallas, pp.157–171 in Pielowski, Z. & Pucek, Z. (eds.) *Ecology and management of European hare populations.* Polish Hunting Association, Warsaw.

53 Broekhuizen, S. & Maaskamp, F. (1980) Behaviour of does and leverets of the European hare (*Lepus europaeus*) whilst nursing. *Journal of Zoology,* **191**, 487–501.

54 Broekhuizen, S. & Maaskamp, F. (1981) Annual production of young in European hares (*Lepus europaeus*) in the Netherlands. *Journal of Zoology,* **193**, 499–516.

55 Broekhuizen, S. & Maaskamp, F. (1982) Movement, home range and clustering in the European hare (*Lepus europaeus* Pallas) in the Netherlands. *Zeitschrift für Säugtierkunde,* **47**, 22–32.

56 Broekhuizen, S. & Martinet, L. (1979) Growth of embryos of the European hare (*Lepus europaeus* Pallas). *Zeitschrift für Säugtierkunde,* **44**, 175–179.

57 Broekhuizen, S. & Mulder, J.L. (1983) Differences and similarities in nursing behaviuor of hares and rabbits. *Acta Zoologica Fennica,* **174**, 61–63.

58 Broekhuizen, S. *et al.* (1986) Variation in timing of nursing in the brown hare (*Lepus europaeus*) and the European rabbit (*Oryctolagus cuniculus*). *Mammal Review,* **16**, 139–144.

59 Brown, L.H. & Watson, A. (1964) The golden eagle in relation to its food supply. *Ibis,* **106**, 78–100.

60 Brüll, U. (1976) Nahrungsbiologische Studien am Feldhasen in Schleswig-Holstein. Ein Beitrag zu Asungsverbesserung, pp. 93–99 in Pielowski, Z. & Pucek, Z. (eds.) *Ecology and management of European hare populations.* Polish Hunting Association, Warsaw (in German)

61 Bukovjan, K. *et al.* (1992) Ruckstande bei Hasenwild. Vorkommen von Organochlorverbindungen und poly-chlorierten Biphenylen im Fettgewebe von Feldhasen aus Mittelbohmen. *Fleischwirtschaft,* 72, 339–341 (in German).

62 Bull, P.C. (1958) Incidence of coccidia (Sporozoa) in wild rabbit *Oryctolagus cuniculus* (L.) in Hawke's Bay, New Zealand. *New Zealand Journal of Science,* **1**, 289–329.

63 Caillol, M. *et al.* (1991) Pituitary and ovarian responses to luteinizing-hormone-releasing hormone during pregnancy and after parturition in brown hares (*Lepus europaeus*). *Journal of Reproduction and Fertility,* **91**, 89–97.

64 Caldow, G. *et al.* (1997) *Johne's disease in cattle.* SAC technical note, T467. Scottish Agricultural College, Edinburgh.

65 Capucci, L. *et al.* (1991) Diagnosis of viral haemorrhagic disease of rabbits and the European brown hare syndrome. *Revue Scientifique et Technique, Office Internationale des Epizooties,* **10**, 347–370.

66 Chapman, J.A. & Flux, J.E.C. (eds.) (1990) *Rabbits, hares and pikas: status survey and conservation action plan.* IUCN, Gland.

67 Chapple, P.J. & Lewis, N.D. (1965) Myxomatosis and the rabbit flea. *Nature,* **207**, 388–389.

68 Chapuis, J.L. (1990) Comparison of the diets of two sympatric lagomorphs, *Lepus europaeus* (Pallas) and *Oryctolagus cuniculus* (L.) in an agroecosystem of the Ile-de-France. *Zeitschrift für Säugetierkunde,* **55**, 176–185.

69 Chasey, D. (1994) Possible origins of rabbit haemorrhagic disease in the United Kingdom. *Veterinary Record,* **135**, 496–499.

70 Chasey, D. (1997) Rabbit haemorrhagic disease: the new scourge of *Oryctolagus cuniculus. Laboratory Animals,* **31**, 33–44.

71 Chasey, D. & Trout R.C. (1995) Rabbit haemorrhagic disease in Britain. *Mammalia,* **59**, 599–603.

72 Church B.M. *et al.* (1953) Surveys of rabbit damage to wheat in England and Wales 1950–1952. *Plant Pathology,* **2**, 107–112.

73 Church B.M. *et al.* (1956) Surveys of rabbit damage to winter cereals, 1953–1954. *Plant Pathology,* **5**, 66–69.

74 Cooke, M.M. *et al.* (1993) Tuberculosis in a free-living brown hare (*Lepus europaeus occidentalis*). *New Zealand Veterinary Journal,* **41**, 144–146.

75 Corbet, G.B. (1986) Relationships and origins of the European lagomorphs. *Mammal Review,* **16**, 106–110.

76 Corbet, G.B. (1994) Taxonomy and origins, pp. 1–7 in Thompson, H.V. & King, C.M. (eds.) *The European rabbit. The history and biology of a successful colonizer.* Oxford University Press, Oxford.

77 Corbet, G.B. & Hill, J.E. (1986) *A world list of mammalian species.* British Museum (Natural History), London.

78 Corbett, L. (1978) Current research on wild cats: why have they increased? *Scottish Wildlife,* **14**, 17–21.

79 Cowan, D.P. (1979) *The wild rabbit.* Blandford Press, Dorset.

80 Cowan, D.P. (1984) The use of ferrets *Mustela furo* in the study and management of the European wild rabbit *Oryctolagus cuniculus. Journal of Zoology,* **204**, 570–4.

81 Cowan, D.P. (1985) Coccidiosis in rabbits, pp. 25–27 in Mollison, D. & Bacon, P. (eds.) *Population dynamics and epidemiology of territorial animals: ITE Merlewood research and development paper no.106.* ITE Merlewood, Cumbria.

82 Cowan, D.P. (1987) Aspects of the social organisation of the European wild rabbit O*ryctolagus cuniculus. Ethology,* **75**, 197–210.

83 Cowan, D.P. (1987) Group living in the European rabbit (*Oryctolagus cuniculus*): mutual benefit or resource localisation? *Journal of Animal Ecology,* **56**, 779–795.

84 Cowan, D.P. (1987) Patterns of mortality in a free-living rabbit (*Oryctolagus cuniculus*) population. *Symposia of the Zoological Society of London,* **58**, 59–77.

85 Cowan, D.P. (1991) The availability of burrows in relation to dispersal by the European wild rabbit. *Symposia of the Zoological Society of London,* **63**, 213–230.

86 Cowan, D.P. & Garson, P.J. (1985) Variations in the social structure of rabbit populations: causes and demographic consequences, pp. 537–555 in Sibly, R.M. & Smith, R.H. (eds.) *Behavioural ecology: the ecological consequences of adaptive behaviour.* Blackwell Scientific Publications, Oxford.

87 Cowan, D.P. & Roman, E.A. (1985) On the construction of life tables with special reference to the European wild rabbit O*ryctolagus cuniculus. Journal of Zoology,* **207**, 607–609.

88 Cowan, D.P. *et al.* (1989) Rabbit ranging behaviour and its implications for the management of rabbit populations, pp. 178–185 in Putman, R.J. (ed.) *Mammals as Pests,* Chapman & Hall, London.

89 Crawley, M.J. (1989) Rabbits as pests of winter wheat, pp.168–177 in Putman, R.J. (ed.) *Mammals as pests.* Chapman & Hall, London.

90 Crawley, M.J. (1990) Rabbit grazing, plant competition and seedling recruitment in acid grassland. *Journal of Applied Ecology,* **27**, 803–820.

91 Czaplinska, D. *et al.* (1965) Helminth fauna in the annual cycle. *Acta Theriologica,* **10**, 55–78.

92 Daly, J.C. (1981) Effects of social organisation and environmental diversity on determining the genetic structure of a population of the wild rabbit, *Oryctolagus cuniculus. Evolution,* **35**, 689–706.

93 Davies, P.W. & Davis, P.E. (1973) The ecology and

conservation of the red kite in Wales. *British Birds,* **66**, 183–270.

94 Davis, P.E. & Davis, J.E. (1981) The food of the red kite in Wales. *Bird Study,* **28**, 33–40.

95 Deane, C.D. (1955) Note on myxomatosis in hares. *Bulletin of the Mammal Society of the British Isles,* **3**, 20.

96 Dekker, J.J.A. *et al.* (2006) No effects of dominance rank or sex on spatial behaviour of rabbits. *Lutra,* **49**, 59–66.

97 Dendy, J. *et al.* (2003). Quantifying the costs of crop damage by rabbits, pp. 211–219 in Tattersall, F. & Manly, W. (eds.) *Conservation and conflict: mammals and farming in Britain.* Westbury Press/Linnean Society of London.

98 Dendy, J. *et al.* (2003) The development of a model to assess the effects of rabbit grazing on grass. *Annals of Applied Biology,* **142**, 317–322.

99 Dendy, J. *et al.* (2004) A field trial to assess the effects of rabbit grazing on spring barley. *Annals of Applied Biology,* **145**, 77–80.

100 Dingerkus, S.K. (1997). *The distribution and ecology of the Irish hare* L. t. hibernicus *in Northern Ireland.* PhD thesis, Queen's University of Belfast.

101 Dingerkus, S.K. & Montgomery W.I. (1997) The distribution of the Irish hare (*Lepus timidus hibernicus*) in Northern Ireland and its relationship to land classification. *Gibier Faune Sauvage,* **14**, 325–334.

102 Dingerkus, S.K. & Montgomery, W.I. (2001) The diet and landclass affinities of the Irish hare (*Lepus timidus hibernicus*). *Journal of Zoology,* **253**, 233–240.

103 Dingerkus, S.K. & Montgomery, W.I. (2002) A review of the status and decline in abundance of the Irish Hare (*Lepus timidus hibernicus*) in Northern Ireland. *Mammal Review,* **32**, 1–11.

104 Duff, J.P. *et al.* (1994) European brown hare syndrome in England. *Veterinary Record,* **134**, 669–673.

105 Dunsmore, J.D. (1974) The rabbit in sub-alpine south-eastern Australia. I. Population structure of rabbits and productivity. *Australian Wildlife Research,* **1**, 1–16.

106 Easterbee, N. (1988) The wild cat *Felix silvestris* in Scotland. *Lutra,* **31**, 29–43.

107 Eden, A. (1940) Coprophagy in the rabbit. *Nature,* **145**, 36–37.

108 Eskens, U. *et al.* (1999) Untersuchungen uber mogliche Einflussfaktorum auf die Populationsdichte des Feldhasen. *Zeitschrift für Jadgwissenschaft,* **45**, 60–65 (in German).

109 Fairley, J.S. (1975) *An Irish beast book,* 2nd edn. Blackstaff Press, Belfast.

110 Fairley, J.S. (2001) *A basket of weasels.* Privately published, J.S. Fairley, Belfast.

111 Fargher, S.E. (1977) The distribution of the brown hare (*Lepus capensis*) and the mountain hare (*Lepus timidus*) in the Isle of Man. *Journal of Zoology,* **182**, 164–167.

112 Farrow, E.P. (1917) On the ecology of the vegetation of Breckland. III. General effects of rabbits on the vegetation. *Journal of Ecology,* **5**, 1–18.

113 Fenton, E.W. (1939) The vegetation of 'screes' in certain hill-grazing districts of Scotland. *Journal of Ecology,* **27**, 502–512.

114 Fenton, E.W. (1940) The influence of rabbits on the vegetation of certain hill-grazing districts of Scotland. *Journal of Ecology,* **28**, 438–449.

115 Flux, J.E.C. (1967) Reproduction and body weights of the hare *Lepus europaeus* Pallas, in New Zealand. *New Zealand Journal of Science,* **10**, 357–401.

116 Flux, J.E.C. (1970) Life history of the mountain hare (*Lepus timidus scoticus*) in north-east Scotland. *Journal of Zoology,* **161**, 75–123.

117 Flux, J.E.C. (1970) Colour change of mountain hares (*Lepus timidus scoticus*) in north-east Scotland. *Journal of Zoology,* **162**, 345–358.

118 Flux, J.E.C. (1981) Field observations of behaviour in the genus *Lepus*, pp. 377–394 Myers, K. & MacInnes, C.D. (eds.) *Proceedings of the World Lagomorph Conference,*

University of Guelph, Ontario. IUCN, Gland.

119 Flux, J.E.C. (1987) Moult, condition and body weight in mountain hares (*Lepus timidus*). *Journal of Zoology,* **212**, 365–367.

120 Flux, J.E.C. (1994) World distribution, pp.8–21 in Thompson, H.V. & King, C.M. (eds.) *The European rabbit: the history of a successful colonizer.* Oxford University Press, Oxford.

121 Flux, J.E.C. (1997) Status of rabbits (*Oryctolagus cuniculus*) and hares (*Lepus europaeus*) in New Zealand. *Gibier Faune Sauvage,* **14**, 267–280.

122 Flux, J.E.C. & Angermann, R. (1990) The hares and jackrabbits, pp. 61–94 in Chapman, J.A. & Flux, J.E.C. (eds.) *Rabbits, hares and pikas. Status, survey and conservation action plans.* IUCN, Gland.

123 Flux, J.E.C. & Fullagar, P.J. (1992) World distribution of the rabbit *Oryctolagus cuniculus* on islands. *Mammal Review,* **22**, 151–205.

124 Fredsted, T. *et al.* (2006) Introgression of mountain hares (*Lepus timidus*) mitochondrial DNA into wild brown hares (*Lepus europaeus*) in Denmark. *BMC Ecology,* **6**, 17–21.

125 Frylestam, B. (1980) Reproduction in the European hare in southern Sweden. *Holarctic Ecology,* **3**, 74–80.

126 Frylestam, B. (1986) Agricultural land use effects on the winter diet of brown hares (*Lepus europaeus* Pallas) in southern Sweden. *Mammal Review,* **16**, 157–161.

127 Frylestam, B. (1992) Utilization by brown hares *Lepus europaeus*, Pallas of field habitats and complimentary food stripes in southern Sweden, pp. 259–261 in Bobek, B. *et al.* (eds.) *Global trends in wildlife management.* Swiat Press, Krakow.

128 Frylestam, B. & von Schantz, T. (1977) Age determination of European hares based on periosteal growth lines. *Mammal Review,* **7**, 151–154.

129 Garson, P.J. (1981) Social organisation and reproduction in the rabbit: a review, pp. 256–270 in Myers, K. & McInnes, C.D. (eds.) *Proceedings of the World Lagomorph Conference, University of Guelph, Ontario.* IUCN, Gland.

130 Garson, P.J. (1986) Intraspecific influences on juvenile recruitment rate in rabbits: observational and experimental evidence from a study in costal duneland habitat. *Mammal Review,* **16**, 195–196.

131 Gibb, J.A. (1979) Factors affecting population density in the wild rabbit, *Oryctolagus cuniculus* (L.) and their relevance to small mammals, pp. 33–46 in Stonehouse, B. & Perrins, C. (eds.) *Evolutionary ecology.* Macmillan, London.

132 Gibb, J.A. *et al.* (1978) Natural control of a population of rabbits *Oryctolagus cuniculus* (L.) for ten years in the Kourarau enclosure. *New Zealand DSIR Bulletin,* **223**, 1–89.

133 Goodrich, B.S. *et al.* (1981) Identification of some volatile compunds in the odour of fecal pellets of the rabbit, *Oryctolagus cuniculus. Journal of Chemical Ecology,* **7**, 817–826.

134 Goszczyński, J. & Wasilewski, M. (1992) Predation of foxes on a hare population in central Poland. *Acta Theriologica,* **37**, 329–338.

135 Gough, H.C. (1955) Grazing of winter corn by the rabbit *Oryctolagus cuniculus* (L.). *Annals of Applied Biology,* **43**, 720–734.

136 Graham, I.M. *et al.* (1995) The diet and breeding density of common buzzards *Buteo buteo* in relation to indices of prey abundance. *Bird Study,* **42**, 165–173.

137 Griffiths, I.R. & Whitwell, K.E. (1993) Leporine dysautonomia: further evidence that hares suffer from grass sickness. *Veterinary Record,* **132**, 376–377.

138 Gurnell, J. *et al.* (1994) The food of pine martens (*Martes martes*) in West Scotland. *Journal of Zoology,* **234**, 680–683.

139 Gustafsson, K. *et al.* (1989) Studies on an idiopathic syndrome in the brown hare (*Lepus europaeus* P.) and

mountain hare (*Lepus timidus* L.) in Sweden, with special reference to hepatic lesions. *Journal of Veterinary Medicine* A, **36,** 631–637.

140 Gustavsson, I. (1971) Mitotic and meiotic chromosomes of the variable hare (*Lepus timidus* L.), the common hare (*Lepus europaeus* Pall.) and their hybrids *Hereditas, 67,* 27–34.

141 Hackländer, K. *et al.* (2002) Postnatal development and thermoregulation in the precocial European hare (*Lepus europaeus*). *Journal of Comparative Physiology B,* **172,** 183–190.

142 Hamill, R.M. *et al.* (2006) Spatial patterns of genetic diversity across European subspecies of the mountain hare *Lepus timidus* L. *Heredity,* **97,** 355–365.

143 Hansen, K. (1992) Reproduction in European hare in a Danish farmland. *Acta Theriologica,* **37,** 27–40.

144 Hansen, K. (1996) European hare (*Lepus europaeus*) time budget of nine different nocturnal activities in a Danish farmland, pp. 167–173 in Botev, N. (ed.) *The game and the man.* Pensoft, Sofia.

145 Hansen, K. (1997) Effects of cereal production on the population dynamics of the European hare (*Lepus europaeus*). *Gibier Faune Sauvage,* **14,** 510–511.

146 Hardy, C. *et al.* (1995) Rabbit mitochondrial DNA diversity from prehistoric to modern times. *Journal of Molecular Evolution,* **40,** 227–237.

147 Harris, S. *et al.* (1995) *A review of British Mammals: population estimates and conservation status of British mammals other than cetaceans.* JNCC, Peterborough.

148 Hartl, G.B. *et al.* (1990) Biochemical variation and differentiation in the brown hare (*Lepus europaeus*) of central Europe. *Zeitschrift für Säugtierkunde,* **55,** 186–193.

149 Hartl, G.B. *et al.* (1995) Allozyme heterozygosity and fluctuating asymmetry in the brown hare (*Lepus europaeus*): a test of the developmental homeostasis hypothesis. *Philosophical Transactions of the Royal Society of London, Series B,* **350,** 313–323.

150 Hartley, F.G. (2001) The pest status of the rabbit in Scotland, pp. 98–101 in *Scientific Review 1997–2000.* Scottish Agricultural Science Agency, Edinburgh.

151 Hartman, E.G. & Broekhuizen, S. (1980) Antibodies to Leptospira in European hares (*Lepus europaeus* Pallas) in the Netherlands. *Zentralblatt für Veterinarmedizin* B, **27,** 640–649.

152 Heath, E. (1972) Sexual and related territorial behaviour in the laboratory rabbit. *Laboratory Animal Science,* **22,** 684–691.

153 Hesterman, E.R. & Mykytowycz, R. (1982) Misidentification by wild rabbits, *Oryctolagus cuniculus,* of group members carrying the odour of foreign inguinal gland secretion. I. Experiments with all male groups. *Journal of Chemical Ecology,* **8,** 419–427.

154 Hesterman, E.R. & Mykytowycz, R. (1982) Misidentification by wild rabbits, *Oryctolagus cuniculus,* of group members carrying the odour of foreign inguinal gland secretion. II. Experiments with all female groups. *Journal of Chemical Ecology,* **8,** 723–728.

155 Hesterman, E.R. *et al.* (1976) Behavioural and cardiac responses of the rabbit *Oryctolagus cuniculus* to chemical fractions from anal gland. *Journal of Chemical Ecology,* **2,** 25–37.

156 Hewson, R. (1958) Moults and winter whitening in the mountain hare *Lepus timidus scoticus* Hilzheimer. *Proceedings of the Zoological Society of London,* **131,** 99–108.

157 Hewson, R. (1962) Food and feeding habits of the mountain hare *Lepus timidus scoticus* Hilzheimer. *Proceedings of the Zoological Society of London,* **139,** 515–526.

158 Hewson, R. (1963) Moults and pelages in the brown hare *Lepus europaeus occidentalis* de Winton. *Proceedings of the Zoological Society of London,* **141,** 677–688.

159 Hewson, R. (1964) Reproduction in the brown hare and the mountain hare in north-east Scotland. *Scottish Naturalist,* **71,** 81–89.

160 Hewson, R. (1968) Weights and growth rates in the mountain hare. *Journal of Zoology,* **154,** 249–262.

161 Hewson, R. (1970) Variation in reproduction and shooting bags of mountain hares in north-east Scotland. *Journal of Applied Ecology,* **7,** 243–252.

162 Hewson, R. (1977) Food selection by brown hares (*Lepus capensis*) on cereal and turnip crops in north-east Scotland. *Journal of Applied Ecology,* **14,** 779–785.

163 Hewson, R. (1983) The food of wild cats (*Felis silvestris*) and red foxes (*Vulpes vulpes*) in west and north-east Scotland. *Journal of Zoology,* **200,** 283–289.

164 Hewson, R. (1989) Grazing preferences of mountain hares on heather moorland and hill pastures. *Journal of Applied Ecology,* **26,** 1–11.

165 Hewson, R. (1990) Behaviour, population changes and dispersal of mountain hares (*Lepus timidus*) in Scotland. *Journal of Zoology,* **220,** 287–309.

166 Hewson, R. & Kolb, H.H. (1973) Changes in the numbers and distribution of foxes (*Vulpes vulpes*) killed in Scotland from 1948–1970. *Journal of Zoology,* **171,** 345–365.

167 Hewson, R. & Taylor, M. (1968) Movements of European hares in an upland area of Scotland. *Acta Theriologica,* **13,** 31–34.

168 Hewson, R. & Taylor, M. (1975) Embryo counts and length of the breeding season in European hares in Scotland from 1960–1972. *Acta Theriologica,* **20,** 247–254.

169 Hill, W.C.O. (1948) Rhinoglyphics: epithelial sculpture of the mammalian rhinarium. *Proceedings of the Zoological Society of London,* **118,** 1–35.

170 Hirakawa, H. (2001) Coprophagy in leporids and other mammalian herbivores. *Mammal Review,* **31,** 61–80.

171 Höglund, N.H. (1957) Fortplantningen hos skoghare (*Lepus t. timidus* Lin). *Viltrevy,* **1,** 267–282 (in Swedish).

172 Holley, A.J.F. (1986) A hierarchy of hares: dominance status and access to oestrous does. *Mammal Review,* **16,** 181–186.

173 Holley, A.J.F. (1992) *Studies on the biology of the brown hare (*Lepus europaeus*) with particular refererence to behaviour.* PhD thesis, University of Durham.

174 Holley, A.J.F. (1993) Do brown hares signal to foxes? *Ethology,* **94,** 21–30.

175 Holley, A.J.F. Personal communication.

176 Holley, A.J.F. & Greenwood, P.J. (1984) The myth of the mad March hare. *Nature,* **309,** 549–550.

177 Homolka, M. (1982) The food of *Lepus europaeus* in a meadow and woodland complex. *Folia Zoologica,* **31,** 243–253.

178 Homolka, M. (1987) A comparison of the trophic niches of *Lepus europaeus* and *Oryctolagus cuniculus. Folia Zoologica,* **36,** 307–317.

179 Hörnfeldt, B. (1978) Synchronous population fluctations in voles, small game, owls and tularemia in Northern Sweden. *Oecologia,* **32,** 141–152.

180 Hörnicke, H. & Björnhag, G. (1980) Coprophagy and related strategies for digesta utilization, pp. 707–730 in Ruckebusch, Y & Thivend, P. (eds.) *Digestive physiology and metabolism in ruminants.* MTP Press, Lancaster.

181 Hughes, M. *et al.* (2007) *Population genetic structure and systematics of the Irish hare.* Report Qu03–04 to Heritage Service Northern Ireland. Quercus, Queen's University, Belfast.

182 Hughes, R.L. & Myers, K. (1966) Behavioural cycles during pseudopregnancy in confined populations of domestic rabbits and their relation to the histology of the female reproductive tract. *Australian Journal of Zoology,* **14,** 173–183.

183 Hulbert, I.A.R. & Boag, B. (2001) The potential role of habitat on intestinal helminths of mountain hares *Lepus timidus* L. *Journal of Helminthology,* **75,** 345–349.

184 Hulbert, I.A.R. & Iason, G.R. (1996) The possible effects of landscape change on diet composition and body weight of mountain hares *Lepus timidus. Wildlife Biology,*

2, 269–273.

185 Hulbert, I.A.R. *et al.* (1996) Habitat utilisation in a stratified landscape of two lagomorphs with different feeding strategies. *Journal of Applied Ecology,* **33**, 315–324.

186 Hulbert, I.A.R. *et al.* (1996) Home-range sizes in a stratified landscape of two lagomorphs with different feeding strategies. *Journal of Applied Ecology,* **33**, 1479–1488.

187 Hulbert, I.A.R. *et al.* (2001) The flexibility of an intermediate feeder: dietary selection by mountain hares measured using faecal *n*-alkanes. *Oecologia,* **129**, 197–205.

188 Hutchings, M.R. & Harris, S. (1995) Does hunting pressure affect the flushing behaviour of brown hares (*Lepus europaeus*)? *Journal of Zoology,* **237**, 663–667.

189 Hutchings, M.R. & Harris, S. (1996) *The current status of the brown hare* (Lepus europaeus*) in Britain.* JNCC, Peterborough.

190 Iason, G.R. (1988) Age determination of mountain hares (*Lepus timidus*): a rapid method and when to use it. *Journal of Applied Ecology,* **25**, 389–395.

191 Iason, G.R. (1989) Growth and mortality in mountain hares: the effect of sex and date of birth. *Oecologia,* **81**, 540–546.

192 Iason, G.R. (1989) Mortality of mountain hares in relation to body size and age. *Journal of Zoology,* **219**, 676–680.

193 Iason, G.R. (1990) The effects of size, age and a cost of early breeding on reproduction in female mountain hares. *Holarctic Ecology,* **13**, 81–89.

194 Iason, G.R. & Ebling, F.J.P. (1989) Seasonal variation in the daily patterns of plasma melatonin in a wild mammal: the mountain hare (*Lepus timidus*). *Journal of Pineal Research,* **6**, 157–167.

195 Iason, G.R. & Waterman, P.G. (1988) Avoidance of plant phenolics by juvenile and reproducing female mountain hares in summer. *Functional Ecology,* **2**, 433–440.

196 Iason, G.R. *et al.* (2002) The functional response does not predict the local distribution of European rabbits (*Oryctolagus cuniculus*) on grass swards: experimental evidence. *Functional Ecology,* **16**, 394–402.

197 Irvin, A.D. (1970) A note on the gastro-intestinal parasites of British hares (*Lepus europaeus* and *L. timidus*). *Journal of Zoology,* **162**, 544–546.

198 Jackes, A.D.& Watson A. (1975) Winter whitening of Scottish mountain hares (*Lepus timidus scoticus*) in relation to day length, temperature and snow-lie. *Journal of Zoology,* **176**, 403–409.

199 Jarman, P. (1986) The brown hare a herbivorous mammal in a new ecosystem, pp. 63–76 in Kitching, R.L. (ed.) *Ecology of exotic animals and plants: some Australian case histories.* Wiley, Brisbane.

200 Jeffery, R. (1996) *Aspects of the ecology and behaviour of the Irish hare,* Lepus timidus hibernicus *(Bell, 1837) on lowland farmland.* PhD thesis, Trinity College Dublin.

201 Jones, L.D. *et al.* (1999) Transmission of louping ill virus between infected and uninfected ticks co-feeding on mountain hares. *Medical and Veterinary Entomology,* **11**, 172–176.

202 Kasapidis, P. *et al.* (2005) The shaping of mitochondrial DNA phylogeographic patterns of the brown hare (*Lepus europaeus*) under the combined influence of Late Pleistocene climatic fluctuations and anthropogenic translocations. *Molecular Phylogenetics and Evolution,* **34**, 55–66.

203 Keith, L.B. (1981) Population dynamics of hares, pp. 395–440 in Myers, K. & MacInnes, C.D. (eds.) *Proceedings of the World Lagomorph Conference, University of Guelph, Ontario.* IUCN, Gland.

204 King, J.E. (1962) Report on animal bones. In Wymer, J. (ed.) Excavations at the Maglemosian sites at Thatcham, Berkshire, England, *Proceedings of the Prehistoric Society,* **28**, 355–361.

205 Kirkham, G. (1981) Economic diversification in a marginal economy: a case study. In Roebuck, P. (ed.) *Plantation to partition: essays in Ulster history.* Blackstaff Press, Belfast.

206 Kolb, H.H. (1991) Use of burrows and movements by wild rabbits (*Oryctolagus cuniculus*) on an area of sand dunes. *Journal of Applied Ecology,* **28**, 879–891.

207 Kolb, H.H. (1992) The effect of moonlight on activity in the wild rabbit (*Oryctolagus cuniculus*). *Journal of Zoology,* **228**, 661–665.

208 Kolb, H.H. (1992) The supraorbital ridge as an indicator of age in wild rabbits (*Oryctolagus cuniculus*). *Journal of Zoology,* **227**, 334–338.

209 Kolb, H.H. (1994) Rabbit (*Oryctolagus cuniculus*) populations in Scotland since the introduction of myxomatosis. *Mammal Review,* **24**, 41–48.

210 Kovács, G. & Búza, C. (1988) A mezeinyúl (*Lepus europaeus* Pallas) mozgáskörzetének jellemzöi egy erdösült és egy intenziven müvelt mezögazdasági élöhelyen. I. A mozgáskörzet nagysága. *Vadbiológia* 1988, 67–84 (in Hungarian).

211 Kovács, G. & Heltay, I. (1981) Study of a European hare population mosaic in the Hungarian lowland, pp. 508–528 in Myers, K. & MacInnes, C.D. (eds.) *Proceedings of the World Lagomorph Conference, University of Guelph, Ontario.* IUCN, Gland.

212 Kunkele, J. (1992) Infanticide in wild rabbits (*Oryctolagus cuniculus*). *Journal of Mammalogy,* **73**, 317–320.

213 Kunkele, J.& von Holst, D. (1996) Natal dispersal in the European wild rabbit. *Animal Behaviour,* **51**, 1047–1059.

214 Langbein, J. *et al.* (1999) Techniques for assessing the abundance of brown hares *Lepus europaeus.* *Mammal Review,* **29**, 93–116.

215 Laurenson, M.K., *et al.* (2003) Identifying disease reservoirs in complex systems: mountain hares as reservoirs of ticks and louping-ill virus, pathogens of red grouse. *Journal of Animal Ecology,* **72**, 177–185.

216 Lello, J. *et al.*(2005) The effect of single and concomitant pathogen infections on condition and fecundity of the wild rabbit (*Oryctolagus cuniculus*). *International Journal for Parasitology,* **35**, 1509–1515.

217 Lever, C. (1994) *Naturalized animals: the ecology of successfully introduced species.* Poyser, London.

218 Lever, R.J.A.W. (1959) The diet of the fox since myxomatosis. *Journal of Animal Ecology,* **58**, 359–375.

219 Lincoln, G.A. (1974) Reproduction and 'March madness' in the brown hare, *Lepus europaeus.* *Journal of Zoology,* **174,** 1–14.

220 Lindlöf, B. (1978) Aggressive dominance rank in relation to feeding in the European hare. *Viltrevy,* **10,** 145–157.

221 Lindlöf, B. & Lemnell, P.A. (1981) Differences in island and mainland populations of mountian hare. Pp 478–484 in Myers, K. & MacInnes, C.D. (eds.) *Proceedings of the World Lagomorph Conference, University of Guelph, Ontario.* IUCN, Gland.

222 Lindstrom, E. *et al.* (1986) Influence of predators on hare populations in Sweden: a critical review. *Mammal Review,* **16,** 151–156.

223 Lindstrom, E. *et al.* (1994) Disease reveals the predator: sarcoptic mange, red fox predation, and prey populations. *Ecology,* **75,** 1042–1049.

224 Lloyd, H.G. (1963) Intra-uterine mortality in the wild rabbit, *Oryctolagus cuniculus* (L.) in population of low density. *Journal of Animal Ecology,* **32,** 549–563.

225 Lloyd, H.G. (1967) Variations in fecundity in wild rabbit populations. *CIBA Foundation Study Group,* **26,** 81–88.

226 Lloyd, H.G. (1968) Observations on breeding in the brown hare (*Lepus europaeus*) during the first pregnancy of the season. *Journal of Zoology,* **156,** 521–528.

227 Lloyd, H.G. (1970) Post-myxomatosis rabbit populations in England and Wales. *EPPO Publicity Series* A, **58,** 197–215.

228 Lloyd, H.G. (1970) Variation and adaptation in reproductive performance. *Symposia of the Zoological Society of London,* **26**, 165–188.

229 Lloyd, H.G. (1980) *The red fox.* Batsford, London.

230 Lloyd, H.G. & McCowan, D. (1968) Some observations on the breeeding burrow of the wild rabbit, *Oryctolagus cuniculus* on the island of Skokholm. *Journal of Zoology,* **156**, 540–549.

231 Lockley, R.M. (1961) Social structure and stress in the rabbit warren. *Journal of Animal Ecology,* **30**, 585–423.

232 Lockley, R.M. (1964) *The private life of the rabbit.* André Deutsch, London.

233 Lumeij, J.T. (1997) Syphilis in European brown hares (*Lepus europaeus*). *Gibier Faune Sauvage,* **14**, 517–519.

234 Macdonald, D.W. *et al.* (1999) The impact of American mink *Mustela vison* as predators of native species, pp. 5–23 in Cowan, D.P. & Feare, C.J. (eds.) *Advances in vertebrate pest management.* Filander Verlag, Fürth.

235 Madsen, O. *et al.* (2001) Parallel adaptive radiations in two major clades of placental mammals. *Nature,* **409**, 610–614.

236 Main, N.S. (1968) Pseudotuberculosis in free-living wild animals. *Symposia of the Zoological Society of London,* **24**, 107–177.

237 Mallon, D.P. (2001) *The mountain hare in the Peak District.* Derbyshire Wildlife Trust, Belper.

238 Mallon, D.P. *et al.* (2003) Mountain hares in the Peak District. *British Wildlife,* **15**, 110–116.

239 Marboutin, E. & Aebischer, N.J. (1996) Does harvesting arable crops influence the behaviour of the European hare *Lepus europaeus*? *Wildlife Biology,* **2**, 83–91.

240 Marboutin, E. & Hansen, K. (1998) Survival rates in a nonharvested brown hare population. *Journal of Wildlife Management,* **62**, 772–779.

241 Marboutin, E. & Peroux, R. (1995) Survival pattern of European hare in a decreasing population. *Journal of Applied Ecology,* **32**, 809–816.

242 Marboutin, E. *et al.* (1990) Survival patterns in wild and captive-reared leverets (*Lepus europaeus* Pallas) determined by telemetry. *Gibier Faune Sauvage,* **7**, 325–342.

243 Marcström, V. *et al.* (1989) Demographic responses of arctic hares (*Lepus timidus*) to experimental reductions of red foxes (*Vulpes vulpes*) and martens (*Martes martes*). *Canadian Journal of Zoology,* **67**, 658–668.

244 Martinet, L. (1976) Seasonal reproduction cycles in the European hare, *Lepus europaeus*, raised in captivity. The role of photoperiodicity, pp. 55–57 in Pielowski, Z. & Pucek, Z. (eds.) *Ecology and management of European hare populations.* Polish Hunting Association, Warsaw.

245 McDiarmid, A. (1965) Modern trends in animal health and husbandry; some infectious diseases of free-living wildlife. *British Veterinary Journal,* **121**, 265–257.

246 McKillop, I.G. (1987) The effectiveness of barriers to exclude the European wild rabbit from crops. *Wildlife Society Bulletin,* **15**, 394–401.

247 McKillop, I.G. *et al.* (1986) Specifications for wire mesh fences used to exclude the European wild rabbit from crops, pp.147–152 in Salmon, T.P. (ed.) *Proceedings of the 12th Vertebrate Pest Conference, University of California, Davis.*

248 McKillop, I.G. *et al.* (1998) Long-term cost-effectiveness of fences to manage European wild rabbits. *Crop Protection,* **17**, 393–400.

249 McLaren, G.W. (1996) *Resource limitation in brown hare (*Lepus europaeus*) populations.* PhD thesis, University of Bristol.

250 McLaren, G.W. *et al.* (1997) Why are brown hares (*Lepus europaeus*) rare in pastoral landscapes in Great Britain? *Gibier Faune Sauvage,* **14**, 335–348.

251 Mead-Briggs, A.R. (1964) The reproductive biology of the rabbit flea *Spylopsyllus cuniculi* (Dale) and the dependence of this species upon the breeding of its host. *Journal of Experimental Biology,* **41**, 371–402.

252 Mead-Briggs, A.R. & Hughes A.M. (1965) Records of mites and lice from wild rabbits collected throughout Great Britain. *Annals and Magazine of Natural History,* (**13**)8, 695–708.

253 Mead-Briggs, A.R. & Page, R.J.C. (1964) Fleas other than *Spilopsyllus cuniculi* Dale from a collection of rabbits, predominantly myxomatous, obtained throughout Great Britain. *Entomologist's Gazette,* **15**, 60–65.

254 Mead-Briggs, A.R. & Page, R.J.C. (1967) Ectoparasites from hares collected throughout the United Kingdom, January–March, 1964. *Entomologist's Monthly Magazine,* **103**, 26–34.

255 Mead-Briggs, A.R. & Page, R.J.C. (1975) Records of anoplocephaline cestodes from wild rabbits and hares collected throughout Great Britain. *Journal of Helminthology,* **49**, 49–56.

256 Mead-Briggs, A.R. & Vaughan J.A. (1975) The differential transmissibility of myxoma virus strains of differing virulence grades by the rabbit flea *Spilopsylla cunicili* (Dale). *Journal of Hygiene,* **75**, 237–247.

257 Mead-Briggs, A.R. & Vaughan, J.A. (1980) The importance of the European rabbit flea *Spilopsyllus cuniculi* (Dale) in the evolution of myxomatosis in Britain. In Traub, R. & Starcke, H (eds.) *Proceedings of the International Conference on Fleas, Peterborough, 1977.* Balkema, Rotterdam.

258 Mead-Briggs A.R. *et al.* (1975) Seasonal variation in numbers of the rabbit flea on the wild rabbit. *Parasitology,* **70**, 103–118.

259 Melo-Ferreira, J. *et al.* (2005) Invasion from the cold past: extensive introgression of mountain hare (*Lepus timidus*) mitochondrial DNA into three other hare species in Northern Iberia. *Molecular Ecology,* **14**, 2459–2464.

260 Meriggi, A. & Alieri, R. (1989) Factors affecting brown hare density in northern Italy. *Ethology, Ecology & Evolution,* **1**, 255–264.

261 Meriggi, A. & Verri, A. (1990) Population dynamics and habitat selection of the European hare on poplar monocultures in northern Italy. *Acta Theriologica,* **35**, 69–76.

262 Middleton, A.D. (1932) Syphilis as a disease of wild rabbits and hares. *Journal of Animal Ecology,* **6**, 84–85.

263 Milanov, Z. & Bonchev, S. (1996) Lead, cadmium and copper in inner organs of game mammals from Bulgaria, pp. 502–505 in Botev, N. (ed.) *The game and the man.* Pensoft, Sofia.

264 Miller, G.S. (1912) *Catalogue of the mammals of Western Europe.* British Museum (Natural History), London.

265 Mitchell-Jones, A.J. *et al.* (1999) *Atlas of European mammals.* Poyser, London.

266 Monaghan, P. & Metcalfe, N.B. (1985) Group foraging in wild brown hares: effects of resource distribution and social status. *Animal Behaviour,* **33**, 993–999.

267 Moore, N.W. (1956) Rabbits, buzzards and hares. Two studies on the indirect effects of myxomatosis. *Terre et La Vie,* **103**, 220–225.

268 Moore, N.W. (1957) The past and present status of the buzzard in the British Isles. *British Birds,* **5**, 173–197.

269 Moseby, K.E. *et al.* (2005) Home range, activity and habitat use of European rabbits (*Oryctolagus cuniculus*) in arid Australia: implications for control. *Wildlife Research,* **32**, 305–311.

270 Moss, R. & Hewson, R. (1985) Effects on heather of heavy grazing by mountain hares. *Holarctic Ecology,* **8**, 280–284.

271 Muirhead-Thomson, R.C. (1956) The part played by woodland mosquitoes of the genus *Aedes* in the transmission of myxomatosis in England. *Journal of Hygiene,* **54**, 461–471.

272 Muirhead-Thomson, R.C. (1956) Field studies of the role of *Anopheles atroparvus* in the transmission of

myxomatosis in England. *Journal of Hygiene,* **54**, 472–477.

273 Mulder, J.L. & Wallage-Dress, J.M. (1979) Red fox predation on young rabbits in breeding burrows. *Netherlands Journal of Zoology,* **29**, 144–145.

274 Myers, K. & Poole, W.E. (1958) Sexual behaviour cycles in the wild rabbits, *Oryctolagus cuniculus* (L.). *CSIRO Wildlife Research,* **4**, 144–145.

275 Myers, K. & Poole, W.E. (1959) A study of the biology of the wild rabbit, *Oryctolagus cuniculus* (L.) in confined populations I: the effects of density on home range and formation of breeding groups. *CSIRO Wildlife Research,* **4**, 14–26.

276 Myers, K. & Poole, W.E. (1961) A study of the biology of the wild rabbit *Oryctolagus cuniculus* (L.) in confined populations II: the effects of season and population increase on behaviour. *CSIRO Wildlife Research,* **6**, 1–41.

277 Myers, K. & Schneider, E.C. (1964) Observations on reproduction, mortality and behaviour in a small, free-living population of wild rabbits. *CSIRO Wildlife Research,* **9**, 138–143.

278 Mykytowycz, R. (1959) Social behaviour of an experimental colony of wild rabbits. *Oryctolagus cuniculus* (L.) II: first breeding season. *CSIRO Wildlife Research,* **4**, 1–13.

279 Mykytowycz, R. (1960) Social behaviour of an experimental colony of wild rabbits. *Oryctolagus cuniculus* (L.) III: second breeding season. *CSIRO Wildlife Research,* **5**, 1–20.

280 Mykytowycz, R. & Dudzinski, M.L. (1972) Aggressive and protective behaviour of adult rabbits, *Oryctolagus cuniculus* (L.), towards juveniles. *Behaviour,* **43**, 97–120.

281 Mykytowycz, R. & Gambale, S. (1969) The distribution of dung-hills and the behaviour of free-living rabbits, *Oryctolagus cuniculus* (L.) on them. *Forma et Functio,* **1**, 333–349.

282 Mykytowycz, R. & Hesterman, E.R. (1970) The behaviour of captive wild rabbits, *Oryctolagus cuniculus* (L.) in response to strange dung-hills. *Forma et Functio,* **2**, 1–12.

283 Mykytowycz, R. *et al.* (1976) A comparison of the effectiveness of the odours of rabbits in enhancing territorial confidence. *Journal of Chemical Ecology,* **2**, 13–24.

284 Myrcha, A. (1968) Winter food intake in European hare (*Lepus europaeus* Pallas, 1775) in experimental conditions. *Acta Theriologica,* **13**, 453–459.

285 Neal, E. & Cheeseman, C. (1996) *Badgers.* Poyser, London.

286 Newey, S. (2005) *Population fluctuations in mountain hares: a role for parasites?* Doctoral thesis, Swedish University of Agricultural Science, Umeå.

287 Newey, S. & Thirgood, S.J. (2004) Parasite mediated reduction of fecundity of mountain hares. *Proceedings of the Royal Society of London, Series B,* **271** (Supplement 6), S413–S415.

288 Newey, S. *et al.* (2004) Do parasite burdens in spring influence condition and fecundity of female mountain hares *Lepus timidus. Wildlife Biology,* **10**, 171–176.

289 Newey, S. *et al.* (2005) Prevalence, intensity and aggregation of intestinal parasites in mountain hares and their potential impact on population dynamics. *International Journal for Parasitology,* **35**, 367–373.

290 O'Mahony, D. & Montgomery, W. I (2001) *The distribution, abundance and habitat use of Irish hare in upland and lowland areas of Co. Antrim and Co. Down.* Report by Queen's University Belfast for the Environment and Heritage Service, Department of the Environment Northern Ireland.

291 Oberwalder, U. & Steineck, T. (1997) Observations on the occurrence of psuedotuberculosis in the European brown hare (*Lepus europaeus*) in Austria. *Gibier Faune Sauvage,* **14**, 521–522.

292 Palomares, F. (2003) Warren building by European rabbits (*Oryctolagus cuniculus*) in relation to cover availability in a sandy area. *Journal of Zoology,* **259**, 63–67.

293 Panek, M. & Kamieniarz, R. (1999) Relationships between density of brown hare *Lepus europaeus* and landscape structure in Poland in the years 1981–1995. *Acta Theriologica,* **44**, 67–75.

294 Parer, I. (1977) The population ecology of the wild rabbit *Oryctolagus cuniculus* (L.) in a Mediterranean type climate in New South Wales. *Australian Wildlife Research,* **4**, 171–205.

295 Parer, I. (1982) Dispersal of the wild rabbit, *Oryctolagus cuniculus* (L.), at Urana in New South Wales. *Australian Wildlife Research,* **9**, 427–441.

296 Parker, B.S. *et al.* (1976) The distribution of rabbit warrens at Mitchell, Queensland in relation to soil and vegetation characteristics. *Australian Wildlife Research,* **3**, 129–148.

297 Parkes, J.P. (1984) Home ranges of radio-telemetered hares (*Lepus capensis*) in a sub-alpine population in New Zealand: implications for control. *Acta Zoologica Fennica,* **171**, 279–281.

298 Pehrson, Å. (1983) Caecotrophy in caged mountain hares (*Lepus timidus*). *Journal of Zoology,* **199**, 563–574.

299 Pépin, D. (1987) Dynamics of a heavily exploited population of brown hare in a large-scale farming area. *Journal of Applied Ecology,* **24**, 725–734.

300 Pépin, D. (1989) Variation in survival of brown hare (*Lepus europaeus*) leverets from different farmland areas in the Paris basin. *Journal of Applied Ecology,* **26**, 13–23.

301 Pépin, D. & Birkan, M. (1981) Comparative total- and strip-census estimates of hares and partridges. *Acta Oecologica,* **2**, 151–160.

302 Pepper, H.W. (1978) *Chemical repellents.* Forestry Commission Leaflet 73, HMSO, London.

303 Pérez-Suarez, G. *et al.* (1994) Speciation and paraphyly in western Mediterranean hares (*Lepus castroviejoi, L. europaeus, L. granatensis,* and *L. capensis*) revealed by mitochondrial DNA phylogeny. *Biochemical Genetics,* **32**, 423–436.

304 Péroux, R. (1995) *Le lièvre d'Europe.* Bulletin Mensuel de l'Office National de la Chasse, Paris.

305 Péroux, R. *et al.* (1997) Point transect sampling: a new approach to estimate densities or abundances of European hare (*Lepus europaeus*) from spotlight counts. *Gibier Faune Sauvage,* **14**, 525–529.

306 Petter, F. (1961) Eléments d'une révision des lièvres européens et asiatiques du sous-genre *Lepus. Zeitschrift für Säugetierkunde,* **26**, 30–40 (in French).

307 Philips, W.M. (1953) The effect of rabbit grazing on reseeded pasture. *Annals of the British Grassland Society,* **8**, 16–181.

308 Philips, W.M. (1955) The effect of commercial trapping on rabbit populations. *Annals of Applied Biology,* **43**, 247–57.

309 Pielowski, Z. (1969) Sex ratio and weight of hares in Poland. *Acta Theriologica,* **14**, 119–131.

310 Pielowski, Z. (1971) Length of life of the hare. *Acta Theriologica,* **16**, 89–94.

311 Pielowski, Z. (1976) The role of foxes in the reduction of the European hare population, pp. 135–148 in Pielowski, Z. & Pucek, Z. (eds.) *Ecology and management of European hare populations.* Polish Hunting Association, Warsaw.

312 Pierpaoli, M. *et al.* (1999) Species distinction and evolutionary relationships of the Italian hare (*Lepus corsicanus*) as described by mitochondrial sequencing. *Molecular Ecology,* **8**, 1805–1817.

313 Poelma, F.G. & Broekhuizen, S. (1972) *Pneumocystis carinii* in hares, *Lepus europaeus* Pallas, in the Netherlands. *Zeitschrift für Parasitenkunde,* **40**, 195–202.

314 Poole, D.W. *et al.* (2003) Developing a sight count based

census method to estimate rabbit (*Oryctolagus cuniculus*) numbers. *Wildlife Research, 30,* 487–493.

315 Raczynski, J. (1964) Studies on the European hare V. Reproduction. *Acta Theriologica, 9,* 305–352.

316 Ranwell, D.S. (1960) Newborough Warren, Anglesey, III. Changes in the vegetation on parts of the dune system after the loss of rabbits by myxomatosis, *Journal of Ecology, 48,* 385–395.

317 Rao, S. *et al.* (2003) The effect of establishing native woodland on habitat selection and ranging of moorland mountain hares (*Lepus timidus*): a flexible forager. *Journal of Zoology, 260,* 1–9.

318 Rao, S. *et al.* (2003) The effect of sapling density, heather height and season on browsing by mountain hares on birch. *Journal of Applied Ecology, 40,* 626–638.

319 Rao, S. *et al.* (2003) Estimating diet composition for mountain hares in newly established native woodland: development and application of plant-wax faecal markers. *Canadian Journal of Zoology, 81,* 1047–1056.

320 Rao, S. *et al.* (2003) Tree browsing by mountain hares (*Lepus timidus*) in young Scots pine (*Pinus sylvestris*) and birch (*Betula pendula*) woodland. *Forest Ecology and Management, 176,* 459–471.

321 Rattenborg, E. (1997) Diseases in the Danish brown hare population (*Lepus europaeus*). *Gibier Faune Sauvage, 14,* 530–531.

322 Rees, W.A. *et al.* (1985) Humane control of rabbits, pp.96–104 in Britt, D.P. (ed.) *Humane control of land mammals and birds.* Universities Federation for Animal Welfare, London.

323 Reid, N. (2006) *Conservation ecology of the Irish hare* (Lepus timidus hibernicus). PhD thesis, Queen's University, Belfast.

324 Reid, N. & Montgomery, W.I. (2007) Naturalisation of the brown hare in Ireland: a threat to the endemic Irish hare? *Biology and Environment, Proceedings of the Royal Irish Academy, 107B,* 129–138.

325 Reitz, F. & Leonard, Y. (1994) Characteristics of European hare *Lepus europaeus* use of space in a French agricultural region of intensive farming. *Acta Theriologica, 39,* 143–157.

326 Reynolds, J.C. & Tapper, S.C. (1995) Predation by foxes *Vulpes vulpes* on brown hares *Lepus europaeus* in central southern England, and its potential impact on annual population growth. *Wildlife Biology, 1,* 145–158.

327 Robinson, T.J. & Matthee, C.A. (2005) Phylogeny and evolutionary origins of the Leporidae: a review of cytogenetics, molecular analyses and a supramatrix analysis. *Mammal Review, 35,* 231–247.

328 Rödel, H.G. (2005) Winter feeding behaviour of European rabbits in a temperate zone habitat. *Mammalian Biology, 70,* 300–306.

329 Rödel, H.G. *et al.* (2005) Timing of breeding and reproductive performance of female European rabbits in response to winter temperature and body mass. *Canadian Journal of Zoology, 83,* 935–942.

330 Rogers, P.M. (1979) *Ecology of the European wild rabbit in the Camargue.* PhD thesis, University of Guelph, Ontario.

331 Rogers, P.M. (1981) Ecology of the European wild rabbit, *Oryctolagus cuniculus* (L.) in Mediterranean habitats. II. Distribution in the landscape of the Camargue, southern France. *Journal of Applied Ecology, 18,* 355–371.

332 Rogers, P.M. & Myers, K. (1979) Ecology of the European wild rabbit *Oryctolagus cuniculus* (L.) in Mediterranean habitats. I. Distribution in the landscape of Coto Donana, southern Spain. *Journal of Applied Ecology, 16,* 691–703.

333 Rogers, P.M. *et al.* (1994) The rabbit in continental Europe, pp.22–63 in Thompson, H.V. & King, C.M. (eds.) *The European rabbit: the history of a successful colonizer.* Oxford University Press, Oxford.

334 Ross, J. (1982) Myxomatosis: the natural evolution of the disease. *Symposia of the Zoological Society of London, 50,* 77–95.

335 Ross, J. (1986) Comparison of fumigant gases used for rabbit control in Great Britain, pp. 153–157 in Salmon, T.P. (ed.) *Proceedings of the 12th Vertebrate Pest Conference, University of California, Davis.*

336 Ross, J. & Sanders, M.F. (1984) The development of genetic resistance to myxomatosis in wild rabbits in Britain. *Journal of Hygiene, 92,* 255–261.

337 Ross, J & Sanders, M.F. (1987) Changes in the virulence of myxoma virus strains in Britain. *Epidemiology and Infection, 98,* 113–117.

338 Ross, J. & Tittensor, A.M. (1981) Myxomatosis in selected rabbit populations in southern England and Wales, pp. 830–833 in Myers, K. & McInnes, C.D. (eds.) *Proceedings of the World Lagomorph Conference, University of Guelph, Ontario.* IUCN, Gland.

339 Ross, J & Tittensor, A.M. (1986) Influence of myxomatosis in regulating rabbit numbers. *Mammal Review, 16,* 163–168.

340 Ross, J. *et al.* (1998) The development of a carbon monoxide producing cartridge for rabbit control. *Wildlife Research, 25,* 305–314.

341 Rothschild, M. & Ford, B. (1973) Factors influencing the breeding of the rabbit flea (*Spilopsyllus cuniculi*): a spring-time accelerator and a kairomone in nestling rabbit urine, with notes on *Cediopsylla simplex*, another 'hormone bound' species. *Journal of Zoology, 170,* 87–137.

342 Rutin, J. (1992) Geomorphic activity of rabbits on a coastal sand dune, De Blink Dunes, the Netherlands. *Earth Surface Processes and Landforms, 17,* 85–94.

343 Salzmann-Wandeler, I. (1976) Feldhasen-Abschusszahlen in der Schweiz, pp. 35–40 in Pielowski, Z. & Pucek, Z. (eds.) *Ecology and management of European hare populations.* Polish Hunting Association, Warsaw (in German).

344 Scaife, H.R. *et al.* (2006) Wild rabbits (*Oryctolagus cuniculus*) as potential carriers of VTEC. *Veterinary Record, 159,* 175–178.

345 Schneider, E. & Maar, S. (1997) Survey on the situation of the hare (*Lepus europaeus*) population in the 'Wetterau' area (FRG). *Gibier Faune Sauvage, 14,* 534–535.

346 Schröder, J. *et al.* (1987) Hybrids between *Lepus timidus* and *Lepus europaeus* are rare although fertile. *Hereditas, 107,* 185–189.

347 Sheail, J. (1971) *Rabbits and their history.* David & Charles, Newton Abbott.

348 Sibly, R.M. *et al.* (1990) Seasonal changes in the gut morphology of the wild rabbit (*Oryctolagus cuniculus*) in southern England. *Journal of Zoology, 221,* 605–619.

349 Slamecka, J. (1991) The influence of ecological arrangements on brown hare population, pp. 340–346 in Csanyi, S. & Ernhaft, J. (eds.) *XXth congress of the International Union of Game Biologists.* Gödöllő, Hungary.

350 Smith, C.J. (1980) *Ecology of English chalk.* Academic Press, London.

351 Smith, G.C. & Trout, R.C. (1994) Using Leslie matrices to determine wild rabbit population growth and the potential for control. *Journal of Applied Ecology, 31,* 223–230.

352 Smith, G.C. *et al.* (1995) Age and sex bias in samples of wild rabbits, *Oryctolagus cuniculus* from wild populations in southern England. *New Zealand Journal of Zoology, 22,* 115–121.

353 Smith, G.C. *et al.* (2006). Rabbit control in Great Britain, pp. 165–186 in Feare, C.J. & Cowan, D.P. (eds.) *Advances in Vertebrate Pest Management IV,* Filander Verlag, Fürth.

354 Smith, R.K. *et al.* (2004). Conservation of European hares *Lepus europaeus* in Britain: is increasing habitat heterogeneity the answer? *Journal of Applied Ecology, 41,* 1092–1102.

355 Smith, R.K. *et al.* (2005). A quantitative analysis of the

abundance and demography of European hares *Lepus europaeus* in relation to habitat type, intensity of agriculture and climate. *Mammal Review*, **35**, 1–24.

356 Sneddon, I.A. (1991) Latrine use by the European rabbit (*Oryctolagus cuniculus*). *Journal of Mammalogy*, **72**, 769–775.

357 Šoštaric, B. *et al.* (1991) Disappearance of free living hares in Croatia: European brown hare syndrome. *Veterinarski Arkiv*, **61**, 133–150.

358 Southern, H.N. (1940) The ecology and population dynamics of the wild rabbit *Oryctolagus cuniculus* (L.). *Annals of Applied Biology*, **26**, 509–526.

359 Southern, H.N. (1942) Periodicity of refection in the wild rabbit. *Nature*, **149**, 553–554.

360 Southern, H.N. (1948) Sexual and aggressive behaviour in the wild rabbit. *Behaviour*, **1**, 173–194.

361 Southern, H.N. (1970) The natural control of a population of tawny owls (*Strix aluco*). *Journal of Zoology*, **162**, 197–285.

362 Stoate, C. & Tapper, S.C. (1993) The impact of three hunting methods on brown hare (*Lepus europaeus*) populations in Britain. *Gibier Faune Sauvage*, **10**, 229–240.

363 Stoate, C. *et al.* (1994) Hares, farming and foxes. *Game Conservancy Review*, **26**, 108–110.

364 Stoddart, E. (1968) Coccidiosis in wild rabbits at four sites in different climatic regions in eastern Australia I. Relationship with age of rabbit. *Australian Journal of Zoology*, **16**, 69–85.

365 Strandgaard, H. & Asferg, T. (1980) The Danish bag record II. Fluctuations and trends in the game bag record in the years 1941–1976 and the geographical distribution of the bag in 1976. *Danish Review of Game Biology*, **11**, 1–112.

366 Strevens, T.C. & Rochford, J. M (2004) The diet and impact of the Irish hare (*Lepus timidus hibernicus* Bell 1837) in a young plantation. *Biology and Environment. Proceedings of Royal Irish Academy*, **104B**, 89–94.

367 Suchentrunk, F. *et al.* (1991) On eye lens weights and other age criteria of the brown hare (*Lepus europaeus* Pallas, 1778). *Zeitschrift für Säugtierkunde*, **56**, 365–374.

368 Suchentrunk, F. *et al.* (2001). Little allozyme variation and mtDNA variability in brown hares (*Lepus europaeus*) from New Zealand and Britain – a legacy of bottlenecks? *Mammalian Biology*, **66**, 48–59.

369 Suchentrunk, F. *et al.* (2005). Introgressive hybridization in wild living mountain hares (*Lepus timidus varronis*) and brown hares (*L. europaeus*) and morphological consequences. *Mammalian Biology*, **70**, supplement, 39–40.

370 Sumption, K.J. & Flowerdew, J.R. (1985) The ecological effects of the decline in rabbits (*Oryctolagus cuniculus* L.) due to myxomatosis. *Mammal Review*, **15**, 151–186.

371 Surridge, A.K. *et al.* (1999) Fine-scale genetic structuring in a natural population of European wild rabbits (*Oryctolagus cuniculus*). *Molecular Ecology*, **8**, 299–307.

372 Swann, R.L. & Etheridge, B. (1995) A comparison of breeding success and prey of the buzzard *Buteo buteo* in two areas of northern Scotland. *Bird Study*, **42**, 37–43.

373 Tangney, D. *et al.* (1995) Food of Irish hares *Lepus timidus hibernicus* in Western Connemara, Ireland. *Acta Theriologica*, **40**, 403–413.

374 Tansley, A.G. & Adamson, R.S. (1925) Studies of the vegetation of English chalk III. the chalk grasslands of the Hampshire-Sussex border. *Journal of Ecology*, **13**, 177–223.

375 Tapper, S. (1980) The status of some predatory mammals. *Game Conservancy Annual Review*, **11**, 48–54.

376 Tapper, S. (1987) Cycles in game-bag records of hares and rabbits in Britain. *Symposia of the Zoological Society of London*, **58**, 79–98.

377 Tapper, S. (1987) *The brown hare*. Shire Natural History, Aylesbury.

378 Tapper, S. (1992) *Game heritage. An ecological review from shooting arid game keeping records*. Game Conservancy, Fordingbridge.

379 Tapper, S. Personal communication.

380 Tapper, S.C. & Barnes, R.F.W. (1986) Influence of farming practice on the ecology of the brown hare (*Lepus europaeus*). *Journal of Applied Ecology*, **23**, 39–52.

381 Tapper, S. & Cox, R. (1990) Selection for double zero oilseed rape crops by rabbits, hares and deer grazing at night, pp. 152–161 in Askew, M.F. (ed.) *Agriculture. Rapeseed 00 and intoxication of wild animals*. Commission of the European Communities, Luxembourg.

382 Tapper, S. & Parsons, N. (1984) The changing status of the brown hare (*Lepus capensis* L.) in Britain. *Mammal Review*, **14**, 57–70.

383 Tapper, S. & Stoate, C. (1992) Surveys galore – but how many hares? *Game Conservancy Review*, **23**, 63–64.

384 Thirgood, S.T. & Hewson, R. (1987) Shelter characteristics of mountain hare resting sites. *Holarctic Ecology*, **10**, 294–298.

385 Thomas, A.S. (1956) Botanical effects of myxomatosis. *Bulletin of the Mammal Society of the British Isles*, **5**, 16–17.

386 Thomas, A.S. (1963) Further changes in vegetation since the advent of myxomatosis. *Journal of Ecology*, **51**, 151–186.

387 Thomas, J.A. (1980) Why did the Large Blue become extinct in Britain? *Oryx*, **15**, 243–247.

388 Thompson, H.V. (1956) The origin and spread of myxomatosis with particular reference to Great Britain. *Terre et la Vie*, **103**, 137–151.

389 Thompson, H.V. (1994) The rabbit in Britain, pp.64–107 in Thompson, H.V. & King, C.M. (eds.) *The European rabbit: the history of a successful colonizer*. Oxford University Press, Oxford

390 Thompson, H.V. & Armour, C.J (1951) Control of the European rabbit *Oryctolagus cuniculus* (L.). An experiment to compare the efficiency of gin trapping, ferreting and cyanide gassing. *Annals of Applied Biology*, **38**, 464–474.

391 Thompson, H.V. & King, C.M. (1994) *The European rabbit: the history of a successful colonizer*. Oxford University Press, Oxford.

392 Thompson, H.V. & Worden, A.N. (1956) *The rabbit*. Collins, London.

393 Thulin, C.-G. (2003) The distribution of mountain hares *Lepus timidus* in Europe: a challenge from brown hares *L. europaeus*? *Mammal Review*, **33**, 29–42.

394 Thulin, C.-G. & Tegelström, H. (2002) Biased geographical distribution of mitochondrial DNA that passed the species barrier from mountain hares to brown hares (genus *Lepus*) : an effect of genetic incompatibility and mating behaviour ? *Journal of Zoology*, **258**, 299–306.

395 Thulin, C.-G. *et al.* (1997) The occurrence of mountain hare mitochondrial DNA in wild brown hares. *Molecular Ecology*, **6**, 463–467.

396 Tittensor, A.M. (1981) Rabbit population trends in southern England, pp. 629–632 in Myers, K. & McInnes, C.D. (eds.) *Proceedings of the World Lagomorph Conference, University of Guelph, Ontario*. IUCN, Gland

397 Tittensor, A.M. & Lloyd, H.G. (1983) *Rabbits*. Forestry Commission Record 125, HMSO, London.

398 Tosh, D. *et al.* (2004) *Northern Ireland Irish Hare Survey 2004*. Report by Quercus (Queen's University Belfast) for the Environment and Heritage Service, Department of the Environment Northern Ireland.

399 Trout, R.C. (1999) Results from field studies of rabbit haemorrhagic disease in Britain, pp. 67–71 in *Rabbit Control, RCD; Dilemmas and Implications. Wellington, N.Z. March 1998*. Miscellaneous Series 55, Royal Society of New Zealand, Wellington.

400 Trout, R. (2003) Rabbits in the farmland ecosystem,

pp.198–210 in Tattersall, F. & Manly, W. (eds.) *Conservation and conflict: mammals and farming in Britain.* Westbury Press/ Linnean Society of London.

401 Trout, R.C. & Lelliot, L.M. (1992) Ageing wild rabbits (*Oryctolagus cuniculus*) from southern England by determining epiphyseal ossification in the lumbar vertebrae. *Journal of Zoology,* **228**, 653–687.

402 Trout, R.C. & Smith G.C. (1995) The reproductive productivity of the wild rabbit (*Oryctolagus cuniculus*) in southern England on sites with different soils. *Journal of Zoology,* **237**, 411–422.

403 Trout, R.C. & Smith, G.C. (1998) Long term study of litter size in relation to populations density in rabbits (*Oryctolagus cuniculus*) in Lincolnshire, England. *Journal of Zoology,* **246**, 347–350.

404 Trout, R.C. & Tittensor, A.M. (1989) Can predators regulate wild rabbit *Oryctolagus cuniculus* population density? *Mammal Review,* **19**, 153–173.

405 Trout, R.C. *et al.* (1986) Recent trends in the rabbit population in Britain. *Mammals Review,* **16**, 117–123.

406 Trout, R.C. *et al.* (1992) The effect on a British wild rabbit population (*Oryctolagus cuniculus*) of manipulating myxomatosis. *Journal of Applied Ecology,* **29**, 679–686)

407 Trout, R.C. *et al.* (1997) Seroepidemiology of rabbit haemorrhagic disease (RHD) in wild rabbits *(Oryctolagus cuniculus)* in the United Kingdom. *Journal of Zoology,* **243**, 846–853.

408 Trout, R.C. *et al.* (2000) Factors affecting the abundance of rabbits (*Oryctolagus cuniculus*) in England and Wales. *Journal of Zoology,* **252**, 227–238.

409 Tubbs, C.R. (1974) *The buzzard.* David & Charles, Newton Abbot.

410 Twigg, G.I. *et al.* (1968) Leptospirosis in British wild mammals. *Symposia of the Zoological Society of London,* **24**, 75–98.

411 Van der Merwe, M. & Racey, P.A. (1991) Body composition and reproduction in mountain hares (*Lepus timidus scoticus*) in north-east Scotland. *Journal of Zoology,* **225**, 676–682.

412 Vaughan, J.A. & Mead-Briggs, A.R. (1970) Host finding behaviour of the rabbit flea, *Spilopsylla cuniculi,* with special reference to the significance of urine as an attactant. *Parasitology,* **61**, 397–409.

413 Verkaik, A.J. & Hewson, R. (1986) Moult and rank in male mountain hares (*Lepus timidus*). *Journal of Zoology,* **207**, 628–630.

414 Walhovd, H. (1965) Age criteria of the mountain hare (*Lepus timidus* L.) with analysis of age and sex ratios and growth in some Norwegian populations. *Meddelelser fra Statens Viltunders,* **22**, 1–57.

415 Walhovd, H. (1966) Reliability of age criteria for Danish hares (*Lepus europaeus* Pallas). *Danish Review of Game Biology,* **4**, 105–128.

416 Walker, J. & J.S. Fairley (1968) Winter food of Irish hares in Co. Antrim, Northern Ireland. *Journal of Mammalogy,* **49**, 783–785.

417 Waltari, E & Cook J.A. (2005) Hares on ice: phylogeography and historical demographics of *Lepus arcticus, L. othus* and *L. timidus* Mammalia: Lagomorpha). *Molecular Ecology,* **14**, 3005–3016.

418 Watson, A. (1963) The effect of climate on the colour changes of mountain hares in Scotland, *Proceedings of the Zoological Society of London,* **41**, 823–835.

419 Watson, A. & Hewson, R. (1973) Population densities of mountain hares (*Lepus timidus*) on western Scottish and Irish moors and on Scottish hills. *Journal of Zoology,* **170**, 151–159.

420 Watson, A. *et al.* (1973) Population densities of mountain hares compared with red grouse on Scottish moors. *Oikos,* **24**, 225–230.

421 Watson, J.S. & Tyndale-Biscoe, C.H. (1953) The apophyseal line as an age indicator for the wild rabbit *Oryctolagus cuniculus. New Zealand Journal of Science &*

Technology B, **34**, 427–435.

422 Watson, J. *et al.* (1992) The diet of sea eagles (*Haliaeetus albicilla*) and golden eagles (*Aquila chrysaetos*) in western Scotland. *Ibis,* **134**, 27–31.

423 Watson, J. *et al.* (1993) The diet of golden eagles (*Aquila chrysaetos*) in Scotland. *Ibis,* **135**, 387–393.

424 Watt, A.S. (1919) On the causes of failure of natural regeneration in British oakwoods. *Journal of Ecology,* **7**, 173–203.

425 Watt, A.S. (1957) The effect of excluding rabbits. from Grassland B (*Mesobrometum*) in Breckland. *Journal of Ecology,* **45**, 861–878.

426 Watt, A.S. (1981) Further observations on the effects of excluding rabbit from Grassland A in East Anglian Breckland: the pattern of change and factors affecting it (1936–1973). *Journal of Ecology,* **69**, 509–536.

427 Webb, N.J. (1993) Growth and mortality in juvenile European wild rabbits (*Oryctolagus cuniculus*). *Journal of Zoology,* **230**, 665–677.

428 Webb, N.J. *et al.* (1995) Natal dispersal and genetic structure in a population of the European rabbit *Oryctolagus cuniculus. Molecular Ecology,* **4**, 239–247.

429 Welch, D. & Kemp, E. (1973) A *Callunetum* subjected to intensive grazing by mountain hares. *Transactions of the Botanical Society of Edinburgh,* **42**, 89–99.

430 Wheeler, P.J.W. (2002) *The distribution of mammals across the upland landscape.* PhD thesis, University of Manchester.

431 Wheeler, S.H. & King, D.R. (1980) The use of eyelens weight for ageing wild rabbits *Oryctolagus cuniculus. Australian Wildlife Research,* **7**, 79–84.

432 Wheeler, S.H. *et al.* (1981) Habitat and warren utilisation by the European rabbit, *Oryctolagus cuniculus* (L.) as determined by radio-tracking. *Australian Wildlife Research,* **8**, 581–588.

433 Whelan, J. (1985) The population and distribution of the mountain hare (*Lepus timidus* L.) on farmland. *Irish Naturalists' Journal,* **21**, 532–534.

434 White, P.J. *et al.* (2001) The emergence of rabbit haemorrhagic disease virus: will a non-pathogenic strain protect the UK? *Philosophical Transactions of the Royal Society of London, Series B,* **356**, 1087–1095.

435 Whitwell, K. (1997) Natural causes of mortality in wild hares (*Lepus europaeus*) in Britain, 1993–95. *Gibier Faune Sauvage,* **14,** 544–545.

436 Whitwell, K.E. & Tennent, G.A. (1999) Amyloid deposits in the tissues of wild hares in the UK, p. 85 in *Proceedings of the 17th Meeting of the European Society of Veterinary Pathology, Nantes, France.*

437 Wildman, L. *et al.* (1998) The diet and foraging behaviour of the red kite in northern Scotland. *Scottish Birds,* **19**, 134–140.

438 Williams, J.M. (1985) A possible basis for economic rabbit control. *Proceedings of the New Zealand Ecological Society,* **24**, 132–135.

439 Williams, O.B. *et al.* (1974) Grazing management of Woodwalton Fen: seasonal changes in the diet of cattle and rabbits. *Journal of Applied Ecology,* **11**, 499–516.

440 Wilson, D.E. & Reeder, D.M. (eds) (2005) *Mammal species of the world, a taxonomic and geographic reference,* 3nd edn. Smithsonian Institution Press, Washington, DC

441 Wilson, J.M. (1979) *Encephalitozoon cuniculi* in wild European rabbits and a fox. *Research in Veterinary Science,* **26**, 114.

442 Wolfe, A. (1995) *A study of the ecology of the Irish mountain hare (*Lepus timidus hibernicus) *with some considerations to its management and that of the rabbit (*Oryctolagus cuniculus) *on North Bull Island, Dublin Bay.* PhD Thesis, University College Dublin.

443 Wolfe, A. *et al.* (1996) The diet of the mountain hare (*Lepus timidus hibernicus*) on coastal grassland. *Journal of Zoology,* **240**, 804–810.

444 Wood, D.H. (1980) The demography of a rabbit

population in an arid region of New South Wales, Australia. *Journal of Animal Ecology,* **49**, 55–79.

445 Wood, D.H. (1984) The rabbit (*Oryctolagus cuniculus* L.) as an element in the arid biome of Australia, pp. 273–87 in Cogger, H.G. & Cameron, E.E. (eds.) *Arid Australia.* Australian Museum, Sydney.

446 Woodman, P. *et al.* (1997) The Quaternary fauna project. *Quaternary Science Reviews,* **16**, 129–159.

447 Wray, S. (1992) *The ecology and management of European hares* (Lepus europaeus) *in commercial coniferous forestry.*

PhD thesis, University of Bristol.

448 Yalden, D.W. (1971) The mountain hare in the Peak District. *Naturalist,* **91**, 81–92.

449 Yalden, D.W. (1984) The status of the mountain hare *Lepus timidus* in the Peak District. *Naturalist,* **109**, 55–59.

450 Yalden, D.W. (1999) *The history of British mammals.* Poyser, London.

451 Yalden, D.W. Personal communication.

452 Zorner, H. (1996) *Der Feldhase.* Spektrum Akademischer Verlag, Heidelberg.

Two generations of young rabbits accompanying presumed mother reflect colonial living and rapid reproductive cycle in this species (*photo B.Phipps*).

Plate 5

A Hedgehog *Erinaceus europaeus* **B** Water shrew *Neomys fodiens* **C** Common shrew *Sorex araneus*
D Pygmy shrew *S. minutus* **E** Greater white-toothed shrew *Crocidura suaveolens*
F Lesser white-toothed shrew *C. russula* **G** Mole *Talpa europaea*

7

Insectivores
Orders Erinaceomorpha and Soricomorpha

Compiled by S. Churchfield

Hedgehogs, moles and shrews were previously assigned to the order Insectivora, together with other small, ground-dwelling insectivorous small mammals such as tenrecs, golden moles and solenodons. It was long argued that these mammals were united by the possession of certain primitive features which gave them closer affinity to the ancestral stock of mammals than any other living group. However, the composition of the group and the phylogenetic relationships of its members have been hotly debated. There is accumulating evidence from anatomical and molecular studies for the paraphyletic nature of the former clade Insectivora (e.g. [6–8, 39, 108, 313]) and alternative groupings have been proposed. Currently [353], the order Insectivora is replaced by 3 orders: the Erinaceomorpha (hedgehogs, gymnures and moonrat), the Soricomorpha (including moles, shrews, and solenodons), both represented in Europe, and the Afrosoricida (golden moles, otter-shrews and tenrecs of Africa).

Erinaceomorphs and soricomorphs are mainly small, ground-dwelling or subterranean mammals that feed principally upon invertebrates. They are found throughout the world except in Australasia and most of South America (where they are replaced ecologically by marsupials). In spite of diverse external form and certain specialisations, especially of the anterior teeth (Fig. 7.1), they retain many conservative characters: plantigrade feet, 5 clawed digits on each foot, small brain, continuous tooth-rows with relatively few, pointed cusps on the low-crowned molars, long muzzle and abdominal (but ventral) testes.

In GB, the Erinaceomorpha is represented by the hedgehog (family Erinaceidae) and the Soricomorpha by the mole (Talpidae) and the 6 shrews (Soricidae)(Plate 5), but only 2 of these occur in Ireland.

FAMILY ERINACEIDAE

A small family of about 24 species, confined to the Old World. Divided between 2 subfamilies: spiny hedgehogs (subfamily Erinaceinae), 5 closely related genera with 16 species, occur in the deciduous woodland, steppe and desert zones of Eurasia and Africa; hairy hedgehogs (subfamily Galericinae), 5 genera with 8 species, live in the evergreen forest zones of SE Asia [75]. All Erinaceidae are ground-dwelling, nocturnal and predominantly insectivorous. The family is well represented in the fossil record, back to the Eocene. All spiny hedgehogs have the dental formula 3.1.3.3/2.1.2.3; front incisors enlarged, caniniform, but true canines small, resembling small premolars.

GENUS *Erinaceus*

Woodland hedgehogs with smaller ears than desert or steppe hedgehogs *Hemiechinus, Paraechinus*. Includes the W European *E. europaeus* and 3 other Palaearctic hedgehogs, *E. concolor* and *E. roumanicus* in E Europe and W Asia, and *E. amurensis* in China and Korea. The closely related African genus *Atelerix* includes 4 species which have sometimes been placed in Erinaceus [75].

Hedgehog *Erinaceus europaeus*
Erinaceus europaeus Linnaeus, 1758; Wamlingbo, S Gothland Island, Sweden.

Urchin, hedgepig, *draenog* (Welsh), *graineag* (Scottish Gaelic), *gráinneog* (Irish Gaelic).

RECOGNITION
Unmistakable – the only British mammal with spiny pelage (Plate 5). Tooth-rows continuous but without enlarged canines, distinctive forward-projecting enlarged i^1, wide diastema between i_1 pair. Skull shows widely flared, robust zygomatic arches (Fig. 7.1).

SIGN
Footprints: Fairly distinctive, with 5 claw marks but need careful comparison with those of rats, squirrels and water vole, which are usually smaller and have 4-toed foreprints.

Faeces: Normally long (15–50 mm), cylindrical (10 mm diameter), usually firmly compressed, dark grey or black and often studded with shiny fragments of insects.

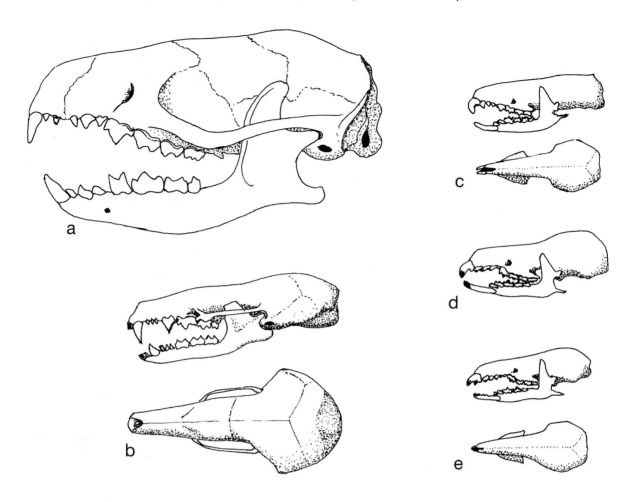

Fig. 7.1 Insectivore skulls: (a) hedgehog, (b) mole, (c) greater white-toothed shrew, (d) water shrew (lateral only) and (e) common shrew. Shrews lack the zygomatic arches, present in hedgehogs and moles; hedgehogs and shrews have the enlarged incisors, replaced functionally by an enlarged upper canine and lower p₁ in the mole *(drawn by D.W. Yalden).*

Nests: Typically dome-shaped structures constructed of tightly packed broad leaves, usually well concealed under low cover, e.g. bramble bushes.

Other field signs: Presence in area often revealed by road casualties. Active animals can be found by searching after dark with a torch, especially in moist grassy areas.

DESCRIPTION

Pelage: Several thousand sharply pointed spines completely replace hair on dorsal surface except for face and a narrow median naked patch on the crown. Spines of adults *c.*22 mm long, pale creamy brown with darker brown band near pale tip. Pelage on face and ventral surface sparse and coarse, usually uniform light brown but variable. Facial vibrissae well developed. No seasonal moult; spines long-lasting, replaced irregularly; individual marked spines still present after 18 months.

Anatomy: Feet plantigrade with 5 well-developed, clawed toes. Legs quite long but normally hidden by fur on flanks. Tail short. Sexes similar, but in male penis sheath opens well forward on belly; in female, vagina opens very close to anus. Skeleton unremarkable. Musculature of skin highly specialised to erect spines, and enable animal to flex into ball and pull spiny part of skin down over rest of body, chief muscle being the orbicularis which encircles body at limit of spines. Anatomy of soft parts described in [44].

Nipples: 5 pairs in both sexes, evenly spaced from axilla to groin.

Scent glands: No specialised external scent glands and no territorial scent-marking behaviour reported but secretions from variously located sebaceous and eccrine sweat glands, a proctodeal gland [140], sexual accessory glands and saliva in 'self-anointing' (see Fig. 7.4) are likely to be important in olfactory communication [262].

Teeth: 3.1.3.3/2.1.2.3. i_1 procumbent (Fig. 7.1), fits into gap inside enlarged caniniform i^1. i^2 and i^3 resemble premolars. Canines and first premolars small, last premolars and molars larger with low-cusped crowns.

Reproductive tract: Ventral testes permanently abdominal; elaborate male accessory reproductive organs enlarge to about 5% of total body weight in early spring [2]. Female tract unremarkable [83].

Chromosomes: 2n = 48 [287].

Relationships: DNA analysis (of mitochondrial cytochrome *b* gene sequences) has indicated that *E. europaeus* and *E. concolor* diverged in the late Miocene–early Pliocene, about 5.8 million years ago [276]. *E. europaeus* subdivides into a western clade (Spain, France, SW Netherlands, GB and Ireland) and an eastern clade distributed from Italy northwards through Austria, Switzerland, Germany to the Netherlands, Scandinavia and Estonia. A third clade is restricted to Sicily. These 3 clades show a clear separation of mitotypes [290]; eastern and western clades probably separated *c.*2.7 million years ago, with isolation enforced by retreat to refugia in Iberia and Italy during Pleistocene glaciations [276].

MEASUREMENTS
See Table 7.1.

Head and body *c.*160 mm at weaning, increasing to 260 mm or more in large adults. Tail short, 20–30 mm. Condylobasal length of skull similarly increases from *c.*40 to *c.*58 mm. Ear length 20–30 mm. Males usually bigger than females, but sex differences obscured by seasonal variations and age. Weight increases from *c.*120 g at weaning to >1100 g (exceptionally >1600 g; captives can exceed 2 kg); adult summer weight typically about 800 g [91]; males at 2 study sites, means 850±30, 950±21 g [97]. Age and sex differences in body weight overshadowed by enormous seasonal fluctuation: massive accu-mulation of fat reserves in early autumn, followed by *c.*25% [118, 223] loss of body weight during hibernation as reserves are depleted. Weight loss *c.*40% in Scandinavia, but hedgehogs larger and winters longer [184, 186].

VARIATION
Extent to which processes of premaxillae and frontal bones approach each other variable. These meet in 11 out of 16 skulls (69%) from British mainland and 12 out of 44 (27%) from continental Europe. This character the basis for description of British subspecies (*E. e. occidentalis* Barrett-Hamilton, 1900, Haddington, Scotland), but British population not sufficiently distinctive to justify recognition as a subspecies.

Individuals vary in facial shape, the degree to which they show a dark facial mask, and shade of hair colour. Spine colour variable, a few all-white spines commonly present. Full albinos with pink eyes, nose and feet not infrequent, also white specimens are known with black nose and eyes. Leucistic animals (with pale pelage, pink nose and paws but normal eye colour) also occasionally found; 25% of introduced population on Alderney are leucistic [231]. Melanics not recorded. Abnormal partial or complete loss of spines sometimes occurs.

DISTRIBUTION
W Europe, from Spain and Italy N to Scandinavia (Fig 7.2). In GB and Ireland, in suitable habitat throughout up to treeline (Fig 7.3). Present on the following islands (known introductions marked*, but many others probably introduced also): Shetland Mainland*, Unst*,Yell*, Foula*, Fetlar*, Muckle Roe*, Bressay*, Whalsay*, E Burra*, W Burra*, Vementry*, Orkney Mainland*, Hoy*, S Ronaldsay*, Shapinsay*, Stronsay*, Westray*, Papa Westray*, Eday*, Sanday*, N Ronaldsay* [23, 172]; Lewis*, Harris*, Scalpay*, N Uist*, Benbecula*, Grimsay*, S Uist* (mid 1970s), Skye, Soay, Canna*, Coll, Tiree*, Mull, Ulva, Luing, Islay*, Arran, Bute [172, 173]; Man (probably*), Anglesey, Wight, Alderney, Guernsey, Jersey; Beginish (Kerry). Successful introduction (1985) to St Mary's (Isles

Table 7.1 Measurements of British hedgehogs [15]; mean weights vary with season [117]

	Males (n = 7)		Females (n = 10)	
	Mean	Range	Mean	Range
Head and body (mm)	230	188–263	217	179–257
Tail (mm)	26	17–35	23.5	17–31
Weight (g)		900–1200		800–1025

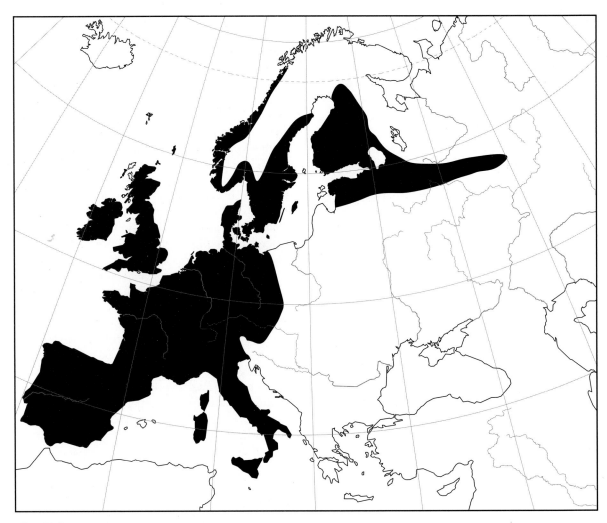

Fig. 7.2 Hedgehog *Erinaceus europaeus:* world distribution.

Fig. 7.3 Hedgehog *Erinaceus europaeus:* distribution in the British Isles.

of Scilly) and Sark (where population expanded rapidly in 1990s). British hedgehogs introduced to New Zealand late 19th century, very abundant there now.

HISTORY
Genus *Erinaceus* known from Early Miocene. Late Glacial, confined to Spain and Italy. Spread N quickly, probably indigenous to GB, where present since Mesolithic, *c.*9500 bp at Star Carr, Yorkshire [121, 363]. Probably introduced to Ireland (a Norman date has been suggested [336]), and to most of the smaller islands where it occurs.

HABITAT
Most abundant where grassland in close proximity to woodland, scrub or hedgerow, e.g. edge of woods, hedgerows in meadowland, or sand dunes with shrubs. Present in virtually all lowland habitats where there is sufficient cover for nesting. However, much farmland has become less suitable for hedgehogs because of a shift during the last 50 years to larger-scale intensive agriculture, use

of pesticides, loss of hedgerows and reduction of permanent grassland and rough grazing (rich in macroinvertebrates) [227]. More common in suburban areas; in 10 paired sites, only seen in 3 of 82 pasture fields (4%), but in 14 of 23 amenity grasslands (61%) [366]. Generally scarce in coniferous woodland, marshy and moorland areas. The availability of suitable sites and materials for summer nests (daytime refuges and breeding nests) and winter nests (hibernacula) is likely to be a factor limiting distribution. Amenity grasslands rich in earthworms and other invertebrate food, but also argued to be a refuge habitat from badger predation [366].

SOCIAL ORGANISATION AND BEHAVIOUR

General behaviour fairly well known from field and captive studies (review in [262]). Hibernates from about November to March. Activity almost entirely nocturnal but may be seen at dawn and dusk; forages during daylight in periods of food shortage, e.g. drought. Essentially a solitary species but with overlapping home ranges; does not defend territories but shows evidence of mutual avoidance [218, 261].

Home range: Several field studies have shown sexually active males to range more widely and over longer distances than females [262]. Distance travelled per night in suburban golf-course habitat averaged 1690 m (males) and 1006 m (females). Seasonal ranges average 32 ha (males), 10 ha (females). The ranges of both females and males may overlap completely; male's range typically overlaps that of several females [261]. Similar range data obtained from a farmland study in which one male covered as much as 3140 m in one night [226]. In less open, forest-edge habitat, nightly distances travelled are less, averaging 868 m for a male, 570 m, 693 m for 2 females [225]. These data are based on intensive radio-tracking studies; mark–recapture or short-duration radio-tracking result in smaller estimates of range size. Distance travelled is a more reliable measure of activity per night than nightly range area [226]. Home range not significantly affected by provision of supplementary food, at least in summer [224].

Nesting: Summer nests, used as daytime refuges, typically located and constructed in the same way as hibernacula (winter nests) but, except for breeding nests, may be less substantial [264]. Often occupied for only a few days before moving to another. Previously used nests may be used again and may sometimes be used by other individuals. Males change nests more frequently than females [264].

For hibernation, builds a hibernaculum, a nest 30–60 cm diameter usually constructed from broad leaves constrained by cover, e.g. bramble or brushwood, sometimes in rabbit burrow or under garden shed. In machair habitat on S Uist, rabbit burrows are the principal nest sites [173]. More than one hibernaculum usually built; most animals move at least once during winter. Some evidence of territoriality; hibernacula are rarely in very close proximity [221]. Hibernaculum serves to maintain optimal temperature for hibernation [228]. Arousals during winter normal and fairly regular, though hedgehog often does not leave its nest before resuming torpor. Hibernation usually begins about October, induced at least partly by low temperature. Adult males begin earliest, females later; younger animals (especially late litters) may remain active into December. Hibernation ends from March to April in S England; males earlier than females. On S Uist, most emerged late April, subadults about 5 days earlier than adults, but no difference between sexes [172]. Hibernation preceded by accumulation of white fat under the skin and around the viscera, and deposits of brown fat (thermogenic tissue important for arousal) mainly around the thorax. During hibernation, body temperature falls from normal 35 °C to match that of the environment. Heart beat slows from normal sleeping rate of around 147 beats/min to 2–12 beats/min at 4 °C, the optimum hibernation temperature [185]; breathing rate drops to average 13 breaths/min [183]. Other physiological changes much studied, reviewed in [262].

Scent-marking: No evidence of scent-marking objects or locations, or systematic deposition of urine or faeces. Self-anointing is an intriguing activity in which the hedgehog is stimulated to produce frothy saliva which is liberally plastered

Fig. 7.4 Hedgehog self-anointing – applying copious saliva to its spines *(photo P. Morris)*.

over its body (Fig. 7.4) [37]. Nature of stimulus and purpose remain a mystery (see review [262]) but likely to be a means of spreading odours over body for self-advertisement (e.g. to facilitate individual recognition).

Vocalisations: Normally silent except for snuffling sounds during foraging, but distressed adults can emit loud scream; nestlings may make bird-like chirping sounds if separated from family. Rapid, repeated snorting during aggressive and courtship interactions.

Other communication: Unlikely to be by acoustic or visual means except perhaps at short range. Olfactory communication likely to be important, especially during prolonged courtship encounters, but poorly known.

Aggressive behaviour: Captives, especially males, may fight and establish a 'peck order' [193] but wild hedgehogs seem to avoid each other and do not defend exclusive territories. Fighting or overt aggression (other than courtship encounters) rarely witnessed in field studies.

Dispersal: Little known, but young may disperse from natal area in the first few months of life [17]; once established seem to remain in same area for life [261]. However, translocated animals may disperse more than 2 km, perhaps as much as 15 km [1], but most settled at *c.*1 km in Oxfordshire [97], 300–500 m in Bristol [214].

Activity: Gait rather hesitant, with frequent stops to sniff the air. Snuffle and snort regularly when searching for food. Smell and hearing acute, eyesight relatively poor. Crouch and erect spines at least sign of danger, reacting especially to noise; will jerk upwards to spike dog's nose [1]. Roll up tightly when disturbed, head and extremities completely protected by spines. Swim and climb surprisingly well. Some homing instinct, and ability to recognise landmarks; may follow well-used paths [193].

Grooming: Scratching of spines (with hindfoot) frequently observed during activity, especially soon after leaving nest. Fur may also be licked vigorously.

FEEDING

Food almost entirely ground-living invertebrates; in Britain (% occurrence), beetles (mainly carabids 60% and scarabeids 20%), caterpillars (49%) and earthworms (34%) are principal prey [91, 356, 360]; frequently eaten prey include earwigs, slugs and snails, dipteran larvae, centipedes, millipedes, harvestmen and spiders. Smaller prey, arachnids, woodlice and myriapods, eaten more frequently by young animals; molluscs, beetles and caterpillars eaten more by adults [91]. Nightly food requirement probably 60–80 g wet weight [186, 356]. Food caught and dealt with entirely by the mouth. Food never cached, not even for winter.

Occasionally take carrion and predate eggs or chicks of ground-nesting birds [173, 187]. Despite the low importance of eggs in the diet, egg predation by hedgehogs on S Uist accounted for between 36% and 64% of nest failures of lapwing, dunlin, snipe and redshank in 1996–1997 [173]. Elsewhere hedgehogs account for about 10% of game-bird clutches lost to predators.

Folk tales of hedgehogs carrying fruit (usually apples) on spines frequently repeated. Validity disputed, though stories of wide currency. Similarly, often-repeated tales of hedgehogs taking milk from cows. Frequently claimed to kill snakes for food, but little evidence for this in Britain. Spines observed to protect skin from puncture by fangs. Hedgehogs have some degree of immunity to adder venom; proteinase inhibitors in the blood plasma counteract the haemorrhagic effect of the venom [354].

BREEDING

Breeding season: 2 peaks of pregnancies, May–July and September. Gestation: 31–35 days. Litter size: 2–7, generally 4–5. Weight at birth: 10–25 g. Duration of lactation: 4–6 weeks.

Males fertile early April to late August, pregnant females found May–October with early peak May–July and later peak September [216] (Fig. 7.5). Seasonally polyoestrous, spontaneous ovulation; early cycles often infertile [83]. Pregnancy 31–35 days, embryos typically 2–7, litter of *c.*4–6 young born usually in June; means recorded 5.0 (n = 10) [83] and 4.6 (n = 42) [216]. Few embryos lost (3.3%) but postnatal mortality

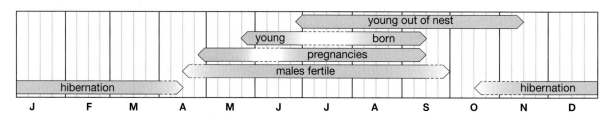

Fig. 7.5 Hedgehog: annual cycle.

Fig. 7.6 Baby hedgehogs, *c*.10 days old, showing the soft white spines with which they are born *(photo P. Morris)*.

c.20% prior to weaning [222]. Under favourable conditions in Britain could potentially raise 2 litters in a season [83] but only demonstrated in wild for S Uist [172]. 3rd litter possible under captive conditions. Promiscuous; both sexes may each have several partners in a season [172, 265].

Males: Marked seasonal changes in size of testes and sexual accessory organs, peak weights in late April and May [2]. Spermatogenesis virtually ceases October–December [119]. Seasonal hormonal changes described in [118].

Females: Seasonal changes in size of sexual organs described in [83]. Duration of oestrus cycle unknown but probably similar to the average of 8–10 days reported for long-eared hedgehogs (*Hemiechinus collaris*) [5]. Infertile matings may result in a 7–10 day period of pseudopregnancy [83]. Courtship consists of the male approaching and circling the female, who repulses him aggressively with much snorting and butting with bristling spines. Circling may continue for hours before the female allows copulation. Birth in large, specially built nest. Mother eats young if disturbed soon after birth, later reacts to interference by carrying litter to safer place. Later may lead young on foraging trips. Male takes no part in rearing family.

Development of young: Young suck for about 4 weeks; blind at birth, weighing 10–25 g; sex ratio about equal. First coat of white spines appears soon after birth (Fig. 7.6), second pelage of dark spines with white tips visible by 36 hours among first white spines. Capable of rolling up from day 11. Eyes open at day 14, begin to leave nest at about day 22. Replacement of milk teeth begins about day 24, weaned at 4–6 weeks. Young disperse to lead solitary lives thereafter. Young from early summer litters are fully grown before hibernation in autumn; those from later litters must hibernate at a subadult size and are unlikely to survive the winter: a weight of 450 g or more is required to survive hibernation [223], heavier animals probably have higher survival rate [36]. First breed in year following birth, at not less than 9 months old [2, 83].

POPULATION

Numbers: Total pre-breeding population estimated at 1 555 000 (England 1 100 000; Scotland 310 000; Wales 14 000 [149]) but based on very limited information. Reported densities vary with habitat: 0.21/ha to 1.23/ha in small-scale mixed farmland and pasture [89, 100, 226]; suburban areas 0.83/ha [260] and 1.79/ha [97]. In 10 paired study sites, only 0.09/ha in pasture but 1.54/ha in amenity grasslands [366]. No reliable data about national population trends, although most data suggest either stable or in long-term decline [227]. Steady decline in numbers killed by gamekeepers, 1961–1999, to less than 50% [323], but may reflect less trapping rather than fewer hedgehogs. Numbers killed per 100 miles of road fell by 20–30% in 1990s [29]. Widespread and consistent anecdotal evidence of decline in gardens. Increases in badger numbers may pose significant threat due to predation and competition for food [96, 97]; sett density of >10/km^2 predicted to result in no hedgehogs, even in favoured amenity grasslands [366].

Sex ratio: Among juveniles 1:1; higher proportions of males observed in spring and of females in autumn reflect sexual differences in seasonal activity.

Age determination: Most reliably determined by growth lines in jaw [219] and epiphyseal fusion in the forefoot [220], but a combination of methods is recommended (review in [262]).

Age structure: Population samples taken in autumn show preponderance of juveniles, but partly because adults already hibernating. At beginning of breeding season 40–45% of population comprises 1-year-old animals. Mortality of 60–70% in 1st year is suggested by preliminary studies, with good survival over next 2 years, and decline in survival rate after 4th or 5th year [1]. May achieve 7 years of age in wild; maximum lifespan probably *c*.10 years.

MORTALITY

Spines protect against most predators, although some (especially the sick and young) may be killed by foxes, dogs or other ground predators, e.g. mink [102] or polecat. Very occasionally taken by tawny owl and golden eagle, regularly (in Europe) by eagle owl. Badgers peel off spiny skin using strong claws and are a significant predator; foxes may also peel hedgehogs. In areas of high badger density (20/km²) predation pressure may locally eliminate hedgehogs but they persisted in an area with 5 badgers/km² [96]. Many die in hibernation, especially during first winter; no reliable data from GB, but 28% p.a. adults and 28% juveniles died in hibernation in S Sweden [184]. Large numbers killed on roads; again no reliable British data, but 10% p.a. of adults, only 2% of juveniles killed in S Sweden [184]; would extrapolate to around 150 000–170 000 killed annually on British roads, could cause loss of isolated populations. Hedgehogs account for 54% of mammal casualties received by wildlife rescue centres (BWRC data, mean for 1993–1997). In a survey of fatalities (n = 856) from the admissions to 3 hedgehog rescue centres, 11.8% had traumatic injuries (e.g. from mowers), 8.8% died from road traffic accidents, 4.3% were poisoned, 2.3% were injured by dogs and cats [263]. Some also incinerated through nesting or hibernating in garden bonfire heaps. Despite ability to swim, many drown in garden ponds through inability to climb out. Cattle grids a similar hazard, but many now fitted with escape ramps.

PARASITES AND PATHOGENS
See Table 7.2.

Ectoparasites: Flea *Archaeopsylla erinacei* is highly specific and sometimes present in large numbers. Lice have not been recorded. Tick *Ixodes hexagonus* frequent and *I. ricinus* common, as are parasitic mites *Caparinia tripilis* and *Demodex erinacei*; *Sarcoptes* spp. and others may also occur. Blowfly maggots (Family Calliphoridae) may infest wounds, ears and other orifices, especially of sick, weakened individuals.

Helminths: Reported incidences of *Brachylaemus erinacei* (Trematoda) 2.7% [177], 16.4% [263]. Lungworms, *Crenosoma striatum* and *Capillaria aerophila* (Nematoda), commonly fatal in hedgehogs, may occur in mixed infections [199]. *C. striatum* found in 39% and *C. aerophila* in 20.9% of animals [263]. Intestinal *Capillaria* also common; reported incidences 49.6% [263], 79% [22]. *Rodentolepis erinacei* (Cestoda) less common; reported incidences 2.6% [22], 1.4% [177], 3.7% [263]. Thorny-headed worms (Acanthocephala) little studied in Britain; 1.6% incidence reported in [263].

Others: Foot-and-mouth disease [204] and paramyxovirus have been reported [337]. Bacteria include *Leptospira* [333] and *Salmonella* [325]. Coccidia, principally *Isospora rastegaivae*, found in 15.2% of animals [263]. A ringworm fungus, *Trichophyton erinacei*, is specific to hedgehogs and infects the skin of 20–25% of British animals; more prevalent in older animals and those living at higher densities [230]. *Candida albicans* ('thrush') has been found in over 87% of European hedgehogs in New Zealand [307].

RELATIONS WITH HUMANS
Traditionally persecuted for predation on eggs of game birds, although damage is relatively insignificant compared with that done by foxes and crows. Nevertheless, hundreds killed annually in the past on some shooting estates. Blamed for decline of seabirds on N Ronaldsay, but collapse of sandeel supply a more likely cause. Caused significant declines in breeding success of waders in Hebrides [174], leading to attempted eradication; some rescued by supporters, released on mainland Scotland. Combined efforts removed <500 per year (2003–2005), so unlikely to eradicate population estimated at 5000.

Formerly eaten in some areas, especially by gypsies who baked them in mud. Has been used for experimental work on viruses (foot-and-mouth disease, influenza, yellow fever) and the physiology of hibernation. Easy to keep, will breed in captivity [22]. Popular with general public, witness support given to British Hedgehog Preservation Society. Often encouraged to visit food bowls put out in gardens, perhaps contributing to apparent abundance of hedgehogs in suburban habitats, where reported from 70% of gardens [4]. Regarded as a useful predator of horticultural pests such as slugs, although also threatened by widespread use of slug pellets. Several thousand sick, injured and abandoned animals taken into care annually, often by specialist hedgehog carers. Large numbers subsequently released with a high survival rate (even among inexperienced juveniles) [214, 229].

Afforded partial protection on Schedule 6 of the Wildlife and Countryside Act 1981 and the Wild Mammals (Protection) Act 1996; trapping or invasive procedures require a licence (see Chapter 4).

LITERATURE
Morris [228] gives a comprehensive popular account. Bullen [34] is a useful manual for carers of hedgehogs. The monograph by Reeve [262] includes study methods.

PRINCIPAL AUTHORS
P.A. Morris & N.J. Reeve

Table 7.2 Principal endoparasites and pathogens of hedgehogs. A large number of less commonly found species are excluded. Adapted from [261, 262, 366] with further example of British studies as indicated

Organism	Notes
Trematoda	
Brachylaemus erinacei	Intestinal fluke specific to hedgehogs; snails e.g. Helicidae are intermediate hosts [177]
Nematoda	
Crenosoma striatum	Lungworm specific to hedgehogs infesting trachea, bronchi, bronchioles and alveolar ducts [22, 199]. Molluscan intermediate hosts
Capillaria aerophila	Lungworms infesting the epithelium of the trachea, bronchi and bronchioles [199] direct transmission or via earthworms and possibly carabid beetles
Capillaria erinacei, c. ovoreticulata and at least one other *Capillaria* spp.	Intestinal worms [22, 199]
Cestoda	
Rodentolepis (=Hymenolepis) erinacei	Intestinal tapeworm with arthropod intermediate hosts; insects, myriapods, etc. [177].
Acanthocephala	
Moniliformis erinacei, M. major and others	Intestinal thorny-headed worm, insects are likely intermediate hosts
Viruses	
Paramyxoviruses of the morbilli group	Symptoms include poor coordination, lesions of eyes mouth, feet, lungs, brain [337]
Foot and mouth disease	Vesicular lesions on feet, perineum and around mouth or asymptomatic [162, 204]
Bacteria	
Leptospira interrogans (serovar bratislava)	Blood system and urinary tract [194]
Salmonella enteriditis	The commonest of several *Salmonella* spp. that may be found in the gut; may cause enteritis [177]
Bordetella bronchiseptica	Affects respiratory tract [162] may complicate lungworm infections [177]
Pasteurella spp.	Respiratory tract [105]
Protozoa	
Isospora rastegaivae and other coccidia	Intestinal; usually asymptomatic but may lead to diarrhoea and emaciation
Toxoplasma gondii	General effects: infects blood and other tissues
Fungi	
Trichophyton erinacei [109]	'Ringworm'; affects skin, especially of the head
Candida albicans	Affects mouth, gastrointestinal and genitourinary tract

FAMILY TALPIDAE

A family of about 16 genera, 39 species of fossorial, semi-fossorial and semi-aquatic insectivores, found in moist soils and riparian habitats throughout Palaearctic and Nearctic. Besides true moles *Talpa, Scapanus, Scalopus* etc., includes several species of shrew-moles, *Urotrichus* in E Asia and *Neurotrichus* in N America, and the semi-aquatic desmans, *Desmana* of Russia and *Galemys* of Iberia.

GENUS *Talpa*

The moles of the Palaearctic comprise some 9 very similar species, occurring from GB to Siberia. Highly adapted for a subterranean life, combine tubular body, reduced extremities and large, laterally placed spade-like hands. The most widespread, *T. europaea*, alone occurs in GB. Relatives in E Asia, 5 species of *Mogera*, sometimes included in *Talpa*. The dental formula is 3.1.4.3/3.1.4.3 (the maximum found in placental mammals); lower canine small, replaced functionally by enlarged caniniform p_1.

Mole *Talpa europaea*
Talpa europaea Linnaeus, 1758; S Sweden.

Moldwarp, want, taupe; *gwadd, twrch daear* (Welsh), *famh* (Scottish Gaelic).

RECOGNITION
Elongate cylindrical body with uniformly short, usually black, fur. Prominent features are broad, spade-like forelimbs, pink fleshy snout and short tail (Plate 5). Ears without pinnae, eyes minute, hidden in fur (Fig. 7.7); tapering head deeply set into the main body giving the appearance of no proper neck. Seldom seen above ground, but unlikely to be confused with any other mammal.

Skull, *c.*35 mm in length, has continuous tooth-rows, each with 11 teeth, enlarged upper canines and very slender zygomatic arches (Fig 7.1).

Short humerus and broad forefeet are distinctive features of the skeleton, often found in owl pellets and mammalian scats.

SIGN
Most evident from the molehills, spoil heaps formed during the excavation of permanent tunnels; usually conical in shape with no opening to ground surface. Beneath each molehill there is a vertical or sloping tunnel through which soil has been pushed to the surface. Molehills are not permanent features, are eroded by weather and other animals, rapidly colonised by vegetation. In some areas molehills may be confused with more permanent, and usually larger, steep-sided hills of the yellow ant *Lasius flavus*; these usually firmer, composed of finer grains, partially vegetated. When moles are colonising new areas, or feeding in newly cultivated fields, temporary surface tunnels, which appear as slightly raised ridges of soil, may be formed.

Under some circumstances, particularly in low-lying areas prone to flooding or on very shallow soils, more permanent hills may be constructed. Often termed 'fortresses', these usually contain a nest chamber above the level of the surrounding ground and several radiating tunnels. Function is probably thermal insulation and protection for the nest which, in other circumstances, is constructed at some depth beneath the ground surface. Not all moles build these structures. Built throughout the year, but chiefly in winter, and by both sexes. Often contain a large store of decapitated earthworms, serve as a food reserve during periods of flooding or when shallow soils are hard-frozen in the winter [135].

DESCRIPTION
Anatomy: Highly specialised for a fossorial life. Body cylindrical and external features, including ears, much reduced in size to facilitate movement through tunnels. Forelimbs adapted for digging: broad, flat hand equipped with 5 large, strong claws, faces sideways, cannot be placed flat on ground. An extra bone, the radial sesamoid, '6th finger', further increases surface area of hand. Much-enlarged humerus strongly attached to scapula, clavicle and deep sternum [137, 359]. In contrast, hind limbs slender, simple in structure, though '6th toe', tibial sesamoid, broadens foot. Primarily used for movement, but also brace body against tunnel walls whilst digging. Tail short, with constriction at base, usually carried erect. Eyes reduced in size, concealed by thick pelage, but are functional [256]. Canal lumen area, major determinant of sensitivity in the vertebrate

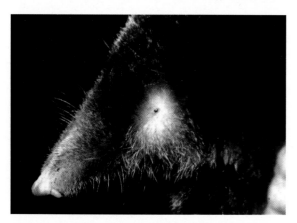

Fig. 7.7 Mole, portrait showing the minute eye, normally hidden in the fur *(photo P. Morris)*.

Table 7.3 Measurements of moles from Suffolk [135]

	Males (n = 42)		Females (n = 57)	
	Mean	Range	Mean	Range
Head and body (mm)	143	121–159	135	113–144
Tail (mm)	33	26–40	32	25–38
Weight (g)	110	87–128	85	72–106

semicircular canals, is significantly enlarged in *T. europaea* and may adapt it to life underground [205].

Pelage: Uniformly short over the whole body, *c.*6 mm in summer, and 9 mm in winter. Velvet texture, no lie, so unaffected by frequent backing down tunnels. Only feet and snout are largely devoid of fur. Colour usually velvet black, but variable (see Variation); no sexual dimorphism. Yellow-brown secretions from skin glands form obvious midventral staining in both sexes, particularly during breeding season. Skin on chest thicker than elsewhere, serving to protect the body while digging [308]. Naked snout covered with touch-sensitive, microscopic receptors (Eimer's organs). Coarse vibrissae on face, forelimbs and tail are all sensory.

Moult: At least twice per year. Spring moult, April–May in females, May–June in males, begins on rump, spreads around flanks and sides to back, eventually to head and shoulders. Autumnal moult, September–December, about a week earlier in males, proceeds in the reverse order. May also be partial, patchy, summer moult [302].

External genitalia: Males and non-breeding females are similar, easily confused. Testes located outside the abdomen, not in external scrotum but in sacs near base of tail, producing no external swelling. Sexes best distinguished by length of the prepuce (>6 mm in males and <6 mm in females), and by length of the perineum (>5 mm in males, <4 mm in females) [203]. Vagina and uterus merge to form a long, S-shaped median uterovaginal canal into which the 2 uterine horns open at right angles. Vulva perforates only during breeding season.

Nipples: 4 pairs, inguinal.

Scent glands: Paired anal glands, containing both holocrine and apocrine elements, are involved in scent-marking behaviour [137].

Skull: Long and narrow, tapering forward from middle of brain case, the widest point, to just behind the canines. Zygomatic arches slender, tympanic bullae flattened. Surface of skull smooth apart from a slight sagittal crest, which becomes more marked in older animals. Viewed laterally, skull has long wedge-shaped outline, rounded off posteriorly. Incisors small and simple in structure, followed in upper jaw by large canines, but in lower jaw by smaller canines, resembling 4th incisors, and large caniniform 1st premolars. The other anterior premolars are small, almost rudimentary. Deciduous dentition is rudimentary, does not erupt, and is not detectable after birth except for dp^1, which persists as the functional tooth and is not replaced.

Chromosomes: 2n = 34; FNa = 64 (European data) [368].

RELATIONSHIPS
T. europaea very similar to *T. romana* (Italy and Balkans) and the smaller *T. caeca* of S Europe. *T. caeca* has a different karyotype (2n = 36) from both *T. europaea* and *T. romana* (both 2n = 34 [368]). Further east, *T. europaea* is replaced by the more distinctive *T. altaica*.

MEASUREMENTS
Males generally larger than females (Table 7.3), but body weights and sizes highly variable, not recommended as characters for distinguishing between the sexes.

VARIATION
British animals not distinguishable from European specimens, and no evidence of clear regional variation in Britain. Abnormal coat colour, including albino, cream, apricot, rust coloured, piebald and grey or silver grey, more frequent than in other British mammals, but no figure for frequencies available.

Premolars variable, at least one upper absent in 0.3% of 8184 animals collected throughout the species' range (0 out of 880 from England). Some lower premolars absent in 0.6% of 8653 (0.2% of 978

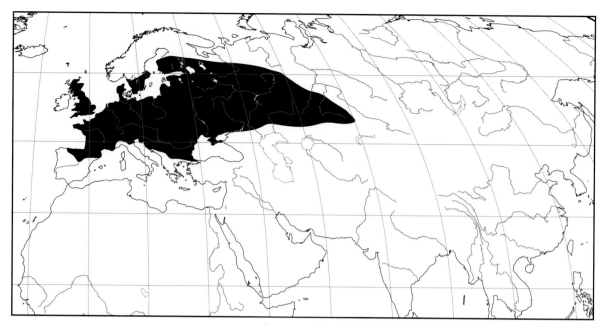

Fig. 7.8 Mole *Talpa europaea:* world distribution.

from England); 0.1% of 8184 had supplementary, or bicuspid, upper premolars (0.34% of 880 from England); and supplementary lower premolars present in 2.1% of 8653 (1.7% of 978 from England) [315].

DISTRIBUTION

From GB east to W Siberia, about 70° E; in middle latitudes, absent from most of Scandinavia (too cold) and Mediterranean (too dry) (Fig. 7.8). Throughout mainland GB, and on Skye, Mull,

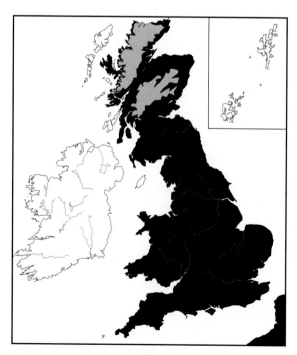

Fig. 7.9 Mole *Talpa europaea:* distribution in GB.

Anglesey, Wight, Alderney and Jersey, wherever habitat is suitable. Absent from Ireland, Man and outer islands (Fig. 7.9).

HISTORY

Recorded from early Pleistocene (Cromerian interglacial), and from last glaciation at Tornewton Cave, Devon [321]. Likely to have been a natural Postglacial colonist, but records unreliable because of intrusive burrowing. Present at Thatcham, Berkshire and Steetley Cave, Derbyshire, both Mesolithic sites [363].

HABITAT

Highly adaptable; present in most habitats where soil is sufficiently deep to allow tunnel construction. Originally inhabitants of deciduous woodland, moles have taken advantage of agriculture and thrive in pastures and on arable land. Live at low densities in coniferous forests, on moorland and in sand-dune systems, probably because of the paucity of suitable prey [137]. Recorded up to 1000 m asl in Wales [211].

SOCIAL ORGANISATION AND BEHAVIOUR

Burrow system: Moles spend almost their whole lives in an extensive and elaborate system of tunnels in various depths, from just below the surface to well over 1 m down [137]. Digging performed exclusively with forelimbs, using alternate strokes. Limb is thrust sideways and backwards, by rotation of the humerus, pushing loosened soil into tunnel behind the mole. While digging, hindlimbs are braced against the sides of the tunnel, providing support [301]. When earth has accumulated behind, mole turns towards the displaced earth, scoops it up with forelimbs and pushes it along tunnel to a previously dug vertical or sloping shaft leading to ground surface.

Usually a single nest, which may be situated anywhere within the home range, but usually away from the range boundary. Females may use 2 or more nests during breeding season [137]. Composed of dry grass, leaves or even paper, all gathered from ground surface; lies in a chamber formed by enlarging a section of tunnel.

Social dispersion: Males and females solitary for most of the year, occupying largely exclusive territories. If resident removed, territory quickly taken over by neighbours, sometimes within a few hours. During non-breeding season, male's territory may overlap slightly with those of one or more females but not with those of other males. With onset of breeding, males tunnel over extensive areas in search of receptive females and ranges of neighbouring males may overlap considerably [137].

Home-range size: For the female 1300–2100 m², does not vary seasonally. During the non-breeding season, males occupy ranges about twice as large (2700–3400 m²), increase *c*.3-fold during breeding season (to 7300–7700 m²). Size of home range is a function of habitat and food availability [137].

Scent: Deposited from anal glands during routine daily movements. Advertises presence of a resident animal, but short-lived, must be renewed frequently. Secretions experimentally placed in tunnels will repel other moles. Anal glands larger in males than females, show marked seasonal changes in weight in both sexes: largest during the breeding season, regress thereafter [137].

Secretions dominated by C5–C10 carboxylic acids. Female glands regress as they enter pro-oestrus, accompanied by profound changes in chemical composition of the secretion with early disappearance of carboxylic acids. In juveniles, composition changes as the animal matures, carboxylic acids become dominant only at maturity [178].

Dispersal: Adults rarely disperse once established in territory, but may do so following flooding or other disturbance [137]. Dispersal of young follows weaning and is a time of major mortality by predation.

Aggressive behaviour: Takes form of chasing through tunnels and fighting with the forelimbs and teeth. Encounters rarely fatal since subordinate usually withdraws. Both sexes apparently equally aggressive towards intruders. Agonistic encounters rare because moles appear to show temporal avoidance of neighbours; only one uses any area of overlap between adjacent territories at any given time [320]. Radiotelemetry revealed that, on average, moles spent only 0.9% of their time within 6 m of another mole [198]. However, no evidence from simultaneous movement patterns of neighbouring moles avoiding each other. Tend to return to same part of range at the same time on successive days, but some indication of gradual changes in spatial pattern of daily home-range use.

Activity: For most of year, both sexes have 3 periods of activity every 24 h, each lasting for 3–4 h, followed by a rest period of similar duration spent in nest. During breeding season, males may not return to their nests for several days at a time, sleeping at irregular intervals in the tunnel system. Lactating females return to their nests 4–6 times each 24 h, but show no change in the total time spent foraging [137]. During autumn, males show only 2 active periods per 24 h [320]. Males generally spend more time active each day than females. Become active at about the same time each day, regardless of season, with no clear relationship between onset of activity and sunrise. Onset and cessation of activity is closely synchronised between neighbouring animals, at least in NE Scotland [137]. Elsewhere, may be sudden start of activity at dawn and cessation shortly before dusk, at all times of year [357]. Differences between these studies may reflect the fact that the latter moles were in captivity without competing neighbours. In other areas may show tetraphasic pattern of daily activity under drought conditions [198].

Grooming: By hindfeet and teeth only.

FEEDING

Moles obtain most food by foraging along the tunnel system, eating soil invertebrates that they encounter, either in the tunnel or in the tunnel walls. Incidental food may be obtained whilst digging; very occasionally, are seen scavenging on the surface [144]. Earthworms, particularly *Lumbricus terrestris*, are the single most important prey, present in 50–100% of stomachs. Insect larvae (Elateridae, Tipulidae, Scarabaeidae) also taken in large numbers, myriapods and molluscs less so. Composition of diet reflects local abundance and availability of prey species, insects more important in acid soils. Earthworms predominate in winter (in 90–100% of stomachs), less in summer (50%) when insects more important [123, 137, 191, 303].

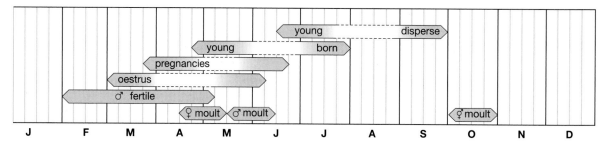

Fig. 7.10 Mole: annual cycle.

From rates of energy expenditure, a 100 g mole requires about 62 g of earthworms daily, which provide c.185 kJ.

Food, particularly earthworms with anterior segments mutilated, commonly stored at all times of the year, but particularly in spring and autumn. Up to 1500 g of worms have been recorded in a store, sufficient to nourish a mole for around 24 days [111, 137].

BREEDING

Litter of usually 3–4 young born in spring, sometimes, especially in S England and Europe, followed by a 2nd later in the summer (Fig. 7.10). Gestation c.4 weeks, weaning 4–5 weeks.

Breeding season short, with rapid enlargement and regression of gonads and accessory organs. Onset of breeding varies with latitude, strongly suggesting regulation by changes in photoperiod [137]. 1st pregnancies recorded in March in England [135] and in May–June in NE Scotland [137, 257].

Moles exceptional among female mammals in possession of bilateral ovotestes [257]. Ovotestis contains a morphologically normal ovarian component that develops during spring breeding season and a histologically defined testicular region, the interstitial gland, which enlarges during autumn when ovarian component decreases in size. Female mole also displays a penile clitoris traversed by a urethral canal. Clear evidence of seasonal variation in plasma testosterone concentrations in female moles, which parallel the growth and regression of the 'testicular' interstitial gland [352].

Oestrus probably lasts <24 h. Promiscuous. Gestation c.4 weeks. Average number of embryos in Britain 3.8, means of 5.7 recorded in continental European samples [137]. Rate of embryo resorption is variable; in one study 6% [191], in another 25%, including 20% of litters totally resorbed [216]. 2nd litters occur in S England and are common in continental populations.

Young born naked, c.3.5 g. Fur starts to grow at 14 days and eyes open at 22 days, when young weigh c.40 g. Lactation lasts 4–5 weeks. Juveniles start leaving nest at c.33 days and finally disperse at 5–6 weeks [132]. Dispersal occurs above ground. By 3 months old, juveniles are difficult to distinguish from adults on the basis of body proportions. Moles become sexually mature in the spring following their birth.

POPULATION

Sex ratio: In adults 1:1, but during breeding season males outnumber females in captured samples due to increased movement [320].

Densities: 8/ha in winter and 16/ha in summer reported for English pastures [191]. In NE Scotland densities in woodland and pasture remain similar throughout the year, 4–5/ha [137]. Density of molehills is not an accurate measure of population size. Extrapolating densities, British population estimated at 31 million (England 19.75 million, Scotland 8 million, Wales 3.25 million) [149].

Population structure: Can be accurately aged by counting incremental growth rings in teeth [195]. Generally, once established in a territory, mortality rates relatively constant, around 50–60% p.a., regardless of age. Consequently, most are aged 1 year or less, few live beyond 3 years, although some attain 6 years [137].

MORTALITY

Mortality most severe during surface dispersal of juveniles in early summer. Major causes of mortality at this time are starvation, for those failing to find a vacant territory, and predation, by tawny owls, buzzards, stoats, domestic cats and dogs, and vehicles. May contribute 45% by weight of tawny owl diet in June–July. About 68% mortality in 1st year [137, 144, 310].

Territorial adults relatively safe from predation, about 50% p.a. mortality; oldest 1% may reach 6 years. However, persecution by humans still a major source of adult mortality, although much less than formerly when moles were trapped for their skins. In 1905, >1 million skins p.a. were traded on London market alone and by 1920s

>12 million skins a year were being sent from Europe to America to satisfy fashion market. Today, market for moleskins practically non-existent, although moles still widely persecuted because of perceived pest status [137].

PARASITES AND PATHOGENS

Ectoparasites: Infestation enhanced by use of permanent nest. Fleas include *Palaeopsylla minor, P. kohauti, Ctenophthalmus bisoctodentatus, C. nobilis* and *Hystrichopsylla talpae* [304]. Fur mite *Labidophorus soricis* and tick *Ixodes hexagonus* often present.

Six species of fleas and 13 species of mites collected from 9 mole nests in Leicestershire and 1 nest in Surrey [104]; mean of 127.8 adult fleas collected per nest; an appreciably higher figure than previously reported for mole nests in Europe. *Ctenophthalmus nobilis* most abundant (901 specimens) followed by *C. bisoctodentatus* (288), *Hystrichopsylla talpae* (72), *Palaeopsylla minor* (8), *Rhadinopsylla pentacantha* (8) and *R. isacantha* (1). Mites included 4 species of facultative parasites, 4 predatory species and 5 species of soil-associated saprophages/fungivores. Samples suggested that species composition of mites in English mole nests impoverished compared with that for mole nests in continental Europe.

No lice recorded.

Endoparasites: Include trematode *Ityogonimus* spp. [120] and blood protozoans *Trypanosoma talpae* and *Babesia microti* [77]. Fungi *Emmonsia crescens* and *Aspergillus fumigatus* have been found in the lungs, may be pathogenic [14]. Recent study [267] of helminths from 269 moles in 39 localities in France and Spain revealed 12 species: 2 digeneans – *Ityogonimus lorum* and *Nephrotrema truncatum*; 1 cestode – *Multitesticulata* sp., and 9 nematodes – *Capillaria talpae, Eucoleus oesophagicola, Liniscus incrassatus, Trichuris feliui, Parastrongyloides winchesi, Porrocaecum* spp., *Spirura talpae, Tricholinstowia linstowi* and *T. mornanti*. *S. talpae* was the most prevalent helminth (43.9%) and had highest infection intensity. Prevalences of *I. lorum*, L. *incrassatus, Porrocaecum* spp. and *T. mornanti* ranged from 9.7 to 17.5% and mean intensities between 1.4 and 2.3.

Serological evidence of bacterial infection with *Leptospira* reported [334]. *Mycobacterium bovis* isolated from 1.3% of sample of moles from SW England [212].

RELATIONS WITH HUMANS

Pest status of mole rarely adequately quantified, but widely perceived as a pest of agricultural and amenity land; widely persecuted, either by trapping or by (formerly legal) poisoning with strychnine. Perception that strychnine poisoning cruel, and open to abuse, leading annually to the death of many other wild and domestic animals. Since 1 September 2006, strychnine (strychnine hydrochloride) is no longer authorised for mole control in the UK.

'Sonic' mole scarers widely advertised for use in gardens and other high amenity areas, but radio-tracking studies have shown them to be totally ineffective [136]. It is possible to repel moles with a formulation based on bone oil [11]. However, such methods raise their own problems of legality and animal welfare.

Questionnaire study revealed that most farmers perceived moles as pests, but damage attributed to them slight on most farms [12]. Control of moles nonetheless common and widespread, undertaken by 49.5% of respondents in 1992. Perceived pest status and favoured method of control (trapping or poisoning) varied regionally, perhaps related to soil quality and cultivation type. Silage pollution by soil from molehills the most widely cited agricultural problem, but <1% of respondents reported that 10% or more of their silage was seriously affected by mole activity.

LITERATURE

Godfrey & Crowcroft [135], Gorman & Stone [137] and Mellanby [207] are excellent general accounts. Quilliam [256] is a research symposium on many aspects of mole biology. Smith [306] discusses mole control.

AUTHOR

M.L. Gorman

FAMILY SORICIDAE (SHREWS)

A widespread family in Palaearctic, Oriental, Afrotropical and Nearctic regions, marginal in Neotropical; absent only polar regions and Australasia. Contains small, insectivorous or carnivorous forms which live mainly on the ground amongst vegetation and leaf litter. Among the most speciose of all mammal families, about 374 living species in 28 genera [353]. Geological range in Europe extends back to the Eocene, some 39 million years ago, with a rapid increase in number of species and genera in the Oligocene and early Miocene [266, 275, 365]. Gross form of shrews has changed little.

Characterised externally by narrow pointed snout, small eyes, short, rounded ears with complex lobes in the conch, short legs, plantigrade feet with 5 digits, slender tail, and short, dense pelage (Plate 5). Scent glands on flanks.

No functional milk dentition. First incisors very

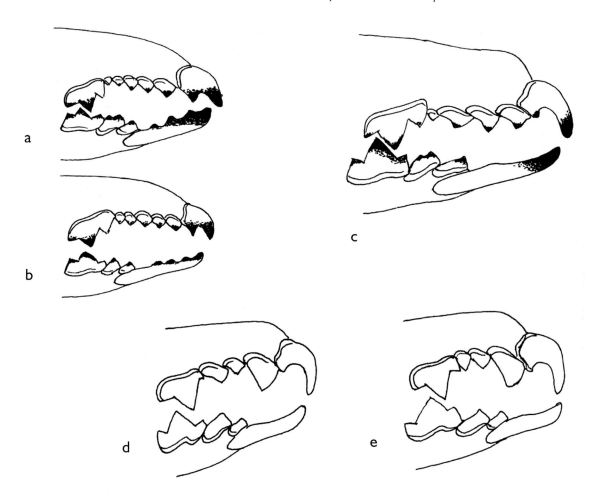

Fig 7.11 Anterior teeth of (a) common shrew; (b) pygmy shrew; (c) water shrew, (d) greater and (e) lesser white-toothed shrews. Note 5 unicuspids in *Sorex*, 4 (but 4th very small) in *Neomys*, 3 in *Crocidura* (drawn by D.W. Yalden).

large, followed in upper jaw by 3–5 small, single-cusped (unicuspid) teeth (Fig. 7.11). Remaining premolars and molars (p^3_3–m^3_3) large, with high, pointed cusps. Tympanic bone annular and loosely attached to skull, zygomatic arches lacking (Fig. 7.1), mandibles with double articulating surfaces.

Prominent, very large lymph gland in abdomen: the 'pancreas of Aselli' [330, 332]. Testes ventral but internal; female tract T-shaped; no pubic symphysis.

Shrews are voracious with high energy requirements; need to feed frequently and have little resistance to starvation, so are active day and night and in all seasons. Do not hibernate, but some species can enter daily torpor. An important element of many terrestrial communities through impact on invertebrates.

Divided into two subfamilies, the Soricinae ('red-toothed shrews') and the Crocidurinae ('white-toothed shrews') [266]. Red-tipped teeth of soricine shrews due to the deposition of iron in the outer layer of enamel, may increase resistance to wear [82, 98, 345]. Both represented in the British Isles. *Sorex* shrews, which have a more northerly distribution than *Crocidura*, are characterised by a higher metabolic rate, shorter lifespan and associated life history traits [343, 344]. The characteristics of the three genera of shrews in the British Isles are compared in Table 7.4.

GENUS *Sorex*

The dominant genus of shrews in northern parts of Eurasia and N America, about 77 extant species [353] almost equally divided between the 2 landmasses. Teeth red-tipped, although this may not be obvious in very old animals with worn teeth. Five pairs of unicuspid teeth behind the large 1st incisors. The tail lacks the long, prominent tactile hairs found in *Crocidura*.

The two species found in GB can be distinguished as in Fig. 7.11 and Table 7.4. Third species, *Sorex coronatus*, Millet's shrew (also known

Table 7.4 Characteristics of the three genera of shrews in the British Isles

	Sorex	*Neomys*	*Crocidura*
Dorsal colour	Brown	Black	Greyish brown
Thin scatter of long hairs on tail	No	No	Yes
Keel of stiff hairs on tail	No	Yes	No
Fringe of stiff hairs on hind feet	Slight	Prominent	Slight
Colour of teeth	Red-tipped	Red-tipped	White
Upper unicuspids	5	4	3
Lower first incisor	4-cusped	Smooth	Smooth

as French shrew or Jersey shrew), found on Jersey but not on mainland Britain, barely distinguishable externally from common shrew.

Common shrew *Sorex araneus*
Sorex araneus Linnaeus, 1758; Uppsala, Sweden.
Sorex vulgaris Nilsson, 1848.
Sorex tetragonurus Hermann, 1780; France.
Sorex grantii Barrett-Hamilton & Hinton, 1913; Islay, Inner Hebrides, Scotland.

Shrew mouse, ranny; *llygoden goch, chwistl* (Welsh); *beathacan feior, luch shith, feornachan* (Scottish Gaelic).

RECOGNITION
Easily distinguished from water shrew by brown (never black) upper surface, smaller size and, in the hand, by the evenly haired tail, lobed i_1 and the presence of a very small, 5th upper unicuspid tooth on each side. More difficult to distinguish from pygmy shrew but sharp contrast between pelage colour on the back and flank is distinctive as are relatively shorter, thinner tail and larger overall size. Length of hind foot and skull, and smaller 3rd unicuspid tooth relative to the 2nd (Fig 7.11), reliable indicators to species (Table 7.5).

SIGN
Footprints: 5 toes on both forefeet and hindfeet, but rarely seen. Smaller than those of water shrew or small rodents. Stance plantigrade.

Faeces: Almost black in colour, 3–4 mm in length and rather moist in texture. Occasionally found deposited at random or in groups in runways through vegetation. Heterogeneous, granular consistency due to presence of chewed pieces of chitinous exoskeleton of arthropods and snail shells.

Calls: Produce a high-pitched, rapid 'chee-chee-chee' sound, just audible to the human ear, when in contact with another shrew or otherwise alarmed. Often heard during the breeding season.

Burrows: Make small holes for runways through ground vegetation and excavate burrows or modify those of other small mammals; not very distinctive.

Presence: Can be determined by hair-tube survey [89, 327] and bait tubes [70].

DESCRIPTION
Pelage: In immatures during winter and in adults during summer, dark brown dorsally, contrasting sharply with pale brown flanks and grey, yellow-tinged ventral surface (Plate 5). In summer before their first moult, immatures have lighter brown dorsal pelage. This and features of the tail make immatures and adults caught during the summer easy to distinguish. Tail bicoloured (pale below), of even width; well-haired with a prominent terminal pencil of hairs in young animals, but hairs are lost without renewal, and adults tend to have bare, often scarred, tails.

Sexes: Adults distinguished externally by prominent inguinal bulges containing the testes and large lateral flank glands in males, or presence of obvious nipples in females. May be hair loss on inguinal bulges and around flank glands in males and around nipples in females. Breeding females may also have a bare or white-haired patch on the head or nape of the neck where held during copulation. Immature shrews lack all these features, but can be sexed externally by the presence of a patch of intensely pigmented fur at the position of the nipples in females and its absence in males [78, 284].

In skeleton, adult males can be distinguished

Table 7.5 Distinctions between *Sorex* species in GB. Millet's shrew (Jersey only) is indistinguishable in the field from common shrew.

	Common shrew	**Pygmy shrew**
Pelage	Tricoloured, flanks buff, contrasting with back and belly	Bicoloured, flanks not distinct
Head and body (mm)	48–80	40–60
Tail (mm)	24–44	32–46
Tail : head and body (%)	50–60	65–70
Hind foot (mm)	12–13	10–11
Weight (g)	5–14	2.4–6.1
Upper tooth-row (mm)	8.0–8.8	6.2–6.6
3rd upper unicuspid	Smaller than 2nd	Larger than 2nd

unequivocally from adult females by size and shape of the pelvis [30].

Moult: In autumn after birth, starting at the rump and moving forward to the head, dorsal surface ahead of ventral. Moult the following spring proceeds in the opposite direction, starting on head, completed earlier in males. Length of hair on back varies from *c*.3.5 mm in summer to 6–7 mm in winter [24]; coefficient of heat conductivity of skin 27% lower in the winter [170].

Nipples: 3 pairs, inguinal.

Scent glands: Lateral flank glands, midway between forelimbs and hindlimbs on a line separating lighter belly fur from dark upper pelage. Small, well-vascularised oval areas bordered by short, stiff hairs. Present in both sexes throughout their lifetime but most prominent in males at sexual maturity when they produce a slightly greasy, highly odoriferous secretion. Scent probably significant in social interactions. Scent also produced with the faeces.

Teeth: Unicuspid teeth decrease rather evenly in size from front to back.

Reproductive tract: In males, testes abdominal, 1.5–2.0 mm long in immatures, 7–8 mm in mature individuals when they show as large inguinal swellings. Female tract T-shaped; vagina and uterus thicken and widen greatly in maturity; combined length of uterine horns increases from 4–7 mm in immatures to >17 mm in breeding condition [26, 59].

Seasonal changes: Undergo seasonal changes in size and body weight, marked decrease during winter of 12–20% in Britain and up to 45% in N and E Europe, brought about by shrinkage of the skeleton, notably the cranium, and of certain internal organs including the adrenal bodies, as well as reduction in body water content: the 'Dehnel effect' [52, 67, 84, 255]. Smaller shrews have lower absolute energy requirements. In spring, rapid growth and sexual development, generating adult individuals that are considerably larger than preceding immature phases. Seasonal weight changes not correlated with prevailing ambient temperature in England [67].

Chromosomes: Diploid number varies over species; range 21–33 in males, 20–32 in females, due to Robertsonian fusion of variable numbers of ancestral acrocentric chromosomes to generate metacentrics. NF = 40; multiple sex chromosomes: females XX and males XY_1Y_2 [116, 289, 291].

Within GB, 6 races which differ consistently in chromosome complement [280, 284, 289]. At hybrid zones between these races, intermediate and novel karyotypes are found [283, 289].

RELATIONSHIPS
Common shrew belongs to a monophyletic group of species with the XX/XY_1Y_2 sex chromosomes, including *S. coronatus* (W Europe and Jersey), *S. granarius* (NW Spain), *S. asper, S. daphaenodon, S. satunini* (Asia), *S. tundrensis* (Asia and N America), and *S. arcticus* (N America) [369].

MEASUREMENTS
See Table 7.5.

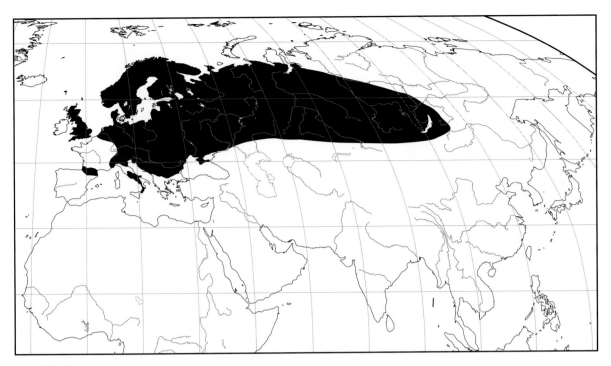

Fig. 7.12 Common shrew *Sorex araneus:* world distribution.

VARIATION

Common shrews on British mainland not distinguishable morphologically from those elsewhere. No good evidence of discrete subspecies within the continental range of the species, British mainland animals therefore allocated to *Sorex araneus araneus*.

Also, no strong differences between GB and the rest of N Eurasia on the basis of molecular variation [19]. Although distinctive karyotypic races found in GB, these are closely related to forms found in Europe [289].

No evidence for geographical variation within GB except in karyotype [289], but some island populations rather distinctive, particularly on Islay and Jura (*S. a. grantii*), characterised by very grey flanks, frequent lack of 5th unicuspid teeth. These absent on at least one side in 52% of shrews on Islay (n = 23); 5% on island of Skomer (n = 126); 1.1% on British mainland (n = 465). On Bardsey (Wales), where pygmy shrew absent, common shrew significantly smaller than on mainland [76]. On many of the Scottish islands, however, the species is larger than on the mainland [351]. These Scottish island populations have reduced genetic diversity relative to the mainland, presumably due to small founding populations and subsequent genetic drift [351].

Gross colour variation rare: melanism extremely rare, albinos more frequent. Minor albinism of the ear tufts is frequent, e.g. 30% [81]; albinism of the tail tip seems to vary geographically: 4.5% in England and Wales, 8.8.% in Scotland [73]. Other types of partial albinism also seen, with extreme case of a white belt all around the abdomen [124].

Studies with molecular variants have shown that common shrew may form large interbreeding populations, with substantial gene flow between karyotypic races [3, 259, 358].

DISTRIBUTION

Widely distributed in the Palaearctic (Fig 7.12): most of Europe except for much of the Mediterranean region; replaced in W Europe (France, N Spain, part of Switzerland, Netherlands and neighbouring countries) and on Jersey by closely similar Millet's shrew *S. coronatus* [213]. North to the Arctic coast and east into Siberia as far as Lake Baikal.

Throughout GB at all altitudes (Fig 7.13) and on following islands: Anglesey, Arran, Bardsey, Bute, Gigha, Great Cumbrae, Holy Island (Anglesey), Islay, Isle of Wight, Jura, Lismore, Luing, Mull, Piel Island (Walney), Raasay, Ramsey, Sanda (Kintyre), Scalpay (Skye), Scarba, Seil, Shuna, Skomer, Skye, Soay (Skye), Ulva, Walney. Definitely absent from Ireland, Shetland, Orkney, Outer Hebrides, Isle of Man, Lundy, Isles of Scilly, from the remaining larger islands of the Inner Hebrides, and from the Channel Islands.

HISTORY

Known from Early Pleistocene (*c.*1.5 million years bp) in Europe and various sites in England of

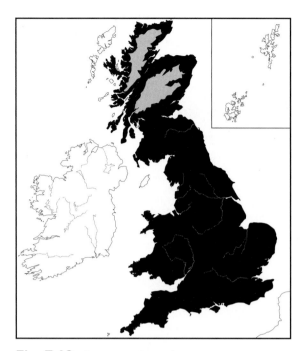

Fig. 7.13 Common shrew *Sorex araneus*: distribution in GB.

Middle and Late Pleistocene age, including Hoxne, Suffolk (Hoxnian Interglacial) [275, 363]. Found in Cat Hole, Glamorgan, during Bolling Inter-stadial, Late Glacial, around 13 000–12 500 years bp when an equable, warm temperate climate with open birch scrub was prevalent [362]. Impact on common shrew of subsequent climatic deterioration, Younger Dryas, 11 000–10 000 years bp unclear, but species was certainly present in GB in the earliest Holocene; well-dated remains from the Mesolithic site at Thatcham, Berkshire at 10050–9600 years bp.

Presence of common shrews in GB in Late Glacial and early Holocene reflects colonisation from mainland Europe. At the Last Glacial Maximum, the coldest time of the Devensian (c.20 000 years bp), common shrews surely absent, so colonisation of GB from continental Europe would have been over a land bridge, that to offshore islands via land bridges or ice bridges [351]. Absence of common shrews from Ireland, Isle of Man and Orkney suggests that the species is not easily spread by humans. Molecular data show that common shrews throughout GB, N Europe and Siberia are closely related, suggesting colonisation over a large area from a single glacial refugium [19, 155, 351]. Distribution of chromosomal races suggests that these colonised sequentially, later colonisers displacing earlier ones [288].

HABITAT

Found in most terrestrial habitats provided some low vegetation cover available. Most abundant in thick grass, bushy scrub, hedgerows and deciduous woodland. Rapidly colonises fallow land, roadside verges and urban habitats [69, 93]. At high altitudes, found occasionally among heather and more frequently in stable scree (to at least 1000 m asl in Britain and >2000 m in continental Europe). Climb quite well and occasionally found amongst aerial vegetation [237], even occupying nests of harvest mice in bushes. Rarely, may enter houses, damage stored foods.

SOCIAL ORGANISATION AND BEHAVIOUR

Social organisation: Essentially solitary except when mating and rearing young, and extremely aggressive towards each other [59, 81, 215]. After leaving the nest, young may disperse although many stay close to the site of their birth [1]. Immatures appear to establish territories where strangers not tolerated; immatures may oust old adults, over which they are socially dominant [79, 215]. Socially inferior immatures may also be excluded [146]. Territories are largely exclusive but may overlap at peripheries [33, 79, 294]. At maturity, females expand their home ranges and appear to defend them from other females. Breeding males roam over even larger areas, overlapping with females and other males. Early-maturing males occupy areas with a high density of females, increasing their mating opportunities [319]. Later-maturing males occupy more peripheral areas and may move large distances in search of mates.

Home ranges: Vary considerably in size according to habitat and season. Typically 360–630 m^2 but extend from 90 m^2 to 2800 m^2 [33, 78, 79, 171].

Active: About 10 periods of 1–2 h almost continuous activity alternating with shorter periods of rest, both day and night. Most active during darkness and least in the early afternoon; peaks of activity at about 1000 and 2200 h [50, 80, 175, 240]. Less active on ground surface in winter than in summer [54, 295]. Periods of complete inactivity last only a few minutes at a time. Usually return to the nest to rest but will cat-nap away from nest.

Aggressive behaviour: Very aggressive and pugnacious towards each other at all times, once independence from the mother achieved, regardless of age or sex. Intruders immediately rebuffed. On meeting, both individuals freeze momentarily, then commence loud squeaking and rearing on hind legs. One may retreat and a chase ensues, sometimes resulting in a scuffle; aim bites at each other's heads and tails, and kick out with the forelegs. One may throw itself on to its back while kicking and squeaking, when other rushes off [59, 81]. Often lash tails rapidly from side to side when excited.

Movements: Swift and bustling, using mobile snout to probe amongst vegetation, leaf litter and soil. Occasionally rear up on hind legs, appear to sniff the air. Swim well, but do not dive underwater.

Long-distance movements over water (hundreds of metres) and across ice (several kilometres) recorded in Scandinavia [146, 328]. Homing from 900 m has been recorded [188].

Burrowing: Make own surface runways through the vegetation, also use those of voles and mice. Keen but not expert burrowers, readily use and modify burrows of other small mammals or naturally occurring crevices.

Nests: Usually below ground in burrows, but also on the ground surface under logs or patches of dense cover; rounded, made of dried grass and leaves, with several entrances. Nests made for bearing young are particularly large and dome-shaped.

Groom: By scratching vigorously with hindfeet and by licking fur.

Rectum-licking: Will occasionally curl up on side or back, particularly during daytime rest period, and lick the anal area and the everted rectum which produces a milky-white fluid [81, 160]. Also termed refection, this may function like coprophagy to extract nutrients, but composition of the licked substance unknown.

Sense: Olfactory, auditory and tactile senses well developed but sight poor. Can distinguish between light and dark but unable to discern moving objects; eyes possess many retinal cones and show evidence of colour discrimination, but visual acuity very limited [28]. Able to produce and perceive high-frequency sounds. Can use echo-location to detect obstacles [117] but analysis of echoes too crude for echolocating to be useful in hunting [28]. Large vibrissae on the snout may assist prey detection by tactile means. Locate prey by probing with snout and digging, using a combination of smell and touch. Able to locate prey hidden 12 cm deep in soil [51].

Vocalisation: Produce soft, high-pitched but audible twitters intermittently during foraging and exploring. Use similar sounds in interactions between female and young. Very young shrews produce loud bark when separated from the mother. Characteristic raucous, high-pitched, staccato shrieks punctuated by harsh 'churls', just audible to the human ear, emitted when alarmed or threatened, and used in aggressive interactions.

FEEDING

Opportunistic predators, feeding on a wide variety of common invertebrates, particularly earthworms, slugs, snails, beetles, spiders, woodlice and insect larvae. Prey range in size from small mites and springtails to large earthworms. In Britain 60–82% of prey >6 mm in body length, most 6–10 mm, matching preponderance of small invertebrates available amongst soil and ground vegetation [59]. Positive correlation between the availability of certain prey (including beetles, earthworms, woodlice and molluscs) and their incidence in the diet [53, 272]. Small quantities of plant material including seeds are also taken.

Shrews discriminate between prey and show preference for some and distaste for others. Millipedes and some molluscs (e.g. *Oxychilus alliarius* and *Arion hortensis*) not favoured; amongst woodlice, *Philoscia muscorum* highly preferred to other species [81, 244, 272]. Attack prey head first to immobilise it, usually eat it from the head down. Large wings, legs and other unpalatable parts normally discarded. In captivity, readily caches surplus food in nest or a small depression in the soil which is covered by leaves.

Much dietary overlap between common shrew and other coexisting shrew species, but reduced by each species taking different proportions of major prey types and adopting different foraging modes [59, 64, 65]. Common shrew makes greater use of subterranean prey, e.g. earthworms, than either the pygmy or water shrew.

Require 80–90% of their body weight in food daily or 6.7–9.7 kJ/g per day, rising to 1.5 times body weight when lactating [49, 81, 154]. Common shrew of 8–9 g estimated to require >570 prey captures per day [60, 62]. High food intake often attributed to high water content of prey and the quantity of indigestible chitinous exoskeleton ingested, but metabolic rate high, BMR 6.9–8.7 ml O_2/g/h, 3–4.5 × that of rodent [59, 238, 344].

BREEDING

Gestation: 20 days (up to 27 days if pregnant following postpartum oestrus). Litter size: 1–11, generally 4–8. Weight at birth: 0.4 g. Duration of lactation: 22–25 days.

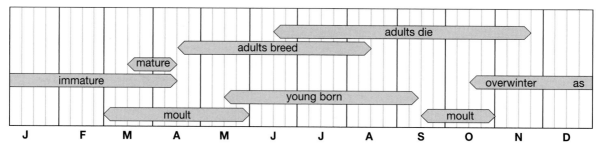

Fig. 7.14 Common shrew: annual cycle.

Season: Shrews overwinter as immatures, rapidly mature in March–April, males slightly earlier than females (Fig. 7.14). Breeding season April–September but mortality of adults high, numbers decline rapidly through summer. Number of litters per female per season is variable, commonly 2 but potentially up to 4–5. First oestrus is rather synchronous within a site and results in pregnancy of most females [317]. A 2nd, post-partum, oestrus also generally leads to a pregnancy. Later in the breeding season, pregnancies become more erratic. Embryo number and litter size decline as the season progresses, first through a decrease in the ova shed and later through increased fetal mortality [26, 246, 324]. Rare in Britain for females to become sexually mature in their year of birth, occasional in continental Europe [254, 314].

Mating: Males seeking to mate frequently rebuffed by females. Female only receptive for a short period of oestrus, perhaps only 2 h [81, 86]. Ovulation probably follows copulation [26]. Little courtship, and mating brief; male mounts female and uses his teeth to hold her by the scruff of the neck or top of the head [81, 86]. Recently mated females easily recognised by bare patch on head or scruff. Both males and females highly promiscuous, so possibility of mating with close relatives. Litters sired by up to 6 different males (mean 3), possibly to reduce inbreeding [286, 318, 319]. No paternal care; male shows no further interest in female after mating.

Sex ratio: *c*.1:1 but bias towards males is common in trapped samples, particularly early in the breeding season. Presumably reflects greater activity of males then.

Development of young: Born naked and blind. Growth very rapid and linear for first 14 days. At 9 days, pelage is evident as a soft, grey down; by 11 days teeth have developed characteristic red tips; by 14 days weigh 5–7 g and eyes beginning to open. By 16 days, eyes fully open. Young first venture outside nest at about 18 days old. Take first invertebrate prey at *c*.21 days, weaned at 22–25 days and fully independent thereafter. Full accounts in [59, 341]. Caravanning behaviour of wild young (the mother leading the young in a line, each grasping the base of the tail of the one in front), just prior to weaning, has been observed, apparently resulting from disturbance of the nest [148], less usual than by *Crocidura*.

POPULATION

Densities: Very variable but regular seasonal cycles of abundance; peak in summer breeding season, decline in autumn and winter as old individuals die and young disperse [67]. Summer peaks of 43–98/ha recorded in grassland [63], 7–21/ha in scrub-grassland and dune scrub [59, 78] and up to 69/ha in deciduous woodland [284]. Winter densities 5–27/ha. High densities often found along roadside verges [16, 279] and grassy field margins generated under agri-environment schemes [299], particularly those grassy margins cut infrequently to maintain high swards of >20 cm [11]. Total population estimated at 41.7 million (England 26 million, Scotland 11.5 million, Wales 4.2 million [149]).

Age structure: Young born during summer carry the population over ensuing winter as immatures. Mature the following spring and breed during summer, then die off in late summer–autumn. Young animals distinguished from parental generation in summer by smaller size, paler colour, hairier tails and unworn teeth.

Survival: Lifespan 15–18 months [26, 67]. Life tables and survivorship curves calculated [50, 54, 78, 246]. Immature cohort reduced by 50% during first 2 months of life, *c*.40–50% survive 6 months and 20–30% survive to breed. Overwintering survival relatively high, 80–100% [50, 78]. Mortality of old adults following breeding has been attributed to tooth wear, incomplete moult affecting thermoregulation, competition with immatures for food and nest sites, and inability to maintain a territory. Monthly survival and winter mortality not affected by weather conditions, but early-born cohorts have higher survival rates at all stages of life than late-born cohorts [67].

MORTALITY

Main predators are owls, but kestrels, buzzards, stoats, weasels, badgers, mink and foxes occasionally take shrews. In large surveys across Britain, constituted 28% of mammalian prey taken by barn owls in 1974, 19% in 1997; ranked 2nd or 3rd in frequency of mammalian prey eaten in different years/seasons [131, 197]. Constituted 13% of mammalian prey items in diets of tawny owls in deciduous woodland in S England, caught most frequently in summer and autumn [310]. Shrews are taken most by avian predators when densities of preferred prey (rodents) are low [182]. Adult barn owls preferentially feed rodents to their young, while their own diet has relatively more

shrews [11]. Frequently killed by domestic cats, but distasteful to them and rarely eaten.

PARASITES

Fleas: *Palaeopsylla soricis* and *Doratopsylla dasycnema* most abundant, found only on shrews. Rodent flea *Ctenophthalmus nobilis* is regular, large 'mole' flea *Hystrichopsylla talpae* less frequent. Several other rodent fleas are found occasionally (Table 7.6).

Mites and ticks: Fur mite *Labidophorus soricis* frequent, and nest mites such as *Euryparasitus emarginatus* and *Haemogamasus horridus* are commonly carried in pelage (Table 7.6). Larval ticks e.g. *Ixodes ricinus* and *I. trianguliceps* common, and capable of transmitting tick-borne encephalitis in continental Europe. Seasonal dynamics of *I. trianguliceps* studied in [258].

Table 7.6 Ectoparasites recorded from shrews in the British Isles. x, present; xx, particularly common

	Common shrew	Pygmy shrew	Water shrew	White-toothed shrews	
				Lesser	Greater
Fleas					
Ctenophthalmus nobilis	x	x	x	x	x
Doratopsylla dasycnema	xx	xx	xx		
Hystrichopsylla talpae	x	x			
Nosopsyllus fasciatus				x	x
Palaeopsylla soricis	xx	xx	xx		
Typhloceras poppei					x
Mites					
Euryparasitus emarginatus	xx	xx	x		
Haemogamasus arvicolorum		x			
Haemogamasus hirsutus		x			
Haemogamasus horridus	xx				
Labidophorus soricis	xx		x		
Myobia blairi				x	
Myobia michaeli					x
Ticks					
Ixodes dorriensmithi				x	
Ixodes ricinus	xx	x			
Ixodes trianguliceps	xx	x			

Table 7.7 Helminth parasites recorded in common, pygmy and water shrews in Britain (after [192, 270, 271]). x, present; xx, particularly common

	Common shrew	Pygmy shrew	Water shrew
Cestoda			
Choanotaenia crassiscolex	xx	x	x
Choanotaenia hepatica	x		
Hymenolepis diaphana	x	x	
Hymenolepis furcata	x	xx	
Hymenolepis infirma	x	x	
Hymenolepis jacutensis	x	x	
Hymenolepis prolifera	x		
Hymenolepis schaldybini	xx	xx	
Hymenolepis scutigera	xx	x	
Hymenolepis singularis	x	x	x
Digenea			
Brachylaemus fulvus	xx	x	x
Dicrocoelium soricis	x	xx	x
Opisthoglyphe sobolevi	x		
Nematoda			
Calodium cholidicola	x		
Eucoleus oesophagicola	xx	x	
Eucoleus kutori	x	xx	
Liniscus incrassatus	xx	x	x
Parastrongyloides winchesi	xx	xx	
Porrocaecum sp.	xx	x	
Stammerinema soricis	x	x	
Stefanskostrongylus soricis		xx	
Longistriata depressa	xx	xx	
Longistriata didas	xx	xx	
Longistriata thomasi	x	x	
Longistriata trus	x	xx	
Acanthocephala			
Gordiorhynchus aluconis	xx	xx	x
Prosorhynchus sp.	x		

Endoparasites: Diverse fauna, intermediate hosts of which are usually invertebrate prey of shrews, particularly molluscs and beetles. Encysted larvae of nematode *Porrocaecum* sp. very common, curled up in the mesenteries of the body cavity and under the skin; the final hosts are predatory birds, particularly owls. Tapeworms and flukes numerous in stomach, alimentary canal and bladder (Table 7.7). No pathological effects evident from high endoparasite loads [270].

In Britain carry bacteria *Mycoplasma* [46, 138], *Leptospira* [333], *Mycobacterium tuberculosis* var *muris*, *Campylobacter jejuni* and *Yersinia enterocolitica* [156] and several other species of common enteric bacteria [157]. Infections with the virus causing louping ill in sheep [305] and with the ringworm fungus *Trichophyton persicolor* [110] also detected.

RELATIONS WITH HUMANS
Source of many myths and superstitions [59]. Despite harbouring a range of parasites, poses low risk of disease transmission to humans and domestic animals compared with rodents [59]. Generally beneficial to humans by preying on large numbers of potential pest invertebrates, including leatherjackets (tipulid larvae), caterpillars and plant bugs [66]. Occasionally enters human dwellings.

Abundant throughout most of range, quite resistant to habitat modification and degradation, so no special requirements for conservation. As with all species of British shrews, afforded partial protection on Schedule 6 of the Wildlife and Countryside Act 1981, and by the Wild Mammals (Protection) Act 1996. Trapping, killing and use of invasive procedures requires a licence (see Chapter 4). Because of its high densities in grassy field margins and similar habitat, the species is likely to benefit from agri-environment schemes such as 'Environmental Stewardship' [10, 300]. Also able to prosper in agroforestry [179].

A valuable model to study the exposure to, accumulation and effects of pesticides, heavy metals and radionuclides in the environment; high position in food chain, invertebrate prey (good bioaccumulators), high metabolism, high abundance and short-range movements all contribute to its value [88, 94, 95, 241, 273]. Evidence of unusual resistance to high levels of cadmium [297].

Common shrew also used as key comparative model for understanding the molecular evolution of humans, and genome of a female from Piel Island (Walney) has been sequenced [161].

Easy to trap but quickly dies of cold, starvation and stress in unattended traps. Use of well-insulating bedding (hay, cotton waste, shredded newspaper) and appropriate food (blowfly pupae,

fresh meat), plus frequent visits to traps (*c.* every 3 h) highly recommended for minimising fatalities during live trapping. With care can be maintained and bred in captivity [208, 281] and can survive a 2nd winter.

LITERATURE
Crowcroft [81] and Churchfield [57–59] provide general, illustrated accounts of biology, ecology and behaviour of common shrews. For a detailed scientific review, see Hausser *et al.* [153].

AUTHORS
S. Churchfield & J.B. Searle

Millet's shrew *Sorex coronatus*
Sorex coronatus Millet, 1828; Blou, Maine-et-Loire, France.
Sorex fretalis Miller, 1909; Trinity, Jersey, Channel Islands.
'*Sorex araneus* chromosome type A', Meylan, 1964.
Sorex gemellus Ott, 1968; Rhone Valley, Switzerland.

French shrew, Jersey shrew.

DESCRIPTION
Sibling species to *S. araneus*, but differing in karyotype. No evidence of hybridisation between them. Small morphological differences detected but not possible to distinguish them reliably in the hand. Common shrew generally has darker pelage with a broad back band while Millet's shrew has a narrower back band with lighter flanks and more defined tricolour. These pelage differences a useful guide but not wholly reliable [233].

Clear differences between Millet's shrew and common shrew have been found in mandible morphology, and Millet's shrew slightly smaller than common shrew in continental Europe [145, 150, 152]. Discriminant function using 4 measurable skull characteristics also proves useful for distinguishing the species [331]. On Jersey, Millet's shrew appears to differ from common shrew of mainland Britain by a longer rostrum (upper tooth-row and mandible) relative to length of skull, but data few. Millet's shrew can also be distinguished from common shrew by molecular markers [234, 236, 322].

Chromosomes: 2n = 22 (female)/23 (male); NF = 44 [116, 209]. Belongs to the monophyletic group of *Sorex* which share an XX/XY_1Y_2 sex chromosome system [369].

VARIATION
Show some geographic variation in size, which may relate to climate, but no evidence of character displacement in areas of sympatry with common shrew [331]. Very striking uniformly dark form coexists with those of normal pelage in marshland in W France [38].

DISTRIBUTION
W Europe only: widely distributed through most of France, Belgium and Netherlands, extending into parts of Switzerland, Germany and N Spain [213] (Fig. 7.15). In British Isles, confined to Jersey (Channel Islands) where common shrew absent. Millet's shrew and common shrew have a parapatric distribution in C and W Europe, with narrow contact zones and some altitudinal differences in distribution [31, 235].

HISTORY
Apparently colonised W Europe from an Iberian glacial refugium at the end of the last (Devensian) glaciation, crossing a land bridge from N France to Jersey [280, 362].

HABITAT
Much as for common shrew. On Jersey, found in coastal habitats of sand dunes, heath and scrub as well as inland in deciduous woodland, hedgebanks and gardens [133]. In continental Europe, evidence that Millet's shrew prefers areas of medium soil humidity with Atlantic climates, while common shrew occupies areas of dry or wet soils with more continental climates [31, 206]. In sympatry, in Switzerland, coexist over a limited zone of overlap by some habitat segregation: common shrew in areas with a thicker litter layer and wetter soils [235]. Exist in 'competitive parapatry' in this area, and presumably elsewhere where they make contact.

SOCIAL ORGANISATION AND BEHAVIOUR
Social organisation: Strictly territorial during non-breeding season, with little overlap between home ranges. In breeding season, females territorial while males have large home ranges overlapping with females and other males. Promiscuous mating system like that observed in common shrew might be expected, but data from one site in Switzerland suggests a monogamous mating system with polygamous tendencies [41].

Home ranges: Mean home range of males 221 (autumn, immatures), 199 (winter) and 586 m^2 (spring, adults). Equivalent values for females 261, 268 and 357 m^2. Measured intensively at one site in Switzerland [41].

Activity: Radioisotope tracking in wild in Switzerland [126] produced results similar to those for common shrew in laboratory [81].

FEEDING
Feeding habits much as for common shrew; diet includes range of common terrestrial invertebrates [48]. Also similar high metabolic rate to common shrew [127, 311].

BREEDING
Litter size may be smaller by 1–2 offspring than common shrew, but data limited [151, 196].

OTHER ASPECTS
Resembles common shrew in all other aspects of biology, population dynamics and ecology.

RELATIONS WITH HUMANS
Partially protected by law, as common shrew.

LITERATURE
Comprehensive scientific review [151].

AUTHORS
S. Churchfield & J.B. Searle

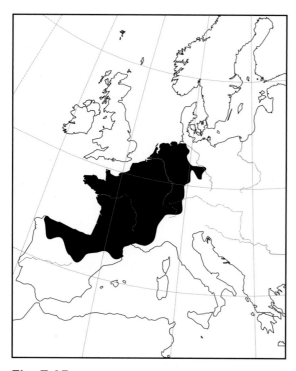

Fig. 7.15 Millet's shrew *Sorex coronatus:* world distribution; in British Isles, present only on Jersey.

Pygmy shrew *Sorex minutus*
Sorex minutus Linnaeus, 1766; Barnaul, W Siberia.
Sorex pygmaeus Laxmann, 1769; Barnaul, Siberia.
Sorex rusticus Jenyns, 1838; near Cambridge, England.

Lesser shrew; *luch féir* (Irish Gaelic); *thollag-airhey* (Manx).

RECOGNITION
Much smaller than common shrew ((Table 7.5) but tail proportionately longer, thicker and more hairy. Lacks sharp contrast between colour of back and flank; dorsal surface never as dark as adult common shrew (Plate 5).

Unicuspid teeth distinctive, 3rd being larger than or at least as large as 2nd (in common shrew it is smaller than 2nd) (Fig. 7.11).

SIGN
Footprints: As for common shrew, smaller, rarely seen.

Faeces: Similar to those of common shrew but smaller, and not easily distinguishable.

Calls: Not often heard in the wild but a high-pitched, very short 'chit' when threatened or alarmed.

Burrows: Use burrows of other small mammals, but less subterranean than common shrew.

Presence: Can be determined by hair-tube survey [89, 327].

DESCRIPTION
Pelage: Medium brown above, similar to immature common shrews in their first summer, separated by a rather obscure dividing line from the dirty-white ventral pelage (Fig. 7.16). Tail as in common shrew but longer relative to body length, and thicker. Tail of immature pygmy shrews also very hairy, although much or all of this hair lost by adulthood.

Sexes: As for common shrew; adult males distinguished externally by inguinal bulges containing the testes and large lateral glands, and adult females by nipples. Live immatures difficult to sex reliably.

Moult: Similar to common shrew, but no seasonal variation in colour of pelage [25, 139]. In winter, length and density of pelage increases and coefficient of heat conductivity of skin decreases [170].

Nipples: 3 pairs, inguinal.

Scent glands: On flanks, as in common shrew.

Teeth: As in common shrew except for large size of 3rd unicuspids.

Reproductive tract: As in common shrew and

Fig. 7.16 Pygmy shrew, juvenile, with bluebottle *Calliphora (photo P. Morris)*.

with similar seasonal changes. Testes 6 mm in mature individuals, visible as inguinal bulges; 0.8–1.2 mm in immatures. Combined length of uterine horns 4–7 mm in immatures, up to 15 mm in breeding condition [1, 139].

Seasonal changes: Changes in size and weight of body and certain internal organs as in common shrew. Decrease in weight in winter but may be less pronounced than in common shrew: 26% in Ireland [139] but only 3–6% in Netherlands [78].

Chromosomes: 2n = 42; NF = 56 in GB, Isle of Man and Ireland, and in continental Europe [1, 285, 369]. Unlike other *Sorex* in British Isles, has standard mammalian XX/XY sex chromosome system.

MEASUREMENTS
See Table 7.5.

VARIATION
Very little geographical variation in morphology, and none between British Isles and continental Europe nor within British mainland. Comparison of jaw length of pygmy shrews in areas where common shrews present (Scotland, S Sweden) or absent (Ireland, Outer Hebrides, Orkney, Gotland) showed that pygmy shrews in allopatry larger than those in sympatry, except in Orkney [200]. No evidence of body weight differences between pygmy shrews in Netherlands (common shrews present) and Ireland [106].

Albino and cream-coloured individuals rare; albinism of the tail-tip less frequent than in common shrew: 2 out of 75 (2.7%) [73]; white ear tufts never found.

DISTRIBUTION
Widely distributed through the Palaearctic (Fig. 7.17): the whole of Europe except for parts of the Mediterranean region, eastwards through Siberia to Lake Baikal [213].

Throughout GB and Ireland at all altitudes (Fig. 7.18). Absent from Shetland, Lewis, Isles of Scilly and Channel Islands, but present on all other islands larger than 10 km² and on the following smaller islands: Orkney: Flotta, Holm of Grimbister, Graemsay, Copinsay; Hebrides: Muck, Pabay (Skye), Soay (Skye), Verran, Ceann Ear, Iona, Sanda (Kintyre); Inchmarnock, Davaar, Holy Island (Arran), Little Cumbrae, Ailsa Craig, Calf of Man, Skomer, Lundy, Brownsea; Ireland: Rathlin, Tory, Aranmore, Inishkea South, Achill, Clare, Inishmore, Inishmaan, Great Blasket, Cape Clear, Sherkin, Great Saltee, North Bull.

HISTORY
Has the oldest fossil record of extant European shrews, dating back to early Pliocene (*c.*4.5 million years bp) in Poland. Earliest fossils in Britain are Early Pleistocene, *c.*0.5 million years bp, from West Runton, Norfolk and Westbury-sub-Mendip in Cromerian Interglacial [275, 363].

Its mode of colonising Britain at the end of the last (Devensian) glaciation probably parallels that of the common shrew. Molecular markers show similarity between British pygmy shrews and those from elsewhere in C and N Europe [19]. However, pygmy shrew also present in Ireland, Isle of Man, Outer Hebrides and Orkney, where common shrew absent. Presence in Ireland, unaccompanied by other shrew species, particularly difficult to explain, though temporary land bridge has been suggested [361–363]. Recent

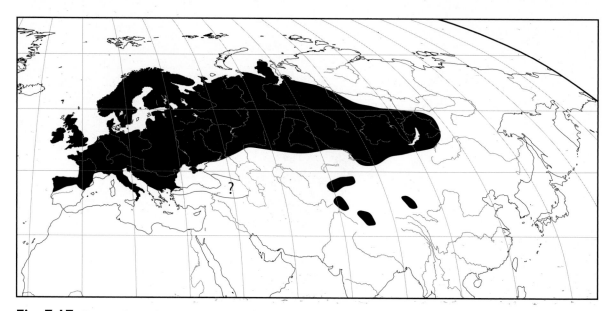

Fig. 7.17 Pygmy shrew *Sorex minutus*: world distribution.

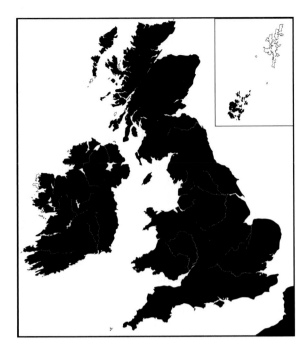

Fig. 7.18 Pygmy shrew *Sorex minutus*: distribution in British Isles.

molecular data suggest that introduced to Ireland from S (Spain or France?) by humans [202]. This fits with presence on other islands (Orkney, Outer Hebrides) that were certainly not attached to Britain at end of Devensian.

HABITAT
Widespread in all types of habitat, with preference for sites offering plenty of ground cover [239]. Generally more abundant in grassland than woodland although not in Ireland where common shrew absent [81, 139, 239]. Less abundant than common shrew in most habitats, except in moorland and blanket bog [40, 361]. Seem to fare best in very wet or very dry habitats, relative to common shrew [78]. Largely ground-dwelling but readily climb up into aerial vegetation.

SOCIAL ORGANISATION AND BEHAVIOUR
Social organisation: Solitary, and aggressive towards others of the same species. Territorial behaviour much as common shrew [79]. Territories of immatures are largely mutually exclusive but strict territoriality abandoned at sexual maturity, particularly by males as they search for mates [79].

Home ranges: As in common shrew but generally significantly larger. Mean size 1400–1700 m² in grassland in England [246]; 530–1860 m² in dune scrub in Netherlands [79]; 200–600 m² in a variety of habitats in Ireland and Netherlands [106]. Territories increase in size in winter [79, 246]. Territories large in Ireland despite absence of other shrews, and not significantly different between Irish and Dutch habitats [106].

Activity: About equal by day and night. More frequent alternation of rest and activity periods than in common shrew and relatively more active during the day [80, 139]. Two main peaks of activity in captivity, at 0800–1000 h and 2100–2300 h [80]. Spend relatively more time on surface than underground compared with common shrew [59, 79, 107]: in Netherlands in winter, spent *c*.50% of their time above ground compared with only 20% for common shrew.

Aggressive behaviour: Aggressive and intolerant of others of the same species, but not as pugnacious as common shrew [292]. Tend to avoid contact with other individuals. On meeting, they produce a single short 'chit' sound and immediately move off in different directions. Lash tail rapidly from side to side when angry, like common shrew.

Locomotion: Dart rapidly over the ground, movements and reactions even faster than common shrew. Use snout to probe amongst ground vegetation. Climb and swim well. In Finland, shown to be remarkably effective at colonising small islands in freshwater lakes [242].

Burrowing: Make surface tunnels through moss and grass, and through snow, but poor burrowers, instead use burrows and runways of other small mammals together with natural crevices.

Nests, grooming and refection or rectum-licking: As for common shrew [81, 112, 160].

Senses: Olfactory, auditory and tactile senses well developed, as in common shrew, but do not dig for prey.

Vocalisations: Much less vocal than common shrew and infrequently heard. Unlike common shrew, do not emit audible twitters during foraging and exploration. Produce a short, audible 'chit' when threatened or alarmed and on meeting another individual.

FEEDING
Feeding habits very similar to those of common shrew. Most important food items in study of Irish pygmy shrews from various habitats were beetles (20% by composition), woodlice and adult flies

Calls: Produce loud audible squeaks and rolling 'churr-churr' as a threat or alarm signal when calling to each other. Most frequently heard in summer.

Burrows: Made in banks of streams, rivers and drainage ditches, *c.*2 cm in diameter at entrance. Entrances are rounded in cross-section and, unlike those of bank voles, have little disturbance of vegetation around them, and no chopped-up plant material nearby. Also use burrows of bank voles and wood mice.

Presence: Can be determined by scat analysis in bait tubes [70, 122, 141]; difficult to distinguish from other shrews in hair tubes [89, 165].

DESCRIPTION

Pelage: Upper surface black, often with a small tuft of white hairs on ears and/or white hairs around eyes. Underside usually silvery grey, with sharp line of demarcation; variable wash of yellow or brown in the midline; melanic forms with dark undersides are quite common. Tail dark brown/black above, white below with hairs on the midventral line elongate and stiff, forming a continuous keel. Similar fringes of stiff, white hairs on the margins of the fore and hind feet, probably aid propulsion during swimming. Pelage longer and denser than in terrestrial shrews.

Moult: Autumn and spring moults similar to *Sorex araneus*, with hair changing from rump to head in autumn and reverse in spring [85]. Also occasionally a summer moult, proceeding from head to tail [296].

Nipples: 5 pairs, inguinal (cf. *Sorex*, only 3 pairs).

Scent glands: On flanks, highly developed in adult males only, fringed with white hairs. Situated on thorax, further forward than in *Sorex* spp.

Teeth: 1st upper incisors large with very long, curved anterior cusps while posterior cusps are shorter than in other species (see Fig. 7.11). Front 3 unicuspids large, 4th much smaller. Large, lower incisors have smooth upper surface with only a single, ill-defined lobe.

Reproductive tract: Poorly developed out of breeding season. Testes abdominal and large (7–9 mm) in breeding condition; only 2.5–3 mm in immatures. Female tract T-shaped, vagina and uterus enlarging greatly in breeding season [1, 251].

Viscera: A vascular plexus in interscapular adipose tissue resembles typical, if poorly developed, rete mirabilia of diving mammals [169].

Seasonal changes: Evidence of decrease in size and weight of body and internal organs in winter, similar to common shrew [85, 253, 296].

Chromosomes: 2n = 52; NF = 98 in Britain and Europe [1, 369]

MEASUREMENTS
Head and body: 67–96 mm. Tail: 45–77 mm. Hind foot: 15–16 mm. Weight: 12–18 g (pregnant females up to 28 g). Upper tooth-row: 8.5–9.4 mm.

VARIATION
British population not distinguishable from continental. Colour of ventral pelage very variable, melanism being quite frequent. Few data available on insular populations, but some may be distinctive, e.g. those on Shuna (Argyll & Bute) are small with uniformly pale grey ventral pelage [74]. Albinism very rare.

DISTRIBUTION
Widely distributed across Europe and Asia [213] (Fig. 7.20). Widely distributed in GB, particularly C and S England, but probably rather local in N Scotland (Fig. 7.21); status confirmed by recent survey [45]. Absent from Ireland and many of the small islands, but present on Hoy (Orkney), Raasay, Skye, Pabay (Skye), Mull, S Shuna (Argyll & Bute), Garvellachs (all 4 main islands), Islay, Kerrera, Arran, Anglesey, Isle of Wight and possibly on others. Recorded at 420 m asl in Wales [71].

HISTORY
Species known in fossil record from Early–Middle Pleistocene (*c.*1.5 million years bp) in Europe, and Middle–Late Pleistocene in England, including Tornewton Cave and Stutton, dating to Ipswichian Interglacial. Could not have survived permafrost of last glaciation, no evidence for Late Glacial, but present at Dog Holes Cave and Igtham Fissure, believed to be early Postglacial [275, 363]. Present Broken Cavern and Three Holes Cave, Devon (Neolithic), also Merlin's Cave, Hereford, but date there uncertain [250].

HABITAT
Typically inhabits temperate deciduous forest and coniferous taiga zones over much of its Palaearctic range [61]. In GB, mainly the banks of clear, fast-flowing, unpolluted rivers and streams, but also ponds, lakes, canals and drainage ditches, and in reed beds, fens, marshes and bogs [45, 141]. Often found in man-made habitats including gardens, especially numerous in watercress beds. In NW

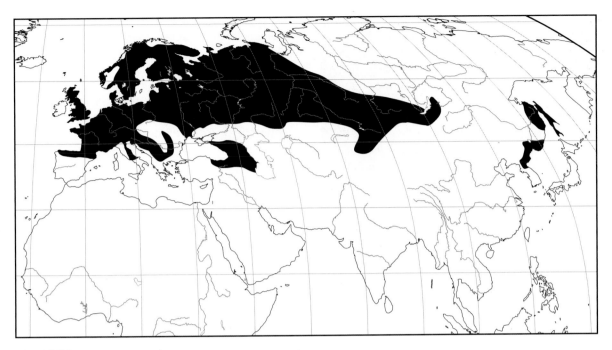

Fig. 7.20 Water shrew *Neomys fodiens*: world distribution.

Scotland occurs amongst boulders on rocky beaches. Occur sporadically far from water (up to 3 km) in deciduous woodland, hedgerows and grassland.

SOCIAL ORGANISATION AND BEHAVIOUR

Social organisation: Essentially solitary except when mating and rearing young, but live quite close to neighbours. Evidence of territoriality, at least during non-breeding season. Defends a portion of stream but with some overlap of home ranges which is greater between than within sexes. Females territorial during breeding season while males wander in search for mates, suggesting a promiscuous mating system. Juveniles disperse quickly after weaning and become territorial until following breeding season [41]. May use faecal deposits to delineate territories, in addition to scent from flank glands in males.

Home ranges: Generally small, 60–509 m² in stream-side or canal-side habitats [41, 168, 190, 335], often smaller in winter than summer; may overlap at peripheries. Several water shrews may inhabit burrow systems in close proximity.

Activity: Day and night, but mostly during darkness. Peak activity just before dawn, least active in late morning [80]. Less active on ground surface in winter than spring and summer [54]. Activities mostly restricted to small stretch of bank and nearby water, occasional sorties away from the bank. Daily movement around 10–60 m, rarely 150–200 m [54, 168, 350]. Move less in winter

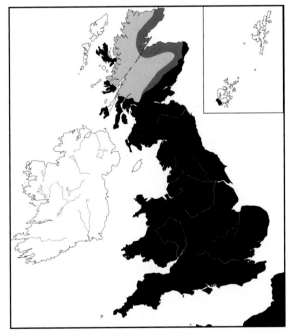

Fig 7.2 Water shrew *Neomys fodiens*: distribution in GB.

than summer. Appear to spend only a brief time (a few months) in one area before passing on, exhibiting intermittent nomadic existence with frequent shifts of home range [54, 249, 296].

Aggressive behaviour: More tolerant of each other than are common and pygmy shrews. Introduction of a stranger provokes strident squeaking and 'churr-churr' sound (in captivity

273

Fig. 7.22 Water shrew, portrait, showing wide net formed by vibrissae *(photo S. Furness)*.

and in wild), may be accompanied by chases and scuffles [35, 49]. Resident usually victorious, but pugnacity gradually diminishes, will coexist particularly if they can establish separate nests.

Locomotion: On land, as for common shrew. When swimming, use all four limbs in dog-paddle fashion. Dive frequently, when propulsion mainly from hindfeet. Dive up to 2 m in river in the wild [277], up to 2.6 m in captivity [348] but body very buoyant with air trapped in the dense coat and dives brief: usually 3–10 s, up to 24 s, in wild [277]. Often anchor against rocks and plant stems to remain submerged.

Burrowing: Inhabit extensive burrow systems in banks of streams, usually with entrance above water; may take over and modify burrows of other small mammals. Burrow using forefeet and teeth to loosen soil, and hindfeet and mouth to remove soil and small stones [49, 81].

Nests: Usually below ground in burrows. Make rounded sleeping nests of moss, dried leaves and grass, even small stones, with 1–2 entrances. Nests for young are much larger.

Grooming: Mostly after swimming. Water removed from pelage by frequent shaking, scratching with hindfeet and squeezing through narrow burrows. Fur of healthy shrew remains completely water repellent, even after repeated dives, probably due to the special grooved structure of the curly overhair [101, 167, 346].

Senses: Olfactory, auditory and tactile senses well developed, but sight poor. Sensitive, mobile vibrissae on snout may assist in prey detection (Fig. 7.22).

Vocalisation: High-pitched twitters while exploring and foraging; loud squeaks and rolling 'churrs' in aggressive interactions.

FEEDING

Forage on land and underwater throughout the year, on a wide variety of terrestrial and aquatic invertebrates plus frogs, newts and small fish [32, 55, 64, 103, 245, 355]. In S England, 33–67% (mean 50%) of prey taken were aquatic, and dominant prey in all months were freshwater crustaceans (*Gammarus* and *Asellus*) and cased caddis larvae [55]; aquatic prey up to 80% of diet in Pyrenees [47] and Switzerland [102]. Other major prey are terrestrial beetles, spiders, millipedes, centipedes, molluscs and earthworms. Terrestrial diet overlaps considerably with those of common and pygmy shrews but, unlike them, water shrews frequently eat millipedes [64]. Water shrews can subsist entirely on terrestrial prey when living away from water. Feeding habits reviewed [55, 56]. Consume *c*.50% of their body weight daily, amounting to 3.8–5.9 kJ/g body weight per day [49, 154].

Aquatic prey usually brought ashore to be eaten, partially eaten prey sometimes cached [32, 143]. Prey usually attacked at or just behind the head. Take prey, particularly amphibians, considerably larger than themselves. Immobilisation of prey apparently assisted by a venom produced in the saliva by the submaxillary glands, which affects the nervous, respiratory and blood systems when experimentally injected into mice [252]. In humans, bite produces a burning sensation, tingling and reddening of the skin at the site which persists for a few days.

BREEDING

Gestation: 19–21 days. Litter size: 3–15, mean 6. Weight at birth: *c*.1 g. Duration of lactation: 38–40 days.

Breeding season: April–September, reaching a peak in May–June [251] (Fig 7.23). Some females may breed in their 1st calendar year, but most commence breeding in their 2nd calendar year. Generally 1–2 litters per breeding season (max. 3). Litter size declines as season advances. Seasonally polyoestrous; female can become pregnant at postpartum oestrus. Ovulation probably stimulated by coitus.

Mating: Similar to common shrew, with a

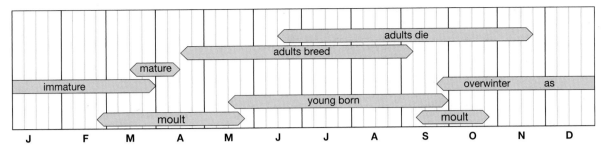

Fig. 7.23 Water shrew: annual cycle.

promiscuous mating strategy and no paternal care. Males utter pure tone calls during courtship, possibly to reduce female aggression [164].

Sex ratio: *c.*1:1, but slight bias towards males common in trapped samples.

Development of young: Born blind and naked. Dorsal pigment apparent on day 4, and fur develops by day 10. Young first leave nest at 23–25 days old, but retain close bonds with mother. Weaned and reach independence at day 27–28 in captivity, but remain together with mother for about 40 days. First signs of aggression within the family at *c.*50 days old. Full accounts of breeding and social behaviour [180, 210].

POPULATION
Densities: Vary greatly according to site and season, but always lower than those of common shrew, even in continental Europe. Constituted 31% of shrew captures in watercress beds in S England [55]; >30% in wet areas in Poland [13]; 6–8.5% in marshland, France and Germany [316, 364]; 0.5% in Russian taiga [293]. Maximum of 3–5/ha recorded in watercress beds in S England [1, 54]. Peak numbers in summer, lowest in winter. Spring population estimated at 1.9 million (England 1.2 million, Scotland 0.4 million, Wales 0.3 million [149]).

Age structure: Overwintering population largely made up of immatures born in the preceding summer, which themselves mature and breed the following spring and summer. Some may survive into a 2nd winter. Juveniles have hairier tails than adults.

Survival: Lifespan 14–19 months [85, 251], most adults dying at conclusion of the breeding season. In S England, *c.*55% of summer-born cohorts die or disperse during the first 2 months of life, but survival rate remains fairly steady from 3–8 months of age (equivalent to the overwintering period) followed by a steep decline in adult survival during the breeding season [54].

MORTALITY
Predators mainly carnivorous birds (owls, kestrels, buzzards), occasionally mammals and fish. Contribute 2–6% of total number of shrews recovered in tawny and barn owl pellets [131, 197, 310, 316], 9% in eagle owl and 0.4% in kestrel pellets [182], but only about 0.2–0.8% of the total prey.

PARASITES
As with common shrew, host to many ectoparasites and helminths (Tables 7.6, 7.7). Known to carry *Trypanosoma* sp. [77] and the bacteria *Campylobacter jejuni* and *Yersinia frederiksenii,* both capable of causing enteric infections in humans [157].

RELATIONS WITH HUMANS
As with other shrews, useful in preying upon potential pest invertebrates. Surveys of 1998 and 2004–2005 found them to be widespread in mainland Britain, occupying many different aquatic habitats [45, 141], but may be threatened by habitat destruction, particularly in S and C England, through pollution of streams, reduction in aquatic prey and modification of river banks. Will tolerate considerable habitat disturbance and management (including periodic mowing of river banks and clearance of emergent plants). Occasionally found around garden ponds. Partially protected by law, as common shrew (see Chapter 4).

LITERATURE
General, illustrated accounts by Crowcroft [81], Churchfield [57–59]. Social, breeding and swimming behaviour, Michalak [210], Köhler [180, 181]; habitat occurrence, Churchfield [61], Greenwood *et al.* [141].

AUTHOR
S. Churchfield

GENUS *Crocidura*

A very large, homogeneous genus containing *c.*164 species distributed throughout the Afrotropical, Oriental and S Palaearctic regions [349]. Distinguished by unpigmented teeth, 3 upper unicuspids, long scattered hairs on the tail, and more prominent ears than *Sorex* or *Neomys*. Represented in the British Isles only on the Isles of Scilly and Channel Islands. The 2 species found here are rather difficult to distinguish, but have not been found to occupy the same islands. Distinguishing dental characters are shown in Table 7.8.

Lesser white-toothed shrew *Crocidura suaveolens*
Sorex suaveolens Pallas, 1811: Crimea, Russia.
Crocidura cassiteridum Hinton, 1924; Isles of Scilly.

Scilly shrew; garden shrew.

RECOGNITION
In British Isles, is the only species of shrew on the islands on which it occurs, except on Jersey where Millet's shrew (*S. coronatus*) also found. Lesser white-toothed shrew slightly smaller and paler than Millet's shrew, has characteristic long, scattered hairs on the tail and wholly white teeth.

SIGN
Footprints: Similar to common shrew.

Faeces: Similar to common shrew, but have a characteristic sweet, musky odour. Often deposited in piles in prominent places.

Calls: Produce high-pitched squeaks when threatened or alarmed, soft twittering sounds when exploring.

Burrows: Not clearly distinguishable from those of other small mammals.

Food remains: Remains of invertebrate prey, particularly littoral amphipods (sandhoppers), sometimes found under rocks and among seaweed on islands.

DESCRIPTION
Pelage: Greyish or reddish brown above, and slightly paler ventrally (Plate 5). Little seasonal variation; slightly longer and thicker in winter and in spring when ventral fur may be lighter coloured. Ears short-haired, prominent (Fig 7.24). Tail covered with short bristly hairs interspersed with fine, long, white hairs.

Sexes: Very similar externally except for inguinal bulges containing the testes and prominent lateral glands in adult males, prominent nipples in oestrous and lactating females. Immature animals very difficult to sex reliably.

Moult: Males tend to moult before females, and some show successive moults. Spring moult usually

Table 7.8 Identification of greater and lesser white-toothed shrews

	Lesser	Greater
Head and body length (mm)	50–75	60–90
Tail length (mm)	24–44	33–46
Hindfoot length (mm)	10.0–13.0	10.5–14.0
Body weight (g)	3.0–7.0	4.5–14.5
Upper tooth-row length (mm)	7.4–8.0	7.7–8.5
Ratio, length of upper unicuspids (at cingula): labial length of large premolar	<1.3	>1.3
2nd unicuspid smaller than 3rd (in crown view)	Markedly	Slightly
Lingual part of large upper premolar	Smaller	Larger

Fig. 7.24 Lesser white-toothed shrew, showing long tail hairs characteristic of *Crocidura* (*photo P. Morris*).

begins on ventral surface of head, spreading dorsally and posteriorly. Autumn moult more rapid and proceeds in reverse direction, commencing on posterior and moving anteriorly and ventrally [268].

Nipples: 3 pairs, inguinal.

Scent glands: On flanks, marked by fringe of short white hairs, present in both sexes in all seasons, but better developed in males. Caudal glands at base of tail are absent (cf. greater white-toothed shrew). Exude a sweet, musky odour.

Teeth: Unpigmented; 3 upper unicuspids, with 2nd markedly smaller than 3rd.

Reproductive tract: Similar to that of common shrew.

Seasonal changes: Young born in late summer and autumn show slackening of development during winter, but body weight continues to increase, albeit very slowly. Winter decrease in size and body weight of immatures, so characteristic of *Sorex* and *Neomys*, not found in *Crocidura*, but adults undergo weight reduction and slight regression of testes in autumn after breeding [268, 338].

Chromosomes: No data from British island populations; 2n = 39–40; NF = 50 in continental Europe [368, 369].

RELATIONSHIPS
Most similar to *C. russula* with which extensively

sympatric in continental Europe.

MEASUREMENTS
See Table 7.8.

VARIATION
Animals from Isles of Scilly have been described as a distinct subspecies (*C. s. cassiteridum*) [159] on basis of darker colour, but subsequent evidence suggests this separation is invalid. Populations from various Scilly Islands are more alike than those from Jersey or Sark, but, on the basis of skull and tooth-row lengths, are intermediate in size between Sark populations (largest) and those from Jersey (smallest) [87].

DISTRIBUTION
Very widely distributed in Europe, Asia and Africa (Fig. 7.25); occupies most of Palearctic from N Spain to S Korea [213]. Also on some Mediterranean islands (Crete, Corsica, Menorca). Absent from GB, NW France and most of Spain, but present on Atlantic islands of Scilly, Jersey and Sark (Channel Islands), Sein, Ouessant and Yeu. In the Isles of Scilly, found on all larger islands (certainly occurs on St Mary's, St Martin's, Tresco, Bryher, St Agnes, Gugh, Samson and Tean) (Fig. 7.26).

HISTORY
Known from Early Pleistocene in Italy, Middle and Late Pleistocene elsewhere in Europe and possibly S England (Pre-Ipswichian, Aveley) [275]. In Europe, has essentially southern distribution, likely to have been introduced to the British Isles

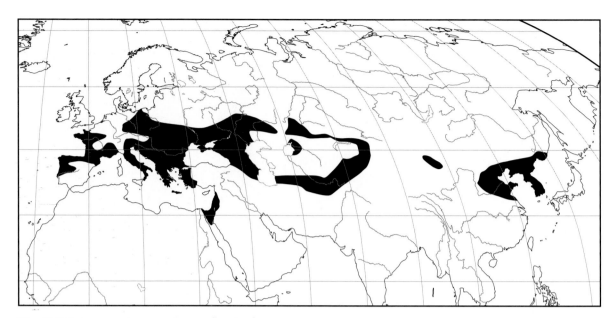

Fig 7.25 Lesser white-toothed shrew *Crocidura suavolens:* world distribution.

by humans. Iron Age or earlier traders from France or N Spain probably introduced it to the Isles of Scilly when they came to the Cornish coast in search of tin; present Nornour in supposed Bronze Age deposits [248].

HABITAT

Found in most habitats offering adequate cover, commonly in tall vegetation including bracken and

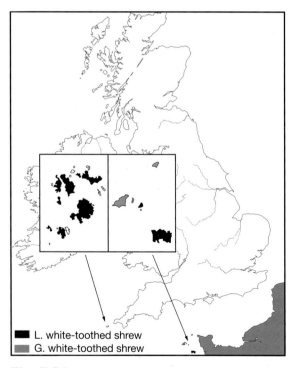

Fig. 7.26 Lesser and greater white-toothed shrew *Crocidura suavolens* and *C. russula*: distribution in the British Isles distribution.

also in hedgebanks and woodland. In France, common in olive groves, vineyards, abandoned terraces, oak forests and especially numerous in maquis scrub [115]. Frequent inhabitants of gardens in continental Europe. Occur among boulders and vegetation on the shores of the Isles of Scilly, especially on sheltered boulder beaches and close to the high-tide line where shrews can retreat to terrestrial vegetation [329]. Even found among rotting seaweed on tidelines. On Jersey, found mostly in coastal habitats on sand dunes, scrub, heath and in the boulder zone [133].

SOCIAL ORGANISATION AND BEHAVIOUR

Social organisation: Essentially solitary, but not nearly as pugnacious as *Sorex*. Home ranges of individuals overlap, so probably not highly territorial. Can be kept together in groups in captivity where they generally ignore each other, but will share nests. Males are apparently dominant to females, and old to young. Indulge in 'belly marking' both in home range and, more often, in unfamiliar areas: hindfeet are spread, belly and anal area are pressed to the ground and dragged forward using forefeet. Both lateral flank glands and anal area touch the ground during marking, so scent could be deposited from either or both. 'Chinning' has also been observed, but less frequently: underside of chin is rubbed several times against prominent objects. Defecate in prominent places, possibly also to mark out home range [247].

Home ranges: In Isles of Scilly, males tend to have larger home ranges (average length 50 m, maximum 80 m) than females (27 m) or juveniles, although home ranges are smaller on Bryher [269, 312]. Adults have firmly established home ranges but juveniles shift theirs sometimes; individual home ranges often overlap considerably [269].

Activity: Day and night, but generally less diurnal than greater white-toothed shrew, with 80% of activity occurring at night [134]. In captivity, peaks of activity at 0400–0500 h and 1800–1900 h [247]. Well-marked feeding rhythms with mean cycle length 30–50 min [134]. Diurnal activity increases during summer months. Can be induced to reduce metabolism and become quite torpid [232].

Aggressive behaviour: When disturbed or threatened, assumes a crouched posture with head raised and teeth bared, while emitting a single, sharp metallic squeak. On meeting, intruder rears on to hind legs while resident lunges towards its neck; this results in the flight of the intruder and a chase by resident [247].

Locomotion: As for common shrew, but less agile and quick.

Burrowing: Able to excavate own burrows but often uses those of other small mammals. Tunnels through loose humus and leaf litter, often active under fallen logs and heaps of brushwood or stone.

Nests: Constructed of dried grass and twigs amongst thick grass or under logs, rocks or boulders. Spherical in shape with a tightly woven roof and a single chamber with several exits.

Grooming: As in common shrew.

Rectum-licking: Observed to take place as in common shrew, in the nest while animal lies on its side.

Senses: As in common shrew; vision probably not very important; smell well developed.

Vocalisation: Soft, continuous twittering is emitted while foraging and exploring. Sharp, metallic squeaks produced when threatened or alarmed.

FEEDING

Mostly preys on arthropods, especially beetles, flies, insect larvae and centipedes, also earthworms and gastropods [189]. On shores of Isles of Scilly, feeds predominantly on crustaceans, especially littoral amphipod *Talitroides dorrieni*, introduced to the islands on plants from New Zealand, which is particularly abundant on boulder beaches [329]. Also feeds on millipedes, adult and larval flies (particularly *Thoracochaeta zosterae* among rotting seaweed), adult and larval beetles (including *Cercyon littoralis*), spiders and mites [243, 312]. In captivity, will readily take various insects including grasshoppers, butterflies and moths; spiders and woodlice, fresh fish, meat and grain are also eaten. Metabolic rate is relatively low compared with *Sorex* and *Neomys*. Food intake is 4.2–8.0 kJ/g per day or 55% of body weight [49, 154].

BREEDING

Gestation: 24–32 days. Litter size: 1–5, mean 3 (on Scillies). Weight at birth: *c*.0.5 g. Duration of lactation: *c*.22 days.

Breeding season: March–September (Fig. 7.27). Females have postpartum oestrus which permits lactation and pregnancy to occur simultaneously, give birth about once a month in captivity. Produce 2–4 litters per year in wild, up to 6 in captivity [338]. Some breed in calendar year of their birth (on Scillies, few young males found in breeding condition but 24% of young females were pregnant in year of birth), but most do not reach sexual maturity until spring of following year; occasionally survive into a second breeding season [268, 338].

Mating: Much as in common shrew [338].

Sex ratio: Significant bias towards males in trapped samples [268].

Young: Litter size significantly smaller on average than in *Sorex* and *Neomys*; young are born blind and hairless, but are slightly better developed. Remain hairless for 7–9 days after birth, but growth rapid and linear for 10–15 days. Eyes open at 10–13 days, young fully haired by 16 days old when they take solid food [49, 338]. Show caravanning behaviour from day 7, particularly when they first leave the nest [147,

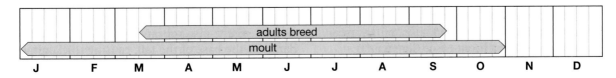

Fig. 7.27 Lesser white-toothed shrew: annual cycle.

REFERENCES

1 Author's data.

2 Allanson, M. (1934) The reproductive process of certain mammals. VII. Seasonal variation in the reproductive organs of the male hedgehog. *Philosophical Transactions of the Royal Society of London Series B*, **223**, 277–303.

3 Andersson, A.-C. *et al.* (2004) No apparent reduction of gene flow in a hybrid zone between the west and north European karyotypic groups of the common shrew, *Sorex araneus*. *Molecular Ecology*, **13**, 1205–1215.

4 Ansell, R. *et al.* (2001) The value of gardens for wildlife – lessons from mammals and herpetofauna. *British Wildlife*, **13**, 77–84.

5 Asawa, S.C. & Mathur, R.S. (1986) Influence of annual cycle on the acid phosphatase activity in certain endocrine glands of hedgehog, *Hemiechinus auritus collaris* (Gray). *Uttar Pradesh Journal of Zoology*, **6**, 207–214.

6 Asher, R.J. (1999) A morphological basis for assessing the phylogeny of the 'Tenrecoidea' (Mammalia, Lipotyphla). *Cladistics*, **15**, 231–252.

7 Asher, R.J. (2001) Cranial anatomy of tenrecid insectivores: character evolution across competing phylogenies. *American Museum Novitates*, **3352**, 1–54.

8 Asher, R.J. *et al.* (2002) Morphology and relationships of *Apternodus* and other extinct, zalambdodont, placental mammals. *Bulletin of the American Museum of Natural History*, **273**, 1–117.

9 Askew, N.P. Personal communication.

10 Askew, N.P. *et al.* (2007) Agri-environment schemes and foraging of barn owls *Tyto alba*. *Agriculture, Ecosystems and Environment*, **118**, 109–114.

11 Atkinson, R.P.D. & Macdonald, D.W. (1994) Can repellents function as a non-lethal means of controlling moles (*Talpa europaea*)? *Journal of Applied Ecology*, **31**, 731–736.

12 Atkinson, R.P.D. *et al.* (1994) The status of the European mole *Talpa europaea* as an agricultural pest and its management. *Mammal Review*, **24**, 73–90.

13 Aulak, W. (1970) Small mammal communities of the Białowieża National Park. *Acta Theriologica*, **15**, 465–515.

14 Austwick, P.K.C. (1968) Mycotic infections. *Symposia of the Zoological Society of London*, **24**, 249–271.

15 Barrett-Hamilton, G.E.H. & Hinton, M.A.C. (1911–1921) *A history of British mammals*, Vol. 2. Gurney & Jackson, London.

16 Bellamy, P.E. *et al.* (2000) Road verges as habitat for small mammals in Britain. *Mammal Review*, **30**, 131–139.

17 Berthoud, G. (1978) Note préliminaire sur les déplacements du hérisson européen (*Erinaceus europaeus*). *Terre et la Vie*, **32**, 73–82 (in French).

18 Bever, K. (1983) Zur Nährung der Hausspitzmaus, *Crocidura russula* (Hermann, 1780). *Säugetierkundliche Mitteilungen*, **31**, 13–26 (in German).

19 Bilton, D.T. *et al.* (1998) Mediterranean Europe as an area of endemism for small mammals rather than a source for northwards postglacial colonization. *Proceedings of the Royal Society of London Series B*, **265**, 1219–1226.

20 Bishop, I.R. (1962) *Studies on the life histories, ecology and systematics of small mammals inhabiting the Channel Islands.* MSc thesis, University of Southampton.

21 Bishop, I.R. & Delany, M.J. (1963) Life histories of small mammals in the Channel Islands in 1960–61. *Proceedings of the Zoological Society of London*, **141**, 515–526.

22 Boag, B. & Fowler, P.A. (1988) The prevalence of helminth parasites from the hedgehog *Erinaceus europaeus* in Great Britain. *Journal of Zoology*, **215**, 379–382.

23 Booth, C. & Booth, J. (1994) *The mammals of Orkney.* The Orcadian, Kirkwall.

24 Borowski, S. (1968) On the moult in the common shrew. *Acta Theriologica*, **13**, 483–498.

25 Borowski, S. (1973) Variations in coat and colour in representatives of the genera *Sorex* L. and *Neomys* Kaup. *Acta Theriologia*, **18**, 247–279.

26 Brambell, F.W.R. (1935) Reproduction in the common shrew (*Sorex araneus* Linnaeus). I. The oestrous cycle in the female. II. Seasonal changes in the reproductive organs of the male. *Philosophical Transactions of the Royal Society of London Series B*, **225**, 1–62.

27 Brambell, F.W.R. & Hall, K. (1937) Reproduction of the lesser shrew (*Sorex minutus* Linnaeus). *Proceedings of the Zoological Society of London*, **1936**, 967–969.

28 Braniš, M. & Burda, H. (1994) Visual and hearing biology of shrews, pp189–200 in Merritt, J.F. *et al.* (eds) *Advances in the biology of shrews.* Carnegie Museum of Natural History, Pittsburgh, PA.

29 Bright, P. (2005) Personal communication.

30 Brown, J.C. & Twigg, G.I. (1970) Sexual dimorphism in the pelvis of the common shrew. *Mammal Review*, **1**, 78–79.

31 Brünner, H. & Neet, C.R. (1991) A parapatric scenery: distribution and ecology of *Sorex araneus* and *S. coronatus* (Insectivora, Soricidae) in southwestern Germany. *Zeitschrift für Säugetierkunde*, **56**, 1–9.

32 Buchalczyk, T. & Pucek, Z. (1963) Food storage of the European water-shrew, *Neomys fodiens* (Pennant, 1771). *Acta Theriologica*, **7**, 376–377.

33 Buckner, C.H. (1969) Some aspects of the population ecology of the common shrew, *Sorex araneus*, near Oxford, England. *Journal of Mammalogy*, **50**, 326–332.

34 Bullen, K. (2002) *Hedgehog rehabilitation.* British Hedgehog Preservation Society, Ludlow.

35 Bunn, D.S. (1966) Fighting and moult in shrews. *Journal of Zoology*, **148**, 580–582.

36 Bunnell, T. (2002) The assessment of British hedgehog (*Erinaceus europaeus*) casualties on arrival and determination of optimum release weights using a new index. *Journal of Wildlife Rehabilitation*, **4**, 11–21.

37 Burton, M. (1957) Hedgehog self-anointing. *Proceedings of the Zoological Society of London*, **129**, 452–453.

38 Butet, A. & Leroux, A. (1993) Polymorphisme phénotypique de *Sorex coronatus* dans des marais de l'ouest de la France. *Mammalia*, **57**, 367–373 (in French).

39 Butler, P.M. (1988) Phylogeny of the insectivores, pp. 117–141 in Benton, M.J. (ed.) *The phylogeny and classification of the tetrapods: mammals*, vol. 2. Clarendon Press, Oxford.

40 Butterfield, J. *et al.* (1981) Studies on the distribution, food, breeding biology and relative abundance of the pygmy and common shrews (*Sorex minutus* and *S. araneus*) in upland areas of northern England. *Journal of Zoology*, **195**, 169–180.

41 Cantoni, D. (1993) Social and spatial organization of free-ranging shrews, *Sorex coronatus* and *Neomys fodiens* (Insectivora, Mammalia). *Animal Behaviour*, **45**, 975–995.

42 Cantoni, D. & Vogel, P. (1989) Social organization and mating system of free-ranging, greater white-toothed shrews, *Crocidura russula*. *Animal Behaviour*, **38**, 205–214.

43 Cantoni, D. *et al.* (1996) Intra- and interindividual variation in flank gland secretions of free-ranging shrews *Crocidura russula*. *Journal of Chemical Ecology*, **22**, 1669–1688.

44 Carlier, E.W. (1893) Contributions to the histology of the hedgehog (*Erinaceus europaeus*). *Journal of Anatomy and Physiology*, **27**, 85–178, 354–360, 508–518.

45 Carter, P. & Churchfield, S. (2006) *Distribution and habitat occurrence of water shrews in Great Britain.* Environment Agency, Almondsbury, Bristol.

46 Cassell, G.H. & Hill, A. (1979) Murine and other small animal mycoplasmas, pp. 233–273 in Tully, G.H. & Whitcomb, R.F. (eds) *The mycoplasmas, Vol. II. Human and other animal mycoplasmas.* Academic Press, New York.

47 Castién, E. (1995) The diet of *Neomys fodiens* in the Spanish western Pyrenees. *Folia Zoologica*, **44**, 297–303.

48 Castién, E. & Gosalbez, J. (1995) Diet of *Sorex coronatus* in the western Pyrenees. *Acta Theriologica*, **40**, 113–121.

49 Churchfield, S. (1979) *Studies on the ecology and behaviour of British shrews.* PhD thesis, University of London.

50 Churchfield, S. (1980) Population dynamics and the seasonal fluctuations in numbers of the common shrew in

Britain. *Acta Theriologica*, **25**, 415–424.

51 Churchfield, S. (1980) Subterranean foraging and burrowing activity of the common shrew. *Acta Theriologica*, **25**, 451–459.

52 Churchfield, S. (1981) Water and fat contents of British shrews and their role in the seasonal changes in body weight. *Journal of Zoology*, **194**, 165–173.

53 Churchfield, S. (1982) Food availability and the diet of the common shrew, *Sorex araneus*, in Britain. *Journal of Animal Ecology*, **51**, 15–28.

54 Churchfield, S. (1984) An investigation of the population ecology of syntopic shrews inhabiting water-cress beds. *Journal of Zoology*, **204**, 229–240.

55 Churchfield, S. (1984) Dietary separation in three species of shrew inhabiting water-cress beds. *Journal of Zoology*, **204**, 211–228.

56 Churchfield, S. (1985) The feeding ecology of the European water shrew. *Mammal Review*, **15**, 13–21.

57 Churchfield, S. (1986) *Shrews*. Anthony Nelson, Oswestry.

58 Churchfield, S. (1988) *Shrews of the British Isles*. Shire Publications, Princes Risborough.

59 Churchfield, S. (1990) *The natural history of shrews*. Christopher Helm, London.

60 Churchfield, S. (1993) Foraging strategies of shrews: interactions between small predators and their prey. *Symposia of the Zoological Society of London*, **65**, 235–252.

61 Churchfield, S. (1998) Habitat use by water shrews, the smallest of amphibious mammals. *Symposia of the Zoological Society of London*, **71**, 49–68.

62 Churchfield, S. (2002) Why are shrews so small? The costs and benefits of small size in northern temperate *Sorex* species in the context of foraging habits and prey supply. *Acta Theriologica*, **47**, Suppl. 1, 169–184.

63 Churchfield, S. & Brown, V.K. (1987) The trophic impact of small mammals in successional grasslands. *Biological Journal of the Linnean Society*, **31**, 273–290.

64 Churchfield, S. & Rychlik, L. (2006) Diets and coexistence in *Neomys* and *Sorex* shrews in Białowieża Forest, eastern Poland. *Journal of Zoology*, **269**, 381–390.

65 Churchfield, S. & Sheftel, B.I. (1994) Food niche overlap and ecological separation in a multi-species community of shrews in the Siberian taiga. *Journal of Zoology*, **234**, 105–124.

66 Churchfield, S. *et al.* (1991) The effects of small mammal predators on grassland invertebrates, investigated by field exclosure experiment. *Oikos*, **60**, 283–290.

67 Churchfield, S. *et al.* (1995) Population dynamics and survivorship patterns in the common shrew *Sorex araneus* in southern England. *Acta Theriologica*, **40**, 53–68.

68 Churchfield, S. *et al.* (1997) Habitat occurrence and prey distribution of a multi-species community of shrews in the Siberian taiga. *Journal of Zoology*, **241**, 55–71.

69 Churchfield, S. *et al.* (1997) Community structure and habitat use of small mammals in grasslands of different successional age. *Journal of Zoology*, **242**, 519–530.

70 Churchfield, S. *et al.* (2000) A new survey method for water shrews (*Neomys fodiens*) using baited tubes. *Mammal Review*, **30**, 249–254.

71 Condry, W.M. (1981) *The natural history of Wales*. Collins, London.

72 Cooke, D. *et al.* (1996) The diet of the barn owl *Tyto alba* in County Cork in relation to land-use. *Proceedings of the Royal Irish Academy*, **96B**, 97–111.

73 Corbet, G.B. (1963) The frequency of albinism of the tail-tip in British mammals. *Proceedings of the Zoological Society of London*, **140**, 327–330.

74 Corbet, G.B. (1966) Records of mammals and their ectoparasites from four Scottish islands. *Glasgow Naturalist*, **18**, 426–434.

75 Corbet, G.B. (1988) The family Erinaceidae: a synthesis of its taxonomy, phylogeny, ecology and zoogeography. *Mammal Review*, **18**, 117–172.

76 Corbet, G.B. & Critchlow, M. (1986) The shrews and mice

of Bardsey – a comparison with mainland animals. *Bardsey Observatory Report*, **29**, 138, 141.

77 Cox, F.E.G. (1970) Parasitic protozoa of British wild mammals. *Mammal Review*, **1**, 1–28.

78 Croin Michielsen, N. (1966) Intraspecific and interspecific competition in the shrews *Sorex araneus* L. and *S. minutus* L. *Archives Néerlandaises de Zoologie*, **17**, 73–174.

79 Croin Michielsen, N. (1991) A field experiment on minimum territory size in the common shrew *Sorex araneus*. *Netherlands Journal of Zoology*, **41**, 85–98.

80 Crowcroft, P. (1954) The daily cycle of activity in British shrews. *Proceedings of the Zoological Society of London*, **123**, 715–729.

81 Crowcroft, P. (1957) *The life of the shrew*. Max Reinhardt, London.

82 Dannelid, E. (1998) Dental adaptations in shrews, pp. 157–174 in Wójcik, J.M. & Wolsan, M. (eds.) *Evolution of shrews*. Mammal Research Institute, Polish Academy of Sciences, Białowieża.

83 Deanesly, R. (1934) The reproductive processes of certain mammals. Part VI – the reproductive cycle of the female hedgehog. *Philosophical Transactions of the Royal Society of London Series B*, **223**, 239–276.

84 Dehnel, A. (1949) [Studies on the genus *Sorex* L]. *Annales Universitatis Mariae Curie-Skłodowska*, **C 4**, 17–102 (in Polish).

85 Dehnel, A. (1950) [Studies on the genus *Neomys* Kaup]. *Annales Universitatis Mariae Curie-Skłodowska*, **C 5**, 1–63 (in Polish).

86 Dehnel, A. (1952) [The biology of breeding of common shrew *Sorex araneus* L.]. *Annales Universitatis Mariae Curie-Skłodowska*, **C 6**, 359–376 (in Polish).

87 Delany, M.J. & Healy, M.J.R. (1966) Variation in white-toothed shrews (*Crocidura* spp.) in the British Isles. *Proceedings of the Royal Society of London Series B*, **164**, 63–74.

88 Dell'Omo, G. *et al.* (1997) Effects of exposure to an organophophate on behaviour and acetylcholinesterase activity in the common shrew, *Sorex araneus*. *Environmental Toxicology and Chemistry*, **16**, 272–276.

89 Dickman, C.R. (1986) A method for censusing small mammals in urban habitats. *Journal of Zoology*, **210A**, 631–636.

90 Dickman, C.R. (1988) Body size, prey size, and community structure in insectivorous mammals. *Ecology*, **69**, 569–580.

91 Dickman, C.R. (1988) Age-related dietary change in the European hedgehog, *Erinaceus europaeus*. *Journal of Zoology*, **215**, 1–14.

92 Dickman, C.R. (1991) Mechanisms of competition among insectivorous mammals. *Oecologia*, **85**, 464–471.

93 Dickman, C.R. & Doncaster, C.P. (1987) The ecology of small mammals in urban habitats. I. Populations in a patchy environment. *Journal of Animal Ecology*, **56**, 629–640.

94 Dodds-Smith, M.E. *et al.* (1992) Trace metal accumulation by the shrew *Sorex araneus*, I. Total body burden, growth, and mortality. *Ecotoxicology and Environmental Safety*, **24**, 102–117.

95 Dodds-Smith, M. *et al.* (1992) Trace metal accumulation by the shrew *Sorex araneus*, II. Tissue distribution in kidney and liver. *Ecotoxicology and Environmental Safety*, **24**, 118–130.

96 Doncaster, C.P. (1992) Testing the role of intraguild predation in regulating hedgehog populations. *Proceedings of the Royal Society of London Series London Series B*, **249**, 113–117.

97 Doncaster, C.P. (1994) Factors regulating local variations in abundance: field tests on hedgehogs, *Erinaceus europaeus*. *Oikos*, **69**, 182–192.

98 Dötsch, C. & von Koenigswald, W. (1978) Zur Rotfärbung von Soricidenzähen. *Zeitschrift für Säugetierkunde*, **43**, 65–70 (in German).

99 Dowie, M. (1987) Rural hedgehogs – many questions to answer. *Game Conservancy Annual Review*, **18**, 126–129.

100 Dowie, M. (1988) Radio-tracking hedgehogs. *Game Conservancy Annual Review*, **19**, 122–124.

101 Ducommun, M.-A. *et al.* (1994) Shield morphology of curly overhair in 22 genera of Soricidae (Insectivora, Mammalia). *Revue Suisse de Zoologie*, **101**, 623–643.

102 Dunstone, N. (1993) *The mink*. Poyser, London.

103 DuPasquier, A. & Cantoni, D. (1992) Shifts in benthic microinvertebrate community and food habits of the water shrew, *Neomys fodiens* (Soricidae, Insectivora). *Acta Oecologia*, **13**, 81–99.

104 Durden, L.A. *et al.* (1991) Fleas (Siphonaptera) and mites (Acari) collected from mole (*Talpa europaea*) nests in England. *Entomologist*, **110**, 43–48.

105 Edwards, J.T.G. (1957) The European hedgehog *(Erinaceus europaeus* L.), pp. 450–460 in Worden, A.N. & Lane-Petter, W. (eds.) *The UFAW handbook on the care and management of laboratory animals*, 2nd edn. Churchill Livingstone, Edinburgh.

106 Ellenbroek, F.J.M. (1980) Interspecific competition in the shrews *Sorex araneus* and *Sorex minutus* (Soricidae, Insectivora): a population study of the Irish pygmy shrew. *Journal of Zoology*, **192**, 119–136.

107 Ellenbroek, F.J.M. & Hamburger, J. (1991) Interspecific interactions between the shrews *Sorex araneaus* [sic] L. and *Sorex minutus* L. (Soricidae, Insectivora) and the use of habitat: a laboratory study. *Netherlands Journal of Zoology*, **41**, 32–62.

108 Emerson, G.L. *et al.* (1999) Phylogenetic relationships of the order Insectivora based on complete 12S rRNA sequences from mitochondria. *Cladistics*, **15**, 221–230.

109 English, M.P. & Morris, P.A. (1969) *Trichophyton mentagrophytes* var. *erinacei* in hedgehog nests. *Sabouraudia*, **7**, 118–121.

110 English, M.P. & Southern, H.N. (1967) *Trichophyton persicolor* infection in a population of small wild mammals. *Sabouraudia*, **5**, 302–309.

111 Evans, A.C. (1948) The identity of earthworms stored by moles. *Proceedings of the Zoological Society of London*, **118**, 356–359.

112 Fairley, J. (1984) *An Irish beast book*, 2nd edn. Blackstaff Press, Belfast.

113 Favre, L. *et al.* (1997) Female-biased dispersal in the monogamous mammal *Crocidura russula*: evidence from field data and microsatellite patterns. *Proceedings of the Royal Society of London Series B*, **264**, 127–132.

114 Fons, R. (1972) La musaraigne musette *Crocidura russula* (Hermann, 1780). *Science et Nature*, **112**, 23–28 (in French).

115 Fons, R. (1975) Première données sur l'écologie de la pachyure étrusque *Suncus etruscus* (Savi, 1822) et comparaison avec deux autres Crocidurinae: *Crocidura russula* (Hermann, 1780) et *Crocidura suaveolens* (Pallas, 1811) (Insectivora, Soricidae). *Vie Milieu*, **25**, 315–360 (in French).

116 Ford, C.E. & Hamerton, J.L. (1970) Chromosome polymorphism in the common shrew, *Sorex araneus*. *Symposia of the Zoological Society of London*, **26**, 223–236.

117 Forsman, K.A. & Malmquist, M.G. (1988) Evidence for echolocation in the common shrew, *Sorex araneus*. *Journal of Zoology*, **216**, 655–662.

118 Fowler, P.A. (1988) Seasonal endocrine cycles in the European hedgehog, *Erinaceus europaeus*. *Journal of Reproduction and Fertility*, **84**, 259–272.

119 Fowler, P.A. & Racey, P.A. (1987) Relationship between body and testis temperatures in the European hedgehog, *Erinaceus europaeus*, during hibernation and sexual reactivation. *Journal of Reproduction and Fertility*, **81**, 567–573.

120 Frankland, H.M.T. (1959) The incidence and distribution in Britain of the trematodes of *Talpa europaea*. *Parasitology*, **49**, 132–142.

121 Fraser, F.C. & King, J.E. (1954) Faunal remains, pp. 70–89 in Clark, J.G.D. (ed.) *Excavations at Star Carr, an early Mesolithic site at Seamer near Scarborough, Yorkshire.*

Cambridge University Press, Cambridge.

122 French, B.I. *et al.* (2001) Habitat variables affecting the occurrence of *Neomys fodiens* (Mammalia, Insectivora) in Kent, UK. *Folia Zoologica*, **50**, 90–105.

123 Funmilayo, O. (1979) Food consumption, preferences and storage in the mole. *Acta Theriologica*, **25**, 379–389.

124 Gelling, M. (2003) Partial albinism in the common shrew *Sorex araneus*. *Mammal Review*, **33**, 189–190.

125 Genoud, M. (1978) Étude d'une population urbaine de musaraignes musettes (*Crocidura russula* Hermann, 1780). *Bulletin de la Société Vaudoise des Sciences Naturelle*, **74**, 25–34 (in French).

126 Genoud, M. (1984) Activity of *Sorex coronatus* (Insectivora, Soricidae) in the field. *Zeitschrift für Säugetierkunde*, **49**, 74–78.

127 Genoud, M. (1985) Ecological energetics of two European shrews: *Crocidura russula* and *Sorex coronatus* (Soricidae: Mammalia). *Journal of Zoology*, **207A**, 63–85.

128 Genoud, M. & Hausser, J. (1979) Écologie d'une population de *Crocidura russula* en milieu rural montagnard (Insectivora, Soricidae). *Terre et la Vie*, **33**, 539–554 (in French).

129 Genoud, M. & Hutterer, R. (1990) *Crocidura russula* (Hermann, 1780) – Hausspitzmaus, pp. 429–452 in Neithammer, J. & Krapp, F. (eds.) *Handbuch der Säugetiere Europas 3(1)*. AULA, Wiesbaden (in German).

130 Genoud, M. & Vogel, P. (1981) The activity of *Crocidura russula* (Insectivora, Soricidae) in the field and in captivity. *Zeitschrift für Säugetierkunde*, **46**, 222–232.

131 Glue, D.E. (1974) Food of the barn owl in Britain and Ireland. *Bird Study*, **21**, 200–210.

132 Godfrey, G.K. (1957) Observations on the movements of moles (*Talpa europaea* L.) after weaning. *Proceedings of the Zoological Society of London*, **128**, 287–295.

133 Godfrey, G.K. (1978) The ecological distribution of shrews (*Crocidura suaveolens* and *Sorex araneus fretalis*) in Jersey. *Journal of Zoology*, **185**, 266–270.

134 Godfrey, G.K. (1978) The activity pattern in white-toothed shrews studied with radar. *Acta Theriologica*, **23**, 381–390.

135 Godfrey, G. & Crowcroft, P. (1960) *The life of the mole*. Museum Press, London.

136 Gorman, M. & Lamb, A. (1994) An investigation into the efficacy of mechanical mole scarers. *Animal Welfare*, **3**, 3–12.

137 Gorman, M.L. & Stone, R.D. (1990) *The natural history of moles*. Christopher Helm, London.

138 Gourlay, R.N. & Wyld, S.G. (1976) Ilsley-type and other mycoplasmas from the alimentary tracts of cattle, pigs and rodents. *Proceedings of the Society for General Microbiology*, **3**, 142.

139 Grainger, J.P. & Fairley, J.S. (1978) Studies on the biology of the pygmy shrew *Sorex minutus* in the west of Ireland. *Journal of Zoology*, **186**, 109–141.

140 Grassé, P-P. (1955) *Traité de zoologie, anatomie systematique: Vol. 17 Mammalia, Fasc IIA*. Masson, Paris (in French).

141 Greenwood, A. *et al.* (2002) Geographical distribution and habitat occurrence of the water shrew (*Neomys fodiens*) in the Weald of south-east England. *Mammal Review*, **32**, 40–50.

142 Grünwald, A. (1969) Untersuchungen zur Orientierung der Weisszahnspitzmäuse (Soricidae – Crocidurinae). *Zeitschrift für Vergleichende Physiologie*, **65**, 191–217 (in German).

143 Haberl, W. (2002) Food storage, prey remains and notes on occasional vertebrates in the diet of the Eurasian water shrew, *Neomys fodiens*. *Folia Zoologica*, **51**, 93-102.

144 Haeck, J. (1969) Colonization of the mole (*Talpa europaea* L.) in the Ijsselmeer Polders. *Netherlands Journal of Zoology*, **19**, 145–248.

145 Handwerk, J. (1987) Neue Daten zur Morphologie, Verbreitung und Ökologie der Spitzmause *Sorex araneus* und *S. coronatus* im Rheinland. *Bonner Zoologische Beiträge*, **38**, 273–297 (in German).

146 Hanski, I. *et al.* (1991) Natal dispersal and social dominance in the common shrew *Sorex araneus*. *Oikos*, **62**, 48–58.

147 Hanzák, J. (1966) Zur Jugendentwicklung der Gartenspitzmaus, *Crocidura suaveolens* (Pallas, 1821). *Lynx*, **6**, 67–74 (in German).

148 Harper, R.J. (1977) 'Caravanning' in *Sorex* species. *Journal of Zoology*, **183**, 541.

149 Harris, S. *et al.* (1995) *A review of British mammals: population estimates and conservation status of British mammals other than cetaceans.* JNCC, Peterborough.

150 Hausser, J. (1984) Genetic drift and selection: their respective weights in the morphological and genetic differentiation of four species of shrews in southern Europe (Insectivora, Soricidae). *Zeitschrift für Zoologische Systematik und Evolutionsforschung*, **22**, 302–320.

151 Hausser, J. (1990) *Sorex coronatus* Millet, 1882 – Schabrackenspitzmaus, pp. 279–286 in Neithammer, J. & Krapp, F. (eds.) *Handbuch der Säugetiere Europas 3(1)*. AULA, Wiesbaden (in German).

152 Hausser, J. & Jammot, D. (1974) Étude biometrique des machoires chez les *Sorex* du groupe *araneus* en Europe continentale. *Mammalia*, **38**, 324–343 (in French).

153 Hausser, J. *et al.* (1990) *Sorex araneus* Linnaeus 1758 – Waldspitzmaus, pp. 237–278 in Neithammer, J. & Krapp, F. (eds.). *Handbuch der Säugetiere Europas 3(1)*. AULA, Wiesbaden (in German).

154 Hawkins, A.E. & Jewell, P.A. (1962) Food consumption and energy requirements of captive British shrews and the mole. *Proceedings of the Zoological Society of London*, **138**, 137–155.

155 Haynes, S. (2000) *The history of wild and domesticated vertebrates deduced from modern and ancient DNA sequences.* DPhil thesis, University of York.

156 Healing, T.D. Personal communication.

157 Healing, T.D. *et al.* (1980) A note on some Enterobacteriaceae from the faeces of small wild British mammals. *Journal of Hygiene*, **85**, 343–345.

158 Hellwing, S. (1973) The postnatal development of the white-toothed shrew *Crocidura russula monacha* in captivity. *Zeitschrift für Säugetierkunde*, **38**, 257–270.

159 Hinton, M.A.C. (1924) On a new species of *Crocidura* from Scilly. *Annals and Magazine of Natural History*, **14**, 509–510.

160 Hirakawa, H. & Haberl, W. (1998) The behaviour of licking the everted rectum in shrews (Soricidae, Insectivora). *Acta Theriologica*, **43**, 113–120.

161 Hitte, C. *et al.* (2005) Facilitating genome navigation: survey sequencing and dense radiation-hybrid gene mapping. *Nature Reviews Genetics*, **6**, 643–648.

162 Hulse, E.C. & Edwards, J.T. (1937) Foot-and-mouth disease in hibernating hedgehogs. *Journal of Comparative Pathology and Therapeutics*, **50**, 421–430.

163 Hutterer, R. (1976) Beobachtungen zur Geburt und Jugendentwicklung der Zwergspitzmaus, *Sorex minutus* L. (Soricidae-Insectivora*). Zeitschrift für Säugetierkunde*, **41**, 1–22 (in German).

164 Hutterer, R. (1978) Paarungsrufe der Wasserspitzmaus (*Neomys fodiens*) und verwandte Laute weiterer Soricidae. *Zeitschrift für Säugetierkunde*, **43**, 330–336 (in German).

165 Hutterer, R. (1985) Anatomical adaptations of shrews. *Mammal Review*, **15**, 43–55.

166 Hutterer, R. (1990) *Sorex minutus* Linnaeus, 1766 – Zwergspitzmaus, pp. 183–206 in Neithammer, J. & Krapp, F. (eds.). *Handbuch der Säugetiere Europas 3(1)*. AULA, Wiesbaden (in German).

167 Hutterer, R. & Hürter, T. (1981) Adaptive Haarstrukturen bei Wasserspitzmausen (Insectivora, Soricinae). *Zeitschrift für Säugetierkunde*, **46**, 1–11 (in German).

168 Illing, K. *et al.* (1981) Freilandbeobachtungen zur Lebensweise und zum Revierverhalten der Europäischen Wasserspitzmaus, *Neomys fodiens* (Pennant, 1771). *Zoologische Beitrage*, **27**, 109–122 (in German).

169 Ivanovna, E.I. (1967) [New data on the nature of the rete mirabile and derivative apparatuses in some semi-aquatic mammals.] *Doklady Academia Nauka SSSR*, **173**, 1–3 (in Russian).

170 Ivanter, E.V. (1994) The structure and adaptive peculiarities of pelage in soricine shrews, pp. 441–454 in Merritt, J.F. *et al.* (eds.) *Advances in the biology of shrews*. Carnegie Museum of Natural History, Pittsburgh, PA.

171 Ivanter, E.V. *et al.* (1994) The territorial and demographic structures of a common shrew population, pp. 89–95 in Merritt, J.F. *et al.* (eds.) *Advances in the biology of shrews*. Carnegie Museum of Natural History, Pittsburgh, PA.

172 Jackson, D.B. (2006) The breeding biology of introduced hedgehogs (*Erinaceus europaeus*) on a Scottish island: lessons for population control and bird conservation. *Journal of Zoology*, **268**, 303–314.

173 Jackson, D.B. & Green, R.E. (2000) The importance of the introduced hedgehog (*Erinaceus europaeus*) as a predator of the eggs of waders (Charadrii) on machair in South Uist, Scotland. *Biological Conservation*, **93**, 333–348.

174 Jackson, D.B. *et al.* (2004) Long-term population changes among breeding shorebirds in the Outer Hebrides, Scotland, in relation to introduced hedgehogs (*Erinaceus europaeus*). *Biological Conservation*, **117**, 151–166.

175 Jánský, L. & Hanák, V. (1960) Studien über Kleinsäuger populationen in Südböhmen. II. Aktivität der Spitzmäuse unter natürlichen Bedingungen. *Säugetierkundliche Mitteilungen*, **8**, 55–63 (in German).

176 Jeanmaire-Besançon, F. (1986) Estimation de l'âge et de la longevité chez *Crocidura russula* (Insectivora: Soricidae). *Acta Oecologia*, **7**, 355–366 (in French).

177 Keymer, I.F. *et al.* (1991) Zoonoses and other findings in hedgehogs (*Erinaceus europaeus*): a survey of mortality and review of the literature. *Veterinary Record*, **128**, 245–249.

178 Khazanehdari, C. *et al.* (1996) Anal gland secretion of European mole: volatile constituents and significance in territorial maintenance. *Journal of Chemical Ecology*, **22**, 383–392.

179 Klaa, K. *et al.* (2005) Distribution of small mammals in a silvoarable agroforestry system in Northern England. *Agroforestry Systems*, **63**, 101–110.

180 Köhler, D. (1984) Zum verhaltensinventar der Wasserspitzmaus (*Neomys fodiens*). *Säugetierkundliche Informationen*, **2**, 175–199 (in German).

181 Köhler, D. (1991) Notes on the diving behaviour of the water shrew *Neomys fodiens* (Mammalia, Soricidae). *Zoologischer Anzeiger*, **227**, 218–228.

182 Korpimäki, E. & Norrdahl, K. (1989) Avian and mammalian predators of shrews in Europe: regional differences, between-year and seasonal variation, and mortality due to predation. *Annales Zoologici Fennici*, **26**, 389–400.

183 Kramm, C. *et al.* (1975) Respiratory function of blood in hibernating and non–hibernating hedgehogs. *Respiration Physiology*, **25**, 311–318.

184 Kristiansson, H. (1990) Population variables and causes of mortality in a hedgehog (*Erinaceous* [*sic*] *europaeus*) population in southern Sweden. *Journal of Zoology*, **220**, 391–404.

185 Kristoffersson, R. & Soivio, A. (1964) Hibernation of the hedgehog (*Erinaceus europaeus* L.). The periodicity of hibernation of undisturbed animals during the winter in a constant ambient temperature. *Annales Academiae Scientarium Fennicae A, IV, Biologica*, **80**, 1–22.

186 Kristoffersson, R. & Suomalainen, P. (1964) Studies on the physiology of the hibernating hedgehog. 2. Changes of body weight of hibernating and non–hibernating animals. *Annales Academiae Scientarium Fennicae A, IV, Biologica*, **76**, 1–11.

187 Kruuk, H. (1964) Predators and anti-predator behaviour of the black-headed gull (*Larus ridibundus* L.). *Behaviour Suppl.*, **11**, 1–129.

188 Kuptsov, A.V. & Shchipanov, N.A. (2004) [Homing in the shrews *Sorex araneus*, *S. caecutiens*, *S. minutus*, and *S. isodon*

298.

284 Searle, J.B. (1988) Karyotypic variation and evolution in the common shrew, pp. 97–107 in Brandham, P.E. (ed.) *Sorex araneus. Kew chromosome conference III.* HMSO, London.

285 Searle, J.B. (1989) Genetic studies of small mammals from Ireland and the Isle of Man. *Irish Naturalists' Journal,* **23**, 112–113.

286 Searle, J.B. (1990) Evidence for multiple paternity in the common shrew (*Sorex araneus*). *Journal of Mammalogy,* **71**, 139–144.

287 Searle, J.B. & Erskine, I. (1985) Evidence for a widespread karyotypic race of hedgehog (*Erinaceus europaeus*) in Britain. *Journal of Zoology,* **206A**, 276–278.

288 Searle, J.B. & Wilkinson, P.J. (1987) Karyotypic variation in the common shrew (*Sorex araneus*) in Britain – a 'Celtic fringe'. *Heredity,* **59**, 345–351.

289 Searle, J.B. & Wójcik, J.M. (1998) Chromosomal evolution: the case of *Sorex araneus*, pp. 219–268 in Wójcik, J.M. & Wolsan, M. (eds.) *Evolution of shrews.* Mammal Research Institute, Polish Academy of Sciences, Białowieża.

290 Seddon, J.M. *et al.* (2001) DNA footprints of European hedgehogs, *Erinaceus europaeus* and *E. concolor*: Pleistocene refugia, postglacial expansion and colonization routes. *Molecular Ecology,* **10**, 2187–2198.

291 Sharman, G.B. (1956) Chromosomes of the common shrew. *Nature,* **177**, 941–942.

292 Shchipanov, N.A. *et al.* (1998) [General characteristics of *Sorex araneus, Sorex caecutiens, Sorex minutus* and *Sorex isodon* (Insectivora, Soricidae) behaviour.] *Zoologicheskï Zhurnal,* **77**, 444–458 (in Russian).

293 Sheftel, B.I. (1989) Long-term and seasonal dynamics of shrews in Central Siberia. *Annales Zoologici Fennici,* **26**, 357–369.

294 Shillito, J.F. (1963) Observations on the range and movements of a woodland population of the common shrew *Sorex araneus* L. *Proceedings of the Zoological Society of London,* **140**, 533–546.

295 Shillito, J.F. (1963) Field observations on the growth, reproduction and activity of a woodland population of the common shrew *Sorex araneus* L. *Proceedings of the Zoological Society of London,* **140**, 99–114.

296 Shillito, J.F. (1963) Field observations on the water shrew (*Neomys fodiens*). *Proceedings of the Zoological Society of London,* **140**, 320–322.

297 Shore, R.F. & Douben, P.E.T. (1994) The ecotoxicological significance of cadmium intake and residues in terrestrial small mammals. *Ecotoxicology and Environmental Safety,* **29**, 101–112.

298 Shore, R.F. & Mackenzie, S. (1993) The effects of catchment liming on shrews *Sorex* spp. *Biological Conservation,* **64**, 101–111.

299 Shore, R.F. *et al.* (1995) Capture success for pygmy and common shrews (*Sorex minutus* and *S. araneus*) in Longworth and pitfall traps on upland blanket bog. *Journal of Zoology,* **237**, 657–662.

300 Shore, R.F. *et al.* (2005) Will Environmental Stewardship enhance small mammal abundance on intensively managed farmland? *Mammal Review,* **35**, 277–284.

301 Skoczén, S. (1958) Tunnel digging by the mole (*Talpa europaea* Linne). *Acta Theriologica,* **2**, 235–249.

302 Skoczén, S. (1966) Seasonal changes in the pelage of the mole, *Talpa europaea* Linnaeus, 1758. *Acta Theriologica,* **11**, 537–549.

303 Skoczén, S. (1966) Stomach contents of the mole, *Talpa europaea* Linnaeus, 1758 from southern Poland. *Acta Theriologica,* **11**, 551–575.

304 Smit, F.G.A.M. (1957) *Handbook for the identification of British insects. Siphonaptera.* Royal Entomological Society, London.

305 Smith, C.E.G. *et al.* (1964) Isolation of louping ill virus from small mammals in Ayrshire, Scotland. *Nature,* **203**, 992–993.

306 Smith, G.N. (1980) *Moles and their control.* Saiga Publishing, Hindhead.

307 Smith, J.M.B. (1968) Diseases of hedgehogs. *Veterinary Bulletin,* **38**, 425–430.

308 Sokolov, V.E. (1982) *Mammal skin.* University of California Press, Berkeley.

309 Soroker, V. *et al.* (1982) Parental behaviour in male and virgin white toothed shrews *Crocidura russula monacha* (Soricidae, Insectivora). *Zeitschrift für Säugetierkunde,* **47**, 321–324.

310 Southern, H.N. (1954) Tawny owls and their prey. *Ibis,* **96**, 384–410.

311 Sparti, A. & Genoud, M. (1989) Basal rate of metabolism and temperature regulation in *Sorex coronatus* and *Sorex minutus* (Soricidae: Mammalia). *Comparative Biochemistry and Physiology A,* **92**, 359–363.

312 Spencer-Booth, Y. (1963) A coastal population of shrews (*Crocidura suaveolens cassiteridum*). *Proceedings of the Zoological Society of London,* **140**, 322–326.

313 Stanhope, M.J. *et al.* (1998) Molecular evidence for multiple origins of Insectivora and for a new order of endemic African insectivore mammals. *Proceedings of the National Academy of Sciences of the USA,* **95**, 9967–9972.

314 Stein, G.H.W. (1961) Bezeihung zwischen Bestandsdichte und Vermehrung bei der Waldspitzmaus, *Sorex araneus,* und weiteren Ratzahnspizmäusen. *Zeitschrift für Säugetierkunde,* **26**, 13–28 (in German).

315 Stein, G.H.W. (1963) Anomolien der Zahnzahl und ihre geographische Variabilität bei Insectivoren: I. Maulwurf, *Talpa europaea* L. *Mitteilungen aus dem Zoologischen Museum in Berlin,* **39**, 223–240 (in German).

316 Stein, G.H.W. (1975) Über die Beststandsdichte und ihre Zusammenhänge bei der Wasserspitzmaus, *Neomys fodiens* (Pennant). *Mitteilungen aus dem Zoologischen Museum in Berlin,* **51**, 187–198 (in German).

317 Stockley, P. (1996) Synchrony of estrus in common shrews. *Journal of Mammalogy,* **77**, 383–387.

318 Stockley, P. *et al.* (1993) Female multiple mating behaviour in the common shrew as a strategy to reduce inbreeding. *Proceedings of the Royal Society of London Series B,* **254**, 173–179.

319 Stockley, P. *et al.* (1994) Alternative reproductive tactics in male common shrews: relationships between mate-searching behaviour, sperm production, and reproductive success as revealed by DNA fingerprinting. *Behavioral Ecology and Sociobiology,* **34**, 71–78.

320 Stone, R.D. & Gorman, M.L. (1985) The social organization of the European mole (*Talpa europaea*) and the Pyrenean desman (*Galemys pyrenaicus*). *Mammal Review,* **15**, 35–42.

321 Stuart, A.J. (1974) Pleistocene history of the British vertebrate fauna. *Biological Reviews,* **49**, 225–266.

322 Taberlet, P. *et al.* (1994) Chromosomal versus mitochondrial DNA evolution: tracking the evolutionary history of the southwestern European populations of the *Sorex araneus* group (Mammalia, Insectivora). *Evolution,* **48**, 623–636.

323 Tapper, S. (1992) *Game heritage.* Game Conservancy, Fordingbridge.

324 Tarkowski, A.K. (1957) [Studies on reproduction and prenatal mortality of the common shrew (*Sorex araneus* L.) Part II. Reproduction under natural conditions.] *Annales Universitatis Mariae Curie-Skłodowska,* **10 C**, 177–244 (in Polish).

325 Taylor, J. (1968) Salmonella in wild animals. *Symposia of the Zoological Society of London,* **24**, 51–73.

326 Taylor, J.R.E. (1998) Evolution of energetic strategies in shrews, pp. 309–346 in Wójcik, J.M. & Wolsan, M. (eds.) *Evolution of shrews.* Mammal Research Institute, Polish Academy of Sciences, Białowieża.

327 Teerink, B.J. (1991) *Hair of west-European mammals.* Cambridge University Press, Cambridge.

328 Tegelström, H. & Hansson, L. (1987) Evidence of long distance dispersal in the common shrew (*Sorex araneus*). *Zeitschrift für Säugetierkunde,* **52**, 52–54.

329 Temple, R. & Morris, P. (1997) The lesser white-toothed

shrew on the Isles of Scilly. *British Wildlife*, **9**, 94–99.

330 Tsiperson, V.P. (1997) Pancreas of Aselli in some species of the shrews (*Sorex araneus & Neomys fodiens*) as an analogue of the Bursa of Fabricius in birds. *Cell Biology International*, **21**, 359–365.

331 Turni, H. & Muller, E.F. (1996) Discrimination of the shrew species *Sorex araneus* L., 1758 and *Sorex coronatus* Millet, 1828 by help of a new discriminance function. *Zeitschrift für Säugetierkunde*, **61**, 73–92.

332 Twigg, G.I. & Hughes, D.M. (1970) The 'pancreas of Aselli' in shrews. *Journal of Zoology*, **162**, 541–544.

333 Twigg, G.I. *et al.* (1968) Leptospirosis in British wild mammals. *Symposia of the Zoological Society of London*, **24**, 75–98.

334 Twigg, G.I. *et al.* (1969) The leptospirosis reservoir in British wild mammals. *Veterinary Records*, **84**, 424–426.

335 van Bemmel, A.C. & Voesenek, L.A.C.J. (1984) The home range of *Neomys fodiens* (Pennant, 1771) in the Netherlands. *Lutra*, **27**, 148–153.

336 van Wijngaarden-Bakker, L.H. (1985) Littletonian faunas, pp. 233–349 in Warren, K.J. & Warren, W.P. (eds.) *The Quaternary history of Ireland*. Academic Press, London.

337 Vizoso, A.D. & Thomas, W.E. (1981) Paramyxoviruses of the morbilli group in the wild hedgehog *Erinaceus europaeus*. *British Journal of Experimental Pathology*, **62**, 79–86.

338 Vlasak, P. (1970) The biology of reproduction and postnatal development of *Crocidura suaveolens* Pallas, 1811 under laboratory conditions. *Acta Universitatis Carolinae, Biologica*, **1970**, 207–292.

339 Vlasak, P. & Niethammer, J. (1990) *Crocidura suaveolens* (Pallas, 1811) – Gartenspitzmaus, pp. 397–428 in Neithammer, J. & Krapp, F. (eds.) *Handbuch der Säugetiere Europas*, **3(1)**. AULA, Wiesbaden (in German).

340 Vogel, P. (1969) Beobachtungen sum intraspezifischen Verhalten der Hausspitzmaus (*Crocidura russula* Hermann, 1870). *Revue Suisse de Zoologie*, **76**, 1079–1086 (in German).

341 Vogel, P. (1972) Vergleichende Untersuchungen zum Ontogenesemodus einheimischer Soriciden (*Crocidura russula, Sorex araneus* und *Neomys fodiens*). *Revue Suisse de Zoologie*, **79**, 1201–1332 (in German).

342 Vogel, P. (1972) Beitrag zur Fortpflanzungsbiologie der Gattung *Sorex, Neomys* und *Crocidura* (Soricidae). *Verhandlungen der Naturforschenden Gesellschaft in Basel*, **82**, 165–192 (in German).

343 Vogel, P. (1976) Energy consumption of European and African shrews. *Acta Theriologica*, **21**, 195–206.

344 Vogel, P. (1980) Metabolic levels and biological strategies in shrews, pp. 170–180 in Schmidt-Nielsen, K. *et al.* (eds.) *Comparative physiology: primitive mammals*. Cambridge University Press, Cambridge.

345 Vogel, P. (1984) Verteilung des roten Zahnschmelzes im Gebiss der Soricidae (Mammalia, Insectivora). *Revue Suisse de Zoologie*, **91**, 699–708 (in German).

346 Vogel, P. (1990) Body temperature and fur quality in swimming water-shrews, *Neomys fodiens* (Mammalia, Insectivora). *Zeitschrift für Säugetierkunde*, **55**, 73–80.

347 Vogel, P. *et al.* (1979) Influence de la température et de la nourriture disponsible sur la torpeur chez la musaraigne musette (*Crocidura russula*) en captivité. *Bulletin de la Société Vaudoise de Sciences Naturelles*, **74**, 325–332 (in French).

348 Vogel, P. *et al.* (1998) Diving capacity and foraging behaviour of the water shrew (*Neomys fodiens*). *Symposia of*

the Zoological Society of London, **71**, 31–47.

349 Wolsan, M. & Hutterer, R. (1998) Appendix: A list of the living species of shrews. Pp. 425–448 in Wójcik, J.M. & Wolsan, M. (eds.) *Evolution of Shrews*. Mammal Research Institute, Polish Academy of Sciences, Białowieża.

350 Weissenberger, T. *et al.* (1983) Observations de populations marquées de la musaraigne aquatique *Neomys fodiens* (Insectivora, Mammalia). *Bulletin de la Société Vaudoise de Sciences Naturelles*, **76**, 381–390 (in French).

351 White, T.A. Personal communication.

352 Whitworth, D.J. *et al.* (1999) Testis-like steroidogenesis in the ovotestis of the European mole, *Talpa europaea*. *Biology of Reproduction*, **60**, 413–418.

353 Wilson, D.E. & Reeder, D.M. (eds.) (2005) *Mammal species of the world*, 3rd edn. Johns Hopkins University Press, Baltimore, MD.

354 Wit, C.A. de & Weström, B.R. (1987) Venom resistance in the hedgehog, *Erinaceus europaeus*: purification and identification of macroglobulin inhibitors as plasma antihemorrhagic factors. *Toxicon*, **25**, 315–323.

355 Wołk, K. (1976) The winter food of the European water-shrew. *Acta Theriologica*, **21**, 117–129.

356 Wroot, A.J. (1984) *Feeding ecology of the European hedgehog*, Erinaceus europaeus. PhD Thesis, University of London.

357 Woods, J.A. & Mead-Briggs, A.R. (1978) The daily cycle of activity in the mole (*Talpa europaea*) and its seasonal changes, as revealed by radio-active monitoring of the nest. *Journal of Zoology*, **184**, 563–572.

358 Wyttenbach, A. *et al.* (1999) Microsatellite variation reveals low genetic subdivision in a chromosome race of *Sorex araneus* (Mammalia, Insectivora). *Journal of Heredity*, **90**, 323–327.

359 Yalden, D.W. (1966) The anatomy of mole locomotion. *Journal of Zoology*, **149**, 55–64.

360 Yalden, D.W. (1976) The food of the hedgehog in England. *Acta Theriologica*, **21**, 401–424.

361 Yalden, D.W. (1981) The occurrence of the pigmy shrew *Sorex minutus* on moorland, and the implications for its presence in Ireland. *Journal of Zoology*, **195**, 147–156.

362 Yalden, D.W. (1982) When did the mammal fauna of the British Isles arrive? *Mammal Review*, **12**, 1–57.

363 Yalden, D. (1999) *The history of British mammals*. Poyser, London.

364 Yalden, D.W. *et al.* (1973) Studies on the comparative ecology of some French small mammals. *Mammalia*, **37**, 257–276.

365 Yates, T.L. (1984) Insectivores, elephant shrews, tree shrews and dermopterans, pp. 117–144 in Anderson, S. & Jones, J.K. (eds.) *Orders and families of recent mammals of the world*, 2nd edn. Wiley, New York.

366 Young, R.P. *et al.* (2006) Abundance of hedgehogs (*Erinaceus europaeus*) in relation to the density and abundance of badgers (*Meles meles*). *Journal of Zoology*, **269**, 349–356.

367 Zaltenbach-Hanßler, B. *et al.* (1998) *Igel in der Tierarztpraxis*. ProIgel e.V, Neumünster (in German).

368 Zima, J. & Kral, B. (1984) Karyotypes of European mammals 1. *Acta Scientiarum Naturalium Brno*, **18**, 1–51.

369 Zima, J. *et al.* (1998) Chromosomal evolution in shrews, pp.175–218 in Wójcik, J.M. & Wolsan, M. (eds.) *Evolution of shrews*. Mammal Research Institute, Polish Academy of Sciences, Białowieża.

Plate 6

A Leisler's *Nyctalus leisleri*   **B** Noctule *N. noctula*   **C** Barbastelle *Barbastella barbastellus*   **D** Serotine *E. serotinus*
E Parti coloured *Vespertilio murinus*   **F** Bechstein's *Myotis bechsteini*   **G** Northern *Eptesicus nilsonii*
H Mouse-eared *M. myotis*   **I** Daubenton's *M. daubentonii*   **J** Brandt's *M. brandtii*   **K** Whiskered *M. mystacinus*
L Nathusius' pipistrelle *Pipistrellus nathusii*   **M** Common pipistrelle *P. pipistrellus*   **N** Natterer's *M. nattereri*
O Soprano pipistrelle *P. pygmaeus*   **P** Brown long-eared *Plecotus auritus*   **Q** Grey long-eared *Pl. austriacus*
R Greater horseshoe *Rhinolophus ferrumequinum*   **S** Lesser horseshoe *R. hipposideros*

8

Bats
Order Chiroptera

Compiled by P.A. Racey

A large, speciose order of flying mammals, with *c.*1033 species (second in numbers only to rodents), found mainly in tropical and subtropical climates. Only 3 (out of 18) families occur in Europe, and only 2, Rhinolophidae and Vespertilionidae, in British Isles. Traditionally divided into suborders Megachiroptera (Old World fruit bats, Pteropodidae) and Microchiroptera (all other families, mostly insectivorous); some discussion in the 1990s that these 2 suborders not closely related to each other, but that Pteropodidae might be more closely related to Primates, Microchiroptera to insectivores. Recent molecular phylogenies confirm Chiroptera as a monophyletic group, divided instead into Yinpterochiroptera and Yangochiroptera. Former include both Pteropodidae and Rhinolophidae, while Vesper-tilionidae belong with other mostly insectivorous bats in Yangchiroptera, so modern view has insectivorous bats diphyletic, echo-location possibly evolved twice (alternatively, Ptero-podidae have lost that ability [636].

Elongation of forearm, hands and fingers provides skeletal frame for double layer of skin forming the wing; attached to side of body and hind limbs, usually extending between them to include the tail (Fig. 8.1). This allows great manoeuvrability in flight, at some expense of mobility when landed, but also risks loss of heat and water through extensive skin surface. In combination, bats very dependent on safe, usually dark but humid, roost sites. Regularly use torpor and, outside tropics, hibernation, to reduce losses when at roost. Bats very sensitive to weather, when both roosting and hunting. Flight is energetically demanding, and catching insects in flight, usually using echolocation, demands great agility; this is hampered in late pregnancy, so bats typically have only 1 young per litter, and long lifespan (up to 40 years). Young normally left in roost when mothers foraging (though can be carried to new roost when small), also requiring safe roost sites. Mothers typically collect in large maternity roosts, clustering to save energy in cool weather. Prolonged mating season, from autumn through winter, but sperm stored, fertilisation delayed until spring (see Fig. 8.34).

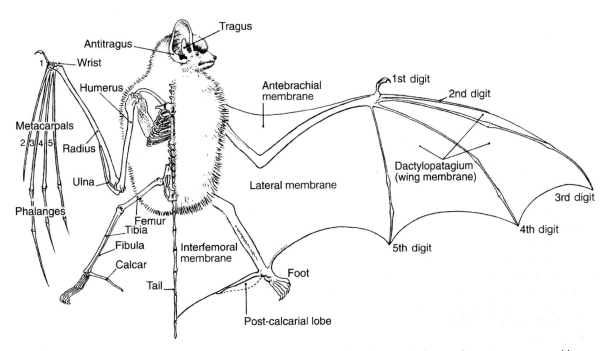

Fig. 8.1 A generalised vespertilionid bat, showing features referred to in the key and species accounts *(drawn by R. Gillmor)*.

293

Longevity, low reproductive rate, dependence on limited number of roosts, clustering into maternity roosts and hibernacula and dependence on human sites (buildings, tunnels, etc.) render bats very sensitive to human disturbance, therefore priorities for conservation. All bats protected under relevant legislation (e.g. Wildlife and Countryside Act 1981, EU directives on migratory species, see Chapter 4); roosts also legally protected. Licences required to handle or disturb bats, and prior permission from the statutory conservation agencies to alter buildings where work might affect bat roosts.

Echolocation such an important element of bat behaviour that specific identification often possible, and anatomical features related to it also important. Ear shape varies with loudness of calls and hunting mode (very large in bats that hunt quietly). Vespertilionids have an extra lobe, the tragus, in the base of the ear that varies in size and shape, and helps the bat determine the direction of returning echoes (Plate 6). Horseshoe bats, which call through their nostrils, have an elaborate noseleaf that directs the outgoing call, but lack the tragus. Availability of improved bat detectors and associated software to analyse the calls makes bat detector surveys increasingly important. The following section summarises this information.

Echolocation and social calls of British bats

All British bats use echolocation to orientate themselves and, in most cases, to locate and capture food; calls emitted from the bat's nose or mouth reflect off objects and return as echoes. By analysing these, the bats can gain information on an object's distance, size, and wing-beat rate (if flying). Most species also produce so-called 'social calls' that function in communication; they may reinforce territoriality, attract females for mating, communicate information about food availability to other bats, and repel others from foraging areas when prey is scarce [48]. Infant bats emit 'isolation calls' to attract their mothers. Social calls are often audible to humans, but the echolocation calls of most species are inaudible (ultrasonic).

Echolocation calls are highly variable in their frequency–time structure. Calls vary within species according to habitat [313], foraging ecology [311, 415], individual identity [397], family affiliation [364], and sex and age [294, 303]. Different species of bat produce different echolocation calls [44]. In general, larger bats produce calls of lower frequency, longer duration, and at lower repetition rates than smaller bats

[290]. For the functional significance of different pulse types, see [538].

Echolocation calls contain 2 basic components. Frequency-modulated (FM) components sweep down (or up) in frequency over time; constant frequency (CF) components do not vary in frequency over time. Most calls consist mainly of one component, but both may be combined and pure CF calls are rare.

Despite their inherent variability, echolocation calls produced by many bats are species-specific. Bats flying in confined spaces often produce broadband sweeps, making identification difficult. Several species of British bats also produce social calls that can be used for identification in the field. Identification using echolocation calls may be possible using narrow-band heterodyne bat detectors to find the frequency of a call that is loudest. However, identification of bats in flight based solely on echolocation calls is not a precise art. Some species, especially within the genus *Myotis*, can be extremely difficult to identify because the frequencies they use overlap. Identification using broadband detectors, which 'listen' to a broad range of frequencies simultaneously, is only possible in combination with software that allows calls to be visualised on a computer. For a detailed review of detection methods, see [317].

In this section we present information on the echolocation calls produced by 14 of the 16 species of bat known to breed in GB. More detail is provided in [654, 655]. For species where social calls are also useful for identification, these are presented. All calls were detected using a broadband bat detector and subsequently time-expanded before being recorded using a high-quality audio tape recorder. The recorded calls were then digitised and analysed using either specialised computer software or a digital spectrum analyser. For each species we present the means and standard deviations of 5 call parameters (start frequency, end frequency, frequency with most energy, duration, and inter-pulse interval; Table 8.1) and spectrograms detailing the frequency–time structure of several calls from each species (Fig. 8.2a–f). Inter-pulse intervals shown in the spectrograms are not to scale, to simplify the diagrams. However, within the social calls, which are made up of several components, inter-component time intervals are correct. Call sequences for each species (where available) can be viewed and downloaded via the Internet(*www.bio.bris.ac.uk/research/bats/calls*).

AUTHORS

S. Parsons, N. Jennings & G. Jones.

Table 8.1 Call parameters for British bats: mean and standard deviation

Species	Start frequency	End frequency	Frequency with most energy	Duration	Inter-pulse interval
	(kHz)	(kHz)	(kHz)	(ms)	(ms)
Barbastella barbastellus (Barbastelle)	40.3 (±3.4)	30.2 (±4.1)	34.9 (±3.5)	3.1 (±0.7)	63.8 (±-)
Eptesicus serotinus (Serotine)	59.5 (±7.1)	27.6 (±1.9)	32.2 (±2.8)	6.9 (±2.3)	116.0 (±26.2)
Myotis bechsteinii (Bechstein's bat)	109.2 (±11.9)	33.8 (±3.9)	51.0 (±3.1)	2.1 (±0.4)	96.4 (±13.1)
Myotis brandtii (Brandt's bat)	85.5 (±13.3)	33.7 (±3.8)	47.9 (±8.3)	3.1 (±0.8)	88.0 (±18.3)
Myotis daubentonii (Daubenton's bat)	84.2 (±4.8)	29.4 (±3.7)	46.2 (±4.5)	2.9 (±1.0) (±1.0)	78.6 (±22.6)
Myotis mystacinus (Whiskered bat)	80.3 (±12.1)	32.2 (±3.4)	47.5 (±5.9)	2.2 (±0.9)	87.8 (±23.8)
Myotis nattereri (Natterer's bat)	98.5 (±19.6)	22.5 (±5.1)	51.2 (±11.3)	2.3 (±1.1)	76.8 (±24.8)
Nyctalus leisleri (Leisler's bat)	36.3 (±10.3)	25.5 (±1.6)	28.9 (±2.0)	10.7 (±1.7)	177.0 (±71.6)
Nyctalus noctula (Noctule)	25.9 (±7.2)	18.2 (±2.1)	20.3 (±2.0)	19.6 (±4.4)	336 (±138.0)
Pipistrellus pipistrellus (Common pipistrelle)	71.3 (±14.0)	43.3 (±1.8)	46.0 (±1.8)	4.8 (±1.3)	98.2 (±32.1)
Pipistrellus pygmaeus (Soprano pipistrelle)	83.2 ±17.0)	52.2 (±1.7)	53.8 (±1.7)	5.0 (±1.1) (±1.1)	95.2 (±27.5)
Pipistrellus nathusii (Nathusius' pipistrelle)	49.8 (±6.8)	36.7 (±1.0)	39.3 (±1.0)	6.1 (±1.2)	134.0 (±55.9)
Plecotus auritus (Brown long-eared bat)	49.9 (±3.1)	27.1 (±1.8)	53.1 (±14)	1.8 (±0.5)	71.3 (±25.0)
Plecotus austriacus (Grey long-eared bat)	41.4 (±2.08)	23.6 (±2.87)	32.6 (±8.67)	3.8 (±1.36)	105.0 (±32.90)
Rhinolophus ferrumequinum (Greater horseshoe bat)	69.4 (±1.7)	67.5 (±3.4)	82.1 (±0.5)	51.6 (±12.4)	83.0 (±18.9)
Rhinolophus hipposideros (Lesser horseshoe bat)	97.5 (±1.6)	96.1 (±9.3)	111.5 (±1.1)	40.8 (±10.5)	82.4 (±12.3)

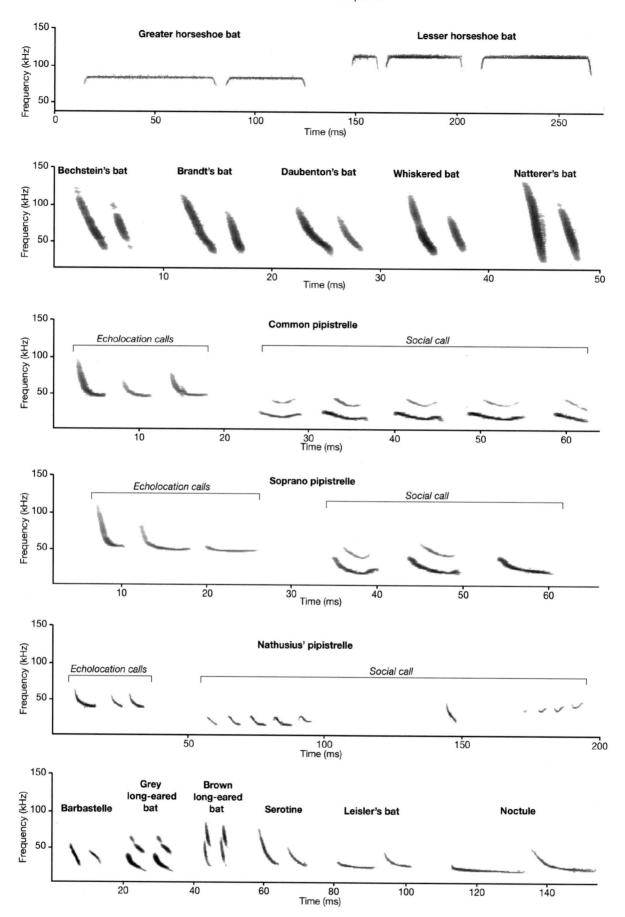

Fig. 8.2 Sonagrams of echolocation calls of British bats. Social calls are also shown for *Pipistrellus* species, where they are valuable diagnostically (see text). *(devised by S. Parsons, G. Jones & N. Jennings)*.

Identification of breeding bats

For rare vagrants, see text and general identification guides, e.g. [194, 539]. See Fig. 8.1 and Plate 6 for details of characters. An identification key for bats breeding in the British Isles is given in Table 8.2 (simplified from [609]). Generic features of skulls are shown in Fig 8.3.

FAMILY RHINOLOPHIDAE

A family of only 1 genus, with *c.*77 species; widely distributed in warmer parts of Old World, especially Afrotropical and Oriental regions, but 5 species in S Europe; 2 reach British Isles, at extreme N edge of family range. Long fossil history, back to Late Eocene, one of oldest modern bat

Table 8.2 Simplified key to bats breeding in the British Isles (cf. [609])

1	(a) Complex noseleaf present	2
	(b) No noseleaf, but ear with tragus	3
2	(a) Larger, forearm >50 mm	Greater horseshoe bat
	(b) Smaller, forearm <43 mm	Lesser horseshoe bat
3	(a) Ears separate, at sides of head	4
	(b) Ears joined over head	15
4	(a) With postcalcarial lobe; tragus blunt	5
	(b) No postcalcarial lobe; tragus pointed	10
5	(a) Smaller, forearm <35 mm	6
	(b) Larger, forearm >39 mm	8
6	(a) Tail membrane furred dorsally to half length of tail	Nathusius' pipistrelle
	(b) Tail membrane not furry	7
7	(a) Face usually dark, echolocates strongly at 45 kHz	Common pipistrelle
	(b) Face usually pink, echolocates strongly at 55 kHz	Soprano pipistrelle
8	(a) Tragus longer, blunt; tail tip extends 5–7 mm	Serotine
	(b) Tragus short, mushroom shaped	9
9	(a) Smaller, forearm <47 mm; fur darker, bicoloured	Leisler's bat
	(b) Larger, forearm >47 mm; fur uniformly golden	Noctule
10	(a) Larger, forearm >57 mm	Mouse-eared bat
	(b) Smaller, forearm <45 mm	11
11	(a) Ears long, >20 mm	Bechstein's bat
	(b) Ears shorter, <17 mm	12
12	(a) Tail membrane with fringe of stiff 1mm long bristles	Natterer's bat
	(b) Tail membrane without bristles, though may be fine fur	13
13	(a) Hind feet large, >½ length of shin	Daubenton's bat
	(b) Hind feet small, about 1/3 length of shin	14
14	(a) Tragus sharply pointed,; face usually black	Whiskered bat
	(b) Tragus bluntly pointed; face usually dark brown	Brandt's bat
15	(a) Ears very long, >29 mm (but may be folded away under wing when resting)	16
	(b) Ears short, <20 mm, triangular shape	Barbastelle
16	(a) Thumb longer, > 6 mm; face usually pink or brown	Brown long-eared bat
	(b) Thumb shorter, <6 mm; face usually black	Grey long-eared bat

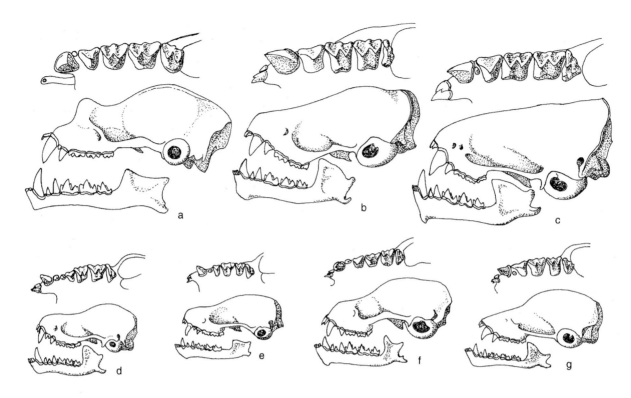

Fig. 8.3 *Rhinolophus* (a) is readily distinguished by the bulbous nose. *Myotis* (d) has 3 pairs of premolars, 4 genera have 2, and *Eptesicus* (b) only 1. These are probably p^2, p^3 and p^4 in *Myotis*, p^4 in *Eptesicus*, and p^2 with p^4 in *Nyctalus* (c), *Pipistrellus* (e), *Plecotus* (f) and *Barbastella* (g). Note that p^2 is very small, hidden inside the other teeth, in *Nyctalus* (c) and *Barbastella* (g) *(drawn by D.W. Yalden).*

families. Characterised by prominent noseleaf; lack tragus. Echolocate through nostrils, placed 1/2 wavelength apart, with noseleaf forming a megaphone; use long pulses, mostly CF, which overlap returning echoes. Roost by hanging freely by hindfeet, usually wrap wings tightly round body (see Fig. 8.7). Wings rounded, flight highly manoeuvrable, hunt within and between tree canopies (see Fig 8.4). Will land, take food from ground, but unable to walk because hind limbs slender, permanently directed backwards, adapted to hanging. Skull with characteristic profile, bulbous muzzle supporting noseleaf. Dentition $i^1/_2c^1/_1p^2/_3m^3/_3$; upper incisors tiny, born on slender forwardly directed premaxillae, often lost in preparation or fossilisation; only 2 pairs of lower incisors distinguish jaws from vespertilionids (3 pairs).

GENUS *Rhinolophus*

A genus of *c.*77 species, 2 of which occur in British Isles.

Greater horseshoe bat *Rhinolophus ferrumequinum*

Vespertilio ferrum-equinum Schreber, 1774; France.

RECOGNITION

Readily distinguished from lesser horseshoe, without disturbance, by size (Plate 6). Body about tablespoon size (lesser is teaspoon size). When active or in tight clusters, wings folded alongside body. Noseleaf and size then permits recognition (forearm 50.6–59.0 mm in adults). Fur fairly evenly buff-brown above and below. Juveniles have greyish fur until the following June moult.

Total length of skull >20 mm (cf. <16 mm for lesser horseshoe); p^2 very small, outside tooth row, canine touches p^4 (see Fig. 8.3).

SIGN

Territorial sites of adult males often show yellow-brown stain on projections used for hanging, visible only on light-coloured stone. Dismembered insect remains beneath perches.

Faeces: *c.*9–13 × 2.5 mm, vary in colour and texture according to diet: black after *Melolontha* and *Geotrupes* beetles; dark brown after *Aphodius*, ichneumonids and tipulids; grey to light brown after moths.

Food remains often within a short distance of the entrance of a cave, mine, porch, etc., below a vertical hollow used to cluster after foraging, and beneath trees used as nocturnal perches. Insect remains usually wings, heads or legs, but even

Fig. 8.4 Greater horseshoe bat in flight, showing characteristic broad inner wing, small dactylopatagium of rhinolophids *(photo F. Greenaway).*

thoraxes of large beetles may be dropped.

DESCRIPTION

Fur thick, fluffy; pale buff with buff tips that darken and turn reddish with age; barely paler ventrally (Fig. 8.4). In juveniles, grey fur may develop buff tips ventrally in 1st year. Moult begins late May–early June. Usually complete by late June–early July, but delayed by severe spring weather.

Eyes small; field of view partly obscured by noseleaf. Nostrils open within the parabolic horseshoe (*c.*14 mm high × 8 mm wide). A few vibrissae occur beneath the horseshoe and on lower lip. Ears large, triangular, lacking a tragus but with broad antitragus.

Nipples: 1 pair functional, pectoral, but also a pair of pelvic teats which develop slightly anterior to the vulva during late pregnancy in females breeding for 1st time. These lack milk supply, but are sucked by the young between suckling periods, facilitate close attachment. In summer, pink and swollen when in use; but turn white and regress during weaning and in following winter. If breeding omitted for a summer, shrink further.

Chromosomes: 2n = 58, Fna = 60, European data [685].

Relationships: Most closely related to *R. clivosus* (Africa), *R. bocharicus* (Iran, etc.), *R. affinis* (SE Asia); probably derived from an African ancestor [118].

MEASUREMENTS

Head and body 56–68 mm, forearm 50.6–59.0 mm, wingspan 330–395 mm, ear 21–26 mm, weight 13–34 g. Males *c.*2% smaller than females as measured by forearm, but considerable overlap. Mean forearm length 54.8 mm (n = 228) for males and 55.5 mm (n = 222), both SD *c.*1.0 mm, for females occupying unheated roosts. Males 2–15% lighter than non-pregnant females, according to age and season. Mature males show greatest variability

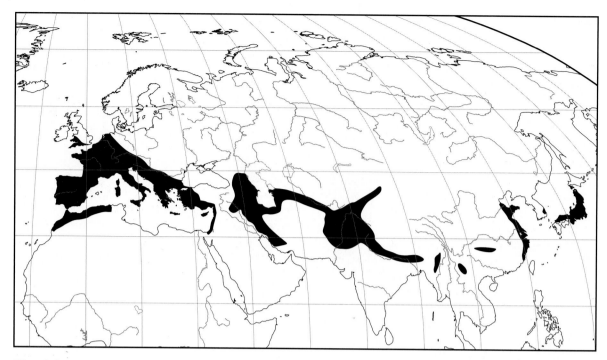

Fig. 8.5 Greater horseshoe bat *Rhinolophus ferrumequinum*: presumed world distribution. Former range further east (to China, Japan) perhaps assigned to related species.

(see Table 6.1 in [459]).

Incubators installed to maintain temperature at *c*.27 °C [464] only affected mean size of female forearm, which rose to 56.5 mm.

VARIATION

British animals slightly smaller on average than in some continental populations, e.g. mean forearm length of 55.7–56.7 mm in Italy [135], not enough to justify recognition as discrete subspecies. (The name *R. f. insulanus* Barrett-Hamilton, 1910 (Cheddar, Somerset) [55] is based on this size difference.)

DISTRIBUTION

Widely in S half of W Palaearctic, from GB to Israel; perhaps across across Palaearctic (*R. f. irani*) to Japan, but *R. f. nippon* (Japan) perhaps a distinct species [118] (Fig. 8.5).

In GB, limited by climate to SW England and Wales (Fig. 8.6). Winter severity affects winter foraging by 1st-year and mature males. Time of birth and juvenile growth affected by cold springs [468]. No cross-channel movements recorded, despite extensive ringing studies in England and France over 4 decades. Warmer climate since late 1980s has facilitated spread into more northerly and easterly counties.

HISTORY

Rhinolophus known as early as Late Eocene, France, and *R.* cf. *ferrumequinum* from Lower Pleistocene, Hungary. No fossil record from British Isles, despite cave-dwelling habits. Earliest certain records Roman, may have awaited creation of farmland before able to colonise [677].

Range and numbers significantly reduced this century, e.g. present in Kent and Isle of Wight until *c*.1900 [55], but degree of population decline

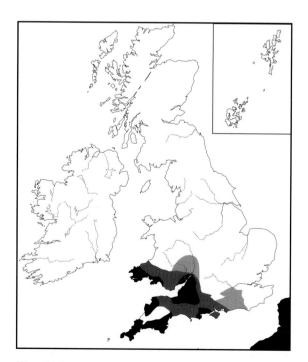

Fig. 8.6 Greater horseshoe bat *Rhinolophus ferrumequinum*: range in GB.

disputed [215, 376]. In areas lacking caves, distribution benefited from hibernacula created by mining industries after mines fell into disuse, early 20th century. However, subsequent closure of many disused mines for safety reasons may have seriously depressed numbers in Dorset, and to lesser extent elsewhere.

HABITAT

Maternity roosts normally in sun-warmed attics of large old buildings, but also in underground sites. Numbers greatest in colonies with close access to sheltered south-facing slopes, covered by blocks of deciduous woodland, interspersed with permanent pastures grazed primarily by cattle, but also sheep and horses. Such habitats generate large numbers of insect prey. Hunts mainly along linear features, such as substantial hedgerows and woodland edge, usually within *c*.3–4 km of the roost [145], so woodland blocks ideally linked. Early flights and feeding by young bats occur within 1 km of the roost [304]. Also needs a series of suitable hibernacula, which must offer range of airflow patterns and hence temperature regimes [451, 452]. Hibernacula should be dispersed among suitable feeding areas, and free from excessive human disturbance.

SOCIAL ORGANISATION AND BEHAVIOUR

Ringed bats provide data on social organisation, subsequent movements and life histories of individuals. DNA sampling and subsequent microsatellite analysis has revealed further details of breeding behaviour and its implication for social structure and gene flow. Most summer studies refer to the colony in Woodchester Mansion, near Stroud, Gloucestershire [453, 454, 460, 498–503]. Infrared video and DVD film from roosts, and radiotelemetry field studies, have revealed new aspects of behaviour.

Highly gregarious in summer, especially immature and breeding females, possibly because need to cluster after foraging to reduce thermoregulatory costs. Breeding females more solitary and widespread in midwinter. Solitary mature males occupy mating territories with 1–8 mature females in autumn, but largely absent from maternity roosts. Large winter clusters in hibernacula consist mostly of 1st-year bats, immature males and mature males. Females show strong philopatry to their natal colony [460], regularly occur in maternity roost as immatures [1]. Male young usually return to the natal roost in their 2nd summer, but presence erratically declines in subsequent summers. Immigrant females rarely stay to breed, and may breed at lower frequencies than local females [1].

During winter, activity remains largely nocturnal, with bats typically arousing from torpor at dusk [408]. Torpor bouts within hibernation last up to 12 days, and euthermic activity after arousal increases in duration only above 10 °C external temperature, when likely to feed [405, 409]. Bats normally synchronise arousals with dusk; synchrony greatest in bats with lowest body weight [409].

TERRITORIES

Summer: Colonies may occupy a single traditional summer roost over many decades, using the same roost space, provided conditions remain favourable. In mid July, 150–350 adults typically congregate in UK roosts. Roost destruction can result in occupation of alternative roosts in the same foraging region [464]. Other colonies regularly switch during the summer [465].

At Woodchester, immatures and younger mothers form active clusters in spring whenever weather permits regular feeding. Return to hibernacula and use torpor during cold spells [453]. Older mothers return in June–early July; some just before giving birth [1]. Some adult males return in May and June, usually leaving by mid July, when segregate from females [340, 453, 534]. By August, roost contains mainly lactating females, juveniles and immatures of both sexes. In early September, mothers and most immatures depart, leaving mainly juveniles in October.

The pattern above may be flexible, especially with regard to adult male occupation. The proportions of non-breeding bats present among roosts [464], and limited captures at other roosts, suggest that many adult males may remain throughout the summer, possibly due to higher habitat quality around the roost.

Winter: Bats from different colonies disperse to widespread hibernacula and share sites. 3 types of hibernacula recognised, based on age and sex groups of occupants.

- **Type 1:** Mainly 1st-year animals of both sexes plus older immatures throughout the winter, with mature males in mid to late winter. Clusters of up to 350 torpid bats may occur in a single hibernaculum, but normally a cluster contains 30–80 bats.
- **Type 2:** Few 1st-year bats, mainly 2nd- and 3rd-year immatures with surplus adult males. The latter seem to accumulate after a series of mild winters. Clusters of torpid bats can also occur. Solitary older females may also be present.
- **Type 3:** Single breeding male, occupying territorial site in spring and autumn, for up to 12 years. Up to 8 breeding females may

annually visit his territory. One female visited the same roost for 19 years. Small sites, providing little protection against cold midwinter weather, mainly occupied only in autumn and spring. Larger ones may be occupied all through the hibernation period, if they provide suitable temperature and airflow regimes [451, 452]. Function both as mating territories and as roosts where much of pregnancy takes place.

A few type 1, several type 2 and many type 3 hibernacula serve the winter population of bats in a region [465].

Roosting behaviour: Infrared video studies of active bats in clusters show little aggression and no evidence of hierarchy [1]. In unheated roosts, clusters form and disperse largely in relation to ambient temperatures and the need to conserve energy for reproduction. After an incubator was fitted in the Woodchester roost, bats used it whenever feeding conditions were good.

Minor disputes may occur as individuals enter or leave tight clusters for defecation or urination. However, aggressive chasing behaviour has been seen in corridors outside the maternity attic in May and June. Possibly immigrant animals, which are sometimes found in the colony in May, but not later in summer, are involved in these chases. No aggressive interactions while foraging away from the roost have been observed [143].

Scent-marking: Yellow-brown stains on projections used for hanging in type 3 hibernacula (see Sign) are believed to be produced by facial glands of the adult male occupying the territory, may be scent-marks.

Vocalisations: Echolocation calls are long (45–55 ms), dominated by a CF component at *c.*83 kHz, with FM sweeps initiating and terminating them [299]. Call frequency changes slightly with season and age [297]. Adults also may emit distress calls when handled. Young emit isolation calls on separation from their mothers.

Social calls are complex and varied, suggesting that communication among colony members is important. 12 different calls were identified at a maternity roost, mostly between 20 and 29 kHz [14], and a further 2 types from a hibernaculum [15]. For captive Chinese greater horseshoe bats, in free-flight facility, social calls classified into 17 syllable types (10 simple, 7 composite) [358]. Most syllables lasted >100 ms, with multiple harmonics and fundamental frequencies normally >20 kHz. Behavioural observations suggested many calls produced in non-contact situations, responding to social calls from conspecifics.

Dispersal: Type 1 hibernacula are usually within 10 km, type 2 within 20 km and type 3 within 40 km of the maternity roost of origin. 1st year bats occasionally travel 40 km, and exceptionally 158 km, to a type 1 hibernaculum in their 1st winter [467]. Bats occupying a given type 1 or 2 hibernaculum may move up to 55 km to a type 3 hibernaculum [465]. Limit for regular returns to natal roost may be *c.*40 km; longer movements seem to result in permanent shifts. Hence a colony may disperse over an area of some 5000 km². This

Table 8.3 Greater horseshoe bat: mean diet between late April and early October at 7 UK maternity roosts

Prey item	% diet by volume	Standard deviation
Moths	38.6	6.45
Aphodius rufipes	21.7	3.31
Tipulidae	14.3	8.92
Ichneumonids (*Ophion* complex)	9.4	5.18
Melolontha melolontha	8.0	2.94
Trichoptera (caddisflies)	5.7	3.74
Geotrupes sp.	1.5	1.59
Small Diptera	0.4	0.55
Other insects	0.4	0.34

5 roosts were within 40 km of Bristol, 2 in SW Wales. Data refer to summer 1996. In some years moth consumption is lower, and *Aphodius* much higher [462].

area not normally occupied exclusively by a given colony, but shared among others. Such overlaps permit gene flow among colonies during mating within type 3 hibernacula.

FEEDING

Insectivorous; eat live prey caught mainly on the wing. Lactating females may consume their lean body mass of insects in a single night. Faecal analysis shows this bat is a selective feeder, preferring larger insect prey, such as beetles (Coleoptera, especially Scarabaeidae), and moths (Lepidoptera, especially Noctuidae). Crane flies (Diptera, Tipulidae), caddisflies (Trichoptera) and ichneumonoid parasitic wasps (Hymenoptera, Ichneumonoidea) are taken in decreasing order of preference [286, 461, 462] (Table 8.3.)

Beetle prey include cockchafers (May bugs) *Melolontha melolontha*, small dung beetles *Aphodius rufipes* and large dung beetles *Geotrupes* spp. (important in winter). Cockchafers preferred spring prey when abundant, and may promote rapid pregnancy of breeding females. From June until early August, females eat various types of large noctuid moths, e.g. the yellow underwing moth *Noctua pronuba*, and occasionally sphingid (hawk) moths. Mothers usually eat moths during lactation; their young prey almost exclusively upon *Aphodius* when begin to feed at 28–30 days of age. If *Aphodius* absent, young eat tipulids. When reach 45 days, juveniles can feed on moths, but *Aphodius* usually preferred [461].

Winter diet (October–mid April) consists mainly of *Geotrupes* spp. and *Ophion* spp. at sites within good habitats. Also small amounts of dung flies *Scatophaga stercoraria*, moths, tipulids and caddisflies [466]. 1st-year bats and adult males are frequent winter foragers, but individuals of other sex/age groups also feed if body reserves are low. Amounts per foraging bout eaten by some individuals can approach summer levels.

Many grazing animals slaughtered in foot-and-mouth disease (FMD) outbreak, spring 2001; had significant impact upon consumption of dung beetles at 2 roosts in Gloucestershire. One roost (Dean Hall) was within an FMD slaughter area, other (Woodchester Mansion) some 12 km outside the affected area. During the summers of 2001 and 2002 consumption of *Aphodius* beetles fell at both roosts compared with 1997 [469]. At Dean Hall, consumption fell most (by 31.5%) and juvenile mortality rose in both summers, confirming the importance of *Aphodius* to this species.

HUNTING BEHAVIOUR

Hunting bouts last 1–2.5 h, within a foraging area [143]. Separated by periods of resting, when rapid digestion and egestion of faeces occurs, allowing the consumption of more food. Inter-bout periods may be spent in daytime roosts, or in temporary night roosts. Females from specific matrilines share foraging areas and night roosts in summer [501].

Radiotelemetry studies of many colonies in 3 European countries [62, 72, 143, 293, 295, 426, 488, 599] show a consistent specialised hunting technique, using foraging areas with similar structure. Commute from roost to a foraging area, flying c.1–2 m above grassland, along the side of linear features such as tall hedgerows and woodland edges. Foraging areas may be close to a maternity roost or up to 14 km away (mean 3–4 km). Whatever the commuting range, the bats normally fly up to 21–25 km total distance in a night [143].

Within foraging area (mean 6–7 ha), mainly use localised favoured spots, or core areas, of c.0.35 ha. Hunting mainly involves either hawking along the edges of linear habitat features, or perching on a bare twig some 2 m from the ground, scanning for passing prey which they intercept like a flycatcher [145].

Most prey are caught close to the ground as they emerge from the soil beneath short grassland, oviposit in it, or feed on the dung of domestic animals. Besides hawking and perch-feeding, some studies report regular gleaning of prey from vegetation [426], during which may hover briefly.

Perches may also be used whilst large prey items are dismembered, and the less digestible parts discarded. Occasionally groups of bats hunt together from perches within the same core area.

Foraging occurs 1–3 times a night according to weather, season and reproductive class, normally for c.3 h each night. Foraging bout length varies with sex, reproductive condition and climatic factors [143]. Foraging concentrates soon after dusk when conditions are usually most favourable for prey flight. Emergence timing relative to dusk, and hence to light levels at emergence, seems to reflect a conflict between the need to forage and the avoidance of predators [146, 301]. Sparrowhawks *Accipiter nisus* and some owls are known to catch greater horseshoe bats. Adults usually leave roost to forage 13–22 min after sunset. However, females emerge later as pregnancy advances, and bats under energetic stress, e.g. lactating females during poor summer weather, emerge relatively early. Juveniles emerge later than adults for the 1st fortnight of initial foraging. Emergence from bright, exposed roosts later than from darker, tree-sheltered ones [304].

IMPACT OF PREY AVAILABILITY

Climatic conditions (temperature, rainfall and wind speed) and prey population densities interact to control insect availability to bats during a specific foraging bout and their foraging success [463]. Temperature important throughout the year. Above 14 °C all insect prey can fly. As temperature falls, certain insects unable to fly, thus unavailable to foraging bats. Most moths require at least 12 °C to fly, whereas some ichneumonids fly down to *c*.3 °C. Above *c*.10 °C maximum day temperature, foraging potentially profitable at dusk. Above *c*.7–8 °C minimum night temperature, foraging also profitable at dawn [453]. Foraging time increases with increasing night-time temperatures in summer, and lactating females usually also feed in the middle of the night [143]. Cold, or wet and windy, weather prevents or seriously reduces foraging success at any time of the summer [463]. Hence ability to enter torpor at any time of year minimises starvation risk.

BREEDING

Monoestrous, mating from late August–possibly May; both sexes store sperm; flexible pregnancy length with peak births early July; always single births. Normally breed first at either 2 or 3 years [460], but 5 years in Dorset [606]. Mating system is resource defence polygyny. Sequential matings by individual females returning to the same territory leads to full siblings and increased kinship within summer colony matrilines, and favours social group cooperation, such as sharing foraging areas and night roosts [501, 502]. However, inbred bats, especially males, suffer reduced survival [500]. Female relatives often share sexual partners across different years, although serious inbreeding limited by the avoidance of matings between close relatives, such as father/daughter [502].

Males: Develop sperm during June and July from age 2 or 3. Viable sperm stored in epididymes from late summer to following spring. Copulation occurs in male territory, normally in September–October, but may occur in winter or be delayed until spring. Male mounts female, who may be semi-torpid, from rear and bites nuchal fur. May last for 50 min and leads to formation of a vaginal plug (coagulated secretion of male urethral gland), with sperm storage in oviducts. Retained plug may ensure male's reproductive success as further copulations seem physically impossible [365]. Plug incidence rises as winter progresses [1]. Plugs not site of sperm storage, although some trapped inside [433].

Females: Meiosis starts in single (right) ovary in October, is suspended in winter and completed by early April in Japan [398]. Ovulation and fertilisation of single egg occurs at time of plug ejection [534], mid March–early May; peak usually early April in Gloucestershire [1]. Delayed in cold springs. Implantation follows a week later [365].

Periods of torpor in pregnancy [453] delay births until July (individual range 10 June–10 August in Gloucestershire; mean annual birth date over 21 years from 6–26 July). Later in cold springs [468], probably due to poor foraging success.

Birth occurs inside roost, often at dusk. Female hangs from feet and baby emerges into overlapping wings. Afterbirth eaten. Babies parked by mothers within roost on 1st day while mothers forage. Females can breed successfully every year up to 24 years, and achieve lifetime reproductive output up to 19 births [460]. Those breeding earlier (age 2 years) breed at *c*.96% of opportunities, cf. 85% for later breeders (age 3 or more), which live longer.

Lactation lasts up to 45 days, including 2-week overlap with insect capture by the young. Mammary glands bald only during suckling; hair regrowth rapid. 1st-time breeders give birth later than experienced breeders [460], and their young are often stunted [1].

Development: Young born blind with sparse, short grey fur dorsally; naked abdomen; milk teeth shed before birth. Wing membranes pink with soft flexible bones. Forearm *c*.26 mm, mass *c*.6.2 g (both sexes); increase to 50 mm and 13 g in *c*.17 days. Peak radius growth rate occurs after *c*.4 days [373, 464], faster in females, but complete in both by 40 days to give slightly larger females. Forearm length is best judge of overall growth, but digits take up to 60 days to ossify. Female forearm length is largely influenced by early growth rate, mother's forearm length and birth timing, but also by thermal conditions within the roost [464]. Eyes open at 9 days. Although body mass rises, faster growth of the wing area results in wing loading declining with age [248]. This promotes flight from 15 days; increasingly skilful from 3 weeks, and successful foraging from 4 weeks; initially close to roost [304].

Ultrasonic calls emitted from birth: initially isolation calls, to attract mother, and emitted orally. By 11–19 days, precursors of echolocation calls emitted nasally. These lose harmonics and increase in frequency as grow. Frequency of echolocation calls emitted by weaned juveniles correlates with those of their mothers; learning may play a role in echolocation development [297]. Young can compensate for Doppler shift after 45 days [125, 331]. Food consumption rises rapidly from age 30 to 55 days, then rate slows as skeletal growth ceases at 60 days. Foraging range reaches adult levels by this age [304].

Table 8.4 Greater horseshoe bat: survival of females from Gloucestershire breeding colony, 1980–1983 [1]

Age group (years)	n caught year t	% surviving year t + 1
1	92	53
2	57	72
3	42	79
4	35	66
5	21	71
6	24	87
7	22	91
8–12	56	86
13–17	39	82
18–25	12	58
Overall	**400**	**73**

Parental care: Mothers remain with young for 10–22 days after weaning at Woodchester. In winter separate, but rejoin in spring. Survival of female offspring may depend upon mother's survival through its 2nd summer [1], but precise form of extended maternal care unknown.

POPULATION

Numbers: Total UK population estimated at 4000–5000 [215], may have been too high. Peak exit counts and juvenile numbers at 8 colonies [462] produced estimates of 1600 bats total in midsummer. Currently *c.*24 colonies known, numbers of bats either stable or increasing [465]. In stable habitat conditions, numbers within colony strongly regulated and stable for long periods (1–2 decades) until periodic, climate-induced crashes [456].

Sex ratio: Normally 1:1 at birth, but may favour males during prolonged severe climatic conditions [468], and roosts with incubators show female-dominated births during favourable climates during population recovery [464]. Females outnumber males at maternity roosts and in nearby hibernacula. Males outnumber females in type 1 and 2 hibernacula, especially after a series of mild winters.

Age determination: Juveniles and 1st-year bats separable from all older ones by grey fur and smoothly tapered finger joints of 5th digit. Older bats have brownish fur and knobbly joints. Maturity may occur at 2 or 3 years in either sex.

Tooth wear unreliable guide to age [1]. Only ringing of juveniles or 1st-years and subsequent recapture allows exact ageing.

Age structure: See descriptions of hibernacula and social organisation and behaviour. In summer 28–35% of population consists of breeding females and another 25–32% juveniles. Rest are immature older males and females, with varying numbers of adult males.

Survival: Reliable data only from maternity roost captures. Young show few (3%) perinatal deaths; 13% in early flights and another 15% just after weaning [457]. More young reach hibernacula after early mean births [456], and survival varies with winter severity. Also true of adult males. Hence sex ratios in hibernacula fluctuate. Some live beyond 25 years and still breed; upper limit of *c.*30 years for both males [102] and females [117]. See Tables 8.4 and 8.5.

MORTALITY

Predation by aerial raptors [304], but rarely observed. Sparrowhawks *Accipiter nisus* seen to catch greater horseshoe bats [143]. Skeletal remains reported from barn and tawny owl pellets [598]. Cats also sometimes catch them [1]. Cars can kill bats crossing rural roads as they fly at low levels. Greatest threat to populations is mass starvation in late, cold springs [456].

PARASITES AND PATHOGENS

Most common ectoparasite is wing mite

Table 8.5 Greater horseshoe bat: survival from birth to age 1 year

Years of births	Total no. of young born	No. of 1st-year bats known to reach hibernacula	No. alive 1 year after birth
		(% of no. born)	(% of no. born)
1984–1988	171	77 (45)	48 (28)
1989–1993	126	62 (49)	49 (39)
1994–1997	116	70 (60)	60 (52)

All data from the Woodchester colony. During 1984–1988, suffered severe population crash [456]. During 1994–1997, incubator set at 27 °C in the roost to improve growth rates [464]. These data suggest the incubator also improves survival rates to age 1 year ($\chi^2 = 5.47$, df = 1, P = 0.019; with incubator versus without).

Eyndhovenia euryalis (Acarina: Mesostigmata). Most common on young infants and in larger maternity colonies [404], disperse into bat's fur in winter [133]. In France, another mite, *Paraperiglischrus rhinolophinus* (Acarina: Mesostigmata), found mainly in winter. Male mites live on wing membranes, females plus nymphs on tail membrane. In UK, tick *Ixodes vespertilionis* (Acarina: Ixodidae) regularly found in winter [17] and nycteribiid fly *Phthiridium biarticulum* occasionally occurs on this species [255]. Flea *Rhinolophopsylla unipectinata* not recorded in GB, despite widespread occurrence in Europe.

RELATIONS WITH HUMANS
As most insect prey species are pests of either agriculture or forestry, their control is likely to have made a major contribution to bat declines. Endangered species, classified as conservation dependent by IUCN, and assisted by English Nature under its species recovery programme. Potential for continued survival in the UK has been questioned [602]. Grills installed at entrances to disused mines protect bats from disturbance and owners from liability. About 23% of known hibernacula, containing an estimated 72% of bats, now protected as sites of special scientific interest (SSSIs) [380]. Landowners near maternity roosts received grant aid for complying with environmental prescriptions favouring their populations under Countryside Stewardship Scheme of Ministry of Agriculture [379]. Scheme now discontinued, but farmers now paid graded subsidies according to the wildlife value of their land, and their land management practices.

LITERATURE
A general account for school students [455]; a review of hibernating bats, much relevant to this species [457]. Major research reports for English Nature [461, 462, 464, 465]; see also [304].

AUTHORS
R.D. Ransome, with contributions from G. Jones

Lesser horseshoe bat *Rhinolophus hipposideros*
Vespertilio hipposideros Bechstein, 1800; France.
Vespertilio minutus Montagu, 1808; Wiltshire, England.
Ystlum pedol lleiaf (Welsh); *mion-ialtóg chrúshrónach* (Irish Gaelic).

RECOGNITION
Whole animal: Generally similar to greater horseshoe bat, but *c.*1/3 the size (Plate 6). Easily distinguished by forearm length, 34.4–42.5 mm in adults. Fur greyish from birth to 1st moult in August of their 2nd year, thereafter buff brown. When torpid, wing membranes almost entirely enclose body (Fig. 8.7).

Skull and teeth: Skull similar in shape to that of the greater horseshoe bat (Fig. 8.3) but *c.*1/3 the size and much more delicate, condylobasal length 13.5–15.2 mm. 1st upper premolar (p^2) larger than in greater horseshoe bat.

Field signs: Faeces *c.*3.4 × 1.7 mm, ovoid, often occurring as joined pair, triplet or occasionally quadruplet. Vary in texture and colour, from black to golden, according to diet. In summer, faeces accumulate in piles in day roosts under nursery clusters; smaller accumulations form in night roosts, frequently in porches, outbuildings, underground sites and heated cellars. In winter,

Fig. 8.7 Lesser horseshoe bat, hanging in a cave with its wings furled round it, characteristic of hibernating rhinolophids *(photo P. Morris)*.

often scattered throughout hibernacula but larger accumulations may occur in sites in areas where extensive winter feeding occurs and at mating roosts. Culled insect legs and wings often present, particularly tipulids and moths.

DESCRIPTION
Fur similar in texture to greater horseshoe bat but relatively longer and does not develop reddish tips with age. Moult occurs in August. Anatomically similar to greater horseshoe bat but 1/3 smaller, wing membranes darker and body more elongated

in profile. Noseleaf <12 mm long × 8 mm wide, forearm 34.4–42.5 mm.

Skull has a bulbous projection above the snout. Condylobasal length 13.5–15.2 mm. Upper tooth-row 5.2–5.6 mm. Of 2 premolars, p^2 larger, lies within tooth-row, separates canine from p^4 (cf. greater horseshoe).

CHROMOSOMES
2n = 56, Fna = 60 [684].

RELATIONSHIPS
Very distinct species within *Rhinolophus*, sole member of subgenus *R. (Phyllorhina)*; perhaps distantly related to Malaysian *R. trifoliatus* [118].

MEASUREMENTS
See Table 8.6. No size variation between GB, Ireland and W Europe; e.g. in France, mean forearm length males 37.0 mm (n = 171), females 38.0 (n = 110). However, populations in C Europe may be significantly larger. In Poland, female forearms 40.1 mm (SD = 0.62, n = 16) [329].

DISTRIBUTION
Widely distributed across W Palaearctic from Ireland to Iran, southwards through Arabia to Ethiopia (Fig. 8.8). At beginning of 20th century, found in Yorkshire, Derbyshire and Kent. Currently restricted to Wales, W Midlands and SW England. Highest densities found in Forest of Dean, Gloucestershire and Gwynedd (Fig. 8.9).

In Ireland, along W coast from Co. Cork to Co. Mayo. Highest densities in Co. Clare and Co. Kerry.

HISTORY
Possibly known from Middle Pleistocene, Hungary and Germany. No early history in British Isles. In Postglacial, recorded from Wetton Mill Rockshelter, Staffordshire (?Mesolithic), Dowel Cave, Derbyshire (Neolithic), Ossom's Eyrie Cave

Table 8.6 Lesser horseshoe bat: measurements

Head and body (mm)	35.0–39.0	
Forearm (mm)	34.4–42.5	Mean male 37.0 (SD 0.86, n = 99)
		Mean female 37.9 (SD 0.86, n = 128)
Wingspan (mm)	225–250	
Ear (mm)	10–12	
Mass (g)	4.0–9.4	

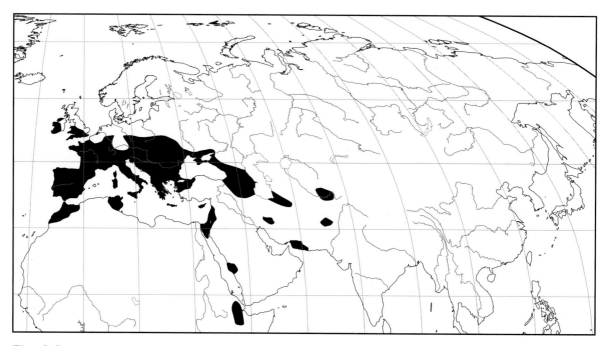

Fig. 8.8 Lesser horseshoe bat *Rhinolophus hipposideros*: world distribution.

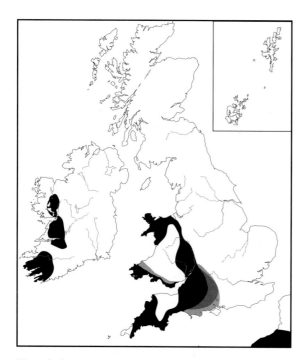

Fig. 8.9 Lesser horseshoe bat *Rhinolophus hipposideros*: range in British Isles.

(Romano-British) and Pin Hole Cave, Derbyshire (date uncertain) [678].

HABITAT
Roosts in disused or undisturbed old buildings, caves and mines. Usually in areas of extensive deciduous woodland, well connected with tree lines and hedgerows. Summer maternity roosts generally in pre-20th-century building built of stone with slate roofs, especially those associated with old country estates but also in churches and farm outbuildings. Prefer large entrances that allow uninterrupted flight into roosting areas (usually in roof spaces, attics and heated cellars). Satellite roosts may occur within 2 km of main maternity roost. Night roosts in porches, cellars and open buildings. Hibernates in underground structures such as caves, mines, cellars and icehouses [540]. Winter night roosts often where heat available, such as heated cellars.

Forages in deciduous woodland, riparian trees, along hedgerows and tree lines. Generally within 2.5 km radius of day roost, may travel >4 km [81]. In winter mean foraging distance is 1.2 km radius from hibernacula but may travel >2.1 km [673]. Avoids flying across open areas, uses linear landscape features such as hedgerows and tree lines as commuting routes [540].

SOCIAL ORGANISATION AND BEHAVIOUR
Little known of social organisation, probably similar to greater horseshoe bat but winter clusters do not occur, deep hibernation period shorter. In mild areas, carry out more foraging activity throughout the winter than greater horseshoe bat.

Territories: Summer colonies form in buildings from late April until September [369, 540]. Size variable, *c.*30–500 animals. Select microclimates within roosts depending on sex and reproductive condition. Breeding females select warmer areas,

308

e.g. roof apex and heated cellars; non-breeding females and males cooler areas. Shift position during day to select most energetically advantageous places. Females cluster during pregnancy and lactation when roost temperatures are below *c.*30 °C [540]. Summer colonies are predominantly breeding females, with smaller numbers of young of both sexes from previous year and mature males. Demography of these colonies may vary with size. Large colonies often found in buildings with a large number of microhabitats and so more non-breeders and males. Smaller colonies predominantly breeding females, with males and non-breeders in surrounding satellite roosts.

Emergence characterised by some bats 'light sampling' (brief emergence/return) but not correlated to light levels so maybe a zeitgeber [369, 540]. Similar behaviour also noted at dawn return. Emergence time earlier at roosts where entrance has vegetative cover compared to more exposed sites. Timing of emergence related to light levels, so earlier on cloudy nights. Emergence delayed in wet weather [369].

Use night roosts in porches, cellars and open buildings. Level of use of night roosts related to reproductive condition. More used when females heavily pregnant [540].

Winter hibernacula range from cave and mine systems to underground pipes; usually within 5 km of maternity roost, can be up to 22 km. Exceptional movements of 150 km [63, 212]. Generally occupied October–March. In early hibernation, adult females have most fat and adult males least. Females lose *c.*23% of original mass in winter, males *c.*13%. Temperatures recorded near hibernating animals range 5–11°C; higher until late December [458]. Most sites occupied by >5 animals but winter colonies of up to 400 occur; no clustering (cf. greater horseshoe). In some sites, where evidence of extensive winter feeding, highest numbers are recorded in early winter [540]. In Cornwall, greatest numbers in midwinter when least activity occurs; many hibernacula used by <5 animals [673]. Similar emergence behaviour as at summer roosts but main dusk activity period shorter: *c.*1–2 h [1].

During December–February, winter feeding at lowest level, bats emerging only on mild nights [540]. During this period of deepest torpor, far fewer arousals at dusk, but low levels of activity frequently recorded even during this period in milder counties, e.g. Cornwall.

Vocalisations: Echolocates at frequencies of 105–115 kHz [299, 303] but produces audible clicks when disturbed in roosts.

FEEDING

Most foraging is associated with deciduous woodland or broadleaf tree species. Occurs in or below tree canopy, by aerial hawking or gleaning. Occasionally take prey from the ground. Females perch-hunt when heavily pregnant [540].

Summer diet, W Ireland, mainly craneflies, window midges, moths, caddisflies and lacewings, with nematoceran Diptera predominant. Small beetles, ichneumon flies and spiders also eaten. Some seasonal variation in prey: more nematoceran Diptera and Trichoptera at beginning and end of season, more moths and lacewings present July–August [371].

Analysis of winter diet in Cornwall over 2 years showed predominance of Diptera, much more than in summer in Cornwall or Ireland. The main prey items were craneflies, lesser dung flies, yellow dung flies, fungus gnats, winter gnats, window midges and blackflies. The most frequently taken insects were tipulids and lesser dung fly. A difference in diet between years was due to the varying importance of the suborders and families of Diptera, rather than between orders of insects [673].

BREEDING

Mating September–April, sperm stored in uterus until ovulation in mid–late April, pregnancy *c.*78 days, peak births 20 July–10 August, single young, females first breed when 15 months.

Males: Spermatogenesis occurs May–October, with peak in July–August. Sexual glands never free of spermatozoa. Attain sexual maturity at 1 year [163].

Females: Most females enter 1st oestrus at 15 months, but a few reproduce in 1st year, some not until 3 years. Follicle development starts in September, then rests over winter before completing oogenesis early April. Ovulation mid–late April, but may be delayed by poor weather. Normally a single egg released, but 1 record of 2 embryos. No direct evidence of twins [163]. Pregnancy lasts *c.*78 days but periods of torpor due to poor climate and food supplies may influence final birth date [434]; e.g. significantly colder weather, May 1991, resulted in mean birth date 12 days later than in 1992 [540].

Newborn young attach to mother by holding pelvic nipples with teeth and grasping neck with feet. Disappearance of marked young from maternity roost suggests they may be moved by mother to different roosts overnight [540]. Pups left in maternity roost do not cluster (cf. greater horseshoe). Lactation lasts *c.*4–5 weeks.

Productivity: Evidence from Czech Republic suggests 100% of females inseminated, but mean productivity in UK only 38% of adults in maternity roosts, indicating that not all mature females give birth every year.

Development of young: In Wales births occur over 3 weeks, late June–early July, maybe earlier in S England. At birth, mean forearm length 16.7 mm, mean mass 1.8 g (n = 17, Wales). No differences found in the mass and forearm length of males and females at birth. Pups approach adult proportions, mean forearm length 37.5 mm and mean lean adult mass 4.2 g, after 40 days [540].

At *c*.10 days, when forearm is *c*.28 mm, young start vigorous wing-flapping exercises usually while hanging from the mother's chest or head. Young with forearms of *c*.34 mm can fly short distances but sustained flight only demonstrated by young with a forearm length of 36 mm at *c*.23 days. At this time they make short excursion flights out of the roost but continue suckling until they become independent after 4–5 weeks [540]. Young often remain in the maternity roost until the end of September following the departure of females.

POPULATION
Population in GB currently estimated at 15 000 [215], Ireland 12 000 [395]. Highest population densities in GB are in Forest of Dean, Gloucestershire, and Gwynedd, both with extensive lowland deciduous woodlands. Population in Wales stable 1992–1998 [661].

MORTALITY
Cats most frequent predators; attacks by sparrowhawks also reported. Starvation seems to be major cause of death. In some years up to 40% of young have died [1]. In severe cold spells, in late winter, low-weight dead individuals found still hanging on walls of hibernacula.

PARASITES AND PATHOGENS
Principle host of nycteribiid fly *Phthiridium biarticulatu,* but no recent records from British Isles. Often host to the tick *Ixodes vespertilionis* [253].

RELATIONS WITH HUMANS
Very difficult to maintain in captivity, even for a few days. Have benefited from the reduced disturbance at hibernation sites by the installation of grills and from improved roost conditions by repairs and alteration of buildings. Numbers increase in buildings repaired and protected specifically in the interests of nursery colonies [541]. Dependence on old buildings makes them vulnerable to dereliction or unsympathetic renovation.

LITERATURE
General account of hibernating bats, comparisons of 2 *Rhinolophus* [457]. Recent research review [541].

PRINCIPAL AUTHORS
H.W. Schofield & K. McAney

FAMILY VESPERTILIONIDAE

The most speciose family of bats, *c*.42 genera with 364 species. Widely distributed, up to 65° N and 50° S, on all continents. 29 species in 8 genera listed for Europe, of which 15 species in 6 genera breed in British Isles, and a few more have occurred as vagrants. Do not have the ornate noseleaves of Rhinolophidae, but have a characteristically shaped lobe, tragus, in ear opening, which plays a role in determining direction of returning echo, and is useful in identification (Plate 6). Echolocate using short pulses, each changing in frequency (FM pulses); usually call through mouth, await echo before calling again (Fig. 8.2). Can furl wings at side of body, feet point sideways, and can scramble around on ground or vertical surfaces; often roost in small crevices, especially in hibernation, but some can hang from roof beams and cave roofs, more like horseshoe bats.

GENUS MYOTIS

The most widely distributed and speciose genus of bats; *c*.104 species, of which 10 occur in Europe; 5 breed in British Isles, and 6th has bred, now probably only a vagrant. Characterised by dental formula of 2.1.3.3/3.1.3.3 (more teeth than any other vespertilionid, which have fewer premolars; Fig. 8.3). Ears modest length, longer than broad; tragus long, usually pointed. No postcalcarial lobe.

Whiskered bat *Myotis mystacinus*
Vespertilio mystacinus Kuhl, 1819; Germany.
Selysius mystacinus.
Ialtóg ghiobach (Irish Gaelic).

RECOGNITION
Whole animal: Smallest of the British *Myotis* bats. Easily confused with Daubenton's bat, very similar to Brandt's bat. Distinguished from Daubenton's bat by small feet, shaggy dorsal fur, darker face, shorter calcar, 1/2 length of tail membrane (cf. 2/3 in Daubenton's bat) and a straight or concave outer margin of its long, pointed tragus.

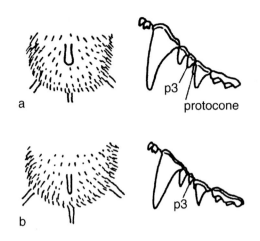

Fig. 8.10 Comparison of teeth and penis of (a) Brandt's and (b) whiskered bats. In Brandt's bat, the penis is usually club-shaped, and p^3 is large relative to both p^2 and the large protocone on p^4 (*after [609]*).

Interspecific differences between whiskered and Brandt's bats insufficient to allow absolute separation of these cryptic species. Until an identification feature with no overlap has been detected (or identification verified by molecular analysis), all identifications of whiskered and Brandt's bats tentative. Past literature attributed to whiskered might be, or include, Brandt's; identified by * in following account.

Penis shape generally believed to be a good identification feature, at least for adults. Whiskered bats typically have a thin, straight penis, while Brandt's bats have a bell- or club-shaped penis. However, in England [68], testing commonly used identification features against identification based on sequencing of the cytochrome *b* gene found this to be uncertain. While all whiskered males had a thin penis, so did 30% of the Brandt's bats, though 70% had a club-shaped penis. So, not completely safe to assume that a bat with a thin penis is a whiskered bat. The same study found that tragus shape, upper dentition, lower dentition (see Skull and dentition) and length of claw on thumb could separate between the 2 species with 100% certainty in a backward stepwise logistic regression model of 13 whiskered and 10 Brandt's males (χ^2 = 31.492, df = 7, P = 0.001). Put into logistic regression separately, each of these features could classify 80–91% to correct species [68]. For illustrations of penis shape for whiskered and Brandt's bats, see Fig. 8.10.

Skull and dentition: Distinguished from Brandt's bat by size of conspicuous cusp (protocone) on anterior inner angle of p^4. This cusp lacking or smaller than p^3 in whiskered bats (same

height or larger than p^3 in Brandt's bats). This visible in live animal when viewed from the side and slightly forward or perpendicular to the maxilla. In lower jaw, ratio of p_2 to p_3 useful:. Whiskered bats generally have p_3 <1/2 height of p_2 (Brandt's bats generally have p_3 >1/2 height of p_2). However, both species can have p_2 and p_3 of similar sizes. Dentition may even differ between sides, i.e. one jaw with 'whiskered' and one with 'Brandt's' dentition (see Fig. 8.10).

Echolocation: In English study, mean values for echolocation call parameters: peak frequency 47.5 kHz, start frequency 80.3 kHz, end frequency 32.2 kHz, pulse interval 87.8 ms, duration 4.5 ms. Using artificial neural networks on a range of echolocation call parameters, 78% of the whiskered bats were correctly identified [414].

Field signs: Faeces cylindrical, black, 2.0–2.3 × 6.0–9.0 mm with medium particle size [601]. Most commonly found under roost exits or in roosts. Contain many fragments of small dipterans, visible when faeces crushed and viewed under a microscope.

Bats may begin vocalising audibly soon before emerging.

DESCRIPTION
Dorsal pelage dark or reddish brown, with golden bronze tips. Ventral parts light greyish brown. Fur quite long and shaggy compared to other British bats. Juveniles <12 months often darker than adults (Fig. 8.11). Adults often have pronounced yellowish-brown fur around the neck, forming a sort of ruff [134]. Face, ears and membranes usually dark brown or black, darker than Brandt's bats. Ears moderately long (*c*.15 mm.) and narrow. Tragus little more than 1/2 length of conch. Anterior border of tragus straight and posterior border straight or slightly concave, narrowing to a blunt point (Plate 6). For further description see [134].

Chromosomes: 2n = 44, FNa = 50–52, European data [684].

RELATIONSHIPS
Whiskered and Brandt's bats were only separated in 1970; earlier information on whiskered bats may refer to either species.

Given great similarity in appearance, assumed that whiskered and Brandt's bats closely related. However, sequence divergence of 16% in the cytochrome *b* gene of mitochondrial (mt) DNA (1140 bp) indicates that they are in fact not closely related. Phylogeny based on genetic differences shows both species to be more closely related to

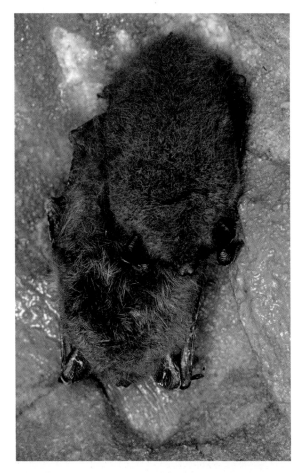

Fig. 8.11 Whiskered or Brandt's bats, adult and juvenile hibernating together, with their wings furled by their sides as typical of vespertilionids. Juveniles are greyer than adults in most bat species *(photo F. Greenaway)*.

other *Myotis* species than to each other. Brandt's bat belongs in a clade with American *Myotis*, but the whiskered bat belongs to a Palaearctic clade of uncertain origins [508].

Despite similar appearances, seems to be little overlap in ecological niches in either diet or habitat use [65, 67, 632–634]. No clear link between morphological differences between the species and any differences in habitat use, although Brandt's bats tend to have lower wing loadings than whiskered bats, perhaps allowing Brandt's bats to be more manoeuvrable in more forested environments [287].

Recently, further cryptic species and subspecies of whiskered and Brandt's bats have been discovered in Europe, e.g. *M. alcathoe* and *M. ikonnikovi*; genetic and ecological relationships of *mystacinus* complex much investigated [6, 244, 321, 367, 368, 647]. *M. alcathoe* has recently been discovered as far north as N France [510]. Molecular study of English specimens found no evidence of further cryptic species among the 33 *M. mystacinus* and *M. brandtii* sequences analysed [68]. Taxonomic and biogeographic review of *mystacinus* complex given by [244].

MEASUREMENTS

Head and body length 35–48 mm; forearm length 30–37 mm; wingspan 210–240 mm; ear length 14–15 mm; weight in hibernation 4–8 g. Males smaller than females on average: mean forearm length of 36 males 32.4 mm (range 32.0–35.3 mm), of 11 females 33.7 mm (range 32.5–34.9 mm) [605]. For additional measurements see Table 8.7.

Table 8.7 Whiskered bats: measurements (mm) of genetically sequenced individuals (n = 16, males n = 13, females n = 3) [68]

Feature	Minimum	Maximum	Mean	SD
Forearm length	32.9	35.1	33.8	0.7
Tragus width	1.2	2.0	1.8	0.2
Tragus length	5.0	8.4	6.6	0.9
Thumb length	4.0	6.3	5.3	0.5
Thumb claw length	1.2	2.1	1.6	0.3
5th finger length	38.3	41.2	40.0	1.0
Calcar length	10.2	16.6	13.0	2.2
Foot length	5.0	8.2	7.3	0.8
Foot claw length	1.0	2.3	1.7	0.3
Body mass	4.0	6.5	5.1	0.6

DISTRIBUTION

Mainly Palaearctic: from Ireland, N Iberia and Morocco to Korea and Japan, W Himalayas and S China, but distribution may not be accurate because of recent discoveries of cryptic species (Fig. 8.12). Widely distributed in Europe up to 64° N. Distribution reviewed in [175, 381]. Generally, ratio of whiskered:Brandt's bats increases from E to W and from N to S. Probably found throughout England and Wales (Fig. 8.13), but more common in N and W [474]. Status in Scotland uncertain, but found throughout Ireland [381].

HABITAT

Foraging habitat: Wing morphology and echolocation calls indicate that whiskered bats forage in edge or cluttered habitats [393]. Currently no radio-tracking studies of whiskered bats have been published. However, in Germany, habitat survey concluded that whiskered bats choose maternity sites surrounded by meadows and fields bordered by hedgerows and coppices [632]. Also found over flowing water, woodland paths and in woodland [539]. In Spain and Greece, also caught in woodland [6, 231]. Swedish study concluded they were negatively affected by increased forest patchiness [284].Whiskered bats tend to fly along edges, preferring to forage in dense parts such as tree crowns [539]. In Finland, changed hunting grounds as nights became darker, towards the end of summer. Habitat type, size of hunting ground and number of individuals using the area changed. Suggested that this

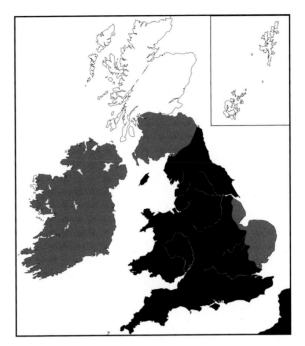

Fig. 8.13 Whiskered bat *Myotis mystacinus*: range in British Isles.

behaviour may be linked to change in lighting conditions and not insect availability [394]*.

Summer roosts: Mostly in buildings, more rarely in trees, in Scandinavia, continental Europe and the UK [539, 682]. In Finland, used 75% manmade structures [394]*. Roost occasionally in bat boxes and bridges [539]. Colonies of whiskered and Brandt's bats may use separate parts of the same

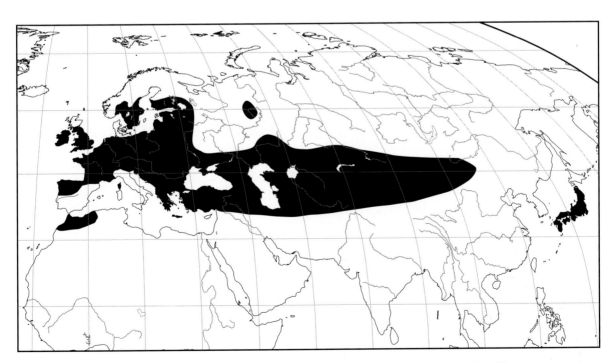

Fig. 8.12 Whiskered bat *Myotis mystacinus*: suggested world distribution; possibly confused by cryptic species.

313

roof [171], may also occur with *Pipistrellus* spp. or *Plecotus auritus* [394]*. Usually fewer than 100 roosting together [1]. In N England, mean size of maternity roosts 23.3 individuals (n = 15) [306].

Winter roosts: Hibernates in disused mines and caves; starts in December, generally leaves around March in Denmark and UK [131, 287, 682]. Occasionally found hibernating in cellars [539].

SOCIAL ORGANISATION AND BEHAVIOUR

Summer: Adult males seem to be solitary, adult females form large nursery colonies to give birth and raise young. Emerge within 0.5 h of sunset, active intermittently throughout the night [66]. Maximum foraging distance from maternity sites in the UK 2.2 km [66]. Frequently flies along a regular beat or flight path at foraging grounds [66, 539]. In Finland, 2 distinct periods of activity in summer – after sunset and before sunrise; interrupted at intervals during the night when hang off tree trunk, dry branch stump, vertical rock wall or live branch. Lengths of these breaks irregular [394]*. Usually sedentary, but longest movement recorded 1936 km, from Russia SW to Bulgaria [337]*.

Can be found swarming at underground sites from August until October. Purpose not fully understood; mating or information transfer possible explanations [412]. At swarming site, disused mine, in SW England, captures 80% males, only 20% females [411].

Winter: Sometimes observed flying in daylight in winter and spring [539]*. Within caves, usually found in cold areas close to the entrance, but occasionally roost in warmer interior. Whiskered bats choose more humid situations than Brandt's bats, but no difference in temperature requirements between them [287].

FEEDING

In SW England Anisopodidae (window midges) almost 1/3 of the diet. Lepidoptera (moths) 17%, Muscidae (houseflies and dung flies), Calliphoridae (bluebottles) and Hemerobiidae (brown lacewings) each *c*.10% (percentage occurrences, defined as the number of items of each prey group as a percentage of the total number of identified remains) [65]. Suggest that whiskered bats glean some prey including diurnal groups such as Brachycera and Cyclorrhapha flies and non-flying arthropods such as Araneida (spiders). In same study, Simpson's index of 0.140 indicates that whiskered bats have a broad diet. Most diverse in May, July and August, but these are only minor fluctuations. Other studies support

these findings: diet mostly comprised of Lepidoptera and Diptera and some prey gleaned [61, 478, 633, 634]. Earlier (pre-2000) dietary studies reviewed in [652]. However, differences of 50% in diet between whiskered colonies suggests that a flexible forager [478]. May reflect different foraging habitats around the colonies, could explain differences between studies.

Laboratory study showed that chose Lepidoptera [394]*. Also ate midges, flies, craneflies, dragonflies, mayflies, beetles and bedbugs; concluded that these captive animals not particularly selective. Individual differences in choice of foods noted, but no difference for young bats. Preferred live prey.

BREEDING

Sexual maturity in some females at 3 months, but majority at 15 months [585]*. In Dutch cave, copulation observed January [390]*, increasing proportion found to be inseminated as hibernation progressed [612]*. Females ovulate in spring, give birth to single young in mid-June. Unfavourable weather may delay birth. Forearm lengths reach adult size by time of 1st flight due to fast growth. Adults start dispersing in mid–late July and onwards after weaning. Nursery roosts vacated by early September [1].

POPULATION

During hibernation, sex ratio usually male biased: in Suffolk 60% males (n = 68) [590]*, in Netherlands 62% males (n = 1377) [70]*, in Czechoslovakia 59% males (n = 42) recorded for individually roosting bats, but 93% (n = 213) for winter colonies [163]*. Several population parameters estimated from studies in hibernacula [70]*. Adult survival rate 0.75, giving lifespan of 16 years and mean longevity of 4.0 years. In Surrey, one found 23 years after banding [258], a male >18 years old in Netherlands [227]*. Minimum population density *c*.1.5/km^2 estimated in N England, based on counts from maternity colonies (n = 15) [306].

Total GB population estimated 40 000 (England 30 500, Scotland 1500, Wales 8000). No estimate for Ireland, considered scarcer there, perhaps 10 000.

MORTALITY

Shrews or mice ate several whiskered bats during hibernation in caves in Suffolk [605]. Several reported killed by domestic dogs or cats [1]. One found in stomach of edible frog *Rana esculenta* in Slovakia [399].

PARASITES

Some ectoparasites reported before separation of

whiskered from Brandt's, unknown whether host similar parasite faunas. Flea *Ischnopsyllus simplex* common; the mites *Spinturnix myoti, Steatonyssus periblepharus* and *Neomyobia mystacinalis* recorded. Parasite load low on male whiskered bats, highest on both sexes in August (Spinturnicidae: mean 4.2 ± 1.71; Ischnopsyllidae mean $= 1.6 \pm 1.1$) [682].

RELATIONS WITH HUMANS
Has been maintained in captivity for several months.

Conservation status 'Vulnerable' in the UK [261], but worldwide classed as 'Lower Risk Least Concern' by the IUCN [275], currently poorly understood. Action Plan for the Conservation of Bats in the United Kingdom [261] emphasises need, for both whiskered and Brandt's bats, for further research to establish their ecological and conservation requirements.

Vulnerable to effects of modern forestry and agriculture, which result in habitat loss and especially feeding habitat, hedgerows and suitable roosting trees. Also susceptible to pesticides. Disturbance and vandalism of their swarming and hibernating sites, caves and tunnels is an additional threat. Research, especially on habitat use and feeding ecology, therefore important for the design of effective conservation measures.

PRINCIPAL AUTHORS
L. Berge with G. Jones. Based on the account in the 2nd edition by R.E. Stebbings, with additional data from P.W. Richardson & A.M. Hutson.

Brandt's bat *Myotis brandtii*
Vespertilio brandtii Eversmann, 1845; Russia.
Myotis mystacinus (part).

RECOGNITION
Whole animal: Easily confused with Daubenton's bat, very similar to whiskered bat. Distinguished from Daubenton's bat by its shaggy dorsal fur, darker face, smaller feet, a convex outer margin of its long pointed tragus and a shorter calcar, 1/2 length of tail membrane (cf. 2/3 in Daubenton's bat).

Interspecific differences between whiskered and Brandt's bats insufficient to allow full separation; see account under whiskered bat, also Plate 6 and Fig. 8.10.

Skull and dentition: Presence of cusp on the anterior angle of p^4 distinguishes the skull from whiskered bat; is same height or larger than p^3 (lacking or smaller than p^3 in whiskered bat)(Fig 8.10). When viewed slightly forward and from the side, perpendicular to maxilla, can be seen in live animal. The ratio of p_2 to p_3 useful in distinguishing lower jaw. Brandt's bats generally have $p_3 > 1/2$ height of p_2 (whiskered bats generally have $p_3 < 1/2$ of the height of the p_2, though both species can have p_2 and p_3 of similar sizes).

Echolocation: In England, mean values of echolocation call parameters are: frequency of most energy 47.9 kHz, start frequency 85.5 kHz, end frequency 33.7 kHz, pulse interval 88.0 ms, duration 4.7 ms (Fig. 8.2). Using artificial neural networks and a range of echolocation call parameters, 84% of Brandt's bats correctly identified [414].

DESCRIPTION
A small bat closely resembling the whiskered bat. Fur shaggy and quite long compared to other British bats. Dorsal pelage dark or reddish brown with golden bronze tips. Ventral parts light greyish brown. Juveniles up to 12 months often darker than adults. Membranes and ears usually dark brown or black. Face usually brown or dark brown, but often lighter coloured [605]. Penis generally distinctly club-shaped, but may be thin and straight, in both juveniles and adults. Further description in [134].

Chromosomes: $2n = 44$, FNa $= 50$, European data [684].

RELATIONSHIPS
Separated as a distinct species from whiskered bat in 1970, information prior to 1970 may therefore also refer to Brandt's bats: see account under whiskered bat. Phylogenetic studies show both species to be more closely related to other *Myotis* species than to each other. Brandt's bat belongs in a clade with several American bat species [508].

Little overlap has been detected in their ecological niches [67, 632–634]. May be explained by tendency for Brandt's bats to have lower wing loadings than whiskered bats, allowing them to be more manoeuvrable in more forested environments; this link is not clear, however [287].

Further cryptic species (e.g. *M. alcathoe* and *M. ikonnikovi*) have recently been revealed, leading to investigations of the genetic and ecological relationship of the *mystacinus* complex [6, 244, 321, 368, 647]. No evidence of any further cryptic species among 33 English *M. mystacinus* and *M. brandtii* sequences analysed [68], although *M. alcathoe* recently discovered as near as N France [510]. Detailed review of taxonomy and biography of the *mystacinus* complex in [244].

MEASUREMENTS
Head and body length 37–48 mm; forearm length

Table 8.8 Brandt's bats: measurements (mm) of genetically sequenced individuals [68]

Feature	Minimum	Maximum	Mean	SD
Forearm length	33.4	36.0	34.8	0.9
Tragus width	1.6	2.4	2.0	0.3
Tragus length	5.8	7.8	6.7	0.6
Thumb length	5.5	6.4	5.9	0.3
Thumb claw length	1.5	2.3	1.9	0.2
5th finger length	39.6	42.6	41.0	0.7
Calcar length	10.2	18.2	15.4	1.8
Foot length	6.8	8.3	7.7	0.5
Foot claw length	1.7	2.5	1.9	0.2
Body mass	4.0	8.0	5.7	1.0

n = 16, males n = 10, females n = 3.

31–38 mm; wingspan 210–255 mm; ear length 11–13 mm; condylobasal length of skull 13.0–14.5 mm [605]. In Devon 21 adult females had a mean forearm length of 34.8 mm and a mean wingspan of 240 mm [605]. For additional measurements, see Table 8.8.

DISTRIBUTION

Uncertain because of confusion with whiskered bat, but widespread and occur in sympatry in Europe and Palaearctic Asia [381, 617], from S Scotland, England and E France to Korea and Japan (Fig. 8.14). In Europe up to 65° N, common in C Europe as far south as SE France, C Italy, Bulgaria [381]. Generally, ratio of Brandt's bats to whiskered bats increases from W to E and S to N. Probably found throughout England, Wales and S Scotland, but more common in N and W of GB (Fig 8.15) [474]. Only recently recorded in Ireland [214].

HABITAT

Habitat use: Wing morphology and echolocation calls suggest it forages in edge or cluttered habitats [393]. In Germany, principal foraging habitat

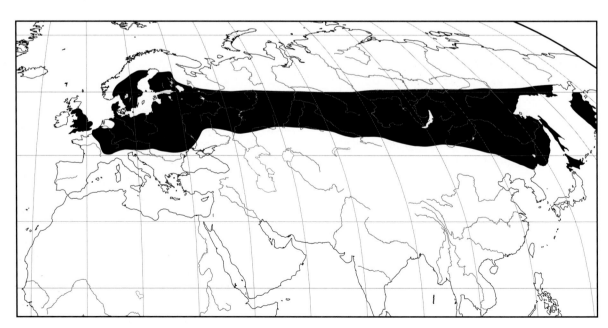

Fig. 8.14 Brandt's bat *Myotis brandtii*: world range.

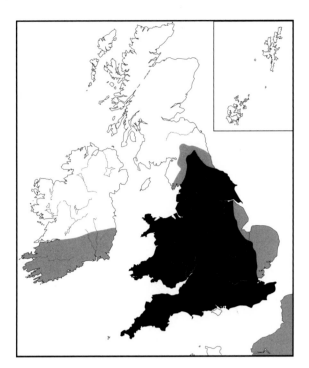

Fig. 8.15 Brandt's bat *Myotis brandtii*: range in British Isles.

broadleaf forest with particularly damp areas, close to water [632]. Coniferous woodland, forest edges and clearings also frequently used. Disagreement in literature on importance of coniferous forest [151, 632]. In Germany, radio-tracking study of 9 females found that hunt along hedges, rows of trees and in various forest habitats including deciduous, coniferous and mixed stands [132]. In Sweden, found to be negatively affected by habitat isolation; suggests particular vulnerability to increased forest patchiness. Hypotheses failed to explain why Brandt's bat avoids open habitats and is thus negatively affected by isolation [151].

Summer roosts: Occasionally in bridges and bat boxes [539], but mostly in buildings and more rarely in trees in Scandinavia, continental Europe and the UK [539, 682]. Colonies usually <100 individuals [1]. In N England, mean size of maternity roosts of 28.3 individuals (n = 5) [306]. May roost together with *Pipistrellus* spp., *Plecotus auritus* or whiskered bats [171, 394] often using separate parts of same roof.

Winter roosts: Commonly in disused mines and caves, occasionally in cellars [539]. Brandt's males hibernate for longer than whiskered bats, until May and March respectively [287].

SOCIAL ORGANISATION AND BEHAVIOUR
Summer: Females form nursery colonies, but adult males seem solitary.

Emerge within 30 min of sunset, may remain active intermittently throughout the night [66]. Reported to be less skilful in confined spaces than whiskered bats [539]. In Germany, radio-tracking study of 9 females found single extended period of activity from dusk until dawn. Weather conditions had almost no influence on activity patterns. Main hunting grounds within 1.5 km to >10 km away from maternity colony [132]. In England, radio-tracking study found maximum foraging distance of 2.3 km [66]. Frequently flies regular beat or flight path at foraging grounds [66, 539]. Usually sedentary; longest reported movement 230 km [539].

Swarms at underground sites August–October, peak in early August [412]. Purpose not fully understood, but mating or information transfer possible explanations [410]. At disused mine in SW England, swarms 60% males and 40% females [411].

Winter: Movements of 2.5 km recorded, Suffolk [605].

Commonly found in cold areas close to the cave entrances, occasionally in warmer interior: no difference in temperature requirements between the 2 species, but Brandt's choose drier situations than whiskered bats [287].

FEEDING
In SW England (Table 8.9), Anisopodidae (window midges) made up 15% of diet and Lepidoptera (moths) 12%. Araneida (spiders), Hemerobiidae (brown lacewings), Ichneumonidae (ichneumon flies) and Psychodidae (owl midges) each made up around 10% (percentage occurrence, defined as the number of items of each prey group as a percentage of the total number of identified remains) [65]. A German dietary study matched these findings [633, 634]. Results provide strong evidence that Brandt's bats glean some prey, including diurnal groups such as Brachycera and Cyclorrhapha flies and non-flying arthropods such as Araneida (spiders). Although Brandt's bats often hunt close to water [632], not particularly reliant on aquatic insects and many of the insects eaten are found in woodland [65, 652].

In England, Simpson index of 0.088 [65], indicating that Brandt's bats have a broad diet, slightly narrower than whiskered bat (Simpson index 0.140). Diet most diverse in June and September, and fluctuates more throughout summer than that of whiskered bat. Significant statistical differences between diet of 2 Brandt's colonies as well as between whiskered and Brandt's bats [65].

Table 8.9 Whiskered bats and Brandt's bats: differences in total diet shown in % items, data combined from 2 maternity colonies for each species

	% of total diet			% of total diet	
	M. mystacinus (n=757)	*M. brandtii* (n=681)		*M. mystacinus* (n=757)	*M. brandtii* (n=681)
Dermaptera (Earwigs)	0.3		Cyclorrhapha		
Hemiptera (True bugs)			Syrphidae	0.6	0.3
Delphacicae	0.2		Sphaeroceridae	1.0	
Psylloidea		0.1	Ephydridae		0.1
Aphidoidea		2.8	Drosophilidae	0.2	
Neuroptera (Lacewings, etc.)			Calliphoridae	8.3	5.2
Hemerobiidae	5.6	9.6	Scathophagidae	9.2	3.8
Coleoptera (Beetles)			Fanniidae		0.1
Unidentified Coleoptera	1.3	2.1	Lepidoptera (Butterflies and moths)	17.0	12.2
Carabidae	0.2	0.1	Trichoptera (Caddisflies)		
Scarabaeoidea	2.7	1.7	Limnophilidae	0.2	0.3
Diptera (True flies)			Hydropsychidae		2.7
Unidentified Diptera	5.6	12.1	Hymenoptera (Bees, ichneumons, etc.)		
Nematocera			Ichneumonidae	2.1	9.0
Anisopodidae	27.3	16.0	Chalcicoidea	1.0	0.4
Tipulidae	3.5	1.0	Proctotrupidae	0.2	
Psychodidae	2.3	5.8	Araneida (Spiders)	2.3	9.3
Culicidae	1.7	0.7	Argasidae	0.8	0.1
Chironomidae/Ceratopogonidae	3.2	3.8	Acari	0.5	
Mycetophilidae	0.8		Psocoptera (Booklice)		0.1
Scatopsidae	0.8		Ephemeroptera (Mayflies)		
Cecidomyiidae	0.2		Siphlonuridae		0.2
Brachycera					
Rhagionidae		0.3			
Empididae	0.7	0.3			

318

BREEDING

Little known. Females ovulate in spring and give birth to a single young in mid June. Unfavourable weather conditions may delay birth. Forearm lengths reach adult proportions at time of 1st flight due to fast growth of young. Adults start dispersing from mid–late July onwards, after weaning. Nursery roosts vacated by early September [1].

POPULATION

Little known. Greatest longevity 41 years, currently the oldest bat on record (from the Siberian region of Russia [427]). Minimum population density $c.1.7/km^2$ in N England, based on counts from maternity colonies (n = 5) [306].

Total GB population estimated as $c.30\ 000$ (England 22 500, Scotland 500, Wales 7000) [215], but very uncertain. Irish population presumed very small, but perhaps overlooked.

PARASITES

Flea *Ischnopsyllus simplex* common. Some ectoparasites observed on whiskered bats (q.v.) prior to the separation of the species, unknown whether whiskered and Brandt's bats host similar parasite faunas.

MORTALITY

Sometimes killed by cats, especially around houses [1].

RELATIONS WITH HUMANS

Worldwide classed as 'Lower Risk Least Concern' by the IUCN [275], but has conservation status of 'Vulnerable' in the UK [261]. Little precise information on conservation status. Population ecology of whiskered and especially Brandt's bats barely studied. *Action Plan for the Conservation of Bats in the United Kingdom* [261] emphasises that 'further research is needed to establish ecological and conservation requirements of either species'.

Brandt's bats vulnerable to pesticides, and to other effects of modern forestry and agriculture such as habitat loss; especially feeding habitat, hedgerows and suitable roosting trees. Vandalism and disturbance to hibernation and swarming sites an added threat. Important for research to be carried out to establish their ecology so that the correct management recommendations can be made.

PRINCIPAL AUTHORS

L. Berge with G. Jones. Based on the account in the 2nd edition by R.E. Stebbings, with additional data from A.M. Hutson.

Daubenton's bat *Myotis daubentonii*

Vespertilio daubentoni Kuhl, 1819; Germany.
Vespertilio emarginatus Flemming, 1828 (not of Geoffroy, 1806).
Vespertilio aedilis Jenyns, 1839; Durham, England.
Water bat; *ialtóg uisce* (Irish Gaelic).

RECOGNITION

Distinguished from other species of *Myotis* by size, even-length fur, uniform colour of dorsal fur from bases to tips, and large feet (>1/2 length of tibia) with bristle-like hairs on toes (Fig. 8.18). Posterior margin of tragus strongly convex with rounded tip.

Characteristic echolocation calls consist of ultrasonic FM calls beginning at 90 kHz and sweeping down to $c.30$ kHz with a weak peak of frequency at $c.50$ kHz. Call duration $c.2$–3 ms, as recorded from oscillograms, with an interpulse interval of 70–80 ms [414, 654, 655]. On a heterodyne bat detector, sound like short, fairly sharp clicks which are evenly spaced ('machine-gun rattle'), with little change as the frequency dial is turned.

In flight, characteristically flies steadily within a few centimetres of still water surface, likened to hovercraft.

SIGN

Faeces when first voided generally wetter than faeces of other British bats. Located in tunnels and under bridges, usually by water.

DESCRIPTION

Upper parts medium to dark brown; underside pale buff-grey. Head blunt and rounded (Plate 6). Ears situated more to sides of head than pointing above it, and rounded rather than long. Inside of ear pale at base, darker brown distally. Pink, bare skin around lips and eyes, especially in spring and autumn. Wing and tail membranes dark brown, never black. Juveniles have a black 'chin spot' (actually lower lip) which becomes greyer and paler with age; lost after 1–2 years (males later than females) [472].

Chromosomes: 2n = 42–44, Fna 50–52, European data [685].

MEASUREMENTS

See Table 8.10.

VARIATION

Several albino/partial albino specimens described [55].

DISTRIBUTION

Widespread across Palaearctic from Spain and Ireland to Japan (Fig. 8.16); found throughout GB and Ireland (Fig. 8.17), regularly seen over water (see Fig. 8.18).

HISTORY
M. cf. daubentonii recorded from Early Pleistocene, *M. daubentonii* from Middle and Upper Pleistocene, Hungary, Romania, etc. [78, 278]. Known from ?Late Glacial, Pin Hole Cave and Neolithic, Dowel Cave, both Derbyshire [282, 677].

HABITAT
Predominately associated with still or slow-moving freshwater habitats, in open countryside [669] and less commonly in urban areas [168]. Foraging areas may consist of riverine corridors [533], canals [471], open water [670] and occasionally woodland close to water [394]. Appears to select sections of rivers with trees on the riverbank, avoids areas with turbulent water [663]. Summer roosts in crevices in bridges [73, 567], buildings [580], holes in trees [394], artificial roost boxes [635] and very occasionally caves [681] with 2 examples in N Ireland [1]. Tree holes selected are narrow, long vertical splits; uses small crevices in branches as well as cavities in the main trunk [447]. Woodpecker holes used less than by some other species [83]. Favoured trees are oak, beech and ash [83, 314, 447]. Most roosts in close proximity (<200 m) to water [394], 1 study showing an average distance of 1.3 km (1.0–2.3 km) [477], but recorded up to 8 km away [21].

Hibernation recorded in all types of underground sites used by hibernating bats, also use crevices in bridges [483].

SOCIAL ORGANISATION AND BEHAVIOUR
During the summer, sexually segregated in roosts, females occupying maternity roosts of <15 to >100 individuals [394, 629]. In N England, mean size of maternity roosts 16 [306]. Male roosts, often small, in bridges [662], tunnels [1] and trees [477]. Both male and female roosts highly mobile, large numbers of bats regularly move between roost sites [476]. Night-roosts in trees and tunnels used regularly [1], especially during rainfall or low temperatures [507]. Audible chattering often heard from roosts during the day, especially towards evening [1].

Begin to leave roost 11 min after sunset, median emergence 45–84 min after sunset [301, 473]. Occasionally bats do not emerge to feed [394, 473].

Commute to foraging areas along linear landscape elements such as hedges [348]. Flew up to 2 km from a roost centred in woodland to small ponds and a river in Scotland [629] and up to 10 km along canals in Northamptonshire [471]. In Yorkshire, males fly >4.5 km to use the same small foraging area each night [662]. Aggressive behaviour at feeding areas noted when bats apparently defending feeding patch [659], although may arrive at same foraging patch

Table 8.10 Daubenton's bats: forearm lengths (mm) in GB. In all populations, females are larger on average

Population	Mean	Range	n	Source
Inverness-shire				[598]
Males	37.3		37	
Females	37.6		18	
Scottish Highlands				[580]
Males	37.1	35.8–38.4	21	
Females	38.3	36.2–40.2	22	
C Scotland				[198]
Males	37.0	32.9–40.3	161	
Females	37.6	34.2–40.3	143	
Northamptonshire				[475]
Males	36.7	33.3–40.3	327	
Females	37.6	34.7–40.4	725	
Suffolk				[598]
Males	36.6		87	
Females	37.3		76	

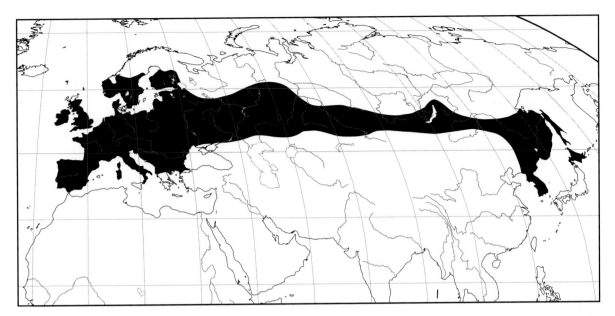

Fig. 8.16 Daubenton's bat *Myotis daubentonii*: supposed world range, but confused by cryptic species *M.petax*, in E.

together, then forage singly or in pairs [629]. Marked sexual segregation at some feeding areas: males occupy upper reaches of river systems, females occupy lower reaches [346, 524].

In August–September, bats congregate at mine entrances and engage in 'swarming', flying repeatedly in and out of cave and mine entrances; sex ratio heavily skewed towards males [412].

In GB, bats hibernate singly, in a crevice or against the wall. Few found before December, most present January–February. Only very small numbers are ever located at any site, usually single figures. Bats may emerge during winter [337].

Longest recorded movements in GB 27 km [410], 19 km [475] and 14.5 km [57], but longer distances recorded on mainland Europe, both under natural conditions (260 km [650]; 215 km [165] or homing after displacement (132 km [394].

Flight speed 4–8 m/s, faster when commuting [298, 471, 477].

FEEDING

Insectivorous, locating flying prey by echolocation. Hunt by flying low (usually <30 cm) over the surface of still water, locating prey ahead by echolocation and gaffing from surface with feet or taking smaller prey directly into mouth (Fig. 8.18) [89, 298]. Gaffing captures up to 70% of all prey, but only 20% if water surface cluttered with detritus; remainder aerial captures, made within 1 m of water surface [648]. Up to 15 capture attempts per minute recorded, Germany [312]. Show preference for foraging over nutrient-enriched water [653] with increased populations of pollution-tolerant Diptera, e.g. Chironomidae [328]. In Ireland, diet (by percentage frequency)

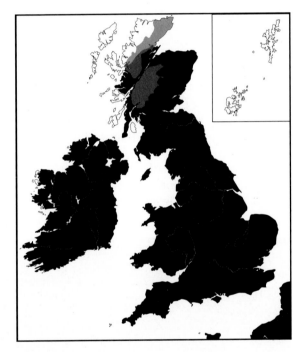

Fig. 8.17 Daubenton's bat *Myotis daubentonii*: range in British Isles.

1/3 Trichoptera and 1/3 nematoceran Diptera, mainly Chironomidae/Ceratopogonidae [621]. Hemiptera and non-nematoceran Diptera also formed 9% and 8% of the number of identifiable fragments respectively. Later in year, specialise less, include a greater proportion of other insect groups including more non-nematoceran Diptera [621]. In Scotland, 55–70% of identifiable insect fragments from faeces were nematoceran Diptera, remainder Trichoptera and small percentages of Lepidoptera, Coleoptera and Ephemeroptera [629].

BREEDING

Most copulation observed in October [220, 651], but mating continues into winter: increasing proportion of females in hibernation found inseminated as hibernation progresses [612].

A few males reach sexual maturity in year of birth [330], others at least 2 years old before able to breed. Higher proportion of females able to breed in 1st year [1].

A marked female, E Midlands, produced young when 1 year old, and each subsequent year until 8. In 9th, 10th and 11th years, also 14th, she was not captured in summer, but seen to have young again in her 12th, 13th and 15th years. Another had young in 5 years, did not breed in 2 subsequent years, but was successful in following 3 years [1].

POPULATION

Population (GB) estimated as 150 000 (95 000 England, 40 000 Scotland, 15 000 Wales) with a reliability rating of 4 (1–5, 5 least reliable) [215]. Equally common and widespread in Ireland, expect *c*.62 000 *pro rata*. In N England, density of 1/km² estimated [306], 2.4/km² in Scotland [580]. Population increases recorded, hibernacula in Netherlands [121] and Poland [328]; attributed to eutrophication of many inland rivers with corresponding increase in small Diptera [447]. More open water sites in GB in the 20th century (flooded gravel pits, reservoirs for drinking water) likely to have had a positive effect.

The sex ratio in winter is variable between sites, with values between 44% male (n = 920) [69] and 61% male (n = 2820) [148]. Annual survival, Netherlands, estimated as 80% [69], gives a predicted longevity of 20 years. Greatest recorded longevity, 20 years for a male in the E Midlands [1].

PARASITES

3 ectoparasites common: the fly *Nycteribia kolenatii* in the body fur, and the mites *Spinturnix myoti* and *Macronyssus flavus* on the wing membrane. For *N. kolenatii* an infestation rate of 78% (n = 167) with an average 2.3 flies per bat was found in GB [274] with a greater infestation rate and density on females. *Spinturnix* numbers relate to sex and age of bat, with greatest numbers on pregnant females in midsummer (average of 9.9 per bat) and on juveniles (average of 10.7 per bat), an incidence rate of well over 80% in summer. It seems that the mites select the pregnant females early in the active season then move to the babies when born. Males and non-pregnant females have a steady, low level of infestation [1]. The mite *Nycteridocoptes poppei* may also be found as pustule-like lumps on the wings. Of the bigger ectoparasites the bug *Cimex pipistrelli* is infrequently recorded.

Of 108 bats examined, 27 contained the malaria parasite *Polychromophilus murinus* and 57 the bacterium *Grahamella* sp. [170]. *P. murinus* may be transmitted to Daubenton's bats by *N. kolenatii* [255].

RELATIONS WITH HUMANS

Recently reported to carry European bat lyssavirus 2 (EBLV2) which is transmissible to humans through bites [285, 668].

Fig. 8.18 Daubenton's bat uses its large hindfeet to snatch prey from the surface of the water *(photo F. Greenaway).*

Has been kept successfully in captivity for several months, fed on mealworms.

AUTHORS
P.W. Richardson, D. Waters & R. Waters

Pond bat *Myotis dasycneme*
Vespertilio dasycneme Boie, 1825; Denmark.

DESCRIPTION
Similar to *M. daubentonii* and *M. capaccinii*, formerly grouped with them in subgenus *M. (Leuconoe)*. Like *M. daubentonii*, but larger, more domed forehead, tragus shorter (<1/2 ear length) and blunter, fine white hairs along inside of tarsus on underside of tail membrane, with large hairy feet; dorsal fur sometimes pale-tipped; calcar to 2/3 or 3/4 distance to tail; penis conical (widest at base); m^1–m^3 with protoconules, p^2 much smaller than p^1, p_2 no smaller than p_1.

Chromosomes: 2n = 44, NF = 52.

Measurements: Head and body 57–67 mm; tail 46–51 mm, forearm 41–49 mm; wingspan 200–230 mm; ear length 16–19 mm; condylobasal length 15.7–17.4 mm; c–m^3 6.0–6.5 mm; weight 14–20 g. Single UK specimen (adult male), forearm length 46.7 mm [497].

DISTRIBUTION
Boreal species, occurring from lowlands of NW Europe in Netherlands and Denmark to the R. Yenisei (Russia), south to N France, Hungary, Slovakia, Moldova and eastwards through Kazakhstan (approximately 48–60° N, 2–90° E) [381].

Single UK record: adult male, found on a wall close to ground in Ramsgate, Kent, September 2004; taken into care, died next day [1].

HABITATS/HABITS
Rarely abundant. Forages mainly over water (including artificial aquatic habitats) and in woodland [350, 497]. Roosts in trees and buildings (principally larger buildings, such as churches) in summer, underground sites in winter. Summer colonies usually <100, but can reach 500. In winter sites, usually roost singly or small groups of up to 10, few sites with >200 individuals (maximum 700). Medium-range migrant to 350 km [276].

AUTHOR
A.M. Hutson

Natterer's bat *Myotis nattereri*
Vespertilio nattereri Kuhl, 1817; Hessen, Germany.
Red-armed bat; *ystlum natterer* (Welsh); *ialtóg nattereir* (Irish Gaelic).

RECOGNITION
Whole animal: Medium-sized bat, distinguished by its S-shaped calcar (Fig. 8.19) and conspicuous fringe of stiff hairs, *c*.1 mm long, along the edge of tail membrane. Long ears, would reach beyond tip of muzzle if folded forwards (although not as long as Bechstein's bat). Tragus long, more sharply pointed than other *Myotis* sp. (Plate 6) [194, 539].

FIELD SIGNS
Faeces: Medium sized (mean 9.3 × 2.8 mm; range 13.5–6.2 × 3.5–2.3 mm; n = 98; from maternity roost near Hereford) and chunky; irregular outline, blunt/rounded at one end and often tapered to a point at other end; typically composed of 3–4 distinct segments joined together in a manner that gives a twisted or plaited appearance [570].

Roosts: Largely in trees [382, 571] but most known summer colonies in older buildings (e.g. churches, barns, castles, large houses) with large wooden beams and/or stone walls [194, 571]. Generally summer roosts within crevices and cavities in trees and buildings [382, 625], though attic ridges [571] and bat boxes [382, 407] also used. Winters in underground sites, usually in crevices [194, 309]. Night roosts in a tunnel, culvert and barn regularly used in C Scotland [625] whereas shrubs and trees the main night roosts in Herefordshire and Monmouthshire [570].

Other field signs: Fly up to 16 m above ground; usually seen around trees and amongst canopy, and near water [55, 366]. Often fly within 1 m of ground as leave roost or cross open ground [630]. Echolocation calls generally quieter than other *Myotis* sp.; short (2.3 ms call with 76.8 ms interpulse interval) [654]. Calls (FM) cover wide bandwidth, peak energy *c*.50 kHz [555]. On a heterodyne bat detector, sound like the fine crackle of burning stubble [88]. Analysis of echolocation calls of British bats shows Natterer's bats not always clearly distinguishable from other *Myotis* sp. or brown long-eared bats, using bat detectors [655].

DESCRIPTION
Pelage: Long, fluffy with dark grey base to hairs; upper parts light brown, underside white or very light buff. Juveniles light greyish brown for 1st year.

Anatomy: Forearms pinkish; wing membranes

Fig. 8.19 Natterer's bat in flight, showing well the baggy interfemoral membrane with its characteristic fringe of stiff bristles (*photo F. Greenaway*).

pinkish to mid-brown; wings broad but long. Muzzle long, pink to light brown, largely bare. Ears well separated, splayed, shade from pink basally to light brown distally, but occasionally all dark; relatively narrow and long (14–17 mm), slightly reflexed at tip. Tragus pale, narrow, straight-sided, finely pointed and approximately 2/3 of ear-length. Foot *c.*1/3 length of tibia [11, 194, 539, 677].

Skull and teeth: Condylobasal length 14.0–15.6 mm; c–m^3 5.6–6.4 mm. Dental formula 2.1.3.3/3.1.3.3; crowns of upper incisors slightly splayed; premolars in line (i.e. p^3 fully in tooth-row); p^3 slightly lower than p^2 [194]. p^4 (large premolar) lacking well-developed protocone on inner shelf; upper molars usually without protoconules [609].

Chromosomes: 2n = 44; FNa = 50–52, European data [684].

Table 8.11 Natterer's bat: measurements

	Range	95% confidence intervals	
	Adults	Adult males (n = 167)	Adult females (n = 167)
Head & body length (mm)	40–50	–	–
Forearm length (mm)	36–43	38.52–39.28	39.32–39.66
Wingspan (mm)	250–300	–	–
Ear length (mm)	14–18	–	–
Weight in hibernation (g)	7–12	–	–
Weight in summer (g)	5–10	6.66–7.22	7.40–7.60

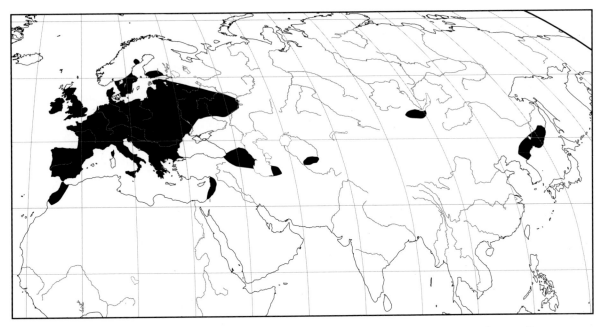

Fig. 8.20 Natterer's bat *Myotis nattereri*: supposed world range, but confused by *M. bombinus* in E.

RELATIONSHIPS

In Armenia and Iran occurs sympatrically with larger sibling species *M. schaubi*. In Japan and E Asia, represented by *M. bombinus* [161], formerly considered a subspecies [243, 679]. Some authorities consider *M. schaubi, M. bombinus* and *M. nattereri* to comprise subgenus *Isotus* [113, 679], but this not recognised in [674]. Populations of Turkmenistan, Transcaucasia, N Iran, N Iraq and E Turkey separated as subspecies *M. n. tschuliensis* [64, 244]. *M. thysanodes* (North America) morphologically very similar [55] but recent genetic studies suggest this due to convergence rather than close relationships [508].

MEASUREMENTS

Males smaller than females [1, 570]. Forearm lengths, males 39.2 mm (95% CI 39.4–39.7 mm, n = 274), females 39.6 mm (95% CI 39.0–39.3 mm, n = 321). See Table 8.11.

VARIATION

Rarely, in Germany, partial albinism and partial melanism recorded [202, 430].

DISTRIBUTION

Widespread from Ireland to Turkmenistan (Fig. 8.20) [112, 381, 674], but not common anywhere in Europe [104] and UK population is internationally significant [261]. Recognition of *M. bombinus* in E Asia and Japan makes Turkmenistan the eastern limit for *M. nattereri* [64, 243, 244]. Widespread in GB and Ireland (Fig. 8.21); also found on Arran, Isle of Wight, Isle of Man [23] and Islay [441].

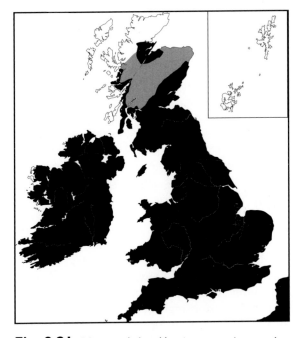

Fig. 8.21 Natterer's bat *Myotis nattereri*: range in British Isles.

HISTORY

Found in Middle Pleistocene, Westbury Quarry Cave, Westbury-sub-Mendip, Somerset [119]; also Late Glacial, Pin Hole Cave, Mesolithic (9960 BP), Dog Hole Cave, and Neolithic, Dowel Cave, all Derbyshire [282, 677, 678].

HABITAT

Colonies in Herefordshire/Monmouthshire foraged preferentially in semi-natural broadleaved woodland and tree-lined river corridor; avoided arable and coniferous plantation. Improved grassland used more than any other habitat category in the study, though avoided relative to availability [570]. Using radio-tracking, stable estimates of habitat use attained after 22 h of foraging time [572]. Radio-tracking in S England, autumn, revealed preference for arable, pasture and broadleaved woodland [411]. In N England, radio-tracked individuals showed varying individual habitat preferences including open arable fields [2]. In a commercial coniferous (Corsican and Scots pine) plantation in Fife, mature Corsican pine trees and land adjacent to water bodies were preferred for foraging over arable land and grazing meadows. The predominant Scots pine was underused relative to abundance [382]. In C Scotland, of 35 observations of foraging Natterer's bats, 18 were in woodland edges or treelines, 8 were around bushes or single trees in parkland, 6 were over part of a small loch sheltered by vegetation and the other 3 were over open pasture or in woodland clearings; on roadsides, observed to forage over grass and thistles [625].

SOCIAL ORGANISATION AND BEHAVIOUR

Territories: Territorial behaviour not observed, but radio-tracking study of 2 adjacent colonies, Monmouthshire, suggests that each colony occupies exclusive summer home range of *c*.14 km² [572]. Home ranges considerably smaller than this, population densities higher, in commercial plantation, Fife, where core foraging areas did not overlap [382].

Roosting behaviour: Maternity colonies comprise 25–200 adults, mostly females, in buildings and hollow trees [572]. Male summer colonies of 8–28 bats known from Scotland [625] but adult males likely to be roosting near maternity roosts singly or in small groups [570] and can be difficult to locate. Categorised as a low roost-fidelity species [347]; 2 British studies show bats frequently moving between several roosts used by the colony [382, 572]. Arrive in underground hibernation sites November–December, leave in March–April [482, 604]. In Poland, hibernate at 8–14 °C in autumn, falling to 6–10 °C in winter [211]. Preference for cool entrance areas; is, with brown long-eared bat, the species most frequently found in any small exposed cave-like site. Usually solitary, small groups not uncommon; cluster of *c*.150 recorded at the Hampshire site that has perhaps highest overall count of hibernating bats in UK (including the highest count of 484 Natterer's bats) [604]. However, observations of autumn swarming

suggest that larger numbers hibernate in caves, go undetected in crevices [11, 482].

Vocalisations: During late summer swarming, Germany, vocalisations audible without aid of bat detector [644]; however, rarely audible at UK swarming sites and, with many species swarming together, difficult to attribute vocalisation to specific species [480]. Sometimes make a buzzing sound when held in the hand [1].

Dispersal: Analysis of a 17-year data set from a bat box scheme in Dorset indicates limited juvenile dispersal by both sexes for summer roosting; seasonal movements more important [481].

Migration: Usually regarded as sedentary in Europe [276, 613], but movements up to 63 km recorded in GB during seasonal migrations between summer roosts and underground sites [411, 482]. Longest European movements 266 km and 325 km [276].

Activity: In C Scotland, emerge late in evening (55.9±1.8 min after sunset; n = 10) at an average light intensity of 3.5 lux (±0.9 lux; n = 7), in groups of 2–6, then circle in sheltered areas before departing along flyways towards foraging areas; circling behaviour repeated on return to roost, take up to 10 attempts to land before crawling into access hole [625]. During pregnancy, remained away from roost for 3–4.5 h, with the last returning by sunrise. During lactation, returned to roost before making further foraging flight(s), with between 1.84 and 1.74 flights per bat being recorded. Earlier pattern largely resumed during weaning [625]. In Herefordshire and Monmouthshire, also made at least 1 return to the roost while foraging during lactation, typically staying up to 10 min before resuming foraging [570].

Locomotion: Mean flight speed in the field, 4.5 m/s (16.2 km/h) in a straight line in Scandinavia [30] but only 5.7 km/h in Germany; but German bats also recorded flying at 15.5 km/h using photographs under stroboscopic illumination [556]. Both in a flight room and in the wild, seen to pursue prey by quadrupedal locomotion and to take off easily from the ground [630].

FEEDING

Hunting behaviour: Arthropods caught and eaten both in flight and gleaned off foliage. In Ireland [550] 68% and in Germany [173] 81% of the diet was presumed to have been gleaned from surfaces. Gleaning using echolocation and associative learning considered to contribute to resource partitioning between Natterer's and related bat species [555, 630]. Forage using a sequence of low searching flight, hovering, capture using the interfemoral membrane and prey consumption at a perch or on the wing [20, 630].

Food: Wide array of arthropods taken [652]; dipteran flies (42.9–60.2%), caddisflies (12.7–16.1%), bees and wasps (0.0–10.7%), beetles (4.9–12.3%) and arachnids (6.8–18.1%) the most common prey, using faecal analysis, in Ireland and Scotland [550, 625]; Table 8.12.

BREEDING

Copulation observed during December in a cave [182]. Genetic and behavioural evidence suggests that most copulations occur at underground sites, most likely in the autumn [481].

Males: Swarming behaviour, sometimes involving large numbers of bats at entrances to underground sites, late summer and autumn (August–November) [412, 482] interpreted as mating behaviour [411, 482]. Recapture and genetic data, England, show that *M. nattereri* travel from several summer colonies to mate at the same swarming site [481].

Productivity: Single young, born end of June–early July [56, 366]; parturition, Herefordshire/Monmouthshire, 22 June–13 July [570].

Development of young: In captive colony, maintained in a flight room, mean birthweight 3.4 g, mean forearm length 17.0 mm. First flights occurred at 20 days of age, when forearm length was 98% that of adults; by 58–60 days, mean body mass and forearm length were respectively 89% and 98% of adult values [627]. Young recorded dropping to the floor, or from flying mothers, in several British roosts; some were retrieved by adults, others died on the floor and others (such as premature neonates) are likely to have died in the roost [56, 254, 570].

Table 8.12 Natterer's bat: prey, determined as percentage of fragments from faecal analysis

	C Scotland [625]	Co. Limerick [550]
Midges (Chironomidae)	23.5	0.0
Crane flies (Tipulidae)	7.9	3.4
Other longhorn flies (Nematocera)	16.0	5.4
Other flies (Brachycera and Cyclorrapha)	12.8	34.1
Moths (Lepidoptera)	1.2	5.4
Lacewings (Neuroptera)	0.3	0.0
Caddisflies (Trichoptera)	16.1	12.7
Mayflies (Ephemeroptera)	0.1	0.0
Bees and wasps (Hymenoptera)	0.0	10.7
Earwigs (Dermaptera)	1.9	1.3
True bugs (Hemiptera)	1.1	3.2
Beetles (Coleoptera)	12.3	4.9
Centipedes (Chilopoda)	0.0	0.8
Spiders (Araneae)	2.2	12.0
Harvestmen (Opiliones)	4.3	5.4
Mites (Acarina)	0.3	0.7
Total	**100**	**100**

POPULATION
Numbers: Pre-breeding GB population estimated at 100 000 (70 000 England, 17 500 Scotland, 12 500 Wales); based on very limited information [215], as relatively few roost sites known [18, 569]. Increased counts during swarming and hibernation suggest these figures are underestimates, due to the crevice-dwelling nature of the species [18, 482]. Ireland, no estimate available, expected to be *c.*40 000.

Sex ratio: Volant juveniles captured at maternity colonies in Herefordshire and Monmouthshire were 52% males (n = 60) [570] and in Yorkshire 54% males (n = 103) [482]. In hibernation (Suffolk) 59% were males (n = 261) [590]. During autumn swarming, captures are heavily sex-biased towards males: 76% in N Yorkshire [482] and 75% in S England [411].

Age determination: After the ossification of wing bones of juveniles in the autumn, young of current year difficult to differentiate from adults although nipple development can be an indication [274]; characteristics such as tartar on teeth and frostbite on ear tips used in Germany [645].

Survival: Survival rates (calculated from mark–recapture) approximately 0.8 for adults, much lower for juveniles [382, 481]. Greatest recorded longevity in GB 12 years [590]; in Netherlands 17 years [227].

Species interactions: In England and Wales, shares summer roosts with brown long-eared bats [1, 570], Brandt's bats [570], Daubenton's bats [274] and lesser horseshoe bats [570]. In Scotland, frequently share roosts with brown long-eared bats [198, 628] and with pipistrelles [628]. Swarm in autumn with various other species, primarily other *Myotis* and brown long-eared bats [411, 482].

MORTALITY
Predation: Found at low frequency in barn owl pellets [338, 352].

PARASITES AND PATHOGENS
Ectoparasites: 2 species of flea, *Ischnopsyllus simplex* and the rare winter flea *Nycteridopsylla longiceps,* regular [274]. 6 species of mites, including *Spinturnix myoti, Macronyssus ellipticus* and *M. diversipilis,* recorded in GB [36]. A range of other parasites recorded in continental Europe [344].

RELATIONS WITH HUMANS
Has survived in captivity several months [431]. Adapted well to living in a flight room and successfully re-released into the wild after 3–4 weeks [628].

PRINCIPAL AUTHORS
P.G. Smith & N.M. Rivers. Additional data and comments from A.M. Hutson & S.M. Swift, and based on material in earlier editions by R.E. Stebbings, D.J. Bullock & P.W. Richardson.

Bechstein's bat *Myotis bechsteinii*
Vespertilio bechsteinii Kuhl, 1818; Germany.
Selysius bechsteini.
Ystlum Bechstein (Welsh).

RECOGNITION
Whole animal: Medium-sized bat (forearm 38–45 mm), similar in general characteristics to Natterer's bat. Ears conspicuously long and broad (Plate 6), reaching 8–10 mm beyond tip of nose (relatively longer than in any British bat except brown and grey long-eared, but not joined at the base and not folded beneath the wings during hibernation).

Skull and teeth: Similar to other British *Myotis* spp., dental formula 21.3.3/3.1.3.3 but distinguished by condylobasal length of 16.0–17.0 mm.

Field signs: None.

DESCRIPTION
Medium sized, weighing 7–14 g, forearm length 38–45 mm. Face long, pointed, bare and slightly pink in colour. Dorsal fur long, pale brown to reddish brown, darker at the base. Ventral fur pale grey. Wing and ear membranes opaque, mid to dark grey brown. Wings comparatively broad and short. Ears longer than face (Fig. 8.22). Tragus straight sided, long and slender, nearly 1/2 length of the ear.

Skull: Condylobasal length 16.0–17.0 mm, upper tooth row 7.2–7.6 mm. Similar to *M. nattereri,* slightly larger, and with premolars less crowded, p³ fully in tooth-row (p³ displaced inside p⁴ in *M. nattereri*).

CHROMOSOMES
2n = 44, FNa = 52 [684].

RELATIONSHIPS
Traditionally included in subgenus *Myotis,* along with e.g. *M. myotis, M. blythii, M. nattereri,* so presumed related to them, rather than to *M. mystacinus* or *M. daubentonii.* However, molecular

Fig. 8.22 Bechstein's bat, showing longer ears, differently shaped interfemoral membrane (cf. Fig. 8.19) *(photo F. Greenaway)*.

phylogeny shows that closest to *M. daubentonii* [508], and morphological similarities responsible for assignment to *M. (Myotis)* evolved by convergence.

MEASUREMENTS
See Table 8.13. Forearm of males *c*.2% shorter than females (Avon, Dorset, Surrey, Sussex and Wiltshire)

VARIATION
Partial albino individuals recorded.

DISTRIBUTION
Essentially S European, from England to Caucasus, S to Mediterranean (Fig. 8.23). Restricted to S England, Kent west to Devon and north to Gloucestershire (Fig 8.24). 2 possible records from Wales [1, 213].

HISTORY
Known from Lower and Middle Pleistocene, Hungary [278]. Present Late Glacial?, Pin Hole Cave, Derbyshire. Commonest bat species recorded from Neolithic, Grimes Graves, Norfolk and at Ightham Fissures, Kent (date uncertain). Likely to have been more common when deciduous woodland widespread, declined as woodlands cleared for farmland [678].

HABITAT
Roosts in holes and cracks in old trees [103, 536,

Table 8.13 Bechstein's bat: measurements

Head and body length (mm)	43.0–50.0	
Forearm length (mm)	38.0–45.0	Mean male 41.1 (SD 0.95, n = 34)
		Mean female 41.8 (SD 0.75, n = 42)
Wingspan (mm)	250–300	
Ear length (mm)	20–26	
Mass (g)	7.00–13.0	

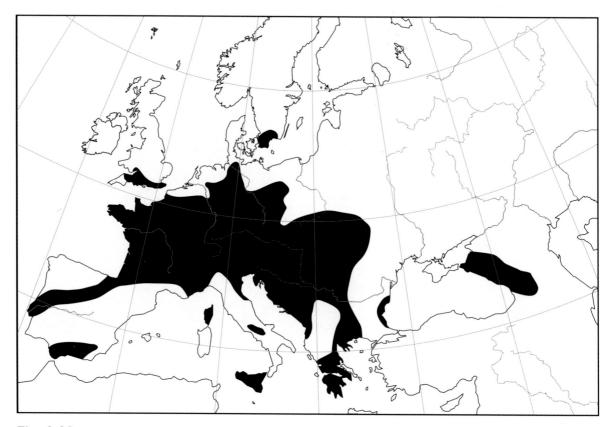

Fig. 8.23 Bechstein's bat *Myotis bechsteinii:* world range.

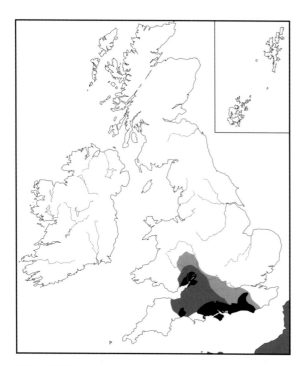

Fig. 8.24 Bechstein's bat *Myotis bechsteinii:* range in GB.

542] but readily uses concrete and sawdust bat boxes [676]; occasionally found in buildings [34, 595]. Usually associated with broadleaved woodland containing veteran trees, particularly oak. Nursery colonies favour old woodpecker holes. Tree holes probably main hibernacula, but occasionally found in caves and mines.

Usually forages in deciduous woodland, particularly where water bodies are present; occasionally along treelines and hedgerows. Breeding females select areas with closed canopy structure, close (<1 km) to day roosts and have a small foraging range (1–10 ha). Although commutes along treelines and hedgerows, occasionally recorded flying directly across open fields to reach foraging area or to return to roost at dawn [1].

SOCIAL ORGANISATION AND BEHAVIOUR

Little known of the social structure of this species in GB. Evidence from monitoring bat boxes suggests a near-complete separation of adult males and females during the summer [1]. Genetic studies from the continent indicate that females in maternity colonies are a socially closed unit that frequently splits into subgroups occupying different roosts. Although fission and fusion frequent between these groups throughout the summer months, their composition is not completely random; females associate according to their reproductive status [322]. During autumn, mating groups of a single male and up to 5 females reported from Europe [34]. Males in summer mostly spread out in suboptimal habitats between nursery colonies.

TERRITORIES

Summer: Males roost singularly or in small groups. Females form maternity colonies from May to September; varying in size, 20–130 adults dispersed in subgroups in different roosts within a small area (<15 ha). Groups shift roost every few days, splitting and reforming into new groups. At dawn, colony members swarm around the roost and then fly between different roosts before selecting the next roost to be occupied. Subgroup size varied from 3 to 80 adults [1].

Emergence time related to ambient light levels: in exposed roosts, *c.*20 min after sunset but earlier within dark woodlands.

Winter: Probably hibernates in tree holes but small numbers (>5) found in caves and mines; these tend to be predominantly males [1, 592]. Ringing studies, Europe, suggest that relatively sedentary during winter, most recorded movements <10 km, although exceptionally long flights (39 km) recorded [200].

VOCALISATIONS

Produces very quiet echolocation calls, difficult to detect unless within a few metres of the bat. Call parameters vary with location but consist of steep FM sweeps from 112 to 31 kHz, ranging in duration from 2.1 to 5.1 ms with peak frequency at *c.*51 kHz. [34, 82, 413, 654]. Also loud, low social calls emitted close to the roost.

FEEDING

Most foraging in closed canopy woodland or above woodland streams within and below the canopy, and sometimes just above the woodland floor. Prey taken by aerial hawking, gleaning, passive listening, and by perch hunting. Bats frequently return to individual trees or groups of trees with their foraging range [1].

Prey mainly moths, but also include Diptera (Tipulidae and Brachycera), Planipennia and Coleoptera [633, 676].

BREEDING

Reproductive biology very little known. Up to 30 different animals have been caught in an evening, swarming at the entrance to underground hibernation sites during late summer and early autumn [1]. Non-pregnant female young from previous year present in maternity colonies, indicating that sexual maturity may not be reached until 2nd year of life [1, 103]. Probably females give birth to singletons (no records of twins).

Births in UK, late June–mid July [1]. Longevity, Europe, 21 years [232].

POPULATION

Population estimated at 1500 [215] but with only 13 extant maternity colonies known from GB, true population difficult to assess. May be as great as 20 000–25 000 [1].

MORTALITY

Reported from pellets of *Strix aluco* and *Tyto alba* in Europe [338, 512].

PARASITES AND PATHOGENS

Nycteribiid fly *Basilia nana* specific to Bechstein's bat, occurs on most individuals.

RELATIONS WITH HUMANS

Has been successfully maintained in captivity for up to 6 years [141]. High levels of Bechstein's bats in fossil records suggest that woodland clearance is likely to be the main reason for population decline. In areas where veteran trees have been cleared and suitable tree holes scarce, may benefit from provision of concrete and sawdust bat boxes.

PRINCIPAL AUTHORS

H.W. Schofield & F. Greenaway

Greater mouse-eared bat *Myotis myotis*

Vespertilio myotis Borkhausen, 1797; Germany. *Vespertilio murinus*, of Schreber, 1774 *et al.* (not of Linnaeus, 1758; widely but incorrectly used for this species throughout 19th century, now correctly applied to particoloured bat (see account below).

RECOGNITION

Very large (forearm >57 mm), distinguished from noctule and serotine by pointed tragus (Plate 6) and lack of postcalcarial lobe.

DESCRIPTION

Upper parts medium to light brown; underside white or greyish white with distinct line of demarcation along side of neck. Juveniles and subadults up to 12 months are greyer. Face almost bare, pinkish or brown. Ears and flight membranes brown, the latter thick, leathery and broad.

Ears large, extending *c.*5 mm beyond tip of muzzle when laid forward. Tragus *c.*1/2 height of conch with both anterior and posterior sides more or less straight.

Chromosomes: 2n = 44; FNa = 50–52, European data [684].

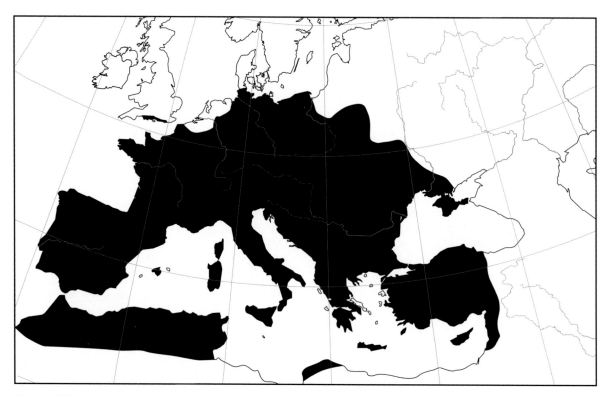

Fig. 8.25 Mouse-eared bat *Myotis myotis*: world range.

MEASUREMENTS

Head and body 65–80 mm; forearm 57–68 mm; wingspan 365–450 mm; ear 24–28 mm; weight 20–40 g. Males smaller than females: average length of forearm (in Sussex): males 59.9 mm (n = 10), females 62.4 mm (n = 21) [1].

DISTRIBUTION

Widely distributed in Europe north to *c*.54º N, extinct Netherlands (Fig. 8.25). Well studied in Europe [197]. Effectively extinct in British Isles, but perhaps never well established. Recent records from Dorset, W Sussex and Kent.

HISTORY

2 old records, London and Epping (pre 1850), are doubtful [55]. Another from Cambridge, 1888, more likely the southern European lesser mouse-eared bat (*Myotis blythii*). Small hibernating population discovered in Dorset, 1956 [76] probably never much exceeded 10, extinct by 1980. Last hibernating population in W Sussex, discovered in 1969 [424], maximum of *c*.30 bats but reduced to 1 male from 1985 to 1990 [603].

One in Kent, winter 1985 [256]; extensive subsequent search suggested this was probably a stray migrant. Old female, found dying Bognor, W Sussex, January 2001 [1]. Juvenile male, ringed December 2002 in the same W Sussex hibernation site used previously by this species, still wintering there early 2006 [1].

HABITAT

Open, lightly wooded country and pasture/meadow [19, 197]. Roosts in buildings in summer and caves in winter in N Europe; more regular in caves in summer in S Europe.

SOCIAL ORGANISATION AND BEHAVIOUR

Summer: Males solitary or in small groups, usually in buildings with large roofs; females form large nursery colonies in buildings or caves. Interchange between adjacent nursery colonies seems frequent [560]. In the Netherlands, 312 bats in a nursery cave roost included 156 adult females, 121 juveniles and 35 post-juvenile males [63]. The latter may have been 1 year old and just reaching sexual maturity [563]. Nursing colonies in Czechoslovakia [164] comprised 86% adult females, 2% adult males and 12% immature (n = 933). Females visit solitary males for mating in the autumn [165]. In Hungary, emerge very late, when quite dark, and return an hour before sunrise, again when still dark; apparently unaffected by weather conditions [643]. Flight slow, heavy and generally straight, low to medium height, up to 20 m.

Winter: Generally solitary but also found in groups, sometimes of mixed species. Preferred temperature 7–8 ºC in Poland [210]. In mainland Europe, preference for internal areas of caves at beginning of winter, moving towards entrance by spring [122, 139]. The few observations in GB conform to this pattern; most found hanging in high exposed parts of tunnels.

Movements of 7.5 km noted in Dorset. Regular movements, up to 200 km, between summer and winter roosts recorded in Czechoslovakia [165], but usually <50 km and rarely >100 km in Germany or elsewhere [276, 560]. Greatest movement 436 km [560].

FEEDING
Mostly larger ground beetles (Carabidae, 36–65% by volume), lepidopteran larvae (15–24%), melolonthids and ground-dwelling orthopteroids [19].

BREEDING
Females may achieve sexual maturity at 3 months of age [564], but more usually in their 2nd year [197] and males at 15 months [563]. Gestation period 46–59 days [561].

POPULATION
During hibernation, Netherlands, sex ratio biased to males (58%; n = 2914) [63], but in Czechoslovakia, predominance of females (55%; n = 1251) [164]. In Sussex 32% (n = 31) were females (Fig. 8.26)[1]. Greatest longevity in GB, a male at 18 years [16]; a male also caught > 18 years after banding in Europe [425], and 22 years recorded [539].

MORTALITY
In Poland, frequently taken by owls, notably barn owls [209, 512].

PARASITES
No records from British specimens, although a wide range of parasites recorded from Europe [344].

RELATIONS WITH HUMANS
Given special protection by Conservation of Wild Creatures and Wild Plants Act, 1975 before such protection extended to all bats under Wildlife and Countryside Act, 1981 (see Chapter 4).

AUTHOR
A.M. Hutson, based on the account in the 2nd edition by R.E. Stebbings.

Fig. 8.26 Mouse-eared bat, the largest but rarest of British bats *(photo. F. Greenaway)*.

GENUS *Lasiurus*

A New World genus of *c.*17 species; accidental in Europe.

Hoary bat *Lasiurus cinereus*
Vespertilio cinereus Palisot de Beauvois, 1796; Philadelphia, Pennsylvania, USA.

A very distinctive, large bat (forearm 50.7–56.8 mm); ears short, rounded, furry with black edges, dorsal fur extending completely over uropatagium. Dark-brown to greyish pelage, frosted by pale tips to hairs; pale patches on wrists, elbows and shoulders, throat yellowish.

Measurements: Males, head and body 80.5±0.51 mm; forearm 52.5±0.3 mm; condylocanine length 16.7± 0.7 mm; c–m³ 6.1±0.07 mm; females *c.*4% larger [553].

A woodland bat. Roosts among leaves in canopy, at least in summer. Migrates from higher latitudes towards subtropical zone in both N and S hemisphere.

Only recorded 5 times in Europe, all in autumn (known migration period in N America): 4 records, Iceland, (Octobers 1943, 1957, 1964, December 1957) and from S Ronaldsay, Orkney, in September 1847 [236], an autumn when at least 2 American landbirds were also recorded in Europe. Presumed storm-blown.

AUTHOR
D.W. Yalden

GENUS *Nyctalus*

A Palaearctic genus of 8 species; medium–large bats with very short, mushroom-shaped tragus. Typically woodland bats, living in woodpecker holes, etc.

Leisler's bat *Nyctalus leisleri*
Vespertilio leisleri, Kuhl, 1818; Hanau, Hessen-Nassau, Germany.
Hairy-armed bat; *ialtóg Leisler* (Irish Gaelic).

RECOGNITION
In flight: A medium-sized, high-flying bat, first to appear in evening in Ireland. Flight while commuting high, fast and straight with occasional dives. Flight while foraging, generally lower with more turns and dives.

In hand: Similar to noctule but distinguished by smaller size (forearm <48 mm) and distinctly bicoloured fur, individual hairs much darker at base than tips (Plate 6).

With bat detector: Echolocation calls loud, picked up on detector up to 100m; consist of both FM and CF components. In open areas, pulses are shallowly FM, with or without an initial steep FM component. Call duration in open areas 9–14 ms, with peak energy 24–28 kHz. [664]. Echolocation calls shorter (<4 ms) with broader bandwidth when flying in confined spaces [654]. Detailed call parameters: frequency of maximum energy 26.9 kHz (range 21.1–36.6 kHz); call duration 10.9 ms (range 10.6–27.1 ms); interpulse interval 226.0 ms (range 69.0–880.0 ms) [516]. 2 main types of social call: mating call, most commonly emitted by a stationary bat in a tree, a long, shallow FM sweep down from *c.*20 kHz, repeated every 0.5–1 s; 2nd social call appears to be aggressive [516].

Skull: Smaller than noctule (condylobasal length 15–16 mm), relatively smaller incisors (Fig 8.27). p¹ not as reduced as in noctule, and visible from side.

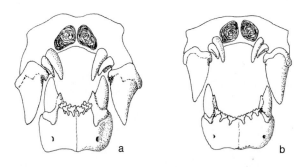

Fig. 8.27 Anterior teeth of noctule (a) and Leisler's bats (b). i³ is relatively larger in the noctule, and lower incisors overlap *(drawn by D.W. Yalden).*

Field signs: Droppings accumulate below exit hole from roost site. Faecal pellets 2–3 × 9–11 mm.

DESCRIPTION
Medium-large bat, upper parts varying from golden to dark rufous brown, very dark brown bases to hairs. Under parts lighter and slightly grey-brown. Facial skin, ears and patagium very dark brown, sometimes blackish. Wings narrow and pointed with thick opaque membranes. Fur extends on to wing membrane and along forearm, hence old name 'hairy-armed bat' (Fig. 8.28). Ears short (12 mm), broad and rounded. Tragus very short, mushroom-shaped, as in noctule. Prominent postcalcarial lobe. Males have enlarged buccal glands during mating season [229].

Chromosomes: 2n = 46, FNa = 50; European data [684].

Fig. 8.28 Leisler's bat, echolocating through its wide-open mouth, like most vespertilionids *(photo F. Greenaway).*

RELATIONSHIPS

Noctule and Leisler's bats appear to occupy similar ecological niches, with comparable flight styles, activity patterns and habitat preferences.

MEASUREMENTS

See Table 8.14. Mean forearm length of adult females in Ireland 43.8 mm (n = 128) and in Worcestershire 43.7 mm (n = 8) [598]. Mean and range of forearm length of adult females in Ireland 42.7 mm, range 41–44 mm (n = 23), of recently volant juveniles 42.4 mm, range 41–44 mm (n = 12). Mean and range of body weights of adult females on emergence 15.6 g, range 14–19.5 g (n =

23), of recently volant juveniles 13.1 g, range 11.5–14.5 g (n = 12) [552]. Males slightly smaller than females in Switzerland: mean forearm lengths of males 43.8 mm (n = 11), of females 44.3 mm (n = 14) [3]. Body mass changes over the reproductive cycle, Slovakia, described in [316].

VARIATION

Currently 2 recognised subspecies, *N. l. leisleri* (Kuhl, 1818) and *N. l. verrucosus* (Bowdich, 1825) [401], latter restricted to Madeira. A 3rd subspecies, described as *N. l. azoreum* [112], Azores, now regarded as distinct species *Nyctalus azoreum* [401, 579].

Table 8.14 Leisler's bat and noctule: measurements

	Leisler's bat	Noctule
Head and body length (mm)	54–64	70–82
Forearm length (mm)	39–47	47–55
Wingspan (mm)	280–340	330–450
Ear length (mm)	12–13	15–18
Skull length (condylobasal length) (mm)	15.2–16.0	17.6–19.0
Upper tooth-row (c–m^3) (mm)	5.8–6.0	7.0–7.4
Lower tooth-row (c–m^3) (mm)	6.0–6.2	7.2–8.2
Weight (g)	11–20	15–49

DISTRIBUTION

Largely restricted to Europe, though patchily recorded E to C Asia (Fig. 8.29). Widespead and common throughout Ireland; nursery roosts of up to 100 adult females relatively common [395]. Fewer records from GB, but new records of small numbers of individuals reported each year. Most English records from C–S counties, significant breeding populations in Bristol, Kent, Suffolk, Oxfordshire, Sheffield, S Yorkshire, Essex and Worcestershire areas (Fig 8.30). Recently found in bat boxes, Galloway, Scotland [107]. One record from Gwynedd, Wales, 1992. Largest known roost in England, urban Bristol, with up to 320 bats after young fly.

HISTORY

N. cf. *leisleri* recorded Lower Pleistocene, Hungary [278]. *N. leisleri* recorded Late Glacial?, Pinhole Cave [282] and Neolithic, Dowel Cave [677], both Derbyshire.

HABITAT

Although considered tree roosting in Europe [495], in Ireland and GB nursery colonies chiefly located in roof spaces of buildings. Non-maternity roosts in tree cavities and bat boxes. Radio-tracking studies, Polish forest, showed lactating females roosting in tree holes often at considerable heights above ground level (17–26 m) [506]. In Poland, roosts mainly in natural cavities, characteristics described [505].

Foraging concentrated over open areas. In Ireland, radiotelemetry revealed 2/3 of recorded foraging time over pasture and canal, but mostly pasture. Neighbourhood of lights also important (both street lights and floodlights) [552]. Also been recorded foraging around mercury vapour (but not sodium) street lights in England [669], Switzerland [687] and France [41]. In England, radio-tracked bats foraged preferentially along woodland and scrub-lined roads in Kent, and over pasture near Bristol; urban and arable areas avoided as foraging sites in both [665]. Bat detector surveys found bats feeding especially over lakes and improved pasture in SW England [655]. Transects using bat detectors in cars, N Ireland, detected highest numbers in July (presumably when young began to fly); found similar numbers of bat passes in all habitat types studied, no seasonal trends in habitat selection [522]. Spot sampling with bat detectors in N Ireland revealed selection for parkland/amenity grassland, deciduous woodland edge and rivers/canals; avoided improved grassland and hedgerows [517]. During the pre-hibernal period, foraging bats selected improved grassland in N Ireland [239]. No records of winter foraging after mid-November in Ireland.

A radiotelemetry study, N Ireland, recorded hibernacula mainly in mature deciduous trees (chiefly in splits in oak *Quercus* spp. and beech *Fagus sylvaticus*, although rot holes and exfoliating bark also used), fewer in buildings. Roosted in both trees and buildings, August–early November, but thereafter exclusively in

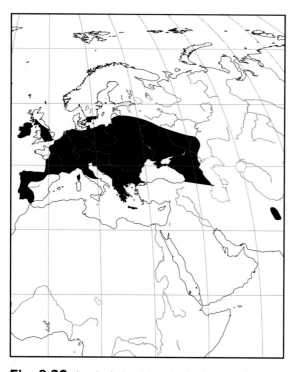

Fig. 8.29 Leisler's bat *Nyctalus leisleri*: world range.

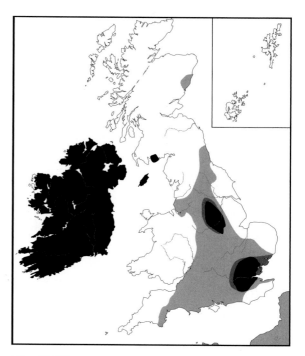

Fig. 8.30 Leisler's bat *Nyctalus leisleri*: range in British Isles.

trees. Time spent roosting increased from August to October, bats alternating between periods of torpor and activity. Temperature-sensitive radio transmitters revealed bats always entered torpor when ambient temperature dropped below 6 °C. Roosting continuous from early November, with onset of true hibernation [239]. In Europe, hibernacula thought to be in hollow trees, buildings and occasionally rock crevices [339, 495, 539, 586].

SOCIAL ORGANISATION AND BEHAVIOUR

Nursery colonies begin to form in April. Numbers stabilise before parturition, display high degree of site fidelity throughout lactation.

Position of roosts often advertised by loud vocalisations before emergence at dusk. Emerges early, often before sunset. At nursery roost in Ireland, the first bat often, and >1/2 the colony exceptionally, left before sunset. Departure, in some colonies at least, earlier during lactation. Emergence earlier on overcast nights and delayed with increased light intensity. Departure mainly in pulses, rate of emergence increased with colony size [548]. In England, typically emerge *c.*18 min after sunset [301, 665].

Radiotelemetry studies in Ireland and England revealed unimodal or bimodal activity patterns for nursery colonies prior to parturition, all bats taking main foraging flight at dusk but occurrence of shorter flight towards dawn temperature-dependent [547, 665]. Timing of flights thought to coincide with flight periodicity of insect prey. During lactation, activity multimodal, lactating females taking up to 5 flights per night. Percentage of the night spent flying also peaked during lactation. Straight-line distance to foraging site greatest early in season (max. 13.4 km), lowest during lactation when foraged local to the nursery roost. Emergence and subsequent foraging inhibited by heavy rain [552]. Foraging distances averaged 4.2 km straight-line distance from roost in England [665]. No information on behaviour of adult males during summer. During pre-hibernal period, both males and females exhibited bimodal activity patterns.

Considered migratory in Europe [5, 613]. Longest recorded movements, 810 km from Switzerland to Germany [5], 975 km from Germany to France [387], 1245 km from Voronezh reserve in Russia to Ordu, Turkey [403] and 1567 km for a bat ringed in Germany and recaptured in Spain [398a]. A female in poor condition, accidentally trapped in a house in NW Germany, rehabilitated and found alive 10 months later in C Spain, had covered 1534 km [675]. 25 individuals caught at 1923 m asl in Swiss Alps considered to be migrating [3]; 1 found dead on glacier in Alps at 2600 m asl in 1945. Maximum documented rate of travel 8.1 km/day [230] and a juvenile recorded travelling 29 km (straight-line distance) in an evening before contact was lost [552]. No evidence of long-distance migration between summer and winter quarters in Ireland.

FEEDING
Strictly aerial, diet comprising mainly medium-sized and small insects caught and eaten in flight, many probably from swarms. Extensive dropping analyses in Ireland revealed major pastoral component, indicated by yellow dung fly *Scathophaga stercoraria* (single most frequent item), Scarabaeoidea and associated mites. Insects with aquatic larvae (Chironomidae/Ceratopogonidae, Trichoptera, Culicidae, Ephemeroptera), presumably caught near water, also significant component. Results from roost in pastoral land in England similar, but Chironomidae/Ceratopogonidae most important, as they were at English roost on mainly arable land, but there followed by Lepidoptera, Anisopodidae, Chrysopodidae, Sphaeroceridae and Scathophagidae. Diet dominated by small nematoceran Diptera at roosts in Kent and Bristol. Coleoptera were the second most frequent prey by volume, and more Lepidoptera were eaten in Kent than in Bristol during June, showing regional differences in diet in England [665]. Analysis of droppings from 3 forest sites in Germany indicated very diverse diets. Prey groups Lepidoptera, Neuroptera, and Ichneumonidae may indicate feeding near trees [551]. In Switzerland, Lepidoptera, Diptera and Trichoptera most often taken [61]. In Slovakia, Lepidoptera and Diptera main prey by both volume and frequency [316].

BREEDING
Harems, a single male with several females, recorded in bat boxes until mid October in N Ireland [239]. Mating calls of male Leisler's bats commence from late July in Ireland, issued mainly from mature deciduous trees, especially beech *Fagus sylvaticus*. These calls initially described from beech forests (Vernon mountains, N Greece). Adult males recorded singing from perches or in songflight. Perches not associated with tree holes, but on exposed beech trunks at height of 6–9 m at edge of forest. Same perches used repeatedly night after night. Song consists of one type of call, with repetition rate *c.*1/s, sweeping down in range from 18 to 10.5 kHz; peak amplitude 12.4 kHz; duration *c.*29 ms. Mating not observed [229]. Such calls since also described in Ireland [516]. Copulation presumed to take place throughout autumn and winter.

Females ovulate in spring, give birth to single young in mid-June. Unfavourable weather conditions may delay birth date until late June [543, 549]. Parturition recorded typically between mid and late June in Slovakia and Austria [316]. Young commence flying *c*.30 days after birth. Newly volant young initially forage in vicinity of roost site, move progressively further as they mature [552].

Grow rapidly, forearm lengths reaching adult proportions around time of 1st flight. Young females may mate in their 1st year. After weaning, adults disperse from mid–late July onwards, leaving juvenile colonies, composed of progressively more young males as season progresses [549]. Nursery roosts vacated by mid September.

POPULATION
Ireland considered stronghold of world distribution; 3rd most frequently recorded species, after pipistrelle and brown long-eared. Initial investigations suggest that Irish population stable. Much scarcer in GB, pre-breeding population estimated at 10 000 [215]. Sex ratio of unweaned bats apparently 1:1 (n = 107) [598]. Survival rates unknown.

SPECIES INTERACTIONS
Throughout most of its geographic range, Leisler's bat sympatric with its larger congener, the noctule. Sometimes roosts with this species in Poland [506]. Relative abundance of Leisler's bat in Ireland may reflect absence of noctule as potential competitor. Both species are fast fliers, have similar echolocation calls and emerge early. Significant overlap in diet of the 2 species reported in England [1].

MORTALITY
Remains of Leisler's bats found in barn owl pellets, Poland [512]. In N Ireland, long-eared owls observed attempting to catch Leisler's bats in flight and a sparrowhawk regularly observed waiting for Leisler's bats to emerge from their roost at dusk [490].

PARASITES
Fleas, *Ichnopsyllus elongatus, I. intermedius, I. octactenus, Nycteridopsylla longiceps* and the bug *Cimex pipistrelli* have been recorded. In Slovakia, ectoparasites found on 57% of examined bats; mites *Spinturnix helvetiae* and *Steatonyssus spinosus* most frequent, and 2 species of fly *Nycteribia* found [316].

RELATIONS WITH HUMANS
Nursery roosts in buildings threatened by exclusion and remedial timber treatment. Unsympathetic tree surgery and tree felling may reduce the availability of suitable roosts. Mature deciduous trees are particularly important for this species. Widespread use of the anthelmintic drug ivermectin may have implications for foraging success, given the importance of pastoral prey.

PRINCIPAL AUTHORS
C.B. Shiel, with G. Jones & D. Waters

Noctule *Nyctalus noctula*
Vespertilio noctula Schreber, 1774; France.
Vespertilio magnus Berkenhout, 1789; Cambridge, England.
Vespertilio altivolans White, 1789; Selborne, Hants, England.
Great bat.

RECOGNITION
In flight: The largest, highest-flying, bat of the British Isles, and often the first to appear, strikingly silhouetted against the evening sky. Compared with other British bats has a long, narrow wing with pointed tip, flying purposefully with deep wing beats. 2 distinct flight patterns observed, one just before sunset when bats fly high, fast and straight with occasional rapid diversions; the other of fast flight up to 30 m high with repeated deep dives and occasional glides.

In hand: Fills the hand. Short, sleek, golden, ginger or reddish fur with pronounced 'set'. Short, stout brown ears and mushroom-shaped tragus (Plate 6). Postcalcarial lobe present. Differs from Leisler's in that forearm >47 mm (Table 8.14), and hair shorter, of uniform colour from base to tip. Fur quite greasy.

With bat detector: Very loud. Pulse repetition rate slow. Short, steep, FM sweep used when bats hunting closer to ground [7, 683], or long, almost CF pulse (*c*.20 kHz, audible to young people without detector) used together with 1st call type when hunting higher [7, 288]. Alternation between the 2 call types explains the 'plip-plop' sound from the detector; uses both calls together more often than Leisler's [360]. Sonographic analysis demonstrates call sequences can be distinguished from Leisler's with high degree (>98%) of certainty [360]. When using only the short FM sweep, it may be confused with serotine. Constant frequency call harmonics at 40 kHz and 60 kHz may also cause confusion.

During aerial chases and when circling the roost, social calls used, sounding like an undulating whistle to the ear under time expansion, and like a rattle through heterodyne bat detector (Fig. 8.2). Most varied social calls of any Palaearctic bat [667].

Skull: Large, c–m³ 7.0–7.4 mm; i³ larger in crown area than i²; p¹ very small, invisible from side. Some geographic variation across range matching genetic isolation of regional populations [618].

At roost: Often betrays location of tree roosts by shrill vocalisation towards dusk and during the day in warm weather. Tree roosts may be recognised by dark streak of faeces and urine which drains from exit hole or by droppings below hole, scattered as bats exit. When occupied, insects can be seen swarming around hole. Faecal pellets tubular, 3.0–3.5 × 11–15 mm.

DESCRIPTION
Dorsal fur golden, ginger or reddish; ventral fur similar, often slightly paler (Fig. 8.31). Adult males brightest. Juveniles slightly darker and usually duller. Face, ears and wing membrane dark brown, almost black. Fur extends on to wing membrane. Ears short and broad, 15 mm long and wide. Tragus mushroom-shaped, height roughly equal to width, broader at tip than at base. Muzzle broad and glandular; conspicuous white buccal glands in corners of mouth, more prominent in males than in females [219, 327]; produce white fatty material with a conspicuous odour [574]. Postcalcarial lobe present; tip of tail emerges *c.*2 mm from interfemoral membrane. Wings quite narrow and pointed with average aspect ratio [392].

Fig. 8.31 Noctules roosting in a woodcrete Schwegler hibernation box *(photo F. Greenaway)*.

Skull: Heavy muzzle, no obvious 'forehead' in profile; dentition 2.1.2.3/3.1.2.3; differs from *N. leisleri* in larger i³ relative to i² (not so tall, but crown areas nearly equal), and lower incisors large, overlap (Fig. 8.27) (in *N. leisleri*, i³ much more slender, smaller than i²; lower incisors smaller, placed side by side).

Chromosomes: 2n = 42; FNa = 50, European data [684].

RELATIONSHIPS
Sympatric with *N. leisleri* over much of range, and little dietary or roost site separation evident. In Białowieża, Poland, mixed colonies frequent. Abundance in British Isles assumed to depress numbers of *N. leisleri* (cf. Ireland, where absent, and *N. leisleri* relatively common), but this speculative.

MEASUREMENTS
See Table 8.14. In Suffolk mean weight of 21 adult males caught while feeding in June and July was 30.2±1.7 g (range 25–34 g) and of 12 in October was 33.2±3.2 g (range 28–38 g) [116]. Higher weights recorded in captivity where food provided *ad libitum* [385, 442]. Slight sexual dimorphism; in GB mean forearm length of males 51.9 mm (n = 41), of females 53.0 mm (n = 34) [1], in Romania mean forearm length of males 53.9 mm (n = 83), of females 54.3 mm (n = 145) [43].

DISTRIBUTION
Widespread across Palaearctic from Wales and Spain in W to Himalayas, China and Japan in E (Fig. 8.32). In British Isles, local in England and Wales, N to C Scotland [1]; absent Ireland (Fig 8.33). May be limited by availability of broad-leaved woodland [10]. Several vagrants recorded on Orkney [438], Shetland and North Sea oil rigs, presumably blown from Europe [1].

HISTORY
Known from Middle Pleistocene, Germany. Poor record in GB, but present Cromerian, West Runton, Norfolk [218].

HABITAT
Roosts: Predominantly a tree bat; will use rot holes but consistently prefers cavities excavated by woodpeckers that are larger, further from the ground, in more open situations and warmer than other available cavities; usually in mature deciduous trees and Scots pine [360, 504, 505]; even roosts in trees in suburban areas. Buildings rarely used in GB, though more frequently outwith the nursing season [1]; in Europe, buildings used more frequently [71, 166, 613]. In GB commonly

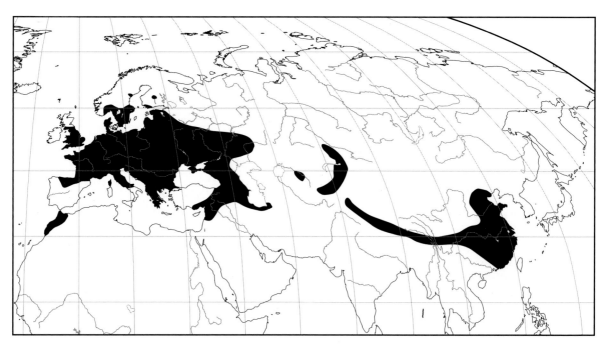

Fig. 8.32 Noctule *Nyctalus noctula*: world range (but bats in E now segregated as *N. plancxi*).

co-roost in trees with Daubenton's bats (*Myotis daubentonii*) and in buildings with pipistrelles (*Pipistrellus pipistrellus*) [1]. Although seldom found in caves, in Europe hibernate in crevices in rock faces [43, 166, 172], with up to 100 individuals recorded in a single fissure.

SOCIAL ORGANISATION AND BEHAVIOUR

Summer: In Europe mixed-sex pre-maternity colonies first appear in March and females migrate back to place of birth where maternity colonies have formed by June [63, 420]. Colonies may move between roosts throughout summer, some carrying their young during lactation [1, 166, 565], but roosting within a specific area of woodland; others remain faithful to a single roost during lactation [360]. Non-lactating females (n = 10) changed roosts significantly more frequently (median 3 changes) than simultaneously radio-tracked lactating females (median no changes, n = 10) from the same colony [360]. Bats frequently observed entering roosts just before residents first emerge, suggesting a colony may occupy several roosts at the same time [1]. Nursery roosts cluster significantly on emergence, with 73 bats taking just over 4.5 min to emerge [360]. Nursery roosts may exceed 100 bats in Europe but only occasionally reach that size in GB; mean roost size in one study, 14 [246].

Adult males solitary or in small groups while the females nurse; similarly change roosts frequently. In August–September, individual males establish territorial mating roosts between which

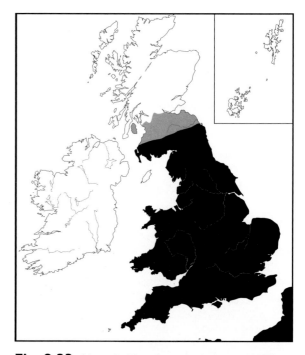

Fig. 8.33 Noctule *Nyctalus noctula*: range in GB.

females move. Up to 18 females found with a single male [565]. Individual males will defend the same roost in subsequent years [1, 335, 565]. In Switzerland, males predominate for most of the year, particularly during June–August. During this time most roosts either abandoned or inhabited by males only, suggesting that although noctules mate and hibernate in Switzerland, birth and lactation occur elsewhere, probably at lower altitudes [620]. Males predominate in all winter samples from W and C Europe [166], suggesting that many females migrate to E and S parts. European distribution and breeding range have been mapped [614, 615].

Foraging behaviour: Feed by fast aerial hawking over pasture next to woodland, over water and in brightly lit areas [360a]. The first bat to emerge in N Europe [301], often before sunset in male [335, 620] and female colonies [288]. Non-lactating females emerge slightly later (11 min after sunset, n = 10) than simultaneously tracked lactating females (7 min after sunset, n = 10) [360a]. Peaks of foraging activity at dusk, for just over an hour, and at dawn, for c.1/2 an hour, coinciding with flight periodicity of insects [360, 449, 620]. Individual bats make 1–6 foraging bouts per night; lactating females make significantly more (median 3, n = 10 individuals) than non-lactating females (median 2, n = 10), although little difference in total nightly foraging duration (mean 115 min, n = 20)[360a]. Where insects were attracted to mercury vapour lamps, bats foraged throughout the night [335]. Bats mist-netted in light rain or thick mist, but not during heavy rain [116], and dawn foraging suppressed by inclement weather [620]. Group foraging is observed at preferred feeding sites, which are traditionally used in consecutive years [1, 335]. Average maximum distance to foraging grounds 4.5 km (n = 20 individuals); average area 8.23 km^2 (minimum convex polygon, n = 20) in cultural landscape in SW England where broadleaved woodland and pasture were habitats consistently preferred [360a]. In heavily forested landscapes, open areas over large rivers, villages and meadows preferred [449]. Some evidence that population regulation linked to habitat availability; non-lactating females foraged over less preferred habitats significantly more than lactating bats [360a]. Prey selection has been reported [53, 116, 188]; passive listening and gleaning may be adopted with suitable prey [53, 54, 335].

Migration: Migratory in former USSR, with ringing recoveries 500–2347 km S and SW; individuals move 20–44 km/day [203, 612]. Noctules also travelled 45 km in 24 h in homing experiments, in one case returning to the same roost after being translocated 237 km the previous year [528]. In W Europe probably less migratory; in Holland most hibernated close to summer roosts but some long-distance movements recorded, up to 900 km SW from Holland to Bordeaux [565]. In Europe several large, mixed-sex hibernation colonies are known [646], genetic analysis shows they are composed of individuals from several different summer colonies [421]. Differential migration in distance and direction observed between age classes and sexes: juvenile males hibernate with juvenile and adult females from the same maternity colony [421, 423] but adult males disperse randomly to occupy mating territories [420]. However, not all females from same maternity colony found in same hibernaculum [565]. Not known to move out of England in winter, and recorded hibernating even in most severe winters.

Winter: Form large mixed-sex colonies of up to 1000 [613] in buildings or trees in Europe, although colony sizes in GB much smaller [611]. Tree holes occupied during winter occur S of the line delineating January isotherm –2 to –4 °C [166].

With an ambient air temperature of –7 °C, the outer individuals of a cluster of 150 were at +1 °C and those at the centre +2 °C [43]. Insulating capacity of tree hole with large cavity poor [227], although most of a colony of 100 bats survived for 53 days when the temperature in their tree hole was permanently below zero, occasionally falling to –16 °C. The minimum recorded skin temperature was –9 °C. Abrupt rises or falls in temperatures resulted in arousal [566]. Nevertheless, very severe winters are thought to result in heavy mortality [613]. In England (52° N) foraging activity observed throughout winter but greatly reduced [28] and in Switzerland flight recorded in winter at an ambient temperature of +2 °C [172].

FEEDING
Broad dietary range. From faecal analysis, flies (Diptera), beetles (Coleoptera) and moths (Lepidoptera) equally prevalent [61, 359, 652] with variation reflecting their seasonal abundance [188, 288] even in winter [315]. Caddisflies rarely found in diet of noctules in England but frequently eaten in Europe [532]. In Russia, small flies were the main constituents of the diet, together with a wide variety of beetles [440].

BREEDING
See Fig. 8.34. Single males disperse randomly to establish mating territories in tree holes during August–September where vocalisations used to attract conspecifics [166, 221, 422, 565, 687]. Mating occurs mainly September–October in the wild [565] but also during winter and spring in captivity [432, 434]; spermatozoa retain their fertilising capacity after storage by both male and female bats for up to 7 months [433]. During winter, uterus distended with semen, the result of several inseminations by the same or different males [221, 433].

Only European species of several maintained in

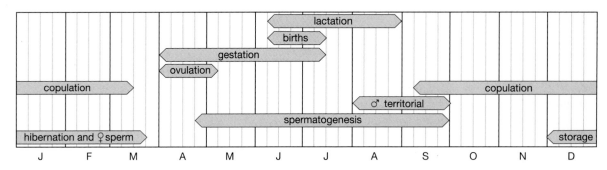

Fig. 8.34 Noctule annual cycle. This cycle applies essentially to all British bats.

captivity to breed routinely there, with fertile F_1 and F_2 generations [327, 431, 442]. Summer period of spermatogenesis characterised by increased aggression [436]. When males are caged together at this time, one assumes dominance, drives others from the nest box and signifies occupation by prolonged high-pitched vocalisations, which sometimes answered by cage mates. He will repel intruders, but may be ousted if he loses one of the occasional but vicious fights. During winter, aggressive behaviour of caged males much reduced.

Females ovulate in spring, and after a gestation period of 70–73 days [149] give birth to a single young in June and July. Twins recorded in captivity in UK [327], rarely in wild [283], and on the European mainland, where triplets also exceptionally occur [63, 402]. In S Bohemia most females older than 1 year have 2 young (mean 1.8) [166]. Segregation of sexes generally occurs when females give birth but mixed colonies may be encountered during summer. Maternal care, growth and development of young described in captivity [326].

Young generally born 1st half of June–early July, begin to fly in 1st half of July, but are not weaned before August [166, 565]. In England some young may not fly until September [116] if inclement spring weather delays ovulation. A proportion of females achieve sexual maturity and mate in their 1st autumn and give birth as yearlings, both in the wild [116] and in captivity [327]. A small proportion of males may also achieve sexual maturity and mate in their 1st autumn [332]. However, spermatogenesis more commonly occurs first in their 2nd summer both in the wild and in captivity as judged by distension of the epididymis with sperm in August [116, 166, 327].

POPULATION

Sex ratio at birth is equal (n = 214) [63], but biased towards females in juvenile samples and in feeding populations. Survival rates unknown, but greatest recorded longevity 8 years [63]. In 2 areas of optimum roosting habitat in Europe, average population density during summer was 0.32/ha, in

Yorkshire 0.015/ha [306]. Estimated British population 50 000 (45 000 England, 250 Scotland, 4750 Wales) [215].

MORTALITY

Low temperatures result in mortality in severe winters [43, 613] and bats die when roosts blown down or when trees felled. Starlings drive out (and possibly kill) noctules from roost holes [246, 363] and grey squirrels successfully compete for cavities [1]. Remains found in pellets from both barn and tawny owls [512], and taken by peregrines in Germany [336].

PARASITES

Ectoparasites include the bug *Cimex pipistrelli* (common); the fleas *Ischnopsyllus elongatus* (common), *Nycteridopsylla eusarca* (a rare winter flea) and *I. intermedius*; the mites *Spinturnix acuminatus*, *Macronyssus flavus*, *M. kolenati*, *'Radfordia' noctulia*, *Leiognathus uncinatus*, *Macrocheles glaber* and *Glycyphagus domesticus*. A median of 5 *Spinturnix acuminatus* (range 0–25) were obtained, per individual, from 75 bats emerging from 10 different roosts in August 1998 [1]. In captivity, a single case of phoresy by the mite *Notoedres chiropteralis* recorded [327].

The blood protozoan *Trypanosoma vespertilionis* has also been recorded [37]. Commonest cause of death in a laboratory colony was pneumonia of unknown aetiology, perhaps the result of lack of flight [431]. Helminth eggs may be present in faeces [1].

RELATIONS WITH HUMANS

Of several tried, this species adapted best to captivity; breeding colony successfully maintained in close confinement for 6 years [327, 431, 442]. A large outdoor flight chamber ($12 \times 7 \times 4$ m) has also been used [221]. Very dependent on woodland management for supply of roost sites and foraging habitat. Will use bat boxes where natural holes lacking.

AUTHORS

I.J. Mackie & P.A. Racey

GENUS *Pipistrellus*

A diverse genus of around 31 species; formerly much larger, but former subgenera *Hypsugo, Neoremicia* now separated as distinct genera. In Europe, 4 species, of which 3 breed in British Isles, other recorded as vagrant. Small bats, with blunt tragus, of moderate length. Possess postcalcarial lobe (contrast *Myotis*). Dentition $i^2/_3c^1/_1p^2/_2m^3/_3$ (same as *Nyctalus*) (Fig. 8.3).

Common pipistrelle *Pipistrellus pipistrellus*
Vespertilio pipistrellus Schreber, 1774; France.
Bandit pipistrelle, *ialtóg fheascrach* (Irish Gaelic).

Soprano pipistrelle *Pipistrellus pygmaeus*
Vespertilio pygmaeus Leach, 1825; Dartmoor, Devon, England.
Ialtóg fheascrach sopránach (Irish Gaelic).

Since previous edition of this handbook, has become clear that pipistrelles previously identified as *P. pipistrellus* comprise 2 cryptic species. First evidence for this separation came from analysis of echolocation signals. Echolocation calls emitted by pipistrelles searching for prey or leaving roosts are 5–10 ms in duration. Each pulse starts at high frequency and falls rapidly to a 'tail' that is almost constant in frequency. Calls emitted by pipistrelles had tails that were bimodal in distribution: one group with most energy at *c*.46 kHz, the other averaging 55 kHz. The 2 distributions of call frequencies show little overlap (<5%). In many areas, the 2 echolocating types were sympatric, yet bats in any maternity colony contained only 1 'phonic type' [296]. Became known as '45 kHz' and '55 kHz' pipistrelles while scientific names were being researched. More recently, differences were found in geographic range [289], habitat use [123, 388, 517, 654], diet [45], 'social' calls [47, 48] (see Fig. 8.2, Table 8.1), mating groups [406] and roost size [49]. Interspecific differences in skull morphology [50], but insufficient to allow absolute separation of the cryptic species. Large genetic differences confirm existence of cryptic species, with a sequence divergence of 11% in a 630-bp region of the cytochrome *b* gene of mtDNA [52, 448].

In 2003 the International Commission on Zoological Nomenclature accepted the proposition that the '45 kHz' cryptic species retain the name *Pipistrellus pipistrellus*, and that *Pipistrellus pygmaeus* be used for the slightly smaller species that calls at a higher frequency (the '55 kHz' cryptic species). Neotypes for both species lodged at the Natural History Museum, London, with molecular data to confirm their identities [292]. Below we refer to information on 'pipistrelles' *Pipistrellus* sp. before the cryptic species were recognised, adding specific detail on each species where available. Studies that are presumed to apply to one or the other (usually on distribution) are identified as *P. pipistrellus?*, *P. pygmaeus?*.

RECOGNITION
Whole animal: Among the smallest British bats, forearm length <35 mm. Ears short, with short, curved, blunt tragus (Plate 6). Postcalcarial lobe present (unlike small *Myotis*). Distinguished from *P. nathusii* by smaller size, lack of pale or white tips to dorsal hair, and shorter relative length of 5th digit divided by forearm length, <1.25 (>1.25 in *P. nathusii* [597]. Fur extends little on to wing and tail membranes (cf. *P. nathusii*, which also shows more pronounced dentition of apical hair scales in the fur on the breast and back than seen in Dutch pipistrelles (almost certainly *P. pipistrellus*), visible in scanning electron micrographs [195].

P. pipistrellus tends to be slightly larger than *P. pygmaeus* (Table 8.15). Dorsal fur typically dark brown with a black base, whereas *P. pygmaeus* hairs tends to be lighter brown over entire length. *P. pipistrellus* usually has a dark pigment over the face, giving it a masked appearance (hence 'bandit pipistrelle'). *P. pygmaeus* often has exposed pink flesh on face. In Germany, *P. pipistrellus* often has a light-coloured, hairless band across the width of its grey-coloured penis, while the penis of *P. pygmaeus* is uniformly brown [223]. The 2nd and 3rd phalanges of the 3rd finger tend to be of similar length in *P. pygmaeus*, while the 2nd is shorter than the 3rd phalanx in *P. pipistrellus* in Germany [223]. Bacula of the 2 species have similar morphology, though that of *P. pygmaeus* looks more angular [1, 235].

Skull and teeth: Detailed accounts of skull and dental morphology given for Dutch pipistrelles (almost certainly *P. pipistrellus*) and *P. nathusii* [195], which can be separated by multivariate analyses of morphological parameters (see Fig. 8.41). Relative length of i^2 the most important dental character: in 73% of *P. nathusii* but only 8% of *P. pipistrellus*, i^2 reaches beyond the caudal cusp of i^1. Overall, skulls larger in *P. pipistrellus* than *P. pygmaeus*, and *P. pipistrellus* has longer lower jaw, longer upper canines and larger gape. Overall, however, only 88% of skulls could be classified to correct species by multivariate analysis of skull measurements [50].

FIELD SIGNS
Both species: Faeces, cylindrical, black and *c*.6–9 mm long, often found on walls or on ground under roost exits. When crushed and viewed under

Table 8.15 Measurements of *Pipistrellus pipistrellus* and *P. pygmaeus*. Forearm and wingspan data from [49], representing bats from 16 roosts of each species throughout mainland Britain. To facilitate comparisons, all data on forearm length and wingspan are for pregnant and lactating adult females – males are slightly smaller. Means ± SD (n) are cited. Skull data for males and females from [50], showing range of measurements. Echolocation call frequencies are frequencies of most energy (FMAXE) derived from power spectra of time-expanded calls

Measurement	*P. pipistrellus*	*P. pygmaeus*	Source
Forearm length (mm)	32.0±0.82 (178)	31.7±0.77 (220)	[49]
Range	29.9–33.9	29.9–33.7	
Wingspan (mm)	217±6.7 (226)	215±7.2 (253)	[49]
Range	(200–234)	(192–232)	
Skull length (condylobasal) (mm)	10.8–12.2 (20)	10.9–11.9 (35)	[50]
Dentary length (mm)	7.98–8.54 (20)	7.56–8.40 (35)	[50]
Upper tooth-row (c–m^3) (mm)	4.06–4.48 (20)	3.78–4.48 (35)	[50]
Lower tooth-row (c–m_3) (mm)	4.34–4.76 (20)	4.06–4.48 (35)	[50]
Body mass (pregnant–post-lactating females)	4.8–6.5	4.3–6.8	[291]
FMAXE of echolocation calls (kHz)	45.1±1.77 (181)	53.2±1.76 (220)	[49]
	46.3±1.97 (174)	55.1±2.62 (398)	[296]
	46.0±1.77 (60)	53.8±1.7 (59)	[655]
Range from all studies	41.6–53.0	49.2–58.0	

a microscope, contain many fragments of small dipterans. Roost exits may be characterised by scratch marks; in large and frequently occupied roosts, dark stain, yellow-brown to black, may develop directly beneath the exit. Bats in large colonies may begin vocalising audibly soon before evening emergence, and often 'swarm' around roosts in large numbers immediately before the morning return. Signs may be more obvious at roosts of *P. pygmaeus*, which tend to be larger [49].

DESCRIPTION

Both species are dark brown dorsally, often with slightly lighter underparts. Fur tends to be dense, soft and silky in *P. pygmaeus*, appearing shorter in length than in *P. pipistrellus*. Dorsal fur appears shaggier in *P. pipistrellus*. *P. pygmaeus* tends to have lighter-coloured fur (almost sand coloured), but coloration can be variable, especially in *P. pipistrellus*. Bare skin usually pink around eyes in *P. pygmaeus*, whereas *P. pipistrellus* often has dark face mask (Plate 6). Ears of both species short, 7–8 mm in *P. pygmaeus* and 8–9 mm in *P. pipistrellus* (German data) [223]. For both, tragus <1/2 height

of pinna, anterior border concave but posterior convex, with round, blunt tip. Short muzzle with glandular swellings. Flight membranes dark brown to black, opaque. Wings narrow, and arm wing of *P. pygmaeus* may have narrow white border between 5th digit and foot in German specimens [223]. Some bats may begin to moult at beginning of August [594]. Parous females can be distinguished from nulliparous females by protuberant keratinised nipples, sometimes with short, crinkly, emergent hair. In contrast, nipples of nulliparous females diminutive and have emergent body hair [436].

Chromosomes: 2n = 41–44, Fna = 48–52, European data [684]. One pipistrelle, Yorkshire (sp.?), had karyotype 2n = 44 [545].

RELATIONSHIPS

Large sequence divergence (11%) in portions of the cytochrome *b* gene of mtDNA between the cryptic species [50, 51]. Phylogenetic tree based on genetic differences showed both species to be more closely related to *P. kuhlii* than *P. nathusii* [50].

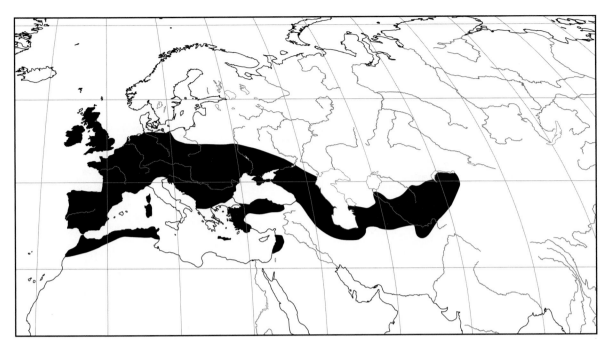

Fig. 8.35 Common pipistrelle *Pipistrellus pipistrellus*: world range.

MEASUREMENTS
Head and body length of both species 35–45 mm. Morphological and echolocation call parameters of the 2 species described in Table 8.15. Pregnant female pipistrelles (sp.?) may weigh up to 9.5 g [29]. Juvenile *P. pygmaeus* captured on exit from roost with forearm lengths as small as 28.1 mm, and mass as little as 3.4 g. Volant juvenile *P. pipistrellus* caught with forearm length of 29.4 mm, mass 3.4 g [1]. In Sweden, male pipistrelles (*P. pygmaeus*?) increase in mass over summer, then lose mass late July–late August when spend much time in songflight. Mass increases again towards hibernation [357]. For pipistrelles (sp.?), body mass lowest late April, highest September, linear mass loss over winter [29].

VARIATION
Colour variation extensive, with upper parts varying from orange-brown to very dark brown. Variation in colour may be greater in *P. pipistrellus* than *P. pygmaeus*. Average forearm lengths of females in maternity colonies varied from 31.5 to 32.8 mm in *P. pipistrellus*, 31.0 to 32.5 mm in *P. pygmaeus*, with neither latitude nor longitude affecting mean forearm length in GB for either species [49]. Variation in echolocation call frequency (FMAXE – see Table 8.15) among roosts of *P. pygmaeus* but not *P. pipistrellus*, though by far the most variation in call frequency in both species is among individuals within roosts [49]. Echolocation call frequency is not related to forearm length in females of either cryptic species [49, 296, 302]. In both cryptic species, males call at slightly higher frequencies than females, perhaps because males are on average smaller and echolocation call frequency scales inversely with body size [177, 406].

DISTRIBUTION
Now clear that both *P. pipistrellus* and *P. pygmaeus* occur across a wide geographic range throughout Europe (Figs. 8.35, 8.36). Largely overlap in

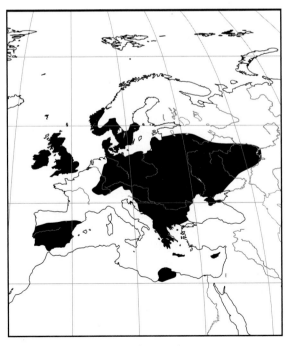

Fig. 8.36 Soprano pipistrelle *Pipistrellus pygmaeus*: world range.

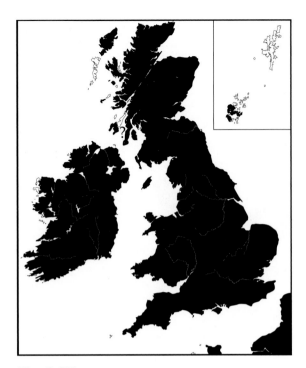

Fig. 8.37 Common pipistrelle *Pipistrellus pipistrellus*: range in British Isles.

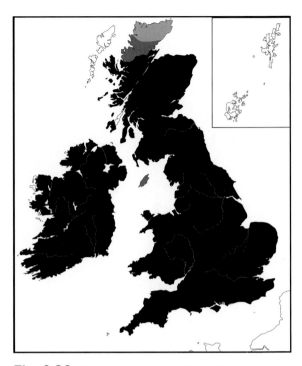

Fig. 8.38 Soprano pipistrelle *Pipistrellus pygmaeus*: range in British Isles.

distribution, although relative abundance varies locally. Both are widespread and abundant in N Ireland [514] and Switzerland [688]; more recently have been recorded in Germany [222, 367], Spain [367, 509]), Greece [367] and Italy [525]. Although *P. pipistrellus* is the most common species in C Europe it is rare or even absent in Scandinavia and the Netherlands and is less common than *P. pygmaeus* along the Mediterranean coast. The overall impression is that the middle latitudes of the range of these 2 species are dominated by *P. pipistrellus* with *P. pygmaeus* dominating in the outer margins. However, since the separation of these 2 species is still relatively recent, more evidence from mainland Europe is essential before firm conclusions can be drawn about their relative distribution. Both species are common throughout the British Isles, though one species may be rare or perhaps absent in particular regions (Figs. 8.37, 8.38). For example, most roosts in Yorkshire appear to be of *P. pipistrellus* [641]. Pipistrelles are generally found on Orkney but not on Shetland, where a probable vagrant occurred in 1974 [23]. They are also recorded on most of the Inner Hebrides, but only on Lewis in the Outer Hebrides.

HABITAT

Female pipistrelles (*P. pygmaeus?*) in Scotland fed mainly among riparian trees and in parkland. Travelled on average 1.8 km from roost when pregnant (maximum 5.1 km), and 1.3 km in lactation (maximum 3.7 km) [445]. Acoustic surveys carried out in SW England [652] and N Ireland [517] identified differential patterns of habitat use by the 2 species. *P. pygmaeus* foraged preferentially in habitats associated with water: rivers, lakes and riparian woodland. *P. pipistrellus* was widespread over broad range of habitat types including rivers and lakes, unimproved grassland, improved cattle pasture, coniferous plantations and mixed plantations. *P. pygmaeus* may be a riverine specialist and *P. pipistrellus* a more generalist forager. This pattern of habitat use recently corroborated by radiotelemetry studies carried out contemporaneously in England [123] and Scotland [388]. In both studies, *P. pygmaeus* foraging activity was highest over open water and adjacent riparian woodland. *P. pipistrellus* foraged over a broader range of habitat categories in England, although with a slight preference for deciduous woodland [123]. In Scotland, foraging activity of *P. pipistrellus* only limited by the distribution of linear landscape elements: foraging activity highest along woodland edge, both deciduous and coniferous, and along short isolated tree lines. However this pattern by no means consistent. In historic national parks in England [187], pattern reversed, *P. pipistrellus* feeding predominantly over water and *P. pygmaeus* selecting for treelines and semi-natural woodland. Similarly, several studies along R. Wharfe, Yorkshire Dales National Park, recorded higher incidence of *P. pipistrellus*, *P. pygmaeus* recorded in substantially smaller numbers [648, 663]. Both *P. pipistrellus* and *P. pygmaeus* less active along river stretches polluted by sewage outputs [653].

Pipistrelle roosts usually found in human habitations (Fig. 8.39), ranging from mediaeval churches to modern houses. Maternity roosts of *P. pygmaeus* in Scotland in buildings 13–750 years old [281]. May form maternity colonies in bat boxes (probably *P. pygmaeus* [177]. Tree roosts of pipistrelles rarely found. Usually roost out of sight in cracks or crevices, and often in cavity walls. Occasionally found in apex of roof. Rare in caves, though may occur occasionally at tunnels or mine entrances during autumn. Pipistrelles are the bat species found most frequently in churches and chapels [535]. Roost in crevices behind wooden beams in churches, behind noticeboards, and throughout church buildings, especially old ones. *P. pipistrellus* and *P. pygmaeus* maternity roosts have both been found in old and modern residential dwellings, amenity buildings, and churches. Maternity colonies of the 2 species occur in the same complex of buildings at 2 sites, but appear to use different parts of the buildings [124]. Maternity roosts often face S or SW, presumably chosen for warmth, may occur close to artificial sources of heat. *P. pygmaeus* does not appear to select roosts with particular structural features, though maternity roosts tend to occur close to tree cover, and with linear features leading from them. In Scotland, roosts of *P. pygmaeus* often surrounded by more deciduous and coniferous woodland than is in the area in general, and likely to be close to a major river [281]. Habitat around maternity roosts of *P. pygmaeus* in SW England includes more water (especially riparian habitats with woodland or

Fig. 8.39 Common pipistrelle, leaving a typical roost site beneath a broken tile *(photo F. Greenaway).*

hedgerow on banks), and linear features such as continuous hedgerow with emergent trees compared with random points in the same region [396]. Both species use bat boxes, especially during mating season. The 2 species have been found together under a window frame during hibernation [142].

SOCIAL ORGANISATION AND BEHAVIOUR

Although pipistrelles have been much studied in Europe, knowledge regarding similarities or differences in behaviour between the 2 cryptic species remains sparse. Almost certain that Swedish studies on behaviour [177–179, 181, 355–357] were of *P. pygmaeus*, whereas long-term studies in Yorkshire mainly *P. pipistrellus* [638–640].

In summer, females congregate in large maternity colonies to give birth and raise young. Maternity roosts of *P. pygmaeus* are typically larger (median = 203 bats before young fly in late May–early July, range 30–605, n = 40 roosts) than those of *P. pipistrellus* (median = 76, range 20–223, n = 33 roosts) [49]. *P. pygmaeus* maternity colonies often occupy the same site over the summer or even over years, whereas *P. pipistrellus* maternity colonies seem to move more frequently. Many *P. pygmaeus* appear to leave the nursery roost immediately before the peak birth time [666]. Males scarce in maternity roosts; those that occur mainly immature [29]. In winter, pipistrelles of different sex and age groups roost together in small groups; much time spent in torpor, with body temperature close to ambient temperature. Median temperature in a church hibernaculum was 3.4 °C [435]; bats started to arrive there in late November–early December [434]. *Pipistrellus* sp. hibernates in caves in continental Europe [335], but rare in caves in GB. Females may also become torpid in pregnancy and lactation when food scarce [443, 444].

Male pipistrelles may remain in churches throughout the year, joined by females during September–April [29]. Sometimes active in winter, especially when ambient temperature exceeds 8 °C and feeding on aerial insects is possible [26].

Individual male pipistrelles of both species occupy roost sites, often bat boxes [406] or sometimes under bridges [533] from early summer; are joined by up to 10 females during the autumn [178, 406]. Males defend these roosts against other adult males by advertising their presence to conspecifics with a songflight display at night [181, 357]. Mating system described as resource defence polygyny. Non-territorial males (*P. pygmaeus*?) may be excluded from roosts during the mating period, though they may try to sneak matings with females. Yearlings may occupy bat boxes with territorial males, which are usually older, and may eventually inherit their territory [356]. During mating period, male pipistrelles (both species) fly fixed routes and emit low-frequency (*c*.14–40 kHz) vocalisations that resemble the 'social calls' emitted during defence of feeding patches, though the repetition rate of songflight calls is higher [47]. Songflight calls differ between the 2 cryptic species, and are individually distinctive. Those of *P. pipistrellus* typically have 4 components (range 3–5) and a lower frequency; those of *P. pygmaeus* typically contain 3 components (range 2–4) and have a higher frequency [47]. Presumably these differences facilitate reproductive isolation between the cryptic species. A male (*P. pygmaeus*?) in Sweden that spent the most time in songflight was visited by the most females [357]. Female reproductive tract of *Pipistrellus* sp. is distended with semen during winter, female-produced plug blocks the vagina after copulation [439].

Mating groups contain only bats of 1 cryptic species. Composition of females in mating groups is dynamic, though females of *P. pipistrellus* may remain with the same male for at least 6 weeks in some cases, and same female has been found with a male in successive years. Number of females in mating groups averaged 1.2 in *P. pipistrellus*, 1.8 in *P. pygmaeus* [406]. Range is 1–10 females in mating groups (*P. pygmaeus*?), Sweden; yearling females join mating groups later in the year than older females [181].

Some continental populations of pipistrelles show sudden 'invasions' of roosts by up to 800 bats during August–September [334, 400]. Function of this behaviour unknown.

Both species produce audible vocalisations before evening emergence. First emergence usually *c*.20 min after sunset [29, 623]. Males typically emerge before females in mixed-sex roosts [27]. *P. pipistrellus* median emergence time 29 min after sunset during pregnancy (n = 3 roosts), *P. pygmaeus* 32 min after sunset (n = 7 roosts) during pregnancy, 20 mins after sunset during lactation (n = 3 roosts) [305]. *P. pygmaeus* exits from roosts in small groups or clusters [93, 584], and bats may coordinate the use of separate exit points to increase clustering [583]. Most recent analyses of clustering patterns in *P. pygmaeus* suggest that clustering reduced at large roosts and in the middle of emergences [584]. Both species commonly swarm around roost entrances in large numbers before returning to the roost shortly before dawn. Bats may follow each other in large numbers on circular flight paths, but function of this dawn 'swarming' behaviour remains unknown.

Females (*P. pipistrellus*?) strongly philopatric to maternity roosts, only 1.2% found away from their colony of origin over 8 years [640]. Of females that moved, most found within the 500 km² study area in Yorkshire; maximum distance moved to a new colony, 34 km [640]. Longest recorded movement of a pipistrelle in GB, 69 km [598]. Females (*P. pygmaeus*?) show strong philopatry in Sweden, with only 0.38% moving away from colony of origin; maximum distance moved to a new colony 30 km [355]. Bats (*P. pipistrellus*?) from a single 'colony' may occupy several roosts, with frequent splitting and rejoining of subcolonies [638]. Pipistrelles can home over distances of *c*.80 km within a week in Scotland [29] and up to at least 143 km in Germany [494]. Pipistrelles may be migratory in continental Europe; movement of 1150 km recorded between Russia and Bulgaria [613].

During pregnancy, females of both species leave the roost on average once per night, returning between midnight and dawn. After parturition, activity generally bimodal, females returning once during the night to suckle. However, activity of female *P. pygmaeus* in NE Scotland was more typically trimodal [388], females returning to the roost twice during the night. Once young weaned, gradual return to unimodal pattern, and on average bats make only a single flight per night.

Bats (*P. pygmaeus*?) at roosts in Scotland and England can spend 2.5–5 h outside the maternity roost in summer. Time spent away increased with air temperature [362]. However, from radio-tracking, individual *P. pipistrellus* during summer months spend approximately an hour longer outside the roost than *P. pygmaeus* [123, 388].

In NE Scotland, core foraging areas of *P. pipistrellus* were much further from the roost than those of *P. pygmaeus* (mean 1.44 km and 0.69 km respectively); consequently *P. pipistrellus* home ranges were approximately 3 times larger than those of *P. pygmaeus* [389]. However a similar study in England revealed *P. pygmaeus* foraging further from the roost than *P. pipistrellus* but found no significant difference in home range size [123]. Differences may reflect latitudinal differences between the 2 studies and predominant land classes under investigation.

Individuals of both cryptic species commonly recorded foraging at the same location, but foraging ranges of adjacent colonies of *P. pipistrellus* and *P. pygmaeus*, NE Scotland, were spatially segregated and core foraging areas of either species were mutually exclusive [389].

Pipistrelles often forage on regular flight paths, or 'beats', at foraging grounds. May move from one beat to another and back again during a night, may use the same foraging site from night to night

[445]. Agonistic encounters occur at low insect availabilities [445]. Both species produce social calls to defend foraging patches; resemble the songflight calls emitted by males, but emitted at lower repetition rates. Are emitted at a higher rate when insects scarce, and playbacks warn off bats of the same species, but have no obvious effect on the activity of the other cryptic species [48]. Distress calls sweeping down from 40 to 18 kHz produced by caged *P. pygmaeus* attract conspecifics, probably to mob predators [519]. Infant *P. pygmaeus* produce individually distinct isolation calls when separated from their mothers [302], these facilitate recognition of offspring by mothers [128]. In *P. pygmaeus*, infants >8 days of age may choose their mother's scent in preference to that of other females [128]. Adult female *P. pygmaeus* can recognise colony members by scent in laboratory conditions, prefer scent of females from their own colony to that of females from another colony [126].

Flight speed when foraging averages 6.3 m/s for *P. pipistrellus*, 4.2 m/s for *P. pygmaeus* [311], though *P. pygmaeus* may reach 7.4 m/s when leaving the roost [300]. Flight speed decreases during prey capture [311].

FEEDING

Pipistrelles in Scotland [631] and Ireland [621] eat mainly small nematoceran Diptera and Trichoptera (caddisflies), with some mayflies, lacewings and moths. Dipterans of the family Cecidomyiidae were mainly eaten in Kent during October–November [237]. 2 studies [237, 631] suggest that many aerial insect families are eaten in proportion to their abundance (Fig. 8.40). Main prey of *P. pipistrellus*, June–July, were Diptera: Pyschodidae, Anisopodidae and Muscidae (latter all yellow dung flies *Scathophaga stercoraria*) [45]. Main prey of *P. pygmaeus* were Chironomidae and Ceratopogonidae [45], and dietary differences between them may reflect the greater use of riparian habitats by *P. pygmaeus* [654]. No difference in average size of eyes from Diptera eaten by the 2 species [45]. Presence of more dung flies in diet of *P. pipistrellus* than *P. pygmaeus* may be because *P. pipistrellus* feeds more frequently over cattle pasture [654]. Feeding activity of *P. pipistrellus* was lower over pasture where cattle had been treated with the antihelminthic ivermectin than over pastures where cattle had not been treated [144], presumably because ivermectin reduces the abundance of dung fly larvae in cowpats [619].

Fig. 8.40 Soprano pipistrelle, catching geometrid moth in its tail pouch *(photo F. Greenaway)*.

Almost all prey captured on the wing with tail or wing membrane [311]. Feeding rates (measured by rate of feeding buzzes heard on bat detector) rise with increasing abundance of aerial insects, levelling off at 10 buzzes/min (exceptionally 20 buzzes/min over short time periods) when insects are abundant [445]. Feeding rate increases with ambient temperature in winter [26]. No sex differences apparent in feeding behaviour, but young are initially less efficient at flight (*P. pygmaeus* [249]) and prey capture [445] than adults. Echolocation calls of both species change during prey captures, but pipistrelles avoid overlap between prey echo and outgoing pulse until the end of the terminal phase of the feeding buzz. Detection occurs at 1.14–2.10 m within search cone of up to 150° relative to body axis [311].

BREEDING

Female pipistrelles can copulate in their 1st autumn whereas males do not undergo spermatogenesis until *c.*12 months old [436]. No difference in body condition of mature and immature yearlings (of *P. pygmaeus?*) in Sweden [181]. Pipistrelles copulate in spring [25], summer [178], autumn (earliest recorded inseminated female 23 September [439]) and possibly in winter. Most inseminations probably September–November. Sperm stored throughout winter until ovulation and fertilisation in April–May [434, 439]. Gestation *c.*44 days [129, 433] but depends on environmental conditions, partly as a consequence of females using torpor during pregnancy when insects are scarce [431, 433, 445]. Only a minority of female *Pipistrellus pipistrellus* became pregnant in each year of a long-term study [639]. However, because all parous females and 85% of nulliparous pipistrelles are inseminated [436], pregnancy rates may often be higher.

Pipistrelles give birth to single young (occasionally twins) as early as the 2nd week of June in S England, later in Scotland. Parturition of some females may extend into August, though 81% of births occurred within 6 days at 1 colony of *P. pygmaeus* in Scotland [666]. Young can fly at 3 weeks, though flight speed increases and wing-beat frequency decreases as young develop in *P. pygmaeus* [249]. Suckling restricted to own offspring in some studies of *P. pygmaeus* in captivity [74, 247], though allosuckling of relatively old infants observed in other captive studies [128, 147]. Whether allosuckling occurs in the wild unknown for either species.

In *P. pygmaeus*, infants first found apart from mothers at 4 days, eyes open at 4–6 days, and downy fur develops at 6–8 days in captivity. Growth curves (*Pipistrellus* sp. [85], *P. pygmaeus* [249] show mean mass of neonates 1.2–1.3 g,

forearm length *c.*11 mm [249]. Volant juveniles have darker pelage than adults.

POPULATION

Pre-breeding population of pipistrelles in GB estimated at 2 million, although validity of estimate low [215]. Bat detector surveys in SW England show *P. pipistrellus* and *P. pygmaeus* to be about equally abundant [654]. Estimated to have undergone substantial population declines, around 55%, since the 1960s [607]. Annual surveys of house roosts in 1987 revealed colonies to be 38% of the average size in 1978, with regional differences in colony size apparent [607]. However, population estimates and trends do not separate the 2 species, difficult to interpret historic trends accurately. Results of National Bat Monitoring Programme (NBMP) field survey reveal 63.5% increase in the British population of *P. pipistrellus* from 1998 to 2004. The same survey identified no significant change in the population of *P. pygmaeus* for the same time period; survey sequence too short, longer time series needed to confirm initial trends.

2 populations of pipistrelle (*P. pygmaeus?*), S Sweden, studied for 8 consecutive breeding seasons using bat boxes. One adjacent to intensively farmed area declined relative to the more rural site comprising substantial pine forests [177]. Bats in the intensively farmed area had higher levels of organochlorine residues and cadmium than rural bats, though proximate cause of decline may have been deteriorating feeding conditions caused by drainage and water pollution.

Sex ratios of weaned pipistrelles close to unity [591]. Long-term studies at maternity roosts, Yorkshire, (*P. pipistrellus?*) showed annual survival rate, females, 0.64/year. Survival in 1st year may be lower. 8 bats survived to at least 10 years, 7 bats to 11 years [639]. 1 in Czechoslovakia reached 16 years 7 months [251]. Survival and longevity of males little studied, but some live at least 5 years [29]. Mean survival rate of adult females (40–60%, average 54%) exceeded that of males (28–75%, average 44%) in Sweden (*P. pygmaeus?*) [179].

MORTALITY

Pipistrelles vulnerable to chlorinated hydrocarbons [280], particularly to organochlorine insecticides and some fungicides used for timber treatment [87, 446]. Organochlorine residues higher in adult males and juveniles than in adult females in Sweden (*P. pygmaeus?*) [177] and Germany [384], though in Spain (*P. pygmaeus?*) juveniles show higher amounts of residues than adults throughout the year [196]. Adult female *Pipistrellus* sp. have lower concentrations of organochlorine residues than suckling young [384]. Sublethal effects of these chemicals recently established in *P.*

pygmaeus [622]. Most highly toxic timber-treatment insecticides now withdrawn, and fungicides with high toxicity to mammals rarely used [377]. Can be injured by hooks used in fly-fishing [562]. Often killed by cats, especially around houses.

PARASITES AND PATHOGENS

Not known whether *P. pipistrellus* and *P. pygmaeus* host different parasite faunas, following refers to pipistrelles of unknown species.

Bug *Cimex pipistrelli* and flea *Ischnopsyllus octactenus* common; winter flea *Nycteridopsylla longiceps* found regularly [252]. Tick *Argas vespertilionis* recorded most commonly on ventral surface; present on minority of hosts but up to 57 recorded on one bat, and females more infested than males which may lose ticks as they age. At one maternity roost mean parasite load, including tick incidence, increased over spring [29]. Mites *Spinturnix acuminatus*, *Macronyssus kolenatii*, *M. uncinatus* (not preferred host), *Steatonyssus periblepharus*, *Pteracarus pipistrellia*, *Acanthophthirius etheldrae* and *Leptotrombidium russicum* [252]. Endoparasitic protozoans include *Trypanosoma incertum*, *T. dionisii*, *Babesia vesperuginis* and *Polychromophilus murinus* [37]. Blood parasites also include the bacterium *Grahamella* sp. [169].

RELATIONS WITH HUMANS

Pipistrelles are the bats most often found in and around human habitation. Maternity colonies often create problems with unsympathetic householders. Colonies of *P. pygmaeus* tend to be larger and more odorous than roosts of *P. pipistrellus*, potentially cause more problems.

PRINCIPAL AUTHORS

G. Jones & P.A. Racey, based on the account in the 3rd edition (pipistrelle sp.) by M.I. Avery; with acknowledgements to K.E. Barlow, C. Maier, B. Nicholls & M.J.A. Thompson.

Nathusius' pipistrelle *Pipistrellus nathusii*

Vespertilio nathusii Keyserling & Blasius, 1839; Germany.

RECOGNITION

Whole animal: Similar appearance to *P. pipistrellus* and *P. pygmaeus*, except slightly larger; ratio of 5th digit (not including the wrist) to forearm generally >1.25 (<1.25 for *P. pipistrellus* and *P. pygmaeus*); 3rd digit (including wrist) >60 mm; penis often has distinct fringe of white hairs [194, 597, 601]. Shaft of baculum curved concavely on dorsal side [235] (slightly convex in *P. pipistrellus* and *P. pygmaeus* [291]).

Skull and teeth: Condylobasal length 11.6–14.2 mm, mean 13.4 mm [195], upper tooth-row 4.4–5.0 mm [194]; canines noticeably narrow; length of lower canine (length of cingulum) $c.1/2$ width of anterior edge of crown; upper canine similarly with short cingulum length; i^3 nearly reaching height of i^2; i_3 well separated from i_2 [194]; p^3 large, fully in tooth-row and extending well above cingulum of the canine (Fig. 8.41) [609]. I^2 reaches beyond caudal cusp of i^1 in > 72% of skulls of *P. nathusii* (only 8% of *P. pipistrellus*) from Holland and Belgium [195]. Gap between i_2 and i_3 present in 84% of jaws of *P. nathusii* (only 21% of jaws of *P. pipistrellus*) [195].

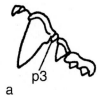 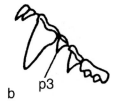

Fig. 8.41 Anterior teeth of (a) common/soprano pipistrelle and (b) Nathusius' pipistrelle. The p³ is relatively larger in Nathusius' pipistrelle, and the incisors are taller and slimmer (*after [609]*).

FIELD SIGNS

Faeces: Black, cylindrical, $c.7$ mm in length. Common under roosts.

Roosts: 4 known maternity roosts in British Isles all situated in walls of traditionally built buildings of stone or red brick, in wall cavities and under roof slates. Maternity roosts frequently shared with soprano pipistrelles. Individual males located in cracks in tree hollows, spaces in buildings such as under soffit boards, cracks between bricks and under plaster. One male roost in a building. Majority of summer and autumn roosts located close to large freshwater lakes. No winter roosts known. In Europe, summer roosts (maternity roosts) usually located in tree holes, bat boxes and cracks in tree trunks, but rarely in buildings. Winter roosts located in fissures in rocks, cracks in walls, caves, as well as tree holes [539].

DESCRIPTION

Small species; dorsal fur longer than for *P. pipistrellus* and *P. pygmaeus*, often giving a shaggy appearance, occasionally with pale frosted tips, otherwise mid-brown. Ventrally distinctly pale and well differentiated from upper fur. Juveniles dark brown, without grey tones. Ears medium rounded, slightly longer than broad; tragus with distinctly blunt rounded tip, $c.4$ times as long as broad,

Fig. 8.42 Nathusius' pipistrelle in flight, showing postcalcarial lobe characteristic of *Pipistrellus* *(photo F. Greenaway).*

curved forward. Calcar reaching about halfway to tail; distinct postcalcarial lobe present (Fig. 8.42). Thumb with claw equal to or greater than width of closed wrist. Face, ears and membranes generally dark, nose more prominent, less snub-nosed, than *P. pipistrellus*; dorsal surface of tail membrane well haired on basal half and beside tibia. Fur on underside of tail membrane, and sometimes extended obviously along forearm to wrist [194].

Chromosomes: 2n = 44, FNa = 48–50, European data [684].

RELATIONSHIPS
Analysis of a portion of the cytochrome *b* gene of

mtDNA suggested that *Pipistrellus nathusii* is less closely related to *P. pipistrellus* and *P. pygmaeus* than is *P. kuhlii* [52].

MEASUREMENTS
See Tables 8.16, 8.17. Body masses were higher in N Ireland because data were from pregnant females only.

DISTRIBUTION
Occurs across Europe E to Caucasus, population strongest in S Russia; more scattered but increasing in W (Fig. 8.43). Widely recorded throughout British Isles, but rare: 170 records of individuals found to 2006, ranging from North Sea

Table 8.16 Nathusius' pipistrelle: measurements of pregnant females in N Ireland [1]

	Mean	SD	n
Head and body length (mm)	51.3	4.31	18
Forearm length (mm)	34.51	1.14	20
3rd digit length (mm)	64.32	2.77	20
5th digit length (mm)	45.25	1.82	20
Ear length (mm)	12.31	1.19	19
Mass (g)	8.43	2.44	20

Table 8.17 Nathusius' pipistrelle: measurements from the British Isles. Data from [39, 96, 199, 233, 581, 582, 597, 680]

	Male			Female		
	Mean	SD	n	Mean	SD	n
Forearm length (mm)	33.95	0.79	11	35.70	0.82	17
5th digit length (mm)	43.36	1.21	11	44.66	1.61	13
Body mass (g)	6.28	0.79	6	6.37	0.94	4

oil platforms, Shetland and Orkney, Jersey and Guernsey, Isle of Wight, to GB and Ireland (Fig. 8.44) [521]. First recorded in GB, Whalsay, Shetland, 1940 [233]. Clusters of records in N Ireland, NE Scotland/North Sea oil platforms, S England probably result from concentrated sampling effort. Also 4 maternity roosts known: 2 in Co. Antrim, N Ireland [520, 521], 1 in Avon and 1 in Lincolnshire [268]. First occurrence in Ireland in 1996 [520]. Recent increase in records from British Isles reflects increased sampling effort, but possibly also range expansion [521].

HABITAT
In N Ireland, feeds in riparian habitats, broadleaved and mixed woodland and parkland. Occasionally found in farmland but nearly always near water; SW England, found over lakes and rivers [655]; Germany, hunts in wet deciduous woodland and over farmed land [308]; Netherlands, hunts mainly above water, but also seen in woodlands and along lines of trees in agricultural areas [318, 319].

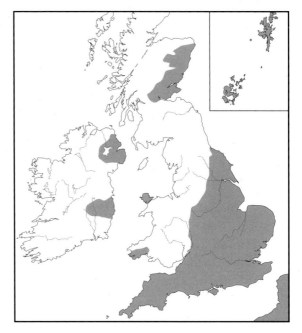

Fig. 8.44 Nathusius' pipistrelle *Pipistrellus nathusii*: range in British Isles.

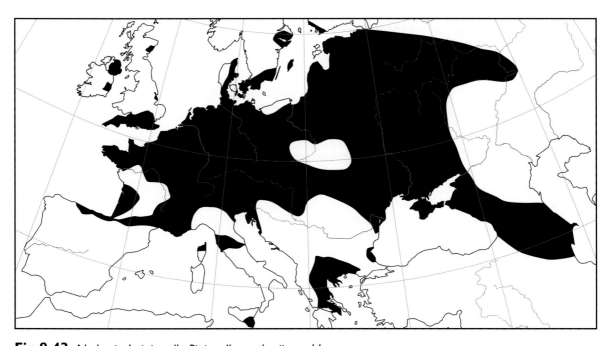

Fig 8.43 Nathusius' pipistrelle *Pipistrellus nathusii*: world range.

SOCIAL ORGANISATION AND BEHAVIOUR

Little known in British Isles, most information comes from Europe.

During summer, females form large maternity colonies where they give birth and raise their young [181]. Similar colonies found in British Isles [268, 520]. Occasionally, maternity colonies may temporarily move location [1]. During July–August, after weaning young, adult females join territorial males. Often there are many male roosts located close to the maternity roosts (often within 30 m). During autumn mating period, males defend roost sites to obtain harems [181, 320], spend a large proportion of their time emitting a complex vocalisation from a perch or roost site [181, 355] (in contrast to *P. pipistrellus* and *P. pygmaeus*, which emit their calls on the wing). In SW Poland, vocal activity is lowest April–June, begins to rise July, peaks in August–September [162]. Song structure different between individual males; *P. nathusii* are attracted to the song of conspecifics but not of congeners [518].

Males defend roost singly, July–end August, forming mating groups with females; maximum number of territorial males occurs August–early September [181]. During this time, adult females found within mating groups are gradually outnumbered by yearlings [181]. A mating group, Somerset, contained 1 male and 1 female [46], though average of 4.5 females more typical in Sweden [181]. In N Poland, distribution of *P. nathusii* harem sizes extremely right-skewed; majority of male roosts contain 0 (45%) or 1 (22%) female; only 13% had >2 females, to maximum of 9 in 1 roost [105]. Songflighting males have been recorded in both England and N Ireland [46, 520]. Some evidence that songflighting may also occur during spring [520]. Hibernation poorly studied. Records of grounded bats on British offshore islands indicate that some are active during winter.

Vocalisations: Echolocation calls are typically FM, sweeping from *c*.50 kHz to narrowband tails typically around 37 kHz (see Fig. 8.2). Frequency of most energy, in that tail, therefore lower than for *P. pipistrellus* and *P. pygmaeus*, and pulse repetition rate slower. *P. nathusii* also emits distinctive social calls [46]: main part of this call consists of 5–8 components, and lasts *c*.50 ms; then a brief FM sweep, followed by a 'trill' of 3–7 components, between 48 and 31 kHz. Trill lower in amplitude than main part of call, may be missed in some recordings. Social calls differ from those of *P. pipistrellus* and *P. pygmaeus* in containing more components in their main part, and in having the trill. Trill often followed by a series of FM elements, highly variable in duration and inter-element interval [518]. These often not recorded, 16 times less intense than the main call type. Social calls emitted at a low repetition rate in defence of feeding patches, and more regularly in the male advertisement display.

P. nathusii emit distress calls when under physical duress; consist of a high-intensity, downward FM sweep of short duration, usually repeated in rapid succession, with a strong harmonic content [523]. These calls attract congeners, which perform mobbing behaviour as an antipredator response [523].

Migration: In Europe, *P. nathusii* migrates during autumn and winter from its stronghold in NE Europe in a SW direction [8, 496, 613–615] to W–C Europe, returning to traditional breeding areas in E Europe during late spring [4, 279, 320, 349]. Bats ringed in N and E Germany, Latvia, Lithuania and Russia recaptured in France during winter [90, 537]. In SW Germany, resident population augmented during winter by migrating bats returning from summer sites in E Europe [22], as also in Switzerland and Austria [496], possibly the Netherlands [320, 349]. Hence, may be a transitional area in W–C Europe where migrating populations mix with resident populations.

Migration not well documented in the British Isles; some data suggest that *P. nathusii* migrates from Scandinavia in autumn, returns in spring [521, 581]. Peak numbers occur in September (Fig. 8.45), the time of peak migration in Europe. Likely that in GB, and especially Ireland, with milder winters, *P. nathusii* may have relinquished its migratory behaviour [520], but resident bats are augmented during winter by migrants from the NE [521].

ACTIVITY

First emergence around 18 min after sunset, median emergence *c*.27 min after sunset [1]. At 2 maternity roosts, N Ireland, males roost singly within 50 m of the maternity roost entrance. Social calls and chasing behaviour are evident, throughout the non-hibernation period, close to the maternity roosts. Males may call within close vicinity to each other [1].

FEEDING

Mainly feed on aquatic Diptera [652]. Remains of Chironomidae found in 100% of pellets [61, 62]. All prey probably caught by aerial hawking [311].

Foraging behaviour consist of 4 stages: search flight (before detection of prey), approach flight (pursuit after detection of prey), capture and retrieval of prey [311]. Unlikely that bats forage by flying through dense swarms of insects [311]. Flight speed averages 6.4–7.1 m/s [30, 311].

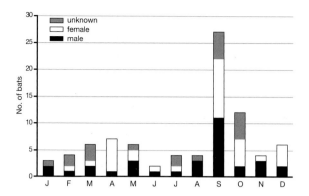

Fig 8.45 Nathusius' pipistrelle: seasonal occurrence in British Isles [521].

BREEDING

Females attain sexual maturity during their 1st autumn, aged *c*.3 months [181]. In Sweden, 8 males with unfused phalangeal epiphyses found with distended cauda epididymides, so had reached puberty during their season of birth. On same occasion, juvenile males (n = 8) with diminutive testes and black tunica vaginalis also found. Size of epididymides begins to increase end of July, peaks 1st week in September, then decreases. Males attract females to mating groups by defending roost sites [181, 228, 575, 576]. Main mating period, end July–end August [228, 576], prior to migration by both sexes, which completed by 2nd half of September [176, 419]. However, mating may possibly also occur during May, after hibernation [520]. In N Ireland, young are born after the 1st week in June [573].

During mating period, advertising males lose *c*.16% of their mass; regained after the 1st week in September. Mass of cauda epididymides increases during this period [181].

POPULATION

4 maternity roosts in the British Isles holding up to 200 individuals each. No population estimates exist for GB. Estimated N Ireland population 6317–18 579, based on bat detector surveys [515]. Presumably numbers in GB increase during late winter and decrease at the start of spring due to migration [521].

MORTALITY

No predation information for GB. In W Poland, remains of *P. nathusii* found in pellets of both barn owl (*Tyto alba*) and tawny owl (*Strix aluco*) [513].

PRINCIPAL AUTHORS

J.M. Russ, G. Jones, P.A. Racey & A.M. Hutson

Kuhl's pipistrelle *Pipistrellus kuhlii*
Vespertilio kuhlii Kuhl, 1817; Italy.

DESCRIPTION

Small pipistrelle, usually pale sandy-coloured dorsally, creamy- or grey-white ventrally, with white band along wing margin between 5th digit and ankle; i^2 large and unicuspid, i^3 very small and barely visible, p^2 very small, barely visible between c^1 and p^4 which are almost in contact. Might be confused with Savi's pipistrelle, but dentition of *P. kuhlii* is characteristic.

Chromosomes: 2n = 44, NFa = 50.

Measurements: Head and body 40–50 mm, forearm 31–36 mm, wingspan 210–250 mm, ear length 10–14 mm, tail 30–40 mm, weight 5–10 g; condylobasal length 12–13.2 mm, c–m³ 4.7–5.4 mm.

DISTRIBUTION

In Europe, generally southern (Mediterranean) species to *c*.45° N, but expanding northwards and more recently recorded to 50° N in France and Ukraine [489]. Wide non-European distribution in Africa and Asia, although populations in the African part of the range may be a separate species, *P. hesperidus* (tropical Africa) which probably includes *P. deserti* (parts of North Africa).

In British Isles, not recorded until 2 in October 1991: Felixstowe Docks, Suffolk, perhaps accidental, and Jersey, Channel Isles. Since then, 6 records in England, 3 perhaps natural and 3 accidental: adult female, St Leonards, Sussex, August 1992; St Blazey, Cornwall, April 1994; Waterlooville, Hampshire (emerged from luggage of holidaymaker on return from Cyprus), October 1994; Shropshire, September 1995, in container shipped from France; a female, Southampton Docks, Hampshire, April 1996, found on board ship from Rotterdam; a female, Appley, Ryde, Isle of Wight, August 2002 [1, 234, 260, 263, 264, 266, 267].

Also recurred Channel Isles, and breeding there. Adult female, Guernsey, May 2003; low-density but widespread, Jersey, from bat detector survey, and one maternity colony discovered [361].

HABITATS/HABITS

Relatively abundant species in Mediterranean region and Middle East. Forages over variety of habitats, including disturbed agricultural and urban (including around street lights) [79]. Feeds on small insects, including Diptera, Psocoptera, Coleoptera. Summer maternity colonies in crevices in buildings; colonies normally 30–100. Winter sites include rock crevices and cellars. Altitude to 2000 m asl, but generally lower. Probably sedentary [276].

AUTHOR

A.M. Hutson

GENUS *Hypsugo*

Old World genus of *c*.18 species, recently separated from *Pipistrellus*, initially as subgenus [235], now as genus [242, 674].

Savi's pipistrelle *Hypsugo savii*
Vespertilio savii Bonaparte, 1837; Italy.

DESCRIPTION

Ears relatively short and broad, tragus broadening towards apex and almost as broad at widest point as long. Ears and face black-brown, flight membranes also dark. Dorsal fur relatively long, variable in colour from yellow- or gold-brown to dark brown but usually retaining gold tips. Ventral fur pale, more or less white, distinctly contrasting with upper fur. Narrow postcalcarial lobe, last 1–2 vertebrae of tail extending beyond membrane by 3–5 mm.

Dental formula 2.1.2.3/3.1.2.3. Inner upper incisor with 2 cusps, 1st (small) premolar not visible from outside, very small and sometimes absent, upper canine and large premolar more or less in contact.

May be confused with *E. nilssonii*, which larger, has widest point of tragus near base.

Chromosomes: 2n = 44, NF = 50 [242].

Measurements: Head and body 40–54 mm; tail 34–44 mm; forearm 32–37.5 mm; wingspan 220–225 mm; ear length 11.5–16 mm; condylobasal length 11.9–14.0 mm; c–m^3 4.6–4.8 mm; weight 4.5–9.0 g.

DISTRIBUTION

Generally S Europe/Mediterranean area, north to *c*.45° N (extending to 48° N in E France, Switzerland and Czech Republic), east to Kyrgyzstan and Tajikistan, south to North Africa, Middle East, North India, Burma. Canary and Cape Verde islands. Possibly expanding northwards in Europe [587].

First UK record, a juvenile male, clearly an import, emerged from a punnet of nectarines imported from Italy, bought in a supermarket in Wick, Caithness, Scotland, July 1990. Apparent natural occurrence: female found on S coast at Pevensey Bay, near Eastbourne, East Sussex, January 1993; found exhausted, subsequently died [262]. Further record, one rescued from a cat at a house in Wallasey, Wirral, Merseyside, February 1996 [158]. Unsubstantiated additional records from Jersey and UK [158].

HABITATS/HABITS

Rocky areas where forages over open woodland, pasture and wetland. Also feeds at lights. Often in towns and cities. Roosts in rock crevices, occasionally buildings, under bark, rarely in underground habitats. Summer maternity colonies usually 20–70 individuals. Generally low density, but abundant in some Mediterranean areas. Altitude to 2600 m asl. Quoted movements of up to 250 km appear to be without foundation [276].

AUTHOR
A.M. Hutson

GENUS *Eptesicus*

A genus of *c*.20 species, distributed throughout the Palaearctic, the Americas and parts of Africa and S Asia. Very closely related to *Pipistrellus*, with similar short, blunt tragus, but generally larger and has short, broad baculum [235, 674]. Dentition 2.1.1.3/3.1.2.3, differs from *Pipistrellus* by loss of p^3 (Fig. 8.3). 2 species in Europe, serotine *E. serotinus*, found in S–C Europe including England, and northern bat *E. nilssonii*, found in C–N Europe. Latter not highly migratory but has recently been reported in GB. A 3rd species, *E. bottae*, is recorded from Greece (Rhodes) and further east.

The N and C American *E. fuscus* (big brown bat) has been recorded in UK [1] and elsewhere in Europe [656], following accidental transport by ship or aircraft (see below, p. 375).

Serotine *Eptesicus serotinus*
Vespertilio serotinus Schreber, 1774; France.

RECOGNITION

Large, robust, dark brown bat (Fig. 8.46), with slight postcalcarial lobe, blunt-tipped tragus just under 1/2 height of ear, tail extending beyond margin of interfemoral membrane and conspicuously large teeth (Fig. 8.46). Leisurely flapping flight of deep wing-beats on broad wings, up to a height of 30 m. Free tip of tail sometimes visible; occasional short glides or steep descents. Forages in open pasture or in open parkland and gardens, around tree canopies and open spaces. Often flies low and sometimes takes insects from the ground.

SIGNS

Faeces often abundant in breeding roosts in buildings, at gable ends or around base of chimney, but some traditional breeding sites may exhibit few droppings. Faeces 3.5–4.0 × 8–11 mm, blunt-

356

ended, more oval longitudinal section than in other large bats. Fresh droppings always black and glistening, quite coarse. Usually a few droppings outside the point of access, which is otherwise not well marked.

Frequently very active chattering at roost entrance for up to 30 min before emergence. Sometimes audible during the day, including occasional short, very loud penetrating squeaks.

DESCRIPTION
Ears about twice as long as wide. Tragus blunt-tipped, <1/2 height of conch, widest at *c*.1/3 of its length, apical half more or less parallel-sided but slightly curved anteriorly (Plate 6). Muzzle distinctly bulbous. Wings broad, membranes thick and opaque. Postcalcarial lobe long but narrow and ill defined. Last and part of penultimate caudal vertebrae free from interfemoral membrane, giving *c*.6 mm of free tail.

Pelage: Upper parts with long dark brown hair, sometimes tinged slightly purple (plum coloured) or chestnut, often with paler tips. Underparts paler but no clear demarcation. Face, ears and flight membranes very dark brown-black. Distinct glandular swellings on muzzle; gland under chin. Juveniles are very dark brown.

Teeth: Dental formula: 2.1.1.3/3.1.2.3 (fewer premolars than any other British bat); outer incisor distinctly >1/2 height of inner; canines and upper premolar (p^4) conspicuously large (Fig. 8.3); m^3 much reduced; p_3 small, less that 1/2 crown area of p_4.

Baculum: Short and triangular, with proximal notch.

Chromosomes: $2n = 50$, $Fna = 48–50$ [684].

MEASUREMENTS
Head and body 58–80 mm; tail 34–65 mm, tail beyond membranes 5–8 mm; forearm 48–55 mm; wingspan 320–380 mm; ear length 14–21 mm; condylobasal length 19–22 mm; c–m^3 7.4–8.2 mm; weight 15–35 g (adult, summer, non-pregnant *c*.20–24 g).

VARIATION
British populations not distinguishable from European and no variation has been recognised within British range.

DISTRIBUTION
Palaearctic between *c*.58° and 30° N in west; east to China (Fig. 8.47) [31, 381]. Recent expansion in Denmark suggested [35], but later considered a

longer-term change [32]; first recorded Sweden 1982 [9].

In GB, main range in SE England, Dorset to Suffolk; recent records from Wales (Fig. 8.48) [374], C and NW England, and increase in records from Norfolk and SW England, suggest expansion [474, 660].

HISTORY
Eptesicus known from Europe, Early Pleistocene, and *E. serotinus* from Mid Pleistocene. Known from Lower/Mid Pleistocene, Westbury, Somerset [119]. No Late Glacial or Postglacial history in British Isles; perhaps a late coloniser, after creation of farmland.

HABITAT
Mainly in lowland open flat country of pasture, parkland and woodland edge or hedgerow.

Fig. 8.46 Serotine in the hand; current advice is to handle all bats wearing gloves, but the temperament and large size of the serotine has always made that advisable *(photo F. Greenaway)*.

Roosts: Mainly in buildings, frequently in those constructed around 1900 with high gable end and cavities in walls. Rarely in modern houses, often in older buildings. Access usually 6–8 m or higher, at or near gable apex or from lower eaves. Roost in crevices around chimneys, in cavity walls, between felt/boarding and tiles/slates, sometimes in open roof space at ridge ends or occasionally elsewhere along ridge. Individuals or small colonies have been found irregularly behind window shutters [241, 386]. Occasionally in tree hollows [206, 386] and in bird and bat boxes in summer [183].

SOCIAL ORGANISING AND BEHAVIOUR

Summer: Some species of *Eptesicus* have a harem structure throughout the breeding season; this has not been recorded in *E. serotinus*. Colonies usually number 15–30, occasionally up to 60 (exceptionally >100, to 300); (3 estimates of mean size, 18.4, 19.6, 21.4 [59, 378, 608]. Males probably solitary or in small groups (e.g. in older buildings, especially churches); occasionally with females in spring and autumn [38].

Activity starts around mid-April. Bats emerge early in evening, especially at the beginning of the season [99, 130, 150]. Often much active squeaking before emergence. Main emergence within 10 min, total emergence never >40 min. Flight at emergence often directly towards feeding ground at about treetop level (to *c*.30 m), sometimes very low along lee of hedges, etc. Early in the season bats return to roost *c*.30–40 min after emergence. As season progresses, more time spent away from roost, some passage of bats in and out

of roost at all times of night and secondary peak of activity around dawn (often returning well after first light) [99]. On return to roost, single bats may enter without pause; others, particularly if several bats are returning at about the same time, circle around the roost entrance for several minutes (swarming) before entering. Activity patterns differ in different parts of England [486].

Roost building often shared with pipistrelles and/or long-eared bats [1]. Has associated with

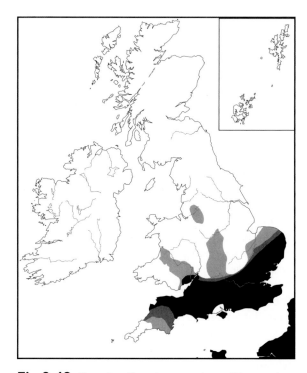

Fig 8.48 Serotine *Eptesicus serotinus*: GB range.

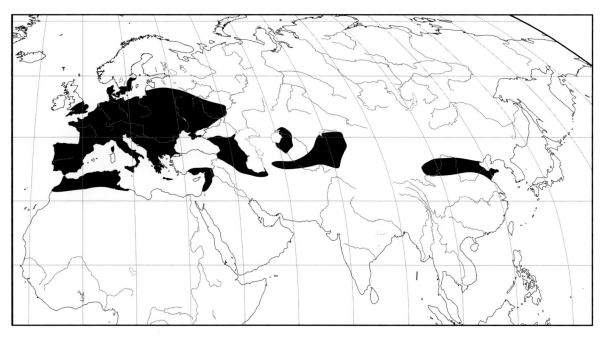

Fig 8.47 Serotine *Eptesicus serotinus*: world range.

Natterer's [1] and shared access with noctules when this species present in a building until late May [38].

Colony structure, roost use, activity, food and foraging also studied elsewhere in Europe [31, 59, 207, 323, 560].

Results from DNA analysis support ringing studies in showing that maternity colonies generally discrete entities; regional differences in structure can be identified, but slight over wide areas of the distribution [24, 172, 310, 560].

Winter: Frequently hibernate in buildings, occasionally in caves, dungeons and cellars, particularly in E Europe [120, 183, 613]. In caves, usually singly and close to entrance, but in European Russia recorded at 22 of 91 cave sites (17 with <10 individuals; 4 with 10–50; 1 with 50–100) [613]. Only twice recorded from caves in British Isles [594]. A hardy species [224], preferring temperatures of 5–11 °C in autumn and 0.5–6 °C in winter [210]. Tolerant of dry air [613]. Relatively sedentary in winter, but occasionally hunt on warm winter days [209].

Movement: Generally regarded as a sedentary, non-migratory, species, with local movements of up to 50 km [32, 276], but movements of up to 330 km [224, 613], 201 km [610] and 145 km [642] have been recorded in Europe. The latter (one of only 20 ringed) moved NW between July 1954 and August 1955. Supposed that these are longer range 'dispersal movements' [276], may account for observations of serotines flying straight and purposefully at 90 m in Surrey [206]. Of *c*.600 ringed in Sussex and Kent, no recovery >10 km from the ringing site [1].

Echolocation calls: A frequency sweep from 60 to 25 kHz; longer cries are produced by extending the lower frequency, and a V-shaped sweep is often used when circling outside roost during mating season [31, 375].

Most identifiable at *c*.28 kHz. Most typical call in cruising flight is a simple 'tock-tock-tock' (as heard through bat detector) at *c*.4–5 pulses/s. Occasionally when cruising in the open, call slightly extended into a short 'whip-like' sound reminiscent of but much shorter than noctule. Identifiable feeding buzzes relatively few, extremely short.

FEEDING

Fly around trees, particularly the canopy, very close to and often touching the vegetation. In open pasture etc., often fly very close to the ground or up to *c*.10 m, with sudden steep dives. Slow and highly manoeuvrable in flight. Often feed along roads and around street lights. Cooler weather limits feeding activity more than with noctule [115]. Occasionally feed well within beech woods [375].

Feed mainly on large beetles, e.g. *Aphodius*, Melolonthinae, *Nicrophorus* and larger moths [652]. Many flies (Diptera, Nematocera) eaten, particularly early in the season [99, 342]. Also in England, a range of smaller, more delicate prey taken early in the year [1]. Lepidoptera were the 2nd most frequent prey item in one study [485]. In all studies, dung beetles (and other dung fauna) are of major importance [271]. Prey taken on wing, occasionally from the ground [137] and probably directly from vegetation. Ingestion occurs in flight, discarding legs and wings of moths and elytra of larger beetles. Feeding perches unrecorded.

Commuted on average 6.5 km to and from foraging sites, used up to 5 sites per night [101] in a predominantly woodland and pasture area. Would exploit temporary sites, such as recently mown areas or areas occupied by cattle, and white street lights. Foraging range notably higher in mainly arable areas [487].

BREEDING

Mating recorded (in captivity) in September and October (occasionally later). 3 captive males and 1 female showed no sexual activity in 1st autumn, but yearling males developed enlarged testes and epididymides, and mating occurred in the 2nd autumn at *c*.15 months. Mating can be protracted, recorded coition lasting for several hours, even during torpor [326, 442]. Mating strategy in the wild unknown.

Nursery colonies start to build up in May, with numbers very stable in some (mainly smaller) colonies from late May; other colonies rather variable in number throughout season. Maternity colonies usually show a high level of site fidelity [101], but some frequently change roosts during breeding season. Roost switching may be more common in colonies using more modern buildings or larger building complexes [1, 560].

The number of nulliparous individuals in breeding colonies is low, suggesting maturation in the 1st year; the number of non-breeding females in breeding colonies is also low, suggesting regular parturition, but samples are small. Despite high level of parturition at breeding colonies, up to 80% [183], relatively small increase of colony size (±30%) follows weaning of young. Juvenile mortality up to 30%, mostly in 1st week [183, 208]; mortality often associated with inclement weather. Nothing known of post-weaning mortality.

Females can increase weight by nearly 60% in pregnancy [326]. Single young born at *c*.5 g in early July (mid-June in Netherlands and

Germany) [183, 208]. Occasional births as late as mid-August [1]. Sex ratio at birth is 1:1 [224]. Infants possibly carried by mother for first few days [1, 114]. Young fly at 4–5 weeks. Suckling discouraged at 5–6 weeks (at *c.*16 g weight), but may be maintained for 2 months [114, 326]. Development and behaviour of juvenile described from a captive animal in Germany [470]. Juvenile epiphyses fuse at 50–70 days [326]. Adults begin to leave colony as soon as young become volant, early August [1]; mother–young bond lasts only a day or two once the young flying [353]. Most of colony disperses by early September, but some bats continue to be active at breeding roosts (or return to maternity colony sites) until early October.

Maternity sites may be used for communal night roosting outside the maternity season [354] and small groups will collect at winter swarming sites (e.g. in a church [1]); not known if any of these activities related to mating.

POPULATION

Sharp population declines were recorded in Germany [492, 493] and GB [607]; average colony size declined 15% in 10 years in the Netherlands [183, 186], though overall populations recorded as unaffected during last 20 years [121, 185]. Data scarce and conflicting, but GB and other European populations thought to be currently stable [59, 607].

Away from Kent, Surrey, Sussex and Hampshire, few recorded roosts. Of *c.*50 known roost sites in Sussex, only *c.*15 are thought likely to be regular breeding sites, but the species appears to be widespread [1]. Colonies not large (see above), so overall density likely to be low. Apparent range extension not associated with obvious increase in density in main range. Several colonies known to be very well established, with a history of up to 70 years, but many sites show evidence that once present with no evidence of recent occupation. Insect diet similar to other large bats supposed to be declining, noctule and greater horseshoe, and serotine seems more dependent on occupied buildings than either of them. If it is expanding its range, reasons suggested for decline of these other large species, e.g. reduction of large beetles, loss of roost sites, use of highly toxic timber treatment chemicals, may be questioned. However, the number of abandoned sites within its well established range suggest a local decline similar to theirs. No clear evidence. Certainly large bats believed to be this species are still widespread and relatively common in Kent, Sussex, and possibly Essex.

GB population estimated at 15 000 (England 14 500, Wales 500) [215], but possibly underestimated [59].

MORTALITY

One of the species more frequently taken by owls [208, 338, 671]; no regular predators known.

2 Sussex individuals have been recovered at 16 years [1]; longest recorded survivals to 19 years [205] and 21 years [450].

PARASITES

Flea *Ischnopsyllus intermedius* regular and common [174, 568]. Bug *Cimex pipistrelli* occasionally found in the roost [1]. Tick *Argas vespertilionis* rarely associated with this species [1] but a number of other acarines are commonly found including *Spinturnix kolenatii, Steatonyssus occidentalis* (and *nyassae*), and *Ornithonyssus pipistrelli* [36]. Laelapidae, other Macronyssidae, Trombiculidae and various sarcoptiform mites have also been found on the continent [157, 344].

2 rabies-related viruses reported from bats in Europe: EBLV1 and EBLV2 [160, 216, 273, 351, 383]. Both have caused isolated human fatalities; EBLV1 recorded, rarely, in species other than bats. Of >800 recorded cases of EBLV in bats in Europe, all but *c.*20 are of EBLV1, and >95% of these in serotine. This virus widely distributed; most frequently recorded in Denmark, N Germany and Netherlands where long-term surveillance established [428]. EBLV1 not found so far in British bats, despite extensive surveillance [217] and proximity to positive cases across the English Channel and North Sea.

RELATIONS WITH HUMANS

In GB, appears to be dependent on buildings.

AUTHOR

A.M. Hutson

Northern bat *Eptesicus nilssonii*

Vespertilio nilssonii Keyserling & Blasius, 1839; Sweden.

DESCRIPTION

Smaller than *E. serotinus*, with dark golden-tipped dorsal fur, well-demarcated from somewhat yellow-brown ventral fur especially around throat (Plate 6); tragus broadest about middle, post-calcarial lobe narrow. Single upper premolar in contact with canine, i^2 >1/2 height of i^3, m^3 reduced. Similar to Savi's pipistrelle (which is smaller, has tragus broadest towards tip, under fur paler). Particoloured bat has broadly blunt tragus, silver-tipped upper fur, white underside.

Chromosomes: 2n = 50, NFa = 48.

Measurements: Head and body 54.5–63.5 mm,

forearm 38–43 mm, wingspan 240–280 mm, ear length 13–17 mm, tail 35–40 mm, tail beyond membrane by 3–5 mm, weight 8–17 g; condylobasal length 14–15.5 mm, c–m³ 5–5.8 mm [180].

DISTRIBUTION

Across Palaearctic, from N Europe E to Pacific seaboard and N Japan. In Europe, N to above Arctic Circle; absent or occasional in W (Netherlands, Belgium, UK, W France, Iberia), scarce in mountains of S Europe. Small isolated population in Caucasus. Widespread and relatively common in northern areas of distribution [381].

Only 4 UK records, 2 presumed natural: 1 found hibernating, Betchworth, Surrey, January 1987 [192, 193], 1 on North Sea oil platform, August 1996 [268]; 2 likely accidental imports: Tyneport, Tyne & Wear, September 1993, off a ship (from Europe?); Barwell, Leicestershire, May 1995, pregnant immature female, from lorry from Bergamo, Italy, via Belgium [265].

HABITATS/HABITS

Forages in open areas of diverse habitats, including woodland edge (or above woodland), small-scale farmland, over lakes and rivers and at street lights. Diet small insects, such as Diptera. Summer roosts mainly in houses, occasionally tree holes. May change roost sites during summer. Summer maternity colonies usually 10–100. Winter roosts mainly in houses, cellars, underground habitats, singly or in small groups (2–4). Altitude to 2300 m asl. Generally considered sedentary, but longer-range movements, to 450 km, recorded [276].

AUTHOR
A.M. Hutson

GENUS *Vespertilio*

A genus of 1 widespread Palaearctic species, which occurs as a vagrant in GB, and 2 species in E Asia. Similar to *Eptesicus* but ears short and square, more like *Nyctalus*. Dental formula 2.1.1.3/3.1.2.3. Generally found in hollow trees and in buildings, occasionally in caves. Rare throughout their range and therefore little known.

Particoloured bat *Vespertilio murinus*

Vespertilio murinus Linnaeus,1758; Sweden (in the 19th century, this name erroneously but widely used for *Myotis myotis*).
Vespertilio discolor Natterer, 1819.

DESCRIPTION

Middle-sized bat with short, broad, rounded ears; tragus short, broadest towards tip; dorsal fur long, dark brown or black towards base and with silvery tips, giving frosted appearance; contrasts strongly with bright creamy white underside; skin very dark brown; ears short, slightly wider than high; tragus short and bean-shaped, concave along anterior margin and strongly convex posteriorly (Plate 6). Wings narrow and pointed. Unusually for vespertilionid, 2 pairs of nipples; penis elongate. Calcar extending about halfway to tail, postcalcarial lobe distinct. i^2 <1/2 height of i^1, p_1 very much smaller than p_2, m^3 not compressed (3-lobed). Might be confused with northern bat (which has different tragus, gold-tipped dorsal fur, 1 pair of nipples or broad short blunt penis, i^2 >1/2 height of i^1).

Chromosomes: 2n = 38, NFa = 50.

Measurements: Head and body 48–64 mm, forearm 40–50 mm (mean 44.5 mm for males, n = 17 [3], wingspan 260–330 mm, ear length 12–18 mm, tail 37–45 mm, tail beyond membrane 3–5 mm, weight 11–24 g; condylobasal length 13.9–15.8 mm, c–m³ 4.9–6.2 mm.

DISTRIBUTION

Mainly northern distribution, from 50° N to 60° N in Europe; extending south to c.45°N in Alps, further south in Balkans, Greece, W Russia, Middle East. Ranges E from Norway, Germany to Pacific seaboard. Rare W of c.5° E, scattered records from Netherlands, France, British Isles and many S European records likely to be migrants or vagrants.

Occasional but increasing in British Isles: only 4 records to 1980, but 16 since, almost annual since 2000. Found at Plymouth and Yarmouth in early 19th century [56]. Shetland: at Whalsay, March 1927 [479], Lerwick, September 1981, Mid Yell, September 1984 [416], and November 2001 [1]. In S and E England: Cambridge, November 1985; Essex, Ilford, October 1994, and Colchester, June 1996; E Yorkshire, Hornsea, March 2002; Isle of Wight, Ryde, May 2001 and Freshwater, April 2006 ; Sussex, Brighton, March 1986, Mayfield, May 2001, and Eastbourne July 2005; Wiltshire, Savernake Forest, May 2002 [1, 17, 138, 257, 265, 266].

Also in North Sea, on ships or oil rigs: 270 km E of Berwick, June 1965 [589]; 190 km ENE of Fraserburgh (Forties Charlie oil rig), July 1992; 256 km E of Newcastle, November 2001; 128 km E of Aberdeen, December 2001; Ocean Nomad oil rig, January 2002; and 64 km NE of Fraserburgh, November 2004.

A migratory species with recorded movements

of 360, 800 and 850 km [613–616], maximum of 1780 km [276]. Predominance of autumn and spring records suggest that migrants sometimes deflected towards GB, but enough summer records to suggest may colonise [17].

HABITATS/HABITS

Widespread and abundant species, particularly in northern parts of range. Forages in open areas over various habitat types (forest, urban, steppe, agricultural land), including around street lights in towns [33, 530]. Feeds on moths and beetles. Summer roosts mostly in houses or other buildings; also rarely hollow trees, nest boxes, rock crevices. Maternity colonies 30–50 (–100); males may also form large colonies in summer. Males have characteristic autumn songflight. Winter roosts in rock fissures, often (as substitute) in tall buildings (especially in cities), occasionally tree holes, cellars. Usually in colder sites exposed to temperature changes, singly or in small groups (but up to 30 recorded). Altitude to >1900 m asl.

AUTHORS

P.A. Racey, I.J. Mackie & A.M. Hutson

GENUS *Barbastella*

A small Palaearctic genus of only 2 species, the more northern *B. barbastellus* which occurs in Europe, including GB, and the more easterly *B. leucomelas*. Related to *Plecotus*; ears similarly joined at base across head, but much shorter, distinctive triangular shape.

Barbastelle *Barbastella barbastellus*
Vespertilio barbastellus Schreber, 1774; France.

RECOGNITION

Short broad, black angular ears joined across the forehead and almost black colour distinguish this from all other British species (Plate 6).

DESCRIPTION

A medium-sized species. Dorsal fur almost black and glossy, with creamy or golden tips; extends on to wing, tail and back of ear; ventral fur dark grey brown. Juveniles similar but brighter. Face squat and pug-like (Fig. 8.49). Face, ears and membranes very dark brownish black; ears almost meet over the top of the head and are connected by a small flap of skin; a lobe occasionally present on the rear ear margin. Tragus very broad near the base, with a fine parallel-sided tip; *c*.1/2 height of ear. Hind feet very small. Tail membrane broad, with calcar reaching rather less than halfway to the tail; small postcalcarial lobe; tail protrudes slightly beyond membrane. Wings broad and pointed, membrane reaches down to base of 1st toe [194].

Chromosomes: 2n = 32, FNa = 50–52, European data [684]

VARIATION

Rare white, partially white and golden-brown examples recorded [56].

MEASUREMENTS

Head and body 40–52 mm, forearm 35–43 mm, wingspan 245–280 mm, ear 12–18 mm, condylobasal length 12.9–13.8 mm, weight 6–13 g [194]. Males smaller than females: mean forearm lengths, GB, males 38.5 mm (n = 11), females 39.5 mm (n = 14) [1].

DISTRIBUTION

Restricted to Europe, from Iberia and Italy N to S Scandinavia, E to Caucasus (Fig 8.50). In British Isles, probably restricted to England and Wales, S of line between Humber and Dovey (Fig 8.51).

HISTORY

Known from ?Lower Pleistocene (*B.* cf. *barbastellus*), Middle and Upper Pleistocene, Hungary, Romania, Czechoslovakia [278, 531]. In GB, from Middle Pleistocene, Westbury [75, 119] and Aveley, Essex [544]; also Late Pleistocene, Pin Hole Cave, Derbyshire [282]. Recorded N to Cumbria, Durham, Anglesey before 1970 [23, 56] but recent records more southerly.

HABITAT

Prefers largely wooded riverine habitats with plenty of connecting features. Can exist in more open environments, will cross extensive open areas to reach suitable foraging habitat. Old woodland with abundance of dead trees, complex understorey, much preferred [191]. In Italy, unmanaged beechwood preferred over harvested/shelterwood areas, and those over wood-pasture [526].

BEHAVIOUR

Little known until 1997 when nursery roosts discovered in Norfolk and Sussex.

In prime habitat, S England, summer roosts almost exclusively in trees, often within ancient woodland; either behind loose bark, for individuals, or in vertical cracks in dead stumps and broken branches, for nursery roosts [191]; in Italy, favour large, dead, beech *Fagus sylvatica* [526]. Maternity colonies small, <30 females; males usually solitary during summer. Roosts, including

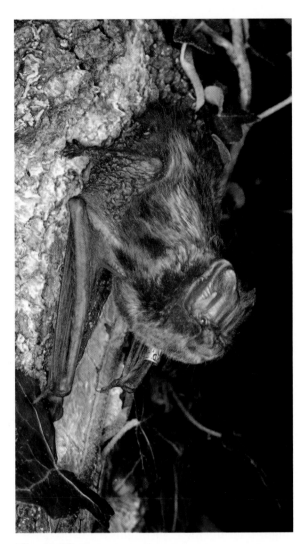

Fig. 8.49 Barbastelle about to leave its roost tree. Note numbered ring on left forearm (*photo F. Greenaway*).

nursery roosts, move frequently but are loyal to a general area [1, 527]. In areas with less wooded habitat, nursery roosts recorded from barns and similar buildings [190, 213]. Trees also utilised in mid-winter when massive hollow or cracked trunks are used; unheated structures such as barns, churches, tunnels, mines and grottoes may also be used [1]. Severe cold produces a slight increase in records from such sites. Temperatures down to 0 °C or lower are tolerated; preference for *c.*4.5 °C [210]. Hibernation conditions often similar to and shared by pipistrelle species [1, 649]. Rarely, very small clusters composed largely of males found in hibernation. Males solitary for most of year, appear in small numbers at underground sites during summer [412]. In E Europe, large numbers, 100s–1000s, gather in suitable cave/mine hibernacula [531]; much rarer in W Europe, never in large numbers. Recorded movements up to 145 km (Germany), 180 km (Czechoslovakia), 290 km (Austria–Hungary) [531], presumed more sedentary in England.

FEEDING

Heavily reliant on small moths (>99% of diet) throughout the year [1, 558], though diet more diverse in winter when also eat flies, earwigs, spiders [531]. Forage amongst woodland canopy and margins, hedgerows and landscape features, with a continual forward progression. Foraging path typically within 200 m of water features. Colony of 13 radio-tracked females, Sussex, spread out over 240 km², but each had own hunting patch of *c.*5 km²; some close to roost, within same woodland, but others in isolated woods up to 18 km distant [191]. In more wooded habitat,

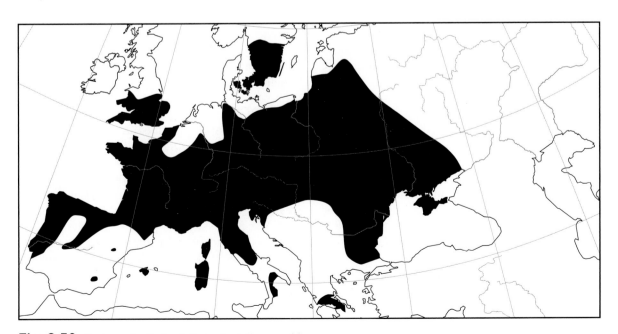

Fig. 8.50 Barbastelle *Barbastella barbastellus*: world range.

363

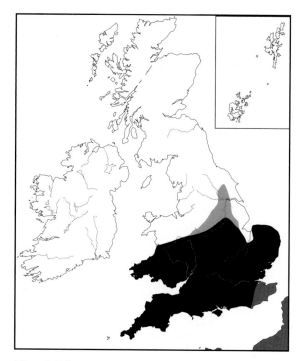

Fig. 8.51 Barbastelle *Barbastella barbastellus*: GB range

Switzerland, whole colony hunting range only 59 ha for 11 tagged females [557]. Winter foraging lower and in denser cover. Flight fast and agile, hunting at 4–5 m along trees, often at low (<2 m) level crossing open ground; food items both caught and consumed on the wing; some gleaned from vegetation. Barbastelles will emerge early under canopy [1].

3 types of echolocation used. When commuting, a short, loud CF–FM sweep with a peak frequency of 32 kHz alternates with a quieter call at 34 kHz. When foraging, a longer CF–FM sweep, peaking at 38 and 32 kHz, is often used as well as a *Myotis*-like FM sweep. In light conditions, will fly with no discernible echo-location. Call intensity can be greatly varied [1].

BREEDING
Single young born early July, S England; births spread out over 2–3 weeks. Juveniles are flying at 3 weeks. At this age the pelage resembles a very bright adult. Nursery colonies disperse during the latter half of August [191]. Autumn mating roosts, 1 adult male with up to 6 adult females and their young of the year, recorded in S England. Recorded longevity, Europe, 21 years 9 months [531].

POPULATION
British population widely but very thinly spread, estimated at 5000 (England 4500, Wales 500) [215]. Given that Sussex colony, approximately 30 breeding females, exploited 250 km², and extent

of unsuitable habitat, broader estimates of 5000–10 000 [215] seem reasonable.

PARASITES
The flea *Ischnopsyllus hexactenus* and mite *Neomyobia pantopus* have been recorded. During hibernation, pinkish eggs of a mite often visible, embedded in and protruding from hinder margin of ear.

RELATIONS WITH HUMANS
Conservation will require cooperative habitat management across the very large areas of nursery colony's foraging territory. In areas with a history of records, retention of storm-damaged deciduous woodland and groups of broken tree stumps should be a priority.

AUTHOR
F. Greenaway

GENUS *Plecotus*

A small genus of *c*.8 species, mostly Palaearctic but extending to Oriental and Afrotropical Regions; closely related to Nearctic *Corynorhinus*, which sometimes included as a subgenus. 2 species occur in GB, but only separated *c*.1970, earlier literature might refer to either. Distinguished by long ears *c*.2/3 body length. Dentition 2.1.2.3/3.1.3.3, so differ from *Myotis* by loss of 1 upper premolar.

Brown long-eared bat *Plecotus auritus*
Vespertilio auritus Linnaeus 1829; Sweden.
Plecotus brevimanus Jenyns, 1829; Grunty Fen, Cambridgeshire, England.
Common long-eared bat; *ialtog fhad-chluasach* (Irish Gaelic).

RECOGNITION
Whole animal: A medium-sized bat distinguished from all other species, except grey long-eared, by very large ears (at least 28 mm), approximately 3/4 of body length (Plate 6). Identity less obvious when ears tucked away, at rest (Fig. 8.54). Similar to grey long-eared bat, but generally smaller, with narrower tragus, paler face, and fur with distinctive banding on individual hairs. The 2 species can be separated by these characteristics, along with a suite of measurements (Table 8.18).

Skull and teeth: Condylobasal length 13.0–15.5 mm; upper tooth-row 4.8–5.6 mm; diameter of tympanic bulla <4.5 mm; canines <1.8 mm; p^2 short but distinct, higher than cingulum of canine and >1/2 height of p^4 (Fig 8.52) [194].

FIELD SIGNS

Faeces: Relatively coarse grained, 8–10 mm long, brown to black, often shiny as a result of moth scales in them.

Roosts: Sites detected from faeces, often scattered or distributed along central axis of attic roosts below apex. Bats often visible in small groups within the apex of attic spaces or in tight corners of gables. Well-used attics frequently free from cobwebs.

Other field signs: Feeding perches identifiable from piles of discarded insect remains, often including moth wings, along with faeces [637]; frequently found in outbuildings or porches [429]. Calls difficult to distinguish on bat detector, due to low intensity, sometimes detected at 45–50 kHz. In flight, distinctive silhouette, extended ears may be visible. Flight slow (2–3 m/s) and fluttering [391].

DESCRIPTION

Pelage: Light brown or beige dorsally, creamy or white underparts. Individual hairs banded, with dark base, pale middle region and brown tips [194]. Juveniles have dark grey dorsal fur and white underparts; greyish colour may be retained for up to a year.

Anatomy: Face pinkish to pale brown, with little hair. Snout pointed, relatively long, with slit-like nostrils opening laterally on top. There may be yellow discharge from glands around the face. Eyes large, round and bright. Ears long and rounded, with folds along edges. Tragus almost half as long as conch, narrows distally to a rounded tip. Ears joined by a low flap of skin at the base; may be folded and tucked under the wings, especially in torpor; in this case, only tragus visible (Fig. 8.53, Fig 8.54). Ears may also be held halfway in a 'ram's horn'. Wings broad with low aspect ratio [393]; consist of a dark, semi-transparent membrane. Thumbs relatively long and slender.

Skull: Upper canine small and rounded in section just below cingulum. Dental formula $i^2/_3c^1/_1p^2/_3m^3/_3$.

Reproductive tract: Y-shaped baculum, with slender limbs, c.3 times as long as wide and with axis length 0.8 mm [109].

Chromosomes: 2n = 32; FNa = 50–54; European data [684].

RELATIONSHIPS

Very similar to *P. austriacus*, and confusion may occur. The 2 species show some differences in roost selection and habitat use. Much wider northerly distribution than *P. austriacus*, mirrored in Europe by its occurrence at higher altitudes [240].

MEASUREMENTS

Females on average have forearm 2.5% longer than males (Table 8.19). Weight varies dramatically with season and reproductive condition. Over summer, average male weight increases from 6 to 8 g. Females, on average, 0.5 g heavier; mean weight 7–9 g during summer. Pregnant females reaches 12 g. Weight in winter lower, and up to 22% of body weight may be lost during hibernation [596].

VARIATION

Some variation in size reported both between GB

Table 8.18 Long-eared bats: distinguishing brown from grey [593]. Grey long-eared bats are generally larger, but have shorter thumbs. However, there is some overlap, especially between male grey and female brown long-eared bats. In both species, males are slightly smaller than females (Table 8.19)

	Brown		Grey	
	Mean	Range	Mean	Range
Forearm length (mm)	<40	36.0–40.0	>39	39.1–42.0
Thumb length (mm) (exc. claw)	>6.3	5.4–7.6	<6.3	5.1–7.0
Tragus length (mm)	<15	13.4–16.0	>15	13.7–17.8
Tragus width (mm)	<5.5	4.5–5.7	>5.5	5.5–6.4

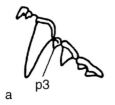 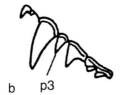

Fig. 8.52 Anterior teeth of (a) grey and (b) brown long-eared bats. The p³ is taller, over ¹/2 the height of p⁴ behind it, in the brown long-eared bat (*after [609]*).

and Europe and within GB. Average forearm lengths differ for both males and females between different roost sites [152].

DISTRIBUTION
Widespread across Europe, but absent from southernmost parts of the continent. Rare beyond 64° N (Fig 8.55) [539]. Widespread in GB except for exposed N and NW regions of Scotland (Fig. 8.56). Distribution appears to reflect tree cover in general pattern. Apparently absent from most offshore islands round Scotland, although reported from Orkney [84].

HISTORY
Of old European origin, and present back to the Pliocene [240]. Appears to have been common in the Pleistocene [546]. Recorded, from Westbury-sub-Mendip, Somerset (Mid Pleistocene) [75], Pin

Hole Cave (?Late Glacial) and Dog Hole Fissure (Mesolithic), Derbyshire [282].

HABITAT
Strongly associated with tree cover, prefers light woodland, particularly deciduous. Frequently flies among foliage of different heights. Besides deciduous woodland, also forages in mixed woodland edge and among native conifers such as Scots pine [153], but rarely uses any parts of non-native coniferous plantations except the edge.

Found in villages and suburban areas, but rarely in urban zones. In GB, predominantly roosts in buildings (houses, churches and barns) during summer, but also uses trees and bat boxes [86]. In Scotland, selected large, old houses (average age 150 years) located close to abundant woodland [154]. Temporary roosts located in farm buildings and trees. In autumn, transitional colonies formed in buildings, trees or bat boxes. In winter, hibernation sites include caves, mine tunnels, underground constructions, buildings (particularly cellars and outbuildings) and trees.

SOCIAL ORGANISATION AND BEHAVIOUR
Roosting behaviour: Main summer roosts occupied May–October by small colonies. Number of bats visible averages 15–20; however, mark–recapture estimates indicate that actual colony size averages significantly more (30–50) [156]; this

Fig 8.53 Brown long-eared bat waking from hibernation, with ears partially unrolled (*photo P. Morris*).

Fig. 8.54 Brown long-eared bat in hibernation, with its ears tucked under its wings and only the tragus projecting (*photo P. Morris*).

Table 8.19 Long-eared bats: variation in forearm length (mm). Across their range, and in both species, females average *c*.1 mm larger.

	Males		Females	
	Mean	Range	Mean	Range
Brown long-eared bats				
Dorset	37.5	38	38.3	46
Suffolk	37.6	32	38.5	35
Northamptonshire	38.1	57	39.2	77
Nottinghamshire	–	–	39.3	31
Inverness	38.2	28	39.2	23
Czechoslovakia	39.5	37	40.2	58
Grey long-eared bats				
Dorset	39.9	22	41.1	35
Czechoslovakia	39.8	131	41.0	151

reinforced by genetic data [95]. However, numbers of bats visible provide reliable indication of relative colony size. Larger colonies are associated with roosts close to abundant woodland [1]. Colonies consist of both adult males and females; number of males increases through the summer. Colonies show long-term associations with their roost sites; site fidelity appears high in both sexes, both within and between years [156].

Enters hibernation relatively late (usually November) and emerges late March–early April. Hibernates singly or in small groups, generally relatively deep within crevices [240], within caves, tunnels, icehouses, cellars and trees. Preferred temperatures low (−3 to 11 ºC; average 7 ºC) [211], and stable conditions selected. Appears to fly relatively frequently during winter [226], may arouse on nights when temperature rises above 4 ºC, when able to catch non-flying arthropods by gleaning.

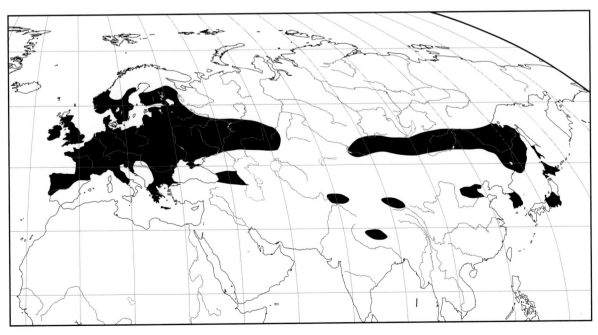

Fig. 8.55 Brown long-eared bat *Plecotus auritus*: supposed world range, but confounded by cryptic species in E.

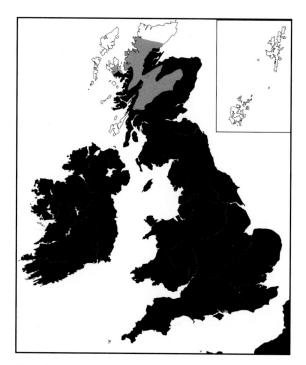

Fig. 8.56 Brown long-eared bat *Plecotus auritus*: range in British Isles.

Vocalisations: Audible communication calls [7] may be heard in foraging sites and around roosts.

Dispersal: Roost sites used traditionally, often for decades. Inter-colony movement rare (<1%) and only between adjacent colonies [156]. Colonies using different roost sites appear to represent discrete units, and genetic structuring between regions is evident through isolation by distance [94]. Some evidence for natal recruitment within colonies.

Migration: Does not appear to undertake long-distance migrations to hibernacula, and is a relatively sedentary species [165, 613]. In GB, there is evidence that this species may remain within, or in the vicinity of, summer roosts during winter [274]. However, flights of up to 60 km have been noted, and there are a number of reported incidents where bats have been found offshore during autumn [110].

Activity: Becomes active up to 80 min before emergence, preparatory flights made within roost space [629]. Emergence begins relatively late compared with most other species (around 50 min after sunset in NE Scotland, although this varies with length of twilight). Emergence earlier at roosts closer to woodland or other cover [153]. Remain active all night, returning around 50 min before dawn in Scotland (earlier at lower latitudes). Swarming behaviour noted outside roosts when bats return at dawn. Foraging may be interrupted by rain, but continues at temperatures as low as 3.5 °C. Individuals also take periodic rests from flight, perhaps as larger prey items are dismembered. Lactating females return to roost during night to suckle young; frequency of returns declines as lactation progresses [153]

FEEDING

Gleans prey directly from foliage and other surfaces, but also catches insects in flight. Broad wings allow flight in cluttered environments and hovering in front of foliage. In addition, short (*c*.2 ms) FM echolocation calls [7] allow insects to be detected in cluttered habitats. Hunt in short twisting beats which incorporate several trees [629]. Around 1/2 prey captures made by gleaning and 1/2 in flight. During gleaning, insects may be located at close range by passive listening rather than echolocation [12, 13]

Foraging occurs at a series of areas to which individuals return within or between nights. Move to and between sites using flyways (including hedgerows, treelines, banks, fences and forest rides), along which they fly low and relatively fast (up to 6 m/s) [245]. Evidence of simultaneous use of feeding sites by more than one individual from the same roost. Generally forage close to the roost (within 1.5 km, often within 0.5 km; maximum recorded 3 km). Males forage further from the roost than females [153].

Food requirements: Prey consists mainly of moths, beetles and flies [629] (Table 8.20). Flexible diet, which changes through the summer [658], although smaller insects (<3 mm body

Table 8.20 Brown long-eared bat: diet composition in Inverness-shire, determined by faecal analysis [626]

	% identified fragments
Lepidoptera (moths)	41
Coleoptera (beetles)	22
Trichoptera (caddisflies)	16
Nematocera (craneflies, midges etc.)	10
Other Diptera (houseflies, etc.)	3
Hemiptera (bugs)	1
Neuroptera (lacewings)	1
Dermaptera (earwigs)	1
Araneae (spiders)	1

length) are rarely eaten. Noctuid moths frequently consumed [333, 429, 484, 491], discarded noctuid wings often accumulate under feeding perches. Non-flying prey such as earwigs, spiders and centipedes also eaten (Table 8.21); some of these may be caught within roost [491, 629].

BREEDING

Monoestrous, producing single young in summer. Mate in autumn and winter through to early spring [596], sperm stored until ovulation. Mating system appears to be promiscuous, little potential for female defence during mating period; existence of multi-male polygyny also suggested [407]. Evidence of swarming in autumn prior to hibernation.

Males: Spermatogenesis initiated late spring, reaches peak August. During this period, testes first swell and later regress as spermatozoa are released into caudae epididymides, which become extended. Testes regress completely during autumn. Copulation begins in autumn, in nursery and transitory sites [407]. Mating continues throughout the hibernation period, number of inseminated females increases [612].

Females: Appear to ovulate on arousal from hibernation, are palpably pregnant by end of May. Gestation 60–70 days. Births occur late June–end of July, dependent on latitude and weather during pregnancy. Infants cling to mother's nipple for first 10 days of life, except when mother foraging; then left in groups within the roost. Females recognise their own infant through vocal signals and olfactory cues [624], and suckle only their own young [128,372].

Productivity: In GB, 2 studies suggest that, on average, 63–70% of females breed each year, but in some years only 1/2 of females may produce young [152, 600]. Higher fecundity recorded at roosts closer to abundant woodland [1].

Development of young: Average birthweight 1.76 g. Weight stabilises at 60–70% of adult mass by 40 days, forearm length is 97% that of adults by 30 days [128]; at this age, practice flights inside roosts occur [624]. Isolation calls emitted from birth, orientation pulses from 12–14 days and echolocation calls by 20 days [128]. Eyes open and hair covering complete by 6 days; young first leave roost to forage at around 30 days [128, 624]; are weaned when *c*.6 weeks old.

Sexual maturity: Most females give birth for first time at 2 years old, some not until their 3rd year [152, 591]. A few males show signs of maturity in the autumn following birth but most undertake spermatogenesis for first time during 2nd summer; maturity appears related to body condition [578]. Relative size and shape of caudae epididymides are the most reliable indicators of sexual maturity in males of this species [155].

POPULATION

Numbers: Overall population in GB estimated at around 200 000 (England 155 000, Scotland 27 500, Wales 17 500) [215], based on assumption of average colony size of 16.8 [580]. If actually >30 (see above), population may be double this estimate. No estimate available for Ireland, but 300 roosts known [225], likely *pro rata* to be around 130 000. Availability of foraging habitat may limit both population size and distribution of this species.

Population structure: Although both sexes show strong roost loyalty (and some degree of natal philopatry), genetic data indicate that inter-colony mating occurs, and most offspring are fathered by males from different colonies; within colony relatedness therefore low [95]. Populations show a degree of exchange, are not inbred, but some indication of genetic isolation by distance, suggesting increased likelihood of mating between adjoining colonies [94].

Fluctuations: Some indication of population decline over the last 200 years in GB [580].

Sex ratio: Approximately 1:1 at birth; in adults, recorded sex ratios biased towards females (33–44% males) in GB. Higher proportions of males found further north.

Survival: Annual survival rates 0.76 and 0.78 for females, 0.60 and 0.70 for males [86, 152]. Estimates of lifespan, 3–17 years. Longevity records include bats recaught after 13 years, GB, 30 years in Europe [345].

Species interactions: May share roosts with *P. austriacus*, frequently found in the same roof spaces as colonies of *Myotis nattereri*. Also shares roosts with other species, including *Pipistrellus pipistrellus* and *Myotis daubentonii*.

MORTALITY

Predation: In GB, avian predators include owls and kestrels [189, 559]. In Poland, also captured by barn owls and tawny owls [511]. However, in GB, domestic cat appears to be greater cause of mortality; captures bats as they emerge from roosts, resulting in high losses in some colonies; may also hunt within roosts [91].

Other sources of mortality: Timber treatment chemicals (see below).

PARASITES
Adult generally carry few ectoparasites, although heavy infestations of juveniles reported. Mites (*Spincturnix plecotina, Ornithonyssus pipistrelli, Neomyobia plecotia*) frequently recorded, flea *Ischnopsyllus hexactenus* also found. Another flea *Nycteridopsylla longiceps* has been found occasionally in winter. Internal parasites are not well documented – one study showed the presence of a bacterium *Grahamella* in the blood of this species [170].

RELATIONS WITH HUMANS
An attractive and appealing bat, often used to promote public awareness and as a symbol for bat conservation. Some declines in populations have been recorded [121, 580], but not considered threatened. Because of strong association with buildings, is frequent subject of conservation/ planning consultations. Timber treatment chemicals a particular risk, given the use of open attic spaces by this species [446]; use of chemicals with low toxicity essential, now legal requirement.

Preservation of mature woodland and maintenance of flyways likely to be important for conservation. Woodland in the vicinity of roosts may be of particular importance, so roosts and surrounding woodland should be managed as a single unit. Exclusion from traditional roost sites may be detrimental. Often returns to roosts despite significant disturbance. Bat boxes frequently occupied, can provide roosts in previously unpopulated areas.

Has been maintained in captivity fairly successfully, although pregnant females tend to abort. Young have been born and reared under laboratory conditions [126, 372]. Difficult to provide conditions suitable for hibernation in captivity [431]. Appears to tolerate repeated captures and handling in the wild without abandoning roosts.

PRINCIPAL AUTHORS
A.C. Entwistle & S.M. Swift

LITERATURE
Popular account of the natural history of *P. auritus*, including detailed observations of a colony in a house in England [245]. Comprehensive review of the biology, ecology and behaviour of *P. auritus* and its sibling species *P. austriacus* in Europe [626].

Grey long-eared bat *Plecotus austriacus*
Vespertilio auritus austriacus Fischer, 1829; Austria

RECOGNITION
Whole animal: A medium-sized bat, distinguished from all other species except brown long-eared bat by its very long ears (30 mm or longer) joined at the base; from brown long-eared by its slightly larger size (Table 8.19), short, thick thumbs (<6 mm) and therefore lower thumb length/forearm ratio (14%), broader tragus (>5.5 mm), uniformly dark colour along dorsal hairs and dark brown face (Plate 6).

Skull and teeth: Upper canine >1.9 mm long, relatively narrow when viewed from the side and angular in section below cingulum. p^2 small, barely extending beyond the cingulum of the canine and not reaching 1/2 height of p^4 (Fig. 8.52) [109]. Condylobasal length 16.6–17.0 mm, maximum diameter of tympanic bulla 4.8–5.0 mm, average length of c–m^3 5.9 mm and of c–m_3 6.6 mm.

FIELD SIGNS
Faeces: Similar to brown long-eared.

Roosts: Scattered droppings, particularly under ridge, and absence of cobwebs characterize roosts, but signs not distinguishable from those of *P. auritus*.

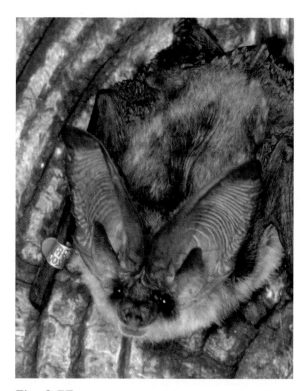

Fig. 8.57 Grey long-eared bat at rest *(photo F. Greenaway)*.

Table 8.21 Grey long-eared bat: measurements from a colony in Dorset [593, 596]

Measurement	Range	Adult males (n = 6)		Adult females (n = 13)	
		Mean	Range	Mean	Range
Head and body length (mm)	44.0–52.0	47.2	44.0–51.0	48.4	40.0–52.0
Forearm length (mm)	39.1–42.0	40.1	39.5–40.7	41.0	39.1–42.0
Thumb length (mm)	5.1–7.0	5.6	5.1–6.0	6.0	5.1–7.0
Wingspan (mm)	265–292	276	270–283	281	265–292
Tragus width (mm)	5.5–6.4	5.9	5.5–6.2	6.0	5.6–6.4
Tragus length (mm)	13.7–17.8	15.4	14.4–16.4	15.6	13.7–17.8
Ear length (mm)	30.0–38.0	34.0	33.0–36.0	34.2	30.0–38.0
Mean body weight (g)					
August	10.0				
October	11.3				
April	8.0				

Other field signs: Echolocation calls as for *P. auritus,* characterized by quietness combined with very fast pulse rate [98]. Huge, erect ears can be seen in flight. Feeding perches used [60], similar to those of brown long-eared.

DESCRIPTION

Pelage: Dorsally, mid to dark grey, sometimes almost black, with hairs uniformly dark along most of their length (Fig. 8.57) [194]. Ventrally, usually whitish grey, occasionally cream.

Anatomy: Face dark to very dark brown, ears and membranes dark brown. Ears may be curved in 'ram's horn' position or folded and tucked beneath wings when at rest; tragus remains erect. Tragus broad, with anterior edge straight and posterior edge strongly convex in proximal half, concave distally. Eyes relatively large, nostrils elongate and open laterally. Wings broad, with propatagium well developed.

Skull: Dental formula 2.1.2.3/3.1.3.3; p^2 very small.

Reproductive tract: Baculum Y-shaped with stout proximal limbs, shorter than wide and with axis length 0.6 mm [109].

Chromosomes: 2n = 32; Fna = 50–52; European data [684].

RELATIONSHIPS

Very similar to *P. auritus,* with which sympatric over much of Europe and with which frequently confused. 2 species recognised in Europe in 1959–1962 and in GB in 1964 [109]. Also closely related to *P. teneriffae,* endemic to the Canary Islands, and to *P. taivanus* from Taiwan. *P. kolombatovici* [140], formerly considered a subspecies of *P. austriacus,* from Adriatic coast of former Yugoslavia and adjacent islands, now recognised as a full species [325, 588]; another closely related species, *P. macrobullaris (alpinus),* described recently [324, 325].

MEASUREMENTS

Males slightly smaller than females, as indicated by forearm length (Table 8.21).

VARIATION

Little subspecific variation, matching low intraspecific genetic diversity [588]. Slight geographic variation in colouration and skull measurements recorded [588].

DISTRIBUTION

Commoner than *P. auritus* in Mediterranean and Middle Eastern countries. Recorded Egypt, Jordan, Algeria and Malta, reaches southern limit in Cape Verde islands. Range extends northwards to Poland and Germany at around 53° N (Fig. 8.58).

8 Bats: Order Chiroptera

Confined to the extreme S of British Isles (Fig. 8.59); recorded Somerset, Dorset, Devon, Hampshire, Isle of Wight and all Channel Islands except Herm [23]. Also records from Sussex: Brighton [259] and Chichester [267].

HISTORY

From absence of fossils in Europe, considered to be Asian in origin and to have spread through Europe in historical period [240]. Heavy reliance on buildings as both summer roosts and hibernacula, so perhaps unable to colonise Europe until such sites available.

HABITAT

In England and Channel Islands, known roosts in house roofs in open, lightly wooded country. In continental Europe, lives almost exclusively in cultivated lowland areas [240, 307, 511] and nursery roosts are in attics or church lofts, often in villages or small towns. Foraging habitats include woodland [40], as well as open meadows [60] and, in the Channel Islands, pasture containing trees [343]. Single radio-tracked female in Germany [159] foraged in gardens, open meadows, orchards, forest edge and mixed woodland. Hibernates in caves as well as cellars [201, 240] and other synanthropic structures such as brick kilns [184].

SOCIAL ORGANISATION AND BEHAVIOUR

Roosting behaviour: In summer, always roosts in attics – use of tree holes unknown and only one report of occupation of a bat box attached to a building [331a]. Selects warm, old houses or

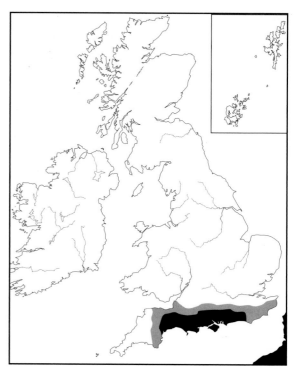

Fig 8.59 Grey long-eared bat *Plecotus austriacus*: range in GB.

churches [211, 307], frequently roosts on ridge beam, in spaces between rafters [164, 240]. Colony size 10–30 in both England and mainland Europe; average 10.4 [167]. Number of males in nursery colonies increases through summer to a peak in September [596], but many roost solitarily within attic spaces.

Hibernation begins late October and ends late March–early April [596]. In Europe, select slightly

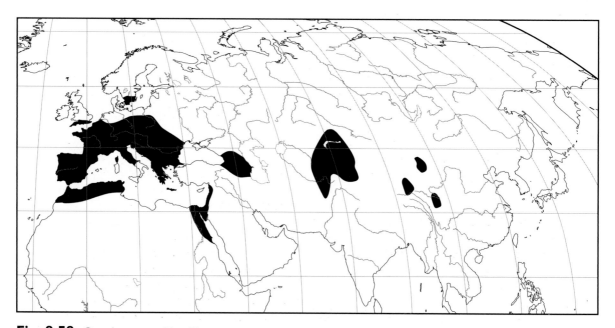

Fig. 8.58 Grey long-eared bat *Plecotus austriacus*: supposed world range may include cryptic species in E.

372

Table 8.22 Grey long-eared bat: diet composition (% frequency) in the Czech Republic, determined by faecal analysis [60]

Insect order	% frequency in faecal pellets							
	April	May	June	July	Aug	Sept	Oct	Whole summer
Lepidoptera (moths)	67	50	73	90	75	86	64	72.1
Diptera (flies)	14	2	5	2	11	6	32	10.3
Coleoptera (beetles)	19	48	20	8	9	2	0	15.1
Hemiptera (true bugs)	0	0	0	0	2	5	0	1.0
Other groups	0	0	2	0	3	1	4	1.5

warmer sites than *P. auritus* [240, 250]; range 2–9 °C. Hibernate singly or in groups of 2 or 3, either on walls or at entrances to crevices, but not deep in crevices [240]. Hibernation weight loss high (29%), attributed to frequent arousals and unsuitable conditions in British Isles for hibernation of this species [596].

Aggressive behaviour: Large number of healed injuries suggests high degree of intraspecific aggression [596]. Relatively aggressive when handled. Presence of only 1 male per roof section in nursery colonies interpreted as territorial behaviour [596].

Dispersal: Considered to be a stationary species, with longest recorded flight 62 km in Czech Republic [165]. 1 found on a lightship 18 km off Sussex coast, followed by another dead on adjacent coast 11 days later [111], suggesting immigration from mainland Europe.

Activity: In Europe, emerges *c*.30 min after sunset, when almost dark [60, 159]. Activity pattern unimodal [159], with individuals remaining intermittently active all night.

FEEDING

Foraging behaviour: Not studied in GB. In Europe, reported to show 2 distinct forms of behaviour: slow, hovering flight involving gleaning in cluttered environments, and aerial capture during fast flight in more open situations [159]. Landscape features such as hedges used as flyways [40], along which commute between a series of regularly-used feeding sites [97, 159].

Food requirements: Lepidoptera by far the most important group in diet, although other arthropods taken (Table 8.22). Remains of centipedes, spiders, earwigs and booklice ([61]; European data) in faecal pellets indicates that gleans part of its diet, although probably much less than *P. auritus*. Large noctuid moths selected; these and large chafers and bugs caught mainly in free flight [60].

BREEDING

Mate in autumn, beginning mid September [596], but no evidence of winter or spring copulation. All mating observed was at summer roosts; swarming at transitory roosts, as reported for *P. auritus*, does not appear to occur [240]. Presence of only one male per section of roof space in autumn [596] may indicate a system of female group defence. Ovulation probably late April–early May. Males become sexually mature at 1 year and females first give birth in their 2nd or 3rd year [591].

Productivity: Single young, born July.

Development of young: Not known in detail – probably similar to *P. auritus*. Weaning at around 6 weeks.

POPULATION

Numbers: Total British population (from counts at all known roosts) estimated at between 1000 [215] and 1500 [607].

Fluctuations: In Dorset [597], colony size suffered sharp decline during a severe winter.

Survival: Lifespan estimated as 5 years (males) and 9 years (females), Dorset [597]. Oldest recorded, 11.75 years, Czech Republic [165].

Species interactions: Frequently shares roosts with *P. auritus*.

MORTALITY

Predation: In Europe, occurred in 9.3% of barn owl pellets [512]. Probably also vulnerable to predation by domestic cats.

PARASITES

Unknown, probably similar to those of *P. auritus.*

RELATIONS WITH HUMANS

Has not been kept in captivity. Aggressive and difficult to handle; suffers relatively high degree of ring damage due to chewing [417]. Heavy reliance on buildings, so vulnerable to poisoning by inappropriate timber treatment; colonies in Channel Islands have been adversely affected [343]. In Europe, has been found to feed opportunistically on large moths flying round street lamps [60].

LITERATURE

Review of current knowledge of the biology, ecology and behaviour of both European *Plecotus* species [626].

PRINCIPAL AUTHORS

S.M. Swift & A.C. Entwistle

FAMILY MOLOSSIDAE

A largely tropical and subtropical family of insectivorous bats, with tails that extend beyond uropatagium when at rest, hence free-tailed bats. Heavy wrinkled muzzles result in alternative name mastiff bats. About 99 species in 16 genera, but only 1 reaches Europe, and that only a vagrant to British Isles. Accidental record of 1 American species (see below).

European free-tailed bat *Tadarida teniotis*
Cephalotes teniotis Rafinesque, 1814; Italy (Sicily).

DESCRIPTION

Very large, comparable with mouse-eared bat; fur short and dense, dorsally smoky grey to almost black, ventrally lighter grey; ears joined over head and projecting forwards beyond eyes; sides of muzzle with vertical folds (wrinkles); tail membrane short, tail extending beyond membrane by 30–50% of its length, no postcalcarial lobe, legs short and strong with hairy feet; wing membranes long and narrow. Strong smell. No similar European species, smaller American *T. brasiliensis* (forearm 36–46 mm) recorded as accidental (see below).

Chromosomes: $2n = 48$, $NF = 76$.

Measurements: Head and body 81–92 mm, forearm 57–64 mm, wingspan *c.*410 mm, ear length 27–33 mm, tail 44–57 mm, tail beyond membrane, weight 25–50 g; condylobasal length 20.9–24 mm, c–m^3 9–10 mm.

DISTRIBUTION

Widely distributed in Mediterranean basin [381] to N Spain and S Alps. Also Arabian Peninsula and E from Afghanistan to China. Vagrant to British Isles, only 2 records: 19th century, Jersey [136] and a male, found grounded, March 2003, Helston, Cornwall [1].

HABITATS/HABITS

Common in suitable habitats. Forages high, usually 10–50 m, over range of temperate to sub-desert habitats [277]. Echolocation calls audible, down to 11 kHz [529]. Feeds on aerial drifts of insects (mainly moths, plus neuropterans and other insects). Summer and winter roosts in fissures and hollows in rock outcrops, quarries and sea cliffs. Also in artificial structures, including old and modern bridges and buildings, sometimes in roof of high caves. Summer and winter colonies of 5–100 individuals, up to 300–400. Altitude up to 3100 m asl. Some evidence of migration (e.g. seasonal in Malta), but probably largely sedentary [276].

AUTHOR

A.M. Hutson

Accidental imports from America

4 species have been accidentally imported from America. Records of 3 species are from or close to docks, presumably bats that 'jumped ship' after docking, having crossed the Atlantic. 3 records are from consignments of timber imported from North America and found at the destination timber yard (NB 2 records of *E. fuscus* from same timber yard, see below), 1 from a military aircraft from N America, 1 from box of fruit opened at a distribution depot. Some of the European species have been found in similar circumstances.

The traffic of such bats around the world is probably quite frequent. Though none appears to have become established, exotic diseases could be translocated by such bats [108]. With this in mind, and the possibility that foreign species could be overlooked or mistaken for European bats, it seems worth listing them here. They are generally relatively common and widespread species [42], and while 2 of them are relatively distinct species, occurrences of *Eptesicus fuscus* or *Myotis lucifugus* here could be overlooked.

Big brown bat *Eptesicus fuscus* (Palisot de Beauvois, 1796)

Very similar to European *E. serotinus*, but smaller (forearm 42–51 mm, tragus relatively shorter and broader). Widespread and abundant in N America, south through Caribbean and C America to northern S America [341]. Primarily a house bat, occasionally in trees or underground habitats. More or less sedentary. Colonies 20–200, twins common in parts of range. Also recorded imported to the Netherlands [657].

2 records, November 1996 and December 2000, both in Atkins & Cripps' timber yard, Bishops Stortford, Hertfordshire [1, 270].

Silver-haired bat *Lasionycteris noctivagans* (Le Conte, 1831)

Similar to *Eptesicus*, but very dark with silver frosted-tipped dorsal fur; tragus short, almost as broad as long and ear relatively longer than in *Eptesicus*; dorsal surface of tail membrane well-furred on upper half, forearm 37–44 mm. Widespread but of erratic occurrence across North America and considered to be generally scarce. Mainly breeding in the north, noted migrant sometimes reaching the Caribbean and N Mexico. A forest bat, usually solitary or small groups roosting in trees, occasionally buildings, twins frequent.

3 records: 1995, in USAF transport plane, Mildenhall, Suffolk; January 1996, in container of wood (no location); October 2005, near Seaforth Dock, near Bootle, Merseyside [1, 264, 265].

Little brown bat *Myotis lucifugus* (Le Conte, 1831)

Very similar to European *M. daubentonii* (forearm 34–41 mm). Very common and widespread through N America except for southern states. Closely associated with water, where feeds on aquatic insects. Maternity colonies usually 300–800. Much more building-oriented in summer than Daubenton's bat, occasionally under bridges or in caves. Medium-range migrant with movements of >300 km to underground hibernation sites. Also recorded from Iceland [418].

One record, September 1992, Ipswich docks, Suffolk [1].

Mexican free-tailed bat *Tadarida brasiliensis* (I. Geoffroy, 1824)

Similar to European *Tadarida teniotis* but much smaller, forearm 36–46 mm. Ears not quite joined above head, wings long and narrow, 1/3 of tail extending beyond tail membrane, feet with long hairs, wrinkles on sides of muzzle, fur generally dull brown to grey coloured. Widespread from southern states of USA, south though Caribbean and C America almost to the cone of S America [672]. Forms huge colonies in caves, but will also form quite small colonies in buildings in some areas. Some populations highly migratory, especially the females, to >1800 km, with frequent stopover points.

2 records, August 1998, Kent, imported from Martinique; March 2003, in docks, Isle of Grain, Kent, presumed from USA [1].

AUTHOR
A.M. Hutson

Serotine pup, a few days old. All bats are born naked, blind and with short wings, but their hindfeet are well developed, allowing them to cling to their mother, or to the roost site (*photo P. Morris*).

REFERENCES

1   Author's data.

2   Aegerter, J. Personal communication.

3   Aellen, V. (1962) La baguement des chauves-souris au Col de Bretolet (Valais). *Archives des Sciences, Genève,* **14,** 365–392 (in French).

4   Aellen, V. (1983) Migrations of bats in Switzerland. *Bonner Zoologische Beiträge,* **34,** 3–27.

5   Aellen, V. (1983–84) Migrations des chauves-souris en Suisse. Note complementaire. *Myotis,* **21/22,** 185–189 (in French).

6   Agirre-Mendi, P.T. *et al.* 2004. Presence of *Myotis alcathoe* Helversen & Heller, 2001 (Chiroptera: Vespertilionidae) in the Iberian Peninsula. *Acta Chiropterologica,* **6,** 49–57.

7   Ahlén, I. (1981) Field identification of bats and survey methods based on sounds. *Myotis,* **19,** 128–136.

8   Ahlén, I. (1997) Migratory behaviour of bats at south Swedish coasts. *Zeitschrift für Säugetierkunde,* **62,** 375–380.

9   Ahlén, I. (2004) Fladdermusfaunan i Sverige – Artenas utbredning och status. Kunskapslaget 2004. *Fauna och Flora,* **99**(2), 2–11 (in Swedish).

10 Ahlén, I. & Gerell, R. (1987) Distribution and status of bats in Sweden, pp. 317–319 in Hanak, V. *et al.* (eds.) *European bat research 1987.* Charles University Press, Prague.

11 Altringham, J.D. (2003) *British bats.* HarperCollins, London.

12 Anderson, M.E. & Racey, P.A. (1991) Feeding behaviour of captive brown long-eared bats, *Plecotus auritus. Animal Behaviour,* **42,** 489–493.

13 Anderson, M.E. & Racey, P.A. (1993) Discrimination between fluttering and non-fluttering moths by brown long-eared bats *Plecotus auritus. Animal Behaviour,* **46,** 1151–1155.

14 Andrews, M.M. & Andrews, P.T. (2003) Ultrasound social calls made by greater horseshoe bats (*Rhinolophus ferrumequinum*) in a nursery roost. *Acta Chiropterologica,* **5,** 221–234.

15 Andrews, M.M. *et al.* (2006) Ultrasound social calls of greater horseshoe bats (*Rhinolophus ferrumequinum*) in a hibernaculum. *Acta Chiropterologica,* **5,** 221–234.

16 Anon. (1991) Britain's last mouse-eared bat missing. *Bat News* **20,** 1.

17 Anon. (2002) Parti-coloureds pose population question. *Bat News* **66,** 2.

18 Anon. (2005) *The National Bat Monitoring Programme Annual Report 2003.* Bat Conservation Trust, London.

19 Arlettaz, R. (1995) *Ecology of the sibling mouse-eared bats* (Myotis myotis *and* Myotis blythii*): zoogeography, niche, competition, and foraging.* Horus, Martigny, Switzerland.

20 Arlettaz, R. (1996) Foraging behaviour of the gleaning bat *Myotis nattereri* (Chiroptera, Vespertilionidae) in the Swiss Alps. *Mammalia,* **60,** 181–186.

21 Arnold, A. & Braun, M. (1995) Untersuchungen zum Raumnutzungsverhalten der Wasserfledermause in den Rhienauen bei Philippsburg. *Der Flatterman, Regionalbeilage Baden-Württemberg,* **7,** 7–8.

22 Arnold, A. *et al.* (1996) The Nathusius' bats in flood plain forests in Nordbaden (SW-Germany). *Carolinea,* **54,** 149–158.

23 Arnold, H.R. (1993) *Atlas of mammals in Britain.* HMSO, London.

24 Atterby *et al.* (in press) DNA of serotine bats.

25 Aubert, A. (1963) Observations sur l'accouplement des Chiroptères. *Acta Theriologica,* **6,** 300–301.

26 Avery, M.I. (1985) Winter activity of pipistrelle bats. *Journal of Animal Ecology,* **54,** 721–38.

27 Avery, M.I. (1986) Factors affecting the emergence of pipistrelle bats. *Journal of Zoology,* **209,** 293–296.

28 Avery, M.I. (1986) The winter activity of noctule bats (*Nyctalus noctula*). *Journal of Zoology,* **209,** 296–299.

29 Avery, M.I. (1991) Pipistrelle *Pipistrellus pipistrellus,* pp. 124–128 in Corbet, G.B. & Harris, S. (eds.) *The handbook of British mammals.* Blackwell, Oxford.

30 Baagøe, H.J. (1987) The Scandinavian bat fauna: adaptive wing morphology and free flight in the field, pp. 57–74 in Fenton, M.B. *et al.* (eds.) *Recent advances in the study of bats.* Cambridge University Press, Cambridge.

31 Baagøe, H.J. (2001). *Eptesicus serotinus (Schreber, 1774) – Breitflugelfledermaus,* pp. 519–559 in Krapp, F. (ed.) *Handbuch der Säugetiere Europas,* Band 4: Fledertiere, Tiel I: Chiroptera 1: Rhinolophidae, Vespertilionidae I. AULA-Verlag, Wiesbaden.

32 Baagøe, H.J. (2001). Danish bats (Mammalia: Chiroptera): atlas and analysis of distribution, occurrence, and abundance. *Steenstrupia,* **26**(1), 1–117.

33 Baagøe, H.J. (2001). *Vespertilio murinus* Linnaeus, 1758 – *Zweifarbfledermaus,* pp. 473–514 *in* Krapp, F. (ed.) *Handbuch der Säugetiere Europas,* Band 4: Fledertiere, Tiel I: Chiroptera 1: Rhinolophidae, Vespertilionidae I. AULA-Verlag, Wiesbaden.

34 Baagøe, H.J. (2001). Bechsteins Fledermaus (*Myotis bechsteinii*). In Niethammer, J. & Krapp, F. (eds.) *Handbuch der Säugetiere Europas,* Vol. 3. AULA-Verlag, Wiesbaden.

35 Baagøe, H.J. & Jensen, B. (1973) The spread and present occurrence of the serotine (*Eptesicus serotinus*) in Denmark. *Periodicum Biologorum,* **75,** 107–109.

36 Baker, A.S. & Craven, J.C. (2003) Checklist of the mites (Arachnida: Acari) associated with bats (Mammalia: Chiroptera) in the British Isles. *Systematic and Applied Acarology, Special Publications,* **14,** 1–20.

37 Baker, J.R. (1974) Protozoan parasites of the blood of British wild birds and mammals. *Journal of Zoology,* **172,** 161–190.

38 Banks, C. *et al.* (1980) Observations on an unusual mixed roost of serotine and noctule bats in East Hertfordshire. *Transactions of the Hertfordshire Natural History Society and Field Club,* **29,** 15–18.

39 Banks, C. *et al.* (1983) A second Nathusius' Pipistrelle (*Pipistrellus nathusii*) in Britain, caught in flight in Hertfordshire. *Transactions of the Hertfordshire Natural History Society,* **29,** 15–18.

40 Barataud, M. (1990) Elements sur le comportement alimentaire des oreillards brun et gris, *Plecotus auritus* (Linnaeus, 1758) et *Plecotus austriacus* (Fischer, 1829). *Le Rhinolophe,* **7,** 3–10 (in French).

41 Barataud, M. (1992) L'activité crépusculaire et nocturne de 18 espèce de chiroptères, révélée par marquage luminescent et suivi acoustique. *Le Rhinolophe,* **9,** 23–57 (in French).

42 Barbour, R.W. & Davis, W.H. (1969) *Bats of America.* University Press of Kentucky, Lexington, KY.

43 Barbu, P. & Sin, G. (1985) Observatii asupra hibernarii speciei *Nyctalus noctula* (Schreber 1774) in Faleza Lacului Razelm-Capul Dolosman-Dobrogea. *Studii si Cercetari de Biologie, Seria Zoologie,* **20,** 291–297. (in Romanian).

44 Barclay, R.M.R. & Brigham, R.M. (1991) Prey detection, dietary niche breadth, and body size in bats: why are aerial insectivorous bats so small. *American Naturalist,* **137,** 693–703.

45 Barlow, K.E. (1997) The diets of two phonic types of *Pipistrellus pipistrellus* (Chiroptera: Vespertilionidae) in Britain. *Journal of Zoology,* **243,** 597–609.

46 Barlow, K.E. & Jones, G. (1996) *Pipistrellus nathusii* (Chiroptera: Vespertilionidae) in Britain in the mating season. *Journal of Zoology,* **240,** 767–773.

47 Barlow, K.E. & Jones, G. (1997) Differences in songflight calls and social calls between two phonic types of the vespertilionid bat *Pipistrellus pipistrellus. Journal of Zoology,* **241,** 315–324.

48 Barlow, K.E. & Jones, G. (1997) Function of pipistrelle social calls: field data and a playback experiment. *Animal Behaviour,* **53,** 991–999.

49 Barlow, K.E. & Jones, G. (1999) Roosts, echolocation calls and wing morphology of two phonic types of *Pipistrellus pipistrellus. Zeitschrift für Säugetierkunde,* **64,** 257–268.

50 Barlow, K.E. *et al.* (1997) Can skull morphology be used to predict ecological relationships between bat species? A test using two cryptic species of pipistrelle. *Proceedings of the Royal Society of London, Series B,* **264**, 1695–1700.

51 Barratt, E.M. *et al.* (1995) Characterization of mitochondrial DNA variability within the microchiropteran genus *Pipistrellus*: approaches and applications. *Symposia of the Zoological Society of London,* **67**, 377–386.

52 Barratt, E.M. *et al.* (1997) DNA answers the call of pipistrelle bat species. *Nature, London,* **387**, 138–139.

53 Barrett, H.G. & Cranbrook, Earl of (1961) Feeding habits of bats. *Transactions of the Suffolk Naturalists' Society,* **11**, 528.

54 Barrett, H.G. & Cranbrook, Earl of (1964) Noctule bats (*Nyctalus noctula*) feeding on cockchafers. *Transactions of the Suffolk Naturalists' Society,* **12**, 347–349.

55 Barrett-Hamilton, G.E.H (1910–11) *A history of British mammals. I. Bats.* Gurney & Jackson, London.

56 Barrett-Hamilton, G.E.H. & Hinton, M.A.C. (1911–1921) *A history of British mammals,* Vol. 2. Gurney & Jackson, London.

57 Barrington, R.M. (1891) Quoted in Barrett-Hamilton (1910–1911).

58 Battersby, J.E. (1999) *A comparison of the roost ecology of the brown long-eared bat* Plecotus auritus *and the serotine bat* Eptesicus serotinus. PhD thesis, University of Sussex.

59 Battersby, J. (ed.) & Tracking Mammals Partnership (2005) *UK Mammals: species status and population trends. First report by the Tracking Mammals Partnership.* JNCC/Tracking Mammals Partnership, Peterborough.

60 Bauerova, Z. (1982) Contribution to the trophic ecology of the grey long-eared bat, *Plecotus austriacus. Folia Zoologica,* **31**, 113–122.

61 Beck, A. (1995) Faecal analysis of European bat species. *Myotis,* **32–33**, 109–119.

62 Beck, A. *et al.* (1994) Jagdhabitatwahl und nächtliche Aufenhaltsgebiete der Grossen Hufeisennase (*Rhinolophus ferrumequinum*) in Raum Castrich/GR. *Report from a Swiss study on habitat use by greater horseshoe bats.* Arbeitsgruppe zum Schutz der Hufeisennasen Graubündens ASHG, Encarden 51, 7152 Sagogn, Switzerland (in German).

63 Bels, L. (1952) Fifteen years of bat banding in the Netherlands. *Publicaties van het Natuurhistorisch Genootschap in Limburg,* **5**, 1–99.

64 Benda, P. & Horácek, I. (1998) Bats (Mammalia: Chiroptera) of the Eastern Mediterranean. Part 1. Review of distribution and taxonomy of bats in Turkey. *Acta Societatis Zoologicae Bohemicae,* **62**, 255–313.

65 Berge, L. and Jones, G. (in prep. a) Diet of the cryptic species *Myotis mystacinus* and *Myotis brandtii.*

66 Berge, L. and Jones, G. (in prep. b) Foraging behaviour of the cryptic species *Myotis mystacinus* and *Myotis brandtii.*

67 Berge, L. and Jones, G. (in prep. c) Habitat use of the cryptic species *Myotis mystacinus* and *Myotis brandtii.*

68 Berge, L. *et al.* (in prep.) Morphology, identification and genetics of the cryptic species *Myotis mystacinus* and *M. brandtii.*

69 Bezem, J.J. *et al.* (1960) Population statistics of five species of the bat genus *Myotis* and one of the genus *Rhinolophus,* hibernating in caves of South Limburg. *Archives Néerlandaises de Zoologie,* **13**, 511–539.

70 Bezem, J.J. *et al.* (1964) Some characteristics of the hibernating locations of various species of bats in South Limburg. I and II. *Proceedings, Koninklijke Nederlandse Akademie van Wetenschappen,* **67**, 235–350.

71 Bihari, Z. (2004) The roost preference of *Nyctalus noctula* (Chiroptera, Vespertilionidae) in summer and the ecological background of their urbanization. *Mammalia* **68**, 329–336.

72 Billington, G.E. (2000) Radio tracking study of greater horseshoe bats at Mells, near Frome, Somerset. *English Nature Research Reports,* No. **403**, 1–24.

73 Billington, G.E. & Norman, G.M. (1997) *The conservation of bats in bridges project – a report of the survey and conservation of bat roosts in bridges in Cumbria.* English Nature, Peterborough.

74 Bishop, C.M. *et al.* (1992) Discriminate suckling in pipistrelle bats is supported by DNA fingerprinting. *Molecular Ecology,* **1**, 255–258.

75 Bishop, M.J. (1982) The mammal fauna of the Early Middle Pleistocene Cavern infill site at Westbury-sub-Mendip, Somerset. *Special Papers in Palaeontology,* **28**, 1–108. Palaeontological Association, London.

76 Blackmore, M. (1956) An occurrence of the mouse-eared bat *Myotis myotis* (Borkhausen) in England. *Proceedings of the Zoological Society of London,* **127**, 201–203.

77 Blake, D. *et al.* (1994) Use of lamplit roads by foraging bats in southern England. *Journal of Zoology,* **234**, 453–462.

78 Bogdanowicz, W. (1994) *Myotis daubentonii. Mammalian Species,* **475**, 1–9.

79 Bogdanowicz, W. (2004) *Pipistrellus kuhlii (Kuhl, 1817) – Weissrandfledermaus,* pp. 875–910 *in* Krapp, F. (ed.). *Handbuch der Säugetiere Europas,* Band **4**, Fledertiere, Teil II: Chiroptera II: Vespertilionidae 2, Molossidae, Nycteridae. AULA-Verlag, Wiesbaden (in German).

80 Bogdanowicz, W. & Ruprecht, A.L. (1998) *Nyctalus leisleri.* In Niethammer, J. & Krapp, F. (eds.) *Handbuch der Säugetiere Europas.* Fledermause. AULA-Verlag, Wiesbaden.

81 Bontadina, F. *et al.* (2002) Radio-tracking reveals that lesser horseshoe bats (*Rhinolophus hipposideros*) forage in woodland. *Journal of Zoology,* **258**, 281–290.

82 Boonman, A. Personal communication.

83 Boonman, M. (2000) Roost selection by noctules (*Nyctalus noctula*) and Daubenton's bats (*Myotis daubentonii*). *Journal of Zoology,* **251**, 385–389.

84 Booth, C. & Booth, J. (1994) *The mammals of Orkney.* Orcadian Ltd, Kirkwall.

85 Boyd, I.L. & Myhill, D.G. (1987) Variations in the post-natal growth of pipistrelle bats (*Pipistrellus pipistrellus*). *Journal of Zoology,* **213**, 750–755.

86 Boyd, I.L. & Stebbings, R.E. (1989) Population changes of brown long-eared bats (*Plecotus auritus*) in bat boxes at Thetford forest. *Journal of Applied Ecology,* **26**, 101–112.

87 Boyd, I.L. *et al.* (1988) Uptake of gamma-HCH (Lindane) by pipistrelle bats and its effect on survival. *Environmental Pollution,* **51**, 95–111.

88 Briggs, B. & King, D. (1998) *The bat detective: a field guide for bat detection.* Bat Box Ltd, Steyning.

89 Britton, A.R.C. & Jones, G. (1999) Echolocation behaviour and prey-capture success in foraging bats: laboratory and field experiments on *Myotis daubentonii. Journal of Experimental Biology,* **202**, 1793–1801.

90 Brosset, A. (1990) The migrations of *Pipistrellus nathusii* in France – possible implication on the spreading of rabies. *Mammalia,* **54**, 207–212.

91 Bruijn, Z. (1990) Domestic cat *Felis catus* as a predator of bats. *Lutra,* **33**, 30–34.

92 Buckley, D.J. (2005) *The emergence behaviour and foraging habitat preferences of the whiskered bat* (Myotis mystacinus) *in a lowland landscape in mid-Cork.* BSc thesis, National University of Ireland, Cork.

93 Bullock, D.J. *et al.* (1987) Analysis of the timing and pattern of emergence of the pipistrelle bat (*Pipistrellus pipistrellus*). *Journal of Zoology,* **211**, 267–274.

94 Burland, T.M. *et al.* (1999) Population genetic structure and gene flow in a gleaning bat, *Plecotus auritus. Proceedings of the Royal Society of London, Series B,* **266**, 975–980.

95 Burland, T.M. *et al.* (2001) Mating patterns, relatedness and the basis of natal philopatry in the brown long-eared bat, *Plecotus auritus. Molecular Ecology,* **10**, 1309–1321.

96 Carroll, J.B. (1988) Nathusius' pipistrelle *Pipistrellus nathusii* in the Channel Islands. *Bat News,* **14**, 2.

97 Castor, C. *et al.* (1993) Von Tagesmenu zum Gestamptfarbspectrum des Grauen Langohrs (*Plecotus austriacus*) – 2 Jahre Freilandar beit furden Fledermausschutz. *Nyctalus,* **4**, 495–538 (in German).

98 Catto, C. (1994) *Bat detector manual*. Bat Conservation Trust, London.

99 Catto, C.M.C. *et al.* (1994) The diet of *Eptesicus serotinus* in southern England. *Folia Zoologica*, **43**, 307–314.

100 Catto, C.M.C. *et al.* (1995) Activity patterns of the serotine bat (*Eptesicus serotinus*) at a roost in southern England. *Journal of Zoology*, **235**, 635–644.

101 Catto, C.M.C. *et al.* (1996) Foraging behaviour and habitat use of the serotine bat (*Eptesicus serotinus*) in southern England. *Journal of Zoology*, **238**, 623–633.

102 Caubere, B. *et al.* (1984) Un record mondial de longevité in nature pour une chiroptère insectivore? *La Terre et la Vie* **39**, 351–353 (in French).

103 Červený, J & Bürger, P (1989) Bechstein's bat, *Myotis bechsteinii* (Kuhl 1818) in the Šumava Region, pp. 591–592 in Hanák, V. *et al.* (eds.) *European bat research 1987.* Charles University Press, Prague.

104 Červený, J. & Horácek I. (1981) Comments on the life history of *Myotis nattereri* in Czechoslovakia. *Myotis*, **18–19**, 156–162.

105 Ciechanowski, M. & Jarzembowski, T. (2004) The size and number of harems in the polygynous bat *Pipistrellus nathusii* (Keyserling and Blasius, 1839) (Chiroptera: Vespertilionidae). *Mammalian Biology*, **69**, 277–280.

106 Clarkson, K. & Whiteley, D. (1985) The distribution of the Daubenton's bat in Sheffield. *Sorby Record*, **3**, 17–20.

107 Collin, P.N. (1995) Leisler's bats from Galloway. *Scottish Bats*, **3**, 8.

108 Constantine, D.G. (2003) Geographic translocation of bats: known and potential problems. *Emerging Infectious Diseases*, **9**, 17–21.

109 Corbet, G.B. (1964) The grey long-eared bat *Plecotus austriacus* in England and the Channel Islands. *Proceedings of the Zoological Society of London*, **143**, 511–515.

110 Corbet, G.B. (1970) Vagrant bats in Shetland and the North Sea. *Journal of Zoology*, **161**, 281–282.

111 Corbet, G.B. (1971) Provisional distribution maps of British mammals. *Mammal Review*, **1**, 95–142.

112 Corbet, G.B. (1978) *The mammals of the Palaearctic region: a taxonomic review*. British Museum (Natural History), London.

113 Corbet, G.B. & Hill J.E. (1991) *A world list of mammalian species*, 3rd edn. Natural History Museum Publications, Oxford University Press, Oxford.

114 Cranbrook, Earl of (1960) Birth of a serotine bat (*Eptesicus serotinus* Schreber) in captivity. *Transactions of the Suffolk Naturalists' Society*, **11**, 387–389.

115 Cranbrook, Earl of (1965) Notes on a foraging group of serotine bats (*Eptesicus serotinus* Schreber) in captivity. *Transactions of the Suffolk Naturalists' Society*, **13**, 14–19.

116 Cranbrook, Earl of & Barrett, H.G. (1965) Observations on noctule bats (*Nyctalus noctula*) captured while feeding. *Proceedings of the Zoological Society of London*, **144**, 1–24.

117 Cropper, R.S. & Ransome, R.D. Personal communication.

118 Csorba, G. *et al.* (2003) *Horseshoe bats of the World*. Alana Books, Bishop's Castle, Shropshire.

119 Currant, A. (1999) A brief review of the Westbury Cave small mammal faunas. Appendix 6. 1: Bats from the pink breccia (unit 11/4) in sample WSM 1978 W2 94, pp. 135–137 in Andrews, P. *et al.* (eds.) *Westbury Cave. The Natural History Museum excavations 1976–1984.* Western Academic Press, Bristol.

120 Daan, S. (1973) Activity during natural hibernation in three species of vespertilionid bats. *Netherlands Journal of Zoology*, **23**, 1–71.

121 Daan, S. (1980) Long term changes in bat populations in the Netherlands: a summary. *Lutra*, **22**, 95–105.

122 Daan, S. & Wichers, H.J. (1968) Habitat selection of bats hibernating in the Netherlands. *Zeitschrift für Säugetierkunde*, **33**, 262–287.

123 Davidson-Watts, I. & Jones, G. (2006) Differences in foraging behaviour between *Pipistrellus pipistrellus* (Schreber, 1774) and *Pipistrellus pygmaeus* (Leach, 1825).

Journal of Zoology, **268**, 55–62.

124 Davidson-Watts, I. *et al.* Personal communcation.

125 De Fanis, E. (1994) *Cues used in communication by microchiropteran bats.* PhD thesis, University of Bristol.

126 De Fanis, E. & Jones, G. (1995) The role of odour in the discrimination of conspecifics by pipistrelle bats. *Animal Behaviour*, **49**, 835–39.

127 De Fanis, E. & Jones, G. (1995) Post-natal growth, mother-infant interactions and development of vocalizations in the vespertilionid bat *Plecotus auritus*. *Journal of Zoology*, **235**, 85–97.

128 De Fanis, E. & Jones, G. (1996) Allomaternal care and recognition between mothers and young in pipistrelle bats (*Pipistrellus pipistrellus*). *Journal of Zoology*, **240**, 781–787.

129 Deansley, R. & Warwick, T. (1939) Observations on pregnancy in the common bat (*Pipistrellus pipistrellus*). *Proceedings of the Zoological Society of London*, **109**, 57–60.

130 Degn, H.J. (1983) Field activity of a colony of Serotine bats. *Nyctalus*, **1**, 521–530.

131 Degn, H.J. *et al.* (1995) Automatic registration of bat activity through the year at Monsted limestone mine, Denmark. *Zeitschrift für Säugetierkunde* 60 (3): 129–135.

132 Dense, C. & Rahmel, U. (2002) Untersuchungen zur Habitatnutzung der Grossen Bartfledermaus (*Myotis brandtii*) im nordwestlichen Niedersachsen. *Landschaftspflege Naturschutz*, **71**, 51–68.

133 Deuff, J. & Beaucornu, J-C. (1981) Phènologie et variations du dermecos chez quelques espèces de Spinturnicidae. *Annales de Parasitologie (Paris)*, **56**, 203–224 (in French).

134 Dietz, C. & von Helversen, O. (2004) *Illustrated identification key to the bats of Europe*. Electronic publication. http://www. unituebingen.de/tierphys/Kontakt/mitarbeiter_seiten/dietz .htm.

135 Dinale, G. (1969) Studi sui Chirotteri Italiani: X. Biometria di una collezione di *Rhinolophus ferrumequinum* Schreber catturati in Liguria (Italy). *Annali del Museo Civic di Storia Naturale di Genova*, **77**, 574–590 (in Italian).

136 Dobson, G.E. (1878) *Catalogue of the Chiroptera in the collection of the British Museum*. Trustees of the British Museum, London.

137 Dobson, J. (1985) Serotine feeding on ground, p. 13 in Dobson, J. (ed.) *Essex Bat Group Report* 1985.

138 Dobson, J. (1999) *The mammals of Essex*. Lopinga Books, Wimbish.

139 Dorcelo, J. & Punt, A. (1969) Abundance and internal migration of hibernating bats in an artificial limestone cave. *Lynx*, **10**, 101–125.

140 Dulic, B. (1980) Morphological characteristics and distribution of *Plecotus auritus* and *Plecotus austriacus* in some regions of Yugoslavia, pp. 151–161 in Wilson, D.E. & Gardner, A.L. (eds.) *Proceedings of the 5th International Bat Research Conference.* Texas Technical Press, Lubbock, TX.

141 Durn, A. Personal communication.

142 Durose, M. & Jones, G. Personal communication.

143 Duvergé, P.L. (1996) *Foraging activity, habitat use, development of juveniles, and diet of the greater horseshoe bat (*Rhinolophus ferrumequinum *– Schreber 1774) in south-west England*. PhD thesis, University of Bristol.

144 Duvergé, P.L. Personal communication.

145 Duvergé, P.L. & Jones, G. (2003) Use of farmland habitats by greater horseshoe bats, pp. 64–81 in Tattersall, F. & Manley, W. (eds) *Conservation and conflict: mammals and farming in Britain.* Occasional Publications of the Linnean Society **4**.

146 Duvergé, P.L. *et al.* (2000) Functional significance of emergence timing in bats. *Ecography*, **23**, 32–40.

147 Eales, L.A. *et al.* (1988) Shared nursing in captive pipistrelles (*Pipistrellus pipistrellus*)? *Journal of Zoology*, **216**, 584–587.

148 Egsbaek W. & Jensen B. (1963) Results of bat banding in Denmark. *Videnskabelig Meddelelser fra Dansk Naturhistorisk Forening*, **125**, 269–296.

149 Eisentraut, M. (1936) Zur Fortpflanzungsbiologie der

Fledermause. *Zeitschrift für Morphologie und Okologie der Tiere*, **31**, 27–63.

150 Eisentraut, M. (1952) Beobachtungen über Jagdroute und Flugbeginn bei Fledermäusen. *Bonner Zoologische Beiträgen*, **3**, 1–22.

151 Ekman, M. & De Jong, J. (1996) Local patterns of distribution and resource utilization of four bat species (*Myotis brandti, Eptesicus nilssoni, Plecotus auritus* and *Pipistrellus pipistrellus*) in patchy and continuous environments. *Journal of Zoology*, **238**, 571–580.

152 Entwistle, A.C. (1994) *Roost ecology of the brown long-eared bat (Plecotus auritus, Linnaeus 1758) in north-east Scotland.* PhD thesis, University of Aberdeen.

153 Entwistle, A.C. *et al.* (1996) Habitat exploitation by a gleaning bat, *Plecotus auritus. Philosophical Transactions of the Royal Society of London*, **351**, 921–931.

154 Entwistle, A.C. *et al.* (1997) Roost selection by the brown long-eared bat *Plecotus auritus. Journal of Applied Ecology*, **34**, 399–408.

155 Entwistle, A.C. *et al.* (1998) The reproductive cycle and determination of sexual maturity in male brown long-eared bats, *Plecotus auritus* (Chiroptera: Vespertilionidae). *Journal of Zoology*, **244**, 63–70.

156 Entwistle, A.C. *et al.* (2000) Social and population structure of a gleaning bat, *Plecotus auritus. Journal of Zoology*, **252**, 11–17.

157 Faveaux, M.A. de (1971) Catalogue des acariens parasites et commensaux des chiroptères. *Documents de Travail, Institut Royal des Sciences Naturelles de Belgique, Studiedocumenten*, **7**, 1–451 (in French).

158 Fisher, C. (1998) Savi's pipistrelle *Pipistrellus savii* in Britain. *Myotis*, **36**, 77–81.

159 Fluckiger, P.F. & Beck, A. (1995) Observations on the habitat use for hunting by *Plecotus austriacus* (Fischer, 1829). *Myotis*, **32–33**, 121–122.

160 Fooks, A.R. *et al.* (2003) Review article: European bat lyssaviruses: an emerging zoonosis. *Epidemiology of Infection*, **131**, 1029–1039.

161 Funakoshi, K. (1991) Reproductive ecology and social dynamics in nursery colonies of the Natterer's bat *Myotis nattereri bombinus. Journal of the Mammal Society of Japan*, **15**, 61–71.

162 Furmankiewicz, J. (2003) The vocal activity of *Pipistrellus nathusii* (Vespertilionidae) in SW Poland. *Acta Chiropterologica*, **5**, 97–105.

163 Gaisler, J. (1966) Reproduction in the lesser horseshoe bat (*Rhinolophus hipposideros hipposideros* Bechstein 1800). *Bijdragen tot de Dierkunde*, **36**, 45–64.

164 Gaisler, J. (1966) A tentative ecological classification of colonies of the European bats. *Lynx*, **6**, 35–39.

165 Gaisler, J. & Hanák, V. (1969) Summary of the results of bat banding in Czechoslovakia, 1948–1967. *Lynx*, **10**, 25–34.

166 Gaisler, J. *et al.* (1979) A contribution to the population ecology of *Nyctalus noctula* (Mammalia: Chiroptera). *Acta Scientiarum Naturalium Brno*, **13**, 1–38.

167 Gaisler, J. *et al.* (1990) The bats of south Moravian Lowlands (Czechoslovakia) over thirty years. *Prirodvedne Prace Ustavu Ceskovenske Academie ved V Brne*, **24**, 1–50.

168 Gaisler, J. *et al.* (1998) Habitat preference and flight activity of bats in a city. *Journal of Zoology*, **244**, 439–445.

169 Gardner, R.A. (1983–84) Blood parasites of British bats. *Myotis*, **21–22**, 190.

170 Gardner, R.A. *et al.* (1987) Studies on the prevalence of haematozoa of British bats. *Mammal Review*, **17**, 75–80.

171 Gauckler, A. and Kraus, M. (1970) Kennzeichen und Verbreittung von *Myotis brandti* (Eversmann, 1845). *Zeitschrift für Säugertierkunde*, **35**, 113–124 (in German).

172 Gebhard, G. (1983–84) *Nyctalus noctula* – Beobachtungen an einem traditionellen Winter-quartier im Fels. *Myotis*, **21–22**, 163–170 (in German).

173 Geisler, H. & Dietz, M. (1999) Zur nahrungsökologie einer wochenstubenkolonie der Fransenfledermaus (*Myotis*

174 George, R.S. (1974) Siphonaptera: Fleas. *Provisional atlas of the insects of the British Isles* 4. Biological Records Centre, Huntingdon.

175 Gerell, R. (1987) Distribution of *Myotis mystacinus* and *Myotis brandti* (Chiroptera) in Sweden. *Zeitschrift für Säugertierkunde*, **52**, 338–341.

176 Gerell, R. (1987) Do Swedish bats migrate? *Fauna et Flora*, **82**, 79–83.

177 Gerell, R. & Gerell Lundberg, K. (1993) Decline of a bat *Pipistrellus pipistrellus* population in an industrialized area in south Sweden. *Biological Conservation*, **65**, 153–157.

178 Gerell, R. & Lundberg, K. (1985) Social organization in the bat *Pipistrellus pipistrellus. Behavioral Ecology and Sociobiology*, **16**, 177–184.

179 Gerell, R & Lundberg, K (1990) Sexual differences in survival rates of adult pipistrelle bats (*Pipistrellus pipistrellus*) in south Sweden. *Oecologia*, **83**, 401–404.

180 Gerell, R. & Rydell, J. (2001) *Eptesicus nilssonii (Keyserling et Blasius, 1839) – Nordfledermaus*, pp. 561–581 in Krapp, F. (ed.) *Handbuch der Säugetiere Europa*s, Band 4: Fledertiere, Tiel I: Chiroptera 1: Rhinolophidae, Vespertilionidae I. AULA-Verlag, Wiesbaden (in German).

181 Gerell-Lundberg, K. & Gerell, R. (1994) The mating behaviour of the pipistrelle and the Nathusius' pipistrelle (Chiroptera) – a comparison. *Folia Zoologica*, **43**, 315–324.

182 Gilbert, O. & Stebbings, R.E. (1958) Winter roosts of bats in West Suffolk. *Proceedings of the Zoological Society of London*, **131**, 321–33.

183 Glas, G.H. (1981) Activities of serotine bats (*Eptesicus serotinus*) in a 'nursing roost'. *Myotis*, **18–19**, 164–167.

184 Glas, G.H. (1982) Records of hibernating barbastelle and grey long-eared bats in the Netherlands outside the southern Limberg cave areas. *Lutra*, **25**, 15–16.

185 Glas, G.H. (1986) Atlas van de Nederlandse vleermuizen 1970–1984. *Zoologischen Bijdragen*, **34**, 1–97 (in Dutch).

186 Glas, G.H. & Braaksma, S. (1980) Aantalsontwikkelingen in zomerverblijfplaatsen van vleermuizen in kerken. *Lutra*, **22**, 84–95 (in Dutch).

187 Glendell, M. & Vaughan, N. (2002) Foraging activity of bats in historic landscape parks in relation to habitat composition and management. *Animal Conservation*, **5**, 309–316.

188 Gloor, S. *et al.* (1995) Nutritional habits of the noctule bat, *Nyctalus noctula*, (Schreber, 1774) in Switzerland. *Myotis*, **32–33**, 231–242.

189 Glue, D.E. (1970) Avian predator pellet analysis and the mammalogist. *Mammal Review*, **1**, 53–62.

190 Goldsmith, J. Personal communication.

191 Greenaway, F. (2001) The Barbastelle in Britain. *British Wildlife*, **12**, 327–334.

192 Greenaway, F. & Hill, J.E. (1987) British record of the northern bat (*Eptesicus nilssonii*). *Bat News*, **10**, 1–2.

193 Greenaway, F. & Hill, J.E. (1988) First British record of the northern bat (*Eptesicus nilssonii*). *Journal of Zoology*, **215**, 357–358.

194 Greenaway, F. & Hutson, A.M. (1990) *A field guide to British bats.* Bruce Coleman Books, Uxbridge.

195 Grol, B.P.F.E. (1985) Multivariate analysis of morphological characters of *Pipistrellus pipistrellus* (Schreber, 1774) and *P. nathusii* (Keyserling & Blasius, 1839) (Mammalia: Chiroptera) from the Netherlands. *Zoologische Verhandelingen, Leiden*, **221**, 1–62.

196 Guillén, A. *et al.* (1994) Organochlorine residues in Spanish common pipistrelle bats (*Pipistrellus pipistrellus*). *Bulletin of Environmental Contamination and Toxicology*, **52**, 231–237.

197 Güttinger, R. *et al.* (2001) *Myotis myotis* (Borkhausen, 1797) – Großes Mausohr, Großmausohr, pp. 123–207 in Krapp, F. (ed.): *Handbuch der Säugetiere Europas. Band 4, Fledertiere. Teil I: Chiroptera I. Rhinolophidae, Vespertilionidae 1.* AULA-Verlag, Wiebelsheim (in German).

198 Haddow, J.F. Personal communication.

199 Haddow, J.F. & Herman, J.S. (1997) New record of Nathusius' pipistrelle from Scotland. *Scottish Bats,* **4,** 6–7.

200 Haensel, J. (1991) Vorkommen, Überwinterungsverhalten und Quartierwechsel der Bechsteinfledermaus (*Myotis bechsteinii*) in Land Brandenburg. *Nyctalus,* **4,** 67–78 (in German).

201 Haensel, J. & Nafe, M. (1993) Flavismus bei einem Braunen Langohr *(Plecotus auritus)* erhebliche Farbaufhellung bei einem Grauen Langohr *(Plecotus austriacus). Nyctalus,* **4,** 465–468 (in German).

202 Haensel, J. & Nest, R. (1989) Partiell-albinotische Fransenfledermaus (*Myotis nattereri*) in Frankfurt/Oder gefunden. *Nyctalus (N.F.),* **3,** 67–69 (in German).

203 Hanák, V. (1966) Ergebnisse der Fledermausberingung in der Sowjet union. *Myotis,* **4,** 12–18 (in German).

204 Hanák, V. (1969) Okologische Bemerkungen zur Verbreitung der Langohnen (Gattung *Plecotus* Geoffroy, 1818) in der Tschechoslowakei. *Lynx,* **10,** 35–39 (in German).

205 Hanák, V. (1976) Hochstalter einer Breitflugelfledermaus (*Eptesicus serotinus*). *Myotis,* **14,** 53–54 (in German).

206 Hancock, B.D. (1963) Some observations on bats in East Surrey and recent records for the London area. *London Naturalist,* **42,** 26–41.

207 Harbusch, C. (2003) *Aspects of the ecology of serotine bats (*Eptesicus serotinus, *Schreber 1774) in contrasting landscapes in southwest Germany and Luxembourg.* PhD thesis, University of Aberdeen.

208 Harbusch, C. & Racey, P.A. (2006) The sessile serotine: the influence of roost temperature on philopatry and reproductive phenology of *Eptesicus serotinus* (Schreber, 1774) (Mammalia: Chiroptera). *Acta Chiropterologica,* **8,** 213–229.

209 Harmata, W. (1962) Seasonal rhythmicity of behaviour and the ecology of bats (Chiroptera) living in some buildings in the district of Krakow. *Zeszyty Naukowe Uniwersytetu Jagionellonskiego (Prace Zoologiczne),* **58,** 149–179.

210 Harmata, W. (1969) The thermopreferendum of some species of bats (Chiroptera). *Acta Theriologica,* **14,** 49–62.

211 Harmata, W. (1973) The thermopreferendum of some species of bats (Chiroptera) in natural conditions. *Zeszyty Naukowe Uniwersytetu Jagiellonskiego,* **19,** 127–141.

212 Harmata, W. (1992) Movements and migrations of lesser horseshoe bat, *Rhinolophus hipposideros* (Bechst.) (*Chiroptera, Rhinolophidae*) in southern Poland. *Prace Zoologiczne,* **39,** 47–60.

213 Harrington, L.A. *et al.* (1995) The status and distribution of barbastelle bat (*Barbastella barbastellus*) and Bechstein's bat (*Myotis bechsteinii*) in the UK, with recovery plans. Unpublished report, Bat Conservation Trust, London.

214 Harris, S. (2006) *European bat lyssaviruses (EBLVs) – exposure and pathogenesis in British bats.* PhD thesis, University of Bristol.

215 Harris, S. *et al.* (1995) *A review of British mammals: population estimates and conservation status of British mammals other than cetaceans.* JNCC, Peterborough.

216 Harris, S.L. *et al.* (2006). European bat lyssaviruses: distribution, prevalence and implications for conservation. *Biological Conservation,* 1**31,** 193–210.

217 Harris, S.L. *et al.* (2006). Passive surveillance (1987 to 2004) of United Kingdom bats for European bat lyssaviruses. *Veterinary Record,* 159, 439–446.

218 Harrison, D.L. & Bates, P.J.J. (1984) Occurrence of *Nyctalus noctula* Schreber, 1774 (Chiroptera: Vespertilionidae) in the Cromerian Interglacial of England. *Mammalia,* **48,** 603–606.

219 Harrison, D.L. & Davies, D.V. (1949) A note on some epithelial structures in Microchiroptera. *Proceedings of the Zoological Society of London,* **119,** 351–357.

220 Harrje, C. (1994) Etho-ökologische Untersuchung der ganzjähringen Aktivität von Wasserfledermäusen (*Myotis daubentoni,* Kuhl, 1819) am Winterquartier. *Mitteilungen der naturforschenden Gesellschaft Schaffhausen,* **39,** 15–52 (in German).

221 Häussler, U. & Nagel, A. (1984) Remarks on seasonal group composition turnover in captive noctules, *Nyctalus noctula* (Schreber 1774). *Myotis,* **21–22,** 172–178.

222 Häussler, U. *et al.* (1999) '*Pipistrellus pygmaeus/mediterraneus*' in SW-Deutschland: ein fast perfekter Doppelgänger der Zwergfledermaus *Pipistrellus pipistrellus. Der Flattermann,* **21,** 13–19 (in German).

223 Häussler, U. *et al.* (1999) External characteristics discriminating species of European pipistrelles, *Pipistrellus pipistrellus* (Schreber, 1774) and *P. pygmaeus* (Leach, 1825). *Myotis,* **37,** 7–40.

224 Havekost, H. (1960) Die Beringung der Breitflugelfledermaus (*Eptesicus serotinus* Schreber) im Oldenbergerland. *Bonner Zoologische Beiträgen,* **11,** 222–233 (in German).

225 Hayden, T. & Harrington, R. (2001) *Exploring Irish mammals.* Duchas, The Heritage Service, Dublin.

226 Hays, G.C. *et al.* (1992) Why do long-eared bats (*Plecotus auritus*) fly in winter? *Physiological Zoology,* **65,** 554–567.

227 Heerdt, P.F. van & Sluiter, J.W. (1961) New data on longevity in bats. *Natuurhistorisch Maandblad,* **3–4,** 36.

228 Heise, G. (1982) Zu Vorkommen, Biologie und Ökologie der Rauhautfledermaus (*Pipistrellus nathusii*) in der Umgebung von Prenzlau (Vekermark), Bezirk, Neubrandenburg. *Nyctalus (N.F.),* **1,** 281–300 (in German).

229 Helversen, O. von & Helversen, D. von (1994) The 'advertisement song' of the lesser noctule bat (*Nyctalus leisleri*). *Folia Zoologica,* **43,** 331–338.

230 Helversen, O. von *et al.* (1987) *Die fledermäuse Sudbadens. Mitteilungen der Badischen Landesvereins für Naturkunde* N.F., **14,** 409–475 (in German).

231 Helversen, O. von *et al.* (2001) Cryptic mammalian species: a new species of whiskered bat (*Myotis alcathoe* sp) in Europe. *Naturwissenschaften,* **88,** 217–233.

232 Henze, O. (1979) 20 und 21 jährige Bechstein-Fledermäuse (*Myotis bechsteinii*) in Bayerischen Giebel-kästen. *Myotis,* **17,** 44 (in German).

233 Herman, J.S. (1992) The earliest record of Nathusius' pipistrelle from the British Isles. *Scottish Bats,* **1,** 48.

234 Hill, J.E. (1992) British reports of Kuhl's pipistrelle. *Bat News,* **26,** 4.

235 Hill, J.E. & Harrison, D.L. (1987) The baculum in the Vespertilioninae (Chiroptera: Vespertilionidae) with a systematic review, a synopsis of *Pipistrellus* and *Eptesicus,* and the descriptions of a new genus and subgenus. *Bulletin of the British Museum (Natural History), Zoology,* **52,** 225–305.

236 Hill, J. & Yalden, D.W. (1990) The status of the hoary bat, *Lasiurus cinereus,* as a British species. *Journal of Zoology,* **222,** 694–697.

237 Hoare, L.R. (1991) The diet of *Pipistrellus pipistrellus* during the pre-hibernal period. *Journal of Zoology,* **225,** 665–670.

238 Hooper, J.H.D. & Hooper, W.M. (1956) Habits and movements of cave dwelling bats in Devonshire. *Proceedings of the Zoological Society of London,* **127,** 1–26.

239 Hopkirk, A. & Russ, J. (2004) *Pre-hibernal and hibernal activity and dispersal patterns of Leisler's bat* Nyctalus leisleri *in Northern Ireland.* Final Report to the Environment and Heritage Service of Northern Ireland.

240 Horácek, I. (1975) Notes on the ecology of bats of the genus *Plecotus* Geoffroy, 1818 (Mammalia, Chiroptera). *Vestnik Cestoslovenske Spolecnosti Zoologiche,* **39,** 195–210.

241 Horácek, I. (1981) Comparative notes on the population structure in several European bat species. *Myotis,* **18–19,** 48–53.

242 Horácek, I. & Benda, P. (2004) *Hypsugo savii (Bonaparte, 1837) – Alpenfledermaus,* pp. 911–941 in Krapp, F. (ed.). *Handbuch der Säugetiere Europas,* Band 4, Fledertiere, Tiel II: Chiroptera II: Vespertilionidae 2, Molossidae, Nycteridae. AULA-Verlag, Wiesbaden.

243 Horácek, I. & Hanák, V. (1984) Comments on the systematics and phylogeny of *Myotis nattereri* (Kuhl, 1818).

Myotis, **21–22,** 20–29.

244 Horácek, I. *et al.* (2000) Bats of the Palaearctic Region: a taxonomic and biogeographical review, pp. 11–157 in Woloszyn, B.W. (ed.) *Proceedings of the VIIIth EBRS. Vol. 1, Approaches to biogeography and ecology of bats.* Institute of Systematics and Evolution of Animals, Krakow.

245 Howard, R.W. (1995) *Auritus. A natural history of the brown long-eared bat.* William Sessions, York.

246 Howes, C.A. (1979) The noctule bat, *Nyctalus noctula* (Schr.) in Yorkshire. *Naturalist,* **104,** 31–38.

247 Hughes, P.M. *et al.* (1989) Suckling behaviour in the pipistrelle bat (*Pipistrellus pipistrellus*). *Journal of Zoology,* **219,** 665–70.

248 Hughes, P.M. *et al.* (1989) Aerodynamic constraints on flight ontogeny in free-living greater horseshoe bats, *Rhinolophus ferrumequinum,* pp. 255–262 in Hanák, V. *et al.* (eds.) *European bat research 1987.* Charles University Press, Prague.

249 Hughes, P.M. *et al.* (1995) Ontogeny of 'true' flight and other aspects of growth in the bat *Pipistrellus pipistrellus. Journal of Zoology,* **235,** 291–318.

250 Hurka, L. (1971) Zur Verbreitung und Okologie der Fledermäuse der Gattung *Plecotus* (Mammalia, Chiroptera) in Westböhmen. *Folia Musei Rerum Naturalium Bohemiae Occidentalis,* **1,** 1–24 (in German).

251 Hurka, L. (1986) Wanderungen und Alter der Fledermaus-artenpopulationen in Westböhmen. *Zpravy Muzei Zapodoceskeho Kraje, Priroda,* **32–3,** 105–109 (in German).

252 Hutson, A.M. (1964) Parasites from mammals in Suffolk. *Transactions of the Suffolk Naturalists' Society,* **12,** 451–452.

253 Hutson, A.M. (1971) Ectoparasites of British bats. *Mammal Review,* **1,** 143–150.

254 Hutson, A.M. (1981) Observations on host-finding by bat-fleas, with particular reference to *Ischnopsyllus simplex* (Siphonaptera; Ischnopsyllidae) in Great Britain. *Journal of Zoology,* **195,** 546–549.

255 Hutson, A.M. (1984) Keds, flat-flies and bat flies, Diptera, Hippoboscidae and Nycteribiidae, pp. 1–40 in *Handbook for identification of British insects,* vol. 10, part 7. Royal Entomological Society, London.

256 Hutson, A. (1985) The mouse-eared bat in Britain. *Bat News,* **4,** 2.

257 Hutson, A.M. (1986) Parti-coloured bats, *Vespertilio murinus,* in Britain. *Bat News,* **7,** 4.

258 Hutson, A.M. (1987) Whiskered bats in south-east Britain. *Bat News,* **11,** 2–3.

259 Hutson, A.M. (1991) Grey long-eared bat at Brighton. *Bat News,* **23,** X.

260 Hutson, A.M. (1992) A Kuhl's pipistrelle in Sussex. *Bat News* **27,** 3.

261 Hutson, A.M. (1993) *Action plan for the conservation of bats in the United Kingdom.* Bat Conservation Trust, London

262 Hutson, A.M. (1993) The British record of Savi's pipistrelle *Pipistrellus savii. Bat News,* **30,** 6.

263 Hutson, A.M. (1995) Recent records. *Bat News,* **36,** 7.

264 Hutson, A.M. (1995) Recent records. *Bat News,* **37,** 6.

265 Hutson, A.M. (1995) Recent records. *Bat News,* **38,** 6.

266 Hutson, A.M. (1996) Recent records. *Bat News,* **43,** 6–7.

267 Hutson, A.M. (1996) Recent reports and news. *Bat News,* **41,** 6.

268 Hutson, A.M. (1997) Recent reports. *Bat News,* **45,** 6.

269 Hutson, A.M. (1997) Recent reports. *Bat News,* **46,** 6.

270 Hutson, A.M. (1997) Two species of bat new to the UK. *Bat News,* **46,** 2.

271 Hutson, A.M. (1999) Bats and dung, pp. 40–45 in Cox, J. (ed.), *The biodiversity of animal dung.* Hampshire and Isle of Wight Trust, Hants.

272 Hutson, A.M. (2002) *DNA from faecal pellets used to assess relationships within and between colonies of serotine bat* Eptesicus serotinus, p. 4 in *Abstracts, IXth European Bat Research Symposium, 26–30 August 2002,* University of Le Havre.

273 Hutson, A.M. (2004) Occurrence, distribution and incidence of Lyssavirus in bats, pp. 40–70 in Racey, P.A. *et al.* (eds) *A review of European Bat Lyssavirus (EBLV) and the status of bats in Scotland.* Commissioned Report No. 063 (ROAME No. FO3AC318). Scottish Natural Heritage, Edinburgh.

274 Hutson, A.M. Personal communication.

275 Hutson, A.M. *et al.* (2001) *Microchiropteran bats: global status survey and conservation action plan.* IUCN/SCC Chiroptera Specialist Group, Gland, Switzerland.

276 Hutterer, R. *et al.* (2005) *Bat migrations in Europe; a review of banding data and literature.* Naturschutz und Biologische Vielfalt 28. BfN, Bonn.

277 Ibanez, C. & Perez-Jorda, J.L. (2004) *Tadarida teniotis (Rafinesque, 1814) – Bulldoggfledermaus,* pp. 1125–1143 in Krapp, F. (ed.). *Handbuch der Säugetiere Europas,* Band 4, Fledertiere, Tiel II: Chiroptera II: Vespertilionidae 2, Molossidae, Nycteridae. AULA-Verlag, Wiesbaden (in German).

278 Janossy, D. (1986) Pleistocene vertebrate faunas of Hungary. *Developments in Palaeontology and Stratigraphy,* **8,** 1–208. Elsevier, Amsterdam.

279 Jarzembowski, T. & Stepniewska, A. (1998) Migration of the Nathusius' pipistrelle *Pipistrellus nathusii* along Baltic coast, p. 41 in *11th International Bat Research Conference,* Departamento de Zoologia, Universidade de Brasilia. Pirenopolis–GO, Brazil.

280 Jefferies, D.J. (1972) Organochlorine insecticide residues in British bats and their significance. *Journal of Zoology,* **166,** 245–263.

281 Jenkins, E.V. *et al.* (1998) Roost selection in the pipistrelle bat, *Pipistrellus pipistrellus* (Chiroptera: Vespertilionidae), in northeast Scotland. *Animal Behaviour,* **56,** 909–917.

282 Jenkinson, R. (1984) *Creswell Crags. Late Pleistocene sites in the East Midlands.* British Archaeological Reports British Series **122,** 1–371. Archaeopress, Oxford.

283 Jenyns, L. (1846) *Observations in natural history.* van Voorst, London.

284 Johansson, M. & De Jong, J. (1996) Bat species diversity in a lake archipelago in central Sweden. *Biodiversity and Conservation,* **5,** 1221–1229.

285 Johnson, N. *et al.* (2003) European bat lyssavirus type 2 RNA in *Myotis daubentonii. Emerging Infectious Diseases,* **12,** 1142–1144.

286 Jones, G. (1990) Prey selection by the greater horseshoe bat (*Rhinolophus ferrumequinum*): optimal foraging by echolocation? *Journal of Animal Ecology,* **59,** 587–602.

287 Jones, G. (1991) Hibernal ecology of whiskered bats (*Myotis mystacinus*) and Brandt's bats (*Myotis brandti*) sharing the same roost site. *Myotis,* **29,** 121–128.

288 Jones, G. (1995) Flight performance, echolocation and foraging behaviour in noctule bats *Nyctalus noctula. Journal of Zoology,* **237,** 303–312.

289 Jones, G. (1997) Acoustic signals and speciation: the roles of natural and sexual selection in the evolution of cryptic species. *Advances in the Study of Behaviour,* **26,** 317–354.

290 Jones, G. (1999) Scaling of echolocation call parameters in bats. *Journal of Experimental Biology,* **202,** 3359–3367.

291 Jones, G. Personal communication.

292 Jones, G. & Barratt, E.M. (1999) *Vespertilio pipistrellus* Schreber, 1774 and *V. pygmaeus* Leach, 1825 (currently *Pipistrellus pipistrellus* and *P. pygmaeus;* Mammalia, Chiroptera): proposed designation of neotypes. *Bulletin of Zoological Nomenclature,* **56,** 182–186.

293 Jones, G. & Billington, G.E. (1999) Radio tracking study of greater horseshoe bats at Cheddar, north Somerset (unpublished). Contract No. F14/01/572, English Nature.

294 Jones, G. & Kokurewicz, T. (1994) Sex and age variation in echolocation calls and flight morphology of Daubenton's bats *Myotis daubentonii. Mammalia,* **58,** 41–50.

295 Jones, G. & Morton, M. (1992) Radio-tracking studies on habitat use by greater horseshoe bats (*Rhinolophus ferrumequinum*), pp. 521–537 in Priede, I.G. & Swift, S.M. (eds.) *Wildlife telemetry: remote monitoring and tracking of*

animals. Ellis Horwood, Chichester.

296 Jones, G. & Parijs, S.M. van (1993) Bimodal echolocation in pipistrelle bats: are cryptic species present? *Proceedings of the Royal Society of London, Series B,* **251,** 119–125.

297 Jones, G. & Ransome, R.D. (1993) Echolocation calls of bats are influenced by maternal effects and change over a lifetime. *Proceedings of the Royal Society of London, Series B,* **252,** 125–128.

298 Jones, G. & Rayner, J.M.V. (1988) Flight performance, foraging tactics and echolocation in free-living Daubenton's bats *Myotis daubentoni* (Chiroptera: Vespertilionidae). *Journal of Zoology,* **215,** 113–132.

299 Jones, G. & Rayner, J.M.V. (1989) Foraging behaviour and echolocation of wild horseshoe bats *Rhinolophus ferrumequinum* and *R. hipposideros* (Chiroptera, Rhinolophidae). *Behavioural Ecology and Sociobiology,* **25,** 183–191.

300 Jones, G. & Rayner J.M.V. (1989) Optimal flight speed in pipistrelle bats, *Pipistrellus pipistrellus,* pp. 247–253 in Hanák, V. *et al.* (eds.) *European bat research 1988.* Charles University Press, Prague.

301 Jones, G. & Rydell, J. (1994) Foraging strategy and predation risk as factors influencing emergence time in echolocating bats. *Philosophical Transactions of the Royal Society of London, Series B,* **346,** 445–455.

302 Jones, G. *et al.* (1991) The development of vocalizations in *Pipistrellus pipistrellus* (Chiroptera: Vespertilionidae) during post-natal growth and the maintenance of individual vocal signatures. *Journal of Zoology,* **225,** 71–84.

303 Jones, G. *et al.* (1992) Sex and age differences in the echolocation calls of the lesser horseshoe bat, *Rhinolophus hipposideros. Mammalia,* **56,** 189–193.

304 Jones, G. *et al.* (1995) Conservation biology of an endangered species: field studies of greater horseshoe bats. *Symposium of the Zoological Society of London,* **67,** 309–324.

305 Jones, G. *et al.* Personal communication.

306 Jones, K.E. *et al.* (1996) Distribution and population densities of seven species of bat in northern England. *Journal of Zoology,* **240,** 788–798.

307 Jooris, R. (1980) Additional data on the distribution of *Plecotus austriacus* (Fischer, 1829) in the low lying districts of Belgium, with a critical assessment of biometrical data of the two *Plecotus* species. *Lutra,* **23,** 3–11.

308 Jüdes, U. (1987) Analysis of the distribution of flying bats along line-transects, pp. 311–318 in Hanák, V. *et al.* (eds.) *European bat research 1987.* Charles University Press, Prague.

309 Jurczyszyn, M. (1998) The dynamics of *Myotis nattereri* and *M. daubentoni* (Chiroptera) observed during hibernation season as an artefact in some type of hibernacula. *Myotis,* **36,** 85–91.

310 Juste, J. *et al.* (2004) Genetic structure in serotine bats, *Eptesicus serotinus,* at two different geographical scales for mtDNA sequences, p. 23 in *Programme and Abstracts for the 13th International Bat Research Conference,* Mikolajki, Poland, 23–27 August 2004. Museum and Institute of Zoology PAS, Warsaw.

311 Kalko, E.K.V. (1995) Insect pursuit, prey capture and echolocation in pipistrelle bats (Microchiroptera). *Animal Behaviour,* **50,** 861–80.

312 Kalko, E.K.V. & Braun M. (1991) Foraging areas as an important factor in bat conservation: estimated capture attempts and success rate of *Myotis daubentonii. Myotis,* **29,** 55–60.

313 Kalko, E.K.V. & Schnitzler, H-U. (1993) Plasticity in echolocation signals of European pipistrelle bats in search flight: implications for habitat use and prey detection. *Behavioral Ecology and Sociobiology,* **33,** 415–428.

314 Kaňuch, P. (2005) Roosting and population ecology of three synoptic tree-dwelling bat species (*Myotis nattereri, M. daubentonii* and *Nyctalus noctula*). *Biologia,* **60,** 579–587.

315 Kaňuch, P. *et al.* (2005) Winter diet of the noctule bat *Nyctalus noctula. Folia Zoologica,* **54,** 53–60.

316 Kaňuch, P. *et al.* (2005) Phenology, diet, and ectoparasites

of Leisler's bat (*Nyctalus leisleri*) in the Western Carpathians (Slovakia). *Acta Chiropterologica,* **7,** 249–257.

317 Kapteyn, K. (ed.) (1993) *Proceedings of the First European Bat Detector Workshop.* Netherlands Bat Research Foundation, Amsterdam.

318 Kapteyn, K. (1993) Intraspecific variation in the echolocation calls of vespertilionid bats, and its implication for identification, pp. 45–57 in Kapteyn, K. (ed.) *Proceedings of the First European Bat Detector Workshop.* Netherlands Bat Research Foundation, Amsterdam.

319 Kapteyn, K. (1995) *Vleermuizen in het landschap. Over hun ecologie, gedrag en verspreiding.* Schuyt & Co, Haarlem (in Dutch).

320 Kapteyn, K. & Lina, P.H.C. (1994) First record of a nursery roost of Nathusius' pipistrelle, *Pipistrellus nathusii,* in the Netherlands. *Lutra,* **37,**106–109.

321 Kawai, K. *et al.* (2003) Distinguishing between the cryptic species *Myotis ikonnikovi* and *M. brandtii* in Hokkaido, Japan: evaluation of a novel diagnostic morphological feature using molecular methods. *Acta Chiropterologica,* **8,** 95–102.

322 Kerth, G. & König, B. (1999) Fission, fusion and non-random associations in female Bechstein's bats (*Myotis bechsteinii*). Unpublished report to Biozentrum der Universität Würzburg, Germany.

323 Kervyn, T. (2001) *Ecology and ethology of the serotine bat, Eptesicus serotinus (Chiroptera, Vespertilionidae): Perspectives for the conservation of bats.* DSc thesis, Université de Liège, Belgium.

324 Kiefer, A. & Vieth, M. (2001) A new species of long-eared bat from Europe (Chiroptera: Vespertilionidae). *Myotis,* **39,** 5–16.

325 Keifer, A. *et al* (2002) Conflicting molecular phylogenies of European long-eared bats (*Plecotus*) can be explained by cryptic diversity. *Molecular Phylogeny and Evolution,* **25,** 557–566.

326 Kleiman, D.G. (1969) Maternal care, growth rate and development in the noctule (*Nyctalus noctula*), pipistrelle (*Pipistrellus pipistrellus*), and serotine (*Eptesicus serotinus*) bats. *Journal of Zoology,* **157,** 187–211.

327 Kleiman, D.G. and Racey, P.A. (1969) Observations on noctule bats (*Nyctalus noctula*) breeding in captivity. *Lynx,* **10,** 65–77.

328 Kokurewicz T. (1995) Increased population of Daubenton's bats (*Myotis daubentonii*) (Kuhl, 1818) (Chiroptera: Vespertilionidae) in Poland. *Myotis,* **32–33,** 155–161.

329 Kokurewicz, T. Personal communication.

330 Kokurewicz, T. & Bartmanska, J. (1992) Early sexual maturity in male Daubenton's bats *Myotis daubentoni* (Kuhl, 1819) (Chiroptera: Vespertilionidae); field observations and histological studies on the genitalia. *Myotis,* **30,** 95–107.

331 Konstantinov, A.I. (1989) The ontogeny of echolocation functions in horseshoe bats, pp. 271–280 in Hanák, V. *et al.* (eds.) *European bat research 1987.* Charles University Press, Prague.

331a Kowalski, M. & Lesinski, G. (1994) Bats occupying nest boxes for birds and bats in Poland. *Nyctalus,* **5,** 19–26.

332 Kozhurina, E.I. and Morozov, P.N. (1994) Can males of *Nyctalus noctula* successfully mate in their first year? *Acta Theriologica,* **39,** 93–97.

333 Krauss, A. (1978) Materialien zur kenntnis de ernahrungsbiologie des braunen langohrs (*Plecotus auritus* L.). *Zoologische Abhandlungen (Staatliches Museum für Tierkunde in Dresden),* **34,** 325–337 (in German).

334 Kretzschmar, F. & Heinz, B. (1995) Social behaviour and hibernation of a large population of *Pipistrellus pipistrellus* (Schreber, 1774) (Chiroptera: Vespertilionidae) and some other bat species in the mining-system of a limestone quarry near Heidelberg (south west Germany). *Myotis,* **32–33,** 221–229.

335 Kronwitter, F. (1988) Population structure, habitat use and activity patterns of the noctule bat, (*Nyctalus noctula*)

Schreb. 1774 (Chiroptera: Vespertilionidae) revealed by radio tracking. *Myotis*, **26**, 23–85.

336 Kroymann, L. (1994) Abendsengler *Nyctalus noctula* als Beute des Wanderfalken *Falco peregrinus* in der Neckartalaue bei Stuttgart-Hofen. *Nyctalus*, **42**, 53–54 (in German).

337 Krzanowski, A. (1961) Weight dynamics of bats wintering in the cave at Pulawy (Poland). *Acta Theriologica*, **4**, 249–264.

338 Krzanowski, A. (1973) Numerical comparison of Vespertilionidae and Rhinolophidae (Chiroptera, Mammalia) in owl pellets. *Acta Zoologica Cracoviensia*, **18**, 249–264.

339 Kuhnert-Ryser, C. (1990) Wissenschaftliche Kurzmitteilung: Herbsfund von fünf wieblichen kleinabendseglern (*Nyctalus leisleri*) im Kanton Bern (Schweiz). *Myotis*, **28**, 131–132 (in German).

340 Kuramoto, T. (1979) Nursery colony of the Japanese greater horseshoe bat, *Rhinolophus ferrumequinum nippon*. *Bulletin Akiyoshi-dai Science Museum*, **14**, 27–44.

341 Kurta, A. & Baker, R.H. (1990) *Eptesicus fuscus*. *Mammalian Species*, **356**, 1–10.

342 Labee, A.M. & Voûte, A.M. (1983) The diet of a nursing colony of serotine bats in the Netherlands. *Lutra*, **26**, 12–19.

343 Laffoley, D. Personal communication.

344 Lanza, B. (1999) I parassiti dei pipistrelli (Mammalia, Chiroptera) della fauna italiana. *Museo Regionale di Scienze Naturali Torino, Monographie*, **30**, 1–318 (in Italian).

345 Lehmann, J. *et al.* (1992) A new longevity record for the long-eared bat (*Plecotus auritus*, Chiroptera). *Mammalia*, **56**, 316–318.

346 Leuzinger, Y. & Brossard, C. (1994) Répartition de *M. daubentonii* en fonction du sexe et de la période de l'année dans le Jura bernois. Résultats préliminaires. *Mitteilungen Naturforschenden Gesellschaft Schaffhausen*, **39**, 135–143 (in French).

347 Lewis, S.E. (1995) Roost fidelity of bats – a review. *Journal of Mammalogy*, **76**, 481–496.

348 Limpens, H.J.G. & Kapteyn K. (1991) Bats: their behaviour and linear landscape elements. *Myotis*, **29**, 39–48. .

349 Limpens, H. *et al.* (1997) *Atlas van de Netherlandse vleermuizen*. KNNV, Utrecht (in Dutch).

350 Limpens, H.J.G.A. *et al.* (2000) Action plan for the conservation of the pond bat in Europe (*Myotis dasycneme*). *Nature and Environment*, no. 108, Council of Europe, Strasbourg.

351 Lina, P.H.C. & Hutson, A.M. (2006) Bat rabies in Europe: a review, pp. 245–254 in Dodet, B. *et al.* (eds.) *Rabies in Europe. Developmental Biology, Basel* **125**.

352 Love, R.A. *et al.* (2000) Changes in the food of British barn owls (*Tyto alba*) between 1974 and 1997. *Mammal Review*, **30**, 107–129.

353 Lubeley, S. (2005) Juvenile exploration behavior and philopatry in the serotine bat, *Eptesicus serotinus*. *Programme abstracts, Xth European Bat Research Symposium*, Galway, Ireland, 21–26 August 2005.

354 Lubeley, S. (2005) Communal night roosting of serotine bats, *Eptesicus serotinus*, in vacant maternity roosts. *Programme abstracts, Xth European Bat Research Symposium*, Galway, Ireland, 21–26 August 2005.

355 Lundberg, K. (1989) *Social organisation and survival of the pipistrelle bat* Pipistrellus pipistrellus *and a comparison of advertisement behaviour in three polygynous bat species*. PhD thesis, University of Lund, Sweden.

356 Lundberg, K. (1990) The occurrence of non-territorial adult and yearling males on the mating ground in the pipistrelle bat (*Pipistrellus pipistrellus*). *Zeitschrift für Säugetierkunde*, **55**, 226–232.

357 Lundberg, K. & Gerell, R. (1986) Territorial advertisement and mate attraction in the bat *Pipistrellus pipistrellus*. *Ethology*, **71**, 115–24.

358 Ma, J. *et al.* (2006) Vocal communication in adult greater horseshoe bats, *Rhinolophus ferrumequinum*. *Journal of Comparative Physiology A*, **192**, 535–550.

359 Mackenzie, G.A. & Oxford, G.S. (1995) Prey of the noctule bat (*Nyctalus noctula*) in east Yorkshire. *Journal of Zoology*, **236**, 322–327.

360 Mackie , I.J. (2002) *Aspects of the conservation biology of the noctule bat* (Nyctalus noctula). PhD thesis, University of Aberdeen.

360a Mackie , I.J. & Racey, P.A. (2007) Habitat use varies with reproductive state of noctule bats *(Nyctalus noctula)* implications for conservation. *Biological Conservation*, **140**, 70-77.

361 Magris, L. (2003) *The Jersey bat survey*. Environment and Public Services Committee, Jersey.

362 Maier, C (1992) Activity patterns of pipistrelle bats (*Pipistrellus pipistrellus*) in Oxfordshire. *Journal of Zoology*, **228**, 69–80.

363 Mason, C.F. (1972) Noctules and starlings competing for roost holes *Journal of Zoology*, **166**, 467.

364 Masters, W.M. *et al.* (1995) Sonar signals of big brown bats, *Eptesicus fuscus*, contain information about individual identity, age, and family affiliation. *Animal Behaviour*, **50**, 1243–1260.

365 Matthews, L.H. (1937) The female sexual cycle in the British horseshoe bats. *Transactions of the Zoological Society of London*, **23**, 224–267.

366 Matthews, L.H. (1952) *British mammals*. Collins, London.

367 Mayer, F. & von Helversen, O. (2001) Sympatric distribution of two cryptic bat species across Europe. *Biological Journal of the Linnaean Society*, **74**, 365–374.

368 Mayer, F. & von Helversen, O. (2001) Cryptic diversity in European bats. *Proceedings of the Royal Society of London Series B*, **268**, 1825–1832.

369 McAney, C.M. & Fairley, J.S. (1988) Activity patterns of the lesser horseshoe bat *Rhinolophus hipposideros* at summer roosts. *Journal of Zoology*, **216**, 352–338.

370 McAney, C.M. & Fairley, J.S. (1989) Observations at summer roosts of the lesser horseshoe bat in Co. Clare, *Irish Naturalist's Journal*, **23**, 1–6.

371 McAney, C.M. & Fairley, J.S. (1989). Analysis of the diet of the lesser horseshoe bat *Rhinolophus hipposideros* in the west of Ireland. *Journal of Zoology*, **217**, 491–498.

372 McLean, J.A. & Speakman, J.R. (1996) Suckling behaviour in the brown long-eared bat (*Plecotus auritus*). *Journal of Zoology*, **239**, 411–416.

373 McOwat, T.P. & Andrews, P.T. (1994) The influence of climate on the growth rate of *Rhinolophus ferrumequinum* in west Wales. *Myotis*, **32**, 69–79.

374 Messenger, J. (1985) The serotine (*Eptesicus serotinus*), a species new to Wales. *Bat News*, **5**, 7.

375 Miller, L.A. & Degn, H.J. (1981) The acoustic behaviour of four species of vespertilionid bats studied in the field. *Journal of Comparative Physiology*, **142**, 76–74.

376 Mitchell-Jones, A.J. (1995) The status and conservation of horseshoe bats in Britain. *Myotis*, **32/33**, 271–284.

377 Mitchell-Jones, A.J. (1999) *The bat workers' manual*. JNCC, Peterborough.

378 Mitchell-Jones, A.J. Personal communication.

379 Mitchell-Jones, A.J. & Ransome, R.D. (1998) Conserving greater horseshoe bat feeding areas: II. Environmental prescriptions. *Myotis*, **36**, 71–76.

380 Mitchell-Jones, A.J. *et al.* (1993) The growth and development of bat conservation in Britain. *Mammal Review*, **23**, 139–148.

381 Mitchell-Jones, A.J. *et al.* (1999) *The atlas of European mammals*. Poyser Natural History/Academic Press, London.

382 Mortimer, G. (2005) *Foraging, roosting and survival of Natterer's bats* Myotis nattereri, *in a commercial coniferous plantation*. PhD thesis, University of St Andrews.

383 Müller, W.W. (2000) Review of reported rabies case data in Europe to the WHO collaborating centre Tübingen from 1977 to 2000. *Rabies Bulletin Europe*, **24**, 11–19.

384 Nagel, A. & Disser, J. (1990) Rückstände von Chlor-kohlenwasserstoff-Pestiziden in einer Wochenstube der

Zwergfledermaus (*Pipistrellus pipistrellus*). *Zeitschrift für Säugetierkunde,* **55**, 217–225 (in German).

385 Nagel, A. & Haussler, U. (1981) Bemerkungen zur Haltung und Zucht von Abendseglern (*Nyctalus noctula*). *Myotis* **18–19**, 1286–1289 (in German).

386 Natuschke, G. (1960) Ergebnisse der Fledermausberingung und biologishe Beobachtungen an Fledermausen in der Oberlausitz. *Bonner Zoologische Beiträgen,* **11**, 77–98 (in German).

387 Néri, F. & Aulagnier, S. (1996) Première reprise d'une noctule de Leisler, *Nyctalus leisleri* (Mammalia: Chiroptera) en France. *Mammalia,* **60**, 317–319 (in French).

388 Nicholls, B. & Racey, P.A. (2006) Habitat selection as a mechanism of resource partitioning in two cryptic bat species *Pipistrellus pipistrellus* and *Pipistrellus pygmaeus*. *Ecography,* **29**, 1–12.

389 Nicholls, B. & Racey, P.A. (2006) Contrasting home-range size and spatial partitioning in cryptic and sympatric pipistrelle bats. *Behavioral Ecology and Sociobiology,* **61**, 131–142.

390 Nieuwenhoven, P.J. van (1956) Ecological observation of hibernation-quarter of cave dwelling bats in South Limberg. *Publicaties van het Natuurhistorisch Genootschap in Limburg,* **9**, 1–55.

391 Norberg, U.M. (1976) Aerodynamics, kinematics and energetics of horizontal flapping flight in the long-eared bat *Plecotus auritus. Journal of Experimental Biology,* **65**, 179–212.

392 Norberg, U.M. (1981) Allometry of bat wings and legs and comparison with bird wings. *Philosophical Transactions of the Royal Society of London, Series B,* **292**, 359–398.

393 Norberg, U.M. & Rayner, J.M.V. (1987) Ecological morphology and flight in bats (Mammalia: Chiroptera): wing adaptations, flight performance, foraging strategy and echolocation. *Philosophical Transactions of the Royal Society of London, Series B,* **316**, 335–427.

394 Nyholm, E.S. (1965) Zur Okologie von *Myotis mystacinus* (Leisl.) und *M. daubentoni* (Leisl.) (Chiroptera). *Annales Zoologici Fennici,* **2**, 77–123 (in German).

395 O'Sullivan, P (1994) Bats in Ireland. *Irish Naturalist's Journal,* **24**, Special Zoological Supplement, 1–21.

396 Oakeley, S.F. & Jones, G. (1998) Habitat around maternity roosts of the 55 kHz phonic type of pipistrelle bats (*Pipistrellus pipistrellus*). *Journal of Zoology,* **245**, 222–228.

397 Obrist, M.K. (1995) Flexible bat echolocation: the influence of individual, habitat and conspecifics on sonar signal design. *Behavioral Ecology and Sociobiology,* **36**, 207–219.

398 Oh, Y.K. *et al.* (1985) Prolonged survival of the Graafian follicle and fertilization in the Japanese greater horseshoe bat, *Rhinolophus ferrumequinum nippon. Journal of Reproduction and Fertility,* **73**, 121–126.

398a Ohlendorf, B. *et al.* (2000). Ferfund eines kleinabendseglers (*Nyctalus leisleri*) in Spanien. *Nyctalus,* **7**, 239–242.

399 Orszaghova, Z. *et al.* (2003) Whiskered bat (*Myotis mystacinus*) as a prey of the edible frog (*Rana esculenta*). *Biologia,* **58**, 291–293.

400 Palasthy, J. & Gaisler, J. (1965) Otazce tak zvanych 'Invazi' a zimnich Koloni netopyra hvizdaveho (*Pipistrellus pipistrellus* Schr. 1774). *Zoologicke Listy,* **14**, 9–14 (in Czech).

401 Palmeirim, J.M. (1991) A morphometric assessment of the systematic position of the *Nyctalus* from Azores and Madeira (Mammalia: Chiroptera). *Mammalia,* **55**, 381–388.

402 Panyutin, K.K. (1963)[Reproduction in the common noctule.] *Uchenye Zapiski Moskovo, Obl. Pedagog. Inst.* **126**, 63–66 (in Russian; see *Biological Abstracts* (1965) **46**, 21, No 96256).

403 Panyutin, K.K. (1980) Rukokrylye, pp. 23–46 in Kuceruk, V. (ed.) *Voprosy teriogii. Itogi mecenija mlekopitajuscich.* Nauka, Moskow (in Russian; cited in [80]).

404 Paresce, C. *et al.* Personal communication.

405 Park, K.J. (1998) *Roosting ecology and behaviour of four temperate bat species.* PhD thesis, University of Bristol.

406 Park K.J. *et al.* (1996) Assortative roosting in the two phonic types of *Pipistrellus pipistrellus* during the mating season. *Proceedings of the Royal Society of London, Series B,* **263**, 1495–1499.

407 Park, K.J. *et al.* (1998) Social structure of three sympatric bat species (Vespertilionidae). *Journal of Zoology,* **244**, 379–389.

408 Park, K.J. *et al.* (1999) Winter activity of a population of greater horseshoe bats (*Rhinolophus ferrumequinum*). *Journal of Zoology,* **248**, 419–427.

409 Park, K.J. *et al.* (2000) Torpor, arousal and activity of hibernating greater horseshoe bats (*Rhinolophus ferrumequinum*). *Functional Ecology,* **14**, 580–588.

410 Parsons, K.N. & Jones G. (2003) Dispersion and habitat use by *Myotis daubentonii* and *Myotis nattereri* during the swarming season: implications for conservation. *Animal Conservation,* **6**, 283–290.

411 Parsons, K.N. *et al.* (2003) Swarming of bats at underground sites in Britain – implications for conservation. *Biological Conservation,* **111**, 63–70.

412 Parsons, K.N. *et al.* (2003). Swarming activity of temperate zone microchiropteran bats: effects of season, time of night and weather conditions *Journal of Zoology,* **261**, 257–264.

413 Parsons, S. Personal communication.

414 Parsons, S. & Jones, G. (2000) Acoustic identification of twelve species of echolocating bat by discriminant function analysis and artificial neural networks. *Journal of Experimental Biology,* **203**, 2641–2656.

415 Parsons, S. *et al.* (1997) Echolocation calls of the long-tailed bat – a quantitative analysis of types of call. *Journal of Mammalogy,* **78**, 964–976.

416 Pennington, M.G. (1992) Vagrant bats and seals in Shetland. *Shetland Bird Club, Shetland Bird Report for 1991,* 76–79.

417 Perez-Barberia, F.J. (1991) Evaluation of damages produced by ringing in *Plecotus austriacus,* Fischer, 1829 (Chiroptera, Vespertilionidae). *Miscellania Zoologica (Barcelona),* **15**, 209–213.

418 Petersen, A. (1994) Leðurblökur á Íslandi. *Natturufraedingurinn* **64**, 3–12 (in Icelandic with English summary).

419 Petersons, G. (1990) Die Rauhautfledermaus, *Pipistrellus nathusii* (Keyserling & Blasius, 1839), in Lettland: Vorkommon, Phänologie und Migration. *Nyctalus (N.F.)* **3**, 81–98 (in German).

420 Petit, E. & Mayer, F. (1999) Male dispersal in the noctule bat (*Nyctalus noctula*): where are the limits? *Proceedings of the Royal Society of London Series B,* **266**, 1717–1722.

421 Petit, E. & Mayer, F. (2000) A population genetic analysis of migration: the case of the noctule bat (*Nyctalus noctula*). *Molecular Ecology,* **9**, 683–690.

422 Petit, E. *et al.* (1999) No evidence of bottleneck in the postglacial recolonization of Europe by the noctule bat (*Nyctalus noctula*). *Evolution,* **53**, 1247–1258.

423 Petit, E. *et al.* (2001) Sex-biased dispersal in a migratory bat: a characterization using sex-specific demographic parameters. *Evolution,* **55**, 635–640.

424 Phillips, W.W.A. & Blackmore, M. (1970) Mouse-eared bats *Myotis myotis* in Sussex. *Journal of Zoology,* **162**, 520–521.

425 Pieper, H. (1968) Neues Hochstalter für die Mauseohrfledermaus. *Myotis,* **6**, 29–30.

426 Pir, J.B. (1994) *Etho-Ökologische untersuchung einer wochenstubenkolonie der grossen hufeisennase (*Rhinolophus ferrumequinum, *Schreber 1774) in Luxemburg.* MSc thesis, University of Giessen, Germany.

427 Podlutsky, A.J. *et al.* (2005) A new field record for bat longevity. *Journals of Gerontology Series A – Biological Sciences and Medical Sciences,* **60**, 1366–1368.

428 Poel, W.H.M. van der *et al.* (2005) European bat lyssaviruses, the Netherlands. *Emerging Infectious Diseases,* **11**, 1854–1859.

429 Poulton, E.B. (1929) British insectivorous bats and their prey. *Proceedings of the Zoological Society of London,* **1929(1)**, 277–303.

430 Pryswitt, K-P. (1997) Eine partiell-albinotische Fransenfledermaus (*Myotis nattereri* Kuhl, 1818) bei Rodewald. *Nyctalus,* **6**, 315–317 (in German).

431 Racey, P.A. (1970) The breeding, care and management of vespertilionid bats in the laboratory. *Laboratory Animals,* **4**, 171–183.

432 Racey, P.A. (1972) Viability of bat spermatozoa after prolonged storage in the epididymis. *Journal of Reproduction and Fertility,* **28**, 171–183.

433 Racey, P.A. (1973) The viability of spermatozoa after prolonged storage by male and female bats. *Periodicum Biologorum,* **75**, 201–205.

434 Racey, P.A. (1973). Environmental factors affecting the length of gestation in heterothermic bats. *Journal of Reproduction and Fertility,* Supplement **19**, 175–189.

435 Racey, P.A. (1974) The temperature of a pipistrelle hibernaculum. *Journal of Zoology,* **173**, 260–262.

436 Racey, P.A. (1974) Aging and assessment of reproductive status in the pipistrelle bat (*Pipistrellus pipistrellus*) *Journal of Zoology,* **173**, 263–271.

437 Racey, P.A. (1974). The reproductive cycle of male noctule bats, *Nyctalus noctula. Journal of Reproductive Fertility,* **41**, 169–182.

438 Racey, P.A. (1977) A vagrant noctule in Orkney. *Journal of Zoology* **183**, 555–556.

439 Racey, P.A. (1979) The prolonged storage and survival of spermatozoa in Chiroptera. *Journal of Reproduction and Fertility,* **56**, 391–402.

440 Racey, P.A. (1991) *Nyctalus noctula.* In Corbet, G.B. & Harris, S. (eds) *The handbook of British mammals.* Blackwell, Oxford.

441 Racey, P.A. Personal communication.

442 Racey, P.A. & Kleiman, D.G. (1970) Maintenance and breeding in captivity of some vespertilionid bats with special relevance to the noctule, *Nyctalus noctula. International Zoo Yearbook,* **10**, 65–70.

443 Racey, P.A. & Speakman J.R. (1987) The energy costs of pregnancy and lactation in heterothermic bats. *Symposia of the Zoological Society of London,* **57**, 107–127.

444 Racey, P.A. & Swift S.M. (1981) Variations in gestation length in a colony of pipistrelle bats (*Pipistrellus pipistrellus*) from year to year. *Journal of Reproduction and Fertility,* **61**, 123–129.

445 Racey, P.A. & Swift, S.M. (1985) Feeding ecology of *Pipistrellus pipistrellus* (Chiroptera: Vespertilionidae) during pregnancy and lactation. I. Foraging behaviour. *Journal of Animal Ecology,* **54**, 205–215.

446 Racey, P.A. & Swift, S.M. (1986) The residual effects of remedial timber treatments on bats. *Biological Conservation,* **35**, 205–214.

447 Racey, P.A. *et al.* (1998) Bats and insects over two Scottish rivers with contrasting nitrate status. *Animal Conservation,* **1**, 195–202.

448 Racey, P.A. *et al.* (2007) Microsatellite DNA polymorphism confirms reproductive isolation and reveals differences in population genetic structure of cryptic pipistrelle bat species *Biological Journal of the Linnean Society,* **90**, 539–550.

449 Rachwald, A. (1992) Habitat preference and activity of the noctule bat *Nyctalus noctula* in the Białowieża primeval forest. *Acta Theriologica* **37**, 413–422.

450 Rakhmatulina, I.K. (1992) Major demographic characteristics of populations of certain bats from Azerbaijan, pp. 127–141 in Horacek, I & Vohralik, V. (eds.) *Prague studies in mammalogy, Collection of papers dedicated to Prof. Dr. Vladimir Hanak on occasion of his 60th birthday.* Carolinum – Charles University Press, Prague.

451 Ransome, R.D. (1968) The distribution of the greater horseshoe bat, *Rhinolophus ferrum-equinum,* during hibernation, in relation to environmental factors. *Journal of Zoology,* **154**, 77–112.

452 Ransome, R.D. (1971) The effect of ambient temperature on the arousal frequency of the hibernating greater horseshoe bat, *Rhinolophus ferrumequinum,* relation to site selection and the hibernation state. *Journal of Zoology,* **164**, 357–371.

453 Ransome, R.D. (1973) Factors affecting the timing of births of the greater horseshoe bat (*Rhinolophus ferrumequinum*). *Periodicum Biologorum,* **75**, 169–175.

454 Ransome, R.D. (1978) Daily activity patterns of the greater horseshoe bat, *Rhinolophus ferrumequinum,* from April to September, pp. 259–274 in Olembo, R.J. *et al.* (eds.) *Proceedings of the Fourth International Bat Research Conference.* Kenya National Academy for Advancement of Arts and Sciences, Kenya Literature Bureau, Nairobi.

455 Ransome, R.D. (1980) *The greater horseshoe bat.* Mammal Society Series, Blandford, Poole.

456 Ransome, R.D. (1989) Population changes of greater horseshoe bats studied near Bristol over the past twenty-six years. *Biological Journal of the Linnean Society,* **38**, 71–82.

457 Ransome, R.D. (1990) *The natural history of hibernating bats.* Christopher Helm, London.

458 Ransome, R.D. (1991) Lesser horseshoe bat. In Corbet, G.B. & Harris, S. (eds.) *The handbook of British mammals.* Blackwell, Oxford.

459 Ransome, R.D. (1991). Greater horseshoe bat, pp. 88–94 in Corbet, G.B. & Harris, S. (eds.) *The handbook of British mammals.* Blackwell, Oxford.

460 Ransome, R.D. (1995) Earlier breeding shortens life in female greater horseshoe bats. *Philosophical Transactions of the Royal Society of London, Series B,* **350**, 153–161.

461 Ransome, R.D. (1996) The management of feeding areas for greater horseshoe bats. *English Nature Research Report,* No. **174**, 1–74.

462 Ransome, R.D. (1997). The management of greater horseshoe bat feeding areas to enhance population levels. *English Nature Research Reports,* **241**, 1–62.

463 Ransome, R.D. (1997). Climatic effects upon foraging success and population changes of female greater horseshoe bats, pp. 129–132 in Ohlendorf, B. (ed.) *Proceedings of the Nebra Rhinolophid Bat Conference 1995.* IF-A Verlages, Berlin.

464 Ransome, R.D. (1998) The impact of maternity roost conditions on populations of greater horseshoe bats. *English Nature Research Reports,* **292**, 1–80.

465 Ransome, R.D. (2000) Monitoring diets and population changes of greater horseshoe bats in Gloucestershire and Somerset. *English Nature Research Reports,* **341**, 1–55.

466 Ransome, R.D. (2002) Winter feeding studies on greater horseshoe bats. *English Nature Research Reports,* **449**, 1–47.

467 Ransome, R. D. & Flanders, J. Personal communication.

468 Ransome, R.D. & McOwat, T.P. (1994) Birth timing and population changes in greater horseshoe bat colonies are synchronised by climatic temperature. *Zoological Journal of the Linnean Society,* **112**, 337–351.

469 Ransome, R.D. & Priddis, D.J. (2005) The effects of FMD-induced mass livestock slaughter on greater horseshoe bats in the Forest of Dean. *English Nature Research Reports,* **646**, 1–67.

470 Reumpler, G. (1980) Handaufzucht und Jungendentwicklung einer Breitflugelfledemaus (*Eptesicus serotinus*). *Zeitschrift Kölner Zoo,* **23**, 25–30 (in German).

471 Richardson, P.W. (1985) Nightly dispersal of Daubenton's bats (*Myotis daubentonii*) from a summer roost site. *Bat Research News,* **28**, 71.

472 Richardson, P.W. (1994) A new method for distinguishing Daubenton's bats (*Myotis daubentonii*) up to one year old from adults. *Journal of Zoology,* **233**, 307–309.

473 Richardson, P. (2000) *Bats.* Whittet Books, London.

474 Richardson, P. (2000) *Distribution atlas of bats in Britain and Ireland.* Bat Conservation Trust, London.

475 Richardson, P.W. Personal communication.

476 Rieger, I. (1996) Tagesquartiere von Wasserfledermäusen *Myotis daubentonii* (Kuhl, 1819) in hohlen Bäumen.

Schweizerischen Zeitschrift für Forstwesen, **147**, 1–20 (in German).

477 Rieger, I. & Alder, H. (1993) Weitere Beobachtungen an Wasserfledermäuse, *Myotis daubentonii,* auf Flugstrasse. *Mitteilungen der Naturforschenden Gesellschaft Schaffhausen,* **38**, 1–34 (in German).

478 Rindle, U. & Zahn, A. (1997) Untersuchungen zum Nahrungsspektrum der Kleinen Bartfledermaus (*Myotis mystacinus*). *Nyctalus,* **6**, 304–308 (in German).

479 Ritchie, J. (1927) A long-flight – the European particoloured bat *Vespertilio murinus* in Scotland. *Scottish Naturalist,* **1927**, 101–103.

480 Rivers, N.M. (2005) *Seasonal changes in population structure and behaviour of the Natterer's bat* (Myotis nattereri). PhD thesis, University of Leeds.

481 Rivers, N.M. *et al.* (2005) Genetic population structure of Natterer's bats explained by mating at swarming sites and philopatry. *Molecular Ecology,* **14**, 4299–4312.

482 Rivers, N.M. *et al.* (2006) Autumn swarming behaviour of Natterer's bats in the UK: population size, catchment area and dispersal. *Biological Conservation,* **127**, 215–226.

483 Roberts, D. (1989) Bats under bridges in North Yorkshire. *Bat News,* **16**, 6–7.

484 Robinson, M.F. (1990) Prey selection by the brown long-eared bat (*Plecotus auritus*). *Myotis,* **28**, 5–18.

485 Robinson, M.F. & Stebbings, R.E. (1993) Food of the serotine bat, *Eptesicus serotinus* – is faecal analysis a valid qualitative and quantitative technique? *Journal of Zoology,* **231**, 239–248.

486 Robinson, M.F. & Stebbings, R.E. (1997) Activity of the serotine bat, *Eptesicus serotinus* in England. *Myotis,* **35**, 5–16.

487 Robinson, M.F. & Stebbings, R.E. (1997) Home range and habitat use by the serotine bat, *Eptesicus serotinus*, in England. *Journal of Zoology,* **243**, 117–136.

488 Robinson, M.F. *at al.* (2000) Dispersal and foraging behaviour of greater horseshoe, Brixham, Devon. *English Nature Research Reports,* **344**, 1–56.

489 Robinson, R.A. *et al.* (2005) *Climate change and migratory species.* British Trust for Ornithology Research Report 414, Defra, London.

490 Robson, B. Personal communication.

491 Roer, H. (1969) Zur ernahurungsbiologie von *Plecotus auritus* (L.) (Mammalia: Chiroptera). *Bonner Zoologische Beiträge,* **20**, 278–283 (in German).

492 Roer, H. (1977) Zur Populationsentwicklung der Fledermäuse (Mammalia, Chiroptera) in der Bundesrepublik Deutschland unter besonderer Berucksicktigung der Situation im Rheinland. *Zeitschrift für Säugertierkunde,* **42**, 265–278 (in German).

493 Roer, H. (1979) Zur Bestandsentwicklung der Breitflugelfledemaus (*Eptesicus serotinus* Schreber) und des Mausohrs (*Myotis myotis* Borkhausen) in Oldenbeger Land. *Myotis,* **17**, 23–30 (in German).

494 Roer, H. (1989). Field experiments about the homing behaviour of the common pipistrelle (*Pipistrellus pipistrellus* Schreber), pp. 551–558 in Hanák, V. *et al.* (eds.) *European bat research 1987.* Charles University Press, Prague.

495 Roer, H. (1989). Zum vorkommen und migrationsverhalten des kleinen Abendseglers (*Nyctalus leisleri* Kuhl, 1818) in Mitteleuropa. *Myotis,* **27**, 99–109 (in German).

496 Roer, H. (1995) 60 years of bat-banding in Europe – results and tasks for future research. *Myotis,* **32–33**, 251–261.

497 Roer, H. (2001) *Myotis dasycneme (Boie, 1825) – Teichfledermaus,* pp. 303–319 *in* Krapp, F. (ed.). *Handbuch der Säugetiere Europas,* Band 4, Fledertiere, Tiel I: Chiroptera 1, Rhinolophidae, Vespertilionidae I. AULA-Verlag, Wiesbaden (in German).

498 Rossiter, S.J. (2000) *The causes and consequences of genetic structure in the greater horseshoe bat (*Rhinolophus ferrumequinum*).* PhD thesis, University of Bristol.

499 Rossiter, S.J. *et al.* (2000) Parentage, reproductive success, and breeding behaviour in the greater horseshoe bat (*Rhinolophus ferrumequinum*). *Proceedings of the Royal Society of London Series B,* **267**, 545–551.

500 Rossiter, S.J. *et al.* (2001) Outbreeding increases offspring survival in wild greater horseshoe bat (*Rhinolophus ferrumequinum*). *Proceedings of the Royal Society of London Series B,* **268**, 1055–1061.

501 Rossiter, S.R. *et al.* (2002) Relatedness structure and kin-biased foraging in the greater horseshoe bat *Rhinolophus ferrumequinum. Behavioural Ecology and Sociobiology,* **51**, 510–518.

502 Rossiter, S.R. *et al.* (2005) Mate fidelity and intra-lineage polygyny in greater horseshoe bats. *Nature,* **437**, 408–411.

503 Rossiter, S.R. *et al.* (2006) Causes and consequences of genetic structure in the greater horseshoe bat, *Rhinolophus ferrumequinum, pp.* 213–226 in Zubaid, A. *et al.* (eds.) *Functional and evolutionary ecology of bats.* Oxford University Press, Oxford.

504 Ruczynski, I. (2006) Influence of temperature on maternity roost selection by noctule bats (*Nyctalus noctula*) and Leisler's bats (*N. leisleri*) in Białowieża Primeval Forest, Poland. *Canadian Journal of Zoology – Revue Canadienne de Zoologie,* **84**, 900–907.

505 Ruczyuski, I. & Bogdanowicz, W. (2005) Roost cavity selection by *Nyctalus noctula* and *N. leisleri* (Vespertilionidae, Chiroptera) in Białowieża primeval forest, eastern Poland. *Journal of Mammalogy,* **86**, 921–930.

506 Ruczynski, I. & Ruczynska, I. (2000) Roosting sites of Leisler's bat *Nyctalus leisleri* in Białowieża Forest – preliminary results. *Myotis,* **37**, 55–60.

507 Ruedi, M. (1993) Variations de la fréquentation de gîtes nocturnes par *Myotis daubentoni* pendant la période de reproduction. Rôle des précipitations de la température. *Mammalia,* **57**, 307–315 (in French).

508 Ruedi, M. & Mayer, F. (2001) Molecular systematics of bats of the genus *Myotis* (Vespertilionidae) suggests deterministic ecomorphological convergences. *Molecular Phylogenetics and Evolution,* **21**, 436–448.

509 Ruedi, M. *et al.* (1998) First breeding record for the noctule bat (*Nyctalus noctula*) in the Iberian peninsula. *Mammalia,* **62**, 301–304.

510 Ruedi, M. *et al.* (2002) DNA reveals the existence of *Myotis alcathoe* in France (Chiroptera: Vespertilionidae). *Revue Suisse de Zoologie,* **109**, 643–652.

511 Ruprecht, A.L. (1971) Distribution of *Myotis myotis* (Borkhausen, 1797) and representatives of the genus *Plecotus* (Geoffroy, 1818) in Poland. *Acta Theriologica,* **16**, 96–104.

512 Ruprecht, A.L. (1979) Bats (Chiroptera) as constituents of the food of barn owls *Tyto alba* in Poland. *Ibis,* **121**, 489–494.

513 Ruprecht, A.L. (1990) Bats (Chiroptera) in the food of the Owls in the Nadnotecka Forest. *Przegląd Zoologiczny,* **34**, 349–358.

514 Russ, J.M. (1996) First record of bimodality in the echolocation calls of the common pipistrelle *Pipistrellus pipistrellus* in Ireland. *Irish Naturalists' Journal,* **25**, 225–226.

515 Russ, J.M. (1999) *The Microchiroptera of Northern Ireland: community composition, habitat associations and ultrasound.* PhD thesis, Queen's University, Belfast.

516 Russ, J. (1999) *The bats of Britain and Ireland – echolocation calls, sound analysis and species identification.* Alana Books, Powys.

517 Russ, J.M. & Montgomery, W.I. (2002) Habitat associations of bats in Northern Ireland: implications for conservation. *Biological Conservation,* **108**, 49–58.

518 Russ, J.M. & Racey, P.A. (2007) Species-specificity and individual variation in the song of male Nathusius' pipistrelles (*Pipistrellus nathusii*). *Behavioral Ecology and Sociobiology,* **61**, 669–677.

519 Russ, J.M. *et al.* (1998) Intraspecific responses to distress calls of the pipistrelle bat, *Pipistrellus pipistrellus. Animal Behaviour,* **55**, 705–13.

520 Russ, J.M. *et al.* (1998) Nathusius' pipistrelle (*Pipistrellus nathusii* (Keyserling & Blasius, 1839)) breeding in Ireland. *Journal of Zoology,* **245,** 345–349.

521 Russ, J.M. *et al.* (2001) The status of Nathusius' pipistrelle, *Pipistrellus nathusii* (Keyserling & Blasius, 1839), in the British Isles. *Journal of Zoology,* **254,** 91–100.

522 Russ, J.M. *et al.* (2003) Seasonal patterns in activity and habitat use by bats (*Pipistrellus* spp. and *Nyctalus leisleri*) in Northern Ireland, determined using a driven transect. *Journal of Zoology,* **259,** 289–299.

523 Russ, J.M. *et al.* (2004) Interspecific responses to distress calls in bats (Chiroptera: Vespertilionidae): a function for convergence in call design? *Animal Behaviour,* **67,** 1005–1014.

524 Russo, D. (2002) Elevation affects the distribution of the two sexes in Daubenton's bats *Myotis daubentonii* in Italy. *Mammalia,* **66,** 543–551.

525 Russo, D. & Jones, G. (2000) The two cryptic species of *Pipistrellus pipistrellus* (Chiroptera: Vespertilionidae) occur in Italy: evidence from echolocation and social calls. *Mammalia,* **64,** 187–197.

526 Russo, D. *et al.* (2004) Spatial and temporal patterns of roost selection by barbastelle bats (*Barbastella barbastellus,* Chiroptera: Vespertilionidae) in beech woodlands of central Italy: consequences for conservation. *Biological Conservation,* **117,** 73–81.

527 Russo, D. *et al.* (2005) Spatial and temporal patterns of roost use by tree-dwelling barbastelle bats *Barbastella barbastellus. Ecography,* **28,** 769–776.

528 Ryberg, O. (1947) *Studies on bats and bat parasites.* Svensk Naturvetenskap, Stockholm.

529 Rydell, J. & Arlettaz, R. (1994) Low-frequency echolocation enables the bat *Tadarida teniotis* to feed on tympanate insects. *Proceedings of the Royal Society of London, Series B,* **257,** 175–178.

530 Rydell, J. & Baagøe, H.J. (1994) *Vespertilio murinus. Mammalian Species,* **467,** 1–6.

531 Rydell, J. & Bogdanowicz, W. (1997) *Barbastella barbastellus. Mammalian Species,* **557,** 1–8.

532 Rydell, J. & Petersons, G. (1998) The diet of the noctule bat *Nyctalus noctula* in Latvia. *Zeitschrift für Säugetierkunde International Journal of Mammalian Biology,* **63,** 79–83.

533 Rydell, J.R. *et al.* (1994) Habitat use by bats along rivers in north east Scotland. *Folia Zoologica,* **43,** 417–434.

534 Saint Girons, H. *et al.* (1969) Contribution à la connaissance du cycle annuel de la chauve-souris *Rhinolophus ferrumequinum* (Schreber, 1774). *Mammalia,* **33,** 357–470.

535 Sargent, G. (1995) *The Bats in Churches project.* Bat Conservation Trust, London.

536 Schlapp, G. (1990) Populationsdichte und habitat-ansprüche der Bechsteinfledermaus *Myotis bechsteinii* (Kuhl 1818) im Steigerwald (Forstamt Ebrach). *Myotis,* **28,** 39–58 (in German).

537 Schmidt, A. (1991) Überflüge von Rauhhautfledermäusen (*Pipistrellus nathusii*) zwischen Ostbrandenburg und Lettland. *Nyctalus,* **2,** 381–385 (in German).

538 Schnitzler, H-U. & Kalko, E.K.V. (1998) How echolocating bats search for and find food, pp. 183–196 in Kunz, T.H. & Racey, P.A. (eds.) *Bat biology and conservation.* Smithsonian Institution Press, Washington, DC.

539 Schober, W. & Grimmberger, E. (1989) *Bats of Britain and Europe.* Hamlyn, London.

540 Schofield, H.W. (1996) *The ecology and conservation biology of* Rhinolophus hipposideros, *the lesser horseshoe bat.* PhD thesis, University of Aberdeen.

541 Schofield, H.W. *et al.* (1997) Research and conservation work on the lesser horseshoe bat. In *The Vincent Wildlife Trust Review of 1996 (and an overview of the Trust's mammal work since its inception).* Vincent Wildlife Trust, London.

542 Schofield, H.W. *et al* (1997). Preliminary studies on Bechstein's bat. In *The Vincent Wildlife Trust Review of 1996 (and an overview of the Trust's mammal work since its inception).*

Vincent Wildlife Trust, London.

543 Schorcht, W. (1994) Beobachtungen zur ökologie des kleinen abendseglers (*Nyctalus leisleri*) in einem südthüringischen vorkommen. *Naturschutz Report,* **7,** 405–408 (in German).

544 Schreve, D.C. (2004) The mammalian fauna of the penultimate (MIS 7) interglacial in the Lower Thames Valley. Table 6 in Schreve, D.C. (ed.) *The Quaternary mammals of southern and eastern England. Field guide.* Quaternary Research Association, London.

545 Searle, J.B. Personal communication.

546 Sese, C. & Ruiz-Bustos, A. (1992) New small mammal faunas from the Pleistocene of the north of the province of Madrid (Spain). *Boletín de la Real Sociedad Española de Historia Natural Sección Geológica,* **87,** 115–139.

547 Shiel, C.B. & Fairley, J.S. (1998) Activity of Leisler's bat *Nyctalus leisleri* (Kuhl) in the field in south-east County Wexford, as revealed by a bat detector. *Biology and Environment: Proceedings of the Royal Irish Academy,* **98B,** 105–112.

548 Shiel, C.B. & Fairley, J.S. (1999) Evening emergence of two nursery colonies of Leisler's bat (*Nyctalus leisleri*) in Ireland. *Journal of Zoology,* **247,** 439–447.

549 Shiel, C.B. & Fairley, J.S. (2000) Observations at two nursery roosts of Leisler's bat *Nyctalus leisleri* (Kuhl, 1817) in Ireland. *Myotis,* **37,** 41–53.

550 Shiel, C.B. *et al.* (1991) Analysis of the diet of Natterer's bat *Myotis nattereri* and the common long-eared bat *Plecotus auritus* in the west of Ireland. *Journal of Zoology,* **223,** 299–305.

551 Shiel, C.B. *et al.* (1998) Analysis of the diet of Leisler's bat (*Nyctalus leisleri*) in Ireland with some comparative analyses from England and Germany. *Journal of Zoology,* **246,** 417–425.

552 Shiel, C.B. *et al.* (1999) Seasonal changes in the foraging behaviour of Leisler's bat *Nyctalus leisleri* in Ireland as revealed by radio-telemetry. *Journal of Zoology,* **249,** 347–358.

553 Shump, K.A. & Shump, A.U. (1982) *Lasiurus cinereus. Mammalian Species,* **185,** 1–5.

554 Siemers, B.M. & Schnitzler, H.U. (2000) Natterer's bat (*Myotis nattereri* Kuhl, 1818) hawks for prey close to vegetation using echolocation signals of very broad bandwidth. *Behavioral Ecology and Sociobiology,* **47,** 400–412.

555 Siemers, B.M & Swift, S.M. (2006) Differences in sensory ecology contribute to resource partitioning in the bats *Myotis bechsteinii* and *Myotis nattereri* (Chiroptera: Vespertilionidae). *Behavioral Ecology and Sociobiology,* **59,** 373–380.

556 Siemers, B.M. *et al.* (1999) The use of day roosts and foraging grounds by Natterer's bats (*Myotis nattereri* Kuhl, 1818) from a colony in southern Germany. *Zeitschrift für Säugetierkunde,* **64,** 241–245.

557 Sierro, A. (1999) Habitat selection by barbastelle bats (*Barbastella barbastellus*) in the Swiss Alps (Valais). *Journal of Zoology,* **248,** 429–432.

558 Sierro, A. & Arlettaz, R. (1997) Barbastelle bats (*Barbastella* spp.) specialise in the predation of moths: implications for foraging tactics and conservation. *Acta Ecologica,* **18,** 91–106.

559 Simms, C. (1977) Kestrels hunting long-eared bats. *British Birds,* **70,** 499–500.

560 Simon, M. *et al.* (2004) Ecology and conservation of bats in villages and towns. *Schriftenreihe für Landschaftspflege und Naturschutz,* **77,** 1–263.

561 Sklenar, J. (1963) The reproduction of *Myotis myotis* Borkh. *Lynx,* **2,** 29–37.

562 Sleeman, D.P. (1996) Pipistrelle bats *Pipistrellus pipistrellus* Schreber injured during fly-fishing. *Irish Naturalist,* **25,** 225.

563 Sluiter, J.W. (1961) Sexual maturity in males of the bat *Myotis myotis. Proceedings, Koninklijke Nederlandse Akademie van Wetenschappen, Series C,* **64,** 243–249.

564 Sluiter, J.W. & Bouman, M. (1951) Sexual maturity in bats of the genus *Myotis* I. Size and histology of the reproductive organs during hibernation in connection with the age and the wear of the teeth in female *Myotis myotis* and *Myotis emarginatus*. *Proceedings, Koninklijke Nederlandse Akademie van Wetenschappen*, **54,** 594–601.

565 Sluiter, J.W. & Heerdt, P.F. van (1966) Seasonal habits of the noctule bat (*Nyctalus noctula*). *Archives Néerlandaises de Zoologie*, **16**, 423–439.

566 Sluiter, J.W. *et al.* (1973) Hibernation of *Nyctalus noctula*. *Periodicum Biologorum* **75**, 181–188.

567 Smiddy, P. (1991) Bats and bridges. *Irish Naturalist's Journal*, **23**, 425–426.

568 Smit, F.G.A.M. (1957) Siphonaptera. *Handbooks for the identification of British insects* **1**(16), 1–94. Royal Entomological Society, London.

569 Smith, P.G. (1995) *Summer roost monitoring of lesser horseshoe bats, Natterer's bats and serotine bats during 1995 in the UK.* Report for the JNCC. Bat Conservation Trust, London.

570 Smith, P.G. (2000) *Habitat preference, range use and roosting ecology of Natterer's bat* (Myotis nattereri) *in a grassland–woodland landscape.* PhD thesis, University of Aberdeen.

571 Smith, P.G. & Racey P.A. (2005). Optimum effort to estimate habitat use when the individual animal is the sampling unit. *Mammal Review,* **35**, 295–301.

572 Smith, P.G. & Racey P.A. (2005). The itinerant Natterer: physical and thermal characteristics of summer roosts of *Myotis nattereri* (Mammalia: Chiroptera). *Journal of Zoology,* **266**, 171–180.

573 Smyth, M. Personal communication.

574 Sokolov, V. E & Cernova, O.F. (1984) [Systematic review of topography and structure of bat's specific skin glands], pp. 55–59 in *Signalizatsiya i ehkologiya mlekopitayuschikh i ptits*. Nauka, Moscow (in Russian).

575 Sosnovtzena, V.A. (1974) [Ecological differences between *Pipistrellus pipistrellus* Schreb. and *Pipistrellus nathusii* Keys. et Blas., in their cohabitation areas], pp. 98–100 in *Conference materials on the bats*. Leningrad (in Russian).

576 Sosnovtzena, V.A. (1974) [Phenomenon of autumn mating in *Pipistrellus nathusii* Keys. et Blas.], pp. 100–101 in *Conference materials on the bats*. Leningrad (in Russian).

577 Speakman, J.R. (1991) Daubenton's bat, p. 109 in Corbet, G.B. & Harris S. (eds.) *The handbook of British mammals*, 3rd edn. Blackwell, Oxford.

578 Speakman, J.R. & Racey, P.A. (1986) The influence of body condition on sexual development of male brown long-eared bats (*Plecotus auritus*) in the wild. *Journal of Zoology,* **233**, 318–321.

579 Speakman, J.R. & Webb, P.I. (1993) Taxonomy, status and distribution of the Azorean bat (*Nyctalus azoreum*). *Journal of Zoology,* **231**, 27–38.

580 Speakman, J.R. *et al.* (1991) Minimum population estimates and densities of bats in N.E. Scotland, near to the northern borders of their distributions, during summer. *Journal of Zoology,* **225**, 327–345.

581 Speakman, J.R. *et al.* (1991) Status of Nathusius' pipistrelle (*Pipistrellus nathusii*) in Britain. *Journal of Zoology,* **225**, 685–690.

582 Speakman, J.R. *et al.* (1993) Six new records of Nathusius' pipistelle *Pipistrellus nathusii* for Scotland. *Scottish Bats,* **2**, 14–16.

583 Speakman, J.R. *et al.* (1995) Emergence patterns of pipistrelle bats (*Pipistrellus pipistrellus*) are consistent with an anti-predator response. *Animal Behaviour,* **50**, 1147–56.

584 Speakman, J.R. *et al.* (1999) Effect of roost size on the emergence behaviour of pipistrelle bats. *Animal Behaviour,* **58**, 787–795.

585 Spitzenberger, E. (1986) Die Nord Fledermaus (*Eptesicus nilssoni*, Keyserling & Blasius, 1839) in Osterreich. *Annals of the Natural History Museum, Vienna,* **87**, 117–130 (in German).

586 Spitzenberger, F. (1992) The lesser noctule (*Nyctalus leisleri* Kuhl, 1818) in Austria, pp. 189–192 in Horácek, I. &

Vohralik, V. (eds.) *Prague studies in mammalogy*. Charles University Press, Prague.

587 Spitzenberger, F. (2001) *Die Säugetierfauna Osterreichs*. Bundersministerium für Land-und Forstwirtschaft, Umwelt and Wasserwirtschaft, Graz (in German).

588 Spitzenberger, F. *et al* (2006) A preliminary revision of the genus *Plecotus* (Chiroptera, Vespertilionidae) based on genetic and morphological results. *Zoologica Scripta,* **35,** 187–230.

589 Stansfield, G. (1966) The parti-coloured bat (*Vespertilio murinus*) from a North Sea drilling rig. *Journal of Zoology,* **150**, 491–492.

590 Stebbings, R.E. (1965) Observations during 16 years on winter roosts of bats in West Suffolk. *Proceedings of the Zoological Society of London,* **144**, 137–143.

591 Stebbings, R.E. (1966). A population study of bats of the genus *Plecotus*. *Journal of Zoology,* **150**, 53–75.

592 Stebbings, R.E. (1966) Bechstein's bat, *Myotis bechsteinii*, in Dorset, 1960–1965. *Journal of Zoology,* 14**8**, 574–576.

593 Stebbings, R.E. (1967) Identification and distribution of bats of the genus *Plecotus* in England. *Journal of Zoology,* **153,** 291–310.

594 Stebbings, R.E. (1968) Measurements, composition and behaviour of a large colony of the bat *Pipistrellus pipistrellus*. *Journal of Zoology,* **156**, 15–33.

595 Stebbings, R.E. (1968) Bechstein's bat (*Myotis bechsteinii*) in Dorset 1966–67. *Journal of Zoology,* **155**, 228–231.

596 Stebbings, R.E. (1970). A comparative study of *Plecotus auritus* and *P. austriacus* (Chiroptera, Vespertilionidae) inhabiting one roost. *Bijdragen tot de Dierkunde,* **40**, 91–94.

597 Stebbings, R.E. (1970) A bat new to Britain, *Pipistrellus nathusii*, with notes on its identification and distribution in Europe. *Journal of Zoology,* **161**, 282–286.

598 Stebbings, R.E. (1977) Order Chiroptera, pp. 68–128 in Corbet, G.B. & Harris, S. (eds.) *The handbook of British mammals*, 2nd edn. Blackwell, Oxford.

599 Stebbings, R.E. (1982) Radio tracking greater horseshoe bats with preliminary observations on flight patterns. *Symposia of the Zoological Society of London*, **49**, 161–173.

600 Stebbings, R.E. (1986). Rare cave bats – how rare are they? *Bat News* **6**, 2–3.

601 Stebbings, R. (1986). *Which bat is it?* Mammal Society, London.

602 Stebbings, R.E. (1990) Is the long-term survival of the greater horseshoe bat a viable concept? *British Wildlife,* **1**, 14–19.

603 Stebbings, R.E. (1992) Mouse-eared bat – extinct in Britain? *Bat News,* **26**, 2–3.

604 Stebbings, R.E. (1993) *The Greywell Tunnel: an internationally important haven for bats*. English Nature (South Region), Newbury, Berkshire.

605 Stebbings, R.E. Personal communication.

606 Stebbings, R.E. & Arnold, H.R. (1987) Assessment of trends in size and structure of a colony of the greater horseshoe bat. *Symposia of the Zoological Society of London,* **58**, 7–24.

607 Stebbings, R.E. & Griffiths, F. (1986) *Distribution and status of bats in Europe*. Institute of Terrestrial Ecology, Monks Wood, Abbots Ripton.

608 Stebbings, R.E. & Robinson, M.F. (1991) The enigmatic serotine bat – a case of human dependency. *British Wildlife,* 2, 261–265.

609 Stebbings, R.E. *et al.* (2007) *Which bat is it?* Mammal Society, London.

610 Steffens, R. *et al.* (2005) *40 Jahre Fledermausmark-ierungszentrale Dresden – methodische Hinweise und Ergeb-nisubersicht*. Sachsisches Landesamt für Umwelt und Geologie, Dresden (in German).

611 Strachan, R. (1986) Noctule bats returned to hibernation. *Batchat* **7**, 10–12.

612 Strelkov, P. (1962) The peculiarities of reproduction in bats (Vespertilionidae) near the northern border of their distribution, pp. 306–311 in *International Symposium on*

Methods of Mammal Investigations, Brno, 1960.

613 Strelkov, P. (1969) Migratory and stationary bats (Chiroptera) of the European part of the Soviet Union. *Acta Zoologica Cracoviensia,* **14,** 393–439.

614 Strelkov, P.P. (1997). Breeding area and its position in range of migratory bats species (Chiroptera, Vespertilionidae) in East Europe and adjacent territories. Communication 1. *Zoologicheskii Zhurnal,* **76,** 1073–1082.

615 Strelkov, P.P. (1997). Breeding area and its position in range of migratory bats species (Chiroptera, Vespertilionidae) in East Europe and adjacent territories. Communication 2. *Zoologicheskii Zhurnal,* **76,** 1381–1390.

616 Strelkov, P.P. (2001) Materials on wintering of migratory bat species (Chiroptera) on the territory of the former USSR and adjacent regions. Part 1. *Vespertilio murinus* L. *Plecotus et al.,* **4,** 25–40.

617 Strelkov, P.P. & Buntova, E.G. (1982) *Myotis mystacinus* and *M. brandti,* inter-relations of these species, part I. *Zoologischeskii Zhurnal,* **61,**1227–1241.

618 Strelkov, P.P. *et al.* (2002) Geographic variation of craniometric characteristics in the noctule bat *Nyctalus noctula* (Chiroptera) related to its life history. *Zoologichesky Zhurnal,* **81,** 850–863.

619 Strong, L. & Wall, R. (1994) Effects of ivermectin and moxidectin on the insects of cattle dung. *Bulletin of Entomological Research* **84,** 403–409.

620 Stutz, H.P. & Haffner, M. (1986) Activity patterns of non-breeding populations of *Nyctalus noctula* (Mammalia, Chiroptera) in Switzerland. *Myotis,* **23–24,** 149–155.

621 Sullivan, C.M. *et al.* (1993) Analysis of the diets of Leisler's *Nyctalus leisleri,* Daubenton's *Myotis daubentoni* and pipistrelle *Pipistrellus pipistrellus* bats in Ireland. *Journal of Zoology,* **231,** 656–663.

622 Swanepoel, R.E. *et al.* (1999) Energetic effects of sublethal exposure to lindane on pipistrelle bats (*Pipistrellus pipistrellus*). *Environmental Pollution,* **104,** 169–177.

623 Swift, S.M. (1980) Activity patterns of pipistrelle bats (*Pipistrellus pipistrellus*) in north-east Scotland. *Journal of Zoology,* **190,** 285–295.

624 Swift, S.M. (1981) *Foraging, colonial and maternal behaviour of bats in north-east Scotland.* PhD thesis, University of Aberdeen.

625 Swift, S.M. (1997) Roosting and foraging behaviour of Natterer's bats (*Myotis nattereri*) close to the northern border of their distribution. *Journal of Zoology,* **242,** 375–384.

626 Swift, S.M. (1998) *Long-eared bats.* Poyser, London.

627 Swift, S.M. (2001) Growth rate and development in infant Natterer's bats (*Myotis nattereri*) in a flight room. *Acta Chiropterologica,* **3,** 217–223.

628 Swift, S.M. Personal communication.

629 Swift, S.M. & Racey, P.A. (1983) Resource partitioning in two species of vespertilionid bats (Chiroptera) occupying the same roost. *Journal of Zoology,* **200,** 249–259.

630 Swift, S.M. & Racey P.A. (2002) Gleaning as a foraging strategy in Natterer's bat *Myotis nattereri. Behavioral Ecology and Sociobiology,* **52,** 408–416.

631 Swift, S.M. *et al.* (1985) Feeding ecology of *Pipistrellus pipistrellus* (Chiroptera: Vespertilionidae) during pregnancy and lactation. 2. Diet. *Journal of Animal Ecology,* **54,** 217–25.

632 Taake, K.H. (1984) Strukturelle Untersciede zwischen den Sommerhabitaten von Kleiner und Großer Bartfledermaus (*Myotis mystacinus* und *M. brandti*) in Westfalen. *Nyctalus,* **2,** 16–32 (in German).

633 Taake, K.H. (1992) Strategien der resourcennutzung an Waldgewässern jagender Fledermäuse (Chiroptera: Vespertilionidae). *Myotis,* **30,** 7–74 (in German).

634 Taake, K.H. (1993) Zur Nahrungsokologie waldwohnender Fledermäuse- ein Nachtrag. *Myotis,* **31,** 163–165 (in German).

635 Taake, K.H. & Hilddenhagen, U. (1989) Nine years inspections of different artificial roosts for forest-dwelling bats in Northern Westfalia: some results. In Hanak, V. *et al.* (eds.) *European bat research 1987.* Charles University Press, Prague.

636 Teeling, E. *et al.* (2005) A molecular phylogeny for bats illuminates biogeography and the fossil record. *Science,* **307,** 580–584.

637 Thompson, M.J.A. (1982) A common long-eared bat *Plecotus auritus* – moth predator–prey relationship. *Naturalist,* **107,** 87–98.

638 Thompson, M.J.A (1987) Longevity and survival of female pipistrelle bats (*Pipistrellus pipistrellus*) on the Vale of York, England. *Journal of Zoology,* **211,** 209–214.

639 Thompson, M.J.A. (1990) The pipistrelle bat *Pipistrellus pipistrellus* Schreber in the Vale of York. *Naturalist,* **115,** 41–56.

640 Thompson, M.J.A (1992) Roost philopatry in female pipistrelle bats *Pipistrellus pipistrellus. Journal of Zoology,* **228,** 973–979.

641 Thompson, M.J.A. Personal communication.

642 Topal, G. (1956) The movements of bats in Hungary. *Annales Historico-Naturales Musei Nationalis Hungarici,* **7,** 477–488.

643 Topal, G. (1966) Some observations on the nocturnal activity of bats in Hungary. *Vertebratica Hungarica,* **8,** 139–165.

644 Trappmann, C. (1997) Aktivitätsmuster einheimischer fledermäuse as einem bedeutenden winterquartier in den Baumbergen. *Abhandlungen aus dem Westfälischen Museum für Naturkunde,* **59,** 51–62 (in German).

645 Trappmann, C. (1999) Anmerkungen zur altersbestimmung bei der Fransenfledermaus, *Myotis nattereri* (Kuhl, 1817). *Nyctalus,* **7,** 121–135 (in German).

646 Trappman, C. & Ropling, S. (1996) Bemerkenswerte winterquartierfunde des abendseglers, *Nyctalus noctula* (Schreber, 1774), in Westfalen. *Nyctalus (N.F.),* **6,** 114–120 (in German).

647 Tsytsulina, K. (2001). *Myotis ikonnikovi* (Chiroptera, Vespertilionidae) and its relationship with similar species. *Acta Chiropterologica,* **3,** 11–19.

648 Turner, V.L.T. (2002) *Aspects of the ecology of Daubenton's bat* (Myotis daubentonii), *the common pipistrelle* (Pipistrellus pipistrellus), *the soprano pipistrelle* (P. pygmaeus) *and their potential prey in relation to altitude.* PhD thesis, University of Leeds.

649 Uhrin, M. (1995) The finding of a mass winter colony of *Barbastella barbastellus* and *Pipistrellus pipistrellus* in Slovakia. *Myotis,* **32–33,** 131–133.

650 Urbanczyk, Z. (1990) Northern Europe's most important hibernation site. *Oryx,* **24,** 30–34.

651 Urbanczyk, Z. (1991) Hibernation of *Myotis daubentoni* and *Barbastella barbastellus* in Nietoperek bat reserve. *Myotis,* **29,** 115–120.

652 Vaughan, N. (1997) The diets of British bats (Chiroptera). *Mammal Review,* **27,** 77–94.

653 Vaughan, N. *et al.* (1996) Effects of sewage effluent on the activity of bats (Chiroptera: Vespertilionidae) foraging along rivers. *Biological Conservation,* **78,** 337–343.

654 Vaughan, N. *et al.* (1997) Identification of British bat species by multivariate analysis of echolocation call parameters. *Bioacoustics,* **7,** 189–207.

655 Vaughan, N. *et al.* (1997) Habitat use by bats (Chiroptera) assessed by means of a broad-band acoustic method. *Journal of Applied Ecology,* **34,** 716–730.

656 Voûte, A.M. (1982) First recorded accidental transatlantic bat transport. *Bat Research News,* **23,** 16–18.

657 Voûte, A.M. (1983) De twintigste vleermuisssort voor Nederland? *Lutra,* 20–23 (in Dutch).

658 Waldhovd, H. & Hoegh-Guildberg, O. (1984) On the feeding habits of the common long-eared bat, *Plecotus auritus* (Chiroptera: Vespertilionidae). *Flora og Fauna,* **90,** 115–118.

659 Wallin, L. (1961) Territorialism on the hunting ground of *Myotis daubentonii. Säugetierkundliches Mitteilungen,* **9,** 156–159.

660 Walsh, A. *et al.* (2001) *The UK's national bat monitoring programme, final report 2001.* Department for the Environment, Food and Rural Affairs, Bristol.

661 Warren, R. (1999) Lesser horseshoe bat summer roost monitoring, 29 May to 17 June 1998. CCW Natural Science Report 98/9/2. Unpublished Report to the Countryside Council for Wales.

662 Warren, R.D. *et al.* (1997) The ecology and conservation of Daubenton's bats *Myotis daubentonii*, in Mainstone, C.P. (ed.) *Species management in aquatic habitats. Compendium of project outputs – research and survey reports on non-mollusc species 1998.* R&D Project Record W1/i640/2/m. Environment Agency.

663 Warren, R. *et al.* (2000) The influence of small scale habitat features in the distribution of Daubenton's bats in riverine habitats. *Biological Conservation,* **92**, 85–91.

664 Waters, D.A. *et al.* (1995) Echolocation call design and limits on prey size: a case study using the aerial hawking bat *Nyctalus leisleri. Behavioural Ecology and Sociobiology,* **37**, 321–328.

665 Waters, D. *et al.* (1999) Foraging ecology of Leisler's bat (*Nyctalus leisleri*) at two sites in southern Britain. *Journal of Zoology,* **249**, 173–180.

666 Webb, P.I. *et al.* (1996) Population dynamics of a maternity colony of the pipistrelle bat (*Pipistrellus pipistrellus*) in north-east Scotland. *Journal of Zoology,* **240**, 777–80.

667 Weid, R. (1994) Sozialrufe mannlicher Abendsegler (*Nyctalus noctula*). *Bonner Zoologische Beiträge,* **45**, 33–38 (in German).

668 Whitby, J.E. *et al.* (2000) First isolation of a rabies-related virus from a Daubenton's bat in the United Kingdom. *Veterinary Record,* **147**, 250–254.

669 Whiteley, D. & Clarkson, K. (1985) Leisler's bats in the Sheffield area – 1985. *Sorby Record,* **23**, 12–16.

670 Whiteley, D & Johnson, S. (1984) Daubenton's bat in the Sheffield area. *Sorby Record,* **22**, 24–27.

671 Wijngaarden, A. van, *et al.* (1971) De verspreiding van de Nederlandse zoogdieren. *Lutra,* **13**, 1–41 (in Dutch).

672 Wilkins, K.T. (1989) *Tadarida brasiliensis. Mammalian Species,* **331**, 1–10.

673 Williams, C. (2001) *The winter ecology of* Rhinolophus hipposideros, *the lesser horseshoe bat.* PhD thesis, Open University.

674 Wilson, D.E. & Reeder, D.M. (2005) *Mammal species of the world; a taxonomic and geographical reference,* 3rd edn. John Hopkins University Press, Baltimore, MD.

675 Wohlgemuth, R. *et al.* (2004) Long-distance flight of a lesser noctule (*Nyctalus leisleri*) after rehabilitation. *Myotis,* **41–42**, 69–73.

676 Wolz, I. (1992) *Zur Ökologie der Bechsteinfledermaus* Myotis bechsteinii *(Kuhl, 1818) (Mammalia: Chiroptera).* PhD thesis, University of Erlangen (in German).

677 Yalden, D.W. (1986) Neolithic bats from Dowel Cave, Derbyshire. *Journal of Zoology* A, **210**, 616–619.

678 Yalden, D. (1999) *The history of British mammals.* Poyser, London.

679 Yoshiyuki, M. (1989) *A systematic study of the Japanese Chiroptera.* National Science Museum, Tokyo.

680 Young, H.G. (1989) *Report of Jersey Natural History Society.* Jersey Natural History Society, Jersey.

681 Zahn, A. & Hager, I. (2005) A cave-dwelling colony of *Myotis daubentonii* in Bavaria, Germany. *Mammalian Biology,* **70**(4), 250–254.

682 Zahn, A. & Rupp, D. (2004) Ectoparasite load in European vespertilionid bats. *Journal of Zoology,* **262**, 383–391.

683 Zbinden, K. (1989) Field observations on the flexibility of the acoustic behavior of the European bat *Nyctalus noctula* (Schreber, 1774). *Revue Suisse de Zoologie,* **96,** 335–343.

684 Zima, J. & Horácek, I. (1985) Synopsis of karyotypes of vespertilionid bats (Mammalia: Chiroptera). *Acta Universitatis Carolinae Biologica,* **1981**, 311–329.

685 Zima, J. & Kral, B. (1984) Karyotypes of European mammals I. *Acta Scientiarium, Brno* **18**(7), 1–51.

686 Zingg, P.E. (1988) A conspicuous cry of the noctule bat *Nyctalus noctula* (Schreber) (Mammalia, Chiroptera) in the mating season. *Revue Suisse de Zoologie,* **95,** 1057–1062.

687 Zingg, P.E. (1988) Search calls of echolocating *Nyctalus leisleri* and *Pipistrellus savii* (Mammalia: Chiroptera) recorded in Switzerland. *Zeitschrift für Saügetierkunde,* **53**, 281–293.

688 Zingg, P.E. (1990) Akustische Artidentifikation von Fledermäusen (Mammalia: Chiroptera) in der Schweiz. *Revue Suisse de Zoologie* **97**, 263–294 (in German).

hazy, since many pet cats live partly (even largely) independent of their 'owners'. Distinctions may lie more in attitude of owner than behaviour of cat. Convenient to use the adjective 'dependent' (on people) to describe those domestic cats that are not feral (or independent). Feral or domestic cats are readily identified throughout most of British Isles except in N Scotland, where can be confused with wildcats. May be impossible to distinguish between a striped tabby feral domestic cat and a wildcat from a brief sighting [229, 704] (see wildcat account, below).

Typically, smaller than wildcats, but much variation and considerable overlap; castrated male domestic cats often very large [135]. Striped tabby domestic cats usually distinguished from wildcats by their tapering tails with pointed tips, rings on tails joined by a dorsal stripe from back, and more stripes on body and legs, which tend to break up into spots especially on rump (see further discussion under wildcat). Blotched tabby pattern (circular whorls on the flanks) is a domestic variant, wild type being a striped tabby pattern (vertical stripes or spots on the flanks).

Skull: Width of brain case (mastoid width) >75% of zygomatic width. Very similar to wildcat skull, but traditionally differs in 4 key characters (see Fig. 9.1): (a) the medial junction of the nasals and frontal is usually in a pit (in one plane in wildcat) (b) anterior nasals are angular (smooth in wildcat) (c) sagittal suture straight (convoluted in wildcat) (d) angular process of the mandibles poorly developed (well developed in wildcat) [704, 710, 1427, 1428]. Differences also in cranial volume and overall length (see wildcat).

Chromosomes: 2n = 38; FNa = 68 as in wildcat [1441].

SIGN

Cat tracks are readily distinguishable due to 4 toes, lack of claw marks and similarly rounded shape of both fore- and hind-paw prints (Fig. 9.2). Toe prints compact, arranged in an arc, and all 4 point forward. Great size variation, but print on soft ground *c.*3.5 cm long × 4.0 cm wide. Hind pad 3-lobed. Tracks distinguished from those of canids by very different shape and, generally, absence of claw marks, and from those of mustelids by absence of claw marks and 4 rather than 5 toes. When walking, hindfoot placed in front of corresponding forefoot track; stride 30 cm and straddling the midline (cf. fox). When trotting, stride lengthens to 35–40 cm and becomes straighter.

Will use paths and tracks such as those of fox, badger, rabbits, but does so with less regularity

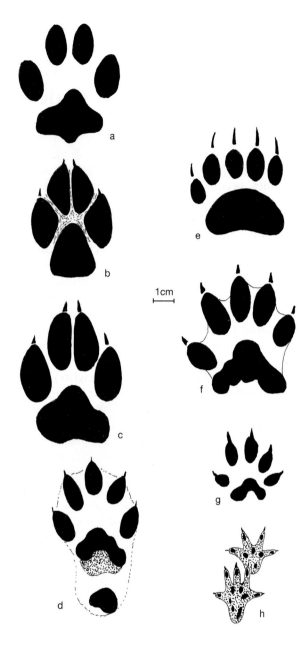

Fig. 9.2 Carnivore footprints are useful for recognising the species' identity and presence. Cats (a), foxes (b) and dogs (c) show only 4 toe pads; cats rarely show claw marks, but like dogs, and unlike foxes, have a 3-lobed main pad. Mustelids (d–g) usually show 5 toes, though the 'thumb' sometimes fails to register. Badgers (e) show 4 toes in a row ahead of the wide main pad, and usually show long claw marks. The webbing does not always show on otter prints (f), but is diagnostic when it does, and note the irregular main pad. Martens (d), mink (g), and the smaller *Mustela* spp. (whose tracks are rarely detected) usually show 5 evenly-spaced toes, whereas rodents (e.g. water vole (h)) have only 4 front toes, arranged in a star-like pattern, though 5 hind toes, arranged as 3 ahead of 2 lateral ones. (*drawn by D.W. Yalden, approximately to scale*).

than either of these species, and does not normally form its own network of trails. Generally travels along hedgerows, woodland edges and other borders. Characteristically coloured fur caught on barbed-wire fences at crossing places. Dens often in outbuildings, hay stores, woodpiles, rock piles or other natural shelters in the countryside; in urban areas dens in crevices in buildings. Claw-sharpening scratch marks sometimes on trees (often elder), fence posts and other wooden uprights [390].

Faeces and scent: Pungent urine sprayed backwards by adult males on to upright surfaces, e.g. fence posts and grassy tussocks; this behaviour much less frequent for females [390]. Cats associated with farms tend to bury faeces when in vicinity of farmyard, as do house cats, but leave them atop conspicuous objects along trails when further afield in their home ranges, as do wildcats [859, 1020]. Faeces 6–8 cm long × 1.5 cm diameter.

Food remains: Difficult to distinguish from those of other carnivores. Chews through feather quills, as does fox; unlike fox, tends not to break bones of larger prey such as rabbits, rarely chews heads off rabbits or birds. Bite marks of upper canine teeth *c*.1.8 cm apart. Food sometimes, but not often, cached beneath loose covering of leaf litter, or dragged into cover and off the ground, but never buried as by fox.

MEASUREMENTS
Weight: Females 2.5–4.5 k g, males 3.5–7.0 kg, newborn 80–140 g, 5 weeks *c*.450 g, 8 weeks *c*.1 kg.

VARIATION
Selective breeding has produced a large number of varieties. Coat colours may be associated with other qualities (pleiotropic effects) affecting survival of feral cats; blotched tabby and black gene are common in urban feral populations [1112]; dark mutant that occurs commonly among feral cats on Marion I., S Ocean, is associated with small adrenal glands [3]. Distribution of some varieties (e.g. sex-linked orange, non-agouti) reflects ancient shipping and overland trade routes [1302, 1303]. See under wildcat for hybridisation, consequent difficulties of identification.

DISTRIBUTION
Feral cats with various degrees of dependence on humans probably numerous throughout the British Isles, but in unknown numbers and distribution. Most conspicuously associated with urban development, especially hospitals, warehouses, dockyards and urban centres, but also found in the countryside. Introductions to many islands, e.g. to St Kilda in 1930 and to Noss, South Havra and Holm of Melly in Shetland in the 1890s to control rats. In 1950, 36 cats released on Great Saltee I. off Ballyteige Bay, Co. Wexford, for rabbit control [785]. Wherever there are crofters, e.g. Western Isles, there are cats living feral in some degree, and there are feral populations on some uninhabited islands, e.g. Monach I., where they were initially released to control rabbits [228]. Distribution of feral cats in urban areas reviewed in [1082], but little is known on the extent of their independence from provisioning by people and this survey is out of date. There are probably >9 million cats in the British Isles, of which *c*.20% have been classed as feral [1262].

HISTORY
Ancient Egyptian paintings, *c*.2000 BC, are earliest certain records of cats in domestic circumstances; appear subsequently in the art of India and China [211, 1303]. Possible very early domestic cats recorded, Cyprus: skeleton from Shillourokambos, 7000 BC, and mandible from Khirokitia, 6000 BC; similar size to *lybica*, wildcats not recorded from Cyprus, so these presumed early domestic introductions [266, 775]. Recorded from Iron Age sites in GB [499, 1206], still scarce in Roman period, only became common in Middle Ages [1420]. Wild ancestor probably *Felis silvestris lybica* [211, 217], which may have begun its own domestication by exploiting rodents associated with early grain stores.

HABITAT
Found in varying degrees of independence from people, in wide variety of habitats, from urban docklands [260, 261] to wooded valleys [400] and farmland [788, 845].

SOCIAL ORGANISATION AND BEHAVIOUR
Structure: Social organisation varies between habitats: more solitary where food dispersed and fluctuating in abundance, more sociable where it is clumped and abundant, e.g. farms and rubbish tips [671]. Social relationships within a group of farm cats have been described [859, 865]. Groups seem to develop as matrilines, successive generations of daughters sharing a home range with broadly amicable relationships [1, 865]. Social structure of these groups involves a net flow of social greetings from socially peripheral, and perhaps subordinate, females to a central one which is perhaps the original female of the matriline. Larger colonies are probably not integrated social units, but composed of a central, and reproductively successful, matriline which

Fig. 9.3 Skins of wildcat (a), hybrid (b) and feral tabby cat (c), showing head, nape and flank striping, separate bands on tail, and clubbed tip to tail that characterise wildcats (*photo © The Trustees of the National Museums of Scotland*).

domestic cat >2.75 [1149, 1342]. Although skulls of castrated male domestic cats may be as big as those of wildcats [135], they always have a much higher cranial index. 4 skull characters allow separation of wildcats from domestic cats (see above, Fig. 9.1). Wildcat skull is more robust and the cranium is much broader (reflected by greater cranial volume) than domestic cat (Fig. 9.4). Skull morphometrics can distinguish samples of wildcats, domestic cats and their hybrids [414, 710], but some discriminant functions may give false identifications for individual cat skulls.

398

Table 9.1 Feral cats, hybrids and wildcats: key pelage characters [871]

	Feral cat	Hybrid	Wildcat
Dorsal stripe	Absent/extends down tail	Continues on to tail	Stops at base of tail
Tail tip	Tapered to point	Intermediate	Blunt
Tail bands	Absent/joined by dorsal stripe	Indistinct/fused	Distinct
Stripes on flanks/hindquarters	>50% broken, or absent	25–50% broken	<25% broken
Spots on flanks/hindquarters	Many, or absent	Some	None
Stripes on nape	Thin/none	Intermediate	4, thick
Stripes on shoulders	Indistinct/none	Intermediate	2, thick

SIGN

Footprints: 4 toes and a 3-lobed main pad; 5th toe on front foot and metacarpal pad do not normally register, except in very soft ground (Fig. 9.2). Print roughly circular in outline, usually larger than that of domestic cat, more delicate than that of fox; overprinting often occurs. Claws protractile so do not usually register, except in very soft ground, but toe pads extended further from foot pad than in those of dogs and foxes (Fig. 9.2) [152].

Faeces: Dark and variable in colour, from brown to grey-green; strong musty odour when fresh. Roughly cylindrical in shape, 15 mm diameter × 40–80 mm long [228, 1223], but may be formless depending on diet. Sometimes buried, but usually left exposed and often deposited in conspicuous areas on rocks, tussocks of vegetation and along animal trails [228, 569].

Communication: Scratch marks left on trees and saplings when removing cornified layers on claws are probably also visual and olfactory cues for other cats. Also exposed faeces in prominent positions along trails (see above), which may include anal gland and/or anal sac scretions, and sprays of urine against trees and other objects at nose height.

Feeding remains: Lagomorphs typically have skin everted, with muscle cleaned from bones, and ribs and scapulae chewed [228]. However, same signs left by domestic cats when feeding on similar prey. Caching of uneaten prey observed, remains hidden under vegetation and covered with debris [228, 1304], in holes and in trees [741].

DESCRIPTION

See Table 9.1. Fur thick, length *c.*50 mm on sides and up to 70 mm along the back in winter coat (20–30 mm in summer coat), and very dense (10 000–30 000/cm^2 in winter, 5500–24 000/cm^2 in summer) [1032, 1040, 1223]. Agouti patterned, giving an overall general coat colour of buff grey or yellowish brown, occasionally silvery grey [1038, 1040, 1287]. Up to 12 dark brown or black body stripes, 4–7 transverse bands on the hind legs and 2–3 more or less distinct bands on the forelegs below the elbow. Tail thickly furred and club-like, with 3–5 distinct black rings and a blunt black tip [710]. Ground colour of tail usually greyer and paler than body. 4 longitudinal stripes with a distinctive wave (always straight in domestic cats and most hybrids) [710] extend from the nape up and over the forehead, where they may become confused, and down on to the shoulders where they disappear. On shoulders, 2 usually well-defined longitudinal stripes *c.*60 mm in length and 10–20 mm apart [710, 942, 1040]. The dorsal stripe begins behind the shoulder stripes and terminates at the base of the tail [228, 710]. On the cheeks, 3 stripes, 2 of which are fused [710]. Small patches of white fur on belly (at umbilicus), chest and throat may or may not be present in any combination [228, 703]. Muzzle and upper lips buff, but often a white edge to upper lips. Chin off-white or buff [228, 703]. Ears coloured as body, often with ochre or rusty wash, darkening towards the tip. Underparts lighter, large distinct dark spots on belly; buff to ochreous fur in groin, inside hind legs and underside of tail base. Foot pads black with variable amount of black fur running from foot to ankle on hindfeet [1032]. Eyes amber, pupils narrow to vertical slit in bright light. Nose pink with dark line running up centre. Whiskers mostly white. Kittens and juveniles darker and more distinctly marked than adults, with less bushy tail.

Moult: Little information available. Seasonal moults recorded: winter coat persists from October until mid–end March, takes 6 weeks to be replaced by summer coat, which lasts until end September [564, 1032, 1223]; more research required.

Senses: Good vision at night; retinal ganglion cell densities 20–100% higher than in domestic cat, total number of retinal ganglion cells 70% greater [1385], reflective tapetum lucidum present. Good vision in daylight (possibly colour vision); density of cone receptors more than 100% higher than in domestic cat [1385]. Sense of smell keen; under favourable conditions has been reported to detect meat at up to 200 m [1304]. Vibrissae mostly on upper lips, a few on each cheek and over the eyes. Short bristle-like whiskers found on the chin.

Ears erect, cone shaped, can be moved through 180° to locate source of sound. Hearing very sensitive; in domestic cat extends from 30 Hz to 65 kHz [372, 1416].

Nipples: 4 pairs; axillary pair sometimes absent [904].

Scent glands: Apocrine and sebaceous scent glands on head, chin and base of tail, and sebaceous glands between toes.

Teeth: Dental formula $i^3/_3c^1/_1p^3/_2m^1/_1$. Incisors small and rather weak; canines and carnassials (p^4 and m_1) well developed. 1st and 2nd upper premolars (p^2 and p^3) vestigial or absent; p_2 occasionally present [1040].

Chromosomes: 2n = 38, FNa = 68 (European data) [1441], as in domestic cat.

RELATIONSHIPS

Most closely related to sand cat *Felis margarita* of the Sahara, etc., Chinese mountain cat *F. bieti* (which may be conspecific), jungle cat *F. chaus* of S Asia and black-footed cat *F. nigripes*, of southern Africa [226, 665, 898, 1135]. African (*lybica* group) and Asian (*ornata* group) wildcats treated either as subspecies of a polytypic *F. silvestris* or as one or more separate species [704]. Recent craniometric study showed that skulls of *F. s. lybica* and *F. s. ornata* groups are very similar, but distinctly differentiated from European *F. s. silvestris* [1427].

MEASUREMENTS

See Table 9.2.

VARIATION

Wildcats in Scotland have been considered as a subspecies (*F. s. grampia*) on the basis of general darker coloration, with extensive, well-defined dark markings on flanks and legs [941, 942]. However, there is considerable variation within the Scottish population [1040] and a distinction between British and European forms may not be justified [715]. Recent research suggests that the boldness of flank stripes is clinal with a decrease from W (Scotland, Spain) to E (Russia) [708].

Hybridisation with domestic cats occurs, producing fertile offspring [215, 1035]. Hybrids can closely resemble *F. silvestris*, making identification difficult in the field. However, tails of hybrids tend to resemble those of *F. catus*, being tapered and less distinctly marked; the dorsal stripe continues on to the tail; there are spots on the rump; and the nape stripes are straight [228, 7803, 708, 1341]. *F. silvestris* is distinguishable from *F. catus* on basis of cranial volume [1149], cranial characters [703, 704], pelage characters [1341] and gut length [1151]. Hybrids can be distinguished from wildcats by skull and pelage characters [1341], and skull morphometrics [414].

Recent morphological study of wild-living cats in Scotland unable to distinguish groups of cats that corresponded to wildcats and domestic cats [67, 254], but identified 2 groups; group 1 cats had short guts and long standardised limb bone lengths, whereas group 2 cats had long guts and short limb bone lengths. Although group 1 cats might be equated with wildcats, they showed much greater variation in pelage markings and coloration than usually associated with the wildcat; 31% were non-tabby. Recent analyses of microsatellites (nuclear DNA) showed greatest genetic distances occur between wildcats and domestic cats (as defined by 5 key pelage characters), and group 1 and 2 cats respectively [80]. Therefore, these 2 approaches overlap extensively, but further research required to resolve current differences in interpretation.

An alternative multivariate statistical analysis of 21 pelage characters provided a diagnosis of the wildcat that is consistent with the traditional description given above [710]. It also suggests that hybridisation has been occurring in Scotland for at least 150 years [1341]. 7 key pelage characters were identified in wildcats (Fig. 9.3) including (1) 3 stripes on the cheeks, 2 of which are fused; (2) 4 thick wavy stripes extending from crown to nape of neck; (3) 2 distinct shoulder stripes; (4) a dorsal stripe extending only to root of tail; (5) stripes on flank and rump continuous or discontinuous, but never break up

Table 9.2 Wildcats and domestic cats from Scotland: measurements. Only specimens which have been identified by the skull and pelage characters of [1341] are included.

	Wildcats		Domestic cats	
	Male	**Female**	**Male**	**Female**
Head and body length (mm)				
n	19	10	10	16
Mean	587.0	539.9	498.6	479.9
Range	547–655	473–575	435–555	435–527
Tail length (mm)				
n	19	10	10	16
Mean	305.4	283.8	284.2	270.2
Range	276–326	257–320	264–325	234–340
Hindfoot length (mm)				
n	17	11	8	13
Mean	136.3	125.0	115.6	116.4
Range	120–154	111–140	100–129	107–134
Weight (kg)				
n	20	11	10	16
Mean	5.30	3.73	3.72	3.72
Range	3.77–7.26	2.35–4.68	2.10–4.90	2.90–6.60

into distinct spots; (6) 3–5 rings on tail that do not overlap; and (7) blunt black tip to tail (Table 9.1) [710]. 8 subsidiary characters may also help distinguish wildcats from other cats.

Melanistic cats reported from Scotland, where commonly called 'Kellas cats' [409]. Most specimens so far studied are melanistic hybrids, although one appears to be the first melanistic Scottish wildcat [702, 708]. 2 studies on wild-living cats in Scotland found that 16–17% of the animals were black, although their taxonomic status was uncertain [254, 708]; similar to gene frequencies of non-agouti gene in rural populations of *F. catus* in Scotland [205]. The status of apparently similar melanistic forms in E Europe is also unclear [17, 1004, 1143].

It has been suggested that there is much greater variation in wildcat coat colour and markings than currently recognised, e.g. *c.*31% of group 1 cats were non-tabby [67]. However, this proportion seems very high compared with populations in Slovakia (1.2%; [1194]), implying that hybridisation may be the main cause.

DISTRIBUTION

In Europe, found mainly in woodland, but distribution highly fragmented [1222]. Elsewhere, in savannah and steppe zones from W China to the Middle East, except in India, and throughout Africa, except in desert and tropical forest areas (Fig. 9.5) [226, 489, 995, 1040]. Modern and historical global distributions modelled using GIS environmental data [1]. In GB, range confined to C and N Scotland (Fig. 9.6); absent from Scottish islands, although there are historical records from Skye and fossil remains from Bute [703, 1101]. The most recent survey of the wildcat in Scotland [336, 337] failed to find any evidence that this species was present S of the central industrial belt of Scotland, although it is recorded S of here in the Kyle of Lochalsh. Reports of wildcats further S probably refer to feral cats, although the possibility of an unofficial release of this species cannot be ruled out. The central industrial belt appears to be acting as a physical barrier to the natural southward movement of the wildcat into S Scotland.

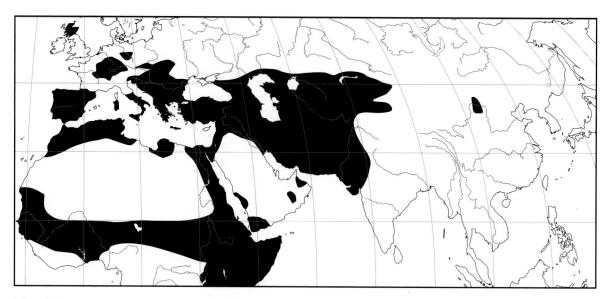

Fig. 9.5 Wildcat *Felis silvestris*: northern part of world range, which extends to S Africa.

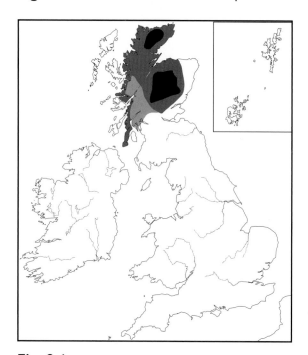

Fig. 9.6 Wildcat *Felis silvestris*: range in GB.

HISTORY

Present in Europe, including Swanscombe, England, at least since Hoxnian Interglacial, common in cave faunas of Last Glaciation; extensive refugium, Last Glaciation, across S Europe, Spain to Romania [763, 1218]. Present Late Glacial, Sun Hole, Somerset, and early in Postglacial British Isles; recorded Mesolithic, Thatcham, Berkshire, *c.*9000 bp and in Ireland [1217]. Known only from Mesolithic to Late Bronze Age sites in Ireland, probably became extinct by Late Bronze Age or Iron Age [912]. Cause of early extinction in Ireland unknown.

More recent history documented in [769].

Steady reduction in range from the Middle Ages through hunting and habitat destruction. Disappeared from S England probably during 16th century. Lost from N England and Wales by 1880, and also last heard of in S Scotland at about this time. Population minimum occurred *c.*1914, when thought confined to Inverness-shire, parts of Argyllshire, Ross-shire and Sutherland. However, this restricted relict distribution recently questioned [67, 767] on basis of literature records. Possible that small numbers of wildcats survived over a wide area, would explain rapidity of apparent recolonisation between the wars [296]. Freedom from persecution during World War I (1914–1918) and reduced persecution levels since then have allowed the wildcat to expand its range, aided by increased reafforestation, particularly of coniferous woodland [337, 769].

Recently, identification of wildcat has become contentious, because of hybridisation with domestic cats, which have been in GB for *c.*3000 years [67, 236, 254, 704, 1206, 1274]; but see [491, 492]. Some authors believe that the definition of a wildcat may rest on its lifestyle rather than a strict physical definition [67]. Uncertainty over appearance of indigenous wildcat, because no specimens or other reference exist from before arrival of domestic cat. Argued therefore that characteristics currently recognised as indicating hybridisation may be part of natural variation in the wild population, or that today's wildcat may be the result of natural selection on a variably introgressed population. Contradicted by other recent research, suggesting that pelage and skull characters used to distinguish wildcat (see above) have been consistent across Europe for 100–200 years, do provide basis for defining hybrids, even though wildcat populations small in comparison with those of introgressed hybrids and feral domestic cats [710, 1079, 1221, 1341].

HABITAT

Found in the margins of mountains and moorland with rough grazing and most often with forests and crops [337]. Regional differences; marginal agricultural areas with moorlands, pastureland and woodlands in E; uplands with rough grazing and moorland, and some pastures in W [337]. Avoids high mountain areas, exposed coasts, fertile lowlands with intensive agriculture, and industrialised/urbanised areas. Recorded from >800 m asl, but usually found <500 m. Onset of bad weather in winter may drive wildcats from exposed moorland and hill ground to areas containing more woodland and scrub [228]. However, recent study of wild-living cats in the Angus glens found that cats remained at an altitude of *c.*380 m throughout the year, even during a severe winter [253]. Forestry plantations, especially in the early years after planting, important habitat because they are freed from grazing pressure by fencing, offer shelter and prey such as small mammals and rabbits [228].

SOCIAL ORGANISATION AND BEHAVIOUR

Solitary and territorial except when mating [228]. Social groups as in other felids, i.e. male and female in oestrus, female and kittens, and dispersing siblings [705]. Home-range size varies geographically, depending on availability of food, quality of habitat and age structure of population. Heavily persecuted population, NE Scotland, comprised 85% juveniles; where there were abundant rabbit populations in woodland habitats, male (n = 2) and female (n = 2) ranges similar in size, mean annual areas 1.75 km^2 [228]. In Angus glens, median home range for male cats was more than double that for females (males 4.59 km^2, n = 7; females 1.77 km^2, n = 6) [253]. However, non-persecuted population, W Scotland, comprised 80% adults; had a low population density of rabbits, consisted mainly of heathland and rough grassland, home ranges were much larger; male winter home ranges (mean 14.3 km^2, n = 3 (range 9–18 km^2)) exceeded those of females (mean 9 km^2, n = 2 (range 8–10 km^2)) [1160]. Male and female ranges overlapped, but core areas of an individual's range avoided by other cats; least overlap of range between animals of same sex. Females more sedentary and exclusively territorial, probably related to the need for exclusive hunting areas when raising young in years of poorest food availability. Young animals have smallest ranges (females (n = 3) average 0.77 km^2; males (n = 3) average 0.54 km^2) in NE Scotland. Juvenile wild-living cats in the Angus glens had smaller home ranges than adult females (males median = 1.59 km^2, n = 3; females median = 0.63 km^2) [253]. Many males, particularly young animals, nomadic [228], probably trying to find vacant areas to establish home ranges. Little information on hierarchy, but older cats dominant to young animals [228].

Scent-marking: Territorial marking achieved by spraying urine on trees, vegetation and boulders and by depositing faeces (with or without anal sac/gland secretion) in prominent places, e.g. tussocks of vegetation. Scratching of trees and saplings may also serve as a visual marker and as an olfactory sign by the deposition of scent from interdigital glands on paws. Exhibit flehmen reaction, using vomeronasal organ to sample scent [369].

Vocal communication: Little information; mostly silent, but have been heard to scream during the mating season [1153, 1304]. Vocalisation frequent between mother and kittens; purring by mother and kittens recorded during suckling [218]. Yowling was heard 4 times when tracking 3 different adult male wild-living cats in the Angus glens during winter and spring; one was recorded with an adult female who shared the male's home range [253].

Aggressive behaviour: Rarely recorded except between males during mating season over access to females. Aggressive encounters possibly not common because of mutual avoidance. Young animals failed to settle in areas that were already occupied [228]; whether as a result of direct aggression not known.

Activity: Mainly crepuscular and nocturnal, although may be active at any hour of the day [228]. More strictly nocturnal in summer, but in winter active throughout 24 h, probably in response to food shortage, but remained in thick cover during daylight hours [1159]. Remained inactive for periods up to 28 h during heavy snowfall and rain [228]; also inactive during strong winds which upset ability to hunt [1304]. Wild-living female cats were more active than males during the day, Angus glens (55% of daylight fixes active for females, 36% for males), but both sexes showed similar activity at night (66% of nocturnal fixes active for females, 68% for males) [253].

Dens: Situated amongst large rocks and boulders and rocky cairns on hill ground, old fox earths, badger setts and amongst tree roots. Little attempt at nest building in den, though some effort may be made by female to rake in dry grass and heather before giving birth [1304].

Locomotion: Walking, running and leaping. Swims well when necessary and climbs well, but usually descends trees backwards unlike true arboreal animals.

Grooming: Uses barbed tongue and forepaws, with teeth and claws, to remove debris in fur.

FEEDING

Carnivorous, taking small rodents, lagomorphs and birds. Composition of diet related to availability of prey; up to 70% lagomorphs in E and up to 47% small mammals in W [228, 569]. Hunting organised in circuit, with different habitats visited [228]. Mobile and stationary hunting strategies used to hunt small rodents [228, 1153]. Larger prey, e.g. lagomorphs, stalked from behind cover when possible, before final rush and seizure of prey, which is killed by bite to back of neck, dislocating cervical vertebrae with canines and severing spinal cord. May also sit over rabbit holes waiting for prey to emerge [228]. Carrion (sheep and deer) rarely taken [228, 1304]; scavenges road casualties, e.g. lagomorphs. Other species taken include amphibians, reptiles, insects and a variety of small mammals and birds. Vegetation, including grass and bracken, also eaten possibly as source of roughage [1304].

BREEDING

One litter produced, usually in April–May, but kittens can be born March–August (Fig. 9.7) [219, 220, 228]. Oestrus lasts 5–9 days, gestation 65 days (range 60.5–68.5) [1223]; if no conception, recycles in *c*.14 days. Mean litter size in captivity 3.4, range 1–8 [219], in wild 3.4, range 1–7 [1223]. Weight at birth 65–163 g [1150], duration of lactation 6–7 weeks [1304].

In captivity, females able to breed at 1 year of age; males begin to show signs of sexual activity from 9–10 months [219], but unlikely to breed successfully until established in home range. Males fertile from mid December to beginning of August [219, 220, 228], but possibly all year round [904]. Females seasonally polygynous, come into oestrus in spring, usually February–March in Scotland [228, 904], but may be fertile December–August [1223]. Wildcats, like other felids, are believed to be induced ovulators, but there is also evidence for spontaneous ovulation in domestic cats and lynxes, so possible in wildcats too [700]; more research needed. Single litter produced, usually in April–May (59% in E Scotland, n = 27 [228]); reports of repeated breeding in same year [904], but may be confusion with late-born litters or the early loss of a litter, allowing female to recycle and give birth later in the year. Reports of several males attending oestrous female, but also records of male and female alone together, having formed temporary pair [1304]. Male and female observed to share same range and occasionally to move about together over 2-week period at mating time [228]. Sex ratio 1:1 at birth [220], but road casualties, trapped and shot samples usually show bias towards males.

Young: Blind at birth but covered in fur, weigh *c*.135 g (range 65–163 g, but <90 g do not usually survive) [1150, 1329]. Pads pink, darkening almost to black at 3 months [228]. Eyes open at 7–13 days, blue at first, but change from 7 weeks to final amber colour at *c*.5 months [228, 793, 1329]. Kittens begin to walk at 16–20 days [793], play at 4–5 weeks, and may follow female hunting or change den sites from 10–12 weeks [1223]. Lactation completed mostly by 6–7 weeks, but continues sporadically up to 4 months [793]. Female brings live prey to den from 3 weeks. Some evidence of males bringing prey to female and kittens [1305]. Milk teeth all erupted by 6–7 weeks [939], permanent dentition complete at 175–195 days [219]. 4 upper canines present for limited period as permanent canines erupt before deciduous ones are lost [219]. Largely grown by 10 months, with skeletal growth continuing to 18–19 months, when epiphyses of long bones close [1152].

Family breaks up from *c*.5 months [781, 792], and young enter roaming stage while attempting to establish home range [228]. However, females may stay within part of mother's home range during winter for up to 6 months [1223]. May disperse up to 55 km [1032].

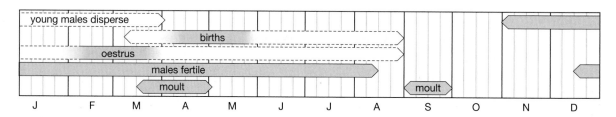

Fig. 9.7 Wildcat: annual cycle.

POPULATION

In NE Scotland 30.3 cats/100 km² [228] but in W only 8 cats/100 km² [1160]; density varies with quality of habitat and availability of prey, and note differences in persecution levels on age structure of populations below. In Europe estimates vary: 1 cat/0.7–10 km² [1153].

Age structure little known, but 2 samples of cats from a persecuted population in NE Scotland indicated essentially young population, containing 15% and 25% adult animals respectively [228]. Age structure of group 1 cats shows most (93%) <6 years old [67]. In a non-persecuted population in W Scotland, 80% were adults (n = 5) [1159].

Population size for 1990s estimated at 3500 [536], but because only 18% of a sample from the 1990s considered to be pure wildcats [67], population of true wildcats then perhaps as low as 400, would make the wildcat a critically endangered species in GB [710, 1428].

MORTALITY

Persecution by snaring and shooting (most often by lamping) a major cause of death in many areas of Scotland; 83% in NE Scotland [228]. Golden eagles and foxes may take kittens; reports from Europe of stoats taking young kittens from the den, and martens taking young cats [1153]. Starvation during winter has been recorded in Scotland [228] and in Germany [781]. Road accidents also contribute to mortality; anecdotal evidence of shot animals being placed on roads to simulate road accidents. In radio-tracking study, wild-living cats, Angus glens, 42% suffered human-induced mortality [253].

PARASITES AND DISEASES

Ectoparasites: Mites *Otodectes* sp. recorded from captive-bred animals in GB [350], and a probable case of *Notodectes cati* recorded [336]; fleas, probably cat flea, *Ctenocephalides felis*, occur but other recorded species, e.g. *Spilopsyllus cuniculi* (from rabbits), *Ceratophyllus s. sciurorum* (from red squirrels) and *Hystrichopsylla talpae* (from small rodents) are casual from prey items [1, 228]; ticks *Ixodes ricinus*; lice *Felicola subrostratus*.

Endoparasites: Include roundworms *Toxacara cati* [165]; tapeworms *Taenia taeniaeformis* (intermediate hosts small rodents, shrews and lagomorphs), *T. pisiformis* (intermediate hosts lagomorphs and occasionally rodents), *Mesocestoides litteratus* (intermediate hosts mites followed by birds and rodents) [165], *M. lineatus* (intermediate hosts mites followed by rodents and possibly birds). Very high prevalence of roundworms (*T. cati*; 96%) and tapeworms (*T. taeniformis*; 80%)

found in group 1 cats (n = 51) [288].

Very little known about diseases. FeLV was recorded in 2 of 23 wildcats from Scotland, and 'cat flu' was recorded in another, whereas toxoplasmosis was recorded in all cats [930]. Feline infectious peritonitis (FIPV) was recorded in 5 of 17 captive wildcats, all of which resulted in death [1349]. Feline panleukopenia, cat flu (FCV and FHV) also recorded in captive wildcats [931]. Injuries from snares and illegal gin traps have been reported. May receive burns during heather burning [228].

Recently, prevalence of commoner domestic cat viral diseases assessed in 50 wild-living cats in Scotland; FIV 0%, FeLV 10%, FCV 16% (n = 26), FHV 16% (n = 49), feline coronavirus (FCoV) 6% (n = 49), and feline foamy virus (FFV) 33% (n = 18) [255].

RELATIONS WITH HUMANS

More enlightened attitudes reduced overall persecution in the late 20th century [1268]. However, anecdotal evidence that confusion over identification has probably resulted in more persecution in recent years in some areas [67,253, 704]. Although take many rabbits and small rodents considered as pests of forestry and agriculture, still regarded by gamekeeping interests (pheasant, red grouse) as vermin, and many illegally killed every year, although evidence for wildcats as a major predator of grouse is poor [655].

Legislation: Included on Schedule 5 of the Wildlife and Countryside Act 1981 since 1988, which grants full protection since animals on Schedule 5 may only be 'taken' under licence if causing serious damage or for scientific purposes (see Chapter 4). Also on Annex IV of European Directive 92/43/EEC on the conservation of natural habitats and of wild fauna and flora (the Habitats and Species Directive), which lists species in need of strict protection.

Protection currently ineffective due to poor implementation and confusion between wildcats and unprotected hybrids, especially since 1990 [67, 236]. However, recent morphological and genetic studies [80, 315, 710] may help to resolve identification problems, although further research required to find reliable genetic markers.

Conservation: A number of threats face wildcats today [704, 931], including persecution (despite legal protection), habitat loss and fragmentation (particularly due to economic development and upgrading roads), habitat deterioration (e.g. maturation of conifer plantations making them unsuitable for small mammals), toxic chemicals (dieldrin and DDE found in wildcats), domestic cat diseases and hybridisation. Has been suggested that group 1 cats (which have traits associated with wildcats and survive at higher altitudes than group 2 cats) should be conserved by protecting all cats within areas identified by GIS (mainly E Scotland); would be areas where group 1 cats predominate and appear to have a competitive advantage over group 2 (hybrid/feral) cats [67, 253]. However, this approach could be abused by illegally killed wildcats being moved into unprotected areas.

A series of measures would probably assist wildcat conservation, including protection of key habitats and corridors, proscribing control methods for feral domestic cats (i.e. banning non-discriminatory methods, e.g. snares and lamping, and allowing only live trapping), neutering and microchipping of domestic cats within the wildcat's distributional range, vaccination of domestic cats against common viral diseases, and education of gamekeepers, farmers and schoolchildren about the heritage and ecological value of the indigenous wildcat [704, 871].

Techniques for study: A difficult animal to study, but radio-tagging has been successful [228, 253]. Faecal analysis a useful technique for dietary information [228, 569]. Road casualties can provide much information on hybridisation, ageing, sex, growth, diet, reproduction etc. [67, 253], but samples may be biased towards males, juveniles, domestic cats and hybrids. Camera trapping has only been carried out on an *ad hoc* basis, but may provide important data for field surveys, etc.

LITERATURE
Review of ecology [1153]; recent major work in Scotland [228] (brief report in [229]). Study of wild-living cat population in the Angus glens [253]. Most recent study of wild-living cats in Scotland based on road casualties and persecuted animals [67]. Popular account of wildcats in semi-captivity [1304]; non-technical reviews [703, 1306]. Recent comprehensive review summarises significant research in Scotland over the last 20–30 years [871]. 3 monographs in German [489, 781, 1032], 1 in French [1223]. Populations in the former USSR covered in [564].

AUTHORS
A.C. Kitchener & M.J. Daniels

Lynx *Lynx lynx*
Felis lynx L. 1758. Sweden

RECOGNITION
A large cat (head and body length 80–130 cm) with tufted ears and a short tail with a black tip (Plate 1). Fur yellowish-brown in summer, sometimes with distinct black spots, especially in the south; paler and greyer in winter. Skull 108–144 mm long, and lower carnassial 14–16 mm long (compared with 81–90 mm and 8–10 mm for wildcat). Other bones of skeleton equally large and distinctive.

DESCRIPTION
Identification of fossil remains usually possible on size; much smaller than cave lion *Panthera leo spelaea*, but larger than wildcat. Typical felid skull with reduced muzzle (Fig. 9.8). Appreciably larger than wildcat in all elements, and further distinguished by absence of small upper premolar; dental formula $i^3/_3c^1/_1p^2/_2m^1/_1$ (cf. $i^3/_3c^1/_1p^3/_2m^1/_1$ for *Felis*).

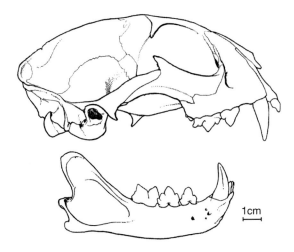

Fig. 9.8 Lynx skull *(from [942])*.

DISTRIBUTION
Palaearctic (replaced in N America by *Lynx canadensis*, and in Iberia by *L. pardinus*) (Fig. 9.9). Once widespread across W Europe, but much reduced by habitat loss and persecution; survived in N Scandinavia, Pyrenees and the Balkans, and eastwards from E Poland. Subject of active reintroduction campaigns to Austria, France, Germany, Italy, Slovenia and Switzerland [137].

HISTORY
Extinct in GB and Ireland. Scarce in the Late Glacial (only 3 records) and only 16 records from Postglacial, including 1 in Ireland [657].

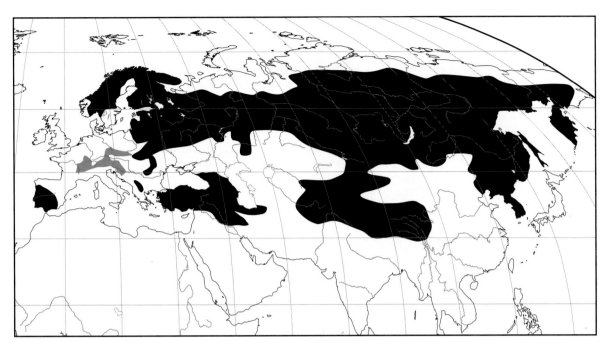

Fig. 9.9 Lynx *Lynx lynx*, native range (black) and reintroduced range (grey). The Iberian population is usually considered a distinct species, pardel lynx *Lynx pardina*.

Radiocarbon dates of 8875 bp for Kilgreany Cave and indirect dating for other specimens indicate present in Mesolithic. Latest dates 1842 bp (*c.*160 AD), Moughton Fell Cave, N Yorkshire; 1770 bp (*c.*180 AD), Creag nan Uamh, Sutherland; 1550 bp (*c.*450 AD), Kinsey Cave, N Yorkshire [568, 707]. These much later than previously supposed, suggesting a human-caused extinction rather than natural climatic/habitat change; thus growing interest in reintroducing the lynx to GB [567a].

GENERAL ECOLOGY

Primarily a predator of deer, lagomorphs and game birds. In Sweden, preys on reindeer and roe deer [481]; in Austria takes mostly yearlings and adult female red deer in poor condition [452]. In Poland, Białowieża Forest, roe deer, calves of red deer and brown hares (respectively 62%, 22% and 9% of 172 kills found by radio-tracking) were main prey [1006]. In France, reintroduced lynx reputed to be a serious predator of sheep, but this a less serious problem in Switzerland [136]. Territorial: radio-tracked territories around 250 km² for males and 130 km² for females [1156]. Secretive, heavily dependent on woodland cover for ambushing prey and for dens. Success of reintroductions to Switzerland and Slovenia suggests that could survive elsewhere if roe deer are readily available; some evidence from Switzerland that is valuable in limiting damage to forestry [136].

AUTHORS
A.C. Kitchener & D.W. Yalden

FAMILY CANIDAE

A small family of *c.*36 species of foxes, dogs, wolves and jackals. Distribution worldwide, even (by human introduction) Australia. Primarily predators of other mammals and birds, often hunt by running down their prey. Elongate muzzles, dentition usually $i^1/1c^1/1p^4/4m^3/3$, canines and carnassials well developed. Rely extensively on sense of smell both for hunting and social communication, though eyesight and hearing also well developed. Represented in British Isles only by red fox (and domestic dog) though historically also by wolf, more distantly also by Arctic fox.

Fox *Vulpes vulpes*
Canis vulpes Linnaeus 1758; Sweden.
Canis crucigera Bechstein 1789; Germany.
Tod; *llwynog*, *cadno* (Welsh); *madadh ruaidh*, *sionnach* (Scottish Gaelic); *sionnach*, *madra rua* (Irish Gaelic).

Male – dog; female – vixen; young – cub.

RECOGNITION
Whole animal: Conspicuous characters are the erect, black-backed ears, slender muzzle, long, horizontally held, bushy tail, white muzzle, usually white bib of throat and often white tail tip, and black socks and ears (Plate 7).

Skull and teeth: Skull dog-like but narrower, with more sharply pointed, prominent, slender

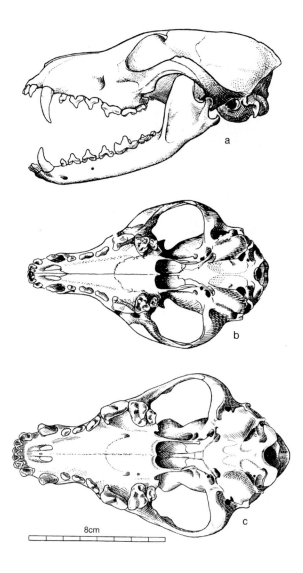

Fig. 9.10 Skulls of fox (a, b) and domestic dog (c). Note narrower muzzle, less crowded premolars, of fox. The canines are also much longer, more slender, in the fox, and dorsally the postorbital process is concave (convex in dog) (*drawn by R. Gillmor*).

canine teeth (Fig. 9.10); concave upper surfaces to postorbital processes distinguish it readily from that of dog.

FIELD SIGNS

Tracks and trails: Footprints with 4 toes on fore- and hindfeet readily observed in mud or snow (Fig. 9.2). In soft mud, hairs between toes may register, especially in winter when fur thicker. Print typically more oval than in small dogs, 2 central toes extending well ahead of others. Forefoot larger (5 cm long × 3–4 cm wide) than hindfoot, which is more slender. When walking or trotting, overprinting of foreprints by hindfeet usually occurs, sometimes gives mistaken impression of 5 toes being in contact with ground. Footprints of trotting fox form a straighter line than those of dog, although this is not an infallible identification. When walking, prints *c.*30 cm apart; when galloping, groups of prints up to 250 cm apart. Runs through hedges smaller than those of badger, but larger than brown hare and without the jump pattern of the latter. Regular passage through hedges, rusty fences, bramble patches, under chestnut palings, etc., often identifiable by snagged hairs.

Faeces: Very variable; if much indigestible material, e.g. fur or feathers, usually pointed, may be linked together by hairs; length 5–20 cm. When fresh, usually black with characteristic odour; may persist for several months after small inclusions have been leached. If few indigestible hard parts, faeces may be indistinguishable from dogs', except, if fresh, by odour; often deposited on prominent objects: stones, fallen branches, molehills, rabbit spoil heaps. Other scent stations, where drops of urine sprinkled on prominent objects, even long stalks of grass, detectable by smell. Characteristic smell of fox may be readily detected e.g. at earth, but also on wind, albeit apparently not by everyone.

Dens (earths): Presence of cubs indicated by unconsumed food remnants at entrance. Outside breeding season, use of dens erratic; except in worst weather, will lie out above ground in thick cover. Even in breeding season, vixen progressively spends less time below ground with cubs. In winter, many earths or disused rabbit burrows may be 'cleaned out', fresh soil evident, and possibly with strong smell of fox, though this not indicative of occupancy. May share sett with badgers, sometimes emerging from same entrance.

Other field signs: Food items cached, buried singly. Eggs frequently cached, cached corpses often buried with legs or wings projecting [349]. Caching behaviour described in [560, 561, 831]. Once food consumed, location often marked with urine [560, 561].

Primary wing feathers sheared close to bases indicate fox kills (Fig. 9.11). Manner of killing and subsequent treatment also often characteristic: lambs may have teeth marks over shoulder and crushed cervical vertebrae; lambs and poultry often decapitated, heads sometimes buried. Hind legs of adult rabbits sometimes stripped to bones, left with feet intact. Gap between upper canines 30 mm, between lower canines 26 mm, equivalent to medium-sized dog [1260], so not reliable as sole evidence of fox predation. Skins of mammals, e.g. rabbits, hedgehogs, picked clean and turned inside out, but similar signs also left by badgers.

Fig. 9.11 Fox-predated birds have primary feathers bitten off, whereas avian predators pluck each feather individually (*photo P. Morris*).

At night, fox eyes highly reflective, blue/white when viewed head-on, but pink when not looking directly at light source; eye-shine difficult to distinguish from domestic cat. Vocalisations characteristic.

DESCRIPTION

Pelage: Overall colour yellow-brown, but much variation from sandy colour to (rarely) henna red. White foxes, with normal-coloured eyes, and albinos reported very rarely. Melanic forms common in N America, where called black, silver or cross foxes, depending on degree of blackness; very rare in British Isles. Guard hairs composed of black, yellow-brown and white bands, but much variation in proportions of these according to parts of body. Underfur grey. Backs of ears, socks and sometimes entire leading edge of limb usually black, but black on limbs may be much reduced; also a black stripe from eye to muzzle; lips and nose dark brown; belly white, pale or deep slate grey; no age distinction. Tail less colourful than shoulders and back; white tip may be conspicuous or reduced to a few white hairs; white tag not confined to males. Caudal scent gland usually marked by a conspicuous black patch. Mandible, upper lips and throat white. White flecking may occur throughout pelage, even in juveniles; white

spots on ears of cubs frequent, but lost with age. Pads naked, but much interdigital fur. Scrotum covered in cream-coloured hair, usually lost during rut. Belly fur of vixens, sometimes dog foxes, assumes pinkish tinge in March–April, and in vixens may be brick red during lactation. Many colour mutants bred commercially; genetics of fox coat colours described in [1111].

Moult: 2 moulting periods, but only that of spring clearly visible. During autumn moult, only fine hair grows; this thickens the summer coat [908]. From April, significant loss of guard and fine hairs; new coat appears on extremities of legs and progresses dorsally, late April. By late June, summer coat covers legs, abdomen and flanks; elsewhere guard hairs still being shed. Finally reaches tail late August–early September. In October–November, further growth of fine hairs, again in ventrodorsal direction. Moult coincides with seasonal decrease in testicular endocrine function and seasonal hyperthyroidism [906].

Anatomy: Eyes blue until 4 weeks old, thereafter yellow; pupil, when contracted, a vertical slit. Nictitating membrane present but moves only when eye closed. Has binocular vision. Vibrissae on snout black, with a total span of 255–280 mm; also shorter vibrissae on underside of lower jaw and elsewhere on head, and on forelimbs just above dew claws. 5 digits on forefeet, but only 4 in contact with ground; 4 on hindfeet, which lack dew claws. Seasonal changes in thymus gland [1317].

Nipples: Usually 4 pairs, inguinal, but some variation, and 7, 9 or 10 not uncommon.

Scent glands: Paired anal sacs, each opening through a single duct; the 2 openings clearly visible on circumanal skin. Lined by sebaceous glands. Anal sac acts as fermentation chamber in which aerobic and anaerobic bacteria convert sebum into aliphatic acids and other odorous compounds [14–16]. Caudal gland *c*.75 mm from root of tail on dorsal side; oval in shape, 25 mm long × 13 mm wide. Reported to smell of violets. Evidence of increased secretory activity in males during spermatogenesis, which may tie in with reported steroid-metabolising properties [12, 13, 842]. Presence of foot glands equivocal; interdigital cavities deep, skin with reddish tinge, smelling strongly and heavily glandular [842], but difficult to decide if the feet have a scent-marking function [804]. Skin at angle of jaw and mandible richly endowed with sebaceous glands; this maxillary gland perhaps important to female foxes in the rut [842].

Skull: Adult males and females differentiated in *c.*70% of cases by prominent sagittal crest in male; males up to 10 months old resemble females. Frontal silhouette of head and ears has been used to identify sex in the field [164]. Sequence and timing of closure of cranial sutures described in [202, 509], eruption of permanent teeth in [509], age-related changes in cranial measurements in [611].

Reproductive tract: Testes scrotal at all times, enlarge 6-fold seasonally with spermatogenic activity [509, 907]. Cowper's gland and seminal vesicles absent; prostate gland not large. Primitive bicornuate uterus with direct continuity between 2 horns; ovaries in bursa. Vulva swollen, often pinkish, at oestrus; corpora lutea large and persistent throughout pregnancy. Placenta zonary, endotheliochorial, with prominent lateral haematomata. Placental scars persist from birth to next oestrus, can be used to estimate litter size [795, 797]. Embryos visible at 20 days as delicate

Table 9.3 Fox: measurements

	Males		Females	
	Mean	Range	Mean	Range
England [545]	(n = 31–35)		(n = 39)	
Head and body length (mm)	671	600–755	627	570–700
Tail length (mm)	412	375–470	385	335–420
Hindfoot length (mm)	152	135–170	141	125–150
Ear length (mm)	93	85–100	89	90–95
Weight (kg)	6.7	5.5–8.2	5.4	3.5–6.7
Scotland [722]	(n = 30)		(n = 34–41)	
Head and body length (mm)	712	659–700	679	574–732
Tail length (mm)	436	388–493	411	277–491
Hindfoot length (mm)	167	143–178	159	143–168
Ear length (mm)	96	87–106	94	89–102
Weight (kg)	7.3	5.7–9.3	6.2	4.2–7.8
Wales [804]	(n = 50; weight n = 463)		(n = 50; weight n = 610)	
Head and body length (mm)	666	570–747	622	560–730
Tail length (mm)	411	350–465	380	330–420
Hindfoot length (mm)	154	130–172	142	130–155
Ear length (mm)	90	83–102	86	82–98
Weight (kg)	6.4	–	5.5	–
N Ireland [379]	(n = 42; weight n = 207)		(n = 42; weight n = 281)	
Head and body length (mm)	723	635–777	677	614–744
Tail length (mm)	367	222–429	348	289–410
Hindfoot length (mm)	161	109–173	151	134–166
Ear length (mm)	104	94–113	99	56–110
Weight (kg)	6.9	4.0–9.2	5.8	4.0–6.9

streak of cells within fetal membranes, and can be aged from 33 days by weight or crown–rump length [804].

Chromosomes: 2n = 34 [1441]. Variation in chromosome number discussed in [156].

RELATIONSHIPS

Generally considered conspecific with *V. fulva* of N America [201], although taxonomy needs to be reconsidered [669]. Phylogenetic relationships based on different morphological and molecular approaches equivocal [71, 89, 212, 422, 1443]. Allometry and phylogeny of sexual dimorphism of carnivore skulls [438], life-history traits [423, 437, 953], and social organisation and behaviour [241, 423].

MEASUREMENTS

See Table 9.3. Males slightly larger than females (*c.*1.2:1) but considerable overlap, not reliable for identifying sex. Seasonal variations of body weight [804, 1144] and fat deposits [513, 724]. Suggestions that foxes from Scotland are a distinct

subspecies or race [545, 1286] on basis of larger size not accepted. Skull measurements given in [610–612, 804]. Multivariate analysis shows sex differences in skull measurements [610].

VARIATION

British foxes formerly ascribed to subspecies *V. v. crucigera* Bechstein 1789 (Thuringia, Germany); said to be slightly smaller, with distinctly smaller teeth, premolars widely spaced and rarely or never in contact [942]. However, many British skulls show a high degree of tooth compaction, particularly in some populations [1]. Continuity of range of red fox such that doubtful whether any discrete, definable subspecies can be recognised [226].

In Europe and N America, northern animals have larger white tip to tail and longer coat than southern animals. In Scotland, foxes larger from S to N but variation independent of climate, prey taken or productivity of areas in which each population lives; suggested that N–S cline in size results from increased hunting hours at higher latitudes during winter [716]. Hill foxes of

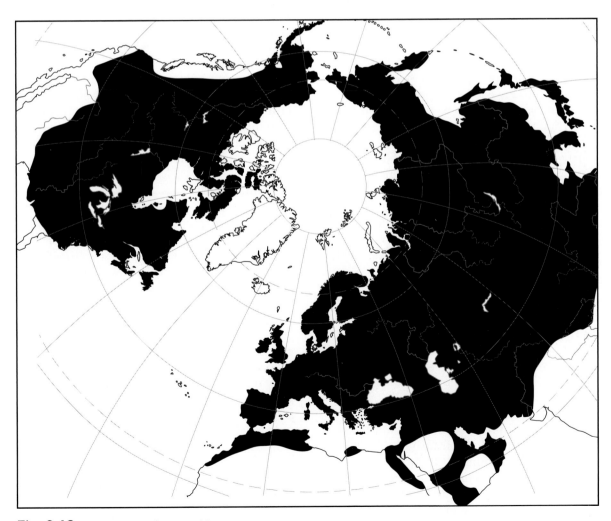

Fig. 9.12 Fox *Vulpes vulpes*: world range.

411

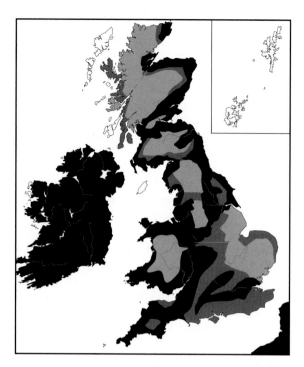

Fig. 9.13 Fox *Vulpes vulpes*: estimated densities of > 2/km² (black), > 1/km² (dark grey) and < 1/km² (pale grey) (*based on [858, 1356]*).

Westmorland said to be larger than lowland foxes, but opposite tendency in Wales. In Israel, foxes increased in size towards end of Pleistocene, then declined [265, 266]. Geographical variation in cranial measurements from 6 counties in Wales [612], and Ireland [387].

Non-metrical variation described [1193], but genetic polymorphisms not described from British foxes. Syndactyly with 2 different genetic origins described [506], and 3 cases with a 3rd genetic origin reported from vixens caught at the same earth in different years [1]. Sporadic individuals lack guard hairs locally (often only on tail) or completely, giving a woolly appearance; called 'Samson' foxes.

DISTRIBUTION
Present throughout most of N hemisphere (Fig. 9.12). Introduced from GB to E USA in mid-18th century, whence spread westward and interbred with native stocks, and to Australia *c.*1850 [785]. Illegally introduced into Tasmania *c.*2001, eradication being attempted.

Almost ubiquitous in GB and Ireland (Fig. 9.13); absent or uncommon until recently in many parts of Norfolk, and coastal areas of NE Scotland [578]. Probably continuing to increase in areas where previously uncommon. Common in many urban areas in S England and parts of Scotland [522, 853], where new low-density residential suburbs colonised late 1930s–1940s [517, 524].

Marked changes in urban populations during 1980s–1990s; variously, growth of existing populations, colonisation of new towns and cities, deaths due to sarcoptic mange [1381]. Occurs to >1300 m asl in Cairngorms. Absent from all Scottish islands except Skye, and Harris where illegally introduced [536]; present some years on Scalpay. Absent from Anglesey until 1962. Absent from Scilly Isles and Channel Isles; present on Isle of Wight. Purportedly introduced to Isle of Man during the 1980s, population in 1990 estimated to be 200–400 [849]; however, erroneous [1091], no evidence that foxes ever established there. Single carcass reported Shetland, 1996, a hoax.

HISTORY
Antecedent probably *Vulpes alopecoides*, appeared in middle Villafranchian [764]. *V. vulpes* found in middle Pleistocene deposits 400 000 years old; probably present in Late Glacial (Gough's Cave, Somerset), present early in Postglacial (Star Carr, Thatcham); foxes probably an important food item for Neolithic hunters. History in GB discussed in [1420]. Ireland, earliest records Bronze Age, Haughey's Fort, Co. Armagh and Lough Gur, Co. Limerick, probably introduced [912].

Bounty payments recorded in churchwardens' accounts in 1700s–early 1800s suggest foxes were uncommon [804] but widely persecuted [826]. In late 19th century, foxes introduced from Europe to reinforce local populations for hunting [785, 1101]. Vermin bags record increases in E Anglia, parts of NE Scotland, since 1950 [804, 1268]; overall population stable in GB from 1980 to date [1356].

HABITAT
A highly adaptable, unspecialised, versatile species; lack of specific habitat requirements [805] is key to success. Most abundant in fragmentary habitats offering wide variety of cover and food, but also found on large expanses of hill land, sand dunes, etc. Small woodlands, especially conifers, afford good shelter in upland areas; large coniferous plantations are good habitat while ground vegetation remains, but poor foraging areas subsequently. Most movements and foraging on habitat edges, hence most abundant where habitat diverse. Habitat requirements of urban foxes determined from surveys of 7 cities [522]; favoured areas are 1930s–1940s low-density residential suburbs; data used to predict numbers of foxes in different types of urban habitat [523]. Habitat utilisation during night determined by radio-tracking in Edinburgh [719], Oxford [306] and Bristol before [1145] and after [983] mange outbreak. In Oxford, preferred habitats were woodland, scrub, detached housing, flats and long

grass; in Bristol, back gardens, woodland, rough ground and allotment gardens; in Edinburgh, no preferences evident. In Bristol, similar habitat preferences for daytime rest sites.

SOCIAL ORGANISATION AND BEHAVIOUR

Much information in recent years, largely from studies in GB – popular account [843] and reviews in relation to spread of rabies [835, 857]; international reviews [182, 984]. In GB, much information about urban foxes; rural fox populations poorly studied.

Territories: Live in family groups that share a joint territory. In areas of higher population density (i.e. more favourable habitats) and/or low hunting pressure, subordinate animals may be present on range [836]. Typically, subordinates believed to be female, but study in Bristol reported equal numbers of subordinate males [56]; may number up to 8 [56], usually 1–2 [512, 836]. May be former dominants, are usually young from previous year. Have been described as 'helpers', assisting in rearing the dominant vixen's cubs, alternatively, argued that these groups form in response to temporary food surpluses, unrelated to helping reproductive efforts [1148]. Captive studies show that non-breeding vixens will guard, groom, play with cubs and retrieve strays, and provision them; same thought to occur in wild [833]. In Bristol, most subordinate males and females helped to feed cubs to same extent as dominant animals but this did not increase the number of cubs that survived [56]. Role of these extra vixens in terms of kin selection discussed in [836, 852].

Size of territory varies with habitat; in hill areas of Scotland up to 4000 ha [811]; averaged 270 ha in rural Dorset [1092] and 520 ha in Sitka spruce plantations [999]. In urban areas, may be as small as 8.5 ha, although mean 27 ha in Bristol [57, 512, 1372], 39 ha in Oxford [305, 839] and *c*.100 ha in Edinburgh [720].

In Bristol, ranges very stable until mange epizootic [57, 1372]; this reflected by longevity of dominant animals [56]. Prior to mange outbreak, territories decreased in size in response to increased food availability [57]. During mange epizootic, ranges expanded only when neighbouring group disappeared [57]. In Oxford, territories reportedly less stable, pronounced changes in spatial location each year [305]; believed to reflect high levels of mortality and unstable food sources.

In areas of very high population density, appears to be minimum size below which territories do not fall, but degree of overlap between adjacent territories increases [1309]. Nor

is there any relationship between territory size and fox family group size [840]. In Bristol, mean group size remained constant in areas of different population density [525]; however, group size increased and territory size reduced in a high-density region in response to increased food availability [57].

Fox social systems variable and adaptable to habitat type [840]. Resource dispersion used to explain group-living strategies [839, 840]. Mathematical models for relationship between territory size and evolution of group living [42, 43, 179, 664, 847]; relationship between dispersion of habitat patches and territory size in Oxford documented [306]. Alternative explanations proposed [796, 1148].

Denning behaviour: Very variable. Outside breeding season many (perhaps most) animals lie up above ground in dense cover, and use earths only in particularly bad weather. Earths dug in wide variety of habitats: extensive earths dug in banks; old rabbit burrows enlarged; disused or occupied badger setts utilised; also natural holes in rock crevices, drains and turbaries (peatlands), when often very little sign of occupation by foxes. In urban areas, under sheds, under buildings, overgrown gardens, cemeteries, rubbish heaps, cemeteries etc., are favoured sites for earths; foxes may spend the day on roofs of buildings if they can gain access by sloping roofs or walls [507, 517]; following outbreak of mange, larger proportion of breeding dens located in woodlands [1]. Habitat preferences for daytime rest sites documented in [1144]; pattern of sharing within group in [57, 1370]. Rest-site fidelity decreased after mange outbreak, possibly as mechanism to reduce disease spread [983]. Den sites used by foxes in Scotland described in [573, 575].

No bedding in breeding den, cubs born on bare ground. Vixen stays with very young cubs, but progressively lies up above ground nearby, only returning to feed cubs. Dog fox rarely remains in natal earth; occasionally 1–2 dog foxes may be in earth with young cubs, sometimes without the vixen, more usually with 1 or more adult vixens also present [1]. Except in urban areas, cubs moved to another earth at slightest disturbance from people or dogs; several earths available to vixen on each territory.

Earths occupied by cubs recognised by fresh food debris around and inside earth, often accompanied by putrid smell and flies in hot weather. Play items such as food wrappings, balls and clothes also brought back to earth [513]. During first 4 months, cub activity focused around den sites [1106]; as cubs grow, range further, but centred on den sites. With hot weather in late

May–June, most cubs lie up above ground in dense vegetation. At this stage, or sometimes while still living underground, litters split into groups of 1–2 and only come together at night to play. By autumn, movement patterns of juveniles and adults similar [1106].

Occasional reports of >1 litter of cubs on a territory, sometimes in earths only a few metres apart, when 2nd vixen in family group breeds; probably also explains pooling of litters, when found sharing an earth; may stay together semipermanently, or for only a few days [1].

Scent-marking: Territories marked with urine and faeces. Small urine marks left on conspicuous objects at nose height; both sexes may cock leg to do this but vixens normally squat [834]. Urine marks left on main travel routes in proportion to frequency with which each path travelled, irrespective of location of path within range. Number of sites marked drops rapidly to zero towards border of range; socially dominant animals in group mark more frequently than subordinates [834, 837]. May urine-mark inedible food remnants or empty caching holes where odour of food lingers; avoids wasting search time on unproductive sites [560]. Faeces usually single, often on or near conspicuous objects, and scattered throughout territory [837]. Foxes may mark some sites with urine and faeces, and may rub perioral region along site before/after urinating.

Vocalisations: Wide range; 28 groups of sounds based on 40 forms of sound production described [1280] but more recent analysis identifies 12 adult and 8 cub vocalisations [988]. Most characteristic are the triple bark and 'scream' heard particularly during the rut. Sound recordings listed in [520].

Other communication: Wide range of facial and body postures used to describe dominant/submissive status, and many of these – e.g. threat gape – used by young cubs. Also a range of visual cues [406].

Aggressive behaviour: When fighting, stand with forelegs on each other's chest/shoulders, and use open-mouthed threats. Such fights usually between juveniles or adults of same sex.

Dispersal: Occurs principally at 6–12 months old, but some older or younger animals will disperse [528]. Tagging study, Bristol, showed that by end of December in 1st year, 59% of males and 33% of females had dispersed; by end of March 67% and 32%, and by end of following March 73% and 32%. Proportion dispersing depends on density of population, and possibly also level of control; in some populations up to 100% of males and 77% of females disperse [1307]. Factors affecting decision to disperse unknown; for males, small cubs from large litters more likely to disperse, and females that disperse come from larger litters [528]. Indirect measures suggest negative relationship between social interaction as cub and subsequent dispersal tendency [529]. For males that disperse, life expectancy only 85% that of non-dispersers; for both males and females, those that disperse further have shorter life expectancy [528].

Most disperse relatively short distances. In Bristol, mean and maximum for males 2.3 and 18.0 km, for females 0.8 and 6.3 km [528]. For mid-Wales comparable figures for males 13.7 and 52.0 km, for females 2.3 and 24.0 km [804], for Ireland mean distances for males and females 14.8 and 7.5 km [376, 378, 379]. Occasional movements >300 km in USA, and 100 km in Europe. Distance moved positively correlated with home-range size but negatively with population density; simulation model, derived from mean and maximum dispersal distances, predicted from simple population parameters [1309] used to predict pattern of dispersal in urban fox populations [1307].

Disturbance, particularly by fox hunts, may stimulate dispersal [804]. Actual pattern of movements very variable; animals may make a number of exploratory movements before finally moving, slowly drift into a neighbouring range, or make a sudden one-off movement [597, 1328, 1414]. Similar variation shown by rehabilitated juvenile foxes [1103].

Dispersal may last only a few days; exceptionally, several weeks or even months [1]. Few barriers deter a dispersing fox; tidal stretches of R. Avon swum regularly [517], and in urban areas disperse across gardens, etc.; do not necessarily follow railways or other corridors [1308]. Direction of dispersal random, although littermates tend to disperse in the same general direction [528].

Activity: Mainly nocturnal and crepuscular; amount of diurnal activity depends on degree of persecution. In summer, may remain active long after dawn, especially if vixen feeding young cubs. Activity during night punctuated by periods of rest. In one study, urban foxes most active after midnight [1414]; in another, activity declined after midnight [307]; but much individual variation; even in city centres, daylight sightings quite frequent. In rural study, activity peaked in the hours before sunrise and after sunset [1092]. Activity influenced by weather, reduced on cold, wet nights, although warm, wet weather provides an ideal opportunity for 'worming' [838].

Influence of other weather conditions on activity not quantified. Except for lactating females, no seasonal variation in amount of time spent active but number of activity bouts varied [307]. In Oxford, excluding lactating females, duration of activity averaged 6.9 h/night [307]; in Bristol, 8.2 h/day [1144].

Ranging behaviour: Well documented for urban foxes; very little information for rural foxes. Many parts of territory used only infrequently, mainly for travel between key foraging areas [804]. In Edinburgh, railway lines used as travel routes, between foraging areas, by dog foxes [718, 719]. Core areas may form small proportion of territories; in Bristol, core areas encompassing 60% of radio fixes often only 10% of total territory [1414]. In Bristol, many activity foci shared between individuals from same group [50, 1372] with high retention of foci between seasons [1372].

During mating season, males range beyond their territorial boundaries in search of receptive females [718, 1372]. During lactation, area ranged by female generally much reduced [307], but often trapped off their normal home range [58]. In Oxford, excluding lactating females, mean area travelled per night was 17.6 ha [307]; in Bristol, excluding winter season, 19.4 ha [1369]. These figures relate to *c*.45% and 70% of total home-range area [305, 1372]. Mean distance travelled in Oxford 4.4 km [307]; in Bristol, 6.1 km [1144]. In one study, animals tended to use similar areas from night to night, those in same group followed each other around [307].

Contact behaviour increasingly well studied because of importance in rabies transmission. Dynamic interaction calculated from radio-tracking data, using defined separation distances to denote contact. In Oxford, using maximum separation distance of 50 m, foxes from same group in contact for 18% of active period; corresponding figure for foxes in neighbouring groups, 1% [307]. In Bristol, foxes averaged 2.1 intra-group and 0.3 inter-group encounters per day, using maximum separation distance of 25 m [1370]. Majority of intra-group encounters non-aggressive, but of inter-group encounters aggressive; inter-group encounters increased during winter [1370]. Simulation model of movement showed that foxes in neighbouring groups avoid each other at close quarters, while those in the same group actively interact [1370]. Interaction rates between dominant and subordinate animals similar to those for dominant pairs [51]. Rabies simulation models developed [1207–1209, 1211, 1371].

Locomotion: Usually walks when hunting or

investigating; when moving unhurriedly, travels at slow trot of 6–13 km/h, at slightly greater speed lopes or canters, and when pursued will gallop; speeds of >65 km/h reported but probably unrealistic [804]. In Oxford, average speed of movement 0.6 km/h [307]; in Bristol, averaged 2.0 km/h, marked differences between habitat types [1144].

FEEDING

A highly adaptable omnivore; lack of specialised food requirements one of keys to success. Many British food studies, in both rural [62, 164, 170, 314, 402, 412, 569, 570, 572, 574, 579, 581, 603–605, 624, 662, 723, 72, 374, 375, 379, 778, 786, 804, 808, 810, 811, 999, 1090, 1092, 1097, 1109, 1220, 1235, 1344, 1345, 1394] and urban environments [309, 513, 531, 839, 1144]. Most studies presented as percentage occurrence or percentage volume, but methodology for estimating mass of prey ingested given in [1090, 1092]. Rural studies summarised in [52]; nationwide study in [1357].

Most show that mammals, e.g. lagomorphs, wood mice or field voles, most frequently eaten; bank voles and insectivores uncommon due to food preferences [832]. Pronounced differences between different regions and seasons (e.g. [52, 309, 1144, 1357]), between neighbouring territories [1092] and between adults and cubs (e.g. [62, 170, 379, 412, 513, 531, 804, 1092, 1097]). Cannibalism of littermates [1041], or predation by vixens on other litters, may occur [1, 832, 1092].

Fig. 9.14 Fox raiding dustbin; this distinctive individual was raiding bins in Epsom, Surrey, in the 1960s (*photo I. Beames/Ardea*).

Of birds, passerines, pigeons and various galliformes (hens, game birds) most frequent, but in coastal areas scavenged or predated gulls and waders common [170, 604, 605]. Beetles and a wide variety of invertebrates common, as is fruit (windfall apples, pears and plums, and black-berries) in autumn. In most habitats scavenging important (Fig. 9.14); in upland areas sheep and deer carcasses are main food supply in winter [570]. Non-food items frequent in stomachs (e.g. [513]) and fish may be caught in warm weather when active near the surface [662]. Assumption that food eaten reflects prey availability equivocal, e.g. studies on black-headed gull and eider duck colonies show that when nesting these species not used in proportion to their abundance, probably because they are not a preferred food item [412, 737]; predation on nesting game birds often high relative to their abundance [62]. Proportion of field vole in fox diet related to density of voles in a cyclic population [999]. Following myxomatosis [1258], importance of rabbits in diet decreased, and field voles increased [786] (in Ireland, brown rats [375]), but in recent years importance of rabbit has increased in most areas. In Scotland, availability of field voles in winter shown to be factor most likely associated with population fluctuations [724]. In W Scotland, breeding delayed when compared with NE Scotland, due to more intermittent food supply in W [724, 725].

Hunting behaviour: Very variable. Predation at

nesting colonies of gulls described in [737, 739]; results of sand-tracking foxes through colonies in [349]; potential impact of different foraging patterns on predation on ground-nesting birds in [1166]. In some months earthworms provide over 60% of calorific intake [838]; hunted probably by hearing, grasped by incisor teeth, and dislodged from burrow by slow but accelerating head movement. Young may be taught to hunt earthworms, low-status or younger foxes may exploit earthworms more frequently than adults [838].

Impact on prey: Relatively few species, mainly ground-nesting birds, game species and livestock, considered to date. Examined using predator control experiments, natural reductions in fox numbers through e.g. disease outbreaks, and by comparing estimated number killed to prey abundance and productivity. Experimental manipulation usually controls full suite of predators, thus impact of foxes alone uncertain.

Electric fences used to reduce depredation on nesting colonial birds, e.g. terns [928, 944]. Predation on lapwing nests incidental [1165] but foxes probably contributed to decline of curlew in N Ireland [461]. Can be a significant predator of brooding hen partridges, although post-hatching fox predation less important [1056]; where foxes and other predators experimentally removed, partridge numbers increased by 75% [1271]. Fox predation on recently released pheasants and breeding hens can be significant [62, 586, 1092,

Fig. 9.15 Fox carrying prey back to its den – a feature of fox behaviour that is not shown by badgers (*photo B. Phipps*).

1107, 1108]. Many wild pheasant populations possibly unsustainable in presence of fox predation (e.g. [62]). For moorland, concluded that foxes limited neither numbers of breeding red grouse nor surplus available for shooting, because predated mostly non-territorial birds [655]; these conclusions refuted in [606]. Habitat changes, and associated changes in predator distribution and density, likely to have been a significant factor affecting grouse populations [264]. Experimental study concluded that predation by foxes may depress black grouse and capercaillie in Scotland [47, 1257]. Potential beneficial effects of fox control by gamekeepers on hen harrier breeding success on grouse moors considered marginal relative to deleterious effects of human persecution [470].

Computer simulation model predicted elimination of fox predation should increase hare densities 3–6-fold [1093], but increase in fox numbers, E Anglia, not paralleled by decline in hares [1268]. Fox predation unlikely to have regulatory effect on high-density rabbit populations, even though large numbers of rabbits may be consumed [62, 1092], but rabbits more abundant where predators absent [1310]. One study suggested that foxes should have stabilising effect on vole populations, yet voles show 3–4 year cycles [999]. In survey of householders, hedgehogs 1.4 times less likely to be seen in gardens with foxes [30]. Rats may increase diurnal activity to avoid predation risk from foxes [391].

Actual and perceived predation rates on lambs, free-range pigs and poultry typically average <10% of total mortality [570, 574, 582, 921, 950–952, 1373], but highly variable between farms. Estimated annual direct cost to agriculture from fox predation £12 million [949]; of this, sheep producers £9.4 m, egg producers £0.7 m, turkey producers £0.2 m, goose producers £0.4 m, pig producers £1 m. These losses partially offset by predation on rabbits, which may save £7 million [63, 868].

Losses to urban foxes minimal; estimated that 0.7% of cats and 7% of other pets killed by foxes each year in one area of high fox density, Bristol [514]; most losses could be avoided by improved housing.

Food caching: An important strategy; food may be cached even when fox still hungry, to protect it from competitors or increase time available for food capture (Fig. 9.15). Surplus food scatter-hoarded, preferred food items more likely to be cached; caches probably found by memory and most likely to be found by the fox that makes them, although may be found by other foxes [560, 661, 831, 1300].

Surplus killing: Occasionally kill large numbers of easy prey, leave many uneaten [738]. In 1 breeding season c.200 black-headed gulls were killed by each of 4 foxes, with 230 killed in 1 night; most likely to be killed on dark nights. Losses of poultry and penned game birds can be substantial; 75 pheasants killed in 1 night in damaged release pen [1092]. Biological significance of behaviour discussed in [738].

Food requirements: Daily requirement 121 kcal (507 kJ)/kg body weight, based on captive US foxes; requirements of carbohydrates, fats, proteins and vitamins for growth and various stages of life history given in [28], as are main features of deficiency diseases. Allometric model used to estimate energy expenditure from radio-tracking data [1144]; daily energy expenditure c.2000 kJ/day. British male and female foxes weighing 6.50 kg and 5.50 kg estimated to consume 2.86 and 2.53 kg prey per week [52]; female requires additional 0.66 kg prey per week to support each cub during lactation.

BREEDING
Monoestrous, mating December–February (Fig. 9.16), spontaneous ovulation, pregnancy 53 days, peak births March, mean litter size 4–5, breeds when 10 months old. Largely monogamous, but DNA evidence from one population indicated high levels of polygyny with intra- and inter-group cuckoldry, as well as mixed-paternity litters [56, 60].

Males: Seasonally fecund, November–March, spermatogenesis peaks December–February [804]. Later onset of breeding with increasing latitudes, correlated with day length [807]. During quiescent period, testes still scrotal, but scrotum far less conspicuous than during breeding season. During 1st breeding season, growth of testes of juveniles slightly delayed relative to older males. Seasonal variations in plasma testosterone, luteinising hormone and prolactin [907]. Average volume of semen ejaculated by adult males 6 ml, 2.5 ml in young animals, and total number of spermatozoa on average >300 million [804].

Females: Single oestrus period lasting 3 weeks but fertilisation possibly only during 3 days, although mating may occur outside this period [804]. During oestrus, male closely attends female, and as peak receptivity approaches, male shadows every move of female, with his tail held higher than usual. 1st attempts to mate usually rejected by female. Mating may occur during day or night. Successful mountings may last only a few seconds, with ejaculation occurring quickly, or the pair may

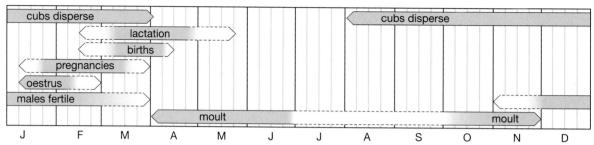

Fig. 9.16 Fox: annual cycle.

'tie' or 'lock' back to back, with tails curved over each other's rump. Once tied, the male cannot withdraw his penis, pair may stay tied for up to 90 min. Pair may mate several times, and between matings lie close together.

During oestrus, cervix very firm and round, vulva swollen and slightly pink. In anoestrus, uterus thin-walled and flaccid; following oestrus, rapidly elongates, becomes round and turgid. Implantation 10–14 days; implantation sites evenly spaced throughout 2 horns of uterus, due to transmigration of ova between them. Swelling of uterine horns follows implantation; pregnancy lasts 52–53 days, age of embryos can be determined from 33 days [804]. Variations in circulating hormone levels in anoestrus and pregnancy [127, 956].

Polyovular follicles common in cubs, but frequency decreases at approach of oestrus, and functional polyovular follicles probably uncommon in wild foxes [804]. In London, 3.6% of follicles released 2 ova [507]. Corpora lutea develop rapidly, persist throughout pregnancy. Pseudo-pregnancy lasts *c*.40 days; corpora lutea develop, and uterus becomes turgid in condition similar to that at implantation; mammary glands may develop, milk may even be visible microscopically [1130].

In wild, subordinate females often become pregnant but fail to whelp, or cubs may be killed postpartum by either dominant or subordinate female [1327]. In captive study, pre-parturition losses associated with reduced prolactin levels, as consequence of social stress [539]. In later stages of pregnancy, vixen digs out several earths before selecting one as natal den. Cubs born on bare soil; soon after birth, fur lost from vixen's belly; peak lactation lasts on average 7 weeks [240], but cubs will try to suck up to 14 weeks. At 28–35 days, milk 18.1% dry matter, 5.8% fat, 6.7% protein, 4.6% sugar, 0.9% ash [1000]. At end of lactation, nipples regress but usually still possible to recognise breeding from barren animals on size of regressed nipple [1029]. Ovarian activity during anoestrus described in [956].

Productivity: Mean number of corpora lutea 5.5 in Kent, 5.7 in Wales [804]; losses from ovulation to birth calculated to be 10.2% in London [507], but no data to show whether loss pre- or post-implantation.

Litters of up to 10 reported from placental scar counts, e.g. [511]; larger litters of emergent cubs reported, but these may be pooled litters. Mean number of implanted embryos in 3 rural areas, England and Wales, 6.95–7.56; with 11–32% intrauterine losses, litter sizes at birth 4.85–6.38 cubs [583]. Mean number of placental scars in London 4.77, mean litter size of cubs <6 weeks old 3.97, hence 16.8% natural mortality in cubs below ground [507]. In London, litter size significantly reduced in vixens >4 years old [511], but not observed in Bristol [525].

Number of barren vixens very variable: in rural study, only present in population subject to lightest control [583]. In London, Bristol, placental scars most frequently absent from 1st-year vixens and those >4 years; few 2–4-year old vixens lack scars [525]. Additional breeding failures from some vixens which undergo full-term pregnancy but do not produce viable cubs; this late-term failure possibly associated with social stress [539], occurs in 17.6% of vixens in London, 22.7% in Bristol. Including all vixens in population, mean productivity per vixen 3.22 London, 2.61 Bristol [525], 3.70 Wales [804], 6.38 mid-Wales, 4.49 E Midlands and 6.24 E Anglia [583].

Development of young: Born blind and deaf, with short black fur; white tag to tail evident from birth; weigh 80–120 g. Eyes and ears open 11–14 days; eyes slate-blue in colour, change to adult amber colour at 4–5 weeks. For 2–3 weeks, unable to thermoregulate effectively, and vixen spends most of her time with cubs but may make short foraging trips; during this period, vixen may be fed by dog fox or possibly a barren vixen (Fig. 9.15). From 3 weeks onwards, vixen spends increasing amounts of time away from cubs, and by 4–5 weeks often only comes back to earth to feed cubs.

Coat colour starts to change at 3 weeks, when

black eye streak appears. White muzzle and red patches on face apparent at 4 weeks, when ears become erect, muzzle starts to elongate from snub shape. By 6 weeks, fur colour similar to adult, but appears woolly. Facial proportions much more fox-like, and full complement of milk teeth by 7–8 weeks. By 8 weeks, woolly coat begins to be covered by shiny guard hairs, and colour and pattern very like that of adult. Thereafter, growth rapid but no significant changes in appearance, reach adult size by end of September, weight continues slight increase to end of year [1].

Sexual dimorphism in average body proportions evident from 6 weeks, but considerable overlap between sexes. In large litters, growth rates lower, may be considerable variation in both size and developmental age between littermates [1]; such variations in speed of development may produce some erroneous reports of pooled litters.

Cubs suckled until 4 weeks, when progressively weaned on to solids. First emerge above ground at this age. By 5–6 weeks, eating wide variety of solid items, even catching earthworms and insects for themselves. During summer, cubs become progressively independent, but may hunt with vixen until July–August. How cubs learn to hunt unclear, but probably largely by trial and error.

POPULATION

Numbers: Pre-breeding rural population, GB, of 225 000 adults estimated by faecal counts [1356]; this agrees closely with previous estimates based on habitat characteristics [536, 858]. In Ireland, pro rata, 150 000–200 000 [548]; limited in N Ireland by high cub mortality caused by various diseases [381]. Prior to outbreak of sarcoptic mange, estimated pre-breeding population of 33 000 adults in urban areas [536]. Subsequently, numbers of urban foxes increased due to colonisation of towns and cities, and growth of established populations [1381] but both urban and rural populations reduced by mange epizootic in mid–late 1990s [1219].

Density very variable; dependent on habitat and degree of persecution. In hill areas of Scotland, 1 pair/40 km^2 [811]. Area per breeding den in various Scottish habitats: 32 km^2 in deer forest, 23 km^2 on grouse moors, 10 km^2 on agricultural land [573]. For mid-Wales 1 breeding pair per 1.2–4.8 km^2, for parts of Pembrokeshire 0.4–0.8/km^2 [804]. In New Forest, 0.76 family groups per km^2 [616]. Based on spotlight counts, pre-breeding density in mid-Wales, E Midlands and E Anglia 0.41, 1.17 and 0.16 foxes/km^2 [584]; post-breeding abundance, 0.90, 2.62 and 0.59 foxes/km^2 respectively. Using faecal transect counts, density in arable, pasture, marginal upland and upland landscapes estimated as 0.79–2.23, 1.39–1.88, 0.82 and 0.21 foxes/km^2 respectively [1356]. Relative density in different regions illustrated in [1269], in different landscapes in [1356].

In urban areas, mean fox density in 14 cities ranged from 0.19 family groups/km^2 (Wolverhampton) to 2.24 (Cheltenham) [526]; local densities up to 5.0 family groups/km^2; highest density ever recorded 37.0 adults/km^2 in NW Bristol immediately before outbreak of mange [57].

Fluctuations: If numbers killed annually reflect population density, suggest periodic fluctuations in numbers [376, 377, 573, 578], and trend of increasing numbers in Scotland 1953–1978 [571, 578]. Trends in game bags [1268] do not reflect population changes, which overall are stable [1356]. Most significant recent change was decline due to sarcoptic mange epidemic.

Sex ratio: In most populations 1:1 at birth [1307]; males preponderate in caught samples, especially in winter; where heavily controlled, large excess of itinerant males. In Bristol, a high-density population, birth sex ratio overall 1 male: 0.83 females, but 1 male: 0.76 females in areas of highest fox density [1307]. Adult sex ratio in Bristol 1 male: 0.83 females [525]. During 1980s, the city had 211 fox family groups with 383 adult males and 333 adult females, i.e. 1.8 adult males and 1.6 adult females per group [514].

Age determination: Eye-lens weight, baculum weight, epiphyseal and suture closure differentiate young-of-year from older animals. Thereafter only reliable method is incremental lines in cementum of teeth [509, 660]; are laid down in late winter, associated with physiological changes during sexual cycle [441, 717]. Importance of reproductive abstinence and non-formation of cementum lines discussed in [441]. Using known-age animals from the same population as a standard, incisor tooth wear gives useful guide to age of live adults [509]. Age-related variability in skull measurements [611]: skulls of male foxes appear to change more with age than females, but relationships inadequate for age determination.

Age structure: Various examples shown in Table 9.4; no significant differences between sexes, although very old animals more likely to be males. Maximum survival in wild 10–11 years, but in captivity >14 years not unusual [1]. Proportion <1 year old in sample reflects intensity of control, varies from 0.98 to 5.6 per adult [507]; most British samples towards low end of this range.

Table 9.4 Fox: age structure of several British populations, both sexes combined. The figures are percentages; ages were determined from incremental lines in the teeth

Age (years) Source	Bristol [525]	London [525]	E Anglia [583]	Midlands [583]	NE Scotland [724]	W Scotland [724]	W Wales [804]	Mid-Wales [583]	Mid-Wales [804]	Isle of Skye [804]
0–1	50	57	55	57	62	56	43	59	53	67
1–2	24	24	23	28	21	27	23	25	24	19
2–3	13	10	17	9	9	6	13	11	17	10
3–4	7	5	4	3	5	6	11	5	3	3
4–5	4	3	<1	1	1	1	3	2	3	1
5–6	2	1	<1	1	1	2	5	1	1	
6–7	1	<1	<1	<1	1	1	1			
7–8	<1	<1	<1	<1	<1	1	1			
8–9	<1				<1	1	1			
9–10	<1									

Survival: Low; including an estimate for mortality of cubs <4 weeks old, mean life expectancy in London, where level of control low, 12.1 months for males, 12.4 months for females; for Bristol, where no control, comparable figures 16.6 and 17.8 months [525]. Age-specific mortality rates for different populations given in [525, 583]. Annual mortality rates vary for both adults and juveniles, 50–60%.

High rate of annual turnover means that survival of both members of a pair unlikely; in mid-Wales, adult mortality 57% and so probability of both members of pair dying is 32.5%, of 1 member dying 49%, and of both members surviving 18.5% [804]. In uncontrolled population, Bristol, age at death of dominant adult animals 4.5 years, compared to 2.1 years for subordinates [56].

MORTALITY

Predation: Few natural predators; cubs killed at earths by golden eagles, and cubs (rarely adults) killed by badgers. In urban areas, dogs significant predators of young cubs, occasionally kill adults [514]. Adults occasionally killed by conspecifics [318, 525].

Persecution: Most mortality believed to be human-induced. Few samples of foxes adequate to represent true levels of mortality; numbers killed in a small area, late autumn–early winter, not representative because of large numbers of itinerants (e.g. Pembrokeshire, over 8 weeks in winter on 3.2 km², an average of 1 fox/4 ha killed [806]). In rural Dorset, 58% deliberately killed by people, 7% killed accidentally by people, 31% cubs killed by vixen and 5% natural mortality [1092]. In comprehensive sample from Bristol, causes of death for adults: road accidents 61%, shot, snared, etc. 18%, disease 10%, fights 3%, parturition death <1%, trains 1%, misadventure (trapped in fences, falling into pits, etc.) 2%, and unknown causes 5%. Significant increase in the number of foxes dying from disease and fights with other foxes as population density increased [525]. Cull intensity (foxes killed/km² per year) in mid-Wales 0.71–1.90, E Midlands 0.37–1.85 and E Anglia 0.41–2.66 [582].

In early 1960s, large numbers died in E Anglia through eating birds killed by seed dressings [110]. In GB, the fox is the most commonly recorded mammalian victim of accidental and deliberate poisoning [1173]; poisons include agricultural pesticides, biocides and rodenticides.

Major single cause of death is road traffic (e.g. 58% in Bristol [61]). Annual shooting mortality thought to total 80 000 individuals [1073]; 12 000 killed by 544 gamekeepers in 1995–1997 [583]; c.30 000 animals snared and killed annually [1073]. Before implementation of Hunting Act 2004, hunting with dogs took variety of forms: c.200 registered packs of foxhounds killed 21 000–25 000 annually [163]; 50 000 dug out with terriers introduced into dens and 10 000 killed by lurchers [1073]. Foxes culled on 50–62% of farms in nationwide surveys [1321, 1374] and 70–95% of farms in survey of 3 regions [582].

Intense debate on welfare standards of hunting with dogs vs shooting as result of legislative changes. Post-mortem examination indicates hounds do not always kill foxes by cervical dislocation as commonly stated [163, 340, 341]. Estimates of wounding rates arising from shooting discussed in [407], but see [53, 54].

Impact of high anthropogenic mortality on fox numbers equivocal. At local scale (e.g. individual farm) intensive culling can eliminate breeding and/or all foxes, but effects short term because of dispersal from surrounding area [1094]. Number killed substantial relative to estimated density in E Anglia [583], yet vermin bag records still increasing [1268]. Culling in commercial forests, Wales, produced no decline in index of fox numbers [55]. Similarly, cessation of hunting in 2001 due to outbreak of foot-and-mouth disease did not lead to widespread increases in regional fox abundance indices [59]. Comparing fox populations in Bristol (uncontrolled) and London (some control), control did not significantly reduce number of family groups in an area, but did reduce total number of adult foxes and cubs in the population, hence mean family group size [525]. In N Ireland, hunting (encouraged by a bounty system) did not limit fox population [381].

Disease: Most important disease rabies, for which fox is main vector throughout much of Europe [670, 857]. Government contingency plans for dealing with a rabies event outlined in [534, 879]; public preferences for different strategies in [231]. Mathematical models used to predict disease spread, culling strategies and vaccination [523, 1207–1209, 1211, 1371].

Foxes prone to traumatic injuries. In London, 32.4% of foxes >6 months old had one or more broken bones, probably the result of road accidents. Healing often involved shortening or distortion of long bones [510]. Other frequent injuries include loss of part or all of the tail, and some or all of a limb; 3-legged foxes occasional, particularly in urban areas where their mobility and reproductive capabilities seem little impaired [1].

In London, arthritis frequent, particularly in the spine, whole lengths fused in badly affected animals [508]; some evidence that badly affected animals were in poorer condition, and debilitating levels accelerated mortality in older age groups.

PARASITES
Parasite monitoring and surveillance studies in GB and Ireland in [1188, 1212, 1399].

Ectoparasites: Fleas mostly stragglers, mean infestation low [155, 1128]. Some, e.g. *Spilopsyllus cuniculi*, probably from prey, others, e.g. *Archaeopsylla e. erinacei*, from travelling around range. *Pulex irritans, Ctenocephalides canis* and *Paraceras melis* believed to feed on foxes; no host-specific flea in GB [155]. Ticks *Ixodes ricinus* and *I. hexagonus* common, particularly on nursing vixens and juveniles still using earths [527]; very large infestations only rarely recorded, when extensive fur loss from scratching may occur. *I. canisuga* more frequent in N.

Louse *Trichodectes vulpis* specific to fox but recorded infrequently, e.g. only 3 foxes infested in over 3000 examined in Bristol [1] but each had many hundreds or thousands; small infestations may be overlooked. *T. melis* occurs, straggler from badgers.

Mite *Sarcoptes scabiei* most important, causes sarcoptic mange. Burrows into skin, causes extensive hair loss, first on base of tail and hindfeet, then rump, finally spreading forward to cover whole body. Fox scratches infected areas, causing excessive fluid exudation, dries on body as thick crust, exceptionally >1 cm thick. In final stages, may number many millions [1], fox loses up to 50% of body weight, most of fur, and may gnaw at infested limbs and tail. In urban areas, infected animals increasingly seek shelter in sheds, garages, etc. Mean time from infestation until death 4 months in epizootic phase of disease [1238]. Mange may be transferred to domestic dogs and humans [1238, 1239]; in Bristol, appeared in dogs 1 month after appearance in foxes [1219]. Until recently, sarcoptic mange not widespread in GB. One epidemic recorded, S England, late 19th century, resulting in some hunts restocking with healthy foxes [1265]. Mange widespread in parts of London since before 1970s [1]; since mid 1990s, has spread over much of England [1219], locally may exterminate fox populations; in Bristol, first case recorded in spring 1994; in 2 years, had reduced population by >95% [57].

Other skin mites *Demodex folliculorum* and *Notoderes* sp. reported, frequency of occurrence unknown. *Otodectes cyanotis* frequent in ear canal, >70% of foxes in Bristol infested [1]. Pentastomid mite *Linguatula serrata*, in nasal passages, recorded twice in GB [804]. Ringworm *Microsporum* recorded occasionally [1128].

Helminths: Variety reported in GB and Ireland [845, 804, 1099, 1128, 1212, 1383, 1399]. Nematoda: *Toxocara canis* and *Uncinaria stenocephala* most common species in gut; *Capillaria aerophila* and *Crenosoma vulpis* in lungs, and *Capillaria plica* in bladder. *Angiostrongylus vasorum* reported in foxes, SW England [1187]. Formerly, cases in domestic dogs also confined to this region but recently identified elsewhere [967]; role of foxes in expansion of disease unknown, but possible link with sarcoptic mange noted [1187, 1188]. *Trichinella spiralis* not detected in 587 foxes sampled, GB [1212], but in 1% of foxes from Ireland [1075]. Cestoda: *Taenia serialis* and *T. pisiformis* most common. *Echinococcus granulosus* formerly recorded in 8% of foxes [225], not detected in most recent national survey [1212]. *E. multilocularis* significant zoonosis in Europe, but absent from GB. Trematoda: 11 species recorded [804], frequency of occurrence or effects on host little known.

Prevalence of main parasites in surveys [1099, 1212]: Nematoda – *T. canis* 55.9–61.6%, *T. leonina* 0.3–1.5%, *U. stenocephala* 41.3–68.0%, *Trichuris vulpis* 0.3–0.5%; Cestoda – *T. pisiformis* 2.0–13.8%, *E. granulosus* 0.0–0.1%, *Dipylidium caninum* 0.7–3.8%. Additionally: Nematoda – *C. aerophila* 0.2%; Cestoda – *Taenia hydatigena* 2.5%; Trematoda – *Brachylaima recurva* 2.9%, *Cryptocotyle lingua* 2.3%; Acanthocephala – *Prosthorhynchus transversus* 0.7%, *Macracanthorhynchus catulinus* 0.1% [1099]. In Bristol, of 521 foxes, 58.2% of males and 44.1% of females infected with *T. canis* [1098]. Cubs had higher rates of prevalence than subadults, which had higher prevalence rates than adults [1098]. Cubs likely to be infected *in utero*.

Diseases: Little information; sporadic reports, discussed in [804]. No record of distemper in wild foxes in GB, although locally common in Europe [804]. In urban areas, antibodies to various pet diseases (e.g. parvovirus) recorded, but no information on the effects of such diseases on the fox population [1]. *Brucella abortus* recorded in Ireland [910] and *Salmonella infantes* in GB [1273]. 10 serotypes of *Leptospira* recorded [1318], 1 more in [110]. Of these, *L. icterohaemorrhagiae* (likely to be obtained from eating infected rodents) and *L. canicola* most common; in old foxes, extensive nephritis thought to be associated with former may be an important cause of mortality, but no firm data [1, 1128].

Protozoans *Toxoplasma gondii* and *Neospora caninum* recorded in 20% and 1% of foxes examined [490], but little evidence of *N. caninum* in foxes on dairy farm where present in cattle [1191]. Oocysts of *Cryptosporidium parvum* detected in 2 of 23 faecal samples [1254].

Mycobacterium bovis found in 12/993 [291] and 9/9 [902] foxes examined. *Mycobacterium avium* subspecies *paratuberculosis*, which causes paratuberculosis or Johne's disease, recently reported in foxes from Scotland [81, 82]. Further work needed to identify role of foxes in epidemiology of these diseases.

RELATIONS WITH HUMANS

Very mixed. Much mythology and folklore surrounds the fox [1320]. A 'beast of the chase'; formerly >200 packs of hounds in GB. In 1982, estimated that nearly 200 000 people hunted foxes with hounds, at total annual expenditure of about £80 million [213]; these figures refuted in [1342]. Questionnaire survey describing functioning of hunts given in [851]. Detailed account of economic, social and environmental aspects of hunting with hounds in W Somerset and Exmoor [883]; impact in Wiltshire discussed in [48]. Governmental review [163] led to Hunting Act 2004, which only permits the use of ≤2 dogs to drive foxes from cover to waiting guns. Potential implications for changes in the prevalence of different management practices outlined in [1374].

Generally, foxes unpopular with rural communities; unwelcome to gamekeepers, shepherds, and many farmers. Review of fox control in game management and conservation in [1094]. Questionnaire surveys of the perceived pest status, attitudes, of urban and rural dwellers in [48, 582, 841, 851, 992, 1066].

Average value of pelt increased dramatically in 1970s, reached a peak of £27.80 in 1979; trade in GB pelts via major auctioneers in London up to 30 000/year in late 1970s [846]. Some sources speculated that GB total then nearer 100 000 pelts. In 1980s, price of pelts decreased considerably. Effects of trade on British fox population unknown, but decrease reported in Ireland [1393].

In urban areas, welcomed by most residents [516, 531]; popular pressure during 1970s and 1980s, particularly in London, reduced numbers of foxes killed by local authorities. In one area of Bristol, c.10% of householders fed foxes [57]; changes in amount of food supplied closely mirrored by changes in group size. Damage caused by foxes in urban areas generally slight [514, 848]. No evidence that foxes pose significant direct risk to people; none of occasional press reports of bitten babies appear typical fox bites.

Large numbers of orphaned and injured foxes reared and treated annually by wildlife rehabilitators. Condition and survival of foxes following release discussed in [1103, 1104]. Pest control agencies also known to move problem foxes from urban areas and release them in rural areas but extent of activity unknown.

Techniques for study: A medium-sized, elusive carnivore, difficult to study until advent of radio-tracking and night-viewing equipment [843]. Expanding radio-collars used to study growing cubs [1105]. Other methods include capture–mark–recapture [528]; studies on captive foxes [832]; urban surveys [516]; molecular techniques

[60, 1339]; radio-isotope analysis [772]. Census methods reviewed in [84, 1134]. In remote areas, N America, habituation of foxes to observer used successfully to study detailed aspects of behaviour [561]. Field and laboratory techniques [804]; methods of rearing orphaned fox cubs [521].

LITERATURE
Current overview of foxes in GB [63]; extensive review of literature in [804], now dated. Symposia on behaviour and ecology [1065, 1442]. Rural study [164, 721]; urban foxes [517, 518]; photographic study, Japan [1264]; long-term study [843]; long-term field study, N America [561, 562]. Popular accounts with emphasis on urban foxes [530, 558, 589, 1234].

AUTHORS
P.A. Baker & S. Harris

GENUS *Canis*

A genus of 7 species of wolves, dogs and jackals; occurs across most of N. hemisphere, S into Oriental and African regions. One, wolf *Canis lupus*, has wide Holarctic range, formerly occurred in British Isles (and domestic descendent, dog *C. familiaris*, occurs worldwide). All larger, more robust, than *Vulpes*, but anatomically similar; broader muzzles and stronger canines; postorbital processes convex on top, not dimpled, concave, as in *Vulpes*.

Wolf *Canis lupus*
Canis lupus L. 1758. Sweden.
Bleidd (Welsh), *madadh allaidh*, *madadh* (Scottish Gaelic), *faol*, *faol-chu* (Irish Gaelic), *bleit* (Cornish).

RECOGNITION
The wild ancestor of, and fully interfertile with, the domestic dog *Canis familiaris*. Usually looks like a large greyish-fawn dog (head and body length 90–150 cm) with reddish-brown tinge to head, ears, shoulders and legs, somewhat larger than a husky or Alsatian (Plate 1). Erect, slightly rounded, ears, a full bushy, straight but shortish tail, and large feet, by dog standards.

Skull not always separable from dog of comparable size (Fig. 9.17), but larger than most dogs, and with larger carnassial teeth [267]. Premolars usually sit neatly behind each other along the jaws (cf. dogs where reduced length of the muzzle results in premolars overlapping somewhat [210]). These distinctions most marked for larger breeds of dogs, so these usually recognisable from skulls. Postcranial remains are indistinguishable, except by size.

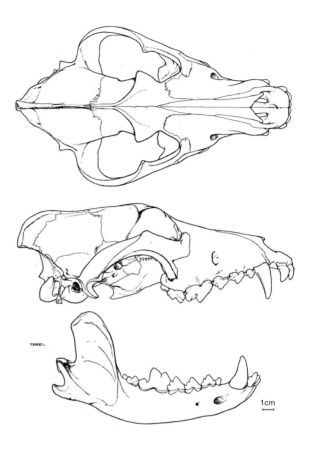

Fig. 9.17 Wolf skull *(from [942])*.

HISTORY
Preceded by an ancestral form, *Canis mosbachensis*, in the Cromerian Interglacial; *C. lupus* common as a fossil from the Hoxnian Interglacial onwards. Common in GB in cave sites of Devensian Glacial age, present in the Windermere Interstadial, and common in Late Glacial sites (e.g. Sun Hole, Soldier's Hole and Gough's Cave, Cheddar Gorge). Also present early in the Holocene (e.g. at Star Carr) and may well have survived through the Younger Dryas. Rare in Scotland, although numerous remains of cubs in the caves at Creag nan Uamh, of Late Glacial and/or Holocene age. Also certainly present in Ireland in Devensian (at Shandon and Castlepook Caves) and Late Glacial (Plunkett Cave) times [1420].

Later archaeological record poor, because of uncertain identity of bones. Anglo-Saxon and Norse placenames demonstrate that widely known in England through to 11th century [41]. Documentary evidence of attempts at extermination demonstrates its survival in England at least to end of 13th century, by which time probably limited to N (Cumbria, N Pennines). In Scotland, certainly survived through Stuart times, but declared extinct around 1680–1700 by contemporary writers. Very doubtful claim that last killed 1743. In Ireland likewise survived through

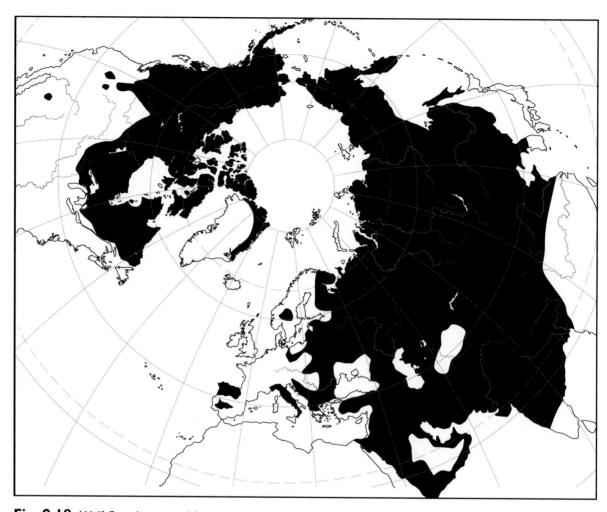

Fig. 9.18 Wolf *Canis lupus*: world range.

to 17th century, but active persecution documented by laws of 1614, 1652 and 1653, led to perceptible scarcity by 1680s and 'last wolves' claimed for various counties between 1692 and 1786 [385, 1036, 1420].

Wolves widely distributed across Holarctic (Fig. 9.18), but range severely reduced by persecution; successfully reintroduced to Yellowstone National Park, Wyoming, USA, have naturally recolonised Sweden and E Europe from Russia, also France from Italy [929, 1057]. Reintroduction to GB often proposed in recent years (e.g. [1418]), but no feasibility study published; outline study [446] suggests that the Scottish Highlands could hold up to 200 packs; thorough statistical model suggests density stabilising at 25 wolves/1000 km², benefits to estates of reduced expenditure on hind cull [989]. Conflict with hill farmers and hill walkers seen as major obstacles to any reintroduction. However, reintroduction of captive-bred wolves to Georgia in 1974, using electric collars to train wolves not to attack people and livestock [44], may offer a potential model for GB and other areas in W Europe.

GENERAL ECOLOGY

Lives in packs of 2–14 or more adults, plus young-of-year. Packs occupy territories, typically 150–200 km² in Poland [618] but as large as 600–2600 km² in Alaska [935]; where not limited by human persecution, aggressive rejection of intruders a major cause of mortality. Cubs born in den to alpha pair, tended by whole pack which brings food back to den; feed pups by regurgitation; litter typically 5–6 pups [934]. Predators especially of large ungulates; in Europe, usually rely on red deer, though roe, reindeer and wild boar also killed [618, 1005], elsewhere moose, bison, even musk ox. Density and breeding success strongly related to abundance and vulnerability of main prey, pack size more likely related to size of prey (larger where prey on moose or bison). Domestic stock, especially sheep, vulnerable when native prey absent. Will scavenge. Occurs in very wide range of habitats, from Arctic tundra to Arabian semi-desert; main requirement likely to be few or tolerant humans, because heavily persecuted; in part, reaction to predation on livestock, but also historically, in Eurasia, a much-feared carrier of rabies; also evidently in part cultural [1036]; Europeans much less tolerant of wolves than e.g. native Americans.

AUTHORS
A.C. Kitchener & D.W. Yalden

FAMILY MUSTELIDAE

A diverse and versatile family of small to medium-sized carnivores, *c.*59 species arranged in 22 genera; 4 genera with 8 species present in British Isles, including *Martes* (pine marten), *Mustela* (stoat, weasel, polecat, ferret, mink), *Meles* (badger) and *Lutra* (otter). Typically slender, elongate hunters, able to enter burrows of prey, climb trees and swim; heavier, less agile badgers and wolverines retain the bounding gait of their smaller relatives. Short limbs bear 5 toes on all feet, leave characteristic 5-toed footprints. Dental formula varies from $i^3/_3c^1/_1p^4/_4m^2/_2$ (*Martes*) to $i^3/_3c^1/_1p^3/_3m^1/_2$ (*Mustela*); canines and carnassials usually well developed, but badgers have large flattened molars, an adaptation to more omnivorous diet, carnassials small, not very evident.

GENUS *Meles*

Included in subfamily Melinae (true badgers) with *Taxidea, Arctonyx, Melogale*; basal subfamily within Mustelidae. Usually considered a monospecific genus, containing only Eurasian badger *M. meles*. Possible that eastern forms *M. leucura* (Tibet) and *M. anakuma* (Japan) should be regarded as separate species. Heavy-bodied with short tail and distinctive face pattern. Distinguished among European mustelids by flattened molars; dentition usually $i^3/_3c^1/_1p^3/_3m^1/_1$, but vestigial p^1/p_1 sometimes present, giving $i^3/_3c^1/_1p^4/_4m^1/_1$.

Badger *Meles meles*
Ursus meles Linnaeus, 1785; Uppsala, Sweden.
Meles taxus Boddaert, 1785.

Brock, grey pate, bawson, baget; *mochyn daeaar, broch, pryf penfrith, pryf llwyd* (Welsh); *brochlach* (Scottish Gaelic); *broc* (Irish Gaelic).

Male – boar; female – sow; young – cub.

RECOGNITION
Whole animal: Unlike any other British mammal in having a white head with conspicuous dark stripes through eyes (Plate 8).

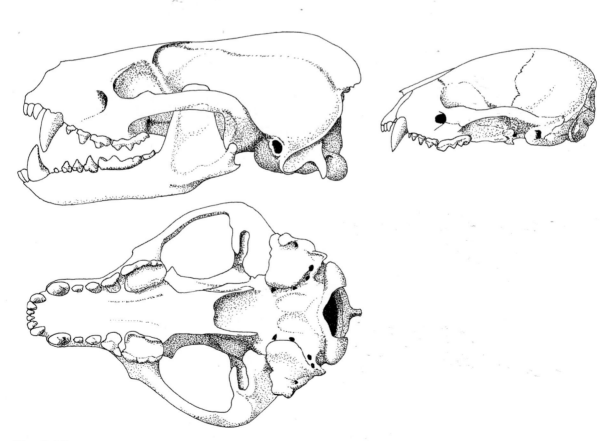

Fig. 9.19 Skull of old male badger, from side to show enlarged sagittal crest, and palate to show teeth, especially the enlarged, flattened m¹; the cub, right, has a rounded braincase with no crest (*drawn by D.W. Yalden*).

Plate 8

A Pine marten *Martes martes* female, summer **B** male, winter **C** Ferret *Mustela furo*
D Polecat *Mu. putorius* female, summer **E** male, winter
F Mink *Mu. vison* female, wet, sleek **G** male, dry **H** Stoat *Mu. erminea* male, summer **I** female, winter, ermine
J Irish stoat *Mu. e. hibernica* **K** Weasel *Mu. nivalis* (female) **L** male

Skull and teeth: Distinguished as adult by prominent interparietal ridge (sagittal crest), prominent canines and flattened molars (Fig. 9.19).

FIELD SIGNS

Tracks and trails: Paths leading from the sett often well worn, may be followed for long distances; conspicuous where they cross linear features and often run alongside them, but may also extend out into fields. Hairs often caught in lowest strand of barbed wire where a badger passes under it. Footprints typically show 5 toes and impression of broad, fused plantar pads (Fig. 9.2); the longer claw marks of the forefeet show up well in soft ground; in mud and snow the heel (normally raised slightly) may leave an impression. Print of forefoot is broader than hind and inner toe set further back. Overprinting often occurs, but not when travelling fast.

Faeces: Looser than those of dog, but consistency varies with food eaten; appear muddy after consuming earthworms. Beetle elytra and cereal husks may be conspicuous; purplish colour often indicates blackberries, bilberries. Usually placed in shallow pits which are not covered after use, but occasionally deposited on the ground surface. Aggregations of pits form latrines.

Dens: Burrow system (sett) can be extensive. Typically 3–10 large entrances (range 1–80), >25 cm in diameter (often much greater). Large spoil heaps outside, may be deeply grooved from digging activity; contain discarded bedding: plant debris, hay, bracken, straw, etc. (spoil at fox earth contains no plant material). Scratching tree (frequently elder), with claw marks and mud up *c*.1 m, often nearby. Underground, labyrinth of tunnels and chambers, sometimes large and complex [1122]: one large sett, Cotswolds, extended over 35 × 15 m, had 12 entrances, tunnels totalling 310 m, total volume of 15.28 m³, equivalent to 25 t of soil [1122]. Tunnels known to extend around hillside up to 100 m, but typically 10–20 m; may be at several levels. Social group usually has single main sett, the focus of its social and breeding behaviour, and several smaller, less frequently used, outlier setts. Levels of visible activity at setts indicate whether badgers are resident, but are poor predictors of numbers [1390].

Other field signs: Occasionally sleep above ground in day nests or night couches of bedding material, often in thick cover. When feeding on tall cereals, may leave bundles of trampled stalks in a characteristic criss-cross pattern. Aggregations of shallow pits (sometimes over an extensive area) may result from digging for insect larvae and plant storage organs.

DESCRIPTION

Pelage: Appears grey from a distance owing to colour of dorsal and lateral guard hairs; are light at the base and tip, with dark subterminal patch between. Legs and underside covered by uniformly dark hairs, often sparse ventrally. Underfur thick in winter, uniformly pale.

Moult: Single prolonged moult, begins in spring when underfur shed, followed by guard hairs. Begins on withers and shoulders, spreads along back and flanks. New guard hairs grow in late summer, followed by new underfur [908, 994]. Yearlings moult earlier than adults, lactating females moult last [1229].

Anatomy and physiology: Powerfully built with a rather small head, thick short neck, stocky wedge-shaped body and short tail. Low-slung body carried on short powerful limbs. Feet are digitigrade but short; 5 toes on each foot, especially large claws on front feet.

Snout flexible, muscular, used in probing and digging. Eyes small; ears short, tipped with white. Vibrissae present on snout and above eye. Senses of smell and hearing very acute. Eyesight poor, particularly in cubs; because rods predominant, is best in poor light. Tapetum present, white eye-shine at night. Difficult to sex in the field, except for most extreme cases. Typically, male has broader head, thicker neck and a relatively pointed, narrow, white tail; females sleeker, have narrower, less domed head and more tufty tail (Plate 8). Tail not a reliable feature on its own. When adult males sit up and scratch, scrotal sacs conspicuous; penis not visible, lies under skin, pointing forward, but protrudes when in use. Males have larger canines and wider skulls than females [663].

Gut longer than that of fox; mean length of small intestine 5.36 m [1224]; no caecum.

Preliminary haematological and blood bio-chemistry values available for wild badgers [971]. Blood biochemistry levels vary in relation to physical condition and season, suggest that badgers do not conserve protein during periods of food scarcity [301]. Basic metabolic rate of 10 kg badger estimated at 500 kcal (*c*.2000 kJ)/day [617].

Nipples: 3 pairs in both sexes, well developed in adult females. Always longer in females that have produced cubs than in non-breeding females.

Scent glands: Subcaudal gland is an invagination of skin just below base of tail; secretes a cream-coloured fatty substance with a faint musky smell. Pair of anal glands, just beneath skin on either side of tail; open by short ducts, just internal to the anus; secrete a yellowish-brown fatty fluid with a powerful, rank, musky odour.

Skull: Prominent interparietal ridge starts growth at 10 months, may reach 15 mm tall in old males (Fig. 9.19); lacking in juvenile skulls, but have temporal ridges (lines) marking upper limits of temporalis muscles on either side of cranium; gradually migrate nearer to midline with age, coalesce to form the interparietal ridge. In adults, lower jaw articulates firmly, dislocation impossible without fracturing skull.

Dentition: Well suited for an omnivorous diet: incisors small and chisel-like, canines prominent, no specialised carnassial teeth, molars considerably flattened for grinding. Deciduous teeth usually $di^3/_3dc^1/_1dp^3/_3$, sometimes with additional $dm^1/_1s$; adult dentition usually $i^3/_3c^1/_1p^3/_3m^1/_1$, sometimes with additional $p^1/_1s$. Incisors sometimes reduced in number, di_1 and di_2 often never penetrate the gums – an adaptation for sucking.

Reproductive tract: Weights of paired testes in mature males reach mean maximum of 11 g in February–March; decrease slowly to mean minimum of 5 g in October–November, increase rapidly thereafter [9].

Uterus bicornuate, mean length of each horn in mature females during delayed implantation 86 mm, with a mean flat diameter of 6.6 mm [1015]. Ovaries partly embedded in fat, may reach maximum of 15 × 10 × 8 mm; can only be examined by removing the wall of the bursa; surface is smooth up to time of maturity. Corpora of delay cream-coloured, nearly flush with the surface; those during pregnancy may project prominently, are well vascularised. Tube much convoluted. Placental scars persist as dark patches for a considerable time, sometimes difficult to distinguish between old and new scars.

Chromosomes: 2n = 44; FNa = 72 (European data) [1441].

RELATIONSHIPS

Either the only member of genus *Meles*, or very close to Tibetan *M. leucura* and Japanese *M. anakuma*, if these distinct. Genetically next closest to *Arctonyx* of SE Asia.

Body weight may vary between regions: in Scotland females averaged 6.5 kg on W coast but 10 kg on E coast (see Table 9.5) [753]. Positively related to amount of earthworms in diet and their availability [753], hence with access to agricultural grasslands [292], but negatively related to population density [866, 1116]. Seasonal variation in weight [742, 752] follows food abundance; lowest in summer when food scarcest, highest in autumn. Breeding females generally show widest fluctuations [195, 742, 1116]. Growth rate during 1st year varies with food availability: mean weight of cubs in spring was 3.0 kg, summer 4.0 kg, autumn 6.9 kg and winter 8.0 kg [1116]. Artificial provisioning of food may substantially affect suburban badgers; a female cub, caught September, Essex garden, weighed 11.3 kg [286].

VARIATION

Recognition of British population as subspecies (*M. m. britannicus* Satunin 1906, based on cranial measurements) not justified, although do have larger skulls than those from mainland Europe [830]. Badger populations within the British Isles can be distinguished on both cranial measurements and genetic structure [828]. Colour variations described, genetical basis unclear. Include albinos (no melanin), semi-albinos (eye-stripes visible), erythristic (gingery) and melanistic (very dark). Much staining of fur from soil surrounding setts, e.g. in red sandstone regions [978]. Tail patterns may vary between individuals [299].

Table 9.5 Badger: measurements of individuals > 1 year old [978][a] and >21 months old [1017][b] from SW England

	Males			Females		
	Mean	Range	n	Mean	Range	n
Head and body length (mm)[a]	753	686–803	31	724	673–787	31
Tail length (mm)[a]	150	127–178	31	150	114–190	31
Tibia length (mm)[b]	103	91–119	635	99	88–121	910
Weight (kg)[a]	11.6	9.1–16.7	33	10.1	6.6–13.9	84

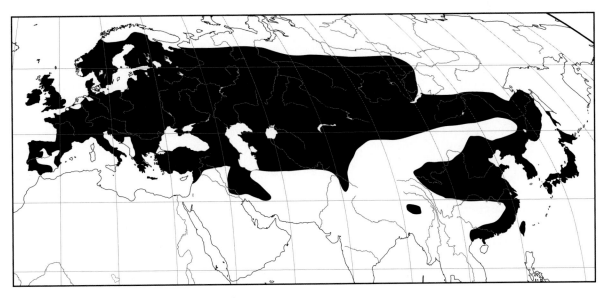

Fig. 9.20 Badger *Meles meles*: Palaearctic range, mapped assuming that eastern forms *leucura* and *anakuma* are conspecific.

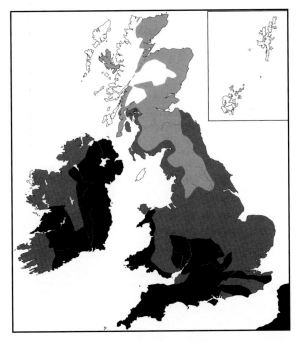

Fig. 9.21 Badger *Meles meles*: estimated densities of >1.2/km² (black), >0.3/ km² (dark grey), < 0.3/ km² (pale grey) (*after [241a, 1389]*). Abundance in central Ireland is currently much reduced from the potential density indicated by a prolonged eradication campaign.

DISTRIBUTION

Distributed across temperate Palaearctic from Ireland to Siberia, perhaps to Japan (Fig. 9.20).

Widespread in GB and Ireland (Fig. 9.21). Absent only in regions of high altitude (usually >500 m asl), most (although not all) large conurbations, some intensively farmed areas, extensive lowlands liable to flooding and most offshore islands. Present Anglesey, Arran, Canvey, Wight, Sheppey and Skye. Attempts to introduce badgers to islands including Jura and Ailsa Craig failed [541].

HISTORY

Meles apparently evolved in temperate forests of Asia, spread into Europe. Thoral's badger, *M. thoralis*, present in the Early Pleistocene, Europe, *c.*1 mya. By early Middle Pleistocene, *M. meles* present in Europe, very similar to modern form. Sporadically present in GB since Hoxnian interglacial (300 000–440 000 years ago); earliest records, 2 teeth from ancient tufa deposits at Hitchen, Hertfordshire, and a single record from the lower Brickearth at Boxgrove, Sussex [474]. Survived Last Glaciation in S Europe (Spain–Italy–Ukraine), spread N into C Europe in Late Glacial, but not into GB until Postglacial; present early in Mesolithic, Kendrick's Cave, N Wales, 9945 bp, and Star Carr, Yorkshire [1217]. Construction of ancient earthworks, Avebury, Wiltshire, filled in 3-hole badger sett, dated when excavated to *c.*2600 BC [474]. Earliest records from Ireland, Bronze Age, Lough Gur, Co. Limerick and Ballinderry, Co. Cork; possibly a human introduction [912].

HABITAT

Optimal habitat a mixture of deciduous woodland and earthworm-rich pasture in a region with a mild wet climate. Areas of high badger density often associated with cattle farming where short grass provides ideal habitat for earthworm foraging [977, 979].

Setts dug in wide variety of places: often woodland, scrub, hedgerows, quarries, sea cliffs, moorland, open fields; occasionally, in embankments, Iron Age forts, mines, caves, coal tips, rubbish dumps and under buildings. May also occur in urban environments [515]. National badger survey of GB, main setts preferably located in deciduous and mixed woodland (44%); 23% were in hedgerows and scrub, 6% in coniferous woods and 13% in open situations [1389]. Favourable factors were presence of adequate cover, well-drained, easily dug soil, little disturbance by humans or domestic animals and a varied and plentiful food supply (particularly earthworms) nearby [207]. Latter assured where deciduous woodland, pasture and arable land all occur within the territory [593]. Low-lying marshy areas and regions of high altitude are avoided.

SOCIAL ORGANISATION AND BEHAVIOUR

Territories: Form social groups comprising, on average, 6 (range 2–23) adults (Fig. 9.22) [195, 519, 740, 754]. Group size, particularly numbers of females and cubs, may be related to habitat composition [292]. Territory size ranges from *c.*30 ha in optimal habitat to >150 ha in marginal habitat; territories less pronounced in areas of low density [242] or where populations have been disturbed (e.g. [198]). Territorial boundaries characterised by the presence of well-worn paths and shared latrines. Territory size and config-

uration arguably related to distribution of food resources [111, 179] or setts [304, 308]. Can remain remarkably stable in undisturbed populations [195].

Commonly stated that usually a dominant male in each group, but existence of dominance hierarchy within groups not established; evidence of considerable tolerance between animals of same and neighbouring groups [867]. Males tend to play more active role in demarcating territory than females, have correspondingly larger ranges within the territory [194, 740, 1125]. Territorial activity peaks in early spring, coinciding with main mating period [978, 979, 1124], with a minor peak in autumn [1125]. Large proportion of cubs fathered by the resident males in their group, but up to 54% sired by males from neighbouring groups [178, 370, 1410]. Group living in badgers postulated to be the most efficient way to exploit irregularly dispersed food resources [593, 751].

Denning behaviour: Digging and bedding collection take place throughout year, but particularly in autumn and spring. Resident adult females and dominant males carry out most sett maintenance [1231]. Chambers frequently lined with large amounts of bedding (e.g. grass, bracken, straw, leaves or moss) brought in on dry nights. May bring 20–30 bundles on a single night; works backwards to sett, keeping bundle in

Fig. 9.22 Badgers maintain group cohesion by mutual grooming and marking each other with scent (*photo D. Hunford*).

Fig. 9.23 Badgers gather bedding beneath the chin, and drag it backwards into the sett (*photo D. Hunford*).

place with chin and forepaws (Fig. 9.23). old bedding discarded periodically; in winter, bedding may be taken outside near entrance on sunny mornings, retrieved later. Often sleep together in chambers, particularly in winter [1126]. Space use within setts and a tendency to move to outliers in summer may help reduce ectoparasite burdens [171, 1126].

Scent-marking: Scent probably the most important means of communication, both within and between social groups. Secretions from both subcaudal and anal glands thought to be important in territoriality: contain information about group identity, subcaudal gland secretions also allow individual recognition within group [157, 263, 449, 755]. Individual may set scent on a fellow group member by smearing it with subcaudal gland, or they may press subcaudal glands together, reinforcing group scent [158, 980]. Persistent and strong-smelling, orange-coloured, anal gland secretion frequently deposited with faeces. Faeces probably serve to pass anal gland secretion into the environment. Urine probably also important in scent communication, explaining complex patterns of urine deposition, which vary with sex, age and season [150, 1164]. Urine may establish oestrous condition of female, contains excreted sex hormones [980].

Possession of interdigital glands not established; paw scraping on trees and near latrines suggests presence.

Vocalisations: Most vocal February–June. Extensive repertoire [887, 1019, 1186, 1401]; sound recordings can be heard at *http://www.wildcru.org/research/ecol/badgercalls.htm*. Include a deep growl when threatened, a bark when surprised and the whickering of playing or distressed cubs [980].

Other communication: Males may raise the tail and fluff up body fur when sexually excited. Cubs also fluff up their fur when excited or threatened; adults may do so if attacked by dogs [980].

Aggressive behaviour: Mainly associated with territorial defence and mating activity. Bite wounds most frequent in spring and mostly on males [417]. Wounding can be common but rates vary over time and in response to local conditions [293, 869, 1119]. Badgers typically bite each other around neck and rump, while running and chasing, uttering low 'kekkering' sounds. Wounding can be severe, occasionally fatal [417]. Females aggressively defend cubs against potential predators such as foxes [978].

Evidence for cannibalism and infanticide is largely circumstantial. Dominant females may sometimes kill cubs of subordinate members of own social group, or adult males may kill and eat cubs while female away [980]. Early cessation of lactation in a high proportion (35%) of females [244] and high cub mortality (42%) during lactation [1017] suspected to result from infanticide by dominant females. Anecdotal support from a female, that had produced cubs earlier in the year, later found as a road casualty with cub remains in the stomach [827].

Black and white mask probably a warning coloration. Cub's defence is to face attacker, showing facial pattern to best advantage, fluff up its fur and make menacing noises. An adult faces an aggressor in the same way but keeps its body and head low. If attacked, will slash upwards with its teeth or use its front claws with rapid raking movements.

Dispersal: Rates of permanent dispersal from natal social group relatively low in medium–high density rural populations, but temporary visits to other social groups may be common [178, 199, 1118]. Most permanent dispersers move into neighbouring social groups; process can take several months. Badgers may move in coalitions of males [1127] or females [1410]. Some studies report that males move most [196, 742, 1118], others show female-biased dispersal [250, 1410]. In one study permanent group changes exclusively involved mature females [199]. Disturbance to population increases the likelihood of movements occurring [198, 1123, 1314]. More frequent dispersal has been reported in urban habitats [196].

Excessive inbreeding avoided by transfer of sexually mature adults between groups and matings between members of different groups [178, 370]. This mating system, unusual among mammals, may not occur where badgers do not form distinct social groups [742].

Activity: Mainly crepuscular and nocturnal. Emergence from the sett usually around dusk; varies according to sex, age, season, environmental conditions and levels of human disturbance [979, 1315]; usually before dark in May–August, after dark at other times, but much less regular in November–February. Emergence and activity reduced in winter, especially in N [405], but no true hibernation. Effects of weather on activity of suburban badgers have been described [243]. Badgers can go without food for long periods, may remain below ground for many days, e.g. during periods of severe frost. Disturbance, such as earth-stopping by fox hunts, may delay or prevent emergence [794].

Diurnal activity not unusual in secluded places. Sometimes lies out, away from sett, in bracken, brambles or cereal crops, particularly in August–September. Shortage of food, as in severe drought, a common cause of diurnal behaviour.

Locomotion: When travelling, moves at an ambling trot, head down with hindquarters swaying from side to side, pausing frequently to listen. Moves at a slow walk when foraging, but when alarmed, can travel at up to 30 km/h over short distances. May climb wire-netting fences and sloping trees, gripping the bark like a bear. Can swim, but usually avoids doing so.

Grooming: Frequently takes place after emergence, very thorough, using claws and teeth. Mutual grooming occurs, may have a social function (Fig. 9.22). Both breeding and non-breeding females may groom cubs [1405]. Also lick fur; mutual licking has been observed [947].

Defecation: Usually into shallow pits, several of which form a latrine, although single defecations may also occur, particularly in lower-density populations [613]. Latrines concentrated in vicinity of setts, and at strategic places near territory boundaries and abundant food sources. In a stable high-density population, Gloucester-shire, *c.*50–60% of latrines located on or near territorial boundaries [1]. Faeces may also be deposited underground in a side chamber and occasionally on the spoil heap. Urination occasionally takes place in empty dung pits, but usually random. Latrines and urination points may be more frequent near linear features such as hedges and fences. Latrines are dynamic, with much overmarking and incidental burial of droppings [289, 1125]; tendency for neighbouring groups to match the quantities deposited at boundary latrines [1232].

FEEDING

Highly adaptable opportunistic foragers; omnivorous, exploit wide range of animal and plant food (detailed analyses in [129, 515, 752, 753]). Earthworms often the most important item in the diet. Foods taken according to availability, hence diet varies according to geographical location, types of habitat present within territory, season of year and prevailing weather. Apart from earthworms, main food categories are larger insects, small mammals (mainly their young), carrion (particularly in winter), cereals, fruit and underground storage organs. Mammals include rabbits, rats, mice, voles, shrews, moles and hedgehogs. Insects: chafers, dung and ground beetles, caterpillars, leatherjackets, wasps' and bumble bees' nests. Cereals: wheat, oats and maize, occasionally barley. Fruit: windfall apples, pears, plums, blackberries, bilberries, raspberries, strawberries, acorns and beechmast; also pignut and wild arum corms. Occasional foods include birds, mainly ground nesters and ground roosters; frogs, toads and newts; snakes and lizards; snails and slugs; fungi; green food such as clover and grass occasionally taken in winter and during drought.

Foraging behaviour: Mild, damp nights most productive for worming on pasture. When encountered on the surface, earthworm is gripped in incisors, steadily pulled to release tail from burrow; if it breaks, badger will dig the tail out. Takes worms and other invertebrates from beneath cowpats, and digs for invertebrate larvae, plant storage organs and small mammals. May also take stored foodstuffs or grain from farm buildings [419] and will climb into troughs to take cattle feed [420].

Impact on prey: Predation unlikely to have any significant effect on earthworm numbers: usually superabundant in optimal badger habitat. Predation may control wasps locally by destroying large numbers of nests [172], may regulate hedgehog abundance or even result in their local absence [302, 303, 1432]. Analysis of published diet studies suggests that impact on bird populations minimal [598].

Food caching: Prey usually eaten on the spot, items rarely taken back to the sett [980].

Surplus killing: Eyewitness accounts of badgers surplus killing in chicken coops.

BREEDING

Oestrus may occur throughout year, but mating peaks in spring, postpartum. Implantation delayed until December, active pregnancy 6–7 weeks. Majority of births February, litter size 1–5, peak emergence of cubs in April (Fig. 9.24).

Males: Most males mature at 12–15 months but some at 8–9 months [1017], others take up to 2 years [9]. Normally fecund January–May, testosterone secretion and spermatogenesis decline through summer, testicles then ascend out of the scrotum [1410, 1411], although breeding males sustain testicular activity later into the summer [1406] and in some animals high concentrations of sperm remain in the epididymis throughout the year [455, 1017]. Maintenance of high testosterone levels into autumn observed in immigrant breeding males [1411].

Females: Usually begin to ovulate in spring of 2nd year, when 12–15 months old, but some begin a few months later [9, 1017]. Exceptionally, some become sexually mature at *c*.9 months [195, 388, 397]. Induced ovulators. Mating can take place during any month; main peak February–May, when mature females in postpartum oestrus, and younger animals experience their 1st oestrus. Matings at other times may involve females which did not conceive at earlier matings, and those late in maturing. Some females may have 2nd oestrus during the period of delay before implantation of the blastocysts, causing further matings [9, 244, 981]. Some of these further matings lead to fertilisation, with new blastocysts being added to existing ones. Genetic studies [178, 370] show mixed-paternity litters are common. Mating prolonged (15–60 min), although brief copulations (<2 min) also occur when female not in full oestrus. Oestrus lasts 4–6 days, frequent copulations may occur during this period, sometimes with >1 male [200, 981, 1018].

Long period of delay before fertilised eggs implant in wall of uterus (2–9 months), except that December matings probably followed by immediate implantation [397]. Implantation usually occurs during December, followed by true gestation of *c*.7 weeks. Physiological control of delayed implantation largely unresolved, although implantation probably triggered by day length [174, 176, 177], and limited evidence of possible relationship between seasonal changes in body temperature and implantation [405]. Females in good condition implant earlier [1407].

Although fertilisation takes place at any time, births are synchronised by delayed implantation. Usually occur mid January–mid March, peak in 1st

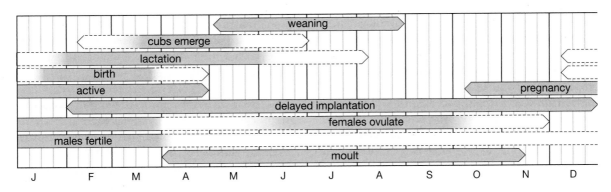

Fig. 9.24 Badger: annual cycle.

3 weeks of February (slightly later in N) [980, 1017]. Occurs in an underground chamber containing bedding. Breeding above ground, sometimes in buildings, recorded where surrounding countryside waterlogged [979, 980].

Productivity: >75% of females may carry blastocysts, but most do not implant and fetal losses of >35% have been recorded [1017]. Suspected due to reproductive suppression, only dominant females produce litters [1408]. High rate of reproductive failure may be a cost of group living for female badgers [250]. Litter size is 1–5; average for Europe, based on fetuses and placental scars, 2.7 [24]; estimates deduced from observations on families seen above ground, SW England, averaged 2.3 (50 families): 9 singles, 23 twins, 11 triplets, 7 quadruplets [979]. Both litter sizes and pregnancy rates tend to be lower in yearlings. Cub mortality high, estimates of pre-emergence mortality range from 24% [1117] to 38.4% [519]; an estimated 42% lost during lactation [1017]. Numbers, growth rates and survival of cubs are linked to food availability; high mortality may occur in dry summers [1409]. Population productivity estimated at 11% [1017] to 30% [244] below the potential. Quality of the group territory [1408], body condition [244, 1407] and availability of annex setts [244] may influence whether more than one female in a social group can successfully breed.

Development of young: Newborn cubs have pink skin covered with greyish, silky fur; darker eye stripe is usually visible. Eyelids fused, usually open at *c.*5 weeks. Average head and body length 120 mm; weight variable (75–132 g), those from large litters being smaller.

Milk teeth erupt over period of 2 weeks, when *c.*4–6 weeks old. First permanent incisors appear at *c.*10 weeks, and full transition to permanent dentition occurs during the following 6 weeks. Some milk teeth may be present, functional, after corresponding permanent teeth have come through; possible because canines and premolars do not emerge through same sockets as their milk precursors [978, 979].

Cubs emerge above ground for the first time at *c.*8 weeks. Weaning usually starts at 12 weeks, but some suckling may continue until 4–5 months [979]. By end of lactation, female's condition may have markedly deteriorated [1406]. During weaning, female observed to provide cubs with solid food [600, 979]. Alloparental behaviour recorded, related individuals cooperating with mother in raising her young. Non-breeding females observed to groom cubs, and guard them while mother away from sett [1405].

POPULATION

Numbers: Adult densities up to 25/km² [1117] and 38/km² [854] recorded in optimal habitats where social groups contiguous; <1–2/km² in unfavourable areas with a discontinuous, patchy distribution [740, 751]. Highest densities in SW England [1389]. Typical density where badgers common is *c.*10 adults/km².

Indirect estimates suggest a 77% increase in badger numbers in GB from the mid 1980s to the mid 1990s [1389]. Intensively studied populations have exhibited increases, from 7.8 to 25.3 adults/km² 1978–1993 at Woodchester Park, Gloucestershire [1117], and from 10 to 38 adults/km² 1987–1996 at Wytham Woods, Oxfordshire [854]. Both populations showed signs of density-dependent constraints on population growth [198, 854, 1116, 1117].

In GB, estimated to be 250 000 (England 190 00, Scotland 25 000, Wales 35 000) [536]. Re-examination suggests perhaps only 190 000 in 1980s, increased to 302 900 by 1990s [1388]. Ireland, estimated *c.*250 000 in 1990s [1204], perhaps reduced by culling to control bovine TB.

Fluctuations: Population recovery in GB facilitated by introduction of comprehensive protective legislation ensuring full protection for badgers and their setts [980] (see Chapter 4). Widespread in GB, 17th–18th centuries, but declined considerably in 19th century because of persecution and extensive predator control by gamekeepers. Intensity of predator control declined after World War I, numbers steadily increased, peaked in *c.*1960. Subsequently, numbers fell in some regions (road accidents, persecution, keepering). Legislation (1973 and later) helped recovery, but persecution may still depress numbers in some areas (e.g. parts of N England, E Anglia, S Scotland [1389] and N Ireland [1133]). Recent population growth also linked to increasingly mild winters [854].

Sex ratio: 1:1 in fetuses [1017] but in high-density population, Oxfordshire, post-emergent cub sex ratios male-biased when adult females in good body condition [319]. Adult sex ratios reported as 1:1 [854] or female biased [519, 1117]; latter may reflect higher adult mortality among males [195, 1382].

Age determination: In live animals, radiographic detection of fusion of the epiphyses in the forelimbs can distinguish yearling badgers from older animals up to *c.*18 months of age [388, 1014]. Growth rings seen in sectioned teeth [8] but can be poorly developed, may not correspond to age in years [10]. Tooth wear, compared with reference collection of known age material, provided correct estimates of age to within 1 year with >89% accuracy [533]. Baculum length and weight attain adult proportions during the 2nd year of life, but as time of maturity varies considerably, baculum an unreliable indicator of age [456].

Age structure: Pyramidal age structure, greater number of badgers in younger age classes. Heavy cub loss and consistent losses each year thereafter result in reduced numbers of badgers in each age class [1117].

Survival: Mortality of cubs is high, with 50–65% dying in their 1st year [195, 519, 979, 1117]. In high-density population, annual mortality rates of healthy adults 30% for males, 24% for females [1382]. Wild badgers seldom >6 years of age, although have reached 14 years; in captivity, live up to 19 years [980].

Species interactions: Foxes, rabbits and small rodents may live in separate parts of occupied badger setts. Foxes often seen near setts; although fighting observed [980] and badgers generally dominant, often tolerate each others' company [870]. Foxes have been observed following badgers to foraging areas [843]. Both aggressive and playful interactions with domestic dogs have been observed [980]. Badgers and cattle generally indifferent to each other, although cattle will investigate sett entrances and badger carcasses.

MORTALITY

Roads: Major reported cause of death in many parts of GB is road traffic [979, 1117]; estimated to kill *c.*50 000 badgers/year [532], expected to increase in future as traffic levels rise [206].

Predation: Adult badgers have no natural enemies in GB apart from humans. Young cubs sometimes killed by dogs, foxes and even adult badgers.

Persecution: Illegal hunting estimated to account for deaths of up to 10 000 badgers/year [532]. Evidence that persecution decreased, mid 1980s–mid 1990s, may remain a problem in some areas [1389]

Disease: TB not a major cause of mortality in badgers [197]; infected individuals can live and breed successfully for several years [1]. In GB MAFF culled *c.*1000–2000 badgers annually 1992–1996, to control TB in cattle [734]; extensive culls in Ireland also [371]. Arteriosclerosis, pneumonia, pleurisy, nephritis, enteritis, polyarthritis and lymphosarcoma have been ascribed as the cause of death in a small number of badgers [417].

PARASITES AND PATHOGENS
Reviewed in [495].

Ectoparasites: Fleas *Paraceras melis* (very common), *Chaetopsylla trichosa* (very rare), *Pulex irritans* (occasional) [1293]; biting lice *Trichodectes melis* (very common) [1293]; ticks *Ixodes ricinus* (occasional), *I. canisuga* (common), *I. hexagonus* (common), *I. reduvius* (occasional), *I. melicola* (occasional) [1292]. Mange (*Sarcoptes scabiei*) has been reported in badgers (e.g. [979]) but there are no confirmed cases in the literature.

Helminths: Trematodes: *Itygonimus lorum*; nematodes: *Molineus patens* (intestinal), *Uncinaria stenocephala* (intestinal), *Capillaria erinacei* (stomach), *Aelurostrongylus falciformis* (lungs); tapeworms: *Mesocestoides lineatus, Dilepis undula* [667].

Others: Viruses: mustelid herpesvirus-1 common in British badgers [698]. Rabies found in badgers in Europe, but not in GB. Widely believed to be spillover hosts in Europe [1338], could potentially be involved in the initial spread and maintenance of infection when present at higher densities [844, 1210]. Canine distemper also found in badgers in Europe (e.g. [954]) but not in GB [287]. Bacteria: salmonellosis [1392, 1415] and leptospirosis [1136] recorded. *Mycobacterium bovis* (bovine TB) found in badgers, and they are implicated in its transmission to cattle [734]. Infection is widespread, particularly in S England and Wales, also Ireland, but can be highly locally clustered [290]. Protozoa: *Eimeria melis* and *Isopora melis* (Coccidea) identified [31]. *Trypanosoma pestanai* [1025], and 2 unconfirmed forms of intra-erythrocytic parasite [862, 1026] found in the blood of British badgers. Antibodies to *Toxoplasma gondii* detected in populations in S England [32]. Fungi: Adiospiromycosis of the lungs has been observed in British badgers [494].

Commensals: Invertebrate fauna of badger setts described in [495].

RELATIONS WITH HUMANS
Exploitation: Badger body parts have been used for clothing, culinary, medicinal, cosmetic and occult purposes (reviewed in [473]). Badger digging and baiting, shooting with the use of lamps at night, snaring and gassing still occur, despite full legal protection.

Problems and their management: A survey of badger damage to agriculture in England and

Wales [959] found crop damage widespread but generally of little economic consequence. Commonest forms included flattening of cereals and maize, and digging damage to grassland. Damage to high-value crops such as grapes, sweetcorn and strawberries can also be a problem. Badgers can be excluded by use of electric fencing [1042, 1043]. Occasionally badgers open up holes in fields; can be hazardous especially to heavy machinery, as tunnel roofs collapse. In agricultural environments, burrowing damage to fences and buildings the most widely reported and costly types of damage [959]. In residential areas, can cause problems from undermining gardens and houses [901]. Attempts to manage such problems (under licence; see Chapter 4) involve sett closure, usually by exclusion using one-way gates, sometimes with provision of artificial setts; on rare occasions badgers have been translocated [149, 535]. Badgers do not trouble foresters, helpful because destroy many small rodents, wasps' nests and other pests. May force up wire netting around plantations, letting rabbits in; alleviated by use of badger gates [699]. Poultry killing occasionally a nuisance, usually confined to individuals which acquire the habit. Eggs of ground-nesting birds can form an occasional item in the badger diet, but rarely take a significant proportion of nests. Historically, rates of badger predation on game birds low (2–3% of pheasant *Phasianus colchicus* and partridge *Perdix* spp. nests) [586, 1055]. More recently, rates include 13% of grey partridge *Perdix perdix* [1095] and >10% of corn bunting *Miliaria calandra* nests, W Sussex [138]. Bird remains present in only *c.*8% of British diet samples [598].

Locally, badgers culled by MAFF, 1975–1997, in areas where suspected of transmitting bovine TB to cattle. In 1998, MAFF (now the Department for Environment, Food and Rural Affairs, DEFRA) began a large-scale field experiment, to compare incidence of infection in cattle herds in areas where badgers culled with unculled areas [615.] Reactive culling of badgers (i.e. after TB found in local cattle herd) increased the incidence of infection in cattle [310]; proactive culling over a 100 km² area reduced the incidence of TB in cattle within that area, but increased it at the periphery [311]. Presumed that observed increases in incidence of cattle TB due to disrupted badger social organisation caused by culling [1412], i.e. 'social perturbation' (reviewed in [181]), enhancing movements of badgers, increasing opportunities for spread of infection amongst badgers and to cattle.

Benefits: Badgers undoubtedly play a role in the breakdown and cycling of materials in woodland ecosystems through their sett building and foraging activities; may reduce the local abundance of perceived pests such as wasps and rabbits. One of the most popular of British mammals; badger watching and feeding them in gardens are popular pastimes.

Conservation: The best way to conserve badgers is to leave them alone. Many badger conservation groups have been formed to protect setts from diggers and report persecution to the police.

Legislation: Any unauthorised killing or taking of badgers is illegal and it is an offence to keep them as pets. Badger baiting became illegal in 1835; legal protection was introduced in the Badger Act of 1973, amended by the Wildlife and Countryside Act 1981, followed by further amendment and the introduction of related acts, culminating in comprehensive protective legislation for badgers and their setts in The Protection of Badgers Act 1992. Licences to interfere with badgers or their setts may be available from either DEFRA or Natural England, depending on the purpose (see Chapter 4).

Techniques for study: Radiotelemetry [194], infrared/image intensifying binoculars and video surveillance [1230] are invaluable aids in behavioural and ecological studies, although a powerful torch with a red filter can be effective for observation. Capture–mark–recapture techniques valuable in population studies [854, 1117]; distance sampling using spotlights along transects can be used to estimate population density [599]. Individual badgers have been marked by tattooing [193], electronic tags [1120] and fur clipping [1229], and their movements traced using a spool of fine line fitted to a collar [546]. Coloured markers presented in food at main setts, recovered in perimeter latrines, valuable to delineate territories [289]. Recovery of DNA from faeces and hair shows promise as a non-invasive technique for studying badgers [413, 1391].

LITERATURE
Comprehensive review [980].

PRINCIPAL AUTHORS
R. Delahay, G. Wilson, S. Harris & D.W. Macdonald

GENUS *Lutra*

A small genus of 1–3 species; widespread Eurasian otter *Lutra lutra*, found in British Isles, with Japanese *L. nippon*, Indonesian *L. sumatrana* usually considered conspecific. Molecular analysis confirms that otters, subfamily Lutrinae, a small monophyletic group, bracketed by Melinae and Mustelinae, but casts doubt on current taxonomy. American otters *Lontra* (formerly included in *Lutra*) confirmed as distinct, but clawless otters *Aonyx* and African *L. maculicollis* (= *Hydrictis maculicollis*) genetically very close to *Lutra*, probably should be merged with it [888]. All otters have sleek bodies, webbed feet, with stout, tapered, dorso-ventrally flattened tails. Skull more *Mustela*-like than badger, broad and flat but with elongated braincase and short jaws; dentition $i^3/_3c^1/_1p^4/_3m^1/_2$, strong carnassials and crushing areas on molars.

Otter *Lutra lutra*

Mustela lutra Linnaeus, 1758; Uppsala, Sweden.
Lutra vulgaris Erxleben, 1777.
Lutra roensis Ogilby, 1834; Roe Mills, near Newton Limnavaddy, Londonderry, Ireland.
Dyfrigi, dwr-gi (water dog) (Welsh); *balgaire, cudoun* (burn dog), *matadh* (hound) (Scottish Gaelic); *tek, dafi, dratsi* (Shetland); *madrirga, madra uisce* (water dog), *dobharchu* (Irish Gaelic).
Male – dog; female – bitch; young – cubs.

RECOGNITION

Whole animal: A distinctively large (terrier-sized) aquatic carnivore, with a long tapered tail; dark brown, appearing black when wet (swimming mink sometimes misidentified as otter, but much smaller, ferret-sized). Otter swims low in water with a V-shaped bow wave (Fig. 9.25) (mink swim buoyantly, with much of body showing). Long tapering tail lies along surface when swimming rapidly (mink has shorter, cylindrical fluffy tail). In common with other mustelids, otters will stand upright to get a better view; when walking or running on land, has a marked 'hump-back' appearance (Plate 7). When only head and neck above the surface, can look like common seal (which also travels up rivers), but shape finer, not so thickset.

Skull and teeth: Distinguished from all other mustelids by large size, narrow postorbital constriction and 5 upper and lower postcanine teeth (Fig. 9.26).

Coastal and freshwater otters: On Shetland, W Isles and W coast of Scotland, otters live along coasts, are active during daylight. Described as coastal otters (not to be confused with Pacific sea otter *Enhydra lutris*), are the same species as those inhabiting inland freshwater systems but distinction necessary because of behavioural differences.

Fig. 9.25 Otters swim very low in the water, with only the top of the head and back showing (*photo S. Searle*).

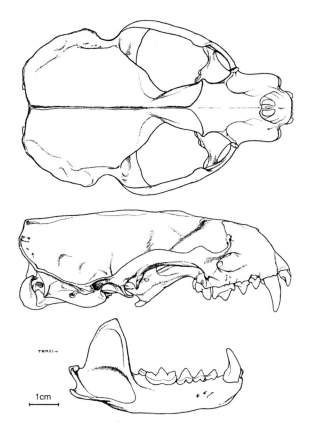

Fig. 9.26 Skull and lower jaw of otter from side and skull from above. The skull is very elongate and shallow, with a very pronounced interorbital constriction (*from [942]*).

FIELD SIGNS
Tracks: Good, clear footprints with 5 toes arching around the front of a large pad only found in soft substances (Fig. 9.2). Webbing and claw marks only occasionally visible. Often inner toe does not 'print'. Width 5–7 cm (adults) and 4.5 cm or less (cubs) [1351] (mink prints in same environment smaller, with pear-shaped toe pads with claws).

Trails: Coastal otters make trails linking the shore with freshwater pools and lochs. Well marked on Shetland and W Isles. Trails also occasionally found by rivers cutting across meanders. Marked at intervals by 'spraint stations' [1311].

Faeces (spraints): Most commonly found survey sign. Often black, with pleasant sweet-musky odour when fresh. Size and shape varies from tiny blob or 'tarry' smear to complete, cylindrical dropping 10 × 1 cm; like cigar ash when dry. Show fish bones and otoliths [223] (scats of mink foul smelling, narrower with twisted ends, often contain fur). Spraints and sometimes jelly-like secretions deposited at prominent places; on large rocks, logs, fallen tree trunks, under bridges, entrances to holts, exits from water, river con-

fluences. May scrape up soil or sand to form 'sign heaps' and spraint on top. Significance unknown.

Dens (holts): Often situated in natural cavities. Extensive holts with large entrances may be dug in peat banks in the W Isles [644]. In Shetland, usually constructed their own holts, digging extensive systems of tunnels and chambers which they furnished with bedding [744]. Bankside holts found within interlaced roots of adjacent trees [465], under heaps of boulders, stick piles, culverts, drain pipes, upturned roots of windfall trees [744].

Other signs: Partially eaten remains of prey sometimes found; difficult to distinguish from those of other predators unless other signs also present.

DESCRIPTION
Pelage: Fur medium to rich dark brown, except for grey throat and underparts. White 'moustaches' on upper lip and patches under chin. 2 types of hair: dense underfur of fine hairs 10–15 mm long; longer, coarser guard hairs 25 mm long. Underfur traps insulating layer of air, helps keep body warm and dry during swimming. Pelage smooth and glossy when wet; guard hairs give 'spiky' appearance after shaking.

Moult: 1 extended moult per year [994].

Anatomy: Flat head, small eyes and ears, broad muzzle with long stiff vibrissae. Naked rhinarium with upper border diagnostically W-shaped (Fig. 9.26). Short legs, elongated sinuous body and long flattened tail, tapering to a point from broad base. 5 clawed digits on fore- and hindfeet; webbing extends to toe pads. Baculum >60 mm long and 2 g or more in weight in adults; curves upwards at tip [134]. Paired uterine horns.

Nipples: 6 nipples (3 pairs), but only 4 may be visible and functional [905].

Scent glands: Pair of anal scent glands discharge on either side of anus [448], and proctodeal glands discharge into rectum [1251, 1311].

Skull: Large and broad with short rostrum and narrow postorbital constriction. Full development of skull not until >2 years old [1251]. Jaw hinged to move in 1 plane only. Dental formula i^3/₃c^1/₁p^4/₃m^1/₂. Tooth wear not usually apparent until 3rd year [1251].

Chromosomes: 2n = 38, as in all Lutrinae except African *L. maculicollis* (where 2n = 40).

Table 9.6 Otter: measurements, from 3 samples

	Males			Females		
	Mean	Range	n	Mean	Range	n
Measurements and weight [a]						
Head and body length (mm)	722	35.9	21	654	24.4	23
Tail length (mm)	419	22.5	21	381	20.2	23
Ear length (mm)	20.4	1.4	21	19.3	1.1	23
Hindfoot length (mm)	125	5.8	21	112	3.2	23
Weight of above sample (kg)	8.75	0.97	21	6.07	0.55	23
Weight (kg) [b]						
	10.1	1.37	433	7.0	1.03	220
Skull dimensions[c]						
Condylobasal length (mm)	114.80	3.88	25	108.25	4.73	20
Zygomatic breadth (mm)	70.37	3.32	25	66.06	3.25	20
Postorbital breadth (mm)	14.32	1.12	25	14.22	1.14	20

[a]Small British sample collected 1983–1990 [642]; [b]Large sample from GB and Ireland collected over 20th century [188]; [c]Adult sample from mainland Scotland [829].

As in [188], female otters <5.0 kg and males <7.25 kg excluded from the calculations (probably juvenile, though females of lower weight known to have bred). Formulae in [627] used to correct weights for missing parts of bodies.

RELATIONSHIPS

Molecular phylogenetic analysis confirms otters Lutrinae as monophyletic group, placed between Melinae and Mustelinae; shows 9 species of otters divided between 3 primary clades. Eurasian otter most closely related to (African) Cape clawless *Aonyx capensis* and (Asian) short-clawed otters *A. cinerea* with (African) spotted-necked otter *Lutra maculicollis* and sea otter *Enhydra lutris* in the same clade. 3 New World *Lontra* otters, including the N American river otter *L. canadensis*, form a 2nd clade, giant otter *Pteronura brasiliensis* a 3rd [714].

MEASUREMENTS

See Table 9.6. Much older literature [382, 659, 1226] contains skinned or incomplete weights because of fur trade; equation derived for predicting whole body weight with correction factors for missing head/feet/tail [627].

VARIATION

White 'moustaches' on upper lip variable in size, shape and presence [646], as are pale patches on throat [642]. Dorsal pelage of British specimens usually rich dark brown but Irish animals much darker, approaching black [251], hence suggestion of separate species *L. roensis* [1001] or subspecies [590]. Irish otters cranially distinct from British counterparts (more so than British animals are from those of Europe), sexual dimorphism significantly greater, providing stronger evidence for validity of *L. l. roensis* [829]. Albinism is known [505]. Genetic diversity (microsatellite polymorphism) studied in Scotland [252] and in England [966].

DISTRIBUTION

Original range covers whole of Palaearctic and into Indo-Malaya (Fig. 9.27), from Ireland to Kamchatka and Norway to Java [505]. Has declined or disappeared from parts of European range [894, 948]. Recent status in European countries reviewed in [221]. Extinct in Laos and Malaysia, status/ presence in many parts of Asia unknown [224].

In British Isles, currently well but unevenly distributed (Fig. 9.28). Occurs throughout Ireland [192, 548], present in all but 13 hectads in Scotland [469]. In Wales, found in 65% of hectads, mainly in Clywd, Wye, Teifi and Cleddau regions [25, 668]. England, surveyed by 50 ×

over time with regional recovery, so does mean number of spraints per survey site [1245]. Spraint density also decreases with increasing altitude [463, 464, 1245, 1375], as does otter density [759]. Useful as fine adjustment on percentage site occupancy at survey (see Fluctuations); England surveys of 1984–1986 and 1991–1994 showed increased mean spraints per occupied site (4.52 to 5.14), implying higher otter density with time. DNA fingerprinting may eventually prove valuable for calibrating spraint density [232].

Fluctuations: Numbers thought severely reduced in 19th century, through gamekeeping. Population low but still widespread, 1895 [631]. Effect of persecution, by gamekeepers and hunting, revealed by their cessation in World War I. Hunting success of Border Counties Otterhounds low, means of 64.2±4.8 otters found/100 days hunting and 24.2±3.3% blank days (with no scent), 1909–1913. By 1919–1923, significant increases to 86.7±4.5 otters found, only 4.9±0.8% blank days [631]. Fewer gamekeepers after 1918 [1268], allowed numbers to increase 1918–1939 [190, 631, 1245]; desk survey 1952–1954 [1226] suggested otters very numerous/numerous in 66% of river boards.

Severe decline followed, starting suddenly 1957 [190, 1245]; widespread across GB, most severe SE England and SE Scotland. Timing correlated with introduction, 1956, of highly toxic cyclodiene organochlorine insecticides, e.g. dieldrin; likewise, regions of greatest effect, 2 wheat-bulb fly areas with highest usage of dieldrin for cereal seed dressings and sheep dips [190, 641] In NW, density of otters remaining 1977–1979 negatively correlated with density of sheep, thus with amount of dieldrin used in sheep dips [641]. Residues of dieldrin, DDT, DDE and mercury (from fungicide use) found in otter bodies and spraints 1960s–1990s [633, 641, 645, 760, 892, 896, 897,

1192, 1245]. By 1977, most otters had been lost from SE Scotland, Midlands, S, SE, N England. Disappearance probably caused by high mortality of breeding-age adults from dieldrin poisoning [641] (cf. contemporary decline of the peregrine falcon *Falco peregrinus* [643, 1081]); detrimental sublethal effects, including reduced vitamin A storage, also possible [625, 634, 1192]. PCBs also found in large concentrations from 1966 onwards; however, largest amounts found in Shetland, where otters remained numerous; PCB levels were increasing when otters were recovering [641].

Use of organochlorines and PCBs banned, following research on their environmental damage [625, 635, 641]. Decline of otter slowed with the first (1962) ban on use of dieldrin on spring-sown cereals [641, 1245]. Recovery started in W (dieldrin banned in sheep dip), followed later in E (final ban on seed dressing 1975) [641, 1245]. However, E Anglian population too fragmented to recover, would have disappeared by 1986 but for release of captive-bred stock [647, 652]. Similarly very low N Yorkshire population reinforced by rehabilitated otters [1375, 1403].

Changing status during decline determined from otter hunt data [190, 1245] to 1976 (legal protection 1978), during recovery by spraint surveys [635, 636]. 8926 riparian sites, each 600 m, examined for spraints in GB (= 5356 km; 1.73% of total riparian length) and 2373 in Ireland; has become standard European survey method [626, 635, 1089]. Occupation lowest in England, high in Scotland, highest in Ireland: 5.8% England 1977–1979 [780], compared with 91.7% Ireland 1980–1981 [192], where organochlorine use had been minimal. Repeat surveys at 7504 sites (Table 9.8) showed increases in England, Scotland and Wales; overall, 56.5% increase in occupied sites in 14 years [636]. Recovery curve sigmoid; predicted that English population will only reach 75% occupation around 2025 (68 years after crash) [1245].

Table 9.8 Otter: summary of results of 11 surveys, GB 1977–2002

Country	Sites visited	% occupied			
		1977–1979	1984–1986	1991–1994	2000–2002
England	2940	5.8	9.7	23.4	36.3
Wales	1008	20.5	39.0	52.5	73.8
Scotland	3556	67.0	73.0	87.2	–
GB	7504	36.8	43.6	57.5	–

Sources: England [237, 780, 1245, 1246]; Wales [25, 26, 238, 668]; Scotland: [463, 464, 469]; GB [636]. Occupation in Ireland (Irish Republic and Northern Ireland) was 91.7% in 1980–1981 [192].

Spraint surveys, 1997, of Essex, Norfolk, Suffolk [159, 874, 1430] update and provide more detail for E Anglia. Together showed 1.2 (1984–1986), 12.1 (1991–1994) and 30.3% (1997) occupation; rapid recovery achieved by releasing otters [652, 1245].

Sex ratio: 1:1 in young and adults [1251].

Age determination: By counting incremental lines in cementum of sectioned incisors [552]. 1st line deposited at 1 year old, Shetland [450]. Cubs usually with mother until 10 months, age estimated on size and weight.

Age structure: Dependent young 25–38% of population, Sweden [352]. 42% in 1st year, 33% in 2nd year, Germany (n = 91; aged by skull dimensions/tooth wear) [1253]. If violent deaths (road accidents) are a random sample of population, on Shetland 28% were in 1st, dependent, year, 17% in 2nd year, 27% aged 2–4 years, 20% 4–6 years, 7% 6–8 years and 1% >8 years (n = 83; aged by tooth section) [450].

Survival: Different survival/age patterns in otters suffering violent and non-violent deaths. Age-specific survival not constant: relatively high in early years, decreases with age [450]. Oldest wild otter, GB, (n = 391) 16 years, on cementum lines, but median age at death only 4 years on Shetland/mainland Scotland, 3 years in England/Wales [450]. Senility shown by captive otters at 9–10 years [216, 629]. Lower median age in England may reflect rapidly increasing population and greater litter size, so larger 0–2 year group available to be killed.

Species interactions: Competition with American mink (*Mustela vison*) for food [209] and dens apparently much greater than originally envisaged [1397]. Areas of SW England, with high density of mink sites 1984–1986, became areas with highest density of otter sites 1991–1994, suggesting closely similar preferences [1245]. Absence of otter from riparian predator niche after 1957 (see Fluctuations) apparently allowed rapid colonisation of GB by mink from 1960s [633, 637].

Water vole/mink surveys [1243, 1244] confirm decline of mink occupancy from 1989–1990 to 1996–1998 to 51.8% in England, 44.9% in Scotland. Mink did not colonise otter-occupied areas [637], and otters obliterated mink scent-marking sites [1377]. Expansion and recovery of otter population tracked by mink decline [637], rate of loss suggests lethal intraguild aggression (see Aggressive behaviour); otters known to kill mink [637, 994, 1203]. Depends on otter density,

interference greater at medium densities (30–70% occupation) than at highest densities (70–100% occupation) e.g. in Scotland [637]. Some apparent decline may be due to a change in mink activity away from water [126].

MORTALITY

Most known mortality caused by humans (Table 9.9). Of 113 dead otters, Shetland, 60 (53%) died violent deaths and 53 (47%) died natural deaths, though 29 of latter too decomposed to examine. Natural deaths most frequent (73%) March–June, when prey biomass lowest and otters underweight. At autopsy, 37% of 24 natural deaths had haemorrhaging stomachs/intestines, indicating starvation [749, 757]. Non-violent deaths (all causes) on mainland Scotland only 14% of total (n = 76) [744]. Starvation not known in low-density otters, southern GB [642].

Predation: Unimportant in British Isles. Sea eagles *Haliaeetus albicilla*, wolves *Canis lupus* and lynx *Lynx lynx* have attacked otters, Europe [894]. Golden eagle *Aquila chrysaetos* takes young otters especially around coasts, islands, W Scotland [1345]; also attacked by skuas *Stercorarius* sp. [188], possibly mink [632].

Persecution: Cull by otterhounds increased after World War I, peaked at 434 otters killed by 23 packs in 1933 [631]. Only 11 main packs hunted after World War II, killed 1212 otters 1950–1955 [631]. Mean total catch, all hunts in England, Wales and S Scotland 199/year 1950–1959, reducing to 100 1960–1969, only 11 1970–1976, as population declined [188, 190]. Numbers killed by gamekeepers for fishery protection unknown, probably much larger (see History), e.g. 13 trapped at 1 English locality during 12 weeks of 1964 [1402]. Bodies of snared otters still received in 1980s [642].

Accidental mortality: Road mortality the major cause of death in otters autopsied 1980s–1990s [642]. Difficult to evaluate against other causes because of detection bias but serious; 1800 British casualties known [639]. 50 road kills recorded from recovering population of Devon and Cornwall alone, 1987–1994 [1245]. Numbers increase as otter population increases [639, 1245]. 61% of otters examined (n = 66) 1981–1992, for organochlorines, parasites or killed after release, were road casualties [650, 896, 1245]; higher than the 34% found in the 1970s [187]. Mortality pattern analysed [1030].

During 1975–1992, 136 otters known to have drowned in eel fyke nets (69), lobster creels (66) and fish traps (1) in GB [651]; 32 found drowned

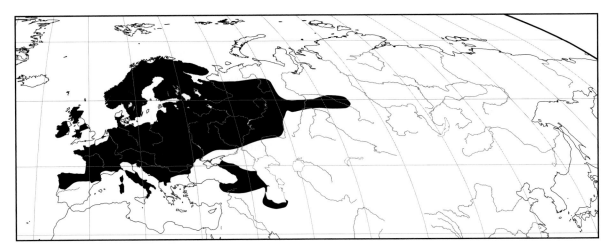

Fig. 9.30 Pine marten *Martes martes*: world range.

Scottish females (405–473 mm; n = 93) although lighter (670–1050 g), females from USSR proportionally smaller again [563]. Martens in continental Europe generally smaller and lighter (e.g. [885, 1155]), though N–S gradient of increasing skull size suggested [1083]. Skull of a recent British marten larger than those from 11 European countries (n = 137) [23, 638, 942], comparable with European Postglacial specimens [638].

DISTRIBUTION

European distribution (Fig. 9.30), status and population trends reviewed in [1067].

Scotland: Expanding population, estimated to have doubled in 12 years between 1982 [1322] and 1994 [70]. Now found throughout wooded and mountainous areas of Highland region, actively recolonising Grampian, Tayside, Central and Strathclyde regions [70]. Carcasses and sightings are not uncommon well outside these areas (Fig. 9.31). Reintroduced to Galloway Forest, S Scotland (n = 12) 1980–1981, resulting in small but apparently viable population that may be expanding [141, 1167].

England and Wales: Much reduced to remnant pockets, mainly confined to rugged upland landscapes [769, 937, 1247]. Viability of these populations questioned, perhaps extinct [140]; record confused by escapes and perhaps illicit releases, e.g. of *M. americana*. 5 areas (4 in N England, 1 in N Wales) seem to have persistent records (sightings, carcasses, skulls) 1800–1988 [1247]. Subsequent sightings [96, 102, 104, 936, 937, 1058], occasional photographs [239], specimens [103, 638, 765, 1182, 1183] and faecal DNA [270] suggest persistence of sparse populations in these areas, also in SW–mid Wales

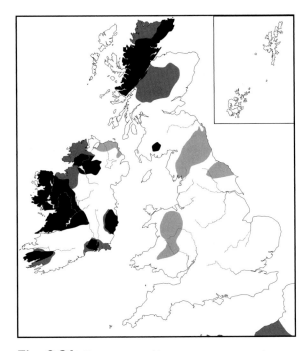

Fig. 9.31 Pine marten *Martes martes*: range in British Isles.

[966]. Occasional specimens from S England, likely to be releases or escapees from captivity [108, 403, 1058, 1247].

Ireland: From scat survey 1978–1980, distribution mainly confined to wood and scrub areas of mid-W, strongholds in Cos. Galway and Clare; smaller outlier populations on Slieve Bloom Mountains, C Ireland, and in Cos. Louth, Meath and Waterford [1010]. Range now expanding following reduced use of strychnine; new population established by reintroduction to Killarney in 1980s [386]. In N Ireland, found in Fermanagh and Tyrone, with small pockets elsewhere; in E Fermanagh, now regarded as quite common [29].

HISTORY

Conditions in British Isles too severe for pine marten during the last glacial stage *c.*18 000 bp; glacial refuge in C Europe (Pyrenees–Romania) [1217]. Mitochondrial phylogeography suggests pine martens spread to GB from a single southern refugium post-glaciation [765]. In Late Glacial, spread N to France, Denmark; apparently not GB, but early Postglacial immigrant, present Star Carr and Thatcham (10 050–9600 bp). Present in Ireland since 'before historic times' [385], but origins probably different from GB population [765], possibly introduced for its fur [769]. Skull from late Neolithic/early Bronze Age site, Westray, Orkney [911]; possibly native, but probably animals imported and traded for their skins. Mesolithic population estimated at 147 474, pine marten perhaps more abundant than any other British carnivore except weasel [889]; now, only wildcat less abundant [536].

Woodland clearance probably major cause of decline [96]. By 14th century, becoming scarce in England, high prices paid for pelts from Wales and Scotland [538]; still hunted for sport in parts of England during 18th–19th centuries [940]. By 1800, apparently rare in many lowland areas of GB and Ireland [769, 1010]. Rate of extinction accelerated through 1800s; county losses most rapid 1850–1915, associated with heavy predator control by gamekeepers [769]. By early 20th century, confined to NW Scotland, N Wales, Lake District, parts of Northumberland, N Yorkshire and Ireland [393, 940]. Trapping pressure much reduced after World War I, and large areas planted in trees following Forest Act 1919; both favoured martens. By 1959, population in NW Scotland had consolidated, spread S and E though still confined NW of Loch Ness. By 1982, range had extended further S and E into Argyll and Grampian [1322] By contrast, populations in England and Wales showed no signs of recovery 1900–1988 [140, 1247], though scatter of records since 1995 may be response to full legal protection 1988 [1058].

HABITAT

Adapted to exploit structurally complex, 3-dimensional habitats, especially woodland; can exist in more open ground provided there are some pockets of tree or scrub cover. Strong avoidance of open areas in Scotland [65, 141, 486, 1322] and elsewhere [131, 885, 1070, 1233, 1241]. Areas devoid of tree or shrub cover, e.g. open moor, pasture, alpine tundra, young plantations (0–8 years old), either excluded from territory or little used. In Scotland, 5-fold difference in territory sizes between study areas (Table 9.11), yet area of woodland per breeding pair similar. *M. americana* vulnerable to forest fragmentation [502], and *M. martes* predicted to be similar [139]. Rugged, rocky or mountainous terrain offers alternative 3-dimensional habitat where woodland scarce and fragmented [609, 1367].

'Old growth' woodland features and associated tree cavities preferred [132]; scarcity of cavities suitable as natal dens may limit breeding success in managed woodlands [106, 107, 132]. Arboreal cavities preferred [5, 65, 132, 1435]. Females more likely than males to select insulated den sites, and both sexes more likely to select sheltered dens in poor weather [298, 1435]. In European woodlands, nesting chambers of black woodpecker *Dryocopus martius* important as den sites [132]. In Scotland, natal dens most often in buildings, hollow trees, bird boxes or burrows under tree roots, although rabbit burrows and rock piles also used [65, 107]; diversity of den types may reflect scarcity of suitable cavities in British woodlands [106, 107], artificial den boxes may improve woodland habitat for martens [938]. Bracken, moss and *Molinia* grass

Table 9.11 Pine marten: population densities in Scotland

Study area	Density (adult martens/km^2)	Average woodland area (ha/breeding pair)	Source
Novar	0.82	194	[486]
Strathglass	0.45	274	[65]
Galloway Forest (lowland mixed conifers)	0.34	–	[141]
Galloway Forest (upland spruce)	0.12	–	[141]
Kinlochewe	0.12	234	[65]

have been used as bedding material in rock dens; in tree dens only woody debris has been found [65]. Bowls of moss and other vegetation twice found at rock den entrances visited in fine weather [68].

No clear preference for coniferous over deciduous woodland or mature native forest over commercial plantations. Habitat preferences may reflect prey base; preference for spruce-dominated forests, Scandinavia and Russia, where squirrels reach high densities [131, 460, 1069, 1331]. Diet sometimes dominated by grassland voles *Microtus* sp., seems to contradict dependence on woodland and avoidance of open spaces. However, *Microtus* may be abundant in grassy areas within woodland [167], so fire breaks, harvesting tracks, river banks, etc. may be critical habitat where field voles dominate the diet [65, 167]. Structure of forest floor also very important; martens use fallen trees extensively while hunting [621, 997]. In America, coarse woody debris at ground level, especially during periods of deep snow cover, facilitates access to subnivean spaces to capture prey [501] and to resting sites [168]. Large-scale contiguous clear felling (>1000 ha) can adversely affect marten populations [460, 1297]. However, small (<10 ha) cuts may be beneficial by increasing food supplies [130].

SOCIAL ORGANISATION AND BEHAVIOUR

Radio-tracking (e.g. [66, 141, 486, 885, 1071, 1240, 1438]) confirms that martens are solitary foragers living in intrasexual territories; adult males exclude other adult males from their territories and adult females exclude other adult females, although male's territory may overlap with one or two females'. Subadults may remain within territory of breeding male or female [66]. Interactions between adult males and females often aggressive; rarely use the areas where their territories overlap simultaneously [646, 1228, 1276], not reported to den together. Likely that mother–young group is most extensive social contact.

Home range: In Białowieża Forest, Poland, mean home-range size 2.23 km² for males and 1.49 km² for females [1438]. Home-range size within Scotland may vary 5-fold, mainly dependent on area of woodland within territory (Table 9.11). Home ranges may remain stable for >3 years [68] and longer than one marten's residence [66]. Where woodland highly fragmented, requirement for woodland most important for breeding females; immature animals living outwith the range of breeding pairs and solitary adult males had access on average to only 50 ha of woodland [66]. In expanding population, new recruits settle close to areas already occupied, even though sightings suggest that travelling much further afield [70, 141].

Scent-marking: Urine, scats and secretions from the anal and abdominal glands are used to mark objects [1070, 1323]. Plantar glands also present on fore- and hindfeet [958]. Secretions from anal glands deposited with scats. Several factors influence patterns of scat abundance (reviewed [105]); in Scotland, marked reduction in number of scats found along tracks in winter compared with summer [486, 1323]. Typically placed at intersections between tracks and/or streams or at bridges over rivers, often in prominent positions on the ground or on a low wall or stone. Fox droppings are often found at same spots; some sites accumulate large numbers of scats.

Vocalisations: Mother approaching cubs makes deep, repeated, chugging sound. Young emit tremulous, high-pitched squeaks; lost cubs call for mother with sharp rasping sound like paper being torn. Growling and high-pitched chattering, squealing or snarling noises heard from adults, particularly during the breeding season. Captured animals usually quiet but may growl or snarl. Full range of sounds described in [609].

Aggressive behaviour: In captivity, threat shown by low growl, progressing to deep huffing noise when extremely agitated. Growling may be followed by fighting, which may involve biting and a high-pitched squealing/screaming noise. Aggression reaches its peak during the breeding season between both the same and opposite sexes [1154, 1155]. Fighting in wild martens not directly recorded, although some males trapped during the summer had scars around their head and neck [66]; similar scarring reported for *M. americana* [547]. Some adult females captured July–August had scars or patches of bare skin on the neck behind the head, possibly result of mating [1].

Dispersal: Little known. Approximately adult size by 6 months but dispersal may be at any time before maturity due to tolerance of pre-breeding age animals within territories of adult animals [66].

Activity: Generally nocturnal in winter [885, 997, 1070, 1436] with resting periods during the night lasting from 30 min to 4 h [66, 68]. In summer, significant increase in number of hours spent active [68, 885, 1436] and distance travelled during the night [66]; thus martens frequently active before dusk and after dawn. Females with young cubs active any time throughout the day,

452

active periods lasting *c.*2 h; daylight activity strictly confined to areas with good canopy cover [65]. Adult females most active June–July (12.7 h activity/day) and males June–September (11–12 h); both sexes least active February–March (females 2.8 and males 4.6 h/day) [1436].

Locomotion: Well adapted for climbing; broad scapula and powerful, highly differentiated muscles of forelimbs, long tail to aid balance [682]. Climbs using claws and clutching the surface of the tree with one pair of legs while moving the other [608]. Reported downhill leaps of 4 m [682] and falling 20 m and landing on all fours safely [609] Summing distances between radio-fixes, average distance travelled per night in Galloway Forest, Scotland, 7.33 km; sexes similar; greatest distance travelled was 15.8 km [141]. Usual distance travelled, Switzerland, 5–7 km/night, average speed 0.5 km/h [885].

Grooming: Similar to cat with stroking or scratching with fore- and hindfeet accompanied by licking and biting motions. Fur balls may be coughed up after grooming [1181].

Table 9.12 Pine marten: components of diet from scat study in NW Scotland [65]

Food type	Estimated % of total total weight of food eaten per annum
Field vole	34.3
Woodmice, shrews, bank voles	2.6
Deer carrion	31.2
Sheep carrion	0.7
Rabbit and brown hare	3.2
Passerines (40% = wren)	11.4
Birds other than passerines	0.6
Birds' eggs	0.8
Frogs and toads	5.3
Berries (mainly rowan and blaeberry)	1.5
Honey	7
Invertebrates	1.1
Fungi	0.3

FEEDING

Opportunistic generalist, taking whatever is available from the following: small mammals (voles, mice and shrews), ungulate carrion, rabbits, hares, squirrels, birds (usually passerines and tetraonids), eggs, insects, honey, fruit, nuts, fungi, frogs, toads, lizards and leftovers from bird tables and rubbish bins. Throughout Europe, microtine rodents among the most important prey [453, 454, 486, 809, 885, 1241]; review [1437]. In most of range *Myodes* preferred over *Microtus* [1347], except Scotland, where *Microtus agrestis* a key prey species (Table 9.12). Larger mammals and carrion may be important in winter–early spring and when voles scarce. Berries and insects frequent in scats in summer and autumn, may be relatively unimportant in terms of biomass [65, 453, 486, 809, 1085]. Honey from bumblebee and wasp nests may be an important item in late summer [65].

Hunting behaviour: Most foraging believed to take place on the ground [997, 1072], although canopy-nesting birds and squirrels are taken [486].

Food caching: Not convincingly recorded for wild marten in GB; readily observed in tame and captive Scottish martens, reported for wild martens in snow in Finland [1069].

Surplus killing: Attributed to pine martens in Scotland; 20 or more game birds, ducks or domestic hens killed overnight; occurs when game birds and ducks are being slowly released into the wild from enclosure which they cannot readily escape but which marten can enter, or, similarly, hen house.

Food requirements: On average 140–160 g food/night [1069] or *c.*10% of body weight [1155].

BREEDING

Polyestrous, mating in June–August, probably induced ovulator, delayed implantation, birth usually in April, mean litter size 3, unlikely to breed successfully until >2 years old, probably promiscuous (Fig. 9.32).

Males: Permanently scrotal testes, distinct seasonal testicular cycle, discontinuous spermatogenesis. During October–December, paired testes weight small, *c.*0.5 g; during breeding season reach maximal weight of 3.2 g [933]. Testosterone levels peak in May [39, 66]. Free sperm present April–September [146]. Changes in testicular cycle probably controlled by photoperiod [933]. Can reach sexual maturity at 12–15 months yet most captive martens do not breed until 27 months

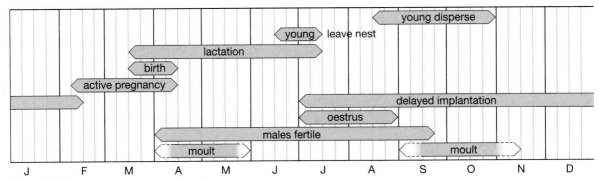

Fig. 9.32 Pine marten: annual cycle.

[933]; in wild, Scotland, males <36 months did not exhibit scent-gland activity or testosterone levels associated with breeding condition [66].

Females: Can mate at 15 months but generally do not successfully breed in captivity until 27 months [933]. For *M. americana*, numbers of breeding yearlings fluctuate [1248]; lower ovulation rates and reduced productivity in 1- and 2-year olds than older females, when prey scarce [1296]. Mating late June–early August, probably controlled by photoperiod [933] Vulva swells during oestrus. Usually promiscuous in captivity; multiple oestrus usually lasting 1–4 days, recurring at 6–17 day intervals. Ovulation presumed to be induced, oestrus thought to reoccur because of failure to ovulate during previous matings [933]. Blastocyst implantation delayed until spring, controlled by seasonal increase in daylight [176]; post-implantation gestation 30–35 days [175]. Young born late March–early April, litter size 2–6, averaging 3 (summary in [933]). 2 reports of *M. americana* breeding at 15 years old [1248].

Mating: Precopulatory behaviour includes following and playful chasing, with purring and growling vocalisations. Female then restrained by neck bite and dragged about by male. She assumes the mating posture (presentation); copulation lasts 15–75+ min. Females emit a clucking or piping noise as they approach oestrus [1154, 1155]. Mating usually occurs on the ground, but has been reported in the branches of a tree [1180].

Development of young: 30 g at birth, eyes open at 34–38 days; begin consuming solid food at 36–45 days, lactation ceases at *c.*6 weeks, young emerge from den at 7–8 weeks [933, 1155]. Born with whitish fur; soft woolly brown pelage fringed with white guard hairs developed by 3 weeks; tail originally thin and tapering, becomes bushier in autumn. Sexes show size differentiation from 8 weeks, males 950–1150 g, females 800–900 g at 12 weeks, approximately adult weight by 6 months

[480]. Natal dens occupied by breeding females for 50–60 days, before litters relocated [712].

POPULATION
Numbers: Pre-breeding population, GB, *c.*3650 (England <100, Scotland 3500, Wales <50) [536]. Population densities in Scotland in Table 9.11. Ireland, densities 1–10/km², population size unknown. In Russia, density increased from 0.06/km² to 0.37/km² as plantations matured. In pristine mixed lowland Białowieża Forest, Poland, winter density was 0.36–0.76 martens/km² [1438]. In the Swiss Jura, density higher in low-altitude deciduous forests (0.3–0.8 martens/km²) than in mountain coniferous forests (0.1–0.2 martens/km²) [885].

Fluctuations: Slight, birth rate low, longevity high and territories contiguous and stable over years and between territory holders, thus likely that numbers of breeding animals in long-colonised areas are stable. In Białowieża Forest, Poland, numbers fluctuated year to year, correlated with those of woodland rodent prey with a 1-year time lag [1438].

Age determination: Measurement of the pulp cavity in canines, temporal muscle coalescence and baculum weight separates juveniles (<1) from older *M. americana*, cementum annuli in premolars and canines used to age adults (techniques reviewed in [1044]. Cementum annuli in incisor teeth used in Scottish study [66]. During the breeding season, breeding males have active abdominal scent glands and higher testosterone levels than non-breeding animals [66]. Nipple size and appearance separated 86% of parous from non-parous females [1248]. Juvenile pelage until end of 1st summer.

Age structure: Life expectancy, captive martens, to 17–18 years [1, 608]. Longevity of 17–18 years reported in Lithuania in the wild; 45% of animals <1 year, 29% 1–3 years, 26% >3 years [682].

However, in Swiss study, juveniles <30% of any sample, 50% were of reproductive age and 1 gravid female aged at 11 years by cementum annuli [885].

Species interactions: Within woodland, high dietary overlap with foxes and wild-living cats, these species could limit marten density. Predation by fox known in Scandinavia [798, 1011] and the Netherlands [1340], but this does not determine spatial abundance of pine marten in Finland [762]. Distribution, from scat collections, does not appear to be limited by foxes either [70]. However, decrease in foxes due to mange, Sweden, was associated with an increase in martens [555, 798]. Fox impact likely to be greatest where fox abundance high and woodland cover low and fragmented [96]. In Europe where standing deadwood scarce, may depend upon black woodpecker for natal dens [132]. Competition between pine marten and beech marten reduced by greater nocturnality of beech marten, enabling it to exploit urban habitats avoided by pine marten [145].

MORTALITY
Predation: Few data on predation in GB; juvenile found as prey in eagle eyrie [65]. Snow tracking, Scandinavia, found 2 main predators to be red fox and golden eagle [997, 1070, 1256]. Avoidance of open areas, especially during daylight, possibly response to aerial predation, may be an innate behaviour for *M. martes* [1241]; also allows avoidance of attack from larger mammals by climbing trees.

Persecution: Formerly trapped, snared and poisoned; now has full legal protection. Easily trapped, readily caught in snares/traps set for other species unless precautions taken. Predator control may be curbing the expansion of martens into forests in NE Scotland. Elsewhere (e.g. Netherlands), road casualties are a major cause of mortality [975].

Disease: No information for *M. martes*. *M. americana* sensitive to canine distemper in captivity [75] and a vector of bubonic plague in USA [1439].

PARASITES
No specific ectoparasites. Siphonaptera picked up at resting sites, Ixodidae while travelling on the ground [885]. Biting louse *Trichodectes salfi* recorded from Europe [681]. Nematode *Skrjabingylus nasicola*, infesting nasal cavity, frequent in Russia: up to 90% of animals <1 year and 50% of animals >3 years infested, yet only 5% population in Scandinavia [681]. Lungworm *Filaroides* sp. frequent in Russia.

RELATIONS WITH HUMANS
Persecuted by humans for centuries. Marten pelts were valuable [538], have been harvested for centuries, e.g. Chester paid *c*.150 marten pelts as part of tax in 1086 [1419]). Lucrative import/export trade by 14th century. Hunted with packs of hounds for sport in Wales and Lake District [538] and trapped for game preservation in 19th century [1247]. Was considered destructive to lambs [538] and killed by strychnine baits set in sheep areas [1010]. Conflicts with game management resurgent as range expands in Scotland. However, electric fencing sufficient to deter pine martens from entering release pens [69]. Readily takes domestic hens; unlikely to do so during daylight, securing birds in sound hen house at dusk should safeguard poultry at night. May visit houses and bird tables for food but does not enter towns or dwellings as readily as *M. foina*. Tendency to den and breed in buildings in Scotland and Ireland [107], leading to conflicts with householders and requests for relocation of marten families [148].

M. martes, *M. americana* and *M. foina* have been bred for fur on farms in England [75]; a possible source of escapes [1247].

First attempts at conservation [393] in the 1920s. Initially protected under Schedule 6 of the Wildlife and Countryside Act 1981; gained full protection under Schedule 5 in 1988 (see Chapter 4).

LITERATURE
Detailed reviews of the biology, taxonomy, management, study techniques and life requirements of marten species [169, 537, 1067, 1141]. Review of changes in distribution in GB [1247] and Europe [1067]. Popular accounts [96, 1197].

PRINCIPAL AUTHORS
E. Balharry, D.J. Jefferies & J.D.S. Birks

GENUS *Mustela*

A genus containing some of the smallest carnivores, 17 species of stoats, weasels and polecats; widely distributed in N and S America and Eurasia; mostly northern, but extend S as far as C Brazil and Indonesia. Of 4 wild species in Europe, 3 (*M. erminea*, *M. nivalis*, *M. putorius*) occur in British Isles, plus 1 feral (*M. furo*) and 1 introduced (*M. vison*). Latter genetically the most distinct species in genus, separated as *Neovison* in some recent accounts, but not well justified. Slender body form and skull enable *Mustela* spp. to follow prey down burrows. Canines and carnassials well developed, premolars reduced;

dental formula i³/₃c¹/₁p³/₃m¹/₂; jaws short, barely ¹/₂ length of skull, braincase elongated well behind jaw joint.

Stoat *Mustela erminea*

Mustela erminea Linnaeus, 1758; 'Europa and Asia frigidiore'. Restricted to Uppsala, Sweden.

Putorius hibernicus Thomas & Barrett-Hamilton 1895; Enniskillen, Co. Fermanagh, Ireland.

Stot, stat, clubtail, royal hunter, ermine, short-tailed weasel (N. America); hob (English); whittret (Scots); whitrit (Shetland); whutret (Ulster Scots); whitnick (Cornish, white neck also weasel); white weasel, weasel (Ireland and Isle of Man); *carlwm* (Welsh), *neas, nios* (Scottish Gaelic); *eas, easóg* (Irish Gaelic), *conna-gwyn* (Cornish, literally white-throat), *assag* (Manx).

Male – dog, hob, jack; female – bitch, jill; young – kit; collective – gang, pack.

RECOGNITION

Whole animal: Long, thin body (209–318 mm), short legs and long tail (55–127 mm) with distinctive black tip that bristles in moments of excitement (Plate 8). Weasel *M. nivalis* generally smaller (169–248 mm), shorter tail (28–62 mm) with no black tip. Sandy-brown on back and head but cream on belly (weasels slightly darker, chestnut-brown on back and head, whiter belly). Division between brown and cream fairly straight line in stoats but irregular and spotted in weasels, except in Ireland where some stoats also have irregular pattern. Only stoats sometimes turn white in winter in GB (British weasels very rarely, if ever, turn white).

Skull and teeth: Skull flattened with broad, delicate zygomatic arch and large brain case, rounded in young animals (Fig. 9.33). In older stoats, sagittal and nuchal crests and postorbital constriction more pronounced than in younger animals. Small incisors, large canines, 4 premolars and molars in upper jaw, 5 on lower jaw. Carnassial teeth (p⁴, m₁) form close shear. Skull visually distinguishable from weasel only by larger size (total skull length >42 mm, lower jaw >21 mm). However, smallest females can be as small as largest male weasels.

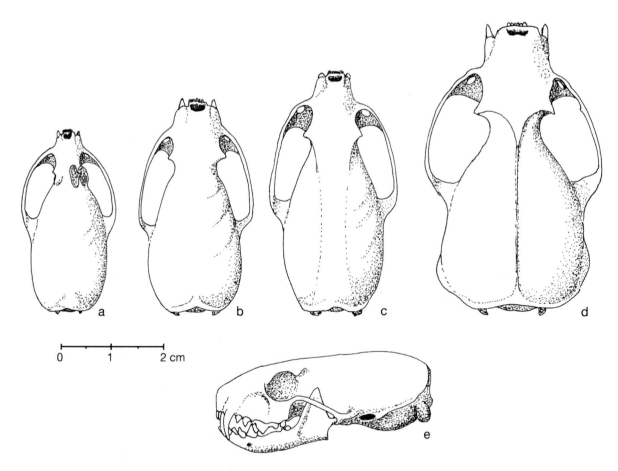

Fig. 9.33 Skulls, from above, of (a) female weasel, (b) male weasel, (c) female stoat, (d) male stoat; (e), lateral view of female stoat skull. Note that the female weasel skull shows modest deformation following infestation with *Skrjabingylus nasicola*. Recalling the badger (Fig. 9.19), the male stoat shows a slight sagittal crest *(drawn by D.W. Yalden)*.

FIELD SIGNS

Tracks and trails: 5 toes on each foot: tracks of forefoot *c.*20 × 22 mm, hindfoot *c.*42 × 25 mm. Stride when bounding *c.*300–500 mm between each group of 4 prints (average for smaller Finnish animals – 300 mm in female, 560 mm in male) [996]. Weaving paths along hedgerows and stone walls sometimes visible in snow.

Faeces: Scats long (40–80 mm), thin and twisted. Contain fur, feathers but rarely any bone fragments. Often drawn into characteristic twists of fur at each end. Distinguished from smaller weasel or larger polecat or marten only by size or smell if fresh, but no reliable distinction, except by genetic methods. May be piled in dens, occasionally found singly on prominent stones in the middle of a track.

Dens: Usually occupy nests of prey: rabbit or rodent burrows, even squirrel dreys. Dens often lined with fur from prey [882] and may contain or be recognised by prey remains including the teeth, feet and tails of rodents, flight feathers or beaks of birds and whole shrews [399]. Territories contain several (2–10) dens and temporary resting places [996, 1059].

Other field signs: Rarely observed. Caches of prey may occasionally be found in burrows or cavities.

DESCRIPTION

Pelage: In summer sandy-brown on the back and head, creamy-white below (Plate 8). Division of dark back from pale belly always straight, except in parts of Ireland where only 13.5% of 170 *M. e. hibernica* had straight colour pattern [380, 942].

Moult: Twice a year. Spring moult slow, progressing from head across back towards belly. Autumn moult faster, progressing in reverse direction [413]. Initiation of moult controlled by photoperiod. At higher latitudes, moult cycle starts earlier in autumn and later in spring, regardless of climate or altitude [694].

In winter, N of range, adopts white coat, except for black tip of tail. White coat, known as ermine, valued for regalia of nobility and judiciary. Further S, winter coat stays brown but is denser and sometimes paler than in the summer. In temperate regions with variable climates, including GB and New Zealand, intermediate stages of moult can be found, varying with minimum temperature and snow lie [580] and frost and altitude, but not day length [694]. Stoats in full ermine commonplace in Scotland and N England. Piebald or mottled coats regularly recorded elsewhere in England and Wales. In Russia, do not turn white in regions where snow cover lasts for <40 days/year [415]. Females more often found in ermine than males [401, 484, 970], so winter whitening probably controlled by sex-linked genetic polymorphism [614]. Histology of moult and colour change illustrated in [1158]. White winter fur has larger upper shaft medullas with more air cavities than brown summer fur, presumably provides better insulation [1132]. White fur, in combination with black tail tip, has role in protecting stoats from other predators (see below), but none in camouflage from potential prey.

Anatomy: Eyes round, black and slightly protruding; tapetum, eye-shine green. Vibrissae brown or white, very long. Ears short and rounded, lie almost flat to head. Feet furred between small pads. Claws large relative to digits and non-retractile. Males have curved baculum with proximal knob, which increases in weight with age [477]. Fat deposited in several sites successively; first along spine and kidneys, then on gut mesenteries, in cavities under limbs and finally around shoulders [696].

Nipples: Usually 4 or 5 pairs, visible only in adult females.

Scent glands: Large (8.5 × 5 mm in males, smaller in females) anal glands under tail emit strong musky scent produced by several sulphur-containing compounds. Identified as mixtures of thietanes and dithiolanes [143, 246]. Composition of scent varies between sexes, distinct from closely related species such as weasels [143, 246]. Histology and anatomy of anal glands described in [1252]. Scent glands also on cheeks, belly and flanks.

Reproductive tract: Uterus simple, bicornate. Rarely or never shows durable placental scars, but unimplanted blastocysts can be flushed from the uterus and counted [21]. Ovaries often surrounded by fat. Yellow corpora lutea of delay visible on ovary surface for 9–10 months of year. Scrotum furred. Testes of mature adults clearly visible during external examination. Regressed October–March but still readily visible. Testes of young males scarcely apparent externally.

Chromosomes: 2n = 44, FNa = 60. Data from Sweden, Japan and Ontario [1441].

RELATIONSHIPS

Similar in appearance to weasels but quite different in ecology [695]. In GB, both species found in similar habitats, though stoats more

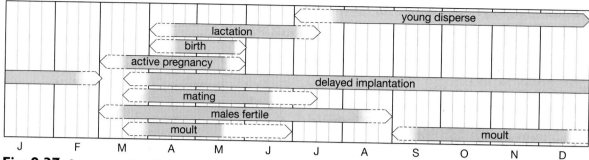

Fig. 9.37 Stoat: annual cycle.

>43 million *M. agrestis*, 4.4% of total annual impact of predators on vole population in GB [332], though this estimate not translated to impact on population dynamics.

Predation by small mustelids suggested as driving force in microtine population cycles in Nordic regions [732, 1431]. Removal of predators, mainly small mustelids, can reverse crash phase of rodent cycles [731] and increase growth rate of *Microtus* populations [713]. Mobility of voles also reduced under higher predation risk from mustelids [730, 933] Role of predation and predation risk in population dynamics remains a contentious area [367, 368, 676, 768, 1431].

Surplus killing and food caching: Occur when prey is abundant; an adaptive response to small size, high metabolic needs and the demands of living in a cold climate, as well as a strategy for utilising unpredictable and/or otherwise indefensible resources [1007, 1008].

Food requirements: In GB, minimum estimates for males 57 g/day (23% body weight), females 33 g/day (14%) [271]. In Germany 19–32% of body weight for males and 23–27% for females daily [970]. During lactation, females require 2–3 times more, and while feeding weaned young 5–10 times more [970]. Long, thin shape allows efficient pursuit of prey, but at high cost in energetic inefficiency [151].

BREEDING
Mating April–July (Fig. 9.37), induced ovulation, delayed implantation 9–10 months, active pregnancy 4 weeks, total gestation *c.*280 days, embryos 8.8 (range 6–13) [918], peak birth April, litter size *c.*6–9, females reproductively mature soon after birth and usually fertilised before weaning; postpartum oestrus.

Males: Sexually mature at 10–11 months. Weight of baculum remains at 20–30 mg until that age, doubles at puberty, then probably increases throughout adult life [477, 1214]. In spring, rapid

enlargement of testes of all males accompanied by increased concentration of testosterone in plasma [478]. Fertile May–August, then testes regress, quiescent until November [277, 1129]. Regressed testes of adults still distinctly larger than undeveloped testes of younger males [694]. Spermatogenesis begins in December, but spermatozoa not found in the epididymides until May [478].

Females: Sexually mature at 2–3 weeks while still blind, deaf and hairless. Mated by adult males. Kit weighing 18 g mated at 17 days, gave birth after 337 days to 13 kits, reared them successfully [1283]. Lack of pair bonds and rapid turnover of population reduces chances that adult male is serving his own young [696], though levels of inbreeding not tested. Evidence of multiple paternity within litters [595]. Postpartum oestrus [1129]. Ovulation induced by repeated and vigorous mating [970, 1283]. Artificial insemination always unsuccessful, even after injection of gonadotropin [1129].

Initial development of corpora lutea and blastocysts rapid, interrupted after 2–3 weeks by an obligate delay in implantation of 9–10 months. Corpora lutea remain small and plasma progesterone levels low until March [277, 278, 479]. Implantation controlled by increasing day length in spring, mediated by rise in plasma progesterone, produced by reactivated corpora lutea [479]. Critical day length stimulating implantation reached earlier in lower latitudes, births earlier, e.g. difference of *c.*10 days between N and S New Zealand, 7° latitude apart [694]. Active gestation 4 weeks [129]. Young born in April–May.

Productivity: Mean ovulation rate 10, range 6–17 [1129]. In New Zealand 10, range 3–20 [694]. Inverse correlation between counts for 2 ovaries in any individual [694]. Fecundity not related to female age when corrected for inter-annual variation in food availability [1062]. Mean embryo count 8.8, n = 33, range 6–13 [277, 380, 694, 918]. 25% of 17 pregnancies showed some resorptions

464

[1129], but resorption rate can vary markedly with year and location of collection. General mean litter size not known; 9 young born in one litter in captivity [334], 13 in another [1102]. Productivity not related to fecundity because of resorption and nestling mortality, which vary from 0–100% of available blastocysts. Depends on food availability during season of implantation and lactation, not season of fertilisation. Highest reproductive success is in areas [360] or years [687, 697] with highest density of favoured prey. Mortality rates of cohorts born in years with high food availability are higher than those in low food years, due to high density-dependent mortality [1062].

Development of young: Females rear young alone. Young born blind, deaf, toothless, covered with fine white or pinkish down. Birth weight in GB 3–4 g [277]. At 3 weeks milk teeth erupt and prominent but temporary mane develops [109], 4 weeks solid food taken, 5–6 weeks eyes open (females first), 6–7 weeks black tail tip appears, 7–12 weeks lactation ends, 10–12 weeks innate killing behaviour fully developed, >12 weeks family groups break up [334, 451, 493, 970].

Before 5–7 weeks kits have poor thermoregulatory ability. When female away, kits huddle together for warmth. Below 10–12 °C enter reversible torpor with reduced cardiac and respiratory function; fully homeothermic down to 0 °C when fur fully grown at 8 weeks [1162].

POPULATIONS

Numbers: Estimated pre-breeding population, GB, 462 000 (England 245 000, Scotland 180 000, Wales 37 000), but estimate could be changed by >50% with more information on population densities [536]; based on assumption of 1–6 stoats/km² depending on habitat. Estimate for Ireland 160 000 pro rata. Densities highly variable with food supply, and no field studies conducted in GB to gauge accuracy of density estimates. In New Zealand beech forests, density estimated from live trapping to be 4.2/km² (2.9–7.7/km² 95% CI) in a good summer for mice, and 2.5/km² (2.1–3.5/km²) in the following winter [20]; probably less in beech forests in other years, and in other habitats in all years [696].

Fluctuations: Populations highly volatile. Productivity varies with food supply in year of implantation, not year of fertilisation [687]. Postnatal mortality also variable, dependent on food supply and density dependence [1062]. Declined dramatically during myxomatosis epidemics in 1950s and 1960s [685, 1258]. Game bags showed decline, recovery until 1975 then slow decline thereafter continuing to 1998 [1268].

However, trends in game bags affected by reduction in trapping effort and overall populations may not be declining [917].

Sex ratio: 1:1 at birth [970]. Trapped and road-killed samples, but not shot samples, usually biased towards males, reflecting differences in ranging behaviour, trap density and susceptibility to capture rather than genuine bias in wild populations [166, 696, 918, 1195].

Age determination: Reviewed in [691]. Most reliable method is sectioning and counting annual layers in cementum [477, 691]. If date of death is known, development of postorbital constriction, sagittal crest and other skull features, together with weight of baculum in males, can be used to identify young males up to *c.*10 months and young females up to *c.*5 months [691]. Over 99% of adult males have enlarged testes in summer, but young-of-year do not. Adult females have visible nipples, small if they have not borne young, larger if they have, but nipples of young-of-year are not readily visible.

Age structure: Depends on breeding success in previous year. Proportion of young (0–1 years) can vary from to 0 to 90%. Lifespan short, especially where kill-trapping pressure is continuous [280, 918]. Data on undisturbed populations obtainable only by live trapping, hence none from GB. Over 5 years in S Sweden, the proportion of young varied from 31% to 76%; average further life expectancy from age of independence (3–4 months), 1.4 years in males, 1.1 years in females; maximum age observed 4.5 years (n = 47) in males, 3.5 years (n = 48) in females [361]. Over 3 years in Switzerland, the proportion of young from August to December was 55–67%, mean age 14.4 months [280]. Maximum age attained (infrequently) by wild stoats in temperate countries 6–8 years [477], less in the far north [727].

Survival: Correlated with food supplies [1062]. Actual mortality rates in undisturbed populations measured in the field variable: 0.40–0.78 (males) and 0.54–0.83 (females), according to age and year, in Sweden [361], 0.68 (both sexes) in Switzerland [280]; i.e. 2/3 of all live adults in one year will die before the next year. Population turnover very high (0.93/year) [280], i.e. only 7% of adults remained resident a 2nd year, but that study area rather small relative to dispersal capabilities of stoats.

MORTALITY

Predation: Small enough to be considered prey by a range of other predators. Foxes thought to cause extinction of stoats in restricted area of sand dunes in Netherlands [969] and implicated in decline of stoats in areas of Russia [774]. Occasionally killed by domestic cats [1413]. Raptors may have large impact on small mustelid populations [729, 730]. Black tip on tail thought to be predator deflection mark [1061].

Persecution: Rarely victim of deliberate persecution. Legally trapped and shot by gamekeepers as part of predator control programmes (see Relations with humans).

Disease: Reviewed in [919]. Mortality due to disease largely unknown. TB recorded in former USSR [773]. None of 33 stoats examined in GB 1971–1986 positive for *Mycobacterium bovis* [880], but 1 of 62 stoats from an area in New Zealand with endemic TB showed tuberculous lesions [1077]. Resistant to tularaemia, but thought to cause mortality [773]. Reputed to suffer from distemper [1052], detected in captivity [673]. Symptoms of mange also recorded [774].

PARASITES AND PATHOGENS
Reviewed in [919].

Ectoparasites: Specific louse *Trichodectes (Stachiella) ermineae* recorded in Canada, Ireland and New Zealand [658, 696, 1197]. Specific flea *Nearctopsylla brooksi* not recorded in GB [594, 680]. Host to several ectoparasites associated with prey and nest parasites from species that are not eaten; European records total 26 flea species [281]. *Rhadinopsylla pentacantha*, an uncommon flea specific to vole nests, *Megabothris rectangulatus* specific to voles, *Orchopeas howardi*, squirrels and *Spilopsyllus cuniculus* rabbits, recorded in GB [680, 886]. *Ctenophthalamus nobilis, Dasypsyllus gallinulae, Nosopsyllus fasciatus* and *S. cuniculi* recorded in Ireland [1197]. In New Zealand, rat fleas *N. fasciatus* make up 97% of records, but *Leptopsylla segnis, Ceratophyllus gallinae* and *Parapsyllus n. nestoris* also recorded [694]. *Amphipsylla kuznetzovi* and *Ctenopsyllus bidentatus* collected in Kazakhstan [773]. In Ireland, host to ticks *Ixodes canisuga, I. hexagonus* and *I. ricinus*, lice *Mysidea picae* and *Polyplax spinulosa* and the mite *Neotrombicula autumnalis* [1198]. In New Zealand tick *Haema-physalis longicornis* and mites *Demodex erminae, Eulaelaps stabulans, Gymnolaelaps annectans, Hypoaspis nidicorva* and *Listrophorus mustelae* also recorded [696].

Endoparasites: Nematode parasitism identified in intestines of 14% and lungs of 11% of sample of 44 British stoats [924]. Nematode *Skrjabingylus nasicola* common in GB; causes skull deformity by eroding bones of nasal sinuses. Rates of sinus infestation 17–31% in GB [787, 1215]; up to 50% in Ireland [1196]. Obligate intermediate hosts are terrestrial snails. Invasive 3rd-stage *S. nasicola* larvae found encapsulated in *Apodemus*, which readily eats molluscs both in the wild and in captivity, and can experimentally infect stoats within 24 days [1365]. Heavy infestations believed to affect skull size adversely on Terschelling [1215] and density and fertility in Russia [773, 1052], but stunting of infested individuals not detected in sample of 1492 in New Zealand [694]. Not thought to cause significant mortality, but may induce fits or spasms otherwise associated with 'dancing' behaviour or playing dead under stress [696].

Survey of common helminths in Russian sample included nematodes *Capillaria putorii, Molineus patens* and *Strongyloides martis*; cestodes *Taenia tenuicollis* and *Mesocestoides lineatus*; and, rarely, Acanthocephala *Acanthocephalus* sp. [773].

Others: Not thought to host dermatophytes, e.g. *Trichophyton*, that cause ringworm, though only small samples tested [348]. See [919] and Disease above.

RELATIONS WITH HUMANS
Reviewed in [915, 920].

Fur: Pelts (ermine) rarely in prime condition in GB, but commonly harvested in Siberia, Canada and Alaska. Formerly large market in pelts, e.g. 80 000 pelts traded in London fur sales in March 1906; demand and prices now low.

Pest status and control: Commonly regarded as vermin, at least since 16th century. Regarded as pest by gamekeepers, because of predation on game birds, including nesting females [1270]. Regarded as less serious pest than foxes, feral cats, mink and corvids, but more serious than polecats, rats, hedgehogs [1013] or weasels [915]. Perceived as greater pest to gamekeepers promoting wild game than to those rearing game [917]. Legally shot and trapped, using live traps or approved metal spring traps, most commonly Fenn or Springer, that must be set in tunnels and checked at least once a day [418]. Gin trap [78] now illegal in GB. In 1997, typical wild-partridge keeper ran *c*.90 traps for 9 months of the year and caught *c*.34 stoats. In contrast, reared-bird keeper ran 40 traps for 6 months and caught 19 stoats [917]. Bag strongly related to trapping effort and not beat area or region [917]. Trapping generally thought to have only temporary and local effect on populations [1270]. Empirical data and models suggest reduction of population growth rate due to mortality of dependent young when females trapped or shot [918], hence trapped populations dependent on immigration.

Occasionally regarded as beneficial because of predation on rodents and rabbits, though effects probably overstated [696]. Gamekeepers' trapping records best existing method of monitoring populations in GB, though require correction for trapping effort to be meaningful [917]. Major conservation pest in New Zealand, where there are extensive campaigns for control of predation on endangered ground- and hole-nesting birds [920].

Conservation and protection: Not protected under UK conservation legislation (see Chapter 4) but protected in Republic of Ireland. Included in Appendix III of Bern Convention, hence status and exploitation subject to consideration by signatory states. No proposals to give protection from control measures [920, 1269]. Some concern about conservation status [536, 860] (see Populations above), though records detailing population trends [1268] biased in part by decreasing trapping effort [917]. Potentially large numbers exposed to anticoagulant rodenticides, though effects at population level unknown [860]. May also suffer from intra-guild predation from increasing fox populations [1269].

Techniques for study: Not well studied in GB. Few published data on social and spatial behaviour; well described by live trapping and telemetry elsewhere (see above), but these techniques problematic because of variable populations, large ranges and habit of hunting underground and in thin cover. Gut, skull and tissue samples readily available from gamekeepers and used in wide range of studies of diet, toxicology, morphology, etc. Studies relating trapping records to population densities required [917], also efficacy of control measures [918], parasitology [919] and impact on prey populations still to be described in detail.

LITERATURE
Monograph on stoats and weasels [696]. Shorter, detailed account of stoats and weasels in [916]. *Mammalian Species* account [688]. Popular account of small mustelids [1198].

PRINCIPAL AUTHORS
R.A. McDonald & C.M. King

Weasel *Mustela nivalis*
Mustela nivalis, Linnaeus 1766; 'province of Vesterbotten, Sweden'.
Mustela vulgaris Erxleben, 1777; 'near Leipzig, Germany'.
Kine, cane, beale, rassel, mousehunter, grass weasel (English); whittret (Scots); *gwenci* (Welsh); *neas* (*bheag*), *nios* (Scottish Gaelic); *bronwen, lovennan* (Cornish).
Male – dog, hob, jack; female – bitch, jill; young – kit; collective – gang, pack.

RECOGNITION
Whole animal: Smallest member of Carnivora. Small size, short legs and long slender body (175–248 mm) distinguish it from all other British mammals except stoat (Plate 8). Can be difficult

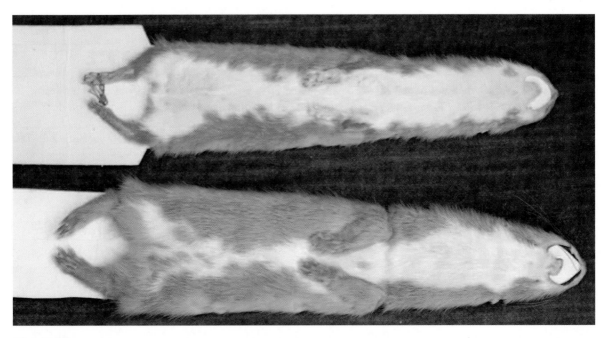

Fig. 9.38 Weasels have individually recognisable ventral patterns (*photo P. Morris*).

to distinguish live weasels from stoats in the field, though weasels have noticeably shorter tail (32–62 mm) lacking black tip. Sandy-chestnut brown on back and white belly. Irregular and spotted margin between dark back and pale belly in *M. n. vulgaris* (in GB and W Europe): straight margin in *M. n. nivalis* (in Scandinavia, parts of E Europe and most of Russia). *M. n. vulgaris* very rarely, if ever, turns white in winter; *M. n. nivalis* usually does.

Skull and teeth: Similar to stoat (Fig. 9.33), distinguishable only by size (skull 32–44 mm, lower jaw 15–22 mm), though largest male weasels overlap with smallest female stoats. Nasal bones and postorbital area frequently damaged by *Skrjabingylus* infestation (see Parasites and pathogens).

FIELD SIGNS
Inconspicuous and hard to find.

Tracks and trails: 5 toes on each foot: forefoot *c*.13 × 10 mm, hindfoot *c*.15 × 13 mm. Stride when bounding *c*.200–300 mm between each group of 4 prints.

Faeces: Long, thin and twisted, very similar to stoat but smaller (30–60 mm). Feeding sign likely to be found only in dens, then indistinguishable from stoat.

Dens: Does not make runways or dens. Takes over dens of prey and other mammals, complete with nest parasites [680]. Each home range includes many dens and resting places visited at intervals [1059]. In cold climates usually lined with fur of prey [245].

DESCRIPTION
Pelage: Chestnut brown on back and head with white belly. Prominent gular spots. Margin between dorsal and ventral surfaces irregular and spotted. Pattern of margin and spots can be used to distinguish individuals [802] (Fig. 9.38). Fur *c*.10 mm long in summer, 15–16 mm in winter.

Moult: Twice yearly, similar sequence and pattern to stoat [683].Winter whitening extremely rare in GB [401]. Lack of genes for whitening distinguishes *M. n. vulgaris* from *M. n. nivalis* [411, 416, 1237, 1440], suggesting different sources of Postglacial recolonisation [696]. Occasional albinos, recognisable by pink eyes. Winter fur in *M. n. vulgaris* generally paler brown and new spring fur may appear as distinct dark stripe [683].

Anatomy: Generally (eyes, ears, vibrissae, paws, etc.) similar to stoat, but smaller. Baculum short with a thick, straight shaft (length 16–20 mm, weight 7–67 mg according to age), proximal knob and distal hook; increases in weight with age [684]. Sequential deposition of fat along spine, kidneys, gut mesenteries and around limbs [696].

Nipples: Usually 4 pairs, visible only in adult females [553].

Scent glands: Muscular anal glands under tail, 7 × 5 mm [1252]. Contents made up of sulphurous volatiles, including thietanes and dithiacyclopentanes. Smell and chemistry distinct from stoat [143].

Reproductive tract: Scrotum furred; no seminal vesicles or prostate gland in males [587]. Testes regressed but still visible in adults November–January [587]. Uterus bicornate and similar to stoat, but smaller [279]. Ovaries show corpora lutea only in breeding season.

Table 9.14 Weasel: measurements. Data are from animals that are at least 12 months old, collected from throughout GB 1995–1997. Measurements do not include pregnant females [1]

	Males					**Females**				
	Mean	SD	Min	Max	n	Mean	SD	Min	Max	n
Head and body length (mm)	216	10	195	248	102	184	6	175	194	24
Tail length (mm)	49	5	32	62	101	39	3	35	46	24
Hind foot length (mm)	31	2	26	36	102	25	2	22	29	24
Weight (g)	125	22	81	195	102	68	13	48	107	24
Condylobasal length (mm)	39.6	1.5	36.7	44.5	94	34.6	1.1	32.45	36.6	20
Upper canine diameter (mm)	1.74	0.13	1.35	2.03	100	1.33	0.10	1.01	1.46	24

Chromosomes: 2n = 42 in both subspecies, throughout Europe and N America [1440, 1441].

RELATIONSHIPS
M. nivalis closely related to *M. frenata*, but also to *M. erminea* and *M. altaica* [89]. *M. nivalis* previously considered distinct from Nearctic least weasel, *M. rixosa* Bangs 1896 (Osler, Saskatchewan) [484] but latter generally given subspecies status *M. n. rixosa* [485, 1444]. However, variation in skull shape between regions of N America may justify full specific status of *M. rixosa* [1084]. Skulls of Egyptian weasels, formerly recognised as sub-species *M. n. subpalmata* Hemprich & Ehrenberg 1833; (Cairo, Egypt) distinct in size and shape from all other groups of *M. nivalis* [4, 1084, 1444], hence recent recognition as full species *M. subpalmata* [914, 1387].

In GB, only similar species is stoat. Both species found in similar habitats, though stoats more likely to be found in upland areas than weasels, and weasels more likely than stoats to be found in commercial conifer plantations, where vole populations are high [458]. Competition with stoat partially avoided by specialist foraging on small rodents and ability to enter smaller tunnels [1059, 1185]. Encounters with stoats actively avoided by weasels, though female weasels less likely to abandon foraging in presence of stoat than males, perhaps because they can always escape into a tunnel [1059]. Stoat scent avoided by weasels in arena trials [364], though perhaps not in field [1059]. Coexist in heterogeneous environment where balance alternately favours exploitation competitor, weasel, and interference competitor, stoat [695], though relative importance of exploitation and interference debated [40]. As part of guild of British mustelids, excepting otters and badgers, weasels exhibit community-wide character displacement [274], but this may not be related to partitioning of food resources by size among species [913].

MEASUREMENTS
See Table 9.14. Pronounced sexual size dimorphism; males much larger than females; ratio of body weights 1.8–2.2:1 [964]. In GB, size of males appears to increase with latitude [689]. However, size variation may also be influenced by age structure, season and year of collection.

VARIATION
British weasels indistinguishable from W European forms of *M. n. vulgaris* Erxleben 1777 (near Leipzig, Germany). Distinguished from Scandinavian and Eurasian least weasel *M. n. nivalis* Linnaeus 1766 (Vesterbotten, Sweden) by latter's smaller size, straight flank line and winter whitening [1237]. The 2 subspecies are interfertile [410, 411]. In Europe, pronounced trend for increasing body size with decreasing latitude, contrary to predictions of Bergmann's rule [735]. Variation within GB principally in body size. Male weasels appear to be larger in Scotland than in S England, though females do not appear to vary in size between regions [689]. Reports of smaller British species of weasel, commonly referred to as mouse-hunter, are unfounded, probably based on markedly smaller size of females or late-born young.

DISTRIBUTION
Circumboreal in distribution. Sympatric with stoat over much of range in N Holarctic, though weasel extends further S into Mediterranean and N Africa (Fig. 9.39). Introduced from GB to New Zealand in 1880s, now much less common and widespread there than stoat [692]. Introduced to various Mediterranean islands and the Azores, possibly to North Africa [275, 300, 914, 948]. Egyptian weasels now recognised as separate species (see Relationships above).

Occurs throughout mainland GB; absent Ireland (Fig. 9.40). Gamekeepers in SW of GB appear to catch fewer weasels, when trapping effort is taken into account [917]; other records of regional variation in keeper harvests affected by uncorrected variation in effort [1268]. No other extensive survey data on populations.

Distribution on British islands described in [695], updated and clarified here. Weasels established on Sheppey, Skye, Wight, Ynys Môn (Holy Island and Anglesey) [36, 88]. Bute also has long-established population, omitted from previous accounts [434, 940]. Recent records from Scalpay (Skye) [1434], though weasels may not be established there. Records of weasels on Mull [88] and Jura [36] not confirmed recently and may stem from the common habit of referring to stoats, which are resident on both islands, as 'weasels' [1003]. Old records from Raasay [542] and Islay [940] not confirmed recently. Further records from Brownsea (Dorset), Hilbre (Wirral), Lindisfarne, Ramsey (Dyfed) and Tiree probably stem from incidental visitors [36, 695].

HISTORY
Derived from *M. pliocaenica*, middle Pliocene, and descended gradually from *M. praenivalis*, late Pliocene through early Pleistocene [764]. Recent form recorded among temperate forest fauna at West Runton, Norfolk, Cromerian Interglacial [1249] and at Westbury-sub-Mendip, probably slightly later [1420]. Common in European cave deposits dating from the late Pleistocene [764], widely distributed across S–C Europe in Last

Glaciation [1217]. Date of recolonisation of GB after glaciation uncertain; may have survived in S of GB near glacial front by eating lemmings [1420], but no records [1217]. Absence of weasel from Ireland implies weasel returned to GB later than stoat, i.e. after Ireland was cut off. Alternatively both species may have reached Ireland in early Holocene, together with cold-tolerant fauna including lemmings, then weasels died out when lemmings became extinct and were not replaced by voles [695]. Recent range unchanged by human intervention. Common and widespread throughout mainland GB.

HABITAT

Occupies wide range of habitats offering food and cover. On temperate farmland, strongly associated with hedgerows, stone walls and other linear features, rarely ventures into open habitat [961, 1059]. Less common where small mammals are scarce, e.g. higher mountains or woodland with sparse ground cover [354, 678], though common in coniferous woodlands with dense *Microtus* populations. In Arctic or montane regions may spend entire winter under snow [876]. Dens found in nests

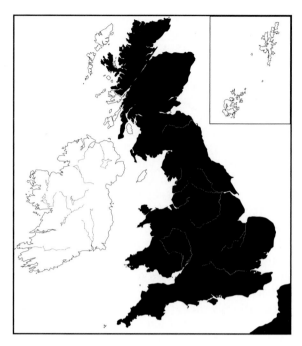

Fig. 9.40 Weasel *Mustela nivalis*: range in GB.

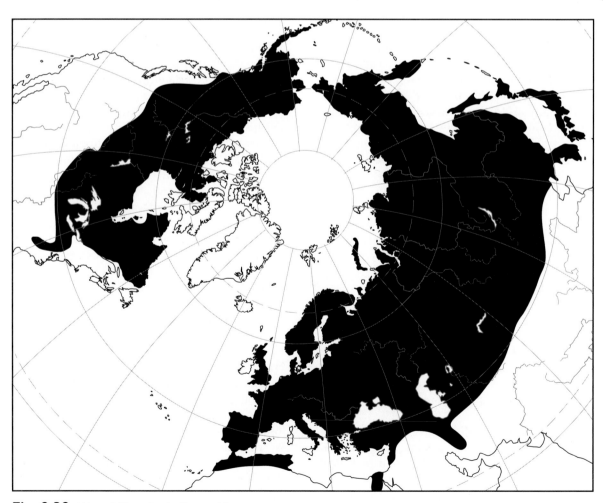

Fig. 9.39 Weasel *Mustela nivalis*: world range.

of prey and other species, including mole tunnels, rabbit burrows, stone walls, under trees, etc. [680].

SOCIAL ORGANISATION AND BEHAVIOUR

In GB, reasonably well studied by live trapping [679, 812, 961] and radio-tracking [133, 872, 1059]. Other substantial work from Sweden [364] and Poland [622].

Territories: Usual mustelid pattern, exclusive male territories enclosing female territories [1060]. Population density dependent on food supply and consequent success of most recent breeding season, hence great instability and flexibility in social structure and population density. In rank grassland in young plantation, Stirlingshire, where *Microtus* density was 110–540/ha, 10 males occupied 1–5 ha each; when *Microtus* density crashed, territorial system broke down [812]. In mature deciduous woodland near Oxford, where *Apodemus* and *Myodes* density was 21–39/ha, 7 males occupied 7–15 ha each, 3 females 1–4 ha [678]. In the same area when *Myodes* density was especially low, resident weasels were absent [551]. On farmland, Aberdeenshire, winter ranges of 5 males were 9–16 ha, summer ranges of 3 males 10–25 ha, range of 2 females *c.*7 ha [961]. In same area in winter/spring 1977–1978, ranges of 7 males estimated by radio-tracking averaged 34 ha, of 2 females 39 and 12 ha [1059]. Large parts of total range in farmland (i.e. open fields) normally unexploited; when these areas excluded, ranges reduced to average of 2.4 ha for males, 1.2 ha for females [1059]. On farmland, Oxfordshire, weasels rarely moved >5 m from linear features, hence total range sizes of up to 190 ha (mean 113 ha in 4 adult males, 28 ha in 2 females) contained much smaller areas (5–10%) of exploited habitat [972].

Like stoats, male weasels extend ranges in spring [354, 961], probably to increase access to potential mates. Ranges also extended during periods of food shortage, e.g. in Poland during a post-seedfall rodent peak, mean range of 5 radio-tracked males 24.2±11.9 ha, expanding to 117 and 216 ha in 2 males during the vole crash year [622].

Denning behaviour: Do not make dens of their own. Nest and lie up in burrows of prey and other species, e.g. mole and rat holes. Hence infestation by ectoparasites from non-prey species [680].

Scent-marking: Behaviour similar to stoat, though scents and chemistry distinct [143]. Use faeces, urine, anal and dermal gland secretions, deposited by anal dragging and body rubbing. Can rapidly expel stored anal gland scent when stressed.

Vocalisations: Described and analysed in [451, 607]. 4 basic sounds: guttural hiss when alarmed, interspersed with short screaming barks or shrieks when provoked; shrill defensive wail or squeal; and high-pitched trilling during encounters between mates or between mother and young.

Aggressive behaviour: Social hierarchy, mutual avoidance and territory-marking behaviour much like stoat [154, 443]. Dominant individual in aggressive interaction exhibits lunges and shrieks; subdominant emits submissive squeal [355]. When dominant male removed experimentally, subdominant male in adjacent range expanded into vacated area [355]. Interactions between 2 males of equal status characterised by few vocalisations, brief fights and simultaneous retreat [355].

Dispersal: No data in GB. Like stoat, probably moves large distances relative to body size.

Activity: Mostly diurnal. Several (1–7) daily activity bouts of 12–130 min separated by similar rest periods [133]. Radio-tracked excursions away from nest mainly by day [133, 623, 872, 1059], hence greater trapping success by day [678, 961]. Activity levels positively related to food availability, varying with habitat, possibly related to more time spent on intraspecific relations such as territory defence or foraging for a litter [133]. In captivity, activity pattern often nocturnal, strongly influenced by feeding regime [1064]. In spring, females less active, saving energy for pregnancy by remaining in nest and feeding from cache, but males more active in spring, as in stoat [154]. Time spent out of nest correlated with ambient temperature and sunny/rainy conditions [133, 551].

Locomotion: Characteristic mustelid gaits; bounding run, low dash with straight back, 'periscoping' on hind legs. Able swimmer and climber.

Other behaviour: Like stoat, 'dances' to 'mesmerise' prey. Also reported to 'play dead' or to experience convulsions when stressed, possibly associated with infestations of *Skrjabingylus* [689]. Very curious, responds to simulated squeaking.

FEEDING

Small-mammal specialist, but also commonly eats rabbits (probably mostly young ones), birds and birds' eggs (Fig. 9.41). Only rarely eats other items such as shrews, rats, water voles, reptiles, amphibians and invertebrates, including earthworms [272, 686, 923, 962, 1267]. Males eat

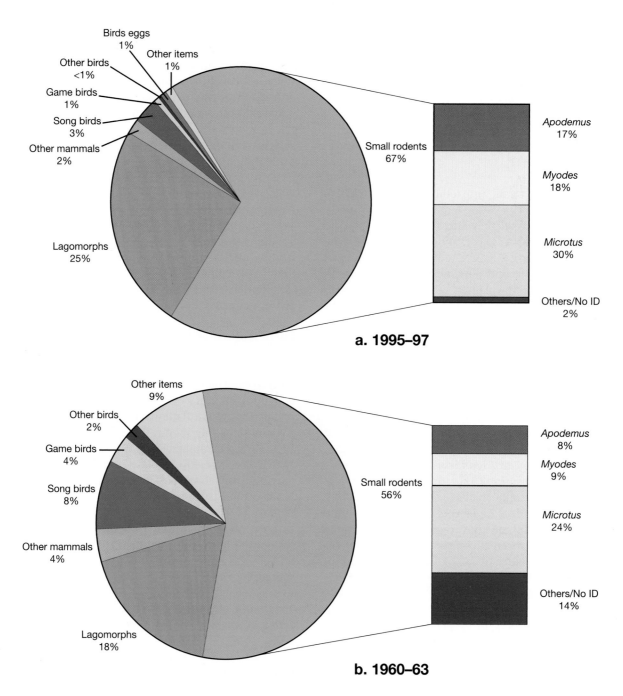

Fig. 9.41 Weasel diet [1].

higher proportion of rabbits than females, which depend almost entirely on small rodents [923, 1267]. Males also take a greater variety of prey than females, related to their ability to take a greater range of prey sizes and larger home ranges, so encountering greater diversity of prey [686, 1267]. Small rodents most important prey type in all seasons, to the near exclusion of all other prey in summer and autumn. Importance of rabbits greatest in spring, when rodents scarce and juvenile rabbits available [923, 962, 1267].

Hunting behaviour: Forage under cover, to avoid predation by foxes and raptors. Adapted for pursuing rodents down tunnels, though may also attempt to bolt prey from tunnels to kill them in the open. Males spent 50%, females 90%, of active time moving under matted grass [1059]. On farmland, of time recorded near stone walls, weasels spent 19% inside the walls, compared to 6% in stoats [1059]. Also hunt rodents under snow. Commonly raid bird nest boxes, and in some studies major cause of nestling mortality [320, 686]. Reported to kill birds caught in mist nets [35] and small mammals caught in Longworth traps [790].

Fig. 9.42 Weasel raiding bird nest-box – an indication that rodents are scarce (*photo B. Bevan /Ardea*).

Pattern of movement, localised foraging in favourable areas, especially <100 m from den, interspersed with longer straight-line excursions [1059]. When foraging intensively, males travel *c.*8.8 m/min, females 7.7 m/min [1059]. Longer straight-line excursions more rapid, e.g. 1.3 km in 55 min [961]. Mean distances travelled in foraging bouts, males 840 m, females 549 m [1059.] On farmland, usually restricted to linear features, rarely forage in the open, though one male observed in turnip field during harvest, working along rows, hunting for wood mice disturbed by labourers [1059].

In enclosures, no preferences shown for prey types. In captive trials, all offered prey attacked when encountered, in line with opportunistic foraging strategy, though capture efficiency of mice *Peromyscus* lower than voles, varied between *Microtus* spp. [297]. In another, male weasels preferred *Microtus* whereas females preferred *Myodes*, but both sexes selected juvenile *Myodes* as

the first prey to eat [1027]. Attack prey much larger than themselves, usually rabbits and rats, but occasionally even as large as hares [160]. In captivity, search, chasing and handling times were similar for all prey types, but capture success rate is lower and killing time is higher for larger prey [297]. Small prey killed by bite to neck dislocating cervical vertebrae with large canines [451, 554]. Kills of larger prey probably assisted by shock of attack and blood loss.

Impact on prey: Substantial, can eat high proportion of rodents in any population. In deciduous woodland, 7.8% of *Myodes* and 9.7% of *Apodemus* eaten by weasels per month [686]. In Poland, 2–28% of autumn numbers of rodents, or 1.6–9.5 rodents/ha, removed between October and April [622]. In Kielder Forest, weasel predation decreased adult vole survival and increased juvenile vole survival rates, though impact on overall vole population dynamics negligible, since population growth rate so much higher for rodents than for weasels [459] Apparent functional and numerical response to rodent populations, though shape of response is not well described [1267]. Switch diet from voles to birds when vole availability low [1267], hence impact on tit *Parus* spp. populations nesting in boxes greatest when rodent populations low or nest density high (Fig. 9.42) [320]. Not regarded as a serious pest by most gamekeepers [915, 920], though impact on wild-breeding game birds could theoretically be substantial [1266].

Predation by small mustelids postulated as driving factor in vole population cycles [498], though in Kielder Forest weasel predation was neither sufficient nor necessary to drive cyclic dynamics [459] and question remains controversial [733]. Sublethal effects of predation risk also demonstrated. Weasel scent avoided by voles, influences vole foraging decisions [128, 1236]. Scent invokes arboreal escape response and causes reduced mobility in bank voles [620]. In captive trials, distribution of voles, except breeding females and juveniles, affected for several days after visit by weasel [619].

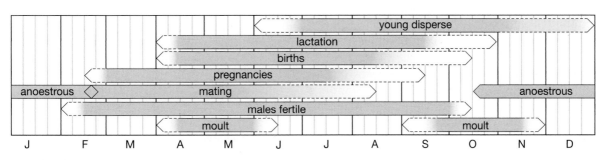

Fig. 9.43 Weasel: annual cycle.

Surplus killing and food caching: Common as response to increased prey availability and adaptation to small size and high metabolic requirements [1007, 1008]. In Russia, 15 caches held on average 30 carcasses of wide range of prey [1023].

Food requirements: *c.*1/3 of body weight per day, males 0.33 g/g, females 0.36 g/g [963] in 5–10 meals of 2–4 g each [436]. Meals pass through gut in 3–4 h [1175]. Assimilation efficiency *c.*80%, higher for larger prey, i.e. avoid fur and feathers [963]. Generally high metabolic costs, though reproduction very expensive. At 12–13 °C, 2 captive females required an additional 6–7% of normal intake during gestation, then 80–100% more during lactation [551].

BREEDING
Mating April–July (Fig. 9.43), induced ovulation, direct implantation, gestation 34–37 days, embryos 5.7 (n = 44, range 4–9), births April–August in N hemisphere, litter size 6.0 (n = 16), mature 3–4 months, can breed in 1st year, postpartum oestrus.

Males: Sexually mature at 3–4 months. May mate in the year of their birth, though usually unsuccessfully [279]. Fecund February–October, though early stages of spermatogenesis present throughout winter [587].

Females: Sexually mature at 3–4 months. In adults, anoestrus lasts September–February; heat (indicated by a swollen vulva; implantation is direct), and pregnancies may be observed at any time March–September [279, 685, 918]. Can continue pregnancy through moult, after temporary pause during oestrus [683] and at below-zero temperatures [876].

Productivity: Mean ovulation rate 7.1, range 4–11 (n = 32); embryo count 5.7 (n = 44 range 4–9); number of young born 6.2, range 4–8 (17 litters) [279, 685, 918]. During vole peaks, may produce 2nd litter and young-of-year can breed for 1st time. Large number of young weasels born July–August in peak years mostly produced by the early-born young [685]. Conversely, during poor vole years, breeding may fail completely [1267]. Minimum vole density for successful breeding calculated as 10/ha [354], 14/ha [1267], 15/ha [295].

Development of young: Females rear young alone. Birth weight 1.5–4.5 g, male kits slightly heavier [551]. Born pink, naked, blind and deaf; at 4 days, covered in white downy fur, at 10 days margin between dark back and pale belly clearly visible; at 2–3 weeks deciduous teeth erupt, 3–4 weeks weaned, though lactation may last to 12 weeks; 3–4 weeks ears open, 4 weeks eyes open (females first), 5 weeks canines emerge, 8 weeks killing behaviour developed; 10 weeks permanent dentition complete, 9–12 weeks family group breaks up; 12–16 weeks adult weight attained [118, 333, 540, 551, 553]. Development of 2nd litters slower than 1st.

POPULATION
Numbers: Estimated GB pre-breeding population 450 000 (England 308 000, Scotland 106 000, Wales 36 000), but estimate could be changed by >50% [536]: based on species range described in [36] and abundance in game bags relative to bags of stoats [1268]. Actual densities extremely variable, related to food supply, and few field studies conducted in GB.

Fluctuations: Populations volatile. Productivity, density, territoriality and mobility vary greatly with food supply [685]. National population increased following myxomatosis epidemics in 1950s and 1960s, due to flush of grassland and more voles, due to reduced grazing by rabbits [685, 1258]. Downward trend in national game bags since 1961 may reflect return to pre-myxomatosis populations, reduction in trapping effort or genuine decline in abundance [917, 1268, 1269].

Sex ratio: 1:1 at birth [679]. Trapped samples vary from 2.59–6.00:1 [271, 279, 685, 918, 962, 1332]. Skew ascribed to sampling error variously resulting from greater ranges of males and greater trap encounter rate [679]; lighter weight and lower likelihood of capture in spring trap [1268]; and behavioural differences between the sexes [166].

Age determination: Best described and verified method uses combination of date of death, skull morphology and baculum weight in males (DSB method) to separate young from old weasels [684]. Only effective to 8–9 months, dependent on large, well-documented samples from specific areas. Otherwise, cementum analysis is most likely accurate method, though not tested on specimens of known age [903].

Age structure: Known mainly from samples of trapped animals from game estates. Most large samples have 67–87% of animals <1 year [685, 918]. One sample from previously untrapped population 59% <1 year [685]. Proportion of young varies with month and between sites, but does not differ between sexes [685]. Few individuals apparently >2 years [685]. In sample of 38 individuals, aged by cementum analysis, maximum age was 2 [918]. No individuals >3 years observed [812].

Survival: Mean expectation of life <1 year in most populations. Preliminary life tables suggest *c.*15–20% survival between independence and 1 year in males, 3–25% in females, though difference not significant [685, 918]. Period of highest mortality is March–May, though confounded by greatest trapping effort in this season [685, 918].

MORTALITY

Predation: Small enough to be considered prey by a range of other predators. Occasionally killed by foxes and domestic cats. Raptors may have large impact on populations of small mustelids [729, 730]. Weasel lacks stoat's black tip on tail as predator deflection mark, because tail is too short to deflect predator sufficiently to avoid being caught [1061].

Persecution: Rarely victim of deliberate persecution. Legally trapped and shot by game-keepers as part of predator control programmes (see Relations with humans). In several years' sampling in Wildlife Incident Investigation Scheme, only 1 case of deliberate poisoning using organophosphate mevinphos [472], though small carcasses rarely recovered.

Disease: Reviewed in [919]. Susceptible to sarcosporidiosis [1263]. Reputed to suffer from distemper, though undiagnosed. None of 33 weasels examined in GB 1971–1986 tested positive for *Mycobacterium bovis* [880]. 2 of 4 individuals positive for *M. avium paratuberculosis* [82].

PARASITES AND PATHOGENS
Reviewed in [919].

Ectoparasites: Specific biting louse, *Trichodectes mustelae* and mites *Demodex* spp., and *Psorergates mustela* recorded in New Zealand, so presumably present in GB [1281]. Picks up fleas from prey species, nest parasites from dens and tunnels of other species. 11 species recorded at Wytham, near Oxford [680]; 6 of these plus additional 2 recorded in Aberdeenshire [886]. Of the 13 species, 8 are normally found on voles and mice, or in their nests; 2 are monoxenous on moles *Ctenophthalmus bisoctodentatus* and *Palaeopsylla m. minor*, 1 on shrews *P. s. soricis*, 1 on rats and other rodents *Nosopsyllus fasciatus* and 1 on birds *Dasypsyllus gallinulae*. Conversely, prey such as birds that have uninviting nests seldom passed their fleas to weasels.

Helminths: Poorly documented in GB, though several genera recorded elsewhere, including trematode *Alaria*, nematodes *Capillaria, Filaroides, Trichinella* and cestode *Taenia* [1259]. Nematode *Skrjabingylus nasicola* common in GB and elsewhere [681, 787]. Causes conspicuous lesions of nasal sinuses and distortion of postorbital area in 69–100% of samples in GB [681]. Incidence of damage particularly high in areas with higher rainfall, correlated to higher mollusc populations [681]. Transmitted via paratenic host *Apodemus*, in which larvae encyst in mouth area [1365]. No effects of infestation on body weight or condition detected in several large trapped samples [681].

Others: Host to sporozoan *Sarcocystis* [1263]. Of 14 weasels examined, 1 was host to *Trichophyton persicolor*, a dermatophyte that causes ringworm [348].

RELATIONS WITH HUMANS
Reviewed in [920].

Fur: Once exploited for white fur (lettice) but not in GB due to lack of whitening. Rarely trapped commercially.

Pest status and control: Considered pest of game [1268], though regarded as less serious problem on all types of shoot than stoats [915]. Perceived as greater pest to gamekeepers promoting wild game than to those rearing game [917]. Legally trapped and shot in the same way as stoats, using same approved traps. Less likely to be shot than stoat, because of smaller size and tendency to forage under cover [918, 1268]. In 1997, typical wild-partridge keeper ran *c.*90 traps for 9 months of the year and caught *c.*28 weasels. In contrast, average reared-bird keeper ran 40 traps for 6 months and caught 11 weasels [917]. Bag strongly related to trapping effort and not beat area [917]. SW region has lower average bags than elsewhere in GB, after controlling for effort [917]. Trapping generally thought to have only temporary and local effect on populations [685, 918, 1270]. Much less common than stoat in New Zealand, hence lesser status as pest [692, 920].

Conservation and protection: Same protection status as stoat. Listed under Appendix III of Bern Convention, but not protected under UK conservation legislation (see Chapter 4). Concern about conservation status [536, 860] (see Populations above), based on pronounced decline in game bags [1268]. Susceptible to poisoning by warfarin [1306] and potentially large numbers exposed to 2nd-generation rodenticides [922], though population-level effects are unknown. Habitat improvement and reduction of rabbit abundance suggested as methods of increasing populations [1269].

Techniques for study: Live trapping and telemetry effective when populations at high density [678, 1059], though both techniques highly problematic otherwise [551]. Most substantial studies of diet, morphology, parasitology, demography, etc., based on cadavers collected by gamekeepers [279, 681, 684, 685, 917, 918, 922–924, 1267]. Live trapping and camera trapping advocated as survey techniques [860]. Gamekeeper records best existing method of surveying trends in populations, though data on trapping effort and calibration to real densities required [917].

LITERATURE
Monograph on stoats and weasels [696]; shorter, detailed account of stoats and weasels [916]; *Mammalian Species* account [1168]; popular account of small mustelids [1198].

PRINCIPAL AUTHORS
R.A. McDonald & C.M. King

Polecat *Mustela putorius*
Mustela putorius Linnaeus, 1758; Sweden.
Putorius vulgaris Griffith, 1827.
Putorius foetidus Gray, 1843.
Foulmarten, fulimart, foulmart, foumart, foumaire, fummet (English vernaculars); fitchuke, fitchew, fitcher, fitchet, fitch (in fur trade); *ffwlbart* (Welsh); *kayt ny giark* (Manx Gaelic).
Male – hob; female – jill or jen; young – kits or (pole) kittens.

RECOGNITION
Whole animal: Creamy underfur over most of body, dark facial mask, white fur on muzzle and white ear margins (Plate 8); these readily distinguish it from similar-sized mink (which uniformly dark). Distinguished from escaped ferrets by (usually) darker appearance, absence of pale marten-like throat patch or other markings on throat and more restricted white facial band; dark polecat–ferret hybrids difficult to distinguish from polecats in the field (Fig. 9.44).

Skull: Has broader postorbital constriction and greater cranial volume than ferret (Fig. 9.45), though overlap in these measurements between polecats, ferrets and polecat–ferret hybrids makes classification of individuals unreliable, especially from wild-living ferret populations [37, 38, 99]. At population level, greater postorbital breadth and cranial volume in polecat correlates with darker pelage and shorter throat patch length [100].

FIELD SIGNS
Footprints: Difficult to distinguish from those of mink [1177], and identical to ferret. Commonest gait, arched-back gallop, in which hindfeet placed in same position as forefeet and tracks in groups of 2. Average stride in this gait 40–60 cm. When walking, feet placed singly astride median line with 20–25 cm between each track. When bounding at speed, body stretches out more and pattern of 4 prints rectangular, rhomboid or irregular.

Faeces: Scats long, cylindrical, twisted and

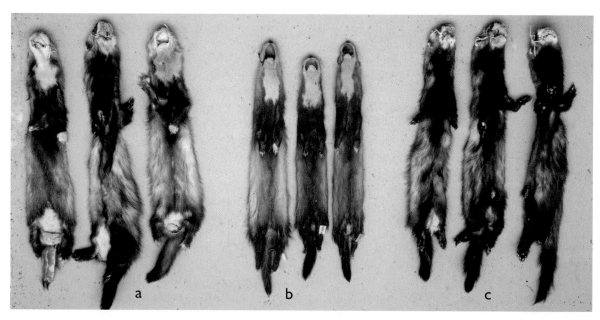

Fig. 9.44 Skins of polecats from Cumbria (a) and Herefordshire (c) compared with captive-bred polecat–ferret hybrids (b); hybrids usually have an extensive cream chin patch (*photo © The Trustees of the National Museums of Scotland*).

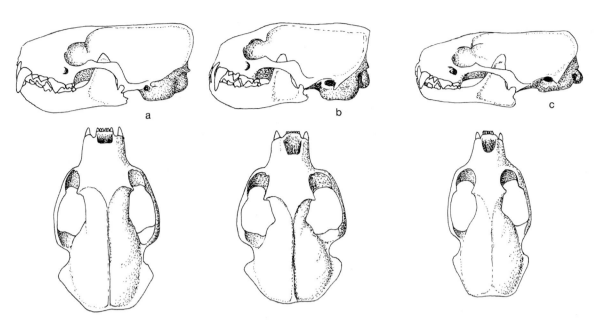

Fig. 9.45 Skulls of (a) polecat, (b) ferret and (c) American mink, showing 'waisted' interorbital region of ferret and mink, and narrower muzzle, more elongate, shallower skull in mink (*drawn by D.W. Yalden*).

tapering to one end, coiling slightly as dropped, 5–9 mm in diameter and up to 70 mm long; looser if polecat has fed on frogs. Blackish, especially when fresh, but colour varies with diet. Fresh droppings bear characteristic musky odour, but not used as markers. Deposited inconspicuously in latrine associated with den [100]. Pungent anal scent-marks (sometimes visible as smears) of independent origin. Distinguished from faeces of stoats and weasels by greater size; difficult to distinguish from mink faeces because size, smell and contents similar (except where mink prey heavily on fish).

Dens usually simple and occupied opportunistically; vary from casual resting places above ground to self-excavated lairs (unrecorded in GB) with compartments [443]. Opportunistically used dens (e.g. rabbit burrows in GB) typically show no evidence of polecat occupation [100]. Collection of dried vegetation as bedding occasionally observed. In winter, often dens in buildings and haystacks. Latrines associated with winter haystack dens, uncovered as hay removed to feed stock [100].

Feeding remains: Cranium of prey often bitten through at base. Heads of toads not eaten because of poison glands. Frog ovary masses also rejected. Birds' eggs opened in characteristic way (large, jagged, square opening bitten in side) and eggshells may bear marks of canines. Prey usually carried to nearest burrow but may be cached among vegetation. Some feeding remains of mink may be indistinguishable from polecat due to similar size and predatory behaviour.

DESCRIPTION

Long, sinuous, cylindrical body, relatively short legs, long neck, small, flattish head, blunt face and small, broadly rounded ears. During autumn–early winter lays down subcutaneous fat and appears tubby. Marked sexual dimorphism in size (male larger) and some difference in shape of muzzle (thicker in male), sexes otherwise alike. Eyes small with dark brown iris; facial vibrissae long; tail furry, slightly bushy and comparatively short. Hind toes long, slightly webbed and bear weakly curved, non-retractile claws 4 mm long; front claws 6 mm long, strongly curved and partially retractile. Plantar and palmar tubercles bare in summer and furred in winter; soles always thickly furred.

Pelage: Coat contains both underfur and guard hairs. Proportion of these types of hairs varies between juvenile and summer coats, when density of underfur and guard hairs reduced, and adult winter coat. Underfur mostly buff but greyish over shoulders and forelimbs, rump and hindlimbs and on tail. Coarser guard hairs pigmented (dark brown to purplish black with iridescent sheen) almost to base. Fine structure illustrated in [281, 1279]. Guard hair width 100–125 μm (cf. 8–20 μm for underfur), with medullary index of 0.70–0.85.

In winter coat underfur much longer (25 mm vs 15 mm), denser and whiter, except over extremities. Guard hairs much longer (up to 40 mm), distal half pigmented and basal half white. Also denseness of wool forces guard hairs to stand out and expose underfur. Back assumes whitish hue that may have camouflage value.

Contrasting light and dark facial markings

Table 9.15 Polecat: measurements of adults from study sites in Powys, upland mid-Wales (P) [113] and lowland W Midlands, England (WM) [1]

		Males			Females		
		Mean	Range	n	Mean	Range	n
Head and body length (mm)	P	398	330–450	28	367	335–385	14
	WM	418	362–450	40	357	318–388	30
Tail length (mm)	P	149	125–165	28	133	125–145	14
	WM	173	140–190	39	147	130–169	29
Ear length (mm)	P	26.1	22–29	28	22.7	21–24	14
	WM	26.2	21–29	40	24.0	19–27	20
Hindfoot length (mm)	P	60.4	53–68	28	53.1	51–58	14
	WM	63.3	57–69	40	53.9	57–69	20
Weight (g)	P	1111	800–1710	28	689	530–915	14
	WM	1439	995–1913	39	787	500–1123	30

distinctive. All polecats have white ear margins, white chin patch extending on to muzzle and white cheek patches (Plate 8). Mask appears in young *c*.9th week, firstly as 2 white patches between eyes and ears which elongate towards jaw angle as animal grows older. In winter, both adults and juveniles show variation in development of white frontal band that appears across forehead to unite cheek patches. Sometimes cheek patches join but more often remain separated by grizzled area. May also develop downwards to join up with chin patch and form complete ring, although this may be common and often more extensive in feral ferrets and introgressive hybrids.

Moult: 2 main moult periods, in spring and autumn, but cyclic moulting continues through summer months [117]. Winter coat normally replaced by darker summer pelage by May–June; winter coat re-grown fully by late October–early November [1045].

Skull: Robust and rather flat, with short rostrum, short, broad braincase and long, nearly parallel-sided, postorbital constriction (Fig. 9.44) [942, 1400]. Juvenile cranium pear-shaped, with greater cranial capacity, slight postorbital constriction, short nasal region, small tympanic bullae, rough surface, poorly developed crests and obvious sutures. May not reach final dimensions until 3rd year [563].

Teeth: Upper canines long, narrow and almost

straight; lower canines recurved at front. A proportion of adult skulls have asymmetrical dentition, most often supernumerary incisors [1131], perhaps due to recent addition of ferret genes [77]. Tooth wear can be severe in older animals, may prevent proper feeding; 2 patterns of attrition have been identified [86].

Baculum: Weight and shape used to separate male juveniles up to age 7 months from adults [1333]. In adult, has expanded knobbly base, tapering shaft and hooked tip. Shape and size of baculum differs considerably in juveniles but above *c*.300 mg becomes indistinguishable from that of adults.

Scent glands: Anal glands are paired spherical bodies at base of tail; secrete foetid creamy musk.

Chromosomes: 2n = 40, FNa = 64 [1441].

RELATIONSHIPS
Analysis of mtDNA reveals limited interspecific variation between *Mustela putorius*, ferret *M. furo*, steppe polecat *M. eversmannii*, and European mink *M. lutreola*, with possible recent speciation of *lutreola* and *putorius*; outside this Palearctic group, American black-footed ferret *M. nigripes* another close relative with *c*.1% sequence divergence in the cytochrome b gene. Molecular phylogeny within this group unclear [268], might even be considered conspecific [888]. Possible hybrids between *eversmannii* and *putorius* reported [994] with diploid

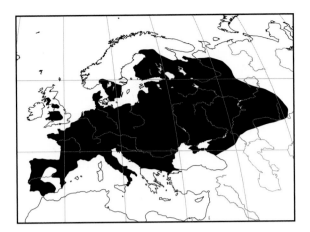

Fig. 9.46 Polecat *Mustela putorius*: world range.

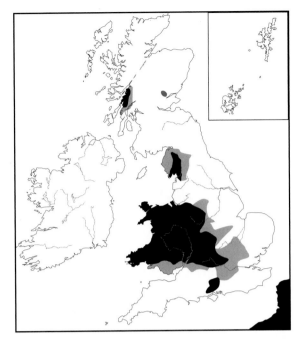

Fig. 9.47 Polecat *Mustela putorius*: range in GB.

chromosome number 39 [457]. Hybridisation between *putorius* and *lutreola* in E Europe implicated in decline of latter [269, 822, 884].

In GB, polecat cytochrome *b* haplotype differs by single base transition substitution from ferret haplotype. Geographical distribution suggests 2 mitochondrial lineages, derived from Welsh polecat and domestic ferret respectively [268]. Introgressive hybrids frequent in some areas; presence of the ferret cytochrome *b* gene in polecats indicates matings generally between male polecats and female ferrets. However, natural selection expected to favour polecat phenotype because ferret poorly equipped to survive in wild following domestication [100, 1049]. Genetic structure of European populations described [1028].

MEASUREMENTS

See Table 9.15. Body weight varies seasonally; males are in poorest condition from April to June, females lightest from July to September [1358]. Mean male:female dimorphism in body weight is 1.61. Further skull dimensions and proportions quoted in [38, 942, 1039].

VARIATION

Overall, geographic variability slight, subspecies not recognised [153]. In GB, larger in lowland landscapes (Table 9.15). Some difference in average size between British and European samples [259, 439]. Formerly 2 endemic subspecies described from British Isles, *Putorius p. anglius* Pocock 1936 and *P. p. caledoniae* Tetley 1939, but distinctions not valid [251, 1045].

Occasionally black pigment in guard hairs replaced by reddish tone ('red' or erythristic variety). Initially most British erythristic records from a restricted area of W Wales, 1st record 1903 [404]; several reported by 1950s [899] but few since: only 3 recorded in 1990s, one from Carmarthenshire and 2 from Oxfordshire [711]. Erythristic animals noted in other parts of European range, e.g. Bulgaria, W Russia [1299, 1400]. Red and normal colour varieties may occur together in same litter [1031]; red genetically recessive to normal black [1034]. Dark, mink-like form reported from France [814, 816], where genetic divergence linked to habitat diversity [821].

In GB, regional variation in pelage colour especially from introgression with feral ferrets. Animals with one or more hybrid features (e.g. generally paler pelage, broad pale frontal band, extended pale throat patches, pale fur on toes and a scattering of white guard hairs on hind limbs and tail) encountered especially at fringes of range and in isolated populations where polecats may fail to encounter wild mates [99].

DISTRIBUTION

Widespread in W Europe (Fig. 9.46), though distribution more patchy in S [948]. In several parts of range, status uncertain or evidence of population decline (e.g. [45]; review [99]). Overlaps with and replaced by steppe polecat in E Europe and European Russia. Despite earlier claims [173], European polecat does not appear to occur in Africa [1012].

In GB, formerly widespread; range currently restricted following heavy persecution in late 19th–early 20th centuries. Accurate mapping of distribution in late 20th century hindered by occurrence of dark feral ferrets and assumptions that polecats confined to Wales. Naturally recovering range now covers most of Wales (including Anglesey, recolonised from mid-1990s) and English Midlands east to Peak District and the Home Counties (Fig. 9.47). Reintroductions since 1970 have re-established populations in Argyll [235], Perthshire, Cumbria, the Chilterns and central S England. Now more abundant, and occupies greater range, in England than in Wales [100]. Recent specimens from Caithness are probably reintroduced polecats or hybrids; unlikely to indicate survival since beginning of 20th century [1216]. Apparently never present in Ireland.

HISTORY

Oldest finds of *M. putorius* from Middle Pleistocene, Mosbach, Germany and Tornewton, England; also France [764, 1400]. Believed to be a relatively prompt Late Glacial recoloniser of C and N Europe [1217], though earliest genuine British fossils Neolithic [476], and linguistic evidence casts some doubt on native status [147]. Large Late Pleistocene form, originally regarded as full species *Mustela robusta*, with skull 12% bigger than modern polecat, reported from cave deposits in Kent and Derbyshire [985, 986, 1420]. History prior to 1800 poorly documented, but evidently widespread and common throughout England, Scotland and Wales. Despite various pressures, maintained distribution until middle 19th century, when numbers fell and range reduced. Decline correlated with development of sporting estates [769] rather than clearance of woodland. Decline probably hastened by demand for fur, resulting in increasing prices as polecat became scarcer [1101]. Last definite record for Scotland 1914 at Inverpolly, Wester Ross (NMS specimen), but later unconfirmed records in 1916 (Rhidorroch, Wester Ross) 1928 (Morvern, Argyll) 1941 (Brahan, Easter Ross) and 1959 (Braemore, Wester Ross); most of these may have been feral ferrets or hybrids [926, 1285]. A few possibly survived in isolated parts of England until the 1930s. Population minimum probably reached 1915. Survived in C Wales and Herefordshire/Shropshire, where little game-keeping. Even there suffered heavy losses in gin traps used for commercial rabbit-trapping. World War I led to decline in gamekeeping, to which polecat responded with increase in numbers and range [899].

Sustained range expansion followed changes in 1950s: commercial rabbit trapping no longer economic after arrival of myxomatosis, and associated trapping-out of ground predators stopped. Gin traps banned by 1958 legislation. The Wildlife and Countryside Act 1981 afforded further, limited protection (see Chapter 4). Recovering rabbit populations fuelled faster recovery from 1970s, with main British range expanding at estimated 3–4 km/year [95], augmented by translocations which re-established populations elsewhere (see Distribution above). Continued recolonisation of former range anticipated, though rate and pattern of expansion may be influenced by threats from road traffic, lethal trapping, intensive agriculture and rodenticide poisoning [92–95, 99, 987, 1013, 1171, 1172, 1174]. Present distribution in GB more than double the area recorded in 1980 [99].

HABITAT

Occupies wide range of habitats, with no strong selection apparent in GB, though general association with lowlands apparent. Commonly associated with wetlands and riparian vegetation in Europe [815, 1121]. Radio-tracking on lowland farmland, W England, revealed greatest preference for woodland edge, farm buildings and field boundaries; least preferred were open fields and suburban areas [100]. Innate preference for habitats providing dense cover and shelter from view suggested by one study [1359]. Some evidence of association with areas of high rabbit abundance [100].

Association with farm buildings in winter linked to abundance of rodent prey (rats and mice), may lead to secondary rodenticide poisoning [94]. Rubbish tips similarly favoured habitat. In extreme climates, may use buildings in winter as response to thermoregulatory problems [1361]. May visit buildings on edge of settlements and, occasionally, enter small towns. Found near the centre of Aberystwyth [1048], Bangor [115] and Llandrindod Wells [113]; in Europe, even found in cities. However, high traffic-related mortality may prevent establish-ment of populations near British towns and cities [100].

SOCIAL ORGANISATION AND BEHAVIOUR

European polecat, ferret and hybrids differ in behaviour [1049]. Polecats are quick, nervous, easily frightened by people but habituate quickly to rustling noises, whereas ferrets easy to handle, resemble juvenile polecats in behaviour. Hybrids show intermediate characteristics.

Home range and denning: Studied by live trapping and radio-tracking in C Wales [113] and W England [94, 100]. Home-range characteristics variable according to season, habitat (prey availability), sex and social status. Breeding females settle into discrete home range; breeding males and dispersing juveniles more mobile, with fluid home ranges. Dispersal movements up to 10 km recorded. Mean home range 101 ha in C

Table 9.16 Polecat: home-range characteristics of individuals radio-tracked in mid-Powys (P) [113] and Herefordshire/Worcestershire, W England (HW) [99]

| | Males | | | | Females | | | |
| | P (n = 14) | | HW (n = 9) | | P (n = 7) | | HW (n = 4) | |
	Mean	Range	Mean	Range	Mean	Range	Mean	Range
Home range area (ha)	119	18–355	212	16–500	64	29–83	125	25–375
Max. linear distance within home range (km)	1.8	0.7–4.3	2.3	1.2–4.3	1.3	1.1–1.5	1.65	0.7–2.9
Number of dens	5.3	2–11	10.75	4–22	4.6	1–6	10	7–12

Wales, 183 ha in Herefordshire/Worcestershire. Male home ranges typically larger than female (Table 9.16). Each individual uses several dens distributed throughout home range. One radio-tagged male used 22 dens in 27 days [100]. Rabbit warrens most frequently used category of den (see Table 9.17), often associated with predation on occupants. In the English study, rabbit warrens a major focus of polecat activity, accounting for 50% of all radio fixes. In winter, farm buildings and haystacks commonly used for foraging and as daytime resting sites. Dens occupied either temporarily or for long periods. Breeding females limited to single den when rearing young.

Intrasexual spacing of home ranges, although territorial behaviour weakly developed compared with other small mustelids [115, 813]; intrasexual tolerance occasionally recorded at sites with high prey density [100]. Intersexual territory overlap ascribed to breeding factors.

Table 9.17 Polecat: den types used by radio-tracked individuals in mid Powys (P) (n = 20) [113] and Herefordshire/Worcestershire (HW) (n = 13) [99]. Figures are percentages

	P (n = 106)	HW (n = 186)
Rabbit warren	49	80
Badger sett/ other burrow	24	–
Log/brushwood pile	12	–
Couch in vegetation	6	–
Tree base/rock crevice	5	2
Human artefact (barn, haystack etc.)	5	18

Otherwise solitary with no direct contact. Limited cohesive behaviour established in captivity but no hierarchy. Little evidence of active marking of territories with scats. Territories vacated voluntarily and often not refilled [113]. Play, fighting and other interactions well studied in captives (e.g. [1046, 1047]).

Movements and activity: Movements categorised into short foraging excursions (usually concentrated around one den), inter-den movements and more extensive shifts/expansions of range. Most stays at one den about 1 day (mean 26.6 h). Males undertook longer inter-den movements. Nightly foraging routes typically covered 3–4 km (max. *c*.8 km). Home ranges rarely regularly patrolled. Radio-tracked polecats predominantly or exclusively nocturnal [46, 100], although bouts of diurnal behaviour reported [566]. Limited diurnal activity in English study, mainly involved animals underground in rabbit warrens or above ground in dense cover [100]. Activity correlated principally with that of prey [817, 820]; suppressed by availability of food surpluses, also modified by weather. Average time spent foraging greater for females (4.2 h/day) than males (mean 3.0 h/day) [115]. Male activity increases February–April during mating season. Females show increased activity and greater diurnality in midsummer when feeding young. Both sexes less active in midwinter [45, 100].

Normally walks with ambling gait, body fully stretched out, almost level, and head held low. Heels placed flat on ground, tail trails downwards and pelvic region is highest point of body. When moving faster, back repeatedly arched, giving sinuous appearance to gait. When hunting, moves with large jumps. Can penetrate relatively small openings owing to flexibility of body. Can climb, but rarely does; has little springing agility and judges distance poorly. Sometimes described as semi-aquatic and good swimmer, but in GB at least

Table 9.18 Polecat: diet in GB, based on 558 scats from 20 radio-tagged animals in mid Powys, Wales [113] and the stomach contents of 83 road casualties from the English Midlands [99]

Prey category	Percentage bulk estimate in diet	
	Wales	**English Midlands**
Lagomorphs[a]	36.5	85.4
Wood mouse	14.8	1.0
Bank vole	10.6	0.3
Field vole	5.7	1.7
Other mammals[b]	6.9	2.4
Total mammals	74.5	90.8
Galliformes	7.6	-
Passeriformes	4.2	0.03
Columbiformes	2.3	2.4
Other birds[c]	5.2	0.1
Total birds	19.3	2.6
Amphibians	6.0	4.6
Fish	–	0.01
Invertebrates	0.3	1.8

[a]All lagomorphs in stomach samples were rabbits.
[b]Includes hedgehog, shrew, mole, bat, common rat, squirrel, polecat.
[c]Includes Anseriformes, Gruiformes, waders, gulls.

rarely ventures directly into water.

Olfaction: Relative amount of the active constituents of anal gland secretions species-specific to polecat [143]. Odour strong and unpleasant, used for scent-marking and defence [343]. Volatile, pungent scent extruded as reflex action if frightened or injured.

Vocalisations: Adults normally silent but possess wide variety of calls. Divided into threat and molesting calls, squeal/shriek defensive/submissive calls and begging, greeting and appeasement calls [451]. Make clucking and chattering sounds when relaxed. Hiss and scream when frightened to disconcert enemy. Young emit distress calls.

Senses: Capable of localising sounds very accurately, reacts quickly to slight noises. Keen sense of smell used in hunting, recognising territory and finding mate [1417]. Picks up and follows scent trails on ground, but also sensitive to windborne scents [974]. Eyesight in daytime not good; better at night, particularly in relation to moving objects [974, 1169]. More sensitive to light intensity than colour but can distinguish red from blue or green [429]; 15 rods/cone [1048].

FEEDING

Diet: Studied in C Wales and Herefordshire by analysis of scats from radio-tagged animals [94, 113], and in Wales and English Midlands through analysis of stomach contents [100] Winter diet of animals using Herefordshire farmyards dominated by common rats. Diet more heavily dominated by rabbits in lowland England (Table 9.18). Food very varied but mainly vertebrate and dominated by mammals. Some food taken as carrion. Birds' eggs, fish and a variety of invertebrates, notably earthworms, recorded. Plant material taken only incidentally. Eels may be caught by polecats in GB. Feeding strategy opportunistic, prey taken roughly in proportion to season and relative abundance. Variations in diet of different age classes insignificant. High degree of association between male and female diets but dietary overlap varies seasonally; greatest in spring and least in summer [113]. European studies confirm polecat as a generalist feeder with the flexibility to specialise on particular groups (notably rodents, lagomorphs and anurans) where prey abundance permits (review [818]).

Predatory behaviour: Movement of prey is important stimulus [33]. Smell may also serve as stimulus for prey selection [34]. Prey stalked and seized with canines, then killed by neck bite that is instinctive [442, 1417] but perfected by practice [343]. Commonly kills adult rabbits and rats, is capable of killing animals as large as a goose or hare. Caches food [1074], often large numbers of frogs or toads, in times of excess [443]; these are bitten at base of skull so that paralysed but not killed, remain fresh; this may be a special technique [1417] or a chance effect.

BREEDING

Seasonal breeder, 1 litter of 5–10 kits born usually in May–June, after gestation of 40–43 days (Fig. 9.48). Both sexes sexually mature and begin to breed in year following birth. Wild females probably in oestrus from late March. Captive females have remained in oestrus for up to 6 weeks when unmated, but this unlikely in the wild. Climate and latitude may affect the timing of breeding [258]. Lips of vulva become engorged.

Spermatogenesis: In England, January–September [112]. Testes heaviest and sperm most abundant March–May [1336] Mature corpora lutea recorded in ovaries of females in England March–August, but sample size small [112]. There is no courtship.

Mating behaviour: Vigorous, male grasping female by neck and dragging her about. This acts as a stimulus to induced ovulation. Copulation lasts up to 1 h. Probably promiscuously polygamous, each male mating with several females. No delayed implantation. Gestation 40–43 days [550]. Most born late May–early June, though some records from early May, W England [99]. Exceptionally, births may occur as early as March or as late as October [1362]. Although only 1 litter usual, there is the potential to reproduce again if litter lost and this may explain late births [1284].

Nipples: Difficult to locate in non-lactating animals. Number of active nipples (max. 10) does not correspond to number of offspring [113]. Litter size 2–12 (usually 5–10), <7 on average surviving to weaning. 69% of May–July female road casualties in W England lactating [99].

Young: Weigh 9–10 g at birth, head and body length 55–70 mm, tail length 14–15 mm [480]. Eyelids and ears closed. Week-old kits have thin covering of silky, white hair. Replaced when 3–4 weeks old with cinnamon brown-greyish woolly coat. Ear tips and parts of muzzle retain whiteness. By 50 days, have assumed more typical appearance with characteristic facial markings.

Weaning: Begins at 3 weeks. Eyes open at beginning of 5th week, when sexes of equal size. Subsequently, the males grow faster. Eruption of permanent dentition begins at 7–8 weeks and completed by 11–13 weeks [480]. Juveniles reach adult proportions in the late autumn of the year of birth. Achieve independence when 2–3 months old. Usually first appearance of young is when 'families' of mother and dependent young appear (typically June–July in GB).

POPULATION

Sampling of British populations by live trapping suggests mean winter density of $0.9/km^2$. Populations apparently sparser or more patchy towards fringes of current GB range [93, 99, 1268]. European data indicate similar range of population densities, with sparser populations at high altitude [1360]. Population density estimates (Table 9.19) combined with distribution data suggest minim-um GB population of >38 000 in late 1990s, numbers in England now greater than in Wales (Table 9.20) (estimate of 15 000 [536] considered low even then, and range since expanded further). Life expectation of males at birth, 8.1 months [1334], 80% dying before reproducing [1362]. Lifespan 8–10 years, rarely 13–14 years, in captivity; 4–5 years more probable in wild. For wild polecats of known age in Switzerland, very few >4 years, up to max. 8 years [1362]. Some suggestion that polecats susceptible to cold, but not supported by thermoregulatory properties: polecat's reaction to cold similar to that of mink and stoat, which have more northerly distributions [728].

MORTALITY

Ferocity and powerful scent protect polecat from most larger predators. Sometimes killed by dogs, possibly also by foxes and raptors [408, 969]. Most recorded mortality in GB due to humans: in one sample, 86% were killed by road traffic or trapping, the remaining 14% by dogs, snares or shooting [1334]. Road casualties comprised 68% of 1990s records from English Midlands [95].

Most gamekeepers questioned within current range of species report killing up to 10 (exceptionally >40) polecats/year, often in tunnel traps set for other species [1013, 1268]. This level of mortality unlikely to affect population in core of range, where gamekeeper numbers low; could become significant towards fringes of range.

Secondary poisoning by anticoagulants probably common: up to 45% of animals vulnerable to exposure in one study in W England, up to 31% of road casualties contained detectable rodenticide residues [94, 987, 1171, 1172, 1174]. No evidence of serious contamination by organo-

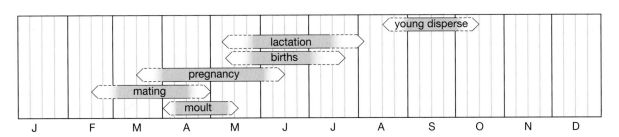

Fig. 9.48 Polecat: annual cycle.

Table 9.19 Polecat: population density data based on live trapping in 136 1-km squares in Wales, the English Midlands and Cumbria in the 1990s [99]

	Individuals trapped /km²		% of 1km squares in which polecats (+ve squares)		Individuals trapped/+ve1km²	
	Mean	Range	Mean	Range	Mean	Range
Core of range[a]	1.01	0–6	57.1	33.3–68.75	1.8	1–6
Fringe of range[b]	0.69	0–4	31.1	0.0–50	2.2	1–4
Whole range	0.9	0–6	48.5	0.0–68.75	1.86	1–6

[a] Caernarvon, Denbigh, Flint, Cheshire, Merioneth, Montgomery, Salop, Cardigan, Radnor, Brecon, Carmarthen and Hereford.
[b] The remaining counties within the polecat's range in S Wales, the English Midlands and Cumbria.

Table 9.20 Polecat: minimum GB population estimate, based on 2 mean population densities across the 473 hectads (10-km squares) recorded as occupied in 1997 [99]

	N 'core' hectads @ 101 polecats/square	N 'fringe' hectads @ 69 polecats/square	Min. population
Scotland	0	6 (+2 at 50%)[a]	483
Wales	134 (+ 27 at 50%)[a]	36 (+9 at 50%)[a]	17 691
England	73	186	20 207
Total	207 (+ 27 at 50%)[a]	228 (+11 at 50%)[a]	38 381

[a] 10-km squares containing substantial areas of sea are assigned a population estimate reduced by 50%.

chlorines or heavy metals in GB [1, 633], though high PCB concentrations reported from polecats elsewhere [895]. Fumigation ('gassing') of rabbit burrows with toxic gas likely to kill polecats using them as resting sites [94], though impossible to monitor population effects.

Polecats especially vulnerable to road traffic in GB, perhaps due to association with lowland landscapes where traffic densities highest, combined with tendency to forage for carrion and live prey along relatively prey-rich roadside habitat corridors through intensive farmland. Road casualties peak in March (breeding males) and September–October (dispersing juveniles). Sex ratio of road casualties over whole year 2.4 males:1 female. Only in June (main lactation and weaning period) did females outnumber male road casualties in one study [100]. Typically >50% of deaths occur in 4 months August– November [100, 1335], when young recruited to population and suffer heavy mortality. Some evidence that mortality in areas of high traffic density hinders establishment of populations [100].

PARASITES

Ectoparasites: Fleas: cat flea *Ctenocephalides felis* is very common on captive animals, including ferrets. *Archaeopsylla erinacei, Nosopsyllus fasciatus, Paraceras melis* are among several species recorded infrequently but none specific [1337]. Tick *Ixodes hexagonus* is commonest ectoparasite, sometimes in large numbers, especially on neck and behind ears; *I. canisuga* also recorded [1337]. Biting louse *Trichodectes jacobi* is known from polecat, but not in GB.

Endoparasites: Cestodes *Taenia tenuicollis, T. martis* (stomach and intestine); nematodes *Molineus patens, Strongyloides papillosus, Capilliaria putorii* (intestine/stomach), *Filaroides martis* (lungs), *Skjrabingylus nasicola* (nasal and ethmoid sinuses, causing abnormal bone growth) [787].

Diseases: Suffers from distemper, influenza, colds and pneumonia; occasionally malignant tumours [440] or hydrocephaly [591]. Broken teeth common. Abscesses on jaw and around head and neck rarer but often fatal. In Europe, carrier of trichinosis [875], leptospirosis [389], toxoplasmosis [1225] and adiaspiromycosis [736]. High incidence of rabies in polecats in localised areas of Europe [6].

RELATIONS WITH HUMANS

Awareness and understanding of species in GB limited, due to nocturnal habit, long-term absence from most populous areas, lack of representation in popular culture and confusion with ferret. Even where well established, many farmers and landowners unaware of presence [92, 99, 1013].

Unsavoury image rooted in Middle Ages, when the term 'polecat' was used to describe vile persons and prostitutes. Reputation as vermin and a wanton killer of poultry led to bounty payments for polecats and other predators, and many records appear in parish accounts [596]. Society now generally more tolerant, though antipathy persists in some sectors. Polecats may cause damage if poor husbandry allows access to poultry houses or pheasant pens. Greatest conflict with game-rearing: most gamekeepers regard polecat as a pest and wish to be free to control it. Impact on agriculture negligible, and positive role in controlling rabbits and rodents recognised. Farmers' concerns relate mainly to threat to game; associated intolerance greater towards fringe of species' range. Methods of killing or taking now restricted (see Chapter 4), although there is no ban on disturbing the animal or destroying dens. Trapping illegal without licence, although licensing system ignored and polecats still trapped in many areas [1013].

Formerly hunted with hounds in Wales, Devon and Westmorland. Large numbers were once caught in GB for the fur trade and in Europe to supply London auctions [1101]. Pelts highly valued when polecat made scarce.

Many 'polecats' in zoos and in photographs in field guides and magazines etc. are hybrids with ferrets, adding to confusion about recognition of the species. Ferret-keepers show great interest in the polecat as the wild ancestor of their domestic stock. Many ferret shows have a 'polecat' class for polecat-like ferrets. Wild-caught polecats increasingly available, and commonly crossed with ferrets to produce very dark, polecat-like animals that may be difficult to handle.

Focus on biodiversity restoration has led to recognition of polecat's recovery as a conservation success story.

LITERATURE

Comprehensive bibliography and review of all aspects of biology [114]; summary of recent studies in GB of distribution, abundance, relations with ferrets, and basic ecology in lowland England [99]; popular account [1198].

AUTHORS

J.D.S. Birks & A.C. Kitchener

Feral ferret *Mustela furo*

Mustela furo Linnaeus, 1758; 'Africa'.
'Polecat' (sometimes) when dark coloured; polecat-ferret when dark or hybrid with *M. putorius*; fitch, etc. (see section on polecat, above); *ffured* (Welsh); *feòcullan* (Scottish Gaelic).

Male – dog or hob; female – bitch or jill; young – kits.

RECOGNITION

Similar in size and proportions to polecat [27, 99, 114–116]. Darkest forms may be indistinguishable in the field. Generally pelage either albino, or like that of polecat but much paler, as if the pigment has been washed out (Plate 8), and with more extensive white or cream on face and throat [99]. Many feral ferrets and hybrids have a distinctive throat patch (Fig. 9.44), like that of pine marten, one or more white feet, white hairs interspersed among the body fur; dark fur does not reach the nose, often a broad pale frontal band which produces a discrete mask of darker fur sur-rounding the eyes [99]. Eyes of albinos are pink.

Skull: Narrower postorbital constriction and smaller cranial volume (Fig. 9.45), although these measurements overlap with polecat skulls [99].

SIGN AND DESCRIPTION

Similar to polecat except for pelage coloration and skull characteristics described above [99, 114–116]. However, distinct behavioural differences from polecat: not fearful of people, does not habituate to rustling sounds, slow and docile [1049].

Moult: Twice per year; summer coat shed in October and winter coat shed in April, but cyclic moulting continues through summer months [117, 1045].

MEASUREMENTS

See Table 9.21.

RELATIONSHIPS

Domesticated from western polecat, *M. putorius*, based on morphological, cytological and molecular studies [268, 1037, 1087, 1330]; frequently suggested in past that eastern or steppe polecat, *M. eversmannii*, could also have been ancestral [114, 211, 942, 943, 1012]; denied by more recent data. Ferrets treated formally as a distinct species [227, 424], distinguished from western polecat, but could be considered conspecific, differences probably due entirely to selective breeding.

Table 9.21 Ferret: measurements of feral animals from South Uist and Shetland. All specimens are in National Museums of Scotland collections

		South Uist		Shetland	
		Male	Female	Male	Female
n		10	12	57	29
Head and body length (mm)	Mean	407.8	338.0	403.4	355.0
	Range	390–430	305–366	350–432	319–406
Tail length (mm)	Mean	139.8	120.2	168.5	145.1
	Range	123–156	101–135	140–188	125–161
Hindfoot length (mm)	Mean	61.7	50.6	62.6	53.3
	Range	58–67	46–57	53–70	50–60
Ear length (mm)	Mean	26.7	21.4	26.2	23.6
	Range	20–33	19–25	21–30	20–27
Weight (g)	Mean	1512	740	1276	706
	Range	1288–1789	496–972	711–1816	512–1094

VARIATION

Feral populations very variable in pelage coloration. For example, in Shetland, vary from albino to very dark, but always distinguishable from polecats [99]. Little or no evidence to suggest that long-standing populations develop greater morphological uniformity as has happened in New Zealand [909], and no evidence for reversion to the wild type [99]. Supernumerary upper incisors are not unusual [1, 87].

DISTRIBUTION

Ferrets are widely kept; escaped or abandoned animals could be found almost anywhere, so it is often difficult to determine whether feral populations have become established [99]. Many released animals probably have poor ability to survive. Most self-sustaining populations occur on islands, e.g. Sardinia, Sicily, New Zealand [784]. In British Isles, feral populations still viable 1990s, on Mull [1037, 1288], Lewis [394], North Uist, Benbecula and South Uist [503], Bute [432, 434], Arran [433, 434], Islay (10–15 introduced in 1979 to control rabbits [1002]), Shetland [1], Isle of Man [1051] and Jersey [881]. On mainland GB, apparently populations in N Yorkshire, Speyside, Renfrewshire, Argyll and possibly Caithness, but many records over the last 30 years, particularly in C England, are probably recolonising or reintroduced polecats [1, 99]. Ireland, 1 feral ferret population reported, Co. Monaghan [1202].

HISTORY

First mentioned, 350 BC, by Aristotle [1298]. In 1st century AD, Greek and Roman writers first mention the use of ferrets for bolting rabbits from their burrows, in the Balearics [1298]. Arrived in GB with the Normans, perhaps 11th century, certainly by 13th century, well established in 14th century [1012, 1298, 1420]. Widely kept today as pets or show animals and to hunt rabbits [1053].

HABITAT

Similar to polecat on mainland, and more probable as escapees in urban areas. On islands, on moorland, heathland, shores and other more open habitats than polecats on mainland.

SOCIAL ORGANISATION AND BEHAVIOUR

Probably similar to polecat [114–116]. Captive studies indicate that ferrets are not afraid of humans, do not habituate to sounds and show no fear or disorientation when introduced to unfamiliar environments, in contrast to polecats [1049]. Little studied as a feral animal in GB, except for diet, reproductive biology and variation in skulls and pelages from trapped animals or road casualties [99, 112, 711]; trapping used to investigate population dynamics in New Zealand [771].

FEEDING

In Shetland, stomach contents mainly ground-nesting birds (29% volume; 31% of stomachs), rabbits (29% volume; 21% of stomachs) and small mammals (19% volume; 17% of stomachs) [711]. In New Zealand, 87% of scats contained rabbit, and birds and invertebrates were other significant prey items [1076].

BREEDING
In Shetland males fecund February–September, females pregnant February–September [112]. A single oestrus, March–September, if no mating [312]. Ovulation 30 h after mating [313], and only 1 litter/year [771]. Gestation 40–43 days, usual litter size 6–7 (range 1–15) [27, 550]. Young born blind, covered in fine white fur; replaced after 3 days by grey hair in fitch ferrets and white hair in albinos; sensitive to sounds at 32 days, eyes begin to open at 34 days, begin to take solid food at 4–5 weeks, weaned at 6–8 weeks [27]. Young independent at 5–7 months [27].

RELATIONS WITH HUMANS
Ferrets have been bred for bolting rabbits for >2000 years [1298]. Introduced to New Zealand since 1870 to control rabbits; many thousands were shipped from London between 1882 and 1884; these possibly included some polecats from Europe [909]. Feasibility of using ferrets in the biological control of rabbits investigated, but found to be of value only at a local level [430, 431]. Ferrets introduced to Islay 1979 [1002], and Shetland 1986, to control rabbits, although present in Shetland before then (specimens in NMS). Suspected to be important vectors of bovine TB in New Zealand, with an incidence of 11.9% [1077, 1078].

Traditional unsavoury image countered in UK by growing ferret welfare movement and interest in keeping animals as pets. Ferret-breeders often produce hybrids with wild polecats to increase their aggressiveness for hunting rabbits and also to improve the wild characteristics for the polecat class at ferret shows [927]. These hybrids often difficult to handle, may not be suited to captivity in ferret cages. Many ferrets are abandoned or escape each year; prospects for survival poor, especially where sympatric with polecats [99].

AUTHORS
A.C. Kitchener & J.D.S. Birks

American mink *Mustela vison*
Mustela vison Schreber, 1777; E Canada.

RECOGNITION
Medium-sized mustelid, dark chocolate brown, may appear almost black (Plate 8). Usually a white chin patch; white patches on chest, belly and in groin. Tail slightly bushy, *c*.1/2 body length. Semi-aquatic. Similar size to polecat, but uniformly darker; much smaller than otter. (Not easily distinguished from European mink *Mustela lutreola* where co-occur, although *M. lutreola* generally smaller with more reddish fur, frequently possesses a white muzzle).

Skull: Similar to polecat (Fig. 9.45). Width of postorbital constriction <15 mm in the mink, greater in the polecat. Several features of skull and teeth larger in males than in females, the difference being greater than simply due to underlying difference in body size [1289].

FIELD SIGNS
Footprints: The most useful indicator of presence [120], because animal habitually follows soft margins of waterways: 2.5–4.0 cm long × 2–4 cm wide, depending upon softness of substrate and sex (male prints larger than female) (Fig. 9.2). Toes radiate from a lobed, central pad, giving prints a characteristic splayed 'star' shape, best seen in soft mud. Often only 4 of 5 toes show. Each toe pad, with associated claw, leaves a slim, pear-shaped impression. Bounding gait often results in over-printing. Prints similar to polecat, usually more splayed.

Faeces: Cylindrical, with tapered ends, 5–8 cm long and usually 1 cm or less in diameter. Colour and consistency of faeces (known as scats) vary according to freshness and food taken; many dark green or brown. Fresh scats have an unpleasant fetid odour due to a covering of secretions from the proctodeal glands [142, 143]; deposited at dens and on prominent objects (rocks, tree roots, etc.) possibly to effect scent dissemination [1110]. Known to affect the behaviour of some prey species, e.g. water voles [72]. Otter faeces (spraints) found at similar sites, but have a looser consistency and a sweeter smell. Faeces of polecats very similar to those of mink, but unlikely to contain fish remains.

Prey remains: Larger prey items (e.g. birds, rabbits, fish) often stored in hollow trees or beneath rocks by the waterside. Dens may contain partly eaten remains of several prey items [97, 338, 1142]. Vertebrate prey usually killed by a bite to the back of the head or neck. The upper canines leave puncture marks 9–11 mm apart.

Table 9.22a Mink: measurements (excluding kits), from 2 study sites [186, 331]

	Males				Females			
	Mean	SD	Range	n	Mean	SD	Range	n
Rivers Otter, Teign, Devon								
Head and body length (mm)	397	24	330–450	39	338	10	320–360	29
Tail length (mm)	193	16	150–220	39	168	12	135–190	29
Ross Peninsula, S Scotland								
Head and body length (mm)	395	18	360–430	43	343	11	330–370	20
Tail length (mm)	181	19	150–220	43	157	10	140–180	20

DESCRIPTION

Pelage: Dark brown, appearing almost black, in wild type. Dark guard hairs protrude through slightly lighter underfur. White patches, spots, and sometimes only a few white hairs at chin, throat and on ventral surface. Experimental breeding from mutated individuals on fur farms has produced a variety of pelage colours such as Aleutian (white), Breath of Spring, Black Cross, light and dark Pastel, Palomino, Pearl, Platinum, Silver-Blue and Topaz. Offspring of later generations of wild mink vary in colour but most approximate to the wild, dark-brown type. Silver-Blue, a pale silvery grey colour, is 2nd most common colour in feral populations; comprised 3% of population trapped in Devon and 9% in S Scotland [91]. Older animals may develop areas of white flecking amongst the darker fur around the cheeks and nape of the neck, thought to grow from the sites of scars received during fighting and mating activity.

Moult: Twice per year, regulated by photoperiod. Development of summer pelage begins late March, completed mid July; shorter, less dense fur remains intact until mid August when development of winter pelage initiated. During succeeding 3 months, summer coat is shed and animals reach winter prime by about mid November [76, 317, 324].

Nipples: Difficult to detect outside breeding season; 1–8 palpable teats detected in lactating wild mink; number related to number of kits being suckled [186, 324].

Scent glands: Anal glands with paired sacs opening just inside the anus, and proctodeal glands which open into the rectum [142]. Suggested that odour of faeces due to secretion of proctodeal glands, since ducts from anal sacs close during defecation. Behaviour during scent-marking suggests ventral glands also present.

Teeth: Can show considerable variation in wear, particularly in coastal populations; hence not a useful indicator of age.

Chromosomes: 2n = 30, FNa = 54 [1441]. Assessment of genetic variability in captive and wild American mink has been made using microsatellite markers [83]. Identification of mink possible from DNA in faecal samples [497].

RELATIONSHIPS

Although the American and European mink are superficially very similar, studies [888, 1433] indicate that *M. lutreola* is more closely related to *M. sibirica* than to *M. vison*, and that *M. vison* the most distinctive species in the genus. Hybridisation (in captivity) with *M. lutreola*, and with polecat *M. putorius*, has been reported [1433,] although recorded that hybrid embryos between *M. vison* and *M. lutreola* are reabsorbed [1282]. Molecular studies suggest most isolated of *Mustela* spp., some recent accounts (including [1387]) assign to distinct genus *Neovison* (with extinct sea mink *N. macrodon*); this not considered justified, confirm *Mustela* as a distinctive monophyletic genus [888].

MEASUREMENTS

See Table 9.22. Males larger than females, sexual dimorphism ratio *c.*1.66–1.88:1 [1289]. Can be approximately aged using bacula [344], dentition [1024] and osteology [471]. Morphometric details have been presented for ranch-bred specimens [1021] and for feral animals [324, 855, 1378].

VARIATION

Feral mink in GB are derived from those bred on

Table 9.22b Mink: weights (g),from 3 sites in GB [186, 331]

Sex	Age	Mean	SD	Range	n
R. Otter, Devon					
Male	Adult	1232	–	1024–1439	2
	Juvenile	1009	187	685–1329	14
Female	Adult	665	94	559–778	7
	Juvenile	605	98	437–738	8
R. Teign, Devon					
Male	Adult	1153	–	850–1805	48
Female	Adult	619	–	450–810	32
Ross Peninsula, S Scotland					
Male	Adult	1121	172	840–1500	23
	Juvenile	987	157	690–120	17
Female	Adult	676	62	560–805	23
	Juvenile	630	66	500–745	11

fur farms in N America, thought to have been derived from 6 or more subspecies.

DISTRIBUTION

Native range covers most of N America, including the deciduous and coniferous zones and extending into the tundra (Fig. 9.49). Translocations associated with the fur trade have led to the establishment of feral populations widely across the Palaearctic, including Iceland, GB, Ireland, France, Spain, Germany, all Scandinavian countries and former USSR [122, 324]. American mink also been reported in Chile and Argentine Patagonia [1063]. Widespread in mainland GB and Ireland, though some areas remain incompletely colonised (Fig. 9.50). Occurs on a few islands, e.g. Harris, Lewis and Arran.

HISTORY

Imported to GB and bred on fur farms from 1929 onwards [91, 323, 1294]. Escapes or releases led to establishment of a self-sustaining feral population, Devon, by late 1950s [803] and others by early 1960s [248, 1294]. Not farmed in Ireland until early 1950s, so feral populations established there later [276, 383].

HABITAT

Normally associated with aquatic habitats, but may spend time elsewhere where suitable prey, such as rabbits, abundant [799, 1426]. Favours eutrophic streams and rivers with abundant bankside cover, and eutrophic lakes fringed with reedbeds and carr [18, 90, 183]. Less abundant on oligotrophic waters or where waterside cover sparse or absent [18, 91, 183]. Relatively dense populations may occur in undisturbed rocky coastal habitat with a broad littoral zone and nearby cover [123, 326.] Also may occur on estuaries [91], and on rivers and canals near urban areas if sufficient cover and prey available [90, 101]. Habitat requirements reviewed and evaluated [18] (although that model has been criticised [825]).

SOCIAL ORGANISATION AND BEHAVIOUR

Based on individual territories with minimal intrasexual overlap, often much overlap of territories held by animals of opposite sex [90, 185, 1422]. Territorial system appears to be unstable in suboptimal habitat [90, 183, 185]. Non-territorial transient individuals especially common during the spring mating season when many males vacate territories [90, 184, 428, 1429]. Mating system promiscuous, no pair-bonding [891, 1290]. Fighting between males common during mating season; this may result in loose, temporary dominance hierarchy governing access to receptive females [90].

Home range: Tends to be linear because activity is

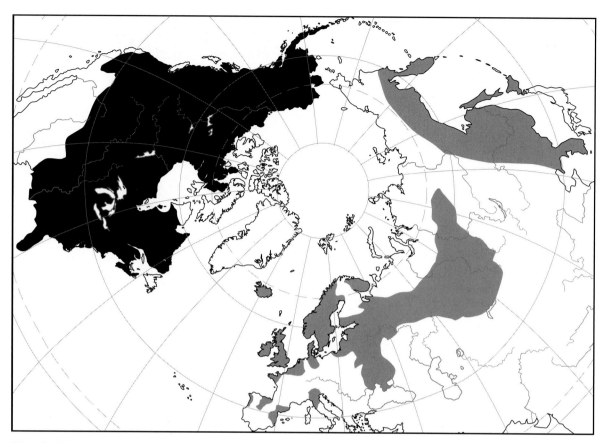

Fig. 9.49 American mink *Mustela vison*, native (black) and introduced (grey) range.

concentrated on water's edge [101, 326, 1422]. Ranges 1–6 km long, those occupied by males generally larger than those of females. Home ranges largest where social environment unstable due to absence of, or frequent removal of, neighbouring territory holders [101, 427, 1422]. Evidence suggests home-range size inversely related to habitat productivity [326]. Use of home range uneven, activity concentrated where prey season-ally abundant [90, 101]. May utilise several dens within home range, often located close to foraging area [101, 123, 1425]. Dens commonly situated within or beneath waterside trees, in rabbit burrows, among rocks or above ground in scrub or brush-piles; mink rarely excavate their own dens [90, 101, 1425]. Most dens <10 m from water [90, 1425]. Availability of den sites may limit populations [487].

Activity: Predominantly nocturnal or crepuscular, but may occur at any time [101, 324, 326, 426]. In one study, mink spent only 16% of time outside dens, though there were seasonal deviations from this mean [326]. Frequency and timing of foraging activity probably influenced by the activity and availability of prey [101, 123, 324, 426]. Level of activity generally depressed in winter relative to summer [101, 427].

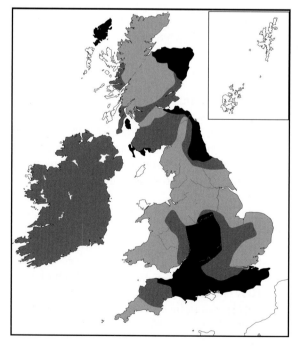

Fig. 9.50 American mink *Mustela vison*: density indicated by presence of sign in >20% (black), >10% (dark grey) and <10% of survey sites (*from [637]*).

490

Fig. 9.51 American mink, swimming very buoyantly, with half the body above water (cf. much larger otter, Fig. 9.25) (*photo B. Bevan/Ardea*).

Movements: Tends to show a patrolling pattern within the home range, with regular visits to boundaries [101, 427]. Insufficient data exist to determine dispersal distances accurately. However, one American study recorded a juvenile moving >50 km in <4 months [7]; studies in GB suggest that juveniles commonly disperse >10 km from birth places from August onwards [90, 183]. Movements made by rutting males during January–March also poorly understood, but available information suggests they may be extensive [ ]90].

Communication: Largely achieved by scent-marking involving jelly-like anal gland secretions which coat the faeces, and may also be deposited alone as a blob or smear by anal dragging on water [90, 142]. Behavioural observations suggest that glands in skin of throat and chest also used in scent-marking [90]. Volatile odours released from anal glands of alarmed animals may serve as an antipredator defence mechanism [142] and as a means of intimidating conspecifics during aggressive interactions [90].

Vocalisations: Normally confined to close encounters with conspecifics or threatening predators. Basic vocalisations analysed [435]; include piercing shrieks (fundamental frequency 325 Hz with overtones rising to 3 kHz, mean duration 1 s, max. intensity 20 dB) and hisses (fundamental frequency 600 Hz, mean duration 0.8 s) in response to threat [90, 435, 877]. During

mating season, both sexes may emit a muffled 'chuckling' sound (ranging up to 800 Hz) on meeting [347, 435]. Juvenile mink squeak repeatedly when separated from their mothers [90].

Aggressive behaviour: Range of threatening behaviour patterns shown during aggressive interactions described, including back-arching, erecting hairs on tail ('bottle-brushing') and lashing of the tail, stamping and scraping of the feet, 'broadside' threat postures and an open-mouth display [90, 877]. If dominance not established by threat displays, fighting may result, especially between males during mating season when aggression levels are high [877]. Fights may result in wounds to the head and neck region [90, 186], rarely fatal (e.g. [824]).

Locomotion: Commonest form on land is a bounding gait, speeds up to 6.5 km/h attained [1386]. Also climbs trees [770] and swims well. Fish and other aquatic prey are caught during underwater dives with chases of 5–20 s duration [322, 1050]. Underwater foraging efficiency investigated in laboratory studies [322, 328, 329]. More recently, time-depth data recorders have documented diving behaviour in the wild [549]. Generally dives to depths of *c.*30 cm, for *c.*10 s, but dives of up to 3 m and 60 s in duration have been recorded; some individuals dived 100 times/day [549]. Aquatic locomotion involves alternate use of all 4 limbs when swimming under water,

REFERENCES

1 Author's data.

2 Aarde, R.J. van (1980) The diet and feeding behaviour of feral cats, *Felis catus*, at Marion island. *South African Journal of Wildlife Research,* **10,** 123–128.

3 Aarde, R.J. van & Blumenberg, B. (1980) Genotypic correlates of body and adrenal weight in a population of feral cats *Felis catus. Carnivore,* **2**(4), 37–45.

4 Abramov, A.V. & Baryshnikov, G.F. (2000) Geographic variation and intraspecific taxonomy of weasel *Mustela nivalis* (Carnivora, Mustelidae). *Zoosystematica Rossica,* **8,** 365–402.

5 Achterberg, C. *et al.* (2000) Inventarisatie Van Boom-marternestbomen op de Utrechtse Heuvelrug 1992–1999. *Lutra,* **43,** 93–99 (in Dutch).

6 Adamovich, V.L. (1978) Landscape-ecological foundations of the local foci of rabic infection. *Zoologicheskii Zhurnal,* **57,** 260–271.

7 Adams, A.W. (1965) Mink movement study. *North Dakota State Game and Fish Department Report* No. 524.

8 Ahnlund, H. (1976) Age determination in the European badger *Meles meles* L. *Zeitschrift für Säugetierkunde,* **41,** 119–125.

9 Ahnlund, H. (1980) Sexual maturity and breeding season of the badger, *Meles meles,* in Sweden. *Journal of Zoology,* **190,** 77–95.

10 Ahnlund, H. (1980) *Aspects of the population dynamics of the badger* (Meles meles L.). Department of Zoology, University of Stockholm.

11 Akande, M. (1972) The food of feral mink (*Mustela vison*) in Scotland. *Journal of Zoology,* **167,** 475–479.

12 Albone, E.S. (1975) Dihydroactinidiolide in the supra-caudal scent gland secretions of the red fox. *Nature,* **256,** 575.

13 Albone, E.S. & Flood, P.F. (1976) The supracaudal scent gland of the red fox *Vulpes vulpes. Journal of Chemical Ecology,* **2,** 167–175.

14 Albone, E.S. & Fox, M.W. (1971) Anal gland secretion of the red fox. *Nature,* **233,** 569–570.

15 Albone, E.S. & Perry, G.C. (1975) Anal sac secretion of the red fox, *Vulpes vulpes;* volatile fatty acids and diamines: implications for a fermentation hypothesis of chemical recognition. *Journal of Chemical Ecology,* **2,** 101–111.

16 Albone, E.S. *et al.* (1974) The anal sac secretion of the red fox (*Vulpes vulpes*); its chemistry and microbiology. A comparison with the anal sac secretion of the lion (*Panthera leo*). *Life Sciences,* **14,** 387–400.

17 Aliev, F. (1974) The Caucasian black cat, *Felis silvestris caucasica* Satunin 1905. *Säugetierkundliche Mitteilungen,* **22,** 142–145.

18 Allen, A.W. (1983) *Habitat suitability index models: mink.* United State Department of Interior, Fisheries, and Wildlife Service Report No. FWS/OBS-83/10/61.

19 Allen, M. & Magris, L. Personal communication.

20 Alterio, N. *et al.* (1999) Trappability and densities of stoats (*Mustela erminea*) and ship rats (*Rattus rattus*) in a South Island *Nothofagus* forest, New Zealand. *New Zealand Journal of Ecology,* **23,** 95–100.

21 Amstislavsky, S. & Ternovskaya, Y. (2000) Reproduction in mustelids. *Animal Reproduction Science* **60–61,** 571–581.

22 Andersen, J. (1978) Mængdemæssige forhold i for-ekomsten af brud (*Mustela nivalis*) i forhold til lækat (*Mustela erminea*) i Danmark. *Natura Jutlandica,* **20,** 123–128 (in Danish).

23 Anderson, E. (1970) Quaternary evolution of the genus *Martes* (Carnivora, Mustelidae). *Acta Zoologica Fennica,* **130,** 1–132.

24 Anderson, R.M. & Trewhella, W.J. (1985) Population dynamics of the badger (*Meles meles*) and the epidemiology of bovine TB (*Mycobacterium bovis*). *Philosophical Transactions of the Royal Society of London Series B,* **310,** 327–381.

25 Andrews, E.M. & Crawford, A.K. (1986) *Otter survey of Wales 1984–85.* Vincent Wildlife Trust, London.

26 Andrews, E. *et al.* (1993) *Otter survey of Wales 1991.* Vincent Wildlife Trust, London.

27 Andrews, P.L.R. & Illman, O. (1987) The ferret, pp. 436–455 in Poole, T.B. (ed.) *UFAW handbook on the care and management of laboratory animals.* Longman, London.

28 Anon. (1968) *Nutrient requirements of mink and foxes.* National Academy of Sciences, Washington DC.

29 Anon. (1993) *Mammal survey of 5 species.* Ulster Wildlife Trust and Forest Service, Department of Agriculture of Northern Ireland, Belfast.

30 Ansell, R. *et al.* (2001) The value of gardens for wildlife – lessons from mammals and herpetofauna. *British Wildlife,* **13,** 77–84.

31 Anwar, M.A. *et al.* (2000) Coccidiosis in the European badger (*Meles meles*) from England, an epidemiological study. *Parasitology,* **120,** 255–260.

32 Anwar, M.A. *et al.* (2006) The presence of antibodies to *Toxoplasma gondii* in European badgers. *Journal of Wildlife Diseases,* **42,** 179–181.

33 Apfelbach, R. (1973) Woran erkennt ein Raubtier seine Beute? *Umschau,* **73,** 453–457 (in German).

34 Apfelbach, R. (1973) Olfactory sign stimulus for prey selection in polecats (*Putorius putorius* L.). *Zeitschrift für Tierpsychologie,* **33,** 270–273.

35 Armitage, J.S. (1980) Notes on hunting techniques and prey of the weasel. *Sorby Record,* **18,** 83.

36 Arnold, H.R. (1993) *Atlas of mammals in Britain.* HMSO, London.

37 Ashton, E.H. (1955) Some characters of the skulls and skins of the European polecat, the Asiatic polecat, and the domestic ferret (Addendum). *Proceedings of the Zoological Society of London,* **125,** 807–809.

38 Ashton, E.H. & Thomson, A.P.D. (1955) Some characters of the skulls and skins of the European polecat, the Asiatic polecat, and the domestic ferret. *Proceedings of the Zoological Society of London,* **125,** 317–333.

39 Audy, M.C. (1976) Le cycle sexuel saisonnier du male des mustelides européens. *General and Comparative Endocrinology,* **30,** 117–127 (in French).

40 Aunapuu, M. & Oksanen, T. (2003) Habitat selection of coexisting competitors: a study of small mustelids in northern Norway. *Evolutionary Ecology,* **17,** 371–392.

41 Aybes, C. & Yalden, D.W. (1995) Place-name evidence for the former status of wolves and beavers in Britain. *Mammal Review,* **24,** 73–90.

42 Bacon, P.J. *et al.* (1991) Analysis of a model of group territoriality based on the Resource Dispersion Hypothesis. *Journal of Theoretical Biology,* **148,** 433–444.

43 Bacon, P.J. *et al.* (1991) A model for territory and group formation in a heterogeneous habitat. *Journal of Theoretical Biology,* **148,** 445–468.

44 Badridze, J. *et al.* (1992) Pp. 1–12 in *The reintroduction of captive-raised large mammals into their natural habitat: Problems and method.* Institute of Zoology of the Academy of Sciences, Republic of Georgia.

45 Baghli, A. & Verhagen, R. (2003) The distribution and status of the polecat *Mustela putorius* in Luxembourg. *Mammal Review,* **33,** 57–68.

46 Baghli, A. & Verhagen, R. (2005) Activity patterns and use of resting sites by polecats in an endangered population. *Mammalia,* **69,** 211–222.

47 Baines, D. *et al.* (2004) Capercaillie breeding success in relation to forest habitat and predator abundance. *Journal of Applied Ecology,* **41,** 59–71.

48 Baines, R. *et al.* (1995) *The impact of foxes and fox hunting on the management of Wiltshire County Farms Estate.* Report to

Wiltshire County Council. Centre for Rural Studies, Royal Agricultural College, Cirencester.

49 Baker, P. *et al.* (2001) Bristol's foxes – 40 years of change. *British Wildlife*, **12**, 411–417.

50 Baker, P.J. (1995) *Factors affecting group formation in an urban fox* (Vulpes vulpes) *population.* PhD thesis, University of Bristol.

51 Baker, P.J. & Harris, S. (2000) Interaction rates between members of a group of red foxes (*Vulpes vulpes*). *Mammal Review*, **30**, 239–242.

52 Baker, P.J. & Harris, S. (2003) A review of the diet of foxes in rural Britain and a preliminary assessment of their impact as a predator, pp. 120–140 in Tattersall, F. & Manly, W. (eds.) *Conservation and conflict – mammals and farming in Britain.* Linnean Society Occasional Publication No. 4, London.

53 Baker, P.J. & Harris, S. (2005) Shooting in the dark. *Animal Welfare*, **14**, 275–278.

54 Baker, P.J. & Harris, S. (2006) Still shooting in the dark. *Animal Welfare*, **15**, 89–90.

55 Baker, P.J. & Harris, S. (2006) Does culling reduce fox (*Vulpes vulpes*) density in commercial forests in Wales, UK? *European Journal of Wildlife Research*, **52**, 99–108.

56 Baker, P.J. *et al.* (1998) Potential fitness benefits of group living in the red fox, *Vulpes vulpes. Animal Behaviour*, **56**, 1411–1424.

57 Baker, P.J. *et al.* (2000) Flexible spatial organization of urban foxes, *Vulpes vulpes*, before and during an outbreak of sarcoptic mange. *Animal Behaviour*, **59**, 127–146.

58 Baker, P.J. *et al.* (2001) Differences in the capture rate of cage-trapped red foxes *Vulpes vulpes* and an evaluation of rabies control measures in Britain. *Journal of Applied Ecology*, **38**, 823–835.

59 Baker, P.J. *et al.* (2002) Effect of British hunting ban on fox numbers. *Nature*, **419**, 34.

60 Baker, P.J. *et al.* (2004) Polygynandry in a red fox population: implications for the evolution of group living in canids? *Behavioral Ecology*, **15**, 766–778.

61 Baker, P.J. *et al.* (2004) Is it possible to monitor mammal population changes from counts of road traffic casualties? An analysis using Bristol's red foxes *Vulpes vulpes* as an example. *Mammal Review*, **34**, 115–130.

62 Baker, P.J. *et al.* (2006) The potential impact of red fox predation in agricultural landscapes in lowland Britain. *Wildlife Biology*, **12**, 39–50.

63 Baker, P.J. *et al.* (n.d.) *After the hunt: the future for foxes in Britain.* IFAW, London.

64 Bakeyev, Y.N. (1994) Stone martens in the Commonwealth of Independent States, pp. 243–245 in Buskirk, S.W *et al.* (eds.) *Martens, sables and fishers, biology and conservation.* Cornell University Press, Ithaca, NY.

65 Balharry, D. (1993) *Factors affecting the distribution and population density of pine martens* (Martes martes L.) *in Scotland.* PhD thesis, University of Aberdeen.

66 Balharry, D. (1993) Social organisation in martens: an inflexible system? *Symposia of the Zoological Society of London*, **65**, 321–345.

67 Balharry, D. & Daniels, M. (1998) Wild living cats in Scotland. *Scottish Natural Heritage Research, Survey and Monitoring Report* No. 23.

68 Balharry, E.A. (1994) *The energetics of territoriality in the pine marten* (Martes martes L.) *and its relevance to a hypothesis on delayed implantation.* MSc thesis, University of Aberdeen.

69 Balharry, E.A. & Macdonald, D.W. (1999) Cost effective electric fencing for protecting gamebirds against pine marten (*Martes martes*) predation. *Mammal Review*, **29**, 67–72.

70 Balharry, E.A. *et al.* (1996) *Distribution of pine martens in Scotland as determined by field survey and questionnaire.* Scottish Natural Heritage Research, Survey and Monitoring Report.

No. 48. Edinburgh.

71 Bardeleben, C. *et al.* (2005) A molecular phylogeny of the Canidae based on six nuclear loci. *Molecular Phylogenetics and Evolution*, **37**, 815–831.

72 Barreto, G.R. & Macdonald, D.W. (1999) The response of water voles, *Arvicola terrestris*, to the odours of predators. *Animal Behaviour*, **57**, 1107–1112.

73 Barreto, G.R. *et al.* (1998) The role of habitat and mink predation in determining the status and distribution of declining populations of water voles in Britain. *Animal Conservation*, **1**, 129–137.

74 Baruš, V. & Zejda, J. (1981) The European otter (*Lutra lutra*) in the Czech Socialist Republic. *Prirodovedné Práce ústavu Ceskoslovenske Akademie Ved v Brne*, **15**(12), 1–41.

75 Bassett, C. (1957) The marten, pp. 575–587 in Worden A.N. & Lane-Petter, W. (eds.) *UFAW handbook on the care and management of laboratory animals*, 2nd edn. Universities Federation for Animal Welfare, London.

76 Bassett, C.F. & Llewellyn, L.M. (1949) The moulting and fur growth pattern in the adult mink. *American Midland Naturalist*, **42**, 751–755.

77 Bateman, J.A. (1970) Supernumerary incisors in mustelids. *Mammal Review*, **1**, 81–86.

78 Bateman, J.A. (1979) *Trapping: a practical guide.* David & Charles, Newton Abbot.

79 BBONT (1995) *Restoring land for otters.* Wildlife Trust for Berkshire, Buckinghamshire and Oxfordshire, Oxford.

80 Beaumont, M. *et al.* (2001) Genetic diversity and introgression in the Scottish wildcat. *Molecular Ecology*, **10**, 319–336.

81 Beard, P.M. *et al.* (1999) Evidence of paratuberculosis in fox (*Vulpes vulpes*) and stoat (*Mustela erminea*). *Veterinary Record*, **145**, 612–613.

82 Beard, P.M. *et al.* (2001) Paratuberculosis infection of nonruminant wildlife in Scotland. *Journal of Clinical Microbiology*, **39**, 1517–1521.

83 Belliveau, A.M. *et al.* (1999) Assessment of genetic variability in captive and wild American mink (*Mustela vison*) using microsatellite markers. *Canadian Journal of Animal Science*, **79**(1), 7–16.

84 Beltrán, J.F. *et al.* (1991) Methods of censusing red fox (*Vulpes vulpes*) populations. *Hystrix*, **3**, 199–214.

85 Beresford-Jones, W.P. (1961) Observations on the helminths of British wild red foxes. *Veterinary Record*, **73**, 882–883.

86 Berkovitz, B.K.B. & Poole, D.F.G. (1977) Attrition of the teeth in ferrets. *Journal of Zoology*, **183**, 411–418.

87 Berkovitz, B.K.B. & Thomson, P. (1973) Observations on the aetiology of supernumerary upper incisors in the albino ferret (*Mustela furo*). *Archives of Oral Biology*, **18**, 457–463.

88 Berry, R.J. (1983) Evolution of animals and plants. *Proceedings of the Royal Society of Edinburgh B*, **83**, 433–447.

89 Bininda-Emonds, O.R.P. *et al.* (1999) Building large trees by combining phylogenetic information: a complete phylogeny of the extant Carnivora (Mammalia). *Biological Review*, **74**, 143–175.

90 Birks, J.D.S. (1981) *Home range and territorial behaviour of the feral mink (*Mustela vison *Schreber) in Devon.* PhD thesis, University of Exeter.

91 Birks, J. (1986) *Mink.* Anthony Nelson, Oswestry, Shropshire.

92 Birks, J. (1993) The return of the polecat. *British Wildlife*, **5**, 16–25.

93 Birks, J.D.S. (1997) A volunteer-based system for sampling variations in the abundance of polecats (*Mustela putorius*). *Journal of Zoology*, **243**, 857–863.

94 Birks, J.D.S. (1998) Secondary rodenticide poisoning risk arising from winter farmyard use by the European polecat *Mustela putorius. Biological Conservation*, **85**, 233–240.

95 Birks, J.D.S. (2000) The recovery of the polecat (*Mustela*

putorius) in Britain, pp. 141–152 in Griffiths, H.I. (ed.) *Mustelids in a modern world: management and conservation aspects of small carnivore: human interactions.* Backhuys, Leiden.

96 Birks, J. (2002) *The pine marten.* The Mammal Society, London.

97 Birks, J.D.S. & Dunstone, N. (1984) A note on prey remains collected from the dens of feral mink (*Mustela vison*) in a coastal habitat. *Journal of Zoology.* **203**, 279–281.

98 Birks, J.D.S. & Dunstone, N. (1985) Sex-related differences in the diet of the mink *Mustela vison.* *Holarctic Ecology*, **8**, 245–252.

99 Birks, J.D.S. & Kitchener, A.C. (1999) *The distribution and status of the polecat* Mustela putorius *in Britain in the 1990s.* Vincent Wildlife Trust, London.

100 Birks, J.D.S. & Kitchener, A.C. (1999) Ecology of the polecat in lowland England, pp. 111–130 in Birks, J.D.S. & Kitchener, A.C. (eds.) *The distribution and status of the polecat* Mustela putorius *in Britain in the 1990s.* Vincent Wildlife Trust. London.

101 Birks, J.D.S. & Linn, I.J. (1982) Studies of home range of the feral mink, *Mustela vison. Symposia of the Zoological Society of London*, **49**, 231–57.

102 Birks, J.D.S. & Messenger, J.E. (2000) The pine marten (*Martes martes*) in Cumbria in the late twentieth century. *Carlisle Naturalist*, **8**(1), 6–10.

103 Birks, J.D.S. *et al.* (1997) A 1994 pine marten *Martes martes* (L.) record for Lancashire, including a preliminary genetic analysis. *Naturalist*, **122**, 13–18.

104 Birks, J. *et al.* (2002) The pine marten in Wales – our greatest enigma? *Natur Cymru* No. 5 (Winter), 4–8.

105 Birks, J.D.S. *et al.* (2004) Are scat surveys a reliable method for assessing distribution and population status of pine martens? pp. 235–252 in Harrison, D.J. *et al.* (eds.) *Marten and fishers* (Martes) *in human-altered environments: an international perspective.* Springer, Norwell, MA.

106 Birks, J.D.S. *et al.* (2004) Reintroducing pine martens – habitat constraints and enhancement opportunities, pp. 37–40 in Quine, C.P., *et al* (eds.) *Managing woodlands and their mammals: proceedings of a joint Mammal Society/Forestry Commission symposium.* Forestry Commission, Edinburgh.

107 Birks, J.D.S. *et al.* (2005) Diversity of den sites used by pine martens *Martes martes:* a response to the scarcity of arboreal cavities? *Mammal Review*, **35**, 313–320.

108 Birks, J. *et al.* (2005) A 2003 pine marten record for Hampshire. *Newsletter of the Hampshire Mammal Group*, **6**, 9.

109 Bishop, S.C. (1923) Note on the nest and young of the small brown weasel. *Journal of Mammalogy*, **4**, 26–27.

110 Blackmore, D.K. (1964) A survey of disease in British wild foxes (*Vulpes vulpes*). *Veterinary Record*, **76**, 527–533.

111 Blackwell, P.G. & Macdonald, D.W. (2000) Shapes and sizes of badger territories. *Oikos*, **89**, 392–398.

112 Bland, K.P. *et al.* Personal communication..

113 Blandford, P.R.S. (1986) *Behavioural ecology of the polecat in Wales.* PhD thesis, University of Exeter.

114 Blandford, P.R.S. (1987) Biology of the polecat *Mustela putorius*: a literature review. *Mammal Review*, **17**, 155–198.

115 Blandford, P.R.S. & Walton, K.C. (1991) Polecat *Mustela putorius*, pp. 396–405 in Corbet, G.B. & Harris, S. (eds.) *The handbook of British mammals*, 3rd edn. Blackwell Scientific Publications, Oxford.

116 Blandford, P.R.S. & Walton, K.C. (1991) Ferret *Mustela furo*, pp. 405–406 in Corbet, G.B. & Harris, S. (eds.) *The handbook of British mammals*, 3rd edn. Blackwell Scientific Publications, Oxford.

117 Blomstedt, L. (1995) Pelage cycle and hair bundle structure in the young and adult ferret, *Mustela putorius. Canadian Journal of Zoology*, **73**, 1937–1944.

118 Blomquist, L. *et al.* (1981) Breeding the least weasel (*Mustela rixosa*) in Helsinki Zoo. *Zoologische Garten Jena*, **5/6**, 363–368.

119 Bonesi, L. & Macdonald, D.W. (2004) Differential habitat use promotes sustainable coexistence between the specialist otter and the generalist mink. *Oikos*, **106**, 509–519.

120 Bonesi, L. & Macdonald, D.W. (2004) Evaluation of sign surveys as a way to estimate the relative abundance of American mink (*Mustela vison*). *Journal of Zoology*, **262**, 65–72.

121 Bonesi, L. & Macdonald, D.W. (2004) Impact of released Eurasian otters on a population of American mink: a test using an experimental approach. *Oikos*, **106**, 9–18.

122 Bonesi, L. & Palazon, S. (2007) The American mink in Europe: status, impacts, and control. *Biological Conservation*, **134**(4), 470–483.

123 Bonesi, L. *et al.* (2000) Winter selection of habitats within intertidal foraging areas by mink (*Mustela vison*). *Journal of Zoology*, **250**, 419–424.

124 Bonesi, L. *et al.* (2004) Competition between Eurasian otter *Lutra lutra* and American mink *Mustela vison* probed by niche shift. *Oikos*, **106**, 19–26.

125 Bonesi, L. *et al.* (2006) Demography of three populations of American mink, *Mustela vison*, in Europe. *Mammal Review*, **36**, 98–106.

126 Bonesi, L. *et al.* (2006) Why are there fewer signs of mink in England? Considering multiple hypotheses. *Biological Conservation*, **130**, 268–277.

127 Bonnin, M. *et al.* (1978) Oestrogen and progesterone concentrations in peripheral blood in pregnant red foxes (*Vulpes vulpes*). *Journal of Reproduction and Fertility*, **54**, 37–41.

128 Borowski, Z. (1998) Influence of predator odour on the feeding behaviour of the root vole (*Microtus oeconomus*, Pallas, 1776). *Canadian Journal of Zoology*, **76**, 1791–1794.

129 Bradbury, K. (1974) The badger's diet, pp. 113–125 in Paget, R.J. & Middleton, A.L.V. (eds.) *Badgers of Yorkshire and Humberside.* William Sessions, York.

130 Brainerd, S.M. (1990) The pine marten and forest fragmentation: a review and synthesis. In Myrberget, S. (ed.) *Transactions of the Nineteenth International Congress of Game Biology*, NINA, Norwegian Institute for Nature Research, Trondheim.

131 Brainerd, S.M. *et al.* (1994) Eurasian pine martens and old industrial forest in southern boreal Scandinavia, pp. 343–354 in Buskirk, S.W. *et al.* (eds.) *Martens, sables and fishers, biology and conservation.* Cornell University Press, Ithaca, NY.

132 Brainerd, S.M. *et al.* (1995) Pine marten (*Martes martes*) selection of resting and denning sites in Scandinavian managed forests. *Annales Zoologici Fennici*, **32**, 151–157.

133 Brandt, M.J. & Lambin, X. (2005) Summertime activity patterns of common weasels *Mustela nivalis vulgaris* under differing prey abundances in grassland habitats. *Acta Theriologica*, **50**, 67–79.

134 Bree, P.J.H. van *et al.* (1966) Skull dimensions and the length/weight relationship of the baculum as age indications in the common otter *Lutra lutra* (Linnaeus, 1758). *Danish Review of Game Biology*, **4**, 97–104.

135 Bree, P.H. van *et al.* (1970) Biometric analysis of the effect of castration on the skull of the male domestic cat (*Felis catus* L., 1758). *Publicaties van het Hatuurhistorisch Genootschap in Limburg* **20**(3/4): 11–14.

136 Breitenmoser, U. (1998) Large predators in the Alps: the fall and rise of Man's competitors. *Biological Conservation*, **83**, 279–289.

137 Breitenmoser, U. & Breitenmoser-Würsten, C. (1990) *Status, conservation needs and reintroduction of the lynx* (Lynx lynx) *in Europe.* Council of Europe, Strasbourg.

138 Brickle, N.W. (1999) *The effect of agricultural intensification on the decline of the corn bunting* Miliaria calandra. DPhil thesis, University of Sussex.

139 Bright, P.W. (1993) Habitat fragmentation – problems and predictions for British mammals. *Mammal Review*, **23**, 101–111.

140 Bright, P.W. & Halliwell, E.C. (1999) *Species recovery programme for the pine marten in England: 1996–1998*. Research Reports No. 306, English Nature, Peterborough.

141 Bright, P.W. & Smithson, T.J. (1997) *Species recovery programme for the pine marten in England: 1995–1996*. Unpublished report to the People's Trust for Endangered Species, London and English Nature, Peterborough.

142 Brinck, C. *et al.* (1978) Anal pouch secretion in mink *Mustela vison*. *Oikos*, **30**, 68–75.

143 Brinck, C. *et al.* (1983) Anal sac secretion in mustelids: a comparison. *Journal of Chemical Ecology*, **9**, 727–745.

144 Brodie, J. (1988) Mammalian predation on Norway rats (*Rattus norvegicus*) living in a rural environment. *Journal of Zoology*, **216**, 582–583.

145 Broekhuizen, S. & Müskens, G.J.D.M. (2000) Utilization of rural and suburban habitat by pine marten *Martes martes* and beech marten *M. foina*: species-related potential and restrictions for adaptation. *Lutra*, **43**, 223–228.

146 Broekhuizen, S. & Müskens, G.J.D.M. (2000) Voortplanting bij de boommarter *Martes martes* in Nederland. *Lutra*, **43**, 205–214 (in Dutch).

147 Brown, D. (1997) The foulmart: what's in a name? *Mammal Review*, **32**, 145–149.

148 Brown, H. & Birks, J.D.S. (2006) Resolving conflicts generated by pine martens denning in buildings in Scotland, pp. 125–133 in Santos-Reis, M. *et al.* (eds.) *Martes in carnivore communities*. Alpha Wildlife Publications, Sherwood Park, Alberta, Canada.

149 Brown, J.A. & Cheeseman, C.L. (1996) The effect of translocation on a social group of badgers (*Meles meles*). *Animal Welfare*, **5**, 289–309.

150 Brown, J.A. *et al.* (1993) The development of field techniques for studying potential modes of transmission of bovine tuberculosis from badgers *Meles meles* to cattle, pp. 139–153 in Hayden, T.J. (ed.) *The badger*. Royal Irish Academy, Dublin.

151 Brown, J.H. & Lasiewski, R.C. (1972) The metabolism of weasels: the cost of being long and thin. *Ecology*, **53**, 939–943.

152 Brown, R.W. *et al.* (1992) *Animal tracks, trails and signs*. Hamlyn, London.

153 Buchalczyk, T. & Ruprecht, A.L. (1977) Skull variability of *Mustela putorius* Linnaeus, 1758. *Acta Theriologica*, **22**, 87–120.

154 Buckingham, C.J. (1979) *The activity and exploratory behaviour of the weasel*, Mustela nivalis. PhD thesis, University of Exeter.

155 Buckle, A. & Harris, S. (1980) The flea epifauna of a suburban fox (*Vulpes vulpes*) population. *Journal of Zoology*, **190**, 431–439.

156 Buckton, K.E. & Cunningham, C. (1971) Variations in the chromosome number in the red fox (*Vulpes vulpes*). *Chromosoma (Berlin)*, **33**, 268–272.

157 Buesching, C.D. *et al.* (2002) Variations in colour and volume of the subcaudal gland secretion of badgers (*Meles meles*) in relation to sex, season and individual-specific parameters. *Mammalian Biology*, **67**, 147–156.

158 Buesching, C.D., *et al.* (2003) The social function of allo-marking in the European badger (*Meles meles*). *Behaviour*, **140**, 965–980.

159 Bullion, S. (1997) *East Anglian otter survey: the Suffolk rivers 1996–1997*. Suffolk Wildlife Trust/Environment Agency, Ipswich/Huntingdon.

160 Bullock, D. & Pickering, S. (1982) Weasels (*Mustela nivalis*) attacking a young and an adult brown hare (*Lepus capensis*). *Journal of Zoology*, **197**, 307–308.

161 Burleigh, R. *et al.* (1976) British Museum natural radiocarbon measurements VIII. *Radiocarbon*, **18**, 16–42.

162 Burns, J.J. (1964) Movements of a tagged weasel in Alaska. *Murrelet*, **45**, 10.

163 Burns, L. *et al.* (2000) *Report of the committee of inquiry into hunting with dogs in England & Wales*. Stationery Office, London.

164 Burrows, R. (1968) *Wild fox: a complete study of the red fox*. David & Charles, Newton Abbot.

165 Burt, M.D.B. *et al.* (1980) Helminth parasites of wild cats in north-east Scotland. *Journal of Helminthology*, **54**, 303–308.

166 Buskirk, S.W. & Lindstedt, S.L. (1989) Sex biases in trapped samples of Mustelidae. *Journal of Mammalogy*, **70**, 88–97.

167 Buskirk, S.W. & MacDonald, S.O. (1984) Seasonal food habits of marten in south central Alaska. *Canadian Journal of Zoology*, **62**, 944–950.

168 Buskirk, S.W. *et al.* (1989) Winter resting site ecology of marten in the central Rocky mountains. *Journal of Wildlife Management*, **53**(1), 191–196.

169 Buskirk, S.W. *et al.* (1994) *Martens, sables and fishers, biology and conservation*. Cornell University Press, Ithaca, NY.

170 Butler, D.J. (1980) *Feeding ecology and management of foxes* (Vulpes vulpes) *in coastal Aberdeenshire*. PhD thesis, University of Aberdeen.

171 Butler, J.M. & Roper, T.J. (1996) Ectoparasites and sett use in European badgers. *Animal Behaviour*, **52**, 621–629.

172 Butterworth, W.C.J.R. (1905) *Victoria History of the County of Sussex*. Constable, London.

173 Cabrera, A. (1932) Los mamíferos de Marruecos. *Trabajos del Museo Nacional de Ciencias Naturales, Madrid*, **57**, 1–361.

174 Canivenc, R.(1966) A study of progestation in the European badger (*Meles meles* L.). *Symposia of the Zoological Society of London*, **15**, 15–26.

175 Canivenc, R. (1970) Contrôle de la biologie lutéale chez les espèces à ovo-implantation différée. *Colloques du CNRS*, **927**, 223–233 (in French).

176 Canivenc, R. & Bonnin, M. (1975) Les facteurs écophysiologiques de régulation de la fonction lutéale chez les mammifères a ovo-implantation différée. *Journal de Physiologie*, **70**, 533–538 (in French).

177 Canivenc, R. & Bonnin-Laffargue, M. (1981) Environmental control of delayed implantation in the European badger (*Meles meles*). *Journal of Reproduction and Fertility, Suppl.*, **29**, 25–33.

178 Carpenter, P.J. *et al.* (2005) Mating system of the Eurasian badger, *Meles meles*, in a high density population. *Molecular Ecology* , **14**, 273–284.

179 Carr, G.M. & Macdonald, D.W. (1986) The sociality of solitary foragers: a model based on resource dispersion. *Animal Behaviour*, **34**, 1540–1549.

180 Carss, D.N. *et al.* (1990) Predation on adult Atlantic salmon, *Salmo salar*, by otters *Lutra lutra* within the River Dee system, Aberdeenshire, Scotland. *Journal of Fish Biology*, **37**, 935–944.

181 Carter, S.P. *et al.* (submitted) Culling-induced social perturbation in Eurasian badger *Meles meles* populations and the management of TB in cattle: a review and a simulation model. *Journal of Applied Ecology*.

182 Cavallini, P. (1996) Variation in the social system of the red fox. *Ethology, Ecology and Evolution*, **8**, 323–342.

183 Chanin, P.R.F. (1976) *The ecology of the feral mink (*Mustela vison *Schreber) in Devon*. PhD thesis, University of Exeter.

184 Chanin, P. (1981) The diet of the otter and its relations with the feral mink in two areas of south-west England. *Acta Theriologica*, **26**, 83–95.

185 Chanin, P. (1981) The feral mink – natural history, movements and control. *Nature in Devon*, **2**, 33–54.

186 Chanin, P. (1983) Observations of two populations of feral mink in Devon, U.K. *Mammalia*, **47**, 463–476.

187 Chanin, P. (1985) *The natural history of otters*. Croom Helm, Beckenham.

188 Chanin, P. (1991) Otter *Lutra lutra*, pp. 424–431 in Corbet, G.B. & Harris, S. (eds.) *The handbook of British mammals*, 3rd edn. Blackwell Scientific Publications, Oxford.

189 Chanin, P. (1993) *Otters*. Whittet Books, London.

190 Chanin, P.R.F. & Jefferies, D.J. (1978) The decline of the otter *Lutra lutra* L. in Britain: an analysis of hunting records and discussion of causes. *Biological Journal of the Linnean Society*, **10**, 305–328.

191 Chanin, P.R.F. & Linn, I. (1980) The diet of the feral mink (*Mustela vison*) in southwest Britain. *Journal of Zoology*, **192**, 205–223.

192 Chapman, P.J. & Chapman, L.L. (1982) *Otter survey of Ireland 1980–81*. Vincent Wildlife Trust, London.

193 Cheeseman, C.L. & Harris, S. (1982) Methods of marking badgers *Meles meles*. *Journal of Zoology*, **197**, 289–292.

194 Cheeseman, C.L. & Mallinson, P.J. (1979) Radiotracking in the study of bovine TB in Badgers. pp. 649–656 in Amlaner, C.J. & MacDonald, D.W. (eds.) *A handbook on biotelemetry and radio-tracking*. Pergamon Press, Oxford.

195 Cheeseman, C.L. et al. (1987) Badger population dynamics in a high density area. *Symposium of the Zoological.Society of London*, **58**, 279–294.

196 Cheeseman, C.L. et al. (1988) Comparison of dispersal and other movements in two badger (*Meles meles*) populations. *Mammal Review*, **18**, 51–59.

197 Cheeseman, C.L et al. (1988) Dynamics of tuberculosis in a naturally infected badger population. *Mammal Review*, **18**, 61–72.

198 Cheeseman, C.L. et al. (1993) Recolonisation by badgers in Gloucestershire, pp. 78–93 in Hayden, T.J. (ed.) *The badger*. Royal Irish Academy, Dublin.

199 Christian, S.F. (1994) Dispersal and other inter-group movements in badgers, *Meles meles*. *Zeitschrift für Säugetierkunde*, **59**, 218–223.

200 Christian, S.F. (1995) Observations of extra-group mating and mate-defence behaviour in badgers, *Meles meles*. *Journal of Zoology*, **237**, 668–670.

201 Churcher, C.S. (1959) The specific status of the New World red fox. *Journal of Mammalogy*, **40**, 513–520.

202 Churcher, C.S. (1960) Cranial variation in the North American red fox. *Journal of Mammalogy*, **41**, 349–360.

203 Churcher, J.B. & Lawton, J.H. (1987) Predation by domestic cats in an English village. *Journal of Zoology*, **212**, 439–455.

204 Cijnak, L. & Ruff, R.L. (1990) Human-bear conflicts in Yougoslavia [sic], pp. 573–580 in Myrberget, S. (ed.) *Transactions of the 19th International Congress of Game Biology*. NINA, Trondheim.

205 Clark, J.M. (1976) Variation in coat colour gene frequencies and selection in the cats of Scotland. *Genetica*, **46**, 401–412.

206 Clarke, G.P. et al. (1998) Effects of roads on badger *Meles meles* populations in south-west England. *Biological Conservation*, **86**, 117–124.

207 Clements, E.D. et al. (1988) The national badger sett survey. *Mammal Review*, **18**, 1–19.

208 Clements, F.A. & Dunstone, N. (1984) Comparative aerial and underwater motion perception capability of the mink (*Mustela vison*) as a function of stimulus radiant intensity and discrimination distance. *Animal Behaviour*, **32**, 790–797.

209 Clode, D. & Macdonald, D.W. (1995) Evidence for food competition between mink (*Mustela vison*) and otter (*Lutra lutra*) on Scottish islands. *Journal of Zoology*, **237**, 435–444.

210 Clutton-Brock, J. (1969) The origin of the dog, pp. 303–309 in Brothwell, D. & Higgs, E. (eds) *Science and archaeology* (revised ed.) Thames & Hudson, London.

211 Clutton-Brock, J. (1999) *The natural history of domesticated mammals*, 2nd edn. Cambridge University Press, Cambridge.

212 Clutton-Brock, J. et al. (1976) A review of the family Canidae, with a classification by numerical methods. *Bulletin of the British Museum (Natural History) Zoology*, **29**, 119–199.

213 Cobham Resource Consultants (1983) *Countryside sports – their economic significance. Summary report*. Standing Conference on Countryside Sports, Reading.

214 Cocks, A.H. (1881) Note on the breeding of the otter. *Proceedings of the Zoological Society of London*, **1881**, 249–250.

215 Cocks, A.H. (1881) Wild cat breeding in confinement. *Zoologist, 3rd series*, **5**, 307.

216 Cocks, A.H. (1905) Mammals, pp 153–176 in Page, W. (ed.) *The Victoria History of the county of Buckingham*, vol. 1. Archibald Constable, London.

217 Collier, G.E. & O'Brien, S.J. (1985) A molecular phylogeny of the Felidae: immunological distance. *Evolution*, **39**, 473–487.

218 Condé, B. (1970) Ronronnement et empreinte chez un félidé sauvage. *Compte Rendu des Séances de la Société de Biologie*, **164**, 1392–1394 (in French).

219 Condé, B. & Schauenberg, P. (1969) Reproduction du chat forestier d'Europe (*Felis silvestris* Schreber) en captivité. *Revue Suisse de Zoologie*, **76**, 183–210 (in French).

220 Condé, B. & Schauenberg, P. (1974) Reproduction du chat forestier (*F. silvestris* Schr.) dans le nord-est de la France. *Revue Suisse de Zoologie*, **81**(1), 45–52 (in French).

221 Conroy, J.W.H. & Chanin, P.R.F. (2002) The status of the Eurasian otter (*Lutra lutra*) in Europe – a review, pp. 7–28 in Conroy, J.W.H. et al (eds.) *Proceedings of the First Otter Toxicological Conference*, Skye, September 2000. The International Otter Survival Fund, Skye.

222 Conroy, J.W.H. & French, D.D. (1987) The use of spraints to monitor populations of otters (*Lutra lutra* L.). *Symposia of the Zoological Society of London*, **58**, 247–262.

223 Conroy, J.W.H. et al. (1993) *A guide to the identification of prey remains in otter spraint*. Occasional publication No. 16, The Mammal Society, London.

224 Conroy, J. et al. (1998) The distribution and status of the Eurasian otter (*Lutra lutra*) in Asia – a preliminary review. *IUCN Otter Specialist Group Bulletin*, **14**, 15–30.

225 Cook, B.R. (1965) *Incidence and epidemiology of* Echinococcus granulosis *in Great Britain*. PhD thesis, University of Liverpool.

226 Corbet, G.B. (1978) *The mammals of the Palaearctic region: a taxonomic review*. British Museum (Natural History), London.

227 Corbet, G.B. & Hill, J.E. (1991) *A world list of mammalian species*, 2nd edn. Natural History Museum, London/Oxford University Press, Oxford.

228 Corbett, L.K. (1979) *Feeding ecology and social organization of wildcats* (Felis silvestris) *and domestic cats* (Felis catus) *in Scotland*. PhD thesis, University of Aberdeen.

229 Corbett, L.K. (1981) The wildcat, pp. 185–189 in Boyle, C.L. (ed.) *The RSPCA book of British mammals*. Collins, London.

230 Council of Europe (1989) *Workshop on the situation and protection of the brown bear (*Ursus arctos*) in Europe*. Council of Europe, Strasbourg.

231 Cox, M. et al. (1999) Public preferences regarding rabies-prevention policies in the UK. *Preventive Veterinary Medicine*, **41**, 257–270.

232 Coxon, K. et al. (1998) *The use of DNA fingerprinting to study the population dynamics of otters* (Lutra lutra) *in southern Britain: a feasibility study*. R&D Technical report W202, Environment Agency, Swindon.

233 Craik, C. (1997) Long-term effects of North American Mink *Mustela vison* on seabirds in western Scotland. *Bird Study*, **44**, 303–309.

234 Craik, J.C.A. (1998) Recent mink related declines of gulls and terns in west Scotland and the beneficial effects of mink control. *Argyll Bird Report*, **14**, 98–110.

235 Craik, J.C.A. & Brown, D. (1997) Polecats in the West of Scotland. *Glasgow Naturalist*, **23**, 50–53.

236 Cramb, A. (1994) Claws out in the wildcat debate. *The*

Scotsman (Edinburgh), 15 August, pp. 1 & 6.

237 Crawford, A. (2003) *Fourth otter survey of England 2000–2002*. Environment Agency, Bristol.

238 Crawford, A. *et al.* (1979) *Otter survey of Wales 1977–78*. Society for the Promotion of Nature Conservation, Nettleham, Lincoln.

239 Crawley, D. & Birks, J. (2004) Pine marten confirmed in Staffordshire! *Mammal News,* **138**, 13.

240 Creed, R.F.S. (1972) *Aspects of reproduction and early development in* Vulpes vulpes. PhD thesis, University of London.

241 Creel, S. & Macdonald, D. (1995) Sociality, group size, and reproductive suppression among carnivores. *Advances in the Study of Behavior,* **24**, 203–257.

241a Cresswell, P. *et al.* (1990) *The history, status and habitat requirements of the badger in Britain*. Nature Conservancy Council, Peterborough.

242 Cresswell, W.J. & Harris, S. (1988) Foraging behaviour and home-range utilization in a suburban badger (*Meles meles*) population. *Mammal Review,* **18**, 37–49.

243 Cresswell, W.J. & Harris, S. (1988) The effects of weather conditions on the movements and activity of badgers (*Meles meles*) in a suburban environment. *Journal of Zoology,* **216**, 187–194.

244 Cresswell, W.J. *et al.* (1992) To breed or not to breed: an analysis of the social and density-dependent constraints on the fecundity of female badgers (*Meles meles*). *Philosophical Transactions of the Royal Society of London Series B,* **338**, 393–407.

245 Criddle, S. (1947) A nest of the least weasel. *Canadian Field Naturalist,* **61**, 69.

246 Crump, D.R. (1980) Thietanes and dithiolanes from the anal gland of the stoat (*Mustela erminea*). *Journal of Chemical Ecology,* **6**, 341–347.

247 Cummins, J. (1988) *The hound and the hawk: the art of medieval hunting*. Weidenfeld & Nicolson, London.

248 Cuthbert, J.H. (1973) The origin and distribution of feral mink in Scotland. *Mammal Review,* **3**, 97–103.

249 Cuthbert, J.H. (1979) Food studies of feral mink *Mustela vison* in Scotland. *Fish Management,* **10**, 17–25.

250 da Silva, J. *et al.* (1994) Net costs of group living in a solitary forager, the Eurasian badger (*Meles meles*). *Behavioural Ecology,* **5**, 151–158.

251 Dadd, M.N. (1970) Overlap of variation in British and European mammal populations. *Symposia of the Zoological Society of London,* **26**, 117–125.

252 Dallas, J.F. *et al.* (1999) Genetic diversity in the Eurasian otter, *Lutra lutra* in Scotland. Evidence from microsatellite polymorphism. *Biological Journal of the Linnean Society,* **68**, 73–86.

253 Daniels, M.J. (1997) *The biology and conservation of the wildcat in Scotland*. D.Phil thesis, University of Oxford.

254 Daniels, M.J. *et al.* (1998) Morphological and pelage characteristics of wild living cats in Scotland: Implications for defining the 'wildcat'. *Journal of Zoology,* **244**, 231–247.

255 Daniels, M.J. *et al.* (1999) Feline viruses in wildcats from Scotland. *Journal of Wildlife Diseases,* **35**(1), 121–124.

256 Daniels, M.J. *et al.* (2001) Ecology and genetics of wild-living cats in the north-east of Scotland and the implications for the conservation of the wildcat. *Journal of Applied Ecology,* **38**, 146–161.

257 Danilov, P.I. (1990) The brown bear in Soviet Karelia, pp. 566–572 in Myberget, S. (ed) *Transactions of the 19th IUGB Congress, Trondheim*. NINA, Trondheim.

258 Danilov, P.I. & Rusakov, O.S. (1969) [Peculiarities of the ecology of *Mustela putorius* in the north-west districts of the European part of the USSR.] *Zoologicheskii zhurnal,* **48**, 1383–1394 (in Russian).

259 Danilov, P.I. & Tumanov, I.L. (1976) [*Mustelids of northwestern USSR.*] Nauka, Leningrad (in Russian).

260 Dards, J.L. (1978) Home ranges of feral cats in Portsmouth dockyard. *Carnivore Genetics Newsletter,* **3**, 242–255.

261 Dards, J.L. (1981) Habitat utilisation by feral cats in Portsmouth dockyard, pp. 30–46 in *The ecology and control of feral cats*. UFAW, Potters Bar.

262 Davies, J. (1988) Otter spotter. *Radio Times,* 17–30 December 1988, 17.

263 Davies, J.M. *et al.* (1988) The anal gland secretion of the European badger (*Meles meles*) and its role in social communities. *Journal of Zoology,* **216**, 455–463.

264 Davies, R. (2005) Predation and the profitability of grouse moors. *British Wildlife,* **16**, 339–347.

265 Davis, S.J.M. (1977) Size variation of the fox, *Vulpes vulpes,* in the Palaearctic region today, and in Israel during the late Quartenary. *Journal of Zoology,* **182**, 343–351.

266 Davis, S.J.M. (1987) *The archaeology of animals*. Batsford, London.

267 Davis, S.J.M. & Valla, F.R. (1978) Evidence for domestication of the dog 12,000 years ago in the Natufian of Israel. *Nature,* **276**, 608–610.

268 Davison, A. *et al.* (1998) Hybridization and the phylogenetic relationship between polecats and domestic ferrets in Britain. *Biological Conservation,* **87**, 155–162.

269 Davison, A. *et al.* (2000) Conservation implications of hybridization between polecats, ferrets and European mink (*Mustela* spp.), pp. 153–162 in Griffiths, H.I. (ed.) *Mustelids in a modern world: Management and conservation aspects of small carnivore: human interactions*. Backhuys, Leiden.

270 Davison, A. *et al.* (2002) On the origin of faeces: morphological versus molecular methods for surveying rare carnivores from their scats. *Journal of Zoology,* **257**, 141–143.

271 Day, M.G. (1963) *An ecological study of the stoat (*Mustela erminea L.*) and the weasel (*Mustela nivalis L.*) with particular reference to their food and feeding habits*. PhD thesis, University of Exeter.

272 Day, M.G. (1968) Food habits of British stoats (*Mustela erminea*) and weasels (*Mustela nivalis*). *Journal of Zoology,* **155**, 485–497.

273 Day, M.G. & Linn, I. (1972) Notes on the food of feral mink *Mustela vison* in England and Wales. *Journal of Zoology,* **167**, 463–73.

274 Dayan, T. & Simberloff, D. (1994) Character displacement, sexual dimorphism and morphological variation among British and Irish mustelids. *Ecology,* **75**, 1063–1071.

275 De Marinis, A.M. & Masseti, M. (2003) The weasel (*Mustela nivalis*) on the Mediterranean islands. *Mammalian Biology,* **68**, 181–186.

276 Deane, C.D. & O'Gorman, F. (1969) The spread of feral mink in Ireland. *Irish Naturalists' Journal,* **16**, 198–202.

277 Deanesly, R. (1935) The reproductive processes of certain mammals: Part IX – Growth and reproduction in the stoat (*Mustela erminea*). *Philosophical Transactions of the Royal Society of London Series B,* **225**, 459–492.

278 Deanesly, R. (1943) Delayed implantation in the stoat (*Mustela mustela* [sic]). *Nature,* **151**, 365–366.

279 Deanesly, R. (1944) The reproductive cycle of the female weasel *Mustela nivalis*. *Proceedings of the Zoological Society of London,* **114**, 339–349.

280 Debrot, S. (1984) Dynamique du renouvellement et structure d'age d'une population d'hermines (*Mustela erminea*). *La Terre et la Vie,* **39**, 77–88 (in French).

281 Debrot, S. & Mermod, C. (1982) Quelques siphonaptères de mustélidés, dont *Rhadinopsylla pentacantha* (Rothschild, 1897), nouvelle espèce pour la Suisse. *Révue Suisse de Zoologie,* **89**, 27–32 (in French).

282 Debrot, S. & Mermod, C. (1983) The spatial and temporal distribution pattern of the stoat (*Mustela erminea* L.). *Oecologia,* **59**, 69–73.

283 Debrot, S. *et al.* (1982) *Atlas des poils de mammifères d'Europe*. Institut de Zoologie, Université de Neuchâtel (in French).

284 Debrot, S. *et al.* (1985) The day and night activity pattern of the stoat (*Mustela erminea* L.). *Mammalia*, **49**, 13–17.

285 Degerbøl, M. (1933) Danmarks Pattedyr I Fortiden I Sammenligning med recente former, I. *Vidensk Meddelelse Dansk Naturhist Foreningen,* **96**, 357–641 (in Danish).

286 Delahay, R.J. Personal communication.

287 Delahay, R.J. & Froelich, K. (2000) Absence of antibodies against canine distemper virus infection in free ranging British populations of the Eurasian badger (*Meles meles*). *Journal of Wildlife Diseases,* **36**, 576–579.

288 Delahay, R.J. *et al.* (1998) Do patterns of helminth parasitism differ between groups of wild-living cats in Scotland? *Journal of Zoology,* **245,** 175–183.

289 Delahay, R.J. *et al.* (2000) The use of marked bait in studies of the territorial organisation of the European badger (*Meles meles*). *Mammal Review,* **30**, 73–87.

290 Delahay, R.J. *et al.* (2000) The spatio-temporal distribution of *Mycobacterium bovis* (bovine tuberculosis) infection in a high density badger (*Meles meles*) population. *Journal of Animal Ecology,* **69**, 1–15.

291 Delahay, R.J. *et al.* (2001) Wildlife disease reservoirs: the epidemiology of *Mycobacterium bovis* infection in the European badger (*Meles meles*) and other British mammals. *Tuberculosis,* **81**, 43–49.

292 Delahay, R.J. *et al.* (in press a). Habitat correlates of group size, bodyweight and reproductive performance in a high-density Eurasian badger (*Meles meles*) population. *Journal of Zoology.*

293 Delahay, R.J. *et al.* (in press b) Demographic correlates of bite wounding in Eurasian badgers (*Meles meles* L.) in stable and perturbed populations. *Animal Behaviour.*

294 Delattre, P. (1983) Density of weasel (*Mustela nivalis* L.) and stoat (*Mustela erminea* L.) in relation to water vole abundance. *Acta Zoologica Fennica,* **174**, 221–222.

295 Delattre, P. (1984) Influence de la pression de prédation exercée par une population de belettes (*Mustela nivalis* L.) sur un peuplement de microtidae. *Acta Œcologica,* **5**, 285–300 (in French).

296 Dent, G. (1935) British wild cat. Notes on status in Scotland. *Society for the Preservation of the Fauna of the Empire. Journal,* **26**, 48–51.

297 Derting, T.L. (1989) Prey selection and foraging characteristics of least weasels (*Mustela nivalis*) in the laboratory. *American Midland Naturalist,* **122**, 394–400.

298 Dijkstra, V.A.A. (2000) Het gebruik van boomholten op de Veluwezoom door de boommarter *Martes martes. Lutra,* **43**, 171–184 (in Dutch).

299 Dixon, D.R. (2003) A non-invasive technique for identifying individual badgers. *Mammal Review,* **33**, 92–94.

300 Dobson, M. (1998) Mammal distributions in the western Mediterranean: the role of human intervention. *Mammal Review,* **28**, 77–88.

301 Domingo-Roura, X. *et al.* (2001) Blood biochemistry reflects seasonal nutritional and reproductive constraints in the Eurasian badger (*Meles meles*). *Physiological and Biochemical Zoology,* **74**, 450–460.

302 Doncaster, C.P. (1992) Factors regulating local variations in abundance: field tests on hedgehogs, *Erinaceus europaeus. Oikos,* **69**, 182–192.

303 Doncaster, C.P. (1994) Testing the role of intraguild predation in regulating hedgehog populations. *Proceedings of the Royal Society of London Series B,* **249**, 113–117.

304 Doncaster, C.P. (2001) What determines territory configuration of badgers? *Oikos,* **93**, 497–498.

305 Doncaster, C.P. & Macdonald, D.W. (1991) Drifting territoriality in the red fox *Vulpes vulpes. Journal of Animal Ecology,* **60**, 423–439.

306 Doncaster, C.P. & Macdonald, D.W. (1992) Optimum group size for defending heterogenous distributions of resources: a model applied to red foxes, *Vulpes vulpes*, in Oxford city.

307 Doncaster, C.P. & Macdonald, D.W. (1997) Activity patterns and interactions of red foxes (*Vulpes vulpes*) in Oxford city. *Journal of Zoology,* **241**, 73–87.

308 Doncaster, C.P. & Woodroffe, R. (1993) Den site can determine shape and size of badger territories: implications for group-living. *Oikos,* **66**, 88–93.

309 Doncaster, C.P. *et al.* (1991) Feeding ecology of red foxes (*Vulpes vulpes*) in the city of Oxford, England. *Journal of Mammalogy,* **71**, 188–194.

310 Donnelly, C.A. *et al.* (2003) Impact of localized badger culling on tuberculosis incidence in British cattle. *Nature,* **426**, 834–837.

311 Donnelly, C.A. *et al.* (2005) Positive and negative effects of widespread badger culling on tuberculosis in cattle. *Nature,* **439**, 843–846.

312 Donovan, B.T. (1956) Regulation of the reproductive cycle of the ferret. *Proceedings of the III International Congress on Animal Reproduction,* Cambridge.

313 Donovan, B.T. (1967) Light and the control of the oestrous cycle in the ferret. *Journal of Endocrinology,* **39,** 105–113.

314 Douglas, M.J.W. (1965) Notes on the red fox *Vulpes vulpes* near Braemar, Scotland. *Journal of Zoology,* **147**, 228–233.

315 Driscoll, C. Personal communication.

316 Dubnitskii, A.A. (1956) [A study of the development of the nematode *Skrjabingylus nasicola*, a parasite of the frontal sinuses of mustelids.] *Karakulevodstvo i Zverovodstvo,* **1**, 59–61 (in Russian).

317 Duby, R.T. & Travis, H.F. (1972) Photoperiodic control of fur growth and reproduction in the mink (*Mustela vison*). *Journal of Experimental Zoology,* **182**, 217–225.

318 Duff, J.P. & Hunt, B. (1995) Courtship and mortality in foxes (*Vulpes vulpes*). *Veterinary Record,* **136**, 367.

319 Dugdale, H.L. *et al.* (2003) Offspring sex ratio variation in the European badger (*Meles meles*). *Ecology,* **84**, 40–45.

320 Dunn, E. (1977) Predation by weasels (*Mustela nivalis*) on breeding tits (*Parus* spp.) in relation to density of tits and rodents. *Journal of Animal Ecology,* **46**, 633–652.

321 Dunstone, N. (1976) *Vision in relation to subaquatic predatory behaviour in the mink.* PhD thesis, University of Wales.

322 Dunstone, N. (1978) The fishing strategy of the mink (*Mustela vison*); time-budgeting of hunting effort? *Behaviour,* **67**, 157–177.

323 Dunstone, N. (1986) Exploited animals: the mink. *Biologist, Institute of Biology,* **33**, 69–75.

324 Dunstone, N. (1993) *The mink.* Poyser, London.

325 Dunstone, N. & Birks, J.D.S. (1983) Activity budget and habitat usage by coastal-living mink (*Mustela vison* Schreber). *Acta Zoologica Fennica,* **174**, 189–191.

326 Dunstone, N. & Birks, J.D.S. (1985) The comparative ecology of coastal, riverine and lacustrine mink *Mustela vison* in Britain. *Zeitschrift für Angewandte Zoologie,* **72**, 59–70.

327 Dunstone, N. & Birks, J.D.S. (1987) The feeding ecology of mink (*Mustela vison*) in coastal habitat. *Journal of Zoology,* **212**, 69–83.

328 Dunstone, N. & O'Connor, R.J. (1979) Optimal foraging in an amphibious mammal. I. The aqualung effect. *Animal Behaviour,* **27**, 1182–94.

329 Dunstone, N. & O'Connor, R.J. (1979) Optimal foraging in an amphibious mammal. II. A study using principal component analysis. *Animal Behaviour,* **27**, 1195–2001.

330 Dunstone, N. & Sinclair, W. (1978) Comparative aerial and underwater visual acuity of the mink, *Mustela vison* Schreber, as a function of discrimination distance and stimulus luminance. *Animal Behaviour,* **26**, 6–13.

331 Dunstone, N. *et al.* Personal communication.

332 Dyczkowski, J. & Yalden, D.W. (1998) An estimate of the impact of predators on the British Field Vole *Microtus agrestis* population. *Mammal Review,* **28**, 165–184.

333 East, K. & Lockie, J.D. (1964) Observations on a family of

Journal of Theoretical Biology, **159**, 189–198.

weasels (*Mustela nivalis*) bred in captivity. *Proceedings of the Zoological Society of London*, **143**, 359–363.

334 East, K. & Lockie, J.D. (1965) Further observations on weasels (*Mustela nivalis*) and stoats (*Mustela erminea*) born in captivity. *Journal of Zoology,* **147**, 234–238.

335 Easterbee, N. (1988) The wild cat *Felis silvestris* in Scotland: 1983–1987. *Lutra,* **31**, 29–43.

336 Easterbee, N. Personal communication.

337 Easterbee, N. *et al.* (1991) *Survey of the status and distribution of the wildcat in Scotland 1983–1987.* Nature Conservancy Council for Scotland, Edinburgh.

338 Eberhardt, R.T. & Sargeant, A.B. (1977) Mink predation on prarie marshes during waterfowl breeding season. In Phillips, R.L. & Jonkel, C. (eds.) *Proceedings of the 1975 Predator Symposium*, Montana Forest and Conservation Experimental Station, University of Montana, Missoula.

339 Edgington, S.B. (1981) Vermin in Buckden 1627–1774. *Huntingdonshire Fauna & Flora Society Annual Report*, **33**, 31–37.

340 Edwards, R. (1999) Findings in a fox rescued from hounds. *Veterinary Record*, **144**, 243–244.

341 Edwards, R. (1999) Findings in a fox rescued from hounds. *Veterinary Record*, **144**, 424.

342 Eger, J.L. (1989) Patterns of geographic variation in the skull of Nearctic ermine (*Mustela erminea*). *Canadian Journal of Zoology*, **68**, 1241–1249.

343 Eibl-Eibesfeldt, I. (1956) Angeborenes und Erworbenes in der Technik des Beutetötens (Versuche am Iltis, *Putorius putorius* L.). *Zeitschrift für Säugetierkunde,* **21**, 135–137 (in German).

344 Elder, W.H. (1951) The baculum as an age criterion in mink. *Journal of Mammalogy*, **32**, 43–50.

345 Elliott, G. (1996) Productivity and mortality of mohua (*Mohoua ochrocephala*). *New Zealand Journal of Zoology*, **23**, 229–237.

346 Elton, C.S. (1953) The use of cats in farm rat control. *Journal of Animal Behaviour,* **1**, 151–155.

347 Enders, R.K. (1952) Reproduction in the mink (*Mustela vison*). *Proceedings of the American Philosophical Society*, **96**, 691–755.

348 English, M.P. (1969) Ringworm in wild mammals: further investigations. *Journal of Zoology*, **159**, 515–522.

349 Ennion, E.A.R. & Tinbergen, N. (1967) *Tracks.* Clarendon Press, Oxford.

350 Ensley, P.K. (1979) *Otodectes* sp. infection in Scottish wildcats – a case report. *Journal of Zoo Animal Medicine,* **10**, 92–93.

351 Erlinge, S. (1967) Home range of the otter *Lutra lutra* L. in southern Sweden. *Oikos*, **18**, 186–209.

352 Erlinge, S. (1968) Territoriality of the otter *Lutra lutra* L. *Oikos,* **19,** 81–98.

353 Erlinge, S. (1968) Food studies on captive otters *Lutra lutra* L. *Oikos*, **19,** 259–270.

354 Erlinge, S. (1974) Distribution, territoriality and numbers of the weasel *Mustela nivalis* in relation to prey abundance. *Oikos*, **25**, 308–314.

355 Erlinge, S. (1975) Feeding habits of the weasel *Mustela nivalis* in relation to prey abundance. *Oikos*, **26**, 378–383.

356 Erlinge, S. (1977) Agonistic behaviour and dominance in stoats (*Mustela erminea* L.). *Zeitschrift für Tierpsychologie*, **44**, 375–388.

357 Erlinge, S. (1977) Home range utilisation and movements of the stoat, *Mustela erminea*. *International Congress of Game Biologists*, **13**, 31–42.

358 Erlinge, S. (1977) Spacing strategy in stoat *Mustela erminea*. *Oikos*, **28**, 32–42.

359 Erlinge, S. (1979) Movements and daily activity pattern of radio-tracked male stoats, *Mustela erminea*, pp. 703–710 in Amlaner, C.J. & Macdonald, D.W. (eds.) *A handbook on biotelemetry and radio-tracking.* Pergamon Press, Oxford.

360 Erlinge, S. (1981) Food preference, optimal diet and reproductive output in stoats *Mustela erminea* in Sweden.

Oikos, **36**, 303–315.

361 Erlinge, S. (1983) Demography and dynamics of a stoat *Mustela erminea* population in a diverse community of vertebrates. *Journal of Animal Ecology*, **52**, 705–726.

362 Erlinge, S. (1987) Why do European stoats *Mustela erminea* not follow Bergmann's Rule? *Holarctic Ecology*, **10**, 33–39.

363 Erlinge, S. & Sandell, M. (1986) Seasonal changes in the social organisation of male stoats *Mustela erminea*: an effect of shifts between two decisive resources. *Oikos*, **47**, 57–62.

364 Erlinge, S. & Sandell, M. (1988) Coexistence of stoat, *Mustela erminea*, and weasel, *Mustela nivalis*: social dominance, scent communication, and reciprocal distribution. *Oikos*, **53**, 242–246.

365 Erlinge, S. *et al.* (1982) Scent-marking and its territorial significance in stoats, *Mustela erminea*. *Animal Behaviour*, **30**, 811–818.

366 Erlinge, S. *et al.* (1983) Predation as a regulating factor on small rodent populations in southern Sweden. *Oikos*, **40**, 36–52.

367 Erlinge, S. *et al.* (1984) Can vertebrate predators regulate their prey? *American Naturalist*, **123**, 125–133.

368 Erlinge, S. *et al.* (1988) More thoughts on vertebrate predator regulation of prey. *American Naturalist*, **132**, 148–154.

369 Estes, R.D. (1972) The role of the vomeronasal organ in mammalian reproduction. *Mammalia,* **36**, 315–341.

370 Evans, P.G.H. *et al.* (1989) Social structure of the Eurasian badger *(Meles meles)*: genetic evidence. *Journal of Zoology,* **218**, 587–595.

371 Eves, J.A. (1999) Impact of badger removal on bovine tuberculosis in east County Offaly. *Irish Veterinary Journal*, **52,** 199–203.

372 Ewer, R.F. (1973) *The carnivores.* Cornell University Press, Ithaca, NY.

373 Fahmy, M.A.M. (1954) On some helminth parasites of the otter, *Lutra lutra. Journal of Helminthology*, **28**, 189–204.

374 Fairley, J.S. (1965) The food of the fox, *Vulpes vulpes* (L.), in Co. Down. *Irish Naturalists' Journal*, **15**, 2–5.

375 Fairley, J.S. (1967) An indication of the food of the fox in Northern Ireland after myxomatosis. *Irish Naturalists' Journal*, **15**, 149–151.

376 Fairley, J.S. (1969) Tagging studies of the red fox *Vulpes vulpes* in north-east Ireland. *Journal of Zoology,* **159**, 527–532.

377 Fairley, J.S. (1969) The fox as a pest of agriculture. *Irish Naturalists' Journal*, **16**, 216–219.

378 Fairley, J.S. (1970) More results from tagging studies of foxes *Vulpes vulpes* (L.). *Irish Naturalists' Journal*, **16**, 392–393.

379 Fairley, J.S. (1970) The food, reproduction, form, growth and development of the fox *Vulpes vulpes* (L.) in north-east Ireland. *Proceedings of he Royal Irish Academy*, **69B**, 103–137.

380 Fairley, J.S. (1971) New data on the Irish stoat. *Irish Naturalists' Journal*, **17**, 49–57.

381 Fairley, J.S. (1971) The control of the fox *Vulpes vulpes* (L.) population in Northern Ireland. *Scientific Proceedings of the Royal Dublin Society*, **3**, 43–47.

382 Fairley, J.S. (1972) Food of otters (*Lutra lutra*) from Co. Galway, Ireland, and notes on other aspects of their biology. *Journal of Zoology*, **166**, 469–474.

383 Fairley, J.S. (1980) Observations on a collection of feral Irish mink *Mustela vison* Schreber. *Proceedings of the Royal Irish Academy*, **80B,** 79–80.

384 Fairley, J.S. (1981) A north-south cline in the size of the Irish stoat. *Proceedings of the Royal Irish Academy*, **81B**, 5–10.

385 Fairley, J. (1984) *An Irish beast book: a natural history of Ireland's furred wildlife.* Blackstaff Press, Belfast.

386 Fairley, J. (2001) *A basket of weasels.* Privately published, Belfast.

387 Fairley, J.S. & Bruton, T. (1984) Some observations on a collection of fox skulls from north-east Ireland. *Irish Naturalists' Journal*, **21**, 349–351.

388 Fargher, S. & Morris, P. (1975) *An investigation into methods of age determination in the badger* (Meles meles). University of London, unpublished report on an ARC research grant.

389 Farina, R. & Andreani, E. (1970) Leptospirosi degli animali selvatici in Italia. *Archivo Veterinario Italiano,* **21,** 127–141 (in Italian).

390 Feldman, H.N. (1994) Methods of scent marking in the domestic cat. *Canadian Journal of Zoology,* **72,** 1093–1099.

391 Fenn, M.G.P. & Macdonald, D.W. (1995) Use of middens by red foxes: risk reverses rhythms of rats. *Journal of Mammalogy,* **76,** 130–136.

392 Ferguson, S.H. *et al.* (2006) Does seasonality explain the evolution and maintenance of delayed implantation in the family Mustelidae (Mammalia : Carnivora)? *Oikos,* **114,** 249–256.

393 Fergusson, E.J. (1939) The pine marten in northern Scotland. *Journal for the Preservation of the Fauna of the Empire,* **36,** 27–30.

394 Fergusson, J. Personal communication.

395 Fernandez-Galiano, E. Personal communication.

396 Ferreras, P. & Macdonald, D.W. (1999) The impact of American mink *Mustela vison* in the upper Thames. *Journal of Applied Ecology,* **36,** 701–708

397 Ferris, C. (1986) Mating and early maturity of badgers in Kent. *Journal of Zoology,* **209,** 282.

398 Fiennes, J. Personal communication.

399 Fitzgerald, B.M. (1977) Weasel predation on a cyclic population of the montane vole, *Microtus montanus* in California. *Journal of Animal Ecology,* **46,** 367–397.

400 Fitzgerald, B.M. & Karl, B.J. (1979) Food of feral house cats (*Felis catus* L.) in forest of the Orongorongo Valley, Wellington. *New Zealand Journal of Zoology,* **6,** 107–126.

401 Flintoff, R.J. (1935) Stoats and weasels, brown and white. *North Western Naturalist,* **10,** 214–229.

402 Forbes, T.O.A. & Lance, A.N. (1976) The contents of fox scats from western Irish blanket bog. *Journal of Zoology,* **179,** 224–226.

403 Forrest, G. *et al.* (2002) A 2002 pine marten record for Worcestershire? *Worcestershire Record,* **13,** 23–24.

404 Forrest, H.E. (1904) Varieties of polecat and badger. *Zoologist (4th series),* **8,** 227.

405 Fowler, P.A. & Racey, P.A. (1988) Overwintering strategies of the badger, *Meles meles,* at 57°N. *Journal of Zoology,* **214,** 635–651.

406 Fox, M.W. (1971) *Behaviour of wolves, dogs and related canids.* Jonathan Cape, London.

407 Fox, N.C. *et al.* (2005) Wounding rates in shooting foxes (*Vulpes vulpes*). *Animal Welfare,* **14,** 93–102.

408 Fozzer, F. (1981) Distribuzione e biologia di 22 specie di mammiferi in Italia, pp. 89–94 in *Collana del progretto finalizzato 'Primozione della qualita' del l'ambiente'.* Pubblicazioni AQ/1/142–164, Consiglio Nazionale delle Ricerche, Rome (in Italian).

409 Francis, D. (1993) *My Highland Kellas cats.* Jonathan Cape, London.

410 Frank, F. (1974) Wurfzahl and Wurffolge beim nordischen Wiesel (*Mustela nivalis rixosa* Bangs, 1896). *Zeitschrift für Säugetierkunde,* **39,** 248–250 (in German).

411 Frank, F. (1985) Zur evolution und systematik der kleinen wiesel (*Mustela nivalis* Linnaeus, 1766). *Zeitschrift für Säugetierkunde,* **50,** 208–225 (in German).

412 Frank, L.G. (1979) Selective predation and seasonal variation in the diet of the fox (*Vulpes vulpes*) in N.E. Scotland. *Journal of Zoology,* **189,** 526–532.

413 Frantz, A.C. *et al.* (2004) Estimating population size by genotyping remotely plucked hair: the Eurasian badger. *Journal of Applied Ecology,* **41,** 985–995.

414 French, D.D. *et al.* (1988) Morphological discriminants of Scottish wildcats (*Felis silvestris*), domestic cats (*F. catus*) and their hybrids. *Journal of Zoology,* **214,** 235–259.

415 Gaiduk, V.E. (1977) [Control of moulting and winter whitening in the ermine, (*Mustela erminea*)]. *Zoologicheskii Zhurnal,* **56,** 1226–1231 (in Russian).

416 Gaiduk, V.E. (1980) [Seasonal and geographical variations in the time of moult and change of hair cover in the weasel (*Mustela nivalis*)]. *Zoologicheskii Zhurnal,* **59,** 113–119 (in Russian).

417 Gallagher, J. & Nelson, J. (1979) Causes of ill health and natural death in badgers in Gloucestershire. *Veterinary Record,* **105,** 546–551.

418 Game Conservancy (1994) *Predator control.* Game Conservancy, Fordingbridge.

419 Garnett, B.T. *et al.* (2002) Use of cattle farm resources by badgers (*Meles meles*) and risk of bovine tuberculosis (*Mycobacterium bovis*) transmission to cattle. *Proceedings of the Royal Society Series B,* **269,** 1487–1491.

420 Garnett, B.T. *et al.* (2003) Use of cattle troughs by badgers (*Meles meles*). A potential route for the transmission of bovine tuberculosis (*Mycobacterium bovis*) to cattle. *Applied Animal Behaviour Science,* **80,** 1–8.

421 Garrad, L.S. (1972) *The naturalist in the Isle of Man.* David & Charles, Newton Abbott.

422 Geffen, E. *et al.* (1992) Phylogenetic relationships of the fox-like canids: mitochondrial DNA restriction fragment, site and cytochrome *b* sequence analyses. *Journal of Zoology,* **228,** 27–39.

423 Geffen, E. *et al.* (1996) Size, life-history traits, and social organization in the Canidae: a reevaluation. *American Naturalist,* **147,** 140–160.

424 Gentry, A. *et al.* (1996) Case 3010. Proposed conservation of usage of 15 mammal specific names based on wild species which are antedated by or contemporary with those based on domestic animals. *Bulletin of Zoological Nomenclature,* **53,** 28–37.

425 Gerell, R. (1967) Food selection in relation to habitat in mink (*Mustela vison* Schreber) in Sweden. *Oikos,* **18,** 233–246.

426 Gerell, R. (1969) Activity patterns of the mink *Mustela vison* Schreber in southern Sweden. *Oikos* 20, 451–460.

427 Gerell, R. (1970) Home ranges and movements of the mink *Mustela vison* Schreber in Sweden. *Oikos,* **21,** 160–173.

428 Gerell, R. (1971) Population studies on mink (*Mustela vison* Schreber) in southern Sweden. *Viltrevy,* **8,** 83–114.

429 Gewalt, W. (1959) Beiträge zur Kenntnis des optischen Differentzierungsvermögens einiger Musteliden mit besonderer Berücksichtigug des Farbensehens. *Zoologische Beiträge,* **5,** 117–175 (in German).

430 Gibb, J A. *et al.* (1969) An experiment in the control of a sparse population of wild rabbits (*Oryctolagus c. cuniculus* L.) in New Zealand. *New Zealand Journal of Science,* **12,** 509–534.

431 Gibb, J.A. *et al.* (1978). Natural control of a population of rabbits (*Oryctolagus cuniculus* L.) for 10 years in the Kourarau enclosure. *DSIR Bulletin* **223.**

432 Gibson, J. (1970) The mammals of the Island of Bute. *Transactions of the Buteshire Natural History Society,* **18,** 5–20.

433 Gibson, J. (1970) Additional mammal notes from the Island of Arran. *Transactions of the Buteshire Natural History Society,* **18,** 45–47.

434 Gibson, J.A. Personal communication.

435 Gilbert, F.F. (1969) Analysis of basic vocalizations of the ranch mink. *Journal of Mammalogy,* **50,** 625–7.

436 Gillingham, B.J. (1984) Meal size and feeding rate in the least weasel (*Mustela nivalis*). *Journal of Mammalogy,* **65,** 517–519.

437 Gittleman, J.L. (1993) Carnivore life histories: a re-analysis in the light of new models. *Symposia of the Zoological Society of London,* **65,** 65–86.

438 Gittleman, J.L. & van Valkenburgh, B. (1997) Sexual dimorphism in the canines and skulls of carnivores: effects of size, phylogeny, and behavioural ecology. *Journal of Zoology,* **242,** 97–117.

439 Glas, G.H. (1974) Over lichaamsmaten en gewichten van de bunzing *Mustela putorius* Linnaeus, 1758, in Nederland.

Lutra, **16,** 13–19 (in Dutch).

440 Glas, G.H. (1977) [Two unusual polecats from the Netherlands.] *Lutra,* **19,** 64–65 (in Dutch).

441 Goddard, H.N. & Reynolds, J.C. (1993) Age determination in the red fox (*Vulpes vulpes* L.) from tooth cementum lines. *Gibier Faune Sauvage,* **10,** 173–187.

442 Goethe, F. (1940) Beiträge zur Biologie des Iltis. *Zeitschrift für Säugetierkunde,* **15,** 180–223 (in German).

443 Goethe, F. (1964) Das Verhalten der Musteliden. *Handbuch der Zöologie,* **VIII**(10), 1–80 (in German).

444 Gormally, M.J. & Fairley, J. (1982) Food of otters *Lutra lutra* in a freshwater lough and an adjacent brackish lough in the West of Ireland. *Journal of Zoology,* **197,** 313–321.

445 Gorman, M.L. (1984) Response of prey to stoat (*Mustela erminea*) scent. *Journal of Zoology,* **202,** 419–423.

446 Gorman, M.L. Personal communication.

447 Gorman, M.L. & Trowbridge, B.J. (1989) The role of odor in the social lives of carnivores, pp. 57–88 in Gittleman, J.G. (ed.) *Carnivore behaviour, ecology, and evolution.* Cornell University Press, Ithaca, NY.

448 Gorman, M.L. *et al.* (1978) The anal scent sacs of the otter (*Lutra lutra*). *Journal of Zoology,* **186,** 463–474.

449 Gorman, M.L. *et al.* (1984) Social functions of the sub-caudal scent gland secretion of the European badger (*Meles meles,* Carnivora, Mustelidae). *Journal of Zoology,* **204,** 549–559.

450 Gorman, M.L. *et al.* (1998) The demography of European otters *Lutra lutra. Symposia of the Zoological Society of London,* **71,** 107–118.

451 Gossow, H. (1970) Vergleichende Verhaltensstudien an Marderartigen I. Über Lautäusserungen und zum Beuteverhalten. *Zeitschrift für Tierpsychologie,* **27,** 405–480 (in German).

452 Gossow, H. & Honsig-Erlenberg, P. (1986) Management problems with reintroduced lynx in Austria, pp. 77–83 in Miller, S.D. & Everett, D.D. (eds.) *Cats of the world.* National Wildlife Federation, Washington, DC.

453 Goszczynski, J. (1976) Composition of the food of martens. *Acta Theriologica,* **21,** 527–534.

454 Goszczynski, J. (1986) Diet of foxes and martens in Central Poland. *Acta Theriologica,* **31,** 491–506.

455 Graf, M. & Wandeler, A.I. (1982) The reproductive cycle of male badgers (*Meles meles* L.) in Switzerland. *Revue Suisse de Zoo*logie, **89,** 1005–1008.

456 Graf, M. & Wandeler, A.I. (1982) Age determination in badgers, (*Meles meles* L.). *Revue Suisse de Zoo*logie, **89,** 1017–1023.

457 Grafodatskii, A.S. *et al.* (1978) [Cytogenetics of albinism in ferrets of the genus *Putorius* (Carnivora, Mustelidae)] *Genetika,* **14,** 68–71 (in Russian).

458 Graham, I.M. (2002) Estimating weasel *Mustela nivalis* abundance from tunnel tracking indices at fluctuating field vole *Microtus agrestis* density. *Wildlife Biology,* **8,** 279–287.

459 Graham, I.M. & Lambin, X. (2002) The impact of weasel predation on cyclic field-vole survival: the specialist predator hypothesis contradicted. *Journal of Animal Ecology,* **71,** 946–956.

460 Grakov, N.N. (1972) Effect of concentrated clearfellings on the abundance of the pine marten (*Martes martes* L.). *Biulleten – Moskovskoe obshchestvo ispytatelei prirdy otdel biologicheskii,* **77,** 14–23 (in Russian; English summary).

461 Grant, M.C. *et al.* (1999) Breeding success and causes of breeding failure of curlew *Numenius arquata* in Northern Ireland. *Journal of Applied Ecology,* **36,** 59–74.

462 Green, J. (1978) Sensory perception in hunting otters, *Lutra lutra* L. *Otters 1977,* **1**(1), 13–16.

463 Green, J. & Green, R. (1980) *Otter survey of Scotland 1977–79.* Vincent Wildlife Trust, London.

464 Green, J & Green, R. (1987) *Otter survey of Scotland 1984–85.* Vincent Wildlife Trust, London.

465 Green, J. *et al.* (1984) A radio-tracking survey of otters *Lutra*

lutra on a Perthshire river system. *Lutra,* **27,** 85–145.

466 Green, J. *et al.* (1986) Interspecific use of resting sites by mink *Mustela vison* and otter *Lutra lutra. Vincent Wildlife Trust Report 1985,* 20–26.

467 Green, R. (1999) Otter speed on land. *IUCN Otter Specialist Group Bulletin,* **16**(2), 102–103.

468 Green, R. Personal communication.

469 Green, R. & Green, J. (1997) *Otter survey of Scotland 1991–1994.* Vincent Wildlife Trust, London.

470 Green, R.E. & Etheridge, B. (1999) Breeding success of the hen harrier *Circus cyaneus* in relation to the distribution of grouse moors and the red fox *Vulpes vulpes. Journal of Applied Ecology,* **36,** 472–483.

471 Greer, K.R. (1957) Some osteological characters of known-age ranch minks. *Journal of Mammalogy,* **38,** 319–330.

472 Greig-Smith, P.W. *et al.* (1990) *Pesticide poisoning of animals 1989: investigations of suspected incidents in Great Britain.* MAFF, London.

473 Griffiths, H.I. (1993) The Eurasian badger, *Meles meles,* as a commodity species. *Journal of Zoology,* **230,** 340–342.

474 Griffiths, H.I. (1994) Pre- and early historic records of the Eurasian badger, *Meles meles* (L., 1758) (Carnivora, Mustelidae), in Britain. *Studies in Speleology,* **9,** 27–36.

475 Grigor'ev, N.D. & Egorov, Y.E. (1969) [On the biocenotic connections of the mink with the common otter in the Bashkirian SSR.] *Sbornik trudov Nauchno-issledovatel' skogo instituta zhivotnovodstva Syr'ya Pushniny,* **22,** 26–32 (in Russian).

476 Grigson, C. (1978) The Late Glacial and Early Flandrian ungulates in England and Wales – an interim review, pp. 46–56 in Limbrey, S & Evans, J.G. (eds.) *The effect of man on the landscape: the lowland zone.* CBA Research Report no. 21, London.

477 Grue, H.E. & King, C.M. (1984) Evaluation of age criteria in New Zealand stoats (*Mustela erminea*) of known age. *New Zealand Journal of Zoology,* **11,** 437–443.

478 Gulamhusein, A.P. & Tam, W.H. (1974) Reproduction in the male stoat, *Mustela erminea. Journal of Reproduction and Fertility,* **41,** 303–312.

479 Gulamhusein, A.P. & Thawley, A.R. (1974) Plasma progesterone levels in the stoat. *Journal of Reproduction and Fertility,* **36,** 405–408.

480 Habermehl, K.H. & Röttcher, D. (1967) Die Möglichkeiten der Alterbestimmung beim Marder und Iltis. *Zeitschrift für Jagdwissenschaft,* **13,** 89–102 (in German).

481 Haglund, B. (1966) Winter habits of the lynx (*Lynx lynx* L.) and wolverine (*Gulo gulo* L.) as revealed by tracking in the snow. *Viltrevy,* **4,** 81–310.

482 Hagmeier, E.M. (1961) Variation and relationships in North American marten. *Canadian Field Naturalist,* **75,** 122–138.

483 Halbrook, R.S. *et al.* (1999) Ecological risk assessment in a large river-reservoir: 8. Experimental study of the effects of polychlorinated biphenyls on reproductive success in mink. *Environmental Toxicology and Chemistry,* **18**(4), 649–654.

484 Hall, E.R. (1951) *American weasels.* University of Kansas Press, Lawrence.

485 Hall, E.R. (1981) *The mammals of North America,* 2nd edn. Wiley, New York.

486 Halliwell, E.C. (1997) *The ecology of red squirrels in Scotland in relation to pine marten predation.* PhD thesis, University of Aberdeen.

487 Halliwell, E.C. & Macdonald, D.W. (1996) American mink *Mustela vison* in the Upper Thames catchment: relationship with selected prey species and den availability. *Biological Conservation,* **76**(1), 51–56.

488 Haltenorth, T. (1953) *Die Wildkatzen der alten Welt: Eine Übersicht über die Untergattung Felis.* Geest & Portig, Leipzig (in German).

489 Haltenorth, T. (1957) *Die Wildkatze.* Die Neue Brehm Bücherei no.189. Ziemsen, Wittenberg Lutherstadt (in German).

490 Hamilton, C.M. *et al.* (2005) Prevalence of antibodies to *Toxoplasma gondii* and *Neospora caninum* in red foxes (*Vulpes vulpes*) from around the UK. *Veterinary Parasitology*, **130**, 169–173.

491 Hamilton, E. (1896) *The wildcat in Europe.* Porter, London.

492 Hamilton, E. (1897) The wild cat of Scotland. *Annals of Scottish Natural History*, **21**, 65–78.

493 Hamilton, W.J. (1933) The weasels of New York: their natural history and economic status. *American Midland Naturalist*, **14**, 289–344.

494 Hancox, M. (1980) Parasites and infectious diseases of the Eurasian badgers (*Meles meles*): a review. *Mammal Review*, **10**, 151–162.

495 Hancox, M. (1988) The nidicolous fauna of badger setts. *Entomologist's Monthly Magazine*, **124**, 93–95.

496 Hannson, I. (1970) Cranial helminth parasites in species of Mustelidae. 2. Regional frequencies of damage in preserved crania from Denmark, Finland, Sweden, Greenland and the northeast of Canada compared with the helminth invasion of fresh mustelid skulls from Sweden. *Arkiv för Zoologi*, **22**, 571–594.

497 Hansen, M.M. & Jacobsen, L. (1999) Identification of mustelid species: otter (*Lutra lutra*), American mink (*Mustela vison*) and polecat (*Mustela putorius*), by analysis of DNA from faecal samples. *Journal of Zoology*, **247**(2), 177–181.

498 Hanski, I. *et al.* (2001) Small-rodent dynamics and predation. *Ecology*, **82**, 1505–1520.

499 Harcourt, R. (1979) The animal bones, pp. 150–160 in Wainwright, G.J. (ed.) *Gussage All Saints: an Iron Age settlement in Dorset*. HMSO, London.

500 Harding, L.E. *et al.* (1999) Reproductive and morphological condition of wild mink (*Mustela vison*) and river otters (*Lutra canadensis*) in relation to chlorinated hydrocarbon contamination. *Environmental Health Perspectives*, **107**(2), 141–147.

501 Hargis, C.D. & McCullough, D.R. (1984) Winter diet and habitat selection of marten in Yosemite National Park. *Journal of Wildlife Management*, **48**, 140–146.

502 Hargis, C.D. *et al.* (1999) The influence of forest fragmentation and landscape pattern on American martens. *Journal of Applied Ecology*, **36**, 157–172.

503 Harman, M. Personal communication.

504 Harper, R.J. & Jenkins, D. (1981) Mating behaviour in the European otter (*Lutra lutra*). *Journal of Zoology*, **195**, 556–558.

505 Harris, C.J. (1968) *Otters: a study of the recent Lutrinae.* Weidenfeld & Nicolson, London.

506 Harris, S. (1975) Syndactyly in the red fox, *Vulpes vulpes. Journal of Zoology*, **176**, 282–287.

507 Harris, S. (1977) Distribution, habitat utilization and age structure of a suburban fox (*Vulpes vulpes*) population. *Mammal Review*, **7**, 25–39.

508 Harris, S. (1977) Spinal arthritis (spondylosis deformans) in the red fox, *Vulpes vulpes*, with some methodology of relevance to zooarchaeology. *Journal of Archaeological Science*, **4**, 183–195.

509 Harris, S. (1978) Age determination in the red fox (*Vulpes vulpes*) – an evaluation of technique efficiency as applied to a sample of suburban foxes. *Journal of Zoology*, **184**, 91–117.

510 Harris, S. (1978) Injuries to foxes (*Vulpes vulpes*) living in suburban London. *Journal of Zoology*, **186**, 567–572.

511 Harris, S. (1979) Age-related fertility and productivity in red foxes, *Vulpes vulpes*, in suburban London. *Journal of Zoology*, **187**, 195–199.

512 Harris, S. (1980) Home ranges and patterns of distribution of foxes (*Vulpes vulpes*) in an urban area, as revealed by radio tracking, pp. 685–690 in Amlaner, C.J. & Macdonald, D.W. (eds.) *A handbook on biotelemetry and radio tracking.* Pergamon Press, Oxford.

513 Harris, S. (1981) The food of suburban foxes (*Vulpes vulpes*), with special reference to London. *Mammal Review*, **11**, 151–168.

514 Harris, S. (1981) An estimation of the number of foxes (*Vulpes vulpes*) in the city of Bristol, and some possible factors affecting their distribution. *Journal of Applied Ecology*, **18**, 455–465.

515 Harris, S. (1984) Ecology of urban badgers *Meles meles*: Distribution in Britain and habitat selection, persecution, food and damage in the city of Bristol. *Biological Conservation*, **28**, 349–375.

516 Harris, S. (1985) Surveying the urban fox. *Biologist*, **32**, 259–264.

517 Harris, S. (1986) *Urban foxes.* Whittet, London.

518 Harris, S. & Baker, P. (2001) *Urban foxes*, 2nd edn. Whittet, London.

519 Harris, S. & Cresswell, W.J. (1987) Dynamics of a suburban badger (*Meles meles*) population. *Symposium of the Zoological Society of London*, **58**, 295–311.

520 Harris, S. & Lloyd, H.G. (1991) Fox, pp. 351–367 in Corbett, G.C. & Harris, S. (eds.) *Handbook of British Mammals*, 3rd edn. Blackwell Scientific Publications, Oxford.

521 Harris, S. & Macdonald, D. (1987) *Orphaned foxes.* RSPCA, Horsham, W Sussex.

522 Harris, S. & Rayner, J.M.V. (1986) Urban fox (*Vulpes vulpes*) population estimates and habitat requirements in several British cities. *Journal of Animal Ecology*, **55**, 575–591.

523 Harris, S. & Rayner, J.M.V. (1986) Models for predicting urban fox (*Vulpes vulpes*) numbers in British cities and their applications for rabies control. *Journal of Animal Ecology*, **55**, 593–603.

524 Harris, S. & Rayner, J.M.V. (1986) A discriminant analysis of the current distribution of urban foxes (*Vulpes vulpes*) in Britain. *Journal of Animal Ecology*, **55**, 605–611.

525 Harris, S. & Smith, G.C. (1987) Demography of two urban fox (*Vulpes vulpes*) populations. *Journal of Applied Ecology*, **24**, 75–86.

526 Harris, S. & Smith, G.C. (1987) The use of sociological data to explain the distribution and numbers of urban foxes (*Vulpes vulpes*) in England and Wales. *Symposia of the Zoological Society of London*, **58**, 313–328.

527 Harris, S. & Thompson, G.B. (1978) Populations of the ticks *Ixodes* (*Pholeoixodes*) *hexogonus* and *Ixodes* (*Pholeoixodes*) *canisuga* infesting suburban foxes, *Vulpes vulpes. Journal of Zoology*, **186**, 83–93.

528 Harris, S. & Trewhella, W.J. (1988) An analysis of some of the factors affecting dispersal in an urban fox (*Vulpes vulpes*) population. *Journal of Applied Ecology*, **25**, 409–422.

529 Harris, S. & White, P.C.L. (1992) Is reduced affiliative rather than increased agonistic behaviour associated with dispersal in red foxes? *Animal Behaviour*, **44**, 1085–1089.

530 Harris, S. & White, P. (1994) *The red fox.* The Mammal Society, London.

531 Harris, S. & Woollard, T. (1990) Bristol's foxes. *Proceedings of the Bristol Naturalists' Society*, **48**, 3–15.

532 Harris, S. *et al.* (1992) An integrated approach to monitoring badger (*Meles meles*) population changes in Britain, pp. 945–953 in McCullough, D.R. & Barrett, R.H. (eds.) *Wildlife 2001: populations.* Elsevier Applied Science, London.

533 Harris, S., *et al.* (1992) Age determination of badgers (*Meles meles*) from tooth wear: the need for a pragmatic approach. *Journal of Zoology*, **228**, 679–684.

534 Harris, S. *et al.* (1992) Rabies contingency planning in Britain, pp. 63–77 in O'Brien, P. & Berry, G. (eds.) *Wildlife rabies contingency planning in Australia.* Bureau of Rural Resources Proceeding No. 11, AGPS, Canberra.

535 Harris, S. *et al.* (1994) *Problems with badgers*, 3rd edn. RSPCA, Horsham, W Sussex.

536 Harris, S. *et al.* (1995) *A review of British mammals: population estimates and conservation status of British mammals other than cetaceans.* JNCC, Peterborough.

537 Harrison, D.J. *et al.* (eds.) (2004) *Martens and fishers* (Martes) *in human-altered environments: an international perspective.* Springer, Norwell, MA.

538 Harting, J.E. (1891–93) The British marten *Martes sylvatica*, Nilsson. *Zoologist* (series 3), **15**, 401–409, 450–459; **16**, 131–138; **17**, 161–163.

539 Hartley, F.G.L. *et al.* (1994) The endocrinology of gestation failure in foxes. *Journal of Reproduction and Fertility*, **100**, 341–346.

540 Hartman, L. (1964) The behaviour and breeding of captive weasels (*Mustela nivalis* L.). *New Zealand Journal of Science*, **7**, 147–156.

541 Harvie-Brown, J.A. (1882) The past and present distribution of the rarer animals of Scotland. *Zoologist*, 3rd series, **6**, 41–45.

542 Harvie-Brown, J.A. & MacPherson, H.A. (1904) *A vertebrate fauna of the Northwest Highlands and Skye.* David Douglas, Edinburgh.

543 Harvey, P. Personal communication.

544 Hatler, D.F. (1976) *The coastal mink of Vancouver Island, British Columbia.* PhD thesis, University of British Columbia.

545 Hattingh, I. (1956) Measurements of foxes from Scotland and England. *Proceedings of the Zoological Society of London*, **127**, 191–199.

546 Hawkins, C.E. & Macdonald, D.W. (1992) A spool-and-line method for investigating the movements of badgers, *Meles meles. Mammalia*, **56**, 322–325.

547 Hawley, V.D. & Newby, F.E. (1957) Marten home ranges and population fluctuations. *Journal of Mammalogy*, **38**, 174–184.

548 Hayden, T. & Harrington, R. (2000) *Exploring Irish mammals.* Duchas, The Irish Heritage Service, Dublin.

549 Hays, G.C. *et al.* (2007) Recording the free-living behaviour of small-bodied, shallow diving animals with data-loggers. *Journal of Animal Ecology*, **76**, 183–190.

550 Hayssen, V. *et al.* (1993) *Asdell's patterns of mammalian reproduction.* Comstock/Cornell University Press, Ithaca, NY.

551 Hayward, G.F. (1983) *The bio-energetics of the weasel,* Mustela nivalis *L.* D Phil thesis, University of Oxford.

552 Heggberget, T.M. (1984) Age determination in the European otter *Lutra lutra lutra. Zeitschrift für Säugetierkunde*, **49**, 299–305.

553 Heidt, G.A. (1970) The least weasel, *Mustela nivalis* Linnaeus. Developmental biology in comparison with other North American *Mustela. Publications of Michigan State University, Museum (Biological Series)*, **4**, 227–282.

554 Heidt, G.A. (1972) Anatomical and behavioral aspects of killing and feeding by the least weasel *Mustela nivalis* L. *Arkansas Academy of Science Proceedings*, **26**, 53–54.

555 Helldin, J-O. (1998) *Pine marten* (Martes martes) *population limitation: food, harvesting or predation?* Doctoral thesis, Swedish University of Agricultural Sciences, Uppsala.

556 Hellstedt, P. & Henttonen, H. (2006) Home range, habitat choice and activity of stoats (*Mustela erminea*) in a subarctic area. *Journal of Zoology*, **269**, 205–212.

557 Hemming, F. & Noakes, D. (1958) Opinion 465. p.136 in *Official list of specific names in zoology.* International Commission on Zoological Nomenclature, London.

558 Hemmington, M. (1997) *Foxwatching.* Whittet, London.

559 Henry, C.J. *et al.* (1981) PCBs and organochlorine pesticides in wild mink and river otters from Oregon, pp. 1763–1780 in Chapman, J.A. & Pursely, D. (eds.) *Proceedings of the first worldwide furbearer conference.* Worldwide Furbearer Conference, Frostburg, MD.

560 Henry, J.D. (1977) The use of urine marking in the scavenging behavior of the red fox (*Vulpes vulpes*). *Behavior*, **61**, 82–106.

561 Henry, J.D. (1986) *Red fox: the catlike canine.* Smithsonian Institution Press, London.

562 Henry, J.D. (1993) *How to spot a fox.* Chapters Publishing, Shelburne, VT.

563 Heptner, V.G. & Nuamov, N.P. (eds.) (1967) [*Mammals of the Soviet Union. Vol. 2. Sirenia and Carnivora.*] Vysshaya Shkola, Moscow (in Russian).

564 Heptner, V.G. & Sludskii, A.A. (1992) *Mammals of the Soviet Union. Vol. II, Part 2. Carnivora (hyaenas and cats).* Brill, Leiden.

565 Herfst, M. (1984) Habitat and food of the otter *Lutra lutra* in Shetland. *Lutra*, **27**, 57–70.

566 Herrenschmidt, V (1982) Note sur les déplacements et le rythme d'activité d'un putois, *Mustela putoriu* L., suivi par radiotracking. *Mammalia*, **46**, 544–546 (in French).

567 Herter, K. & Klaunig, J.R. (1956) Untersuchungen an der Retina amerikanischer Nerze (*Mustela lutreola vison* Schreb.) *Zoologische Beiträge*, **2**, 127–143 (in German).

567a Hetherington, D. (2006) The lynx in Britain's past, present and future. *Ecos*, **27**, 66–74.

568 Hetherington, D. *et al.* (2006) New evidence for the occurrence of Eurasian lynx (*Lynx lynx*) in medieval Britain. *Journal of Quaternary Science*, **21**, 3–8.

569 Hewson, R. (1983) The food of wild cats (*Felis silvestris*) and red foxes (*Vulpes vulpes*) in west and north-east Scotland. *Journal of Zoology*, **200**, 283–289.

570 Hewson, R. (1984) Scavenging and predation upon sheep and lambs in west Scotland. *Journal of Applied Ecology*, **21**, 843–868.

571 Hewson, R. (1984) Changes in the number of foxes in Scotland. *Journal of Zoology*, **204**, 561–569.

572 Hewson, R. (1985) Lamb carcasses and other food remains at fox dens in Scotland. *Journal of Zoology*, **206**, 291–296.

573 Hewson, R. (1986) Distribution and density of fox breeding dens and the effects of management. *Journal of Applied Ecology*, **23**, 531–538.

574 Hewson, R. (1990) *Victim of myth.* A report to the League Against Cruel Sports, London.

575 Hewson, R. (1994) The use of dens by hill foxes (*Vulpes vulpes*). *Journal of Zoology*, **233**, 331–335.

576 Hewson, R. (1995) Use of salmonid carcasses by vertebrate scavengers. *Journal of Zoology*, **235**, 53–65.

577 Hewson, R. & Healing, T.D. (1971) The stoat *Mustela erminea* and its prey. *Journal of Zoology*, **164**, 239–244.

578 Hewson, R. & Kolb, H.H. (1973) Changes in the number and distribution of foxes (*Vulpes vulpes*) killed in Scotland from 1948–1970. *Journal of Zoology*, **171**, 345–365.

579 Hewson, R. & Leitch, A.F. (1983) The food of foxes in forests and the open hill. *Scottish Forestry*, **37**, 39–50.

580 Hewson, R. & Watson, A. (1979) Winter whitening of stoats (*Mustela erminea*) in Scotland and north-east England. *Journal of Zoology*, **187**, 55–64.

581 Hewson, R. *et al.* (1975) The food of foxes in Scottish forests. *Journal of Zoology*, **176**, 287–292.

582 Heydon, M.J. & Reynolds, J.C. (2000) Fox (*Vulpes vulpes*) management in three contrasting regions of Britain, in relation to agricultural and sporting interests. *Journal of Zoology*, **251**, 237–252.

583 Heydon, M.J. & Reynolds, J.C. (2000) Demography of rural foxes (*Vulpes vulpes*) in relation to cull intensity in three contrasting regions of Britain. *Journal of Zoology*, **251**, 265–276.

584 Heydon, M.J. *et al.* (2000) Variation in abundance of foxes (*Vulpes vulpes*) between three regions of rural Britain, in relation to landscape and other variables. *Journal of Zoology*, **251**, 253–264.

585 Highways Agency (1999) *Design manual for roads and bridges. Vol. 10 Environmental design, Section HA 81/99 Nature Conservation advice in relation to otters.* The Stationery Office, London.

586 Hill, D.A. & Robertson, P.A. (1988) *The pheasant: ecology, management and conservation.* Blackwell Scientific Publications, Oxford.

587 Hill, M. (1939) The reproductive cycle of the male weasel *Mustela nivalis. Proceedings of the Zoological Society of London*, **109B**, 481–512.

588 Hillegaart, V. *et al.* (1985) Area utilisation and marking behaviour among two captive otter (*Lutra lutra* L.) pairs. *Otters 1984*, **1**(8), 64–74.

589 Hillel, A. (2003) *The suburban timeshare*. Privately published.

590 Hinton, M.A.C (1920) The Irish otter. *Annals and Magazine of Natural History*, **5**, 464.

591 Hoekstra, B. (1975) Een geval van hydrocephalie bij de bunzing, *Putorius putorius* (Linnaeus, 1758). *Lutra*, **17**, 1–6 (in Dutch).

592 Hofer, H. (1986) *Patterns of resource distribution and exploitation by the red fox (*Vulpes vulpes*) and the Eurasian badger* (Meles meles): *a comparative study*. DPhil thesis, University of Oxford.

593 Hofer, H. (1988) Variation in resource presence, utilization and reproductive success within a population of European badgers (*Meles meles*). *Mammal Review*, **18**, 25–36.

594 Holland, G.P. (1964) Evolution, classification and host relationships of Siphonaptera. *Annual Review of Entomology*, **9**, 123–146.

595 Holland, O.J. & Gleeson, D.M. (2005) Genetic characterisation of blastocysts and the identification of an instance of multiple paternity in the stoat (*Mustela erminea*). *Conservation Genetics*, **6**, 855–858.

596 Hope Jones, P. (1974) Wildlife records from Merioneth parish documents. *Nature in Wales*, **14**, 35–43.

597 Hough, N.G. (1980) The ranging behavior of a maturing female red fox, *Vulpes vulpes*, pp. 691–696 in Amlaner, C.J. & Macdonald, D.W. (eds.) *A handbook on biotelemetry and radio tracking*. Pergamon Press, Oxford.

598 Hounsome, T.D. & Delahay, R.J. (2005) Birds in the diet of the Eurasian badger (*Meles meles*). A review and a meta-analysis. *Mammal Review*, **35**, 199–209.

599 Hounsome, T.D. *et al.* (2005) Estimating badger abundance by distance sampling: an evaluation study on a intensively studied, high density population. *Journal of Zoology*, **266**, 81–87.

600 Howard, R.W. & Bradbury, K. (1979) Feeding by regurgitation in the badger (*Meles meles*). *Journal of Zoology*, **188**, 299.

601 Howes, C. (1981) What the cat brought in. *Bird Life*, March–April, 18–19.

602 Howes, C. (1982) What the cat brought in. *Bird Life*, January–February, 26.

603 Howes, C.A. (1974) Notes on the food of foxes on Spurn Peninsula. *Naturalist, Leeds*, **99**, 131–133.

604 Howes, C.A. (1978) Notes on the food of foxes at Gibraltar Point, Lincolnshire. *Naturalist, Leeds*, **103**, 25–26.

605 Howes, C.A. (1980) The seasonal food of foxes on Spurn Peninsula. *Spurn Bird Observatory Report for 1980*, pp. 74–75.

606 Hudson, P.J. (1992) *Grouse in space and time. The population biology of a managed game bird*. Game Conservancy, Fordingbridge.

607 Huff, J.N. & Price, E.O. (1968) Vocalizations of the least weasel *Mustela nivalis*. *Journal of Mammalogy*, **49**, 548–550.

608 Hurrell, H.G. (1968) *Wildlife tame but free*. David & Charles, Newton Abbot.

609 Hurrell, H.G. (1968) *Pine martens*. Forest Record No. 64. HMSO, London.

610 Huson, L.W. & Page, R.J.C. (1979) A comparison of fox skulls from Wales and south-east England. *Journal of Zoology*, **187**, 465–470.

611 Huson, L.W. & Page, R.J.C. (1980) Age related variability in cranial measurements in the red fox (*Vulpes vulpes*). *Journal of Zoology*, **191**, 427–429.

612 Huson, L.W. & Page, R.J.C. (1980) Multivariate geographical variation of the red fox (*Vulpes vulpes*) in Wales. *Journal of Zoology*, **191**, 453–459.

613 Hutchings, M.R. *et al.* (2002) Is population density correlated with faecal and urine scent marking in European badgers (*Meles meles*) in the UK? *Mammalian Biology*, **67**, 286–293.

614 Hutchinson, G.E. & Parker, P.J. (1978) Sexual dimorphism in the winter whitening of the stoat *Mustela erminea*. *Journal of Zoology*, **186**, 560–563.

615 Independent Scientific Group on Cattle TB (1998) *Towards a sustainable policy to control TB in cattle*. First Report of the Independent Scientific Group on Cattle TB. MAFF, London.

616 Insley, H. (1977) An estimate of the population density of the red fox (*Vulpes vulpes*) in the New Forest, Hampshire. *Journal of Zoology*, **183**, 549–553.

617 Iverson, J.A. (1972) Basal energy metabolism of mustelids. *Journal of Comparative Physiology*, **81**, 341–344.

618 Jędrzejewska, B. & Jędrzejewski, W. (1998) *Predation in vertebrate communities. The Białowieża Primeval Forest as a case study*. Springer, Berlin.

619 Jędrzejewski, W. & Jędrzejewski, B. (1990) Effect of a predator's visit on the spatial-distribution of bank voles – experiments with weasels. *Canadian Journal of Zoology*, **68**, 660–666.

620 Jędrzejewska, W. *et al.* (1993) Responses of bank voles to odours of seven species of predators: experimental data and their relevance to natural predator-vole relationships. *Oikos*, **68**, 251–257.

621 Jędrzejewska, W. *et al.* (1993) Foraging by pine marten *Martes martes* in relation to food resources in Białowieża National Park, Poland. *Acta Theriologica*, **38**, 405–426.

622 Jędrzejewska, W. *et al.* (1995) Weasel population response, home-range and predation on rodents in a deciduous forest in Poland. *Ecology*, **76**, 179–195.

623 Jędrzejewska, W. *et al.* (2000) Activity patterns of radio-tracked weasels *Mustela nivalis* in Białowieża National Park (E. Poland). *Annales Zoologici Fennici*, **37**, 161–168.

624 Jefferies, D.J. (1974) Earthworms in the diet of the red fox (*Vulpes vulpes*). *Journal of Zoology*, **173**, 251–252.

625 Jefferies, D.J. (1975) The role of the thyroid in the production of sublethal effects by organochlorine insecticides and polychlorinated biphenyls, pp. 131–230 in Moriarty, F. (ed.) *Organochlorine insecticides: persistent organic pollutants*. Academic Press, London.

626 Jefferies, D.J. (1980) Programme of research, pp 71–72 in Lenton, E.J. *et al.* Otter Survey of England 1977–79. Nature Conservancy Council, London.

627 Jefferies, D.J. (1986) Estimation of complete body weights for skinned European otters *Lutra lutra* (L.). *Journal of Zoology* A, **209**, 282–285.

628 Jefferies, D.J. (1987) The effects of angling interests on otters, with particular reference to disturbance, pp. 23–30 in Maitland, P.S. & Turner, A.K. (eds.) *Angling and wildlife in fresh waters, ITE Symposium no. 19*. Institute of Terrestrial Ecology, Grange-over-Sands.

629 Jefferies, D.J. (1988) Dimensions and weights of some known-aged otters *Lutra lutra*, with notes on continuous growth during maturity, the largest weights achieved and a possible recent reduction in longevity. *Otters 1987*, **2**(1), 10–18.

630 Jefferies, D.J. (1989) Otters crossing watersheds. *Otters 1988*, **2**(2), 17–19.

631 Jefferies, D.J. (1989) The changing otter population of Britain 1700–1989. *Biological Journal of the Linnean Society*, **38**, 61–69.

632 Jefferies, D.J. (1991) Predation of otters *Lutra lutra* by American mink *Mustela vison*. *Otters 1990*, **2**(4), 33–35.

633 Jefferies, D.J. (1992) Polecats *Mustela putorius* and pollutants in Wales. *Lutra*, **35**, 28–39.

634 Jefferies, D.J. (1996) Blindness in British otters: further incidence, possible causes and correlation with the period of organochlorine pollution. *Otters 1995*, **2**(9), 14–22.

635 Jefferies, D.J. (1996) Decline and recovery of the otter – a personal account. *British Wildlife*, **7**, 353–364.

636 Jefferies, D.J. (1997) The changing status of the otter in the British Isles as revealed by spraint surveys. *Vincent Wildlife Trust Review 1996*, 19–23.

637 Jefferies, D.J. (2003) *The water vole and mink survey of Britain 1996–1998 with a history of the long term changes in the status of both species and their causes.* Vincent Wildlife Trust, Ledbury.

638 Jefferies, D.J. & Critchley, C.H. (1994) A new pine marten *Martes martes* record for the North Yorkshire Moors: skull dimensions and confirmation of species. *Naturalist,* **119,** 145–150.

639 Jefferies, D.J. & Green, R. Personal communication.

640 Jefferies, D.J. & Hanson, H.M. (1991) Evidence of fighting in a juvenile male otter road casualty bred from the otters released at Minsmere in 1985 and 1987. *Otters 1990,* **2**(4), 13–24.

641 Jefferies, D.J. & Hanson, H.M. (2002) The role of dieldrin in the decline of the otter in Britain : the analytical data, pp. 95–144 in Conroy, J.W.H. *et al.* (eds.) *Proceedings of the First Otter Toxicological Conference,* Skye, September 2000. International Otter Survival Fund, Skye.

642 Jefferies, D.J. & Hanson, H.M. Personal communication.

643 Jefferies, D.J. & Prestt, I. (1966) Post-mortems of Peregrines and Lanners with particular reference to organochlorine residues. *British Birds,* **59,** 49–64.

644 Jefferies, D.J. & Twelves, J. Personal communication.

645 Jefferies, D.J. *et al.* (1974) Pollution and mammals, pp. 13–15 in *Monks Wood Experimental Station Report for 1972–73.* Natural Environment Research Council, Huntingdon.

646 Jefferies, D.J. *et al.* (1985) The composition, age, size and pre-release treatment of the groups of otters *Lutra lutra* used in the first releases of captive-bred stock in England, *Otters 1984,* **1**(8), 11–16.

647 Jefferies, D.J. *et al.* (1986) Reinforcing the native otter *Lutra lutra* population in East Anglia: an analysis of the behaviour and range development of the first release group. *Mammal Review,* **16,** 65–79.

648 Jefferies, D.J. *et al.* (1989) A further record of *Lutridia exilis* (Nitzsch) (Phthiraptera, Trichodectidae) in Britain, with notes of the presence and absence of lice on otters. *Entomologist's Monthly Magazine,* **125,** 245–249.

649 Jefferies, D.J. *et al.* (1989) Entanglement with monofilament nylon fishing net: a hazard to otters. *Otters 1988,* **2**(2), 11–16.

650 Jefferies, D.J. *et al.* (1990) The prevalence of *Pseudoterranova decipiens* (Nematoda) and *Corynosoma strumosum* (Acanthocephala) in otters *Lutra lutra* from coastal sites in Britain. *Journal of Zoology,* **221,** 316–321.

651 Jefferies, D.J. *et al.* (1993) Otter mortalities due to commercial fishing 1975–1992, pp. 25–29 in Morris, P.A. (ed.) *Proceedings of the National Otter Conference,* Cambridge, September 1992. The Mammal Society, Bristol.

652 Jefferies, D.J. *et al.* (2001) A brief history of the Otter Trust's successful programme of repopulating lowland England with otters bred in captivity with a special emphasis on East Anglia. *Otters 2000,* **3**(4), 105–117.

653 Jenkins, D. (1980) Ecology of otters in northern Scotland I. Otter (*Lutra lutra*) breeding and dispersion in mid-Deeside, Aberdeenshire in 1974–79. *Journal of Animal Ecology,* **49,** 713–735.

654 Jenkins, D. & Harper, R.J. (1980) Ecology of otters in northern Scotland II. Analyses of otter (*Lutra lutra*) and mink (*Musela vison*) faeces from Deeside, N.E. Scotland in 1977–78. *Journal of Animal Ecology,* **49,** 737–754.

655 Jenkins, D. *et al.* (1964) Predation and red grouse populations. *Journal of Applied Ecology,* **1,** 183–195.

656 Jenkins, D. *et al.* (1979) Analyses of otter (*Lutra lutra*) faeces from Deeside, N.E. Scotland. *Journal of Zoology,* **187,** 235–244.

657 Jenkinson, R. (1983) The recent history of the Northern Lynx (*Lynx lynx* Linné) in the British Isles. *Quaternary Newsletter,* **41,** 1–7.

658 Jennings, D.H. *et al.* (1982) Metazoan parasites and food of short-tailed weasels and mink in Newfoundland, Canada. *Canadian Journal of Zoology,* **60,** 180–183.

659 Jensen, A. (1964) Odderen i Danmark. *Danske Vildtundersogelser,* **11,** 1–48 (in Danish).

660 Jensen, B. & Nielsen, L.B. (1968) Age determination in the red fox (*Vulpes vulpes* L.) from canine tooth sections. *Danish Review of Game Biology,* **5,** 1–15.

661 Jeselnik, D.L. & Brisbin, Jr, I.L. (1980) Food-caching behaviour of captive-reared red foxes. *Applied Animal Ethology,* **6,** 363–367.

662 Johnson, C.E. (1980) An unusual food source of the red fox (*Vulpes vulpes*). *Journal of Zoology,* **192,** 561–562.

663 Johnson, D.P. & Macdonald, D.W. (2001) Why are group-living badgers (*Meles meles*) sexually dimorphic? *Journal of Zoology,* **255,** 199–204.

664 Johnson, D.P. *et al.* (2002) Does the resource dispersion hypothesis explain group living? *Trends in Ecology and Evolution,* **17,** 563–570.

665 Johnson, W.E. & O'Brien, S.J. (1997) Phylogenetic reconstruction of the Felidae using 16S rRNA and NADH-5 mitochondrial genes. *Journal of Molecular Evolution,* **44**(Suppl. 1), S98–S116.

666 Jones, E. (1977) Ecology of the feral cat, *Felis catus* (L.). (Carnivora: Felidae) on Macquarie Island. *Australian Wildlife Research,* **4,** 249–262.

667 Jones, G.W. *et al.* (1980) The helminth parasites of the badger (*Meles meles*) in Cornwall. *Mammal Review,* **10,** 163–164.

668 Jones, I. & Jones, D. (2004) *Otter Survey of Wales* 2002. Environment Agency, Bristol.

669 Kamler, J.F. & Ballard, W.B. (2002) A review of native and non-native foxes in North America. *Wildlife Society Bulletin,* **30,** 370–379.

670 Kaplan, C. (1985) Rabies: a worldwide disease, pp. 1–21 in Bacon, P.J. (ed.) *Population dynamics of rabies in wildlife.* Academic Press, London.

671 Kerby, G. & Macdonald, D.W. (1988) Cat society and the consequences of colony size, pp. 67–82 in Turner, D.C. & Bateson, P. (eds.) *The domestic cat: the biology of its behaviour.* Cambridge University Press, Cambridge.

672 Keymer, I.F. (1993) Diseases of the otter (*Lutra lutra*), pp. 30–33 in Morris, P.A. (ed.) *Proceedings of the National Otter Conference,* Cambridge, September 1992. The Mammal Society, Bristol.

673 Keymer, I.F. & Epps, H.B.G. (1969) Canine distemper in the family Mustelidae. *Veterinary Record,* **85,** 204–205.

674 Keymer, I.F. *et al.* (1981) Urolithiasis in otters (Family Mustelidae, Subfamily Lutrinae) and other species. *Verhandlungsbericht des XXIII Internationalen Symposiums über die Erkrankungen der Zootiere,* **23,** 391–401.

675 Keymer, I.F. *et al.* (1988) Pathological changes in wild otters (*Lutra lutra*) and organochlorine tissue residues. *Veterinary Record,* **122,** 153–155.

676 Kidd, N.A.C. & Lewis, G.B. (1987) Can vertebrate predators regulate their prey? A reply. *American Naturalist,* **130,** 448–453.

677 Kildemoes, A. (1985) The impact of introduced stoats (*Mustela erminea*) on an island population of the water vole, *Arvicola terrestris. Acta Zoologica Fennica,* **173,** 193–195.

678 King, C.M. (1975) The home range of the weasel (*Mustela nivalis*) in an English woodland. *Journal of Animal Ecology,* **44,** 639–668.

679 King, C.M. (1975) The sex ratio of trapped weasels *Mustela nivalis. Mammal Review,* **3,** 1–8.

680 King, C.M. (1976) The fleas of a population of weasels in Wytham Woods, Oxford. *Journal of Zoology,* **180,** 525–535.

681 King, C.M. (1977) The effects of the nematode parasite *Skrjabingylus nasicola* on British weasels (*Mustela nivalis*). *Journal of Zoology,* **182,** 225–249.

682 King, C.M. (1977) Pine marten *Martes martes,* pp. 323–330. In Corbet, G.B. & Southern, H.N. (eds.) *The handbook of British mammals,* 2nd edn. Blackwells, Oxford.

683 King, C.M. (1979) Moult and colour change in English

weasels (*Mustela nivalis*). *Journal of Zoology,* **189**, 127–134.

684 King, C.M. (1980) Age determination in the weasel (*Mustela nivalis*) in relation to the development of the skull. *Zeitschrift für Säugetierkunde,* **45**, 153–173.

685 King, C.M. (1980) Population biology of the weasel *Mustela nivalis* on British game estates. *Holarctic Ecology,* **3**, 160–168.

686 King, C.M. (1980) The weasel (*Mustela nivalis*) and its prey in an English woodland. *Journal of Animal Ecology,* **49**, 127–159.

687 King, C.M. (1981) The reproductive tactics of the stoat (*Mustela erminea*) in New Zealand forests, pp. 443–468 in Chapman, J.A. & Pursley, D. (eds.) *Proceedings of the First Worldwide Furbearer Conference.* Worldwide Furbearer Conference, Frostburg, MD.

688 King, C.M. (1983) *Mustela erminea. Mammalian Species,* **195**, 1–8.

689 King, C.M. (1989) The advantages and disadvantages of small size to weasels, *Mustela* species, pp. 302–334 in Gittleman, J.L. (ed.) *Carnivore behaviour, ecology and evolution.* Cornell University Press, Ithaca, NY.

690 King, C.M. (1991) Body size–prey size relationships in European stoats *Mustela erminea*: a test case. *Holarctic Ecology,* **14**, 173–185.

691 King, C.M. (1991) A review of age-determination methods for the stoat *Mustela erminea. Mammal Review,* **21**, 31–49.

692 King, C.M. (ed.) (2005) *The handbook of New Zealand mammals,* 2nd edn. Oxford University Press, Melbourne.

693 King, C.M. & McMillan, C.D. (1982) Population structure and dispersal of peak year cohorts of stoats (*Mustela erminea*) in two New Zealand forests, with especial reference to control. *New Zealand Journal of Ecology,* **5**, 59–66.

694 King, C.M. & Moody, J.E. (1982) The biology of the stoat (*Mustela erminea*) in the national parks of New Zealand. *New Zealand Journal of Zoology,* **9**, 49–144.

695 King, C.M. & Moors, P.J. (1979) On co-existence, foraging strategy and the biogeography of weasels and stoats (*Mustela nivalis* and *M. erminea*) in Britain. *Oecologia,* **39**, 129–150.

696 King, C.M. & Powell, R.A. (2007) *The natural history of weasels and stoats: ecology, behavior and management,* 2nd edn. Oxford University Press, New York.

697 King, C.M. *et al.* (2003) Matching productivity to resource availability in a small predator, the stoat (*Mustela erminea*). *Canadian Journal of Zoology,* **81**, 662–669.

698 King, D.P. *et al.* (2004) Detection of mustelid Herpesvirus-1 infected European badgers (*Meles meles*) in the British Isles. *Journal of Wildlife Diseases,* **40**, 99–102.

699 King, R.J. (1958) The training of badgers in Pershore Forest. *Journal of the Forestry Commission,* **2**, 45–50.

700 Kitchener, A. (1991) *The natural history of the wild cats.* Comstock, Ithaca, NY.

701 Kitchener, A. (1992) The Scottish wildcat *Felis silvestris*: decline and recovery, pp. 21–41 in Mansard, P. (ed). *Cats.* Ridgeway Trust for Endangered Cats, Hastings.

702 Kitchener, A. (1993) Appendix. Investigating the identity of the Kellas cats, pp. 211–213 in Francis, D. *My Highland Kellas cats.* Jonathan Cape, London

703 Kitchener, A. (1995) *Wildcats.* The Mammal Society, London.

704 Kitchener, A.C. (1998) The Scottish wildcat: a cat with an identity crisis? *British Wildlife,* **9,** 232–242.

705 Kitchener, A.C. (1999) Watch with mother: a review of social learning in the Felidae. *Symposia of the Zoological Society of London,* **72**, 236–258.

707 Kitchener, A.C. & Bonsall, C. (1997) AMS radiocarbon dates for some extinct Scottish mammals. *Quaternary Newsletter,* **83**, 1–11.

708 Kitchener, A.C. & Easterbee, N. (1992) The taxonomic status of black felids in Scotland. *Journal of Zoology,* **227**, 342–346.

709 Kitchener, A.C. & Ward, J. Personal communication.

710 Kitchener, A.C. *et al.* (2005) A diagnosis for the Scottish wildcat: a tool for conservation action for a critically-endangered felid. *Animal Conservation,* **8**, 223–237.

711 Kitchener, A.C. *et al.* Personal communication.

712 Kleef, H. (2000) Natal den attendance of two female pine martens *Martes martes* related to kitten development. *Lutra,* **43**, 137–149.

713 Klemola, T. *et al.* (1997) Small mustelid predation slows population growth of *Microtus* voles: a predator reduction experiment. *Journal of Animal Ecology,* **66**, 607–614.

714 Koepfli, K-P. & Wayne, R.K. (1998) Phylogenetic relationships of otters (Carnivora: Mustelidae) based on mitochondrial cytochrome b sequences. *Journal of Zoology,* **246**, 401–416.

715 Kolb, H.H. (1977) Wildcat *Felis silvestris*, pp. 275–282 in Corbet, G.B. & Southern, H.N. (eds.) *The handbook of British mammals.* Blackwell Scientific Publications, Oxford.

716 Kolb, H.H. (1978) Variation in the size of foxes in Scotland. *Biological Journal of the Linnean Society,* **10**, 291–304.

717 Kolb, H.H. (1978) The formation of lines in the cementum of the premolar teeth in foxes. *Journal of Zoology,* **185**, 259–263.

718 Kolb, H.H. (1984) Factors affecting the movements of dog foxes in Edinburgh. *Journal of Applied Ecology,* **21**, 161–173.

719 Kolb, H.H. (1985) Habitat use by foxes in Edinburgh. *Revue d'Ecologie (Terre et la Vie),* **40**, 139–143.

720 Kolb, H.H. (1986) Some observations on the home range of vixens (*Vulpes vulpes*) in the suburbs of Edinburgh. *Journal of Zoology,* **210A**, 636–639.

721 Kolb, H. (1996) *Country foxes.* Whittet, London.

722 Kolb, H.H. & Hewson, R. (1974) The body size of the red fox (*Vulpes vulpes*) in Scotland. *Journal of Zoology,* **173**, 253–255.

723 Kolb, H.H. & Hewson, R. (1979) Variation in the diet of foxes in Scotland. *Acta Theriologica,* **24**, 69–83.

724 Kolb, H.H. & Hewson, R. (1980) A study of fox populations in Scotland from 1971 to 1976. *Journal of Applied Ecology,* **17**, 7–19.

725 Kolb, H.H. & Hewson, R. (1980) The diet and growth of fox cubs in two regions of Scotland. *Acta Theriologica,* **25**, 325–331.

726 Kontrimavichus, V.L. (1966) *Helminths of mustelids and trends in their evolution.* Amerind Publishing, New Delhi.

727 Kopein, K.I. (1967) Analysis of the age structure of ermine populations, pp. 158–169 in King, C.M. (ed.) *Biology of mustelids: some Soviet research.* British Library Lending Division, Boston Spa.

728 Korhonen, H. *et al.* (1983) Thermoregulation of polecat and racoon dog: a comparative study with stoat, mink and blue fox. *Comparative Biochemistry and Physiology* A, **74**, 225–230.

729 Korpimäki, E. & Norrdahl, K. (1989) Avian predation on mustelids in Europe 1: occurrence and effects on body size variation and life traits. *Oikos,* **55,** 205–215.

730 Korpimäki, E. & Norrdahl, K. (1989) Avian predation on mustelids in Europe 2: impact on small mustelid and microtine dynamics – a hypothesis. *Oikos,* **55**, 273–276.

731 Korpimäki, E. & Norrdahl, K. (1998) Experimental reduction of predators reverses the crash phase of small-rodent cycles. *Ecology,* **79**, 2448–2455.

732 Korpimäki, E. *et al.* (1991) Responses of stoats and least weasels to fluctuating food abundances – is the low phase of the vole cycle due to mustelid predation? *Oecologia,* **88**, 552–561.

733 Korpimäki, E. *et al.* (2005) Vole cycles and predation in temperate and boreal zones of Europe *Journal of Animal Ecology,* **74,** 1150–1159.

734 Krebs, J.R. (1997) *Bovine tuberculosis in cattle and badgers.* Report to the Rt Hon Dr Jack Cunningham MP. Ministry of Agriculture, Fisheries and Food, London.

735 Kratochvíl, J. (1977) Studies on *Mustela erminea* (Mammalia, Mustelidae) I. of metric and mass traits. *Folia*

Zoologica, **26,** 291–304.

736 Krivanec, K. *et al.* (1975) The role of polecats of the genus *Putorius* Cuvier, 1817 in natural foci of adiaspiromycosis. *Folia Parasitologica,* **22,** 245–249.

737 Kruuk, H. (1964) Predators and anti-predator behaviour of the black-headed gull (*Larus ridibundus* L.). *Behaviour, Supplement,* **11,** 1–130.

738 Kruuk, H. (1972) Surplus killing by carnivores. *Journal of Zoology,* **166,** 233–244.

739 Kruuk, H. (1976) The biological function of gulls' attraction towards predators. *Animal Behaviour,* **24,** 146–153.

740 Kruuk, H. (1978) Spatial organization and territorial behaviour of the European badger *Meles meles. Journal of Zoology,* **184,** 1–19.

741 Kruuk, H. (1986) Interactions between Felidae and their prey species, pp. 353–374 in Miller, S.D. & Everett, D.D. (eds.) *Cats of the world.* National Wildlife Federation, Washington, DC.

742 Kruuk, H. (1989) *The social badger – ecology and behaviour of a group-living carnivore.* Oxford University Press, Oxford.

743 Kruuk, H. (1992) Scent marking by otters (*Lutra lutra*): signalling the use of resources. *Behavioural Ecology,* **3,** 133–140.

744 Kruuk, H. (1995) *Wild otters: predation and populations.* Oxford University Press, Oxford.

745 Kruuk, H. (2006) *Otters: ecology, behaviour and conservation.* Oxford University Press, Oxford.

746 Kruuk, H. & Balharry, D. (1990) Effects of seawater on thermal insulation of the otter, *Lutra lutra* L. *Journal of Zoology,* **220,** 405–415.

747 Kruuk, H. & Carss, D.N. (1996) Costs and benefits of fishing by a semi-aquatic carnivore, the otter *Lutra lutra,* pp. 10–16 in Greenstreet, S.T.R. & Tasker, M. (eds.) *Aquatic predators and their prey.* Fishing News Books, Blackwell, Oxford.

748 Kruuk, H. & Conroy, J.W.H. (1987) Surveying otter *Lutra lutra* populations: a discussion of problems with spraints. *Biological Conservation,* **41,** 179–183.

749 Kruuk, H. & Conroy, J.W.H. (1991) Mortality of otters *Lutra lutra* in Shetland. *Journal of Applied Ecology,* **28,** 83–94.

750 Kruuk, H. & Moorhouse, A. (1990) Seasonal and spatial differences in food selection by otters *Lutra lutra* in Shetland. *Journal of Zoology,* **221,** 621–637.

751 Kruuk, H. & Parish, T. (1982) Factors affecting population density, groups and territory size of the European badger, *Meles meles. Journal of Zoology,* **196,** 31–39.

752 Kruuk, H. & Parish, T. (1983) Seasonal and local differences in the weight of European badgers (*Meles meles* L.) in relation to food supply. *Zeitschrift für Säugetierkunde,* **48,** 45–50.

753 Kruuk, H. & Parish, T. (1985) Food, food availability and weight of badgers (*Meles meles*) in relation to agricultural changes. *Journal of Applied Ecology,* **22,** 705–715.

754 Kruuk, H. & Parish, T. (1987) Changes in the size of groups and ranges of the European badger (*Meles meles*) in an area in Scotland. *Journal of Animal Ecology,* **56,** 351–364.

755 Kruuk, H. *et al.* (1984) Scent-marking with the subcaudal gland by the European badger, (*Meles meles*). *Animal Behaviour,* **32,** 899–907.

756 Kruuk, H. *et al.* (1986) The use of spraints to survey populations of otters *Lutra lutra. Biological Conservation,* **35,** 187–194.

757 Kruuk, H. *et al.* (1987) Seasonal reproduction, mortality and food of otters (*Lutra lutra* L.) in Shetland. *Symposia of the Zoological Society of London,* **58,** 263–278.

758 Kruuk, H. *et al.* (1989) An estimate of numbers and habitat preference of otters *Lutra lutra* in Shetland. *Biological Conservation,* **49,** 241–254.

759 Kruuk, H. *et al.* (1993) Otter (*Lutra lutra* L.) numbers and fish productivity in rivers in N.E. Scotland. *Symposia of the Zoological Society,* **65,** 171–191.

760 Kruuk, H. *et al.* (1993) *Otters, eels and contaminants.* Institute of Terrestrial Ecology, Report to Scottish Natural Heritage.

761 Kryštufek, B. *et al.* (2003) *Living with bears. A large European carnivore in a shrinking world.* Ecological Forum, Liberal Democracy of Slovenia, Ljubljana.

762 Kurki, S. *et al.* (1998) Abundances of red fox and pine marten in relation to the composition of boreal forest landscapes. *Journal of Animal Ecology,* **67,** 874–886.

763 Kurtén, B. (1965) On the evolution of the European wildcat, *Felis silvestris* Schreber. *Acta Zoologica Fennica,* **111,** 1–29.

764 Kurtén, B. (1968) *Pleistocene mammals of Europe.* Weidenfeld & Nicolson, London.

765 Kyle, C.J. *et al.* (2003) Genetic structure of European pine martens (*Martes martes*), and evidence for introgression with *M americana* in England. *Conservation Genetics,* **4,** 179–188.

766 Kyne, M.J. *et al.* (1989) The food of otters *Lutra lutra* in the Irish Midlands and a comparison with that of mink *Mustela vison* in the same region. *Proceedings of the Royal Irish Academy B,* **89,** 33–46.

767 Lamb, A. Personal communication.

768 Lambin, X. *et al.* (1995) Vole cycles. *Trends in Ecology and Evolution,* **10,** 204.

769 Langley, P.J.W. & Yalden, D.W. (1977) The decline of the rarer carnivores in Great Britain during the nineteenth century. *Mammal Review,* **7,** 95–116.

770 Lariviere, S. (1996) The American mink, *Mustela vison,* (Carnivora, Mustelidae) can climb trees. *Mammalia,* **60,** 485–486.

771 Lavers, R.B. (1973) Aspects of the ecology of the ferret *Mustela putorius* forma *furo* L. at Pukepuke Lagoon. *Proceedings of the New Zealand Ecological Society,* **20,** 7–12.

772 Lavin, S.R. *et al.* (2003) Prey use by red foxes (*Vulpes vulpes*) in urban and rural areas of Illinois. *Canadian Journal of Zoology,* **81,** 1070–1082.

773 Lavrov, N.P. (1944) Effect of helminth invasions and infectious disease on variations in numbers of the ermine, pp. 170–187 in King, C.M. (ed.) *Biology of mustelids: some Soviet research.* British Library Lending Division, Boston Spa.

774 Lavrov, N.P. (1956) Characteristics and causes of the prolonged depression in numbers of the ermine in forest steppe and steppe zones of USSR, pp. 188–215 in King, C.M. (ed.) *Biology of mustelids: some Soviet research.* British Library Lending Division, Boston Spa.

775 le Brun, A. *et al.* (1987) Le néolithique preceramique de Chypre. *L'Anthropologie,* **91,** 283–316 (in French).

776 Le Cren, E.D. (1951) The length-weight relationship and seasonal cycle in gonad weight and condition in the perch *Perca fluviatilis. Journal of Animal Ecology,* **20,** 201–219.

777 Le Sueur, F. (1976) *A natural history of Jersey.* Phillimore & Co., London.

778 Leckie, F.M. *et al.* (1998) Variation in the diet of red foxes on Scottish moorland in relation to prey abundance. *Ecography,* **21,** 599–604.

779 Lenton, E. (1982) Otters and the Otter Haven Project. *Nature in Devon,* **3,** 27–43.

780 Lenton, E.J. *et al.* (1980) *Otter survey of England 1977–79.* Nature Conservancy Council, London.

781 Leuw, A. de (1957) *Die Wildkatze.* Merkblatt Nieder-wildausschuss Deutschland Jagdschutzverband, Munich (in German).

782 Lever, C. (1978) The not so innocuous mink? *New Scientist,* **78,** 812–814.

783 Lever, C. (1978) Are wild mink a threat? *New Scientist,* **80,** 712.

784 Lever, C. (1985) *Naturalized mammals of the world.* Longman, Harlow.

785 Lever, C. (1994) *Naturalized animals: the ecology of successfully introduced species.* Poyser, London.

786 Lever, R.J.A.W. (1959) The diet of the fox since

myxomatosis. *Journal of Animal Ecology,* **28**, 359–375.

787 Lewis, J.W. (1967) Observations on the skull of Mustelidae infected with the nematode, *Skrjabingylus nasicola. Journal of Zoology,* **153**, 561–564.

788 Liberg, O. (1981) *Predation and social behaviour in a population of domestic cats – an evolutionary approach.* PhD thesis, University of Lund.

789 Liberg, O. (1983) Home range and territoriality in free-ranging cats. *Acta Zoologica Fennica,* **171**, 283–285.

790 Lightfoot, V.M.A. & Wallis, S.J. (1982) Predation of small mammals inside Longworth traps by a weasel. *Journal of Zoology,* **198**, 521.

791 Liles, G. Personal communication.

792 Lindemann, W. (1955) Über die Jugendentwicklung beim Luchs (*Lynx l. lynx* Kerr) und bei der Wildkatze (*Felis s.silvestris* Schreber, 1777). *Behaviour,* **8**, 1–45 (in German).

793 Lindemann, W. & Rieck, W. (1953) Beobachtungen bei der Aufzucht von Wildkazten. *Zeitschrift für Tierpsychologie,* **10**, 92–119 (in German).

794 Lindsay, I.M. & Macdonald, D.W. (1985) The effects of disturbance on the emergence of Eurasian badgers in winter. *Biological Conservation,* **34**, 289–306.

795 Lindström, E. (1981) Reliability of placental scar counts in the red fox (*Vulpes vulpes* L.) with special reference to the fading of scars. *Mammal Review,* **11**, 137–149.

796 Lindström, E. (1986) Territory inheritance and the evolution of group-living in carnivores. *Animal Behaviour,* **34**, 1825–1835.

797 Lindström, E.R. (1994) Placental scars in the red fox (*Vulpes vulpes* L.) revisited. *Zeitschrift für Säugetierkunde,* **59**, 169–173.

798 Lindström, E. *et al.* (1995) Pine marten–red fox interactions: a case of intraguild predation? *Annales Zoologicae Fennici,* **32**, 123–130.

799 Linn, I.J. & Birks, J.D.S. (1981) Observations on the home ranges of feral American mink (*Mustela vison*) in Devon, England, as revealed by radio-tracking, pp. 1088–1102 in Chapman, J.A & Pursely, D. (eds.) *Proceedings of the First Worldwide Furbearer Conference.* Worldwide Furbearer Conference, Frostburg, MD.

800 Linn, I. & Chanin, P. (1978) Are mink really pests in Britain? *New Scientist,* **77**, 560–562.

801 Linn, I. & Chanin, P. (1978) More on the mink 'menace'. *New Scientist,* **80**, 38–40.

802 Linn, I. & Day, M.G. (1966) Identification of individual weasels *Mustela nivalis* using the ventral pelage pattern. *Journal of Zoology,* **148**, 583–585.

803 Linn, I. & Stevenson, J.H.F. (1980) Feral mink in Devon. *Nature in Devon,* **1**, 7–27.

804 Lloyd, H.G. (1980) *The red fox.* Batsford, London.

805 Lloyd, H.G. (1980) Habitat requirements of the red fox, pp. 7–25 in Zimen, E. (ed.) *The red fox: symposium on behaviour and ecology.* Junk, The Hague.

806 Lloyd, H.G. Personal communication.

807 Lloyd, H.G. & Englund, J. (1973) The reproductive cycle of the red fox in Europe. *Journal of Reproduction and Fertility, Supplement,* **19**, 119–130.

808 Lockie, J.D. (1956) After myxomatosis: notes on the food of some predatory animals in Scotland. *Scottish Agriculture,* **36**, 65–69.

809 Lockie, J.D. (1961) The food of the pine marten *Martes martes* in West Ross-shire, Scotland. *Proceedings of the Zoological Society of London,* **136**, 187–195.

810 Lockie, J.D. (1963) Eagles, foxes and their food supply in Wester Ross, Scotland. *Scottish Agriculture,* **42**, 1–4.

811 Lockie, J.D. (1964) The breeding density of the golden eagle and fox in relation to food supply in Wester Ross, Scotland. *Scottish Naturalist,* **71**, 67–77.

812 Lockie, J.D. (1966) Territory in small carnivores. *Symposia of the Zoological Society of London,* **18**, 143–165.

813 Lodé, T. (1993) Stratégies d'utilisation de l'espace chez le putois Européen *Mustela putorius* L. dans l'Ouest de la France. *Revue d'Ecologie (Terre et Vie),* **48**, 305–322 (in French).

814 Lodé, T (1994) Polymorphisms in the European polecat, *Mustela putorius,* in France. *IUCN Small Carnivore Conservation Newsletter,* **11**, 10.

815 Lodé, T. (1994) Environmental factors influencing habitat exploitation by the polecat *Mustela putorius* in western France. *Journal of Zoology,* **234**, 75–88.

816 Lodé, T. (1995) Convergences morphologiques du putois (*Mustela putorius*) et du vison Americain (*M. vison*) avec le vison d'Europe (*M. lutreola*). *Gibier Faune Sauvage,* **12**, 147–158 (in French).

817 Lodé, T. (1995) Activity pattern of polecats *Mustela putorius* L. in relation to food habits and prey activity. *Ethology,* **100**, 295–308.

818 Lodé, T. (1997) Trophic status and feeding habits of the European Polecat *Mustela putorius* L. 1758. *Mammal Review,* **27**, 177–184.

819 Lodé, T. (1999) Comparative measurements of terrestrial and aquatic locomotion in *Mustela lutreola* and *M. putorius. Zeitschrift für Säugetierkunde–International Journal of Mammalian Biology,* **64**, 110–115.

820 Lodé, T. (2000) Functional response and area-restricted search in a predator: seasonal exploitation of anurans by the European polecat, *Mustela putorius. Australian Ecology,* **25**, 223–231.

821 Lodé, T. (2001) Genetic divergence without spatial isolation in polecat *Mustela putorius* populations. *Journal of Evolutionary Biology,* **14**, 228–236.

822 Lodé, T. *et al.* (2005) European mink–polecat hybridization events: hazards from natural process? *Journal of Heredity,* **96**, 89–96.

823 Lodge, D. *et al.* Personal communication.

824 Long, C.A. & Howard, T. (1976) Intra-specific overt fighting in the wild mink. *Reports on Fauna and Flora of Wisconsin,* **11**, 4–5.

825 Loukmas, J.J. & Halbrook, R.S. (2001) A test of the mink habitat suitability index model for riverine systems. *Wildlife Society Bulletin,* **29**, 821–826.

826 Lovegrove, R. (2007) *Silent fields: the long decline of a nation's wildlife.* Oxford University Press, Oxford.

827 Lüps, P. & Roper, T.J. (1990) Cannibalism in a female badger (*Meles meles*): infanticide or predation? *Journal of Zoology,* **221**, 314–315.

828 Lynch, J.M. *et al.* (1993) Morphometric and genetic variation among badger populations, pp. 94–107 in Hayden, T. (ed.) *The badger.* Royal Irish Academy, Dublin.

829 Lynch, J.M. *et al.* (1996) Variation in cranial form and sexual dimorphism among five European populations of the otter, *Lutra lutra. Journal of Zoology,* **238**, 81–96.

830 Lynch, J.M. *et al.* (1997) Craniometric variation in the Eurasian badger, *Meles meles. Journal of Zoology,* **242**, 31–44.

831 Macdonald, D.W. (1976) Food caching by red foxes and some other carnivores. *Zeitschrift für Tierpsychologie,* **42**, 170–185.

832 Macdonald, D.W. (1977) On food preference in the red fox. *Mammal Review,* **7**, 7–23.

833 Macdonald, D.W. (1979) 'Helpers' in fox society. *Nature,* **282**, 69–71.

834 Macdonald, D.W. (1979) Some observations and field experiments on the urine marking behaviour of the red fox, *Vulpes vulpes* L. *Zeitschrift für Tierpsychologie,* **51**, 1–22.

835 Macdonald, D.W. (1980) *Rabies and wildlife – a biologist's perspective.* Oxford University Press, Oxford.

836 Macdonald, D.W. (1980) Social factors affecting reproduction amongst red foxes, Vulpes vulpes, pp. 123–175 in Zimen, E. (ed.) *The red fox: symposium on behaviour and ecology.* Junk, The Hague.

837 Macdonald, D.W. (1980) Patterns of scent marking with urine and faeces amongst carnivore communities. *Symposia of the Zoological Society of London,* **45**, 107–139.

References

838 Macdonald, D.W. (1980) The red fox, *Vulpes vulpes*, as a predator upon earthworms, *Lumbricus terrestris. Zeitschrift für Tierpsychologie*, **52**, 171–200.

839 Macdonald, D.W. (1981) Resource dispersion and the social organization of the red fox (*Vulpes vulpes*), pp. 918–949 in Chapman, J.A & Pursely, D. (eds.) *Proceedings of the First Worldwide Furbearer Conference*. Worldwide Furbearer Conference, Frostburg, MD.

840 Macdonald, D.W. (1983) The ecology of carnivore social behaviour. *Nature*, **301**, 379–384.

841 Macdonald, D.W. (1984) A questionnaire survey of farmers' opinions and actions towards wildlife on farmlands, pp 171–177 in Jenkins, D. (ed.) *Agriculture and the environment*. ITE Monks Wood, Huntingdon.

842 Macdonald, D.W. (1985) The carnivores: order Carnivora, pp. 619–722 in Brown, R.E. & Macdonald, D.W. (eds.) *Social odours in mammals*. Clarendon Press, Oxford.

843 Macdonald, D.W. (1987) *Running with the fox*. Unwin Hyman, London.

844 Macdonald, D.W. (1995) Wildlife rabies: the implications for Britain. Unresolved questions for the control of wildlife rabies: social perturbation and interspecific interactions, pp. 33–48. in Beynon, P.H. & Ednay, A.T.B. (eds.) *Rabies in a changing world*. British Small Animal Veterinary Association, Cheltenham.

845 Macdonald, D.W. & Apps, P.J. (1978) The social behaviour of a group of semi-dependent farm cats, *Felis catus*: A progress report. *Carnivore Genetics Newsletter*, **3**, 256–268.

846 Macdonald, D.W. & Carr, G.M. (1981) Foxes beware: you are back in fashion. *New Scientist*, **89**, 9–11.

847 Macdonald, D.W. & Carr, G.M. (1989) Food security and the rewards of tolerance, pp. 75–99 in Standen, V. & Foley, R.A. (eds.) *Comparative socioecology: the behavioural ecology of humans and other mammals*. Blackwell Scientific Publications, Oxford.

848 Macdonald, D.W. & Doncaster, P. (1985) *Foxes in your neighbourhood?* RSPCA, Horsham, W Sussex.

849 Macdonald, D.W. & Halliwell, E.C. (1994) The rapid spread of red foxes, *Vulpes vulpes*, on the Isle of Man. *Global Ecology and Biogeography Letters*, **4**, 1–8.

850 Macdonald, D.W. & Harrington, L.A. (2003) The American mink: the triumph and tragedy of adaptation out of context. *New Zealand Journal of Zoology*, **30**, 421–441.

851 Macdonald, D.W. & Johnson, P.J. (1996) The impact of sport hunting: a case study, pp. 160–207 in Taylor, V.J. & Dunstone, N. (eds.) *The exploitation of mammal populations*. Chapman & Hall, London.

852 Macdonald, D.W. & Moehlman, P.D. (1982) Cooperation, altruism, and restraint in the reproduction of carnivores. *Perspectives in Ethology*, **5**, 433–467.

853 Macdonald, D.W. & Newdick, M.T. (1982) The distribution and ecology of foxes, *Vulpes vulpes* (L), in urban areas, pp. 123–135 in Bornkamm, R. *et al.* (eds) *Urban ecology*. Blackwell Scientific, Oxford.

854 Macdonald, D.W. & Newman, C. (2002) Population dynamics of badgers (*Meles meles*) in Oxfordshire, U.K.: numbers, density and cohort life histories, and a possible role of climate change in population growth. *Journal of Zoology*, **256**, 121–138.

855 Macdonald, D.W. & Strachan, R. (1999) *The mink and the watervole: analyses for conservation*. Wildlife Conservation Unit, Oxford.

856 Macdonald, D.W. & Thom, M.D. (2001) Alien carnivores: unwelcome experiments in ecological theory, pp. 93–122 in Gittleman, J. *et al.* (eds.) *Carnivore conservation*: Cambridge University Press, Cambridge.

857 Macdonald, D.W. & Voigt, D.R. (1985) The biological basis of rabies models, pp. 71–108 in Bacon, P.J. (ed.) *Population dynamics of rabies in wildlife*. Academic Press, London.

858 Macdonald, D.W. *et al.* (1981) Fox populations, habitat characterization and rabies control. *Journal of Biogeography*, **8**, 145–151.

859 Macdonald, D.W. *et al.* (1987) Social dynamics, nursing coalitions and infanticide among farm cats, *Felis catus*. *Advances in Ethology*, **28**, 1–64.

860 Macdonald, D.W. *et al.* (1998) *Proposals for future monitoring of British mammals*. HMSO, London.

861 Macdonald, D.W. *et al.* (1998) The health, haematology and blood biochemistry of free-ranging farm cats in relation to social status. *Animal Welfare*, **7**, 243–256.

862 Macdonald, D.W. *et al.* (1999) Inter-annual differences in the age-related prevalences of *Babesia* and *Trypanosoma* parasites of European badgers (*Meles meles*). *Journal of Zoology*, **247**, 65–70.

863 Macdonald, D.W. *et al.* (1999) The impact of American Mink, *Mustela vison*, as predators of native species in British freshwater systems, pp. 5–23 in Cowand, D.P. & Feare, C.J. (eds.) *Advances in vertebrate pest management*. Filander Verlag, Fürth.

864 Macdonald, D.W. *et al.* (2000) Measuring the dynamics of mammalian societies: an ecologist's guide to ethological methods, pp. 332–388 in Boitani, L. & Fuller, T. (eds.) *Research techniques in animal ecology: controversies and consequences*. Columbia University Press, New York.

865 Macdonald, D.W. *et al.* (2000) Group-living in the domestic cat: its sociobiology and epidemiology, pp. 95–118 in Turner, D.C. & Bateson, P. (eds.) *The domestic cat: the biology of its behaviour*, 2nd edn. Cambridge University Press, Cambridge.

866 Macdonald, D.W. *et al.* (2002) Density-dependent regulation of body mass and condition in badgers (*Meles meles*) from Wytham Woods. *Ecology*, **83**, 2056–2061.

867 Macdonald, D.W. *et al.* (2002) No evidence of social hierarchy amongst feeding badgers, *Meles meles. Ethology*, **108**, 613–628.

868 Macdonald, D.W. *et al.* (2003) The bio-economics of fox control, pp. 220–236 in Tattersall, F. & Manly, W. (eds.) *Conservation and conflict – farming and mammals*. Westbury Publishing, Otley, W Yorks.

869 Macdonald, D.W. *et al.* (2004) Increasing frequency of bite wounds with increasing population density in Eurasian badgers, *Meles meles. Animal Behaviour*, **67**, 745–751.

870 Macdonald, D.W. *et al.* (2004) Encounters between two sympatric carnivores: red foxes (*Vulpes vulpes*) and European badgers (*Meles meles*). *Journal of Zoology*, **263**, 385–392.

871 Macdonald, D.W. *et al.* (2004) *The Scottish wildcat. Analyses for conservation and an action plan*. Wildlife Conservation Research Unit, Oxford.

872 Macdonald, D.W. *et al.* (2004) The ecology of weasels (*Mustela nivalis*) on mixed farmland in southern England. *Biologia, Bratislava*, **59**, 235–241.

873 Macdonald, S.M. & Mason, C.F. (1994) *Status and conservation needs of the otter (Lutra lutra) in the western Palaearctic*. Nature and Environment Series no 67, Council of Europe, Strasbourg.

874 Macdonald, S.M. & Mason, C.F. (1997) *Otter survey of Essex: first and second reports*. World Wide Fund for Nature, London.

875 Machinskii, A.P. & Semov, V.N. (1973) [Trichinellosis of wild animals in Mordovia.] *Meditsinskaya Parazitologiya i Parazitarnye Bolezni* 40:532–534 (in Russian).

876 MacLean, S.F. *et al.* (1974) Population cycles in Arctic lemmings: winter reproduction and predation by weasels. *Arctic and Alpine Research*, **6**, 1–12.

877 MacLennan, R.R. & Bailey, E.D. (1969) Seasonal changes in aggression, hunger, and curiosity in ranch mink. *Canadian Journal of Zoology*, **47**, 1395–1404.

878 Madsen, A.B. & Prang, A. (2001) Habitat factors and the presence or absence of otters *Lutra lutra* in Demark. *Acta Theriologica*, **46**, 171–179.

879 MAFF (1985) *Rabies prevention and control – the risk to Great Britain from rabies. Government policy*. HMSO, London.

880 MAFF (1987) *Bovine tuberculosis in badgers, 11th report.* MAFF, London.

881 Magris, L. Personal communication.

882 Maher, W.J. (1967) Predation by weasels on a winter population of lemmings, Banks Island, Northwest Territories. *Canadian Field Naturalist,* **81,** 248–250.

883 Manley, W. *et al.* (1999) *Economics, social and environmental aspects of hunting with hounds in west Somerset and Exmoor.* Report to the Rural Economy Working Group of West Somerset District Council. Centre for Rural Studies, Royal Agricultural College, Cirencester.

884 Maran, T. & Henttonen, H. (1995) Why is the European mink, *Mustela lutreola,* disappearing? – a review of the process and hypothesis. *Annales Zoologici Fennici,* **32,** 47–54.

885 Marchesi, P. (1989) *Ecologie et comportement de la martre (Martes martes L.) dans le Jura Suisse.* PhD thesis, Université de Neuchâtel (in French).

886 Mardon, D.K. & Moors, P.J. (1977) Records of fleas collected from weasels (*Mustela nivalis*) in North-east Scotland. (Siphonaptera: Hystrichopsyllidae and Ceratophyllidae). *Entomologist's Gazette,* **28,** 277–280.

887 Margoschis, R. (1985) *Mammal haunts.* Sound recording on one cassette. R. Margoschis, 80 Manchester Road, Atherstone, Warwickshire.

888 Marmi, J. *et al.* (2004) Phylogeny, evolutionary history and taxonomy of the Mustelidae, based on sequences of the cytochrome *b* gene and a complex repetitive flanking region. *Zoologica Scripta,* **33,** 481–499.

889 Maroo, S. & Yalden, D.W. (2000) The Mesolithic mammal fauna of Great Britain. *Mammal Review,* **30,** 243–248.

890 Marshall, H. (1991) Recent ottter records in Devon. *Report and Transactions of the Devonshire Association for the advancement of Science,* **123,** 137–148.

891 Marshall, W.H. (1936) A study of the winter activities of the mink. *Journal of Mammalogy,* **17,** 382–92.

892 Mason, C.F. (1988) Concentrations of organochlorine residues and metals in tissues of otters *Lutra lutra* from the British Isles 1985–1986. *Lutra,* **31,** 62–67.

893 Mason, C.F. & Macdonald, S.M. (1980) The winter diet of otters (*Lutra lutra*) on a Scottish sea loch. *Journal of Zoology,* **192,** 558–561.

894 Mason, C.F. & Macdonald, S.M. (1986) *Otters: ecology and conservation.* Cambridge University Press, Cambridge.

895 Mason, C.F. & Weber, D. (1990) Organochlorine residues and heavy metals in kidneys of polecats (*Mustela putorius*) from Switzerland. *Bulletin of Environmental Contamination and Toxicology,* **45,** 689–696.

896 Mason, C.F. *et al.* (1986) Organochlorine residues in British otters. *Bulletin of Environmental Contamination and Toxicology,* **36,** 656–661.

897 Mason, C.F. *et al.* (1986) Mercury, cadmium and lead in British otters. *Bulletin of Environmental Contamination and Toxicology,* **37,** 844–849.

898 Masuda, R. *et al.* (1996) Molecular phylogeny of mitochondrial cytochrome b and 12S rRNA sequences in the Felidae: Ocelot and domestic cat lineages. *Molecular Phylogenetics and Evolution,* **6**(3), 351–365.

899 Matheson, C. (1932) *Changes in the fauna of Wales within historic times.* National Museum of Wales, Cardiff.

900 Matheson, C. (1963) The distribution of the red polecat in Wales. *Proceedings of the Zoological Society of London,* **140,** 115–120.

901 Mathews, A.J. & Wilson, C.J. (2005) *The management of problems involving badgers (*Meles meles*): protection of Badgers Act 1992 licensing cases 1997–1999.* Department for Environment, Food and Rural Affairs, London.

902 Mathews, F. *et al.* (2006) Bovine tuberculosis (*Mycobacterium bovis*) in British farmland wildlife: the importance to agriculture. *Proceedings of the Royal Society of London Series B,* **273,** 357–365.

903 Matson, G. Personal communication.

904 Matthews, L.H. (1941) Reproduction in the Scottish wildcat, *Felis silvestris grampia* Miller. *Proceedings of the Zoological Society of London,* **111,** 59–77.

905 Matthews, L.H. (1952) *British mammals.* Collins, London.

906 Maurel, D. & Boissin, J. (1983) Comparative mechanisms of physiological, metabolical and eco-ethological adaptation to winter season in two wild European mammals: the European badger (*Meles meles* L.) and the red fox (*Vulpes vulpes* L.), pp. 219–233 in Margaris, N.S. *et al.* (eds.) *Adaptations to terrestrial environment.* Plenum Press, New York.

907 Maurel, D. *et al.* (1984) Seasonal reproductive endocrine profiles in two wild mammals: the red fox (*Vulpes vulpes* L.) and the European badger (*Meles meles* L.) considered as short-day mammals. *Acta Endocrinologica,* **105,** 130–138.

908 Maurel, D. *et al.* (1986) Seasonal moulting patterns in three fur bearing mammals: the European badger (*Meles meles* L.), the red fox (*Vulpes vulpes* L.), and the mink (*Mustela vison*). A morphological study. *Canadian Journal of Zoology,* **64,** 1757–1764.

909 McCann, C. (1956) Observations on the polecat (*Putorius putorius* Linn.) in New Zealand. *Records of the Dominion Museum, Wellington,* **2,** 151–165.

910 McCaughey, W.J. & Fairley, J.S. (1969) Serological reactions to *Brucella* and *Leptospira* in foxes. *Veterinary Record,* **84,** 542.

911 McCormick, F. (1984) Large mammal bones, in Sharples, N.M. (ed.) Excavations at Pierowall Quarry, Westray, Orkney. *Proceedings of the Society of Antiquaries of Scotland,* **114,** 75–125.

912 McCormick, F. (1999) Early evidence for wild animals in Ireland, in Benecke, N. (ed.) The Holocene history of the European vertebrate fauna. *Archäologie in Eurasien,* **6,** 355–371.

913 McDonald, R.A. (2002) Resource partitioning among British and Irish mustelids. *Journal of Animal Ecology,* **71,** 185–200.

914 McDonald, R.A. (2007) *Mustela nivalis* and *Mustela subpalmata,* in Kingdon, J.S.& Hoffmann, M. (eds.) *The mammals of Africa Vol 5. Carnivora, Pholidota, Perissodactyla.* Academic Press, Amsterdam.

915 McDonald, R.A. & Birks, J.D.S. (2003) Effects of farming practice and wildlife management on small mustelid carnivores, pp. 106–119 in Tattersall, F. & Manley, W. (eds.) *Conservation and conflict: mammals and farming in Britain.* Linnean Society, London.

916 McDonald, R. & Harris, S. (1998) *Stoats and weasels.* The Mammal Society, London.

917 McDonald, R.A. & Harris, S. (1999) The use of trapping records to monitor populations of stoats *Mustela erminea* and weasels *M. nivalis*: the importance of trapping effort. *Journal of Applied Ecology,* **36,** 679–688.

918 McDonald, R.A. & Harris, S. (2002) The population biology of stoats *Mustela erminea* and weasels *Mustela nivalis* on game estates in Great Britain. *Journal of Applied Ecology,* **39,** 793–805.

919 McDonald, R.A. & Larivière, S.C. (2001) Diseases and pathogens of *Mustela* spp., with special reference to the biological control of introduced stoat *Mustela erminea* populations in New Zealand. *Journal of the Royal Society of New Zealand,* **31,** 721–744.

920 McDonald, R.A. & Murphy, E.C. (2000) A comparison of the management of stoats and weasels in Great Britain and New Zealand, in Griffiths, H.I. (ed.) *Mustelids in a modern world,* pp. 21–40. Backhuys, Leiden.

921 McDonald, R. *et al.* (1997) *Is the fox a pest?* Electra Publishing, Cheddar.

922 McDonald, R.A. *et al.* (1998) Anticoagulant rodenticides in stoats (*Mustela erminea*) and weasels (*M. nivalis*) in England. *Environmental Pollution,* **103,** 17–23.

923 McDonald, R.A. *et al.* (2000) The diet of stoats (*Mustela erminea*) and weasels (*Mustela nivalis*) in Great Britain. *Journal of Zoology,* **252**, 363–371.

924 McDonald, R.A. *et al.* (2001) Histological evidence of disease in wild stoats *Mustela erminea* in England. *Veterinary Record,* **149**, 671–675.

925 McFadden, Y.M.T. & Fairley, J.S. (1984) Food of otters *Lutra lutra* (L.) in an Irish limestone river system with special reference to the crayfish *Austropotamobius pallipes* (Lereboullet). *Journal of Life Sciences, Royal Dublin Society,* **5**, 65–76.

926 McGhie, H. (2002) Changes in distribution and persecution of carnivores in north Scotland 1912–1970 as evidenced by taxidermists' records. *Scottish Naturalist,* **114**, 45–83.

927 McKay, J. (1995) *Complete guide to ferrets.* Swan Hill Press, Shrewsbury.

928 McKillop, I.G. & Sibly, R.M. (1988) Animal behaviour at electric fences and the implications for management. *Mammal Review,* **18**, 91–103.

929 McNamee, T. (1997) *The return of the wolf to Yellowstone.* H. Holt, New York.

930 McOrist, S. (1992) Diseases of the European wildcat (*Felis silvestris* Schreber, 1777) in Great Britain. *Revue Scientifique et Technique (International Office of Epizootics),* **11**(4), 1143–1149.

931 McOrist, S. & Kitchener, A.C. (1994) Current threats to the European wildcat, *Felis silvestris,* in Scotland. *Ambio,* **23**, 243–245.

932 Mead, C.J. (1982) Ringed birds killed by cats. *Mammal Review,* **12**, 183–186.

933 Mead, R.A. (1994) Reproduction in *Martes,* pp. 243–245 in Buskirk, S.W. *et al.* (eds.) *Martens, sables and fishers, biology and conservation.* Cornell University Press, Ithaca, NY.

934 Mech, D. & Boitani, L. (2003) *Wolves. Behavior, ecology and conservation.* University of Chicago Press, Chicago.

935 Mech, D. *et al.* (1998) *The wolves of Denali.* University of Minnesota Press, Minneapolis.

936 Messenger, J.E. & Birks, J.D.S. (2000) Monitoring the very rare: pine marten populations in England and Wales, pp. 217–230 in Griffiths, H.I. (ed.) *Mustelids in a modern world.* Backhuys, Leiden.

937 Messenger, J. *et al.* (1997) What is the status of the pine marten in England and Wales? *British Wildlife,* **8**, 273–279.

938 Messenger, J.E. *et al.* (2006) An artificial natal den box for pine martens *Martes martes,* pp. 87–96 in Santos-Reis, M. *et al.* (eds.) *Martes in carnivore communities.* Alpha Wildlife Publications, Sherwood Park, Alberta, Canada

939 Meyer-Holzapfel, M. (1968) Breeding the European wild cat *Felis s. silvestris* at Berne Zoo. *International Zoo Yearbook,* **8**, 31–39.

940 Millais, J.G. (1905) *The mammals of Great Britain and Ireland,* vol. 2. Longmans Green & Co., London.

941 Miller, G.S. (1907) Some new European Insectivora and Carnivora. *Annals and Magazine of Natural History, 7th series,* **20**, 389–398.

942 Miller, G.S. (1912) *Catalogue of the mammals of western Europe (exclusive of Russia) in the collections of the British Museum.* British Museum (Natural History), London.

943 Miller, G.S. (1933) The origin of the ferret. *Scottish Naturalist,* **203**, 153–154.

944 Minsky, D. (1980) Preventing fox predation at a least tern colony with an electric fence. *Journal of Field Ornithology,* **51**, 180–181.

945 Mitchell, J.L. (1958) *Mink population study.* Report W49-R-7, Montana Fish Game Project.

946 Mitchell, J.L. (1961) Mink movements and populations on a Montana river. *Journal of Wildlife Management,* **25**, 48–54.

947 Mitchell, J.L. Personal communication.

948 Mitchell-Jones, A.J. *et al.* (1999) *The atlas of European mammals.* Poyser, London.

949 Moberly, R.L. *et al.* (2002) *The costs of foxes to agricultural interests in Britain.* Report to the RSPCA, Southwater, W Sussex.

950 Moberly, R.L. *et al.* (2003) Factors associated with fox (*Vulpes vulpes*) predation of lambs in Britain. *Wildlife Research,* **30**, 1–9.

951 Moberly, R.L. *et al.* (2004) Mortality due to fox predation in free-range poultry flocks in Britain. *Veterinary Record,* **155**, 48–52.

952 Moberly, R.L. *et al.* (2004) Modelling the costs of fox predation and preventive measures on sheep farms in Britain. *Journal of Environmental Management,* **70**, 129–143.

953 Moehlman, P.D. & Hofer, H. (1997) Cooperative breeding, reproductive suppression, and body mass in Canids, pp. 76–128 in Solomon, N.G. & French, J.A. (eds.) *Cooperative breeding in mammals.* Cambridge University Press, Cambridge.

954 Moll, P. van *et al.* (1995) Distemper in wild carnivores: an epidemiological, histological and immunocytochemical study. *Veterinary Microbiology,* **44**, 193–199.

955 Moller, H. & Alterio, N. (1999) Home range and spatial organisation of stoats (*Mustela erminea*), ferrets (*Mustela furo*) and feral house cats (*Felis catus*) on coastal grasslands, Otago Peninsula, New Zealand: implications for yellow-eyed penguin (*Eudyptes antipodes*) conservation. *New Zealand Journal of Zoology,* **26**, 165–174

956 Mondain-Monval, M. *et al.* (1979) Androgens in the peripheral blood of the red fox (*Vulpes vulpes* L.) during the reproductive season and the anoestrus. *Journal of Steroid Biochemistry,* **11**, 1315–1322.

957 Mönnig, H.O. (1950) *Veterinary helminthology and entomology: The diseases of domesticated animals caused by helminth and arthropod parasites,* 3rd edn. Baillière, Tindall and Cox, London.

958 Monte, M. & Roeder, J.J. (1990) Histological structure of the abdominal gland and other body regions involved in olfactory communication in pine martens (*Martes martes*). *Zeitschrift für Säugetierkunde,* **55**, 425–427.

959 Moore, N. *et al.* (1999) Survey of badger *Meles meles* damage to agriculture in England and Wales. *Journal of Applied Ecology,* **36**, 974–988.

960 Moorhouse, A. (1988) *Distribution of holts and their utilisation by the European otter (Lutra lutra L.) in a marine environment.* MSc thesis, University of Aberdeen.

961 Moors, P.J. (1974) *The annual energy budget of a weasel (Mustela nivalis) population in farmland.* PhD dissertation, University of Aberdeen.

962 Moors, P.J. (1975) The food of weasels (*Mustela nivalis*) on farmland in north east Scotland. *Journal of Zoology,* **177**, 455–461.

963 Moors, P.J. (1977) Studies of metabolism, food consumption and assimilation efficiency of a small carnivore, the weasel (*Mustela nivalis* L.). *Oecologia,* **27**, 185–202.

964 Moors, P.J. (1980) Sexual dimorphism in the body size of mustelids (Carnivora): the roles of food habits and breeding systems. *Oikos,* **34**, 147–158.

965 Moors, P.J. (1983) Predation by stoats (*Mustela erminea*) and weasels (*M. nivalis*) on nests of New Zealand forest birds. *Acta Zoologica Fennica,* **174**, 193–196.

966 Morgan, C.A. (2002) *Studies on a reinforced population of the Eurasian otter (Lutra lutra).* PhD thesis, University of York.

967 Morgan, E.R. *et al.* (2005) *Angiostrongylus vasorum;* a real heartbreaker. *Trends in Parasitology,* **21**, 49–51.

968 Morgan, I.K. (1992) Interim notes on the status of the pine marten in south-west and mid-Wales. *Llanelli Naturalists Newsletter,* Winter 1992–93, 11–22.

969 Mulder, J.L. (1990) The stoat *Mustela erminea* in the Dutch dune region, its local extinction, and a possible cause: the arrival of the fox *Vulpes vulpes. Lutra,* **33**, 1–21.

970 Müller, H. (1970) Beiträge zur Biologie des Hermelins,

Mustela erminea Linné 1758. *Säugetierkundliche Mitteilungen,* **18**, 293–380 (in German).

971 Mullineaux, E. (2003) Badgers, pp. 123–136 in Mullineaux, E. *et al.* (eds.) *BSAVA manual of wildlife casualties.* British Small Animal Veterinary Association, Gloucester.

972 Murphy, E.C. & Dowding, J.E. (1994) Range and diet of stoats (*Mustela erminea*) in a New Zealand beech forest. *New Zealand Journal of Ecology,* **18**, 11–18.

973 Murphy, E.C. & Dowding, J.E. (1995) Ecology of the stoat in *Nothofagus* forest: Home range, habitat use and diet at different stages of the beech mast cycle. *New Zealand Journal of Ecology,* **19**, 97–109.

974 Murphy, M.J. (1985) *Behavioural and sensory aspects of predation in mustelids.* PhD thesis, University of Durham.

975 Müskens, G.J.D.M. & Broekhuizen, S. (2000) De boommarter *Martes martes* als verkeersslachtoffer. *Lutra,* **43**, 229–235 (in Dutch).

976 Nams, V.O. & Beare, S.S. (1982) Use of trees by ermine, *Mustela erminea. Canadian Field Naturalist,* **96**, 89–90.

977 Neal, E.G. (1972) The national badger survey. *Mammal Review,* **2**, 55–64.

978 Neal, E.G. (1977) *Badgers.* Blandford Press, Poole.

979 Neal, E.G. (1986) *The natural history of badgers.* Croom Helm, London.

980 Neal, E.G. & Cheeseman, C.L. (1996) *Badgers.* Poyser, London.

981 Neal, E.G. & Harrison, R.J. (1958) Reproduction in the European badger (*Meles meles,* L.). *Transactions of the Zoological Society of London,* **29**, 67–131.

982 Neville, P.F. & Remfrey, J. (1984) Effect of neutering on two groups of feral cats. *Veterinary Record,* **114**, 447–450.

983 Newman, T.J. *et al.* (2003) Changes in red fox habitat preference and rest site fidelity following a disease-induced decline. *Acta Theriologica,* **48**, 79–91.

984 Newsome, A.E. (1995) Socio-ecological models for red fox populations subject to fertility control in Australia. *Annales Zoologica Fennici,* **32**, 99–110.

985 Newton, E.T. (1894) The Vertebrate fauna collected by Mr. Lewis Abbott from the Fissure near Ightham, Kent. *Quarterly Journal of the Geological Society,* **50**, 189–211.

986 Newton, E.T. (1899) Additional notes on the vertebrate fauna of the rock-fissure at Ightham (Kent). *Quarterly Journal of the Geological Society,* **55**, 419–429.

987 Newton, I. *et al.* (1999) Empirical evidence of side-effects of rodenticides on some predatory birds and mammals, pp. 347–367 in Cowan, D.P. & Feare, C.J. (eds.) *Advances in vertebrate pest management.* Filander Verlag, Fürth.

988 Newton-Fisher, N. *et al.* (1993) Structure and function of red fox *Vulpes vulpes* vocalisations. *Bioacoustics,* **5**, 1–31.

989 Nilson, E.B. *et al.* (2007) Wolf reintroduction to Scotland: public attitudes and consequences for red deer management. *Philosophical Transactions of the Royal Society of London Series B,* **274**, 995–1002.

990 Nolet, B.A. & Kruuk, H. (1989) Grooming and resting of otters *Lutra lutra* in a marine habitat. *Journal of Zoology,* **218**, 433–440.

991 Nolet, B.A. *et al.* (1993) Diving of otters (*Lutra lutra*) in a marine habitat: use of depths by a single-prey loader. *Journal of Animal Ecology,* **62**, 22–32.

992 NOP (1974) *Facts about foxes and farming.* NOP Consumer Market Research, London.

993 Norrdahl, K. & Korpimäki, E. (1998) Does mobility or sex of voles affect risk of predation by mammalian predators? *Ecology,* **79**, 226–232.

994 Novikov, G.A. (1962) *Carnivorous mammals of the fauna of the USSR.* Israel Program for Scientific Translations, Jerusalem.

995 Nowell, K. & Jackson, P. (1996) *Wild cats: status surveys and conservation action plans.* IUCN, Gland.

996 Nyholm, E.S. (1959) Stoats and weasels in their winter habitat, pp. 118–131 in King C.M. (ed.) *Biology of mustelids: some Soviet research.* British Library Lending Division, Boston Spa.

997 Nyholm, E.S. (1970) [On the ecology of the pine marten in eastern and northern Finland.] *Suomen Riista,* **13**, 106–116 (in Finnish).

998 O'Donnell, C.F.J. & Phillipson, S.M. (1996) Predicting the incidence of mohua predation from the seedfall, mouse, and predator fluctuations in beech forests. *New Zealand Journal of Zoology,* **23**, 287–293.

999 O'Mahoney, D. *et al.* (1999) Fox predation on cyclic field vole populations in Britain. *Ecography,* **22**, 575–581.

1000 Oftedal, O.T. (1984) Milk composition, milk yield and energy output at peak lactation: a comparative review. *Symposia of the Zoological Society of London,* **51**, 33–85.

1001 Ogilby, W. (1834) Notice of a new species of otter from the north of Ireland. *Proceedings of the Zoological Society of London,* **1834**, 110–111.

1002 Ogilvie, M. Personal communication.

1003 Ogilvie, M. & Wright, G. Personal communication.

1004 Ognev, S.I. (1962) *Mammals of the USSR and adjacent countries Vol. 3. Carnivora.* Israel Program for Scientific Translations, Jerusalem.

1005 Okarma, H. *et al.* (1995) The roles of predation, snow cover, acorn crop, and man-related factors on ungulate mortality in Białowieża Primeval Forest, Poland. *Acta Theriologica,* **40**, 197–217.

1006 Okarma, H. *et al.* (1997) Predation of Eurasian lynx on roe deer and red deer in Białowieża Primeval Forest, Poland. *Acta Theriologica,* **42**, 203–224.

1007 Oksanen, T. (1983) Prey caching in the hunting strategy of small mustelids. *Acta Zoologica Fennica,* **174**, 197–199.

1008 Oksanen, T. *et al.* (1985) Surplus killing in the hunting strategy of small predators. *American Naturalist,* **126**, 328–346.

1009 Östman, J. *et al.* (1985) Behavioural changes in captive female otters (*Lutra lutra* L.) around parturition. *Otters 1984,* **1**(8), 58–63.

1010 O'Sullivan, P.J. (1983) The distribution of the pine marten (*Martes martes*) in the Republic of Ireland. *Mammal Review,* **13**, 39–44.

1011 Overskaug, K. (2000) Pine marten *Martes martes* versus red fox *Vulpes vulpes* in Norway: an inter-specific relationship? *Lutra,* **43**, 215–221.

1012 Owen, C. (1984) Ferret. pp. 225–228 in Mason, I.L. (ed.) *Evolution of domesticated animals.* Longman, London.

1013 Packer, J.J. & Birks, J.D.S. (1999) An assessment of British farmers' and gamekeepers' experiences, attitudes and practices in relation to the European Polecat *Mustela putorius. Mammal Review,* **29**, 75–92.

1014 Page, R.J.C. (1993) X-Ray method for determination of the age of live badgers (*Meles meles*) in the field. *Mammalia,* **57**, 123–126.

1015 Page, R.J.C. Personal communication.

1016 Page, R.J.C. & Langton, S.D. (1996) The occurrence of ixodid ticks on wild mink *Mustela vison* in England and Wales. *Medical and Veterinary Entomology,* **10**(4), 359–364.

1017 Page, R.J.C. *et al.* (1994) Seasonality of reproduction in the European badger *Meles meles* in south-west England. *Journal of Zoology,* **233**, 69–91.

1018 Paget, R.J. & Middleton, A.L.F. (1974) Some observations on the sexual activities of badgers in Yorkshire in the months December–April. *Journal of Zoology,* **173**, 256–260.

1019 Palmer, S. & Boswall, J. (1975) *A field guide to the mammal voices of Europe.* Sound recording on two 30 cm 33.3 rpm discs, RFLP 5016–17. Swedish Broadcasting Corporation, Stockholm, Sweden.

1020 Panaman, R. (1981) Behaviour and ecology of free-ranging female farm cats (*Felis catus* L.). *Zeitschrift für Tierpsychologie* **56**: 59–73.

1021 Park, A.W. & Nowosielski-Slepowron, B.J.A. (1981) Aspects of the skull and dentition morphology of the mink, *Mustela vison*. *Acta Morphologica*, **18**, 47–65.

1022 Park, K.J. *et al.* (2002) Breeding losses of red grouse in Glen Esk (NE Scotland): comparative studies, 30 years on. *Acta Zoologica Fennica*, **39**, 21–28.

1023 Parovshikov, V.Y. (1963) A contribution to the ecology of *Mustela nivalis* Linnaeus, 1766 of the Archangel'sk North, pp. 84–97 in King, C.M. (ed.) In: *Biology of mustelids: some Soviet research* (1975), British Library Lending Division, Boston Spa.

1024 Pascal, M. & Delattre, P. (1981) Comparaison de différentes méthodes de détermination de l'âge chez le vison (*Mustela vison* Schreber). *Canadian Journal of Zoology*, **59** 202–211 (in French).

1025 Peirce, M.A. & Neal, C. (1974) *Trypanosoma* (*megatryparum*) *pestania* in British badgers (*Meles meles*). *International Journal of Parasitology*, **4**, 439–440.

1026 Peirce, M.A. & Neal, C. (1974) Piroplasmosis in British badgers (*Meles meles*). *Veterinary Record*, **94**, 493–494.

1027 Pekkarinen, P. & Heikkila, J. (1997) Prey selection of the least weasel *Mustela nivalis* in the laboratory. *Acta Theriologica*, **42**, 179–188.

1028 Pertoldi, C. *et al.* (2006) Genetic structure of the European polecat (*Mustela putorius*) and its implication for conservation strategies. *Journal of Zoology*, **270**, 102–115.

1029 Petrides, G.A. (1950) The determination of sex and age ratios in fur animals. *American Midland Naturalist*, **43**, 355–382.

1030 Philcox, C.K. *et al.* (1999) Patterns of otter *Lutra lutra* road mortality in Britain. *Journal of Applied Ecology*, **36**, 748–761.

1031 Phillips, E.C. (1921) The red polecat of Cardiganshire. *Transactions of the Woolhope Club* 1918–1920, LXXVIII and 60–61.

1032 Piechocki, R. (1990) *Die Wildkazte*. Die Neue Brehm-Bücherei no.189. Ziemsen, Wittenberg Lutherstadt (in German).

1033 Pilbeam, T.E. *et al.* (1979) The annual reproductive cycle of mink (*Mustela vison*). *Journal of Animal Science*, **48**, 578–584.

1034 Pitt, F. (1921) Notes on the genetic behaviour of certain characters in the polecat, ferret and in polecat-ferret hybrids. *Journal of Genetics*, **11**, 99–115.

1035 Pitt, F. (1939) *Wild animals in Britain*. Batsford, London.

1036 Pluskowski, A. (2006) *Wolves and the wilderness in the Middle Ages*. Boydell Press, Woodbridge, Suffolk.

1037 Pocock, R.I. (1932) Ferrets and polecats. *Scottish Naturalist*, **196**, 97–108.

1038 Pocock, R.I. (1934) The races of the European wild cat (*Felis silvestris*). *Journal of the Linnean Society of London*, **39**, 1–14.

1039 Pocock, R.I. (1936) The polecats of the genera *Putorius* and *Vormela* in the British Museum. *Proceedings of the Zoological Society of London, 1936*, 691–723.

1040 Pocock, R.I. (1951) *Catalogue of the genus* Felis. British Museum (Natural History), London.

1041 Polis, G.A. *et al.* (1984) A survey of intraspecific predation within the class Mammalia. *Mammal Review*, **14**, 187–198.

1042 Poole, D.W. & McKillop, I.G. (1999) Comparison of the effectiveness of two types of electric fences to exclude badgers. *Crop Protection.* **18**, 61–66.

1043 Poole, D.W. *et al.* (2002) Effectiveness of an electric fence to reduce badger (*Meles meles*) damage to field crops. *Crop Protection, 21*, 409–417.

1044 Poole, K.G. *et al.* (1994) Age and sex determination for American martens and fishers, pp. 243–245 in Buskirk, S.W. *et al.* (eds.) *Martens, sables and fishers, biology and conservation*. Cornell University Press, Ithaca, NY.

1045 Poole, T.B. (1964) Observations on the facial pattern of the polecat (*Putorius putorius* Linn.). *Proceedings of the Zoological Society of London, 143*, 350–352.

1046 Poole, T.B. (1966) Agressive play in polecats. *Symposia of the Zoological Society of London*, **18**, 23–44.

1047 Poole, T.B. (1967) Aspects of aggressive behaviour in polecats. *Zeitschrift für Tierpsychologie*, **24,** 351–369.

1048 Poole, T.B. (1970) *Polecats*. HMSO, London.

1049 Poole, T.B. (1972) Some behavioural differences between the European polecat *Mustela putorius*, the ferret, *M. furo*, and their hybrids. *Journal of Zoology*, **166**, 25–35.

1050 Poole, T.B. & Dunstone, N. (1976) Underwater predatory behaviour of the American mink (*Mustela vison*). *Journal of Zoology*, **178**, 395–412.

1051 Pooley, E. Personal communication.

1052 Popov, V.A. (1943) Numerosity of *Mustela erminea* as affected by *Skrjabingylus* worms invasion. *Comptes Rendus de l'Académie des Sciences, Paris*, **39**, 160–162.

1053 Porter, V. & Brown, N. (1997) *The complete book of ferrets*. D & M Publications, Bedford.

1054 Potts, G.R. (1980) The effects of modern agriculture, nest predation and game management on the population ecology of partridges (*Perdix perdix* and *Alectoris rufa*). *Advances in Ecological Research*, **11**, 1–79.

1055 Potts, G.R. (1986) *The partridge: pesticides, predation and conservation*. Collins, London.

1056 Potts, G.R. & Vickerman, G.P. (1974) Studies on the cereal ecosystem. *Advances in Ecological Research*, **8**, 107–197.

1057 Poulle, M.L. *et al.* (1997) Significance of ungulates in the diet of recently settled wolves in the Mercantour Mountains (southeastern France). *Revue d' Ecologie (Terre et Vie)*, **52,** 357–368.

1058 Poulton, S. *et al.* (2006). A quality-scoring system for using sightings data to assess pine marten distribution at low densities, pp. 175–202 in Santos-Reis, M. *et al.* (eds.) *Martes in carnivore communities*. Alpha Wildlife Publications, Sherwood Park, Alberta, Canada.

1059 Pounds, C.J. (1981) *Niche overlap in sympatric populations of stoats* (Mustela erminea) *and weasels* (Mustela nivalis) *in northeast Scotland*. PhD thesis, University of Aberdeen.

1060 Powell, R.A. (1979) Mustelid spacing patterns variations on a theme by *Mustela*. *Zeitschrift für Tierpsychologie*, **50**, 153–163.

1061 Powell, R.A. (1982) Evolution of black-tipped tails in weasels – predator confusion. *American Naturalist*, **119**, 126–131.

1062 Powell, R.A. & King, C.M. (1997) Variation in body size, sexual dimorphism and age-specific survival in stoats, *Mustela erminea* (Mammalia: Carnivora), with fluctuating food supplies. *Biological Journal of the Linnean Society*, **62**, 165–194.

1063 Previtali, A. *et al.* (1998) Habitat use and diet of the American mink (*Mustela vison*) in Argentinian Patagonia. *Journal of Zoology*, **246**(4), 482–486.

1064 Price, E.O. (1971) Effect of food deprivation on activity of the least weasel. *Journal of Mammalogy*, **52**, 636–640.

1065 Prigioni, C. (1991) Biologia, ecologia e gestione della volpe. *Hystrix*, **3,** 1–257 (in Italian).

1066 Produce Studies (1995) *Farmers' attitudes to fox control*. Produce Studies, Newbury, Berkshire.

1067 Proulx, G. *et al.* (eds.) (1997) *Martes: taxonomy, ecology, techniques, and management*. Provincial Museum of Alberta, Edmonton.

1068 Proulx, G. *et al.* (2004) World distribution and status of the genus *Martes* in 2000, pp. 21–76 in Harrison, D.J. *et al.* (eds.) *Marten and fishers* (Martes) *in human altered environments: an international perspective*. Springer, Norwell, MA.

1069 Pulliainen, E. (1981) Food and feeding habits of the pine marten in Finnish forest Lapland in winter, pp. 580–598 in Chapman, J.A. & Pursley, D. (eds.) *Proceedings of the First Worldwide Furbearer Conference*. Worldwide Furbearer Conference, Frostburg, MD.

1070 Pulliainen, E. (1981) Winter habitat selection, home range, and movements of the pine marten (*Martes martes*) in Finnish Lapland Forest, pp. 1068–1086 in Chapman, J.A.

& Pursley, D. (eds.) *Proceedings of the First Worldwide Furbearer Conference*. Worldwide Furbearer Conference, Frostburg, MD.

1071 Pulliainen, E. (1984) The predation system seed-squirrel-marten under subarctic conditions. *Zeitschrift für Säugetierkunde*, **49**, 121–126.

1072 Pulliainen, E. & Hiekkenen, H. (1980) [Behaviour of the pine marten (*Marrtes martes*) in E Finnish Forest Lapland in winter.] *Suomen Riista*, **28**, 30–36 (in Finnish).

1073 Pye-Smith, C. (1997) *Fox-hunting – beyond the propaganda*. Wildlife Network, Oakham, Rutland.

1074 Räber, H. (1944) Versuche zur Ermittlung des Beuteschemas an einem Iltis (*Putorius putorius*). *Revue Suisse de Zoologie*, **51**, 293–332 (in German).

1075 Rafter, P. *et al.* (2005) Rediscovery of *Trichinella spiralis* in red foxes (*Vulpes vulpes*) in Ireland after 30 years of oblivion. *Journal of Infection*, **50**, 61–65.

1076 Ragg, J.R. (1998) Intraspecific and seasonal differences in the diet of feral ferrets (*Mustela furo*) in a pastoral habitat, East Otago, New Zealand. *New Zealand Journal of Ecology*, **22**, 113–119.

1077 Ragg, J.R. *et al.* (1995) The prevalence of bovine tuberculosis (*Mycobacterium bovis*) infections in feral populations of cats (*Felis catus*), ferrets (*Mustela furo*) and stoats (*Mustela erminea*) in Otago and Southland, New Zealand. *New Zealand Veterinary Journal*, **43**, 333–337.

1078 Ragg, J.R. *et al.* (1995) The distribution of gross lesions of tuberculosis caused by *Mycobacterium bovis* in feral ferrets (*Mustela furo*) from Otago, New Zealand. *New Zealand Veterinary Journal*, **43**, 338–341.

1079 Ragni, B. & Possenti, M. (1996) Variability of coat-colour and markings system in *Felis silvestris*. *Italian Journal of Zoology*, **63**, 285–292.

1080 Ralls, K. & Harvey, P.H. (1985) Geographic variation in size and sexual dimorphism of North American weasels. *Biological Journal of the Linnean Society*, **25**, 119–167.

1081 Ratcliffe, D. (1993) *The peregrine falcon*, 2nd edn. Poyser, Calton.

1082 Rees, P. (1981) The ecological distribution of feral cats and the effects of neutering a hospital colony, pp. 12–22 in *The ecology and control of feral cats*. UFAW, Potters Bar.

1083 Reig, S. (1992) Geographic variation in pine marten (*Martes martes*) and beech marten (*M. foina*) in Europe. *Journal of Mammalogy*, **73**, 744–769.

1084 Reig, S. (1997) Biogeographic and evolutionary implications of size variation in North American least weasels (*Mustela nivalis*). *Canadian Journal of Zoology*, **75**, 2036–2049.

1085 Reig, S. & Jędrzejewski, W. (1988) Winter and early spring food of some carnivores in the Białowieża National Park, Eastern Poland. *Acta Theriologica*, **33**, 57–65.

1086 Reig, S. *et al.* (2001) Craniometric differentiation within wild-living cats in Scotland using 3D morphometrics. *Journal of Zoology*, **253**, 121–132.

1087 Rempe, U. (1970) Morphometrische Untersuchungen an Iltisschädeln zur Klärung der Verwandtschaft von Steppeniltis, Waldiltis und Frettchen. Analyse eines 'Grenzenfalles' zwischen Unterart und Art. *Zeitschrift für wissenschaftliche Zoologie*, **180**, 185–367 (in German).

1088 Rensburg, P.J.J. van *et al.* (1987) Effects of feline panleucopaenia on the population characteristics of feral cats on Marion Island. *Journal of Applied Ecology*, **24**, 63–73.

1089 Reuther, C. *et al.* (2000) Surveying and monitoring distribution and population trends of the Eurasian otter (*Lutra lutra*): Guidelines and evaluation of the standard method for surveys as recommended by the European Section of the IUCN/SSC Otter Specialist Group. *Habitat*, **12**, 1–148.

1090 Reynolds, J.C. & Aebischer, N.J. (1991) Comparison and quantification of carnivore diet by faecal analysis: a critique, with recommendations, based on a study of the fox *Vulpes vulpes*. *Mammal Review*, **21**, 97–122.

1091 Reynolds, J.C. & Short, M.J. (2003) The status of foxes *Vulpes vulpes* on the Isle of Man in 1999. *Mammal Review*, **33**, 69–76.

1092 Reynolds, J.C. & Tapper, S.C. (1995) The ecology of the red fox *Vulpes vulpes* in relation to small game in rural southern England. *Wildlife Biology*, **1**, 105–119.

1093 Reynolds, J.C. & Tapper, S.C. (1995) Predation by foxes *Vulpes vulpes* on brown hares *Lepus europaeus* in central southern England, and its potential impact on annual population growth. *Wildlife Biology*, **1**, 145–158.

1094 Reynolds, J.C.& Tapper, S.C. (1996) Control of mammalian predators in game management and conservation. *Mammal Review*, **26**, 127–156.

1095 Reynolds, J.C. *et al.* (1992) Tracking partridge predation. *Game Conservancy Annual Review*, **23**, 60–62.

1096 Reynolds, J.C. *et al.* (1993) The impact of local fox (*Vulpes vulpes*) removal on fox populations at two sites in southern England. *Gibier Faune Sauvage*, **10**, 319–334.

1097 Richards, D.F. (1977) Observations on the diet of the red fox (*Vulpes vulpes*) in south Devon. *Journal of Zoology*, **183**, 495–504.

1098 Richards, D.T. *et al.* (1993) Epidemiology of *Toxocara canis* in red foxes (*Vulpes vulpes*) from urban areas of Bristol. *Parasitology*, **107**, 167–173.

1099 Richards, D.T. *et al.* (1995) Epidemiological studies on intestinal helminth parasites of rural and urban red foxes (*Vulpes vulpes*) in the United Kingdom. *Veterinary Parasitology*, **59**, 39–51.

1100 Richardson, M.G. (1979) *The environmental effects of the Esso Bernicia fuel oil spill, Sullom Voe, Shetland, January 1979*. Report to Nature Conservancy Council, Lerwick.

1101 Ritchie, J. (1920) *The influence of man on animal life in Scotland. A study in faunal evolution*. Cambridge University Press, Cambridge.

1102 Roberts, J. Personal communication.

1103 Robertson, C.P.J. & Harris, S. (1995) The behaviour after release of captive-reared fox cubs. *Animal Welfare*, **4**, 295–306.

1104 Robertson, C.P.J. & Harris, S. (1995) The condition and survival after release of captive-reared fox cubs. *Animal Welfare*, **4**, 281–294.

1105 Robertson, C.P.J. & Harris, S. (1996) An expandable, detachable radio-collar for juvenile red foxes (*Vulpes vulpes*). *Journal of Zoology*, **239**, 382–387.

1106 Robertson, C.P.J. *et al.* (2000) Ranging behaviour of juvenile red foxes and its implications for management. *Acta Theriologica*, **45**, 525–535.

1107 Robertson, P.A. (1988) Survival of released pheasants, *Phasianus colchicus*, in Ireland. *Journal of Zoology*, **214**, 683–695.

1108 Robertson, P.A. (1991) Estimating the nesting success and productivity of British pheasants *Phasianus colchicus* from nest-record schemes. *Bird Study*, **38**, 73–79.

1109 Robertson, P.A. & Whelan, J. (1987) The food of the red fox (*Vulpes vulpes*) in Co. Kildare, Ireland. *Journal of Zoology*, **213**, 740–743.

1110 Robinson, I.H. (1987) *Olfactory communication and social behaviour in the mink* (Mustela vison). PhD thesis, University of Aberdeen.

1111 Robinson, R. (1975) The red fox, pp. 399–419 in King, R.C. (ed.) *Handbook of genetics, volume 4: vertebrates*. Plenum Press, New York.

1112 Robinson, R. (1980) Evolution of the domestic cat. *Carnivore Genetics Newsletter*, **4**, 46–65.

1113 Robitaille, J.-F. & Baron, G. (1987) Seasonal changes in the activity budget of captive ermine, *Mustela erminea* L. *Canadian Journal of Zoology*, **65**, 2864–2871.

1114 Robitaille, J.F. & Raymond, M. (1995) Spacing patterns of ermine, *Mustela erminea* L., in a Quebec agrosystem.

Canadian Journal of Zoology, **73,** 1827–1834.

1115 Robson, G. (1998) *The breeding ecology of curlew* Numenius arquata *on north Pennine moorland*. PhD dissertation, University of Sunderland.

1116 Rogers, L.M. *et al.* (1997) Body weight as an indication of density dependent population regulation in badgers (*Meles meles*) at Woodchester Park, Gloucestershire. *Journal of Zoology,* **242,** 597–604.

1117 Rogers, L.M. *et al.* (1997) The demography of a high-density badger (*Meles meles*) population in the west of England. *Journal of Zoology,* **242,** 705–728.

1118 Rogers, L.M. *et al.* (1998) Movement of badgers (*Meles meles*) in a high density population: Individual, population and disease effects. *Proceedings of the Royal Society Series B,* **265,** 1269–1372.

1119 Rogers, L.M. *et al.* (2000) Changes in badger (*Meles meles*) social organisation in response to increasing population density at Woodchester Park, south west England, pp. 267–279 in Griffiths, H.I. (Ed.) *Mustelids in a modern world*. Backhuys, Leiden.

1120 Rogers, L.M. *et al.* (2002) An evaluation of passive integrated transponders (PITs) as a means of permanently marking badgers (*Meles meles*). *Mammal Review,* **32,** 63–65.

1121 Rondinini, C. *et al.* (2006) Habitat use and preference by polecats (*Mustela putorius* L.) in a Mediterranean agricultural landscape. *Journal of Zoology,* **269,** 213–219.

1122 Roper, T.J. (1992) Badger *Meles meles* setts – architecture, internal environment and function. *Mammal Review,* **22,** 43–53.

1123 Roper, T.J. & Lups, P. (1993) Disruption of territorial behaviour in badgers *Meles meles*. *Zeitschrift für Säugetierkunde,* **58,** 252–255.

1124 Roper, T.J. *et al.* (1986) Scent marking with faeces and anal secretion in the European badger (*Meles meles*): seasonal and spatial characteristics of latrine use in relation to territoriality. *Behaviour,* **97,** 94–117.

1125 Roper, T.J. *et al.* (1993) Territorial marking with faeces in badgers (*Meles meles*): a comparison of boundary and hinterland latrine use. *Behaviour,* **127,** 289–307.

1126 Roper, T.J. *et al.* (2001) Sett use in European badgers *Meles meles*. *Behaviour,* **138,** 173–187.

1127 Roper, T.J. *et al.* (2003) The process of dispersal in badgers *Meles meles*. *Mammal Review,* **33,** 314–318.

1128 Ross, J.G. & Fairley, J.S. (1969) Studies of disease in the red fox (*Vulpes vulpes*) in Northern Ireland. *Journal of Zoology,* **157,** 375–381.

1129 Rowlands, I.W. (1972) Reproductive studies in the stoat. *Journal of Zoology,* **166,** 574–576.

1130 Rowlands, I.W. & Parkes, A.S. (1935) The reproductive processes of certain mammals – VIII. Reproduction in foxes (*Vulpes* spp.). *Proceedings of the Zoological Society of London,* **1935,** 823–841.

1131 Ruprecht, A.L. (1978) Dentition variations in the common polecat in Poland. *Acta Theriologica,* **23,** 239–245.

1132 Russell, J.E. & Tumlison, R. (1996) Comparison of microstructure of white winter fur and brown summer fur of some Arctic mammals. *Acta Zoologica,* **77,** 279–282.

1133 Sadlier, L. & Montgomery, I. (2004) The impact of sett disturbance on badger *Meles meles* numbers; when does protective legislation work? *Biological Conservation,* **119,** 455–462.

1134 Sadlier, L.M.J. *et al.* (2004) Methods of monitoring foxes (*Vulpes vulpes*) and badgers (*Meles meles*): are field signs the answer? *Mammal Review,* **34,** 75–98.

1135 Salles, L. (1992) Felid phylogenetics: Extant taxa and skull morphology. *American Museum Novitates,* **3047,** 1–67.

1136 Salt, G.F.H. & Little, T.W.A. (1977) Leptospires isolated from wild mammals caught in the south west of England. *Research in Veterinary Science,* **22,** 126–127.

1137 Samson, C. & Raymond, M. (1995) Daily activity pattern

and time budget of stoats (*Mustela erminea*) during summer in southern Quebec. *Mammalia,* **59,** 501–510.

1138 Samson, C. & Raymond, M. (1998) Movement and habitat preference of radio tracked stoats, *Mustela erminea*, during summer in southern Quebec. *Mammalia,* **62,** 165–174.

1139 Sandell, M. (1986) Movement patterns of male stoats *Mustela erminea* during the mating season: differences in relation to social status. *Oikos,* **47,** 63–70.

1140 Sandell, M. & Liberg, O. (1992) Roamers and stayers : a model on mating tactics and mating systems. *American Naturalist,* **139,** 177–189.

1141 Santos-Reis, M. *et al.* (eds.) (2006). Martes *in carnivore communities*. Alpha Wildlife Publications, Sherwood Park, Alberta, Canada.

1142 Sargeant, A.B. *et al.* (1973) Selective predation by mink on waterfowl. *American Midland Naturalist,* **89,** 208–214.

1143 Satunin, C. (1904) The black wild cat of Transcaucasia. *Proceedings of the Zoological Society of London,* **11,** 162–163.

1144 Saunders, G. *et al.* (1993) Urban foxes (*Vulpes vulpes*): food acquisition, time and energy budgeting of a generalized predator. *Symposia of the Zoological Society of London,* **65,** 215–234.

1145 Saunders, G. *et al.* (1997) Habitat utilisation by urban foxes (*Vulpes vulpes*) and the implications for rabies control. *Mammalia,* **61,** 497–510.

1146 Say, L. *et al.* (1999) High variation in multiple paternity of domestic cats (*Felis catus* L.) in relation to environmental conditions. *Proceedings of the Royal Society of London Series B,* **266,** 2071–2074.

1147 Scales, H. (1969) *Fur farm guide book*. American Fur Breeder, Duluth, MN.

1148 Schantz, T. von (1984) 'Non-breeders' in the red fox *Vulpes vulpes*: a case of resource surplus. *Oikos,* **42,** 59–65.

1149 Schauenberg, P. (1969) L'identification du chat forestier d'Europe, *Felis s. silvestris* Schreber 1777, par une méthode ostéométrique. *Revue Suisse de Zoologie,* **76,** 433–441 (in French).

1150 Schauenberg, P. (1976) Poids et taille de naissance du chat forestier *Felis silvestris* Schreber, 1777. *Mammalia,* **40,** 687–689 (in French).

1151 Schauenberg, P. (1977) Longueur de l'intestin du chat forestier *Felis silvestris* Schreber. *Mammalia,* **41,** 357–360 (in French).

1152 Schauenberg, P. (1980) Note sur le squelette et la maturité physique du chat forestier *Felis silvestris* Schreber. *Revue Suisse de Zoologie,* **87,** 549–556 (in French).

1153 Schauenberg, P. (1981) Éléments d'écologie du chat forestier d'Europe *Felis silvestris* Schreber, 1777. *Terre et la Vie,* **35,** 3–36 (in French).

1154 Schmidt, F. (1934) Über die Fortpflanzungsbiologie von sibirischen Zobel (*Martes zibellina* L.) und europäischen Baummarder (*Martes martes* L.). *Zeitschrift für Säugetierkunde,* **9,** 392–402 (in German).

1155 Schmidt, F. (1943) Naturgeschichte des Baum- und des Steinmarders. *Monographien der Wildsäugetiere,* **10,** 1–258 (in German).

1156 Schmidt, K. *et al.* (1997) Spatial organization and social relations in the Eurasian lynx population in Białowieża Primeval Forest, Poland. *Acta Theriologica,* **42,** 289–312.

1157 Schreber, J.C.D. von (1777) *Die Säugethiere in Abbildungen nach der Natur mit Beschreibungen*. Vol. 3, Part 23. Walther, Erlangen (in German).

1158 Schwalbe, G. (1893) Über den Ferbenwechsel winterweissen Thiere. *Morphologische Arbeiten,* **2,** 483–606 (in German).

1159 Scott, R. Personal communication.

1160 Scott, R. *et al.* (1993) A radio-tracking study of wildcats in western Scotland, pp. 94–97 in *Seminar on the biology and conservation of the wildcat* (Felis silvestris). Council of Europe, Strasbourg.

1161 Sealander, J.A. (1943) Winter food habits of mink in southern Michigan. *Journal of Wildlife Management*, **7**, 411–417.

1162 Segal, A.N. (1975) Postnatal growth, metabolism, and thermoregulation in the stoat. *Soviet Journal of Ecology*, **1**, 38–44.

1163 Serpell, J. (1991) It's the elephant by a nose. *BBC Wildlife*, **9**, 849–851.

1164 Service, K.M. *et al.*(2001) Analysis of badger urine volatiles using gas chromatography-mass spectrometry and pattern recognition techniques. *Analyst*, **126**, 615–623.

1165 Seymour, A. *et al.* (2003) Factors influencing the nesting success of lapwings *Vanellus vanellus* and behaviour of red fox *Vulpes vulpes* in lapwing nesting sites. *Bird Study*, **50**, 39–46.

1166 Seymour, A. *et al.* (2004) Potential effects of reserve size on incidental nest predation by red foxes *Vulpes vulpes*. *Ecological Modelling*, **175**, 101–114.

1167 Shaw, G. & Livingstone, J. (1992) The pine marten: its reintroduction and subsequent history in the Galloway Forest Park. *Transactions of the Dumfriesshire and Galloway Natural History and Antiquarian Society,* **67**, 1–7.

1168 Sheffield, S.R. & King, C.M. (1994) *Mustela nivalis*. *Mammalian Species*, **454**, 1–10.

1169 Shepeleva, V.K. (1957) [Responsiveness of nerve processes in the motor analysor of the Forest polecat.] *Doklady Akademii nauk SSSR, Seriya Biologiya*, **106**, 941–944 (in Russian).

1170 Shimalov, V.V. *et al.* (2000) Helminths of the Eurasian otter (*Lutra lutra*) in Belorussian Polesie. *IUCN Otter Specialist Group Bulletin*, **17**(2), 89–90.

1171 Shore, R.F. *et al.* (1996) Second-generation rodenticides and polecats (*Mustela putorius*) in Britain. *Environmental Pollution*, **91**, 279–282.

1172 Shore, R.F. *et al.* (1999) Exposure of non-target vertebrates to second-generation rodenticides in Britain, with particular reference to the polecat *Mustela putorius*. *New Zealand Journal of Ecology,* **23**, 199–206.

1173 Shore, R.F. *et al.* (2003) Agricultural pesticides and mammals in Britain, pp. 37–50 in Tattersall, F. & Manly, W. (eds.) *Conservation and conflict – mammals and farming in Britain*. Linnean Society Occasional Publication No. 4, London.

1174 Shore, R.F. *et al.* (2003) Spatial and temporal analysis of second-generation anticoagulant rodenticide residues in polecats (*Mustela putorius*) from throughout their range in Britain 1992–1999. *Environmental Pollution,* **122**, 183–193.

1175 Short, H.L. (1961) Food habits of a captive least weasel *Mustela rixosa*, Bangs. *Journal of Mammalogy*, **42**, 273–274.

1176 Shuter, R. (1996) Road deaths as an indicator of the otter's revival. *Otters 1995*, **2**(9), 22–23.

1177 Sidorovich, V.E. (1994) How to identify the tracks of the European mink (*Mustela lutreola*), the American mink (*M. vison*) and the Polecat (*M. putorius*) on waterbodies. *IUCN Small Carnivore Conservation Newsletter*, **10**, 8–9.

1178 Sidorovich, V. & Anisimova, E.I.G. (1999) Comparative analysis of the helminthocenoses of the native semiaquatic mustelids (*Lutra lutra, Mustela lutreola*) in connection with the width of food spectra. *IUCN Otter Specialist Group Bulletin*, **16**(2), 76–78.

1179 Sidorovich, V. *et al.*(1998) Diets of semi-aquatic carnivores in northern Belarus, with implications for population changes, pp. 177–189 in Dunstone, N. & Gorman, M. (eds.) *Behaviour and ecology of riparian mammals*. Cambridge University Press, Cambridge.

1180 Siefke, A. (1960) Baummarder-Paarung. *Zeitschrift für Säugetierkunde*, **25**, 178 (in German).

1181 Simms, C. (1973) Aspects of grooming in wild mustelids in northern England. *Roebuck,* **1973**, 33–35.

1182 Simms, C. (1973) *Pine marten, seven prints*. Genera 14, York.

1183 Simms, C. (2004) *Otters and martens*. Shearsman Books, Exeter.

1184 Simms, D.A. (1979) North American weasels: resource utilization and distribution. *Canadian Journal of Zoology*, **57**, 504–520.

1185 Simms, D.A. (1979) Studies of an ermine population in southern Ontario. *Canadian Journal of Zoology*, **57**, 824–832.

1186 Simms, E. (1969) *British mammals and amphibians*. Sound recording on one 30-cm 33.3 rpm disc, BBC RED 42M. BBC Records, London.

1187 Simpson, V.R. (1996) *Angiostrongylus vasorum* infection in foxes (*Vulpes vulpes*) in Cornwall. *Veterinary Record*, **139**, 443–445.

1188 Simpson, V.R. (2002) Wild animals as reservoirs of infectious diseases in the UK. *Veterinary Journal*, **163**, 128–146.

1189 Simpson, V.R. (2006) Patterns and significance of bite wounds in Eurasian otters (*Lutra lutra*) in Southern and South East England. *Veterinary Record*, **158**, 113–119.

1190 Simpson, V.R. & Coxon, K.E. (2000) Intraspecific aggression, cannibalism and suspected infanticide in otters. *British Wildlife*, **11**, 423–426.

1191 Simpson, V.R. *et al.* (1997) Foxes and neosporosis. *Veterinary Record*, **141**, 503.

1192 Simpson, V.R. *et al.* (2000) A long-term study of vitamin A and polychlorinated hydrocarbon levels in otters (*Lutra lutra*) in South West England. *Environmental Pollution*, **110**, 267–275.

1193 Sjovold, T. (1977) Non-metrical divergence between skeletal populations. The theoretical foundation and biological importance of C.A.B. Smith's mean measure of divergence. *Ossa, Supplement*, **4**, 1–33.

1194 Sladek, J. (1976) Farbené anomálie v západokarpatskej populácii macky divej (*Felis silvestris* Schreber, 1777). *Lynx*, **18,** 73–83 (in Slovak).

1195 Sleeman, D.P. (1988) Irish stoat road casualties. *Irish Naturalists' Journal*, **22**, 527–529.

1196 Sleeman, D.P. (1988) *Skrjabingylus nasicola* (Leuckhart *sic*) (Metastrongylidae) as a parasite of the Irish stoat. *Irish Naturalists' Journal*, **22**, 525–527.

1197 Sleeman, D.P. (1989) Ectoparasites of the Irish stoat. *Medical and Veterinary Entomology*, **3**, 213–218.

1198 Sleeman, P. (1989) *Stoats and weasels, polecats and pine martens*. Whittet, London.

1199 Sleeman, D.P. (1990) Dens of Irish stoats. *Irish Naturalists' Journal*, **23,** 202–203.

1200 Sleeman, D.P. (1991) Home ranges of Irish stoats. *Irish Naturalists' Journal*, **23**, 486–488.

1201 Sleeman, D.P. (1992) Diet of Irish stoats. *Irish Naturalists' Journal*, **24**, 151–153.

1202 Sleeman, P. Personal communication.

1203 Smal, C. (1991) *Feral American mink in Ireland*. Office of Public Works, Dublin.

1204 Smal, C. (1995) *The badger and habitat survey of Ireland*. Stationery Office, Dublin.

1205 Smal, C.M. (1991) Population studies on feral American mink *Mustela vison* in Ireland. *Journal of Zoology*, **224,** 233–249.

1206 Smith, C. *et al.* (1994) Animal bone report, pp. 139–153 in Smith, B.B. (ed.) *Four millennia of Orkney prehistory,* Monograph Series No. 9, Society of Antiquaries of Scotland, Edinburgh.

1207 Smith, G.C. (1995) Modelling rabies control in the UK: the inclusion of vaccination. *Mammalia*, **59**, 629–637.

1208 Smith, G.C. & Cheeseman, C.L. (2002) A mathematical model for the control of diseases in wildlife populations: culling, vaccination and fertility control. *Ecological Modelling*, **150**, 45–53.

1209 Smith, G.C. & Harris, S. (1991) Rabies in urban foxes (*Vulpes vulpes*) in Britain: the use of a spatial stochastic simulation model to examine the pattern of spread and evaluate the efficacy of different control regimes. *Philosophical Transactions of the Royal Society of London Series B,* **334**, 459–479.

1210 Smith, G.C. & Wilkinson, D. (2002) Modelling disease spread in a novel host: rabies in the European badger *Meles meles. Journal of Applied Ecology,* **39**, 865–874.

1211 Smith, G.C. & Wilkinson, D. (2003) Modeling control of rabies outbreaks in red fox populations to evaluate culling, vaccination, and vaccination combined with fertility control. *Journal of Wildlife Diseases,* **39**, 278–286.

1212 Smith, G.C. *et al.* (2003) Prevalence of zoonotic important parasites in the red fox (*Vulpes vulpes*) in Great Britain. *Veterinary Parasitology,* **118**, 133–142.

1213 Soest, R.W.M. van & Bree, P.J.H. van (1969) On the moult in the stoat, *Mustela erminea* Linnaeus, 1758, from the Netherlands. *Bijdragen tot de Dierkunde,* **39**, 63–68.

1214 Soest, R.W.M. van & Bree, P.J.H. van (1970) Sex and age composition of a stoat population (*Mustela erminea* Linnaeus, 1758) from a coastal dune region of the Netherlands. *Beaufortia,* **17**, 51–77.

1215 Soest, R.W.M. van *et al.* (1972) *Skrjabingylus nasicola* (Nematoda) in skulls of *Mustela erminea* and *Mustela nivalis* (Mammalia) from the Netherlands. *Beaufortia,* **20**, 85–97.

1216 Solow, A.R. *et al.* (2006) Rediscovery of the Scottish polecat, *Mustela putorius*: survival or reintroduction? *Biological Conservation,* **128**, 574–575.

1217 Sommer, R. & Benecke, N. (2004) Late- and Post-Glacial history of the Mustelidae in Europe. *Mammal Review,* **34**, 249–284.

1218 Sommer, R.S. & Benecke, N. (2006) Late Pleistocene and Holocene development of the felid fauna (Felidae) of Europe: a review. *Journal of Zoology,* **269**, 7–19.

1219 Soulsbury, C.D. *et al.* (2007) The impact of sarcoptic mange *Sarcoptes scabiei* on the British fox *Vulpes vulpes* population. *Mammal Review.*

1220 Southern, H.N. & Watson, J.S. (1941) Summer food of the red fox (*Vulpes vulpes*) in Great Britain: a preliminary report. *Journal of Animal Ecology,* **10**, 1–11.

1221 Spassov, N. *et al.* (1997) The wild cat (*Felis silvestris* Schr.) and the feral domestic cat: Problems of the morphology, taxonomy, identification of the hybrids and purity of the wild population. *Historia Naturalia Bulgarica,* **8**, 101–120.

1222 Stahl, P. & Artois, M. (1995) *Status and conservation of the wildcat (*Felis silvestris*) in Europe and around the Mediterranan rim.* Nature and Environment 69. Council of Europe, Strasbourg.

1223 Stahl, P. & Leger, F. (1992) *Le chat sauvage d'Europe (*Felis silvestris* Schreber, 1777).* Encyclopédie des carnivores de France no. 17. SFEPM, Nort s/Edre (in French).

1224 Stark, R. *et al.* (1987) Gastrointestinal anatomy of the European badger (*Meles meles*). *Zeitschrift für Säugetierkunde,* **52**, 88–96.

1225 Starzyk, J. *et al.* (1973) Studies on the frequency of occurrence of *Toxoplasma gondii* in fur-bearing animals. *Acta Biologica Cracoviensia, Série Zoologique,* **16**, 229–33.

1226 Stephens, M.N. (1957) *The otter report.* UFAW, Potters Bar.

1227 Stephenson, R. *et al.* (1988) Heart rate and gas exchange in freely diving American mink (*Mustela vison*). *Journal of Experimental Biology,* **134**, 435–442.

1228 Steventon, J.D. & Major, J.T. (1982) Marten use of habitat in a commercially clear-cut forest. *Journal of Wildlife Management,* **46**, 175–182.

1229 Stewart, P.D. & Macdonald, D.W. (1997) Age, sex, and condition as predictors of moult and the efficacy of a novel fur-clip technique for individual marking of the European badger (*Meles meles*). *Journal of Zoology,* **241**, 543–550.

1230 Stewart, P.D. *et al.* (1997) Remote video-surveillance of wildlife – an introduction from experience with the European badger *Meles meles. Mammal Review,* **27**, 185–204.

1231 Stewart, P.D. *et al.* (1999) Individual differences in den maintenance effort in a communal dwelling mammal: the Eurasian badger. *Animal Behaviour,* **57**, 153–161.

1232 Stewart, P.D. *et al.* (2001) Boundary faeces and matched advertisement in the European badger (*Meles meles*): a potential role in range exclusion. *Journal of Zoology,* **255**, 191–198.

1233 Stier, N. (2000) Habitat use of the pine marten *Martes martes* in small-scale woodlands of Mecklenburg (Germany). *Lutra,* **43**, 185–203.

1234 Stocker, L. (1994) *The complete fox.* Butler & Tanner, London.

1235 Stoddart, D.M. (1974) Earthworms in the diet of the red fox (*Vulpes vulpes*). *Journal of Zoology,* **173**, 251–275.

1236 Stoddart, M. (1975) Effect of the odour of weasels (*Mustela nivalis* L.) on trapped samples of their prey. *Oecologia,* **22**, 439–441.

1237 Stolt, B.-O. (1979) Colour pattern and size variation of the weasel *Mustela nivalis* L. in Sweden. *Zoon,* **7**, 55–61.

1238 Stone, W.B. *et al.* (1972) Experimental transfer of sarcoptic mange from red foxes and wild canids to captive wildlife and domestic animals. *New York Fish and Game Journal,* **19**, 1–11.

1239 Stone, W.B. *et al.* (1976) Spontaneous and experimental transfer of sarcoptic mange mites from red foxes to humans. *New York Fish and Game Journal,* **23**, 183–184.

1240 Storch, I. (1988) Home range utilisation by pine martens. *Zeitschrift für Jagdwissenschaft,* **34**, 115–119.

1241 Storch, I. *et al.* (1990) Diet and habitat selection of the pine marten in relation to competition with the red fox. *Acta Theriologica,* **35**, 311–320.

1242 Strachan, C. *et al.* (1998) The rapid impact of resident American mink on water voles: case studies in lowland England. *Symposia of the Zoological Society of London,* **71**, 339–357.

1243 Strachan, C. *et al.* (2000) *Preliminary report on the changes in the water vole population of Britain as shown by the National Surveys of 1989–1990 and 1996–1998.* Vincent Wildlife Trust, London.

1244 Strachan, R. & Jefferies, D.J. (1993) *The water vole (*Arvicola terrestris*) in Britain 1989–1990: its distribution and changing status.* Vincent Wildlife Trust, London.

1245 Strachan, R. & Jefferies, D.J. (1996) *Otter survey of England 1991–1994.* Vincent Wildlife Trust, London.

1246 Strachan, R. *et al.* (1990) *Otter survey of England 1984–1986.* Nature Conservancy Council, Peterborough.

1247 Strachan, R. *et al.* (1996) *Pine marten survey of England and Wales 1987–1988.* JNCC, Peterborough.

1248 Strickland, M.A. & Douglas, C.W. (1987) Marten, pp. 530–546 in Novak, M. *et al.* (eds.) *Wild furbearer management and conservation in North America.* Ontario Trappers Association, North Bay, Ontario.

1249 Stuart, A.J. (1982) *Pleistocene vertebrates in the British Isles.* Longman, London.

1250 Stubbe, M. (1968) Zur Populationnsbiologie der Martes-Arten, pp. 195–203 in *13th Working Fellowship for Game and Wildlife Research, Gatersleben, January 1968.* Germany Academy for Agricultural Science, Berlin (in German).

1251 Stubbe, M. (1969) Zur Biologie und zum Schutz des Fischotters *Lutra lutra* (L.). *Archiv für Naturschutz und Landschaftsforschung,* **9**, 315–324 (in German).

1252 Stubbe, M. (1972) Die analen Markierungsorgane der *Mustela*-Arten. *Zoologische Garten N.F. Leipzig,* **42**, 176–188 (in German).

1253 Stubbe, M. (1977) Der Fischotter *Lutra lutra* (L., 1758) in der DDR. *Zoologischer Anzeiger,* **199**, 265–285 (in German).

1254 Sturdee, A.P. *et al.* (1999) Detection of *Crytosporidium* oocysts in wild mammals of mainland Britain. *Veterinary Parasitology,* **80**, 273–280.

1255 Stuttard, R.M. (ed.). (1986) *Predatory mammals in Britain: a code of practice for their management.* British Field Sports Society, London.

1256 Sulkava, S. *et al.* (1984) Diet and breeding success of the golden eagle in Finland 1958–82. *Annales Zoologici Fennici,* **21**, 283–286.

1257 Summers, R.W. *et al.* (2004) An experimental study of the effects of predation on the breeding productivity of capercallie and black grouse. *Journal of Applied Ecology,* **41**, 513–525.

1258 Sumption, K.J. & Flowerdew, J.R. (1985) The ecological effects of the decline in rabbits (*Oryctolagus cuniculus* L.) due to myxomatosis. *Mammal Review,* **15**, 151–186.

1259 Svendsen, G.E. (2003) Weasels and black-footed ferret (*Mustela* species), pp. 650–661 in Feldhamer, G.A. *et al.* (eds.) *Wild mammals of North America: biology, management, and conservation.* Johns Hopkins University Press, Baltimore, MD.

1260 Swire, P.W. (1978) Laboratory observation on the fox (*Vulpes vulpes*) in Dyfed during the winters of 1974/75 and 1975/76. *British Veterinary Journal,* **134**, 398–405.

1261 Taberlet, P. & Bouvet, J. (1994) Mitochondrial DNA polymorphism, phylogeography, and conservation genetics of the brown bear *Ursus arctos* in Europe. *Proceedings of the Royal Society of London Series B,* **255**, 195–200.

1262 Tabor, R. (1981) General biology of feral cats, pp. 5–11 in *The ecology and control of feral cats.* UFAW, Potters Bar.

1263 Tadros, W. & Laarman, J.J. (1979) Muscular sarcosporidiosis in the common European weasel, *Mustela nivalis. Zeitschrift für Parasitenkunde,* **58**, 195–200.

1264 Taketazu, M. (1979) *Fox family – four seasons of animal life.* Weatherhill, New York.

1265 Talbot, J.S. (1906) *Foxes at home.* Horace Cox, London.

1266 Tapper, S.C.(1976) The diet of weasels, *Mustela nivalis,* and stoats, *Mustela erminea* during early summer, in relation to predation on game birds. *Journal of Zoology,* **179**, 219–224.

1267 Tapper, S. (1979) The effect of fluctuating vole numbers (*Microtus agrestis*) on a population of weasels (*Mustela nivalis*) on farmland. *Journal of Animal Ecology,* **48**, 603–617.

1268 Tapper, S. (1992) *Game heritage: an ecological review from shooting and gamekeeping records.* Game Conservancy, Fordingbridge.

1269 Tapper, S. (ed.) (1999) *A question of balance.* Game Conservancy, Fordingbridge.

1270 Tapper, S.C. *et al.* (1982) Effects of mammalian predators on partridge populations. *Mammal Review,* **12**, 159–167.

1271 Tapper, S. *et al.* (1996) The effect of an experimental reduction in predation pressure on the breeding success and population density of grey partridges (*Perdix perdix*). *Journal of Applied Ecology,* **33**, 965–978.

1272 Tarasoff, F.J. *et al.* (1972) Locomotory patterns and external morphology of the river otter, sea otter, and harp seal (Mammalia). *Canadian Journal of Zoology,* **50**, 915–929.

1273 Taylor, J. (1968) *Salmonella* in wild animals. *Symposia of the Zoological Society of London,* **24**, 51–73.

1274 Taylor, K. (1994) Does the wildcat really exist? *Scottish Wildlife,* **24**, 20–23.

1275 Taylor, P.S. & Kruuk, H. (1990) A record of an otter (*Lutra lutra*) natal den. *Journal of Zoology,* **222**, 689–692.

1276 Taylor, R.H. & Abrey, N. (1982) Marten, *Martes americana,* movements and habitat use in Algonquin Provincial Park, Ontario. *Canadian Field Naturalist,* **96**, 439–447.

1277 Taylor, R.H. & Tilley, J.A.V. (1984) Stoats (*Mustela erminea*) on Adele and Fisherman Islands, Abel Tasman National Park, and other offshore islands in New Zealand. *New Zealand Journal of Ecology,* **7**, 139–145.

1278 Teall, N. (1982) A natural survivor? The polecat in Britain. *Country Life,* 9 December.

1279 Teerink, B.J. (1991) *Hair of West European mammals: atlas and identification key.* Cambridge University Press, Cambridge.

1280 Tembrock, G. (1963) Acoustic behaviour of mammals, pp. 751–786 in Busnel, R.G. (ed.) *Acoustic behaviour of animals.* Elsevier, Amsterdam.

1281 Tenquist, J.D. & Charleston, W.A.G. (1981) An annotated checklist of ectoparasites of terrestrial mammals in New Zealand. *Journal of the Royal Society of New Zealand,* **11**, 257–285.

1282 Ternosvkij, D.V. (1977) *Biologia kuniceobraznyh (Mustelidae).* Nauka, Novosibirsk (in Russian).

1283 Ternovskii, D.V. (1983) [The biology of reproduction and development of the stoat *Mustela erminea* (Carnivora, Mustelidae)]. *Zoologicheskii Zhurnal,* **62**, 1097–1105 (in Russian).

1284 Ternovskii, D.V.& Ternovskaya, Yu.G. (1978) [Potential reproductive ability in Mustelidae.] *Izvestiya Sibirskogo Otdeleniya Akademii Nauk SSSR, Seriya Biologicheskikh Nauk,* **5**, 88–91(in Russian).

1285 Tetley, H. (1939) On the British polecats. *Proceedings of the Zoological Society of London,* **109B**, 37–39.

1286 Tetley, H. (1941) On the Scottish fox. *Proceedings of the Zoological Society of London,* **111B**, 25–35.

1287 Tetley, H. (1941) On the Scottish wild cat. *Proceedings of the Zoological Society of London,* **111B**, 13–23.

1288 Tetley, H. (1945) Notes on British polecats. *Proceedings of the Zoological Society of London,* **115**, 212–217.

1289 Thom, M.D. *et al.* (2004) Why are American mink sexually dimorphic? A role for niche separation. *Oikos,* **105**, 525–535.

1290 Thom, M.D. *et al.* (2004) Female American mink, *Mustela vison,* mate multiply in a free-choice environment. *Animal Behaviour,* **67**, 975–984.

1291 Thom, M.D. *et al.* (2004) The evolution and maintenance of delayed implantation in the Mustelidae (Mammalia: Carnivora). *Evolution,* **58**, 175–183.

1292 Thompson, G.B. (1961) The parasites of British birds and mammals; the ectoparasites of the badger *Meles meles. Entomologist's Monthly Magazine,* **97**, 156–158.

1293 Thompson, G.B. (1972) Badger fleas and lice. *Entomologist's Monthly Magazine,* **108**, 51.

1294 Thompson, H.V. (1962) Wild mink in Britain. *New Scientist,* **13**, 130–132.

1295 Thompson, H.V. (1971) British wild mink – a challenge to naturalists. *Agriculture, London,* **78**, 421–425.

1296 Thompson, I.D. & Colgan, P.W. (1987) Numerical responses of marten to a food shortage in northcentral Ontario. *Journal of Wildlife Management,* **51**, 824–835.

1297 Thompson, I.D. & Harested, A.S. (1994) Effects of logging on American martens and models for habitat management, pp. 243–245 in Buskirk, S.W. *et al.* (eds.) *Martens, sables and fishers, biology and conservation.* Cornell University Press, Ithaca, NY.

1298 Thomson, A.P.D. (1951) A history of the ferret. *Journal of the History of Medicine and Allied Sciences,* **6**(4), 471–480.

1299 Timofeeff-Ressovsky, N. (1940) Mutations and geographical variations, pp. 73–136 in Huxley, J. (ed.) *The new systematics.* Clarendon Press, Oxford.

1300 Tinbergen, N. (1972) Food hoarding by foxes (*Vulpes vulpes*) L., pp. 315–328 in *The animal in its world – explorations of an ethologist, volume 1.* George Allen & Unwin, London.

1301 Tjernberg, M. (1981) Diet of the golden eagle *Aquila chrysaetos* during the breeding season in Sweden. *Holarctic Ecology,* **4**, 12–19.

1302 Todd, N.B. (1977) Cats and commerce. *Scientific American,* **237**(5), 100–107.

1303 Todd, N.B. (1978) An ecological, behavioural genetic model for the domestication of the cat. *Carnivore,* **1**, 52–60.

1304 Tomkies, M. (1977) *My wilderness wildcats.* Macdonald & Jane, London.

1305 Tomkies, M. (1991) *Wildcats.* Whittet, London.

1306 Townsend, M.G. *et al.* (1984) Assessment of secondary poisoning hazard of warfarin to least weasels. *Journal of Wildlife Management,* **48**, 628–632.

1307 Trewhella, W.J. & Harris, S. (1988) A simulation model of the pattern of dispersal in urban fox (*Vulpes vulpes*) populations and its application for rabies control. *Journal of Applied Ecology*, **25,** 435–450.

1308 Trewhella, W.J. & Harris, S. (1990) The effect of railway lines on urban fox (*Vulpes vulpes*) numbers and dispersal movements. *Journal of Zoology*, **221,** 321–326.

1309 Trewhella, W.J. *et al.* (1988) Dispersal distance, home-range size and population density in the red fox (*Vulpes vulpes*): a quantitative analysis. *Journal of Applied Ecology*, **25,** 423–434.

1310 Trout, R.C. & Tittensor, A.M. (1989) Can predators regulate wild rabbit *Oryctolagus cuniculus* population density in England and Wales? *Mammal Review*, **19,** 153–173.

1311 Trowbridge, B.J. (1983) *Olfactory communication in the European otter* Lutra lutra *L.* PhD thesis, University of Aberdeen,.

1312 Turner, D.C. & Bateson, P. (eds.) (2001) *The domestic cat: the biology of its behaviour*, 2nd edn. Cambridge University Press, Cambridge.

1313 Turner, D. & Mertens, C. (1986) Home range overlap and exploitation in domestic farm cats (*Felis catus*). *Behaviour*, **99,** 22–45.

1314 Tuyttens, F.A.M. *et al.* (2000) Comparative study on the consequences of culling badgers (*Meles meles*) on biometrics, population dynamics and movement. *Journal of Animal Ecology*, **69,** 567–580.

1315 Tuyttens, F.A.M. *et al.* (2001) Vigilance in badgers *Meles meles*: the effects of group size and human persecution. *Acta Theriologica*, **46,** 79–86.

1316 Twelves, J. (1983) Otter (*Lutra lutra*) mortalities in lobster creels. *Journal of Zoology*, **201,** 585–588.

1317 Twigg, G.I. & Harris, S. (1982) Seasonal and age changes in the thymus gland of the red fox, *Vulpes vulpes*. *Journal of Zoology*, **196,** 355–370.

1318 Twigg, G.I. *et al.* (1968) Leptospirosis in British wild mammals. *Symposia of the Zoological Society of London*, **24,** 75–98.

1319 Vaisfel'd, M.A. (1972) [A contribution to the ecology of the stoat in the cold season in the European north]. *Zoologicheskii Zhurnal*, **51,** 1705–1714 (in Russian).

1320 Varty, K. (1967) *Reynard the fox: a study of the fox in Medieval English art*. Leicester University Press, Leicester.

1321 Vaughan, N. *et al.* (2003) Habitat associations of European hares *Lepus europaeus* in England and Wales: implications for farmland management. *Journal of Applied Ecology*, **40,** 163–175.

1322 Velander, K.A. (1983) *Pine marten survey of Scotland, England and Wales 1980–1982*. Vincent Wildlife Trust, London.

1323 Velander, K.A. (1986) *A study of pine marten ecology in Inverness-shire*. Nature Conservancy Council CSD Report 651. JNCC, Peterborough.

1324 Velander, K.A. (1991) Pine marten *Martes martes*, pp. 367–376 in Corbet G.B. & Harris, S. (eds.) *The handbook of British mammals*, 3rd edn. Blackwell Scientific Publications, Oxford.

1325 Venables, L.S.V. & Venables, U.M. (eds.) (1955) *Birds and mammals of Shetland*. Oliver & Boyd, Edinburgh.

1326 Venge, O. (1973) Reproduction in the mink. *Kongelige Veterinaer-og Landbohoiskøles Aarsskrift*, **1973,** 95–146.

1327 Vergara, V. (2000) Two cases of infanticide in a red fox, *Vulpes vulpes*, family in southern Ontario. *Canadian Field Naturalist*, **115,** 170–173.

1328 Voigt, D.R. & Macdonald, D.W. (1984) Variation in the spatial and social behaviour of the red fox, *Vulpes vulpes*. *Acta Zoologica Fennica*, **171,** 261–265.

1329 Volf, J. (1968) Breeding the European wild cat at Prague Zoo. *International Zoo Yearbook*, **8,** 38–42.

1330 Volobuev, V.T. *et al.* (1974) The taxonomic status of the white African polecat or ferret in the light of karyological data. *Zoologicheskii Zhurnal*, **53,** 1738–1740.

1331 Wabakken, P. 1985. *Vinternaering, habitatbruk og jaktatferd hos mar* (Martes martes) *i sorost-norsk barskog*. MS thesis,

University of Oslo (in Norwegian).

1332 Walker, D.R.G. (1972) Observations on a collection of weasels (*Mustela nivalis*) from estates in South-west Hertfordshire. *Journal of Zoology*, **166,** 474–480.

1333 Walton, K.C. (1968) The baculum as an age indicator in the polecat *Putorius putorius*. *Journal of Zoology*, **156,** 533–536.

1334 Walton, K.C. (1968) *Studies on the biology of the polecat* Putorius putorius *(L.)*. MSc. thesis, University of Durham.

1335 Walton, K.C. (1970) The polecat in Wales. In Lacey, W.S. (ed.) *Welsh wildlife in trust*. North Wales Wildlife Trust, Bangor.

1336 Walton, K.C. (1976) The reproductive cycle in the male polecat *Putorius putorius* in Britain. *Journal of Zoology*, **180,** 498–503.

1337 Walton, K.C. & Page, R.J.C. (1970) Some ectoparasites found on polecats in Britain. *Nature in Wales*, **12,** 32–34.

1338 Wandeler, A. *et al.* (1974) Rabies in wild carnivores in central Europe I. Epidemiological studies. *Zentralblatt für Veterinaermedizin B*, **21,** 735–756.

1339 Wandeler, P. *et al.* (2003) The city-fox phenomenon: genetic consequences of a recent colonization of urban habitat. *Molecular Ecology*, **12,** 647–656.

1340 Wansink, D. (1997) Bedreigingen van de boommarter in Nederland, pp. 45–51 in Canters, K. & Wijsman, H. (eds.) *Wat doen we met de Boommarter?* Wetenschappelijke Mededeling KNNV No. 219 (in Dutch).

1341 Ward, J. & Kitchener, A. Personal communication.

1342 Ward, N. (1999) Foxing the nation: the economic (in)significance of hunting with hounds in Britain. *Journal of Rural Studies*, **15,** 389–403.

1343 Warren, P.K. & Baines, D. (2002) Dispersal, survival and causes of mortality in black grouse *Tetrao tetrix* in northern England. *Wildlife Biology*, **8,** 91–97.

1344 Watson, A. (1955) The winter food supply of six highland foxes. *Scottish Naturalist*, **67,** 123–124.

1345 Watson, A. (1976) Food remains in the droppings of foxes (*Vulpes vulpes*) in the Cairngorms. *Journal of Zoology*, **180,** 495–496.

1346 Watson, J. (1997) *The golden eagle*. Poyser, London.

1347 Watt, J.P. (1991) *Prey selection by coastal otters* (Lutra lutra L.). PhD thesis, University of Aberdeen.

1348 Watt, J.P. (1993) Ontogeny of hunting behaviour of otters (*Lutra lutra* L.) in a marine environment. *Symposia of the Zoological Society of London*, **65,** 87–104.

1349 Watt, N.J. *et al.* (1993) An extended outbreak of infectious peritonitis in a closed colony of European wildcats (*Felis silvestris*). *Journal of Comparative Pathology*, **108,** 73–79.

1350 Wayre, P. (1972) Breeding the Eurasian otter *Lutra lutra* at the Norfolk Wildlife Park. *International Zoo Yearbook*, **12,** 116–117.

1351 Wayre, P. (1979) *The private life of the otter*. Batsford, London.

1352 Wayre, P. (1979) Report of Council 1978. *Otters 1978*, **1**(2), 1–13.

1353 Wayre, P. (1981) Report of Council 1980. *Otters 1980*, **1**(4), 5–9.

1354 Wayre, P. (1982) Report of Council 1981. *Otters 1981*, **1**(5), 5–11.

1355 Webb, J.B. (1975) Food of the otter (*Lutra lutra*) on the Somerset levels. *Journal of Zoology*, **177,** 486–491.

1356 Webbon, C.C. *et al.* (2004) Faecal density counts for monitoring changes in red fox numbers in rural Britain. *Journal of Applied Ecology*, **41,** 768–779.

1357 Webbon, C.C. *et al.* (2006) Macroscopic prey in the winter diet of foxes in Britain. *Mammal Review*, **36,** 85–97.

1358 Weber, D. (1987) *Zur Biologie des Iltisses* (Mustela putorius L.) *und den Ursachen seines Rückganges in der Schweiz*. PhD thesis, Naturhistorisches Museum Basel (in German).

1359 Weber, D. (1988) Experiments on microhabitat preference of polecats. *Acta Theriologica*, **33,** 403–413.

1360 Weber, D. (1988) Die aktuelle Verbreitung des Iltisses

Fig. 10.3 Grey seals clustered together in middle of mixed haul-out with common seals *(photo SMRU)*.

fetal coat. Occasional reports of red seals, perhaps due to deposition of ferric oxide on pelage [4] or heavy infestations of sucking lice.

Moult: Undergoes a complete moult each year at end of breeding season. Hair loss normally starts around the face and genitals, ends in the mid-dorsal region, and lasts about 3–4 weeks. Timing of moult differs with sex and age classes. Yearlings moult first, sometimes as early as June. Other seals start moulting from mid-July, with females

moulting before males; in males (no data for females) immatures before matures. By late September all are fully moulted [162].

Anatomy: Typically a rather stubby 'seal-shaped' torpedo. Adult males with heavier build, particularly around the neck. Forelimbs paddle shaped; digits 1 and 2 nearly equal, others shorter in order, all digits bound together in a common integument. Hind limbs fan-like with digits joined by hair-covered web; digits 1 and 5 nearly equal,

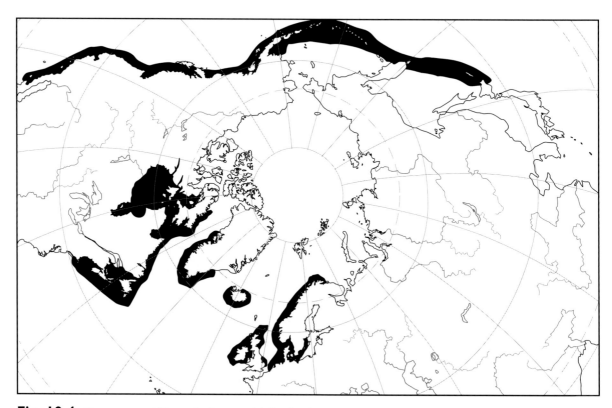

Fig. 10.4 Common seal *Phoca vitulina*: world distribution.

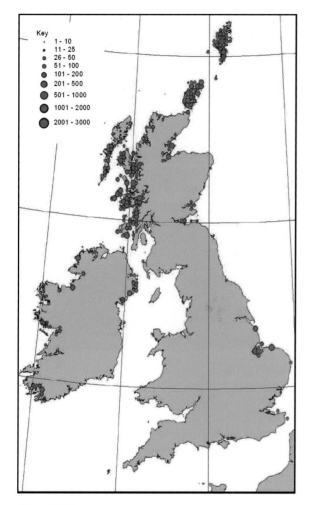

Fig. 10.5 Common seal *Phoca vitulina*: breeding season distribution and status, based on aerial counts of adults at haulouts *(map courtesy of SMRU, St Andrews).*

2–4 shorter. Nails present on all digits, though sometimes lost and often heavily worn.

Nipples: 1 (rarely 2) abdominal pairs in both sexes; inconspicuous in males, most obvious in females during breeding season and moult. Position lateral and slightly anterior to navel.

Skull: Anterior part of palate on maxilla, posterior border of palate ⌃-shaped; lacunae often present in basioccipital and exoccipital. Nasals extend beyond posterior margin of maxillae. Permanent dentition 3.1.5 (postcanines)/2.1.5 (postcanines). Milk teeth usually resorbed or shed before birth and permanent dentition erupted at birth or shortly after. Cheek-teeth much longer than broad, set obliquely in jaw, with 3–4 cusps. First lower postcanine usually with 4 cusps, of which 2nd (from anterior end) largest.

Reproductive tract: *Male:* testes internal, penile aperture fairly obvious even in juveniles; prostate immediately below bladder at junction with urethra; simple baculum present. *Female:* vulva and anus in common furrow, vulva often obviously swollen in adult females; reproductive tract bicornuate with short common uterus; vagina opening into urinogenital sinus which in turn opens to exterior by a bursa including the anus; ovaries ovulate alternately.

Chromosomes: 2n = 32, Fna = 60 [13], as in most phocids (except *Erignathus*, 2n = 34).

RELATIONSHIPS
Closest relative is the largha seal, *P. largha*, an ice-breeding species in NW Pacific, once regarded as a subspecies of *P. vitulina*. Also close to ringed and grey seals [14].

MEASUREMENTS
See Table 10.2. Adult body length varies between populations [79]. Within a population, body weight is highly variable depending upon age and season. Length and weight of yearling seals also differ in relation to between-year changes in food availability [46, 79].

VARIATION
Single subspecies occurs throughout NE Atlantic (*P. v. vitulina*), with 4 other subspecies recognised: *P. v. concolor* (W Atlantic), *P. v. richardii* (E Pacific), *P. v. stejnegeri* (W Pacific) and *P.v. mellonae* (in freshwater lakes, E Canada). Only minor

Table 10.2 Measurements of common seals. Data for adult seals are for seals of at least 6 years old from the Moray Firth, Scotland [46]. Length was measured as nose–tail. Weights of pups are from the Wash, England [182]

	Males				**Females**			
	Mean	SD	Range	n	Mean	SD	Range	n
Adult length (cm)	150	4	138–158	23	139	4	125–150	12
Adult weight (kg)	88	15	68–125	23	71	11	50–98	12
Weight at birth (kg)	12.5	1	10–16	11	12	1		

Fig. 10.6 Common seals hauled out. Note characteristic 'head-up, tail-up' pose of the animal at front left. *(Photo P. M. Thompson)*

morphological differences recorded, but genetic studies have confirmed that subspecies are highly differentiated, while different European populations of *P. v. vitulina* diverged only after the last ice age [149]. In contrast to grey seals, North Sea common seal populations show low levels of genetic variation [98].

DISTRIBUTION
Holarctic, in coastal waters mainly between 40° and 70° N (Fig. 10.4). In Europe, breeds around Iceland, in Norway south from Finnmark, sparsely in Baltic S of Stockholm, more abundantly in Denmark, German Frisian coast and Dutch Wadden Sea. Occurs sporadically along Channel coast and Biscay as far south as Portugal.

In GB, widespread along the W coast of Scotland and throughout the Hebrides and N Isles. On E coast, more restricted, occurring in estuaries such as the Moray Firth, the Tay and the Wash, with smaller groups on sandbanks off SE England (Fig. 10.5). Vagrants or remnant populations in S coast estuaries, Bristol Channel and Menai Straits. Occasionally move up inland waterways, notably Thames above Tower Bridge, East Anglian Ouse and Loch Ness [187]. In Ireland, occurs on E and NE coast in sheltered sea loughs and estuaries, especially Strangford and Carlingford loughs, and in scattered locations along W coast.

HISTORY
Hunted at Mesolithic Oronsay, Bronze Age to Viking Jarlshof, but less numerous than grey seal [191]. Historical records poor at differentiating the 2 species until the 20th century, but were once more widely distributed around British coasts; colonies present Isle of Wight, 19th century, Bristol Channel to mid 20th century.

HABITAT
Most observations relate to seals at terrestrial haul-out sites. These are generally in shallow, sheltered waters, sea lochs and around island archipelagos. Is the characteristic (though not exclusive) seal of sandbanks, mudbanks and estuaries (e.g. Wash, Abertay Sands). In such situations, uses banks that allow immediate access to deep water for ease of escape. In Shetland, Orkney, W Isles and W coast of Scotland, found on rocky shores and shingle or sandy beaches of small islands (e.g. Eynhallow, Orkney; see Fig. 10.6); in remote sea lochs (e.g. Loch Teacuis, Argyll); or on isolated skerries (Ve Skerries, Shetland). However, not restricted to remote localities, and may haul out close to roads or piers when undisturbed. Elsewhere in their range, will haul out on ice floes, log booms, etc.

Less is known about foraging habitats. Telemetry studies indicate mostly feed relatively locally to haul-out sites [168, 174]. Together with information on the habitat preferences of known prey, suggests that they exploit a wide range of coastal habitats.

Generally feed on the seabed in shallow waters around Britain, often over sandy sediments, rocky reefs and submarine banks [174]. Elsewhere in their range (e.g. NE Pacific), may feed pelagically.

SOCIAL ORGANISATION AND BEHAVIOUR

Common seals are one of the most aquatic pinnipeds, yet most information on their behaviour remains based on terrestrial observations. Come ashore throughout the year at highly predictable haul-out sites, forming groups that range from singletons to several hundred individuals. Some segregation by age and sex, notably during the breeding season when females and pups predominate at some sites and males at others [3, 102, 159]. Choice of haul-out site varies with weather conditions, season and between-year changes in local food availability [159]. Probably solitary when feeding, but often form loose aggregations in water off haul-out sites.

Home range: Move regularly from inshore haul-out areas to feed in more open waters. Summer foraging ranges, NE Scotland, vary from 4 to 106 km, and are positively related to body size [168]. Individuals favour predictable foraging areas within a season, travelling directly to them and spending much of their time at sea in a relatively local area. Not known whether individuals continue to use same foraging areas over longer periods. No regular migratory movements known in UK waters; longer distance seasonal movements between alternative haul-out sites are seen elsewhere in range.

Individuals generally faithful to particular haul-out areas within a season; few data on longer-term site fidelity or social structuring of haul-out groups. No evidence of territoriality on land, but adult males in NE Scotland defend small (<200 m²) dispersed aquatic 'territories' in which they display repeatedly during the mating season. Analyses of vocal characteristics indicate that males return repeatedly to these areas within and between breeding seasons [181].

Communication and senses: Vision good in both air and water, though less effective at low light intensities in air [96, 184]. As sensitive to waterborne sound as terrestrial mammals to airborne sound. Hearing not as sensitive in air, but still quite good. Auditory range to 180 kHz, with directional hearing in both media [115]. Scent characteristic, and sense of smell acute. Vibrissae capable of detecting vibrations in water, such as those set up by swimming fish.

Not very vocal on land. Growling threats occasionally heard, and pups call to mothers with an almost human 'waa waa' cry. Under water, adult males produce powerful low-frequency vocalisations during mating season; associated with stereotypic dive displays, which seem characteristic of different regions [22, 77, 179]. Early in the breeding season, males also slap water surface with fore flipper, to produce 'rifle-shot' sound, and 'snort' at the surface. These displays also form an element of play by juveniles [188].

Aggressive behaviour: Disputes over space at haul-out sites may lead to a series of threat gestures: growls, head thrusts and fore-flipper waves [152]. The frequency of aggressive interactions is related to availability of space at haul-out sites [118], and dominance hierarchies may form where space is very restricted. Similar aggressive gestures are made by females when defending the area around their young pups and, in all age classes of common seals, in response to approaches by grey seals. Fights on land are rare, but may be seen during the breeding season when oestrous females repel advances by adult males. Male–male competition is intense during June and July, and mature bulls are often seen with multiple bite wounds around the neck [157]. Serious fighting between males appears to occur only in the water.

Dispersal: Some pups, tagged in the Wash and Orkney, have dispersed several hundred km to other parts of the North Sea, but most recoveries within 50 km [31, 165]. Tagging recoveries are usually within the first year of life; unknown what proportion of pups return to recruit to their natal sites in the UK. Longer-term studies of >150 pups branded in the Kattegat–Skaggerak recorded no dispersal >32 km; females became increasingly site-faithful with age, but the opposite was true of males [78]. Genetic data from different North Sea populations suggest that dispersal rates between these areas are very low [63].

Activity: Varies markedly in relation to season and local environmental conditions as well as sex, age of individuals [81]. Females must come ashore to give birth and suckle young, but primary reason for hauling out outside the breeding season remains unclear. May be energetic advantages to being ashore, though may cause heat stress in some conditions [185]. Hauling out may also lower predation risk and infection by ectoparasites, or enhance skin maintenance and hair growth.

Females spend more time ashore in breeding season with their young pups, while males increase their time ashore during the annual moult. Outside these periods, time spent hauled-out related to body size; from 40% for a juvenile to as low as 10% for a large adult [168]. Timing of haul-out usually restricted to low tide period on sandbanks, but on rocky shores seals are found hauled out at all stages on the tide, sometimes for periods exceeding 24 h. At such sites, haul-out behaviour can be diurnal, nocturnal or tidal; likely to be related to local or individual differences in feeding activity. Where rich feeding areas close inshore, seals may make short feeding trips and haul out daily. In UK waters, typically alternate periods of several days near haul-out sites with foraging trips of <1 to 12 days [163, 168].

Locomotion: Swim by side-to-side sweeps of hind flippers; forelimbs used only for manoeuvring or very slow progression. Typical swimming speed when travelling is *c*.5 km/h [186]. In coastal UK waters, seals appear to swim along the seabed during periods of travel. On land, move by characteristic body hitching, with forelimbs on ground, hind limbs trailing or held together and lifted clear of ground. Can hitch forward with forelimbs folded against sides, or may progress in this way with one flank against ground.

Diving: While at sea, spend 70–80% of time under water. Dives typically last 2–6 min and are very regular. Less regular dives seen when playing in shallows. Longer dives, >30 min, may occur occasionally [51, 141]. Dive duration strongly related to body size: larger seals make longest dives, spend higher proportion of dive cycle under water. Often seen 'bottling', with body held vertical in the water and face above the surface, apparently asleep. When resting like this may sink down for as long as 8 min before resurfacing at the same spot. Pups can dive for up to 2 min when a few days old; dive performance gradually increases with age [20]. Around the UK, rarely dive deeper than 75 m, but dives down to 200 m recorded in Norwegian waters [22] and to >400 m off the Californian coast [51].

Play: Pairs sometimes seem engaged in erotic rolling behaviour, particularly in the pre-pupping period and in late summer [183]. Originally thought to be precopulatory display, but more likely to be play between immatures [157, 188]. Sometimes 'porpoise', jumping repeatedly clear of the water while swimming fast, often when disturbed from, or arriving at, a haul-out site; significance of this unknown.

FEEDING

Appear to be opportunistic feeders, taking species that are locally or seasonally abundant, or easy to catch. Older information on diet composition based on analyses of prey from stomach samples, but more recent studies have identified fish ear bones (otoliths) and cephalopod beaks from faecal samples. Reliance on faecal samples can risk under-representation of prey species with fragile hard parts, or where heads are not eaten, but provides a good indication of variation in the frequency of key prey. Wide variety of prey species taken, but a few groups predominate in most studies; notably sandeels *Ammodytes*, gadoids (e.g. cod and whiting), clupeids (herring and sprat), cephalopods (octopus and squid) and pleuronectids (e.g. flounder). Differences in diet composition often found between regions; within a region, diet can differ both in different seasons and in different years. Differences in foraging ranges and diving capabilities of different sized seals may cause age- and sex-related differences in diet, but data to assess this possibility are currently unavailable.

Most fish consumed tend to be small (10–30 cm) but larger prey are also taken [34, 172]. Comparisons with fishing surveys indicate that seals generally take the most abundant species and size classes available [173]. Large fish brought to the surface, broken up by shaking, but most prey items (up to at least 30 cm) presumably swallowed whole underwater.

Hunting behaviour: Direct observations of feeding behaviour rarely possible, but recent Canadian studies using animal-mounted video have identified different foraging strategies involving capture of cryptic benthic or schooling prey [37]. In typical UK shallow waters, diving patterns recorded from computer data loggers indicate that most foraging is on the bottom. Seals typically descend quickly to the seabed, at *c*.1 m/s. Occasionally, dives are only to mid-water, possibly in pursuit of schooling prey such as sandeels [174].

Impact on prey: Much debate about potential impact of seals upon prey stocks, particularly those of commercial importance such as salmon and cod. Currently, data insufficient to evaluate the impact of common seals on prey populations in UK waters. In particular, uncertain how seal predation upon key prey species varies relative to relative abundances of that species and alternative prey (but see [114]).

Daily food requirements: Adults lose considerable mass during the summer, when pupping and mating activity constrain foraging [79]. Food requirements therefore differ markedly with age, sex and season. Averaged over whole year, per capita requirements estimated at 3.6–4.15 kg of fish daily, depending on the diet composition [23, 80].

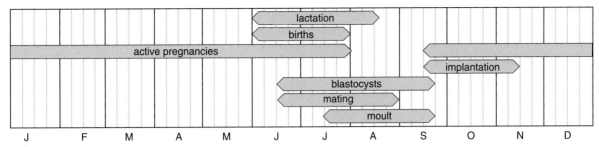

Fig. 10.7 Common seal: annual cycle.

BREEDING

Monoestrus, mating in July. Pregnancy 10–11 months, including delayed implantation. Single pup born in June–July. Mature at 3–6 years old. Polygynous. See Fig. 10.7.

Males: Sexually mature at 4–6 years, based on presence of sperm in epididymis and increase in testes weight [21, 33, 79, 83]; not known at what age males first compete socially for mating opportunities.

Females: Sexually mature at 3–4 years [21, 33, 83]. Single pup, born at intertidal haul-out site, each year, in June–early July. Peak pupping occurs in 2nd half of June. Twin fetuses known, but no records of twins surviving. Mothers and pups usually move quickly into water when disturbed (Fig. 10.8). Much of detailed information on reproductive behaviour and physiology comes from Sable Island, Canada, where common seals exhibit greater tolerance of humans. Studies of lactation difficult due to mobility of mothers and pups; on Sable Island, lactation lasts 3–4 weeks [116]. At intertidal sandbank sites, Scotland,

Fig. 10.8 Common seal: mother with pup on sandbank *(photo P. M. Thompson)*.

mothers spent 10–15% of their time suckling over the low tide period, with peaks at the beginning and end of haul-out [46]. Mothers and pups maintain close contact during the first half of lactation, both in and out of the water. Females fast during this period, may lose 33% of body weight [36]. Later in lactation, females resume feeding [25, 166]; extent to which pups join them on these longer foraging trips not known. Mating occurs around the time of weaning. After several cell divisions, implantation is delayed for 5–12 weeks [55].

Productivity: Aquatic behaviour of mothers and young pups currently prevents a comparison of levels of pup production either within or between different UK regions.

Development of young: Weigh 9–11 kg at birth. White fetal pelage (lanugo) usually moulted in the uterus but a few pups, generally of younger mothers, may be born with lanugo [35]. Male pups tend to be slightly heavier than females [35, 182], and larger and older mothers produce heavier pups [35]. Pups more than double their birth weight during the lactation period, but this followed by a post-weaning fast of 15–17 days, resulting in a 20% reduction in weaning weights [116]. In late July–mid September weaned pups rarely seen at haul-out sites; may be dispersing or spending much of their time in local waters learning to feed. Between-year differences in the availability of key prey can result in marked differences in growth rates during the subsequent winter [46].

Mating patterns: Copulation rarely seen on land, approaches by males usually successfully rebuffed by females [2, 159]. Mating therefore appears to occur almost exclusively in the water. In Scotland, adult males continue foraging until late June. Subsequently, restrict their range and make stereotypic dive and acoustic displays at dispersed sites throughout females' ranges [179]. Detailed picture of mating pattern remains elusive, but increasing evidence for a lek-type system in this species [26, 89], highest density of display sites found on transit routes between female haul-out sites and foraging areas [180]. Genetic studies in Canada indicate both a low level of polygyny [43, 44] and alternative male mating strategies [45].

POPULATION

Population size: Abundance estimates based on counts at haul-out sites, usually during either the pupping season or moult. Provide a minimum estimate and index of population size, but an unknown proportion of population remains in the water. Telemetric studies across a range of habitats indicate that haul-out counts during these periods represent 60–70% of the population of animals aged 1 year or older [142, 161, 167]. Synoptic aerial surveys across the whole UK produce minimum population count of 34 200, of which >85% were in Scotland (Table 10.3). This suggests a total population of *c*.50 000–60 000 [146]. An aerial survey of the coastline of the Republic of Ireland in 2003 produced a minimum population count of nearly 3000 [48]. Less precise estimates for Irish population suggest at least 3000 [88].

Fluctuations: Populations were dramatically reduced (by 40–60%) in parts of the southern North Sea after the 1988 morbillivirus (PDV) outbreak, but mortality appeared lower (10–20%) around Scotland [90]. Subsequently, populations in the Wash and areas such as the Dutch Wadden Sea, Kattegat and Skaggerak increased steadily, before the second PDV outbreak in 2002 [156]. Again, populations in many parts of Europe

Table 10.3 UK and Irish common seals: minimum population estimates, based on aerial counts made during the August moult between 1996 and 2005. Irish data from [48], all other data from [146]

Area	Peak count
Scotland, W coast and Inner Hebrides	12 507
Outer Hebrides	2 098
Shetland	4 883
Orkney	7 752
Scotland, E coast	1 819
England, E coast	3 617
N Ireland	1 248
Ireland	2 905
Total	**33 944**

markedly reduced, but less evidence of mortality in Scottish waters [82]. However, several populations appear to have declined as a result of other, largely unknown, factors in recent years [106, 170]. Assessments of trends complicated by uncertainty over movements between different regions and the possibility that behavioural changes influence the index of abundance.

Sex ratio: At birth apparently 1:1 [52], but becomes increasingly biased towards females after sexual maturity.

Age determination: Seals in their 1st year can be aged by measuring the width of individual hairs [47]. Canines or incisors can be used to estimate age from cementum growth rings [49]. Anomalies in growth rings can indicate females' age at sexual maturity [79].

Age structure: Few data for British population. Information based on samples from culls in Canada [21], and mortalities from the 1988 morbillivirus epizootic [79]; both techniques likely to provide biased samples. Maximum age for females 36 and for males 31 years. Differing mortality due to epizootics [160], as well as marked regional and between-year variability in prey supplies, suggest that age-structure likely to vary between different populations. In Canada, also evidence of temporal variation in age-structure in relation to population declines [38].

Survival: Data limited in all areas. On Sable Island, a minimum of 12% of all pups died in their 1st month of life [32]. Estimates of 1st-year mortality are highly variable (25–65%) probably reflecting both temporal and spatial variation in mortality rates and the extreme difficulty of producing precise estimates for this parameter [21, 137]. Analyses of the age structure of seals dying during the 1988 outbreak of phocine distemper virus (PDV) produced estimates for adult survival of 0.89–0.91 for males and 0.91–0.95 for females in an increasing Scandinavian population [79] Photographically based mark–recapture estimate of adult survival in one Scottish population was 0.9815 (95% PI = 0.9382–0.9995) [107].

MORTALITY

Predation: Killer whales and sharks can cause significant levels of mortality in some N American populations [52, 97]. Killer whale attacks recorded around Scotland, and potential shark predators occasional in British waters; uncertain that these predators affect UK common seals.

Persecution: Legal shooting occurs, particularly in Scotland to protect fish farms, netting stations and salmon rivers. Levels of shooting in some areas may be sufficient to drive local population declines [171].

Disease: Occasional mass mortalities have occurred periodically in British waters [85]. The 1988 PDV outbreak killed 18 000 individuals in the North Sea, became one of the best studied wildlife disease incidents (see [85] for review). Second outbreak occurred in 2002; comparisons of pattern of spread of these 2 outbreaks suggest that grey seals act as reservoir host for the disease [82]. Increased interest in marine mammal diseases following the 1988 outbreak led to the identification of various other pathogens in British populations. Many of these, such as *Brucella* sp., are likely to be endemic [58]. Others, such as certain *Salmonella* sp. may result from contact with human or agricultural waste [19]. Uncertain whether these different disease agents cause mortality.

Contaminants: Accumulating evidence that common seals particularly sensitive to adverse immunosuppressive and reproductive effects of persistent organic pollutants [135, 143]. Despite the ban on production and use of many compounds such as PCBs and DDT, levels in some populations remain high. Effects of exposure on the endocrine system such as thyroid function [153] and the impact of mixtures of compounds, including newer brominated flame retardants, are ongoing.

PARASITES

Ectoparasites: Louse *Echinophthirius horridus* widespread, particularly on young seals [169], believed to be an intermediate host for nematode heartworms [60]. When seals in poor condition, lice may occur in tens of thousands all over the body.

Endoparasites: Nematode lungworms *Otostrongylus circumlitus* and *Parafilarioides gymnurus* frequent, thought to be a significant cause of mortality of young seals. *Parafilaroides* may also have a commensal relationship with *Brucella* [59]. Nematode heartworms *Skrjabinaria spirocauda* also occur. Stomach nematodes *Contracaecum osculatum* and *Pseudoterranova (Porrocaecum) decipiens* are almost universal. Acanthocephalan worm *Corynosoma strumosum* found in posterior part of ileum and large intestine. Cestodes, mostly *Diphyllobothrium spp.,* and trematodes recorded from both gut and liver [27].

RELATIONS WITH HUMANS

Traditionally exploited for food, oil and skins in many parts of Britain. Local hunting of pups for skin trade continued in Shetland, Orkney, W coast of Scotland and Wash until 1960s, but this trade now minimal (though common seal skin is still a traditional covering for sporrans). Regarded as a serious pest of salmon fisheries in some areas, particularly because haul out in river estuaries and occasionally move into fresh water. Establishment of fish farms in Scotland has also led to problems in some areas with seals damaging fish in cages. Common seals more frequently implicated than grey seals, since most farms in sheltered waters. However, damage often occurs at night, not always clear which species to blame. Seals commonly play with, and puncture, plastic creel buoys, incurring resentment of lobster fishermen.

Important tourist attraction in several localities: seals become very accustomed to tourist boats and allow close approach. Also good viewing opportunities from many land-based sites in Scotland. Common seals kept in captivity at several aquaria in the UK, and several centres rehabilitate pups. Pups or sick seals found by the public should not be approached or touched because of the risk of injury and zoonoses. Such animals should be reported to the local RSPCA or SSPCA office.

Protected in GB by a close season, 1 June–31 August, under Conservation of Seals Act 1970, during which common seals can be killed only under licence or in the vicinity of fishing nets to protect catch. Protection has been extended throughout the year in certain areas such as the Moray Firth through special conservation orders. Unprotected in Northern Ireland but protected in the Irish Republic at all times by the Wildlife Act 1976. Special Areas of Conservation have been developed for common seals under the EC Habitats and Species Directive, providing new opportunities to protect key marine habitats in addition to haul-out sites.

LITERATURE

Good general accounts of seals in [29, 93, 134, 140]. Popular account focusing on British seals by Anderson [8]. Monograph on common seals by Thompson [158]. Results of annual surveys are presented in the report of the NERC Special Committee on Seals (available at *http://smru.st-and.ac.uk/*)

PRINCIPAL AUTHOR
P.M. Thompson

Fig. 10.9 Grey seal: mother nuzzling white-coated pup (cf. Fig. 10.8) *(photo P. M. Thompson).*

GENUS *Halichoerus*

Contains only the grey seal; molecular data suggests that should be incorporated in *Phoca* [14]. Differs from *Phoca* in details of skull and teeth (see Fig. 10.2).

Grey seal *Halichoerus grypus*

Phoca grypus Fabricius, 1791; Greenland.
Atlantic seal, great seal; *morlo llwyd* (Welsh); *selchie* or *selkie* (Scots; also used for common seal), *ron mor* (Gaelic); haaf-fish (obsolete, Shetland); horse head (Canada).

RECOGNITION

Whole animal: Difficult to distinguish from common seal, especially in water. Colour variable and not useful as a field character. Spots, where recognisable, larger and less numerous than in common seal. Head large and muzzle elongated, giving 'Roman nose' or equine appearance to face; top of head fairly flat (see Fig. 10.1). Head shape of young grey seal similar to that of common seal. Nostrils almost parallel and separated ventrally (see Fig 10.1). In some areas, frequently hauls out with common seals (see Fig. 10.3).

Skull and teeth: Postcanine teeth large, usually with single conical cusp; secondary cusps when present insignificant (Fig.10.2). Interorbital region of skull wide, snout high, so that axis of nasals approximately parallel to tooth-row. Anterior part of palate deeply concave.

FIELD SIGNS

Tracks and trails: Rocks or non-tidal beaches used regularly for hauling out may show traces of hair, particularly in spring. Breeding males particularly have characteristic musky odour. Occur on sandy beaches in some areas, leaving tracks similar to common seal, but wider.
Faeces: Sometimes found on rocks or sandbanks. Consistency highly variable; when firm, dog-like, 4–4.5 cm diameter. Colour variable: brown, black, putty coloured, even orange (which may be indicative of fasting during breeding or moulting season).

DESCRIPTION

Pelage: Older males generally uniformly dark grey or brown background with few pale patches, belly slighter paler. Juvenile males and females very difficult to distinguish by pelage alone (Plate 9). Adult females typically medium grey on back, shading to pale grey or cream on belly, with dark patches sparsely scattered on this lighter background; enormous variation in colour and patterning, from very pale uniform colour with almost no spots to very dark females whose patches nearly coalesce (see Fig. 10.9). All shades of light and dark grey, brown and silver occur; a few adults of both sexes may be completely black; some individuals may have a ginger coloration, particularly on the head. Approaching moult, worn hair gives brown or fawn coloration, especially when pelage dries.

Moult: All except young of the year undergo

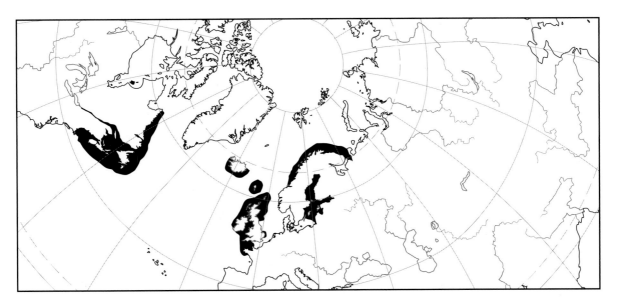

Fig. 10.10 Grey seal *Halichoerus grypus*: world distribution.

complete annual moult: females January–March; males February–June. Pups born in white natal fur (lanugo), shed after 2–3 weeks revealing first adult coat (Fig. 10.9). Their next moult is not until after *c*.15 months.

Anatomy: Marked sexual dimorphism; adult male half as large again as female, with heavy neck and shoulders, usually scarred. Head profile of male convex, with heavy muzzle, contrasted with much flatter profile and more slender muzzle of female (see Fig. 10.1). Other external characteristics similar to common seal, but note long slender claws on fore flipper of grey seal.

Skull: Most noticeable feature of skull is long and wide snout with elevated frontonasal region; particularly marked in male, associated with the 'roman nose' (see Fig. 10.1). Posterior margin of palate evenly rounded, posterior palatal foramen opens on palatines, anterior part of palate strongly concave. Posterior margin of nasals approximately level with that of maxilla. Interorbital region wide. Permanent dentition 3.1.5 (often 6) (postcanines) /2.1.5 (postcanines). Milk teeth shed before birth, permanent dentition erupts shortly after. Upper incisors larger than lower. Canines massive, cone-shaped, postcanines are undifferentiated, large and strong, some nearly circular in cross-section with single conical cusp. Small secondary cusps sometimes present on 5th upper and 4th and 5th lower postcanines. First upper postcanine pushed inwards out of line in old animals.

Reproductive tract: Similar to common seal but penile opening in males not as obvious.

Chromosomes: 2n = 32, Fna = 60 [13].

RELATIONSHIPS
Molecular data suggest most closely related to species of *Pusa*, notably Caspian and Baikal seals *P. caspica, P. sibirica*, but that all these belong in the genus *Phoca* [14].

MEASUREMENTS
Adult males bigger than females. Adult body weight varies seasonally (see Breeding). See Table 10.4.

Table 10.4 Measurements of grey seals. Standard length is measured as nose–tail. All data are from North Rona [146]

	Males				**Females**			
	Mean	SD	Range	n	Mean	SD	Range	n
Adult length (cm)	207	10	195–230	25	168	9	143–197	511
Adult weight (kg)	233	40	170–440	25	190	23	131–251	184
Weight at birth (kg)	16.4	1.94		57	15.8	2.09		52

VARIATION

No subspecies recognised, but 3 reproductively isolated populations: western N Atlantic, eastern N Atlantic and Baltic. Around GB, significant genetic variation between animals at sites around Scotland [1] and between Scotland and SW Britain [146].

DISTRIBUTION

Restricted to N Atlantic and adjacent waters. NW Atlantic, range from Labrador to New York State; main breeding sites include Sable Island and the Gulf of St Lawrence. NE Atlantic, from the White Sea to Brittany (Fig. 10.10); breeding sites include the Murmansk coast, Iceland, Norway (N of Møre), Faroe Islands, Baltic Sea (in gulfs of Bothnia, Riga and Finland), British Isles and Brittany.

Most of NE Atlantic population breeds around the British Isles (Fig. 10.11), particularly in the Inner and Outer Hebrides, Orkney and Shetland. Other important breeding colonies include mainland Scotland (at Loch Eriboll, Helmsdale and Fast Castle), the Isle of May (Firth of Forth), the Farne Islands, Donna Nook (Humberside) and the Pembroke coast and islands in SW Wales. Smaller breeding sites are interspersed between these including Isles of Scilly, Lundy and various sites scattered along Norfolk, Devon and Cornwall coasts. Around Ireland, at least 50 breeding sites, main ones Inishkea, Co. Mayo and Blasket islands, Co. Kerry.

Distribution more widespread outside breeding season, may be seen almost anywhere around the British coast, particularly in Scotland. Studies using satellite telemetry [108, 111, 146] show distribution at sea to include most of continental shelf area to N and W of Scotland, the western North Sea, the Channel (Fig. 10.12), and the Irish Sea.

HISTORY

Molecular data suggest diverged from other *Phoca/Pusa* seals only within last 3 my, in late Pliocene. Hunted at Mesolithic Oronsay, Hebrides and Bronze Age–Viking Jarlshof, Shetland; also Mesolithic Dalkey Island, Dublin, dated to 6400 bp [88, 191]. Heavily hunted during more recent centuries, claimed that only 500 remained around GB in 1914, certainly restricted to a few remote sites. Has expanded range and population as humans have evacuated islands and protection of breeding colonies has had effect; increase about 6%/year at best-studied colonies, 1950–2000; complex interplay of hunting, legal protection and changing human attitudes during 20th century [103, 191].

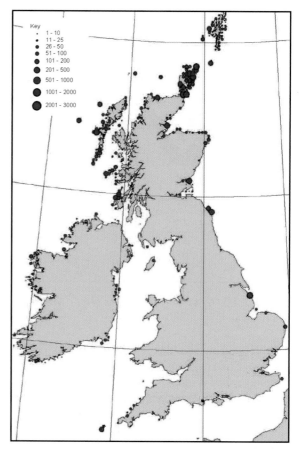

Fig. 10.11 Grey seal: breeding distribution and colony size, based on estimated production of pups *(map courtesy of SMRU, St Andrews)*.

HABITAT

While all foraging occurs at sea, grey seals haul out for prolonged periods during breeding and moulting seasons, and for shorter intervals throughout the remainder of the year, when they appear to take 'rests' or 'breaks' from their foraging trips.

Type of terrestrial habitat used by grey seals during breeding season differs from that used through the remainder of the year, when either moulting or resting. Breeding colonies typically on remote undisturbed islands or coastlines, usually with good access to open sea; in Gulf of St Lawrence and Baltic Sea, breed on ice. In the British Isles, breeding sites are above the high-water mark on sandy, shingle or rocky beaches or in sea caves. Where access is available, grey seals spread inland from the coast on to grassy swards as colony size increases, but remain within approximately 300 m of access to the sea. Certain breeding colonies are found on islands without beaches. Here seals use particular gullies or rocky slopes to gain access to the interior of the island (e.g. North Rona, Gasker, Coppay and Haskeir in the Outer Hebrides). Breeding colonies vary greatly

Table 10.6
North Sea [7(

Cod	
Whiting	
Haddock	
Ling	
Herring	
Plaice	
Sandeel	
All species	

Wide vari
species inclu
whiting, had
(mainly plai
such as drag
Myoxocephalus
(e.g. southern
but not maj
seasonally an
In 2002, a
some notabl
average, in 20
haddock and
in 2002 ate le:
same amount
haddock than
Consume
small fish (e.g
(e.g. cod up
Sometimes s
particularly in

Hunting bel
out sites usua
areas, genera
[111]. These f
seals and ir
associated wi
preferred habi
Telemetry
dives are to
foraging, cons
that energy-sa
role in grey se
'sit and wait' :
searching for
seabed for san

in size from those producing single figures of pups to Ceann Iar, Monach Isles, which produces over 6000 pups per year.

Outside breeding season, haul-out sites considerably closer to or below the high-water mark, include intertidal sandbanks, rocky coasts and skerries, sea caves and sandy, shingle or rocky beaches. Non-breeding haul-out sites are more widespread, much less remote, than breeding sites. Numbers of seals at non-breeding haul-out sites fluctuate greatly from day to day and between locations.

Around Britain, foraging habitats are at or near the seabed in shelf waters [108, 111, 146]. Off Farne Islands, forage over submarine banks of gravelly sand [111], the preferred habitat of sandeels, a major prey item. Wide variety of prey taken (see Feeding) indicates that these seabed foraging habitats also include sand/mud (flatfish) and rocky substrates (gadoids, etc.).

SOCIAL ORGANISATION AND BEHAVIOUR
Spend extended periods ashore while breeding and moulting. Social organisation during pupping and mating described under Breeding, below. Outside these times, they spend up to 40% of their time on or adjacent to haul-out sites; the remaining time is spent foraging at sea or travelling between haul-out sites.

Senses: As for common seals, few data. Blind seals typically found in good condition, so can forage successfully without sight. Sense of smell acute, particularly used in mother/pup recognition during breeding period [113]. Seals often smell haul-out areas repeatedly before leaving water. Vibrissae used as tactile organs.

Vocalisations: Interactions frequently include some vocalisations; females may howl, moan and hiss at each other and males. Males produce low hissing, growling and throbbing noises on land. Males on Sable Island, Nova Scotia produce characteristic loud ululation or yodelling. Pups' calls to mothers resemble human baby cries. Adult males produce loud low-frequency vocalisation underwater during the mating season, females also produce sounds in water [112].

Aggressive behaviour: During breeding, females maintain separation of 3 m. Vocalise, flipper aggressively, threaten using an open-mouth display and lunge or bite. Actual contact rare but occurs most when intruding pups or females come close to initiator's offspring. Female responses to male advances before oestrus vigorously aggressive, do involve contact. On land, males use

a repertoire of stereotypic sound and display behaviours, often over distances of 50 m or more, to establish dominance relationships [175]. Male–male competition particularly intense during later part of breeding season. Fights on land during breeding season rare, occur between closely matched competitors, may result in serious injury to either or both participants.

Dispersal: Pups tagged at breeding colonies in the UK have dispersed several hundred km away from natal sites, e.g. N Rona to Iceland, Ireland, Shetland, Norway; Farne Islands to Faroe Islands, Minches, Norway, Holland, Denmark; Ramsey (W Wales) to Ireland, France, Spain. Comparison of genetic data and tagging returns from N Rona and Isle of May breeding colonies suggests a low level of recruitment from non-natal sites into established breeding colonies [1, 127]. No known migratory movements.

Activity: Varies markedly in relation to season. Come ashore throughout the year at predictable haul-out sites to form groups of a few to several thousand individuals. Segregation of different ages and sexes can occur, notably around the time of moult. All-female groups seen less frequently than all-male groups. Juveniles and yearlings may occupy peripheral locations in some haul-out sites. Choice of haul-out site varies in relation to weather conditions and season. Spacing of individuals at haul-out sites much denser than in breeding colonies.

At sea, grey seals range widely in coastal waters, but rarely cross edge of continental shelf. (Fig.10.12) Movements range from short-range return trips from haul-out sites to local foraging areas, to extended journeys between distant haul-out sites. Spend approximately 40% of their time near or at haul-out sites, 12% of their time foraging and the remainder travelling between foraging areas and haul-out sites [110, 111]. Variability in foraging movements is greater between individuals than within individuals; a good description might be 'population generalist, individual specialist'.

Locomotion: Swim by side-to-side sweeps of hind flippers, with forelimbs used only for manoeuvring or very slow progression. Travelling speed typically about 4 km/h. Appears ungainly on land, but may move with surprising speed. Moves by characteristic body hitching, with forelimbs on ground, hind limbs trailing or held together and lifted clear of ground. Can hitch forward with forelimbs folded against sides, or may progress in this way with one flank against ground. Adults capable of climbing over vertical rock ledges >1 m high.

Diving: E
154, 155]
water. Div
variable w
Diving be
Travelling
consist of
V- or U-s
(typically
swim direc
not at all
32 min, de
speed unc
surface. H
and rhyth
about 45 b
to about 1

Play: Mo
behaviour;
objects su
between ju

Table 10

Prey typ

Sandeel

Gadoids

 Cod

 Whiting

 Haddock

 Saithe

 Ling

Flatfish

 Dover so

 Plaice

 Lemon s

Pelagics

 Herring

Benthic spe

 Dragone

 Bullrout

 Trisopter

Others

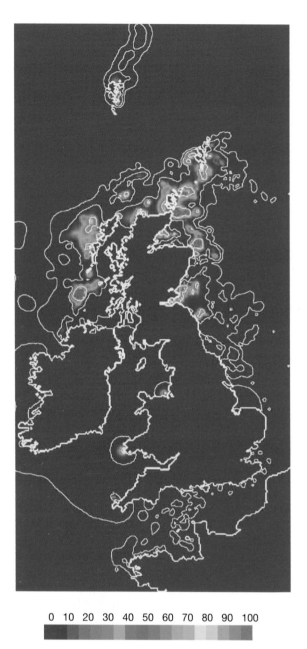

0 10 20 30 40 50 60 70 80 90 100

Fig. 10.12 Grey seal: intensity of usage of sea areas. The scale is in 5% segments of total usage (red sea areas host the top 5% of all use by grey seals at sea) *(map courtesy of SMRU, after [108]).*

to particular breeding sites, and may return to within 10–100 m of previous breeding sites [125, 128]. This breeding site fidelity persists over many seasons, thus some animals occur together repeatedly in the same areas. Canadian greys show no sign of such fidelity on Sable Island. Evidence of social affiliation between adult females on North Rona [131] (Fig. 10.14).

Males: Sexually mature at 4–6 years, but most males only begin to compete for mating opportunities from 8 years or later [61, 92]. A few males have bred successfully at the same colony for >10 years [175, 189]; attempt to defend shifting areas around female groups within breeding colonies, though some may occupy and try to control topographical features such as access to gullies or pools of water.

Females: Most are sexually mature at 3–5 years [40, 92]. Single pup born each year, mostly in September–November in Britain. Peak date of pupping varies according to locality and even within islands. Established breeding females vary little in date of pupping in different years; younger females tend to breed later, pupping dates get earlier as they age [126].

Twin fetuses are known and rare, but energetic constraints mean that mothers unlikely to raise 2 pups successfully. Maternal attendance pattern on pup varies: on North Rona, all mothers tend to remain ashore for duration of lactation, at Isle of May, some mothers return to tidal pools or inlets between suckling bouts [12, 42, 101, 125]. Mothers spend 2–6% of their time suckling [11, 101]. Milk has a high fat content (55%) and very little lactose (1%); composition varies as lactation proceeds, fat increasing and water decreasing [9]. Females fast during lactation and may lose 40% of their body weight [53, 126]. Mating occurs around days 14–16 of the 18–20 day lactation period.

Productivity: Adult female pregnancy rate 83% at the Hebrides and 94% at the Farne Islands in shot

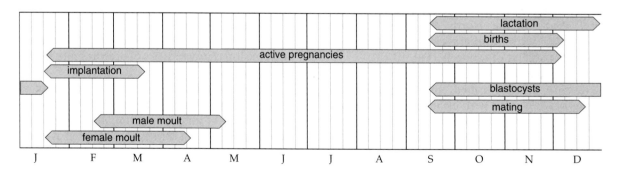

Fig. 10.13 Grey seal: annual cycle.

Fig. 10.14 Grey seal: white-coated pups with their mothers on breeding beach, Muckle Greenholm, Orkney. The nearest cow is suckling her pup *(photo P.M. Thompson)*.

samples [40]. Natality rate for known females over a 20-year period at North Rona estimated at 80–98% [126]. Females breed successfully till mid-30s at least. Evidence of reproductive senescence [38, 124].

Development of young: Characteristic white natal pelage (lanugo) retained until pup at least 10 days old (Fig 10.14), when begins moulting to 'weaner' coat. Weaner pelage may vary from typical adult pattern to uniform black coloration, persists until first juvenile moult around 15 months later. Weigh 12–20 kg at birth, male pups slightly heavier than females [53, 126] (see Table 10.4). Larger and older mothers produce heavier pups [126]. Pups may reach masses of 60+ kg at weaning (on average, 18 days after birth), then abandoned. Post-weaning fast of up to 3 weeks may result in a 20% reduction in weight [138]. Between December and March, weaned pups rarely seen at adult haul-out sites.

Mating patterns: Males maintaining positions within groups of females in the colony have highest mating success. Generally are large, experienced animals but other males achieve matings using alternative strategies [6, 24, 61, 175, 189]. Most successful copulations appear to occur within the breeding colony, but some matings also occur around the fringes of the colony or in the water [177]. Males that stay ashore longest have greatest mating success, but must bear average daily mass loss of 2.2 kg/day. Approaches by males to females before oestrus usually aggressively and

successfully rejected by females. Evidence of female mate choice is beginning to emerge. Genetic studies show that, within seasons, dominant males gain fewer paternities than expected by observations of mating success [5], but a moderate level of polygyny is indicated [175, 189].

POPULATION

Size of British Isles population derived from annual estimates of pup production at the main breeding sites (see Fig. 10.11), but uncertainties over nature of density-dependence preclude the use of simple multipliers previously used to extrapolate from pup production to total population size.

Numbers: The British Isles holds about 40% of the world population of grey seals. Based on data from 2005, the best estimate of size of the UK population is 97 000–159 000. [146]. Most, c.90%, are in Scotland; remaining 10% in England and Wales [146]. Irish population c.4000 [119].

Fluctuations: Grey seal pup production at UK sites has increased markedly over the past five decades but rate of increase may be slowing down; pattern varies between regions (Table 10.7). Pup production in Inner and Outer Hebrides levelled off in the mid 1990s. Orkney population also apparently approaching an asymptote, effect less pronounced and more recent. By contrast, most recent data (2005) shows North Sea population continuing to increase exponentially [146].

Table 10.7 Pup production of grey seals at different sites around the UK and Ireland. Irish data from 2001 [119], other data from 2005, except where annual surveys are not conducted (SW England, Wales, Shetland, mainland Scotland) [146]

Area	Pups born
Inner Hebrides	3 387
Outer Hebrides	12 297
Orkney	17 644
Isle of May and Fast Castle	3 586
All other Scottish sites	3 586
England, east coast	2 414
South-west	1 750
Ireland	1 000
Total	**45 664**

Sex ratio: At birth close to unity, but more male pups are born early in pupping season and more females later [10].

Age determination: Age can be estimated from growth rings in cementum of canines or incisors [92].

Age structure: Data for grey seals in Britain limited to samples from culls at the Farne Islands,1970s. Females sexually mature at 3–5 years [39]; maximum recorded age of females 46, but few live beyond 35 years. Males mature at *c.*6 years old, do not participate successfully in breeding until age 10. Few survive beyond age 20; maximum recorded in Britain 26 years [123].

Survival: Estimates of pre-weaning mortality from counts of dead pups in aerial photographs are less than 5% for most open colonies and up to 15% at colonies such as North Rona, Gasker, Isle of May [146]. Annual survival rates estimated at 93.5% (adult females) and 80% (males), based on age structure of animals culled at the Farne Islands in 1972 and 1975 [86]. Annual survival from weaning to age 1 estimated as *c.*60% in female pups, significantly lower in males [68]. Survival from weaning to age 5 must be *c.*50% to be consistent with observed growth rate of Farne Islands population.

MORTALITY
Predation and persecution: Humans remain the only serious predator of adult grey seals, but hunting now rare. Some shot by fishermen around fishing gear but no recent figures exist. Killer whales have been observed taking young seals in Scotland (especially Shetland). Seals, particularly juveniles, may be caught in fishing nets; mortality rates vary with area and fishery type; 1–2% of returns from pups tagged at the Farne Islands and Orkney are from seals entangled in fishing gear.

Disease: Diseases of the respiratory system, e.g. pneumonia and pleurisy, are the most commonly reported, followed by alimentary tract disorders, trauma and sepsis [15]. Females may suffer puerperal disease leading to death. Viral infections include herpes, ortho- and parapoxvirus and calicivirus [120, 148]. Young seals particularly vulnerable to poxvirus and can be seen with many lesions on the skin. Juveniles also appear susceptible to a mycotic dermatitis [121] which causes alopecia, but these skin conditions alone are not likely to be fatal. Starvation and infection are major causes of pre-weaned pup mortality, often following failure of the mother–pup bond [16, 18]. Causes of post-weaning juvenile mortality are largely unknown, although many have high lungworm infestations.

Grey seals were also exposed to phocine distemper during the 1988 and 2002 European epidemics [66, 74, 87, 130]. Serological studies found widespread exposure to the virus but no overt disease, suggesting this species is very resistant to PDV. Pup production the following year was reduced by approximately 12% [146], suggesting some effect on female reproduction.

PARASITES
Ectoparasites: Mite *Halarachne halichoeri*, found in the nasal tract and trachea, and louse *Echinophthirius horridus,* found less frequently than on common seals.

Endoparasites: High infestation rates of gastric nematodes *Contracaecum osculatum* and codworm *Pseudoterranova decipiens* recorded [17]. Grey seals are definitive host for codworm, which passes its final larval stage in gadoid fish. Although killed by freezing or cooking, codworm reduces the marketability of fish and increases processing costs. Infestation requires the presence of seals but levels not obviously related to numbers. Seal size is important in determining individual burdens, adult males carrying most [150]. Substantial seasonal variation is reported, declines during the breeding season fast, as burden levels are maintained by ingesting immature worms from prey. *Anisakis simplex* infection (anisakiasis) is less common; infests herring and can be a source of zoonotic infection from raw or lightly cured herring. Other marine mammals, e.g. porpoises (*Phocoena phocoena*), are more important as final hosts to *Anisakis* than either grey or common seals.

Lung nematodes *Otostrongylus spp.* and *Parafilaroides spp.* often found, particularly in young animals. Acanthocephalans are largely *Corynesoma* spp. [17].

Bacterial pathogens include *Streptococcus* and *Corynebacterium. Salmonella* also reported [16] and antibodies to *Brucella*, although no isolates have been obtained from grey seals.

Contaminants: Heavy metals such as mercury and lead reported in livers of grey seals from around the UK, highest levels in animals from Liverpool Bay [104]. Similarly PCBs and pesticides, such as DDT and dieldrin, can be concentrated in the blubber. Levels in UK animals seem to be declining in line with a ban on the production of the chemicals, but newer contaminants, such as polybrominated flame retardants, appear to be associated with thyroid hormone disruption, although the nature and consequences of such effects are still uncertain [69]. Evidence for adverse effects of environmental contaminants on the immune and reproductive systems in the wild remains equivocal; grey seals appear to be much less susceptible to effects than common seals [67, 73, 91].

RELATIONS WITH HUMANS

Exploitation: Grey seals were hunted extensively in the past, kept numbers at low levels. During most of the 20th century, exploitation was largely restricted to commercial hunting of pups for skins.

Conservation/legislation: Protected in GB under the Conservation of Seals Act 1970. During the close season (1 September–31 December), licence required to kill a seal, licences to shoot grey seals around fishing nets regularly issued in Scotland. Protected during the same season in Northern Ireland by the Grey Seal Protection Act and throughout the year in the Irish Republic under the Wildlife Act 1976. Special Areas of Conservation (SACs) being established under EC Habitats and Species Directive provide new opportunities to protect key habitats.

Seals may remove fish from nets or cause them damage; levels may vary annually, seasonally and from site to site. Significance of grey seal predation on salmon outside nets unknown. Fixed nets and long lines set for whitefish may also be affected by seal predation. Previous attempts to develop an effective method of seal control at nets include poisoning with strychnine-baited fish (now illegal). Current methods used are shooting and acoustic scaring devices. Grey seals may also cause problems at fish farms (see Common seal).

Competition with humans: Whitefish fishermen consider them to be competitors for commercial fish stocks. Comparison of estimates of the amount of prey consumed by seals with fish catches indicates seal predation typically an order of magnitude less than commercial catch limits in the North Sea [70], but much higher in W of Scotland [71]. In the past, various attempts made to reduce seal numbers, aiming to reduce damage to fisheries, including experimental culls of pups in Orkney, 1962, and at Farne Islands, 1963–1965. Annual pup quotas set in Orkney 1963–1982, in Outer Hebrides 1972–1979, and in Shetland 1962–1982. A plan to reduce grey seal numbers in Scotland to the levels of the early 1960s by a combination of adult and pup culls was initiated in 1977 but abandoned in 1978 because of widespread public concern [105]. No licences have been issued in Britain for commercial hunting or large-scale control measures since 1982.

Competition with other wildlife: At the Farne Islands, adult seals and pups were culled, 1972–82, in attempts to lessen damage by seals to fragile soil and vegetation used as breeding habitat by seabirds. Since 1982, management has discouraged seals from accessing vulnerable sites.

PRINCIPAL AUTHORS
P.S. Hammond, C.D. Duck, A.J. Hall & P.P. Pomeroy

LITERATURE
See under common seal for general accounts. Anderson [7] is a monograph on grey seals; Hickling [95] relates specifically to the Farne Islands.

VAGRANT SEALS

Five species normally confined to higher latitudes have been reported irregularly around the British Isles.

GENUS *Pusa*

Ringed seal *Pusa hispida*
Phoca hispida Schreber, 1775; Greenland and Labrador.
Floe rat, jar seal, silver jar (moulted pup).

DESCRIPTION
Adults grow to 140–150 cm nose–tail length, 45–

95 kg; females generally slightly smaller than males. Very similar in shape and colouring to common (harbour) seal, but perhaps generally darker. Colour very variable, usually a pale grey background with a number of black spots, particularly on the back (Plate 9). Many spots surrounded by ring-shaped lighter markings (hence common name), although mid-dorsally the dark spots may be close enough to run together, may form dark vertebral stripe. Belly silver grey. Common seals may also occasionally have ring markings, but these are smaller than in ringed seal.

Dentition weaker than common seal, mandibular teeth always aligned with the axis of the jaw; inner side of mandible between middle postcanines concave (cf. common seal, where convex).

Ringed seals produce their pups in snow lairs, dug out with claws, March–April. Feed on a variety of pelagic crustaceans, particularly in the summer, and fish such as cod. Preyed upon by polar bears and Arctic foxes [140].

DISTRIBUTION
Commonest seal in the Arctic. Found in circumpolar Arctic coasts, wherever there is open water, from near the ice edge to the Pole. Normally solitary, rarely found in the open sea or in floating pack ice, but common in fjords and bays where ice is firm [99]. Found in Iceland in the winter and along Pacific Japanese coasts as far south as 35° N. Also found in the Baltic, with subspecies in some freshwater lakes (e.g. Lake Saimaa, Finland and Lake Ladoga, Russia).

Although largely non-migratory [100], ringed seals show long-distance seasonal movements, moving N in summer and S in autumn with melting and expanding pack ice [144]. However occasional, especially young, animals, move S and have been recorded from Atlantic coasts of several European countries. Numbers reported increasing slightly, taken into the many seal rescue and rehabilitation centres around European and British coasts: 14 records on the W European coast between 1970 and 1980, 21 between 1980 and 1990 [178]. Most southerly record in Portugal [50]. In March 1995 a female found on Brittany coast of France, rehabilitated, tagged and released in the English Channel in September, was found in May 1996 in the stomach of a Greenland shark *Somniosus microcephalus* caught off the coast of Iceland, a straight-line distance of 2600 km from its release [139]. GB records suggest ringed seals may be regular visitors around Shetland [28] although probably under-recorded due to resemblance to common seal, occasionally taken by hunters in Shetland in 1960s. Records in

British Isles include: 1846, Norfolk coast; 1889, Lincolnshire coast; 1897, Collieston, Aberdeenshire; 1901, Aberdeen; 1940, Isle of Man; 1990, Northumberland; 1994, Scarborough; 1991, and 1995, Norfolk; 1999, Mablethorpe, Lincolnshire; 2006, one seen, hauled out close to Bonar Bridge, Kyle of Sutherland, Scotland.

Fossil specimens recorded from 8 sites, Scottish lowlands, dated to Late Glacial; one dated *c.*12 000 bp.

Harp seal *Pagophilus groenlandica*
Phoca groenlandica Erxleben, 1777; Greenland and Newfoundland.
Greenland seal, saddleback seal, saddle seal; bedlamer (immature seal).

DESCRIPTION
Adults up to 170 cm nose–tail length, weight *c.*130 kg. Sexes very similar in size. Easily recognised by the dark face and broad dark band starting on shoulders, dividing and spreading over flanks to form two roughly harp-shaped patches (hence common name). In adult males, ground colour a light silvery grey (almost white) and the 'harp' and face to just behind the eyes, nearly black; in females, the face and 'harp' are paler, may be broken into spots (Plate 9). Juveniles are grey with black spots and blotches. Markings develop through successive annual moults though some females never develop a full pattern [30].

Harp seals breed in the spring on ice floes in the pack. They feed on pelagic crustaceans such as *Thysanoessa* sp. and *Themisto* sp. and on fish, notably capelin *Mallotus villosus*, polar cod *Arctogadus glacialis*, Arctic cod *Boreogadus saida* and herring *Clupea harengus*.

DISTRIBUTION
A highly migratory and gregarious species, found in the open sea of the Arctic Atlantic; nowhere is it resident throughout the year. Range extends N to open waters of the Arctic in summer and early autumn, come S in late autumn and winter in time for the spring breeding. While on migration, leap and jump out of the water like dolphins [99].

There are three breeding regions: (1) off the NE coast of Newfoundland (the Front) and in the Gulf of St Lawrence (the Gulf); (2) Greenland Sea around Jan Mayen Island; (3) White Sea. In the summer, after breeding, seals from the first region move to W Greenland coast and the Canadian E Arctic; those from Jan Mayen move to the E Greenland coast and W of Svalbard; and those from the White Sea move to the Barents Sea following the pack-ice belt. Occasionally animals visit N coast of Iceland.

Harp seals can extend their range further S into N North Sea, occurring in large numbers along the Norwegian coasts. Many were caught in fishing nets in 1987 and 1988 in N Norway [117], suspected to be responsible for the introduction of PDV into the European common and grey seal populations, producing the epidemic in 1988 [62]. However, no such invasion occurred in 2001 before a second outbreak of PDV in 2002 [82]. Extralimital movements have also been reported in the NW Atlantic [109]. Reasons for such movements not clear but population increases, food shortages and climate change have all been suggested. Moderate invasions into European waters continue to occur, with higher numbers reported around W Europe in 1994 and 1995 [178]. In these years, sightings from British coasts also more frequent. Records kept since about 1800 from the UK include: 1868 one killed Lancashire; 1873, one in fishing net, Argyll; 1899, two in nets, Ayrshire; 1902, Teignmouth, Devon; 1903, one in Firth of Forth; 1968, adult in Shetland; 1987, one live and one dead in Shetland; 1987, adult male River Humber; 1988, one very sick Medway, Kent; 1988, one seen off Flamborough Head, Yorkshire; 1994, adult, Holkham, Norfolk, taken into rescue centre; 1994, E Scotland, taken into rescue centre. One possible record from Co. Galway, Eire.

GENUS *Erignathus*

Bearded seal *Erignathus barbatus*
Phoca barbata Erxleben, 1977; North Atlantic.
Square flipper, sea hare, *oogruk* (Inuit).

DESCRIPTION
Adults of both sexes *c*.220–270 cm nose–tail length, weight 235–340 kg; females slightly smaller than males. Disproportionately small head. Main characteristic is great profusion of long, very sensitive, glistening white mystacial vibrissae, recognisable from some distance (moustache rather than beard). Vibrissae unlike those of most other phocids in being straight and not beaded; they also curl, sometimes forming tight spirals at the tips, particularly when dry [99]. The 3rd digit on the fore flipper slightly longer than the others, giving a square-ended appearance to the flipper. Have 2 pairs of nipples, brown-coated pups, chromosomes 2n = 34, all considered primitive traits for phocids.

Colour the same for both sexes and not distinctive; usually grey ground colour, slightly darker down the midline, with a brownish or reddish tinge on the head, and paler grey ventrally (Plate 9). Occasionally faint spots on the back or dark spots on the flank.

Dentition very weak; teeth in adults loose-rooted, may be worn down or entirely missing. Postcanines widely spaced.

Breed on pack-ice floes from mid-March to May. Pups can enter the water soon after birth, helping to protect them from polar bear predation [30]. Mostly benthic feeding, food items include benthic invertebrates (bivalves, crabs, shrimps, polychaete worms) with some fish and cephalopods.

DISTRIBUTION
Circumpolar distribution, found in shallow waters all along the American, European and Asiatic Arctic and on all the associated islands, occasionally as far south as Hokkaido. Not migratory but a few reach the Gulf of St Lawrence and as far south as Cape Cod. Occasional animals found on N Norwegian coasts.

Records of sightings in British waters largely from N and W Isles: 1892, Norfolk young male; 1977, 2 from Shetland; 1981, Mid Yell Shetland; 1986, Ronas Voe, Shetland; 1987, 2 records from Shetland, one from Orkney (same animal as seen in Shetland 2 days earlier?); 1988, one in Orkney, one in Shetland; 1993, Shetland; 1998, Lincolnshire taken into rescue centre and released in Shetland; 1999, January, Hartlepool Fish Quay, Teesside; 1999, April, one seen in Loch Scavaig, Isle of Skye, 7 days later 2 hauled out in bay Camas Mo'r, seen intermittently separately, then together on Eilean Mo'r, hauled out with grey seals, May.

GENUS *Cystophora*

Hooded seal *Cystophora cristata*
Phoca cristata Erxleben, 1777; S Greenland and Newfoundland.
Crested seal, bladdernose seal; blueback (pup).

DESCRIPTION
Adult males reach 220–250 cm nose–tail length, weigh >400 kg; females 220 cm long, weigh *c*.300 kg. Most conspicuous feature is inflatable crest or hood in adult male, about twice the size of a football, on top of the head. Is enlargement of nasal cavity, inflated during confrontations with other males during breeding season. Starts to develop when male about 4 years old, and grows with age and increasing body size. When not inflated, tip of hood hangs down in front of mouth. Pelage with grey background, lighter on sides and belly. Many dark patches of irregular size scattered over the body, smaller on the neck and

abdomen. Females less strongly marked than males and lighter in colour (Plate 9).

Dentition distinguishable from all other seals found in British waters by presence of only one pair of lower incisors. Postcanines peg-like and widely spaced.

Pups born March–April, when widely scattered family groups found drifting on ice floes. Lactation shortest of all phocids at only 4 days. Pup coat slate grey on back, paler beneath, known as 'bluebacks'. Feed pelagically on demersal fish such as Greenland halibut, redfish, polar cod and squid *Gonatus fabricii*. Young seals take smaller prey, such as capelin and amphipod shrimps [30].

DISTRIBUTION
Solitary, found in deep waters of the Arctic regions of the Atlantic on drifting ice. Occur mainly from Bear Island and Svalbard to Jan Mayen Island, Iceland, Denmark Strait, Greenland, E coast of Baffin Island and Labrador. Breeding areas similar to harp seal: the Gulf and the Front on the Canadian Arctic, W Ice near Jan Mayen and in the Davis Strait.

Extralimital records in NW Atlantic and W European waters on the increase, e.g. 4 records for W Europe 1970–1980; 17, 1981–1990; 16, 1990–1996 [109, 178]. Telemetry studies of animals from Jan Mayen (W Ice) stock showed them spending time around the Faroe Islands and N and W of Shetland [56]; thus not surprising to see animals in N and W of British Isles, but some seen surprisingly far south. About 14 records: 1892, one killed River Orwell, Suffolk; 1872 one killed St Andrews, Fife; 1873 one caught in Frodsham, Cheshire; 1890, one shot and one seen on Sanday, Orkney; 1891, uncertain record from Benbecula, Hebrides; 1903, Elgin, mouth of River Lossie; 1980, pup seen Haaf Gruney, Shetland; 1989, pup taken to rescue centre from Felixstowe; 1996, juvenile, taken to rescue centre from River Mersey; 2000, one juvenile rehabilitated from Lincolnshire coast; 2001, one juvenile and one immature taken into rescue centre from Norfolk coast; 2005, one seen, mouth of R. Conon, Ross-shire, Scotland.

FAMILY ODOBENIDAE

A distinctive family, including only one modern genus and species but with a long and diverse fossil record. More closely allied to Otariidae than Phocidae, diverged from them in Late Oligocene, about 28 mya. Oldest fossil odobenids about 14 mya, mid Miocene.

GENUS *Odobenus*

Walrus *Odobenus rosmarus*
Phoca rosmarus Linnaeus, 1758; Arctic Ocean.
Sea cow, sea horse.

DESCRIPTION
One of the largest pinnipeds, 3rd only behind the 2 elephant seals. Adult males 365 cm nose–tail and up to 1270 kg; females 300 cm, 850 kg. Appearance distinctive; head truncated, appears rather small for the large body; large array of stiff whiskers. Skin rough, wrinkled and nearly naked in old animals but covered with short brown hair in young ones. Colour largely uniformly greyish, flushing reddish when hauled out or basking (Plate 9).

Dentition unique. Large tusks (upper canines) present in both sexes, but more slender in females. Remaining teeth (upper: 3 incisors and 3 postcanines; lower: canine and 3 postcanines) all reduced to flattened pads of dentine.

Young born in May, usually on sea ice. Calf feeds from female for at least 6 months, separates from mother at 2 years old. Highly selective feeders, mostly clams and other molluscs (excavated from the sea bottom at depths of up to 75 m), sometimes young seals (bearded, ringed, hooded and spotted seals).

DISTRIBUTION
Found in shallow water around Arctic coasts. Prefer moving pack ice in areas where sea is *c*.80–100 m deep. If no ice available, will haul out on small rocky islands. Atlantic and Pacific walrus each occur in 2 geographically isolated groups. Still occasionally occur off Iceland; 31 records on the Norwegian coast between 1900 and 1967 [41]. Occasionally found as far south as Germany, the Netherlands and Belgium. Between 1815 and 1986, 29 records of walrus seen or killed in British waters, largely off the Scottish coasts, except one shot in the Severn in 1839 and one seen in the river Shannon, Ireland in 1897 [99]. Since 1954, about 20 records: 1954, immature female Aberdeenshire coast [57]; 1981, animals seen off Donegal, in Shetland, Arran and the Wash; 1984, Pentland Firth; 1986, two in Shetland, one in Orkney; 1994, one dead, Sybil Head , Co. Kerry; 1998, one seen ashore, Old Head, Co. Mayo; also several sightings, 1980–2000, at sea off the Donegal coast [88].

Fossils recovered Jarlshof, Shetland, Bronze Age [191].

PRINCIPAL AUTHOR
A.J. Hall

REFERENCES

1 Allen, P.J. *et al.* (1995) Microsatellite variation in grey seals (*Halichoerus grypus*) shows evidence of genetic differentiation between two British breeding colonies. *Molecular Ecology*, **4**, 653–662.

2 Allen, S.G. (1985) Mating behaviour in the harbor seal. *Marine Mammal Science*, **1**, 84–87.

3 Allen, S.G. *et al.* (1988) Herd segregation in harbor seals at Point Reyes, California. *California Fish and Game*, **74**, 55–59.

4 Allen, S.G. *et al.* (1993) Red-pelaged harbour seals of the San Francisco Bay region. *Journal of Mammalogy*, **74**, 588–593.

5 Amos, W. *et al.* (1993) Male mating success and paternity in the grey seal (*Halichoerus grypus*): a study using DNA fingerprinting. *Proceedings of the Royal Society of London Series B*, **252**, 199–207.

6 Amos, W.A. *et al.* (1995) Evidence for mate fidelity in the gray seal. *Science*, **268**, 1897–1899.

7 Anderson, S.S. (1988) *The grey seal*. Shire Natural History Series 26, Shire Publications, Aylesbury.

8 Anderson, S. (1990) *Seals*. Whittet, London.

9 Anderson, S.S. & Fedak, M.A. (1985) Grey seal males: energetic and behavioural links between size and sexual success. *Animal Behaviour*, **33**, 829–838.

10 Anderson, S.S. & Fedak, M.A. (1987) The energetics of sexual success of grey seals and comparison with the costs of reproduction in other pinnipeds. *Symposia of the Zoological Society of London*, **57**, 319–341.

11 Anderson, S.S. & Harwood, J. (1985) Time budgets and topography: how energy reserves and terrain determine the breeding behaviour of grey seals. *Animal Behaviour*, **33**, 1343–1348.

12 Anderson, S.S. *et al.* (1979) Mortality in grey seal pups: incidence and causes. *Journal of Zoology*, **189**, 407–417.

13 Arnason, U. (1974) Comparative chromosome studies in Pinnipedia. *Hereditas*, **76**, 179–226.

14 Arnason, U. *et al.* (2006) Pinniped phylogeny and a new hypothesis for their origin and dispersal. *Molecular Phylogenetics and Evolution*, **41**, 345–354.

15 Baker, J.R. (1980) The pathology of the grey seal *Halichoerus grypus*. II. Juveniles and adults. *British Veterinary Journal*, **136**, 443–447.

16 Baker, J.R. (1984) Mortality and morbidity in grey seal pups (*Halichoerus grypus*). Studies on its causes, effects of environment, the nature and sources of infectious agents and the immunological status of pups. *Journal of Zoology*, **203**, 23–48.

17 Baker, J.R. (1987) Causes of mortality and morbidity in wild juvenile and adult grey seals (*Halichoerus grypus*). *British Veterinary Journal*, **143**, 203–220.

18 Baker, J.R. *et al.* (1980) The pathology of the grey seal (*Halichoerus grypus*). I. Pups. *British Veterinary Journal*, **136**, 401–412.

19 Baker, J.R. *et al.* (1995) Isolation of salmonellae from seals from UK waters. *Veterinary Record*, **136**, 471–472.

20 Bekkby, T. & Bjørge, A. (2000) Diving behaviour of harbour seal *Phoca vitulina* pups from nursing to independent feeding. *Journal of Sea Research*, **44**, 267–275.

21 Bigg, M.A. (1969) The harbour seal in British Columbia. *Fisheries Research Board of Canada, Bulletin* **172**.

22 Bjørge, A. *et al.* (1995) Habitat use and diving behaviour of harbour seals in a coastal archipelago in Norway, pp 211–223 in Blix, A.S., Walløe, L. & Ulltang, Ø. (ed.) *Whales, seals, fish and man*. Elsevier Science, Amsterdam.

23 Bjørge, A. *et al.* (2002) Interactions between harbour seals, *Phoca vitulina*, and fisheries in complex coastal waters explored by combined Geographic Information System (GIS) and energetics modelling. *Ices Journal of Marine Science*, **59**, 29–42.

24 Boness, D.J. & James, H. (1979) Reproductive behaviour of the grey seal (*Halichoerus grypus*) on Sable Island, Nova Scotia. *Journal of Zoology*, **188**, 477–500.

25 Boness, D.J. *et al.* (1994) Evidence of a maternal foraging cycle resembling that of otariid seals in a small phocid, the harbor seal. *Behavioural Ecology and Sociobiology*, **34**, 95–104.

26 Boness, D.J. *et al.* (2006) Mating tactics and mating system of an aquatic-mating pinniped: the harbor seal, *Phoca vitulina*. *Behavioral Ecology and Sociobiology*, **61**, 119–130.

27 Bonner, W.N. (1972) The grey seal and common seal in European waters. *Oceanography and Marine Biology Annual Review*, **10**, 461–507.

28 Bonner, W.N. (1982) The status of seals in the United Kingdom, pp. 253–265 in *Mammals in the seas* 4. FAO Fisheries Series 5, FAO, Rome.

29 Bonner, W.N. (1990) *The natural history of seals*. Christopher Helm, London.

30 Bonner, W.N. (1994) *Seals and sea lions of the world*. Blandford Press, London.

31 Bonner, W.N. & Witthames, S.R. (1974) Dispersal of common seals (*Phoca vitulina*), tagged in the Wash, East Anglia. *Journal of Zoology*, **174**, 528–531.

32 Boulva, J. (1971) Observations on a colony of whelping harbour seals, *Phoca vitulina concolor*, on Sable Island, Nova Scotia. *Journal of the Fisheries Research Board of Canada*, **28**, 755–759.

33 Boulva, J. & McClaren, I.A. (1979) Biology of the harbor seal, *Phoca vitulina*, in Eastern Canada. *Bulletin of the Fisheries Research Board of Canada*, **200**, 1–24.

34 Bowen, W.D. & Harrison, G.D. (1996) Comparison of harbour seal diets in two inshore habitats of Atlantic Canada. *Canadian Journal of Zoology*, **74**, 125–135.

35 Bowen, W.D. *et al.* (1994) The effect of maternal age and other factors on birth mass in the harbour seal. *Canadian Journal of Zoology*, **72**, 8–14.

36 Bowen, W.D. *et al.* (2001) Foraging effort, food intake and lactation performance depend on maternal mass in a small phocid seal. *Functional Ecology*, **15**, 325–334.

37 Bowen, W.D. *et al.* (2002) Prey-dependent foraging tactics and prey profitability in a marine mammal. *Marine Ecology – Progress Series*, **244**, 235–245.

38 Bowen, W.D. *et al.* (2003) Maternal and newborn life-history traits during periods of contrasting population trends: implications for explaining the decline of harbour seals (*Phoca vitulina*), on Sable Island. *Journal of Zoology*, **261**, 155–163.

39 Boyd, I.L. (1982) *Reproduction of grey seals with reference to factors influencing fertility*. PhD thesis. University of Cambridge.

40 Boyd, I.L. (1985) Pregnancy and ovulation rates in grey seals (*Halichoerus grypus*) on the British coast. *Journal of Zoology*, **205**, 265–272.

41 Brun *et al.* (1968) Hvalross, *Odobenus rosmarus*, på norskekysten. *Fauna*, **21**, 7–20.

42 Caudron, A. (1998) *Behavioural plasticity in function of the breeding environment in a marine mammal, the grey seal* Halichoerus grypus. PhD thesis, University of Liège, Belgium.

43 Coltman, D.W. *et al.* (1998) The energetics of male reproduction in an aquatically mating pinniped, the harbour seal. *Physiological Zoology*, **71**, 387–399.

44 Coltman, D.W. *et al.* (1998) Male mating success in an aquatically mating pinniped, the harbour seal (*Phoca vitulina*), assessed by microsatellite DNA markers. *Molecular Ecology*, **7**, 627–638.

45 Coltman, D.W. *et al.* (1999) A multivariate analysis of phenotype and paternity in male harbor seals, *Phoca vitulina*, at Sable Island, Nova Scotia. *Behavioural Ecology*, **10**, 169–177.

46 Corpe, H.M. (1996) *The behavioural ecology of young harbour seals in the Moray Firth, NE Scotland*. PhD thesis, University of Aberdeen.

47 Corpe, H.M. *et al.* (1998) A rapid non-invasive technique for distinguishing harbour seals (*Phoca vitulina*) in their first year from older age classes. *Marine Mammal Science*,

14, 372–379.

48 Cronin, M. *et al.* (2007) An assessment of population size and distribution of harbour seals in the Republic of Ireland during the moult season in August 2003. *Journal of Zoology* (in press).

49 Dietz, R. *et al.* (1991) Age determination of European harbour seal, *Phoca vitulina* L. *Sarsia*, **76,** 17–21.

50 Duguy, R. (1988) Les phoques des côtes de France. *Annales de la Société de Sciences Naturelles de la Charente-Maritime,* supplément, 1–52 (in French).

51 Eguchi, T. & Harvey, J.T. (2005) Diving behavior of the Pacific harbor seal *(Phoca vitulina richardii)* in Monterey Bay, California. *Marine Mammal Science,* **21,** 283–295.

52 Ellis, S.L. (1998) *Maternal effects on offspring traits from birth through weaning in the harbour seal,* Phoca vitulina. PhD thesis, Dalhousie University.

53 Fedak, M.A. & Anderson, S.S. (1982) The energetics of lactation: accurate measurements from a large wild mammal, the grey seal (*Halichoerus grypus*). *Journal of Zoology,* **198,** 473–479.

54 Fedak, M.A. & Thompson, D. (1993) Behavioural and physiological options in diving seals. *Symposium of the Zoological Society of London,* **66,** 333–348.

55 Fisher, H.D. (1954) Delayed implantation in the harbour seal (*Phoca vitulina*). *Nature,* **173,** 879–880.

56 Folkow, L.P. *et al.* (1996) Annual distribution of hooded seals (*Cystophora cristata*) in the Greenland and Norwegian Seas. *Polar Biology,* **16,** 179–189.

57 Forman, J. (1954) Walrus at Collieston. *Scottish Naturalist,* **66,** 56–57.

58 Foster, G. *et al.* (1996) Isolation of brucella species from cetaceans, seals and an otter. *Veterinary Record,* **138,** 583–586.

59 Garner, M.M. *et al.* (1997) Evidence of *Brucella* infection in *Parafilaroides* lungworms in a Pacific harbour seal (*Phoca vitulina richardsi*). *Journal of Veterinary Diagnosis and Investigation,* **9,** 298–303.

60 Geraci, J.R. *et al.* (1981) The seal louse, *Echinophthirius horridus*: an intermediate host of the seal heartworm, *Dipetalonema spirocauda* (Nematoda). *Canadian Journal of Zoology,* **59,** 1457–1459.

61 Godsell, J. (1991) The relative influence of age and weight on the reproductive behaviour of male grey seals, *Halichoerus grypus. Journal of Zoology,* **224,** 537–551.

62 Goodhart, C.B. (1988) Did virus transfer from harp seals to common seals? *Nature,* **336,** 21.

63 Goodman, S.J. (1998) Patterns of extensive genetic differentiation and variation among European harbour seals (*Phoca vitulina vitulina*) revealed using microsatellite DNA polymorphisms. *Molecular Biological Evolution,* **15,** 104–118.

64 Grellier, K & Hammond, P.S. (2005) Feeding method affects otolith digestion in captive grey seals: implications for diet composition estimation. *Marine Mammal Science,* **21,** 296–306.

65 Grellier, K. & Hammond, P.S. (2006) Robust digestion and passage rate estimates for hard parts of grey seal (*Halichoerus grypus*) prey. *Canadian Journal of Fisheries and Aquatic Sciences,* **63,** 1982–1998.

66 Hall, A.J. *et al.* (1992) The descriptive epizootiology of phocine distemper in the UK during 1988/89. *Science of the Total Environment,* **115,** 31–44.

67 Hall, A.J. *et al.* (1997) Infection, haematology and biochemistry in grey seal pups exposed to chlorinated biphenyls. *Marine Environmental Research,* **43,** 81–98.

68 Hall, A. *et al.* (2001) Factors affecting first-year survival in grey seals and their implications for life history strategy. *Journal of Animal Ecology,* **70,** 138–149.

69 Hall, A. *et al.* (2003) Polybrominated diphenyl ethers (PBDEs) in grey seal pups during their first year of life – are they thyroid hormone endocrine disrupters? *Environmental Pollution,* **126,** 29–37.

70 Hammond, P.S. & Grellier, K. (2006) *Grey seal diet composition and prey consumption in the North Sea.* Final report to Department for Environment Food and Rural Affairs on project MF0319.

71 Hammond, P.S. & Harris, R.N. (2006) *Grey seal diet composition and prey consumption off western Scotland and Shetland.* Final report to Scottish Executive Environment and Rural Affairs Department and Scottish Natural Heritage.

72 Hammond, P.S. & Prime, J.H. (1990) The diet of British grey seals (*Halichoerus grypus*). In Bowen, W.D. (ed.) Population biology of sealworm (*Pseudoterranova decipiens*) in relation to its intermediate and seal hosts. *Canadian Bulletin of Fisheries and Aquatic Sciences,* **222,** 243–254.

73 Hammond, J.A. *et al.* (2005) Comparison of poly-chlorinated biphenyl (PCB) induced effects on innate immune functions in harbour and grey seals. *Aquatic Toxicology,* **74,** 126–138.

74 Hammond J.A. *et al.* (2005) Identification and real-time PCR quantification of phocine distemper virus from two colonies of Scottish grey seals in 2002. *Journal of General Virology,* **86,** 2563–2567.

75 Hammond, P.S. *et al.* (1994) The diet of grey seals around Orkney and other island and mainland sites in north-eastern Scotland. *Journal of Applied Ecology,* **31,** 340–350.

76 Hammond, P.S. *et al.* (1994) The diet of grey seals in the Inner and Outer Hebrides. *Journal of Applied Ecology,* **31,** 737–746.

77 Hanggi, E. & Schusterman, R. (1994) Underwater acoustic displays and individual variation in male harbour seals, *Phoca vitulina. Animal Behaviour,* **48,** 1275–1283.

78 Härkönen, T. & Harding, K.C. (2001) Spatial structure of harbour seal populations and the implications thereof. *Canadian Journal of Zoology,* **79,** 2115–2127.

79 Härkönen, E. & Heide-Jorgensen, M.P. (1990) Comparative life histories of East Atlantic and other harbour seal populations. *Ophelia,* **32,** 211–235.

80 Härkönen, T. & Heide-Jorgensen, M.-P. (1991) The harbour seal *Phoca vitulina* as a predator in the Skagerrak. *Ophelia,* **34,** 191–207.

81 Härkönen, T. *et al.* (1999) Age- and sex-specific behaviour in harbour seals *Phoca vitulina* leads to biased estimates of vital population parameters. *Journal of Applied Ecology,* **36,** 825–841.

82 Härkönen, T. *et al.* (2006) A review of the 1988 and 2002 Phocine Distemper Virus seal epidemics in European Harbour Seals. *Diseases in Aquatic Organisms,* **68,** 115–130.

83 Harrison, R.J. (1960) Reproduction and reproductive organs in common seals (*Phoca vitulina*) in the Wash, East Anglia. *Mammalia,* **24,** 372–385.

84 Harwood, J. & Croxall, J.P. (1988) The assessment of competition between seals and commercial fisheries in the North Sea and Antarctic. *Marine Mammal Science,* **4,** 13–33.

85 Harwood, J. & Hall, A.J. (1990) Mass mortality in marine mammals: its implications for population dynamics and genetics. *Trends in Ecology and Evolution,* **5,** 254–257.

86 Harwood, J. & Prime J.H. (1978) Some factors affecting the size of British grey seal populations. *Journal of Applied Ecology,* **15,** 401–411.

87 Harwood, J. *et al.* (1989) Seal diseases predictions. *Nature,* **339,** 670.

88 Hayden, T. & Harrington, R. (2000) *Exploring Irish mammals.* Duchas: The Heritage Service, Dublin.

89 Hayes, S.A. *et al.* (2004) Aquatic mating strategies of the male Pacific harbor seal (*Phoca vitulina richardii*): Are males defending the hotspot? *Marine Mammal Science,* **20,** 639–656.

90 Heide-Jorgensen, M.-P. *et al.* Retrospective of the 1988 European seal epizootic. *Diseases of Aquatic Organisms,* **13,** 37–62.

91 Helle, E. *et al.* (1976) PCB levels correlated with pathological changes in seal uteri. *Ambio,* **5,** 261–263.

92 Hewer, H.R. (1964) The determination of age, sexual maturity and a life-table in the grey seal (*Halichoerus*

grypus). *Proceedings of the Zoological Society of London*, **142**, 593–624.

93 Hewer, H.R. (1974) *British seals*. Collins, London.

94 Hiby, A.R. *et al.* (1996) Seal stocks in Great Britain. *NERC News, January*, 20–22.

95 Hickling, G. (1962) *Grey seals and the Farne Islands*. Routledge & Kegan Paul, London.

96 Jamieson, G.S. & Fisher, H.D. (1972) The pinniped eye: a review, pp. 245–261 in Harrison, R.J. (ed.) *Functional anatomy of marine mammals*, Vol. 1. Academic Press, London.

97 Jefferson, T.A. *et al.* (1991) A review of killer whale interactions with other marine mammals: predation to co-existence. *Mammal Review*, **21**, 151–180.

98 Kappe, A.L. *et al.* (1995) Genetic variation in *Phoca vitulina* (the harbour seal) revealed by DNA fingerprinting and RAPDs. *Heredity*, **74**, 647–653.

99 King, J.E. (1983) *Seals of the world*. Oxford University Press, Oxford.

100 Kingsley, M.C.S. (1990) Status of the ringed seal, *Phoca hispida*, in Canada. *Canadian Field Naturalist*, **104**, 138–145.

101 Kovacs K.M. (1987) Maternal behaviour and early behavioural ontogeny of grey seals (*Halichoerus grypus*) on the Isle of May, UK. *Journal of Zoology*, **213**, 697–715.

102 Kovacs, K.M. *et al.* (1990) Sex and age segregation by *Phoca vitulina concolor* at haul-out sites during the breeding season in the Passamaquoddy Bay region, New Brunswick. *Marine Mammal Science*, **6**, 204–214.

103 Lambert, R.A. (2002) The grey seal in Britain: a twentieth century history of a nature conservation success. *Environment and History*, **8**, 449–474.

104 Law, R.J. *et al.* (1991) Concentrations of trace metals in the livers of marine mammals (seals, porpoises and dolphins) from waters around the British Isles. *Marine Pollution Bulletin*, **22**, 183–191.

105 Lister-Kaye, J. (1979) *Seal cull: the grey seal controversy*. Penguin Books, London.

106 Lonergan, M.C. et al. (2007) Using sparse survey data to investigate the declining abundance of British harbour seals. *Journal of Zoology*, **271**, 261–269.

107 Mackey, B.L. *et al.* (in press) A Bayesian estimate of harbour seal survival using sparse photo-identification data. *Journal of Zoology*, in press.

108 Matthiopoulos, J. *et al.* (2004) Using satellite telemetry and aerial counts to estimate space use by grey seals around the British Isles. *Journal of Applied Ecology*, **41**, 476–491.

109 McAlpine, D.F. *et al.* (1999) Increase in extralimital occurrences of ice-breeding seals in the northern Gulf of Maine region: more seals or fewer fish? *Marine Mammal Science*, **15**, 906–911.

110 McConnell, B.J. *et al.* (1992) Satellite tracking of grey seals (*Halichoerus grypus*). *Journal of Zoology*, **226**, 271–282.

111 McConnell, B.J. *et al.* (1999) Movements and foraging areas of grey seals in the North Sea. *Journal of Applied Ecology*, **36**, 573–590.

112 McCulloch, S. Personal communication.

113 McCulloch, S. *et al.* (1999) Individually distinctive pup vocalisations fail to prevent allo-suckling in grey seals. *Canadian Journal of Zoology*, **77**, 716–723.

114 Middlemas, S. *et al.* (2005) Functional and aggregative responses of harbour seal predators to changes in salmonid abundance. *Proceedings of the Royal Society, Series B*, **273**, 193–198.

115 Mohl, B. (1968) Auditory sensitivity of the common seal in air and water. *Journal of Auditory Research*, **8**, 27–38.

116 Muelbert, M.M.C. & Bowen, W.D. (1993) Duration of lactation and postweaning changes in mass and body composition of harbour seal, *Phoca vitulina*, pups. *Canadian Journal of Zoology*, **71**, 1405–1414.

117 Nilssen K.T. *et al.* (1992) The effect of invading harp seals (*Phoca groenlandica*) on local coastal fish stocks of North Norway. *Fisheries Research*, **13**, 25–37.

118 Neumann, D.R. (1999) Agonistic behaviour of harbor seals

119 Ó'Cadhla, O. & Mackey, M. (2002) Out of sight, out of mind? Marine mammals and seabirds on Ireland's Atlantic margin, pp.423–426 in Covery, F. & Feehan, J. (eds) *Achievement and challenge – Rio+10 and Ireland*. Environmental Institute, University College Dublin.

120 Osterhaus, A.D.M.E. *et al.* (1990) Isolation of an orthopoxvirus from pox-like lesions of a grey seal (*Halichoerus grypus*). *Veterinary Record*, **127**, 91–92.

121 Paterson, T. Personal communication.

122 Pierce, G.J. *et al.* (1991) Prey remains in grey seal, *Halichoerus grypus*, faeces from the Moray Firth, north-east Scotland. *Journal of Zoology*, **224**, 337–341.

123 Platt, N.E. *et al.* (1975) The age of the grey seal at the Farne Islands. *Transactions of the Natural History Society of Northumberland, Durham and Newcastle-upon-Tyne*, **42**, 99–106.

124 Pomeroy, P.P. Personal communication.

125 Pomeroy, P.P. *et al.* (1994) Dispersion and site fidelity of breeding female grey seals (*Halichoerus grypus*) on North Rona, Scotland. *Journal of Zoology*, **233**, 429–447.

126 Pomeroy, P.P. *et al.* (1999) Consequences of maternal size for reproductive expenditure and pupping success of grey seals at North Rona, Scotland. *Journal of Animal Ecology*, **68**, 235–253.

127 Pomeroy, P.P. *et al.* (2000) Philopatry, site fidelity and local kin associations within grey seal breeding colonies. *Ethology*, **106**, 899–919.

128 Pomeroy, P.P. *et al.* (2000) Expansion of a grey seal breeding colony – changes in pupping site use at the Isle of May, Scotland. *Journal of Zoology*, **250**, 1–12.

129 Pomeroy, P.P. *et al.* (2001) Reproductive performance links to fine scale spatial patterns of female grey seal relatedness. *Proceedings of the Royal Society of London Series B*, **268**, 711–717.

130 Pomeroy, P.P. *et al.* (2005) Morbillivirus neutralizing antibodies in Scottish grey seals: assessing the effects of the 1988 and 2002 PDV epizootics. *Marine Ecology Progress Series*, **287**, 241–250.

131 Pomeroy, P.P. *et al.* (2005) Breeding site choice fails to explain interannual associations of female grey seals. *Behavioural Ecology and Sociobiology*, **57**, 546–556.

132 Prime, J.H. & Hammond, P.S. (1987) Quantitative assessment of gray seal diet from fecal analysis, pp. 161–181 in Huntley, A.C. *et al.* (eds.) *Approaches to marine mammal energetics*. Society of Marine Mammalogy Special Publication No. 1. Allen Press, Lawrence, KS.

133 Prime, J.H. & Hammond, P.S. (1990) The diet of grey seals from the south-western North Sea assessed from analyses of hard parts found in faeces. *Journal of Applied Ecology*, **27**, 435–447.

134 Reeves, R.R. *et al.* (1992) *The Sierra Club handbook of seals and sirenians*. Sierra Club Books, San Francisco.

135 Reijnders, P.J.H. (1986) Reproductive failure in common seals feeding on fish from polluted coastal waters. *Nature, London*, **324**, 456–457.

136 Reijnders, P.J.H. *et al.* (1993) *Seals, fur seals, sea lions and walrus. Status survey and conservation action plan*. IUCN, Gland.

137 Reijnders, P.J.H. *et al.* (1997) Population development of harbour seals, *Phoca vitulina*, in the Wadden Sea after the 1988 virus epizootic. *Journal of Sea Research*, **38**, 161–168.

138 Reilly, J.J. & Fedak, M.A. (1990) Measurement of the body composition of living gray seals by hydrogen isotope dilution. *Journal of Applied Physiology*, **69**, 885–891.

139 Ridoux V. *et al.* (1998) An inadvertent homing experiment with a young ringed seal, *Phoca hispida*. *Marine Mammal Science*, **14**, 883–888.

140 Riedman, M (1990) *The pinnipeds, seals, sea lions and walruses*. University of California Press, Berkeley, CA.

141 Ries, E.H. *et al.* (1997) Diving patterns of harbour seals (*Phoca vitulina*) in the Wadden Sea, the Netherlands and

(*Phoca vitulina*) in relation to availability of haul-out space. *Marine Mammal Science*, **15**, 507–525.

Germany, as indicated by VHF telemetry. *Canadian Journal of Zoology*, **75**, 2063–2068.

142 Ries, E.H. *et al.* (1998) Maximum likelihood population size estimation of harbour seals in the Dutch Wadden Sea based on a mark-recapture experiment. *Journal of Applied Ecology*, **35**, 332–339.

143 Ross, P.S. *et al.* (1996) Suppression of natural killer cell activity in harbour seals (*Phoca vitulina*) fed Baltic Sea herring. *Aquatic Toxicology*, **34**, 71–84.

144 Smith, T.G. (1973) Population dynamics of the ringed seal in the Canadian eastern Arctic. *Fisheries Research Board Canada, Bulletin* No. 181.

145 Smout, S.C. (2006) *Modelling the multispecies functional response of generalist marine predators.* PhD thesis, University of St Andrews.

146 NERC Sea Mammal Research Centre, unpublished data.

147 Sparling, C.E. (2003) *Causes and consequences of variation in the energy expenditure of grey seals* (Halichoerus grypus). PhD thesis, University of St Andrews.

148 Stack, M.J. *et al.* (1993) Mixed poxvirus and calicivirus infections of grey seals (*Halichoerus grypus*) in Cornwall. *Veterinary Record*, **132**, 163–165.

149 Stanley, H.F. *et al.* (1996) Worldwide patterns of mitochondrial DNA differentiation in the harbour seal, *Phoca vitulina. Journal of Molecular Biology and Evolution*, **13**, 368–382.

150 Stobo, W.T. *et al.* (1990) Seasonal sealworm (*Pseudoterraova decipiens*) abundance in grey seals (*Halichoerus grypus*), pp. 147–162 in Bowen, W.D. (ed.) *Population biology of sealworm* (Pseudoterranova decipiens) *in relation to its intermediate and seal hosts. Canadian Bulletin of Fisheries and Aquatic Scienc*es 222. Department of Fisheries and Oceans, Ottawa.

151 Strong, P.G. (1995) Grey seal pup production monitoring, Ramsey Island and North Pembrokeshire, 1995. Coutryside Commision for Wales, Bangor.

152 Sullivan, R.M. (1982) Agonistic behaviour and dominance relationships in the Harbor seal, *Phoca vitulina. Journal of Mammalogy*, **63**, 554–569.

153 Tabuchi, M. *et al.* PCB-related alteration of thyroid hormones and thyroid hormone receptor gene expression in free-ranging harbor seals (*Phoca vitulina*). *Environmental Health Perspectives*, **114**, 1024–1031.

154 Thompson, D. & Fedak, M.A. (1993) Cardiac responses of grey seals during diving at sea. *Journal of Experimental Biology*, **174**, 139–164.

155 Thompson, D. *et al.* (1991) Movements, diving and foraging behaviour of grey seals (*Halichoerus grypus*). *Journal of Zoology*, **224**, 223–232.

156 Thompson, D. *et al.* (2005) Population dynamics of harbour seals *Phoca vitulina* in England: monitoring growth and catastrophic declines. *Journal of Applied Ecology,* **42**, 638–648.

157 Thompson, P.M. (1988) Timing of mating in the common seal (*Phoca vitulina*). *Mammal Review*, **18**, 105–112.

158 Thompson, P.M. (1989) *The common seal.* Shire Publications, Aylesbury.

159 Thompson, P.M. (1989) Seasonal changes in the distribution and composition of common seal (*Phoca vitulina*) haul-out groups. *Journal of Zoology*, **217**, 281–94.

160 Thompson, P.M. & Hall, A.J. (1993) Seals and epizootics – what factors might affect the severity of mass mortalities? *Mammal Review*, **23**, 147–152.

161 Thompson, P.M. & Harwood, J. (1990) Methods for estimating the population size of common seals *Phoca vitulina. Journal of Applied Ecology*, **27**, 924–938.

162 Thompson, P.M. & Rothery, P. (1987) Age and sex differences in the timing of moult in the common seal, *Phoca vitulina. Journal of Zoology*, **212**, 597–603.

163 Thompson, P.M. *et al.* (1989) Seasonal and sex-related variation in the activity patterns of common seals (*Phoca vitulina*). *Journal of Applied Ecology*, **26**, 521–535.

164 Thompson, P.M. *et al.* (1991) Winter foraging by common seals (*Phoca vitulina*) in relation to food availability in the inner Moray Firth, N.E. Scotland. *Journal of Animal Ecology*, **60**, 283–294.

165 Thompson, P.M. *et al.* (1994). Natal dispersal of harbour seals (*Phoca vitulina*) from breeding sites in Orkney. *Journal of Zoology*, **234**, 668–673.

166 Thompson, P.M. *et al.* (1994) Changes in the distribution and activity of female harbour seals during the breeding season: implications for their lactation strategy and mating patterns. *Journal of Animal Ecology*, **63**, 24–30.

167 Thompson, P.M. *et al.* (1997) Estimating harbour seal abundance and status in an estuarine habitat in north-east Scotland. *Journal of Applied Ecology*, **34**, 43–52.

168 Thompson, P.M. *et al.* (1998). The influence of body size and sex on the characteristics of harbour seal foraging trips. *Canadian Journal of Zoology*, **76**, 1044–1053.

169 Thompson, P.M. *et al.* (1998). Prevalence and intensity of the parasite *Echinophthirius horridus* on harbour seals (*Phoca vitulina*); effects of host age and inter-annual variability in host food availability. *Parasitology*, **117**, 393–403.

170 Thompson, P.M. *et al.* (2001) Local declines in the abundance of harbour seals; implications for the designations and monitoring of protected areas. *Journal of Applied Ecology,* **38**, 117–125.

171 Thompson, P.M. *et al.* (2007) Assessing the potential impact of salmon fisheries management on the conservation status of harbour seals in NE Scotland. *Animal Conservation,* **10**, 48–56.

172 Tollit, D.J. & Thompson, P.M. (1996) Seasonal and between-year variations in the diet of harbour seals in the Moray Firth, Scotland. *Canadian Journal of Zoology*, **74**, 1110–1121.

173 Tollit, D.J. *et al.* (1997) Prey selection by harbour seals, *Phoca vitulina*, in relation to variations in prey abundance. *Canadian Journal of Zoology*, **75**, 1508–1518.

174 Tollit, D.J. *et al.* (1998) Variations in harbour seal, *Phoca vitulina*, diet and dive-depths in relation to foraging habitat. *Journal of Zoology*, **244**, 209–222.

175 Twiss, S.D. *et al.* (1998) Limited intra specific variation in male grey seal (*Halichoerus grypus*) dominance relationships in relation to variation in male mating success and female availability. *Journal of Zoology*, **246**, 259–267.

176 Twiss, S.D. *et al.* (2001) Topographic spatial character-isation of grey seal breeding habitat at a sub-seal size spatial grain. *Ecography,* 24, 257–266.

177 Twiss, S.D. *et al.* (2006) Finding fathers – spatio-temporal analysis of paternity assignment in grey seals (*Halichoerus grypus*). *Molecular Ecology*, **15**, 1939–1953.

178 Van Bree, P.J.H. (1997) On extralimital records of Arctic seals (Mammalia, Pinnipedia) on the West European continental coast in the past and at present – a summary. *Beaufortia*, **47**, 153–156.

179 Van Parijs, S.M. *et al.* (1997) Distribution and activity of male harbour seals during the mating season. *Animal Behaviour*, **54**, 35–43.

180 Van Parijs, S.M. *et al.* (1999) Geographic variation in temporal and spatial vocalisation patterns of male harbour seals, *Phoca vitulina*, during the mating season. *Animal Behaviour*, 58, 1231–1239.

181 Van Parijs, S.M. *et al.* (2000) Display area size, tenure length and site fidelity in the aquatically mating male harbour seal. *Canadian Journal of Zoology*, **78**, 2209–2217.

182 Vaughan, R.W. (1978) A study of common seals in the Wash. *Mammal Review*, **8**, 25–34.

183 Venables, U.M. & Venables, L.S.V. (1957) Mating behaviour of the seal, *Phoca vitulina*, in Shetland. *Proceedings of the Zoological Society of London*, **128**, 387–396.

184 Walls, G.L. (1942) *The vertebrate eye and its adaptive radiation.* Cranbrook Institute of Science, Bloomfield Hills, MI.

185 Watts, P. (1992) Thermal constraints on hauling out by harbour seals (*Phoca vitulina*). *Canadian Journal of Zoology*, **70**, 553–560.

186 Williams, T.M. & Kooyman, G.L. (1985) Swimming performance and hydrodynamic characteristics of harbor seals, *Phoca vitulina*. *Physiological Zoology*, **58**, 576–589.

187 Williamson, G.R. (1988) Seals in Loch Ness. *Scientific Reports of the Whales Research Institute*, **39**, 151–157.

188 Wilson, S. (1974) Juvenile play of the common seal *Phoca vitulina vitulina* with comparative notes on the grey seal *Halichoerus grypus*. *Behaviour*, **48**, 37–60.

189 Worthington Wilmer, J. *et al.* (1999) Where have all the fathers gone? An extensive microsatellite analysis of paternity in the grey seal (*Halichoerus grypus*). *Molecular Ecology*, **8**, 1417–1429.

190 Wynne-Edwards, V.C. (1954) Field identification of the common and grey seals. *Scottish Naturalist*, **66**, 192.

191 Yalden, D. (1999) *The history of British mammals*. Poyser, London.

Fig. 10.15 Common seals hauled out, Orkney, shortly after being attacked by killer whales, July 2007. Both grey and common seals are taken by killer whales (*photo S.Thompson*).

Plate 10

A Park cattle *Bos taurus* Chillingham bull   B Feral goat *Capra hircus* nanny   C billy
D Wild boar *Sus scrofa*   E Sheep *Ovis aries* Soay ram   F Red-necked wallaby *Macropus rufogriseus*
G Sheep *O. aries* Boreray ram   H New Forest pony *Equus caballus*

Ungulates
Orders Perissodactyla and Artiodactyla

Compiled by R.J. Putman

The term ungulate covers various unrelated herbivorous mammals that have hooves rather than claws. 2 orders extant; various other fossil groups have been recognised. Divided legally into feral ungulates (horse, cattle, sheep, goats) and wild deer; latter covered by legislation including Deer Act 1991 (England and Wales), Deer (Scotland) Act 1996, Wildlife and Countryside Act 1981 (UK), Wildlife Act 1976 (Republic of Ireland), Wildlife Order 1985 (N Ireland), defining close seasons and methods of culling (see Chapter 4 and species accounts).

ORDER PERISSODACTYLA (ODD-TOED UNGULATES)

A small order of *c*.19 extant species, in 3 families: tapirs Tapiridae, rhinoceroses Rhinocerotidae, and horses and asses Equidae. Much more diverse and abundant in the fossil record, including Titanotheriidae and Chalicotheriidae, as well as numerous forms assigned to the 3 modern families. Only one family now represented in the British Isles, and that only as domestic or semi-feral, but others formerly present (see Chapter 3).

FAMILY EQUIDAE

A small family with a single extant genus, *Equus.*

GENUS *Equus*

A genus of *c*.10 species, including 3 zebras, 4 wild asses, Przewalski's horse, domestic horse and donkey, native to Africa and Asia. Other species once numerous also in N America, extinct there until reintroduced (domestic, since become feral) from Europe. Characterised by single functional toe on each foot, with enlarged hoof. Monogastric, enlarged caecum instead of rumen.

Horse *Equus caballus*
Equus caballus Linnaeus, 1758; Europe (Sweden?).

Male – stallion; female – mare; young – foal.

STATUS
Wild horses, *Equus ferus*, were present in GB during the last glaciation and as late as the Boreal phase of the postglacial period (10 000–9000 bp); there is no good evidence to suggest that they survived beyond that time (see Chapter 3). Domestic horses have been present since the Neolithic, *c*.4000 bp [813]. Within British Isles there are a number of free-ranging populations of relatively unimproved stock. None is truly feral and self-sustaining: all are managed to some degree.

SIGN
Tracks and trails: Free-ranging horses are typically unshod and individual footprints are of a single digit. On harder ground only the forward edge indents, leaving a characteristic crescent-shaped mark.

Dung: Deposited in piles formed of discrete balls *c*.5–7 cm diameter, dark brown in colour. When weathered can be seen to be extremely fibrous in texture. Free-ranging populations often dung in specific area away from preferred feeding areas, establishing latrines. On favoured grasslands, a clear mosaic may result, patches of closely cropped sward devoid of any dung alternating with ungrazed latrine patches with an abundance of dung and taller, ranker vegetation [251, 594, 596]. Latrine sites are grazed by horses only when feed elsewhere becomes very scarce. Both grazing and latrine areas maintained from year to year; as a result of differences in nutrient availability and grazing pressure, pronounced vegetational differences develop [594, 602].

Grazing: Unlike ruminants, horses have both upper and lower incisors, so may crop a sward more tightly. Results in a dominance of dwarf, rosette-forming or prostrate-growing species in characteristically species-poor sward [252, 594, 602, 619].

DESCRIPTION
All free-ranging populations similar: bay or dark brown ponies with thick coats, dark manes and tails (Plate 10); frequently lighter on belly and around muzzle (mealy-mouthed). Stockily built with short necks and rather heavy heads; ears small and erect.

Pelage: Grows in 2 phases within the year, thick insulatory underfur grows into the summer coat to provide distinct heavy winter pelage. Insulation remarkably efficient: in winter ponies may be 'thatched' with snow because insufficient body heat is lost to melt it. Pattern of guard hairs claimed to maximise surface drainage and disperse water away from parts of the body vulnerable to chilling: thus tail, mane, forelock and beard and a special fan of short hairs near the root of the tail all show water-shedding specialisations [287].

Winter coat shed in April–May (depending on local conditions); regrows, into summer coat, from late autumn.

Digestive system: Monogastric, i.e. a simple stomach, not the 4-chambered stomach of ruminants. Instead, caecum greatly enlarged to house the symbiotic microorganisms required to break down cellulose.

Nipples: 2 on pronounced udder in lactating mares, inguinal.

Chromosomes: 2n = 32 in all populations.

RELATIONSHIPS

All domestic horses derived from the wild horse, *Equus ferus*, of which Przewalski's horse in C Asia the sole surviving population. Herds of primitive domestic strains (e.g. Polish pony or 'konik') maintained in some reserves; unmanaged population, free-ranging at Oostervaardersplassen, Netherlands, taken as model [425].

MEASUREMENTS

Size dependent on breeding history. 'Pure-bred' Exmoors *c*.127 cm at withers (range 117–137 cm), New Foresters up to 147 cm. Most breeds 115–150 cm.

VARIATION

Differences in origin and extensive later attempts at breed improvements by introduction of, variously, thoroughbred, Hackney, carthorse, Arab and cob blood have led to extensive variation both within and between populations. Major groups can be recognised: Fell ponies (Lake District, Northumberland), dark colours, dark manes and tails, height up to *c*.125–130 cm; Dartmoor ponies, bay, black or brown, height to 125 cm; Exmoor ponies, bay or dark brown with black points and pronouncedly mealy muzzle, *c*.127 cm; Welsh ponies, dark colours, variable heights dependent on breeding history; New Forest ponies, very variable in both height and colour due to extensive 'mongrelisation'; traditionally bay with dark manes and tails. Scottish Highland ponies now free-ranging only in some of the Western Isles; tend to be smaller than the mainland (garron) type: height to 134 cm, colour dun, with dorsal stripe, usually black points, silver mane and tail.

DISTRIBUTION

Free-ranging populations are found in New Forest (Hampshire), Dartmoor and Exmoor (Devon), Gower peninsula (South Wales), Carneddau hills (Gwynedd), Lundy, Lake District, Northumberland, Shetland, certain Hebridean islands and W Ireland.

HISTORY

Wild horse *Equus ferus* present in British Isles in Late Glacial times (see Chapter 3); commonly claimed that some semi-wild ponies (e.g. Exmoor) are direct descendants but little evidence to support this. Domestic horse introduced in Neolithic, *c*.4000 bp: some ponies, Exmoor, Dartmoor and New Forest especially, thought by some to descend from early domestic breeds [287, 713, 714], but others have more recent origins. Few populations have remained 'pure'; successive introductions attempting to 'improve' the commercial quality of breeds have resulted almost universally in a completely mongrel stock [285, 296]. Genetic analysis shows all breeds very diverse, but little breed structure in domestic horses, Exmoor not genetically distinct [770].

HABITAT

All British populations of free-ranging ponies use essentially marginal habitat: open moorland and rough grassland, access to woodland cover usually limited. Pattern of habitat use dictated by relative availability of different habitat types. New Forest ponies show strong positive preference for grasslands throughout the year (Fig. 11.1), a weak preference for woodlands and other cover communities – more evident during winter months – and strong avoidance of heathland areas. Despite the low availability of favoured grasslands (<7% of the area available) the ponies spend more than 50% of their time on these communities throughout the year [588]. Woodlands and other shelter communities used primarily at night, more open communities occupied during daylight: in summer, a pronounced shift in habitat occupance at dusk as animals leave open grasslands and seek shelter of woodland or gorsebrake. Such a shift less obvious during winter when animals make more use of cover communities at all times [588, 596, 602].

SOCIAL ORGANISATION AND BEHAVIOUR

Social structure usually grossly distorted by management. Studies of free-living horses

Fig. 11.1 New Forest ponies, showing browse line on trees, and tightly grazed ground vegetation *(photo R.J. Putman)*.

elsewhere, primarily in the USA [41, 42, 264, 664, 789, 790] suggest normal social 'unit' is a stallion-maintained harem of mares and subadults, maintained throughout year. Stallions aggressively territorial, defend both their group of mares and an exclusive home range [41, 42, 264]. Such groups observed in many British populations although they do not always appear strictly territorial and often occupy (at least for part of the year) overlapping home ranges.

Where populations more closely managed (e.g. New Forest), stallions may be removed from open range during winter months, only returned in summer. Here females develop a matriarchal organisation, with permanent groups of adult mares and their followers [765]. A stallion may join such a group over the summer months, but plays little role in social structuring. The groups are not true harems; social order is essentially matriarchal.

Group size: Harem groups usually a single adult stallion with 8–18 mares and their offspring. Male offspring >2 years usually excluded from group; female offspring also appear to leave group when they reach breeding age and join the harem of some other stallion [663, 765].

In matriarchal groups, e.g. in the New Forest, most commonly an adult mare with her offspring of the current and possibly previous year. Larger groups may be formed as associations of these basic units, but both size and degree of persistence of these social groups varies [596, 765].

Home range: Little studied in British Isles

(although extensive literature from N America, above). Two harem groups of Exmoor ponies had ranges of 240–290 ha but most activity was restricted to only 45–60 ha [285]. In the New Forest, range sizes of 125, 140 ha for 2 stallion-led groups [584]; ranges of all-female units tend to be larger [596]. Range size determined by 4 major factors: an area of good grazing, an area for shelter, supplies of fresh water, and a 'shade' (see below). Where vegetation communities occur in relatively large, homogeneous blocks, these components widely separated and ranges much larger. Where vegetation mosaic is of finer grain, home ranges are <100 ha. Range size often reduced over the winter months, when ponies range less widely for forage and water more readily available [596].

Social behaviour: Essentially group-living animals, maintain social cohesiveness by frequently nuzzling each other or mutual grooming. Clear dominance hierarchy among mares in both mare-only and harem groups; position determined primarily by age [41, 175, 664, 765]. Dominant females, and stallions in harem groups, frequently 'cover' dung and urine of other group members.

A characteristic group behaviour is 'shading' [765], when individuals and social groups form large congregations (in New Forest, commonly 20–30 animals, occasionally up to 100). This behaviour particularly common in mid–late summer, and shade sites are traditional (maintained both day to day and year to year). While shading, animals stand close together, largely inactive, merely whisking their tails or occasionally shifting position; may be maintained for up to 6 h. The term 'shade' is misleading: animals do not necessarily seek shelter from sun, and many sites in exposed locations. Function uncertain: believed to minimise attacks of biting insects [244].

Aggressive interactions: Rare within a social group; more commonly displayed to individuals of other social units [294, 765]. Ear-threats and head-threats (head moved towards opponent with ears laid back) are most common. Teeth may be bared, mares sometimes bite at each other. If these displays ineffective, may turn and kick out at opponent with hind legs. Territorial stallions show far more overt aggression; although preliminary displays similar to those used by mares, stallions more frequently escalate to actual combat, biting at each others' necks and withers, rearing onto hind legs and striking with one or both forefeet.

FEEDING

Preferential grazers. Both dentition and gut physiology suggest they should be relatively unselective bulk feeders [243]. Diet composition or foraging behaviour, studied in detail in 3 of the British populations [286, 287, 294, 306, 594, 620], support this expectation. Marked seasonal variation as availability of grass declines during hot, dry summer months and during winter: animals then compensate by increasing intake of other forages. Almost identical changes recorded for both New Forest and Exmoor ponies. In summer >80% of the diet is grass. As availability declines over the autumn, falls to *c*.50%; animals then increase intake of gorse and tree leaves. Proportion of moss in diet also increases, and heather, avoided during summer, regularly recorded in winter. However, winter diet is often supplemented with artificial feeding of hay, straw or roots.

Within any population, variation in diet related to local availability of forages and individual feeding patterns. These small variations in diet composition may significantly affect condition and reproductive performance [294, 295].

BREEDING
Males become sexually active at 2–3 years, but do not usually win dominance over a harem until much later. Females receptive from *c*.2 years but do not necessarily breed in every successive season; most breed 2 years in every 3. Females come into oestrus at any time May–October, but most matings in early summer, when stallion especially assiduous in maintaining harem and territory, continuously circling his mares, rounding up stragglers and herding them back to centre of his domain. Attempted theft of oestrous mares by other stallions is not uncommon, and is when most serious fights occur. Gestation 11 months (329–345 days), foals born any time late April–September; unless removed from their mothers by human intervention, usually continue to suck until following spring.

POPULATION
Both size and structure of populations of free-ranging horses in British Isles are controlled by humans; for example, most stallions removed from the New Forest over winter and returned only between May and September [594, 765]. Thus sex structure of the population skewed. Similarly, natural age structure is rarely realised: foals or yearlings are commonly removed each autumn for sale, and age structure of the residual population grossly distorted. Likewise, old animals are commonly shot or removed from common grazing.

MORTALITY
Natural mortality generally low, although severe winters may cause severe losses of both adults and juveniles. In many populations (New Forest, Exmoor, Dartmoor, Gower), road accidents may be a significant cause of death.

PARASITES
Free-ranging horse populations susceptible to the same range of parasites and diseases as confined domestic horses. Detailed information available from New Forest [96] where regular infestation with lice *Damalinia equi* and *Haemotopinus asini* and biting flies *Hippobosca equina*, *Haematopota* spp. and *Tabanus* spp.

Internal parasites: Although most New Forest ponies are regularly treated with anthelminthics, post-mortems and larval culture from dung reveal high numbers of nematode cyathostomes, and larger strongyles (*Strongylus vulgaris*, *S. edentatus*, *S. equinus*) present in up to 50% of animals. Other nematodes include *Gyalocephalus capitatus*, *Oesophagodontus robustus*, *Oxyuris equi*, *Parascaris equorum* (in 50% of sample), *Poteriostomum* sp., *Trichostrongylus axei* and *Triodontophora* sp., Cestodes *Anoplocephala perfoliata* and *Paranoplocephala mamillana* each recorded in 30% of animals. All animals examined were infested with botflies (*Gasterophilus intestinalis* and *G. nasalis*). Lungworm *Dictyocaulus arnfieldi* not recorded [96].

INTERACTIONS WITH OTHER SPECIES
Free-ranging horse populations may show competitive or facilitative relationships with other large ungulates. On Rum, high overlap in vegetation community use with cattle and red deer hinds in summer, when food resources relatively abundant, but relatively exclusive resource use during periods of low availability over winter [306, 307]. In New Forest, ponies show similar high overlap in both habitat use and diet with free-ranging cattle year-round, with some small separation in microhabitat selection within grasslands [594, 602, 620]. Some overlap in diet with roe and fallow deer [602]; analyses of long-term trends in numbers suggest that population performance of roe deer in particular may be related to pony grazing levels [602, 616, 693]. Effects of intensive grazing on vegetation structure and composition documented in the New Forest [594]; consequent indirect effects of vegetation change on species diversity and abundance of small rodents [382, 620] and on density and breeding performance of dependent predators [384, 594, 760].

LITERATURE
Few scientific reviews cover all free-range populations; popular account in [296]. Social

organisation in New Forest [594, 765] and Exmoor [285, 286, 287]. Habitat use and feeding behaviour in New Forest [294, 295, 588, 596, 620]; Exmoor [287]; Rum [306, 307].

AUTHOR
R.J. Putman

ORDER ARTIODACTYLA (EVEN-TOED UNGULATES)

An order of medium–large ungulates containing *c*.228 species in 8 smaller families (Suidae, Tayassuidae, Camelidae, Hippopotamidae, Tragulidae, Moschidae, Antilocapridae, Giraffidae) and 2 larger ones (Cervidae, 47 species; Bovidae, 141 species). Have toes 3 and 4 enlarged and central in foot (hence 'even-toed'), with toes 2 and 5 smaller or absent; also have characteristic double-pulleyed astragalus in ankle. Traditionally split between Suiformes (Suidae, Tayassuidae, Hippopotamidae) with 4-toed feet, simple stomach, Tylopoda (Camelidae) and Ruminantia (other families), with side toes reduced or absent, elongated metapodials 3 and 4 fused into a cannon bone, and complex stomachs with 3 (Camelidae) or 4 (Ruminantia) chambers. Ruminants in particular show many parallels with horses (elongate limbs, reduced toes, diastema, complex molar teeth for dealing with herbage), but these result from convergent evolution; artiodactyls, especially Hippopotamidae, are more closely related to Cetacea than to Perissodactyla.

FAMILY SUIDAE (PIGS)

A small family, native to the Old World, with 17 species in 5 genera. Of these, 3 (*Potamochoerus, Phacochoerus, Hylochoerus*) confined to Africa; 1, *Sus*, widespread in Palaearctic and Oriental regions, and 1, *Babyrousa*, confined to Indonesia.

GENUS *Sus*

An Old World genus of *c*.11 species, mostly found in SE Asia. Wild boar *S. scrofa* found throughout Palaearctic, and its domestic descendant *S. domestica* introduced worldwide, often feral (e.g. in USA, Australia).

Wild boar *Sus scrofa*
Sus scrofa Linnaeus, 1758; Germany.
Twyrch (Welsh), *tuirc allaidh, tuirc, torc; fiadh tuirc* (Scottish Gaelic), *eofor* (Anglo-Saxon); *muc fhiadhaich, muc allta, fiadh mhuc* (Irish Gaelic); wild pigs, swine (collective).

RECOGNITION
Powerfully built animal with body weight carried forwards on strong shoulders, tapering down to small rump (shoulder height *c*.700 mm). Head large with a long narrow snout, small ears held erect. Coarse coat has brindled appearance, with a mane of bristles from the neck down to middle of back and thick brown underlying pelage (Plate 10). Tail straight with long hairs, tassled at tip. Males larger than females and only males grow tusks, when 2 years old. Piglets have characteristic coat of longitudinal brown and cream stripes (Fig. 11.3).

Skull distinctive, continuous tooth row with bunodont molars and large canines (Fig. 11.2).

Signs distinctive; side toes almost as large as central toes (other artiodactyls have reduced side toes that only show on soft ground), so tracks routinely 4-toed. Snuffling creates extensive disturbed soil and vegetation. Wallows also evident [315].

DISTRIBUTION
Palaearctic, from W Europe across to Japan, and from N Africa to S Scandinavia; further S in Asia, to Sri Lanka and Malaya. Largely confined to deciduous forest zone, *c*.40–60° N (Fig. 11.4).

HISTORY
Present in GB in Cromerian, Hoxnian and Ipswichian Interglacials (see Chapter 3). Not recorded from Late Glacial, but arrived in GB and Ireland early in Mesolithic (e.g. at Star Carr,

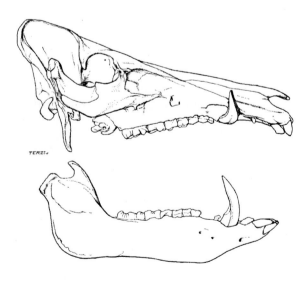

Fig. 11.2 Wild boar: skull and lower jaw of male from the side (*from [520]*).

Fig. 11.3 Wild boar with striped piglet *(photo S. Searle)*.

Thatcham, Mt Sandel; and dated to 8340 bp at Kilgreany Cave). Apparently extinct in Ireland by Neolithic, though archaeological record obscured everywhere by arrival of domestic pigs *Sus domestica*. In England, survived certainly to *c.*1300, on documentary evidence, but supposed evidence of later survival probably confused by reintroductions to parks for hunting; status in Scotland after *c.*1300 also doubtful [813].

Between 17th century and 1980s, when wild boar farming began, only a handful of captive wild boar, imported from the continent as exhibits in

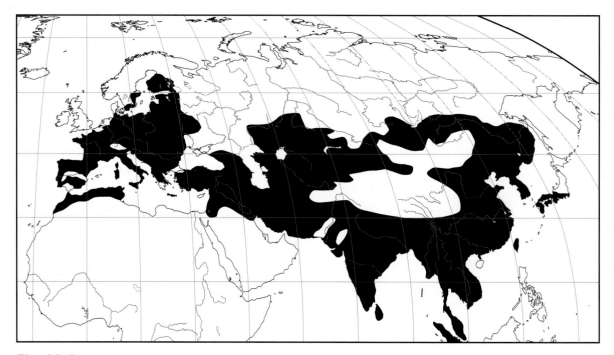

Fig. 11.4 Wild boar *Sus scrofa*: world distribution (extends further SE through Sumatra to Java).

Fig. 11.6 Wild boar rooting up grassland – damaged vegetation is one of the obvious signs of their presence *(photo B. Phipps)*.

zoos and wildlife collections, were present in GB [63]. Until very recently, no free-living wild boar had been present in GB for *c*.300 years.

In 1990s, sightings of wild boar outside captivity increased and escapes from captivity have been recorded 23 times, involving at least 198 animals (see Table 13.1). By 1998 2 viable populations existed, 1 in Dorset, 1 in Kent/E Sussex [316]. By 2005 several other substantial escapes had been reported and a 3rd population recognised, in Herefordshire [801] (Fig 11.5). Origin of animals uncertain, although the increase in escapes of wild boar coincided with the increase in the number of farms rearing wild boar for meat [1].

Genetic make-up of wild boar populations in GB unclear [314]. Numerous subspecies have been described [506]. Animals exhibited in zoo collections were from W Europe and their descendants became part of the breeding stock in the first wild boar farms [62]. Recently wild boar farmers began importing and breeding from the larger E European wild boars to increase the amount of meat [76]. Some farmers mate domestic pig sows with male wild boar, to give increased litter sizes while retaining some of the flavour of wild boar meat; hybrids have the typical appearance of wild boar [62]. Thus unclear whether feral pigs in GB are pure-bred wild boar.

GENERAL ECOLOGY

Largely herbivorous (90%), eating a large variety of herbage, roots, seeds and fruits, but also carrion,

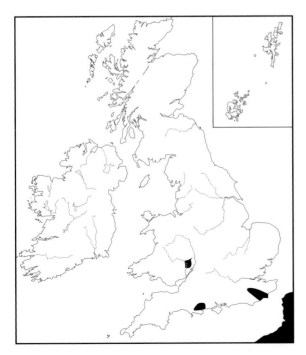

Fig. 11.5 Wild boar *Sus scrofa*: distribution in GB.

young mammals, eggs and chicks of ground-nesting birds. In summer, eat a variety of broadleaved grasses [324]. In agricultural areas turn to roots (sugar beet, potatoes) and maize [290, 682], but level of damage can be limited by supplementary feeding. Mast (beech, acorns) in autumn particularly important for overwintering, and winter mortality strongly related to severity of winter and size of autumn seed crop [560]. Almost immune to predation, except from humans and wolves.

POPULATION AND MORTALITY

Number of animals in free-living populations uncertain. In 2004 estimated to be 200 animals in Kent and E Sussex, up to 30 in Dorset [801] and a 'significant number' in Herefordshire [803]. Numbers are predicted to increase [540] as wild boar have a high reproductive potential and no natural predators in GB. Additions to the free-living populations from further escapes from captivity likely. Population growth and spread affected by unregulated hunting, populations likely to be restricted to areas of high woodland cover and low hunting pressure [540].

RELATIONSHIP WITH HUMANS

As a former native species, deliberate re-introduction into Scotland has been considered [394]. Could be regarded as a species with high biodiversity value, forming an integral part of woodland ecology, and a sporting quarry providing flavoursome meat. Important game species throughout Europe, with a harvest estimated at 0.4 million annually from spring population of 0.5 million [551]. If reintroduced, would be expected to exercise some control of bracken (the rhizomes are an important winter food) and other forest weeds.

Conversely, could be an undesirable agricultural pest [802] (Fig. 11.6), a danger to the public (a licence issued under the Dangerous Wild Animals Act 1976 is required by all those keeping wild boar; see Chapter 4) and a route for transmitting disease to domestic pigs. Farmed stock, and therefore their descendants, disease-free, but could catch various diseases from domestic swine, and then act as a reservoir for further infection. Potentially, several serious viral diseases (foot and mouth, Aujeszki's, classical swine fever, African swine fever) and bovine TB could be spread by wild boar [803]. Management options discussed in [540].

LITERATURE

Popular account [315]; reviews of status [803]; management options [540].

AUTHORS

M. Goulding, A.C. Kitchener & D.W. Yalden

FAMILY CERVIDAE (DEER)

Ruminant artiodactyls with short-crowned teeth, adapted to browsing, and with complex branched horns (antlers) that are shed annually. About 47 species, distributed in N and S America and Eurasia. 2 native and 4 introduced species established in wild in British Isles, plus 2 species extinct since last glaciation, one of them reintroduced in semi-domestic state. 2 subfamilies: Odocoileinae, mostly American deer, plus *Rangifer, Alces, Hydropotes* and *Capreolus*, with the splints of the lateral (vestigial) metapodial bones distally placed (telemetacarpal) and Cervinae, mostly Old World deer, including *Muntiacus, Dama* and *Cervus,* with the splints proximally placed (plesio-metacarpal). As in all ruminants, upper incisors lost; lower canines incisiform and lie alongside lower incisors, all bite against pad in upper jaw. Upper canines usually also reduced or absent, leaving gap (diastema) in front of cheek-teeth.

GENUS *Muntiacus*

Oriental genus of 9 species of small forest deer, distributed from Pakistan and China through SE Asia to Borneo. Have small, backwardly directed antlers and enlarged canine tusks in bucks. Occupy basal position within Cervinae [581]. Indian muntjac (*M. muntjak*) and Reeves' muntjac (*M. reevesi*) introduced to London Zoo in 1820s–1830s, subsequently to Woburn Park and Whipsnade Zoo. Reeves' muntjac now well established and widespread in GB. Suggestion that the wild populations are Indian × Reeves' hybrids refuted [123].

Reeves' muntjac *Muntiacus reevesi*
Cervus reevesi Ogilby, 1839; Canton, S China.
Chinese muntjac, barking deer.

Male – buck; female – doe; young – fawn.

RECOGNITION

Small reddish-brown deer with conspicuous white underside to tail, held vertically and very prominent when alarmed (Plate 12). Males have short simple antlers with or without small brow tines. Upper canine teeth protrude below lip in males but not as long as in Chinese water deer. Facial markings unlike any other deer in British Isles, black frontal stripes on ginger face. Sometimes stand with back arched and commonly hold head down so rump appears higher than withers.

Skull: Distinguished at any age by pair of

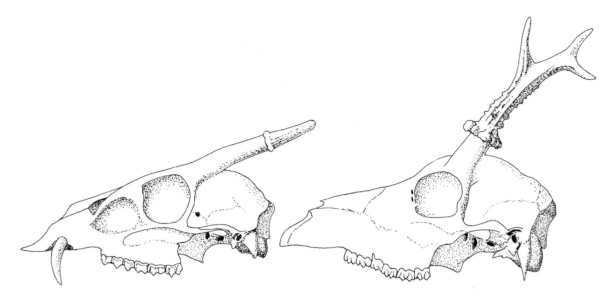

Fig. 11.7 Skulls of buck muntjac (left) and roe (right), showing the long antler pedicle, tusk and large depression for the preorbital scent gland of the muntjac *(drawn by D. W. Yalden)*.

preorbital pits, almost as large as orbits. In male, pedicle arises from elongation of ridge on frontal bone (Fig. 11.7).

FIELD SIGNS

Footprints: Smaller (*c.*3 cm long × 2 cm wide) than any other adult ungulate in British Isles. When walking, hindfeet register on prints made by forefeet. Prints *c.*30 cm apart.

Faecal pellets: Black, shiny, striated, may be nearly spherical or cylindrical. Most weigh 0.1–0.2 g; 6–12 × 5–11 mm. Shape variable: pointed at both ends, pointed at one end, rounded, concave or flat at other, or rounded at both ends. Deposited in heaps (mostly 20–120 pellets). Same spot sometimes used frequently to form a regular latrine, probably by neighbours in high-density populations. Defecation rate for captives on diet of browse 7.0–8.2 groups/day [141].

Scrapes: Well defined (*c.*30 cm) in ground vegetation, exposing bare soil, mostly seen in habitats with high density of muntjac where territorial disputes between adult bucks most likely. Scraping by vigorous pawing with forefeet usually accompanied by aggressive behaviour to neighbouring male.

Fraying of bark on saplings not easily distinguished from roe deer damage but occurs at low level, *c.*10–40 cm above ground level: usually fuzzy threads remain attached. Mostly done by lower incisor teeth or tusks, occasionally when cleaning velvet. Saplings/coppice shoots sometimes partly bitten through, mostly at 50–70 cm, to form an inverted V, bringing upper leaves within reach [203].

Browse line on shrubs, trees, climbers (ivy, honeysuckle, clematis) *c.*96 cm but can reach to *c.*114 cm by standing on hind legs [1].

DESCRIPTION

Pelage in summer a rich red-brown over most of body, with buff belly. Extent of white on inside of thighs and chin variable. Tail rich chestnut dorsally, white below. Winter coat, developed by September–October, is duller, greyer brown, forelegs often almost black on front, especially in adult males. Head sandy ginger, neck of male sometimes almost golden. Males have black stripes, almost forming a V, up frontal ridges and pedicles. Females have dark or black kite-shaped pattern on forehead. Fawns have female face pattern, males develop their characteristic pattern by *c.*9 months of age. At birth, pelage heavily spotted with buff: spots gradually fade, usually disappeared by *c.*8 weeks. Cuticle pattern of guard hairs described in [518].

Moult in April–June conspicuous, sometimes not completed until August. Usually begins on head, followed by shoulder or rump.

For field observations the following age/sex categories have proved useful. Fawns: <8 weeks old, coat spotted or spots fading. Juveniles: indeterminate sex, 2–5 months, up to 3/4 grown. Immature females: 5–8 months, 3/4 to full-grown. Mature females: >8 months, full size, breeding age. Subadult males: from 5–26 months; antler status varies from having only pedicle bumps to having hard 1st set of antlers. Adult males: enter this class from 12–26 months, after casting the 1st head of antlers [1].

ANATOMY

Skull: Very narrow between preorbital pits. Mean measurements (mm) for animals >2 years (males n = 23, females n = 19): greatest length, males 167 (range 162–176), females 162 (range 154–169); zygomatic breadth, males 78 (range 73–82), females 74 (range 71–78); mandibles, greatest length, males 129 (range 123–135); females 127 (range 122–133).

Antlers: 1st head a simple spike or knob with no coronet. 2nd and subsequent heads have coronets and may have small brow tine. Presence of brow tine one year does not necessarily mean it will be present in successive heads. In mature bucks, distal portion of each antler typically curves backwards and usually terminates in a hooked point. Length seldom >10 cm nor weight >17 g.

Pedicles first recognisable from 20–31 weeks of age. At 32–46 weeks, small velvet-covered antlers appear. Period in velvet variable: cleaning occurs when 46–76 weeks old. Young males subsequently synchronise with the cycle of adult males by casting 1st antlers in May or June (median date 26 May) when they may be 51–112 weeks old [135]. Thereafter a regular cycle [122]; new antlers grow through the summer (growing period 79–130 days, mean 106 days), with velvet cleaned August–October (median date September 14) and remain in hard antler until late April–mid July (median date 27 May).

Scent glands: A slit opening below the corner of each eye leads to large preorbital sac composed of 2 pockets; posterior pocket contains a paste of sloughed epidermal cells and lipids, anterior pocket has fewer sebaceous and sweat glands and lacks paste (Fig. 11.8). A functional connection is suspected between preorbital sac and Harderian gland; latter has 2 lobes of which the large red lobe lies deep within the orbit and is much larger in males than females [645]. Pair of frontal glands on forehead form shallow grooves, almost meeting as a small V. Hindfeet have interdigital gland. Preputial gland consists of modified sebaceous glands ([558], but misreported as *M. muntjak*).

Teeth: Deciduous formula 0.1.3.0/3.1.3.0: permanent 0.1.3.3/3.1.3.3. As in other cervids, p^1/p_1 lost in evolution, so survivors numbered p^2/p_2, p^3/p_3, p^4/p_4 [649]. Lower canine incisiform, abuts 3rd incisor. The deciduous premolar dp_4 has 3 cusps but p_4 replacing it has only 2. All of dp_2, p_2, dp_3, p_3 and p_4 are lophodont. but dp_4 and all permanent upper premolars and molars are selenodont. Permanent lower teeth erupt in order: molars, 1st and 2nd incisors, premolars, 3rd incisor and canine. Permanent upper teeth erupt in order:

1st molar, canine in males *c.*21 weeks, 2nd and 3rd molars, canine in females 53–57 weeks, premolars, so full complement of functional permanent teeth by 83–92 weeks [130, 160]. Wear pattern on mandibular molars useful guide to age [160].

Marked sexual dimorphism of permanent upper canines; in male, is a slightly mobile tusk, curved, with posterior cutting edge, sharp point and up to 60 mm long (of which 1/3 within alveolus)(Fig. 11.7); important as weapon. Root usually closed by 5 years. One or both upper canines broken in 51% of 83 bucks aged 3–5 years [1]. In female, canine small, insignificant: length 17 mm (2/3 within alveolus), 1 or both absent in 0.02% (n = 247) [138].

Nipples: 2 pairs, inguinal.

Reproductive tract: Male accessory glands comprise a disseminate prostate gland, paired seminal vesicles, ampullae and large Cowper's (bulbourethral) glands. Latter have a homologue of similar size in the female (bulbovesticular or Bartholin's glands). For both sexes, these have been termed paraurethral glands [223]. Seasonal changes in accessory glands very small [146]. Female, bicornuate uterus; most pregnancies occur in right horn [125].

Thymus consists of cervical and thoracic portions [150]; ultrastructure described [815].

Chromosomes: 2n = 46, all acrocentric except for small submetacentric Y chromosome. Identification of feral muntjac present in England confirmed by chromosome number [127].

Fig. 11.8 Reeves' muntjac: young buck, with antlers still in velvet and short canines, licking its preorbital gland *(photo N.G. Chapman)*.

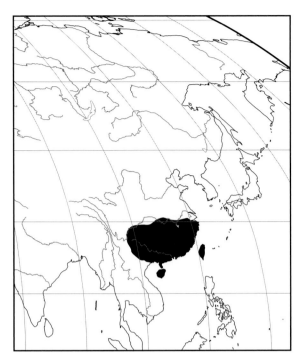

Fig. 11.9 Reeves' muntjac *Muntiacus reevesi*: native (black) range.

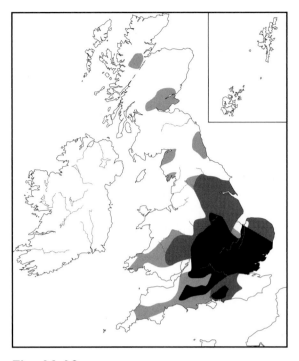

Fig. 11.10 Reeves' muntjac *Muntiacus reevesi*: distribution in GB.

Tandem fusion of chromosomes during the evolution of *Muntiacus* facilitates hybridisation between species with widely differing chromosome number [814]. Reeves' muntjac can hybridise with Indian muntjac (*M. muntjak*) [699] but the progeny are infertile [698]. Claims for wild hybrids in England unsubstantiated; could only have occurred during the brief period when the two species might have cohabited in Woburn woods. Muntjac now established in England are all Reeves' [123, 127].

MEASUREMENTS
See Table 11.1.

VARIATION
M. reevesi reevesi on mainland China (introduced to GB) poorly differentiated from *M. r. micrurus* on Taiwan. Reeves' muntjac in GB: minor variation in pelage, some darker brown, some more ginger, rarely very pale. Darkness of forehead pattern in females variable. Facial stripes of male vary from jet black to dark brown, do not always extend full length of pedicles. Black nape stripe present or absent in either sex. Ears may be same colour as head (golden/sandy brown), almost black with sharp demarcation at base, or gradually darken towards tip. Scattering of white hairs above cleaves sometimes present, rarely white 'socks'. Antlers sometimes with pearling at base or somewhat flattened blade-like form. Pedicles characteristically long but shorten with age. Some non-metric

variation in skulls including time (prenatal or perinatal) of fusion of bones of parietal region [140]. Number of caudal vertebrae variable (10–13), congenital absence of tail reported [142].

DISTRIBUTION
Native to SE China and Taiwan, where inhabits scrub and dense forest at 200–400 m asl (Fig. 11.9). Well established over much of England, especially southern half (Fig. 11.10). By 1993 recorded in 745 10-km squares; only 5 counties lacked any records [155]. Some further expansion since then, expected to continue with increase in suitable habitats [137]. A few records from Wales and Scotland. Wandering individuals, usually subadult males, sometimes reported in urban areas [149, 155, 156].

HISTORY
2 species of muntjac introduced to Woburn Park, Bedfordshire: Indian (in 1893) and Reeves' (1894). In 1901 11 Reeves' and 31 Indian released into neighbouring woods, but Indian died out. Contemporary documentation fragmentary, many written accounts incorrect; many translocations, escapes and releases 1930s–1990s, as well as natural spread, contributed to such wide establishment [155]. Genetic variation also provides strong evidence that muntjac have not attained present wide distribution by natural spread from single centre of origin (i.e. Woburn) [800] as previously believed [794].

HABITAT

Prefer dense habitat with diversity of vegetation, e.g. deciduous woodland with year-round understorey, coppice, young unthinned plantations, scrub, overgrown and undisturbed gardens, cemeteries. Frequently present in commercial coniferous woodlands with some deciduous trees and ground cover, where they select areas with diverse ground and shrub layers, bramble and mature nut-bearing trees [152, 158].

SOCIAL ORGANISATION AND BEHAVIOUR

Basically solitary; most sightings are of single adults or subadults of either sex. Next most common sightings are mature female and her most recent offspring, adult male and adult female, or the latter plus the doe's latest fawn. Other combinations are much less common and seldom are 4 or more together, though a larger number may assemble temporarily at a favoured feeding area (e.g. for acorns) without being a cohesive group.

Observations and radio-tracking of marked animals have shown that a particular mature male and adult female frequently may be together over several years but this does not indicate a life-bond as changes in associations occur, or several may occur concurrently.

Ranges: Generally larger for adult males than females, but range size varies with habitat quality/diversity [154, 428, 731]. Ranges of adult males 20–28 ha, females 11–14 ha, in a 5-year radio-tracking study, within mainly coniferous woodland. Subsequent to a gale which initiated greater diversity of habitat, the population doubled and ranges halved [428]. Similar mean range sizes in other areas: females in Rockingham woods (low-density population) 13.1 ha but in Monks Wood National Nature Reserve (high density) 6.1 ha: adult males at both sites 19.6 ha [731]; 14 ha for both sexes in Wytham Wood, Oxfordshire [351].

Adult males territorial, ranges defended, seldom overlap but encompass the ranges of several does. Does less territorial, permitting overlap, but core areas exclusive; aggressive chasing toward intruding does [154].

Tenure remarkably stable from year to year; in long-term study, King's Forest, Thetford, does held ranges for 9 years, bucks for 3.5 years [159]. Methods of home-range analysis discussed [359].

Communication: Scent-marking most important. Males use facial glands more than females, and dominant males more than subordinates [35] (Fig. 11.11). During courtship, defecation and urination, preorbital glands frequently opened, even everted, under control of several muscles [34] and may be wiped against twigs [242]. Deer then sometimes licks its own preorbital area (Fig. 11.8), presumably reinforcing recognition of its own scent. Preorbital secretions extremely complex, individually distinctive, although some common

Table 11.1 Muntjac: measurements for individuals ≥2 years old, shot or killed on roads within King's and Thetford Forests, Suffolk/Norfolk

	Males			Females		
	Mean	Range	n	Mean	Range	n
Whole body wt (kg)	14.9	12.3–17.0	41	13.3	10.0–16.0	30
Carcass wt (kg)	9.8	8.5–12.25	32	8.5	6.75–10.25	25
Carcass wt (% of whole wt)	65.5	–	–	–	–	–
Head and body length (cm)	84	78–91	34	82	77–91	23
Tail to end vertebra (cm)	13	10.3–17.0	36	12.0	10–14.5	25
Tail inc. terminal hairs (cm)	16	13–17.5	31	15	13–18	22
Ear length (cm)	8.2	7.5–9.0	43	8.1	7–8.5	29
Hindfoot length (cm)	22.7	21.5–24.5	40	22.4	20–23.5	28
Shoulder height (cm)	49.5	46–52	27	47	45–50	20
Girth (cm)	58	29–65	29	55	50–61	20

Carcass wt = head off, feet off (at proximal ends of cannon bones), all viscera removed, skin on.

Fig. 11.11 Muntjac: buck scent-marking with frontal glands on sapling *(photo B. Phipps)*.

characteristics link animals within the same population; consistent differences between the sexes [456, 457].

Frontal glands produce a slightly waxy secretion, are frequently placed in contact with the ground. Secretion from deep pocket of interdigital gland on hindfeet deposited as deer walks.

Vocalisation: Loud, single barks, repeated a few or hundreds of times, most usually heard after birth when doe in oestrus or following unfamiliar disturbance. Occasionally more a shriek than a bark. Loud scream emitted when alarmed, e.g. caught in fence. Young fawns squeak; does pursued by amorous bucks give plaintive squeaks.

Other communication: When alarmed, run off with tail vertical, displaying white underside. If less frightened, move off without raising tail [194].

If apprehensive of a strange object, e.g. observer, stamp forefeet several times (like other deer). Vibrations may signal to conspecifics.

Dispersal: Age of natal dispersal variable. Males sometimes disperse before growing their pedicles, others not until much later. Some young females remain in the mother's area and establish an overlapping range. Adults of either sex sometimes disperse from area where they have been established for several years. Longest known dispersal of a marked (adult) muntjac, 21 km [651].

Aggressive behaviour: Fighting strategy described in [36, 536]. Sparring matches involve antler-to-antler contact, usually between unequal males; such engagements harmless, may end in mutual grooming. Fights between equally matched bucks preceded by low, deliberate walk towards the opponent and often grinding of cheek-teeth. Head-on clash ensues, using antlers to unbalance the opponent, and deliver a downward blow with a tusk on face or neck. Wounds can be deep and liable to infection [54]. Adults of either sex will pursue well-grown offspring, presumably driving it from its natal range. Neck fighting seen between doe and subadult offspring, and between adult does. One doe sometimes rushes aggressively towards or chases another, the pursued sometimes squealing [164, 166].

Activity: Main feeding periods early morning, dusk and middle of the day but may be active at any time. Mean of 5 active periods/24 h in one study [276]. After a feeding session, usually lies up in cover to ruminate.

Movement: When undisturbed, usual travels at walking gait, head held low, or trots purposefully. If disturbed, runs short distance before stopping to investigate source of disturbance; rarely bounds – only if passing through extensive long grass. Occasionally stands on hind legs to reach browse. Several reports of swimming, even in sea.

Fawns a few weeks old indulge in playful rushing about. A buck, usually a subadult, sometimes has a 'bucking bronco' session lasting several minutes on one spot during which leaps vertically, twists and almost stands on head.

Grooming: Self-grooming from 1 day old, tongue and incisiform teeth used. Both parents will groom a fawn all over, especially round the anus, while suckling. Mutual grooming important social behaviour: occurs between animals of the same or different sex, within the same or different age class and concentrates on neck, head and ears,

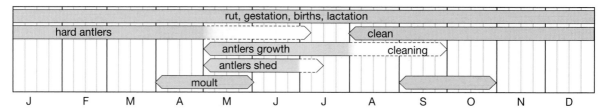

Fig. 11.12 Muntjac: annual cycle.

especially during the spring moult, and on antlers when in velvet. Evidently mutually beneficial, and reinforces social bonds [35].

FEEDING

Concentrate selectors [385], i.e. primarily browsers rather than grazers, as confirmed by direct observations, rumen content analysis [402], faecal pellet analysis [358], anatomy of alimentary tract [385], digestive studies [19] and size of salivary glands [426]. In deciduous woods, leaves and flowers of many species (e.g. bluebells, primroses, orchids) and shoots selected, causing changes in composition of flora and structure of habitat, with loss of biodiversity [195, 200, 740, 742]; see also Relations with humans, below).

Analysis of faecal pellets collected over 2-year period in a mainly coniferous wood in Suffolk recorded 85 species of plants [358]. Most important was *Rubus* (bramble and raspberry), accounting for 30–40% of diet in all months, but not all varieties of bramble palatable to muntjac [86, 166]. Other foods changed seasonally with ivy, ferns, fungi, broad-leaved trees and shrubs, nuts and other fruits all being important. Grasses a significant food only briefly in spring and in some winters when preferred foods in short supply [358, 428].

Frequently coexist with one or more other cervids, usually fallow and/or roe. Considerable niche overlap between muntjac and roe (also a concentrate selector) so there may be competition in winter [276, 366, 808].

BREEDING

Polygynous. Buck has opportunity to mate with any doe coming into oestrus whose range overlaps his. Uncertain whether either sex makes short-term excursions further afield to seek mating opportunities. Breed throughout the year (Fig. 11.12); fawns born in any month with no obvious peak [129]. First conception in captive animals can occur at 5–6 months, more usually at 7 months or later.

Single fawn: twin fetuses rare, one report of triplet fetuses [12]. Postpartum oestrus, so female often conceives within few days of parturition. Of 36 known interbirth periods, shortest was 211 days, 50% were 216 days and 31% were 220–250 days. A female can be almost continuously pregnant over many years, e.g. one captive doe had 16 live births (plus 1 aborted fetus) in 9 years 10 months. Productivity likely to be 1.6 fawns/year [159].

Testes less active in summer, but buck still capable of fertilising even when antlers just cast and while antlers growing [146].

Gestation 210 days. Mating follows period of male pursuing doe, often chasing her relentlessly, with frequent sniffing, licking of vulval area and her urine, exhibiting flehmen and mounting many times. Oestrous female frequently walks with tail raised and often barking.

Sex ratio at birth 1:1. Of 53 captive births, 27 males:26 females. Of 80 pregnant uteri from wild animals with sexable fetus, 42 male and 38 female. Mean weight (within day of birth) 1209 g (range 900–1500 g, n = 30 captive animals). Lactation observed in captivity up to 17 weeks.

POPULATION

Densities vary with habitat. In a coniferous forest with some deciduous woodland, 30 muntjac (excluding fawns) in 206 ha, a density of 1/6.8 ha [165]. When this same habitat improved, density doubled [428]. Density as high as 1.2/ha estimated for a Cambridgeshire deciduous wood in the summer preceding a die-off [211].

Numbers: Estimated as 52 000 in England, 250 in Wales assuming densities of 30/km² in prime habitats, 15/km² in less favourable areas [360], with population doubling in <8 years; current population likely to be double these figures.

Because of year-round breeding, at any time a population will include animals in all age categories. In one winter population of 30 muntjac, 3 were juveniles, 3 immature females, 14 mature females, 4 subadult males, 6 adult males [165].

Survival: Potentially long-lived; 16 years for a male in captivity [1]; >20 years for a female [85]. In wild (marked individuals): 13 years (female); 10 years (male) but some unmarked animals, from tooth wear, judged to be older. Demographic data from several sites in S England: mortality 56% by

1 year, 69%by 2 years, 75% by 3 years, 81% by 4 years, 88% by 5 years and 100% by15 years. In a sample of 35 female road kills from the Breckland forests, only 20% were estimated to be 5 years old or more, and mean age was 2.95 years [149].

DISEASE
Generally healthy and disease-free. Can be infected with foot-and-mouth disease, but no cases recorded in the wild. Reports of erysipelas [53], hydromelia [249], bovine TB [230], meningitis [1]. Wasting disease, including polycystic renal disease, reported from Whipsnade Animal Park [258]. Joint disease of limbs [318], scoliosis, spondylosis, degenerative joint disease, mandibular and maxillary bone lesions and intervertebral disc disease also observed [491].

Occasional reports of carcinomas, e.g. liver. One case of possible poisoning by oxalic acid after eating sugar beet leaves [134].

MORTALITY
From disease, as above, and predation by dogs and foxes. Carcasses found partly eaten by foxes may have been carrion, but foxes definitely take some live fawns. In one study area, although fox population was at low density, estimated total loss of 47% fawns (<2 months old), probably mostly predation but some abortions and perinatal deaths [360].

Heavy mortality reported after severe winter with prolonged periods of deep snow [155]. Debilitation from starvation, often with pneumonia, accounted for deaths of c.50% of a high-density population [211]. Human-inflicted mortality by shooting and many road traffic accidents.

PARASITES
Endoparasites: Very few recorded. No lungworm found in 90 animals, no bladderworm cysts in 169. Incidence of gastrointestinal nematodes very low. *Nematodirus battus*, *Oesphagostomum* sp. and *Trichostrongylus* sp. (primarily parasites of sheep) recorded from eggs in muntjac faeces collected in a park [362]. Intestinal protozoan *Eimeria* sp. recorded [555].

Ectoparasites: One biting louse *Cervicola indica (= Damalinia* or *Tricholipeurus indica*) and one sucking louse *Selenopotes muntiacus. C. indica* more common but rarely a heavy burden. Related *C. muntiacus* not recorded in GB. Tick *Ixodes ricinus* frequently present in some localities but many fewer than on roe in the same habitat. Orange larvae of mite *Trombicula autumnalis* also recorded.

RELATIONS WITH HUMANS
Muntjac became well established before need for control widely accepted [149, 155]. Shooting carried out for control, also fee-paying trophy shooting of bucks. Very little if any damage to conifers. The small mouth cannot bite a lump from large carrots, potatoes or sugar beets, but pieces or riddlings readily taken from fields after harvest. May take oilseed rape or field beans [206]; some market-garden crops vulnerable. Shoots and flowers of many deciduous trees and garden plants are selected [156, 188].

Impacts in conservation woodland can be serious where muntjac densities are high [199] with direct effects noted on woody vegetation [200, 201, 203, 206] and ground flora [191, 193, 210, 233, 742], and with indirect effects on other fauna [206, 583]. Coppice stems vulnerable until >1.6 m [195, 203]. Limited success at exclusion with chestnut paling [741] and electric fencing [209]. Wire fencing to exclude muntjac should have 75 mm mesh and be >1.5 m high [574]. Scoring system devised to monitor change in muntjac presence or damage [192, 197, 199, 743]. Culling can reduce density and therefore damage in conservation woodlands, but some impacts may be irreversible [198–201]. Exclusion from gardens difficult as muntjac can push under fences or through small holes: many species of garden plant are eaten [156, 188]. Road traffic takes a toll and an errant muntjac in a town creates hazards.

Legislation: No close seasons defined for muntjac because they breed throughout the year. When females are to be culled, selection should be for immature females (which will not have a dependent fawn) or heavily pregnant does whose previous fawn will be at least 7 months old. Licences to catch/transport muntjac for specific purposes, as for other deer, at the discretion of Natural England (see Chapter 4). Translocation prohibited since 1997 except for rehabilitators within 12 named counties who hold licences from Natural England (Wildlife and Countryside Act, 1981, Schedule 9).

Techniques for study: Animals individually marked with ear-tags, coloured collars and radio-collars [54, 165]. Captured using long nets [153] and immobilising drugs [213].

LITERATURE
Early information on distribution in England [794]. Popular account of the deer which colonised a Hertfordshire garden [712]. Observations on captive and wild deer [163]. Natural history and biology [148]. natural history and stalking [711].

AUTHOR
N.G. Chapman

Plate 11

A Red deer *Cervus elaphus* calf   B hind, summer   C stag, winter
D Reindeer *Rangifer tarandus* bull   E Fallow deer *Dama dama* fawn   F doe, winter   G buck, summer
H Sika *Cervus nippon* fawn   I doe, summer   J buck, winter

GENUS *Cervus*

A genus of *c*.10 species, mostly Oriental in distribution, but 1 widespread Holarctic species (*C. elaphus*) is native and another introduced species occurs in British Isles. Medium–large deer, stags have cylindrical branching antlers (Fig. 11.13).

Red deer *Cervus elaphus*

Cervus elaphus Linnaeus, 1758; Southern Sweden.
Carw coch (Welsh); *fiadh* (Scottish Gaelic); *fia rua* (Irish Gaelic).
Male – stag (also hart, obsolete); *craw* (Welsh); *damh* (Scottish and Irish Gaelic). Female – hind; *hydd* (Welsh); *eilid* (Scottish Gaelic); *eilit* (Irish Gaelic). Mature female with calf – milk hind; adult without calf – yeld, rarely blue or eild hind; young-of-year – calf.

Other names used to describe different ages/types of animal derived from hunting vocabulary [794, 798].

RECOGNITION

Whole animal: Only large red-brownish deer in British Isles that does not have spots as adult.

Rump patch creamy coloured extending dorsally above short, beige tail; rump patch not clearly outlined with black as in sika and fallow deer (Plate 11). Tail shorter than ear [482]. Can be mistaken for much smaller roe, which similar colour in summer, but ears proportionately smaller, muzzle much longer.

Skull and teeth: Large head with elongated snout. In male, large antlers consisting of a main stem (beam) with up to 3 branches, usually in the same plane and with a fork or cup at the top; not palmate as in fallow or rugose as in roe deer. Antlers larger than sika antlers and 1st (brow) point, when present, generally arises at an angle >90° to the main antler stem (cf. *c*.55° in sika).

FIELD SIGNS

Tracks and trails: Footprints (slots) oval, 5 cm wide in calves and 7 cm in adult males, size of slot dependent on substrate and gait, larger on snow or soft ground, or when animal is running [746]. Overlap in size and shape with other medium–large deer and sheep and goats.

Faeces: Variable according to age, size and diet. Droppings ('fewmets') acorn-shaped, up to 3 cm

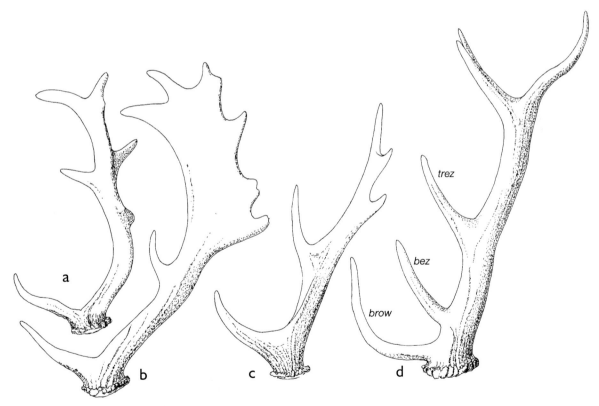

Fig. 11.13 Antlers of fallow deer (a,b), sika (c) and red deer (d). The red deer stag typically has a low sweeping brow tine and both bez and trez tines, as well as a variable number of 'tops'. Sika and fallow deer have brow and trez, but no bez; their brow tines are angled more acutely. In all deer, younger males have less elaborate antlers than mature ones, and the young fallow buck (a) shows little sign of the palmation characteristic of older bucks *(drawn by D.W. Yalden)*.

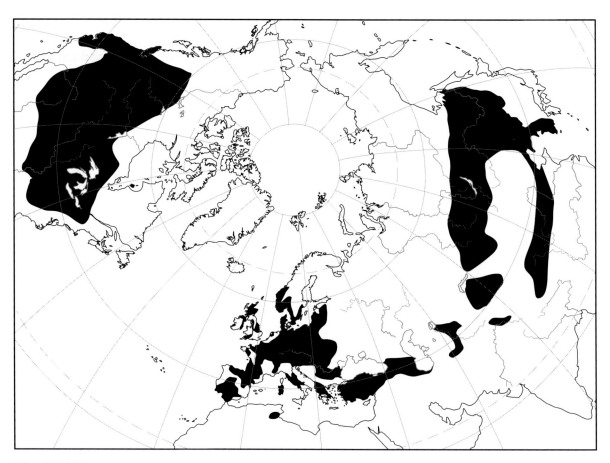

Fig. 11.15 Red deer *Cervus elaphus*: world distribution.

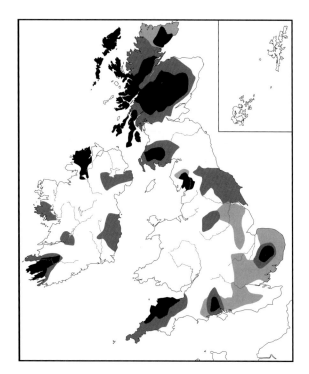

Fig. 11.16 Red deer *Cervus elaphus*: distribution in British Isles.

Asia and N America [585]. N American and NE Asiatic races (wapitis) very large. Molecular evidence [581] suggests that red deer more distinct from wapiti than from sika, and that *C. elaphus* contains 3 distinct species.

British race described as *C. e. scoticus* Lönnberg, 1907 (type locality Glenquoich Forest, Invernessshire) on basis of skull shape, but not clearly distinguishable from continental animals [485]; thought to be confined to Scotland N of the central belt, NW England, SW Ireland (Co. Kerry) and possibly Exmoor and Galloway [485]. Other populations believed feral, established from introductions or deer escaping from deer parks or farms, of multiple or unknown genetic origins. Introductions into Scotland and elsewhere direct from continental Europe. In Ireland, introductions from England and Scotland.

DISTRIBUTION

Widespread in Palaearctic from Ireland and Hebrides eastwards to Manchuria and N America. Found just S of Arctic Circle in Norway (65° N) to N Africa (33° N) (Fig. 11.15) [798]. In British Isles, main concentrations in Scottish highlands and islands and SW Scotland, SW England (especially Exmoor and Quantocks) and SW Ireland (Fig. 11.16). Elsewhere in England and Wales, scattered populations with

578

reasonable numbers in NW England, Hampshire and E Anglia. Smaller populations established in Peak District/N Staffordshire moors, Yorkshire (around Sheffield and Doncaster) and Sherwood Forest; isolated pockets in Wales. In Ireland, main populations in Cos. Kerry (including Innisvicillane Island), Wicklow (probably now all red/sika hybrids [356, 632]), Meath, Donegal, Tyrone, Fermanagh and Down.

Found on the following Scottish islands: Arran, Bute, Islay, Jura, Mull, Pabbay, Raasay, Rum, Scalpay, Scarba, Seil, Skye, N and S Uist, N Harris and S Lewis [360, 731].

HISTORY

See [469, 478, 794, 813]. Probably evolved from sika-like form, perhaps *Cervus perrieri* [469]. Occurred first in Middle Pleistocene Cromerian interglacial (*c*.400 000 bp) of Europe. Earliest deer found associated with woodlands, but some evidence of them occupying treeless areas where there was topographical shelter [469]. Occurred in GB and Ireland before maximum of last glacial (40 000–26 000 bp), and in Late Glacial interstadial (13 000–11 000 bp), but died out in Younger Dryas cold spell; returned to GB (e.g. Star Carr, Thatcham) early in Postglacial, but not to Ireland where probably an ancient introduction [807, 813].

Decline in body size throughout European range since prehistoric times [478]. In Scotland, decline in size since last Ice Age [478, 650] influenced initially by climatic effects on habitats, subsequently by deforestation and disturbance by humans, obliging red deer to occupy treeless, exposed, poor-quality hill land. Range and numbers greatly reduced in historic times; extinct in much of England, Wales and Scottish lowlands by the end of the 18th century. Increased in Scotland during 19th century due to interest in deer stalking; high and increasing numbers maintained over last 40 years through under-culling of females, less overwinter mortality, reduced competition with hill sheep and colonisation of forestry plantations.

Similarly in Ireland, numbers declined due to deforestation and disturbance from humans, so that extinct in all parts but the SW by end of 19th century [794]. Killarney red deer thought to be the only remnant of the ancient population [262, 354, 794] although some introductions from deer parks in England and Ireland, and of wild deer from England and Scotland, have occurred over last 100 years [794]. Numbers increasing in established populations due to colonisation of conifer plantations and lowland deciduous woods.

HABITAT

Highly adaptable, associated with many climatic and vegetation types from semi-arid Mediterranean areas such as Sardinia and Atlas mountains of N Africa to rich flood plains of the Danube, alpine meadows of Switzerland and former Yugoslavia and high-snowfall areas of Norway and former USSR. Primarily an ecotone species associated with forest edge or the interface between woodland and grassland [250, 532]. In Europe, 1000–2000 ha of forest thought necessary to sustain permanent populations [6, 532]; vary from pure deciduous or coniferous to mixed woodlands. Rarely occupy large tracts of dense forest [250, 262].

In GB, most widespread, and highest numbers found, on open moorland ('deer forest') in Scottish highlands and islands. Also occupy treeless areas in some parts of Ireland, SW England and Cumbria; elsewhere associated with woodland as in remainder of world range. In SW England, highest densities found in woodland and farmland fringes; actively select broadleaved woodland and areas with cover over upland heath and conifer forest [439].

Has colonised many conifer plantations established during last century, and other woodlands, especially in Scotland, SW England, E Anglia and Ireland. Plantation age and structure important, highest densities being found in open thicket where good cover and food are in close proximity, rather than in older forests (Table 11.6). Selection of forest structures in conifer plantations follows: open thicket > re-stock > pre-thicket > high forest > pole stage. Young stands and open areas within forest (forest rides, checked areas) used as feeding areas [109, 383, 728]. Improved pastures and crops next to woodland extensively used, especially in S and E England.

SOCIAL ORGANISATION AND BEHAVIOUR

Social organisation: Throughout range adult males and females segregate for most of year to varying degrees, except during the rut [532]. In Scotland, in winter, areas occupied often traditional and geographically separate [785]; hinds tend to occupy areas overlying richer rocks and soils with proportionately more grassland; adjacent stag populations found on poorer ground often with more heather [729, 785]. Differences in habitat selection between sexes greatest at high population densities [171].

Hind organisation appears generally to be based on matriarchy, group consisting of dominant hind and dependent offspring; mature daughters and offspring have adjacent, overlapping ranges with her; individual family groups coalesce around favourable resources (see Dominance) [176, 479].

Stag groups less stable, with unrelated

individuals forming semi-permanent groups for varying periods. Ranges apparently undefended.

Group size varies according to habitat and weather (particularly snowfall) and sex. In woodlands, usually individuals or small numbers of stags, or family groups of hinds and dependent offspring; different groups may join together when venturing on to open ground but split up again into family groups when returning to cover. On open moorland, larger groups may persist but group size varies according to distribution and abundance of local feeding and resting areas and to disturbance, especially from heavy shooting [532, 718, 727]; average *c*.9–11 on Rum [176, 479], 6–10 in Exmoor [446] to *c*.40 in C and E Scottish Highlands [532, 718]; largest groups in a local population generally of females and young except where stags are concentrated for supplementary winter feeding. Groups of <600 hinds and followers recorded in C Scottish Highlands in winter [1].

Stag groups on open ground may be composed of all old, all young or of mixed ages. Within stag groups, nearest neighbours tend to be of similar age, with young and subdominants occupying peripheral positions [532]. Hind groups sometimes predominantly milk hinds with calves or predominantly yeld hinds [479, 532].

Dominance hierarchy approximately linear in stag groups on open hill; related mainly to age and body size; role of antler size in dominance problematic, being confounded by correlation with age and body size [176]. In females, on Rum where groups relatively stable, hierarchy age-related but not clearly linear and causes obscure [176]; unlikely to be the case where larger aggregations may occur and are less stable in composition, nor in woodlands where the family forms the group. During rut, males usually defend a harem of females and young or the area around them ('moving territory' [224]), although in some areas this may be a stag defending a specific area or rutting stand [220, 269].

Table 11.6 Red deer: estimated densities in different habitats in the British Isles

Area	Habitat	Density (deer/km2)	Method	Source
Scotland				
Cairngorms	Open hill	13.9	Visual counts	[735]
E Grampians	Open hill	14.1	Visual counts	[735]
Glenartney	Open hill	26.9	Visual counts	[735]
N Ross	Open hill	6.8	Visual counts	[735]
Galloway	Plantation	8	Dung counts	[633]
Glenbranter, S Argyll	Plantation	10	Dung counts	[728]
Glencrippesdale, N Argyll	Plantation	40	Dung counts	[633]
SW England				
Exmoor	Open hill	3, 6	Visual/dung counts	[439]
NE Exmoor	Woodland	14	Dung counts	[439]
Quantocks	Woodland	9	Dung counts	[439]
Ireland				
Donegal	Open hill	6–8.	Visual	[95]
Kerry	Open hill	17	Visual	[95]
	Woodland	18–20	Visual	[95]
Wicklow	Open hill	<5	Visual	[95]
Meath	Woodland	6	Visual	[95]

Home range: Size varies according to habitat; largest in open country. Hind ranges 200–400 ha on Rum [176, 479]; 900–2400 ha in E Highlands, with one recorded range >8000 ha [717, 719]. In SW England, hind ranges average 430 ha (range 275–711 ha) with 1 core area; adult stags tend to have 2, seasonal, core areas totalling 1000–1200 ha [440]. In forestry plantations in Scotland, range size related to forest structure, 400 ha in open habitats with intimate mixtures of food and cover to >1000 ha when ranges include more unplanted ground or older forest [109, 383].

No seasonal differences in range locality found in hinds in Scottish plantations [109, 383] nor Exmoor [439, 440] but found in Exmoor stags (see above) [440]. By contrast, on open hill country in Scotland, marked seasonal ranges for both sexes: lower ground used in winter and higher ground in summer. In winter largely affected by weather, snow cover and food availability. Males often found lower than females in winter, higher during July–September; both may be found at altitudes >1000 m asl in winter during temperature inversions [785].

Stags often have distinct winter, summer and rutting ranges [176, 460, 532] (see Breeding).

Dispersal: Exploratory behaviour starts within 6 months of birth, earlier in stag than hind calves. Strong fidelity to home area in females and no evidence of widespread or long-distance dispersal [176]. Many young stags leave natal area, age of dispersal varying from 1 year old in plantations to 2 or more on open ground; usually occurs at rut or just before dam next calves. Young stags wander widely and do not settle for several years until mature, when seasonal ranges are established.

Activity: Active throughout 24 h; 5–9 feeding cycles daily, 2/3 during day with longest activity periods around dusk and dawn [84, 383, 472]. When frequently disturbed, become more nocturnal [6, 240]. In open hill country, usually found at higher elevations during the day, descending to lower levels at dusk and returning to higher ground again by dawn; may cover 10 km and 750 m in altitude [224]. In forests remain in, or close to, woodland cover during daylight, venturing on to open areas from dusk to dawn [109, 383, 439, 751].

Communication: Best-known sound is the roar, made by stags during rut; in SW England called 'balving'. Roar sometimes preceded or followed by several grunts. By contrast, wapiti 'bugle': starts as a squeal followed by a prolonged bellow. Alarm call by hinds a gruff bark or series of barks. Hinds also make a low 'mooing' sound when trying to locate young calves; calf gives nasal bleat or, if alarmed, high-pitched squeal. When close together, such as at winter feeding places, both sexes give low-pitched soft grunts when approaching each other; significance uncertain. Scent produced by hinds in season detectable only at short range. Role of other scent glands unclear, but as above, scent secretions of preorbital and metatarsal glands are individually distinct and odour profile may also contain coded information on age and sex [456, 457].

Visual communication important. Rump patch flared as warning signal. If suddenly alarmed, may move off with series of stiff-legged jumps, sometimes all 4 feet together (pronking), although less common than in sika.

Low-intensity aggressive behaviour by hinds and stags by raising chin and exposing pale chin patch with ears laid flat. Stags may tilt head and antlers on one side. If warning not heeded, hinds and stags in velvet go on to back legs and box quickly with forefeet. When antlers are hard, stags fight and spar by locking antlers and twisting and pushing.

Movement: Usually slow stride or trot; when chased or disturbed, gallops for short distances; in woodlands, may lie down in cover rather than leave area when disturbed. Swims well; moves between mainland and offshore islands in Scotland and crosses rivers and lakes.

FEEDING

Versatile feeder, depending on availability of plants in various habitats, yet selective within these areas. Classified as 'intermediate' feeder from digestive anatomy and physiology and feeding style [385, 597]. In GB, best studied in Scotland [171, 427, 453, 532, 719, 728], New Forest [596] and SW England [439]. Throughout the year, grasses most important item in diet. In winter, heather, blaeberry and other dwarf shrubs more important, with brambles, holly and ivy when available. Ferns, lichens, shoots of deciduous and coniferous trees and, in coastal areas, seaweeds (especially the stipes of kelps) eaten in autumn and winter (Fig. 11.18) [453, 725, 728]. Can browse up to 180 cm by rearing up on hind legs. Eats bark of some trees, especially rowans, willows, Norway spruce and lodgepole pine. Differences in food selection between stags and hinds on open ground in Scotland [176, 725, 729]; in winter, stags eat more heather, hinds more grasses; quality of winter food eaten by hinds higher than by stags [725, 729, 785]. Some evidence that smaller-bodied hinds can displace stags from favoured feeding areas by reducing average sward height below that at which stags

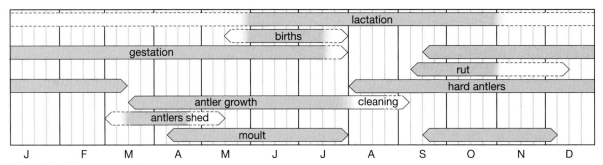

Fig. 11.17 Red deer: annual cycle.

may forage effectively; due to allometry of jaw size with body size, stags may be forced to take larger quantities of coarser forage to gain adequate dry matter intake, but have ruminal volume to cope with foods of poorer digestibility [176, 178, 398].

Estimations for energy requirements rudimentary; vary seasonally ranging from 3.5 (hinds) to 4.5 (stags) Mcal/day (15–19 MJ/day) in winter to *c*.9 Mcal/day (38 MJ/day) for lactating hinds and *c*.11.5 Mcal/day (50 MJ/day) for stags in summer [15]. Voluntary reduction in food intake in winter [427]. Hind more than doubles food intake during early lactation [23].

BREEDING

Polygynous. Sexual cycle seasonal, driven by photoperiod, secondarily affected by body condition (Fig. 11.17). Oestrus cycle *c*.18 days, gestation 225–245 days. Secondary corpora lutea found, especially in 1st breeders [717]; significance unknown. Single young, twins rare; sex ratio at birth *c*.1:1.

Rut: Usually end September–November. Stags fecund by end of 1st year and throughout the year as adults, except June. Mature stags leave bachelor groups in September and seek out hinds. Rutting areas of adult stags traditional, often several km

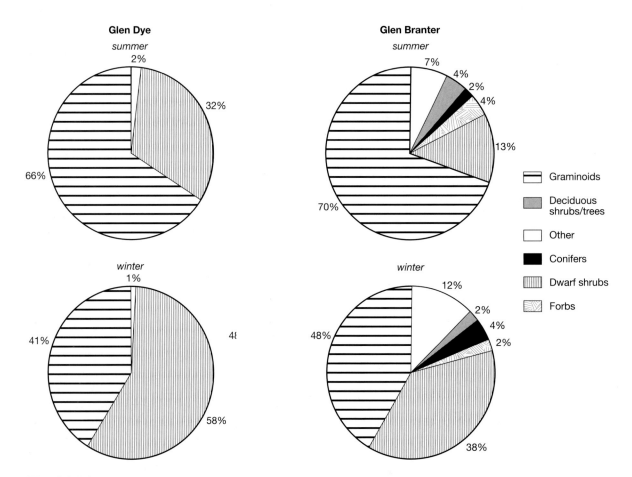

Fig. 11.18 Red deer: diet in Glen Dye and Glen Branter, summer and winter [1].

Fig. 11.19 Red deer: stag roaring – the span of the antlers, their white tips, the mane and especially the deep pitch and sustained roaring all impress both hinds and rivals. Ex-park deer, and those in wooded habitats (here, in the New Forest) develop larger antlers than those on moorland in Scotland *(photo B. Phipps)*.

Fig. 11.20 Red deer: hind suckling well-grown calf which has already shed its spotted coat *(photo B. Phipps)*.

from summer and wintering areas [719, 794]; perhaps places where stags first successful in rut [176].

Usually, stag rounds up hinds into harems which he defends against other stags. Harem size variable, according to habitat; small family groups in woodlands, 10–15 usual on hill ground with >70 recorded [717]. Larger and older stags usually rut first. Stags do not usually hold harems until 5–6 years old, although a particularly big 3-year stag was observed holding large harem [717]. Groups of unsuccessful adult and young stags (bachelor groups) gather around harems; on hill ground, usually found above dominant ('master') stag and his harem [532]. All stags have greatly reduced food intake during rut and lose *c*.14% of their pre-rut body weight [531].

Much ritualised display during rut (Fig. 11.19); wallow and spray with own urine and ejaculum, thrash vegetation and roar. Frequency and duration of roaring linked to dominance [176]. Serious fighting only between animals of comparable size. After roaring contest, animals walk side by side (parallel walk), one lowers and turns head and the pair lock antlers; fight by pushing and twisting; following fight, loser runs off and winner usually roars. Serious injuries and deaths can occur.

Fertility in females, and birthweight and viability of calves, depends on age coupled with body weight as affected by habitat quality and density [9, 10, 176, 531, 534, 633, 720]. Hinds <55 kg live weight rarely calve [55].

In most (high-quality) areas, hinds reach puberty at 15 months. In England, yearling pregnancies vary: 65% in Grizedale, Cumbria [527]; 72% in the S Exmoor fringe and 74% in Quantocks, N Exmoor and the Exe valley; 83% in the S Lake District [442]; in Suffolk all yearlings shot found to be pregnant [655]. In most Scottish woodlands, majority of hinds fertile at 15–16 months [631]; a few fertile calves and lactating yearlings found in plantations in W and SW Scotland [633]. On Scottish hill land, hinds do not usually reach threshold body weight for ovulation until 2 years 4 months or 3 years 4 months [10, 532, 717, 720]; *c*.35% of milk hinds fail to breed the following year [532].

Usual number of calves reared by females over lifetime is 4 (range 0–13); number sired by individual stags, 6 (range 0–24). Variability of fertility in hinds related to quality of home range and group size; hinds associated with smaller groups produce more calves than those in larger groups [171, 176]. Evidence that hinds in better condition dominant [177], and older hinds [481, 717] more likely to produce male calves.

Birth from mid–late May, peaking during 1st–2nd week of June, to end of July; occasionally calving observed as late as December [1]. Before giving birth, hind goes off on own, chasing away young of previous year, at times violently. Calf left lying alone for several days except during feeds; on open hill ground mother can be several kilometres away. When disturbed, newborn calves lie quite still, neck, head and ears flat out, and may remain motionless even if disturbed. Accompany mother after *c*.7–10 days. Young calves often form 'crèches' with frequent playing [224]. Weight at birth on Scottish hill ground 6.7 kg (males), 6.4 kg (females) [525]. Weaning variable; usually over by 8 months (Fig. 11.20).

POPULATION

Densities variable; most reliable data from Scotland. Varies with quality and structure of habitat and with management, especially level of culling (Table 11.7). Over some 30 000 km² of open hill land, averages 9/km² [735] with 10–15/km² common on major deer forests; >100/km² on some winter ranges [724]. In plantations, 5–15/km² common, reaching as high as 40/km² [631].

Over some 675 km² of Exmoor National Park, densities derived from sightings averaged 3.5/km² whereas dung counts suggested nearer 6/km² [439, 446]. Highest densities in wooded valleys and E fringes of the moor, lowest on more exposed W plateau. For some 95 km² of the Quantock Hills

Table 11.7 Red deer: density related to forest structure in Scottish plantations [631]

Forest structure	Density/km²		
	Galloway	Glenbranter	Glen Crippesdale
Establishment	2	2	
Pre-thicket	5	8	
Open thicket	10	12	40
Pre-felling	2	2	2

Table 11.8 Red deer: population estimates for major populations in the British Isles

Locality	Numbers	Source
Scotland (hill land)	300 000	[722]
Scotland (plantations)	20 000–50 000	[726]
SW England	10 000	[360]
East Anglia	350	[360]
Peak District	200	[360]
Hampshire	300	[360]
Cumbria	1 000	[360]
Donegal	1500–2000	[95]
Kerry	1750–2000	[95]
Wicklow	50–60	[95]
Meath/Donegal/Tyrone/Fermanagh	200	[95]

Area of Outstanding Natural Beauty, densities of 9/km² suggested from sightings [441], with concentrations of 50/km² in parts of the region based on dung counts and remote video surveillance [665]. In Ireland, on open hill in Co. Donegal, 6–8 deer/km², with 20–25/km² in coniferous woodland [1].

Scottish population increased greatly in last 40 years [722, 726], estimated to be >300 000 on hill ground [722] with 27 000–50 000 in plantations [726]. For other main populations, believed to be at least 10 000 in SW England, 1000 in Cumbria [360], <2000 in Co. Donegal and <2000 in Co. Kerry [1]. Population estimates for major populations given in Table 11.8.

Structure: Adult sex ratio variable, averaging *c.*1:1.3 to 1:1.6 stags to hinds [172]. Population structure related to density, habitat but especially to culling regimes. High-performance populations have greater proportion of young. In Scottish hill populations, calves form *c.*15% of population of each sex, and animals >8 years *c.*10%; in Exmoor, calves are *c.*25–30% of the spring population. Maximum longevity *c.*20 years [524] but few deer >16 years; a 27-year-old recorded in Richmond Park [151].

Survival: Overwinter mortality highest in calves and very old [528, 530]. Varies annually from 5 to 65% in calves; related to initial birthweight, population density, heavy rainfall during the preceding autumn, and late winter temperatures and prolonged snow cover [170, 171, 178, 179, 528, 784].

Overwinter mortality in adults related to tooth wear; associated with low winter temperatures and population density in milk hinds and yearlings of both sexes [171]. Some hinds die giving birth. Perinatal mortality of calves varies annually, can be as high as 44% [720]; related to weather during calving period [171], low birthweight and nutrition of mother during pregnancy; highest in 1st breeders [720]. Occasional mortality due to snow avalanches, lightning, fights during rut. Road traffic accidents less common than with other British deer, although locally serious; overall, thought to be *c.*1% of the population annually (National Deer Collision Project – preliminary findings [442]). Golden eagles known to predate on young calves [212]; foxes also suspected. In Europe, adults a main prey of wolves, and calves important to lynx [408].

PARASITES AND DISEASES
See [13, 266, 271, 272, 532]. Free-ranging deer thought to be relatively free of major diseases. Studied more in farmed situations.

Ectoparasites: Ticks *Ixodes ricinus* are common; also deer ked *Lipoptena cervi*, deer warble maggot *Hypoderma diani*, nostril maggot *Cephenomyia auribarbis*, a sucking louse *Solenopotes burmeisteri* and biting lice *Bovicola longicornis, B. concavifrons* and *Damalinia* spp. Effects on individuals can be important if linked to other stresses such as winter starvation; effects on populations thought to be minor [272].

Endoparasites: Wide range of gastrointestinal parasites but rarely a cause of disease. Occasionally type II ostertagiasis can occur. The tissue worm *Elaphostrongylus cervi,* lungworm *Dictyocaulus* spp. and liver fluke *Fasciola hepatica* are widely distributed in Scottish Highlands but level of parasitism generally low [59, 548]. Main tapeworms include adult stage of *Moniezia benedeni* and the cysticercus stage of *Taenia hydatigena* (adult parasite in carnivores).

Viruses: Serological evidence of infections with infectious bovine rhinotracheitis, bovine virus diarrhoea, reoviruses 1 and 2 and adenovirus A [450], but not likely that red deer form an important reservoir of these diseases of cattle and sheep in the UK. Ocular disease due to bovine herpesvirus 1 has been recorded in farmed red deer calves [555a]. Antibodies to this virus are common in free-living deer and probably account for the serological reactions to infectious bovine rhinotracheitis [548]. Tick-borne viruses such as louping ill have been detected in both wild and farmed red deer but do not appear to cause clinical illness [272, 647] unless other predisposing stresses present, such as tick-borne fever *Ehrlichia phagocytophilia.* Farmed deer particularly susceptible to malignant catarrhal fever, which is thought to be carried by sheep. Antibodies to rickettsial disease tick-borne fever and *Borrelia burgdorferi* (cause of Lyme disease) also detected. Red deer not directly involved in the transmission of Lyme disease to humans, but act as a reservoir for adult ticks [272].

Bacteria: Those isolated include *Mycobacterium avium* [503] and *M. avium paratuberculosis* (responsible for Johne's disease), *M. bovis* [215, 272] and *Salmonella* spp.; infections uncommon [512]. Bovine TB only occasional in wild red deer, with one hotspot in SW England in an area of unnaturally high density [232]; only 1 reported from Scotland, 10/78 N Ireland and 9/340 in the Irish Republic [625]. Other bacteria include *Yersinia pseudotuberculosis, Clostridium* spp. and *Sarcocystis* spp. Infections common but mortality rare unless under other stress.

Antibodies to the protozoan parasites *Babesia* and *Toxoplasma gondii* have been found [4]. At least 7 genera of commensal intestinal ciliates are known to occur [217].

Tumours occur sporadically in wide range of organs and tissues.

SPECIES INTERACTIONS

Compete with hill sheep in Scotland [102, 171, 562] but complementary grazers with cattle [102, 305]. In Scottish plantations, red and roe densities inversely related; high red deer numbers thought to depress roe performance and density [451, 452]. Red deer thought to be adversely affected by high numbers of sika [113, 632]. In the New Forest, evidence of niche overlap in food use between red deer and sika (all seasons), also red and fallow during winter and spring [594, 602]; high overlap in habitat use with fallow [66] but no direct evidence of competitive effects on behaviour or population dynamics. In deer parks, fallow deer performance is lower when red deer are present [438, 611].

Red deer and sika hybridise, with fertile offspring [3, 31, 354, 640]. See p.594 for more details. In Scotland, thought that hybridisation occurs when sika stags colonise forestry plantations and mate with red deer hinds [573]. F_1 hybrids probably a rare event, but backcrossing common, leading to rapid introgression [569]. After F_1 generation, hybrids difficult to detect in the field. There are more 'sika-like' than 'red-like' hybrids in Scotland [572].

RELATIONS WITH HUMANS

Long association with humans. Red deer the commonest ungulate in Mesolithic and Neolithic middens [407]. Important food of early humans; antlers and bones used for tools, weapons and ornaments, skins for clothing.

In early historical times, hunting reserved for nobility. Deer-stalking in Scotland became fashionable in 19th and 20th centuries [797]. Hunting deer with hounds and on horseback now only practised in Republic of Ireland, where 'carted' deer are hunted (park deer kept for hunting with hounds, returned alive afterwards to the park, under licence from the National Parks and Wildlife Service; see Chapter 4).

Competition with livestock, agriculture and forestry, especially since World War I. Can have a major impact on commercial forestry and conservation of some native plants, especially woodland [298, 302, 532, 721, 730]. Serious damage to agricultural crops (especially cereals) [610, 615, 686]; mostly localised within individual fields, and in SW England found not to be significant when considered at whole farm or regional level [238, 447, 665].

Over the last 30 years or so red deer have been farmed commercially [56].

Legislation: See Chapter 4 for details of animal welfare and management, poaching controls and appropriate firearms; also close seasons.

Red and sika sympatric in many deer parks for a long time, so there is doubt over genetic 'purity' of both species, many may be hybrids. This has consequences for introductions of park or non-native deer into populations. Both sika and red deer therefore placed on Schedule 9 of Wildlife and Countryside Act 1981 (Variation of Schedule 9, Order 1999 No. 1002); this makes it illegal for either species to be introduced to particular Hebridean islands where only red deer occur, in order to preserve the 'red deer genotype'.

Deer Commission for Scotland (successor to the Red Deer Commission) is the lead agency there, under the Deer (Scotland) Act 1997, to advise on the protection of agriculture, forestry and the natural heritage and on the welfare and management of all deer species. No single body has comparable responsibility in England and Wales or N Ireland, although the 'Deer Initiative' (a broad partnership of statutory and voluntary organisations) has been set up to promote greater cooperation in deer management. In Republic of Ireland, deer are the responsibility of the National Parks and Wildlife Service.

LITERATURE

Popular accounts of local herds include [273, 514, 515, 666]. Good general references on deer [794, 798]. Scientific reviews [171, 176, 532].

AUTHORS

B.W. Staines, J. Langbein & T.D. Burkitt

Sika *Cervus nippon*
Cervus nippon Temminck, 1838; Japan.

Male – stag; female – hind; young-of-year – calf.

RECOGNITION

Medium-sized deer, intermediate between red and roe, but with considerable variation between populations in both size and appearance. Summer coat chestnut or fawn, marked with distinct white spots (Plate 11). Formosan sika retain spotted pelage throughout the year, but other races lose spotting in winter. The winter coat is grey to almost black, notably thick and dense, and mature stags develop pronounced cape or mane.

Characteristic white caudal patch, outlined in black; may be erected or flared in alarm. This 'target' very similar to fallow deer, hinds readily confused with fallow does. However, the black-striped tail of sika extends only about halfway across the target (tail of fallow deer extends right across the caudal patch, and is almost always in motion). Facial appearance of sika is also distinctive, a 'frown', with dark lines above the eyes and a contrasting paler area between them emphasising the anterior raised margins of the frontal bones.

Sika stags have relatively simple antlers, with no more than 4–5 points each (a clear field character); brow tine more acute than in red stag, bez tine absent (Fig. 11.13).

SIGN

Footprints: Not a good diagnostic sign, easily confused with those of roe or fallow or yearling red deer if also present.

Faeces: Likewise very similar to those of roe and young red deer. Defecation rate estimated at 25 pellet groups/day [508].

Wallows and rutting pits are established by mature males during the breeding season.

Other sign: As other deer, stags thrash and fray trees with their antlers both to remove velvet and in territorial advertisement during the rut. Perhaps the most characteristic (and persistent) sign of sika is scarring of tree trunks with deep vertical grooves with antlers by mature males (bole-scoring), associated primarily with the rut, but scars persist throughout the year and rarely associated with other deer.

DESCRIPTION

Very variable (see Measurements, below). 2 main forms occur within British Isles: a larger race originating in mainland Asia and the island of Taiwan and a smaller race introduced from Japan. Only Japanese form has established successfully in the wild; show marked variation in size, some populations extremely small and stocky (females as little as 50 cm at the shoulder, males 70–80 cm) and others more nearly size of fallow deer (100–120 cm at the shoulder). Matched by variation in body weight (see Measurements, below). Sexual dimorphism well marked, adult males 30–40% larger than females.

Pelage: In all sika, the summer coat is chestnut or fawn, marked with distinct white spots either side of dark vertebral stripe; in the mainland Manchurian race, base colour is a very distinct deep chestnut red. Taiwanese sika retain their spotted pelage throughout the year; in other races the spotting is lost in winter coat, which is grey to almost black. Winter coat notably thick and dense, mature stags develop a pronounced cape or mane (Fig. 11.21). Newborn calves are various shades of brown, from dark chocolate to nearly yellow, marked with white spots; this calf coat is partially retained until the 1st winter moult in October–November.

White caudal patch, outlined in black, characteristic; may be erected or flared in alarm. Tail, white with a black stripe of variable thickness, extends only partway across this caudal patch (cf. fallow deer). Facial appearance of sika also distinctive, dark lines above the eyes and contrasting paler area between them emphasising the anterior raised margins of the frontal bones. Metatarsal glands on hock (see Scent glands, below) usually white and very distinct.

Moult: Starts in May and complete by July. Winter coat develops in September and coat change complete by early November. Stags develop thick manes during the rut which persist throughout winter. The 1st, calf, moult occurs from 2–3 months after birth, but is inconspicuous and calf coat may be partially retained till 1st winter coat develops in October–November.

Nipples: 2 pairs, inguinal.

Scent glands: Pronounced metatarsal gland (hock gland) exuding a waxy material which impregnates surrounding hair. Also very obvious preorbital gland, which appears particularly active in rutting males, when it secretes a milky fluid that may appear clearly on cheeks. No interdigital gland, but whole tail is believed to be glandular.

Skull: Much shorter than red deer, with short pointed rostrum.

Teeth: Milk teeth 0.1.3.0/3.1.3.0; permanent dentition 0.1.3.3/3.1.3.3. Eruption sequence identical to red deer, and as with that species, used to estimate age.

Antlers: Relatively simple, characteristically develop up to 4 points only on each side; bez tine absent. Brow tines characteristically present at an acute angle to the main beam (cf. red deer, where angle between brow tine and main beam is >90°). Stag calves begin to develop pedicles at 6–7 months, and simple spiked antlers in 2nd year. These replaced in the 3rd year by antlers bearing brow, trez and top tines; full head of 8 points developed in following season. Antlers are cast each year around April–May and the new growth remains in velvet through May–August. Antlers are cleaned during late August–early September; older stags tend to finish slightly earlier than younger males.

Chromosomes: 2n = 64–68 in both pure sika and red × sika hybrids; number variable due to Robertsonian fusions [823].

MEASUREMENTS

Marked variation between populations in body size, recorded differences in shoulder height for Japanese sika of females 50–100 cm; males 70–120 cm. All races and subspecies show pronounced sexual dimorphism with adult males some 30–40% larger than females. Similar variation in recorded weights for Japanese sika (Table 11.9). Such variation in weight is not atypical; weights of Killarney [1] and Dorset animals [608] are very similar to those reported from populations at Mohnesee, Germany [433], or from N Moravia in the Czech Republic [819], while the weights of animals from the New Forest, or from Scottish forests [635], are very similar to published weights for sika in Maryland, USA [265].

Comparisons of body weights of animals of known age suggest that hinds may not reach full body size until 2–3 years old. Stags continue to gain weight for a further 2 years, maturing fully at 5 years [424, 433].

Table 11.9 Sika: mean weights from different British populations

	Males		Females	
	Yearlings	Mature	Yearlings	Mature
Age in months	16–20	>20	16–20	>20
Lulworth, Dorset	42	63	35	40
New Forest, Hants	33	50	–	31
Killarney, Ireland	39	57	34	44
Scotland		40		31

Average whole body weights (kg), recalculated from cull statistics (either carcass weights, measured after the removal of the viscera; or dressed carcass weights, after removal of viscera, head and feet). Dressed carcass weight (New Forest, Scotland) c.87% of whole carcass weight for males, 90% for females; whole carcass weight (Dorset, Killarney) c.76% of live body weight for both sexes.

TAXONOMY AND RELATIONSHIPS

Native to Japan and Taiwan, and adjacent mainland of E Asia (Fig. 11.22), where a number of distinct geographical races, such as Chinese, Manchurian, Taiwanese and Japanese forms, recognised; up to 13 distinct subspecies by some authorities [256]. However, the taxonomy is confused. Also much mixing of stocks, particularly on the mainland, so now a continuum of intermediate forms. Some evidence that many of the mainland forms themselves ancient hybrids between sika and red deer or sika and Chinese wapiti [304, 486]. Many of the putative subspecies are thus poorly defined; general consensus now that all sika broadly grouped into 2 main forms: the rather smaller sika *Cervus nippon nippon* from the Japanese islands, and *C. n. hortulorum*, comprising the mainland Asiatic and Taiwanese forms [605, 632, 635]. Sika of both races have been introduced to GB, but only the Japanese subspecies has successfully established in the wild [486, 573, 632].

Sika are congeneric with red deer *(Cervus elaphus)* and the 2 species produce fertile hybrids (see p. 594).

VARIATION

Extensive variation is recorded between populations in size and body weight (above; Measurements). Reflects differences between founder population, extent of hybridisation with red deer, effects of habitat and density [605].

DISTRIBUTION

Despite introduction to numerous deer parks in 19th century, sika are not widely established in

Fig. 11.21 Sika: stags, in dark winter coats, producing the browse line that is typical of any area where deer densities are high *(photo B. Phipps)*.

the wild in England, restricted to a few localised populations. Strong populations in New Forest,

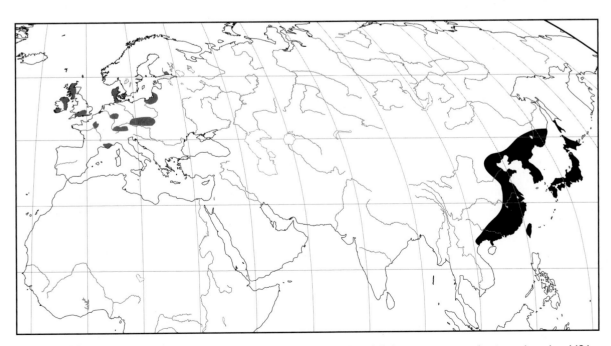

Fig. 11.22 Sika *Cervus nippon*: native (black) and introduced (grey) Palaearctic range; also introduced to USA and New Zealand.

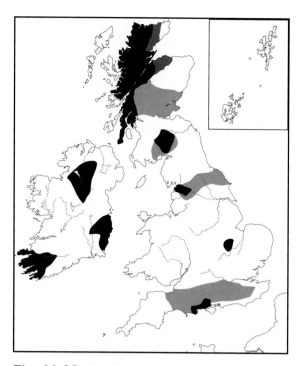

Fig. 11.23 Sika *Cervus nippon*: range in the British Isles; populations in the Wicklow Mountains, S Lake District and elsewhere are now hybrid populations of red × sika.

Poole basin (SE Dorset), Bowland (Lancashire) and Lake District (Fig. 11.23). Smaller populations in Northamptonshire and Bedfordshire, recently colonised areas around Oxfordshire/Buckinghamshire and Oxfordshire/Wiltshire/Gloucestershire borders. Also on Lundy island, and Brownsea island in the Poole basin.

New Forest population currently 150–200 animals, Bowland also *c.*200 animals [360], <100 maintained on Lundy. Most extensive population in England, in Dorset, now extending into Devon, probably <2000 [360, 723]. Absent from Wales. In Scotland, extremely well-established and widespread, with some 14 000 km² colonised by *c.*10 000 individuals. Main populations in Argyll, Inverness-shire, Peebles-shire, Ross and Cromarty, and Sutherland, although actively extending their range [3, 360].

In S Ireland, major populations in Killarney (believed to be pure Japanese sika), Limerick, Donegal and Wicklow. In N Ireland, significant populations associated with the old deer park of Colebrooke, Co. Fermanagh, and in Tyrone, probably continuous with populations in Donegal. Smaller populations were established as escapes from deer parks in Monaghan and Down, but the current status of these is unknown.

In addition, sika still widely maintained in deer parks, with *c.*1000 Japanese sika and 500 Manchurian or Taiwanese sika [360].

HISTORY

Widely introduced to much of C Europe (including Austria, Czech Republic, France, Germany, Poland), New Zealand and a number of states of the USA, where feral populations remain in Maryland, Virginia, Texas and North Carolina. Introduced into British Isles in 1860 when Zoological Society of London presented with both *C. n. nippon* and *C. n. hortulorum* [794]. In the same year Viscount Powerscourt introduced Japanese sika into his deer park at Enniskerry in Ireland [587]. Numerous further introductions were made up until the 1930s, but few of these came directly from Asia; most were derived from Powerscourt [632].

Only 2 later populations are known to derive directly from Japan, at Dawyck (Peebles-shire) and Pixton Park (Devon) [632], although the origins of some other populations are not recorded; those in the New Forest appear possibly also of pure, non-hybrid status [235, 609]. Sika from deer parks and private collections escaped or were deliberately released to establish feral populations; their history and subsequent spread in England and Scotland is reviewed in [632].

HABITAT

Primarily associated with acid soils, most populations being established in areas of coniferous plantations and adjacent heath. The relative preference for different forest structures is reflected in the range of densities recorded (Table 11.10) [113]. Adaptable, and may be encountered in a wide range of other conditions including estuarine reed beds (e.g. at Arne, Dorset). Appear to be dependent on woodland cover, however, and less able to adapt to completely treeless conditions than red deer [723].

In acid coniferous woodland, have predictable pattern of habitat use, lying up in dense thickets during the day and moving out to feed at night in

Table 11.10 Sika: densities of in different growth stages of coniferous forests in Scotland, from direct observation [113]

Forest type	Density (deer/km²)
Young plantation	2.3–4.0
Pre-thicket	4.0–14.0
Thicket	10.3–29.8
Pre-felling	
(pole stage and mature)	8.0–11.0

Table 11.11 Sika: patterns of habitat use (% time in each habitat type) for in an area of coniferous woodland (Wareham, Dorset) and in more mixed woodland (New Forest, Hampshire) [496]

	% time in each habitat type			
	Winter	**Spring**	**Summer**	**Autumn**
Wareham				
Deciduous woodland	4	2	0	7
Young growth conifer				
(thicket and prethicket)	35	46	51	36
Mature conifer	0	0	0	0
Rides and clearings	3	2	4	2
Agricultural fields and heaths	58	50	45	55
New Forest				
Deciduous woodland	48	41	30	53
Young growth conifer				
(thicket and pre-thicket)	35	46	52	28
Polestage/mature conifer	6	4	7	7
Rides and clearings	9	7	9	11
Agricultural fields and heaths	2	2	2	1

the more open communities within forest or on open ground beyond, with little change in the overall pattern of use of available habitats between seasons (Table 11.11; [496]).

In New Forest, occupy more varied environment of acid grasslands, heathland, broadleaved and coniferous woodland. General pattern of habitat use much the same, but make greater use of deciduous woodlands for feeding, use open fields and heaths less [496].

SOCIAL ORGANISATION AND BEHAVIOUR

Social organisation: Outside rut, sexes strongly segregated; in most populations stags and hinds occupy distinct geographical ranges for much of the year. Although commonly considered a 'herding' species, sika are one of the less social deer [614]. From the end of winter to September, the majority of animals solitary or (hinds) a single animal accompanied by a calf and perhaps a yearling; in Dorset and Hampshire, 95% of females seen through spring and summer were solitary hinds or single females and followers, most stags were also solitary individuals [495, 614]. In September, rut causes aggregation and more groups contain adults of both sex; these larger aggregations persist until March or April, when females drift away to calve. Even during this winter period however, sika rarely observed in groups of >5–6. Groups appear very temporary associations formed as animals coincide in favoured feeding areas. Observations on marked sika hinds in Wareham Forest, Dorset, showed little consistency of group composition or individual association from one day to the next [391, 392]; these social 'groups' are thus extremely fluid in composition.

Group size very responsive to habitat; mean group size in denser habitats, such as coniferous woodland or closed oak woods, usually 1–2 individuals, with larger groupings generally being encountered in more open habitats (Table 11.12). Group size even varies in relation to density of different growth stages within commercial coniferous plantations [113].

Home range: Individual deer have relatively small home ranges. In Killarney National Park in Ireland, mature hinds used ranges of only 18–22 ha, adult stags 45–55 ha and young stags 60–70 ha. Little work has been done on ranging

Table 11.12 Sika: typical group sizes recorded in a range of different habitat types in England [496]

	Winter	Spring	Summer	Autumn
Deciduous woodlands	2–3	2	1–2	2–3
Plantation conifer	1–2	2–3	1–2	1–2
Pre-thicket conifer	2	2	1–2	1–2
Polestage conifer	2	1–2	1–2	1–2
Rides and clearings	2	2–3	1–2	1–2
Heathland	2–6	2–4	2	2–3
Agricultural fields	2–7	2–7	2–5	2–7

behaviour elsewhere in the British Isles, but preliminary radio-tracking studies in 2 areas of N Scotland suggest similar range areas [490].

Active: Throughout the 24 h where undisturbed, with peaks of activity at dawn and dusk. Become more markedly crepuscular or nocturnal in areas of high disturbance [614].

Senses and communication: Both sexes utter a brief, high-pitched squeal when alarmed, with call directed towards object of suspicion. At the same time, alerted animal often moves gradually towards source of alarm to investigate more closely; a deeper alarm 'bark' precedes immediate flight. Young calves use high-pitched wavering bleat, not unlike the mewing of a buzzard, when calling for mothers, and hinds use a deeper, stronger bleat when searching for their calves. Young stags also make a submissive bleat when threatened by the approach of a dominant male, while mature stags may make a subdued 'mee-mee-mee' call as they approach and follow hinds during rut [710].

Male vocalisations peak in rut, when stags produce a characteristic high-pitched whistle, audible up to 1 km away (very different from roaring of red stags or belching of fallow bucks). Whistles repeated, 3–5 in a bout lasting 7–10 s overall. Stags may commonly also make a deeper, moaning call during the rut (more like that of fallow or red deer) which does not carry so far.

Preorbital gland of males particularly active during rut, when may visibly secrete a white milky fluid which trickles down the cheeks; also secretes a simple series of volatiles at other times of year. Odours from preorbital and metatarsal gland are individually distinct; secretions from metatarsal gland contain coded information about sex and probably age of signaller [455, 456, 457].

FEEDING

Sika from coniferous forest and heathland habitat have a high intake of grasses and heather in all seasons, proportion of grasses to heather ranging from 30:50 to 70:20 [495, 497, 626]. A variety of other items contribute the remainder of the diet (pine needles, bark, gorse) but no single item comprises >8% at any time [497]. Few comparable data are available for (e.g.) reedbed populations or others (but see [234]).

In New Forest, consume considerable quantities of both deciduous and coniferous browse, particularly in winter when up to 23% of the total food intake. In spring and summer, New Forest sika feed extensively on grasses and heather, but diet far more varied, includes significant amounts of forbs, deciduous browse, gorse and conifer needles. In autumn, only 25% of diet composed of heather and grass, bulk of intake being coniferous browse, gorse, holly and acorns. In winter, there is a further increase in the intake of pine needles, when <20% of the diet consists of grasses [497].

BREEDING

Rut: Begins towards the end of September or early October (depending on location and latitude). Often more protracted than other deer; whistling stags may be heard from the end of August to mid December, exceptionally as late as mid February (Fig. 11.24). Early studies suggested that stags mark and defend mating territories in woodland within hind range [391, 392]. Marked by fraying and bole-scoring of perimeter trees and thrashed ground vegetation such as heather bushes. More recently shown that mating strategy within sika extremely flexible, stags adopting different strategies depending on circumstances [598, 614, 752]. Males may defend rutting territories, but may collect and defend a harem, as do red deer, or simply patrol areas of superior food quality within

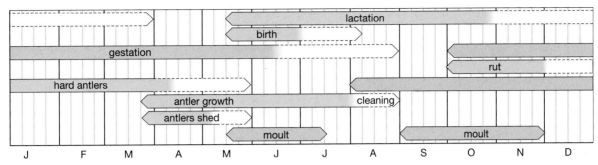

Fig. 11.24 Sika: annual cycle.

the female range and cover oestrus hinds when encountered [598, 614]. Simple breeding lek has also been reported in certain C European populations [37]. Probably, as in other deer, the mating strategy depends on the male's own age and dominance status, density and distribution of females and degree of competition experienced from other breeding males [448, 598, 752].

Calves born early May–late June, after 220 days gestation. Poorly synchronised breeding cycle means that not uncommonly newborn calves found in August or September; infrequently as late as October. Single calf usual, but infrequently twins [167, 225].

Most hinds first breed as yearlings, and thereafter each year. In 3 English populations (New Forest, Lulworth and Bovington) conception rates amongst yearling females were *c*.80%; for adult hinds, *c*.80% (New Forest) and 90% (Dorset populations) respectively [1, 608]. In 6 Scottish populations, yearling conception rates 80% or above, pregnancy rates among adults mostly 85–100% [113]. Pregnant calves not uncommon in culled sika from most Scottish and many English populations [113, 126]; uncertain whether these precocious breeders would have been able to maintain the pregnancy to term, or successfully rear the resultant calf.

No clear evidence for any density-dependent reduction in fecundity among British sika [113, 608, 623] with recorded densities up to 35/km². Recruitment rates to the adult population are not, however, as high as such high fecundity rates might suggest, since high early juvenile mortality and only 40–50% of calves born may survive to the beginning of their 1st winter [557].

POPULATION

Population density: Tends to be lower in GB than reported from Japan (40/km², with peak winter densities of 57.5/km² [424]; densities in a managed population at Lulworth in Dorset *c*.11–12/km² [608]). Substantial populations may build up in suitable habitat: in 2nd rotation forests in Co. Wicklow, densities of sika 14–44/km²; in younger forest, 42–45/km² [477].

Numbers: Estimated at 11 500 in GB (2500 England, 9000 Scotland) [360], but increased substantially, perhaps doubled, since then; estimated at 20 000–25 000 in Ireland [363].

Population dynamics and dispersal: Most sika populations in GB are closely managed and rates of increase slow. Even at highest densities in British Isles, no evidence for density-dependent suppression of fertility or survival; potential rates of increase in areas of continuous habitat in Scotland *c*.20% per year [723]. While populations in N Scotland are expanding rapidly in both numbers and distribution, populations in England and in some parts of W Scotland are spreading only slowly. This difference seems to reflect availability of suitable habitat for colonisation, particularly availability of young coniferous plantations. In areas of continuous good habitat, sika show a steady expansion in range, estimated in Argyll at 3–5 km/year, whereas localised populations occupy small pockets of suitable habitat for long periods with no movement beyond the established range, followed by a sudden and rapid irruption [605].

Young males disperse first. At the leading edge of a wave of expansion, may be encountered up to 50 km from the main population, and stags may become established in an area 10–15 years before the first hinds [632, 723].

Most free-living populations managed, and culling mortality imposed is probably major source of death amongst adults. Very occasional involvement in road traffic accidents has been reported from England. Maximum recorded lifespan in the wild 15–16 years, up to 26 years in captivity [559].

PARASITES AND DISEASES

Ectoparasites: Of 139 from New Forest, 127 were infested by tick *Ixodes ricinus*, and 45 carried ked *Liptotena cervi*. In Ireland, sika also commonly infested with ticks and keds; infestations of sucking and biting lice *Solenopotes bumeisteri* and *Damalinia meyeri sikae* have been recorded [705].

Endoparasites: 47 different gastrointestinal helminths recorded from British sika [246, 362] although animals rarely carry a heavy individual burden. Most commonly recorded species is *Ostertagia asymmetrica*. Liver fluke *Fasciola hepatica* recorded in 2/139 carcasses from New Forest [5].

Bacteria: Both bovine and avian TB recorded; 2 cases of bovine TB identified in Knapdale, Argyll, 1990–2000, and in 5/240 sika culled in S England, 1971–1996 [231]. 6 positives/153 carcasses taken in Co. Tyrone (N Ireland) (3.9%) in 1996/97 season and 5 (3.8% of sample) of sika shot in 1984 in Co. Wicklow but 0/28 from Co. Fermanagh [231, 237].

British sika seem prone to a form of white-muscle disease, a wasting dystrophy of the muscles, appearing in its most acute form as a post-traumatic myopathy following physical stress such as chases by dogs or live-capture operations [1, 5]. Mortality may result up to 48 h after the incident.

INTERACTIONS WITH OTHER SPECIES

Hybridisation with red deer: Occurs where distribution overlaps with that of congeneric red deer, produces fertile offspring [2, 3, 31, 354, 356, 640], thereby threatening the genetic integrity of native red deer stocks. Where substantial populations of both red and sika occur in the wild, hybridisation appears to be rather uncommon; [354, 356, 486]. However, once a 1st cross has been established (perhaps in captivity), further hybridisation or back-crossing to either parental type is rapid.

Most of the 'sika' populations of England and Scotland are in fact hybrids [235, 303, 485, 609, 640]. The only remaining populations that may be pure Japanese sika are in the New Forest and around Peebles and Moray in Scotland.

Hybridisation is now also widespread in Ireland, with populations in Wicklow mountains entirely hybrid status and only the animals of the Muckross peninsula, Killarney believed to be pure sika stock [363].

Competition with other species of ungulates: Sika sympatric with red deer in most areas; exceptions are the Scottish Borders and parts of England; generally sympatric with roe deer in England and Scotland, and with fallow deer in most of their English range, N Argyll and Perthshire. In all these cases there is potential for feeding competition, and with red–sika populations there is also the possibility of mate competition. Very few objective studies. For New Forest, analyses of overlap in both habitat use and diet with other deer (red, roe and fallow), also

cattle and horses [594, 602], show considerable potential for competition with fallow, yet no evidence that affect numbers [616], perhaps because all species strongly managed. Recent analysis of overlap in habitat use and diet between red deer and sika, as well as assessment of effects of sika numbers on red deer population dynamics in Killarney National Park, shows no significant effect [95].

RELATIONS WITH HUMANS

Impact on forestry, agriculture and conservation habitats: Considerable impact where sika at high density. So far, little significant damage has been reported to conservation habitats, but local populations have damaged agricultural crops in England. May cause considerable damage to commercial forestry through browsing of both lateral and leading shoots, much as by red deer in similar contexts, and by bark-stripping in hard winters [3, 113, 477, 634]. Mature trees may suffer additional damage through bole-scoring (see above), which appears to be a peculiarity of sika [108, 449], more severe on coniferous than deciduous trees [108].

In areas of high density, sika may also have significant impacts on ground vegetation on open heathland and/or wetland areas (reed beds, salt marshes), changing vegetational structure and species composition [234].

Management and legal status: Covered by same legislation as other deer; close seasons as red deer (see Chapter 4). Because of damage to forestry once populations reach higher densities, there is growing concern about control of sika populations within GB. Many populations already closely managed in an attempt to maintain population sizes, prevent further increases or actively reduce numbers. In Scotland, sika regarded as a considerable threat, particularly to forestry; rigorous control, with 'every practicable measure taken to reduce populations' [3]. Recently added to Schedule 9 of the Wildlife and Countryside Act 1981, so translocation to areas outside their existing range now illegal. Additionally, because of hybridisation with red deer, cannot be introduced to specified Hebridean islands that have 'pure' red deer.

LITERATURE
Major reviews of origins and British status [3, 632]; genetics [303]; social organisation and behaviour, diet, habitat use [113, 496, 497, 597]. General overview [605].

AUTHOR
R.J. Putman

GENUS *Dama*

A small genus of 2 closely related species, sometimes regarded as subspecies, European fallow deer *D. dama* and the Mesopotamian (Persian) fallow, *D. mesopotamica*. The latter is larger and differs in antler morphology [139], but the two hybridise in captivity. Characterised by palmate antlers (Fig. 11.13), and by details of skeleton. Sometimes included in *Cervus*, but closer phylogenetically to extinct 'Irish elk' *Megaloceros giganteus* [470].

Fallow deer *Dama dama*

Cervus dama Linnaeus, 1758; Sweden (introduced). European fallow deer; *gafrdanas* (Welsh).

Male – buck; female – doe; young – fawn.

RECOGNITION

Only British deer with palmate antlers (Plate 11). Intermediate between red and roe in size. Colour ranges from white to nearly black. Typically, reddish fawn with white spots along flanks and back in summer coat, turning dull brown to grey with indistinct or no spots in winter; black vertebral stripe extends along dorsal surface of long (*c*.14–24 cm) tail. Other colour varieties (especially black) may predominate in some geographical areas.

Confusion most likely with sika (similar size): in summer coat, spots less apparent on sika; sika winter coat dark, similar to black fallow. Both have white rump patch edged with black and black line down tail; however, tail extends well below the rump in fallow (only 2/3 down the rump in sika) and twitches continuously when feeding. Hair over metatarsal gland on hock similar colour to surrounding hair (not conspicuous, white, as in sika).

FIELD SIGNS

Tracks and trails: Cloven footprints intermediate in size and shape between red and roe deer, and similar to sika: may also be confused with those of sheep and goats, but narrower and with stronger crescent shape than roe deer or domestic stock. Size of prints varies with age, sex, substrate and gait.

Faeces: Variable, similar to those of other deer. Black, cylindrical pellets up to 2 × 1.5 cm, usually with one end pointed and one indented. Deposited in piles (crotties) or clumped together, but may appear as a string if the animal is moving. Number of daily defecations varies from 22–28 in spring/summer to 14–18 over winter [507].

Other field signs: Bucks fray trees when cleaning velvet from their antlers, and during rut thrash branches and ground vegetation, but these signs not species-specific and difficult to distinguish from those of other deer. Bark also eaten by either sex from trunks, exposed roots of trees, and fallen branches, mainly in winter and spring if food resources are scarce. Scraped areas, often beneath

Fig. 11.25 Fallow deer: a park herd with a mixture of white, dark, menil and typical spotted bucks. The menil buck (3rd rump from left) shows the characteristically paler markings on tail and rump, which are black on typical bucks. These bucks, in high summer, show still-growing antlers, in velvet, and illustrate the variation in size and shape that goes with age (*photo J. Langbein*).

mature trees, and with trampled-in dung and pungent urine are indicative of rutting bucks in the area, but several smaller scrapes (e.g.50 × 25 cm) may also occur some way from their main rutting stands.

DESCRIPTION

Pelage: Common colour variety has rich fawn summer coat with many prominent white spots on flanks and back, and black vertebral stripe. Tail white underneath, black line on top. White rump patch bordered by black curved line. In winter, coat becomes dull grey-brown with spots indistinct or absent. Menil variety paler, retains spots in winter and lacks black border to rump patch (Fig. 11.25). Black variety usually slightly dappled but has no white at all. Many intermediate colour varieties. In all, belly is always paler than flanks. True albinos very rare but animals with white or off-white coats are common; most of these animals are sandy coloured at birth, becoming white when about a year old. Spots are dominant to no spots, black is dominant to brown, black and brown are dominant to white [47].

Male has prominent brush of hairs from penis sheath visible from *c.*3 months, and female has tuft of long (*c.*12 cm) hairs below the vulva. Ears prominent, eyes relatively large. Dew claws present.

Moult occurs May–June; winter coat regained late September–October.

ANATOMY

Neck: Position of larynx always prominent on a buck; girth of buck's neck increases during rut.

Skeleton: Skull described in [269]; less elongated than red deer (Fig. 11.26). Average condylobasal length *c.*255 mm adult females, 275 mm adult males [438]; cf. Table 11.2 for red deer). Mandibles fully grown by *c.*3 years in females, 5 years in males [432].

Teeth: Milk teeth 0.0.3.0/3.1.3.0; permanent teeth 0.0.3.3./3.1.3.3. Incisors and incisiform canine are spatulate; 1st permanent incisor twice as wide as others. Large diastema between canine and premolar. 1–2 incisiform teeth may be absent or 1–2 upper canines may be present in either dentition [116, 119]. Molars all bicuspid except m_3 which usually has 3 cusps. Mandibular tooth eruption occurs by 5–6 months (m_1), 9–12 (i_1), 13–16 (m_2, i_2), 17–20 (i_3, c), 21–24 (m_3, p_4, p_3), 25–26 months (p_2). Deciduous 3rd cheek-tooth (dp_4) has 3 pairs of cusps, its permanent replacement has only 2 pairs. Scoring schemes devised to assess age from development and wear [81, 82].

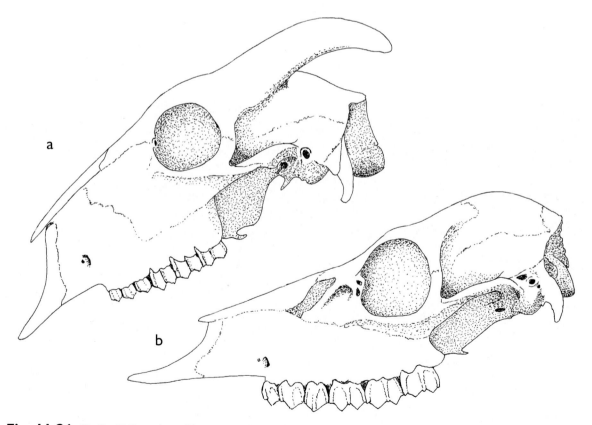

Fig. 11.26 Skull of fallow deer (b) compared with sheep (a), drawn with braincase floor orientated in the same plane. The sheep's muzzle is turned down more (grazing adaptation), and lacks the depression for a preorbital gland *(drawn by D.W. Yalden)*.

Table 11.13 Fallow deer: body measurements (mm)

	Adult males >2 years			Adult females >2 years		
	Mean	Range	n	Mean	Range	n
Total length head–rump	1660	1550–1790	14	1490	1380–1570	25
Height at shoulder	900	840–940	14	810	730–910	26
Head length	282	256–303	72	257	238–282	362
Ear length	140	130–150	14	140	120–180	25
Hindfoot length	410	400–430	14	380	360–410	26
Tail length	210	180–240	14	180	140–210	24

Table 11.14 Fallow deer: average body weight (kg) of males and females, by age class (n in brackets)

	Males			Females			Source
	5–9 months	17–21 months	>2 years	5–9 months	17–21 months	>2 year	
Live entire weights during winter (November–March)							
Survey of 11 British park populations:							[438]
Highest 'park' average	31.8	54.5	70.3	28.9	42.6	48.9	
	(26)	(5)	(34)	(20)	(17)	(23)	
Lowest 'park' average	21.4	39.8	54.5	19.3	32.4	37.5	
	(17)	(7)	(10)	(11)	(9)	(22)	
New Forest, Hampshire:	24.3	46.5	–	24.5	35	45.1	[1]
mixed forest/heath	(2)	(2)	–	(3)	(1)	(6)	
Suffolk:	34.4	55.6	65.2	30.5	43.4	44.3	[1]
agricultural land and							
conifer plantations	(8)	(6)	(1)	(4)	(1)	(6)	
Carcass weights hog-dressed[a]							
New Forest, Hants:							
mixed forest/heath	15.4	28.6	41.3	14.2	22.1	25.2	[613]
	(324)	(201)	(74)	(417)	(158)	(1008)	
Brendon Hills, Somerset:	15.9	25.3	40.2	13.1	20.2	25.1	[1]
mixed deciduous/							
coniferous woodland	(7)	(26)	(9)	(9)	(13)	(39)	
South Downs, Surrey:	–	–	–	–	22.7	24.3	[423]
mixed deciduous/							
coniferous woodland				(>30)	(>30)		
Margam Forest, S. Wales:	–	–	–		19.8	22.3	[423]
upland coniferous woodland				–	(>30)	(>30)	

[a] Live weight in skin but minus head, feet, heart, lung, abdominal viscera and blood.

Antlers: Size variable, depending on age, condition and genotype. Pedicles usually start to develop from 5–7 months. First antlers vary from 3 cm knobs to spikes up to 23 cm, and are clean of velvet at *c*.15 months. Some 2nd and 3rd sets of antlers have porous tips because velvet shed before mineralisation of the antler complete [132]. Size and complexity increases with age, length up to *c*.76 cm and inside span up to *c*.70 cm [794]. When fully developed, antlers have broad flattened 'palm'. Some palmation may occur in 3rd year, but more pronounced later (Fig. 11.13). Antlers cast April–June, older animals casting before younger ones; regrown and clean of velvet August–September. Antler development related to sexual cycle, with casting and re-growth while bucks are sexually quiescent. Mechanism of casting described [313]. Velvet shed late summer–early autumn when spermatogenesis is increasing. Directional asymmetry in antler size [14], or fluctuating asymmetry, have been reported [493, 568, 624]; degree of asymmetry related to environmental stress and decreasing with age [624].

Reproductive tract: Uterus bicornuate; paired pea-sized ovaries.

Testes: Scrotal. Annual changes in weight and histology of testes [118] and the male accessory glands described [143, 144]. Bulbourethal glands absent.

Nipples: 2 pairs, inguinal. Udder prominent in lactating females.

Sense organs: Orientation chiefly by sight, but appears fairly short-sighted; discrimination of distant stationary objects poor, though any movement quickly detected. Colour vision limited to short (blue) and middle (green) wavelength, so red–green colour blind [52, 406]. Large mobile ears give acute hearing; sense of smell also acute.

Scent glands: Preorbital, rear interdigital and metatarsal. Males also have scent gland associated with penis sheath [429], which becomes active during the rut. Preorbital gland of males may also be active during the rut, but releases no detectable volatiles in females or males at other times of year [455, 456]. Rear interdigital glands active within few weeks of birth and throughout the year. Scent of metatarsal glands individually distinct [456] but does not appear to contain specific information about age, sex or rank [457]; possibly warns conspecifics of danger [20].

Thymus: Intra- and extrathoracic parts, each of 2 lobes [150].

Chromosomes: 2n = 68, NF = 70 [338]. Karyotype illustrated in [468]; chromosomal evolution discussed in [657].

RELATIONSHIPS

Distinguished from *Cervus* by palmate antlers, lack of mane and absence of upper canine teeth. Most closely related to Mesopotamian fallow with which European fallow may hybridise [824]; not known to hybridise with any other species. Closest relative extinct 'Irish elk' *Megaloceros giganteus* [471].

MEASUREMENTS

Summarised by age and sex class in Tables 11.13, 11.14. For adults >2.5 years old, head length 260–300 mm (males), 240–280 mm (females); body length 1550–1790 mm (male), 1350–1570 (female); whole weight 50–105 kg (male), 36–55 kg (female). Tail longer than for any other British deer species. Most data available are from park populations [120, 438]. Few data on entire body weights or sizes for wild fallow in GB; but converted clean carcass weights generally intermediate within range of mean weights determined for differing park populations [423, 438]. Average weights vary among populations in relation to density and habitat, and also between years in relation to food supply (especially mast crop) [401, 613]. Growth and winter live weights of park fallow also shown to vary widely in relation to supplementary winter feeding [438, 612].

VARIATION

Conspicuous variation in coat colour: 4 main varieties known as common, menil, black and white, but many other minor variations [120]. A long-haired variety, known only from Mortimer Forest, Shropshire, has body hairs more than twice the usual length with even longer, often curly, hairs on the tail, inside the ears and on the forehead [715]. Long hair is dominant over normal-length hair and occurs in various colour varieties [709]. The hairs grow faster and over a longer period, but the character declines with age [419].

Variation in mandible size, independent of age, has been recorded [117]. Absence of 1–2 incisiform teeth noted in some populations: e.g. 18.7% (n = 107) in Richmond Park [116]. 1–2 upper canines may be present at birth but are usually lost at an early age [119].

Electrophoretic studies of blood proteins in GB revealed no evidence of polymorphism: fallow are the least variable of our cervids [571]. In Europe, polymorphisms of 5 proteins (1 from each of 5 populations) have been reported [684].

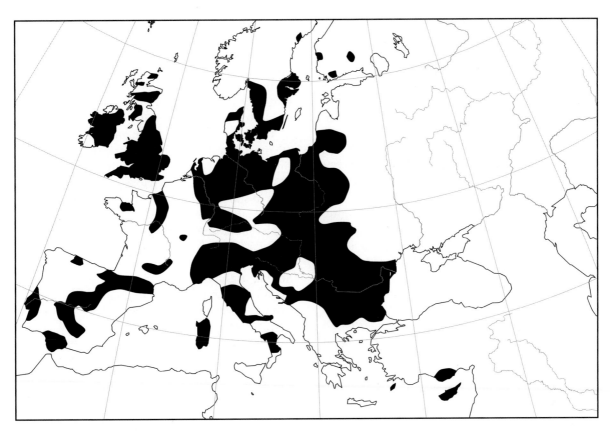

Fig. 11.27 Fallow deer *Dama dama*: native only to Anatolia, but introduced widely in Europe, and in many other parts of the world.

DISTRIBUTION

Original range believed to have been Turkey–Iran (Fig. 11.27). Introduced early in Neolithic to Mediterranean region; widely introduced elsewhere since, now established in 38 countries between 61° N and 46° S. Most widespread species of deer in British Isles (Fig. 11.28), including the islands of Anglesey, Islay, Mull, Lambay and Scarba [121]; further increases in distribution and numbers in mainland populations noted over last 30 years [360, 731, 780].

HISTORY

A large form of fallow deer (*D. d. clactoniana*) lived in GB during the Hoxnian period, 250 000 bp. By the Ipswichian period, 100 000 bp, they were only slightly larger than the present-day deer. Became extinct during the last (Würm) glaciation and survived only further S in Europe [813]. Late Pleistocene and Early Holocene evidence in Aegean and Mediterranean regions [501, 502]. Fallow reintroduced to GB and released in forests by the Normans in 11th century [739]. By 14th century there were >1800, perhaps 3200, parks where fallow were hunted [628]. From these extensive wild tracts of land evolved the landscaped deer park adjacent to a stately home, many of which remain today. All free-living fallow in the British Isles

descend from mediaeval introductions to a forest or subsequent escapees from parks, especially during and between the two World Wars [794].

Fig. 11.28 Fallow deer *Dama dama*: range in British Isles.

HABITAT

Characteristic of mature woodland, which need not be large as it is used primarily for shelter. Prefers deciduous or mixed woodland with established understorey but will colonise coniferous plantations with some open areas. Although the deer may increasingly feed within the woodlands at the time of the autumn mast crop, or overwinter when the diet includes a greater proportion of woody browse, they are not usually dependent on the woodland's food supplies. Fallow are preferential grazers [101, 402, 622], so feed on woodland rides or ground vegetation between the trees, and frequently forage in adjacent open land [749, 783]. Woodland cover used more by day both in extensive forests and in agricultural landscapes with small copses [401, 749, 783, 811]; open habitats used more at night [747]. Habitat use changes seasonally with availability of different forages. Populations based on extensive woodlands feed in open, grassland habitats most during spring and summer [401, 596, 750]. In agricultural landscapes arable and grassland habitats are grazed all year, with small woodlands used mostly for cover [749].

SOCIAL ORGANISATION AND BEHAVIOUR

Social organisation: Herding species, sometimes forms aggregations of 70–200 individuals at favoured feeding grounds, but large aggregations mostly transient. More stable groups mostly composed of 1–5 individuals, i.e. 1–2 adult females with their current and sometimes previous year's offspring [401, 593, 598, 750]. Adult male groups less stable, with unrelated individuals forming open bachelor groups for varying periods. Neither sex defends territories outside rut.

Groups of adult males and female groups (which include males <20 months of age) separate for much of the year in most populations but degree of social and spatial segregation very variable [22, 162, 274, 594, 750]. In many populations, adult males remain in female areas only during the rut, then move to distinct geographical ranges where they may associate in bachelor groups; in the New Forest >95% of groups December–September were either females with males <20 months old or exclusively male [747, 750]. Strict segregation of sexes does not occur in all cases. In some populations, males remain in the female areas up to April–May; in largely open habitats, or in populations with few adult males, aggregations containing adults of both sexes more common throughout the year.

Male–male aggression increases once antler cleaning is completed (Fig. 11.25), leading to break-up of bachelor groups. Males come into

female areas early in autumn to breed. Mature bucks compete to establish display grounds and call to attract females. Groups containing adults of both sexes are observed most frequently from autumn into early winter; rutting groups then break up and adult males drift off to re-establish single-sex groups or remain solitary.

Group size varies according to habitat and stage of annual cycle. Female groups tend to be 2–4 times larger in more open habitats than in woodland, and larger in winter/spring (mean = 4) than in summer (mean = 2) or autumn [564, 679, 750]. Males largely solitary; groups >6 rare at all times, but all-male aggregations >100 recorded in New Forest.

Social behaviour: Female groups generally hierarchical and led by a dominant doe, but social dynamics very variable, affected by population density and environmental structure. In heterogeneous environments, group sizes frequently change as animals move between closed and more open habitat types, thus few permanent social associations develop. In more homogenous environments, changes in group size are less apparent, more permanent groupings may persist, and dominance hierarchies form [254, 587].

Social interactions such as mutual grooming are relatively rare, except between does and their fawns. Play behaviour, such as sudden chases, jumps and pronking, common among young fawns in summer, when they may form small nursery groups apart or on the edge of main (feeding) herd [1]. Inter-male mounting, usually the subordinate mounting the dominant, occurs [360].

Home range: Fallow are non-territorial and home ranges overlap extensively. Long-term direct observation of individuals identified by their spot patterns in the New Forest suggest summer ranges of 50–90 ha for females, mean 110 ha for adult males; winter ranges *c.*50% larger [594]. In the Wyre Forest, ranges of some bucks estimated at only 50 ha [72]. In predominantly agricultural landscapes, interspersed with small woodlands, in Northamptonshire radio-tracking studies have shown total (year-round) ranges of 178 ha for females and 202 ha for males [811].

Dispersal: No evidence of widespread or long-distance dispersal; tolerate build-up to very high local densities, hence colonisation of new areas fairly gradual. Dispersal movements are primarily juvenile males leaving family groups prior to birth of next fawn. Although sex ratios in most populations are female biased, far more males killed in road traffic accidents [437, 604, 689].

Main peaks in crossing major roads February–April and September–November [437, 575]; latter associated mainly with increased movement of bucks to and from rutting areas.

Aggressive behaviour: Most obvious when males compete for display grounds in rut. Many contests resolved by display behaviours: groaning (see below), parallel walk, displaying antlers, or thrashing antlers against vegetation. Direct fights usually preceded by parallel walk, lowering of heads leading into clashing and locking of antlers, followed by pushing and twisting for several minutes. Serious fighting only between animals of comparable size, but deaths and serious injuries can occur, especially towards later stages of the rut as the most actively rutting bucks lose condition [438, 539, 541]. Lateral palm presentation serves to de-escalate fighting between mature bucks [409].

Movement: Gait usually a walk [221] or trot; when alarmed, will bound stiff-legged on all 4 feet (pronk), stop, look around to detect source of disturbance and then run away. Jumps well to *c.*1.7 m, but unless disturbed will usually go under or through a hedge or fence rather than over. Can swim well.

Activity: Mainly crepuscular, tending to lie up by day in cover, where they doze and ruminate. If disturbed, move off quickly and quietly. At dusk they move to foraging areas. This pattern of activity seems in part imposed by disturbance. In less disturbed areas fallow are more diurnal, grazing and lying to ruminate in the open at all hours, alternating between feeding and rumination every 3–4 h. Activity rhythms change seasonally.

Communication: Usually silent for much of the year. When rutting, male repeatedly makes a deep loud belching noise called 'groaning' which may also serve for individual recognition [642]. When suspicious of danger, especially if near young,

female gives short bark, sometimes repeated several times. Fawns <*c.*6 months bleat when disturbed or when searching for female. Female may respond with quieter bleat or whicker.

Communication and recognition among adults within social groups apparently makes use of whole body odour as well as visual cues. 79% of interactions between adults involve scent and 22% visual cues; indirect interactions between mothers and fawns mainly by sight (97%), though 22% also involved vocal cues and 18% used scent [455].

FEEDING

Gut structure suggests that fallow should be relatively unselective bulk feeders [385]. Field studies confirm they are preferential grazers. Grasses contribute >60% of forage intake from March to September, and >20% even in winter [101, 402, 783, 810]. Herbs and broadleaf browse also make a significant contribution and fallow readily browse some species of young broadleaved trees [542]. Acorns, chestnuts, beech mast and other fruits eaten in autumn–early winter. Increasing amounts of browse, e.g. bramble, holly, ivy, heather and conifer, taken in autumn and winter if grazing limited [101, 402, 596, 783]. In New Forest, does take more grass, less rushes, sedges, dwarf shrubs and browse, than bucks [622].

BREEDING

Seasonal breeder, polygynous, rut October–November, most fawns born June–July. Usually single fawn born after 234 days gestation (Fig. 11.29).

Mating system and courtship: In most populations, males move into the female areas September–October and begin to create scrapes in the ground, scent-mark trees and thrash bushes. Usually mature bucks compete to establish fairly widely separated display grounds (rutting stands). Groans attract females and reflect social status [432]. However, mating system shows considerable flexibility, with bucks adopting a

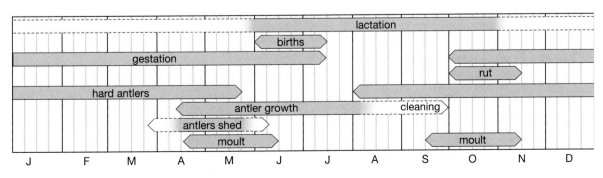

Fig. 11.29 Fallow deer: annual cycle.

number of different strategies in differing situations. While males in some areas/years establish the traditional, discrete 'rutting' stand or breeding territory, others defend only very temporary stands and thereafter consort with the harem they have attracted; others simply patrol areas offering superior forage within the females' range and cover oestrous hinds when they encounter them [448, 598, 748]. In some circumstances bucks establish leks [21, 180, 181, 448, 570, 680; reviewed in [752]. Form of mating system adopted in any population or year appears to be determined primarily by the male's own age and dominance status, the density and degree of aggregation of females, and the degree of competition experienced from other breeding males [448, 676].

Locations used for rutting may be traditional and a buck may return to the same area in successive years. Does may also be faithful to a particular rutting stand year after year, often accompanied by their daughters, making it possible for a buck to cover his own daughters. Implications of potential inbreeding considered in [709], but for this to happen a buck would need to maintain a high rank in 3 or more consecutive years which is unlikely in most populations [438, 539, 747].

Breeding bucks frequently herd females attracted to the rutting area to retain them as a compact group. The buck periodically moves among them nuzzling either neck or anogenital region. Immediately before copulation, the male will follow one doe more persistently at a slow walking pace, often tilting his head to one side, groaning, nuzzling and pushing his muzzle into her flanks or placing his neck across her back. Actual copulation is preceded by 3–20 or more attempted mountings, before successful intromission and ejaculation [438]. After intromission the buck dismounts, stands to emit a rapid series of deep groans, then takes little further interest in that doe. Although other bucks may attempt to mount the same doe later, very few does appear to be served more than once by either the same or another buck [438, 539].

Birth rate and maternal behaviour: Gestation 234±5 days [28]. Single fawn, born June or early July, although occasionally fawns born as late as November following a late, post-rut mating. Twin fetuses recorded rarely, e.g. 2/326 (0.6%) uteri examined [133]. Mean birthweight of female fawns 4.3 kg, males 4.7 kg. Yearlings mate, give birth an average of 11 days later than older does, and produce lighter offspring (mean 3.7 kg compared to 4.8 kg) [438, 444]. Lactation sometimes lasts 9 months [120], 90% of New

Forest fallow still lactating after 7 months [402]. Growth of fawns in an enclosure has been described [49], and there have been several studies on relative maternal investment in male and female fawns [48, 50, 74]. Allosuckling sometimes occurs in captive populations [51] or relatively isolated wild populations with a high level of interrelatedness among mothers (43% of all observed suckling bouts [252]). Fawns left lying in cover for several days after birth except during feeds. When disturbed, newborn fawns lie quite still. Accompany mother after *c*.10 days.

Females polyoestrous; commonly 1st breed at 16 months and then annually. Oestrous cycle *c*.22 days [27] and doe in oestrus for *c*.15 h. Ovulation and fetal development described in [25, 27] and reproductive biology reviewed in [732]. Breeding success of both adult and yearling does related to resources available in their year of birth. Where food availability is low (or population density high), proportion conceiving, especially yearling does, may be reduced from >90% in some to <15% in other populations; fawning success also closely related to body weight; few yearling does <32 kg live weight become pregnant [438, 444].

Males attain puberty at 7–14 months but social hierarchy usually prevents mating. Spermatozoa present August–March/April but spermatogenesis peaks October–November.

POPULATION

Density: Very variable; in most places controlled by humans. Overall density estimates range from <5 to 75 deer/km^2 for feral populations, with densities of >35/km^2 in agricultural and forested regions [360, 507, 731]. Often kept at densities of 100–800/km^2 in traditional deer parks, but supplementary feed necessary in winter [444, 612].

Numbers: In wild, GB, estimated as *c*.100 000 (England 95 000, Scotland 4000, Wales 1000 [360]). In Ireland *c*.2000/year legally shot, size of source population not estimated [363].

Sex ratio: Usually close to 1:1 at birth. In managed populations, selective culling usually aims towards an adult sex ratio of 1 male:3 females.

Survival and age-structure: Highest mortality amongst neonates; moderate overwinter mortality of fawns, but may be heavy (*c*.25%) during severe weather. Natural mortality of adults usually relatively low until old age. Oldest recorded female in wild 16 years, >20 years recorded in captivity. Few males in wild >8–10 years. Of 87 wild deer (45 males, 42 females) killed in road accidents or through other injuries in Essex, 21% females were <1 year; 42% males and 29% females were <2 years [120].

In park populations, mortality rates density dependent [612, 623], and populations with a higher proportion of males suffer heavier losses. Degree of cover available also important.

Most fallow populations managed by humans, who thus impose most adult mortality. Road traffic accidents significant in some areas. Foxes sometimes predate neonates, and chases by unsupervised domestic dogs occasionally cause injuries and deaths [445]. Some bucks die as result of injuries and general loss of condition towards the end of the rut.

PARASITES AND DISEASES
Reviewed in [5, 13].

Diseases: Wild deer appear generally free of disease; studied more in farmed situations. Among wild fallow, some reports of avian and bovine TB, brucellosis, tickborne fever, yersiniosis and leptospirosis. Fallow deer may be a potential, but localised, source of bovine TB infection for cattle [231, 232]. Show little clinical sign of foot and mouth disease but can become carriers. Lesions seen in deer described in [270].

Pasteurellosis has been described in park herds [422, 621]. Serological evidence of infection with bovine diarrhoea virus, reoviruses 1 and 2 and adenovirus A recorded [450]. Fallow deer, first in the New Forest [544], and subsequently in wild and park populations elsewhere in England and Wales, seropositive for *Borrelia burgdorferi* (causing Lyme disease).

Bone lesions similar to ringbone reported in 50% of fallow sample from Epping Forest [116] and abscess in jaws associated with erosion of bone not uncommon in older animals. High incidence (males 59%, females 21%) of deviation of at least one epiphysis of metapodial bones examined from one park population: also some cases of bowing of the shaft and deformity of the epiphyseal growth plate [128]. Brachygnathia [147] and chondrodystrophy [30] reported.

Ectoparasites: Biting louse, *Bovicola tibialis*, often numerous on debilitated animals. Deer keds *Lipoptena cervi* and ticks *Ixodes ricinus* also occur. The warble fly, *Cephanomyia auribarbis*, is rare in this species; the related *Hypoderma diana* may also occur.

Endoparasites: Commonly include liver fluke *Fasciola hepatica* and lungworm *Dictyocaulus viviparus*, found in 16% and 4% respectively of carcasses from S and E England [5]. Also *c.*18 species of gastrointestinal nematodes, but burden usually very slight compared with domestic stock [38] which are the prime host of most species that occur in fallow, e.g. *Capillaria bovis*, *Trichostrongylus vitrinus* and species of *Cooperia*, *Oesophagostomum*, *Ostertagia* and *Nematodirus*; 3 (*Apteragia quadrispiculata*, *Spiculopteragia spiculoptera*, *S. asymmetrica*) are predominantly deer parasites. Wild Essex fallow whose range included cattle pastures had fewer species and smaller numbers of nematodes than a park herd that grazed with sheep and red deer [39]. Park animals aged 8–9 months dying in winter had much higher burdens than comparable animals killed at that time; clinical signs suggested parasitic gastroenteritis contributed to mortality. The bladderworm cyst *Cysticercus tenuicollis* of the dog tapeworm *Taenia hydatigena* was observed in 12.3% of fallow deer in SE England [145], but only among 2% in wider survey [5].

SPECIES INTERACTIONS
In deer parks, fallow deer performance is lower when red deer are present [612], probably due to direct competition at supplementary feeding sites. Fallow, as preferential grazers, show relatively low dietary overlap with other British deer species except sika [596, 602] and, in some areas, red deer. However, where population densities of deer and other grazers are particularly high, reduction in shrub and field layers may lead to reduced suitability of the habitat for roe and muntjac. Inverse correlations between fallow and roe deer numbers in New Forest [275, 616, 693]. Fallow and red deer coexist in several parts of GB, but usually one species much more abundant at local level.

RELATIONS WITH HUMANS
Very closely associated with humans for long period, having been reintroduced to GB by the Normans primarily for hunting. Numerous hunting reserves and parks stocked with fallow deer were established throughout England (lesser extent Wales, Scotland and Ireland), from which feral populations descend. In addition to wild fallow, some 17 000 fallow are kept in deer parks [360] and a few thousand on farms.

Fallow may damage young plantings or prevent regeneration of coppice [297, 298, 599, 600]; bark-stripping of mature trees (both coniferous and deciduous) can be a problem in hard winters. Severe damage to ground flora reported in some places, e.g. to oxslip *Primula elatior* in Hayley Wood, Cambridgeshire [627]. Bucks may also inflict considerable damage on trees by thrashing them with their antlers in late summer.

Fallow established in woodlands adjoining

agricultural land can damage pastures and crops, particularly cereals [238, 615] but significant damage to agriculture is mostly localised, mainly in areas with very large herds [563].

Where fallow numbers thought to be excessive, control is undertaken largely by shooting, which controls populations at an appropriate level and yields annual harvest of venison or revenue from stalking. Hunting of fallow on horseback following a pack of hounds, last practised in the New Forest, ceased in 1997.

Commercial fallow deer farms for the production of venison were mostly established in early 1980s. Marketed for meat, but also for skins, antlers, sinews, penis, and testes. Removal of growing antlers for velvet, used as traditional medicine in China, prohibited in UK.

Legislation: Covered by same legislation as other deer (see Chapter 4); covers animal welfare and management, capture and handling, poaching controls, permitted firearms for killing deer and close seasons (see Tables 4.10, 4.11). In Scotland, the Deer Commission for Scotland (see above) advises on the welfare and management of all deer species, including fallow. No single body has responsibility in England and Wales or N Ireland, although the Deer Initiative, a partnership of statutory and voluntary organisations, promotes and assists deer management groups. In Republic of Ireland, deer are the responsibility of the National Parks and Wildlife Service.

LITERATURE
Popular general introductions [131, 443]. Definitive reviews [120, 124]. Additional material, on food, social organisation and behaviour [596, 597, 606]; fallow deer farming [648].

MAIN AUTHORS
J. Langbein, N.G. Chapman & R.J. Putman

GENUS *Rangifer*

Reindeer form a distinct genus which is usually considered to be monospecific although Nearctic (caribou *R. tarandus groenlandicus*) and Palaearctic (reindeer *R. t. tarandus*) populations are sometimes given specific status. The only deer in which females also bear antlers. Nearer to *Capreolus* and American deer (Odocoileinae) than to *Cervus* [470].

Reindeer *Rangifer tarandus*
Cervus tarandus Linnaeus, 1758; Swedish Lapland.

Caribou (N America).

Male – bull, female- cow, young-of-year – calf.

RECOGNITION
A medium-sized deer with relatively robust build (Plate 11). Both sexes bear antlers, more slender in cows than bulls. Antlers are multi-branched and with both main beam and brow tine showing branching; tines and beams somewhat flattened, with brow tines asymmetrical, left usually larger, palmate [312]. Pelage dense and long, greyish-brown to fawn with upper parts commonly lighter than underparts. Feet noticeably large, with digits splayed to facilitate walking on snow or soft ground.

DESCRIPTION
Coat dense with thick underfur; denser over shoulders such that males develop a distinct cape and hairy 'dewlap'. Greyish-brown or fawn, commonly with flanks and legs darker; belly pale, ash-grey. White rump patch, with short tail; white feet and mane. Lighter in winter. Within British population, approximately 20% are light or white-coloured; 17% have completely dark pelage, the remaining 63% the usual grey-brown. Calves are born unspotted but can be a range of colours from white, through slate-grey, brown or black.

Nipples: 1 pair, inguinal.

Chromosomes: 2n = 70.

Woodland populations are larger, with heavier antlers than tundra forms, while High Arctic populations are smallest; 6 subspecies recognised [326]. Using molecular evidence, 3 main groupings recognised, presumed to represent 3 separate populations during the last glacial period [267]. The main population (extending across most of Eurasia into Beringia) has contributed to the gene pool of all supposed subspecies. Smaller refugial populations postulated for E North America and W Europe. Scandinavian, therefore presumably Scottish, reindeer are a mix of the W European and main populations.

MEASUREMENTS
British population, males *c.*100–130 cm at the shoulder; weight 100–220 kg. Sexually dimorphic; females smaller, 95–115 cm tall, 65–150 kg.

DISTRIBUTION
Widespread through Nearctic (Alaska, Canada, Greenland) and Palaearctic (Scandinavia, Russia), north from *c.*50° N. Typically present on open

tundra habitats, but, especially in Nearctic, migrate southwards into open boreal woodland in winter. Many Palaearctic herds semi-domesticated. Reintroduced to GB in 1952; current populations restricted to 2 units of a managed herd in E Cairngorms.

HISTORY

Abundant in W Europe as far south as the Pyrenees in the Devensian. In the Late Glacial, common and widespread in British Isles [813], recorded from 30/33 sites of that period in GB [104]. Also numerous in Ireland at that time: 25 records from 22 sites [535]. Latest in Ireland 10 250 bp, but survived in GB into the Mesolithic, latest confirmed dates include 9940–9750 bp (Dead Man's Cave, Yorkshire) and 8300 bp (Inchnadamph, Sutherland) [813]. No evidence for popular notion (based mostly on a reference in a 12th-century Norse text, the *Orkneyinga saga*) that the species survived in Scotland until medieval times [173].

Domesticated reindeer reintroduced to Cairngorms by Mikel Utsi in 1952. Original stock from Sweden, since supplemented with additional deer from Norway and Russia. Until 1990, confined to the original 2400 ha site in the Cairngorms E of Aviemore. Secondary herd since established in a 1200 ha site near Tomintoul. While free-ranging within their areas, the herds are privately owned and closely managed.

HABITAT

At both sites, are relatively free-ranging over upland heather moorland (wet heath, dry heath and blanket bog), remaining well above the treeline.

SOCIAL STRUCTURE

Social organisation and structure in British populations strongly influenced by management. Group sizes and structures dependent on what animals are released to open range; many males are castrates.

FEEDING

In GB, graze primarily on hill vegetation: heathers, other dwarf shrubs (bilberry, cowberry), sedges (largely *Scirpus*), grasses and lichens (mainly *Cladonia* spp.). Strong seasonal variation, lichens more important during winter. Natural diet supplemented year-round with artificial feed.

BREEDING

Rut extends from mid September into early October. After gestation period of approximately 214 days, a single calf, usually born in May. Twins recorded only once in history of the herd. Calves weigh 4.5–7 kg at birth.

Mature bulls are first to cast their antlers, at the end of rut (usually November), and the first to begin growing new antlers, from late February–early March. Cows keep their antlers longest, often not casting until after calving in May. A few females lack antlers throughout their lives. Cows may calve at 2 years.

POPULATION

Both populations of reindeer in GB are owned and managed by the Reindeer Company Limited. Total numbers between the 2 herds are maintained at 140–150.

PARASITES/MORTALITY

As part of the management of Cairngorm herds, some culled annually; the other main causes of mortality are road traffic accidents and dogs.

AUTHORS

E. Dansie, R.J. Putman & D.W. Yalden

GENUS *Capreolus*

A distinctive Palaearctic genus of 2 species, European roe *Capreolus capreolus* and Siberian roe *C. pygargus*. Short, 3-tined antlers characteristic. Unusual among deer in that has summer rut, and delayed implantation of resulting embryos.

European roe deer *Capreolus capreolus*

Cervus capreolus Linnaeus, 1758; Southern Sweden.

Male – buck; *iwrch* (Welsh); *boc* (Scottish and Irish Gaelic); female – doe; *ewig* (Welsh); *earb* (Scottish Gaelic); *earb*, *fearb* (Irish Gaelic); young-of-year – kid, less commonly fawn.

RECOGNITION

Small to moderate-sized deer, body comparatively short with long legs and neck. Apparently tailless except that anal tuft of hair in females is prominent in winter coat. Distinctive black nose with white chin and also, commonly, black chinstrap. Also distinguished from muntjac by upright stance and pointed ears (Plate 12). When disturbed, characteristic bounding gait with white-cream rump patch (target) flared, while often giving dog-like barks. In reddish summer coat can be mistaken for red deer, but much smaller, shorter muzzle.

Skull: Head relatively short and broad. In male, small rugose antlers, no more than 3 tines; well-developed pearling; pedicles close together relative to orbital width (Fig. 11.7).

Plate 12

A Roe deer *Capreolus capreolus* buck, summer B kids C doe, winter
D Reeves' muntjac *Muntiacus reevesi* buck, winter E kid F doe, summer
G Chinese water deer *Hydropotes inermis* buck, winter H kids I doe, summer

FIELD SIGNS

Tracks (slots): Small, up to 4.5 cm long × 3.5 cm wide, typical of cloven-hoofed mammals. Can be confused with other small deer, sheep or goats. Cleaves generally close together along whole length, but varies according to animal's gait and substrate.

Faeces: Pellets typically elongated, cylindrical, black and shiny; size variable, in adults approximately 14 mm long × 8 mm in diameter, but overlap with other species in size and shape, even the larger red deer [508, 746]. In summer or when animals have been feeding on highly digestible foods, often stick together. Defecation rates 17–23 pellet groups per day, generally higher in winter than in summer [507, 508, 533].

Other field signs: Ground patches may be scraped for bedding sites, possibly leaving hair; bucks may mark territories in spring and summer by fraying or rubbing saplings with antlers and forehead, usually 10–80 cm from ground [543] and side branches broken; prefer plants 1–3 cm diameter [418]; *Pinus* spp. together with rare and exotic species are frayed more than dominant or native trees, but preference differs between studies [112]; often also scrape ground to clear vegetation at base of tree as territory mark. Rubs and scrapes may each occur at up to 100 marks/ha [418].

Well-trodden tracks or 'rings' around natural features such as trees, bushes or rocks, particularly during rut, but not of widespread occurrence.

DESCRIPTION

Pelage: Summer coat reddish-brown, uniform dorsally but paler underneath; hair 35 mm long. Winter coat colour variable, usually pale or olive-grey, greyish brown to almost black, especially in SW Scotland and N England [590]; hair 55 mm long. Kids at birth generally pale or dark reddish-brown, flecked with black; dappled with white spots on sides and flanks and with a row of spots on either side of spine; spots fade after *c*.6 weeks, disappearing by 1st moult. Face distinctive with short muzzle and black nose, often with a white rim above which sometimes extends on to upper part of muzzle; characteristic 'moustache stripe'; white chin. 1–2 pale patches on throat common in winter coat. Rump patch very distinct, especially in winter in females, which have a white, inverted heart-shaped patch, with a backward projecting anal tush of hair; in males, rump patch kidney-shaped, cream, with no tush; rump patch flared when alarmed. In summer, rump patch smaller, cream to buff in both sexes; anal tush of females generally absent.

Moult: To summer coat April–June, earlier in S, later in N; to winter coat September–October, later in S, earlier in N.

Anatomy: Ears large, prominent and rounded; eyes rounded with slanted pupils. Dew claws present; also vestigial splint bones on forelegs (teleometacarpalian condition).

Nipples: 2 pairs, inguinal.

Scent glands: Metatarsal on outer side of hind leg just below hock; interdigital with distal glandular complex on metacarpus and metatarsus; glandular area between, and anterior to, antler pedicles in males [222]; preorbital glands absent [470].

Skull: Detailed description in [269]. Small to medium sized, with a blunt rostrum, arched nasals and high frontals (cf. red deer). Distinguishing feature is reduction in the lachrymal bone and the ethmoid fissure relative to other deer [467]. 3 morphological types identified in GB, one of which, currently restricted to Scotland, may be the native British phenotype [372].

Teeth: Milk teeth usually 0.0.3.0/3.1.3.0 and permanent 0.0.3.3/3.1.3.3; lower canine modified to resemble an extra incisor, upper canines rare (2–17% of population) [590]. Permanent teeth erupt between 8 and 15 months; little eruption after 2 years (cf. red deer). Tooth wear often used to estimate age of adults, but unreliable due to variation between populations, individuals and observers [379]. Annual layers in dental cement may give better estimate of age [8]. Age determination of kids easy due to presence of milk teeth and obvious tripartite (3-cusped) last premolar; replaced in adult dentition by bicuspid tooth.

Antlers: Short, usually <30 cm and placed more or less vertically in a lyre shape. 3 tines on each antler usual in adults; the 3rd central tine (the 'true' brow tine is missing [269]) faces forwards and upwards. Main beam branches dichotomously at top; posterior tine faces backwards. Lower part of antler beam covered in variable amounts of large tubercles (pearling) with well-developed burr, or coronet, at base (Fig. 11.7).

Pedicles develop at *c*.3–4 months; small button antlers of a few cm may then form, to be shed around January; 1st true antlers subsequently develop during late winter and early spring as simple spikes up to 10 cm long, or with 1 or both extra points according to habitat quality. Antlers generally of adult size by 3 years, but antler size and number of tines poor indicators of age [373]. Unlike most other deer, antlers cast from October to December, adults possibly casting before juveniles; regrown immediately in velvet and fully formed by March (Fig. 11.30); velvet shed in March–April by adults, possibly later in young animals or those in poor condition ([590, 736], but see [415, 416]. Infrequently, antlers retained in velvet with the addition of further layers each year (called 'perruques'); thought to be due to low androgen levels, possibly caused by damage to testes or their remaining in body cavity (cryptorchidism), preventing 'cleaning' of velvet [115].

Short antlers (5–10 cm) rarely observed in females; usually remain in velvet, but not invariably. These females may be true hermaphrodites or male pseudohermaphrodites (freemartins) [115, 590]. Antlered females, both in 'hard horn' and pregnant, known.

Alimentary system: Typical of selective feeders, with relatively small omasum and larger abomasum (cf. red deer [385, 386]); rumen capacity 4.0–5.8 l. Specific adaptations to concentrate diet: extremely large salivary glands (up to 0.38% of body weight) producing large quantities of saliva, apparently for inactivation of free tannins; bypass mechanism allowing soluble carbohydrates to avoid fermentation and to be absorbed in the small intestine; large liver (2.6% of body weight), possibly for detoxification of plant secondary metabolites [245].

Chromosomes: 2n = 70 [222]; FNa = 72 (68 acrocentric autosomes and submetacentric X chromosomes) [470].

Previously thought to be monospecific genus,

Fig. 11.30 Roe deer: buck in velvet, and in its grey winter coat; unlike other British deer, roe grow their antlers during the winter months *(photo B. Phipps)*.

but 2 allopatric species now widely recognised, the 'European' roe deer (*C. capreolus*, Linnaeus 1758), the species native to the British Isles, and the larger 'Siberian' roe deer (*C. pygargus*, Pallas 1771); the latter carries 1–14 additional accessory B

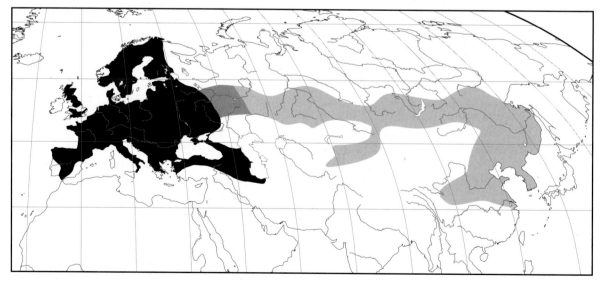

Fig. 11.31 Roe deer: Palaearctic distribution of European roe *Capreolus capreolus* (black), Siberian roe *C. pygargus* (grey) and putative hybrid or overlap zone (dark grey) in Russia.

Table 11.15 Roe deer: measurements of wild European adults (>2 years old)

	Locality	Males				Females			
		Range	Range of population means	Mean	n	Range	Range of population means	Mean	n
Head and body length (mm)	Europe[a]	900–1380	1082–1265	1170		850–1385	1071–1257	1165	
Jaw length (mm)	Europe[a]		153–167				147–168		
Hindfoot length (mm)	Europe[a]	280–470	350–390	370		250–475	345–395	370	
Ear length (mm)	Europe[a]	100–175	120–160	140		110–180	130–170	150	
Weight (whole body) (kg)	Dorset			24.5	81			23.1	63

[a] Data from the entire European range [222].

chromosomes [222, 374, 470]. Small overlap zone in the Volgograd region (Fig. 11.31); hybridisation possible, but high rate of birth complications leading to death of kid and/or mother and partial or reduced infertility among F_1 hybrid bucks [222]. Closer phylogenetically to odocoileine (American) deer, *Rangifer* and *Alces* than other Palaearctic deer [470].

MEASUREMENTS
Birth weight of 900–2260 g (average generally *c*.1500 g), no sex differences apparent [17]. Adult size dimorphism between sexes <10%, males being larger than females (Table 11.15). Mean

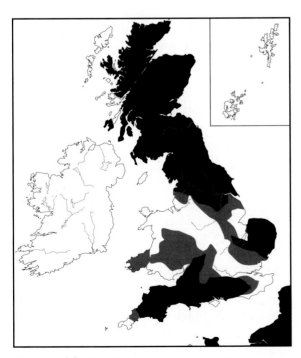

Fig. 11.32 Roe deer *Capreolus capreolus*: range in GB.

height at shoulder 60–70 cm. Body weight variations are given in Tables 11.15 (live) and 11.16 (carcass). Seasonal variation in body weight and fat deposits; females lose weight and fat during spring and early summer, probably due to gestation and lactation; males lightest in autumn due to costs of rutting [377], but weight and fat loss may occur during winter in northern climates [388].

VARIATION
British race (*C. c. thotti* Lönnberg, 1910; Craigellachie, Morayshire), described on basis of darker colour, especially of the face, but is not generally recognised; some support from variation in cranial characteristics [372]. 3 morphological types identified in GB on basis of skull structure, one of which (currently restricted to Scotland) may represent the native British phenotype [372], the rest undoubtedly derived from European introductions (see History, below). Native deer reported to retain white target in summer coat, whereas that of introduced European deer is pale brown to yellow [590]. Introductions from continental Europe may have resulted in novel allelic variant in S GB [370]. Melanistic (in Dumfriesshire), white and skewbald roe deer occasionally recorded in GB [590]. Genetic differentiation between populations across Europe considered high [361], but reduced in GB, possibly due to bottleneck in historic times [370].

DISTRIBUTION
Widespread throughout Scotland and N GB; range increasing (Fig. 11.32). In S England, present from W Kent to Cornwall, spreading north in Gloucestershire. Populations also in Essex, Norfolk and Suffolk, now spreading into the Midlands. Roe in N England are spreading southwards into

Table 11.16 Roe deer: carcass weight[a] (kg) of kids, yearlings and adults (>2 years old) across GB (from [639])

		Kids			Yearlings			Adults		
		Range	Mean	n	Range	Range	n	Range	Mean	n
Pickering (North Yorkshire)	Bucks	11–20	15.8	20	14–19	16.3	16	12–21	17.7	35
	Does	10–15	12.8	20	13–19	16.3	13	14–20	16.2	37
Alice Holt (Hampshire)	Bucks	14–16	14.4	4	12–17	14.4	5	15–19	17.7	8
	Does	10–15	12.8	10	16–22	18.2	10	15–22	19.0	20
Thetford (Norfolk)	Bucks	10–18	13.7	20	10–17	13.4	20	11–22	15.9	40
	Does	7–13	9.9	20	12–17	14.6	20	11–19	14.4	35
Craigellachie (Morayshire)	Bucks	8–16	10.6	6	8–18	13.2	17	7–20	14.9	34
	Does	5–16	9.9	12	8–19	12.9	20	8–18	13.4	27

[a] Carcass weight = live weight minus blood, abdominal and thoracic viscera.
Female and kid weights from October to March; adult males from May to October.

region around Leeds, Manchester, Sheffield and N Lincolnshire. Recently appeared in Wales around Llandrindod Wells. Absent from Ireland, Isle of Wight and most Scottish islands except Bute, Islay, Seil and Skye; recently colonised Arran.

HISTORY

Descended from *Procapreolus* (Schlosser 1924) present from the Miocene; earliest known fossil *Capreolus* from the Late Pliocene (*c*.3 mya); true roe deer first appeared in the Middle Pleistocene (Cromerian), differing only slightly from modern *Capreolus capreolus* [470]. From fossil evidence, widespread during Pleistocene, always remained in temperate zone of Eurasia. Absent from GB during cold stages of Pleistocene, its range probably restricted to S Europe [469], perhaps due to lack of suitable woodland cover; snow depth defines northern limits of current range [222]. Briefly recolonised during Late Glacial (one record, Kendrick's Cave, Conwy, 11 795 bp) [405]. Abundant fossil evidence of continuous occupation of GB from 10 000 bp until the present; some indication of fluctuations in population size and distribution, possibly in relation to landscape changes following cultivation [396,590].

In historical times became extinct throughout much of GB (e.g. since c.1600 AD in Wales); by *c*.1700, thought to survive only in remnant woodlands in parts of the C and NW Highlands of Scotland [650, 795]. Increase in woodlands during 18th century led to range expansion in Scotland, reached Scottish Borders by 1840. Roe in S England all considered to be derived from reintroductions [794]. Roe of debated origin

introduced into Milton Abbas, Dorset, in 1800 [590] and subsequently colonised much of SE England; deer from German stock introduced into E Anglia c.1884 [152]; roe in Lake District thought to be of Austrian origin [483]. Roe never present in Ireland, except for introductions during 1860s–1870s, shot out during 1st half of 20th century [590].

HABITAT

Occur in a wide variety of habitats, but generally associated with open mixed, coniferous or deciduous woodland; density lower in purely coniferous habitat, higher in rich, agricultural–woodland mosaics [222]. Early successional habitats generally preferred and food requirements best met by mosaic landscapes with high proportion of forest edge [222]; often favour interface of habitat types such as forest rides or clearings [787]; cover also important [761]. In plantations, density highest in young stands 5–15 years old where both food and cover abundant [368, 452, 453, 728]. Also occupy agricultural land in continental Europe if sufficient topographic or ground cover available [378]; apparently more dependent on small woods in agricultural areas in GB (cf. [381]). In some parts of Scotland, occupy open moorland [219] and farmland [397] without access to woodland cover. Also found in many urban and suburban situations such as parks, golf courses and rough ground where sufficient woodland or scrub cover [395, 509].

Tolerant of climatic extremes (Mediterranean to Arctic Circle), but snow depth defines N European range limit [222].

Table 11.17 Roe deer: home range size related to habitat

Habitat type	Range area[a] (ha)	n
Forest or woodland >75% land area	37	128
Farmland and woodland	70	15
Farmland >75% land area	172	8

[a] Mean of mean range areas reported in each study. Data compiled from 151 studies from Europe [299].

SOCIAL ORGANISATION AND BEHAVIOUR

Some information from GB on ranging behaviour, but most comes from European studies. Reviews available of social organisation [378], mating system [459] and behaviour [222, 389, 467].

Social organisation: In summer, usually solitary or in small groups of females with young and perhaps an associated male [43, 222]. Larger, but unstable, groups occur in winter, up to 8 deer in forest habitat [43, 73], but 10–100 in open agricultural areas [75, 818]; group of >60 recorded in Scotland [639]. Average winter group size increases with population density, habitat openness and landscape homogeneity [378, 381].

Home ranges and territories: Males territorial March–September. Territories exclusive at low density [73, 736], increasingly overlap as density increases [46, 421], but core range remains constant and exclusive [112, 154]. Territory size varies according to habitat and population density [222, 299, 383, 421, 430], 5.2±2.5 ha at Chedington [420]. Ranges of non-territorial males (mostly subadults) may be larger (means 7.7 ha (2nd year), 12.3 ha (3rd year, range 0.8–28.1 ha), overlapping those of several territorial bucks [73, 420], or very small, situated in buffer zone between 2 territories; satellites sharing territory of a dominant buck also recorded [378, 415].

First territory obtained at 2–4 years old [73, 459]; retained year to year by same or replacement buck for 6 years or more [73, 415, 736]; old bucks may lose territory, becoming nomadic or restricted to a small area [459]. Territorial boundaries stable, frequently natural features such as streams, woodland rides or roads [378]. Males may tolerate each other outside their territories. Winter ranges not defended, roughly the same size and location as summer territories in forest habitat [43, 73, 771], but may be much larger in more open landscapes [107, 378, 504].

Female ranges apparently undefended, except for some agonistic activity within a reduced range at parturition [260, 420]; retained annually [73].

Ranges of 3–4 does may overlap considerably [420, 772], potentially giving rise to clans of related females; can also overlap with one or several territorial males. Range size generally similar to male territories, e.g. 4.55±2.5 ha, Chedington (Table 11.17) [154, 420, 421]. Seasonal ranges of females in winter generally larger than in summer although core areas may remain similar to those in winter [154, 222].

Young females in 2nd or 3rd year may take up own ranges overlapping with that of mother, or may emigrate.

Bedding: Sites chosen for proximity to feeding grounds, but also for cover, particularly when bedding for a long period and in cold weather; may also seek to lower chance of visual detection; humid substrates sought on warm days to aid thermal regulation [552, 553].

Scent-marking: During period of territoriality, when rubbing stems and scraping the ground, bucks scent mark substrate with secretions from glandular area on forehead and interdigital glands [222]; possibly acts as territorial signal [417]. Scent secretions from metatarsal and interdigital glands individually characteristic [456] with consistent differences also between sexes [457]. Metatarsal secretion may be important in entraining following of dam by kids, and may be significant in signalling alarm [545].

Vocalisations: From 6 months old, roe give short (average 0.32 s) repeated barks (average 14/min) in response to disturbance, particularly at dawn and dusk [378]; not extended as in muntjac. More frequent among males or solitary animals; neighbouring deer may respond, indicating role in range surveillance [643]. Differences in vocal characteristics between sexes and individuals [644]. Male also makes rasping noises, especially when courting or exhibiting aggressive behaviour. Squeals are used for mother–offspring contact; kids bleat or squeal when alarmed or hungry; females squeal when searching for offspring or (louder) when in season [222].

Stamping may be used to communicate alarm [222].

Aggressive behaviour: By males (mainly during territorial period) is generally ritual demonstration, including barking, chasing, rubbing, fraying, butting and scent-marking vegetation, scraping and stamping with forefeet; more rarely leads to fighting by locking antlers and pushing and twisting; deaths may occur [222]. Females aggressive (stamping, hissing, chasing, butting) towards predators, humans and other deer around parturition [260].

Dispersal: By both sexes; generally 20–75% of yearlings disperse a few km [467], although distances >20 km recorded in Scottish farmland [397]; may preferentially disperse along woodland corridors in agricultural landscapes [216]. Near N limit, Europe, 95% dispersed 100 km or more [777]; dispersal reduced at high density due to poor body condition [778]. Breakdown of mother–young associations during April–May prior to birth period [44] when yearlings make excursions and may disperse, but many, particularly females, later rejoin mother until next spring [467, 778]. Otherwise, males may disperse in spring *c.*2nd or 3rd birthday [45, 736]. If female does not disperse as yearling, will probably remain philopatric for life [467]. Female dispersal thought to be voluntary [467]; male dispersal may be enforced by aggression from territorial males, particularly towards heavy yearlings with large antlers which may be potential competitors [776].

Activity: Active throughout 24 h; highest during rut due to social interactions [762]. Usually 4–12 feeding periods/day, with longest bouts around dusk and dawn [383]; feeding bouts longer in spring, rest up to 60% of time in winter, varying with weather [410]. Does move more than bucks. Activity rhythm of group highly synchronised, particularly in winter. Grazing bouts longer and locomotor activity shorter in large groups. Kid activity synchronised with mother by 2.5–3 months [222].

Locomotion: Usually walk; mean speed of 0.57 km/h in winter and 1.26 km/h during period of territoriality, maximum of 6.2 km/h during rut

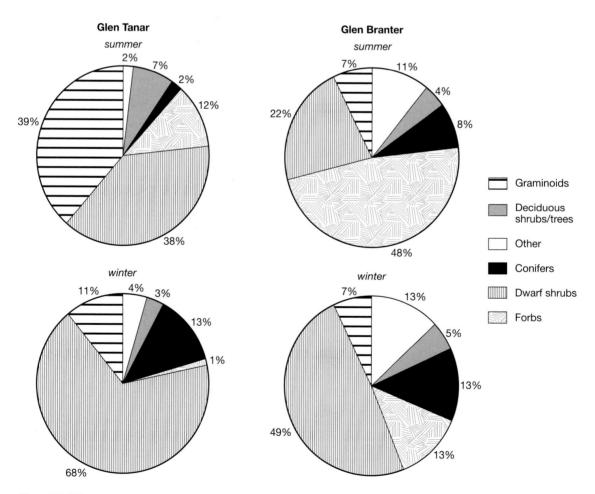

Fig. 11.33 Roe deer: diet in summer and winter, in 2 Scottish forests: a native pinewood (Glen Tanar, Aberdeenshire) and planted spruce plantation (Glen Branter, Argyll).

[687]. Bound when alarmed, flaring rump patch, often barking. If disturbed often cut back behind source, or lie flat and hide until disturbance has passed. Will swim.

FEEDING

Versatile and opportunistic, diet varies according to food availability in different habitats and seasons. Selective feeders [754, 755], with buds, shoots and leaves of deciduous trees and shrubs, and non-graminaceous herbs (forbs) important throughout world range [222, 753]. As concentrate-selectors [385], prefer plants with high soluble carbohydrates and high tannin concentrations [754]; diet selectivity appears to be largely a learned behaviour based on post-ingestive consequences [755]. Switch to seasonally abundant fruits, seeds (e.g. acorns) or mushrooms when available.

Feed from ground level to 120 cm, mostly *c*.75 cm when browsing; shoot diameter generally 2–4 mm; bite size is small (50–500 mg dry matter/bite), but largest mouthful taken first, increasing bite-rate compensating for declining bite-size when depletion occurs [399]. Intake rate is higher in summer (57–80 $g/kg^{0.75}/day$) than winter (21–55 $g/kg^{0.75}/day$) [245]. Requirement for assimilable protein estimated as 70–150 g/day; water requirement up to 135 ml/kg body weight, mostly obtained from vegetation [222]. Sometimes use natural salt licks or eat soil as source of mineral salts.

Food: Diet of roe in GB studied in E England [364], S England [393, 403], NE England [367] and Scotland [100, 397, 728] (Fig. 11.33). In S and E England, brambles (*Rubus* spp.) especially selected throughout year; in summer, deciduous browse and forbs more important; in winter, ivy, conifers, ferns and dwarf shrubs taken. In Scotland, in summer, forbs selected when available, sorrels and rosebay willowherb prominent; also shoots of conifers and deciduous trees, especially

at bud-burst [728, 786]. In winter, heather, blaeberry and other woody browse important. Grasses eaten in small amounts throughout year; only taken in appreciable quantities in early spring or where preferred foods are not available. Roe in agricultural habitats take mostly cultivated crops, especially cereals in all seasons [100], but may supplement diet by browsing in any adjacent woodlands [596].

BREEDING

Females apparently monoestrous; rut mostly mid July–end August (Fig. 11.34). Evidence for 2nd 'false' rut in October and November debatable. Some authors suggest 2nd surge of sexual activity in autumn, perhaps due to precocious sexual behaviour of kids (e.g. [590]) but this disputed [310, 436, 688]. Spontaneous ovulation [688], cotyledonous placentation, pregnancy *c*.300 days including 5 months of embryonic diapause [310, 435, 700]; birth peak May–mid June; twins most common litter size; most females breed for 1st time at 15 months but occasional fertile [636] or pregnant kids recorded ([371] – but see arguments in [436]); probably low level of polygyny (reviewed in [17, 467, 688]). Males thought generally to mate with females residing within their territory, but female excursions during rut possibly allow females to select, and mate with, other partners [459]; towards the end of rut, males may raid neighbouring territories to gain additional matings [222]. Bucks locate oestrous females primarily through scent, e.g. urine [434], several days before they are receptive [459].

Mating: Characterised by vigorous rutting chases which are frequent and long, often describing a circle or figure of eight; 'roe rings' common in Scotland but less so elsewhere, often traditional [746]; mounts are short and repeated (>15 times in 30 min recorded), generally involving a single male, continuing for 2–5 days [222].

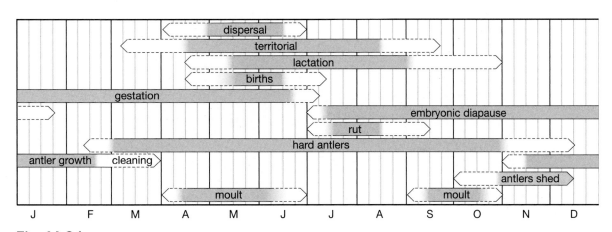

Fig. 11.34 Roe deer: annual cycle.

Males: Testicular activity March–late August; spermatozoa present May–November; testes fully regressed by January [701]; endogenous rhythm of steroid hormones (testosterone) with 6-month periodicity; territorial behaviour initiated by testosterone and maintained by long photoperiod; full sexual activity with 2nd testosterone peak by July [688]; 1st active spermatazoa generally observed in yearlings; spermatogenesis maximum during July [222].

Females: High progesterone concentrations August–May in pregnant females and August–March in non-pregnant females indicating no recycling (monoestry) when fertilisation does not occur; long photoperiod inhibits sexual cycle and ovarian activity [688]. Follicles may contain 1 or 2 ova, each of which can contain 2 nuclei, giving up to 4 corpora lutea in a single ovary [222].

Only artiodactyl with embryonic diapause: after fertilisation, blastocyst does not implant into uterine endometrium until late December or early January; normal embryonic development then proceeds, so active gestation of *c.*4.5 months [700]; delay probably under control of endogenous rhythm [688].

Births: Highly synchronised [279]; in Chedington Woods, Dorset, most births occurred in May, but mean birth date was later with declining habitat quality [299]; doe often gives birth in same place in consecutive years [421]. Lactation lasts *c.*3 months, but most intense during 1st month when maternal metabolic rate increases by 27% [505]. Roe young are 'hiders' for up to 3 months (Fig. 11.35): mother leaves offspring hidden alone while foraging and resting 50–150 m away; siblings lie separately for 1st month; kids moved 100–200 m overnight [467]. Highest known postnatal maternal care among ungulates [586].

Productivity: Practically all (>98%) adult (>2 years) does ovulate and are fertilised, proportion implanting fetus generally high [278], but variable between populations and years across GB (Table 11.18) [371]. Most females produce twins in good habitat, but triplets common in some populations [17, 369]; average litter size also varies (Table 11.18) in relation to female body weight; sex ratio at birth and postnatal maternal investment also dependent on female body weight (see below).

Fig. 11.35 Roe deer: kid hidden in the grass; typical behaviour for young of all deer in their first few days *(photo B. Phipps)*.

Table 11.18 Roe deer: variation in female fecundity of yearlings and adults (> 2 years) across GB (from [369, 371])

Study site	Ovulation				Pregnancy				Embryos per reproductive doe				Potential litter size per doe			
	Yearlings		Adults		Yearlings		Adults		Yearlings		Adults		Yearlings		Adults	
	%	n	%	n	%	n	%	n	$\bar{x}$	n	$\bar{x}$	n	$\bar{x}$	n	$\bar{x}$	n
Alice Holt, Hampshire	100	51	99	186	96	27	91	117	1.88	26	1.89	104	1.80	26	1.72	104
Thetford, Norfolk	98	181	99	344	81	118	90	216	1.70	81	1.75	170	1.38	81	1.58	170
Ringwood, Hampshire	100	12	99	171	71	7	84	110	2.00	4	1.67	91	1.42	4	1.40	91
Spadeadam, Kielder	92	25	99	188	56	16	75	115	1.25	8	1.52	86	0.70	8	1.14	86
Kershope, Kielder	95	38	99	206	35	23	67	116	1.38	8	1.64	77	0.48	8	1.10	77
Pickering, N Yorks	99	67	99	368	74	39	79	239	1.82	28	1.98	188	1.35	28	1.56	188
Craigellachie, Morayshire	97	107	100	219	62	34	70	81	1.38	21	1.63	56	0.86	21	1.14	56
Queens, Inverness	74	19	99	76	55	11	68	37	1.00	1	1.12	8	0.55	1	0.76	8
S Strome, Ross-shire	100	11	98	92	100	1	81	37	2.00	1	1.45	29	2.00	1	1.17	29

Fecundity generally lower and more variable among yearlings [278, 371], and decreases from the age of 12 [283]; females average 8 breeding attempts (maximum recorded = 16) [283].

Development of young: Data on Siberian roe deer indicate may suckle within 30 min of birth, walk within 40 min and move away from birth site within 2–3 h [222]. May take some vegetation from 5–10 days; taste all plants; preference/avoidance pattern similar to adults from 2–6 weeks [755]; diet similar to adults from 3 months when suckling ceases [222]. Early juvenile linear growth rate 113–155 g/day; growth of triplets and early-borns slower than twins/singles and later-borns [17]; siblings have similar growth rates [284], no differences between sexes ([16, 280, 379], but see [299]). Males slightly heavier by 8 months due to differential growth post-weaning [299, 475]. Females achieve adult size by 18 months, males continue growth through to 30 months [376].

Permanent molars erupt at *c.*2, 6 and 10 months, then milk premolars replaced by 15 months [590]. Independence and dispersal possible in spring at 1st birthday (see above).

POPULATION
Numbers: Total in GB *c.*500 000 (350 000 in Scotland, 150 000 in England, 50 in Wales) [360].

Densities: Vary from 0.5–25 deer/km² in conifer forests in Scotland and Borders [451, 476] and pine forests of E Anglia [638]. Related to forest structure, greatest in stands 5–15 years old, reaching lowest point in close-canopy thickets, but increasing again in mature stands prior to felling [301, 451, 452, 728, 787]. In richer habitats of S England, densities of 34–76 deer/km² observed in individual woods [299]. In Scotland, density lower in areas of higher rainfall; also affected by culling levels and density of red deer [452].

Fluctuations: Maximum annual population growth rate of *c*.1.4, largely dependent on summer kid survival (see below); *c*.25% of individuals replaced annually [283]. Decrease across GB in average jaw length of successive cohorts suggests that either population densities are increasing or habitat quality is declining (with canopy closure) [376].

Sex ratio: European data for adult sex ratio vary from 1.03 to 2.52 females/male [222]. Sex ratio at birth depends on maternal condition: heavier mothers produce more daughters, lighter mothers produce more sons [375, 380].

Age structure: Average age of population generally 2–4 years; kids constitute 20–45% of the population in autumn, yearlings 15–25%, adults (2–6 years) *c*.35% and old animals (>6 years) <10% [222]. Maximum recorded age in wild 14 for males and 18 for females, but most die before 8–10 years [283].

Survival: Kid survival over 1st summer low and highly variable between years (20–100% in England) [299]; related to summer rainfall, positively [282] or negatively [636]; 1st winter survival less variable, dependent on achieving 60% of adult body weight for males, 65% for females, by onset of winter [283]. Annual survival of yearlings and prime-age adults high, although may be lower during harsh winters; female adults survive better (95%) than males (85%), the difference increasing with age; survival decreases from 7 years old, possibly due to tooth wear [281, 284, 420].

European data indicate foxes (main predator of roe in GB) can take 40% or more of kids (<2 months old), mostly male kids lying in open habitat [1a]; golden eagle predation on kids also recorded in GB [637]. Otherwise, humans main predator in GB (see below).

Species interactions: Roe densities lower than expected when coexist with red, fallow and sika deer, suggesting some interaction. Red and roe deer densities inversely correlated in Scottish conifer plantations; competitive exclusion of roe possible, but dietary differences evident [364, 451, 452]. Diet and habitat overlap probably greatest with muntjac, some evidence for competition; roe densities can be lowered 20% where muntjac present [154, 808].

PARASITES AND PATHOGENS
Reviews in [13, 259, 272].

Ectoparasites: Keds (*Lipoptena cervi*), sucking louse *Solenopotes burmeisteri,* biting louse *Damalinia meyeri* and ticks *Ixodes ricinus* are common in many British populations. *Cephenomyia stimulator* is a nasal botfly specific to roe deer in Bitish Isles. Warble fly *Hypoderma diana* uncommon [272].

Endoparasites: Lungworms *Dictyocaulus* spp. cause significant mortality in roe in some areas [546] and malignant catarrhal fever has been recorded [97]. Many gastrointestinal parasites present; liver fluke *Fasciola hepatica* very common in some areas and effects can be serious [247], perhaps limiting populations [272]. *Babesia capreoli*, a blood haemoprotozoon (redwater) transmitted by ticks, is common in Scotland although clinical signs are rare [272]; deaths known [805]. The protostrongylid *Elaphostrongylus cervi* (tissue worm) regularly found (cf. other deer species); heavy infestations may cause loss of lung function [272].

Viruses and bacteria: Subclinical louping ill common in wild Scottish deer although clinical louping ill seems only to occur when there are other predisposing factors such as infection with *Ehrlichia phagocytophilla* [272]. Several *Myco-bacterium* spp. recorded [272, 547, 591, 654]. *M. bovis* detected at low levels in S England and Wales (6/695 carcasses sampled [231], see also [654]), and in SW England (3/236 carcasses sampled [591], 4/903 [227]); no evidence in 732 examined in Scotland [646] but 1 subsequently reported W Argyll [272]. *M. avium, M. kansasii* also found [272, 591]. *M. avium paratuberculosis* (Johne's disease) particularly prevalent in E Scotland, causing significant mortality in some places [272].

Serological evidence of infection with bovine virus diarrhoea, reovirus 1 and 2 and adenovirus A [450]. Roe susceptible to foot-and-mouth disease under experimental conditions [277] but none found in 2001 outbreak. Antibodies to *Leptospira* and *Borrelia burgdorferi* (the agent involved in Lyme disease) have been detected in roe from the New Forest [511, 544]. *B. burgdorferi* cannot be sustained in roe, but they support disease cycle by providing food for adult ticks (see red deer section) [272]. Roe considered to be an important mammalian reservoir of *Ehrlichia phagocytophila*, a bacterium (rickettsia) causing tick-borne fever in sheep and cattle; not thought to cause disease in deer but may have an immunosuppresive effect on other infections [272].

Lymphosarcoma recorded in a roe deer from Dorset [806].

RELATIONS WITH HUMANS
Hunted from prehistoric times. Damage forestry through browsing and fraying young trees (Fig. 11.36); can be very important, delaying tree

Fig. 11.36 Sapling frayed by roe buck. All deer can cause serious damage in commercial forestry by fraying saplings, eating them, or eating bark off older trees *(photo D.W. Yalden)*.

Fig. 11.37 Roe doe killed by motor traffic. Collisions between deer and vehicles are an important cause of mortality for deer, and other large mammals, but also increasingly a serious concern for drivers and insurers *(photo J. Langbein)*.

regeneration or establishment, particularly conifers [297, 298, 302, 641, 686, 782, 788]; selective browsing may alter forest species composition [112]. Before 1960 generally treated as vermin but since 1970s increasing interest in exploitation as game species. Around 30 000 culled annually in recent years in Scotland [228], and many more unreported kills for home consumption. May also cause significant damage to agricultural crops [563, 596, 615, 686] although impacts highly localised, at farm or field level, not of regional or national economic significance [238, 563, 606, 610].

Roe is the commonest deer involved in road traffic accidents in the UK (Fig. 11.37), as elsewhere in Europe [323, 441].

Covered by several Acts of Parliament but legislation differs between Scotland, England and Wales (see Chapter 4 for details). For close seasons, see Tables 4.10, 4.11.

LITERATURE
Multi-authored collection of chapters synthesising results of primary research studies across Europe [18]; in-depth description of behaviour and ecology of the European and Siberian species [222]; important case study contributions [255, 420, 589, 736]; popular overviews [263, 289, 590, 794, 798].

AUTHORS
A.J.M. Hewison & B.W. Staines.

GENUS *Hydropotes*

A distinctive genus with a single species, notable as one of the two species of deer without antlers. Relationship with other deer discussed in [326]. Phylogenetic studies have since shown *Hydropotes* to be nested within the subfamily Odocoileinae, being particularly closely related to *Capreolus* spp. [241, 629]. Divergence occurred *c*.10 mya, with antlers being lost secondarily.

Chinese water deer *Hydropotes inermis*
Hydropotes inermis Swinhoe 1870; R. Yangtze, China.

Water deer; *ke, zhang* (Chinese).

RECOGNITION
Small deer with reddish-brown summer coat; thick, paler winter coat. No antlers, but adult males have long curved upper canines (Plate 12). Large ears, usually held upright. Black, beady eyes. Slightly taller than muntjac and differ in having a straight or concave back (muntjac often hunched). Further distinguished from muntjac by short tail, which is never held erect but may stick out, especially on males in winter. Lack black facial markings of muntjac. Stance and movement more like roe, but roe larger and has conspicuous white caudal patch.

SIGN

Slot: In soft mud measures 4–5 cm long × 3–4 cm wide. Cleaves even with straight inner edges. Dew claws leave mark when running in soft mud or snow. Stride length when walking typically *c*.35 cm.

Faeces: Usually 1.0–1.5 cm long × 0.5–1.0 cm wide; not normally aggregated, black or dark brown, cylindrical, pointed at one end, rounded at other.

DESCRIPTION

Thick winter coat of hollow hairs, 40–55 mm long, white at base, buff or ginger at tip and black in between. Individual deer vary in appearance from pale fawn to grey-brown. Muzzle may have white, grey or black band, last type especially in males. Summer coat sleek and reddish-brown. Deer with rough, transitional coats seen mainly March–May; by May most in summer coat. Fawns have pale spots in lines at birth but lose these after 2 months. Large, hairy ears held erect. Eyes rounded, black and button-like. Tail short, stumpy, occasionally sticks out. Although no conspicuous caudal patch, rump can appear paler below tail. Hind legs muscular and longer than front ones, so hindquarters higher than shoulders.

Skeleton: Skull described in [269] (Fig. 11.38). Lateral metacarpals (splint bones) at distal end of cannon bone, the teleometacarpalian condition.

Teeth: Dental formula 0.1.3.3/3.1.3.3. Long, curved, hinged upper canine (tusk) in adult male protruding well below jaw line [7]. Upper canine small in female (<8 mm), not visible in field. Maximum recorded length of tusk protruding from gum in Cambridgeshire males was 72 mm with mean of 56 mm (Table 11.19); mean for sample of males from Whipsnade in 1990s was 44 mm [822]). In young males, canines erupt in autumn and by end of winter are *c*.1/2 final length.

Scent glands: Preorbital glands small; secretions individually distinct and composition varies with age [456]. Interdigital glands more obvious on hindfeet. Only deer with inguinal glands. Territorial marking includes rubbing vegetation with the forehead, but forehead glands not reported [716].

Nipples: 2 pairs, inguinal.

Chromosomes: 2n = 70; Fna = 68 [823].

MEASUREMENTS

Body measurements for feral animals from Cambridgeshire in Table 11.19; skull measurements in Table 11.20. Mean weights for Cambridgeshire samples similar to weights in China, where adult males 14.8 kg, adult females 15.1 kg [696]. Enclosed population, Whipsnade, lighter: mean weights of adult males 11.1–11.7 kg, adult females 11.7–13.4 kg, for samples taken at

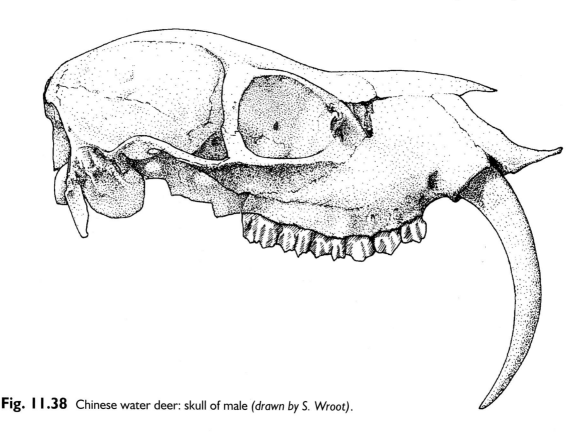

Fig. 11.38 Chinese water deer: skull of male *(drawn by S. Wroot).*

618

Table 11.19 Chinese water deer: measurements of adults found dead in Cambridgeshire

	Males			Females		
	Mean	Range	n	Mean	Range	n
Weight (kg)	14.3	12.0–18.5	11	15.6	14.0–17.4	7
Tusk length in socket (mm)	56.3	44–72	16	4.6	4–8	8
Body length (cm)	95.6	82–106	15	95.6	90–105	6
Height at shoulder (cm)	52.3	42–65	14	50.3	42–61	7
Ear (cm)	9.9	9–11	10	11.0	10–12	5
Tail (cm)	6.7	4.5–9.0	10	6.2	2.4–8.0	6

various times [820]. Comparing Cambridgeshire water deer with muntjac in same area, males of similar weight, but female water deer c.30% heavier than female muntjac. Water deer usually stand c.50–55 cm at the shoulder.

VARIATION

2 subspecies described, Chinese water deer *H. inermis inermis* (the form found in GB) and Korean water deer *H. i. argyropus* Heude 1984, but latter not recognised by some authors [269].

DISTRIBUTION

Native to E China and Korea (Fig. 11.39). In GB, established in the wild in Bedfordshire, Cambridgeshire, Norfolk and Suffolk, but distribution discontinuous [136]. Relatively few populations between main centres in W Bedfordshire, Cambridgeshire Fens and Norfolk Broads, although has spread away from the Broads towards the NW (Fig. 11.40). Also introduced to France [458].

HISTORY

First kept in GB in London Zoo in 1873, but not subsequently. Kept in Woburn Park from 1896. During 1929 and 1930, some transferred to Whipsnade Zoo. Later kept in a range of parks and collections. First reported in the wild in 1945, Buckinghamshire. First reports in the wild from counties making up main current range: Bedfordshire 1954, Norfolk 1968, Cambridgeshire 1971 (though misidentified as muntjac in 1960s), Suffolk 1987. Dispersal rate in Cambridgeshire not >1 km/year [204].

HABITAT

In China, near rivers, lakes and coasts with reed and other tall grasses for cover, and grassland in hills [694]. In GB, reed beds and woodland, where prefers mixed vegetation, open areas for feeding and denser vegetation for cover. Also occurs at low densities in arable environments. At Whipsnade, lives in open parkland and downland with some

Table 11.20 Chinese water deer: skull measurements (mm) of adults at Woodwalton Fen, Cambridgeshire [535a]

	Males			Females		
	Mean	Range	n	Mean	Range	n
Greatest length	167.2	163.7–171.0	5	167.0	166.5–167.5	2
Zygomatic width	70.0	68.6–71.5	5	66.1	64.0–67.0	3
Length of palate	95.0	91.6–98.2	5	96.4	96.0–96.9	2
Length of maxillary tooth row	49.7	48.4–51.4	5	49.3	48.6–50.0	3
Length of mandible	137.8	135.2–140.6	5	136.7	136.0–137.0	3
Length of extracted canine (round curve)	86.9	81.5–95.1	4	16.4	15.9–17.0	

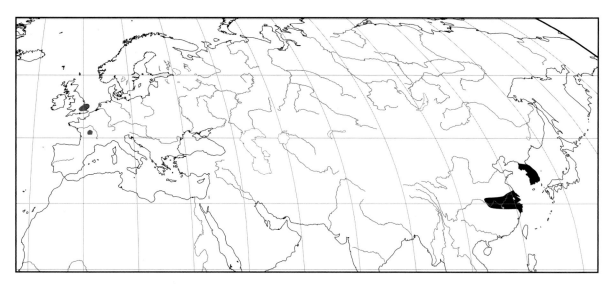

Fig. 11.39 Chinese water deer *Hydropotes inermis*: native (black) and introduced (grey) range.

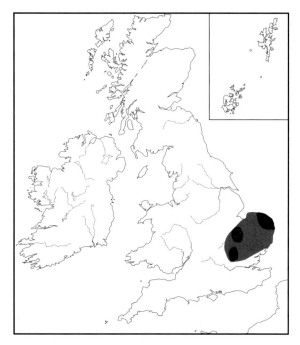

Fig. 11.40 Chinese water deer *Hydropotes inermis*: range in GB.

woodland, where it survives despite lack of wetland, albeit with low body weight. At Woodwalton Fen (Cambridgeshire) and in the Norfolk Broads, the mixed fen and woodland appear more similar to its native habitat.

SOCIAL ORGANISATION AND BEHAVIOUR

Tendency to be solitary, in part because of aggressive nature of males. At Woodwalton Fen, most sightings of single deer; even at Whipsnade tend to be individuals or pairs [204]. Groups most likely to be seen foraging on arable land in early months of the year, when natural food is scarce [202], or early autumn when family groups of mothers and young become most apparent. Sometimes loose associations of females outside fawning period. Play behaviour observed in all age and sex categories although fawns of 1–2 months seem most playful.

Territories: May be established and retained by males throughout the year, but spatial arrangement flexible, varies according to local conditions [204]. At Whipsnade, many males fail to hold territories, and range size of those with territories through the year was only 2 ha [716], whereas range size for females >2 years was 25 ha. At Woodwalton Fen, range sizes during the rut varied between 5 and 15 ha [204].

In China, mean home ranges varied from 18 to 46 ha with season and methodology [812], but during rut, bucks followed does to better feeding grounds, established territories *c*.0.5 ha [738].

Mark territories with glandular secretions, urine or faeces. Plant stems and thin saplings held behind the male's tusk and rubbed past the preorbital gland; vegetation also rubbed against forehead. No noticeable fraying of saplings. Piles of faeces often litter territorial boundaries during rut, when pellet group size reduced [207, 737]. Females may be territorial before and after giving birth.

Communication: By sight and sound as well as scent. Emit a range of sounds: alarm call is a bark, although more of a growl than the briefer bark of the muntjac. Barking more frequent in summer. One deer chasing another often makes a mechanical sound described as clicking, whickering or chittering. Male in rut pursuing

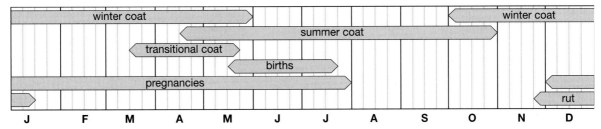

Fig. 11.41 Chinese water deer: annual cycle.

female utters a bird-like squeak or whistle. Other sounds include a loud scream by deer in pain or distress and a gentle whistle by a mother to her fawn. Odour profiles from preorbital glands individually distinct and change with age [456].

Rutting: Behaviour seen mainly during December [207, 820]. Males attempt to associate with females in their territories with increasing intensity as oestrus nears. Rival males approach with necks below horizontal, rotating head movements result in ear-slapping. Males will attempt to mate with more than one female. Encounters between 2 males start with one approaching with a ritualised stiff gait. Might then walk parallel, 10–20 m apart, followed by a chase or fight. Males use tusks to stab and tear; many males carry scars to ears, neck or flanks. Tufts of hair can frequently be found on ground during winter.

Activity: Active at any time of day or night, but mainly around dawn and dusk. Usually move with leisurely walk. Stare fixedly at human intruders, and sometimes bark. 'Neck-bobbing' mainly by does when disturbed. When frightened run off, often flinging up hind legs. May stop, turn round and assess danger. Will crouch when threatened. Good swimmers.

FEEDING
During daytime at least, spend *c.*1/2 time feeding; bouts of *c.*20 min feeding punctuated by resting and ruminating [820]. Peaks in feeding activity early morning and evening [821]. Selective feeder on tender parts of a range of grasses, sedges, herbs and woody species; proportions of each group taken depend on availability [204, 337]. Feed on crops such as carrots (especially the green tops), winter wheat and potatoes left after harvest [202]. When seen on arable land, often eating weeds rather than crop plants. Drink occasionally, obtaining most of their requirements from food and dew.

BREEDING
Polygynous, rut occurs mainly in December in

England [207, 820] (Fig. 11.41). In China, rut November–January [697]. Estimates of gestation period vary, 165–210 days. Up to 7 fetuses recorded in single female in China, but in GB, twins most usual, up to 4 recorded [114, 204, 519, 820]. Young born mainly May–June, some in July. At birth, most weigh 0.6–1.0 kg, weight gain 0.1 kg per day [114, 820]. Young left in sheltered places by female which returns at regular intervals to suckle and groom them [820]. Fawns usually hide singly, but sometimes 2–3 found together. Weaned after 3 months or less, remain with doe till early autumn (Fig. 11.42). Sexually mature by time of 1st rut when 5–8 months old [519, 695], but 1st-winter deer less successful at holding territory or mating. Body weight at 6 months *c.*80% that of adults [694].

POPULATION
Numbers: England, 2100 in 2004, of which 1500 were free-living and the remainder confined to parks [780]. China 10 000–30 000 [697].

Density: Woodwalton Fen and Norfolk Broads 10/km² or more, Whipsnade up to 240/km², farmland outside Woburn <2/km² [204]. Sex

Fig. 11.42 Chinese water deer: doe simultaneously suckling kid and cleaning its rear *(photo P. Morris)*.

ratio 1:1. At Woodwalton Fen, most young deer either died or dispersed before their 1st winter [205]. Known to live at least 6 years [695]. Population declines documented in large woodland areas where muntjac at high density or increasing [196, 207, 208]. However, populations can persist for many years under suitable conditions [205], and range continues to expand in England [781].

MORTALITY

Over 6-year period at Woodwalton Fen, 35 found dead, 83% in October–March, associated with harder weather and rutting season. Annual survival of adults at Woodwalton Fen 52–99% over 22 years, mortality greatest in cold wet winters [205]. Can suffer from starvation during hard weather, even on parkland. Fawns eaten by foxes. Adult males shot by trophy hunters, but some stalkers do not shoot this species, to encourage populations to establish. Over same 6-year period at Woodwalton Fen, 16 recorded shot on adjacent farmland. Road casualties a major cause of mortality; first identified in Norfolk as road casualty.

PARASITES

Demodex mites cause mange. Ticks *Ixodes* spp., keds *Lipoptena* sp. and lice *Cervicola meyeri* and *Damalinia* sp. all recorded. More parasites on park deer than wild ones [114]. Nematode *Oesophagostomum venulosum* found in colon at Whipsnade. Haemolytic streptococci recorded in subcutaneous pustules. Suffer from pulmonary congestion and respiratory diseases. Reovirus 1 and 2 and adenovirus A recorded by serological evidence [450].

RELATIONS WITH HUMANS

Root crops and sprouting grain eaten when other food scarce, but impact slight and localised [202]. Does not fray trees. May, in time, be shown to cause occasional conservation problems, but does not reach such high densities as muntjac, is not such an extreme concentrate selector, and is found in more robust habitats. Easily raised in captivity but a tendency to fight and escape. Close season (15 March–31 October) for both sexes under consideration, and inclusion on Schedule 9 of the Wildlife and Countryside Act 1981 being discussed [229].

LITERATURE

General account [204]; behaviour at Whipsnade [716, 820]; general accounts from China [694, 695].

AUTHORS

A.S. Cooke & L. Farrell

FAMILY BOVIDAE (CATTLE, SHEEP, GOATS, ANTELOPES)

A large and diverse family of *c*.141 species, mostly in Africa and Asia, a few in N America and Europe. Differ from Cervidae in structure of horns, which have bony core and keratin sheath; not shed annually, usually present in both sexes. Tend to have higher-crowned cheek-teeth, and to be grazers rather than browsers, but much variation in structure and diet. Represented in British Isles only by feral or semi-feral populations of 3 domestic ungulates: sheep, goats and cattle.

GENUS *Ovis*

A genus of *c*.7 closely related species of sheep, distributed in mountainous regions of Asia and N America, from Turkey and Iran to the Rocky Mountains as far south as Mexico. Domestic sheep *Ovis aries* derive from W Asian population of urial *O. orientalis*. Accepted convention that different specific names used for ancestral and descendant forms [291]. Skeleton very similar to *Capra*, but skull, horns and fighting methods different; sheep butt head-on into each other, and have stout battering-ram horns in rams (more slender in ewes), while goats meet cross-horned, and have longer, curved horns.

Feral sheep *Ovis aries*

Ovis aries Linnaeus, 1758; Sweden.

Male – ram, tup; female – ewe; juvenile – lamb.

RECOGNITION

Two forms of feral sheep, Soay and Boreray, occur in GB, each named from islands of St Kilda group (Plate 10). The Soay is the most primitive domestic sheep, resembling wild sheep in brown coat, relatively long legs, short tail and narrow body. Brown coat variable, dimorphic – very dark or tan (Table 11.21). Soays are smallest of all sheep, wild or domestic, *c*.50 cm at the shoulder [672]; only likely to be confused with unimproved sheep breeds such as Hebridean and North Ronaldsay. Boreray is a primitive form of Scottish Blackface, but smaller and variable in colour, ranging from cream-white to blackish [87, 90].

Skull and skeleton: For distinctions between sheep and goats, see under feral goat (cf. Figs. 11.26, 11.44). All Boreray sheep have one pair of horns; most Soay rams and about 1/3 Soay ewes are horned, other ewes are polled or carry distinctive deformed horns called 'scurs' (Table 11.21; [239]).

Table 11.21 Soay sheep on Hirta: percentage of in each coat and horn class

Sex	Horns (n = 1343)			Coat (n = 1288)			
	Normal	Scurred	Polled	Dark Wild	Dark Self	Light Wild	Light Self
Male	87.1	12.9	–	70.5	4.7	23.8	0.01
Female	35.5	21.0	43.5	67.1	4.8	26.5	0.02

Deviation from 100% results from rounding and unclassified individuals with anomalous coats.

FIELD SIGNS

Tracks: Typical cloven hoofprint, very similar to feral goat.

Faeces: Very similar to feral goat, but less regular. Deposited throughout home range but large accumulations occur in resting and sheltering places [71].

DESCRIPTION

Pelage: Soay fleece is classed as either 'Dark' or 'Light' phase with 'Wild' or 'Self' markings (Table 11.21). Dark individuals vary from russet-brown to dark chocolate, and Light from pale buff to gingery-fawn. Wild-type marking similar to mouflon: whitish belly, extending onto the inside of limbs, scrotum or udder, and forming a prominent rump patch; a pale ring may surround the eyes in dark animals. In Self-marked sheep, white markings absent, replaced by main colouring, though in Light Self individuals often with slightly darker gingery-fawn [239]. Less hairy than wild sheep, particularly in Light sheep; c.4–5% have anomalous white patches [239]. 'Hairy' Soays have longer coats than 'woolly', Dark are longer than Light, males longer than females [239, 667]. Males develop large throat ruffs and manes before the rut in autumn.

Colour of Boreray varies from white to blackish.

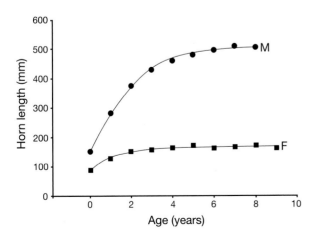

Fig. 11.43 Soay sheep: growth pattern of horns.

In 1980, approximately 67% had cream/off-white fleeces, 20% grey/grey-brown and the remainder tan or darker. 4–7% have wholly blackish coats. Often a dark collar extending from nape to front legs. Fleece shorter, finer than modern Scottish Blackface sheep [670].

Moult: In both breeds, fleece cast during late spring–early summer, males starting and finishing earlier [71, 669, 670]. In Soays, new fibres start growing from March–April (males) or April–May (females), growth finishing in September–October under the influence of shortened daylength [669, 675]. Moulted fleece may not be shed properly, especially by females [239].

Horns: Strong, laterally placed, forming full-turn spiral in mature rams; lighter, gentle arc in ewes (Fig. 11.43).

Nipples: 1 functional pair, often rudimentary 2nd pair.

Scent glands: In rams, antorbital gland swells and opens during the rut. Caudal, circumanal, inguinal and interdigital glands also present [311].

Teeth: In most Soays, eruption of successive pairs of incisiform teeth, from the central pair outwards, annually spaced, can be used to age sheep approximately up to 4 years (Table 11.22) [327]. Can also be aged by counting cementum lines in cross-sections of the 1st incisor [182, 659]. Dentition remains in good condition until advanced age, with very few 'broken mouths', in part due to the high mineral input from sea spray [33, 169].

Skeleton: In Soays, skeleton fully formed (including metacarpal and metatarsal fusion) by 6 years [169]. In general, Soays on St Kilda show slower skeletal development than mainland improved breeds. Broken limbs are uncommon, but c.60% of males show damage to the cervical vertebrae, probably due to head-butting during the rut [169].

Table 11.22 Soay sheep on Hirta: distribution of incisiform teeth with age, recorded in August, 1985–1995. Sheep with 'rising' teeth were assigned to the same category as those with fully erupted teeth [169a]

Age	Milk	2	4	6	Full
0	100%				
1	50	50			
2		60	40		
3		Trace	40	50	10
4				50	50
5+					100%

Reproductive tract: Female: bicornate uterus; corpus luteum active for *c.*14 days, uterine epithelium frequently with black pigment; cotyledonary placenta. Male: testes and epididymes develop less quickly than in goat; mature spermatozoa first recorded at 147 days. Average ejaculate volume 1.18–1.46 ml. Soays have possibly the largest testes for their body size of any ungulate [462, 733].

Chromosomes: 2n = 54 as in *O. orientalis* [554]. *O. aries, O. orientalis* and *O. musimon* produce fertile hybrids.

Domestic sheep are descended from Asiatic mouflon *O. orientalis*, whose range extends from SW to C Asia [681]. This is the only wild sheep with the same chromosomal complement; urial *Ovis vignei*, previously thought to be ancestral, has 2n = 58 chromosomes (although it will hybridise with *O. aries*) [672].

Measurements
See Table 11.23.

VARIATION
Founding stock for non-St Kilda populations often lack variation in coat and horn morphs, and may have different allele frequencies e.g. for blood proteins. The Cheddar Gorge population has only horned females, and probably lacks Self type markings. Managed mainland 'park' Soays are typically Dark-wild, woolly, with all-horned females; scurring does exist, but is rare (possibly selected against by breeders).

DISTRIBUTION
Soays originally on Soay, some transferred to Hirta (St Kilda); more recently, introduced to various offshore islands: Lundy, Cardigan Island, Holy Isle (Arran), Sheep Island (Sanda Is., Kintyre). A mainland feral population appeared in Cheddar Gorge in 1990s, now numbers >130. Small population on Ailsa Craig, Firth of Clyde, removed late 1950s–early 1960s. The Boreray is confined to Boreray, St Kilda.

Worldwide, feral sheep occur on *c.*20 islands (less frequent than feral goats) [662], including Arapawa, Campbell and Pitt Is. of New Zealand [561, 661, 804], Kerguelen in the Southern Ocean [65], Hawaii [757] and Santa Cruz I., California [767].

HISTORY
Sheep introduced to British Isles as domestic

Table 11.23 Soay and Boreray sheep: live measurements for males and females

	Birthweight (single/twin) (kg)		Adult weight (range) (kg)		Height at shoulder (mm)		Foreleg length[a] (mm)		Max horn basal length[b] (mm)		Max horn circumference (mm)	
	M	F	M	F	M	F	M	F	M	F	M	F
Soay	2.0/1.6	1.9/1.5	35.6	23.7	56[f]	52[f]	347	321	615	237	215	111
n	109/21[c]	83/37[c]	135[d]	707[d]			11[c]	98[c]	118[d]	98[d]	358[d]	237[d]
Boreray	2.9/–	2.2/–	45	30	60	55	–	–	750	–	–	–
n	3[c]	3[c]	3[f]	3[f]	3[f]	3[f]	–	–	?[de]–	–	–	–

All from feral sheep except those for Boreray marked f.

[a] Foreleg measured from olecranon process to top of hoof.

[b] Horn length outer circumference.

Sources: [c] Hirta [239]; [d] Hirta/ Boreray [169a]; [e] Boreray [87]; [f] Edinburgh [670].

stock by Neolithic peoples by 4000 BC [672]; exact date uncertain, due to confusion between goat/sheep bones in archaeological sites, but earliest claimed to be 5635 bp, Lambourn Downs, Berkshire [813]. First evidence of domestication comes from SE Turkey, N Syria and Iraq, *c.*8500 BC (9300 bp) [576, 672]. *O. musimon* (Corsica and Sardinia) and *O. ophion* (Cyprus) ('wild mouflon') are feral relics of early domestic sheep imported soon after their domestication [325, 769]. Typical results of domestication include short legs, long tail, smaller or absent horns, finer white coat, lack of moult and a brain 20% smaller, despite similar body size [325, 672].

Horn shape, short tail, coat colour and moult all suggest affinity of Soays with wild *Ovis* species. Soay bones are very like those discovered in late Neolithic, Bronze Age and Iron Age sites [70, 672]. The Soay may have reached St Kilda in the Bronze Age, as early as 2000 BC [673], and there is evidence of farmers living there around that time [268]. Introduction later than Early Iron Age unlikely, based on fleece colours [673], despite suggested introduction by the Vikings [70].

Sheep on Soay were first distinguished from others on St Kilda in the 1830s [353], when population estimated to vary from 200 to 500 [352]. Little management then, though some evidence for occasional introduction of rams of 'improved' breeds [257]. In 1932, following the evacuation of the St Kildans and their sheep in 1930, 107 Soays (20 rams, 44 ewes, 21 ewe lambs and 22 castrate ram lambs) were transferred to Hirta [67]. Since then, have been unmanaged.

The Boreray represents the 19th century Scottish Blackface, formed by crossing the Old Scottish Shortwool (now extinct) and Blackface introduced from England in the 18th century [90, 672]; were abandoned on Boreray when the islanders were evacuated in 1930 [106].

HABITAT
On St Kilda, both breeds select *Agrostis–Festuca*, *Holcus–Agrostis, Festuca, Poa* grassland and *Plantago* sward during summer. In autumn–early winter, Soays on Hirta make more use of *Calluna* wet heath [339, 522]. (*Calluna* heath does not occur on Boreray.)

Shelter affects the distribution of animals, particularly in winter. On St Kilda, cleits (dry-stone chambers) are used during poor weather and at night. In summer, Soays may also take refuge in cleits to escape the sun. Input of nutrients around cleits strongly influences the vegetation, which becomes denser and more vigorous [340].

SOCIAL ORGANISATION AND BEHAVIOUR
Considerable information available for Soays, covering social groupings, ranging behaviour, and breeding behaviour [174, 414]. Patterns are similar in domestic hill breeds and wild sheep [387, 454, 691].

Territories: Soay ewes on Hirta maintain matriarchal relationships in ewe home-range groups. Individual ewes may occupy ranges of 2–25 ha, usually smallest March–April [331]. Typical size of group was 27–37 between 1964 and 1967. Home ranges are not overtly defended, but 'core areas' tend to be used exclusively. Ram lambs leave these ewe groups by 2 years of age, and join, or form, separate ram groups, usually with similar-aged males. These ram groups break down shortly before the rut when males move individually and may cover large distances, appearing anywhere on the island. No territory defence by rams at any time of year.

Vocalisations: Contact call between lamb and ewes is the familiar bleat. Alarm call a snort or whistle in response to danger (as also in hill sheep). During rut, males make low growling/rumbling vocalisation during aggressive interactions with other males, or when investigating oestrous ewes

Aggressive behaviour: Peaks in the month before, and during, rut as rams groups disperse [328]. Aggression is particularly marked between rams which are unknown to each other. Typically males stand parallel, head to tail or head to head, leaning heavily on each other and kicking with a stiff foreleg; head may be twisted to side and the tongue flicked rapidly in and out; often aim sideways blows with horns at shoulder or rump of the opponent [328]. Fights may escalate into head-butting; males walk backwards before charging, but do not rear up as do some wild sheep [288]. Bouts of head-butting may be particularly prolonged in ram lambs, lasting for tens of minutes. Head-butting may very occasionally be fatal [1]. Ewes occasionally butt one another at any time of year (whether horned or polled), may also butt small ram lambs which harass them during the rut.

Dispersal: On Hirta, all rams have left their natal ewe home-range group before 2 years. Ewes usually remain in natal group or close by. Occasionally both rams and ewes will disperse longer distances to areas widely separated from their normal range.

Activity: On Hirta, typically spend night in shelter or uphill. Move downhill at dawn and begin grazing. Bouts of rumination occur throughout day, but especially around midday. Often start moving uphill again during afternoon [331]. In winter, most of the day spent grazing, rumination less frequent than summer.

FEEDING

Predominantly or exclusively grazers. Soay on Hirta show a marked seasonal variation in diet similar to that shown by hill sheep on the mainland of Scotland: in summer, grasses predominate with an increasing proportion of heather towards and through the winter [522]. In summer, food is unlikely ever to be limiting, but energy intake is likely to be below maintenance levels during some of the winter [522]. On Boreray, where there is no *Calluna*, sheep graze the year round. This diet is probably typical of most island populations of Soays; in the only mainland population, in Cheddar Gorge, Soays browse on yew and ivy [1].

BREEDING

Polyoestrous, mating November–early December on St Kilda (earlier at lower latitudes), spontaneous ovulation, gestation 148–155 days (mean 151), peak birth April (on St Kilda), singletons or twins. Mating system promiscuous.

Males: Minimum levels of testosterone, smallest testes, occur March–May. Seasonal testicular increase begins June–September, followed by increase in testosterone concentrations [466]. Seasonal cycle in testes size is larger than observed in mouflon or 'improved' breeds, varying by 171% [462]. Seasonal cycles controlled by the effect of daylength on melatonin production, but rise in testicular activity can occur while days are still lengthening, before midsummer [463, 464]. Rams take part in their 1st rut at 7 months of age [734]. Rams start to show interest in ewes in early summer, sniffing their urine and displaying flehmen [261]. In October, males move widely outside their home range, investigating ewes for oestrus [328]. Aggression between males peaks late October–early November, before peak of oestrous females.

Mating behaviour: Males do not defend harems, but search for individual ewes in oestrus. Large dominant rams form consorts with oestrous ewes and attempt to defend them from other males [328, 330]. Consorting may last from a few minutes to many hours, and include repeated bouts of mating. Consort pairs often surrounded by subordinate males, which are small, young or have scurred horns; attempt to separate female from consort. If successful, chase often results, with ewe fleeing from pursuing subordinates and

dominant male, which tries to regain control. During these chases, many different subordinates may mate with the female; if chase prolonged, dominant male likely to give up. Amongst adult males, these 2 types of mating behaviour are associated with horn type. Large-horned males defend females and may invest significant time in individual consorts; scurred males spend little time with each female, but follow an opportunistic strategy of rapid investigation and hurried mating with many females [174]. Sperm competition likely to be important, particularly for subordinates, since females mate with many males during a single oestrus.

Male reproductive success: Large adult males are most successful in fathering lambs [32, 189], but success of young males and scurred adults can be quite high in the rut following a population crash, when less competition from dominant adults [32, 572, 733]. Success of large-horned adults declines relative to scurred males as population density increases; at high density, more difficult to successfully defend an oestrous ewe in consort, consequently dominant males must adopt a more opportunistic strategy akin to that of scurred males [174].

Females: Oestrus may last 1–4 days, most commonly 1–2; juvenile females often have shorter oestrus, later in the rut [413]. Most only display 1 oestrus, but if conception fails, cycle again about 15 days later. Ewes in same home-range group tend to show synchronised oestruses. The timing and synchrony of oestrus depends on population latitude [411]. On St Kilda, females are more synchonous, peaking in mid November, but in Cheddar Gorge females may be in oestrus late July–October [1]. Females often actively avoid mating with subordinate males.

Productivity: (St Kilda) proportion of females conceiving in 1st year reduced by high population density; varies 6–81%. Twinning only by females 2 years or older, is reduced by high population density, varying from 3% to 23% in adult ewes [182]; twinning is commonest in heavy females (corrected for age) [184]. In captive Soays with good feeding, twins are common, triplets occur, 1 case of quads reported [510]. Birth weight declines as population density increases. Males are heavier than females at low population density, but show a tendency to be lighter at high density [653]. Sex ratio at birth 1:1 [413].

Development of young: Twins are lighter than singletons, grow more slowly (twins 75 g/day; singletons 120 g/day). Weight of lambs at

4 months also declines with increasing population density. By 4 weeks, suckling is reduced to 20 s/h, and by 6 weeks lambs are effectively weaned [329], spend >40% of the day grazing [653] (lambs will occasionally still attempt to suck at 7 months, in the rut).

POPULATION

St Kilda: Between 1952 and 1999, total number on Hirta fluctuated dramatically (Table 11.24). Irregular 'crashes', when 30–70% of the population may die [174, 182, 321], occur at intervals of 3–15 years. Fluctuations correlate with those of Boreray sheep (between 200 and 699), 6 km away from Hirta. Poor weather greatly increases mortality at high population density, leading to entrainment of their population dynamics [322]. Pattern seems similar for 3rd population, Soay sheep on Soay, but counts poorer, island inaccessible. Exceptionally high peak density of Boreray sheep possibly reflects high quality pastures, fertilised by seabird guano [68].

Other populations: Cheddar Gorge 138 (March 1998); Lundy *c.*188 (October 1998); Sheep I., Sanda *c.*35 (1998).

MORTALITY

On Hirta, most deaths occur early February–early April. In crashes, male lamb mortality may reach 99% [174, 182]. Males generally suffer much higher mortality rates, resulting in a highly skewed adult sex ratio which may reach 1:14 (M:F) after particularly high mortality [733]. Males die earlier in the year than females, whose peak mortality occurs in late gestation and parturition [734]. Heavier animals survive better over winter [182, 183], Dark coats survive better than Light [538], and scurred individuals better than polled or normal-horned [185]. Survival also declines with degree of inbreeding [189]. Neonatal survival is highest for prime-aged mothers [183]. Reproductive activity reduces overwinter survival: breeding in 1st year of life increases mortality for

both sexes [184, 500, 734], and twinning females show higher mortality, particularly those with low weight [184, 500]. Castration at birth removes all reproductive costs and increases male lifespan over that for both intact males and females [412]. Oldest recorded ram on Hirta was aged 10, oldest ewe almost 17 years of age. Average lifespans are much lower: at 6 months of age, average life expectancy for a ram is only 2 years [733].

Disease: Rare at low population density on St Kilda, and only causes death in association with undernutrition at high population density [334]. On Boreray, overgrown hooves cause 3% of adult sheep to limp [87]; such lameness may precipitate falls from cliffs; neither this nor footrot found in Soays on Hirta.

PARASITES

Ectoparasites: Lice *Damalinia ovis*, keds *Melophagus ovinus*. Sheep tick *Ixodes ricinus* not recorded from St Kilda; seabird tick *I. rothschildi* occurs on Boreray [87], may accidentally occur on sheep.

Helminths: Nematodes *Teladosagia circumcincta*, *Nematodirus filicollis*, *N. battus*, *Bunostomum trigonocephalum*, *Trichuris ovis* and *Chabertia ovina* (intestines); *Dictyocaulus filaria* (trachea, lungs), *Muelleris capillaris* (lungs). Tapeworms: *Taenia hydatigena*, *Monieza* spp. [81, 333, 334, 758]. No definitive host (carnivore) for *T. hydatigena* on St Kilda; possible that egg dispersal by birds maintains the population [758].

No antibody for louping ill recorded for Soay sheep on Hirta. Coccidial oocysts recorded for Boreray sheep: *Eimeria weybridgensis*, *E. ninakohlyakimoriae*, *E. ovina* and *E. parva*. Detailed parasite lists in [90, 161, 174, 334].

Parasites increase mortality of Soay sheep, especially in winter [335], and play a role in the maintenance of genetic diversity [189, 336, 567]. Nematode burdens higher in younger sheep, in males than females, in ewes at time of birth than rest of year [174].

Table 11.24 Soay sheep: counts from the 3 islands in the St Kilda group; those for Soay are subject to high error

Island	Hirta	Boreray	Soay
Island area (ha)	638	77	99
Sheep breed	Soay	Boreray	Soay
Max. pop. (year)	2022 (2000)	699 (1980)	c.360
Min. pop. (year)	610 (1985)	215 (1990)	c.100

RELATIONS WITH HUMANS

Present management policy for Soay and Boreray sheep on St Kilda is for minimal interference, while at the same time watching for serious damage to the ecosystem. Soay sheep scatter, cannot be herded by sheepdogs. Both classified by the Rare Breeds Survival Trust as 'Rare Breeds'. Many consider the St Kildan sheep a valuable heritage (note that the name 'St Kilda' used to be given to the 4-horned breed now called the Hebridean). May also have genetic and historical importance; feral sheep occur in British Isles and Mediterranean, share with 'wild mouflon' on Cyprus, Corsica, Sardinia ancestry from earliest Neolithic sheep [325], perhaps of European significance [360]. The Soay, in particular, is regarded as an important link with the sheep type that was first introduced to the British Isles in prehistoric times [70].

A long-term study of the behaviour and ecology of Soay sheep on Hirta has been conducted since 1959 [174, 414]. This study, supported by Scottish Natural Heritage and the National Trust for Scotland, is one of the most detailed for any free-living population, continues to yield new insights into population dynamics, maintenance of genetic diversity, parasite–host relationships and plant–herbivore interactions.

LITERATURE

Comprehensive accounts of the ecology of Soay sheep on St Kilda [174, 414]; a comprehensive account of the natural history of Boreray, including its sheep [87].

AUTHORS

I.R. Stevenson & D.J. Bullock.

GENUS *Capra*

A genus of 6 or 7 closely related species of ibex and goats [494], distributed mostly in mountainous regions of Asia, extending to Europe and NE Africa. Domestic goats *Capra hircus* derive from W Asian population of bezoar *C. aegagrus*. Accepted convention that different specific names used for ancestral and descendant forms [291]. Skeleton very similar to *Ovis*, but skull, horns and fighting methods different; goats meet cross-horned, and have longer, curved horns.

Feral goat *Capra hircus*

Capra hircus Linnaeus, 1758; Sweden.
Wild goat; *gafr wyllt* (Welsh); *gabhar fhiadhain* (Scottish Gaelic); *gabhar fia* (Irish Gaelic); *goayr cheoie* (Manx).

Male – billy; female – nanny; juvenile – kid.

RECOGNITION

Whole animal: Only likely to be confused with certain unimproved breeds of sheep (Plate 10). Goats distinguished from sheep by the presence of a callus on the knee, a beard and a potent body odour (especially in billies); have flat, rather long tails, bare underneath (sheep have more rounded, hairy tails). Smaller, lighter and longer haired than 'improved' (modern) goat breeds (billies usually <70 cm at the shoulder and <65 kg). Colour varies from white through to faded black; most are grey, grey-brown or black with paler patches. Both sexes usually horned and with dished faces. A few are polled (genetically hornless), especially in N Wales and Ireland. Ears normally erect.

Skull and teeth: Distinguishable from sheep by convex frontals and nasals (Fig. 11.44). Horn cores arise from frontals vertically (laterally in sheep). Lower jaw thinner and more acutely angled than in sheep. Distal end of metapodials (cannon bones) characterised by 2 converging sagittal ridges (cf. sheep which have parallel sagittal ridges) [58, 592]. Otherwise, bones of goats and sheep are very similar. Ageing accurate to 1 year possible by counting annual rings on horn sheaths for all except nannies >3 years [94]. Ring formed in winter, becomes conspicuous at the base of the horn when growth recommences in spring [319].

FIELD SIGNS

Tracks and trails: Very similar to sheep. Sometimes distinguishable because hoofs tend to be more splayed and smaller in goats than sheep. Both species may use the same tracks, but some goat tracks cross very steep terrain inaccessible to sheep.

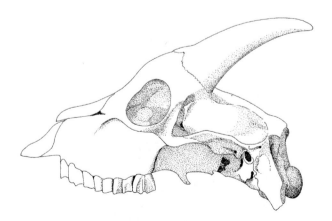

Fig. 11.44 Goat skull, showing short muzzle, strong boss carrying the horns (cf. sheep, Fig. 11.26) *(drawn by D.W. Yalden).*

Faeces: Very similar to sheep, roe deer and red deer. Pellets 1–2 cm long, cylindrical with pointed or concave ends. Tend to be more symmetrical and drier than either sheep or deer. Deposited throughout home range but large accumulations occur in traditional shelter sites.

Other field signs: Bark-stripping frequent where goats have access to woodland. Bark stripped from a central vertical line splaying to either side moving up the trunk and interspersed with long rips of bark. Difficult to separate bark-stripping by goats from that of deer or sheep. Bark-stripping usually to maximum height of 2 m, but may climb trees, cause higher damage [1, 365].

DESCRIPTION

Pelage: Colour variable; ranges from pure black to white; fawns and greys most common, latter due to mixture of black and white fibres [668]. Black goats often have a fringe of long, ginger hair along the back and on hindquarters. Many Welsh ferals have dark forequarters and whitish hindquarters [78]. Dark stripe on front of forelegs frequent. Some goats in SW Scotland show a dark eel stripe, 'Jesus' saddle and brown and black pattern similar to the true wild goat. Goats from SW Scotland are paler and greyer than those from further east [708].

Moult: Once a year; in late spring–early summer, when winter hair and underwool are shed. Thicker winter coat due to increase in length of underwool [668].

Horns: Grow backwards and then outwards in a smooth curve. Wide spreading ('dorcas') horns frequent in Wales, E of Southern Uplands and in some Highland and Irish populations. In SW Scotland close set, backward-sweeping horns ('scimitar') are more frequent.

Nipples: 1 pair, inguinal.

Scent glands: Postcornual 'musk' glands found in both sexes, situated immediately behind and along inside edge of horn. These are apparently activated by testosterone and usually are only active in males [489]. Interdigital and caudal glands also present [311].

Teeth: Eruption sequence and degree of wear used to assign individuals to broad age classes. Incisiform teeth: in 11 nannies tracked throughout life, 9 had erupted all 4 pairs by the age of 3.5 years. For a similar sample of 9 billies, 'full-mouthed' condition attained later: 3 by 3.5 years, 5 by 4.5 years and 1 by 5.5 years [1]. Cheek-teeth (data from billies): deciduous premolars shed by 1.5 years. m_1 already erupted at birth, m_2 by 1.5 years, m_3 by 3.5 years. Cusps on all cheek-teeth well worn to flat surfaces by 6.5 years [92].

Excessive tooth wear and tooth loss can occur after 4 years old. By 7 years, frequently lose molars and show signs of diseased teeth. Incisiform teeth usually wear evenly and are rarely lost in life (although frequently fall out after death) [88].

Table 11.25 Feral goats: measurements of adult (4 years or older) feral goats from S Scotland. Weights from late autumn–winter when goats are heaviest

	Males			Females		
	Mean	Range	n	Mean	Range	n
Head and body (cm)	129.7	118–152	10	120.9	106–136	30
Tail (cm)	11.3	8–14	10	10.7	7–14	30
Ear (cm)	10.7	9.5–11.5	20	10.8	10–11.5	29
Weight (kg)	52.4	39–65	10	41.1	29–52	30
Jaw length (mm)	174	157–198	14	172	151–190	13
Condylobasal length (mm)	226	208–241	10	221	209–243	17
Horn length (mm)	607	465–755	20	249	93–385	30
Heart girth (cm)	99.3	91–108	10	93.6	80–106	30
Height at shoulder (cm)	69.0	60–75	20	64.2	56–74	30
Beard length (cm)	26.5	26–27	2	19.6	17–22	10

Skeleton: In billies, frontal, nasofrontal and nasal sutures fused by 4.5 years. In nannies, fusion occurs at approximately twice this age. In billies, all postcranial epiphyses fused by the age of 6.5 years, apparently similar for nannies [92].

Reproductive tract: Female: bipartite Y-shaped uterus; syndesmochorial placentation. Villi from fetal placenta clustered into groups called fetal caruncles. Male: testes and epididymides develop rapidly from 30–40 days until 140–150 days, when fully mature and weigh 90–136 g. Spermatozoa first recorded at 88–95 days. Average ejaculate into artificial vagina 0.10–1.25 ml [26].

Chromosomes: 2n = 60, as other members of the genus, all of which appear to interbreed freely in captivity.

MEASUREMENTS
See Table 11.25.

VARIATION
Goats from SE Scotland/NE England significantly larger and heavier than those from SW Scotland and N Wales [88, 365]. Variation may have a genetic basis, but density and range quality may also be important.

DISTRIBUTION
Mainly hilly and mountainous areas of Scotland, Wales, Ireland and N England (Fig. 11.45), including the following islands: Achil, Bute, Cara,

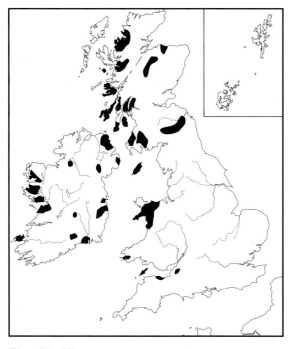

Fig. 11.45 Feral goat *Capra hircus*: range in British Isles.

Colonsay, Great Blasket , Holy Island (Arran), Islay, Jura, Lundy, Mull, Rathlin, Rum, Skelligs. Recently introduced to the Isle of Wight. Populations often small and discrete rather than scattered over a wide area of apparently suitable ground. In France, only one small (*c*.20 goats) population on sea cliffs at Jobourg, Normandy [40].

Feral goats occur elsewhere in Eurasia and Far East (e.g. S Norway, Spain, Japan, Canada, USA). Australia and New Zealand have large populations. Worldwide, feral goats occur on at least 111 islands [105, 662].

HISTORY
Not native. Wholly or largely descended from wild goat *Capra aegagrus* [226, 487] whose range extends from E Mediterranean to C Asia. Domestic goats arose *c*.11 000 bp in SW Asia, perhaps SE Turkey or W Iran [226, 487, 816, 817]; 3 genetic lineages recognisable, but feral goats in British Isles likely to belong only to main lineage. In GB, first introduced as domestic stock by Neolithic peoples [703]; date uncertain due to confusion of archaeological goat/sheep bones, but earliest record at Windmill Hill, Wiltshire, 4530 bp [813].

Most feral goats in GB and Ireland show characters – presence of horns, lack of neck tassels, coat pattern, prick ears and foreleg stripe – that apparently fit those of the old breeds 'Old English', 'Old Irish', 'Old Scottish' or 'native goat' . These became extinct in domestication in the early 1900s as improved breeds were imported and sheep farming became increasingly popular. Most feral populations were established at least a century ago [319]. Domestic goats continue to be liberated or escape and become feral in the Burren (Co. Clare), S Uplands (Scotland) and elsewhere [1].

Until 18th century, as important in the rural economies of N Wales, W Scotland as other livestock. Goats grazed steep rocky ledges, thereby removing tempting herbage that would result in cattle or sheep getting stuck or falling. Goat grease is translucent and was highly valued for candles [516, 652]. Dry-stone wall pens for goat kids (*cwt myn*) in Snowdonia, designed to lure and trap their nursing dams and take half her milk for human consumption, point to a long association between feral (as opposed to captive) goats and farmers [99].

HABITAT
Mostly restricted to hilly, mountainous or coastal areas where cliffs are available. Steep ground, often above 300 m asl in hills, used for refuge, shelter and for feeding in associated dwarf shrub communities. Prefer dry, well-drained ground. At night, and during persistent rain, use shelter such as crags, caves, rank heather and gullies

extensively. During severe winters, goats tend to move downhill to lower altitudes.

Many populations use scrub (e.g. the Burren) or woodland (native and planted coniferous e.g. Wicklow Mountains, SW and W Scotland, N Wales). Where co-occur with hill sheep, frequently occur on steeper, rockier terrain [88, 218].

SOCIAL ORGANISATION AND BEHAVIOUR

Matriarchal relationships within nanny groups. Adult billies often group together, may range separately from nanny groups. Within billy groups, peers usually associate more closely with each other than with other age classes. In S Uplands and N Wales, group size varies seasonally between 1 and 70, depending on population size. Median group size of 2 in spring as nannies near term isolate themselves from home-range group; rises to 8 in the autumn and winter when rut occurs [88]. Similar seasonal variation in group size occurs in Wales [80]. In the Burren, median group sizes can be much larger [1].

Some evidence for optimal group size for foraging feral goats: in S Uplands, as group size increases up to 9, the amount of time individuals spent scanning decreases and foraging time increases, but collective time spent vigilant increases [492].

Degree of sexual segregation variable; in some (but not all) populations, outside the rut, home-range groups of billies may be geographically distinct from those of nannies (Rum [69]; N Wales [80]; S Uplands [88]; Wicklow Mountains [678]). Sex differences in habitat use reported on Rum (males use plant communities with poorer quality forage than females [306]), N Wales and Wicklow Mountains (males use woodland more than females [236, 678]).

Dispersion: In many populations, dispersed in home-range groups, consisting of one to several matrilines and associated billies. In many populations, nannies rarely disperse from their natal home-range groups. Billies may disperse to join billy home-range group [88, 579]. Home-range groups can have clearly defined boundaries with little overlap between neighbouring group ranges [69, 88]. Area used by home-range group 0.3–6.5 km² (mean 3.0 km²) depending partly on the number of goats in the group (6–62), and the quality of the range [69, 78, 88].

Billies wander widely during the rut in search of nannies in oestrus, usually returning to their non-breeding range by the summer. In GB and Ireland, dispersal from known population range has never been documented. In New Zealand, dispersal rate *c.*4 km/year [565]. Lack of dispersal probably related to need for known shelter sites.

Behaviour: Few differences between behavioural repertoires of feral and wild goats [691]. Social hierarchy exists amongst nannies and amongst billies in billy groups with dominant individuals tending to be the largest and oldest. Billies >1 year are dominant in encounters to nannies. Dominance exerted by 'stare threat', through 'horn-lowering', escalating to the 'clash' where 2 goats crash their heads and horns together with great force. Bouts of clashing by same-sized billies may last several hours. Dominance and mating success in billies related to pre-rut body weight and horn length [579].

Billies (unlike rams) urinate over forequarters; resulting odour possibly used in communicating dominance rank [186]. During rut, billies 'test' the reproductive state of nannies: odours in her urine 'tasted' by vomeronasal organ during lip-curling (flehmen). Flehmen also given by billies in response to their own urine, and by nannies after sniffing kids [556].

Communication: Contact call, a series of bleats, often used by dam searching for kid when it is 'hiding out'. Also used by adults when separated from group. Alarm call an abrupt, nasal snort which immediately alerts most of the group. Potentially dangerous threats cause a walking retreat or, if necessary, a run to steep ground such as cliffs. Distress call a loud, wavering scream.

Activity: Predominantly diurnal. Day spent alternatively feeding and ruminating (and resting). In winter, typically one long (*c.*2 h) rumination period, during the middle of the day. Goats in a group tend to ruminate synchronously. In summer, several rumination periods during the course of the day. May feed at dusk and at dawn during the summer and autumn. Billies feed relatively little during the rut [88].

Movement is by walking, running or leaping. Extremely agile, an able climber of trees and near-vertical cliff faces provided there are footholds. Frequently browse on hind legs to bring branches within reach of mouth. Apparently avoid swimming.

FEEDING

A highly selective but versatile feeder, adapting diet to season and local conditions. Goats may browse or graze (typically to a minimum of 6 cm into the sward, approximately twice as high as hill sheep [521]). In the uplands, show a seasonal pattern of diet selection similar to hill sheep but more diverse: in summer, grasses, sedges and rushes predominate, increased use of dwarf shrubs and gorse in winter. Browse more than sheep or cattle, and where dwarf shrubs scarce, also feed more on rushes, ferns, herbs and bog myrtle. In woodlands, browse and bark can make up 75% of diet [89, 98, 236, 365, 706, 707]. On Rum and Holy Island, seaweed eaten extensively in winter [319, 582]. In winter, where goats have access to woodland, bark-stripping is common. In oakwoods on base-poor soils, W GB, trees with a dbh of 1–15 cm were the most vulnerable to stripping. In order of selection, species stripped were: (holly, ash, willow), (oak), (alder, hazel); birch avoided [365, 677].

Estimated daily intake rates (summer and winter) for feral goats in Scottish uplands are: nanny (40 kg) 1.2 and 0.6; billy (50 kg) 1.4 and 0.7 kg dry matter respectively. These values are similar to those for hill sheep of comparable weight [24].

BREEDING

Mate during autumn rut; gestation 151 days in large series of goats of several breeds; 86% of observations from 147 to 155 days [26]; 1–2 kids born January–April.

Rut: Autumn, cued by decreasing photoperiod [26]. Mating system polygynous; mating takes place following a courtship and tending period where billy guards the nanny from intrusion by other, subordinate individuals. Tending period up to 2 days.

Oestrus cycle: 20 days in domestic dairy goats; 72% of observations from 15 to 24 days [26]. Nannies in oestrus are conspicuous: frequently bleat and lift and shake their tails. Main behavioural elements in courtship of nanny by billy are 'low stretch', 'gobble' and 'foreleg kick' [692], identical to those of wild goat [681]. Dominant billies tend and mate nannies at peak of oestrus. Other matings attempted by young, subordinate billies occur outside peak of oestrus, may result in successful copulations [579].

Births: Mostly March, S Uplands (mean birth dates vary between 5 March and 8 April in Moffat Hills) [579], February–March in Wales [79] and January–February on Rum [308]. In N Scotland, occasionally elsewhere, some kids born July–August, may have been conceived in a postpartum oestrus by nannies that lost kids in January. Alternatively, may be from 1st-year nannies, breeding for the 1st time in January.

Number of fetuses: 1 or 2; up to 5 recorded in domestic stock [26].

Incidence of twinning probably under-estimated due to early death of 1 twin. In S Uplands and Wales proportion of nannies with twins at heel in summer varies between 1% and 20% depending on population and year [80, 88]. Weight at birth 1.5–2.7 kg [319, 513]; lactation 5–6 months; male kids suck for longer and probably obtain more milk than do female kids [579].

Sex ratio at birth 1:1 [319]. Population bias towards females typical, arises from higher mortality rates of males from 1st year onwards [88].

Young uses a hiding place for 2 to several days after birth, then follows its mother. Maternal attachment specific, rapidly formed and fairly stable. Mother labels kid indirectly via the milk or directly by licking it [332]. While hiding out, kid is periodically suckled by mother [579, 658]. Hiding-out site chosen by kid; typically sheltered and dry, often amongst dwarf shrubs, rocks or gorse.

POPULATION

Densities (number, excluding kids, in area enclosed by outermost sightings of the population) vary from 1.5 to 11.8/km^2 depending on the population and the year. Typical density c.2/km^2, similar to feral goats in Australian pastoral areas (1.6–3.6/km^2 [566]) and wild goat in Pakistan (0.8–4.1/km^2 [681]). Highest densities of free-ranging feral goats in GB and Ireland recorded from the Burren [61] and SW Scotland [88]. Exceptionally reach very high density, such as 1000/km^2 on Macauley Island, New Zealand [799].

In GB and Ireland, total population 5000–10 000 (estimates from 1990 to 1999), higher than previous decade [91]. Wide range reflects variation in kid and adult (especially male) survival rate (inversely related to severity of winter weather) and culling intensity (related to population size). Minimum counts as follows: S Scotland/Scottish border, 2265; Clyde area, 355; Rum, 200; Islay, Jura, Mull and W coast mainland of Scotland, 400+; C and N Scottish Highlands, 500+; Wales, 675 (mainly Snowdonia – Glyderiau and Rhinogau, including 60 on Great Orme); Devon and Somerset, 135 (including 25 on Lundy Island); Isle of Wight, 40. Estimates for Irish populations mostly unavailable; all are probably less than 300 except for the Burren where 2000+. Estimated Scottish total in 1969, 4000 [319]; recently higher because of long series of mild winters but heavy culls now reducing population sizes [1, 69, 236, 293, 365, 580, 708].

Population structure: Most mortality occurs in 1st year of life. After 1st year, survivorship relatively high for c.6 years in nannies. Billies have lower survival rates. In S Scotland, after the 1st 6 months of life, median age at death is 3.25 for billies and 6.25 for nannies. Maximum ages recorded are 13 (billy) and 11 (nanny) [88]. Claims of feral goats aged >20 years are unsubstantiated.

MORTALITY

Kid mortality probably caused by hypothermia associated with starvation. In adults, mortality associated with low marrow fat index [704] indicating that starvation was an important contributory cause of death. Most billies die before their teeth are particularly worn; in contrast, nannies die at an age where their teeth are heavily worn and often diseased [88].

Apart from culling by humans, predators (of kids) include golden eagles, probably ravens, foxes and wild cats. Important source of carrion for ravens and the few remaining golden eagles in S Scotland [499].

PARASITES

British records from feral goats in [77, 88, 103, 218, 248, 488, 764].

Sucking louse *Linognathus stenopsis* and biting lice *Damalinia limbata, D. caprae* (all regularly recorded), also *D. ovis*. Ticks: *Ixodes ricinus* common. Mites: *Chorioptes bovis*.

Parasite egg counts from goat faeces, S Uplands and Holy Island, low, within range from healthy domestic (dosed) sheep. Tapeworms: *Monieza expansa*, Roundworms: *Dictyocaulus filaria* in lungs; *Haemonchus contortus, Ostertagia circumcincta, O. leptospicularis, O. trifurcata, O. lasensis, Teladorsagia davtiana, Trichostrongylus axei, Spiculopteragia spiculoptera* in abomasum; *Bunostomum trigoncephalum, Cooperia* spp., *Nematodirus filicollis, N. battus, T. capricola, T. colubriformis, T. vitrinus* in small intestine; *Chabertia ovina, Oesophagostomum venulosum, Skrjabinema ovis, Trichuris globulosa* in colon; *Trichuris ovis, Skrjabinema ovis* in caecum.

Positive reactions for louping ill, Q fever (*Coxiella burnetti*), leptospirosis (*Leptospira grippotyphosa, L. icterohamorrhagiae, L. autumnalis*) and toxoplasmosis (*Toxoplasma gondii*).

RELATIONS WITH HUMANS

Have tourist value as one of the few large 'wild' mammals on British and Irish uplands and sea cliffs. May also have genetic and historical importance; feral goats occur in British Isles and Mediterranean, share with 'wild goats' on Crete ancestry from earliest Neolithic goats [325]. Feral goats in British Isles have phenotypic characters of old breeds now extinct in domestication (see History, above), appear to be unique in Europe [360].

Regularly culled as pests, and IUCN Caprinae Specialist [690] recommends extermination of feral Caprinae unless good reasons (as above) presented for making an exception. Foresters and nature conservationists note damage to plantations and semi-natural woodlands respectively; farmers claim that they compete with sheep, and damage walls and crops. Standard livestock fencing to exclude sheep from woodlands is no barrier to goats. Bark-stripping and browsing by goats may cause more economic damage to trees and prohibit regeneration to a greater extent than either sheep or deer at equivalent densities, but no comparative study yet undertaken. On tropical islands, feral goats destroy habitats, leading to extinction of native species [105, 187]; eradication attempted from many islands, e.g. Isabella, Galapagos. In semi-arid pastoral areas of Australia, compete with sheep for food and water [566].

Used to restore grassland invaded by scrub [93, 763], and control weed species on hill pastures such as soft rush *Juncus effusus* and mat grass *Nardus stricta* [317, 517]. Also produce high-quality cashmere wool [671], whose economic potential is being evaluated [537]. Occasionally harvested for food (e.g. roast kid is eaten at Easter in the Burren, and goat, some from feral stock, by Asian and Afro-Caribbean communities). Some billies stalked for their trophy heads.

Practical management of feral goats is usually straightforward: except on steep rocky ground, goats bunch together when gathered and can usually be controlled by sheepdogs. Alternatively, they are relatively easy to stalk. Several authors [320, 660, 791] have stressed the historical and genetic value of feral goats. Not listed as either a Rare or Minority breed by the Rare Breeds Survival Trust but some populations (e.g. Valley of Rocks, Devon, and Great Orme, N Wales) are managed to preserve certain bloodlines [792].

Legally, feral goats are believed to be owned by whosoever's land they are on, unless marked by another landowner. Readily (re)adapt to captivity provided that shelter from rain, sufficient dry ground and diverse food are available; difficult to enclose if these conditions are not met.

LITERATURE

Comprehensive description plus detailed distribution maps, now well out of date [796]; feral goats on Rum [308]; review updating status, distribution, conservation and management [91].

AUTHOR

D.J. Bullock (with thanks for information on status and culling from statutory agencies (Countryside Council for Wales, Forest Enterprise, Scottish Natural Heritage, Parks & Wildlife Service, Ireland), NGOs (National Trust, National Trust for Sccotland) and private estates/individuals).

GENUS *Bos*

A Palaearctic genus of 8 species of wild and domestic cattle, including yak, gaur, aurochs, kouprey and their domestic descendants; closely related to, probably congeneric with, *Bison*. Large grazers with wide muzzles, characterised by relatively short, stout, curved horns in both sexes.

Cattle *Bos taurus*

Bos taurus Linnaeus 1758. Uppsala, Sweden.

Male – bull; multiparous female – cow; primiparous female – heifer; young – calf; castrated male – bullock.

DESCRIPTION

Most cattle in the British Isles belong to one of about 70 pure breeds [756], or are well-characterized crossbreds, though crossing can lead to animals that lack clear breed affinity. Cattle used in extensive grazing systems are usually beef suckler cows [578] whose calves will be sold for finishing for beef elsewhere (attainment of market weight and conformation often requires more intensive feeding than can be achieved on extensive grazings). Swona, Orkney, has herd of commercial beef cattle (based on Shorthorn–Aberdeen Angus crosses), run feral since 1978, with no winter supplementation. They receive no special care or attention.

Main interest is semi-feral park cattle. Chillingham cattle: white cattle with red ears and sweeping horns (Plate 10). White Park: typically white with black ears, but variable with some calves white with red ears and others coloured. Such sports usually selected out. British White, superficially similar to the White Park but polled (genetically hornless), traces its ancestry to the Middleton Park herd (18th century, Lancashire) [793].

Chromosomes: 2n = 60 for all breeds. All breeds freely interfertile. White Park cattle have a C-band chromosomal polymorphism (absence of a centromeric block of heterochromatin) [656]. A chromosomal translocation is prevalent in the British White but has not been found in White Park nor Chillingham cattle [474].

Blood grouping studies, examining 12 mendelian loci, show Chillingham cattle to be remarkably homozygous. DNA from Chillingham samples was scored for 25 microsatellite markers [733]; 1 was found to be heterozygous. These markers are highly polymorphic in cattle, heterozygosity typically 70%; the remarkable homozygosity at Chillingham is consistent with recorded bottlenecks and a long history of inbreeding.

Skull: Frontal part of skull expanded, with air cells communicating with those of horn cores. Frontals form greater part of cranial vault, parietals small and confined to occipital area. Orbits prominent, completely closed at rear. Facial axis is bent at an angle to basicranial axis so nose is directed downwards. Occipital area is small, sloping forward and there are large paraoccipital processes [214].

Horns: Permanent, hollow horns, in both sexes, though those of male are much larger. Supported on bony outgrowths of frontal bones, the horn cores [214]. Allele for polled (genetically hornless) condition is dominant though inheritance complex [292]. Most horned commercial cattle have the horns removed and the wounds cauterized while still young.

Teeth: Dental formula 0.0.3.3/3.1.3.3. Upper incisors and canines absent. Lower canine is closely associated with the 3 true incisors. The lower incisiform teeth bear on a hard fleshy pad on the premaxilla. Ages of cattle can be estimated from number of fully erupted incisiform teeth: 2, 2 years of age; 4, 2.5 years; 6, 3 years; 8, 3.5 years [214]. A high proportion of commercial cattle show dental defects [400].

Moult: Thick, woolly coat generally shed in spring, summer coat shorter and sleeker. Daylength major factor in timing, also temperature and to lesser extent nutrition (poor diet delays shedding) [550].

Nipples: 2 pairs, inguinal, yet cows seldom produce twins (*c.*1% of all calvings). Reasons for this are a matter of speculation.

Scent glands: Perineal skin glands may produce a pheromone inducing oestrus in the cow [57]. May also be pheromone in bull's urine which stimulates early puberty [431]. Some studies have suggested a bull's presence can shorten postpartum anoestrus in cows, but this response seems not to be reliable [64]. Both sexes show prominent flehmen behaviour [342].

MEASUREMENTS

Chillingham cattle: Only partial data available because impractical to handle live animals; height at shoulder approximately 110 cm. Maximum adult weight for bulls 300 kg, for cows 280 kg (recorded for 'thin but not emaciated' animals collected after death in winter) [341] but 430 kg recorded for the only mature male in the reserve herd in N Scotland. Slow-growing; 18-month-old bulls weigh *c.*100 kg [341], cf. normal target weight at 400 days for commercial beef animal, at least 400 kg.

White Park cattle: Cows weigh *c.*610 kg for lowland herds and *c.*450 kg in upland conditions [11], are 131 cm at the shoulder [685].

Commercial beef cattle: Body weights given in [756] for pure breeds; comparative data on cattle shoulder heights are not readily available. Sample body weights for some crossbreds [809]: Hereford–Friesian 462–474 kg; Aberdeen Angus–Friesian 464–472 kg; Welsh Black 486–497 kg. Cattle shoulder height and mature female body weight are highly heritable [702].

DISTRIBUTION

Chillingham herd held at Chillingham Park, Northumberland, with a reserve herd established in N Scotland in 1970 [349]. Numbers in main herd, May 2006, 33 males and 29 females. Reserve herd 17 animals. Semen has been stored from the latter and a programme of embryo recovery is under way [349].

Swona cattle only found on that island [347], numbers currently 13.

Other well-established and well-studied herds of free-ranging domestic cattle occur on Rum (e.g. [305, 307]) and in New Forest (e.g. [588, 596, 602, 620]). Locations of several herds of other breeds, used for conservation grazing, given in [756].

HISTORY

Husbanded cattle are descended from aurochs *Bos primigenius*, but domestication took place separately in India (zebu, *Bos taurus indicus*) and the Near East (*Bos taurus taurus*) [168, 344, 473]. British cattle derived from Near East domestications [759], British aurochs not involved. Accepted convention that different specific names used for ancestral and descendant forms [291]. Neolithic people brought farming and livestock, including cattle, to GB *c.*5500 bp, though earliest apparently Sutton, Dublin, Ireland, 6660 bp [807]. Aurochs remains have been found in deposits where remains of domesticated cattle predominate. The latest aurochs specimen is dated 3245 bp (see Chapter 3). Aurochs has never been reported from Ireland.

Populations of relatively primitive breeds of medieval cattle are maintained in a number of old hunting parks. Fanciful notion of a distinct line of descent from (British) aurochs not sustainable. First documented in 17th century [345], catalogued by Whitehead [793]. Best known are Chartley, Cadzow and Chillingham; later herds, 19th century establishment, include Vaynol (Glan Faenol) and Dynevor (Dinefwr). Modern White Park breed a mixture of these stocks, with some contribution from other breeds. Chillingham herd has been kept pure since records began in the early 18th century and is a distinct breed; Vaynol also accepted as a distinct breed because isolated for most of 20th century. Apart from Chillingham, all are managed herds. In addition, fully modern husbanded cattle are turned out to graze free-range in some areas.

HABITAT

Much recent interest in habitat usage by aurochs and the extent that this can be replicated by currently extant species including free-ranging, or 'dedomesticated' ('feralized') cattle, because of the hypothesis [768] that aurochs and other wild grazers drove a cyclic turnover of vegetation types leading to a shifting mosaic of open grassland, scrub, and 'woodland groves' which might perhaps be replicated in modern conservation management.

Chillingham Park is a medieval wood pasture of 135 ha in total, overlain by a designed landscape of the early 1800s, with woods mostly of 18th and early 19th century establishment [342]. Swona comprises 113 ha maritime heath with abandoned arable land and pasture [347]. On Rum, range over a mosaic of wet heath, *Calluna* heath, herb-rich heath, *Juncus* marshes and *Agrostis–Festuca* grasslands [306]. In New Forest, restricted to unenclosed, open forest areas, which offer mosaic of open-based ancient deciduous woodlands, heathlands and valley mires with grazing on *Agrostis curtisii*-dominated acid grasslands, alluvial streamside grasslands and areas of artificially improved pasture (areas reseeded and/or fertilised specifically to improve grazing for livestock) [588, 596, 620].

Patterns of habitat use: Detailed studies for New Forest cattle [588, 617, 618]. Various improved grasslands and stream margins provided over 40% of all sightings throughout the year, and over 70% during summer (July–September). Heathland communities also used extensively throughout the year, except in midwinter; deciduous woodland showed peak use in spring and autumn. Overall, patterns of habitat use throughout the year showed relatively little variation [588]. Although no pronounced seasonal variation in habitat use, marked diurnal shift: daytime habitats selected primarily for feeding, night-time communities offering some degree of cover. In all seasons, spend most of the daylight hours on open vegetation communities, deliberately move into shelter communities at dusk and back to open grazing areas at dawn [596].

On Rum, grazing cattle concentrate on the more mesotrophic communities (*Agrostis–Festuca* grasslands and *Juncus* marsh) during summer months when forage availability and digestibility high. Over winter, when these grasslands are depleted, associate more with *Schoenus* fens and *Molinia* flushes [306, 307].

At Chillingham, similar pattern observed; apparently most productive *Festuca–Agrostis–Galium* grasslands most favoured earlier in the grazing season. Later, exploit more typical *Festuca–Agrostis–Galium* grassland, *Holcus lanatus–Trifolium repens* subcommunity and the *Luzula multiflora–Rhytidiadelphus loreus* subcommunity.

SOCIAL ORGANISATION AND BEHAVIOUR
General review in [343].

Social behaviour: Only UK study in a herd of natural sex ratio and age distribution is at Chillingham [342]. Some sexual segregation, with mature bulls over 4–5 years of age living in discrete groups of 2–3, each within a defined home range. Cows, calves and young bulls roam apparently freely in a group or a number of subgroups of variable size throughout the entire park (135 ha). In most other free-ranging herds, sex and age distribution artificially managed, few mature bulls depastured. Social organisation thus strongly influenced by management. Highland cattle on Rum [175], Camargue cattle in France [683, 774] and cattle in New Forest in Hampshire [596, 602] all have all-female herds organised on the basis of a clear dominance hierarchy and matriarchal affinities.

In New Forest, most cattle spend winter on their owners' holdings, turned out on to open grazings in spring. Dispersion of herds across the Forest reflects location of the farmsteads, since typically released nearby. Herds belonging to different owners thus range widely over the Forest in relatively discrete units, each having a home range centred on one or more primary grazing areas; areas may be used in turn over the course of several days, daily movements of 4–5 km not uncommon. Over summer, herds fragment into smaller groups which range independently but encounter each other frequently on grazing sites, commonly aggregate in 'camps' overnight. These small subunits are not cohesive, individuals regularly move from one to another. Spend most of daylight on primary grazing areas, although make frequent visits to water supplies; at night, generally move to vegetation types offering cover, particularly deciduous woodland, although groups will spend the night out on dry heathland when weather mild.

In autumn, most cattle removed from the Forest; those few herds that remain are generally fed hay and straw. This practice radically alters the entire activity pattern and ranging behaviour: subunits of the herd are drawn together at the feeding site and herd cohesiveness is markedly higher over the winter months than during summer. Feeding usually takes place at a fixed site, 1–2 h after dawn. Animals congregate at the site over this period and stand around ruminating or resting; little foraging occurs. About 1 h before dusk, general departure from feeding site to selected overnight area. Route taken may vary, but site selected to spend the night is usually the same, often involves considerably greater movement than during summer months; round trips of 11.5–12 km recorded [596, 617].

Vocalisations: Lowing of Chillingham cow not greatly differentiated from call of calf, while bull has at least 3 quantitatively and qualitatively different vocalisations [348].

In cattle generally, behavioural study suggests that calves recognise their mothers by sight rather than by scent and sound [549, 683].

FEEDING
Species composition of the diet has not been studied at Chillingham.

New Forest cattle feed throughout the year on a restricted range of grasses, make up balance with heathers [620]. Consistent with constancy of seasonal use of habitat, diet similar throughout year: only minor changes in relative proportion of these 2 main components. Throughout summer (May–August), approximately 80% of diet grasses (primarily *Agrostis capillaris, A. canina, A. curtisii* and *Festuca rubra*); heathers (both *Calluna* and *Erica*) contributed a further 14% overall. No other items contributed more than 1–2% of the summer diet. Through autumn, small reduction in percentage of grasses, with corresponding increase in heather intake. New Forest cattle fed hay or straw from November to March; these supplements together with natural grasses continue to provide 70–75% of the diet through winter, with heather contributing further 20–25% [620].

On Rum, again, cattle are preferential grazers and concentrate feeding on available *Agrostis–Festuca* grasslands during the summer; over winter reduced forage availability on these shorter grasslands leads to increased intake of coarser species such as *Juncus, Molinia, Scirpus* and heather [306].

BREEDING
Cattle are not seasonal breeders and their tendency to spring or summer calving is due to the lengthening effect of winter on postpartum oestrus [350]). Cattle in most free-ranging populations consist solely of cows and calves, heifers and

castrated males; natural breeding systems are therefore not apparent. At Chillingham, receptive cows appear to be mated by the bull of highest rank in the male group occupying the area where she is at the time [1].

Herd records for the periods 1862–1899 and 1953–1985 show consistent levels of fertility (with no apparent decline due to continued inbreeding). Calving rates approximately 0.3 calves per breeding female per year; 73% of calves survive to 1 month of age and about 50% survive to maturity.

Onset of puberty in Chillingham bulls is at *c.*18–20 months of age [349]. Adult bulls have small testes, total weight being about 167 g (thus 0.06% of body weight). In commercial cattle breeds, combined testicular weight is about 0.10% of total body weight. Chillingham bulls probably have rather low fertility and a short reproductive life, from onset of home-range establishment at 4 years to perhaps 7 years of age, depending on level of competition [341].

POPULATION

Population size and dynamics of most free-ranging herds closely controlled by management. In Chillingham, population size was controlled by culling up to the end of the 19th century at an average of 60. Since culling stopped, numbers have fluctuated widely (to low of 13 in 1947 [349]) but now range between 40 and 65.

MORTALITY

At Chillingham, mortality has been correlated with population number at the start of winter and with spring rainfall [346]. Mortality is higher in males than females and thus adult sex ratio is usually biased towards females [346].

PARASITES AND DISEASE

Free-ranging populations are susceptible to all the major parasites and diseases of domestic cattle [578, 756]. Incidences of disease at Chillingham, and management steps taken to limit these, summarised in [349].

INTERACTIONS WITH OTHER SPECIES

Preferential grazers and bulk feeders, with intakes of 8–10 kg herbage organic matter per day on short (4–5 cm) swards, and 13–15 kg/day on tall (7–8 cm) [809], cattle have major impact upon vegetation, particularly grassland, in areas where free-ranging (though grazing alone is not sufficient to maintain diversity in some grasslands [744]). Consequently deliberately exploited for management of open vegetation types in conservation areas [29, 60, 309, 766, 775, 779]. This grazing impact may have significant effects on other wild ungulates. Summer grazing by cattle on Rum shown to increase quality of grass swards available to feeding red deer hinds [305]; over winter, however, changes in patterns of resource use and partitioning of resources by red deer, cattle, ponies and goats strongly suggest potential competition during the period of limited forage availability [307]. High degree of overlap in resource use recorded between all species over summer, when forage abundant; over winter period of low food availability, far stricter partitioning of diets observed. In New Forest, high dietary overlap apparent year-round between cattle and ponies, also between cattle and fallow deer [594, 596, 602]. Analyses of changes in population size of all deer species over 25–30 years indicate negative effects of grazing by cattle and ponies on densities of roe [616] and fallow deer [693].

Grazing in the New Forest, through its effects on forage availability and vegetation architecture, has also been shown to affect species diversity and population densities of voles and mice, and their predators [382, 594]. Similar results in response to cattle grazing in the uplands [577].

AUTHORS

S.J.G. Hall & R.J. Putman.

REFERENCES

1   Author's data

1a   Aanes, R. & Andersen, R. (1996) The effects of sex, time of birth, and habitat on the vulnerability of roe deer fawns to red fox predation. *Canadian Journal of Zoology,* **74**, 1857–1865.

2   Abernethy, K. (1994) The establishment of a hybrid zone between red and sika deer (genus *Cervus*). *Molecular Ecology,* **3**, 551–562.

3   Abernethy, K. (1998) *Sika deer in Scotland.* Deer Commission for Scotland, Inverness/The Stationery Office, Edinburgh.

4   Adam, K.M.G. *et al.* (1977) The occurrence of antibody to *Babesia* and to the louping-ill virus in deer in Scotland. *Research in Veterinary Science,* **23**, 133–138.

5   Adams, J.C. & Dannatt, N. (1989) *The culling and processing of wild deer.* Arun District Council/Forestry Commission.

6   Ahlen, I. (1965) Studies on the red deer *Cervus elaphus* L. in Scandinavia. III Ecological investigations. *Viltrevy,* **3**, 177–376.

7   Aitchison, J. (1946) Hinged teeth in mammals: a study of tusks of muntjacs (*Muntiacus*) and Chinese water deer (*Hydropotes inermis*). *Proceedings of the Zoological Society of London,* **116**, 329–338.

8   Aitken, R.J. (1975) Cementum layers and tooth wear as criteria for ageing roe deer (*Capreolus capreolus*). *Journal of Zoology,* **175**, 15–28.

9   Albon, S.D. *et al.* (1983) Fertility and body weight in female red deer: a density dependent relationship. *Journal of Animal Ecology,* **52**, 969–980.

10   Albon, S.D. *et al.* (1986) Fertility in female red deer (*Cervus elaphus*):the effects of body composition, age and reproductive status. *Journal of Zoology,* **209**, 447–460.

11   Alderson, G.L.H. (1982) White Park cattle. *Ark,* **9**, 168–170.

12   Alexander, J. Personal communication.

13   Alexander, T.L. & Buxton, D. (eds.) (1994) *Management and diseases of deer – a handbook for the veterinary surgeon.* Veterinary Deer Society, London.

14   Alvarez, F. (1995) Functional directional asymmetry in fallow deer. *Journal of Zoology,* **236**, 563–569.

15   Anderson, J. (1976) Food energy requirements of wild Scottish red deer, pp. 220–221 in Clutton-Brock, T.H. *et al.* 1982, *Red deer: behaviour and ecology of two sexes.* Edinburgh University Press, Edinburgh.

16   Andersen, R. & Linnell, J.D.C. (1997) Variation in maternal investment in a small cervid; the effects of cohort, sex, litter size and time of birth in roe deer (*Capreolus capreolus*) fawns. *Oecologia,* **109**, 74–79.

17   Andersen, R. *et al.* (1998) Variation in life-history parameters in roe deer, pp. 285–307 in Andersen, R. *et al.* (eds.) *The European roe deer: the biology of success.* Scandinavian University Press, Oslo.

18   Andersen, R. *et al.* (eds.) (1998) *The European roe deer: the biology of success.* Scandinavian University Press, Oslo.

19   Anderson, J.M. (1981) *Studies on digestion in* Muntiacus reevesi. MPhil thesis, University of Cambridge.

20   Apollonio, M. & Vailati, G. (1996) Functional morphology of metatarsal glands in fallow deer. *Zeitschrift für Säugetierkunde,* **61**, 321–326.

21   Apollonio, M. *et al.* (1992) To lek or not to lek: mating strategies of male fallow deer. *Behavioural Ecology,* **3**, 25–31.

22   Apollonio, M. *et al.* (2005) Long-term influence of human presence on spatial sexual segregation in fallow deer (*Dama dama*). *Journal of Mammalogy,* **86**, 937–946.

23   Arman, P. *et al.* (1974) The composition and yield of milk from captive red deer (*Cervus elaphus* L.). *Journal of Reproduction and Fertility,* **37**, 67–84.

24   Armstrong, H. (1998) Appendix 6, pp. 101–110 in Stewart, F. & Eno, S. (eds.) *Grazing management planning for uplands Natura 2000 sites: a practical manual.* National Trust for Scotland, Aberdeen.

25   Armstrong, N. *et al.* (1969) Observation on the reproduction of female wild and park fallow deer (*Dama dama*) in southern England. *Journal of Zoology,* **158**, 27–37.

26   Asdell, S.A. (1964) *Patterns in mammalian reproduction.* Cornell University Press, New York.

27   Asher, G.W. (1985) Oestrus cycle and breeding season of farmed fallow deer. *Journal of Reproduction and Fertility,* **75**, 521–529.

28   Asher, G.W. (1993) Reproduction of fallow deer, pp. 101–112 in Asher, G.W. (ed.) *Proceedings of the First World Forum on Fallow Deer Farming,* Mudgee, Australia.

29   Bakker, J.P. (1989) *Nature management by grazing and cutting.* Kluwer, Dordrecht.

30   Baker, J.R. *et al.* (1979). Four cases of chondrodystrophy in fallow deer. *Veterinary Record,* **104**, 450–453.

31   Balharry, E. *et al.* (1994) *Hybridisation in British mammals.* Report 154, JNCC, Peterborough.

32   Bancroft, D. (1993) *Genetic variation and fitness in Soay sheep.* PhD thesis, University of Cambridge.

33   Benzie, D. & Gill, J.C. (1974) Radiography of the skeletal and dental condition of the Soay sheep, pp. 131–159, 326–337 in Jewell, P.A. *et al.* (eds.) *Island survivors: the ecology of the Soay sheep of St Kilda.* Athlone Press, London.

34   Barrette, C. (1976) Musculature of facial glands scent glands in the muntjac. *Journal of Anatomy,* **122**, 61–66.

35   Barrette, C. (1977) Scent-marking in captive muntjacs, *Muntiacus reevesi. Animal Behaviour,* **25,** 536–541.

36   Barrette, C. (1977) Fighting behavior of muntjac and the evolution of antlers. *Evolution,* **31**, 169–176.

37   Bartos, L. *et al.* (1992) Lekking behaviour in sika deer. In Maruyama, N. *et al.* (eds.) *International Symposium on Wildlife Conservation – present trends and perspectives for the 21st century.* Japan Wildlife Research Center, Tokyo.

38   Batty, A.F. & Chapman, D.I. (1970) Gastro-intestinal parasites of wild fallow deer (*Dama dama* L.) *Journal of Helminthology,* **44**, 57–61.

39   Batty, A.F. *et al.* (1987) Prevalence of nematode parasites in wild fallow deer (*Dama dama*). *Veterinary Record,* **120**, 599.

40   Bellec, F. & Froissart, A. (1997) *Contribution a l'etude du troupeau de chevres ferals de Jobourg.* Maitrise de Biologie des Populations et des Ecosystèmes. Université du Havre, France (in French).

41   Berger, J. (1977) Organisational systems and dominance in feral horses in the Grand Canyon. *Behavioural Ecology and Sociobiology,* **2**, 131–146.

42   Berger, J. (1986) *Wild horses of the Great Basin.* Chicago University Press, Chicago.

43   Bideau, E. *et al.* (1983) Evolution saisonnière de la taille des groupes chez le chevreuil en milieu forestier. *Revue d'Ecologie (Terre et Vie),* **37**, 161–169 (in French).

44   Bideau, E. *et al.* (1983) Note sur l'évolution de l'association mère-jeune chez le chevreuil (*Capreolus capreolus* L., 1758) étudiés par la technique du radio-tracking. *Mammalia,* **47**, 477–482 (in French).

45   Bideau, E. *et al.* (1987) Dispersion chez le jeune chevreuil (*Capreolus capreolus* L.): étude sur une population en milieu forestier. *Acta Oecologica Oecologia Applicata,* **8**, 135–148 (in French).

46   Bideau, E. *et al.* (1993) Effects of age and sex on space occupation by European roe deer. *Journal of Mammalogy,* **74**, 745–751.

47   Bignell, J. (1993) Genetics of coat colour inheritance in fallow deer, pp. 173–179 in Asher G.W. (ed.) *Proceedings of the First World Forum on Fallow Deer Farming,* Mudgee, Australia.

48   Birgersson, B. (1997) *Maternal investment in male and female offspring in the fallow deer.* PhD thesis, University of Stockholm.

49   Birgersson, B. & Ekvall, K. (1994) Suckling time and fawn growth in fallow deer (*Dama dama*). *Journal of Zoology,* **232**, 641–650.

50   Birgersson, B. & Ekvall, K. (1997) Early growth in male and female fallow deer fawns. *Behavioral Ecology,* 8, 493–499.

51   Birgersson, B. *et al.* (1991) Allosuckling in fallow deer, *Dama dama. Animal Behaviour* **42**, 326–327.

52   Birgersson, B. *et al.* (2001) Colour vision in fallow deer; a

behavioural study. *Animal Behaviour,* **61,** 367–371.

53 Blackmore, D.K. & Gallagher, G.L. (1964) An outbreak of erysipelas in captive and wild birds and mammals. *Veterinary Record,* **76,** 1161–1164.

54 Blakeley, D. *et al.* (1997) Studying muntjac in the King's Forest, Suffolk. *Deer,* **10,** 156–161.

55 Blaxter, K.L. & Hamilton, W.J. (1980) Reproduction in farmed deer. 2. Calf growth and mortality. *Journal of Agricultural Science, Cambridge,* **95,** 275–284.

56 Blaxter, K.L. *et al.* (1988) *Farming the red deer – the first report of an investigation by the Rowett Research Institute and the Hill Farming Research Organisation.* HMSO, Edinburgh.

57 Blazquez, N.B. *et al.* (1988) A pheromonal function for the perineal skin glands in the cow. *Veterinary Record,* **123,** 49–50.

58 Boessneck, J. (1969) Osteological differences between sheep (*Ovis aries* Linné) and goat (*Capra hircus* Linné), pp. 331–358 in Brothwell, D. & Higgs E. (eds.) *Science in archaeology.* Thames & Hudson, London.

59 Bohm, B. *et al.* (2002) *The health of wild red and sika deer in Scotland: an analysis of key endoparasites and recommendations for monitoring disease.* Report to the Deer Commission for Scotland, Inverness.

60 Bokdam, J. (2003) *Nature conservation and grazing management.* PhD thesis, University of Wageningen.

61 Bonham, F.R.H. & Fairley, J.S. (1984) Observations on a herd of feral goats *Capra* (domestic) in the Burren. *Irish Naturalists' Journal,* **21,** 208–212.

62 Booth, W.D. (1988) Wild boar farming. *State Veterinary Journal,* **42,** 1167–1175.

63 Booth, W.D. (1995) Wild boar farming in the United Kingdom. *IBEX Journal of Mountain Ecology,* **3,** 245–248.

64 Booth, W.D. & Signoret, J.P. (1992) Olfaction and reproduction in ungulates. *Oxford Reviews of Reproductive Biology,* **14,** 263–301.

65 Boussès, P., *et al.* (1991) The Corsican mouflon (*Ovis ammon musimon*) on Kerguelen archipelago: structure and dynamics of the population, p. 91 in *Proceedings of the International Symposium, Ongulés/Ungulates,* Toulouse, France.

66 Boxall, M, R. (1990) *Patterns of habitat use and spatial separation of four deer species living in sympatry in Roydon Woods Nature Reserve, Hampshire.* Dissertation submitted for Certificate in Field Biology, Birkbeck College, University of London.

67 Boyd, J.M. (1953) The sheep population of Hirta, St Kilda, 1952. *Scottish Naturalist,* **65,** 25–28.

68 Boyd, J.M. (1981) The Boreray sheep of St. Kilda, Outer Hebrides, Scotland: the natural history of a feral population. *Biological Conservation,* **20,** 215–227.

69 Boyd, I.L. (1981) Population changes and the distribution of a herd of feral goats (*Capra* sp.) on Rhum, Inner Hebrides, 1960–1978. *Journal of Zoology,* **193,** 287–304.

70 Boyd, J.M. & Jewell, P.A. (1974) The Soay sheep and their environment: a synthesis, pp. 360–373 in Jewell, P.A. *et al.* (eds.) *Island survivors: the ecology of the Soay sheep of St Kilda.* Athlone Press, London.

71 Boyd, J.M. *et al.* (1964) The Soay sheep of the island of Hirta, St Kilda. A study of a feral population. *Proceedings of the Zoological Society of London,* **142,** 129–163.

72 Bradley, C. (1996) *The realm of the fallow buck.* Published by C. Bradley.

73 Bramley, P.S. (1970) Territoriality and reproductive behaviour of roe deer. *Journal of Reproduction and Fertility,* Supplement, **11,** 43–70.

74 Braza, F. *et al.* (2000) Variation of male-biased maternal investment in fallow deer (*Dama dama*) *Journal of Zoology,* **250,** 237–241.

75 Bresinski, W. (1982) Grouping tendencies in roe deer under agrocenosis conditions. *Acta Theriologica,* **27,** 427–447.

76 British Wild Boar Association. Personal communication.

77 Britt, D. & Bullock, D.J. Personal communication.

78 Brown, D.J. (1983) *The Rhinog goats: 2 Social and spatial organisation.* Unpublished report to the Nature Conservancy Council, North Wales Region.

79 Brown, D.J. Personal communication.

80 Brown, D.J. & Lloyd, M.G. (1981) *The Rhinog goats: 1. A survey and management review.* Unpublished report to the Nature Conservancy Council, North Wales Region.

81 Brown, W.A.B. & Chapman, N.G. (1990) The dentition of fallow deer (*Dama dama* L.): a scoring scheme to assess age from wear of the permanent molariform teeth. *Journal of Zoology,* **221,** 659–682.

82 Brown, W.A.B. & Chapman, N.G. (1991) Age assessment of fallow deer (*Dama dama*): from a scoring scheme based on radiographs of developing permanent molariform teeth. *Journal of Zoology,* **224,** 367–379.

83 Bryant, L.D. & Maser, D. (1982) Classification and distribution, pp. 1–59 in Thomas, J.W. & Toweill, D.E. (eds.) *Elk of North America.* Stackpole Books, Harrisburg, PA.

84 Bubenik, A.B. & Bubenikova, J.M. (1967) 24-hour periodicity in red deer (*Cervus elaphus* L.). *Proceedings of the International Congress of Game Biology,* **7,** 343–349.

85 Buckingham, B. Personal communication

86 Bull, E. Personal communication

87 Bullock, D. (1981) Aspects of the ecology of Boreray sheep. In Duncan, N. *et al.* (eds.) *Boreray 1980 expedition.* Unpublished report, University of Durham.

88 Bullock, D.J. (1982) *Aspects of the ecology of feral goats (Capra (domestic)) in the Southern Uplands.* PhD thesis, University of Durham.

89 Bullock, D.J. (1985) Annual diets of hill sheep and feral goats in southern Scotland. *Journal of Applied Ecology,* **22,** 423–33.

90 Bullock, D.J. (1985) Borerays, the other rare breed on St Kilda. *Ark,* **10,** 274–278.

91 Bullock, D.J. (1995) The feral goat – conservation and management. *British Wildlife,* **6,** 152–159.

92 Bullock, D.J. & Rackham, J. (1982) Epiphysial fusion and tooth eruption of feral goats from Moffatdale, Dumfries and Galloway, Scotland. *British Archaeological Reports British Series,* **109,** 73–80.

93 Bullock, D.J. & Kinnear, P.K. (1988) The use of goats to control birch in dune systems: an experimental study. *Aspects of Applied Biology,* **16,** 163–168.

94 Bullock, D.J. & Pickering, S.P. (1984) The validity of horn ring counts to determine the age of Scottish feral goats (*Capra* (domestic)). *Journal of Zoology,* **202,** 561–564.

95 Burkitt, T. (2006) Personal communication.

96 Burton, D. (1992) *The effects of parasitic nematode infection on body condition of New Forest ponies.* PhD thesis, University of Southampton.

97 Buxton, D. (1986) Malignant catarrhal fever, pp. 86–88 in Alexander, T.L. (ed.) *Management and diseases of deer.* Veterinary Deer Society, London.

98 Byrne, D. Personal communication.

99 Caffell, G. (1995) Pen up your kids! *Current Archaeology,* **12,** 385–386.

100 Calder, C.J. (1994) *Population performance and feeding ecology of roe deer in farm woodland.* PhD thesis, University of Aberdeen.

101 Caldwell, J.F. *et al.* (1983) Observations on the autumn and winter diet of fallow deer (*Dama dama*). *Journal of Zoology,* **201,** 559–563.

102 Cameron, A.G. (1923) *The wild red deer of Scotland.* Blackwood & Sons, Edinburgh.

103 Cameron, T.W.M. & Parnell, I.W. (1993) Internal parasites of land mammals in Scotland. *Proceedings of the Royal Physiological Society of Edinburgh,* **22,** 133–154.

104 Campbell, J.B. (1977) *The Upper Palaeolithic of Britain.* Clarendon Press, Oxford.

105 Campbell, K. *et al.* (1999) Feral goats on islands – a request for help. *Caprinae News.* Newsletter of the IUCN/SSC Caprinae Specialist Group, January, 6–7.

106 Campbell, R.N. (1974) St Kilda and its sheep, pp. 8–35 in Jewell, P.A. *et al.* (eds.) *Island survivors: the ecology of the Soay sheep of St Kilda.* Athlone Press, London.

107 Cargnelutti, B. *et al.* (2002) Space use by roe deer in a

fragmented landscape – some preliminary results. *Revue d'ecologie (Terre Vie)*, **57**, 29–37.

108 Carter, N.A. (1984) Bole scoring by sika deer (*Cervus nippon*) in England. *Deer*, **6**, 77–78.

109 Catt, D.C. & Staines, B.W. (1987) Home range use and habitat selection by red deer (*Cervus elaphus*) in a Sitka spruce plantation as determined by radio-tracking. *Journal of Zoology*, **211**, 681–693.

110 Caughley, G. (1971) An investigation of hybridisation between free-ranging wapiti and red deer in New Zealand. *New Zealand Journal of Science*, **13**, 209–219.

111 Cederlund, G. (1983) Home range dynamics and habitat selection by roe deer in a boreal area in central Sweden. *Acta Theriologica*, **28**, 443–460.

112 Cederlund, G. *et al.* (1998) Managing roe deer and their impact on the environment: maximising benefits and minimising costs, pp. 337–372 in Andersen, R. *et al.* (eds.) *The European roe deer: the biology of success.* Scandinavian University Press, Oslo.

113 Chadwick, A.H. *et al.* (1996) Sika deer in Scotland: density, population size, habitat use and fertility – some comparisons with red deer. *Scottish Forestry*, **50**, 8–16.

114 Chaplin, R.E. (1977) *Deer.* Blandford Press, Poole.

115 Chapman, D.I. (1975) Antlers – bones of contention. *Mammal Review*, **5**, 121–172.

116 Chapman, D.I. & Chapman, N.G. (1969) The incidence of congenital abnormalities in the mandibular denition of fallow deer (*Dama dama*). *Research in Veterinary Science*, **10**, 485–7.

117 Chapman, D.I. & Chapman, N.G. (1969) Geographical variation in fallow deer (*Dama dama* L.). *Nature*, **221**, 59–60.

118 Chapman, D.I. & Chapman, N.G. (1970) Preliminary observations on the reproductive cycle of the male fallow deer (*Dama dama* L.). *Journal of Reproduction and Fertility*, **21**, 1–8.

119 Chapman, D.I. & Chapman, N.G. (1973) Maxillary canine teeth in fallow deer (*Dama dama* L.). *Journal of Zoology*, **170**, 143–147.

120 Chapman, D.I. & Chapman, N.G. (1975) *Fallow deer: their history, distribution and biology.* Terence Dalton, Lavenham.

121 Chapman, D.I. & Chapman, N.G. (1980) Morphology of the male accessory organs of reproduction in immature fallow deer (*Dama dama* L.) with particular reference to puberty and antler development. *Acta Anatomica*, **108**, 51–59.

122 Chapman, D.I. & Chapman, N.G. (1982) The antler cycle of Reeves' muntjac. *Acta Theriologica*, **27**, 107–114.

123 Chapman, D.I. & Chapman, N.G. (1982) The taxonomic status of feral muntjac (*Muntiacus* sp.) in England. *Journal of Natural History*, **16**, 381–387.

124 Chapman, D.I. & Chapman, N.G. (1997) *Fallow deer: their history, distribution and biology.* Coch-y-bonddu Books, Machynlleth.

125 Chapman, D.I. & Dansie, O. (1969) Unilateral implantation in muntjac deer. *Journal of Zoology*, **159**, 534–536.

126 Chapman, D.I. & Horwood, M.T. (1968) Pregnancy in a sika deer calf (*Cervus nippon*). *Research in Veterinary Science*, **29**, 105–107.

127 Chapman, D.I. *et al.* (1983) Chromosome studies of feral muntjac deer (*Muntiacus* sp.) in England. *Journal of Zoology*, **201**, 557–559.

128 Chapman, D.I. *et al.* (1984) Deformities of the metacarpus and metatarsus in fallow deer (*Dama dama* L.). *Journal of Comparative Pathology*, **94**, 77–91.

129 Chapman, D.I. *et al.* (1984) The periods of conception and parturition in feral Reeves' muntjac (*Muntiacus reevesi*) in southern England, based upon age of juvenile animals. *Journal of Zoology*, **204**, 575–578.

130 Chapman, D.I. *et al.* (1985) Tooth eruption in Reeves' muntjac (*Muntiacus reevesi*) and its use as a method of age estimation (Mammalia: Cervidae). *Journal of Zoology* A, **205**, 205–221.

131 Chapman, N.G. (1984) *Fallow deer.* Anthony Nelson, Oswestry.

132 Chapman, N.G. (1986) An explanation for the porous tips of

133 Chapman, N.G. (1986) Fallow deer twins. *Deer*, **7**, 46.

134 Chapman, N. (1988) Oxalic acid in the urine of wild muntjac deer (*Muntiacus reevesi*). *Publication of the Veterinary Deer Society*, **3**, 18–22.

135 Chapman, N. (1991) The first antler cycle of Chinese muntjac deer, pp. 303–305 in Bobek, B. *et al.* (eds.) *Global trends in wildlife management, Vol.1.* Swiat Press, Krakow.

136 Chapman, N. (1995) Our neglected species. *Deer*, **9**, 360–362.

137 Chapman, N. (1996) Are deer a problem? *Journal of Practical Ecology and Conservation, Special publication No.1,* 4–10.

138 Chapman, N.G. (1997) Upper canine teeth of *Muntiacus* (Cervidae) with particular reference to *M. reevesi. Zeitschrift für Saugetierkunde Supplementum* 2, **62,** 32–36.

139 Chapman, N. (2003) Cast in Iran. *Deer*, **12**, 455–457.

140 Chapman, N.G. (2003) Observations on the parietal region of the skull of *Muntiacus reevesi. Zeitschrift für Jagdwissenschaft,* **49,** 237–241.

141 Chapman, N.G. (2004) Faecal pellets of Reeves' muntjac, *Muntiacus reevesi*: defecation rate, decomposition period, size and weight. *European Journal of Wildlife Research,* **50,** 141–145.

142 Chapman, N.G. (2005) Congentital absence of a tail in a Reeves' muntjac (*Muntiacus reevesi*). *European Journal of Wildlife Research,* **51,** 131–132.

143 Chapman, N.G. & Chapman, D.I. (1979) Seasonal changes in the male accessory glands of reproduction in the male fallow deer (*Dama dama* L.). *Journal of Zoology*, **189**, 259–273.

144 Chapman, N.G. & Chapman, D.I. (1980) The distribution of fallow deer: a worldwide review. *Mammal Review* **10**, 61–138.

145 Chapman, N.G. & Chapman, D.I. (1987) Cysticercosis in fallow deer in England. *Acta Theriologia*, **32**, 105–113.

146 Chapman, N. & Harris, S. (1991) Evidence that the seasonal antler cycle of adult Reeves' muntjac (*Muntiacus reevesi*) is not associated with reproductive quiescence. *Journal of Reproduction and Fertility*, **92**, 361–369.

147 Chapman, N.G. & Harris, S. (1992) Brachygnathia in fallow deer. *Journal of Zoology*, **227**, 323–326.

148 Chapman, N. & Harris, S. (1996) *Muntjac.* The Mammal Society, London/British Deer Society, Fordingbridge.

149 Chapman, N. & Harris, S. (1997) Muntjac: where do we go from here? pp. 32–37 in Goldspink, C.R. *et al.* (eds.) *Population ecology, management and welfare of deer.* Manchester Metropolitan University.

150 Chapman, N. & Twigg, G.I. (1990) Studies on the thymus gland of British Cervidae, particularly muntjac, *Muntiacus reevesi*, and fallow, *Dama dama*, deer. *Journal of Zoology*, **222**, 653–675.

151 Chapman, N. & Whitwell, K. (1998) Skeletal and dental changes in the old lady of Richmond Park. *Deer*, **10**, 405–408.

152 Chapman, N.G. *et al* (1985) Distribution and habitat selection by muntjac and other species of deer in a coniferous forest. *Acta Theriologica*, **30,** 287–303.

153 Chapman, N.G. *et al.* (1987) Techniques for the safe and humane capture of free-living muntjac deer (*Muntiacus reevesi*). *British Veterinary Journal*, **143,** 35–43.

154 Chapman, N.G. *et al.* (1993) Sympatric populations of muntjac (*Muntiacus reevesi*) and roe deer (*Capreolus capreolus*): a comparative analysis of their ranging behaviour, social organizational activity. *Journal of Zoology*, **229**, 623–640.

155 Chapman, N. *et al.* (1994) Reeves' muntjac *Muntiacus reevesi* in Britain: their history, spread, habitat selection, and the role of human intervention in accelerating their dispersal. *Mammal Review.* **24**, 113–160.

156 Chapman, N. *et al.*(1994) What gardeners say about muntjac. *Deer* **9**, 302–306.

158 Chapman, N. *et al* (1997) History and habitat preferences of muntjac in the King's Forest, Suffolk. *Deer*, **10**, 289–294.

159 Chapman, N.G. *et al* (1997) Reproductive strategies and the influence of date of birth on growth and sexual development of an aseasonally breeding ungulate: Reeves'

muntjac (*Muntiacus reevesi*). *Journal of Zoology,* **241,** 551–570.

160 Chapman, N.G. *et al.* (2005) Assessing the age of Reeves' muntjac (*Muntiacus reevesi*) by scoring wear of the mandibular molars. *Journal of Zoology,* **267,** 233–247.

161 Cheyne, I.A., *et al.* (1974) The incidence of disease and parasites in the Soay sheep population of Hirta, pp. 338–359 in Jewell, P.A. *et al.* (eds.) *Island survivors: the ecology of the Soay sheep of St Kilda.* Athlone Press, London.

162 Ciuti, S. *et al.* (2004) Could the predation risk hypothesis explain large-scale spatial sexual segregation in fallow deer (*Dama dama*)? *Behavioral Ecology and Sociobiology,* **56,** 552–564.

163 Clark, M. (1981) *Mammal Watching.* Severn House, London.

164 Claydon, K. Personal communication.

165 Claydon, K. *et al.* (1986) Estimating the number of muntjac deer (*Muntiacus reevesi*) in a commercial coniferous forest. *Bulletin of the British Ecological Society,* **17,** 185–189.

166 Claydon, M. Personal communication.

167 Clinton, T. *et al.* (1992) A case of twin foetuses in a sika hind (*Cervus nippon*) from County Wicklow, Ireland. *Deer,* **8,** 437–438.

168 Clutton-Brock, J. (1987) *A natural history of domesticated mammals.* Cambridge University Press, Cambridge/British Museum (Natural History), London.

169 Clutton-Brock, J. *et al.* (1990) Osteology of the Soay sheep. *Bulletin of the British Museum of Natural History (Zoology),* **56,** 1–56.

169a Clutton-Brock, T.H. Personal comunication.

170 Clutton-Brock, T.H. & Albon, S.D. (1982) Winter mortality in red deer (*Cervus elaphus*). *Journal of Zoology* **56,** 515–520.

171 Clutton-Brock, T.H. & Albon, S.D. (1989) *Red deer in the Highlands.* BSP Professional Books, Oxford.

172 Clutton-Brock, T.H. & Lonergan, M.E. (1994) Culling regimes and sex ratio biases in Highland red deer. *Journal of Animal Ecology,* **31,** 521–527.

173 Clutton-Brock, J. & MacGregor, A. (1988) An end to medieval reindeer in Scotland. *Proceedings of the Society of Antiquaries of Scotland,* **118,** 23–35.

174 Clutton-Brock, T.H. & Pemberton, J.M. (2004) *Soay sheep. Dynamics and selection in an island population.* Cambridge University Press, Cambridge.

175 Clutton-Brock, T.H. *et al.* (1976) Ranks and relationships in Highland ponies and Highland cows. *Zeitschrift für Tierpsychologie,* **41,** 202–216.

176 Clutton-Brock, T.H. *et al.* (1982) *Red deer: behaviour and ecology of two sexes.* Edinburgh University Press, Edinburgh.

177 Clutton-Brock, T.H. *et al.* (1984) Maternal dominance, breeding success and birth sex ratios in red deer. *Nature,* **308,** 358–360.

178 Clutton-Brock, T.H. *et al.* (1987) Interactions between population density and maternal characteristics affecting fecundity and juvenile survival in red deer. *Journal of Animal Ecology,* **56,** 857–871.

179 Clutton-Brock, T.H. *et al.* (1987) Early development and population dynamics in red deer. 1. Density-dependent effects on juvenile survival. *Journal of Animal Ecology,* **56,** 53–67.

180 Clutton-Brock, T.H. *et al.* (1988) Passing the buck: resource defence, lek breeding and mate choice in fallow deer. *Behavioural Ecology and Sociobiology,* **23,** 281–296.

181 Clutton-Brock, T.H. *et al.* (1989) Mate choice on fallow deer leks. *Nature, London,* **340,** 463–465.

182 Clutton-Brock, T.H. *et al.* (1991) Persistent instability and population regulation in Soay sheep. *Journal of Animal Ecology,* **60,** 593–608.

183 Clutton-Brock, T.H. *et al.* (1992) Early development and population fluctuations in Soay sheep. *Journal of Animal Ecology,* **61,** 381–396.

184 Clutton-Brock, T.H. *et al.* (1996) Population fluctuations, reproductive costs and life history tactics in female Soay sheep. *Journal of Animal Ecology,* **65,** 675–689.

185 Clutton-Brock, T.H. *et al.* (1997) Density-dependent selection on horn phenotype in Soay sheep. *Philosophical Transactions of the Royal Society of London Series B,* **352,** 839–850.

186 Coblentz, B.E. (1976) Functions of scent-urination in ungulates with special reference to feral goats (*Capra hircus* L.). *American Naturalist,* **110,** 549–57.

187 Coblentz, B.E. (1978) The effects of feral goats (*Capra hircus*) on island ecosystems. *Biological Conservation,* **13,** 279–286.

188 Coles, C. (1997) *Gardens and deer: A guide to damage limitation.* Swan Hill Press, Shrewsbury.

189 Coltman, D.W. *et al.* (1999) Male reproductive success in a promiscuous mammal: behavioural estimates compared with genetic paternity. *Molecular Ecology,* **8,** 1199–1209.

190 Coltman, D.W. *et al.* (1999) Parasite-mediated selection against inbred Soay sheep in a free-living, island population. *Evolution,* **53,** 1259–1267.

191 Cooke, A.S. (1994) Colonisation by muntjac deer *Muntiacus reevesi* and their impact on vegetation, pp. 45–61 in Massey, M.E. & Welch, R.C. (eds.) *Monks Wood National Nature Reserve. The experience of 40 years 1953–93.* English Nature, Peterborough.

192 Cooke, A.S. (1996) Conservation, muntjac deer and woodland reserve management. *Journal of Practical Ecology and Conservation, Special publication* **1,** 43–52.

193 Cooke, A.S. (1997) Effects of grazing by muntjac (*Muntiacus reevesi*) on bluebells (*Hyacinthoides non-scripta*) and a field technique for assessing feeding activity. *Journal of Zoology,* **242,** 365–369.

194 Cooke, A.S. (1998) Some aspects of muntjac behaviour. *Deer,* **10,** 464–466.

195 Cooke, A.S. (1998) Survival and regrowth performance of coppiced ash (*Fraxinus excelsior*) in relation to browsing damage by muntjac deer (*Muntiacus reevesi*). *Quarterly Journal of Forestry,* **92,** 286–290.

196 Cooke, A.S. (1998) Colonisation of Holme Fen National Nature Reserve by Chinese water deer and muntjac, 1976–1997. *Deer,* **10,** 414–416.

197 Cooke, A.S. (2001) Information on muntjac from studying ivy. *Deer,* **12,** 46–47.

198 Cooke, A.S. (2002) Signs of ground flora recovering in Monks Wood in response to deer management. *Deer,* **12,** 141–144.

199 Cooke, A.S. (2004) Muntjac and conservation woodland, pp. 65–69 in Quine, C.P. *et al.* (eds.) *Managing woodlands and their mammals: proceedings of a joint Mammal Society/Forestry Commission Symposium.* Forestry Commission, Edinburgh.

200 Cooke, A.S. (2005) Muntjac deer *Muntiacus reevesi* in Monks Wood NNR: their management and changing impact, pp. 65–74 in Gardiner, C. & Sparks, T. (eds.) *Ten years of change: woodland research at Monks Wood NNR, 1993–2003.* Research Report 613, English Nature, Peterborough.

201 Cooke, A.S. (2006) Monitoring muntjac deer *Muntiacus reevesi* and their impacts in Monks Wood National Nature Reserve, pp. 1–174 in Research Report No. 681. English Nature, Peterborough.

202 Cooke, A.S. & Farrell, L. (1987) The utilisation of neighbouring farmland by Chinese water deer (*Hydropotes inermis*) at Woodwalton Fen National Nature Reserve. *Huntingdonshire Fauna & Flora Society Report 1986,* **39,** 28–38.

203 Cooke, A.S. & Farrell, L. (1995) Establishment and impact of muntjac (*Muntiacus reevesi*) on two national nature reserves, pp. 48–62 in Mayle, B.A. (ed.) *Muntjac deer. Their biology, impact and management in Britain.* Forestry Commission, Edinburgh.

204 Cooke, A. & Farrell, L. (1998) *Chinese water deer.* The Mammal Society, London and British Deer Society, Fordingbridge.

205 Cooke, A.S. & Farrell, L. (2000) A long-term study of a population of Chinese water deer. *Deer,* **11,** 232–237.

206 Cooke, A.S. & Farrell, L. (2001) Impact of muntjac deer (*Muntiacus reevesi*) at Monks Wood National Nature Reserve, Cambridgeshire, eastern England. *Forestry,* **74,** 241–250.

207 Cooke, A.S. & Farrell, L. (2001) Timing of the rut in a wild population of Chinese water deer. *Deer,* **12,** 22–25.

208 Cooke, A.S. & Farrell, L. (2002) Colonisation of Woodwalton Fen by muntjac. *Deer,* **12,** 250–253.

209 Cooke, A.S. & Lakhani, K.H. (1996) Damage to coppice regrowth by muntjac deer *Muntiacus reevesi* and protection

with electric fencing. *Biological Conservation,* **75,** 231–238.

210 Cooke, A.S. *et al.* (1995) Changes in abundance and size of dog's mercury apparently associated with grazing by muntjac. *Deer,* **9,** 429–433.

211 Cooke, A.S. *et al.* (1996) Mortality in a feral population of muntjac *Muntiacus reevesi* in England. *Acta Theriologica,* **41,** 277–286.

212 Cooper, A.B. (1969) Golden eagle kills red deer calf. *Journal of Zoology,* **158,** 215–216.

213 Cooper, J.E. *et al.* (1986) A comparison of xylazine and methohexitone for the chemical immobilization of Reeves' muntjac (*Muntiacus reevesi*). *British Veterinary Journal,* **142,** 350–357.

214 Cornwall, I.W. (1974) *Bones for the archaeologist.* J.M. Dent & Sons, London.

215 Corrigal, W. (1978) Naturally occurring leptospirosis (*Leptospira ballum*) in a red deer (*Cervus elaphus*). *Veterinary Record,* **103,** 75–76.

216 Coulon, A. *et al.* (2004) Landscape connectivity influences gene flow in a roe deer population inhabiting a fragmented landscape: an individual-based approach. *Molecular Ecology,* **13,** 2841–2850.

217 Cox, F.E.G. (1970) Parasitic protozoa of British wild mammals. *Mammal Review,* **1,** 1–28.

218 Crook, I.G. (1969) *Ecology and behaviour of feral goats in North Wales.* MSc thesis, University College of North Wales, Bangor.

219 Cumming, H.G. (1966) *Behaviour and dispersion in roe deer* (Capreolus capreolus). PhD thesis, University of Aberdeen.

220 Da Fonesca, M.M.S.P.P. (1998) *Plasticity of mating behaviour in red deer* (Cervus elaphus) *in a Mediterranean environment.* PhD thesis, University of London.

221 Dagg, A.I. & de Vos, A. (1958) The walking gaits of some Pecora. *Journal of Zoology,* **155,** 103–110.

222 Danilkin, A. (1996) *Behavioural ecology of Siberian and European roe deer.* Chapman & Hall, London.

223 Dansie, O. & Williams, J. (1973) Paraurethral glands in Reeves' muntjac deer, *Muntiacus reevesi. Journal of Zoology,* **171,** 469–471.

224 Darling, F.F. (1937) *A herd of red deer.* Oxford University Press, London.

225 Davidson, M.M. (1990) Sika deer, pp. 468–477 in King, C.M. (ed) *The handbook of New Zealand mammals.* Oxford University Press, Auckland.

226 Davis, S.J.M. (1987) *The archaeology of animals.* Batsford, London.

227 Davis, R. (2004) Roe deer and TB. *Deer,* **13**(2), 23–24.

228 DCS (1998–2005) Deer Commision for Scotland, annual reports. The Stationery Office, Edinburgh.

229 Defra (2004) *The sustainable management of wild deer populations in England: an action plan.* The Deer Initiative, Wrexham.

230 Delahay, R.J. *et al.* (2001) First report of *Mycobacterium bovis* in a muntjac deer. *Veterinary Record,* **149,** 95–96.

231 Delahay, R.J. *et al.* (2002) The status of *Mycrobacterium bovis* infection in UK wild mammals: a review. *Veterinary Journal,* **164,** 90–105.

232 Delahay, R.J. *et al.*(2006) Bovine tuberculosis infection in wild mammals in south-west England: a survey of prevalence and semi-quantitative assessment of the relative risks to cattle. *Veterinary Journal,* **173,** 287–301.

233 Diaz, A. & Burton, R.J. (1996) The impact of predation by Muntjac deer *Muntiacus reevesi* on sexual reproduction of the woodland herb, lords & ladies *Arum maculatum. Deer,* **10,** 14–19.

234 Diaz, A. *et al.* (2005) Ecological impacts of sika deer on Poole Harbour saltmarshes, pp. 175–188 in Humphreys, J. & May, V. (eds.) *The ecology of Poole Harbour.* Elsevier, Amsterdam.

235 Diaz, A. *et al.* (2006) A genetic study of sika (*Cervus nippon*) in the New Forest and in the Isle of Purbeck, Southern England: is there evidence of recent or past hybridisation with red deer? *Journal of Zoology,* **270,** 227–235.

236 Dickinson, B.G. (1993*) A study of the diets of feral goat*

populations in the Snowdonia National Park. MSc thesis, University of Wales.

237 Dodd, K. (1984) Tuberculosis in free-living deer. *Veterinary Record,* **115,** 592–3.

238 Doney, J. & Packer, J. (1998) An assessment of the impact of deer on agriculture, pp. 38–43 in Goldspink, C.R. *et al.* (eds.) *Population ecology, management and welfare of deer.* British Deer Society/Universities' Federation for Animal Welfare/ Manchester Metropolitan University.

239 Doney, J.M. *et al.* (1974) Colour, conformation, affinities, fleece and patterns of inheritance of the Soay sheep, pp. 88–125 in Jewell, P.A. *et al.* (eds.) *Island survivors: the ecology of the Soay sheep of St Kilda.* Athlone Press, London.

240 Douglas, M.J.W. (1971) Behaviour responses of red deer and chamois to cessation of hunting. *New Zealand Journal of Science,* **14,** 507–518.

241 Douzery, E. & Randi, E. (1997) The mitochondrial control region of Cervidae: evolutionary patterns and phylogenetic content. *Molecular Biology and Evolution,* **14,** 1154–1166.

242 Dubost, G. (1971) Observations éthologiques sur le Muntjak (*Muntiacus muntjak* Zimmermann 1789 et *M.reevesi* Ogilby 1839) en captivité et semi-liberté. *Zeitschrift für Tierpsychologie,* **28,** 387–427 (in French).

243 Duncan, P. (1992) *Horses and grasses: the nutritional ecology of equids and their impact on the Camargue.* Springer-Verlag, New York.

244 Duncan, P. & Vigne, N. (1979) The effect of group size in horses on the rate of attacks by blood-sucking flies. *Animal Behaviour,* **27,** 623–625.

245 Duncan, P. *et al.* (1998) Feeding strategies and the physiology of digestion in roe deer, pp. 91–116 in Andersen, R. *et al.* (eds.) *The European roe deer: the biology of success.* Scandinavian University Press, Oslo.

246 Dunn, A.M. (1967) Endoparasites of deer. *Deer,* **1,** 85–90.

247 Dunn, A.M. (1986) Nasal bots, pp. 70–71 in Alexander, T.L. (ed.) *Management and diseases of deer.* Veterinary Deer Society, London.

248 Dunn, A.M. Personal communication.

249 Dutton, C.J. *et al.* (2002) Hydromyelia in a Reeves' muntjac (*Muntiacus reevesi*). *Journal of Zoo and Wildlife Medicine,* **33,** 256–262.

250 Dzieciolowski, R. (1979) *The quantity, quality and seasonal variation of food resources in various environmental conditions of forest management.* Polish Academy of Sciences Forest Research Institute, Warsaw.

251 Edwards, P.J. & Hollis, S. (1982) The distribution of excreta on New Forest grasslands used by cattle, ponies and deer. *Journal of Applied Ecology,* **19,** 953–964.

252 Ekins, J.R. (1989) *Forage resources of cattle and ponies in the New Forest, southern England.* PhD thesis, University of Southampton.

253 Ekvall, K. (1998) Effects of social organisation, age and aggressive behaviour on allosuckling in wild fallow deer. *Animal Behaviour,* **56,** 695–703.

254 Ekvall, K. (1999) *Alloparental care and social dynamics in the fallow deer* (Dama dama). PhD thesis, University of Stockholm.

255 Ellenberg, H. (1978) Zur populationsökologie des rehes (*Capreolus capreolus* L.) in Mitteleuropa. *Spixiana – Zeitschrift für Zoologie,* Supplement, **2,** 1–211 (in German).

256 Ellerman, J.R. & Morrison-Scott, T.C.S. (1951) *Check list of Palearctic and Indian mammals.* British Museum (Natural History), London.

257 Elwes, H.J. (1912) Notes on the primitive breeds of sheep in Scotland. *Scottish Naturalist,* **1,** 1–7, 25–32, 49–52.

258 Emanuelson, K. *et al.* (1987) Chronic wasting disease in muntjac and hog deer: a nephropatholohy and arthropathy. *Proceedings of International Conference of Zoological and Avian Medicine,* **1,** 495.

259 English, A.W. (1988) *Diseases of deer.* T.G. Hungerford Vade Mecum Series for Domestic Animals, No. 11. University of Sydney, Sydney, Australia

260 Espmark, Y. (1969) Mother-young relations and

development of behaviour in roe deer (*Capreolus capreolus* L.). *Viltrevy,* **6,** 461–531.

261 Estes, R.D. (1972) The role of the vomeronasal organ in mammalian reproduction. *Mammalia,* **36,** 315–341.

262 Fairley, J. (1984) *An Irish beast book.* Blackstaff Press, Belfast.

263 Fawcett, J.K. (1997) *Roe deer.* The Mammal Society, London and British Deer Society, Fordingbridge.

264 Feist, J.D. & McCullough, D.R. (1976) Behaviour patterns and communication in feral horses. *Zeitschrift für Tierpsychologie,* **41,** 337–371.

265 Feldhamer, G.A. *et al.* (1985) Body morphology and weight relationships of sika deer (*Cervus nippon*) in Maryland. *Zeitchrift für Säugetierkunde,* **50,** 88–106.

266 Fennesey, P.F. & Drew, K.R. (eds.) (1985) *Biology of deer production.* Royal Society of New Zealand, Wellington.

267 Flagstad, O. & Røed, K.H. (2003) Refugial origins of reindeer (*Rangifer tarandus* L.) inferred from mitochondrial DNA sequences. *Evolution,* **57,** 658–670.

268 Fleming, A. (1995) St Kilda: stone tools, dolerite quarries and long-term survival. *Antiquity,* **69,** 25–35.

269 Flerov, K.K. (1952) *Fauna of the USSR. Mammals Vol. 1, No. 2 Musk deer and deer.* Moscow, Academy of Sciences of the USSR. (English translation: Israel Program for Scientific Translations, Jerusalem, 1960).

270 Fletcher, J. (2001) Foot and mouth disease in British deer. *Deer,* **12,** 54–57.

271 Fletcher, T.J. (1982) Management problems and disease in farmed deer. *Veterinary Record,* **111,** 219–23.

272 Fletcher, T.J. (2002) *Diseases of deer relevant to Scotland.* Contract Report to the Deer Commission for Scotland, Inverness.

273 Floyd, G.C. (1998) *All his rights: a study of the wild red deer of Exmoor.* West Somerset Free Press, Williton.

274 Focardi, S. & Pecchioli, E. (2005). Social cohesion and foraging decrease with group size in fallow deer (*Dama dama*). *Behavioural Ecology and Sociobiology,* **59,** 84–91.

275 Focardi, S. *et al.* (2006) Inter-specific competition from fallow deer *Dama dama* reduces habitat quality for the Italian roe deer *Capreolus capreolu.* *Ecography,* **29,** 407–417.

276 Forde, P. (1989) *Comparative ecology of muntjac* Muntiacus reevesi *and roe deer* Capreolus capreolus *in a commercial coniferous forest.* PhD thesis, University of Bristol.

277 Forman, A.J. & Gibbs, E.P.J. (1974) Studies with foot-and-mouth disease virus in British deer (red, fallow and roe) I. Clinical disease. *Journal of Comparative Pathology,* **84,** 215–220.

278 Gaillard, J.M. *et al.* (1992) Effects of age and body weight on the proportion of females breeding in a population of roe deer (*Capreolus capreolus*). *Canadian Journal of Zoology,* **70,** 1541–1545.

279 Gaillard, J.M. *et al.* (1993) Timing and synchrony of births in roe deer. *Journal of Mammalogy,* **74,** 738–744.

280 Gaillard, J.M. *et al.* (1993) Effects of cohort, sex and birth date on body development of roe deer (*Capreolus capreolus*) fawns. *Oecologia,* **94,** 57–61.

281 Gaillard, J.M. *et al.* (1993) Roe deer survival patterns: a comparative analysis of contrasting populations. *Journal of Animal Ecology,* **62,** 778–791.

282 Gaillard, J.M. *et al.* (1997) Early survival in roe deer: causes and consequences of cohort variation in two contrasted populations. *Oecologia,* **112,** 502–513.

283 Gaillard, J.M. *et al.* (1998) Population dynamics of roe deer, pp. 309–335 in Andersen, R. *et al.* (eds.) *The European roe deer: the biology of success.* Scandinavian University Press, Oslo.

284 Gaillard, J.M. *et al.* (1998) Family effects on growth and survival of juvenile roe deer. *Ecology,* **79,** 2878–2889.

285 Gates, S. (1979) A study of the home ranges of free-ranging Exmoor ponies. *Mammal Review,* **9,** 3–18.

286 Gates, S.A. (1980) *Studies of the ecology of the free-ranging Exmoor pony.* PhD thesis, University of Exeter.

287 Gates, S.A. (1981) The Exmoor pony – a wild animal? *Nature in Devon (Journal of the Devon Trust for Nature Conservation),* **2,** 7–30.

288 Geist, V. (1971) *Mountain sheep. A study in behavior and evolution.* University of Chicago Press, Chicago.

289 Geist, V. (1998) *Deer of the world: their evolution, behaviour and ecology.* Stackpole Books, Mechanicsburg, PA.

290 Genov, P. (1981) Food composition of wild boar in north-eastern and western Poland. *Acta Theriologica,* **26,** 185–205.

291 Gentry, A. *et al.* (2004) The naming of wild animal species and their domestic derivatives. *Journal of Archaeological Science,* **31,** 645–651.

292 Georges, M. *et al.* (1993) Microsatellite mapping of a gene affecting horn development in *Bos taurus. Nature Genetics,* **4,** 206–210.

293 Gibson, J.A. (1972) The wild goats of the Clyde area. *Western Naturalist,* **1,** 6–25.

294 Gill, E.L. (1988) *Factors affecting body condition of New Forest ponies.* PhD thesis, University of Southampton.

295 Gill, E.L. (1991) *Factors affecting body condition in free-ranging ponies.* Technical Report, Royal Society for the Prevention of Cruelty to Animals, London.

296 Gill, E.L. (1994) *Ponies in the wild.* Whittet Books, London.

297 Gill, R.M.A. (1992) A review of damage by mammals in north temperate forests. I. Deer. *Forestry,* **65,** 145–169.

298 Gill, R.M.A. (1992) A review of damage by mammals in north temperate forests: 3. Impact on trees and forests. *Forestry,* **65,** 363–388.

299 Gill, R.M.A. (1994) *The population dynamics of roe deer* (Capreolus capreolus L.) *in relation to forest habitat succession.* PhD thesis, Open University, Milton Keynes.

301 Gill, R.M.A. *et al.* (1996) Changes in roe deer (*Capreolus capreolus* L.) population density in response to forest habitat succession. *Forest Ecology and Management,* **88,** 31–41.

302 Gill, R. *et al.* (2000) The economic implications of deer damage: a review of current evidence. *DCS Annual Report 1999–2000,* 48–49.

303 Goodman, S. *et al.* (1999) Introgression through rare hybridization: A genetic study of a hybrid zone between red and sika deer (Genus *Cervus*) in Argyll, Scotland. *Genetics,* **152,** 355–371.

304 Goodman, S. *et al.* (2001) Bottlenecks, drift and different-iation: the population genetic structure and demographic history of sika deer (*Cervus nippon*) in the Japanese archipelago. *Molecular Ecology,* **10,** 1357–1370.

305 Gordon, I. (1988) Facilitation of red deer grazing by cattle and its impact on performance. *Journal of Applied Ecology,* **25,** 1–10.

306 Gordon, I.J. (1989) Vegetation community selection by ungulates on the Isle of Rhum. II. Vegetation community selection. *Journal of Applied Ecology,* **26,** 53–64.

307 Gordon, I.J. & Illius, A.W. (1989) Resource partitioning by ungulates on the Isle of Rhum. *Oecologia,* **79,** 383–90.

308 Gordon, I.J. *et al.* (1987) Ponies, cattle and goats, pp. 110–125 in Clutton-Brock, T.H. & Ball, M.E. (eds.) *Rhum: the natural history of an island.* Edinburgh University Press, Edinburgh.

309 Gordon, I.J. *et al.* (1990) The use of domestic herbivores in the conservation of the biological richness of European wetlands. *Bulletin Ecologique,* **21,** 49–60.

310 Goritz, F. *et al.* (1999) Experimental investigations on embryonic diapauses and seasonality of spermatogenesis in the European roe deer (*Cervus elaphus*). *Abstracts of the 1999 European Roe Deer Meeting Chize,* CNRS, Paris.

311 Gosling, L.M. (1985) The even-toed ungulates: Order Artiodactyla, pp. 550–618 in Brown, R.E. & Macdonald, D.W. (eds.) *Social odours in mammals.* Oxford University Press, Oxford.

312 Goss, R.J. (1983) *Deer antlers. Regeneration, function and evolution.* Academic Press, London.

313 Goss, R. *et al.* (1992) The mechanisms of antler casting in fallow deer. *Journal of Experimental Zoology,* **264,** 429–436.

314 Goulding, M.J. (2001) Possible genetic sources of free-living wild boar (*Sus scrofa*) in southern England. *Mammal Review,* **31,** 245–248.

315 Goulding, M. (2003) *Wild boar in Britain.* Whittet Books, Stowmarket.

316 Goulding, M.J. *et al.* (1998) *Current status and potential impact*

of Wild Boar (Sus scrofa) *in the English countryside: A risk assessment.* Central Science Laboratory report to the Ministry of Agriculture, Fisheries and Food.

317 Grant, S.A. *et al.* (1984) The utilisation of sown and indigenous plant species by sheep and goats grazing hill pastures. *Grass and Forage Science, 39, 361–370.*

318 Green, P. & Chapman, N. (1993) Joint disease in wild deer. *Deer, 9, 30–31.*

319 Greig, J.C. (1969) *The ecology of feral goats in Scotland.* MSc thesis, University of Edinburgh.

320 Greig, J.C. (1977) Feral goat *Capra* (domestic), pp. 455–459 in Corbet, G.B.& Southern, H.N. (eds.) *The handbook of British mammals.* Blackwell Scientific Publications, Oxford.

321 Grenfell, B.T. *et al.* (1992) Overcompensation and population cycles in an ungulate. *Nature, 355, 823–826.*

322 Grenfell, B.T. *et al.* (1998) Noise and determinism in synchronized sheep dynamics. *Nature, 394, 674–677.*

323 Groot Bruinderink, G.W.T.A. & Hazebroek, E. (1996) Ungulate traffic collisions in Europe. *Conservation Biology, 10, 1059–1067.*

324 Groot Bruinderink, G.W.T.A. *et al.* (1994) Diet and condition of wild boar, *Sus scrofa scrofa,* without supplementary feeding. *Journal of Zoology, London, 233, 631–648.*

325 Groves, C.P. (1989) Feral mammals of the Mediterranean islands. Document of early domestication, pp. 46–57 in Clutton-Brock, J. (ed.) *The walking larder.* Unwin Hyman, London.

326 Groves, C.P. & Grubb, P. (1987) Relationships of living deer, pp. 21–59 in Wemmer, C.M. (ed.) *Biology and management of the Cervidae.* Smithsonian Institution Press, Washington, DC.

327 Grubb, P. (1974) Population dynamics of the Soay sheep, pp 242–272 in Jewell, P.A. *et al.* (eds.) *Island survivors: the ecology of the Soay sheep of St Kilda.* Athlone Press, London.

328 Grubb, P. (1974) The rut and behaviour of Soay rams, pp 195–223 in Jewell, P.A. *et al.* (eds.) *Island survivors: the ecology of the Soay sheep of St Kilda.* Athlone Press, London.

329 Grubb, P. (1974) Social organization of Soay sheep and the behaviour of ewes and lambs, pp 131–159 in Jewell, P.A. *et al.* (eds.) *Island survivors: the ecology of the Soay sheep of St Kilda.* Athlone Press, London.

330 Grubb, P. & Jewell, P.A. (1973) The rut and the occurrence of oestrus in the Soay sheep on St Kilda. *Journal of Reproduction and Fertility, Supplement, 19, 491–502.*

331 Grubb, P. & Jewell, P.A. (1974) Movement, daily activity and home range of Soay sheep, pp 160–194 in Jewell, P.A. *et al.* (eds.) *Island survivors: the ecology of the Soay sheep of St Kilda.* Athlone Press, London.

332 Gubernick, D.J. (1981) Mechanisms of maternal 'labelling' in goats. *Animal Behaviour, 29, 305–6.*

333 Gulland, F.M.D. (1991) *Nematodirus* species on St Kilda. *Veterinary Record, 128, 576.*

334 Gulland, F.M.D. (1991) *The role of parasites in the population dynamics of Soay sheep on St Kilda.* PhD thesis, University of Cambridge.

335 Gulland, F.M.D. (1992) The role of nematode parasites in Soay sheep (*Ovis aries* L.) mortality during a population crash. *Parasitology, 105, 493–503.*

336 Gulland, F.M.D. *et al.* (1993) Parasite-associated polymorphism in a cyclic ungulate population. *Proceedings of the Royal Society of London, Series B, 254, 7–13.*

337 Guo, G. & Zhang, E. (2005) Diet of Chinese water deer (*Hydropotes inermis*) in Zhoushan Archipelago, China. *Acta Theriologica Sinica, 25, 122–130.*

338 Gustavsson, I. & Sundt, C.O. (1968) Karyotypes of five species of deer (*Alces alces* L., *Capreolus capreolus* L., *Cervus elaphus* L., *Cervus nippon* Temm. and *Dama dama* L.) *Hereditas, 60, 233–248.*

339 Gwynne, D.C. & Boyd, J.M. (1970) Relationship between numbers of Soay sheep and pastures at St Kilda, pp. 289–300 in Watson, A. (ed.) *Animal populations in relation to their food resources.* Blackwells, Oxford.

340 Gwynne, D. *et al.* (1974) The vegetation and soils of Hirta, pp. 36–87 in Jewell, P.A. *et al.* (eds.) *Island survivors: the ecology*

341 Hall, S.J.G. (1985) The Chillingham white cattle. *British Cattle Breeders Club Digest, 40, 24–28.*

342 Hall, S.J.G. (1989) Chillingham cattle: social and maintenance behaviour in an ungulate which breeds all year round. *Animal Behaviour, 38, 215–225.*

343 Hall, S.J.G. (2002) Behaviour of cattle, pp. 131–143 in Jensen, P. (ed.) *The ethology of domestic animals. An introductory text.* CABI, Wallingford.

344 Hall, S.J.G. (2004) *Livestock biodiversity. Genetic resources for the farming of the future.* Blackwell Science, Oxford.

345 Hall, S.J.G. & Clutton-Brock, J. (1988) *Two hundred years of British farm livestock.* British Museum (Natural History), London.

346 Hall, S.J.G. & Hall, J.G. (1988) Inbreeding and population dynamics of the Chillingham cattle (*Bos taurus*). *Journal of Zoology, 216, 479–493.*

347 Hall, S.J.G. & Moore, G.F. (1986) Feral cattle of Swona, Orkney Islands. *Mammal Review, 16, 89–96.*

348 Hall, S.J.G. *et al.* (1988) Vocalisations of the Chillingham cattle. *Behaviour, 104, 78–104.*

349 Hall, S.J.G. *et al.* (2005) Management of the Chillingham wild cattle. *Government Veterinary Journal, 15, 4–11.*

350 Hansen, P.J. (1985) Seasonal modulation of puberty and the postpartum anestrus in cattle: a review. *Livestock Production Science, 12, 309–327.*

351 Harding, S.P.(1986) *Aspects of the ecology and social organisation of the muntjac deer* (Muntiacus reevesi). DPhil thesis, University of Oxford.

352 Harman, M. (1997) *An isle called Hirte. History and culture of the St Kildans to 1930.* Maclean Press, Waternish, Isle of Skye.

353 Harman, M. Personal communication.

354 Harrington, R. (1973) Hybridisation among deer and its implications for conservation. *Irish Forestry Journal, 30, 64–78.*

355 Harrington, R. (1974) The hybridization of red deer and sika deer in Northern Ireland. *Irish Forestry Journal, 31, 2.*

356 Harrington, R. (1982) The hybridization of red deer (*Cervus elaphus* L., 1758) and Japanese sika deer (*Cervus nippon* Temmink, 1838). *International Congress of Game Biologists, 14, 559–571.*

357 Harrington, R. Personal communication.

358 Harris, S.& Forde, P. (1986) The annual diet of muntjac (*Muntiacus reevesi*) in the King's Forest, Suffolk. *Bulletin of the British Ecological Society, 17, 19–22.*

359 Harris, S. *et al.* (1990) Home-range analysis using radio-tracking data – a review of problems and techniques particularly as applied to the study of mammals. *Mammal Review, 20, 97–123.*

360 Harris, S. *et al.* (1995) *A review of British mammals: population estimates and conservation status of British mammals other than cetaceans.* JNCC, Peterborough.

361 Hartl, G.B. *et al.* (1998) Genetics of European roe deer, pp. 71–90 in Andersen, R. *et al.* (eds.) *The European roe deer: the biology of success.* Scandinavian University Press, Oslo.

362 Hawkins, D. (1988) The parasitic interrelationships of deer and sheep on the Knebworth Park estate, near Stevenage. *Deer, 7, 296–300.*

363 Hayden, T. & Harrington, R. (2000) *Exploring Irish mammals.* Duchas – The Heritage Service, Dublin.

364 Hearny, A.W. & Jennings, T.J. (1983) Annual foods of the red deer (*Cervus elaphus*) and the roe deer (*Capreolus capreolus*) in the east of England. *Journal of Zoology, 201, 565–570.*

365 Hellawell, T.C. (1991) *Aspects of the ecology and management of the feral goat* (Capra hircus L.) *populations of the Rhinogau and Maentwrog areas, north Wales.* PhD thesis, University of Wales.

366 Hemami, M.R. (2003) The ecology of roe deer (*Capreolus capreolus*) and muntjac (*Muntiacus reevesi*) in a forested landscape in eastern England. PhD thesis, University of East Anglia.

367 Henry, B.A.M. (1978) Diet of the roe deer in an English conifer forest. *Journal of Wildlife Management, 42, 937–940.*

368 Henry, B.A.M. (1981) Distribution patterns of roe deer (*Capreolus capreolus*) related to the availability of food and cover. *Journal of Zoology,* **194,** 271–275.

369 Hewison, A.J.M. (1993) *The reproductive performance of roe deer in relation to environmental and genetic factors.* PhD thesis, University of Southampton.

370 Hewison, A.J.M. (1995) Isozyme variation in roe deer in relation to their population history in Britain. *Journal of Zoology,* **235,** 279–288.

371 Hewison, A.J.M. (1996) Variation in the fecundity of roe deer in Britain: effects of age and body weight. *Acta Theriologica,* **41,** 187–198.

372 Hewison, A.J.M. (1997) Evidence for a genetic component of female fecundity in British roe deer from studies of cranial morphometrics. *Functional Ecology,* **11,** 508–517.

373 Hewison, A.J.M. Personal communication.

374 Hewison, A.J.M. & Danilkin, A. (2001) Evidence for separate specific status of European (*Capreolus capreolus*) and Siberian (*Capreolus pygargus*) roe deer. *Mammalian Biology,* **66,** 13–21.

375 Hewison, A.J.M. & Gaillard, J.M. (1996) Birth sex ratios and local resource competition in roe deer. *Behavioural Ecology,* **7,** 461–464.

376 Hewison, A.J.M. *et al.* (1996) Variation in cohort mandible size as an index of roe deer (*Capreolus capreolus*) densities and population trends. *Journal of Zoology,* **239,** 573–581.

377 Hewison, A.J.M. *et al.* (1996) Annual variation in body composition of roe deer (*Capreolus capreolus*) in moderate environmental conditions. *Canadian Journal of Zoology,* **74,** 245–253.

378 Hewison, A.J.M. *et al.* (1998) Social organisation of European roe deer, pp. 189–219 in Andersen, R. *et al.* (eds.) *The European roe deer: the biology of success.* Scandinavian University Press, Oslo.

379 Hewison, A.J.M. *et al.* (1999) Contradictory findings in studies of sex-ratio variation in roe deer. *Behavioral Ecology and Sociobiology,* **45,** 339–348.

380 Hewison, A.J.M. *et al.* (1999) Tests of age estimation from tooth wear on roe deer of known age: variation within and between populations. *Canadian Journal of Zoology,* **77,** 58–67.

381 Hewison, A.J.M. *et al.* (2001) The effects of woodland fragmentation and human activity on roe deer distribution in agricultural landscapes. *Canadian Journal of Zoology,* **79,** 679–689.

382 Hill, S.D. (1985) *Influences of large herbivores on small rodents in the New Forest.* PhD thesis, University of Southampton.

383 Hinge, M.D.C. (1986) *Ecology of red and roe deer in a mixed-aged conifer plantation.* PhD thesis, University of Aberdeen.

384 Hirons, G.J.M. (1984) The diet of tawny owls (*Strix aluco*) and kestrels (*Falco tinnunculus*) in the New Forest, Hampshire. *Proceedings of the Hampshire Field Club and Archaeological Society,* **40,** 21–26.

385 Hofmann, R.R. (1985) Digestive physiology of the deer – their morphophysiological specialisation and adaptation. *Bulletin of the Royal Society of New Zealand,* **22,** 393–407.

386 Hofmann, R.R. (1989) Evolutionary steps of ecophysiological adaptation and diversification of ruminants: a comparative view of their digestive system. *Oecologia,* **78,** 449–457.

387 Hogg, J.T. (1984) Mating in bighorn sheep: multiple creative strategies. *Science,* **225,** 526–529.

388 Holand, O. (1992) Seasonal variation in body composition of European roe deer. *Canadian Journal of Zoology,* **70,** 502–504.

389 Holand, O. *et al.* (1998) Roe deer in northern environments: physiology and behaviour, pp. 117–137 in Andersen, R. *et al.* (eds.) *The European roe deer: the biology of success.* Scandinavian University Press, Oslo.

390 Holecková, J. *et al.* (2000) Inter-male mounting in fallow deer, *Dama dama* – its seasonal pattern and social meaning. *Folia Zoologica,* **49,** 175–181.

391 Horwood, M.T. & Masters, E.H. (1970) *Sika deer.* British Deer Society, Reading.

392 Horwood, M.T. & Masters, E.H. (1981) *Sika deer,* 2nd edn. British Deer Society, Reading.

393 Hosey, G.R. (1981) Annual foods of the roe deer (*Capreolus capreolus*) in the south of England. *Journal of Zoology,* **194,** 276–278.

394 Howells, O. & Edwards-Jones, G. (1977) A feasibility study of reintroducing wild boar (*Sus scrofa*) to Scotland: are existing woodlands large enough to support a minimum viable population? *Biological Conservation,* **81,** 77–89.

395 Howes, C.A. (1996) The history and spread of roe deer in southern Yorkshire – a review, pp. 39–42 in Jones, M. *et al.* (eds.) *Deer or the new woodlands? Journal of Practical Ecology and Conservation, spec. pub.* **1**.

396 Hufthammer, A.K. & Aaris-Sorensen, K. (1998) Late- and postglacial European roe deer, pp. 47–69 in Andersen, R. *et al.* (eds.) *The European roe deer: the biology of success.* Scandinavian University Press, Oslo.

397 Idris, A.B.H. (1990) *The ecology of roe deer (*Capreolus capreolus L*) inhabiting farmland in north-east Scotland.* PhD thesis, University of Aberdeen.

398 Illius, A.W. & Gordon, I.J. (1987) The allometry of food intake in grazing ruminants. *Journal of Animal Ecology,* **56,** 989–999.

399 Illius, A.W. *et al.* (2002) Mechanisms of functional response and resource exploitation in browsing roe deer. *Journal of Animal Ecology,* **71,** 723–734.

400 Ingham, B. (2001) Abattoir survey of dental defects in cull cows. *Veterinary Record,* **148,** 739–742.

401 Jackson, J.E. (1974) *The feeding ecology of fallow deer in the New Forest.* PhD thesis, University of Southampton.

402 Jackson, J.E. (1977) The annual diet of the fallow deer (*Dama dama*) in the New Forest, Hampshire, as determined by rumen content analysis. *Journal of Zoology,* **181,** 465–473.

403 Jackson, J.E. (1980) The annual diet of the roe deer (*Capreolus capreolus*) in the New Forest, Hampshire, as determined by rumen content analysis. *Journal of Zoology,* **192,** 71–84.

404 Jackson, J.E. *et al.* (1977) A note on the food of muntjac deer (*Muntiacus reevesi*). *Journal of Zoology,* **183,** 546–548.

405 Jacobi, R. Personal communication.

406 Jacobs, G.H. *et al.* (1994) Electrophysiological measurements of spectral mechanisms in the retina of two cervids: white-tailed deer (*Odocoileus virginianus*) and fallow deer (*Dama dama*). *Journal of Comparative Physiology A,* **174,** 551–557.

407 Jarman, M.R. (1972) European deer economies and the advent of the Neolithic, pp. 125–147 in Higgs, E.S. (ed.) *Papers in economic history.* Cambridge University Press, Cambridge.

408 Jedrzejewska, B. & Jedrzejewski, W. (1998) *Predation in vertebrate communities.* Springer-Verlag, Berlin.

409 Jennings, D.J. *et al.* (2002) Does lateral presentation of the palmate antlers during fights by fallow deer (*Dama dama* L.) signify dominance or submission? *Ethology,* **108,** 389–401.

410 Jeppesen, J.L. (1989) Activity patterns of free-ranging roe deer (*Capreolus capreolus*) at Kalo. *Danish Review of Game Biology,* **13,** 1–30.

411 Jewell, P.A. (1989) Factors that affect fertility in a feral population of sheep. *Zoological Journal of the Linnean Society,* **95,** 163–174.

412 Jewell, P.A. (1997) Survival and behaviour of castrated Soay sheep (*Ovis aries*) in a feral island population on Hirta, St Kilda, Scotland. *Journal of Zoology,* **243,** 623–636.

413 Jewell, P.A. & Grubb, P. (1974) The breeding cycle, the onset of oestrus and conception in Soay sheep, pp. 224–241 in Jewell, P.A. *et al.* (eds.) *Island survivors: the ecology of the Soay sheep of St Kilda.* Athlone Press, London.

414 Jewell, P.A. *et al.* (eds.) (1974) *Island survivors: the ecology of the Soay sheep of St Kilda.* Athlone Press, London.

415 Johansson, A. (1996) Territory establishment and antler cycle in male roe deer. *Ethology,* 102, 549–559.

416 Johansson, A. (1996) *Territory dynamics and marking behaviour in male roe deer.* PhD thesis, Stockholm University.

417 Johansson, A. & Liberg, O. (1996) Functional aspects of marking behaviour by male roe deer (*Capreolus capreolus*). *Journal of Mammalogy,* **77,** 558–567.

418 Johansson, A. *et al.* (1995) Temporal and physical characteristics of scraping and rubbing in roe deer (*Capreolus capreolus*). *Journal of Mammalogy,* **76,** 123–129.

419 Johnson, E. & Hornby, J. (1980) Age and seasonal coat changes in long haired and normal fallow deer (*Dama dama*). *Journal of Zoology,* **192,** 501–509.

420 Johnson, A.L. (1982) Notes on the behaviour of roe deer (*Capreolus capreolus* L.) at Chedington, Dorset, 1970–1980. *Forestry Commission Research and Development Paper,* **130,** 1–87.

421 Johnson, T.H. (1984) *Habitat and social organisation of roe deer* (Capreolus capreolus). PhD thesis, University of Southampton.

422 Jones, T.O. (1982) Outbreak of *Pasteurella multocida* septicaemia in fallow deer (*Dama dama*). *Veterinary Record* **110,** 451–2.

423 Jowett, C (1995) *The reproductive status of four wild populations of fallow deer occupying distinct woodland habitats.* MSc thesis, University of Surrey.

424 Kaji, K. *et al.* (1988) Effects of resource limitation on the physical and reproductive condition of sika deer on Nakanoshima Island, Hokkaido. *Acta Theriologica,* **33,** 187–208.

425 Kampf, H. (2000) The role of large grazing animals in nature conservation – a Dutch perspective. *British Wildlife,* **12,** 37–46.

426 Kay, R.N.B. (1987) Weights of salivary glands in some ruminant animals. *Journal of Zoology,* **211,** 431–436.

427 Kay, R.N.B. & Staines, B.W. (1981) The nutrition of the red deer (*Cervus elaphus*). *Nutrition Abstracts and Reviews B,* **51,** 601–622.

428 Keeling, J.G.M. (1995) *Ecological determinants of muntjac deer* Muntiacus reevesi *behaviour.* PhD thesis, University of Bristol.

429 Kennaugh, J.H. *et al.* (1977) Seasonal changes in the prepuce of adult fallow deer (*Dama dama*) and its probable function as a scent organ. *Journal of Zoology,* **183,** 301–310.

430 Kjellander, P. *et al.* (2004) Experimental evidence for density-dependence of home range size in roe deer. *Oecologia,* **139,** 478–485.

431 Knight, T.W. (1985) Pheromones in farm animals. *Trends in Pharmacological Sciences,* **6,** 171–173.

432 Komers, P.E. *et al* (1997) Age at first reproduction in male fallow deer: age-specific versus dominance-specific behaviors. *Behavioral Ecology,* **8,** 456–462.

433 Konig, R. & Eick, E. (1989) Variations due to growth and seasonal changes in the body weights of sika deer (*Cervus nippon*) of the Mohnesee population in West Germany. *Symposium on Wildlife in Japan,* April. Japan Hunters' Association.

434 Kurt, F. (1991) *Das reh in der Kulturlandschaft.* Verlag Paul Parey, Hamburg.

435 Lambert, R. (1998) Delayed implantation. The enigma of the female roe deer (*Capreolus capreolus*). *Deer,* **10**(7), 409–413.

436 Lambert, R. (1999) Monoestry in the European roe deer and are pregnant roe kids an illusion. *Deer,* **11**(2), 67–69.

437 Langbein, J. (1985) *North Staffordshire Deer Survey 1983–84, I. Research and development.* British Deer Society, Fordingbridge.

438 Langbein, J. (1991) *Effects of density and age on body condition, reproductive performance, behaviour and survival of fallow deer.* PhD thesis, University of Southampton.

439 Langbein, J. (1997) *The ranging behaviour, habitat-use and impact of deer in oak woods and heather moors of Exmoor and the Quantock Hills.* British Deer Society, Fordingbridge.

440 Langbein, J. (1997) The ranging behaviour, habitat-use and impact of deer in oak woods and heather moors on Exmoor. *Deer,* **10,** 516–521.

441 Langbein, J. (2006) *Sustainable management and conservation of deer on the Quantocks.* Quantock Deer Management and Conservation Group, Bridgwater.

442 Langbein, J. Personal communication

443 Langbein, J. & Chapman, N. (2003) *Fallow deer.* The Mammal Society, London/British Deer Society, Fordingbridge.

444 Langbein, J. & Putman, R.J. (1992) Reproductive success of female fallow deer in relation to age and condition, pp. 293–299 in Brown, R. (ed.) *The biology of deer.* Springer-Verlag, New York.

445 Langbein, J. & Putman, R.J. (1992) Behavioural responses of park red and fallow deer to disturbance and effects on population performance. *Animal Welfare,* **1,** 19–38.

446 Langbein, J. & Putman, R.J. (1992) *Conservation and management of deer on Exmoor and the Quantocks.* National Trust, London.

447 Langbein, J. & Rutter, S.M. (2003) Quantifying the damage wild deer cause to agricultural crops and pastures, pp. 32–39 in Goldberg, E. (ed.) *Proceedings of the Future of Deer conference.* Research Report 548, English Nature, Peterborough.

448 Langbein, J. & Thirgood, S.J. (1989) Variation in mating systems of fallow deer in relation to ecology. *Ethology,* **83,** 195–214.

449 Larner, J.B. (1977) Sika deer damage to mature woodlands of southwestern Ireland. *Proceedings of the 13th International Congress of Game Biology,* 192–202.

450 Lawman, M.J.P. *et al.* (1978) A preliminary survey of British deer for antibody to some virus diseases of farm animals. *British Veterinary Journal,* **134,** 85–91.

451 Latham, J. *et al.* (1996) The relative densities of red (*Cervus elaphus*) and roe (*Capreolus capreolus*) deer and their relationship in Scottish plantation forests. *Journal of Zoology,* **240,** 285–299.

452 Latham, J. *et al.* (1997) Correlations of red (*Cervus elaphus*) and roe (*Capreolus capreolus*) deer in Scottish forests with environmental variables. *Journal of Zoology,* **242,** 681–704.

453 Latham, J. *et al.* (1999) Comparative feeding ecology of red (*Cervus elaphus*) and roe deer (*Capreolus capreolus*) in Scottish plantation forests. *Journal of Zoology,* **247,** 409–418.

454 Lawrence, A.B. & Wood-Gush, D.G.M. (1988) Home-range behaviour and social organisation of Scottish blackface sheep. *Journal of Applied Ecology,* **25,** 25–40.

455 Lawson, R.E. (1996) *The influences of evolution, habitat and social organisation upon chemical signalling in deer.* PhD thesis, University of Southampton.

456 Lawson, R.E. *et al.* (2000) Individual signatures in scent gland secretions of Eurasian deer. *Journal of Zoology,* **251,** 399–410.

457 Lawson, R.E. *et al.* (2001) Chemical communication in Eurasian deer: do individual odours also code for attributes? *Journal of Zoology,* **253,** 91–99.

458 Lever, C. (1985) *Naturalized mammals of the world.* Longman, London.

459 Liberg, O. *et al.* (1998) Mating system, mating tactics and the function of male territoriality in roe deer, pp. 221–256 in Andersen, R. *et al.* (eds.) *The European roe deer: the biology of success.* Scandinavian University Press, Oslo.

460 Lincoln, G. (1970) History of a hummel 2. *Deer,* **1,** 630–632.

461 Lincoln, G. (1978) History of a hummel. *Deer,* **4,** 274–275.

462 Lincoln, G.A. (1989) Seasonal cycles in testicular activity in mouflon, Soay sheep and domesticated breeds of sheep: breeding seasons modified by domestication. *Zoological Journal of the Linnean Society,* **95,** 137–147.

463 Lincoln, G.A. & Davidson, W. (1977) The relationship between sexual and aggressive behaviour, and pituitary and testicular activity during the seasonal sexual cycles of rams, and the influence of photoperiod. *Journal of Reproduction and Fertility,* **49,** 267–276.

464 Lincoln, G.A. & Ebling, F.J.P. (1985) Effect of constant-release implants of melatonin on seasonal cycles in reproduction, prolactin secretion and moulting in rams. *Journal of Reproduction and Fertility,* **73,** 241–253.

465 Lincoln, G. & Fletcher, T. (1984) History of a hummel Part

VII. Nature vs. nurture. *Deer,* **6,** 127–131.

466 Lincoln, G.A. *et al.* (1990) Seasonal cycles in the blood plasma concentrations of FSH inhibin and testosterone, and testicular size in rams of wild, feral and domesticated breeds of sheep. *Journal of Reproduction and Fertility,* **88,** 623–633.

467 Linnell, J.D.C *et al.* (1998) From birth to independence: birth, growth, neonatal mortality, hiding behaviour and dispersal, pp. 257–283 in Andersen, R. *et al.* (eds.) *The European roe deer: the biology of success.* Scandinavian University Press, Oslo.

468 Lioi, M.B. *et al.* (1994) The RBA-banded karyotype of the fallow deer (*Dama dama* L.). *Cytogenetics and Cell Genetics,* **67,** 75–80.

469 Lister, A.M. (1984) Evolutionary and ecological origins of British deer. *Proceedings of the Royal Society of Edinburgh,* **82B,** 205–229.

470 Lister, A. *et al.* (1998) Taxonomy, morphology and evolution of European roe deer, pp. 23–46 in Andersen, R. *et al.* (eds.) *The European roe deer: the biology of success.* Scandinavian University Press, Oslo.

471 Lister, A.M. *et al.* (2005) The phylogenetic position of the 'giant deer' *Megaloceros giganteus. Nature, London,* **438,** 850–853.

472 Lochman, I.J. (1967) (The feeding rhythm and daily regime of red and roe deer.) *Proceedings of the International Congress of Game Biology,* **7,** 231–234.

473 Loftus, R.T. *et al.* (1994) Evidence for two independent domestications of cattle. *Proceedings of the National Academy of Sciences of the USA,* **91,** 2757–2761.

474 Long, S.E. (1993) Incidence of the rob.t (1;29) centric fusion translocation in British White cattle in Britain. *Veterinary Record,* **132,** 165–166.

475 Loudon, A.S.I. (1978) The control of roe deer populations: a problem in forest management. *Forestry,* **51,** 73–83.

476 Loudon, A.S.I. (1982) Too many deer for the trees? *New Scientist,* **93,** 708–711.

477 Lowe, R. (1994) *Deer management: developing the requirements for the establishment of diverse coniferous and broadleaf forests.* Unpublished report, Coilte, Bray, Co. Wicklow.

478 Lowe, V.P.W. (1961) A discussion on the history, present status and future conservation of red deer (*Cervus elaphus,* L.) in Scotland. *Terre et la vie,* **1,** 9–40.

479 Lowe, V.P.W. (1966) Observations on the dispersal of red deer on Rhum. *Symposia of the Zoological Society of London,* **18,** 211–228.

480 Lowe, V.P.W. (1967) Teeth as indicators of age with special reference to red deer (*Cervus elaphus*) of known age from Rhum. *Journal of Zoology,* **152,** 137–153.

481 Lowe, V.P.W. (1969) Population dynamics of the red deer (*Cervus elaphus*) on Rhum. *Journal of Animal Ecology,* **38,** 425–458.

482 Lowe, V.P.W. (1977) Red deer, pp. 411–423 in Corbet, G.B. & Southern, H.N. (eds.) *The handbook of British mammals,* 2nd edn. Blackwell Science, Oxford.

483 Lowe, V.P.W. (1979) Wild and feral deer in Great Britain. Unpublished NERC contract report HF3/05/43, Institute of Terrestrial Ecology, Merlewood Research Station.

484 Lowe, V.P.W. Personal communication.

485 Lowe, V.P.W. & Gardiner, A.S. (1974) A re-examination of the subspecies of red deer (*Cervus elaphus*) with particular reference to the stocks in Britain. *Journal of Zoology* **174,** 185–201.

486 Lowe, V.P.W. & Gardiner, A.S. (1975) Hybridisation between red deer and sika deer, with reference to stocks in north-west England. *Journal of Zoology,* **177,** 553–566.

487 Luikart, G. *et al.* (2001) Multiple origins and weak phylogeographic structure in domestic goats. *Proceedings of the National Academy of Sciences of the USA,* **98,** 5927–5932.

488 MacArthur, J. (1981) *A disease study of feral goats in a closed population.* Unpublished report to the Universities Federation for Animal Welfare, Potters Bar.

489 Mackenzie, D. (1980) *Goat husbandry,* 4th edn. Faber and Faber, London.

490 Maclean, C. Personal communication.

491 Mahen, P. & Chapman, N. Skeletal abnormalities in Reeves' muntjac. In preparation

492 Maisels, F.G. (1982) *Grazing and vigilance behaviour of feral goats.* MSc thesis, University of Edinburgh.

493 Malyon, C. & Healy, S. (1994) Fluctuating asymmetry in antlers of fallow deer, *Dama dama,* indicates dominance. *Animal Behaviour,* **48,** 248–250.

494 Manceau, V. *et al.* (1999) Systematics of the genus *Capra* inferred from mitochondrial DNA sequence data. *Molecular Phylogenetics and Evolution,* **13,** 504–510.

495 Mann, J.C.E. (1983) *The social organisation and ecology of the Japanese sika deer* (Cervus nippon) *in southern England.* PhD thesis, University of Southampton.

496 Mann, J.C.E. & Putman, R.J. (1989) Habitat use and activity patterns of British sika deer (*Cervus nippon* Temminck) in contrasting environments. *Acta Theriologica,* **34,** 83–96.

497 Mann, J.C.E. & Putman, R.J. (1989) Diet of British sika deer (*Cervus nippon* Temminck) in contrasting environments. *Acta Theriologica,* **34,** 97–110.

499 Marquiss, M. *et al.* (1985) The numbers, breeding success and diet of golden eagles in southern Scotland in relation to changes in land use. *Biological Conservation,* **34,** 121–40.

500 Marrow, P. *et al.* (1996) State-dependent life history evolution in Soay sheep: dynamic modelling of reproductive scheduling. *Philosophical Transactions of the Royal Society of London, Series B,* **351,** 17–32.

501 Masseti, M. (1996) The post-glacial diffusion of the genus *Dama* Frisch, 1775, in the Mediterranean region. *Supplemento alle Ricerche di Biologia della Selvaggina,* **XXV,** 7–29.

502 Masseti, M. (1999) The European fallow deer *Dama dama* L., 1758, in the Aegean region. *Contributions to the Zoogeography and Ecology of the Eastern Mediterranean Region,* **1**(*suppl.*), 17–30.

503 Matthews, P.R.J. *et al.* (1981) Mycobacterial infections in various species of deer in the United Kingdom. *British Veterinary Journal,* **137,** 60–66.

504 Maublanc, M.L. *et al.* (1987) Flexibilite de l'organisation sociale du chevreuil en function des characteristiques de l'environnment. *Revue d'Ecologie,* **42,** 109–133 (in French).

505 Mauget, C. *et al.* (1997) Metabolic rate in female European roe deer (*Capreolus capreolus*): incidence of reproduction. *Canadian Journal of Zoology,* **75,** 731–739.

506 Mayer, J.J. & Brisbin, I.L. (1991) *Wild pigs in the United States: their history, comparative morphology and current status.* University of Georgia Press, Athens.

507 Mayle, B.A. & Staines, B.W. (1998) An overview of methods used for estimating the size of deer populations in Great Britain, pp. 19–31 in Goldspink, C.R. *et al.* (eds.) *Population ecology, management and welfare of deer.* Manchester Metropolitan University.

508 Mayle, B.A. *et al.* (1999) *How many deer? A field guide to estimating deer population size.* Field Book 18, Forestry Commission, Edinburgh.

509 McCarthy, A. *et al.* (1996) Urban deer, community forests and control. *Deer,* **10**(1), 26–27.

510 McCulloch, A.P. (1996) Soay sheep 1– Proflicacy. *Ark,* **24,** 6.

511 McDiarmid, A. (1965) Some infectious diseases of free-living wildlife. *British Veterinary Journal,* **121,** 245–257.

512 McDiarmid, A. (1975) Some disorders of wild deer in the United Kingdom. *Veterinary Record,* **97,** 6–9.

513 McDougall, P. (1975) The feral goats of Kielderhead Moor. *Journal of Zoology,* **176,** 215–246.

514 McNally, L. (1970) *Highland deer forest.* J.M. Dent & Sons, London.

515 McNally, L. (1975) *The year of the red deer.* J.M. Dent & Sons, London.

516 Megaw, B.R.S. (1963) Goat keeping in the old Highland economy. *Scottish Studies,* **7,** 201–209.

517 Merchant, M. (1993) The potential for control of the soft rush *Juncus effusus* in grass pastures by grazing goats. *Grass and Forage Science,* **48,** 395–409.

518 Meyer, W. *et al.* (2001) Subgroup differentiation in the Cervidae by hair cuticle analysis. *Zeitschrift für Jagdwissenschaft,* **47,** 253–258.

519 Middleton, A.D. (1937) Whipsnade ecological survey, 1936–7. *Proceedings of the Zoological Society of London A,* **107,** 471–481.

520 Miller, G.S. (1912) *Catalogue of the mammals of western Europe.* British Museum (Natural History), London.

521 Milne, J.A. *et al.* (1998) The impact of vertebrate herbivores on the natural heritage of the Scottish uplands – a review. *Scottish Natural Heritage Review,* No. 95. Battleby, Scotland.

522 Milner, C. & Gwynne, D. (1974) The Soay sheep and their food supply, pp. 273–325 in Jewell, P.A. *et al.* (eds.) *Island survivors: the ecology of the Soay sheep of St Kilda.* Athlone Press, London.

523 Mitchell, B. (1967) Growth layers in dental cement for determining the age of red deer (*Cervus elaphus*). *Journal of Animal Ecology,* **36,** 279–93.

524 Mitchell, B. (1970) Notes on two old red deer. *Deer,* **2,** 568–570.

525 Mitchell, B. (1971) The weights of new-born to one-day-old red deer calves in Scottish moorland habitats. *Journal of Zoology,* **164,** 250–254.

526 Mitchell, B. & Crisp, J.M. (1981) Some properties of Red deer (*Cervus elaphus*) at exceptionally high population-density in Scotland. *Journal of Zoology,* **193,** 157–169.

527 Mitchell, B., & Grant, W. (1981) Notes on the performance of red deer, *Cervus elaphus,* in a woodland habitat. *Journal of Zoology,* **194,** 279–284.

528 Mitchell, B. & Staines, B.W. (1976) An example of natural winter mortality in Scottish red deer. *Deer,* **3,** 549–552.

529 Mitchell, B. & Youngson, R.W. (1969) Teeth and age in Scottish red deer – a practical guide to the determination of age, pp. 14–15 in *Red Deer Commission Annual Report for 1968.* HMSO, Edinburgh.

530 Mitchell, B. *et al.* (1973) Some characteristics of natural mortality among wild Scottish red deer (*Cervus elaphus*), pp. 437–450 in *Proceedings of the International Congress of Game Biologists,* **10,** 1971.

531 Mitchell, B. *et al.* (1976) Annual cycles of condition in Scottish red deer. *Journal of Zoology,* **180,** 107–127.

532 Mitchell, B. *et al.* (1977) *Ecology of red deer: a research review relevant to their management in Scotland.* Institute of Terrestrial Ecology, Cambridge.

533 Mitchell, B. *et al.* (1985) Defecation frequency in roe deer (*Capreolus capreolus*) in relation to the accumulation rates of faecal deposits. *Journal of Zoology,* **207,** 1–7.

534 Mitchell B. *et al.* (1986) Performance and population dynamics in relation to management of red deer *Cervus elaphus* at Glenfeshie, Inverness-shire, Scotland. *Biological Conservation,* **37,** 237–267.

535 Mitchell, G.F. (1941) The reindeer in Ireland. *Proceedings of the Royal Irish Academy,* **46B,** 183–188.

535a Mitchell-Jones, A.J. Personal communication.

536 Miura, S. (1984) Dominance hierarchy and space use pattern in male captive muntjacs. *Muntiacus reevesi. Journal of Ethology,* **2,** 69–75.

537 MLURI (1993) *Annual Report 1992.* Macauley Land Use Research Institute, Aberdeen.

538 Moorcroft, P.R. *et al.* (1996) Density-dependent selection in a fluctuating ungulate population. *Proceedings of the Royal Society of London, Series B,* **263,** 31–38.

539 Moore, N.P. (1993) *Mating success in fallow bucks in Phoenix Park, Ireland.* PhD thesis. National University of Ireland.

540 Moore, N.P. & Wilson, C.J. (2005) *Feral wild boar in England. Implications of future management options.* A report on behalf of Defra European Wildlife Division.

541 Moore, N.P. *et al.* (1995) Mating strategies and mating success of fallow bucks in a non-lekking population. *Behavioural Ecology and Sociobiology,* **36,** 91–100.

542 Moore, N.P. *et al.* (2000) Browsing by fallow deer (*Dama dama*) in young broadleaved plantations: seasonality, and the effects of previous browsing and bud eruption. *Forestry,* **73,** 437–445.

543 Motta, R. & Nola, P. (1996) Fraying damages in the subalpineforests of Panveggio (Trento, Italy): a dendrocroecological approach. *Forest Ecology and Management,* **88,** 81–86.

544 Muhlemann, M.F. & Wright, D.J.M. (1987) Emerging pattern of Lyme disease in the United Kingdom and Irish Republic. *Lancet,* **8527,** 260–262.

545 Muller-Schwarze, D. (1987) Evolution of cervid olfactory communication, pp. 223–234 in Wemmer, C.M. (ed.) *Biology and management of the Cervidae.* Smithsonian Institution Press, Washington, DC.

546 Munro, R. (1986) *Dictyocaulus,* pp. 71–74 in Alexander, T.L. (ed.) *Management and diseases of deer.* Veterinary Deer Society, London.

547 Munro, R. (1986) Tuberculosis, pp. 157–160 in Alexander, T.L. (ed.) *Management and diseases of deer.* Veterinary Deer Society, London.

548 Munro, R. Personal communication.

549 Murphey, R.M. *et al.* (1990) Maternal recognition in Gyr (*Bos indicus*) calves. *Applied Animal Behavioural Science,* **27,** 183–191.

550 Murray, D.M. (1965) A field study of coat shedding in cattle under conditions of equal day-length but different temperatures. *Journal of Agricultural Science, Cambridge,* **65,** 295–300.

551 Myrberget, S. (1990) Wildlife management in Europe outside the Soviet Union. *NINA Utreding,* **018,** 1–47.

552 Mysterud, A. (1996) Bed-site selection by adult roe deer *Capreolus capreolus* in southern Norway during summer. *Wildlife Biology,* **2,** 101–106.

553 Mysterud, A. & Ostbye, E. (1995) Bed-site selection by European roe deer (*Capreolus capreolus*) in southern Norway during winter. *Canadian Journal of Zoology,* **73,** 924–932.

554 Nadler, C.F. (1973) Cytogenetic differentiation, geographic distribution, and domestication in palaearctic sheep (*Ovis*). *Zeitschrift für Säugetierkunde,* **38,** 109–125.

555 Nelson, G. (1966) A note on the internal parasites of the muntjac. *Deer,* **1,** 16–17.

555a Nettleton, P.H. *et al.* (1986) Prevalence of herpesvirus infection in British red deer and investigation of further disease outbreaks. *Veterinary Record,* **118,** 267–270.

556 O'Brien, P.H. (1982) Flehmen: its occurrence and possible function in feral goats. *Animal Behaviour,* **30,** 1015–1019.

557 O'Donoghue, A. (1991) *Growth, reproduction and survival in a feral population of Japanese sika deer* (Cervus nippon). PhD thesis, University College, Dublin.

558 Odend'hal, S. *et al.* (1996) Preputial glands in artiodactyla. *Journal of Mammalogy,* **72,** 417–421.

559 Ohtaishi, N. (1978) Ecological and physiological longevity in mammals – from the age structures of Japanese deer. *Journal of the Mammal Society of Japan,* **3,** 130–134.

560 Okarma, H. *et al.* (1995) The roles of predation, snow cover, acorn crop, and man-related factors on ungulate mortality in Białowieża Primeval Forest, Poland. *Acta Theriologica,* **40,** 197–217.

561 Orwin, D.F.G. & Whitaker, A.H. (1984) Feral sheep (*Ovis aries* L.) of Arapawa Island, Marlborough Sound, and a comparison of their wool characteristics with those of four other feral flocks in New Zealand. *New Zealand Journal of Zoology,* **11,** 201–224.

562 Osborne, B.C. (1984) Habitat use by red deer (*Cervus elaphus* L.) and hill sheep in the West Highlands. *Journal of Applied Ecology,* **21,** 497–506.

563 Packer, J.J. *et al.* (1998) *Field and desk studies to assess tolerable damage levels for different habitats and species of deer.* Final project report to Ministry of Agriculture, Fisheries and Food, London on contract VC 0315.

565 Parkes, J. Personal communication.

566 Parkes, J. *et al.* (1996) *Managing vertebrate pests: Feral goats.* Australian Government Publishing Service, Canberra.

567 Paterson, S. *et al.* (1998) Major histocompatibility complex variation associated with juvenile survival and parasite resistance in a large unmanaged ungulate population (*Ovis*

aries L.). *Proceedings of the National Academy of Sciences of the USA,* **95**, 3714–3719.

568 Pélabon, C. & Joly, P. (2000) What, if anything, does visual asymmetry in fallow deer antlers reveal? *Animal Behaviour,* **59**, 193–199.

569 Pemberton, J. Personal communication.

570 Pemberton, J.M. & Balmford, A.P. (1987) Lekking in fallow deer. *Journal of Zoology,* **213**, 762–765.

571 Pemberton, J.M. & Smith, R.H. (1985) Lack of chemical biochemical polymorphism in British fallow deer. *Heredity,* **55**, 199–207.

572 Pemberton, J.M. *et al.* (1996) The maintenance of genetic polymorphism in small island populations: large mammals in the Hebrides. *Philosophical Transactions of the Royal Society of London, Series B,* **351**, 745–752.

573 Pemberton, J. *et al.* (2006) Hybridisation between red and sika deer in Scotland. *Deer,* **14,** 22–26.

574 Pepper, H. (1992) *Forest fencing.* Forestry Commission Bulletin 102, HMSO, Edinburgh.

575 Pepper, H.W. *et al.* (1998) Deer reflectors and road traffic accidents through Forestry Commission roads. In Pepper, H.W. & Hartley, S. (eds.) *Lowland deer: the development and testing of deterrents for deer in both rural and urban fringe areas.* Final Report to Ministry of Agriculture, Fisheries and Foods, London, on contract VC 0317.

576 Peters, J. *et al.* (2004) The upper Euphrates-Tigris basin: cradle of agro-pastoralism?, pp. 96–124 in Vigne, J.D. *et al.* (eds.) *First steps of animal domestication.* Oxbow Books, Oxford.

577 Petty, S.J. & Avery, M.I. (1990) *Forest bird communities.* Occasional Paper **26**, Forestry Commission, Edinburgh.

578 Phillips, C.J.C. (2001) *Principles of cattle production,* CABI, Wallingford.

579 Pickering, S.P.C. (1983) *Aspects of the behavioural ecology of feral goats* (Capra *domestic*). PhD thesis, University of Durham.

580 Pinchen, B. (1992) *Feral goats on the Great Orme.* Unpublished report, Aberconwy Borough Council, Wales.

581 Pitra, C. *et al.* (2004) Evolution and phylogeny of Old World deer. *Molecular Phylogenetics and Evolution,* **33**, 880–895.

582 Plumb, J. Personal communication.

583 Pollard, E. & Cooke, A.S. (1994) Impact of muntjac deer *Muntiacus reevesi* on egg-laying sites of the white admiral butterfly *Ladoga camilla* in a Cambridgeshire wood. *Biological Conservation,* **70**, 189–191.

584 Pollock, J.I. (1980) *Behavioural ecology and body condition changes in New Forest ponies.* RSPCA Scientific Publications No. 6, Royal Society for the Prevention of Cruelty to Animals, Horsham.

585 Polziehn, R.O. & Strobeck, C. (1998) Phylogeny of wapiti, red deer, sika deer, and other North American cervids as determined by mitochondrial DNA. *Molecular Phylogenetics and Evolution,* **10**, 249–258.

586 Portier, C. (1997) *Soins maternels et dynamique des populations d'ongulés: approches aux niveaux intra- et interspécifiques.* PhD thesis, University of Paris VI, Paris, France (in French).

587 Powerscourt, Viscount (1884) On the acclimatisation of the Japanese deer at Powerscourt. *Proceedings of the Zoological Society of London,* 1884, 207–209.

588 Pratt, R.M. *et al.* (1986) Habitat use of free-ranging cattle and ponies in the New Forest of southern England. *Journal of Applied Ecology,* **23**, 539–557.

589 Prior, R. (1968) *The roe deer of Cranborne Chase: an ecological survey.* Oxford University Press, London.

590 Prior, R. (1995) *The roe deer: conservation of a native species.* Swan Hill Press, Shrewsbury.

591 Proud, A.J. & Davis, R. (1998) Tuberculosis in roe deer, cattle and badgers. *Deer* **10**(7), 417–419.

592 Prummel, W. & Frisch, H-J. (1986) A guide for the distinction of species, sex and body size in bones of sheep and goat. *Journal of Archaeological Science* **13**, 567–577.

593 Putman, R.J. (1981) Social systems of deer: a speculative review. *Deer,* **5**, 186–188.

594 Putman, R.J. (1986) Competition and coexistence in a multispecies grazing community: the large herbivores of the New Forest. *Acta Theriologica,* **31**, 271–291.

595 Putman, R.J. (1986) Foraging by roe deer in agricultural areas and impact on arable crops. *Journal of Applied Ecology,* **23**, 91–99.

596 Putman, R.J. (1986) *Grazing in temperate ecosystems: large herbivores and the ecology of the New Forest.* Croom Helm, Beckenham.

597 Putman, R.J. (1988) *The natural history of deer.* Christopher Helm/Academic Press, London.

598 Putman, R.J. (1993) Flexibility of social organisation and reproductive strategy in deer. *Deer,* **9**, 23–28.

599 Putman, R.J. (1994) Effects of grazing and browsing by mammals in woodlands. *British Wildlife,* **5**, 205–213.

600 Putman, R.J. (1994) Damage by deer in coppice woodlands: an analysis of factors affecting the severity of damage and options for management. *Quarterly Journal of Forestry,* **88**, 45–54.

602 Putman, R.J. (1996) *Competition and resource partitioning in temperate ungulate assemblies.* Chapman & Hall, London.

603 Putman, R.J. (1996) *Deer on National Nature Reserves: problems and practices.* Research Report 173, 1–50. English Nature, Peterborough.

604 Putman, R.J. (1997) Deer and road traffic accidents: options for management. *Journal of Environmental Management,* **51**, 43–57.

605 Putman, R.J. (2000) *Sika deer.* British Deer Society, Fordingbridge and the Mammal Society, London.

606 Putman, R.J. (2004) *The deer manager's companion: a guide to deer management in the wild and in parks.* Swan Hill Press, Shrewsbury.

607 Putman, R. (2005) *Selection of animals for culling: age and condition.* Research Contract RP41, Deer Commission, Scotland.

608 Putman, R.J. & Clifton-Bligh, J.R. (1997) Age-related bodyweight, density and fecundity in a south Dorset sika population (*Cervus nippon*), 1985–93. *Journal of Natural History,* **31**, 649–660.

609 Putman, R.J. & Hunt, E.J. (1994) Patterns of hybridisation and introgression between red and sika deer in different populations of the North of Scotland and Argyll. *Deer,* **9**, 104–110.

610 Putman, R.J. & Kjellander, P. (2002) Deer damage to cereals: economic significance and predisposing factors, pp. 186–197 in Tattersall, F. & Manley, W. (eds.) *Conservation and conflict – Mammals and farming in Britain.* Linnean Society Occasional Publication 4, London.

611 Putman, R.J. & Langbein, J. (1990) *Factors affecting performance of deer in parks.* Report PECD 7/2/65 to Deptrtment of Environment.

612 Putman, R.J. & Langbein, J. (1992) Effects of stocking density, feeding and herd management on mortality of park deer, pp.180–188 in Brown, R. (ed.) *The biology of deer.* Springer-Verlag, New York.

613 Putman, R.J. & Langbein, J. (1999) *Deer and their management in the New Forest.* Consultation report on behalf of the Deputy Surveyor of the New Forest. Forest Enterprise, Lyndhurst, Hampshire.

614 Putman, R.J. & Mann, J.C.E. (1990) Social organisation and behaviour of British sika deer in contrasting environments. *Deer,* **8**, 90–94.

615 Putman, R.J. & Moore, N.P. (1998) Impact of deer in lowland Britain on agriculture, forestry and conservation habitats. *Mammal Review,* **28**, 141–164.

616 Putman, R.J. & Sharma, S.K. (1987) Long term changes in New Forest deer populations and correlated environmental change. In Harris, S. (ed.) *Mammal population studies, Symposia of the Zoological Society of London,* **58**, 167–179.

617 Putman, R.J. *et al.* (1981) *Interrelationships between large herbivores of the New Forest and the Forest vegetation.* Report HF3/03/127 to Chief Scientist's Team, Nature Conservancy Council.

618 Putman, R.J. *et al.* (1982) Habitat use and grazing by free-

ranging cattle and ponies, and impact on vegetation in the New Forest, Hampshire. *Acta Theriologica Fennica*, **173,** 183–186.

619 Putman, R.J. *et al.* (1984) Patterns of habitat use and grazing by cattle and ponies and impact upon vegetation. *Proceedings of the 3rd International Theriological Congress, Helsinki, 1982. Acta Zoologica Fennica*, **172**, 183–186.

620 Putman, R.J. *et al.* (1987) Food and feeding behaviour of cattle and ponies in the New Forest, Hampshire. *Journal of Applied Ecology*, **24**, 369–380.

621 Putman, R.J. *et al.* (1992) Pasteurella-related mortality in park fallow deer (abstract), p. 152 in Brown, R. *(*ed.) *The biology of deer*. Springer-Verlag, New York.

622 Putman, R.J. *et al.* (1993) Sexual differences in composition and quality of the diets of male and female fallow deer in sympatry and in allopatry. *Journal of Zoology*, **229**, 267–275.

623 Putman, R.J. *et al.* (1996) Relative roles of density-dependent and density-independent factors in population dynamics of British deer. *Mammal Review*, **26**, 81–101.

624 Putman, R.J. *et al.* (2000) Fluctuating asymmetry in antlers of fallow deer (*Dama dama*): the relative roles of environmental stress and sexual selection. *Biological Journal of the Linnean Society*, **70**, 27–36.

625 Quigley, F.C. *et al.* (1997) Isolation of mycobacteria from lymph node lesions in deer. *Veterinary Record*, **141**, 516–518.

626 Quirke, K. (1991) *The diet of red deer, sika deer and Scottish blackface sheep in Killarney National Park, Co. Kerry*. MSc thesis, National University of Ireland, Dublin.

627 Rackham, O. (1975) *Hayley Wood: its history and ecology*. Cambridgeshire and Isle of Ely Naturalists' Trust, Cambridge.

628 Rackham, O. (1986) *The history of the countryside*. J.M. Dent & Sons, London.

629 Randi, E. *et al.* (1998) New phylogenetic perspectives on the Cervidae (Artiodactyla) are provided by the mitochondrial cytochrome b gene. *Proceedings of the Royal Society of London, Series B*, **265**, 793–801.

630 Ratcliffe, P.R. (1977) Age determination in red deer. *Deer*, **4,** 88–89.

631 Ratcliffe, P.R. (1984) Population dynamics of red deer (*Cervus elaphus* L) in Scottish commercial forests. *Proceedings of the Royal Society of Edinburgh*, **82B**, 291–302.

632 Ratcliffe, P.R. (1987) Distribution and current status of sika deer, *Cervus nippon*, in Great Britain. *Mammal Review*, **17**, 39–58.

633 Ratcliffe, P.R. (1987) *The management of red deer in the commercial forests of Scotland related to population dynamics and habitat changes*. PhD thesis, University of London.

634 Ratcliffe, P.R. (1989) The control of red and sika deer populations in commercial forests, pp. 98–115 in Putman, R.J. (ed.) *Mammals as pests*. Chapman & Hall, London.

635 Ratcliffe, P.R. (1991) Sika deer, pp. 504–508 in Corbet, G.B. & Harris, S. (eds.) *The handbook of British mammals*. Blackwell Scientific Publications, Oxford.

636 Ratcliffe, P.R. & Mayle, B. (1992) *Roe deer biology and management*. Forestry Commission Bulletin 105, HMSO, London.

637 Ratcliffe, P.R. & Rowe, J.J. (1979) A golden eagle (*Aquila chrysaetus*) kills an infant roe deer (*Capreolus capreolus*). *Journal of Zoology*, **189**, 532–535.

638 Ratcliffe, P.R. & Rowe, J.J. (1985) A biological basis for managing red and roe deer in British commercial forests. *International Congress of Game Biologists*, **17**, 917–925.

639 Ratcliffe, P.R. & Staines, B.W. (1991) Roe deer *Capreolus capreolus*, pp. 518–525 in Corbet, G.B. & Harris, S. (eds.) *The handbook of British mammals*. Blackwell Scientific Publications, Oxford.

640 Ratcliffe, P.R. *et al.* (1992) The origins and characterizations of Japanese sika deer populations in Great Britain, pp. 185–190 in Maruyama, N. et al. (eds.) *International Symposium on Wildlife Conservation - present trends and perspectives for the 21st century*. Japan Wildlife Research Center, Tokyo.

641 Ratcliffe, P.R. *et al.* (2001) Comparison of the financial value

of deer damage and the related costs of deer control, pp. 42–45 in *Deer Commission for Scotland Annual Report 2000–2001*. DCS, Inverness.

642 Reby, D *et al.* (1998) Individuality in the groans of fallow deer (*Dama dama*) bucks. *Journal of Zoology*, **245**, 79–84.

643 Reby, D. *et al.* (1999) Contexts and possible functions of barking in roe deer. *Animal Behaviour*, **57,** 1121–1128.

644 Reby, D. *et al.* (1999) Spectral acoustic structure of barking in roe deer: sex-, age-, and individual related variations. *Comptes Rendus de l'Académie des Sciences (Life Sciences)*, **322,** 271–279.

645 Rehorek, S.J.*et al.* (2005) The gland and the sac – the preorbital apparatus of muntjacs, pp. 152–158 in Mason, R. *et al.* (eds.) *Chemical signals in vertebrates* **10**. Springer-Verlag, New York.

646 Reid, H.W. (1999) The ecology of deer as it relates to domestic animal husbandry and the possible spread of tuberculosis and pathogenic mycobacteria, pp. 38–40 in *Deer Commission for Scotland Annual Report 1998–1999*. The Stationery Office, Edinburgh.

647 Reid, H.W. *et al.* (1978) Isolation of louping-ill virus from red deer (*Cervus elaphus*). *Veterinary Record*, **102,** 463–464.

648 Reineken, G. (1990) *Deer farming: a practical guide to German techniques*. Farming Press Books, Ipswich.

649 Riney, T. (1951) Standard terminology for deer teeth. *Journal of Wildlife Management*, **15,** 99–101.

650 Ritchie, J. (1920) *The influence of man on animal life in Scotland*. Cambridge University Press, Cambridge.

651 Rivett, A. Personal communication.

652 Roberts, R.A. (1959) Ecology of human occupation and land use in Snowdonia. *Journal of Ecology*, **47**, 317–323.

653 Robertson, A. *et al.* (1992) Early growth and sucking behaviour of Soay sheep in a fluctuating population. *Journal of Zoology*, **227**, 661–671.

654 Rose, H.R. (1987) Bovine tuberculosis in deer. *Deer*, **7**, 78.

655 Rose, H.R. Personal communication.

656 Royle, N.J. (1986) New C-band polymorphism in the White Park cattle of Great Britain. *Journal of Heredity*, **77**, 366–367.

657 Rubini, M. *et al.* (1990) Standard karyotype and chromosomal evolution of the fallow deer (*Dama dama* L.). *Cytobos*, **64,** 155–161.

658 Rudge, M.R. (1970) Mother and kid behaviour in feral goats (*Capra hircus* L.). *Zeitschrift für Tierpsychologie*, **27**, 687–692.

659 Rudge, M.R. (1976) Ageing domestic sheep (*Ovis aries* L.) from growth lines in the cementum of the first incisor. *New Zealand Journal of Zoology*, **3**, 421–424.

660 Rudge, M.R. (1982) Feral goats in New Zealand. *Oryx*, **16**, 230–231.

661 Rudge, M.R. (1983) A reserve for feral sheep on Pitt Island, Chatham group, New Zealand. *New Zealand Journal of Zoology*, **10**, 349–363.

662 Rudge, M.R. (1984) The occurrence and status of populations of feral goats and sheep throughout the world, pp. 55–84 in Munton, P.N. (ed.) *Feral mammals: problems and potential*. IUCN, Gland.

663 Rutberg, A.T. (1990) Inter-group transfer in Assateague pony mares. *Animal Behaviour*, **40**, 945–952.

664 Rutberg, A.T. & Greenberg, S.A.(1990) Dominance, aggression frequencies and modes of aggressive competition in feral pony mares. *Animal Behaviour*, **40**, 322–331.

665 Rutter, S.M. & Langbein, J. (2005) *Quantifying the damage wild deer cause to agricultural crops and pastures*. DEFRA, contract report VC0327.

666 Ryan, S. (1998) *The wild deer of Killarney*. Mount Eagle Publications, Dingle, Co. Kerry.

667 Ryder, M.L. (1966) Coat structure in Soay sheep. *Nature*, **211**, 1092–1093.

668 Ryder, M.L. (1970) Structure and seasonal change of the coat in Scottish wild goats. *Journal of Zoology*, **161**, 355–361.

669 Ryder, M.L. (1971) Wool growth cycles in Soay sheep. *Journal of Agricultural Science, Cambridge*, **76**, 183–197.

670 Ryder, M.L. (1975) Development, structure and seasonal change in the fleeces of unimproved Scottish blackface

sheep from the Hebrides. *Journal of Agricultural Science, Cambridge,* **85**, 85–92.

671 Ryder, M.L. (1983) Will cashmere grow on Scottish hills? *Wool Record,* September, 89, 93.

672 Ryder, M.L. (1984) Sheep, pp. 63–85 in Mason, I.L. (ed.) *Evolution of domesticated animals.* Longman, London.

673 Ryder, M.L. (1995) When did the Soay sheep reach St Kilda? *The Ark,* **22**, 293–294.

674 Ryder, M.L. & Kay, R.N.B. (1973) Structure and seasonal change in the coat of red deer (*Cervus elaphus*). *Journal of Zoology,* **170**, 69–77.

675 Ryder, M.L. & Lincoln, G.A. (1976) A note on the effect of changes in daylength on the seasonal wool growth cycle in Soay sheep. *Animal Production,* **23**, 257–260.

676 San Jose, C. & Braza, F. (1997) Ecological and behavioural variables affecting the fallow deer mating system in Donana. *Ethology, Ecology and Evolution,* **9**, 133–148.

677 Sater, R.J. (1983) *Bark stripping and browsing at Loch Lomond: the involvement of feral goats* (Capra *sp.*). BSc Hons Thesis, University of St Andrews.

678 Saunders, F. Personal communication.

679 Schaal, A. (1982) Influence de l'environnement sur les composantes du groupe social chez le daim, *Cervus (Dama) dama* L. *Terre et Vie; Revue d'Ecologie,* **36**, 161–174 (in French).

680 Schaal, A. (1986) Mise en evidence d'un comportement de réproduction en arène chez le daim d'Europe (*Dama d. dama*). *Comptes Rendues de l'Academie des Sciences, Paris, Series III,* **18**, 729–732 (in French).

681 Schaller, G.B. (1977) *Mountain monarchs: wild sheep and goats of the Himalaya.* University of Chicago Press, Chicago.

682 Schley, L. & Roper, T.J. (2003) Diet of the wild boar in Western Europe, with particular reference to consumption of agriculturaL crops. *Mammal Review,* **33**, 43–56.

683 Schloeth, V.R.(1961) Das Sozialleben des Camargue-Rindes. *Zeitschrift für Tierpsychologie* **18**, 547–627 (in German).

684 Schreiber, A. & Fakler, P. (1996) NADH diaphorase polymorphisms in European fallow deer. *Biochemical Genetics,* **34**, 61–65.

685 Schwabe, A.E. & Hall, S.J.G. (1989) Dystocia in nine British breeds of cattle and its relationship to the dimensions of the dam and calf. *Veterinary Record,* **125**, 636–639.

686 Scott, D. & Palmer, S.C.F. (2000) Damage by deer to agriculture and forestry. *DCS Annual Report* 1999–2000, 50–53.

687 Sempéré, A.J. (1982) *Fonction de réproduction et caractères sexuels secondaires chez le chevreuil* (Capreolus capreolus)*: variations saisonnières et incidences sur l'utilisation du budget temps-espace.* PhD thesis, University of Tours (in French).

688 Sempéré, A.J. *et al.* (1998) Reproductive physiology of roe deer, pp. 161–188 in Andersen, R. *et al.* (eds.), *The European roe deer: the biology of success.* Scandinavian University Press, Oslo.

689 SGS Environment (1998) *The prevention of wildlife casualties on roads through the use of deterrents: prevention of casualties among deer populations.* Final project report to the Highways Agency, London.

690 Shackleton, D.M. (ed.) and the IUCN/SSC Caprinae Specialist Group (1997) *Wild sheep and goats and their relatives. Status survey and conservation action for Caprinae.* IUCN, Gland.

691 Shackleton, D.M. & Shank, C.C. (1984) A review of the social behaviour of feral and wild sheep. *Journal of Animal Science,* **58**, 500–509.

692 Shank, C.C. (1972) Some aspects of social behaviour in a population of feral goats (*Capra hircus* L.). *Zeitschrift für Tierpsychologie,* **30**, 488–528.

693 Sharma, S.K. (1994) *The decline of the roe deer (*Capreolus capreolus *L.) in the New Forest, Hampshire.* PhD thesis, University of Southampton.

694 Sheng, H. (1992) Chinese water deer, pp. 96–110 in Sheng, H. (ed.) *The deer in China.* East China Normal University, Shanghai.

695 Sheng, H. & Lu, H. (1984) A preliminary study on the river deer population of Zhoushan Island and adjacent islets. *Acta*

Theriologica Sinica, **4**, 161–166.

696 Sheng, H. & Lu, H. (1985) A preliminary study on the Chinese river deer population of Zhoushan Island and adjacent islets, pp. 6–9 in Kawamichi, T. (ed.) *Contemporary mammalogy in China and Japan.* Mammalogical Society of Japan, Tokyo.

697 Sheng, H. & Ohtaishi, N. (1993) The status of deer in China, pp. 1–11 in Ohtaishi, N.& Sheng, H. (eds.) *Deer of China: biology and management.* Elsevier, Amsterdam.

698 Shi, L. & Pathak, S. (1981) Gametogenesis in a male Indian muntjac × Chinese muntjac hybrid. *Cytogenetics and Cell Genetics,* **30**, 152–156.

699 Shi, L. *et al.* (1980) Comparative cytogenetic studies on red muntjac, Chinese muntjac and their F1 hybrids. *Cytogenetics and Cell Genetics,* **26**, 22–27.

700 Short, R.V. & Hay, M.F. (1966) Delayed implantation in the roe deer *Capreolus capreolus. Symposium of the Zoological Society of London,* **15**, 173–194.

701 Short, R.V. & Mann, T. (1966) The sexual cycle of a seasonally breeding mammal, the roe-buck (*Capreolus capreolus*). *Journal of Reproduction and Fertility,* **12**, 337–351.

702 Simm, G. (1998) *Genetic improvement of cattle and sheep.* Farming Press, Ipswich.

703 Simmons, I.G. & Tooley, M.J. (eds.) (1981) *The environment in British prehistory.* Duckworth, London.

704 Sinclair, A.R.E. & Duncan, P. (1972) Indices of condition in tropical ruminants. *East African Wildlife Journal,* **10**, 143–149.

705 Sleeman, D.P. (1983) Parasites of deer in Ireland. *Journal of Life Sciences, Royal Dublin Society,* **4**, 203–9.

706 Smith, J.E. (1989) *Aspects of the foraging ecology and management of feral goats* (Capra hircus) *at Coed Allt Wen and Dinorwic Quarries, North Wales: A pilot study.* MSc thesis, University of Wales.

707 Smith, J.E. & Bullock, D.J. (1993) A note on the summer feeding behaviour and habitat use of free ranging goats (*Capra hircus*) in the Cheddar Gorge SSSI. *Journal of Zoology,* **231**, 683–688.

708 Smith, J.E. & Bullock, D.J. (1993). *Phenotypic characters, conservation and management of feral goats on northern England and southern Scotland.* Report to the Rare Breeds Survival Trust, Stoneleigh, Warks.

709 Smith, R.H. (1980) The genetics of fallow deer and their implications for management. *Deer,* **5**, 79–83.

710 Smith, S. (1996) New Forest sika deer. II. Vocal behaviour. *Deer,* **9**, 643–645.

711 Smith-Jones, C. (2004) *Muntjac: managing an alien species.* Coch-y-Bonddu Books, Machynlleth.

712 Soper, E.A. (1969) *Muntjac.* Longmans, Green & Co, London.

713 Speed, J.G. & Etherington, M.G. (1952) The Exmoor pony – and a survey of the evolution of horses in Britain. I. Exmoor ponies. *British Veterinary Journal,* **108**, 329–338.

714 Speed, J.G. & Etherington, M.G. (1953) The Exmoor pony – and a survey of the evolution of horses in Britain. II. The Celtic pony. *British Veterinary Journal,* **109**, 315–320.

715 Springthorpe, G. (1969) Long-haired fallow deer at Mortimer Forest. *Journal of Zoology,* **159**, 537.

716 Stadler, S.G. (1991) *Behaviour and social organisation of Chinese water deer* (Hydropotes inermis) *under semi-natural conditions.* PhD dissertation, Universität Bielefeld.

717 Staines, B.W. (1970) *The management and dispersion of a red deer population at Glen Dye, Kincardineshire.* PhD thesis, University of Aberdeen.

718 Staines, B.W. (1974) A review of factors affecting deer dispersion and their relevance to management. *Mammal Review,* **4**, 79–91.

719 Staines, B.W. (1977) Factors affecting the seasonal distribution of red deer (*Cervus elaphus*) at Glen Dye, north-east Scotland. *Annals of Applied Biology,* **87**, 495–512.

720 Staines, B.W. (1978) The dynamics and performance of a declining population of red deer (*Cervus elaphus*). *Journal of Zoology* **184**, 403–19.

721 Staines, B.W. (1995) The impact of red deer on the regeneration of native pinewoods, pp. 107–114 in Aldhous,

J.R. (ed.) *Our pinewood heritage.* Forestry Commission, Wrecclesham.

722 Staines, B.W. (1998) The management of red deer (*Cervus elaphus*) in the context of other land uses in Scotland, pp. 385–400 in Milne, J. (ed.) *Recent developments in deer biology.* Macaulay Land Use Research Institute, Aberdeen and Moredun Research Institute, Edinburgh.

723 Staines, B.W. (1998) Sika deer: their status, distribution and ranging behaviour. In Staines, B.W. *et al.* (eds.) *Desk and limited field studies to analyse the major factors influencing regional deer populations and ranging behaviour.* Final project report to Ministry of Agriculture, Fisheries and Food, London on contract VC 0314.

724 Staines, B.W. & Balharry, R. (2002) Red deer and their management in the Cairngorms, pp. 130–138 in Gimmingham, C.H. (ed.) *The ecology, land use and conservation of the Cairngorms.* Packard Publishing, Chichester.

725 Staines, B.W. & Crisp, J. (1978) Observations on food quality in Scottish red deer (*Cervus elaphus*) as determined by chemical analysis of the rumen contents. *Journal of Zoology,* **185,** 253–259.

726 Staines, B.W. & Ratcliffe, P.R. (1987) Estimating the abundance of red (*Cervus elaphus* L.) and roe (*Capreolus capreolus* L.) deer and their current status in Great Britain. *Symposia of the Zoological Society of London,* **58,** 131–152.

727 Staines, B.W. & Scott, D. (1994) *Recreation and red deer; a preliminary review of the issues.* Scottish Natural Heritage Review 31.

728 Staines, B.W. & Welch, D. (1984) Habitat selection and impact of red (*Cervus elaphus* L.) and roe (*Capreolus capreolus* L.) deer in a sitka spruce plantation. *Proceedings of the Royal Society of Edinburgh,* **82B,** 303–319.

729 Staines, B.W. *et al.* (1982) Differences in the quality of food eaten by red deer (*Cervus elaphus*) stags and hinds in winter. *Journal of Applied Ecology,* **19,** 65–77.

730 Staines, B.W. *et al.* (1995) The impact of red deer and their management on the natural heritage in the uplands, pp. 294–308 in Thompson, D.B.A. *et al.* (eds.) *Heaths and moorlands: cultural landscapes.* HMSO, Edinburgh.

731 Staines, B. *et al.* (1998) *Desk and limited field studies to analyse the major factors influencing regional deer populations and ranging behaviour.* MAFF Contract report VC 0314.

732 Šterba, O. & Klusák, K. (1984) Reproductive biology of fallow deer (*Dama dama*). *Acta Scientiarum Naturalium Academiae Scientiarum Bohemoslovacae Brno,* **18**(6), 1–52.

733 Stevenson, I.R. (1994) *Male-biased mortality in Soay sheep.* PhD thesis, University of Cambridge.

734 Stevenson, I.R. & Bancroft, D.R. (1995) Fluctuating trade-offs favour precocial maturity in male Soay sheep. *Proceedings of the Royal Society of London, Series B,* **262,** 267–275.

735 Stewart, L.K. (1985) Red deer, pp. 45–50 in Murray, R.B. (ed.) *Vegetation management in northern Britain.* British Crop Protection Council, Croydon.

736 Strandgaard, H. (1972) The roe deer (*Capreolus capreolus*) population at Kalo and the factors regulating its size. *Danish Review of Game Biology,* **7,** 1–205.

737 Sun, L. *et al.* (1994) Scent marking behaviour in male Chinese water deer. *Acta Theriologica,* **39,** 177–184.

738 Sun, L. & Xiao, B. (1995) The effect of female distribution on male territoriality in Chinese water deer. *Zeitschrift für Säugetierkunde,* **60,** 33–40.

739 Sykes, N. (2005) Zooarchaeology of the Norman Conquest. *Anglo-Norman Studies,* **27,** 185–197.

740 Symonds, R.(1985) A comparison of the food preferences of fallow deer (*Dama dama*) and muntjac (*Muntiacus reevesi*) in Hayley Wood SSSI, Cambridgeshire: with special reference to the effects of browsing on coppice regrowth. *British Ecological Society Bulletin,* **16,** 97–98.

741 Tabor, R.C.C. (1993). Control of deer in a managed coppice. *Quarterly Journal of Forestry,* **87,** 308–313.

742 Tabor, R.C.C. (1999) The effects of muntjac deer, *Muntiacus reevesi,* and fallow deer *Dama dama,* on the oxslip *Primula elatior. Deer,* **11,** 14–19.

743 Tabor, R. (2004) Assessing deer activity and damage in woodlands. *Deer,* **13,** 27–29.

744 Tallowin, J.R.B. *et al.* (2005) Impact of grazing management on biodiversity of grasslands. *Animal Science,* **81,** 193–198.

745 Tate, M.L. *et al.* (1998) Genetic analysis of farmed deer hybrids. *Acta Veterinaria Hungarica,* **46,** 329–340.

746 Taylor Page, F.J. (1982) *Field guide to British deer,* 3rd edn. Blackwell Scientific Publications, Oxford.

747 Thirgood, S.J. (1990) *Variation in social and sexual strategies of fallow deer.* PhD thesis, University of Southampton.

748 Thirgood, S.J. (1991) Alternative mating strategies and reproductive success in fallow deer. *Behaviour,* **116,** 1–10.

749 Thirgood, S.J. (1995) The effects of sex, season and habitat availability on patterns of habitat use by fallow deer. *Journal of Zoology,* **235,** 645–659.

750 Thirgood, S.J. (1996) Ecological factors influencing sexual segregation and group size in fallow deer (*Dama dama*). *Journal of Zoology,* **239,** 783–797.

751 Thirgood, S. & Staines, B.W. (1989) Summer use of young stands of restocked sitka spruce by red and roe deer. *Scottish Forestry,* **43,** 183–191.

752 Thirgood, S.J. *et al.* (1998) Intraspecific variation in ungulate mating strategies: the case of the flexible fallow deer. *Advances in the Study of Behavior,* **28,** 333–361.

753 Tixier, H. & Duncan, P. (1996) Are European deer browsers? A review of variations in the composition of their diets. *Revue d'Ecologie (Terre et Vie),* **51,** 3–17.

754 Tixier, H. *et al.* (1997) Food selection by European roe deer (*Capreolus capreolus*): effects of plant chemistry, and consequences for the nutritional value of their diets. *Journal of Zoology,* **242,** 229–245.

755 Tixier, H. *et al.* (1998) The development of feeding selectivity in roe deer. *Behavioural Processes,* **43,** 33–42.

756 Tolhurst, S. & Oates, M. (2001) *The breed profiles handbook. A guide to the selection of livestock breeds for grazing wildlife sites.* Grazing Animals Project/English Nature, Norwich, UK.

757 Tomich, P.Q. (1969) *Mammals in Hawaii.* Bernice P. Bishop Museum Press, Oahu.

758 Torgerson, P.R. *et al.* (1992) Observations on the epidemiology of *Taenia hydatigena* in Soay sheep on St Kilda. *Veterinary Record,* **131,** 218–219.

759 Troy, C.S. *et al.* (2001) Genetic evidence for Near-Eastern origins of European cattle. *Nature,* **410,** 1088–1091.

760 Tubbs, C.R. &Tubbs, J.M. (1985) Buzzards (*Buteo buteo*) and land use in the New Forest, Hampshire, England. *Biological Conservation,* **31,** 46–65.

761 Tufto, J. *et al.* (1996) Habitat use and ecological correlates of home range size in a small cervid: the roe deer. *Journal of Animal Ecology,* **65,** 715–724.

762 Turner, D.C. (1980) A multi-variate analysis of roe deer (*Capreolus capreolus*) population activity. *Revue Suisse de Zoologie,* **87,** 991–1002.

763 Tutton, T. (1994) Goats versus holm oak. *Enact,* **2,** 8–9.

764 Twigg, G.I. *et al.* (1973) Antibodies to *Leptospira grippotyphosa* in British wild mammals. *Veterinary Record,* **92,** 119.

765 Tyler, S. (1972) The behaviour and social organisation of the New Forest ponies. *Animal Behaviour Monographs,* **5,** 87–194.

766 van Wieren, S.E. (1991) The management of populations of large mammals, pp. 103–127 in Spellerberg, I.F. *et al.* (eds.) *The scientific management of temperate communities for conservation.* Blackwell, Oxford.

767 Van Vuren, D. & Coblentz, B.E. (1991) Population characteristics of feral sheep on Santa Cruz Island. *Journal of Wildlife Management,* **53,** 306–313.

768 Vera, F.W.M. (2000) *Grazing ecology and forest history.* CABI, Wallingford.

769 Vigne, J.D. (1992) Zooarchaeology and the biogeographical history of the mammals of Corsica and Sardinia since the last Ice Age. *Mammal Review,* **22,** 87–96.

770 Vilà, C. *et al.* (2001). Widespread origins of domestic horse lineages. *Science,* **291,** 474–477.

771 Vincent, J. P. *et al.* (1983) Occupation de l`espace chez le chevreuil (*Capreolus capreolus*) II. Cas des femelles. *Acta Oecologica – Oecologica Applicata,* **4,** 379–389.

772 Vincent, J.P. *et al.* (1995) The influence of increasing density on body weight, kid production, home range size and winter grouping in roe deer. *Journal of Zoology,* **236,** 371–382.

773 Visscher, P.M. *et al.* (2001) A viable herd of genetically uniform cattle. *Nature,* **409,** 303.

774 von Sambraus, H.H. (1977) Observations and experiments on social behaviour in a herd of cattle during an 11-year period. *Applied Animal Ethology,* **3,** 199–200.

775 Vulink, J.T. (2001) *Hungry herds: management of temperate lowland wetlands by grazing (by cattle and horses).* PhD thesis, University of Groningen.

776 Wahlström, L.K. (1994) The significance of male-male aggression for yearling dispersal in roe deer (*Capreolus capreolus*). *Behavioral Ecology and Sociobiology,* **35,** 409–412.

777 Wahlström, L.K. & Liberg, O. (1995) Contrasting dispersal patterns in two Scandinavian roe deer (*Capreolus capreolus*). *Wildlife Biology,* **1,** 159–164.

778 Wahlström, L.K. & Liberg, O. (1995) Patterns of dispersal and seasonal migration in roe deer *Capreolus capreolus* populations. *Journal of Zoology,* **235,** 455–467.

779 Wallis de Vries, M.F. (1998) Large herbivores as key factors for nature conservation, pp. 1–20 in Wallis de Vries, M.F. *et al.* (eds.) *Grazing and conservation management.* Kluwer, Dordrecht.

780 Ward, A. (2005) New population estimates for British mammals. *Deer,* **13,** 8.

781 Ward, A.I. (2005) Expanding ranges of wild and feral deer in Great Britain. *Mammal Review,* **35,** 165–173.

782 Ward, A.I. *et al.* (2004) Modelling the cost of roe deer browsing damage to forestry. *Forest Ecology and Management,* **191,** 301–310.

783 Waterfield, M.R. (1986) *Observations on the ecology and behaviour of fallow deer (*Dama dama *L.)* PhD thesis, University of Exeter.

784 Watson, A. (1971) Climate and the antler shedding and performance of red deer in north-east Scotland. *Journal of Applied Ecology,* **8,** 53–67.

785 Watson, A. & Staines, B.W. (1978) Differences in the quality of wintering areas used by male and female red deer (*Cervus elaphus*) in Aberdeenshire. *Journal of Zoology,* **186,** 544–550.

786 Welch, D. *et al.* (1988) Roe-deer browsing on spring-flush growth of Sitka spruce. *Scottish Forestry,* **42,** 33–43.

787 Welch, D. *et al.* (1990) Habitat usage by red (*Cervus elaphus*) and roe (*Capreolus capreolus*) deer in a Sitka spruce plantation. *Journal of Zoology,* **221,** 453–476.

788 Welch, D. *et al.* (1992) Leader browsing by red and roe deer on young Sitka spruce trees in Western Scotland. 2. Effects on growth and tree form. *Forestry,* **65,** 309–330.

789 Wells, S. & von Goldschmidt-Rothschild, B. (1979) Social behaviour and relationships in a group of Camargue horses. *Zeitschrift für Tierpsychologie,* **49,** 363–80.

790 Welsh, D. (1975) *Population, behavioural and grazing ecology of the horses of Sable Island, Nova Scotia.* PhD thesis, Dalhousie University.

791 Werner, R. (1998) *The British goat and the Northern Breed Group.* Unpublished report.

792 Werner, R. Personal communication.

793 Whitehead, G.K. (1953) *The ancient white cattle of Britain and their descendants.* Faber and Faber, London.

794 Whitehead, G.K. (1964) *The deer of Great Britain and Ireland.* Routledge & Kegan Paul, London.

795 Whitehead, G.K. (1972) *Deer of the world.* Constable, London.

796 Whitehead, G.K. (1972) *The wild goats of Great Britain and Ireland.* David & Charles, Newton Abbot.

797 Whitehead, G.K. (1980) *Hunting and stalking deer in Britain through the ages.* B.T. Batsford, London.

798 Whitehead, G.K. (1993) *The Whitehead encyclopedia of deer.* Swan Hill Press, Shrewsbury.

799 Williams, G. & Rudge, M. (1969) A population study of feral goats (*Capra hircus* L.) from Macauley Island, New Zealand. *Proceedings of the New Zealand Ecological Society,* **16,** 17–28.

800 Williams, T. *et al* (1995) A molecular analysis of the introduced Reeves' muntjac in southern England: genetic variation in the mitochondrial genome, pp. 6–20 in Mayle, B. (ed.) *Muntjac deer, their biology, impact and management in Britain.* Forestry Commission, Edinburgh.

801 Wilson, C.J. (2003) Distribution and status of wild boar *Sus scrofa* in Dorset, southern England. *Mammal Review,* **33,** 302–307.

802 Wilson, C.J. (2004) Rooting damage to farmland in Dorset, southern England, caused by wild boar *Sus scrofa. Mammal Review,* **34,** 331–335.

803 Wilson, C.J. (2005) *Feral wild boar in England. Status, impact and management.* A report on behalf of Defra European Wildlife Division.

804 Wilson, P.R. & Orwin, D.F.G. (1964) The sheep population of Campbell Island. *New Zealand Journal of Science,* **7,** 460–489.

805 Wood, D.A. & Munro, R. (1986) Babesiosis, p. 105 in Alexander, T.L. (ed.) *Management and diseases of deer.* Veterinary Deer Society, London.

806 Woodford, M. (1966) Lymphosarcoma in a wild roe deer. *Veterinary Record,* **79,** 74.

807 Woodman, P. *et al.* (1997) The Irish Quaternary fauna project. *Quaternary Science Reviews,* **16,** 129–159.

808 Wray, S. (1994) Competition between muntjac and other herbivores in a commercial coniferous forest. *Deer,* **9,** 237–245.

809 Wright, I.A. *et al.* (1994) The effect of genotype × environment interactions on biological efficiency in beef cows. *Animal Production,* **58,** 197–207.

810 Wright, K. (1996) *The winter diet of Fallow deer,* Dama dama, *in the Northants Forest District, as determined by rumen content analysis.* HND project, Sparsholt College, Hampshire.

811 Wyllie, I. *et al.* (1998) Radio-telemetry studies of muntjac and fallow deer. In Staines, B.W. *et al.* (eds.) *Desk and limited field studies to analyse the major factors influencing regional deer populations and ranging behaviour.* Final project report to Ministry of Agriculture, Fisheries and Food, London on contract VC 0314.

812 Xiao, B. & Sheng, H. (1990) Home range and activity patterns of Chinese water deer *(Hydropotes inermis)* in Poyang Lake Region. *Journal of East China Normal University (Mammalian Ecology Supplement),* **9,** 27–36.

813 Yalden, D. (1999) *The history of British mammals.* Poyser, London.

814 Yang, F. *et al.* (1995) A comparative study of karyotypes of muntjacs by chromosome painting. *Chromosoma,* **103,** 642–652.

815 Young, B.A.(1976) Some observations on the ultrastructure of the thyroid of certain Cervidae. *Journal of Zoology,* **180,** 175–183.

816 Zeder, M.A. (2004) A view from the Zagros: new perspectives on livestock domestication in the Fertile Crescent, pp. 125–147 in Vigne, J.D. *et al.* (eds.) *First steps of animal domestication.* Oxbow Books, Oxford.

817 Zeder, M.A. & Hesse, B. (2000) The initial domestication of goats (*Capra hircus*) in the Zagros Mountains 10,000 years ago. *Science,* **287,** 2254–2257.

818 Zejda, J. (1978) Field groupings of roe deer (*Capreolus capreolus*) in a lowland region. *Folia Zoologica,* **27,** 111–122.

819 Zedja, J. & Horakova, M. (1988) Three kinds of weights in sika deer (*Cervus nippon*). *Folia Zoologica, Brno,* **37,** 289–299.

820 Zhang, E. (1996) *Behavioural ecology of the Chinese water deer at Whipsnade Wild Animal Park, England.* PhD dissertation, University of Cambridge.

821 Zhang, E. (2000) Daytime activity budget in Chinese water deer. *Mammalia,* **64,** 163–172.

822 Zhang, E. Personal communication.

823 Zima, J. & Kral, B. (1984) Karyotypes of European mammals, part III. *Acta Scientiarum Naturalium, Brno,* **18,** 1–51.

824 Zuckerman, S. (1953) The breeding season of mammals in captivity. *Proceedings of the Zoological Society of London,* **122,** 827–950.

Plate 13

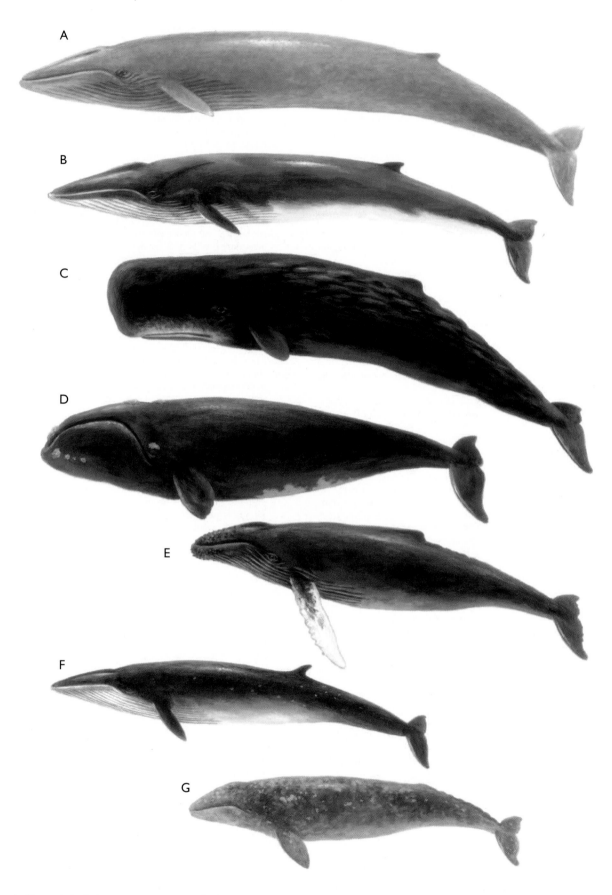

A Blue whale *Balaenoptera musculus* **B** Fin whale *B. physalus* **C** Sperm whale *Physeter macrocephalus*
D Northern right whale *Eubalaena glacialis* **E** Humpback whale *Megaptera novaeangliae*
F Sei whale *B. borealis* **G** Gray whale *Eschrichtius robustus*

12

Whales, porpoises and dolphins
Order Cetacea

Compiled by P.G.H. Evans

An order of mostly marine mammals, with a few freshwater species, distributed throughout the oceans of the world: 84 species arranged in *c*.40 genera [558, 922, 989, 1245]. Divided into 2 suborders: Mysticeti, baleen whales, mostly very large marine mammals, filter feeders with baleen plates but no teeth; Odontoceti, a more varied group of small (porpoise), medium (dolphin) and large (whale) species, mostly toothed, some of which occur in fresh water. Phylogenetically, Cetacea are very closely related to Artiodactyla, especially (among extant mammals) Hippopotamidae, and could formally be classified as a family of Artiodactyla; phylogenetic classifications group them as an Order Cetartiodactyla. This relationship is indicated not only by genetic analyses (e.g. [733, 962]) but also by a series of fossils (Pakicetidae) from the early Eocene–Oligocene of Pakistan which show limb reduction, skull and dental changes bridging the transition from terrestrial ungulates to aquatic whales [1145]. The conservative retention of an Order Cetacea for this handbook is a compromise between practical and theoretical mammalogy.

Cetaceans are highly modified in all aspects, physiological, anatomical and ecological, from the basic mammalian form. The skin is essentially naked (a few whiskers may remain on the snout of juveniles), and cetaceans rely on a subcutaneous fat layer (blubber) for insulation. Their front limbs are reduced to flippers, the wrist bones are reduced to small unrecognisable discs of bone and the hind limbs are apparently absent (tiny internal vestiges of their skeleton in baleen whales are all that remain). Vertical undulation of the elongate body provides the propulsion for their swimming, aided by horizontal tail flukes that contain no skeleton. Most species have a mid-dorsal fin, which also lacks any skeletal support.

The skull is elongate, the nostrils relocated mid-dorsally as a blowhole, and the braincase compressed anteroposteriorly, so that the occipital (posterior) surface meets the frontal bones. The eyes are very low on the side of the head. Mysticetes have long, toothless jaws, and keratinous (compressed hair) baleen plates hanging from the upper jaws. These are frayed internally, producing a filtering fringe that separates plankton or fish from a mouthfull of water. Most

odontocetes have numerous identical teeth (up to 210, 45–65 in each jaw, in *Stenella longirostris*), strongly contrasting with the differentiated teeth (incisors, canines, premolars, molars) that characterise most mammals, and indeed pakicetids and early whales; some (females) are essentially toothless, and their males have only a pair of tusks (modified canines?). The snouts are usually elongate, but the jaws are slender, for cetaceans swallow their food whole, do not (cannot) chew it, so have simple-looking jaws, slender jaw muscles and loose jaw joints with slight condyles and shallow glenoids.

Odontocetes, at least, use echolocation to locate their prey, producing clicks that are transmitted out through the bones of the snout, and perhaps concentrated (beamed) by a fatty melon on top of the face. Returning echoes are transmitted well through water, poorly through air, but because soft tissue is essentially water, their bodies are 'transparent'; to overcome this problem, and give directional hearing, the inner ear is encased in dense bone but separated from the rest of the skeleton by pockets of air. Sound travels into the inner ear through a solid ear canal, thus left and right ears hear sounds differently. There is no evidence that mysticetes use echolocation, but they certainly use sounds extensively in communication, and their inner ears are modelled similarly.

Externally, most cetaceans have no obvious neck, the body being smoothly tapered, and internally the neck vertebrae are compressed, often partially or completely fused. The thoracic vertebrae and ribs are about as numerous as in terrestrial mammals (9–16 pairs, but usually 12–13 pairs), but the lumbar and caudal vertebrae are more numerous, flat-ended, with tall dorsal spines on most of them. The large whales suffocate when stranded because their rib cages are too slight to support their weight; compression of their chests, forcing air from the lungs into the more rigid bronchii, is one of their adaptations to diving.

Many species, baleen whales in particular, move to higher latitudes to feed in summer on the rich plankton and the fish associated with it, but travel to tropical waters to calf during the winter. Tropical waters are largely devoid of plankton, so little feeding is possible, but the warmer waters are more suitable for young calves. This means that southern and northern populations are 6 months out of phase. Atlantic and Pacific populations are also somewhat isolated, though contact is possible through the Indian and Southern Oceans. This has permitted a degree of separation of stocks, allowing partial or complete speciation. However, conventional taxonomy of such large, elusive mammals has been and remains challenging, though molecular markers are yielding valuable insights. It is often still uncertain whether populations in tropical or higher latitudes, Pacific or Atlantic, N or S hemispheres, are in complete genetic contact, partially isolated or separated into several species. Specific taxonomy is therefore uncertain in many genera, and changing rapidly as new genetic techniques reveal unsuspected differences.

The larger whales, in part because of their thick blubber, have been severely persecuted by humans since at least the Middle Ages, and commercial whaling in the late 19th–early 20th centuries reduced all the larger, more vulnerable species to commercial extinction. This was successively true of the right and bowhead whales, then in turn the gray whale, humpback, blue, fin and sei whales [342]; the sperm whale was also severely persecuted, but its largely tropical range and deep-diving behaviour offered it some sanctuary. International agreements made by the International Whaling Commission (IWC) successively gave them protection from 1935 (right whale), 1966 (humpback), 1967 (blue whale), 1985 (sperm whale) and 1986 (fin, sei, minke), though even that was, we now know, flouted by some whaling fleets [87, 1255]. Some stocks of most species have shown a modest recovery over the last 40 years, but this has prompted renewed pressure from some whaling nations, who wish the IWC to allow some reopening of commercial whaling. A small amount of scientific whaling was in any case permitted, and Iceland, Norway and Japan in particular have availed themselves of this exemption; coastal whaling in national waters seems likely to resume in the N Atlantic, facilitated by the establishment amongst whaling nations of the North Atlantic Marine Mammal Commission (NAMMCO) in 1992.

From the Middle Ages, cetaceans stranded on British coasts were legally 'Royal Fish', and belonged to the crown; originally, they provided a source of meat, oil and other products, but latterly became a nuisance; their legal status was exploited to require the notification of strandings to the British Museum (Natural History), resulting in a valuable sequence of reports on stranded cetaceans for most of the 20th century

[404, 406–408, 485, 1073, 1074]. This recording system persists, but is now supplemented by routine sea-watch surveys from headlands, dedicated cruises and survey flights, and the results of commercial as well as impromptu whale-watching, so that the distribution of live, as well as dead, cetaceans is better documented [973]. Distributions around the British Isles have been mapped specially for this account by P.G.H. Evans. Other study techniques for cetaceans include, for live animals at sea: direct observations [354, 477], photo-ID [354, 477], and acoustic monitoring [450]; and for stranded, bycaught and captured individuals: pathology, toxicology, morphometrics, genetic and dietary methods (see [661] for reviews of post-mortem methods for sample collection).

Legislation has also progressed. Several of the coastal species are now protected within national and European waters, while larger species, once hunted commercially off the W coast of Ireland [367] and off NW Scotland [181, 1148], are now protected by a moratorium on commercial hunting under IWC auspices. International protection for cetaceans includes Appendix I or II of the CMS Agreement on the Conservation of Migratory Species of Wild Animals (Bonn Convention, 1983); Appendix II or III of the Bern Convention on the Conservation of European Wildlife and Natural Habitats; and Annex IV Animal and Plant Species of Community Interest in Need of Strict Protection of the EC Habitats Directive (1992). Species are listed on List C1 of Council Regulation and since 1985, have largely been treated by the European Community as if on CITES Appendix II (trade controlled to prevent overexploitation). See Table 12.1.

Cetaceans are protected under the Wildlife and Countryside Act 1981 and the Wildlife (Northern Ireland) Order 1985. The international Agreement on the Conservation of Small Cetaceans in the Baltic and North Seas (ASCOBANS) (1992) applies to all odontocetes besides the sperm whale (see Chapter 4).

Table 12.1

Conservation status of cetacean species recorded around the British Isles

Species	Bonn Convention	Bern Convention	CITES	EU Habitats	ASCOBANS	IWC	IUCN
Northern right whale	I[a]	II	I	IV	–	Protected	EN
Minke whale	–	III	Ic	IV	–	Lim Catch	LR/nt
Sei whale	I[a]	III	I	IV	–	Protected	EN
Blue whale	I	II	I	IV	–	Protected	EN
Fin whale	Ia	II	I	IV	–	Protected	EN
Humpback	I	II	I	IV	–	Protected	VU
Sperm whale	I & II[a]	III	I	IV	–	Protected	VU
Pygmy sperm	–	II	II	IV	–	–	LR/lc
Northern bottlenose	–	II	I	IV	+	–	LR(cd)
Sowerby's	–	II	II	IV	+	–	DD
Blainville's	–	II	II	IV	+	–	DD
True's beaked whale	–	II	II	IV	+	–	DD
Cuvier's beaked whale	–	II	II	IV	+	–	DD
Beluga	II	III	II	IV	+	–	VU
Narwhal	II	II	II	IV	+	–	DD
Long-finned pilot whale	II	II	II	IV	+	–	LR/lc
Killer whale	–	II	II	IV	+	–	LR(cd)
False killer whale	–	II	II	IV	+	–	LR/lc
Melon-headed whale	–	III	II	IV	+	–	LR/lc
Risso's dolphin	II[b]	II	II	IV	+	–	DD
Common dolphin	I[a]	II	II	IV	+	–	LR/lc
Striped dolphin	–	II	II	IV	+	–	LR(cd)
Fraser's dolphin	–	III	II	IV	+	–	DD
Atlantic white-sided dolphin	II[b]	II	II	IV	+	–	LR/lc
White-beaked dolphin	II[b]	II	II	IV	+	–	LR/lc
Bottlenose dolphin	II[b]	II	II	II & IV	+	–	DD
Harbour porpoise	II[b]	II	II	II & IV	+	–	VU

[a] The species, or a separate population of that species, or a higher taxon which includes that species is included in Appendix II of the Convention.

[b] North Sea and Baltic populations.

[c] Except population of West Greenland.

IUCN Categories: DD, Data Deficient; EN, Endangered; VU, Vulnerable; LR, Lower Risk; nt, near threatened; cd, conservation dependent; lc = least concern.

SUBORDER MYSTICETI (BALEEN WHALES)

A small group of *c.*13 species, nowadays arranged in 4 families: right whales Balaenidae, pygmy right whale, Neobalaenidae, gray whale Eschrichtiidae and rorquals Balaenopteridae [989, 1245]. Validity of Eschrichtiidae in question [494].

FAMILY BALAENIDAE (RIGHT WHALES)

A small family of 2 genera, 2–4 species [1245], the Arctic bowhead *Balaena mysticetus* and 1–3 species of right whale, *Eubalaena*, one of which occurs, now rarely, in the NE Atlantic. Pygmy right whale *Caperea marginata* (S hemisphere) sometimes included. Have very long baleen plates, suspended from highly arched upper jaws; sieve plankton by swimming slowly, at surface.

Northern right whale *Eubalaena glacialis*
Balaena glacialis Müller 1776, North Cape, Norway.
Balaena britannica Gray 1870, Dorset, England.

Fiormhiol mór na bioscáine (Irish Gaelic).

RECOGNITION
Large head, narrow rostrum with highly arched lower jaws, dark skin and absence of dorsal fin render them unmistakable (Plate 13). Have light-coloured callosities on their heads (see below). Seen along animal's axis, blow distinctively V shaped, can reach 7 m high. Feeding, occurring at surface, may lead to reports of sea monsters, as these whales skim with their mouths wide open, narrow rostrums raised in the air, and baleen plates partially exposed above the water. Broad all-black flukes are raised above the water on diving (Fig. 12.1).

DESCRIPTION
Relatively rotund, squarish in the chin, generally black, occasionally with white belly and chin patches. Head forms 25% of the total body length in adults, up to 35% in juveniles. Narrow, strongly arched rostrum and strongly bowed lower jaws are characteristic of the species. The skull can be up to 5 m in length and weigh as much as 1000 kg, with a distinctive supraoccipital bony shield. Vertebral formula C7, D14, and L11 (10–12) [1163].

Grey or black thickened skin patches, callosities, found on rostrum, behind the blowholes, over the eyes, on the corners of the chin, and variably along the lower lip and jawlines. Their arrangement is unique to each right whale, can be used for individual recognition [475].

Callosities appear light yellow or cream coloured due to large infestations of whale lice *Cyamus*; consist of spikes of columnar epithelial tissue, appearing barnacle-like, but no barnacles have ever been found on N Atlantic right whales. Baleen plates black or brown, 205–270 plates on each side; very long, average 2–2.8 m long but relatively narrow (up to 18 cm) (Fig. 12.2). No grooves along the throat. Tail broad (up to 6 m tip to tip), all black.

MEASUREMENTS
Length: newborn *c.*4.4–4.8 m; on reaching maturity *c.*13.0–16.0 m; adult typically 14–16 m (max. 18 m), females averaging *c.*1 m longer than males [27, 967]. Weight *c.*50–56 t, occasionally to 90 t. Blubber layer up to 20 cm thick, provides both insulation and energy storage.

RELATIONSHIPS
Genetic data [1013] clearly separate *Eubalaena* (right whales) from *Balaena* (bowhead), identify 3 *Eubalaena* species (*japonica*, N Pacific; *australis*, S hemisphere; and *glacialis*, N Atlantic), and suggest that *Eubalaena* populations in N and S Atlantic have been separated for *c.*1 million years [1044].

VARIATION
Morphological variation between populations in different ocean basins, with differences in callosity patterns and maximum adult sizes reported. However, within N Atlantic, genetic data from historical samples suggest ocean-wide interbreeding [1014], Recent re-sighting off Norway of known individual from New England demonstrates the relative ease with which this whale can traverse large distances [561]. Suggests that local variation within N Atlantic population likely to be confined to coloration (white vs black ventral patterns) and callosity patterns.

DISTRIBUTION
In N hemisphere, normally restricted to between 20° and 70° N (mainly temperate zone) [651]. In E North Atlantic, once ranged from NW Africa, Azores and Mediterranean, N to Bay of Biscay, W Ireland, Hebrides, Shetland, Faroes, Iceland, and Svalbard. Since 1920s, sightings sporadic: from Canaries, Madeira, Spain, Portugal, British Isles and Iceland [182, 346, 353, 1168]. Historically, good evidence that E North Atlantic right whales calved in Cintra Bay, W Sahara during winter [964]. Whaling records indicate occurred off Hebrides and Ireland in early summer (mainly June), possibly having spent winter in Bay of Biscay (the Basque fishery operated mainly between October and February); may have moved on to Scandinavian feeding areas later [11, 273,

Fig. 12.1 Flukes of four large whales that usually show them on diving: (a) Northern right *(photo S.Kraus)*, (b) blue *(photo P.G.H. Evans)*, (c) humpback *(photo P.G.H. Evans)* and (d) sperm *(photo F. Ugarte)* whales. The pattern of black and white under the humpback whale's tail is very variable, and used for individual identification.

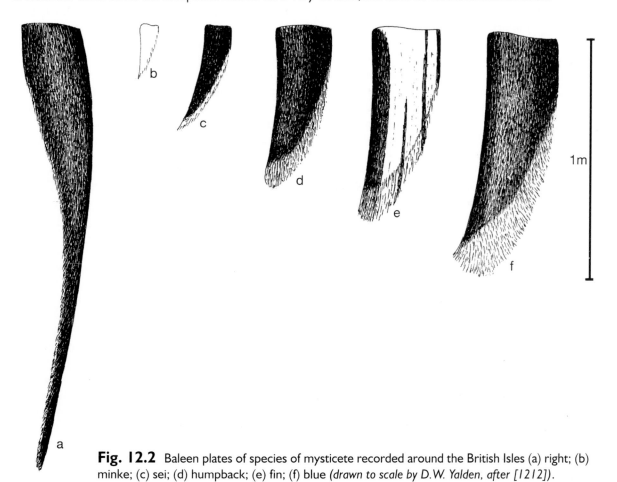

Fig. 12.2 Baleen plates of species of mysticete recorded around the British Isles (a) right; (b) minke; (c) sei; (d) humpback; (e) fin; (f) blue *(drawn to scale by D.W. Yalden, after [1212])*.

367, 1148]. Recent findings identify an historic right whaling ground off Norway in the 1600s [1103]. The few recent sightings in British and Irish waters have all occurred May–September [346, 360].

In W North Atlantic, range extended from Texas, Florida, and Bermuda in S, to the Gulf of St Lawrence and the coasts of Nova Scotia, Newfoundland and S Greenland in N. Most cows give birth in coastal waters of SE USA during winter [656]. Males and adult females without calves rarely seen there; whereabouts during winter remain unknown. In spring, aggregations observed in the Great South Channel, E of Cape Cod, and in Massachusetts Bay [1046, 1249]. In summer and autumn, observed in the Bay of Fundy, between Maine and Nova Scotia, and in an area on the continental shelf 50 km S of Nova Scotia [651, 652, 1127].

Individuals seen off Iceland and Norway matched animals seen in W North Atlantic [641], and preliminary genetic data indicate that separation between E and W Atlantic stocks unlikely. Given few sightings in E, best hope for the return of right whales to European waters is re-colonisation from W North Atlantic population

HISTORY

Little fossil material is available on *Eubalaena* from the N Atlantic.

Hunting right whales, started by the Basques >1000 years ago [972], led to development of all whaling [11]. Continued until 1935, when international protection given to this species by the League of Nations [967] (see Relations with humans, below).

HABITAT

No specific contemporary habitat identified in E North Atlantic. Historical whaling data suggest that most taken off GB and Ireland were <40 km from land, over the continental shelf [340, 972, 1148]. Historical whaling records identify a former right whale summering ground off Norway [1103]. Some calving certainly occurred in the coastal waters of Morocco (formerly W Sahara) in winter months, late 1800s [966]. Northern areas presumed to be feeding habitats for the few right whales that survive.

In W North Atlantic, several habitat types recognised. Feeding grounds have been identified as areas with high concentrations of copepods [615, 764]. Scotian shelf hypothesised to be a breeding ground because of the high proportion of courtship groups present there [1127]. Coastal waters of SE USA have been shown to be a calving habitat, with few males present, and no feeding

activity [654].

Although nearly all right whale cows in W North Atlantic give birth off SE USA, substructuring evident within population. From genetic and photo-ID data inferred that one group of cows (representing about 1/3 of the population) does not bring its calves to Bay of Fundy nursery area [1044]. Subsequent work suggested strong maternally directed site fidelity in right whales [737], with offspring returning to the mother's summer habitat. Implies another, unknown, summer–autumn nursery area; most of coastal zone of E North America has been surveyed over the past 25 years, so this unknown location is probably offshore and/or further N. Suggests a group of whales under-represented in photo-ID surveys, could alter population estimates.

SOCIAL ORGANISATION AND BEHAVIOUR

Poorly understood. Seen either singly or in pairs, except for courtship activity. Pairs of apparently unrelated individuals sometimes associate for several weeks at a time. In feeding areas, large aggregations of whales sometimes seen, but these appear to be acting independently, with few interactions. Echelon feeding in Cape Cod Bay of 2 skimming right whales reported. Engage in many typical whale behaviours, such as breaching, fluking upon diving, flipper slapping, and lobtailing (slamming the tail down on the water surface).

Courtship groups can be large and boisterous (up to 40 animals), appear to be multiple males competing for access to a single female. Courtship and mating activities occur at the surface, with associated underwater acoustic signals [899].

Speculation that males engage in sperm competition [185], and that females actively solicit competition among males to ensure the best mate [650, 898]. Mature males (n = 11, N Pacific population) had testes with a combined average weight of 972 kg, and penis lengths that averaged 2.3 m [185]. Mother–calf bonds strong for the first 10 months; subsequent interactions appear to be rare.

Vocalisations: Relatively vocal; substantial information on N Atlantic right whale [899, 900, 1149, 1173]; see also [1205]. Produce mainly moans in the range 400–3200 Hz, lasting 0.5–6.0 s, often with both pulsive and tonal components [254, 907]. Maximum source level 182 dB re 1 μPa @ 1 m [1204]. More complex calls are often associated with sexual activity; described as usually very harsh, strident or like a growl [254, 898]. These are AM moans, with major energy around 0.05–0.2 kHz. 3 classes of right whale sounds have been described: blows, gunshots, and tonal calls [898]. Most common call is an FM upsweep with major energy around 0.05–0.2 kHz; thought to be a contact call because all whales produce it, but only when separated. Also common is the high call, an FM sweep with major energy at 0.2–0.5 kHz, with multiple frequency shifts, and greater harmonic structure, made during social activity. During social interactions, other broadband sounds made, including blows (with major energy 0.1–0.4 kHz) and slaps (major energy 0.05–1 kHz); only made during social interaction, and may serve as threats [255, 899, 900].

FEEDING
Skim feeders on zooplankton, both at the surface and at depth, depending on patch locations and density [106]. Feed primarily on copepods but also occasionally on euphausiids [616, 764, 881, 1206]. In N Atlantic, identified feeding grounds are areas of high concentrations of copepod *Calanus finmarchius*, specifically the larger stages (C4, C5, and adult) [106, 627]. Feeding documented by observing open-mouth skimming at the surface, or defecation, in all 4 of the northern habitats in W North Atlantic, but not in the calving grounds off the SE USA. No feeding documented recently in E North Atlantic.

BREEDING
Calves born in winter, early December–late March, although newborn calves occasionally reported outside this season [656]. Gestation estimated at 12–13 months [128]. Infants born at 4–5 m, grow rapidly, attain 8–9 m by end of their 1st year [473]. Lactation lasts 10–12 months, although juveniles may rarely suck up to 17 months. Average age at sexual maturity for females is probably 9–10 years, although one female gave birth at 5 years [474, 656].

Cows give birth to a single calf every 3–5 years. Calving intervals increased from slightly over 3 years in the 1980s to >5 years by the late 1990s, but returned to *c.*3 years after 2001 [656]. Causes of this variation unknown.

POPULATION
Since 1980, have been studied using photographic identification of individuals from both aerial and shipboard surveys [180, 475]. Individually identifiable from their callosity patterns. In total, 500 right whales are catalogued in the N Atlantic population, but because of known and estimated mortality, currently estimated to number *c.*400 animals. Despite increases in survey effort, few new adult individuals have been added each year to the catalogued population since 1985, suggesting that most of W North Atlantic population is currently documented.

In E North Atlantic, scattered sightings suggest that the eastern stock, if it survives, is represented at most by a few tens of individuals. At least 134 right whales killed in whaling activities 1900–1926, mostly around the British Isles [182]. One cow and calf killed off Madeira, 1967 [762]. Sightings few; comprise 23 sightings of 48 whales reported, 1901–1980 [182], and a few additional sightings reported to right whale researchers over the last 20 years. Special efforts should be made to photograph any observed in E North Atlantic, for comparison with W North Atlantic catalogue.

Right whales have been sexed on appearance of the genital area, or, for cows, the long-term association with a newborn calf, and by using genetic techniques [179]. Of 60 calves sexed since 1980, 28 were females and 32 males, not significantly different from 1:1. Is seasonal segregation by sex in this population. Primarily adult females use the calving ground off SE USA, and males are rarely observed there; cows with calves rarely observed in the summering Scotian shelf area, which is dominated by males [179].

MORTALITY
Mortality rates estimated at 26–31% in year 1, 10% in year 2, 5% in year 3, and 1–4% for the next 7 years [808]. Adult mortality rates apparently very low; only 3 adults are known to have died of natural causes in this population since 1970. Longevity remains unknown, although at least one N Atlantic female had a sighting history extending over 60 years. Over 50% of mortality in this population caused by human activities, primarily ship collisions and entanglements in fishery gear [649, 655, 808].

May be low levels of predation by killer whales; *c.*7% of the N Atlantic population displays scars from their attacks, but anecdotal reports of orca/right whale encounters suggest that right whales can defend themselves adequately. No fatal diseases or epizootics reported, although lesions and parasites, thought to be related to illness, have been reported [472, 1010, 1011].

PARASITES
3 species of cyamids reported: *Cyamus ovalis*, *C. gracilis* and *C. erraticus*. Appear to have no long-term effect, although living on the sloughing skin of the whales [1020]. Both *Giardia* spp. and *Cryptosporidium* spp. reported [1010]. Diatom *Cocconeis ceticola* common on baleen plates. No recent review of endoparasites, but 3 species of helminths reported from N Pacific right whales [637].

RELATIONS WITH HUMANS
Right whales so called from being the right whale

to kill: gave high yields of oil and baleen, slow moving and floated after death. During early 20th century, Scottish whale fishery took 94 off Outer Hebrides and 6 off Shetland, 1903–1928, although only 3 after 1918 [1148]. None obtained when whaling resumed 1950–1951 [181]. In W Ireland, 18 caught 1908–1914, but none in 1920 or 1922 [367]. Right whaling in the N Atlantic well reviewed in [972].

Contemporary threats to right whales more insidious, but no less devastating. Over 50% of all mortality due to collisions with large ships and entanglement in fishing gear [639, 649, 655, 808]. Almost 75% of all right whales in N Atlantic display scars from entanglement in fishing gear some time in their lives. Lines from lobster or crab pots and groundfish gill nets appear to be primarily responsible, although all fixed gear presents a risk [581]. Extensive efforts in USA currently under way to develop alternative fishing methods and strategies for managing shipping to reduce kills. Cumulative impacts of all human activities not well understood, may be affecting health and reproduction of this species [651]. In addition, consequences to right whales from global climate changes may be anticipated [612].

Studies currently under way worldwide to gain better understanding of biology and conservation needs of *Eubalaena* spp. Most rely on individual identification [475, 653, 908]. Aerial and shipboard photographic surveys, as well as studies on life history, genetics, feeding behaviour and habitat use, are all currently used in research on N Atlantic right whales [106, 180, 410, 475, 617, 642, 737, 764, 1044, 1095].

Listed by IUCN as Endangered and has full international and national legal protection (see Table 12.1), including complete protection under IWC; large-scale violations of this protection in the 1960s by the Soviet whaling fleet apparently did not occur in the N Atlantic.

Where locally abundant (S Africa; Argentina; Bay of Fundy, Canada), thriving whale-watching businesses have developed. Concerns over disturbance from boats remain untested. Is an icon of humanity's failure to manage any marine 'resources'.

LITERATURE
Good overviews of historical topics [186]. Habitat and feeding reviewed in [615]. Up-to-date review of the conservation status and biology of N Atlantic right whales [651].

PRINCIPAL AUTHORS
S.D. Kraus & P.G.H. Evans

FAMILY ESCHRICHTIIDAE (GRAY WHALE)

Nominally, a family with 1 genus and species. Genetic evidence clusters this species within *Balaenoptera*, closer to big rorquals than minke whale [494].

Gray whale *Eschrichtius robustus*
Balaenoptera robustus Lilljeborg 1866; Gräsö, Sweden.
Rachianectes glaucus Cope 1869.

Californian gray whale, scrag whale.

RECOGNITION
A moderately large baleen whale (males average 12.2 m, females 12.8 m) with a grey back, mottled white (Plate 13). Baleen plates short (40–50 cm), grey with a white fringe. Throat with just 2 grooves. Skull without the high arched rostrum of a right whale, but with a narrower snout than a rorqual.

DISTRIBUTION
Confined to N hemisphere. Found in both W and E Pacific. E Pacific population migrates from winter breeding grounds in warmer waters off Baja California, N up Pacific coasts of USA and Canada to feed in summer in shallow seas of Bering Strait and further N. W Pacific population less well known, but may have bred off S Korea, and summered in the Sea of Okhotsk. Atlantic population extinct; may have bred off Florida and in the Bay of Biscay, feeding in summer in the Gulf of St Lawrence and the Baltic Sea, but too few records to do more than speculate.

HISTORY
Extinct in Atlantic, and nearly exterminated in the Pacific as well. As a coastal species, was very vulnerable to hunting, during migration and on S breeding grounds. In Pacific, believed to have recovered now to *c.*20 000 in American waters, but only 2000 in Asian waters.

Evidence for former presence in Atlantic derives partly from some rather uncertain descriptions by early whalers of the 'scrag whale', which had no dorsal fin but several knobs along its back – features of this but no other baleen whale; better descriptions from early Norse writings [697]. Definite subfossil remains of 10 specimens from American E coast [777] and 7 from European coasts [189], most of which now radiocarbon dated; another, Dutch, specimen currently under study. Latest in America dated 275 bp, i.e. 1675 AD. The 2 latest from Europe are from Pentewan, Cornwall (1329 bp) and Babbacombe Bay, Devon (340 bp, i.e. 1610 AD). These strongly support notion that the species just survived into era of commercial whaling; uncertain whether a longer history of aboriginal hunting contributed to its decline.

Original description of *(E.) robustus* based on European subfossil, acceptance that Pacific *Rachianectes glaucus* was conspecific required about a century [990].

Reintroduction barely feasible, but global warming and opening up of NW passage round N Canada may offer opportunity for natural recolonisation.

GENERAL ECOLOGY
Unusual among baleen whales in feeding largely on bottom fauna, especially amphipods. W Pacific population feeds for 4 months in summer in shallow Arctic waters. Migrates S, starting late September, passing Californian coast in December, to reach shallow lagoons on the coasts of Baja California. Calves born January, accompany mothers on migration back N starting February. Mating also takes place January, gestation lasts 12 months. Females breed at 2 years old, have 1 calf every other year [585, 990].

Presumed that European population would have fed in Baltic or White Sea, migrating S to breed in Bay of Biscay or along Moroccan coast.

AUTHORS
A.C. Kitchener, J.M. Mead & D.W. Yalden

FAMILY BALAENOPTERIDAE (RORQUALS)

A small family, usually accorded 2 genera, *Megaptera* and *Balaenoptera*, which includes the largest known mammals. Shorter baleen, less bowed upper jaws, than Balaenidae (Fig. 12.2), but strongly pleated throat which expands to allow intake of large volumes of water containing prey; water squeezed out through baleen plates by large muscular tongue, leaving prey caught on baleen.

GENUS *Megaptera*

A monospecific genus [494, 1021]; morphologically distinguished from *Balaenoptera* by very long pectoral flippers, bulkier body.

Humpback whale *Megaptera novaeangliae*
Balaena Novae Angliae Borowski, 1781; type locality coast of New England, USA.
Megaptera longimanna moorei Gray, 1866; R. Dee estuary, Cheshire, England.

Miol mór dronnach (Irish Gaelic).

RECOGNITION
At close range, impossible to mistake for any other whale. Flippers, 1/3 body length, are the longest of any cetacean; knobs (tubercles) on the head are diagnostic (Plate 13). At a distance can be confused with any large rorqual; however, habit of raising tail before a deep dive separates it from all rorquals except blue whale (typically larger, bluish, not black) (Fig. 12.1). Trailing edge of tail prominently serrated, frequently has much white on underside (cf. sperm, right whales, which also raise their tails on diving; right whale lacks a dorsal fin, sperm whale differs in colour and overall form, and usually in habitat). Back is prominently arched before a dive, accentuating the dorsal fin. Blow often bushier than for other large rorquals, and lacks V-shape of right whales.

DESCRIPTION
Flippers very long and narrow, generally all or largely white; rounded knobs (tubercles) present on rostrum, on both upper and lower jaws; 270–400 baleen plates per side (up to 70 cm long × 30 cm wide), generally black with black or olive-black bristles (Fig. 12.2). Skin generally black dorsally; ventrally varies from white to mottled to black. Flukes scalloped on trailing edge. Dorsal fin highly variable in size and shape, from almost absent to high and falcate. Body more robust than other balaenopterids. From 14 to 35 ventral grooves, up to 38 cm wide, extending almost from tips of lower jaws to umbilicus. Females and males are not distinguishable dorsally, but females possess a grapefruit-sized lobe at rear end of genital slit, absent in males.

Tail flukes butterfly-shaped, more rounded (less obviously triangular) than those of right or sperm whales. Flukes distinctly notched, with distinctive serrations on trailing edge (Fig. 12.1). Pigmentation of underside of tail variable, from all white to all black; these markings unique to each whale, widely used for individual identification. A large catalogue of identified individuals exists for N Atlantic and other oceans.

MEASUREMENTS
Length: newborn calf 4.0–4.6 m; at independence (*c.*1 year) 8–10 m [251]; at sexual maturity 13.9 m (females), 13.0 m (males) [236]. Females *c.*1–1.5 m longer than males [236]. Reliably recorded maximum lengths 15.5 m (female) and 14.75 m (male), though pre-whaling populations may have contained some larger individuals. Adult weights to *c.*45 t.

DISTRIBUTION
Worldwide, occasionally to ice edge. Highly migratory; feeds in summer in high latitudes, mates and calves in winter, in tropical waters,

though a few overwinter on feeding grounds. Strong individual fidelity to feeding areas; in N Atlantic, include the Gulf of Maine, Gulf of St Lawrence, Newfoundland/Labrador, Greenland, Iceland and Norway. Matching of photographically and genetically identified individuals indicates E North Atlantic population migrates primarily to West Indies [740, 1121], though some animals winter near Cape Verde islands [565, 980]; genetic analysis suggests a 3rd, unknown, breeding area. Despite fidelity to specific feeding grounds, whales from all N Atlantic areas mix spatially and genetically in the W Indies in winter.

Sightings from around the British Isles have increased markedly since the early 1980s; occur in 3 main areas – N Isles, S to E Scotland; N Irish Sea to W Scotland; and Celtic Sea between S Ireland, W Wales and SW England [340, 346, 360]. Since 1980, have also been 7 strandings around British Isles, all but one (Kent) in those same regions [120, 574, 1074]. In shelf waters, humpbacks occur mainly May–September, but some sightings extend through winter (November–March), confirmed by acoustic detection with SOSUS hydrophone arrays in the Atlantic W of the British Isles [235, 256]. Sightings in Ireland, mainly along S coast, increase through summer to peak in September, rapidly declining thereafter [122].

Regional whaling catches (76 animals, 1903–1929) occurred off Shetland, Outer Hebrides and NW Ireland, all on continental shelf, mainly in July–August [181, 1148]. The small number taken may reflect unimportance of the region to the species, or depletion from earlier exploitation.

HISTORY
The frequently coastal distribution of the humpback made it easy prey for whalers; often the first species to be depleted in an area. Most populations under study appear to be recovering well. Catches in the Scottish whale fishery amounted to 51 (Shetland) and 19 (Outer Hebrides), 1903–1929 [181], but none taken in the latter area in 1950–1951. In W Ireland, 6 humpbacks were taken 1908–1914, but none 1920, 1922 [367]. No subsequent records around British Isles until 1966. Many more humpbacks taken off Norway in the late 19th century, may have affected the local stock.

SOCIAL ORGANISATION AND BEHAVIOUR
No strongly organised social structure [247]. Typically found in small unstable groups or alone, though large feeding aggregations can occur in summer and large competitive groups of males can form around females in breeding areas. Group size

in summer often correlated with size of exploited prey patch.

Vocalisations: Produce 3 kinds of sounds: (1) songs produced solitarily, ranging from <20 Hz to 4 kHz (occasionally to 8 kHz) with source levels estimated at 144–174 dB re 1 μPa @ 1 m; (2) group or 'social' sounds often associated with agonistic behaviour among males, ranging from 50 Hz to >10 kHz (though mainly below 3 kHz); (3) sounds made in summer during feeding bouts, at c.20 Hz– 2 kHz, and 0.2–0.8 s duration, with estimated source levels of 175–192 dB re 1 μPa @ 1 m [993]. In winter (and occasionally at other times), males sing long, complex songs, the primary purpose of which is probably to attract females [906, 1166]. Songs change markedly over time in length, form and content, yet all whales within a population sing essentially the same song. Song regularly recorded in recent years during winter in deep water off W Scotland and Ireland, and probably originates from humpbacks migrating SW from Norwegian waters [235]. Breeding males frequently engage in aggressive contests with each other over females, but mating almost never observed, thus details of female mate choice remain unclear.

Humpbacks are known for their frequent high-energy aerial displays, which include breaching, lobtailing and flippering; these behaviours occur at all times of year and in widely different contexts; likely to perform a variety of social or other functions.

FEEDING
Diet: Euphausiids (krill) (*Meganyctiphanes, Thysanöessa, Euphausia* and *Pseudoeuphasia*), also small schooling fish, notably herring and sprat *Clupea* spp., sandeel *Ammodytes*, and capelin *Mallotus*.

Feeding methods: Vary with prey type, but always end with lunges of varying speed. Humpback blows clouds or nets of bubbles to entrap prey (especially fish). Specialised variations on this technique are often individual-specific; a common example is lobtail feeding, in which the whale slaps the water surface, perhaps to create bubbles or stun fish. No feeding on breeding grounds in winter.

BREEDING
Strongly seasonal, with most births in low latitudes in winter (peak January–March). Gestation period c.12 months. Lactation up to a year. Calving intervals typically 2–3 years, with occasional annual calving [247]. Age at sexual maturity varies by population, from 4 to >10 years for both sexes [236, 246, 414].

POPULATION

Longevity at least 48 years [236]; possibly much longer. Annual population growth rate *c*.3.1–6.5% in W North Atlantic, annual juvenile/adult mortality *c*.4% [98, 1122]. Overall, N Atlantic population has recovered well from exploitation, estimated at 10 400–11 570 in 1992 [1102, 1122]. Status of E North Atlantic population unclear, although clearly larger than was once thought. However, remains relatively uncommon around British Isles [360, 973].

PARASITES/COMMENSALS

Heavily invested with barnacles *Coronula* and *Conchoderma* spp. and whale lice *Cyamus* spp. Large number of endoparasites recorded, including trematodes, cestodes, nematodes and acanthocephalans [288]. Nematode *Ogmogaster ceti* commensal on baleen plates.

RELATIONS WITH HUMANS

Heavily exploited by whaling, population reduced by >90%. Little whaling in British waters. Protected in N Atlantic since 1955, and worldwide from 1966 (though USSR continued to hunt humpbacks illegally until 1973) (see Table 12.1). Vulnerable to ship strikes, entanglement in fishing gear and disturbance from industrial noise [668, 694, 971].

LITERATURE

Detailed species review [249].

AUTHORS

P.J. Clapham & P.G.H. Evans

GENUS *Balaenoptera*

A genus currently comprising 7 species, 4 of which occur in NE Atlantic, but perhaps more species if some S populations distinct from N. Genetic evidence clusters *Eschrichtius* within *Balaenoptera*, possibly also *Megaptera* [494, 1021]. Differs from *Megaptera* in shorter flippers, more streamlined body, from *Eschrichtius* by many more pleats on throat (85–90).

Minke whale *Balaenoptera acutorostrata*

Balaenoptera acutorostrata Lacépède, 1804; Cherbourg, France.

Lesser rorqual; little piked whale; *morfil pigfain* (Welsh); *muc-mhara-mhionc* (Scottish Gaelic); *miol mór mince* (Irish Gaelic).

RECOGNITION

Smallest baleen whale around British Isles. Blow low (2 m), inconspicuous, not always visible; typically seen at same time as 30 cm tall, re-curved dorsal fin situated 2/3 along back. Typical breathing sequence 3–6 blows at intervals of <1 min, followed by a longer dive typically lasting 6–12 min. Flippers have diagonal white band on upper surface (Plate 14). Head slender, pointed, triangular, with straight rather than curved borders to rostrum. Pale chevrons sometimes seen between blowhole and dorsal fin.

DESCRIPTION

General form similar to fin and sei whales, but sharply pointed snout. Baleen plates short (max.

Fig. 12.3 Minke whale lunging through surface, showing distended throat typical of feeding rorquals. Note also white blaze on flipper showing through the water splash *(photo P. Anderwald)*.

20 cm long × 12 cm wide), yellowish white; 230–342 on each side of upper jaw (Fig. 12.2). Plates sometimes with black streaking; fringed with fine white bristles. General body colour dark grey to black on back, lightening to white on belly and undersides of flippers. Light chevron across dorsal surface in 2 parts: one thin and crescent-shaped, just above and behind flippers, the other larger and usually more diffuse, between flippers and dorsal fin. Flippers approximately 1/8 body length, narrow, have distinctive white band on upper surface. 50–70 throat grooves, ending just behind flippers, but in front of navel. Dorsal fin a little more than 1/3 anterior to tail flukes, tall relative to body (compared to fin and blue whales), and usually distinctly sickle shaped (Plate 14). Tail flukes broad with small median notch.

RELATIONSHIPS
Smallest of 7 nominal species of *Balaenoptera*; molecular phylogenies suggest may be basal to rest of family (*Eschrichtius, Megaptera* and the larger *Balaenoptera*) [494, 1021].

MEASUREMENTS
Length: newborn *c.*2.4–2.8 m; at sexual maturity *c.*7.3–7.45 m (female), 6.8–7.0 m (male); adult *c.*8.5 m (female), *c.*8.0 m (male). Adult weight 5–14 t (data from Norwegian/Icelandic specimens).

VARIATION
In N hemisphere, average *c.*0.5 m smaller than in Antarctic. On morphological [879, 1032] and genetic evidence [526, 1188, 1189], Antarctic form now recognised as separate species, *B. bonaerensis* [187, 945]. Dwarf form in S hemisphere more closely related to N hemisphere animals than to *B. bonaerensis* [542, 1189]; *B. acutorostrata* thus divided into 3 subspecies: *B. a. acutorostrata* in N Atlantic, *B. a. scammoni* (formerly *davidsoni*) in N Pacific and dwarf form (unnamed) in S hemisphere [37, 187, 526, 542, 758, 931, 932].

In N Atlantic, morphometric differences between minke whales from W Greenland, Icelandic and Norwegian waters [243], supported by isozyme and microsatellite evidence [47, 291, 292]. However, microsatellite analyses [55] suggest only weak genetic differentiation between areas, and DNA studies of minkes from Iceland and N Norway suggested mixing of these breeding stocks [90, 891]. Mixing of breeding stocks on feeding grounds clearly demonstrated in N Pacific, where Korean (= Asian coastal) and W North Pacific stocks mix seasonally in Sea of Okhotsk [452, 1188].

DISTRIBUTION
Commonest of all baleen whales, both in N Atlantic and around British Isles, mainly in temperate and polar regions. Widely distributed along Atlantic seaboard of GB and Ireland, W and N Norway, Faroes and Iceland, often seen close to coast. Also in N and C North Sea, regularly S to Yorkshire coast. Small numbers in Irish Sea, but rare in S North Sea, Channel, and Bay of Biscay [340, 346, 360, 857, 973].

Is the baleen whale most likely to be observed from land, particularly from headlands along coasts of W Scotland and N Isles (Fig. 12.4). Most sightings July–September, but can be seen any time May–October, and some remain in coastal waters year-round [360, 973]. General offshore movement in autumn, possibly associated with breeding, although breeding locations unknown. Unknown whether extensive migrations occur, although one satellite-tagged immature individual entrapped in fishing gear in Danish waters travelled to N and W of British Isles, then to Azores, Canaries and finally into W Mediterranean [1140].

HISTORY
Fossils of balaenopteroid whales discussed in [1118], but none known of this species.

HABITAT
Occurs mainly over continental shelf of temperate and subarctic regions, often very close to land, sometimes entering estuaries, bays or inlets. Often feeds around banks and in areas of upwelling or strong currents around headlands and small islands, primarily during summer. In Scottish waters, feeding minke whales in late summer commonly associated with flocks of auks, Manx shearwaters, kittiwakes and various *Larus* gulls. Breeding areas unknown.

SOCIAL ORGANISATION AND BEHAVIOUR
Usually seen singly or in pairs, sometimes aggregates into larger groups of *c.*10–20 individuals when feeding. Evidence from recognisable individuals indicates seasonal site fidelity over small geographic range [326, 327, 443]. Genetic data indicate some differentiation among populations at small geographical scale [452, 1188, 1189].

Moderately fast swimmer, cruises at 5–26 km/h, capable of bursts >40 km/h. Often arches tail stock when beginning long dive, without raising flukes above surface. Frequently approaches vessels, will both bow- and stern-ride. Breaching not uncommon. Frequently feeds near other cetacean species, e.g. harbour porpoises, white-beaked and Atlantic white-sided dolphins, and humpback whales [341, 353].

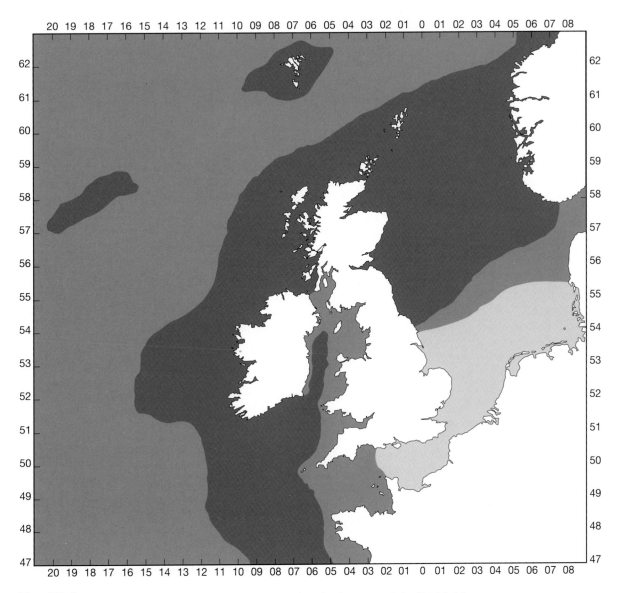

Fig. 12.4 Minke whale *Balaenoptera acutorostrata*: distribution around the British Isles.

Vocalisations: Involve intense low-frequency broadband (0.5–1 kHz bandwidth) and harmonic down-sweeps with maximum source level of 165 dB re 1 μPa. These include short broadband downsweeps (mainly 0.13–0.06 kHz lasting 200–300 ms); 'grunts' (mainly between 0.08–0.14 kHz, but up to 2 kHz, lasting 165–320 ms); and thumps (often downsweeps; mainly 0.1–0.2 kHz, lasting 50–70 ms) [337, 1047, 1149, 1247].

FEEDING

Diet: Most catholic feeder of the rorquals; in N hemisphere takes more fish (sandeels, herring, sprat, cod, capelin, haddock, saithe and whiting) than others, but euphausiids and pteropods also taken, especially in higher latitudes [157, 497, 498, 844, 852, 878, 927, 1085].

Feeding methods: Like humpback and fin whale,

minke whale uses variety of methods depending on nature of prey: engulfing prey with open mouth from behind, or side- and lunge-feeding using surface to trap fish shoals (Fig.12.3). Known individuals revisiting same bank or bay over period of several years fed at same site using same feeding strategy [529]: 2 types of foraging specialisations, used exclusively by individual whales; some fed on ephemeral patches of herring, brought to surface by feeding auks, others pursued prey in deeper water, herding them against air/water interface. Similar feeding specialization not observed off W coast of Scotland [56].

BREEDING

Births mainly around December, probably in temperate offshore waters, possibly in subtropics. Gestation 10 months. Lactation <6 months, calving interval of 1–2+ years. Sexual maturity at *c.*7–10 years, at least in Antarctic minkes [544, 706, 1080, 1123]. However, difficult to read ear plugs of N Atlantic minkes, due to indistinct layering.

POPULATION

Only published population estimate for minke whales in British waters is from North Sea, English Channel and Celtic Sea; line transect survey (SCANS), July 1994, estimated 8450 (95% CI 5000–13 500) [481]. More extensive line transect survey (SCANS II) over NW European continental shelf, July 2005, gave overall estimate of 16 395 (including 10 500 in area equivalent to 1994 study) [478]. Population estimate for entire C/NE North Atlantic (based on data from 1996–2001) 174 000 (95% CI 125 000–245 000) [559]. Previously, stock seasonally inhabiting Norwegian and Barents Seas estimated at 86 700 individuals (95% CI 61 000–117 000) [1052]. Assessing minke whale numbers difficult and controversial since inconspicuous at sea and may react to survey vessels.

Population changes in NE Atlantic uncertain; effort-related sightings surveys hint that increased in British shelf waters during 1980s–1990s [152, 346, 360].

Spatial and temporal segregation by sex and maturity [240, 587, 588, 1064]; of 225 minke whales caught during Norwegian scientific whaling programme (1992–1994), 45.8% males, 54.2% females [852]. Lifespan *c.*40–50 years, but 1 individual 57.5 years. Annual adult mortality 9–10% [873], but likely to vary between populations and times.

MORTALITY

Besides humans, main predator of minke whale is killer whale. In Antarctic waters, remains of minke whales identified in 70–85% of killer whale stomachs [196, 325, 1075]. Transient killer whales in E North Pacific also observed preying on minkes in recent years. Extent of this in N Atlantic unknown, but scars seen apparently from killer whale teeth [590, 591]. Serological investigation of 129 minke whales from NE Atlantic revealed no evidence of morbillivirus antibodies [1131].

PARASITES AND PATHOGENS

Ectoparasites: Rare, but some carry whale lice *Cyamus* spp., mostly at posterior ends of ventral grooves or around umbilicus, and parasitic copepod *Pennella balaenopterae* sometimes embedded in skin, on dorsal surface or near urinogenital opening.

Endoparasites: Include 3 trematodes (*Fasciola skrajabini, Lecithodesmus goliath, Ogomogaster plicatus*, 3 nematodes (*Anisakis simplex, Crassicauda crassicauda, Porrocaecum decipiens*), 3 acanthocephalans

(*Bolbosoma balaena, B. brevicolle, B. nipponicum*), and at least 1 cestode (*Tetrobothrius affinis*) [107, 127, 302, 442, 670, 874].

RELATIONS WITH HUMANS

Because of small size, not a target of Scottish and Irish whale fisheries in early 20th century. Only exploited more recently, when stocks of larger rorquals depleted and, in some cases, protected. Since late 1920s, whaling for this species carried out along Norwegian coast, expanding just before World War II to Spitsbergen and Shetland–Faroes, later extending to Barents Sea, Iceland, Jan Mayen, W Greenland and Labrador. Most whaling currently by Norway, but limited commercial fishery resumed by Iceland, 2006, after some years of scientific whaling completed in 2007. In August 2007, Iceland decided not to issue a new commercial quota for the time being. Since 1993, Norway gradually increased its catch limit year by year, taken under objection to IWC's commercial whaling moratorium; has been 1052 whales since 2006, but fewer actually caught.

Latest of baleen whales exploited by whaling industry, previously considered too small to be worth hunting. Stock reduced by whaling to 45–70% of pre-exploitation abundance [971]. In 1984, NE Atlantic Stock considered depleted by IWC, declared Protection stock. In 1986, IWC moratorium on commercial whaling came into effect with zero catch limits for all species. Legally protected in European, British and Irish waters (Table 12.1).

Sometimes gets entangled in fishing gear, mainly gillnets set for salmon and creel lines [555]. Several reports from British Isles; one photographed off W Ireland managed to get inside a salmon cage [347].

Pollutant levels of PCBs in blubber of minke whales relatively high [636, 1094]. Concentrations of PCB and DDT across N Atlantic generally increase from W to E, highest PCB levels in animals from Barents Sea [523]. Highest ^{137}Cs levels found in North Sea [156].

Now focus of British whale-watching industry, mainly off W coast of Scotland; also off Iceland, is most common species near Husavik, centre of Icelandic whale-watching industry. May suffer from sounds made by ship traffic (and particularly whale-watching) and seismic testing from oil and gas exploration in certain regions [338, 1202]. Collisions with vessels occur (e.g. one struck by ship in Firth of Forth, E Scotland [1]. Active sonar used by military may have killed 2 minke whales off Bahamas.

LITERATURE

Review [1123], updated in [914]; monograph

[544]; detailed research analyses [139, 1179]; popular account [528].

AUTHORS
P. Anderwald, P.G.H. Evans, A.R. Hoelzel & V. Papastavrou

Fin whale *Balaenoptera physalus*
Balaena physalus Linnaeus, 1758; Svalbard.

Common rorqual, finback; *muc-an-scadain* (Scottish Gaelic); *miol mór eiteach* (Irish Gaelic).

RECOGNITION
2nd largest of all whales, females up to 24 m in length. Uniform slate grey (Plate 13) (blue whale lighter, mottled). Generally does not show tail flukes when diving, but rolls in high arch. Relatively small dorsal fin with little curvature. White on right lower lip and palate diagnostic (all other balaenopterids symmetrically dark). Tall (4–6 m) blow, shaped like an inverted cone, followed by long shallow roll showing fin, repeated up to 7 times at intervals of 10–20 s (50 s when feeding at surface) before dive, commonly of 5–15 min, sometimes as short as 25 s (similar sei whale often rises to surface at shallow angle, does not arch its back, and dives more frequently).

DESCRIPTION
General form slender. Slender head, V-shaped and flattened from above but with prominent median ridge (cf. 3 ridges in Bryde's whale). Baleen plates relatively short (maximum 72 cm long × 30 cm wide), 260–480 on each side of upper jaw (Fig. 12.2). Plates on right side usually yellowish-white for 75–100 cm from front end. Remaining plates

of right side, and all of left side, slaty grey alternating with longitudinal yellowish bands. Fringes brownish grey to greyish white. General body colour uniformly dark grey to brownish grey above, grading to white below including lower surface of flukes and inner surfaces of flippers (cf. sei whale). Most have pale grey chevron on each side behind head, and may have dark stripe or blaze running up and back from eye, light stripe arching down to where flipper joins body. Fairly slender pointed flippers, about 1/7 body length. Throat grooves 56–100, ending posterior to maximum cross-section of body (i.e. around navel). Dorsal fin 1/3 along back from tail, *c.*60 cm tall (i.e. taller than in much larger blue whale) though appears relatively small compared with sei and minke whale (Fig. 12.5). Behind fin, back is ridged to tail flukes, which are broad, triangular, with slight median notch and slightly concave trailing edge.

RELATIONSHIPS
Of 7 species of *Balaenoptera*, 4 (not tropical Bryde's whale) regularly occur in European seas. Blue, fin and sei whales tend to live in deep waters, smaller minke whale occurs primarily over the continental shelf. Molecular (mtDNA) phylogeny suggests closer to humpback than blue whale [494], though rare hybrids with blue whale known [123, 1112].

MEASUREMENTS
Length: newborn *c.*6.4 m, but considerably smaller (5.3 m) in the Mediterranean; at sexual maturity *c.*18.3 m (female), *c.*17.7 m (male); adult usually *c.*20.0 m (female), *c.*18.5 m (male); maximum, N Atlantic, 24.0 m (female), 22.0 m (male). Weight *c.*20 t (15 m whale) to 80 t (25 m whale, S hemisphere) [863].

Fig. 12.5 Fin whale rolling into dive, showing small fin, placed far back *(photo P.G.H. Evans)*.

VARIATION

In N hemisphere, average c.1–2 m smaller than in S hemisphere. DNA studies indicate genetic differences between populations in W and E North Atlantic and resident Mediterranean population [124, 894].

DISTRIBUTION

Worldwide, mainly in temperate and polar seas, both hemispheres. Although fin whales may show seasonal latitudinal migration, remaining in polar seas only during summer, those further S around the British Isles appear to be present year-round [256, 360]. The commonest large whale in E North Atlantic, Bay of Biscay and Mediterranean. Distributed around British Isles mainly along Atlantic seaboard, along or beyond edge of continental shelf (Fig. 12.6). Most sightings in coastal waters come from Shetland, Outer Hebrides, SW Ireland and the Celtic Sea between S Ireland and SW England [340, 346, 360, 941, 1125, 1126]. Most sightings in northern GB June–August, further S September–February. Some indication from sightings that move generally northwards off NW Scotland June–October [1125] when numbers may concentrate in areas like Rockall Trough and Faroe-Shetland Channel.

Of 50 verified strandings around British Isles, 1913–1992, 27 (1.35/year) occurred 1913–1932, dropping to 5 (0.25/year) 1933–1952 and 4 (0.20/year) 1953–1972, before rising again to 14 (0.70/year) 1973–1992 [120, 404, 406–408, 485, 1073, 1074]. Paucity of strandings 1932–1972 attributed to decline following intense human exploitation [408].

HISTORY

No fossil or archaeological material known.

HABITAT

Most commonly recorded in deep waters (400–2000 m depth) off the edge of the continental shelf, in some localities (e.g. lower Bay of Fundy) occurs in shallow areas (<200 m depth). Appears to favour areas with high topographic variation – underwater sills or ledges, upwellings and frontal zones between mixed and stratified waters with high zooplankton concentrations [345, 981, 982, 1252].

SOCIAL ORGANISATION AND BEHAVIOUR

Usually seen singly or in pairs (mainly mother with dependent calf), can form larger pods of 3–20, perhaps part of broader group of hundreds of individuals spread over wide area, especially on feeding grounds [794, 1233]. Aggregations usually associated with feeding; differences in group size result from different feeding situations or from geographical segregation by sex or age class [9, 1233]. Individuals may change associations with one another over short time period, suggesting fluid relationships at least on feeding grounds [338, 1233]. Lunging behaviour frequently observed, mainly when groups present [218, 338]. Breaching occasional, whale typically landing on its belly [743]; surface sexual behaviour involving excited chases also described [1128].

Fast swimmers: 2–6.5 km/h when feeding, 6–9 km/h during normal travel, up to 30 km/h in short bursts when migrating or cruising, and up to 41 km/h when alarmed [563, 666, 704]. Tagged fin whales tracked at 4.1–12.6 km/h [1207, 1233], and averaged 6–9 km/h when tracked by laser rangefinder [861]. May dive to depths >470 m [895].

Vocalisations: Mainly low-frequency pulses (moans), usually FM downsweeps (though sometimes constant frequency, upsweeps or wavers) from c.4 to 17 Hz (but can reach 125 Hz) lasting 0.5–1 s, often repeated in series with regular interpulse intervals (5–45 s) [257, 337, 1150, 1203]. Maximum source level is 186 dB re 1 μPa @ 1 m [1209]. Short sequences (2–30 repetitions) produced by both sexes, probably serve for communication over distances up to 30 km, possibly more, between widely spaced individuals [1203]. Long (up to 30 h) patterned sequences of single or paired pulses with stereotyped repetition patterns (often interrupted by 20 min rest periods) produced by slow-swimming adult males, mainly October–April, thought to be reproductive song displays. Additional sounds include rumbles of very long duration (*c.*30 s), 10–30 Hz with extensive frequency and amplitude modulation, thought to be agonistic [337]; and high-frequency clicks (16–28 kHz, duration 8.8 s) recorded at close range [1149].

FEEDING

Diet: Feeds mainly on planktonic crustacea (mainly euphausiids, e.g. *Meganyctiphanes norvegica,* also copepods), but also take fish (e.g. herring, capelin, sandeels, mackerel, and blue whiting), and cephalopods [589, 610, 791, 1080]. Relationship between fin whale distribution and *Meganyctiphanes* abundance demonstrated in W Mediterranean [982].

Feeding methods: Uses variety of methods: engulfing prey from behind by distending the throat grooves and taking large gulp of water and prey, to side- and lunge-feeding involving some herding of prey into tight concentration. Coordinated swimming among several whales,

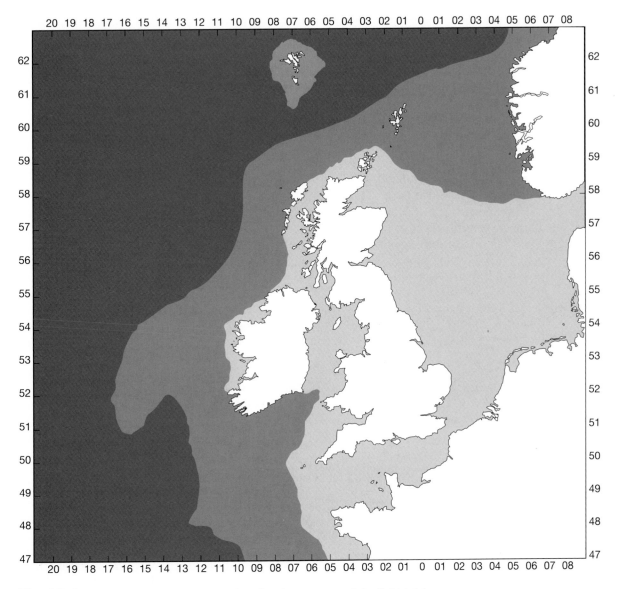

Fig. 12.6 Fin whale *Balaenoptera physalus*: distribution around the British Isles.

surface-feeding on the euphausiid *Nyctiphanes couchii*, observed in S Mediterranean [218]. In NW Atlantic, fin whale's consumption of prey estimated at 533 kg/day [470].

BREEDING
Births occur mainly in autumn–winter. Gestation period 11–12 (mean 11.25) months; lactation period 6–7 months. Age at sexual maturity 6–10 years (females) and 8–12 years (males), with indication that exploited populations (such as Iceland) mature earlier [705, 1080]. Calving interval now estimated to be *c*.3 years [706]; photo-ID studies, Gulf of Maine, indicate average time between consecutive births is 2.71 years [9].

POPULATION
No current estimates for whole N Atlantic population, but recent sightings surveys suggest >46 000 (still below its former size), including 17 000 for British Isles–Spain–Portugal stock [193, 554]. Estimate of 3500 for W Mediterranean, from sightings surveys [388]. IWC estimate for C/NE North Atlantic, 1996–2001, is 30 000 (95% CI 23 000–39 000) [559].

Can live to 85–90 years [342]. Average annual mortality estimated at 4% [873], but this varies between areas and over time.

MORTALITY
Killer whales may sometimes attack and kill fin whales [501, 573, 933, 1157].

PARASITES AND PATHOGENS
External parasites, e.g. copepod *Pennella* sp., amphipods *Cyamus*, and cirripeds including *Coronula* sp., *Conchoderma auritum*, *C. virgatum*, and *Xenobalanus globicipitis*, tend to infect whales in

671

warmer waters but are lost in polar regions. Diatoms, e.g. *Cocconeis,* appear as surface films over skin of animals summering in high latitudes. Often infected by nematode *Crassicauda crassicauda;* severe infections thought to cause congestion of kidney and renal failure [669]. Other internal parasites include cestodes and acanthocephalans [416].

One stranded, Belgium, 1997, showed positive antibodies to morbillivirus [568].

RELATIONS WITH HUMANS
Heavily exploited, at least 75 000 taken (mostly S oceans) since invention of steam catcher boats and explosive harpoon gun in mid-19th century, but given full protection from commercial whaling in 1986. Original (pre-exploitation) population estimate for N hemisphere, 58 000 [342].

In 1903–1928, Scottish catches of 4536 (Shetland) and 1492 (Outer Hebrides) [1148]; further 46 caught, Outer Hebrides, 1950–1951 [181]. Irish catches 435, 1908–1914, and 157, 1920 and 1922 [367]. Seem to have depleted local stocks, species scarce in region thereafter. Most catches made off edge of continental shelf, particularly N and W of Shetlands. Until mid-1980s, whaling in Spanish waters may have reduced occurrences off SW GB and Ireland. Intense whaling conducted in Strait of Gibraltar, from 1921 to late 1950s, mostly targeting fin whales, ended with collapse of local stock [863]. Small numbers (from population numbering *c.*3000 in 2005) still taken by subsistence whale fishery in Greenland, but protected from commercial whaling since 1986.

Occasionally caught accidentally in fishing gear in E Canada and Mediterranean (<1 per year [555, 863]). Collapse of capelin stocks off Newfoundland, late 1970s, thought to have reduced summering populations [1234].

Levels of pollutants including heavy metals (such as mercury), PCBs and other organohalogen compounds usually low, compared to other marine mammals [13, 17, 108, 378, 379, 1027]; levels higher in North Atlantic and Mediterranean than elsewhere (DDT in blubber 0.2–10 μg/g, PCBs 0.5–8 μg/g [12].

Noise and disturbance from vessels and industrial activities may also have negative impact in some coastal areas [336, 338, 1128], and concerns expressed about impact of seismic sounds from oil and gas exploration along NE Atlantic shelf break [352]. Collisions between fin whales and vessels, particularly ferries, known, including reports in British waters, but most serious concern is in Mediterranean, in areas of heavy traffic [198, 896].

Legally protected in European, British and Irish waters and listed by IUCN as Endangered, with the Mediterranean population proposed as Data Deficient (Table 12.1).

LITERATURE
Good reviews [12, 415].

AUTHORS
G. Notarbartolo di Sciara & P.G.H. Evans

Sei whale *Balaenoptera borealis*
Balaenoptera borealis Lesson, 1828; Lubeck Bay, Schleswig-Holstein, Germany.

Muc-mhara-sei (Scottish Gaelic); *miol mór an tuaisceart* (Irish Gaelic).

RECOGNITION
Dark steely-grey back, often with grey or white round scars. Right lower lip and mouth cavity usually uniformly grey (unlike fin whale) and no white on undersides of flippers or tail flukes (Plate 13). Prominent dorsal fin, strongly re-curved and more erect than fin whale, often visible simultaneously with blow. Blow moderately tall (*c.*3 m), inverted cone shape. Along with dorsal fin, remains in view for relatively long periods before typically making shallow dive. May blow 2–3 times at 20 s intervals followed by dive of 5–6 min duration, or 5–6 times at 30–40 s intervals before longer dive of 15–30 min. Slender head with slightly arched forehead, though not as rounded as blue whale, with single prominent median ridge (cf. Bryde's whale which has 3 distinct ridges). Baleen plates relatively narrow (length:breadth ratio typically >2.2 whereas always less than this in Bryde's whale).

DESCRIPTION
Slender, streamlined body. Baleen plates relatively short, 300–410 on each side of upper jaw, uniformly grey-black but with fine (0.1 mm in diameter at base), almost silky white fringes (Fig. 12.2). Generally dark grey on back and sides, and rear part of belly, but greyish white on middle part of throat grooves. Relatively small pointed flippers, about 1/11 body length; *c.*30–60 throat grooves (averaging *c.*50), all ending well before navel (in fin and Bryde's whale they end at or beyond navel). Dorsal fin fairly erect, usually 25–60 cm high, strongly re-curved and located a little more than 1/3 along back from tail (i.e. slightly further forward than in fin whale and much further forward than in blue whale) (Fig. 12.7). Relatively small tail flukes, broad and triangular, with median notch.

MEASUREMENTS
Length: newborn *c.*4.4 m; at sexual maturity

Fig. 12.7 Sei whale rolling into dive, showing recurved dorsal fin *(photo S. Kraus)*.

*c.*14.0 m (female), *c.*13.6 m (male); adult *c.*14.5 m (female), *c.*14.0 m (male); maximum 19.5 m. Weight: newborn 680 kg, adult *c.*20–30 t.

VARIATION

N hemisphere animals average *c.*0.5–1.0 m smaller than those found in S hemisphere. Closely related to Bryde's whale [42, 313, 315, 494, 1021, 1189], from which it was only relatively recently distinguished. Genetic studies indicate little mixing between populations of N and S hemispheres, but apparently little differentiation within ocean basins [314, 597, 1189].

DISTRIBUTION

Worldwide, mainly offshore in deep waters. Seasonal migrations from polar and cold temperate regions (mainly around Iceland, in Greenland Sea and W Barents Sea) in summer, to warm temperate and subtropical waters (off Spain, Portugal and NW Africa) in winter.

Summering populations are concentrated in deep waters of central N Atlantic, N to Iceland. In W North Atlantic, reported from 2 main locations: Scotian shelf and Labrador in summer, off Florida, Gulf of Mexico and Caribbean in winter, although some of latter may be misidentified Bryde's whales [543, 571, 592]. In E North Atlantic, thought to winter off NW Africa, Spain and Portugal and in Bay of Biscay, migrating N to summering grounds off Shetland, the Faroes, Norway, and Svalbard [346, 352, 360, 543].

Rarely seen in coastal waters of British Isles, though probably under-recorded because difficult to identify (Fig. 12.8). Most records come from waters >200 m deep, between N Isles and Faroes, and in Rockall Trough; occurs occasionally in coastal waters off Shetland, Hebrides and between S Ireland and SW England [346, 360, 973, 1216].

Around GB, off Outer Hebrides was caught mainly in June along the shelf edge near St Kilda; off Shetland waters, also from the shelf edge, mainly July–August. Recent sightings around British Isles generally in summer, July–October, particularly in August [360]. Off S Ireland, most casual sightings July–November [122]; to S, seen regularly in Bay of Biscay in autumn–winter [267].

HABITAT

Favours pelagic, temperate deep waters, 500–3000 m deep. Seems to have a more offshore distribution than fin whales or other balaenopterids [543, 1080].

HISTORY

No fossil or archaeological material known. Heavily exploited in the past; see Relations with humans, below.

SOCIAL ORGANISATION AND BEHAVIOUR

Relatively non-social species, usually seen singly or in pairs; otherwise in groups of up to 5.

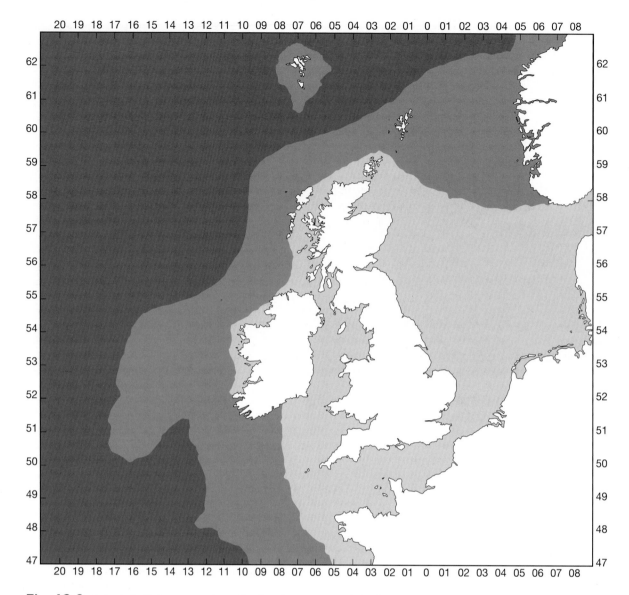

Fig. 12.8 Sei whale *Balaenoptera borealis*: distribution around the British Isles.

Occasional larger aggregations, up to 30, generally associated with feeding [195]. Some segregation by age and reproductive status likely; in S Ocean, pregnant females migrate first, and younger individuals rarely reach highest latitudes [415, 543].

Very fast swimmer (possibly fastest of all rorquals), attaining 55 km/h, though usually travels at 3.6–30 km/h [704]. Usually does not dive very deeply, and so generally surfaces and dives again at shallow angle. Sometimes breaches clear of water.

Vocalisations: Little studied, but include 3 kHz pulsed clicks each <1 s long. Recorded sounds consisted of 2 phrases of 0.5–0.8 s duration, spaced 0.4–1 s apart. Each phrase consisted of 210–220 FM sweeps in 1.5–3.5 kHz range [640, 1149].

FEEDING
Diet: In N Atlantic, mainly copepods (*Calanus, Eucalanus, Metridia,* and *Temora*); also euphausiids (*Thysanoessa* and *Meganyctiphanes*). Small schooling fishes and squid important in some areas [610, 840, 985, 1157].

Feeding methods: Prey taken near surface, captured either by taking large mouthfuls of water with plankton or by skimming close to surface with half-open mouth and then swallowing [543, 609, 610, 836, 837].

BREEDING
Reproductive biology reviewed in [417, 706, 1080]. Births mainly in winter (particularly November–December), possibly offshore from NW Africa or W of Iberia. Gestation 10.5–13 months; lactation 6–9 months; calving interval 2–3 years. Age at

sexual maturity 5.6–11.7 years (females) and 7–11.7 years (males), although in places has declined from 10–11 years to 6–8 years, following exploitation.

POPULATION

Longevity *c.*65 years [342]. Annual adult mortality *c.*9–10% in exploited Icelandic population [714]. Main natural predator is probably killer whale: lethal attacks witnessed, mainly in Pacific [848].

No current estimates exist for the N Atlantic population; recent sightings surveys indicate >13 500, evident depletion of stocks from some of former whaling grounds [230, 244, 594, 1079, 1080].

PARASITES/COMMENSALS

White scars in skin may be caused by copepod crustaceans of genus *Pennella*, or lesions made by the shark *Isistius* or by lampreys. Copepods *Balaenophilus* and *Haematophagus* commonly infest baleen.

Internal parasites very prevalent; acanthocephalan *Bolbosoma turbinella* common in intestine, along with cestodes *Tetrabothrius affinis* and *Diplogonoporus balaenopterae*. Nematodes frequent in kidney and in erectile tissue of penis and urethra of males [417]. In N Pacific, often heavily infected with stomach nematode *Anisakis simplex* and trematode *Lecithodesmus spinosus*; 7% of individuals infected with a disease causing loss of baleen plates [986].

RELATIONS WITH HUMANS

Heavily exploited wherever it was common, particularly 1955–1975. Original (pre-exploitation) population, N hemisphere, estimated at 66 000 [417]. Off N Norway alone, 4000 killed, 1885–1900 [543]. Total commercial protection since 1986, but recent scientific take off Iceland, and limited subsistence whaling off Greenland.

Catches in Scottish and Irish waters earlier this century suggest that sei whales were less abundant than fin whales – still true. Off Scotland, catches of 1839 (Shetland) and 375 (Outer Hebrides), 1903–1928 [1148] with 3 more 1950–1951 (Outer Hebrides) [181]. Off W Ireland, 88 caught, 1908–1914, and a further 3, 1920, 1922 [367]. Off Outer Hebrides, caught particularly along the shelf edge near St Kilda, mainly in June; N of Shetland, mainly taken July–August.

No information exists on fisheries interactions or pollutant levels. Noise and disturbance from vessels and industrial activities potentially damaging in more heavily used areas, and seismic soundings for oil and gas exploration along Atlantic Frontier also a potential problem [352].

Legally protected in European, British and Irish waters, listed by IUCN as Endangered (Table 12.1)

LITERATURE

Detailed account [543]; valuable summaries [417, 545].

PRINCIPAL AUTHOR

P.G.H. Evans

Blue whale *Balaenoptera musculus*

Balaena musculus Linnaeus, 1758; Firth of Forth, Scotland.
Physalus sibbaldii Gray, 1847; Yorkshire.

Sulphur-bottomed whale, Sibbald's rorqual; *muc-mhara-mhor* (Scottish Gaelic); *miol mór gorm* (Irish Gaelic).

RECOGNITION

Largest whale, reaching 28 m length. Distinctly pale bluish grey over most of body, mottled with grey or greyish white (Plate 13). Very small dorsal fin, variable in shape but usually with little curvature, distinctly more than 2/3 along back so that seen only just prior to dive, some time after blow. Tall (to 10–12 m) vertical blow, denser and broader than fin whale. Typically, makes several shallow dives at intervals of *c.*20 s. Very broad, long body with broad, flat U-shaped head and single ridge extending from raised area forwards of blowholes towards tip of snout to form prominent 'splash guard'.

DESCRIPTION

Largest and heaviest mammal known. Body form robust with broad snout and large head up to 25% of total length. Baleen plates relatively short (90 cm long × 50 cm wide), 260–400 on each side of upper jaw, stiff and coarsely fringed, and jet black in colour (Fig. 12.2). Body generally bluish grey, mottled with grey or greyish white; sometimes has mustard yellow coloration mainly on belly (caused by diatoms from periods spent in high latitudes). Pigmentation patterns sufficiently variable to allow some individual recognition; 2 main types: dark blue-grey, mottled with sparse pale patches, or pale background mottled with sparser dark patches. Sometimes has distinct chevrons, curving down and angled back from apex on both sides of back behind blowholes. Young animals usually paler grey. Flippers long (up to 15% of body length), slim, with underside and pointed tips white or pale greyish-blue. 55–88 throat grooves, extending more than 1/2 way along body to navel. Dorsal fin >1/3 along towards tail; very small, usually <33 cm high; variable in shape from nearly triangular to moderately falcate (Fig.

Fig. 12.9 Blue whale rolling into dive, showing small dorsal fin *(photo P.G.H. Evans)*.

12.9). Tail flukes predominantly grey on both sides and broad, triangular with slight median notch, usually lifted only slightly before diving (Fig. 12.1). May have white patches on ventral surface of tail, also useful for individual identification.

MEASUREMENTS

Length: newborn *c*.6–7 m; at sexual maturity *c*.21–23.0 m (female), 20–21.6 m (male); adult *c*.26.0 m (female), 24.0 m (male); larger in S hemisphere, to max. 33.6 m. Weight: newborn 2–3 t, adult 80–150 t [1257].

VARIATION

3 subspecies designated: Antarctic form *B. m. intermedia* is a few metres larger than N hemisphere *B. m. musculus*. Taxonomic status of small 3rd subspecies, pygmy blue whale *B. m. brevicauda*, in sub-Antarctic zone of S Indian Ocean and SW Pacific, requires confirmation. In N Atlantic, E and W subpopulations recognised for purpose of management [416]; also need confirmation by genetic studies, although photo-ID suggests that whales from Iceland and Azores do not mix with those from NE USA, E Canada or W Greenland [1058].

RELATIONSHIPS

Of 7 species of *Balaenoptera*, 4 (not tropical Bryde's whale) occur regularly in European seas. Blue, fin and sei whales tend to live in deep waters, smaller minke whale occurs primarily over the continental shelf. Molecular (nuclear and mtDNA) phylogeny suggests closer to Bryde's and sei than fin or humpback whale [62, 494, 1021], though rare hybrids with humpback and fin whales known [123, 1112].

DISTRIBUTION

Worldwide in all seas, mainly in warm temperate–subtropical waters during winter, summering in cold temperate and polar seas.

In N Atlantic, occurs from Caribbean to Davis Strait S Greenland in W, and from Canaries, Cape Verdes and W Africa to Jan Mayen, Svalbard and Barents Sea in E. Best-known population lives in St Lawrence, April–January, where 350 individuals have been photographed [1056–1058].

Presence around British Isles evident primarily from whale fisheries of early 20th century; small numbers regularly passed W of GB and Ireland during summer in deep waters off edge of continental shelf [181, 1148]. More recently, sightings [346, 360, 973, 1216] and acoustic monitoring [234, 256] reveal small numbers in deep waters of Faroe-Shetland Channel and Rockall Trough, S to Bay of Biscay. Thought to winter in tropical and subtropical seas where they breed, then migrate to feed during summer months in cold temperate and polar waters. Supported by recent sightings in Azores and Canaries during winter–spring, and in high latitudes, May–September; but recent monitoring using SOSUS acoustic arrays suggests that some remain in high latitudes throughout winter [234, 256].

4 strandings on British/Irish coasts, 1913–1923,

676

but none since [408, 1072]. Only 1 recent well-documented sighting, one off NW coast of Ireland, May 1977, although also sighted over Wyville Thompson Ridge and in Faroe-Shetland Channel [346, 358, 360]. Also a few sightings in Bay of Biscay, N of Spain [20, 267, 1026].

HABITAT
Usually found in deep waters (100–1000 m); in some regions, occurs regularly close to land, in depths of 200 m or less [1055, 1080]. In Iceland, tends to be seen closer to the coast than fin or sei whales [1080].

HISTORY
No fossil or archaeological material known.

SOCIAL ORGANISATION AND BEHAVIOUR
Relatively non-social; usually seen singly or in pairs; larger aggregations of >50 occasionally occur around concentrations of food [1056, 1257]. Mother–calf pairs often observed away from schools of males and non-reproductive females [838]. Extended associations between males for as long as 3 weeks observed in St Lawrence estuary [1056]. When male–female pair approached by another whale, vigorous surface displays lasting 5–15 min observed; all 3 may race high out of water, almost breaching, and porpoising forward in explosive manner.

Fast swimmer, 2–6.5 km/h while feeding, 3–33 km/h while travelling or migrating, and >30 km/h when being pursued [704, 997].

When diving, lifts tail stock only slightly, generally dives at a shallow angle. Rarely dives to >100 m, but may go down to 500 m [416]. Only occasionally breaches clear of water.

Vocalisations: Throughout year, but with peaks from midsummer into winter. Include 17–30 Hz moans lasting 15–38 s, sometimes with higher-pitched pulses, and clicks at 6–8 or 21–31 kHz. Low-frequency sounds are very loud (c.188 dB re 1 μPa @ 1 m); thought to allow communication over great distances (possibly even across ocean basins) [256, 1056, 1257].

FEEDING
Diet: Feeds almost exclusively on planktonic crustaceans, mainly euphausiids (*Thysanoessa*, *Nemotoscelis* and *Meganyctiphanes*; and, in Antarctic, *Euphausia* species), although will also take copepods (e.g. *Temora*), and, less frequently, amphipods, cephalopods, and occasionally small fish (perhaps accidentally) [610, 836, 839, 1157, 1257]. Observed feeding on pelagic red crabs *Pleuroncodes planipes* off Baja California [987].

Feeding methods: Thought to feed in deep waters, primarily at 100–200 m [839]. During deep dives, typically remains below surface for 8–15 min (max. 36 min). Feeding occurs primarily during summer, at higher latitudes. Although surface feeding often seen during day, more usually dives deep to plankton swarms during daylight hours, feeding near surface in evening, following ascent of prey in water column [1056]. When feeding just below surface, often surfaces slowly, belly first, exposing throat grooves of ventral pouch, rolling to breathe and expelling water from mouth before diving again. In high krill concentrations, feeds by lunging with mouth wide open, gulping large mouthfuls of plankton and water, before closing mouth and expelling water by muscular action of throat grooves and tongue through still-exposed baleen plates. If prey close to surface, lunges vigorously on sides or vertically, projecting massive lower jaw several metres up through surface [1055].

BREEDING
Reproductive biology summarised in [706, 1257]. Mating thought to occur late autumn–winter, with births during winter. Breeding grounds not known, thought to be in tropical Atlantic off NW Africa. In N Pacific, adults with young seen regularly in winter, Gulf of California. Gestation 10–11 months. Lactation 6–8 months (weaned at c.16 m long), calving interval c.2–3 years. Sexual maturity reached at 5–15 years, but mainly 8–10 years for both sexes.

POPULATION
Lifespan estimated at 30 years [1096], 80–90 years [849]. Annual adult mortality possibly c.10–12%.

Main natural predator is probably killer whale. No reports of attacks in N Atlantic, but 25% of blue whales photographed in Gulf of California have raked scars of killer whale teeth [1056].

Populations everywhere seriously depleted by whaling. N Atlantic population severely reduced by over-exploitation, thought to be no more than 1500, mostly in W where are some signs of recent recovery [971]. No precise estimates for whole region; recent line-transect surveys suggested a maximum of 442 whales [1082], later extrapolated to overall population estimate of 1000–2000 animals [1080], but without details of how derived. These surveys did not cover entire N Atlantic range of species, may be misleading to extrapolate from high-density areas around Iceland. Long-term photo-ID study identified 350 individuals in Gulf of St Lawrence [1056, 1057], but not possible to derive an abundance estimate from this [480].

PARASITES/COMMENSALS

Ectoparasites/commensals: Copepod *Penella balaenopterae* found embedded in the skin; commensal copepod *Balaenophilus unisetus* found on baleen. Diatom *Cocconeis ceticola* may cover part or all of body when in cold waters [1257].

Endoparasites: Nematode *Crassicauda crassicauda*, cestodes *Tetrobothrius affinis*, *T. wilsoni*, *T. schaeferi*, *Priapocephalus grandis*, *Diplogonoporus balaenopterae* and acanthocephalan *Bolbosoma nipponicum*.

RELATIONS WITH HUMANS

Prime target of over-exploitation late 19th–mid 20th century; numbers killed worldwide greatest 1920–1940, peaking at 30 000 in 1930–1931 season. In N Atlantic, 11 000 were taken over this period, mainly off Iceland.

Off Scotland, 85 taken, 1903–1928, from Shetland and 310 from Outer Hebrides [1148]. In 1950–1951, a further 6 captured off Outer Hebrides [181]. Off Ireland, 98 killed 1908–1914, and 27 in 1920, 1922 [367]. Most captures from deep waters beyond edge of continental shelf.

Despite protection from commercial whaling in 1966, catches by USSR continued into the 1970s in secret [184, 248]. Only now is there any sign of a slight recovery of stocks, mainly in E North Pacific [250] but also possibly N Atlantic [965, 971].

Persistent contaminants such as PCBs found in blue whales off E Canada may have impact on reproduction [1056]. Little information on incidental capture in fishing gear but thought to be relatively unimportant. Sound from shipping, including whale-watching boats, may have a negative effect [338]. Collisions with ships reported, California [99]; in St Lawrence, 25% of blue whales photographed have scars attributable to vessel strikes [1056]. Seismic testing during oil and gas exploratory activities also has potential to disturb blue whales in areas like Atlantic Frontier W of British Isles, although this has yet to be demonstrated [352]. With their restricted diet of euphausiid crustaceans, could be particularly vulnerable to climate change [250, 719].

Has strong international and local legal protection (Table 12.1); completely protected since 1994 by IWC, listed by IUCN as Endangered.

LITERATURE

No detailed scientific review since [1257]. Popular reviews include [199, 416], with overview in [1056].

AUTHOR

P.G.H. Evans

SUBORDER ODONTOCETI (TOOTHED WHALES)

FAMILY PHYSETERIDAE (SPERM WHALES)

A family of only 2 genera and 3 species, 2 of which occur, occasionally, in NE Atlantic. Sperm whale *Physeter* is much the largest odontocete, but the 2 species of *Kogia* are small whales, *c*.3 m long. Distinguished by narrow lower jaws with numerous teeth, but toothless upper jaws. Squid specialists. Blunt heads containing spermaceti organ: large bladder full of special liquid wax. Genetically isolated within Odontoceti, perhaps closest to Ziphiidae.

GENUS PHYSETER

Monospecific. Linnaeus used both *P. macrocephalus* and *P. catodon*; former given priority by first reviser (ICZN Code Article 24) [548, 945].

Sperm whale *Physeter macrocephalus*
Physeter macrocephalus Linnaeus, 1758; European Sea, restricted to Berckhey near Wassenaar, The Netherlands [548].
Physeter catodon Linnaeus, 1758, Northern (= N Atlantic) Ocean, restricted to Scheldt Estuary, The Netherlands [548].

Muc-mhara-sputach (Scottish Gaelic); *caisealóid* (Irish Gaelic).

RECOGNITION

Readily distinguished at sea by single blowhole at apex of head, displaced to left, producing low (1.5–5 m), bushy, obliquely left, forward-facing blow (Fig. 12.10). Dark, smooth barrel-shaped 'head', disproportionately large, behind which is low dorsal fin (Plate 13). Forepart of head may show pronounced swollen hump, particularly on left side around blowhole. Usually raises large, triangular, flexible flukes above surface to initiate dives (fluking-up). Ashore, easily distinguished by massive head, long, thin tooth-bearing lower-jaw, with corresponding tooth sockets in upper jaw, and single S-shaped blowhole at front left side of head.

Skull: The only asymmetrical skull of this size (the left naris is much larger, and offset left) with concave premaxilla, frontal region rising to a high, basin-like structure. Mandibles very characteristic; long, narrow fused region indented with sockets for up to 25 pairs of large, peg-like or slightly re-curved teeth. Posterior end of each mandible extends to form broad, relatively thin pan bone. Each mandible resembles an upside-down rifle in shape.

Fig. 12.10 Sperm whale, showing asymmetrical blow through left nostril (*photo P.G.H. Evans*).

DESCRIPTION

Most striking feature is huge, barrel-shaped head; may account for up to 1/3 of body length in males, has long, thin lower jaw slung below (Plate 13). General body colour dark grey or brownish grey. Paler patches on belly in genital area. Inside of mouth, and skin on upper and lower jaw pale cream or white; particularly striking when viewed underwater. Head of male often marked by numerous pale scratches and scars inflicted by teeth of other sperm whales; round impressions due to suckers and tentacles of squid sometimes visible on head. Scarring particularly common on sexually mature males, may lead to anterior portion of head acquiring a very pale coloration with white, callous-like patches on tip of snout. After-part of the body often deeply corrugated. Short, ill-defined grooves in throat region diagnostic of Physeteridae. Large, rounded paddle-like flippers. Small dorsal fin (often topped by white or yellowish rough callus, particularly in mature females); often, several pronounced bumps along spinal ridge running back to insertion of triangular and deeply-notched tail flukes. Flukes quite stiff, with straight or slightly convex trailing edge (Fig. 12.1); have uniform, plain coloration, unlike patterned flukes of humpbacks. Pronounced keel runs along underside of tailstock. Lower jaw contains *c.*20–26 pairs of large (up to 25 cm and 1 kg) peg-like teeth (declining in size towards the front and back). Each fits into a deep matching socket in upper jaw; rudimentary teeth sometimes found between these sockets, vestigial teeth sometimes just erupting. Teeth apparently not essential for feeding, erupt some time after weaning, and not at all in some females. Disproportionate size of head is due to development of 2 huge fatty bodies, spermaceti organ, and, between it and upper jaws, the 'junk' (also containing spermaceti chambers, surrounded by connective tissue), both of which are unique to Physeteridae and thought to be involved in sound production, and possibly also in buoyancy; in addition, the large head in adult males serves as a fighting organ.

RELATIONSHIPS

Closest living relatives are 2 much smaller *Kogia* sp. Despite suggestion that sperm whales more closely related to baleen whales than to other odontocetes [785], current genetic and morphological evidence supports traditional view that they belong within odontocetes, though occupying basal position; separated early in modern cetacean evolution, *c.*20 mya [434, 518, 763, 779].

MEASUREMENTS

Length: newborn 4 m; at sexual maturity 9 m (female), 12 m (male); at physical maturity 11 m, rarely up to 12.5 m (female), 15.8 m, rarely up to 18.5 m (male), though large bulls have become rare after selection by whalers. Weight at physical maturity 13.5 t (female), 44 t (male) [130, 988].

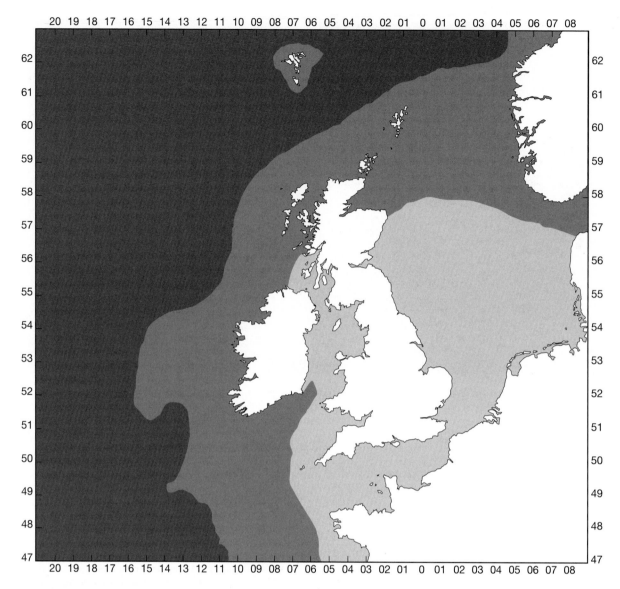

Fig. 12.11 Sperm whale *Physeter macrocephalus*: distribution around British Isles.

VARIATION

Limited understanding of stock structure. Genetic studies fail to identify distinct stocks within ocean basins [725, 727]. Surprisingly little variation even globally (using maternally inherited mtDNA); variously explained by one or more of following interpretations: historical population bottleneck, stronger selection on mitochondrial genome, the demographic consequence of matrilineal social system, or indirect effects of selection of cultural traits transmitted from mothers [725, 726, 1230, 1232].

DISTRIBUTION

Worldwide, in deep waters of all seas. Females and juvenile males have a more limited range than adolescent and mature males, confined to warmer waters, generally with sea surface temperatures (SST) >15° C, between *c.*45° N and *c.*45° S. Young

males accompany females in tropical and subtropical waters but from ages of 14–21 years move increasingly to higher latitudes. Only large males found in highest latitudes, sometimes even close to ice edge, but generally in most productive deep waters.

In E North Atlantic, widely distributed in deep waters off continental shelf, along Mid-Atlantic Ridge and around mid-Atlantic islands (Azores, Madeira, Canaries, Cape Verdes), from Iceland and Norway S to Iberian peninsula and E into Mediterranean. Some known preferred feeding areas for males include deeper waters along continental slope W of Portugal and N of Spain, W and N of British Isles, off Iceland, and Lofoten I. in Norway [360, 973, 1081, 1084]. Areas with aggregations of mixed groups of females with immature males include Azores, Madeira, and Canaries. Calving and mating are known to occur there, as well as in the Caribbean and Mediterranean.

Have been no systematic surveys for sperm whales in British and Irish waters (Fig. 12.11). Some areas of predictable abundance identified, but to some extent reflect patchy distribution of survey effort. Generally, only males come as far N as British Isles; virtually all sightings come from deep waters off continental shelf. Waters around Rockall, to N of Outer Hebrides, N and W of Shetland in Faroe-Shetland Channel, and in Bay of Biscay all have relatively high densities [282, 346, 350, 360, 941, 973, 1135, 1216]. Formerly, sightings off British Isles were almost exclusively of larger males, singly or in small groups; more recently, more records of smaller individuals in larger groups noted, including mass strandings of immature males [350, 360].

Often stray into North Sea when travelling S; causes of such 'navigational errors' still unknown; often become disorientated and eventually stranded, thought to be due to poor navigation abilities in shallow water and lack of food: the North Sea has been called a 'sperm whale trap'. Strandings may concern single animals or groups of up to 16, though groups and hence strandings may become scattered in place and time. Most strandings in the North Sea occur November–February [569, 1100, 1158]; peaks recorded late 18th century and 1990s–early 21st century; poorly understood, but may partly be related to higher sea temperatures, possibly affecting the distribution of squid [928]. Number of strandings on British and Irish coasts increased markedly: 12 in 1913–1948, 31 in 1949–1986 and 53 in 1987–1994 [121, 350]. Unclear whether due to changes in whale distribution, or to increased mortality due to unknown causes. In recent years, have been several well-publicised occurrences of sperm whales (all mature or adolescent males) entrapped in enclosed waters: 2 groups in Scapa Flow (Orkney), 1 in Hebrides, and 1 in the Firth of Forth.

Sightings in British and Irish waters mainly July–December, but increasing evidence of small groups remaining at high latitudes into winter, when most coastal sightings and mass strandings take place [121, 346, 350, 360, 1100, 1158]. During Scottish and Irish whaling, early 20th century, most sperm whales caught June–August [367, 1148]. Some indication of southwards movement in late summer [360].

HABITAT

Mainly offshore either in mid ocean or over submarine canyons at edges of continental shelf or beyond; can occur close to coasts of volcanic and oceanic islands in waters >200 m (and usually 500–2000 m) depth. Concentrations occur in areas a few hundred km across, characterised by relatively high deep-water biomass resulting from increased primary productivity due to upwellings [566]. Occasionally stray into shallow waters; see above.

SOCIAL ORGANISATION AND BEHAVIOUR

Most social of the great whales. In high latitudes, typical group size is 1–2 but tight coordinated groups of 6–10 (occasionally more) may be encountered. Core social units are called 'mixed groups', believed to be matrilines, comprising around 12 adult females plus their calves, and immature male and female offspring [1229, 1232]. Sometimes, 2 or more such groups may travel together for a few days, forming a larger group of *c*.20–30. Typically, females remain to become long-term members of these family units, but young males leave as they reach puberty (from 14–15 years onwards), forming bachelor herds. Members of mixed groups stay together for extended periods (probably for life in the case of females); show communal care (baby-sitting) of young (which possibly extends to communal suckling). Mixed groups may number tens of animals, but are usually spread over several miles while still in contact, so rarely seen together at the surface. Groups of males too, may consist of widely scattered subgroups, which join and split up frequently.

Groupings of sperm whales also spaced out over the ocean at scales of up to *c*.700 km (320 nm), associated with the presence of high relief features [566]. As males get older, form smaller and smaller bachelor groups, and range to higher latitudes. Socially mature adult males associate briefly with matrilineal groups to breed, occasionally fighting with other males. Photo-ID studies (using mainly tail-fluke margins) and radio telemetry have helped understand movement patterns. Females have home ranges generally *c*.1000 km across whereas males roam more widely, and largely seem to forage independently.

Adults spend *c*.75% of their lives in making deep dives for feeding; this continues day and night. Typically spend 10–12 min at the surface (termed 'logging'), blowing strongly and regularly every 10–15 s and moving very slowly (1–4 km/h), before fluking-up to initiate a long deep dive. Dives typically last 25–50 min, exceptionally to 138 min [448, 449, 897, 1043, 1208]. Usually reach depths of 300–1000 m; dives of >2000 m observed [1210]; depths of 3195 m inferred from observation and stomach contents [258, 703]. Members of mixed groups come together at the surface *c*.once a day forming tight socialising/resting aggregations of 6–30 whales. Individuals, particularly juveniles, may breach clear of the surface, or lobtail [1201].

Patterns of migration not well known. In temperate waters, females appear to show a poorly defined seasonal N–S migration; some mature males migrate from high latitudes to join female groups to breed. Recent acoustic surveys indicate that sperm whales are common off the British Isles in winter [234, 1135].

Vocalisations: Very vocal [448, 734, 1213], but makes only short, impulsive, broadband (*c*.0.1–30 kHz) click-type vocalisations. These can be very powerful – up to 223 dB re 1 μPa @ 1 m [804]. Long, regular click sequences, produced at rates of around 2/s during deep dives, are probably used for echolocation; stereotyped patterns of clicks (3 to *c*.20 clicks lasting 0.2–2 s), termed 'codas', heard from socialising female groups, may be more important for communication. Groups of females have distinctive coda repertoires, probably acquired culturally from within family units. Slow, ringing clicks or 'clangs' repeated every 6–8 s are produced almost entirely by large males; function unclear, may be to attract females or repel other males. Accelerating series of clicks, called 'creaks', are thought to represent foraging attempts towards potential prey. Typically quiet at the surface, except during periods of social activity.

FEEDING

Diet: Varied, dominated by medium-sized mesopelagic squid; males tend to take larger items than females, and more likely to eat demersal fish, from high latitudes [608, 988]. Most prey have mantle lengths of 20–100 cm; in N Atlantic, are mostly Onychoteuthidae and Ommastrephidae, although giant *Architeuthis* and bottom-living octopus also taken. In some areas (e.g. Iceland) deep-living fish, including rays, sharks, lantern fish, lump-suckers, red fish *Sebastes* and gadids, are the dominant prey [262, 747]. Crustaceans very occasionally eaten, including giant mysids and benthic crabs [608]. Stomach contents from recent European mass strandings often empty, but otherwise revealed squid *Gonatus* sp. the most important prey (likely ingested in N Atlantic); both deep-sea octopus and coastal species also frequent [1033]. *Loligo forbesi* and octopus also found in Scottish specimens, *Histioteuthis bonnellii* and *Teuthowenia megalops* in one of the Danish animals.

Sperm whales apparently dominate this deep ocean trophic level in terms of biomass removed, estimated globally at *c*.100 million t/year, and comparable with current annual catch by all human marine fisheries [1232].

BREEDING

Mating system poorly understood. For most of their lives, mature males and females live hundreds or thousands of miles apart. Mating takes place over an extended season (probably February–June in N Atlantic); believed that largest 'prime' males account for most matings, migrate to lower latitudes to achieve this, but not all mature males migrate to female areas each year. Tooth scars suggest fierce competitions take place between males. Males join mixed groups for short periods, when breeding presumably takes place. In N Atlantic, single young born mainly June–September, after 16–17 months gestation. Fetal sex ratio is *c*.1:1. Lactation extended, at least 19–42 months, but some young continue to take milk up to 13 years; late sucking apparently primarily for social reasons ('comfort' behaviour). Solid food generally first taken after 1 year. Sperm whales have one of the lowest breeding rates of any mammal, with calving intervals of 3–15 years (generally around 5 years, but varying with region and history of exploitation, and declining with age). Sexual maturity reached around 18–19 years by males, 7–12 years by female, but males generally do not play active role in breeding before their late 20s. Growth rates very slow, physical maturity not reached until around age 30 years (female) and 50 years (male). Breeding parameters reviewed in [130, 988].

POPULATION

Longevity estimated as 65–70 years, and annual adult mortality low at *c*.5–8% (slightly higher in males) [956, 988]. Once a common, ecologically dominant, animal in offshore waters. Numbers substantially reduced by whaling. In N Atlantic alone, over 20 000 animals have been taken since 1950. Numbers now recovering, though at an unknown rate. No reliable estimates for current N Atlantic or world populations; likely to be a few hundred thousand globally.

MORTALITY

Although killer whale and sharks are potential predators, and harassment by pilot whales has been observed, sperm whales are largely capable of driving them away. Females rapidly form a cluster either in 'marguerite' or 'wagon wheel' formation where members of group either place their heads together to form a circle or face their attackers in a tight group facing out, using their jaws for defence [1232]. Young calves remain protected in the centre, and adults may assist one another in defence.

PARASITES/COMMENSALS

Remarkably clear of external parasites. Cyamids

(notably *Neocyomus physeter*) usually occur. Remora frequently attach to calves and juveniles. 24 species of parasitic helminths reported [988], though air-sinus flukes *Nasitrema*, lungworms Pseudaliidae and kidney worms *Crassicauda* surprisingly absent. Cestodes include *Phyllobothrium*, *Monorygma*, and *Tetrabothrius*; nematodes include *Anisakis simplex* and *A. physeteris*; and acanthocephalans include *Bolbosoma* and *Corynosoma*.

RELATIONS WITH HUMANS

Since early 18th century, sperm whales have been especially valuable to whaling industry for waxy spermaceti (used originally for lamps and candles, later as a lubricant in engineering and textile industries), blubber, meat for fertiliser, and ambergris (an intestinal deposit highly valued as a fixative in cosmetic industry). Sperm whale populations, including those W of GB, were the target of devastating worldwide, open-boat whaling by 'Yankee' whalers in the 18th–19th centuries. Later, after populations of most baleen whale species had become depleted, sperm whales formed main target of modern whaling industry. In 1903–1929, Scottish whale fishery took 19 sperm whales off Shetland, and 76 off Outer Hebrides; 1 taken off Hebrides in 1950–1951 [181, 1148]. Off Ireland, 48 taken 1908–1914, and a further 15 1920–1922 [367]. Most catches occurred in deep waters, just off the edge of the continental shelf. Recent whaling for this species in N Atlantic occurred around Iceland, Spain, Madeira and Azores. The last catches were made in 1987.

Sperm whales are known to interact with some fisheries, including long lines and deep water trawls; in Mediterranean, young sperm whales sometimes caught in drift nets or set nets, and may be victims of ship strikes, particularly fast ferries, in areas such as the Canaries and W Mediterranean. Some killed by ingesting plastic. Contaminant levels usually somewhat higher than in baleen whales. Relatively high cadmium levels probably natural [534].

Nowadays, sperm whales are the mainstay of 2 commercial whale-watching operations in the NE Atlantic. Large males can be observed off Lofoten I., and mixed groups in Azores, Madeira and Canaries. Legally protected in European, British and Irish waters (Table 12.1).

LITERATURE

Most detailed treatment is [1232], which updates and expands upon [988]; popular introduction [449]; succinct overview [1231].

PRINCIPAL AUTHORS

J.C.D. Gordon & P.G.H. Evans

GENUS *Kogia*

Contains 2 closely related species, pygmy sperm whale *K. breviceps* and dwarf sperm whale *K. sima*. Are among the least known cetaceans and were only recently separated [482]. Only pygmy sperm whale has been recorded from British and Irish waters.

Pygmy sperm whale *Kogia breviceps*
Physeter breviceps Blainville, 1838; S Africa.

Caisealóid beag (Irish Gaelic).

RECOGNITION

Both *Kogia* spp. have robust bodies. Surface slowly, with indistinct blow. May lie still at surface, showing back and dorsal fin. *Kogia* sp. difficult to tell apart at sea. Both have falcate dorsal fins but that of pygmy sperm whale proportionally smaller: typically 5–9% of snout–fin length (9–16% in dwarf sperm whale) [745]. May be confused with blunt-headed dolphins of similar size; distinguished by slower movements and square head (Plate 16). Noticeably smaller than similar-looking beaked whales. Usually has crescent-shaped, light marking on side of head between eye and flippers ('false gill'), giving head a shark-like appearance.

Skull resembles miniature sperm whale. Blowhole slightly left of midline, placed further back in pygmy than dwarf sperm whale; tip of snout to blowhole is 10.5–13% of body length (in dwarf sperm whale, <10% of body length). Lower jaw narrow, underslung, ends well behind the tip of the snout, carries 10–16 pairs of sharp pointed teeth; no upper teeth (dwarf sperm whale sometimes has 1–3 pairs of teeth in upper jaw). No reported sexual dimorphism.

DESCRIPTION

Conical head, 1/6 of body length (cf. 1/3 in sperm whale), which becomes squarer with age. No beak. Blowhole on top of head, but right naris passes through a valve structure ('museau de singe') unique to Physeteridae, thought to be used for sound production. Oil-filled spermaceti organ in *Kogia* is small, lies above skull behind a large melon [203]. Short, ill-defined grooves in throat region. Body dark blue-grey on back, outer margins of flippers and upper surface of tail flukes, lightening to pale grey on flanks and dull white belly (sometimes with pinkish tinge). Skin may have wrinkled appearance. Flippers relatively long (up to 14% of body length), wide at the base tapering to rounded point. Low, slightly re-curved dorsal fin placed just behind centre of back. Tail with concave trailing edge, distinct median notch. Low and inconspicuous blow during slow sluggish roll. Unlike sperm whale, no obvious sexual dimorphism. Skull of both *Kogia* spp. has an unusually short rostrum (the shortest among living cetaceans), and marked asymmetry with no independent jugal, a well-developed facial depression, and a pronounced sagittal septum extending from the narial aperture to the vertex. In pygmy sperm whale, this is broad near its apex and slopes gradually into cranial fossae on each side (dwarf sperm whale has a narrow steep-sided septum, often pinched posteriorly) [203, 1016]. Cranial fossae are elongated anterioposteriorly, posterior walls slope gradually from the dorsal rim of the skull (in dwarf sperm whale, dorsal rim of each fossa is steep, giving a cupped appearance to the skull).

RELATIONSHIPS

Dwarf sperm whale *K. sima* is closely related, only recently distinguished as a separate species; tends to inhabit warmer waters [203], in E North Atlantic, recorded from Senegal [203], Spain [1172], and France [283, 331], as well as W Mediterranean [78]; might yet occur off British Isles.

MEASUREMENTS

Length: newborn *c*.1.2 m; at sexual maturity *c*.2.3–2.7 m (both sexes); adult maximum *c*.3.30 m (both sexes) [203, 937]. Typical weight 300–400 kg, but 450 kg male reported from E Canada [766].

VARIATION

No information.

DISTRIBUTION

Poorly known; apparently worldwide in tropical, subtropical and temperate seas of both hemispheres. Rarely sighted, most information from strandings, mostly on coasts of N America. Records in N Atlantic range from equatorial waters N to Nova Scotia in W and British Isles in E.

On Atlantic coasts of British Isles, 12 strandings: singles in Co. Clare, in April 1966; Co. Galway, October 1985; Glamorgan, October 1980; Devon, October 1993 and January 1997; a live stranding in Pembrokeshire, October 1997; singles in Co. Mayo, sometime in 1998 and in July 1999; an adult and calf, live stranded in Loch Ryan, Wigtownshire, October 1999; singles in Co. Galway in June 2000; Devon, January 2002; and Co. Kerry, July 2002 [120, 360, 408, 1040, 1073]. Also strandings from Netherlands [883], Atlantic coasts of France [330, 333], Spain [853], Portugal [978, 1060, 1061], and the Azores [759, 1143]. Also 3 sightings reported from waters around British Isles: 1 in North Sea off NE England, August 1979;

2 in deep waters off NW Ireland, on successive days in June 1982 [346, 360].

HISTORY

No fossils attributable to this species, but Kogiinae is represented in the Pliocene [53]; a few, incomplete, fossils listed in [828].

HABITAT

Occurs in deep waters; dietary analysis indicates feeding in deep zone of continental shelf and slope waters [938, 1040].

SOCIAL ORGANISATION AND BEHAVIOUR

Poorly known. Apparently not gregarious, observations mainly of single individuals or small groups of 3–4, rarely up to 6 animals [937]. Slight sexual size dimorphism, small group size and small relative testis size all suggest a promiscuous mating system [937]. Relatively easy to approach, although it rarely approaches vessels [607, 787]. Occasionally breaches, but more usually lies apparently motionless on the surface. A relatively slow swimmer, perhaps *c*.5–6 km/h, although capable of much more rapid bursts of speed [814].

Vocalisations: Not studied in detail; echolocation clicks recorded at 60–200 kHz (dominant frequency 120 kHz) [204, 1028]. Possible sound production mechanisms suggested in [260].

FEEDING

Diet: Predominantly mesopelagic squid, such as *Histioteuthis, Chiroteuthis,* and *Lycoteuthis,* also fish and crustacea [759, 766, 938, 1040]. Females with calves take more inshore species whereas adult males consume cephalopods that inhabit continental shelf edge and slope [938].

BREEDING

Breeding season unknown in N Atlantic. Off S Africa, conceptions occur April–September, with prolonged calving season March–August [937]. Gestation period thought to be *c*.11 months [787, 937]. Age at sexual maturity estimated at *c*.4 years (both sexes), with ovulation in females occurring every *c*.1.5 years (17.7 months, assuming 1 dentinal growth layer group = 1 year) [937]. 24% of all mature animals examined along coast of S Africa found to be simultaneously pregnant and lactating, indicating a postpartum oestrus [937]. Lactation thought to last *c*.12 months [937]. Lifespan unknown.

POPULATION

No estimates for population size or status, nor on sex ratio, age structure or mortality rates.

MORTALITY

A few reports of evidence of attacks by killer whales and sharks, although the species of shark was not identified [1040]; false killer whale also a possible predator.

PARASITES AND PATHOGENS

Cyamid whale lice have been reported attached to infected tissue from a wound on the flanks of an individual [206]; nematodes have been found in abundance in the forestomach, and trematodes encysted in the blubber, particularly ventrally and in anal region [203, 288, 828]. Heart failure and pneumonia have each been noted in stranded animals, although their role in mortality is rarely known [166, 203, 870].

RELATIONS WITH HUMANS

The status of the species is unknown but there are reports of mortality caused by a variety of human activities. Occasionally in various harpoon fisheries, e.g. E Caribbean, Indonesia, Japan [203]. Found in fish markets in Sri Lanka [677], estimated >80/year die there in fishing gear [679]. Fisheries-related mortality also reported Caribbean coast of Colombia, coastal Brazil; Japanese squid gillnets may take incidentally, N Pacific [882, 919]. Stranded animals frequently show evidence of collisions with vessels [766]; may move away from or dive to avoid aircraft or large vessels [818, 993]. Very little information on pollutant levels; high zinc levels (163 mg/kg wet weight) in 1 female, Argentina, but generally low levels of other metals and organochlorines (DDT, PCBs) from this and 5 other individuals from SE USA, S Africa and Australia [622, 643, 673, 741]. Plastic bags in stomachs of some individuals may have prevented feeding, led to death [203, 1016, 1117].

Legally protected in European, British and Irish waters (Table 12.1).

LITERATURE

Most recent reviews [203, 765]; original biological data [1016]; genetic variation [237].

AUTHORS

R. Leaper & P.G.H. Evans

FAMILY ZIPHIIDAE (BEAKED WHALES)

A small family of 6 genera, 21 species [1245], of which 3 genera and 6 species occur in NE Atlantic. Characterised by obvious elongate beak, sharply demarcated from prominent melon, and most species have few or no teeth – none in most females, 1–2 pairs of lower tusks in males (only the southern *Tasmacetus* has numerous teeth, like other odontocetes). Mostly occur in deep water, specialise in eating squid. Occupy position in Odontoceti above Physeteridae, but basal to all others.

GENUS *Hyperoodon*

A genus of 2 species, the southern *H. planifrons* and northern *H. ampullatus*. Largest ziphiid, distinguished by enlarged, bulbous head. Males have a single pair of lower tusks at the tip of the jaws (as also in *Ziphius*, some *Mesoplodon*) (Fig. 12.12).

Northern bottlenose whale *Hyperoodon ampullatus*

Balaena ampullatus Forster, 1770; Maldon, Essex, England.
Balaena rostrata Muller, 1776.
Delphinus butskopf Bonnaterre, 1789; R. Thames.
Hyperoodon butskopf Lacépède, 1804; near London.
Hyperoodon bidens Fleming, 1828; Essex.
Hyperoodon latifrons Gray, 1846; Orkney (based on different skull morphology of males).

Bottle-nosed whale or bottlenose whale, latter favoured [551]; *miol bolgshrónach* (Irish Gaelic).

RECOGNITION

Large bulbous head (particularly in male) and short bottle-nosed beak. Usually 1 pair of teeth in lower jaw (of male, rarely visible on live animals), no teeth visible in mouth of female. Solid bony maxillary crests on sides of skull becoming larger and heavier with age, especially in males.

DESCRIPTION

Largest of British beaked whales, distinguished from other ziphiids by large bulbous forehead and distinct short dolphin-like beak (Plate 14). Older males have single pair of conical teeth (up to 41 mm long), erupting at tip of lower jaw; in females, these rarely appear through gum. 2nd pair sometimes buried in gums behind 1st; minute vestigial teeth may be embedded in gums of upper and lower jaws. Pair of V-shaped throat grooves. Coloration very variable, from chocolate brown to yellowish-brown above, caused by diatom coating on skin; lighter on flanks and belly, with irregular patches or blotches; male forehead becomes lighter with age [145, 458].

Plate 14

A Minke whale *Balaenoptera acutorostrata* **B** Northern bottlenose whale *Hyperoodon ampullatus*
C Killer whale *Orcinus orca* **D** Cuvier's beaked whale *Ziphius cavirostris* **E** Long-finned pilot whale *Globicephala melas*

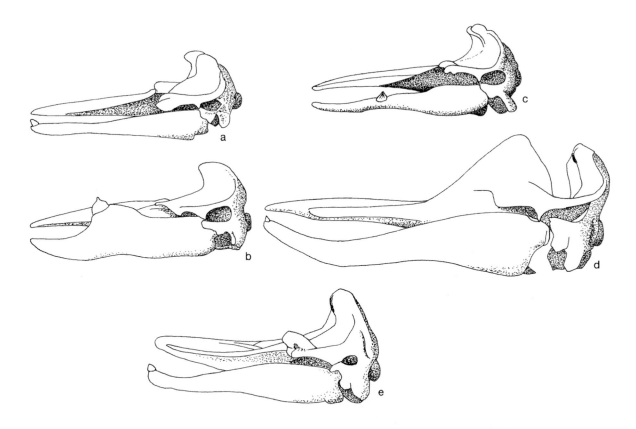

Fig. 12.12 Skulls of male beaked whales, to show position of tusks (a) True's; (b) Blainville's; (c) Sowerby's; (d) Bottlenose; (e) Cuvier's *(drawn to scale by D.W. Yalden, after [1212]).*

Newborn calves grey, with dark eye-patches and light-coloured head. Long, fairly robust, cylindrical body. Single crescent-shaped blowhole in depression behind forehead giving single low (<2 m) bushy blow, slightly forward-pointing. Short tapering flippers, can fold into underlying indentation in body. Falcate dorsal fin of moderate height (30 cm), 2/3 along back. Broad, un-notched tail flukes with concave trailing edge. At sea, usually seen in groups of 1–4, sometimes up to 14. Dives generally 30–40 min, max. 70 min [536]. May be confused with Cuvier's or Sowerby's beaked whales, minke whale, or sperm whale. Main distinguishing feature is shape of head.

RELATIONSHIPS

Anti-tropical distribution of northern and southern bottlenose whales prevents interbreeding; relationships to other ziphiids unresolved [763]. Supposed equatorial Indo-Pacific bottlenose whales [935] confirmed as Longman's beaked whales *Indopacetus pacificus* [289].

MEASUREMENTS

Dimorphic, males larger than females. Length: newborn *c*.3.4 m; at sexual maturity *c*.6.9 m (female), *c*.7.5 m (male); adult 7.0–8.5 m (female), 8.0–9.5 m (male). Weight *c*.6–8 t.

DISTRIBUTION

Temperate and Arctic N Atlantic, from ice-edge to Azores, particularly in deep waters. Main regions of concentration, identified from former whaling activities, appear to be W of Norway, W of Spitsbergen, N of Iceland, Davis Strait off Labrador, off Faroes and in the Gully off E Canada [968]. Majority of sightings and strandings off British coasts, July–September [352, 360, 407]. Strandings recorded on all coasts of GB and Ireland [404, 406–408, 485, 1073]. One immature female famously swam up R. Thames, London, 19–21 January 2006. In adjacent waters, sighted primarily in waters >1000 m depth, such as Faroe–Shetland Channel, Rockall Trough, and S Bay of Biscay [340, 346, 360, 973, 1194, 1215, 1236] (Fig. 12.13).

Increased stranding frequency in British waters in late summer–autumn cited as evidence of S migration from polar regions [407, 872], reported most commonly between Iceland and Jan Mayen late April–early June, then off Scotland June–July [145, 1148] However, alternative explanations equally plausible, and S migration hypothesis contradicted by sightings also off Azores during summer [264]; stomach contents of one off Faroes, August, suggested that had recently been much further S [261]. Genetic studies also show little

687

link between populations that might be caused by seasonal migration [290].

HISTORY

Commercial whaling of bottlenose whales began in 1850 by Scottish whalers [776]. Commercial fishery ceased in 1973, when GB banned import of whale meat for pet food [968]. See Relations with humans, below.

HABITAT

Primarily found in waters >500 m [110, 111, 540, 973, 1194]. Perhaps associated with submarine canyons [540, 1246], possibly due to influx of squid or other food [539].

SOCIAL ORGANISATION AND BEHAVIOUR

British populations little known; most information from 10-year study in the Gully, E Canada. Groups may contain any mix of age and sex classes. Juvenile whales (from newborn to 3 years old) seen with different escorts, although mostly associated with presumed mother. Most associations between individuals appear to be brief, but males sometimes form bonds that last for years [459]. Aggressive behaviour rare, although conflict between mature males observed [456].

Often curious, will approach vessels. Also show caring behaviour, will remain beside wounded companions, making them particularly vulnerable to hunting. Dive deeply, to at least 1450 m, for up to 70 min [536]. After a long dive, remain at the surface for >10 min, blowing regularly, but may remain at surface for hours at a time. Rarely show tail flukes at onset of dive. Rarely exhibit percussive behaviour; lobtailing seen more often than breaching.

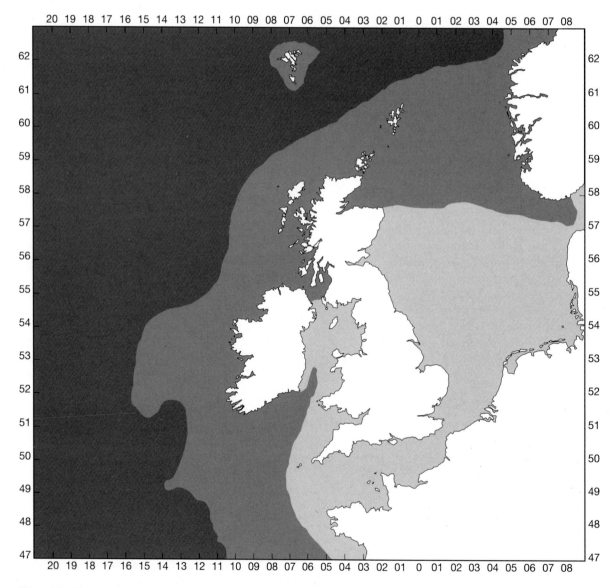

Fig. 12.13 Northern bottlenose whale *Hyperoodon ampullatus*: distribution around British Isles.

Fig. 12.14 Northern bottlenose whale, adult female and calf *(photo S. Hooker)*.

Vocalisations: Includes high-frequency (24 kHz) echolocation clicks [537]. Whistles (3–16 kHz) and chirps (3–16 kHz) lasting 115–850 ms recorded from one encounter [1248], but nearby pilot whales may have confounded this, since not found in a more detailed study [537].

FEEDING
Diet: Mainly adult squid *Gonatus*, off British Isles likely to be *G. fabricii* [261, 538, 693, 1034]. Other squid and fish (including herring *Clupea harengus* and redfish *Sebastes* sp.) occasionally eaten [111].

Feeding methods: Appears to forage largely at or near sea floor [536].

BREEDING
Mating system unknown, though possibly some male territoriality [540]. Young born late spring–summer; gestation period >12 months [110]. Lactation period uncertain, at least 1 year, calving interval at least 2–3 years (Fig. 12.14). Sexual maturity reached at 7–11 years in male, *c*.11 years in female [239].

POPULATION
No detailed population estimates for N Atlantic; IWC N Atlantic sightings surveys (NASS), 1987 and 1989, suggested *c*.40 000 [829, 1178]. Still locally abundant [466, 968]. Former N Atlantic stock poorly estimated, but surely heavily depleted by whaling. Sex ratio likely to be 1:1. Longevity at least 37 years [239], probably much more.

MORTALITY
Causes of mortality little known; killer whales and sharks likely predators, especially of young animals. Norwegian whalers observed attacks by killer whales on a free-swimming animal, as well as 2 harpooned animals [590, 591].

PARASITES AND PATHOGENS
Include lice and barnacles [461, 872] and several species of endoparasites mainly from the digestive system [288, 302].

RELATIONS WITH HUMANS
Previously hunted for oil and animal food. Scottish and Norwegian whalers took in total 60 000 throughout N Atlantic, 1850–1920 [535]. Since 1920, yearly catches, primarily by Norwegian whalers, much reduced and total of *c*.5900 taken [776]. Small numbers taken off Scotland early in 1900s, though preference given to larger rorquals. In 1908–1927, 26 captured around Shetland and 1 in Outer Hebrides [1148]. Most catches in deep waters off edge of continental shelf.

As yet no attempt at commercial whale-watching, due to offshore nature of distribution.

Contaminant load investigated for one stranded specimen in North Sea; PCB and DDT levels similar to other local cetaceans [541], relatively high levels of cadmium in liver [486]. Oil and gas development off Hebrides and in N North Sea may present acoustic and contaminant threats; like other beaked whales, *Hyperoodon* may be susceptible to trauma induced by mid-frequency active sonar and other loud sound sources [281, 757]. Ship collisions implicated in some strandings [120].

Legally protected in European, British and Irish waters (Table 12.1). Designated as 'Lower Risk (conservation dependent)' [971], and 'completely protected' under management procedures of IWC.

LITERATURE
Review of species [776]; summary for genus [455]; review of past exploitation and current conservation status, N Atlantic [968].

AUTHORS
S.K. Hooker, S. Gowans & P.G.H. Evans

GENUS *Ziphius*

A monospecific genus, a large whale with a single pair of tusks at the tip of the lower jaws (as also in *Hyperoodon*), head much less bulbous, skull without the huge maxillary 'wings'. (Fig. 12.12). Short beak when compared to *Mesoplodon*, leading to alternative name, goose-beaked whale.

Cuvier's beaked whale *Ziphius cavirostris*
Ziphius cavirostris G. Cuvier, 1823; mouth of the Rhône, France.

Cuvier's whale, goose-beaked whale; *miol mór le gob gé* (Irish Gaelic).

RECOGNITION
Is 2nd-largest beaked whale in European waters, with the typical ziphiid pattern (small fin located in the middle 1/3 of the back), and often pale body. In addition, it has a sloping (or slightly bulbous) forehead with short, indistinct beak and upcurved mouth line. This not easy to distinguish, can be confused with *Mesoplodon* because both tend to break the surface beak-first, making it look longer. Often pale head and anterior back (entire back sometimes white in older animals); body often scarred (Plate 14), and sometimes covered with patches of yellow diatoms. One pair of small conical teeth at tip of lower jaw in males.

DESCRIPTION
Long stout body with small head; concave or slightly S-shaped mouth line (likened to goose beak) (Fig. 12.15). Beak generally shorter than in other ziphiids, mostly ill-defined, with slightly protruding lower jaw. Single pair of conical teeth (up to c.60 mm long and c.35 mm in diameter) at tip of lower jaw, erupting only in adult males and then protruding forward from mouth. 2nd pair of teeth or tiny rudimentary teeth sometimes present [165]. Converging pair of throat grooves. Coloration variable; most commonly brownish grey but sometimes blue-grey; paler grey or even white head and (anterior) back (particularly in older males); often has linear pale scars on back and sides and cream or white oval blotches on

Fig. 12.15 Cuvier's beaked whale. Note pale body and distinctive shape of head *(photo N. Aguilar)*.

690

sides and posterior abdomen. Sometimes yellow diatoms in patches over body. Distance from snout to blowhole less than in *Hyperoodon*, forehead far less bulbous. Low, inconspicuous blow that can be heard at a distance in calm weather. Small, narrow flippers with pointed tip, located low down on flanks, fitting in a depression of the body. Dorsal fin varying from small, triangular to relatively tall (up to 38 cm), sickle-shaped, situated about 2/3 along back. Somewhat concave tail flukes, like other beaked whales, normally lacking distinct median notch.

Skull relatively short and broad, with well-developed cranial vertex and enlarged, asymmetrical nasal bones overhanging the bony nares (Fig. 12.12). No bony maxillary crests on rostrum, but (in adult males) a densely ossified mesorostral canal and a characteristic prenarial basin.

RELATIONSHIPS
No congeners, relationships to other ziphiids unresolved [763, 962].

MEASUREMENTS
Length: newborn *c.*2.7 m; at sexual maturity *c.*5.8 m (female), *c.*5.5 m (male); max. recorded length 7.0 m (both sexes). Weight up to *c.*3 t.

VARIATION
No information on geographical variation or genetic polymorphisms.

DISTRIBUTION
Most widespread of beaked whales, probably worldwide in warm and warm–temperate seas. Like other beaked whales, appears to favour deeper waters, occurring off continental shelf edges. Apparently prefers warmer waters, rarely recorded as far N as British Isles (1 record from Iceland). Further S, is the most common ziphiid off the Iberian peninsula, in the Bay of Biscay, and the only species occurring regularly in the Mediterranean. Seen year-round in the Canaries.

Around British Isles, only 6 well-documented sightings: singles in the N North Sea, E of Orkney, August 1980; off Co. Cork, S Ireland, August 1984; SW of Mizen Head, Co. Cork, July 1987; 2–3 individuals with a mixed pod of long-finned pilot whales and bottlenose dolphins off NW Ireland, August 1987; 3 off Skye, September 1988; and 2 off Co. Cork, June 1998 [340, 346, 360]. By contrast, at least 12 sightings 1995–1998, (total of 36 individuals) from ferry surveys in Bay of Biscay (S of 46° N), 75% in February–May [1237].

On coasts of British Isles, 65 strandings in 1913–2005, of which 41 since 1963 [120, 360, 408, 1073, 1022, 1074]. All but 2 of these from the Atlantic seaboard – SW England, S and W Ireland, W Scotland and the N Isles. Almost 50% occurred January–March. Only 6 well-documented records from the North Sea – 2 strandings on Swedish W coast, April 1867 and August 1872; 1 stranded, Scheldt Estuary, Netherlands, July 1914; 1 near Wells, Norfolk, August 1989; another at Walcott near Happisburgh, Norfolk; and 1 near Dunkerque, France in March 1980 [360, 1192].

HISTORY
Frequent fossil remains of the early ziphiid, *Choroeziphius*, found in the Tertiary North Sea area, but supposed fossil ziphiid *Ziphius* (*Dolichodon*) *geelongensis*, early Pliocene, Australia, is erroneous [397].

HABITAT
Mainly found in deep waters, possibly favouring continental or island slopes at depths of 500–3000 m. Sightings from Greece along shelf slope in waters 650–1000 m deep [943, 944]; in NW Mediterranean, most sightings from depths of 750–2000 m [815].

SOCIAL ORGANISATION AND BEHAVIOUR
Not often seen; most sightings are singletons or small groups of 2–12 (occasionally up to 25) [403, 517, 678, 685, 815]. Mean group size, NW Mediterranean, 2.3; larger groups partially segregated by age and sex [815]. Social organisation unknown; extensive scarring on dorsal surface and flanks of males, presumed due to intraspecific aggression [806].

Vocalisations: D-tag studies reveal main vocalizations to be echolocation clicks and buzzes [582]. Usual clicks are FM, have a characteristic upward sweep shape, with most energy at 30–50 kHz [1265]. Mostly restricted to deep, long foraging dives, up to 85 min and to depths of 1990 m; average foraging dives 58 min, to 1070 m [1167]. Echolocation used in the deepest part of the dives, normally >500 m; vocal phase averages 33 min [582, 1167]. Foraging dives are usually interspersed by series of shorter (mean 15 min) and shallower (mean 250 m) dives with no vocal activity. Function of these intermediate dives still unknown; may relate to processing lactic acid produced during long foraging dives [1167]. Average duration of surfacing intervals 2 min; occasionally may stay on surface for long periods and before foraging dives usually surfaces for 4–5 min. Rarely breaches, but often shows head when surfacing, presumably after a deep dive.

FEEDING
Diet: Mainly a great variety of squid; particularly

Histioteuthis reversa and *H. bonnellii*, also *Gonatus* spp., *Todarodes sagittatus, Ancistoteuthis lichtensteini, Heteroteuthis dispar, Chiroteuthis veranyi, Octopoteuthis sicula, Ommastrephes bartramii,* and members of the families Brachioteuthidae, Cranchiidae, Lycoteuthidae, Onychoteuthidae, and Pholidoteuthidae; sometimes crustaceans and fish, including Gadiformes such as *Antimora* sp. and blue whiting *Micromesistius poutassou,* but the latter may not be primary prey [137, 221, 259, 304, 374, 378, 400, 685, 806, 850, 880, 939, 1035, 1017, 1157, 1197].

Feeding methods: During the vocal phase of each foraging dive, performs *c.*30 buzzes that are interpreted as prey capture attempts [582, 1167]. Average of 12 foraging dives/24 h performed during day and night.

BREEDING
Little information. Possibly protracted breeding season. No seasonal pattern found [517]. Length of largest reported fetus 267 cm; shortest calf 269 cm [774]. No information on gestation or lactation periods.

POPULATION
No population estimates. Longevity >36 years for males and *c.*30 years for females, assuming that 1 dentinal growth layer group in teeth = 1 year [1017].

Photo-ID studies suggest territorial fidelity to certain areas (Hawaii, Canaries); also observed off Bahamas, although individuals identified there not re-sighted since mass mortality in 2000, related to the use of mid-frequency military sonar [252].

MORTALITY
Killer whale observed feeding on a fresh carcass, Mediterranean [860]; oval scars, thought to be due to cookie-cutter shark *Isistius brasiliensis,* found on skin of many specimens from the Canaries [806].

PARASITES AND PATHOGENS
Commensals include barnacles *Xenobalanus* from the flukes and dorsal fin [96, 168, 806] and *Conchoderma* on erupted apical teeth [398, 435, 787]; parasitic copepods *Pennella* found in blubber of flanks [806]. Nematodes *Anisakis* [398, 618, 806, 889] and *Crassicauda* [302, 806], and cestodes *Phyllobothrium* encysted in the blubber [620, 806, 1157] recorded.

RELATIONS WITH HUMANS
Occasionally taken in fisheries for small cetaceans off Japan [850, 880] and E Caribbean [200, 205, 311]. Incidentally caught in many types of fisheries [311, 555].

Few specimens analysed for pollutants. A mature male, stranded New Zealand, had low levels of pesticides and mercury [398]. 4 mature animals, stranded Bermuda, contained moderate levels of PCBs and pesticides [638]. Single animals in S Adriatic (Italy) and W Mediterranean (Corsica) had relatively high levels of total mercury in the liver and cadmium in the kidney [411, 1129]. In 10 *Ziphius* stranded in Kyparissiakos Gulf (SE Ionian Sea, Greece) in May 1996, DDT 11.2–35.1 μg/g wet wt (mean value 20.9 μg/g), PCBs (sum of 13 congeners) 3.0–12.4 μg/g wet wt (mean value 7.5 μg/g) [495].

Military sonar in mid-frequency range (1–10 kHz) shown to cause mass strandings of ziphiids, particularly Cuvier's beaked whale [355, 369, 402, 403, 757].

Legally protected in European, British and Irish waters (Table 12.1).

LITERATURE
General review [517]; European information well reviewed in [1000].

AUTHORS
P.G.H. Evans, C.S. Smeenk & K. Van Waerebeek

GENUS *Mesoplodon*

A genus of *c.*14 poorly known species, found in deeper waters of all oceans, but mostly known from occasional strandings: many known from only a handful of specimens. All morphologically rather similar. Differ from other ziphiids in more slender (less bulbous) head and smaller size. A single pair of teeth in the lower jaws, erupting from the gum only in mature males, their shape and position diagnostic for the species; may be near the tip or up to 1/2 way back, flattened or re-curved (Fig. 12.12). Believed to take mesopelagic squid and fish [775], thought to employ a sucking action when feeding; have pleated throats [520]. Phylogenetic relationships within family unresolved [763, 942].

Sowerby's beaked whale *Mesoplodon bidens*
Physeter bidens Sowerby, 1804; Moray, Scotland.

Sowerby's whale, North Sea beaked whale; *miol mór gobach an tuaisceart* (Irish Gaelic).

RECOGNITION
Rarely seen at sea, difficult to distinguish from other *Mesoplodon*, but usually dark brown or grey uniform coloration on back. Shares their prominent forehead bulge, sickle-shaped dorsal fin almost 2/3 along back, and inconspicuous blow. Diagnostic features are long, slender beak and

Fig. 12.16 Sowerby's beaked whale, showing narrow elongate beak characteristic of *Mesoplodon*, posteriorly placed tusks of this species *(photo J. Benney)*.

moderately arched lower jaw, with 1 pair of laterally compressed triangular teeth (only visible in adult male) placed slightly behind midpoint of gape (Fig. 12.16).

DESCRIPTION

Long, slender, spindle-shaped body, small head with bulge in front of crescent-shaped blowhole and well-defined slender beak, pair of deep grooves forming V-shape below (Plate 15). Relatively small flippers, 1/7–1/9 body length, often tucked into flipper pockets. Dorsal fin triangular or slightly sickle-shaped, almost 2/3 along back. Un-notched tail flukes have trailing edge slightly concave. Dark grey coloration, paler on belly, with light spots and, especially in adult males, single linear scars scattered over back and flanks. Young animals have lighter bellies and fewer spots. Pair of teeth extruding outside of mouth in adult males, set on rising curve of lower jawline slightly behind midpoint of gape; project backwards, then slightly forwards at tip, up to 3 cm exposed above gum. In females and young, are smaller, concealed beneath gum.

Premaxillae project anteriorly to nasals at vertex of skull, when viewed from above, rostrum slender, not dorsoventrally deepened. Teeth located at posterior limit of mandibular symphysis: no other N Atlantic beaked whale species has tooth sockets overlapping posterior limit of symphysis (Fig. 12.12).

RELATIONSHIPS
One of 5 species of *Mesoplodon* in N Atlantic; relationships unresolved [962].

MEASUREMENTS
Length: newborn *c*.2.4 m; adult *c*.4.5–5 m. Weight: a 2.7-m calf weighed 185 kg; adult estimated *c*.1000–1400 kg [328].

VARIATION
No information on geographical variation, intra-population differences or genetic polymorphisms.

HISTORY
No archaeological or fossil material known, but fragments of *Mesoplodon*-like animals found in Red Crag and Suffolk Crag in E England (Upper Miocene) and from the phosphate beds of N and S Carolina [775].

DISTRIBUTION
Known only from the temperate N Atlantic, mainly in European waters; distribution presumably centred on deep waters of mid and E North Atlantic, mostly N of other *Mesoplodon* species [360, 728, 973]. Although many stranded in North Sea, most probably a consequence of passive drift of carcasses. In N European waters, confirmed sightings S of Iceland, in the Norwegian Sea, W of Norway, around the Faroes, N and W of

British Isles, in the Channel Approaches and Bay of Biscay [140, 223, 346, 360, 695, 762, 1215, 1236]. Further S and W, recorded from Madeira [1260] and the Azores [979, 1088].

Although rarely seen (or at least specifically identified), have been *c.*80 strandings around British Isles, 1913–2007, with 55 of these since 1963 [120, 360, 408, 974, 1073, 1074]. Occurred mainly in N Isles, N & W Scotland and along the E coast of GB, but also from English Channel, W Ireland, and other European coasts of North Sea. Occurred in all months but mostly July–November.

HABITAT
Although most strandings from North Sea, bycatches on shelf edge of NW Atlantic and distribution of sightings suggest that, like other beaked whales, mostly inhabits deep ocean basins and trenches with depths of 700 m or more.

SOCIAL ORGANISATION AND BEHAVIOUR
Very poorly known. Strandings generally of single individuals or mothers with calves; once, 3 juveniles [974]. Most sightings either singles or pairs, but with groups of 4–10 recorded [346, 353, 360, 678, 696, 1236].

Intraspecific combat between adult males inferred from development of teeth and higher incidence of scarring, as for Blainville's beaked whale [730, 731].

Fast swimmer, often at surface, and clearly mainly pelagic. Echolocating sound pulses recorded from young animals kept in a dolphinarium for a few hours. One stranded alive was reported as lowing like a cow.

FEEDING
Diet: Very poorly known, but believed to favour mesopelagic squid (e.g. members of family Ommastrephidae). Small numbers of otoliths from fish (Gadidae, Merlucciidae and Ammodytidae) found in stomachs of 3 stranded on E coast of Scotland, 1992–1996 [1030].

BREEDING
Virtually unknown. Mating and birth possibly occur in late winter and spring [678]. No data on gestation or lactation periods, or calving interval.

POPULATION
No population estimates; like other *Mesoplodon*, pelagic distribution and difficulty of observing and identification at sea mean the species may be more common than the few records suggest. No information on age structure or mortality rates.

MORTALITY
No information; killer whale and false killer whale potential predators (cf. [775]).

PARASITES AND PATHOGENS
Little information. Gooseneck barnacles *Conchoderma* found attached to teeth of males stranded on Scottish coasts [974, 1165]. Cestode *Tetrabothrius* sp. found in one stranded on English coast [442].

RELATIONS WITH HUMANS
Formerly hunted off Newfoundland [1065]. Occasionally captured accidentally in fishing gear such as gillnets [775, 792, 1050]. 12 mesoplodonts of unknown species (but probably this one) recorded as bycatches in one year in swordfish gillnet fishery along shelf edge of E USA [1219].

Oil and gas exploration W of British Isles (along Atlantic Frontier) may pose a threat [349, 352], although military sonar in mid-frequency range (1–10 kHz) likely to be more important (cf. Cuvier's whale) [355]. One washed up, Belgium, was a victim of a ship strike [632].

Legally protected in European, British and Irish waters (Table 12.1).

LITERATURE
Useful general review of *Mesoplodon* [775] but no comprehensive treatise on this species. Variation in the genus as a whole considered in [729].

AUTHORS
P.G.H. Evans, J.S. Herman & A.C. Kitchener

True's beaked whale *Mesoplodon mirus*
Mesoplodon mirum True, 1913; Beaufort Harbour, North Carolina, USA.

Miol mór gobach le clár-fiacla (Irish Gaelic).

RECOGNITION
Not yet identified with certainty at sea, because of the great difficulty in distinguishing it from other *Mesoplodon* species. Back slate grey, often with pale spots and linear scars, which may be in closely spaced pairs (Plate 15). Like others of genus, may have a prominent bulge on forehead, with sickle-shaped dorsal fin, inconspicuous blow. Diagnostic feature is short but clearly defined beak sloping into slightly bulbous forehead, with single pair of teeth (exposed above gum only in adult male) at extreme tip of lower jaw.

DESCRIPTION
Long spindle-shaped body, more robust than Sowerby's and more similar to Cuvier's beaked

whale. Small head with bulge in front of crescent-shaped blowhole; short but pronounced beak, pair of throat grooves forming V-shape below. Relatively small narrow flippers often tucked into flipper pockets and triangular or slightly sickle-shaped dorsal fin situated almost 2/3 along back. Tail flukes have trailing edge slightly concave; usually no notch, but some show slight median notch. Coloration bluish-grey on back, lighter on belly, with light spots and, especially in adult males, linear scars which may be paired; pale patches may be present in anal and genital regions. Single pair of teeth, slightly compressed laterally (25 × 13 mm), oval in cross-section, directed forward and upward at extreme tip of lower jaw; exposed above gum and outside mouth in adult males (Fig. 12.12). In females and young, are smaller and concealed below gum. Premaxillae project anteriorly to nasals at vertex of skull, when viewed from above; teeth slightly laterally compressed, ratio of antero-posterior to transverse breadth >1.66 (cf. rounded oval teeth in Cuvier's beaked whale, with which it can be confused).

RELATIONSHIPS
One of 5 *Mesoplodon* spp. recorded from N Atlantic; relationships unresolved [763, 942].

MEASUREMENTS
Length *c*.4.5–5.5 m; shortest reported calf 2.33 m. Weight *c*.800–1400 kg.

VARIATION
No information on geographical variation, intra-population differences or genetic polymorphisms.

DISTRIBUTION
Range very poorly known; may be widespread in deep waters of temperate Atlantic extending to SW Indian Ocean; records from E North America, NW Europe, NW Africa and S Africa [75, 728, 769, 776, 1015].

Of 10 strandings from Europe since 1899, 9 from W Ireland (Killadoon, Co. Mayo to Long Strand, Co. Cork) [51, 120, 360, 406, 483, 484, 1002, 1181]. This includes 2 specimens, one in University College Museum, Galway [51], thought to be from a stranding in Galway Bay around 1899, and another washed ashore in 1903/1904 on Aran Is., Co. Galway, in Galway Museum [52]. Variously identitified as Hector's beaked whale and Cuvier's beaked whale, reassessed as *M. mirus* [483, 484] (both omitted in [120]). No definite records from GB; supposed skull from S Uist, Outer Hebrides, 1931, proved to be *Ziphius* [404, 633, 768].

One other European record, France [104], although also reported from Canaries [1187]. Sightings thought to be of this species on the basis

of uniform bluish grey coloration and short but prominent beak, October 1993, N of Canaries [1134]; July 1997, Bay of Biscay [1193]; and off Azores [1119]. Irish strandings occurred February–November, mostly June–July.

HISTORY
No archaeological or fossil material attributable to this species is known, but see *M. bidens* (cf. [775]).

HABITAT
Not known, but presumably deep ocean basins and trenches.

SOCIAL ORGANISATION AND BEHAVIOUR
No information. Putative sightings have been of singles or pairs. Intraspecific combat between adult males inferred from development of teeth and higher incidence of scarring, as for Blainville's beaked whale [731].

FEEDING
Diet: No data, believed to take mesopelagic squid and fish [775].

Feeding methods: Thought to employ suction when feeding [520].

BREEDING
No information.

POPULATION
No information; like other *Mesoplodon*, probably under-recorded, because of pelagic distribution and difficulties of observing and identifying it at sea.

MORTALITY
No information; killer whale or false killer whale potential predators (cf. [775]).

PARASITES AND PATHOGENS
A few parasitic copepods *Pennella* sp. found on flanks of 2 specimens, USA [775]. Unidentified trematodes found in liver and bile duct, and nematodes in stomach and intestine [775]. Male, stranded Co. Mayo, November 1987, had many commensal barnacles, *Conchoderma*, growing around its teeth [1180]. *Conchoderma* (usually in blubber of flanks) and cestode cysticerci *Monorhygma* (between the peritoneal membrane and the body wall in the posterior abdomen) frequent [775]. *Xenobalanus globicipitis* reported, attached to flukes of 2 from S Africa [1017].

RELATIONS WITH HUMANS
No information. Legally protected in European, British and Irish waters (Table 12.1).

695

LITERATURE
Useful general review of *Mesoplodon* [775], but no detailed treatise on this species.

AUTHORS
P.G.H. Evans, J.S. Herman & A.C. Kitchener

Gervais' beaked whale *Mesoplodon europaeus*
Dioplodon europaeus Gervais, 1855; English Channel.

Gulf Stream beaked whale, Gervais' beaked whale, Antillean beaked whale, European beaked whale.

RECOGNITION
Rarely seen at sea, when it would be difficult to distinguish from other *Mesoplodon* species. Back usually uniformly dark grey, sometimes with pale linear scars. Like other *Mesoplodon*, may have a prominent bulge on forehead, sickle-shaped dorsal fin situated almost 2/3 along back, and inconspicuous blow. Diagnostic features are moderately long, slender beak, relatively straight mouthline, and 1 pair of laterally compressed, triangular teeth in lower jaw (exposed above gum only in adult male) about 1/3 along gape from tip of snout. In transverse section, rostrum ventrally flattened (cf. dorsally flattened in Blainville's).

DESCRIPTION
Long spindle-shaped body, proportionately small head with slight bulge in front of crescent-shaped blowhole and on forehead; pronounced, slender beak, with pair of deep grooves forming V-shape below. Relatively small narrow flippers often tucked into flipper pockets. Triangular or slightly sickle-shaped dorsal fin situated almost 2/3 along back. Un-notched tail flukes may have a small (*c*.3 cm) median projection on the slightly concave trailing edge. Coloration dark grey or indigo dorsally, sometimes becomes medium or light grey on lower flanks and belly, with single pair of scars, especially in adult males. Juveniles have a white belly. In some adult females, white patch, *c*.15 cm diameter, extends from just before genital slit to just behind anus. Rosy patch under the flipper in the freshly stranded Spanish specimen [1172a]. Single pair of flattened, triangular teeth (c.7–8 cm × 3–5 cm), set 1/3 of gape from tip of lower jaw, exposed above gum and outside mouth only in adult males. In females and young, teeth usually smaller, concealed below gum.

Premaxillae project anteriorly to nasals at vertex of skull, when viewed from above, rostrum slender, not dorsoventrally deepened. Teeth set back from tip of mandible, but anterior to posterior limit of symphysis. Gray's beaked whale, *M. grayi*, a Southern Ocean species recorded once from the Netherlands, has teeth similarly placed but very long and slender rostrum.

RELATIONSHIPS
One of 5 *Mesoplodon* spp. recorded from N Atlantic; relationships unresolved [763, 942].

MEASUREMENTS
Length: newborn thought to be *c*.2.1 m; physically mature adults usually 4.2–4.8 m (max. probably 5 m). Weight *c*.600–1200 kg.

VARIATION
No information on geographical variation, intra-population differences, or genetic polymorphisms.

DISTRIBUTION
Known only from the Atlantic; apparently favours warm temperate and subtropical waters. Type specimen found floating in the English Channel, 1848, but most records come from W Atlantic, between Long Island, New York and E Caribbean; most records S of North Carolina. Is the most common *Mesoplodon* in E USA, Gulf of Mexico [570, 775].

Several recent strandings in E North Atlantic [360]. In W Ireland, a male stranded, Ballysadare, Co. Sligo, January 1989 [1007]. In Canaries, 5 strandings involving 11 specimens, 1985–1997, and 3 sighted, January 1998 [226]. Other strandings in Portugal [1061], S Spain [1172a], Azores [1119], Mauritania [999] and Guinea-Bissau [977].

HISTORY
No archaeological or fossil material known, but fragments of *Mesoplodon*-like animals in phosphate beds of N and S Carolina, and also from Red Crag and Suffolk Crag in E England (Upper Miocene) [775].

HABITAT
Not well known, but apparently deep ocean basins and trenches.

SOCIAL ORGANISATION AND BEHAVIOUR
Very little information on behaviour: nearly all records are of strandings. The 3 seen off Tenerife, Canaries (in 1700 m depth) approached the vessel and swam around it for about 10 min [226]. May associate at times with Cuvier's [1187], and Blainville's beaked whales [756].

FEEDING
Diet: Very poorly known, presumably mesopelagic squid and fish, like other *Mesoplodon* [775]. Traces of squid beaks (but no fish remains) found in

stomachs of 3 stranded specimens [775]. Those from the Canaries contained squid beaks and mandibles of the deep-sea fish *Chauliodus sloani* [756].

BREEDING
Negligible information. One specimen 48 years old (assuming 1 dentine tooth growth layer = 1 year) [775].

POPULATION
Unknown; pelagic distribution, and difficulty in observation and identification at sea, mean that may be more common than few records imply.

MORTALITY
No information for this species, but see Blainville's beaked whale.

PARASITES AND PATHOGENS
Numerous parasitic cyamids, *Isocyamus delphini*, found on a healing wound on the flank of an adult male [775]. Nematode *Anisakis* found in the stomach, and cestode cysticerci *Monorhygyma* and *Phyllobothrium* found in the posterior abdomen (between the peritoneal membrane and body wall) and the blubber (mainly of the flanks) respectively [756, 775]. Unidentified trematodes have also been found in the liver and bile duct of specimens [775]. Teeth of adult males often bear commensal barnacles: *Conchoderma* cf. *C. auritum* identified [775].

RELATIONS WITH HUMANS
Hunted off New Jersey coast, 19th century, and more recently in Jamaica [807]. Occasionally taken in the local small cetacean fisheries, E Caribbean [792]. One individual, later identified as *M. europaeus*, entangled in a pound net off New Jersey, 1905 [26] Legally protected; see Table 12.1 and Chapter 4.

LITERATURE
Useful general review of *Mesoplodon* [775] but no detailed treatise on this species.

AUTHORS
P.G.H. Evans, J.S. Herman & A.C. Kitchener

Blainville's beaked whale *Mesoplodon densirostris*
Delphinus densirostris Blainville, 1817; Seychelles, Indian Ocean.

Dense beaked whale, Atlantic beaked whale, tropical beaked whale; *miol mór gobach na h-Eorpa* (Irish Gaelic).

RECOGNITION
More commonly seen at sea than other N Atlantic *Mesoplodon* species: either quite common in some areas, or more coastal and easier to identify to species. High-arching lower jaw distinctive, surmounted in adult males by massive pair of flattened, triangular teeth; these tilt slightly forward, are often encrusted with barnacles (Plate 15). Usually dark grey or brown on the back, lighter grey on the abdomen, and commonly with large grey or pale blotches (sometimes described as pinkish) dorsally, may disappear after death. Head often flattened directly in front of blowhole, with moderately long, slender beak (in Gervais' beaked whale, the rostrum is ventrally flattened). The long beak is the first part of the body to break the surface, and its curved shape readily distinguishes this from other *Mesoplodon* species.

DESCRIPTION
Long spindle-shaped body, small head with slight bulge in front of crescent-shaped blowhole; pronounced slender beak and highly arched mouthline, with pair of deep grooves forming V-shape below. Relatively small narrow flippers often tucked into flipper pockets; triangular or slightly sickle-shaped dorsal fin situated almost 2/3 along back. Un-notched tail flukes. Coloration dark grey or brown on back and pale grey on belly; juveniles and adult females may be lighter grey on dorsal surface with white belly. Greyish white or pink blotches over back and flanks; linear scars and scratches (sometimes paired), at least in adult males, which are often covered with intricate network of pale scars, mainly between dorsal fin and blowhole. Younger males and females may also have scars, but less numerous. All sexes/ages may have yellowish patches of diatoms on the body. Lower mandible sometimes white. Brownish hue may show on the head, shading to light grey on the edge of the upper lip and on the lateral and ventral lower jaw. In adult males, single pair of flattened, triangular teeth (*c.*12 × 8 cm) set anteriorly on apex of arch of lower jaw, up to 4 cm erupted from gum and exposed outside mouth (Fig. 12.17). In females and young, teeth smaller (*c.*6 × 3–5 cm), usually concealed below gum [126, 515, 1171].

Premaxillae project anteriorly to nasals at vertex of skull, when viewed from above, rostrum dorsoventrally deepened. Teeth located on upward arch of stepped mandible, well behind posterior limit of symphysis (Fig. 12.12).

RELATIONSHIPS
One of 5 *Mesoplodon* spp. recorded from the N Atlantic; relationships unresolved [763, 942].

MEASUREMENTS

Limited to very few specimens. Length at birth thought to be *c*.2.1 m; maximum probably *c*.4.8 m; physically mature adults usually 4.1–4.8 m. Apparent age at sexual maturity *c*.9 years (based on data from related species *M. europaeus*). Weight *c*.700–1100 kg.

VARIATION

No information on geographical variation, intra-population differences or genetic polymorphisms.

DISTRIBUTION

One of the most widely distributed species of *Mesoplodon*, recorded from tropical and warm temperate seas of all oceans. In the Atlantic, mostly recorded from SE USA, Gulf of Mexico and Caribbean; records range from Nova Scotia to S Brazil [229, 351, 546, 570, 775, 782].

In E North Atlantic, recorded from France [219], Portugal [976, 1061], Spain [228, 1172] and Madeira [484], but most records come from the Canaries where sightings frequent [22, 224, 998]. Here, occur year-round, with individuals identified over several years, suggesting site fidelity [24, 58] as also recorded in Bahamas [252] and Hawaii [772].

Only 1 record from British Isles: adult female, stranded July 1993 at Aberaeron, W Wales [360, 515]. Considered to have a more offshore distribution than some other *Mesoplodon* [807], Welsh and another, Icelandic, extralimital record [926], perhaps carried on North Atlantic Drift. The type specimen described by De Blainville in 1817 now thought to be from Seychelles, not France [377, 462].

HISTORY

No archaeological or fossil material attributable to this species known, but see under *M. bidens* (cf. [775]).

HABITAT

Poorly known, likely to be deep ocean basins and trenches of >700 m depth. Frequently seen near oceanic archipelagos such as Hawaii, Bahamas and Canaries, where great depths occur near shore. Sightings around Hawaii were made over 700–1000 m, with depths of up to 5000 m occurring nearby [775, 1067]. In the Canaries, may approach coast near the slope, and follow this to forage at depths usually >500 m [22].

SOCIAL ORGANISATION AND BEHAVIOUR

Most sightings have been of singles or pairs [225]. Pods of 3–7 (off Hawaii) [1067], 1–7 (off Canaries) [58]. Calves or juveniles never observed alone at the surface, groups strongly synchronous. Typically only 1 adult male, accompanied by 1 or more adult female–calf pairs and juveniles, suggests harem structure [58]. Support similar observations in Bahamas [252, 253]. Sometimes approach vessels; may lie on the surface during calm weather. Scarring incidence much higher in adult males than other sex/age groups, suggesting that males are aggressive to each other, perhaps compete for mates [731].

Spend on average only 2 min at the surface between dives. Make deep foraging dives to 800–1300 m, commonly for 45–60 min (revealed by time–depth recorders) [22, 1167]. Employ stereotyped diving and foraging behaviour, with long, deep foraging dives undertaken day and night, separated on average by 1.5 h, during which they make shallow, silent, short dives (mean 20 min) with no foraging function [22].

Vocalisations: Before 2003, only recordings came from 2 stranded animals that produced short whistles and chirps which when analysed were definitely pulsed, at frequencies ranging from <1 kHz to >6 kHz [201]. Use of attached D-tags that record sounds emitted by diving whales has revolutionised our knowledge [22, 582, 583, 736, 1167]. Uses echolocation to forage, producing long series of ultrasonic clicks interspaced by pauses and buzzes. Buzzes during dives indicate prey capture attempts; performs some 30 of these per deep foraging dive.Mostly silent <200 m depth, vocalising only in deep parts of foraging dives.

FEEDING

Diet: Little information on food preferences; presumed to favour mesopelagic and benthopelagic squid and fish [775]. Traces of squid beaks (but no fish remains) found in stomachs of 3 stranded specimens [775]. The female stranded in Wales contained the lower beak of a squid, *Histioteuthis reversa* [515]. However, S African specimens contained remains of fish *Cepola*, *Lampanyctus*, and *Scopelogadus*, and one had 2 squid beaks, *Todarodes sagittatus* and *Octopoteuthis* spp. [1017]. One stranded, in Canaries, had remains of squids *Octopoteuthis sicula, Histioteuthis meleagroteuthis, H. reversa* and *Histioteuthis* Type A, as well as myctophid and gadid fishes [1041].

Feeding methods: Thought to employ suction when feeding [520]. Tagging studies suggest that catches around 30 prey per foraging dive, with little variation in swimming speed, suggesting that targeted prey are relatively small, scarcely mobile relative to whale [22].

BREEDING

Very little information. Presumed minimum age at sexual maturity 9 years (based on data from one individual *M. europaeus* [1017]). The Welsh specimen was 21 years old, assuming 1 tooth growth layer = 1 year, and was considered to have borne a number of calves [515].

POPULATION

Unknown; recent sightings indicate that, at least in some localities (e.g. Canaries, Bahamas, Hawaii), the species concentrates in certain areas with site fidelity for many years. May be locally abundant, but populations do not seem numerous, and calves few relative to adults, suggesting slow recruitment [23].

MORTALITY

Virtually no information, but tooth scars on a female thought to have been caused by killer whale or false killer whale [775].

PARASITES AND PATHOGENS

Unidentified adult cestodes present in proximal intestine of juvenile male, New Jersey [775]; nematode *Anisakis simplex* and cestode *Tetrabothrius* sp. found in female stranded, Wales [442]. Clumps of stalked barnacle *Conchoderma* sp. recorded on teeth of male animals [353, 775, 787]. *Xenobalanus* sp. and unidentified balanoid barnacle found deeply embedded on the flank of one, S Africa [775].

Two vaginal fibromas described from a stranded specimen [376].

RELATIONS WITH HUMANS

No commercial fishery, but occasionally taken in small cetacean fisheries of Taiwan, Japan and Korea [553, 605, 775, 792]. Accidentally killed in fishing gear off Sri Lanka, Seychelles, and W coast of Australia [679, 775].

Pollutants (PCBs, DDT) present in blubber of stranded animals from NW Atlantic [1138], Wales [673] and Mediterranean [19], but levels all comparatively low.

Live-stranded individuals occasionally held in captivity for limited periods but have invariably died [775].

Major threat probably comes from use of military sonar in mid-frequency range (1–10 kHz), has been responsible for mass strandings of ziphiids, including Blainville's beaked whale [355, 369, 757].

Legally protected in European, British and Irish waters (Table 12.1).

LITERATURE

Useful general review of *Mesoplodon* [775]; for this species, most detailed information in unpublished PhD thesis [22]. Additional information on population analysis in [252, 772].

AUTHORS

P.G.H. Evans, N. Aguilar Soto, J.S. Herman & A.C. Kitchener

FAMILY MONODONTIDAE

Currently considered to comprise 2 monospecific genera, *Monodon* and *Delphinapterus*; both occur as rare vagrants in British waters. No biological data collected from these occasional visitors, so accounts below derived from their normal range. Closest to Phocoenidae [763]. Irrawaddy dolphin *Orcaella brevirostris* once assigned to Monodontidae, but similarities superficial, genetic evidence places it clearly in Delphinidae [684, 700].

GENUS *Delphinapterus*

Beluga *Delphinapterus leucas*
Delphinapterus leucas Pallas, 1776; mouth of R. Ob, Siberia.

White whale; *míol mór bán* (Irish Gaelic).

RECOGNITION

Only medium-sized cetacean lacking dorsal fin and with uniform white body colour (Plate 15) (whiteness only achieved in adulthood, but all British records are of adults). Smaller animals varying shades of grey. Stout body with small head and pronounced melon. Upper profile of skull broad and flat, distinguished from narwhal by having erupted teeth in both upper and lower jaws. Unique among cetaceans in having all, or almost all, of the neck vertebrae unfused.

DESCRIPTION

Head has slight beak, looks unusually small compared with body, due to great thickness (up to 15 cm) of blubber covering thorax and abdomen. Neck uniquely flexible and visually distinct. 8–11 pairs of simple peg-like teeth in upper jaw, 8–9 pairs in lower jaw, often curved and worn, maximum 40 in total; in old adults, may be worn flat to gumline. Melon bulbous and malleable. Skin soft, often with small transverse ridges, and frequently scarred. Adults pure white or (in early summer) yellowish. Calves grey or grey-brown, often blotched. Juveniles become progressively lighter with age (becoming pure white by age 9 years in males and 7 years in females), although females often still light grey at sexual maturity.

Pectoral fins short, rounded; progressively turned up at their tips in adulthood. Tail fluke is deeply notched and changes shape with age, developing a lobe on each side of trailing edge. A distinct ridge takes the place of a dorsal fin.

RELATIONSHIPS

Only close relative is *Monodon*. Within species, variations in beluga body size and growth parameters [317, 1124], mtDNA and microsatellite analysis [740], contaminant patterns [550], and vocal dialects suggest some geographical differentiation, although evidence for limited gene exchange weak [865] and may be result of sampling separate stable pods comprising family units [893]. However, mtDNA confirms that belugas tend to return to their natal areas year after year, dispersal among summering concentrations limited even where there are few geographical barriers [183, 866]; satellite tracking supports this [991].

MEASUREMENTS

Size varies geographically, larger further N [1124]. Vagrants to GB probably derive from either Svalbard or White Sea populations, which contain some of largest individuals. Length: newborn *c.*1.6 m [176]; at sexual maturity (varies between geographical areas) *c.*270–379 cm (female), *c.*310–415 cm (male) [505]; adult female typically 3–4 m (max. 4.7 m), male 4–5 m (max. 5.7 m) [317, 505]. Weight: newborn 79 kg [176]; adult typically 400–1000 kg (female), 1000–1700 kg (male) [317, 505].

DISTRIBUTION

Arctic, circumpolar. Normally occurs at or near ice-edge, seasonal distributions largely dictated by annual sea-ice cycle. Most S population resident in Gulf of St Lawrence, Canada.

Only stranding on British coast, October 1932, in R. Forth near Stirling. Most reliable sightings from N North Sea. Singletons off Clare Island, Co. Mayo, September 1948; off Soay, Skye, in 1950; between Orkney and Burray, October 1960; in Gourock Bay, late summer 1964, and possibly same individual at Arrochar, Loch Long; off Yorkshire coast, Whitby, June 1987, with possibly the same animal off Northumberland, March 1988; in Cork harbour, June 1988; off Applecross, W Scotland, April 1995; and singles in Shetland, September 1996 and August 1997 [360].

Single belugas also seen from mainland European North Sea coasts. Some may involve the same individuals of this highly visible and unmistakable species.

HISTORY

Fossils in Pleistocene clays in NE North America reflect successive range expansions and contractions associated with glacial maxima and minima. Earliest monodontid is extinct beluga *Deuebola brachycephala* from late Miocene, Baja California, Mexico, indicating that this family once occupied temperate zone [100].

HABITAT

Cold marine waters near or within sea ice. Enters estuaries and river mouths for brief periods in summer, probably linked to annual synchronised epidermal moult. In many Arctic regions (e.g. E Canadian Arctic and W Greenland), believed to migrate ahead of advancing polar ice front [373], but in some areas (e.g. White, Barents and Kara Seas) occurs year-round, remaining in polynyas in deeper water during winter [635].

SOCIAL ORGANISATION AND BEHAVIOUR

Gregarious, rarely seen alone, so single vagrants to temperate waters are geographically and socially abnormal. Basic social unit is mother–calf pair, but previous calf also sometimes present. Medium-term associations between adult males shown by radio-tracking [755]. Aggregations often hundreds, even thousands of whales, but within these are smaller groups of 2–20, often of similar ages or reproductive status. Mating system not known; probably promiscuous, since no indication of any long-term male–female relationships. Mature males and females appear to mix only during breeding season on winter grounds [1106].

Unusually among cetaceans, has an annual moult; enters sheltered shallow coastal and estuarine waters, actively rubs its skin on gravel substrates [1105, 1115]. Never breaches, but in aggregations may spyhop, tail wave, or tail slap. Facial expression and physical contact, including biting, appear to be important forms of communication within herd [176].

Swims slowly, typically 1–3 km/h but up to 6 km/h during prolonged migration [1104, 1133], which may extend 1100 km from shore and penetrate 700 km into dense polar ice cap with 90% ice cover [1133]. Contrary to expectations, now known to be a capable diver; routinely submerges to seabed, maximum recorded depth >1100 m for up to 25 min [746, 749, 752, 754, 991].

Forages individually, between bouts of resting, beginning with slow directed movement combined with passive acoustic localisation, followed by short sprints and rapid changes of direction using echolocation for orientation and prey capture [108a].

Vocalisations: Known as the 'sea canary', the

Plate 15

A True's beaked whale *Mesoplodon mirus* B Blainville's beaked whale *M. densirostris*
C Sowerby's beaked whale *M. bidens* D False killer whale *Pseudorca crassidens* E Beluga *Delphinapterus leucas* (adult)
F Risso's dolphin *Grampus griseus* G Narwal *Monodon monoceros* (female)

701

beluga is very vocal during periods of socialisation, a great variety of whistles, chirps and grunts being clearly heard both above and below water, with as many as 50 call types recognised [1093]. Communicative and emotive calls broadly divided into whistles and pulsed calls typically at frequencies of 0.1–12 kHz. Excellent echolocation system, well adapted to ice-covered waters, and capable of detecting targets at some distance and in high levels of ambient noise and backscatter [69, 70].

FEEDING

Diet: Catholic. Mainly fish, both benthic and pelagic, depending upon seasonal habitat (including arctic cod *Arctogadus glacialis*, polar cod *Boreogadus saida*, salmon *Oncorhynchus* spp., herring *Clupea harengus*, capelin *Mallotus villosus*, smelt *Osmerus nordax* and saffron cod *Eleginus gracilis*), with squid and invertebrates also taken in various parts of range [505, 635, 1054, 1186].

Feeding methods: Feeds both near surface and on seabed, in depths up to 550 m [754].

BREEDING

Single calf born in late spring–early summer, at time of entry to warmer coastal waters or before. Gestation period uncertain, but most likely 13–15 months. Lactation period 2 or more years. Modal calving interval probably 3 years. Mating believed to occur mainly in late winter–early spring, whilst still on wintering grounds or during spring migration.

On assumption of 2 pairs of tooth laminae deposited per year (cf. 1 pair in other odontocetes), both sexes reach sexual maturity around 5–8 years of age, males probably a year or two later than females in same population.

POPULATION

Possibly 30 different stocks around the Arctic [556], though estimate will change with better information on movements and genetics. Population sizes range from a few tens in stocks that have been subjected to over-hunting, to tens of thousands. Total world population probably *c.* 150 000 [556, 830].

Longevity difficult to establish because tooth wear affects age estimation, but probably few animals reach 30 years, and a 40-year-old is exceptional.

MORTALITY

Due to difficulties in determining age and biases in harvest data, no reliable estimates of mortality rates.

Killer whale, walrus and polar bear are natural predators [635]. Belugas also prone to ice entrapment; may starve, suffocate and become easy prey to humans and polar bears [176, 1078].

RELATIONS WITH HUMANS

Most populations have been hunted; native harvests continue in several areas, sometimes unsustainably. Maintained in many captive facilities; trained by U.S. and Soviet navies for submarine warfare roles. One in Brighton aquarium, 1878, was one of the first cetaceans in captivity. Legally protected in European, British and Irish waters (Table 12.1).

Increasing human activities in areas that are occupied seasonally by belugas (e.g. St Lawrence R., Canada) have caused habitat destruction, disturbance from vessel traffic, incidental capture in fishing gear and pollution [176, 624, 625, 690, 781].

LITERATURE

Popular introduction to the species [745]. Most detailed academic review available is [176], now somewhat dated. More recent academic reviews [155, 506]; popular account [865].

AUTHORS

A.R. Martin & P.G.H. Evans

GENUS *Monodon*

Narwhal *Monodon monoceros*
Monodon monoceros Linnaeus, 1758; Arctic seas.

RECOGNITION

Body shape similar to beluga: blunt head, no dorsal fin, and pectoral fins which turn up distally with age, especially in males (Plate 15). Age-related change in tail-fluke shape similar to, but even more marked than, beluga. All but youngest males have an unmistakable tusk. Skull similar to beluga, but no erupted teeth in upper jaw (except tusk in males) and none at all in lower.

DESCRIPTION

Stout body with small rounded head, bulbous forehead and very slight beak. One pair of teeth in upper jaw only, left tooth of male greatly extended as spiralled tusk (up to 2.7 m long) pointing forwards and erupting through upper lip. Extremely rarely, both teeth are thus elongated; frequency of this abnormality greatly exaggerated in museum collections. In females, teeth are embedded in skull and rarely or never erupt. Body mottled grey-green, cream and black; older males look lighter, partly because of accumulation of white scar tissue. Newborn are blotchy slate grey or bluish grey; mottling increases in juveniles. Pectoral fins short, have upturned tip in adults; in very old males, may describe a complete circle, almost touching dorsal surface of fin.

MEASUREMENTS

Length: newborn *c.*1.6 m; at sexual maturity 3.6 m (females), 4.2 m (males); adult female 4.0 m (max. 4.15 m), male (excluding tusk) 4.2 m (max. 4.75 m). Tusk erupts at body length of 2.6 m, reaches 1.5 m at sexual maturity, and *c.*2.0 m at physical maturity (max. 2.67 m). Weight: newborn 80 kg, adult 500–1600 kg (males considerably larger than females).

VARIATION

Low genetic (nucleotide and haplotype) diversity revealed by mtDNA, suggests rapid expansion from small founder population after last glaciation [892]. Some genetic differences between populations in Baffin Bay and E Greenland, but also between 2 summering and 1 autumn ground in W Greenland; suggests fidelity to feeding localities [892].

DISTRIBUTION

Discontinuous, (mainly high) Arctic, circumpolar (60–85° N). Rare outside Arctic. Centres of distribution are E Canada/W Greenland and E Greenland/Svalbard/Franz Josef Land. Recorded only 6 times in British waters, presumably involving vagrants from this latter population. Single animals were stranded in 1648, 1800 and 1808, and 2 in Thames estuary, 1949. Only live sighting, 2 off Orkney, also in 1949. No verified records since then [360].

HISTORY

Fossils from Pleistocene, England and Germany, also along Russian Arctic coasts; suggests different range before or during most recent glaciation, as do remains from early Postglacial both N (Ellesmere I.) and S (Gulf of St Lawrence) of present range [503].

HABITAT

Usually in deep offshore waters near or within sea ice. In summer, ventures N into fjords and bays as they become ice-free, occasionally using waters <10 m deep; in autumn, moves S offshore into shelf slope waters of 1000–2000 m depth as coastal areas freeze up. In winter, remains in highly consolidated ice, usually in leads or holes [312, 504].

SOCIAL ORGANISATION AND BEHAVIOUR

Presence of tusk, scarring of adult males, and sexual dimorphism in body size imply polygyny, though not confirmed directly. Social, group-forming species, rarely seen alone; usually small groups, 5–10, migrating together, but sometimes coalesce into larger herds. Vagrants to GB presumably usually aberrant individuals, but multiple records in 1949 show that not always so. Structure of pods similar to those of belugas: small, tightly-knit groups of whales of similar age/sexual status identifiable within often much larger aggregations. These aggregations may cover several km, move as a unit, and can comprise thousands of whales. Adult males usually segregated from groups of females with calves (sometimes accompanied by immature males).

Deep divers, can dive to >1000 m (max. recorded 1164 m) [504], and probably actively chasing prey at these depths [753]. On surface, swim slowly (*c.*5 km/h) [312].

Vocalisations: Include whistles of 300 Hz–18 kHz, often rising or falling in pitch, lasting 0.5–1 s; pulsed tones of 500 Hz–5 kHz; and echolocating clicks of 500 Hz–48 kHz at 3–10 clicks/s at 48 kHz, and faster click rates (110–150 clicks/s) at 19 kHz [392, 786]. Whistles may be social signals between individuals within groups.

FEEDING

Diet: Mainly squid and fish (both pelagic and demersal), with some invertebrates. Common prey include polar cod *Boreogadus saida*, arctic cod *Arctogadus glacialis*, redfish *Sebastes marinus*, Greenland halibut *Reinhardtius hippoglossoides*, and squid *Gonatus fabricii* [372, 507].

Feeding methods: Little feeding apparently takes place during period in open water (August).

BREEDING

Little known. Calving (single calf) occurs in summer (July–August) in both Greenland and Canada, with mating in early spring, and gestation length *c.*13–16 months. Modal inter-birth interval is, by inference, probably *c.*3 years. Lactation *c.*2 years.

No reliable method for ageing from either protruding tusk or embedded teeth: contain distinctive growth layers in both dentine and cementum, but these merge and become unreadable with age.

POPULATION

Probably 3 main populations – E Canada/ Baffin Bay, Foxe Basin/N Hudson Bay and E

Greenland/Svalbard/Franz Josef Land. No precise estimates of abundance; aerial surveys suggest low tens of thousands, low thousands and low thousands respectively for these 3 stocks [556, 830].

MORTALITY
Little known. Annual adult mortality probably <10% [623]. Occasional large-scale mortality of whales trapped in savssats (open water in sea ice), which then freeze over (as in Disko Bay, W Greenland [1078]). Like belugas, when entrapped in ice, large numbers may asphyxiate, may then be exploited by Inuit and polar bear.

PARASITES AND COMMENSALS
Whale lice *Cyamus monodontis* and *C. nodosus* found in fold of skin at the base of the tusk, and in any deep wounds. Among endoparasites are *Stenurus alatus*, *Pseudalius alatus*, *Torynurus alatus* and *Pharurus alatus* in middle ear sinuses, *Anisakis simplex* in stomach and intestine, *Ascaris simplex* in the stomach, *Terranova decipiens* and *Porrocaecum decipiens* in the intestine, and *Halocercus monoceris* in the lungs [500].

RELATIONS WITH HUMANS
Hunting for tusks and skin (muktuk) continues in Canada and Greenland. Harvest averaged 550/year in Greenland and 280/year in Canada, 1993–1995 [503]. Some international trade in tusks. No known threats from other human activity, although some have relatively high levels of organochlorines and heavy metals. Legally protected in European, British and Irish waters (Table 12.1).

Mythical horse-like unicorn, with spiralled horn on its forehead, derived from traded narwhal tusks, brought S from Arctic. Long viewed as having healing properties.

LITERATURE
Good academic review [500]; modern ecological study [155]; more recent general account [503].

AUTHORS
A.R. Martin & P.G.H. Evans

FAMILY PHOCOENIDAE (PORPOISES)

A small family of small cetaceans: 3 genera with 6 species of porpoises, only 1 of which occurs in N Atlantic. Distinguished from dolphins by short face, lacking a beak, and by spade-shaped teeth. Possibly closer to Monodontidae than Delphinidae [763].

GENUS *Phocoena*

A small genus of 4–5 species: spectacled porpoise *P. dioptrica* (S hemisphere), vaquita *P. sinus* (Gulf of California), Burmeister's porpoise *P. spinipinnis* (S America) and harbour porpoise *P. phocoena* (N Pacific and N Atlantic), probably also Dall's porpoise *Phocoenoides dalli* (N Pacific).

Harbour porpoise *Phocoena phocoena*
Delphinus phocoena Linnaeus, 1758; Swedish seas.

Llamhidydd (Welsh); *peileag* (Scottish Gaelic); *neesic, pellach* (Shetland); *much mhara* (Irish Gaelic).

RECOGNITION
Smallest British cetacean, <2 m in length (usually *c.*1.5 m) (Plate 16). Rarely leaps clear of water, as do dolphins. Short blunt head, no beak, and dorsal fin small, triangular, situated in centre of back. Upper and lower jaws contain spade-shaped teeth (conical in all delphinids) (Fig. 12.17).

DESCRIPTION
Small rotund body with small head, no obvious forehead or beak. 19–28 pairs of small spade-shaped teeth in each jaw. Dark grey back with paler grey patch on flanks and white belly, though coloration of back and sides variable. Grey line from flippers to jawline. Short, slightly rounded flippers. Upper and lower jaws, chin, flippers and flukes grey or blackish. Low triangular dorsal fin centrally placed on back (Fig. 12.18). Central notch in tail flukes.

RELATIONSHIPS
No congeners in N Atlantic; closest to Dall's porpoise *Phocaenoides dalli*, N Pacific, which belongs within *Phocoena* [763].

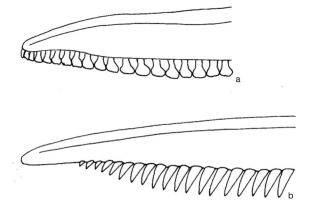

Fig. 12.17 Spade-shaped teeth of harbour porpoise (a) compared with those of common dolphin (b) (*drawn by D.W. Yalden*).

704

Fig. 12.18 Harbour porpoise rolling, showing short triangular fin (*photo M.E. Baines*).

MEASUREMENTS

Length: newborn 65–85 cm (max. *c*.90 cm); at sexual maturity typically 138–147 cm (female), 127–135 cm (male); adult *c*.160 cm (female), *c*.145 cm (male), max. 189 cm (female), 163 cm (male) [708, 711]. Adult weight 50–55 kg (max. 81 kg in females, 54 kg in males).

VARIATION

Using skull material, differences between samples from Denmark and the Netherlands indicate some geographical segregation of Baltic and North Sea populations [627]; Dutch, German and Danish North Sea specimens differ, as do North Sea, Skagerrak, Kattegat and Baltic samples, indicating some degree of separation [628]. Additional studies of tooth ultrastructure [709] and genetics (using mtDNA, nuclear DNA, microsatellites and allozymes) indicate some differentiation in North Sea and adjacent waters, with possible subpopulations occurring in Irish Sea, N vs S North Sea, and E (Danish) vs W (English) North Sea [43, 45, 46, 709, 710, 1151, 1156, 1157, 1196]. Contrarily, extensive micro-satellite study of 752 porpoises from locations throughout E North Atlantic range (including Black Sea) imply continuous population structure, with significant isolation only by distance, except in SE part (on a large scale, Black Sea; on a smaller scale, Portuguese waters) where isolation and/or major changes in oceanographic features occur [380].

DISTRIBUTION

Occurs from cool (sub)tropical to subarctic seas of N hemisphere. In E North Atlantic, widely distributed over continental shelf from Barents Sea, S to coasts of Portugal and Spain, and off W Africa from Morocco to Senegal. Isolated population in Black Sea. During 1960s, became scarce in S North Sea, English Channel and Bay of Biscay [6, 346, 1099]. Nevertheless, remained the most frequently observed, and stranded, cetacean around British Isles; most abundant around Scotland, parts of Wales, and off W and S Ireland [340, 346, 360, 481, 857, 973, 1004] (Fig. 12.19). Since late 1980s, particularly late 1990s, sharp increase in sightings and strandings in Dutch and Belgian waters, rising to spectacular peak in 2005/06. This sudden change not well understood; probably reflects a shift in distribution, maybe caused by a decrease in sandeels, a known important prey, further N [210, 211], a recovery in some North Sea herring stocks [344], or a combination of the two. Similar increases in sightings rates off SE England from 1990s [360]. SCANS II survey of NW European shelf waters, July 2005, also indicated a distributional shift with higher densities in S North Sea compared with N North Sea, reversing situation from SCANS I in July 1994 [478].

Occurs year-round in coastal waters of British Isles; distinct seasonal peaks, July–October, in

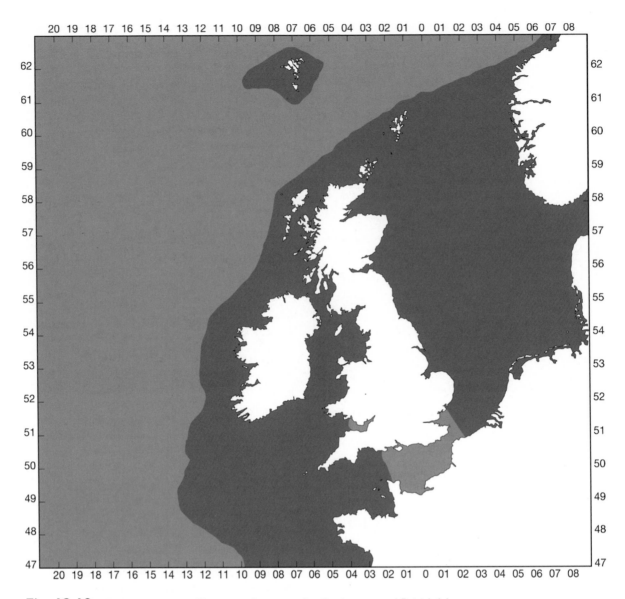

Fig. 12.19 Harbour porpoise *Phocoena phocoena*: distribution around British Isles.

some places [340, 346, 360, 857], but along S English coast and in Dutch waters, is a distinct peak January–April [6, 210, 360]; suggests a seasonal shift in distribution [212].

HISTORY

No fossil or archaeological material known in GB, although there are archaeological finds in the Netherlands and elsewhere in Europe.

HABITAT

Occupies (sub)tropical to cool temperate and subarctic (mainly 11–14 °C) waters, usually (but not exclusively) over the continental shelf at depths of 20–100 m. Consequently is commonly found in coastal bays and estuaries, around headlands, and within tidal channels; in most parts of NW Europe, is the most common cetacean within 10 km of the coast.

SOCIAL ORGANISATION AND BEHAVIOUR

Only a few detailed studies of social organisation or behaviour. Due to their small size and inconspicuous habits, difficult to observe for extended periods. Rarely bow-ride and only in certain circumstances approach moving vessels. Few individuals bear marks that allow recognition of individuals. Most detailed behavioural observations are of captive animals (e.g. [49]), although surface behaviour described for Denmark [1108], Scotland [348], Wales [929] and Germany [1049].

In British waters (as elsewhere), usually solitary or in small loose groups of 2–10 [340, 346, 960]; in most months, median group size is 2, rising to 3 August–October [346]. Larger aggregations of several hundreds observed, but these appear to be temporary coalitions of smaller groups; off GB, occur primarily in February–April and August–October, either associated with long-distance movements or at feeding concentrations [346, 348, 689]. Group size of Dutch animals from 13 years of observations averaged 1.2–1.6 [1250]. Group composition appears fluid, except for adult females with dependent calves. Patterns of strandings and bycatches suggest segregation by age and sex. Individuals extremely mobile, often travelling >50 km/day [961]; some satellite-tagged in N Danish waters made seasonal movements to winter around Shetland [1139]. Genetic evidence from GB and elsewhere indicates that males disperse more widely than females [45, 709, 1155, 1196].

Surfacing behaviour varies with environmental conditions. In calm weather, rolls slowly at the surface, occasionally resting at or just below the surface for a minute or more, when sexual activity may also be observed [39, 348]. Swims at 6–12 km/h; can reach 22 km/h when pursued. Usually swims unobtrusively, rarely showing more than the upper back. However, in rough seas or in tidal rips, surfaces rapidly, almost clearing the water to breathe. Can remain submerged for up to 5 min and usually takes a series of breaths between long dives. In Bay of Fundy, recorded diving to 226 m [1226]. Off Denmark, 14 with satellite-linked dive recorders averaged 29 dives/h, April–August, and 43 October–November [1142]. Dived day and night, but with peak activity during daylight hours, spending 55% of time in upper 2 m during April–August. Max. dive depths were to sea bottom (30–50 m) in Belt seas and Kattegat, and 132 m in deeper Skagerrak; most frequent depths 14–32 m. Dive durations typically 4–6 min, but possibly up to 10–15 min [1142]. Unlike dolphins, does not bow-ride, but sometimes approaches sterns of slower vessels, particularly in late summer [348].

Does not associate with other species, but may co-occur with minke whale, fin whale or humpback in a restricted area, presumably at food aggregations; seabirds (e.g. shags, gannets, auks and gulls) often aggregate nearby as well [341, 348]. Where bottlenose dolphins and harbour porpoises co-occur (e.g. E Scotland, W Wales), dolphins have been known to kill porpoises [575, 1018], possibly as a result of interspecific competition for food.

Vocalisations: Produces high-frequency sounds for echolocation and communication, but not the frequency-modulated whistles typical of delphinids. High-frequency sounds are comprised entirely of click trains, produced in 2 narrow frequency bands: one weaker and of longer duration (*c*.0.2 ms) at 1–20 kHz [447, 1048], the other at 120–160 kHz (peaking around 130 kHz) of shorter duration (*c*.0.02 ms) [40, 447, 595, 803]. Repetition rates of pulses range between 0.5 and 1000 clicks/s [40]. Maximum source level in captivity 149–177 re 1 μPa at 1m [25]. but in the wild 178–205 dB [1179a]. More intense bursts of clicks used during foraging [1175, 1176].

FEEDING

Diet: Can vary both geographically and seasonally. Primarily small (mainly 75–200 mm) schooling fish, found in the water column or on the sea floor. Small cephalopods (mainly Sepiolidae) also consumed, but less frequently than fish. Analyses of tissues from porpoises bycaught at 4 Scandinavian localities (from North Sea to Barents Sea), using stable isotopes and trace element cadmium, correlated well with both bathymetry and latitude, indicating a shift in feeding habits from pelagic prey species in deep N waters to more coastal and/or demersal prey in relatively shallow North Sea and Skagerrak [381]. This supports dietary studies from various geographical regions using stomach contents. In France, mainly blue whiting *Micromesistius poutassou*, scad *Trachurus trachurus*, and hake *Merluccius merluccius* [304]. In Germany, mainly sole *Solea solea* and cod *Gadus morhua* [692] or sandeels (Ammodytidae) and sole [112]. Herring *Clupea harengus*, sprat *Clupea sprattus* and gadoids (particularly cod and whiting *Merlangius merlangus*) predominated in large samples (n = 179, n = 145 stomachs) from Denmark and Scandinavia respectively [2, 117, 154, 1039]; gadoids (particularly whiting and *Trisopterus* spp.), sandeel and gobies Gobiidae predominated in large samples (n = 100, n = 58) from GB [746]; gadoids (mainly whiting) and gobies were the main species in a sample of 62 from the Netherlands [1039]. From 188 stomach samples, Scotland (mostly E coast) main prey were whiting and sandeels, although there were differences between regions, seasons and years [1037]. Off Ireland, mainly *Trisopterus* spp., whiting, and herring [119]. Echosounder survey of porpoise–prey associations, Shetland, found significant spatiotemporal associations only with sandeel, despite abundance of gadoid fish (whiting and saithe *Pollachius virens*), which presumably not favoured when sandeels abundant [348].

In much of North Sea, herring became scarcer in the 1970s. Where herring present, frequently major component of diet [2, 423, 698, 950, 951, 963], presumably because fatty and energy rich [344]. In parts of North Sea and in Baltic, stomach contents include gobies as well as cephalopods (Sepiolidae), crustaceans, polychaetes and other molluscs [113, 692, 738, 1039].

Feeding methods: Little is known of how porpoises find and catch their prey in the wild (although several recent captive studies [599, 1176]). Circumstantial evidence that seasonal movements into coastal waters of British Isles, and longer-term status changes in North Sea, related to timing of spawning of herring, sandeels and gadoids [344, 348, 975].

Food requirements: Not well understood; preliminary work with captive animals suggests that adult porpoises require a daily ration of 4–9.5% of body mass, and juveniles up to 15% [599, 645, 717]. Porpoises increase food consumption in the late summer and increase their body weight, reach peak weight with increased fat storage by mid-winter [712, 717]. This aids insulation in the cold months and provides a temporary energy surplus.

BREEDING
Young born mainly May–August though some as early as March; peak in June [6, 375, 598, 708, 711, 805, 1108]. Some evidence for seasonal movements nearshore in various areas around British Isles, may be related to parturition or calf-rearing during summer [346, 348, 357].

Mating season April–September, with a peak in July–August; gestation period *c*.10–11 months; calving interval 1–2 years [375, 598, 708, 713, 1108]. Lactation period may last up to 10 months [711, 713, 805], with calves starting to feed independently after *c*.2–3 months [348]. Age at sexual maturity 3–5 years, little difference between sexes [7, 708, 711, 713].

POPULATION
From line transect surveys (SCANS I) conducted July 1994 [481], population estimated at 341 366 (CV = 0.14; 95% CI 260 000–449 000) from North Sea (*c*.250 000), Baltic (33 000 in Kattegat/Skagerrak), Channel (0) and Celtic Sea (36 000). In Norwegian waters, estimates of 11 000 (95% CI: 4 790–25 200) for Barents Sea and Norwegian waters N of 66° N, and 82 600 (95% CI 52 100–131 000) for S Norway and N North Sea, made during July 1989 [136]. Repeat survey, July 2005 (SCANS II), covering a wider area (continental shelf seas from SW Norway, S to Atlantic Portugal), gave an estimate of 386 000 (CV = 0.20) [478].

Longevity relatively short, usually up to 12 years, but maximum of 24 years in both sexes [708, 711, 713].

MORTALITY
Suffers predation from sharks (including Greenland shark, great white shark and mako) [63, 1144, 1239], and killer whales [340, 547, 573]. In Moray Firth, NE Scotland, and Cardigan Bay, W Wales, also attacked by bottlenose dolphins [575, 1018].

PARASITES AND PATHOGENS
Whale-lice *Isocyamus delphinii* found on Dutch animals [401]. 22 helminths reported [955]. Internal parasites include the nematodes *Anisakis simplex* (stomach), *Stenurus minor* (cranial sinuses), *Pseudalius inflexus* (bronchi, lung, and heart), *Torynurus convolutus* (bronchi), *Halocercus invaginatus* and *H. tauricus* (in lungs); trematode *Campula oblonga* (bile and pancreatic ducts); *Crassicauda* sp. (subdermally in blubber); cestode *Diphylobothrium stemmacephalum* (intestine) [48, 89, 92, 93, 304, 441, 442, 487, 713, 955, 1097].

HEALTH STATUS
Some from British waters had morbillivirus infection, although not thought to be cause of death [611, 1222]; antibodies to morbillivirus found in porpoises from Bay of Fundy [334] and British Isles [173] although its significance as a cause of mortality remains uncertain. In a large sample, 32% had positive antibodies to *Brucella* [576], and a Dutch sample gave 27% positive (n = 70) [1]. Lung infections a common cause of death [577]. Frequent pox lesions on skin [88].

RELATIONS WITH HUMANS
Living in Europe mainly on the continental shelf, is exposed to a variety of human activities. Was formerly hunted in drive fisheries in the Baltic and off Faroes. However, major threats currently appear to be fishery conflicts. Incidentally caught in a variety of fishing gear: bottom-set gillnets for hake, cod, turbot and sole; fixed nets or traps for cod or salmon; herring weirs; trawls, drift nets, and purse seines for cod, herring or plaice. Recent independent observer schemes estimate annual bycatches in English and French bottom-set gillnet fisheries of at least 6% of the harbour porpoise population (2237 out of an estimated population of 36 280) in the Celtic Sea W of Cornwall; Danish bottom-set gillnet fishery killed 4% of the population in C and N North Sea (6785 out of an estimated 185 000) [481, 1162, 1182], though have decreased recently [1183]. Bycatches also identified as main cause of mortality (at least 28%) for stranded porpoises in England and Wales [631]. Autopsies similarly showed that bycatch caused at least 50% of stranded porpoises in the Netherlands, 1990s [425], and even higher recently [687]; similar figure for German porpoises [1077].

Examined for pollutants in many areas (reviewed in [16, 1226]). High levels of particular pollutants (notably organohalogen compounds such as DDT and PCBs, heavy metals such as mercury, copper, and zinc) found in small samples from certain locations (e.g. the Netherlands [644]; Sweden [886]; NW England [672], but levels of some compounds (particularly DDT) have decreased recently in parts of the North Sea and Baltic [16, 460]. Both organochlorine and heavy metal levels generally low in British and Irish waters [671a, 672, 770, 1003, 1218], but PCB levels still high enough to cause concern in some localities, early 1990s [16], including Moray Firth, NE Scotland [1218], and the Netherlands [1045]. Despite slight decrease over the last 20 years, PCB concentrations in many GB-stranded porpoises, 1989–2002 high enough to cause adverse physiological effects in other mammals [580, 928]. Brominated flame-retardants highest in N Irish Sea (median value 2.9 µg/g lipid, Irish and Scottish coasts), and W coast of Scotland (5.1 µg/g lipid) [1264].

Effects of these pollutants not clearly known; PCBs cause immunosuppression as well as reproductive impairment [16, 1136]. Females can transfer organochlorine compounds to their fetuses. Whereas no correlation initially found between PCB levels, body condition and cause of death in GB porpoises [663], nor in organochlorine levels and adrenocortical hyperplasia [662], mortality from infectious diseases considered to be associated with chronic exposure to both PCBs [471, 579] and mercury [114] in a much larger sample.

Often live in the vicinity of vessel traffic, may experience sound disturbance as well as danger of ship strikes. Off Shetland, porpoises showed short-term avoidance of speedboats and large ferries, although reactions varied with group size, social status, and season [348, 349, 359]. Pile-driving activities during windfarm construction shown to result in both short-term and longer-term avoidance by porpoises [227, 1141].

Legally protected in European, British and Irish waters (Table 12.1). Listed by IUCN [971] as 'vulnerable'.

LITERATURE
General review [960]; aspects of biology, diet, management and conservation well covered in special IWC issue [135] and a NAMMCO volume [499]; anatomy and physiology reviewed in [827, 962] and feeding in [1031].

PRINCIPAL AUTHORS
P.G.H. Evans, C.H. Lockyer, C.S. Smeenk, M. Addink & A.J. Read

FAMILY DELPHINIDAE (DOLPHINS)

The most diverse family of cetaceans, with 34–36 species in 17–18 genera [558, 971, 945, 1245]. Relationships within Delphinidae poorly understood [962]. Mostly small, fast-swimming, predators of fish, though largest take other mammals and birds. In British waters, 7 species, each in a different genus, occur regularly, and another 4 occur irregularly.

Bottlenose dolphin *Tursiops truncatus*
Delphinus truncatus Montagu, 1821; R. Dart, Devon.

Dolffin trwyn potel (Welsh); *muc-bhiorach* (Scottish Gaelic); *deilf bolgshrónach* (Irish Gaelic).

RECOGNITION
Robust dolphin (Plate 16) with short, stout beak. Melon clearly distinct from beak. Coloration generally counter-shaded tones of grey. Some subtle patterning but no strongly contrasting colour patches (cf. other dolphins). Dorsal fin tall, slender, sickle-shaped, placed midway along back. Usually identified by eliminating other species first. Can be confused with harbour porpoise and white-beaked dolphin. Key features are coloration, dorsal fin, blunt beak and demarcated melon.

Behaviour at sea variable. May swim alone or in schools of up to 50 individuals; rarely, schools of hundreds. Often boisterous, with leaps and splashing, readily approach boats and ride pressure waves.

DESCRIPTION
Body: Robust, torpedo-shaped; stout head with blunt bottle-end beak. Abrupt junction between upper jaw and beak. Dorsal fin central on back, tall, generally sickle-shaped, but can be triangular, particularly in young animals. Flippers pointed. Moderately keeled tail stock, tail flukes with deep median notch.

Coloration: Variable. Generally counter-shaded; black, brown or dark grey on back, lighter grey flanks and white or cream on belly. Calves generally paler, often light grey, cream or olive. Neonates marked with several vertical pale bars at intervals along body. Adults may have indistinct cape from apex of melon broadening from blowhole to dorsal fin. Skin frequently marked with pale scars, particularly around jaws. Discoloured skin patches from disease common in British waters.

Skull: Broad with short rostrum. Teeth stout and conical, 19–26 per quadrant (Fig. 12.20). Tooth

Plate 16

A Pygmy sperm whale *Kogia breviceps* B Bottlenose dolphin *Tursiops truncatus* C Atlantic white-sided dolphin *Leucopleurus acutus* D White-beaked dolphin *Lagenorhynchus albirostris* E Fraser's dolphin *Lagenodelphis hosei* F Striped dolphin *Stenella coeruleoalba* G Melon-headed whale *Peponocephala electra* H Harbour porpoise *Phocoena phocoena* I Short-beaked common dolphin *Delphinus delphis*

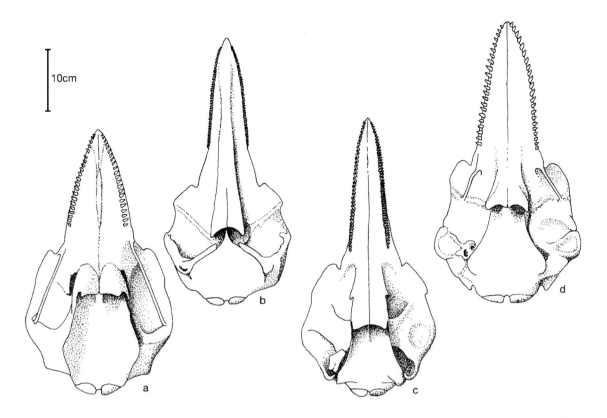

Fig. 12.20 Palates of (a) white-beaked, (b) common, (c) striped and (d) bottlenose dolphins, to show longer beaks with more (*c.*45) teeth of common and striped dolphins, and the characteristic grooves in the palate of common dolphin (*drawn by D.W. Yalden*).

enamel smooth, tips often worn flat. Morphology variable between regions and habitats, typically larger and more robust in colder climates.

RELATIONSHIPS

Tursiops recently split into 2 species: bottlenose dolphin *T. truncatus* widespread, in tropical and temperate waters worldwide, including around British Isles; Indo-Pacific bottlenose dolphin *T. aduncus,* restricted to coastal waters of warm temperate–tropical Indo-Pacific. Genus remains under review, may be split further in future. Genetically close to *Stenella* and *Delphinus*, though phylogeny within Delphinidae not well resolved [962].

MEASUREMENTS

Highly variable between regions. Animals around British Isles perhaps amongst world's largest. Length: newborn c.1.20–1.30 m, adult *c.*3.20 m (female), *c.*3.42 m (male) [1024]. Weight to 365 kg. Age and length at sexual maturity unknown for European populations. Likewise, level of sexual dimorphism unknown, but adult males in W Atlantic 10% longer than females [1154].

VARIATION

Highly variable in morphology, pigmentation and behaviour across range and habitats. Distinct ecotypes identified in adjacent inshore and offshore areas off E USA and S Africa. Ecotypic and other variation not described for NE Atlantic but other differences include ranging patterns, social organisation and disease [701, 1242, 1251]. Significant genetic variation found in coastal dolphins in British and European waters, boundaries coinciding with transitions in environmental features such as surface salinity, productivity and temperature [832, 901]. Local populations (e.g. off NE Scotland) have lower genetic diversity [901].

DISTRIBUTION

Worldwide in coastal and offshore tropical and temperate waters. In NE Atlantic, locally common from N Africa to N Scotland (Fig. 12.21). Degree of site fidelity in coastal habitats variable: groups apparently resident in Scottish NE coast, Sound of Barra (Scotland), Cardigan Bay (Wales) and Shannon estuary (Ireland) [360], but other groups off Cornwall, Devon (England) and W Isles (Scotland) more mobile. Probably once common in S North Sea [1177]. Current N limit of coastal range, N Scotland. Frequent sightings at or beyond the continental shelf break, offshore distribution extends N at

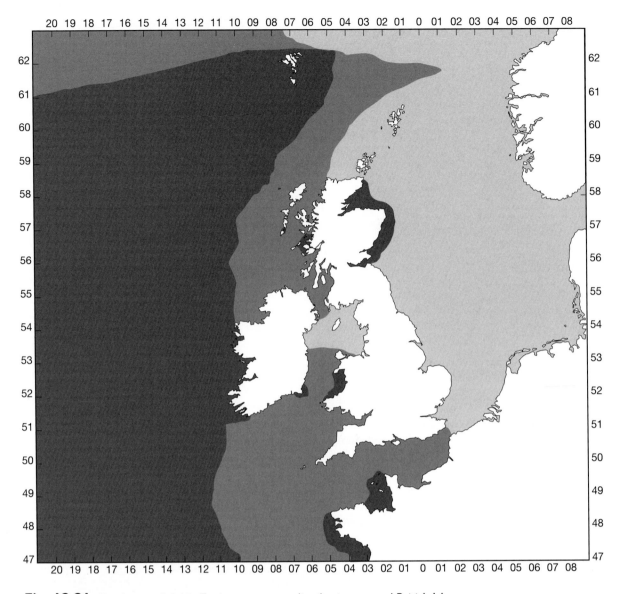

Fig. 12.21 Bottlenose dolphin *Tursiops truncatus*: distribution around British Isles.

least to Faroes [767, 973]. Little known about ecology of offshore animals though often associated with pilot whales *Globicephala melas*. Relationship between offshore and coastal bottlenose dolphins unknown. Local migrations in coastal areas probably driven by prey availability [1251, 1241]. Lone animals occasionally resident in small coastal areas, may associate with humans [707].

HISTORY

Genus *Tursiops* arose *c.*5 mya. *T. truncatus* in fossil record from Pleistocene, recovered from Atlantic and Pacific basins and coastal habitats. Most evidence from area around Mediterranean but specific point of origin unknown [101].

Known in British waters from Anglo-Saxon era (7th–10th centuries AD), when archaeological evidence indicates targeted fishery of population near the Humber estuary [514]. This population now apparently extinct, other similar changes elsewhere: dolphins in S North Sea became increasingly rare during 20th century, new groups appeared to have settled during the 19th or 20th century (Moray Firth, Scotland; Cornwall, Devon) [342, 1159, 1177, 1240, 1251]. Thus coastal communities can be dynamic and result from extinctions or changes in distribution. Such range shifts may be rapid or gradual, taking a decade or more [1244].

HABITAT

Cosmopolitan in British waters: found offshore, at the shelf break and close inshore. Inshore distribution includes estuaries and harbours; brief forays into fresh water. Areas of strong tidal currents and steep bottom relief particularly favoured [492].

SOCIAL ORGANISATION AND BEHAVIOUR

Most often found in small schools (2–50); sightings of single animals or hundreds comparatively rare. School size generally correlated with habitat; larger schools in more open and offshore environments (Fig. 12.22). School composition best studied in coastal areas where schools dynamic, change composition frequently, forming 'fission–fusion' societies. Small groups (20 animals) more stable, typically a mixture of males, females, calves and adults. Seem to show longer-term associations. Studies in N America, Australia suggest that adult females with young preferentially associate with other females and their calves, subadults with other subadults, and adult males form stable alliances with other males of similar age [275, 1107, 1221]. Male alliances thought to influence female movements and mating partners; this not observed in British dolphin communities, males may adopt a different mating strategy [1240].

Cooperation between individuals common, includes baby-sitting and coordinated hunting; with increased defence against predators and infanticide [904], probably main reasons for sociality of this species. Relationships between individuals complex, suggest high degree of individual recognition, long-term memory of previous encounters [275].

Generally slow swimmers (*c*.4 km/h), can reach 54 km/h [716]. Frequently approach boats to ride pressure waves. Surface behaviour diverse, includes breaches, slapping tails on the surface, side-rolls and a variety of exhalations including rapid loud exhalations and blowing raspberries. Functions of these behaviours poorly understood.

Vocalisations: Diverse. Echolocation clicks (used for orientation and foraging) are intense, short duration, broadband clicks (40–130 kHz) [68]; broadcast in episodic trains, can continue for duration of dive, culminate in buzzes and whines as approach target. Burst pulse vocalisations (barks, yelps and donkey brays, 0.2–16 kHz,) may have a variety of social and feeding-related functions [564]. Whistles, pure-tone frequency-modulated calls ranging from 2–20 kHz, produced in social contexts.

FEEDING

Diet: Generally considered selective opportunistic; includes a wide variety of benthic and pelagic, solitary and schooling, fish and cephalopods. Individuals may specialise on particular prey species or switch as availability changes particularly with area and season. Documented prey in British waters include gadoids (cod, saithe, whiting, haddock), salmon, sprats, sandeels, flatfish and cephalopods [1034].

Fig. 12.22 Cetaceans often form mixed schools, here long-finned pilot whales (foreground) and bottlenose dolphins (*photo D. Stroud*).

713

Feeding methods: Independent and cooperative feeding observed. Local topography, shore line, water surface or tidal interfaces, may be used to herd prey [493, 701, 715]. Exploits human fisheries in several parts of the world, particularly trawling and gillnets. Other than direct competition for prey and accidental capture in fishing nets, few interactions between human fisheries and bottlenose dolphins in British waters are known. Echolocation undoubtedly important for prey detection, may also use passive listening and vision. Probably feeds day and night.

Food requirements: Captive dolphins consume 3–6% of body weight in food per day.

BREEDING

Mating system unclear but violent interactions between males, heavy body scarring, subtle size dimorphism and formation of male–male alliances suggest competition for access to females. In addition, large testis size and high concentrations of spermatozoa in ejaculate imply polygamy. Thus probably a promiscuous system, each sex mating with several partners, but plasticity in behaviour and morphology suggests that mating systems may vary between populations.

Females are spontaneous sporadic ovulators, cycling repeatedly within season. Males may be sexually active throughout the year with prolonged elevation of testosterone during the mating season(s). Single calf (twins exceptionally rare), gestation *c.*12 months. Extended season for births, though peak May–November in British waters [340, 1240], may be timed to coincide with warmest water temperatures. Sex ratio of births *c.*1:1. Specifics of female behaviour associated with the birth unclear. Frequent claims of nursery areas, but evidence lacking. Calves dependent on milk for 18–20 months. Weaning gradual, suckling may last several years. Mating and pregnancy occur while previous calf still associating with mother. Calf may leave mother at birth of subsequent calf or remain in association. Interbirth interval variable from 2 to 5 years, generally shorter if calf dies prematurely.

Neonates swim and breathe without aid immediately after birth, gain hydrodynamic advantage from mother by positioning just below and behind her dorsal fin. Breaths taken during awkward lunges through the water surface. Sucking frequent when mother stationary or swimming. Calves gradually become more adept at swimming and gain independence, interacting with males and females from a wide range of age groups. Levels of independence displayed by calf thought to be a compromise between increased social learning and elevated chances of predation

or infanticide. Fathers probably play no part in raising young.

Growth rates greatest during period of suckling, i.e. first 1.5–2 years. Asymptotic size reached around or shortly after puberty. Age at sexual maturity varies regionally, around 5–13 years (females), 10–15 years (males) [1220]. Males may reach >20 years before attaining breeding status [1220]. Females appear to reproduce throughout life, without reproductive senescence. Precise ageing possible by examining tooth sections. Off Florida, females may live to 50 and males to 40–45 years.

POPULATION

Estimates of inshore dolphins around the British Isles total at least 490 individuals [80, 465, 549, 1228, 1243]; at least 85 occur coastally in the English Channel and off W France [702]. Wide-scale SCANS-II survey, 2005, W European continental shelf waters (W Baltic, North Sea and Atlantic margin as far as S Spain) estimated 12 600 bottlenose dolphins in this area (CV=27%), mostly offshore. Numbers W of continental shelf break unknown.

MORTALITY

Causes of death diverse. Disease probably most common cause, killer whale or shark predation less frequent in British waters than elsewhere. Death from attack by other bottlenose dolphins, physical injury, hypothermia, natural poisoning, starvation and mother–calf separation recorded. Eventual mortality often the result of several factors in combination.

PARASITES/COMMENSALS

Of all cetaceans, parasites and diseases of bottlenose dolphins best known due to worldwide distribution, prevalence in captivity and frequency of stranding. Range of organisms diverse [1220]. Ectoparasites including barnacles and remoras generally common, but rare off NW Europe. Endoparasites diverse and common, include trematodes, cestodes and nematodes. Viral, bacterial, protozoan and fungal pathogens frequently described [1220].

RELATIONS WITH HUMANS

The best-known and most widely exhibited of all dolphins in aquaria. Lone wild individuals sometimes associate with bathers and small vessels [707]. Coastal populations increasingly targeted for dolphin-watching activities. Anthropogenic threats diverse. Hunts outlawed but direct physical injury from boat strikes, underwater explosions, and entanglement in fishing equipment occur [147, 856, 993]. Organochlorines, heavy metals, petrochemicals and other toxins thought to affect immune and reproductive abilities [584]. Habitat alteration and overfishing may reduce prey abundance [905], and noise disturbance may disrupt social communication and foraging [993].

Legally protected in European, British and Irish waters (Table 12.1). Key bottlenose dolphin habitats in the Moray Firth and Cardigan Bay designated as Special Areas of Conservation under EU Habitats Directive (see Chapter 4).

LITERATURE
General review [1220], see also species account in [922].

AUTHOR
B. Wilson

GENUS *Stenella*

Coined by Gray in 1866, *Stenella* considered a subgenus of *Steno* until Oliver raised it to a genus in 1922. Widely distributed, mainly in warm and temperate waters. *Stenella* generally considered to include 5 species of long-beaked slender dolphins [910, 917]: only 1, *S. coeruleoalba* in European waters; pantropical spotted dolphin *S. attenuata*, worldwide in tropical waters; spinner dolphin *S. longirostris*, also worldwide in tropical waters; clymene dolphin *S. clymene*, in tropical and subtropical Atlantic; Atlantic spotted dolphin *S. frontalis*, also in tropical and warm temperate Atlantic. Also a number of poorly differentiated forms; taxonomy has been very confused.

Striped dolphin *Stenella coeruleoalba*
Delphinus coeruleo-albus Meyen, 1833; off Rio del Plata, E coast of S America
Delphinus styx Gray, 1846; S Africa.
Delphinus euphrosyne Gray, 1846 N Pacific.

Euphrosyne or blue-white dolphin; *deilf riabach* (Irish Gaelic).

RECOGNITION
Small, swift dolphin (Plate 16) with slender beak, superficially resembling common dolphin but shorter beak. Always in groups. Frequently breaches clear of water, showing black lateral stripes from eye to flipper and eye to anus that give its name; distinctive light grey blaze on upper flanks, above and behind eye to side of dorsal fin; lacks yellow patches of common dolphin. Skull with similarly numerous teeth but lacking deep palatal grooves of common dolphin (Fig. 12.20).

DESCRIPTION
Slender torpedo-shaped body with elongated beak (to *c*.10–12 cm). In each jaw, 39–50 pairs of sharp, slightly incurved teeth (*c*.3 mm in diameter). Distinct groove separates beak from forehead. Coloration variable, dark grey or bluish grey on back, lighter grey flanks, and white belly. 2 distinctive black stripes on flanks, 1 from eye to anus (often doubled by a secondary thinner and lighter stripe originating from this band and turning downwards towards the flippers) and a 2nd thick black stripe from below eye to flippers (Fig. 12.23). Conspicuous light grey blaze originates above and behind eye, narrowing to point below dorsal fin; posterior part of flanks light grey sometimes upwards over dorsal surface of tail stock. Tapering, black flippers inserted in white region, although some individuals show rather pale flippers towards base; slender sickle-shaped, centrally-placed, black dorsal fin. Narrow tail-stock with no obvious keel; dark tail flukes with median notch.

RELATIONSHIPS
Molecular evidence suggests that *S. coeruleoalba* closest to *S. clymene*, then *S. frontalis*; also close to *Delphinus*. Spotted and spinner dolphins *S. attenuata, S. longirostris* should probably be in a different genus [763].

MEASUREMENTS
Length: newborn *c*.0.80–0.95 m; at sexual maturity 1.94–1.97 m (female), 2.01–2.28 m (male); adult female 1.85 m (mean) to 2.25 m (max.), male 2.0 (mean) to 2.4 m (max.) Weight: newborn 7–10 kg, adult mean 70–90 kg, max. *c*.130 kg [310, 674, 948].

VARIATION
Some intraspecific variation in pigmentation [59, 409, 1169]. Specimens from NE Atlantic longer, heavier than those from Mediterranean [60, 310]; these 2 populations are genetically distinct [167, 426, 1170]. Within Mediterranean population, specimens from S seem to be longer than those from N [208], and inshore and offshore dolphin groups significantly differentiated genetically [430]. No skeletal differences detected between E and W Atlantic populations [60]. Nuclear and mtDNA indicate Atlantic population more genetically diverse than Mediterranean one, the latter having significant heterozygote deficiency [167, 1170]. Bycaught striped dolphins from Celtic Sea showed no significant genetic differentiation (using 13 microsatellite loci) from ones stranded on SW coast of Ireland; both had similar low levels of genetic diversity to Mediterranean population [788].

Fig. 12.23 Striped dolphins, showing the eponymous stripes (*photo M. Reichelt*).

DISTRIBUTION

Worldwide, mainly in tropical and warm temperate waters. In NE Atlantic, occurs mainly offshore from the continental shelf of Spain, Portugal and France (also in W Mediterranean). An occasional visitor around British Isles, recorded mainly from SW [120, 346, 358, 360]; occasionally strays in shelf waters further N to Scotland, where both sightings and live strandings recorded [346, 360, 1074] (Fig. 12.24). Records in mid Atlantic to 62° N suggest that distribution offshore extended northward by Gulf Stream [346, 358, 360].

Only 5 strandings (average 0.09/year) on British and Irish coasts 1913–1969; 9 strandings (average 0.60/year) 1970–1984; sharp increase, to 145 strandings (average 9.67/year), 1985–1999 [120, 188, 408, 816, 1002, 1072, 1074]. Some earlier *Stenella* may have been misidentified as *Delphinus*, as possible also with some Irish specimens [120, 867], but recent increase in both strandings and sightings, including records since mid 1980s from Scotland, indicate that species is ranging further N, possibly reflecting warmer sea temperatures [346, 360]. Has also been recorded recently from Icelandic, Danish, Swedish and Norwegian waters (with sightings up to 66.5° N) [144, 560].

Around British Isles (Fig. 12.24), most sightings July–September, whereas strandings mainly December–March [120, 346, 360, 864, 1074].

HISTORY

No fossil material found. Often depicted in ancient Greek and Roman art.

HABITAT

An oceanic species of warm and temperate waters (modal SST, NE Atlantic, 19 °C); mainly occurs well beyond continental shelf in depths of >1000 m; occasionally comes on to the shelf, where recorded in waters of 60 m depth or less [360, 384, 386]. From Sea Watch database, 75% of sightings in NW European seas recorded at SSTs of 12.5–16.5 °C (total range including outliers 9.5–18 °C), but upper limits likely to be skewed low since data come from N part of its range [54].

SOCIAL ORGANISATION AND BEHAVIOUR

Sightings in British and Irish waters either single individuals (sometimes in mixed herds with common dolphins) or more usually groups up to 30 individuals [346, 358, 973]. Elsewhere, group size may number hundreds or even low thousands of animals; in European Atlantic waters, groups of 6–60 most common [973], modal group size 30 [384]. May show strong segregation by age, some

716

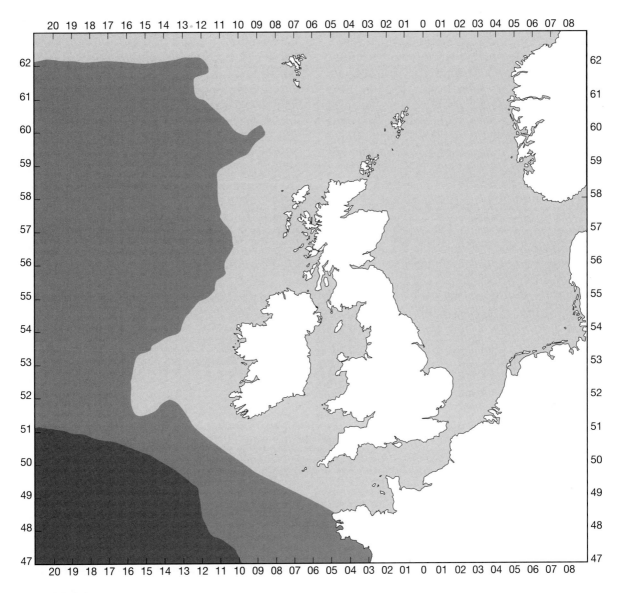

Fig. 12.24 Striped dolphin *Stenella coeruleoalba*: distribution around British Isles.

schools entirely comprising immatures, and others mixed with mature and immature males and females [799]. Some evidence of segregation of sexes outside breeding season, especially around British Isles, where recent strandings predominantly males [120, 834, 1022, 1074]. Fast swimmer (13–25 km/h [665]); frequently breaches clear of water. May also bow-ride, although less inclined than common dolphins to approach vessels.

Vocalisations: Emits clicks from 0.3 to >100 kHz (max. source level 168 dB) at repetition rates of up to 900 clicks/s, and FM whistles from 3.5 to 28.5 kHz (mainly around 10 kHz, max. source level 170 dB) [1204, 1263].

FEEDING

Diet: In E North Atlantic, feeds on a variety of meso- and benthopelagic fish, including sprat *Sprattus sprattus,* blue whiting *Micromesistius poutassou, Trisopterus* spp., *Atherina* spp., silvery pout *Gadiculus argenteus,* whiting *Merlangius merlangus,* hake *Merluccius merluccius,* scad *Trachurus trachurus,* bogue *Boops boops,* anchovy *Engraulis encrasicholus, Chauliodus sloanei,* garfish *Belone belone,* myctophids and gobies. Squid are also frequently taken, including *Chirotheutis* spp., *Loligo* spp., *Histioteuthis reversa* and *H. bonnelli, Alloteuthis subulata, Todarodes sagittatus, T. eblanae, Ancistroteuthis lichtensteini, Illex coindetii, Abraliopsis pferrei, Onychoteuthis banksii, Brachioteuthis riisei, Sepietta oweniana,* and *Heteroteuthis dispar* and crustaceans such as *Pasiphaea multidentata,* and *P. sivado, Acanthephyra pelagica* and *Sergetes spp.* [119, 138, 304, 675, 945, 996, 1032, 1113, 1253].

Fatty acid profiles from tissues of stranded animals along Scottish, Irish, French and Spanish

Atlantic coasts show no clear geographical separation, suggesting broadly similar diets [675]. However, stable isotope analysis of stranded animals from French Channel and Irish Atlantic coasts indicates a more oceanic diet for Irish specimens [296]. Stomach contents also differ geographically: haddock/saithe/pollack *Trisopterus* spp. and whiting more than 1/2 estimated prey weight in Scottish strandings; *Trisopterus* spp. and hake most frequently recorded from Irish strandings; in French Atlantic waters, 61% of estimated prey weight comprised a wide variety of fish, whereas squid *Todarodes sagittatus* and gobies together made up *c.*70% of prey weight in Galician strandings [675], and cephalopods comprised 56% of prey weight in bycaught animals from oceanic waters, Bay of Biscay, with fish (39%), particularly lanternfish, next in importance [996]. Probably change their diet as they move over the shelf [1113].

BREEDING

Reproductive parameters found to vary with exploitation pressure and populations [21, 309, 602]. Gestation period *c.*12 months, but lactation period between 8 and 20 (probably usually 12–14) months. Calving interval *c.*2–4 years. Sexual maturity reached at *c.*12/14 years and 182/180 cm (males/females) in Mediterranean; at 7–14 years, 211–228 cm (males) and 15–18 years, 194–197 cm (females) in E North Atlantic [309, 675]. In sample (n = 60) of Irish strandings and bycaught animals, age at sexual maturity was 15+ years (males) and 6–10 years (females) [621, 948]; asymptotic lengths were 233 cm (males) and 203 cm (females), although males exhibited a slower growth rate than females [1008]. Breeding season extended and probably variable: July–October in Mediterranean, mainly April–May in NE Atlantic [309].

POPULATION

Only population estimate for NE Atlantic covered continental shelf off SW Ireland and NW France (excluding Bay of Biscay) and NW Spain, extending up to 20° W: 73 843 (36 113–150 990) [454]. In NW Mediterranean, population estimated at 50 634 (32 254–79 488) [387], and for whole W Mediterranean basin, 225 000 (131 000–386 000) [385].

In NE Atlantic, sex ratio varied from 1:1.08 male:female in sample from tuna drift net bycatches (n = 406, 1992–1993 seasons), to 1:0.75 in a sample of stranded specimens (n = 761 from 1970 to 1999); both samples possibly unrepresentative because of age/sex segregation [269–271]. No significant variation in sex ratio from Irish strandings [621].

Longevity *c.*30–35 years, maybe up to 58 years

[918]. No mortality rates calculated for European populations.

MORTALITY

Severe die-off due to morbillivirus infection in C and W Mediterranean, 1990–1992. Over 1100 carcasses were collected on Spanish, French and Italian coasts; nevertheless, not possible to evaluate impact on total population [18, 149, 903]. Most significant pathologies were subacute to chronic pneumonia, encephalitis and lymphoid depletion [323]. Did not affect all age classes equally: fully mature dolphins (11–20 years old) most affected [209]. Those that died during initial stages of morbillivirus outbreak (1990–1992) were significantly more inbred than those that died later [1170].

Possible predators are sharks and killer whale [271, 676].

PARASITES

Many parasites recorded, including 10 trematodes, 6 cestodes, 8 nematodes, 2 acanthocephalans and 9 crustaceans [952]. In European waters, frequently infested with nematodes, notably *Anisakis simplex* (which may provoke gastric ulceration [77]), *Stenurus ovatus*, *Skrjabinalius guevarai*, and *Crassicauda* spp. Other endoparasites include tapeworms (mainly *Phyllobothrium delphini* and *Monorygma grimaldii*, but also *Strobilocephalus triangularis*, *Scolex pleuronectis* and *Tetrabothrium forsteri*), and trematodes *Pholeter gastrophilus*, *Nasitrema* sp., *Zalophotrema atlanticum*, *Campula rochebruni*, *C. palliata*, *Oschmarinella mascomai* and acanthocephalan *Bolbosoma vasculosum* [4, 304, 308, 370, 442, 739, 869]. Ectoparasitic crustaceans *Conchoderma auritum*, *Isocyamus delphini*, and *Xenobalanus globicipites*, *Lepas* spp., *Syncyamus aequus* and *Penella* spp. [4, 75, 304, 308, 370, 442, 739, 869, 1109]. Oval or circular scars on skin caused by lampreys or remoras.

RELATIONS WITH HUMANS

Occasionally hunted in S Europe (including Mediterranean). Substantial bycatch in French tuna drift net fishery operating in an area from 44–51.5° N, includes Bay of Biscay from 6° to 21° W; annual catches around 1200, representing *c.*1.6% of estimated population in area [272, 453, 454]. Much smaller GB albacore driftnet fishery, 1995, caused estimated bycatch of 104 striped dolphins [1053]. Irish albacore driftnet fishery, 1996, caused estimated bycatch of 134 striped dolphins, extrapolated to 964 in 1998 due to increased effort [489]; these caught mainly on N edge of Porcupine Seabight, a gently sloping area of relatively high productivity, 500–2000 m in depth [1006]. Overall, estimated *c.*12 635 striped dolphins killed incidentally by combined French, Irish and GB tuna driftnet fisheries, 1990–2000 [1005]. With recent ban on driftnets and change to pelagic trawls, number of Irish bycaught striped dolphins has declined (8 striped dolphins out of 145 cetaceans in 1999 [153].

High pollutant levels (max. 833 μg/g wet weight PCBs and 706 μg/g wet weight total DDT) found in blubber of striped dolphins from French Mediterranean [30]; mean levels much lower, show slight decrease over 1987–1993 [162]. Mercury levels up to 2272 μg/g dry weight in liver, W Mediterranean specimens [74], up to 42.6 μg/g dry weight of cadmium in kidney [744]. Total PCB concentration may be twice as high in adult males as females, which transfer contaminants to offspring during gestation and lactation; pollutant concentrations therefore decline with age in females [161]. Mediterranean die-off due to morbillivirus infection probably facilitated by known immunosupressive capacity of PCBs; casualties contained high levels (up to 778 μg/g wet weight in blubber) of PCBs and 440 μg/g wet weight of DDT [14, 15, 160].

Never maintained successfully in captivity. Legally protected in European, British and Irish waters (Table 12.1).

LITERATURE
Worldwide review [918]; recent overview [61].

AUTHORS
P.G.H. Evans & A. Collet

GENUS *Delphinus*

Differs from all other delphinids by the deep lateral grooves in the palate (Fig. 12.20).

Common dolphin *Delphinus delphis*
Delphinus delphis Linnaeus, 1758; European seas.

Short-beaked common dolphin; *dolffin cyffredin* (Welsh); *deilf cyffredin* (Scottish Gaelic).

RECOGNITION
Small, swift dolphin with long slender beak (Plate 16). Often attracted to moving vessels; frequently leaps clear of water revealing distinctive hourglass pattern of yellow and light grey intersecting patches on flanks. In stranded specimens, when colour pattern has disappeared, presence of deep palatal grooves in lateral-posterior part of palate distinguishes it from striped dolphin (Fig. 12.20).

DESCRIPTION
Slender torpedo-shaped body, with long (23–34 cm) dark beak; 41–56 pairs of small, sharp-pointed teeth (diameter c.3 mm) in each jaw. Chevron-shaped groove separates beak from low, receding forehead. Dorsal fin centrally located on back, slender and sickle-shaped to erect. Coloration variable both within and between populations [362, 521, 790, 913]. Species best identified by unique 'hourglass' or crisscross colour pattern formed from interaction of dorsal overlay and cape, resulting in distortions of the usual delphinine lateral and ventral fields. Lower margin of dorsal overlay passes high anteriorly and dips to cross ventral margin of low-riding cape, yielding four-part pattern of dark grey to black uppermost portion or spinal field (cape under dorsal overlay); yellow thoracic patch, dirty grey posterior portion or flank patch (undiluted dorsal overlay/lateral field), and white abdominal field [922]. Accessory abdominal stripes more common on animals from N Atlantic; distal flank blaze is either absent or less conspicuous on animals from the N Pacific [31, 521]. Dorsal fin black, but often with large creamy central patch; flipper variable, from black to light grey, particularly in E North Atlantic. Tail flukes dark grey or black, with distinct median notch. Anomalous pigmented forms described in several regions including NE Atlantic [921].

Distinct stripe runs parallel to lower margin of cape, from flipper to anus, passing below corner of gape and fusing with lip patch at >1/2 of gape length in NE Atlantic population [31]. Coloration of area adjacent to genital blaze is sexually dimorphic, males displaying prominent black blaze just above the genital opening, and females a narrower band of black and grey counter-shading [363].

RELATIONSHIPS
Both morphological and genetic data suggest 2 species: short-beaked common dolphin *Delphinus delphis* and long-beaked common dolphin *Delphinus capensis*; latter possibly contains 2 subspecies in Indo-Pacific region, nominate *D. c. capensis* and the extremely long-beaked *D. c. tropicalis* [521, 572, 833, 1012]. Recent research fails to confirm reciprocal monophyly of *D. delphis* vs *D. capensis* [33, 684]; have perhaps only very recently diverged [33, 626]. Overall, *D. delphis* populations, although highly morphologically variable, show low genetic differentiation (with evidence of gene flow across oceans), reflecting high mobility and a fluid social structure (by contrast, *D. capensis* exhibits high differentiation [833]). Closest to some of *Stenella* spp. (see above).

In N Atlantic, anatomical and genetic evidence concur that only short-beaked common dolphin present [33, 824, 833, 1184, 1224].

MEASUREMENTS

Length: newborn 90–110 cm [268, 821], average 93 cm [1]. *D. delphis* in NE Atlantic among largest documented, with maximum body lengths 250–270 cm [404, 406, 408, 485]. However, since 1980s max. body lengths of 250 cm (males) and 230 cm (females) reported, with most individuals <230 cm [268, 919, 821, 1087]. Weight: newborn 8–10 kg; mature individuals up to 135 kg.

Sexual size dimorphism evident, with ratio of 1.06 (male:female) for body length in NE Atlantic; some cranial and other body measurements also exhibit sexual dimorphism [820, 821]. Mature males have prominent postanal hump [821].

DISTRIBUTION

Occurs worldwide, in both temperate and tropical waters. In NE Atlantic, ranges widely from subtropical waters off Africa to 70° N [217, 345, 360, 363, 496, 1216]. Occurs along mid-Atlantic ridge S of Charlie Gibbs Fracture Zone, in areas of higher SST (14 °C), and from E North Atlantic to 35 °W [217, 1200]. In W North Atlantic mostly reported between the coast and continental shelf; suggests that during summer may be distributed across entire N Atlantic. Majority of on-shelf sightings reported below 60° N latitude, and more northerly incursions offshore likely to be influenced by warm currents of N Atlantic Drift [360, 973]. On GB continental shelf, common in W half of English Channel and S Irish Sea (particularly around Celtic Deep); in smaller numbers N to Sea of Hebrides and S part of Minch [360]. Also common S and W of Ireland [122]. In some years (e.g. since *c.*2000), occurs further N and E in shelf seas – in N Hebrides, around Shetland and Orkney, and in N North Sea [360, 732], probably due to stronger flow of N Atlantic

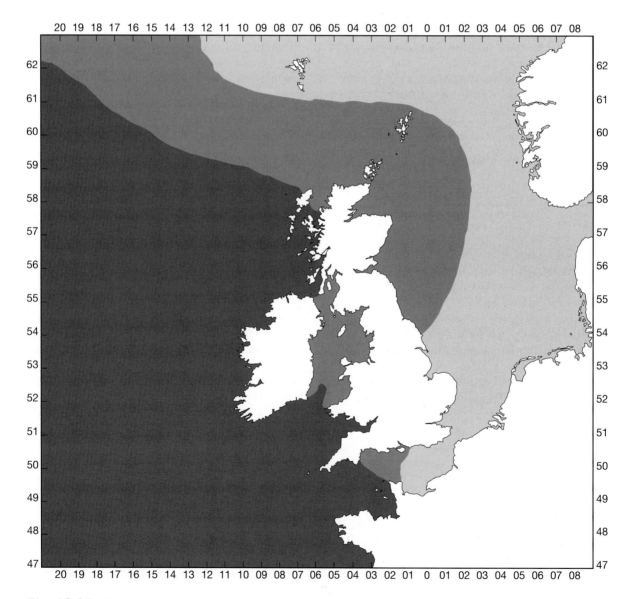

Fig. 12.25 Common dolphin *Delphinus delphis*: distribution around British Isles.

current. Generally rare in C–S North Sea and E English Channel [360, 973] (Fig. 12.25).

Distribution patterns in European seas show long-term changes. During 1930s–1970s, more strandings along Dutch and Danish coasts [91, 629], coinciding with decline along Irish and English coasts; strongly suggests a shift in general distribution [345, 356, 404, 406, 819, 824, 1071]. Decrease in strandings along English coastline appeared to coincide with changes in fish stocks off SW coast of England, and an increase in SST (Russell cycle) between 1920s and 1960s; result was that herring and whiting (along with other fish) became scarcer in English Channel, shifted their distribution northwards, with common dolphins following [356, 404, 824, 1111]. Since 1965, conditions of 1920s have returned, and have been more strandings of common dolphins along SW coast of England [361], S and W coasts of Ireland [819].

In W Scotland, sightings peak in June–July, then decline markedly; in Irish Sea, numbers peak in summer but continue to be present through winter, particularly in S [353, 360]. In W English Channel, S to Bay of Biscay, also occurs year-round, but numbers highest in winter [172, 360, 859].

HABITAT
Distribution correlated with prominent undersea topography such as seamounts and sea escarpments [362, 363], and continental slope waters [429, 1059]. From Sea Watch database, 75% of sightings in NW European waters occurred at SSTs of 11.5–15 °C (total range including outliers 6–19 °C [54].

VARIATION
Using genetic (mtDNA and microsatellite) and morphometric analyses of cranial specimens, low genetic differentiation reported between NE and NW Atlantic *D. delphis* populations, suggesting either recent separation or at least some gene flow [833, 1224].

Cranial morphometric analysis reveals population differentiation within E North Atlantic; female Portuguese common dolphins segregated from more northerly regions, may mix with those in the Mediterranean or further S [824]. No significant variation between W Mediterranean and adjacent North Atlantic (Straits of Gibraltar, Portugal), indicating gene flow [831]. Little differentiation between areas within NE Atlantic, suggesting high levels of gene flow [833, 789, 1184], with low or non-significant F_{ST} values and high number of shared haplotypes, although significant F_{ST} values reported using cytochrome *b* gene for both males and females within NE Atlantic [33], but sample sizes small.

Contaminant studies (cadmium levels) suggest 2 ecological stocks, in neritic and oceanic waters, Bay of Biscay, but also based on small sample sizes (from oceanic stock) [667].

Fig. 12.26 Common dolphins leaping (*photo P.G.H. Evans*).

SOCIAL ORGANISATION AND BEHAVIOUR

In NE Atlantic, usually travel in schools of 6–15 individuals (Fig 12.26); larger concentrations, hundreds or even thousands, sometimes observed, associated with feeding or large-scale movements [217, 340, 453, 721, 973, 1174].

Commonly bow-rides; exhibits a variety of above-surface activities, including forward and side breaches, somersaults, and tail-smacking. One, radio-tagged in NE Pacific, travelled 270 nautical miles (500 km) from capture site in 10 days [362], and even greater movements documented in E tropical Pacific [293]. Generally very agile and active, travelling at 15–20 km/h, sometimes twice as fast. Maximum recorded dive depth 280 m [362].

Evidence of age and sex segregation from sightings, mass live strandings and bycatch observed during both summer [353, 444] and winter [284, 819, 826]. In Portuguese bycatches, spring–summer, sexually mature females found only with young calves; sexually immature males either formed separate groups or joined mature male groups, with complete absence of sexually immature female groups [1087]. Elsewhere in Pacific [371] and off New Zealand [842], nursery groups and male bachelor groups reported, although large mixed groups comprising juveniles, mature males, mature females and their calves also observed [843].

Vocalisations: Include whistles of 1–50 kHz (mainly 5–20 kHz, duration 0.05–2.02 s, max. source level 172 dB); echolocation clicks, not adequately described but may reach 150 kHz (max. source levels 170 dB) at repetition rates of 30–200 clicks/s; pulsed calls, i.e. 'buzzes' and 'barks' [57, 361, 809, 1132, 1204]. Clicks and whistles may be produced simultaneously [335].

FEEDING

Diet: Includes variety of fish and squid. Reported to be opportunistic feeder [1259], but in NE Atlantic diet predominately comprises a few main species, which vary depending on season and region. Horse mackerel, mackerel, Norway pout and sardines dominant in stomachs of stranded specimens from British Isles, but other species included whiting, herring, scad, sprat and sandeel [119, 280, 451, 663, 902, 1029]. Cephalopods included mainly *Loligo* spp., *Alloteuthis subulata*, *Ancistroteuthis lichtensteini*, *Todarodes sagittatus*. *T. eblane* and *Sepiola atlantica*, although other squid species, octopus and cuttlefish also consumed. In French inshore waters, 4 taxa contributed to majority of dietary remains: anchovy, sardine, horse mackerel, and *Trisopterus* spp. [780]. Diet

displayed strong inter-annual and seasonal variations, reflecting prey availability in area [780]. In Portuguese waters, sardine, blue whiting, *Atherina* sp., *Trachurus* and scombrid species comprised 84% of total estimated weight, with *Sardina pilchardus* most important [1086]. In Galician waters, blue whiting and sardine together comprised >56% of prey weight consumed; main cephalopods *Loligo vulgaris* and *L. forbesi*; signs of opportunistic feeding, with higher numbers of sardines consumed in years of higher sardine abundance and lower recruitment of blue whiting; other species included scad, sandeels, scaldfish, sole, gobies, garfish, and *Atherina* sp. [1038].

Feeding methods: Food-herding behaviour frequently observed with apparent cooperation between school members [342, 344]. Where preferred prey species are very abundant, tend to be selective for those species. Thus, in inshore areas during winter, mainly prey upon small pelagic fish, whereas beyond continental shelf edge in summer, apparently feed predominantly nocturnally (when deep scattering layer near surface) on squids and mesopelagic fishes, e.g. myctophids [177, 178, 491, 947a].

BREEDING

In NE Atlantic, reproduction seasonal; mating and calving May–September as indicated both by marked seasonal changes in testes mass, cellular activity, in males and by presence of ovulating and recently pregnant females [819, 823]. Newborn calves sighted or stranded in W European waters May–September [268, 340, 360, 864, 928, 1022]. In Irish waters, gestation period *c*.11.5 months, with annual pregnancy rate (APR) 28.2%, calving interval 42.5 months, lactation period 10.4 months and resting period 20.7 months [819]. Low APR of 25% for NE Atlantic confirmed by data collected for EU BIOCET project, from stranded animals along Irish, French and Galician (N Spain) coasts, over a 2 year period.

Although lactation may last up to 10 months after parturition, dietary studies showed that while calves aged 0–3 months had only milk in their stomachs (n = 8), those aged 3–6 months had both milk and solid food (n = 3) [178, 819].

Average age at sexual maturity (ASM) for males 11.86 years. Mature males ranged from 8 to 28 years, and 195 to 233 cm in length (Irish and French data) [823]. Combined testes mass for mature males 0.45–5 kg – relatively large considering overall size, suggesting sperm competition and promiscuous mating system [823]. Females off Irish coast attained sexual maturity between 9 and 10 years of age. Immatures ranged in body length from 93 to

184 cm, pubertal individuals from 189 to 206 cm and sexually matures from 183 to 216 cm [819]. ASM of 8 years (SE = 0.69) calculated for BIOCET project, but with 89% of mature individuals >10 years [674].

POPULATION

Several surveys using line transect methods have estimated population abundance levels in the NE Atlantic. MICA survey, summer 1993, estimated population of 61 888 (95% CI 35 461–108 010) in area where French tuna driftnet fishery operated (Bay of Biscay, continental shelf W to *c.*20° W, and S to *c.*43° N) [454]. SCANS I survey, July 1994, included the Celtic shelf to *c.*11° W and 48° S, gave estimate of 75 450 (CV = 0.67; 95% CI 23 000–249 000) [481]. Where surveys overlapped in area along shelf edge (11° W–51° N to 8° W–48° N), total summer population estimated at *c.*120 000 [453]. During August 2002, the ATLANCET aerial survey covered 140 000 km² of continental shelf and shelf break in Bay of Biscay; overlapped with SCANS I survey area in S Celtic Sea, gave estimate of 17 639 (95% CI 11 253–27 652) [994, 1227]. NASS Faroese ship-based survey, 1995, covering 2 large areas to N and W of Ireland (NASS east and NASS west), gave estimate of 273 159 (95% CI 153 392–435 104) for western block [217], whereas SIAR survey estimated only 4496 (95% CI 2414–9320) within area *c.*120 000 km² off W Ireland during 30 July–22 August 2000. Differences may have resulted from survey design and/or precise area covered [864].

MICA and SCANS I did not use a double-platform method, nor correct for animals missed on track line (g(0)) and responsive movements; estimates from these surveys may therefore be inaccurate. In 2005, SCANS II surveyed same area as SCANS I, but increased to include Irish Sea, waters off W and N Ireland, W Scotland, and continental shelf waters off France, Spain and Portugal. Total summer abundance for those NE Atlantic shelf waters *c.*63 400 (CV = 0.46) [478].

MORTALITY

Possible predators are sharks, and killer or false killer whales, although no cases reported in European waters [676]. Bottlenose dolphins reported to attack common dolphins in NE Atlantic; carcass of sexually mature lactating female stranded on W coast of Ireland extensively bruised, especially along ventral abdomen between both pectoral fins, and had >25 sets of recent bottlenose dolphin rake marks along body [822].

Maximum age reported in NE Atlantic, 28 years [823]. No mortality rates calculated for this population.

HEALTH STATUS

In British waters, overall increase in numbers stranded since early 1990s, with 3-fold increase since 1999. Most reported in January–March, along SW coast of GB [579]. Increase in strandings attributed to increase in reporting effort, and/or increase in numbers caught in fishing gear, and/or increase in relative density of animals in W English Channel during winter [1023]. During 2000–2004, 61.1% (116/190) of autopsied stranded *D. delphis* diagnosed as incidentally caught in fishing gear, with 15.3% dying as result of a live stranding event, and 3.7% from starvation [1023]. In previous 10 years (1990–1999), data from 212 autopsies found that 56% of individuals died as result of entanglement in fishing gear, 8.9% from a live stranding event, 3.7% from pneumonia, with cause of death in 22.2% of cases undetermined [114, Table 3.3].

In general, common dolphins caught in fishing nets were in good health, and in good nutritional condition. Overall, mortality due to infectious disease rare. A few recent cases of fatal *Brucella* sp. meningoencephalitis in common dolphins in Scottish waters [580]. Overall, low seroprevalence of antibodies to morbilliviruses in common dolphins and other GB-stranded cetaceans examined 1989–1999, and probably therefore only accidental host to cetacean morbillivirus [1023]. [173, 174]. Pathological evidence that common dolphins (and other cetaceans) can suffer *in vivo* gas bubble formation [580]; 5 common dolphins stranded on British coasts 1992–2004 showed acute and chronic systemic gas and fat embolism, which caused acute and chronic lesions in various organs including liver, spleen, kidneys, and lymph nodes [580, 1023].

PARASITES

Often infested with nematodes, including lungworm *Halocerus delphini*, stomach worm *Anisakis simplex,* which may provoke gastric ulceration, and tissue worm *Crassicauda* sp. [77, 488]. Cestodes, e.g. *Phyllobothrium delphini* and *Monorygma* sp., and trematodes, e.g. liver fluke *Campula* sp. and stomach fluke *Pholeter gastrophilus*, also reported [488]. Whale lice and barnacles *Xenobalanus globicipites* observed only rarely.

RELATIONS WITH HUMANS

Main current cause of concern for NE Atlantic population is large-scale but poorly documented incidental capture in fishing nets [489, 813, 1160, 1161]. In 1990s, extensive bycatch by W European tuna driftnet fisheries [489] led to closure of these fisheries in 2002. Recent PETRACT project estimated total bycatch of common dolphins in GB, Irish, French, Dutch and Danish pelagic trawls, December 2003–May 2005. Incidental captures reported only in bass and tuna fisheries, with <*c*.1000 dolphins/year, *c*.95% identified as common dolphins [859]. Also reported bycaught in following fisheries in NE Atlantic: French, Irish and GB hake fisheries [813, 1161]; Dutch horse-mackerel fishery [279]; and also in Spanish trawls, gillnets and seine nets [720]; and Portuguese gill, beach seine and trawl nets [1087]; consequent bycatch mortality rates not determined.

Numerous contaminants investigated in NE Atlantic, including mercury [533], cadmium [295, 667], lead [232], hexabromocyclododecane [1264], DDT and PCBs [10, 30, 163, 164, 663]. A Σ-PCB level of 17 µg/g lipid reported as threshold level for effects on reproduction in bottlenose dolphin [1051]. However, in W European waters, 40% of the *D. delphis* sample exceeded this threshold value [928]. Highest PCB concentrations in blubber were generally in resting mature females with high numbers of corpora albicantia on their ovaries; unclear whether high contaminant burdens prevented them from reproducing, and inhibited ovulation, or females not reproducing for some other reason, either physical or social, and therefore accumulated high contaminant levels, as unable to pass burdens on to their offspring via placenta or through lactation.

Legally protected in European, British and Irish waters (Table 12.1).

LITERATURE
Worldwide review [363]; overview [913].

AUTHORS
S. Murphy, P.G.H. Evans & A. Collet

GENUS *Lagenorhynchus*

Conventionally a genus of about 6 species of slender dolphins with fewer, larger teeth than *Delphinus* or *Stenella*. However, taxonomy uncertain, molecular data suggest that may not be monophyletic on current taxonomy [962], and *L. acutus* certainly belongs in a different genus from *L. albirostris* (see below).

White-beaked dolphin *Lagenorhynchus albirostris*
Lagenorhynchus albirostris Gray, 1846; Great Yarmouth, England.

Deilf-gheal-ghobach (Scottish Gaelic); *deilf na ngoba bána* (Irish Gaelic).

RECOGNITION
Large, very stout dolphin (Plate 16) with short (5–8 cm) beak (often white in colour), black back except behind dorsal fin, where pale grey to whitish area extends from flanks, forming a distinctive pale 'saddle'; also grey to whitish blaze on flanks forward of dorsal fin. Black and whitish pattern very distinctive in the field, less obvious in dead animals. Large, often erect, sickle-shaped dorsal fin, centrally placed. Flippers larger, less clearly sickle-shaped than in white-sided dolphin, with fairly straight front margin.

Adult skull distinguished from that of white-sided dolphin by being larger and broader, with wider and clearly tapering rostrum and with fewer and larger teeth.

Fig. 12.27 Dorsal view of a white-beaked dolphin, showing both the beak and the characteristic black/white pattern on the flanks (*photo D. Burn*).

DESCRIPTION

Very stout torpedo-shaped body, rounded snout with short, fairly stubby beak and 22–28 pairs of small (*c.*7 mm diameter), sharp-pointed teeth in each jaw. Dark grey or black on back, tail and top of head; dark flank patch of varying extent below dorsal fin, separated from dark back by paler grey coloration of flanks. Pale grey to whitish area extending from flanks over dorsal surface behind fin and back to tail stock ('saddle': less distinct in young animals); pale grey to whitish blaze extending from below dorsal fin forward, sometimes forming pale 'chevron' over head or back (and sometimes passing over the blowhole) (Fig. 12.27). Beak generally white (not always easy to see in the field), but often blotched or spotted with dark grey; sometimes nearly all grey, always paler and contrasting with blackish dorsal surface. Pale eye ring, sometimes connected to beak by

thin, white line. Flippers and tail blackish; front edge of flippers near base and lower surface of tail often freckled with white. Ventral surface white; on central part of abdomen restricted to narrow band between greyish flank patches. Centrally placed, tall (*c.*15% body length), sickle-shaped dorsal fin. Thick tail stock, gradually tapering towards the slightly notched tail flukes, with concave trailing edges.

Adult skull larger, broader, than Atlantic white-sided dolphin, with wider, clearly tapering rostrum, fewer and larger teeth (Fig. 12.20). Lachrymal short and thick, not extending backward below frontal; ramus of lower jaw high, upper margin ascending behind tooth row, ending in a prominent coronoid process. Scapula much wider than high, more or less mushroom-shaped, with clearly concave hind margin. Upper process (acromion) directed nearly horizontally forward;

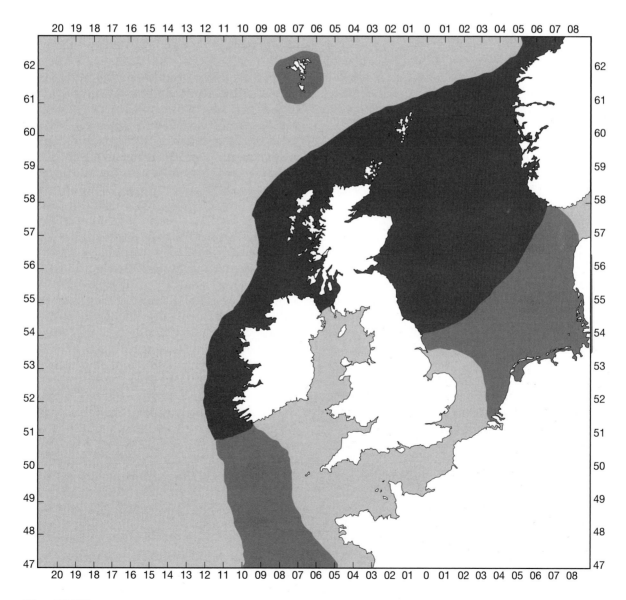

Fig. 12.28 White-beaked dolphin *Lagenorhynchus albirostris*: distribution around British Isles.

ventral margin of lower process (coracoid) clearly projecting downward below glenoid fossa. Front margin of flipper skeleton nearly straight, particularly the radius; combined width of radius/ulna at their distal end about equal to length of radius. These skeletal characters more similar to bottlenose dolphin than to Atlantic white-sided dolphin [1, 112, 800, 969].

RELATIONSHIPS
Analysis of cytochrome *b* [684], osteological characters including skeletal pathology (see below) and occurrence of apparently unique ectoparasite (see below) evidence that white-beaked dolphin not closely related to Atlantic white-sided dolphin, best placed in different genus. Generic name *Lagenorhynchus* thereby restricted to *L. albirostris*, type species for the genus.

MEASUREMENTS
Length: newborn 110–120 cm; at sexual maturity 230–250 cm (female), 250–260 cm (male); adults generally 240–270 cm (female), 250–280 cm (male); max. *c*.3.0 m (female), 3.1 m (male). Weight: newborn *c*.40 kg, adult max. 306 kg (female) (although one pregnant female, Netherlands, weighed 387 kg), 354 kg (male) [413, 630, 970].

VARIATION
Specimens from E and W Atlantic differ in skull characters [783]. Animals in British waters and North Sea may be partially separated from other populations [857, 858]; see also [876].

DISTRIBUTION
Restricted to northern N Atlantic, from SW and CE Greenland, Svalbard and Barents Sea, S to about Cape Cod (USA) and Bay of Biscay. Occurs over much of N European continental shelf; common in British and Irish waters, most abundantly in C and N North Sea across to W Scotland and Ireland; occasional off S Ireland, in the Irish Sea, W Channel, and N Bay of Biscay [97, 340, 345, 346, 360, 481, 857, 858, 973, 1236] (Fig 12.28). Similar distribution to the Atlantic white-sided dolphin, though less pelagic, generally more abundant on the continental shelf [340, 346, 360, 481, 857, 858, 973].

General decline (numbers sighted per unit effort), NW Scotland, since early 1980s; may reflect distributional change [346, 360]. Strandings significantly increased in S North Sea since 1960s, now regularly occur in S Bight [91, 630]. Other important concentrations occur off N Norway [876].

Recorded throughout the year in British waters, but largest numbers seen in late summer, July–September. May move offshore in winter, though poorer coverage may explain lower numbers seen then in nearshore waters [340, 341, 360, 857, 858].

HISTORY
No fossil or archaeological material known.

HABITAT
Found in cool and subarctic waters, usually over the continental shelf in waters 50–100 m deep. From Sea Watch database, 75% of sightings in NW European waters occurred at SSTs of 11–13 °C (total range including outliers 3–17 °C) [54].

SOCIAL ORGANISATION AND BEHAVIOUR
Most groups <10 individuals, but herds up to 50 not uncommon off NW Scotland, and a few sightings of groups numbering 100–500. Some segregation by age and sex, and, within larger aggregations, subgroups of 2–5 individuals commonly observed. Strandings of small groups (2–7 animals) not uncommon [970]. Otherwise, social structure poorly known. Groups of juveniles may be separated from groups of adults with calves [970]. Apparently adult males generally stay further offshore: of white-beaked dolphins stranded in the Netherlands, juveniles (<2.2 m) show a sex ratio of 1:1, but larger animals predominantly females. Predominance of females among stranded animals also found Denmark, Germany [630].

Moderately fast swimmer, usually travels at 6–12 km/h, attains bursts of 30 km/h [353]. Frequently approaches boats and bow-rides. Often breaches clear of the surface, leaping vertically, falling back into the water usually on its back or side, sometimes directly on to belly [97, 353]. Sometimes associates with fin, sei, and humpback whales, as well as with long-finned pilot and killer whales. Sometimes mixed herds with Atlantic white-sided dolphins, occasionally also with bottlenose dolphin, Risso's dolphin or common dolphin [148, 213, 340, 353, 467, 586, 970].

Vocalisations: Poorly known. Include whistles of 6.5–15 kHz (often *c*.8 kHz), with average source levels (SL) of 180 dB re 1 μPa @ 1 m. Echolocation clicks up to at least 325 kHz, with click bursts of 100–750 pulses/s, and maximum SL of 214 dB re 1 μPa @ 1 m (mean SL = 204 dB, mean inter-click interval = 51 ms) [795, 796, 957, 970, 1204].

FEEDING
Diet: Great variety of fish (including *Clupea, Mallotus, Gadus, Merlangius, Melanogrammus, Trisopterus, Eleginus, Merluccius, Trachurus, Scomber,* various species of Ammodytidae, Gobiidae,

Soleidae, Pleuronectidae and Bothidae), snow crab *Chionoecetes opilio* and octopus *Eledone cirrhosa*. Analyses of stomach contents, North Sea and Newfoundland, reveal cod *Gadus morhua*, whiting *Merlangius merlangus* and hake *Merluccius merluccius* as dominant prey [1, 340, 630, 970, 1032] [324, 428, 1101].

Feeding methods: Herds fish cooperatively. Groups seen hunting in a broad front, dolphins swimming parallel to each other at regular distances; fish shoals then encircled and trapped near the surface. Seabirds, particularly northern gannet, kittiwake, and other gull species often closely associate with feeding white-beaked dolphin groups [1, 341, 342].

BREEDING
Data limited. Births mainly in late spring-summer (May–August), with some in September–October [340, 346, 360, 408, 630, 970]. Gestation period *c.*10–11 months. Lactation period, calving interval and age at sexual maturity unknown. 3 pregnant animals, Newfoundland, at least 7 years old [324].

POPULATION
SCANS I survey, North Sea and adjacent waters, June–July 1994, gave estimate of 7856 (95% CI 4032–13 301) white-beaked dolphins, or of 11 760 (95% CI 5587–18 528) combining white-beaked and unidentified *Lagenorhynchus* (great majority probably white-beaked). All records were from North Sea and directly NW of Scotland, between *c.*54–60° N, 6° W–7° E [481]. Repeat survey (SCANS II), July 2005, covering a wider area (continental shelf seas from SW Norway, S to Atlantic Portugal), gave estimate of 22 700 (CV = 0.42) [478].

MORTALITY
Observed fleeing from pod of killer whales; frequently have scars thought to be caused by sharks and killer whales, but direct evidence of predation lacking [340, 970, 353]. Longevity at least 32 years (males) and 39 years (females) [413]. No information on mortality rates.

PARASITES AND PATHOGENS
2 whale-lice recorded: *Scutocyamus parvus* found on animals from North Sea; unknown from other dolphin species; a few records of *Isocyamus delphinii,* also from North Sea [1, 401].

Endoparasites: Nematodes *Anisakis simplex* (digestive tract) and *Halocercus lagenorhynchi* (bronchi) [170, 324, 441, 1065]; also *Pseudoterranova* sp. (stomach) [64], with trematode *Pholeter gastrophilus* also found [442].

Dystocia (birth trauma in mother, rather uncommon in other dolphins) found several times [424, 631]. Pneumonia occasional [424, 631]; in 1 animal stranded on Dutch coast, dystocia was associated with morbillivirus, in another with rhabdovirus [630, 885]; morbilli- and rhabdovirus also found in other animals from Dutch coast; 1 stranded in Suffolk had antibodies to morbillivirus [173]. Poxvirus in the skin reported [88]. Diseased jaws and teeth frequent in older animals [646, 970]. Discarthrosis (spondylosis deformans) and spondyloarthritis (spondyloarthropathy: reactive arthritis of the vertebrae) much more common in white-beaked dolphins than in other cetaceans; in one study, discarthrosis reported in 54% of 22 adult females and in 42% of 7 males [646–648]. A few animals found with kyphosis (S-shaped vertebral column) [646, 970]

RELATIONS WITH HUMANS
Organochlorine levels in blubber, kidney and muscle of 27 white-beaked dolphins from Newfoundland were high, considering that all <7 years old; also high levels of lead in kidney, liver and muscle. May have been overwintering in highly polluted Gulf of St. Lawrence [817]. Organochlorine levels in animals from GB generally low [770], as also in Denmark [50], E USA [619], although sample sizes small. Except for lead, heavy metals examined in an adult female, Liverpool Bay, also low [671a, 672]; same true for 7 stranded along Belgian and N French coasts [294].

Other threats poorly known, although small numbers reported bycaught from midwater trawls and driftnets set mainly for cod, mackerel, salmon or herring [347, 855].

Legally protected in European, British and Irish waters (Table 12.1).

LITERATURE
Most recent scientific review [970].

AUTHORS
P.G.H. Evans & C.S. Smeenk

GENUS *Leucopleurus*

Included in *Lagenorhynchus* by most authors, but molecular and genetic evidence argue for separation (see below). Since *L. albirostris* is type species for *Lagenorhynchus*, the generic name *Leucopleurus* (Gray 1866) is applicable to *L. acutus.*

Atlantic white-sided dolphin *Leucopleurus acutus*
Delphinus (Grampus) acutus Gray, 1828; type locality probably North Sea.

Deilf-chliathaich-ghil (Scottish Gaelic); *deilf le cliathán bán* (Irish Gaelic).

RECOGNITION

Similar to white-beaked dolphin but somewhat smaller. Large, robust dolphin (Plate 16) with short beak, black back; distinctive long, white patch on flanks; narrow, yellow-ochre band extending backwards on tail stock. Large, sickle-shaped dorsal fin, centrally placed. Flippers smaller, much more clearly sickle-shaped than in white-beaked dolphin, with strongly curved front margin. Skull smaller, narrower, with more but smaller teeth.

DESCRIPTION

Stout, torpedo-shaped body, rounded snout with short (*c*.5 cm) beak. Black on back including tail, top of head and upper jaw; dark grey flanks and side of head; long and narrow, sharply demarcated white patch on flanks from below front edge of dorsal fin to about halfway between dorsal fin and tail (Fig. 12.29), but not extending over back (as often in white-beaked dolphin). Sharply demarcated, long, narrow yellow-ochre band extending on to tail stock, starting as a thin line above the white flank patch and widening towards the tail, set off from grey flanks below by a black line originating from the tail stock. White belly and lower jaw. Flippers pointed and strongly re-curved, black; narrow dark stripe extends from angle of mouth to flipper insertion. Black eye patch, from which a thin black line extends forward to the dark upper jaw, and very thin black line from eye patch to ear opening (not visible in the field). Clearly demarcated black patch around genital/anal opening. Relatively tall (*c*.12% body length), centrally placed, sickle-shaped dorsal fin. Very high tail stock, parallel-sided, particularly in adult males, in which it suddenly narrows close to the slightly notched tail flukes, which have a concave trailing edge.

Adult skull smaller and narrower than in white-beaked dolphin, with narrower and only slightly tapering rostrum and with more (29–40) and smaller (*c*.4 mm diameter) teeth. Lachrymal long and narrow, extending far backward below frontal. Ramus of lower jaw low, upper margin behind tooth row nearly horizontal over about 2/3 of its length, no pronounced coronoid process. Scapula only slightly broader than high, with nearly straight hind margin. Upper process (acromion) directed more or less upward, ventral margin of lower process (coracoid) not or only slightly projecting below glenoid fossa (joint socket). Flipper skeleton strongly curved, particularly the radius; combined width of radius/ulna at the distal end greater than height of radius [1, 112, 800, 969, 970].

RELATIONSHIPS

Previously thought closely related to white-beaked dolphin *Lagenorhynchus albirostris*, and thus placed in same genus. Cytochrome *b* sequences indicate that not closely related, best placed in separate

Fig. 12.29 Atlantic white-sided dolphins rolling, showing distinctive white and yellow-ochre band on flanks. (*photo P.H.G. Evans*).

genera [684]. Corroborated by considerable skeletal differences, and occurrence of seemingly unique ectoparasite on white-beaked dolphin (see above).

MEASUREMENTS
Length: newborn 108–122 cm; at sexual maturity 2.0–2.2 m (female), 2.3–2.4 m (male); adult, generally 210–240 cm (female), 210–260 cm (male); max. *c.*253 cm (female), *c.*274 cm (male). Weight: newborn *c.*25 kg; max 182 kg (female), 234 kg (male) [8, 1007, 1066].

VARIATION
No differences in skull characters between specimens from E and W Atlantic [783].

DISTRIBUTION
Restricted to N North Atlantic, mainly in offshore waters, from SW Greenland, Iceland and W Barents Sea S to Virginia (USA) and the Bay of Biscay. Less common than white-beaked dolphin on European continental shelf [346, 360, 481, 858, 876, 973]. Off British Isles, concentrated around Hebrides, N Isles and N North Sea, but extends S along Atlantic seaboard, mainly outside or near the continental shelf (*c.*200 m depth), W and S of Ireland and Bay of Biscay; rare in the Irish Sea, English Channel and S North Sea (Fig. 12.30) [279, 340, 346, 360, 630, 688, 858, 969, 973, 1236].

HISTORY
No fossil or archaeological material known.

HABITAT
More pelagic than white-beaked dolphin, occurring mainly along edges or seaward of continental shelves, over depths of 100–300 m. Sometimes comes on to continental shelf, may

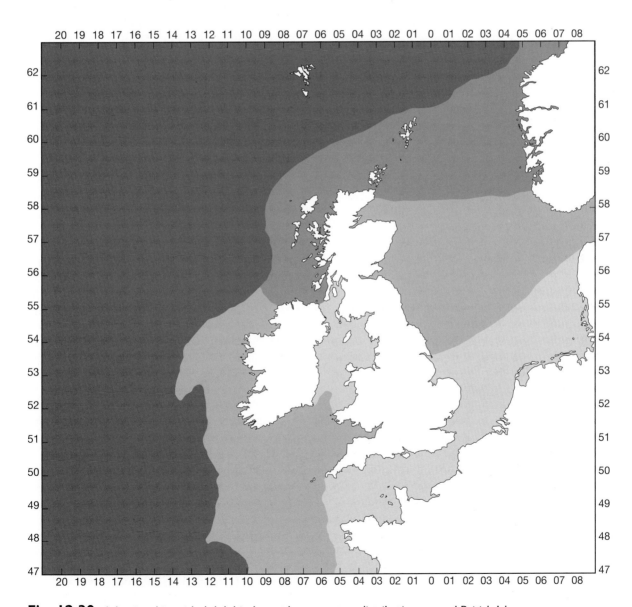

Fig. 12.30 Atlantic white-sided dolphin *Leucopleurus acutus*: distribution around British Isles.

enter fjords and inlets with depths <50 m. From Sea Watch database, 75% of sightings in NW European seas recorded at SSTs of 7–13 °C (total range including outliers 6–17.5 °C) [54]. In European seas, occur mainly in SSTs of *c*.7–12 °C [360]. In E USA, occupies waters of 1–13 °C in spring and autumn, but most occur in waters of *c*.5–11 °C [1059].

SOCIAL ORGANISATION AND BEHAVIOUR

Very gregarious; groups in E North Atlantic frequently 10s–100s, particularly offshore [340, 346, 360]. Groups up to 1000 recorded on American continental shelf and at shelf edge W and S of Ireland [688, 969]. Within large aggregations, subgroups of 2–15 animals may be distinguished [148, 353, 428, 467, 688]. Groups include both sexes, ages mixed, but possibly with some age segregation, since in 2 mass strandings, immatures aged 3–6 years (assuming 1 dentinal growth layer = 1 year) were absent from breeding groups consisting of adults and calves [1007, 1066]. However, immatures found with adults in bycatches W and S of Ireland [8]. Otherwise, social structure poorly known.

Fast swimmer, travelling over long distances at 14 km/h [760]. Bow-rides occasionally. Frequently breaches, though not as much as white-beaked, bottlenose or common dolphins. Mixed herds frequently formed with white-beaked dolphins, less often with bottlenose and common dolphins; sometimes associate with long-finned pilot whales, northern bottlenose whales, sperm whales, fin whales, and humpback whales [148, 213, 457, 467, 606, 969].

Vocalisations: Include whistles of 7–16 kHz frequency, with mean peak frequencies of 8–12 kHz, and mean duration 0.5 s, and broadband echolocation clicks at 0.2–180 kHz with peak frequencies of 60–80 kHz and single pulse duration of 0.25–1 ms [1204].

FEEDING

Diet: Wide variety of fish (including *Clupea, Osmerus, Gadus, Merlangius, Micromesistius, Trisopterus, Merluccius, Scomber* and Salmonidae), squid (*Illex, Loligo*) and shrimps [1, 304, 340, 427, 969, 1066, 1101, 1195].

Stomachs of 17 animals in a mass stranding, Co. Mayo, Ireland, September 1994, contained otoliths of gadoid fishes including *Trisopterus* sp., herring *Clupea harengus*, horse mackerel (scad) *Trachurus trachurus*, as well as an argentine *Argentina sphyraena* and a squid beak [1007]. Stomachs of 50 white-sided dolphins from bycatch of Dutch mesopelagic trawl fishery for mackerel

and horse-mackerel, 1992–1994, at shelf edge (near 200 m depth contour) W and S of Ireland, revealed mainly mackerel *Scomber scombrus* (67% prey weight) and Gadidae (mainly silvery pout *Gadiculus argenteus*: 9% prey weight), various other fish including lantern fish *Notoscopelus kroeyerii*, and cephalopods (13% prey weight, at least 12 species). Nearly all collected in February–March, when mackerel arrive in the area on southward migration, probably attracting white-sided dolphins from deeper waters. One animal, same area, September, showed Gadidae (45% prey weight: mainly silvery pout and blue whiting *Micromesistius poutassou*) and cephalopods (52% prey weight: nearly all Ommastrephidae). In all cases, horse-mackerel was conspicuously absent from stomachs, despite being important target of Dutch fisheries [279, 280].

Feeding methods: Small groups frequently seen herding fish by surface-rushing in a crescent-shaped configuration [353, 688].

BREEDING

Data limited. Births mainly late spring–summer (May–August) [340, 358, 408, 969, 1066], sometimes as early as February and as late as September [8, 1007]. Gestation period *c*.11 months [1007, 1066]. Lactation period *c*.18 months [1066]. Calving interval 2–3 years, some animals being both lactating and pregnant [1007, 1114]. Age at sexual maturity 7–11 years (males) and 6–12 years (females), assuming 1 dentine layer/year [8, 1066].

POPULATION

No comprehensive population estimates; estimate of 5587–18 528 *Lagenorhynchus* includes an unknown proportion of white-sided dolphins [481]. Most commonly observed over GB continental shelf July–September; apparently concentrated in deep waters off shelf edge November–May [340, 346, 360, 688, 857, 858, 973].

Greatest number of dentine layers reported so far is 27 in a female, implying age of at least 27 years, and 22 in a male [1066]. Population structure unknown.

MORTALITY

Sharks and killer whales are likely predators, but no attacks reported.

PARASITES AND PATHOGENS

Internal parasites (with body locations where known) found in stranded specimens [79, 131, 438, 441, 442, 1007, 1195] include:

Trematodes: *Pholeter gastrophilus* (stomach and

duodenum), *Oschmarinella laevicaecum* (bile ducts and hepatopancreatic ducts).

Cestodes: *Tetrabothrius forsteri* (upper intestine), *Phyllobothrium delphini* (blubber), *Strobilocephalus triangularis, Monorygma grimaldii* (abdomen, peritoneum and testes).

Nematodes: *Anisakis simplex* (trachea and stomach), *Stenurus globicephalae* (stomach and cranial sinuses), *Crassicauda grampicola* (subcutaneous tissue, mammary glands, see below), *Crassicauda* sp. (subcutaneous tissue; frequently observed, with over 50% of the animals affected in some studies [424, 437, 438, 1007]), *Pseudalius inflexus* (bronchi and lungs), *Torynurus convolutus* (head sinuses), and *Bolbosoma* sp. (intestine).

In 2 mass strandings, Maine (USA), September 1974 and Ireland, September 1994, high incidence of parasitic mastitis caused by the nematode *Crassicauda grampicola* [437, 438, 1007]: 14/30 females in Maine, 5/7 adult females in Ireland, also recorded in bycatch victims [424]. Can severely damage the mammary glands and thus affect milk production [438]. From Irish stranding, neoplasia found in 3/19 animals; 2 cases of benign intestinal leiomyomas and 1 of intestinal fibroma [1007]. In Maine, 4/41 animals had various papillomas, 5 had intestinal leiomyomas. Adrenal lesions such as nodular hyperplasia and cyst formation were found in 20 /23 females (and in 1 male) of Maine sample [437]. 2 cases of adrenal adenoma [438]. *Brucella* sp. isolated from a male stranded, Scotland [399].

RELATIONS WITH HUMANS
Not hunted commercially, though taken opportunistically by drive fisheries for small whales in Faroes, up to 500 taken some years [141], formerly also in Norway and Canada. Probably hunted in small numbers off SW Greenland [502]. Incidental mortality in fishing gear reported from British Isles, Ireland and Canada [279, 347, 969]. Numerous in bycatches from former Dutch trawl fishery for mackerel and horse-mackerel near the shelf edge W and S of Ireland. About 90% of this mortality in February–March [279].

Few examined for pollutants, and few details given (e.g. [158, 294]). 17 animals from mass stranding, Ireland, and 5 stranded, Scotland, analysed for chlorobiphenyls (CBs) and organochlorine pesticides [660, 770]. Levels generally low, but 2 adult males had CB levels of >40 and >60 μg/g in blubber. Similar concentrations in 2 bycaught males (1 adult) from Canada. Some of Irish animals also had relatively high levels of pesticides, particularly *p,p'*-DDE,

dieldrin and HCB, as had the 2 males from Canada [660, 770]. Juvenile stranded, NW Ireland, had a high concentration (44 μg/g wet weight) of mercury in the liver [672], much higher than in adult male from Canada [660]. High levels of cadmium in the kidneys of 2 stranded, Belgium, perhaps related to diet [294].

Legally protected in European, British and Irish waters (Table 12.1).

LITERATURE
Good review [969], brief popular overview [245].

AUTHORS
P.G.H. Evans & C.S. Smeenk

GENUS *Lagenodelphis*

Described by Fraser in 1956 from a skeleton brought back from Sarawak over 50 years previously, holotype in NHM, London; external morphology and colour pattern not described until early 1970s [916]; a monospecific genus, intermediate between *Lagenorhynchus* and *Delphinus* in characters.

Fraser's dolphin *Lagenodelphis hosei*
Lagenodelphis hosei Fraser, 1956; mouth of Lutong R., Baram, Borneo.

RECOGNITION
Small, stocky dolphin with a short but distinct beak, small flippers and dorsal fin (Plate 16). Deep palatal grooves; 34–44 teeth in each jaw. Usually in groups, frequently leaps clear of water, showing dark grey to black back, grey flanks and white to pink belly with broad darker stripes from beak to flipper and from eye to genital area. At a distance, eye-to-anus stripe may resemble striped dolphin, and not always visible, but body shape distinctive.

DESCRIPTION
Small dolphin with very short beak (3–6 cm), general shape not as slender as *Delphinus* sp. but not as stocky as *Lagenorhynchus* sp. Forehead slopes gradually to short beak; 34–44 pointed teeth in each jaw; deep palatal grooves. Small flippers; small pointed subtriangular dorsal fin, placed centrally on back. Coloration variable [918]: greybrown back and appendages, pale grey flanks separated from whitish or pinkish belly by a thick dark stripe running from eye to genital area (although dark stripe sometimes missing on juveniles), giving appearance of 'masked' dolphin (possibly a feature of adult males). Sometimes another dark thick stripe from beak to flipper, but both dark stripes may be faint or absent in some

populations. Dorsal fin slightly falcate in calves and females, more erect or canted in adult males. Similarly, postanal hump either absent or slight in females and young, well developed in adult males.

RELATIONSHIPS
Member of subfamily Delphininae. Cytochrome *b* mtDNA sequences suggest closer to *Stenella*, *Tursiops*, *Delphinus*, and *Sousa* than to *Lagenorhynchus* [684]. Morphologically, skull structure similar to common dolphin *D. delphis* in possessing deep palatal grooves but to *S. longirostris*, *S. coeruleoalba*, and *S. clymene* in several other characteristics.

MEASUREMENTS
Length: newborn *c*.0.9–1.1 m; at sexual maturity *c*.2.1–2.2 m (female), *c*.2.2–2.3 (male) [918]; adult mean 2.2 m, max. 2.64 m (female), mean 2.4 m, max. 2.70 m (male); weight up to 209 kg. Body size may vary over range, Atlantic animals larger than E Pacific [171, 419].

HABITAT
Primarily found in open oceans, particularly warm equatorial waters (between 30° N and 30° S), such as deep waters around oceanic islands where sometimes come very close to coast. Extensions into higher latitudes may be associated with incursion of warm oligotrophic waters. Depth preferences apparently *c*.500–5000 m, although can occur in shallower waters adjacent to continental shelf.

DISTRIBUTION
Poorly known: worldwide in tropical pelagic waters, with rare intrusions into temperate coastal waters (South Australia, Uruguay, British Isles, France). Live sightings in N Atlantic reported from Caribbean (e.g. Dominica, Martinique), Azores and Canaries. First record in European waters, from mass stranding, N Brittany coast, 1984 [171]. Only 1 confirmed record in British waters; a single male stranded on S Uist, Scotland, 1996 [150].

SOCIAL ORGANISATION AND BEHAVIOUR
Most schools 100–1000 individuals but small groups of 4–15 seen. Social structure unknown, groups of mixed sexes and ages reported. Fast, very active swimmers (*c*.20 km/h and more), making low-angle splashy leaps. May approach boats to bow-ride but can also actively avoid boats. Breaches are common. Often associates with other cetaceans, particularly *Peponocephala electra,* but also others (*Globicephala macrorhynchus, Pseudorca crassidens, Stenella attenuata, S. longirostris, S. coeruleoalba, Grampus griseus, Tursiops truncatus* and *Physeter macrocephalus*).

Vocalisations: Information limited, but sounds include at least 2 types of whistles similar in frequency to those produced by *Stenella* (0.5 s and 0.2 s duration), burst pulse vocalisations and echolocation clicks [683, 1211].

FEEDING
Diet: Unknown while in British waters. Specimens stranded on N Brittany coast had fed on blue whiting *Micromesistius poutassou, Trisopterus spp.,* whiting *Merlangius merlangus* and *Sepia* sp. [171]. In tropical E Pacific and Sulu Sea, feeds on mesopelagic fishes (Myctophidae and Chauliodontidae), shrimps (Oplophoridae), and (in Sulu Sea) squid [319, 1001].

Feeding methods: Takes prey from near surface to depths of at least 500 m; in S Indian Ocean and W Pacific, it may also feed far below the surface [1017, 1153]. In French Polynesia, during daylight hours mainly observed travelling or resting, so possibly feeding largely nocturnally at least in some regions [418]. Myoglobin levels comparable to levels in deepest divers like northern bottlenose whale and sperm whale [321].

BREEDING
Only sparse data available; suggest no strong breeding seasonality. Births may occur year-round, but in Japanese waters peaks in spring and autumn, whereas in S Africa peak in summer. Males reach sexual maturity from 7–10 years of age, and females from 5–8 years. Single testis weight 1–2 kg in mature specimens, which suggests polyandrous or promiscuous breeding strategy [918]. Annual ovulation rate *c*.0.49, gestation period *c*.12.5 months. No information on lactation period. Calving interval *c*.2 years.

POPULATION
Presumably only transient in British waters; no confirmed sightings of live animals despite extensive sighting efforts. Abundance elsewhere in Atlantic unknown; not uncommon in Caribbean, occurs in large groups. Only data on sex ratio and age structure comes from 2 mass strandings, France, Japan [32, 171]. Both schools comprised juveniles and adults of both sexes (aged 5–16 years, France; up to 17.5 years, Japan).

MORTALITY
Probable predators are large sharks, killer whales and false killer whales. Cookie-cutter sharks (*Isistius brasiliensis*) thought to inflict circular wounds.

PARASITES
As many other delphinids, often infested by

Phyllobothrium delphini and *Monorygma grimaldii*, other cestodes found: *Strobicephalus triangularis* and *Tetrabothrius* sp.; trematode *Campula* sp.; nematodes *Anisakis simplex* and *Stenurus ovatus*; acanthocephalan *Bulbosoma* sp. [918]. External parasite, *Xenobalanus* sp. also reported.

RELATIONS WITH HUMANS

Those captured for exhibition died within 14–100 days [476]. Small numbers harpooned in Lesser Antilles and W Pacific, incidental captures in various nets in tropical E Pacific and Philippines, S Africa, Japan and Sri Lanka [265, 318, 679]. Levels of organochlorine pollutants reported for 1 specimen [868].

Legally protected in European, British and Irish waters (Table 12.1).

LITERATURE

General reviews for the species [320, 918].

AUTHOR

P.G.H. Evans

Melon-headed whale *Peponocephala electra*

Lagenorhynchus electra Gray, 1846; N Pacific.

RECOGNITION

Very dark, almost black, with slender form. (Plate 16) Triangular head with rounded forehead but with very indistinct beak, often white lips. Dark mask-like eye patch distinct in good light or under water. Centrally placed sickle-shaped dorsal fin. Flippers have pointed tips (in very similar pygmy killer whale, are usually rounded at tip, more sinuous along rear margin). At close range, and from above, an important distinguishing feature is longer, less-rounded head (in pygmy killer whale, is much shorter and more rounded).

Skull resembles *Lagenorhynchus* but with more rounded cranium, much larger antorbital notches, and much shorter tooth row relative to total length of rostrum. From 20–26 teeth in each half of upper and lower jaw (cf. pygmy killer whale, <15). High tooth count separates skull from other small beakless whales.

DESCRIPTION

Torpedo-shaped body with triangular head and rounded forehead, and slightly underslung jaw presenting a very indistinct beak. In each jaw, 20–26 small, sharply pointed teeth. Mouth terminal to subterminal, angles slightly upward towards eyes. Posterior segment of gape turns slightly downward, ending just below or forward of eye, and thickened at base of lower lips. Body moderately robust in front half, tapering to slender

peduncle. Coloration dark grey but with paler belly, particularly around anus and genital region; lips often white, light grey or pink. Indistinct pale grey anchor-shaped throat patch, and, in some populations, indistinct downward-pointing darker triangle or cape below dorsal fin. Cape is narrow over the head, thorax, and anterior half of tail stock, but dips downward near dorsal fin to form dark triangular region with its apex pointing ventrally, lower limit ill-defined (unlike pygmy killer whale). Dark eye patch broadens as extends from eye to melon, giving appearance of wearing a mask. Long (to 52 cm or more), dark, narrow, tapered flippers, generally pointed at tips, with relatively straight rear edges. Tall (to *c*.30 cm) centrally placed sickle-shaped dorsal fin, pointed at tip. Slender tail stock, but some males have pronounced ventral keel posterior to anus. Males also have proportionately longer flippers and broader tail flukes than females [129, 802].

Skull typically delphinid in shape but with very broad rostrum and deep antorbital notches; resembles bottlenose dolphin in size, shape and tooth count, but teeth of melon-headed whale much smaller and more delicate looking, distance between antorbital notch and end of tooth row proportionally greater, and premaxillaries do not converge at midlength of rostrum.

RELATIONSHIPS

No congeners. Considered closely allied to false killer whale *Pseudorca crassidens* and pygmy killer whale *Feresa attenuata* [849], but morphological [601] and genetic [1076] evidence indicate the species is most closely related to the pilot whales *Globicephala* spp.; these 4 genera a distinct clade [962].

MEASUREMENTS

Length: newborn *c*. 1 m [191]; adults *c*.2.3–2.8 m (males possibly slightly larger than females, asymptotic lengths 2.52 m and 2.43 m). Appears smaller (*c*.2.0–2.4 m) in French Polynesia and Caribbean [419]. Weight *c*.160–228 kg.

VARIATION

No information except that dorsal cape clearly visible in E tropical Pacific, Gulf of Mexico, and Philippines, but not around Hawaii [925]. No obvious variation between French Polynesia and Caribbean, however, with cape clearly visible in both regions under suitable light conditions [419].

DISTRIBUTION

Poorly known; occurs around the world in deep offshore tropical and subtropical waters, mainly between 40° N and 35° S. In N Atlantic, most frequently reported from E coast USA (Maryland),

Gulf of Mexico (Texas, Louisiana), and Caribbean (St Vincent, Dominica, Puerto Rico). Rather few sightings or strandings reported from E North Atlantic: include strandings from Senegal and sightings off Sierra Leone and Cape Verde, Western Africa. Stranding near Charlestown, Cornwall, September 1949, previously identified as *Lagenorhynchus albirostris* [408], found on re-examination to be *Peponocephala electra* [784]; is first record for GB and Europe. Since then, 2 live stranded in France near La Rochelle, August 2003. Such extralimital records may reflect incursions of warmer water further N.

HISTORY
No fossil or archaeological material known.

HABITAT
Occurs mainly in deep warm waters (>1000 m depth), seaward of the edge of continental shelves; can be observed around oceanic islands, where schools may aggregate during daylight hours [419].

SOCIAL ORGANISATION AND BEHAVIOUR
Little information, but groups often very large, 150–1500 individuals [190, 925, 1067, 1191]. Schools tend to be highly packed, travel rapidly with frequent course changes, creating a crescent of water that may obscure clear view of the animals. Is reported to bow-ride slow-moving vessels; sometimes breaches. Relatively inconspicuous at sea, has been recorded swimming just under the surface with dorsal fins exposed, occasionally coming above the surface sufficiently to expose the head and upper body. On diving, tail stock strongly arched. Like pilot whales, sometimes spy-hops with head above the water. During fast porpoising, a pair of 'water moustaches' escape from each side of the head during expiration [419.

Social organisation not known, stranded groups include both sexes and varying ages. Mass strandings reported on several occasions, and one exhibited a female preponderance of 2:1, implies some sexual segregation [718], supported by observation of male-only groups of 10–15 [419, 476]. Associations with Fraser's dolphin frequently reported [298, 682, 801, 925], but may also associate with spinner dolphins and bottlenose dolphins [319]. Scavenging seabirds (e.g. Parkinson's petrels) may associate with herds of melon-headed whales [936].

Vocalisations: Poorly known.

FEEDING
Diet: Small fish, larger ommastrephid squid (e.g. *Dosidicus gigas*), and shrimps [129, 207, 513, 571, 925, 916].

Feeding methods: Has been reported herding and possibly attacking small dolphins (*Stenella* spp.) escaping from tuna seine nets in the tropical Pacific [678], although possibility of confusion with *Feresa*.

BREEDING
Season poorly known, but, in N hemisphere, a neonate was found in July and a near-term (80 cm) fetus collected in October [925], and in S hemisphere, newborn calves also observed during warm season [419]. Gestation period *c.*12 months [191]. Lactation period and calving interval unknown. Males mature somewhere between 3 and 7 years; females between 4 and 12 years (assuming 1 dentinal/cemental growth layer group = 1 year) [191]. Smallest mature female 230 cm [925]; smallest mature male 248 cm [129].

POPULATION
Only population estimate is 45 000 from a recent survey of E tropical Pacific [1191]; no information on abundance in N Atlantic, but large herds may be seen in E Caribbean [353]. Longevity up to 47 years (on growth layers) [191].

MORTALITY
Mass strandings reported in Australia, Vanuatu, Seychelles, Japan, Brazil, Kwajalein Atoll, Hawaii and Costa Rica [925, 1111], with suggestion that may be caused by panic response in the school when a few members accidentally strand [802], or in case of Hawaii stranding, possibly use of mid-frequency sonar in the vicinity [1111]. No information on predation on this species, but scars thought to be caused by sharks observed, and those of the cookie-cutter shark *Isistius brasiliensis* found on stranded specimen [129].

PARASITES AND PATHOGENS
Remoras observed attached to free-swimming animals in tropical E Pacific [925]. Cyamid whale lice have been found on the exterior [801], and traces of barnacles possibly of the genus *Xenobalanus* on the tail flukes [190].

Internal parasites include trematode *Nastrema gondo* (tympanic cavity); nematodes *Stenurus globicephalae* (tympanic cavity), *Anisakis simplex* and *A. typica* (stomach); acanthocephalan *Bolbosoma* sp. (rectum); and cestodes *Monorygma* (intestines) and *Halocercus* (host tissue not specified), *Phyllobothrium chamissoni* (blubber, intestines, and between peritoneum and abdominal muscles) [129, 190, 220, 288, 811].

RELATIONS WITH HUMANS

Rarely encountered by humans. Taken opportunistically in various drive fisheries, particularly off Japan [798]. A herd of *c.*500 animals came into Sturga Bay, Japan, March 1965, half driven ashore and consumed [849]; further 200 animals were trapped in Taiji Bay, Japan, 1980 [797]. Elsewhere, 4 animals landed by small whale fishery on St Vincent, Lesser Antilles [207]; a male calf caught in a tuna net off Guatemala, tropical E Pacific [911]; occasionally harpooned or netted near Sri Lanka and in the Philippines [476, 679, 682]. Specimens from a mass stranding in E Australia, 1973, used as bait in lobster pots [190]. More systematically, melon-headed whales have been taken in the well-established harpoon fishery for sperm whales and various small cetaceans near Lamalera, Indonesia [102, 681]. Focus of opportunistic commercial whale-watching operations in the Marquesas [419].

Sometimes bycaught in various fisheries, including harpoon and drift net fisheries in Philippines [318], Indonesia, Malaysia, and Caribbean; in N Indian Ocean off Sri Lanka [681], and occasionally in E Pacific tuna purse seine fishery [911]. Has been held in captivity in the Philippines, on Hawaii, and in Japan, but generally has not thrived [476, 1067]. In Hawaiian waters, said to have aggressively approached divers [923], but many non-aggressive interactions with divers reported from French Polynesia [419].

Legally protected in European, British and Irish waters (Table 12.1).

LITERATURE

Reviews [923, 925].

AUTHOR

P.G.H. Evans

GENUS *Globicephala*

A genus of 2 closely related species, only 1 of which occurs in NE Atlantic; other has a tropical to warm temperate distribution.

Long-finned pilot whale *Globicephala melas*
Delphinus melas Traill, 1809; Scapa Bay, Orkney.
Globicephala melaena Thomas, 1898.

Pilot whale, blackfish, caa'ing whale (Shetland), pothead whale; *muc-mhara-chinn-mhoir* (Scottish Gaelic); *miol phiolótach* (Irish Gaelic).

RECOGNITION

Black or dark grey medium-sized whale (Plate 14), with square bulbous head; low dorsal fin, sickle-shaped in subadults and females but more broad-based in adult males, situated slightly forward of centre of back. Long slender flippers. Male larger, with broader dorsal fin and more bulbous head, than female. Skull similar in shape to killer and false killer but has much smaller teeth.

DESCRIPTION

Long slender body becoming more robust with age, with square bulbous head extending over upper lip, particularly in old males. In each jaw, 8–12 pairs of small (<13 mm diameter) peg-like teeth. Flippers long (usually >15% of body length), pointed and sickle-shaped (in short-finned pilot whales and similar false killer whales, <15% of body length [143, 909, 1063, 1258]. Coloration black or dark grey on back and flanks (young born lighter grey) with 3 areas of lighter pigmentation which are variable in extent and intensity: the throat patch (an anchor-shaped area of greyish white on chin extending to grey on belly, also called the throat chevron), the postdorsal saddle patch (a grey area behind and below the dorsal fin extending down to the midpoint of the body), and the postocular (or postorbital) blaze (a light grey stripe extending backwards from behind the eye, often connecting with the leading edge of the dorsal patch). Fairly low dorsal fin, slightly forwards of midpoint (to the front 1/3 on longer adult males), with long base, sickle-shaped (in adult females and immatures) to broad, with hump on leading edge (in adult males), usually black, but sometimes grey. As changes shape with age, dorsal fin becomes more rounded and less dolphin-like. Thick keel on tail stock, more pronounced on adult males. Tail flukes have concave trailing edge, are deeply notched in centre. Sexual dimorphism of individual features (e.g. dorsal fin, melon overhang) are all related to larger body size in males [143], i.e. there is no indication of allometric growth patterns.

RELATIONSHIPS

2 closely related species of pilot whale: long-finned, *G. melas*, and short-finned, *G. macrorhynchus*; differ in a few morphological features, principally pectoral fin length, but also skull features. Their primary difference is distributional: short-finned is found in tropical waters (>25° C), while long-finned has antitropical distribution in temperate waters of N and S hemispheres [297]. Relationships to other Globicephalinae uncertain, seem closest to *Peponocephala*, then *Feresa* and *Pseudorca* [962].

MEASUREMENTS

Length: newborn *c.*175–178 cm (weighing 60–

80 kg); at sexual maturity *c.*3.0–4.0 m (female), *c.*5.0 m (male); adult *c.*4.0–5.0 (max. 6.0) m (female), *c.*5.5–6.0 (max. 8.5) m (male).

VARIATION

Pigmentation patterns noted to vary between N and S hemisphere populations of long-finned pilot whales in the Atlantic, separated by tropical short-finned pilot whale *G. macrorhynchus*, when they were first proposed as separate species [959]. Later suggested that indicated subspecific variation [297], but even this has been questioned [985]. Morphometric differences have been reported between pilot whales of E and W North Atlantic [142]. Genetic studies showing differences between pilot whales off Greenland and elsewhere in Atlantic suggest SST as an isolating mechanism, perhaps through temperature-dependent distribution of favoured prey [412]. Variability in

pigmentation patterns was noted between individual Faroese pilot whales, but this could not be related to school membership [143], and thus was unlikely to be genetic. Variation in isozyme frequencies suggest that there may be restricted gene flow between certain pods [41, 42]. Analyses of pollutant levels and profiles in Faroese pilot whales showed pod-specific variability, implying 2 subpopulations with 2 different food resources [160, 231]. Genetic analyses of numerous loci have revealed high levels of variation between pods because of the high degrees of relatedness within pods [35, 38].

DISTRIBUTION

Widespread in temperate regions of the world, mainly in offshore waters. Common and widely distributed in NE Atlantic from Iberian peninsula and Bay of Biscay, N to Faroes and Iceland; also

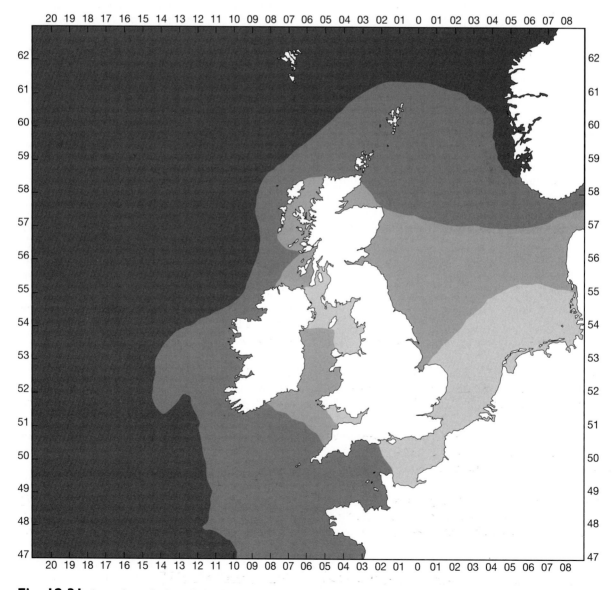

Fig. 12.31 Long-finned pilot whale *Globicephala melas*: distribution around British Isles.

common in Mediterranean. (Short-finned pilot whale overlaps this distribution, with strandings in N Spain [446, 854].) Around British Isles, during 1970s–early 1980s, was the most commonly observed whale species [340, 358], but has since become relatively uncommon [346, 358, 360]. Mainly pelagic, seaward of continental shelf edge, with main concentrations occurring in Faroe-Shetland Channel, Rockall Trough, Porcupine Bight and SW approaches to English Channel [360, 973, 1216]. Thus, most sightings over the shelf occur in northern GB (NW and N Scotland), W of Ireland, and in W English Channel [358, 360, 973]. Rare throughout North Sea, except northern-most sector (Fig. 12.31).

Sighted in all months of the year, but numbers in shelf waters highest November–January; possibly associated with an autumn inshore movement following their prey [358, 360]. Sightings offshore from weather ships, 700 km W of Scotland, showed lowest numbers over same period [340, 358].

HABITAT
In E North Atlantic, usually occurs in deep temperate and subpolar waters of 200–3000 m depth (particularly around 1000 m isobath) seaward and along edges of continental shelf where bottom relief is greatest; may occasionally venture into coastal waters, entering fjords and bays [360].

SOCIAL ORGANISATION AND BEHAVIOUR
Gregarious; herds of 20–40 common, sometimes may number hundreds–low thousands (though probably representing temporary coalitions of social groups, particularly during mating/breeding period) [340, 346, 358]. Samples from mass strandings and coastal drive fisheries have revealed herd structure [41, 42, 306, 748, 751, 1062]. Most groups comprise females with calves, immatures and 1 or more adult males. Sex ratio of groups often biased 3:1 in favour of females. All individuals within a pod, including adult males, related [36]; however, males were not the fathers of the calves in their pod, and so mating must be occurring between males and females from different pods [44]. Paternal alleles suggest that fetuses within a cohort may share same father or have related fathers [36], indicating some degree of variability in male mating success. Adult males may serve a defensive role for the pod, often position themselves between a vessel approaching a herd and females with young.

Photo-ID has been attempted with this species [215, 885a, 1214], but use limited by low recognisability of individuals [73].

Relatively slow swimmer, travelling at *c*.5–15 km/h, though may attain *c*.40 km/h. Rarely bow-rides although may allow boats to approach. Usually moves through water in undemonstrative manner, scarcely ever breaching clear of water (generally only young animals), though may slap surface with tail. Frequently lies vertically in water with head and top of flippers above surface. On occasions, observed resting motionless on surface. Dolphins (mainly bottlenose and Atlantic white-sided) may associate with pilot whale herds (Fig. 12.22).

Tracking studies reveal very variable travel patterns. Off the Faroes, one small group of 4 related individuals averaged 70–111 km/24 h, but the maximum distance travelled was 200 km/24 h [146]. Other studies have tracked pilot whales for 3144 km over 94.5 days in NW Atlantic [761].

Diving behaviour characterised by short, shallow daytime dives (<16 m), with longer (mean *c*.8 min, deep dives occurring at night [85]. Maximum dive durations *c*.26 min [506, 761, 835], and maximum depth 648 m [85].

Vocalisations: Include variety of whistles mainly at 3.4–4.7 kHz lasting 0.65–1.0 s, and echo-location clicks of 0.1–100 kHz [1137], [1214]. Comparisons found vocalisations of long-finned pilot whales to be lower in frequency, longer in duration, and over a narrower frequency range than for short-finned pilot whale [984, 1120, 1137].

FEEDING
Diet: Mainly squid (notably *Todarodes*, but also *Ommastrephes*, *Loligo*, *Gonatus* and *Sepia*), but also variety of fish (*Anguilla*, *Conger*, *Dicentrarchus*, *Gadus*, *Merluccius*, *Molva*, *Pollachius*, *Scomber*, *Solea*, *Trachurus* and *Trisopterus*) [3, 118, 259, 304, 305, 344, 421, 422, 887, 930]. Diet varies with reproductive condition: lactating females ate a greater proportion of fish off the Faroes [305].

Feeding methods: Observations of captive animals show they can use suction feeding [123].

BREEDING
No distinct breeding season, although some evidence for slight peak in births, late winter–early spring (January–March) [340, 346, 751]. Further N, in Faroes, conceptions peak April–July, most births July–September [306, 748], though differences may only reflect variation between pods. Gestation period *c*.14–16 months. Lactation *c*.22 months. Calving interval 3–4 years. Various estimates of age at sexual maturity: 10–12 years (male) and 6–7 years (female) for shore-driven specimens, Newfoundland [1062]; 9–14 years

(male) and *c*.7 years (female) from British mass strandings [751]; and 15–20 years (male) and 9–10 years (female) for shore-driven specimens from Faroes [306, 307, 748].

POPULATION
Surveys across the N Atlantic estimated 778 000 (CV 0.295) long-finned pilot whales in 1989, but coverage did not extend fully into British waters, accuracy of estimates limited by difficulty of estimating group size and distance to centre of group [194]. Longevity at least 20 years (male) and 25 years (female), possibly higher due to difficulty in reading dentine layers in teeth of older animals [751]. Lifespan estimated elsewhere at 40–50 years [1063]. Although segregation of sexes in herds may occur, skewed sex ratios (*c*.60% females) suggest higher mortality rates for males than females.

PARASITES AND COMMENSALS
Studied intensively in 125 Faroese specimens [953]; 15 species were recorded: whale louse *Isocyamus delphini* common around natural openings and wounds; barnacle *Xenobalanus globicipitis* rare, around natural openings or on edge of dorsal fin and flukes; 3 trematodes, mainly *Pholeter grastrophilus*, also *Leucasiella* sp., and rarely *Odhneriella* sp., in stomach and intestine; 4 cestodes *Trigonocotyle* sp., *Phyllobothrium delphini, Diphyllobothrium* sp., *Monorygma grimaldii*, either within blubber or in intestine; 5 nematodes, mainly *Anisakis simplex* and 3 *Sternus* spp., also *Crassicauda* sp., in gut (*Anisakis*), lungs, air sinuses, and tympanic bullae (*Sternus* spp.), and within mammary glands (*Crassicauda* sp.); and one acanthocephalan *Bolbosoma* sp. in intestine.

RELATIONS WITH HUMANS
Organised drives have taken place for at least 11 centuries in Faroes, average annual catch of 850 from 1709 to 1992 [1262]; still continue. Other drive fisheries have operated opportunistically, mainly in Shetland and Orkney, but also in Outer Hebrides and W Ireland, until early 20th century. Extensive fishery in Newfoundland, Canada, 1947–1972. Otherwise, small numbers taken by the coastal Norwegian small whale fishery, off W Greenland and Iceland. Legally protected in European, British and Irish waters (Table 12.1).

Accidental capture in fishing nets is also a problem: off France, 50–100/year were estimated killed in nets [912]; off USA, incidentally caught in mackerel trawl fishery and in a variety of squid fisheries [366, 1198]. Bycatch mortality also reported in British waters, mainly in English Channel during 1960s and 1970s [340, 356].

Relatively high levels (up to 95 μg/g wet weight in blubber) of PCBs found in stranded animals in GB [751] and up to 995 μg/g PCBs in an immature from W Mediterranean [30]. PCB levels generally similar between animals in Faroes [1091] and W Atlantic [778, 1152]. High levels of DDT, PBDE, mercury and cadmium also recorded from Faroes [160, 231, 686, 699, 841, 845]. Pollutant levels in pilot whale meat consumed by Faroese may exceed 'safe' levels of toxicity allowed for human consumption [1091]. Faroese pilot whales have adapted to high cadmium levels by increasing levels of metallothionein, a known aid to detoxification [34].

Pilot whales change vocalisations in vicinity of military sonar [983], increasing number of whistles; significance currently unknown. Exposure to military sonar previously implicated in some cetacean deaths [578]. Ship strikes may also pose a threat, as has been suggested for the related short-finned pilot whale [22].

AUTHORS
J.R. Boran, P.G.H. Evans & A.R. Martin

GENUS *Pseudorca*

A monospecific genus, resembling *Orcinus* in few, robust, teeth (7–12 in each jaw) but these circular in cross-section.

False killer whale *Pseudorca crassidens*
Phocoena crassidens Owen, 1846; Lincolnshire Fens (subfossil).

Blackfish; *cráin dubh bréagach* (Irish Gaelic).

RECOGNITION
Almost all black, form slender (Plate 15). No beak. Small, slender, tapered head with rounded snout projecting beyond extremity of lower jaw. Tall sickle-shaped dorsal fin, centrally placed. Skull with large teeth, proportionately somewhat smaller than those of killer whale and circular (not oval) in cross-section.

DESCRIPTION
Long slender body with small, tapered head; underslung jaw contains 7–12 pairs of large (25 mm diameter) teeth, circular in cross-section [1116]; slightly fewer (6–10) similar teeth in upper jaw. Melon extends further forward on adult males [773]. Coloration all black except for a blaze of grey (variable from indistinct to nearly white) known as the throat patch or throat chevron [790] on belly between flippers. Sometimes also a light grey postorbital blaze on sides of face. Black, narrow tapered flippers (1/10

body length) with broad hump on front margin near middle, giving distinctive 'elbowed' appearance. Tall (to 40 cm), sickle-shaped (rounded to sharply pointed) dorsal fin just behind midpoint of back [1116].

RELATIONSHIPS
Most closely related to killer whale *Orcinus*, pygmy killer whale *Feresa* and long- and short-finned pilot whales *Globicephala*, often grouped as subfamily Globicephalinae [846, 847], though other studies have placed these in a subfamily Orcininae [192]. Seems closest to *Feresa*, then *Globicephala* [962], placement of *Orcinus* less certain.

MEASUREMENTS
Length: newborn *c*.160–190 cm; at sexual maturity *c*.3.3–4.3 m (female), *c*.3.7–4.6 m (male); adult *c*.4.5 m (max. 5.1) (female), *c*.5.4 m (max. 6.1) (male). Weight *c*.1200–2000 kg.

VARIATION
Morphological comparisons of false killer whales stranded in Australia, S Africa and Scotland [634] showed the 3 groups to be distinct in various features (e.g. overall width and length of the skull, rostrum and mandible). Skulls larger in Scottish animals; differences also noted in growth rates and extent of sexual dimorphism; greatest differences between Scotland and the 2 southern populations, which were more similar. All 3 populations distinct, should be managed as separate stocks [634].

DISTRIBUTION
Worldwide, but mainly in tropical and warm temperate offshore waters. In NE Atlantic, only occasionally N of the British Isles, and records here confined to a few mass strandings: in 1927 (*c*.150 at Dornoch Firth, NE Scotland) [522]; 1934 (*c*.25 in S Wales); 1935 (*c*.75 in S Wales and 41 in SE Scotland) [343, 360, 909]. No strandings since 1935 [408, 1072]. Pelagic, usually occurring in deep waters off the continental shelf edge, so rarely observed at sea; 5 sightings since 1976, variously between 5 and 54 km from land: 2 off W Scotland, 1 S of Cornwall towards the French coast, and 2 off NE Scotland [358, 360]. The first 3 involve single individuals, but the 2 sightings in N North Sea were herds of 10–20 and 100–150 animals. 4 sightings were in July and August [360].

HISTORY
Known from subfossil material from the upper Pleistocene [742, 888]

HABITAT
Found primarily in deep offshore waters, although populations off Hawaii, Costa Rica and Japan reported in waters of *c*.200 m depth [5, 600, 871]. Migrations into cooler, northern waters have been reported in the NW Pacific [84, 600].

SOCIAL ORGANISATION AND BEHAVIOUR
Mass strandings and observations at sea indicate that may form large herds up to *c*.300 animals, though groups of 10–30 more common. Herds are of mixed age and sex.

Very fast swimmer, up to 55 km/h, and very manoeuvrable. Captive speed tests found a maximum 8.0 m/s [1009]. May breach clear of water; may bow-ride vessels. Often associates with other dolphin species.

Photo-ID of individuals, exploiting naturally occurring marks and scars, conducted off W coast of Costa Rica [5]; 59 identified at 2 sites, and same ones seen over 2 years.

Vocalisations: Comprise whistles ranging 5.3–8.2 kHz (significantly higher than for pilot whales and killer whales [984]) and echolocation clicks with peak frequencies *c*.100 kHz [71, 175, 197, 586, 825, 1146]. Able to discriminate between complex harmonic whistles and simpler ones, suggesting that can understand complex vocalisations [1261]. Characteristics of echolocation signals from wild animals suggest that *Pseudorca* should be able to detect fish prey up to 210 m and small squid up to 80 m [735]. Hearing sensitivity is best around 16–64 kHz [1147].

In captivity, false killer whales reported to be as 'trainable' as bottlenose dolphins, although also considered the most aggressive species [300]. Can recognise themselves in mirrors, indicating a high degree of self-awareness [301].

FEEDING
Diet: Primarily squid (e.g. *Berryteuthis* and *Gonatopsis* in NE Pacific [84]; *Ommastrephes* in SW Atlantic [28, 1042]; *Thysanoteuthis*, *Argonauta* in central E Atlantic [516] and large fish (e.g. *Seriola*, *Thunnus*, *Sarda*) [1116]. Has been known to prey on dolphins (*Stenella*, *Delphinus*), for example during tropical E Pacific tuna purse seine fishery [924] and has also been reported attacking sperm whales [890].

BREEDING
Females are spontaneous ovulators and seasonally polyestrous, but with no obvious calving peak [65]. Gestation period 15.5 months (but possibly down to 11). 1 captive birth documented at 14 months gestation, using urine and blood serum hormone analyses [871]. 1 birth observed, central E Atlantic, in May [862].

Lactation period 18–24 months [603, 947]. Calving interval reported in one population at almost 7 years [82]. Sexual maturity at *c*.8–14 years (both sexes) [946, 947]. Hybrids reported with bottlenose dolphins [851].

POPULATION

No estimates of population size in the Atlantic. Sex ratio in Scottish mass strandings around 0.8:1 (male:female). Longevity averages 30–40 years [946, 947], with the oldest female reported at 63 years (measured by dentinal growth layer groups) and the oldest male 58 years [604].

Recent study of genetic variability and population structure suggests at least 'ocean-basin-scale population structure' between the NE Atlantic and the Indian Ocean, but additional samples needed to refine this definition [238]. Better sampling in the tropical and subtropical Pacific between 15° S and 40° N found at least 2 distinct populations around Hawaii: one small island-associated population (100–200 animals) and a much larger pelagic one, suggesting local adaptations to specific island habitats via a matrilineal social structure [238].

MORTALITY

No detailed information on mortality rates, but age structure suggests fairly high immature mortality.

PARASITES AND PATHOGENS

Known parasites collected from stranded animals include trematodes *Nasitrema* sp., nematodes *Stenurus*, *Anisakis* and the acanthocephalan *Bolbosoma* [871]. Trematode infestation has been suggested as the cause for at least one mass stranding via damage to the 8th cranial nerve [812]. Scars caused by shark-suckers *Remora*, a commensal fish, are frequently found on the body.

Morbillivirus has been found in false killer whales stranded along E coast of America [334].

RELATIONS WITH HUMANS

Has been actively hunted off Japan [603], and from St Vincent, W Indies, in the 1970s [202]. Caught live off Florida for display as performing animals in many dolphinaria [792]. Accidental bycatch reported from gill net fishery off Australia [490]. Legally protected in European, British and Irish waters (Table 12.1).

Pollutant levels of 728 μg/g wet weight of mercury in liver and 1400 μg/g wet weight DDE in blubber reported from stranded animals off British Columbia [84], where high levels of PCB and DDT also reported [567].

AUTHORS

J.R. Boran & P.G.H. Evans

Risso's dolphin *Grampus griseus*

Delphinus griseus Cuvier, 1812; Brest, France.

Grampus; *Dolffin risso* (Welsh); *deilf-risso* (Scottish Gaelic); *deilf liath* (Irish Gaelic).

RECOGNITION

Large, robust dolphin (Plate 15) with blunt rounded head, slight melon but no beak; greyish (whitening with age), often with numerous white scars on flanks; tall sickle-shaped dorsal fin in midpoint of back. Few teeth, all in lower jaw.

DESCRIPTION

Stout torpedo-shaped body narrowing behind dorsal fin to quite narrow tail stock, blunt snout, rounded with slight melon and no beak. Deep V-shaped crease down middle and front of head from blowhole to top lip, seen only at close range. Has 2–7 (usually 4) peglike teeth at tip of each lower jaw, often badly worn and sometimes lost; no upper teeth. Coloration dark to light grey on back and flanks (Fig. 12.32), palest in older individuals so that head and anterior portion of dorsal surface may be pure white; many conspicuous white scars on flanks of adults; white belly enlarging to oval or anchor-shaped patch on chest and chin (cf. pilot whale). Newborn young overall light grey, changing to chocolate brown as juveniles. Long (17% body length), narrow, pointed flippers, usually dark. Tall, centrally placed, re-curved dorsal fin (taller, more erect in adult males); dark, but may lighten with age, particularly along leading edge. Dark tail flukes with median notch and concave trailing edge.

RELATIONSHIPS

No congeners. Cytochrome *b* sequences place *Grampus* with *Globicephala*, *Feresa*, *Pseudorca*, and *Peponocephala* in distinct subfamily Globicephalinae, supporting earlier inferences from anatomy and blood proteins [684, 763], but relationships between these 5 uncertain.

MEASUREMENTS

Length: newborn *c*.1.35 m; at physical maturity *c*.2.31 m [949]; at sexual maturity 2.60–2.84 m (females), 2.62–2.97 m (males) [915]; adult *c*.3.3–3.8 m. Male slightly larger than female: maxima 3.83 m (male) and 3.66 m (female). Weight 350–400 kg.

VARIATION

Both morphometric [60] and genetic variation demonstrated between regions and ocean basins. Strong significant genetic differentiation found between animals sampled in British waters and those from the Mediterranean, using both

Fig. 12.32 Risso's dolphins, showing the grey colour (paler in older dolphins) and taller fin that distinguishes them from the similarly blunt-headed pilot whale (*photo P.G.H. Evans*).

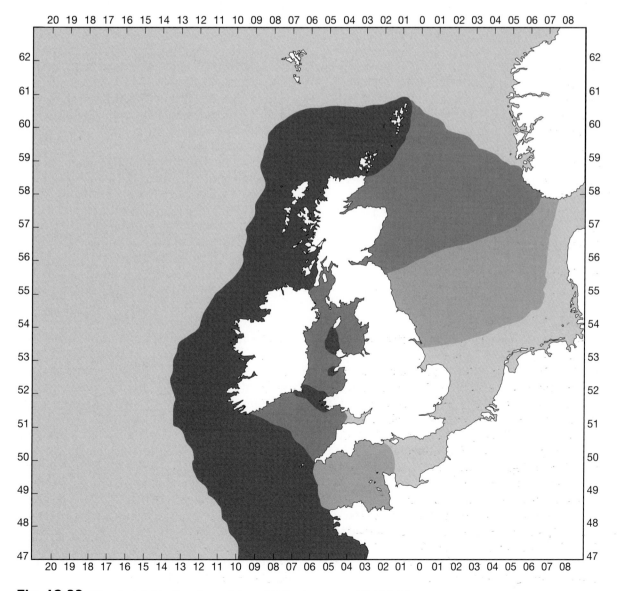

Fig. 12.33 Risso's dolphin *Grampus griseus*: distribution around British Isles.

741

microsatellite and mtDNA analysis [433]. The British sample also showed lower genetic diversity.

DISTRIBUTION

Worldwide in tropical and temperate seas in both hemispheres. In W North Atlantic, occurs from Newfoundland to Lesser Antilles. In E North Atlantic, reaches N limits of its regular range in Northern Isles of Scotland (though has been recorded off Norway), S to Iberia and Mediterranean. Also occurs around oceanic islands like the Azores, Canaries and Cape Verde.

Widely distributed in coastal waters of British Isles, primarily on Atlantic seaboard but also in N North Sea [340, 346, 358, 360, 973]. Major British/Irish populations around Hebrides, but regular also off Northern Isles, in Irish Sea (particularly St George's Channel and around N Wales and Isle of Man), and off W Ireland [346, 360, 973]. Elsewhere, rare in C and S North Sea, and all but W end of English Channel (Fig. 12.33). Regular again in W France, Bay of Biscay, around Iberian Peninsula, and in Mediterranean. On occasions (as in recent years), ranges further into C North Sea, apparently following cephalopod prey. Occurs in much of Mediterranean, most frequently in NW in deep pelagic waters, particularly over steep shelf slopes and submarine canyons [76, 216]. However, estimates of abundance are available only for few regions, and information on their distribution is generally lacking.

Around British Isles, nowhere common; seen most frequently May–September, peaking in July–September [360].

HISTORY

No fossil or archaeological material known.

HABITAT

A widespread pelagic species, preferring warm water (range 7.5–28 °C, but mainly 5–20 °C, and rarely <10 °C [83, 659]), generally favouring continental slope waters. In E Pacific, typically occurs seaward of 180 m isobath, seen in coastal areas only where continental shelf relatively close to shore [657, 680]; depth averaged 1000 m. Steep sections along edge of continental shelf also identified as high-use areas in E USA and Gulf of Mexico [105, 468, 613, 614].

Over continental shelf around British Isles, seen mainly over slopes of 50–100 m depth [66, 67, 358, 360]. In Mediterranean, recorded mainly from 500–1000 m depth in Ligurian Sea [76, 365, 420], and at depths of 400–1200 m (particularly 800–1000 m) off SE Spain [215, 216].

SOCIAL ORGANISATION AND BEHAVIOUR

Form small to medium-sized pods of 2–50 animals (most commonly 6–12 in British waters, 15–20 in Spain, and 5–20 in Ligurian Sea) (Fig. 12.33), although they may be seen singly or in groups of several hundreds or even thousands. Photo-ID studies indicate that groups can be stable over the long term, individuals associating from one year to the next [66, 67, 342, 353, 430, 657], although associations mostly weak [430]. Limited evidence on genetic similarity among individuals within and among groups in NW Mediterranean, suggests a fluid social structure [430]. Sex and age composition of groups not well known; segregation by age and sex known to occur, with groups of calfless adults, juveniles, and females with calves [353, 657]. Aggressive behaviour frequently observed, is assumed to cause the intense scarring seen on some older animals [66, 67, 342]. Caring behaviour reported around animal wounded by a harpoon [934].

A relatively slow swimmer. When travelling, swims at *c.*4–12 km/h, but when frightened can speed up to 20–25 km/h [353, 934a, 940]. Usually slightly wary of vessels; occasionally bow-rides (mainly juveniles), and regularly engages in a variety of surface behaviours including breaching (particularly juveniles), spyhopping, tail-slapping, and communal diving.

In N Atlantic, Risso's dolphins sometimes seen swimming with other cetaceans, including long-finned pilot whales, white-beaked, Atlantic white-sided dolphins, common and bottlenose dolphins [66, 67, 233, 340, 353, 659]; in N Pacific, even observed bow-riding and apparently harassing gray whales [1070], as well as showing aggressive behaviour towards long-finned pilot whales [1068, 1069]. In Mediterranean, occa-sionally seen swimming with striped dolphins [431].

Vocalisations: Include a variety of clicks, whistles, and pulsed calls. Whistles, rarely heard, range over 2.5–20 kHz, usually 8–12 kHz, average duration 0.67 s, and maximum source level of 170 dB re 1 μPa @ 1 m [1204]. Clicks have peak frequency 65 kHz, last 40–100 s [68]. Click frequencies are from 0.2 to >100 kHz, with repetition rates of 4–200/s. Click-bursts last 0.2–1.5 s, maximum source level 175 dB re 1 μPa @ 1 m [1204]. 8 different kinds of sounds in 3 main categories recognised in Hebridean Risso's dolphins: clicks in discrete series (echolocation clicks, creaks, grunts) with repetition rates of 37–167 pulses/s; fast sequences of pulses (buzzes, squeaks, squeals, moans) with high repetition rates of 187–3750 pulses/s, resulting in harmonics; and whistles of 9–13.2 kHz [115, 116].

FEEDING

Diet: Mainly cephalopods, particularly octopus *Eledone cirrhosa,* cuttlefish *Sepia officinalis* and squids *Todarodes sagittatus, Loligo forbesi* and *L. vulgaris, Gonatus* spp., *Histioteuthis reversa* and *H. bonnellii, Ancistroteuthis lichtensteinii, Sepiola oweniana* and various Cranchiidae; occasionally small fish (e.g. cod *Gadus morhua*) [67, 109, 222, 259, 263, 266, 304, 339, 792, 939, 1164, 1254, 1266].

Feeding methods: Limited information on diel patterns of activity; off Santa Catalina, California, feeding mainly nocturnal [1068].

BREEDING

Poorly known. Off British Isles (from records of fetuses and newborn calves), births mainly from early spring to summer (March–July) [340, 346, 353, 408], although suggested elsewhere that occur mainly in winter (December–February) [316, 1157]. Examination of 51 stranded animals, NW Mediterranean, indicated calving between end of winter and early summer [949], but number of calves there peaks in July, despite proportion of adults to calves largely the same throughout year [430]. Possible that calves born in most months of the year [233]. Gestation lasts *c.*13–14 months (recently estimated at 13.87 months [949]); lactation period and calving interval unknown. Age at sexual maturity 3–4 years [680, 1017]. Suspected hybrids from mating with bottlenose dolphin found on Irish coast [405], and hybrid calf of these species successfully produced in captivity in Japan.

POPULATION

In W North Atlantic, 29 000 estimated off E USA and 2700 in N Gulf of Mexico [1199]. No population estimates for any region in E North Atlantic. Study in N Minches, Scotland, identified at least 142 individuals [66, 67]. Similarly, at least 345 individuals photo-identified in NW Mediterranean, 1990–2004 [432].

Oldest individual (male) examined estimated at >29 years (on basis that 1 tooth growth layer = 1 year [949]). One recognisable individual, 'Pelorus Jack', accompanied vessels over 24 years from 1888 [29, 680].

MORTALITY

No instances of predation known [573], but have been observed fleeing from a pod of killer whales [353]. No information on mortality rates.

PARASITES AND PATHOGENS

External parasites include *Isocyamus delphini* and *Xenobalanus globicipitis* [691, 1017]. Internal parasites include the trematode *Nasitrema* spp.,

cestodes *Phyllobothrium delphini, Monorygma grimaldii,* and *Tetrabothrius,* and nematodes *Stenurus minor* and *Crassicauda grampicola* [304, 659, 954].

RELATIONS WITH HUMANS

Hunted in small numbers in several regions of world [552, 553, 792, 965, 971], and previously including Mediterranean [332] and Lesser Antilles [205]. Widely caught incidentally in fishing gear [792, 659, 919]; killed deliberately in Japan to reduce competition with fisheries; has been observed stealing fish from longlines [603]. Recent annual takes estimated at *c.*250–500 [971]. Bycatches off Sri Lanka thought to be unsustainable [658].

Pollutant burdens are only poorly known; levels of total PCBs very high (466 and 2061 μg/g wet weight) in blubber of 2 animals stranded on Spanish Mediterranean coast [276]. DDT levels in one of them also high (670 μg/g wet weight), but much lower in a Welsh specimen, which also had low levels of heavy metals (with exception of cadmium and zinc) [671]. One stranded, S Adriatic Sea (Italy), had relatively high levels of total mercury in the liver and cadmium in the kidney [1129]. Effects of disturbance from oil and gas exploration, other industrial activities, and shipping largely unknown [469, 659].

Small numbers live-captured for dolphinaria, particularly in Japan [552, 965]. Legally protected in European, British and Irish waters (Table 12.1).

LITERATURE

General review [659].

AUTHOR

P.G.H. Evans

GENUS *Orcinus*

A monospecific genus, characterised by few (10–12) pairs of robust, oval-sectioned, teeth.

Killer whale *Orcinus orca*

Delphinus orca Linnaeus, 1758; European seas.

Orca, grampus, blackfish; swordfish, pied whal' (Shetland); *lleiddiad* (Welsh) *mada-chuain* (Scottish Gaelic); *cráin dubh, orc* (Irish Gaelic).

RECOGNITION

Striking black and white pattern (white patch near eye, large white patch extending from belly to flanks, and less distinct pale grey saddle behind dorsal fin). Tall dorsal fin, triangular or sickle-shaped, centrally placed (Fig. 12.34). Broad

Fig. 12.34 Killer whales, showing taller fin of adult male (foreground), as well as characteristic pale saddle and white eye-spot (*photo F. Ugarte*).

rounded flippers. Teeth large, pointed and anterioposteriorly compressed.

DESCRIPTION
Powerfully built, robust torpedo-shaped body with conical head, and indistinct beak (Plate 14). 10–12 pairs of large conical teeth. Coloration very striking: black on back and sides, white ventrally from chin and underside of flippers narrowing rearward along the belly and expanding as a 3-pointed lobe around the urogenital region and along the sides up the flanks. Distinctive, conspicuous white oval patch above and behind eye ('eye spot'). Lighter grey saddle over back behind dorsal fin often shows individual variation. Large, rounded, paddle-shaped flippers; conspicuous centrally-placed dorsal fin, sickle-shaped in adult females and immatures, but very tall (to 1.8 m) and erect (triangular, sometimes tilted forwards) in adult male. Tail flukes black above, white below, with shallow median notch and concave trailing edge.

RELATIONSHIPS
The largest member of Delphinidae. Often grouped with false killer whale *Pseudorca*, pygmy killer whale *Feresa*, Irrawaddy dolphin *Orcaella* and the 2 pilot whales *Globicephala* in a subfamily Globicephalinae [846, 847] or Orcininae [601, 773]; current view has *Orcinus* outside Globicephalinae, but nearest relatives uncertain [192, 962].

MEASUREMENTS
Length: newborn 208–220 cm; at sexual maturity *c*.4.5–4.9 m (female), *c*.5.7–5.8 m (male); adult 5.6–5.7 m (female), *c*.9.4–9.5 m (male). Weight 2500–3000 kg (female), 4000–5000 kg (male).
VARIATION
Regional variation in E North Pacific attributed to existence of 2 'forms' or 'types', specialising on either fish or marine mammal prey (originally termed 'residents' and 'transients', respectively) based on long-term studies along the coasts of W Canada and NW USA [133, 134, 877]. Variation in genetics, morphology, social organisation, feeding ecology and acoustic behaviour all well documented (e.g. [299, 395, 396, 530, 995, 1217]). Genetic studies indicate ongoing gene flow between 'resident' and 'transient' types in E North Pacific, but at rate low enough to maintain differentiation between all putative populations in that region [531]. Fish-feeding populations similar to 'resident' type have been reported in N Atlantic off Norway [1089, 1090, 1130], but in British waters, same pod observed hunting both fish and marine mammals on same day [1]. Worldwide variability in pigmentation and body size suggest further regional phenotypes [125, 364, 1185], yet worldwide genetic diversity is low [530].

DISTRIBUTION
Worldwide, from tropical to polar seas. In NE Atlantic, apparently most numerous around Iceland, Faroes, and in localised regions off W

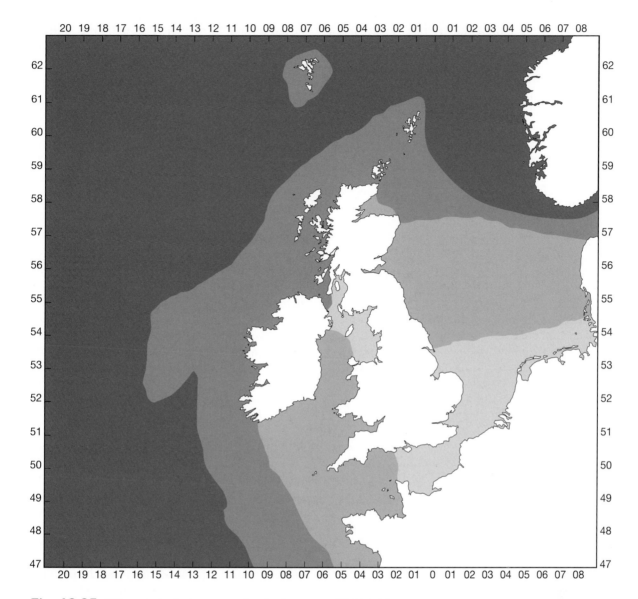

Fig. 12.35 Killer whale *Orcinus orca*: distribution around British Isles.

Norway. Widely distributed in small numbers around British Isles (Fig. 12.35), mainly Atlantic seaboard and in N North Sea [340, 358, 360, 973]. Regularly sighted off Scotland, in N Isles and Hebrides; rare in Irish Sea, C and S North Seas and English Channel. Recorded in British waters in all months, but most sightings in coastal waters May–September [360]. Offshore, between Shetland and Norway and in N North Sea, regularly occurs November–March, associates with pelagic trawling for mackerel [277, 278, 723]. In April–June, concentrates along continental slope N of Shetland, making onshore movements around N Isles and Caithness coast [343, 360, 1216].

HISTORY
Earliest fossils attributed to *Orcinus* from Pliocene, Italy [220a, 519]. Fossil teeth reported from Suffolk [724].

HABITAT
Found in a wide variety of habitats: common in cold, nearshore waters, but also reported from the polar ice pack to tropical oceanic islands. Individual populations often develop feeding specialisations which restrict distribution, e.g. on pinnipeds, bringing them near breeding rookeries, or on spawning fish, bringing them to spawning grounds.

SOCIAL ORGANISATION AND BEHAVIOUR
Sightings around British Isles mainly of single individuals or small groups <15, but groups of 100–300 sighted in N North Sea and E of Shetland, generally associated with trawling activities [343, 358, 360, 723]. Elsewhere, groups commonly up to 40, sometimes >100, although these probably represent temporary coalitions. Social structure

intensively studied along the Pacific coast of USA and Canada [94, 132]. Groups often matriarchal, basic social unit being mothers with calves, including immatures of both sexes and one or more adult males. Single animals are mainly subadults and adult males [132, 343, 511]. 'Resident' groups seem to form extended family units; certainly members remain within the pod for many years [94, 287, 396]. Other evidence that pods remain stable from one generation to the next comes from presence of distinct, pod-specific vocal dialects (even among pods in a localised area), with some shared call-types, but always including predominant calls unique to the pod [169, 389–391, 393, 394, 527, 995, 1130]. The smaller 'transient' pods have a less predictable home range in E North Pacific and smaller vocal repertoire [94, 132] Some transient individuals photographically identified in California and Alaska, 2300 km apart [445].

'Resident' killer whale pods apparently maintain communal, seasonal territories with large home ranges that may extend for 320–480 km, and even within a single day can range 120–160 km [95]. Fast swimmers, travelling at 14–22 km/h, can attain 50 km/h. No particular diurnal pattern of behaviour has been observed but foraging activities were related to tidal cycle, and amounted to 53% of time spent [368]. Spent 20% of time in percussive foraging; 13% in more obvious play; 12% in rest or sleep; 2% in intermingling behaviour [510, 525, 884].

Average maximum dive depth 140.8 m (max. 264 m, n = 34 individuals) in the inland waters of the NE Pacific; max. depth 330 m [86]. No significant differences in diving rates by age or sex, but adult males had higher rates of deep dives than adult females, perhaps due to sex-based differences in feeding patterns. Also, most deep diving occurred during the day, perhaps due to diurnal vertical migrations of favoured salmon prey, vision-dependent feeding or preferences for resting at night with lower levels of vessel noise [86].

Vocalisations: Well studied; include a variety of whistles of variable duration, mainly of 6–12 kHz frequency, a tonal call primarily in the frequency range 1–6 kHz, and very short (41 μs) broadband echolocation clicks, some with low- and high-frequency peaks near 29 kHz and 105 kHz [169, 390, 527, 810, 1092]. Source level of clicks made by Norwegian and Icelandic killer whales was 199 dB re 1 μPa @ 1 m [1092]. A specific high-intensity call, peak frequency 680 Hz and duration 3.1 s, recorded from foraging killer whales off Iceland but never off Norway [1092]; usually heard just prior to sound of underwater

tail slap, thought to be used as an aid to herding herring prey into tight schools before using tail slaps [1092]. Underwater tail slaps produce broadband, multi-pulsed sounds with source level of 191 dB re 1 μPa @ 1 m, which can be heard by other whales at distances of up to 3–4 km [1092]. Mammal-eating killer whales often hunt silently, perhaps adapting to the hearing sensitivity of their mammalian prey [103, 299]. Suggested to be one of the few animals capable of vocal learning [383].

FEEDING

Diet: Highly varied; includes fish, squid, marine mammals and even occasionally turtles and birds, though individuals (or social groups) typically specialise [340, 343, 395, 1157, 1235]. Fish prey include *Salmo*, *Clupea*, *Gadus*, *Scomber*, *Pleurogrammus*, *Hippoglossus*, *Sardinella* and *Sarda*. Marine mammals include minke, humpback and long-finned pilot whales, harbour porpoise, and various seals including grey seal. Auks and kittiwakes have also been taken in Faroese waters. Squid include members of Loliginidae (e.g. *Loligo*).

Feeding methods: Often use tidal rips in which to capture fish such as salmon, cooperatively herding them into tight clusters, at the same time breaching, lobtailing and slapping the water with their flippers [274, 509, 562]. Cooperative feeding on grey seal seen off N Scotland: adult male made the kill, then moved aside for other pod members to feed [340]. Intentional stranding on beach to capture seals (off Argentina and Crozet Is.) suggests a large degree of social learning [151, 524, 722], involved single individuals dominant in provisioning other pod members [524]. Cooperative feeding on schooling herring well documented off Norway [322, 1089, 1090, 1092]; cooperative foraging on salmon in E North Pacific suggested by way subgroups converged [525]. Echolocation studies show that can detect individual large fish at ranges up to 100 m [72], and herring schools within a few km [1092]. Males tend to dive deeper than females; most deep diving occurs during the day [86].

BREEDING

Births probably mainly in late autumn and winter (October–January), may be associated with offshore movement at this time [343, 358, 360]. Fetal lengths from Norwegian specimens suggest that mating peaks around October–November [241, 242]. Precise breeding areas not known. Gestation period *c*.12 (possibly up to 16) months. Lactation period unknown, but at least 12 months. Calving interval at least 3, maybe sometimes up to 8–9 years. Age at sexual maturity 15–16 years in male, 8–10 years in female [132, 241, 242, 593].

POPULATION

Population estimates incomplete; 1987 survey of N Atlantic from Icelandic and Faroese vessels estimated 6618 animals (95% confidence limits 3500–12 500) [466]. Longevity, based on life history table analysis, was 60 years for males and 90 years for females [877]. Individuals up to 35 years found off Norway [241]. One population had a finite annual rate of increase of 2.92%, relatively high for such a long-lived mammal [877]. Although subject to cropping (for display in oceanaria) and natural population increase, no evidence of density dependence in any life history parameters [877]. However, one population has not recovered from captures for oceanaria, is on list of endangered species, USA [532].

MORTALITY

Has no known predators. Mortality curves U-shaped for both sexes, but narrower for males [877]. Annual mortality estimates in the wild (based on horizontal estimates following individuals over time) low, perhaps 3.9% for mature males and as low as 1.1% for mature females [877]. Mortality in captivity variously estimated at 6.2–8.9%, significantly higher than for wild populations [303, 329, 1098]. Sex differences in mortality for captive animals (males 8.5%, females 5%) not significantly different, possibly due to a small sample size [1098]. Diseases reported from captivity and strandings include pneumonia, systemic mycosis, bacterial infections (of the tooth pulp cavity and of the vestigial hair follicles), atherosclerosis and Chidiak–Higashi syndrome [285, 464, 519] Depleted populations may be more susceptible to infectious diseases [436].

PARASITES AND PATHOGENS

Endoparasites: Include cestodes *Trigonocotyle spasskyi* and *Phyllobothrium* sp., a nematode *Anasakis simplex* and trematode *Fasciola skriabini* [288].

Ectoparasites: Rare, but barnacles *Xenobalanus globicipitus* and *Cryptolepas rhachianecti*, remoras Echeneididae and whale-louse *Cyamus antarcticensis* reported [285, 1025].

RELATIONS WITH HUMANS

Has been hunted opportunistically in E Canadian Arctic, W Greenland and Faroes (in latter case using similar driving methods as used on pilot whales). Commercial catches primarily by Norway both in coastal waters and offshore [593]; total catch 1938–1981, 2455 whales [875]. Live capture fishery conducted sporadically off Iceland since 1975, for dolphinaria [1083]. One animal ('Keiko', star of the film *Free Willy*) returned to Iceland for potential reintroduction to the wild in 1998. In 2002, he 'escaped' during open ocean training, was found 2 months later 1400 km away in Norway. He was held in a Norwegian bay until 2003, when he died of pneumonia.

Sometimes perceived as threat to herring, halibut, tuna and salmon, and bottomfish fisheries, but no evidence for any serious effects on these businesses. For example, in Prince William Sound, Alaska, only a few specific pods developed habits of stealing fish off longlines and this predation amounted to <3% of the overall monetary value of the fishery [1256].

In E North Pacific, various pollutants (PCBs, PBDEs, PBBs and PCNs) collected from known animals; similar high concentrations in fish-eating, southern 'resident' populations that live around the industrialised areas of Seattle and Vancouver and the mammal-eating 'transients' who feed at high trophic levels [958]. Toxicity information non-existent for cetaceans, but levels of PCBs (mean for male transient whales 251.2±54.7 μg/kg) were 3 times those correlated with immunotoxicity in captive harbour seals [1019]. Off Prince William Sound, Alaska, the site of the *Exxon Valdez* oil spill, killer whales had 237.7 μg/g PCB and 346 μg/g DDT, levels similar to those found in the belugas of the heavily industrialised St Lawrence River. Of individually identified killer whales, 25 last seen in Prince William Sound swimming through oil slicks from the spill have disappeared, presumed dead [286].

Whale-watching now so popular that some populations may be suffering acoustic threats through masking of natural communication [382, 1238].

Legally protected in European, British and Irish waters (Table 12.1).

LITERATURE

Succinct review [519]; more extensive one [285]; studies of Pacific coast population [81, 396].

AUTHORS

J.R. Boran, A.R. Hoelzel & P.G.H. Evans

REFERENCES

1 Author's data.

2 Aarefjord, H. *et al.* (1995) Diet of the harbour porpoise (*Phocoena phocoena*) in Scandinavian waters. *Report of the International Whaling Commission* (Special Issue No. **16**), 211–222.

3 Abend, A.G. & Smith, T.D. (1997) Differences in stable isotope ratios of carbon and nitrogen between long-finned pilot whales (*Globicephala melas*) and their primary prey in the western north Atlantic. *ICES Journal of Marine Science*, **54**(3), 500–503.

4 Abril, E. *et al.* (1991) A new species of the genus *Zalophotrema* (Digenea: Campulidae), *Zalophotrema atlanticum* n. sp., from the liver of the striped dolphin *Stenella coeruleoalba* (Meyen, 1833) (Cetacea: Delphinidae) in Atlantic waters. *Systematic Parasitology,* **18**, 133–138.

5 Acevedo-Gutierrez, A. *et al.* (1997) Resightings and behavior of false killer whales (*Pseudorca crassidens*) in Costa Rica. *Marine Mammal Science*, **13**(2), 307–314.

6 Addink, M. & Smeenk, C.S. (1999) The harbour porpoise *Phocoena phocoena* in Dutch coastal waters: analysis of stranding records for the period 1920–1994. *Lutra*, **41**, 55–80.

7 Addink, M.J. *et al.* (1995) *The harbour porpoise* Phocoena phocoena *in Dutch waters: life history, pathology and historical records.* IWC document SC/47/SM 5.

8 Addink, M. *et al.* (1997) A note on life-history parameters of the Atlantic white-sided dolphin (*Lagenorhynchus acutus*) from animals bycaught in the northeastern Atlantic. *Report of the International Whaling Commission*, **47**, 637–639.

9 Agler, B.A. *et al.* (1993) Reproduction of photographically identified fin whales, *Balaenoptera physalus*, from the Gulf of Maine. *Journal of Mammalogy*, **74**, 577–587.

10 Aguilar, A. (1983) Spain progress report on cetacean research, June 1981 to May 1982. *Report of the International Whaling Commission,* **33,** 245–248.

11 Aguilar, A. (1986) A review of old Basque whaling and its effect on the right whales (*Eubalaena glacialis*) of the North Atlantic. *Report of the International Whaling Commision* (Special Issue 10), 191–200.

12 Aguilar, A (2002) Fin whale *Balaenoptera physalus*, pp. 435–438 in Perrin, W.F. *et al.* (eds.) *Encyclopaedia of marine mammals*. Academic Press, San Diego, CA.

13 Aguilar, A. & Borrell, A. (1988) Age and sex related changes in organochlorine compound levels in fin whales from the eastern north Atlantic. *Marine Environmental Research*, **25**, 195–211.

14 Aguilar, A. & Borrell, A. (1993) A possible link between striped dolphin mass mortality and toxic contaminents in the Mediterranean Sea, p. 36 in Miyazaki, N. (ed.) *Mammals and toxic contaminants*. International Marine Biological Institute, Kamogawa, Japan.

15 Aguilar, A. & Borrell, A. (1994) Abnormally high polychlorinated biphenyl levels in striped dolphins (*Stenella coerulealba*) affected by the 1990–92 Mediterranean epizootic. *Science of the Total Environment*, **154**, 237–247.

16 Aguilar, A. & Borrell, A. (1995) Pollution and harbour porpoises in the eastern North Atlantic. *Report of the International Whaling Commission, Special Issue* **16**, 231–242.

17 Aguilar, A. & Jover, L. (1982) DDT and PCB residues in the fin whale, *Balaenoptera physalus*, of the North Atlantic. *Report of the International Whaling Commission*, **32**, 299–301.

18 Aguilar, A. & Raga, J.A. (1993) The striped dolphin epizootic in the Mediterranean Sea. *Ambio*, **22**, 524–528.

19 Aguilar, A. *et al.* (1982) A note on the organochlorine contamination in a Blainville's beaked whale, *Mesoplodon densirostris* (de Blainville, 1817) from the Mediterranean Sea. *Departmento de Zoologia, Universidad de Barcelona, Publications*, **7**, 85–90.

20 Aguilar, A. *et al.* (1983) Report of the 'Ballena 1' whale marking and sighting cruise in the waters off western Spain. *Report of the International Whaling Commission*, **31**, 457–459.

21 Aguilar, A. *et al.* (1994) Striped dolphins from Mediterranean and the Sea of Japan: two sides of the same coin? p. 127 in Evans P.G.H. (ed.) *European research on cetaceans – 8.* European Cetacean Society.

22 Aguilar de Soto, N. (2006) *Acoustic and diving behaviour of the short-finned pilot whale* (Globicephala macrorhynchus) *and Blainville's beaked whale* (Mesoplodon densirostris) *in the Canary Islands. Implications on the effects of man-made noise and boat collisions.* PhD thesis, University of La Laguna, Tenerife.

23 Aguilar de Soto, N. Personal communication.

24 Aguilar de Soto, N. *et al.* (2004) High concentrations of beaked whales observed close to the shore of El Hierro (Canary Islands). In Evans, P.G.H. (ed.) *European research on cetaceans – 18.* European Cetacean Society.

25 Akamatsu, T. *et al.* (1992) The rate with which a harbor porpoise uses echolocation at night, pp. 299–316 in Thomas, J.A. *et al.* (eds.) *Marine mammal sensory systems*. Plenum Press, New York.

26 Allen, G.M. (1906) Sowerby's whale on the American coast. *American Naturalist*, **40**, 357–370.

27 Allen, J.A. (1908) The north Atlantic right whale and its near allies. *Bulletin of the American Museum of Natural History*, **24**(18), 227–329.

28 Alonso, M.K. *et al.* (1999) Stomach contents of false killer whales (*Pseudorca crassidens*) stranded on the coasts of the Strait of Magellan, Tierra del Fuego. *Marine Mammal Science*, **15**(3), 712–724.

29 Alpers, A. (1963) *Dolphins*. John Murray, New Zealand.

30 Alzieu, C. & Duguy, R. (1979) Teneurs en composes organochlores chez les cétacés et pinnipèdes frequentant les côtes françaises. *Oceanologia Acta*, **2**, 107–120 (in French).

31 Amaha, A. (1994) *Geographic variation of the common dolphin,* Delphinus delphis *(Odontoceti: Delphinidae)*. PhD thesis, Tokyo University of Fisheries, Tokyo.

32 Amano, M. *et al.* (1996) Life history of Fraser's dolphin *Lagenodelphis hosei*, based on a school captured off Pacific coast of Japan. *Marine Mammal Science*, **12**, 199–214.

33 Amaral, A.R. *et al.* (2007) New insights on population genetic structure of *Delphinus delphis* from the northeast Atlantic and phylogenetic relationships within the genus inferred from two mitochondrial markers. *Marine Biology*, **151** (5).

34 Amiard Triquet, C. & Caurant, F. (1997) Adaptation of the delphinids *Globicephala melas* (Traill, 1809) to cadmium contamination. *Bulletin de la Societé Zoologique de France – Evolution et Zoologie*, **122**(2), 127–136.

35 Amos, B. *et al.* (1991) Breeding behaviour of pilot whales revealed by DNA fingerprinting. *Heredity*, **67**, 49–55.

36 Amos, B. *et al.* (1993) A review of molecular evidence relating to social organisation and breeding system in the long-finned pilot whale. *Report of the International Whaling Commission, Special Issue,* **14**, 209–217.

37 Amos, W. & Dover, G.A. (1991) The use of satellite DNA sequences in determining population differentiation in the minke whale. *Report of the International Whaling Commission Special Issue,* **13**, 235–244.

38 Amos, W. *et al.* (1993) Social structure of pilot whales revealed by analytical DNA profiling. *Science*, **260**, 670–672.

39 Amundin, M. (1974) Functional analysis of the surfacing behaviour in the harbour porpoise, *Phocoena phocoena* (L.). *Zeitschrift für Säugetierkunde*, **39**, 313–318.

40 Amundin, M. (1991) *Sound production in odontocetes withg emphasis on the harbour porpoise* Phocoena phocoena. Doctoral dissertation, University of Stockholm.

41 Andersen, L.W. (1988) Electrophoretic differentiation

among local populations of the long-finned pilot whale, *Globicephala melaena*, at the Faroe Islands. *Canadian Journal of Zoology*, **66**, 1884–1892.

42 Andersen, L.W. (1993) Further studies on the population structure of the long-finned pilot whale, *Globicephala melas*, off the Faroe Islands. *Report of the International Whaling Commission, Special Issue* **14**, 219–231.

43 Andersen, L.W. (2003) Harbour porpoises (*Phocoena phocoena*) in the North Atlantic: Distribution and genetic population structure, pp. 11–29 in Haug, T. *et al.* (ed) *Harbour porpoises in the North Atlantic*. NAMMCO Scientific Publications, Volume 5, Tromsø.

44 Andersen, L.W. & Siegismund, H.R. (1994) Genetic-evidence for migration of males between schools of the long-finned pilot whale, *Globicephala melas*. *Marine Ecology Progress Series*, **105**(1–2), 1–7.

45 Andersen, L.W. *et al.* (1997) A combined DNA-microsatellite and isozyme analysis of the population structure of the harbour porpoise in Danish waters and West Greenland. *Heredity*, **78**, 270–276.

46 Andersen, L.W. *et al.* (2001) Conservation genetics of the harbour porpoise, *Phocoena phocoena*, in eastern and central North Atlantic. *Conservation Genetics*, **2**, 309–324.

47 Andersen, L.W. *et al.* (2003) Genetic population structure of minke whales *Balaenoptera acutorostrata* from Greenland, the North East Atlantic and the North Sea probably reflects different ecological regions. *Marine Ecology Progress Series*, **247**, 263–280.

48 Andersen, S.H. (1965) L'alimentation du marsouin (*Phocoena phocoena*) en captivité. *Vie et Milieu*, **16**, 799–810 (in French).

49 Andersen, S. and Dziedzic, A. (1964) Behaviour patterns of captive harbour porpoises *Phocaena phocaena* (L.). *Bulletin Institution Océanographie, Monaco*, **63**, 1–20.

50 Andersen, S.H. & Rebsdorff, A. (1976) Polychlorinated hydrocarbons and heavy metals in harbour porpoise (*Phocoena phocoena*) and white-beaked dolphin (*Lagenorhynchus albirostris*) from Danish waters. *Aquatic Mammals*, **4**, 14–20.

51 Anderson, R.J. (1901) A note on a beaked whale. *Irish Naturalist*, **10**, 117–119.

52 Anderson, R.J. (1904) The teeth in '*Mesoplodon hectori*'. *Irish Naturalist*, **13**, 126.

53 Anderson, S. & Jones, J.K. (1967) *Recent mammals of the world. A synopsis of families*. Ronald Press, New York.

54 Anderwald, A. (2002) *Niche differentiation of cetaceans in the northeast Atlantic*. MSc thesis, University of Zurich.

55 Anderwald, P. *et al.* (2007) Do North Atlantic minke whales show population sub-structuring? p. 35 in *European research on cetaceans –21*. European Cetacean Society.

56 Anderwald, P. *et al.* Personal communication.

57 Ansmann, I. *et al.* (2007) Variation in the whistle characteristics of short-beaked common dolphins, *Delphinus delphis*, at two locations around the British Isles. *Journal of the Marine Biological Association of the UK*, **87**, 19–26.

58 Aparicio, C. *et al.* (2006) Resident and reproductive populations of beaked whales in El Hierro, Canary Islands, in Evans, P.G.H. & Ridoux, V. (eds.) *European research on cetaceans – 19*. European Cetacean Society.

59 Aquarone, M. & Notarbartolo di Sciara, G. (1992) Pigmentation patterns of the striped dolphin, *Stenella coeruleoalba* (Meyen, 1933), in the central Mediterranean Sea, pp. 203–204 in Evans, P.G.H. (ed.) *European Research on Cetaceans – 6*. European Cetacean Society.

60 Archer, F.I. (1996) *Morphological and genetic variation of striped dolphins (*Stenella coeruleoalba, *Meyen 1833)*. PhD Thesis, Scripps Institution of Oceanography, University of California San Diego.

61 Archer, F.I. (2002) Striped dolphin *Stenella coeruleoalba*, pp. 1201–1203 in Perrin, W.F. *et al.* (eds.) *Encyclopaedia of marine*

mammals. Academic Press, San Diego, CA.

62 Árnason, Ú. & Gullberg, A. (1994) Relationships of baleen whales established by cytochrome b gene sequence comparison. *Nature*, **367**, 726–728.

63 Arnold, P.W. (1972) Predation on harbour porpoise *Phocoena phocoena* by white shark, *Carcharodon carcharias*. *Journal of the Fisheries Research Board of Canada*, **29**, 1213–1214.

64 Arvy, L. (1982) Phoresies and parasitism in cetaceans: a review. *Investigations on Cetacea*, **14**, 233–335.

65 Atkinson, S. *et al.* (1999) Monitoring of progesterone in captive female false killer whales, *Pseudorca crassidens*. *General and Comparative Endocrinology*, **115**(3), 323–332.

66 Atkinson, T. *et al.* (1997) Notes on the natural markings on Risso's dolphins (*Grampus griseus*) photographed in the coastal waters around the Eye Peninsula, Isle of Lewis, Scotland, p. 209 in Evans, P.G.H. *et al.* (eds.) *European research on cetaceans – 11*. European Cetacean Society.

67 Atkinson, T. *et al.* (1998) A photo-identification study of Risso's dolphins in the Outer Hebrides, Northwest Scotland, p. 102 in Evans, P.G.H. & Parsons, E.C.M. (eds.) *European research on cetaceans – 12*. European Cetacean Society.

68 Au, W.L. (1993) *The sonar of dolphins*. Springer-Verlag, New York.

69 Au, W.W.L. *et al.* (1985) Demonstration of adaptation in beluga whale *Delphinapterus leucas* echolocation signals. *Journal of the Acoustical Society of America*, **77**, 726–730.

70 Au, W.W.L. et al. (1987) Propagation of beluga echolocation signals. *Journal of the Acoustical Society of America*, **82**, 807–813.

71 Au, W.W.L. *et al.* (1995) Echolocation signals and transmission beam pattern of a false killer whale (*Pseudorca crassidens*). *Journal of the Acoustical Society of America*, **98**(1), 51–59.

72 Au, W.W.L. *et al.* (2004) Echolocation of free-ranging killer whales (*Orcinus orca*) and modeling of foraging for chinook salmon (*Onchorhynchus tshawytscha*). *Journal of the Acoustic Society of America*, **115**(2), 901–909.

73 Auger-Methe, M. & Whitehead, H. (2007) The use of natural markings in studies of long-finned pilot whales (*Globicephala melas*). *Marine Mammal Science*, **23**(1), 77–93.

74 Augier, H. *et al.* (1993) Mercury contamination of the striped dolphin *Stenella coeruleoalba* Meyen from the French Mediterranean coasts. *Marine Pollution Bulletin*, **26**, 306–310.

75 Aznar, F.J. *et al.* (1994) On the identity and emigration of *Scolex pleuronectis* lavae (Cestoda) in the striped dolphin, pp. 243–246 in Evans, P.G.H. (ed.) *European research on cetaceans – 8*. European Cetacean Society.

76 Azzellino, A. *et al.* (2007) Habitat use and preference of cetaceans along the continental slope and the adjacent pelagic waters in the Western Ligurian Sea. *Deep-Sea Research Part I* (in press).

77 Babin, P. *et al.* (1994) Ulcères parasitaires gastriques chez les cétacés odontocètes échoués sur les côtes de France. *Le Point Vétérinaire*, **26**, 77–81 (in French).

78 Bacetti, N. *et al.* (1991) First record of *Kogia simus* (Cetacea, Physeteridae) from the Mediterranean Sea. *Mammalia*, **55**, 152–154.

79 Baer, J.G. (1932) Contribution à l'étude des cestodes de cétacés. *Revue suisse de Zoologie*, **39**, 195–228 (in French).

80 Baines, M.E. *et al.* (2002) Comparison of the abundance and distribution of harbour porpoises (*Phocoena phocoena*) and bottlenose dolphins (*Tursiops truncatus*) in Cardigan Bay, UK. *European research on cetaceans – 16*. European Cetacean Society.

81 Baird, R.W. (2000) The killer whale: foraging specializations and group hunting, pp. 127–153 in Mann, J. *et al.* (eds.) *Cetacean societies: field studies of whales and dolphins*. University of Chicago Press, Chicago.

82 Baird, R.W. (2002) False killer whale *Pseudorca crassidens*, pp.

12 Whales, porpoises and dolphins: Order Cetacea

411–412 in Würsig, B. *et al.* (eds.) *Encyclopaedia of marine mammals*. Academic Press, San Diego.

83 Baird, R.W. & Stacey, P.J. (1991) Status of Risso's dolphin, *Grampus griseus*, in Canada. *Canadian Field Naturalist*, **105**, 233–242.

84 Baird, R.W. *et al.* (1989) First records of false killer whales (*Pseudorca crassidens*) in Canada. *Canadian Field Naturalist*, **103**, 368–371.

85 Baird, R.W. *et al.* (2002) Diving and night-time behavior of long-finned pilot whales in the Ligurian Sea. *Marine Ecology Progress Series*, **237**, 301–305.

86 Baird, R.W. *et al.* (2005) Factors influencing the diving behaviour of fish-eating killer whales: sex differences and diel and interannual variation in diving rates. *Canadian Journal of Zoology*, **83**, 257–267.

87 Baker, C.S. & Clapham, P.J. (2004) Modelling the past and future of whales and whaling. *Trends in Ecology and Evolution*, **19**, 365–371.

88 Baker, J.R. (1992) Causes of mortality and parasites and incidental lesions in dolphins and whales from British waters. *Veterinary Record*, **130**, 569–572.

89 Baker, J.R. & Martin, A.R. (1992) Causes of mortality and parasites and incidental lesions in harbour porpoises (*Phocoena phocoena*) from British waters. *Veterinary Record*, **130**, 554–558.

90 Bakke, I. *et al.* (1996) Lack of population subdivision among the minke whales from Icelandic and Norwegian waters based on mitochondrial DNA sequences. *Marine Biology*, **125**, 1–9.

91 Bakker, J. & Smeenk, C. (1987) Time-series analysis of *Tursiops truncatus*, *Delphinus delphis*, and *Lagenorhynchus albirostris* strandings on the Dutch coast, pp. 14–19 in Broekema, J.W. & Smeenk, C. (eds.) *European research on cetaceans – 1*. European Cetacean Society.

92 Balbuena, J.A. *et al.* (1987) Some data on parasites of the harbour porpoise *Phocoena phocoena* in French Atlantic waters, pp. 56–58 in Broekema, J.W. & Smeenk, C. (eds.) *European research on cetaceans – 1*. European Cetacean Society.

93 Balbuena, J.A. *et al.* (1994) Lung-worms (Nematoda: Pseudaliidae) of harbour porpoises (*Phocoena phocoena*) in Norwegian waters: patterns of colonization. *Parasitology*, **108**, 343–349.

94 Balcomb, K.C. & Bigg, M.A. (1986) Population biology of the three resident killer whale pods in Puget Sound and off southern Vancouver Island, pp. 85–95 in Kirkevold, B. & Lockard, J.S. (eds.) *Behavioral biology of killer whales*. A.R. Liss, New York.

95 Balcomb, K.C. *et al.* (1982) Killer whales in Greater Puget Sound. *Report of the International Whaling Commission*, **32**, 681–685.

96 Bane, G.W. & Zullo, V.A. (1981) Observation on a stranded goosebeaked whale (*Ziphius cavirostris*, Cuvier, 1823) and its ectocommensal barnacles (*Xenobalanus globicipitis*). *Journal of the Elisha Mitchell Scientific Society*, **96**, 1–3.

97 Baptist, H.J.M. (1987) Waarnemingen van zeezoogdieren in de Nederlandse sector van de Noordzee. *Lutra*, **30**, 93–104 (in Dutch).

98 Barlow, J. & Clapham, P.J. (1997) A new birth-interval approach to estimating demographic parameters of humpback whales. *Ecology*, **78**, 535–546.

99 Barlow, J. *et al.* (1995) *US Pacific marine mammal stock assessments*. NOAA Technical Memorandum NMFS-SWFSC-219.

100 Barnes, L.G. (1984) *Fossil Odontocetes (Mammalia: Cetacea) from the Almejas Formation, Isla Cedros, Mexico*. Paleobios, Museum of Paleontology, University of California.

101 Barnes, L.G. (1990) The fossil record and evolutionary relationships of the genus *Tursiops*, pp. 3–26 in Leatherwood, S. & Reeves, R.R. (eds.) *The bottlenose dolphin*.

Academic Press, San Diego.

102 Barnes, R.H. (1991) Indigenous whaling and porpoise hunting in Indonesia, pp. 99–106 in Leatherwood, S. & Donovan, G.P. (eds.) *Cetaceans and cetacean research in the Indian Ocean sanctuary*. UNEP Marine Mammal Technical Report No. 3.

103 Barrett-Lennard, L.G. *et al.* (1996) The mixed blessing of echolocation: differences in sonar use by fish-eating and mammal-eating killer whales. *Animal Behaviour*, **51**, 553–565.

104 Barriety, L. (1962) Echouage a Bidart d'un *Mesoplodon mirus*. *Centre de Recherches scientifiques, Biarritz, Bulletin*, **4**, 93–94 (in French).

105 Baumgartner, M.F. (1997) The distribution of Risso's dolphin (*Grampus griseus*) with respect to the physiography of the northern Gulf of Mexico. *Marine Mammal Science*, **13**, 614–628.

106 Baumgartner, M.F., *et al.* (2007) Enormous carnivores, microscopic food, and a restaurant that's hard to find, pp. 138–171 in Kraus, S.D. & Rolland, R.M. (eds.) *The urban whale: North Atlantic right whales at the crossroads*. Harvard University Press, Cambridge, MA.

107 Bayliss, H.A. (1932) A list of worms parasitic in Cetacea. *Discovery Reports*, **6**, 393–418.

108 Beland, P. *et al.* (1992) *Toxicology and pathology of St. Lawrence marine mammals*. Final report, Wildlife Toxicology Fund, WWF, St Lawrence National Institute of Ecotoxicology, Quebec, Canada.

108a Bel'kovitch, V.M. & Sh'ekotov, M.N. (1990) *The belukha whale – belukha: natural behavior and bioacoustics*. Akademiia Nauk, Moscow. English translation (1993) by M.A. Svanidze, Woods Hole Oceanographic Institution, Woods Hole, MA.

109 Bello, G. & Pulcini, M. (1989) On a Risso's dolphin (*Grampus griseus*) stranded off the coast of the Gulf of Taranto. *Atti Simposio Nazionale Cetacei*, June 1989, Mola di Bari.

110 Benjaminsen, T. (1972) On the biology of the bottlenose whale, *Hyperoodon ampullatus* (Forster). *Norwegian Journal of Zoology*, **20**, 233–241.

111 Benjaminsen, T. & Christensen, I. (1979) The natural history of the bottlenose whale, *Hyperoodon ampullatus*, pp. 143–164 in Winn, H.E. & Olla, B.L. (eds.) *Behaviour of marine animals: current perspectives in research*. Plenum Press, New York.

112 Benke, H. (1993) Investigations on the osteology and the functional morphology of the flipper of whales and dolphins (Cetacea). *Investigations on Cetacea*, **24**, 9–252.

113 Benke, H. & Siebert, U. (1996) The current status of harbour porpoises (*Phocoena phocoena*) in German waters. *International Whaling Commission*, document SC/47/SM 49.

114 Benhett, P.M. *et al.* (2001) Exposure to heavy metals and infectious disease mortality in harbour porpoises from England and Wales. *Environmental Pollution*, **112**, 33–40.

115 Benoldi, C. *et al.* (1997) Risso's dolphin acoustic survey in the Hebridean waters, Scotland, pp. 232–236 in Evans, P.G.H. *et al.* (eds.) *European research on cetaceans – 11*. European Cetacean Society.

116 Benoldi, C. *et al.* (1998) Comparison between Risso's dolphin vocal repertoire in Scottish waters and in the Mediterranean Sea, pp. 235–239 in Evans, P.G.H. & Parsons, E.C.M. (eds.) *European research on cetaceans – 12*. European Cetacean Society.

117 Berggren, P. (1996) *A preliminary assessment of the status of harbour porpoises* (Phocoena phocoena) *in the Swedish Skagg-erak, Kattegat and Baltic Seas*. IWC document SC/47/SM **50**.

118 Bernard, H.J. & Reilly, S.B. (1998) Pilot whales *Globicephala* Lesson, 1828, pp. 245–279 in Ridgway, S.H. & Harrison, R.J. (eds.) *Handbook of marine mammals*, Vol. 6. Academic Press, London.

119 Berrow, S.D. & Rogan, E. (1995) Stomach contents of harbour porpoise and dolphins in Irish waters, pp. 179–181 in Evans, P.G.H. (ed.) *European research on cetaceans – 9*. European Cetacean Society.

120 Berrow, S.D. & Rogan, E. (1997) Review of cetaceans stranded on the Irish coast, 1901–95. *Mammal Review*, **27**, 51–76.

121 Berrow, S. *et al.* (1993) An analysis of sperm whale *Physeter macrocephalus* stranding and sighting records from Britain and Ireland. *Journal of Zoology*, **230**, 333–337.

122 Berrow, S. *et al.* (2001) *Irish Whale and Dolphin Group cetacean sighting schemes*. Irish Whale & Dolphin Group, Final Report to the Heritage Council.

123 Berubé, M. & Aguilar, A. (1998) A new hybrid between a blue whale, *Balaenoptera musculus*, and a fin whale, *B. physalus*. Frequency and implications of hybridization. *Marine Mammal Science*, **14**, 82–98.

124 Bérubé, M. *et al.* (1998) Population genetic structure of North Atlantic, Mediterranean Sea and Sea of Cortez fin whales, *Balaenoptera physalus* (Linnaeus, 1758): analysis of mitochondrial and nuclear loci. *Molecular Ecology*, **7**, 585–599.

125 Berzin, A.A. & Vladimirov, V.L. (1983) A new species of killer whale (*Cetacea, Delphinidae*) from Antarctic waters. *Zoologicheskii Zhurnal*, **62**, 287–295.

126 Besharse, J.C. (1971) Maturity and sexual dimorphism in the skull, mandible and teeth of the beaked whale *Mesoplodon densirostris*. *Journal of Mammalogy*, **52**, 297–314.

127 Best, P.B. (1982) Seasonal abundance, feeding, reproduction, age, and growth in minke whales off Durban. *Report of the International Whaling Commission*, **32**, 759–786.

128 Best, P.B. (1994) Seasonality of reproduction and the length of gestation in southern right whales *Eubalaena australis*. *Journal of Zoology*, **232**, 175–189.

129 Best, P.B. & Shaughnessy, P.D. (1981) First record of the melon-headed whale (*Peponocephala electra*) from South Africa. *Annals of the South African Museum*, **83**, 33–47.

130 Best, P.B. *et al.* (1984) Patterns of reproduction in sperm whales, *Physeter macrocephalus*. *Report of the International Whaling Commission, Special Issue*, **6**, 51–79.

131 Beverley-Burton, M. (1978) Helminths of the alimentary tract from a stranded herd of Atlantic white-sided dolphin, *Lagenorhynchus acutus*, *Journal of the Fisheries Research Board of Canada*, **35**, 1356–1359.

132 Bigg, M.A. (1982) An assessment of killer whale (*Orcinus orca*) stocks off Vancouver Island, British Columbia. *Report of the International Whaling Commission*, **32**, 655–666.

133 Bigg, M.A. *et al.* (1987) *Killer whales: a study of their identification, genealogy and natural history in British Columbia and Washington state*. Phantom Press, Nanaimo, Canada.

134 Bigg, M.A. *et al.* (1990) Social organization and genealogy of resident killer whales (*Orcinus orca*) in the coastal waters of British Columbia and Washington State. *Report of the International Whaling Commission, Special Issue*, **12**, 383–405.

135 Bjørge, A. & Donovan, G. (eds.) (1995) Biology of the Phocoenids. *Report of the International Whaling Commission, Special Issue*, **16**, 1–552.

136 Bjørge, A. & Øien, N. (1995) Distribution and abundance of harbour porpoise, *Phocoena phocoena*, in Norwegian waters. *Report of the International Whaling Commission, Special Issue*, **16**, 89–98.

137 Blanco, C. & Raga, J.A. (2000) Cephalopod prey of two *Ziphius cavirostris* (Cetacea) stranded on the western Mediterranean coast. *Journal of the Marine Biological Association of the UK*, **80**, 381–382.

138 Blanco, C. *et al.* (1994) Food habits of *Stenella coeruleoalba* in the western Mediterranean during the 1990 die-off, with special reference to squids, pp. 196–198 in Evans, P.G.H. (ed.). *European research on cetaceans – 8*. European Cetacean Society.

139 Blix, A.S. *et al.* (1995) *Whales, seals, fish and man*. Elsevier, Amsterdam.

140 Bloch, D. (1998) Cetaceans of the Faroe Islands. *Shetland Sea Mammal Group Annual Report*.

141 Bloch, D. & Hoydal, K. (1990) Denmark. Progress report on cetacean research, June 1988 to May 1989. Part 2. Faroe Islands. *Report of the International Whaling Commission*, **40**, 192–194.

142 Bloch, D. & Lastein, L. (1993), Morphometric segregation of long-finned pilot whales in eastern and western North Atlantic, *Ophelia*, **38**, 55–68.

143 Bloch, D. *et al.* (1993) Some external characters of the long-finned pilot whale off the Faroe Islands and a comparison with the short-finned pilot whale. *Report of the International Whaling Commission, Special Issue*, **14**, 117–135.

144 Bloch, D. *et al.* (1996) Strandings of striped dolphins (*Stenellacoeruleoalba*) in Iceland and the Faroe Islands and sightings in the Northeast Atlantic, north of 50°N latitude. *Marine Mammal Science*, **12**, 125–132.

145 Bloch, D. *et al.* (1996) The northern bottlenose whale in the Faroe Islands. *Journal of Zoology*, **239**, 123–140.

146 Bloch, D. *et al.* (2003) Short-term movements of long-finned pilot whales *Globicephala melas* around the Faroe Islands. *Wildlife Biology*, **9**(1), 47–58.

147 Bloom, P.R.S. & Jager, M. (1994) The injury and subsequent healing of a serious propeller strike to a wild bottlenose dolphin (*Tursiops truncatus*) resident in cold waters off the Northumberland coast of England. *Aquatic Mammals*, **20**, 59–64.

148 Boer, R. de (1989) Waarneming van een gemengde groep witflankdolfijnen *Lagenorhynchus acutus* en witsnuit-dolfijnen *L. albirostris* in de centrale Noordzee. *Lutra*, **32**, 181–184 (in Dutch).

149 Bompar, J.M. *et al.* (1992) *Stenella coeruleoalba* affected by morbillivirus. Preliminary study for the French Mediterranean continental coast, pp. 27–32 in *Proceedings of the Mediterranean striped dolphin mortality*, international workshop, Palma de Mallorca, 4–5 November 1991. Greenpeace.

150 Bones, M. *et al.* (1998) Fraser's dolphin (*Lagenodelphis hosei*) stranded in South Uist: first record in U.K. waters. *Journal of Zoology*, **246**, 460–461.

151 Boran, J.R. & Heimlich, S.L. (1999) Social learning in cetaceans: hunting, hearing and hierarchies, pp. 282–307 in Box, H. & Gibson, K. (eds.) *Mammalian social learning: comparative and ecological perspectives*. Cambridge University Press, Cambridge.

152 Boran, J.R. *et al.* (1999) Cetaceans of the Hebrides: seven years of surveys. In Evans, P.G.H. *et al.* (eds.) *European research on cetaceans – 13*. European Cetacean Society.

153 Bord Iascaigh Mhara (2000) *Diversification trials with alternative tuna fishing techniques including the use of remote sensing technology*. No. 98/010. Bord Iascaigh Mhara (Irish Sea Fisheries Board), Dun Laoghaire, Co. Dublin.

154 Børjesson, P. & Berggren, P. (1996) Seasonal variation in the diet of harbour porpoises (*Phocoena phocoena*) from the Kattegat and Skaggerak seas, p. 261 in Evans, P.G.H. (ed.) *European research on cetaceans – 10*. European Cetacean Society.

155 Born, E.W. *et al.* (eds.) (1994) Studies of white whales (*Delphinapterus leucas*) and narwhals (*Monodon monoceros*) in Greenland and adjacent waters. *Meddr Grønland, Biosciences*, **39**, 1–259.

156 Born, E. *et al.* (2002) Regional variation of caesium-137 in minke whales *Balaenoptera acutorostrata* from West Greenland, the Northeast Atlantic and the North Sea. *Polar Biology*, **25**, 907–913.

157 Born, E. *et al.* (2003) Population substructure of North Atlantic minke whales (*Balaenoptera acutorostrata*) inferred from regional variation of elemental and stable isotopic

signatures in tissues. *Journal of Marine Systems*, **43**, 1–17.

158 Borrell, A. (1993) PCB and DDTs in blubber of cetaceans from the northeastern North Atlantic. *Marine Pollution Bulletin*, **26**, 146–151.

159 Borrell, A. & Aguilar, A. (1991) Were PCBs levels abnormally high in striped dolphins affected by the western Mediterranean die-off? pp. 88–90 in Evans, P.G.H. (ed.) *European research on cetaceans – 5*. European Cetacean Society.

160 Borrell, A. & Aguilar, A. (1993) DDT and PCB pollution in blubber and muscle of long-finned pilot whales off the Faroe Islands. *Report of the International Whaling Commission, Special Issue*, **14**, 351–358.

161 Borrell, A. et al. (1994) Evaluation of toxicity and age-related variation of coplanar PCB levels in Mediterranean striped dolphin, pp. 222–225 in Evans, P.G.H. (ed.) *European research on cetaceans – 8*. European Cetacean Society.

162 Borrell, A. et al. (1996) Organochlorine compound levels in striped dolphins from the western Mediterranean Sea during the period 1987–93, pp. 281–285 in Evans, P.G.H. (ed.) *European research on cetaceans – 10*. European Cetacean Society.

163 Borrell, A. et al. (1998) Organochlorine compound levels in common dolphins from the Atlantic and Mediterranean waters off Spain, pp. 328–331 in Evans, P.G.H. & Parsons, E.C.M. (eds.) *European research on cetaceans– 12*. European Cetacean Society.

164 Borrell, A. et al. (2001) Organochlorine compounds in common dolphins (*Delphinus delphis*) from the Atlantic and Mediterranean waters of Spain. *Environmental Pollution*, **114**, 265–274.

165 Boschma, H. (1951) Rows of small teeth in ziphioid whales. *Zoologische Mededelingen* Leiden, **31**, 139–148.

166 Bossart, G.D. et al. (1985) Cardiomyopathy in stranded pygmy and dwarf sperm whales. *Journal of the American Veterinary Medical Association*, **187**, 1137–1140.

167 Bourret, V.J.R. et al. (2007) Genetic variation and population structure of western Mediterranean and northern Atlantic *Stenella coeruleoalba* populations inferred from microsatellite data. *Journal of the Marine Biological Association of the UK*, **87**, 265–269.

168 Boutiba, Z. et al. (1997) A stranding record of the Cuvier's beaked whale in Algerian waters, pp. 173–175 in *European research on cetaceans – 10*. European Cetacean Society.

169 Bowles, A.E. et al. (1988) Ontogeny of stereotyped calling of a killer whale calf, *Orcinus orca*, during her first year. *Rit Fiskideildar*, **11**, 251–275.

170 Brattey, J. & Clark, K.J. (1992) Effect of temperature on egg hatching and survival of larvae of *Anisakis simplex* B (Nematoda: Ascaroidea). *Canadian Journal of Zoology*, **70**, 274–279.

171 Bree, P.J.H. van et al. (1986) Le dauphin de Fraser *Lageodelphis hosei* (Cetacea, Odontoceti), espèce nouvelle pour la faune d'Europe. *Mammalia*, **50**, 57–86 (in French).

172 Brereton, T. et al. (2005) Ecology and status of the common dolphin *Delphinus delphis* in the English Channel and Bay of Biscay 1995–2002, pp 15–22 in Stockin, K. et al. (eds.) *Proceedings of the workshop on common dolphins: current research, threats and issues, Kolmarden, Sweden*. European Cetacean Society.

173 Bressem, M.F. van et al. (1998) Further insight on the epidemiology of cetacean morbillivirus in the northeastern Atlantic. *Marine Mammal Science*, **14**, 605–613.

174 Bressem, M.F. van et al. (2001) An insight into the epidemiology of dolphin morbillivirus worldwide. *Veterinary Microbiology*, **81**, 287–304.

175 Brill, R.L. et al. (1992) Target detection, shape-discrimination, and signal characteristics of an echolocating false killer whale (*Pseudorca crassidens*). *Journal of the Acoustical Society of America*, **92**(3), 1324–1330.

176 Brodie, P.F. (1989) The white whale *Delphinapterus leucas*, pp. 119–144 in Ridgway, S.H. & Harrison, R. (eds.) *Handbook of marine mammals, Volume 4: River dolphins and the larger toothed whales*. Academic Press, San Diego, CA.

177 Brophy, J.T. (2003) *Diet of the common dolphin* (Delphinus delphis) *in Irish waters*. MSc thesis, University College Cork.

178 Brophy, J. et al. (2004) Feeding ecology of common dolphins (*Delphinus delphis*) in the North east Atlantic, p. 44 in *European research on cetaceans – 19*. European Cetacean Society.

179 Brown, M.W. et al. (1994) Sexual composition and analysis of reproductive females in the North Atlantic right whale (*Eubalaena glacialis*) population. *Marine Mammal Science*, **10**(3), 253–265.

180 Brown, M.W. et al. (2007) Surveying for discovery, science nd management, pp. 105–136 in Kraus, S.D. & Rolland, R.M. (eds.) (2007) *The urban whale: North Atlantic right whales at the crossroads*. Harvard University Press, Cambridge, MA.

181 Brown, S.G. (1976) Modern whaling in Britain and the North-east Atlantic Ocean. *Mammal Review*, **6**, 25–36.

182 Brown, S.G. (1986) Twentieth-century records of right whales (*Eubalaena glacialis*) in the northeast Atlantic Ocean, pp. 121–127 in Brownell, R.L. et al. (eds.) *Right whales: past and present status*. International Whaling Commission, Cambridge.

183 Brown Gladden, J.G. et al. (1997) Matriarchal genetic population structure of North American beluga whales *Delphinapterus leucas* (Cetacea: Monodontidae). *Molecular Ecology*, **6**, 1033–1046.

184 Brownell, R.L., Jr (1995) Japanese and Soviet exploitation of pygmy blue whales. *IBI Reports*, **5**, 25–29.

185 Brownell, R.L. & Ralls, K. (1986) Potential for sperm competition in baleen whales, pp. 97–112 in Donovan, G.P. (ed.) *Behavior of whales in relation to management*. International Whaling Commission, Cambridge.

186 Brownell, R. et al. (eds.) (1986) Report of the workshop on the status of right whales. *Report of the International Whaling Commission, Special Issue* **10**.

187 Brownell, R.L. et al. (2000) Worldwide taxonomic status and geographic distribution of minke whales (*Balaenoptera acutorostrata* and *B. bonaerensis*). *Report of the International Whaling Commission* SC/52/O27.

188 Bruton, T. & Greer, J. (1985) Euphrosine dolphin *Stenella coeruleoalba* (Meyen). *Irish Naturalists' Journal*, **21**, 538–540.

189 Bryant, P.J. (1995) Dating remains of gray whales from the eastern North Atlantic. *Journal of Mammalogy*, **76**, 857–861.

190 Bryden, M.M. et al. (1977) Melon-headed whale, *Peponocephala electra*, on the east coast of Australia. *Journal of Mammalogy*, **58**, 180–187.

191 Bryden, M.M. et al. (1977) Some aspects of the biology of *Peponocephala electra* (Cetacea: Delphinidae). I. General and reproductive biology. *Australian Journal of Marine and Freshwater Research*, **28**, 703–15.

192 Buchholtz, E.A. & Schur, S.A. (2004) Vertebral osteology in Delphinidae (Cetacea). *Zoological Journal of the Linnean Society*, **140**, 383–401.

193 Buckland, S.T. et al. (1992) Fin whale abundance in the eastern North Atlantic, estimated from Spanish NASS-89 data. *Report of the International Whaling Commission*, **42**, 457–460.

194 Buckland, S.T. et al. (1993) Distribution and abundance of long-finned pilot whales in the north Atlantic, estimated from NASS-87 and NASS-89 data. *Report of the International Whaling Commission, Special Issue*, **14**, 33–49.

195 Budylenko, G.A. (1977) Distribution and composition of sei whale schools in the southern hemisphere. *Report of the International Whaling Commission, Special Issue*, **1**, 121–123.

196 Budylenko, G.A. (1981) Distribution and some aspects of the biology of killer whales in the South Atlantic. *Report of*

the International Whaling Commission, **31**, 523–526.

197 Busnel, R.G. & Dziedzic, A. (1968) Characteristiques physiques des signaux acoustiques de *Pseudorca crassidens*. *Mammalia*, **32**, 1–6 (in French).

198 Cagnolaro, L. & Notarbartolo di Sciara, G. (1992) Research activities and conservation status of cetaceans in Italy. *Bollettino dei Musei e degli Istituti Biologica dell'Universita di Genova*, **56–7**, 53–85.

199 Calambokidis, J. & Steiger, G. (1997) *Blue whales*. Colin Baxter Photography, Grantown-on-Spey, Scotland.

200 Caldwell, D.K. & Caldwell, M.C. (1971) Beaked whales, *Ziphius cavirostris*, in the Bahamas. *Florida Academy of Sciences Quaternary Journal*, **34**, 157–160.

201 Caldwell, D.K. & Caldwell, M.C. (1971) Sounds produced by two rare cetaceans stranded in Florida. *Cetology*, **4**, 1–6.

202 Caldwell, D.K. & Caldwell, M.C. (1975) Dolphin and small whale fisheries of the Caribbean and West Indies: occurrence, history, and catch statistics – with special reference to the Lesser Antillean island of St. Vincent. *Journal of the Fisheries Research Board of Canada*, **32**, 1105–1110.

203 Caldwell, D.K. & Caldwell, M.C. (1989) Pygmy sperm whale *Kogia breviceps* (de Blainville, 1838): Dwarf sperm whale *Kogia simus* Owen, 1866, pp. 235–260 in Ridgway, S.H. & Harrison, R. (eds.) *Handbook of marine mammals, Volume 4: River dolphins and the larger toothed whales*. Academic Press, San Diego, CA.

204 Caldwell, D.K. *et al.* (1966) Production of pulsed sounds by the pigmy sperm whale, *Kogia breviceps*. *Bulletin of Southern Californian Academy of Sciences*, **65**(4), 245–248.

205 Caldwell, D.K. *et al.* (1971) Cetaceans from the Lesser Antillean island of St. Vincent. *Fishery Bulletin*, **69**, 303–312.

206 Caldwell, D.K. *et al.* (1971) A preliminary report on some ectoparasites and nasal-sac parasites from small odontocete cetaceans from Florida and Georgia. *Marineland (Florida) Research Laboratory Technical Reports*, **5**, 1–7.

207 Caldwell, D.K. *et al.* (1976) First records for Fraser's dolphin (*Lagenodelphis hosei*) in the Atlantic and the melon-headed whale (*Peponocephala electra*) in the western Atlantic. *Cetology*, **25**, 1–4.

208 Calzada, N. & Aguilar, A. (1994) Geographical variation in body size in western Mediterranean striped dolphins *Stenella coeruleoalba*, pp. 128–131 in Evans, P.G.H. (ed.) *European research on cetaceans – 8*. European Cetacean Society.

209 Calzada, N. *et al.* (1991) Age and sex composition of striped dolphin die-off in the western Mediterranean, pp. 81–83 in Evans, P.G.H. (ed.).*European research on cetaceans – 5*. European Cetacean Society.

210 Camphuysen, C.J. (2004) The return of the harbour porpoise (*Phocoena phocoena*) in Dutch coastal waters. *Lutra*, **47**, 113–122.

211 Camphuysen, C.J. (2006) A marked increase in harbour porpoises in the southern North Sea. *Shetland Sea Mammal Report 2004*, 20–24.

212 Camphuysen, C.J. & Leopold, M.F. (1993) The harbour porpoise *Phocoena phocoena* in the southern North Sea, particularly the Dutch sector. *Lutra*, **36**, 1–24.

213 Camphuysen, C.J. *et al.* (1995) Distant feeding and associations with cetaceans of gannets *Morus bassanus* from Bass Rock, May 1994. *Seabird*, **17**, 36–43.

214 Cañadas, A.M. & Sagarminaga, R. (1996) Preliminary results of photo-identification studies on Risso's dolphins (*Grampus griseus*) undertaken during surveys of cetacean distribution and dynamics along the south-east coast of Spain: 1992–1995, pp. 221–224 in Evans, P.G.H. (ed.) *European research on cetaceans – 10*. European Cetacean Society.

215 Cañadas, A. & Sagarminaga, R. (2000) The northeastern Alboran Sea, an important breeding and feeding ground for the long-finned pilot whale (*Globicephala melas*) in the Mediterranean Sea. *Marine Mammal Science*, **16**(3), 513–529.

216 Cañadas, A. *et al.* (2002) Cetacean distribution related with depth and slope in the Mediterranean waters off southern Spain. *Deep Sea Research*, **I 49**, 2053–2073.

217 Cañadas, A. *et al.* (in press) *Distribution of short-beaked common dolphins* (Delphinus delphis) *in the central and eastern North Atlantic with an abundance estimate for part of this area.* NAMMCO Scientific Publications, Tromsø.

218 Canese, S. *et al.* (2006) The first identified winter feeding ground of fin whales (*Balaenoptera physalus*) in the Mediterranean Sea. *Journal of the Marine Biological Association of the UK*, **86**(5119), 1–5.

219 Canneyt, O. van. Personal communication.

220 Cannon, L.R.G. (1977) Some aspects of the biology of *Peponocephala electra* (Cetacea: Delphinidae). II Parasites. *Australian Journal of Marine and Freshwater Research*, **28**, 717–722.

220a Capellini, G. (1883) Di un'orca fossile scoperta a cetona in Toscana. *Memorie dell'Accademia delle Scienze dell'Instituto di Bologna*, **4**, 1–25.

221 Carlini, R. *et al.* (1992) Cephalopods from the stomachs of Cuvier's beaked whale (*Ziphius cavirostris* Cuvier, 1823) stranded at Fiumino, Central Tyrrhenian Sea, pp. 190–191 in Evans, P.G.H. (ed.) *European research on cetaceans – 6*. European Cetacean Society.

222 Carlini, R. *et al.* (1992) Cephalopods from the stomachs of Risso's dolphins, *Grampus griseus*, (Cuvier, 1812) stranded along the central Tyrrhenian coast, pp. 196–198 in Evans, P.G.H. (ed.) *European research on cetaceans – 6*. European Cetacean Society.

223 Carlstrom, J. *et al.* (1997) Record of a new northern range of Sowerby's beaked whale (*Mesoplodon bidens*). *Polar Biology*, **17**, 459–461.

224 Carrillo, M. & Lopez-Jurado, L.F. (1998) Structure and behaviour of a Blainville's beaked whale (*Mesoplodon densirostris*) group in Tenerife (Canary Islands), p. 74 in Evans, P.G.H. & Parsons, E.C.M. (eds.) *European research on cetaceans – 12*. European Cetacean Society.

225 Carrillo, M. & Lopez-Jurado, L.F. Personal communication.

226 Carrillo, M. & Martin, V. (1999) First sighting of Gervais' beaked whale (*Mesoplodon europaeus* Gervais, 1855) (Cetacea; Ziphiidae) from the North Oriental Atlantic coast, p. 53 in *European research on cetaceans –13*. European Cetacean Society.

227 Carstensen, J. *et al.* (2006) Impacts on harbour porpoises from offshore wind farm construction: acoustic monitoring of echolocation activity using porpoise detectors (T-PODs). *Marine Ecology Progress Series*, **321**, 295–308.

228 Casinos, A. & Filella, S. (1981) Notes on cetaceans of the Iberian coasts: IV. A specimen of *Mesoplodon densirostris* (Cetacea, Hyperoodontidae) stranded on the Spanish Mediterranean coast. *Säugetierkundliche Mitteilungen*, **29**, 61–67.

229 Castello, H.P. & Pinedo, M.C. (1980) *Mesoplodon densirostris* (Cetacea: Ziphiidae), primeiro registro para o Atlantico Sul Occidental. *Boletino Instituto Oceanografico S. Paulo*, **29**, 91–94 (in Portuguese).

230 Cattanach, K.L. *et al.* (1993) Sei whale abundance, estimated from Icelandic and Faroese NASS-87 and NASS-89 data. *Report of the International Whaling Commission*, **43**, 315–321.

231 Caurant, F. *et al.* (1993) Factors influencing the accumulation of metals in pilot whales (*Globicephala melas*) off the Faroes Islands. *Report of the International Whaling Commission, Special Issue*, **14**, 369–390.

232 Caurant, F. *et al.* (2006) Lead contamination of small cetaceans in European waters – the use of stable isotopes for identifying the sources of lead exposure. *Marine Environmental Research*, **62**, 131–148.

233 CETAP (1982) *A characterisation of marine mammals and turtles in the mid and North Atlantic areas of the US outer continental shelf.* Final Report of the Cetacean and Turtle Assessment Program to the US Dept. Interior under contract AA551-CT8–48. Department of the Interior, Washington, DC.

234 Charif, R.A. & Clark, C.W. (2000) *Acoustic monitoring of large whales off north west Britain and Ireland: a two-year study, October 1996–September 1998.* Report No. 313, JNCC, Aberdeen.

235 Charif, R. *et al.* (2001) Acoustic detections of singing humpback whales in deep waters off the British Isles. *Marine Mammal Science,* **17**, 751–768.

236 Chittleborough, R.G. (1965) Dynamics of two populations of the humpback whale, *Megaptera novaeangliae* (Borowski). *Australian Journal of Marine and Freshwater Research,* **16**, 33–128.

237 Chivers, S.J. *et al.* (2005) Genetic variation of *Kogia* spp. with preliminary evidence for two species of *Kogia sima*. *Marine Mammal Science,* **21**(4), 619–634.

238 Chivers, S.J. *et al.* (2007) Genetic variation and evidence for population structure in eastern North Pacific false killer whales (*Pseudorca crassidens*). *Canadian Journal of Zoology,* **85**, 783–794.

239 Christensen, I. (1973) Age determination, age distribution and growth of bottlenose whales, *Hyperoodon ampullatus*, in the Labrador Sea. *Norwegian Journal of Zoology,* **21**, 331–340.

240 Christensen, I. (1975) Preliminary report on the Norwegian fishery for small whales: expansion of Norwegian whaling to Arctic and Northwest Atlantic waters, and Norwegian investigations of the biology of small whales. *Journal of the Fisheries Research Board of Canada,* **32**(7), 1083–1094.

241 Christensen, I. (1982) Killer whales in Norwegian coastal waters. *Report of the International Whaling Commsion,* **32**, 633–642.

242 Christensen, I. (1984) Growth and reproduction of killer whales, *Orcinus orca*, in Norwegian coastal waters. *Report of the International Whaling Commission, Special Issue,* **6**, 253–258.

243 Christensen, I. *et al.* (1990) Morphometric comparison of minke whales (*Balaenoptera acutorostra*) from different areas of the North Atlantic. *Marine Mammal Science,* **6**, 327–338.

244 Christensen, I. *et al.* (1990) *Review of the biology, exploitation and present abundance of large baleen whales and sperm whales in Norwegian and adjacent waters.* IWC/SC/42/O5, presented to the Scientific Committee of the International Whaling Commission.

245 Cipriano, F. (2002) Atlantic white-sided dolphin *Lagenorhynchus acutus*, pp. 49–51 in Perrin, W.F. *et al.* (eds.) *Encyclopaedia of marine mammals.* Academic Press, San Diego, CA.

246 Clapham, P.J. (1992) The attainment of sexual maturity in humpback whales. *Canadian Journal of Zoology,* **70**, 1470–1472.

247 Clapham, P.J. (1996) The social and reproductive biology of humpback whales: an ecological perspective. *Mammal Review,* **26**, 27–49.

248 Clapham, P.J. & Brownell, R.J., Jr (1996) Potential for interspecific competition in baleen whales. *Report of the International Whaling Commission,* **46**, 361–367.

249 Clapham, P.J. & Mead, J.G. (1999) *Megaptera novaeangliae.* *Mammalian Species,* **604**, 1–9.

250 Clapham, P.J. *et al.* (1999) Baleen whales: conservation issues and the status of the most endangered populations. *Mammal Review,* **29**(1), 35–60.

251 Clapham, P.J. *et al.* (1999) Length at birth and at independence in humpback whales. *Journal of Cetacean Research and Management,* **1**, 141–146.

252 Claridge, D.E. (2005) *Social structure of Blainville's beaked whale in Bahamas.* MSc thesis, University of Aberdeen.

253 Claridge, D.E. *et al.* (1999) Harem society identified in dense-beaked whales (*Mesoplodon densirostris*) from the Bahamas. *13th Biennial Conference on the Biology of Marine Mammals.* Hawaii.

254 Clark, C.W. (1982) The acoustic repertoire of the southern right whale: a quantitative analysis. *Animal Behaviour,* **30**, 1069–1071.

255 Clark, C.W. (1990) Acoustic behaviour of mysticete whales, pp. 571–583 in Thomas, J. & Kastelein, R. (eds.) *Sensory abilities of cetaceans.* Plenum Press, New York.

256 Clark, C.W. & Charif, R.A. (1998) *Acoustic monitoring of large whales to the west of Britain and Ireland using bottom-mounted hydrophone arrays, October 199–September 1997.* JNCC Report No. 281.

257 Clark, C.W. *et al.* (2002) Vocal activity of fin whales, *Balaenoptera physalus*, in the Ligurian Sea. *Marine Mammal Science,* **18**(1), 286–295.

258 Clarke, M.R. (1976) Observations on sperm whale diving. *Journal of the Marine Biological Association of the UK,* **56**, 809–810.

259 Clarke, M.R. (1986) Cephalopods in the diet of odontocetes, pp. 281–322 in Bryden, M.M. & Harrison, R.J. (eds.) *Research on dolphins.* Clarendon Press, Oxford.

260 Clarke, M.R. (2003) Production and control of sound by the small sperm whales, *Kogia breviceps* and *K. sima* and their implications for other Cetacea. *Journal of the Marine Biological Association of the UK,* **83**, 241–263.

261 Clarke, M.R. & Kristensen, T.K. (1980) Cephalopod beaks from the stomachs of two northern bottlenosed whales (*Hyperoodon ampullatus*). *Journal of the Marine Biological Association of the UK,* **60**, 151–156.

262 Clarke, M.R. & MacLeod, N. (1976) Cephalopod remains from sperm whales caught off Iceland. *Journal of the Marine Biological Association of the UK,* **56**, 733–749.

263 Clarke, M.R. & Pascoe, P.L. (1985) The stomach contents of a Risso's dolphin (*Grampus griseus*) stranded at Thurlestone, South Devon. *Journal of the Marine Biological Association of the UK,* **65**, 663–665.

264 Clarke, R. (1981) Whales and dolphins of the Azores and their exploitation. *Report of the International Whaling Commission,* **31**, 607–615.

265 Cockcroft, V.G. (1990) Catches of dolphins in the Natal shark nets, 1980 to 1988. *South African Journal of Wildlife Research,* **20**, 44–51.

266 Cockcroft, V.G. *et al.* (1993) The diet of Risso's dolphin (*Grampus griseus*) from the east coast of South Africa. *Zeitschrift für Säugetierkunde,* **58**, 286–293.

267 Coles, P. *et al.* (2001) A report on the whales, dolphins and porpoises of the Bay of Biscay and English Channel, 2000. *Orca,* **2**, 9–61.

268 Collet, A. (1981) *Biologie du dauphin commun Delphinus delphis L. en Atlantique Nord-Est.* Thèse de doctorat de troisième cycle, Université de Poitiers (in French).

269 Collet, A. (1992) *Age et statut reproducteur des cétacés capturés, programme GERDAU, données 1992.* Unpublished report, IFREMER-DRV/PE-92.2.511145 (in French).

270 Collet, A. (1993) *Age et statut reproducteur des cétacés capturés, programme GERDAU, données 1993.* Unpublished report, IFREMER-DRV/PE-92.2.511145 (in French).

271 Collet, A. Personal communication.

272 Collet, A. & Mison, V. (1995) Analyse des échouages de cétacés sur le littoral français, in Morisur, Y. *et al.* (eds.). *By-catch and discarding in pelagic trawl fisheries.* Final report, contract EC DG XIV-C-1, study BIOECO/93/017 (in French).

273 Collett, R. (1909) A few notes on the whale *Balaena glacialis* and its capture in recent years in the North Atlantic by Norwegian whalers. *Proceedings of the Zoological Society of London,* **7,** 91–97.

274 Condy, P.R. *et al.* (1978) The seasonal occurrence and behaviour of killer whales, *Orcinus orca*, at Marion Island.

Journal of Zoology, **184**, 449–464.

275 Connor, R.C. *et al.* (1992) Dolphin alliances and coalitions, pp. 415–443 in Harcourt, A.H. & De Waal, F.B.M. (eds.) *Coalitions and alliances in humans and other animals*. Oxford University Press, Oxford.

276 Corsolini, S. *et al.* (1995) Toxicity assessment of polychlorinated biphenyl isomers including non-ortho coplanar PCBs in cetaceans from the Mediterranean Sea, pp. 269–272 in Evans, P.G.H. & Nice, H. (eds.) *European research on cetaceans – 9*. European Cetacean Society.

277 Couperus, A.S. (1993) Killer whales and pilot whales near trawlers east of Shetland. *Sula*, **7**, 41–52.

278 Couperus, A.S. (1994) Killer whales (*Orcinus orca*) scavenging on discards of freezer trawlers north-east of the Shetland islands. *Aquatic Mammals*, **20**, 47–51.

279 Couperus, A.S. (1997) Interactions between Dutch midwater trawl and Atlantic white-sided dolphins (*Lagenorhynchus acutus*) southwest of Ireland. *Journal of Northwest Atlantic Fishery Science*, **22**, 209–218.

280 Couperus, A.S. (1999) Diet of Atlantic white-sided dolphins southwest of Ireland, p. 107 in Evans, P.G.H. & Parsons, E.C.M. (eds.) *European research on cetaceans – 12*. European Cetacean Society.

281 Cox, T.M. *et al.* (2006) Understanding the impacts of anthropogenic sound on beaked whales. *Journal of Cetacean Research and Management*, **7**, 177–187.

282 Cresswell, G. & Walker, D. (2001) *A report on the whales, dolphins and seabirds of the Bay of Biscay and English Channel*. Organisation Cetacea (ORCA), Cambridge.

283 Creton, P. *et al.* (1992) A dwarf sperm whale, *Kogia simus*, stranded in Brittany: second record from Atlantic European waters, pp. 100–102 in Evans, P.G.H. (ed.) *European research on cetaceans – 6*. European Cetacean Society.

284 Dabin, W. *et al.* (2003) Reconstructing individual female reproductive histories from the examination of ovarian scars in cetaceans: challenging results from the common dolphin, pp. 77–78 in *European research on cetaceans – 17*. European Cetacean Society.

285 Dahlheim, M.E. & Heyning, J. (1999) Killer whale *Orcinus orca* (Linnaeus, 1738), pp. 281–322 in Ridgway, S.H.& Harrison, R.J. (eds.) *Handbook of marine mammals, Vol. 6, The second book of dolphins*. Academic Press, London.

286 Dahlheim, M.E. & Matkin, C.O. (1994) Assessment of injuries to Prince William Sound killer whales, pp. 163–171 in Laughlin, T.R. (ed.) *Impacts of the Exxon Valdez oil spill on marine mammals*. Academic Press, San Diego, CA.

287 Dahlheim, M.E. *et al.* (1997) *Killer whales of southeast Alaska*. Day Moon Press, Seattle, WA.

288 Dailey, M.D. & Brownell, R.L. Jr (1972) A checklist of marine mammal parasites, pp. 528–589 in Ridgway, S.H. (ed.) *Mammals of the sea, biology and medicine*. C.C. Thomas, Springfield, IL.

289 Dalebout, M.L. *et al.* (2003) Appearance, distribution, and genetic distinctiveness of Longman's beaked whale, *Indopacetus pacificus*. *Marine Mammal Science*, **19**, 421–461.

290 Dalebout, M.L. *et al.* (2006) Nuclear and mitochondrial markers reveal distinctiveness of a small population of bottlenose whales (*Hyperoodon ampullatus*) in the western North Atlantic. *Molecular Ecology*, **15**, 3115–3129.

291 Daníelsdóttir, A.K. *et al.* (1992) Genetic variation at enzyme loci in North Atlantic minke whales, *Balaenoptera acutorostrata*. *Biochemical Genetics*, **30**, 189–202.

292 Daníelsdóttir, A.K. *et al.* (1995) Genetic variation in northeastern Atlantic minke whales (*Balaenoptera acutorostrata*), pp. 105–118 in Blix, A.S. *et al.* (eds.) *Whales, seals, fish and man*. Elsevier, Amsterdam.

293 Danil, K. & Chivers, S.J. (2006) Habitat-based spatial and temporal variability in life history characteristics of female common dolphins *Delphinus delphis* in the eastern tropical Pacific. *Marine Ecology Progress Series*, **318**, 277–286.

294 Das, K. (2002) *Trace metal contamination and detoxification processes in marine mammals from European coasts*. PhD thesis, University of Liège.

295 Das, K. *et al.* (2000) Tuna and dolphin associations in the North-east Atlantic: Evidence of different ecological niches from stable isotope and heavy metal measurements. *Marine Pollution Bulletin*, **40**, 102–109.

296 Das, K. *et al.* (2003) Marine mammals from northeast Atlantic: relationship between their trophic status as determined by δ^{13}C and δ^{15}N measurements and their trace metal concentrations. *Marine Environmental Research*, **56**, 349–365.

297 Davies, J.L. (1960) The southern form of the pilot whale. *Journal of Mammalogy*, **41**, 29–34.

298 Dawbin, W.H. (1974) *Cetacea of the S.W. Pacific*. Report, FAO/ACMRR Working Party on Marine Mammals. Ad hoc group II – Small Cetaceans and Sirenians, La Jolla, CA.

299 Deecke, V.B. *et al.* (2005) The vocal behaviour of mammal-eating killer whales: communicating with costly calls. *Animal Behaviour*, **69**, 395–405.

300 Defran, R.H. & Pryor, K. (1980) The behavior and training of cetaceans in captivity, pp. 247–305 in Herman, L. (ed.) *Cetacean behavior: mechanisms and functions*. Wiley-Interscience, New York.

301 Delfour, F. & Marten, K. (2001) Mirror image processing in three marine mammal species: killer whales (*Orcinus orca*), false killer whales (*Pseudorca crassidens*) and California sea lions (*Zalophus californianus*). *Behavioural Processes*, **53**(3), 181–190.

302 Delyamure, S.L. (1968) *Helminthofauna of marine mammals (ecology and phylogeny)*. Israel Program for Scientific Translations, Jerusalem (Original Russian edition Akademii Nauk, Moscow, 1955).

303 DeMaster, D.P. & Drevenak, D.J. (1988) Survivorship patterns in three species of captive cetaceans. *Marine Mammal Science*, **4**, 297–311.

304 Desportes, G. (1985) *La nutrition des odontocètes en Atlantique Nord-Est (côtes Françaises – Iles Feroë)*. PhD thesis, University of Poitiers.

305 Desportes, G. & Mouritsen, R. (1993) Preliminary results on the diet of long-finned pilot whales off the Faroe Islands. *Report of the International Whaling Commission, Special Issue*, **14**, 305–324.

306 Desportes, G. *et al.* (1993) Reproductive maturity and seasonality of long-finned pilot whales, off the Faroe Islands. *Report of the International Whaling Commission, Special Issue*, **14**, 233–262.

307 Desportes, G. *et al.* (1994) Growth-related changes in testicular mass and plasma testosterone concentrations in long-finned pilot whales, *Globicephala melas*. *Journal of Reproduction and Fertility*, **102**(1), 237–244.

308 Di Cave, D. *et al.* (1993) Parasitic metazoa of striped dolphin (*Stenella coeruleoalba* Meyen, 1833) (Cetacea: Delphinidae), stranded along Central Italian coast, p. 188 in Evans, P.G.H. (ed.) *European research on cetaceans – 7*. European Cetacean Society.

309 Di-Méglio, N. & Collet, A. (1994) Reproductive parameters in striped dolphins from the Mediterranean and Atlantic coast of France, pp. 145–147 in Evans, P.G.H (ed.) *European research on cetaceans – 8*. European Cetacean Society.

310 Di-Méglio, N. *et al.* (1996) Growth comparison in striped dolphins, *Stenella coeruleoalba*, from the Atlantic and Mediterranean coast of France. *Aquatic Mammals*, **22**, 11–21.

311 Di Natale, A. (1995) Driftnets impact on protected species: observers data from the Italian fleet and proposal for a model to assess the number of cetaceans in the by-catch. *International Commission for the Conservation of Atlantic Tunas Collective Volume of Scientific Papers*, **44**, 255–263.

312 Dietz, R. & Heide-Jørgensen, M.P. (1995) Movements and swimming speed of narwhals, *Monodon monoceros*, equipped

with satellite transmitters in Melville Bay, Northwest Greenland. *Canadian Journal of Zoology*, **73**, 2120–2132.

313 Dizon, A. *et al.* (1996) An interim phylogenetic analysis of sei and Bryde's whale mitochondrial DNA control region sequences. *Report of the International Whaling Commission*, **46**, 669.

314 Dizon, A. *et al.* (eds.) (1997) *Molecular genetics of marine mammals.* Special Publication No. 3, Society for Marine Mammalogy, San Francisco, CA.

315 Dizon, A. *et al.* (1998) Molecular phylogeny of the Bryde's whale/sei whale complex. Separate species status for the pygmy Bryde's form? *Report of the International Whaling Commission*, **47**, 398.

316 Dohl, T.P. *et al.* (1983) *Cetaceans of central and northern California 1980–1983. Status, abundance and distribution.* Final report submitted to Pacific OCS Region, Minerals Management Service, US Department of the Interior, LA. OCS Study MMS-84-0045.

317 Doidge, D.W. (1990) Age-length and length-weight comparisons in the beluga, *Delphinapterus leucas*, pp. 59–68 in Smith, T.G. *et al.* (eds.) *Advances in research on the beluga whale,* Delphinapterus leucas. *Canadian Bulletin of Fisheries and Aquatic Sciences,* **224.**

318 Dolar, M.L.L. (1994) Incidental takes of small cetaceans in fisheries in Palawan, Central Visayas and Northern Mindanao in the Philippines. *Report of the International Whaling Commission, Special Issue,* **15**, 355–363.

319 Dolar, M.L.L. (1999) *Abundance, distribution and feeding ecology of small cetaceans in the eastern Sulu Sea and Tañon Strait, Philippines.* PhD dissertation, University of California, San Diego, CA.

320 Dolar, M.L.L. (2002) Fraser's dolphin *Lagenodelphis hosei*, pp. 485–487 in Würsig, B. *et al.* (eds.) *Encyclopaedia of marine mammals.* Academic Press, San Diego, CA.

321 Dolar, M.L.L. *et al.* (1999) Myoglobin in pelagic small cetaceans. *Journal of Experimental Biology*, **202**, 227–236.

322 Domenici, P. *et al.* (2000) Killer whales (*Orcinus orca*) feeding on schooling herring (*Clupea harengus*) using underwater tail-slaps: kinematic analyses of field observations. *Journal of Experimental Biology*, **203**, 283–294.

323 Domingo, M. *et al.* (1991) Morbillivirus infection in striped dolphins *Stenella coeruleoalba* in the Mediterranean Sea, p. 97 in Evans, P.G.H. (ed.) *European research on cetaceans – 5* European Cetacean Society.

324 Dong, J.H., *et al.* (1996) A contribution to the biology of the white-beaked dolphin, *Lagenorhynchus albirostris*, in waters off Newfoundland. *Canadian Field Naturalist*, **110**, 278–287.

325 Doroshenko, N.W. (1978) On inter-relationship between killer whales (predator-prey) in the Antarctic. *Marine Mammals Abstract Report of the 7th All-Union Meeting Moscow*, **3**, 107–109.

326 Dorsey, E.M. (1983) Exclusive adjoining ranges in individually identified minke whales (*Balaenoptera acutorostrata*) in Washington State. *Canadian Journal of Zoology*, **61**, 174–81.

327 Dorsey, E.M. *et al.* (1990) Minke whales (*Balaenoptera acutorostrata*) from the west coast of North America: individual recognition and small-scale site fidelity. *Report of the International Whaling Commission, Special Issue,* **12**, 357–368.

328 Dudok van Heel, W.H. (1974) Remarks on a live ziphiid baby (*Mesoplodon bidens*). *Aquatic Mammals*, **2**, 3–7.

329 Duffield, D.A. & Miller, K.W. (1988) Demographic features of killer whales in oceanaria in the United States and Canada. *Rit Fiskideildar*, **11**, 297–306.

330 Duguy, R. (1966) Quelques données nouvelles sur un Cétacé rare sur les côtes d'Europe: Le Cachalot à tête courte, *Kogia breviceps* (Blainville, 1838). *Mammalia*, **30**(2), 259–269 (in French).

331 Duguy, R. (1987) Deux espèces nouvelles pour les côtes de France: *Kogia simus* (Physetridae) et *Phoca groenlandica* (Phocidae). ICES 75th meeting, Santander, C.M. 1987/N, 6 (in French).

332 Duguy, R. & Hussenot, E. (1982) Occasional captures of delphinids in the northeast Atlantic. *Report of the International Whaling Commission,* **32**, 461–462.

333 Duguy, R. & Robineau, R. (1973) Cétacés et phoques des côtes de France. Guide d'identification. *Annales de la Société d'Histoire Naturelle de la Charente-Maritime*, Supplement, 1–93 (in French).

334 Duignan, P.J. *et al.* (1995) Morbillivirus infection in cetaceans of the western North Atlantic. *Veterinary Microbiology*, **44**, 241–249.

335 Dziedzic, Z.A. (1978) *Etude expérimentale des émissions sonar de certains delphinidés et notamment D. delphis et T. truncatus.* Thèse de doctorat d'etat es sciences appliquées, Université de Paris VII (in French).

336 Edds, P.L. (1980) *Variations in the vocalisations of fin whales,* Balaenoptera physalus, *in the St. Lawrence river.* MSc thesis, University of Maryland.

337 Edds, P.L. (1988) Characteristics of finback *Balaenoptera physalus* vocalizations in the St. Lawrence Estuary. *Bioacoustics*, **1**, 131–149.

338 Edds, P.L. & Macfarlane, J.A.F. (1987) Occurrence and general behavior of balaenopterid cetaceans summering in the St. Lawrence Estuary, Canada. *Canadian Journal of Zoology*, **65**, 1363–1376.

339 Eggleton, J. (1905) The occurrence of Risso's dolphin, *Grampus griseus* Cuv., in the Forth. *Transactions of the Natural History Society of Glasgow*, **7**, 253–257.

340 Evans, P.G.H. (1980) Cetaceans in British waters. *Mammal Review*, **10**, 1–52.

341 Evans, P.G.H. (1982) Associations between seabirds and cetaceans – a review. *Mammal Review*, **12**, 187–206.

342 Evans, P.G.H. (1987) *The natural history of whales and dolphins.* Christopher Helm/Academic Press, London.

343 Evans, P.G.H. (1988) Killer whales (*Orcinus orca*) in British and Irish waters. *Rit Fiskideildar* **11**, 42–54.

344 Evans, P.G.H. (1990) European cetaceans and seabirds in an oceanographic context. *Lutra*, **33**, 95–125.

345 Evans, P.G.H. (ed.) (1990) Report of the European Cetacean Society sightings workshop, Palma de Mallorca, 1 March. *European Cetacean Society Newsletter Special Issue*, **10**, 1–10.

346 Evans, P.G.H. (1992) *Status review of cetaceans in British and Irish waters.* Report to UK Department of Environment. Sea Watch Foundation, Oxford.

347 Evans, P.G.H. (1994) *Cetacean bycatches in UK and Ireland.* Discussion Paper for Ministry of Agriculture, Fisheries & Food Bycatch Working Group, London.

348 Evans, P.G.H. (1996) *Ecological studies of the harbour porpoise in Shetland, North Scotland.* Report for WWF-UK. Sea Watch Foundation, Oxford.

349 Evans, P.G.H. (1996) Human disturbance of cetaceans, pp. 376–394 in Dunstone, N. & Taylor, V. (eds.) *The exploitation of mammals – principles and problems underlying their sustainable use.* Cambridge University Press, Cambridge.

350 Evans, P.G.H. (1997) Ecology of sperm whales (*Physeter macrocephalus*) in the eastern North Atlantic, with special reference to sightings and strandings records from the British Isles, pp. 37–46 in Jacques, T.G. & Lambertsen, R.H. (eds.) *Sperm whale deaths in the North Sea: science and management. Bulletin de L'Institut Royal des Sciences Naturelles de Belgique. Biologie,* **67** – Supplement.

351 Evans, P.G.H. (1997) *Guide to dive sites and other marine life.* Dominica Nature Island Series, vol. 4. Dominica Ministry of Tourism, Government Headquarters, Roseau.

352 Evans, P.G.H. (1998) Biology of cetaceans of the northeast Atlantic (in relation to seismic energy). *Proceedings of the seismic and marine mammal workshop*, June 23–25, London.

353 Evans, P.G.H. Personal communication.

354 Evans, P.G.H. & Hammond, P.S. (2004) Monitoring cetaceans in European waters. *Mammal Review*, **34**, 131–156.

355 Evans, P.G.H. & Miller, L. (eds.) (2004) *Active sonar and cetaceans*. Proceedings of workshop held at the ECS 17th annual conference, Las Palmas, Gran Canaria, 8 March 2003. European Cetacean Society.

356 Evans, P.G.H. & Scanlan, G. (1989) *Historical review of cetaceans in British and Irish waters*. Unpublished report to Greenpeace Environmental Trust, Cetacean Group, Mammal Society, Oxford.

357 Evans, P.G.H. & Wang, J. (2002) *Re-examination of distribution data for the harbour porpoise around Wales and the UK with a view to site selection for this species*. Countryside Council for Wales Scientific Publication Series, Bangor.

358 Evans, P.G.H. *et al.* (1986) *Analysis of cetacean sightings in the British Isles, 1958–1985*. Nature Conservancy Council, Peterborough.

359 Evans, P.G.H. *et al.* (1994) A study of the reactions of harbour porpoises to various boats in the coastal waters of SE Shetland, pp. 60–64 in Evans, P.G.H. (ed.) *European research on cetaceans – 8*. European Cetacean Society.

360 Evans, P.G.H. *et al.* (2003) *UK cetacean status review*. Report to English Nature and Countryside Council for Wales. Sea Watch Foundation, Oxford.

361 Evans, W.E. (1973) Echolocation by marine delphinids and one species of freshwater dolphin. *Journal of the Acoustical Society of America*, **54**, 191–199.

362 Evans, W.E. (1975) *Distribution, differentiation of populations, and other aspects of the natural history of* Delphinus delphis *Linnaeus in the northeastern Pacific*. PhD thesis, University of California, Los Angeles, CA.

363 Evans, W.E. (1994) Common dolphin, white-bellied porpoise *Delphinus delphis* Linnaeus, 1758, pp. 191–224 in Ridgway, S.H. & Harrison, R. (eds.) *Handbook of marine mammals, Vol. 5*. Academic Press, London.

364 Evans, W.E. *et al.* (1982) Geographic variation in the color pattern of killer whales. *Report of the International Whaling Commission*, **32**, 687–694.

365 Fabbri, F. *et al.* (1992) A preliminary investigation into the relationship between the distribution of Risso's dolphin and depth, pp. 146–151 in Evans, P.G.H. (ed.). *European research on cetaceans – 6*. European Cetacean Society.

366 Fairfield, C.P. *et al.* (1993) Pilot whales incidentally taken during the distant water fleet Atlantic mackerel fishery in the Mid-Atlantic Bight, 1984–1988. *Report of the International Whaling Commission, Special Issue*, **14**, 107–116.

367 Fairley, J.S. (1981) *Irish whales and whaling*. Longstaff Press, Dublin.

368 Felleman, F.L. *et al.* (1991) Feeding ecology of the killer whale (*Orcinus orca*), pp. 113–147 in Pryor, K. & Norris, K.S. (eds.) *Dolphin societies*. University of California Press, Berkeley, CA.

369 Fernández, A. *et al.* (2005) 'Gas and fat embolic syndrome' involving a mass stranding of beaked whales (family Ziphiidae) exposed to anthropogenic sonar signals. *Veterinary Pathology*, **42**, 446–457.

370 Fernandez, M. *et al.* (1991) Parasites collected in the striped dolphin die-off in the Spanish Mediterranean, pp. 101–104 in Evans, P.G.H. (ed.) *European research on cetaceans – 5*. European Cetacean Society.

371 Ferrero, R.C. & Walker, W.A. (1995) Growth and reproduction of the common dolphin, *Delphinus delphis* Linnaeus, in the offshore waters of the North Pacific Ocean. *Fishery Bulletin*, **93**, 483–494.

372 Finley, K.J. & Gibb, E.J. (1982) Summer diet of the narwhal (*Monodon monoceros*) in Pond Inlet, northern Baffin Island. *Canadian Journal of Zoology*, **60**, 3353–3363.

373 Finley, K.J. & Renaud, W.E. (1980) Marine mammals inhabiting the Baffin Bay North Water in winter. *Arctic*, **33**, 724–738.

374 Fiscus, C.H. (1997) Cephalopod beaks in a Cuvier's beaked whale (*Ziphius cavirostris*) from Amchitka Island, Alaska. *Marine Mammal Science*, **13**, 481–486.

375 Fisher, H.D. & Harrison, R.J. (1970) Reproduction in the common porpoise (*Phocoena phocoena*) of the North Atlantic. *Journal of Zoology*, **161**, 471–486.

376 Flom, J.O. *et al.* (1980) Vaginal fibromas in a beaked whale. *Journal of Wildlife Diseases*, **16**, 99–102.

377 Flower, W.H. (1878) A further contribution to the knowledge of the existing ziphioid whales. *Transactions of the Zoological Society of London*, **10**, 415–437.

378 Focardi, S. *et al.* (1991) Subcutaneous organochlorine levels in fin whales (*Balaenoptera physalus*) from the Ligurian Sea, pp. 93–96 in Evans, P.G.H. (ed.) *European research on cetaceans – 5*. European Cetacean Society.

379 Focardi, S. *et al.* (1992) Organochlorines and trace elements in skin biopsies of *Balaenoptera physalus* and *Stenella coeruleoalba*, pp. 230–233 in Evans, P.G.H. (ed.) *European research on cetaceans – 6*. European Cetacean Society.

380 Fontaine, M.C. *et al.* (2007) Rise of oceanographic barriers in continuous populations of a cetacean: the genetic structure of harbour porpoises in Old World waters. *BMC Biology*, **5**, 30.

381 Fontaine, M.C. *et al.* (2007) Long-term feeding ecology and habitat use in harbour porpoises *Phocoena phocoena* from Scandinavian waters inferred from trace elements and stable isotopes. *BMC Ecology*, **7**, 1.

382 Foote, A.D. *et al.* (2004) Whale-call response to masking boat noise. *Nature, London*, **428**, 910.

383 Foote, A.D. *et al.* (2006) Killer whales are capable of vocal learning. *Biology Letters*, **2**, 509–512.

384 Forcada, J. *et al.* (1990) Distribution of common and striped dolphins in the temperate waters of the eastern North Atlantic, pp. 64–66. in Evans, P.G.H. *et al.* (eds.) *European Research on cetaceans – 4*. European Cetacean Society.

385 Forcada, J. *et al.* (1992) Population abundance of striped dolphins inhabiting the western Mediterranean sea, pp. 105–107 in Evans, P.G.H. (ed.) *European research on cetaceans – 6*. European Cetacean Society.

386 Forcada, J. (1994) Striped dolphin habitats in the Northwest Mediterranean, p. 95 in Evans, P.G.H. (ed.). *European research on cetaceans – 8*. European Cetacean Society.

387 Forcada, J. *et al.* (1994) Striped dolphin abundance in the Northwestern Mediterranean, pp. 96–98 in Evans, P.G.H. (ed.). *European research on cetaceans – 8*. European Cetacean Society.

388 Forcada J. *et al.* (1996) Distribution and abundance of fin whales (*Balaenoptera physalus*) in the western Mediterranean sea during the summer. *Journal of Zoology*, **238**, 23–34.

389 Ford, J.K.B. (1984) *Call traditions and dialects of killer whales* (Orcinus orca) *in British Columbia*. PhD thesis, University of British Columbia.

390 Ford, J.K.B. (1989) Acoustic behavior of resident killer whales (*Orcinus orca*) off Vancouver Island, British Columbia. *Canadian Journal of Zoology*, **67**, 727–745.

391 Ford, J.K.B. (1991) Vocal traditions among resident killer whales (*Orcinus orca*) in coastal waters of British Columbia. *Canadian Journal of Zoology*, **69**, 1454–1483.

392 Ford, J.K.B. & Fisher, H.D. (1978) Underwater acoustic signals of the narwhal (*Monodon monoceros*). *Canadian Journal of Zoology*, **56**, 552–560.

393 Ford, J. & Fisher, H. (1982) Killer whale (*Orcinus orca*) dialects as an indicator of stocks in British Columbia. *Report of International Whaling Commission*, **32**, 671–679.

394 Ford, J.K.B. & Fisher, H.D. (1983) Group-specific dialects of killer whales (*Orcinus orca*) in British Columbia, pp. 129–161 in Payne, R.S. (ed.) *Communication and behavior of*

whales. Westview Press, Boulder, CO.

395 Ford, J.K.B. *et al.* (1998) Dietary specialization in two sympatric populations of killer whales *(Orcinus orca)* in coastal British Columbia and adjacent waters. *Canadian Journal of Zoology*, **76**, 1456–1471.

396 Ford, J.K.B. *et al.* (2000) *Killer whales: the natural history and genealogy of* Orcinus orca *in British Columbia and Washington State*. UBC Press, Vancouver.

397 Fordyce, R.E. (1982) A review of Australian fossil Cetacea. *Memoirs of the National Museum of Victoria*, **43**, 43–58, pl. 2.

398 Fordyce, R.E. *et al.* (1979) Stranding of a Cuvier's beaked whale *Ziphius cavirostris* Cuvier, 1823, at New Brighton, New Zealand. *Mauri Ora*, **7**, 73–82.

399 Foster, G. *et al.* (1996) Isolation of *Brucella* species from cetaceans, seals and an otter. *Veterinary Record*, **138**, 583–586.

400 Foster, N.R. & Hare, M.P. (1990) Cephalapod remains from a Cuvier's beaked whale (*Ziphius cavirostris*) stranded in Kodiak, Alaska. *Northwestern Naturalist*, **71**, 49–51.

401 Fransen, C.H.J.M. & Smeenk, C. (1991) Whale-lice (Amphipoda: Cyamidae) recorded from the Netherlands. *Zoologische Mededelingen Leiden*, **65**, 393–405.

402 Frantzis, A. (1998) Does acoustic testing strand whales? *Nature, London*, **392**, 29.

403 Frantzis, A. & Cebrian, D. (1999) A rare, atypical mass stranding of Cuvier's beaked whales: Cause and implications for the species' biology, pp. 332–335 in Evans, P.G.H. & Parsons, E.C.M. (eds.) *European research on cetaceans – 12*. European Cetacean Society.

404 Fraser, F.C. (1934) *Report on Cetacea stranded on the British coasts from 1927 to 1932*. No. **11**. British Museum (Natural History), London.

405 Fraser, F.C. (1940) Three anomalous dolphins from Blacksod Bay, Ireland. *Proceedings of Royal Irish Academy* (B), **45**, 413–455.

406 Fraser, F.C. (1946) *Report on Cetacea stranded on the British coasts from 1933 to 1937*. No. **12**. British Museum (Natural History), London.

407 Fraser, F.C. (1953) *Report on Cetacea stranded on the British coasts from 1938 to 1947*. No. **13**. British Museum (Natural History), London.

408 Fraser, F.C. (1974) *Report on Cetacea stranded on the British coasts from 1948 to 1966* No. **14**. British Museum (Natural History), London.

409 Fraser, F.C. & Noble, B.A. (1970) Variation of pigmentation pattern in Meyen's dolphin, *Stenella coeruleoalba* (Meyen). *Investigation on Cetacea*, **2**, 147–163.

410 Frasier, T.R. *et al.* (2007) Right whales past and present as revealed by their genes, pp. 200–231 in Kraus, S.D. & Rolland, R.M. (eds.) *The urban whale: North Atlantic right whales at the crossroads*. Harvard University Press, Cambridge, MA.

411 Frodello, J.P. *et al.* (2002) Metal levels in a Cuvier's beaked whale (*Ziphius cavirostris*) found stranded on a Mediterranean coast, Corsica. *Bulletin of Environmental Contamination and Toxicology*, **69**, 662–666.

412 Fullard, K.J. *et al.* (2000) Population structure of long-finned pilot whales in the North Atlantic: a correlation with sea surface temperature? *Molecular Ecology*, **9**(7), 949–958.

413 Galatius, A. & Kinze, C.C. (2007) Aspects of life history of white-beaked dolphins (*Lagenorhynchus albirostris*) from Danish waters, p. 75 in *European research on cetaceans – 21*. European Cetacean Society.

414 Gabriele, C.M. *et al.* (2007) Age at first calving of female humpback whales in Southeastern Alaska. *Marine Mammal Science*, **23**, 226–239.

415 Gambell R. (1985) Fin whale *Balaenoptera physalus* (Linnaeus, 1758), pp. 171–192 in Ridgway, S.H. & Harrison, R. (eds.) *Handbook of marine mammals. Vol. 3. The sirenians and baleen whales*. Academic Press, London.

416 Gambell, R. (1979) The blue whale. *Biologist*, **26**(5), 209–215.

417 Gambell, R. (1985) Sei whale, pp. 155–170 in Ridgway, S.H. & Harrison, R. (eds.) *Handbook of marine mammals. Vol. 3. The sirenians and baleen whales*. Academic Press, London.

418 Gannier, A. (2000) Distribution of Cetaceans off the Society Islands (French Polynesia) as obtained from dedicated survey. *Aquatic Mammals*, **26**(2), 111–126.

419 Gannier, A. Personal communication.

420 Gannier, A. & Gannier, O. (1994) Abundance of *Grampus griseus* in northwestern Mediterranean, pp. 99–102 in Evans, P.G.H. (ed.) *European research on cetaceans – 8*. European Cetacean Society.

421 Gannon, D.P. *et al.* (1997) Feeding ecology of long-finned pilot whales *Globicephala melas* in the western north Atlantic. *Marine Ecology Progress Series*, **148**(1–3), 1–10.

422 Gannon, D.P. *et al.* (1997) Stomach contents of long-finned pilot whales (*Globicephala melas*) stranded on the US mid-Atlantic coast. *Marine Mammal Science*, **13**(3), 405–418.

423 Gannon, D.P. *et al.* (1998) Autumn food habits of harbor porpoises, *Phocoena phocoena*, in the Gulf of Maine. *Fishery Bulletin*, **96**, 428–437.

424 García Hartmann, M. Personal communication.

425 García Hartmann, M. *et al.* (2004) *The diagnosis of by-catch: Examining harbour porpoises* Phocoena phocoena *stranded on the Dutch coast from 1990 to 2000*. Report, National Museum of Natural History (Naturalis), Leiden, The Netherlands/Zoo Duisburg, Duisburg, Germany.

426 García-Martinez, J. *et al.* (1999) Genetic differentiation in the striped dolphin *Stenella coeruleoalba* from European waters according to mitochondrial DNA (mtDNA) restriction analysis. *Molecular Ecology*, **8**, 1069–1073.

427 Gaskin, D.E. (1982) *The ecology of whales and dolphins*. Heinemann, London.

428 Gaskin, D.E. (1992) Status of the Atlantic white-sided dolphin, *Lagenorhynchus acutus*, in Canada. *Canadian Field Naturalist*, **106**, 64–72.

429 Gaskin, D.E. (1992) Status of the common dolphin, *Delphinus delphis*, in Canada. *Canadian Field Naturalist*, **106**, 55–63.

430 Gaspari, S. (2004) *Social and population structure of striped and Risso's dolphins in the Mediterranean Sea*. PhD thesis, University of Durham.

431 Gaspari, S. Personal communication.

432 Gaspari, S. *et al.* (2007) Risso's dolphins (*Grampus griseus*) in UK waters are differentiated from a population in the Mediterranean Sea and genetically less diverse. *Conservation Genetics*, **8**, 727–732.

433 Gaspari, S. *et al.* (in prep.) Individual associations and kin social structure of Risso's dolphins (*Grampus griseus*) in the Northwest Mediterranean Sea.

434 Gatesy, J. (1998) Molecular evidence for the phylogenetic affinities of Cetacea, pp. 63–111 in Thewissen, G.M. (ed.)*The emergence of whales: evolutionary patterns in the origin of cetacea*. Plenum Press, New York.

435 Gauthier, H. (1938) Observations sur un cétacé du genre *Ziphius* mort au large d'Alger. *Bulletin du Station d'Aquiculture et Pêche, Castiglioni*, **1**, 181–204 (in French).

436 Gaydos, J.K. *et al.* (2004) Evaluating potential infectious disease threats for southern resident killer whales, *Orcinus orca*: a model for endangered species. *Biology and Conservation*, **117**(3), 253–262.

437 Geraci, J.R. *et al.* (1978) *A mass stranding of the Atlantic white-sided dolphin,* Lagenorhynchus acutus: *a study into pathobiology and life history*. Marine Mammal Commission, Washington, DC.

438 Geraci, J.R. *et al.* (1978) Parasitic mastitis in the Atlantic white-sided dolphin, *Lagenorhynchus acutus*, as a probable factor in herd productivity. *Journal of the Fisheries Research Board of Canada*, **35**, 1350–1355.

439 Geraci, J.R. *et al.* (1987) Tumors in cetaceans: analysis and new findings. *Canadian Journal of Fisheries and Aquatic Sciences*, **44**, 1289–1300.

440 Gervais, P. (1855) *Histoire naturelle des mamifères*. L. Curmer, Paris (in French).

441 Gibson, D.I. & Harris, E.A. (1979) The helminth parasites of cetaceans in the collection of the British Museum (Natural History). *Investigations on Cetacea*, **10**, 309–324.

442 Gibson, D.I. *et al.* (1998) A survey of the helminth parasites of cetaceans stranded on the coast of England and Wales during the period 1990–1994. *Journal of Zoology*, **244**, 563–574.

443 Gill, A. & Fairbairns, R.S. (1995) Photo-identification of the minke whale *Balaenoptera acutorostrata* off the Isle of Mull, Scotland, pp. 129–132 in Blix, A.S. *et al.* (eds.) *Whales, seals, fish and man*. Elsevier, Amsterdam.

444 Glanville, E. *et al.* (2003) Common dolphin *Delphinus delphis* (L.). *Irish Naturalists' Journal*, **27**, 241–242.

445 Goley, P.D. & Straley, J.M. (1994) Attack on gray whales (*Eschrichtius robustus*) in Monterey Bay, California, by killer whales (*Orcinus orca*) previously identified in Glacier Bay, Alaska. *Canadian Journal of Zoology*, **72**, 1528–1530.

446 Gonzalez, A.F. *et al.* (2000) First recorded mass stranding of short-finned pilot whales (*Globicephala macrorhynchus* Gray, 1846) in the northeastern Atlantic. *Marine Mammal Science*, **16**(3), 640–646.

447 Goodson, A.D. *et al.* (1995) Source levels and echolocation signal characteristics of juvenile harbour porpoises *Phocoena phocoena*, pp. 41–54 in Nachtigall P.E. *et al.* (eds.) *Harbour porpoises, laboratory studies to reduce bycatches*. De Spil, Woerden, The Netherlands.

448 Gordon, J.C.D. (1987) *The behaviour and ecology of sperm whales off Sri Lanka*. PhD dissertation, University of Cambridge.

449 Gordon, J.C.D. (1998) *Sperm whales*. Colin Baxter Photography, Grantown-on-Spey.

450 Gordon, J.C.D. & Tyack, P. (2001) Acoustic techniques for studying cetaceans, pp. 293–324 in Evans, P.G.H. & Raga, J.A. (eds.) *Marine mammals: biology and conservation*. Kluwer Academic/Plenum Press, London.

451 Gosselin, M. (2001) *Aspects of the biology of common dolphins* (Delphinus delphis) *subject to incidental capture in fishing gears in the Celtic Sea and Channel*. MSc thesis, Heriot-Watt University, Edinburgh.

452 Goto, M. & Pastene, L.A. (1996) Population genetic structure in the western North Pacific minke whale examined by two independent RFLP analyses of mitochondrial DNA. *Report of the International Whaling Commission*, **47**, 531–537 (SC/48/NP5).

453 Goujon, M. (1996) *Captures accidentelles du filet maillant derivant et dynamique des populations da dauphins au large du Golfe de Gascogne*. PhD thesis, Laboratoire Halieutique, D.E.E.R.N., Ecole Nationale Superieure Agronomique de Rennes, France (in French).

454 Goujon, M. *et al.* (1994) A study of the ecological impact of the French tuna driftnet fishery in the North-East Atlantic, pp. 47–48 in Evans, P.G.H. (ed.) *European research on cetaceans – 8*. European Cetacean Society.

455 Gowans, S. (2002) Bottlenose whales *Hyperoodon ampullatus* and *H. planifrons*, pp.128–129 in Perrin, W.F. *et al.* (eds.). *Encyclopaedia of marine mammals*. Academic Press, San Diego, CA.

456 Gowans, S. & Rendell, L. (1999) Head-butting in northern bottlenose whales (*Hyperoodon ampullatus*): a possible function for big heads? *Marine Mammal Science*, **13**, 1342–1350.

457 Gowans, S. & Whitehead, H. (1995) Distribution and habitat partitioning by small odontocetes in the Gully, a submarine canyon on the Scotian Shelf. *Canadian Journal of Zoology*, **73**, 1599–1608.

458 Gowans, S. *et al.* (2000) Reliability of photographic and molecular techniques for sexing northern bottlenose whales (*Hyperoodon ampullatus*). *Canadian Journal of Zoology*, **78**, 1224–1229.

459 Gowans, S. *et al.* (2001) Social organization in northern bottlenose whales (*Hyperoodon ampullatus*): not driven by deep-water foraging. *Animal Behaviour*, **62**, 369–377.

460 Granby, K. & Kinze, C.C. (1991) Organochlorines in Danish and West Greenland harbour porpoises (*Phocoena phocoena*). *Marine Pollution Bulletin*, **22**, 458–462.

461 Gray, D. (1882) Notes on the characteristics and habits of the bottlenose whale (*Hyperoodon rostratus*). *Proceedings of the Zoological Society of London*, **1882**, 726–731.

462 Gray, J.E. (1846) On the cetaceous animals. pp. vxii, 1353, pls 37 in Volume I, part III, Mammalia of Richardson, J. & Gray, J.E. (eds.) *The zoology of the voyage of H.M.S. Erebus and Terror, under the command of Captain Sir James Clark Ross during the years 1839 to 1843 . . .* 2 vols, quarto, 1844–1875. Longmans, Brown, Green and Longmans, London.

463 Gray, J.E. (1866) *Catalogue of seals and whales in the British Museum,* 2nd ed. British Museum, London.

464 Greenwood, A.G. & Taylor, D.C. (1985) Captive killer whales in Europe. *Aquatic Mammals*, **1**, 10–12.

465 Grellier, K. & Wilson, B (2003) Bottlenose dolphins (*Tursiops truncatus*) in the Sound of Barra: a resident community off the Scottish west coast. *Aquatic Mammals*, **29**, 378–382.

466 Gunnlaugsson, T. & Sigurjónsson, J. (1990) NASS-87: estimation of whale abundance based on observations made onboard Icelandic and Faeroese survey vessels. *Report of the International Whaling Commission*, **40**, 571–580.

467 Haase, B.J.M. (1987) A mixed herd of white-beaked dolphins *Lagenorhynchus albirostris* and white-sided dolphins *L. acutus* in the southern North Sea. *Lutra*, **30**, 105–106.

468 Hain, J.H. *et al.* (1981) General distribution of cetaceans in the continental shelf waters of the NE United States, pp. 11.1–11.345 in *A characterisation of marine mammals and turtles in the mid and North Atlantic areas of the US outer continental shelf*. Cetacean and Turtle Assessment Program, Annual Report for 1979, contract AA551-CT8-48. US Department of the Interior, Washington, DC.

469 Hain, J.H. *et al.* (1985) The role of cetaceans in the shelf edge region of the northeast U.S. *Marine Fisheries Review*, **47**, 13–17.

470 Hain, J.H. *et al.* (1992) The fin whale (*Balaenoptera physalus*) in waters of the northeastern United States continental shelf. *Report of the International Whaling Commission*, **42**, 653–669.

471 Hall, A.J. *et al.* (2006) The risk of infection from polychlorinated biphenyl exposure in harbour porpoise (*Phocoena phocoena*) – a case-control approach. *Environmental Health Perspectives*, **114**, 704–711.

472 Hamilton, P.K. & Marx, M.J. (2005) Skin lesions on North Atlantic right whales: categories, prevalence, and change in occurrence in the 1990's. *Diseases of Aquatic Organisms*, **68**, 71–82.

473 Hamilton, P.K. *et al.* (1995) Weaning in North Atlantic right whales. *Marine Mammal Science*, **11**(3), 386–390.

474 Hamilton, P.K. *et al.* (1998) Age structure and longevity in North Atlantic right whales *Eubalaena glacialis* and their relation to reproduction. *Marine Ecology Progress Series*, **171**, 285–292.

475 Hamilton, P.K.A. *et al.* (2007) Right whales tell their own stories: the photo-identification catalog; pp. 75–104 in Kraus, S.D. & Rolland, R.M. (eds.) *The urban whale: North Atlantic right whales at the crossroads*. Harvard University Press, Cambridge, MA.

476 Hammond, D.D. & Leatherwood, S. (1984) Cetaceans live-captured for Ocean Park, Hong Kong April 1974–February 1983. *Report of the International Whaling Commission*, **34**, 491–495.

477 Hammond, P.S. (2001) Assessment of marine mammal population size and status, pp. 269–291 in Evans, P.G.H. & Raga J.A. (eds.) *Marine mammals: biology and conservation*. Plenum Press/Kluwer Academic, London.

478 Hammond, P.S. Personal communication.

479 Hammond, P.S. *et al.* (1990) Individual recognition of cetaceans: use of photo-identification and other techniques to estimate population parameters. *Report of the International Whaling Commission, Special Issue,* **12.**

480 Hammond, P.S. *et al.* (1990) A note on problems in estimating the number of blue whales in the Gulf of St Lawrence from photo-identification data. *Report of the International Whaling Commission,* **12,** 141–142.

481 Hammond, P.S. *et al.* (2002) Abundance of harbour porpoises and other cetaceans in the North Sea and adjacent waters. *Journal of Applied Ecology,* **39,** 361–376.

482 Handley, C.O., Jr (1966) A synopsis of the genus *Kogia* (pygmy sperm whales), pp. 62–69. in Norris, K.S. (ed.) *Whales, dolphins and porpoises*. University of California Press, Berkeley, CA.

483 Harmer, S.F. (1918) Notes on Cetacea stranded on the British coasts during 1913–1917. *Proceedings of the Zoological Society of London,* 147–161.

484 Harmer, S.F. (1924) On *Mesoplodon* and other beaked whales. *Proceedings of the Zoological Society of London,* 541–587.

485 Harmer, S.F. (1927) *Report on Cetacea stranded on British coasts from 1913 to 1926.* Report No. 10. British Museum (Natural History), London.

486 Harms, U. *et al.* (1978) Further data on heavy metals and organochlorines in marine mammals from German coastal waters. *Meeresforschung,* **26,** 153–161.

487 Harreras, V. *et al.* (1997) Helminth parasites of the digestive tract of the harbour porpoise *Phocoena phocoena* in Danish waters: a comparative geographical analysis. *Diseases of Aquatic Organisms,* **28,** 163–167.

488 Harris, E.A. *et al.* (1995) Parasites of stranded cetaceans, p. 39 in *Studies on the biology of cetacea.* A report to the Welsh office. WEP/100/154/6. Natural History Museum, London.

489 Harwood, J. *et al.* (1999) *Assessment and reduction of the bycatch of small cetaceans (BYCARE).* Final report to the European Commission under FAIR contract CT05-0523.

490 Harwood, M.B. *et al.* (1984) Incidental catch of small cetaceans in a gillnet fishery in northern Australian waters. *Report of the International Whaling Commission* **34,** 555–559.

491 Hassani, S. *et al.* (1997) Diets of albacore, *Thunnus alalunga*, and dolphins, *Delphinus delphis* and *Stenella coerulaeoalba*, caught in the Northeast Atlantic albacore drift-net fishery: a progress report. *Journal of Northwest Atlantic Fishery Science,* 119–123.

492 Hastie, G.D. *et al.* (2004) Functional mechanisms underlying cetacean distribution patterns: hotspots for bottlenose dolphins are linked to foraging. *Marine Biology,* **144,** 397–403.

493 Hastie, G.D. *et al.* (2006) Diving deep in a foraging hotspot: acoustic insights into bottlenose dolphin dive depths and feeding behaviour. *Marine Biology,* **148,** 1181–1188.

494 Hatch, L. *et al.* (2006) Phylogenetic relationships among the baleen whales based on maternally and paternally inherited characters. *Molecular Phylogenetics and Evolution,* **41,** 12–27.

495 Hatzianestis, J. *et al.* (1998) Organochlorine levels in Cuvier's goosebeaked whales from Ionian Sea, Hellas. *Fresenius Environmental Bulletin,* **7,** 345–350.

496 Haug, T. (1981) On some reproduction parameters in fin whales, *Balaenoptera physalus* (L.) caught off Norway. *Report of the International Whaling Commission,* **31,** 373–378.

497 Haug, T. *et al.* (1995) Spatial and temporal variations in northeast Atlantic minke whale *Balaenoptera acutorostrata* feeding habits, pp. 225–239 in Blix, A.S. *et al.* (eds.) *Whales, seals, fish and man*. Elsevier, Amsterdam.

498 Haug, T. *et al.* (2002) Variations in minke whale (*Balaenoptera acutorostrata*) diet and body condition in response to ecosystem changes in the Barents Sea. *Sarsia,* 87, 409–422.

499 Haug, T. *et al.* (2003) *Harbour porpoises in the North Atlantic.* Scientific Publications Volume 5, NAMMCO, Tromsø.

500 Hay, K.A. & Mansfield, A.W. (1989) Narwhal *Monodon monoceros* Linnaeus, 1758, pp. 145–176 in Ridgway, S.H. & Harrison, R. (eds.) *Handbook of marine mammals, Volume 4: River dolphins and the larger toothed whales*. Academic Press, San Diego, CA.

501 Heide-Jørgensen M.P. (1988) Occurrence and hunting of killer whales in Greenland. *Rit Fiskideildir,* **11,** 115–135.

502 Heide-Jørgensen, M.P. (1990) Small cetaceans in Greenland: hunting and biology. *North Atlantic Studies,* **2,** 55–58.

503 Heide-Jørgensen, M.P. (2002) Narwhal. *Monodon monoceros,* pp. 783–787 in Perrin, W.F. *et al.* (eds.) *Encyclopaedia of marine mammals*. Academic Press, San Diego, CA.

504 Heide-Jørgensen, M.P. & Dietz, R. (1995) Some characteristics of narwhal, *Monodon monoceros,* diving behaviour in Baffin Bay. *Canadian Journal of Zoology,* **73,** 2120–2132.

505 Heide-Jørgensen, M.P. & Teilmann, J. (1994) Growth, reproduction, age structure and feeding habits of white whales (*Delphinapterus leucas*) in West Greenland. *Meddr Grønland, Biosciences,* **39,** 195–212.

506 Heide-Jørgensen, M.P. & Wing, Ø. (eds.) (2002) *Belugas in the North Atlantic and the Russian Arctic*. NAMMCO Scientific Publications, Volume 4, Tromsø.

507 Heide-Jørgensen, M.P. *et al.* (1994) A note on the diet of narwhals (*Monodon monoceros*) in Inglefield Bredning (NW Greenland). *Meddr Grønland, Biosciences,* **39,** 213–216.

508 Heide-Jørgensen, M.P. *et al.* (2002) Diving behaviour of long-finned pilot whales *Globicephala melas* around the Faroe Islands. *Wildlife Biology,* **8**(4), 307–313.

509 Heimlich-Boran, J.R. (1986) Fishery correlations with the occurrence of killer whales in greater Puget Sound, pp. 113–131 in Kirkevold, B.C. & Lockard, J.S. (eds.) *Behavioral biology of killer whales*. A.R. Liss, New York.

510 Heimlich-Boran, J.R. (1988) Behavioral ecology of killer whales (*Orcinus orca*) in the Pacific Northwest. *Canadian Journal of Zoology,* **66,** 565–578.

511 Heimlich-Boran, S.L. (1986) Cohesive relationships among Puget Sound killer whales, pp. 251–284 in Kirkevold, B. & Lockard, J.S. (eds.) *Behavioral biology of killer whales*. A.R. Liss, New York.

512 Heimlich-Boran, S.L. (1988) *Association patterns and social dynamics of killer whales* (Orcinus orca) *in Greater Puget Sound*. MA Thesis, Moss Landing Marine Laboratories, San Jose State University, CA.

513 Hembree, D. (1984) Cetacean catch during 1982 by aboriginal subsistence fishery in Lembata, Indonesia. *Report of the International Whaling Commission,* PS/WP 3.

514 Herman, J.S. & Dobney, K.M. (2001) Evidence for an Anglo-Saxon dolphin fishery in the North Sea. European Cetacean Society Annual Conference, Rome.

515 Herman, J.S. *et al.* (1994) The most northerly record of Blainville's beaked whale, *Mesoplodon densirostris*, from the eastern Atlantic. *Mammalia,* **58,** 657–661.

516 Hernandez-Garcia, V. (2002) Contents of the digestive tract of a false killer whale (*Pseudorca crassidens*) stranded in Gran Canaria (Canary Islands, central east Atlantic). *Bulletin of Marine Science,* **71**(1), 367–369.

517 Heyning, J.E. (1989) Cuvier's beaked whale *Ziphius cavoirostris* G. Cuvier, 1823, pp. 289–308 in Ridgway, S.H. & Harrison, R. (eds.) *Handbook of marine mammals, Volume 4: River dolphins and the larger toothed whales*. Academic Press, San Diego, CA.

518 Heyning, J.E. (1997) Sperm whale phylogeny revisited:

analysis of the morphological evidence. *Marine Mammal Science*, **13**, 596–613.

519 Heyning, J.E. & Dahlheim, M.E. (1988) *Orcinus orca*. *Mammalian Species*, **304**, 1–9.

520 Heyning, J.E. & Mead, J. (1996) Suction feeding in beaked whales: morphological and observational evidence. *Natural History Museum of Los Angeles City, Contributions to Science*, **464**, 1–12.

521 Heyning, J.E. & Perrin, W.F. (1994) Evidence of two species of common dolphins (genus *Delphinus*) from the eastern North Pacific. *Natural History Museum of Los Angeles City, Contributions to Science*, **442**.

522 Hinton, M.A.C. (1928) Stranded whales at Dornoch Firth. *Natural History Magazine*, **1**, 131–138.

523 Hobbs, K.E. *et al.* (2003) Levels and patterns of persistent organochlorines in minke whale (*Balaenoptera acutorostrata*) stocks from the North Atlantic and European Arctic. *Environmental Pollution*, **121**, 239–252.

524 Hoelzel, A.R. (1991) Killer whale predation on marine mammals at Punta Norte, Argentina; foraging strategy, provisioning and food sharing. *Behavioural Ecology and Sociobiology*, **29**, 197–204.

525 Hoelzel, A.R. (1993) Foraging behaviour and social group dynamics in Puget Sound killer whales. *Animal Behaviour*, **45**, 581–591.

526 Hoelzel, A.R. & Dover, G.A. (1991) Mitochondrial D-loop DNA variation within and between populations of the minke whale. *Report of the International Whaling Commission, Special Issue*, **13**, 171–182.

527 Hoelzel, A.R. & Osborne, R.W. (1986) Killer whale call characteristics; implications for cooperative foraging strategies, pp. 373–406 in Kirkevold, B.C. & Lockard, J.S. (eds.) *Behavioral biology of killer whales*. A.R. Liss, New York.

528 Hoelzel, R. & Stern, J. (2000) *Minke whales*. Colin Baxter Photography, Grantown-on-Spey.

529 Hoelzel, A.R. *et al.* (1989) The foraging specialisations of individual minke whales. *Animal Behaviour*, **38**, 786–794.

530 Hoelzel, A.R. *et al.* (2002) Low worldwide genetic diversity in the killer whale (*Orcinus orca*): implications for demographic history. *Proceedings of the Royal Society of London Series B*, **269**, 1467–1473.

531 Hoelzel, A.R. *et al.* (2007) Evolution of population structure in a highly social top predator, the killer whale. *Molecular Biology and Evolution*, **24**(6), 1407–1415.

532 Hogarth, W.M. (2005) Endangered and threatened wildlife and plants: Endangered status for southern resident killer whales. *Federal Register*, **70**(222), 69903–69912.

533 Holsbeek, L. *et al.* (1998) Heavy metals in dolphins stranded on the French Atlantic coast. *Science of the Total Environment*, **217**, 241–249.

534 Holsbeek, L. *et al.* (1999) Heavy metals, organochlorines and polycylic aromatic hydrocarbons in sperm whales stranded in the southern North Sea during the 1994/1995 winter. *Marine Pollution Bulletin*, **38**, 304–313.

535 Holt, S.J. (1977) Does the bottlenose whale necessarily have a sustainable yield, and if so is it worth taking? *Reports of the International Whaling Commission*, **27**, 206–208.

536 Hooker, S.K. & Baird, R.W. (1999) Deep-diving behaviour of the northern bottlenose whale, *Hyperoodon ampullatus* (Cetacea: Ziphiidae). *Proceedings of the Royal Society of London Series B*, **266**, 671–676.

537 Hooker, S.K. & Whitehead, H. (2002) Click characteristics of northern bottlenose whales (*Hyperoodon ampullatus*). *Marine Mammal Science*, **18**, 69–80.

538 Hooker, S.K. *et al.* (2001) Diet of northern bottlenose whales inferred from fatty-acid and stable-isotope analyses of biopsy samples. *Canadian Journal of Zoology*, **79**, 1442–1454.

539 Hooker, S.K. *et al.* (2002) Ecosystem consideration in conservation planning: energy demand of foraging bottlenose whales (*Hyperoodon ampullatus*) in a marine protected area. *Biological Conservation*, **104**, 51–58.

540 Hooker, S.K. *et al.* (2002) Fluctuations in distribution and patterns of individual range use of northern bottlenose whales. *Marine Ecology Progress Series*, **225**, 287–297.

541 Hooker, S.K. *et al.* (2007) Changes in persistent contaminant concentration and CYP1A1 protein expression in biopsy samples from northern bottlenose whales, *Hyperoodon ampullatus*, following the onset of nearby oil and gas development *Environmental Pollution* (in press).

542 Hori, H. *et al.* (1994) *World-wide population structure of minke whales deduced from mitochondrial DNA control region sequences*. Paper SC/46/SH14 presented to the IWC Scientific Committee, May 1994.

543 Horwood, J. (1987) *The sei whale*. Academic Press, London.

544 Horwood, J.W. (1990) *Biology and exploitation of the minke whale*. CRC Press, Boca Raton, FL.

545 Horwood, J. (2002) Sei whale *Balaenoptera borealis*, pp. 1069–1071 in Perrin, W.F. *et al.* (eds.) *Encyclopaedia of marine mammals*. Academic Press, San Diego, CA.

546 Houston, J. (1990) Status of Blainville's beaked whale, *Mesoplodon densirostris*, in Canada. *Canadian Field Naturalist*, **104**, 117–120.

547 Hoyt, E. (1984) *Orca: the whale called killer*. Camden House Publishing, Camden East, Ontario.

548 Husson, A.M. & Holthuis, L.B. (1974) *Physeter macrocephalus* Linnaeus, 1758, the valid name for the sperm whale. *Zoologische Mededelingen Leiden*, **48**, 205–217, pls 1–3.

549 Ingram, S.N. (2000) *The ecology and conservation of bottlenose dolphins in the Shannon estuary*. PhD thesis, University College Cork.

550 Innes, S. *et al.* (2002) Stock identity of belugas (*Delphinapterus leucas*) in eastern Canada and West Greenland based on organochlorine contaminants in their blubber, pp. 51–68 in Heide-Jørgensen, M.P. & Wing, Ø. (eds.) *Belugas in the North Atlantic and the Russian Arctic*. NAMMCO Scientific Publications, Volume 4, Tromsø.

551 International Whaling Commission (1975) Report of the meeting on smaller cetaceans, Montreal, April 1–11, 1974, Subcommittee on Small Cetaceans, Scientific Committee, International Whaling Commission. *Journal of the Fisheries Research Board of Canada*, **32**, 889–983.

552 International Whaling Commission (1984) Report of the sub-committee on small cetaceans. *Report of the International Whaling Commission*, **34**, 144–160.

553 International Whaling Commission (1989) Report of the subcommittee on small cetaceans. *Report of the International Whaling Commission*, **39**, 117–129.

554 International Whaling Commission (1992) Report of the comprehensive assessment special meeting on north Atlantic fin whales. *Report of the International Whaling Commission*, **42**, 595–644.

555 International Whaling Commission (1994) Report of the workshop on mortality of cetaceans in passive fishing nets and traps. *Report of the International Whaling Commission, Special Issue*, **15**, 1–71.

556 International Whaling Commission (2000) Report of the standing sub-committee on small cetaceans. *Journal of Cetacean Research and Management*, **2** (Suppl.), 235–263.

557 International Whaling Commission (2000) Report of the Scientific Committee. *Journal of Cetacean Research and Management*, **2**(suppl.), 1–367.

558 International Whaling Commission (2001) Report of the working group on nomenclature. *Journal of Cetacean Research and Management*, **3**(suppl.), 363–367.

559 International Whaling Commission. *www.iwcoffice.org*

560 Isaksen, K. & Syvertsen, P.O. (2002) Striped dolphins, *Stenella coeruleoalba*, in Norwegian and adjacent waters. *Mammalia*, **66**, 33–41.

561 Jacobsen, K.-O. *et al.* (2004) Two-way trans-Atlantic migration of a North Atlantic right whale (*Eubalaena*

glacialis). *Marine Mammal Science,* **20**, 161–166.

562 Jacobson, J. (1986) The behavior of *Orcinus orca* in Johnstone Strait, British Columbia, pp. 135–185 in Kirkevold, B.C. & Lockard, J.S. (eds.) *Behavioral biology of killer whales.* A.R. Liss, New York.

563 Jahoda, M. *et al.* (2003) Mediterranean fin whale's (*Balaenoptera physalus*) response to small vessels and biopsy sampling assessed through passive tracking and timing of respiration. *Marine Mammal Science,* **19**(1), 96–110.

564 Janik, V.M. (2000) Food-related bray calls in wild bottlenose dolphins (*Tursiops truncatus*). *Proceedings of the Royal Society of London Series B,* **267**, 923–927.

565 Jann, B. Personal communication.

566 Jaquet, N. (1996) How spatial and temporal scales influence understanding of sperm whale distribution: a review. *Mammal Review,* **26**, 51–65.

567 Jarman, W.M. *et al.* (1996) Levels of organochlorine compounds, including PCDDS and PCDFS, in the blubber of cetaceans from the west coast of North America. *Marine Pollution Bulletin,* **32**(5), 426–436.

568 Jauniaux, T. *et al.* (1998) Lesions of morbillivirus infection in a fin whale (*Balaenoptera physalus*) stranded along the Belgian coast. *Veterinary Record,* **143**, 423–424.

569 Jauniaux, T. *et al.* (1998) Postmortem investigations on winter stranded sperm whales from the coasts of Belgium and the Netherlands. *Journal of Wildlife Diseases,* **34**, 99–109.

570 Jefferson, J.A. & Schiro, A.J. (1997) Distribution of cetaceans in the offshore Gulf of Mexico. *Mammal Review,* **27**, 27–50.

571 Jefferson, T.A. & Barros, N.B. (1997) *Peponocephala electra.* *Mammalian Species,* **553**, 1–6.

572 Jefferson, T.A. & Van Waerebeek, K. (2002) The taxonomic status of the nominal dolphin species, *Delphinus tropicalis* van Bree, 1971. *Marine Mammal Science,* **18**, 787–818.

573 Jefferson, T.A. *et al.* (1991) A review of killer whale interactions with other marine mammals: predation to co-existence. *Mammal Review,* **22**, 151–180.

574 Jepson, P.D. (ed.) (2006) *Cetacean strandings investigation and co-ordination in the UK 2000–2004.* Final report to Defra. *www.defra.gov.uk/wildlife-countryside/resprog/findings/cetaceanar/index.htm*

575 Jepson, P.D. & Baker, J.R. (1998) Bottlenosed dolphins (*Tursiops truncatus*) as a possible cause of acute traumatic injuries in porpoises (*Phocoena phocoena*). *Veterinary Record,* **143**, 614–615.

576 Jepson, P.D. *et al.* (1997) Antibodies to *Brucella* in marine mammals around the coast of England and Wales. *Veterinary Record,* **141**, 513–515.

577 Jepson, P. *et al.* (2000) Pulmonary pathology of harbour porpoises (*Phocoena phocoena*) stranded in England and Wales between 1990 and 1996. *Veterinary Record,* **146**, 721–728.

578 Jepson, P.D. *et al.* (2003) Gas-bubble lesions in stranded cetaceans – was sonar responsible for a spate of whale deaths after an Atlantic military exercise? *Nature,* **425** (6958), 575–576.

579 Jepson, P.D. *et al.* (2005) Relationships between PCBs and health status in UK-stranded harbour porpoises (*Phocoena phocoena*). *Environmental Toxicology and Chemistry,* **24**, 238–248.

580 Jepson, P.D. *et al.* (2005) Acute and chronic gas bubble lesions in cetaceans stranded in the United Kingdom. *Veterinary Pathology,* **42**, 291–305.

581 Johnson, A.J. *et al.* (2007) The entangled lives of right whales and fishermen: can they coexist? pp. 380–408 in Kraus, S.D. & Rolland, R.M. (eds.) *The urban whale: North Atlantic right whales at the crossroads.* Harvard University Press, Cambridge, MA.

582 Johnson, M. *et al.* (2004) Beaked whales echolocate on prey. *Proceedings of the Royal Society of London Series B,* **271**, S383–S386.

583 Johnson, M. *et al.* (2006) Foraging Blainville's beaked whales (*Mesoplodon densirostris*) produce distinct click types matched to different phases of echolocation. *Journal of Experimental Biology,* **209**, 5038–5050.

584 Johnston, P.A. *et al.* (1996) Cetaceans and environmental pollution: the global concerns, pp. 219–263 in Simmonds, M.P. & Hutchinson, J.D. (eds.) *The conservation of whales and dolphins.* Wiley, Chichester,.

585 Jones, M.L. *et al.* (eds) (1984) *The gray whale* Eschrichtius robustus. Academic Press, Orlando, FL.

586 Jones, P.H. (1984) Cetaceans seen in the Irish Sea and approaches, late summer 1983. *Nature in Wales,* **3**, 62–64.

587 Jonsgård, Å. (1951) Studies on the little piked whale or minke whale (*Balaenoptera acuto-rostrata* Lacépède). *Norsk Hvalfangsttidsskrift,* **40**, 80–95.

588 Jonsgård, Å. (1962) Population studies on the minke whale *Balaenoptera acuto-rostrata* Lacépède , pp. 159–167 in LeCren, E.O. & Holdgate, M.W. (eds.) *The exploitation of natural animal populations.* Blackwell Scientific Publications, Oxford.

589 Jonsgård, Å. (1966) Biology of the North Atlantic fin whale (*Balaenoptera physalus*). Taxonomy, distribution, migration and food. *Hvalraad Skrift,* **49**, 1–62.

590 Jonsgård, Å. (1968) A note on the attacking behaviour of the killer whale (*Orcinus orca*). *Norsk Hvalfangst Tidende,* **57**, 84–85.

591 Jonsgård, Å. (1968) Another note on the attacking behaviour of killer whale (*Orcinus orca*). *Norsk Hvalfangst Tidende,* **57**, 175–176.

592 Jonsgård, Å. & Darling, K. (1977) On the biology of the eastern North Atlantic sei whale, *Balaenoptera borealis* Lesson. *Report of the International Whaling Commission, Special issue,* **1**, 121–123.

593 Jonsgård, Å. & Lyshoel, P.B. (1970) A contribution to the biology of the killer whale, *Orcinus orca* (L.). *Norwegian Journal of Zoology,* **18**, 41–48.

594 Joyce, G.G. *et al.* (1990) *The Faroese NASS-89 sightings cruise.* Paper SC/42/O 11 presented to the Scientific Committee of the International Whaling Commission.

595 Kamminga, C. (1990) Echolocation signal types of odontocetes, pp. 9–21 in *Animal sonar.* Vol. A156. NATO Advanced Studies Institute, Brussels.

596 Kamminga, C. & van Velden, J.G. (1987) Investigations on cetacean sonar VIII: sonar signals of *Pseudorca crassidens* in comparison with *Tursiops truncatus*. *Aquatic Mammals,* **13**, 43–49.

597 Kanda, N. *et al.* (2006) Genetic characteristics of Western North Pacific sei whales, *Balaenoptera borealis*, as revealed by microsatellites. *Marine Biotechnology,* **8**, 86–93.

598 Karakosta, C.V. *et al.* (1999) Testicular and ovarian development in the harbour porpoise (*Phocoena phocoena*). *Journal of Zoology,* **111**, 111–121.

599 Kastelein, R.A. *et al.* (1997) Food consumption and body weight of harbour porpoises (*Phocoena phocoena*), pp. 217–233 in Read, A.J. *et al.* (eds.) *The biology of the harbour porpoise.* De Spil, Woerden, Netherlands.

600 Kasuya, T. (1971) Consideration of distribution and migration of toothed whale off the Pacific coast of Japan based on aerial sighting records. *Scientific Report of the Whales Research Institute,* **25**, 1–103.

601 Kasuya, T. (1973) Systematic consideration of recent toothed whales based on the morphology of tympano-periotic bone. *Scientific Report of the Whales Research Institute,* **25**, 1–103.

602 Kasuya, T. (1985) Effect of exploitation on reproductive parameters of spotted and striped dolphins off the Pacific coast of Japan. *Scientific Reports of the Whales Research Institute,* **36**, 107–138.

603 Kasuya, T. (1985) Fishery-dolphin conflict in the Iki Island area of Japan, pp. 253–272 in Beddington, J.R. *et al.* (eds.)

Marine mammals and fisheries. Allen & Unwin, London.

604 Kasuya, T. (1986) False killer whales, pp. 178–187 in Tamura, T. *et al.* (eds.) *Report of investigation in search of solution for dolphin-fishery conflict in the Iki Island area.* Japan Fisheries Agency, Tokyo.

605 Kasuya, T. & Nishiwaki, M. (1971) First record of *Mesoplodon densirostris* from Formosa. *Scientific Report of the Whales Research Institute,* **23,** 129–137.

606 Katona, S. *et al.* (1978) Observations on a white-sided dolphin, *Lagenorhynchus acutus,* probably killed in gillnets in the Gulf of Maine. *Fisheries Bulletin US,* **76,** 475–476.

607 Katona, S. *et al.* (1983) *A field guide to the whales, porpoises and seals of the Gulf of Maine and Eastern Canada, Cape Cod to Newfoundland,* 3rd ed. Charles Scribner's Sons, New York.

608 Kawakami, T. (1980) A review of sperm whale food. *Scientific Reports of the Whales Research Institute,* **32,** 199–218.

609 Kawamura, A. (1974) Food and feeding ecology in the southern sei whale. *Scientific Reports of the Whales Research Institute,* **26,** 25–144.

610 Kawamura, A. (1980) A review of food of balaenopterid whales. *Scientific Reports of the Whales Research Institute,* **32,** 155–197.

611 Kennedy, S. *et al.* (1988) Viral distemper now found in porpoises. *Nature, London,* **336,** 21.

612 Kenney, R.D. (2007) Right whales and climate change: Facing the prospect of a greenhouse future, pp. 436–459 in Kraus, S.D. and Rolland, R.M. (eds.) *The urban whale: North Atlantic right whales at the crossroads.* Harvard University Press, Cambridge, MA.

613 Kenney, R.D. & Winn, H.E. (1986) Cetacean high use habitats of the NE United States continental shelf. *Fisheries Bulletin, US,* **84,** 345–357.

614 Kenney, R.D. & Winn, H.E. (1987) Cetacean biomass densities near submarine canyons compared to adjacent shelf/slope areas. *Continental Shelf Research,* **7,** 107–114.

615 Kenney, R.D. & Wishner, K.F. (1995) The South Channel Ocean Productivity Experiment. *Continental Shelf Research,* **15,** 373–384.

616 Kenney, R.D. *et al.* (1986) Estimation of prey densities required by western North Atlantic right whales. *Marine Mammal Science,* **2**(1), 1–13.

617 Kenney, R.D. *et al.* (1995) Cetaceans in the Great South Channel, 1979–1989: right whale (*Eubalaena glacialis*). *Continental Shelf Research,* **15**(4/5), 385–414.

618 Kenyon, K.W. (1961) Cuvier beaked whales stranded in the Aleutian Islands. *Journal of Mammalogy,* **42,** 71–76

619 Kerkshoff, M. *et al.* (1981) Heptachlor epoxide in marine mammals. *Science of the Total Environment,* **19,** 41–50.

620 Kikuchi, S. *et al.* (1995) Morphology of *Crassicauda giliakiana* (Nematoda; Spiruridae) from a Cuvier's beaked whale *Ziphius cavirostris. Japanese Journal of Parasitology,* **44,** 228–237.

621 Kilgallen, N. (2003) *Age determination and the analysis of tooth anomalies in the dentine of striped dolphins,* Stenella coeruleoalba *(Meyen, 1833), in the northeast Atlantic.* BSc thesis, University College Cork.

622 King, C.A. (1987) *Organochlorines in bottlenose dolphins* (Tursiops truncatus) *and pygmy sperm whales* (Kogia breviceps) *from southeastern Florida.* MSc thesis, University of Miami, FL.

623 Kingsley, M. (1989) Population dynamics of the narwhal *Monodon monoceros:* an initial assessment (Odontoceti: Monodontidae). *Journal of Zoology,* **219,** 201–208.

624 Kingsley, M.C.S. (2001) Beluga surveys in the St Lawrence: a reply to Michaud and Béland. *Marine Mammal Science,* **17,** 213–218.

625 Kingsley, M.C. (2002) Status of the belugas of the St. Lawrence estuary, Canada, pp. 239–258 in Heide-Jørgensen, M.P. & Wing, Ø. (eds.) *Belugas in the North Atlantic and the Russian Arctic.* NAMMCO Scientific Publications, Volume 4, Tromsø.

626 Kingston, S.E. & Rosel, P.E. (2004) Genetic differentiation among recently diverged delphinid taxa determined using AFLP markers. *Journal of Heredity,* **95,** 1–10.

627 Kinze, C.C. (1985) Intraspecific variation in Baltic and North Sea harbour porpoises (*Phocoena phocoena* (L. 1758)) *Vidensjabelige Meddelelser fra Dansk Naturhistirisk Forening,* **146,** 63–67.

628 Kinze, C.C. (1990) Non-metric analyses of harbour porpoises (*Phocoena phocoena*) from the North and Baltic seas: implications for stock identity. *International Whaling Commission,* document SC/42/SM 35.

629 Kinze, C.C. (1995) Danish whale records 1575–1991 (Mammalia, Cetacea). *Steenstrupia,* **21,** 155–196.

630 Kinze, C.C. *et al.* (1997) The white-beaked dolphin (*Lagenorhynchus albirostris*) and the white-sided dolphin (*Lagenorhynchus acutus*) in the North and Baltic Seas: review of available information. *Report of the International Whaling Commission,* **47,** 675–681.

631 Kirkwood, J.K. *et al.* (1997) Entanglement in fishing gear and other causes of death in cetaceans stranded on the coasts of England and Wales. *Veterinary Record,* **141,** 94–98.

632 Kiszka, J. & Jauniaux, T. (2002) Suspicion of collision in a Sowerby's beaked whale (*Mesoplodon bidens*) stranded on the northern French coast, p. 59 in *European research on cetaceans – 16.* European Cetacean Society.

633 Kitchener, A.C. & Herman, J.S. (1995) Re-identification of the supposed True's beaked whale *Mesoplodon mirus* from Scotland. *Journal of Zoology,* **236,** 353–357.

634 Kitchener, D.J. *et al.* (1990) Variation in skull and external morphology in the false killer whale, *Pseudorca crassidens,* from Australia, Scotland and South Africa. *Mammalia,* **54,** 119–135.

635 Kleinenberg, S.E. *et al.* (1964) *Beluga* (Delphinapterus leucas): *investigations of the species.* Academy of Sciences of the USSR, Moscow. [Translated by Israel Program for Scientific Translations, 1969].

636 Kleivane, L. & Skaare, J.U. (1998) Organochlorine contaminants in northeast Atlantic minke whales (*Balaenoptera acutorostrata*). *Environmental Pollution,* **101,** 231–239.

637 Klumov, S.K. (1962) [The northern right whales in the Pacific Ocean.] *Trudy Instituta Okeanologii,* **58,** 202–297 (in Russian).

638 Knap, A.H. & Jickells, T.D. (1983) Trace metals and organochlorines in the goosebeaked whale. *Marine Pollution Bulletin,* **14,** 271–274.

639 Knowlton, A.R. & Brown, M.W. (2007) Running the gauntlet: right whales and vessel strikes, pp. 409–443 in Kraus, S.D. & Rolland, R.M. (eds.) *The urban whale: North Atlantic right whales at the crossroads.* Harvard University Press, Cambridge, MA.

640 Knowlton, A.R. *et al.* (1991) Sounds recorded in the presence of sei whales, *Balaenoptera borealis,* p. 40 in *Abstracts, 9th Biennial Conference on Biology of Marine Mammals,* Chicago, IL, December 1991.

641 Knowlton, A.R. *et al.* (1992) Long-distance movements of North Atlantic right whales, (*Eubalaena glacialis*). *Marine Mammal Science,* **8**(4), 397–405.

642 Knowlton, A.R. *et al.* (1994) Reproduction in North Atlantic right whales. *Canadian Journal of Zoology,* **72,** 1297–1305.

643 Kock, A.C. de *et al.* (1994) Persistent organochlorine residues in small cetaceans from the east and west coasts of southern Africa. *Science of the Total Environment,* **154,** 153–162.

644 Koeman, J.H. *et al.* (1972) Persistant chemicals in marine mammals. *TNO-Nieuws,* **27,** 570–578.

645 Koga, T. (1991) Relationship between food consumption and growth of harbour porpoises *Phocoena phocoena* in captivity. *International Marine Biology Research Institute Reports,* **2,** 71–73.

646 Kompanje, E.J.O. (1995) On the occurrence of spondylosis deformans in white-beaked dolphins *Lagenorhynchus albirostris* (Gray, 1846) stranded on the Dutch coast. *Zoologische Mededelingen Leiden*, **69**, 231–250.

647 Kompanje, E.J.O. (1996) Intervertebral disc degeneration and discarthrosis in white-beaked dolphins *Lagenorhynchus albirostris*, pp. 21–25 in *European Association of Zoo and Wildlife Veterinarians (EAZWV) 1st scientific meeting, May 16–18.* Rostock, Germany.

648 Kompanje, E.J.O. (1999) Considerations on the comparative pathology of the vertebrae in Mysticeti and Odontoceti; evidence for the occurrence of discarthrosis, zygarthrosis, infectious spondylitis and spondyloarthritis. *Zoologische Mededelingen Leiden*, **73**, 99–130.

649 Kraus, S.D. (1990) Rates and potential causes of mortality in North Atlantic right whales *(Eubalaena glacialis)*. *Marine Mammal Science*, **6**(4), 278–291.

650 Kraus, S.D. & Hatch, J.J. (2001) Mating strategies in the North Atlantic right whale *(Eubalaena glacialis)*. *Journal of Cetacean Research and Management*, Special Issue **2**, 237–244.

651 Kraus, S.D. & Rolland, R.M. (eds.) (2007) *The urban whale: North Atlantic right whales at the crossroads.* Harvard University Press, Cambridge, MA.

652 Kraus, S.D. *et al.* (1982) Preliminary notes on the occurrence of the north Atlantic right whale *(Eubalaena glacialis)* in the Bay of Fundy. *Report of the International Whaling Commission*, **32**, 407–411

653 Kraus, S.D. *et al.* (1986) Migration and calving of right whales *(Eubalaena glacialis)* in the western North Atlantic, pp. 139–144 in Brownell, R.L. Jr *et al.* (eds.) *Right whales: past and present status, Reports of the International Whaling Commission, Special Issue,* **10**.

654 Kraus, S.D. *et al.* (1986) The use of photographs to identify individual north Atlantic right whales *(Eubalaena glacialis)*, pp. 145–151 in Brownell, R.L. Jr *et al.* (eds.) *Right whales: past and present status, Reports of the International Whaling Commission, Special Issue,* **10**.

655 Kraus, S.D. *et al.* (2005) North Atlantic right whales in crisis. *Science*, **309**, 561–562.

656 Kraus, S.D. *et al.* (2007) High investment, low return: the strange case of reproduction in *Eubalaena glacialis*, pp. 172–199 in Kraus, S.D. & Rolland, R.M. (eds.) *The urban whale: North Atlantic right whales at the crossroads.* Harvard University Press, Cambridge, MA.

657 Kruse, S. (1989) *Aspects of the biology, ecology and behaviour of Risso's dolphin* (Grampus griseus) *off the Californian coast.* MSc thesis, University of California.

658 Kruse, S. *et al.* (1991) Records of Risso's dolphins, *Grampus griseus*, in the Indian Ocean, 1891–1986, pp. 66–77 in Leatherwood, S. & Donovan, G. (eds.) *Cetaceans and cetacean research in the Indian Ocean Sanctuary.* United Nations Environmental Programme, Nairobi.

659 Kruse, S. *et al.* (1999) The Risso's dolphin, pp.183–212 in Ridgway, S.H. & Harrison, R. (eds.) *Handbook of marine mammals. Vol. 6. The second book of dolphins.* Academic Press, London.

660 Kuehl, D.W. *et al.* (1991) Chemical residues in dolphins from the U.S. Atlantic coast including Atlantic bottlenose obtained during 1987/88 mass mortality. *Chemosphere*, **22**, 1071–1084.

661 Kuiken, T. & García Hartmann, M. (1992) Proceedings of 1st ECS workshop on cetacean pathology: dissection techniques and tissue sampling. *European Cetacean Society Newsletter, Special Issue,* **17**, 1–39.

662 Kuiken, T. *et al.* (1993) Adrenocortical hyperplasia, disease, and chlorinated hydrocarbons in the harbour porpoise (*Phocoena phocoena*). *Marine Pollution Bulletin*, **26**, 440–446.

663 Kuiken, T. *et al.* (1994) PCBs, cause of death and body condition in harbour porpoises (*Phocoena phocoena*) from British waters. *Aquatic Toxicology*, **28**, 13–28.

664 Kuiken, T. *et al.* (1994) Mass mortality of common dolphins (*Delphinus delphis*) in south west England due to incidental capture in fishing gear. *Veterinary Record*, **134**, 81–89.

665 Lafortuna C.L. *et al.* (1993) Respiratory pattern in free-ranging striped dolphins, pp. 241–246 in Evans, P.G.H. (ed.) *European research on cetaceans – 7.* European Cetacean Society.

666 Lafortuna C.L. *et al.* (1998) Locomotor behaviour and respiratory patterns in Mediterranean fin whales (*Balaenoptera physalus*) tracked in their summer feeding grounds, pp. 156–160 in Evans, P.G.H. & Parsons E.C.M. (eds.) *European research on cetaceans – 12.* European Cetacean Society.

667 Lahaye, V. *et al.* (2005) Long-term dietary segregation of common dolphins *Delphinus delphis* in the Bay of Biscay, determined using cadmium as an ecological tracer. *Marine Ecology Progress Series*, **305**, 275–285.

668 Laist, D.W. *et al.* (2001) Collisions between ships and great whales. *Marine Mammal Science*, **17**(1), 35–75.

669 Lambertsen, R.H. (1986) Disease of the common fin whale (*Balaenoptera physalus*): crassicaudiosis of the urinary system. *Journal of Mammalogy*, **67**, 353–366.

670 Larsen, F. & Kapel, F. (1981) Collection of biological material of minke whales off west Greenland 1979. *Report of the International Whaling Commission*, **31**, 279–287.

671 Law, R.J. (1994) Collaborative UK Marine Mammal Project: summary of data produced 1988–1992. *Fisheries Research Technical Report*, MAFF Direct. Fish. Res., Lowestoft, **97**, 1–42.

671a Law, R.J. *et al.* (1991) Concentrations of trace metals in the livers of marine mammals (seals, porpoises and dolphins) from waters around the British Isles. *Marine Pollution Bulletin*, **22**, 183–191.

672 Law, R.J. *et al.* (1992) Trace metals in the livers of marine mammals from the Welsh coast and the Irish Sea. *Marine Pollution Bulletin*, **24**, 296–304.

673 Law, R.J. *et al.* (1997) Metals and chlorobiphenyls in tissues of sperm whales (*Physeter macrocephalus*) and other cetacean species exploiting similar diets, pp. 79–90 in Jacques, T.G. & Lambertsen, R.H. (eds.) *Sperm whale deaths in the North Sea. Science and Management. Bulletin de L'Institut Royal des Sciences Naturelles de Belgique. Biologie,* **67**, supplement, 1–133.

674 Learmonth, J.A. *et al.* (2004) *Measurement of reproductive output in small cetaceans from the Northeast Atlantic.* BIOCET workpackage 5 – Final Report. Project Reference EVK3-2000-00027.

675 Learmonth, J.A. *et al.* (2004) *Dietary studies on small cetaceans in the NE Atlantic using stomach contents and fatty acid analyses.* BIOCET workpackage 6 – Final Report. Project Reference EVK3-2000-00027.

676 Leatherwood, J.S. *et al.* (1973) *Observations of sharks attacking porpoises* (Stenella *spp.* and Delphinus cf D. delphis*)*. Unpublished report no. 908 of the Naval Undersea Center, San Diego, CA.

677 Leatherwood, S. (1985) Further notes on cetaceans of Sri Lanka. *Cetology*, **50**, 1–12.

678 Leatherwood, S. & Reeves, R.R. (1983) *Sierra Club handbook of whales and dolphins.* Sierra Club books, San Francisco, CA

679 Leatherwood, S. & Reeves, R.R. (1989) Marine mammal research and conservation in Sri Lanka 1985–1986. *UNEP Marine Mammal Technical Report*, **1**, 1–138.

680 Leatherwood, S. *et al.* (1980) Distribution and movements of Risso's dolphin, *Grampus griseus*, in the eastern North Pacific. *Fisheries Bulletin, U.S.*, **77**, 951–963.

681 Leatherwood, S. *et al.* (1991) Records of the 'blackfish' (killer, false killer, pygmy killer and melon-headed whales) in the Indian Ocean, pp. 33–65 in Leatherwood, S. & Donovan, G.P. (eds.) *Cetaceans and cetacean research in the Indian Ocean sanctuary.* UNEP Marine Mammal Technical Report No. 3.

682 Leatherwood, S. *et al.* (1992) Marine mammal species confirmed from Philippine waters. *Siliman Journal*, **36**, 65–86.

683 Leatherwood, S. *et al.* (1993) Occurrence and sounds of Fraser's dolphins (*Lageodelphis hosei*) in the Gulf of Mexico. *Texas Journal of Science*, **45**, 349–354.

684 LeDuc, R.G. *et al.* (1999) Phylogenetic relationships among the delphinid cetaceans based on full cytochrome B sequences. *Marine Mammal Science*, **15**, 619–648.

685 Lefkaditou, E. & Poulopoulos, Y. (1998) Cephalopod remains in the stomach-content of beaked whales, *Ziphius cavirostris* (Cuvier, 1823), from the Ionian Sea. *Rapports et Procès-verbaux de la Commission Internationale de la Mer Méditerranée*, **35**, 460–461.

686 Lehman, J.W. & Peterle, T.J. (1971) DDT in Cetacea. *Investigations in Cetacea*, **3**, 349–351.

687 Leopold, M.F. & Camphuysen, C.J. (2006) *Bruinvisstrandingen in Nederland in 2006: achtergronden, leeftijdsverdeling, sexratio, voedselkeuze en mogelijke oorzaken.* Rapport (Ext. rep. C083/06). IJmuiden: IMARES (www.metis.wur.nl/result.cfm) (in Dutch).

688 Leopold, M.F. & Couperus, A.S. (1995) Sightings of Atlantic white-sided dolphins *Lagenorhynchus acutus* near the southeastern limit of the known range in the North-East Atlantic. *Lutra*, **38**, 77–80.

689 Leopold, M. *et al.* (1992) The elusive harbour porpoise exposed: strip transect counts off southwestern Ireland. *Netherlands Journal of Sea Research*, **29**, 395–402.

690 Lesage, V. & Kingsley, M.C.S. (1998) Updated status of the St Lawrence River population of the beluga, *Delphinaperus leucas*. *Canadian Field Naturalist*, **112**, 98–114.

691 Leung, Y.M. (1967) An illustrated key to the species of whale lice (amphipoda. Cyamidae) ectoparasites on Cetacea, with a guide to the literature. *Crustaceana*, **12**, 279–291.

692 Lick, R.R. (1991) Parasites from the digestive tract and food analysis of harbour porpoise *Phocoena phocoena* from German coastal waters, pp. 65–68 in Evans, P.G.H. (ed.). *European research on cetaceans – 5*. European Cetacean Society.

693 Lick, R. & Piatkowski, U. (1998) Stomach contents of a northern bottlenose whale (*Hyperoodon ampullatus*) stranded at Hiddensee, Baltic Sea. *Journal of the Marine Biological Association of the UK*, **78**, 643–650.

694 Lien, J. (1994) Entrapments of large cetaceans in passive inshore fishing gear in Newfoundland and Labrador (1979–1990), pp. 149–157 in Perrin, W.F. *et al.* (eds.) *Gillnets and Cetaceans. Report of the International Whaling Commission, Special Issue*, **15.**

695 Lien, J. & Barry, F. (1990) Status of Sowerby's beaked whale, *Mesoplodon bidens*, in Canada. *Canadian Field Naturalist*, **104**, 125–130.

696 Lien, J. *et al.* (1990) Multiple strandings of Sowerby's beaked whales, *Mesoplodon bidens*, in Newfoundland. *Canadian Field Naturalist*, **104**, 414–420.

697 Lindquist, O. (2000) *The North Atlantic gray whale (*Eschrichtius robustus*): an historical outline based on Icelandic, Danish-Icelandic, English and Swedish sources dating from ca 1000 AD to 1792.* Occasional Papers 1, Universities of St Andrews and Stirling.

698 Lindroth, A. (1962) Baltic salmon fluctuations 2: porpoise and salmon. *Report of the Institute of Freshwater Research Drottningholm*, **44**, 105–112.

699 Lindstrom, G. *et al.* (1999) Identification of 19 polybrominated diphenyl ethers (PBDEs) in long-finned pilot whale (*Globicephala melas*) from the Atlantic. *Archives of Environmental Contamination and Toxicology*, **36**(3), 355–363.

700 Lint, D.W. *et al.* (1990) Evolution and systematics of the Beluga whale *Delphinapterus leucas*, and other odontocetes: a molecular approach. *Canadian Bulletin of Fisheries and Aquatic Science*, **224**, 7–22.

701 Liret, C. *et al.* (1994) Foraging activity pattern of bottlenose dolphins, *Tursiops truncatus*, around Ile de Sein, Brittany, France, and its relations with some environmental parameters, pp. 188-191 in Evans, P.G.H. (ed.) *European research on cetaceans – 8*. European Cetacean Society.

702 Liret, C. *et al.* (1998) *English and French coastal* Tursiops *from Cornwall to the Bay of Biscay, 1996.* Photo-Identification Catalogue, Ministère de l'Environnement, France & Sea Watch Foundation, UK.

703 Lockyer, C. (1977) Observations on diving behaviour of the sperm whale *Physeter catodon*, pp. 591–609 in *A voyage of discovery.* Pergamon Press, Oxford.

704 Lockyer, C. (1981) Growth and energy budgets of large baleen whales from the Southern Hemisphere, pp. 379–487 in *Mammals in the seas. Volume III. General papers and large cetaceans.* Fisheries Series No. 5, FAO, Rome.

705 Lockyer, C. (1981) The age at sexual maturity in fin whales off Iceland. *Report of the International Whaling Commission*, **31**, 389–393.

706 Lockyer, C. (1984) Review of baleen whale (Mysticeti) reproduction and implications for management. *Report of the International Whaling Commission, Special Issue*, **6**, 27–50.

707 Lockyer, C.H. (1990) Review of incidents involving wild, sociable dolphins, worldwide, pp. 337–353 in Leatherwood, S. & Reeves, R.R. (eds.) *The bottlenose dolphin*. Academic Press, San Diego, CA.

708 Lockyer, C. (1995) Investigations of aspects of the life history of the harbour porpoise, *Phocoena phocoena*, in British waters. *Report of the International Whaling Commission, Special Issue*, **14**, 189–197.

709 Lockyer, C. (1999) Application of a new method to investigate population structure in the harbour porpoise, *Phocoena phocoena*, with special reference to the North and Baltic Seas. *Journal of Cetacean Research and Management*, **1**, 297–304.

710 Lockyer, C. (2003) A review of methods for defining population structure in the harbour porpoise (*Phocoena phocoena*), pp. 41–69 in Haug, T. *et al.* (ed.) *Harbour porpoises in the North Atlantic.* NAMMCO Scientific Publications, Volume 5, Tromsø.

711 Lockyer, C. (2003) Harbour porpoises (*Phocoena phocoena*) in the North Atlantic: Biological parameters, pp. 71–89. in Haug, T. *et al.* (ed.) *Harbour porpoises in the North Atlantic.* NAMMCO Scientific Publications, Volume 5, Tromsø.

712 Lockyer, C. (2007) All creatures great and smaller: a study in cetacean life history energetics. *Journal of the Marine Biological Assossication of the UK*, **87**, 1035–1045.

713 Lockyer, C. & Kinze, C. (2003) Status, ecology and life history of harbour porpoise *Phocoena phocoena*), in Danish waters, pp. 143–175 in Haug, T. *et al.* (ed.) *Harbour porpoises in the North Atlantic.* NAMMCO Scientific Publications, Volume 5, Tromsø.

714 Lockyer, C. & Martin, A.R. (1983) The sei whale off western Iceland. II. Age, growth and reproduction. *Report of the International Whaling Commission*, **33**, 465–476.

715 Lockyer, C.H. & Morris, R.J. (1986) The history and behaviour of a wild, sociable bottlenose dolphin (*Tursiops truncatus*) off the north coast of Cornwall. *Aquatic Mammals*, **12**, 3–16.

716 Lockyer, C. & Morris, R.J. (1987) Observations on diving behaviour and swimming speeds in a wild juvenile *Tursiops truncatus. Aquatic Mammals*, **13**, 27–30.

717 Lockyer, C. *et al.* (2003) Monitoring growth and energy utilisation of the harbour porpoise (*Phocoena phocoena*) in human care, pp. 107–120 in Haug, T. *et al.* (ed.) *Harbour porpoises in the North Atlantic.* NAMMCO Scientific Publications, Volume 5, Tromsø.

718 Lodi, L.F. *et al.* (1990) Mass stranding of *Peponocephala electra*

(Cetacea Globicephalinae) on Piracanga Beach, Bahia, Brazil. *Scientific Report of Cetacean Research*, **1**, 79–84.

719 Loeb, V. *et al.* (1997) Effects of sea-ice extent and krill or salp dominance in the Antarctic food web. *Nature, London*, **387**, 897–900.

720 López, A. *et al.* (2003) Fishery by-catches of marine mammals in Galician waters: results from on-board observations and an interview survey of fishermen. *Biological Conservation*, **111**, 25–40.

721 López, A. *et al.* (2004) Distribution patterns of small cetaceans in Galician waters. *Journal of the Marine Biological Association of the UK*, **84**, 283–294.

722 Lopez, J.C. & Lopez, D. (1985) Killer whales (*Orcinus orca*) of Patagonia, and their behavior of intentional stranding while hunting nearshore. *Journal of Mammalogy*, **66**, 181–183.

723 Luque, P.L. *et al.* (2006) Opportunistic sightings of killer whales from Scottish pelagic trawlers fishing for mackerel and herring off North Scotland (UK) between 2000 and 2006. *Aquatic Living Resources*, **19**, 403–410.

724 Lydekker, R. (1887) The *Cetacea* of the Suffolk Crag. *Quarterly Journal of the Geological Society of London*, **43**, 7–18.

725 Lyrholm, T. & Gyllensten, U. (1998) Global matrilineal population structure in sperm whales as indicated by mitochondrial DNA sequences. *Proceedings of the Royal Society of London Series B*, **265**, 1679–1684.

726 Lyrholm, T. *et al.* (1996) Low diversity and biased substitution patterns in the mitochondrial DNA control region of sperm whales: Implications for estimates of time since common ancestry. *Molecular Biology and Evolution*, **13**, 1318–1326.

727 Lyrholm, T. *et al.* (1999) Sex-biased dispersal in sperm whales: Contrasting mitochondrial and nuclear genetic structure of global populations. *Proceedings of the Royal Society of London Series B*, **266**, 347–354.

728 MacLeod, C.D. (2000) Review of the distribution of *Mesoplodon* species (order Cetacea, family Ziphiidae) in the North Atlantic. *Mammal Review*, **30**, 1–8.

729 MacLeod, C.D. (2005) *Niche partitioning, distribution and competition in North Atlantic beaked whales*. PhD thesis, University of Aberdeen.

730 MacLeod, C.D. (2006) A review of body length and sexual size dimorphism in the family *Ziphiidae*. *Journal of Cetacean Research and Management*, **7**, 301–308.

731 MacLeod, C.D. & Claridge, D.E. (1998) Scarring in a living population of dense-beaked whales (*Mesoplodon densirostris*) off Great Abaco Island, the Bahamas: levels, causes and insights provided on the natural history of the species, p. 215 in Evans, P.G.H. & Parsons, E.C.M. (eds.) *European research on cetaceans – 12*. European Cetacean Society.

732 MacLeod, C.D. *et al.* (2005) Climate change and the cetacean community of north-west Scotland. *Biological Conservation*, **124**, 477–483.

733 Madsen, O. *et al.* (2001) Parallel adaptive radiation in two major clades of placental mammals. *Nature, London*, **409**, 610–614.

734 Madsen, P.T. (2002) *Sperm whale sound production*. PhD dissertation, University of Aarhus.

735 Madsen, P.T. *et al.* (2004) Echolocation clicks of two free-ranging, oceanic delphinids with different food preferences: false killer whales *Pseudorca crassidens* and Risso's dolphins *Grampus griseus*. *Journal of Experimental Biology*, **207**(11), 1811–1823.

736 Madsen, P. *et al.* (2005) Biosonar performance of foraging beaked whales (*Mesoplodon densirostris*). *Journal of Experimental Biology*, **208**(2), 181–194.

737 Malik, S. *et al.* (1999) Assessment of mitochondrial DNA structuring and nursery use in the North Atlantic right whale (*Eubalaena glacialis*). *Canadian Journal of Zoology*, **77**, 1217–1222.

738 Malinga, M. & Kuklik, I. (1996) Food consumption of harbour porpoises (*Phocoena phocoena*) in Polish waters of the Baltic Sea, p. 260 in Evans, P.G.H. (ed.) *European research on cetaceans – 10*. European Cetacean Society.

739 Mandfredi, M.T. *et al.* (1992) Parasitological findings in striped dolphins, *Stenella coeruleoalba*, pp. 234–237 in Evans, P.G.H. (ed.) *European research on cetaceans – 6*. European Cetacean Society.

740 March, B.G.E. de *et al.* (2002) An overview of genetic relationships of Canadian and adjacent populations of belugas (*Delphinapterus leucas*) with emphasis on Baffin Bay and Canadian eastern arctic populations, pp. 17–38 in Heide-Jørgensen, M.P. & Wing, Ø. (eds.) *Belugas in the North Atlantic and the Russian Arctic*. NAMMCO Scientific Publications, Volume 4, Tromsø.

741 Marcovecchio, J.E. *et al.* (1994) Environmental contamination and marine mammals in coastal waters from Argentina: an overview. *Science of the Total Environment*, **154**, 141–151.

742 Marcuzzi, G. & Pilleri, G. (1971) On the zoogeography of Cetacea. *Investigations on Cetacea*, **3**, 101–170.

743 Marini, L. *et al.* (1996) Aerial behavior in fin whales (*Balaenoptera physalus*) in the Mediterranean Sea. *Marine Mammal Science*, **12**(3), 489–495.

744 Marsili, L. *et al.* (1992) Chlorinated hydrocarbons and heavy metals in tissues of *Stenella coeruleoalba* stranded along the Apulian and Sicilian coasts (summer 1991), pp. 105–107 in Evans, P.G.H. (ed.) *European research on cetaceans – 6*. European Cetacean Society.

745 Martin, A.R. (1990) *Whales and dolphins*. Salamander Books, London.

746 Martin, A.R. (1996) *The diet of harbour porpoises* (Phocoena phocoena) *in British waters*. IWC document SC/47/SM48.

747 Martin, A.R. & Clarke, M.R. (1986) The diet of sperm whales (*Physeter macrocephalus*) captured between Iceland and Greenland. *Journal of the Marine Biological Association of the UK*, **66**, 779–790.

748 Martin, A.R. & Rothery, P. (1993) Reproductive parameters of female long-finned pilot whales (*Globicephala melas*) around the Faroe Islands. *Report of the International Whaling Commission, Special Issue*, **14**, 263–304.

749 Martin, A.R. & Smith, T.G. (1992) Deep diving in wild, free-ranging beluga whales, *Delphinapterus leucas*. *Canadian Bulletin of Fisheries and Aquatic Sciences*, **49**, 462–466.

750 Martin, A.R. *et al.* (1984) Migration of humpback whales between the Caribbean and Iceland. *Journal of Mammalogy*, **65**, 330–333.

751 Martin, A.R. *et al.* (1987) Aspects of the biology of pilot whale (*Globicephala melaena*) in recent mass strandings on the British coast. *Journal of Zoology*, **211**, 11–23.

752 Martin, A.R. *et al.* (1993) Studying the behaviour and movements of high Arctic belugas with satellite telemetry. *Symposia of the Zoological Society of London*, **66**, 195–210.

753 Martin, A.R. *et al.* (1994) Diving behaviour of narwhals (*Monodon monoceros*) on their summer grounds. *Canadian Journal of Zoology*, **72**, 118–125.

754 Martin, A.R. *et al.* (1998) Dive form and function in belugas (*Delphinapterus leucas*) of the Canadian high Arctic. *Polar Biology*, **20**, 218–228.

755 Martin, T. (1996) *Beluga whales*. Colin Baxter Photography, Grantown-on-Spey.

756 Martín, V. *et al.* (1990) Records of Gervais' beaked whale *Mesoplodon europaeus* on the Canary Islands, p. 95 in Evans, P.G.H. *et al.* (eds.) *European research on cetaceans – 4*. European Cetacean Society.

757 Martín, V. *et al.* (2004) Mass stranding of beaked whales in the Canary Islands, p. 78 in Evans, P.G.H. & Miller, L.A. (eds.) *Workshop on active sonar and cetaceans, Gran Canaria*. European Cetacean Society.

758 Martinez, I. & Pastene, L.A. (1999) RAPD-typing of Central

and Eastern North Atlantic and Western North Pacific minke whales, *Balaenoptera acutorostrata*. *ICES Journal of Marine Science*, **56**, 640–651.

759 Martins, H.R. *et al.* (1985) A pygmy sperm whale, *Kogia breviceps* (Blainville, 1838) (Cetacea: Odontoceti) stranded on Faial Island, Azores, with notes on cephalopod beaks in stomach. Universidade dos Açores, Ponta Delgada. *Ciencias Biológicas*, **6**, 63–70.

760 Mate, B.R. & Stafford, M. (1994) Movements and dive behavior of a satellite-monitored Atlantic white-sided dolphin (*Lagenorhynchus acutus*) in the Gulf of Maine. *Marine Mammal Science*, **10**, 116–121.

761 Mate, B.R. *et al.* (2005) Movements and dive habits of a satellite-monitored longfinned pilot whale (*Globicephala melas*) in the northwest Atlantic. *Marine Mammal Science*, **21**(1), 136–144.

762 Maul, G.E. & Sergeant, D.E. (1977) New cetacean records from Madeira. *Bocagiana*, **43**, 1–8.

763 May-Collado, L. & Agnarsson, I. (2006) Cytochrome b and Bayesian inference of whale phylogeny. *Molecular Phylogenetics and Evolution*, **38**, 344–354.

764 Mayo, C.A. & Marx, M.K. (1990) Surface foraging behavior of the North Atlantic right whale and associated plankton characteristics. *Canadian Journal of Zoology*, **68**, 2214–2220.

765 McAlpine, D.F. (2002) Pygmy and dwarf sperm whales (*Kogia breviceps* and *Kogia sima*), pp. 1007–1009 in Perrin, W.F. *et al.* (eds.) *Encyclopedia of marine mammals*. Academic Press, San Diego, CA.

766 McAlpine, D.F. *et al.* (1997) New records for the pygmy sperm whale, *Kogia breviceps* (Physeteridae) from Atlantic Canada with notes on diet and parasites. *Marine Mammal Science*, **13**(4), 701–704.

767 McBrearty, D.A. *et al.* (1986) Observations on small cetaceans in the north-east Atlantic Ocean and the Mediterranean Sea: 1978–1982, pp. 225–249 in Bryden, M.M. & Harrison, R. (eds.) *Research on dolphins*. Clarendon Press, Oxford,.

768 McCann, C. (1964) The supposed occurrence of True's beaked whale (*Mesoplodon mirus*) on the Scottish coast – a correction. *Scottish Naturalist*, **71**, 78–80.

769 McCann, C. & Talbot, F.H. (1963) The occurrence of True's beaked whale (*Mesoplodon mirus* True) in South African waters, with a key to South African species of the genus. *Proceedings of the Linnaean Society of London*, **175**, 137–144.

770 McKenzie, C. *et al.* (1998) Organochlorine contaminants in 13 marine mammal species stranded on the coast of Scotland, 1990–96. *SOAEFD Scottish Fisheries Working Paper, Marine Laboratory, Aberdeen*.

771 McKenzie, C. *et al.* (1998) Concentrations and patterns of organic contaminants in Atlantic white-sided dolphins (*Lagenorhynchus acutus*) from Irish and Scottish coastal waters. *Environmental Pollution*, **98**, 15–27.

772 McSweeney, D. *et al.* (2007) Site fidelity, associations, and movements of Cuvier's (*Ziphius cavirostris*) and Blainville's (*Mesoplodon densirostris*) beaked whales off the island of Hawai'i. *Marine Mammal Science*. In press.

773 Mead, J.G. (1975) Anatomy of the external nasal passages and facial complex of the *Delphinidae*. *Smithsonian Contributions, Zoology*, **207**, 1–72.

774 Mead, J.G. (1984) Survey of reproductive data for the beaked whales (Ziphiidae), pp. 91–96 in Perrin, W.F. *et al.* (eds.) *Reproduction in whales, dolphins and porpoises. Report of the International Whaling Commission, Special Issue*, **6**.

775 Mead, J.G. (1989) Beaked whales of the genus *Mesoplodon*, pp. 349–430 in Ridgway, S.H. & Harrison, R. (eds.) *Handbook of marine mammals. Vol. 4: River dolphins and the larger toothed whales*. Academic Press, London.

776 Mead, J.G. (1989) Bottlenose whales *Hyperoodon ampullatus* (Forster, 1770) and *Hyperoodon planifrons* Flower, 1882, pp. 321–348 in Ridgway, S.H. & Harrison, R. (eds.) *Handbook of marine mammals. Vol. 4: River dolphins and the larger toothed whales*. Academic Press, London.

777 Mead, J.G. & Mitchell, E.D. (1984) Atlantic gray whales, pp. 33–53 in Jones, M.L. *et al.* (eds.) *The gray whale* Eschrichtius robustus. Academic Press, Orlando, FL.

778 Meador, J.P. *et al.* (1993) Toxic metals in pilot whales (*Globicephala melaena*) from strandings in 1986 and 1990 on Cape Cod, Massachusetts. *Canadian Journal of Fisheries and Aquatic Science*, **50**, 2698–2706.

779 Messenger, S.L. & McGuire, J.A. (1998) Morphology, molecules, and the phylogenetics of cetaceans. *Systematic Biology*, **47**, 90–124.

780 Meynier, L. (2004) *Food and feeding ecology of the common dolphin*, Delphinus delphis, *in the Bay of Biscay: intraspecific dietary variation and food transfer modelling*. MSc thesis, University of Aberdeen.

781 Michaud, R. & Béland, P. (2001) Looking for trends in the endangered St. Lawrence beluga population. A critique of Kingsley, M.C.S. 1998. *Marine Mammal Science*, **17**, 206–212.

782 Mignucci-Giannoui, A.A. (1996) *Marine mammal strandings in Puerto Rico and the United States and British Virgin Islands*. PhD thesis, University of Puerto Rico.

783 Mikkelsen, A.M.H. & Lund, A. (1994) Intraspecific variation in the dolphins *Lagenorhynchus albirostris* and *L. acutus* (Mammalia: Cetacea) in metrical and non-metrical skull characters, with remarks on occurrence. *Journal of Zoology*, **234**, 289–299.

784 Mikkelsen, A.M.H. & M. Sheldrick (1992) The first recorded stranding of a melon-headed whale (*Peponocephala electra*) on the European coast. *Journal of Zoology*, **227**, 326–329.

785 Milinkovitch, M.C. *et al.* (1993) Revised phylogeny of whales suggested by mitochondrial ribosomal DNA sequences. *Nature, London*, **361**, 346–348.

786 Miller, L. *et al.* (1995) The click-sounds of narwhals (*Monodon monoceros*) in Inglefield Bay, North-west Greenland. *Marine Mammal Science*, **11**(4), 491–502.

787 Minasian, S.M. *et al.* (1984) *The world's whales; the complete illustrated guide*. Smithsonian Books, Washington, DC.

788 Mirimin, L. (2007) *Molecular genetics of three dolphin species occurring in the eastern North Atlantic*. PhD thesis, University College Cork.

789 Mirimin, L. *et al.* (2007) *Stock structure in the common dolphin* Delphinus delphis *in the Northeast Atlantic: analysis of genetic material*. NECESSITY Contract 501605 Periodic Activity Report No 2 – Annex 8.1.a.

790 Mitchell, E. (1970) Pigmentation pattern evolution in delphinid cetaceans: an essay in adaptive coloration. *Canadian Journal of Zoology*, **48**, 717–740.

791 Mitchell, E.D. (1974) Present status of Northwest Atlantic fin and other whale stocks, pp. 108–169 in Schevill, W.E. (ed.) *The whale problem*. Harvard University Press, Cambridge, MA.

792 Mitchell, E.D. (1975) *Porpoise, dolphin and small whale fisheries of the world*, pp. 1–29 Monograph 3, IUCN, Gland.

793 Mitchell, E. (1977) Evidence that the northern bottlenose whale is depleted. *Reports of the International Whaling Commission*, **27**, 195–203.

794 Mitchell, E.D. (1986) Finner whales, pp. 36–45 in Haley, D. (ed.) *Marine mammals of the eastern North Pacific and Arctic waters*. Pacific Search Press, Seattle, WA.

795 Mitson, R.B. (1990) Very-high-frequency acoustic emissions from the white-beaked dolphin (*Lagenorhynchus albirostris*), pp. 283–294 in Thomas, J.A & Kastelein, R.A. (eds.) *Sensory abilities of cetaceans. Laboratory and field evidence*. Plenum Press, New York.

796 Mitson, R.B. & Morris, R.J. (1988) Evidence of high frequency acoustic emissions from the white-beaked dolphin (*Lagenorhynchus albirostris*). *Journal of the Acoustical Society of America*, **83**, 825–826.

797 Miyazaki, N. (1980) Catch records of cetaceans off the coast of the Kii Peninsula. *Memoirs of the Natural Science Museum,* **12**, 69–82.

798 Miyazaki, N. (1983) Catch statistics of small cetaceans taken in Japanese waters. *Report of the International Whaling Commission,* **33**, 621–631.

799 Miyazaki, N. & Nishiwaki, M. (1978) School structure of the striped dolphin of the Pacific coast of Japan. *Scientific Reports of the Whales Research Institute,* **30**, 65–115.

800 Miyazaki, N. & Shikano, C. (1997) Preliminary study on comparative skull morphology and vertebral formula among the six species of the genus *Lagenorhynchus* (Cetacea: Delphinidae). *Mammalia,* **61**, 573–587.

801 Miyazaki, N. & Wada, S. (1978) Observations on cetacea during whale marking cruise in the western tropical Pacific, 1976. *Scientific Reports of the Whales Research Institute,* **30**, 179–195.

802 Miyazaki, N. *et al* (1998) Biological analysis of a mass stranding of melon-headed whales (*Peponocephala electra*) at Aoshima, Japan. *Bulletin of the National Science Museum, Tokyo, Series A,* **24**, 31–60.

803 Møhl, B. & Andersen, S.H. (1973) Echolocation: high frequency component in the click of the harbour porpoise (*Phocoena phocoena* L.). *Journal of the Acoustical Society of America,* **54**, 1368–1372.

804 Møhl, B.M. *et al.* (2000) Sperm whale clicks: directionality and source level revisited. *Journal of the Acoustical Society of America,* **107**, 638–648.

805 Møhl Hansen, U. (1954) Investigations on reproduction and growth of the porpoise (*Phocoena phocoena*) in the Baltic. *Vidensjabelige Meddelelser fra Dansk Naturhistirisk Forening,* **116**, 369–396.

806 Montero, R. & Martin, V. (1992) First account on the biology of Cuvier's whales, *Ziphius cavirostris*, in the Canary Islands, pp. 97–99 in Evans, P.G.H. (ed. *European research on cetaceans – 6.* European Cetacean Society.

807 Moore, J.C. (1966) Diagnoses and distributions of of beaked whales of the genus *Mesoplodon* known from North American waters, pp. 32–61 in Norris, K.S. (ed.) *Whales, dolphins, and porpoises.* University of California Press, Berkeley, CA.

808 Moore, M.J. *et al.* (2007) Right whale mortality: a message from the dead to the living, pp. 358–379 in Kraus, S.D. & Rolland, R.M. (eds.) *The urban whale: North Atlantic right whales at the crossroads.* Harvard University Press, Cambridge, MA.

809 Moore, S.E. & Ridgway, S.H. (1995) Whistles produced by common dolphins from Southern California Bight. *Aquatic Mammals,* **21**, 51–63.

810 Moore, S.E. *et al.* (1988) Analysis of calls of killer whales, *Orcinus orca*, from Iceland and Norway. *Rit Fiskideildar,* **11**, 225–250.

811 Morimitsu, T. *et al.* (1986) Parasitogenic octavius neuropathy as a cause of mass stranding of Odontoceti. *Journal of Parasitology,* **72**, 469–472.

812 Morimitsu, T. *et al.* (1987) Mass stranding of odontoceti caused by parasitogenic eighth cranial neuropathy. *Journal of Wildlife Diseases,* **23**, 586–590.

813 Morizur, Y. *et al.* (1999) Incidental catches of marine-mammals in pelagic trawl fisheries of the northeast Atlantic. *Fisheries Research,* **41**, 297–307.

814 Mörzer Bruyns, W.F.J. (1971) *Field guide of whales and dolphins.* Mees, Amsterdam.

815 Moulins, A. *et al.* (2007) Aspects of the distribution of Cuvier's beaked whale (*Ziphius cavirostris*) in relation to topographic features in the Pelagos Sanctuary (north-western Mediterranean Sea). *Journal of the Marine Biological Association of the UK,* **87**, 177–186.

816 Muir, A.I. *et al.* (2000) *Trends in cetacean strandings on the British coastline 1994–1999.* Report to DETR. Natural History Museum, London.

817 Muir, D.C.G. *et al.* (1988) Organochlorine chemical and heavy metal contaminants in white-beaked dolphins (*Lagenorhynchus albirostris*) and pilot whales (*Globicephala melaena*) from the coast of Newfoundland, Canada. *Archives of Environmental Contamination and Toxicology,* **17**, 613–629.

818 Mullin, K.D. *et al.* (1991) *Cetaceans on the upper continental slope in the north-central Gulf of Mexico.* OCS Study MMS 91-0027. Report from U.S. National Marine Fisheries Service Pascagoula, MS, for U.S. Minerals Management Service, New Orleans, LA.

819 Murphy, S. (2004) *The biology and ecology of the common dolphin* Delphinus delphis *in the North-east Atlantic.* PhD thesis, University College Cork.

820 Murphy, S. (2006) Species identification, sexual dimorphism and geographical cranial variation of common dolphins (*Delphinus*) in the eastern North Atlantic. *Marine Mammal Science,* **22**(3), 573–599.

821 Murphy, S. & Rogan, E. (2006) External morphology of the short-beaked common dolphin *Delphinus delphis*: growth, allometric relationships and sexual dimorphism. *Acta Zoologica,* **87**, 315–329.

822 Murphy, S. *et al.* (2005) Evidence of a violent interaction between *Delphinus delphis* L. and *Tursiops truncatus* (Montagu). *Irish Naturalists' Journal,* **28,** 42–43.

823 Murphy, S. *et al.* (2005) Mating strategy in the male common dolphin *Delphinus delphis*: what gonadal analysis tells us. *Journal of Mammalogy,* **86**, 1247–1258.

824 Murphy, S. *et al.* (2006) Taxonomic status and geographical cranial variation of common dolphins (*Delphinus*) in the eastern North Atlantic. *Marine Mammal Science,* **22**, 573–599.

825 Murray, S.O. *et al.* (1998) Characterizing the graded structure of false killer whale (*Pseudorca crassidens*) vocalizations. *Journal of the Acoustical Society of America,* **104**(3), 1679–1688.

826 Murray, T. & Murphy, S. (2003) Common dolphin *Delphinus delphis* L. strandings on the Mullet Peninsula. *Irish Naturalists' Journal,* **27**, 240–241.

827 Nachtigall, P.E. *et al.* (eds.) (1995) *Harbour porpoises, laboratory studies to reduce bycatch.* De Spil Publishers, Woerden, Netherlands.

828 Nagorsen, D. (1985) *Kogia simus. Mammalian Species,* **239**, 1–6.

829 NAMMCO (1993) *NAMMCO Scientific Committee. Report from the working group of bottlenose and killer whales.* NAMMCO, Copenhagen.

830 NAMMCO (2000) Report of the NAMMCO Scientific Committee working group on the population status of beluga and narwhal in the North Atlantic, pp. 153–188 in *1999 Annual Report of the North Atlantic Marine Mammal Commission.* Tromsø, Norway.

831 Natoli, A. *et al.* (2003) Patterns of population subdivision and genetic variability of common bottlenose dolphins (*Tursiops truncatus*) and common dolphins (*Delphinus delphis*) in the Black Sea, Mediterranean Sea and eastern North Atlantic. In *Report of the International Whaling Commission SC/55/SM11.*

832 Natoli, A. *et al.* (2005) Habitat structure and the dispersal of male and female bottlenose dolphins (*Tursiops truncatus*). *Proceedings of the Royal Society of London Series B,* **272,** 1217–1226.

833 Natoli, A. *et al.* (2006) Phylogeography and alpha taxonomy of the common dolphin (*Delphinus* sp.). *Journal of Evolutionary Biology,* **19**, 943–954.

834 Natural History Museum, London. Unpublished data

835 Nawojchik, R. *et al.* (2003) Movements and dive behavior of two stranded, rehabilitated long-finned pilot whales (*Globicephala melas*) in the Northwest Atlantic. *Marine Mammal Science,* **19**(1), 232–239.

836 Nemoto, T. (1959) Food of baleen whales with reference to

whale movements. *Scientific Reports of the Whales Research Institute,* **14,** 149–290.

837 Nemoto, T. (1962) Food of baleen whales collected in recent Japanese Antarctic whaling expeditions. *Scientific Reports of the Whales Research Institute,* **16,** 89–103.

838 Nemoto, T. (1964) School of baleen whales in the feeding areas. *Sceintific Reports of the Whales Research Institute,* **18,** 89–110.

839 Nemoto, T. (1970) Feeding pattern of baleen whales in the ocean, pp. 241–252 in Steele, J.H. (ed.) *Marine food chains.* Oliver & Boyd, Edinburgh.

840 Nemoto, T. & Kawamura, A. (1977) Characteristics of food habits and distribution of baleen whales with special reference to the abundance of North Pacific sei and Bryde's whales. *Report of the International Whaling Commission, Special Issue,* **1,** 80–87.

841 NERC (1983) Contaminants in marine top predators. *NERC Publication Series C,* **23,** 1–30.

842 Neumann, D.R. *et al.* (2002) Photo-identification of short-beaked common dolphins (*Delphinus delphis*) in north-east New Zealand: a photo-catalogue of recognisable individuals. *New Zealand Journal of Marine and Freshwater Research,* **36,** 593–604.

843 Neumann, D.R. *et al.* (2002) Identifying sexually mature, male short-beaked common dolphins (*Delphinus delphis*) at sea, based on the presence of a postanal hump. *Aquatic Mammals,* **28,** 181–187.

844 Neve, P.B. (2000) The diet of the minke whale in Greenland – a short review, pp. 92–96 in Víkingsson, G.A. & Kapel, F.O. (eds.) *Minke, harp and hooded seals: major predators in the North Atlantic ecosystem.* Scientific Publications Volume 2, NAMMCO, Tromsø.

845 Nielsen, J.B. *et al.* (2000) Toxic metals and selenium in blood from pilot whales (*Globicephala melas*) and sperm whales (*Physeter catodon*). *Marine Pollution Bulletin,* **40**(4), 348–351.

846 Nishiwaki, M. (1963) Taxonomical consideration on genera of *Delphinidae. Scientific Report of the Whales Research Institute,* **17,** 93–103.

847 Nishiwaki, M. (1964) Revision of 'Taxonomical consideration on genera of *Delphinidae'. Scientific Reports of the Whales Research Institute,* **18,** 171–172.

848 Nishiwaki, M. (1972) General biology, pp. 3–204 in Ridgway, S.H. (ed.) *Mammals of the sea. Biology and medicine.* C.C. Thomas, Springfield, IL.

849 Nishiwaki, M. & Norris, K.S. (1966) A new genus, *Peponocephala,* for the odontocete cetacean species *Electra electra. Scientific Reports of the Whales Research Institute,* **20,** 95–100.

850 Nishiwaki, N. & Oguro, N. (1972) Catch of Cuvier's beaked whales off Japan in recent years. *Scientific Reports of the Whales Research Institute,* **24,** 35–41.

851 Nishiwaki, M. & Tobayama, T. (1982) Morphological study on the hybrid between *Tursiops* and *Pseudorca. Scientific Reports of the Whales Research Institute,* **34,** 109–121.

852 Nordøy, E.S. *et al.* (1995) Food requirements of Northeast Atlantic minke whales, pp. 307–317 in Blix, A.S. *et al.* (eds.) *Whales, seals, fish and man.* Elsevier, Amsterdam.

853 Nores, C. & Pérez, M.C. (1982) Primera cita de un cachalote pigmeo, *Kogia breviceps* (Blainville, 1838) (Mammalia, Cetacea) para las costas peninsulares españolas. *Boletin de Ciencias del Real Istituto de Estudios Asturianos,* **29** (in Spanish).

854 Nores, C. & Pérez, C. (1988) Overlapping range between *Globicephala macrorhynchus* and *Globicephala melaena* in the northeastern Atlantic. *Mammalia,* **52,** 51–55.

855 Northridge, S.P. (1988) *Marine mammals and fisheries.* Unpublished report to Wildlife Link. International Institute for Environment and Development & Marine Resources Assessment Group, Centre for Environmental Technology, Imperial College of Science & Technology, London.

856 Northridge, S.P. (1991) *An updated world review of interactions between marine mammals and fisheries.* FAO Fisheries Technical Paper 251, Suppl. 1, pp.1–58.

857 Northridge, S.P. *et al.* (1995) Distribution and relative abundance of harbour porpoises (*Phocoena phocoena* L.), white-beaked dolphins (*Lagenorhynchus albirostris* Gray), and minke whales (*Balaenoptera acutorostrata* Lacepède) around the British Isles. *ICES Journal of Marine Science,* **52,** 55–66.

858 Northridge, S. *et al.* (1997) White-beaked *Lagenorhynchus albirostris* and Atlantic white-sided dolphin *L. acutus* distributions in Northwest European and US North Atlantic waters. *Report of the International Whaling Commission,* **47,** 707–805.

859 Northridge, S. *et al.* (2006) *Final PETRACET report to the European commission.* Project EC/FISH/2003/09, 1735R07D, June 2006.

860 Notarbartolo di Sciara, G. (1987) Killer whale in the Mediterranean Sea. *Marine Mammal Science,* **3**(4), 356–360.

861 Notarbartolo di Sciara, G. *et al.* (1996) Reactions of fin whales to approaching vessels assessed by means of a laser rangefinder, pp. 38–42 in Evans, P.G.H. (ed.) *European research on cetaceans – 10.* European Cetacean Society.

862 Notarbartolo di Sciara, G. *et al.* (1997) Birth at sea of a false killer whale, *Pseudorca crassidens. Marine Mammal Science,* **13**(3), 508–511.

863 Notarbartolo di Sciara, G. *et al.* (2003) The fin whale, *Balaenoptera physalus* (L. 1758), in the Mediterranean Sea. *Mammal Review,* **33**(2), 105–150.

864 Ó Cadhla, O. *et al.* (2003) *Cetaceans and seabirds of Ireland's Atlantic margin. Volume II – Cetacean distribution and abundance.* Report on research conducted under the 1997 Irish Petroleum Infrastructure Programme: Rockall Studies Group projects 98/6, 99/38 and 00/13.

865 O'Corry-Crowe, G.M. (2002) Beluga whale *Delphinapterus leucas,* pp. 94–99 in Perrin, W.F. *et al.* (eds.) *Encyclopaedia of marine mammals.* Academic Press, San Diego, CA.

866 O'Corry-Crowe, G.M. *et al.* (1997) Phylogeography, population structure and dispersal patterns of the beluga whale *Delphinapterus leucas* in the western Nearctic revealed by mitochondrial DNA. *Molecular Ecology,* **6,** 955–970.

867 O'Riordan C.E. & Bruton, T.E. (1986) Notes on the crania of Euphrosyne dolphin *Stenella coeruleoalba* (Meyen) in the collection of the National Museum of Ireland. *Irish Naturalists' Journal,* **22,** 162–163.

868 O'Shea, T.J. *et al.* (1980) Organochlorine pollutants in small cetaceans from the Pacific and South Atlantic oceans, Nov 1968 – June 1976. *Pesticides Monitoring Journal,* **14,** 35–46.

869 O'Shea, T.J. *et al.* (1991) *Nasitrema sp.*-associated encephalitis in striped dolphin (*Stenella coeruleoalba*) stranded in the Gulf of Mexico. *Journal of Wildlife Diseases,* **27,** 706–709.

870 Odell, D.K. (1987) The mystery of marine mammal strandings. *Cetus,* **7,** 2–6.

871 Odell, D.K. & McClune, K.M. (1999) False killer whale *Pseudorca crassidens* (Owen, 1846), pp. 213–243 in Ridgway, S.H. & Harrison, R.J. (eds.) *Handbook of marine mammals, Vol. 6, The second book of dolphins.* Academic Press, London.

872 Ohlin, A. (1893) Some remarks on the bottlenose-whale (*Hyperoodon*). *Lunds Universitets Arsskrift,* **29,** 1–13.

873 Ohsumi, S. (1979) Interspecies relationships among some biological parameters in cetaceans and estimation of natural mortality coefficient of the southern hemisphere minke whale. *Report of the International Whaling Commission,* **29,** 397–406.

874 Ohsumi, S. *et al.* (1970) Stock of the Antarctica minke whale. *Scientific Reports of the Whales Research Institute,* **22,** 75–125.

875 Øien, N. (1988) The distribution of killer whales (*Orcinus orca*) in the North Atlantic based on Norwegian catches,

1938–1981, and incidental sightings, 1967–1987. *Rit Fiskideildar*, **11**, 65–78.

876 Øien, N. (1996) *Lagenorhynchus* species in Norwegian waters as revealed from incidental observations and recent sighting surveys. *International Whaling Commission*, SC/48/SM **15**, 1–7, figs 1–8.

877 Olesiuk, P.F. *et al.* (1990) Life history and population dynamics of resident killer whales (*Orcinus orca*) in the coastal waters of British Columbia and Washington State. *Report of the International Whaling Commission, Special Issue*, **12**, 209–243.

878 Olsen, E. & Holst, J.C. (2001) A note on common minke whale (*Balaenoptera acutorostrata*) diets in the Norwegian Sea and the North Sea. *Journal of Cetacean Research and Management*, **3**(2), 179–183.

879 Omura H. (1975) Osteological study of the minke whale from the Antarctic. *Scientific Reports of the Whales Research Institute*, **27**, 1–36.

880 Omura, H., *et al.* (1955) Beaked whale *Berardius bairdi* of Japan with notes on *Ziphius cavirostris*. *Scientific Reports of the Whales Research Institute*, **10**, 89–132.

881 Omura, H. *et al.* (1969) Black right whales in the North Pacific. *Scientific Reports of the Whales Research Institute*, **21**, 1–78.

882 Omura, H. *et al.* (1984) A pygmy sperm whale accidentally taken by drift net in the North Pacific. *Scientific Reports of the Whales Research Institute*, **35**, 183–193.

883 Oort, E.D. van (1926) Over eenige aan de kust van Nederland waargenomen cetaceeën-soorten. *Zoologische Mededeelingen Leiden*, **9**, 211-214, pl. II (in Dutch).

884 Osborne, R.W. (1986) A behavioral budget of Puget Sound killer whales, in Kirkevold, B.C. & Lockard, J.S. (eds.) *Behavioral biology of killer whales*, pp. 211–249. A.R. Liss, New York.

885 Osterhaus, A.D.M.E. *et al.* (1993) Isolation of a virus with rhabdovirus morphology from a white-beaked dolphin (*Lagenorhynchus albirostris*). *Archives of Virology*, **133**, 189–193.

885a Ottensmeier, C.A. & Whitehead, H. (2003) Behavioural evidence for social units in long-finned pilot whales. *Canadian Journal of Zoology*, **81**(8), 1327–1338.

886 Otterlind, G. (1976) The harbour porpoise (*Phocoena phocoena*) endangered in Swedish waters. *International Council for the Exploration of the Sea, Doc.C.M.* 1976/N, **16**, 1–7.

887 Overholtz, W.J. & Waring, G.T. (1991) Diet composition of pilot whales *Globicephala* sp. and common dolphins *Delphinus delphis* in the mid-Atlantic bight during spring 1989. *Fisheries Bulletin*, **89**, 723–728.

888 Owen, R. (1846) *A history of British fossil mammals and birds*. London.

889 Paggi, L. *et al.* (1998) A new species of *Anisakis* Dujardin, 1845 (Nematoda, Anisakidae) from beaked whales (Ziphiidae): allozyme and morphological evidence. *Systematic Parasitology*, **40**, 161–174.

890 Palacios, D.M. & Mate, B.R. (1996) Attack by false killer whales (*Pseudorca crassidens*) on sperm whales (*Physeter macrocephalus*) in the Galapagos. *Marine Mammal Science*, **12**, 582–587.

891 Palsbøll, P.J. (1990) Preliminary results of RFLP analysis of mtDNA in minke whales from the Davis Strait, northeast and central Atlantic. *Report of the International Whaling Commission* SC/42/NHMi35.

892 Palsbøll, P. *et al.* (1997) Distributionn of mt DNA haplotypes in narwhals, *Monodon monoceros*. *Heredity*, **78**, 284–292.

893 Palsbøll, P.J. *et al.* (2002) Analysis of mitochondrial control region nucleotide sequences from Baffin Bay belugas (*Delphinapterus leucas*) with emphasis on Baffin Bay and Canadian eastern Arctic populations, pp. 39–50 in Heide-Jørgensen, M.P. & Wing, Ø. (eds.) *Belugas in the North Atlantic and the Russian Arctic*. NAMMCO Scientific

Publications, Volume 4, Tromsø.

894 Palsbøll, P.J. *et al.* (2004) Discerning between recurrent gene flow and recent divergence under a finite-site mutation model applied to North Atlantic and Mediterranean Sea fin whale *(Balaenoptera physalus)* populations. *Evolution*, **58**(3), 670–675.

895 Panigada, S. *et al.* (1999) How deep can baleen whales dive? *Marine Ecology Progress Series*, **187**, 309–311.

896 Panigada, S. *et al.* (2006) Mediterranean fin whales at risk from fatal ship strikes. *Marine Pollution Bulletin*, **52**, 1287–1298.

897 Papastavrou, V. *et al.* (1989) Diving behaviour of the sperm whale, *Physeter macrocephalus*, off the Galapagos Islands. *Canadian Journal of Zoology*, **67**, 839–846.

898 Parks, S.E. & Clark, C.W. (2007) Acoustic communication: social sounds and the potential impacts of noise, pp. 310–332 in Kraus, S.D. & Rolland, R.M. (eds.) (2007) *The urban whale: North Atlantic right whales at the crossroads*. Harvard University Press, Cambridge, MA.

899 Parks, S.E. & Tyack, P.L. (2005) Sound production by North Atlantic right whales *(Eubalaena glacialis)* in surface active groups. *Journal of the Acoustical Society of America*, **117**(5), 3297–3306.

900 Parks, S.E. *et al.* (2005) The gunshot sound produced by male North Atlantic right whales *(Eubalaena glacialis)* and its potential function in reproductive advertisement. *Marine Mammal Science*, **21**(3), 458–475.

901 Parsons, K.M. *et al.* (2002) Mitochondrial genetic diversity and population structuring of UK bottlenose dolphins (*Tursiops truncatus*): is the NE Scotland population demographically and geographically isolated? *Biological Conservation*, **108**, 175–182.

902 Pascoe, P.L. (1986) Size data and stomach contents of common dolphins, *Delphinus delphis*, near Plymouth. *Journal of the Marine Biological Association of the UK*, **66**, 319–322.

903 Pastor, X. & Simmonds, M. (1992) *The Mediterranean striped dolphin die-off*. Proceedings of the Mediterranean striped dolphin mortality, international workshop, Palma de Mallorca, 4–5 November 1991. Greenpeace.

904 Patterson, I.A.P. *et al.* (1998) Evidence for infanticide in bottlenose dolphins: An explanation for violent interactions with harbour porpoises? *Proceedings of the Royal Society of London Series B*, **265**, 1167–1170.

905 Pauly, D *et al.* (1998) Fishing down marine food webs. *Science*, **279**, 860.

906 Payne, R. & McVay, S. (1971) Songs of humpback whales. *Science*, **173**, 585–597.

907 Payne, R. & Payne, K. (1972) Underwater sounds of southern right whales. *Zoologica*, **56**, 159–165.

908 Payne, R. *et al.* (1983) External features in southern right whales (*Eubalaena australis*) and their use in identifying individuals, pp. 371–445 in Payne, R. (ed.) *Communication and behavior of whales*. Westview Press, Boulder, CO.

909 Peacock, A.D. *et al.* (1936) The false killer whales stranded in the Tay Estuary. *The Scottish Naturalist*, **220**, 93–104.

910 Perrin, W.F. (1975) Variation of spotted and spinner porpoise (genus *Stenella*) in the eastern Pacific and Hawaii. *Bulletin of the Scripps Institute of Oceanography*, **21**, 1–206.

911 Perrin, W.F. (1976) First record of the melon-headed whale, *Peponocephala electra* in the eastern Pacific, with a summary of world distribution. *Fisheries Bulletin, U.S.*, **74**, 457–458.

912 Perrin, W.F. (1994) Report of the workshop on mortality of cetaceans in passive fishing nets and traps. *Report of the International Whaling Commission, Special Issue*, **15**, 6–71.

913 Perrin, W.F. (2003) Common dolphins, pp. 245–248 in Perrin, W.F. *et al.* (eds.) *Encyclopedia of marine mammals*. Academic Press, London.

914 Perrin, W.F. & Brownell, R.L. (2002) Minke whales *Balaenoptera acutorostrata* and *B. bonaerensis*, pp. 750–754 in Perrin, W.F. *et al.* (eds.) *Encyclopedia of marine mammals*.

Academic Press, London.

915 Perrin, W.F. & Reilly, S.B. (1984) Reproductive parameters of dolphins and small whales of the family Delphinidae. *Report of the International Whaling Commission, Special Issue,* **6**, 97–133.

916 Perrin, W.F. *et al.* (1973) Rediscovery of Fraser's dolphin *Lagenodelphis hosei. Nature, London,* **241**, 345–350.

917 Perrin, W.F. *et al.* (1987) Revision of the spotted dolphins, *Stenella* spp. *Marine Mammal Science,* **3**, 99–170.

918 Perrin, W.F. *et al.* (1994) Fraser's dolphin *Lagenodelphis hosei* Fraser, 1956, pp. 225–240 in Ridgway, S.H. & Harrison, R. (eds.) *Handbook of marine mammals.* Academic Press, London.

919 Perrin, W.F. *et al.* (1994) *Gillnets and cetaceans. Report of the International Whaling Commission, Special Issue,* **15**.

920 Perrin, W.F. *et al.* (1994) Striped dolphin *Stenella coeruleoalba* (Meyen, 1933), pp. 129–159 in Ridgway, S.H. & Harrison, R. (eds.) *Handbook of marine mammals, Vol. 5.* Academic Press, London.

921 Perrin, W.F. *et al.* (1995) An anomalously pigmented form of the short-beaked common dolphin (*Delphinus delphis*) from the Southwestern Pacific, Eastern Pacific, and the Eastern Atlantic. *Marine Mammal Science,* **11**, 241–247.

922 Perrin, W.F. *et al.* (eds.) (2002) *Encyclopaedia of marine mammals.* Academic Press, San Diego, CA.

923 Perryman, W.L. (2002) Melon-headed whale *Peponocephala electra*, pp. 733–735 in Perrin, W.F. *et al.* (eds.) *Encyclopaedia of marine mammals.* Academic Press, San Diego, CA.

924 Perryman, W.L. & Foster, T.C. (1980) *Preliminary report on predation by small whales, mainly the false killer whale* (Pseudorca crassidens) *on dolphin* (Stenella *spp. and* Delphinus delphis) *in the eastern tropical Pacific.* Southwest Fisheries Center, La Jolla, CA LJ-80-05.

925 Perryman, W.L. *et al.* (1994) Melon-headed whale *Peponocephala electra* Gray, 1846, pp. 363–386 in Ridgway, S.H. & Harrison, R. (eds.) *Handbook of marine mammals, Vol. 5.* Academic Press, London.

926 Petersen, A. Personal communication.

927 Pierce, G.J. *et al.* (2004) Diet of minke whales *Balaenoptera acutorostrata* in Scottish (UK) waters with notes on strandings of this species in Scotland 1992–2002. *Journal of the Marine Biological Association of the UK,* **84**, 1241–1244.

928 Pierce, G.J. *et al.* (in press). Bioaccumulation of persistent organic pollutants in female common dolphins *(Delphinus delphis)* and harbour porpoises *(Phocoena phocoena)* from western European seas: consequences for reproduction, geographical trends and effects of age, maturation and diet. *Environmental Pollution.*

929 Pierpoint, C. Personal communication.

930 Pierrepont, J.F. de *et al.* (2005) Stomach contents of English Channel cetaceans stranded on the coast of Normandy. *Journal of the Marine Biological Association of the UK,* **85**(6), 1539–1546.

931 Pijlen, I.A. van *et al.*(1991) Multilocus DNA fingerprinting applied to population studies of the minke whale, *Balaenoptera acutorostrata. Report of the International Whaling Commission, Special Issue,* **13**, 245–253.

932 Pijlen, I.A. van *et al.* (1995) Patterns of genetic variability at individual minisatellite loci in minke whale *Balaenoptera acutorostrata* populations from three different oceans. *Molecular Biology and Evolution,* **12**, 459–472.

933 Pike, G.C. & MacAskie, A. (1969) Marine mammals of British Columbia. *Fisheries Research Board of Canada Bulletin,* **171**, 1–54.

934 Pilleri, G. & Gihr, M. (1969) On the anatomy and behaviour of Risso's dolphins (*Grampus griseus* G. Cuvier). *Investigations on Cetacea,* **1**, 74–93.

934a Pilleri, G. & Knuckey, J. (1969) Behaviour patterns of some Delphinidae. observed in the western Mediterranean. *Zeitschrift für Tierpsychologie,* **26,** 48–72.

935 Pitman, R.L. *et al.* (1999) Sightings and possible identity of a bottlenose whale in the tropical Indo-Pacific: *Indopacetus pacificus? Marine Mammal Science,* **15**, 531–549.

936 Pitman, W.L. & Ballance, L.T. (1992) Parkinson's petrel distribution and foraging ecology in the eastern tropical Pacific: aspects of an exclusive feeding relationship with dolphins. *Condor,* **94**, 825–835.

937 Plön, S.E.E. *et al.* (1999) Sperm morphology and other aspects of reproduction in *Kogia*, pp. 398–399 in Evans, P.G.H. & Parsons, E.C.M. (eds.) *European research on cetaceans – 12.* European Cetacean Society.

938 Plön, S.E.E. *et al.* (2000) Stomach content analysis of pygmy and dwarf sperm whales and its ecological implications: is there niche partitioning? pp. 336–339 in Evans, P.G.H. *et al.* (eds.) *European research on cetaceans – 13.* European Cetacean Society.

939 Podestà, M. & Meotti, C. (1991) The stomach contents of a Cuvier's beaked whale *Ziphius cavirostris*, and a Risso's dolphin *Grampus griseus*, stranded in Italy, pp. 58–61 in Evans, P.G.H. (ed.) *European research on cetaceans – 5.* European Cetacean Society.

940 Podestá, M. *et al.* (1997) Sightings of Risso's dolphins in the Ligurian waters, pp. 167–169 in Evans, P.G.H. *et al.* (eds.). *European Research on Cetaceans – 11.* European Cetacean Society.

941 Pollock, C. *et al.* (1997) *The distribution of seabirds and cetaceans in the waters around Ireland.* Report No. 267. JNCC, Peterborough.

942 Price, S.A. *et al.* (2005) A complete phylogeny of the whales, dolphins and even-toed hoofed mammals (Cetartiodactyla). *Biological Reviews,* **80**, 445–473.

943 Pulcini, M. (1997) Note about the presence of Cuvier's beaked whale *Ziphius cavirostris* in the Ionian Islands of Greece, p. 176. in Evans, P.G.H. (ed.) *European research on cetaceans – 10.* European Cetacean Society.

944 Pulcini, M. & Angradi, A.M. (1994) Observations of Cuvier's beaked whale *Ziphius cavirostris* (Cetacea, Odontoceti) in the Ionian Islands of Greece, pp. 116–119 in Evans, P.G.H. (ed.) *European Research on Cetaceans – 8.* European Cetacean Society.

945 Pulcini, M. *et al.* (1992) Stomach contents of striped dolphins, *Stenella coeruleoalba* (Meyen, 1933), from the south-central Tyrrhenian coast, pp. 194–195 in Evans, P.G.H. (ed.) *European research on cetaceans – 6.* European Cetacean Society.

946 Purves, P.E. (1977) Order *Cetacea*, pp. 266–309 in Corbet, G.B. & Southern, H.N. (eds.) *The handbook of British mammals,* 2nd edn. Blackwell, Oxford.

947 Purves, P.E. & Pilleri, G. (1978) The functional anatomy and general biology of *Pseudorca crassidens* (Owen) with a review of the hydrodynamics and acoustics in *Cetacea. Investigations on Cetacea,* **9**, 67–227.

947a Pusineri, C. *et al* Food and feeding ecology of the common dolphin (*Delphinus delphis*) in the oceanic northeast Atlantic and comparison with its neritic areas. *Marine Mammal Science,* **23**, 30-47.

948 Quinn, O. (2001) *Reproductive parameters and status of the male striped dolphin* Stenella coeruleoalba *in the North East Atlantic.* BSc thesis, University College Cork.

949 Raduán, A. *et al.* (2007) Some aspects on the life history of Risso's dolphins *Grampus griseus* (Cuvier, 1812) in the Western Mediterranean Sea, p. 74 in *European research on cetaceans – 21.* European Cetacean Society.

950 Rae, B.B. (1965) The food of the common porpoise (*Phocaena phocaena*). *Journal of Zoology,* **146**, 114–122.

951 Rae, B.B. (1973) Additional notes on the food of the common porpoise (*Phocoena phocaena*). *Journal of Zoology,* **169**, 127–131.

952 Raga, J.A. (1994) Parasitismus bei cetacea, pp. 132–179 in Robineau D. *et al.* (eds.) *Handbuch der Saugetiere Europas, Bd.*

6/1A, Wale und delphine 1. Aula-Verlag, Wiesbaden (in German).

953 Raga, J.A. & Balbuena, J.A. (1993) Parasites of the long-finned pilot whale, *Globicephala melas* (Traill, 1809), in European waters. *Report of the International Whaling Commission, Special Issue,* **14**, 391–406.

954 Raga, J.A. *et al.* (1982) Notes on the cetaceans of the Iberian coasts. V. *Crassicauda grampicola* Johnston and Mawson, 1941 (Nematoda) cause of injuries in the pterygoids of some specimens of *Grampus griseus. Säugetierkundliche Mitteilungen,* **30**, 315–318.

955 Raga, J.A. *et al.* (1989) New data on helminth parasites of the harbour porpoise *Phocoena phocoena* in Danish waters, pp. 88–90 in Evans, P.G.H. & Smeenk, C. (eds.) *European research on cetaceans – 3.* European Cetacean Society.

956 Ralls, K. *et al.* (1980) Differential mortality by sex and age in mammals, with special reference to the sperm whale. *Report of the International Whaling Commission, Special Issue,* **2**, 233–243.

957 Rasmussen, M. *et al.* (1999) The sounds and calculated source levels from the white-beaked dolfin reported in Icelandic waters, pp. 43–47 in Evans, P.G.H. *et al. European research on cetaceans – 13.* European Cetacean Society.

958 Rayne, S. *et al.* (2004) PBDEs, PBBs, and PCNs in three communities of free-ranging killer whales (*Orcinus orca*) from the northeastern Pacific Ocean. *Environmental Science and Technology,* **38**, 4293–4299.

959 Rayner, G.W. (1939) *Globobicephala leucosagmaphora,* a new species of the genus *Globicephala. Annals and Magazine of Natural History,* **4**, 543–544.

960 Read, A.J. (1999) Harbour porpoise, pp. 323–355 in *Handbook of Marine Mammals* Vol. 6. Academic Press, London.

961 Read, A.J. & Westgate, A.J. (1997) Monitoring the movements of harbour porpoises (*Phocoena phocoena*) with satellite telemetry. *Marine Biology,* **130**, 315–322.

962 Read, A.J. *et al.* (eds.) (1997) *The biology of the harbour porpoise.* De Spil Publishers, Woerden, Netherlands.

963 Recchia, C.A. & Read, A.J. (1989) Stomach contents of harbour porpoises, *Phocoena phocoena* (L.), from the Bay of Fundy. *Canadian Journal of Zoology,* **67**, 2140–2146.

964 Reeves, R.R. (2001) Overview of catch history, historic abundance and distribution of right whales in the western North Atlantic and in Cintra Bay, West Africa. *Journal of Cetacean Research and Management, Special Issue,* **2**, 187–192.

965 Reeves, R.R. & Leatherwood, S.L. (1994) *1994–1998 Action plan for the conservation of cetaceans: dolphins, porpoises and whales.* IUCN, Gland.

966 Reeves, R.R. & Mitchell, E.D. (1990) Right whales, not humpbacks, taken in Cintra Bay. *The American Neptune,* **L**(2), 119–126.

967 Reeves, R.R. *et al.* (1978) The right whale, *Eubalaena glacialis,* in the western North Atlantic. *Report of the International Whaling Commission,* **28**, 303–312.

968 Reeves, R.R. *et al.* (1993) Status of the northern bottlenose whale, *Hyperoodon ampullatus. Canadian Field Naturalist,* **107**, 490–508.

969 Reeves, R.R., *et al.* (1999) Atlantic white-sided dolphin *Lagenorhynchus acutus* (Gray, 1828), pp. 31–56 in Ridgway, S.H. & Harrison, R. (eds.) *Handbook of marine mammals,* Vol. 6. Academic Press, San Diego, CA.

970 Reeves, R.R. *et al.* (1999) White-beaked dolphin *Lagenorhynchus albirostris* Gray, 1846, pp. 1–30 in Ridgway, S.H. & Harrison, R. (eds.) *Handbook of marine mammals,* Vol. 6. Academic Press, San Diego, CA.

971 Reeves, R.R *et al.* (compilers) (2003) *Dolphins, whales and porpoises.* 2002–2010 Conservation Action Plan for the World's Cetaceans. IUCN/SSC Cetacean Specialist Group, Gland.

972 Reeves, R.R. *et al.* (2007) Near-Annihilation of a species: right whaling in the North Atlantic, pp. 39–74 in Kraus, S.D. & Rolland, R.M. (eds.) *The urban whale: North Atlantic right whales at the crossroads.* Harvard University Press, Cambridge, MA.

973 Reid, J.B. *et al.* (2003) *Atlas of cetacean distribution in north-west European waters.* JNCC, Peterborough.

974 Reid, R.J. Personal communication.

975 Reijnders, P.J.H. (1992) Harbour porpoises, *Phocoena phocoena,* in the North Sea: numerical responses to changes in environmental conditions. *Netherlands Journal of Aquatic Ecology,* **26**, 75–85.

976 Reiner, F. (1979) Nota sobre um raro Ziphioid, *Mesoplodon densirostris,* Blainville 1817, nas costas de Portugal. *Memórias do Museo do Mar, série zoológica,* **1** (in Portuguese).

977 Reiner, F. (1980) First record of an Antillean beaked whale, *Mesoplodon europaeus* Gervais 1855, from Republica Popular da Guine-Bissau. *Museo Marinos, Cascias, Memorias, Serie Zoologie,* **1**, 1–8.

978 Reiner, F. (1981) Nota sobre a ocorrência de um cachalote-anão *Kogia breviceps* Blainville na Praia de Salgueiros – Vila Nova de Gaia. *Memórias do Museo do Mar, série zoológica,* **2**(15), 1–12 (in Portuguese).

979 Reiner, F. (1986) First record of Sowerby's beaked whale from the Azores. *Scientific Reports of the Whales Research Institute,* **37**, 103–107.

980 Reiner, F. *et al.* (1996) Cetaceans of the Cape Verde archipelago. *Marine Mammal Science,* **12**, 434–443.

981 Relini, L.O. *et al.* (1994) *Meganyctiphanes norvegica* and fin whales in the Ligurian Sea: new seasonal pattern, pp. 179–182 in Evans, P.G.H. (ed.) *European research on cetaceans – 8.* European Cetacean Society.

982 Relini, L.O. *et al.* (1998) Notes on ecology of the Mediterranean krill, a mirror of the behaviour of Mediterranean fin whales, p. 119 in Evans, P.G.H. & Parsons, E.C.M. (eds.) *European research on cetaceans – 12.* European Cetacean Society.

983 Rendell, L.E. & Gordon, J.C.D. (1999) Vocal response of long-finned pilot whales (*Globicephala melas*) to military sonar in the Ligurian Sea. *Marine Mammal Science,* **15**(1), 198–204.

984 Rendell, L.E. *et al.* (1999) Quantitative analysis of tonal calls from five odontocete species, examining interspecific and intraspecific variation. *Journal of Zoology,* **249**, 403–410.

985 Rice, D.W. (1977) *A list of marine mammals of the world.* NOAA Technical Report NMFS SSRF, 711, 1–75.

986 Rice, D.W. (1977) Synopsis of biological data on the sei and Bryde's whale in the eastern North Pacific. *Report of the International Whaling Commission, Special Issue,* **1**, 92–97.

987 Rice, D.W. (1978) Blue whale, pp. 170–195 in Haley, D. (ed.) *Marine mammals of eastern North Pacific and Arctic waters.* Pacific Search Press, Seattle, WA.

988 Rice, D.W. (1989) Sperm whale *Physeter macrocephalus* Linnaeus, 1758, pp. 177–233 in Ridgway, S.H. & Harrison, R. (eds.) *Handbook of marine mammals,* Vol. 4. Academic Press, London.

989 Rice, D.W. (1998) *Marine mammals of the world – systematics and distribution.* Special Publication No. 4, Society for Marine Mammalogy, San Francisco, CA.

990 Rice, D.W. & Wolman, A.A. (1971) *The life history and ecology of the gray whale* (Eschrichtius robustus). Special Publication No. 3, American Society of Mammalogists, Stillwater, OK.

991 Richard, P.R. *et al.* (1997) Study of summer and fall movements and dive behaviour of Beaufort Sea belugas: using satellite telemetry, 1992–1995. *Environmental Studies Research Funds* No. 134, 1–38. http://www.esrfunds.org/documents/ESRF_134.pdf

992 Richardson, J. & Gray, J.E. (eds.) (1846) *The zoology of the voyage of H.M.S. Erebus and Terror.* London.

993 Richardson, W.J. *et al.* (1995) *Marine mammals and noise.* Academic Press, New York.

994 Ridoux, V. *et al.* (2003) *Détermination des habitats préférentiels estivaux de prédateurs supérieurs pélagiques du proche Atlantique par observations aeriennes.* Rapport contractuel CRMM-ULR/IFREMER (in French).

995 Riesch, R. *et al.* (2005) Stability and group specificity of stereotyped whistles in resident killer whales, *Orcinus orca*, off British Columbia. *Animal Behaviour,* **71**, 79–91.

996 Ringelstein, J. *et al.* (2006) Food and feeding ecology of the striped dolphin, *Stenella coeruleoalba,* in the oceanic waters of the Northeast Atlantic. *Journal of the Marine Biological Association of the UK*, **86**, 909–918.

997 Ritter, F. & Brederlau, B. (1998) First report of blue whales (*Balaenoptera musculus*) frequenting the Canary Island waters, pp. 95–98 in Evans, P.G.H. & Parsons, E.C.M. (eds.) *European research on cetaceans – 12.* European Cetacean Society.

998 Ritter, F. & Brederlau, B. (1999) Abundance and distribution of cetaceans off La Gomera (Canary Islands), p. 98 in Evans, P.G.H. *et al.* (eds.) *European research on cetaceans – 13.* European Cetacean Society.

999 Robineau, D. (1993) Stranding of a specimen of Gervais' beaked whale (*Mesoplodon europaeus*) on the coast of west Africa (Mauritania). *Marine Mammal Science*, **9**, 438–440.

1000 Robineau, D. & di Natale, A. (1995) *Ziphius cavirostris* – Cuvier-Schnabelwal, pp. 526–543 in Robineau, D. *et al.* (eds.) *Handbuch der Säugetiere Europas. Meeressäuger Teil IB Wale und Delphine 2.* Aula-Verlag, Weisbaden (in German).

1001 Robinson, B.H. & Craddock, J.E. (1983) Mesopelagic fishes eaten by Fraser's dolphin, *Lagenodelphis hosei. Fisheries Bulletin, U.S.,* **81**, 283–289.

1002 Rogan, E. Personal communication.

1003 Rogan, E. & Berrow, S.D. (1995) The management of Irish waters as a whale and dolphin sanctuary, pp. 671–681 in Blix, A.S. *et al.* (eds.) *Whales, seals, fish and man.* Elsevier, Amsterdam.

1004 Rogan, E. & Berrow, S. (1996) A review of harbour porpoises, *Phocoena phocoena*, in Irish waters. *Report of the International Whaling Commission*, **46**, 595–605.

1005 Rogan, E. & Mackey, M. (2007) Megafauna bycatch in driftnets for albacore tuna (*Thunnus alalunga*) in the NE Atlantic. *Fisheries Research* (in press).

1006 Rogan, E. *et al.* (1997) A review of striped dolphins, *Stenella coeruleoalba*, in the waters around Ireland. *Report of the International Whaling Commission* SC/49/SM40.

1007 Rogan, E. *et al.* (1997) A mass stranding of white-sided dolphins (*Lagenorhynchus acutus*) in Ireland: biological and pathological studies. *Journal of Zoology*, **242**, 217–227.

1008 Rogan, E. *et al.* (2004) *Age determination in small cetaceans from the NE Atlantic.* BIOCET workpackage 4 – Final Report. Project Reference: EVK3-2000-00027.

1009 Rohr, J.J. *et al.* (2002) Maximum swim speeds of captive and free-ranging delphinids: Critical analysis of extraordinary performance. *Marine Mammal Science*, **18**(1), 1–19.

1010 Rolland, R.M. *et al.* (2007) The inner whale: hormones, biotoxins, and parasites, pp. 232–272 in Kraus, S.D. & Rolland, R.M. (eds.) *The urban whale: North Atlantic right whales at the crossroads.* Harvard University Press, Cambridge, MA.

1011 Rolland, R.M. *et al.* (2007) External perspectives on right whale health, pp. 273–309 in Kraus, S.D. & Rolland, R.M. (eds.) *The urban whale: North Atlantic right whales at the crossroads.* Harvard University Press, Cambridge, MA.

1012 Rosel, P.E. *et al.* (1994) Genetic analysis of sympatric morphotypes of common dolphins (genus *Delphinus*). *Marine Biology,* **119**, 159–167.

1013 Rosenbaum, H.C. *et al.* (2000) World-wide genetic differentiation of *Eubalaena*: questioning the number of right whale species. *Molecular Ecology*, 9, 1793–1802.

1014 Rosenbaum, H.C. *et al.* (2000) Utility of North Atlantic right whale museum specimens for assessing changes in genetic diversity. *Conservation Biology,* **14**(6), 1837–1842.

1015 Ross, G.J.B. (1969) Evidence for a southern breeding population of True's beaked whale. *Nature, London,* **222**, 585.

1016 Ross, G.J.B. (1979) Records of pygmy and dwarf sperm whales, genus *Kogia*, from southern Africa, with biological notes and some comparisons. *Annals of the Cape Province Museum of Natural History,* **11**, 259–327.

1017 Ross, G.J.B. (1984) The smaller cetaceans of the south east coast of Southern Africa. *Annals of the Cape Province Museum of Natural History,* **15**, 173–410.

1018 Ross, H.M. & Wilson, B. (1996) Violent interactions between bottlenose dolphins and harbour porpoises. *Proceedings of the Royal Society of London*, **263**, 283–286.

1019 Ross, P. *et al.* (2000) High PCB concentrations in free-ranging Pacific killer whales, *Orcinus orca*: effects of age, sex and dietary preference. *Marine Pollution Bulletin,* **40,** 504–515.

1020 Rowntree, V.J. (1996) Feeding, distribution, and reproductive behavior of cyamids (Crustacea: Amphipoda) living on right whales. *Canadian Journal of Zoology,* **74,** 103–109.

1021 Rychel, A.L. *et al.* (2004) Phylogeny of mysticete whales based on mitochondrial and nuclear data. *Molecular Phylogenetics and Evolution*, **32**, 892–901.

1022 Sabin, R. *et al.* (2002) *Trends in cetacean strandings around the UK coastline and marine mammal post-mortem investigations for the year 2002* (contract CRO 238). Report by the Natural History Museum to DEFRA NO. ECM 516F00/03.

1023 Sabin, R.C. *et al.* (2005) *Trends in cetacean strandings around the UK coastline and cetacean and marine turtle investigations 2000 to 2004 inclusive* (Contract CRO 238), Cetaceans Strandings Investigation and Co-ordination in the UK. Report to Defra for the period 1 January 2000–31 December 2004.

1024 SAC Veterinary Services. Unpublished data.

1025 Samaras, W.F. (1994) New host record for the barnacle *Cryptolepas rhachianecti* Dall, 1872 (*Balanomorpha: Cornulidae*). *Marine Mammal Science*, **5**, 84–87.

1026 Sanpera, C. *et al* (1984) Report of the 'Ballena 2' whale marking and sighting cruise in the Atlantic waters off Spain. *Report of the International Whaling Commission*, **34**, 663–666.

1027 Sanpera, C. *et al.* (1992) Total and organic mercury in tissues and organs of fin whales, *Balaenoptera physalus*, pp. 227–229 in Evans, P.G.H. (ed.) *European research on cetaceans – 6.* European Cetacean Society.

1028 Santoro, A.K. *et al.* (1989) Pygmy sperm whale sounds (*Kogia breviceps*), p. 59 in *Abstracts of the 8th Biennial Conference on the Biology of Marine Mammals,* Pacific Grove, CA, December.

1029 Santos, M.B. (1998) *Feeding ecology of harbour porpoises, common dolphins and bottlenose dolphins and sperm whales in the Northeast Atlantic.* PhD thesis, University of Aberdeen.

1030 Santos, M.B. Personal communication.

1031 Santos, M.B. & Pierce, G.J. (2003) The diet of harbour porpoise (*Phocoena phocoena*) in the eastern North Atlantic. *Oceanography and Marine Biology: an Annual Review, 2003,* **41**, 355–390.

1032 Santos, M.B. *et al.* (1994) *Diets of small cetaceans from the Scottish coast.* ICES Marine Mammal Committee, C.M. 1994/No. **11**, 1–16

1033 Santos, M.B. *et al.* (1999) Stomach contents of sperm whales (*Physeter macrocephalus*) stranded in the North Sea, 1990–1996. *Marine Ecology Progress Series*, **183**, 281–294.

1034 Santos, M.B. *et al.* (2001) Stomach contents of northern bottlenose whales *Hyperoodon ampullatus* stranded in the North Sea. *Journal of the Marine Biological Association of the UK*, **81**, 143–150.

1035 Santos, M.B. *et al.* (2001) Feeding ecology of Cuvier's beaked whale (*Ziphius cavirostris*): a review with new information on the diet of this species. *Journal of the Marine Biological Association of the UK,* **81,** 687–694.

1036 Santos, M.B. *et al.* (2001) Stomach contents of bottlenose dolphins (*Tursiops truncatus*) in Scottish waters. *Journal of the Marine Biological Association of the UK,* **81,** 873–878.

1037 Santos, M.B. *et al.* (2004) Variability in the diet of harbor porpoises (*Phocoena phocoena*) in Scottish waters 1992–2003. *Marine Mammal Science,* **20,** 1–27.

1038 Santos, M.B. *et al.* (2004) Variability in the diet of common dolphins (*Delphinus delphis*) in Galician waters 1991–2003 and relationships with prey abundance. ICEM C.M. 2004.

1039 Santos, M.B. *et al.* (2005) Harbour porpoise *(Phocoena phocoena)* feeding ecology in the eastern North Sea. *ICES CM 2005/Theme Session R:15* (Marine Mammals: Monitoring Techniques, Abundance Estimation, and Interaction with Fisheries).

1040 Santos, M.B. *et al.* (2006) Pygmy sperm whales *(Kogia breviceps)* in the Northeast Atlantic: new information on stomach contents and strandings. *Marine Mammal Science,* **22,** 600–616.

1041 Santos, M.B. *et al.* (2007) Insights into the diet of beaked whales from the atypical mass stranding in the Canary Islands in September 2002. *Journal of the Marine Biological Association of the UK,* **87,** 243–251.

1042 Santos, R.A. dos & Haimovici, M. (2001) Cephalopods in the diet of marine mammals stranded or incidentally caught along southeastern and southern Brazil (21–34 degrees S). *Fisheries Research,* **52**(1–2), 99–112.

1043 Sarvas, T.H. & Fleming, V. (1999) The effects of the deep scattering layer on the diving behaviour of sperm whales off Andøya, Norway, pp. 341–345 in Evans, P.G.H. *et al.* (eds.) *European research on cetaceans – 13.* European Cetacean Society.

1044 Schaeff, C.M. *et al.* (1993) Assessment of the population structure of western North Atlantic right whales *(Eubalaena glacialis)* based on sighting and mtDNA data. *Canadian Journal of Zoology,* **71,** 339–345.

1045 Scheppingen, W.B. van *et al.* (1996) Polychlorinated biphenyls, dibenzo-*p*-dioxins, and dibenzofurans in harbor porpoises (*Phocoena phocoena*) stranded on the Dutch coast between 1990 and 1993. *Archives of Environmental Contaminants and Toxicology,* **30,** 492–502.

1046 Schevill, W.E. (1986) Right whale nomenclature. Appendix 5, pp. 221–254 in Brownell, R.L.J. *et al.* (eds). *Right whales: past and present status.* International Whaling Commission, Cambridge.

1047 Schevill, W.E. & Watkins, W.A. (1972) Intense low-frequency sounds from an Antarctic minke whale, *Balaenoptera acutorostrata. Breviora,* **388,** 1–7.

1048 Schevill, W.E. *et al.* (1969) Click structure in the porpoise, *Phocoena phocoena. Journal of Mammalogy,* **50,** 721–728.

1049 Schmidt, R. Personal communication.

1050 Schulze, G. (1973) Die Walfunde aus dem Bereich der Ostseekuste der DDR. *Natur und Naturschutz in Mecklenburg,* **11,** 97–112 (in German).

1051 Schwacke, L.H. *et al.* (2002) Probabilistic risk assessment of reproductive effects of polychlorinated biphenyls on bottlenose dolphins (*Tursiops truncatus*) from the Southeast United States coast. *Environmental Toxicological Chemistry,* **21,** 2752 2764.

1052 Schweder, T. *et al.* (1993) Estimates of abundance of the Northeastern Atlantic minke whales in 1989. *Report of the International Whaling Commission,* **43,** 323–331.

1053 Sea Mammal Research Unit (1995) *Cetacean bycatch in the UK tuna driftnet fishery in 1995.* Sea Mammal Research Unit contract report to the Ministry of Agriculture, Fisheries and Food. SMRU, Cambridge.

1054 Seaman, G.A. *et al.* (1982) Foods of belukha whales (*Delphinapterus leucas*) in western Alaska. *Cetology,* **44,** 1–19.

1055 Sears, R. (1983) A glimpse of blue whale feeding in the Gulf of St. Lawrence. *Whalewatcher,* **17,** 12–14.

1056 Sears, R. (2002) Blue whale *Balaenoptera musculus,* pp. 112–116 in Perrin, W.F. (eds.) *Encyclopaedia of marine mammals.* Academic Press, San Diego, CA.

1057 Sears, R. *et al.* (1990) Photographic identification of the blue whale (*Balaenoptera musculus*) in the Gulf of St. Lawrence, Canada. *Report of the International Whaling Commission, Special Issue,* **12,** 335–342.

1058 Sears, R. *et al.* (1991) The photographic identification of the blue whale (*Balaenoptera musculus*) in the Gulf of St Lawrence, Canada. *Report of the International Whaling Commission, Special Issue,* **12,** 335–342.

1059 Selzer, L.A. & Payne, P.M. (1988) The distribution of white sided (*lagenorhynchus acutus*) and common dolphins (*Delphinus delphis*) vs. environmental features of the continental shelf of the Northeastern United States. *Marine Mammal Science,* **4,**141–153.

1060 Sequeira, M. *et al.* (1992) Arrojamentos de mamíferos marinhos na costa portuguesa entre 1978 e 1988. *Estudos de Biologia e Conversação da Natureza,* **7,** 1–48 (in Portuguese).

1061 Sequeira, M. *et al.* (1996) Arrojamentos de mamíferos marinhos na costa continental Portuguesa entre 1989–1994. *Estudos de Biologia e Conversação da Natureza,* **19,** 1–52 (in Portuguese).

1062 Sergeant, D.E. (1962) The biology of the pilot or pothead whale, *Globicephala melaena* (Traill) in Newfoundland waters. *Bulletin of the Fisheries Research Board of Canada,* **132,** 1–84.

1063 Sergeant, D.E. (1962) On the external characters of the blackfish or pilot whales (genus *Globicephala*). *Journal of Mammalogy,* **43,** 395–413.

1064 Sergeant, D.E. (1963) Minke whales, *Balaenoptera acutorostrata* Lacépède, of the western North Atlantic. *Journal of the Fisheries Research Board of Canada,* **20**(6), 1489–1504.

1065 Sergeant, D.E. & Fisher, H.D. (1957) The smaller cetacea of eastern Canadian waters. *Journal of the Fisheries Research Board of Canada,* **14,** 83–115.

1066 Sergeant, D.E. *et al.* (1980) Life history and Northwest Atlantic status of the Atlantic white-sided dolphin, *Lagenorhynchus acutus. Cetology,* **37,** 1–12.

1067 Shallenberger, E.W. (1981) *The status of Hawaiian cetaceans.* Report MMC-77/23, to the Marine Mammal Commission under contract MM7ACo28.

1068 Shane, S.H. (1995) Behavior patterns of pilot whales and Risso's dolphins off Santa Catalina Island, California. *Aquatic Mammals,* **21,** 195–197.

1069 Shane, S.H. (1995) Relationship between pilot whales and Risso's dolphins at Santa Catalina Island, California, USA. *Marine Ecology Progress Series,* **123,** 5–11.

1070 Shelden, K.E.W. *et al.* (1995) Observations of Risso's dolphins, *Grampus griseus* with gray whales, *Eschrichtius robustus. Marine Mammal Science,* **11,** 231–240.

1071 Sheldrick, M.C. (1976) Trends in the strandings of Cetacea on the British coasts 1913–72. *Mammal Review,* **6,** 15–23.

1072 Sheldrick, M.C. (1979) Cetacean strandings along the coast of the British Isles 1913–77, pp. 35–53 in Geraci, J.R. & St Aubin, D.J. (eds.) *Biology of marine mammals.* US Marine Mammal Commission, Washington, DC.

1073 Sheldrick, M.C. (1989) Stranded whale records for the entire British coastline, 1967–1986. *Investigations on Cetacea,* **22,** 298–329.

1074 Sheldrick, M. *et al.* (1994) Stranded cetacean records for England, Scotland and Wales, 1987–1992. *Investigations on Cetacea,* **25,** 259–283.

1075 Shevchenko, V.I. (1975) The nature of inter-relationships between killer whales and other cetaceans. *Marine Mammals Abstract Report of the 6th All-Union Meeting Moscow,*

2, 173–175.

1076 Shimura, E. & Numachi, K. (1987) Genetic variability and differentiation in the toothed whales. *Scientific Reports of the Whales Research Institute*, **38**, 141–163.

1077 Siebert, U. *et al.* (2001) Post-mortem findings in harbour porpoises (*Phocoena phocoena*) from the German North and Baltic Seas. *Journal of Comparative Pathology*, **124**, 102–114.

1078 Siegstad, H. & Heide-Jørgensen, M.P. (1994) Ice entrapments of narwhals (*Monodon monceros*) and white whales (*Delphinapterus leucas*) in Greenland. *Meddr Grønland, Biosciences,* **39**, 151–160.

1079 Sigurjónsson, J. (1992) Recent studies on abundance and trends in whale stocks in Icelandic and adjacent waters. *Proceedings of the Royal Academy of Overseas Science, Brussels,* 77–111.

1080 Sigurjónsson, J. (1995) On the life history and autecology of North Atlantic rorquals, pp. 425–441 in Blix, A.S. *et al.* (eds.) *Whales, seals, fish and man.* Elsevier, Amsterdam.

1081 Sigurjónsson, J. & Gunnlaugsson, T. (1990) Distribution and abundance of cetaceans in Icelandic and adjacent waters during sightings surveys, July–August 1989. *ICES C.M. 1990/N:5, Marine Mammals Committee, ICES.*

1082 Sigurjónsson, J. & Gunnlaugsson, T. (1990) Recent trends in abundance of blue (*Balaenoptera musculus*) and humpback whales (*Megaptera novaeangliae*) of west and southwest Iceland, with a note on occurrence of other cetacean species. *Report of the International Whaling Commission,* **40**, 537–551.

1083 Sigurjónsson, J. & Leatherwood, S. (1988) The Icelandic live-capture fishery for killer whales, 1976–1988. *Rit Fiskideildar*, **11**, 307–316.

1084 Sigurjónsson, J. *et al.* (1989) NASS-87: shipboard sightings surveys in Icelandic and adjacent waters, June–July 1987. *Report of the International Whaling Commission,* **39**, 395–408.

1085 Sigurjónsson J. *et al.* (2000) A note on stomach contents of minke whales (*Balaenoptera acutorostrata*) in Icelandic waters, pp. 82–90 in Víkingsson, G.A.and Kapel, F.O. (eds.) *Minke, harp and hooded seals: major predators in the North Atlantic ecosystem.* Scientific Publications Volume 2, NAMMCO, Tromsø.

1086 Silva, M.A. (1999) Diet of common dolphins, *Delphinus delphis*, off the Portuguese continental coast. *Journal of the Marine Biological Association of the UK,* **79,** 531–540.

1087 Silva, M.A. & Sequeira, M. (2003) Patterns in the mortality of common dolphins (*Delphinus delphis*) on the Portuguese coast, using strandings records 1975–1998. *Aquatic Mammals*, **29**(1), 88–98.

1088 Simas, E. Personal communication.

1089 Similä, T. & Ugarte, F. (1993) Surface and underwater observations of cooperatively feeding killer whales in northern Norway. *Canadian Journal of Zoology*, **71**, 1494–1499.

1090 Similä, T. *et al.* (1996) Occurrence and diet of killer whales in northern Norway: seasonal patterns relative to the distribution and abundance of Norwegian spring-spawning herring. *Canadian Journal of Fisheries and Aquatic Science,* **53**, 769–779.

1091 Simmonds, M.P. *et al.* (1994) Organochlorines and mercury in pilot whale blubber consumed by Faroe islanders. *Science of the Total Environment*, **149**, 97–111.

1092 Simon, M. (2004) *Sounds produced by foraging killer whales* (Orcinus orca). MSc thesis, University of Southern Denmark, Odense.

1093 Sjare, B.L. & Smith, T.G. (1986) The vocal repertoire of white whales, *Delphinapterus leucas*, summering in Cunningham Inlet, Northwest Territories. *Canadian Journal of Zoology*, **64**, 407–415.

1094 Skaare, J.U. (1995) Organochlorine contaminants in marine mammals from the Norwegian Arctic, pp. 589–598 in Blix, A.S. *et al.* (eds.) *Whales, seals, fish and man.* Elsevier, Amsterdam.

1095 Slay, C.S. & Kraus, S.D. (1999) Right whale tagging in the North Atlantic. *Marine Technology Society Journal*, **32**(1), 102–103.

1096 Slijper, E.J. (1962) *Whales.* Hutchinson, London.

1097 Slob, C.M. *et al.* (2001) Lungworms in harbour porpoises (*Phocoena phocoena*) from Dutch waters. *European Cetacean Society Newsletter, Special Issue,* **27**, 35–40.

1098 Small, R.J. & DeMaster, D.P. (1995) Survival of five species of captive marine mammals. *Marine Mammal Science*, **11**, 209–226.

1099 Smeenk, C.S. (1987) The harbour porpoise *Phocoena phocoena* (L., 1758) in the Netherlands: stranding records and decline. *Lutra*, **30**, 77–90.

1100 Smeenk, C. (1997) Strandings of sperm whales *Physeter macrocephalus* in the North Sea: history and patterns, pp. 15–28 in Jacques, T.G. and Lambertsen, R.H. (eds.) *Sperm whale deaths in the North Sea: science and management. Bulletin de L'Institut Royal des Sciences Naturelles de Belgique. Biologie,* **67**(suppl.).

1101 Smeenk, C. & Gaemers, P.A.M. (1987) Fish otoliths in the stomachs of white-beaked dolphins *Lagenorhynchus albirostris*, pp. 12–13 in Broekema, J.W. & Smeenk, C. (eds.) *European Cetacean Society: Report of the 1987 Meeting*, Hirtshals, Denmark, 26–28 January.

1102 Smith, T.D. *et al.* (1999) An ocean-basin-wide mark-recapture study of the North Atlantic humpback whale (*Megaptera novaeangliae*). *Marine Mammal Science*, **15**, 1–32.

1103 Smith, T.D. *et al.* (2006) Using historical records to relocate a long forgotten summer feeding ground of North Atlantic right whales. *Marine Mammal Science,* **22**(3), 723–734.

1104 Smith, T.G. & Martin, A.R. (1994) Distribution and movements of belugas, *Delphinapterus leucas*, in the Canadian high Arctic. *Canadian Bulletin of Fisheries and Aquatic Sciences,* **51**, 1653–1663.

1105 Smith, T.G. *et al.* (1992) Rubbing behaviour of belugas, *Delphinapterus leucas*, in the Canadian high arctic. *Canadian Journal of Zoology*, **70**, 2405–2409.

1106 Smith, T.G. *et al.* (1994) Herd composition and behaviour of white whales (*Delphinapterus leucas*) in low Canadian arctic estuaries. *Meddr Grønland, Biosciences*, **39**, 175–184.

1107 Smolker, R.A. *et al.* (1992) Sex differences in patterns of association among Indian Ocean bottlenose dolphins. *Behaviour,* **123**, 38–69.

1108 Sørensen, T.B. & Kinze, C.C. (1994) Reproduction and growth in Danish harbour porpoises *Phocoena phocoena*. *Ophelia*, **39**(3), 159–176.

1109 Soulier, L. & Collet, A. (1994) Note on crustaceans recorded on dolphins incidentally caught in the Northeastern Atlantic, pp. 248–250 in Evans, P.G.H. (ed.) *European research on cetaceans – 8.* European Cetacean Society.

1110 Southall, B.L. *et al.* (2006) *Hawaiian melon-headed whale* (Peponocephala electra) *mass stranding event of July 3–4 2004.* NOAA Technical Memorandum NMFS-OPR-31.

1111 Southward, A.J. (1963) The distribution of some plankton animals in the English Channel and Western Approaches. III. Theories about long term biological changes, including fish. *Journal of the Marine Biological Association of the UK*, **43,** 1–29.

1112 Spilliaert, R. *et al.* (1991) Species hybridization between a female blue whale (*Balaenoptera musculus*) and a male fin whale (*B. physalus*): molecular and morphological documentation. *Journal of Heredity*, **82**, 269–274.

1113 Spitz, J. *et al.* (2006) Dietary plasticity of the oceanic striped dolphin, *Stenella coeruleoalba*, in the neritic waters of the Bay of Biscay. *Journal of Sea Research*, **55**, 309–320.

1114 St Aubin, D.J. & Geraci, J.R. (1979) Strandings: a rare look into the biology of the Atlantic white-sided dolphin, *Lagenorhynchus acutus*, pp. 190–206 in Geraci, J.R. & St. Aubin, D.J. (eds.) *Biology of marine mammals: insights through strandings.* U.S. Marine Mammal Commission, Report MMC-77/13.

1115 St Aubin, D.J. *et al.* (1990) Seasonal epidermal molt in beluga whales, *Delphinapterus leucas. Canadian Journal of Zoology,* **68,** 359–367.

1116 Stacey, P.J. *et al.* (1994) *Pseudorca crassidens. Mammalian Species,* **456,** 1–6.

1117 Stamper, M.A. *et al.* (2006) Case study: morbidity in a pygmy sperm whale *Kogia breviceps* due to ocean-borne plastic. *Marine Mammal Science,* **22** (3), 719–722.

1118 Steeman, M.E. (2007) Cladistic analysis and a revised classification of fossil and recent mysticetes. *Zoological Journal of the Linnean Society,* **150,** 875–894.

1119 Steiner, L. *et al.* (1998) Marine mammals of the Azores, p. 79 in Evans, P.G.H. & Parsons, E.C.M. (eds.) *European research on cetaceans – 12.* European Cetacean Society.

1120 Steiner, W.W. (1981) Species-specific differences in pure tonal whistle vocalizations of five western north Atlantic dolphin species. *Behavioral Ecology and Sociobiology,* **9,** 241–246.

1121 Stevick, P.T. *et al.* (2003) Segregation of migration by feeding ground origin in North Atlantic humpback whales *(Megaptera novaeangliae). Journal of Zoology,* **259,** 231–237.

1122 Stevick, P.T. *et al.* (2003) North Atlantic humpback whale abundance and rate of increase four decades after protection from whaling. *Marine Ecology Progress Series,* **258,** 263–273.

1123 Stewart, B.S. & Leatherwood, S. (1985) Minke whale *Balaenoptera acutorostrata,* pp. 91–136 in Ridgway, S.H. & Harrison, R. (eds.) *Handbook of marine mammals,* Vol. 6. Academic Press, London.

1124 Stewart, R.E.A. (1994) Size-at-age relationships as discriminators of white whale (*Delphinapterus leucas*) stocks in the eastern Canadian Arctic. *Meddr Grønland, Biosciences,* **39,** 217–225.

1125 Stone, C.J. (1997) *Cetacean observations during seismic surveys in 1996.* Report No. 228, JNCC, Peterborough.

1126 Stone, C.J. (1998) *Cetacean observations during seismic surveys in 1997.* Report No. 278, JNCC, Peterborough.

1127 Stone, G.S. *et al.* (1988) Significant aggregations of the endangered right whale, *Eubalaena glacialis,* on the Continental Shelf of Nova Scotia. *Canadian Field Naturalist,* **102**(3), 471–474.

1128 Stone, G.S. *et al.* (1992) Respiration and surfacing rates of fin whales, *Balaenoptera physalus,* observed from a lighthouse tower. *Report of the International Whaling Commission,* **42,** 739–745.

1129 Storelli, M.M. *et al.* (1999) Heavy metals and methyl mercury in tissues of Risso's dolphin and Cuvier's beaked whale (*Ziphius cavirostris*) stranded in Italy (South Adriatic Sea). *Bulletin of Environmental Contamination and Toxicology,* **63,** 703–710.

1130 Strager, H. (1995) Pod-specific call repertoires and compound calls of killer whales, *Orcinus orca* Linnaeus, 1758, in the waters of northern Norway. *Canadian Journal of Zoology,* **73,** 1037–1047.

1131 Stuen, S. & Have, P. (1995) Serological investigation of morbillivirus infections in minke whales (*Balaenoptera acutorostrata*), pp. 641–644 in Blix, A.S. *et al.* (eds.) *Whales, seals, fish and man.* Elsevier, Amsterdam.

1132 Sturtivant, C.R. *et al.* (1994) A review of echolocation research on the harbour porpoise *Phocena phocena* and the common dolphin *Delphinus delphis,* pp. 164–168 in Evans, P.G.H. (ed.) *European research on cetaceans – 8.* European Cetacean Society.

1133 Suydam, R.S. *et al.* (2001) Satellite tracking of eastern Chukchi Sea beluga whales in the Arctic Ocean. *Arctic,* **54**(3), 237-243.

1134 Swann, C. Personal communication, with photographs

1135 Swift, R.J. *et al.* (2002) *Studying the distribution and behaviour of cetaceans in the northeast Atlantic using passive acoustic techniques.* Report for the Atlantic Frontier Environmental Network. University of Aberdeen.

1136 Tanabe, S. *et al.* (1988) Capacity and mode of PCB metabolism in small cetaceans. *Marine Mammal Science,* **4,** 103–124.

1137 Taruski, A.G. (1979) The whistle repertoire of the north Atlantic pilot whale (*Globicephala melaena*) and its relationship to behavior and environment, pp. 345–368 in Winn, H.E. & Olla, B.L. (eds.) *Behavior of marine animals, Vol. 3: Cetaceans.* Plenum Press, New York.

1138 Taruski, A.G. *et al.* (1975) Chlorinated hydrocarbons in cetaceans. *Journal of the Fisheries Research Board of Canada,* **32,** 2205–2209.

1139 Teilmann, J. Personal communication.

1140 Teilmann, J. *et al.* (2004) Journey of a minke whale from Denmark to the Mediterranean, p. 70 in *European research on cetaceans –18.* European Cetacean Society.

1141 Teilmann, J. *et al.* (2006) Summary on harbour porpoise monitoring 1999–2006 around Nysted and Horns Rev Offshore Wind Farms. Report to Energi E2 A/S and Vattenfall A/S. National Environmental Research Institute.

1142 Teilmann, J. *et al.* (in press) Time allocation and diving behaviour of harbour porpoises (*Phocoena phocoena*) in Danish waters. *Journal of Cetacean Research and Management.*

1143 Teixeira, A. (1978) Sobre a ocorrência de um exemplar de cachalote-anão, *Kogia breviceps* Blainville, 1838, no mar dos Açores. *Memórias do Museu do Mar, série zoológica,* **1**(3), 1–5 (in Portuguese).

1144 Templeman, W. (1963) Distribution of sharks in the Canadian Atlantic. *Bulletin of the Fisheries Research Board of Canada,* **140,** 1–83.

1145 Thewissen, J.G.M. *et al.* (2001) Skeletons of terrestrial cetaceans and the relationship of whales to artiodactyls. *Nature,* **413,** 277–281.

1146 Thomas, J.A. & Turl, C.W. (1990) Echolocation characteristics and range detection threshold in a false killer whale (*Pseudorca crassidens*), pp. 321-334 in Thomas, J. & Kastelain, R. (eds.) *Sensory abilities of cetaceans.* Plenum Press, New York.

1147 Thomas, J.A. *et al.* (1988) Underwater audiogram of a false killer whale (*Pseudorca crassidens*). *Journal of the Acoustical Society of America,* **84,** 936–940.

1148 Thompson, D'A.W. (1928) On whales landed at the Scottish whaling stations during the years 1908–1914 and 1920–1927. *Scientific Investigations, Fishery Board of Scotland,* **3,** 1–40.

1149 Thompson, P.O. *et al.* (1979) Mysticete sounds, pp. 403–431 in Winn, H.E. & Olla, B.L. (eds.) *Behavior of marine animals, Vol. 3: Cetaceans.* Plenum Press, New York.

1150 Thompson, P.O. *et al.* (1992) 20-Hz pulses and other vocalizations of fin whales, *Balaenoptera physalus,* in the Gulf of California, Mexico. *Journal of the Acoustical Society of America,* **92,** 3051–3057.

1151 Tiedemann, R. (1996) Mitochondrial DNA sequence patterns of harbour porpoises (*Phocoena phocoena*) from the North and the Baltic Sea. *Zeitschrift für Säugetierkunde,* **61,** 104–111.

1152 Tilbury, K.L. *et al.* (1999) Organochlorines in stranded pilot whales (*Globicephala melaena*) from the coast of Massachusetts. *Archives of Environmental Contamination and Toxicology,* **37**(1), 125–134.

1153 Tobayama, T. *et al.* (1973) Records of the Fraser's Sarawak dolphin (*Lagenodelphis hosei*) in the western North Pacific. *Scientific Reports of the Whales Research Institute,* **25,** 251–263.

1154 Tolley, K.A. *et al.* (1995) Sexual dimorphism in wild bottlenose dolphins (*Tursiops truncatus*) from Sarasota, Florida. *Journal of Mammalogy,* **76,** 1190–1198.

1155 Tolley, K.A. *et al.* (1999) Genetic population structure of harbour porpoises (*Phocoena phocoena*) in the North Sea and

Norwegian waters. *Journal of Cetacean Research and Management*, **1**, 265–274.

1156 Tolley, K.A. *et al.* (2001) Mitochondrial DNA sequence variation and phylogeographic patterns in harbour porpoises (*Phocoena phocoena*) from the North Atlantic. *Conservation Genetics*, **2**, 349–361.

1157 Tomilin, A.G. (1967) *Cetacea. Mammals of the USSR and Adjacent Countries*. Vol IX. Israel Program for Scientific Translation, Jerusalem (original edition in Russian, 1957).

1158 Tougaard, J. & Kinze, C.C. (eds.) (1999) *Proceedings from the workshop on sperm whale strandings in the North Sea : the event – the action – the aftermath. Romø, Denmark, 26–27 May 1998.* Biological Papers 1. Fisheries and Maritime Museum, Esbjerg, Denmark.

1159 Tregenza, N.J.C. (1992) 50 years of cetacean sightings from the Cornish coast, SW England. *Biological Conservation*, **59**, 65–70.

1160 Tregenza, N.J.C. & Collet, A. (1998) Common dolphins *Delphinus delphis* bycatch in pelagic trawl and other fisheries in the northeast Atlantic. *Report of the International Whaling Commission*, **48**, 453–459.

1161 Tregenza, N.J.C. *et al.* (1997) Common dolphin, *Delphinus delphis* L., by-catches in set gill nets in the Celtic Sea. *Report of the International Whaling Commission*, **47**, 835–839.

1162 Tregenza, N.J.C. *et al.* (1997) Harbour porpoise (*Phocoena phocoena* L.) by-catch in set gillnets in the Celtic Sea. *ICES Journal of Marine Science*, **54**, 896–904.

1163 True, F.W. (1904) The whalebone whales of the western North Atlantic. *Smithsonian Contributions to Knowledge*, **33**, 1–332.

1164 Tsutsumi, T. *et al.* (1961) Studies on the little toothed whales in the west sea areas of Kyusyu – V. About the food of the little toothed whales. *Bulletin of Faculty of Fisheries, Nagasaki University*, **11**, 10–28.

1165 Turner, W. (1882) On a specimen of Sowerby's whale (*Mesoplodon bidens*) captured in Shetland. *Proceedings of the Royal Society of Edinburgh*, **11**, 443–456.

1166 Tyack, P. (1981) Interactions between singing Hawaiian humpback whales and conspecifics nearby. *Behavioral Ecology and Sociobiology*, **8**, 105–116.

1167 Tyack, P. *et al.* (2006) Extreme diving behaviour of beaked whale species known to strand in conjunction with use of military sonars. *Journal of Experimental Biology*, **209**(21), 4238–4253.

1168 Urquiola, E. Personal communication.

1169 Valentini, T. *et al.*, (1994) Analysis of the variability in the pigmentation of striped dolphins *Stenella coeruleoalba* (Meyen, 1833) in the central Tyrrhenian Sea, pp. 132–135 in Evans, P.G.H. (ed.) *European research on cetaceans – 8.* European Cetacean Society.

1170 Valsecchi, E. *et al.* (2004) The effects of inbreeding on mortality during a morbillivirus outbreak in the Mediterranean striped dolphin. *Animal Conservation*, **7**, 139–146.

1171 Valverde, J.A. (1996) Notes on a specimen of Blainville's beaked whale *Mesoplodon densirostris* (De Blainville, 1817), stranded on the coast of Doñana, Huelva, southern Spain, pp. 184–189 in Evans, P.G.H. (ed.) *European research on cetaceans – 10.* European Cetacean Society.

1172 Valverde, J.A. & Caminas, J.A. (1997) The dwarf sperm whale *Kogia simus* (Owen 1866), Physeteroidea, in Spain: a correction, pp. 168–171 in Evans, P.G.H. (ed.) *European research on cetaceans – 10.* European Cetacean Society.

1172a Valverde, J.A. & Galan, J.M. (1996) Notes on a specimen of Gervais' beaked whale *Mesoplodon europaeus* (Gervais), Ziphioidea, stranded in Andalucia, southern Spain, pp. 177–183 in Evans, P.G.H. (ed.) *European research on cetaceans – 10.* European Cetacean Society.

1173 Vanderlaan, A.S.M. *et al.* (2003) Characterization of North Atlantic right-whale (*Eublalaena glacialis*) sounds in the Bay

of Fundy. *IEEE Journal of Oceanic Engineering*, **28**, 164–173.

1174 Vazquez, R. *et al.* (1996) Varamento masivo de *Delphinus delphis* en Galicia no 1995. *Eubalaena*, **9**, 22–27 (in Spanish).

1175 Verboom, W.C. & Kastelein, R.A. (1997) Structure of harbour porpoise (*Phocoena phocoena*) click train signals, pp. 343–363 in Read, A.J. *et al.* (eds.) *The biology of the harbour porpoise.* De Spil, Woerden, Netherlands.

1176 Verfuß, U.L. *et al.* (2005) Spatial orientation in echolocating harbour porpoises (*Phocoena phocoena*). *Journal of Experimental Biology*, **208**, 3385–3394.

1177 Verwey, J. & Wolff, W.J. (1982) The bottlenose dolphin (*Tursiops truncatus*), in Reijnders, P.J.H. & Wolff, W.J. (eds.) *Marine mammals of the Wadden Sea.* Balkema, Rotterdam.

1178 Vikingsson, G. (1993) Northern bottlenose whale (*Hyperoodon ampullatus*). Availability of data and status of research in Iceland. NAMMCO SC-WG/NBK1/7 1–4.

1179 Vikingsson, G.A. & Kapel, F.O. (eds.) (2000) *Minke, harp and hooded seals: major predators in the North Atlantic ecosystem* Scientific Publications Volume 2, NAMMCO, Tromsø.

1179a Villadsgaard, A. *et al.* (2007) Echolocation signals of wild harbour porpoises, *Phocoena phocoena. Journal of Experimental Biology*, **210**, 56–64.

1180 Viney, M. Personal communication.

1181 Viney, M. & Fairley, J.S. (1983) A stranding of a True's beaked whale *Mesoplodon mirus* in Co. Mayo. *Irish Naturalists' Journal*, **21**, 163–164.

1182 Vinther, M. (1999) Bycatches of harbour porpoise (*Phocoena phocoena*, L.) in Danish set-net fisheries. *Journal of Cetacean Management and Research*, **1**, 123–135.

1183 Vinther, M. & Larsen, F. (2004) Updated estimates of harbour porpoise (*Phocoena phocoena*) bycatch in the Danish North Sea bottom-set gillnet fishery. *Journal of Cetacean Management and Research*, **6**, 19–24.

1184 Viricel, A. (2006) *Spatial and social structure of the common dolphin* Delphinus delphis *in the Northeast Atlantic inferred from genetic data.* MSc thesis, Graduate School of the College of Charleston.

1185 Visser, I.N. & Makelainen, P. (2000) Variation in eye-patch shape of killer whales (*Orcinus orca*) in New Zealand waters. *Marine Mammal Science* **16**, 459–469.

1186 Vladykov, V.D. (1946) Etude sur les mammifères aquatiques. IV. Nourriture du marsouin blanc ou beluga (*Delphinapterus leucas*) du fleuve St Laurent. *Contributions de Department des Pecheries*, Quebec, No. 17 (in French).

1187 Vonk, R. & Martin, V. (1988) First list of odontocetes from the Canaries, pp. 31–35 in Evans, P.G.H. (ed.) *European research on cetaceans – 2.* European Cetacean Society.

1188 Wada, S. (1991) Genetic distinction between two minke whale stocks in the Okhotsk Sea coast of Japan. *Report of the International Whaling Commission* (SC/43/Mi32).

1189 Wada, S. & Numachi, K. (1991) Allozyme analyses of genetic differentiation among the populations and species of the *Balaenoptera. Report of the International Whaling Commission, Special Issue*, **13**, 125–154.

1190 Wada, S. *et al.* (1991) Genetic variability and differentiation of mitochondrial DNA in minke whales. *Report of the International Whaling Commission, Special Issue*, **13**, 203–216.

1191 Wade, P.R. & Gerrodette, T. (1993) Estimates of cetacean abundance in the eastern tropical Pacific. *Report of the International Whaling Commission*, **42**, 533–539.

1192 Waerebeek, K. van *et al.* (1997) Cuvier's beaked whale *Ziphius cavirostris* in the North Sea, with a first record for the Netherlands (Scheldt Estuary). *Lutra*, **40**, 1–8.

1193 Walker, D. *et al.* (2001) True's beaked whale – a first confirmed live sighting for the eastern North Atlantic. *Orca*, **2**, 63–66.

1194 Walker, D. *et al.* (2001) The status and distribution of beaked whales (Ziphiidae) in the Bay of Biscay, pp. 278–282 in Evans, P.G.H. (ed.) *European research on cetaceans – 15.* European Cetacean Society.

1195 Waller, G.H. & Tyler, N.J.C. (1979) Observations on *Lagenorhynchus acutus* stranded on the Yorkshire coast. *The Naturalist*, **104**, 61–64.

1196 Walton, M.J. (1997) Population structure of harbour porpoises *Phocoena phocoena* in the seas around the UK and adjacent waters. *Proceedings of the Royal Society of London Series B*, **264**, 89–94.

1197 Wang, J.Y. *et al.* (1995) Records of Cuvier's beaked whales (*Ziphius cavirostris*) from Taiwan, Republic of China. *Asian Marine Biology*, **12**, 111–118.

1198 Waring, G.T. *et al.* (1990) Incidental take of marine mammals in foreign fishery activities off the northeast United States, 1977–1988. *Fisheries Bulletin, U.S.*, **88**, 347–360.

1199 Waring, G.T. *et al.* (2001) *U.S. Atlantic and Gulf of Mexico marine mammal stock assessments – 2001*. NOAA Technical Memorandum NMFS-NE-168.

1200 Waring, G.T. *et al.* (2005) Distribution and density estimates of cetaceans along the Mid-Atlantic Ridge during summer 2004, pp. 297–298 in *16th Biennial Conference on the Biology of Marine Mammals*, December 12–16, San Diego, CA.

1201 Waters, S. & Whitehead, H. (1990) Aerial behaviour in sperm whales. *Canadian Journal of Zoology*, **68**, 2076–2082.

1202 Watkins, W.A. (1986) Whale reactions to human activities in Cape Cod waters. *Marine Mammal Science*, **2**, 251–262.

1203 Watkins, W.A. (1995) Fin whale sounds, pp. 11–13 in Evans, P.G.H. & Nice, H. (eds.) *European research on cetaceans – 9*. European Cetacean Society.

1204 Watkins, W.A. Personal communication.

1205 Watkins, W.A. & Schevill, W.E. (1972) Sound source location by arrival-times on a non-rigid three-dimensional hydrophone array. *Deep-Sea Research*, **19**, 691–706.

1206 Watkins, W.A. & Schevill, W.E. (1976) Right whale feeding and baleen rattle. *Journal of Mammalogy*, **57**, 58–66.

1207 Watkins, W.A. *et al.* (1984) Fin whale, *Balaenoptera physalus*, tracked by radio in the Irminger Sea. *Rit Fiskideildar*, **8**, 1–14.

1208 Watkins, W.A. *et al.* (1985) Sperm whale acoustic behaviors in the southeast Caribbean. *Cetology*, **49**, 1–15.

1209 Watkins, W.A. *et al.* (1987) The 20-Hz signals of finback whales (*Balaenoptera physalus*). *Journal of the Acoustical Society of America*, **82**, 1901–1912.

1210 Watkins, W.A. *et al.* (1993) Sperm whales tagged with transponders and tracked underwater by sonar. *Marine Mammal Science*, **9**, 55–67.

1211 Watkins, W.A. *et al.* (1994) Fishing and acoustic behavior of Fraser's dolphin (*Lagenodelphis hosei*) near Dominica, southeast Caribbean. *Caribbean Journal of Science*, **30**, 76–82.

1212 Watson, L. (1981) *Sea guide to whales of the world*. Dutton, New York

1213 Weilgart, L.S. (1990) *Vocalizations of the sperm whale* (Physeter macrocephalus) *of the Galapagos Islands as related to behavioural and circumstantial variables*. PhD dissertation, Dalhousie University, Halifax.

1214 Weilgart, L.S. & Whitehead, H. (1990) Vocalizations of the North Atlantic pilot whale (*Globicephala melas*) as related to behavioral contexts. *Behavioral Ecology and Sociobiology*, **26**, 399–402.

1215 Weir, C.R. (2001) Sightings of beaked whale species (Cetacea: Ziphiidae) in the waters to the north and west of Scotland and the Faroe Islands, pp. 239–243 in Evans, P.G.H. *et al.* (eds.) *European research on cetaceans – 14*. European Cetacean Society.

1216 Weir, C.R. *et al.* (2001) Cetaceans of the Atlantic Frontier, north and west of Scotland. *Continental Shelf Research*, **21**, 1047–1071.

1217 Weiss, B.M. *et al.* (2006) Vocal behavior of resident killer whale matrilines with newborn calves: the role of family signatures. *Journal of the Acoustical Society of America*, **119**(1), 627–635.

1218 Wells, D.E. *et al.* (1994) Organochlorine residues in harbour porpoise and bottlenosed dolphins stranded on the coast of Scotland 1988–1991. *Science of the Total Environment*, **151**, 77–99.

1219 Wells, D.E. *et al.* (1997) Patterns of organic contaminants in marine mammals with reference to sperm whale strandings, pp. 91–104 in Jacques, T.G. & Lambertsen, R.H. (eds.) *Sperm whale deaths in the North Sea. Science and management. Bulletin de L'Institut Royal des Sciences Naturelles de Belgique. Biologie*, **67** (suppl.).

1220 Wells, R.S. & Scott, M.D. (1999) Bottlenose dolphin, pp. 137–182 in Ridgway, S.H. & Harrison, R. (eds.) *Handbook of marine mammals*, Vol. 6. Academic Press, London.

1221 Wells, R.S. *et al.* (1987) The social structure of free-ranging bottlenose dolphins, pp. 247–305 in Genoways, H.H. (ed.) *Current mammalogy*, Vol. 1. Plenum Press, London.

1222 Welsh, M.J. *et al.* (1992) Characterization of a cetacean morbillivirus isolated from a porpoise (*Phocoena phocoena*). *Archives of Virology*, **74**, 631–641.

1223 Werth, A. (2000) A kinematic study of suction feeding and associated behavior in the long-finned pilot whale, *Globicephala melas* (Traill). *Marine Mammal Science*, **16**(2), 299–314.

1224 Westgate, A.J. (2005) *Population structure and life history of short-beaked common dolphins* (Delphinus delphis) *in the North Atlantic*. PhD thesis, Duke University, NC.

1225 Westgate, A.J *et al.* (1995) Diving behaviour of harbour porpoises, *Phocoena phocoena*. *Canadian Journal of Fisheries and Aquatic Sciences*, **52**, 1064–1073.

1226 Westgate, A.J. *et al.* (1996) Concentrations and accumulation patterns of organochlorine contaminants in the blubber of harbour porpoises, *Phocoena phocoena*, from the coast of Newfoundland, the Gulf of St Lawrence and the Bay of Fundy/Gulf of Maine. *Environmental Pollution*, **90**, 1–14.

1227 WGMME (2005) *ICES. Report of the working group on marine mammal ecology*. 9–12 May 2005, Savolinna, Finland

1228 White, R. & Webb, A. (1995) *Coastal birds and marine mammals of mid Dorset*. JNCC, Peterborough.

1229 Whitehead, H. (1987) Social organization of sperm whales off the Galapagos: implications for management and conservation. *Report of the International Whaling Commission*, **37**, 195–199.

1230 Whitehead, H. (1998) Cultural selection and genetic diversity in matrilineal whales. *Science*, **282**, 1708–1711.

1231 Whitehead, H. (2002) Sperm whale *Physeter macrocephalus*, pp. 1163–1172 in Perrin, W.F. *et al.* (eds.) *Encyclopaedia of marine mammals*. Academic Press, San Diego, CA.

1232 Whitehead, H. (2003) *Sperm whales. Social evolution in the ocean*. University of Chicago Press, Chicago.

1233 Whitehead, H. & Carlson, C. (1988) Social behavior of feeding finback whales off Newfoundland: comparisons with the sympatric humpback whale. *Canadian Journal of Zoology*, **66**, 217–221.

1234 Whitehead, H. & Carscadden, J.E. (1985) Predicting inshore whale abundance – whales and capelin off the Newfoundland coast. *Canadian Journal of Fisheries and Aquatic Science*, **42**, 976–981.

1235 Whitehead, H. & Glass, C. (1988) Orcas (killer whales) attack humpback whales. *Journal of Mammalogy*, **66**, 183–185.

1236 Williams, A. *et al.* (1999) *Cetaceans in the Bay of Biscay*. Unpublished report, Biscay Research Programme.

1237 Williams, A.D. *et al.* (1999) Seasonal variation in the occurrence of beaked whales in the southern Bay of Biscay, pp. 275–280. In Evans, P.G.H. *et al.* (eds.) *European research on cetaceans – 13*. European Cetacean Society.

1238 Williams, R. *et al.* (2002) Behavioural responses of killer whales (*Orcinus orca*) to whale-watching boats: opportunistic observations and experimental approaches. *Journal of Zoology*, **256**, 255–270.

1239 Williamson, G.R. (1963) Common porpoise from the stomach of a Greenland shark. *Journal of the Fisheries Research Board of Canada*, **20**, 1085–1086.

1240 Wilson, B. (1995) *The ecology of bottlenose dolphins in the Moray Firth, Scotland: a population at the northern extreme of the species' range*. Dissertation, University of Aberdeen.

1241 Wilson, B. *et al.* (1997) Habitat use by bottlenose dolphins: seasonal distribution and stratified movement patterns in the Moray Firth, Scotland. *Journal of Applied Ecology*, **34**, 1365–1374.

1242 Wilson, B. *et al.* (1999) Epidermal diseases in bottlenose dolphins: impacts of natural and anthropogenic factors. *Proceedings of the Royal Society of London Series B*, **266**, 1077–1083.

1243 Wilson, B. *et al.* (1999) Estimating size and assessing trends in a coastal bottlenose dolphin population. *Ecological Applications*, **9**, 288–300.

1244 Wilson, B. *et al.* (2004) Considering the temporal when managing the spatial: a population range expansion impacts protected areas-based management for bottlenose dolphins. *Animal Conservation*, **7**, 331–338.

1245 Wilson, D.E. & Reeder, D.M. (2005) *Mammal species of the world. A taxonomic and geographic reference*. John Hopkins University Press, Baltimore, MD.

1246 Wimmer, T. & Whitehead, H. (2004) Movements and distribution of northern bottlenose whales, *Hyperoodon ampullatus*, on the Scotian Shelf and in adjacent waters. *Canadian Journal of Zoology*, **82**, 1782–1794.

1247 Winn, H.E. & Perkins, P.J. (1976) Distribution and sounds of the minke whale, with a review of mysticete sounds. *Cetology*, **19**, 1–11.

1248 Winn, H.E. *et al.* (1970) Sounds and behavior of the northern bottlenosed whale. *Conference on Biological Sonar and Diving Mammals*, **7**, 53–59.

1249 Winn, H.E. *et al.* (1986) The distributional biology of the right whale *(Eubalaena glacialis)* in the western North Atlantic, pp. 129–138 in Brownell, R.L. Jr. *et al.* (eds.), *Right whales: past and present status*. Special Issue No. 10, International Whaling Commission, Cambridge.

1250 Witte, R.H. *et al.* (1998) Increase of the harbour porpoise *Phocoena phocoena* in the Dutch sector of the North Sea. *Lutra*, **40**, 33–40.

1251 Wood, C.J. (1998) Movement of bottlenose dolphins around the south-west coast of Britain. *Journal of Zoology*, **246**, 155–163.

1252 Woodley, T.H. & Gaskin, D.E. (1996) Environmental characteristics of North Atlantic right and fin whale habitat in lower Bay of Fundy, Canada. *Canadian Journal of Zoology*, **74**, 75–84.

1253 Wurtz, M. & Marrale, D. (1991) On stomach contents of striped dolphins (*Stenella coeruleoalba*, Meyen 1933) from the Ligurian coast, central Mediterranean Sea, pp. 62–64 in Evans, P.G.H. (ed.) *European research on cetaceans – 5*. European Cetacean Society.

1254 Wurtz, M. *et al.* (1992) Cephalopods from the stomachs of a Risso's dolphin (*Grampus griseus* Cuvier, 1812) from the Ligurian Sea, Central Mediterranean. *Journal of the Marine Biological Association of the UK*, **72**, 861–867.

1255 Yablokov, A.V. (1994) Validity of Soviet whaling data. *Nature*, **367**, 108.

1256 Yano, K. & Dahlheim, M.E. (1995) Killer whale, *Orcinus orca*, depredation on longline catches of bottomfish in the southeastern Bering Sea and adjacent waters. *Fishery Bulletin*, **93**, 355–372.

1257 Yochem, P. & Leatherwood, S. (1985) The blue whale, pp. 193–240 in Ridgway, S.H. & Harrison, R. (eds.) *Handbook of marine mammals*, Vol. 3. Academic Press, London.

1258 Yonekura, M. *et al.* (1980) On the external characters of *Globicephala macrorhynchus* off Taiji, Pacific coast of Japan. *Scientific Report of the Whales Research Institute*, **32**, 67–95.

1259 Young, D.D. & Cockcroft, V.G. (1994) Diet of common dolphin (*Delphinus delphis*) off the south east coast of southern Africa: opportunism or specialization? *Journal of Zoology*, **234**, 41–53.

1260 Young, K. *et al.* (1999) Sowerby's beaked whale (*Mesoplodon bidens*) sighting off the Island of Madeira, p. 110 in Evans, P.G.H. *et al.* (eds.) *European research on cetaceans – 13*. European Cetacean Society.

1261 Yuen, M.M.L. *et al.* (2007) The perception of complex tones by a false killer whale (*Pseudorca crassidens*). *Journal of the Acoustical Society of America*, **121**(3), 1768–1774.

1262 Zachariassen, P. (1993) Pilot whale catches in the Faroes, 1709–1992. *Report of the International Whaling Commission, Special Issue*, **14**, 69–88.

1263 Zanardelli, M. *et al.* (1990) Underwater signals by striped dolphins, p. 69 in Evans, P.G.H. *et al.* (eds.) *European research on cetaceans – 4*. European Cetacean Society.

1264 Zegers, B.N. *et al.* (2005) Levels of hexabromo-cyclododecane in harbor porpoises and common dolphins from western European seas, with evidence for stereoisomer-specific biotransformation by cytochrome P450. *Environmental Science and Technology*, **39**, 2095–2100.

1265 Zimmer, W.M.X. *et al.* (2005) Echolocation clicks of free-ranging Cuvier's beaked whales (*Ziphius cavirostris*). *Journal of the Acoustical Society of America*, **117**, 3919–3927.

1266 Zonfrillo, B. *et al* (1988) Notes on a Risso's dolphin from Argyll, with analyses of its stomach contents and mercury levels. *Glasgow Naturalist*, **1988**, 297–303.

Fin whale, showing the characteristic white right jaws *(photo P.G.H. Evans)*.

13

Escapes and introductions

Compiled by S.J. Baker

About a quarter of the terrestrial mammals with well-established populations in the British Isles and covered in earlier chapters were deliberately or accidentally introduced by humans (see Chapter 2). The acclimatisation of exotic species became a popular interest from the middle of the 19th century, resulting in various foreign mammals being deliberately released on private estates around the British Isles. Well-established exotics, such as grey squirrel *Sciurus carolinensis* and muntjac deer *Muntiacus reevesi*, date from this time. The process of introduction and establishment still continues as further species escape or are released into the wild.

The range of species that could get into the wild is large. In 2006, for example, there were 67 zoos and aquaria in the British Isles registered with the British and Irish Association of Zoos and Aquariums, plus many other collections of varying size, between them exhibiting many hundreds of different mammal species from all parts of the world. Such collections must be licensed and follow legislation laid down in the Zoo Licensing Act (Amendment, England and Wales) Regulations 2002. A few additional species of mammal are ranched in the British Isles for their meat, notably various deer, cattle and wild boar *Sus scrofa*. Farming for fur, which led to populations of coypu *Myocastor coypus*, mink *Mustela vison* and muskrat *Ondatra zibethicus* becoming established, was prohibited from 1 January 2003 under the Fur Farming (Prohibition) Act 2000. The Dangerous Wild Animals Act 1976 imposed stricter legal controls on the private keeping of potentially dangerous species, but many unusual exotic pets are still kept in private homes. Various small species are kept as children's pets and laboratory stock [6]. Some species have been unwittingly introduced from abroad in freight or on board vehicles.

This chapter considers those species that have been recorded from the wild in the past 70 years but which have not yet established a free-living population of more than 100 animals that has persisted for more than 10 years. Some species may not have survived, because of the climate or lack of suitable food. In other cases individuals may have had accidents or lacked mates. The muskrat *Ondatra zibethicus* and Himalayan porcupine *Hystrix brachyura* were deliberately eradicated. The wild boar *Sus scrofa,* which may

re-establish itself as a member of the British fauna, has been treated in the main text (Chapter 11), as a former native.

The species are considered in 3 groups that reflect their increasing possibility of ultimately becoming well established. Firstly, there are species with individuals recorded in the wild but which are not known to have survived for 1 year. This helps define a pool of species that could ultimately become established but which have not, so far, demonstrated their ability to survive in the British Isles. Next, there are those species that have escaped and survived for more than 1 year; it is therefore likely that given appropriate circumstances, such as the escape of a breeding group, a free-living population could become established. Finally there are the species that have escaped, survived and bred out of captivity, but, for various reasons, have survived only in low numbers or, so far, for a short time.

Table 13.1 lists at least 58 species (in some cases only the family or genus is known) that have escaped or been released into the wild between January 1970 and May 2006, and the maximum time that any individual has survived in the wild. At least 943 individuals were involved on 239 occasions. Data collection was described in [6]; collecting reports of mammals out of captivity has continued to May 2006. This is only a partial record, biased towards larger and more unusual species, and under-representing species such as wild boar which are breeding out of captivity and frequently seen in certain areas. Species commonly kept as pets are excluded from Table 13.1, but occasions when golden hamster and Mongolian gerbil have bred out of captivity are described in the text, as are details of Himalayan porcupine and muskrat populations, where the original escapes occurred prior to 1970. Introductions into the British Isles are reviewed in [6, 49, 51, 65, 82].

SPECIES THAT HAVE SURVIVED FOR LESS THAN 1 YEAR

Of the species listed in Table 13.1, 86% were not known to have survived out of captivity for more than 1 year. In some cases this may reflect lack of knowledge about what happened to an animal

Table 13.1 Species of exotic mammal recorded out of captivity in England and Wales between January 1970 and May 2006. The number of individuals is the minimum number that could have been present. The longest time free is longest period out of captivity recorded for any individual of the species [1]

Species		Number of occasions	Number of individuals	Longest time free
Marsupialia				
Virginia opossum	*Didelphis virginiana*	1	1	?
Red-necked wallaby[a]	*Macropus rufogriseus*	14	25	2 years
Wallaby	*Macropus* sp.	25	42	1 year
Chiroptera				
Egyptian rousette	*Rousettus aegyptiacus*	1	1	?
Indian flying fox	*Pteropus giganteus*	2	2	?
Big brown bat	*Eptesicus fuscus*	2	2	?
Unidentified exotic bat	Order Chiroptera	1	1	?
Primates				
Fat-tailed dwarf lemur	*Cheirogaleus medius*	1	3	1 week
Ruffed lemur	*Varecia variegata*	1	1	5 days
Capuchin monkey	*Cebus* sp.	2	3	20 days
Squirrel monkey	*Saimiri* sp.	3	6	10 days
Rhesus macaque	*Macaca mulatta*	2	2	3 days
Savanna monkey	*Cercopithecus aethiops*	1	1	11 weeks
Hamadryas baboon	*Papio hamadryas*	1	100	1 day
Baboon	*Papio* sp.	2	101	1 day
Unidentified monkey	Order Primates	1	1	1 day
Carnivora				
Wolf	*Canis lupus*	7	37	10 days
Arctic fox	*Alopex lagopus*	11	27	3 day
Raccoon dog	*Nyctereutes procyonoides*	2	2	?
Raccoon[a]	*Procyon lotor*	32	34	4 years
Coati	*Nasua nasua*	7	10	?
Kinkajou	*Potos flavus*	2	2	?
Red panda	*Ailurus fulgens*	1	1	5 days
Beech marten	*Martes foina*	1	1	1 day
Ratel	*Mellivora capensis*	1	1	?
Canadian otter	*Lutra canadensis*	1	2	?
Short-clawed otter[a]	*Aonyx cinerea*	5	6	5 months
Civet	Family Viverridae	1	1	?
Mongoose	*Herpestes* sp.	1	1	?
Spotted hyaena	*Crocuta crocuta*	1	1	<1 day
Leopard cat	*Felis bengalensis*	4	4	6 months
Caracal	*F. caracal*	1	1	2 weeks

Table 13.1 (*cont.*)		**Number of occasions**	**Number of individuals**	**Longest time free**
Jungle cat	*F. chaus*	2	3	10 months
Ocelot	*F. paradalis*	1	1	?
Asiatic golden cat	*F. temminckii*	1	1	?
Puma	*Puma concolor*	1	1	<1 day
Lynx	*Lynx* sp.	3	5	23 days
Lion	*Panthera leo*	2	5	<1 day
Jaguar	*P. onca*	1	2	<1 day
Leopard	*P. pardus*	1	1	1 day
Tiger	*P. tigris*	1	5	<1 day
Snow leopard	*P. uncia*	1	1	<1 day
Clouded leopard	*Neofelis nebulosa*	2	3	5 months
Sealion	Family Otariidae	1	1	1 day
Artiodactyla				——
European wild boar[a]	*Sus scrofa*	23	198	10 years
Peccary	Family Tayassuidae	1	4	?
Hippopotamus	*Hippopotamus amphibius*	1	1	<1 day
Llama	*Lama glama*	1	1	?
European bison	*Bison bonasus*	1	1	<1 day
Père David's deer[a]	*Elaphurus davidianus*	2	16	2 years
Exotic deer sp.	Family Cervidae	1	1	?
Nilgai	*Boselaphus tragocamelus*	2	3	3 years
Rodentia				——
Prairie dog[a]	*Cynomys ludovicianus*	10	15	15 months
Chipmunk	*Tamias* sp.	14	49	11 months
American Beaver	*Castor canadensis*	2	3	3 months
Beaver[a]	*Castor* sp.	2	3	13 years
Nile Rat	*Arvicanthis niloticus*	1	1	?
Garden dormouse	*Eliomys quercinus*	4	11	1 month
Crested porcupine	*Hystrix cristata*	5	7	2 years
Indian porcupine	*H. indica*	2	2	?
Porcupine	*Hystrix* sp.	1	1	?
Capybara	*Hydrochoerus hydrochoaeris*	7	19	3 months
Agouti	*Dasyprocta* sp.	1	1	?
Chinchilla	*Chinchilla laniger*	2	4	?
Degu	*Octodon* sp.	1	150	?
Total		**239**	**943**	

[a] = bred out of captivity.

once it escaped. The Chiroptera and Primates would generally find the climate and lack of food a bar to becoming established. Of the Carnivora, large cats (Felidae) and wolves *Canis lupus* were usually quickly recaptured or shot after they escaped, so did not get the opportunity to survive in the wild. A female puma *Puma concolor* of unknown origin was caught in Scotland in 1980 and, following her death after several years in captivity, was mounted and displayed in Inverness museum.

Since the 1990s there have been several hundred, often over 1000, reported sightings of 'big cats' out of captivity each year. To the author's knowledge, none of these has been substantiated. Where they have been investigated (e.g. [8, 11]), most reports seem based on mistaken identification. Melanistic leopard and puma are most frequently reported, but black large cats are rare in captivity. A leopard *Panthera pardus* skull and tiger *Panthera tigris* partial maxilla recovered from the Bodmin area were investigated but proved to have come from old hunting trophies [60], presumably planted by persons unknown. With no confirmation of even one individual 'large cat' (Felidae of the genera *Panthera, Neofelis, Acinonyx,* and *Puma*) living in the wild, breeding is highly improbable; reports of hybrids and species as yet unknown to science are science fiction.

The rodents most frequently reported out of captivity are chipmunks. Some are known to have survived over winter, but there are no records of them surviving over 1 year or breeding out of captivity. Although the specific name is rarely reported, most are probably Siberian chipmunks (*Tamias sibiricus*). Isolated introduced populations are established in five Western European countries, originating from escaped pets [57], emphasising the potential for this species to become established here (Fig.13.1). However, it seems to be prone to predation, particularly by cats, and one was caught by a red-tailed hawk *Buteo jamaicensis,* flown for bird control at a landfill site in Yorkshire in 1999.

Another species with clear potential to become established in this country is the garden dormouse *Eliomys quercinus*. It occurs throughout W Europe up to the Channel coast [57] but like the chipmunk this species has not yet been proved to have bred out of captivity or survived over a year. A young male was killed by a cat near Dover in Kent in November 1990; the cat had brought in at least 6 other individuals over several weeks [63]. One specimen had been seen in the area a month earlier, so the animals had been living wild for at least that long. It is likely, but not certain, that animals had been born in the wild. The Channel Tunnel had not been completed at that time so could not have been the route into the country. No further animals have been found, so the colony presumably no longer exists. Two very young garden dormice were brought into an animal hospital in London. They had apparently fallen down a chimney but were too young to have been independent of their mother. A single young adult female was found dead in Carshalton Beeches, Surrey, in June 1991 and another individual in 1992 in a car in London that had just returned from France. This species may come in as an accidental introduction from continental Europe quite frequently and may sometimes be deliberately (but illegally) imported as it is small, appealing, and will quite commonly be seen in houses and gardens. Two archaeological records, from York and South Shields in the Roman period, about 200 AD, are presumed due to deliberate importations for culinary use [62, 84].

SPECIES THAT HAVE SURVIVED FOR MORE THAN 1 YEAR, BUT NOT BRED

These species are considered here in more detail. Survival for 1 year indicates that at least one individual in one location was able to survive through the variations of climate and food supply that occur over a full year. It does not prove that the species would survive in all years, for example through unusually cold winters, or that young could survive. However, as the number that escape is usually small, that even a few of them manage to survive is good evidence that, given appropriate conditions, a viable population could become established.

As well as the following species, each with escapes reported on a number of occasions, there is one record of a nilgai *Boselaphus tragocamelus* (Artiodactyla, Bovidae). A single animal escaped from a zoo in Hampshire in 1972 and was recaptured in 1975, but little else is known about the incident [1].

Raccoon *Procyon lotor*
(Carnivora, Procyonidae)

RECOGNITION
Distinctive-looking carnivore about the size of a cat (head and body *c.*550 mm). Has a plump, grey-furred body, hunched back, pointed nose and ears, and a black mask across the eyes. Tail fairly short and bushy, ringed with a series of black bands, *c.*300 mm.

NATURAL RANGE AND HABITAT
N and C America; prefers woodland near water.

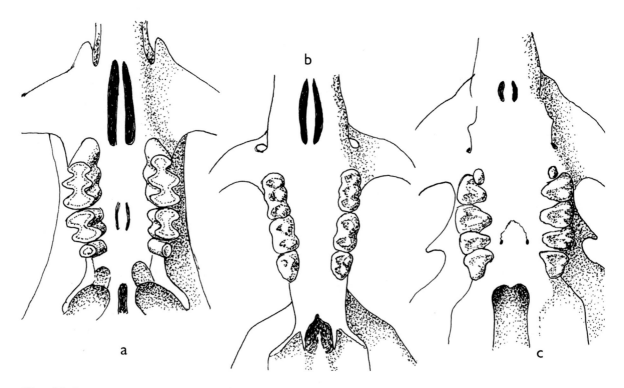

Fig. 13.1 Cheek teeth of (a) gerbil *Meriones unguiculatus*, (b) hamster *Mesocricetus auritus* and (c) chipmunk *Tamias striatus*, species that might occur unexpectedly in owl pellets (*drawn by D.W. Yalden*).

STATUS IN THE BRITISH ISLES

Frequently kept in zoos, and privately as an exotic pet. Has an inquisitive nature and dextrous forepaws which combine to make it an expert escape artist. An opportunistic feeder, able to survive in a wide variety of different habitats. Well established in C Europe including parts of France, Belgium, Netherlands, Germany, Austria, Switzerland and the Czech Republic [51, 57, 61]. No evidence of a breeding population in the British Isles, although a pregnant female escaped near Sheffield in 1984 and is thought to have given birth to 2 cubs in the wild. There have been at least 32 records of free-living individuals from throughout England since 1970, of which 6 are believed to have been at large for more than a year, the longest 4 years [1].

There is evidence to suggest that owners reacted to racoons being included under the Dangerous Wild Animal Act in 1984, and a licence fee being payable, by deliberately releasing them [6]. Although the introduction of this legislation has reduced the incidence of escapes, it has not completely prevented them. There were 22 escapes recorded in the 18 years up to 1988 (i.e. up to 4 years after the Act was passed, given known longevity in the wild) but 10 in the following 18 years. European experience makes it likely that the species could establish in the British Isles; failure, so far, may be due to it being kept singly or in small groups, and on all but 2 of the occasions

raccoons escaped alone, without mates. It is important to distinguish such chance events preventing establishment from ecological ones such as competition from native species. If there are ecological constraints on a species becoming established, it may never happen; if it is a matter of chance, then it may only be a matter of time.

Canadian beaver *Castor canadensis*
(Rodentia, Castoridae)

RECOGNITION

Large, distinctive rodents (body weight to 30 kg) with a large flat scaly tail, webbed hind feet and large incisor teeth.

RANGE AND HABITAT

Native to forested parts of temperate N America; introduced to and well-established in Finland and Russia [51]. The closely related European beaver *Castor fiber* was formerly part of the native British fauna (see Table 3.1).

STATUS IN THE BRITISH ISLES

The Canadian beaver is the species most commonly kept in zoological collections in the British Isles. In the past, captive colonies have been established under semi-natural conditions, on various private estates: at Sotterley Park, near Beccles, Suffolk in 1870; on the Isle of Bute,

Scotland in 1874; and at Leonardslea, Horsham, Sussex, in 1890. A thriving colony existed on Bute for many years, while at Leonardslea there were still beaver present in 1938 some 50 years after the initial foundation, although 2 new animals were added in 1917 [9, 53]. The small group of beaver at Sotterley Park escaped confinement soon after their arrival and were at liberty in the park for 2 seasons, during which time they bred. Their offspring attempted to establish themselves on Benacre Broad, some 7 km from the park but were eventually all either captured or killed [30].

More recently, escaped beaver (believed to be *C. canadensis*) have been recorded in Essex (1984), Surrey (1990, 1998), and in Somerset. That in Somerset was one of two that escaped from a wildlife park in 1977; one was recaptured but the other was likely to be still surviving in 1990 when fresh sign of beaver was present on the river Axe [1].

Crested porcupine *Hystrix cristata*
(Rodentia, Hystricidae)

RECOGNITION
Large rodent, weighing up to 15 kg, 800 mm from nose to tail; blunt face; coarse black bristles cover the front half of the body, long sharp black and white banded spines cover the rear (spines up to 400 mm long). Has crest of thin spines on top of head and neck.

RANGE AND HABITAT
Native to N Africa, probably introduced to Italy and Sicily. Lives in a range of arid habitats, sometimes causes agricultural damage.

STATUS IN THE BRITISH ISLES
In 1972 a pair escaped from Alton Towers, near Stoke-on-Trent, Staffordshire. Subsequently the animals were sighted or signs were found from an area of 7 km² around Alton Towers for at least 2 years. A single male escaped from a private collection in County Durham in 1983 and was recaptured 18 months later when discovered feeding on broad beans in a suburban garden in Durham. Two also escaped from a wildlife collection in Norfolk in 1977 (one of them twice!) but were recaptured within a month.

SPECIES KNOWN TO HAVE ESCAPED, SURVIVED AND BRED

This section considers those species where there has been, or is likely to have been, breeding out of captivity but where a free-living population of more than 100 animals that has persisted for more than 10 years has not yet been established.

Red-necked wallaby *Macropus rufogriseus*
(Marsupialia, Macropodidae)

RECOGNITION
Only this one species of wallaby is known to be at

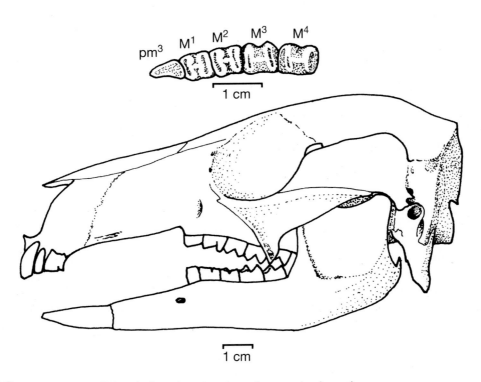

Fig 13.2 Red-necked wallaby: skull, and crown view of upper cheek-teeth.

Table 13.2 Size of red-necked wallabies related to age: mean measurements of samples in New Zealand [14]

Age (years)	Crown–tail tip (cm)		Weight (kg)		n	
	Males	**Females**	**Males**	**Females**	**Males**	**Females**
1	82	85	3.4	3.9	14	10
2	113	109	8.9	7.8	68	45
3	129	120	12.9	10.0	44	32
4	136	125	15.2	11.2	25	18
5	138	126	16.1	11.6	23	19
6	146	130	18.7	12.2	13	7
7	150	129	20.8	12.4	11	16

large in the British Isles. The skull (Fig. 13.2) is immediately recognisable from the combination of three pairs of upper incisors with one pair of procumbent lower incisors. The lophodont molars are also very distinctive.

SIGN

Tracks (e.g. in snow) are unmistakable (Fig. 13.3). Droppings are easier to find than the animals themselves, and fairly distinctive: each pellet is ovoid, *c*.15 × 20 mm (larger than sheep or roe deer pellets), rounded at both ends, and composed of rather coarse material. Pellets are loosely clumped, perhaps 5–6 in a loose string (whereas ruminant pellets are usually in larger piles and composed of finely comminuted fragments).

DESCRIPTION

Generally grizzled greyish-brown above, white below. A rusty patch over the shoulders, variable in intensity. Tail silver-grey, tipped black: the paws, feet and ears are also tipped black, and the face is black in young animals. There is a pale line along the upper lip and a pale spot over each eye; these may spread in older animals to give a white face.

Chromosomes: 2n = 16 [42].

MEASUREMENTS

Males larger than females (Table 13.2). Tail length of adults *c*.67–78 cm in males, 62–68 cm in females; hind foot *c*.22–23 cm in males, 20–21 cm in females [14].

VARIATION

British populations derived from *M. r. rufogriseus*, the Tasmanian race, which differs from *M. r. banksianus* of mainland Australia in its more sombre colouring and in having seasonal breeding [55]. Fawn and silver animals have been reported in the Peak District, the latter possibly very old individuals [83]. Albinos frequent in captivity.

DISTRIBUTION

Native to E Australia from C Queensland to S Australia and Tasmania. Introduced to the S Island of New Zealand, to Germany and to various zoos and parks in the British Isles, notably Whipsnade (Bedfordshire). A feral colony in the Peak District began in 1940 with Whipsnade stock [83] and survived for 60 years but is now dying out. A feral colony in the Weald, Sussex, survived at least from 1940 to 1972, but seems to have died out. A small colony on Inchconnachan island, Loch Lomond, has existed since at least 1975, as has a small colony on the Isle of Man. This is among the most frequently reported of exotics [6], with reports widely scattered across the country, sometimes in

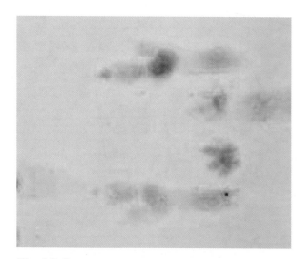

Fig 13.3 Red-necked wallaby: tracks in snow, showing long hind feet, small forefeet and tail drag *(photo D.W. Yalden)*

Fig 13.4 Red-necked wallaby in the Peak District, showing attitude when moving quickly *(photo D.W. Yalden)*.

numbers that suggest other undocumented colonies, e.g. frequent records near Henley-on-Thames. The free-ranging colony at Whipsnade Zoo numbers around 400–600 [17, 23]. A small colony existed on Herm, Channel Isles, from the 1890s to about 1910.

HABITAT

This is a scrub wallaby, lying up in woodland but coming into the open to feed [12, 40]. The Peak District population lives in scrub (mainly birch and pine) and adjoining heather moorland; those on Inchconnan are in open birch–oak–pine woodland [79, 83].

SOCIAL ORGANIZATION AND BEHAVIOUR

Generally solitary, or in loose groups of up to 4–5 individuals, but no herd structure apparent. Usually silent, but faint growling or hissing heard when close to animals disputing food or mates [1, 23]. When alarmed, use foot-slapping (like rabbits) for first 2–3 bounds, presumably to warn other individuals of danger. Sight poor, especially in bright light, but hearing acute, and ears move constantly (and independently) when suspicious.

More active towards dusk and throughout the night than during the day [17], when tend to lie up in dense vegetation or in broken ground [40]. No permanent home site, but may favour depressions between heather tussocks or beneath young birches; in summer, often within bracken stands. No evidence of territoriality; recognisable individuals occupy home ranges of about 500 m diameter [1], comparable with 15 ha reported in Australia [40].

Fast locomotion a bipedal jumping gait, as expected of a kangaroo (Fig. 13.4). At slower speeds, especially when feeding, the hindlimbs alternate as supports with the forelimbs plus tail

[80]. Grooms tail, underside and hindquarters with forefeet, licking them frequently; 'comb' formed from vestigial inner hind toes used for grooming head and shoulders.

Reviews of social behaviour given in [68, 69].

FEEDING

Regarded as a general grazer and browser in Australia, but no details. Peak District population feeds predominately on heather *Calluna* (50% in summer, 90% in winter), but also on grasses and bilberry, sometimes on pine, bracken, oak, rowan and birch [83]. In winter, the Scottish population eats a mixture of heather (35%), bilberry (35%) and grasses (13%) [79]. Whipsnade population feeds on grasses [17]. Like other kangaroos indulge in 'pseudorumination' [58]; i.e. they have a complex stomach, in which fermentation by bacteria takes place, and they may regurgitate food to chew it, though less routinely then ruminants.

BREEDING

Studied in the wild in New Zealand [12], and in captivity both in Australia [55] and in England (Whipsnade) [23].

Breeding seasonal, with peak of births in August–September, and peak emergence from pouch in late May–June (at Whipsnade), but breeding season spread over 6 months (births June–December in the British Isles, January–July in S hemisphere). Less detailed observations of feral population conform to this pattern [81]. Females breed from 1 year old, males from 2. One young per litter (twins very rare – perhaps 1%), but replacement young usually produced if first one lost from pouch early in development. Postpartum oestrus and mating results in blastocyst with delayed development: blastocyst stays quiescent through lactation and non-breeding season for up to 11 months. Active gestation lasts usually

30 days (27–41 days recorded); pouch life lasted 274 (264–286) days in Australia, 247 (185–284) days at Whipsnade. Young stay near mother and suck for another 200–250 days. Mother–young relationship described in detail in [41].

Sex ratio of pouch young biased, 60% male in 2 studies (n = 160); this bias also reported in adults for both Whipsnade population [23] and in wild in New Zealand [13] but difficult to interpret because females with well-grown young tend to remain in cover, thus under-represented in samples.

POPULATION

Peak District population increased from 5 released in 1940 to about 50 in 1962, but then reduced by severe winter. Has varied between 10 and 20 during 1970–1990, occupying about 400 ha of woodland and moorland, but since declined to only 1 in 2006 [1, 81, 83]. Inchconnachan population estimated at 26 in 1992 [79]. Isle of Man colony possibly >20. In New Zealand, reached densities of 0.6–1.3/ha, since reduced by pest control operations. Whipsnade population reached a maximum of about 900 in 200 ha (4.5/ha) in 1979, but then crashed in severe 1978/79 winter.

Pouch young can be aged by length of hind foot; adults can be aged post-mortem from the forward movement of the cheek teeth in the skull, or from growth lines in the jaw [13, 45, 46]. Oldest feral animal examined was 12.25 years old, but Whipsnade animals to 14 and 15 years old, and one of *c*.19 years in Australia [46].

MORTALITY

In the British Isles, New Zealand and Tasmania, suffer heavy mortality in severe snowfalls. Road casualties and other accidents also important; in Australia, an important prey of dingo *Canis familiaris*. Of 32 recorded deaths of Peak District animals, 11 died in road accidents, 10 in snowy weather, 5 in other accidents (drowning, falling over cliffs) and 3 killed by other animals (dog, fox); only 3 died apparently of old age [1]. Suspicion that both road and other accidents result from fleeing in panic from disturbance by dogs or people; certainly very timid.

RELATIONS WITH HUMANS

In parts of Australia, regarded as a pest of forestry, preventing natural regeneration of *Eucalyptus*. In New Zealand likewise a forestry pest, so 70 000 shot 1947–1956 and many more poisoned. No likelihood of such large populations occurring in the British Isles. Does well in captivity, and popular as a small park/zoo animal. Now illegal to release into the wild here, as listed on Schedule 9 of the Wildlife and Countryside Act 1981.

Asian short-clawed otter *Aonyx cinerea*
(Carnivora, Mustelidae)

RECOGNITION

The smallest of the world's otters. Only 43% of weight of male *L. lutra*. Facial shape and reduced claws/webbing on feet diagnostic (see Description).

SIGN

Spraint sites conspicuous in Asia because of crab remains [47]. However, a different diet may make spraints inconspicuous in England and no certain spraints of *A. cinerea* yet found in the wild. In captivity spraints differ from those of *L. lutra* by being unformed and of foul odour [78]. Spraints higher up and further from the river than *L. lutra* where sympatric in Thailand [47, 48].

DESCRIPTION

Dorsal colour variable from pale ashy-brown to dark chocolate-brown according to season and subspecies. Ventrally paler. *A. c. nirnai* from S India darkest [28]. A sharp demarcation line runs from ear to nose below the eye, separating the darker dorsal from pale ventral fur. Face noticeably short and blunt with eyes proportionately closer to the nose on a line from ear to rhinarium than in *L. lutra*. Eye–nose 44% of ear–nose (54% in *L. lutra*) [1]. Digits only webbed to proximal ends of digital pads, i.e. to the 2nd phalanx. Claws on all feet rudimentary and erect [28].

MEASUREMENTS

Size: Head plus body 406–635 mm; tail 246–351 mm [28]. Tail smaller relative to head plus body (54.5%) than in *L. lutra* (62.3%) [1]. Little difference in size between the sexes (see 'Anatomy').

Weight: 2.7–5.4 kg; *A. c. nirnai* type male 4.3 kg [28].

Anatomy: Skull smaller and relatively broader than that of *L. lutra*. Adult condylobasal length (CL) 84.9 mm (male; n = 11) and 84.8 mm (female; n = 7) (data from [4, 16]) compared to 114.5 mm and 107.8 mm for Scottish *L. lutra* [54]. Zygomatic width 68.5% and 56.2% of CL in the two species.

Dentition 3/3, 1/1, 3 (or 4)/3, 1/2 = usually 34. 1st upper premolar generally absent, but not invariably so [28].

DISTRIBUTION

Native range discontinuous: S India, Bengal, Assam, S China, Myanmar (Burma), Thailand, Malay peninsula, Vietnam, Sumatra, Java, Borneo [28]. 3 geographically separated subspecies listed [28]: *A. c. cinerea, A.c concolor, A. c. nirnai.* More than 1 subspecies may have been involved in escapes.

SOCIAL ORGANISATION AND BEHAVIOUR

Playful, climbs well. Largely crepuscular. More social, diurnal and vociferous than *L. lutra* [77]. Pair-bond strong and male helps rear cubs. Couple or family hunt together as a unit with constant chittering and squeaking contact calls [78].

FEEDING

Native diet consists of less fish and more crabs, snails, mussels and other invertebrates than that of other otters [64]. In captivity fed on fish and chickens [78]. Diet when feral unknown. Searches for prey in shallow water with its 'fingers' [47, 77]. Holds food up to the mouth with forepaws when feeding [77].

BREEDING

Gestation as *L. lutra* [15]. No delayed implantation. Births at Otter Trust recorded in all months with peak in June. Capable of breeding at intervals of 6.4 months (6 litters in 32 months by one pair). Mean litter size in captivity 3.43, median 3, range 2–6 with 2.71 reared to maturity (n = 42) ([1], Otter Trust data).

POPULATION

First feral report in British Isles July 1981. Main area around Oxford with six reports between 1983 and 1993. Sightings/photographs/bodies on river Thame, Draycot, 1983 [36]; Bayswater brook, Headington, 1986 [36]; Oxford Canal/river Thames, 1991 [37]; rivers Glyme, Dorn and Cherwell (all 1993) [74]. Twice reported with cubs; August 1983 [36], July 1993 [74]. Span of sightings 17 km in 1986, 25 km in 1993. Single occurrences reported in Kent (July 1981) [36], Gloucestershire (Gloucester; November 1985) [1] and Avon (Bath; January 1987)[1].

MORTALITY

The 2 recorded deaths of feral animals were road casualties [36, 37]. Renal calculi causing kidney failure are a common cause of mortality in captivity [77]. Longevity of 5 years in captivity is known [77].

RELATIONSHIP WITH HUMANS AND NATIVE WILDLIFE

Regarded as an attractive and amenable exotic species, widely kept in wildlife parks and private collections. Not considered to be a fisheries pest where native [64]. No hybridisation problems. Selective feeding on native invertebrates (e.g.

crayfish *Austropotamobius pallipes*) unknown, but unlikely to become a serious conservation problem unless otter densities increase greatly. All areas colonised contained no or few *L. lutra* at time of occupation. Although sympatric with Eurasian otter in parts of native range [47, 48], the interaction between the recovering native otter population and feral American mink *Mustela vison* in the British Isles suggests that *A. cinerea* may be attacked and eliminated on the return of *L. lutra* [38, 73]. Indeed, the lack of records in Thames region since the 1990s may correlate with the release of 17 *L. lutra* at 3 sites on the upper Thames near Oxford by the Otter Trust in 1999 [39]. These animals were released in advance of the recovering native otter population [73] and are known to have eliminated the local American mink population within 2 years [38]. Having spread to the surrounding tributaries by 2000–2002 [19], they could also have reduced the few *A. cinerea* present.

Père David's deer *Elaphurus davidianus* (Artiodactyla, Cervidae)

RECOGNITION

A large, rather inelegant deer similar in size to red deer (shoulder height *c.*1300 mm). Head rather long, hooves large and splayed; distinctive tail, longer than in any other deer (*c.*500 mm), with a dark tasselled tip. Summer coat tawny with a dark dorsal stripe; winter coat consists of coarse, wiry, buff-coloured hair. Males carry antlers composed of 2 shafts, one almost vertical with one or more branches, the other backward-pointing and simple.

NATURAL RANGE AND HABITAT

Formerly in the marshy lowlands of NE China; thought to have been extinct in the wild for more than 2000 years. Preserved by successive Chinese emperors in the imperial hunting park south of Beijing (Peking) where they were 'discovered' by Père Armand David in 1865. During extensive flooding in 1894 the park walls were breached and many of the animals perished; the survivors were destroyed during the following years of civil unrest.

STATUS IN THE BRITISH ISLES

A few years before the loss of the Beijing herd, animals had been procured by various European zoos. During the 1890s, the 11th Duke of Bedford acquired the surviving deer from Paris, Berlin and Cologne to form the nucleus of a successful breeding herd. Their descendants can be seen today in the deer park at Woburn Abbey, at

Whipsnade Zoo, Bedfordshire, and in many other zoos and parks [10].

Some individuals have escaped to the wild. An animal seen near Aston Abbotts, Bucks, between 1963 and 1964, probably came from Woburn [18]; another single deer noted at Balmaha, near Loch Lomond, during 1952 and 1953 was probably one of several deer which escaped from a zoo near Strathblane a few years earlier [56]. Another group of about 12 strayed from a farm near Swindon, Wiltshire, in 1981, and several were known to be still at large over a year later [6]. A herd of 25–30 centred on an unfenced estate at Ashton Wold in Northamptonshire are frequently found within a 16 km radius of the estate. In 1997 2 yearling stags were seen in Monks Wood 13 km from the estate and 2 further stags were shot at Wooley 14 km from the estate. Young calves have been seen some distance from the estate and have almost certainly been born in the wild [27]. Large and easily shot, so may not become readily established out of captivity.

Black-tailed prairie dog *Cynomys ludovicianus* (Rodentia, Sciuridae)

RECOGNITION
Medium-sized rodent, about the size of a grey squirrel; lives colonially in well-developed burrow systems, usually in open grassland.

NATURAL RANGE AND HABITAT
Native to the grasslands of central N America.

STATUS IN THE BRITISH ISLES
A number of wildlife parks have free-living colonies of prairie dogs within their grounds and little to keep them within the perimeter. Colonies have been reported outside the perimeters of three parks, in Cornwall, Isle of Wight and Cambridgeshire. In Cornwall, in 1976, a colony was established 6 km from the wildlife park; at least 6 animals are known to have been killed or caught outside the boundary of the park. On the Isle of Wight, burrows used by free-living prairie dogs were present on agricultural land for several years. Local farmers reported that young had been born outside the park. On two other occasions prairie dogs were found some distance from their presumed source, a known colony kept as described above (Staffordshire, Norfolk). That in Norfolk was knocked over by a car 8 km from the likely source.

Free-living animals have been shot, killed by dogs and gassed (illegally, as there is no product approved for the purpose in GB).

Golden hamster *Mesocricetus auratus*
(Rodentia, Cricetidae, Cricetinae)

RECOGNITION
Soft-furred, plump, blunt-faced rodent with a very short, scarcely visible tail and capacious cheek pouches. Larger than a field vole but smaller than a rat (head and body *c*.150 mm). Common coloration a bright golden brown, with contrasting white undersides; dark cheek stripes, collar mark and white pouch patches are variable. Selective breeding in captivity has produced a wide variety of coat types and colour variants, including long-haired, red-coated, white, cream and particoloured individuals. See also teeth, Fig. 13.1.

NATURAL RANGE AND HABITAT
Known only from N Syria. Very few wild-caught specimens recorded, all from Aleppo and nearby localities. Other species of *Mesocricetus* occur in the steppes of Asia Minor, the S Caucasus, north of the Caucasus, Bulgaria and E Rumania.

STATUS IN THE BRITISH ISLES
The first live specimens, imported from Aleppo in 1880 by retired British consul J.H. Skere, were taken to Edinburgh where a small stock flourished in captivity for *c*.30 years before dying out. All current domestic hamsters are descendants of a single adult female and her 12 young, captured in Aleppo in 1930 and taken to Jerusalem University [2, 29]. This initial group increased to *c*.150 in a single year; today hamsters are one of the commonest and most popular children's pets and are widely kept in private homes, schools and laboratories. There are undoubtedly frequent escapes; as a result several feral populations have been established in protected semi-urban environments such as basements, under floors and in outhouses. Several infestations have been recorded [5, 50, 66, 67]: Bath, Avon 1958 – 52 caught in basement from 6 that had escaped in 1957; Finchley, N London 1962 – 25 caught in a shop from 4 that escaped in 1960; Bootle, Lancashire, 1962 – 17 trapped in a florist's shop; Bury St Edmunds, Suffolk, 1964–1965 – 230 caught in a colony under shops; Burnt Oak, Barnet, N London, 1980–1981 – 150 caught around houses, sheds and allotment gardens on a council housing estate.

Muskrat *Ondatra zibethicus*
(Rodentia, Cricetidae, Arvicolinae)
Castor zibethicus L, 1766; E Canada.

RECOGNITION
A very large amphibious vole, resembling water vole in colour, proportions but much larger (averaging 1000 g (females), 1200 g (males), range 600–1700 g). Small protruding eyes and small ears almost hidden in glossy brown pelage. Rather clumsy on land, hindfeet adapted for swimming, partially webbed with fringes of stiff hairs; smaller forefeet not webbed. Tail laterally compressed. Skull very like large water vole, condylobasal length >45 mm.

DISTRIBUTION
Native to N America, from Gulf of Mexico, Rio Grande and lower Colorado river valleys in the south, north to edge of tundra. Introduced to C Europe, near Prague, 1905; spread from there aided by escapes from fur farms and deliberate introductions. Now widespread from France to Finland, N Sweden, though absent Iberia, Italy, most of Balkans and Scandinavia [57], also in much of Russia. Introduced to British Isles 1920s (Fig. 13.7), established short-lived colonies successfully exterminated by 1937.

HISTORY
Over 87 fur farms established by 1930, escapes soon followed. In GB, resulted in 4 established wild populations: in Tay basin, Scotland; Severn valley, Shropshire; Sussex and Surrey. Keeping of

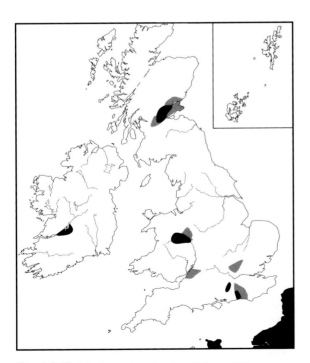

Fig 13.7 Muskrat, distribution 1929–1935.

muskrats prohibited in 1933 under the Destructive Imported Animals Act 1932. From 1932 the Ministry of Agriculture carried out a trapping campaign which at the peak employed 39 trappers. Eradication campaign well documented [75, 76]; 4382 trapped, mostly 1933–1934, stragglers to 1936–1937. In Shropshire, largest population, 2720 trapped 1932–1935; 958 Scotland, 55 Surrey, 162 Sussex. Odd stragglers reported elsewhere. Last killed in England in 1935 and Scotland in 1937 [25, 31, 75, 76]. Trapping used leg-hold traps (now illegal) set with long chains so that animals drowned in deeper water. A large number of non-target species were caught; over 6500 mammals and birds were killed in Scotland alone [59].

In Ireland, 3 individuals imported in 1929 to Annaghbeg, Co. Tipperary; escaped and by 1933 muskrats were established over an area of 50 square miles from Lough Derg south to Nenagh. From September 1933 to May 1934, 487 were killed, and the last individual was killed in 1935 [22].

HABITAT
Lives next to almost any freshwater or brackish water-body, mostly in slow-flowing rivers, canals, lakes and marshes with abundant emergent vegetation.

BEHAVIOUR
Burrows in deep banks where possible; otherwise makes lodges, hollowed-out heaps of vegetation near or at water level; are tall mounds resembling beaver lodges (but unlike them, of marsh plants not of sticks). Runways through marshes, tunnels, much as expected of large vole; digs channels, like beaver, to reach favoured feeding areas.

Active at any time but more nocturnal than diurnal.

FEEDING
Mainly herbivorous, feeding on a wide range of plants, often digging for underground parts; eats some animal material including molluscs and crustaceans. Eats a range of cultivated plants including carrots, maize, peanuts and apples. In England, diet especially of aquatic plants (water crowfoot, water lily, rush, reedmace), also twigs, bark, leaves of willow, poplar; 27 plant species recorded from stomachs [76]; occasionally animal food, including mussels *Anodonta.*

BREEDING
In N America, young born in all months but all breeding parameters strongly influenced by latitude; in Iowa about 90% between April and July [21]. In England, seasonal, pregnancies late March–early August; 2 (possibly 3) litters per year, average 7 young (1–10) [76]. Young blind, naked,

about 21 g at birth; earliest young weaned, trappable, by late May, about 5 weeks old, 250–350 g. Mature after 1st winter. Sex ratio probably 1:1 at birth, but biased, 57% male, in trapped samples [76].

RELATIONS WITH HUMANS

Considered a valuable fur-bearer (musquash) in N America, hence widespread introductions to Europe; also capable of causing severe damage to banks of canals, hence rapid extermination campaigns in British Isles. Latter considered very efficient, in that well-organised, adequately funded, timely; political agreement was difficult [70], but in practice campaigns swiftly concluded, due to good management of trapping (including consulting European and other experts, retaining trappers well past capture of latest muskrats) [25]. Illegal to import muskrat under Destructive Imported Animals Act 1932 and similar legislation in Ireland.

Mongolian gerbil *Meriones unguiculatus*
(Rodentia, Muridae, Gerbillinae)

RECOGNITION

A sleek, speckled yellowish-brown rodent with a well-haired, black-tipped tail and white underparts. Feet pale with black claws, soles of the hindfeet almost entirely covered with fur. Eyes large, upper incisor teeth grooved. Larger than a wood mouse but smaller than a rat (head and body *c*.120 mm, tail *c*.100 mm). Several colour varieties have been bred, including black, white, grey and pale fawn. For teeth, see Fig. 13.1.

NATURAL RANGE AND HABITAT

Arid steppe and desert in Mongolia and adjacent regions of China and former USSR. Lives in small colonies in burrow systems.

STATUS IN THE BRITISH ISLES

First bred in captivity in Japan; 11 pairs from there formed the foundation stock imported into the USA in 1954 [3]. Reached British Isles during the 1960s and soon gained popularity as a children's pet because of their gentle nature and ease of maintenance. More social than hamsters, consequently often kept in pairs or groups; escapees readily establish themselves under the floors of houses and outbuildings but have also survived in less protected environments. There are several records for Yorkshire [32–34]: 2 from isolated areas on Thorne Moor and at Swinfleet Moor early in 1971; at Bradford in 1975 3 animals were found in a burrow under tree roots in woodland near a housing estate. In March 1987 gerbil remains were recovered from a fresh long-eared owl pellet, collected at a roost near Mexborough, S Yorkshire [35]. In a more typical incident, gerbils were found living under sheds at a school in Armthorpe between 1972 and 1973. More escaped from the school science laboratory in 1975 and this colony was still in existence in 1977. The best-documented population existed in burrows in and around a woodyard, under sheds and houses at Fishbourne, Isle of Wight, Hampshire. A colony of >100 animals was estimated in 1976, all descendants of a few gerbils used in a children's TV programme and left behind in 1973 [49]. Melanics common in Netherlands, the likely source of one found (imported with cut flowers?), in a Bolton florist's shop, 1996.

Himalayan porcupine *Hystrix brachyura*
(Rodentia, Hystricidae)

RECOGNITION

Large, stout rodent, weighing up to 12.5 kg and 80 cm from nose to tail; blunt face; coarse black bristles cover the front half of the body, long sharp black and white banded spines cover the rear. Spines erected when feels threatened. Lacks prominent crest of thin spines on top of head and neck of crested porcupine *Hystrix cristata* (more commonly held in captivity, has also escaped in the past). Formerly called *Hystrix hodgsoni* (e.g. on Schedule 9 of Wildlife and Countryside Act 1981), but this now regarded as a synonym of *H. brachyura*.

NATURAL RANGE AND HABITAT

Native range, foothills of the C and E Himalayas, up to 1500 m, and forests of Malaya, Sumatra and Borneo.

BREEDING

Studies on the small sample of animals caught in Devon and held in captivity indicated that breeding could occur throughout the year; gestation period about 105 days; litter size 1 (n = 7) or occasionally 2 (n = 1), weight at birth 261±84 g [24].

STATUS IN THE BRITISH ISLES

Considerable burrowing and gnawing ability can lead to escapes. A feral population became established near Okehampton, Devon, during the 1970s, originating from a single pair which escaped from a wildlife park in 1969 [26]. Numerous records within a 16 km radius of Okehampton. Lived in badger setts, usually disused ones. When found, in 1973, to have caused extensive damage to a spruce plantation, Ministry of Agriculture alerted and a live-trapping programme started. By the time the last animal was caught in 1979, 5 adults and 1 subadult had been accounted for: 4 trapped, 1 killed by a terrier and 1 found dead [71]. Up to 12 individuals could have been at large [26]. With no further evidence for over 20 years, it is certain that the Devon population is no longer extant.

PROBLEMS CAUSED BY INTRODUCED MAMMALS

Some of the best-known British mammals (e.g. rabbit *Oryctolagus cuniculus*, brown hare *Lepus europaeus* and house mouse *Mus domesticus*) were introduced by humans, and introduced species can cause serious ecological damage. The impact of grey squirrels on red squirrels *Sciurus vulgaris* through competition [43] and transmission of disease [44] and the depredations on water vole *Arvicola terrestris* populations by American mink *Mustela vison* [72] are well-known examples. Some introductions might be relatively benign, but ecological damage may be subtle; for example, the hybridisation of red deer *Cervus elaphus* and sika *C. nippon*. By the time problems become apparent it may be highly expensive [6] or practically impossible to eradicate the species causing the problem.

The Bern Convention [20] recognises the potential damage that can be caused to an existing fauna and flora by introduced species. Contracting Parties are required to 'strictly control the introduction of non-native species'. GB has ratified this convention and its obligations are fulfilled under section 14 of the Wildlife and Countryside Act 1981, which makes it an offence to release, or allow to escape, any species which do not have established populations in the wild (and some non-native species which do but are listed on Schedule 9, Part 1 to the 1981 Act). The Natural Environment & Rural Communities Act 2006 gives the Secretary of State powers to prohibit the sale (or advertisement for sale) of specified non-native animal species by order, and to issue or approve Codes of Practice relating to non-native species. Current legislation and its application needs to be kept under review by appropriate government departments to ensure that it is adequate to prevent new species becoming accidentally established; the recent establishment of wild boar indicates that changes are required. The impact of introduced animals is reviewed in [52].

AUTHORS

S.J. Baker & D. Hills, with contributions from D.W. Yalden (red-necked wallaby) and D.J. Jefferies (short-clawed otter).

REFERENCES

1 Author's data.
2 Aharoni, B. (1932) Die Muriden von Palestina und Syrien. *Zeitschrift für Säugetierkunde*, **7**, 173 (in German).
3 Aistrop, J.B. (1968) *The Mongolian gerbil*. Dennis Dobson, London.
4 Allen, J.A. (1922) Carnivora collected by the American Museum Congo expedition. *Bulletin of the American Museum of Natural History*, **47**, 84–108.
5 Baker, S.J. (1986) Free-living golden hamsters (*Mesocricetus auratus*) in London. *Journal of Zoology*, **209**, 285–296.
6 Baker, S.J. (1990) Escaped exotic mammals in Britain. *Mammal Review*, **20**, 75–96.
7 Baker, S.J. Personal communication.
8 Baker, S.J. & Wilson, C.J. (1995) *The evidence for the presence of large exotic cats in the Bodmin area and their possible impact on livestock*. Report PB 2308, Ministry of Agriculture, Fisheries and Food, London.
9 Barrett-Hamilton, G.E.H. & Hinton, M.A.C. (1921) The beaver. In *A history of British mammals*. Gurney & Jackson, London.
10 Beck, B.B. & Wemmer, C.M. (eds.) (1983) *The biology and management of an extinct species, Père David's deer*. Noyes, Park Ridge, NJ.
11 Boyce, N. (1998) Bowels of the beasts. *New Scientist*, 22 August, 36–39.
12 Catt, D.C. (1977) The breeding biology of Bennett's wallaby (*Macropus rufogriseus fruticus*) in South Canterbury, New Zealand. *New Zealand Journal of Zoology*, **4**, 401–411.
13 Catt, D.C. (1979) Age determination in Bennett's wallaby, *Macropus rufogriseus fruticus* (Marsupialia) in South Canterbury, New Zealand. *Australian Wildlife Research*, **6**, 13–18.
14 Catt, D.C. (1981) Growth and condition of Bennett's wallaby (*Macropus rufogriseus fruticus*) in South Canterbury, New Zealand. *New Zealand Journal of Zoology*, **8**, 295–300.
15 Chanin, P. (1993) *Otters*. Whittet Books, London.
16 Chasen, F.N & Kloss, C.B (1931) Mammals from the lowlands and islands of north Borneo. *Bulletin of the Raffles Museum*, **6**, 15, 52.
17 Clarke, J. & Loudon, A.S.I. (1985) The effects of differences in herbage height on the grazing behaviour of lactating Bennett's wallaby (*Macropus rufogriseus rufogriseus*). *Journal of Zoology A*, **207**, 537–544.
18 Cowdy, S. (1965) Mammal report 1958–1965. *Middle Thames Naturalist*, **18**, 8.
19 Crawford, A. (2003) *Fourth otter survey of England 2000–2002*. Environment Agency, Bristol.
20 EEC (1982) *Council decision concerning the conclusion of the convention on the conservation of European Wildlife and natural habitats*. 82/72/EEC(O.J.L. 38 10.2.82).
21 Errington, P.L. (1963) *Muskrat populations*. Iowa State University Press, Ames.
22 Fairley, J.S. (1982) The muskrat in Ireland. *Irish Naturalists' Journal*, **20**, 405–11.
23 Fleming, D. *et al.* (1983) The reproductive biology of Bennett's wallaby (*Macropus rufogriseus rufogriseus*) ranging free at Whipsnade Park. *Journal of Zoology*, **201**, 283–291.
24 Gosling, L.M. (1980) Reproduction of the Himalayan porcupine in captivity. *Journal of Zoology*, **192**, 546–549.
25 Gosling, L.M. & Baker, S.J. (1989) The eradication of muskrats and coypus from Britain. *Biological Journal of the Linnean Society*, **38**, 39–51.
26 Gosling, L.M. & Wright, M. (1975) Feral porcupines. *Report, Pest Infestation Control Laboratory*, **1971–73**, 160–1.
27 Green, P. Personal communication.
28 Harris, C.J (1968) *Otters: a study of the recent Lutrinae*. Weidenfeld & Nicolson, London.
29 Harrison, D.L. (1972) *Mammals of Arabia*, vol. 3. Ernest Benn, London.
30 Harting, J.E. (1880) *British animals extinct within historic*

times. Trubner & Co., London.

31 Hinton, M.A.C. (1932) The muskrat menace. *Natural History Magazine,* **3,** 177–184.

32 Howes, C.A. (1973) *Annual Report, Yorkshire Naturalists' Union,* **1972,** 4–7.

33 Howes, C.A. (1983) An atlas of Yorkshire mammals. *The Naturalist,* **108,** 41–82.

34 Howes, C.A. (1984) Free range gerbils. *Bulletin of the Yorkshire Naturalists' Union,* **1,** 10.

35 Howes, C.A. Personal communication.

36 Jefferies, D.J. (1990) The Asian short-clawed otter *Amblonyx cinerea* (Illiger) living wild in Britain. *Journal of the Otter Trust,* **2**(3), 21–25.

37 Jefferies, D.J. (1992) Another record of an Asian short-clawed otter living free in the Oxford area of England, with notes on its implications. *Journal of the Otter Trust,* **2**(5), 9–12.

38 Jefferies, D.J. (ed.) (2003) *The water vole and mink survey of Britain 1996–1998 with a history of the long term changes in the status of both species and their causes.* Vincent Wildlife Trust, Ledbury.

39 Jefferies, D.J. *et al.* (2001) A brief history of the Otter Trust's successful programme of repopulating lowland England with otters bred in captivity with a special emphasis on East Anglia. *Journal of the Otter Trust,* **3,** 105–117.

40 Johnson, C.N. (1987) Macropod studies at Wallaby Creek. IV Home range and movements of the red-necked wallaby. *Australian Wildlife Research,* **14,** 125–32.

41 Johnson, C.N. (1987b) Relationships between mother and infant red-necked wallabies. *Ethology,* **74,** 1–20.

42 Johnston, P.G. & Sharman, G.B. (1979) Electrophoretic, chromosomal and morphometric studies in the red-necked wallaby, *Macropus rufogriseus* (Desmarest). *Australian Journal of Zoology,* **27,** 433–441.

43 Kenward, R.E. & Holm, J.L. (1989) What future for British red squirrels? *Biological Journal of the Linnean Society,* **38,** 83–89.

44 Keymer, I.F. (1983) Diseases of squirrels in Britain. *Mammal Review,* **13,** 155–158.

45 Kirkpatrick, T.H. (1964) Molar progression and macropod age. *Queensland Journal of Agricultural Science,* **21,** 163–5.

46 Kirkpatrick, T.H. (1965) Studies on Macropodidae in Queensland. 2. Age estimation of the grey kangaroo, red kangaroo, the eastern wallaroo and the red-necked wallaby, with notes on dental abnormalities. *Queensland Journal of Agricultural Science,* **22,** 301–307.

47 Kruuk, H. (1995) *Wild otters: predation and populations.* Oxford University Press, Oxford.

48 Kruuk, H. *et al.* (1993) Identification of tracks and other signs of three species of otter, *Lutra lutra, L. perspicillata* and *Aonyx cinerea. Natural History Bulletin of the Siam Society,* **41,** 28–30.

49 Lever, C. (1977) *Naturalised animals of the British Isles.* Hutchinson, London.

50 Lever, C. (1983) The golden hamster in the London area. *London Naturalist,* **62,** 111.

51 Lever, C. (1985) *Naturalised mammals of the world.* Longman, London.

52 Lever, C. (1994) *Naturalized animals: the ecology of successfully introduced species.* Poyser, London.

53 Loder, E. (1898) On the beaver-pond at Leonardslea. *Proceedings of the Zoological Society of London,* **1898,** 201–202.

54 Lynch, J.M *et al.* (1996) Variation in cranial form and sexual dimorphism among five European populations of the otter *Lutra lutra. Journal of Zoology,* **238,** 81–96.

55 Merchant, J.C. & Calaby, J.H. (1981) Reproductive biology of the red-necked wallaby (*Macropus rufogriseus banksianus* and Bennett's wallaby (*M. r. rufogriseus*) in captivity. *Journal of Zoology,* **194,** 203–17.

56 Mitchell, J. (1983) Strange beasts on bonny banks. *Scottish Wildlife,* **19,** 20.

57 Mitchell-Jones, A.J. *et al.* (1999) *The atlas of European mammals.* Poyser, London.

58 Mollison B.C. (1960) Food regurgitation in Bennett's wallaby *Protemnodon rufogrisea* (Desmarest) and the scrub wallaby *Thylogale billardei* (Desmarest). *CSIRO Wildlife Research,* **5,** 87–88.

59 Munro, T. (1935) Note on musk-rats and other animals killed since the inception of the campaign against musk-rats in October 1932. *Scottish Naturalist,* **4,** 11–16.

60 Natural History Museum, London. Unpublished identification reports.

61 Neithammer, G. (1963) *Die Einburgerung von Säugetieren und Vögeln in Europa.* Paul Parey, Hamburg.

62 O'Connor, T.P. (1986) The garden dormouse *Eliomys quercinus* from Roman York. *Journal of Zoology,* **210,** 620–622.

63 Philp, E. (1991) Notes from Maidstone Museum. *Bulletin of the Kent Field Club,* **36,** 30–31.

64 Prater. S.H. (1971) *The book of Indian animals.*Bombay Natural History Society, Bombay.

65 Roots, C. (1976) *Animal invaders.* David & Charles, Newton Abbot.

66 Rowe, F.P. (1960) Golden hamsters *Mesocricetus auratus* living free in an urban habitat. *Proceedings of the Zoological Society of London,* **134,** 499–503.

67 Rowe, F.P. (1968) Further records of free-living golden hamsters. *Journal of Zoology,* **156,** 529–530.

68 Russell, E.M. (1974) The biology of kangaroos (Marsupialia: Macropodidae). *Mammal Review,* **4,** 14–59.

69 Russell, E.M. (1984) Social behaviour and social organisation of Marsupials. *Mammal Review,* **14,** 101–154.

70 Sheail, J. (1988) The extermination of the muskrat (*Ondatra zibethicus*) in inter-war Britain. *Archives of Natural History,* **15,** 155–170.

71 Smallshire, D. & Davy, J.W. (1989) Feral Himalayan porcupines in Devon. *Nature in Devon,* **10,** 62–69.

72 Strachan, C. *et al.* (1998) The rapid impact of resident American mink on water voles: case studies in Lowland England. *Symposium of the Zoological Society of London,* **71,** 339–357.

73 Strachan, R. & Jefferies, D.J. (1996) *Otter survey of England 1991–1994.* Vincent Wildlife Trust, London.

74 Sykes, T (1995) *Upper Thames otter habitat project: final report.* Bedfordshire, Berkshire, Oxfordshire Wildlife Trust, Oxford.

75 Warwick, T. (1934) Distribution of the muskrat in the British Isles. *Journal of Animal Ecology,* **3,** 250–67.

76 Warwick, T. (1941) Contribution to the ecology of the muskrat in the British Isles. *Proceedings of the Zoological Society of London,* **110,** 165–201.

77 Wayre, P. (1989) *Operation otter.* Chatto & Windus, London.

78 Wayre, P. Personal communication.

79 Weir, A. *et al.* (1995) The winter diet and parasitic fauna of a population of red-necked wallabies *Macropus rufogriseus* recently introduced to Scotland. *Mammal Review,* **25,** 111–16.

80 Windsor, D.E. & Dagg, A.I. (1971) The gaits of the Macropodinae (Marsupialia). *Journal of Zoology,* **163,** 165–73.

81 Yalden, D.W. (1988) Feral wallabies in the Peak District, 1971–1985. *Journal of Zoology,* **215,** 369–374.

82 Yalden, D.W. (1999) *The history of British mammals.* Poyser, London.

83 Yalden, D.W. & Hosey, G.R. (1971) Feral wallabies in the Peak District. *Journal of Zoology,* **165,** 513–520.

84 Younger, D.A. (1994) The small mammals from the forecourt granary and the south west fort ditch. Pp. 266–268 in Bidwell, P. & Speak, S. (eds.) *Excavations at South Shields Roman Fort.* Society of Antiquarians of Newcastle-upon-Tyne Monograph 4(1).

Glossary

Agonistic Competitive (behaviour).

Allopatric Applied to organisms that occupy different geographical areas (cf. *Sympatric*).

Allozymes Genetic variants of enzymes, used as genetic markers.

Altricial Poorly developed and helpless at birth (cf. precocial) e.g. rabbits, mustelids.

Alveolus A socket in a jaw bone occupied by the root of a tooth (plural *alveoli*).

Anoestrus A state of quiescence of the sexual organs in the female, seasonal or between oestrous cycles.

Apocrine glands Secretory glands in which the cells themselves constitute part of the secretion, as in sebaceous and mammary glands.

Aspect ratio Of a wing, the ratio of length to mean width.

Autocoprophagy See *Caecotrophy*.

Awn hairs Projecting guard hairs.

Baculum The bone found in the penis of some mammals, also known as the *os penis*.

Benthic Inhabiting the deep sea or sea bottom.

Blastocyst A stage in the development of a fertilised egg after cell division has begun but before firm attachment to the wall of the uterus. Development may be delayed for a considerable time at this stage.

bp Before the present as determined by radiocarbon dating (capital letters indicate a calibrated, i.e. corrected, date).

Brachycardia Having a very slow heartbeat, e.g. during hibernation, diving.

Caecotrophy Eating the semi-digested products of the caecum straight from the anus as a normal nutritional stratagem (physiologically a more correct term than coprophagy, which implies eating dung). Also referred to as autocoprophagy or refection.

Calcar A cartilaginous or bony rod arising from the ankle of a bat, supporting the trailing edge of the tail membrane.

Carnassials The teeth of carnivores that are specialised for shearing flesh – the last upper premolars and the first lower molars.

Cheek-teeth Molars, with or without rear premolars, behind the diastema.

Chromosomes The thread-like elements in the nucleus of a cell, carrying the genetic material. The number is usually characteristic of a species and is expressed as the *diploid number (2n),* being the number in normal somatic (as distinct from reproductive) cells. Each chromosome may consist of one or two arms and the number of arms may be more constant in a species than the number of chromosomes. It is called the *fundamental number* (FN) more often expressed as *fundamental number of autosomes* (FNa), i.e. excluding the sex chromosomes.

Cline A kind of geographical variation within a species where there is a gradual and progressive change in one or more characters over a large area. The rate of change is not always constant and areas of more abrupt change may demarcate subspecies.

Cohort A group of animals simultaneously recruited to the population, whose subsequent fate is followed; used in analysing population structure and survivorship.

Commensal An animal that benefits by living in close association with another species, without directly harming it as does a parasite.

Condylobasal length The most frequently used measure of the length of a skull, from the anterior point of the premaxillary bones to the back of the occipital condyles.

Dactylopatagium Hand wing of bats: the membrane carried by the fingers, and forming the wing tip.

Diastema Gap in the tooth row, usually between incisors and cheek-teeth.

Dioestrus Sexual quiescence between two oestrous cycles.

Diptera Two-winged flies.

Epigenetic polymorphism Variability in a population caused by the interaction of genetic constitution and development processes.

Epiphyses The terminal parts of a long bone or vertebra; ossify separately from the main shaft of the bone, only become fully fused with it on reaching adult size. The degree of fusion can sometimes be used to estimate age.

Erythrism A condition of the pelage in which red pigment (phaeomelanin) predominates, due usually to absence of the black pigment (eumelanin).

Feral An animal or population that has reverted to the wild from a state of domestication.

Flehmen Use of vomeronasal organ in roof of mouth, by many mammals, best seen in artiodactyls; used to check sexual state of females by males. Rapid passage of air sucks volatilised compounds out of urine by Venturi effect.

FNa Fundamental number of autosomes – see *Chromosomes*.

Fossorial Burrowing (e.g. mole).

F_{ST} A statistical measure of genetic differentiation between populations; high values indicate they are very different, with little gene flow between them.

Hibernaculum Site(s) (nests, caves, etc.) where hibernation occurs. Plural *hibernacula*.

Holarctic Region The biogeographical region comprising the Nearctic Region (North America) and the Palaearctic Region (northern Eurasia).

Home range The area normally utilised by an individual animal.

Hymenoptera The order of insects including sawflies, bees, wasps and ants.

Hypsodont Of teeth, high-crowned (in extreme cases ever-growing) and therefore able to withstand considerable wear by abrasion.

Karyotype The set of chromosomes in a cell, especially when arranged in sequence for description.

Ked A parasitic fly of the family Hippoboscidae.

Kinaesthetic Sensitive to one's own movement or position.

Lek Communal display by males (e.g. some fallow deer).

Lepidoptera moths and butterflies

Leptospire A spirochaete bacterium, genus *Leptospira*, causing the disease leptospirosis, affecting especially the liver and kidneys of many species of mammals.

Lifespan The maximum age to which an animal can live (physiological longevity).

Longevity The average age lived by members of a population under natural conditions. Often given as 'expectation of further life'.

Lophodont Of a tooth, with the cusps elongated to form narrow ridges.

Machair Lime-rich, sandy coastal pasture, especially in the Outer Hebrides.

Matrilines Maternal genetic lineages.

Melon In whales, a fat deposit above the upper lip, sometimes forming a conspicuous rounded protuberance.

Merocrine glands Those in which the secretory cells remain intact during secretion as in most sweat glands (cf. *Apocrine glands*).

Microsatellites Highly variable segments of nuclear DNA, used as genetic markers to study family relationships, the distinctiveness of populations and the level of genetic variation.

Mitochondrial (mt) DNA Genetic material from the mitochondria (not the nucleus), therefore maternally inherited; particularly used for helping to define species and genetic units within species, and to infer colonisation history.

Molars The posterior chewing teeth that are not preceded by milk teeth.

Monogastric Having a single stomach, in contrast to the 3–4-chambered stomachs of ruminants.

Mystacial Of the moustache, or placed equivalently.

Natality Birth rate of a population (cf. mortality).

Nearctic Region The biogeographical region comprising North America.

Neritic Inhabiting shallow coastal waters (cf. *Pelagic*).

Nuclear DNA Genetic material from the nucleus, therefore in duplicate, one maternal and one paternal copy. Used especially in studying family relationships and genetic variability within populations. *Microsatellites* are the segments of nuclear DNA most commonly used as genetic markers.

Occipital The hind surface of the skull.

Oedema A pathological condition involving the excessive accumulation of serum in a tissue.

Orthodont Of rodent upper incisors, pointing downwards, i.e. the most usual situation (cf. *Pro-odont*).

Palaearctic Region The biogeographical region comprising Europe, North Africa and Asia north of the Himalayas.

Parapatry/parapatric (Related) species occurring in adjacent areas, but not, or barely, overlapping.

Paratenic host One that is not essential for a parasite's life cycle.

Parturition The process of giving birth.

PCBs Polychlorinated biphenyls: industrial hydrocarbons which are persistent pollutants in water.

Pelage The hairy coat of a mammal (cf. plumage).

Pelagic Inhabiting the open ocean (cf. *Neritic*).

Pheromone An aromatic secretion that has a specific effect on another animal of the same species.

Philopatry Returning faithfully to the same site (territory, place of birth).

Phoresy Dispersal by external carriage of e.g. mites, pseudoscorpions.

Plesiometacarpal Of deer, having remnant splints of the side-toes present proximally alongside the cannon bones (cf. *Telemetacarpal*).

Polymorphic In genetics, describing a population in which a number of discrete variants of one character are found in considerable numbers (as distinct from one normal condition and rare variants).

Polynya Area of permanent open water within otherwise solid pack-ice.

Polyoestrous Having a number of oestrous cycles per year or per breeding season.

Postcalcarial lobe A small lobe behind the spur (calcar) in bats.

Post-canines Premolars and molars, e.g. when not differentiated, as in seals.

Postpartum, postparturient Immediately after birth (but referring to the mother, not the offspring).

Precocial Well developed at birth (cf. *Altricial*), e.g. deer, hares.

Pro-odont Of rodent incisors, projecting forwards (cf. *Orthodont*), as in those that dig with their teeth (e.g. mole-rats).

Refection See *Caecotrophy*

Riparian Living beside rivers or steams (sometimes extended to include lakes, etc.) (e.g. otter, water shrew).

Rostrum The anterior part of a skull, in front of the orbits (i.e. the skeleton of the muzzle).

SD Standard deviation: a statistical measure of the dispersion of measurements about the mean value.

SE Standard error (of a mean): a statistical measure of the accuracy of the mean value of a sample. The true mean of the population should fall with 95% probability within ±1.96 SE of the observed mean of a subsample.

Selenodont Of teeth, with a crown pattern of longitudinal, crescentic ridges.

SST Sea surface temperature.

Stenopaic Of an eye, with a narrow slit-like pupil.

Superfetation Carrying two sets of embryos of different ages, and from different conceptions.

Sympatry/sympatric (Related) species occurring together in a geographical area.

Telemetacarpal Of deer, having remnant splints of the side toes present distally alongside the cannon bones (cf. *Plesiometacarpal*).

Terete Smoothly rounded.

Thermogenic Able to generate heat by metabolic means.

Tragus A lobe developed from the lower rim of the ear, extending upwards across the conch (especially developed in many bats).

Type locality Location where the original specimen used to describe the species (the *type specimen*) was obtained; may sometimes not be typical of the natural range.

Unicuspid Of teeth, having a single cusp or biting point (especially the simple conical teeth in the upper jaws of shrews).

Uropatagium Tail membrane, stretching between the hind legs of bats and including the tail.

Vibrissae Whiskers, i.e. specialised sensory hairs, usually best developed on the face but also found on other parts of the body.

Index

Index